CCENT/CCNA ICND1
Official Exam Certification Guide, Second Edition

Wendell Odom,
CCIE No. 1624

Cisco Press

800 East 96th Street
Indianapolis, Indiana 46240 USA

CCENT/CCNA ICND1 Official Exam Certification Guide, Second Edition

Wendell Odom

Copyright© 2008 Cisco Systems, Inc.

Published by:
Cisco Press
800 East 96th Street
Indianapolis, IN 46240 USA

Printed in the United States of America

Eighth Printing October 2009

Library of Congress Cataloging-in-Publication Data.

Odom, Wendell.

 CCENT/CCNA ICND1 official exam certification guide / Wendell Odom.

    p. cm.

 ISBN 978-1-58720-182-0 (hardback w/cd) 1. Electronic data processing personnel--Certification. 2. Computer networks--Examinations--Study guides. I. Title.

 QA76.3.O358 2007

 004.6--dc22

2007029241

ISBN-13: 978-1-58720-182-0

ISBN-10: 1-58720-182-8

Warning and Disclaimer

This book is designed to provide information about the Cisco ICND1 (640-822), ICND2 (640-816), and CCNA (640-802) exams. Every effort has been made to make this book as complete and accurate as possible, but no warranty or fitness is implied.

The information is provided on an "as is" basis. The author, Cisco Press, and Cisco Systems, Inc. shall have neither liability nor responsibility to any person or entity with respect to any loss or damages arising from the information contained in this book or from the use of the discs or programs that may accompany it.

The opinions expressed in this book belong to the author and are not necessarily those of Cisco Systems, Inc.

Trademark Acknowledgments

All terms mentioned in this book that are known to be trademarks or service marks have been appropriately capitalized. Cisco Press or Cisco Systems, Inc. cannot attest to the accuracy of this information. Use of a term in this book should not be regarded as affecting the validity of any trademark or service mark.

Corporate and Government Sales

The publisher offers excellent discounts on this book when ordered in quantity for bulk purchases or special sales, which may include electronic versions and/or custom covers and content particular to your business, training goals, marketing focus, and branding interests. For more information, please contact: **U.S. Corporate and Government Sales** 1-800-382-3419   **corpsales@pearsontechgroup.com**

For sales outside the United States please contact: **International Sales**   international@pearsoned.com

Feedback Information

At Cisco Press, our goal is to create in-depth technical books of the highest quality and value. Each book is crafted with care and precision, undergoing rigorous development that involves the unique expertise of members of the professional technical community.

Reader feedback is a natural continuation of this process. If you have any comments about how we could improve the quality of this book, or otherwise alter it to better suit your needs, you can contact us through e-mail at feedback@ciscopress.com. Please be sure to include the book title and ISBN in your message.

We greatly appreciate your assistance.

Publisher: Paul Boger

Associate Publisher: Dave Dusthimer

Cisco Representative: Anthony Wolfenden

Cisco Press Program Manager: Jeff Brady

Executive Editor: Brett Bartow

Managing Editor: Patrick Kanouse

Senior Development Editor: Christopher Cleveland

Senior Project Editor: San Dee Phillips and Meg Shaw

Copy Editor: Gayle Johnson and Bill McManus

Technical Editors: Teri Cook, Brian D'Andrea, and Steve Kalman

Editorial Assistant: Vanessa Evans

Book and Cover Designer: Louisa Adair

Composition: ICC Macmillan Inc.

Indexer: Tim Wright

Proofreader: Suzanne Thomas

Americas Headquarters
Cisco Systems, Inc.
170 West Tasman Drive
San Jose, CA 95134-1706
USA
www.cisco.com
Tel: 408 526-4000
800 553-NETS (6387)
Fax: 408 527-0883

Asia Pacific Headquarters
Cisco Systems, Inc.
168 Robinson Road
#28-01 Capital Tower
Singapore 068912
www.cisco.com
Tel: +65 6317 7777
Fax: +65 6317 7799

Europe Headquarters
Cisco Systems International BV
Haarlerbergpark
Haarlerbergweg 13-19
1101 CH Amsterdam
The Netherlands
www-europe.cisco.com
Tel: +31 0 800 020 0791
Fax: +31 0 20 357 1100

Cisco has more than 200 offices worldwide. Addresses, phone numbers, and fax numbers are listed on the Cisco Website at **www.cisco.com/go/offices.**

©2007 Cisco Systems, Inc. All rights reserved. CCVP, the Cisco logo, and the Cisco Square Bridge logo are trademarks of Cisco Systems, Inc.; Changing the Way We Work, Live, Play, and Learn is a service mark of Cisco Systems, Inc.; and Access Registrar, Aironet, BPX, Catalyst, CCDA, CCDP, CCIE, CCIP, CCNA, CCNP, CCSP, Cisco, the Cisco Certified Internetwork Expert logo, Cisco IOS, Cisco Press, Cisco Systems, Cisco Systems Capital, the Cisco Systems logo, Cisco Unity, Enterprise/Solver, EtherChannel, EtherFast, EtherSwitch, Fast Step, Follow Me Browsing, FormShare, GigaDrive, GigaStack, HomeLink, Internet Quotient, IOS, IP/TV, iQ Expertise, the iQ logo, iQ Net Readiness Scorecard, iQuick Study, LightStream, Linksys, MeetingPlace, MGX, Networking Academy, Network Registrar, Packet, PIX, ProConnect, RateMUX, ScriptShare, SlideCast, SMARTnet, StackWise, The Fastest Way to Increase Your Internet Quotient, and TransPath are registered trademarks of Cisco Systems, Inc. and/or its affiliates in the United States and certain other countries.

All other trademarks mentioned in this document or Website are the property of their respective owners. The use of the word partner does not imply a partnership relationship between Cisco and any other company. (0609R)

About the Author

Wendell Odom, CCIE No. 1624, has been in the networking industry since 1981. He currently teaches QoS, MPLS, and CCNA courses for Skyline Advanced Technology Services (http://www.skyline-ats.com). He has also worked as a network engineer, consultant, systems engineer, instructor, and course developer. He is the author of all previous editions of the *CCNA Exam Certification Guide*, as well as the *Cisco QOS Exam Certification Guide*, Second Edition, *Computer Networking First-Step*, *CCIE Routing and Switching Official Exam Certification Guide*, Second Edition, and *CCNA Video Mentor*—all from Cisco Press.

About the Technical Reviewers

Teri Cook (CCSI, CCDP, CCNP, CCDA, CCNA, MCT, and MCSE 2000/2003: Security) has more than ten years of experience in the IT industry. She has worked with different types of organizations in the private business and DoD sectors, providing senior-level network and security technical skills in the design and implementation of complex computing environments. Since obtaining her certifications, Teri has been committed to bringing quality IT training to IT professionals as an instructor. She is an outstanding instructor who uses real-world experience to present complex networking technologies. As an IT instructor, Teri has been teaching Cisco classes for more than five years.

Brian D'Andrea (CCNA, CCDA, MCSE, A+, and Net+) has 11 years of IT experience in both medical and financial environments, where planning and supporting critical networking technologies were his primary responsibilities. For the last five years he has dedicated himself to technical training. Brian spends most of his time with The Training Camp, an IT boot camp provider. Using his real-world experience and his ability to break difficult concepts into a language that students can understand, Brian has successfully trained hundreds of students for both work and certification endeavors.

Stephen Kalman is a data security trainer. He is the author or tech editor of more than 20 books, courses, and CBT titles. His most recent book is *Web Security Field Guide*, published by Cisco Press. In addition to those responsibilities he runs a consulting company, Esquire Micro Consultants, which specializes in network security assessments and forensics.

Mr. Kalman holds SSCP, CISSP, ISSMP, CEH, CHFI, CCNA, CCSA (Checkpoint), A+, Network+ and Security+ certifications and is a member of the New York State Bar.

Dedication

For Brett Bartow. Thanks for being such a steady, insightful, and incredibly trustworthy guide through the publishing maze.

Acknowledgments

The team who helped produce this book has been simply awesome. Everyone who touched this book has made it better, and they've been particularly great at helping catch the errors that always creep into the manuscript.

Brian, Teri, and Steve all did a great job TEing the book. Besides helping a lot with technical accuracy, Brian made a lot of good suggestions about traps that he sees when teaching CCNA classes, helping the book avoid those same pitfalls. Teri's ability to see each phrase in the context of an entire chapter, or the whole book, was awesome, helping catch things that no one would otherwise catch. Steve spent most of his TE time on the ICND2 book, but he did lend great help with this one, particularly with his reviews of the security-oriented topics, an area in which he's an expert. And more so than any other book I've written, the TEs really sunk their teeth into the specifics of every example, helping catch errors. Thanks so much!

Another (ho-hum) all-star performance from Chris Cleveland, who developed the book. Now I empathize with sports writers who have to write about the local team's star who bats .300, hits 40 homers, and drives in 100 runs, every year, for his whole career. How many ways can you say he does a great job? I'll keep it simple: Thanks, Chris.

The wonderful and mostly hidden production folks did their usual great job. When every time I see how they reworded something, and think, "Wow; why didn't I write that?", it makes me appreciate the kind of team we have at Cisco Press. The final copy edit, figure review, and pages review process required a fair amount of juggling and effort as well – thanks to Patrick's team, especially San Dee, Meg, Tonya, for working so well with all the extra quality initiatives we've implemented. Thanks to you all!

Additionally, several folks who didn't have any direct stake in the book also helped it along. Thanks to Frank Knox for the discussions on the exams, why they're so difficult, and about troubleshooting. Thanks to Rus Healy for the help with wireless. Thanks to the Mikes at Skyline for making my schedule work to get this book (and the ICND2 book) out the door. And thanks to the course and exam teams at Cisco for the great early communications and interactions about the changes to the courses and exams.

Finally, thanks to my wife Kris for all her support with my writing efforts, her prayers, and her understanding when the deadline didn't quite match with our vacation plans this summer. And thanks to Jesus Christ—all this effort is just striving after the wind without Him.

This Book Is Safari Enabled

The Safari® Enabled icon on the cover of your favorite technology book means that the book is available through Safari Bookshelf. When you buy this book, you get free access to the online edition for 45 days.

Safari Bookshelf is an electronic reference library that lets you easily search thousands of technical books, find code samples, download chapters, and access technical information whenever and wherever you need it.

To gain 45-day Safari Enabled access to this book:

- Go to http://www.ciscopress.com/safarienabled.

- Complete the brief registration form.

- Enter the coupon code 6EM9-WNXL-7Z1E-9UL2-KAEC.

If you have difficulty registering on Safari Bookshelf or accessing the online edition, please e-mail customer-service@safari-booksonline.com.

Contents at a Glance

Contents

Part VII   CD-only

Icons Used in This Book

 Web Server

 Web Browser

 PC

 Laptop

 Server

 Printer

 Phone

 IP Phone

 Cable Modem

 CSU/DSU

 Router

 Multiservice Switch

 Switch

 ATM Switch

 Frame Relay Switch

 PBX

 Access Point

 ASA

 DSLAM

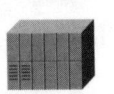 WAN Switch

 Hub

 PIX Firewall

 Bridge

 Wireless Connection

 Network Cloud

Ethernet Connection

Serial Line Connection

Virtual Circuit

Command Syntax Conventions

The conventions used to present command syntax in this book are the same conventions used in the IOS Command Reference. The Command Reference describes these conventions as follows:

- **Bold** indicates commands and keywords that are entered literally as shown. In actual configuration examples and output (not general command syntax), bold indicates commands that the user enters (such as a **show** command).

- *Italic* indicates arguments for which you supply actual values.

- Vertical bars (|) separate alternative, mutually exclusive elements.

- Square brackets ([ ]) indicate an optional element.

- Braces ({ }) indicate a required choice.

- Braces within brackets ([{ }]) indicate a required choice within an optional element.

Foreword

CCENT/CCNA ICND1 Official Exam Certification Guide, Second Edition, is an excellent self-study resource for the CCENT and CCNA ICND1 exam. Passing the ICND1 exam validates the knowledge and skills required to successfully install, operate, and troubleshoot a small branch office network. It is the sole required exam for CCENT certification and the first of two exams required for CCNA certification.

Gaining certification in Cisco technology is key to the continuing educational development of today's networking professional. Through certification programs, Cisco validates the skills and expertise required to effectively manage the modern Enterprise network.

Cisco Press exam certification guides and preparation materials offer exceptional—and flexible—access to the knowledge and information required to stay current in your field of expertise, or to gain new skills. Whether used as a supplement to more traditional training or as a primary source of learning, these materials offer users the information and knowledge validation required to gain new understanding and proficiencies.

Developed in conjunction with the Cisco certifications and training team, Cisco Press books are the only self-study books authorized by Cisco. They offer students a series of exam practice tools and resource materials to help ensure that learners fully grasp the concepts and information presented.

Additional authorized Cisco instructor-led courses, e-learning, labs, and simulations are available exclusively from Cisco Learning Solutions Partners worldwide. To learn more, visit http://www.cisco.com/go/training.

I hope that you find these materials to be an enriching and useful part of your exam preparation.

Erik Ullanderson
Manager, Global Certifications
Learning@Cisco
August 2007

Introduction

Congratulations! If you're reading this Introduction, you've probably already decided to go for your Cisco certification. If you want to succeed as a technical person in the networking industry, you need to know Cisco. Cisco has a ridiculously high market share in the router and switch marketplace—more than 80 percent in some markets. In many geographies and markets around the world, networking equals Cisco. If you want to be taken seriously as a network engineer, Cisco certification makes sense.

Historically speaking, the first entry-level Cisco certification has been the Cisco Certified Network Associate (CCNA) certification, first offered in 1998. The first three versions of the CCNA certification (1998, 2000, and 2002) required that you pass a single exam to become certified. However, over time, the exam kept growing, both in the amount of material covered and the difficulty level of the questions. So, for the fourth major revision of the exams, announced in 2003, Cisco continued with a single certification (CCNA) but offered two certification options: a single exam option and a two-exam option. The two-exam option allowed people to study roughly half the material and then take and pass one exam before moving on to the next.

Cisco announced changes to the CCNA certification and exams in June 2007. This announcement includes many changes; here are the most notable:

- The exams collectively cover a broader range of topics.

- The exams increase the focus on proving the test taker's skills (as compared with just testing knowledge).

- Cisco created a new entry-level certification: Cisco Certified Entry Networking Technician (CCENT).

For the current certifications, announced in June 2007, Cisco created the ICND1 (640-822) and ICND2 (640-816) exams, along with the CCNA (640-802) exam. To become CCNA certified, you can pass both the ICND1 and ICND2 exams, or just the CCNA exam. The CCNA exam simply covers all the topics on the ICND1 and ICND2 exams, giving you two options for gaining your CCNA certification. The two-exam path gives people with less experience a chance to study for a smaller set of topics at one time. The one-exam option provides a more cost-effective certification path for those who want to prepare for all the topics at once.

Although the two-exam option is useful for some certification candidates, Cisco designed the ICND1 exam with a much more important goal in mind. The CCNA certification grew to the point that it tested knowledge and skills beyond what an entry-level network technician would need. Cisco needed a certification that better reflected the skills required for entry-level networking jobs. So Cisco designed its Interconnecting Cisco Networking Devices 1 (ICND1) course, and the corresponding ICND1 640-822 exam, to include the knowledge and skills most needed by an entry-level technician in a small Enterprise network. And so that you can prove that you have the skills required for those entry-level jobs, Cisco created a new certification, CCENT.

Figure I-1 shows the basic organization of the certifications and the exams used to get your CCENT and CCNA certifications. (Note that there is no separate certification for passing the ICND2 exam.)

Figure I-1 *Cisco Entry-Level Certifications and Exams*

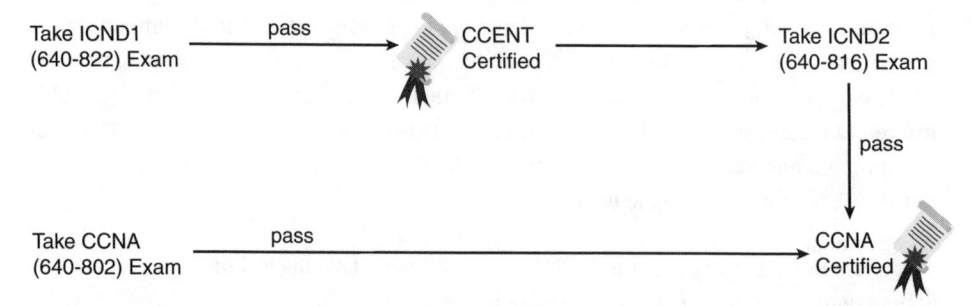

As you can see, although you can obtain the CCENT certification by taking the ICND1 exam, you do not have to be CCENT certified before getting your CCNA certification. You can choose to take just the CCNA exam and bypass the CCENT certification.

The ICND1 and ICND2 exams cover different sets of topics, with a minor amount of overlap. For example, ICND1 covers IP addressing and subnetting, and ICND2 covers a more complicated use of subnetting called variable-length subnet masking (VLSM). Therefore, ICND2 must then cover subnetting to some degree. The CCNA exam covers all the topics covered on both the ICND1 and ICND2 exams.

Although the popularity of the CCENT certification cannot be measured until a few years have passed, certainly the Cisco CCNA is the most popular entry-level networking certification program. A CCNA certification proves that you have a firm foundation in the most important components of the Cisco product line—routers and switches. It also proves that you have broad knowledge of protocols and networking technologies.

Format of the CCNA Exams

The ICND1, ICND2, and CCNA exams all follow the same general format. When you get to the testing center and check in, the proctor gives you some general instructions and then takes you into a quiet room containing a PC. When you're at the PC, you have a few things to do before the timer starts on your exam. For instance, you can take a sample quiz to get accustomed to the PC and the testing engine. Anyone who has user-level skills in getting around a PC should have no problems with the testing environment. Additionally, Chapter 18, "Final Preparation," points to a Cisco website where you can see a demo of Cisco's actual test engine.

When you start the exam, you are asked a series of questions. You answer them and then move on to the next question. *The exam engine does not let you go back and change your answer.* Yes, it's true. When you move on to the next question, that's it for the preceding question.

The exam questions can be in one of the following formats:

- Multiple choice (MC)

- Testlet

- Drag-and-drop (DND)

- Simulated lab (sim)

- Simlet

The first three types of questions are relatively common in many testing environments. The multiple-choice format simply requires that you point and click a circle beside the correct answer(s). Cisco traditionally tells you how many answers you need to choose, and the testing software prevents you from choosing too many. Testlets are questions with one general scenario and several multiple-choice questions about the overall scenario. Drag-and-drop questions require you to click and hold, move a button or icon to another area, and release the mouse button to place the object somewhere else—typically in a list. For some questions, to get the question correct, you might need to put a list of five things in the proper order.

The last two types of questions use a network simulator to ask questions. Interestingly, the two types actually allow Cisco to assess two very different skills. First, sim questions generally describe a problem, and your task is to configure one or more routers and switches to fix it. The exam then grades the question based on the configuration you changed or added. Interestingly, sim questions are the only questions (to date) for which Cisco has openly confirmed it gives partial credit for.

The simlet questions may well be the most difficult style of question. Simlet questions also use a network simulator, but instead of having you answer by changing the configuration, the question includes one or more multiple-choice questions. The questions require that you use the simulator to examine a network's current behavior, interpreting the output of any

show commands you can remember to answer the question. Whereas sim questions require you to troubleshoot problems related to a configuration, simlets require you to analyze both working networks and networks with problems, correlating **show** command output with your knowledge of networking theory and configuration commands.

What's on the CCNA Exam(s)?

Ever since I was in grade school, whenever the teacher announced that we were having a test soon, someone would always ask, "What's on the test?" Even in college, people would try to get more information about what would be on the exams. The goal is to know what to study a lot, what to study a little, and what to not study at all.

Cisco wants the public to know the variety of topics and have an idea of the kinds of knowledge and skills required for each topic, for every Cisco certification exam. To that end, Cisco publishes a set of objectives for each exam. The objectives list the specific topics such as IP addressing, RIP, and VLANs. The objectives also imply the kinds of skills required for that topic. For example, one objective might start with "Describe...", and another might begin with "Describe, configure, and troubleshoot...". The second objective clearly states that you need a thorough understanding of that topic. By listing the topics and skill level, Cisco helps you prepare for the exams.

Although the exam objectives are helpful, keep in mind that Cisco adds a disclaimer that the posted exam topics for all its certification exams are *guidelines*. Cisco makes an effort to keep the exam questions within the confines of the stated exam objectives. I know from talking to those involved that every question is analyzed to ensure that it fits within the stated exam topics.

ICND1 Exam Topics

Table I-1 lists the exam topics for the ICND1 exam. The ICND2 exam topics follow in Table I-2. Although the posted exam topics are not numbered at Cisco.com, Cisco Press numbers them for easier reference. The tables also note the book parts in which each exam topic is covered. Because the exam topics may change over time, it may be worth it to double-check the exam topics listed on Cisco.com (go to http://www.cisco.com/go/ccna). If Cisco does happen to add exam topics at a later date, note that Appendix C, "ICND1 Exam Updates," describes how to go to http://www.ciscopress.com and download additional information about those newly added topics.

> **NOTE**   The table includes gray highlights that are explained in the upcoming section "CCNA Exam Topics."

Table I-1 *ICND1 Exam Topics*

Reference Number	Book Part(s) Where Topic Is Covered	Exam Topic
		Describe the operation of data networks
1	I	Describe the purpose and functions of various network devices
2	I	Select the components required to meet a given network specification
3	I, II, III	Use the OSI and TCP/IP models and their associated protocols to explain how data flows in a network
4	I	Describe common networking applications including web applications
5	I	Describe the purpose and basic operation of the protocols in the OSI and TCP models
6	I	Describe the impact of applications (Voice Over IP and Video Over IP) on a network
7	I–IV	Interpret network diagrams
8	I–IV	Determine the path between two hosts across a network
9	I, III, IV	Describe the components required for network and Internet communications
10	I–IV	Identify and correct common network problems at Layers 1, 2, 3, and 7 using a layered model approach
11	II, III	Differentiate between LAN/WAN operation and features
		Implement a small switched network
12	II	Select the appropriate media, cables, ports, and connectors to connect switches to other network devices and hosts
13	II	Explain the technology and media access control method for Ethernet technologies
14	II	Explain network segmentation and basic traffic management concepts
15	II	Explain the operation of Cisco switches and basic switching concepts
16	II	Perform, save, and verify initial switch configuration tasks including remote access management

continues

Table I-1 *ICND1 Exam Topics (Continued)*

Reference Number	Book Part(s) Where Topic Is Covered	Exam Topic
17	II	Verify network status and switch operation using basic utilities (including: ping, traceroute, Telnet, SSH, ARP, ipconfig), show and debug commands
18	II	Implement and verify basic security for a switch (port security, deactivate ports)
19	II	Identify, prescribe, and resolve common switched network media issues, configuration issues, autonegotiation, and switch hardware failures
		Implement an IP addressing scheme and IP services to meet network requirements for a small branch office
20	I, III	Describe the need for and role of addressing in a network
21	I, III	Create and apply an addressing scheme to a network
22	III	Assign and verify valid IP addresses to hosts, servers, and networking devices in a LAN environment
23	IV	Explain the basic uses and operation of NAT in a small network connecting to one ISP
24	I, III	Describe and verify DNS operation
25	III, IV	Describe the operation and benefits of using private and public IP addressing
26	III, IV	Enable NAT for a small network with a single ISP and connection using SDM and verify operation using CLI and ping
27	III	Configure, verify, and troubleshoot DHCP and DNS operation on a router (including: CLI/SDM)
28	III	Implement static and dynamic addressing services for hosts in a LAN environment
29	III	Identify and correct IP addressing issues
		Implement a small routed network
30	I, III	Describe basic routing concepts (including: packet forwarding, router lookup process)
31	III	Describe the operation of Cisco routers (including: router bootup process, POST, router components)

Table I-1 *ICND1 Exam Topics (Continued)*

Reference Number	Book Part(s) Where Topic Is Covered	Exam Topic
32	I, III	Select the appropriate media, cables, ports, and connectors to connect routers to other network devices and hosts
33	III	Configure, verify, and troubleshoot RIPv2
34	III	Access and utilize the router CLI to set basic parameters
35	III	Connect, configure, and verify operation status of a device interface
36	III	Verify device configuration and network connectivity using ping, traceroute, Telnet, SSH, or other utilities
37	III	Perform and verify routing configuration tasks for a static or default route given specific routing requirements
38	III	Manage IOS configuration files (including: save, edit, upgrade, restore)
39	III	Manage Cisco IOS
40	III	Implement password and physical security
41	III	Verify network status and router operation using basic utilities (including: ping, traceroute, Telnet, SSH, ARP, ipconfig), show and debug commands
		Explain and select the appropriate administrative tasks required for a WLAN
42	II	Describe standards associated with wireless media (including: IEEE, Wi-Fi Alliance, ITU/FCC)
43	II	Identify and describe the purpose of the components in a small wireless network (including: SSID, BSS, ESS)
44	II	Identify the basic parameters to configure on a wireless network to ensure that devices connect to the correct access point
45	II	Compare and contrast wireless security features and capabilities of WPA security (including: open, WEP, WPA-1/2)
46	II	Identify common issues with implementing wireless networks

continues

Table I-1 *ICND1 Exam Topics (Continued)*

Reference Number	Book Part(s) Where Topic Is Covered	Exam Topic
		Identify security threats to a network and describe general methods to mitigate those threats
47	I	Explain today's increasing network security threats and the need to implement a comprehensive security policy to mitigate the threats
48	I	Explain general methods to mitigate common security threats to network devices, hosts, and applications
49	I	Describe the functions of common security appliances and applications
50	I, II, III	Describe security recommended practices including initial steps to secure network devices
		Implement and verify WAN links
51	IV	Describe different methods for connecting to a WAN
52	IV	Configure and verify a basic WAN serial connection

ICND2 Exam Topics

Table I-2 lists the exam topics for the ICND2 (640-816) exam, along with the book parts in the *CCNA ICND2 Official Exam Certification Guide* in which each topic is covered.

Table I-2 *ICND2 Exam Topics*

Reference Number	Book Part(s) Where Topic Is Covered (in ICND2)	Exam Topic
		Configure, verify, and troubleshoot a switch with VLANs and interswitch communications
101	I	Describe enhanced switching technologies (including: VTP, RSTP, VLAN, PVSTP, 802.1q)
102	I	Describe how VLANs create logically separate networks and the need for routing between them
103	I	Configure, verify, and troubleshoot VLANs
104	I	Configure, verify, and troubleshoot trunking on Cisco switches

Table I-2 *ICND2 Exam Topics (Continued)*

Reference Number	Book Part(s) Where Topic Is Covered (in ICND2)	Exam Topic
105	II	Configure, verify, and troubleshoot interVLAN routing
106	I	Configure, verify, and troubleshoot VTP
107	I	Configure, verify, and troubleshoot RSTP operation
108	I	Interpret the output of various show and debug commands to verify the operational status of a Cisco switched network
109	I	Implement basic switch security (including: port security, unassigned ports, trunk access, etc.)
		Implement an IP addressing scheme and IP Services to meet network requirements in a medium-size Enterprise branch office network
110	II	Calculate and apply a VLSM IP addressing design to a network
111	II	Determine the appropriate classless addressing scheme using VLSM and summarization to satisfy addressing requirements in a LAN/WAN environment
112	V	Describe the technological requirements for running IPv6 (including: protocols, dual stack, tunneling, etc.)
113	V	Describe IPv6 addresses
114	II, III	Identify and correct common problems associated with IP addressing and host configurations
		Configure and troubleshoot basic operation and routing on Cisco devices
115	III	Compare and contrast methods of routing and routing protocols
116	III	Configure, verify, and troubleshoot OSPF
117	III	Configure, verify, and troubleshoot EIGRP
118	II, III	Verify configuration and connectivity using ping, traceroute, and Telnet or SSH
119	II, III	Troubleshoot routing implementation issues

continues

Table I-2 *ICND2 Exam Topics (Continued)*

Reference Number	Book Part(s) Where Topic Is Covered (in ICND2)	Exam Topic
120	II, III, IV	Verify router hardware and software operation using show and debug commands
121	II	Implement basic router security
		Implement, verify, and troubleshoot NAT and ACLs in a medium-size Enterprise branch office network
122	II	Describe the purpose and types of access control lists
123	II	Configure and apply access control lists based on network filtering requirements
124	II	Configure and apply an access control list to limit Telnet and SSH access to the router
125	II	Verify and monitor ACLs in a network environment
126	II	Troubleshoot ACL implementation issues
127	V	Explain the basic operation of NAT
128	V	Configure Network Address Translation for given network requirements using CLI
129	V	Troubleshoot NAT implementation issues
		Implement and verify WAN links
130	IV	Configure and verify Frame Relay on Cisco routers
131	IV	Troubleshoot WAN implementation issues
132	IV	Describe VPN technology (including: importance, benefits, role, impact, components)
133	IV	Configure and verify PPP connection between Cisco routers

CCNA Exam Topics

In the previous version of the exams, the CCNA exam covered a lot of what was in the ICND (640-811) exam, plus some coverage of topics in the INTRO (640-821) exam. The new CCNA exam (640-802) covers all the topics on both the ICND1 (640-822) and ICND2 (640-816) exams. One of the reasons for more-balanced coverage in the exams is that some of the topics that used to be in the second exam have been moved to the first exam.

The CCNA (640-802) exam covers all the topics in both the ICND1 and ICND2 exams. The official CCNA 640-802 exam topics, posted at http://www.cisco.com, include all the topics listed in Table I-2 for the ICND2 exam, plus most of the exam topics for the ICND1 exam listed in Table I-1. The only exam topics from these two tables that are not listed as CCNA exam topics are the topics highlighted in gray in Table I-1. However, note that the gray topics are still covered on the CCNA 640-802 exam. Those topics are just not listed in the CCNA exam topics because one of the ICND2 exam topics refers to the same concepts.

ICND1 and ICND2 Course Outlines

Another way to get some direction about the topics on the exams is to look at the course outlines for the related courses. Cisco offers two authorized CCNA-related courses: Interconnecting Cisco Network Devices 1 (ICND1) and Interconnecting Cisco Network Devices 2 (ICND2). Cisco authorizes Certified Learning Solutions Providers (CLSP) and Certified Learning Partners (CLP) to deliver these classes. These authorized companies can also create unique custom course books using this material—in some cases to teach classes geared toward passing the CCNA exam.

About the *CCENT/CCNA ICND1 Official Exam Certification Guide* and *CCNA ICND2 Official Exam Certification Guide*

As mentioned earlier, Cisco has separated the content covered by the CCNA exam into two parts: topics typically used by engineers who work in small Enterprise networks (ICND1), and topics commonly used by engineers in medium-sized Enterprises (ICND2). Likewise, the Cisco Press *CCNA Exam Certification Guide* series includes two books for CCNA—*CCENT/CCNA ICND1 Official Exam Certification Guide* and *CCNA ICND2 Official Exam Certification Guide*. These two books cover the breadth of topics on each exam, typically to a little more depth than is required for the exams, to ensure that the books prepare you for the more difficult exam questions.

This section lists the variety of book features in both this book and the *CCNA ICND2 Official Exam Certification Guide*. Both books have the same basic features, so if you are reading both this book and the ICND2 book, there is no need to read the Introduction to the second book. Also, if you're using both books to prepare for the CCNA 640-802 exam (rather than taking the two-exam option), the end of this Introduction lists a suggested reading plan.

Objectives and Methods

The most important and somewhat obvious objective of this book is to help you pass the ICND1 exam or the CCNA exam. In fact, if the primary objective of this book were different, the book's title would be misleading! However, the methods used in this book to help you pass the exams are also designed to make you much more knowledgeable about how to do your job.

This book uses several key methodologies to help you discover the exam topics on which you need more review, to help you fully understand and remember those details, and to help you prove to yourself that you have retained your knowledge of those topics. So, this book does not try to help you pass the exams only by memorization, but by truly learning and understanding the topics. The CCNA certification is the foundation for many of the Cisco professional certifications, and it would be a disservice to you if this book did not help you truly learn the material. Therefore, this book helps you pass the CCNA exam by using the following methods:

- Helping you discover which exam topics you have not mastered

- Providing explanations and information to fill in your knowledge gaps

- Supplying exercises that enhance your ability to recall and deduce the answers to test questions

- Providing practice exercises on the topics and the testing process via test questions on the CD

Book Features

To help you customize your study time using these books, the core chapters have several features that help you make the best use of your time:

- **"Do I Know This Already?" Quizzes:** Each chapter begins with a quiz that helps you determine how much time you need to spend studying that chapter.

- **Foundation Topics:** These are the core sections of each chapter. They explain the protocols, concepts, and configuration for the topics in that chapter.

- **Exam Preparation Tasks:** After the Foundation Topics section, the "Exam Preparation Tasks" section lists a series of study activities you should perform. Each chapter includes the activities that make the most sense for studying the topics in that chapter. The activities include the following:

  — **Review All the Key Topics:** The key topics icon appears next to the most important items in the Foundation Topics section. The "Review All the Key Topics" activity lists the key topics from the chapter and the page on which they appear. Although the contents of the entire chapter could be on the exam, you should definitely know the information listed in each key topic.

— **Complete the Tables and Lists from Memory:** To help you memorize some lists of facts, many of the more important lists and tables from the chapter are included in Appendix H on the CD. This document lists only some of the information, allowing you to complete the table or list. Appendix I lists the same tables and lists, completed, for easy comparison.

— **Definitions of Key Terms:** Although the exams may be unlikely to ask a question such as "Define this term," the CCNA exams do require that you learn and know a lot of networking terminology. This section lists the most important terms from the chapter, asking you to write a short definition and compare your answer to the glossary at the end of the book.

— **Command Reference tables:** Some book chapters cover a large number of configuration and EXEC commands. These tables list and describe the commands introduced in the chapter. For exam preparation, use this section for reference, but also read through the table when performing the Exam Preparation Tasks to make sure you remember what all the commands do.

■ **CD-based practice exam:** The companion CD contains an exam engine (from Boson software, http://www.boson.com) that includes a large number of exam-realistic practice questions. You can take simulated ICND1 exams, as well as simulated CCNA exams, using this book's CD. (You can take simulated ICND2 and CCNA exams using the CD in the *CCNA ICND2 Official Exam Certification Guide*.)

■ **Subnetting videos:** The companion DVD contains a series of videos that show you how to figure out various facts about IP addressing and subnetting—in particular, using the shortcuts described in this book.

■ **Subnetting practice:** CD Appendix D contains a large set of subnetting practice problems, including the answers and explanations of how they were arrived at. This is a great resource to help you get ready to do subnetting well and fast.

■ **CD-based practice scenarios:** CD Appendix F contains several networking scenarios for additional study. These scenarios describe various networks and requirements, taking you through conceptual design, configuration, and verification. These scenarios are useful for building your hands-on skills, even if you do not have lab gear.

■ **Companion website:** The website http://www.ciscopress.com/title/1587201828 posts up-to-the-minute materials that further clarify complex exam topics. Check this site regularly for new and updated postings written by the author that provide further insight into the more troublesome topics on the exam.

How This Book Is Organized

This book contains 18 core chapters. The final one includes summary materials and suggestions on how to approach the exams. Each chapter covers a subset of the topics on the ICND1 exam. The chapters are organized into parts and cover the following topics:

■ **Part I: Networking Fundamentals**

— **Chapter 1, "Introduction to Computer Networking Concepts,"** provides a basic introduction in case you're new to networking.

— **Chapter 2, "The TCP/IP and OSI Networking Models,"** introduces the terminology used with two different networking architectures— Transmission Control Protocol/Internet Protocol (TCP/IP) and Open Systems Interconnection (OSI).

— **Chapter 3, "Fundamental of LANs,"** covers the concepts and terms used with the most popular option for the data link layer for local-area networks (LANs)—namely, Ethernet.

— **Chapter 4, "Fundamentals of WANs,"** covers the concepts and terms used with the most popular options for the data link layer for wide-area networks (WANs), including High-Level Data Link Control (HDLC), Point-to-Point Protocol (PPP), and Frame Relay.

— **Chapter 5, "Fundamentals of IP Addressing and Routing,"** covers the main network layer protocol for TCP/IP—Internet Protocol (IP). This chapter introduces the basics of IP, including IP addressing and routing.

— **Chapter 6, "Fundamentals of TCP/IP Transport, Applications, and Security,"** covers the main transport layer protocols for TCP/IP— Transmission Control Protocol (TCP) and User Datagram Protocol (UDP). This chapter introduces the basics of TCP and UDP.

■ **Part II: LAN Switching**

— **Chapter 7, "Ethernet LAN Switching Concepts,"** deepens and expands the introduction to LANs from Chapter 3, completing most of the conceptual materials for Ethernet in this book.

— **Chapter 8, "Operating Cisco LAN Switches,"** explains how to access, examine, and configure Cisco Catalyst LAN switches.

— **Chapter 9, "Ethernet Switch Configuration,"** shows you how to configure a variety of switch features, including duplex and speed, port security, securing the CLI, and the switch IP address.

— **Chapter 10, "Ethernet Switch Troubleshooting,"** focuses on how to tell if the switch is doing what it is supposed to, mainly through the use of **show** commands.

— **Chapter 11, "Wireless LANs,"** explains the basic operation concepts of wireless LANs, along with addressing some of the most common security concerns.

■ **Part III: IP Routing**

— **Chapter 12, "IP Addressing and Subnetting,"** completes the explanation of subnetting that was introduced in Chapter 5. More importantly, it describes in detail how to perform the math and processes to find the answers to many varieties of subnetting questions.

— **Chapter 13, "Operating Cisco Routers,"** is like Chapter 8, but with a focus on routers instead of switches.

— **Chapter 14, "Routing Protocol Concepts and Configuration,"** explains how routers forward (route) IP packets and how IP routing protocols work to find all the best routes to each subnet. This chapter includes the details of how to configure static routes and RIP version 2.

— **Chapter 15, "Troubleshooting IP Routing,"** suggests hints and tips about how to troubleshoot problems related to layer 3 routing, including a description of several troubleshooting tools.

■ **Part IV: Wide-Area Networks**

— **Chapter 16, "WAN Concepts,"** completes the conceptual materials for WANs, continuing the coverage from Chapter 4 by touching on Internet access technologies such as DSL and cable. It also covers the concepts of Network Address Translation (NAT).

— **Chapter 17, "WAN Configuration,"** completes the main technical topics, focusing on a few small WAN configuration tasks. It also covers the WAN configuration tasks and NAT configuration using Cisco Security Device Manager (SDM).

■ **Part V: Final Preparation**

— **Chapter 18, "Final Preparation,"** suggests a plan for final preparation after you have finished the core parts of the book. It also explains the many study options available in the book.

■ **Part VI: Appendixes (in the Book)**

— **Appendix A, "Answers to the "Do I Know This Already?" Quizzes,"** includes the answers to all the questions from Chapters 1 through 17.

- **Appendix B, "Decimal to Binary Conversion Table,"** lists decimal values 0 through 255, along with their binary equivalents.

- **Appendix C, "ICND1 Exam Updates,"** covers a variety of short topics that either clarify or expand on topics covered earlier in the book. This appendix is updated from time to time and is posted at http://www.ciscopress.com/ccna. The most recent version available at the time this book was published is included in this book as Appendix C. (The first page of the appendix includes instructions on how to check to see if a later version of Appendix C is available online.)

- The **glossary** defines all the terms listed in the "Definitions of Key Terms" section at the conclusion of Chapters 1 through 17.

■ **Part VII: Appendixes (on the CD)**

The following appendixes are available in PDF format on the CD that accompanies this book:

- **Appendix D, "Subnetting Practice,"** includes a large number of subnetting practice problems. It gives the answers as well as explanations of how to use the processes described in Chapter 12 to find the answers.

- **Appendix E, "Subnetting Reference Pages."** Chapter 12 explains in detail how to calculate the answers to many subnetting questions. This appendix summarizes the process of finding the answers to several key questions, with the details on a single page. The goal is to give you a handy reference page to refer to when you're practicing subnetting.

- **Appendix F, "Additional Scenarios."** One method to improve your troubleshooting and network analysis skills is to examine as many unique network scenarios as possible, think about them, and then get some feedback on whether you came to the right conclusions. This appendix provides several such scenarios.

- **Appendix G, "Subnetting Video Reference."** The DVD includes several subnetting videos that show you how to use the processes covered in Chapter 12. This appendix contains copies of the key elements from those videos, which may be useful when you're watching the videos (so that you do not have to keep moving back and forth in the video).

- **Appendix H, "Memory Tables,"** contains the key tables and lists from each chapter, with some of the content removed. You can print this appendix and, as a memory exercise, complete the tables and lists. The goal is to help you memorize facts that can be useful on the exams.

- **Appendix I, "Memory Tables Answer Key,"** contains the answer key for the exercises in Appendix H.

— **Appendix J, "ICND1 Open-Ended Questions,"** is a holdover from the previous edition of this book. The first edition had some open-ended questions to help you study for the exam, but the newer features make these questions unnecessary. For convenience, the old questions are included here, unedited since the last edition.

How to Use This Book to Prepare for the ICND1 (640–822) Exam and CCENT Certification

This book was designed with two primary goals in mind: to help you study for the ICND1 exam (and get your CCENT certification), and to help you study for the CCNA exam by using both this book and the *CCNA ICND2 Official Exam Certification Guide*. Using this book to prepare for the ICND1 exam is pretty straightforward. You read each chapter in succession and follow the study suggestions in Chapter 18.

For Chapters 1 through 17, you have some choices as to how much of the chapter you read. In some cases, you may already know most or all of the information covered in a given chapter. To help you decide how much time to spend on each chapter, the chapters begin with a "Do I Know This Already?" quiz. If you get all the quiz questions correct, or if you miss just one, you may want to skip to the "Exam Preparation Tasks" section at the end of the chapter and perform those activities. Figure I-2 shows the overall plan.

Figure I-2 *How to Approach Each Chapter of This Book*

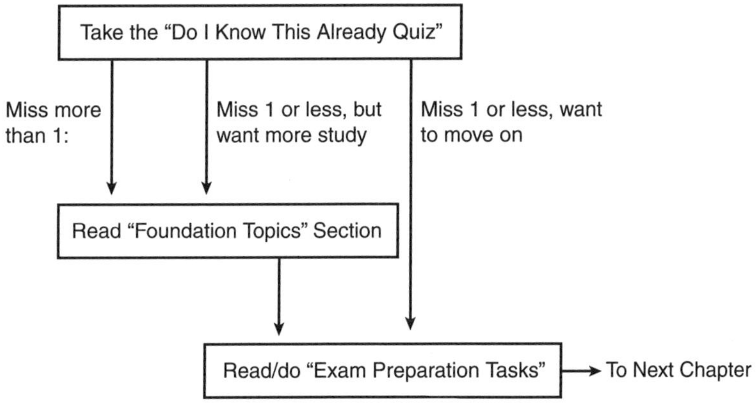

When you have completed Chapters 1 through 17, you can use the guidance listed in Chapter 18 to perform the rest of the exam preparation tasks. That chapter includes the following suggestions:

■   Check http://www.ciscopress.com for the latest copy of Appendix C, which may include additional topics for study.

- Practice subnetting using the tools available in the CD appendixes.

- Repeat the tasks in all the chapters' "Exam Preparation Tasks" chapter-ending sections.

- Review the scenarios in CD Appendix F.

- Review all the "Do I Know This Already?" questions.

- Practice the exam using the exam engine.

How to Use These Books to Prepare for the CCNA 640–802 Exam

If you plan to get your CCNA certification using the one-exam option of taking the CCNA 640-802 exam, you can use this book with the *CCNA ICND2 Official Exam Certification Guide*. If you haven't yet bought either book, you generally can get the pair cheaper by buying both books as a two-book set called the *CCNA Certification Library*.

These two books were designed to be used together when you study for the CCNA exam. You have two good options for the order in which to read the two books. The first and most obvious option is to read this book and then move on to the ICND2 book. The other option is to read all of ICND1's coverage of one topic area, and then read ICND2's coverage of the same topics, and then return to ICND1. Figure I-3 outlines my suggested plan for reading the two books.

Figure I-3 *Reading Plan When You're Studying for the CCNA Exam*

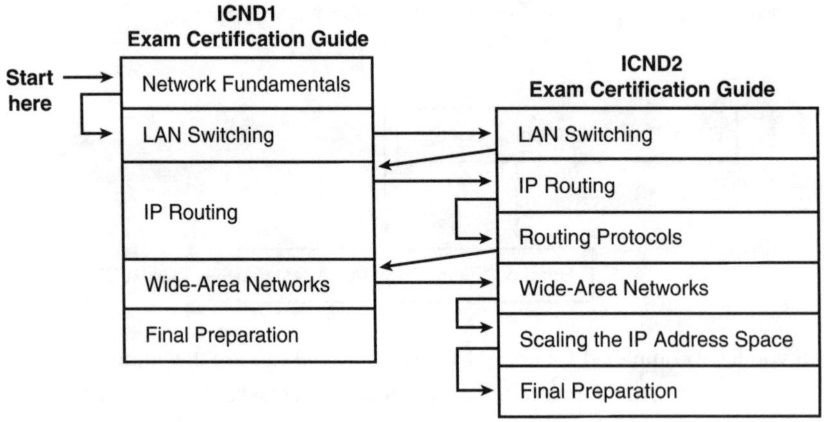

Both reading plan options have some benefits. Moving back and forth between books helps you focus on one general topic at a time. However, note that there is some overlap between the two exams, so there is some overlap between the two books as well. From reader comments about the previous edition of these books, readers who were new to networking tended to do better by completing all of the first book and then moving on to the second. Readers who had more experience and knowledge before starting the books tended to prefer following a reading plan like the one shown in Figure I-3.

Note that for final preparation, you can use the final chapter (Chapter 18) of the ICND2 book rather than the "Final Preparation" chapter (Chapter 18) of this book. Chapter 18 of ICND2 covers the same basic activities as does this book's Chapter 18, with reminders of any exam preparation materials from this book that should be useful.

In addition to the flow shown in Figure I-3, when you study for the CCNA exam (rather than the ICND1 and ICND2 exams), it is important to master IP subnetting before moving on to the IP routing and routing protocol parts of the ICND2 book. The ICND2 book does not review subnetting or the underlying math, assuming that you know how to find the answers. Those ICND2 chapters, particularly Chapter 5 ("VLSM and Route Summarization"), are much easier to understand if you can do the related subnetting math pretty easily.

For More Information

If you have any comments about this book, you can submit them via http://www.ciscopress.com. Just go to the website, select Contact Us, and enter your message.

Cisco might occasionally make changes that affect the CCNA certification. You should always check http://www.cisco.com/go/ccna and http://www.cisco.com/go/ccent for the latest details.

The CCNA certification is arguably the most important Cisco certification, although the new CCENT certification might surpass CCNA in the future. CCNA certainly is the most popular Cisco certification to date. It's required for several other certifications, and it's the first step in distinguishing yourself as someone who has proven knowledge of Cisco.

The *CCENT/CCNA ICND1 Official Exam Certification Guide* is designed to help you attain both CCENT and CCNA certification. This is the CCENT/CCNA ICND1 certification book from the only Cisco-authorized publisher. We at Cisco Press believe that this book can help you achieve CCNA certification, but the real work is up to you! I trust that your time will be well spent.

Cisco Published ICND1 Exam Topics* Covered in This Part:

Describe the operation of data networks

- Describe the purpose and functions of various network devices
- Select the components required to meet a given network specification
- Use the OSI and TCP/IP models and their associated protocols to explain how data flows in a network
- Describe common networking applications including web applications
- Describe the purpose and basic operation of the protocols in the OSI and TCP models
- Describe the impact of applications (Voice Over IP and Video Over IP) on a network
- Describe the components required for network and Internet communications
- Identify and correct common network problems at Layers 1, 2, 3, and 7 using a layered model approach

Implement an IP addressing scheme and IP services to meet network requirements for a small branch office

- Describe the need for and role of addressing in a network
- Create and apply an addressing scheme to a network
- Describe and verify DNS operation

Implement a small routed network

- Describe basic routing concepts (including: packet forwarding, router lookup process)
- Select the appropriate media, cables, ports, and connectors to connect routers to other network devices and hosts

Identify security threats to a network and describe general methods to mitigate those threats

- Explain today's increasing network security threats and the need to implement a comprehensive security policy to mitigate the threats
- Explain general methods to mitigate common security threats to network devices, hosts, and applications
- Describe the functions of common security appliances and applications
- Describe security recommended practices including initial steps to secure network devices

*Always check http://www.cisco.com for the latest posted exam topics.

Part I: Networking Fundamentals

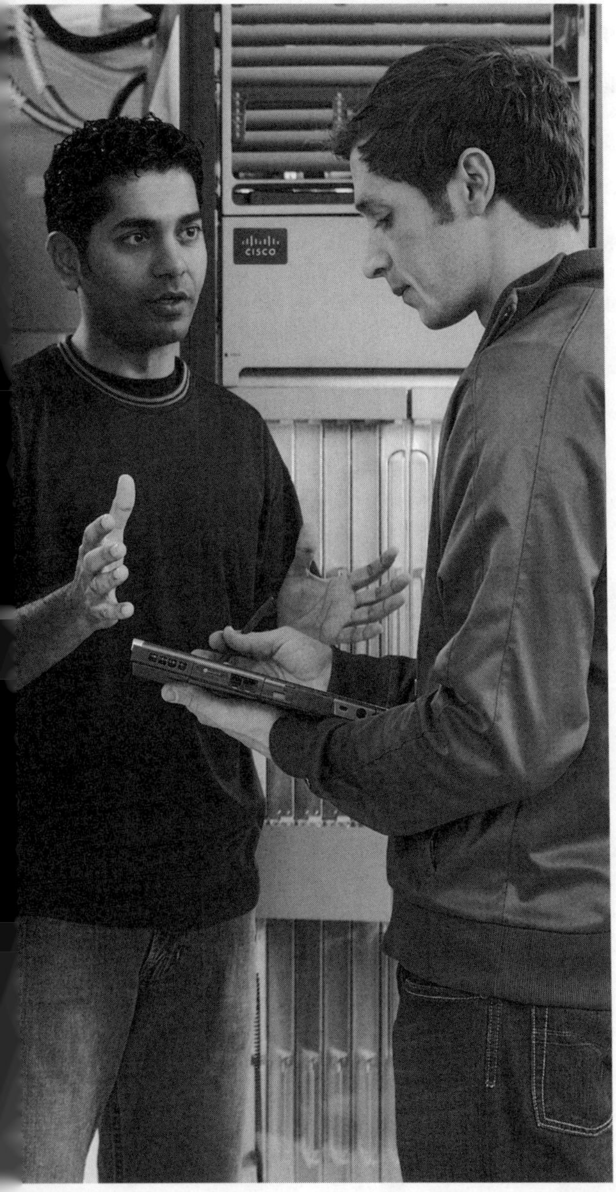
cisco

Introduction to Computer Networking Concepts

This chapter gives you a light-hearted perspective about networks, how they were originally created, and why networks work the way they do. Although no specific fact from this chapter happens to be on any of the CCNA exams, this chapter helps you prepare for the depth of topics you will start to read about in Chapter 2, "The TCP/IP and OSI Networking Models." If you are brand new to networking, this short introductory chapter will help you get ready for the details to follow. If you already understand some of the basics of TCP/IP, Ethernet, switches, routers, IP addressing, and the like, go ahead and skip on to Chapter 2. The rest of you will probably want to read through this short introductory chapter before diving into the details.

Perspectives on Networking

So, you are new to networking. You might have seen or heard about different topics relating to networking, but you are only just now getting serious about learning the details. Like many people, your perspective about networks might be that of a user of the network, as opposed to the network engineer who builds networks. For some, your view of networking might be based on how you use the Internet, from home, using a high-speed Internet connection. Others of you might use a computer at a job or at school, again connecting to the Internet; that computer is typically connected to a network via some cable. Figure 1-1 shows both perspectives of networking.

Figure 1-1 *End-User Perspective on Networks*

The top part of the figure shows a typical high-speed cable Internet user. The PC connects to a cable modem using an Ethernet cable. The cable modem then connects to a cable TV (CATV) outlet on the wall using a round coaxial cable—the same kind of cable used to connect your TV to the CATV wall outlet. Because cable Internet services provide service continuously, the user can just sit down at the PC and start sending e-mail, browsing websites, making Internet phone calls, and using other tools and applications as well.

Similarly, an employee of a company or a student at a university views the world as a connection through a wall plug. Typically, this connection uses a type of local-area network (LAN) called Ethernet. Instead of needing a cable modem, the PC connects directly to an Ethernet-style socket in a wall plate (the socket is much like the typical socket used for telephone cabling today, but the connector is a little larger). As with high-speed cable Internet connections, the Ethernet connection does not require the PC user to do anything first to connect to the network—it is always there waiting to be used, similar to the power outlet.

From the end-user perspective, whether at home, at work, or at school, what happens behind the wall plug is magic. Just as most people do not really understand how cars work, how TVs work, and so on, most people who use networks do not understand how they work. Nor do they want to! But if you have read this much into Chapter 1, you obviously have a little more interest in networking than a typical end user. By the end of this book, you will have a pretty thorough understanding of what is behind that wall plug in both cases shown in Figure 1-1.

The CCNA exams, and particularly the ICND1 (640-822) exam, focus on two major branches of networking concepts, protocols, and devices. One of these two major branches is called enterprise networking. An enterprise network is a network created by one corporation, or enterprise, for the purpose of allowing its employees to communicate. For example, Figure 1-2 shows the same type of PC end-user shown in Figure 1-1, who is now communicating with a web server through the enterprise network (represented by a cloud) created by Enterprise #2. The end-user PC can communicate with the web server to do something useful for the company—for instance, the user might be on the phone with a customer, with the user typing in the customer's new order in the ordering system that resides in the web server.

Figure 1-2 *An Example Representation of an Enterprise Network*

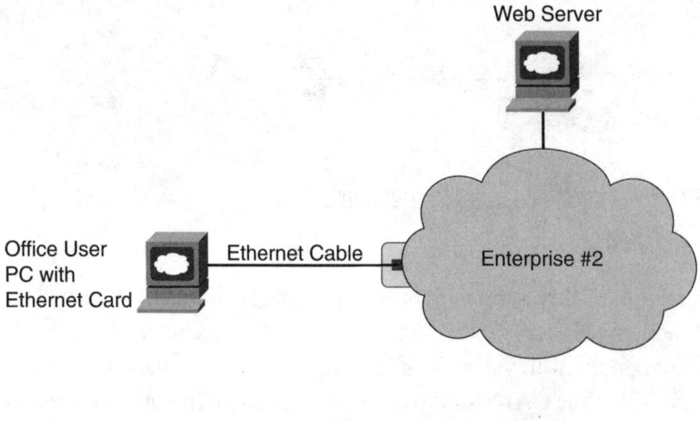

> **NOTE** In networking diagrams, a cloud represents a part of a network whose details are not important to the purpose of the diagram. In this case, Figure 1-2 ignores the details of how to create an enterprise network.

The second major branch of networking covered on the ICND1 exam is called small office/home office, or SOHO. This branch of networking uses the same concepts, protocols, and devices used to create enterprise networks, plus some additional features that are not needed for enterprises. SOHO networking allows a user to connect to the Internet using a PC and any Internet connection, such as the high-speed cable Internet connection shown in Figure 1-1. Because most enterprise networks also connect to the Internet, the SOHO user can sit at home, or in a small office, and communicate with servers at the enterprise network, as well as with other hosts in the Internet. Figure 1-3 shows the concept.

Figure 1-3 *SOHO User Connecting to the Internet and Other Enterprise Networks*

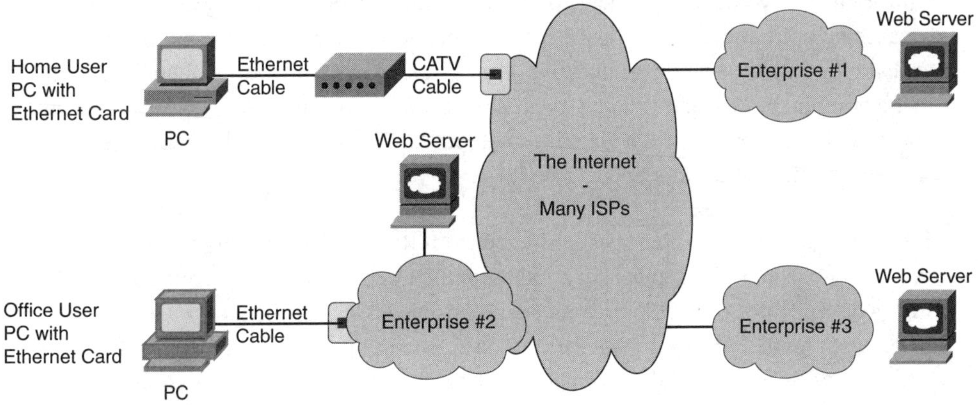

The Internet itself consists of most every enterprise network in the world, plus billions of devices connecting to the Internet directly through Internet service providers (ISPs). In fact, the term itself—Internet—is formed by shortening the phrase "interconnected networks." To create the Internet, ISPs offer Internet access, typically using either a cable TV line, a phone line using digital subscriber line (DSL) technology, or a telephone line with a modem. Each enterprise typically connects to at least one ISP, using permanent connections generally called wide-area network (WAN) links. Finally, the ISPs of the world also connect to each other. These interconnected networks—from the smallest single-PC home network, to cell phones and MP3 players, to enterprise networks with thousands of devices—all connect to the global Internet.

Most of the details about standards for enterprise networks were created in the last quarter of the 20th century. You might have become interested in networking after most of the conventions and rules used for basic networking were created. However, you might understand the networking rules and conventions more easily if you take the time to pause and think about what you would do if you were creating these standards. The next section takes you through a somewhat silly example of thinking through some imaginary early networking standards, but this example has real value in terms of exploring some of the basic concepts behind enterprise networking and some of the design trade-offs.

The Flintstones Network: The First Computer Network?

The Flintstones are a cartoon family that, according to the cartoon, lived in prehistoric times. Because I want to discuss the thought process behind some imaginary initial networking standards, the Flintstones seem to be the right group of people to put in the example.

Fred is the president of FredsCo, where his wife (Wilma), buddy (Barney), and buddy's wife (Betty) all work. They all have phones and computers, but they have no network because no one has ever made up the idea of a network before. Fred sees all his employees exchanging data by running around giving each other disks with files on them, and it seems inefficient. So, Fred, being a visionary, imagines a world in which people can connect their computers somehow and exchange files, without having to leave their desks. The (imaginary) first network is about to be born.

Fred's daughter, Pebbles, has just graduated from Rockville University and wants to join the family business. Fred gives her a job, with the title First-Ever Network Engineer. Fred says to Pebbles, "Pebbles, I want everyone to be able to exchange files without having to get up from their desks. I want them to be able to simply type in the name of a file and the name of the person, and poof! The file appears on the other person's computer. And because everyone changes departments so often around here, I want the workers to be able to take their PCs with them and just have to plug the computer into a wall socket so that they can send and receive files from the new office to which they moved. I want this network thing to be like the electrical power thing your boyfriend, Bamm-Bamm, created for us last year—a plug in the wall near every desk, and if you plug in, you are on the network!"

Pebbles first decides to do some research and development. If she can get two PCs to transfer files in a lab, then she ought to be able to get all the PCs to transfer files, right? She writes a program called Fred's Transfer Program, or FTP, in honor of her father.

The program uses a new networking card that Pebbles built in the lab. This networking card uses a cable with two wires in it—one wire to send bits and one wire to receive bits. Pebbles puts one card in each of the two computers and cables the computers together with a cable with two wires in it. The FTP software on each computer sends the bits that comprise the files by using the networking cards. If Pebbles types a command such as **ftp send filename**, the software transfers the file called filename to the computer at the other end of the cable. Figure 1-4 depicts the first network test at FredsCo.

Figure 1-4 *Two PCs Transfer Files in the Lab*

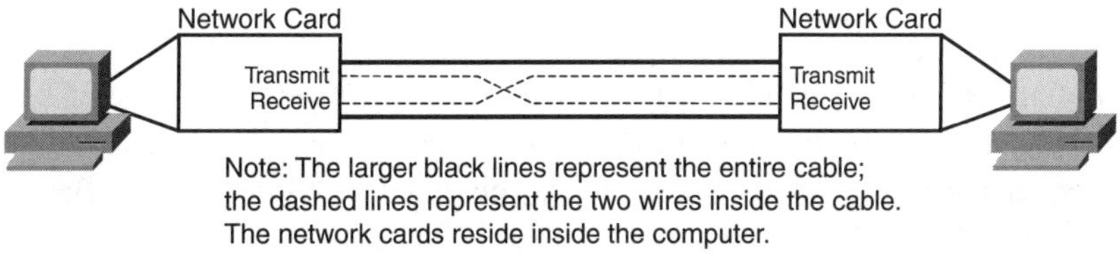

Pebbles' new networking cards use wire 1 to send bits and wire 2 to receive bits, so the cable used by Pebbles connects wire 1 on PC1 to wire 2 on PC2, and vice versa. That way, both cards can send bits using wire 1, and those bits will enter the other PC on the other PC's wire 2.

Bamm-Bamm stops by to give Pebbles some help after hearing about the successful test. "I am ready to start deploying the network!" she exclaims. Bamm-Bamm, the wizened one-year veteran of FredsCo who graduated from Rockville University a year before Pebbles, starts asking some questions. "What happens when you want to connect three computers together?" he asks. Pebbles explains that she can put two networking cards in each computer and cable each computer to each other. "So what happens when you connect 100 computers to the network, in each building?" Pebbles then realizes that she has a little more work to do. She needs a scheme that allows her network to scale to more than two users. Bamm-Bamm then offers a suggestion, "We ran all the electrical power cables from the wall plug at each cube back to the broom closet. We just send electricity from the closet out to the wall plug near every desk. Maybe if you did something similar, you could find a way to somehow make it all work."

With that bit of input, Pebbles has all the inspiration she needs. Emboldened by the fact that she has already created the world's first PC networking card, she decides to create a device that will allow cabling similar to Bamm-Bamm's electrical cabling plan. Pebble's solution to this first major hurdle is shown in Figure 1-5.

Figure 1-5   *Star Cabling to a Repeater*

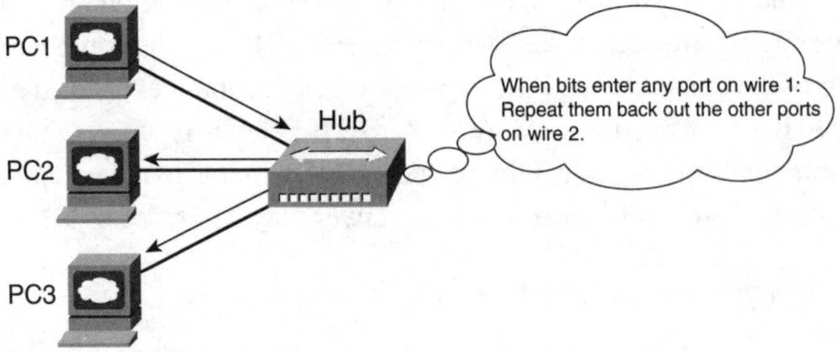

Pebbles follows Bamm-Bamm's advice about the cabling. However, she needs a device into which she can plug the cables—something that will take the bits sent by a PC, and reflect, or repeat, the bits back to all the other devices connected to this new device. Because the networking cards send bits using wire 1, Pebbles builds this new device in such a way that when it receives bits coming in wire 1 on one of its ports, it repeats the same bits, but repeats them out wire 2 on all the other ports, so that the other PCs get those bits on the receive wire. (Therefore, the cabling does not have to swap wires 1 and 2—this new device takes care of that.) And because she is making this up for the very first time in history, she needs to decide on a name for this new device: She names the device a hub.

Before deploying the first hub and running a bunch of cables, Pebbles does the right thing: She tests it in a lab, with three PCs connected to the world's first hub. She starts FTP on PC1, transfers the file called recipe.doc, and sees a window pop up on PC2 saying that the file was received, just like normal. "Fantastic!" she thinks, until she realizes that PC3 also has the same pop-up window on it. She has transferred the file to both PC2 and PC3! "Of course!" she thinks. "If the hub repeats everything out every cable connected to it, then when my FTP program sends a file, everyone will get it. I need a way for FTP to send a file to a specific PC!"

At this point, Pebbles thinks of a few different options. First, she thinks that she will give each computer the same name as the first name of the person using the computer. She will then change FTP to put the name of the PC that the file was being sent to in front of the file contents. In other words, to send her mom a recipe, she will use the **ftp Wilma recipe.doc** command. So, even though each PC will receive the bits because the hub repeats the signal to everyone connected to it, only the PC whose name is the one in front of the file should actually create the file. Then her dad walks in: "Pebbles, I want you to meet Barney Fife, our new head of security. He needs a network connection as well—you are going to be finished soon, right?"

So much for using first names for the computers, now that there are two people named Barney at FredsCo. Pebbles, being mathematically inclined and in charge of creating all the hardware, decides on a different approach. "I will put a unique numeric address on each networking card—a four-digit decimal number," she exclaims. Because Pebbles created all the cards, she will make sure that the number used on each card is unique. Also, with a four-digit number, she will never run out of unique numbers—she has 10,000 (10^4) to choose from and only 200 employees at FredsCo.

By the way, because she is making all this up for the very first time, Pebbles calls these built-in numbers on the cards *addresses*. When anyone wants to send a file, they can just use the **ftp** command, but with a number instead of a name. For instance, **ftp 0002 recipe.doc** will send the recipe.doc file to the PC whose network card has the address 0002. Figure 1-6 depicts the new environment in the lab.

Figure 1-6 *The First Network Addressing Convention*

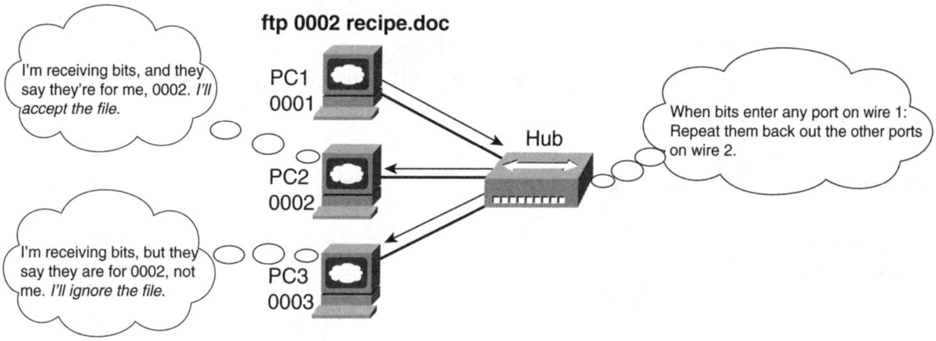

Now, with some minor updates to the Fred Transfer Program, the user can type **ftp 0002 recipe.doc** to send the file recipe.doc to the PC with address 0002. Pebbles tests the software and hardware in the lab again, and although the hub forwards the frames from PC1 to both PC2 and PC3, only PC2 processes the frames and creates a copy of the file. Similarly, when Pebbles sends the file to address 0003, only PC3 processes the received frames and creates a file. She is now ready to deploy the first computer network.

Pebbles now needs to build all the hardware required for the network. She first creates 200 network cards, each with a unique address. She installs the FTP program on all 200 PCs and installs the cards in each PC. Then she goes back to the lab and starts planning how many cables she will need and how long each cable should be. At this point, Pebbles realizes that she will need to run some cables a long way. If she puts the hub in the bottom floor of building A, the PCs on the fifth floor of building B will need a really long cable to connect to the hub. Cables cost money, and the longer the cable is, the more expensive the cable is. Besides, she has not yet tested the network with longer cables; she has been using cables that are only a couple of meters long.

Bamm-Bamm walks by and sees that Pebbles is stressed. Pebbles vents a little: "Daddy wants this project finished, and you know how demanding he is. And I didn't think about how long the cables will be—I will be way over budget. And I will be installing cables for weeks!" Bamm-Bamm, being a little less stressed, having just come from a lunchtime workout at the club, knows that Pebbles already has the solution—she is too stressed to see it. Of course, the solution is not terribly different from how Bamm-Bamm solved a similar problem with the electrical cabling last year. "Those hubs repeat everything they hear, right? So, why not make a bunch of hubs. Put one hub on each floor, and run cables from all the PCs. Then run one cable from the hub on each floor to a hub on the first floor. Then, run one cable between the two main hubs in the two buildings. Because they repeat everything, every PC should receive the signal when just one PC sends, whether they are attached to the same hub or are four hubs away." Figure 1-7 depicts Bamm-Bamm's suggested design.

Figure 1-7 *Per-Floor Hubs, Connected Together*

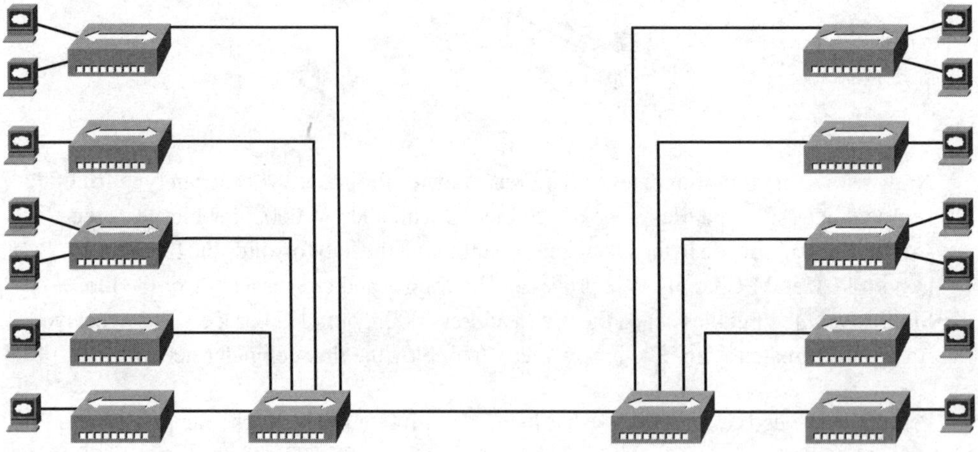

Pebbles loves the idea. She builds and connects the new hubs in the lab, just to prove the concept. It works! She makes the (now shorter) cables, installs the hubs and cables, and is ready to test. She goes to a few representative PCs and tests, and it all works! The first network has now been deployed.

Wanting to surprise Poppa Fred, Pebbles writes a memo to everyone in the company, telling them how to use the soon-to-be-famous Fred Transfer Program to transfer files. Along with the memo, she puts a list of names of people and the four-digit network address to be used to send files to each PC. She puts the memos in everyone's mail slot and waits for the excitement to start.

Amazingly, it all works. The users are happy. Fred treats Pebbles and Bamm-Bamm to a nice dinner—at home, cooked by Wilma, but a good meal nonetheless.

Pebbles thinks she did it—created the world's first computer network, with no problems—until a few weeks pass. "I can't send files to Fred anymore!" exclaims Barney Rubble. "Ever since Fred got that new computer, he is too busy to go bowling, and now I can't even send files to him to tell him how much we need him back on the bowling team!" Then it hits Pebbles—Fred had just received a new PC and a new networking card. Fred's network address has changed. If the card fails and it has to be replaced, the address changes.

About that time, Wilma comes in to say hi. "I love that new network thing you built. Betty and I can type notes to each other, put them in a file, and send them anytime. It is almost like working on the same floor!" she says. "But I really don't remember the numbers so well. Couldn't you make that FTP thing work with names instead of addresses?"

In a fit of inspiration, Pebbles sees the answer to the first problem in the solution to her mom's problem. "I will change FTP to use names instead of addresses. I will make everyone tell me what name they want to use—maybe Barney Rubble will use BarneyR, and Barney Fife will use BarneyF, for instance. I will change FTP to accept names as well as numbers. Then I will tell FTP to look in a table that I will put on each PC that correlates the names to the numeric addresses. That way, if I ever need to replace a LAN card, all I have to do is update the list of names and addresses and put a copy on everyone's PC, and no one will know that anything has changed!" Table 1-1 lists Pebbles' first name table.

Table 1-1 *Pebbles' First Name/Address Table*

Person's Name	Computer Name	Network Address
Fred Flintstone	Fred	0001
Wilma Flintstone	Wilma	0002
Barney Rubble	BarneyR	0011
Betty Rubble	Betty	0012
Barney Fife	BarneyF	0022
Pebbles Flintstone	Netguru	0030
Bamm-Bamm Rubble	Electrical-guy	0040

Pebbles tries out the new FTP program and name/address table in the lab, and it works. She deploys the new FTP software, puts the name table on everyone's PC, and sends another memo. Now she can accommodate changes easily by separating the physical details, such as addresses on the networking cards, from what the end users need to know.

Like all good network engineers, Pebbles thought through the design and tested it in a lab before deploying the network. For the problems she did not anticipate, she found a reasonable solution to get around the problem.

So ends the story of the obviously contrived imaginary first computer network. What purpose did this silly example really serve? First, you have now been forced to think about some basic design issues that confronted the people who created the networking tools that you will be learning about for the CCNA exams. Although the example with Pebbles might have been fun, the problems that she faced are the same problems faced—and solved—by the people who created the original networking protocols and products.

The other big benefit to this story, particularly for those of you brand new to networking, is that you already know some of the more important concepts in networking:

Ethernet networks use cards inside each computer.

The cards have unique numeric addresses, similar to Pebbles' networking cards.

Ethernet cables connect PCs to Ethernet hubs—hubs that repeat each received signal out all other ports.

The cabling is typically run in a star configuration—in other words, all cables run from a cubicle to a wiring (not broom!) closet.

Applications such as the contrived Fred Transfer Program or the real-life File Transfer Protocol (FTP) ask the underlying hardware to transfer the contents of files. Users can use names—for instance, you might surf a website called www.fredsco.com—but the name gets translated into the correct address.

Now on to the real chapters, with real protocols and devices, with topics that you could see on the ICND1 exam.

This chapter covers the following subjects:

The TCP/IP Protocol Architecture: This section explains the terminology and concepts behind the world's most popular networking model, TCP/IP.

The OSI Reference Model: This section explains the terminology behind the OSI networking model in comparison to TCP/IP.

CHAPTER 2

The TCP/IP and OSI Networking Models

The term *networking model*, or *networking architecture*, refers to an organized set of documents. Individually, these documents describe one small function required for a network. These documents may define a protocol, which is a set of logical rules that devices must follow to communicate. Other documents may define some physical requirements for networking, for example, it may define the voltage and current levels used on a particular cable. Collectively, the documents referenced in a networking model define all the details of how to create a complete working network.

To create a working network, the devices in that network need to follow the details referenced by a particular networking model. When multiple computers and other networking devices implement these protocols, physical specifications, and rules, and the devices are then connected correctly, the computers can successfully communicate.

You can think of a networking model as you think of a set of architectural plans for building a house. Sure, you can build a house without the architectural plans, but it will work better if you follow the plans. And because you probably have a lot of different people working on building your house, such as framers, electricians, bricklayers, painters, and so on, it helps if they can all reference the same plan. Similarly, you could build your own network, write your own software, build your own networking cards, and create a network without using any existing networking model. However, it is much easier to simply buy and use products that already conform to some well-known networking model. And because the networking product vendors use the same networking model, their products should work well together.

The CCNA exams include detailed coverage of one networking model—the Transmission Control Protocol/Internet Protocol, or TCP/IP. TCP/IP is the most pervasively used networking model in the history of networking. You can find support for TCP/IP on practically every computer operating system in existence today, from mobile phones to mainframe computers. Almost every network built using Cisco products today supports TCP/IP. Not surprisingly, the CCNA exams focus heavily on TCP/IP.

The ICND1 exam, and the ICND2 exam to a small extent, also covers a second networking model, called the Open System Interconnection (OSI) reference model. Historically, OSI was the first large effort to create a vendor-neutral networking model, a model that was intended to be used by any and every computer in the world. Because OSI was the first major effort to create a vendor-neutral networking architectural model, many of the terms used in networking today come from the OSI model.

"Do I Know This Already?" Quiz

The "Do I Know This Already?" quiz allows you to assess if you should read the entire chapter. If you miss no more than one of these 10 self-assessment questions, you might want to move ahead to the "Exam Preparation Tasks" section. Table 2-1 lists the major headings in this chapter and the "Do I Know This Already?" quiz questions covering the material in those headings so you can assess your knowledge of these specific areas. The answers to the "Do I Know This Already?" quiz appear in Appendix A.

Table 2-1   *"Do I Know This Already?" Foundation Topics Section-to-Question Mapping*

Foundation Topics Section	Questions
The TCP/IP Protocol Architecture	1–6
The OSI Reference Model	7–10

1. Which of the following protocols are examples of TCP/IP transport layer protocols?

    a.   Ethernet

    b.   HTTP

    c.   IP

    d.   UDP

    e.   SMTP

    f.   TCP

2. Which of the following protocols are examples of TCP/IP network access layer protocols?

    a.   Ethernet

    b.   HTTP

    c.   IP

    d.   UDP

    e.   SMTP

   f. TCP

   g. PPP

3. The process of HTTP asking TCP to send some data and make sure that it is received correctly is an example of what?

   a. Same-layer interaction

   b. Adjacent-layer interaction

   c. The OSI model

   d. All the other answers are correct.

4. The process of TCP on one computer marking a segment as segment 1, and the receiving computer then acknowledging the receipt of segment 1, is an example of what?

   a. Data encapsulation

   b. Same-layer interaction

   c. Adjacent-layer interaction

   d. The OSI model

   e. None of these answers are correct.

5. The process of a web server adding a TCP header to a web page, followed by adding an IP header, and then a data link header and trailer is an example of what?

   a. Data encapsulation

   b. Same-layer interaction

   c. The OSI model

   d. All of these answers are correct.

6. Which of the following terms is used specifically to identify the entity that is created when encapsulating data inside data link layer headers and trailers?

   a. Data

   b. Chunk

   c. Segment

   d. Frame

   e. Packet

   f. None of these—there is no encapsulation by the data link layer.

7. Which OSI layer defines the functions of logical network-wide addressing and routing?

    a. Layer 1

    b. Layer 2

    c. Layer 3

    d. Layer 4

    e. Layer 5

    f. Layer 6

    g. Layer 7

8. Which OSI layer defines the standards for cabling and connectors?

    a. Layer 1

    b. Layer 2

    c. Layer 3

    d. Layer 4

    e. Layer 5

    f. Layer 6

    g. Layer 7

9. Which OSI layer defines the standards for data formats and encryption?

    a. Layer 1

    b. Layer 2

    c. Layer 3

    d. Layer 4

    e. Layer 5

    f. Layer 6

    g. Layer 7

10. Which of the following terms are not valid terms for the names of the seven OSI layers?

    a. Application

    b. Data link

    c. Transmission

    d. Presentation

    e. Internet

    f. Session

Foundation Topics

It is practically impossible to find a computer today that does not support the set of networking protocols called TCP/IP. Every Microsoft, Linux, and UNIX operating system includes support for TCP/IP. Hand-held digital assistants and cell phones support TCP/IP. And because Cisco sells products that create the infrastructure that allows all of these computers to talk with each other using TCP/IP, Cisco products also include extensive support for TCP/IP.

The world has not always been so simple. Once upon a time, there were no networking protocols, including TCP/IP. Vendors created the first networking protocols; these protocols supported only that vendor's computers, and the details were not even published to the public. As time went on, vendors formalized and published their networking protocols, enabling other vendors to create products that could communicate with their computers. For instance, IBM published its Systems Network Architecture (SNA) networking model in 1974. After SNA was published, other computer vendors created products that allowed their computers to communicate with IBM computers using SNA. This solution worked, but it had some negatives, including the fact that it meant that the larger computer vendors tended to rule the networking market.

A better solution was to create an open standardized networking model that all vendors would support. The International Organization for Standardization (ISO) took on this task starting as early as the late 1970s, beginning work on what would become known as the Open System Interconnection (OSI) networking model. ISO had a noble goal for the OSI model: to standardize data networking protocols to allow communication between all computers across the entire planet. ISO worked toward this ambitious and noble goal, with participants from most of the technologically developed nations on Earth participating in the process.

A second, less formal effort to create a standardized, public networking model sprouted forth from a U.S. Defense Department contract. Researchers at various universities volunteered to help further develop the protocols surrounding the original department's work. These efforts resulted in a competing networking model called TCP/IP.

By the late 1980s, the world had many competing vendor-proprietary networking models plus two competing standardized networking models. So what happened? TCP/IP won in the end. Proprietary protocols are still in use today in many networks, but much less so than in the 1980s and 1990s. The OSI model, whose development suffered in part because of a slower formal standardization process as compared with TCP/IP, never succeeded in the marketplace. And TCP/IP, the networking model created almost entirely by a bunch of volunteers, has become the most prolific set of data networking protocols ever.

In this chapter, you will read about some of the basics of TCP/IP. Although you will learn some interesting facts about TCP/IP, the true goal of this chapter is to help you understand what a networking model or networking architecture really is and how one works.

Also in this chapter, you will learn about some of the jargon used with OSI. Will any of you ever work on a computer that is using the full OSI protocols instead of TCP/IP? Probably not. However, you will often use terms relating to OSI. Also, the ICND1 exam covers the basics of OSI, so this chapter also covers OSI to prepare you for questions about it on the exam.

The TCP/IP Protocol Architecture

TCP/IP defines a large collection of protocols that allow computers to communicate. TCP/IP defines the details of each of these protocols inside documents called Requests for Comments (RFC). By implementing the required protocols defined in TCP/IP RFCs, a computer can be relatively confident that it can communicate with other computers that also implement TCP/IP.

An easy comparison can be made between telephones and computers that use TCP/IP. You go to the store and buy a phone from one of a dozen different vendors. When you get home and plug in the phone to the same cable in which your old phone was connected, the new phone works. The phone vendors know the standards for phones in their country and build their phones to match those standards. Similarly, a computer that implements the standard networking protocols defined by TCP/IP can communicate with other computers that also use the TCP/IP standards.

Like other networking architectures, TCP/IP classifies the various protocols into different categories or layers. Table 2-2 outlines the main categories in the TCP/IP architectural model.

Table 2-2   *TCP/IP Architectural Model and Example Protocols*

TCP/IP Architecture Layer	Example Protocols
Application	HTTP, POP3, SMTP
Transport	TCP, UDP
Internet	IP
Network access	Ethernet, Frame Relay

The TCP/IP model represented in column 1 of the table lists the four layers of TCP/IP, and column 2 of the table lists several of the most popular TCP/IP protocols. If someone makes up a new application, the protocols used directly by the application would be considered to be application layer protocols. For example, when the World Wide Web (WWW) was first created, a new application layer protocol was created for the purpose of asking for web pages and receiving the contents of the web pages. Similarly, the network access layer includes protocols and standards such as Ethernet. If someone makes up a new type of LAN, those protocols would be considered to be a part of the network access layer. In the next several sections, you will learn the basics about each of these four layers in the TCP/IP architecture and how they work together.

The TCP/IP Application Layer

TCP/IP application layer protocols provide services to the application software running on a computer. The application layer does not define the application itself, but rather it defines services that applications need—such as the capability to transfer a file in the case of HTTP. In short, the application layer provides an interface between software running on a computer and the network itself.

Arguably, the most popular TCP/IP application today is the web browser. Many major software vendors either have already changed or are changing their software to support access from a web browser. And thankfully, using a web browser is easy—you start a web browser on your computer and select a website by typing in the name of the website, and the web page appears.

What really happens to allow that web page to appear on your web browser?

Imagine that Bob opens his browser. His browser has been configured to automatically ask for web server Larry's default web page, or *home page*. The general logic looks like that in Figure 2-1.

Figure 2-1 *Basic Application Logic to Get a Web Page*

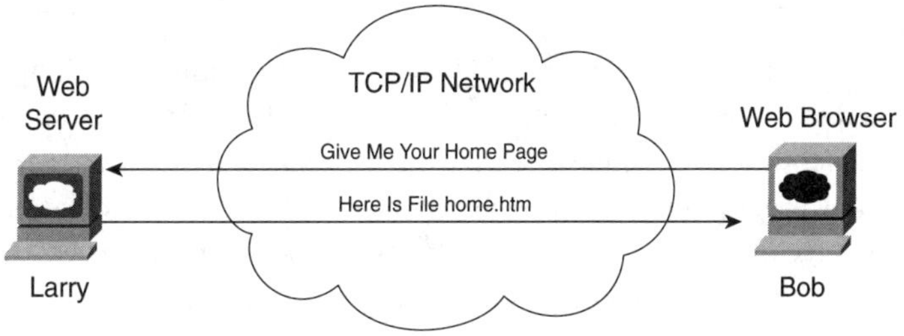

So what really happened? Bob's initial request actually asks Larry to send his home page back to Bob. Larry's web server software has been configured to know that the default web page is contained in a file called home.htm. Bob receives the file from Larry and displays the contents of the file in the web browser window.

Taking a closer look, this example uses two TCP/IP application layer protocols. First, the request for the file and the actual transfer of the file are performed according to the Hypertext Transfer Protocol (HTTP). Many of you have probably noticed that most websites' URLs—universal resource locators (often called web addresses), the text that identifies web pages—begin with the letters "http," to imply that HTTP will be used to transfer the web pages.

The other protocol used is the Hypertext Markup Language (HTML). HTML is one of many specifications that define how Bob's web browser should interpret the text inside the file he just received. For instance, the file might contain directions about making certain text be a certain size, color, and so on. In most cases, the file also includes directions about other files that Bob's web browser should get—files that contain such things as pictures and animation. HTTP would then be used to get those additional files from Larry, the web server.

A closer look at how Bob and Larry cooperate in this example reveals some details about how networking protocols work. Consider Figure 2-2, which simply revises Figure 2-1, showing the locations of HTTP headers and data.

Figure 2-2 *HTTP Get Request and HTTP Reply*

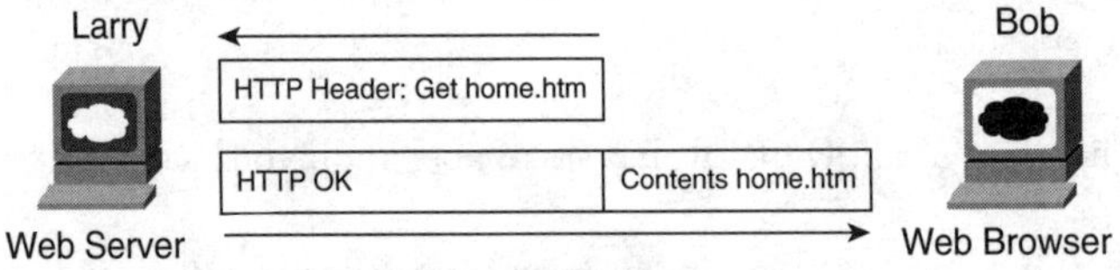

To get the web page from Larry, Bob sends something called an HTTP header to Larry. This header includes the command to "get" a file. The request typically contains the name of the file (home.htm in this case), or, if no filename is mentioned, the web server assumes that Bob wants the default web page.

The response from Larry includes an HTTP header as well, with something as simple as "OK" returned in the header. In reality, the header includes an HTTP return code, which indicates whether the request can be serviced. For instance, if you have ever looked for a web page that was not found, then you received an HTTP 404 "not found" error, which means that you received an HTTP return code of 404. When the requested file is found, the return code is 200, meaning that the request is being processed.

This simple example between Bob and Larry introduces one of the most important general concepts behind networking models: when a particular layer on one computer wants to communicate with the same layer on another computer, the two computers use headers to hold the information that they want to communicate. The headers are part of what is transmitted between the two computers. This process is called *same-layer interaction*.

The application layer protocol (HTTP, in this case) on Bob is communicating with Larry's application layer. They each do so by creating and sending application layer headers to each other—sometimes with application data following the header and sometimes not, as seen in Figure 2-2. Regardless of what the application layer protocol happens to be, they all use the same general concept of communicating with the application layer on the other computer using application layer headers.

TCP/IP application layer protocols provide services to the application software running on a computer. The application layer does not define the application itself, but rather it defines services that applications need, such as the ability to transfer a file in the case of HTTP. In short, the application layer provides an interface between software running on a computer and the network itself.

The TCP/IP Transport Layer

The TCP/IP application layer includes a relatively large number of protocols, with HTTP being only one of those. The TCP/IP transport layer consists of two main protocol options: the *Transmission Control Protocol* (TCP) and the *User Datagram Protocol* (UDP). To get a true appreciation for what TCP/IP transport layer protocols do, read Chapter 6, "Fundamentals of TCP/IP Transport, Applications, and Security." However, in this section, you will learn about one of the key features of TCP, which enables us to cover some more general concepts about how networking models behave.

To appreciate what the transport layer protocols do, you must think about the layer above the transport layer, the application layer. Why? Well, each layer provides a service to the layer above it. For example, in Figure 2-2, Bob and Larry used HTTP to transfer the home page from Larry to Bob. But what would have happened if Bob's HTTP get request had been lost in transit through the TCP/IP network? Or, what would have happened if Larry's response, which included the contents of the home page, had been lost? Well, as you might expect, in either case the page would not have shown up in Bob's browser.

So, TCP/IP needs a mechanism to guarantee delivery of data across a network. Because many application layer protocols probably want a way to guarantee delivery of data across a network, TCP provides an error-recovery feature to the application protocols by using acknowledgments. Figure 2-3 outlines the basic acknowledgment logic.

NOTE The data shown in the rectangles in Figure 2-3, which includes the transport layer header and its encapsulated data, is called a *segment*.

Figure 2-3   *TCP Services Provided to HTTP*

As Figure 2-3 shows, the HTTP software asks for TCP to reliably deliver the HTTP get request. TCP sends the HTTP data from Bob to Larry, and the data arrives successfully. Larry's TCP software acknowledges receipt of the data and also gives the HTTP get request to the web server software. The reverse happens with Larry's response, which also arrives at Bob successfully.

Of course, the benefits of TCP error recovery cannot be seen unless the data is lost. (Chapter 6 shows an example of how TCP recovers lost data.) For now, assume that if either transmission in Figure 2-3 were lost, HTTP would not take any direct action, but TCP would resend the data and ensure that it was received successfully. This example demonstrates a function called *adjacent-layer interaction*, which defines the concepts of how adjacent layers in a networking model, on the same computer, work together. The higher-layer protocol (HTTP) needs to do something it cannot do (error recovery). So, the higher layer asks for the next lower-layer protocol (TCP) to perform the service, and the next lower layer performs the service. The lower layer provides a service to the layer above it. Table 2-3 summarizes the key points about how adjacent layers work together on a single computer and how one layer on one computer works with the same networking layer on another computer.

Table 2-3   *Summary: Same-Layer and Adjacent-Layer Interactions*

Key Topic

Concept	Description
Same-layer interaction on different computers	The two computers use a protocol to communicate with the same layer on another computer. The protocol defined by each layer uses a header that is transmitted between the computers, to communicate what each computer wants to do.
Adjacent-layer interaction on the same computer	On a single computer, one layer provides a service to a higher layer. The software or hardware that implements the higher layer requests that the next lower layer perform the needed function.

All the examples describing the application and transport layers ignored many details relating to the physical network. The application and transport layers work the same way regardless of whether the endpoint host computers are on the same LAN or are separated by the entire Internet. The lower two layers of TCP/IP, the internet layer and the network access layer, must understand the underlying physical network because they define the protocols used to deliver the data from one host to another.

The TCP/IP Internet Layer

Imagine that you just wrote a letter to your favorite person on the other side of the country and that you also wrote a letter to someone on the other side of town. It is time to send the letters. Is there much difference in how you treat each letter? Not really. You put a different address on the envelope for each letter because the letters need to go to two different places. You put stamps on both letters and put them in the same mailbox. The postal service takes care of all the details of figuring out how to get each letter to the right place, whether it is across town or across the country.

When the postal service processes the cross-country letter, it sends the letter to another post office, then another, and so on, until the letter gets delivered across the country. The local letter might go to the post office in your town and then simply be delivered to your friend across town, without going to another post office.

So what does this all matter to networking? Well, the internet layer of the TCP/IP networking model, primarily defined by the *Internet Protocol* (IP), works much like the postal service. IP defines addresses so that each host computer can have a different IP address, just as the postal service defines addressing that allows unique addresses for each house, apartment, and business. Similarly, IP defines the process of routing so that devices called routers can choose where to send packets of data so that they are delivered to the correct destination. Just as the postal service created the necessary infrastructure to be able to deliver letters—post offices, sorting machines, trucks, planes, and personnel—the internet layer defines the details of how a network infrastructure should be created so that the network can deliver data to all computers in the network.

Chapter 5, "Fundamentals of IP Addressing and Routing," describes the TCP/IP internet layer further, with other details scattered throughout this book and the *CCNA ICND2 Official Exam Certification Guide*. But to help you understand the basics of the internet layer, take a look at Bob's request for Larry's home page, now with some information about IP, in Figure 2-4. The LAN cabling details are not important for this figure, so both LANs simply are represented by the lines shown near Bob and Larry, respectively. When Bob sends the data, he is sending an IP packet, which includes the IP header, the transport layer header (TCP, in this example), the application header (HTTP, in this case), and any application data (none, in this case). The IP header includes both a source and a destination

IP address field, with Larry's IP address (1.1.1.1) as the destination address and Bob's IP address (2.2.2.2) as the source.

Figure 2-4 *IP Services Provided to TCP*

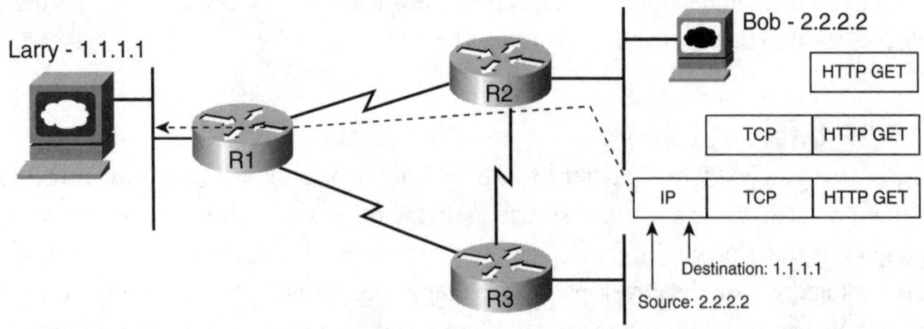

> **NOTE**   The data shown in the bottom rectangle in Figure 2-4, which includes the internet layer header and its encapsulated data, is called a *packet*.

Bob sends the packet to R2. R2 then examines the destination IP address (1.1.1.1) and makes a routing decision to send the packet to R1, because R2 knows enough about the network topology to know that 1.1.1.1 (Larry) is on the other side of R1. Similarly, when R1 gets the packet, it forwards the packet over the Ethernet to Larry. And if the link between R2 and R1 fails, IP allows R2 to learn of the alternate route through R3 to reach 1.1.1.1.

IP defines logical addresses, called *IP addresses*, which allow each TCP/IP-speaking device (called IP hosts) to have an address with which to communicate. IP also defines routing, the process of how a router should forward, or route, packets of data.

All the CCNA exams cover IP fairly deeply. For the ICND1 exam, this book's Chapter 5 covers more of the basics, with Chapters 11 through 15 covering IP in much more detail.

The TCP/IP Network Access Layer

The network access layer defines the protocols and hardware required to deliver data across some physical network. The term *network access* refers to the fact that this layer defines how to physically connect a host computer to the physical media over which data can be transmitted. For instance, Ethernet is one example protocol at the TCP/IP network access layer. Ethernet defines the required cabling, addressing, and protocols used to create an Ethernet LAN. Likewise, the connectors, cables, voltage levels, and protocols used to deliver data across WAN links are defined in a variety of other protocols that also fall into the network access layer. Chapters 3 and 4 cover the fundamentals of LANs and WANs, respectively.

Just like every layer in any networking model, the TCP/IP network access layer provides services to the layer above it in the model. The best way to understand the basics of the TCP/IP network access layer is to examine the services that it provides to IP. IP relies on the network access layer to deliver IP packets across a physical network. IP understands the overall network topology, things such as which routers are connected to each other, which host computers are connected to which physical networks, and what the IP addressing scheme looks like. However, the IP protocol purposefully does not include the details about each of the underlying physical networks. Therefore, the Internet layer, as implemented by IP, uses the services of the network access layer to deliver the packets over each physical network, respectively.

The network access layer includes a large number of protocols. For instance, the network access layer includes all the variations of Ethernet protocols and other LAN standards. This layer also includes the popular WAN standards, such as the Point-to-Point Protocol (PPP) and Frame Relay. The same familiar network is shown in Figure 2-5, with Ethernet and PPP used as the two network access layer protocols.

Figure 2-5   *Ethernet and PPP Services Provided to IP*

NOTE   The data shown in several of the rectangles in Figure 2-5—those including the Ethernet header/trailer and PPP header/trailer—are called *frames*.

To fully appreciate Figure 2-5, first think a little more deeply about how IP accomplishes its goal of delivering the packet from Bob to Larry. To send a packet to Larry, Bob sends the IP packet to router R2. To do so, Bob uses Ethernet to get the packet to R2—a process that requires Bob to follow Ethernet protocol rules, placing the IP packet (IP header and data) between an Ethernet header and Ethernet trailer.

Because the goal of the IP routing process is to deliver the IP packet—the IP header and data—to the destination host, R2 no longer needs the Ethernet header and trailer received from Bob. So, R2 strips the Ethernet header and trailer, leaving the original IP packet. To send the IP packet from R2 to R1, R2 places a PPP header in front of the IP packet and a PPP trailer at the end, and sends this data frame over the WAN link to R1.

Similarly, after the packet is received by R1, R1 removes the PPP header and trailer because PPP's job is to deliver the IP packet across the serial link. R1 then decides that it should forward the packet over the Ethernet to Larry. To do so, R1 adds a brand-new Ethernet header and trailer to the packet and forwards it to Larry.

In effect, IP uses the network access layer protocols to deliver an IP packet to the next router or host, with each router repeating the process until the packet arrives at the destination. Each network access protocol uses headers to encode the information needed to successfully deliver the data across the physical network, in much the same way as other layers use headers to achieve their goals.

> **CAUTION**   Many people describe the network access layer of the TCP/IP model as two layers, the data link layer and the physical layer. The reasons for the popularity of these alternate terms are explained in the section covering OSI, because the terms originated with the OSI model.

In short, the TCP/IP network access layer includes the protocols, cabling standards, headers, and trailers that define how to send data across a wide variety of types of physical networks.

Data Encapsulation Terminology

As you can see from the explanations of how HTTP, TCP, IP, and the network access layer protocols Ethernet and PPP do their jobs, each layer adds its own header (and sometimes trailer) to the data supplied by the higher layer. The term *encapsulation* refers to the process of putting headers and trailers around some data. For example, the web server encapsulated the home page inside an HTTP header in Figure 2-2. The TCP layer encapsulated the HTTP headers and data inside a TCP header in Figure 2-3. IP encapsulated the TCP headers and the data inside an IP header in Figure 2-4. Finally, the network access layer encapsulated the IP packets inside both a header and a trailer in Figure 2-5.

The process by which a TCP/IP host sends data can be viewed as a five-step process. The first four steps relate to the encapsulation performed by the four TCP/IP layers, and the last step is the actual physical transmission of the data by the host. The steps are summarized in the following list:

Step 1   **Create and encapsulate the application data with any required application layer headers.** For example, the HTTP OK message can be returned in an HTTP header, followed by part of the contents of a web page.

Step 2   **Encapsulate the data supplied by the application layer inside a transport layer header.** For end-user applications, a TCP or UDP header is typically used.

Step 3 **Encapsulate the data supplied by the transport layer inside an internet layer (IP) header.** IP is the only protocol available in the TCP/IP network model.

Step 4 **Encapsulate the data supplied by the internet layer inside a network access layer header and trailer.** This is the only layer that uses both a header and a trailer.

Step 5 **Transmit the bits**. The physical layer encodes a signal onto the medium to transmit the frame.

The numbers in Figure 2-6 correspond to the five steps in the list, graphically showing the same concepts. Note that because the application layer often does not need to add a header, the figure does not show a specific application layer header.

Figure 2-6 *Five Steps of Data Encapsulation—TCP/IP*

*The letters LH and LT stand for link header and link trailer, respectively, and refer to the data link layer header and trailer.

Finally, take particular care to remember the terms *segment*, *packet*, and *frame*, and the meaning of each. Each term refers to the headers and possibly trailers defined by a particular layer, and the data encapsulated following that header. Each term, however, refers to a different layer—segment for the transport layer, packet for the internet layer, and frame for the network access layer. Figure 2-7 shows each layer along with the associated term.

Figure 2-7 *Perspectives on Encapsulation and "Data"*

Note that Figure 2-7 also shows the encapsulated data as simply "data." When focusing on the work done by a particular layer, the encapsulated data typically is unimportant. For example, an IP packet may indeed have a TCP header after the IP header, an HTTP header after the TCP header, and data for a web page after the HTTP header—but when discussing IP, you probably just care about the IP header, so everything after the IP header is just called "data." So, when drawing IP packets, everything after the IP header is typically shown simply as "data."

The OSI Reference Model

To pass the ICND1 exam, you must be conversant in a protocol specification with which you are very unlikely to ever have any hands-on experience—the OSI reference model. The difficulty these days when discussing the OSI protocol specifications is that you have no point of reference, because most people cannot simply walk down the hall and use a computer whose main, or even optional, networking protocols conform to the entire OSI model.

OSI is the Open System Interconnection reference model for communications. OSI as a whole never succeeded in the marketplace, although some of the original protocols that comprised the OSI model are still used. So, why do you even need to think about OSI for the CCNA exams? Well, the OSI model now is mainly used as a point of reference for discussing other protocol specifications. And because being either a CCENT or CCNA requires you to understand some of the concepts and terms behind networking architecture and models, and because other protocols (including TCP/IP) are almost always compared to OSI, using OSI terminology, you need to know some things about OSI.

Comparing OSI and TCP/IP

The OSI reference model consists of seven layers. Each layer defines a set of typical networking functions. When OSI was in active development in the 1980s and 1990s, the OSI committees created new protocols and specifications to implement the functions specified by each layer. In other cases, just as for TCP/IP, the OSI committees did not create new protocols or standards, but instead referenced other protocols that were already defined. For instance, the IEEE defines Ethernet standards, so the OSI committees did not waste time specifying a new type of Ethernet; it simply referred to the IEEE Ethernet standards.

Today the OSI model can be used as a standard of comparison to other networking models. Figure 2-8 compares the seven-layer OSI model with the four-layer TCP/IP model. Also, for perspective, the figure also shows some example protocols and the related layers.

Figure 2-8 *Using OSI Layers for Referencing Other Protocols*

Key
Topic

OSI	TCP/IP	NetWare
Application		HTTP, SMTP,
Presentation	Application	POP3, VoIP
Session		
Transport	Transport	SPX
Network	Internet	IPX
Data Link	Network	Mac
Physical	Access	Protocols

Because OSI does have a very well-defined set of functions associated with each of its seven layers, you can examine any networking protocol or specification and make some determination of whether it most closely matches OSI Layer 1, 2, or 3, and so on. For instance, TCP/IP's internet layer, as implemented mainly by IP, equates most directly to the OSI network layer. So, most people say that IP is a network layer protocol, or a Layer 3 protocol, using OSI terminology and numbers for the layer. Of course, if you numbered the TCP/IP model, starting at the bottom, IP would be in Layer 2—but, by convention, everyone uses the OSI standard when describing other protocols. So, using this convention, IP is a network layer protocol.

While Figure 2-8 seems to imply that the OSI network layer and the TCP/IP internet layer are at least similar, the figure does not point out why they are similar. To appreciate why the TCP/IP layers correspond to a particular OSI layer, you need to have a better understanding of OSI. For example, the OSI network layer defines logical addressing and routing, as does the TCP/IP internet layer. While the details differ significantly, because the OSI network layer and TCP/IP internet layer define similar goals and features, the TCP/IP internet layer matches the OSI network layer. Similarly, the TCP/IP transport layer defines many functions, including error recovery, as does the OSI transport layer—so TCP is called a *transport layer*, or *Layer 4*, protocol.

Not all TCP/IP layers correspond to a single OSI layer. In particular, the TCP/IP network access layer defines both the physical network specifications and the protocols used to control the physical network. OSI separates the physical network specifications into the physical layer and the control functions into the data link layer. In fact, many people think of TCP/IP as a five-layer model, replacing the TCP/IP's network access layer with two layers, namely a physical layer and a data link layer, to match OSI.

NOTE For the exams, be aware of both views about whether TCP/IP has a single network access layer or two lower layers (data link and physical).

OSI Layers and Their Functions

Cisco requires that CCNAs demonstrate a basic understanding of the functions defined by each OSI layer, as well as remembering the names of the layers. It is also important that, for each device or protocol referenced throughout the book, you understand which layers of the OSI model most closely match the functions defined by that device or protocol. The upper layers of the OSI reference model (application, presentation, and session—Layers 7, 6, and 5) define functions focused on the application. The lower four layers (transport, network, data link, and physical—Layers 4, 3, 2, and 1) define functions focused on end-to-end delivery of the data. The CCNA exams focus on issues in the lower layers—in particular, with Layer 2, upon which LAN switching is based, and Layer 3, upon which routing is based. Table 2-4 defines the functions of the seven layers.

Table 2-4   *OSI Reference Model Layer Definitions*

Layer	Functional Description
7	Layer 7 provides an interface between the communications software and any applications that need to communicate outside the computer on which the application resides. It also defines processes for user authentication.
6	This layer's main purpose is to define and negotiate data formats, such as ASCII text, EBCDIC text, binary, BCD, and JPEG. Encryption also is defined by OSI as a presentation layer service.
5	The session layer defines how to start, control, and end conversations (called sessions). This includes the control and management of multiple bidirectional messages so that the application can be notified if only some of a series of messages are completed. This allows the presentation layer to have a seamless view of an incoming stream of data.
4	Layer 4 protocols provide a large number of services, as described in Chapter 6 of this book. Although OSI Layers 5 through 7 focus on issues related to the application, Layer 4 focuses on issues related to data delivery to another computer—for instance, error recovery and flow control.
3	The network layer defines three main features: logical addressing, routing (forwarding), and path determination. The routing concepts define how devices (typically routers) forward packets to their final destination. Logical addressing defines how each device can have an address that can be used by the routing process. Path determination refers to the work done by routing protocols by which all possible routes are learned, but the best route is chosen for use.
2	The data link layer defines the rules (protocols) that determine when a device can send data over a particular medium. Data link protocols also define the format of a header and trailer that allows devices attached to the medium to send and receive data successfully. The data link trailer, which follows the encapsulated data, typically defines a Frame Check Sequence (FCS) field, which allows the receiving device to detect transmission errors.
1	This layer typically refers to standards from other organizations. These standards deal with the physical characteristics of the transmission medium, including connectors, pins, use of pins, electrical currents, encoding, light modulation, and the rules for how to activate and deactivate the use of the physical medium.

Table 2-5 lists most of the devices and protocols covered in the CCNA exams, and their comparable OSI layers. Note that many of the devices must actually understand the protocols at multiple OSI layers, so the layer listed in the table actually refers to the highest layer that the device normally thinks about when performing its core work. For example, routers need to think about Layer 3 concepts, but they must also support features at both Layers 1 and 2.

Table 2-5 *OSI Reference Model—Example Devices and Protocols*

Layer Name	Protocols and Specifications	Devices
Application, presentation, session (Layers 5–7)	Telnet, HTTP, FTP, SMTP, POP3, VoIP, SNMP	Firewall, intrusion detection system
Transport (Layer 4)	TCP, UDP	
Network (Layer 3)	IP	Router
Data link (Layer 2)	Ethernet (IEEE 802.3), HDLC, Frame Relay, PPP	LAN switch, wireless access point, cable modem, DSL modem
Physical (Layer 1)	RJ-45, EIA/TIA-232, V.35, Ethernet (IEEE 802.3)	LAN hub, repeater

Besides remembering the basics of the features of each OSI layer (as in Table 2-4), and some example protocols and devices at each layer (as in Table 2-5), you should also memorize the names of the layers. You can simply memorize them, but some people like to use a mnemonic phrase to make memorization easier. In the following three phrases, the first letter of each word is the same as the first letter of an OSI layer name, in the order specified in parentheses:

- All People Seem To Need Data Processing (Layers 7 to 1)

- Please Do Not Take Sausage Pizzas Away (Layers 1 to 7)

- Pew! Dead Ninja Turtles Smell Particularly Awful (Layers 1 to 7)

OSI Layering Concepts and Benefits

Many benefits can be gained from the process of breaking up the functions or tasks of networking into smaller chunks, called *layers*, and defining standard interfaces between these layers. The layers break a large, complex set of concepts and protocols into smaller pieces, making it easier to talk about, easier to implement with hardware and software, and easier to troubleshoot. The following list summarizes the benefits of layered protocol specifications:

- **Less Complex**—Compared to not using a model, network models break the concepts into smaller parts.

Key Topic

- **Standard Interfaces**—The standard interface definitions between each layer allow for multiple vendors to create products that compete to be used for a given function, along with all the benefits of open competition.

- **Easier to learn**—Humans can more easily discuss and learn about the many details of a protocol specification.

- **Easier to develop**—Reduced complexity allows easier program changes and faster product development.

- **Multivendor interoperability**—Creating products to meet the same networking standards means that computers and networking gear from multiple vendors can work in the same network.

- **Modular engineering**—One vendor can write software that implements higher layers—for example, a web browser—and another vendor can write software that implements the lower layers—for example, Microsoft's built-in TCP/IP software in its operating systems.

The benefits of layering can be seen in the familiar postal service analogy. A person writing a letter does not have to think about how the postal service will deliver a letter across the country. The postal worker in the middle of the country does not have to worry about the contents of the letter. Likewise, layering enables one software package or hardware device to implement functions from one layer and assume that other software/hardware will perform the functions defined by the other layers. For instance, a web browser does not need to think about what the network topology looks like, the Ethernet card in the PC does not need to think about the contents of the web page, and a router in the middle of the network does not need to worry about the contents of the web page or whether the computer that sent the packet was using an Ethernet card or some other networking card.

OSI Encapsulation Terminology

Like TCP/IP, OSI defines processes by which a higher layer asks for services from the next lower layer. To provide the services, the lower layer encapsulates the higher layer's data behind a header. The final topic of this chapter explains some of the terminology and concepts related to OSI encapsulation.

The TCP/IP model uses terms such as segment, packet, and frame to refer to various layers and their respective encapsulated data (see Figure 2-7). OSI uses a more generic term: *protocol data unit*, or *PDU*. A PDU represents the bits that include the headers and trailers for that layer, as well as the encapsulated data. For instance, an IP packet, as shown in Figure 2-7, is a PDU. In fact, an IP packet is a *Layer 3 PDU* because IP is a Layer 3 protocol. The term *L3PDU* is a shorter version of the phrase *Layer 3 PDU*. So, rather than use the terms segment, packet, or frame, OSI simply refers to the "Layer x PDU," with "x" referring to the number of the layer being discussed.

OSI defines encapsulation similarly to how TCP/IP defines it. All layers except the lowest layer define a header, with the data from the next higher layer being encapsulated behind the header. The data link layer defines both a header and a trailer and places the Layer 3 PDU between the header and trailer. Figure 2-9 represents the typical encapsulation process, with the top of the figure showing the application data and application layer header, and the bottom of the figure showing the L2PDU that is transmitted onto the physical link.

Figure 2-9 *OSI Encapsulation and Protocol Data Units*

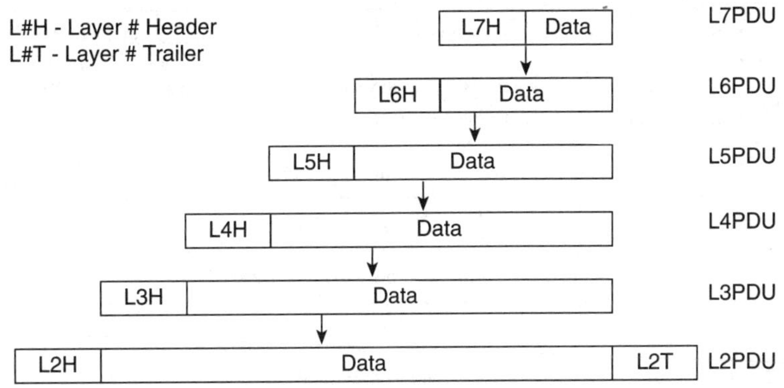

Exam Preparation Tasks

Review all the Key Topics

Key Topic

Review the most important topics from inside the chapter, noted with the key topics icon in the outer margin of the page. Table 2-6 lists a reference of these key topics and the page number on which each is found.

Table 2-6 *Key Topics for Chapter 2*

	Description	Page Number
Table 2-3	Provides definitions of same-layer and adjacent-layer interaction	26
Figure 2-5	Depicts the data-link services provided to IP for the purpose of delivering IP packets from host to host	29
Figure 2-7	Shows the meaning of the terms segment, packet, and frame	31
Figure 2-8	Compares the OSI and TCP/IP network models	33
List	Lists the benefits of using a layered networking model	35-36

Complete the Tables and Lists from Memory

Print a copy of Appendix H (found on the CD), or at least the section for this chapter, and complete the tables and lists from memory. Appendix I includes completed tables and lists to check your work.

Definitions of Key Terms

Define the following key terms from this chapter, and check your answers in the glossary.

adjacent-layer interaction, decapsulation, encapsulation, frame, networking model, packet, protocol data unit (PDU), same-layer interaction, segment

OSI Reference

You should memorize the names of the layers of the OSI model. Table 2-7 lists a summary of OSI functions at each layer, along with some sample protocols at each layer.

Table 2-7 *OSI Functional Summary*

Layer	Functional Description
Application (7)	Interfaces between network and application software. Also includes authentication services.
Presentation (6)	Defines the format and organization of data. Includes encryption.
Session (5)	Establishes and maintains end-to-end bidirectional flows between endpoints. Includes managing transaction flows.
Transport (4)	Provides a variety of services between two host computers, including connection establishment and termination, flow control, error recovery, and segmentation of large data blocks into smaller parts for transmission.
Network (3)	Logical addressing, routing, and path determination.
Data link (2)	Formats data into frames appropriate for transmission onto some physical medium. Defines rules for when the medium can be used. Defines means by which to recognize transmission errors.
Physical (1)	Defines the electrical, optical, cabling, connectors, and procedural details required for transmitting bits, represented as some form of energy passing over a physical medium.

This chapter covers the following subjects:

An Overview of Modern Ethernet LANs:
Provides some perspectives for those who have used Ethernet at the office or school but have not examined the details.

A Brief History of Ethernet: Examines several old options for Ethernet cabling and devices as a point of comparison for today's cabling, devices, and terminology.

Ethernet UTP Cabling: Explains the options for cabling and cable pinouts.

Improving Performance by Using Switches Instead of Hubs: A more detailed examination of the performance improvements made by using switches instead of older Ethernet hubs.

Ethernet Data-Link Protocols: Explains the meaning and purpose of the fields in the Ethernet header and trailer.

CHAPTER 3

Fundamentals of LANs

Physical and data link layer standards work together to allow computers to send bits to each other over a particular type of physical networking medium. The Open Systems Interconnection (OSI) physical layer (Layer 1) defines how to physically send bits over a particular physical networking medium. The data link layer (Layer 2) defines some rules about the data that is physically transmitted, including addresses that identify the sending device and the intended recipient, and rules about when a device can send (and when it should be silent), to name a few.

This chapter explains some of the basics of local-area networks (LAN). The term LAN refers to a set of Layer 1 and 2 standards designed to work together for the purpose of implementing geographically small networks. This chapter introduces the concepts of LANs—in particular, Ethernet LANs. More-detailed coverage of LANs appears in Part II (Chapters 7 through 11).

"Do I Know This Already?" Quiz

The "Do I Know This Already?" quiz allows you to assess whether you should read the entire chapter. If you miss no more than one of these 11 self-assessment questions, you might want to move ahead to the "Exam Preparation Tasks" section. Table 3-1 lists the major headings in this chapter and the "Do I Know This Already?" quiz questions covering the material in those sections. This helps you assess your knowledge of these specific areas. The answers to the "Do I Know This Already?" quiz appear in Appendix A.

Table 3-1 *"Do I Know This Already?" Foundation Topics Section-to-Question Mapping*

Foundation Topics Section	Questions
An Overview of Modern Ethernet LANs	1
A Brief History of Ethernet	2
Ethernet UTP Cabling	3, 4
Improving Performance by Using Switches Instead of Hubs	5–7
Ethernet Data-Link Protocols	8–11

1. Which one of the following answers is most accurate about the cabling of a typical modern Ethernet LAN?

    a. Connect each device in series using coaxial cabling

    b. Connect each device in series using UTP cabling

    c. Connect each device to a centralized LAN hub using UTP cabling

    d. Connect each device to a centralized LAN switch using UTP cabling

2. Which of the following is true about the cabling of a 10BASE2 Ethernet LAN?

    a. Connect each device in series using coaxial cabling

    b. Connect each device in series using UTP cabling

    c. Connect each device to a centralized LAN hub using UTP cabling

    d. Connect each device to a centralized LAN switch using UTP cabling

3. Which of the following is true about Ethernet crossover cables?

    a. Pins 1 and 2 are reversed on the other end of the cable.

    b. Pins 1 and 2 on one end of the cable connect to pins 3 and 6 on the other end of the cable.

    c. Pins 1 and 2 on one end of the cable connect to pins 3 and 4 on the other end of the cable.

    d. The cable can be up to 1000 meters long to cross over between buildings.

    e. None of the other answers is correct.

4. Each answer lists two types of devices used in a 100BASE-TX network. If these devices were connected with UTP Ethernet cables, which pairs of devices would require a straight-through cable?

    a. PC and router

    b. PC and switch

    c. Hub and switch

    d. Router and hub

    e. Wireless access point (Ethernet port) and switch

5. Which of the following is true about the CSMA/CD algorithm?

    a. The algorithm never allows collisions to occur.

    b. Collisions can happen, but the algorithm defines how the computers should notice a collision and how to recover.

    c. The algorithm works with only two devices on the same Ethernet.

    d. None of the other answers is correct.

6. Which of the following is a collision domain?

    a. All devices connected to an Ethernet hub

    b. All devices connected to an Ethernet switch

    c. Two PCs, with one cabled to a router Ethernet port with a crossover cable and the other PC cabled to another router Ethernet port with a crossover cable

    d. None of the other answers is correct.

7. Which of the following describe a shortcoming of using hubs that is improved by instead using switches?

    a. Hubs create a single electrical bus to which all devices connect, causing the devices to share the bandwidth.

    b. Hubs limit the maximum cable length of individual cables (relative to switches)

    c. Hubs allow collisions to occur when two attached devices send data at the same time.

    d. Hubs restrict the number of physical ports to at most eight.

8. Which of the following terms describe Ethernet addresses that can be used to communicate with more than one device at a time?

    a. Burned-in address

    b. Unicast address

    c. Broadcast address

    d. Multicast address

9. Which of the following is one of the functions of OSI Layer 2 protocols?

    a. Framing

    b. Delivery of bits from one device to another

    c. Error recovery

    d. Defining the size and shape of Ethernet cards

10. Which of the following are true about the format of Ethernet addresses?

    a. Each manufacturer puts a unique code into the first 2 bytes of the address.

    b. Each manufacturer puts a unique code into the first 3 bytes of the address.

    c. Each manufacturer puts a unique code into the first half of the address.

    d. The part of the address that holds this manufacturer's code is called the MAC.

    e. The part of the address that holds this manufacturer's code is called the OUI.

    f. The part of the address that holds this manufacturer's code has no specific name.

11. Which of the following is true about the Ethernet FCS field?

    a. It is used for error recovery.

    b. It is 2 bytes long.

    c. It resides in the Ethernet trailer, not the Ethernet header.

    d. It is used for encryption.

    e. None of the other answers is correct.

Foundation Topics

A typical Enterprise network consists of several sites. The end-user devices connect to a LAN, which allows the local computers to communicate with each other. Additionally, each site has a router that connects to both the LAN and a wide-area network (WAN), with the WAN providing connectivity between the various sites. With routers and a WAN, the computers at different sites can also communicate.

This chapter describes the basics of how to create LANs today, with Chapter 4, "Fundamentals of WANs," describing the basics of creating WANs. Ethernet is the undisputed king of LAN standards today. Historically speaking, several competing LAN standards existed, including Token Ring, Fiber Distributed Data Interface (FDDI), and Asynchronous Transfer Mode (ATM). Eventually, Ethernet won out over all the competing LAN standards, so that today when you think of LANs, no one even questions what type—it's Ethernet.

An Overview of Modern Ethernet LANs

The term *Ethernet* refers to a family of standards that together define the physical and data link layers of the world's most popular type of LAN. The different standards vary as to the speed supported, with speeds of 10 megabits per second (Mbps), 100 Mbps, and 1000 Mbps (1 gigabit per second, or Gbps) being common today. The standards also differ as far as the types of cabling and the allowed length of the cabling. For example, the most commonly used Ethernet standards allow the use of inexpensive *unshielded twisted-pair* (UTP) cabling, whereas other standards call for more expensive fiber-optic cabling. Fiber-optic cabling might be worth the cost in some cases, because the cabling is more secure and allows for much longer distances between devices. To support the widely varying needs for building a LAN—needs for different speeds, different cabling types (trading off distance requirements versus cost), and other factors—many variations of Ethernet standards have been created.

The Institute of Electrical and Electronics Engineers (IEEE) has defined many Ethernet standards since it took over the LAN standardization process in the early 1980s. Most of the standards define a different variation of Ethernet at the physical layer, with differences in speed and types of cabling. Additionally, for the data link layer, the IEEE separates the functions into two sublayers:

- The 802.3 Media Access Control (MAC) sublayer

- The 802.2 Logical Link Control (LLC) sublayer

In fact, MAC addresses get their name from the IEEE name for this lower portion of the data link layer Ethernet standards.

Each new physical layer standard from the IEEE requires many differences at the physical layer. However, each of these physical layer standards uses the exact same 802.3 header, and each uses the upper LLC sublayer as well. Table 3-2 lists the most commonly used IEEE Ethernet physical layer standards.

Key Topic

Table 3-2 *Today's Most Common Types of Ethernet*

Common Name	Speed	Alternative Name	Name of IEEE Standard	Cable Type, Maximum Length
Ethernet	10 Mbps	10BASE-T	IEEE 802.3	Copper, 100 m
Fast Ethernet	100 Mbps	100BASE-TX	IEEE 802.3u	Copper, 100 m
Gigabit Ethernet	1000 Mbps	1000BASE-LX, 1000BASE-SX	IEEE 802.3z	Fiber, 550 m (SX) 5 km (LX)
Gigabit Ethernet	1000 Mbps	1000BASE-T	IEEE 802.3ab	100 m

The table is convenient for study, but the terms in the table bear a little explanation. First, beware that the term *Ethernet* is often used to mean "all types of Ethernet," but in some cases it is used to mean "10BASE-T Ethernet." (Because the term Ethernet sometimes can be ambiguous, this book refers to 10-Mbps Ethernet as 10BASE-T when the specific type of Ethernet matters to the discussion.) Second, note that the alternative name for each type of Ethernet lists the speed in Mbps—namely, 10 Mbps, 100 Mbps, and 1000 Mbps. The *T* and *TX* in the alternative names refer to the fact that each of these standards defines the use of UTP cabling, with the *T* referring to the T in *twisted pair*.

To build and create a modern LAN using any of the UTP-based types of Ethernet LANs listed in Table 3-2, you need the following components:

- Computers that have an Ethernet network interface card (NIC) installed

- Either an Ethernet hub or Ethernet switch

- UTP cables to connect each PC to the hub or switch

Figure 3-1 shows a typical LAN. The NICs cannot be seen, because they reside in the PCs. However, the lines represent the UTP cabling, and the icon in the center of the figure represents a LAN switch.

Figure 3-1 *Typical Small Modern LAN*

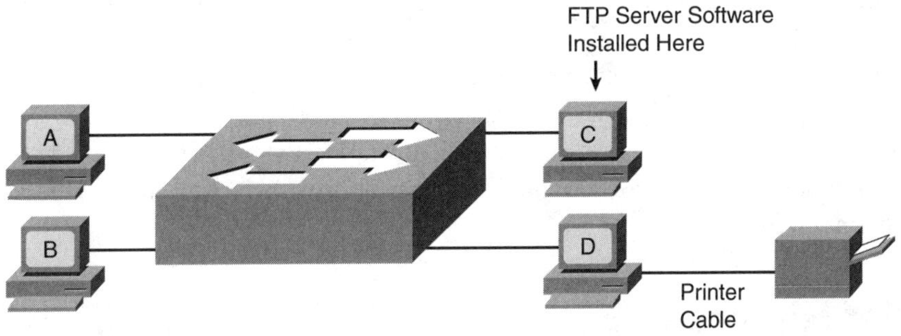

> **NOTE** Figure 3-1 applies to all the common types of Ethernet. The same basic design and topology are used regardless of speed or cabling type.

Most people can build a LAN like the one shown in Figure 3-1 with practically no real knowledge of how LANs work. Most PCs contain an Ethernet NIC that was installed at the factory. Switches do not need to be configured for them to forward traffic between the computers. All you have to do is connect the switch to a power cable and plug in the UTP cables from each PC to the switch. Then the PCs should be able to send Ethernet frames to each other.

You can use such a small LAN for many purposes, even without a WAN connection. Consider the following functions for which a LAN is the perfect, small-scale solution:

File sharing: Each computer can be configured to share all or parts of its file system so that the other computers can read, or possibly read and write, the files on another computer. This function typically is simply part of the PC operating system.

Printer sharing: Computers can share their printers as well. For example, PCs A, B, and C in Figure 3-1 could print documents on PC D's printer. This function is also typically part of the PC's operating system.

File transfers: A computer could install a file transfer server, thereby allowing other computers to send and receive files to and from that computer. For example, PC C could install File Transfer Protocol (FTP) server software, allowing the other PCs to use FTP client software to connect to PC C and transfer files.

Gaming: The PCs could install gaming software that allows multiple players to play in the same game. The gaming software would then communicate using the Ethernet.

The goal of the first half of this chapter is to help you understand much of the theory and practical knowledge behind simple LAN designs such as the one illustrated in Figure 3-1. To fully understand modern LANs, it is helpful to understand a bit about the history of Ethernet, which is covered in the next section. Following that, this chapter examines the physical aspects (Layer 1) of a simple Ethernet LAN, focusing on UTP cabling. Then this chapter compares the older (and slower) Ethernet hub with the newer (and faster) Ethernet switch. Finally, the LAN coverage in this chapter ends with the data-link (Layer 2) functions on Ethernet.

A Brief History of Ethernet

Like many early networking protocols, Ethernet began life inside a corporation that was looking to solve a specific problem. Xerox needed an effective way to allow a new invention, called the personal computer, to be connected in its offices. From that, Ethernet was born. (Go to http://inventors.about.com/library/weekly/aa111598.htm for an interesting story on the history of Ethernet.) Eventually, Xerox teamed with Intel and Digital Equipment Corp. (DEC) to further develop Ethernet, so the original Ethernet became known as *DIX Ethernet*, referring to DEC, Intel, and Xerox.

These companies willingly transitioned the job of Ethernet standards development to the IEEE in the early 1980s. The IEEE formed two committees that worked directly on Ethernet—the IEEE 802.3 committee and the IEEE 802.2 committee. The 802.3 committee worked on physical layer standards as well as a subpart of the data link layer called *Media Access Control (MAC)*. The IEEE assigned the other functions of the data link layer to the 802.2 committee, calling this part of the data link layer the *Logical Link Control (LLC)* sublayer. (The 802.2 standard applied to Ethernet as well as to other IEEE standard LANs such as Token Ring.)

The Original Ethernet Standards: 10BASE2 and 10BASE5

Ethernet is best understood by first considering the two early Ethernet specifications, 10BASE5 and 10BASE2. These two Ethernet specifications defined the details of the physical and data link layers of early Ethernet networks. (10BASE2 and 10BASE5 differ in their cabling details, but for the discussion in this chapter, you can consider them as behaving identically.) With these two specifications, the network engineer installs a series of coaxial cables connecting each device on the Ethernet network. There is no hub, switch, or wiring panel. The Ethernet consists solely of the collective Ethernet NICs in the computers and the coaxial cabling. The series of cables creates an electrical circuit, called a bus, which is shared among all devices on the Ethernet. When a computer wants to send some bits to another computer on the bus, it sends an electrical signal, and the electricity propagates to all devices on the Ethernet.

Figure 3-2 shows the basic logic of an old Ethernet 10BASE2 network, which uses a single electrical bus, created with coaxial cable and Ethernet cards.

Figure 3-2 *Small Ethernet 10BASE2 Network*

The solid lines in the figure represent the physical network cabling. The dashed lines with arrows represent the path that Larry's transmitted frame takes. Larry sends an electrical signal across his Ethernet NIC onto the cable, and both Bob and Archie receive the signal. The cabling creates a physical electrical bus, meaning that the transmitted signal is received by all stations on the LAN. Just like a school bus stops at every student's house along a route, the electrical signal on a 10BASE2 or 10BASE5 network is propagated to each station on the LAN.

Because the network uses a single bus, if two or more electrical signals were sent at the same time, they would overlap and collide, making both signals unintelligible. So, unsurprisingly, Ethernet also defined a specification for how to ensure that only one device sends traffic on the Ethernet at one time. Otherwise, the Ethernet would have been unusable. This algorithm, known as the *carrier sense multiple access with collision detection (CSMA/CD)* algorithm, defines how the bus is accessed.

In human terms, CSMA/CD is similar to what happens in a meeting room with many attendees. It's hard to understand what two people are saying at the same time, so generally, one person talks and the rest listen. Imagine that Bob and Larry both want to reply to the current speaker's comments. As soon as the speaker takes a breath, Bob and Larry both try to speak. If Larry hears Bob's voice before Larry makes a noise, Larry might stop and let Bob speak. Or, maybe they both start at almost the same time, so they talk over each other and no one can hear what is said. Then there's the proverbial "Pardon me; go ahead with what you were saying," and eventually Larry or Bob talks. Or perhaps another person jumps in and talks while Larry and Bob are both backing off. These "rules" are based on your culture; CSMA/CD is based on Ethernet protocol specifications and achieves the same type of goal.

Basically, the CSMA/CD algorithm can be summarized as follows:

- A device that wants to send a frame waits until the LAN is silent—in other words, no frames are currently being sent—before attempting to send an electrical signal.

- If a collision still occurs, the devices that caused the collision wait a random amount of time and then try again.

In 10BASE5 and 10BASE2 Ethernet LANs, a collision occurs because the transmitted electrical signal travels along the entire length of the bus. When two stations send at the same time, their electrical signals overlap, causing a collision. So, all devices on a 10BASE5 or 10BASE2 Ethernet need to use CSMA/CD to avoid collisions and to recover when inadvertent collisions occur.

Repeaters

Like any type of LAN, 10BASE5 and 10BASE2 had limitations on the total length of a cable. With 10BASE5, the limit was 500 m; with 10BASE2, it was 185 m. Interestingly, the 5 and 2 in the names 10BASE5 and 10BASE2 represent the maximum cable length—with the 2 referring to 200 meters, which is pretty close to the actual maximum of 185 meters. (Both of these types of Ethernet ran at 10 Mbps.)

In some cases, the maximum cable length was not enough, so a device called a *repeater* was developed. One of the problems that limited the length of a cable was that the signal sent by one device could attenuate too much if the cable was longer than 500 m or 185 m. *Attenuation* means that when electrical signals pass over a wire, the signal strength gets weaker the farther along the cable it travels. It's the same concept behind why you can hear someone talking right next to you, but if that person speaks at the same volume and you are on the other side of a crowded room, you might not hear her because the sound waves have attenuated.

Repeaters connect to multiple cable segments, receive the electrical signal on one cable, interpret the bits as 1s and 0s, and generate a brand-new, clean, strong signal out the other cable. A repeater does not simply amplify the signal, because amplifying the signal might also amplify any noise picked up along the way.

NOTE   Because the repeater does not interpret what the bits mean, but it does examine and generate electrical signals, a repeater is considered to operate at Layer 1.

You should not expect to need to implement 10BASE5 or 10BASE2 Ethernet LANs today. However, for learning purposes, keep in mind several key points from this section as you move on to concepts that relate to today's LANs:

■   The original Ethernet LANs created an electrical bus to which all devices connected.

■   Because collisions could occur on this bus, Ethernet defined the CSMA/CD algorithm, which defined a way to both avoid collisions and take action when collisions occurred.

■   Repeaters extended the length of LANs by cleaning up the electrical signal and repeating it—a Layer 1 function—but without interpreting the meaning of the electrical signal.

Building 10BASE-T Networks with Hubs

The IEEE later defined new Ethernet standards besides 10BASE5 and 10BASE2. Chronologically, the 10BASE-T standard came next (1990), followed by 100BASE-TX (1995), and then 1000BASE-T (1999). To support these new standards, networking devices called hubs and switches were also created. This section defines the basics of how these three popular types of Ethernet work, including the basic operation of hubs and switches.

10BASE-T solved several problems with the early 10BASE5 and 10BASE2 Ethernet specifications. 10BASE-T allowed the use of UTP telephone cabling that was already installed. Even if new cabling needed to be installed, the inexpensive and easy-to-install UTP cabling replaced the old expensive and difficult-to-install coaxial cabling.

Another major improvement introduced with 10BASE-T, and that remains a key design point today, is the concept of cabling each device to a centralized connection point. Originally, 10BASE-T called for the use of Ethernet *hubs*, as shown in Figure 3-3.

Figure 3-3   *Small Ethernet 10BASE-T Network Using a Hub*

When building a LAN today, you could choose to use either a hub or a switch as the centralized Ethernet device to which all the computers connect. Even though modern Ethernet LANs typically use switches instead of hubs, understanding the operation of hubs helps you understand some of the terminology used with switches, as well as some of their benefits.

Hubs are essentially repeaters with multiple physical ports. That means that the hub simply regenerates the electrical signal that comes in one port and sends the same signal out every other port. By doing so, any LAN that uses a hub, as in Figure 3-3, creates an electrical bus, just like 10BASE2 and 10BASE5. Therefore, collisions can still occur, so CSMA/CD access rules continue to be used.

10BASE-T networks using hubs solved some big problems with 10BASE5 and 10BASE2. First, the LAN had much higher availability, because a single cable problem could, and probably did, take down 10BASE5 and 10BASE2 LANs. With 10BASE-T, a cable connects each device to the hub, so a single cable problem affects only one device. As mentioned earlier, the use of UTP cabling, in a star topology (all cables running to a centralized connection device), lowered the cost of purchasing and installing the cabling.

Today, you might occasionally use LAN hubs, but you will more likely use switches instead of hubs. Switches perform much better than hubs, support more functions than hubs, and typically are priced almost as low as hubs. However, for learning purposes, keep in mind several key points from this section about the history of Ethernet as you move on to concepts that relate to today's LANs:

- The original Ethernet LANs created an electrical bus to which all devices connected.

- 10BASE2 and 10BASE5 repeaters extended the length of LANs by cleaning up the electrical signal and repeating it—a Layer 1 function—but without interpreting the meaning of the electrical signal.

- Hubs are repeaters that provide a centralized connection point for UTP cabling—but they still create a single electrical bus, shared by the various devices, just like 10BASE5 and 10BASE2.

- Because collisions could occur in any of these cases, Ethernet defines the CSMA/CD algorithm, which tells devices how to both avoid collisions and take action when collisions do occur.

The next section explains the details of the UTP cabling used by today's most commonly used types of Ethernet.

Ethernet UTP Cabling

The three most common Ethernet standards used today—10BASE-T (Ethernet), 100BASE-TX (Fast Ethernet, or FE), and 1000BASE-T (Gigabit Ethernet, or GE)—use UTP cabling. Some key differences exist, particularly with the number of wire pairs needed in each case, and in the type (category) of cabling. This section examines some of the details of UTP cabling, pointing out differences among these three standards along the way. In particular, this section describes the cables and the connectors on the ends of the cables, how they use the wires in the cables to send data, and the pinouts required for proper operation.

UTP Cables and RJ-45 Connectors

The UTP cabling used by popular Ethernet standards include either two or four pairs of wires. Because the wires inside the cable are thin and brittle, the cable itself has an outer jacket of flexible plastic to support the wires. Each individual copper wire also has a thin plastic coating to help prevent the wire from breaking. The plastic coating on each wire has a different color, making it easy to look at both ends of the cable and identify the ends of an individual wire.

The cable ends typically have some form of connector attached (typically RJ-45 connectors), with the ends of the wires inserted into the connectors. The RJ-45 connector has eight specific physical locations into which the eight wires in the cable can be inserted, called *pin positions*, or simply *pins*. When the connectors are added to the end of the cable, the ends of the wires must be correctly inserted into the correct pin positions.

> **NOTE**   If you have an Ethernet UTP cable nearby, it would be useful to closely examine the RJ-45 connectors and wires as you read through this section.

As soon as the cable has RJ-45 connectors on each end, the RJ-45 connector needs to be inserted into an RJ-45 receptacle, often called an *RJ-45 port*. Figure 3-4 shows photos of the cables, connectors, and ports.

Figure 3-4   *RJ-45 Connectors and Ports*

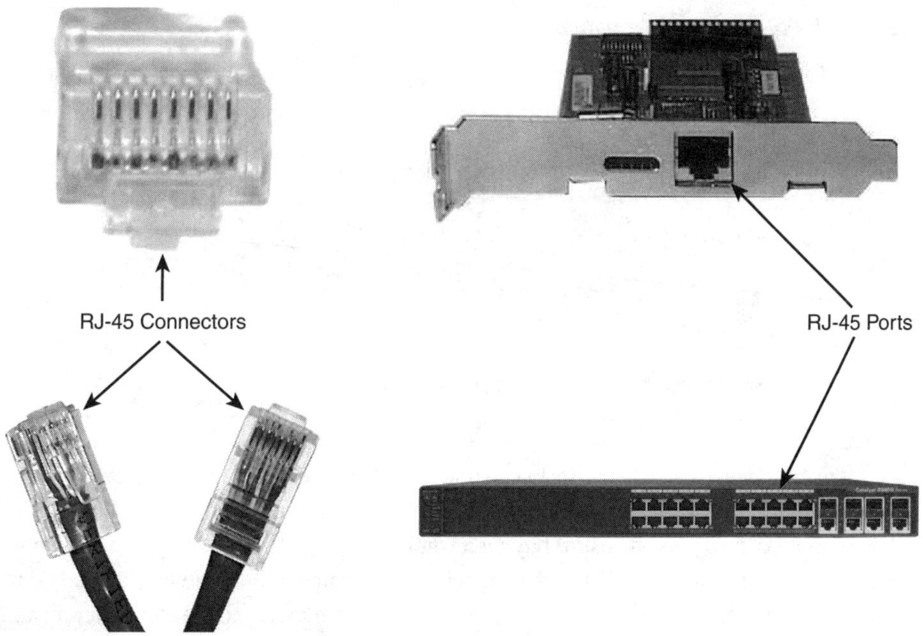

RJ-45 Connectors

RJ-45 Ports

> **NOTE**   The RJ-45 connector is slightly wider, but otherwise similar, to the RJ-11 connectors commonly used for telephone cables in homes in North America.

The figure shows three separate views of an RJ-45 connector on the left. The head-on view in the upper-left part of the figure shows the ends of the eight wires in their pin positions inside the UTP cable. The upper-right part of the figure shows an Ethernet NIC that is not yet installed in a computer. The RJ-45 port on the NIC would be exposed on the side of the computer, making it easily accessible as soon as the NIC has been installed into a computer. The lower-right part of the figure shows the side of a Cisco 2960 switch, with multiple RJ-45 ports, allowing multiple devices to easily connect to the Ethernet network.

Although RJ-45 connectors and ports are popular, engineers might want to purchase Cisco LAN switches that have a few physical ports that can be changed without having to purchase a whole new switch. Many Cisco switches have a few interfaces that use either Gigabit Interface Converters (GBIC) or Small-Form Pluggables (SFP). Both are small removable devices that fit into a port or slot in the switch. Because Cisco manufactures a wide range of GBICs and SFPs, for every Ethernet standard, the switch can use a variety of cable connectors and types of cabling and support different cable lengths—all by just switching to a different kind of GBIC or SFP. Figure 3-5 shows a 1000BASE-T GBIC, ready to be inserted into a LAN switch.

Figure 3-5   *1000BASE-T GBIC with an RJ-45 Connector*

If a network engineer needs to use an existing switch in a new role in a campus network, the engineer could simply buy a new 1000BASE-LX GBIC to replace the old 1000BASE-T GBIC and reduce the extra cost of buying a whole new switch. For example, when using a switch so that it connects only to other switches in the same building, the switch could use 1000BASE-T GBICs and copper cabling. Later, if the company moved to another location, the switch could be repurposed by using a different GBIC that supported fiber-optic cabling, and different connectors, using 1000BASE-LX to support a longer cabling distance.

Transmitting Data Using Twisted Pairs

UTP cabling consists of matched pairs of wires that are indeed twisted together—hence the name *twisted pair*. The devices on each end of the cable can create an electrical circuit using a pair of wires by sending current on the two wires, in opposite directions. When current passes over any wire, that current induces a magnetic field outside the wire; the magnetic field can in turn cause electrical noise on other wires in the cable. By twisting together the wires in the same pair, with the current running in opposite directions on each wire, the magnetic field created by one wire mostly cancels out the magnetic field created by the other wire. Because of this feature, most networking cables that use copper wires and electricity use twisted pairs of wires to send data.

To send data over the electrical circuit created over a wire pair, the devices use an *encoding scheme* that defines how the electrical signal should vary, over time, to mean either a binary 0 or 1. For example, 10BASE-T uses an encoding scheme that encodes a binary 0 as a transition from higher voltage to lower voltage during the middle of a 1/10,000,000th-of-a-second interval. The electrical details of encoding are unimportant for the purposes of this book. But it is important to realize that networking devices create an electrical circuit using each wire pair, and vary the signal as defined by the encoding scheme, to send bits over the wire pair.

UTP Cabling Pinouts for 10BASE-T and 100BASE-TX

The wires in the UTP cable must be connected to the correct pin positions in the RJ-45 connectors in order for communication to work correctly. As mentioned earlier, the RJ-45 connector has eight *pin positions*, or simply *pins*, into which the copper wires inside the cable protrude. The wiring *pinouts*—the choice of which color wire goes into which pin position—must conform to the Ethernet standards described in this section.

Interestingly, the IEEE does not actually define the official standards for cable manufacturing, as well as part of the details of the conventions used for the cabling pinouts. Two cooperating industry groups, the Telecommunications Industry Association (TIA) and the Electronics Industry Alliance (EIA), define standards for UTP cabling, color coding for wires, and standard pinouts on the cables. (See http://www.tiaonline.org and http://www.eia.org.) Figure 3-6 shows two pinout standards from the EIA/TIA, with the color coding and pair numbers listed.

Figure 3-6 *EIA/TIA Standard Ethernet Cabling Pinouts*

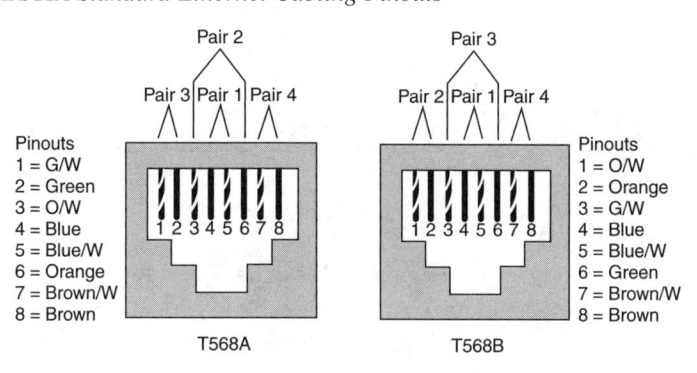

Key
Topic

To understand the acronyms listed in the figure, note that the eight wires in a UTP cable have either a solid color (green, orange, blue, or brown) or a striped color scheme using white and one of the other four colors. Also, a single-wire pair uses the same base color. For example, the blue wire and the blue/white striped wire are paired and twisted. In Figure 3-6, the notations with a / refer to the striped wires. For example, "G/W" refers to the green-and-white striped wire.

> **NOTE**   A UTP cable needs two pairs of wires for 10BASE-T and 100BASE-TX and four pairs of wires for 1000BASE-T. This section focuses on the pinouts for two-pair wiring, with four-pair wiring covered next.

To build a working Ethernet LAN, you must choose or build cables that use the correct wiring pinout on each end of the cable. 10BASE-T and 100BASE-TX Ethernet define that one pair should be used to send data in one direction, with the other pair used to send data in the other direction. In particular, Ethernet NICs should send data using the pair connected to pins 1 and 2—in other words, pair 3 according to the T568A pinout standard shown in Figure 3-6. Similarly, Ethernet NICs should expect to receive data using the pair at pins 3 and 6—pair 2 according to the T568A standard. Knowing what the Ethernet NICs do, hubs and switches do the opposite—they receive on the pair at pins 1,2 (pair 3 per T568A), and they send on the pair at pins 3,6 (pair 2 per T568A).

Figure 3-7 shows this concept, with PC Larry connected to a hub. Note that the figure shows the two twisted pairs inside the cable, and the NIC outside the PC, to emphasize that the cable connects to the NIC and hub and that only two pairs are being used.

Figure 3-7   *Ethernet Straight-Through Cable Concept*

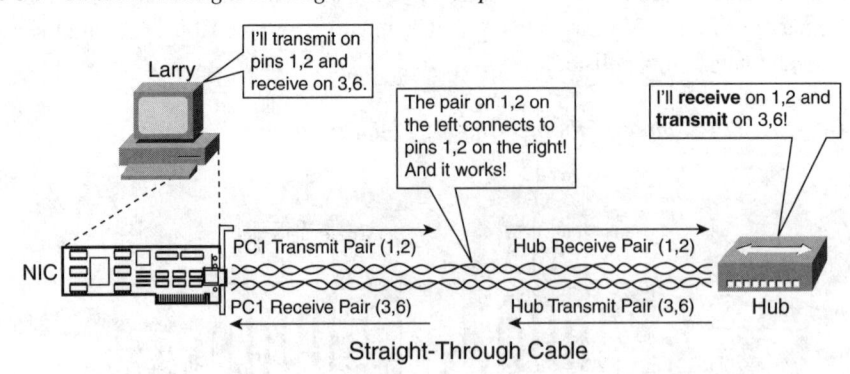

The network shown in Figure 3-7 uses a *straight-through* cable. An Ethernet straight-through cable connects the wire at pin 1 on one end of the cable to pin 1 at the other end of the cable; the wire at pin 2 needs to connect to pin 2 on the other end of the cable; pin 3 on one end connects to pin 3 on the other; and so on. (To create a straight-through cable, both ends of the cable use the same EIA/TIA pinout standard on each end of the cable.)

A straight-through cable is used when the devices on the ends of the cable use opposite pins when they transmit data. However, when connecting two devices that both use the same pins to transmit, the pinouts of the cable must be set up to swap the wire pair. A cable that swaps the wire pairs inside the cable is called a *crossover cable*. For example, many LANs inside an Enterprise network use multiple switches, with a UTP cable connecting the switches. Because both switches send on the pair at pins 3,6, and receive on the pair at pins 1,2, the cable must swap or cross the pairs. Figure 3-8 shows several conceptual views of a crossover cable.

Figure 3-8 *Crossover Ethernet Cable*

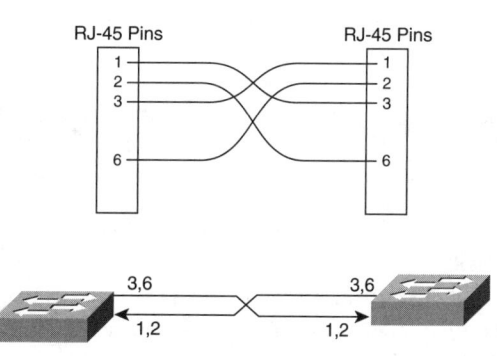

The top part of the figure shows the pins to which each wire is connected. Pin 1 on the left end connects to pin 3 on the right end, pin 2 on the left to pin 6 on the right, pin 3 on the left to pin 1 on the right, and pin 6 on the left to pin 2 on the right. The bottom of the figure shows that the wires at pins 3,6 on each end—the pins each switch uses to transmit—connect to pins 1,2 on the other end, thereby allowing the devices to receive on pins 1,2.

For the exam, you should be well prepared to choose which type of cable (straight-through or crossover) is needed in each part of the network. In short, devices on opposite ends of a cable that use the same pair of pins to transmit need a crossover cable. Devices that use an opposite pair of pins to transmit need a straight-through cable. Table 3-3 lists the devices mentioned in this book and the pin pairs they use, assuming that they use 10BASE-T and 100BASE-TX.

Table 3-3 *10BASE-T and 100BASE-TX Pin Pairs Used*

Devices That Transmit on 1,2 and Receive on 3,6	Devices That Transmit on 3,6 and Receive on 1,2
PC NICs	Hubs
Routers	Switches
Wireless Access Point (Ethernet interface)	—
Networked printers (printers that connect directly to the LAN)	—

For example, Figure 3-9 shows a campus LAN in a single building. In this case, several straight-through cables are used to connect PCs to switches. Additionally, the cables connecting the switches—referred to as *trunks*—require crossover cables.

Figure 3-9 *Typical Uses for Straight-Through and Crossover Ethernet Cables*

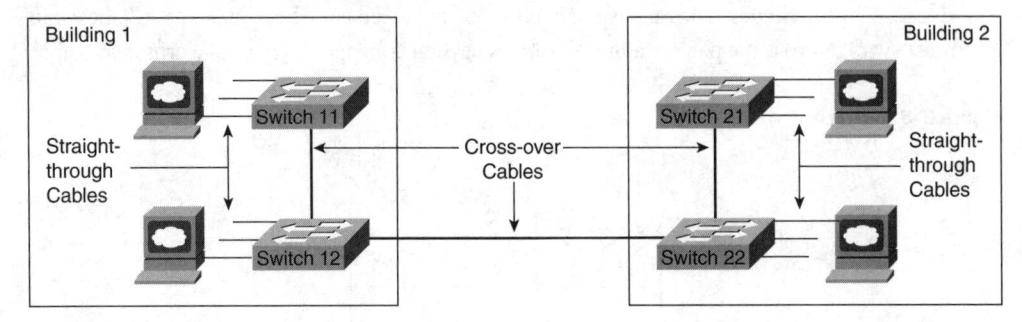

1000BASE-T Cabling

As noted earlier, 1000BASE-T differs from 10BASE-T and 100BASE-TX as far as the cabling and pinouts. First, 1000BASE-T requires four wire pairs. Also, Gigabit Ethernet transmits and receives on each of the four wire pairs simultaneously.

However, Gigabit Ethernet does have a concept of straight-through and crossover cables, with a minor difference in the crossover cables. The pinouts for a straight-through cable are the same—pin 1 to pin 1, pin 2 to pin 2, and so on. The crossover cable crosses the same two-wire pair as the crossover cable for the other types of Ethernet—the pair at pins 1,2 and 3,6—as well as crossing the two other pairs (the pair at pins 4,5 with the pair at pins 7,8).

> **NOTE**   If you have some experience with installing LANs, you might be thinking that you have used the wrong cable before (straight-through or crossover), but the cable worked. Cisco switches have a feature called auto-mdix that notices when the wrong cabling pinouts are used. This feature readjusts the switch's logic and makes the cable work. For the exams, be ready to identify whether the correct cable is shown in figures.

Next, this chapter takes a closer look at LAN hubs and the need for LAN switches.

Improving Performance by Using Switches Instead of Hubs

This section examines some of the performance problems created when using hubs, followed by explanations of how LAN switches solve the two largest performance problems encountered with hubs. To better appreciate the problem, consider Figure 3-10, which shows what happens when a single device sends data through a hub.

> **NOTE** The figure and the logic describing it apply to any hub, whether 10BASE-T, 100BASE-TX, or even 1000BASE-T.

Figure 3-10 *Hub Creates One Shared Electrical Bus*

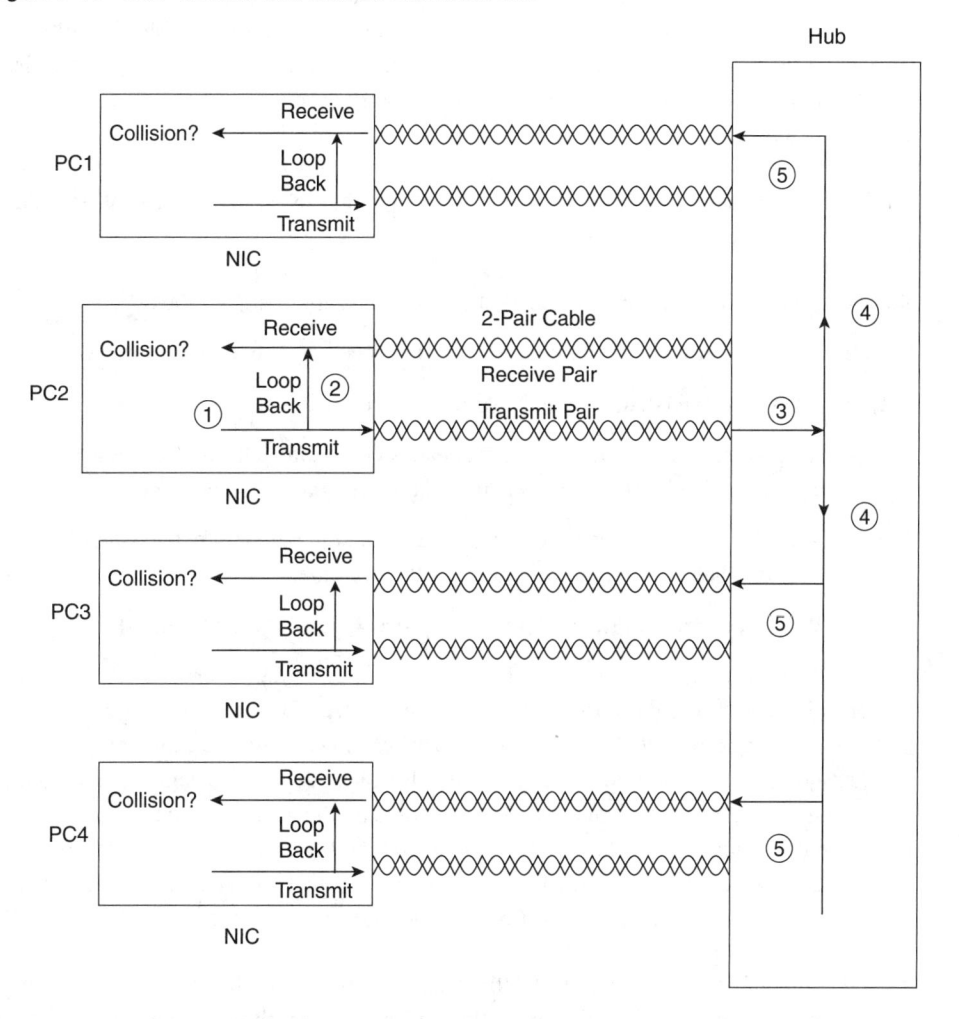

The figure outlines how a hub creates an electrical bus. The steps illustrated in Figure 3-10 are as follows:

Step 1 The network interface card (NIC) sends a frame.

Step 2 The NIC loops the sent frame onto its receive pair internally on the card.

Step 3 The hub receives the electrical signal, interpreting the signal as bits so that it can clean up and repeat the signal.

Step 4   The hub's internal wiring repeats the signal out all other ports, but not back to the port from which the signal was received.

Step 5   The hub repeats the signal to each receive pair on all other devices.

In particular, note that a hub always repeats the electrical signal out all ports, except the port from which the electrical signal was received. Also, Figure 3-10 does not show a collision. However, if PC1 and PC2 sent an electrical signal at the same time, at Step 4 the electrical signals would overlap, the frames would collide, and both frames would be either completely unintelligible or full of errors.

CSMA/CD logic helps prevent collisions and also defines how to act when a collision does occur. The CSMA/CD algorithm works like this:

Step 1   A device with a frame to send listens until the Ethernet is not busy.

Step 2   When the Ethernet is not busy, the sender(s) begin(s) sending the frame.

Step 3   The sender(s) listen(s) to make sure that no collision occurred.

Step 4   If a collision occurs, the devices that had been sending a frame each send a jamming signal to ensure that all stations recognize the collision.

Step 5   After the jamming is complete, each sender randomizes a timer and waits that long before trying to resend the collided frame.

Step 6   When each random timer expires, the process starts over with Step 1.

CSMA/CD does not prevent collisions, but it does ensure that the Ethernet works well even though collisions may and do occur. However, the CSMA/CD algorithm does create some performance issues. First, CSMA/CD causes devices to wait until the Ethernet is silent before sending data. This process helps avoid collisions, but it also means that only one device can send at any one instant in time. As a result, all the devices connected to the same hub share the bandwidth available through the hub. The logic of waiting to send until the LAN is silent is called *half duplex*. This refers to the fact that a device either sends or receives at any point in time, but never both at the same time.

The other main feature of CSMA/CD defines what to do when collisions do occur. When a collision occurs, CSMA/CD logic causes the devices that sent the colliding data frames to wait a random amount of time, and then try again. This again helps the LAN to function, but again it impacts performance. During the collision, no useful data makes it across the LAN. Also, the offending devices have to wait longer before trying to use the LAN. Additionally, as the load on an Ethernet increases, the statistical chance for collisions increases as well. In fact, during the years before LAN switches became more affordable and solved some of these performance problems, the rule of thumb was that an Ethernet's performance began to degrade when the load began to exceed 30 percent utilization, mainly as a result of increasing collisions.

Increasing Available Bandwidth Using Switches

The term *collision domain* defines the set of devices whose frames could collide. All devices on a 10BASE2, 10BASE5, or any network using a hub risk collisions between the frames that they send, so all devices on one of these types of Ethernet networks are in the same collision domain. For example, all four devices connected to the hub in Figure 3-10 are in the same collision domain. To avoid collisions, and to recover when they occur, devices in the same collision domain use CSMA/CD.

LAN switches significantly reduce, or even eliminate, the number of collisions on a LAN. Unlike hubs, switches do not create a single shared bus, forwarding received electrical signals out all other ports. Instead, switches do the following:

■ Switches interpret the bits in the received frame so that they can typically send the frame out the one required port, rather than all other ports

■ If a switch needs to forward multiple frames out the same port, the switch buffers the frames in memory, sending one at a time, thereby avoiding collisions

For example, Figure 3-11 illustrates how a switch can forward two frames at the same time while avoiding a collision. In Figure 3-11, both PC1 and PC3 send at the same time. In this case, PC1 sends a data frame with a destination address of PC2, and PC3 sends a data frame with a destination address of PC4. (More on Ethernet addressing is coming up later in this chapter.) The switch looks at the destination Ethernet address and sends the frame from PC1 to PC2 at the same instant as the frame is sent by PC3 to PC4. Had a hub been used, a collision would have occurred; however, because the switch did not send the frames out all other ports, the switch prevented a collision.

NOTE   The switch's logic requires that the switch look at the Ethernet header, which is considered a Layer 2 feature. As a result, switches are considered to operate as a Layer 2 device, whereas hubs are Layer 1 devices.

Buffering also helps prevent collisions. Imagine that PC1 and PC3 both send a frame to PC4 at the same time. The switch, knowing that forwarding both frames to PC4 at the same time would cause a collision, buffers one frame (in other words, temporarily holds it in memory) until the first frame has been completely sent to PC4.

These seemingly simple switch features provide significant performance improvements as compared with using hubs. In particular:

■ If only one device is cabled to each port of a switch, no collisions can occur.

■ Devices connected to one switch port do not share their bandwidth with devices connected to another switch port. Each has its own separate bandwidth, meaning that a switch with 100-Mbps ports has 100 Mbps of bandwidth *per port*.

Figure 3-11 *Basic Switch Operation*

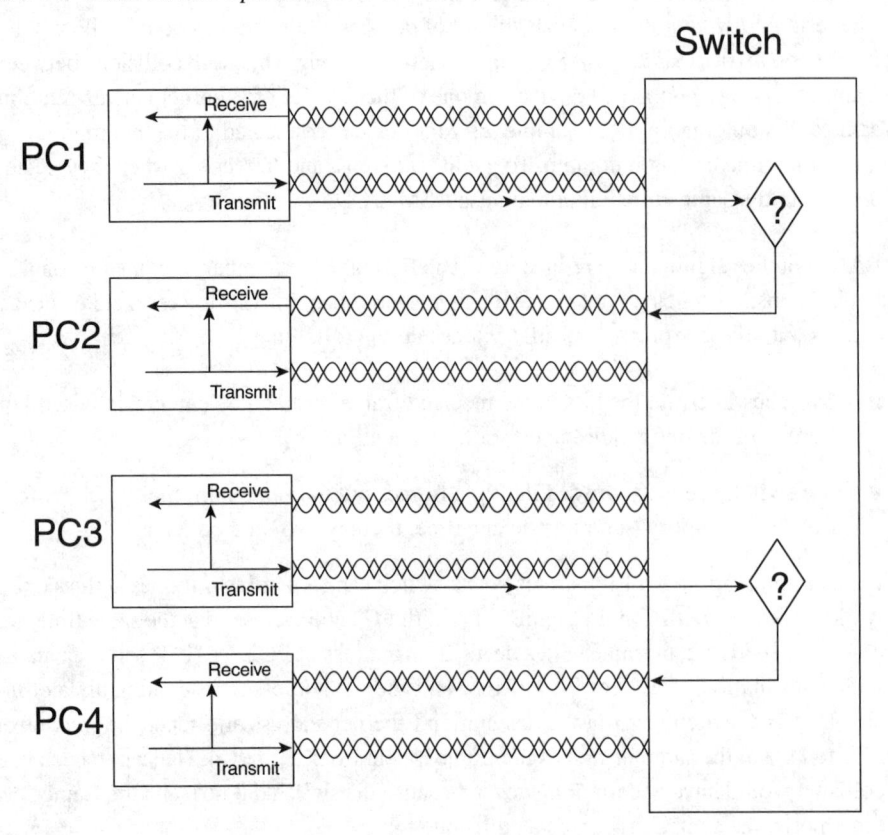

The second point refers to the concepts behind the terms *shared Ethernet* and *switched Ethernet*. As mentioned earlier in this chapter, shared Ethernet means that the LAN bandwidth is shared among the devices on the LAN because they must take turns using the LAN because of the CSMA/CD algorithm. The term switched Ethernet refers to the fact that with switches, bandwidth does not have to be shared, allowing for far greater performance. For example, a hub with 24 100-Mbps Ethernet devices connected to it allows for a theoretical maximum of 100 Mbps of bandwidth. However, a switch with 24 100-Mbps Ethernet devices connected to it supports 100 Mbps for each port, or 2400 Mbps (2.4 Gbps) theoretical maximum bandwidth.

Doubling Performance by Using Full-Duplex Ethernet

Any Ethernet network using hubs requires CSMA/CD logic to work properly. However, CSMA/CD imposes half-duplex logic on each device, meaning that only one device can send at a time. Because switches can buffer frames in memory, switches can completely eliminate collisions on switch ports that connect to a single device. As a result, LAN switches with only one device cabled to each port of the switch allow the use of *full-duplex* operation. Full duplex means that an Ethernet card can send and receive concurrently.

To appreciate why collisions cannot occur, consider Figure 3-12, which shows the full-duplex circuitry used with a single PC's connection to a LAN switch.

Figure 3-12   *Full-Duplex Operation Using a Switch*

With only the switch and one device connected to each other, collisions cannot occur. When you implement full duplex, you disable CSMA/CD logic on the devices on both ends of the cable. By doing so, neither device even thinks about CSMA/CD, and they can go ahead and send data whenever they want. As a result, the performance of the Ethernet on that cable has been doubled by allowed simultaneous transmission in both directions.

Ethernet Layer 1 Summary

So far in this chapter, you have read about the basics of how to build the Layer 1 portions of Ethernet using both hubs and switches. This section explained how to use UTP cables, with RJ-45 connectors, to connect devices to either a hub or a switch. It also explained the general theory of how devices can send data by encoding different electrical signals over an electrical circuit, with the circuit being created using a pair of wires inside the UTP cable. More importantly, this section explained which wire pairs are used to transmit and receive data. Finally, the basic operations of switches were explained, including the potential elimination of collisions, which results in significantly better performance than hubs.

Next, this chapter examines the data link layer protocols defined by Ethernet.

Ethernet Data-Link Protocols

One of the most significant strengths of the Ethernet family of protocols is that these protocols use the same small set of data-link standards. For instance, Ethernet addressing works the same on all the variations of Ethernet, even back to 10BASE5, up through 10-Gbps Ethernet—including Ethernet standards that use other types of cabling besides UTP. Also, the CSMA/CD algorithm is technically a part of the data link layer, again applying to most types of Ethernet, unless it has been disabled.

This section covers most of the details of the Ethernet data-link protocols—in particular, Ethernet addressing, framing, error detection, and identifying the type of data inside the Ethernet frame.

Ethernet Addressing

Ethernet LAN addressing identifies either individual devices or groups of devices on a LAN. Each address is 6 bytes long, is usually written in hexadecimal, and, in Cisco devices, typically is written with periods separating each set of four hex digits. For example, 0000.0C12.3456 is a valid Ethernet address.

Unicast Ethernet addresses identify a single LAN card. (The term *unicast* was chosen mainly for contrast with the terms *broadcast*, *multicast*, and *group addresses*.) Computers use unicast addresses to identify the sender and receiver of an Ethernet frame. For instance, imagine that Fred and Barney are on the same Ethernet, and Fred sends Barney a frame. Fred puts his own Ethernet MAC address in the Ethernet header as the source address and uses Barney's Ethernet MAC address as the destination. When Barney receives the frame, he notices that the destination address is his own address, so he processes the frame. If Barney receives a frame with some other device's unicast address in the destination address field, he simply does not process the frame.

The IEEE defines the format and assignment of LAN addresses. The IEEE requires globally unique unicast MAC addresses on all LAN interface cards. (IEEE calls them MAC addresses because the MAC protocols such as IEEE 802.3 define the addressing details.) To ensure a unique MAC address, the Ethernet card manufacturers encode the MAC address onto the card, usually in a ROM chip. The first half of the address identifies the manufacturer of the card. This code, which is assigned to each manufacturer by the IEEE, is called the *organizationally unique identifier (OUI)*. Each manufacturer assigns a MAC address with its own OUI as the first half of the address, with the second half of the address being assigned a number that this manufacturer has never used on another card. Figure 3-13 shows the structure.

Figure 3-13 *Structure of Unicast Ethernet Addresses*

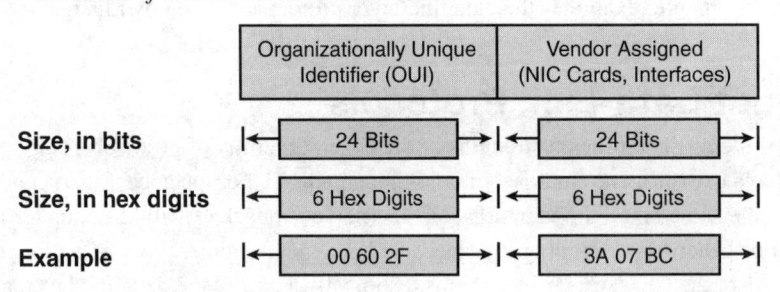

	Organizationally Unique Identifier (OUI)	Vendor Assigned (NIC Cards, Interfaces)
Size, in bits	24 Bits	24 Bits
Size, in hex digits	6 Hex Digits	6 Hex Digits
Example	00 60 2F	3A 07 BC

Many terms can be used to describe unicast LAN addresses. Each LAN card comes with a *burned-in address (BIA)* that is burned into the ROM chip on the card. BIAs sometimes are called *universally administered addresses (UAA)* because the IEEE universally (well, at least worldwide) administers address assignment. Regardless of whether the BIA is used or another address is configured, many people refer to unicast addresses as either LAN addresses, Ethernet addresses, hardware addresses, physical addresses, or MAC addresses.

Group addresses identify more than one LAN interface card. The IEEE defines two general categories of group addresses for Ethernet:

■ **Broadcast addresses:** The most often used of the IEEE group MAC addresses, the broadcast address, has a value of FFFF.FFFF.FFFF (hexadecimal notation). The broadcast address implies that all devices on the LAN should process the frame.

■ **Multicast addresses:** Multicast addresses are used to allow a subset of devices on a LAN to communicate. When IP multicasts over an Ethernet, the multicast MAC addresses used by IP follow this format: 0100.5e*xx.xxxx*, where any value can be used in the last half of the address.

Table 3-4 summarizes most of the details about MAC addresses.

Table 3-4 *LAN MAC Address Terminology and Features*

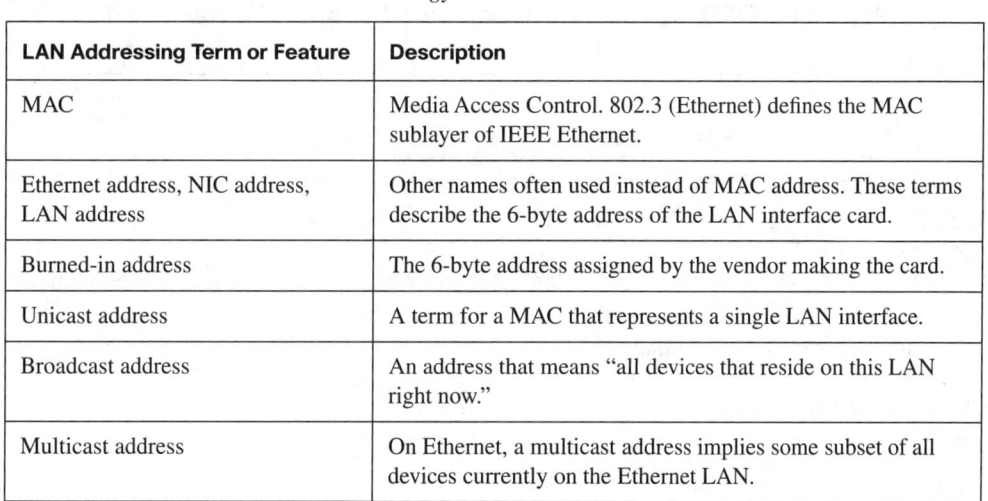
Key
Topic

LAN Addressing Term or Feature	Description
MAC	Media Access Control. 802.3 (Ethernet) defines the MAC sublayer of IEEE Ethernet.
Ethernet address, NIC address, LAN address	Other names often used instead of MAC address. These terms describe the 6-byte address of the LAN interface card.
Burned-in address	The 6-byte address assigned by the vendor making the card.
Unicast address	A term for a MAC that represents a single LAN interface.
Broadcast address	An address that means "all devices that reside on this LAN right now."
Multicast address	On Ethernet, a multicast address implies some subset of all devices currently on the Ethernet LAN.

Ethernet Framing

Framing defines how a string of binary numbers is interpreted. In other words, framing defines the meaning behind the bits that are transmitted across a network. The physical layer helps you get a string of bits from one device to another. When the receiving device gets the bits, how should they be interpreted? The term *framing* refers to the definition of the fields assumed to be in the data that is received. In other words, framing defines the meaning of the bits transmitted and received over a network.

For instance, you just read an example of Fred sending data to Barney over an Ethernet. Fred put Barney's Ethernet address in the Ethernet header so that Barney would know that the Ethernet frame was meant for him. The IEEE 802.3 standard defines the location of the destination address field inside the string of bits sent across the Ethernet.

The framing used for Ethernet has changed a couple of times over the years. Xerox defined one version of the framing, which the IEEE then changed when it took over Ethernet standards in the early 1980s. The IEEE finalized a compromise standard for framing in 1997 that includes some of the features of the original Xerox Ethernet framing, along with the framing defined by the IEEE. The end result is the bottom frame format shown in Figure 3-14.

Figure 3-14 *LAN Header Formats*

DIX

Preamble 8	Destination 6	Source 6	Type 2	Data and Pad 46 – 1500	FCS 4

IEEE 802.3 (Original)

Preamble 7	SFD 1	Destination 6	Source 6	Length 2	Data and Pad 46 – 1500	FCS 4

IEEE 802.3 (Revised 1997)

Bytes

Preamble 7	SFD 1	Destination 6	Source 6	Length/ Type 2	Data and Pad 46 – 1500	FCS 4

Most of the fields in the Ethernet frame are important enough to be covered at some point in this chapter. For reference, Table 3-5 lists the fields in the header and trailer, and a brief description, for reference.

Table 3-5 *IEEE 802.3 Ethernet Header and Trailer Fields*

Field	Field Length in Bytes	Description
Preamble	7	Synchronization
Start Frame Delimiter (SFD)	1	Signifies that the next byte begins the Destination MAC field
Destination MAC address	6	Identifies the intended recipient of this frame
Source MAC address	6	Identifies the sender of this frame
Length	2	Defines the length of the data field of the frame (either length or type is present, but not both)
Type	2	Defines the type of protocol listed inside the frame (either length or type is present, but not both)

Table 3-5 *IEEE 802.3 Ethernet Header and Trailer Fields (Continued)*

Field	Field Length in Bytes	Description
Data and Pad[*]	46–1500	Holds data from a higher layer, typically an L3 PDU (generic), and often an IP packet
Frame Check Sequence (FCS)	4	Provides a method for the receiving NIC to determine if the frame experienced transmission errors

[*]The IEEE 802.3 specification limits the data portion of the 802.3 frame to a maximum of 1500 bytes. The Data field was designed to hold Layer 3 packets; the term maximum transmission unit (MTU) defines the maximum Layer 3 packet that can be sent over a medium. Because the Layer 3 packet rests inside the data portion of an Ethernet frame, 1500 bytes is the largest IP MTU allowed over an Ethernet.

Identifying the Data Inside an Ethernet Frame

Over the years, many different network layer (Layer 3) protocols have been designed. Most of these protocols were part of larger network protocol models created by vendors to support their products, such as IBM Systems Network Architecture (SNA), Novell NetWare, Digital Equipment Corporation's DECnet, and Apple Computer's AppleTalk. Additionally, the OSI and TCP/IP models also defined network layer protocols.

All these Layer 3 protocols, plus several others, could use Ethernet. To use Ethernet, the network layer protocol would place its packet (generically speaking, its L3 PDU) into the data portion of the Ethernet frame shown in Figure 3-14. However, when a device receives such an Ethernet frame, that receiving device needs to know what type of L3 PDU is in the Ethernet frame. Is it an IP packet? an OSI packet? SNA? and so on.

To answer that question, most data-link protocol headers, including Ethernet, have a field with a code that defines the type of protocol header that follows. Generically speaking, these fields in data-link headers are called *Type fields*. For example, to imply that an IP packet is inside an Ethernet frame, the Type field (as shown in Figure 3-14) would have a value of hexadecimal 0800 (decimal 2048). Other types of L3 PDUs would be implied by using a different value in the Type field.

Interestingly, because of the changes to Ethernet framing over the years, another popular option exists for the protocol Type field, particularly when sending IP packets. If the 802.3 Type/Length field (in Figure 3-14) has a value less than hex 0600 (decimal 1536), the Type/Length field is used as a Length field for that frame, identifying the length of the entire Ethernet frame. In that case, another field is needed to identify the type of L3 PDU inside the frame.

To create a Type field for frames that use the Type/Length field as a Length field, either one or two additional headers are added after the Ethernet 802.3 header but before the

Layer 3 header. For example, when sending IP packets, the Ethernet frame has two additional headers:

■   An IEEE 802.2 Logical Link Control (LLC) header

■   An IEEE Subnetwork Access Protocol (SNAP) header

Figure 3-15 shows an Ethernet frame with these additional headers. Note that the SNAP header Type field has the same purpose, with the same reserved values, as the Ethernet Type/Length field.

Figure 3-15 *802.2 SNAP Headers*

	802.3 Header				802.2 LLC Header			SNAP Header			
	Preamble	SFD	Destination	Source	**Length***	DSAP	SSAP	CTL	OUI	**Type**	Data and Pad	FCS
Bytes	7	1	6	6	**2**	1	1	1	3	**2**	46 - 1500	4

* To be a Length field, this value must be less than decimal 1536.

Error Detection

The final Ethernet data link layer function explained here is error detection. Error detection is the process of discovering if a frame's bits changed as a result of being sent over the network. The bits might change for many small reasons, but generally such errors occur as a result of some kind of electrical interference. Like every data-link protocol covered on the CCNA exams, Ethernet defines both a header and trailer, with the trailer containing a field used for the purpose of error detection.

The Ethernet Frame Check Sequence (FCS) field in the Ethernet trailer—the only field in the Ethernet trailer—allows a device receiving an Ethernet frame to detect whether the bits have changed during transmission. To detect an error, the sending device calculates a complex mathematical function, with the frame contents as input, putting the result into the frame's 4-byte FCS field. The receiving device does the same math on the frame; if its calculation matches the FCS field in the frame, no errors occurred. If the result doesn't match the FCS field, an error occurred, and the frame is discarded.

Note that error detection does not also mean error recovery. Ethernet defines that the errored frame should be discarded, but Ethernet takes no action to cause the frame to be retransmitted. Other protocols, notably TCP (as covered in Chapter 6, "Fundamentals of TCP/IP Transport, Applications, and Security"), can notice the lost data and cause error recovery to occur.

Exam Preparation Tasks

Review All the Key Topics

Review the most important topics from this chapter, noted with the key topics icon. Table 3-6 lists these key topics and where each is discussed.

Key Topic

Table 3-6 *Key Topics for Chapter 3*

Key Topic Element	Description	Page Number
Table 3-2	The four most popular types of Ethernet LANs and some details about each	46
List	Summary of CSMA/CD logic	49
Figure 3-6	EIA/TIA standard Ethernet Cabling Pinouts	55
Figure 3-7	Straight-through cable concept	56
Figure 3-8	Crossover cable concept	57
Table 3-3	List of devices that transmit on wire pair 1,2 and pair 3,6	57
List	Detailed CSMA/CD logic	60
Figure 3-13	Structure of a unicast Ethernet address	64
Table 3-4	Key Ethernet addressing terms	65

Complete the Tables and Lists from Memory

Print a copy of Appendix H, "Memory Tables" (found on the CD), or at least the section for this chapter, and complete the tables and lists from memory. Appendix I, "Memory Tables Answer Key," also on the CD, includes completed tables and lists for you to check your work.

Definitions of Key Terms

Define the following key terms from this chapter and check your answers in the glossary.

1000BASE-T, 100BASE-TX, 10BASE-T, crossover cable, CSMA/CD, full duplex, half duplex, hub, pinout, protocol type, shared Ethernet, straight-through cable, switch, switched Ethernet, twisted pair

This chapter covers the following subjects:

OSI Layer 1 for Point-to-Point WANs: This section explains the physical cabling and devices used to create the customer portions of a leased circuit.

OSI Layer 2 for Point-to-Point WANs: This section introduces the data link layer protocols used on point-to-point leased lines, namely HDLC and PPP.

Frame Relay and Packet-Switching Services: This section explains the concept of a WAN packet-switching service, with particular attention given to Frame Relay.

CHAPTER 4

Fundamentals of WANs

In the previous chapter, you learned more details about how Ethernet LANs perform the functions defined by the two lowest OSI layers. In this chapter, you will learn about how wide-area network (WAN) standards and protocols also implement OSI Layer 1 (physical layer) and Layer 2 (data link layer). The OSI physical layer details are covered, along with three popular WAN data link layer protocols: High-Level Data Link Control (HDLC), Point-to-Point Protocol (PPP), and Frame Relay.

"Do I Know This Already?" Quiz

The "Do I Know This Already?" quiz allows you to assess if you should read the entire chapter. If you miss no more than one of these eight self-assessment questions, you might want to move ahead to the "Exam Preparation Tasks" section. Table 4-1 lists the major headings in this chapter and the "Do I Know This Already?" quiz questions covering the material in those headings so you can assess your knowledge of these specific areas. The answers to the "Do I Know This Already?" quiz appear in Appendix A.

Table 4-1   *"Do I Know This Already?" Foundation Topics Section-to-Question Mapping*

Foundation Topics Section	Questions
OSI Layer 1 for Point-to-Point WANs	1–4
OSI Layer 2 for Point-to-Point WANs	5, 6
Frame Relay and Packet-Switching Services	7, 8

1. Which of the following best describes the main function of OSI Layer 1 protocols?

   a. Framing

   b. Delivery of bits from one device to another

   c. Addressing

   d. Local Management Interface (LMI)

   e. DLCI

2. Which of the following typically connects to a four-wire line provided by a telco?

   a. Router serial interface

   b. CSU/DSU

   c. Transceiver

   d. Switch serial interface

3. Which of the following typically connects to a V.35 or RS-232 end of a cable when cabling a leased line?

   a. Router serial interface

   b. CSU/DSU

   c. Transceiver

   d. Switch serial interface

4. On a point-to-point WAN link using a leased line between two routers located hundreds of miles apart, what devices are considered to be the DTE devices?

   a. Routers

   b. CSU/DSU

   c. The central office equipment

   d. A chip on the processor of each router

   e. None of these answers are correct.

5. Which of the following functions of OSI Layer 2 is specified by the protocol standard for PPP, but is implemented with a Cisco proprietary header field for HDLC?

   a. Framing

   b. Arbitration

   c. Addressing

   d. Error detection

   e. Identifying the type of protocol that is inside the frame

6. Imagine that Router1 has three point-to-point serial links, one link each to three remote routers. Which of the following is true about the required HDLC addressing at Router1?

    a. Router1 must use HDLC addresses 1, 2, and 3.

    b. Router1 must use any three unique addresses between 1 and 1023.

    c. Router1 must use any three unique addresses between 16 and 1000.

    d. Router1 must use three sequential unique addresses between 1 and 1023.

    e. None of these answers are correct.

7. What is the name of the Frame Relay field used to identify Frame Relay virtual circuits?

    a. Data-link connection identifier

    b. Data-link circuit identifier

    c. Data-link connection indicator

    d. Data-link circuit indicator

    e. None of these answers are correct.

8. Which of the following is true about Frame Relay virtual circuits (VCs)?

    a. Each VC requires a separate access link.

    b. Multiple VCs can share the same access link.

    c. All VCs sharing the same access link must connect to the same router on the other side of the VC.

    d. All VCs on the same access link must use the same DLCI.

Foundation Topics

As you read in the previous chapter, the OSI physical and data link layers work together to deliver data across a wide variety of types of physical networks. LAN standards and protocols define how to network between devices that are relatively close together, hence the term *local-area* in the acronym LAN. WAN standards and protocols define how to network between devices that are relatively far apart—in some cases, even thousands of miles apart—hence the term *wide-area* in the acronym WAN.

LANs and WANs both implement the same OSI Layer 1 and Layer 2 functions, but with different mechanisms and details. This chapter points out the similarities between the two, and provides details about the differences.

The WAN topics in this chapter describe mainly how enterprise networks use WANs to connect remote sites. Part IV of this book covers a broader range of WAN topics, including popular Internet access technologies such as digital subscriber line (DSL) and cable, along with a variety of configuration topics. The *CCNA ICND2 Official Exam Certification Guide* covers Frame Relay in much more detail than this book, as well as the concepts behind Internet virtual private networks (VPN), which is a way to use the Internet instead of traditional WAN links.

OSI Layer 1 for Point-to-Point WANs

The OSI physical layer, or Layer 1, defines the details of how to move data from one device to another. In fact, many people think of OSI Layer 1 as "sending bits." Higher layers encapsulate the data, as described in Chapter 2, "The TCP/IP and OSI Networking Models." No matter what the other OSI layers do, eventually the sender of the data needs to actually transmit the bits to another device. The OSI physical layer defines the standards and protocols used to create the physical network and to send the bits across that network.

A point-to-point WAN link acts like an Ethernet trunk between two Ethernet switches in many ways. For perspective, look at Figure 4-1, which shows a LAN with two buildings and two switches in each building. As a brief review, remember that several types of Ethernet use one twisted pair of wires to transmit and another twisted pair to receive, in order to reduce electromagnetic interference. You typically use straight-through Ethernet cables between end-user devices and the switches. For the trunk links between the switches, you use crossover cables because each switch transmits on the same pair of pins on the connector, so the crossover cable connects one device's transmit pair to the other device's receive pair. The lower part of Figure 4-1 reminds you of the basic idea behind a crossover cable.

Figure 4-1   *Example LAN, Two Buildings*

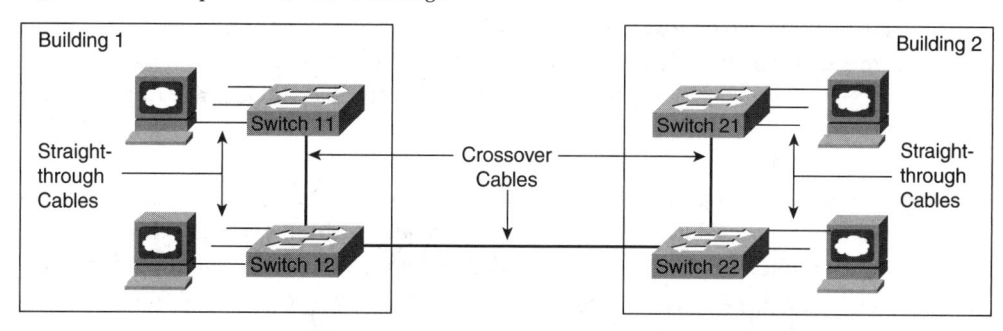

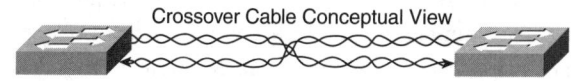

Crossover Cable Conceptual View

Now imagine that the buildings are 1000 miles apart instead of right next to each other. You are immediately faced with two problems:

- Ethernet does not support any type of cabling that allows an individual trunk to run for 1000 miles.

- Even if Ethernet supported a 1000-mile trunk, you do not have the rights-of-way needed to bury a cable over the 1000 miles of real estate between buildings.

The big distinction between LANs and WANs relates to how far apart the devices can be and still be capable of sending and receiving data. LANs tend to reside in a single building or possibly among buildings in a campus using optical cabling approved for Ethernet. WAN connections typically run longer distances than Ethernet—across town or between cities. Often, only one or a few companies even have the rights to run cables under the ground between the sites. So, the people who created WAN standards needed to use different physical specifications than Ethernet to send data 1000 miles or more (WAN).

> **NOTE**   Besides LANs and WANs, the term metropolitan-area network (MAN) is sometimes used for networks that extend between buildings and through rights-of-ways. The term MAN typically implies a network that does not reach as far as a WAN, generally in a single metropolitan area. The distinctions between LANs, MANs, and WANs are blurry—there is no set distance that means a link is a LAN, MAN, or WAN link.

To create such long links, or circuits, the actual physical cabling is owned, installed, and managed by a company that has the right of way to run cables under streets. Because a company that needs to send data over the WAN circuit does not actually own the cable or line, it is called a *leased line*. Companies that can provide leased WAN lines typically started life as the local telephone company, or telco. In many countries, the telco is still a government-regulated or government-controlled monopoly; these companies are sometimes called public telephone and telegraph (PTT) companies. Today, many people use the generic term *service provider* to refer to a company that provides any form of WAN connectivity, including Internet services.

Point-to-point WAN links provide basic connectivity between two points. To get a point-to-point WAN link, you would work with a service provider to install a circuit. What the phone company or service provider gives you is similar to what you would have if you made a phone call between two sites, but you never hung up. The two devices on either end of the WAN circuit could send and receive bits between each other any time they want, without needing to dial a phone number. Because the connection is always available, a point-to-point WAN connection is sometimes called a *leased circuit* or *leased line* because you have the exclusive right to use that circuit, as long as you keep paying for it.

Now back to the comparison of the LAN between two nearby buildings versus the WAN between two buildings that are 1000 miles apart. The physical details are different, but the same general functions need to be accomplished, as shown in Figure 4-2.

Figure 4-2 *Conceptual View of Point-to-Point Leased Line*

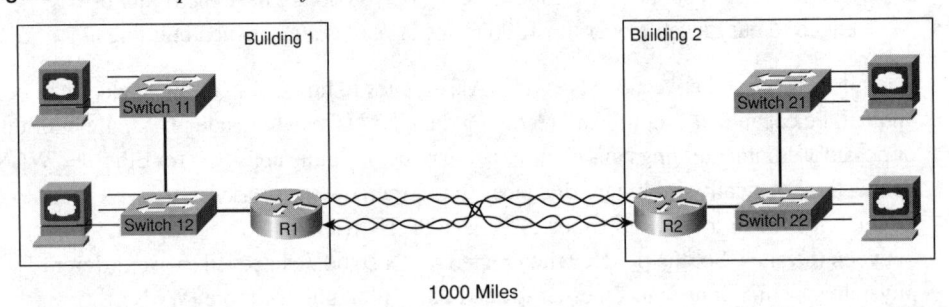

1000 Miles

Keep in mind that Figure 4-2 provides a conceptual view of a point-to-point WAN link. In concept, the telco installs a physical cable, with a transmit and a receive twisted pair, between the buildings. The cable has been connected to each router, and each router, in turn, has been connected to the LAN switches. As a result of this new physical WAN link and the logic used by the routers connected to it, data now can be transferred between the two sites. In the next section, you will learn more about the physical details of the WAN link.

NOTE Ethernet switches have many different types of interfaces, but all the interfaces are some form of Ethernet. Routers provide the capability to connect many different types of OSI Layer 1 and Layer 2 technologies. So, when you see a LAN connected to some other site using a WAN connection, you will see a router connected to each, as in Figure 4-2.

WAN Connections from the Customer Viewpoint

The concepts behind a point-to-point connection are simple. However, to fully understand what the service provider does to build its network to support your point-to-point line, you would need to spend lots of time studying and learning technologies outside the scope of the ICND1 exam. However, most of what you need to know about WANs for the ICND1 exam relates to how WAN connections are implemented between the telephone company and a customer site. Along the way, you will need to learn a little about the terminology used by the provider.

In Figure 4-2, you saw that a WAN leased line acts as if the telco gave you two twisted pairs of wires between the two sites on each end of the line. Well, it is not that simple. Of course, a lot more underlying technology must be used to create the circuit, and telcos use a lot of terminology that is different from LAN terminology. The telco seldom actually runs a 1000-mile cable for you between the two sites. Instead, it has built a large network already and even runs extra cables from the local central office (CO) to your building (a CO is just a building where the telco locates the devices used to create its own network). Regardless of what the telco does inside its own network, what you receive is the equivalent of a four-wire leased circuit between two buildings.

Figure 4-3 introduces some of the key concepts and terms relating to WAN circuits.

Figure 4-3 *Point-to-Point Leased Line: Components and Terminology*

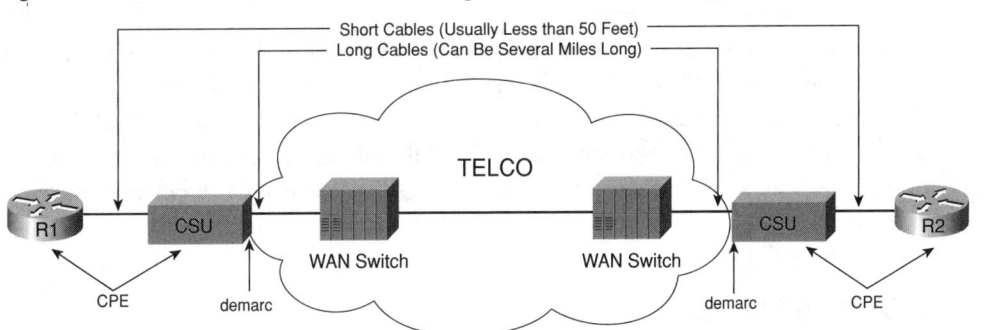

Typically, routers connect to a device called an external channel service unit/data service unit (CSU/DSU). The router connects to the CSU/DSU with a relatively short cable, typically less than 50 feet long, because the CSU/DSUs typically get placed in a rack near the router. The much longer four-wire cable from the telco plugs into the CSU/DSU. That cable leaves the building, running through the hidden (typically buried) cables that you sometimes see phone company workers fixing by the side of the road. The other end of that cable ends up in the CO, with the cable connecting to a CO device generically called a WAN switch.

The same general physical connectivity exists on each side of the point-to-point WAN link. In between the two COs, the service provider can build its network with several competing different types of technology, all of which is beyond the scope of any of the CCNA exams. However, the perspective in Figure 4-2 remains true—the two routers can send and receive data simultaneously across the point-to-point WAN link.

From a legal perspective, two different companies own the various components of the equipment and lines in Figure 4-3. For instance, the router cable and typically the CSU/DSU are owned by the telco's customer, and the wiring to the CO and the gear inside the CO are owned by the telco. So, the telco uses the term *demarc*, which is short for demarcation point, to refer to the point at which the telco's responsibility is on one side and the customer's responsibility is on the other. The demarc is not a separate device or cable, but rather a concept of where the responsibilities of the telco and customer end.

In the United States, the demarc is typically where the telco physically terminates the set of two twisted pairs inside the customer building. Typically, the customer asks the telco to terminate the cable in a particular room, and most, if not all, the lines from the telco into that building terminate in the same room.

The term customer premises equipment (CPE) refers to devices that are at the customer site, from the telco's perspective. For instance, both the CSU/DSU and the router are CPE devices in this case.

The demarc does not always reside where it is shown in Figure 4-3. In some cases, the telco actually could own the CSU/DSU, and the demarc would be on the router side of the CSU/DSU. In some cases today, the telco even owns and manages the router at the customer site, again moving the point that would be considered the demarc. Regardless of where the demarc sits from a legal perspective, the term CPE still refers to the equipment at the telco customer's location.

WAN Cabling Standards

Cisco offers a large variety of different WAN interface cards for its routers, including synchronous and asynchronous serial interfaces. For any of the point-to-point serial links or Frame Relay links in this chapter, the router uses an interface that supports synchronous communication.

Synchronous serial interfaces in Cisco routers use a variety of proprietary physical connector types, such as the 60-pin D-shell connector shown at the top of the cable drawings in Figure 4-4. The cable connecting the router to the CSU/DSU uses a connector that fits the router serial interface on the router side, and a standardized WAN connector type that matches the CSU/DSU interface on the CSU/DSU end of the cable. Figure 4-4 shows a typical connection, with some of the serial cabling options listed.

Figure 4-4 *Serial Cabling Options*

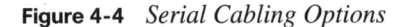

The engineer who deploys a network chooses the cable based on the connectors on the router and the CSU/DSU. Beyond that choice, engineers do not really need to think about how the cabling and pins work—they just work! Many of the pins are used for control functions, and a few are used for the transmission of data. Some pins are used for clocking, as described in the next section.

> **NOTE**   The Telecommunications Industry Association (TIA) is accredited by the American National Standards Institute (ANSI) to represent the United States in work with international standards bodies. The TIA defines some of the WAN cabling standards, in addition to LAN cabling standards. For more information on these standards bodies, and to purchase copies of the standards, refer to the websites http://www.tiaonline.org and http://www.ansi.org.

The cable between the CSU/DSU and the telco CO typically uses an RJ-48 connector to connect to the CSU/DSU; the RJ-48 connector has the same size and shape as the RJ-45 connector used for Ethernet cables.

Many Cisco routers support serial interfaces that have an integrated internal CSU/DSU. With an internal CSU/DSU, the router does not need a cable connecting it to an external CSU/DSU because the CSU/DSU is internal to the router. In these cases, the serial cables shown in Figure 4-4 are not needed, and the physical line from the telco is connected to a port on the router, typically an RJ-48 port in the router serial interface card.

Clock Rates, Synchronization, DCE, and DTE

An enterprise network engineer who wants to install a new point-to-point leased line between two routers has several tasks to perform. First, the network engineer contacts a service provider and orders the circuit. As part of that process, the network engineer specifies how fast the circuit should run, in kilobits per second (kbps). While the telco installs the circuit, the engineer purchases two CSU/DSUs, installs one at each site, and configures each CSU/DSU. The network engineer also purchases and installs routers, and connects serial cables from each router to the respective CSU/DSU using the cables shown in Figure 4-4. Eventually, the telco installs the new line into the customer premises, and the line can be connected to the CSU/DSUs, as shown in Figure 4-3.

Every WAN circuit ordered from a service provider runs at one of many possible predefined speeds. This speed is often referred to as the clock rate, bandwidth, or link speed. The enterprise network engineer (the customer) must specify the speed when ordering a circuit, and the telco installs a circuit that runs at that speed. Additionally, the enterprise network engineer must configure the CSU/DSU on each end of the link to match the defined speed.

To make the link work, the various devices need to synchronize their clocks so that they run at exactly the same speed—a process called synchronization. *Synchronous circuits* impose time ordering at the link's sending and receiving ends. Essentially, all devices agree to try to run at the exact same speed, but it is expensive to build devices that truly can operate at exactly the same speed. So, the devices operate at close to the same speed and listen to the speed of the other device on the other side of the link. One side makes small adjustments in its rate to match the other side.

Synchronization occurs between the two CSU/DSUs on a leased line by having one CSU/DSU (the slave) adjust its clock to match the clock rate of the other CSU/DSU (the master). The process works almost like the scenes in spy novels in which the spies synchronize their watches; in this case, the networking devices synchronize their clocks several times per second.

In practice, the clocking concept includes a hierarchy of different clock sources. The telco provides clocking information to the CSU/DSUs based on the transitions in the electrical signal on the circuit. The two CSU/DSUs then adjust their speeds to match the clocking signals from the telco. The CSU/DSUs each supply clocking signals to the routers so that the routers simply react, sending and receiving data at the correct rate. So, from the routers' perspectives, the CSU/DSU is considered to be *clocking* the link.

A couple of other key WAN terms relate to the process of clocking. The device that provides clocking, typically the CSU/DSU, is considered to be the data communications equipment (DCE). The device receiving clocking, typically the router, is referred to as data terminal equipment (DTE).

Building a WAN Link in a Lab

On a practical note, when purchasing serial cables from Cisco, you can pick either a DTE or a DCE cable. You pick the type of cable based on whether the router is acting like DTE or DCE. In most cases with a real WAN link, the router acts as DTE, so the router must use a DTE cable to connect to the CSU/DSU.

You can build a serial link in a lab without using any CSU/DSUs, but to do so, one router must supply clocking. When building a lab to study for any of the Cisco exams, you do not need to buy CSU/DSUs or order a WAN circuit. You can buy two routers, a DTE serial cable for one router, and a DCE serial cable for the other, and connect the two cables together. The router with the DCE cable in it can be configured to provide clocking, meaning that you do not need a CSU/DSU. So, you can build a WAN in your home lab, saving hundreds of dollars by not buying CSU/DSUs. The DTE and DCE cables can be connected to each other (the DCE cable has a female connector and the DTE cable has a male connector) and to the two routers. With one additional configuration command on one of the routers (the **clock rate** command), you have a point-to-point serial link. This type of connection between two routers sometimes is called a back-to-back serial connection.

Figure 4-5 shows the cabling for a back-to-back serial connection and also shows that the combined DCE/DTE cables reverse the transmit and receive pins, much like a crossover Ethernet cable allows two directly connected devices to communicate.

Figure 4-5 *Serial Cabling Uses a DTE Cable and a DCE Cable*

As you see in Figure 4-5, the DTE cable, the same cable that you typically use to connect to a CSU/DSU, does not swap the Tx and Rx pins. The DCE cable swaps transmit and receive, so the wiring with one router's Tx pin connected to the other router's Rx, and vice versa, remains intact. The router with the DCE cable installed needs to supply clocking, so the **clock rate** command will be added to that router to define the speed.

Link Speeds Offered by Telcos

No matter what you call them—telcos, PTTs, service providers—these companies do not simply let you pick the exact speed of a WAN link. Instead, standards define how fast a point-to-point link can run.

For a long time, the telcos of the world made more money selling voice services than selling data services. As technology progressed during the mid-twentieth century, the telcos of the world developed a standard for sending voice using digital transmissions. Digital signaling inside their networks allowed for the growth of more profitable data services, such as leased lines. It also allowed better efficiencies, making the build-out of the expanding voice networks much less expensive.

The original mechanism used for converting analog voice to a digital signal is called pulse code modulation (PCM). PCM defines that an incoming analog voice signal should be sampled 8000 times per second, and each sample should be represented by an 8-bit code. So, 64,000 bits were needed to represent 1 second of voice. When the telcos of the world built their first digital networks, they chose a baseline transmission speed of 64 kbps because that was the necessary bandwidth for a single voice call. The term digital signal level 0 (DS0) refers to the standard for a single 64-kbps line.

Today, most telcos offer leased lines in multiples of 64 kbps. In the United States, the digital signal level 1 (DS1) standard defines a single line that supports 24 DS0s, plus an 8-kbps overhead channel, for a speed of 1.544 Mbps. (A DS1 is also called a T1 line.) Another option is a digital signal level 3 (DS3) service, also called a T3 line, which holds 28 DS1s. Other parts of the world use different standards, with Europe and Japan using standards that hold 32 DS0s, called an E1 line, with an E3 line holding 16 E1s.

> **NOTE**   The combination of multiple slower-speed lines and channels into one faster-speed line or channel—for instance, combining 24 DS0s into a single T1 line—is generally called time-division multiplexing (TDM).

Table 4-2 lists some of the standards for WAN speeds. Included in the table are the type of line, plus the type of signaling (for example, DS1). The signaling specifications define the electrical signals that encode a binary 1 or 0 on the line. You should be aware of the general idea, and remember the key terms for T1 and E1 lines in particular, for the ICND1 exam.

Table 4-2 *WAN Speed Summary*

Name(s) of Line	Bit Rate
DS0	64 kbps
DS1 (T1)	1.544 Mbps (24 DS0s, plus 8 kbps overhead)
DS3 (T3)	44.736 Mbps (28 DS1s, plus management overhead)
E1	2.048 Mbps (32 DS0s)
E3	34.368 Mbps (16 E1s, plus management overhead)
J1 (Y1)	2.048 Mbps (32 DS0s; Japanese standard)

The leased circuits described so far in this chapter form the basis for the WAN services used by many enterprises today. Next, this chapter explains the data link layer protocols used when a leased circuit connects two routers.

OSI Layer 2 for Point-to-Point WANs

WAN protocols used on point-to-point serial links provide the basic function of data delivery across that one link. The two most popular data link layer protocols used on point-to-point links are High-Level Data Link Control (HDLC) and Point-to-Point Protocol (PPP).

HDLC

Because point-to-point links are relatively simple, HDLC has only a small amount of work to do. In particular, HDLC needs to determine if the data passed the link without any errors; HDLC discards the frame if errors occurred. Additionally, HDLC needs to identify the type of packet inside the HDLC frame so the receiving device knows the packet type.

To achieve the main goal of delivering data across the link and to check for errors and identify the packet type, HDLC defines framing. The HDLC header includes an Address field and a Protocol Type field, with the trailer containing a frame check sequence (FCS) field. Figure 4-6 outlines the standard HDLC frame and the HDLC frame that is Cisco proprietary.

HDLC defines a 1-byte Address field, although on point-to-point links, it is not really needed. Having an Address field in HDLC is sort of like when I have lunch with my friend Gary, and only Gary. I do not need to start every sentence with "Hey Gary"—he knows I am talking to him. On point-to-point WAN links, the router on one end of the link knows that there is only one possible recipient of the data—the router on the other end of the link—so the address does not really matter today.

Figure 4-6 *HDLC Framing*

Standard HDLC (No Type Field)

Bytes	1	1	1	Variable	4
	Flag	Address	Control	Data	FCS

Bytes	1	1	1	2	Variable	4
	Flag	Address	Control	Type	Data	FCS

Proprietary Cisco HDLC (Adds Type Field)

> **NOTE**   The Address field was useful in years past, when the telco would sell multidrop circuits. These circuits had more than two devices on the circuit, so an Address field was needed.

HDLC performs error detection just like Ethernet—it uses an FCS field in the HDLC trailer. And just like Ethernet, if a received frame has errors in it, the device receiving the frame discards the frame, with no error recovery performed by HDLC.

HDLC also performs the function of identifying the encapsulated data, just like Ethernet. When a router receives an HDLC frame, it wants to know what type of packet is held inside the frame. The Cisco implementation of HDLC includes a *Protocol Type* field that identifies the type of packet inside the frame. Cisco uses the same values in its 2-byte HDLC Protocol Type field as it does in the Ethernet Protocol Type field.

The original HDLC standards did not include a Protocol Type field, so Cisco added one to support the first serial links on Cisco routers, back in the early days of Cisco in the latter 1980s. By adding something to the HDLC header, Cisco made its version of HDLC proprietary. So, the Cisco implementation of HDLC will not work when connecting a Cisco router to another vendor's router.

HDLC is very simple. There simply is not a lot of work for the point-to-point data link layer protocols to perform.

Point-to-Point Protocol

The International Telecommunications Union (ITU), previously known as the Consultative Committee for International Telecommunications Technologies (CCITT), first defined HDLC. Later, the Internet Engineering Task Force (IETF) saw the need for another data link layer protocol for use between routers over a point-to-point link. In RFC 1661 (1994), the IETF created the Point-to-Point Protocol (PPP).

Comparing the basics, PPP behaves much like HDLC. The framing looks identical to the Cisco proprietary HDLC framing. There is an Address field, but the addressing does not matter. PPP does discard errored frames that do not pass the FCS check. Additionally, PPP uses a 2-byte Protocol Type field. However, because the Protocol Type field is part of the standard for PPP, any vendor that conforms to the PPP standard can communicate with other vendor products. So, when connecting a Cisco router to another vendor's router over a point-to-point serial link, PPP is the data link layer protocol of choice.

PPP was defined much later than the original HDLC specifications. As a result, the creators of PPP included many additional features that had not been seen in WAN data link layer protocols up to that time, so PPP has become the most popular and feature-rich of WAN data link layer protocols.

Point-to-Point WAN Summary

Point-to-point WAN leased lines and their associated data link layer protocols use another set of terms and concepts beyond those covered for LANs, as outlined in Table 4-3.

Table 4-3 *WAN Terminology*

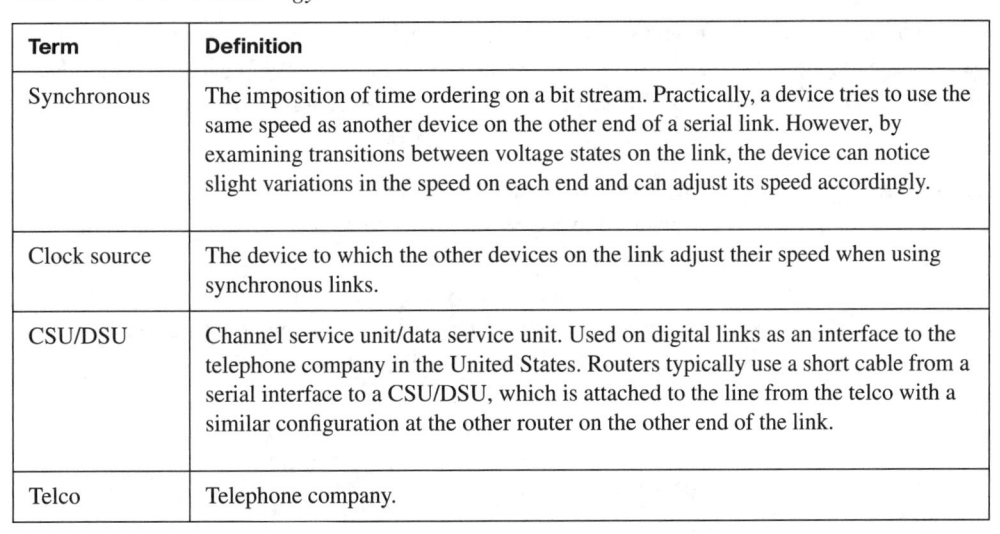

Key
Topic

Term	Definition
Synchronous	The imposition of time ordering on a bit stream. Practically, a device tries to use the same speed as another device on the other end of a serial link. However, by examining transitions between voltage states on the link, the device can notice slight variations in the speed on each end and can adjust its speed accordingly.
Clock source	The device to which the other devices on the link adjust their speed when using synchronous links.
CSU/DSU	Channel service unit/data service unit. Used on digital links as an interface to the telephone company in the United States. Routers typically use a short cable from a serial interface to a CSU/DSU, which is attached to the line from the telco with a similar configuration at the other router on the other end of the link.
Telco	Telephone company.

continues

Table 4-3 *WAN Terminology (Continued)*

Term	Definition
Four-wire circuit	A line from the telco with four wires, composed of two twisted-pair wires. Each pair is used to send in one direction, so a four-wire circuit allows full-duplex communication.
T1	A line from the telco that allows transmission of data at 1.544 Mbps.
E1	Similar to a T1, but used in Europe. It uses a rate of 2.048 Mbps and 32 64-kbps channels.

Also, just for survival when talking about WANs, keep in mind that all the following terms may be used to refer to a point-to-point leased line as covered so far in this chapter:

leased line, leased circuit, link, serial link, serial line, point-to-point link, circuit

Frame Relay and Packet-Switching Services

Service providers offer a class of WAN services, different from leased lines, that can be categorized as *packet-switching services*. In a packet-switching service, physical WAN connectivity exists, similar to a leased line. However, a company can connect a large number of routers to the packet-switching service, using a single serial link from each router into the packet-switching service. Once connected, each router can send packets to all the other routers—much like all the devices connected to an Ethernet hub or switch can send data directly to each other.

Two types of packet-switching service are very popular today, Frame Relay and Asynchronous Transfer Mode (ATM), with Frame Relay being much more common. This section introduces the main concepts behind packet-switching services, and explains the basics of Frame Relay.

The Scaling Benefits of Packet Switching

Point-to-point WANs can be used to connect a pair of routers at multiple remote sites. However, an alternative WAN service, Frame Relay, has many advantages over point-to-point links, particularly when you connect many sites via a WAN. To introduce you to Frame Relay, this section focuses on a few of the key benefits compared to leased lines, one of which you can easily see when considering the illustration in Figure 4-7.

Figure 4-7 *Two Leased Lines to Two Branch Offices*

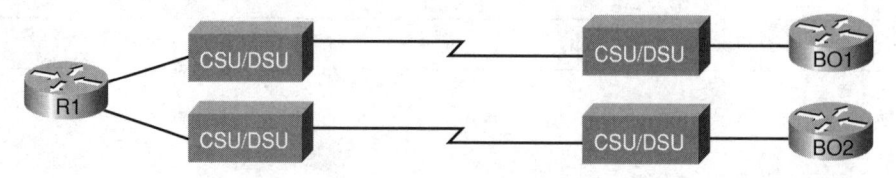

In Figure 4-7, a main site is connected to two branch offices, labeled BO1 and BO2. The main site router, R1, requires two serial interfaces and two separate CSU/DSUs. But what happens when the company grows to 10 sites? Or 100 sites? Or 500 sites? For each point-to-point line, R1 needs a separate physical serial interface and a separate CSU/DSU. As you can imagine, growth to hundreds of sites will take many routers, with many interfaces each, and lots of rack space for the routers and CSU/DSUs.

Now imagine that the phone company salesperson says the following to you when you have two leased lines, or circuits, installed (as shown in Figure 4-7):

> You know, we can install Frame Relay instead. You will need only one serial interface on R1 and one CSU/DSU. To scale to 100 sites, you might need two or three more serial interfaces on R1 for more bandwidth, but that is it. And by the way, because your leased lines run at 128 kbps today, we will guarantee that you can send and receive that much data to and from each site. We will upgrade the line at R1 to T1 speed (1.544 Mbps). When you have more traffic than 128 kbps to a site, go ahead and send it! If we have capacity, we will forward it, with no extra charge. And by the way, did I tell you that it is cheaper than leased lines anyway?

You consider the facts for a moment: Frame Relay is cheaper, it is at least as fast as (probably faster than) what you have now, and it allows you to save money when you grow. So, you quickly sign the contract with the Frame Relay provider, before the salesperson can change their mind, and migrate to Frame Relay. Does this story seem a bit ridiculous? Sure. The cost and scaling benefits of Frame Relay, as compared to leased lines, however, are very significant. As a result, many networks moved from using leased lines to Frame Relay, particularly in the 1990s, with a significantly large installed base of Frame Relay networks today. In the next few pages, you will see how Frame Relay works and realize how Frame Relay can provide functions claimed by the fictitious salesperson.

Frame Relay Basics

Frame Relay networks provide more features and benefits than simple point-to-point WAN links, but to do that, Frame Relay protocols are more detailed. Frame Relay networks are multiaccess networks, which means that more than two devices can attach to the network, similar to LANs. To support more than two devices, the protocols must be a little more detailed. Figure 4-8 introduces some basic connectivity concepts for Frame Relay.
Figure 4-8 reflects the fact that Frame Relay uses the same Layer 1 features as a point-to-point leased line. For a Frame Relay service, a leased line is installed between each router and a nearby Frame Relay switch; these links are called *access links*. The access links run at the same speed and use the same signaling standards as do point-to-point leased lines. However, instead of extending from one router to the other, each leased line runs from one router to a Frame Relay switch.

Figure 4-8   *Frame Relay Components*

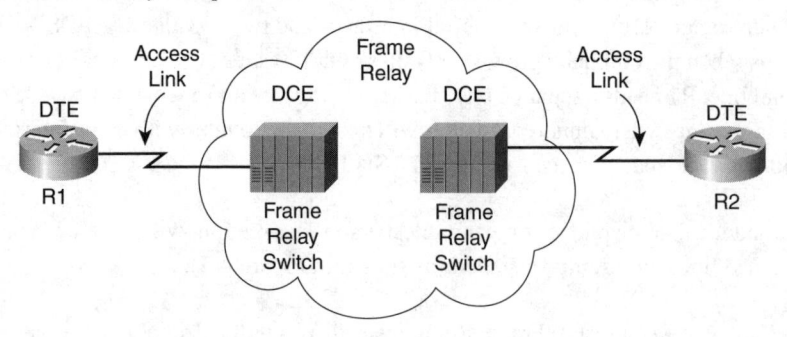

The difference between Frame Relay and point-to-point links is that the equipment in the telco actually examines the data frames sent by the router. Frame Relay defines its own data-link header and trailer. Each Frame Relay header holds an address field called a data-link connection identifier (DLCI). The WAN switch forwards the frame based on the DLCI, sending the frame through the provider's network until it gets to the remote-site router on the other side of the Frame Relay cloud.

> **NOTE**   The Frame Relay header and trailer are defined by a protocol called Link Access Procedure – Frame (LAPF).

Because the equipment in the telco can forward one frame to one remote site and another frame to another remote site, Frame Relay is considered to be a form of *packet switching*. This term means that the service provider actually chooses where to send each data packet sent into the provider's network, switching one packet to one device, and the next packet to another. However, Frame Relay protocols most closely resemble OSI Layer 2 protocols; the term usually used for the bits sent by a Layer 2 device is *frame*. So, Frame Relay is also called a *frame-switching service*, while the term packet switching is a more general term.

The terms DCE and DTE actually have a second set of meanings in the context of any packet-switching or frame-switching service. With Frame Relay, the Frame Relay switches are called DCE, and the customer equipment—routers, in this case—are called DTE. In this case, DCE refers to the device providing the service, and the term DTE refers to the device needing the frame-switching service. At the same time, the CSU/DSU provides clocking to the router, so from a Layer 1 perspective, the CSU/DSU is still the DCE and the router is still the DTE. It is just two different uses of the same terms.

Figure 4-8 depicted the physical and logical connectivity at each connection to the Frame Relay network. In contrast, Figure 4-9 shows the end-to-end connectivity associated with a virtual circuit (VC).

Figure 4-9 *Frame Relay VC Concepts*

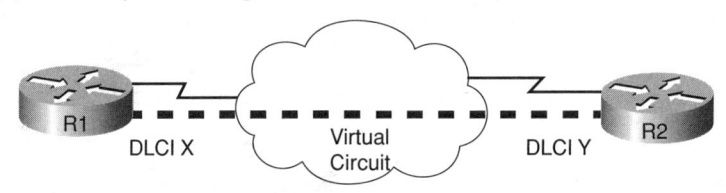

DLCI X   Virtual   DLCI Y
                    Circuit

The logical path that a frame travels between each pair of routers is called a Frame Relay VC. In Figure 4-9, a single VC is represented by the dashed line between the routers. Typically, the service provider preconfigures all the required details of a VC; these VCs are called permanent virtual circuits (PVC). When R1 needs to forward a packet to R2, it encapsulates the Layer 3 packet into a Frame Relay header and trailer and then sends the frame. R1 uses a Frame Relay address called a DLCI in the Frame Relay header, with the DLCI identifying the correct VC to the provider. This allows the switches to deliver the frame to R2, ignoring the details of the Layer 3 packet and looking at only the Frame Relay header and trailer. Recall that on a point-to-point serial link, the service provider forwards the frame over a physical circuit between R1 and R2. This transaction is similar in Frame Relay, where the provider forwards the frame over a logical VC from R1 to R2.

Frame Relay provides significant advantages over simply using point-to-point leased lines. The primary advantage has to do with VCs. Consider Figure 4-10 with Frame Relay instead of three point-to-point leased lines. Frame Relay creates a logical path (a VC) between two Frame Relay DTE devices. A VC acts like a point-to-point circuit, but physically it is not—it is virtual. For example, R1 terminates two VCs—one whose other endpoint is R2 and one whose other endpoint is R3. R1 can send traffic directly to either of the other two routers by sending it over the appropriate VC, although R1 has only one physical access link to the Frame Relay network.

VCs share the access link and the Frame Relay network. For example, both VCs terminating at R1 use the same access link. So, with large networks with many WAN sites that need to connect to a central location, only one physical access link is required from the main site router to the Frame Relay network. By contrast, using point-to-point links would require a physical circuit, a separate CSU/DSU, and a separate physical interface on the router for each point-to-point link. So, Frame Relay enables you to expand the WAN but add less hardware to do so.

Figure 4-10 *Typical Frame Relay Network with Three Sites*

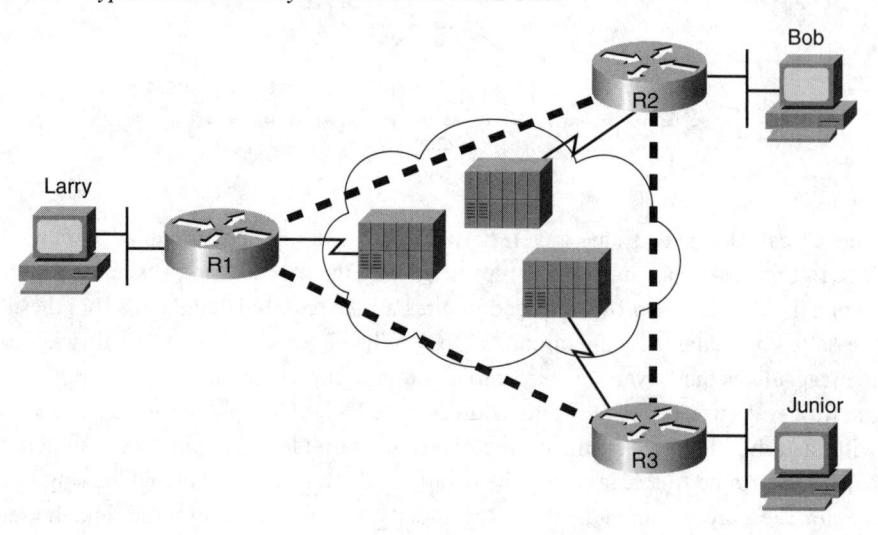

Many customers of a single Frame Relay service provider share that provider's Frame
Relay network. Originally, people with leased-line networks were reluctant to migrate to
Frame Relay because they would be competing with other customers for the provider's
capacity inside the service provider's network. To address these fears, Frame Relay is
designed with the concept of a committed information rate (CIR). Each VC has a CIR,
which is a guarantee by the provider that a particular VC gets at least that much bandwidth.
You can think of the CIR of a VC like the bandwidth or clock rate of a point-to-point circuit,
except that it is the minimum value—you can actually send more, in most cases.

Even in this three-site network, it is probably less expensive to use Frame Relay than to use
point-to-point links. Now imagine a much larger network, with a 100 sites, that needs any-to-
any connectivity. A point-to-point link design would require 4950 leased lines! In addition, you
would need 99 serial interfaces per router. By contrast, with a Frame Relay design, you could
have 100 access links to local Frame Relay switches (1 per router) with 4950 VCs running over
the access links. Also, you would need only one serial interface on each router. As a result, the
Frame Relay topology is easier for the service provider to implement, costs the provider less,
and makes better use of the core of the provider's network. As you would expect, that makes it
less expensive to the Frame Relay customer as well. For connecting many WAN sites, Frame
Relay is simply more cost-effective than leased lines.

Exam Preparation Tasks

Review All the Key Topics

Review the most important topics from inside the chapter, noted with the key topics icon in the outer margin of the page. Table 4-4 lists a reference of these key topics and the page numbers on which each is found.

Table 4-4 *Key Topics for Chapter 4*

Key Topic Element	Description	Page Number
Figure 4-3	Shows typical cabling diagram of CPE for a leased line	77
Table 4-2	Typical speeds for WAN leased lines	83
Figure 4-6	HDLC framing	84
Table 4-3	List of key WAN terminology	85-86
Paragraph	List of synonyms for "point-to-point leased line"	86
Figure 4-10	Diagram of Frame Relay virtual circuits	90

Key
Topic

Complete the Tables and Lists from Memory

Print a copy of Appendix H, "Memory Tables" (found on the CD-ROM), or at least the section for this chapter, and complete the tables and lists from memory. Appendix I, "Memory Tables Answer Key," also on the CD-ROM, includes completed tables and lists to check your work.

Definitions of Key Terms

Define the following key terms from this chapter, and check your answers in the glossary.

access link, back-to-back link, clocking, DTE (Layer 1), CSU/DSU, DCE (Layer 1), DS0, DS1, Frame Relay, HDLC, leased line, packet switching, PPP, serial cable, synchronous, T1, virtual circuit

This chapter covers the following subjects:

Overview of Network Layer Functions: The first section introduces the concepts of routing, logical addressing, and routing protocols.

IP Addressing: Next, the basics of 32-bit IP addresses are explained, with emphasis on how the organization aids the routing process.

IP Routing: This section explains how hosts and routers decide how to forward a packet.

IP Routing Protocols: This brief section explains the basics of how routing protocols populate each router's routing tables.

Network Layer Utilities: This section introduces several other functions useful to the overall process of packet delivery.

CHAPTER 5

Fundamentals of IP Addressing and Routing

The OSI physical layer (Layer 1) defines how to transmit bits over a particular type of physical network. The OSI data link layer (Layer 2) defines the framing, addressing, error detection, and rules for when to use the physical medium. Although they are important, these two layers do not define how to deliver data between devices that exist far from each other, with many different physical networks sitting between the two computers.

This chapter explains the function and purpose of the OSI network layer (Layer 3): the end-to-end delivery of data between two computers. Regardless of the type of physical network to which each endpoint computer is attached, and regardless of the types of physical networks used between the two computers, the network layer defines how to forward, or route, data between the two computers.

This chapter covers the basics of how the network layer routes data packets from one computer to another. After reviewing the full story at a basic level, this chapter examines in more detail the network layer of TCP/IP, including IP addressing (which enables efficient routing), IP routing (the forwarding process itself), IP routing protocols (the process by which routers learn routes), and several other small but important features of the network layer.

"Do I Know This Already?" Quiz

The "Do I Know This Already?" quiz allows you to assess whether you should read the entire chapter. If you miss no more than one of these 13 self-assessment questions, you might want to move ahead to the "Exam Preparation Tasks" section. Table 5-1 lists the major headings in this chapter and the "Do I Know This Already?" quiz questions covering the material in those sections. This helps you assess your knowledge of these specific areas. The answers to the "Do I Know This Already?" quiz appear in Appendix A.

Table 5-1   *"Do I Know This Already?" Foundation Topics Section-to-Question Mapping*

Foundation Topics Section	Questions
Overview of Network Layer Functions	1 – 3
IP Addressing	4 – 8
IP Routing	9, 10
IP Routing Protocols	11
Network Layer Utilities	12, 13

1.   Which of the following are functions of OSI Layer 3 protocols?

   a.   Logical addressing

   b.   Physical addressing

   c.   Path selection

   d.   Arbitration

   e.   Error recovery

2.   Imagine that PC1 needs to send some data to PC2, and PC1 and PC2 are separated by several routers. What are the largest entities that make it from PC1 to PC2?

   a.   Frame

   b.   Segment

   c.   Packet

   d.   L5 PDU

   e.   L3 PDU

   f.   L1 PDU

3.   Imagine a network with two routers that are connected with a point-to-point HDLC serial link. Each router has an Ethernet, with PC1 sharing the Ethernet with Router1, and PC2 sharing the Ethernet with Router2. When PC1 sends data to PC2, which of the following is true?

   a.   Router1 strips the Ethernet header and trailer off the frame received from PC1, never to be used again.

   b.   Router1 encapsulates the Ethernet frame inside an HDLC header and sends the frame to Router2, which extracts the Ethernet frame for forwarding to PC2.

c. Router1 strips the Ethernet header and trailer off the frame received from PC1, which is exactly re-created by R2 before forwarding data to PC2.

d. Router1 removes the Ethernet, IP, and TCP headers and rebuilds the appropriate headers before forwarding the packet to Router2.

4. Which of the following are valid Class C IP addresses that can be assigned to hosts?

a. 1.1.1.1

b. 200.1.1.1

c. 128.128.128.128

d. 224.1.1.1

e. 223.223.223.255

5. What is the range of values for the first octet for Class A IP networks?

a. 0 to 127

b. 0 to 126

c. 1 to 127

d. 1 to 126

e. 128 to 191

f. 128 to 192

6. PC1 and PC2 are on two different Ethernets that are separated by an IP router. PC1's IP address is 10.1.1.1, and no subnetting is used. Which of the following addresses could be used for PC2?

a. 10.1.1.2

b. 10.2.2.2

c. 10.200.200.1

d. 9.1.1.1

e. 225.1.1.1

f. 1.1.1.1

7. Each Class B network contains how many IP addresses that can be assigned to hosts?

   a. 16,777,214

   b. 16,777,216

   c. 65,536

   d. 65,534

   e. 65,532

   f. 32,768

   g. 32,766

8. Each Class C network contains how many IP addresses that can be assigned to hosts?

   a. 65,534

   b. 65,532

   c. 32,768

   d. 32,766

   e. 256

   f. 254

9. Which of the following does a router normally use when making a decision about routing TCP/IP packets?

   a. Destination MAC address

   b. Source MAC address

   c. Destination IP address

   d. Source IP address

   e. Destination MAC and IP address

10. Which of the following are true about a LAN-connected TCP/IP host and its IP routing (forwarding) choices?

   a. The host always sends packets to its default gateway.

   b. The host sends packets to its default gateway if the destination IP address is in a different class of IP network than the host.

   c. The host sends packets to its default gateway if the destination IP address is in a different subnet than the host.

   d. The host sends packets to its default gateway if the destination IP address is in the same subnet as the host.

11. Which of the following are functions of a routing protocol?

   a. Advertising known routes to neighboring routers.

   b. Learning routes for subnets directly connected to the router.

   c. Learning routes, and putting those routes into the routing table, for routes advertised to the router by its neighboring routers.

   d. To forward IP packets based on a packet's destination IP address.

12. Which of the following protocols allows a client PC to discover the IP address of another computer based on that other computer's name?

   a. ARP

   b. RARP

   c. DNS

   d. DHCP

13. Which of the following protocols allows a client PC to request assignment of an IP address as well as learn its default gateway?

   a. ARP

   b. RARP

   c. DNS

   d. DHCP

Foundation Topics

OSI Layer 3-equivalent protocols define how packets can be delivered from the computer that creates the packet all the way to the computer that needs to receive the packet. To reach that goal, an OSI network layer protocol defines the following features:

Routing: The process of forwarding packets (Layer 3 PDUs).

Logical addressing: Addresses that can be used regardless of the type of physical networks used, providing each device (at least) one address. Logical addressing enables the routing process to identify a packet's source and destination.

Routing protocol: A protocol that aids routers by dynamically learning about the groups of addresses in the network, which in turn allows the routing (forwarding) process to work well.

Other utilities: The network layer also relies on other utilities. For TCP/IP, these utilities include Domain Name System (DNS), Dynamic Host Configuration Protocol (DHCP), Address Resolution Protocol (ARP), and ping.

> **NOTE**   The term *path selection* sometimes is used to mean the same thing as routing protocol, sometimes is used to refer to the routing (forwarding) of packets, and sometimes is used for both functions.

This chapter begins with an overview of routing, logical addressing, and routing protocols. Following that, the text moves on to more details about the specifics of the TCP/IP network layer (called the internetwork layer in the TCP/IP model). In particular, the topics of IP addressing, routing, routing protocols, and network layer utilities are covered.

Overview of Network Layer Functions

A protocol that defines routing and logical addressing is considered to be a network layer, or Layer 3, protocol. OSI does define a unique Layer 3 protocol called Connectionless Network Services (CLNS), but, as usual with OSI protocols, you rarely see it in networks today. In the recent past, you might have seen many other network layer protocols, such as Internet Protocol (IP), Novell Internetwork Packet Exchange (IPX), or AppleTalk Datagram Delivery Protocol (DDP). Today, the only Layer 3 protocol that is used widely is the TCP/IP network layer protocol—specifically, IP.

The main job of IP is to route data (packets) from the source host to the destination host. Because a network might need to forward large numbers of packets, the IP routing process is very simple. IP does not require any overhead agreements or messages before sending a packet, making IP a connectionless protocol. IP tries to deliver each packet, but if a router or host's IP process cannot deliver the packet, it is discarded—with no error recovery. The goal with IP is to deliver packets with as little per-packet work as possible, which allows for large packet volumes. Other protocols perform some of the other useful networking functions. For example, Transmission Control Protocol (TCP), which is described in detail in Chapter 6, "Fundamentals of TCP/IP Transport, Applications, and Security," provides error recovery, resending lost data, but IP does not.

IP routing relies on the structure and meaning of IP addresses, and IP addressing was designed with IP routing in mind. This first major section of this chapter begins by introducing IP routing, with some IP addressing concepts introduced along the way. Then, the text examines IP addressing fundamentals.

Routing (Forwarding)

Routing focuses on the end-to-end logic of forwarding data. Figure 5-1 shows a simple example of how routing works. The logic illustrated by the figure is relatively simple. For PC1 to send data to PC2, it must send something to router R1, which sends it to router R2, and then to router R3, and finally to PC2. However, the logic used by each device along the path varies slightly.

Figure 5-1   *Routing Logic: PC1 Sending to PC2*

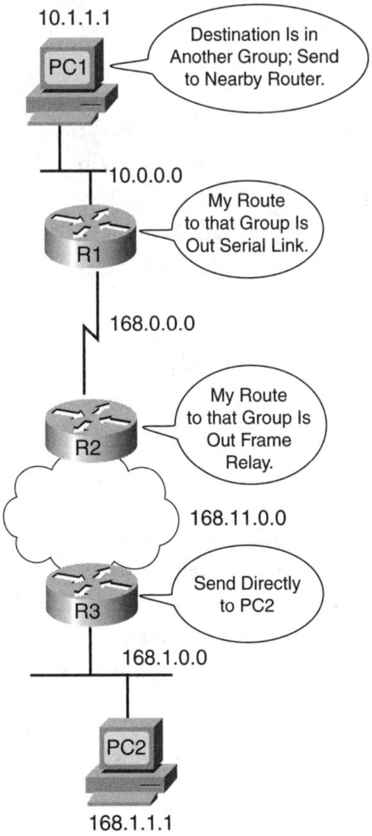

PC1's Logic: Sending Data to a Nearby Router

In this example, illustrated in Figure 5-1, PC1 has some data to send to PC2. Because PC2 is not on the same Ethernet as PC1, PC1 needs to send the packet to a router that is attached to the same Ethernet as PC1. The sender sends a data-link frame across the medium to the nearby router; this frame includes the packet in the data portion of the frame. That frame uses data link layer (Layer 2) addressing in the data-link header to ensure that the nearby router receives the frame.

The main point here is that the computer that created the data does not know much about the network—just how to get the data to some nearby router. Using a post office analogy, it's like knowing how to get to the local post office, but nothing more. Likewise, PC1 needs to know only how to get the packet to R1, not the rest of the path used to send the packet to PC2.

R1 and R2's Logic: Routing Data Across the Network

R1 and R2 both use the same general process to route the packet. The *routing table* for any particular network layer protocol contains a list of network layer address *groupings*. Instead of a single entry in the routing table per individual destination network layer address, there is one routing table entry per group. The router compares the destination network layer address in the packet to the entries in the routing table and makes a match. This matching entry in the routing table tells this router where to forward the packet next. The words in the bubbles in Figure 5-1 point out this basic logic.

The concept of network layer address grouping is similar to the U.S. zip code system. Everyone living in the same vicinity is in the same zip code, and the postal sorters just look for the zip codes, ignoring the rest of the address. Likewise, in Figure 5-1, everyone in this network whose IP address starts with 168.1 is on the Ethernet on which PC2 resides, so the routers can have just one routing table entry that means "all addresses that start with 168.1."

Any intervening routers repeat the same process: the router compares the packet's destination network layer (Layer 3) address to the groups listed in its routing table, and the matched routing table entry tells this router where to forward the packet next. Eventually, the packet is delivered to the router connected to the network or subnet of the destination host (R3), as shown in Figure 5-1.

R3's Logic: Delivering Data to the End Destination

The final router in the path, R3, uses almost the exact same logic as R1 and R2, but with one minor difference. R3 needs to forward the packet directly to PC2, not to some other router. On the surface, that difference seems insignificant. In the next section, when you read about how the network layer uses the data link layer, the significance of the difference will become obvious.

Network Layer Interaction with the Data Link Layer

When the network layer protocol is processing the packet, it decides to send the packet out the appropriate network interface. Before the actual bits can be placed onto that physical interface, the network layer must hand off the packet to the data link layer protocols, which, in turn, ask the physical layer to actually send the data. And as was described in Chapter 3, "Fundamentals of LANs," the data link layer adds the appropriate header and trailer to the packet, creating a frame, before sending the frames over each physical network. The routing process forwards the packet, and only the packet, end-to-end through the network, *discarding data-link headers and trailers along the way.* The network layer processes deliver the packet end-to-end, using successive data-link headers and trailers just to get the packet to the next router or host in the path. Each successive data link layer just gets the packet from one device to the next. Figure 5-2 points out the key encapsulation logic on each device, using the same examples as in Figure 5-1.

Figure 5-2   *Network Layer and Data Link Layer Encapsulation*

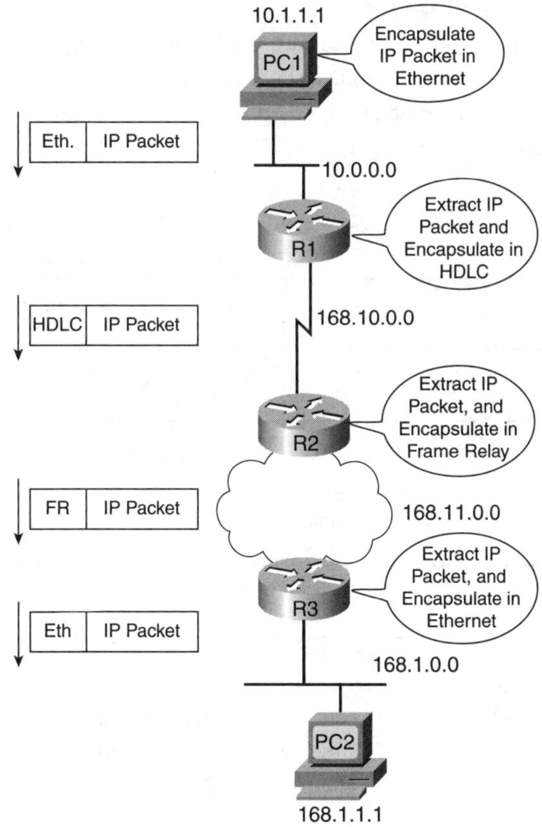

Because the routers build new data-link headers and trailers (trailers not shown in the figure), and because the new headers contain data-link addresses, the PCs and routers must have some way to decide what data-link addresses to use. An example of how the router determines which data-link address to use is the IP Address Resolution Protocol (ARP). *ARP is used to dynamically learn the data-link address of an IP host connected to a LAN.* You will read more about ARP later in this chapter.

Routing as covered so far has two main concepts:

■   The process of routing forwards Layer 3 packets, also called *Layer 3 protocol data units* (*L3 PDU*), based on the destination Layer 3 address in the packet.

■   The routing process uses the data link layer to encapsulate the Layer 3 packets into Layer 2 frames for transmission across each successive data link.

IP Packets and the IP Header

The IP packets encapsulated in the data-link frames shown in Figure 5-2 have an IP header, followed by additional headers and data. For reference, Figure 5-3 shows the fields inside the standard 20-byte IPv4 header, with no optional IP header fields, as is typically seen in most networks today.

Figure 5-3 *IPv4 Header*

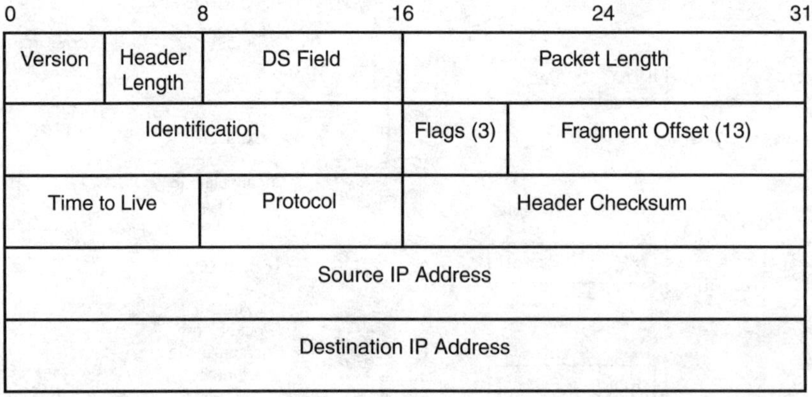

Of the different fields inside the IPv4 header, this book, and the companion *ICND2 Official Exam Certification Guide*, ignore all the fields except the Time-To-Live (TTL) (covered in Chapter 15 in this book), protocol (Chapter 6 of the ICND2 book), and the source and destination IP address fields (scattered throughout most chapters). However, for reference, Table 5-2 briefly describes each field.

Table 5-2 *IPv4 Header Fields*

Field	Meaning
Version	Version of the IP protocol. Most networks use version 4 today.
IHL	IP Header Length. Defines the length of the IP header, including optional fields.
DS Field	Differentiated Services Field. It is used for marking packets for the purpose of applying different quality-of-service (QoS) levels to different packets.
Packet length	Identifies the entire length of the IP packet, including the data.
Identification	Used by the IP packet fragmentation process; all fragments of the original packet contain the same identifier.
Flags	3 bits used by the IP packet fragmentation process.
Fragment offset	A number used to help hosts reassemble fragmented packets into the original larger packet.
TTL	Time to live. A value used to prevent routing loops.
Protocol	A field that identifies the contents of the data portion of the IP packet. For example, protocol 6 implies that a TCP header is the first thing in the IP packet data field.
Header Checksum	A value used to store an FCS value, whose purpose is to determine if any bit errors occurred in the IP header.
Source IP address	The 32-bit IP address of the sender of the packet.
Destination IP address	The 32-bit IP address of the intended recipient of the packet.

This section next examines the concept of network layer addressing and how it aids the routing process.

Network Layer (Layer 3) Addressing

Network layer protocols define the format and meaning of logical addresses. (The term *logical address* does not really refer to whether the addresses make sense, but rather to contrast these addresses with physical addresses.) Each computer that needs to communicate will have (at least) one network layer address so that other computers can send data packets to that address, expecting the network to deliver the data packet to the correct computer.

One key feature of network layer addresses is that they were designed to allow logical grouping of addresses. In other words, something about the numeric value of an address implies a group or set of addresses, all of which are considered to be in the same grouping. With IP addresses, this group is called a *network* or a *subnet*. These groupings work just like USPS zip (postal) codes, allowing the routers (mail sorters) to speedily route (sort) lots of packets (letters).

Just like postal street addresses, network layer addresses are grouped based on physical location in a network. The rules differ for some network layer protocols, but with IP addressing, the first part of the IP address is the same for all the addresses in one grouping. For example, in Figures 5-1 and 5-2, the following IP addressing conventions define the groups of IP addresses (IP networks) for all hosts on that internetwork:

- Hosts on the top Ethernet: Addresses start with 10

- Hosts on the R1-R2 serial link: Addresses start with 168.10

- Hosts on the R2-R3 Frame Relay network: Addresses start with 168.11

- Hosts on the bottom Ethernet: Addresses start with 168.1

> **NOTE**   To avoid confusion when writing about IP networks, many resources (including this one) use the term *internetwork* to refer more generally to a network made up of routers, switches, cables, and other equipment, and the word *network* to refer to the more specific concept of an IP network.

Routing relies on the fact that Layer 3 addresses are grouped. The routing tables for each network layer protocol can have one entry for the group, not one entry for each individual address. Imagine an Ethernet with 100 TCP/IP hosts. A router that needs to forward packets to any of those hosts needs only one entry in its IP routing table, with that one routing table entry representing the entire group of hosts on the Ethernet. This basic fact is one of the key reasons that routers can scale to allow hundreds of thousands of devices. It's very similar to the USPS zip code system. It would be ridiculous to have people in the same zip code live far from each other, or to have next-door neighbors be in different zip codes. The poor postman would spend all his time driving and flying around the country! Similarly, to make routing more efficient, network layer protocols group addresses.

Routing Protocols

Conveniently, the routers in Figures 5-1 and 5-2 somehow know the correct steps to take to forward the packet from PC1 to PC2. To make the correct choices, each router needs a routing table, with a route that matches the packet sent to PC2. The routes tell the router where to send the packet next.

In most cases, routers build their routing table entries dynamically using a routing protocol. Routing protocols learn about all the locations of the network layer "groups" in a network and advertise the groups' locations. As a result, each router can build a good routing table dynamically. Routing protocols define message formats and procedures, just like any other protocol. The end goal of each routing protocol is to fill the routing table with all known destination groups and with the best route to reach each group.

The terminology relating to routing protocols sometimes can get in the way. A *routing protocol* learns routes and puts those routes in a routing table. A *routed protocol* defines the type of packet forwarded, or routed, through a network. In Figures 5-1 and 5-2, the figures represent how IP packets are routed, so IP would be the *routed protocol*. If the routers used Routing Information Protocol (RIP) to learn the routes, RIP would be the *routing protocol*. Later in this chapter, the section "IP Routing Protocols" shows a detailed example of how routing protocols learn routes.

Now that you have seen the basic function of the OSI network layer at work, the rest of this chapter examines the key components of the end-to-end routing process for TCP/IP.

IP Addressing

IP addressing is absolutely the most important topic for the CCNA exams. By the time you have completed your study, you should be comfortable and confident in your understanding of IP addresses, their formats, the grouping concepts, how to subdivide groups into subnets, how to interpret the documentation for existing networks' IP addressing, and so on. Simply put, you had better know addressing and subnetting!

This section introduces IP addressing and subnetting and also covers the concepts behind the structure of an IP address, including how it relates to IP routing. In Chapter 12, "IP Addressing and Subnetting," you will read about the math behind IP addressing and subnetting.

IP Addressing Definitions

If a device wants to communicate using TCP/IP, it needs an IP address. When the device has an IP address and the appropriate software and hardware, it can send and receive IP packets. Any device that can send and receive IP packets is called an *IP host*.

> **NOTE** IP Version 4 (IPv4) is the most widely used version of IP. The *ICND2 Official Exam Certification Guide* covers the newer version of IP, IPv6. This book only briefly mentions IPv6 in Chapter 12 and otherwise ignores it. So, all references to IP addresses in this book should be taken to mean "IP version 4" addresses.

IP addresses consist of a 32-bit number, usually written in *dotted-decimal notation*. The "decimal" part of the term comes from the fact that each byte (8 bits) of the 32-bit IP address is shown as its decimal equivalent. The four resulting decimal numbers are written in sequence, with "dots," or decimal points, separating the numbers—hence the name *dotted decimal*. For instance, 168.1.1.1 is an IP address written in dotted-decimal form; the actual binary version is 10101000 00000001 00000001 00000001. (You almost never need to write down the binary version, but you will see how to convert between the two formats in Chapter 12.)

Each decimal number in an IP address is called an *octet*. The term *octet* is just a vendor-neutral term for *byte*. So, for an IP address of 168.1.1.1, the first octet is 168, the second octet is 1, and so on. The range of decimal numbers in each octet is between 0 and 255, inclusive.

Finally, note that each network interface uses a unique IP address. Most people tend to think that their computer has an IP address, but actually their computer's network card has an IP address. If you put two Ethernet cards in a PC to forward IP packets through both cards, they both would need unique IP addresses. Also, if your laptop has both an Ethernet NIC and a wireless NIC working at the same time, your laptop will have an IP address for each NIC. Similarly, routers, which typically have many network interfaces that forward IP packets, have an IP address for each interface.

Now that you have some idea of the basic terminology, the next section relates IP addressing to the routing concepts of OSI Layer 3.

How IP Addresses Are Grouped

The original specifications for TCP/IP grouped IP addresses into sets of consecutive addresses called *IP networks*. The addresses in a single network have the same numeric value in the first part of all addresses in the network. Figure 5-4 shows a simple internetwork that has three separate IP networks.

Figure 5-4 *Sample Network Using Class A, B, and C Network Numbers*

Network
199.1.1.0

All IP addresses that
begin with 199.1.1

Network
8.0.0.0

All IP addresses
that begin with 8

Network
130.4.0.0

All IP addresses that
begin with 130.4

The conventions of IP addressing and IP address grouping make routing easy. For example, all IP addresses that begin with 8 are in the IP network that contains all the hosts on the Ethernet on the left. Likewise, all IP addresses that begin with 130.4 are in another IP network that consists of all the hosts on the Ethernet on the right. Along the same lines, 199.1.1 is the prefix for all IP addresses on the network that includes the addresses on the serial link. (The only two IP addresses in this last grouping will be the IP addresses on each of the two routers.) By following this convention, the routers build a routing table with three entries—one for each prefix, or network number. For example, the router on the left can have one route that refers to all addresses that begin with 130.4, with that route directing the router to forward packets to the router on the right.

The example indirectly points out a couple of key points about how IP addresses are organized. To be a little more explicit, the following two rules summarize the facts about which IP addresses need to be in the same grouping:

- All IP addresses in the same group must not be separated by a router.

- IP addresses separated by a router must be in different groups.

Key Topic

As mentioned earlier in this chapter, IP addressing behaves similarly to zip codes. Everyone in my zip code lives in a little town in Ohio. If some members of my zip code were in California, some of my mail might be sent to California by mistake. Likewise, IP routing relies on the fact that all IP addresses in the same group (called either a network or a subnet) are in the same general location. If some of the IP addresses in my network or subnet were allowed to be on the other side of the internetwork compared to my computer, the routers in the network might incorrectly send some of the packets sent to my computer to the other side of the network.

Classes of Networks

Figure 5-4 and the surrounding text claim that the IP addresses of devices attached to the Ethernet on the left all start with 8 and that the IP addresses of devices attached to the Ethernet on the right all start with 130.4. Why only one number (8) for the "prefix" on the Ethernet on the left and two numbers (130 and 4) on the Ethernet on the right? Well, it all has to do with IP address classes.

RFC 791 defines the IP protocol, including several different classes of networks. IP defines three different network classes for addresses used by individual hosts—addresses called unicast IP addresses. These three network classes are called A, B, and C. TCP/IP defines Class D (multicast) addresses and Class E (experimental) addresses as well.

By definition, all addresses in the same Class A, B, or C network have the same numeric value *network* portion of the addresses. The rest of the address is called the *host* portion of the address.

Using the post office example, the network part of an IP address acts like the zip (postal) code, and the host part acts like the street address. Just as a letter-sorting machine three states away from you cares only about the zip code on a letter addressed to you, a router three hops away from you cares only about the network number that your address resides in.

Class A, B, and C networks each have a different length for the part that identifies the network:

■ Class A networks have a 1-byte-long network part. That leaves 3 bytes for the rest of the address, called the host part.

■ Class B networks have a 2-byte-long network part, leaving 2 bytes for the host portion of the address.

■ Class C networks have a 3-byte-long network part, leaving only 1 byte for the host part.

For example, Figure 5-4 lists network 8.0.0.0 next to the Ethernet on the left. Network 8.0.0.0 is a Class A network, which means that only 1 octet (byte) is used for the network part of the address. So, all hosts in network 8.0.0.0 begin with 8. Similarly, Class B network 130.4.0.0 is listed next to the Ethernet on the right. Because it is a Class B network, 2 octets define the network part, and all addresses begin with 130.4 as the first 2 octets.

When listing network numbers, the convention is to write down the network part of the number, with all decimal 0s in the host part of the number. So, Class A network "8," which consists of all IP addresses that begin with 8, is written as 8.0.0.0. Similarly, Class B network "130.4," which consists of all IP addresses that begin with 130.4, is written as 130.4.0.0, and so on.

Now consider the size of each class of network. Class A networks need 1 byte for the network part, leaving 3 bytes, or 24 bits, for the host part. There are 2^{24} different possible values in the host part of a Class A IP address. So, each Class A network can have 2^{24} IP addresses—except for two reserved host addresses in each network, as shown in the last column of Table 5-3. The table summarizes the characteristics of Class A, B, and C networks.

Key
Topic

Table 5-3   *Sizes of Network and Host Parts of IP Addresses with No Subnetting*

Any Network of This Class	Number of Network Bytes (Bits)	Number of Host Bytes (Bits)	Number of Addresses Per Network*
A	1 (8)	3 (24)	$2^{24} - 2$
B	2 (16)	2 (16)	$2^{16} - 2$
C	3 (24)	1 (8)	$2^{8} - 2$

*There are two reserved host addresses per network.

Based on the three examples from Figure 5-4, Table 5-4 provides a closer look at the numeric version of the three network numbers: 8.0.0.0, 130.4.0.0, and 199.1.1.0.

Table 5-4   *Sample Network Numbers, Decimal and Binary*

Network Number	Binary Representation, with the Host Part in Bold
8.0.0.0	00001000 **00000000 00000000 00000000**
130.4.0.0	10000010 00000100 **00000000 00000000**
199.1.1.0	11000111 00000001 00000001 **00000000**

Even though the network numbers look like addresses because of their dotted-decimal format, network numbers cannot be assigned to an interface to be used as an IP address. Conceptually, network numbers represent the group of all IP addresses in the network, much like a zip code represents the group of all addresses in a community. It would be confusing to have a single number represent a whole group of addresses and then also use that same number as an IP address for a single device. So, the network numbers themselves are reserved and cannot be used as an IP address for a device.

Besides the network number, a second dotted-decimal value in each network is reserved. Note that the first reserved value, the network number, has all binary 0s in the host part of the number (see Table 5-4). The other reserved value is the one with all binary 1s in the host part of the number. This number is called the *network broadcast* or *directed broadcast* address. This reserved number cannot be assigned to a host for use as an IP address. However, packets sent to a network broadcast address are forwarded to all devices in the network.

Key Topic

Also, because the network number is the lowest numeric value inside that network and the broadcast address is the highest numeric value, all the numbers between the network number and the broadcast address are the valid, useful IP addresses that can be used to address interfaces in the network.

The Actual Class A, B, and C Network Numbers

The Internet is a collection of almost every IP-based network and almost every TCP/IP host computer in the world. The original design of the Internet required several cooperating features that made it technically possible as well as administratively manageable:

■   Each computer connected to the Internet needs a unique, nonduplicated IP address.

■   Administratively, a central authority assigned Class A, B, or C networks to companies, governments, school systems, and ISPs based on the size of their IP network (Class A for large networks, Class B for medium networks, and Class C for small networks).

■   The central authority assigned each network number to only one organization, helping ensure unique address assignment worldwide.

■   Each organization with an assigned Class A, B, or C network then assigned individual IP addresses inside its own network.

By following these guidelines, as long as each organization assigns each IP address to only one computer, every computer in the Internet has a globally unique IP address.

> **NOTE** The details of address assignment have changed over time, but the general idea described here is enough detail to help you understand the concept of different Class A, B, and C networks.

The organization in charge of universal IP address assignment is the Internet Corporation for Assigned Network Numbers (ICANN, www.icann.org). (The Internet Assigned Numbers Authority (IANA) formerly owned the IP address assignment process.) ICANN, in turn, assigns regional authority to other cooperating organizations. For example, the American Registry for Internet Numbers (ARIN, www.arin.org) owns the address assignment process for North America.

Table 5-5 summarizes the possible network numbers that ICANN and other agencies could have assigned over time. Note the total number for each network class and the number of hosts in each Class A, B, and C network.

Key Topic

Table 5-5   *All Possible Valid Network Numbers[*]*

Class	First Octet Range	Valid Network Numbers[*]	Total Number for This Class of Network	Number of Hosts Per Network
A	1 to 126	1.0.0.0 to 126.0.0.0	$2^7 - 2$ (126)	$2^{24} - 2$ (16,777,214)
B	128 to 191	128.0.0.0 to 191.255.0.0	2^{14} (16,384)	$2^{16} - 2$ (65,534)
C	192 to 223	192.0.0.0 to 223.255.255.0	2^{21} (2,097,152)	$2^8 - 2$ (254)

[*]The Valid Network Numbers column shows actual network numbers. Networks 0.0.0.0 (originally defined for use as a broadcast address) and 127.0.0.0 (still available for use as the loopback address) are reserved.

Memorizing the contents of Table 5-5 should be one of the first things you do in preparation for the CCNA exam(s). Engineers should be able to categorize a network as Class A, B, or C with ease. Also, memorize the number of octets in the network part of Class A, B, and C addresses, as shown in Table 5-4.

IP Subnetting

Subnetting is one of the most important topics on the ICND1, ICND2, and CCNA exams. You need to know how it works and how to "do the math" to figure out issues when subnetting is in use, both in real life and on the exam. Chapter 12 covers the details of subnetting concepts, motivation, and math, but you should have a basic understanding of the concepts before covering the topics between here and Chapter 12. IP subnetting takes a single Class A, B, or C network and subdivides it into a number of smaller groups of IP addresses. The Class A, B, and C rules still exist, but now, a single Class A, B, or C network can be subdivided into many smaller groups. Subnetting treats a subdivision of a single Class A, B, or C network as if it were a network itself. In fact, the name "subnet" is just shorthand for "subdivided network."

You can easily discern the concepts behind subnetting by comparing one network topology that does not use subnetting with the same topology but with subnetting implemented. Figure 5-5 shows such a network, without subnetting.

Figure 5-5 *Backdrop for Discussing Numbers of Different Networks/Subnetworks*

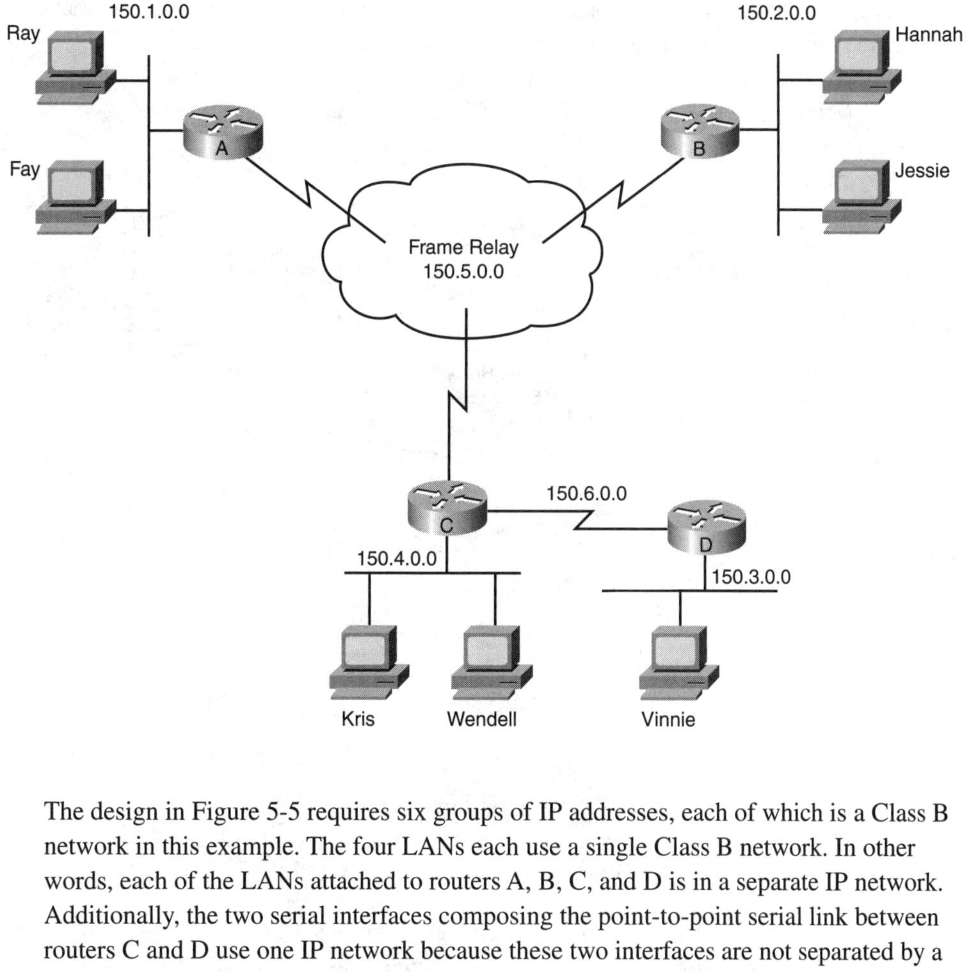

The design in Figure 5-5 requires six groups of IP addresses, each of which is a Class B network in this example. The four LANs each use a single Class B network. In other words, each of the LANs attached to routers A, B, C, and D is in a separate IP network. Additionally, the two serial interfaces composing the point-to-point serial link between routers C and D use one IP network because these two interfaces are not separated by a router. Finally, the three router interfaces composing the Frame Relay network with routers A, B, and C are not separated by an IP router and would use a sixth IP network.

Each Class B network has $2^{16} - 2$ host addresses—far more than you will ever need for each LAN and WAN link. For example, the upper-left Ethernet should contain all addresses that begin with 150.1. Therefore, addresses that begin with 150.1 cannot be assigned anywhere else in the network, except on the upper-left Ethernet. So, if you ran out of IP addresses somewhere else, you could not use the large number of unused addresses that begin with 150.1. As a result, the addressing design shown in Figure 5-5 wastes a lot of addresses.

In fact, this design would not be allowed if it were connected to the Internet. The ICANN member organization would not assign six separate registered Class B network numbers. In fact, you probably would not get even one Class B network, because most of the Class B addresses are already assigned. You more likely would get a couple of Class C networks with the expectation that you would use subnetting. Figure 5-6 illustrates a more realistic example that uses basic subnetting.

Figure 5-6 *Using Subnets*

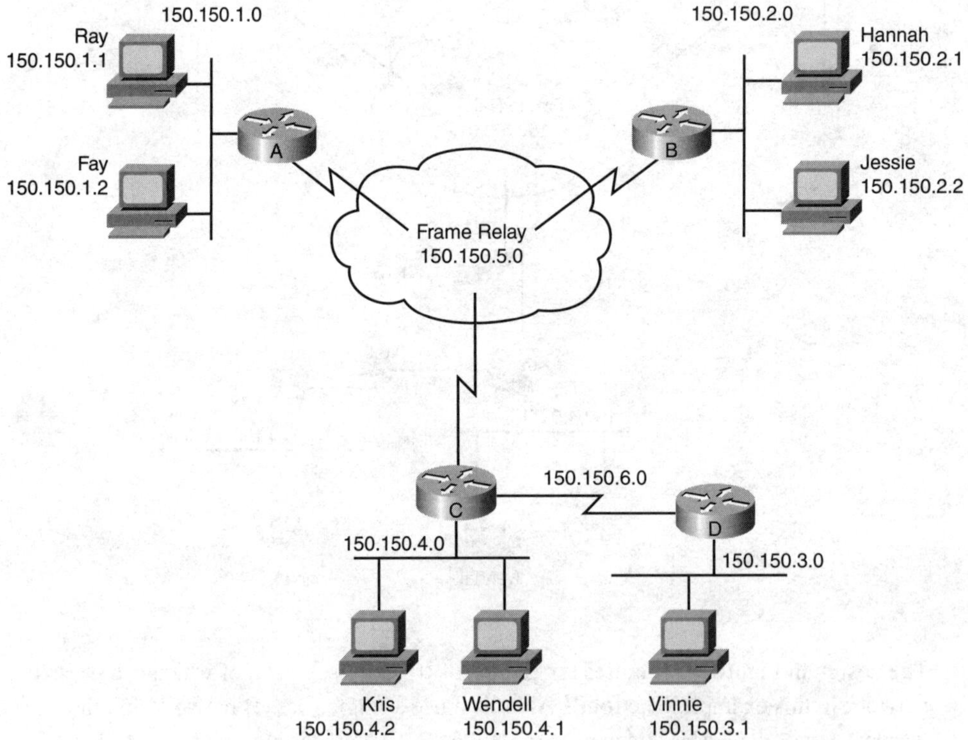

As in Figure 5-5, the design in Figure 5-6 requires six groups. Unlike Figure 5-5, this figure uses six subnets, each of which is a subnet of a single Class B network. This design subdivides the Class B network 150.150.0.0 into six subnets. To perform subnetting, the third octet (in this example) is used to identify unique subnets of network 150.150.0.0.

Notice that each subnet number in the figure shows a different value in the third octet, representing each different subnet number. In other words, this design numbers or identifies each different subnet using the third octet.

When subnetting, a third part of an IP address appears between the network and host parts of the address—namely, the *subnet part* of the address. This field is created by "stealing" or "borrowing" bits from the host part of the address. The size of the network part of the address never shrinks. In other words, Class A, B, and C rules still apply when defining the size of the network part of an address. The host part of the address shrinks to make room for the subnet part of the address. Figure 5-7 shows the format of addresses when subnetting, representing the number of bits in each of the three parts of an IP address.

Figure 5-7 *Address Formats When Subnetting Is Used (Classful)*

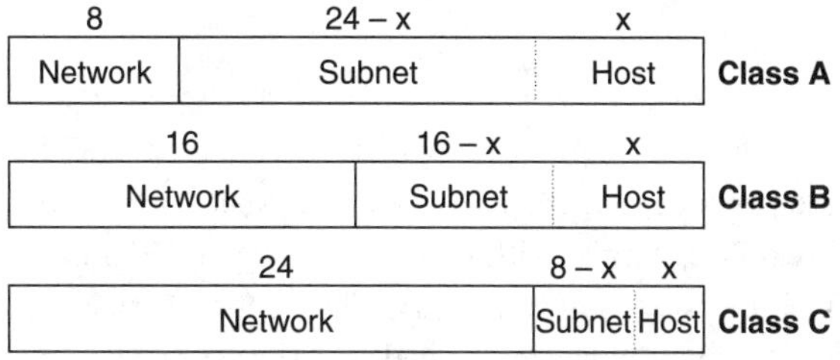

Now, instead of routing based on the network part of an address, routers can route based on the combined network and subnet parts. For example, when Kris (150.150.4.2) sends a packet to Hannah (150.150.2.1), router C has an IP route that lists information that means "all addresses that begin with 150.150.2." That same route tells router C to forward the packet to router B next. Note that the information in the routing table includes both the network and subnet part of the address, because both parts together identify the group.

Note that the concepts shown in Figure 5-7, with three parts of an IP address (network, subnet, and host), are called *classful addressing*. The term *classful addressing* refers to how you can think about IP addresses—specifically, that they have three parts. In particular, classful addressing means that you view the address as having a network part that is determined based on the rules about Class A, B, and C addressing—hence the word "classful" in the term.

Because the routing process considers the network and subnet parts of the address together, you can take an alternative view of IP addresses called *classless addressing*. Instead of three parts, each address has two parts:

■ The part on which routing is based

■ The host part

This first part—the part on which routing is based—is the combination of the network and subnet parts from the classful addressing view. This first part is often simply called the subnet part, or sometimes the *prefix*. Figure 5-8 shows the concepts and terms behind classless IP addressing.

Figure 5-8   *Address Formats When Subnetting Is Used (Classless)*

32 − x	x
Subnet or Prefix	Host

Finally, IP addressing with subnetting uses a concept called a *subnet mask*. A subnet mask helps define the structure of an IP address, as shown in Figures 5-7 and 5-8. Chapter 12 explains the details of subnet masks.

IP Routing

In the first section of this chapter, you read about the basics of routing using a network with three routers and two PCs. Armed with more knowledge of IP addressing, you now can take a closer look at the process of routing IP. This section focuses on how the originating host chooses where to send the packet, as well as how routers choose where to route or forward packets to the final destination.

Host Routing

Hosts actually use some simple routing logic when choosing where to send a packet. This two-step logic is as follows:

Step 1   If the destination IP address is in the same subnet as I am, send the packet directly to that destination host.

Step 2   If the destination IP address is not in the same subnet as I am, send the packet to my *default gateway* (a router's Ethernet interface on the subnet).

For example, consider Figure 5-9, and focus on the Ethernet LAN at the top of the figure. The top Ethernet has two PCs, labeled PC1 and PC11, plus router R1. When PC1 sends a packet to 150.150.1.11 (PC11's IP address), PC1 sends the packet over the Ethernet to PC11—there's no need to bother the router.

Figure 5-9 *Host Routing Alternatives*

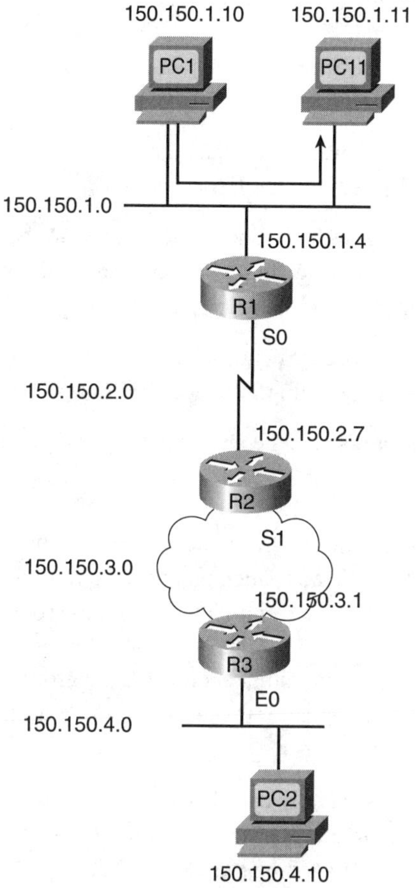

Alternatively, when PC1 sends a packet to PC2 (150.150.4.10), PC1 forwards the packet to its default gateway of 150.150.1.4, which is R1's Ethernet interface IP address according to Step 2 in the host routing logic. The next section describes an example in which PC1 uses its default gateway.

Router Forwarding Decisions and the IP Routing Table

Earlier in this chapter, Figures 5-1 and 5-2 (and the associated text) described generally how routers forward packets, making use of each successive physical network to forward packets to the next device. To better appreciate a router's forwarding decision, this section uses an example that includes three different routers forwarding a packet.

A router uses the following logic when receiving a data-link frame—a frame that has an IP packet encapsulated in it:

Step 1   Use the data-link FCS field to ensure that the frame had no errors; if errors occurred, discard the frame.

Step 2   Assuming the frame was not discarded at step 1, discard the old data-link header and trailer, leaving the IP packet.

Step 3   Compare the IP packet's destination IP address to the routing table, and find the route that matches the destination address. This route identifies the outgoing interface of the router, and possibly the next-hop router.

Step 4   Encapsulate the IP packet inside a new data-link header and trailer, appropriate for the outgoing interface, and forward the frame.

With these steps, each router sends the packet to the next location until the packet reaches its final destination.

Next, focus on the routing table and the matching process that occurs at Step 3. The packet has a destination IP address in the header, whereas the routing table typically has a list of networks and subnets. To match a routing table entry, the router thinks like this:

> Network numbers and subnet numbers represent a group of addresses that begin with the same prefix. In which of the groups in my routing table does this packet's destination address reside?

As you might guess, routers actually turn that logic into a math problem, but the text indeed shows what occurs. For example, Figure 5-10 shows the same network topology as Figure 5-9, but now with PC1 sending a packet to PC2.

NOTE   Note that the routers all know in this case that "subnet 150.150.4.0" means "all addresses that begin with 150.150.4."

The following list explains the forwarding logic at each step in the figure. (Note that all references to Steps 1, 2, 3, and 4 refer to the list of routing logic at the top of this page.)

Step A   **PC1 sends the packet to its default gateway.** PC1 first builds the IP packet, with a destination address of PC2's IP address (150.150.4.10). PC1 needs to send the packet to R1 (PC1's default gateway) because the destination address is on a different subnet. PC1 places the IP packet into an Ethernet frame, with a destination Ethernet address of R1's Ethernet address. PC1 sends the frame onto the Ethernet.

Figure 5-10 *Simple Routing Example, with IP Subnets*

R1 Routing Table

Subnet	Out Interface	Next Hop IP Address
150.150.4.0	Serial0	150.150.2.7

R2 Routing Table

Subnet	Out Interface	Next Hop IP Address
150.150.4.0	Serial1	150.150.3.1

R3 Routing Table

Subnet	Out Interface	Next Hop IP Address
150.150.4.0	Ethernet0	N/A

Step B   R1 processes the incoming frame and forwards the packet to R2.
Because the incoming Ethernet frame has a destination MAC of R1's
Ethernet MAC, R1 copies the frame off the Ethernet for processing. R1
checks the frame's FCS, and no errors have occurred (Step 1). R1 then
discards the Ethernet header and trailer (Step 2). Next, R1 compares the
packet's destination address (150.150.4.10) to the routing table and finds the
entry for subnet 150.150.4.0—which includes addresses 150.150.4.0 through
150.150.4.255 (Step 3). Because the destination address is in this group,
R1 forwards the packet out interface Serial0 to next-hop router R2
(150.150.2.7) after encapsulating the packet in an HDLC frame (step 4).

Step C   R2 processes the incoming frame and forwards the packet to R3.
R2 repeats the same general process as R1 when R2 receives the HDLC
frame. R2 checks the FCS field and finds that no errors occurred (Step 1).
R2 then discards the HDLC header and trailer (Step 2). Next, R2 finds its

route for subnet 150.150.4.0—which includes the address range 150.150.4.0–150.150.4.255—and realizes that the packet's destination address 150.150.4.10 matches that route (Step 3). Finally, R2 sends the packet out interface serial1 to next-hop router 150.150.3.1 (R3) after encapsulating the packet in a Frame Relay header (Step 4).

Step D **R3 processes the incoming frame and forwards the packet to PC2.** Like R1 and R2, R3 checks the FCS, discards the old data-link header and trailer, and matches its own route for subnet 150.150.4.0. R3's routing table entry for 150.150.4.0 shows that the outgoing interface is R3's Ethernet interface, but there is no next-hop router, because R3 is connected directly to subnet 150.150.4.0. All R3 has to do is encapsulate the packet inside an Ethernet header and trailer, with a destination Ethernet address of PC2's MAC address, and forward the frame.

The routing process relies on the rules relating to IP addressing. For instance, why does 150.150.1.10 (PC1) assume that 150.150.4.10 (PC2) is not on the same Ethernet? Well, because 150.150.4.0, PC2's subnet, is different from 150.150.1.0, which is PC1's subnet. Because IP addresses in different subnets must be separated by a router, PC1 needs to send the packet to a router—and it does. Similarly, all three routers list a route to subnet 150.150.4.0, which, in this example, includes IP addresses 150.150.4.1 to 150.150.4.254. What if someone tried to put PC2 somewhere else in the network, still using 150.150.4.10? The routers then would forward packets to the wrong place. So, Layer 3 routing relies on the structure of Layer 3 addressing to route more efficiently.

Chapter 12 covers IP addressing in much more detail. Next, this chapter briefly introduces the concepts behind IP routing protocols.

IP Routing Protocols

The routing (forwarding) process depends heavily on having an accurate and up-to-date IP routing table on each router. IP routing protocols fill the routers' IP routing tables with valid, loop-free routes. Each route includes a subnet number, the interface out which to forward packets so that they are delivered to that subnet, and the IP address of the next router that should receive packets destined for that subnet (if needed) (as shown in the example surrounding Figure 5-10).

Before examining the underlying logic used by routing protocols, you need to consider the goals of a routing protocol. The goals described in the following list are common for any IP routing protocol, regardless of its underlying logic type:

■ To dynamically learn and fill the routing table with a route to all subnets in the network.

■ If more than one route to a subnet is available, to place the best route in the routing table.

■ To notice when routes in the table are no longer valid, and to remove them from the routing table.

■ If a route is removed from the routing table and another route through another neighboring router is available, to add the route to the routing table. (Many people view this goal and the preceding one as a single goal.)

■ To add new routes, or to replace lost routes, with the best currently available route as quickly as possible. The time between losing the route and finding a working replacement route is called *convergence* time.

■ To prevent routing loops.

Routing protocols can become rather complicated, but the basic logic that they use is relatively simple. Routers follow these general steps for advertising routes in a network:

Step 1 Each router adds a route to its routing table for each subnet directly connected to the router.

Step 2 Each router's routing protocol tells its neighbors about all the routes in its routing table, including the directly connected routes and routes learned from other routers.

Step 3 After learning a new route from a neighbor, the router's routing protocol adds a route to its routing table, with the next-hop router typically being the neighbor from which the route was learned.

For example, Figure 5-11 shows the same sample network as in Figures 5-9 and 5-10, but now with focus on how the three routers each learned about subnet 150.150.4.0. Note that routing protocols do more work than is implied in the figure; this figure just focuses on how the routers learn about subnet 150.150.4.0.

Again, follow the items A, B, C, and D shown in the figure to see how each router learns its route to 150.150.4.0. All references to Steps 1, 2, and 3 refer to the list just before Figure 5-11.

Step A R3 learns a route that refers to its own E0 interface because subnet 150.150.4.0 is directly connected (Step 1).

Step B R3 sends a routing protocol message, called a *routing update*, to R2, causing R2 to learn about subnet 150.150.4.0 (Step 2).

Figure 5-11   *Router R1 Learning About Subnet 150.150.4.0*

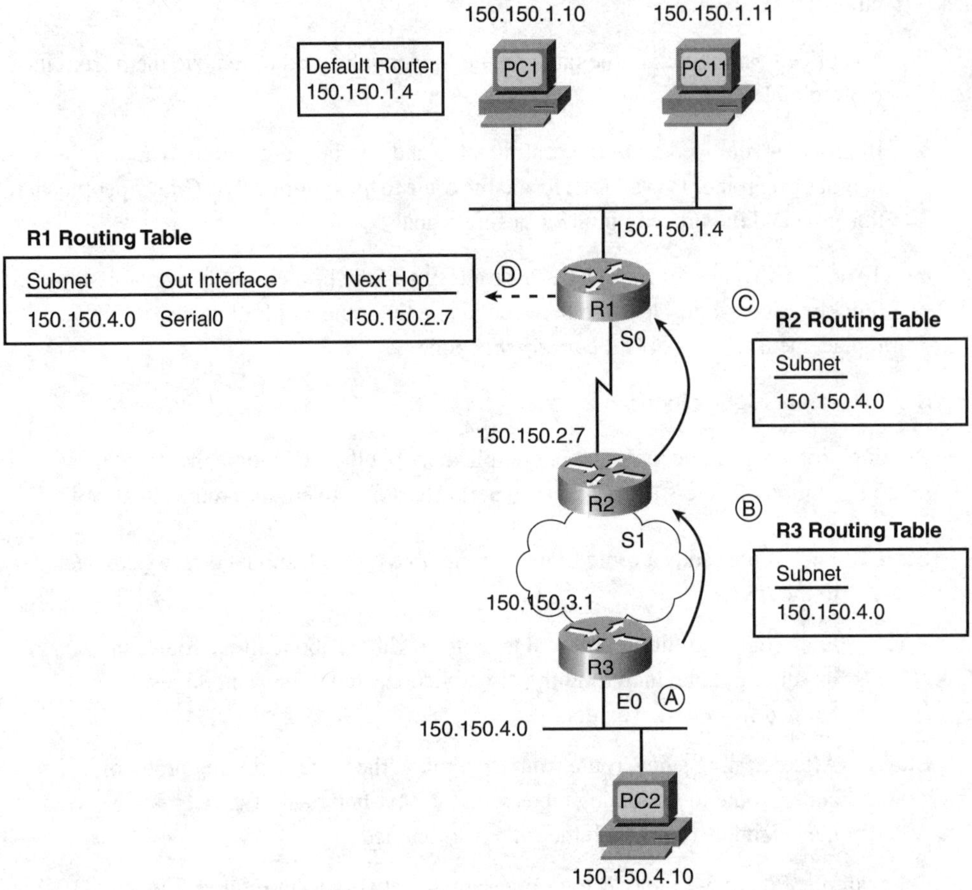

Step C   R2 sends a similar routing update to R1, causing R1 to learn about subnet 150.150.4.0 (Step 2).

Step D   R1's route to 150.150.4.0 lists 150.150.2.7 (R2's IP address) as the next-hop address because R1 learned about the route from R2. The route also lists R1's outgoing interface as Serial0, because R1 learned about the route from the update that came in serial0 (at Step C in the figure).

> **NOTE**   Routes do not always refer to the neighboring router's IP address as the next-hop IP address, but for protocols and processes covered for the ICND1 and CCNA exams, the routes typically refer to a neighboring router as the next hop.

Chapter 14, "Routing Protocol Concepts and Configuration," covers routing protocols in more detail. Next, the final major section of this chapter introduces several additional functions related to how the network layer forwards packets from source to destination through an internetwork.

Network Layer Utilities

So far this chapter has described the main features of the OSI network layer—in particular, the TCP/IP internetwork layer, which defines the same general features as OSI Layer 3. To close the chapter, this section covers four tools used almost every day in almost every TCP/IP network in the world to help the network layer with its task of routing packets from end to end through an internetwork:

- Address Resolution Protocol (ARP)

- Domain Name System (DNS)

- Dynamic Host Configuration Protocol (DHCP)

- Ping

Address Resolution Protocol and the Domain Name System

Network designers should try to make using the network as simple as possible. At most, users might want to remember the name of another computer with which they want to communicate, such as remembering the name of a website. They certainly do not want to remember the IP address, nor do they want to try to remember any MAC addresses! So, TCP/IP needs protocols that dynamically discover all the necessary information to allow communications, without the user knowing more than a name.

You might not even think that you need to know the name of another computer. For instance, when you open your browser, you probably have a default home page configured that the browser immediately downloads. You might not think of that universal resource locator (URL) string as a name, but the URL for the home page has a name embedded in it. For example, in a URL such as http://www.cisco.com/go/prepcenter, the www.cisco.com part is the name of the Cisco web server. So, whether you enter the name of another networked computer or it is implied by what you see on the screen, the user typically identifies a remote computer by using a name.

So, TCP/IP needs a way to let a computer find the IP address of another computer based on its name. TCP/IP also needs a way to find MAC addresses associated with other computers on the same LAN subnet. Figure 5-12 outlines the problem.

In this example, Hannah needs to communicate with a server on PC Jessie. Hannah knows her own name, IP address, and MAC address. *What Hannah does not know are Jessie's IP and MAC addresses.* To find the two missing facts, Hannah uses DNS to find Jessie's IP address and ARP to find Jessie's MAC address.

Figure 5-12 *Hannah Knows Jessie's Name, Needs IP Address and MAC Address*

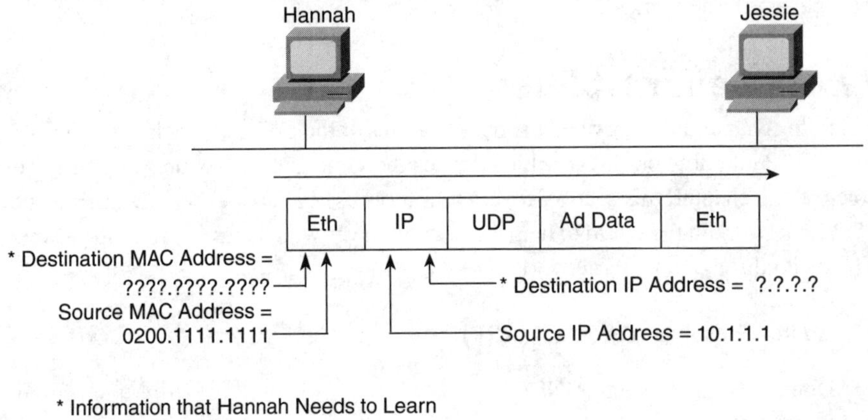

DNS Name Resolution

Hannah knows the IP address of a DNS server because the address was either preconfigured on Hannah's machine or was learned with DHCP, as covered later in this chapter. As soon as Hannah somehow identifies the name of the other computer (for example, jessie.example.com), she sends a *DNS request* to the DNS, asking for Jessie's IP address. The DNS replies with the address, 10.1.1.2. Figure 5-13 shows the simple process.

Figure 5-13 *DNS Request and Reply*

Hannah simply sends a DNS request to the server, supplying the name jessie, or jessie.example.com, and the DNS replies with the IP address (10.1.1.2 in this case). Effectively, the same thing happens when you surf the Internet and connect to any website. Your PC sends a request, just like Hannah's request for Jessie, asking the DNS to resolve the name into an IP address. After that happens, your PC can start requesting that the web page be sent.

The ARP Process

As soon as a host knows the IP address of the other host, the sending host may need to know the MAC address used by the other computer. For example, Hannah still needs to know the Ethernet MAC address used by 10.1.1.2, so Hannah issues something called an *ARP broadcast.* An ARP broadcast is sent to a broadcast Ethernet address, so everyone on the LAN receives it. Because Jessie is on the same LAN, she receives the ARP broadcast. Because Jessie's IP address is 10.1.1.2 and the ARP broadcast is looking for the MAC address associated with 10.1.1.2, Jessie replies with her own MAC address. Figure 5-14 outlines the process.

Figure 5-14 *Sample ARP Process*

Now Hannah knows the destination IP and Ethernet addresses that she should use when sending frames to Jessie, and the packet shown in Figure 5-12 can be sent successfully.

Hosts may or may not need to ARP to find the destination host's MAC address based on the two-step routing logic used by a host. If the destination host is on the same subnet, the sending host sends an ARP looking for the destination host's MAC address, as shown in Figure 5-14. However, if the sending host is on a different subnet than the destination host, the sending host's routing logic results in the sending host needing to forward the packet to its default gateway. For example, if Hannah and Jessie had been in different subnets in Figures 5-12 through 5-14, Hannah's routing logic would have caused Hannah to want to send the packet to Hannah's default gateway (router). In that case, Hannah would have used ARP to find the router's MAC address instead of Jessie's MAC address.

Additionally, hosts need to use ARP to find MAC addresses only once in a while. Any device that uses IP should retain, or cache, the information learned with ARP, placing the information in its *ARP cache*. Each time a host needs to send a packet encapsulated in an Ethernet frame, it first checks its ARP cache and uses the MAC address found there. If the correct information is not listed in the ARP cache, the host then can use ARP to discover the MAC address used by a particular IP address. Also, a host learns ARP information when receiving an ARP as well. For example, the ARP process shown in Figure 5-14 results in both Hannah and Jessie learning the other host's MAC address.

NOTE You can see the contents of the ARP cache on most PC Operating Systems by using the **arp -a** command from a command prompt.

Address Assignment and DHCP

Every device that uses TCP/IP—in fact, every interface on every device that uses TCP/IP—needs a valid IP address. For some devices, the address can and should be statically assigned by configuring the device. For example, all commonly used computer operating systems that support TCP/IP allow the user to statically configure the IP address on each interface. Routers and switches typically use statically configured IP addresses as well.

Servers also typically use statically configured IP addresses. Using a statically configured and seldom-changed IP address helps because all references to that server can stay the same over time. This is the same concept that it's good that the location of your favorite grocery store never changes. You know where to go to buy food, and you can get there from home, on the way home from work, or from somewhere else. Likewise, if servers have a static, unchanging IP address, the users of that server know how to reach the server, from anywhere, consistently.

However, the average end-user host computer does not need to use the same IP address every day. Again thinking about your favorite grocery store, you could move to a new apartment every week, but you'd still know where the grocery store is. The workers at the grocery store don't need to know where you live. Likewise, servers typically don't care that your PC has a different IP address today as compared to yesterday. End-user hosts can have their IP addresses dynamically assigned, and even change their IP addresses over time, because it does not matter if the IP address changes.

DHCP defines the protocols used to allow computers to request a lease of an IP address. DHCP uses a server, with the server keeping a list of pools of IP addresses available in each subnet. DHCP clients can send the DHCP server a message, asking to borrow or lease an IP address. The server then suggests an IP address. If accepted, the server notes that the address is no longer available for assignment to any other hosts, and the client has an IP address to use.

Key Topic

DHCP supplies IP addresses to clients, and it also supplies other information. For example, hosts need to know their IP address, plus the subnet mask to use, plus what default gateway to use, as well as the IP address(es) of any DNS servers. In most networks today, DHCP supplies all these facts to a typical end-user host.

Figure 5-15 shows a typical set of four messages used between a DHCP server to assign an IP address, as well as other information. Note that the first two messages are both IP broadcast messages.

Figure 5-15 shows the DHCP server as a PC, which is typical in an Enterprise network. However, as covered in Chapter 17, "WAN Configuration," routers can and do provide DHCP services as well. In fact, routers can provide a DHCP server function, dynamically assigning IP addresses to the computers in a small or home office, using DHCP client functions to dynamically lease IP addresses from an Internet service provider (ISP). However, the need for these functions is closely related to features most often used with connections to the Internet, so more details about a router's implementation of DHCP server and DHCP client functions are saved for Chapter 17.

Figure 5-15   *DHCP Messages to Acquire an IP Address*

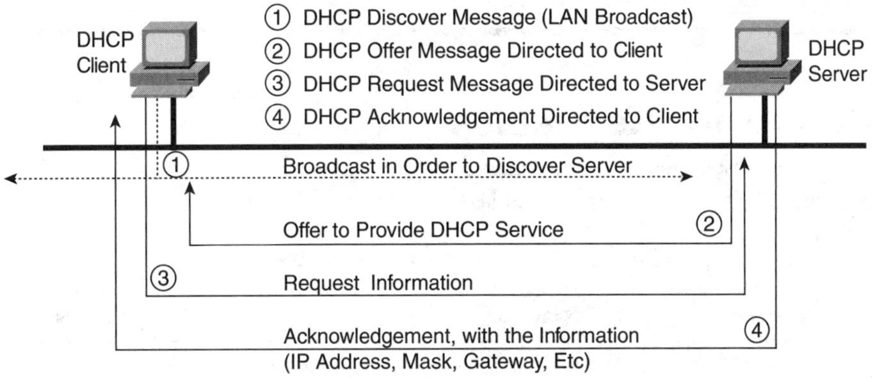

DHCP has become a prolific protocol. Most end-user hosts on LANs in corporate networks get their IP addresses and other basic configuration via DHCP.

ICMP Echo and the ping Command

After you have implemented a network, you need a way to test basic IP connectivity without relying on any applications to be working. The primary tool for testing basic network connectivity is the **ping** command. **ping** (Packet Internet Groper) uses the *Internet Control Message Protocol (ICMP)*, sending a message called an *ICMP echo request* to another IP address. The computer with that IP address should reply with an *ICMP echo reply*. If that works, you successfully have tested the IP network. In other words, you know that the network can deliver a packet from one host to the other, and back. ICMP does not rely on any application, so it really just tests basic IP connectivity—Layers 1, 2, and 3 of the OSI model. Figure 5-16 outlines the basic process.

Figure 5-16   *Sample Network,* **ping** *Command*

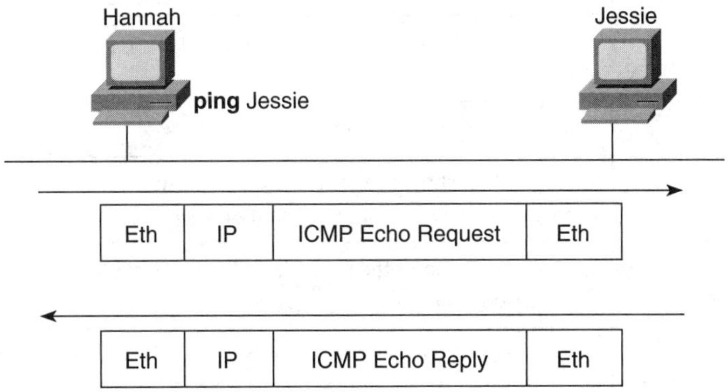

Chapter 15, "Troubleshooting IP Routing," gives you more information about and examples of ping and ICMP.

Exam Preparation Tasks

Review All the Key Topics

Key
Topic

Review the most important topics from this chapter, noted with the key topics icon. Table 5-6 lists these key topics and where each is discussed.

Table 5-6 *Key Topics for Chapter 5*

Key Topic Element	Description	Page Number
List	Two statements about how IP expects IP addresses to be grouped into networks or subnets	107
Table 5-3	List of the three types of unicast IP networks and the size of the network and host parts of each type of network	108
Paragraph	Explanation of the concept of a network broadcast or directed broadcast address	109
Table 5-5	Details about the actual Class A, B, and C networks	110
Figure 5-6	Conceptual view of how subnetting works	112
Figure 5-7	Structure of subnetted Class A, B, and C IP addresses, classful view	113
Figure 5-8	Structure of a subnetted unicast IP address, classless view	114
List	Two-step process of how hosts route (forward) packets	114
List	Four-step process of how routers route (forward) packets	116
Figure 5-10	Example of the IP routing process	117
Figure 5-11	Example that shows generally how a routing protocol can cause routers to learn new routes	120
Figure 5-13	Example that shows the purpose and process of DNS name resolution	122
Figure 5-14	Example of the purpose and process of ARP	123
Paragraph	The most important information learned by a host acting as a DHCP client	124

Complete the Tables and Lists from Memory

Print a copy of Appendix H, "Memory Tables" (found on the CD), or at least the section for this chapter, and complete the tables and lists from memory. Appendix I, "Memory Tables Answer Key," also on the CD, includes completed tables and lists for you to check your work.

Definitions of Key Terms

Define the following key terms from this chapter, and check your answers in the glossary.

ARP, default gateway/default router, DHCP, DNS, host part, IP address, logical address, network broadcast address, network number/network address, network part, routing table, subnet broadcast address, subnet number/subnet address, subnet part

This chapter covers the following subjects:

TCP/IP Layer 4 Protocols: TCP and UDP: This section explains the functions and mechanisms used by TCP and UDP, including error recovery and port numbers.

TCP/IP Applications: This section explains the purpose of TCP/IP application layer protocols, focusing on HTTP as an example.

Network Security: This section provides some perspectives on the security threats faced by networks today, introducing some of the key tools used to help prevent and reduce the impact of those threats.

CHAPTER 6

Fundamentals of TCP/IP Transport, Applications, and Security

The CCNA exams focus mostly on a deeper and broader examination of the topics covered in Chapter 3 (LANs), Chapter 4 (WANs), and Chapter 5 (routing). This chapter explains the basics of a few topics that receive less attention on the exams: the TCP/IP transport layer, the TCP/IP application layer, and TCP/IP network security. Although all three topics are covered on the various CCNA exams, the extent of that coverage is much less compared to LANs, WANs, and routing.

"Do I Know This Already?" Quiz

The "Do I Know This Already?" quiz allows you to assess whether you should read the entire chapter. If you miss no more than one of these ten self-assessment questions, you might want to move ahead to the "Exam Preparation Tasks" section. Table 6-1 lists the major headings in this chapter and the "Do I Know This Already?" quiz questions covering the material in those sections. This helps you assess your knowledge of these specific areas. The answers to the "Do I Know This Already?" quiz appear in Appendix A.

Table 6-1 *"Do I Know This Already?" Foundation Topics Section-to-Question Mapping*

Foundation Topics Section	Questions
TCP/IP Layer 4 Protocols: TCP and UDP	1–6
TCP/IP Applications	7, 8
Network Security	9, 10

1. PC1 is using TCP and has a window size of 4000. PC1 sends four segments to PC2 with 1000 bytes of data each, with sequence numbers 2000, 3000, 4000, and 5000. PC1 does not recieve an acknowledgment within its current timeout value for this connection. What should PC1 do next?

   a. Increase its window to 5000 or more segments

   b. Send the next segment, with sequence number 6000

   c. Resend the segment whose sequence number was 5000

   d. Resend all four previously sent segments

2. Which of the following are not features of a protocol that is considered to match OSI Layer 4?

    a. Error recovery

    b. Flow control

    c. Segmenting of application data

    d. Conversion from binary to ASCII

3. Which of the following header fields identify which TCP/IP application gets data received by the computer?

    a. Ethernet Type

    b. SNAP Protocol Type

    c. IP Protocol Field

    d. TCP Port Number

    e. UDP Port Number

    f. Application ID

4. Which of the following are not typical functions of TCP?

    a. Windowing

    b. Error recovery

    c. Multiplexing using port numbers

    d. Routing

    e. Encryption

    f. Ordered data transfer

5. Which of the following functions is performed by both TCP and UDP?

    a. Windowing

    b. Error recovery

    c. Multiplexing using port numbers

    d. Routing

    e. Encryption

    f. Ordered data transfer

6. What do you call data that includes the Layer 4 protocol header, and data given to Layer 4 by the upper layers, not including any headers and trailers from Layers 1 to 3?

   a. Bits

   b. Chunk

   c. Segment

   d. Packet

   e. Frame

   f. L4PDU

   g. L3PDU

7. In the URL http://www.fredsco.com/name.html, which part identifies the web server?

   a. http

   b. www.fredsco.com

   c. fredsco.com

   d. http://www.fredsco.com

   e. The file name.html includes the hostname.

8. When comparing VoIP with an HTTP-based mission-critical business application, which of the following statements are accurate about the quality of service needed from the network?

   a. VoIP needs better (lower) packet loss.

   b. HTTP needs less bandwidth.

   c. HTTP needs better (lower) jitter.

   d. VoIP needs better (lower) delay.

9. Which of the following is a device or function whose most notable feature is to examine trends over time to recognize different known attacks as compared to a list of common attack signatures?

   a. VPN

   b. Firewall

   c. IDS

   d. NAC

10. Which of the following is a device or function whose most notable feature is to encrypt packets before they pass through the Internet?

   a. VPN

   b. Firewall

   c. IDS

   d. NAC

Foundation Topics

This chapter begins by examining the functions of Transmission Control Protocol (TCP), which are many, as compared to the functions of User Datagram Protocol (UDP), of which there are few. The second major section of the chapter examines the TCP/IP application layer, including some discussion of how DNS name resolution works. Finally, the third major section examines the importance and concepts of network security, introducing some of the core concepts, terminology, and functions important for security today.

TCP/IP Layer 4 Protocols: TCP and UDP

The OSI transport layer (Layer 4) defines several functions, the most important of which are error recovery and flow control. Likewise, the TCP/IP transport layer protocols also implement these same types of features. Note that both the OSI model and TCP/IP model call this layer the transport layer. But as usual, when referring to the TCP/IP model, the layer name and number are based on OSI, so any TCP/IP transport layer protocols are considered Layer 4 protocols.

The key difference between TCP and UDP is that TCP provides a wide variety of services to applications, whereas UDP does not. For example, routers discard packets for many reasons, including bit errors, congestion, and instances in which no correct routes are known. As you have read already, most data-link protocols notice errors (a process called *error detection*) but then discard frames that have errors. TCP provides for retransmission (error recovery) and help to avoid congestion (flow control), whereas UDP does not. As a result, many application protocols choose to use TCP.

However, do not let UDP's lack of services make you think that UDP is worse than TCP. By providing few services, UDP needs fewer bytes in its header compared to TCP, resulting in fewer bytes of overhead in the network. UDP software does not slow down data transfer in cases where TCP may purposefully slow down. Also, some applications, notably today voice over IP (VoIP) and video over IP, do not need error recovery, so they use UDP. So, UDP also has an important place in TCP/IP networks today.

Table 6-2 lists the main features supported by TCP and/or UDP. Note that only the first item listed in the table is supported by UDP, whereas all items in the table are supported by TCP.

Table 6-2 *TCP/IP Transport Layer Features*

Function	Description
Multiplexing using ports	Function that allows receiving hosts to choose the correct application for which the data is destined, based on the port number.
Error recovery (reliability)	Process of numbering and acknowledging data with Sequence and Acknowledgment header fields.
Flow control using windowing	Process that uses window sizes to protect buffer space and routing devices.
Connection establishment and termination	Process used to initialize port numbers and Sequence and Acknowledgment fields.
Ordered data transfer and data segmentation	Continuous stream of bytes from an upper-layer process that is "segmented" for transmission and delivered to upper-layer processes at the receiving device, with the bytes in the same order.

Next, this section describes the features of TCP, followed by a brief comparison to UDP.

Transmission Control Protocol

Each TCP/IP application typically chooses to use either TCP or UDP based on the application's requirements. For instance, TCP provides error recovery, but to do so, it consumes more bandwidth and uses more processing cycles. UDP does not perform error recovery, but it takes less bandwidth and uses fewer processing cycles. Regardless of which of the two TCP/IP transport layer protocols the application chooses to use, you should understand the basics of how each of these transport layer protocols works.

TCP, as defined in RFC 793, accomplishes the functions listed in Table 6-2 through mechanisms at the endpoint computers. TCP relies on IP for end-to-end delivery of the data, including routing issues. In other words, TCP performs only part of the functions necessary to deliver the data between applications. Also, the role that it plays is directed toward providing services for the applications that sit at the endpoint computers. Regardless of whether two computers are on the same Ethernet or are separated by the entire Internet, TCP performs its functions the same way.

Figure 6-1 shows the fields in the TCP header. Although you don't need to memorize the names of the fields or their locations, the rest of this section refers to several of the fields, so the entire header is included here for reference.

Figure 6-1 *TCP Header Fields*

Bit 0			Bit 15	Bit 16			Bit 31

Source Port (16)			Destination Port (16)	
Sequence Number (32)				
Acknowledgement Number (32)				
Header Length (4)	Reserved (6)	Code Bits (6)	Window (16)	
Checksum (16)			Urgent (16)	
Options (0 or 32 If Any)				
Data (Varies)				

20 Bytes

Multiplexing Using TCP Port Numbers

TCP provides a lot of features to applications, at the expense of requiring slightly more processing and overhead, as compared to UDP. However, TCP and UDP both use a concept called *multiplexing*. Therefore, this section begins with an explanation of multiplexing with TCP and UDP. Afterward, the unique features of TCP are explored.

Multiplexing by TCP and UDP involves the process of how a computer thinks when receiving data. The computer might be running many applications, such as a web browser, an e-mail package, or an Internet VoIP application (for example, Skype). TCP and UDP multiplexing enables the receiving computer to know which application to give the data to.

Some examples will help make the need for multiplexing obvious. The sample network consists of two PCs, labeled Hannah and Jessie. Hannah uses an application that she wrote to send advertisements that appear on Jessie's screen. The application sends a new ad to Jessie every 10 seconds. Hannah uses a second application, a wire-transfer application, to send Jessie some money. Finally, Hannah uses a web browser to access the web server that runs on Jessie's PC. The ad application and wire-transfer application are imaginary, just for this example. The web application works just like it would in real life.

Figure 6-2 shows the sample network, with Jessie running three applications:

- A UDP-based ad application

- A TCP-based wire-transfer application

- A TCP web server application

Figure 6-2　*Hannah Sending Packets to Jessie, with Three Applications*

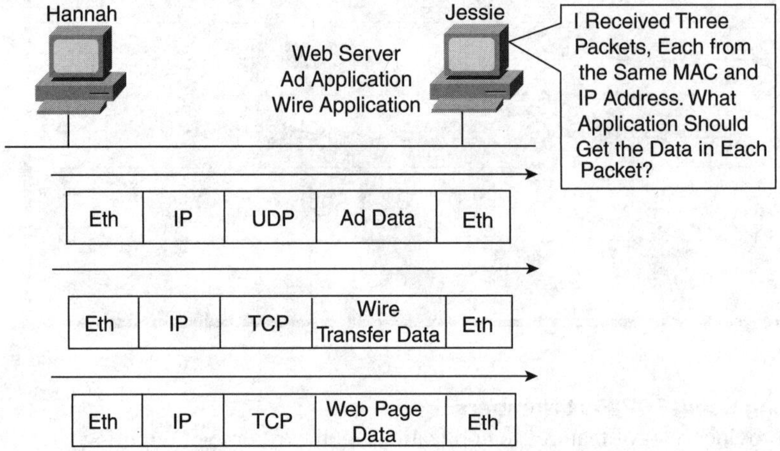

Jessie needs to know which application to give the data to, but *all three packets are from the same Ethernet and IP address*. You might think that Jessie could look at whether the packet contains a UDP or TCP header, but, as you see in the figure, two applications (wire transfer and web) are using TCP.

TCP and UDP solve this problem by using a port number field in the TCP or UDP header, respectively. Each of Hannah's TCP and UDP segments uses a different *destination port number* so that Jessie knows which application to give the data to. Figure 6-3 shows an example.

Multiplexing relies on a concept called a *socket*. A socket consists of three things:

- An IP address

- A transport protocol

- A port number

Figure 6-3 *Hannah Sending Packets to Jessie, with Three Applications Using Port Numbers to Multiplex*

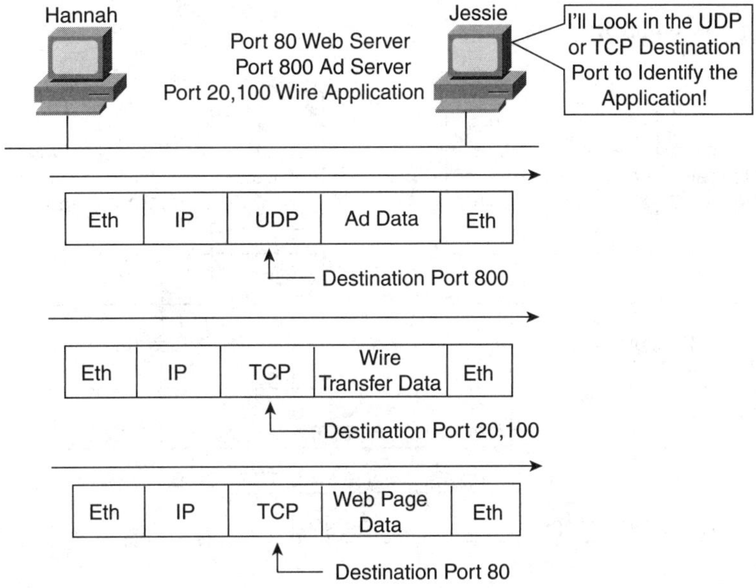

So, for a web server application on Jessie, the socket would be (10.1.1.2, TCP, port 80) because, by default, web servers use the well-known port 80. When Hannah's web browser connects to the web server, Hannah uses a socket as well—possibly one like this: (10.1.1.1, TCP, 1030). Why 1030? Well, Hannah just needs a port number that is unique on Hannah, so Hannah sees that port 1030 is available and uses it. In fact, hosts typically allocate *dynamic port numbers* starting at 1024 because the ports below 1024 are reserved for well-known applications, such as web services.

In Figure 6-3, Hannah and Jessie use three applications at the same time—hence, three socket connections are open. Because a socket on a single computer should be unique, a connection between two sockets should identify a unique connection between two computers. This uniqueness means that you can use multiple applications at the same time, talking to applications running on the same or different computers. Multiplexing, based on sockets, ensures that the data is delivered to the correct applications. Figure 6-4 shows the three socket connections between Hannah and Jessie.

Port numbers are a vital part of the socket concept. Well-known port numbers are used by servers; other port numbers are used by clients. Applications that provide a service, such as FTP, Telnet, and web servers, open a socket using a well-known port and listen for connection requests. Because these connection requests from clients are required to include both the source and destination port numbers, the port numbers used by the servers must be well-known. Therefore, each server has a hard-coded, well-known port number. The well-known ports are listed at http://www.iana.org/assignments/port-numbers.

Figure 6-4   *Connections Between Sockets*

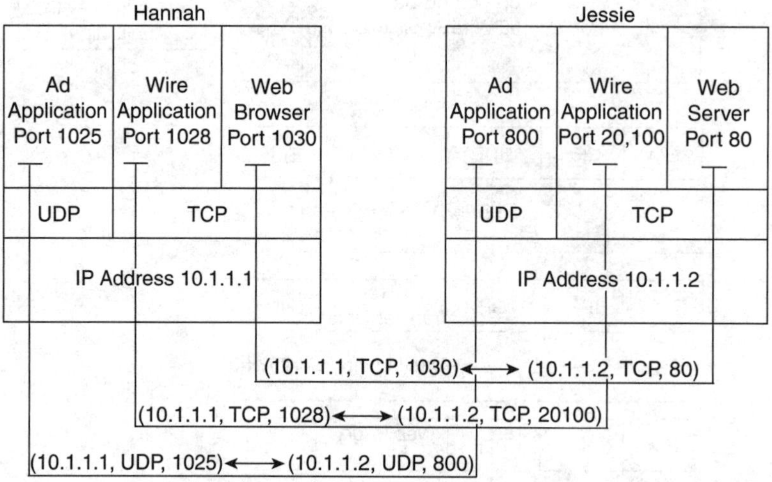

On client machines, where the requests originate, any unused port number can be allocated. The result is that each client on the same host uses a different port number, but a server uses the same port number for all connections. For example, 100 web browsers on the same host computer could each connect to a web server, but the web server with 100 clients connected to it would have only one socket and, therefore, only one port number (port 80 in this case). The server can tell which packets are sent from which of the 100 clients by looking at the source port of received TCP segments. The server can send data to the correct web client (browser) by sending data to that same port number listed as a destination port. The combination of source and destination sockets allows all participating hosts to distinguish between the data's source and destination. Although the example explains the concept using 100 TCP connections, the same port numbering concept applies to UDP sessions in the same way.

> **NOTE**   You can find all RFCs online at http://www.isi.edu/in-notes/rfc*xxxx*.txt, where *xxxx* is the number of the RFC. If you do not know the number of the RFC, you can try searching by topic at http://www.rfc-editor.org/rfcsearch.html.

Popular TCP/IP Applications

Throughout your preparation for the CCNA exams, you will come across a variety of TCP/IP applications. You should at least be aware of some of the applications that can be used to help manage and control a network.

The World Wide Web (WWW) application exists through web browsers accessing the content available on web servers. Although it is often thought of as an end-user application, you can actually use WWW to manage a router or switch. You enable a web server function in the router or switch and use a browser to access the router or switch.

The Domain Name System (DNS) allows users to use names to refer to computers, with DNS being used to find the corresponding IP addresses. DNS also uses a client/server model, with DNS servers being controlled by networking personnel, and DNS client functions being part of most any device that uses TCP/IP today. The client simply asks the DNS server to supply the IP address that corresponds to a given name.

Simple Network Management Protocol (SNMP) is an application layer protocol used specifically for network device management. For instance, Cisco supplies a large variety of network management products, many of them in the CiscoWorks network management software product family. They can be used to query, compile, store, and display information about a network's operation. To query the network devices, CiscoWorks software mainly uses SNMP protocols.

Traditionally, to move files to and from a router or switch, Cisco used Trivial File Transfer Protocol (TFTP). TFTP defines a protocol for basic file transfer—hence the word "trivial." Alternatively, routers and switches can use File Transfer Protocol (FTP), which is a much more functional protocol, to transfer files. Both work well for moving files into and out of Cisco devices. FTP allows many more features, making it a good choice for the general end-user population. TFTP client and server applications are very simple, making them good tools as embedded parts of networking devices.

Some of these applications use TCP, and some use UDP. As you will read later, TCP performs error recovery, whereas UDP does not. For instance, Simple Mail Transport Protocol (SMTP) and Post Office Protocol version 3 (POP3), both used for transferring mail, require guaranteed delivery, so they use TCP. Regardless of which transport layer protocol is used, applications use a well-known port number so that clients know which port to attempt to connect to. Table 6-3 lists several popular applications and their well-known port numbers.

Table 6-3 *Popular Applications and Their Well-Known Port Numbers*

Key Topic

Port Number	Protocol	Application
20	TCP	FTP data
21	TCP	FTP control
22	TCP	SSH

continues

Key Topic

Table 6-3 *Popular Applications and Their Well-Known Port Numbers (Continued)*

Port Number	Protocol	Application
23	TCP	Telnet
25	TCP	SMTP
53	UDP, TCP	DNS
67, 68	UDP	DHCP
69	UDP	TFTP
80	TCP	HTTP (WWW)
110	TCP	POP3
161	UDP	SNMP
443	TCP	SSL
16,384–32,767	UDP	RTP-based Voice (VoIP) and Video

Error Recovery (Reliability)

TCP provides for reliable data transfer, which is also called *reliability* or *error recovery*, depending on what document you read. To accomplish reliability, TCP numbers data bytes using the Sequence and Acknowledgment fields in the TCP header. TCP achieves reliability in both directions, using the Sequence Number field of one direction combined with the Acknowledgment field in the opposite direction. Figure 6-5 shows the basic operation.

Figure 6-5 *TCP Acknowledgment Without Errors*

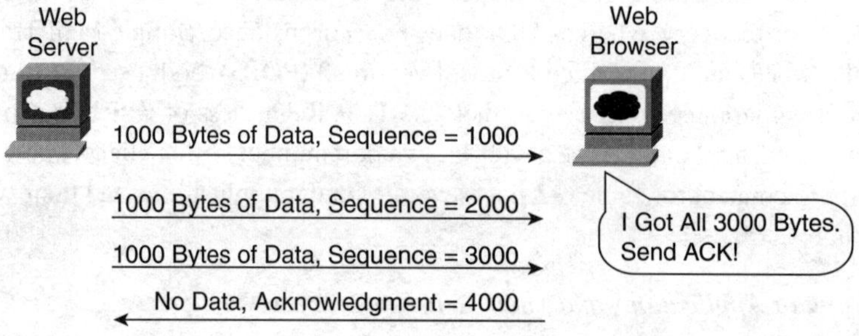

In Figure 6-5, the Acknowledgment field in the TCP header sent by the web client (4000) implies the next byte to be received; this is called *forward acknowledgment*. The sequence number reflects the number of the first byte in the segment. In this case, each TCP segment is 1000 bytes long; the Sequence and Acknowledgment fields count the number of bytes.

Figure 6-6 depicts the same scenario, but the second TCP segment was lost or is in error. The web client's reply has an ACK field equal to 2000, implying that the web client is expecting byte number 2000 next. The TCP function at the web server then could recover lost data by resending the second TCP segment. The TCP protocol allows for resending just that segment and then waiting, hoping that the web client will reply with an acknowledgment that equals 4000.

Figure 6-6   *TCP Acknowledgment with Errors*

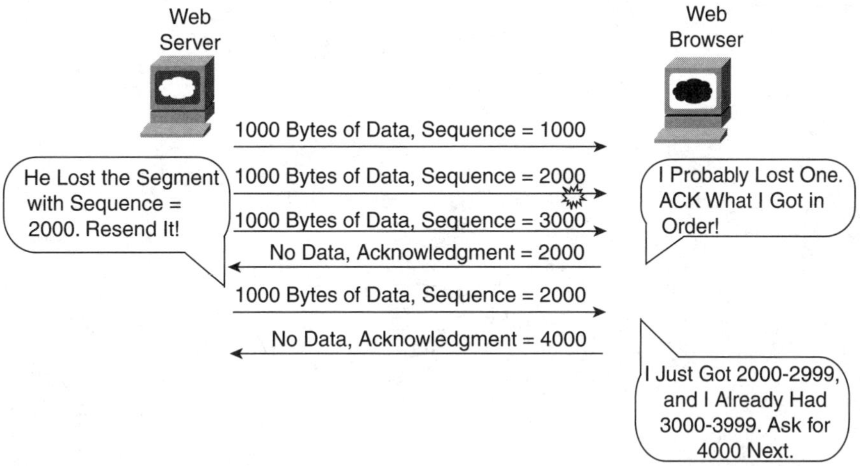

Although not shown, the sender also sets a retransmission timer, awaiting acknowledgment, just in case the acknowledgment is lost or all transmitted segments are lost. If that timer expires, the TCP sender sends all segments again.

Flow Control Using Windowing

TCP implements flow control by taking advantage of the Sequence and Acknowledgment fields in the TCP header, along with another field called the Window field. This Window field implies the maximum number of unacknowledged bytes that are allowed to be outstanding at any instant in time. The window starts small and then grows until errors occur. The size of the window changes over time, so it is sometimes called a *dynamic window*. Additionally, because the actual sequence and acknowledgment numbers grow over time, the window is sometimes called a *sliding window*, with the numbers sliding (moving) upward. When the window is full, the sender does not send, which controls the flow of data. Figure 6-7 shows windowing with a current window size of 3000. Each TCP segment has 1000 bytes of data.

Notice that the web server must wait after sending the third segment because the window is exhausted. When the acknowledgment has been received, another window can be sent. Because no errors have occurred, the web client grants a larger window to the server, so now 4000 bytes can be sent before the server receives an acknowledgment. In other words, the receiver uses the Window field to tell the sender how much data it can send before it must stop and wait for the next acknowledgment. As with other TCP features, windowing is symmetrical. Both sides send and receive, and, in each case, the receiver grants a window to the sender using the Window field.

Key Topic

Figure 6-7   *TCP Windowing*

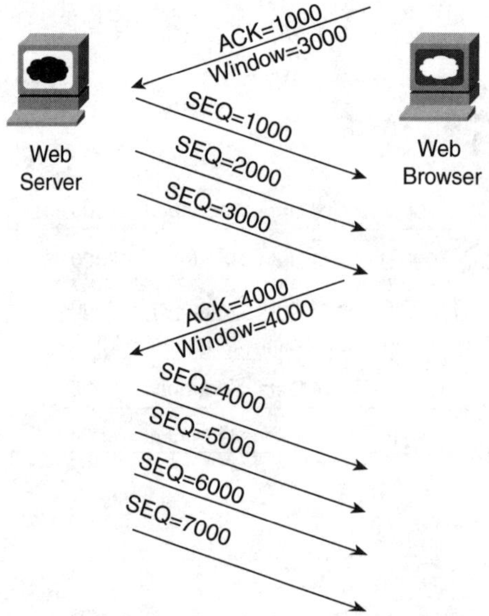

Windowing does not require that the sender stop sending in all cases. If an acknowledgment is received before the window is exhausted, a new window begins, and the sender continues sending data until the current window is exhausted. (The term *Positive Acknowledgment and Retransmission [PAR]* is sometimes used to describe the error recovery and windowing processes that TCP uses.)

Connection Establishment and Termination

TCP connection establishment occurs before any of the other TCP features can begin their work. Connection establishment refers to the process of initializing sequence and acknowledgment fields and agreeing on the port numbers used. Figure 6-8 shows an example of connection establishment flow.

This three-way connection establishment flow must end before data transfer can begin. The connection exists between the two sockets, although the TCP header has no single socket field. Of the three parts of a socket, the IP addresses are implied based on the source and destination IP addresses in the IP header. TCP is implied because a TCP header is in use, as specified by the protocol field value in the IP header. Therefore, the only parts of the socket that need to be encoded in the TCP header are the port numbers.

Figure 6-8 *TCP Connection Establishment*

SEQ=200
SYN, DPORT=80, SPORT=1027

SEQ=1450, ACK=201
SYN, ACK, DPORT=1027, SPORT=80

SEQ=201, ACK=1451
ACK, DPORT=80, SPORT=1027

Web Browser

Web Server

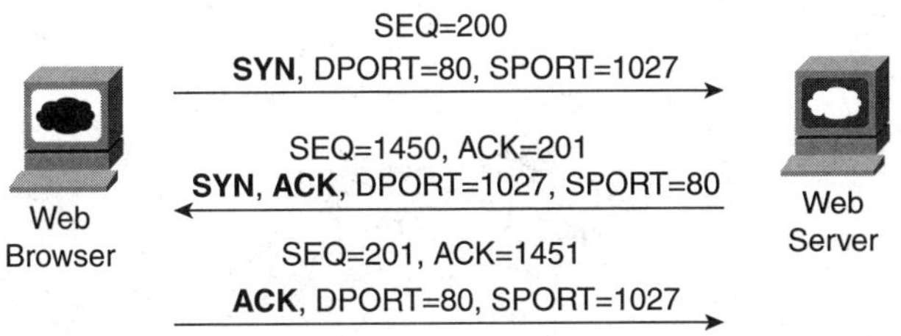

TCP signals connection establishment using 2 bits inside the flag fields of the TCP header. Called the SYN and ACK flags, these bits have a particularly interesting meaning. SYN means "Synchronize the sequence numbers," which is one necessary component in initialization for TCP. The ACK field means "The Acknowledgment field is valid in this header." Until the sequence numbers are initialized, the Acknowledgment field cannot be very useful. Also notice that in the initial TCP segment in Figure 6-8, no acknowledgment number is shown; this is because that number is not valid yet. Because the ACK field must be present in all the ensuing segments, the ACK bit continues to be set until the connection is terminated.

TCP initializes the Sequence Number and Acknowledgment Number fields to any number that fits into the 4-byte fields; the actual values shown in Figure 6-8 are simply sample values. The initialization flows are each considered to have a single byte of data, as reflected in the Acknowledgment Number fields in the example.

Figure 6-9 shows TCP connection termination. This four-way termination sequence is straightforward and uses an additional flag, called the *FIN bit*. (FIN is short for "finished," as you might guess.) One interesting note: Before the device on the right sends the third TCP segment in the sequence, it notifies the application that the connection is coming down. It then waits on an acknowledgment from the application before sending the third segment in the figure. Just in case the application takes some time to reply, the PC on the right sends the second flow in the figure, acknowledging that the other PC wants to take down the connection. Otherwise, the PC on the left might resend the first segment repeatedly.

Figure 6-9 *TCP Connection Termination*

TCP establishes and terminates connections between the endpoints, whereas UDP does not. Many protocols operate under these same concepts, so the terms *connection-oriented* and *connectionless* are used to refer to the general idea of each. More formally, these terms can be defined as follows:

■ **Connection-oriented protocol:** A protocol that requires an exchange of messages before data transfer begins or that has a required preestablished correlation between two endpoints

■ **Connectionless protocol:** A protocol that does not require an exchange of messages and that does not require a preestablished correlation between two endpoints

Data Segmentation and Ordered Data Transfer

Applications need to send data. Sometimes the data is small—in some cases, a single byte. In other cases, such as with a file transfer, the data might be millions of bytes.

Each different type of data-link protocol typically has a limit on the *maximum transmission unit (MTU)* that can be sent inside a data link layer frame. In other words, the MTU is the size of the largest Layer 3 packet that can sit inside a frame's data field. For many data-link protocols, Ethernet included, the MTU is 1500 bytes.

TCP handles the fact that an application might give it millions of bytes to send by *segmenting* the data into smaller pieces, called *segments*. Because an IP packet can often be no more than 1500 bytes because of the MTU restrictions, and because IP and TCP headers are 20 bytes each, TCP typically segments large data into 1460-byte chunks.

The TCP receiver performs reassembly when it receives the segments. To reassemble the data, TCP must recover lost segments, as discussed previously. However, the TCP receiver must also reorder segments that arrive out of sequence. Because IP routing can choose to balance traffic across multiple links, the actual segments may be delivered out of order. So, the TCP receiver also must perform *ordered data transfer* by reassembling the data into the original order. The process is not hard to imagine: If segments arrive with the sequence numbers 1000, 3000, and 2000, each with 1000 bytes of data, the receiver can reorder them, and no retransmissions are required.

You should also be aware of some terminology related to TCP segmentation. The TCP header and the data field together are called a *TCP segment*. This term is similar to a data-link frame and an IP packet in that the terms refer to the headers and trailers for the respective layers, plus the encapsulated data. The term *L4PDU* also can be used instead of the term *TCP segment* because TCP is a Layer 4 protocol.

User Datagram Protocol

UDP provides a service for applications to exchange messages. Unlike TCP, UDP is connectionless and provides no reliability, no windowing, no reordering of the received data, and no segmentation of large chunks of data into the right size for transmission. However, UDP provides some functions of TCP, such as data transfer and multiplexing using port numbers, and it does so with fewer bytes of overhead and less processing required than TCP.

UDP data transfer differs from TCP data transfer in that no reordering or recovery is accomplished. Applications that use UDP are tolerant of the lost data, or they have some application mechanism to recover lost data. For example, VoIP uses UDP because if a voice packet is lost, by the time the loss could be noticed and the packet retransmitted, too much delay would have occurred, and the voice would be unintelligible. Also, DNS requests use UDP because the user will retry an operation if the DNS resolution fails. As another example, the Network File System (NFS), a remote file system application, performs recovery with application layer code, so UDP features are acceptable to NFS.

Figure 6-10 shows TCP and UDP header formats. Note the existence of both Source Port and Destination Port fields in the TCP and UDP headers, but the absence of Sequence Number and Acknowledgment Number fields in the UDP header. UDP does not need these fields because it makes no attempt to number the data for acknowledgments or resequencing.

UDP gains some advantages over TCP by not using the Sequence and Acknowledgment fields. The most obvious advantage of UDP over TCP is that there are fewer bytes of overhead. Not as obvious is the fact that UDP does not require waiting on acknowledgments or holding the data in memory until it is acknowledged. This means that UDP applications are not artificially slowed by the acknowledgment process, and memory is freed more quickly.

Figure 6-10 *TCP and UDP Headers*

2	2	4	4	4 bits	6 bits	6 bits	2	2	2	3	1
Source Port	Dest. Port	Sequence Number	Ack. Number	Offset	Reserved	Flags	Window Size	Checksum	Urgent	Options	PAD

TCP Header

2	2	2	2
Source Port	Dest. Port	Length	Checksum

UDP Header

* Unless Specified, Lengths Shown
Are the Numbers of Bytes

TCP/IP Applications

The whole goal of building an Enterprise network, or connecting a small home or office network to the Internet, is to use applications—applications such as web browsing, text messaging, e-mail, file downloads, voice, and video. This section examines a few issues related to network design in light of the applications expected in an internetwork. This is followed by a much deeper look at one particular application—web browsing using Hypertext Transfer Protocol (HTTP).

QoS Needs and the Impact of TCP/IP Applications

The needs of networked applications have changed and grown significantly over the years. When networks first became popular in Enterprises in the 1970s, the network typically supported only data applications, mainly text-only terminals and text-only printers. A single user might generate a few hundred bytes of data for the network every time he or she pressed the Enter key, maybe every 10 seconds or so.

The term quality of service (QoS) refers to the entire topic of what an application needs from the network service. Each type of application can be analyzed in terms of its QoS requirements on the network, so if the network meets those requirements, the application will work well. For example, the older text-based interactive applications required only a small amount of bandwidth, but they did like low delay. If those early networks supported a round-trip delay of less than 1 second, users were generally happy, because they had to wait less than 1 second for a response.

The QoS needs of data applications have changed over the years. Generally speaking, applications have tended to need more bandwidth, with lower delay as well. From those early days of networking to the present, here are some of the types of data applications that entered the marketplace, and their impact on the network:

■ Graphics-capable terminals and printers, which increased the required bytes for the same interaction as the old text-based terminals and printers

■ File transfers, which introduced much larger volumes of data, but with no significant response time requirements

■ File servers, which allow users to store files on a server—which might require a large volume of data transfer, but with a much smaller end-user response time requirement

■ The maturation of database technology, making vast amounts of data available to casual users, vastly increasing the number of users wanting access to data

■ The migration of common applications to web browsers, which encourages more users to access data

■ The general acceptance of e-mail as both a personal and business communications service, both inside companies and with other companies

■ The rapid commercialization of the Internet, enabling companies to offer data directly to their customers via the data network rather than via phone calls

Besides these and many other trends in the progression of data applications over the years, voice and video are in the middle of a migration onto the data network. Before the mid-to-late 1990s, voice and video typically used totally separate networking facilities. The migration of voice and video to the data network puts even more pressure on the data network to deliver the required quality of network service. Most companies today have either begun or plan on a migration to use IP phones, which pass voice traffic over the data network inside IP packets using application protocols generally referred to as voice over IP (VoIP). Additionally, several companies sell Internet phone service, which sends voice traffic over the Internet, again using VoIP packets. Figure 6-11 shows a few of the details of how VoIP works from a home high-speed Internet connection, with a generic voice adapter (VA) converting the analog voice signal from the normal telephone to an IP packet.

Figure 6-11 *Converting from Sound to Packets with a VA*

A single VoIP call that passes over a WAN typically takes less than 30 kbps of bandwidth, which is not a lot compared with many data applications today. In fact, most data applications consume as much bandwidth as they can grab. However, VoIP traffic has several other QoS demands on the network before the VoIP traffic will sound good:

■ **Low delay:** VoIP requires a very low delay between the sending phone and the receiving phone—typically less than 200 milliseconds (.2 seconds). This is a much lower delay than what is required by typical data applications.

■ **Low jitter:** Jitter is the variation in delay. VoIP requires very low jitter as well, whereas data applications can tolerate much higher jitter. For example, the jitter for consecutive VoIP packets should not exceed 30 milliseconds (.03 seconds), or the quality degrades.

■ **Loss:** If a VoIP packet is lost in transit because of errors or because a router doesn't have room to store the packet while waiting to send it, the VoIP packet is not delivered across the network. Because of the delay and jitter issues, there is no need to try to recover the lost packet. It would be useless by the time it was recovered. Lost packets can sound like a break in the sound of the VoIP call.

Video over IP has the same performance issues, except that video requires either more bandwidth (often time 300 to 400 kbps) or a lot more bandwidth (3 to 10 Mbps per video). The world of video over IP is also going through a bit of transformation with the advent of high-definition video over IP, again increasing demands on the bandwidth in the network.

For perspective, Table 6-4 summarizes some thoughts about the needs of various types of applications for the four main QoS requirements—bandwidth, delay, jitter, and packet loss. Memorizing the table is not important, but it is important to note that although VoIP requires relatively little bandwidth, it also requires low delay/jitter/loss for high quality. It is also important to note that video over IP has the same requirements, except for medium to large amounts of bandwidth.

Table 6-4   *Comparing Applications' Minimum Needs*

Type of Application	Bandwidth	Delay	Jitter	Loss
VoIP	Low	Low	Low	Low
Two-way video over IP (such as videoconferencing)	Medium/high	Low	Low	Low
One-way video over IP (such as security cameras)	Medium	Medium	Medium	Low
Interactive mission-critical data (such as web-based payroll)	Medium	Medium	High	High

Table 6-4 *Comparing Applications' Minimum Needs (Continued)*

Type of Application	Bandwidth	Delay	Jitter	Loss
Interactive business data (such as online chat with a coworker)	Low/medium	Medium	High	High
File transfer (such as backing up disk drives)	High	High	High	High
Nonbusiness (such as checking the latest sports scores)	Medium	High	High	High

To support the QoS requirements of the various applications, routers and switches can be configured with a wide variety of QoS tools. They are beyond the scope of the CCNA exams (but are covered on several of the Cisco professional-level certifications). However, the QoS tools must be used for a modern network to be able to support high-quality VoIP and video over IP.

Next we examine the most popular application layer protocol for interactive data applications today—HTTP and the World Wide Web (WWW). The goal is to show one example of how application layer protocols work.

The World Wide Web, HTTP, and SSL

The *World Wide Web* (WWW) consists of all the Internet-connected web servers in the world, plus all Internet-connected hosts with web browsers. *Web servers*, which consist of web server software running on a computer, store information (in the form of *web pages*) that might be useful to different people. *Web browsers*, which is software installed on an end user's computer, provide the means to connect to a web server and display the web pages stored on the web server.

> **NOTE** Although most people use the term web browser, or simply browser, web browsers are also called *web clients*, because they obtain a service from a web server.

For this process to work, several specific application-layer functions must occur. The user must somehow identify the server, the specific web page, and the protocol used to get the data from the server. The client must find the server's IP address, based on the server's name, typically using DNS. The client must request the web page, which actually consists of multiple separate files, and the server must send the files to the web browser. Finally, for electronic commerce (e-commerce) applications, the transfer of data, particularly sensitive financial data, needs to be secure, again using application layer features. The following sections address each of these functions.

Universal Resource Locators

For a browser to display a web page, the browser must identify the server that has the web page, plus other information that identifies the particular web page. Most web servers have many web pages. For example, if you use a web browser to browse http://www.cisco.com, and you click around that web page, you'll see another web page. Click again, and you'll see another web page. In each case, the clicking action identifies the server's IP address and the specific web page, with the details mostly hidden from you. (These clickable items on a web page, which in turn bring you to another web page, are called *links*.)

The browser user can identify a web page when you click something on a web page or when you enter a *Universal Resource Locator* (URL) (often called a *web address*) in the browser's address area. Both options—clicking a link and entering a URL—refer to a URL, because when you click a link on a web page, that link actually refers to a URL.

NOTE   To see the hidden URL referenced by a link, open a browser to a web page, hover the mouse pointer over a link, right-click, and select **Properties**. The pop-up window should display the URL to which the browser would be directed if you clicked that link.

Each URL defines the protocol used to transfer data, the name of the server, and the particular web page on that server. The URL can be broken into three parts:

- The protocol is listed before the //.

- The hostname is listed between the // and the /.

- The name of the web page is listed after the /.

For example:

http://www.cisco.com/go/prepcenter

In this case, the protocol is *Hypertext Transfer Protocol* (HTTP), the hostname is www.cisco.com, and the name of the web page is go/prepcenter. This URL is particularly useful, because it is the base web page for the Cisco CCNA Prep Center.

Finding the Web Server Using DNS

As mentioned in Chapter 5, "Fundamentals of IP Addressing and Routing," a host can use DNS to discover the IP address that corresponds to a particular hostname. Although URLs may include the IP address of the web server instead of the name of the web server, URLs typically list the hostname. So, before the browser can send a packet to the web server, the browser typically needs to resolve the name in the URL to that name's corresponding IP address.

To pull together several concepts, Figure 6-12 shows the DNS process as initiated by a web browser, as well as some other related information. From a basic perspective, the user enters the URL (http://www.cisco.com/go/prepcenter), resolves the www.cisco.com name into the correct IP address, and starts sending packets to the web server.

Figure 6-12 *DNS Resolution and Requesting a Web Page*

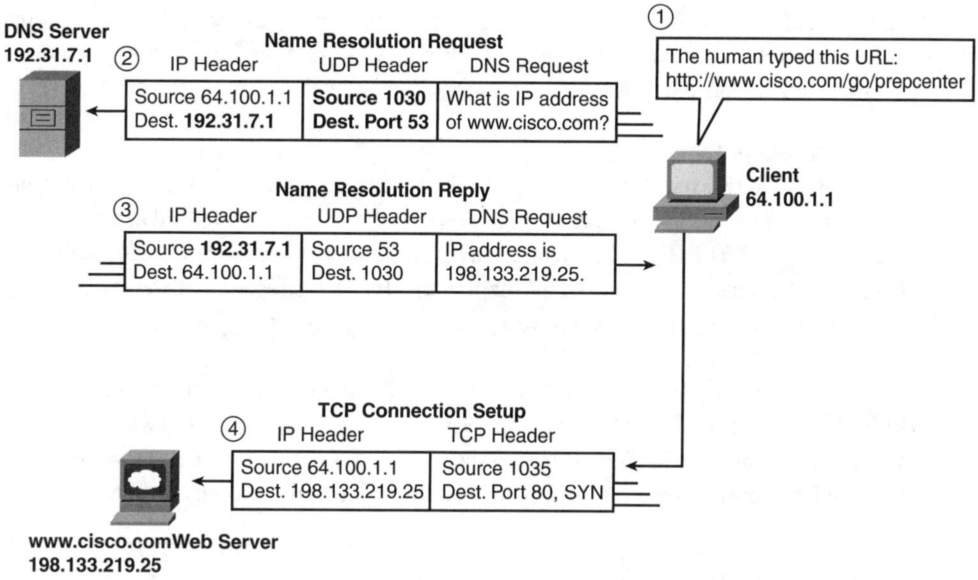

The steps shown in the figure are as follows:

1. The user enters the URL, http://www.cisco.com/go/prepcenter, into the browser's address area.

2. The client sends a DNS request to the DNS server. Typically, the client learns the DNS server's IP address via DHCP. Note that the DNS request uses a UDP header, with a destination port of the DNS well-known port of 53. (See Table 6-3, earlier in this chapter, for a list of popular well-known ports.)

3. The DNS server sends a reply, listing IP address 198.133.219.25 as www.cisco.com's IP address. Note also that the reply shows a destination IP address of 64.100.1.1, the client's IP address. It also shows a UDP header, with source port 53; the source port is 53 because the data is sourced, or sent by, the DNS server.

4. The client begins the process of establishing a new TCP connection to the web server. Note that the destination IP address is the just-learned IP address of the web server. The packet includes a TCP header, because HTTP uses TCP. Also note the destination TCP port is 80, the well-known port for HTTP. Finally, the SYN bit is shown, as a reminder that the TCP connection establishment process begins with a TCP segment with the SYN bit turned on (binary 1).

At this point in the process, the web browser is almost finished setting up a TCP connection to the web server. The next section picks up the story at that point, examining how the web browser then gets the files that comprise the desired web page.

Transferring Files with HTTP

After a web client (browser) has created a TCP connection to a web server, the client can begin requesting the web page from the server. Most often, the protocol used to transfer the web page is HTTP. The HTTP application-layer protocol, defined in RFC 2616, defines how files can be transferred between two computers. HTTP was specifically created for the purpose of transferring files between web servers and web clients.

HTTP defines several commands and responses, with the most frequently used being the HTTP GET request. To get a file from a web server, the client sends an HTTP GET request to the server, listing the filename. If the server decides to send the file, the server sends an HTTP GET response, with a return code of 200 (meaning "OK"), along with the file's contents.

> **NOTE**   Many return codes exist for HTTP requests. For instance, when the server does not have the requested file, it issues a return code of 404, which means "file not found." Most web browsers do not show the specific numeric HTTP return codes, instead displaying a response such as "page not found" in reaction to receiving a return code of 404.

Web pages typically consist of multiple files, called *objects*. Most web pages contain text as well as several graphical images, animated advertisements, and possibly voice or video. Each of these components is stored as a different object (file) on the web server. To get them all, the web browser gets the first file. This file may (and typically does) include references to other URLs, so the browser then also requests the other objects. Figure 6-13 shows the general idea, with the browser getting the first file and then two others.

In this case, after the web browser gets the first file—the one called "/go/ccna" in the URL—the browser reads and interprets that file. Besides containing parts of the web page, the file refers to two other files, so the browser issues two additional HTTP get requests.

Note that, even though it isn't shown in the figure, all these commands flow over one (or possibly more) TCP connections between the client and the server. This means that TCP would provide error recovery, ensuring that the data was delivered.

Figure 6-13 *Multiple HTTP Get Requests/Responses*

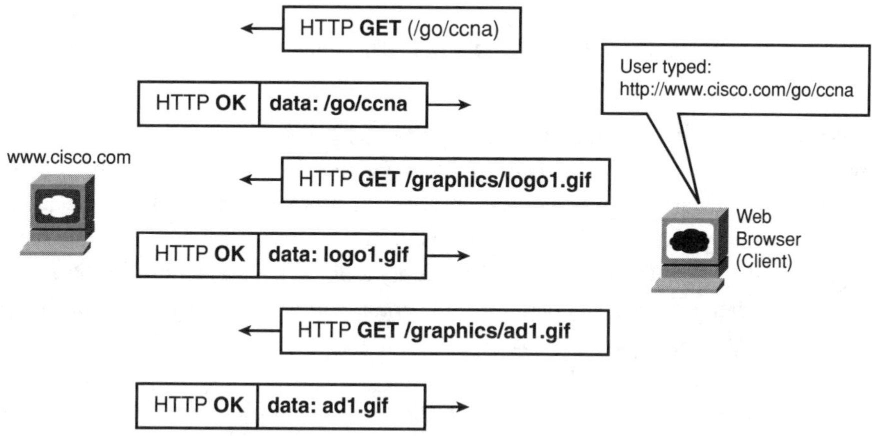

This chapter ends with an introduction to network security.

Network Security

In years past, security threats came from geniuses or nerdy students with lots of time. The numbers of these people were relatively small. Their main motivation was to prove that they could break into another network. Since then, the number of potential attackers and the sophistication of the attacks have increased exponentially. Attacks that once required attackers to have an advanced degree in computing now can be done with easily downloaded and freely available tools that the average junior-high student can figure out how to use. Every company and almost every person connects to the Internet, making essentially the whole world vulnerable to attack.

The biggest danger today may be the changes in attackers' motivation. Instead of looking for a challenge, or to steal millions, today's attackers can be much more organized and motivated. Organized crime tries to steal billions by extorting companies by threatening a denial of service (DoS) attack on the companies' public web servers. Or they steal identity and credit card information for sometimes hundreds of thousands of people with one sophisticated attack. Attacks might come from nation-states or terrorists. Not only might they attack military and government networks, but they might try to disrupt infrastructure services for utilities and transportation and cripple economies.

Security is clearly a big issue, and one that requires serious attention. For the purposes of this book, and for the ICND1 exam, the goal is to know some of the basic terminology, types of security issues, and some of the common tools used to mitigate security risks. To that end, this final section of the chapter gives you some perspectives on attacks, and then it introduces four classes of security tools. Beyond this introduction, this book also examines device security—the securing of access to routers and switches in this case—as part of Chapter 8, "Operating Cisco LAN Switches," and Chapter 13, "Operating Cisco Routers."

Perspectives on the Sources and Types of Threats

Figure 6-14 shows a common network topology with a firewall. Firewalls are probably the best-known security appliance, sitting between the Enterprise network and the dark, cold, unsecure Internet. The firewall's role is to stop packets that the network or security engineer has deemed unsafe. The firewall mainly looks at the transport layer port numbers and the application layer headers to prevent certain ports and applications from getting packets into the Enterprise.

Figure 6-14 *Typical Enterprise Internet Connection with a Firewall*

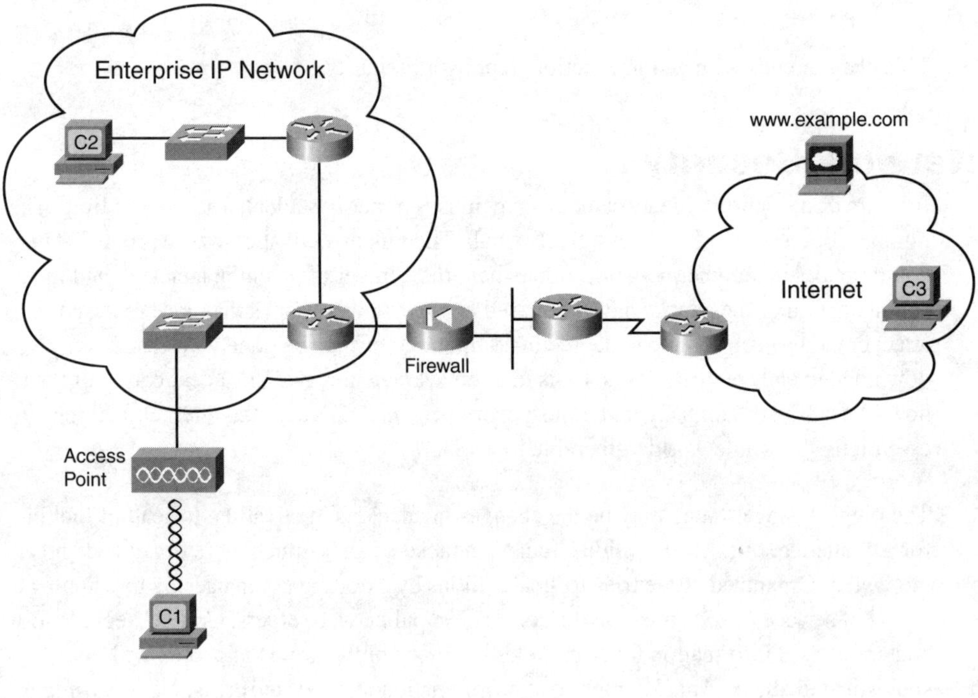

Figure 6-14 might give an average employee of the Enterprise a false sense of security. He or she might think the firewall provides protection from all the dangers of connecting to the Internet. However, a perimeter firewall (a firewall on the edge, or perimeter, of the network) does not protect the Enterprise from all the dangers possible through the Internet connection. Not only that, a higher percentage of security attacks actually come from inside the Enterprise network, and the firewall does not even see those packets.

To appreciate a bit more about the dangers inside the Enterprise network, it helps to understand a bit more about the kinds of attacks that might occur:

- **Denial of service (DoS) attacks:** An attack whose purpose is to break things. DoS attacks called *destroyers* try to harm the hosts, erasing data and software. DoS attacks called *crashers* cause harm by causing hosts to fail or causing the machine to no longer be able to connect to the network. Also, DoS attacks called *flooders* flood the network with packets to make the network unusable, preventing any useful communications with the servers.

Key
Topic

- **Reconnaissance attacks:** This kind of attack may be disruptive as a side effect, but its goal is gathering information to perform an access attack. An example is learning IP addresses and then trying to discover servers that do not appear to require encryption to connect to the server.

- **Access attacks:** An attempt to steal data, typically data for some financial advantage, for a competitive advantage with another company, or even for international espionage.

Computer viruses are just one tool that can be used to carry out any of these attacks. A virus is a program that is somehow transferred onto an unsuspecting computer, possibly through an e-mail attachment or website download. A virus could just cause problems on the computer, or it could steal information and send it back to the attacker.

Today, most computers use some type of anti-virus software to watch for known viruses and prevent them from infecting the computer. Among other activities, the anti-virus software loads a list of known characteristics of all viruses, with these characteristics being known as virus *signatures*. By periodically downloading the latest virus signatures, the anti-virus software knows about all the latest viruses. By watching all packets entering the computer, the anti-virus software can recognize known viruses and prevent the computer from being infected. These programs also typically run an automatic periodic scan of the entire contents of the computer disk drives, looking for any known viruses.

To appreciate some of the security risks inherent in an Enterprise network that already has a quality perimeter firewall, consider Figure 6-15. The list following the figure explains three ways in which the Enterprise network is exposed to the possibility of an attack from within.

Figure 6-15 *Common Security Issues in an Enterprise*

The following types of problems could commonly occur in this Enterprise:

■ **Access from the wireless LAN:** Wireless LANs allow users to access the rest of the devices in the Enterprise. The wireless radio signals might leave the building, so an unsecured wireless LAN allows the user across the street in a coffee shop to access the Enterprise network, letting the attacker (PC1) begin the next phase of trying to gain access to the computers in the Enterprise.

■ **Infected mobile laptops:** When an employee brings his or her laptop (PC2) home, with no firewall or other security, the laptop may become infected with a virus. When the user returns to the office in the morning, the laptop connects to the Enterprise network, with the virus spreading to other PCs, such as PC3. PC3 may be vulnerable in part because the users may have avoided running the daily anti-virus software scans that, although useful, can annoy the user.

■ **Disgruntled employees:** The user at PC4 is planning to move to a new company. He steals information from the network and loads it onto an MP3 player or USB flash drive. This allows him to carry the entire customer database in a device that can be easily concealed and removed from the building.

These attacks are just a few examples; a large number of variations and methods exist. To prevent such problems, Cisco suggests a security model that uses tools that automatically work to defend the network, with security features located throughout the network. Cisco uses the term *security in depth* to refer to a security design that includes security tools throughout the network, including features in routers and switches. Cisco also uses the term "self-defending network" to refer to automation in which the network devices automatically react to network problems.

For example, Network Admission Control (NAC) is one security tool to help prevent two of the attacks just described. Among other things, NAC can monitor when devices first connect to a LAN, be they wireless or wired. The NAC feature, partly implemented by features in the LAN switches, would prevent a computer from connecting to the LAN until its virus definitions were updated, with a requirement for a recent full virus scan. NAC also includes a requirement that the user supply a username and password before being able to send other data into the LAN, helping prevent the guy at the coffee shop from gaining access. However, NAC does not prevent a disgruntled employee from causing harm, because the employee typically has a working username/password to be authenticated with NAC.

Besides viruses, many other tools can be used to form an attack. The following list summarizes some of the more common terms for the tools in an attacker's toolkit:

■ **Scanner:** A tool that sends connection requests to different TCP and UDP ports, for different applications, in an attempt to discover which hosts run which IP services, and possibly the operating system used on each host.

■ **Spyware:** A virus that looks for private or sensitive information, tracking what the user does with the computer, and passing the information back to the attacker in the Internet.

■ **Worm:** A self-propagating program that can quickly replicate itself around Enterprise networks and the Internet, often performing DoS attacks, particularly on servers.

■ **Keystroke logger:** A virus that logs all keystrokes, or possibly just keystrokes from when secure sites are accessed, reporting the information to the attacker. Loggers can actually capture your username and password to secure sites before the information leaves the computer, which could give the attacker access to your favorite financial websites.

- **Phishing:** The attacker sets up a website that outwardly looks like a legitimate website, often for a bank or credit card company. The phisher sends e-mails listing the illegitimate website's URL but making it look like the real company (for example, "Click here to update the records for your credit card to make it more secure."). The phisher hopes that a few people will take the bait, connect to the illegitimate website, and enter information such as their name, address, credit card number, social security number (in the U.S.), or other national government ID number. The best defense for phishing attacks may well be better user training and more awareness about the exposure.

- **Malware:** This refers to a broad class of malicious viruses, including spyware.

The solution to these and the many other security issues not mentioned here is to provide security in depth throughout the network. The rest of this section introduces a few of the tools that can be used to provide that in-depth security.

Firewalls and the Cisco Adaptive Security Appliance (ASA)

Firewalls examine all packets entering and exiting a network for the purpose of filtering unwanted traffic. Firewalls determine the allowed traffic versus the disallowed traffic based on many characteristics of the packets, including their destination and source IP addresses and the TCP and UDP port numbers (which imply the application protocol). Firewalls also examine the application layer headers.

The term firewall is taken from the world of building and architecture. A firewall in a building has two basic requirements. It must be made of fire-resistant materials, and the architect limits the number of openings in the wall (doors, conduits for wires and plumbing), limiting the paths through which the fire can spread. Similarly, a network firewall must itself be hardened against security attacks. It must disallow all packets unless the engineer has configured a firewall rule that allows the traffic—a process often called "opening a hole," again with analogies to a firewall in a building.

Firewalls sit in the packet-forwarding path between two networks, often with one LAN interface connecting to the secure local network, and one to the other, less-secure network (often the Internet). Additionally, because some hosts in the Enterprise need to be accessible from the Internet—an inherently less secure practice—the firewall typically also has an interface connected to another small part of the Enterprise network, called the demilitarized zone (DMZ). The DMZ LAN is a place to put devices that need to be accessible, but that access puts them at higher risk. Figure 6-16 shows a sample design, with a firewall that has three interfaces.

Figure 6-16 *Common Internet Design Using a Firewall*

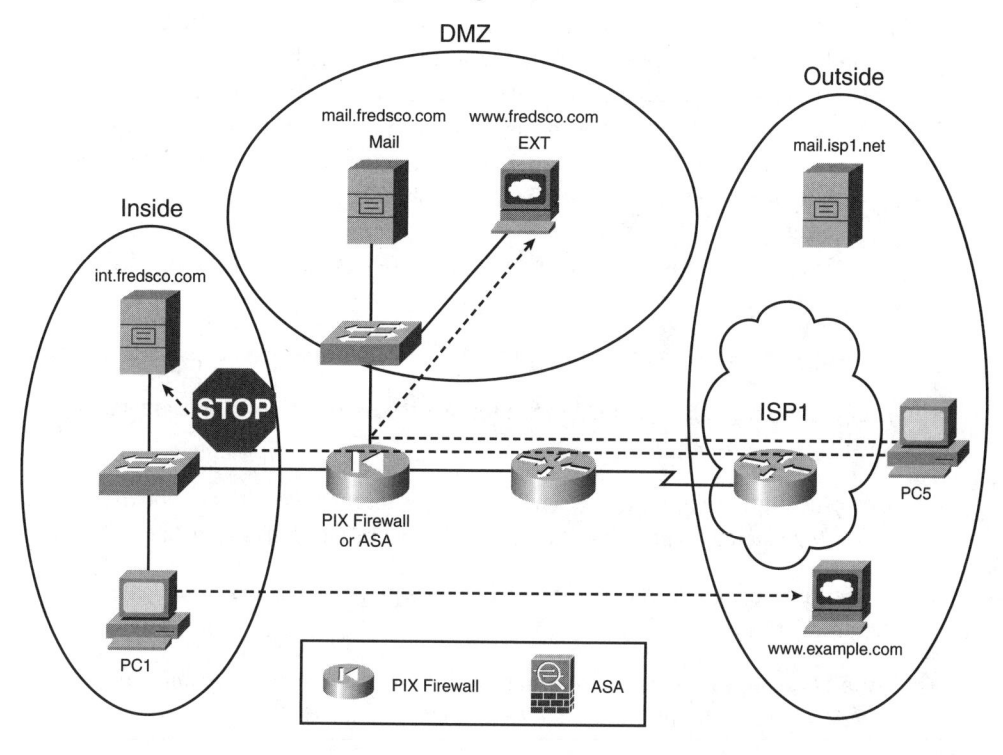

To do its job, the firewall needs to be configured to know which interfaces are connected to the inside, outside, and DMZ parts of the network. Then, a series of rules can be configured that tell the firewall which traffic patterns are allowed and which are not. The figure shows two typically allowed flows and one typical disallowed flow, shown with dashed lines:

- Allow web clients on the inside network (such as PC1) to send packets to web servers (such as the www.example.com web server)

- Prevent web clients in the outside network (such as PC5) from sending packets to web servers in the inside network (such as the internal web server int.fredsco.com)

- Allow web clients in the outside network (such as PC5) to connect to DMZ web servers (such as the www.fredsco.com web server)

In years past, Cisco sold firewalls with the trade name PIX firewall. A few years ago, Cisco introduced a whole new generation of network security hardware using the trade name Adaptive Security Appliance (ASA). ASA hardware can act as a firewall, in other security roles, and in a combination of roles. So, when speaking about security, the term firewall still refers to the functions, but today the Cisco product may be an older still-installed PIX firewall or a newer ASA. (Figure 6-16 shows the ASA icon at the bottom.)

Anti-x

A comprehensive security plan requires several functions that prevent different known types of problems. For example, host-based anti-virus software helps prevent the spread of viruses. Cisco ASA appliances can provide or assist in the overall in-depth security design with a variety of tools that prevent problems such as viruses. Because the names of several of the individual tools start with "anti-," Cisco uses the term *anti-x* to refer to the whole class of security tools that prevent these various problems, including the following:

- **Anti-virus:** Scans network traffic to prevent the transmission of known viruses based on virus signatures.

- **Anti-spyware:** Scans network traffic to prevent the transmission of spyware programs.

- **Anti-spam:** Examines e-mail before it reaches the users, deleting or segregating junk e-mail.

- **Anti-phishing:** Monitors URLs sent in messages through the network, looking for the fake URLs inherent in phishing attacks, preventing the attack from reaching the users.

- **URL filtering:** Filters web traffic based on URL to prevent users from connecting to inappropriate sites.

- **E-mail filtering:** Provides anti-spam tools. Also filters e-mails containing offensive materials, potentially protecting the Enterprise from lawsuits.

The Cisco ASA appliance can be used to perform the network-based role for all these anti-x functions.

Intrusion Detection and Prevention

Some types of attacks cannot be easily found with anti-x tools. For example, if a known virus infects a computer solely through an e-mail attachment of a file called this-is-a-virus.exe, the anti-virus software on the ASA or the end-user computer can easily identify and delete the virus. However, some forms of attacks can be more sophisticated. The attacks may not even include the transfer of a file, instead using a myriad of other, more-challenging methods, often taking advantage of new bugs in the operating system.

The world of network security includes a couple of types of tools that can be used to help prevent the more sophisticated kinds of attacks: Intrusion Detection Systems (IDS) and Intrusion Prevention Systems (IPS). IDS and IPS tools detect these threats by watching for trends, looking for attacks that use particular patterns of messages, and other factors. For instance, an IDS or IPS can track sequences of packets between hosts to look for a file being sent to more and more hosts, as might be done by a worm trying to spread inside a network.

IDS and IPS systems differ mainly in how they monitor the traffic and how they can respond to a perceived threat. IDS tools typically receive a copy of packets via a monitoring port, rather than being part of the packets' forwarding path. The IDS can then rate and report on each potential threat, and potentially ask other devices, such as firewalls and routers, to help prevent the attack (if they can). IPS tools often sit in the packets' forwarding path, giving the IPS the capability to perform the same functions as the IDS, but also to react and filter the traffic. The ability to react is important with some threats, such as the Slammer worm in 2003, which doubled the number of infected hosts every 9 seconds or so, infecting 75,000 hosts in the first 10 minutes of the attack. This kind of speed requires the use of reactive tools, rather than waiting on an engineer to see a report and take action.

Virtual Private Networks (VPN)

The last class of security tool introduced in this chapter is the virtual private network (VPN), which might be better termed a virtual private WAN. A leased line is inherently secure, effectively acting like an electrical circuit between the two routers. VPNs send packets through the Internet, which is a public network. However, VPNs make the communication secure, like a private leased line.

Without VPN technology, the packets sent between two devices over the Internet are inherently unsecure. The packets flowing through the Internet could be intercepted by attackers in the Internet. In fact, along with the growth of the Internet, attackers found ways to redirect packets and examine the contents, both to see the data and to find additional information (such as usernames and passwords) as part of a reconnaissance attack. Additionally, users and servers might not be able to tell the difference between a legitimate packet from an authentic user and a packet from an attacker who is trying to gain even more information and access.

VPNs provide a solution to allow the use of the Internet without the risks of unknowingly accepting data from attacking hosts and without the risk of others reading the data in transit. VPNs authenticate the VPN's endpoints, meaning that both endpoints can be sure that the other endpoint of the VPN connection is legitimate. Additionally, VPNs encrypt the original IP packets so that even if an attacker managed to get a copy of the packets as they pass through the Internet, he or she cannot read the data. Figure 16-17 shows the general idea, with an intranet VPN and an access VPN.

The figure shows an example of two types of VPNs: an *access VPN* and a *site-to-site intranet VPN*. An access VPN supports a home or small-office user, with the remote office's PC typically encrypting the packets. A site-to-site intranet VPN typically connects two sites of the same Enterprise, effectively creating a secure connection between two different parts inside (intra) the same Enterprise network. For intranet VPNs, the encryption could be done for all devices using different kinds of hardware, including routers, firewalls, purpose-built VPN concentrator hardware, or ASAs, as shown in the main site of the Enterprise.

Figure 6-17   *Sample VPNs*

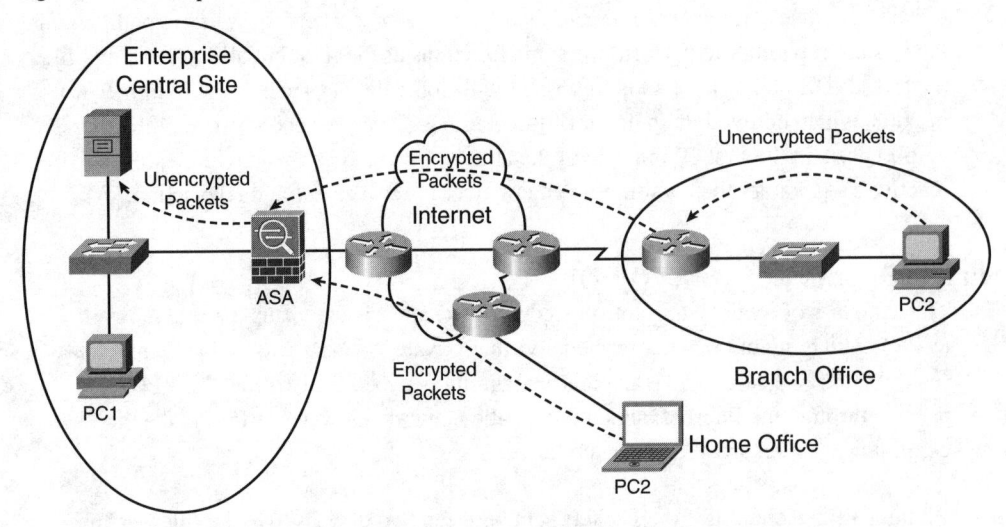

Figure 6-17 shows how VPNs can use end-to-end encryption, in which the data remains encrypted while being forwarded through one or more routers. Additionally, link encryption can be used to encrypt data at the data link layer, so the data is encrypted only as it passes over one data link. Chapter 11, "Wireless LANs," shows an example of link encryption.

Exam Preparation Tasks

Review All the Key Topics

Review the most important topics from this chapter, noted with the key topics icon. Table 6-5 lists these key topics and where each is discussed.

Key Topic

Table 6-5 *Key Topics for Chapter 6*

Key Topic Element	Description	Page Number
Table 6-2	Functions of TCP and UDP	134
Table 6-3	Well-known TCP and UDP port numbers	139-140
Figure 6-6	Example of TCP error recovery using forward acknowledgments	141
Figure 6-7	Example of TCP sliding windows	142
Figure 6-8	Example of TCP connection establishment	143
List	Definitions of connection-oriented and connectionless	144
List	QoS requirements for VoIP	148
List	Three types of attacks	155
Figure 6-15	Examples of common security exposures in an Enterprise	156

Complete the Tables and Lists from Memory

Print a copy of Appendix H, "Memory Tables" (found on the CD), or at least the section for this chapter, and complete the tables and lists from memory. Appendix I, "Memory Tables Answer Key," also on the CD, includes completed tables and lists for you to check your work.

Definitions of Key Terms

Define the following key terms from this chapter and check your answers in the glossary:

Anti-x, connection establishment, DoS, error detection, error recovery, firewall, flow control, forward acknowledgment, HTTP, Intrusion Detection System, Intrusion Prevention System, ordered data transfer, port, Positive Acknowledgment and Retransmission (PAR), segment, sliding windows, URL, virtual private network, VoIP, web server

Cisco Published ICND1 Exam Topics* Covered in This Part:

Describe the operation of data networks.

- Use the OSI and TCP/IP models and their associated protocols to explain how data flows in a network
- Interpret network diagrams
- Determine the path between two hosts across a network
- Identify and correct common network problems at Layers 1, 2, 3, and 7 using a layered model approach
- Differentiate between LAN/WAN operation and features

Implement a small switched network

- Select the appropriate media, cables, ports, and connectors to connect switches to other network devices and hosts
- Explain the technology and media access control method for Ethernet technologies
- Explain network segmentation and basic traffic management concepts
- Explain the operation of Cisco switches and basic switching concepts
- Perform, save, and verify initial switch configuration tasks including remote access management
- Verify network status and switch operation using basic utilities (including: ping, traceroute, Telnet, SSH, ARP, ipconfig), show and debug commands
- Implement and verify basic security for a switch (port security, deactivate ports)
- Identify, prescribe, and resolve common switched network media issues, configuration issues, autonegotiation, and switch hardware failures

Explain and select the appropriate administrative tasks required for a WLAN

- Describe standards associated with wireless media (including: IEEE Wi-Fi Alliance, ITU/FCC)
- Identify and describe the purpose of the components in a small wireless network (including: SSID, BSS, ESS)
- Identify the basic parameters to configure on a wireless network to ensure that devices connect to the correct access point
- Compare and contrast wireless security features and capabilities of WPA security (including: open, WEP, WPA-1/2)
- Identify common issues with implementing wireless networks

Identify security threats to a network and describe general methods to mitigate those threats

- Describe security recommended practices including initial steps to secure network devices

*Always recheck http://www.cisco.com for the latest posted exam topics.

Part II: LAN Switching

This chapter covers the following subjects:

LAN Switching Concepts: Explains the basic processes used by LAN switches to forward frames.

LAN Design Considerations: Describes the reasoning and terminology for how to design a switched LAN that operates well.

CHAPTER **7**

Ethernet LAN Switching Concepts

Chapter 3, "Fundamentals of LANs," covered the conceptual and physical attributes of Ethernet LANs in a fair amount of detail. That chapter explains a wide variety of Ethernet concepts, including the basics of UTP cabling, the basic operation of and concepts behind hubs and switches, comparisons of different kinds of Ethernet standards, and Ethernet data link layer concepts such as addressing and framing.

The chapters in Part II, "LAN Switching," complete this book's coverage of Ethernet LANs, with one additional chapter (Chapter 11) on wireless LANs. This chapter explains most of the remaining Ethernet concepts that were not covered in Chapter 3. In particular, it contains a more detailed examination of how switches work, as well as the LAN design implications of using hubs, bridges, switches, and routers. Chapters 8 through 10 focus on how to access and use Cisco switches. Chapter 8, "Operating Cisco LAN Switches," focuses on the switch user interface. Chapter 9, "Ethernet Switch Configuration," shows you how to configure a Cisco switch. Chapter 10, "Ethernet Switch Troubleshooting," shows you how to troubleshoot problems with Cisco switches. Chapter 11, "Wireless LANs," concludes Part II with a look at the concepts behind wireless LANs.

"Do I Know This Already?" Quiz

The "Do I Know This Already?" quiz allows you to assess whether you should read the entire chapter. If you miss no more than one of these eight self-assessment questions, you might want to move ahead to the "Exam Preparation Tasks" section. Table 7-1 lists the major headings in this chapter and the "Do I Know This Already?" quiz questions covering the material in those sections. This helps you assess your knowledge of these specific areas. The answers to the "Do I Know This Already?" quiz appear in Appendix A.

Table 7-1 *"Do I Know This Already?" Foundation Topics Section-to-Question Mapping*

Foundation Topics Section	Questions
LAN Switching Concepts	1–5
LAN Design Considerations	6–8

1. Which of the following statements describes part of the process of how a switch decides to forward a frame destined for a known unicast MAC address?

   a. It compares the unicast destination address to the bridging, or MAC address, table.

   b. It compares the unicast source address to the bridging, or MAC address, table.

   c. It forwards the frame out all interfaces in the same VLAN except for the incoming interface.

   d. It compares the destination IP address to the destination MAC address.

   e. It compares the frame's incoming interface to the source MAC entry in the MAC address table.

2. Which of the following statements describes part of the process of how a LAN switch decides to forward a frame destined for a broadcast MAC address?

   a. It compares the unicast destination address to the bridging, or MAC address, table.

   b. It compares the unicast source address to the bridging, or MAC address, table.

   c. It forwards the frame out all interfaces in the same VLAN except for the incoming interface.

   d. It compares the destination IP address to the destination MAC address.

   e. It compares the frame's incoming interface to the source MAC entry in the MAC address table.

3. Which of the following statements best describes what a switch does with a frame destined for an unknown unicast address?

   a. It forwards out all interfaces in the same VLAN except for the incoming interface.

   b. It forwards the frame out the one interface identified by the matching entry in the MAC address table.

   c. It compares the destination IP address to the destination MAC address.

   d. It compares the frame's incoming interface to the source MAC entry in the MAC address table.

4. Which of the following comparisons does a switch make when deciding whether a new MAC address should be added to its bridging table?

   a. It compares the unicast destination address to the bridging, or MAC address, table.

   b. It compares the unicast source address to the bridging, or MAC address, table.

   c. It compares the VLAN ID to the bridging, or MAC address, table.

   d. It compares the destination IP address's ARP cache entry to the bridging, or MAC address, table.

5. PC1, with MAC address 1111.1111.1111, is connected to Switch SW1's Fa0/1 interface. PC2, with MAC address 2222.2222.2222, is connected to SW1's Fa0/2 interface. PC3, with MAC address 3333.3333.3333, connects to SW1's Fa0/3 interface. The switch begins with no dynamically learned MAC addresses, followed by PC1 sending a frame with a destination address of 2222.2222.2222. If the next frame to reach the switch is a frame sent by PC3, destined for PC2's MAC address of 2222.2222.2222, which of the following are true?

   a. The switch forwards the frame out interface Fa0/1.

   b. The switch forwards the frame out interface Fa0/2.

   c. The switch forwards the frame out interface Fa0/3.

   d. The switch discards (filters) the frame.

6. Which of the following devices would be in the same collision domain as PC1?

   a. PC2, which is separated from PC1 by an Ethernet hub

   b. PC3, which is separated from PC1 by a transparent bridge

   c. PC4, which is separated from PC1 by an Ethernet switch

   d. PC5, which is separated from PC1 by a router

7. Which of the following devices would be in the same broadcast domain as PC1?

   a. PC2, which is separated from PC1 by an Ethernet hub

   b. PC3, which is separated from PC1 by a transparent bridge

   c. PC4, which is separated from PC1 by an Ethernet switch

   d. PC5, which is separated from PC1 by a router

8. Which of the following Ethernet standards support a maximum cable length of longer than 100 meters?

    a. 100BASE-TX

    b. 1000BASE-LX

    c. 1000BASE-T

    d. 100BASE-FX

Foundation Topics

This chapter begins by covering LAN concepts—in particular, the mechanics of how LAN switches forward Ethernet frames. Following that, the next major section focuses on campus LAN design concepts and terminology. It includes a review of some of the Ethernet types that use optical cabling and therefore support longer cabling distances than do the UTP-based Ethernet standards.

LAN Switching Concepts

Chapter 3 introduced Ethernet, including the concept of LAN hubs and switches. When thinking about how LAN switches work, it can be helpful to think about how earlier products (hubs and bridges) work. The first part of this section briefly looks at why switches were created. Following that, this section explains the three main functions of a switch, plus a few other details.

Historical Progression: Hubs, Bridges, and Switches

As mentioned in Chapter 3, Ethernet started out with standards that used a physical electrical bus created with coaxial cabling. 10BASE-T Ethernet came next. It offered improved LAN availability, because a problem on a single cable did not affect the rest of the LAN—a common problem with 10BASE2 and 10BASE5 networks. 10BASE-T allowed the use of unshielded twisted-pair (UTP) cabling, which is much cheaper than coaxial cable. Also, many buildings already had UTP cabling installed for phone service, so 10BASE-T quickly became a popular alternative to 10BASE2 and 10BASE5 Ethernet networks. For perspective and review, Figure 7-1 depicts the typical topology for 10BASE2 and for 10BASE-T with a hub.

Figure 7-1 *10BASE2 and 10BASE-T (with a Hub) Physical Topologies*

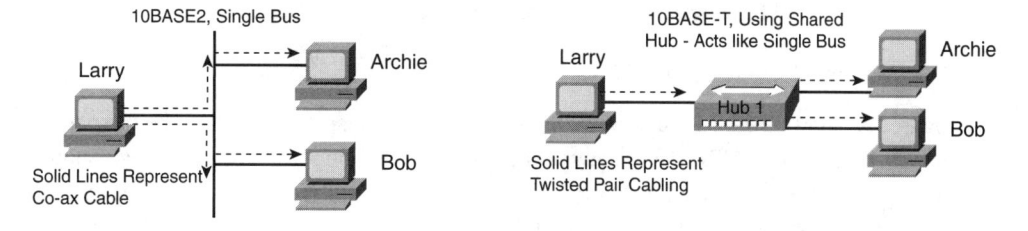

Although using 10BASE-T with a hub improved Ethernet as compared to the older standards, several drawbacks continued to exist, even with 10BASE-T using hubs:

■ Any device sending a frame could have the frame collide with a frame sent by any other device attached to that LAN segment.

■ Only one device could send a frame at a time, so the devices shared the (10-Mbps) bandwidth.

■ Broadcasts sent by one device were heard by, and processed by, all other devices on the LAN.

When these three types of Ethernet were introduced, a shared 10 Mbps of bandwidth was a huge amount! Before the introduction of LANs, people often used dumb terminals, with a 56-kbps WAN link being a really fast connection to the rest of the network—and that 56 kbps was shared among everyone in a remote building. So, in the days when 10BASE-T was first used, getting a connection to a 10BASE-T Ethernet LAN was like getting a Gigabit Ethernet connection for your work PC today. It was more bandwidth than you thought you would ever need.

Over time, the performance of many Ethernet networks started to degrade. People developed applications to take advantage of the LAN bandwidth. More devices were added to each Ethernet. Eventually, an entire network became congested. The devices on the same Ethernet could not send (collectively) more than 10 Mbps of traffic because they all shared the 10 Mbps of bandwidth. In addition, the increase in traffic volumes increased the number of collisions. Long before the overall utilization of an Ethernet approached 10 Mbps, Ethernet began to suffer because of increasing collisions.

Ethernet bridges were created to solve some of the performance issues. Bridges solved the growing Ethernet congestion problem in two ways:

■ They reduced the number of collisions that occurred in the network.

■ They added bandwidth to the network.

Figure 7-2 shows the basic premise behind an Ethernet transparent bridge. The top part of the figure shows a 10BASE-T network before adding a bridge, and the lower part shows the network after it has been *segmented* using a bridge. The bridge creates two separate *collision domains*. Fred's frames can collide with Barney's, but they cannot collide with Wilma's or Betty's. If one LAN segment is busy, and the bridge needs to forward a frame onto the busy segment, the bridge simply buffers the frame (holds the frame in memory) until the segment is no longer busy. Reducing collisions, and assuming no significant change in the number of devices or the load on the network, greatly improves network performance.

Figure 7-2 *Bridge Creates Two Collision Domains and Two Shared Ethernets*

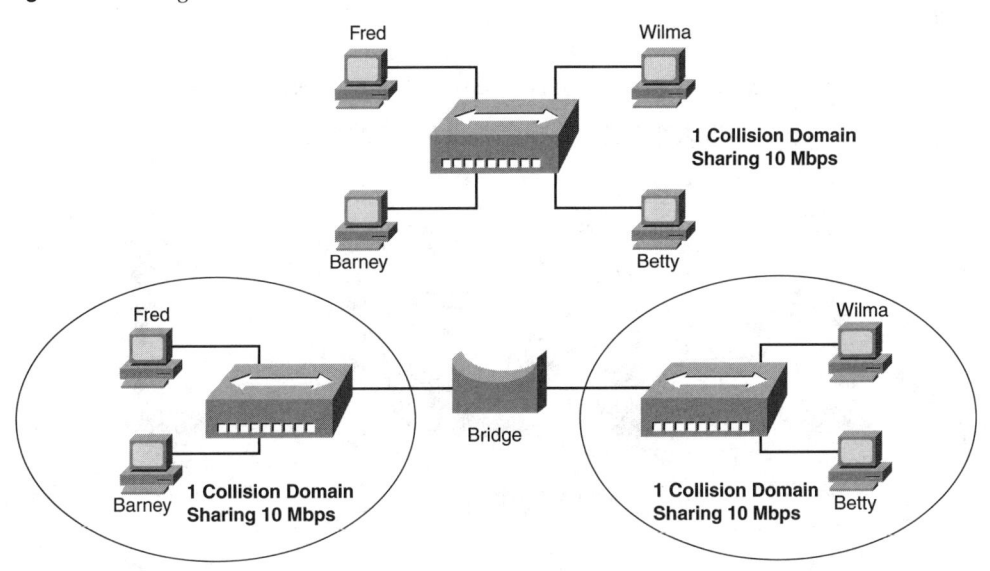

Adding a bridge between two hubs really creates two separate 10BASE-T networks—one on the left and one on the right. The 10BASE-T network on the left has its own 10 Mbps to share, as does the network on the right. So, in this example, the total network bandwidth is doubled to 20 Mbps, as compared with the 10BASE-T network at the top of the figure.

LAN switches perform the same basic core functions as bridges, but with many enhanced features. Like bridges, switches segment a LAN into separate parts, each part being a separate collision domain. Switches have potentially large numbers of interfaces, with highly optimized hardware, allowing even small Enterprise switches to forward millions of Ethernet frames per second. By creating a separate collision domain for each interface, switches multiply the amount of available bandwidth in the network. And, as mentioned in Chapter 3, if a switch port connects to a single device, that Ethernet segment can use full-duplex logic, essentially doubling the speed on that segment.

NOTE   A switch's effect of segmenting an Ethernet LAN into one collision domain per interface is sometimes called *microsegmentation*.

Figure 7-3 summarizes some of these key concepts, showing the same hosts as in Figure 7-2, but now connected to a switch. In this case, all switch interfaces are running at 100 Mbps, with four collision domains. Note that each interface also uses full duplex. This is possible because only one device is connected to each port, essentially eliminating collisions for the network shown.

Figure 7-3 *Switch Creates Four Collision Domains and Four Ethernet Segments*

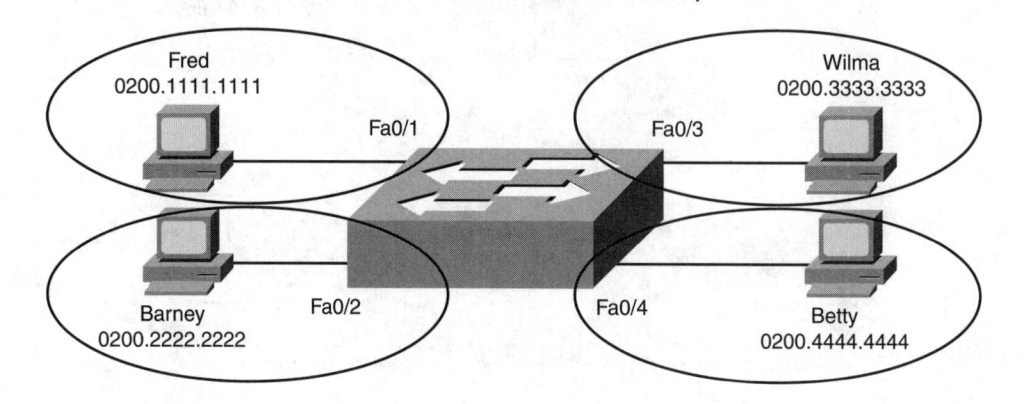

The next section examines how switches forward Ethernet frames.

Switching Logic

Ultimately, the role of a LAN switch is to forward Ethernet frames. To achieve that goal, switches use logic—logic based on the source and destination MAC address in each frame's Ethernet header. To help you appreciate how switches work, first a review of Ethernet addresses is in order.

The IEEE defines three general categories of Ethernet MAC addresses:

- **Unicast addresses:** MAC addresses that identify a single LAN interface card.

- **Broadcast addresses:** A frame sent with a destination address of the broadcast address (FFFF.FFFF.FFFF) implies that all devices on the LAN should receive and process the frame.

- **Multicast addresses:** Multicast MAC addresses are used to allow a dynamic subset of devices on a LAN to communicate.

> **NOTE**   The IP protocol supports the multicasting of IP packets. When IP multicast packets are sent over an Ethernet, the multicast MAC addresses used in the Ethernet frame follow this format: 0100.5e*xx.xxxx*, where a value between 00.0000 and 7f.ffff can be used in the last half of the address. Ethernet multicast MAC addresses are not covered in this book.

The primary job of a LAN switch is to receive Ethernet frames and then make a decision: either forward the frame out some other port(s), or ignore the frame. To accomplish this primary mission, transparent bridges perform three actions:

1. Deciding when to forward a frame or when to filter (not forward) a frame, based on the destination MAC address

2. Learning MAC addresses by examining the source MAC address of each frame received by the bridge

3. Creating a (Layer 2) loop-free environment with other bridges by using Spanning Tree Protocol (STP)

The first action is the switch's primary job, whereas the other two items are overhead functions. The next sections examine each of these steps in order.

The Forward Versus Filter Decision

To decide whether to forward a frame, a switch uses a dynamically built table that lists MAC addresses and outgoing interfaces. Switches compare the frame's destination MAC address to this table to decide whether the switch should forward a frame or simply ignore it. For example, consider the simple network shown in Figure 7-4, with Fred sending a frame to Barney.

Figure 7-4 shows an example of both the forwarding decision and the filtering decision. Fred sends a frame with destination address 0200.2222.2222 (Barney's MAC address). The switch compares the destination MAC address (0200.2222.2222) to the MAC address table, finding the matching entry. This is the interface out which a frame should be sent to deliver it to that listed MAC address (0200.2222.2222). Because the interface in which the frame arrived (Fa0/1) is different than the listed outgoing interface (Fa0/2), the switch decides to forward the frame out interface Fa0/2, as shown in the figure's table.

> **NOTE**   A switch's MAC address table is also called the switching table, or bridging table, or even the Content Addressable Memory (CAM), in reference to the type of physical memory used to store the table.

The key to anticipating where a switch should forward a frame is to examine and understand the address table. The table lists MAC addresses and the interface the switch should use when forwarding packets sent to that MAC address. For example, the table lists 0200.3333.3333 off Fa0/3, which is the interface out which the switch should forward frames sent to Wilma's MAC address (0200.3333.3333).

Figure 7-4 *Sample Switch Forwarding and Filtering Decision*

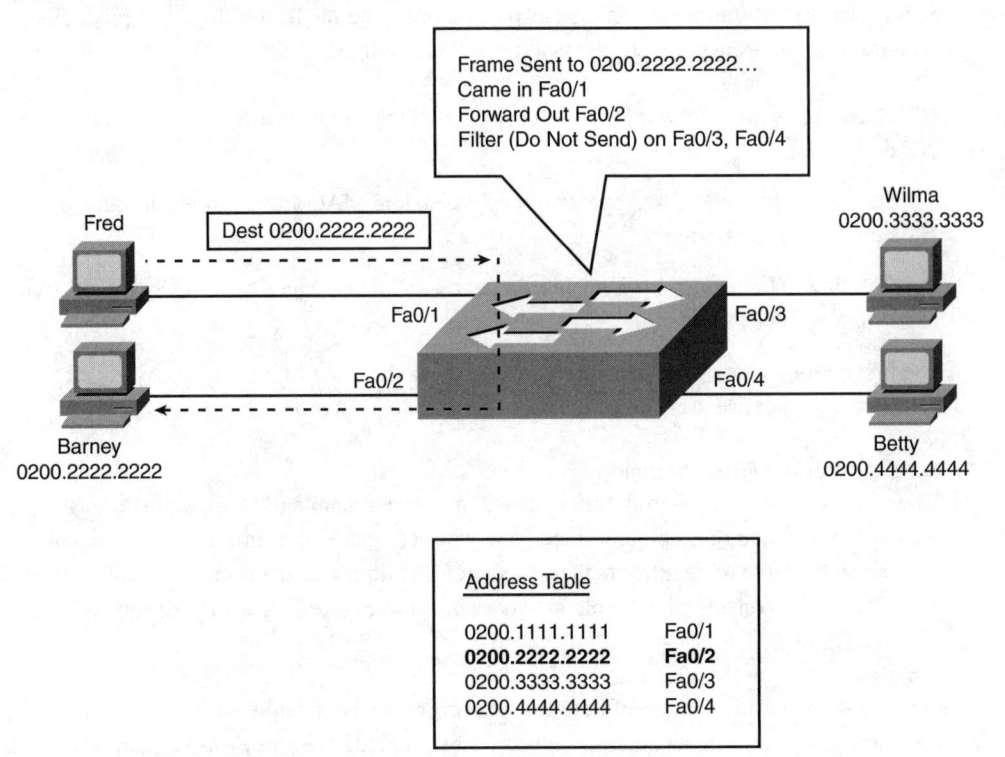

Frame Sent to 0200.2222.2222…
Came in Fa0/1
Forward Out Fa0/2
Filter (Do Not Send) on Fa0/3, Fa0/4

Fred

Dest 0200.2222.2222

Wilma
0200.3333.3333

Fa0/1

Fa0/3

Fa0/2

Fa0/4

Barney
0200.2222.2222

Betty
0200.4444.4444

Address Table

0200.1111.1111	Fa0/1
0200.2222.2222	**Fa0/2**
0200.3333.3333	Fa0/3
0200.4444.4444	Fa0/4

- - - - - - - - - - - - - ▶
Path of Frame Transmission

Figure 7-5 shows a different perspective, with the switch making a filtering decision. In this case, Fred and Barney connect to a hub, which is then connected to the switch. The switch's MAC address table lists both Fred's and Barney's MAC addresses off that single switch interface (Fa0/1), because the switch would forward frames to both Fred and Barney out its FA0/1 interface. So, when the switch receives a frame sent by Fred (source MAC address 0200.1111.1111) to Barney (destination MAC address 0200.2222.2222), the switch thinks like this: "Because the frame entered my Fa0/1 interface, and I would send it out that same Fa0/1 interface, do not send it (filter it), because sending it would be pointless."

Figure 7-5 *Sample Switch Filtering Decision*

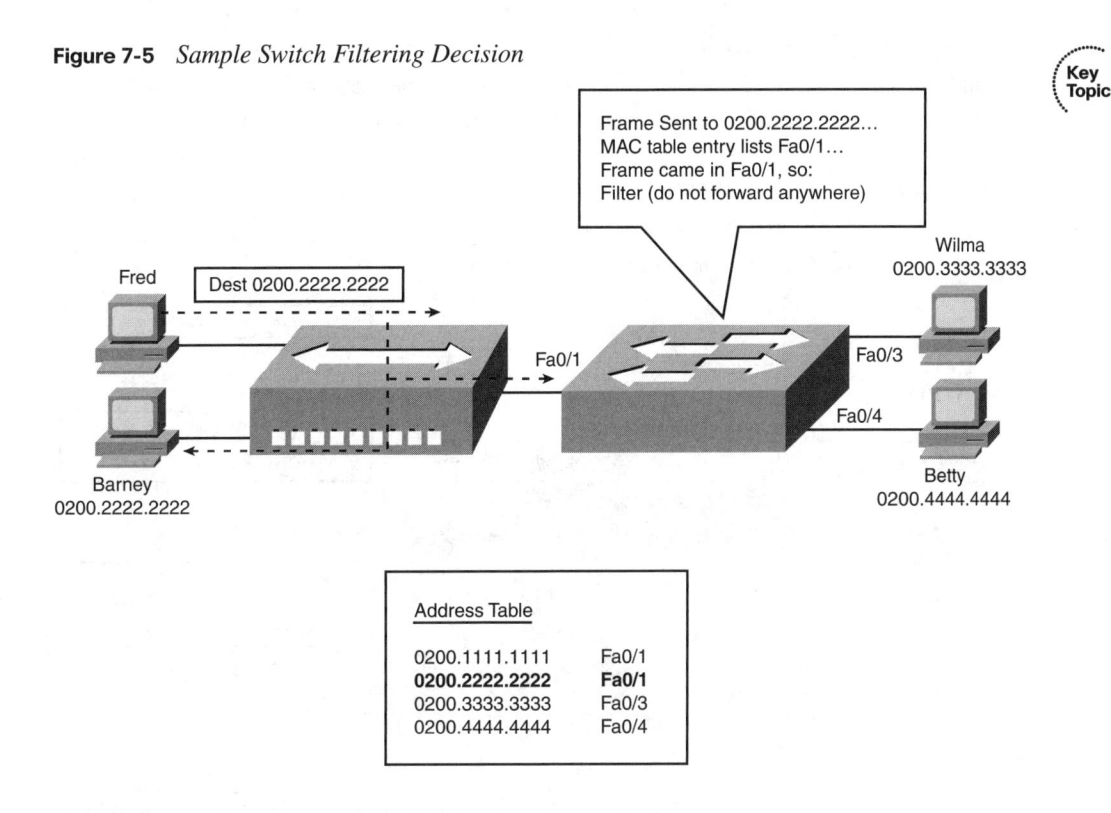

Frame Sent to 0200.2222.2222...
MAC table entry lists Fa0/1...
Frame came in Fa0/1, so:
Filter (do not forward anywhere)

Address Table

0200.1111.1111	Fa0/1
0200.2222.2222	**Fa0/1**
0200.3333.3333	Fa0/3
0200.4444.4444	Fa0/4

- - - - - - - - - - - - - - →
Path of Frame Transmission

Note that the hub simply regenerates the electrical signal out each interface, so the hub forwards the electrical signal sent by Fred to both Barney and the switch. The switch decides to filter (not forward) the frame, noting that the MAC address table's interface for 0200.2222.2222 (Fa0/1) is the same as the incoming interface.

How Switches Learn MAC Addresses

The second main function of a switch is to learn the MAC addresses and interfaces to put into its address table. With a full and accurate MAC address table, the switch can make accurate forwarding and filtering decisions.

Switches build the address table by listening to incoming frames and examining the *source MAC address* in the frame. If a frame enters the switch and the source MAC address is not in the MAC address table, the switch creates an entry in the table. The MAC address is placed in the table, along with the interface from which the frame arrived. Switch learning logic is that simple.

Figure 7-6 depicts the same network as Figure 7-4, but before the switch has built any address table entries. The figure shows the first two frames sent in this network—first a frame from Fred, addressed to Barney, and then Barney's response, addressed to Fred.

Figure 7-6 *Switch Learning: Empty Table and Adding Two Entries*

① Receive Frame with Fred's MAC as Source

② Receive Frame with Barney's MAC as Source

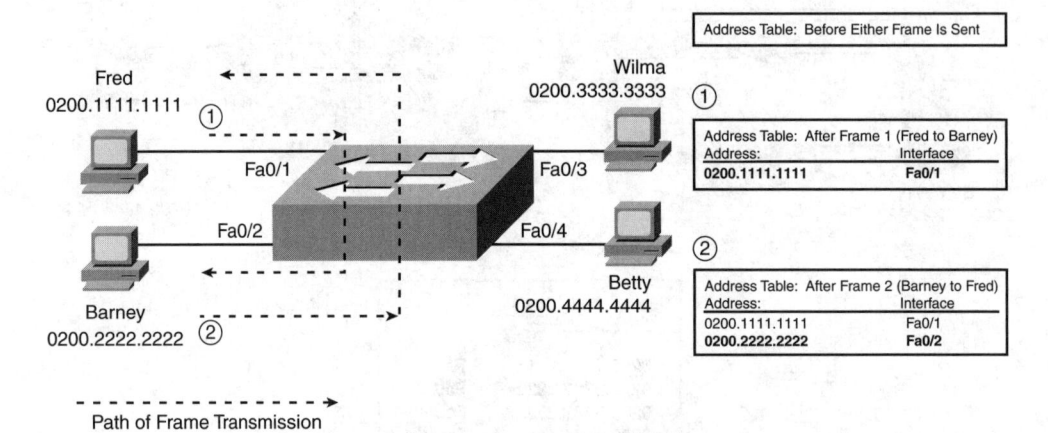

Path of Frame Transmission

As shown in the figure, after Fred sends his first frame (labeled "1") to Barney, the switch adds an entry for 0200.1111.1111, Fred's MAC address, associated with interface Fa0/1. When Barney replies in Step 2, the switch adds a second entry, this one for 0200.2222.2222, Barney's MAC address, along with interface Fa0/2, which is the interface in which the switch received the frame. Learning always occurs by looking at the source MAC address in the frame.

Flooding Frames

Now again turn your attention to the forwarding process, using Figure 7-6. What do you suppose the switch does with Fred's first frame in Figure 7-6, the one that occurred when there were no entries in the MAC address table? As it turns out, when there is no matching entry in the table, switches forward the frame out all interfaces (except the incoming interface). Switches forward these *unknown unicast frames* (frames whose destination MAC addresses are not yet in the bridging table) out all other interfaces, with the hope that the unknown device will be on some other Ethernet segment and will reply, allowing the switch to build a correct entry in the address table.

For example, in Figure 7-6, the switch forwards the first frame out Fa0/2, Fa0/3, and Fa0/4, even though 0200.2222.2222 (Barney) is only off Fa0/2. The switch does not forward the frame back out Fa0/1, because a switch never forwards a frame out the same interface on which it arrived. (As a side note, Figure 7-6 does not show the frame being forwarded out interfaces Fa0/3 and Fa0/4, because this figure is focused on the learning process.) When Barney replies to Fred, the switch correctly adds an entry for 0200.2222.2222 (Fa0/2) to its address table. Any later frames sent to destination address 0200.2222.2222 will no longer need to be sent out Fa0/3 and Fa0/4, only being forwarded out Fa0/2.

The process of sending frames out all other interfaces, except the interface on which the frame arrived, is called *flooding*. Switches flood unknown unicast frames as well as broadcast frames. Switches also flood LAN multicast frames out all ports, unless the switch has been configured to use some multicast optimization tools that are not covered in this book.

Switches keep a timer for each entry in the MAC address table, called an *inactivity timer*. The switch sets the timer to 0 for new entries. Each time the switch receives another frame with that same source MAC address, the timer is reset to 0. The timer counts upward, so the switch can tell which entries have gone the longest time since receiving a frame from that device. If the switch ever runs out of space for entries in the MAC address table, the switch can then remove table entries with the oldest (largest) inactivity timers.

Avoiding Loops Using Spanning Tree Protocol

The third primary feature of LAN switches is loop prevention, as implemented by Spanning Tree Protocol (STP). Without STP, frames would loop for an indefinite period of time in Ethernet networks with physically redundant links. To prevent looping frames, STP blocks some ports from forwarding frames so that only one active path exists between any pair of LAN segments (collision domains). The result of STP is good: frames do not loop infinitely, which makes the LAN usable. However, although the network can use some redundant links in case of a failure, the LAN does not load-balance the traffic.

To avoid Layer 2 loops, all switches need to use STP. STP causes each interface on a switch to settle into either a blocking state or a forwarding state. *Blocking* means that the interface cannot forward or receive data frames. *Forwarding* means that the interface can send and receive data frames. If a correct subset of the interfaces is blocked, a single currently active logical path exists between each pair of LANs.

> **NOTE** STP behaves identically for a transparent bridge and a switch. Therefore, the terms *bridge*, *switch*, and *bridging device* all are used interchangeably when discussing STP.

A simple example makes the need for STP more obvious. Remember, switches flood frames sent to both unknown unicast MAC addresses and broadcast addresses.

Figure 7-7 shows that a single frame, sent by Larry to Bob, loops forever because the network has redundancy but no STP.

Figure 7-7   *Network with Redundant Links But Without STP: The Frame Loops Forever*

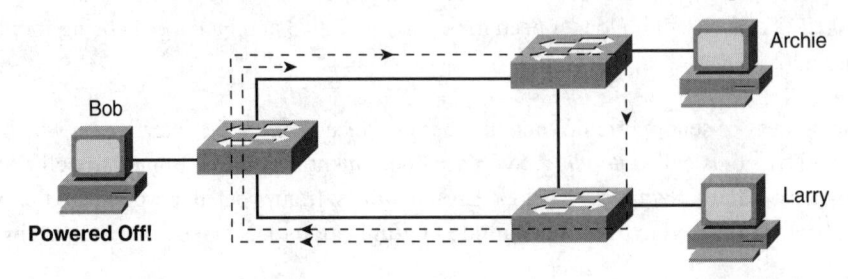

Larry sends a single unicast frame to Bob's MAC address, but Bob is powered off, so none of the switches has learned Bob's MAC address yet. Bob's MAC address would be an unknown unicast address at this point in time. Therefore, frames destined for Bob's MAC address are forwarded by each switch out every port. These frames loop indefinitely. Because the switches never learn Bob's MAC address (remember, he's powered off and can send no frames), they keep forwarding the frame out all ports, and copies of the frame go around and around.

Similarly, switches flood broadcasts as well, so if any of the PCs sent a broadcast, the broadcast would also loop indefinitely.

One way to solve this problem is to design the LAN with no redundant links. However, most network engineers purposefully design LANs to use physical redundancy between the switches. Eventually, a switch or a link will fail, and you want the network to still be available by having some redundancy in the LAN design. The right solution includes switched LANs with physical redundancy, while using STP to dynamically block some interface(s) so that only one active path exists between two endpoints at any instant in time.

Chapter 2, "Spanning Tree Protocol," in the *CCNA ICND2 Official Exam Certification Guide* covers the details of how STP prevents loops.

Internal Processing on Cisco Switches

This chapter has already explained how switches decide whether to forward or filter a frame. As soon as a Cisco switch decides to forward a frame, the switch can use a couple of different types of internal processing variations. Almost all of the more recently released switches use store-and-forward processing, but all three types of these internal processing methods are supported in at least one type of currently available Cisco switch.

Some switches, and transparent bridges in general, use *store-and-forward processing*. With store-and-forward, the switch must receive the entire frame before forwarding the first bit of the frame. However, Cisco also offers two other internal processing methods for switches: *cut-through* and *fragment-free*. Because the destination MAC address occurs very early in the Ethernet header, a switch can make a forwarding decision long before the switch has received all the bits in the frame. The cut-through and fragment-free processing methods allow the switch to start forwarding the frame before the entire frame has been received, reducing time required to send the frame (the latency, or delay).

With *cut-through* processing, the switch starts sending the frame out the output port as soon as possible. Although this might reduce latency, it also propagates errors. Because the frame check sequence (FCS) is in the Ethernet trailer, the switch cannot determine if the frame had any errors before starting to forward the frame. So, the switch reduces the frame's latency, but with the price of having forwarded some frames that contain errors.

Fragment-free processing works similarly to cut-through, but it tries to reduce the number of errored frames that it forwards. One interesting fact about Ethernet carrier sense multiple access with collision detection (CSMA/CD) logic is that collisions should be detected within the first 64 bytes of a frame. Fragment-free processing works like cut-through logic, but it waits to receive the first 64 bytes before forwarding a frame. The frames experience less latency than with store-and-forward logic and slightly more latency than with cut-through, but frames that have errors as a result of collisions are not forwarded.

With many links to the desktop running at 100 Mbps, uplinks at 1 Gbps, and faster application-specific integrated circuits (ASIC), today's switches typically use store-and-forward processing, because the improved latency of the other two switching methods is negligible at these speeds.

The internal processing algorithms used by switches vary among models and vendors; regardless, the internal processing can be categorized as one of the methods listed in Table 7-2.

Table 7-2 *Switch Internal Processing*

Key
Topic

Switching Method	Description
Store-and-forward	The switch fully receives all bits in the frame (store) before forwarding the frame (forward). This allows the switch to check the FCS before forwarding the frame.
Cut-through	The switch forwards the frame as soon as it can. This reduces latency but does not allow the switch to discard frames that fail the FCS check.
Fragment-free	The switch forwards the frame after receiving the first 64 bytes of the frame, thereby avoiding forwarding frames that were errored due to a collision.

LAN Switching Summary

Switches provide many additional features not offered by older LAN devices such as hubs and bridges. In particular, LAN switches provide the following benefits:

- Switch ports connected to a single device microsegment the LAN, providing dedicated bandwidth to that single device.

- Switches allow multiple simultaneous conversations between devices on different ports.

- Switch ports connected to a single device support full duplex, in effect doubling the amount of bandwidth available to the device.

- Switches support rate adaptation, which means that devices that use different Ethernet speeds can communicate through the switch (hubs cannot).

Switches use Layer 2 logic, examining the Ethernet data-link header to choose how to process frames. In particular, switches make decisions to forward and filter frames, learn MAC addresses, and use STP to avoid loops, as follows:

Step 1   Switches forward frames based on the destination address:

    a. If the destination address is a broadcast, multicast, or unknown destination unicast (a unicast not listed in the MAC table), the switch floods the frame.

    b. If the destination address is a known unicast address (a unicast address found in the MAC table):

       i. If the outgoing interface listed in the MAC address table is different from the interface in which the frame was received, the switch forwards the frame out the outgoing interface.

       ii. If the outgoing interface is the same as the interface in which the frame was received, the switch filters the frame, meaning that the switch simply ignores the frame and does not forward it.

Step 2   Switches use the following logic to learn MAC address table entries:

    a. For each received frame, examine the source MAC address and note the interface from which the frame was received.

    b. If they are not already in the table, add the address and interface, setting the inactivity timer to 0.

    c. If it is already in the table, reset the inactivity timer for the entry to 0.

Step 3   Switches use STP to prevent loops by causing some interfaces to block, meaning that they do not send or receive frames.

LAN Design Considerations

So far, the LAN coverage in this book has mostly focused on individual functions of LANs. For example, you have read about how switches forward frames, the details of UTP cables and cable pinouts, the CSMA/CD algorithm that deals with the issue of collisions, and some of the differences between how hubs and switches operate to create either a single collision domain (hubs) or many collision domains (switches).

This section now takes a broader look at LANs—particularly, how to design medium to larger LANs. When building a small LAN, you might simply buy one switch, plug in cables to connect a few devices, and you're finished. However, when building a medium to large LAN, you have more product choices to make, such as when to use hubs, switches, and routers. Additionally, you must weigh the choice of which LAN switch to choose (switches vary in size, number of ports, performance, features, and price). The types of LAN media differ as well. Engineers must weigh the benefits of UTP cabling, like lower cost and ease of installation, versus fiber optic cabling options, which support longer distances and better physical security.

This section examines a variety of topics that all relate to LAN design in some way. In particular, this section begins by looking at the impact of the choice of using a hub, switch, or router to connect parts of LANs. Following that, some Cisco design terminology is covered. Finishing this section is a short summary of some of the more popular types of Ethernet and cabling types, and cable length guidelines for each.

Collision Domains and Broadcast Domains

When creating any Ethernet LAN, you use some form of networking devices—typically switches today—a few routers, and possibly a few hubs. The different parts of an Ethernet LAN may behave differently, in terms of function and performance, depending on which types of devices are used. These differences then affect a network engineer's decision when choosing how to design a LAN.

The terms *collision domain* and *broadcast domain* define two important effects of the process of segmenting LANs using various devices. This section examines the concepts behind Ethernet LAN design. The goal is to define these terms and to explain how hubs, switches, and routers impact collision domains and broadcast domains.

Collision Domains

As mentioned earlier, a *collision domain* is the set of LAN interfaces whose frames could collide with each other, but not with frames sent by any other devices in the network. To review the core concept, Figure 7-8 illustrates collision domains.

Figure 7-8   *Collision Domains*

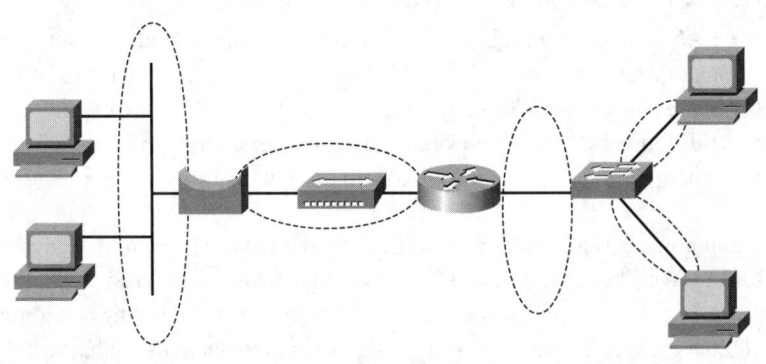

> **NOTE**   The LAN design in Figure 7-8 is not a typical design today. Instead, it simply provides enough information to help you compare hubs, switches, and routers.

Each separate segment, or collision domain, is shown with a dashed-line circle in the figure. The switch on the right separates the LAN into different collision domains for each port. Likewise, both bridges and routers also separate LANs into different collision domains (although this effect with routers was not covered earlier in this book). Of all the devices in the figure, only the hub near the center of the network does not create multiple collision domains for each interface. It repeats all frames out all ports without any regard for buffering and waiting to send a frame onto a busy segment.

Broadcast Domains

The term *broadcast domain* relates to where broadcasts can be forwarded. A *broadcast domain* encompasses a set of devices for which, when one of the devices sends a broadcast, all the other devices receive a copy of the broadcast. For example, switches flood broadcasts and multicasts on all ports. Because broadcast frames are sent out all ports, a switch creates a single broadcast domain.

Conversely, only routers stop the flow of broadcasts. For perspective, Figure 7-9 provides the broadcast domains for the same network depicted in Figure 7-8.

Broadcasts sent by a device in one broadcast domain are not forwarded to devices in another broadcast domain. In this example, there are two broadcast domains. For instance, the router does not forward a LAN broadcast sent by a PC on the left to the network segment on the right. In the old days, the term *broadcast firewall* described the fact that routers did not forward LAN broadcasts.

Figure 7-9 *Broadcast Domains*

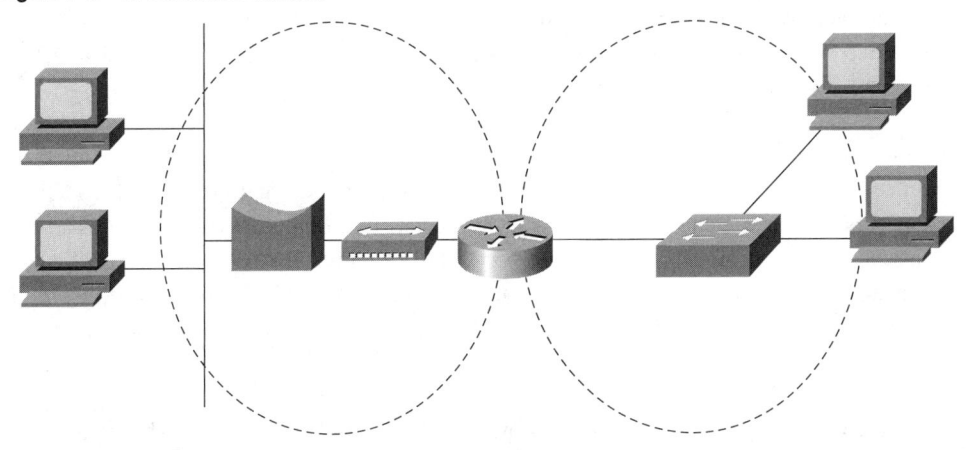

General definitions for a collision domain and a broadcast domain are as follows:

■ A *collision domain* is a set of network interface cards (NIC) for which a frame sent by one NIC could result in a collision with a frame sent by any other NIC in the same collision domain.

■ A *broadcast domain* is a set of NICs for which a broadcast frame sent by one NIC is received by all other NICs in the same broadcast domain.

The Impact of Collision and Broadcast Domains on LAN Design

When designing a LAN, you need to keep in mind the trade-offs when choosing the number of devices in each collision domain and broadcast domain. First, consider the devices in a single collision domain for a moment. For a single collision domain:

■ The devices share the available bandwidth.

■ The devices may inefficiently use that bandwidth due to the effects of collisions, particularly under higher utilization.

For example, you might have ten PCs with 10/100 Ethernet NICs. If you connect all ten PCs to ten different ports on a single 100-Mbps hub, you have one collision domain, and the PCs in that collision domain share the 100 Mbps of bandwidth. That may work well and meet the needs of those users. However, with heavier traffic loads, the hub's performance would be worse than it would be if you had used a switch. Using a switch instead of a hub, with the same topology, would create ten different collision domains, each with 100 Mbps of bandwidth. Additionally, with only one device on each switch interface, no collisions would occur. This means that you could enable full duplex on each interface, effectively giving each interface 200 Mbps, and a theoretical maximum of 2 Gbps of bandwidth—a considerable improvement!

Using switches instead of hubs seems like an obvious choice given the overwhelming performance benefits. Frankly, most new installations today use switches exclusively. However, vendors still offer hubs, mainly because hubs are still slightly less expensive than switches, so you may still see hubs in networks today.

Now consider the issue of broadcasts. When a host receives a broadcast, the host must process the received frame. This means that the NIC must interrupt the computer's CPU, and the CPU must spend time thinking about the received broadcast frame. All hosts need to send some broadcasts to function properly. (For example, IP ARP messages are LAN broadcasts, as mentioned in Chapter 5, "Fundamentals of IP Addressing and Routing.") So, broadcasts happen, which is good, but broadcasts do require all the hosts to spend time processing each broadcast frame.

Next, consider a large LAN, with multiple switches, with 500 PCs total. The switches create a single broadcast domain, so a broadcast sent by any of the 500 hosts should be sent to, and then processed by, all 499 other hosts. Depending on the number of broadcasts, the broadcasts could start to impact performance of the end-user PCs. However, a design that separated the 500 PCs into five groups of 100, separated from each other by a router, would create five broadcast domains. Now, a broadcast by one host would interrupt only 99 other hosts, and not the other 400 hosts, resulting in generally better performance on the PCs.

NOTE   Using smaller broadcast domains can also improve security, due to limiting broadcasts, and due to robust security features in routers.

The choice about when to use a hub versus a switch was straightforward, but the choice of when to use a router to break up a large broadcast domain is more difficult. A meaningful discussion of the trade-offs and options is beyond the scope of this book. However, you should understand the concepts behind broadcast domains—specifically, that a router breaks LANs into multiple broadcast domains, but switches and hubs do not.

More importantly for the CCNA exams, you should be ready to react to questions in terms of the benefits of LAN segmentation instead of just asking for the facts related to collision domains and broadcast domains. Table 7-3 lists some of the key benefits. The features in the table should be interpreted within the following context: "Which of the following benefits are gained by using a hub/switch/router between Ethernet devices?"

Table 7-3 *Benefits of Segmenting Ethernet Devices Using Hubs, Switches, and Routers*

Feature	Hub	Switch	Router
Greater cabling distances are allowed	Yes	Yes	Yes
Creates multiple collision domains	No	Yes	Yes
Increases bandwidth	No	Yes	Yes
Creates multiple broadcast domains	No	No	Yes

Virtual LANs (VLAN)

Most every Enterprise network today uses the concept of virtual LANs (VLAN). Before understanding VLANs, you must have a very specific understanding of the definition of a LAN. Although you can think about and define the term "LAN" from many perspectives, one perspective in particular will help you understand VLANs:

> A LAN consists of all devices in the same broadcast domain.

Without VLANs, a switch considers all interfaces on the switch to be in the same broadcast domain. In other words, all connected devices are in the same LAN. (Cisco switches accomplish this by putting all interfaces in VLAN 1 by default.) With VLANs, a switch can put some interfaces into one broadcast domain and some into another based on some simple configuration. Essentially, the switch creates multiple broadcast domains by putting some interfaces into one VLAN and other interfaces into other VLANs. These individual broadcast domains created by the switch are called virtual LANs.

So, instead of all ports on a switch forming a single broadcast domain, the switch separates them into many, based on configuration. It's really that simple.

The next two figures compare two LANs for the purpose of explaining a little more about VLANs. First, before VLANs existed, if a design specified two separate broadcast domains, two switches would be used—one for each broadcast domain, as shown in Figure 7-10.

Figure 7-10 *Sample Network with Two Broadcast Domains and No VLANs*

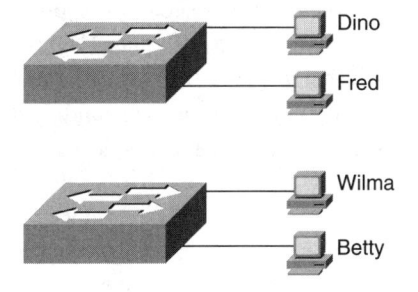

Alternately, you can create multiple broadcast domains using a single switch. Figure 7-11 shows the same two broadcast domains as in Figure 7-10, now implemented as two different VLANs on a single switch.

Figure 7-11 *Sample Network with Two VLANs Using One Switch*

In a network as small as the one shown in Figure 7-11, you might not really need to use VLANs. However, there are many motivations for using VLANs, including the following:

■ To create more flexible designs that group users by department, or by groups that work together, instead of by physical location

■ To segment devices into smaller LANs (broadcast domains) to reduce overhead caused to each host in the VLAN

■ To reduce the workload for STP by limiting a VLAN to a single access switch

■ To enforce better security by keeping hosts that work with sensitive data on a separate VLAN

■ To separate traffic sent by an IP phone from traffic sent by PCs connected to the phones

The *CCNA ICND2 Official Exam Certification Guide* explains VLAN configuration and troubleshooting.

Campus LAN Design Terminology

The term *campus LAN* refers to the LAN created to support larger buildings, or multiple buildings in somewhat close proximity to one another. For instance, a company might lease office space in several buildings in the same office park. The network engineers can then build a campus LAN that includes switches in each building, plus Ethernet links between the switches in the buildings, to create a larger campus LAN.

When planning and designing a campus LAN, the engineers must consider the types of Ethernet available and the cabling lengths supported by each type. The engineers also need to choose the speeds required for each Ethernet segment. Additionally, some thought needs to be given to the idea that some switches should be used to connect directly to end-user devices, whereas other switches might need to simply connect to a large number of these end-user switches. Finally, most projects require that the engineer consider the type of equipment that is already installed and whether an increase in speed on some segments is worth the cost of buying new equipment.

For example, the vast majority of PCs that are already installed in networks today have 10/100 NICs, with many new PCs today having 10/100/1000 NICs built into the PC. Assuming that the appropriate cabling has been installed, a 10/100/1000 NIC can use autonegotiation to use either 10BASE-T (10 Mbps), 100BASE-TX (100 Mbps), or 1000BASE-T (1000 Mbps, or 1 Gbps) Ethernet, each using the same UTP cable. However, one trade-off the engineer must make is whether to buy switches that support only 10/100 interfaces or that support 10/100/1000 interfaces. At the time this book was published (summer 2007), the price difference between switches that support only 10/100 interfaces, versus 10/100/1000 interfaces, was still large enough to get management's attention. However, spending the money on switches that include 10/100/1000 interfaces allows you to connect pretty much any end-user device. You'll also be ready to migrate from 100 Mbps to the desktop device to 1000 Mbps (gigabit) as new PCs are bought.

To sift through all the requirements for a campus LAN, and then have a reasonable conversation about it with peers, most Cisco-oriented LAN designs use some common terminology to refer to the design. For this book's purposes, you should be aware of some of the key campus LAN design terminology. Figure 7-12 shows a typical design of a large campus LAN, with the terminology included in the figure. Explanations of the terminology follow the figure.

Cisco uses three terms to describe the role of each switch in a campus design: *access*, *distribution*, and *core*. The roles differ mainly in two main concepts:

■ Whether the switch should connect to end-user devices

■ Whether the switch should forward frames between other switches by connecting to multiple different switches

Access switches connect directly to end users, providing access to the LAN. Under normal circumstances, access switches normally send traffic to and from the end-user devices to which they are connected. However, access switches should not, at least by design, be expected to forward traffic between two other switches. For example, in Figure 7-12, switch Access1 normally would not forward traffic going from PCs connected to switch Access3 to a PC off switch Access4. Because access layer switches support only the traffic for the locally attached PCs, access switches tend to be smaller and less expensive, often supporting just enough ports to support a particular floor of a building.

Figure 7-12 *Campus LAN with Design Terminology Listed*

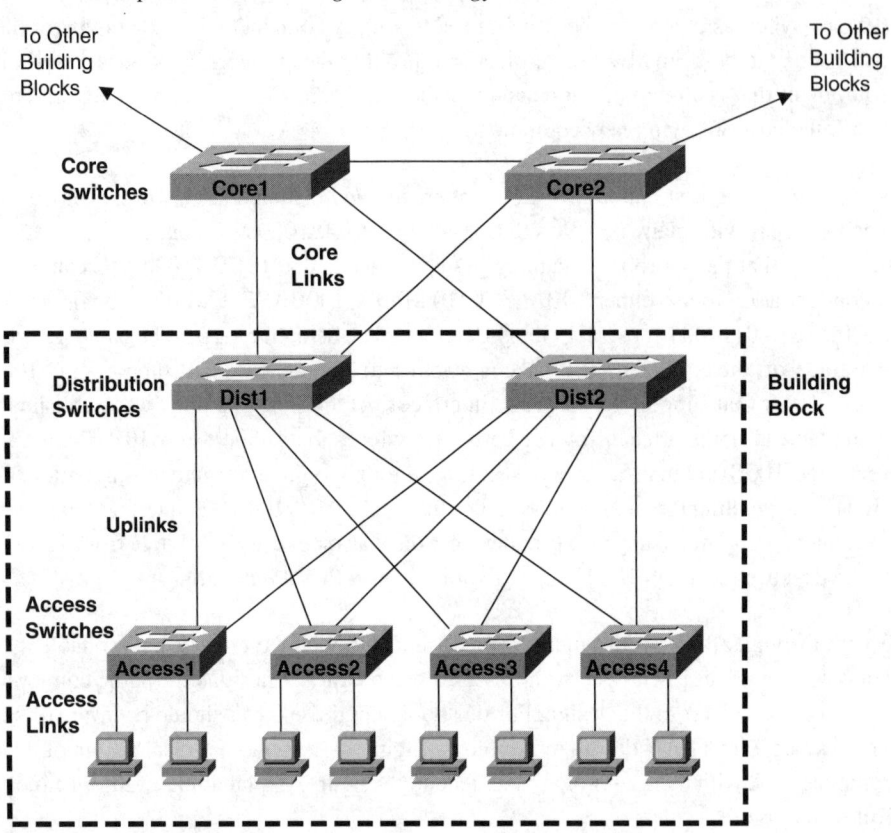

In larger campus LANs, distribution switches provide a path through which the access switches can forward traffic to each other. By design, each of the access switches connects to at least one distribution switch. However, designs use at least two uplinks to two different distribution switches (as shown in Figure 7-12) for redundancy.

Using distribution switches provides some cabling advantages and potential performance advantages. For example, if a network had 30 access layer switches, and the network engineer decided that each access layer switch should be cabled directly to every other access layer switch, the LAN would need 435 cables between switches! Furthermore, that design includes only one segment between each pair of switches. A possibly worse side effect is that if a link fails, the access layer switches may forward traffic to and from other switches, stressing the performance of the access switch, which typically is a less expensive but less powerful switch. Instead, by connecting each of the 30 access switches to two different distribution switches, only 60 cables are required. Well-chosen distribution switches, with faster forwarding rates, can handle the larger amount of traffic between switches. Additionally, the design with two distribution switches, with two uplinks from each access switch to the distribution switches, actually has more redundancy and therefore better availability.

Core switches provide even more aggregation benefits than do the distribution switches. Core switches provide extremely high forwarding rates—these days into the hundreds of millions of frames per second. The reasons for core switches are generally the same as for distribution switches. However, medium to smaller campus LANs often forego the concept of core switches.

The following list summarizes the terms that describe the roles of campus switches:

- **Access:** Provides a connection point (access) for end-user devices. Does not forward frames between two other access switches under normal circumstances.

- **Distribution:** Provides an aggregation point for access switches, forwarding frames between switches, but not connecting directly to end-user devices.

- **Core:** Aggregates distribution switches in very large campus LANs, providing very high forwarding rates.

Ethernet LAN Media and Cable Lengths

When designing a campus LAN, an engineer must consider the length of each cable run and then find the best type of Ethernet and cabling type that supports that length of cable. For example, if a company leases space in five buildings in the same office park, the engineer needs to figure out how long the cables between the buildings need to be and then pick the right type of Ethernet.

The three most common types of Ethernet today (10BASE-T, 100BASE-TX, and 1000BASE-T) have the same 100-meter cable restriction, but they use slightly different cables. The EIA/TIA defines Ethernet cabling standards, including the cable's quality. Each Ethernet standard that uses UTP cabling lists a cabling quality category as the minimum category that the standard supports. For example, 10BASE-T allows for Category 3 (CAT3) cabling or better, whereas 100BASE-TX calls for higher-quality CAT5 cabling, and 1000BASE-TX requires even higher-quality CAT5e or CAT6 cabling. If an engineer plans on using existing cabling, he or she must be aware of the types of UTP cables and the speed restrictions implied by the type of Ethernet the cabling supports.

Several types of Ethernet define the use of fiber-optic cables. UTP cables include copper wires over which electrical currents can flow, whereas optical cables include ultra-thin strands of glass through which light can pass. To send bits, the switches can alternate between sending brighter and dimmer light to encode 0s and 1s on the cable.

Optical cables support a variety of much longer distances than the 100 meters supported by Ethernet on UTP cables. Optical cables experience much less interference from outside sources as compared to copper cables. Additionally, switches can use lasers to generate the light, as well as light-emitting diodes (LED). Lasers allow for even longer cabling distances, up to 100 km today, at higher cost, whereas less-expensive LEDs may well support plenty of distance for campus LANs in most office parks.

Finally, the type of optical cabling can also impact the maximum distances per cable. Of the two types, multimode fiber supports shorter distances, but it is generally cheaper cabling, and it works fine with less-expensive LEDs. The other optical cabling type, single-mode fiber, supports the longest distances but is more expensive. Also note that the switch hardware to use LEDs (often with multimode fiber) is much less expensive than the switch hardware to support lasers (often with single-mode fiber).

Table 7-4 lists the more common types of Ethernet and their cable types and length limitations.

Table 7-4   *Ethernet Types, Media, and Segment Lengths (Per IEEE)*

Ethernet Type	Media	Maximum Segment Length
10BASE-T	TIA/EIA CAT3 or better, two pair	100 m (328 feet)
100BASE-TX	TIA/EIA CAT5 UTP or better, two pair	100 m (328 feet)
100BASE-FX	62.5/125-micron multimode fiber	400 m (1312.3 feet)
1000BASE-CX	STP	25 m (82 feet)
1000BASE-T	TIA/EIA CAT5e UTP or better, four pair	100 m (328 feet)
1000BASE-SX	Multimode fiber	275 m (853 feet) for 62.5-micron fiber 550 m (1804.5 feet) for 50-micron fiber
1000BASE-LX	Multimode fiber	550 m (1804.5 feet) for 50- and 62.5-micron fiber
1000BASE-LX	9-micron single-mode fiber	5 km (3.1 miles)

Most engineers simply remember the general distance limitations and then use a reference chart (such as Table 7-4) to remember each specific detail. An engineer must also consider the physical paths that the cables will use to run through a campus or building and the impact on the required cable length. For example, a cable might have to run from one end of the building to the other, and then through a conduit that connects the floors of the building, and then horizontally to a wiring closet on another floor. Often those paths are not the shortest way to get from one place to the other. So the chart's details are important to the LAN planning process and the resulting choice of LAN media.

Exam Preparation Tasks

Review All the Key Topics

Key
Topic

Review the most important topics from this chapter, noted with the key topics icon.
Table 7-5 lists these key topics and where each is discussed.

Table 7-5 *Key Topics for Chapter 7*

Key Topic Element	Description	Page Number
List	LAN switch actions	175
Figure 7-4	Example of switch forwarding logic	176
Figure 7-5	Example of switch filtering logic	177
Figure 7-6	Example of how a switch learns MAC addresses	178
Table 7-2	Summary of three switch internal forwarding options	181
List	Some of the benefits of switching	182
List	Summary of logic used to forward and filter frames and to learn MAC addresses	182
List	Definitions of collision domain and broadcast domain	185
Table 7-3	Four LAN design feature comparisons with hubs, switches, and routers	187
Figure 7-11	Illustration of the concept of a VLAN	188

Complete the Tables and Lists from Memory

Print a copy of Appendix H, "Memory Tables" (found on the CD), or at least the section for this chapter, and complete the tables and lists from memory. Appendix I, "Memory Tables Answer Key," also on the CD, includes completed tables and lists for you to check your work.

Definitions of Key Terms

Define the following key terms from this chapter, and check your answers in the glossary:

broadcast domain, broadcast frame, collision domain, cut-through switching, flooding, fragment-free switching, microsegmentation, segmentation, Spanning Tree Protocol (STP), store-and-forward switching, unknown unicast frame, virtual LAN

This chapter covers the following subjects:

Accessing the Cisco Catalyst 2960 Switch CLI: This section examines Cisco 2960 switches and shows you how to gain access to the command-line interface (CLI) from which you can issue commands to the switch.

Configuring Cisco IOS Software: This section shows you how to tell the switch different operational parameters using the CLI.

Operating Cisco LAN Switches

LAN switches may be the most common networking device found in the Enterprise today. Most new end-user computers sold today include a built-in Ethernet NIC of some kind. Switches provide a connection point for the Ethernet devices so that the devices on the LAN can communicate with each other and with the rest of an Enterprise network or with the Internet.

Cisco routers also happen to use the exact same user interface as the Cisco Catalyst switches described in this chapter. So, even though this chapter is called "Operating Cisco LAN Switches," keep in mind that the user interface of Cisco routers works the same way. Chapter 13, "Operating Cisco Routers," begins by summarizing the features covered in this chapter that also apply to routers.

"Do I Know This Already?" Quiz

The "Do I Know This Already?" quiz allows you to assess whether you should read the entire chapter. If you miss no more than one of these seven self-assessment questions, you might want to move ahead to the "Exam Preparation Tasks" section. Table 8-1 lists the major headings in this chapter and the "Do I Know This Already?" quiz questions covering the material in those sections. This helps you assess your knowledge of these specific areas. The answers to the "Do I Know This Already?" quiz appear in Appendix A.

Table 8-1 *"Do I Know This Already?" Foundation Topics Section-to-Question Mapping*

Foundation Topics Section	Questions
Accessing the Cisco Catalyst 2960 Switch CLI	1–3
Configuring Cisco IOS Software	4–7

1. In what modes can you execute the command **show mac-address-table**?

    a. User mode

    b. Enable mode

    c. Global configuration mode

    d. Setup mode

    e. Interface configuration mode

2. In which of the following modes of the CLI could you issue a command to reboot the switch?

    a. User mode

    b. Enable mode

    c. Global configuration mode

    d. Interface configuration mode

3. Which of the following is a difference between Telnet and SSH as supported by a Cisco switch?

    a. SSH encrypts the passwords used at login, but not other traffic; Telnet encrypts nothing.

    b. SSH encrypts all data exchange, including login passwords; Telnet encrypts nothing.

    c. Telnet is used from Microsoft operating systems, and SSH is used from UNIX and Linux operating systems.

    d. Telnet encrypts only password exchanges; SSH encrypts all data exchanges.

4. What type of switch memory is used to store the configuration used by the switch when it is up and working?

    a. RAM

    b. ROM

    c. Flash

    d. NVRAM

    e. Bubble

5. What command copies the configuration from RAM into NVRAM?

    a. **copy running-config tftp**

    b. **copy tftp running-config**

    c. **copy running-config start-up-config**

    d. **copy start-up-config running-config**

    e. **copy startup-config running-config**

    f. **copy running-config startup-config**

6. Which mode prompts the user for basic configuration information?

    a. User mode

    b. Enable mode

    c. Global configuration mode

    d. Setup mode

    e. Interface configuration mode

7. A switch user is currently in console line configuration mode. Which of the following would place the user in enable mode?

    a. Using the **exit** command once

    b. Using the **exit** command twice in a row

    c. Pressing the **Ctrl-z** key sequence

    d. Using the **quit** command

Foundation Topics

When you buy a Cisco Catalyst switch, you can take it out of the box, power on the switch by connecting the power cable to the switch and a power outlet, and connect hosts to the switch using the correct UTP cables, and the switch works. You do not have to do anything else, and you certainly do not have to tell the switch to start forwarding Ethernet frames. The switch uses default settings so that all interfaces will work, assuming that the right cables and devices connect to the switch, and the switch forwards frames in and out of each interface.

However, most Enterprises will want to be able to check on the switch's status, look at information about what the switch is doing, and possibly configure specific features of the switch. Engineers will also want to enable security features that allow them to securely access the switches without being vulnerable to malicious people breaking into the switches. To perform these tasks, a network engineer needs to connect to the switch's user interface.

This chapter explains the details of how to access a Cisco switch's user interface, how to use commands to find out how the switch is currently working, and how to configure the switch to tell it what to do. This chapter focuses on the processes, as opposed to examining a particular set of commands. Chapter 9, "Ethernet Switch Configuration," then takes a closer look at the variety of commands that can be used from the switch user interface.

Cisco has two major brands of LAN switching products. The Cisco Catalyst switch brand includes a large collection of switches, all of which have been designed with Enterprises (companies, governments, and so on) in mind. The Catalyst switches have a wide range of sizes, functions, and forwarding rates. The Cisco Linksys switch brand includes a variety of switches designed for use in the home. The CCNA exams focus on how to implement LANs using Cisco Catalyst switches, so this chapter explains how to gain access to a Cisco Catalyst switch to monitor, configure, and troubleshoot problems. However, both the Catalyst and Linksys brands of Cisco switches provide the same base features, as covered earlier in Chapters 3 and 7.

Note that for the rest of this chapter, all references to a "Cisco switch" refer to Cisco Catalyst switches, not Cisco Linksys switches.

Accessing the Cisco Catalyst 2960 Switch CLI

Cisco uses the same concept of a *command-line interface* (CLI) with its router products and most of its Catalyst LAN switch products. The CLI is a text-based interface in which the user, typically a network engineer, enters a text command and presses Enter. Pressing Enter sends the command to the switch, which tells the device to do something. The switch does what the command says, and in some cases, the switch replies with some messages stating the results of the command.

Before getting into the details of the CLI, this section examines the models of Cisco LAN switches typically referenced for CCNA exams. Then this section explains how a network engineer can get access to the CLI to issue commands.

Cisco Catalyst Switches and the 2960 Switch

Within the Cisco Catalyst brand of LAN switches, Cisco produces a wide variety of switch series or families. Each switch series includes several specific models of switches that have similar features, similar price-versus-performance trade-offs, and similar internal components.

Cisco positions the 2960 series (family) of switches as full-featured, low-cost wiring closet switches for Enterprises. That means that you would expect to use 2960 switches as access switches, as shown in Figure 7-12 in Chapter 7, "Ethernet LAN Switching Concepts." Access switches provide the connection point for end-user devices, with cabling running from desks to the switch in a nearby wiring closet. 2960 access switches would also connect to the rest of the Enterprise network using a couple of uplinks, often connecting to distribution layer switches. The distribution layer switches are often from a different Cisco switch family, typically a more powerful and more expensive product family.

Figure 8-1 shows a photo of the 2960 switch series from Cisco. Each switch is a different specific model of switch inside the 2960 series. For example, the top switch in Figure 8-1 (model WS-2960-24TT-L) has 24 RJ-45 UTP 10/100 ports, meaning that these ports can negotiate the use of 10BASE-T or 100BASE-TX Ethernet. The WS-2960-24TT-L switch has two additional RJ-45 ports on the right that are 10/100/1000 interfaces, intended to connect to the core of an Enterprise campus LAN.

Cisco refers to a switch's physical connectors as either *interfaces* or *ports*. Each interface has a number in the style x/y, where x and y are two different numbers. On a 2960, the number before the / is always 0. The first 10/100 interface on a 2960 is numbered starting at 0/1, the second is 0/2, and so on. The interfaces also have names; for example, "interface FastEthernet 0/1" is the first of the 10/100 interfaces. Any Gigabit-capable interfaces would be called "GigabitEthernet" interfaces. For example, the first 10/100/1000 interface on a 2960 would be "interface gigabitethernet 0/1."

Figure 8-1   *Cisco 2960 Catalyst Switch Series*

Cisco supports two major types of switch operating systems: *Internetwork Operating System* (IOS) and *Catalyst Operating System* (Cat OS). Most Cisco Catalyst switch series today run only Cisco IOS, but for some historical reasons, some of the high-end Cisco LAN switches support both Cisco IOS and Cat OS. For the purposes of the CCNA exams, you can ignore Cat OS, focusing on Cisco IOS. However, keep in mind that you might see terminology and phrasing such as "IOS-based switch," referring to the fact that the switch runs Cisco IOS, not Cat OS.

NOTE   For the real world, note that Cisco's most popular core switch product, the 6500 series, can run either Cisco IOS or Cat OS. Cisco also uses the term *hybrid* to refer to 6500 switches that use Cat OS and the term *native* to refer to 6500 switches that use Cisco IOS.

Switch Status from LEDs

When an engineer needs to examine how a switch is working to verify its current status and to troubleshoot any problems, the vast majority of the time is spent using commands from the Cisco IOS CLI. However, the switch hardware does include several LEDs that provide some status and troubleshooting information, both during the time right after the switch has been powered on and during ongoing operations. Before moving on to discuss the CLI, this brief section examines the switch LEDs and their meanings.

Most Cisco Catalyst switches have some LEDs, including an LED for each physical Ethernet interface. For example, Figure 8-2 shows the front of a 2960 series switch, with five LEDs on the left, one LED over each port, and a mode button.

Figure 8-2 *2960 LEDs and a Mode Button*

The figure points out the various LEDs, with various meanings. Table 8-2 summarizes the LEDs, and additional explanations follow the table.

Table 8-2 *LEDs in Figure 8-2*

Number in Figure 8-2	Name	Description
1	SYST (system)	Implies the overall system status
2	RPS (Redundant Power Supply)	Suggests the status of the extra (redundant) power supply
3	STAT (Status)	If on (green), implies that each port LED implies that port's status
4	DUPLX (duplex)	If on (green), each port LED implies that port's duplex (on/green is full; off means half)
5	SPEED	If on (green), each port LED implies the speed of that port, as follows: off means 10 Mbps, solid green means 100 Mbps, and flashing green means 1 Gbps.
7	Port	Has different meanings, depending on the port mode as toggled using the mode button

A few specific examples can help make sense of the LEDs. For example, consider the SYST LED for a moment. This LED provides a quick overall status of the switch, with three simple states on most 2960 switch models:

■ **Off:** The switch is not powered on

■ **On (green):** The switch is powered on and operational (Cisco IOS has been loaded)

■ **On (amber):** The switch's Power-On Self Test (POST) process failed, and the Cisco IOS did not load.

So, a quick look at the SYST LED on the switch tells you whether the switch is working and, if it isn't, whether this is due to a loss of power (the SYST LED is off) or some kind of POST problem (LED amber). In this last case, the typical response is to power the switch off and back on again. If the same failure occurs, a call to the Cisco Technical Assistance Center (TAC) is typically the next step.

Besides the straightforward SYST LED, the port LEDs—the LEDs sitting above or below each Ethernet port—means something different depending on which of three port LED modes is currently used on the switch. The switches have a mode button (labelled with number 6 in Figure 8-2) that, when pressed, cycles the port LEDs through three modes: STAT, DUPLX, and SPEED. The current port LED mode is signified by a solid green STAT, DUPLX, or SPEED LED (the lower three LEDs on the left part of Figure 8-2, labeled 3, 4, and 5). To move to another port LED mode, the engineer simply presses the mode button another time or two.

Each of the three port LED modes changes the meaning of the port LEDs associated with each port. For example, in STAT (status) mode, each port LED implies status information about that one associated port. For example:

■ **Off:** The link is not working.

■ **Solid green:** The link is working, but there's no current traffic.

■ **Flashing green:** The link is working, and traffic is currently passing over the interface.

■ **Flashing amber:** The interface is administratively disabled or has been dynamically disabled for a variety of reasons.

In contrast, in SPEED port LED mode, the port LEDs imply the operating speed of the interface, with a dark LED meaning 10 Mbps, a solid green light meaning 100 Mbps, and flashing green meaning 1000 Mbps (1 Gbps).

The particular details of how each LED works differ between different Cisco switch families and with different models inside the same switch family. So, memorizing the specific meaning of particular LED combinations is probably not required, and this chapter does not attempt to cover all combinations for even a single switch. However, it is important to remember the general ideas, the concept of a mode button that changes the meaning of the port LEDs, and the three meanings of the SYST LED mentioned earlier in this section.

The vast majority of the time, switches power up just fine and load Cisco IOS, and then the engineer simply accesses the CLI to operate and examine the switch. Next, the chapter focuses on the details of how to access the CLI.

Accessing the Cisco IOS CLI

Cisco IOS Software for Catalyst switches implements and controls logic and functions performed by a Cisco switch. Besides controlling the switch's performance and behavior, Cisco IOS also defines an interface for humans called the CLI. The Cisco IOS CLI allows the user to use a terminal emulation program, which accepts text entered by the user. When the user presses Enter, the terminal emulator sends that text to the switch. The switch processes the text as if it is a command, does what the command says, and sends text back to the terminal emulator.

The switch CLI can be accessed through three popular methods—the console, Telnet, and Secure Shell (SSH). Two of these methods (Telnet and SSH) use the IP network in which the switch resides to reach the switch. The console is a physical port built specifically to allow access to the CLI. Figure 8-3 depicts the options.

Figure 8-3 *CLI Access*

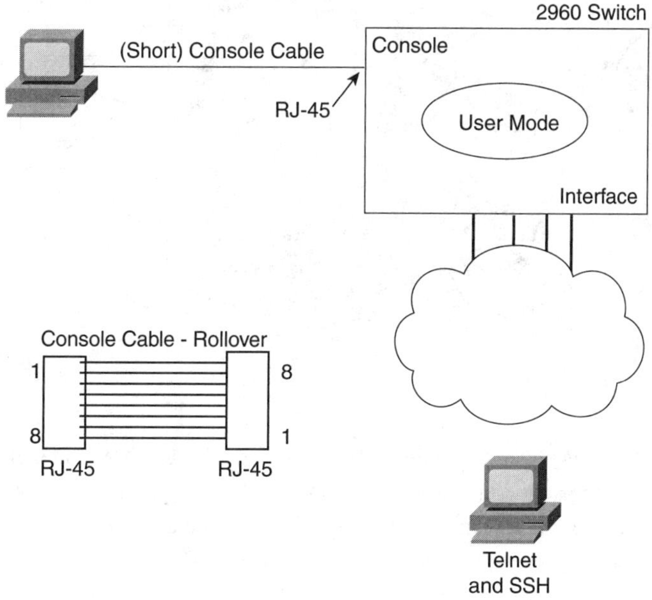

> **NOTE**   You can also use a web browser to configure a switch, but the interface is not the
> CLI interface. This interface uses a tool called either the Cisco Device Manager (CDM)
> or Cisco Security Device Manager (SDM). Some SDM coverage is included in Chapter 17,
> "WAN Configuration," in relation to configuring a router.

Next, this section examines each of these three access methods in more detail.

CLI Access from the Console

The console port provides a way to connect to a switch CLI even if the switch has not been
connected to a network yet. Every Cisco switch has a console port, which is physically an
RJ-45 port. A PC connects to the console port using a UTP rollover cable, which is also
connected to the PC's serial port. The UTP rollover cable has RJ-45 connectors on each
end, with pin 1 on one end connected to pin 8 on the other, pin 2 to pin 7, pin 3 to pin 6, and
pin 4 to pin 5. In some cases, a PC's serial interface does not use an RJ-45 connector, an
adapter must be used to convert from the PC's physical interface—typically either a nine-
pin connector or a USB connector—to an RJ-45. Figure 8-4 shows the RJ-45 end of the
console cable connected to a switch and the DB-9 end connected to a laptop PC.

Figure 8-4   *Console Connection to a Switch*

As soon as the PC is physically connected to the console port, a terminal emulator software
package must be installed and configured on the PC. Today, terminal emulator software
includes support for Telnet and Secure Shell (SSH), which can be used to access the switch
CLI via the network, but not through the console.

Figure 8-5 shows the window created by the Tera Term Pro software package (available free from http://www.ayera.com). The emulator must be configured to use the PC's serial port, matching the switch's console port settings. The default console port settings on a switch are as follows:

■   9600 bits/second

■   No hardware flow control

■   8-bit ASCII

■   No parity bits

■   1 stop bit

Note that the last three parameters are referred to collectively as "8N1."

Figure 8-5   *Terminal Settings for Console Access*

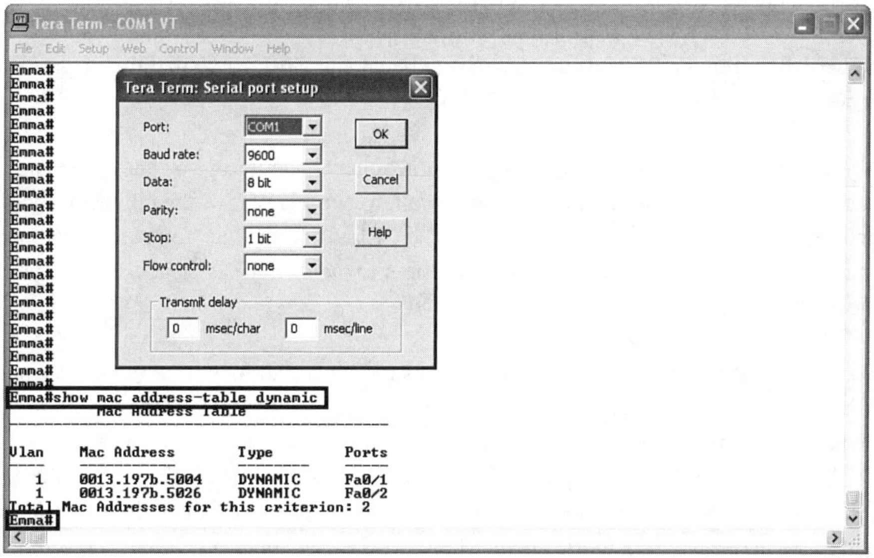

Figure 8-5 shows a terminal emulator window with some command output. It also shows the configuration window for the settings just listed.

The figure shows the window created by the emulator software. Note that the first highlighted portion shows the text **Emma#show mac address-table dynamic**. The **Emma#** part is the command prompt, which typically shows the hostname of the switch (Emma in this case). The prompt is text created by the switch and sent to the emulator. The **show mac address-table dynamic** part is the command that the user entered. The text shown beneath the command is the output generated by the switch and sent to the emulator. Finally, the lower highlighted text **Emma#** shows the command prompt again, as sent to the emulator by the switch. The window would remain in this state until the user entered something else at the command line.

Accessing the CLI with Telnet and SSH

The TCP/IP Telnet application allows a terminal emulator to communicate with a device, much like what happens with an emulator on a PC connected to the console. However, Telnet uses an IP network to send and receive the data, rather than a specialized cable and physical port on the device. The Telnet application protocols call the terminal emulator a *Telnet client* and the device that listens for commands and replies to them a *Telnet server*. Telnet is a TCP-based application layer protocol that uses well-known port 23.

To use Telnet, the user must install a Telnet client software package on his or her PC. (As mentioned earlier, most terminal emulator software packages today include both Telnet and SSH client functions.) The switch runs Telnet server software by default, but the switch does need to have an IP address configured so that it can send and receive IP packets. (Chapter 9 covers switch IP address configuration in greater detail.) Additionally, the network between the PC and switch needs to be up and working so that the PC and switch can exchange IP packets.

Many network engineers habitually use a Telnet client to monitor switches. The engineer can sit at his or her desk without having to walk to another part of the building—or go to another state or country—and still get into the CLI of that device. Telnet sends all data (including any username and password for login to the switch) as clear-text data, which presents a potential security risk.

Secure Shell (SSH) does the same basic things as Telnet, but in a more secure manner by using encryption. Like the Telnet model, the SSH client software includes a terminal emulator and the capability to send and receive the data using IP. Like Telnet, SSH uses TCP, while using well-known port 22 instead of Telnet's 23. As with Telnet, the SSH server (on the switch) receives the text from each SSH client, processes the text as a command, and sends messages back to the client. The key difference between Telnet and SSH lies in the fact that all the communications are encrypted and therefore are private and less prone to security risk.

Password Security for CLI Access

By default, a Cisco switch is very secure as long as the switch is locked inside a room. By default, a switch allows only console access, but no Telnet or SSH access. From the console, you can gain full access to all switch commands, and if so inclined, you can stop all functions of the switch. However, console access requires physical access to the switch, so allowing console access for switches just removed from the shipping boxes is reasonable.

Regardless of the defaults, it makes sense to password-protect console access, as well as Telnet and SSH access. To add basic password checking for the console and for Telnet, the engineer needs to configure a couple of basic commands. The configuration process is covered a little later in this chapter, but you can get a general idea of the commands by looking in the last column of Table 8-3. The table lists the two commands that configure the console and vty passwords. After it is configured, the switch supplies a simple password prompt (as a result of the **login** command), and the switch expects the user to enter the password listed in the **password** command.

Table 8-3 *CLI Password Configuration: Console and Telnet*

Access From	Password Type	Sample Configuration
Console	Console password	**line console 0** **login** **password faith**
Telnet	vty password	**line vty 0 15** **login** **password love**

Cisco switches refer to the console as a console line—specifically, console line 0. Similarly, switches support 16 concurrent Telnet sessions, referenced as virtual terminal (vty) lines 0 through 15. (The term vty refers to an old name for terminal emulators.) The **line vty 0 15** configuration command tells the switch that the commands that follow apply to all 16 possible concurrent virtual terminal connections to the switch, which includes Telnet as well as SSH access.

> **NOTE**   Some older versions of switch software supported only five vty lines, 0 through 4.

After adding the configuration shown in Table 8-3, a user connecting to the console would be prompted for a password, and he or she would have to supply the word **faith** in this case. New Telnet users would also be prompted for a password, with **love** being the required password. Also, with this configuration, no username is required—just a simple password.

Configuring SSH requires a little more effort than the console and Telnet password configuration examples shown in Table 8-3. SSH uses public key cryptography to exchange a shared session key, which in turn is used for encryption. Additionally, SSH requires slightly better login security, requiring at least a password and a username. The section "Configuring Usernames and Secure Shell (SSH)" in Chapter 9 shows the configuration steps and a sample configuration to support SSH.

User and Enable (Privileged) Modes

All three CLI access methods covered so far (console, Telnet, and SSH) place the user in an area of the CLI called *user EXEC mode*. User EXEC mode, sometimes also called *user mode*, allows the user to look around but not break anything. The "EXEC mode" part of the name refers to the fact that in this mode, when you enter a command, the switch executes the command and then displays messages that describe the command's results.

Cisco IOS supports a more powerful EXEC mode called *enable* mode (also known as *privileged* mode or *privileged EXEC* mode). Enable mode is so named because the **enable** command is used to reach this mode, as shown in Figure 8-6. Privileged mode earns its name because powerful, or privileged, commands can be executed there. For example, you can use the **reload** command, which tells the switch to reinitialize or reboot Cisco IOS, only from enable mode.

Figure 8-6 *User and Privileged Modes*

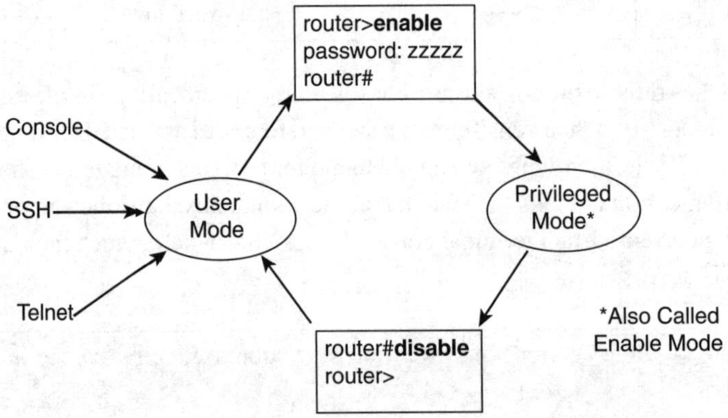

> **NOTE**   If the command prompt lists the hostname followed by a >, the user is in user mode; if it is the hostname followed by the #, the user is in enable mode.

The preferred configuration command for configuring the password for reaching enable mode is the **enable secret** *password* command, where *password* is the text of the password. Note that if the enable password is not configured (the default), Cisco IOS prevents Telnet and SSH users from getting into enable mode, but Cisco IOS does allow a console user to reach enable mode. This default action is consistent with the idea that, by default, users outside the locked room where the switch sits cannot get access without additional configuration by the engineer.

> **NOTE**   The commands that can be used in either user (EXEC) mode or enable (EXEC) mode are called EXEC commands.

So far, this chapter has pointed out some of the first things you should know when unpacking and installing a switch. The switch will work without any configuration—just plug in the power and Ethernet cables, and it works. However, you should at least connect to the switch console port and configure passwords for the console, Telnet, SSH, and the enable secret password.

Next, this chapter examines some of the CLI features that exist regardless of how you access the CLI.

CLI Help Features

If you printed the Cisco IOS Command Reference documents, you would end up with a stack of paper several feet tall. No one should expect to memorize all the commands—and no one does. You can use several very easy, convenient tools to help remember commands and save time typing. As you progress through your Cisco certifications, the exams will cover progressively more commands. However, you should know the methods of getting command help.

Table 8-4 summarizes command-recall help options available at the CLI. Note that, in the first column, *command* represents any command. Likewise, *parm* represents a command's parameter. For instance, the third row lists *command* **?**, which means that commands such as **show ?** and **copy ?** would list help for the **show** and **copy** commands, respectively.

Table 8-4 *Cisco IOS Software Command Help*

What You Enter	What Help You Get
?	Help for all commands available in this mode.
help	Text describing how to get help. No actual command help is given.
command **?**	Text help describing all the first parameter options for the command.
com?	A list of commands that start with **com**.
*command parm***?**	This style of help lists all parameters beginning with **parm**. (Notice that there is no space between *parm* and the **?**.)
command parm<Tab>	If you press the Tab key midword, the CLI either spells the rest of this parameter at the command line or does nothing. If the CLI does nothing, it means that this string of characters represents more than one possible next parameter, so the CLI does not know which one to spell out.
command parm1 **?**	If a space is inserted before the question mark, the CLI lists all the next parameters and gives a brief explanation of each.

When you enter the **?**, the Cisco IOS CLI reacts immediately; that is, you don't need to press the Enter key or any other keys. The device running Cisco IOS also redisplays what you entered before the **?** to save you some keystrokes. If you press Enter immediately after the **?**, Cisco IOS tries to execute the command with only the parameters you have entered so far.

command represents any command, not the word *command*. Likewise, *parm* represents a command's parameter, not the word *parameter*.

The information supplied by using help depends on the CLI mode. For example, when **?** is entered in user mode, the commands allowed in user mode are displayed, but commands available only in enable mode (not in user mode) are not displayed. Also, help is available in configuration mode, which is the mode used to configure the switch. In fact, configuration mode has many different subconfiguration modes, as explained in the section "Configuration Submodes and Contexts." So, you can get help for the commands available in each configuration submode as well.

Cisco IOS stores the commands that you enter in a history buffer, storing ten commands by default. The CLI allows you to move backward and forward in the historical list of commands and then edit the command before reissuing it. These key sequences can help you use the CLI more quickly on the exams. Table 8-5 lists the commands used to manipulate previously entered commands.

Table 8-5 *Key Sequences for Command Edit and Recall*

Keyboard Command	What Happens
Up arrow or Ctrl-p	This displays the most recently used command. If you press it again, the next most recent command appears, until the history buffer is exhausted. (The p stands for previous.)
Down arrow or Ctrl-n	If you have gone too far back into the history buffer, these keys take you forward to the more recently entered commands. (The n stands for next.)
Left arrow or Ctrl-b	This moves the cursor backward in the currently displayed command without deleting characters. (The b stands for back.)
Right arrow or Ctrl-f	This moves the cursor forward in the currently displayed command without deleting characters. (The f stands for forward.)
Backspace	This moves the cursor backward in the currently displayed command, deleting characters.
Ctrl-a	This moves the cursor directly to the first character of the currently displayed command.
Ctrl-e	This moves the cursor directly to the end of the currently displayed command.
Ctrl-r	This redisplays the command line with all characters. It's useful when messages clutter the screen.
Ctrl-d	This deletes a single character.
Esc-b	This moves back one word.
Esc-f	This moves forward one word.

The debug and show Commands

By far, the single most popular Cisco IOS command is the **show** command. The **show** command has a large variety of options, and with those options, you can find the status of almost every feature of Cisco IOS. Essentially, the **show** command lists the currently known facts about the switch's operational status. The only work the switch does in reaction to **show** commands is to find the current status and list the information in messages sent to the user.

A less popular command is the **debug** command. Like the **show** command, **debug** has many options. However, instead of just listing messages about the current status, the **debug** command asks the switch to continue monitoring different processes in the switch. The switch then sends ongoing messages to the user when different events occur.

The effects of the **show** and **debug** commands can be compared to a photograph and a movie. Like a photo, a **show** command shows what's true at a single point in time, and it takes little effort. The **debug** command shows what's true over time, but it requires more effort. As a result, the **debug** command requires more CPU cycles, but it lets you watch what is happening in a switch while it is happening.

Cisco IOS handles the messages created with the **debug** command much differently than with the **show** command. When any user issues a **debug** command, the debug options in the command are enabled. The messages Cisco IOS creates in response to all **debug** commands, regardless of which user(s) issued the **debug** commands, are treated as a special type of message called a *log message*. Any remote user can view log messages by simply using the **terminal monitor** command. Additionally, these log messages also appear at the console automatically. So, whereas the **show** command lists a set of messages for that single user, the **debug** command lists messages for all interested users to see, requiring remote users to ask to view the **debug** and other log messages.

The options enabled by a single **debug** command are not disabled until the user takes action or until the switch is reloaded. A **reload** of the switch disables all currently enabled debug options. To disable a single debug option, repeat the same **debug** command with those options, prefaced by the word **no**. For example, if the **debug spanning-tree** command was been issued earlier, issue the **no debug spanning-tree** command to disable that same debug. Also, the **no debug all** and **undebug all** commands disable all currently enabled debugs.

Be aware that some **debug** options create so many messages that Cisco IOS cannot process them all, possibly resulting in a crash of Cisco IOS. You might want to check the current switch CPU utilization with the **show process** command before issuing any **debug** command. To be more careful, before enabling an unfamiliar **debug** command option, issue a **no debug all** command, and then issue the **debug** that you want to use. Then quickly retrieve the **no debug all** command using the up arrow or Ctrl-p key sequence twice. If the debug quickly degrades switch performance, the switch may be too busy to listen to what you are typing. The process described in this paragraph saves a bit of typing and may be the difference between preventing the switch from failing, or not.

Configuring Cisco IOS Software

You must understand how to configure a Cisco switch to succeed on the exam and in real networking jobs. This section covers the basic configuration processes, including the concept of a configuration file and the locations in which the configuration files can be stored. Although this section focuses on the configuration process, and not on the configuration commands themselves, you should know all the commands covered in this chapter for the exams, in addition to the configuration processes.

Configuration mode is another mode for the Cisco CLI, similar to user mode and privileged mode. User mode lets you issue nondisruptive commands and displays some information. Privileged mode supports a superset of commands compared to user mode, including commands that might harm the switch. However, none of the commands in user or privileged mode changes the switch's configuration. Configuration mode accepts *configuration commands*—commands that tell the switch the details of what to do, and how to do it. Figure 8-7 illustrates the relationships among configuration mode, user EXEC mode, and privileged EXEC mode.

Figure 8-7 *CLI Configuration Mode Versus Exec Modes*

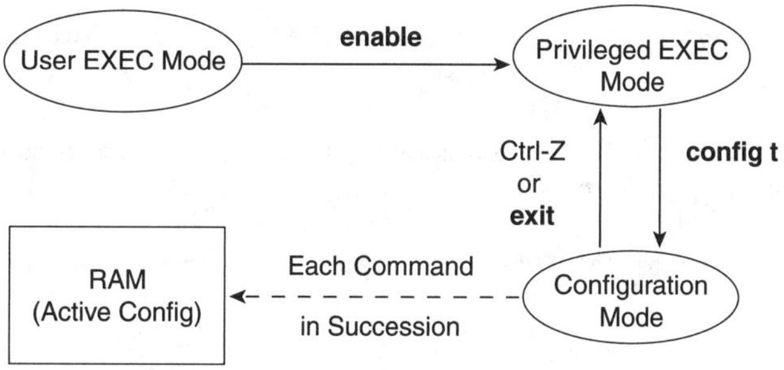

Commands entered in configuration mode update the active configuration file. *These changes to the configuration occur immediately each time you press the Enter key at the end of a command.* Be careful when you enter a configuration command!

Configuration Submodes and Contexts

Configuration mode itself contains a multitude of subcommand modes. *Context-setting commands* move you from one configuration subcommand mode, or context, to another. These context-setting commands tell the switch the topic about which you will enter the next few configuration commands. More importantly, the context tells the switch the topic you care about right now, so when you use the **?** to get help, the switch gives you help about that topic only.

> **NOTE**   Context setting is not a Cisco term—it's just a term used here to help make sense of configuration mode.

The **interface** command is one of the most commonly used context-setting configuration commands. For example, the CLI user could enter interface configuration mode by entering the **interface FastEthernet 0/1** configuration command. Asking for help in interface configuration mode displays only commands that are useful when configuring Ethernet interfaces. Commands used in this context are called *subcommands*—or, in this specific case, *interface subcommands*. When you begin practicing with the CLI with real equipment, the navigation between modes can become natural. For now, consider Example 8-1, which shows the following:

- Movement from enable mode to global configuration mode by using the **configure terminal** EXEC command

- Using a **hostname Fred** global configuration command to configure the switch's name

- Movement from global configuration mode to console line configuration mode (using the **line console 0** command)

- Setting the console's simple password to **hope** (using the **password hope** line subcommand)

- Movement from console configuration mode to interface configuration mode (using the **interface** command)

- Setting the speed to 100 Mbps for interface Fa0/1 (using the **speed 100** interface subcommand)

- Movement from console line configuration mode back to global configuration mode (using the **exit** command)

Example 8-1 *Navigating Between Different Configuration Modes*

```
Switch#configure terminal
Switch(config)#hostname Fred
Fred(config)#line console 0
Fred(config-line)#password hope
Fred(config-line)#interface FastEthernet 0/1
Fred(config-if)#speed 100
Fred(config-if)#exit
Fred(config)#
```

The text inside parentheses in the command prompt identifies the configuration mode. For example, the first command prompt after you enter configuration mode lists (config), meaning global configuration mode. After the **line console 0** command, the text expands to (config-line), meaning line configuration mode. Table 8-6 shows the most common command prompts in configuration mode, the names of those modes, and the context setting commands used to reach those modes.

Table 8-6 *Common Switch Configuration Modes*

Prompt	Name of Mode	Context-setting Command(s) to Reach This Mode
hostname(config)#	Global	None—first mode after **configure terminal**
hostname(config-line)#	Line	**line console 0** **line vty 0 15**
hostname(config-if)#	Interface	**interface** *type number*

No set rules exist for what commands are global commands or subcommands. Generally, however, when multiple instances of a parameter can be set in a single switch, the command used to set the parameter is likely a configuration subcommand. Items that are set once for the entire switch are likely global commands. For example, the **hostname** command is a global command because there is only one hostname per switch. Conversely, the **duplex** command is an interface subcommand to allow the switch to use a different setting on the different interfaces.

Both the Ctrl-z key sequence and the **end** command exit the user from any part of configuration mode and go back to privileged EXEC mode. Alternatively, the **exit** command backs you out of configuration mode one subconfiguration mode at a time.

Storing Switch Configuration Files

When you configure a switch, it needs to use the configuration. It also needs to be able to retain the configuration in case the switch loses power. Cisco switches contain Random Access Memory (RAM) to store data while Cisco IOS is using it, but RAM loses its contents when the switch loses power. To store information that must be retained when the switch loses power, Cisco switches use several types of more permanent memory, none of which has any moving parts. By avoiding components with moving parts (such as traditional disk drives), switches can maintain better uptime and availability.

The following list details the four main types of memory found in Cisco switches, as well as the most common use of each type.

- **RAM:** Sometimes called DRAM for Dynamic Random-Access Memory, RAM is used by the switch just as it is used by any other computer: for working storage. The running (active) configuration file is stored here.

- **ROM:** Read-Only Memory (ROM) stores a bootstrap (or boothelper) program that is loaded when the switch first powers on. This bootstrap program then finds the full Cisco IOS image and manages the process of loading Cisco IOS into RAM, at which point Cisco IOS takes over operation of the switch.

- **Flash memory:** Either a chip inside the switch or a removable memory card, Flash memory stores fully functional Cisco IOS images and is the default location where the switch gets its Cisco IOS at boot time. Flash memory also can be used to store any other files, including backup copies of configuration files.

- **NVRAM:** Nonvolatile RAM (NVRAM) stores the initial or startup configuration file that is used when the switch is first powered on and when the switch is reloaded.

Figure 8-8 summarizes this same information in a briefer and more convenient form for memorization and study.

Figure 8-8 *Cisco Switch Memory Types*

RAM	**Flash**	**ROM**	**NVRAM**
(Working Memory and Running Configuration)	(Cisco IOS Software)	(Bootstrap Program)	(Startup Configuration)

Cisco IOS stores the collection of configuration commands in a *configuration file*. In fact, switches use multiple configuration files—one file for the initial configuration used when powering on, and another configuration file for the active, currently used running configuration as stored in RAM. Table 8-7 lists the names of these two files, their purpose, and their storage location.

Table 8-7 *Names and Purposes of the Two Main Cisco IOS Configuration Files*

Configuration Filename	Purpose	Where It Is Stored
Startup-config	Stores the initial configuration used any time the switch reloads Cisco IOS.	NVRAM
Running-config	Stores the currently used configuration commands. This file changes dynamically when someone enters commands in configuration mode.	RAM

Essentially, when you use configuration mode, you change only the running-config file. This means that the configuration example earlier in this chapter (Example 8-1) updates only the running-config file. However, if the switch lost power right after that example, all that configuration would be lost. If you want to keep that configuration, you have to copy the running-config file into NVRAM, overwriting the old startup-config file.

Example 8-2 demonstrates that commands used in configuration mode change only the running configuration in RAM. The example shows the following concepts and steps:

Step 1   The original **hostname** command on the switch, with the startup-config file matching the running-config file.

Step 2   The **hostname** command changes the hostname, but only in the running-config file.

Step 3   The **show running-config** and **show startup-config** commands are shown, with only the hostname commands displayed for brevity, to make the point that the two configuration files are now different.

Example 8-2   *How Configuration Mode Commands Change the Running-config File, not the Startup-config File*

```
! Step 1 next (two commands)
!
hannah#show running-config
! (lines omitted)
hostname hannah
! (rest of lines omitted)

hannah#show startup-config
! (lines omitted)
hostname hannah
! (rest of lines omitted)
! Step 2 next. Notice that the command prompt changes immediately after
! the hostname command.
!hannah#configure terminal
hannah(config)#hostname jessie
jessie(config)#exit
! Step 3 next (two commands)
!
jessie#show running-config
! (lines omitted)
hostname jessie
! (rest of lines omitted - notice that the running configuration reflects the
!  changed hostname)
jessie# show startup-config
! (lines omitted)
hostname hannah
! (rest of lines omitted - notice that the changed configuration is not
! shown in the startup config)
```

NOTE Cisco uses the term *reload* to refer to what most PC operating systems call rebooting or restarting. In each case, it is a reinitialization of the software. The **reload** exec command causes a switch to reload.

Copying and Erasing Configuration Files

If you reload the switch at the end of Example 8-2, the hostname reverts to Hannah, because the running-config file has not been copied into the startup-config file. However, if you want to keep the new hostname of jessie, you would use the command **copy running-config startup-config**, which overwrites the current startup-config file with what is currently in the running configuration file. The **copy** command can be used to copy files in a switch, most typically a configuration file or a new version of Cisco IOS Software. The most basic method for moving configuration files in and out of a switch is to use the **copy** command to copy files between RAM or NVRAM on a switch and a TFTP server. The files can be copied between any pair, as shown in Figure 8-9.

Figure 8-9 *Locations for Copying and Results from Copy Operations*

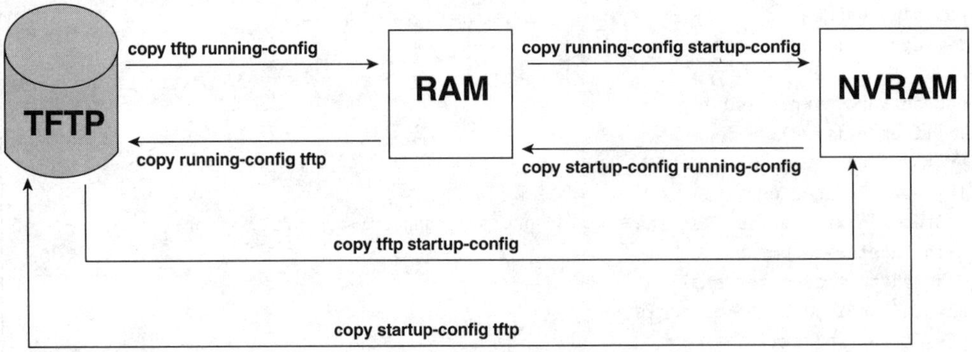

The commands for copying Cisco IOS configurations can be summarized as follows:

```
copy {tftp | running-config | startup-config} {tftp | running-config | startup-config}
```
The first set of parameters enclosed in braces ({}) is the "from" location; the next set of parameters is the "to" location.

The **copy** command always replaces the existing file when the file is copied into NVRAM or into a TFTP server. In other words, it acts as if the destination file was erased and the new file completely replaced the old one. However, when the **copy** command copies a configuration file into the running-config file in RAM, the configuration file in RAM is not replaced, but is merged instead. Effectively, any **copy** into RAM works just as if you entered the commands in the "from" configuration file in the order listed in the config file.

Who cares? Well, we do. If you change the running config and then decide that you want to revert to what's in the startup-config file, the result of the **copy startup-config running-config** command may not cause the two files to actually match. The only way to guarantee that the two configuration files match is to issue the **reload** command, which reloads, or reboots, the switch, which erases RAM and then copies the startup-config into RAM as part of the reload process.

You can use three different commands to erase the contents of NVRAM. The **write erase** and **erase startup-config** commands are older, whereas the **erase nvram:** command is the more recent, and recommended, command. All three commands simply erase the contents of the NVRAM configuration file. Of course, if the switch is reloaded at this point, there is no initial configuration. Note that Cisco IOS does not have a command that erases the contents of the running-config file. To clear out the running-config file, simply erase the startup-config file, and then **reload** the switch.

> **NOTE**   Making a copy of all current switch and router configurations should be part of any network's overall security strategy, mainly so that you can replace a device's configuration if an attack changes the configuration.

Although startup-config and running-config are the most common names for the two configuration files, Cisco IOS defines a few other more formalized names for these files. These more formalized filenames use a format defined by the *Cisco IOS File System* (IFS), which is the name of the file system created by Cisco IOS to manage files. For example, the **copy** command can refer to the startup-config file as nvram:startup-config. Table 8-8 lists the alternative names for these two configuration files.

Table 8-8   *IFS Filenames for the Startup and Running Config Files*

Config File Common Name	Alternative Names
startup-config	nvram: nvram:startup-config
running-config	system:running-config

Initial Configuration (Setup Mode)

Cisco IOS Software supports two primary methods of giving a switch an initial basic configuration—configuration mode, which has already been covered in this chapter, and setup mode. Setup mode leads a switch administrator to a basic switch configuration by using questions that prompt the administrator for basic configuration parameters. Because configuration mode is required for most configuration tasks, most networking personnel do not use setup at all. However, new users sometimes like to use setup mode, particularly until they become more familiar with the CLI configuration mode.

Figure 8-10 and Example 8-3 describe the process used by setup mode. Setup mode is used most frequently when the switch boots, and it has no configuration in NVRAM. You can also enter setup mode by using the **setup** command from privileged mode.

Figure 8-10   *Getting into Setup Mode*

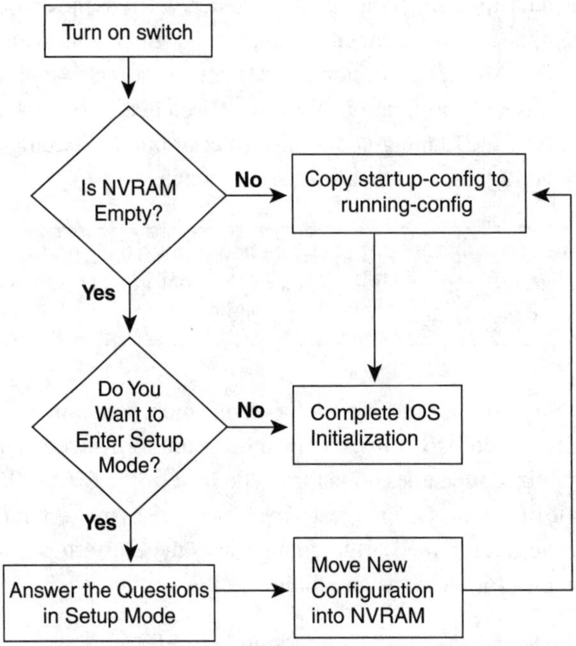

Example 8-3   *Initial Configuration Dialog Example*

```
--- System Configuration Dialog ---

Would you like to enter the initial configuration dialog? [yes/no]: yes

At any point you may enter a question mark '?' for help.
Use ctrl-c to abort configuration dialog at any prompt.
Default settings are in square brackets '[]'.


Basic management setup configures only enough connectivity
for management of the system, extended setup will ask you
```

Example 8-3 *Initial Configuration Dialog Example (Continued)*

```
to configure each interface on the system

Would you like to enter basic management setup? [yes/no]: yes
Configuring global parameters:

  Enter host name [Switch]: fred

  The enable secret is a password used to protect access to
  privileged EXEC and configuration modes. This password, after
  entered, becomes encrypted in the configuration.
  Enter enable secret: cisco

  The enable password is used when you do not specify an
  enable secret password, with some older software versions, and
  some boot images.
  Enter enable password: notcisco

  The virtual terminal password is used to protect
  access to the switch over a network interface.
  Enter virtual terminal password: wilma
  Configure SNMP Network Management? [no]:

Current interface summary

Any interface listed with OK? value "NO" does not have a valid configuration

Interface                IP-Address       OK? Method Status        Protocol
Vlan1                    unassigned       NO  unset  up            up
FastEthernet0/1          unassigned       YES unset  up            up
FastEthernet0/2          unassigned       YES unset  up            up
FastEthernet0/3          unassigned       YES unset  up            up
!
!Lines ommitted for brevity
!
GigabitEthernet0/1       unassigned       YES unset  down          down
GigabitEthernet0/2       unassigned       YES unset  down          down

The following configuration command script was created:

hostname fred
enable secret 5 $1$wNE7$4JSktD3uN1Af5FpctmPz11
enable password notcisco
line vty 0 15
password wilma
no snmp-server
```

continues

Example 8-3 *Initial Configuration Dialog Example (Continued)*

```
!
!
interface Vlan1
shutdown
no ip address
!
interface FastEthernet0/1
!
interface FastEthernet0/2
!
interface FastEthernet0/3
!
interface FastEthernet0/4
!
interface FastEthernet0/5
!
! Lines ommitted for brevity
!
interface GigabitEthernet0/1
!
interface GigabitEthernet0/2
!
end


[0] Go to the IOS command prompt without saving this config.
[1] Return back to the setup without saving this config.
[2] Save this configuration to nvram and exit.

Enter your selection [2]: 2
Building configuration...
[OK]

Use the enabled mode 'configure' command to modify this configuration.
Press RETURN to get started!
```

Setup behaves as shown in Example 8-3, regardless of whether Setup was reached by booting with an empty NVRAM or whether the **setup** privileged EXEC command was used. First, the switch asks whether you want to enter the initial configuration dialog. Answering **y** or **yes** puts you in setup mode. At that point, the switch keeps asking questions, and you keep answering, until you have answered all the setup questions.

When you are finished answering the configuration questions, the switch asks you to choose from one of three options:

0: Do not save any of this configuration, and go to the CLI command prompt.

1: Do not save any of this configuration, but start over in setup mode.

2: Save the configuration in both the startup-config and the running-config, and go to the CLI command prompt.

You can also abort the setup process before answering all the questions, and get to a CLI prompt, by pressing **Ctrl-C**. Note that answer **2** actually writes the configuration to both the startup-config and running-config file, whereas configuration mode changes only the running-config file.

Exam Preparation Tasks

Review All the Key Topics

Key Topic

Review the most important topics from this chapter, noted with the key topics icon. Table 8-9 lists these key topics and where each is discussed.

Table 8-9 *Key Topics for Chapter 8*

Key Topic Element	Description	Page Number
List	A Cisco switch's default console port settings	207
Table 8-6	A list of configuration mode prompts, the name of the configuration mode, and the command used to reach each mode	217
Figure 8-8	Types of memory in a switch	218
Table 8-7	The names and purposes of the two configuration files in a switch or router	218

Complete the Tables and Lists from Memory

Print a copy of Appendix H, "Memory Tables" (found on the CD), or at least the section for this chapter, and complete the tables and lists from memory. Appendix I, "Memory Tables Answer Key," also on the CD, includes completed tables and lists for you to check your work.

Definitions of Key Terms

Define the following key terms from this chapter and check your answers in the glossary:

command-line interface (CLI), Secure Shell (SSH), enable mode, user mode, configuration mode, startup-config file, running-config file, setup mode

Command References

Table 8-10 lists and briefly describes the configuration commands used in this chapter.

Table 8-10 *Chapter 8 Configuration Commands*

Command	Mode and Purpose
line console 0	Global command that changes the context to console configuration mode.
line vty *1st-vty 2nd-vty*	Global command that changes the context to vty configuration mode for the range of vty lines listed in the command.
login	Line (console and vty) configuration mode. Tells IOS to prompt for a password (no username).
password *pass-value*	Line (console and vty) configuration mode. Lists the password required if the **login** command (with no other parameters) is configured.
interface *type port-number*	Global command that changes the context to interface mode—for example, interface Fastethernet 0/1.
shutdown **no shutdown**	Interface subcommand that disables or enables the interface, respectively.
hostname *name*	Global command that sets this switch's hostname, which is also used as the first part of the switch's command prompt.
enable secret *pass-value*	Global command that sets the automatically encrypted enable secret password. The password is used for any user to reach enable mode.
enable password *pass-value*	Global command that sets the clear-text enable password, which is used only when the enable secret password is not configured.
exit	Moves back to the next higher mode in configuration mode.
end	Exits configuration mode and goes back to enable mode from any of the configuration submodes.
Ctrl-Z	This is not a command, but rather a two-key combination (the Ctrl key and the letter z) that together do the same thing as the **end** command.

Table 8-11 lists and briefly describes the EXEC commands used in this chapter.

Table 8-11 *Chapter 8 EXEC Command Reference*

Command	Purpose
no debug all **undebug all**	Enable mode EXEC command to disable all currently enabled debugs.
show process	EXEC command that lists statistics about CPU utilization.
terminal monitor	EXEC command that tells Cisco IOS to send a copy of all syslog messages, including debug messages, to the Telnet or SSH user who issues this command.
reload	Enable mode EXEC command that reboots the switch or router.
copy *from-location to-location*	Enable mode EXEC command that copies files from one file location to another. Locations include the startup-config and running-config files, files on TFTP and RPC servers, and flash memory.
copy running-config startup-config	Enable mode EXEC command that saves the active config, replacing the startup-config file used when the switch initializes.
copy startup-config running-config	Enable mode EXEC command that merges the startup config file with the currently active config file in RAM.
show running-config	Lists the contents of the running-config file.
write erase **erase startup-config** **erase nvram:**	All three enable mode EXEC commands erase the startup-config file.
setup	Enable mode EXEC command that places the user in setup mode, in which Cisco IOS asks the user for input on simple switch configurations.
quit	EXEC command that disconnects the user from the CLI session.
show system:running-config	Same as the **show running-config** command.
show startup-config	Lists the contents of the startup-config (initial config) file.

Table 8-11 *Chapter 8 EXEC Command Reference (Continued)*

Command	Purpose
show nvram:startup-config **show nvram:**	Same as the **show startup-config** command.
enable	Moves the user from user mode to enable (privileged) mode and prompts for an enable password if configured.
disable	Moves the user from enable mode to user mode.
configure terminal	Enable mode command that moves the user into configuration mode.

This chapter covers the following subjects:

Configuration Features in Common with Routers: This section explains how to configure a variety of switch features that happen to be configured exactly like the same feature on Cisco routers.

LAN Switch Configuration and Operation: This section explains how to configure a variety of switch features that happen to be unique to switches, and are not used on routers, or are configured differently than the configuration on Cisco routers.

CHAPTER 9

Ethernet Switch Configuration

Chapter 3, "Fundamentals of LANs," and Chapter 7, "Ethernet LAN Switching Concepts," have already explained the most common Ethernet LAN concepts. Those chapters explained how Ethernet cabling and switches work, including the concepts of how switches forward Ethernet frames based on the frames' destination MAC addresses.

Cisco LAN switches perform their core functions without any configuration. You can buy a Cisco switch, plug in the right cables to connect various devices to the switch, plug in the power cable, and the switch works. However, in most networks, the network engineer needs to configure and troubleshoot various switch features. This chapter explains how to configure various switch features, and Chapter 10, "Ethernet Switch Troubleshooting," explains how to troubleshoot problems on Cisco switches.

"Do I Know This Already?" Quiz

The "Do I Know This Already?" quiz allows you to assess whether you should read the entire chapter. If you miss no more than one of these eight self-assessment questions, you might want to move ahead to the "Exam Preparation Tasks" section. Table 9-1 lists the major headings in this chapter and the "Do I Know This Already?" quiz questions covering the material in those sections. This helps you assess your knowledge of these specific areas. The answers to the "Do I Know This Already?" quiz appear in Appendix A.

Table 9-1 *"Do I Know This Already?" Foundation Topics Section-to-Question Mapping*

Foundation Topics Section	Questions
Configuration of Features in Common with Routers	1–3
LAN Switch Configuration and Operation	4–8

1. Imagine that you have configured the **enable secret** command, followed by the **enable password** command, from the console. You log out of the switch and log back in at the console. Which command defines the password that you had to enter to access privileged mode?

   a. **enable password**

   b. **enable secret**

   c. Neither

   d. The **password** command, if it's configured

2. An engineer had formerly configured a Cisco 2960 switch to allow Telnet access so that the switch expected a password of **mypassword** from the Telnet user. The engineer then changed the configuration to support Secure Shell. Which of the following commands could have been part of the new configuration?

   a. A **username** *name* **password** *password* command in vty config mode

   b. A **username** *name* **password** *password* global configuration command

   c. A **transport input ssh** command in vty config mode

   d. A **transport input ssh** global configuration command

3. The following command was copied and pasted into configuration mode when a user was telnetted into a Cisco switch:

   ```
   banner login this is the login banner
   ```

   Which of the following are true about what occurs the next time a user logs in from the console?

   a. No banner text is displayed.

   b. The banner text "his is" is displayed.

   c. The banner text "this is the login banner" is displayed.

   d. The banner text "Login banner configured, no text defined" is displayed.

4. Which of the following is not required when configuring port security without sticky learning?

   a. Setting the maximum number of allowed MAC addresses on the interface with the **switchport port-security maximum** interface subcommand

   b. Enabling port security with the **switchport port-security** interface subcommand

   c. Defining the allowed MAC addresses using the **switchport port-security mac-address** interface subcommand

   d. All of the other answers list required commands

5. An engineer's desktop PC connects to a switch at the main site. A router at the main site connects to each branch office via a serial link, with one small router and switch at each branch. Which of the following commands must be configured, in the listed configuration mode, to allow the engineer to telnet to the branch office switches?

   a. The **ip address** command in VLAN 1 configuration mode

   b. The **ip address** command in global configuration mode

   c. The **ip default-gateway** command in VLAN 1 configuration mode

   d. The **ip default-gateway** command in global configuration mode

   e. The **password** command in console line configuration mode

   f. The **password** command in vty line configuration mode

6. Which of the following describes a way to disable IEEE standard autonegotiation on a 10/100 port on a Cisco switch?

   a. Configure the **negotiate disable** interface subcommand

   b. Configure the **no negotiate** interface subcommand

   c. Configure the **speed 100** interface subcommand

   d. Configure the **duplex half** interface subcommand

   e. Configure the **duplex full** interface subcommand

   f. Configure the **speed 100** and **duplex full** interface subcommands

7. In which of the following modes of the CLI could you configure the duplex setting for interface fastethernet 0/5?

   a. User mode

   b. Enable mode

   c. Global configuration mode

   d. Setup mode

   e. Interface configuration mode

8. The **show vlan brief** command lists the following output:

```
2    my-vlan                      active    Fa0/13, Fa0/15
```

Which of the following commands could have been used as part of the configuration for this switch?

a. The **vlan 2** global configuration command

b. The **name MY-VLAN** vlan subcommand

c. The **interface range Fa0/13 - 15** global configuration command

d. The **switchport vlan 2** interface subcommand

Foundation Topics

Many Cisco Catalyst switches use the same Cisco IOS Software command-line interface (CLI) as Cisco routers. In addition to having the same look and feel, the switches and routers sometimes support the exact same configuration and **show** commands. Additionally, as mentioned in Chapter 8, some of the same commands and processes shown for Cisco switches work the same way for Cisco routers.

This chapter explains a wide variety of configurable items on Cisco switches. Some topics are relatively important, such as the configuration of usernames and passwords so that any remote access to a switch is secure. Some topics are relatively unimportant, but useful, such as the ability to assign a text description to an interface for documentation purposes. However, this chapter does contain the majority of the switch configuration topics for this book, with the exception of Cisco Discovery Protocol (CDP) configuration commands in Chapter 10.

Configuration of Features in Common with Routers

This first of the two major sections of this chapter examines the configuration of several features that are configured the exact same way on both switches and routers. In particular, this section examines how to secure access to the CLI, plus various settings for the console.

Securing the Switch CLI

To reach a switch's enable mode, a user must reach user mode either from the console or from a Telnet or SSH session, and then use the **enable** command. With default configuration settings, a user at the console does not need to supply a password to reach user mode or enable mode. The reason is that anyone with physical access to the switch or router console could reset the passwords in less than 5 minutes by using the password recovery procedures that Cisco publishes. So, routers and switches default to allow the console user access to enable mode.

> **NOTE**   To see the password recovery/reset procedures, go to Cisco.com and search on the phrase "password recovery." The first listed item probably will be a web page with password recovery details for most every product made by Cisco.

To reach enable mode from a vty (Telnet or SSH), the switch must be configured with several items:

■ An IP address

■ Login security on the vty lines

■ An enable password

Most network engineers will want to be able to establish a Telnet or SSH connection to each switch, so it makes sense to configure the switches to allow secure access. Additionally, although someone with physical access to the switch can use the password recovery process to get access to the switch, it still makes sense to configure security even for access from the console.

This section examines most of the configuration details related to accessing enable mode on a switch or router. The one key topic not covered here is the IP address configuration, which is covered later in this chapter in the section "Configuring the Switch IP Address." In particular, this section covers the following topics:

■ Simple password security for the console and Telnet access

■ Secure Shell (SSH)

■ Password encryption

■ Enable mode passwords

Configuring Simple Password Security

An engineer can reach user mode in a Cisco switch or router from the console or via either Telnet or SSH. By default, switches and routers allow a console user to immediately access user mode after logging in, with no password required. With default settings, Telnet users are rejected when they try to access the switch, because a vty password has not yet been configured. Regardless of these defaults, it makes sense to password protect user mode for console, Telnet, and SSH users.

A user in user mode can gain access to enable mode by using the enable command, but with different defaults depending on whether the user is at the console or has logged in remotely using Telnet or SSH. By default, the **enable** command allows console users into enable mode without requiring a password, but Telnet users are rejected without even a chance to supply a password. Regardless of these defaults, it makes sense to password protect enable mode using the **enable secret** global configuration command.

> **NOTE**   The later section "The Two Enable Mode Passwords" explains two options for configuring the password required by the **enable** command, as configured with the **enable secret** and **enable password** commands, and why the **enable secret** command is preferred.

Example 9-1 shows a sample configuration process that sets the console password, the vty (Telnet) password, the enable secret password, and a hostname for the switch. The example shows the entire process, including command prompts, which provide some reminders of the different configuration modes explained in Chapter 8, "Operating Cisco LAN Switches."

Example 9-1 *Configuring Basic Passwords and a Hostname*

Key Topic

```
Switch>enable
Switch#configure terminal
Switch(config)#enable secret cisco
Switch(config)#hostname Emma
Emma(config)#line console 0
Emma(config-line)#password faith
Emma(config-line)#login
Emma(config-line)#exit
Emma(config)#line vty 0 15
Emma(config-line)#password love
Emma(config-line)#login
Emma(config-line)#exit
Emma(config)#exit
Emma#
! The next command lists the switch's current configuration (running-config)
Emma#show running-config
!
Building configuration...

Current configuration : 1333 bytes
!
version 12.2
no service pad
service timestamps debug uptime
service timestamps log uptime
!
hostname Emma
!
enable secret 5 $1$YXRN$11zOe1Lb0Lv/nHyTquobd.
```

continues

Key Topic

Example 9-1 *Configuring Basic Passwords and a Hostname (Continued)*

```
!
spanning-tree mode pvst
spanning-tree extend system-id
!
interface FastEthernet0/1
!
interface FastEthernet0/2
!
! Several lines have been omitted here - in particular, lines for FastEthernet
! interfaces 0/3 through 0/23.
!
interface FastEthernet0/24
!
interface GigabitEthernet0/1
!
interface GigabitEthernet0/2
!
interface Vlan1
 no ip address
 no ip route-cache
!
ip http server
ip http secure-server
!
control-plane
!
!
line con 0
 password faith
 login
line vty 0 4
 password love
 login
line vty 5 15
 password love
 login
```

Example 9-1 begins by showing the user moving from enable mode to configuration mode by using the **configure terminal** EXEC command. As soon as the user is in global configuration mode, he enters two global configuration commands (**enable secret** and **hostname**) that add configuration that applies to the whole switch.

For instance, the **hostname** global configuration command simply sets the one and only name for this switch (in addition to changing the switch's command prompt). The **enable secret** command sets the only password used to reach enable mode, so it is also a global command. However, the **login** command (which tells the switch to ask for a text password, but no username) and the **password** command (which defines the required password) are shown in both console and vty line configuration submodes. So, these commands are subcommands in these two different configuration modes. These subcommands define different console and vty passwords based on the configuration submodes in which the commands were used, as shown in the example.

Pressing the Ctrl-z key sequence from any part of configuration mode takes you all the way back to enable mode. However, the example shows how to repeatedly use the **exit** command to move back from a configuration submode to global configuration mode, with another **exit** command to exit back to enable mode. The **end** configuration mode command performs the same action as the Ctrl-z key sequence, moving the user from any part of configuration mode back to privileged EXEC mode.

The second half of Example 9-1 lists the output of the **show running-config** command. This command shows the currently used configuration in the switch, which includes the changes made earlier in the example. The output highlights in gray the configuration commands added due to the earlier configuration commands.

> **NOTE**   The output of the **show running-config** command lists five vty lines (0 through 4) in a different location than the rest (5 through 15). In earlier IOS releases, Cisco IOS routers and switches had five vty lines, numbered 0 through 4, which allowed five concurrent Telnet connects to a switch or router. Later, Cisco added more vty lines (5 through 15), allowing 16 concurrent Telnet connections into each switch and router. That's why the command output lists the two vty line ranges separately.

Configuring Usernames and Secure Shell (SSH)

Telnet sends all data, including all passwords entered by the user, as clear text. The Secure Shell (SSH) application provides the same function as Telnet, displaying a terminal emulator window and allowing the user to remotely connect to another host's CLI. However, SSH encrypts the data sent between the SSH client and the SSH server, making SSH the preferred method for remote login to switches and routers today.

To add support for SSH login to a Cisco switch or router, the switch needs several configuration commands. For example, SSH requires that the user supply both a username and password instead of just a password. So, the switch must be reconfigured to use one of two user authentication methods that require both a username and password: one method with the usernames and passwords configured on the switch, and the other with the usernames and passwords configured on an external server called an Authentication, Authorization, and Accounting (AAA) server. (This book covers the configuration using locally configured usernames/passwords.) Figure 9-1 shows a diagram of the configuration and process required to support SSH.

Figure 9-1   *SSH Configuration Concepts*

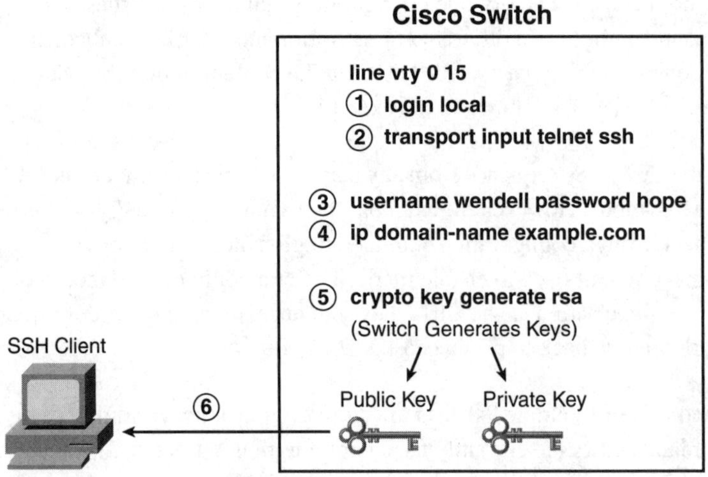

The steps in the figure, explained with the matching numbered list that follows, detail the required transactions before an SSH user can connect to the switch using SSH:

Step 1   Change the vty lines to use usernames, with either locally configured usernames or an AAA server. In this case, the **login local** subcommand defines the use of local usernames, replacing the **login** subcommand in vty configuration mode.

Step 2   Tell the switch to accept both Telnet and SSH with the **transport input telnet ssh** vty subcommand. (The default is **transport input telnet**, omitting the **ssh** parameter.)

Step 3   Add one or more **username** *name* **password** *pass-value* global configuration commands to configure username/password pairs.

Step 4   Configure a DNS domain name with the **ip domain-name** *name* global configuration command.

Step 5   Configure the switch to generate a matched public and private key pair, as well as a shared encryption key, using the **crypto key generate rsa** global configuration command.

Step 6   Although no switch commands are required, each SSH client needs a copy of the switch's public key before the client can connect.

NOTE   This book contains several step lists that refer to specific configuration steps, such as the one shown here for SSH. You do not need to memorize the steps for the exams; however, the lists can be useful for study—in particular, to help you remember all the required steps to configure a certain feature.

Example 9-2 shows the same switch commands shown in Figure 9-1, entered in configuration mode.

Example 9-2 *SSH Configuration Process*

```
Emma#
Emma#configure terminal
Enter configuration commands, one per line.  End with CNTL/Z.
Emma(config)#line vty 0 15
! Step 1's command happens next
Emma(config-line)#login local
! Step 2's command happens next
Emma(config-line)#transport input telnet ssh
Emma(config-line)#exit
! Step 3's command happens next
Emma(config)#username wendell password hope
! Step 4's command happens next
Emma(config)#ip domain-name example.com
! Step 5's command happens next
Emma(config)#crypto key generate rsa
The name for the keys will be: Emma.example.com
Choose the size of the key modulus in the range of 360 to 2048 for your
  General Purpose Keys. Choosing a key modulus greater than 512 may take
  a few minutes.

How many bits in the modulus [512]: 1024
% Generating 1024 bit RSA keys ...[OK]

00:03:58: %SSH-5-ENABLED: SSH 1.99 has been enabled
Emma(config)#^Z
! Next, the contents of the public key are listed; the key will be needed by the SSH
  client.
Emma#show crypto key mypubkey rsa
% Key pair was generated at: 00:03:58 UTC Mar 1 1993
Key name: Emma.example.com
 Usage: General Purpose Key
 Key is not exportable.
 Key Data:
  30819F30 0D06092A 864886F7 0D010101 05000381 8D003081 89028181 00DB43DC
  49C258FA 8E0B8EB2 0A6C8888 A00D29CE EAEE615B 456B68FD 491A9B63 B39A4334
  86F64E02 1B320256 01941831 7B7304A2 720A57DA FBB3E75A 94517901 7764C332
  A3A482B1 DB4F154E A84773B5 5337CE8C B1F5E832 8213EE6B 73B77006 BA8782DE
  180966D9 9A6476D7 C9164ECE 1DC752BB 955F5BDE F82BFCB2 A273C58C 8B020301 0001
% Key pair was generated at: 00:04:01 UTC Mar 1 1993
Key name: Emma.example.com.server
 Usage: Encryption Key
 Key is not exportable.
```

continues

Example 9-2 *SSH Configuration Process (Continued)*

```
Key Data:
  307C300D 06092A86 4886F70D 01010105 00036B00 30680261 00AC339C D4916728
  6ACB627E A5EE26A5 00946AF9 E63FF322 A2DB4994 9E37BFDA AB1C503E AAF69FB3
  2A22A5F3 0AA94454 B8242D72 A8582E7B 0642CF2B C06E0710 B0A06048 D90CBE9E
  F0B88179 EC1C5EAC D551109D 69E39160 86C50122 9A37E954 85020301 0001
```

The example shows a gray highlighted comment just before the configuration commands at each step. Also, note the public key created by the switch, listed in the highlighted portion of the output of the **show crypto key mypubkey rsa** command. Each SSH client needs a copy of this key, either by adding this key to the SSH client's configuration beforehand, or by letting the switch send this public key to the client when the SSH client first connects to the switch.

For even tighter security, you might want to disable Telnet access completely, requiring all the engineers to use SSH to remotely log in to the switch. To prevent Telnet access, use the **transport input ssh** line subcommand in vty configuration mode. If the command is given only the SSH option, the switch will no longer accept Telnet connections.

Password Encryption

Several of the configuration commands used to configure passwords store the passwords in clear text in the running-config file, at least by default. In particular, the simple passwords configured on the console and vty lines, with the **password** command, plus the password in the **username** command, are all stored in clear text by default. (The **enable secret** command automatically hides the password value.)

To prevent password vulnerability in a printed version of the configuration file, or in a backup copy of the configuration file stored on a server, you can encrypt or encode the passwords using the **service password-encryption** global configuration command. The presence or absence of the **service password-encryption** global configuration command dictates whether the passwords are encrypted as follows:

- When the **service password-encryption** command is configured, all existing console, vty, and **username** command passwords are immediately encrypted.

- If the **service password-encryption** command has already been configured, any future changes to these passwords are encrypted.

- If the **no service password-encryption** command is used later, the passwords remain encrypted, until they are changed—at which point they show up in clear text.

Example 9-3 shows an example of these details.

> **NOTE**   The **show running-config | begin line vty** command, as used in Example 9-3, lists the running configuration, beginning with the first line, which contains the text **line vty**. This is just a shorthand way to see a smaller part of the running configuration.

Example 9-3 *Encryption and the* **service password-encryption** *Command*

```
Switch3#show running-config | begin line vty
line vty 0 4
 password cisco
 login
Switch3#configure terminal
Enter configuration commands, one per line.  End with CNTL/Z.
Switch3(config)#service password-encryption
Switch3(config)#^Z
Switch3#show running-config | begin line vty
line vty 0 4
 password 7 070C285F4D06
 login
end
Switch3#configure terminal
Enter configuration commands, one per line.  End with CNTL/Z.
Switch3(config)#no service password-encryption
Switch3(config)#^Z
Switch3#show running-config | begin line vty
line vty 0 4
 password 7 070C285F4D06
 login
end
Switch3#configure terminal
Enter configuration commands, one per line.  End with CNTL/Z.
Switch3(config)#line vty 0 4
Switch3(config-line)#password cisco
Switch3(config-line)#^Z
Switch3#show running-config | begin line vty
line vty 0 4
 password cisco
 login
```

> **NOTE**   The encryption type used by the **service password-encryption** command, as noted with the "7" in the **password** commands, refers to one of several underlying password encryption algorithms. Type 7, the only type used by the **service password-encryption** command, is a weak encryption algorithm, and the passwords can be easily decrypted.

The Two Enable Mode Passwords

The **enable** command moves you from user EXEC mode (with a prompt of hostname>) to privileged EXEC mode (with a prompt of hostname#). A router or switch can be configured to require a password to reach enable mode according to the following rules:

Key
Topic

■   If the global configuration command **enable password** *actual-password* is used, it defines the password required when using the **enable** EXEC command. This password is listed as *clear text* in the configuration file by default.

■   If the global configuration command **enable secret** *actual-password* is used, it defines the password required when using the **enable** EXEC command. This password is listed as *a hidden MD5 hash value* in the configuration file.

■   If *both commands* are used, the password set in the **enable secret** command defines which password is required.

When the **enable secret** command is configured, the router or switch automatically hides the password. While it is sometimes referenced as being encrypted, the enable secret password is not actually encrypted. Instead, IOS applies a mathematical function to the password, called a Message Digest 5 (MD5) hash, storing the results of the formula in the configuration file. IOS references this style of encoding the password as type 5 in the output in Example 9-4. Note that the MD5 encoding is much more secure than the encryption used for other passwords with the **service password-encryption** command. The example shows the creation of the **enable secret** command, its format, and its deletion.

Example 9-4 *Encryption and the* **enable secret** *Command*

```
Switch3(config)#enable secret ?
  0      Specifies an UNENCRYPTED password will follow
  5      Specifies an ENCRYPTED secret will follow
  LINE   The UNENCRYPTED (cleartext) 'enable' secret
  level  Set exec level password

Switch3(config)#enable secret fred
Switch3(config)#^Z
Switch3#show running-config
! all except the pertinent line has been omitted!
enable secret 5 $1$ZGMA$e8cmvkz4UjiJhVp7.maLE1

Switch3#configure terminal
Enter configuration commands, one per line.  End with CNTL/Z.
Switch3(config)#no enable secret
Switch3(config)#^Z
```

When you use the (recommended) **enable secret** command, rather than the **enable password** command, the password is automatically encrypted. Example 9-4 uses the **enable secret fred** command, setting the password text to **fred**. However, the syntax **enable**

secret 0 fred could have been used, with the **0** implying that the password that followed was clear text. IOS then takes the command, applies the encryption type used by the **enable secret** command (type 5 in this case, which uses an MD5 hash), and stores the encrypted or encoded value in the running configuration. The **show running-configuration** command shows the resulting configuration command, listing encryption type 5, with the gobbledygook long text string being the encrypted/encoded password.

Thankfully, to delete the enable secret password, you can simply use the **no enable secret** command, without even having to enter the password value. For instance, in Example 9-4, the command **no enable secret** deletes the enable secret password. Although you can delete the enable secret password, more typically, you will want to change it to a new value, which can be done with the **enable secret** *another-password* command, with *another-password* simply meaning that you put in a new text string for the new password.

Console and vty Settings

This section covers a few small configuration settings that affect the behavior of the CLI connection from the console and/or vty (Telnet and SSH).

Banners

Cisco routers and switches can display a variety of banners depending on what a router or switch administrator is doing. A banner is simply some text that appears on the screen for the user. You can configure a router or switch to display multiple banners, some before login and some after. Table 9-2 lists the three most popular banners and their typical use.

Table 9-2 *Banners and Their Use*

Banner	Typical Use
Message of the Day (MOTD)	Shown before the login prompt. For temporary messages that may change from time to time, such as "Router1 down for maintenance at midnight."
Login	Shown before the login prompt but after the MOTD banner. For permanent messages such as "Unauthorized Access Prohibited."
Exec	Shown after the login prompt. Used to supply information that should be hidden from unauthorized users.

The **banner** global configuration command can be used to configure all three types of these banners. In each case, the type of banner is listed as the first parameter, with MOTD being the default option. The first nonblank character after the banner type is called a beginning delimiter character. The banner text can span several lines, with the CLI user pressing Enter at the end of each line. The CLI knows that the banner has been configured as soon as the user enters the same delimiter character again.

Example 9-5 shows all three types of banners from Table 9-2, with a user login that shows the banners in use. The first banner in the example, the MOTD banner, omits the banner type in the **banner** command as a reminder that **motd** is the default banner type. The first two **banner** commands use a # as the delimiter character. The third **banner** command uses a Z as the delimiter, just to show that any character can be used. Also, the last **banner** command shows multiple lines of banner text.

Example 9-5   *Banner Configuration*

```
! Below, the three banners are created in configuration mode. Note that any
! delimiter can be used, as long as the character is not part of the message
! text.
SW1(config)#banner #
Enter TEXT message.  End with the character '#'.
Switch down for maintenance at 11PM Today #
SW1(config)#banner login #
Enter TEXT message.  End with the character '#'.
Unauthorized Access Prohibited!!!!
#
SW1(config)#banner exec Z
Enter TEXT message.  End with the character 'Z'.
Company picnic at the park on Saturday
 Don't tell outsiders!
Z
SW1(config)#^Z
! Below, the user of this router quits the console connection, and logs back in,
! seeing the motd and login banners, then the password prompt, and then the
! exec banner.
SW1#quit

SW1 con0 is now available

Press RETURN to get started.

Switch down for maintenance at 11PM Today
Unauthorized Access Prohibited!!!!

User Access Verification

Username: fred
Password:
Company picnic at the park on Saturday
don't tell outsiders!
 SW1>
```

History Buffer Commands

When you enter commands from the CLI, the last several commands are saved in the history buffer. As mentioned in Chapter 8, you can use the up-arrow key, or Ctrl-p, to move back in the history buffer stack to retrieve a command you entered a few commands ago. This feature makes it very easy and fast to use a set of commands repeatedly. Table 9-3 lists some of the key commands related to the history buffer.

Table 9-3 *Commands Related to the History Buffer*

Command	Description
show history	Lists the commands currently held in the history buffer.
history size *x*	From console or vty line configuration mode, sets the default number of commands saved in the history buffer for the user(s) of the console or vty lines, respectively.
terminal history size *x*	From EXEC mode, this command allows a single user to set, just for this one connection, the size of his or her history buffer.

The logging synchronous and exec-timeout Commands

The console automatically receives copies of all unsolicited syslog messages on a switch or router; that feature cannot be disabled. The idea is that if the switch or router needs to tell the network administrator some important and possibly urgent information, the administrator may be at the console and may notice the message. Normally a switch or router puts these syslog messages on the console's screen at any time—including right in the middle of a command you are entering, or in the middle of the output of a **show** command.

To make using the console a little easier, you can tell the switch to display syslog messages only at more convenient times, such as at the end of output from a **show** command or to prevent the interruption of a command text input. To do so, just configure the **logging synchronous** console line subcommand.

You can also make using the console or vty lines more convenient by setting a different inactivity timeout on the console or vty. By default, the switch or router automatically disconnects users after 5 minutes of inactivity, for both console users and users who connect to vty lines using Telnet or SSH. When you configure the **exec-timeout** *minutes seconds* line subcommand, the switch or router can be told a different inactivity timer. Also, if you set the timeout to 0 minutes and 0 seconds, the router never times out the console connection. Example 9-6 shows the syntax for these two commands.

Example 9-6 *Defining Console Inactivity Timeouts and When to Display Log Messages*

```
line console 0
 login
 password cisco
 exec-timeout 0 0
 logging synchronous
```

LAN Switch Configuration and Operation

One of the most convenient facts about LAN switch configuration is that Cisco switches work without any configuration. Cisco switches ship from the factory with all interfaces enabled (a default configuration of **no shutdown**) and with autonegotiation enabled for ports that run at multiple speeds and duplex settings (a default configuration of **duplex auto** and **speed auto**). All you have to do is connect the Ethernet cables and plug in the power cord to a power outlet, and the switch is ready to work—learning MAC addresses, making forwarding/filtering decisions, and even using STP by default.

The second half of this chapter continues the coverage of switch configuration, mainly covering features that apply only to switches and not routers. In particular, this section covers the following:

■   Switch IP configuration

■   Interface configuration (including speed and duplex)

■   Port security

■   VLAN configuration

■   Securing unused switch interfaces

Configuring the Switch IP Address

To allow Telnet or SSH access to the switch, to allow other IP-based management protocols such as Simple Network Management Protocol (SNMP) to function as intended, or to allow access to the switch using graphical tools such as Cisco Device Manager (CDM), the switch needs an IP address. Switches do not need an IP address to be able to forward Ethernet frames. The need for an IP address is simply to support overhead management traffic, such as logging into the switch.

A switch's IP configuration essentially works like a host with a single Ethernet interface. The switch needs one IP address and a matching subnet mask. The switch also needs to know its default gateway—in other words, the IP address of some nearby router. As with hosts, you can statically configure a switch with its IP address/mask/gateway, or the switch can dynamically learn this information using DHCP.

An IOS-based switch configures its IP address and mask on a special virtual interface called the *VLAN 1 interface*. This interface plays the same role as an Ethernet interface on a PC. In effect, a switch's VLAN 1 interface gives the switch an interface into the default VLAN used on all ports of the switch—namely, VLAN 1. The following steps list the commands used to configure IP on a switch:

Step 1 Enter VLAN 1 configuration mode using the **interface vlan 1** global configuration command (from any config mode).

Step 2 Assign an IP address and mask using the **ip address** *ip-address mask* interface subcommand.

Step 3 Enable the VLAN 1 interface using the **no shutdown** interface subcommand.

Step 4 Add the **ip default-gateway** *ip-address* global command to configure the default gateway.

Example 9-7 shows a sample configuration.

Example 9-7 *Switch Static IP Address Configuration*

```
Emma#configure terminal
Emma(config)#interface vlan 1
Emma(config-if)#ip address 192.168.1.200 255.255.255.0
Emma(config-if)#no shutdown
00:25:07: %LINK-3-UPDOWN: Interface Vlan1, changed state to up
00:25:08: %LINEPROTO-5-UPDOWN: Line protocol on Interface Vlan1, changed
  state to up
Emma(config-if)#exit
Emma(config)#ip default-gateway 192.168.1.1
```

Of particular note, this example shows how to enable any interface, VLAN interfaces included. To administratively enable an interface on a switch or router, you use the **no shutdown** interface subcommand. To administratively disable an interface, you would use the **shutdown** interface subcommand. The messages shown in Example 9-7, immediately following the **no shutdown** command, are syslog messages generated by the switch stating that the switch did indeed enable the interface.

To verify the configuration, you can again use the **show running-config** command to view the configuration commands and confirm that you entered the right address, mask, and default gateway.

For the switch to act as a DHCP client to discover its IP address, mask, and default gateway, you still need to configure it. You use the same steps as for static configuration, with the following differences in Steps 2 and 4:

Step 2: Use the **ip address dhcp** command, instead of the **ip address** *ip-address mask* command, on the VLAN 1 interface.

Step 4: Do not configure the **ip default-gateway** global command.

Example 9-8 shows an example of configuring a switch to use DHCP to acquire an IP address.

Example 9-8   *Switch Dynamic IP Address Configuration with DHCP*

```
Emma#configure terminal
Enter configuration commands, one per line.  End with CNTL/Z.
Emma(config)#interface vlan 1
Emma(config-if)#ip address dhcp
Emma(config-if)#no shutdown
Emma(config-if)#^Z
Emma#
00:38:20: %LINK-3-UPDOWN: Interface Vlan1, changed state to up
00:38:21: %LINEPROTO-5-UPDOWN: Line protocol on Interface Vlan1, changed state to up
Emma#
Interface Vlan1 assigned DHCP address 192.168.1.101, mask 255.255.255.0
Emma#show dhcp lease
Temp IP addr: 192.168.1.101  for peer on Interface: Vlan1
Temp  sub net mask: 255.255.255.0
   DHCP Lease server: 192.168.1.1, state: 3 Bound
   DHCP transaction id: 1966
   Lease: 86400 secs,  Renewal: 43200 secs,  Rebind: 75600 secs
Temp default-gateway addr: 192.168.1.1
   Next timer fires after: 11:59:45
   Retry count: 0   Client-ID: cisco-0019.e86a.6fc0-Vl1
   Hostname: Emma
Emma#show interface vlan 1
Vlan1 is up, line protocol is up
  Hardware is EtherSVI, address is 0019.e86a.6fc0 (bia 0019.e86a.6fc0)
  Internet address is 192.168.1.101/24
  MTU 1500 bytes, BW 1000000 Kbit, DLY 10 usec,
     reliability 255/255, txload 1/255, rxload 1/255
! lines omitted for brevity
```

When configuring a static interface IP address, you can use the **show running-config** command to see the IP address. However, when using the DHCP client, the IP address is not in the configuration, so you need to use the **show dhcp lease** command to see the (temporarily) leased IP address and other parameters.

> **NOTE**   Some older models of Cisco IOS switches might not support the DHCP client function on the VLAN 1 interface. Example 9-8 was taken from a 2960 switch running Cisco IOS Software Release 12.2.

Finally, the output of the **show interface vlan 1** command, shown at the end of Example 9-8, lists two very important details related to switch IP addressing. First, this **show** command lists the interface status of the VLAN 1 interface—in this case, "up and up." If the VLAN 1 interface is not up, the switch cannot use its IP address to send and receive traffic. Notably, if you forget to issue the **no shutdown** command, the VLAN 1 interface remains in its default shutdown state and is listed as "administratively down" in the **show** command output. Second, note that the output lists the interface's IP address on the third line of the output. If the switch fails to acquire an IP address with DHCP, the output would instead list the fact that the address will (hopefully) be acquired by DHCP. As soon as an address has been leased using DHCP, the output of the command looks like Example 9-8. However, nothing in the **show interface vlan 1** command output mentions that the address is either statically configured or DHCP-leased.

Configuring Switch Interfaces

IOS uses the term *interface* to refer to physical ports used to forward data to and from other devices. Each interface may be configured with several settings, each of which might differ from interface to interface.

IOS uses interface subcommands to configure these settings. For instance, interfaces can be configured to use the **duplex** and **speed** interface subcommands to configure those settings statically, or an interface can use autonegotiation (the default). Example 9-9 shows how to configure duplex and speed, as well as the **description** command, which is simply a text description of what an interface does.

Example 9-9   *Interface Configuration Basics*

```
Emma#configure terminal
Enter configuration commands, one per line.  End with CNTL/Z.
Emma(config)#interface FastEthernet 0/1
Emma(config-if)#duplex full
Emma(config-if)#speed 100
Emma(config-if)#description Server1 connects here
Emma(config-if)#exit
Emma(config)#interface range FastEthernet 0/11 - 20
Emma(config-if-range)#description end-users connect_here
Emma(config-if-range)#^Z
Emma#
Emma#show interfaces status


Port     Name             Status       Vlan      Duplex  Speed Type
Fa0/1    Server1 connects h notconnect  1          full    100 10/100BaseTX
Fa0/2                      notconnect   1          auto   auto 10/100BaseTX
Fa0/3                      notconnect   1          auto   auto 10/100BaseTX
```
continues

Example 9-9 *Interface Configuration Basics (Continued)*

```
Fa0/4                          connected     1     a-full  a-100 10/100BaseTX
Fa0/5                          notconnect    1      auto    auto 10/100BaseTX
Fa0/6                          connected     1     a-full  a-100 10/100BaseTX
Fa0/7                          notconnect    1      auto    auto 10/100BaseTX
Fa0/8                          notconnect    1      auto    auto 10/100BaseTX
Fa0/9                          notconnect    1      auto    auto 10/100BaseTX
Fa0/10                         notconnect    1      auto    auto 10/100BaseTX
Fa0/11    end-users connect    notconnect    1      auto    auto 10/100BaseTX
Fa0/12    end-users connect    notconnect    1      auto    auto 10/100BaseTX
Fa0/13    end-users connect    notconnect    1      auto    auto 10/100BaseTX
Fa0/14    end-users connect    notconnect    1      auto    auto 10/100BaseTX
Fa0/15    end-users connect    notconnect    1      auto    auto 10/100BaseTX
Fa0/16    end-users connect    notconnect    1      auto    auto 10/100BaseTX
Fa0/17    end-users connect    notconnect    1      auto    auto 10/100BaseTX
Fa0/18    end-users connect    notconnect    1      auto    auto 10/100BaseTX
Fa0/19    end-users connect    notconnect    1      auto    auto 10/100BaseTX
Fa0/20    end-users connect    notconnect    1      auto    auto 10/100BaseTX
Fa0/21                         notconnect    1      auto    auto 10/100BaseTX
Fa0/22                         notconnect    1      auto    auto 10/100BaseTX
Fa0/23                         notconnect    1      auto    auto 10/100BaseTX
Fa0/24                         notconnect    1      auto    auto 10/100BaseTX
Gi0/1                          notconnect    1      auto    auto 10/100/1000BaseTX
Gi0/2                          notconnect    1      auto    auto 10/100/1000BaseTX
Emma#
```

You can see some of the details of interface configuration with both the **show running-config** command (not shown in the example) and the handy **show interfaces status** command. This command lists a single line for each interface, the first part of the interface description, and the speed and duplex settings. Note that interface FastEthernet 0/1 (abbreviated as Fa0/1 in the command output) lists a speed of 100, and duplex full, as configured earlier in the example. Compare those settings with Fa0/2, which does not have any cable connected yet, so the switch lists this interface with the default setting of auto, meaning autonegotiate. Also, compare these settings to interface Fa0/4, which is physically connected to a device and has completed the autonegotiation process. The command output lists the results of the autonegotiation, in this case using 100 Mbps and full duplex. The **a-** in **a-full** and **a-100** refers to the fact that these values were autonegotiated.

Also, note that for the sake of efficiency, you can configure a command on a range of interfaces at the same time using the **interface range** command. In the example, the **interface range FastEthernet 0/11 - 20** command tells IOS that the next subcommand(s) apply to interfaces Fa0/11 through Fa0/20.

Port Security

If the network engineer knows what devices should be cabled and connected to particular interfaces on a switch, the engineer can use *port security* to restrict that interface so that only the expected devices can use it. This reduces exposure to some types of attacks in which the attacker connects a laptop to the wall socket that connects to a switch port that has been configured to use port security. When that inappropriate device attempts to send frames to the switch interface, the switch can issue informational messages, discard frames from that device, or even discard frames from all devices by effectively shutting down the interface.

Port security configuration involves several steps. Basically, you need to make the port an access port, which means that the port is not doing any VLAN trunking. You then need to enable port security and then configure the actual MAC addresses of the devices allowed to use that port. The following list outlines the steps, including the configuration commands used:

Step 1   Make the switch interface an access interface using the **switchport mode access** interface subcommand.

Step 2   Enable port security using the **switchport port-security** interface subcommand.

Step 3   (Optional) Specify the maximum number of allowed MAC addresses associated with the interface using the **switchport port-security maximum** *number* interface subcommand. (Defaults to one MAC address.)

Step 4   (Optional) Define the action to take when a frame is received from a MAC address other than the defined addresses using the **switchport port-security violation** {**protect** | **restrict** | **shutdown**} interface subcommand. (The default action is to shut down the port.)

Step 5A   Specify the MAC address(es) allowed to send frames into this interface using the **switchport port-security mac-address** *mac-address* command. Use the command multiple times to define more than one MAC address.

Step 5B   Alternatively, instead of Step 5A, use the "sticky learning" process to dynamically learn and configure the MAC addresses of currently connected hosts by configuring the **switchport port-security mac-address sticky** interface subcommand.

For example, in Figure 9-2, Server 1 and Server 2 are the only devices that should ever be connected to interfaces FastEthernet 0/1 and 0/2, respectively. When you configure port security on those interfaces, the switch examines the source MAC address of all frames received on those ports, allowing only frames sourced from the configured MAC addresses. Example 9-10 shows a sample port security configuration matching Figure 9-2, with interface Fa0/1 being configured with a static MAC address, and with interface Fa0/2 using sticky learning.

Figure 9-2 *Port Security Configuration Example*

Example 9-10 *Using Port Security to Define Correct MAC Addresses of Particular Interfaces*

```
fred#show running-config
(Lines omitted for brevity)

interface FastEthernet0/1
 switchport mode access
 switchport port-security
 switchport port-security mac-address 0200.1111.1111
!
interface FastEthernet0/2
 switchport mode access
 switchport port-security
 switchport port-security mac-address sticky

fred#show port-security interface fastEthernet 0/1
Port Security                : Enabled
Port Status                  : Secure-shutdown
Violation Mode               : Shutdown
Aging Time                   : 0 mins
Aging Type                   : Absolute
SecureStatic Address Aging   : Disabled
Maximum MAC Addresses        : 1
Total MAC Addresses          : 1
Configured MAC Addresses     : 1
Sticky MAC Addresses         : 0
Last Source Address:Vlan     : 0013.197b.5004:1
Security Violation Count     : 1
fred#show port-security interface fastEthernet 0/2
```

Example 9-10   *Using Port Security to Define Correct MAC Addresses of Particular Interfaces (Continued)*

```
Port Security          : Enabled
Port Status            : Secure-up
Violation Mode         : Shutdown
Aging Time             : 0 mins
Aging Type             : Absolute
SecureStatic Address Aging : Disabled
Maximum MAC Addresses  : 1
Total MAC Addresses    : 1
Configured MAC Addresses  : 1
Sticky MAC Addresses   : 1
Last Source Address:Vlan  : 0200.2222.2222:1
Security Violation Count  : 0
fred#show running-config
(Lines omitted for brevity)
interface FastEthernet0/2
 switchport mode access
 switchport port-security
 switchport port-security mac-address sticky
 switchport port-security mac-address sticky 0200.2222.2222
```

For FastEthernet 0/1, Server 1's MAC address is configured with the **switchport port-security mac-address 0200.1111.1111** command. For port security to work, the 2960 must think that the interface is an access interface, so the **switchport mode access** command is required. Furthermore, the **switchport port-security** command is required to enable port security on the interface. Together, these three interface subcommands enable port security, and only MAC address 0200.1111.1111 is allowed to use the interface. This interface uses defaults for the other settings, allowing only one MAC address on the interface, and causing the switch to disable the interface if the switch receives a frame whose source MAC address is not 0200.1111.111.

Interface FastEthernet 0/2 uses a feature called *sticky secure MAC addresses*. The configuration still includes the **switchport mode access** and **switchport port-security** commands for the same reasons as on FastEthernet 0/1. However, the **switchport port-security mac-address sticky** command tells the switch to learn the MAC address from the first frame sent to the switch and then add the MAC address as a secure MAC to the running configuration. In other words, the first MAC address heard "sticks" to the configuration, so the engineer does not have to know the MAC address of the device connected to the interface ahead of time.

The **show running-config** output at the beginning of Example 9-10 shows the configuration for Fa0/2, before any sticky learning occurred. The end of the example shows the configuration after an address was sticky-learned, including the **switchport**

port-security mac-address sticky 0200.2222.2222 interface subcommand, which the switch added to the configuration. If you wanted to save the configuration so that only 0200.2222.2222 is used on that interface from now on, you would simply need to use the **copy running-config startup-config** command to save the configuration.

As it turns out, a security violation has occurred on FastEthernet 0/1 in Example 9-10, but no violations have occurred on FastEthernet 0/2. The **show port-security interface fastethernet 0/1** command shows that the interface is in a *secure-shutdown* state, which means that the interface has been disabled due to port security. The device connected to interface FastEthernet 0/1 did not use MAC address 0200.1111.1111, so the switch received a frame in Fa0/1 with a different source MAC, causing a violation.

The switch can be configured to use one of three actions when a violation occurs. All three configuration options cause the switch to discard the offending frame, but some of the configuration options include additional actions. The actions include the sending of syslog messages to the console and SNMP trap message to the network management station, as well as whether the switch should shut down (err-disable) the interface. The **shutdown** option actually puts the interface in an error disabled (err-disabled) state, making it unusable. An interface in err-disabled state requires that someone manually **shutdown** the interface and then use the **no shutdown** command to recover the interface. Table 9-4 lists the options on the **switchport port-security violation** command and which actions each option sets.

Key Topic

Table 9-4   *Actions When Port Security Violation Occurs*

Option on the switchport port-security violation Command	Protect	Restrict	Shutdown*
Discards offending traffic	Yes	Yes	Yes
Sends log and SNMP messages	No	Yes	Yes
Disables the interface, discarding all traffic	No	No	Yes

*shutdown is the default setting.

VLAN Configuration

Cisco switch interfaces are considered to be either access interfaces or trunk interfaces. By definition, access interfaces send and receive frames only in a single VLAN, called the access VLAN. Trunking interfaces send and receive traffic in multiple VLANs. The concept and configuration for VLAN trunking is beyond the scope of this book, but it is covered in detail in the *ICND2 Official Exam Certification Guide*, Chapters 1 and 3. This book focuses on VLAN configuration for access interfaces, which by definition must be assigned to a single VLAN.

For a Cisco switch to forward frames on access interfaces in a particular VLAN, the switch must be configured to believe that the VLAN exists. Additionally, the switch must have one or more access interfaces assigned to the VLAN. By default, Cisco switches already have VLAN 1 configured, and all interfaces default to be assigned to VLAN 1. However, to add another VLAN, and assign access interfaces to be in that VLAN, you can follow these steps:

Step 1   To configure a new VLAN:

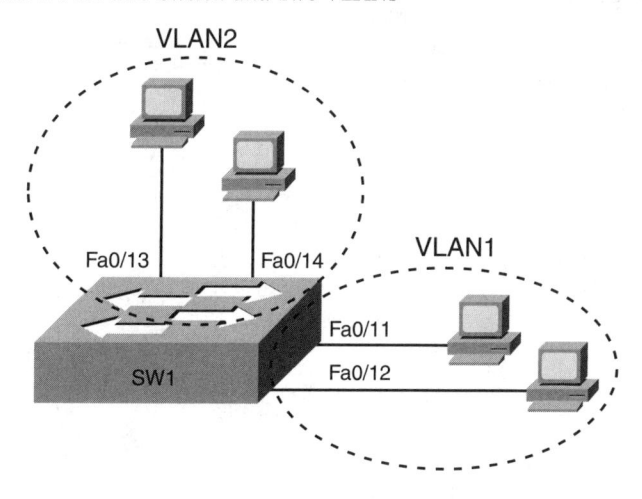

a. From configuration mode, use the **vlan** *vlan-id* global configuration command to create the VLAN and move the user into VLAN configuration mode.

b. (Optional) Use the **name** *name* VLAN subcommand to list a name for the VLAN. If not configured, the VLAN name is VLAN*ZZZZ*, where *ZZZZ* is the four-digit decimal VLAN ID.

Step 2   To configure a VLAN for each access interface:

a. Use the **interface** command to move into interface configuration mode for each desired interface.

b. Use the **switchport access vlan** *id-number* interface subcommand to specify the VLAN number associated with that interface.

c. (Optional) To disable trunking so that the switch will not dynamically decide to use trunking on the interface, and it will remain an access interface, use the **switchport mode access** interface subcommand.

Example 9-11 shows the configuration process to add a new VLAN and assign access interfaces to it. Figure 9-3 shows the network used in the example, with one LAN switch (SW1) and two hosts in each of two VLANs (1 and 2). Example 9-11 shows the details of the two-step configuration process for VLAN 2 and the two access interfaces assigned to VLAN 2.

Figure 9-3   *Network with One Switch and Two VLANs*

Example 9-11 *Configuring VLANs and Assigning Them to Interfaces*

```
! to begin, 5 VLANs exist, with all interfaces assigned to VLAN 1 (default setting)
SW1#show vlan brief
VLAN Name                             Status    Ports
---- -------------------------------- --------- -------------------------------
1    default                          active    Fa0/1, Fa0/2, Fa0/3, Fa0/4
                                                Fa0/5, Fa0/6, Fa0/7, Fa0/8
                                                Fa0/9, Fa0/10, Fa0/11, Fa0/12
                                                Fa0/13, Fa0/14, Fa0/15, Fa0/16
                                                Fa0/17, Fa0/18, Fa0/19, Fa0/20
                                                Fa0/21, Fa0/22, Fa0/23, Fa0/24
                                                Gi0/1, Gi0/2
1002 fddi-default                     act/unsup
1003 token-ring-default               act/unsup
1004 fddinet-default                  act/unsup
1005 trnet-default                    act/unsup
! Above, VLAN 2 did not yet exist. Below, VLAN 2 is added, with name Freds-vlan,
! with two interfaces assigned to VLAN 2.
SW1#configure terminal
Enter configuration commands, one per line.  End with CNTL/Z.
SW1(config)#vlan 2
SW1(config-vlan)#name Freds-vlan
SW1(config-vlan)#exit
SW1(config)#interface range fastethernet 0/13 - 14
SW1(config-if)#switchport access vlan 2
SW1(config-if)#exit
! Below, the show running-config command lists the interface subcommands on
! interfaces Fa0/13 and Fa0/14. The vlan 2 and name Freds-vlan commands do
! not show up in the running-config.
SW1#show running-config
! lines omitted for brevity
interface FastEthernet0/13
 switchport access vlan 2
 switchport mode access
!
interface FastEthernet0/14
 switchport access vlan 2
 switchport mode access
!
SW1#show vlan brief

VLAN Name                             Status    Ports
---- -------------------------------- --------- -------------------------------
1    default                          active    Fa0/1, Fa0/2, Fa0/3, Fa0/4
                                                Fa0/5, Fa0/6, Fa0/7, Fa0/8
                                                Fa0/9, Fa0/10, Fa0/11, Fa0/12
                                                Fa0/15, Fa0/16, Fa0/17, Fa0/18
```

Example 9-11 *Configuring VLANs and Assigning Them to Interfaces (Continued)*

```
                                     Fa0/19, Fa0/20, Fa0/21, Fa0/22
                                     Fa0/23, Fa0/24, Gi0/1, Gi0/2
2    Freds-vlan            active    Fa0/13, Fa0/14
1002 fddi-default          act/unsup
1003 token-ring-default    act/unsup
1004 fddinet-default       act/unsup
1005 trnet-default         act/unsup
```

The example begins with the **show vlan brief** command confirming the default settings of five nondeletable VLANs (VLANs 1 and 1002–1005), with all interfaces assigned to VLAN 1. In particular, note that this 2960 switch has 24 Fast Ethernet ports (Fa0/1–Fa0/24) and two Gigabit Ethernet ports (Gi0/1 and Gi0/2), all of which are listed as being assigned to VLAN 1.

Following the first **show vlan brief** command, the example shows the entire configuration process. The configuration shows the creation of VLAN 2, named "Freds-vlan," and the assignment of interfaces Fa0/13 and Fa0/14 to VLAN 2. Note in particular that the example uses the **interface range** command, which causes the **switchport access vlan 2** interface subcommand to be applied to both interfaces in the range, as confirmed in the **show running-config** command output at the end of the example.

After the configuration has been added, to list the new VLAN, the example repeats the **show vlan brief** command. Note that this command lists VLAN 2, named "Freds-vlan," and the interfaces assigned to that VLAN (Fa0/13 and Fa0/14).

Securing Unused Switch Interfaces

Cisco originally chose the default interface configuration settings on Cisco switches so that the interfaces would work without any overt configuration. The interfaces automatically negotiate the speed and duplex, and each interface begins in an enabled (**no shutdown**) state, with all interfaces assigned to VLAN 1. Additionally, every interface defaults to negotiate to use VLAN features called VLAN trunking and VLAN Trunking Protocol (VTP), which are covered in more detail in Chapter 2 of the *CCNA ICND2 Official Exam Certification Guide*.

The good intentions of Cisco for "plug and play" operation have an unfortunate side effect in that the defaults expose switches to some security threats. So, for any currently unused switch interfaces, Cisco makes some general recommendations to override the default interface settings to make the unused ports more secure. The recommendations for unused interfaces are as follows:

■ Administratively disable the interface using the **shutdown** interface subcommand.

■ Prevent VLAN trunking and VTP by making the port a nontrunking interface using the **switchport mode access** interface subcommand.

■ Assign the port to an unused VLAN using the **switchport access vlan** *number* interface subcommand.

Frankly, if you just shut down the interface, the security exposure goes away, but the other two tasks prevent any immediate problems if someone else comes around and enables the interface by configuring a **no shutdown** command.

Exam Preparation Tasks

Review All the Key Topics

Review the most important topics from this chapter, noted with the key topics icon. Table 9-5 describes these key topics and where each is discussed.

NOTE   There is no need to memorize any configuration step list referenced as a key topic; these lists are just study aids.

Table 9-5   *Key Topics for Chapter 9*

Key Topic Element	Description	Page Number
Example 9-1	Example showing basic password configuration	237-238
Figure 9-1	Five-step SSH configuration process example	240
List	Five-step list for SSH configuration	240
List	Key points about **enable secret** and **enable password**	244
Table 9-3	List of commands related to the command history buffer	247
List	Configuration checklist for a switch's IP address and default gateway configuration	249
List	Port security configuration checklist	253
Table 9-4	Port security actions and the results of each action	256
List	VLAN configuration checklist	257
List	Suggested security actions for unused switch ports	260
Table 9-7	**show** and **debug** command reference (at the end of the chapter). This chapter describes many small but important commands!	265

Complete the Tables and Lists from Memory

Print a copy of Appendix H, "Memory Tables" (found on the CD), or at least the section for this chapter, and complete the tables and lists from memory. Appendix I, "Memory Tables Answer Key," also on the CD, includes completed tables and lists for you to check your work.

Definitions of Key Terms

Define the following key terms from this chapter and check your answers in the glossary:

access interface, trunk interface

Command References

Table 9-6 lists and briefly describes the configuration commands used in this chapter.

Table 9-6 *Chapter 9 Configuration Command Reference*

Command	Mode/Purpose/Description
Basic Password Configuration The following four commands are related to basic password configuration.	
line console 0	Changes the context to console configuration mode.
line vty *1st-vty 2nd-vty*	Changes the context to vty configuration mode for the range of vty lines listed in the command.
login	Console and vty configuration mode. Tells IOS to prompt for a password.
password *pass-value*	Console and vty configuration mode. Lists the password required if the **login** command (with no other parameters) is configured.
Username/Password and SSH Configuration The following four commands are related to username/password and SSH configuration.	
login local	Console and vty configuration mode. Tells IOS to prompt for a username and password, to be checked against locally configured **username** global configuration commands on this switch or router.
username *name* **password** *pass-value*	Global command. Defines one of possibly multiple usernames and associated passwords, used for user authentication. Used when the **login local** line configuration command has been used.

Table 9-6 *Chapter 9 Configuration Command Reference (Continued)*

Command	Mode/Purpose/Description
crypto key generate rsa	Global command. Creates and stores (in a hidden location in flash memory) the keys required by SSH.
transport input {**telnet** l **ssh**}	vty line configuration mode. Defines whether Telnet and/or SSH access is allowed into this switch. Both values can be configured on one command to allow both Telnet and SSH access (the default).
IP Address Configuration **The following four commands are related to IP address configuration.**	
interface vlan *number*	Changes the context to VLAN interface mode. For VLAN 1, allows the configuration of the switch's IP address.
ip address *ip-address subnet-mask*	VLAN interface mode. Statically configures the switch's IP address and mask.
ip address dhcp	VLAN interface mode. Configures the switch as a DHCP client to discover its IP address, mask, and default gateway.
ip default-gateway *address*	Global command. Configures the switch's default gateway IP address. Not required if the switch uses DHCP.
Interface Configuration **The following six commands are related to interface configuration.**	
interface *type port-number*	Changes context to interface mode. The type is typically FastEthernet or gigabitEthernet. The possible port numbers vary depending on the model of switch—for example, Fa0/1, Fa0/2, and so on.
interface range *type port-range*	Changes the context to interface mode for a range of consecutively numbered interfaces. The subcommands that follow then apply to all interfaces in the range.
shutdown **no shutdown**	Interface mode. Disables or enables the interface, respectively.
speed {**10** l **100** l **1000** l **auto**}	Interface mode. Manually sets the speed to the listed speed or, with the **auto** setting, automatically negotiates the speed.

continues

Table 9-6 *Chapter 9 Configuration Command Reference (Continued)*

Command	Mode/Purpose/Description
duplex {**auto** I **full** I **half**}	Interface mode. Manually sets the duplex to half or full, or to autonegotiate the duplex setting.
description *text*	Interface mode. Lists any information text that the engineer wants to track for the interface, such as the expected device on the other end of the cable.
Miscellaneous **The remaining commands are related to miscellaneous configuration topics.**	
hostname *name*	Global command. Sets this switch's hostname, which is also used as the first part of the switch's command prompt.
enable secret *pass-value*	Global command. Sets this switch's password that is required for any user to reach enable mode.
history size *length*	Line config mode. Defines the number of commands held in the history buffer, for later recall, for users of those lines.
switchport port-security mac-address *mac-address*	Interface configuration mode command that statically adds a specific MAC address as an allowed MAC address on the interface.
switchport port-security mac-address sticky	Interface subcommand that tells the switch to learn MAC addresses on the interface and add them to the configuration for the interface as secure MAC addresses.
switchport port-security maximum *value*	Interface subcommand that sets the maximum number of static secure MAC addresses that can be assigned to a single interface.
switchport port-security violation {**protect** I **restrict** I **shutdown**}	Interface subcommand that tells the switch what to do if an inappropriate MAC address tries to access the network through a secure switch port.

Table 9-7 lists and briefly describes the EXEC commands used in this chapter.

Table 9-7 *Chapter 9 EXEC Command Reference*

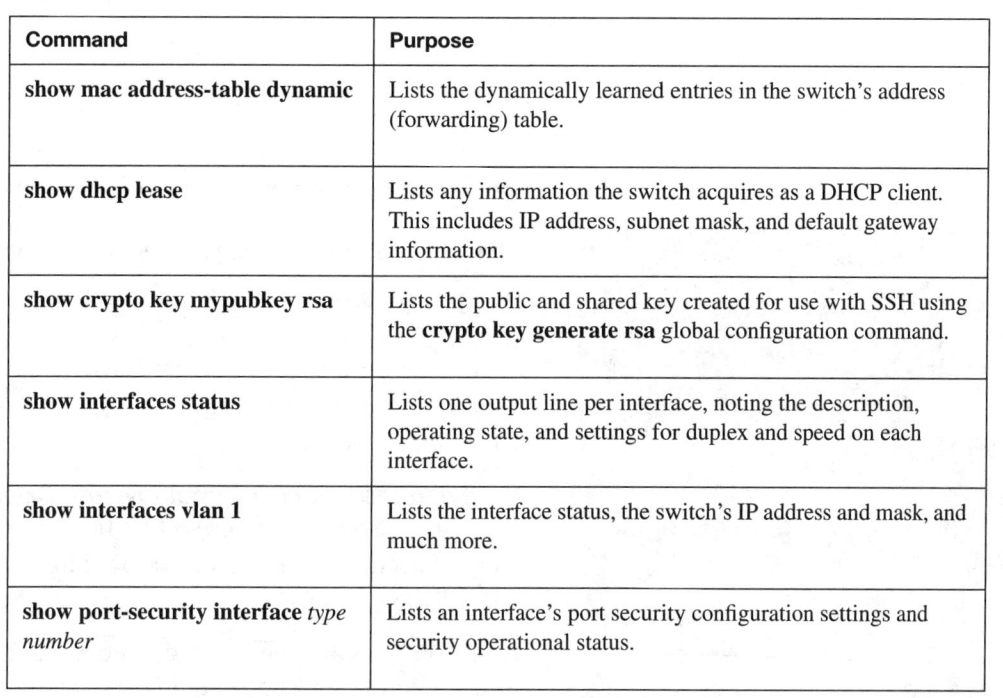

Key
Topic

Command	Purpose
show mac address-table dynamic	Lists the dynamically learned entries in the switch's address (forwarding) table.
show dhcp lease	Lists any information the switch acquires as a DHCP client. This includes IP address, subnet mask, and default gateway information.
show crypto key mypubkey rsa	Lists the public and shared key created for use with SSH using the **crypto key generate rsa** global configuration command.
show interfaces status	Lists one output line per interface, noting the description, operating state, and settings for duplex and speed on each interface.
show interfaces vlan 1	Lists the interface status, the switch's IP address and mask, and much more.
show port-security interface *type number*	Lists an interface's port security configuration settings and security operational status.

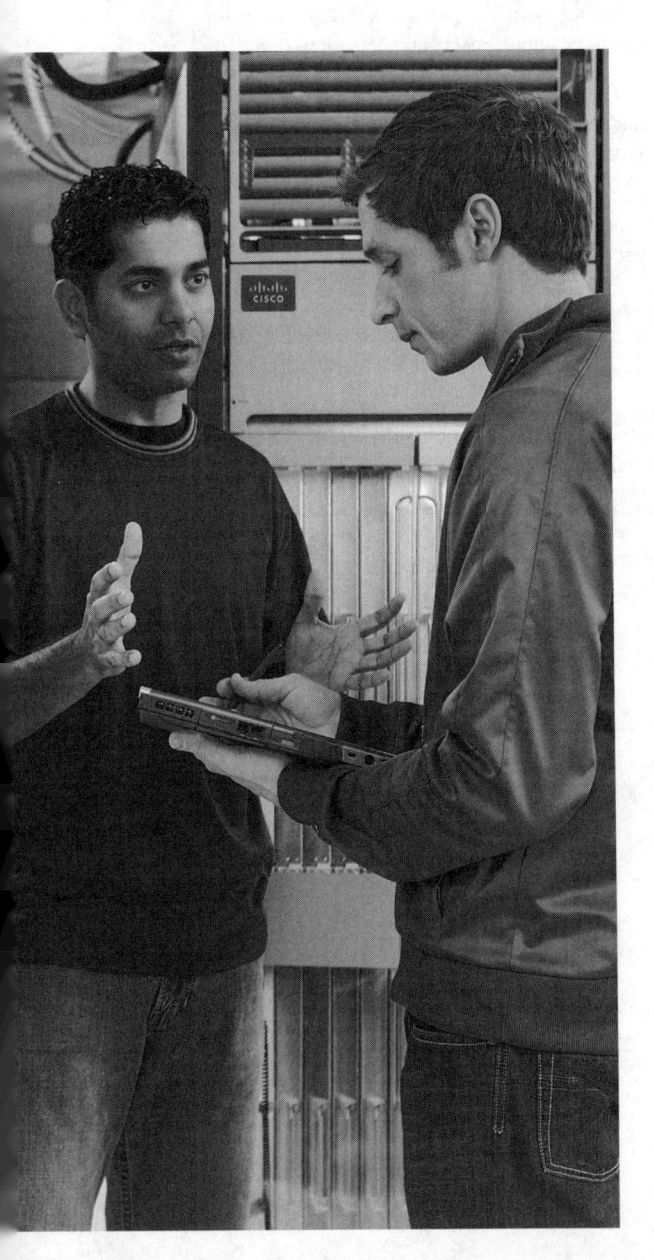

This chapter covers the following subjects:

Perspectives on Network Verification and Troubleshooting: This is the first chapter dedicated to troubleshooting, and this section introduces the concept of troubleshooting computer networks.

Verifying the Network Topology with Cisco Discovery Protocol: This section focuses on CDP—specifically, how it can be used to verify network documentation.

Analyzing Layer 1 and 2 Interface Status: This section explains how to find and interpret interface status and how to find problems even when the interface appears to be working.

Analyzing the Layer 2 Forwarding Path with the MAC Address Table: This section examines how to link the concepts of how switches forward frames with the output of switch **show** commands.

CHAPTER 10

Ethernet Switch Troubleshooting

This chapter has two main goals. First, it covers the remaining Ethernet-oriented topics for this book—specifically, some of the commands and concepts related to verifying that a switched Ethernet LAN works. If the network doesn't work, this chapter suggests tools you can use to find out why. Additionally, this chapter suggests some troubleshooting methods and practices that might improve your troubleshooting skills. Although the troubleshooting processes explained in this book are not directly tested on the exams, they can help you prepare to correctly answer some of the more difficult exam questions.

"Do I Know This Already?" Quiz

The "Do I Know This Already?" quiz allows you to assess whether you should read the entire chapter. If you miss no more than one of these eight self-assessment questions, you might want to move ahead to the "Exam Preparation Tasks" section. Table 10-1 lists the major headings in this chapter and the "Do I Know This Already?" quiz questions covering the material in those sections. This helps you assess your knowledge of these specific areas. The answers to the "Do I Know This Already?" quiz appear in Appendix A.

Table 10-1 *"Do I Know This Already?" Foundation Topics Section-to-Question Mapping*

Foundation Topics Section	Questions
Perspectives on Network Verification and Troubleshooting	—
Verifying the Network Topology with Cisco Discovery Protocol	1, 2
Analyzing Layer 1 and 2 Interface Status	3–6
Analyzing the Layer 2 Forwarding Path with the MAC Address Table	7, 8

1. Imagine that a switch connects via an Ethernet cable to a router, and the router's hostname is Hannah. Which of the following commands could tell you information about the IOS version on Hannah without establishing a Telnet connection to Hannah?

   a. **show neighbor Hannah**

   b. **show cdp**

   c. **show cdp neighbor**

   d. **show cdp neighbor Hannah**

   e. **show cdp entry Hannah**

   f. **show cdp neighbor detail**

2. Which of the following CDP commands could identify a neighbor's model of hardware?

   a. **show neighbors**

   b. **show neighbors Hannah**

   c. **show cdp**

   d. **show cdp interface**

   e. **show cdp neighbors**

   f. **show cdp entry Hannah**

3. The output of the **show interfaces status** command on a 2960 switch shows interface Fa0/1 in a "disabled" state. Which of the following is true about interface Fa0/1?

   a. The interface is configured with the **shutdown** command.

   b. The **show interfaces fa0/1** command will list the interface with two status codes of administratively down and down.

   c. The **show interfaces fa0/1** command will list the interface with two status codes of up and down.

   d. The interface cannot currently be used to forward frames.

   e. The interface can currently be used to forward frames.

4. Switch SW1 uses its gigabit 0/1 interface to connect to switch SW2's gigabit 0/2 interface. SW2's Gi0/2 interface is configured with the **speed 1000** and **duplex full** commands. SW1 uses all defaults for interface configuration commands on its Gi0/1 interface. Which of the following is true about the link after it comes up?

   a. The link works at 1000 Mbps (1 Gbps).

   b. SW1 attempts to run at 10 Mbps because SW2 has effectively disabled IEEE standard autonegotiation.

c.   The link runs at 1 Gbps, but SW1 uses half duplex, and SW2 uses full duplex.

d.   Both switches use full duplex.

5.   The following line of output was taken from a **show interfaces fa0/1** command:

```
Full-duplex, 100Mbps, media type is 10/100BaseTX
```

Which of the following is/are true about the interface?

a.   The speed was definitely configured with the **speed 100** interface subcommand.

b.   The speed may have been configured with the **speed 100** interface subcommand.

c.   The duplex was definitely configured with the **duplex full** interface subcommand.

d.   The duplex may have been configured with the **duplex full** interface subcommand.

6.   Switch SW1, a Cisco 2960 switch, has all default settings on interface Fa0/1, the **speed 100** command configured on Fa0/2, and both the **speed 100** and **duplex half** commands on Fa0/3. Each interface is cabled to a 10/100 port on different Cisco 2960 switches, with those switches using all default settings. Which of the following is true about the interfaces on the other 2960 switches?

a.   The interface connected to SW1's Fa0/1 runs at 100 Mbps and full duplex.

b.   The interface connected to SW1's Fa0/2 runs at 100 Mbps and full duplex.

c.   The interface connected to SW1's Fa0/3 runs at 100 Mbps and full duplex.

d.   The interface connected to SW1's Fa0/3 runs at 100 Mbps and half duplex.

e.   The interface connected to SW1's Fa0/2 runs at 100 Mbps and half duplex.

7.   A frame just arrived on interface Fa0/2, source MAC address 0200.2222.2222, destination MAC address 0200.2222.2222. (The frame was created as part of a security attack; it is not normal to see frames with the same source and destination MAC address.) Interface Fa0/2 is assigned to VLAN 2. Consider the following command output:

```
SW2#show mac address-table dynamic
          Mac Address Table
-------------------------------------------
Vlan    Mac Address       Type        Ports
----    -----------       --------    -----
   1    0200.1111.1111    DYNAMIC     Gi0/2
   1    0200.2222.2222    DYNAMIC     Fa0/13
Total Mac Addresses for this criterion: 2
```

Which of the following describes how the switch will forward the frame if the destination address is 0200.2222.2222?

a. The frame will likely be flooded on all other interfaces in VLAN 2, unless the switch has a static entry for 0200.2222.2222, VLAN 2, in the MAC address table.

b. The frame will be flooded out all other interfaces in VLAN 2.

c. The switch will add an entry to its MAC address table for MAC address 0200.2222.2222, interface Fa0/2, and VLAN 2.

d. The switch will replace the existing entry for 0200.2222.2222 with an entry for address 0200.2222.2222, interface Fa0/2, and VLAN 2.

8. Which of the following commands list the MAC address table entries for MAC addresses configured by port security?

a. **show mac address-table dynamic**

b. **show mac address-table**

c. **show mac address-table static**

d. **show mac address-table port-security**

Foundation Topics

This chapter contains the first specific coverage of topics related to verification and troubleshooting. Verification refers to the process of examining a network to confirm that it is working as designed. Troubleshooting refers to examining the network to determine what is causing a particular problem so that it can be fixed.

As mentioned in the Introduction to this book, over the years, the CCNA exams have been asking more and more questions related to verification and troubleshooting. Each of these questions typically uses a unique topology. They typically require you to apply networking knowledge to unique problems, rather than just being ready to answer questions about lists of facts you've memorized. (For more information and perspectives on these types of exam questions, go back to the Introduction to this book, in the section titled "Format of the CCNA Exams.")

To help you prepare to answer questions that require troubleshooting skills, this book and the *CCNA ICND2 Official Exam Certification Guide* devote several chapters, plus sections of other chapters, to verification and troubleshooting. This chapter is the first such chapter in either book, so this chapter begins with some perspectives on troubleshooting networking problems. Following this coverage, the chapter examines three major topics related to troubleshooting networks built with LAN switches.

Perspectives on Network Verification and Troubleshooting

> **NOTE** The information in this section is a means to help you learn troubleshooting skills. However, the specific processes and comments in this section, up to the next major heading ("Verifying the Network Topology with Cisco Discovery Protocol"), do not cover any specific exam objective for any of the CCNA exams.

You need several skills to be ready to answer the more challenging questions on today's CCNA exams. However, the required skills differ when comparing the different types of questions. This section starts with some perspectives on the various question types, followed by some general comments on troubleshooting.

Attacking Sim Questions

Sim questions provide a text description of a network, a network diagram, and software that simulates the network. Regardless of the details, sim questions can be reduced to the following: "The network is not working completely, so either complete the configuration, or find a problem with the existing configuration and fix it." In short, the solution to a sim question is by definition a configuration change.

One plan of attack for these problems is to use a more formalized troubleshooting process in which you examine each step in how data is forwarded from the sending host to the destination host. However, studies and experience show that when engineers think that the configuration might have a problem, the first troubleshooting step is to look at the various configuration files. To find and solve Sim questions on the exam, quickly comparing the router and/or switch configuration to what you remember about the normal configuration needed (based on the question text) might be all you require.

Sim questions do allow you to have more confidence about whether your answer is correct, at least for the technologies covered on the CCNA exams. The correct answer should solve the original problem. For example, if the sim question essentially states "Router R1 cannot ping router R2; fix it," you can use pings to test the network and confirm that your configuration changes solved the problem.

If you cannot find the problem by looking at the configuration, a more detailed process is required, mainly using **show** commands. The troubleshooting chapters and sections in this book and in the *CCNA ICND2 Official Exam Certification Guide* combine to provide the details of the more complex processes for examining different types of problems.

Simlet Questions

Simlet questions can force the exam taker to interpret the meaning of various **show** and **debug** commands. Simlet questions might not tell you the enable password, so you cannot even look at the configuration, removing the option to simply look at the configuration to find the root cause of a problem. In that case, the question text typically states the details of the scenario, requiring you to remember or find the right **show** commands, use them, and then interpret the output. Also, because simlet questions might not allow you to change the configuration, you do not get the positive feedback that your answer is correct.

For example, a simlet question may show a diagram of a switched LAN, stating that PC1 can ping PC2 but not PC3. You would need to remember the correct **show** commands to use (or take the time to find the commands using the **?** key) to find the root cause of the problem.

You can use several different approaches to attack these types of problems; no single way is necessarily better than another. The first step is to think about what should normally occur in the network, based on any network diagram and information in the question. Then, many people start by trying the **show** commands (that they remember) that are somehow related to the question. The question text probably gives some hints as to the problem area. For example, maybe the problem is related to port security. Many people then just try the commands they know that are related to that topic, such as **show port-security**, just to see if the answer jumps out at them—and that's a reasonable plan of attack. This plan uses common sense, and intuition to some degree, and it can work well and quickly.

If the answer does not become obvious when you look at the most obvious commands, a more organized approach may be useful. The troubleshooting chapters in this book, and large troubleshooting sections of other chapters, review technology and suggest a more organized approach to each topic—approaches that may be useful when the answer does not quickly become obvious.

Multiple-Choice Questions

Like simlets, multiple-choice questions can force the exam taker to interpret the meaning of various **show** and **debug** commands. Multiple-choice questions might simply list the output of some commands, along with a figure, and ask you to identify what would happen. For example, a multiple-choice question might show the **show mac address-table dynamic** command that lists a switch's dynamically learned MAC table entries. The question may then require you to predict how that switch would forward a frame sent by one device, destined for another device. This would require you to apply the concepts of LAN switching to the output shown in the command.

Multiple-choice questions that list **show** and **debug** command output require much of the same thinking as simlet questions. As with simlet questions, the first step for some multiple-choice questions is to think about what should normally occur in the network, based on any network diagram and information in the question. Next, compare the information in the question text, including the sample command output, to see if it confirms that the network is working normally, or if there is a problem. (The network might be working correctly, and the question is designed to confirm that you know why a particular command confirms that a particular part of the network is working well.) The big difference in this case, however, is that the multiple-choice questions do not require you to remember the commands to use. The command output is either supplied in the question, or it is not.

> **NOTE**   Refer to http://www.cisco.com/web/learning/wwtraining/certprog/training/ cert_exam_tutorial.html for a tutorial about the various types of CCNA exam questions.

Approaching Questions with an Organized Troubleshooting Process

If the answer to a sim, simlet, or multiple-choice question is not obvious after you use the more obvious and quicker options just discussed, you need to implement a more thorough and organized thought process. This more organized process may well be what a typical network engineer would do when faced with more complex real-world problems.

Unfortunately, the exams are timed, and thinking through the problem in more detail requires more time.

By thinking through the troubleshooting process as you prepare for the exam, you can be better prepared to attack problems on the exam. To that end, this book includes many suggested troubleshooting processes. The troubleshooting processes are not ends unto themselves, so you do not need to memorize them for the exams. They are a learning tool, with the ultimate goal being to help you correctly and quickly find the answers to the more challenging questions on the exams.

This section gives an overview of a general troubleshooting process. As you progress through this book, the process will be mentioned occasionally as it relates to other technology areas, such as IP routing. The three major steps in this book's organized troubleshooting process are as follows:

Step 1   **Analyzing/predicting normal operation:** Predict the details of what should happen if the network is working correctly, based on documentation, configuration, and **show** and **debug** command output.

Step 2   **Problem isolation:** Determine how far along the expected path the frame/packet goes before it cannot be forwarded any further, again based on documentation, configuration, and **show** and **debug** command output.

Step 3   **Root cause analysis:** Identify the underlying causes of the problems identified in the preceding step—specifically, the causes that have a specific action with which the problem can be fixed.

Following this process requires a wide variety of learned skills. You need to remember the theory of how networks should work, as well as how to interpret the **show** command output that confirms how the devices are currently behaving. This process requires the use of testing tools, such as **ping** and **traceroute**, to isolate the problem. Finally, this approach requires the ability to think broadly about everything that could affect a single component.

For example, imagine a simple LAN with two switches connected to each other, and two PCs (PC1 and PC2) each connected to one of the switches. Originally, PC1 could ping PC2 successfully, but the ping now fails. You could examine the documentation, as well as **show** command output, to confirm the network topology and predict its normal working behavior based on your knowledge of LAN switching. As a result, you could predict where a frame sent by PC1 to PC2 should flow. To isolate the problem, you could look in the switch MAC tables to confirm the interfaces out which the frame should be forwarded, possibly then finding that the interface connected to PC2 has failed. However, knowing that the interface has failed does not identify the root cause of the problem. So you would then need to broaden your thinking to any and all reasons why an interface might fail—from an unplugged cable, to electrical interference, to port security disabling the interface. **show** commands can either confirm that a specific root cause is the problem, or at least give some hints as to the root cause.

Isolating Problems at Layer 3, and Then at Layers 1 and 2

Before moving to the specific topics on Ethernet LAN troubleshooting, it is helpful to consider the larger picture. Most troubleshooting in real IP networks today begins with what the end user sees and experiences. From there, the analysis typically moves quickly to an examination of how well Layer 3 is working. For example, imagine that the user of PC1 in Figure 10-1 can usually connect to the web server on the right by entering www.example.com in PC1's web browser, but the connection to the web server currently fails. The user calls the help desk, and the problem is assigned to a network engineer to solve.

Figure 10-1 *Layer 3 Problem Isolation*

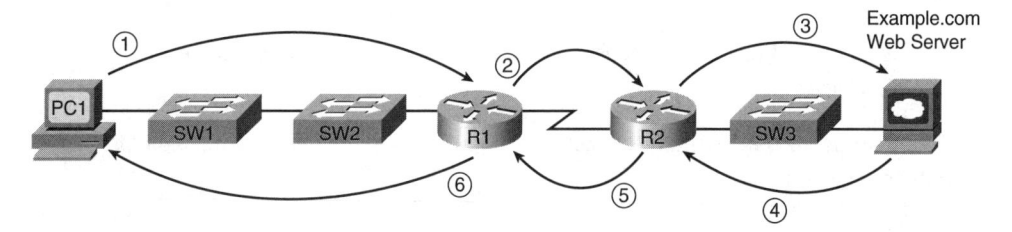

After knowing about the problem, the engineer can work to confirm that PC1 can resolve the hostname (www.example.com) into the correct IP address. At that point, the Layer 3 IP problem isolation process can proceed, to determine which of the six routing steps shown in the figure has failed. The routing steps shown in Figure 10-1 are as follows:

Step 1 PC1 sends the packet to its default gateway (R1) because the destination IP address is in a different subnet.

Step 2 R1 forwards the packet to R2 based on R1's routing table.

Step 3 R2 forwards the packet to the web server based on R2's routing table.

Step 4 The web server sends a packet back toward PC1 based on the web server's default gateway setting (R2).

Step 5 R2 forwards the packet destined for PC1 by forwarding the packet to R1 according to R2's routing table.

Step 6 R1 forwards the packet to PC1 based on R1's routing table.

Chapter 15, "Troubleshooting IP Routing," examines this process in much greater detail. For now, consider what happens if the Layer 3 problem isolation process discovers that Step 1, 3, 4, or 6 is the step that fails. Further isolating the problem would require more Layer 3 analysis. However, at some point, all the potential problems at Layer 3 might be ruled out, so the next problem isolation step would be to figure out why the Layer 1 and 2 details at that routing step do not work.

For example, imagine that the Layer 3 analysis determined that PC1 cannot even send a packet to its default gateway (R1), meaning that Step 1 in Figure 10-1 fails. To further isolate the problem and find the root causes, the engineer would need to determine the following:

- The MAC address of PC1 and of R1's LAN interface

- The switch interfaces used on SW1 and SW2

- The interface status of each interface

- The expected forwarding behavior of a frame sent by PC1 to R1 as the destination MAC address

By gathering and analyzing these facts, the engineer can most likely isolate the problem's root cause and fix it.

Troubleshooting as Covered in This Book

This book has three main troubleshooting chapters or sections, plus a few smaller troubleshooting sections interspersed in other chapters. The main coverage is as follows:

- Chapter 10, "Ethernet Switch Troubleshooting"

- Chapter 15, "Troubleshooting IP Routing"

- Chapter 17, "WAN Configuration"

Essentially, Chapter 15 covers the analysis of problems related to Layer 3, as generally shown in Figure 10-1. This chapter covers some of the details of how to attack problems as soon as you know that the problem may be related to a LAN. Chapter 17 covers the troubleshooting steps in cases where the problem might be with a WAN link.

These three troubleshooting chapters spend some time on the more formalized troubleshooting process, but as a means to an end—focusing on predicting normal behavior, isolating problems, and determining the root cause. The end goal is to help you know the tools, concepts, configuration commands, and how to analyze a network based on **show** commands to solve a problem.

If you have both this book and the *CCNA ICND2 Official Exam Certification Guide*, the ICND2 book provides even more details about troubleshooting and how to use a more formalized troubleshooting process, if needed. The reason for putting more detail in the ICND2 book is that by the time you reach the troubleshooting topics in that book, you will have completed all the CCNA-level materials for a particular technology area. Because troubleshooting requires interpreting a broad range of concepts, configuration, and command output, the ICND2 book's troubleshooting chapters/sections occur at the end of each major topic, summarizing the important materials and helping show how the topics are interrelated.

The rest of this chapter examines three major topics, each of which has something to do with at least one of the three major components of the formalized troubleshooting process:

- **Cisco Discovery Protocol (CDP):** Used to confirm the documentation, and learn about the network topology, to predict normal operation of the network.

- **Examining interface status:** Interfaces must be in a working state before a switch will forward frames on the interface. You must determine if an interface is working, as well as determine the potential root causes for a failed switch interface.

- **Analyzing where frames will be forwarded:** You must know how to analyze a switch's MAC address table and how to then predict how a switch will forward a particular frame.

Verifying the Network Topology with Cisco Discovery Protocol

The proprietary Cisco Discovery Protocol (CDP) discovers basic information about neighboring routers and switches without needing to know the passwords for the neighboring devices. To discover information, routers and switches send CDP messages out each of their interfaces. The messages essentially announce information about the device that sent the CDP message. Devices that support CDP learn information about others by listening for the advertisements sent by other devices.

From a troubleshooting perspective, CDP can be used to either confirm or fix the documentation shown in a network diagram, or even discover the devices and interfaces used in a network. Confirming that the network is actually cabled to match the network diagram is a good step to take before trying to predict the normal flow of data in a network.

On media that support multicasts at the data link layer, CDP uses multicast frames; on other media, CDP sends a copy of the CDP update to any known data-link addresses. So, any CDP-supporting device that shares a physical medium with another CDP-supporting device can learn about the other device.

CDP discovers several useful details from the neighboring Cisco devices:

- **Device identifier:** Typically the hostname

- **Address list:** Network and data-link addresses

- **Local interface:** The interface on the router or switch issuing the **show cdp** command with which the neighbor was discovered

- **Port identifier:** Text that identifies the port used by the neighboring device to send CDP messages to the local device

- **Capabilities list:** Information on what type of device it is (for instance, a router or a switch)

- **Platform:** The model and OS level running in the device

Table 10-2 lists the **show cdp** EXEC commands that include at least some of the details from the preceding list.

Table 10-2   show cdp *Commands That List Information About Neighbors*

Command	Description
show cdp neighbors [*type number*]	Lists one summary line of information about each neighbor, or just the neighbor found on a specific interface if an interface was listed.
show cdp neighbors detail	Lists one large set (approximately 15 lines) of information, one set for every neighbor.
show cdp entry *name*	Lists the same information as the **show cdp neighbors detail** command, but only for the named neighbor (case-sensitive).

Like many switch and router features that are enabled by default, CDP actually creates a security exposure when enabled. To avoid the possibility of allowing an attacker to learn details about each switch, CDP can be easily disabled. Cisco recommends that CDP be disabled on all interfaces that do not have a specific need for it. The most likely interfaces to need to use CDP are interfaces connected to other Cisco routers and switches and interfaces connected to Cisco IP Phones. Otherwise, CDP can be disabled per interface using the **no cdp enable** interface subcommand. (The **cdp enable** interface subcommand re-enables CDP.) Alternatively, the **no cdp run** global command disables CDP for the entire switch, with the **cdp run** global command re-enabling CDP globally.

Figure 10-2 shows a small network with two switches, one router, and a couple of PCs. Example 10-1 shows the **show** commands listed in Table 10-2, as well as several commands that list information about CDP itself, rather than about neighboring devices.

Figure 10-2   *Small Network Used in CDP Examples*

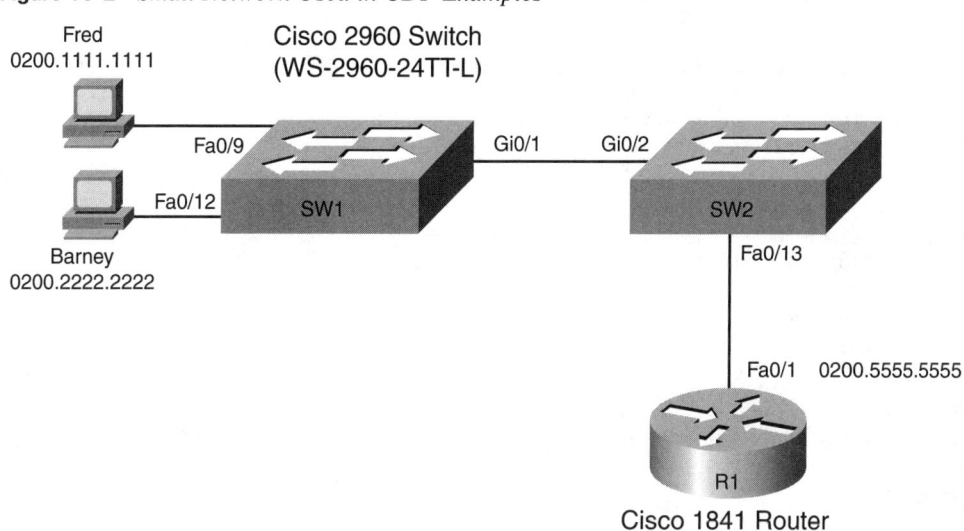

Example 10-1   **show cdp** *Command Examples: SW2*

```
SW2#show cdp ?
  entry      Information for specific neighbor entry
  interface  CDP interface status and configuration
  neighbors  CDP neighbor entries
  traffic    CDP statistics
  |          Output modifiers
  <cr>
! Next, the show cdp neighbors command lists SW2's local interface, and both R1's
! and SW1's interfaces  (in the "port" column), along with other details.
!
SW2#show cdp neighbors
Capability Codes: R - Router, T - Trans Bridge, B - Source Route Bridge
                  S - Switch, H - Host, I - IGMP, r - Repeater, P - Phone


Device ID            Local Intrfce        Holdtme   Capability    Platform    Port ID
SW1                  Gig 0/2              173             S I     WS-C2960-2Gig 0/1
R1                   Fas 0/13             139           R S I     1841       Fas 0/1
SW2#show cdp neighbors detail
------------------------
Device ID: SW1
Entry address(es):
Platform: cisco WS-C2960-24TT-L,  Capabilities: Switch IGMP
Interface: GigabitEthernet0/2,  Port ID (outgoing port): GigabitEthernet0/1
Holdtime : 167 sec
```

continues

Example 10-1 **show cdp** *Command Examples: SW2 (Continued)*

```
Version :
Cisco IOS Software, C2960 Software (C2960-LANBASEK9-M), Version 12.2(25)SEE2, RELEASE
  SOFTWARE (fc1)
Copyright (c) 1986-2006 by Cisco Systems, Inc.
Compiled Fri 28-Jul-06 11:57 by yenanh

advertisement version: 2
Protocol Hello:  OUI=0x00000C, Protocol ID=0x0112; payload len=27,
  value=00000000FFFFFFFF010221FF000
0000000000019E86A6F80FF0000
VTP Management Domain: 'fred'
Native VLAN: 1
Duplex: full
Management address(es):
! The info for router R1 follows.
-------------------------
Device ID: R1
Entry address(es):
   IP address: 10.1.1.1
Platform: Cisco 1841,  Capabilities: Router Switch IGMP
Interface: FastEthernet0/13,  Port ID (outgoing port): FastEthernet0/1
Holdtime : 131 sec

Version :
Cisco IOS Software, 1841 Software (C1841-ADVENTERPRISEK9-M), Version 12.4(9)T, RELEASE
  SOFTWARE (fc1)
Technical Support: http://www.cisco.com/techsupport
Copyright (c) 1986-2006 by Cisco Systems, Inc.
Compiled Fri 16-Jun-06 21:26 by prod_rel_team

advertisement version: 2
VTP Management Domain: ''
Duplex: full
Management address(es):
!
! Note that the show cdp entry R1 command repeats the same information shown in
! the show cdp neighbors detail command, but just for R1.
SW2#show cdp entry R1
-------------------------
Device ID: R1
Entry address(es):
   IP address: 10.1.1.1
Platform: Cisco 1841,  Capabilities: Router Switch IGMP
Interface: FastEthernet0/13,  Port ID (outgoing port): FastEthernet0/1
Holdtime : 176 sec
```

Example 10-1   show cdp *Command Examples: SW2 (Continued)*

```
Version :
Cisco IOS Software, 1841 Software (C1841-ADVENTERPRISEK9-M), Version 12.4(9)T, RELEASE
   SOFTWARE (fc1)
Technical Support: http://www.cisco.com/techsupport
Copyright (c) 1986-2006 by Cisco Systems, Inc.
Compiled Fri 16-Jun-06 21:26 by prod_rel_team


advertisement version: 2
VTP Management Domain: ''
Duplex: full
Management address(es):
SW2#show cdp
Global CDP information:
    Sending CDP packets every 60 seconds
    Sending a holdtime value of 180 seconds
    Sending CDPv2 advertisements is  enabled
SW2#show cdp interfaces
FastEthernet0/1 is administratively down, line protocol is down
  Encapsulation ARPA
  Sending CDP packets every 60 seconds
  Holdtime is 180 seconds
FastEthernet0/2 is administratively down, line protocol is down
  Encapsulation ARPA
  Sending CDP packets every 60 seconds
  Holdtime is 180 seconds
!
! Lines omitted for brevity
!
SW2#show cdp traffic
CDP counters :
    Total packets output: 54, Input: 49
    Hdr syntax: 0, Chksum error: 0, Encaps failed: 0
    No memory: 0, Invalid packet: 0, Fragmented: 0
    CDP version 1 advertisements output: 0, Input: 0
    CDP version 2 advertisements output: 54, Input: 49
```

A little more than the first half of the example shows a comparison of the output of the three commands listed in Table 10-2. The **show cdp neighbors** command lists one line per neighbor, but with lots of key details such as the local device's interface used to connect to the neighbor and the neighboring device's interface (under the Port heading). For example, SW2's **show cdp neighbors** command lists an entry for SW1, with SW2's local interface of Gi0/2, and SW1's interface of Gi0/1 (see Figure 10-2 for reference). The **show cdp neighbors** output also lists the platform, so if you know the Cisco product line to some degree, you know the specific model of the neighboring router or switch. So, even using this basic information, you could either construct a figure like Figure 10-2 or confirm that the details in the figure are correct.

Take a few moments to examine the output of the **show cdp neighbors detail** command
and the **show cdp entry R1** commands in Example 10-1. Both commands supply the exact
same messages, with the first supplying the information for all neighbors, rather than for
one neighbor at a time. Note that the output of these two commands lists additional details,
such as the full name of the model of switch (WS-2960-24TT-L) and the IP address
configured on the 1841 router. (Had SW1's IP address been configured, it would also have
been displayed.)

The bottom portion of Example 10-1 lists sample output from some of the **show cdp**
commands that identify information about how CDP is operating. These commands do not
list any information about neighbors. Table 10-3 lists these commands and their purpose for
easy reference.

Table 10-3   *Commands Used to Verify CDP Operations*

Command	Description
show cdp	States whether CDP is enabled globally, and lists the default update and holdtime timers.
show cdp interface [*type number*]	States whether CDP is enabled on each interface, or a single interface if the interface is listed, and states update and holdtime timers on those interfaces.
show cdp traffic	Lists global statistics for the number of CDP advertisements sent and received.

Analyzing Layer 1 and 2 Interface Status

A Cisco switch interface must be in a working state before the switch will process frames
received on the interface or send frames out the interface. Additionally, the interface might
be in a working state, but intermittent problems might still be occurring. So, a somewhat
obvious troubleshooting step is to examine the interface state, ensure that each interface is
working, and also verify that no intermittent problems are occurring. This section examines
the **show** commands you can use to determine the status of each interface, the reasons why
an interface might not be working, and some issues that can occur even when the interfaces
are in a working state.

Interface Status Codes and Reasons for Nonworking States

Cisco switches actually use two different sets of interface status codes—one set of two
codes (words) that use the same conventions as do router interface status codes, and another
set with a single code (word). Both sets of status codes can determine whether an interface
is working.

The switch **show interfaces** and **show interfaces description** commands list the two-code status just like routers. The two codes are named the *line status* and *protocol status*. They generally refer to whether Layer 1 is working (line status) and whether Layer 2 is working (protocol status). LAN switch interfaces typically show an interface with both codes with the same value, either "up" or "down."

> **NOTE** This book refers to these two status codes in shorthand by just listing the two codes with a slash between them, such as "up/up."

The **show interfaces status** command lists a different single interface status code. This single interface status code corresponds to different combinations of the traditional two-code interface status codes and can be easily correlated to those codes. For example, the **show interfaces status** command lists a "connect" state for working interfaces. It corresponds to the up/up state seen with the **show interfaces** and **show interfaces description** commands.

Any interface state other than connect or up/up means that the switch will not forward or receive frames on the interface. Each nonworking interface state has a small set of root causes. Also, note that the exams could easily ask a question that showed only one or the other type of status code, so be prepared to see both types of status codes on the exams, and know the meanings of both. Table 10-4 lists the code combinations and some root causes that could have caused a particular interface status.

Table 10-4 *LAN Switch Interface Status Codes*

Key
Topic

Line Status	Protocol Status	Interface Status	Typical Root Cause
Administratively Down	Down	disabled	The interface is configured with the **shutdown** command.
Down	Down	notconnect	No cable; bad cable; wrong cable pinouts; the speeds are mismatched on the two connected devices; the device on the other end of the cable is powered off or the other interface is **shutdown**.
Up	Down	notconnect	An interface up/down state is not expected on LAN switch interfaces.
Down	down (err-disabled)	err-disabled	Port security has disabled the interface.
Up	Up	connect	The interface is working.

Most of the reasons for the notconnect state were covered earlier in this book. For example, to troubleshoot problems, you should remember the cabling pinout details explained in Chapter 3, "Fundamentals of LANs." However, one topic can be particularly difficult to troubleshoot—the possibility for both speed and duplex mismatches, as explained in the next section.

Interface Speed and Duplex Issues

Switch interfaces can find their speed and duplex settings in several ways. Many interfaces that use copper wiring are capable of multiple speeds, and duplex settings use the IEEE standard (IEEE 802.3X) autonegotiation process. These same network interface cards (NIC) and interfaces can also be configured to use a specific speed or duplex setting rather than using autonegotiation. On switches and routers, the **speed** {**10** | **100** | **1000**} interface subcommand and the **duplex** {**half** | **full**} interface subcommand set these values. Note that configuring both speed and duplex on a switch interface disables the IEEE-standard autonegotiation process on that interface.

The **show interfaces** and **show interfaces status** commands list both the speed and duplex settings on an interface, as demonstrated in Example 10-2.

Example 10-2 *Displaying Speed and Duplex Settings on Switch Interfaces*

```
SW1#show interfaces status

Port      Name            Status       Vlan      Duplex  Speed Type
Fa0/1                     notconnect   1           auto   auto 10/100BaseTX
Fa0/2                     notconnect   1           auto   auto 10/100BaseTX
Fa0/3                     notconnect   1           auto   auto 10/100BaseTX
Fa0/4                     connected    1         a-full  a-100 10/100BaseTX
Fa0/5                     connected    1         a-full  a-100 10/100BaseTX
Fa0/6                     notconnect   1           auto   auto 10/100BaseTX
Fa0/7                     notconnect   1           auto   auto 10/100BaseTX
Fa0/8                     notconnect   1           auto   auto 10/100BaseTX
Fa0/9                     notconnect   1           auto   auto 10/100BaseTX
Fa0/10                    notconnect   1           auto   auto 10/100BaseTX
Fa0/11                    connected    1         a-full     10 10/100BaseTX
Fa0/12                    connected    1           half    100 10/100BaseTX
Fa0/13                    connected    1         a-full  a-100 10/100BaseTX
Fa0/14                    disabled     1           auto   auto 10/100BaseTX
Fa0/15                    notconnect   3           auto   auto 10/100BaseTX
Fa0/16                    notconnect   3           auto   auto 10/100BaseTX
Fa0/17                    connected    1         a-full  a-100 10/100BaseTX
Fa0/18                    notconnect   1           auto   auto 10/100BaseTX
Fa0/19                    notconnect   1           auto   auto 10/100BaseTX
Fa0/20                    notconnect   1           auto   auto 10/100BaseTX
Fa0/21                    notconnect   1           auto   auto 10/100BaseTX
```

Example 10-2 *Displaying Speed and Duplex Settings on Switch Interfaces (Continued)*

```
Fa0/22                           notconnect  1          auto    auto 10/100BaseTX
Fa0/23                           notconnect  1          auto    auto 10/100BaseTX
Fa0/24                           notconnect  1          auto    auto 10/100BaseTX
Gi0/1                            connected   trunk      full    1000 10/100/1000BaseTX
Gi0/2                            notconnect  1          auto    auto 10/100/1000BaseTX
SW1#show interfaces fa0/13
FastEthernet0/13 is up, line protocol is up (connected)
  Hardware is Fast Ethernet, address is 0019.e86a.6f8d (bia 0019.e86a.6f8d)
  MTU 1500 bytes, BW 100000 Kbit, DLY 100 usec,
     reliability 255/255, txload 1/255, rxload 1/255
  Encapsulation ARPA, loopback not set
  Keepalive set (10 sec)
  Full-duplex, 100Mbps, media type is 10/100BaseTX
  input flow-control is off, output flow-control is unsupported
  ARP type: ARPA, ARP Timeout 04:00:00
  Last input 00:00:05, output 00:00:00, output hang never
  Last clearing of "show interface" counters never
  Input queue: 0/75/0/0 (size/max/drops/flushes); Total output drops: 0
  Queueing strategy: fifo
  Output queue: 0/40 (size/max)
  5 minute input rate 0 bits/sec, 0 packets/sec
  5 minute output rate 0 bits/sec, 0 packets/sec
     85022 packets input, 10008976 bytes, 0 no buffer
     Received 284 broadcasts (0 multicast)
     0 runts, 0 giants, 0 throttles
     0 input errors, 0 CRC, 0 frame, 0 overrun, 0 ignored
     0 watchdog, 281 multicast, 0 pause input
     0 input packets with dribble condition detected
     95226 packets output, 10849674 bytes, 0 underruns
     0 output errors, 0 collisions, 1 interface resets
     0 babbles, 0 late collision, 0 deferred
     0 lost carrier, 0 no carrier, 0 PAUSE output
     0 output buffer failures, 0 output buffers swapped out
```

Although both commands in the example can be useful, only the **show interfaces status** command implies how the switch determined the speed and duplex settings. The command output lists autonegotiated settings with a prefix of **a-**. For example, **a-full** means full duplex as autonegotiated, whereas **full** means full duplex but as manually configured. The example shades the command output that implies that the switch's Fa0/12 interface's speed and duplex were not found through autonegotiation, but Fa0/13 did use autonegotiation. Note that the **show interfaces fa0/13** command (without the **status** option) simply lists the speed and duplex for interface FastEthernet0/13, with nothing implying that the values were learned through autonegotiation.

When the IEEE autonegotiation process works on both devices, both devices agree to the fastest speed supported by both devices. Additionally, the devices use full duplex if it is supported by both devices, or half duplex if it is not. However, when one device has disabled autonegotiation, and the other device uses autonegotiation, the device using autonegotiation chooses the default duplex setting based on the current speed. The defaults are as follows:

■ If the speed is not known, use 10 Mbps, half duplex.

■ If the speed is somehow known to be 10 or 100 Mbps, default to use half duplex.

■ If the speed is somehow known to be 1000 Mbps, default to use full duplex.

> **NOTE** Ethernet interfaces using speeds faster than 1 Gbps always use full duplex.

Cisco switches can determine speed in a couple of ways even when IEEE standard autonegotiation fails. First, the switch knows the speed if the **speed** interface subcommand was manually configured. Additionally, even when IEEE autonegotiation fails, Cisco switches can automatically sense the speed used by the device on the other end of the cable, and can use that speed based on the electrical signals on the cable.

For example, in Figure 10-3, imagine that SW2's Gi0/2 interface was configured with the **speed 100** and **duplex full** commands (not recommended settings on a gigabit-capable interface, by the way). SW2 would use those settings and disable the IEEE-standard autonegotiation process, because both the **speed** and **duplex** commands have been configured. If SW1's Gi0/1 interface did not have a **speed** command configured, SW1 would still recognize the speed (100 Mbps)—even though SW2 would not use IEEE-standard negotiation—and SW1 would also use a speed of 100 Mbps. Example 10-3 shows the results of this specific case on SW1.

Figure 10-3 *Sample Network Showing Ethernet Autonegotiation Defaults*

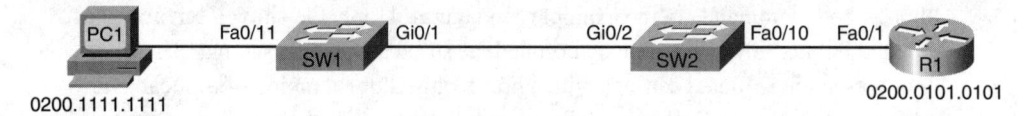

Example 10-3 *Displaying Speed and Duplex Settings on Switch Interfaces*

```
SW1#show interfaces gi0/1 status

Port       Name              Status        Vlan      Duplex  Speed Type
Gi0/1                        connected     trunk     a-half  a-100 10/100/1000BaseTX
```

The speed and duplex still show up with a prefix of **a-** in the output, implying autonegotiation. The reason is that in this case, the speed was found automatically, and the duplex setting was chosen because of the default values used by the IEEE autonegotiation process. SW1 sensed the speed without using IEEE standard autonegotiation, because SW2 disabled autonegotiation. SW1 then defaulted to use half duplex based on the IEEE default recommendation for links running at 100 Mbps.

This example shows one case of a duplex mismatch, because SW1 uses half duplex and SW2 uses full duplex. Finding a duplex mismatch can be much more difficult than finding a speed mismatch, because *if the duplex settings do not match on the ends of an Ethernet segment, the switch interface will still be in a connect (up/up) state.* In this case, the interface works, but it may work poorly, with poor performance, and with symptoms of intermittent problems. The reason is that the device using half duplex uses CSMA/CD logic, waiting to send when receiving a frame, believing collisions occur when they physically do not—and actually stopping sending a frame because the switch thinks a collision occurred. With enough traffic load, the interface could be in a connect state, but it's essentially useless for passing traffic.

To identify duplex mismatch problems, check the duplex setting on each end of the link, and watch for incrementing collision and late collision counters, as explained in the next section.

Common Layer 1 Problems on Working Interfaces

Some Layer 1 problems prevent a switch interface from ever reaching the connect (up/up) state. However, when the interface reaches the connect state, the switch tries to use the interface and keep various interface counters. These interface counters can help identify problems that can occur even though the interface is in a connect state. This section explains some of the related concepts and a few of the most common problems.

First, consider a couple of common reasons why Ethernet frames experience errors during transmission. When an Ethernet frame passes over a UTP cable, the electrical signal may encounter problems. The cable could be damaged, for example, if it lies under carpet. If the user's chair keeps squashing the cable, eventually the electrical signal can degrade. Additionally, many sources of electromagnetic interference (EMI) exist; for example, a nearby electrical power cable can cause EMI. EMI can change the electrical signal on the Ethernet cable.

Regardless of the root cause, whenever the electrical signal degrades, the receiving device may receive a frame whose bits have changed value. These frames do not pass the error detection logic as implemented in the FCS field in the Ethernet trailer, as covered in Chapter 3. The receiving device discards the frame and counts it as some kind of input error.

Cisco switches list this error as a CRC error (cyclic redundancy check [CRC] is an older term referring to the frame check sequence [FCS] concept), as highlighted in Example 10-4.

Example 10-4 *Interface Counters for Layer 1 Problems*

```
SW1#show interfaces fa0/13
! lines omitted for brevity
    Received 284 broadcasts (0 multicast)
    0 runts, 0 giants, 0 throttles
    0 input errors, 0 CRC, 0 frame, 0 overrun, 0 ignored
    0 watchdog, 281 multicast, 0 pause input
    0 input packets with dribble condition detected
    95226 packets output, 10849674 bytes, 0 underruns
    0 output errors, 0 collisions, 1 interface resets
    0 babbles, 0 late collision, 0 deferred
    0 lost carrier, 0 no carrier, 0 PAUSE output
    0 output buffer failures, 0 output buffers swapped out
```

Next, consider the concept of an Ethernet collision versus a late collision, both of which are tracked with interface counters by Cisco switches. Collisions occur as a normal part of the half-duplex logic imposed by CSMA/CD, so a switch interface with an increasing collisions counter may not even have a problem. However, if a LAN design follows cabling guidelines, all collisions should occur by the end of the 64th byte of any frame. When a switch has already sent 64 bytes of a frame, and the switch receives a frame on that same interface, the switch senses a collision. In this case, the collision is a late collision, and the switch increments the late collision counter in addition to the usual CSMA/CD actions to send a jam signal, wait a random time, and try again. (Note that the collision counters are actually listed in the output counters section of the command output.)

Three common LAN problems can be found using these counters: excessive interference on the cable, a duplex mismatch, and jabber. Excessive interference on the cable can cause the various input error counters to keep growing larger, especially the CRC counter. In particular, if the CRC errors grow, but the collisions counters do not, the problem may simply be interference on the cable. (The switch counts each collided frame as one form of input error as well.)

Both duplex mismatches and jabber can be partially identified by looking at the collisions and late collision counters. Jabber refers to cases in which the NIC ignores Ethernet rules and sends frame after frame without a break between the frames. With both problems, the collisions and late collision counters could keep growing. In particular, a significant problem exists if the collision counters show that more than .1% of all the output frames have collided. Duplex mismatch problems can be further isolated by using the **show interface** command options shown in the earlier section "Interface Speed and Duplex

Issues." Isolating jabber problems requires much more effort, typically using more specialized LAN cabling troubleshooting tools.

> **NOTE** To find the percentage of collisions versus output frames, divide the collisions counter by the "packets output" counter, as highlighted in Example 10-4.

Finally, an incrementing late collisions counter typically means one of two things:

■ The interface is connected to a collision domain whose cabling exceeds Ethernet cable length standards.

■ The interface is using half duplex, and the device on the other end of the cable is using full duplex.

Table 10-5 summarizes the main points about these three general types of interface problems that occur even when the interface is in a connect (up/up) state.

Table 10-5 *Common LAN Layer 1 Problem Indicators*

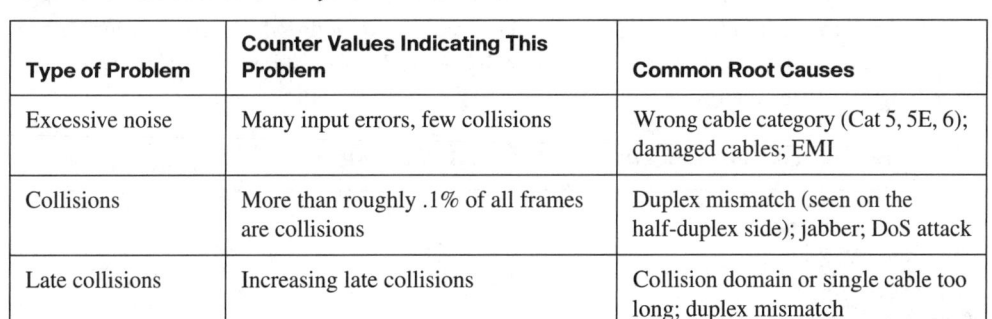

Key
Topic

Type of Problem	Counter Values Indicating This Problem	Common Root Causes
Excessive noise	Many input errors, few collisions	Wrong cable category (Cat 5, 5E, 6); damaged cables; EMI
Collisions	More than roughly .1% of all frames are collisions	Duplex mismatch (seen on the half-duplex side); jabber; DoS attack
Late collisions	Increasing late collisions	Collision domain or single cable too long; duplex mismatch

Analyzing the Layer 2 Forwarding Path with the MAC Address Table

As explained in Chapter 7, "Ethernet LAN Switching Concepts," switches learn MAC addresses and then use the entries in the MAC address table to make a forwarding/filtering decision for each frame. To know exactly how a particular switch will forward an Ethernet frame, you need to examine the MAC address table on a Cisco switch.

The **show mac address-table** EXEC command displays the contents of a switch's MAC address table. This command lists all MAC addresses currently known by the switch. The output includes some static overhead MAC addresses used by the switch and any statically configured MAC addresses, such as those configured with the port security feature. The command also lists all dynamically learned MAC addresses. If you want to see only the dynamically learned MAC address table entries, simply use the **show mac address-table dynamic** EXEC command.

The more formal troubleshooting process begins with a prediction of what should happen in a network, followed by an effort to isolate any problems that prevent the normal expected results. As an exercise, go back and review Figure 10-2, and try to create a MAC address table on paper for each switch. Include the MAC addresses for both PCs, as well as the Fa0/1 MAC address for R1. Then predict which interfaces would be used to forward a frame sent by Fred, Barney, and R1 to every other device. Even though the path the frames should take may be somewhat obvious in this exercise, it might be worthwhile, because it forces you to correlate what you'd expect to see in the MAC address table with how the switches forward frames. Example 10-5 shows the MAC address tables on both switches from Figure 10-2 so that you can check your answers.

The next step in the troubleshooting process is to isolate any problems with forwarding frames. Example 10-5 shows an example using the small network depicted in Figure 10-2, with no problems occurring. This example shows the MAC address table of both SW1 and SW2. Also, for this example, SW1 has been configured to use port security on its Fa0/9 interface, for MAC address 0200.1111.1111 (Fred's MAC address), just so the example can point out the differences between dynamically learned MAC addresses and statically configured MAC addresses.

Example 10-5 *Examining SW1's and SW2's MAC Address Tables*

```
SW1#show mac address-table
          Mac Address Table
-------------------------------------------

Vlan    Mac Address       Type        Ports
----    -----------       --------    -----
 All    0100.0ccc.cccc    STATIC      CPU
 All    0100.0ccc.cccd    STATIC      CPU
 All    0180.c200.0000    STATIC      CPU
 All    0180.c200.0001    STATIC      CPU
 All    0180.c200.0002    STATIC      CPU
 All    0180.c200.0003    STATIC      CPU
 All    0180.c200.0004    STATIC      CPU
 All    0180.c200.0005    STATIC      CPU
 All    0180.c200.0006    STATIC      CPU
 All    0180.c200.0007    STATIC      CPU
 All    0180.c200.0008    STATIC      CPU
 All    0180.c200.0009    STATIC      CPU
 All    0180.c200.000a    STATIC      CPU
 All    0180.c200.000b    STATIC      CPU
```

Example 10-5 *Examining SW1's and SW2's MAC Address Tables (Continued)*

```
 All    0180.c200.000c    STATIC    CPU
 All    0180.c200.000d    STATIC    CPU
 All    0180.c200.000e    STATIC    CPU
 All    0180.c200.000f    STATIC    CPU
 All    0180.c200.0010    STATIC    CPU
 All    ffff.ffff.ffff    STATIC    CPU
   1    0019.e859.539a    DYNAMIC   Gi0/1
! The next three entries are for Fred (statically-configured due to port security),
!  Barney (dynamically learned), and router R1 (dynamically learned)
!
   1    0200.1111.1111    STATIC    Fa0/9
   1    0200.2222.2222    DYNAMIC   Fa0/12
   1    0200.5555.5555    DYNAMIC   Gi0/1
Total Mac Addresses for this criterion: 24
!
! The next command just lists dynamically learned MAC addresses, so it does not list
  Fred's
! MAC address, because it is considered static due to the port security configuration.
!
SW1#show mac address-table dynamic
          Mac Address Table
-------------------------------------------


Vlan    Mac Address      Type      Ports
----    -----------      --------  -----
   1    0019.e859.539a   DYNAMIC   Gi0/1
   1    0200.2222.2222   DYNAMIC   Fa0/12
   1    0200.5555.5555   DYNAMIC   Gi0/1
Total Mac Addresses for this criterion: 3
! The same command on SW2 lists the same MAC addresses, but SW2's interfaces used
! to reach those addresses.
SW2#show mac address-table dynamic
          Mac Address Table
-------------------------------------------


Vlan    Mac Address      Type      Ports
----    -----------      --------  -----
   1    0019.e86a.6f99   DYNAMIC   Gi0/2
   1    0200.1111.1111   DYNAMIC   Gi0/2
   1    0200.2222.2222   DYNAMIC   Gi0/2
   1    0200.5555.5555   DYNAMIC   Fa0/13
Total Mac Addresses for this criterion: 4
! The highlighted line above for 0200.5555.5555 will be used in the explanations
! following this example.
```

When predicting the MAC address table entries, you need to imagine a frame sent by a device to another device on the other side of the LAN and then determine which switch ports the frame would enter as it passes through the LAN. For example, if Barney sends a frame to router R1, the frame would enter SW1's Fa0/12 interface, so SW1 has a MAC table entry that lists Barney's 0200.2222.2222 MAC address with Fa0/12. SW1 would forward Barney's frame to SW2, arriving on SW2's Gi0/2 interface, so SW2's MAC table lists Barney's MAC address (0200.2222.2222) with interface Gi0/2.

> **NOTE**   The MAC table entries in Example 10-5 list several additional entries, entries that list a port of "CPU" and refer to MAC addresses used by the switch for overhead traffic such as CDP and STP. These entries tell the switch to send frames destined for these MAC addresses to the switch's CPU.

After you predict the expected contents of the MAC address tables, you can then examine what is actually happening on the switches, as described in the next section.

Analyzing the Forwarding Path

To analyze the actual path taken by a frame in this network, a few reminders are necessary. As mentioned earlier, this book's coverage of VLANs assumes that no trunks exist, so all interfaces are access interfaces—meaning that they are assigned to be in a single VLAN. So, although it isn't shown in Example 10-5, assume that the **show vlan brief** command lists all the interfaces on each switch as being assigned to default VLAN 1.

The switch forwarding logic can be summarized as follows:

Key Topic

Step 1   Determine the VLAN in which the frame should be forwarded. On access interfaces this is based on the access VLAN associated with the incoming interface.

Step 2   Look for the frame's destination MAC address in the MAC address table, but only for entries in the VLAN identified in Step 1. If the destination MAC is...

   A. **Found (unicast)**, forward the frame out the only interface listed in the matched address table entry.

B. **Not found (unicast)**, flood the frame out all other access ports (except the incoming port) in that same VLAN.

C. **Broadcast or multicast**, flood the frame out all other access ports (except the incoming port) in that same VLAN.

> **NOTE**   Chapter 3 in the *ICND2 Official Exam Certification Guide* includes a more extensive summary of the forwarding process, including comments on the impact of VLAN trunking and STP on the forwarding process.

Using this process as a guide, consider a frame sent by Barney to its default gateway, R1 (0200.5555.5555). Using the same switch forwarding logic steps, the following occurs:

Step 1   SW1 receives the frame on its Fa0/12 interface and sees that it is assigned to access VLAN 1.

Step 2   SW1 looks for its MAC table entry for 0200.5555.5555, in the incoming interface's VLAN (VLAN 1), in its MAC address table.

A. SW1 finds an entry, associated with VLAN 1, outgoing interface Gi0/1, so SW1 forwards the frame only out interface Gi0/1.

At this point, the frame with source 0200.2222.2222 (Barney) is on its way to SW2. You can then pick up SW2's logic, with the following explanation numbered to match the forwarding process summary:

Step 1   SW2 receives the frame on its Gi0/2 interface and sees that Gi0/2 is assigned to access VLAN 1.

Step 2   SW2 looks for its MAC table entry for 0200.5555.5555, in the incoming interface's VLAN (VLAN 1), in its MAC address table.

A. SW2 finds an entry, associated with VLAN 1, outgoing interface Fa0/13, so SW2 forwards the frame only out interface Fa0/13.

At this point, the frame should be on its way, over the Ethernet cable between SW2 and R1.

Port Security and Filtering

Frankly, in real life, you will likely find any switching-related problems before you get to the point of having to think about every possible interface out which a switch forwards a frame. However, the exam can easily test you on the forwarding logic used in switches.

When it appears that all interfaces are up and working, and the switching table would allow a frame to be delivered, but the frame still does not arrive, the problem is likely to be related to some kind of filtering. LAN switches can be configured with access control lists (ACL), which filter frames. Additionally, routers can configure and use ACLs, so if a router is either the sender or receiver of a frame, the router's ACL might be filtering the frame. However, switch ACLs are not covered for the CCNA exams, although router ACLs are covered as part of the *CCNA ICND2 Exam Certification Guide*.

This book does cover one filtering tool that could make it appear that a frame can be delivered (according to the MAC address tables), but the switch discards the frame. With port security enabled with a violate action to shut down the interface, the switch may discard frames. Because of the shutdown violating action, the switch would disable the interface, making it easy to discover the reason why the frame was discarded by simply looking at the interface status. However, with either the **protect** or **restrict** violation action configured, the switch discards the offending traffic, but it leaves the port in a connect (up/up) state. So, a simple **show interface** or **show interface status** command does not identify the reason for the problem.

For example, imagine that Barney (0200.2222.2222) is again sending a frame to router R1 (0200.5555.5555), but SW1 has been configured for port security in a way that disallows traffic from MAC address 0200.2222.2222 on port Fa0/12 of SW1, with a **protect** action. An analysis of the MAC address table on both SW1 and SW2 might well look exactly like it does in Example 10-5, with SW1's entry for 0200.5555.5555 referring out interface Gi0/1, and SW2's entry referring to Fa0/13. However, SW1 never even attempts to forward the frame because of the port security violation based on the source MAC address of Barney's frame as it enters SW1's Fa0/12 interface.

Exam Preparation Tasks

Review All the Key Topics

Review the most important topics from this chapter, noted with the key topics icon. Table 10-6 describes these key topics and where each is discussed.

Key
Topic

Table 10-6 *Key Topics for Chapter 10*

Key Topic Element	Description	Page Number
List	Information gathered by CDP	278
Table 10-2	Three CDP **show** commands that list information about neighbors	278
Table 10-4	Two types of interface state terms and their meanings	283
List	Defaults for IEEE autonegotiation	286
Table 10-5	Common reasons for Layer 1 LAN problems even when the interface is up	289
List	Summary of switch forwarding steps	292

Complete the Tables and Lists from Memory

Print a copy of Appendix H, "Memory Tables" (found on the CD), or at least the section for this chapter, and complete the tables and lists from memory. Appendix I, "Memory Tables Answer Key," also on the CD, includes completed tables and lists for you to check your work.

Definitions of Key Terms

Define the following key terms from this chapter, and check your answers in the glossary:

CDP neighbor, up and up, error disabled, problem isolation, root cause

Command References

Tables 10-7 and 10-8 list only commands specifically mentioned in this chapter, but the command references at the end of Chapters 8 and 9 also cover some related commands. Table 10-7 lists and briefly describes the configuration commands used in this chapter.

Table 10-7 *Commands for Catalyst 2950 Switch Configuration*

Command	Description
shutdown **no shutdown**	Interface subcommands that administratively disable and enable an interface, respectively.
switchport port-security violation **{protect | restrict | shutdown}**	Interface subcommand that tells the switch what to do if an inappropriate MAC address tries to access the network through a secure switch port.
cdp run **no cdp run**	Global commands that enable and disable, respectively, CDP for the entire switch or router.
cdp enable **no cdp enable**	Interface subcommands that enable and disable, respectively, CDP for a particular interface.
speed {10 | 100 | 1000}	Interface subcommand that manually sets the interface speed.
duplex {auto | full | half}	Interface subcommand that manually sets the interface duplex.

Table 10-8 lists and briefly describes the EXEC commands used in this chapter.

Table 10-8 *Chapter 10 EXEC Command Reference*

Command	Description
show mac address-table [dynamic | static] **[address** *hw-addr*] **[interface** *interface-id*] **[vlan** *vlan-id*]	Displays the MAC address table. The security option displays information about the restricted or static settings.
show port-security [interface *interface-id*] **[address]**	Displays information about security options configured on an interface.
show cdp neighbors [*type number*]	Lists one summary line of information about each neighbor, or just the neighbor found on a specific interface if an interface was listed.
show cdp neighbors detail	Lists one large set of information (approximately 15 lines) for every neighbor.
show cdp entry *name*	Displays the same information as the **show cdp neighbors detail** command, but only for the named neighbor.
show cdp	States whether CDP is enabled globally, and lists the default update and holdtime timers.

Table 10-8 *Chapter 10 EXEC Command Reference (Continued)*

show cdp interface [*type number*]	States whether CDP is enabled on each interface, or a single interface if the interface is listed, and states update and holdtime timers on those interfaces.
show cdp traffic	Displays global statistics for the number of CDP advertisements sent and received.
show interfaces [*type number*]	Displays detailed information about interface status, settings, and counters.
show interfaces status [*type number*]	Displays summary information about interface status and settings, including actual speed and duplex, and whether the interface was autonegotiated.

This chapter covers the following subjects:

Wireless LAN Concepts: This section explains the basic theory behind transmitting data with radio waves using wireless LAN standards.

Deploying WLANs: This section lists a set of generic steps for installing small WLANs, with no product-specific details.

Wireless LAN Security: This section explains the various WLAN security options that have progressed through the years.

CHAPTER 11

Wireless LANs

So far, this book has dedicated a lot of attention to (wired) Ethernet LANs. Although they are vitally important, another style of LAN, wireless LANs (WLAN), fills a particularly important role in providing network access to end users. In particular, WLANs allow the user to communicate over the network without requiring any cables, enabling mobile devices while removing the expense and effort involved in running cables. This chapter examines the basic concepts, standards, installation, and security options for some of the most common WLAN technologies today.

As a reminder if you're following the optional reading plan listed in the Introduction to this book, you will be moving on to Chapter 1 of the *CCNA ICND2 Official Exam Certification Guide* following this chapter.

"Do I Know This Already?" Quiz

The "Do I Know This Already?" quiz allows you to assess whether you should read the entire chapter. If you miss no more than one of these nine self-assessment questions, you might want to move ahead to the "Exam Preparation Tasks" section. Table 11-1 lists the major headings in this chapter and the "Do I Know This Already?" quiz questions covering the material in those sections. This helps you assess your knowledge of these specific areas. The answers to the "Do I Know This Already?" quiz appear in Appendix A.

Table 11-1 *"Do I Know This Already?" Foundation Topics Section-to-Question Mapping*

Foundation Topics Section	Questions
Wireless LAN Concepts	1–4
Deploying WLANs	5–7
Wireless LAN Security	8, 9

1. Which of the following IEEE wireless LAN standards uses only the U-NII band of frequencies (around 5.4 GHz)?

    a. 802.11a

    b. 802.11b

    c. 802.11g

    d. 802.11i

2. Which of the following answers is the correct maximum speed at which two IEEE WLAN devices can send data with a particular standard?

    a. 802.11b, using OFDM, at 54 Mbps

    b. 802.11g, using OFDM, at 54 Mbps

    c. 802.11a, using DSSS, at 54 Mbps

    d. 802.11a, using DSSS, at 11 Mbps

3. Which of the following lists the nonoverlapping channels when using 802.1b DSSS in the U.S.?

    a. 1, 2, 3

    b. 1, 5, 9

    c. 1, 6, 11

    d. a, b, g

    e. 22, 33, 44

4. Which of the following terms refers to a WLAN mode that allows a laptop to roam between different access points?

    a. ESS

    b. BSS

    c. IBSS

    d. None of the other answers are correct.

5. When configuring a wireless access point, which of the following are typical configuration choices?

    a. SSID

    b. The speed to use

    c.   The wireless standard to use

    d.   The size of the desired coverage area

6. Which of the following is true about an ESS's connections to the wired Ethernet LAN?

    a.   The AP connects to the Ethernet switch using a crossover cable.

    b.   The various APs in the same WLAN need to be assigned to the same VLAN by the Ethernet switches.

    c.   The APs must have an IP address configured to forward traffic.

    d.   The APs using mixed 802.11g mode must connect via a Fast Ethernet or faster connection to an Ethernet switch.

7. Which of the following are not common reasons why a newly installed WLAN does not allow a client to connect through the WLAN into the wired infrastructure?

    a.   The AP is installed on top of a metal filing cabinet.

    b.   The client is near a fast-food restaurant's microwave oven.

    c.   The client is sitting on top of a big bundle of currently used Cat5 Ethernet cables.

    d.   The AP was configured to use DSSS channel 1 instead of the default channel 6, and no one configured the client to use channel 6.

8. Which of the following WLAN security standards refer to the IEEE standard?

    a.   WPA

    b.   WPA2

    c.   WEP

    d.   802.11i

9. Which of the following security features were not in the original WEP security standard but are now in the WPA2 security standard?

    a.   Dynamic key exchange

    b.   Preshared Keys (PSK)

    c.   802.1x authentication

    d.   AES encryption

Foundation Topics

This chapter examines the basics of WLANs. In particular, the first section introduces the concepts, protocols, and standards used by many of the most common WLAN installations today. The chapter then examines some basic installation steps. The last major section looks at WLAN security, which is particularly important because the WLAN signals are much more susceptible to being intercepted by an attacker than Ethernet LANs.

Wireless LAN Concepts

Many people use WLANs on a regular basis today. PC sales continue to trend toward more laptop sales versus desktop computers, in part to support a more mobile workforce. PC users need to connect to whatever network they are near, whether at work, at home, in a hotel, or at a coffee shop or bookstore. The migration toward a work model in which you find working moments wherever you are, with a need to be connected to the Internet at any time, continues to push the growth of wireless LANs.

For example, Figure 11-1 shows the design of a LAN at a retail bookstore. The bookstore provides free Internet access via WLANs while also supporting the bookstore's devices via a wired LAN.

The wireless-capable customer laptops communicate with a WLAN device called an access point (AP). The AP uses wireless communications to send and receive frames with the WLAN clients (the laptops). The AP also connects to the same Ethernet LAN as the bookstore's own devices, allowing both customers and employees to communicate with other sites.

This section begins the chapter by explaining the basics of WLANs, starting with a comparison of similarities between Ethernet LANs and WLANs. The rest of the section then explores some of the main differences.

Comparisons with Ethernet LANs

WLANs are similar to Ethernet LANs in many ways, the most important being that WLANs allow communications to occur between devices. The IEEE defines standards for both, using the IEEE 802.3 family for Ethernet LANs and the 802.11 family for WLANs. Both standards define a frame format with a header and trailer, with the header including a source and destination MAC address field, each 6 bytes in length. Both define rules about how the devices should determine when they should send frames and when they should not.

Figure 11-1   *Sample WLAN at a Bookstore*

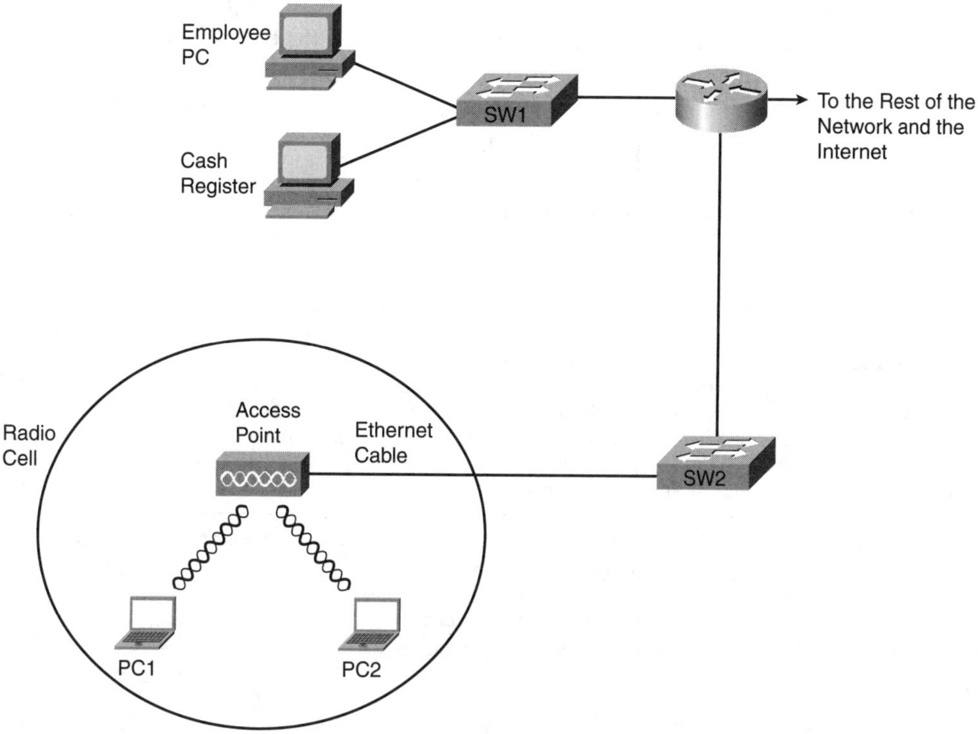

The biggest difference between the two lies in the fact that WLANs use radiated energy waves, generally called radio waves, to transmit data, whereas Ethernet uses electrical signals flowing over a cable (or light on optical cabling). Radio waves pass through space, so technically there is no need for any physical transmission medium. In fact, the presence of matter—in particular, walls, metal objects, and other obstructions—gets in the way of the wireless radio signals.

Several other differences exist as well, mainly as a side effect of the use of wireless instead of wires. For example, Chapter 7, "Ethernet LAN Switching Concepts," explains how Ethernet can support full-duplex (FDX) communication if a switch connects to a single device rather than a hub. This removes the need to control access to the link using carrier sense multiple access collision detect (CSMA/CD). With wireless, if more than one device at a time sends radio waves in the same space at the same frequency, neither signal is intelligible, so a half-duplex (HDX) mechanism must be used. To arbitrate the use of the frequency, WLANs use the carrier sense multiple access with collision avoidance (CSMA/CA) algorithm to enforce HDX logic and avoid as many collisions as possible.

Wireless LAN Standards

At the time this book was published, the IEEE had ratified four major WLAN standards: 802.11, 802.11a, 802.11b, and 802.11g. This section lists the basic details of each WLAN standard, along with information about a couple of other standards bodies. This section also briefly mentions the emerging 802.11n standard, which the IEEE had not yet ratified by the time this book was published.

Four organizations have a great deal of impact on the standards used for wireless LANs today. Table 11-2 lists these organizations and describes their roles.

Key Topic

Table 11-2 *Organizations That Set or Influence WLAN Standards*

Organization	Standardization Role
ITU-R	Worldwide standardization of communications that use radiated energy, particularly managing the assignment of frequencies
IEEE	Standardization of wireless LANs (802.11)
Wi-Fi Alliance	An industry consortium that encourages interoperability of products that implement WLAN standards through their Wi-Fi certified program
Federal Communications Commission (FCC)	The U.S. government agency with that regulates the usage of various communications frequencies in the U.S.

Of the organizations listed in this table, the IEEE develops the specific standards for the different types of WLANs used today. Those standards must take into account the frequency choices made by the different worldwide regulatory agencies, such as the FCC in the U.S. and the ITU-R, which is ultimately controlled by the United Nations (UN).

The IEEE introduced WLAN standards with the creation of the 1997 ratification of the 802.11 standard. This original standard did not have a suffix letter, whereas later WLAN standards do. This naming logic, with no suffix letter in the first standard, followed by other standards with a suffix letter, is like the original IEEE Ethernet standard. That standard was 802.3, with later, more-advanced standards having a suffix, such as 802.3u for Fast Ethernet.

The original 802.11 standard has been replaced by more-advanced standards. In order of ratification, the standards are 802.11b, 802.11a, and 802.11g. Of note, the 802.11n standard is likely to be ratified by the end of 2008, with prestandard products available in 2007. Table 11-3 lists some key points about the currently ratified standards.

Table 11-3 *WLAN Standards*

Feature	802.11a	802.11b	802.11g
Year ratified	1999	1999	2003
Maximum speed using DSSS	—	11 Mbps	11 Mbps
Maximum speed using OFDM	54 Mbps	—	54 Mbps
Frequency band	5 GHz	2.4 GHz	2.4 GHz
Channels (nonoverlapped)*	23 (12)	11 (3)	11 (3)
Speeds required by standard (Mbps)	6, 12, 24	1, 2, 5.5, 11	6, 12, 24

*These values assume a WLAN in the U.S.

This table lists a couple of features that have not yet been defined but that are described in this chapter.

Modes of 802.11 Wireless LANs

WLANs can use one of two modes—ad hoc mode or infrastructure mode. With ad hoc mode, a wireless device wants to communicate with only one or a few other devices directly, usually for a short period of time. In these cases, the devices send WLAN frames directly to each other, as shown in Figure 11-2.

Figure 11-2 *Ad Hoc WLAN*

In infrastructure mode, each device communicates with an AP, with the AP connecting via wired Ethernet to the rest of the network infrastructure. Infrastructure mode allows the WLAN devices to communicate with servers and the Internet in an existing wired network, as shown earlier in Figure 11-1.

NOTE Devices in an infrastructure WLAN cannot send frames directly to each other; instead, they send frames to the AP, which can then in turn forward the frames to another WLAN device.

Infrastructure mode supports two sets of services, called *service sets*. The first, called a Basic Service Set (BSS), uses a single AP to create the wireless LAN, as shown in Figure 11-1. The other, called Extended Service Set (ESS), uses more than one AP, often with overlapping cells to allow roaming in a larger area, as shown in Figure 11-3.

Figure 11-3 *Infrastructure Mode BSS and ESS WLANs*

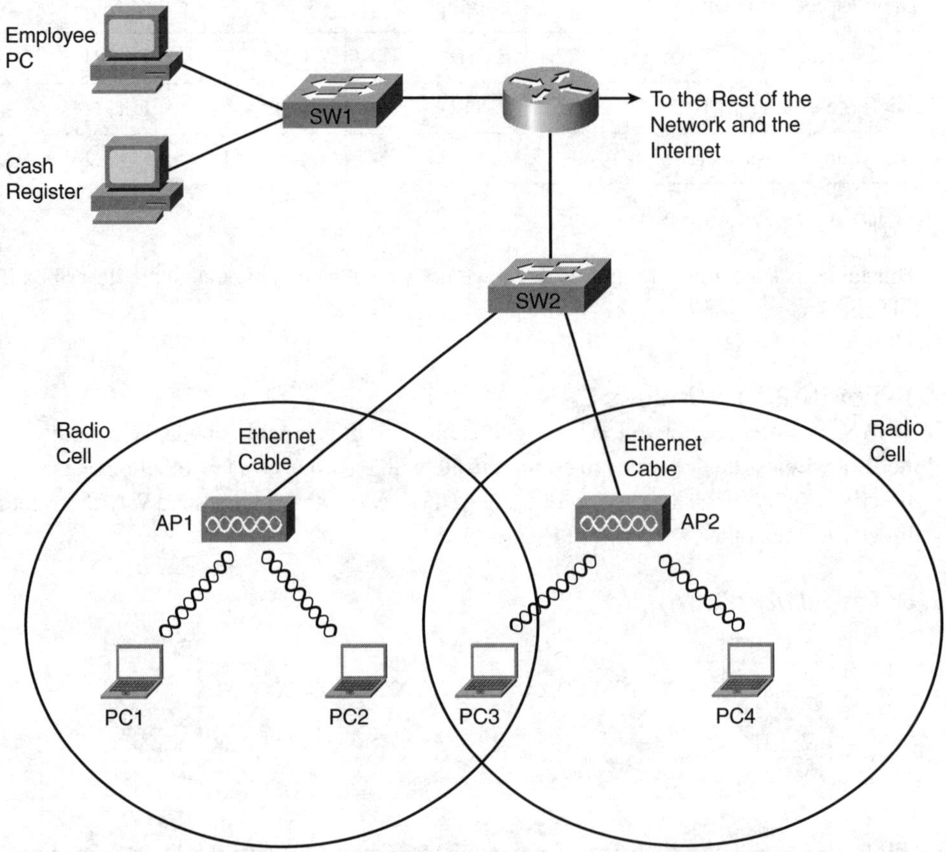

The ESS WLANs allow roaming, which means that users can move around inside the coverage area and stay connected to the same WLAN. As a result, the user does not need to change IP addresses. All the device has to do is sense when the radio signals from the current AP are getting weaker; find a new, better AP with a stronger or better signal; and start using the new AP.

Table 11-4 summarizes the WLAN modes for easy reference.

Table 11-4 *Different WLAN Modes and Names*

Mode	Service Set Name	Description
Ad hoc	Independent Basic Service Set (IBSS)	Allows two devices to communicate directly. No AP is needed.
Infrastructure (one AP)	Basic Service Set (BSS)	A single wireless LAN created with an AP and all devices that associate with that AP.
Infrastructure (more than one AP)	Extended Service Set (ESS)	Multiple APs create one wireless LAN, allowing roaming and a larger coverage area.

Wireless Transmissions (Layer 1)

WLANs transmit data at Layer 1 by sending and receiving radio waves. The WLAN network interface cards (NIC), APs, and other WLAN devices use a radio and its antenna to send and receive the radio waves, making small changes to the waves to encode data. Although the details differ significantly compared to Ethernet, the idea of encoding data by changing the energy signal that flows over a medium is the same idea as Ethernet encoding.

Similar to electricity on copper wires and light over optical cables, WLAN radio waves have a repeating signal that can be graphed over time, as shown in Figure 11-4. When graphed, the curve shows a repeating periodic waveform, with a frequency (the number of times the waveform repeats per second), amplitude (the height of the waveform, representing signal strength), and phase (the particular point in the repeating waveform). Of these items, frequency, measured in hertz (Hz), is the most important in discussions of WLANs.

Figure 11-4 *Graph of an 8-KHz Signal*

.001 Seconds

Frequency = 8000 Hz

Many electronic devices radiate energy at varying frequencies, some related to the device's purpose (for example, a wireless LAN or a cordless telephone). In other cases the radiated energy is a side effect. For example, televisions give off some radiated energy. To prevent the energy radiated by one device from interfering with other devices, national government agencies, regulate and oversee the frequency ranges that can be used inside that country. For example, the Federal Communications Commission (FCC) in the U.S. regulates the electromagnetic spectrum of frequencies.

The FCC or other national regulatory agencies specify some ranges of frequencies, called frequency bands. For example, in the U.S., FM and AM radio stations must register with the FCC to use a particular range (band) of frequencies. A radio station agrees to transmit its radio signal at or under a particular power level so that other radio stations in other cities can use the same frequency band. However, only that one radio station can use a particular frequency band in a particular location.

A frequency band is so named because it is actually a range of consecutive frequencies. An FM radio station needs about 200 kilohertz (KHz) of frequency in which to send a radio signal. When the station requests a frequency from the FCC, the FCC assigns a base frequency, with 100 KHz of bandwidth on either side of the base frequency. For example, an FM radio station that announces something like "The greatest hits are at 96.5 FM" means that the base signal is 96.5 megahertz (MHz), with the radio transmitter using the frequency band between 96.4 MHz and 96.6 MHz, for a total bandwidth of .2 MHz, or 200 KHz.

The wider the range of frequencies in a frequency band, the greater the amount of information that can be sent in that frequency band. For example, a radio signal needs about 200 KHz (.2 MHz) of bandwidth, whereas a broadcast TV signal, which contains a lot more information because of the video content, requires roughly 4.5 MHz.

> **NOTE**   The use of the term bandwidth to refer to speeds of network interfaces is just a holdover from the idea that the width (range) of a frequency band is a measurement of how much data can be sent in a period of time.

The FCC, and equivalent agencies in other countries, license some frequency bands, leaving some frequency bands unlicensed. Licensed bands are used for many purposes; the most common are AM and FM radio, Ultra High Frequency (UHF) radio (for example, for police department communications), and mobile phones. Unlicensed frequencies can be used by all kinds of devices; however, the devices must still conform to the rules set up by the regulatory agency. In particular, a device using an unlicensed band must use power levels at or below a particular setting. Otherwise, the device might interfere too much with other devices sharing that unlicensed band. For example, microwave ovens happen to radiate energy in the 2.4 gigahertz (GHz) unlicensed band as a side effect of cooking food. That same unlicensed band is used by some WLAN standards and by many cordless telephones. In some cases, you cannot hear someone on the phone or surf the Internet using a WLAN when someone's heating up dinner.

The FCC defines three unlicensed frequency bands. The bands are referenced by a particular frequency in the band, although by definition, a frequency band is a range of frequencies. Table 11-5 lists the frequency bands that matter to some degree for WLAN communications.

Table 11-5 *FCC Unlicensed Frequency Bands of Interest*

Key
Topic

Frequency Range	Name	Sample Devices
900 MHz	Industrial, Scientific, Medical (ISM)	Older cordless telephones
2.4 GHz	ISM	Newer cordless phones and 802.11, 802.11b, 802.11g WLANs
5 GHz	Unlicensed National Information Infrastructure (U-NII)	Newer cordless phones and 802.11a, 802.11n WLANs

Wireless Encoding and Nonoverlapping DSSS Channels

When a WLAN NIC or AP sends data, it can modulate (change) the radio signal's frequency, amplitude, and phase to encode a binary 0 or 1. The details of that encoding are beyond the scope of this book. However, it is important to know the names of three general classes of encoding, in part because the type of encoding requires some planning and forethought for some WLANs.

Frequency Hopping Spread Spectrum (FHSS) uses all frequencies in the band, hopping to different ones. By using slightly different frequencies for consecutive transmissions, a device can hopefully avoid interference from other devices that use the same unlicensed band, succeeding at sending data at some frequencies. The original 802.11 WLAN standards used FHSS, but the current standards (802.11a, 802.11b, and 802.11g) do not.

Direct Sequence Spread Spectrum (DSSS) followed as the next general class of encoding type for WLANs. Designed for use in the 2.4 GHz unlicensed band, DSSS uses one of several separate channels or frequencies. This band has a bandwidth of 82 MHz, with a range from 2.402 GHz to 2.483 GHz. As regulated by the FCC, this band can have 11 different overlapping DSSS channels, as shown in Figure 11-5.

Although many of the channels shown in the figure overlap, three of the channels (the channels at the far left and far right, and the channel in the center) do not overlap enough to impact each other. These channels (channels 1, 6, and 11) can be used in the same space for WLAN communications, and they won't interfere with each other.

Figure 11-5 *Eleven Overlapping DSSS Channels at 2.4 GHz*

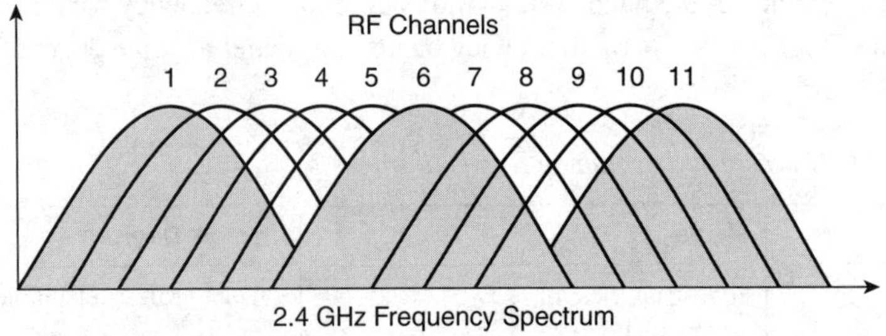

The significance of the nonoverlapping DSSS channels is that when you design an ESS WLAN (more than one AP), APs with overlapping coverage areas should be set to use different nonoverlapping channels. Figure 11-6 shows the idea.

Figure 11-6 *Using Nonoverlapping DSSS 2.4-GHz Channels in an ESS WLAN*

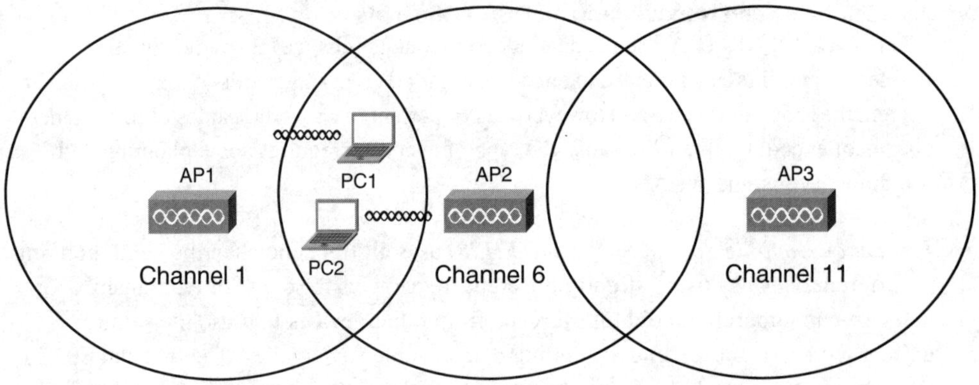

In this design, the devices in one BSS (devices communicating through one AP) can send at the same time as the other two BSSs and not interfere with each other, because each uses the slightly different frequencies of the nonoverlapping channels. For example, PC1 and PC2 could sit beside each other and communicate with two different APs using two different channels at the exact same time. This design is typical of 802.11b WLANs, with each cell running at a maximum data rate of 11 Mbps. With the nonoverlapping channels, each half-duplex BSS can run at 11 Mbps, for a cumulative bandwidth of 33 Mbps in this case. This cumulative bandwidth is called the WAN's *capacity*.

The last of the three categories of encoding for WLANs is called Orthogonal Frequency Division Multiplexing (OFDM). Like DSSS, WLANs that use OFDM can use multiple nonoverlapping channels. Table 11-6 summarizes the key points and names of the main three options for encoding.

Table 11-6 *Encoding Classes and IEEE Standard WLANs*

Name of Encoding Class	What It Is Used By
Frequency Hopping Spread Spectrum (FHSS)	802.11
Direct Sequence Spread Spectrum (DSSS)	802.11b, 802.11g
Orthogonal Frequency Division Multiplexing (OFDM)	802.11a, 802.11g

NOTE The emerging 802.11n standard uses OFDM as well as multiple antennas, a technology sometimes called multiple input multiple output (MIMO).

Wireless Interference

WLANs can suffer from interference from many sources. The radio waves travel through space, but they must pass through whatever matter exists inside the coverage area, including walls, floors, and ceilings. Passing through matter causes the signal to be partially absorbed, which reduces signal strength and the size of the coverage area. Matter can also reflect and scatter the waves, particularly if there is a lot of metal in the materials, which can cause dead spots (areas in which the WLAN simply does not work), and a smaller coverage area.

Additionally, wireless communication is impacted by other radio waves in the same frequency range. The effect is the same as trying to listen to a radio station when you're taking a long road trip. You might get a good clear signal for a while, but eventually you drive far enough from the radio station's antenna that the signal is weak, and it is hard to hear the station. Eventually, you get close enough to the next city's radio station that uses the same frequency range, and you cannot hear either station well because of the interference. With WLANs, the interference may simply mean that the data only occasionally makes it through the air, requiring lots of retransmissions, and resulting in poor efficiency.

One key measurement for interference is the Signal-to-Noise Ratio (SNR). This calculation measures the WLAN signal as compared to the other undesired signals (noise) in the same space. The higher the SNR, the better the WLAN devices can send data successfully.

Coverage Area, Speed, and Capacity

A WLAN coverage area is the space in which two WLAN devices can successfully send data. The coverage area created by a particular AP depends on many factors, several of which are explained in this section.

First, the transmit power by an AP or WLAN NIC cannot exceed a particular level based on the regulations from regulatory agencies such as the FCC. The FCC limits the transmit power to ensure fairness in the unlicensed bands. For example, if two neighbors bought Linksys APs and put them in their homes to create a WLAN, the products would conform to FCC regulations. However, if one person bought and installed high-gain antennas for her AP, and greatly exceeded the FCC regulations, she might get a much wider coverage area—maybe even across the whole neighborhood. However, it might prevent the other person's AP from working at all because of the interference from the overpowered AP.

NOTE   The power of an AP is measured based on the Effective Isotropic Radiated Power (EIRP) calculation. This is the radio's power output, plus the increase in power caused by the antenna, minus any power lost in the cabling. In effect, it's the power of the signal as it leaves the antenna.

The materials and locations of the materials near the AP also impact an AP's coverage area. For example, putting the AP near a large metal filing cabinet increases reflections and scattering, which shrinks the coverage area. Certainly, concrete construction with steel rebar reduces the coverage area in a typical modern office building. In fact, when a building's design means that interference will occur in some areas, APs may use different types of antennas that change the shape of the coverage area from a circle to some other shape.

As it turns out, weaker wireless signals cannot pass data at higher speeds, but they can pass data at lower speeds. So, WLAN standards support the idea of multiple speeds. A device near the AP may have a strong signal, so it can transmit and receive data with the AP at higher rates. A device at the edge of the coverage area, where the signals are weak, may still be able to send and receive data—although at a slower speed. Figure 11-7 shows the idea of a coverage area, with varying speeds, for an IEEE 802.11b BSS.

The main ways to increase the size of the coverage area of one AP are to use specialized antennas and to increase the power of the transmitted signal. For example, you can increase the antenna gain, which is the power added to the radio signal by the antenna. To double the coverage area, the antenna gain must be increased to quadruple the original gain. Although this is useful, the power output (the EIRP) must still be within FCC rules (in the U.S.).

The actual size of the coverage area depends on a large number of factors that are beyond the scope of this book. Some of the factors include the frequency band used by the WLAN standard, the obstructions between and near the WLAN devices, the interference from other sources of RF energy, the antennas used on both the clients and APs, and the options used by DSSS and OFDM when encoding data over the air. Generally speaking, WLAN standards that use higher frequencies (U-NII band standards 802.11a and the future 802.11n) can send data faster, but with the price of smaller coverage areas. To cover all the required space, an ESS that uses higher frequencies would then require more APs, driving up the cost of the WLAN deployment.

Figure 11-7 *Coverage Area and Speed*

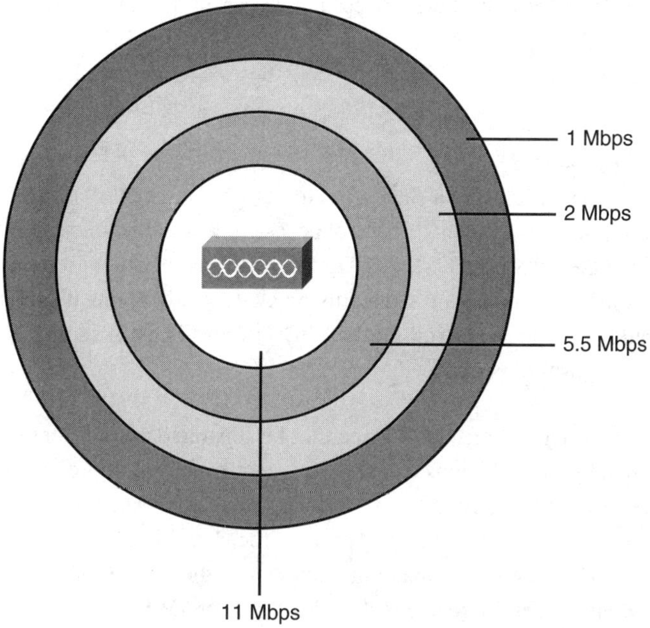

Table 11-7 lists the main IEEE WLAN standards that had been ratified at the time this book was published, the maximum speed, and the number of nonoverlapping channels.

Table 11-7 *WLAN Speed and Frequency Reference*

IEEE Standard	Maximum Speed (Mbps)	Other Speeds* (Mbps)	Frequency	Nonoverlapping Channels
802.11b	11 Mbps	1, 2, 5.5	2.4 GHz	3
802.11a	54 Mbps	**6**, 9, **12**, 18, **24**, 36, 48	5 GHz	12
802.11g	54 Mbps	Same as 802.11a	2.4 GHz	3

*The speeds listed in bold text are required speeds according to the standards. The other speeds are optional.

NOTE The original 802.11 standard supported speeds of 1 and 2 Mbps.

Finally, note that the number of (mostly) nonoverlapping channels supported by a standard, as shown in Figures 11-5 and 11-6, affects the combined available bandwidth. For example, in a WLAN that exclusively uses 802.11g, the actual transmissions could occur at 54 Mbps. But three devices could sit beside each other and send at the same time, using three different channels, to three different APs. Theoretically, that WLAN could support a throughput of 3 * 54 Mbps, or 162 Mbps, for these devices in that part of the WLAN. Along the same line of reasoning, an 802.11a WLAN can transmit data at 54 Mbps, but with 12 nonoverlapping channels, for a theoretical maximum of 12 * 54 Mbps = 648 Mbps of bandwidth capacity.

Media Access (Layer 2)

Ethernet LANs began life using a shared medium (a coaxial cable), meaning that only one device could send data at a time. To control access to this half-duplex (HDX) medium, Ethernet defined the use of the CSMA/CD algorithm. As Ethernet progressed with continually improved standards, it started using switches, with one device cabled to each switch port, allowing the use of full duplex (FDX). With FDX, no collisions can occur, so the CSMA/CD algorithm is disabled.

With wireless communications, devices cannot be separated onto different cable segments to prevent collisions, so collisions can always occur, even with more-advanced WLAN standards. In short, if two or more WLAN devices send at the same time, using overlapping frequency ranges, a collision occurs, and none of the transmitted signals can be understood by those receiving the signal. To make matters worse, the device that is transmitting data cannot concurrently listen for received data. So, when two WLAN devices send at the same time, creating a collision, the sending devices do not have any direct way to know the collision occurred.

The solution to the media access problem with WLANs is to use the *carrier sense multiple access with collision avoidance (CSMA/CA)* algorithm. The collision avoidance part minimizes the statistical chance that collisions could occur. However, CSMA/CA does not prevent collisions, so the WLAN standards must have a process to deal with collisions when they do occur. Because the sending device cannot tell if its transmitted frame collided with another frame, the standards all require an acknowledgment of every frame. Each WLAN device listens for the acknowledgment, which should occur immediately after the frame is sent. If no acknowledgment is received, the sending device assumes that the frame was lost or collided, and it resends the frame.

The following list summarizes the key points about the CSMA/CA algorithm, omitting some of the details for the sake of clarity:

Step 1 Listen to ensure that the medium (space) is not busy (no radio waves currently are being received at the frequencies to be used).

Step 2 Set a random wait timer before sending a frame to statistically reduce the chance of devices all trying to send at the same time.

Step 3 When the random timer has passed, listen again to ensure that the medium is not busy. If it isn't, send the frame.

Step 4   After the entire frame has been sent, wait for an acknowledgment.

Step 5   If no acknowledgment is received, resend the frame, using CSMA/CA logic to wait for the appropriate time to send again.

This concludes the brief introduction to wireless LAN concepts. Next, this chapter covers the basics of what you should do when installing a new wireless LAN.

Deploying WLANs

WLAN security is one of the more important features of WLANs, and for good reason. The same security exposures exist on WLANs as for Ethernet LANs, plus WLANs are exposed to many more vulnerabilities than wired Ethernet LANs. For example, someone could park outside a building and pick up the WLAN signals from inside the building, reading the data. Therefore, all production WLAN deployments should include the currently best security options for that WLAN.

Although security is vitally important, the installation of a new WLAN should begin with just getting the WLAN working. As soon as a single wireless device is talking to an AP, security configuration can be added and tested. Following that same progression, this section examines the process of planning and implementing a WLAN, with no security enabled. The final major section of this chapter, "Wireless LAN Security," examines the concepts behind WLAN security.

Wireless LAN Implementation Checklist

The following basic checklist can help guide the installation of a new BSS WLAN:

Step 1   Verify that the existing wired network works, including DHCP services, VLANs, and Internet connectivity.

Key Topic

Step 2   Install the AP and configure/verify its connectivity to the wired network, including the AP's IP address, mask, and default gateway.

Step 3   Configure and verify the AP's wireless settings, including Service Set Identifier (SSID), but no security.

Step 4   Install and configure one wireless client (for example, a laptop), again with no security.

Step 5   Verify that the WLAN works from the laptop.

Step 6   Configure wireless security on the AP and client.

Step 7   Verify that the WLAN works again, in the presence of the security features.

This section examines the first five tasks. The last major section of this chapter discusses the concepts behind WLAN security but does not explain the large number of detailed options for configuring WLAN security.

Step 1: Verify the Existing Wired Network

Most of the other chapters in this book explain the details of how to understand, plan, design, and implement the switches and routers that create the rest of the network, so there is no need to repeat those details here. However, it can be helpful to consider a couple of items related to testing an existing wired network before connecting a new WLAN.

First, the Ethernet switch port to which the AP's Ethernet port connects typically is a switch access port, meaning that it is assigned to a particular VLAN. Also, in an ESS design with multiple APs, all the Ethernet switch ports to which the APs attach should be in the same VLAN. Figure 11-8 shows a typical ESS design for a WLAN, with the VLAN IDs listed.

Figure 11-8   *ESS WLAN with All APs in Ethernet VLAN 2*

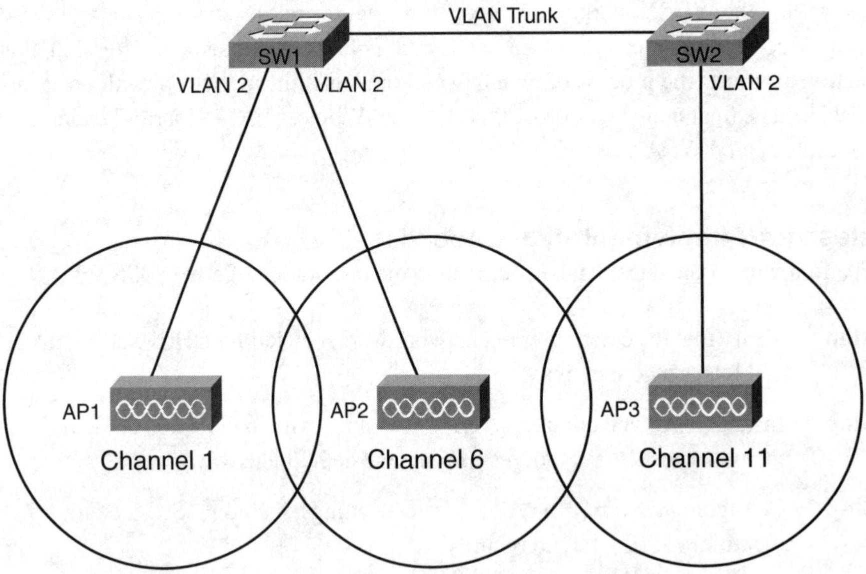

To test the existing network, you could simply connect a laptop Ethernet NIC to the same Ethernet cable that will be used for the AP. If the laptop can acquire an IP address, mask, and other information using DHCP, and communicate with other hosts, the existing wired network is ready to accept the AP.

Step 2: Install and Configure the AP's Wired and IP Details

Just like an Ethernet switch, wireless APs operate at Layer 2 and do not need an IP address to perform their main functions. However, just as an Ethernet switch in an Enterprise network should have an IP address so that it can be easily managed, APs deployed in an Enterprise network should also have an IP address.

The IP configuration details on an AP are the same items needed on an Ethernet switch, as covered in the section "Configuring the Switch IP Address" in Chapter 9, "Ethernet Switch Configuration." In particular, the AP needs an IP address, subnet mask, default gateway IP address, and possibly the IP address of a DNS server.

The AP uses a straight-through Ethernet cable to connect to the LAN switch. Although any speed Ethernet interface works, when using the faster WLAN speeds, using a Fast Ethernet interface on a switch helps improve overall performance.

Step 3: Configure the AP's WLAN Details

Most of the time, WLAN APs can be installed with no configuration, and they work. For example, many homes have consumer-grade wireless APs installed, connected to a high-speed Internet connection. Often, the AP, router, and cable connection terminate in the same device, such as the Linksys Dual-Band Wireless A+G Broadband Router. (Linksys is a division of Cisco Systems that manufactures and distributes consumer networking devices.) Many people just buy these devices, plug in the power and the appropriate cables for the wired part of the connection, and leave the default WLAN settings, and the AP works.

Both consumer-grade and Enterprise-grade APs can be configured with a variety of parameters. The following list highlights some of the features mentioned earlier in this chapter that may need to be configured:

- IEEE standard (a, b, g, or multiple)

- Wireless channel

- Service Set Identifier (SSID, a 32-character text identifier for the WLAN)

- Transmit power

This chapter has already explained most of the concepts behind these four items, but the SSID is new. Each WLAN needs a unique name to identify the WLAN. Because a simple WLAN with a single AP is called a Basic Service Set (BSS), and a WLAN with multiple APs is called an Extended Service Set (ESS), the term for the identifier of a WLAN is the Service Set Identifier (SSID). The SSID is a 32-character ASCII text value. When you configure an ESS WLAN, each of the APs should be configured with the same SSID, which allows for roaming between APs, but inside the same WLAN.

Also note that many APs today support multiple WLAN standards. In some cases, they can support multiple standards on the same AP at the same time. However, these mixed-mode implementations, particularly with 802.11b/g in this same AP, tend to slow down the WLAN. In practice, deploying some 802.11g-only APs and some mixed-mode b/g APs in the same coverage area may provide better performance than using only APs configured in b/g mixed mode.

Step 4: Install and Configure One Wireless Client

A wireless client is any wireless device that associates with an AP to use a WLAN. To be a WLAN client, the device simply needs a WLAN NIC that supports the same WLAN standard as the AP. The NIC includes a radio, which can tune to the frequencies used by the supported WLAN standard(s), and an antenna. For example, laptop computer manufacturers typically integrate a WLAN NIC into every laptop, and you can then use a laptop to associate with an AP and send frames.

The AP has several required configuration settings, but the client may not need anything configured. Typically, clients by default do not have any security enabled. When the client starts working, it tries to discover all APs by listening on all frequency channels for the WLAN standards it supports by default. For example, if a client were using the WLAN shown in Figure 11-6, with three APs, each using a different channel, the client might actually discover all three APs. The client would then use the AP from which the client receives the strongest signal. Also, the client learns the SSID from the AP, again removing the need for any client configuration.

WLAN clients may use wireless NICs from a large number of vendors. To help ensure that the clients can work with Cisco APs, Cisco started the *Cisco Compatible Extensions Program (CCX)*. This Cisco-sponsored program allows any WLAN manufacturer to send its products to a third-party testing lab, with the lab performing tests to see if the WLAN NIC works well with Cisco APs. Cisco estimates that 95 percent of the wireless NICs on the market have been certified through this program.

With Microsoft operating systems, the wireless NIC may not need to be configured because of the Microsoft *Zero Configuration Utility (ZCF)*. This utility, part of the OS, allows the PC to automatically discover the SSIDs of all WLANs whose APs are within range on the NIC. The user can choose the SSID to connect to. Or the ZCF utility can automatically pick the AP with the strongest signal, thereby automatically connecting to a wireless LAN without the user's needing to configure anything.

Note that most NIC manufacturers also provide software that can control the NIC instead of the operating system's built-in tools such as Microsoft ZCF.

Step 5: Verify That the WLAN Works from the Client

The first step to verify proper operation of the first WLAN client is to check whether the client can access the same hosts used for testing in Step 1 of this installation process. (The laptop's wired Ethernet connection should be disconnected so that the laptop uses only its WLAN connection.) At this point, if the laptop can get a response from another host, such as by pinging or browsing a web page on a web server, the WLAN at least works.

If this test does not work, a wide variety of tasks could be performed. Some of the tasks relate to work that is often done in the planning stages, generally called a *site survey*. During a wireless site survey, engineers tour the site for a new WLAN, looking for good AP locations, transmitting and testing signal strength throughout the site. In that same line of thinking, if the new client cannot communicate, you might check the following:

- Is the AP at the center of the area in which the clients reside?

- Is the AP or client right next to a lot of metal?

- Is the AP or client near a source of interference, such as a microwave oven or gaming system?

- Is the AP's coverage area wide enough to reach the client?

In particular, you could take a laptop with a wireless card and, using the NIC's tools, walk around while looking at signal quality measurement. Most WLAN NIC software shows signal strength and quality, so by walking around the site with the laptop, you can gauge whether any dead spots exist and where clients should have no problems hearing from the AP.

Besides the site survey types of work, the following list notes a few other common problems with a new installation:

- Check to make sure that the NIC and AP's radios are enabled. In particular, most laptops have a physical switch with which to enable or disable the radio, as well as a software setting to enable or disable the radio. This allows the laptop to save power (and extend the time before it must be plugged into a power outlet again). It also can cause users to fail to connect to an AP, just because the radio is turned off.

- Check the AP to ensure that it has the latest firmware. AP firmware is the OS that runs in the AP.

- Check the AP configuration—in particular, the channel configuration—to ensure that it does not use a channel that overlaps with other APs in the same location.

This completes the explanations of the first five steps of installing a simple wireless LAN. The final major section of this chapter examines WLAN security, which also completes the basic installation steps.

Wireless LAN Security

All networks today need good security, but WLANs have some unique security requirements. This section examines some of the security needs for WLANs and the progression and maturation of the WLAN security options. It also discusses how to configure the security features.

WLAN Security Issues

WLANs introduce a number of vulnerabilities that do not exist for wired Ethernet LANs. Some of these vulnerabilities give hackers an opportunity to cause harm by stealing information, accessing hosts in the wired part of the network, or preventing service through a denial-of-service (DoS) attack. Other vulnerabilities may be caused by a well-meaning but uninformed employee who installs an AP without the IT department's approval, with no security. This would allow anyone to gain access to the rest of the Enterprise's network.

The Cisco-authorized CCNA-related courses suggest several categories of threats:

- **War drivers:** The attacker often just wants to gain Internet access for free. This person drives around, trying to find APs that have no security or weak security. The attacker can use easily downloaded tools and high-gain directional antennas (easily purchased and installed).

- **Hackers:** The motivation for hackers is to either find information or deny services. Interestingly, the end goal may be to compromise the hosts inside the wired network, using the wireless network as a way to access the Enterprise network without having to go through Internet connections that have firewalls.

- **Employees:** Employees can unwittingly help hackers gain access to the Enterprise network in several ways. An employee could go to an office supply store and buy an AP for less than $100, install the AP in his office, using default settings of no security, and create a small wireless LAN. This would allow a hacker to gain access to the rest of the Enterprise from the coffee shop across the street. Additionally, if the client does not use encryption, company data going between the legitimate employee client PC and the Enterprise network can be easily copied and understood by attackers outside the building.

- **Rogue AP:** The attacker captures packets in the existing wireless LAN, finding the SSID and cracking security keys (if they are used). Then the attacker can set up her own AP, with the same settings, and get the Enterprise's clients to use it. In turn, this can cause the individuals to enter their usernames and passwords, aiding in the next phase of the attacker's plan.

To reduce the risk of such attacks, three main types of tools can be used on a WLAN:

- Mutual authentication

- Encryption

- Intrusion tools

Mutual authentication should be used between the client and AP. The authentication process uses a secret password, called a key, on both the client and the AP. By using some sophisticated mathematical algorithms, the AP can confirm that the client does indeed know the right key value. Likewise, the client can confirm that the AP also has the right key value. The process never sends the key through the air, so even if the attacker is using a network analysis tool to copy every frame inside the WLAN, the attacker cannot learn the key value. Also, note that by allowing mutual authentication, the client can confirm that the AP knows the right key, thereby preventing a connection to a rogue AP.

The second tool is encryption. Encryption uses a secret key and a mathematical formula to scramble the contents of the WLAN frame. The receiving device then uses another formula to decrypt the data. Again, without the secret encryption key, an attacker may be able to intercept the frame, but he or she cannot read the contents.

The third class of tools includes many options, but this class generally can be called intrusion tools. These tools include Intrusion Detection Systems (IDS) and Intrusion Prevention Systems (IPS), as well as WLAN-specific tools. Cisco defines the Structured Wireless-Aware Network (SWAN) architecture. It includes many tools, some of which specifically address the issue of detecting and identifying rogue APs, and whether they represent threats. Table 11-8 lists the key vulnerabilities, along with the general solution.

Table 11-8 *WLAN Vulnerabilities and Solutions*

Key
Topic

Vulnerability	Solution
War drivers	Strong authentication
Hackers stealing information in a WLAN	Strong encryption
Hackers gaining access to the rest of the network	Strong authentication
Employee AP installation	Intrusion Detection Systems (IDS), including Cisco SWAN
Rogue AP	Strong authentication, IDS/SWAN

The Progression of WLAN Security Standards

WLAN standards have progressed over the years in response to a growing need for stronger security and because of some problems in the earliest WLAN security standard. This section examines four significant sets of WLAN security standards in chronological order, describing their problems and solutions.

> **NOTE**   WLAN standards address the details of how to implement the authentication and encryption parts of the security puzzle, and they are covered in this section. The intrusion-related tools (IDS and IPS) fall more into an Enterprise-wide security framework and are not covered in this chapter.

The initial security standard for WLANs, called *Wired Equivalent Privacy (WEP)*, had many problems. The other three standards covered here represent a progression of standards whose goal in part was to fix the problems created by WEP. In chronological order, Cisco first addressed the problem with some proprietary solutions. Then the Wi-Fi Alliance, an industry association, helped fix the problem by defining an industry-wide standard. Finally, the IEEE completed work on an official public standard, 802.11i. Table 11-9 lists these four major WLAN security standards.

Key Topic

Table 11-9   *WLAN Security Standards*

Name	Year	Who Defined It
Wired Equivalent Privacy (WEP)	1997	IEEE
The interim Cisco solution while awaiting 802.11i	2001	Cisco, IEEE 802.1x Extensible Authentication Protocol (EAP)
Wi-Fi Protected Access (WPA)	2003	Wi-Fi Alliance
802.11i (WPA2)	2005+	IEEE

The word *standard* is used quite loosely in this chapter when referring to WLAN security. Some of the standards are true open standards from a standards body—namely, the IEEE. Some of the standards flow from the Wi-Fi Alliance, making them de facto industry standards. Additionally, Cisco created several proprietary interim solutions for its products, making the use of the word more of a stretch. However, all of these standards helped improve the original WEP security, so the text will take a closer look at each standard.

Wired Equivalent Privacy (WEP)

WEP was the original 802.11 security standard, providing authentication and encryption services. As it turns out, WEP provided only weak authentication and encryption, to the point that its authentication and encryption can be cracked by a hacker today, using easily downloaded tools. The main problems were as follows:

- **Static Preshared Keys (PSK):** The key value had to be configured on each client and each AP, with no dynamic way to exchange the keys without human intervention. As a result, many people did not bother to change the keys on a regular basis, especially in Enterprises with a large number of wireless clients.

- **Easily cracked keys:** The key values were short (64 bits, of which only 40 were the actual unique key). This made it easier to predict the key's value based on the frames copied from the WLAN. Additionally, the fact that the key typically never changed meant that the hacker could gather lots of sample authentication attempts, making it easier to find the key.

Because of the problems with WEP, and the fact that the later standards include much better security features, WEP should not be used today.

SSID Cloaking and MAC Filtering

Because of WEP's problems, many vendors included a couple of security-related features that are not part of WEP. However, many people associated these features with WEP just because of the timing with which the features were announced. Neither feature provides much real security, and they are not part of any standard, but it is worth discussing the concepts in case you see them mentioned elsewhere.

The first feature, *SSID cloaking*, changes the process by which clients associate with an AP. Before a client can communicate with the AP, it must know something about the AP—in particular, the AP's SSID. Normally, the association process occurs like this:

Step 1   The AP sends a periodic Beacon frame (the default is every 100 ms) that lists the AP's SSID and other configuration information.

Step 2   The client listens for Beacons on all channels, learning about all APs in range.

Step 3   The client associates with the AP with the strongest signal (the default), or with the AP with the strongest signal for the currently preferred SSID.

Step 4   The authentication process occurs as soon as the client has associated with the AP.

Essentially, the client learns about each AP and its associated SSIDs via the Beacon process. This process aids in the roaming process, allowing the client to move around and reassociate with a new AP when the old AP's signal gets weaker. However, the Beacons allow an attacker to easily and quickly find out information about the APs to begin trying to associate and gain access to the network.

SSID cloaking is an AP feature that tells the AP to stop sending periodic Beacon frames. This seems to solve the problem with attackers easily and quickly finding all APs. However, clients still need to be able to find the APs. Therefore, if the client has been configured with a null SSID, the client sends a Probe message, which causes each AP to respond with its SSID. In short, it is simple to cause all the APs to announce their SSIDs, even with cloaking enabled on the APs, so attackers can still find all the APs.

> **NOTE**   Enterprises often use SSID cloaking to prevent curious people from trying to access the WLAN. Public wireless hotspots tend to let their APs send Beacon frames so that the customers can easily find their APs.

The second extra feature often implemented along with WEP is MAC address filtering. The AP can be configured with a list of allowed WLAN MAC addresses, filtering frames sent by WLAN clients whose MAC address is not in the list. As with SSID cloaking, MAC address filtering may prevent curious onlookers from accessing the WLAN, but it does not stop a real attack. The attacker can use a WLAN adapter that allows its MAC address to be changed, copy legitimate frames out of the air, set its own MAC address to one of the legitimate MAC addresses, and circumvent the MAC address filter.

The Cisco Interim Solution Between WEP and 802.11i

Because of the problems with WEP, vendors such as Cisco, and the Wi-Fi Alliance industry association, looked to solve the problem with their own standards, concurrent with the typically slower IEEE standardization process. The Cisco answer included some proprietary improvements for encryption, along with the IEEE 802.1x standard for end-user authentication. The main features of Cisco enhancements included the following:

■ Dynamic key exchange (instead of static preshared keys)

■ User authentication using 802.1x

■ A new encryption key for each packet

The use of a dynamic key exchange process helps because the clients and AP can then change keys more often, without human intervention. As a result, if the key is discovered, the exposure can be short-lived. Also, when key information is exchanged dynamically, a new key can be delivered for each packet, allowing encryption to use a different key each time. That way, even if an attacker managed to discover a key used for a particular packet, he or she could decrypt only that one packet, minimizing the exposure.

Cisco created several features based on the then-to-date known progress on the IEEE 802.11i WLAN security standard. However, Cisco also added user authentication to its suite of security features. User authentication means that instead of authenticating the device by checking to see if the device knows a correct key, the user must supply a username and password. This extra authentication step adds another layer of security. That way, even if the keys are temporarily compromised, the attacker must also know a person's username and password to gain access to the WLAN.

Wi-Fi Protected Access (WPA)

The Cisco solution to the difficulties of WEP included proprietary protocols as well as IEEE standard 802.1x. After Cisco integrated its proprietary WLAN security standards into Cisco APs, the Wi-Fi Alliance created a multivendor WLAN security standard. At the same time, the IEEE was working on the future official IEEE WLAN security standard, 802.11i, but the WLAN industry needed a quicker solution than waiting on the IEEE standard. So, the Wi-Fi alliance took the current work-in-progress on the 802.11i committee, made some assumptions and predictions, and defined a de facto industry standard. The Wi-Fi Alliance then performed its normal task of certifying vendors' products as to whether they met this new industry standard, calling it *Wi-Fi Protected Access (WPA)*.

WPA essentially performed the same functions as the Cisco proprietary interim solution, but with different details. WPA includes the option to use dynamic key exchange, using the Temporal Key Integrity Protocol (TKIP). (Cisco used a proprietary version of TKIP.) WPA allows for the use of either IEEE 802.1X user authentication or simple device authentication using preshared keys. And the encryption algorithm uses the Message Integrity Check (MIC) algorithm, again similar to the process used in the Cisco-proprietary solution.

WPA had two great benefits. First, it improved security greatly compared to WEP. Second, the Wi-Fi Alliance's certification program had already enjoyed great success when WPA came out, so vendors had great incentive to support WPA and have their products become WPA-certified by the Wi-Fi Alliance. As a result, PC manufacturers could choose from many wireless NICs, and customers could buy APs from many different vendors, with confidence that WPA security would work well.

NOTE   The Cisco-proprietary solutions and the WPA industry standard are incompatible.

IEEE 802.11i and WPA-2

The IEEE ratified the 802.11i standard in 2005; additional related specifications arrived later. Like the Cisco-proprietary solution, and the Wi-Fi Alliance's WPA industry standard, 802.11i includes dynamic key exchange, much stronger encryption, and user authentication. However, the details differ enough so that 802.11i is not backward-compatible with either WPA or the Cisco-proprietary protocols.

One particularly important improvement over the interim Cisco and WPA standards is the inclusion of the *Advanced Encryption Standard (AES)* in 802.11i. AES provides even better encryption than the interim Cisco and WEP standards, with longer keys and much more secure encryption algorithms.

The Wi-Fi Alliance continues its product certification role for 802.11i, but with a twist on the names used for the standard. Because of the success of the WPA industry standard and the popularity of the term "WPA," the Wi-Fi Alliance calls 802.11i WPA2, meaning the second version of WPA. So, when buying and configuring products, you will more likely see references to WPA2 rather than 802.11i.

Table 11-10 summarizes the key features of the various WLAN security standards.

Key Topic

Table 11-10   *Comparisons of WLAN Security Features*

Standard	Key Distribution	Device Authentication	User Authentication	Encryption
WEP	Static	Yes (weak)	None	Yes (weak)
Cisco	Dynamic	Yes	Yes (802.1x)	Yes (TKIP)
WPA	Both	Yes	Yes (802.1x)	Yes (TKIP)
802.11i (WPA2)	Both	Yes	Yes (802.1x)	Yes (AES)

Exam Preparation Tasks

Review All the Key Topics

Review the most important topics from this chapter, noted with the key topics icon.
Table 11-11 lists these key topics and where each is discussed.

Table 11-11 *Key Topics for Chapter 11*

Key Topic Element	Description	Page Number
Table 11-2	WLAN standards organizations and their roles	304
Table 11-3	Comparison of 802.11a, 802.11b, and 802.11g	305
Table 11-4	WLAN modes, their formal names, and descriptions	307
Table 11-5	Unlicensed bands, their general names, and the list of standards to use each band	309
Figure 11-6	DSSS frequencies, showing the three nonoverlapping channels	310
List	WLAN configuration checklist	315
List	Common WLAN installation problems related to the work done in the site survey	319
List	Other common WLAN installation problems	319
Table 11-8	Common WLAN security threats	321
Table 11-9	WLAN security standards	322
Table 11-10	Comparison of WLAN security standards	326

Complete the Tables and Lists from Memory

Print a copy of Appendix H, "Memory Tables" (found on the CD), or at least the section for this chapter, and complete the tables and lists from memory. Appendix I, "Memory Tables Answer Key," also on the CD, includes completed tables and lists for you to check your work.

Definitions of Key Terms

Define the following key terms from this chapter and check your answers in the glossary:

802.11a, 802.11b, 802.11g, 802.11i, 802.11n, access point, ad hoc mode, Basic Service Set (BSS), CSMA/CA, Direct Sequence Spread Spectrum, Extended Service Set (ESS), Frequency Hopping Spread Spectrum, infrastructure mode, Orthogonal Frequency Division Multiplexing, Service Set Identifier (SSID), Wi-Fi Alliance, Wi-Fi Protected Access (WPA), wired equivalent privacy (WEP), WLAN client, WPA2

Cisco Published ICND1 Exam Topics* Covered in This Part:

Describe the operation of data networks

- Use the OSI and TCP/IP models and their associated protocols to explain how data flows in a network
- Interpret network diagrams
- Determine the path between two hosts across a network
- Describe the components required for network and Internet communications
- Identify and correct common network problems at Layers 1, 2, 3, and 7 using a layered model approach
- Differentiate between LAN/WAN operation and features

Implement an IP addressing scheme and IP services to meet network requirements for a small branch office

- Describe the need and role of addressing in a network
- Create and apply an addressing scheme to a network
- Assign and verify valid IP addresses to hosts, servers, and networking devices in a LAN environment
- Describe and verify DNS operation
- Describe the operation and benefits of using private and public IP addressing
- Enable NAT for a small network with a single ISP and connection using SDM and verify operation using CLI and ping
- Configure, verify, and troubleshoot DHCP and DNS operation on a router (including: CLI/SDM)
- Implement static and dynamic addressing services for hosts in a LAN environment
- Identify and correct IP addressing issues

Implement a small routed network

- Describe basic routing concepts (including: packet forwarding, router lookup process)
- Describe the operation of Cisco routers (including: router bootup process, POST, router components)
- Select the appropriate media, cables, ports, and connectors to connect routers to other network devices and hosts
- Configure, verify, and troubleshoot RIPv2
- Access and utilize the router CLI to set basic parameters
- Connect, configure, and verify operation status of a device interface
- Verify device configuration and network connectivity using ping, traceroute, Telnet, SSH, or other utilities
- Perform and verify routing configuration tasks for a static or default route given specific routing requirements
- Manage IOS configuration files (including: save, edit, upgrade, restore)
- Manage Cisco IOS
- Implement password and physical security
- Verify network status and router operation using basic utilities (including: ping, traceroute, Telnet, SSH, ARP, ipconfig), show and debug commands

Identify security threats to a network and describe general methods to mitigate those threats

- Describe security recommended practices including initial steps to secure network devices

*Always recheck http://www.cisco.com for the latest posted exam topics.

Part III: IP Routing

This chapter covers the following subjects:

Exam Preparation Tools for Subnetting: This section lists the various tools that can help you practice your subnetting skills.

IP Addressing and Routing: This section moves beyond the basic concepts in Chapter 5, "Fundamentals of IP Addressing and Routing," introducing the purpose and meaning of the subnet mask.

Math Operations Used When Subnetting: This section explains how to convert between IP address and subnet mask formats.

Analyzing and Choosing Subnet Masks: This section explains the meaning behind subnet masks, how to choose a subnet mask to meet stated design goals, and how to interpret a mask chosen by someone else.

Analyzing Existing Subnets: This section shows how to determine an IP address's resident subnet, broadcast address, and range of addresses in the subnet.

Design: Choosing the Subnets of a Classful Network: This section explains how to find all subnets of a single classful network.

CHAPTER 12

IP Addressing and Subnetting

The concepts and application of IP addressing and subnetting may well be the most important topics to understand both for being a well-prepared network engineer and for being ready to do well on the ICND1, ICND2, and CCNA exams. To design a new network, engineers must be able to begin with some IP address range and break it into subdivisions called subnets, choosing the right size of each subnet to meet design requirements. Engineers need to understand subnet masks, and how to pick the right masks to implement the designs that were earlier drawn on paper. Even more often, engineers need to understand, operate, and troubleshoot pre-existing networks, tasks that require mastery of addressing and subnetting concepts and the ability to apply those concepts from a different perspective than when designing the network.

This chapter begins Part III of the book, which is focused on the role of routers in an internetwork. As introduced in Chapter 5, the network layer defines and uses addressing, routing, and routing protocols to achieve its main goals. After this chapter goes into depth on addressing, the rest of the chapters in Part III focus on how to implement IP addresses, routing, and routing protocols inside Cisco routers.

All the topics in this chapter have a common goal, which is to help you understand IP addressing and subnetting. To prepare you for both real jobs and the exams, this chapter goes far beyond the concepts as covered on the exam, preparing you to apply these concepts when designing a network and when you operate and troubleshoot a network. Additionally, this chapter creates a structure from which you can repeatedly practice the math processes used to get the answers to subnetting questions.

"Do I Know This Already?" Quiz

The "Do I Know This Already?" quiz allows you to assess if you should read the entire chapter. If you miss no more than one of these 14 self-assessment questions, you might want to move ahead to the "Exam Preparation Tasks" section. Table 12-1 lists the major headings in this chapter and the "Do I Know This Already?" quiz questions covering the material in those headings so you can assess your knowledge of these specific areas. The answers to the "Do I Know This Already?" quiz appear in Appendix A.

Table 12-1   *"Do I Know This Already?" Foundation Topics Section-to-Question Mapping*

Foundation Topics Section	Questions
Exam Preparation Tools for Subnetting	None
IP Addressing and Routing	1
Math Operations Used When Subnetting	2, 3
Analyzing and Choosing Subnet Masks	4–8
Analyzing Existing Subnets	9–12
Design: Choosing the Subnets of a Classful Network	13, 14

1. Which of the following are private IP networks?

    a. 172.31.0.0

    b. 172.32.0.0

    c. 192.168.255.0

    d. 192.1.168.0

    e. 11.0.0.0

2. Which of the following is the result of a Boolean AND between IP address 150.150.4.100 and mask 255.255.192.0?

    a. 1001 0110 1001 0110 0000 0100 0110 0100

    b. 1001 0110 1001 0110 0000 0000 0000 0000

    c. 1001 0110 1001 0110 0000 0100 0000 0000

    d. 1001 0110 0000 0000 0000 0000 0000 0000

3. Which of the following shows the equivalent of subnet mask 255.255.248.0, but in prefix notation?

    a. /248

    b. /24

    c. /28

    d. /21

    e. /20

    f. /23

4. If mask 255.255.255.128 were used with a Class B network, how many subnets could exist, with how many hosts per subnet, respectively?

   a. 256 and 256

   b. 254 and 254

   c. 62 and 1022

   d. 1022 and 62

   e. 512 and 126

   f. 126 and 510

5. A Class B network needs to be subnetted such that it supports 100 subnets and 100 hosts/subnet. For this design, if multiple masks meet those design requirements, the engineer should choose the mask that maximizes the number of hosts per subnet. Which of the following masks meets the design criteria?

   a. 255.255.255.0

   b. /23

   c. /26

   d. 255.255.252.0

6. If mask 255.255.255.240 were used with a Class C network, how many subnets could exist, with how many hosts per subnet, respectively?

   a. 16 and 16

   b. 14 and 14

   c. 16 and 14

   d. 8 and 32

   e. 32 and 8

   f. 6 and 30

7. Which of the following subnet masks lets a Class B network have up to 150 hosts per subnet, and supports 164 subnets?

   a. 255.0.0.0

   b. 255.255.0.0

   c. 255.255.255.0

   d. 255.255.192.0

   e. 255.255.240.0

   f. 255.255.252.0

8. Which of the following subnet masks let a Class A network have up to 150 hosts per subnet and supports 164 subnets?

   a. 255.0.0.0

   b. 255.255.0.0

   c. 255.255.255.0

   d. 255.255.192.0

   e. 255.255.252.0

   f. 255.255.255.192

9. Which of the following IP addresses are not in the same subnet as 190.4.80.80, mask 255.255.255.0?

   a. 190.4.80.1

   b. 190.4.80.50

   c. 190.4.80.100

   d. 190.4.80.200

   e. 190.4.90.1

   f. 10.1.1.1

10. Which of the following IP addresses is not in the same subnet as 190.4.80.80, mask 255.255.240.0?

   a. 190.4.80.1

   b. 190.4.80.50

   c. 190.4.80.100

   d. 190.4.80.200

   e. 190.4.90.1

   f. 10.1.1.1

11. Which of the following IP addresses are not in the same subnet as 190.4.80.80/25?

   a. 190.4.80.1

   b. 190.4.80.50

   c. 190.4.80.100

   d. 190.4.80.200

   e. 190.4.90.1

   f. 10.1.1.1

12. Each of the following answers lists a dotted decimal number and a subnet mask. The dotted decimal number might be a valid IP address that can be used by a host or it might be a subnet number or broadcast address. Which of the answers show an address that can be used by a host?

   a.   10.0.0.0, 255.0.0.0

   b.   192.168.5.160, 255.255.255.192

   c.   172.27.27.27, 255.255.255.252

   d.   172.20.49.0, 255.255.254.0

13. Which of the following are valid subnet numbers in network 180.1.0.0 when using mask 255.255.248.0?

   a.   180.1.2.0

   b.   180.1.4.0

   c.   180.1.8.0

   d.   180.1.16.0

   e.   180.1.32.0

   f.   180.1.40.0

14. Which of the following are not valid subnet numbers in network 180.1.0.0 when using mask 255.255.255.0?

   a.   180.2.2.0

   b.   180.1.4.0

   c.   180.1.8.0

   d.   180.1.16.0

   e.   180.1.32.0

   f.   180.1.40.0

Foundation Topics

This chapter is fundamentally different from the other chapters in this book. Like the other chapters, this chapter explains a related set of concepts—in this case, the concepts, thought processes, and math used to attack IP addressing and subnetting questions on the CCNA exams. However, more so than for any other chapter in this book, you must practice the concepts and math in this chapter before you take the exam(s). It is very much like math classes in school—if you do not do the homework, you probably will not do as well on the test.

This chapter begins with a few comments about how to prepare for subnetting questions on the exam. Then the chapter spends a few pages reviewing what has been covered already in regard to IP addressing and routing, two topics that are tightly linked. The rest of the major sections of the chapter tackle a particular type of subnetting question in depth, with each section ending with a list of suggested steps to take to practice your subnetting skills.

Exam Preparation Tools for Subnetting

To help you prepare for the exam, this chapter explains the subnetting concepts and shows multiple examples. Each section also lists the specific steps required to solve a particular type of problem. Often, two sets of steps are provided, one that uses binary math, and another that uses only decimal math.

More so than for any other single chapter in this book, you should also practice and review the topics in this chapter until you have mastered the concepts. To that end, this book includes several tools, some of which are located on the CD-ROM that comes with this book, in addition to this chapter:

- **Appendix D, "Subnetting Practice":** This large appendix lists numerous practice problems, with solutions that show how to use the processes explained in this chapter.

- **Appendix E, "Subnetting Reference Pages":** This short appendix includes a few handy references, including a 1-page summary of each of the subnetting processes listed in this chapter.

- **Subnetting videos (DVD):** Several of the most important subnetting processes described in this chapter are explained in videos on the DVD in the back of this book. The goal of these videos is to ensure that you understand these key processes completely, and hopefully move you quickly to the point of mastering the process.

- **Cisco Binary Game at the Cisco CCNA Prep Center:** If you want to use the processes that use binary math, you can use the Cisco Binary Game to practice your binary-to-decimal and decimal-to-binary conversion accuracy and speed. The CCNA Prep Center is at http://www.cisco.com/go/prepcenter. The binary game is also included on the CD in the back of the book.

- **Subnetting Game at the Cisco CCNA Prep Center:** As of the time of writing this chapter, the CCNA Prep Center had a Beta version of the Subnetting Game available. The game requires that you choose a mask, pick subnets, calculate the subnet number and broadcast address of the subnets, and assign IP addresses in the subnets.

- **Subnetting calculators:** You can make up your own practice problems, and use a subnetting calculator to find the answers to check your work. This allows you to have unlimited amounts of practice to get better and get faster. The CCNA Prep Center also has the Cisco Subnet Calculator for free download.

- **Glossary:** The topics of IP addressing and subnetting use a wide variety of terminology. The glossary in the back of this book includes the subnetting terms used in this book.

Suggested Subnetting Preparation Plan

Over the years, some readers have asked for a suggested subnetting study plan. At the same time, the CCNA exam questions have been getting more difficult. To help you better prepare, the following list outlines a suggested study plan:

Step 1 If you have not done so already, load the CD-ROM and get familiar with its user interface, install the exam engine software, and verify that you can find the tools listed in the preceding list. You may want to go ahead and print Appendix E, and if you expect you will want to use a printed version of Appendix D, print that as well (be warned, Appendix D is almost 100 pages in length).

Step 2 Keep reading this chapter through the end of the second major section, "IP Addressing and Routing."

Step 3 For each subsequent major section, read the section and then follow the instructions in the subsection "Practice Suggestions." This short part of each major section points you to the items that would be of the most help to stop and practice at that point. These suggestions include the use of the tools listed earlier. The following major sections include a "Practice Suggestions" subsection:

- Math Operations Used When Subnetting

- Analyzing and Choosing Subnet Masks

- Analyzing Existing Subnets

- Design: Choosing the Subnets of a Classful Network

Step 4   When finished with the chapter, if you feel the need for more practice, make up your own practice problems, and check your answers using a subnet calculator (more information is provided after this list). I recommend the Cisco Subnet Calculator because its user interface displays the information in a convenient format for doing extra questions.

Step 5   At any point in your study, feel free to visit the CCNA Prep Center (http://www.cisco.com/go/prepcenter) to use both the Cisco Binary Game and the Subnetting Game. Both help you build skills for doing subnetting problems. (The CCNA Prep Center requires you to log in with a Cisco.com User ID; if you do not have one, the preceding URL has a link to Cisco.com registration.) Once in the CCNA Prep Center, you can find the games under the Additional Information tab.

You can certainly deviate from this plan to suit your personal preferences, but at the end of this process, you should be able to confidently answer straightforward subnetting questions, such as those in Appendix D. In fact, you should be able to answer in 10–12 seconds a straightforward question such as, "In what subnet does IP address 10.143.254.17, with mask 255.255.224.0, reside?" That is a subjective time period, based on my experience teaching classes, but the point is that you need to understand it all, and practice to the point of being pretty fast.

However, perfecting your subnetting math skills is not enough. The exams ask questions that require you to prove you have the skills to attack real-life problems, problems such as how to design an IP network by subnetting a classful network, how to determine all the subnets of a classful network, and how to pick subnets to use in an internetwork design. The wording of the exam problems, in some cases, is similar to that of the math word problems back in school—many people have trouble translating the written words into a math problem that can be worked. Likewise, the exam questions may well present a scenario, and then leave it to you to figure out what subnetting math is required to find the answer.

To prepare for these skills-based questions, Chapter 15, "Troubleshooting IP Routing," covers a wide variety of topics that help you analyze a network to solve subnetting-related problems. These extra tips help you sift through the wording in problems, and tell you how to approach the problems, so that you can then find the answers. So, in addition to this chapter, read through Chapter 15 as well, which includes coverage of tips for troubleshooting IP addressing problems.

More Practice Using a Subnet Calculator

If you want even more practice, you can essentially get unlimited practice using a subnet calculator. For the purpose of CCNA study, I particularly like the Cisco Subnet Calculator, which can be downloaded from the Cisco CCNA Prep Center. You can then make up your own problems like those found in this chapter, work the problem, and then check your work using the calculator.

For example, you could pick an IP network and mask. Then, you could find all subnets of that network, using that single mask. To check your work, you could type in the network number and mask in the Cisco Subnet Calculator, and click the **Subnets/hosts** tab, which then displays all the subnet numbers, from which you can check your answers. As another example, you could pick an IP address and mask, try to find the subnet number, broadcast address, and range of addresses, and then check your work with the calculator using the **Subnet** tab. After you have typed the IP address and mask, this tab displays the subnet number, broadcast address, and range of usable addresses. And yet another example: You can even choose an IP address and mask, and try to find the number of network, subnet, and host bits—and again check your work with the calculator. In this case, the calculator even uses the same format as this chapter to represent the mask, with N, S, and H for the network, subnet, and host parts of the address.

Now that you have a study plan, the next section briefly reviews the core IP addressing and routing concepts covered previously in Chapter 5. Following that, four major sections describe the various details of IP addressing and subnetting.

IP Addressing and Routing

This section primarily reviews the addressing and routing concepts found in earlier chapters of this book, particularly in Chapter 5. It also briefly introduces IP Version 6 (IPv6) addressing and the concept of private IP networks.

IP Addressing Review

The vast majority of IP networks today use a version of the IP protocol called IP Version 4 (IPv4). Rather than refer to it as IPv4, most texts, this one included, simply refer to it as IP. This section reviews IPv4 addressing concepts as introduced in Chapter 5.

Many different Class A, B, and C networks exist. Table 12-2 summarizes the possible network numbers, the total number of each type, and the number of hosts in each Class A, B, and C network.

> **NOTE** In Table 12-2, the "Valid Network Numbers" row shows actual network numbers. There are several reserved cases. For example, network 0.0.0.0 (originally defined for use as a broadcast address) and network 127.0.0.0 (still available for use as the loopback address) are reserved.

Table 12-2   *List of All Possible Valid Network Numbers*

	Class A	Class B	Class C
First Octet Range	1 to 126	128 to 191	192 to 223
Valid Network Numbers	1.0.0.0 to 126.0.0.0	128.0.0.0 to 191.255.0.0	192.0.0.0 to 223.255.255.0
Number of Networks in This Class	$2^7 - 2$	2^{14}	2^{21}
Number of Hosts Per Network	$2^{24} - 2$	$2^{16} - 2$	$2^8 - 2$
Size of Network Part of Address (Bytes)	1	2	3
Size of Host Part of Address (Bytes)	3	2	1

NOTE   This chapter uses the term *network* to refer to a *classful network*—in other words, a Class A, B, or C network. This chapter also uses the term *subnet* to refer to smaller parts of a classful network. However, note that many people use these terms more loosely, interchanging the words network and subnet, which is fine for general conversation, but can be problematic when trying to be exact.

Figure 12-1 shows the structure of three IP addresses, each from a different network, when no subnetting is used. One address is in a Class A network, one is in a Class B network, and one is in a Class C network.

Figure 12-1   *Class A, B, and C IP Addresses and Their Formats*

By definition, an IP address that begins with 8 in the first octet is in a Class A network, so the network part of the address is the first byte, or first octet. An address that begins with 130 is in a Class B network. By definition, Class B addresses have a 2-byte network part, as shown. Finally, any address that begins with 199 is in a Class C network, which has a 3-byte network part. Also by definition, a Class A address has a 3-byte host part, Class B has a 2-byte host part, and Class C has a 1-byte host part.

Humans can simply remember the numbers in Table 12-2 and the concepts in Figure 12-1 and then quickly determine the network and host parts of an IP address. Computers, however, use a mask to define the size of the network and the host parts of an address. The logic behind the mask results in the same conventions of Class A, B, and C networks that you already know, but the computer can deal with it better as a binary math problem.

The mask is a 32-bit binary number, usually written in dotted decimal format. The purpose of the mask is to define the structure of an IP address. In short, the mask defines the size of the host part of an IP address, representing the host part of the IP address with binary 0s in the mask. The first part of the mask contains binary 1s, which represents the network part of the addresses (if no subnetting is used), or both the network and subnet parts of the addresses (if subnetting is used).

When subnetting is not used, each class of IP address uses the default mask for that class. For example, the default Class A mask ends with 24 bits of binary 0s, which means that the last three octets of the mask are 0s, representing the 3-byte host part of Class A addresses. Table 12-3 summarizes the default masks and reflects the sizes of the two parts of an IP address.

Table 12-3 *Class A, B, and C Networks: Network and Host Parts and Default Masks*

Key Topic

Class of Address	Size of Network Part of Address in Bits	Size of Host Part of Address in Bits	Default Mask for Each Class of Network
A	8	24	255.0.0.0
B	16	16	255.255.0.0
C	24	8	255.255.255.0

Public and Private Addressing

The ICANN (formerly IANA) and its member organizations manage the process of assigning IP network numbers, or even smaller ranges of IP addresses, to companies that want to connect to the Internet. After a company is assigned a range of IP addresses, only that company can use that range. Additionally, the routers in the Internet can then learn routes to reach these networks, so that everyone in the entire Internet can forward packets to that IP network. Because these IP addresses can be reached by packets in the public Internet, these networks are often called public networks, and the addresses in these networks are called *public addresses.*

Some computers will never be connected to the Internet. So, engineers building a network consisting of only such computers could use IP addresses that are duplicates of registered public IP addresses in the Internet. So, when designing the IP addressing convention for such a network, an organization could pick and use any network number(s) that it wanted, and all would be well. For instance, you can buy a few routers, connect them together in your office, and configure IP addresses in network 1.0.0.0 and make it work, even though some company also uses Class A network 1 as its registered public IP network. The IP addresses that you use might be duplicates of real IP addresses in the Internet, but if all you want to do is learn on the lab in your office, all is well.

However, using the same IP addresses used by another company is unnecessary in this situation, because TCP/IP RFC 1918 defines a set of *private networks* that can be used for internetworks that do not connect to the Internet. More importantly, this set of private networks will never be assigned by ICANN to any organization for use as registered public network numbers. So, when building a private network, like one in a lab, you can use numbers in a range that is not used by anyone in the public Internet. Table 12-4 shows the private address space defined by RFC 1918.

Key Topic

Table 12-4 *RFC 1918 Private Address Space*

Private IP Networks	Class of Networks	Number of Networks
10.0.0.0	A	1
172.16.0.0 through 172.31.0.0	B	16
192.168.0.0 through 192.168.255.0	C	256

In other words, any organization can use these network numbers. However, no organization is allowed to advertise these networks using a routing protocol on the Internet.

Many of you might be wondering, "Why bother reserving special private network numbers when it does not matter whether the addresses are duplicates?" Well, as it turns out, private networks can be used inside a company and that company can still connect to the Internet today, using a function called Network Address Translation (NAT). Chapter 16, "WAN Concepts," and Chapter 17, "WAN Configuration," expand on the concepts of NAT and private addressing, and how the two work together.

IP Version 6 Addressing

IPv6 defines many improvements over IPv4. However, the primary goal of IPv6 is to significantly increase the number of available IP addresses. To that end, IPv6 uses a 128-bit IP address, rather than the 32 bits defined by IPv4. To appreciate the size of the address structure, a 128-bit address structure provides well over 10^{38} possible IP addresses. If you consider the fact that the Earth currently has less than 10^{10} people, you can see that you could have literally billions, trillions, or gazillions of IP addresses per person and still not run out.

> **NOTE**   In case you are wondering, IP Version 5 was defined for experimental reasons but was never deployed. To avoid confusion, the next attempt to update the IP protocol was named IPv6.

IPv6 has been defined since the mid-1990s, but the migration from IPv4 to IPv6 has been rather slow. IPv6 was created to solve an overcrowding problem in the IPv4 address space. Some other short-term solutions in IPv4 (notably, NAT, as covered in Chapter 16) helped relieve the IPv4 overcrowding. However, in 2007, IPv6 deployment has started to quicken. Many large service providers have migrated to IPv6 to support the large number of mobile devices that can connect to the Internet, and the U.S. government has mandated migration to IPv6 for its member agencies.

The 128-bit IPv6 address is written in hexadecimal notation, with colons between each quartet of symbols. Even in hexadecimal, the addresses can be long. However, IPv6 also allows for abbreviations, as is shown in Table 12-5. The table also summarizes some of the pertinent information comparing IPv4 addresses with IPv6.

Table 12-5   *IPv4 Versus IPv6*

Feature	IPv4	IPv6
Size of address (bits or bytes per octets)	32 bits, 4 octets	128 bits, 16 octets
Example address	10.1.1.1	0000:0000:0000:0000:FFFF:FFFF:0A01:0101
Same address, abbreviated	—	::FFFF:FFFF:0A01:0101
Number of possible addresses, ignoring reserved values	2^{32}, (roughly 4 billion)	2^{128}, or roughly 3.4×10^{38}

IP Subnetting Review

IP subnetting creates larger numbers of smaller groups of IP addresses compared with simply using Class A, B, and C conventions. You can still think about the Class A, B, and C rules, but now a single Class A, B, or C network can be subdivided into many smaller groups. Subnetting treats a subdivision of a single Class A, B, or C network as if it were a network itself. By doing so, a single Class A, B, or C network can be subdivided into many nonoverlapping subnets.

Figure 12-2 shows a reminder of the basics of how to subnet a classful network, using the same internetwork shown in Figure 5-6 in Chapter 5. This figure shows Class B network 150.150.0.0, with a need for six subnets.

Figure 12-2 *Same Network Topology Using One IP Network with Six Subnets*

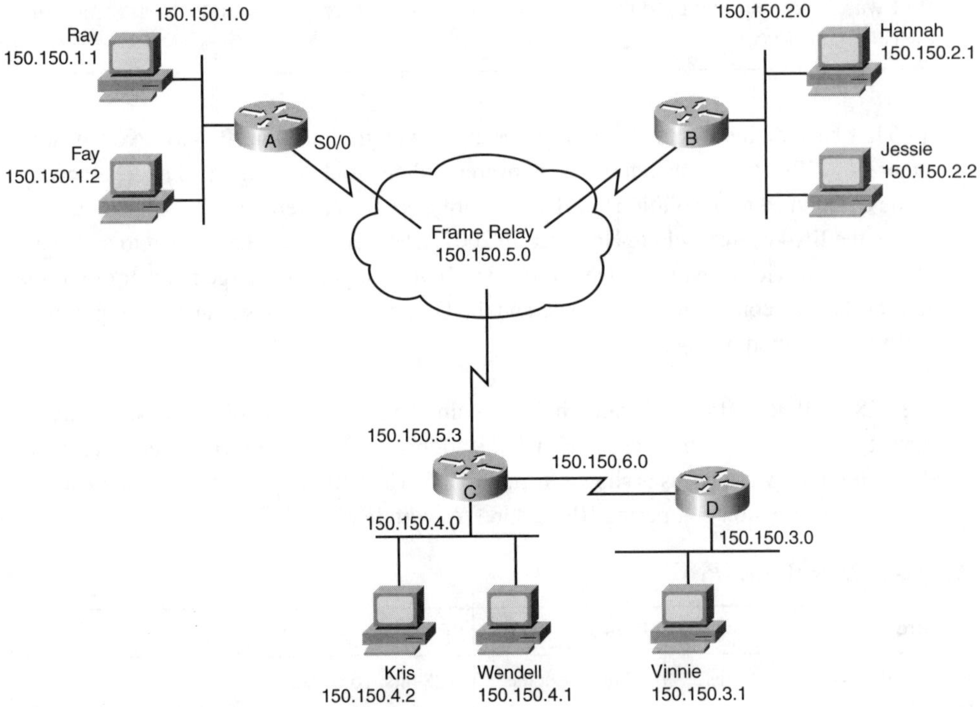

NOTE The term *network* might be used to refer to a Class A, B, or C IP network, or might be used to simply refer to a collection of switches, routers, cables, and end-user devices. To avoid confusion, this chapter uses the term internetwork to refer to the collection of networking devices (internetwork meaning "interconnected networks"), and the term network specifically for a Class A, B, or C IP network.

This design subnets Class B network 150.150.0.0. The IP network designer has chosen a mask of 255.255.255.0, the last octet of which implies 8 host bits. Because it is a Class B network, there are 16 network bits. Therefore, there are 8 subnet bits, which happen to be bits 17 through 24—in other words, the third octet.

NOTE Note that the next major section explains the use and purpose of subnet masks, so do not be concerned at this point if the analysis in this paragraph does not yet make sense.

The network parts (the first two octets in this example) all begin with 150.150, meaning that each of the six subnets is a subnet of Class B network 150.150.0.0.

With subnetting, the third part of an IP address—namely, the subnet part—appears in the middle of the address. This field is created by "stealing" or "borrowing" bits from the host part of the address. The size of the network part of the address never shrinks. In other words, Class A, B, and C rules still apply when you define the size of the network part of an address. However, the host part of the address shrinks to make room for the subnet part of the address. Figure 12-3 shows the format of addresses when subnetting is used.

Figure 12-3 *Address Formats When Subnetting Is Used*

8	24 – x	x	
Network	Subnet	Host	**Class A**

16	16 – x	x	
Network	Subnet	Host	**Class B**

24	8 – x	x	
Network	Subnet	Host	**Class C**

IP Routing Review

IP routing and IP addressing were designed with each other in mind. IP routing presumes the structure of IP subnetting, in which ranges of consecutive IP addresses reside in a single subnet. IP addressing RFCs define subnetting so that consecutively numbered IP addresses can be represented as a subnet number (subnet address) and a subnet mask. This allows routers to succinctly list subnets in their routing tables.

Routers need a good way to list the subnet number in their routing tables. This information must somehow imply the IP addresses in the subnet. For example, the subnet at the bottom of figure 12-2, which contains host Kris, can be described as follows:

> All IP addresses that begin with 150.150.4; more specifically, the numbers 150.150.4.0 through 150.150.4.255.

Although true, the preceding statement is not very succinct. Instead, a router's routing table would list the subnet number and subnet mask as follows:

> 150.150.4.0, 255.255.255.0

The subnet number and mask together means the same thing as the earlier long text statement, but just using numbers. This chapter explains how to examine a subnet number and mask and figure out the range of consecutive IP addresses that comprises the subnet.

One reason you need to be able to figure out the range of addresses in a subnet is to understand, analyze, and troubleshoot routing problems. To see why, again consider router A's route for subnet 150.150.4.0, 255.255.255.0 in Figure 12-2. Each route in a router's routing table lists the destination (a subnet number and mask), plus instructions on how the router should forward packets to that subnet. The forwarding instructions typically include the IP address of the next router to which the packet should be forwarded, and the local router's interface to use when forwarding the packet. For example, router A's route to that subnet would look like the information in Table 12-6.

Table 12-6 *Routing Table Entry in Router A*

Subnet and Mask	Next-hop Router	Outgoing Interface
150.150.4.0, 255.255.255.0	150.150.5.3	S0/0

Now, to see how this information is related to subnetting, consider a packet sent by Ray to Kris (150.150.4.2). Ray sends the packet to router A because Ray knows that 150.150.4.2 is in a different subnet, and Ray knows that router A is Ray's default gateway. Once router A has the packet, it compares the destination IP address (150.150.4.2) to A's routing table. Router A typically will not find the address 150.150.4.2 in the routing table—instead, the router has a list of subnets (subnet numbers and corresponding subnet masks), like the route listed in Table 12-6. So, the router must ask itself the following:

> Of the subnets in my routing table, which subnet's range of IP addresses includes the destination IP address of this packet?

In other words, the router must match the packet's destination address to the correct subnet. In this case, the subnet listed in Table 12-6 includes all addresses that begin with 150.150.4, so the packet destined to Kris (150.150.4.2) matches the route. In this case, router A forwards the packet to router C (150.150.5.3), with router A using its S0/0 interface to forward the packet.

> **NOTE**   The exams might expect you to apply this knowledge to solve a routing problem. For example, you might be asked to determine why PC1 cannot ping PC2, and the problem is that the second of three routers between PC1 and PC2 does not have a route that matches the destination IP address of PC2.

This chapter explains many features of IP addressing and subnetting, as an end to itself. The next section focuses on some basic math tools. The section following that, "Analyzing and Choosing Subnet Masks," examines the meaning of the subnet mask and how it represents the structure of an IP address—both from a design perspective and the perspective of analyzing an existing internetwork. Following that, the next section, "Analyzing Existing

Subnets," explains the processes by which you can analyze an existing IP internetwork, and find the subnet numbers, broadcast addresses, and range of IP addresses in each subnet. Finally, the last section, "Design: Choosing the Subnets of a Classful Network," explains how to go about designing a subnetting scheme for a Class A, B, or C network, including how to find all possible subnets.

Math Operations Used When Subnetting

Computers, especially routers, think about IP addresses in terms of 32-bit binary numbers. This is fine, because technically that is what IP addresses are. Also, computers use a subnet mask to define the structure of these binary IP addresses. Acquiring a full understanding of what this means is not too difficult with a little reading and practice. However, getting accustomed to doing the binary math in your head can be challenging, particularly if you do not do it every day.

In this section, you will read about three key math operations that will be used throughout the discussion of answering CCNA addressing and subnetting questions:

■   Converting IP addresses and masks from binary to decimal, and decimal to binary

■   Performing a binary math operation called a Boolean AND

■   Converting between two formats for subnet masks: dotted decimal and prefix notation

> **NOTE**   This chapter includes many summarized processes of how to do some work with IP addresses and subnets. There is no need to memorize the processes. Most people find that after practicing the processes sufficiently to get good and fast enough to do well on the exams, they internalize and memorize the important steps as a side effect of the practice.

Converting IP Addresses and Masks from Decimal to Binary and Back Again

If you already know how binary works, how binary-to-decimal and decimal-to-binary conversion work, and how to convert IP addresses and masks from decimal to binary and back, skip to the next section, "Performing a Boolean AND Operation."

IP addresses are 32-bit binary numbers written as a series of decimal numbers separated by periods (called *dotted decimal* format). To examine an address in its true form, binary, you need to convert from decimal to binary. To put a 32-bit binary number in the decimal form that is needed when configuring a router, you need to convert the 32-bit number back to decimal 8 bits at a time.

One key to the conversion process for IP addresses is remembering these facts:

Key Topic

When you convert from one format to the other, each decimal number represents 8 bits.

When you convert from decimal to binary, each decimal number converts to an 8-bit number.

When you convert from binary to decimal, each set of 8 consecutive bits converts to one decimal number.

Consider the conversion of IP address 150.150.2.1 to binary. The number 150, when converted to its 8-bit binary equivalent, is 10010110. (You can refer to the conversion chart in Appendix B, "Decimal to Binary Conversion Table," to easily convert the numbers.) The next byte, another decimal 150, is converted to 10010110. The third byte, decimal 2, is converted to 00000010. Finally, the fourth byte, decimal 1, is converted to 00000001. The combined series of 8-bit numbers is the 32-bit IP address—in this case, 10010110 10010110 00000010 00000001.

If you start with the binary version of the IP address, you first separate it into four sets of eight digits. Then you convert each set of eight binary digits to its decimal equivalent. For example, writing an IP address as follows is correct, but not very useful:

10010110100101100000000100000001

To convert this number to a more-convenient decimal form, first separate it into four sets of eight digits:

10010110 10010110 00000010 00000001

Then look in the conversion chart in Appendix B. You see that the first 8-bit number converts to 150, and so does the second. The third set of 8 bits converts to 2, and the fourth converts to 1, giving you 150.150.2.1.

Using the chart in Appendix B makes this much easier, but you will not have the chart at the exam, of course! So, you have two main options. First, you can learn and practice how to do the conversion. This may not be as hard as it might seem at first, particularly if you are willing to practice. The Cisco CCNA Prep Center has a Binary Game that helps you practice the conversions, and its very effective. The second option is to use the decimal-math-only processes listed in this chapter, which removes the need to be good at doing the conversions. However, you do not need to decide right now whether to get really good at doing the conversions—keep reading, understand both methods, and then pick which way works best for you.

Keep in mind that with subnetting, the subnet and host parts of the address might span only part of a byte of the IP address. But when you convert from binary to decimal and decimal to binary, the rule of always converting an 8-bit binary number to a decimal number is always true. However, when thinking about subnetting, you need to ignore byte boundaries and think of IP addresses as 32-bit numbers without specific byte boundaries. This is explained more in the section "Finding the Subnet Number: Binary."

Here are some websites that might help you if you want more information:

■   For a description of the conversion process, try http://doit.ort.org/course/inforep/135.htm.

■   For another, try http://www.wikihow.com/Convert-from-Binary-to-Decimal and http://www.wikihow.com/Convert-from-Decimal-to-Binary.

■   To practice the conversions, use the Cisco Binary Game at the CCNA Prep Center (http://www.cisco.com/go/prepcenter).

Performing a Boolean AND Operation

George Boole, a mathematician who lived in the 1800s, created a branch of mathematics that came to be called Boolean math after its creator. Boolean math has many applications in computing theory. In fact, you can find subnet numbers given an IP address and subnet mask using a Boolean AND.

A *Boolean AND* is a math operation performed on a pair of one-digit binary numbers. The result is another one-digit binary number. The actual math is even simpler than those first two sentences! The following list shows the four possible inputs to a Boolean AND, and the result:

■   0 AND 0 yields a 0

■   0 AND 1 yields a 0

■   1 AND 0 yields a 0

■   1 AND 1 yields a 1

In other words, the input to the equation consists of two one-digit binary numbers, and the output of the equation is one single-digit binary number. The only time the result is a binary 1 is when both input numbers are also binary 1; otherwise, the result of a Boolean AND operation is a 0.

You can perform a Boolean AND operation on longer binary numbers, but you are really just performing an AND operation on each pair of numbers. For instance, if you wanted to

AND together two four-digit numbers, 0110 and 0011, you would perform an AND on the first digit of each number and write down the answer. Then you would perform an AND operation on the second digit of each number, and so on, through the four digits. Table 12-7 shows the general idea.

Table 12-7   *Bitwise Boolean AND Between Two Four-Digit Numbers*

	Four-Digit Binary	First Digit	Second Digit	Third Digit	Fourth Digit
First Number	0110	0	1	1	0
Second Number	0011	0	0	1	1
Boolean AND Result	0010	0	0	1	0

This table separates the four digits of each original number to make the point more obvious. Look at the "First Digit" column. The first digit of the first number is 0, and the first digit of the second number is also 0. 0 AND 0 yields a binary 0, which is listed as the Boolean AND operation result in that same column. Similarly, the second digits of the two original numbers are 1 and 0, respectively, so the Boolean AND operation result in the "Second Digit" column shows a 0. For the third digit, the two original numbers' third digits are 1 and 1, so the AND result this time shows a binary 1. Finally, the fourth digits of the two original numbers are 0 and 1, so the Boolean AND result is 0 for that column.

When you Boolean AND together two longer binary numbers, you perform what is called a *bitwise Boolean AND*. This term simply means that you do what the previous example shows: you AND together the first digits from each of the two original numbers, and then the second digits, and then the third, and so on, until each pair of single-digit binary numbers has been ANDed.

IP subnetting math frequently uses a Boolean AND operation between two 32-bit binary numbers. The actual operation works just like the example in Table 12-7, except it is 32 bits long.

To discover the subnet number in which a particular IP address resides, you perform a bitwise AND operation between the IP address and the subnet mask. Although humans can sometimes look at an IP address and mask in decimal and derive the subnet number, routers and other computers use a bitwise Boolean AND operation between the IP address and the subnet mask to find the subnet number, so you need to understand this process. In this chapter, you will also read about a process by which you can find the subnet number without using binary conversion or Boolean ANDs. Table 12-8 shows an example of the derivation of a subnet number.

Table 12-8 *Bitwise Boolean AND Example*

	Decimal	Binary
Address	150.150.2.1	1001 0110 1001 0110 0000 0010 **0000 0001**
Mask	255.255.255.0	1111 1111 1111 1111 1111 1111 **0000 0000**
Result of AND	150.150.2.0	1001 0110 1001 0110 0000 0010 **0000 0000**

First, focus only on the third column of the table. The binary version of the IP address 150.150.2.1 is listed first. The next row shows the 32-bit binary version of the subnet mask (255.255.255.0). The last row shows the results of a bitwise AND of the two numbers. In other words, the first bit in each number is ANDed, and then the second bit in each number, and then the third, and so on, until all 32 bits in the first number have been ANDed with the bit in the same position in the second number.

The resulting 32-bit number is the subnet number in which 150.150.2.1 resides. All you have to do is convert the 32-bit number back to decimal 8 bits at a time. The subnet number in this case is 150.150.2.0.

While this process may seem long, and make you want to avoid converting all these numbers, do not worry. By the end of this chapter you will see how that, even using binary, you can use a small shortcut so that you only have to convert one octet to binary and back in order to find the subnet. For now, just be aware of the conversion table in Appendix B, and remember the Boolean AND process.

Prefix Notation/CIDR Notation

Subnet masks are actually 32-bit numbers, but for convenience, they are typically written as dotted decimal numbers—for example, 255.255.0.0. However, another way to represent a mask, called *prefix notation*, and sometimes referred to as *CIDR notation*, provides an even more succinct way to write, type, or speak the value of a subnet mask. To understand prefix notation, it is important to know that all subnet masks have some number of consecutive binary 1s, followed by binary 0s. In other words, a subnet mask cannot have 1s and 0s interspersed throughout the mask. The mask always has some number of binary 1s, followed only by binary 0s.

For the purpose of writing or typing the subnet mask, prefix notation simply denotes the number of binary 1s in a mask, preceded by a /. For example, for subnet mask 255.255.255.0, whose binary equivalent is 11111111 11111111 11111111 00000000, the equivalent prefix notation is /24, because there are 24 consecutive binary 1s in the mask.

When talking about subnets, you can say things like "That subnet uses a *slash 24 prefix*" or "That subnet has a 24-bit prefix" instead of saying something like "That subnet uses a mask of two-fifty-five dot two-fifty-five dot two-fifty-five dot zero." As you can tell, the prefix notation alternative—simply saying something like "slash twenty-four"—is much easier.

Binary Process to Convert Between Dotted Decimal and Prefix Notation

To be prepared for both real networking jobs and the exams, you should be able to convert masks between dotted decimal and prefix notation. Routers display masks in both formats, depending on the **show** command, and configuration commands typically require dotted decimal notation. Also, you might see written documentation with different mask formats. Practically speaking, network engineers simply need to be able to convert between the two often.

This section describes the relatively straightforward process of converting between the two formats, using binary math, with the following section explaining how to convert using only decimal math. To convert from dotted decimal to prefix notation, you can follow this simple binary process:

Key Topic

Step 1 Convert the dotted decimal mask to binary.

Step 2 Count the number of binary 1s in the 32-bit binary mask; this is the value of the prefix notation mask.

For example, the dotted decimal mask of 255.255.240.0 converts to 11111111 11111111 11110000 00000000 in binary. The mask has 20 binary 1s, so the prefix notation of the same mask is /20.

To convert from prefix notation to a dotted decimal number, you can follow what is essentially the reverse process, as follows:

Key Topic

Step 1 Write down *x* binary 1s, where *x* is the value listed in the prefix version of the mask.

Step 2 Write down binary 0s after the binary 1s until you have written down a 32-bit number.

Step 3 Convert this binary number, *8 bits at a time*, to decimal, to create a dotted decimal number; this value is the dotted decimal version of the subnet mask.

For example, with a /20 prefix, you would first write:

11111111 11111111 1111

Then, you would write binary 0s, to complete the 32-bit number, as follows:

11111111 11111111 11110000 00000000

At the third step, you would convert this number, 8 bits at a time, back to decimal, resulting in a dotted decimal mask of 255.255.240.0.

Decimal Process to Convert Between Dotted Decimal and Prefix Notation

The binary process for converting masks between dotted decimal format and prefix format is relatively easy, particularly once you can do the binary/decimal conversions quickly. However, due to the time pressure on the exam, practice that process until you can do it quickly. Some people might be able to work more quickly using a decimal shortcut, so this section describes a shortcut. In either case, you should practice using either binary or the decimal process listed here until you can find the answer quickly, and with confidence.

The decimal processes assume you have access to the information in Table 12-9. This table lists the nine possible decimal numbers that can be used in a subnet mask, along with the binary equivalent. And just to make it obvious, the table also lists the number of binary 0s and binary 1s in the binary version of these decimal numbers.

Table 12-9 *Nine Possible Decimal Numbers in a Subnet Mask*

Key Topic

Subnet Mask's Decimal Octet	Binary Equivalent	Number of Binary 1s	Number of Binary 0s
0	00000000	0	8
128	10000000	1	7
192	11000000	2	6
224	11100000	3	5
240	11110000	4	4
248	11111000	5	3
252	11111100	6	2
254	11111110	7	1
255	11111111	8	0

For the exams, you will want to memorize the table. As it turns out, if you practice subnetting problems enough to get really good and fast, then you will probably end up memorizing the table as a side effect of all the practice. So, don't just sit and memorize—wait until you have practiced subnetting, and then decide if you really need to work on memorizing the table or not.

To convert a mask from dotted decimal to prefix format, use the following process:

Step 1 Start with a prefix value of 0.

Step 2 For each dotted decimal octet, add the number of binary 1s listed for that decimal value in Table 12-9.

Step 3 The prefix length is /x, where x is the sum calculated at Step 2.

For example, with a mask of 255.255.240.0 again, for Step 1, you start with a value of 0. At Step 2, you add the following:

Because of the first octet value of 255, add 8.

Because of the second octet value of 255, add 8.

Because of the third octet value of 240, add 4.

Because of the fourth octet value of 0, add 0.

The end result, 20, is the prefix length, written as /20.

Converting from prefix format to dotted decimal may be somewhat intuitive, but the written process is a bit more laborious than the previous process. The process refers to the prefix value as x; the process is as follows:

Step 1 Divide x by 8 (x/8), noting the number of times 8 fully goes into x (the dividend, represented as a d), and the number left over (the remainder, represented as an r).

Step 2 Write down d octets of value 255. (This in effect begins the mask with 8, 16, or 24 binary 1s.)

Step 3 For the next octet, find the decimal number that begins with r binary 1s, followed by all binary 0s. (Table 12-9 will be useful for this step.)

Step 4 For any remaining octets, write down a decimal 0.

The steps may not be so obvious as written, so an example can help. If the prefix length is 20, then at Step 1, 20/8 should be interpreted as "a dividend of 2, with a remainder of 4." At Step 2, you would write down two octets of decimal 255, as follows:

255.255

Then, for Step 3, you will find from Table 12-9 that decimal 240's binary equivalent begins with four binary 1s, so you would write down an octet of value 240:

255.255.**240**

For Step 4, you would complete the subnet mask, 255.255.240.0.

No matter whether you use the binary or decimal shortcut to make these conversions, you should practice until you can make the conversions quickly, confidently, and correctly. To that end, CD-only Appendix D lists some sample questions, with answers.

Practice Suggestions

Before moving on to the next major section, consider taking the time now to practice a few items from this section. First, pick at least one of the processes (binary or decimal) for converting between mask formats, and practice until you can quickly and easily find the right answer. To that end, you can use this chapter, the practice questions in (CD-ROM) Appendix D. Also, if you begin to think that you will want to use the binary process, use the Binary Game at the CCNA Prep Center to refine your skills.

> **NOTE**   For those of you using or intending to use Appendix E, the processes covered in this section are summarized in reference pages RP-1A and RP-1B in that appendix.

Now that the basic tools have been covered, the next section explains how to use these tools to understand and choose subnet masks.

Analyzing and Choosing Subnet Masks

The process of subnetting subdivides a *classful network*—a Class A, B, or C network—into smaller groups of addresses, called subnets. When an engineer designs an internetwork, the engineer often chooses to use a single subnet mask in a particular classful network. The choice of subnet mask revolves around some key design requirements—namely, the need for some number of subnets, and some number of hosts per subnet. The choice of subnet mask then defines how many subnets of that classful network can exist, and how many host addresses exist in each subnet, as well as the specific subnets.

The first part of this section examines how to analyze the meaning of subnet masks once some other network engineer has already chosen the classful network and mask used in an internetwork. The second part of this section describes how an engineer could go about choosing which subnet mask to use when designing a new internetwork. Note that in real life, the first task, analyzing the meaning of the mask someone else chose, is the more common task.

> **NOTE**   This section assumes a single mask in each classful network, a convention sometimes called *static length subnet masking (SLSM)*. The *ICND2 Official Exam Certification Guide* covers the details of an alternative, using different masks in a single classful network, called *variable-length subnet masking (VLSM)*.

Analyzing the Subnet Mask in an Existing Subnet Design

The engineer's choice of using a particular classful network, with a particular single subnet mask, determines the number of possible subnets and number of hosts per subnet. Based on the network number and subnet mask, you should be able to figure out how many network, subnet, and host bits are used with that subnetting scheme. From those facts, you can easily figure out how many hosts exist in the subnet and how many subnets you can create in that network using that subnet mask.

This section begins with a general discussion of how to analyze an IP subnetting design, particularly how to determine the number of network, subnet, and host bits used in the design. Then, the text describes two different formal processes to find these facts, one using binary math, and the other using decimal math. As usual, you should read about both, but you should practice one of these processes until it becomes second nature. Finally, this section ends with the description of how to find the number of possible subnets, and number of possible hosts per subnet.

The Three Parts: Network, Subnet, and Host

You have already learned that Class A, B, and C networks have 8, 16, or 24 bits in their network fields, respectively. Those rules do not change. You have also read that, without subnetting, Class A, B, and C addresses have 24, 16, or 8 bits in their host fields, respectively. With subnetting, the network part of the address does not shrink or change, but the host field shrinks to make room for the subnet field. So the key to answering these types of questions is to figure out how many host bits remain after the engineer has implemented subnetting by choosing a particular subnet mask. Then you can tell the size of the subnet field, with the rest of the answers following from those two facts.

The following facts tell you how to find the sizes of the network, subnet, and host parts of an IP address:

- The network part of the address is always defined by class rules.

- The host part of the address is always defined by the subnet mask. The number of binary 0s in the mask (always found at the end of the mask) defines the number of host bits in the host part of the address.

- The subnet part of the address is what is left over in the 32-bit address.

> **NOTE**   The preceding list assumes a classful approach to IP addressing, which can be useful for learning subnetting. However, a classless view of addressing, which combines the network and subnet fields into one field, can be used as well. For consistency, this chapter uses a classful view of addressing.

Table 12-10 shows an example, with the last three rows showing the analysis of the three parts of the IP address based on the three rules just listed. (If you have forgotten the ranges of values in the first octet for addresses in Class A, B, and C networks, refer to Table 12-2.)

Table 12-10   *First Example, with Rules for Learning the Network, Subnet, and Host Part Sizes*

Step	Example	Rules to Remember
Address	8.1.4.5	
Mask	255.255.0.0	
Number of Network Bits	8	Always defined by Class A, B, C
Number of Host Bits	16	Always defined as the number of binary 0s in the mask
Number of Subnet Bits	8	32 – (network size + host size)

This example has 8 network bits because the address is in a Class A network, 8.0.0.0. There are 16 host bits because 255.255.0.0 in binary has 16 binary 0s—the last 16 bits in the mask. (Feel free to convert this mask to binary as a related exercise.) The size of the subnet part of the address is what is left over, or 8 bits.

Two other examples with easy-to-convert masks might help your understanding. Consider address 130.4.102.1 with mask 255.255.255.0. First, 130.4.102.1 is in a Class B network, so there are 16 network bits. A subnet mask of 255.255.255.0 has only eight binary 0s, implying 8 host bits, which leaves 8 subnet bits in this case.

As another example, consider 199.1.1.100 with mask 255.255.255.0. This example does not even use subnetting! 199.1.1.100 is in a Class C network, which means that there are 24 network bits. The mask has eight binary 0s, yielding 8 host bits, with no bits remaining for the subnet part of the address. In fact, if you remembered that the default mask for Class C networks is 255.255.255.0, you might have already realized that no subnetting was being used in this example.

Binary Process: Finding the Number of Network, Subnet, and Host Bits

You probably can calculate the number of host bits easily if the mask uses only decimal 255s and 0s, because it is easy to remember that decimal 255 represents eight binary 1s and decimal 0 represents eight binary 0s. So, for every decimal 0 in the mask, there are 8 host bits. However, when the mask uses decimal values besides 0 and 255, deciphering the number of host bits is more difficult.

Examining the subnet masks in binary helps overcome the challenge because the binary mask directly defines the number of network and subnet bits combined, and the number of host bits, as follows:

■   The mask's binary 1s define the combined network and subnet parts of the addresses.

■   The mask's binary 0s define the host part of the addresses.

■   The class rules define the size of the network part.

Applying these three facts to a binary mask allows you to easily find the size of the network, subnet, and host parts of addresses in a particular subnetting scheme. For example, consider the addresses and masks, including the binary versions of the masks, shown in Table 12-11.

Table 12-11   *Two Examples Using More-Challenging Masks*

Mask in Decimal	Mask in Binary
130.4.102.1, mask 255.255.252.0	1111 1111 1111 1111 1111 11**00 0000 0000**
199.1.1.100, mask 255.255.255.224	1111 1111 1111 1111 1111 1111 111**0 0000**

The number of host bits implied by a mask becomes more apparent after you convert the mask to binary. The first mask, 255.255.252.0, has ten binary 0s, implying a 10-bit host field. Because that mask is used with a Class B address (130.4.102.1), implying 16 network bits, there are 6 remaining subnet bits. In the second example, the mask has only five binary 0s, for 5 host bits. Because the mask is used with a Class C address, there are 24 network bits, leaving only 3 subnet bits.

The following list formalizes the steps you can take, in binary, to find the sizes of the network, subnet, and host parts of an address:

Step 1   Compare the first octet of the address to the table of Class A, B, C addresses; write down the number of network bits depending on the address class.

Step 2   Find the number of hosts bits by:

a. Converting the subnet mask to binary.

b. Counting the number of binary 0s in the mask.

Step 3   Calculate the number of subnet bits by subtracting the number of combined network and host bits from 32.

Decimal Process: Finding the Number of Network, Subnet, and Host Bits

It is very reasonable to use the binary process to find the number of network, subnet, and host bits in any IP address. With a little practice, and mastery of the binary/decimal conversion process, the process should be quick and painless. However, some people prefer processes that use more decimal math, and less binary math. To that end, this section briefly outlines an alternative decimal process, as follows:

Step 1 (Same as Step 1 in the binary process.) Compare the first octet of the address to the table of Class A, B, C addresses; write down the number of network bits depending on the address class.

Step 2 If the mask is in dotted decimal format, convert the mask to prefix format.

Step 3 To find the number of host bits, subtract the prefix length value from 32.

Step 4 (Same as Step 4 in the binary process.) Calculate the number of subnet bits by subtracting the number of combined network and host bits from 32.

The key to this process is that the mask in prefix format lists the number of binary 1s in the mask, so it is easy to figure out how many binary 0s are in the mask. For example, a mask of 255.255.224.0, converted to prefix format, is /19. Knowing that the mask has 32 bits in it, and knowing that /19 means "19 binary 1s," you can easily calculate the number of binary 0s as $32 - 19 = 13$ host bits. The rest of the process follows the same logic used in the binary process, but these steps do not require any binary math.

Determining the Number of Subnets and Number of Hosts Per Subnet

Both in real networking jobs and for the exams, you should be able to answer questions such as the following:

> Given an address (or classful network number), and a single subnet mask that is used throughout the classful network, how many subnets could exist in that classful network? And how many hosts are there in each subnet?

Two simple formulas provide the answers. If you consider the number of subnet bits to be s, and the number of host bits to be h, the following formulas provide the answers:

Number of subnets $= 2^s$

Number of hosts per subnet $= 2^h - 2$

Both formulas are based on the fact that to calculate the number of things that can be numbered using a binary number, you take 2 to the power of the number of bits used. For example, with 3 bits, you can create $2^3 = 8$ unique binary numbers: 000, 001, 010, 011, 100, 101, 110, and 111.

IP addressing conventions reserve two IP addresses per subnet: the first/smallest number (which has all binary 0s in the host field) and the last/largest number (which has all binary 1s in the host field). The smallest number is used as the subnet number, and the largest number is used as the subnet broadcast address. Because these numbers cannot be assigned to a host to use as an IP address, the formula to calculate the number of hosts per subnet includes the "minus 2."

Number of Subnets: Subtract 2, or Not?

Before seeing more of the math, this chapter needs to explain a bit of related information about which math to use when calculating the number of possible subnets. In some cases, two of the subnets in a single classful IP network are reserved, and should not be used. In other cases, these two subnets are not reserved, and can be used. This section describes these two subnets, and explains when they can be used, and when they cannot be used.

The first of the two possibly reserved subnets in a network is called the *zero subnet*, or *subnet zero*. Of all the subnets of the classful network, it has the smallest numeric value. The subnet number of the zero subnet also happens to always be the exact same number as the classful network number itself. For example, for Class B network 150.150.0.0, the zero subnet number would be 150.150.0.0—which creates a bit of ambiguity at first glance. This ambiguity is one of the reasons that the zero subnet was first reserved.

The other of the two possibly reserved subnets is called the *broadcast subnet*. It is the largest numeric subnet number in a network. The reason why this subnet was not used at one point in time relates to the fact that this subnet's broadcast address—used to send one packet to all hosts in the subnet—happens to be the same number as the network-wide broadcast address. For example, a packet sent to address 150.150.255.255 might mean "send this packet to all hosts in Class B network 150.150.0.0," but in other cases mean that the packet should be delivered to just all the hosts in a single subnet. This ambiguity in the meaning of a broadcast address is the reason why such subnets were avoided.

To succeed in real networking jobs and on the exams, you need to be able to determine when a zero subnet and broadcast subnet can be used. If allowed, the formula for the number of subnets is 2^s, where s is the number of subnet bits; if not allowed, the formula for the number of subnets is $2^s - 2$, which essentially does not count these two special subnets. Also, the exams might ask you to pick subnets to use, and part of that question might require you to figure out which subnets are zero subnets and broadcast subnets, and to know if these should be used.

For the exams, three main factors dictate when you can use these two subnets, and when you cannot. First, if the routing protocol is classless, use these two subnets, but if the routing protocol is classful, do not use these two subnets. (Chapter 14, "Routing Protocol Concepts and Configuration," explains the terms classless routing protocol and classful routing protocol; the details are not important for now.) Additionally, if the question uses VLSM—the practice of using different masks in the same classful network—then the two special subnets are allowed.

The third factor that defines whether the two special subnets should be used is based on a global configuration command: **ip subnet zero**. If configured, this command tells the router that an IP address in a zero subnet can be configured on an interface. If the opposite is configured—the **no ip subnet zero** command—then an IP address in a zero subnet cannot be configured. Note that the **ip subnet zero** command is a default setting in Cisco IOS, meaning that IOS allows the zero subnet by default. So, if the **ip subnet zero** command is configured, or not listed, then the zero subnet and the other special subnet, the broadcast subnet, are both allowed.

For the exams, any time that the zero subnet or broadcast subnet may impact the answer to the question, use the information in Table 12-12 to help you decide whether to allow these two special subnets.

Table 12-12 *When to Use Which Formula for the Number of Subnets*

Key
Topic

Use the $2^s - 2$ formula, and avoid the zero and broadcast subnet, if...	Use the 2^s formula, and use the zero and broadcast subnet, if...
Classful routing protocol	Classless routing protocol
RIP Version 1 or IGRP as the routing protocol	RIP Version 2, EIGRP, or OSPF as the routing protocol
The **no ip subnet zero** command is configured	The **ip subnet zero** command is configured or omitted (default)
	VLSM is used
	No other clues provided

Of particular importance, for the CCNA exams, if a question simply does not give any clues as to whether to allow these two special subnets or not, assume you can use these subnets, and use the 2^s formula.

Now, back to the core purpose of this chapter. The remainder of the chapter will assume that these two special subnets can be used, but it will also point out how to identify these two special subnets to prepare you for the exam.

Practice Examples for Analyzing Subnet Masks

This chapter will use five different IP addresses and masks as examples for various parts of the subnetting analysis. For practice right now, go ahead and determine the number of network, subnet, and host bits, and the number of subnets and the number of hosts per subnet, for each of the following five example problems:

■ 8.1.4.5/16

- 130.4.102.1/24

- 199.1.1.100/24

- 130.4.102.1/22

- 199.1.1.100/27

Table 12-13 lists the answers for reference.

Table 12-13 *Five Examples of Addresses/Masks, with the Number of Network, Subnet, and Host Bits*

Address	8.1.4.5/16	130.4.102.1/24	199.1.1.100/24	130.4.102.1/22	199.1.1.100/27
Mask	255.255.0.0	255.255.255.0	255.255.255.0	255.255.252.0	255.255.255.224
Number of Network Bits	8	16	24	16	24
Number of Host Bits	16	8	8	10	5
Number of Subnet Bits	8	8	0	6	3
Number of Hosts Per Subnet	$2^{16}-2$, or 65,534	2^8-2, or 254	2^8-2, or 254	$2^{10}-2$, or 1022	2^5-2, or 30
Number of Subnets	2^8, or 256	2^8, or 256	0	2^6, or 64	2^3, or 8

Choosing a Subnet Mask that Meets Design Requirements

This chapter's previous discussions about subnet masks assumed that an engineer had already chosen the subnet mask. However, someone has to choose which mask to use. This section describes the concepts related to choosing an appropriate subnet mask, based on a set of design requirements.

When a network engineer designs a new internetwork, the engineer must choose a subnet mask to use, based on the requirements for the new internetwork. The mask needs to define enough host and subnet bits so that the design allows for enough hosts in each subnet (based on the 2^h-2 formula) and enough different subnets (based on the 2^s or the 2^s-2 formula, depending on whether the zero and broadcast subnets can be used). The exams might test this same skill, asking questions like this:

You are using Class B network X, and you need 200 subnets, with at most 200 hosts per subnet. Which of the following subnet masks can you use? (This is followed by some subnet masks from which you choose the answer.)

NOTE   The questions may not be that straightforward, but still ask that you do the same reasoning to find the answers.

To find the correct answers to these types of questions, you first need to decide how many subnet bits and host bits you need to meet the requirements. Basically, the number of hosts per subnet is $2^h - 2$, where h is the number of host bits as defined by the subnet mask. Likewise, the number of subnets in a network, assuming that the same subnet mask is used all over the network, is 2^s, but with s being the number of subnet bits. Alternately, if the question implies that the two special subnets (zero subnet and broadcast subnet) should not be used, you would use the $2^s - 2$ formula. As soon as you know how many subnet bits and host bits are required, you can figure out what mask or masks meet the stated design goals in the question.

In some cases, the design requirements only allow for a single possible subnet mask, whereas in other cases, several masks may meet the design requirements. The next section shows an example for which only one possible mask could be used, followed by a section that uses an example where multiple masks meet the design requirements.

Finding the Only Possible Mask

Next, consider the following question, which happens to lead you to only one possible subnet mask that meets the requirements:

Your network can use Class B network 130.1.0.0. What subnet masks meet the requirement that you plan to allow at most 200 subnets, with at most 200 hosts per subnet?

First you need to figure out how many subnet bits allow for 200 subnets. You can use the formula 2^s and plug in values for s until one of the numbers is at least 200. In this case, s turns out to be 8, because $2^7 = 128$, which is not enough subnets, but $2^8 = 256$, which provides enough subnets. In other words, you need at least 8 subnet bits to allow for 200 subnets.

Similarly, to find the number of required host bits, plug in values for h in the formula $2^h - 2$ until you find the smallest value of h that results in a value of 200 or more. In this case, $h = 8$.

If you do not want to keep plugging values into the formulas based on 2^x, you can instead memorize Table 12-14.

Table 12-14 *Maximum Number of Subnets/Hosts*

Number of Bits in the Host or Subnet Field	Maximum Number of Hosts ($2^h - 2$)	Maximum Number of Subnets (2^s)
1	0	2
2	2	4
3	6	8
4	14	16
5	30	32
6	62	64
7	126	128
8	254	256
9	510	512
10	1022	1024
11	2046	2048
12	4094	4096
13	8190	8192
14	16,382	16,384

As you can see, if you already have the powers of 2 memorized, you really do not need to memorize the table—just remember the formulas.

Continuing this same example with Class B network 130.1.0.0, you need to decide what mask(s) to use, knowing that you must have at least 8 subnet bits and 8 host bits to meet the design requirements. In this case, because the network is a Class B network, you know you will have 16 network bits. Using the letter *N* to represent network bits, the letter *S* to represent subnet bits, and the letter *H* to represent host bits, the following shows the sizes of the various fields in the subnet mask:

NNNNNNNN NNNNNNNN SSSSSSSS HHHHHHHH

In this example, because there are 16 network bits, 8 subnet bits, and 8 host bits already defined, you have already allocated all 32 bits of the address structure. Therefore, only one possible subnet mask works. To figure out the mask, you need to write down the 32-bit subnet mask, applying the following fact and subnet masks:

> The network and subnet bits in a subnet mask are, by definition, all binary 1s. Similarly, the host bits in a subnet mask are, by definition, all binary 0s.

Key Topic

So, the only valid subnet mask, in binary, is

11111111 11111111 11111111 00000000

When converted to decimal, this is 255.255.255.0, or /24 in prefix format.

Finding Multiple Possible Masks

In some cases, more than one mask may meet the design requirements. This section shows an example, with some ideas about how to find all the possible subnet masks. This section also uses an example question, in this case with multiple subnet masks meeting the criteria, as follows:

> Your internetwork design calls for 50 subnets, with the largest subnet having 200 hosts. The internetwork uses a class B network, and will not get any larger. What subnet masks meet these requirements?

For this design, you need 16 network bits, because the design uses a Class B network. You need at least 8 host bits, because $2^7 - 2 = 126$ (not enough), but $2^8 - 2 = 254$, which does provide enough hosts per subnet. Similarly, you now need only 6 subnet bits, because 6 subnet bits allows for 2^6, or 64, subnets, whereas 5 subnet bits only allows for 32 subnets.

If you follow the same process of noting network, subnet, and host bits with the letters N, S, and H, you get the following format:

NNNNNNNN NNNNNNNN SSSSSS_ _ HHHHHHHH

This format represents the minimum number of network (16), subnet (6), and host (8) bits. However, it leaves 2 bit positions empty, namely, the last 2 bits in the third octet. For these bit positions, write an **X** for "wildcard" bits—bits that can be either subnet or host bits. In this example:

NNNNNNNN NNNNNNNN SSSSSS**XX** HHHHHHHH

The wildcard bits, shown as **X** in the structure, can be either subnet or host bits, while still meeting the design requirements. In this case, there are 2 bits, so you might think that four possible answers exist; however, only three valid answers exist, because of a very important fact about subnet masks:

Key Topic

> All masks must start with one unbroken consecutive string of binary 1s, followed by one unbroken consecutive string of binary 0s.

This statement makes more sense by applying the concept to a particular example. Continuing the same example, the following list includes the three correct answers, all of which show consecutive 1s and 0s. The list also includes one invalid combination of wildcard bits—an answer which shows nonconsecutive binary 1s and 0s. Note that the wildcard bits (the bits that could either be subnet bits or host bits) are shown in bold.

11111111 11111111 111111**11** 00000000 (8 subnet, 8 host)

11111111 11111111 111111**10** 00000000 (7 subnet, 9 host)

11111111 11111111 11111**100** 00000000 (6 subnet, 10 host)

11111111 11111111 11111**101** 00000000 illegal (nonconsecutive 1s)

The first three lines maintain the requirement of an unbroken string of binary 1s followed by one unbroken string of binary 0s. However, the last line in the list shows 22 binary 1s, then a binary 0, followed by another binary 1, which makes this value illegal for use as a subnet mask.

The final answer to this problem is to list the three valid subnet masks in decimal or prefix format, as follows:

255.255.255.0   /24   8 subnet bits, 8 host bits

255.255.254.0   /23   7 subnet bits, 9 host bits

255.255.252.0   /22   6 subnet bits, 10 host bits

Choosing the Mask that Maximizes the Number of Subnets or Hosts

Finally, on the exams, a question might ask you to find the subnet mask that meets the stated requirements, but either maximizes or minimizes the number of subnets. Alternately, the question might ask that you pick the mask that either maximizes or minimizes the number of hosts per subnet. To pick among the various subnet masks, simply keep the following in mind when comparing the multiple masks that meet the stated design requirements:

- **The mask with the most subnet bits:** The mask for which the wildcard bits were set to binary 1, thereby making the subnet part of the addresses larger, maximizes the number of subnets and minimizes the number of hosts per subnet.

- **The mask with the most host bits:** The mask for which the wildcard bits were set to binary 0, thereby making the host part of the addresses larger, maximizes the number of hosts per subnet and minimizes the number of subnets.

Completing this same example, with three possible masks, mask 255.255.255.0 (/24)—with 8 subnet bits and 8 host bits—both maximizes the number of subnets and minimizes the number of hosts per subnet (while still meeting the design requirements). Conversely, the mask of 255.255.252.0 (/22)—with 6 subnet bits and 10 host bits—maximizes the number of hosts per subnet and minimizes the number of subnets, again while still meeting the design requirements.

For reference, the following list summarizes the steps to choose a new subnet mask, based on a set of requirements, assuming that the zero and broadcast subnet can be used.

Step 1   Find the number of network bits (N) based on Class A, B, C rules.

Step 2   Find the number of subnet bits (S) based on the formula 2^s, such that 2^s => the required number of subnets.

Step 3   Find the number of host bits (H) based on the formula $2^h - 2$, such that $2^h - 2$ => the required number of hosts per subnet.

Step 4   Write down, starting on the left, N + S binary 1s.

Step 5   Write down, starting on the right, H binary 0s.

Step 6   If the number of binary 1s and 0s together adds up to less than 32:

    a. Fill in the remaining "wildcard" bit positions—between the binary 1s and 0s—with the letter X.

    b. Find all combinations of bits for the wildcard bit positions that meet the requirements for only having one consecutive string of binary 1s in the binary mask.

Step 7   Convert the mask(s) to decimal or prefix format as appropriate.

Step 8   To find the mask that maximizes the number of subnets, pick the mask that has the most binary 1s in it. To find the mask that maximizes the number of hosts per subnet, pick the mask that has the largest number of binary 0s in it.

Key
Topic

Practice Suggestions

Before moving on to the next major section, take a few moments and practice the processes covered in this section. In particular:

- Refer to Appendix E, specifically the following processes, which summarize the processes covered in this section:

    — RP-2: Analyzing Unsubnetted IP Addresses

    — RP-3A: Analyzing an Existing Subnet Mask: Binary Version

    — RP-3B: Analyzing an Existing Subnet Mask: Decimal Version

    — RP-4: Choosing a Subnet Mask

- Do the following problem sets from Appendix D:

    — Problem Set 2, which covers how to analyze an unsubnetted IP address

    — Problem Set 3, which covers how to analyze the meaning of an existing subnet mask

    — Problem Set 4, which covers how to choose a new subnet mask to use

You should practice these problems until you can look at a given IP network and mask and determine the number of hosts per subnet, and the number of subnets, in around 15 seconds. You should also practice the design-oriented process of choosing a new subnet mask, given an IP network and a set of requirements for the number of hosts and subnets, within about 30 seconds. (These timings are admittedly subjective and are meant to give you a goal to help reduce the time pressure you may feel on exam day.)

Analyzing Existing Subnets

One of the most common subnetting-related tasks—both in real networking jobs and for the exams—is to analyze and understand some key facts about existing subnets. You might be given an IP address and subnet mask, and you need to then answer questions about the subnet in which the address resides—sometimes referred to as the *resident subnet*. The question might be straightforward, like "What is the subnet number in which the address resides?" or it might be more subtle, like "Which of the following IP addresses are in the same subnet as the stated address?" In either case, if you can dissect an IP address as described in this chapter, you can answer any variation on this type of question.

This section describes how to find three key facts about any subnet, once you know an IP address and subnet mask for a host in that subnet:

- The subnet number (subnet address)

- The subnet broadcast address for that subnet

- The range of usable IP addresses in that subnet

This section begins by showing how to use binary-based processes to find all three of these facts about a subnet. Following that, the text describes a decimal-based process that helps you find the same answers, but with a little practice, the decimal-based process will help you find these answers much more quickly.

Finding the Subnet Number: Binary

A *subnet number*, or *subnet address*, is a dotted decimal number that represents a subnet. You most often see subnet numbers in written documentation and in routers' routing tables. Each subnet might contain hundreds of consecutively numbered IP addresses, but a router typically represents that range of IP addresses as a subnet number and mask in its IP routing table. Listing the subnet number and mask in the routing table allows a router to concisely refer to the subnet—a consecutive range of IP addresses—without requiring a routing table entry for every individual host address.

Earlier in this chapter, you learned that computers perform a Boolean AND of an IP address and mask to find the resident subnet number. Humans can certainly use the same process, formalized as follows:

Step 1 Convert the IP address from decimal to binary.

Step 2 Convert the subnet mask to binary, writing this number down below the IP address from Step 1.

Step 3 Perform a bitwise Boolean AND of the two numbers. To do so:

   a. AND the first bit of the address with the first bit of the subnet mask, recording the result below those numbers.

   b. AND the second bit of each number, recording the result below those numbers.

   c. Repeat for each pair of bits, resulting in a 32-bit binary number.

Step 4 Convert the resulting binary number, *8 bits at a time*, back to decimal. This value is the subnet number.

Key Topic

Tables 12-15 through 12-19 show the results of all four steps, for five different examples. The tables include the binary version of the address and mask and the results of the Boolean AND.

Table 12-15 *Boolean AND Calculation for the Subnet with Address 8.1.4.5, Mask 255.255.0.0*

Address	8.1.4.5	00001000 00000001 00000100 00000101
Mask	255.255.0.0	11111111 11111111 **00000000 00000000**
AND Result	8.1.0.0	00001000 00000001 00000000 00000000

Table 12-16 *Boolean AND Calculation for the Subnet with Address 130.4.102.1, Mask 255.255.255.0*

Address	130.4.102.1	10000010 00000100 01100110 00000001
Mask	255.255.255.0	11111111 11111111 11111111 **00000000**
AND Result	130.4.102.0	10000010 00000100 01100110 00000000

Table 12-17 *Boolean AND Calculation for the Subnet with Address 199.1.1.100, Mask 255.255.255.0*

Address	199.1.1.100	11000111 00000001 00000001 01100100
Mask	255.255.255.0	11111111 11111111 11111111 **00000000**
AND Result	199.1.1.0	11000111 00000001 00000001 00000000

Table 12-18 *Boolean AND Calculation for the Subnet with Address 130.4.102.1, Mask 255.255.252.0*

Address	130.4.102.1	10000010 00000100 01100110 00000001
Mask	255.255.252.0	11111111 11111111 111111**00 00000000**
AND Result	130.4.100.0	10000010 00000100 01100100 00000000

Table 12-19 *Boolean AND Calculation for the Subnet with Address 199.1.1.100, Mask 255.255.255.224*

Address	199.1.1.100	11000111 00000001 00000001 01100100
Mask	255.255.255.224	11111111 11111111 11111111 111**00000**
AND Result	199.1.1.96	11000111 00000001 00000001 01100000

The last step in the formalized process—converting the binary number back to decimal—causes problems for many people new to subnetting. The confusion typically arises when the boundary between the subnet and host part of the address is in the middle of a byte, which occurs when the subnet mask has a value besides 0 or 255 decimal. For example, with 130.4.102.1, mask 255.255.252.0 (Table 12-18), the first 6 bits of the third octet comprise the subnet field, and the last 2 bits of the third octet, plus the entire fourth octet, comprise the host field. Because of these facts, some people convert the 6-bit subnet part from binary to decimal, and then they convert the 10-bit host part to decimal. However, when converting binary to decimal, to find the dotted decimal IP address, you always convert the entire octet—even if part of the octet is in the subnet part of the address and part is in the host part of the address.

So, in the example shown in Table 12-18, the subnet number (130.4.100.0) in binary is 1000 0010 0000 0100 **0110 0100** 0000 0000. The entire third octet is shown in bold, which converts to 100 in decimal. When you convert the whole number, each set of 8 bits is converted to decimal, giving you 130.4.100.0.

Finding the Subnet Number: Binary Shortcut

Even if you tend to prefer the binary processes for subnetting, you might still find it a bit laborious to convert two dotted decimal numbers to binary, do the Boolean AND for 32 bits, and then convert the result back into dotted decimal. However, as you practice this process, you should start to notice some important trends, which can help you optimize and simplify the binary process. This section specifically notes these trends and shows how you can reduce the Boolean AND process down to a single octet's worth of effort.

First, think about each octet separately. Any single octet of any IP address, when ANDed with a string of eight binary 1s from the mask, yields the same number you started with in the address. Of course, when the mask has an octet of value decimal 255, that number represents eight binary 1s. As a result, for any octet in which the mask shows a decimal value of 255, the result of the Boolean AND leaves the IP address's corresponding octet unchanged.

For example, the first octet of the example in Table 12-19 (199.1.1.100, mask 255.255.255.224) has an IP address value of 199, with a mask value of 255. After converting the IP address value of decimal 199 to binary 11000111, and the mask value of decimal 255 to binary 11111111, and ANDing the two numbers, you still end up with 11000111—or decimal 199. So, although you can convert the whole IP address and mask to binary, for any mask octets of value 255, you can almost ignore that octet, knowing that the subnet number matches the original IP address for this octet.

Similarly, as you consider each octet separately again, you will notice that any IP address octet, ANDed with eight binary 0s, yields an octet of eight binary 0s. Of course, a mask octet of value decimal 0 represents eight binary 0s. As a result, for any octet in which the mask shows a value of decimal 0, the result of the Boolean AND is a decimal 0.

For example, in Table 12-15 (8.1.4.5, mask 255.255.0.0), the last octet has an IP address value of decimal 5, or 00000101 in binary. The fourth octet of the mask has a value of decimal 0, or binary 00000000. The Boolean AND for that octet yields a value of all binary 0s, or decimal 0.

These two facts may help you start developing a few shortcuts of your own. Summarizing, if you want to find the resident subnet by using an AND on the IP address and mask, you could follow this shortcut:

Step 1   Record the decimal mask in the first row of a table and the decimal IP address in the second row.

Step 2   For any mask octets of value decimal 255, copy the IP address's octet value for the same octet of the decimal subnet number.

Step 3   Similarly, for any mask octets of value decimal 0, write down a decimal 0 for the same octet of the subnet number.

Step 4   If the subnet number still has one remaining octet to be filled in, do the following for that one octet:

   a. Convert that one remaining octet of the IP address to binary.

   b. Convert that one remaining octet of the mask to binary.

   c. AND the two 8-bit numbers together.

   d. Convert the 8-bit number to decimal, and place that value in the one remaining octet of the subnet number.

Using this logic, when the mask only has 255s and 0s in it, you can find the subnet number without any binary math. In other cases, you can find three of the four octets easily, and then just Boolean AND the address and mask values for the remaining octet, to complete the subnet number.

Finding the Subnet Broadcast Address: Binary

The subnet broadcast address, sometimes called the *directed broadcast address*, can be used to send a packet to every device in a single subnet. For example, subnet 8.1.4.0/24 has a subnet broadcast address of 8.1.4.255. A packet sent to a destination address of 8.1.4.255 will be forwarded across the internetwork, until it reaches a router connected to that subnet. That final router, when forwarding the packet onto the subnet, encapsulates the packet in a data-link broadcast frame. For instance, if this subnet existed on an Ethernet LAN, the packet would be forwarded inside an Ethernet frame with a destination Ethernet address of FFFF.FFFF.FFFF.

Although interesting as an end to itself, a more interesting use for the subnet broadcast address today is that it helps you more easily calculate the largest valid IP address in the subnet, which is an important part of answering subnetting questions. The next section, "Finding the Range of Valid IP Addresses in a Subnet," explains the details. By definition, a subnet's broadcast address has the same value as the subnet number in the network and subnet parts of the address, but all binary 1s in the host part of the broadcast address.

(The subnet number, by definition, happens to have all binary 0s in the host part.) In other words, the subnet number is the lower end of the range of addresses, and the subnet broadcast address is the high end of the range.

There is a binary math operation to calculate the subnet broadcast address based on the subnet number, but there is a much easier process for humans, especially if you already have the subnet number in binary:

To calculate the subnet broadcast address, if you already know the binary version of the subnet number, change all the host bit values in the subnet number to binary 1s.

You already know how to identify the host bits, based on the mask's bits of value binary 0. You can examine the simple math behind calculating the subnet broadcast address in Tables 12-20 through 12-24. The host parts of the addresses, masks, subnet numbers, and broadcast addresses are in bold.

Table 12-20   *Calculating the Broadcast Address: Address 8.1.4.5, Mask 255.255.0.0*

Address	8.1.4.5	00001000 00000001 **00000100 00000101**
Mask	255.255.0.0	11111111 11111111 **00000000 00000000**
AND Result	8.1.0.0	00001000 00000001 **00000000 00000000**
Broadcast	8.1.255.255	00001000 00000001 **11111111 11111111**

Table 12-21   *Calculating the Broadcast Address: Address 130.4.102.1, Mask 255.255.255.0*

Address	130.4.102.1	10000010 00000100 01100110 **00000001**
Mask	255.255.255.0	11111111 11111111 11111111 **00000000**
AND Result	130.4.102.0	10000010 00000100 01100110 **00000000**
Broadcast	130.4.102.255	10000010 00000100 01100110 **11111111**

Table 12-22   *Calculating the Broadcast Address: Address 199.1.1.100, Mask 255.255.255.0*

Address	199.1.1.100	11000111 00000001 00000001 **01100100**
Mask	255.255.255.0	11111111 11111111 11111111 **00000000**
AND Result	199.1.1.0	11000111 00000001 00000001 **00000000**
Broadcast	199.1.1.255	11000111 00000001 00000001 **11111111**

Table 12-23 *Calculating the Broadcast Address: Address 130.4.102.1, Mask 255.255.252.0*

Address	130.4.102.1	10000010 00000100 01100110 00000001
Mask	255.255.252.0	11111111 11111111 11111100 00000000
AND Result	130.4.100.0	10000010 00000100 01100100 00000000
Broadcast	130.4.103.255	10000010 00000100 01100111 11111111

Table 12-24 *Calculating the Broadcast Address: Address 199.1.1.100, Mask 255.255.255.224*

Address	199.1.1.100	11000111 00000001 00000001 01100100
Mask	255.255.255.224	11111111 11111111 11111111 11100000
AND Result	199.1.1.96	11000111 00000001 00000001 01100000
Broadcast	199.1.1.127	11000111 00000001 00000001 01111111

By examining the subnet broadcast addresses in binary, you can see that they are identical to the subnet numbers, except that all host bits have a value of binary 1 instead of binary 0. (Look for the bold digits in the examples.)

> **NOTE** In case you want to know the Boolean math, to derive the broadcast address, start with the subnet number and mask in binary. Invert the mask (change all the 1s to 0s and all the 0s to 1s), and then do a bitwise Boolean OR between the two 32-bit numbers. (An OR yields a 0 when both bits are 0 and yields a 1 in any other case.) The result is the subnet broadcast address.

For reference, the following process summarizes the concepts described in this section for how to find the subnet broadcast address:

Step 1   Write down the subnet number (or IP address), and subnet mask, in binary form. Make sure that the binary digits line up directly on top of the other.

Step 2   Separate the host part of these numbers from the network/subnet part by drawing a vertical line. Place this line between the rightmost binary 1 in the mask and the leftmost binary 0. Extend this line up and down an inch or two.

Step 3   To find the subnet broadcast address, in binary:

   a. Copy the bits of the subnet number (or IP address) that are to the left of the vertical line.

b. Write down binary 1s for the bits to the right of the vertical line.

Step 4   Convert the 32-bit binary subnet broadcast address to decimal, 8 bits at a time, ignoring the vertical line.

Finding the Range of Valid IP Addresses in a Subnet

You also need to be able to figure out which IP addresses are in a particular subnet and which are not. You already know how to do the hard part of finding that answer. In every subnet, two numbers are reserved and cannot be used as IP addresses by hosts: the subnet number itself and the subnet broadcast address. The subnet number is the numerically smallest number in the subnet, and the broadcast address is the numerically largest number. So, the range of valid IP addresses starts with the IP address that is 1 more than the subnet number, and ends with the IP address that is 1 less than the broadcast address. It is that simple.

Here is a formal definition of the "algorithm" to find the first and last IP addresses in a subnet when you know the subnet number and broadcast addresses:

Step 1   To find the first IP address, copy the subnet number, but add 1 to the *fourth octet*.

Step 2   To find the last IP address, copy the subnet broadcast address, but subtract 1 from the *fourth octet*.

Key
Topic

The math for this process is pretty obvious; however, take care to add 1 (Step 1) and subtract 1 (Step 2) only in the fourth octet—no matter what the class of network and no matter what subnet mask is used. Tables 12-25 through 12-29 summarize the answers for the five examples used throughout this chapter.

Table 12-25   *Subnet Chart: 8.1.4.5/255.255.0.0*

Octet	1	2	3	4
Address	8	1	4	5
Mask	255	255	0	0
Subnet Number	8	1	0	0
First Address	8	1	0	1
Broadcast	8	1	255	255
Last Address	8	1	255	254

Table 12-26   *Subnet Chart: 130.4.102.1/255.255.255.0*

Octet	1	2	3	4
Address	130	4	102	1
Mask	255	255	255	0
Subnet Number	130	4	102	0
First Address	130	4	102	1
Broadcast	130	4	102	255
Last Address	130	4	102	254

Table 12-27   *Subnet Chart: 199.1.1.100/255.255.255.0*

Octet	1	2	3	4
Address	199	1	1	100
Mask	255	255	255	0
Subnet Number	199	1	1	0
First Address	199	1	1	1
Broadcast	199	1	1	255
Last Address	199	1	1	254

Table 12-28   *Subnet Chart: 130. 4.102.1/255.255.252.0*

Octet	1	2	3	4
Address	130	4	102	1
Mask	255	255	252	0
Subnet Number	130	4	100	0
First Address	130	4	100	1
Broadcast	130	4	103	255
Last Address	130	4	103	254

Table 12-29 *Subnet Chart: 199.1.1.100/255.255.255.224*

Octet	1	2	3	4
Address	199	1	1	100
Mask	255	255	255	224
Subnet Number	199	1	1	96
First Address	199	1	1	97
Broadcast	199	1	1	127
Last Address	199	1	1	126

Finding the Subnet, Broadcast Address, and Range of Addresses: Decimal Process

Using the binary math required to find the subnet number and broadcast address forces you to think about subnetting, which really does help you understand subnetting better. However, many people feel too much time pressure on the exam when they have to do a lot of binary math. This section describes some decimal processes for finding the subnet number and subnet broadcast address. From there, you can easily find the range of assignable addresses in the subnet, as described in the previous section.

Decimal Process with Easy Masks

Of all the possible subnet masks, only three masks—255.0.0.0, 255.255.0.0, and 255.255.255.0—use only 255s and 0s. I call these masks "easy masks" because you can find the subnet number and broadcast address easily, without any real math tricks. In fact, many people intuitively see how to find the answers with easy masks, so feel free to skip to the next section, "Decimal Process with Difficult Masks," if you already see how to find the subnet number and broadcast address.

Of these three easy masks, 255.0.0.0 does not cause any subnetting. Therefore, this section describes only how to use the two easy masks that can be used for subnetting—255.255.0.0 and 255.255.255.0.

The process is simple. To find the subnet number when given an IP address and a mask of 255.255.0.0 or 255.255.255.0, do the following:

Step 1 For each *subnet mask octet* of value 255, copy the *IP address* octet value.

Step 2 For the remaining octets, write down a 0.

Yes, it is that easy. Finding the subnet broadcast address is just as easy:

> Perform the same Step 1 as when finding the subnet number, but at Step 2, write down 255s instead of 0s.

As soon as you know the subnet number and broadcast address, you can easily find the first and last IP addresses in the subnet using the same simple logic covered earlier:

- To find the first valid IP address in the subnet, copy the subnet number, but add 1 to the fourth octet.

- To find the last valid IP address in the subnet, copy the broadcast address, but subtract 1 from the fourth octet.

Decimal Process with Difficult Masks

When the subnet mask is not 255.0.0.0, 255.255.0.0, or 255.255.255.0, I consider the mask to be difficult. Why is it difficult? Well, it is difficult only in that most people cannot easily derive the subnet number and broadcast address without using binary math.

You can always use the binary processes covered earlier in this chapter, all the time, whether the mask is easy or difficult—and consistently find the right answers. However, most people can find the correct answer much more quickly by spending some time practicing the decimal process described in this section.

The decimal process uses a table to help organize the problem, an example of which is found in Table 12-30. The text refers to this table as a *subnet chart*.

Table 12-30 *Generic Subnet Chart*

Octet	1	2	3	4
Mask				
Address				
Subnet Number				
First Address				
Last Address				
Broadcast Address				

The following steps list the formal process for finding the subnet number, using a decimal process, assuming a difficult mask is used.

Step 1 Write down the subnet mask in the first empty row of the subnet chart and the IP address in the second empty row.

Step 2 Find the octet for which the *subnet mask's value* is not 255 or 0. This octet is called the *interesting octet*. Draw a dark rectangle around the interesting octet's column of the table, top to bottom.

Step 3 Record the subnet number's value for the uninteresting octets, as follows:

    a. For each octet to the left of the rectangle drawn in Step 2: Copy the *IP address's* value in that same octet.

    b. For each octet to the right of the rectangle: Write down a decimal 0.

Step 4 At this point, the subnet number row of the subnet chart has three octets filled in, with only the interesting octet remaining. To find the subnet number's value for this interesting octet:

    a. Calculate the magic number by subtracting the *subnet mask's interesting octet value* from 256.

    b. Calculate the multiples of the magic number, starting at 0, up through 256.

    c. Find the subnet number's interesting octet's value, as follows: find the multiple of the magic number that is *closest to, but not greater than*, the IP address's interesting octet value.

As you can see, the process itself seems a bit detailed, but do not let the detail deter you from trying this process. The majority of the first three steps—other than drawing a rectangle around the interesting octet—use the same logic used with easy masks. The fourth step is detailed, but it can be learned, mastered, and forgotten once you see the decimal patterns behind subnetting. Also, note that you do not need to memorize the process as an end to itself. If you practice this process long enough to get good and fast at finding the right answer, then you will likely internalize the process to the point that you make the process your own, and then you can ignore the specific steps listed here.

The best way to understand this process is to see it in action. The DVD that comes with this book includes three video examples of how to use the process described here. This would be an excellent place to pause and at least watch subnetting video 1. Video 1 describes a full treatment of the process. You can also watch subnetting videos 2 and 3, which provide additional examples.

You can also learn the process just by reading the examples in this book. For example, consider 130.4.102.1, with mask 255.255.252.0. Because the third octet of the mask is not a 0 or 255, the third octet is where the interesting part of this decimal process takes place. For Step 1, you create a subnet chart and fill in the mask and address in the first two rows. For Step 2, just draw a rectangle around the third octet's column in the subnet chart. For Step 3, fill in the first two octets of the subnet number by copying the IP address's first two octets and writing a zero in the fourth octet. Table 12-31 shows the results of these steps.

Table 12-31 *Subnet Chart: 130.4.102.1/255.255.252.0, Through Step 3A*

Octet	1	2	3	4
Mask	255	255	252	0
Address	130	4	102	1
Subnet Number	130	4		0
First Address				
Last Address				
Broadcast Address				

The last (fourth) step is the only step that may seem a little odd, but at least it lets you use decimal math, and no binary, to find the subnet number. First you find what I call the "magic number": 256 minus the *mask's interesting octet*. In this case, the magic number is 256 – 252, or 4. Then you find the multiple of the magic number that is closest to the *address's interesting octet*, but less than or equal to it. In this example, 100 is a multiple of the magic number (4 × 25), and this multiple is less than or equal to 102. The next-higher multiple of the magic number, 104, is, of course, more than 102, so that is not the right number. So, to complete this example, simply plug in 100 for the third octet of the subnet number in Table 12-30.

As soon as you know the subnet number, you can easily find the first valid IP address in the subnet:

> To find the first valid IP address in the subnet, copy the subnet number, but add 1 to the fourth octet.

That is all. Table 12-32 continues the same example, but with the subnet number and first valid IP address.

Table 12-32 *Subnet Chart: 130.4.102.1/255.255.252.0 with Subnet and First IP Address*

Octet	1	2	3	4	Comments
Mask	255	255	252	1	
Address	130	4	102	1	
Subnet Number	130	4	**100**	**0**	Magic number = 256 – 252 = 4; 100 is the multiple of 4 closest to, but not higher than, 102.
First Address	130	4	**100**	1	Add 1 to the subnet's last octet.
Last Address					
Broadcast Address					

Finding the Broadcast Address: Decimal

If you used the decimal process to find the subnet number, finding the subnet broadcast address using only decimal math is easy. Once you find the broadcast address, you already know how to find the last usable IP address in the subnet: You simply subtract 1 from the fourth octet of the broadcast address. To find the subnet broadcast address after finding the subnet number, assuming a difficult mask, use the following process:

Step 1 Fill in the subnet broadcast address octets to the left of the rectangle by copying the subnet number's same octets.

Step 2 Fill in the subnet broadcast address octets to the right of the rectangle with decimal 255s.

Step 3 Find the value for the interesting octet by adding the *subnet number's* value in the interesting octet to the *magic number, and subtract 1.*

The only possibly tricky part of the process again relates to the interesting octet. To fill in the interesting octet of the broadcast address, you again use the magic number. The magic number is 256 minus the mask's interesting octet. In this example, the magic number is 4 (256 − 252). Then you add the magic number to the interesting octet value of the subnet number and subtract 1. The result is the broadcast address's value in the interesting octet. In this case, the value is

100 (subnet number's third octet) + 4 (magic number) − 1 = 103.

Table 12-33 shows the completed answers, with annotations.

Table 12-33 *Subnet Chart: 130.4.102.1/255.255.252.0 Completed*

Octet	1	2	3	4	Comments
Mask	255	255	252	0	
Address	130	4	102	1	
Subnet Number	130	4	100	0	Magic number = 256 − 252 = 4. 4 × 25 = 100, the closest multiple <= 102.
First Address	130	4	100	1	Add 1 to the subnet's last octet.
Last Address	130	4	103	254	Subtract 1 from the broadcast address's fourth octet.
Broadcast	130	4	103	255	Subnet's interesting octet, plus the magic number, minus 1 (100 + 4 − 1).

> **NOTE**   Subnetting videos 4, 5, and 6 continue the examples shown in videos 1, 2, and 3, respectively, focusing on finding the broadcast address and range of valid addresses. If this process is not clear, take the time now to stop and watch the videos.

Summary of Decimal Processes to Find the Subnet, Broadcast, and Range

The entire process of dissecting IP addresses that use difficult masks is now complete. The following list summarizes the tasks in each step:

Step 1   Write down the subnet mask in the first empty row of the subnet chart and the IP address in the second empty row.

Step 2   Find the octet for which the *subnet mask's value* is not 255 or 0. This octet is called the *interesting octet*. Draw a dark rectangle around the interesting octet's column of the table, top to bottom.

Step 3   Record the subnet number's value for the uninteresting octets, as follows:

   a. For each octet to the left of the rectangle drawn in Step 2: Copy the *IP address's* value in that same octet.

   b. For each octet to the right of the rectangle: Write down a decimal 0.

Step 4   To find the subnet number's value for this interesting octet:

   a. Calculate the magic number by subtracting the *subnet mask's interesting octet value* from 256.

   b. Calculate the multiples of the magic number, starting at 0, up through 256.

   c. Write down the interesting octet's value, calculated as follows: Find the multiple of the magic number that is *closest to, but not greater than*, the IP address's interesting octet value.

Step 5   Find the subnet broadcast address, as follows:

   a. For each *subnet mask octet* to the left of the rectangle: Copy the *IP address* octet value.

   b. For each *subnet mask octet* to the right of the rectangle: Write down 255.

   c. Find the value for the interesting octet by adding the *subnet number's* value in the interesting octet to the *magic number, and subtract 1*.

Step 6   To find the first IP address, copy the decimal subnet number, but add 1 to the fourth octet.

Step 7   To find the last IP address, copy the decimal subnet broadcast address, but subtract 1 from the fourth octet.

NOTE   For those of you using the subnetting reference pages in Appendix E, note that instead of the preceding seven-step process, RP-5C and RP-6C separate the process into two parts—one to find the subnet number (Steps 1–4 from the preceding list), and one to find the rest of the information (Steps 5–7 from the preceding list).

Practice Suggestions

Becoming proficient at both the binary and decimal processes to find the subnet number, broadcast address, and range of valid addresses takes some practice. The binary process is relatively straightforward, but requires conversions between binary and decimal. The decimal process has much easier math, but requires repetition to internalize the details of the many steps.

If you are using the decimal process, please practice it until you no longer think about the process as stated in this book. You should practice it until the concept is obvious, and second nature. It is the same idea as how you learn and master multiplication. For example, as an adult, multiplying 22 times 51 is simple enough that it would take you much longer to explain how to do it than to actually do it. Through practice, you should become equally familiar with the decimal process to find the subnet number.

Appendix D contains practice problems that ask you to find the subnet number, broadcast address, and range of addresses for a given IP address and mask. Regardless of whether you use binary or decimal processes, you should strive to be able to answer each problem within about 10–15 seconds after you have finished reading the problem.

The following list outlines the specific tools that may be useful for practicing the processes covered in this section:

■   Refer to Appendix E, specifically the following processes:

— RP-5A and RP-5A-shortcut, which focus on the binary process to find the subnet number

— RP-5B and RP-5C, which focus on the decimal process to find the subnet number

— RP-6A, which focuses on the binary process to find the broadcast address and range of addresses in a subnet

— RP-6B and RP-6C, which focus on the decimal process to find the broadcast address and range of addresses in a subnet

■ Do Appendix D Problem Set 5, which includes 25 problems that require that you find the subnet number, broadcast address, and range of usable addresses in each subnet.

■ For more practice, make up problems and check your answers using a subnet calculator.

The final major section of this chapter examines the processes by which a network engineer might choose a single subnet mask for a particular classful IP network and determine the subnets that can be used based on that design.

Design: Choosing the Subnets of a Classful Network

The final general type of IP addressing and subnetting question covered in this chapter asks you to list all the subnets of a particular classful network. You could use a long process that requires you to count in binary and convert many numbers from binary to decimal. However, because most people either learn the decimal shortcut or use a subnet calculator in their jobs, I decided to just show you the shortcut method for this particular type of question.

First, the question needs a better definition—or at least a more complete one. The question might be better stated like this:

> If the same subnet mask is used for all subnets of one Class A, B, or C network, what are the valid subnets?

This general type of question assumes that the internetwork uses static-length subnet masking (SLSM), although variable-length subnet masking (VLSM) may also be used. This chapter shows you how to approach questions using SLSM. Chapter 5, "VLSM and Route Summarization," in the *CCNA ICND2 Official Exam Certification Guide* examines this problem in light of VLSM.

The decimal process to find all subnets can be a bit wordy. To make learning a little easier, the text first shows the process with an additional constraint—the process as first explained here only works when there are fewer than 8 subnet bits. This assumption allows the wording in the formal process and upcoming examples to be a bit briefer. Then, once you know the process, the text will describe the more general cases.

Finding All Subnets with Fewer Than 8 Subnet Bits

The following easy decimal process lists all the valid subnets, assuming both that SLSM is used and that fewer than 8 subnet bits are used. First, the process uses another table or chart, called a list-all-subnets chart in this book. Like the subnet chart used earlier in this chapter, the chart is simply a tool to help you organize the information found by a particular process.

Table 12-34 presents a generic version of the list-all-subnets chart.

Table 12-34   *Generic List-All-Subnets Chart*

Octet	1	2	3	4
Mask				
Magic Number				
Network Number/Zero Subnet				
Next Subnet				
Next Subnet				
Last Subnet				
Broadcast Subnet				
Out of Range (Used by Process)				

The process starts with the assumption that you already know the classful network number and subnet mask (dotted decimal format). If the question gives you an IP address and mask instead of the network number and mask, just write down the network number of which that IP address is a member. If the mask is in prefix format, go ahead and convert it to dotted decimal.

The key to this decimal process is the following:

The various subnet numbers' interesting octet values are multiples of the magic number.

For example, as you read in the previous section, with Class B network 130.4.0.0, mask 255.255.252.0, the magic number is 256 − 252 = 4. So, the subnets of 130.4.0.0/ 255.255.252.0, in the third octet, are multiples of 4—namely, 130.4.0.0 (zero subnet), 130.4.4.0, 130.4.8.0, 130.4.12.0, 130.4.16.0, and so on, up through 130.4.252.0 (broadcast subnet).

If that intuitively makes sense to you, great, you are ahead of the game. If not, the rest of this section details the steps of the process, from which you can practice until you master the process. For reference, the process for finding all subnets of a classful network, assuming SLSM with 8 or fewer subnet bits, is as follows:

Key Topic

Step 1   Write down the subnet mask, in decimal, in the first empty row of the table.

Step 2   Identify the interesting octet, which is the one octet of the mask with a value other than 255 or 0. Draw a rectangle around the column of the interesting octet.

Step 3   Calculate the magic number by subtracting the *subnet mask's interesting octet* from 256. (Record this number in the list-all-subnets chart, inside the rectangle, for easy reference.)

Step 4   Write down the classful network number, which is the same number as the zero subnet, in the next empty row of the list-all-subnets chart.

Step 5   To find each successive subnet number:

a. For the three uninteresting octets, copy the previous subnet number's values.

b. For the interesting octet, add the magic number to the previous subnet number's interesting octet.

Step 6   Once the sum calculated in Step 5b reaches 256, stop the process. The number with the 256 in it is out of range, and the previous subnet number is the broadcast subnet.

Again, the written process is long, but with practice, most people can find the answers much more quickly than by using binary math.

> **NOTE**   Subnetting video 7 describes an example of using this process to list all subnets. This would be an excellent time to pause to view that video.

Before you see a few examples, you should know that in every case, the classful network number is the exact same number as the zero subnet number. *Subnet zero*, or the *zero subnet*, is numerically the first subnet, and it is one of the two possibly reserved subnet numbers, as mentioned earlier in this chapter. Interestingly, a network's zero subnet always has the exact same numeric value as the network itself—which is the main reason why the zero subnet was originally avoided.

Now on to some examples. Table 12-35 shows the results of the process for finding all subnets, through Step 4. In particular, at Steps 1 and 2, the subnet mask is recorded, with a box being drawn around the third octet because of the mask's value of 252 in the third octet. At Step 3, the magic number—256 minus the mask's interesting octet value of 252, or 4—is written on the next row. At Step 4, the classful network number, which is also the same number as the zero subnet, is recorded.

Table 12-35 *List-All-Subnets Chart: 130.4.0.0/22—After Finding the Zero Subnet*

Octet	1	2	3	4
Mask	255	255	252	0
Magic Number			4	
Classful Network/Subnet Zero	130	4	0	0

Next, Step 5 continues the process, finding a new subnet number each time Step 5 is repeated. Per Step 5A, octets 1, 2, and 4 are copied from the subnet zero row. For Step 5B, the magic number (4) is added to the zero subnet's interesting octet value of 0, completing the subnet number of 130.4.4.0. By repeating this process, you end up with 130.4.8.0 next, 130.4.12.0 after that, and so on. Table 12-36 lists all the values, including the last few values from which you can determine when to stop the process.

Table 12-36 *List-All-Subnets Chart: 130.4.0.0/22—After Finding Where to Stop the Process*

Octet	1	2	3	4
Mask	255	255	252	0
Magic Number			4	
Classful Network/Subnet Zero	130	4	0	0
First Nonzero Subnet	130	4	4	0
Next Subnet	130	4	8	0
Next Subnet	130	4	12	0
Next Subnet	130	4	16	0
Next Subnet	130	4	20	0
Next Subnet	130	4	24	0
(Skipping many subnets—shorthand)	130	4	X	0
Largest Numbered Nonbroadcast Subnet	130	4	248	0
Broadcast Subnet	130	4	252	0
Invalid—Used by Process	130	4	256	0

The six-step process directs you to create a new subnet by repeating Step 5 continually, but you need to know when to stop. Basically, you keep going until the interesting octet is 256. The number written in that row is invalid, and the number before it is the broadcast subnet.

> **NOTE**   Depending on the exam question, you may or may not be able to use the zero subnet and broadcast subnet. If you do not recall the details, refer to the section "Number of Subnets: Subtract 2, or Not?" earlier in this chapter.

Finding All Subnets with Exactly 8 Subnet Bits

When exactly 8 subnet bits exist, the process of finding all subnets can be somewhat intuitive. In fact, consider Class B network 130.4.0.0, mask 255.255.255.0 for a moment. If you think about what subnets should exist in this network and then check your answers against upcoming Table 12-37, you may realize that you intuitively know how to get the answer. If so, great—move on to the next section in this chapter. However, if not, consider a few brief words that will hopefully unlock the process.

With exactly 8 subnet bits, the mask will be either a 255.255.0.0 mask used with a Class A network or a 255.255.255.0 mask used with a Class B network. In each case, the subnet part of the address is one entire octet. Inside that octet, the subnet numbers begin with a number identical to the classful network number (the zero subnet), and increment by 1 in that one subnet octet. For example, for 130.4.0.0, mask 255.255.255.0, the entire third octet is the subnet field. The zero subnet is 130.4.0.0, the next subnet is 130.4.1.0 (adding 1 in the third octet), the next subnet is 130.4.2.0, and so on.

You can think about the problem in the same terms as the process used when fewer than 8 subnet bits exist. One change is required, however, when exactly 8 subnet bits exist, because the interesting octet is not easily identified. So, with exactly 8 subnet bits, to find the interesting octet:

The interesting octet is the octet in which all 8 subnet bits reside.

For example, consider network 130.4.0.0/255.255.255.0 again. As stated earlier, the entire third octet is the subnet part of the addresses, making the third octet the interesting octet. From that point, just use the same basic process used when fewer than 8 subnet bits exist. For example, the magic number is 1, because 256 minus 255 (the mask's third octet value) is 1. The zero subnet is equal to the Class B network number (130.4.0.0), with each successive subnet being 1 larger in the third octet, because the magic number is 1. Table 12-37 lists the work in progress for this example, with all steps completed.

Table 12-37   *List-All-Subnets Chart: 130.4.0.0/24*

Octet	1	2	3	4
Mask	255	255	255	0
Magic Number			1	
Classful Network/Subnet Zero	130	4	0	0
First Nonzero Subnet	130	4	1	0
Next Subnet	130	4	2	0
Next Subnet	130	4	3	0
(Skipping many subnets—shorthand)	130	4	X	0
Largest Numbered Nonbroadcast Subnet	130	4	254	0
Broadcast Subnet	130	4	255	0
Invalid—Used by Process	130	4	256	0

Practice Suggestions

The process to find all subnets of a network, assuming SLSM is used and assuming more than 8 subnet bits exist, requires some imagination on your part. So, before tackling that problem, it is helpful to master the process to find all subnets when the process is more concise. To that end, take the time now to do Appendix D Problem Set 6, which includes problems about finding all subnets of a network, using a mask that implies fewer than 8 subnet bits. You can refer to Appendix E reference page RP-7A as well, which summarizes the process in this chapter.

Also, if you have not yet done so, feel free to watch subnetting video 7, which explains this same process.

Finding All Subnets with More Than 8 Subnet Bits

When reading this section, particularly for the first time, consider the fact that when more than 8 subnet bits exist, there will be a lot of subnets. Also, note that the subnet part of the addresses exists in at least two different octets, possibly three octets. So, the process will need to work in multiple octets.

The explanation works better by starting with an example. (At your option, you may choose to go ahead and watch subnetting video 8, which also explains the process shown here.) The first example in this written chapter is using Class B network 130.4.0.0 again, now with 10 subnet bits, meaning a mask of 255.255.255.192. The following list notes the first 13 subnets:

- 130.4.0.0 (zero subnet)

- 130.4.0.64

- 130.4.0.128

- 130.4.0.192

- 130.4.1.0

- 130.4.1.64

- 130.4.1.128

- 130.4.1.192

- 130.4.2.0

- 130.4.2.64

- 130.4.2.128

- 130.4.2.192

- 130.4.3.0

You can see some obvious patterns in the subnet numbers. For example, each successive subnet number is larger than the previous subnet number. The last octet's values repeat over time (0, 64, 128, and 192 in this case), whereas the third octet seems to be growing steadily by 1 for each set of four subnets.

Now, consider the following version of the full process for finding all subnets. The process follows the same first five steps of the process used when there are fewer than 8 subnet bits. However, instead of the old Step 6, do the following:

Key
Topic

Step 6   When any step's addition results in a sum of 256:

a. For the octet whose sum would have been 256, write down a 0.

b. For the octet to the left, add 1 to the previous subnet's value in that octet.

    c. For any other octets copy the values of the same octets in the previous subnet number.

    d. Start again with RP-7A Step 5.

Step 7 Each time the process results in a sum of 256, repeat step 6 of this RP-7B process.

Step 8 Repeat until the addition in Step 6b would actually change the value of the network portion of the subnet number.

For example, consider this revised process, now applied to 130.4.0.0/255.255.255.192. In this case, the fourth octet is the interesting octet. Table 12-38 shows the work in progress, up through the point at which a 256 is recorded, triggering the new and revised Step 6.

Table 12-38 *Incorrect Entry in the List-All-Subnets Chart: First Addition to 256*

Octet	1	2	3	4
Mask	255	255	255	192
Magic Number (256 – 192 = 64)				64
Classful Network/Subnet Zero	130	4	0	0
First Nonzero Subnet	130	4	0	64
Next Subnet	130	4	0	128
Next Subnet	130	4	0	192
A 256 in the Fourth Octet...	130	4	0	256

According to Step 6 of the process listed just before the table, you should not have written down the contents in the last row of Table 12-38. Instead, you should have

    Written a 0 in the fourth octet.

    Added 1 to the value in the octet to the left (third octet in this case), for a total of 1.

Table 12-39 shows the revised entry, and the next three subnets (found by continuing Step 5, which adds the magic number *in the interesting octet*). The table lists the subnets up to the point that the next step would again generate a sum of 256.

Table 12-39 *Correct Entry in the List-All-Subnets Chart: First Addition to 256*

Octet	1	2	3	4
Mask	255	255	255	192
Magic Number				64
Classful Network/Subnet Zero	130	4	0	0
First Nonzero Subnet	130	4	0	64
Next Subnet	130	4	0	128
Next Subnet	130	4	0	192
Correct Next Subnet (found by writing 0 in the fourth octet, and adding 1 to the third octet)	130	4	1	0
Next Subnet	130	4	1	64
Next Subnet	130	4	1	128
Next Subnet	130	4	1	192

If you continued the process using the last row in the table, and added the magic number (64) to the interesting (fourth) octet yet again, the sum would total 256 again. With the revised Step 6, that means you would again instead write a 0 for the interesting octet, and add 1 to the octet to the left—in this case resulting in 130.4.2.0.

If you continue with this process, you will find all subnet numbers. However, as usual, it helps to know when to stop. In this case, you would eventually get to subnet 130.4.255.192. Then, when adding the magic number (64) to the interesting (fourth) octet, you would get 256—so instead, you would write down a 0 in the interesting octet, and add 1 to the octet to the left. However, the third octet would then be a value of 256. If you look at the literal wording in the process, any time you try to add, and the result is 256, you should instead write down a 0, and add 1 to the octet to the left. In this case, the next result would then be

130.5.0.0

As you can see, this value is in a totally different Class B network, because one of the two Class B network octets has been changed. So, when the network octets are changed by the process, you should stop. The previous subnet—in this case 130.4.255.192—is the broadcast subnet.

More Practice Suggestions

Now that you have seen the even more involved process when the length of the subnet field is more than 8 bits, you can do a few more practice problems. To practice this process a few times, take the time now to do Appendix D Problem Set 7, which includes problems about finding all subnets of a network, using a mask that implies at least 8 subnet bits. You can refer to Appendix E reference page RP-7B as well, which summarizes the process in this chapter.

Also, if you have not yet done so, feel free to watch subnetting video 8, which explains this same process.

Exam Preparation Tasks

Review All the Key Topics

Key Topic

Review the most important topics from inside the chapter, noted with the key topics icon in the outer margin of the page. Table 12-40 lists a reference of these key topics and the page numbers on which each is found.

This chapter contains a lot of lists that summarize the process used to find a particular answer. These processes do not need to be memorized. Instead, practice your chosen method to find each set of facts about IP addressing, whether it is one of the binary or decimal processes found in this chapter, or elsewhere. The processes are listed here as key topics for easier study and reference. Note that the topics that could be helpful to memorize or study as an end to themselves are shaded in the table.

Table 12-40 *Key Topics for Chapter 12*

Key Topic Element	Description	Page Number
Table 12-2	Reference table for the number of networks, size of the network part, and size of the host part, for Class A, B, and C IP networks	340
Table 12-3	Class A, B, and C networks with their default masks	341
Table 12-4	Reference table of the private (RFC 1918) IP networks	342
List	Tips for doing binary-to-decimal and decimal-to-binary conversion for IP addresses	348
Process list	Binary process for converting a mask from dotted decimal to prefix notation	352
Process list	Binary process for converting a mask from prefix to dotted decimal notation	352
Table 12-9	Nine decimal values allowed in subnet masks, with the binary equivalent values	353
Process list	Decimal process for converting a mask from dotted decimal to prefix notation	354
Process list	Decimal process for converting a mask from prefix to dotted decimal notation	354

Table 12-40 *Key Topics for Chapter 12 (Continued)*

Key Topic Element	Description	Page Number
List	Facts about how to analyze and find the size of the network, subnet, and host parts of an IP address	356
List	Facts about how the subnet mask identifies part of the structure of an IP address	358
Process list	Binary process to find the structure (network, subnet, and host parts) of an IP address	358
Process list	Decimal process to find the structure (network, subnet, and host parts) of an IP address	359
List	Key facts about how to calculate the number of subnets and number of hosts per subnet	359
Table 12-12	How to determine which formula to use to calculate the number of available subnets	361
Paragraph	Important fact about the binary values in subnet masks	365
List	Tips for understanding how to find the mask that provides the most subnets or most hosts per subnet	366
Process list	Summarizes how to choose a subnet mask based on a set of requirements	367
Process list	Binary process, with no binary shortcuts, to find an address's resident subnet by using a Boolean AND	369
Process list	Binary process to find a subnet broadcast address	372
Process list	Decimal process to find the range of addresses in a subnet, after having found the subnet number and subnet broadcast address	374
Process list	Fnding the range of valid IP addresses in a subnet	375
Process list	Decimal process to find the subnet number, broadcast address, and range of addresses in a subnet	382
Paragraph	A note that the subnet numbers of a classful network are multiples of the magic number	385
Process list	Decimal process to find all subnets of a classful network, with one mask and fewer than 8 subnet bits	386
Process list	Decimal process to find all subnets of a classful network, with one mask and more than 8 subnet bits	390

Complete the Tables and Lists from Memory

Print a copy of Appendix H, "Memory Tables" (found on the CD-ROM), or at least the section for this chapter, and complete the tables and lists from memory. Appendix I, "Memory Tables Answer Key," also on the CD-ROM, includes completed tables and lists to check your work.

Definitions of Key Terms

Define the following key terms from this chapter and check your answers in the glossary.

bitwise Boolean AND, Boolean AND, broadcast subnet, classful network, default mask, prefix notation/CIDR notation, private IP address, public IP address, subnet, subnet mask, subnet number/subnet address, zero subnet

Read Appendix F Scenario 1, Part A

Appendix F, "Additional Scenarios," contains two detailed scenarios that give you a chance to analyze different designs, problems, and command output, as well as show you how concepts from several different chapters interrelate. Reviewing Appendix F Scenario 1, Part A, would be useful at this time because it provides an opportunity to practice IP address planning.

Subnetting Questions and Processes

This chapter contains a large number of explanations on how to find a particular piece of information about a subnet, along with formalized processes. These formalized processes provide a clear method for practicing the process to get the correct answer.

The specific processes themselves are not the focus of the chapter. Instead, through practice, you should understand the various tasks, and use the processes to find the right answer, until it begins to become natural. At that point, you probably will not think about the specific steps listed in this chapter—the process will be integrated into how you think about IP addressing and subnetting. By the time you have finished this chapter, and the associated suggested practice throughout the chapter, you should be able to answer the following types of questions. Read over the following questions, and if the process by which you would find the answer is not clear, please refer back to the corresponding section of this chapter, listed with each question, for additional review and practice.

1. For IP address a.b.c.d, what is the classful IP network in which it reside? ("IP Addressing Review")

2. For mask e.f.g.h, what is the same value in prefix notation? ("Prefix Notation/CIDR Notation")

3. For prefix /x, what is the same value in dotted decimal notation? ("Prefix Notation/ CIDR Notation")

4. For IP address a.b.c.d, mask e.f.g.h, how many network bits exist? Subnet bits? Host bits? ("Analyzing the Subnet Mask in an Existing Subnet Design")

5. For a particular classful network, with mask e.f.g.h, how many subnets are supported? How many hosts per subnet? ("Analyzing the Subnet Mask in an Existing Subnet Design")

6. For a given classful network, with a need for X subnets, and Y hosts per subnet, assuming the same mask is used throughout the network, what masks meet the requirements? ("Choosing a Subnet Mask that Meets Design Requirements")

7. For a given classful network, with a need for X subnets, and Y hosts per subnet, of the masks that meet these requirements, which mask maximizes the number of hosts per subnet? Which mask maximizes the number of subnets? ("Choosing a Subnet Mask that Meets Design Requirements")

8. Given IP address a.b.c.d, mask e.f.g.h, what is the resident subnet? Broadcast address? Range of addresses in the subnet? ("Analyzing Existing Subnets")

9. Which of the following subnets are subnets of a given classful network, using mask e.f.g.h for all subnets? ("Design: Choosing the Subnets of a Classful Network")

This chapter covers the following subjects:

Installing Cisco Routers: This section gives some perspectives on the purpose of enterprise-class routers and consumer-grade routers, and how the routers connect users to a network.

Cisco Router IOS CLI: This section examines the similarities between the Cisco IOS router CLI and the Cisco IOS switch CLI (introduced in Chapter 8, "Operating Cisco LAN Switches") and also covers some of the features that are unique to routers.

Upgrading Cisco IOS Software and the Cisco IOS Software Boot Process: This section examines how a router boots, including how a router chooses which Cisco IOS software image to load.

CHAPTER 13

Operating Cisco Routers

Routers differ from switches in terms of their core purposes. Switches forward Ethernet frames by comparing the frame's destination MAC address to the switch's MAC address table, whereas routers forward packets by comparing the destination IP address to the router's IP routing table. Ethernet switches today typically have only one or more types of Ethernet interfaces, whereas routers have Ethernet interfaces, serial WAN interfaces, and other interfaces with which to connect via cable and digital subscriber line (DSL) to the Internet. Routers understand how to forward data to devices connected to these different types of interfaces, whereas Ethernet switches focus solely on forwarding Ethernet frames to Ethernet devices. So, while both switches and routers forward data, the details of what can be forwarded, and to what devices, differ significantly.

Even though their core purposes differ, Cisco routers and switches use the same CLI. This chapter covers the CLI features on routers that differ from the features on switches, particularly features that differ from the switch CLI features as covered in Chapter 8. This chapter also explains more details about the physical installation of Cisco routers, along with some details about how routers choose and load IOS.

"Do I Know This Already?" Quiz

The "Do I Know This Already?" quiz allows you to assess if you should read the entire chapter. If you miss no more than one of these nine self-assessment questions, you might want to move ahead to the "Exam Preparation Tasks" section. Table 13-1 lists the major headings in this chapter and the "Do I Know This Already?" quiz questions covering the material in those headings so you can assess your knowledge of these specific areas. The answers to the "Do I Know This Already?" quiz appear in Appendix A.

Table 13-1 *"Do I Know This Already?" Foundation Topics Section-to-Question Mapping*

Foundation Topics Section	Questions
Installing Cisco Routers	1, 2
Cisco Router IOS CLI	3–7
Upgrading Cisco IOS Software and the Cisco IOS Software Boot Process	8, 9

1.   Which of the following installation steps are typically required on a Cisco router, but not typically required on a Cisco switch?

   a.   Connect Ethernet cables

   b.   Connect serial cables

   c.   Connect to the console port

   d.   Connect the power cable

   e.   Turn the on/off switch to "on"

2.   Which of the following roles does a SOHO router typically play in regards to IP address assignment?

   a.   DHCP server on the interface connected to the ISP

   b.   DHCP server on the interface connected to the PCs at the home/office

   c.   DHCP client on the interface connected to the ISP

   d.   DHCP client on the interface connected to the PCs at the home/office

3.   Which of the following features would you typically expect to be associated with the router CLI, but not with the switch CLI?

   a.   The **clock rate** command

   b.   The **ip address** *address mask* command

   c.   The **ip address dhcp** command

   d.   The **interface vlan 1** command

4.   You just bought two Cisco routers for use in a lab, connecting each router to a different LAN switch with their Fa0/0 interfaces. You also connected the two routers' serial interfaces using a back-to-back cable. Which of the following steps is not required to be able to forward IP on both routers' interfaces?

   a.   Configuring an IP address on each router's FastEthernet and serial interfaces

   b.   Configuring the **bandwidth** command on one router's serial interface

   c.   Configuring the **clock rate** command on one router's serial interface

   d.   Setting the interface **description** on both the FastEthernet and serial interface of each router

5. The output of the **show ip interface brief** command on R1 lists interface status codes of "down" and "down" for interface Serial 0/0. Which of the following could be true?

   a. The **shutdown** command is currently configured for that interface.

   b. R1's serial interface has been configured to use Frame Relay, but the router on the other end of the serial link has been configured to use PPP.

   c. R1's serial interface does not have a serial cable installed.

   d. Both routers have been cabled to a working serial link (CSU/DSUs included), but only one router has been configured with an IP address.

6. Which of the following commands does not list the IP address and mask of at least one interface?

   a. **show running-config**

   b. **show protocols** *type number*

   c. **show ip interface brief**

   d. **show interfaces**

   e. **show version**

7. Which of the following is different on the Cisco switch CLI as compared with the Cisco router CLI?

   a. The commands used to configure simple password checking for the console

   b. The number of IP addresses configured

   c. The types of questions asked in setup mode

   d. The configuration of the device's host name

   e. The configuration of an interface description

8. Which of the following could cause a router to change the IOS that is loaded when the router boots?

   a. **reload** EXEC command

   b. **boot** EXEC command

   c. **reboot** EXEC command

   d. **boot system** configuration command

   e. **reboot system** configuration command

   f. configuration register

9. Which of the following hexadecimal values in the last nibble of the configuration register would cause a router to not look in Flash memory for an IOS?

    a. 0

    b. 2

    c. 4

    d. 5

    e. 6

Foundation Topics

Installing Cisco Routers

Routers collectively provide the main feature of the network layer—the capability to forward packets end-to-end through a network. As introduced in Chapter 5, "Fundamentals of IP Addressing and Routing," routers forward packets by connecting to various physical network links, like Ethernet, serial links, and Frame Relay, and then using Layer 3 routing logic to choose where to forward each packet. As a reminder, Chapter 3, "Fundamentals of LANs," covered the details of making those physical connections to Ethernet networks, while Chapter 4, "Fundamentals of WANs," covered the basics of cabling with WAN links.

This section examines some of the details of router installation and cabling, first from the enterprise perspective, and then from the perspective of connecting a typical small office/home office (SOHO) to an ISP using high-speed Internet.

Installing Enterprise Routers

A typical enterprise network has a few centralized sites as well as lots of smaller remote sites. To support devices at each site (the computers, IP phones, printers, and other devices), the network includes at least one LAN switch at each site. Additionally, each site has a router, which connects to the LAN switch and to some WAN link. The WAN link provides connectivity from each remote site, back to the central site, and to other sites via the connection to the central site.

Figure 13-1 shows one way to draw part of an enterprise network. The figure shows a typical branch office on the left, with a router, some end-user PCs, and a nondescript generic drawing of an Ethernet. The central site, on the right, has basically the same components, with a point-to-point serial link connecting the two routers. The central site includes a server farm with two servers, with one of the main purposes of this internetwork being to provide remote offices with access to the data stored on these servers.

Figure 13-1 purposefully omits several details to show the basic concepts. Figure 13-2 shows the same network, but now with more detail about the cabling used at each site.

Figure 13-1 *Generic Enterprise Network Diagram*

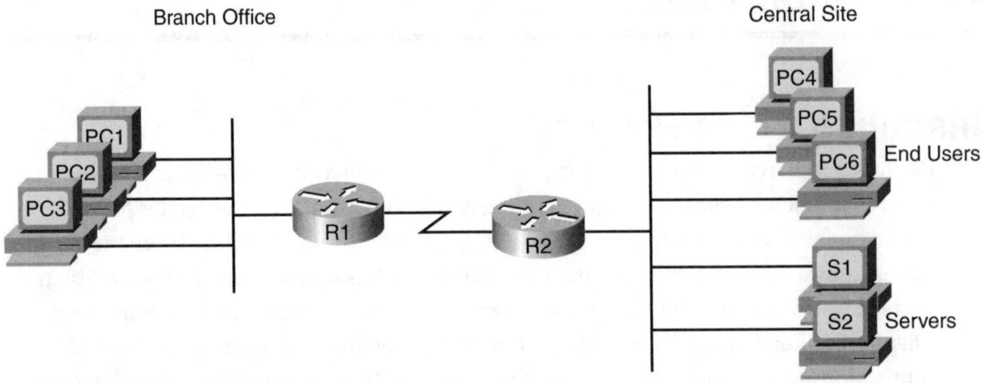

Figure 13-2 *More Detailed Cabling Diagram for the Same Enterprise Network*

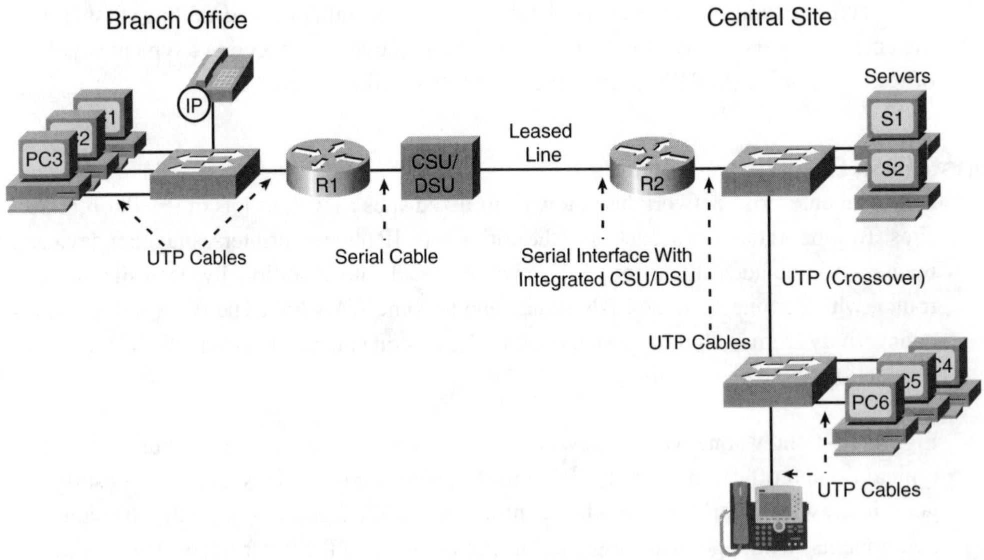

Figure 13-2 shows the types of LAN cables (UTP), with a couple of different WAN cables. The LAN connections all use UTP straight-through cabling pinouts, except for the UTP cable between the two switches, which is a crossover cable.

The serial link in the figure shows the two main options for where the channel service unit/ digital service unit (CSU/DSU) hardware resides: either outside the router (as shown at the branch office in this case) or integrated into the router's serial interface (as shown at the central site). Most new installations today include the CSU/DSU in the router's serial interface. The WAN cable installed by the telco typically has an RJ-48 connector, which is the same size and shape as an RJ-45 connector. The telco cable with the RJ-48 connector inserts into the CSU/DSU, meaning it connects directly into the central site router in this case, but into the external CSU/DSU at the branch office router. At the branch, the external CSU/DSU would then be cabled, using a serial cable, to the branch router's serial port. (See Figure 4-4 in Chapter 4 for a reminder of WAN serial cables.)

Cisco Integrated Services Routers

Product vendors, including Cisco, typically provide several different types of router hardware, including some routers that just do routing, with other routers that serve other functions in addition to routing. A typical enterprise branch office needs a router for WAN/LAN connectivity, and a LAN switch to provide a high-performance local network and connectivity into the router and WAN. Many branches also need Voice over IP (VoIP) services, and several security services as well. (One popular security service, virtual private networking (VPN), is covered in Chapter 6, "Fundamentals of TCP/IP Transport, Applications, and Security.") Rather than require multiple separate devices at one site, as shown in Figure 13-2, Cisco offers single devices that act as both router and switch, and provide other functions as well.

Following that concept further, Cisco offers several router model series in which the routers support many other functions. In fact, Cisco has several router product series called Integrated Services Routers (ISR), with the name emphasizing the fact that many functions are integrated into a single device. If you have not seen Cisco routers before, you can go to http://www.cisco.com/go/isr and click any of the 3D Product Demonstration links to see interactive views of a variety of Cisco ISR routers. However, for the sake of learning and understanding the different functions, the CCNA exams focus on using a separate switch and separate router, which provides a much cleaner path for learning the basics.

Figure 13-3 shows a couple of pictures taken from the interactive demo of the Cisco 1841 ISR, with some of the more important features highlighted. The top part of the figure shows a full view of the back of the router. It also shows a magnified view of the back of the router, with a clearer view of the two FastEthernet interfaces, the console and auxiliary ports, and a serial card with an internal CSU/DSU. (You can find the interactive demo from which these photos were taken at the same ISR web page mentioned in the previous paragraph.)

Figure 13-3   *Photos of a Model 1841 Cisco Integrated Services Router (ISR)*

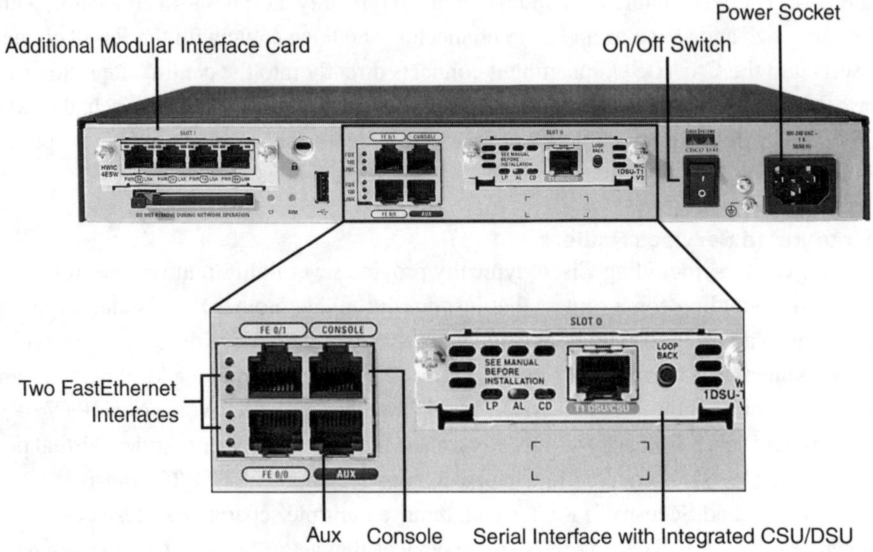

Physical Installation

Armed with the planning information shown in Figure 13-2, and the perspectives shown in Figure 13-3, you can physically install a router. To install a router, follow these steps:

Step 1   Connect any LAN cables to the LAN ports.

Step 2   If using an external CSU/DSU, connect the router's serial interface to the CSU/DSU, and the CSU/DSU to the line from the telco.

Step 3   If using an internal CSU/DSU, connect the router's serial interface to the line from the telco.

Step 4   Connect the router's console port to a PC (using a rollover cable), as needed, to configure the router.

Step 5   Connect a power cable from a power outlet to the power port on the router.

Step 6   Turn on the router.

Note that the steps generally follow the same steps used for installation of LAN switches—install the cables for the interfaces, connect the console (as needed), and connect the power. However, note that most of the Cisco Catalyst switches do not have a power on/off switch—once the switch is connected to power, the switch is on. However, Cisco routers do have on/off switches.

Installing Internet Access Routers

Routers play a key role in SOHO networks, connecting the LAN-attached end-user devices to a high-speed Internet access service. Once connected to the Internet, SOHO users can send packets to and from their enterprise network at their company or school.

As in the enterprise networking market, product vendors tend to sell integrated networking devices that perform many functions. However, in keeping with the CCNA strategy of understanding each function separately, this section first examines the various networking functions needed at a typical SOHO network, using a separate device for each function. Following that, a more realistic example is shown, with the functions combined into a single device.

A SOHO Installation with a Separate Switch, Router, and Cable Modem

Figure 13-4 shows an example of the devices and cables used in a SOHO network to connect to the Internet using cable TV (CATV) as the high-speed Internet service. For now, keep in mind that the figure shows one alternative for the devices and cables, whereas many variations are possible.

Figure 13-4 *Devices in a SOHO Network with High-Speed CATV Internet*

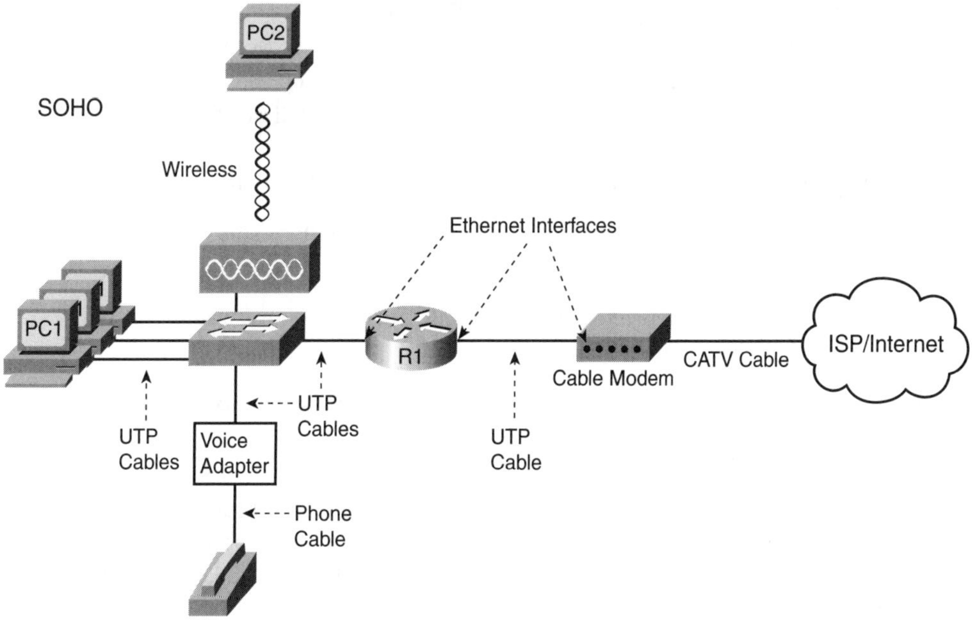

This figure has many similarities to Figure 13-2, which shows a typical enterprise branch office. The end-user PCs still connect to a switch, and the switch still connects to a router's Ethernet interface. The router still provides routing services, forwarding IP packets. The voice details differ slightly between Figure 13-2 and Figure 13-4, mainly because

Figure 13-4 shows a typical home-based Internet phone service, which uses a normal analog phone and a voice adapter to convert from analog voice to IP.

The main differences between the SOHO connection in Figure 13-4 and the enterprise branch in Figure 13-2 relate to the connection into the Internet. An Internet connection that uses CATV or DSL needs a device that converts between the Layer 1 and 2 standards used on the CATV cable or DSL line, and the Ethernet used by the router. These devices, commonly called *cable modems* and *DSL modems*, respectively, convert electrical signals between an Ethernet cable and either CATV or DSL.

In fact, while the details differ greatly, the purpose of the cable modem and DSL modem is similar to a CSU/DSU on a serial link. A CSU/DSU converts between the Layer 1 standards used on a telco's WAN circuit and a serial cable's Layer 1 standards—and routers can use serial cables. Similarly, a cable modem converts between CATV signals and a Layer 1 (and Layer 2) standard usable by a router—namely, Ethernet. Similarly, DSL modems convert between the DSL signals over a home telephone line and Ethernet.

To physically install a SOHO network with the devices shown in Figure 13-4, you basically need the correct UTP cables for the Ethernet connections, and either the CATV cable (for cable Internet services) or a phone line (for DSL services). Note that the router used in Figure 13-4 simply needs to have two Ethernet interfaces—one to connect to the LAN switch, and one to connect to the cable modem. Thinking specifically just about the router installation, you would need to use the following steps to install this SOHO router:

Step 1 Connect a UTP straight-through cable from the router to the switch.

Step 2 Connect a UTP straight-through cable from the router to the cable modem.

Step 3 Connect the router's console port to a PC (using a rollover cable), as needed, to configure the router.

Step 4 Connect a power cable from a power outlet to the power port on the router.

Step 5 Turn on the router.

A SOHO Installation with an Integrated Switch, Router, and DSL Modem

Today, most new SOHO installations use an integrated device rather than the separate devices shown in Figure 13-4. In fact, you can buy SOHO devices today that include all of these functions:

■ Router

■ Switch

■ Cable or DSL modem

- Voice Adapter

- Wireless AP

- Hardware-enabled encryption

The CCNA exams do indeed focus on separate devices to aid the learning process. However, a newly installed high-speed SOHO Internet connection today probably looks more like Figure 13-5, with an integrated device.

Figure 13-5 *SOHO Network, Using Cable Internet and an Integrated Device*

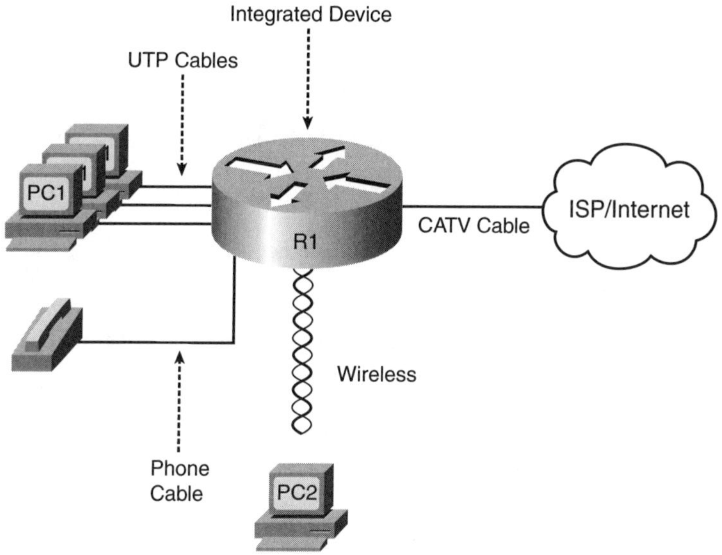

Regarding the SOHO Devices Used in This Book

Cisco sells products to both enterprise customers and consumers. Cisco sells its consumer products using the Linksys brand. These products are easily found online and in office supply stores. Cisco mainly sells enterprise products either directly to its customers or through Cisco Channel Partners (resellers). However, note that the CCNA exams do not use Linksys products or their web-based user interface, instead focusing on the IOS CLI used by Cisco enterprise routing products.

Cisco Router IOS CLI

Cisco routers use the same switch IOS CLI as described in Chapter 8. However, because routers and switches perform different functions, the actual commands differ in some cases. This section begins by listing some of the key features that work exactly the same on both switches and routers, and then lists and describes in detail some of the key features that differ between switches and routers.

Comparisons Between the Switch CLI and Router CLI

The following list details the many items covered in Chapter 8 for which the router CLI behaves the same. If these details are not fresh in your memory, it might be worthwhile to spend a few minutes briefly reviewing Chapter 8.

The configuration commands used for the following features are the same on both routers and switches:

Key Topic

■ User and Enable (privileged) mode

■ Entering and exiting configuration mode, using the **configure terminal**, **end**, and **exit** commands, and the Ctrl-Z key sequence

■ Configuration of console, Telnet, and enable secret passwords

■ Configuration of SSH encryption keys and username/password login credentials

■ Configuration of the host name and interface description

■ Configuration of Ethernet interfaces that can negotiate speed, using the **speed** and **duplex** commands

■ Configuring an interface to be administratively disabled (**shutdown**) and administratively enabled (**no shutdown**)

■ Navigation through different configuration mode contexts using commands like **line console 0** and **interface**

■ CLI help, command editing, and command recall features

■ The meaning and use of the startup-config (in NVRAM), running-config (in RAM), and external servers (like TFTP), along with how to use the **copy** command to copy the configuration files and IOS images

■ The process of reaching setup mode either by reloading the router with an empty startup-config or by using the **setup** command

At first glance, this list seems to cover most everything covered in Chapter 8—and it does cover most of the details. However, a couple of topics covered in Chapter 8 do work differently with the router CLI as compared to the switch CLI, namely:

Key Topic

■ The configuration of IP addresses differs in some ways.

■ The questions asked in setup mode differ.

■ Routers have an auxiliary (Aux) port, intended to be connected to an external modem and phone line, to allow remote users to dial into the router, and access the CLI, by making a phone call.

Beyond these three items from Chapter 8, the router CLI does differ from a switch CLI just because switches and routers do different things. For instance, Example 10-5 in Chapter 10, "Ethernet Switch Troubleshooting," shows the output of the **show mac address-table dynamic** command, which lists the most important table that a switch uses for forwarding frames. The router IOS does not support this command—instead, routers support the **show ip route** command, which lists the IP routes known to the router, which of course is the most important table that a router uses for forwarding packets. As you might imagine, the Cisco Layer 2 switches covered on the CCNA exams do not support the **show ip route** command because they do not do any IP routing.

The rest of this section explains a few of the differences between the router IOS CLI and the switch IOS CLI. Chapter 14, "Routing Protocol Concepts and Configuration," goes on to show even more items that differ, in particular how to configure router interface IP addresses and IP routing protocols. For now, this chapter examines the following items:

- Router interfaces

- Router IP address configuration

- Router setup mode

Router Interfaces

The CCNA exams refer to two general types of physical interfaces on routers: Ethernet interfaces and serial interfaces. The term *Ethernet interface* refers to any type of Ethernet interface. However, on Cisco routers, the name referenced by the CLI refers to the fastest speed possible on the interface. For example, some Cisco routers have an Ethernet interface capable of only 10 Mbps, so to configure that type of interface, you would use the **interface ethernet** *number* configuration command. However, other routers have interfaces capable of 100 Mbps, or even of auto-negotiating to use 10 Mbps or 100 Mbps, so routers refer to these interfaces by the fastest speed, with the **interface fastethernet** *number* command. Similarly, interfaces capable of Gigabit Ethernet speeds are referenced with the **interface gigabitethernet** *number* command.

Serial interfaces are the second major type of physical interface on routers. As you may recall from Chapter 4, point-to-point leased lines and Frame Relay access links both use the same underlying Layer 1 standards. To support those same standards, Cisco routers use serial interfaces. The network engineer then chooses which data link layer protocol to use, such as High-Level Data Link Control (HDLC) or Point-to-Point Protocol (PPP) for leased lines or Frame Relay for Frame Relay connections, and configures the router to use the correct data link layer protocol. (Serial interfaces default to use HDLC as the data link layer protocol.)

Routers use numbers to distinguish between the different interfaces of the same type. On routers, the interface numbers might be a single number, or two numbers separated by a slash, or three numbers separated by slashes. For example, all three of the following configuration commands are correct on at least one model of Cisco router:

```
interface ethernet 0
interface fastEthernet 0/1
interface serial 1/0/1
```

You can view information about interfaces by using several commands. To see a brief list of interfaces, use the **show ip interface brief** command. To see brief details about a particular interface, use the **show protocols** *type number* command. (Note that the **show protocols** command is not available in all versions of Cisco IOS Software.) You can also see a lot of detail about each interface, including statistics about the packets flowing in and out of the interface, by using the **show interfaces** command. Optionally, you can include the interface type and number on many commands, for example, **show interfaces** *type number*, to see details for just that interface. Example 13-1 shows sample output from these three commands.

Example 13-1   *Listing the Interfaces in a Router*

```
Albuquerque#show ip interface brief
Interface                  IP-Address      OK? Method Status                 Protocol
FastEthernet0/0            unassigned      YES unset  up                     up
FastEthernet0/1            unassigned      YES unset  administratively down  down
Serial0/0/0                unassigned      YES unset  administratively down  down
Serial0/0/1                unassigned      YES unset  up                     up
Serial0/1/0                unassigned      YES unset  up                     up
Serial0/1/1                unassigned      YES unset  administratively down  down
Albuquerque#show protocols fa0/0
FastEthernet0/0 is up, line protocol is up
Albuquerque#show interfaces s0/1/0
Serial0/1/0 is up, line protocol is up
  Hardware is GT96K Serial
  MTU 1500 bytes, BW 1544 Kbit, DLY 20000 usec,
     reliability 255/255, txload 1/255, rxload 1/255
  Encapsulation HDLC, loopback not set
  Keepalive set (10 sec)
  CRC checking enabled
  Last input 00:00:03, output 00:00:01, output hang never
  Last clearing of "show interface" counters never
  Input queue: 0/75/0/0 (size/max/drops/flushes); Total output drops: 0
  Queueing strategy: weighted fair
  Output queue: 0/1000/64/0 (size/max total/threshold/drops)
     Conversations  0/1/256 (active/max active/max total)
     Reserved Conversations 0/0 (allocated/max allocated)
     Available Bandwidth 1158 kilobits/sec
```

Example 13-1 *Listing the Interfaces in a Router (Continued)*

```
5 minute input rate 0 bits/sec, 0 packets/sec
5 minute output rate 0 bits/sec, 0 packets/sec
   70 packets input, 6979 bytes, 0 no buffer
   Received 70 broadcasts, 0 runts, 0 giants, 0 throttles
   0 input errors, 0 CRC, 0 frame, 0 overrun, 0 ignored, 0 abort
   36 packets output, 4557 bytes, 0 underruns
   0 output errors, 0 collisions, 8 interface resets
   0 output buffer failures, 0 output buffers swapped out
   13 carrier transitions
   DCD=up  DSR=up  DTR=up  RTS=up  CTS=up
```

NOTE Commands that refer to router interfaces can be significantly shortened by truncating the words. For example, **sh int fa0/0** can be used instead of **show interfaces fastethernet 0/0**. In fact, many network engineers, when looking over someone's shoulder, would say something like "just do a show int F-A-oh-oh command" in this case, rather than speaking the long version of the command.

Interface Status Codes

Each of the commands in Example 13-1 lists two *interface status codes*. For a router to use an interface, the two interface status codes on the interface must be in an "up" state. The first status code refers essentially to whether Layer 1 is working, and the second status code mainly (but not always) refers to whether the data link layer protocol is working. Table 13-2 summarizes these two status codes.

Table 13-2 *Interface Status Codes and Their Meanings*

Key Topic

Name	Location	General Meaning
Line status	First status code	Refers to the Layer 1 status—for example, is the cable installed, is it the right/wrong cable, is the device on the other end powered on?
Protocol status	Second status code	Refers generally to the Layer 2 status. It is always down if the line status is down. If the line status is up, a protocol status of down usually is caused by mismatched data link layer configuration.

Four combinations of settings exist for the status codes when troubleshooting a network. Table 13-3 lists the four combinations, along with an explanation of the typical reasons why an interface would be in that state. As you review the list, note that if the line status (the first status code) is not "up," the second will always be "down," because the data link layer functions cannot work if the physical layer has a problem.

Table 13-3 *Typical Combinations of Interface Status Codes*

Line and Protocol Status	Typical Reasons
Administratively down, down	The interface has a **shutdown** command configured on it.
down, down	The interface has a **no shutdown** command configured, but the physical layer has a problem. For example, no cable has been attached to the interface, or with Ethernet, the switch interface on the other end of the cable is shut down, or the switch is powered off.
up, down	Almost always refers to data link layer problems, most often configuration problems. For example, serial links have this combination when one router was configured to use PPP, and the other defaults to use HDLC.
up, up	All is well, interface is functioning.

Router Interface IP Addresses

As has been mentioned many times throughout this book, routers need an IP address on each interface. If no IP address is configured, even if the interface is in an up/up state, the router will not attempt to send and receive IP packets on the interface. For proper operation, for every interface a router should use for forwarding IP packets, the router needs an IP address.

The configuration of an IP address on an interface is relatively simple. To configure the address and mask, simply use the **ip address** *address mask* interface subcommand. Example 13-2 shows an example configuration of IP addresses on two router interfaces, and the resulting differences in the **show ip interface brief** and **show interfaces** commands from Example 13-1. (No IP addresses were configured when the output in Example 13-1 was gathered.)

Example 13-2 *Configuring IP Addresses on Cisco Routers*

```
Albuquerque#configure terminal
Enter configuration commands, one per line.  End with CNTL/Z.
Albuquerque (config)#interface Fa0/0
Albuquerque (config-if)#ip address 10.1.1.1 255.255.255.0
Albuquerque (config-if)#interface S0/0/1
Albuquerque (config-if)#ip address 10.1.2.1 255.255.255.0
Albuquerque (config-if)#^Z
Albuquerque#show ip interface brief
Interface              IP-Address      OK? Method Status                 Protocol
FastEthernet0/0        10.1.1.1        YES manual up                     up
FastEthernet0/1        unassigned      YES NVRAM  administratively down  down
Serial0/0/0            unassigned      YES NVRAM  administratively down  down
Serial0/0/1            10.1.2.1        YES manual up                     up
Serial0/1/0            unassigned      YES NVRAM  up                     up
Serial0/1/1            unassigned      YES NVRAM  administratively down  down
```

Example 13-2 *Configuring IP Addresses on Cisco Routers (Continued)*

```
Albuquerque#show interfaces fa0/0
FastEthernet0/0 is up, line protocol is up
  Hardware is Gt96k FE, address is 0013.197b.5004 (bia 0013.197b.5004)
  Internet address is 10.1.1.1/24
! lines omitted for brevity
```

Bandwidth and Clock Rate on Serial Interfaces

Ethernet interfaces use either a single speed or one of a few speeds that can be auto-negotiated. However, as mentioned in Chapter 4, WAN links can run at a wide variety of speeds. To deal with the wide range of speeds, routers physically slave themselves to the speed as dictated by the CSU/DSU through a process called *clocking*. As a result, routers can use serial links without the need for additional configuration or autonegotiation to sense the serial link's speed. The CSU/DSU knows the speed, the CSU/DSU sends clock pulses over the cable to the router, and the router reacts to the clocking signal. In effect, the CSU/DSU tells the router when to send the next bit over the cable, and when to receive the next bit, with the router just blindly reacting to the CSU/DSU for that timing.

The physical details of how clocking works prevent routers from sensing and measuring the speed used on a link with CSU/DSUs. So, routers use two different interface configuration commands that specify the speed of the WAN link connected to a serial interface, namely the **clock rate** and **bandwidth** interface subcommands.

The **clock rate** command dictates the actual speed used to transmit bits on a serial link, but only when the physical serial link is actually created with cabling in a lab. The lab networks used to build the examples in this book, and probably in any labs engineers use to do proof-of-concept testing, or even labs you use in CCNA classes, use *back-to-back serial cables* (see the Chapter 4 section "Building a WAN Link in a Lab" for a reminder). Back-to-back WAN connections do not use a CSU/DSU, so one router must supply the clocking, which defines the speed at which bits are transmitted. The other router works as usual when CSU/DSUs are used, slaving itself to the clocking signals received from the other router. Example 13-3 shows an example configuration for a router named Albuquerque, with a couple of important commands related to WAN links.

NOTE Example 13-3 omits some of the output of the **show running-config** command, specifically the parts that do not matter to the information covered here.

Example 13-3 *Albuquerque Router Configuration with **clock rate** Command*

```
Albuquerque#show running-config
! lines omitted for brevity
interface Serial0/0/1
 clock rate 128000
```

continues

Example 13-3 *Albuquerque Router Configuration with* **clock rate** *Command (Continued)*

```
!
interface Serial0/1/0
 clock rate 128000
 bandwidth 128
!
interface FastEthernet0/0
! lines omitted for brevity
Albuquerque#show controllers serial 0/0/1
Interface Serial0
Hardware is PowerQUICC MPC860
DCE V.35, clock rate 128000
idb at 0x8169BB20, driver data structure at 0x816A35E4
! Lines omitted for brevity
```

The **clock rate** *speed* interface subcommand sets the rate in bits per second on the router that has the DCE cable plugged into it. If you do not know which router has the DCE cable in it, you can find out by using the **show controllers** command, which lists whether the attached cable is DCE (as shown in Example 13-3) or DTE. Interestingly, IOS accepts the **clock rate** command on an interface only if the interface already has a DCE cable installed, or if no cable is installed. If a DTE cable has been plugged in, IOS silently rejects the command, meaning that IOS does not give you an error message, but IOS ignores the command.

The second interface subcommand that relates to the speed of the serial link is the **bandwidth** *speed* command, as shown on interface serial 0/1/0 in Example 13-3. The **bandwidth** command tells IOS the speed of the link, in kilobits per second, regardless of whether the router is supplying clocking. However, the **bandwidth** setting does not change the speed at which bits are sent and received on the link. Instead, the router uses it for documentation purposes, in calculations related to the utilization rates of the link, and for many other purposes. In particular, the EIGRP and OSPF routing protocols use the interface **bandwidth** settings to set their default metrics, with the metrics impacting a router's choice of the best IP route to reach each subnet. (The *CCNA ICND2 Official Exam Certification Guide* covers these two routing protocols, including how the **bandwidth** command impacts the routing protocol metrics.)

Every router interface has a default setting of the **bandwidth** command that is used when there is no **bandwidth** command configured on the interface. For serial links, the default bandwidth is 1544, meaning 1544 kbps, or 1.544 Mbps—in other words, the speed of a T1 line. Router Ethernet interfaces default to a bandwidth setting that reflects the current speed of the interface. For example, if a router's FastEthernet interface is running at 100 Mbps, the bandwidth is 100,000 (kbps); if the interface is currently running at 10 Mbps, the router automatically changes the bandwidth to 10,000 kbps. Note that the configuration of the **bandwidth** command on an interface overrides these defaults.

> **NOTE** The **clock rate** command uses a unit of bps, whereas the **bandwidth** command uses a unit of kbps. In other words, a **show** command that lists bandwidth as 10,000 means 10,000 kbps, or 10 Mbps.

Router Auxiliary (Aux) Port

Routers have an auxiliary (Aux) port that allows access to the CLI by using a terminal emulator. Normally, the Aux port is connected via a cable (RJ-45, 4 pair, with straight-through pinouts) to an external analog modem. The modem connects to a phone line. Then, the engineer uses a PC, terminal emulator, and modem to call the remote router. Once connected, the engineer can use the terminal emulator to access the router CLI, starting in user mode as usual.

Aux ports can be configured beginning with the **line aux 0** command to reach aux line configuration mode. From there, all the commands for the console line, covered mostly in Chapter 8, can be used. For example, the **login** and **password** *passvalue* commands could be used to set up simple password checking when a user dials in.

Cisco switches do not have an Aux port.

Initial Configuration (Setup Mode)

The processes related to setup mode in routers follow the same rules as for switches. You can refer to the Chapter 8 section "Initial Configuration Using Setup Mode" for more details, but the following statements summarize some of the key points, all of which are true on both switches and routers:

- Setup mode is intended to allow basic configuration by prompting the CLI user via a series of questions.

- You can reach setup mode either by booting a router after erasing the startup-config file or by using the **setup** enable-mode EXEC command.

- At the end of the process, you get three choices (0, 1, or 2), to either ignore the answers and go back to the CLI (0); ignore the answers but begin again in setup mode (1); or to use the resulting configuration (2).

- If you tire of the process, the Ctrl-C key combination will eject the user out of setup mode and back to the previous CLI mode.

- If you select to use the resulting configuration, the router writes the configuration to the startup-config file, as well as the running-config file.

The main difference between the setup mode on switches and routers relates to the information requested while in setup mode. For example, routers need to know the IP address and mask for each interface on which you want to configure IP, whereas switches have only one IP address. To be complete, Example 13-4 demonstrates the use of setup mode. If you do not have a router with which to practice setup mode, take the time to review the example, and see the kinds of information requested in the various questions.

> **NOTE**   The questions asked, and the default answers, differ on some routers in part due to the IOS revision, feature set, and router model.

Example 13-4   *Router Setup Configuration Mode*

```
--- System Configuration Dialog ---

Would you like to enter the initial configuration dialog? [yes/no]: yes
At any point you may enter a question mark '?' for help.
Use ctrl-c to abort configuration dialog at any prompt.
Default settings are in square brackets '[]'.Basic management setup configures
only enough connectivity
for management of the system, extended setup will ask you
to configure each interface on the system

Would you like to enter basic management setup? [yes/no]: no
First, would you like to see the current interface summary? [yes]:
Any interface listed with OK? value "NO" does not have a valid configuration

Interface                IP-Address      OK? Method Status                Protocol
Ethernet0                unassigned      NO  unset  up                    down
Serial0                  unassigned      NO  unset  down                  down
Serial1                  unassigned      NO  unset  down                  down

Configuring global parameters:

  Enter host name [Router]: R1
      The enable secret is a password used to protect access to
      privileged EXEC and configuration modes. This password, after
      entered, becomes encrypted in the configuration.
      Enter enable secret: cisco
    The enable password is used when you do not specify an
      enable secret password, with some older software versions, and
      some boot images.
      Enter enable password: fred
    The virtual terminal password is used to protect
      access to the router over a network interface.
      Enter virtual terminal password: barney
    Configure SNMP Network Management? [yes]: no
    Configure bridging? [no]:
    Configure DECnet? [no]:
    Configure AppleTalk? [no]:
    Configure IPX? [no]:
```

Example 13-4 *Router Setup Configuration Mode (Continued)*

```
    Configure IP? [yes]:
    Configure RIP routing? [yes]:
Configure CLNS? [no]:
  Configure bridging? [no]:

Configuring interface parameters:
    Do you want to configure Ethernet0  interface? [yes]:
    Configure IP on this interface? [yes]:
    IP address for this interface: 172.16.1.1
    Subnet mask for this interface [255.255.0.0] : 255.255.255.0
    Class B network is 172.16.0.0, 24 subnet bits; mask is /24
    Do you want to configure Serial0  interface? [yes]:
      Configure IP on this interface? [yes]:
    Configure IP unnumbered on this interface? [no]:
    IP address for this interface: 172.16.12.1
    Subnet mask for this interface [255.255.0.0] : 255.255.255.0
    Class B network is 172.16.0.0, 24 subnet bits; mask is /24
    Do you want to configure Serial1  interface? [yes]:
    Configure IP on this interface? [yes]:
    Configure IP unnumbered on this interface? [no]:
    IP address for this interface: 172.16.13.1
    Subnet mask for this interface [255.255.0.0] : 255.255.255.0
    Class B network is 172.16.0.0, 24 subnet bits; mask is /24


    The following configuration command script was created:

    hostname R1
    enable secret 5 $1$VOLh$pkIe0Xjx2sgjgZ/Y6Gt1s.
    enable password fred
    line vty 0 4
    password barney
    no snmp-server
    !
    ip routing
     !
    interface Ethernet0
    ip address 172.16.1.1 255.255.255.0
    !
    interface Serial0
    ip address 172.16.12.1 255.255.255.0
    !
    interface Serial1
    ip address 172.16.13.1 255.255.255.0
    !
    router rip
    network 172.16.0.0
    !
```

continues

Example 13-4 *Router Setup Configuration Mode (Continued)*

```
end

[0] Go to the IOS command prompt without saving this config.
[1] Return back to the setup without saving this config.
[2] Save this configuration to nvram and exit.

Enter your selection [2]: 2
Building configuration...
[OK]Use the enabled mode 'configure' command to modify this configuration.
Press RETURN to get started!
```

NOTE   Although not shown in this example, routers that use an IOS feature set that includes additional security features will also ask the user if they want to configure *Cisco Auto Secure*. This feature automatically configures many router security best practice settings, for example, disabling CDP.

Upgrading Cisco IOS Software and the Cisco IOS Software Boot Process

Engineers need to know how to upgrade IOS to move to a later release or version of IOS. Typically, a router has one IOS image in Flash memory, and that is the IOS image that is used. (The term *IOS image* simply refers to a file containing IOS.) The upgrade process might include steps such as copying a newer IOS image into Flash memory, configuring the router to tell it which IOS image to use, and deleting the old one when you are confident that the new release works well. Alternately, you could copy a new image to a TFTP server, with some additional configuration on the router to tell it to get the new IOS from the TFTP server the next time the router is reloaded.

This section shows how to upgrade IOS by copying a new IOS file into Flash memory and telling the router to use the new IOS. Because the router decides which IOS to use when the router boots, this is also a good place to review the process by which routers boot (initialize). Switches follow the same basic process as described here, with some minor differences, as specifically noted.

Upgrading a Cisco IOS Software Image into Flash Memory

Routers and switches typically store IOS images in Flash memory. Flash memory is rewriteable, permanent storage, which is ideal for storing files that need to be retained when the router loses power. Cisco purposefully uses Flash memory instead of disk drives in its products because there are no moving parts in Flash memory, so there is a smaller chance of failure as compared with disk drives. Additionally, the IOS image can be placed on an external TFTP server, but using an external server typically is done for testing; in production, practically every Cisco router loads an IOS image stored in the only type of large, permanent memory in a Cisco router—Flash memory.

Figure 13-6 illustrates the process to upgrade an IOS image into Flash memory:

Step 1 Obtain the IOS image from Cisco, typically by downloading the IOS image from Cisco.com using HTTP or FTP.

Step 2 Place the IOS image into the default directory of a TFTP server that is accessible from the router.

Step 3 Issue the **copy** command from the router, copying the file into Flash memory.

You also can use an FTP or remote copy (rcp) server, but the TFTP feature has been around a long time and is a more likely topic for the exams.

Figure 13-6 *Complete Cisco IOS Software Upgrade Process*

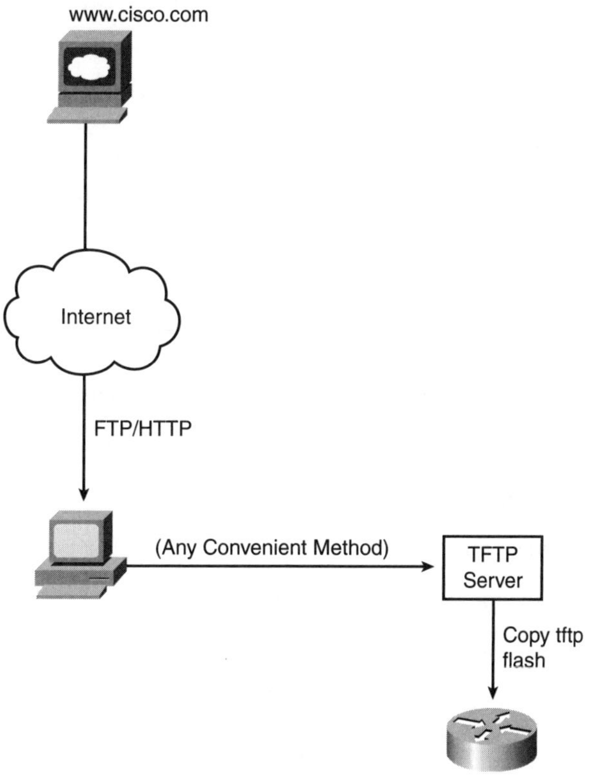

Example 13-5 provides an example of the final step, copying the IOS image into Flash memory. Note that the **copy tftp flash** command shown here works much like the **copy tftp startup-config** command that can be used to restore a backup copy of the configuration file into NVRAM.

Example 13-5   **copy tftp flash** *Command Copies the IOS Image to Flash Memory*

```
R1#copy tftp flash

System flash directory:
File  Length    Name/status
  1   7530760   c4500-d-mz.120-2.bin
[7530824 bytes used, 857784 available, 8388608 total]
Address or name of remote host [255.255.255.255]? 134.141.3.33
Source file name? c4500-d-mz.120-5.bin
Destination file name [c4500-d-mz.120-5.bin]?
Accessing file c4500-d-mz.120-5.bin ' on 134.141.3.33...
Loading c4500-d-mz.120-5.bin from 134.141.3.33 (via Ethernet0): ! [OK]

Erase flash device before writing? [confirm]
Flash contains files. Are you sure you want to erase? [confirm]

Copy 'c4500-d-mz.120-5.bin ' from server
  as 'c4500-d-mz.120-5.bin ' into Flash WITH erase? [yes/no]y
Erasing device... eeeeeeeeeeeeeeeeeeeeeeeeeeeeeeee ...erased
Loading c4500-d-mz.120-5.bin  from 134.141.3.33 (via Ethernet0):
   !!!!!!!!!!!!!!!!!!!!!!!!!!!!!!!!!!!!!!!!!!!!!!!!!!!!!!!!!!!!!!!!!!!!!!!!!!!!
   !!!!!!!!!!!!!!!!!!!!!!!!!!!!!!!!!!!!!!!!!!!!!!! (leaving out lots of exclamation points)
[OK  7530760/8388608 bytes]

Verifying checksum...  OK (0xA93E)
Flash copy took 0:04:26 [hh:mm:ss]
```

During this process of copying the IOS image into Flash memory, the router needs to discover several important facts:

1.   What is the IP address or host name of the TFTP server?

2.   What is the name of the file?

3.   Is space available for this file in Flash memory?

4.   Does the server actually have a file by that name?

5.   Do you want the router to erase the old files?

The router will prompt you for answers, as necessary. For each question, you should either type an answer or press Enter if the default answer (shown in square brackets at the end of the question) is acceptable. Afterward, the router erases Flash memory if directed, copies the file, and then verifies that the checksum for the file shows that no errors occurred in transmission. You can then use the **show flash** command to verify the contents of Flash memory, as demonstrated in Example 13-6. (The **show flash** output can vary among router families. Example 13-6 is output from a 2500 series router.)

Example 13-6   *Verifying Flash Memory Contents with the* **show flash** *Command*

```
fred#show flash
System flash directory:
File  Length    Name/status
  1   13305352  c2500-ds-1.122-1.bin
[13305416 bytes used, 3471800 available, 16777216 total]
16384K bytes of processor board System flash (Read ONLY)
```

The shaded line in Example 13-6 lists the amount of Flash memory, the amount used, and the amount of free space. When copying a new IOS image into Flash, the **copy** command will ask you if you want to erase Flash, with a default answer of [yes]. If you reply with an answer of **no**, and IOS realizes that not enough available Flash memory exists, the copy will fail. Additionally, even if you answer **yes**, and erase all of Flash memory, the new Flash IOS image must be of a size that fits into flash memory; if not, the **copy** command will fail.

Once the new IOS has been copied into Flash, the router must be reloaded to use the new IOS image. The next section, which covers the IOS boot sequence, explains the details of how to configure a router so that it loads the right IOS image.

The Cisco IOS Software Boot Sequence

Cisco routers perform the same types of tasks that a typical computer performs when you power it on or reboot (reload) it. Most computers have a single operating system (OS) installed, and that OS boots by default. However, a router can have multiple IOS images available both in Flash memory and on external TFTP servers, so the router needs to know which IOS image to load. This section examines the entire boot process, with extra emphasis on the options that impact a router's choice of what IOS image to load.

> **NOTE**   The boot sequence details in this section, particularly those regarding the configuration register and the ROMMON OS, differ from Cisco LAN switches, but they do apply to most every model of Cisco router. This book does not cover the equivalent options in Cisco switches.

When a router first powers on, it follows these four steps:

1. The router performs a power-on self-test (POST) to discover the hardware components and verify that all components work properly.

2. The router copies a bootstrap program from ROM into RAM, and runs the bootstrap program.

3. The bootstrap program decides which IOS image (or other OS) to load into RAM, and loads that OS. After loading the IOS image, the bootstrap program hands over control of the router hardware to the newly loaded OS.

4. If the bootstrap program loaded IOS, IOS finds the configuration file (typically the startup-config file in NVRAM) and loads it into RAM as the running-config.

All routers attempt all four steps each time that the router is powered on or reloaded. The first two steps do not have any options to choose; these steps either work or the router initialization fails and you typically need to call the Cisco Technical Assistance Center (TAC) for support. However, Steps 3 and 4 have several configurable options that tell the router what to do next. Figure 13-7 depicts those options, referencing Steps 2 through 4 shown in the earlier boot process.

Figure 13-7 *Loading the Cisco IOS*

As you can see, the router can get the IOS image from three locations and can get the initial configuration from three locations as well. Frankly, routers almost always load the configuration from NVRAM (the startup-config file), when it exists. There is no real advantage to storing the initial configuration anywhere else except NVRAM. So, this chapter will not look further into the options of Step 4. However, there are good reasons for putting multiple IOS images in Flash, and keeping images on external servers, so the rest of this section examines Step 3 in more detail. In particular, the next few pages explain a few facts about some alternate router operating systems besides IOS, and a router feature called the *configuration register*, before showing how a router chooses which IOS image to load.

> **NOTE**   The IOS image is typically a compressed file so that it consumes less space in Flash memory. The router decompresses the IOS image as is it loaded into RAM.

The Three Router Operating Systems

A router typically loads and uses a Cisco IOS image that allows the router to perform its normal function of routing packets. However, Cisco routers can use a different OS to perform some troubleshooting, to recover router passwords, and to copy new IOS files into Flash when Flash has been inadvertently erased or corrupted. In the more recent additions to the Cisco router product line (for example, 1800 and 2800 series routers), Cisco routers use only one other OS, whereas older Cisco routers (for example, 2500 series routers) actually had two different operating systems to perform different subsets of these same functions. Table 13-4 lists the other two router operating systems, and a few details about each.

Table 13-4   *Comparing ROMMON and RxBoot Operating Systems*

Operating Environment	Common Name	Stored In	Used in...
ROM Monitor	ROMMON	ROM	Old and new routers
Boot ROM	RxBoot, boot helper	ROM	Only in older routers

Key
Topic

Because the RxBoot OS is only available in older routers and is no longer needed in the newer routers, this chapter will mainly refer to the OS that continues to be available for these special functions, the ROMMON OS.

The Configuration Register

The configuration register is a special 16-bit number that can be set on any Cisco router. The configuration register's bits control different settings for some low-level operating characteristics of the router. For example, the console runs at a speed of 9600 bps by default, but that console speed is based on the default settings of a couple of bits in the configuration register.

You can set the *configuration register* value with the **config-register** global configuration command. Engineers set the configuration register to different values for many reasons, but the most common are to help tell the router what IOS image to load, as explained in the next few pages, and in the password recovery process. For example, the command **config-register 0x2100** sets the value to hexadecimal 2100, which causes the router to load the ROMMON OS instead of IOS—a common practice when recovering lost passwords. Interestingly, this value is automatically saved when you press Enter at the end of the **config-register** command—you do not need to save the running-config file into the startup-config file after changing the configuration register. However, the configuration register's new value is not used until the next time the router is reloaded.

> **TIP**   The **show version** command, shown near the end of this chapter in Example 13-7, shows the configuration register's current value and, if different, the value that will be used once the router is reloaded.

> **NOTE**   On most Cisco routers, the default configuration register setting is hexadecimal 2102.

How a Router Chooses Which OS to Load

A router chooses the OS to load based on the low-order 4 bits in the configuration register and the details configured in any **boot system** global configuration commands found in the startup-config file. The low-order 4 bits (the 4th hex digit) in the configuration register are called the *boot field*, with the value of these bits being the first value a router examines when choosing which OS to try and load. The boot field's value when the router is powered on or reloaded tells the router how to proceed with choosing which OS to load.

> **NOTE**   Cisco represents hexadecimal values by preceding the hex digit(s) with 0x—for example, 0xA would mean a single hex digit A.

The process to choose which OS to load, on more modern routers that do not have an RxBoot OS, happens as follows (note that "boot" refers to the boot field in the configuration register):

```
Key
Topic
```

Step 1   If boot field = 0, use the ROMMON OS.

Step 2   If boot field = 1, load the first IOS file found in Flash memory.

Step 3   If boot field = 2-F:

   a. Try each **boot system** command in the startup-config file, in order, until one works.

   b. If none of the **boot system** commands work, load the first IOS file found in Flash memory.

NOTE   The actual step numbers are not important—the list is just numbered for easier reference.

The first two steps are pretty straightforward, but Step 3 then tells the router to look to the second major method to tell the router which IOS to load: the **boot system** global configuration command. This command can be configured multiple times on one router, with details about files in Flash memory, and filenames and IP addresses of servers, telling the router where to look for an IOS image to load. The router tries to load the IOS images, in the order of the configured **boot system** commands. Once the router succeeds in loading one of the referenced IOS images, the process is complete, and the router can ignore the remaining **boot system** commands. If the router fails to load an IOS based on the **boot system** commands, the router then tries what Step 1 suggests, which is to load the first IOS file found in Flash memory.

Both Step 2 and Step 3b refer to a concept of the "first" IOS file, a concept which needs a little more explanation. Routers number the files stored in Flash memory, with each new file typically getting a higher and higher number. When a router tries Step 2 or Step 3b from the preceding list, the router will look in Flash memory, starting with file number 1, and then file number 2, and so on, until it finds the lowest numbered file that happens to be an IOS image. The router will then load that file.

Interestingly, most routers end up using Step 3b to find their IOS image. From the factory, Cisco routers do not have any **boot system** commands configured; in fact, they do not have any configuration in the startup-config file at all. Cisco loads Flash memory with a single IOS when it builds and tests the router, and the configuration register value is set to 0x2102, meaning a boot field of 0x2. With all these settings, the process tries Step 3 (because boot = 2), finds no **boot system** commands (because the startup-config is empty), and then looks for the first file in Flash memory at Step 3b.

Figure 13-8 shows a diagram that summarizes the key concepts behind how a router chooses the OS to load.

Figure 13-8 *Choices for Choosing the OS at Boot Time: Modern Cisco Router*

The **boot system** commands need to refer to the exact file that the router should load. Table 13-5 shows several examples of the commands.

Table 13-5 *Sample **boot system** Commands*

Boot System Command	Result
boot system flash	The first file from Flash memory is loaded.
boot system flash *filename*	IOS with the name *filename* is loaded from Flash memory.
boot system tftp *filename* **10.1.1.1**	IOS with the name *filename* is loaded from the TFTP server.

In some cases, a router fails to load on OS based on the three-step process listed earlier in this section. For example, someone might accidentally erase all the contents of Flash, including the IOS image. So, routers need more options to help recover from these unexpected but possible scenarios. If no OS is found by the end of Step 3, the router will send broadcasts looking for a TFTP server, guess at a filename for the IOS image, and load an IOS image (assuming that a TFTP server is found). In practice it is highly unlikely to work. The final step is to simply load ROMMON, which is designed in part to provide tools to recover from these unexpected types of problems. For example, an IOS image can be copied into Flash from a TFTP server while using ROMMON.

For older models of Cisco router that have an RxBoot (boot helper) OS in ROM, the process to choose which OS to load works generally the same, with two differences. When the boot field is 0x1, the router loads the RxBoot OS stored in ROM. Also, in the final efforts to find an OS as described in the previous paragraph, if the effort to find an image from a TFTP server fails, and the router has an RxBoot image, the router first tries to load RxBoot before trying to load the ROM Monitor OS.

The show version Command and Seeing the Configuration Register's Value

The **show version** command supplies a wide variety of information about a router, including both the current value of the configuration register and the expected value at the next reload of the router. The following list summarizes some of the other very interesting information in this command:

1. The IOS version

2. The uptime (the length of time that has passed since the last reload)

3. The reason for the last reload of IOS (**reload** command, power off/on, software failure)

4. The time of the last loading of IOS (if the router's clock has been set)

5. The source from which the router loaded the current IOS

6. The amount of RAM memory

7. The number and types of interfaces

8. The amount of NVRAM memory

9. The amount of Flash memory

10. The configuration register's current and future setting (if different)

Example 13-7 demonstrates output from the **show version** command, highlighting the key pieces of information. Note that the preceding list is in the same order in which the highlighted information appears in the example.

Example 13-7 **show version** *Command Output*

```
Albuquerque#show version
Cisco IOS Software, 1841 Software (C1841-ADVENTERPRISEK9-M), Version 12.4(9)T, RELEASE
  SOFTWARE (fc1)
Technical Support: http://www.cisco.com/techsupport
Copyright (c) 1986-2006 by Cisco Systems, Inc.
                                                              continues
```

Key
Topic

Example 13-7   **show version** *Command Output (Continued)*

```
Compiled Fri 16-Jun-06 21:26 by prod_rel_team

ROM: System Bootstrap, Version 12.3(8r)T8, RELEASE SOFTWARE (fc1)

Albuquerque uptime is 5 hours, 20 minutes
System returned to ROM by reload at 13:12:26 UTC Wed Jan 17 2007
System restarted at 13:13:38 UTC Wed Jan 17 2007
System image file is "flash:c1841-adventerprisek9-mz.124-9.T.bin"


This product contains cryptographic features and is subject to United
States and local country laws governing import, export, transfer and
use. Delivery of Cisco cryptographic products does not imply
third-party authority to import, export, distribute or use encryption.
Importers, exporters, distributors and users are responsible for
compliance with U.S. and local country laws. By using this product you
agree to comply with applicable laws and regulations. If you are unable
to comply with U.S. and local laws, return this product immediately.

A summary of U.S. laws governing Cisco cryptographic products may be found at:
http://www.cisco.com/wwl/export/crypto/tool/stqrg.html

If you require further assistance please contact us by sending email to
export@cisco.com.

Cisco 1841 (revision 4.1) with 354304K/38912K bytes of memory.
Processor board ID FTX0906Y03T
2 FastEthernet interfaces
4 Serial(sync/async) interfaces
1 Virtual Private Network (VPN) Module
DRAM configuration is 64 bits wide with parity disabled.
191K bytes of NVRAM.
125440K bytes of ATA CompactFlash (Read/Write)


Configuration register is 0x2102 (will be 0x2101 at next reload)
```

Most of the information highlighted in the example can be easily found in comparison to
the list preceding Example 13-7. However, note that the amount of RAM, listed as
354304K/38912K, shows the RAM in two parts. The sum of these two parts is the total
amount of available RAM, about 384 MB in this case.

Exam Preparation Tasks

Review All the Key Topics

Review the most important topics from inside the chapter, noted with the key topics icon in the outer margin of the page. Table 13-6 lists a reference of these key topics and the page numbers on which each is found.

Key
Topic

Table 13-6 *Key Topics for Chapter 13*

Key Topic	Description	Page Number
List	Steps required to install a router	406
List	Similarities between router CLI and switch CLI	410
List	Items covered for switches in Chapter 8 that differ in some way on routers	410
Table 13-2	Router interface status codes and their meanings	413
Table 13-3	Combinations of the two interface status codes and the likely reasons for each combination	414
List	Summary of important facts about the initial configuration dialog (setup mode)	417
List	The four steps a router performs when booting	424
Table 13-4	Comparison of ROMMON and RxBoot operating systems	425
List	Steps a router uses to choose which IOS image to load	426
Figure 13-8	Diagram of how a router chooses which IOS image to load	428
List	A list of the many important facts that can be seen in the output from the **show version** command	429

Complete the Tables and Lists from Memory

Print a copy of Appendix H, "Memory Tables" (found on the CD-ROM), or at least the section for this chapter, and complete the tables and lists from memory. Appendix I, "Memory Tables Answer Key," also on the CD-ROM, includes completed tables and lists to check your work.

Definitions of Key Terms

Define the following key terms from this chapter and check your answers in the glossary.

bandwidth, boot field, clock rate, configuration register, IOS image, power-on self-test (POST), ROMMON, RxBoot

Read Appendix F Scenario 2

Appendix F, "Additional Scenarios," contains two detailed scenarios that give you a chance to analyze different designs, problems, and command output, as well as show you how concepts from several different chapters interrelate. At this point in your reading, Appendix F scenario 2, which shows how to use Cisco Discovery Protocol (CDP), would be particularly useful to read.

Command References

Although you should not necessarily memorize the information in the tables in this section, this section does include a reference for the configuration commands (Table 13-7) and EXEC commands (Table 13-8) covered in this chapter. Practically speaking, you should memorize the commands as a complement to reading the chapter and doing all the activities in this exam preparation section. To check to see how well you have memorized the commands, cover the left side of the table with a piece of paper, read the descriptions in the right side, and see if you remember the command.

Table 13-7 *Chapter 13 Configuration Command Reference*

Command	Description
bandwidth *kbps*	Interface command that sets the router's perception of bandwidth of the interface, in a unit of kbps.
clock rate *rate*	Interface command that sets the speed at which the router supplies a clocking signal, applicable only when the router has a DCE cable installed. The unit is bits/second.
config-register *value*	Global command that sets the hexadecimal value of the configuration register.
boot system {*file-url*	*filename*}	Global command that identifies an externally located IOS image using a URL.
boot system flash [*flash-fs:*] [*filename*]	Global command that identifies the location of an IOS image in Flash memory.

Table 13-7   *Chapter 13 Configuration Command Reference (Continued)*

Command	Description
boot system rom	Global command that tells the router to load the RxBoot OS found in ROM, if one exists.
boot system {rcp | tftp | ftp} *filename* [*ip-address*]	Global command that identifies an external server, protocol, and filename to use to load an IOS from an external server.

Table 13-8   *Chapter 13 EXEC Command Reference*

Command	Purpose
show interfaces *[type number]*	Lists a large set of informational messages about each interface, or about the one specifically listed interface.
show ip interface brief	Lists a single line of information about each interface, including the IP address, line and protocol status, and the method with which the address was configured (manual or DHCP).
show protocols *type number*	Lists a single line of information about the listed interface, including the IP address, mask, and line/protocol status.
show controllers *[type number]*	Lists many lines of information per interface, or for one interface, for the hardware controller of the interface. On serial interfaces, this command identifies the cable as either a DCE or DTE cable.
show version	Lists the IOS version, as well as a large set of other useful information (see Example 13-7).
setup	Starts the setup (initial configuration) dialog in which the router prompts the user for basic configuration settings.
copy *source-url destination-url*	Copies a file from the first listed URL to the destination URL.
show flash	Lists the names and size of the files in Flash memory, as well as noting the amount of Flash memory consumed and available.
reload	Enable mode command that reinitializes (reboots) the router.

This chapter covers the following subjects:

Connected and Static Routes: This section covers the basics of how routers learn routes to connected subnets and how to configure static routes.

Routing Protocol Overview: This section explains the terminology and theory related to routing protocols in general and Routing Information Protocol (RIP) in particular.

Configuring and Verifying RIP-2: This section explains how to configure RIP Version 2 (RIP-2) and how to confirm that RIP-2 is working correctly.

CHAPTER 14

Routing Protocol Concepts and Configuration

The United States Postal Service routes a huge number of letters and packages each day. To do so, the postal sorting machines run fast, sorting lots of letters. Then the letters are placed in the correct container and onto the correct truck or plane to reach the final destination. However, if no one programs the letter-sorting machines to know where letters to each ZIP code should be sent, the sorter cannot do its job. Similarly, Cisco routers can route many packets, but if the router does not know any routes—routes that tell the router where to send the packets—the router cannot do its job.

This chapter introduces the basic concepts of how routers fill their routing tables with routes. Routers learn routes by being directly connected to local subnets, by being statically configured with information about routes, and by using dynamic routing protocols.

As you might guess by now, to fully appreciate the nuances of how routing protocols work, you need a thorough understanding of routing—the process of forwarding packets—as well as subnetting. So, this chapter includes a few additional comments on routing and subnetting, to link the ideas from Chapter 5, "Fundamentals of IP Addressing and Routing," Chapter 12, "IP Addressing and Subnetting," and Chapter 13, "Operating Cisco Routers," together so you can better understand dynamic routing protocols.

"Do I Know This Already?" Quiz

The "Do I Know This Already?" quiz allows you to assess if you should read the entire chapter. If you miss no more than one of these ten self-assessment questions, you might want to move ahead to the "Exam Preparation Tasks" section. Table 14-1 lists the major headings in this chapter and the "Do I Know This Already?" quiz questions covering the material in those headings so you can assess your knowledge of these specific areas. The answers to the "Do I Know This Already?" quiz appear in Appendix A.

Table 14-1 *"Do I Know This Already?" Foundation Topics Section-to-Question Mapping*

Foundation Topics Section	Questions
Connected and Static Routes	1, 2
Routing Protocol Overview	3–6
Configuring and Verifying RIP-2	7–10

1. Which of the following must be true for a static route to be installed in a router's IP routing table?

    a. The outgoing interface associated with the route must be in an "up and up" state.

    b. The router must receive a routing update from a neighboring router.

    c. The **ip route** command must be added to the configuration.

    d. The outgoing interface's **ip address** command must use the **special** keyword.

2. Which of the following commands correctly configures a static route?

    a. **ip route 10.1.3.0 255.255.255.0 10.1.130.253**

    b. **ip route 10.1.3.0 serial 0**

    c. **ip route 10.1.3.0 /24 10.1.130.253**

    d. **ip route 10.1.3.0 /24 serial 0**

3. Which of the following routing protocols are considered to use distance vector logic?

    a. RIP

    b. IGRP

    c. EIGRP

    d. OSPF

4. Which of the following routing protocols are considered to use link-state logic?

    a. RIP

    b. RIP-2

    c. IGRP

    d. EIGRP

    e. OSPF

    f. Integrated IS-IS

5. Which of the following routing protocols support VLSM?

    a. RIP

    b. RIP-2

    c. IGRP

    d. EIGRP

    e. OSPF

    f. Integrated IS-IS

6. Which of the following routing protocols are considered to be capable of converging quickly?

    a. RIP

    b. RIP-2

    c. IGRP

    d. EIGRP

    e. OSPF

    f. Integrated IS-IS

7. Router1 has interfaces with addresses 9.1.1.1 and 10.1.1.1. Router2, connected to Router1 over a serial link, has interfaces with addresses 10.1.1.2 and 11.1.1.2. Which of the following commands would be part of a complete RIP Version 2 configuration on Router2, with which Router2 advertises out all interfaces, and about all routes?

    a. **router rip**

    b. **router rip 3**

    c. **network 9.0.0.0**

    d. **version 2**

    e. **network 10.0.0.0**

    f. **network 10.1.1.1**

    g. **network 10.1.1.2**

    h. **network 11.0.0.0**

    i. **network 11.1.1.2**

8. Which of the following **network** commands, following a **router rip** command, would cause RIP to send updates out two interfaces whose IP addresses are 10.1.2.1 and 10.1.1.1, mask 255.255.255.0?

    a. **network 10.0.0.0**

    b. **network 10.1.1.0 10.1.2.0**

    c. **network 10.1.1.1. 10.1.2.1**

    d. **network 10.1.0.0 255.255.0.0**

    e. **network 10**

    f. You cannot do this with only one **network** command.

9. What command(s) list(s) information identifying the neighboring routers that are sending routing information to a particular router?

    a. **show ip**

    b. **show ip protocol**

    c. **show ip routing-protocols**

    d. **show ip route**

    e. **show ip route neighbor**

    f. **show ip route received**

10. Review the snippet from a **show ip route** command on a router:

    ```
    R       10.1.2.0 [120/1] via 10.1.128.252, 00:00:13, Serial0/0/1
    ```

    Which of the following statements are true regarding this output?

    a. The administrative distance is 1.

    b. The administrative distance is 120.

    c. The metric is 1.

    d. The metric is not listed.

    e. The router added this route to the routing table 13 seconds ago.

    f. The router must wait 13 seconds before advertising this route again.

Foundation Topics

Connected and Static Routes

Routers need to have routes in their IP routing tables for the packet forwarding process (routing) to work. Two of the most basic means by which a router adds routes to its routing table are by learning about the subnets connected to its interfaces, and by configuring a route by using a global configuration command (called a static route). This section explains both, with the remainder of the chapter focusing on the third method of learning routes—dynamic routing protocols.

Connected Routes

A router adds routes to its routing table for the subnets connected to each of the router's interfaces. For this to occur, the router must have an IP address and mask configured on the interface (statically with the **ip address** command or dynamically using Dynamic Host Configuration Protocol [DHCP]) and both interface status codes must be "up." The concept is simple: if a router has an interface in a subnet, the router has a way to forward packets into that subnet, so the router needs a route in its routing table.

Figure 14-1 illustrates a sample internetwork that will be used in Example 14-1 to show some connected routes and some related **show** commands. Figure 14-1 shows an internetwork with six subnets, with each of the three routers having three interfaces in use. Each of the LANs in this figure could consist of one switch, one hub, or lots of switches and/or hubs together—but for the purposes of this chapter, the size of the LAN does not matter. Once the interfaces have been configured as shown in the figure, and once each interface is up and working, each of the routers should have three connected routes in their routing tables.

Example 14-1 shows the connected routes on Albuquerque after its interfaces have been configured with the addresses shown in Figure 14-1. The example includes several comments, with more detailed comments following the example.

Figure 14-1   *Sample Internetwork Used Throughout Chapter 14*

Example 14-1   *Albuquerque Connected Routes*

```
! The following command just lists the IP address configuration on Albuquerque.
! The output has been edited to show only the three interfaces used in Figure
! 14-1.
!
Albuquerque#show running-config
interface FastEthernet0/0
 ip address 10.1.1.251 255.255.255.0
!
interface Serial 0/0/1
 ip address 10.1.128.251 255.255.255.0
!
interface Serial 0/1/0
 ip address 10.1.130.251 255.255.255.0
```

Example 14-1 *Albuquerque Connected Routes (Continued)*

```
! Lines omitted for brevity
! The next command lists the interfaces, and confirms that Albuquerque's three
! interfaces shown in Figure 14-1 are in an "up and up" status.
!
Albuquerque#show ip interface brief
Interface                IP-Address      OK? Method Status                Protocol
FastEthernet0/0          10.1.1.251      YES manual up                    up
FastEthernet0/1          unassigned      YES manual administratively down down
Serial0/0/0              unassigned      YES NVRAM  administratively down down
Serial0/0/1              10.1.128.251    YES NVRAM  up                    up
Serial0/1/0              10.1.130.251    YES NVRAM  up                    up
Serial0/1/1              unassigned      YES NVRAM  administratively down down
!
! The next command lists the routes known by Albuquerque – all connected routes
!
Albuquerque#show ip route
Codes: C - connected, S - static, I - IGRP, R - RIP, M - mobile, B - BGP
       D - EIGRP, EX - EIGRP external, O - OSPF, IA - OSPF inter area
       N1 - OSPF NSSA external type 1, N2 - OSPF NSSA external type 2
       E1 - OSPF external type 1, E2 - OSPF external type 2, E - EGP
       i - IS-IS, L1 - IS-IS level-1, L2 - IS-IS level-2, ia - IS-IS inter area
       * - candidate default, U - per-user static route, o - ODR
       P - periodic downloaded static route
Gateway of last resort is not set


     10.0.0.0/24 is subnetted, 3 subnets
C       10.1.1.0 is directly connected, FastEthernet0/0
C       10.1.130.0 is directly connected, Serial0/1/0
C       10.1.128.0 is directly connected, Serial0/0/1
!
! The next command changes the mask format used by the show ip route command
!
Albuquerque#terminal ip netmask-format decimal
Albuquerque#show ip route
Codes: C - connected, S - static, I - IGRP, R - RIP, M - mobile, B - BGP
       D - EIGRP, EX - EIGRP external, O - OSPF, IA - OSPF inter area
       N1 - OSPF NSSA external type 1, N2 - OSPF NSSA external type 2
       E1 - OSPF external type 1, E2 - OSPF external type 2, E - EGP
       i - IS-IS, L1 - IS-IS level-1, L2 - IS-IS level-2, ia - IS-IS inter area
       * - candidate default, U - per-user static route, o - ODR
       P - periodic downloaded static route


Gateway of last resort is not set


     10.0.0.0 255.255.255.0 is subnetted, 3 subnets
C       10.1.1.0 is directly connected, FastEthernet0/0
C       10.1.130.0 is directly connected, Serial0/1/0
C       10.1.128.0 is directly connected, Serial0/0/1
```

To begin, the **show ip interface brief** command in Example 14-1 confirms that Albuquerque's three interfaces meet the requirements to have their connected subnets added to the routing table. Note that all three interfaces are in an "up and up" state and have an IP address configured.

The output of the **show ip route** command confirms that Albuquerque indeed added a route to all three subnets to its routing table. The output begins with a single-letter code legend, with "C" meaning "connected." The individual routes begin with a code letter on the far left—in this case, all three routes have the letter C. Also, note that the output lists the mask in prefix notation by default. Additionally, in cases when one mask is used throughout a single classful network—in other words, static-length subnet masking (SLSM) is used—the **show ip route** command output lists the mask on a heading line above the subnets of that classful network. For example, the lines with 10.1.1.0, 10.1.128.0, and 10.1.130.0 do not show the mask, but the line just above those three lines does list classful network 10.0.0.0 and the mask, as highlighted in the example.

Finally, you can change the format of the display of the subnet mask in **show** commands, for the duration of your login session to the router, using the **terminal ip netmask-format decimal** EXEC command, as shown at the end of Example 14-1.

> **NOTE**   To be well prepared for the exams, you should look at all items in the output of the **show ip interface brief** and **show ip route** commands in each example in this chapter. Example 14-6, later in this chapter, provides more detailed comments about the **show ip route** command's output.

Static Routes

Although the connected routes on each router are important, routers typically need other routes to forward packets to all subnets in an internetwork. For example, Albuquerque can successfully ping the IP addresses on the other end of each serial link, or IP addresses on its local connected LAN subnet (10.1.1.0/24). However, a ping of an IP address in a subnet besides the three connected subnets will fail, as demonstrated in Example 14-2. Note that this example assumes that Albuquerque still only knows the three connected routes shown in Example 14-1.

Example 14-2   *Albuquerque Pings—Works to Connected Subnets Only*

```
! This first ping is a ping of Yosemite's S0/0/1 interface
Albuquerque#ping 10.1.128.252
Type escape sequence to abort.
Sending 5, 100-byte ICMP Echos to 10.1.128.252, timeout is 2 seconds:
!!!!!
Success rate is 100 percent (5/5), round-trip min/avg/max = 4/4/8 ms
```

Example 14-2 *Albuquerque Pings—Works to Connected Subnets Only (Continued)*

```
! This next ping is a ping of Yosemite's Fa0/0 interface
Albuquerque#ping 10.1.2.252
Type escape sequence to abort.
Sending 5, 100-byte ICMP Echos to 10.1.2.252, timeout is 2 seconds:
.....
Success rate is 0 percent (0/5)
```

The **ping** command sends an ICMP echo request packet to the stated destination address. The TCP/IP software at the destination then replies to the ping echo request packet with a similar packet, called an *ICMP echo reply*. The **ping** command sends the first packet and waits on the response. If a response is received, the command displays a "!". If no response is received within the default timeout of 2 seconds, the **ping** command displays a ".". The Cisco IOS software **ping** command sends five of these packets by default.

In Example 14-2, the **ping 10.1.128.252** command works (showing all !'s), because Albuquerque's route to 10.1.128.0/24 matches the destination address of 10.1.128.252. However, the **ping** to 10.1.2.252 does not work, because Albuquerque does not have a route for the subnet in which 10.1.2.252 resides, subnet 10.1.2.0/24. As a result, Albuquerque cannot even send the five ping packets, so the output lists five periods.

The simple and typical solution to this problem is to configure a routing protocol on all three routers. However, you can configure static routes instead. Example 14-3 shows two **ip route** global configuration commands on Albuquerque, which add static routes for the two LAN subnets connected to Yosemite and Seville. The addition of the first of the two **ip route** commands makes the failed ping from Example 14-2 work.

Example 14-3 *Static Routes Added to Albuquerque*

```
Albuquerque#configure terminal
Albuquerque(config)#ip route  10.1.2.0 255.255.255.0  10.1.128.252
Albuquerque(config)#ip route  10.1.3.0 255.255.255.0  10.1.130.253
Albuquerque#show ip route static
      10.0.0.0/24 is subnetted, 5 subnets
S        10.1.3.0 [1/0] via 10.1.130.253
S        10.1.2.0 [1/0] via 10.1.128.252
```

Key Topic

The **ip route** global configuration command supplies the subnet number, mask, and the next-hop IP address. One **ip route** command defines a route to 10.1.2.0 (mask 255.255.255.0), which is located off Yosemite, so the next-hop IP address as configured on Albuquerque is 10.1.128.252, which is Yosemite's Serial0/0/1 IP address. Similarly, Albuquerque's route to 10.1.3.0/24, the subnet off Seville, points to Seville's Serial0/0/1 IP address, 10.1.130.253. Note that the next-hop IP address should be an IP address in a directly connected subnet. Now Albuquerque knows how to forward routes to both subnets.

Whereas you can see all routes using the **show ip route** command, the **show ip route static** command lists only statically configured IP routes. The "S" in the first column means that these two routes were statically configured. Also, to actually be added to the IP routing table, the **ip route** command must be configured, and the outgoing interface implied by the next-hop router IP address must be in an "up and up" state. For example, the next-hop address on the first **ip route** command is 10.1.128.252, which is in the subnet connected to Albuquerque's S0/0/1 interface. If Albuquerque's S0/0/1 interface is not currently in an "up and up" state, this static route would not be listed in the IP routing table.

The **ip route** command allows a slightly different syntax on point-to-point serial links. For such links, you can configure the outgoing interface instead of the next-hop IP address. For instance, you could have configured **ip route 10.1.2.0 255.255.255.0 serial0/0/1** for the first route in Example 14-3.

Unfortunately, adding these two static routes to Albuquerque does not solve all the network's routing problems—you would also need to configure static routes on the other two routers as well. Currently, the static routes help Albuquerque deliver packets to these two remote LAN subnets, but the other two routers do not have enough routing information to forward packets back toward Albuquerque's LAN subnet (10.1.1.0/24). For instance, PC Bugs cannot ping PC Sam in this network yet. The problem is that although Albuquerque has a route to subnet 10.1.2.0, where Sam resides, Yosemite does not have a route to 10.1.1.0, where Bugs resides. The ping request packet goes from Bugs to Sam correctly, but Sam's ping response packet cannot be routed by the Yosemite router back through Albuquerque to Bugs, so the ping fails.

Extended ping Command

In real life, you might not be able to find a user, like Bugs, to ask to test your network by pinging, and it might be impractical to physically travel to some other site just to type a few **ping** commands on some end-user PCs. A better alternative might be to telnet to a router connected to that user's subnet, and use the IOS **ping** command to try similar tests. However, to make the **ping** command on the router more closely resemble a **ping** issued by the end user requires the extended **ping** command.

The extended IOS **ping** command, available from privileged EXEC mode, allows the CLI user to change many options for what the **ping** command does, including the source IP address used for the ICMP echo requests sent by the command. To see the significance of this option, Example 14-4 shows Albuquerque with the working standard **ping 10.1.2.252** command, but with an extended **ping** command that works similarly to a **ping** from Bugs to Sam—a **ping** that fails in this case, because router Yosemite cannot send the ICMP echo reply back to Albuquerque.

Example 14-4 *Albuquerque: Working Ping After Adding Default Routes, Plus Failing Extended ping*

```
Albuquerque#show ip route static
     10.0.0.0/24 is subnetted, 5 subnets
S       10.1.3.0 [1/0] via 10.1.130.253
S       10.1.2.0 [1/0] via 10.1.128.252
Albuquerque#ping 10.1.2.252

Type escape sequence to abort.
Sending 5, 100-byte ICMP Echos to 10.1.2.252, timeout is 2 seconds:
!!!!!
Success rate is 100 percent (5/5), round-trip min/avg/max = 4/4/8 ms

Albuquerque#ping
Protocol [ip]:
Target IP address: 10.1.2.252
Repeat count [5]:
Datagram size [100]:
Timeout in seconds [2]:
Extended commands [n]: y
Source address or interface: 10.1.128.251
Type of service [0]:
Set DF bit in IP header? [no]:
Validate reply data? [no]:
Data pattern [0xABCD]:
Loose, Strict, Record, Timestamp, Verbose[none]:
Sweep range of sizes [n]:
Type escape sequence to abort.
Sending 5, 100-byte ICMP Echos to 10.1.2.252, timeout is 2 seconds:
. . . . .
Success rate is 0 percent (0/5)
```

The simple (standard) **ping 10.1.2.252** command works for one obvious reason and one not-so-obvious reason. First, Albuquerque can forward a packet to subnet 10.1.2.0 because of the static route. The return packet, sent by Yosemite, is sent to address 10.1.128.251— Albuquerque's Serial0/0/1 IP address. Why? Well, the following points are true about the **ping** command on a Cisco router:

■   The Cisco **ping** command uses, by default, the output interface's IP address as the packet's source address, unless otherwise specified in an extended **ping**. The first ping in Example 14-4 uses a source of 10.1.128.251, because Albuquerque's route used to send the packet to 10.1.2.252 refers to interface Serial0/0/1 as the outgoing interface— and Albuquerque's S0/0/1 interface IP address is 10.1.128.251.

■ Ping response packets reverse the IP addresses used in the original ping request. So, in this example, Albuquerque used 10.1.128.251 as the source IP address of the original packet, so Yosemite uses 10.1.128.251 as the destination of the ping response packet—and Yosemite has a connected route to reach subnet 10.1.128.0/24, which includes address 10.1.128.251.

When you troubleshoot this internetwork, you can use the extended **ping** command to act like you issued a **ping** from a computer on that subnet, without having to call a user and ask to enter a **ping** command for you on the PC. The extended version of the **ping** command can be used to refine the problem's underlying cause by changing several details of what the **ping** command sends in its request. In real networks, when a **ping** from a router works, but a **ping** from a host does not, the extended ping could help you re-create the problem without needing to work with the end user on the phone.

For example, in Example 14-4, the extended **ping** command on Albuquerque uses a source IP address of 10.1.1.251 (Albuquerque's Fa0/0 interface IP address), destined to 10.1.2.252 (Yosemite's Fa0/0 IP address). According to the command output, no ping response was received by Albuquerque. Normally, Albuquerque's **ping** would be sourced from the IP address of the outgoing interface. With the use of the extended ping source address option, the source IP address of the echo packet is set to Albuquerque's Fa0/0 IP address, 10.1.1.251. Because the ICMP echo generated by the extended ping is sourced from an address in subnet 10.1.1.0, the packet looks more like a packet from an end user in that subnet. Yosemite builds a reply, with destination 10.1.1.251—but Yosemite does not have a route to subnet 10.1.1.0/24. So, Yosemite cannot send the ping reply packet back to Albuquerque, causing the ping to fail.

The solution in this case is pretty simple: either add a static route on Yosemite for subnet 10.1.1.0/24, or enable a routing protocol on all three routers.

Default Routes

As part of the routing (forwarding) process, a router compares each packet's destination IP address to the router's routing table. If the router does not match any routes, the router discards the packet, and makes no attempt to recover from the loss.

A *default route* is a route that is considered to match all destination IP addresses. With a default route, when a packet's destination IP address does not match any other routes, the router uses the default route for forwarding the packet.

Default routes work best when only one path exists to a part of the network. For example, in Figure 14-2, R1 is a branch office router with a single serial link connecting it to the rest of the enterprise network. There may be hundreds of subnets located outside R1's branch office. The engineer has three main options for helping R1 know routes to reach all the rest of the subnets:

■ Configure hundreds of static routes on R1—but all of those routes would use S0/1 as R1's outgoing interface, with next-hop IP address 172.16.3.2 (R2).

■ Enable a routing protocol on the routers to learn the routes.

■ Add a default route to R1 with outgoing interface S0/1.

Figure 14-2 *Sample Network in Which a Default Route Is Useful*

R1 Routing Table	
Subnet	Outgoing Interface
Subnet 1	**S0/1**
Subnet 2	**S0/1**
Subnet 3	**S0/1**
•	**S0/1**
•	**S0/1**
•	**S0/1**

By coding a special static route called a default route, R1 can have a single route that forwards all packets out its S0/1 interface toward R2. The **ip route** command lists a special subnet and mask value, each 0.0.0.0, which means "match all packets." Example 14-5 shows the default static route on R1, pointing to R2 (172.16.3.2) as the next-hop router.

Example 14-5 *R1 Static Default Route Configuration and Routing Table*

```
R1(config)#ip route  0.0.0.0  0.0.0.0  172.16.3.2
R1#show ip route
Codes: C - connected, S - static, I - IGRP, R - RIP, M - mobile, B - BGP
       D - EIGRP, EX - EIGRP external, O - OSPF, IA - OSPF inter area
       N1 - OSPF NSSA external type 1, N2 - OSPF NSSA external type 2
       E1 - OSPF external type 1, E2 - OSPF external type 2, E - EGP
       i - IS-IS, L1 - IS-IS level-1, L2 - IS-IS level-2, ia - IS-IS inter area
       * - candidate default, U - per-user static route, o - ODR
       P - periodic downloaded static route
```

continues

Example 14-5   *R1 Static Default Route Configuration and Routing Table (Continued)*

```
Gateway of last resort is 172.16.3.2 to network 0.0.0.0

     172.16.0.0/24 is subnetted, 3 subnets
C       172.16.1.0 is directly connected, FastEthernet0/0
C       172.16.3.0 is directly connected, Serial0/1
S*      0.0.0.0/0 [1/0] via 172.16.3.2
```

The **show ip route** command shows a couple of interesting facts about this special default route. The output lists a code of "S" just like other static routes, but with an * as well. The * means that the route might be used as the default route, meaning it will be used for packets that do not match any other routes in the routing table. Without a default route, a router discards packets that do not match the routing table. With a default route, the router forwards packets that do not match any other routes, as in the case in this example.

> **NOTE**   Chapter 4, "IP Routing," in the *CCNA ICND2 Official Exam Certification Guide*, explains default routes in more detail.

You could use static routes, including static default routes, on all routers in an internetwork. However, most enterprises use a dynamic routing protocol to learn all the routes. The next section covers some additional concepts and terminology for routing protocols, with the remainder of the chapter focusing on how to configure RIP-2.

Routing Protocol Overview

IP routing protocols have one primary goal: to fill the IP routing table with the current best routes it can find. The goal is simple, but the process and options can be complicated.

Routing protocols help routers learn routes by having each router advertise the routes it knows. Each router begins by knowing only connected routes. Then, each router sends messages, defined by the routing protocol, that list the routes. When a router hears a routing update message from another router, the router hearing the update learns about the subnets and adds routes to its routing table. If all the routers participate, all the routers can learn about all subnets in an internetwork.

When learning routes, routing protocols must also prevent loops from occurring. A loop occurs when a packet keeps coming back to the same router due to errors in the routes in the collective routers' routing tables. These loops can occur with routing protocols, unless the routing protocol makes an effort to avoid the loops.

This section starts by explaining how RIP-2 works in a little more detail than was covered in Chapter 5. Following that, the various IP routing protocols are compared.

RIP-2 Basic Concepts

Routers using RIP-2 advertise a small amount of simple information about each subnet to their neighbors. Their neighbors in turn advertise the information to their neighbors, and so on, until all routers have learned the information. In fact, it works a lot like how rumors spread in a neighborhood, school, or company. You might be out in the yard, stop to talk to your next-door neighbor, and tell your neighbor the latest gossip. Then, that neighbor sees his other next-door neighbor, and tells them the same bit of gossip—and so on, until everyone in the neighborhood knows the latest gossip. Distance vector protocols work the same way, but hopefully, unlike rumors in a real neighborhood, the rumor has not changed by the time everyone has heard about it.

For example, consider what occurs in Figure 14-3. The figure shows RIP-2 advertising a subnet number, mask (shown in prefix notation), and metric to its neighbors.

Figure 14-3   *Example of How RIP-2 Advertises Routes*

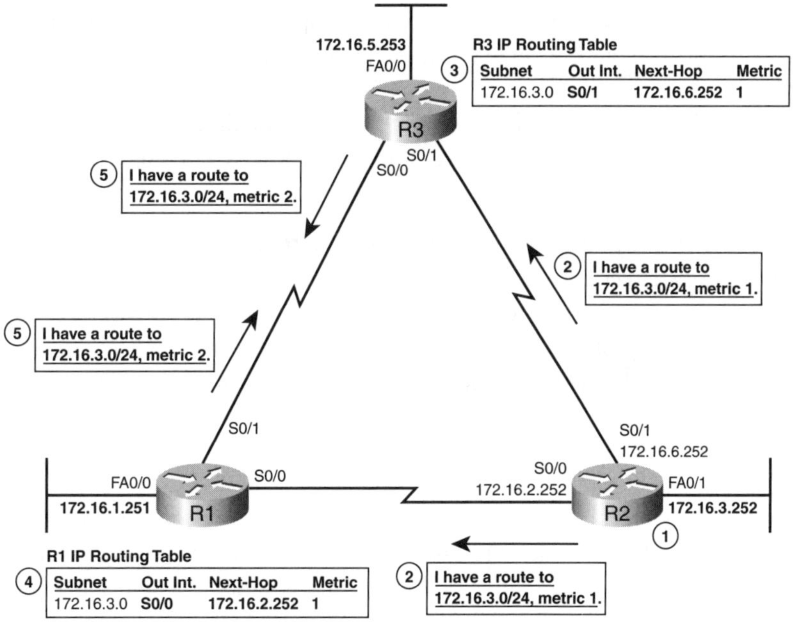

For the sake of keeping the figure less cluttered, Figure 14-3 only shows how the routers advertise and learn routes for subnet 172.16.3.0/24, even though the routers do advertise about other routes as well. Following the steps in the figure:

1.   Router R2 learns a connected route for subnet 172.16.3.0/24.

2.   R2 sends a *routing update* to its neighbors, listing a subnet (172.16.3.0), mask (/24), and a distance, or metric (1 in this case).

3.   R3 hears the routing update, and adds a route to its routing table for subnet 172.16.3.0/24, referring to R2 as the next-hop router.

4.   Around the same time, R1 also hears the routing update sent directly to R1 by R2. R1 then adds a route to its routing table for subnet 172.16.3.0/24, referring to R2 as the next-hop router.

5.   R1 and R3 then send a routing update to each other, for subnet 172.16.3.0/24, metric 2.

By the end of this process, both R1 and R3 have heard of two possible routes to reach subnet 172.16.3.0/24—one with metric 1, and one with metric 2. Each router uses its respective lower-metric (metric 1) routes to reach 172.16.3.0.

Interestingly, distance vector protocols such as RIP-2 repeat this process continually on a periodic basis. For example, RIP routers send periodic routing updates about every 30 seconds by default. As long as the routers continue to hear the same routes, with the same metrics, the routers' routing tables do not need to change. However, when something changes, the next routing update will change or simply not occur due to some failure, so the routers will react and converge to use the then-best working routes.

Now that you have seen the basics of one routing protocol, the next section explains a wide variety of features of different routing protocols for the sake of comparison.

Comparing and Contrasting IP Routing Protocols

IP's long history and continued popularity has driven the need for several different competing routing protocols over time. So, it is helpful to make comparisons between the different IP routing protocols to see their relative strengths and weaknesses. This section describes several technical points on which the routing protocols can be compared. Then, this chapter examines RIP-2 in more detail; the *CCNA ICND2 Official Exam Certification Guide* explains OSPF and EIGRP in more detail.

One of the first points of comparison is whether the protocol is defined in RFCs, making it a public standard, or whether it is Cisco proprietary. Another very important consideration is whether the routing protocol supports variable-length subnet masking (VLSM). Although the details of VLSM are not covered in this book, but instead are covered in the *CCNA ICND2 Official Exam Certification Guide*, VLSM support is an important consideration today. This section introduces several different terms and concepts used to compare the various IP routing protocols, with Table 14-4 at the end of this section summarizing the comparison points for many of the IP routing protocols.

Interior and Exterior Routing Protocols

IP routing protocols fall into one of two major categories:

- **Interior Gateway Protocol (IGP):** A routing protocol that was designed and intended for use inside a single autonomous system

- **Exterior Gateway Protocol (EGP):** A routing protocol that was designed and intended for use between different autonomous systems

Key
Topic

> **NOTE** The terms IGP and EGP include the word *gateway* because routers used to be called gateways.

These definitions use another new term: *autonomous system*. An autonomous system is an internetwork under the administrative control of a single organization. For instance, an internetwork created and paid for by a single company is probably a single autonomous system, and an internetwork created by a single school system is probably a single autonomous system. Other examples include large divisions of a state or national government, where different government agencies may be able to build their own separate internetworks.

Some routing protocols work best inside a single autonomous system, by design, so these routing protocols are called IGPs. Conversely, only one routing protocol, *Border Gateway Protocol (BGP)*, is used today to exchange routes between routers in different autonomous systems, so it is called an EGP.

Each autonomous system can be assigned a number, called (unsurprisingly) an *autonomous system number (ASN)*. Like public IP addresses, the Internet Corporation for Assigned Network Numbers (ICANN) controls the worldwide rights to assign ASNs, delegating that authority to other organizations around the planet, typically to the same organizations that assign public IP addresses. By assigning each autonomous organization an ASN, BGP can ensure that packets do not loop around the global Internet by making sure that packets do not pass through the same autonomous system twice.

Figure 14-4 shows a small view into the worldwide Internet. Two companies and three ISPs use IGPs (OSPF and EIGRP) inside their own networks, with BGP being used between the ASNs.

Figure 14-4   *Comparing Locations for Using IGPs and EGPs*

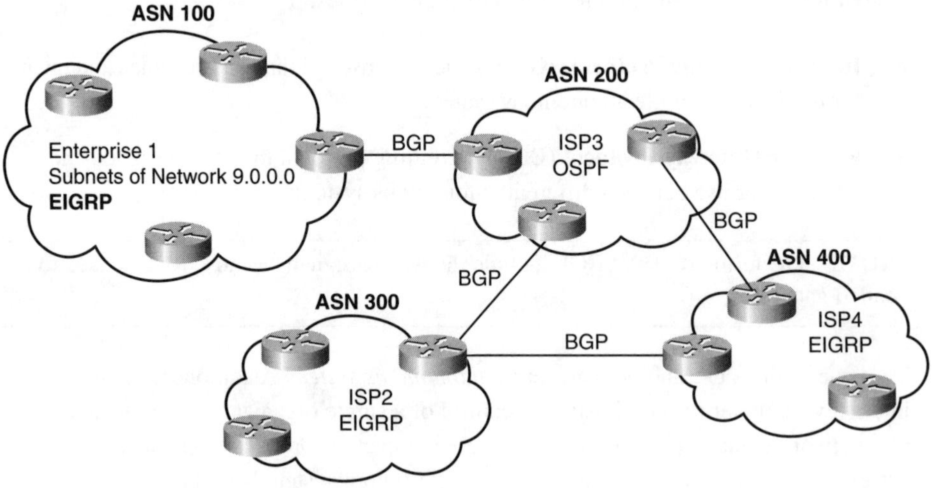

Routing Protocol Types/Algorithms

Each IGP can be classified as using a particular class, or type, of underlying logic. Table 14-2 lists the three options, noting which IGPs use which class of algorithm.

Table 14-2   *Routing Protocol Classes/Algorithms and Protocols that Use Them*

Class/Algorithm	IGPs
Distance vector	RIP-1, RIP-2, IGRP
Link-state	OSPF, Integrated IS-IS
Balanced hybrid (also called advanced distance vector)	EIGRP

The *CCNA ICND2 Official Exam Certification Guide* covers the theory behind each of these classes of routing protocols. However, because the only IGP this book covers to any level of detail is RIP-2, most of the conceptual materials in this chapter actually show how distance vector protocols work.

Metrics

Routing protocols must have some way to decide which route is best when a router learns of more than one route to reach a subnet. To that end, each routing protocol defines a *metric* that gives an objective numeric value to the "goodness" of each route. The lower the metric, the better the route. For example, earlier, in Figure 14-3, R1 learned a metric 1 route for subnet 172.16.3.0/24 from R2, and a metric 2 route for that same subnet from R3, so R1 chose the lower-metric (1) route through R2.

Some metrics work better than others. To see why, consider Figure 14-5. The figure shows two analyses of the same basic internetwork, focusing on router B's choice of a route to reach subnet 10.1.1.0, which is on the LAN on the left side of router A. In this case, the link between A and B is only a 64-kbps link, whereas the other two links are T1s, running at 1.544 Mbps each. The top part of the figure shows router B's choice of route when using RIP (Version 1 or Version 2), whereas the bottom part of the figure shows router B's choice when the internetwork uses EIGRP.

Figure 14-5 *Comparing the Effect of the RIP and EIGRP Metrics*

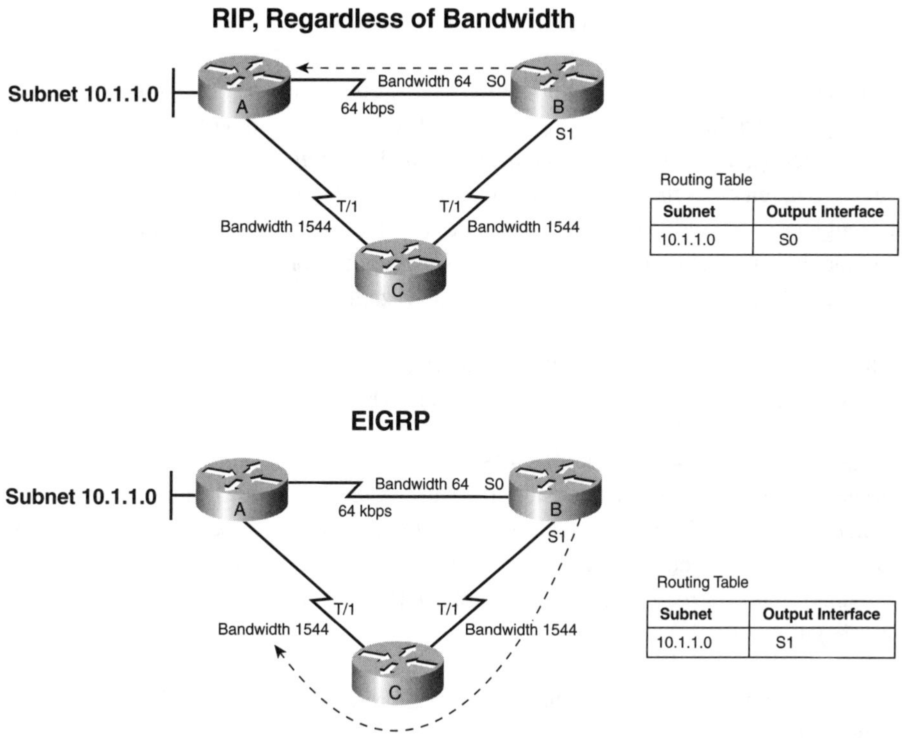

RIP uses a metric called hop count, which measures the number of routers (hops) between a router and a subnet. With RIP, router B would learn two routes to reach subnet 10.1.1.0: a one-hop route through router A, and a two-hop route first through router C and then to router A. So, router B, using RIP, would add a route for subnet 10.1.1.0 pointing to router A as the next-hop IP address (represented as the dashed line in Figure 14-5).

EIGRP, on the other hand, uses a metric that (by default) considers both the interface bandwidth and interface delay settings as input into a mathematical formula to calculate the metric. If routers A, B, and C were configured with correct **bandwidth** interface subcommands, as listed in Figure 14-5, EIGRP would add a route for subnet 10.1.1.0 to its routing table, but with router C as the next-hop router, again shown with a dashed line.

> **NOTE**   For a review of the **bandwidth** command, refer to the section "Bandwidth and Clock Rate on Serial Interfaces" in Chapter 13, "Operating Cisco Routers."

Autosummarization and Manual Summarization

Routers generally perform routing (forwarding) more quickly with smaller routing tables, and less quickly with larger routing tables. Route summarization helps shorten the routing table while retaining all the needed routes in the network.

Two general types of route summarization can be done, with varying support for these two types depending on the routing protocol. The two types, both of which are introduced in this section, are called *autosummarization* and *manual summarization*. Manual summarization gives the network engineer a great deal of control and flexibility, allowing the engineer to choose what summary routes to advertise, instead of just being able to summarize with a classful network. As a result, support for manual summarization is the more useful feature as compared to autosummarization.

Chapter 5 in the *CCNA ICND2 Official Exam Certification Guide* explains both autosummarization and manual summarization in great detail.

Classless and Classful Routing Protocols

Some routing protocols must consider the Class A, B, or C network number that a subnet resides in when performing some of its tasks. Other routing protocols can ignore Class A, B, and C rules altogether. Routing protocols that must consider class rules are called *classful routing protocols*; those that do not need to consider class rules are called *classless routing protocols*.

Classless routing protocols and classful routing protocols are identified by the same three criteria, as summarized in Table 14-3.

Table 14-3   *Comparing Classless and Classful Routing Protocols*

Feature	Classless	Classful
Supports VLSM	Yes	No
Sends subnet mask in routing updates	Yes	No
Supports manual route summarization	Yes	No

Convergence

The term *convergence* refers to the overall process that occurs with routing protocols when something changes in a network topology. When a link comes up or fails, or when a router fails or is first turned on, the possible routes in the internetwork change. The processes used by routing protocols to recognize the changes, to figure out the now-best routes to each subnet, and to change all the routers' routing tables, is called convergence.

Some routing protocols converge more quickly than others. As you might imagine, the capability to converge quickly is important, because in some cases, until convergence completes, users might not be able to send their packets to particular subnets. (Table 14-4 in the next section summarizes the relative convergence speed of various IP routing protocols, along with other information.)

Miscellaneous Comparison Points

Two other minor comparison points between the various IGPs are interesting as well. First, the original routing protocol standards defined that routing updates should be sent to the IP all-local-hosts broadcast address of 255.255.255.255. After those original routing protocols were defined, IP multicast emerged, which allowed newer routing protocols to send routing updates only to other interested routers by using various IP multicast IP addresses.

The earlier IGPs did not include any authentication features. As time went on, it became obvious that attackers could form a denial-of-service (DoS) attack by causing problems with routing protocols. For example, an attacker could connect a router to a network and advertise lots of lower-metric routes for many subnets, causing the packets to be routed to the wrong place—and possibly copied by the attacker. The later-defined IGPs typically support some type of authentication, hoping to mitigate the exposure to these types of DoS attacks.

Summary of Interior Routing Protocols

For convenient comparison and study, Table 14-4 summarizes the most important features of interior routing protocols. Note that the most important routing protocol for the ICND1 exam is RIP, specifically RIP-2. The ICND2 and CCNA exams include more detailed coverage of RIP-2 theory, as well as the theory, configuration, and troubleshooting of OSPF and EIGRP.

Table 14-4 *Interior IP Routing Protocols Compared*

Feature	RIP-1	RIP-2	EIGRP	OSPF	IS-IS
Classless	No	Yes	Yes	Yes	Yes
Supports VLSM	No	Yes	Yes	Yes	Yes
Sends mask in update	No	Yes	Yes	Yes	Yes
Distance vector	Yes	Yes	No[1]	No	No
Link-state	No	No	No[1]	Yes	Yes
Supports autosummarization	Yes	Yes	Yes	No	No
Supports manual summarization	No	Yes	Yes	Yes	Yes
Proprietary	No	No	Yes	No	No
Routing updates sent to a multicast IP address	No	Yes	Yes	Yes	N/A
Supports authentication	No	Yes	Yes	Yes	Yes
Convergence	Slow	Slow	Very fast	Fast	Fast

1. EIGRP is often described as a balanced hybrid routing protocol, instead of link-state or distance vector. Some
   documents refer to EIGRP as an advanced distance vector protocol.

> **NOTE**   For reference, IGRP has the same characteristics as RIP-1 in Table 14-4, with the
> exception that IGRP is proprietary and RIP-1 is not.

Configuring and Verifying RIP-2

RIP-2 configuration is actually somewhat simple as compared to the concepts related to
routing protocols. The configuration process uses three required commands, with only one
command, the **network** command, requiring any real thought. You should also know the
more-popular **show** commands for helping you analyze and troubleshoot routing protocols.

RIP-2 Configuration

The RIP-2 configuration process takes only the following three required steps, with the
possibility that the third step might need to be repeated:

Step 1   Use the **router rip** configuration command to move into RIP configuration mode.

Step 2   Use the **version 2** RIP subcommand to tell the router to use RIP Version
2 exclusively.

Step 3   Use one or more **network** *net-number* RIP subcommands to enable RIP on the correct interfaces.

Step 4   (Optional) As needed, disable RIP on an interface using the **passive-interface** *type number* RIP subcommand.

Of the required first three steps, only the third step—the RIP **network** command— requires much thought. Each RIP **network** command enables RIP on a set of interfaces. The RIP **network** command only uses a classful network number as its one parameter. For any of the router's interface IP addresses in that entire classful network, the router does the following three things:

■   The router multicasts routing updates to a reserved IP multicast IP address, 224.0.0.9.

Key
Topic

■   The router listens for incoming updates on that same interface.

■   The router advertises about the subnet connected to the interface.

Sample RIP Configuration

Keeping these facts in mind, now consider how to configure RIP on a single router. Examine Figure 14-6 for a moment and try to apply the first three configuration steps to this router and anticipate the configuration required on the router to enable RIP on all interfaces.

Figure 14-6 *RIP-2 Configuration: Sample Router with Four Interfaces*

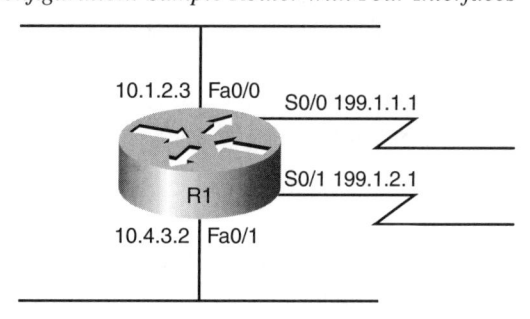

The first two configuration commands are easy, **router rip**, followed by **version 2**, with no parameters to choose. Then you need to pick which **network** commands need to be configured at Step 3. To match interface S0/0, you have to figure out that address 199.1.1.1 is in Class C IP network 199.1.1.0, meaning you need a **network 199.1.1.0** RIP subcommand. Similarly, to match interface S0/1, you need a **network 199.1.2.0** command, because IP address 199.1.2.1 is in Class C network 199.1.2.0. Finally, both of the LAN interfaces have an IP address in Class A network 10.0.0.0, so a single **network 10.0.0.0** command matches both interfaces. Example 14-6 shows the entire configuration process, with all five configuration commands.

Example 14-6 *Sample Router Configuration with RIP Enabled*

```
R1#configure terminal
R1(config)#router rip
R1(config-router)#version 2
R1(config-router)#network 199.1.1.0
R1(config-router)#network 199.1.2.0
R1(config-router)#network 10.0.0.0
```

With this configuration, R1 starts using RIP—sending RIP updates, listening for incoming RIP updates, and advertising about the connected subnet—on each of its four interfaces. However, imagine that for some reason you wanted to enable RIP on R1's Fa0/0 interface, but did not want to enable RIP on Fa0/1's interface. Both interfaces are in network 10.0.0.0, so both are matched by the **network 10.0.0.0** command.

RIP configuration does not provide a way to enable RIP on only some of the interfaces in a single Class A, B, or C network. So, if you needed to enable RIP only on R1's Fa0/0 interface, and not on the Fa0/1 interface, you would actually need to use the **network 10.0.0.0** command to enable RIP on both interfaces, and then disable the sending of RIP updates on Fa0/1 using the **passive-interface** *type number* RIP subcommand. For example, to enable RIP on all interfaces of router R1 in Figure 14-6, except for Fa0/1, you could use the same configuration in Example 14-6, but then also add the **passive-interface fa0/1** subcommand while in RIP configuration mode. This command tells R1 to stop sending RIP updates out its Fa0/1 interface, disabling one of the main functions of RIP.

> **NOTE** The **passive-interface** command only stops the sending of RIP updates on the interface. Other features outside the scope of this book could be used to disable the processing of received updates and the advertisement of the connected subnet.

One final note on the **network** command: IOS will actually accept a parameter besides a classful network number on the command, and IOS does not supply an error message, either. However, IOS, knowing that the parameter must be a classful network number, changes the command. For example, if you typed **network 10.1.2.3** in RIP configuration mode, IOS would accept the command, with no error messages. However, when you look at the configuration, you would see a **network 10.0.0.0** command, and the **network 10.1.2.3** command that you had typed would not be there. The **network 10.0.0.0** command would indeed match all interfaces in network 10.0.0.0.

RIP-2 Verification

IOS includes three primary **show** commands that are helpful to confirm how well RIP-2 is working. Table 14-5 lists the commands and their main purpose.

Table 14-5 *RIP Operational Commands*

Command	Purpose
show ip interface brief	Lists one line per router interface, including the IP address and interface status; an interface must have an IP address, and be in an "up and up" status, before RIP begins to work on the interface.
show ip route [rip]	Lists the routing table, including RIP-learned routes, and optionally just RIP-learned routes.
show ip protocols	Lists information about the RIP configuration, plus the IP addresses of neighboring RIP routers from which the local router has learned routes.

To better understand these commands, this section uses the internetwork shown in Figure 14-1. First, consider the RIP-2 configuration required on each of the three routers. All three interfaces on all three routers are in classful network 10.0.0.0. So each router needs only one **network** command, **network 10.0.0.0**, to match all three of its interfaces. The configuration needs to be the same on all three routers, as follows:

```
router rip
 version 2
 network 10.0.0.0
```

Now, to focus on the **show** commands, Example 14-7 lists a couple of variations of the **show ip route** command, with some explanations in the example, and some following the example. Following that, Example 14-8 focuses on the **show ip protocols** command. Note that Example 14-1, earlier in this chapter, shows the output from the **show ip interfaces brief** command on the Albuquerque router, so it is not repeated here.

Example 14-7 *The **show ip route** Command*

```
Albuquerque#show ip route
Codes: C - connected, S - static, R - RIP, M - mobile, B - BGP
       D - EIGRP, EX - EIGRP external, O - OSPF, IA - OSPF inter area
       N1 - OSPF NSSA external type 1, N2 - OSPF NSSA external type 2
       E1 - OSPF external type 1, E2 - OSPF external type 2
       i - IS-IS, su - IS-IS summary, L1 - IS-IS level-1, L2 - IS-IS level-2
       ia - IS-IS inter area, * - candidate default, U - per-user static route
       o - ODR, P - periodic downloaded static route
Gateway of last resort is not set

     10.0.0.0/24 is subnetted, 6 subnets
R       10.1.3.0 [120/1] via 10.1.130.253, 00:00:16, Serial0/1/0
R       10.1.2.0 [120/1] via 10.1.128.252, 00:00:09, Serial0/0/1
C       10.1.1.0 is directly connected, FastEthernet0/0
```

continues

Example 14-7 *The* **show ip route** *Command (Continued)*

```
C        10.1.130.0 is directly connected, Serial0/1/0

R        10.1.129.0 [120/1] via 10.1.130.253, 00:00:16, Serial0/1/0
                    [120/1] via 10.1.128.252, 00:00:09, Serial0/0/1
C        10.1.128.0 is directly connected, Serial0/0/1
!
! The next command lists just the RIP routes, so no code legend is listed
!
Albuquerque#show ip route rip
     10.0.0.0/24 is subnetted, 6 subnets
R        10.1.3.0 [120/1] via 10.1.130.253, 00:00:20, Serial0/1/0
R        10.1.2.0 [120/1] via 10.1.128.252, 00:00:13, Serial0/0/1
R        10.1.129.0 [120/1] via 10.1.130.253, 00:00:20, Serial0/1/0
                    [120/1] via 10.1.128.252, 00:00:13, Serial0/0/1
!
! The next command lists the route matched by this router for packets going to the
! listed IP address 10.1.2.1.
!
Albuquerque#show ip route 10.1.2.1
Routing entry for 10.1.2.0/24
  Known via "rip", distance 120, metric 1
  Redistributing via rip
  Last update from 10.1.128.252 on Serial0/0/1, 00:00:18 ago
  Routing Descriptor Blocks:
  * 10.1.128.252, from 10.1.128.252, 00:00:18 ago, via Serial0/0/1
      Route metric is 1, traffic share count is 1
!
! The same command again, but for an address that does not have a matching route in
! the routing table.
Albuquerque#show ip route 10.1.7.1
% Subnet not in table
Albuquerque#
```

Interpreting the Output of the show ip route Command

Example 14-7 shows the **show ip route** command, which lists all IP routes, the **show ip route rip** command, which lists only RIP-learned routes, and the **show ip route** *address* command, which lists details about the route matched for packets sent to the listed IP address. Focusing on the **show ip route** command, note that the legend lists "R," which means that a route has been learned by RIP, and that three of the routes list an R beside them. Next, examine the details in the route for subnet 10.1.3.0/24, highlighted in the example. The important details are as follows:

■ The subnet number is listed, with the mask in the heading line above.

■ The next-hop router's IP address, 10.1.130.253, which is Seville's S0/0/1 IP address.

■ Albuquerque's S0/1/0 interface is the outgoing interface.

■ The length of time since Albuquerque last heard about this route in a periodic RIP update, 20 seconds ago in this case.

■ The RIP metric for this route (1 in this case), listed as the second number in the square brackets. For example, between Albuquerque and subnet 10.1.3.0/24, one other router (Seville) exists.

■ The administrative distance of the route (120 in this case; the first number in brackets).

Take the time now to review the other two RIP routes, noting the values for these various items in those routes. As you can see, the **show ip route rip** command output lists the routes in the exact same format, the difference being that only RIP-learned routes are shown, and the legend is not displayed at the top of the command output. The **show ip route** *address* command lists more detailed output about the route that matches the destination IP address listed in the command, with the command output supplying more detailed information about the route.

Administrative Distance

When an internetwork has redundant links, and uses a single routing protocol, each router may learn multiple routes to reach a particular subnet. As stated earlier in this chapter, the routing protocol then uses a metric to choose the best route, and the router adds that route to its routing table.

In some cases, internetworks use multiple IP routing protocols. In such cases, a router might learn of multiple routes to a particular subnet using different routing protocols. In these cases, the metric does not help the router choose which route is best, because each routing protocol uses a metric unique to that routing protocol. For example, RIP uses the hop count as the metric, but EIGRP uses a math formula with bandwidth and delay as inputs. A route with RIP metric 1 might need to be compared to an EIGRP route, to the same subnet, but with metric 4,132,768. (Yes, EIGRP metrics tend to be large numbers.) Because the numbers have different meanings, there is no real value in comparing the metrics.

The router still needs to choose the best route, so IOS solves this problem by assigning a numeric value to each routing protocol. IOS then chooses the route whose routing protocol has the lower number. This number is called the *administrative distance (AD)*. For example, EIGRP defaults to use an AD of 90, and RIP defaults to use the value of 120, as seen in the routes in Example 14-7. So, an EIGRP route to a subnet would be chosen instead of a competing RIP route. Table 14-6 lists the AD values for the most common sources of routing information.

Table 14-6 *IOS Defaults for Administrative Distance*

Route Source	Administrative Distance
Connected routes	0
Static routes	1
EIGRP	90
IGRP	100
OSPF	110
IS-IS	115
RIP (V1 and V2)	120
Unknown or unbelievable	255

While this may be a brief tangent away from RIP and routing protocols, now that this chapter has explained administrative distance, the concept behind a particular type of static route, called a *backup static route*, can be explained. Static routes have a default AD that is better than all routing protocols, so if a router has a static route defined for a subnet, and the routing protocol learns a route to the same subnet, the static route will be added to the routing table. However, in some cases, the static route is intended to be used only if the routing protocol fails to learn a route. In these cases, an individual static route can be configured with an AD higher than the routing protocol, making the routing protocol more believable.

For example, the **ip route 10.1.1.0 255.255.255.0 10.2.2.2 150** command sets this static route's AD to 150, which is higher than all the default AD settings in Table 14-6. If RIP-2 learned a route to 10.1.1.0/24 on this same router, the router would place the RIP-learned route into the routing table, assuming a default AD of 120, which is better than the static route's AD in this case.

The show ip protocols Command

The final command for examining RIP operations is the **show ip protocols** command. This command identifies some of the details of RIP operation. Example 14-8 lists the output of this command, again on Albuquerque. Due to the variety of information in the command output, the example includes many comments inside the example.

Example 14-8 *The* **show ip protocols** *Command*

```
Albuquerque#show ip protocols
Routing Protocol is "rip"
  Outgoing update filter list for all interfaces is not set
  Incoming update filter list for all interfaces is not set
!
! The next line identifies the time interval for periodic routing updates, and when this
! router will send its next update.
  Sending updates every 30 seconds, next due in 22 seconds
  Invalid after 180 seconds, hold down 180, flushed after 240
  Redistributing: rip
!
! The next few lines result from the version 2 command being configured
  Default version control: send version 2, receive version 2
    Interface          Send  Recv  Triggered RIP  Key-chain
    FastEthernet0/0      2    2
    Serial0/0/1          2    2
    Serial0/1/0          2    2
  Automatic network summarization is in effect
  Maximum path: 4
!
! The next two lines reflect the fact that this router has a single network command,
! namely network 10.0.0.0. If other network commands were configured, these networks
! would also be listed.
  Routing for Networks:
    10.0.0.0
!
! The next section lists the IP addresses of neighboring routers from which Albuquerque
! has received routing updates, and the time since this router last heard from the
! neighbors. Note 10.1.130.253 is Seville, and 10.1.128.252 is Yosemite.
  Routing Information Sources:
    Gateway         Distance      Last Update
    10.1.130.253         120      00:00:25
    10.1.128.252         120      00:00:20
  Distance: (default is 120)
```

Of particular importance for real-life troubleshooting and for the exam, focus on both the version information and the routing information sources. If you forget to configure the **version 2** command on one router, that router will send only RIP-1 updates by default, and the column labeled "Send" would list a 1 instead of a 2. The other routers, only listening for Version 2 updates, could not learn routes from this router.

Also, a quick way to find out if the local router is hearing RIP updates from the correct routers is to look at the list of routing information sources listed at the end of the **show ip protocols** command. For example, given the internetwork in Figure 14-1, you should expect Albuquerque to receive updates from two other routers (Yosemite and Seville). The end of Example 14-8 shows exactly that, with Albuquerque having heard from both routers in the last 30 seconds. If only one router was listed in this command's output, you could figure out which one Albuquerque was hearing from, and then investigate the problem with the missing router.

Examining RIP Messages with debug

The best way to understand whether RIP is doing its job is to use the **debug ip rip** command. This command enables a debug option that tells the router to generate log messages each time the router sends and receives a RIP update. These messages include information about every subnet listed in those advertisements as well, and the meaning of the messages is relatively straightforward.

Example 14-9 shows the output generated by the **debug ip rip** command on the Albuquerque router, based on Figure 14-1. Note that to see these messages, the user needs to be connected to the console of the router, or use the **terminal monitor** privileged mode EXEC command if using Telnet or SSH to connect to the router. The notes inside the example describe some of the meaning of the messages, in five different groups. The first three groups of messages describe Albuquerque's updates sent on each of its three RIP-enabled interfaces; the fourth group includes messages generated when Albuquerque receives an update from Seville; and the last group describes the update received from Yosemite.

Example 14-9 *Example RIP Debug Output*

```
Albuquerque#debug ip rip
RIP protocol debugging is on
Albuquerque#

! Update sent by Albuquerque out Fa0/0:
! The next two messages tell you that the local router is sending a version 2 update
! on Fa0/0, to the 224.0.0.9 multicast IP address. Following that, 5 lines list the
! 5 subnets listed in the advertisement.
*Jun  9 14:35:08.855: RIP: sending v2 update to 224.0.0.9 via FastEthernet0/0 (10.1.1.251)
*Jun  9 14:35:08.855: RIP: build update entries
*Jun  9 14:35:08.855:    10.1.2.0/24 via 0.0.0.0, metric 2, tag 0
*Jun  9 14:35:08.855:    10.1.3.0/24 via 0.0.0.0, metric 2, tag 0
*Jun  9 14:35:08.855:    10.1.128.0/24 via 0.0.0.0, metric 1, tag 0
*Jun  9 14:35:08.855:    10.1.129.0/24 via 0.0.0.0, metric 2, tag 0
*Jun  9 14:35:08.855:    10.1.130.0/24 via 0.0.0.0, metric 1, tag 0
```

Example 14-9 *Example RIP Debug Output (Continued)*

```
! The next 5 debug messages state that this local router is sending an update on its
! S0/1/0 interface, listing 3 subnets/masks
*Jun  9 14:35:10.351: RIP: sending v2 update to 224.0.0.9 via Serial0/1/0 (10.1.130.251)
*Jun  9 14:35:10.351: RIP: build update entries
*Jun  9 14:35:10.351:    10.1.1.0/24 via 0.0.0.0, metric 1, tag 0
*Jun  9 14:35:10.351:    10.1.2.0/24 via 0.0.0.0, metric 2, tag 0
*Jun  9 14:35:10.351:    10.1.128.0/24 via 0.0.0.0, metric 1, tag 0

! The next 5 debug messages state that this local router is sending an update on its
! S0/0/1 interface, listing 3 subnets/masks
*Jun  9 14:35:12.443: RIP: sending v2 update to 224.0.0.9 via Serial0/0/1 (10.1.128.251)
*Jun  9 14:35:12.443: RIP: build update entries
*Jun  9 14:35:12.443:    10.1.1.0/24 via 0.0.0.0, metric 1, tag 0
*Jun  9 14:35:12.443:    10.1.3.0/24 via 0.0.0.0, metric 2, tag 0
*Jun  9 14:35:12.443:    10.1.130.0/24 via 0.0.0.0, metric 1, tag 0

! The next 4 messages are about a RIP version 2 (v2) update received by Albuquerque
! from Seville (S0/1/0), listing three subnets. Note the mask is listed as /24.
*Jun  9 14:35:13.819: RIP: received v2 update from 10.1.130.253 on Serial0/1/0
*Jun  9 14:35:13.819:       10.1.2.0/24 via 0.0.0.0 in 2 hops
*Jun  9 14:35:13.819:       10.1.3.0/24 via 0.0.0.0 in 1 hops
*Jun  9 14:35:13.819:       10.1.129.0/24 via 0.0.0.0 in 1 hops

! The next 4 messages are about a RIP version 2 (v2) update received by Albuquerque
! from Yosemite (S0/0/1), listing three subnets. Note the mask is listed as /24.
*Jun  9 14:35:16.911: RIP: received v2 update from 10.1.128.252 on Serial0/0/1
*Jun  9 14:35:16.915:       10.1.2.0/24 via 0.0.0.0 in 1 hops
*Jun  9 14:35:16.915:       10.1.3.0/24 via 0.0.0.0 in 2 hops
*Jun  9 14:35:16.915:       10.1.129.0/24 via 0.0.0.0 in 1 hops

Albuquerque#undebug all
All possible debugging has been turned off
Albuquerque#show process
CPU utilization for five seconds: 0%/0%; one minute: 0%; five minutes: 0%
 PID QTy      PC Runtime (ms)    Invoked    uSecs    Stacks TTY Process
   1 Cwe 601B2AE8          0          1        0 5608/6000   0 Chunk Manager
```

First, if you take a broader look at the five sets of messages, it helps reinforce the expected updates that Albuquerque should both send and receive. The messages state that Albuquerque is sending updates on Fa0/0, S0/0/1, and S0/1/0, on which RIP should be enabled. Additionally, other messages state that the router received updates on interface S0/1/0, which is the link connected to Seville, and S0/0/1, which is the link connected to Yosemite.

Most of the details in the messages can be easily guessed. Some messages mention "v2," for RIP Version 2, and the fact that the messages are being sent to multicast IP address 224.0.0.9. (RIP-1 sends updates to the 255.255.255.255 broadcast address.) The majority of the messages in the example describe the routing information listed in each update, specifically the subnet and prefix length (mask), and the metric.

A close examination of the number of subnets in each routing update shows that the routers do not advertise all routes in the updates. In Figure 14-1, six subnets exist. However, the updates in the example have either three or five subnets listed. The reason has to do with the theory behind RIP, specifically a feature called split horizon. This loop-avoidance feature, which is described in Chapter 8 of the ICND2 book, limits which subnets are advertised in each update to help avoid some forwarding loops.

> **NOTE**   Chapter 8, "Routing Protocol Theory," in the *CCNA ICND2 Official Exam Certification Guide* covers split horizon in greater detail.

Finally, a few comments about the **debug** command itself can be helpful. First, before using the **debug** command, it is helpful to look at the router's CPU utilization with the **show process** command, as shown at the end of Example 14-9. This command lists the router's CPU utilization as a rolling average over three short time periods. On routers with a higher CPU utilization, generally above 30 to 40 percent, be very cautious when enabling debug options, as this may drive the CPU to the point of impacting packet forwarding. Also, you might have noticed the time stamps on the debug messages; to make the router generate time stamps, you need to configure the **service timestamps** global configuration command.

Exam Preparation Tasks

Review All the Key Topics

Review the most important topics in the chapter, noted with the key topics icon in the outer margin of the page. Table 14-7 lists a reference of these key topics and the page numbers on which each is found.

Key Topic

Table 14-7 *Key Topics for Chapter 14*

Key Topic Element	Description	Page Number
Example 14-3	Shows how to configure static routes	443
Definitions	IGP and EGP	451
Table 14-2	List of IGP algorithms and the IGPs that use them	452
Table 14-3	Comparison points for classless and classful routing protocols	454
Table 14-4	Summary of comparison points for IGPs	456
List	RIP-2 configuration checklist	456-457
List	The three things that occur on an interface matched by a RIP network command	457
Table 14-6	List of routing protocols and other routing sources and their default administrative distance settings	462
Example 14-8	Lists the **show ip protocol** command and how it can be used to troubleshoot RIP problems	463

Complete the Tables and Lists from Memory

Print a copy of Appendix H, "Memory Tables" (found on the CD-ROM), or at least the section for this chapter, and complete the tables and lists from memory. Appendix I, "Memory Tables Answer Key," also on the CD-ROM, includes completed tables and lists to check your work.

Definitions of Key Terms

Define the following key terms from this chapter and check your answers in the glossary.

administrative distance, autonomous system, backup static route, balanced hybrid, classful routing protocol, classless routing protocol, convergence, default route, distance vector, Exterior Gateway Protocol (EGP), Interior Gateway Protocol (IGP), link state, metric, routing update, variable-length subnet masking (VLSM)

Command References

Although you should not necessarily memorize the information in the tables in this section, this section does include a reference for the configuration commands (Table 14-8) and EXEC commands (Table 14-9) covered in this chapter. Practically speaking, you should memorize the commands as a side effect of reading the chapter and doing all the activities in this exam preparation section. To check to see how well you have memorized the commands, cover the left side of the table with a piece of paper, read the descriptions in the right side, and see if you remember the command.

Table 14-8 *Chapter 14 Configuration Command Reference*

Command	Description
router rip	Global command that moves the user into RIP configuration mode.
network *network-number*	RIP subcommand that lists a classful network number, enabling RIP on all of that router's interfaces in that classful network.
version {1	2}	RIP subcommand that sets the RIP version.
passive-interface [default] {*interface-type interface-number*}	RIP subcommand that tells RIP to no longer advertise RIP updates on the listed interface.
ip address *ip-address mask*	Interface subcommand that sets the router's interface IP address and mask.
ip route *prefix mask* {*ip-address*	*interface-type interface-number*}	Global command that defines a static route.
service timestamps	Global command that tells the router to put a timestamp on log messages, including debug messages.

Table 14-9 *Chapter 14 EXEC Command Reference*

Command	Purpose
show ip interface brief	Lists one line per router interface, including the IP address and interface status; an interface must have an IP address, and be in an "up and up" status, before RIP begins to work on the interface.
**show ip route [rip	static	connected]**	Lists the routing table, including RIP-learned routes, and optionally just RIP-learned routes.
show ip route *ip-address*	Lists details about the route the router would match for a packet sent to the listed IP address.
show ip protocols	Lists information about the RIP configuration, plus the IP addresses of neighboring RIP routers from which the local router has learned routes.
show process	Lists information about the various processes running in IOS, and most importantly, overall CPU utilization statistics.
terminal ip netmask-format decimal	For the length of the user's session, causes IOS to display mask information in dotted-decimal format instead of prefix format.
debug ip rip	Tells the router to generate detailed messages for each sent and received RIP update.

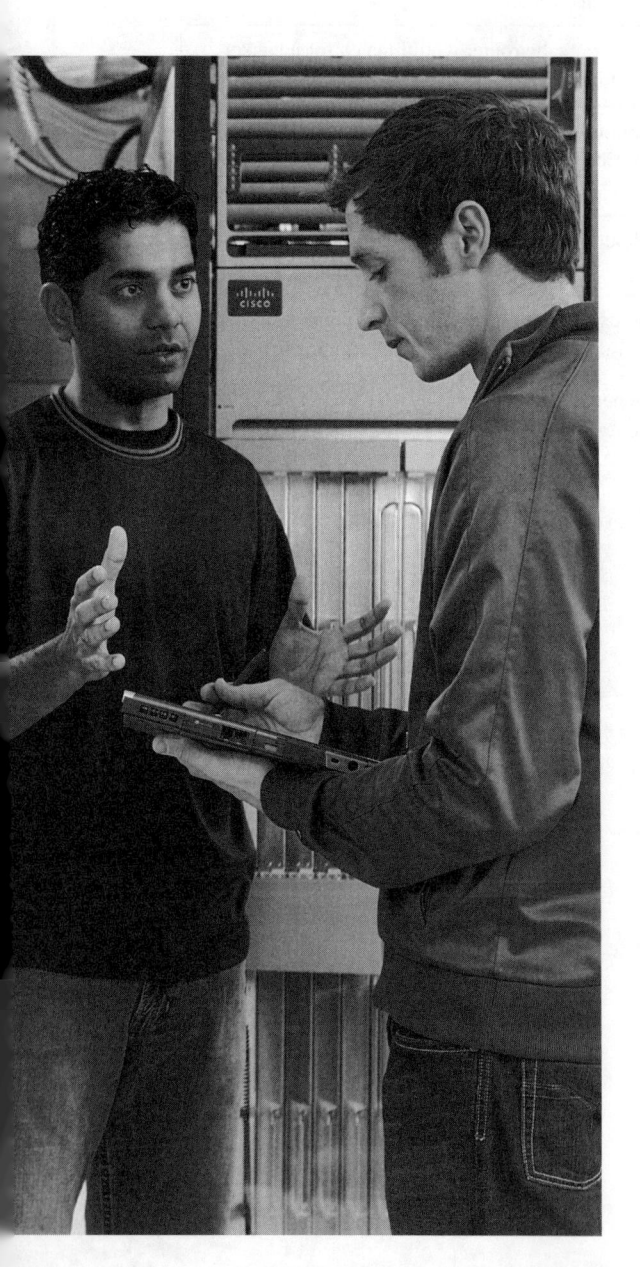

This chapter covers the following subjects:

IP Troubleshooting Tips and Tools: This section suggests some tips for how to approach host routing issues, routing related to routers, and IP addressing problems, including how to use several additional tools not covered elsewhere in this book.

A Troubleshooting Scenario: This section shows a three-part scenario, with tasks for each part that can be performed before seeing the answers.

CHAPTER 15

Troubleshooting IP Routing

This chapter has two main goals. First, this chapter covers some topics that are not covered elsewhere in this book, namely some troubleshooting commands on both hosts and routers. Second, this chapter reviews the core concepts of addressing and routing, but with a focus on how to approach new problems to analyze and understand how to troubleshoot any problems. Additionally, this chapter includes a troubleshooting scenario that shows how to use some of the tools and concepts from earlier in this chapter, with an opportunity for you to try and discover the problems before the text explains the answers.

For those of you following the reading plan using both this book and the *CCNA ICND2 Official Exam Certification Guide*, note that after this chapter, you should proceed to the ICND2 book and read the chapters in Parts II and III.

"Do I Know This Already?" Quiz

The "Do I Know This Already?" quiz allows you to assess if you should read the entire chapter. If you miss no more than one of these nine self-assessment questions, you might want to move ahead to the "Exam Preparation Tasks" section. Table 15-1 lists the major headings in this chapter and the "Do I Know This Already?" quiz questions covering the material in those headings so you can assess your knowledge of these specific areas. The answers to the "Do I Know This Already?" quiz appear in Appendix A.

Table 15-1 *"Do I Know This Already?" Foundation Topics Section-to-Question Mapping*

Foundation Topics Section	Questions
IP Troubleshooting Tips and Tools	1–6
A Routing Troubleshooting Scenario	7–9

1. An internetwork diagram shows a router, R1, with the **ip subnet-zero** command configured. The engineer has typed several configuration commands into a word processor for later pasting into the router's configuration. Which of the following IP addresses could not be assigned to the router's Fa0/0 interface?

    a. 172.16.0.200 255.255.255.128

    b. 172.16.0.200 255.255.255.0

    c. 225.1.1.1 255.255.255.0

    d. 10.43.53.63 255.255.255.192

2. Which of the following is a useful command on some Microsoft OSs for discovering a host's current IP address and mask?

    a. **tracert**

    b. **ipconfig /all**

    c. **arp –a**

    d. **ipconfig /displaydns**

3. Examine the following command output. If the user typed the **resume** command, what would happen?

    ```
    R1#show sessions
    Conn Host                Address            Byte  Idle Conn Name
       1 Fred                10.1.1.1           0     0    Fred
    *  2 Barney              10.1.2.1           0     0    Barney
    ```

    a. The command would be rejected, and the R1 CLI command prompt would be displayed again.

    b. The CLI user would be connected to a suspended Telnet connection to the router with IP address 10.1.1.1.

    c. The CLI user would be connected to a suspended Telnet connection to the router with IP address 10.1.2.1.

    d. The result cannot be accurately predicted from the information shown.

Refer to the following figure for questions 4–9:

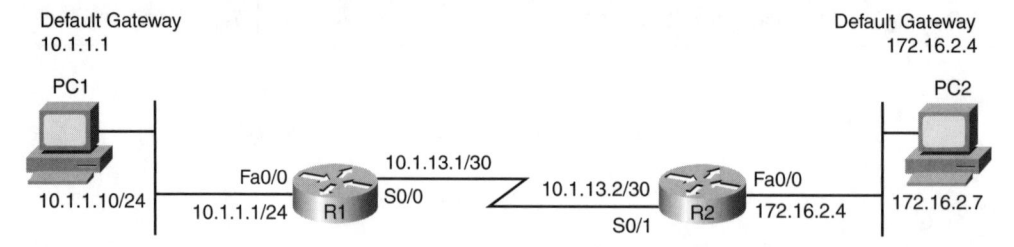

4. If PC3 were added to the LAN on the left, with IP address 10.1.1.130/25, default gateway 10.1.1.1, which of the following would be true?

   a. If PC1 issued a **ping 10.1.1.130** command, PC1 would use ARP to learn PC3's MAC address.

   b. If PC3 issued a **ping 10.1.1.10** command, PC3 would ARP trying to learn PC1's MAC address.

   c. If PC1 issued a **ping 10.1.13.1** command, PC1 would ARP trying to learn the MAC address of 10.1.13.1.

   d. If R1 issued a **ping 10.1.1.130** command, R1 would ARP trying to learn the MAC address of 10.1.1.130.

5. A new network engineer is trying to troubleshoot a problem for the user of PC1. Which of the following tasks and results would most likely point to a Layer 1 or 2 Ethernet problem on the LAN on the left side of the figure?

   a. A **ping 10.1.1.1** command on PC1 did not succeed.

   b. A **ping 10.1.13.3** command from PC1 succeeded, but a **ping 172.16.2.4** did not.

   c. A **ping 10.1.1.1** command from PC1 succeeded, but a **ping 10.1.13.1** did not.

   d. A **ping 10.1.1.10** command from PC1 succeeded.

6. The PC2 user issues the **tracert 10.1.1.10** command. Which of the following IP addresses could be shown in the command output?

   a. 10.1.1.10

   b. 10.1.1.1

   c. 10.1.13.1

   d. 10.1.13.3

   e. 172.16.2.4

7. All the devices in the figure just booted, and none of the devices has yet sent any data frames. Both PCs use statically configured IP addresses. Then PC1 successfully pings PC2. Which of the following ARP table entries would you expect to see?

   a. An entry on PC1's ARP cache for IP address 172.16.2.7

   b. An entry on PC1's ARP cache for IP address 10.1.1.1

   c. An entry on R1's ARP cache for IP address 10.1.1.10

   d. An entry on R1's ARP cache for IP address 172.16.2.7

8. All the devices in the figure just booted, and none of the devices has yet sent any data frames. Both PCs use statically configured IP addresses. Then PC1 successfully pings PC2. Which of the following ARP requests would you expect to occur?

   a. PC1 would send an ARP broadcast looking for R1's MAC address of the interface with IP address 10.1.1.1.

   b. PC2 would send an ARP broadcast looking for R2's MAC address of the interface with IP address 172.16.2.4.

   c. R1 would send an ARP broadcast looking for PC1's MAC address.

   d. R2 would send an ARP broadcast looking for PC2's MAC address.

   e. PC1 would send an ARP broadcast looking for PC2's MAC address.

9. PC1 is successfully pinging PC2 in the figure. Which of the following is true about the packets?

   a. The frame going left-to-right, as it crosses the left-side LAN, has a destination MAC address of R1's MAC address.

   b. The frame going left-to-right, as it crosses the right-side LAN, has a destination MAC address of R2's MAC address.

   c. The frame going left-to-right, as it crosses the serial link, has a destination IP address of PC2's IP address.

   d. The frame going right-to-left, as it crosses the left-side LAN, has a source MAC address of PC2's MAC address.

   e. The frame going right-to-left, as it crosses the right-side LAN, has a source MAC address of PC2's MAC address.

   f. The frame going right-to-left, as it crosses the serial link, has a source MAC address of R2's MAC address.

Foundation Topics

IP Troubleshooting Tips and Tools

The primary goal of this chapter is to better prepare you for the more challenging exam problems that involve potential Layer 3 problems. These problems often require the same thought processes and tools that you would use to troubleshoot networking problems in a real job. The first half of this chapter reviews the main types of problems that can occur, mainly related to addressing, host routing, and a router's routing logic. The second half of the chapter shows a scenario that explains one internetwork that has several problems, giving you a chance to first analyze the problems, and then showing how to solve the problems.

IP Addressing

This section includes some reminders relating to some of the basic features of IP addressing. More importantly, the text includes some tips on how to apply this basic knowledge to a given exam question, helping you know how to attack a particular type of problem.

Avoiding Reserved IP Addresses

One of the first things to check in an exam question that includes a larger scenario is whether the IP addresses are reserved and should not be used as unicast IP addresses. These reserved addresses can be categorized into one of three groups:

- Addresses that are always reserved

- Two addresses that are reserved in each subnet

- Addresses in two special subnets of each classful network, namely the zero subnet and broadcast subnet.

The first category of reserved addresses includes two Class A networks that are always reserved, plus all Class D (multicast) and Class E (experimental) IP addresses. You can easily recognize these IP addresses based on the value of their first octet, as follows:

- 0 (because network 0.0.0.0 is always reserved)

- 127 (because network 127.0.0.0 is always reserved)

- 224–239 (all Class D multicast IP addresses)

- 240–255 (all Class E experimental IP addresses)

Key
Topic

The second category of reserved IP addresses includes the two reserved addresses inside each subnet. When subnetting, each subnet reserves two numbers—the smallest and largest numbers in the subnet—otherwise known as

- The subnet number

- The subnet's broadcast address

So the ability to quickly and confidently determine the subnet number and subnet broadcast address has yet another application, when attempting to confirm that the addresses shown in a question can be legally used.

The third category of reserved IP addresses may or may not apply to a particular internetwork or question. For a given classful network, depending on several factors, the following two subnets may not be allowed to be used:

- The zero subnet

- The broadcast subnet

If an exam question includes an address in the zero subnet or broadcast subnet, you must then consider whether the question allows neither subnet to be used, or both. Table 15-2 summarizes the clues to look for in exam questions to determine whether a question allows the use of both subnets or not.

Table 15-2 *Determining Whether a Question Allows the Use of the Zero and Broadcast Subnets*

Clues in the Question	Subnets Reserved?
Says nothing about it (default for the exam)	No
Lists the **ip subnet-zero** configuration command	No
Uses a classless routing protocol (RIP-2, EIGRP, OSPF)	No
Lists the **no ip subnet-zero** configuration command	Yes
Uses a classful routing protocol (RIP-1)	Yes

One Subnet, One Mask, for Each LAN

The hosts on a single LAN or VLAN (a single broadcast domain) should all be in the same subnet. As a result, each host, each router interface attached to the LAN, and each switch management address in that LAN should also use the same mask.

For the exam, you should check all the details documented in the question to determine the mask used by the various devices on the same LAN. Oftentimes, a question that is intended to test your knowledge will not just list all the information in a nice organized figure. Instead, you might have to look at the configuration and diagrams and use **show** commands to gather the information, and then apply the subnetting math explained in Chapter 12, "IP Addressing and Subnetting."

Figure 15-1 shows an example of a LAN that could be part of a test question. For convenience, the figure lists several details about IP addresses and masks, but for a given question, you might have to gather some of the facts from a figure, a simulator, and from an exhibit that lists command output.

Figure 15-1 *One LAN with Three Different Opinions About the Subnet*

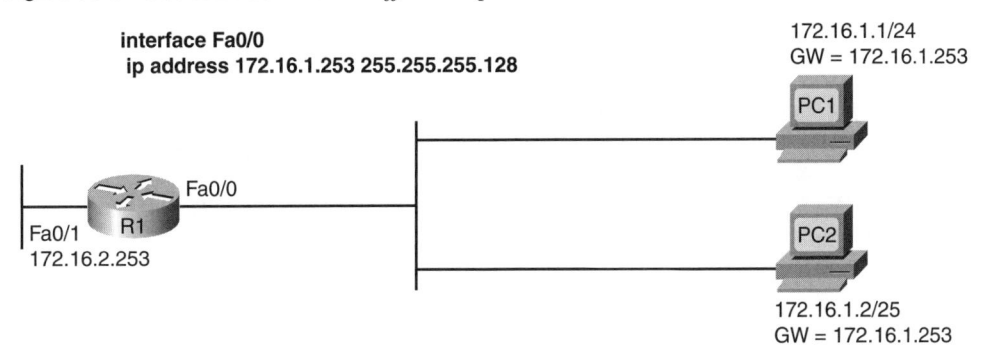

From the information in Figure 15-1, you can quickly tell that the two PCs use different masks (listed in prefix notation). In this case, you would need to know to look in the configuration for the subnet mask in the **ip address** interface subcommand, and then convert that mask to prefix notation to compare it with the other masks in this example. Table 15-3 lists the three differing opinions about the subnet.

Table 15-3 *Different Opinions About the Subnet in Figure 15-1*

	R1 Fa0/0	PC1	PC2
Mask	255.255.255.128	255.255.255.0	255.255.255.128
Subnet number	172.16.1.128	172.16.1.0	172.16.1.0
Broadcast address	172.16.1.255	172.16.1.255	172.16.1.127

In this case, several problem symptoms occur. For example, PC1 thinks 172.16.1.253 (R1) is in the same subnet, and PC1 thinks that it can forward packets to R1 over the LAN. However, R1 does not think that PC1 (172.16.1.1) is in the same subnet, so R1's connected route on the LAN interface (172.16.1.128/25) will not provide a route that R1 can use to forward packets back to PC1. For the exam, recognizing the fact that the hosts on the same LAN do not have the same opinion about the subnet should be enough to either answer the question, or to know what to fix in a Sim question. Table 15-4, found a little later in this chapter, summarizes the router commands that can be used to find the information required to analyze such problems.

Summary of IP Addressing Tips

Generally speaking, keep the following tips and facts in mind when you approach the exam questions that include details about IP addresses:

1. Check the mask used on each device in the same LAN; if different, then the devices cannot have the same view of the range of addresses in the subnet.

2. On point-to-point WAN links, check the IP addresses and masks on both ends of the link, and confirm that the two IP addresses are in the same subnet.

3. When checking to confirm that hosts are in the same subnet, do not just examine the subnet number. Also check the subnet mask, and the implied range of IP addresses.

4. Be ready to use the commands summarized in Table 15-4 to quickly find the IP addresses, masks, and subnet numbers.

The next section, in addition to reviewing a host's routing logic, introduces some commands on Microsoft operating systems that list the host's IP address and mask.

Host Networking Commands

Chapter 5, "Fundamentals of IP Addressing and Routing," explained the simple two-step logic a host uses when forwarding packets, in addition to how a host typically uses DHCP, DNS, ARP, and ICMP. These details can be summarized as follows:

Routing: If the packet's destination is on the same subnet, send the packet directly; if not, send the packet to the default gateway.

Address assignment: Before sending any packets, the host may use DHCP client services to learn its IP address, mask, default gateway, and DNS IP addresses. The host could also be statically configured with these same details.

Name resolution: When the user directly or indirectly references a host name, the host typically uses DNS name resolution requests to ask a DNS to identify that host's IP address unless the host already has that information in its name cache.

IP-to-MAC resolution: The host uses ARP requests to find the other host's MAC address, or the default gateway's IP address, unless the information is already in the host's ARP cache.

Of these four items, note that only the routing (forwarding) process happens for each packet. The address assignment function usually happens once, soon after booting. Name resolution and ARPs occur as needed, typically in reaction to something done by the user.

To analyze how well a host has accomplished these tasks, to troubleshoot problems, and to do the equivalent for exam questions, it is helpful to know a few networking commands on a host. Table 15-4 lists several of the commands on Microsoft Windows XP, but other similar commands exist for other operating systems. Example 15-1 following the table shows the output from some of these commands.

Table 15-4 *Microsoft Windows XP Network Command Reference*

Command	Function
ipconfig /all	Displays detailed IP configuration information for all interfaces, including IP address, mask, default gateway, and DNS IP addresses
ipconfig /release	Releases any DHCP-leased IP addresses
ipconfig /renew	Acquires an IP address and related information using DHCP
nslookup *name*	Sends a DNS request for the listed name
arp –a	Lists the host's ARP cache
ipconfig /displaydns	Lists the host's name cache
ipconfig /flushdns	Removes all DNS-found name cache entries
arp -d	Flushes (empties) the host's ARP cache
netstat -rn	Displays a host's routing table

Example 15-1 shows an example of the **ping www.cisco.com** command on a host running Windows XP, just after the ARP cache and hostname cache have been deleted (flushed). The example first shows the DHCP-learned addressing and DNS details, and then shows the flushing of the two caches. At that point, the example shows the **ping www.cisco.com** command, which forces the host to use DNS to learn the IP address of the Cisco web server, and then ARP to learn the MAC address of the default gateway, before sending an ICMP echo request to the Cisco web server.

> **NOTE**   The **ping** fails in this example, probably due to ACLs on routers or firewalls in the Internet. However, the **ping** command still drives the DNS and ARP processes as shown in the example. Also, the text is from a DOS window in Windows XP.

Example 15-1   *Example Use of Host Networking Commands*

```
C:\>ipconfig /all
! Some lines omitted for brevity
Ethernet adapter Local Area Connection:

        Connection-specific DNS Suffix  . : cinci.rr.com
        Description . . . . . . . . . . . : Broadcom NetXtreme 57xx Gigabit Cont
roller
        Physical Address. . . . . . . . . : 00-11-11-96-B5-13
        Dhcp Enabled. . . . . . . . . . . : Yes
        Autoconfiguration Enabled . . . . : Yes
        IP Address. . . . . . . . . . . . : 192.168.1.102
        Subnet Mask . . . . . . . . . . . : 255.255.255.0
        Default Gateway . . . . . . . . . : 192.168.1.1
        DHCP Server . . . . . . . . . . . : 192.168.1.1
        DNS Servers . . . . . . . . . . . : 65.24.7.3
                                            65.24.7.6
        Lease Obtained. . . . . . . . . . : Thursday, March 29, 2007 6:32:59 AM
        Lease Expires . . . . . . . . . . : Friday, March 30, 2007 6:32:59 AM
! Next, the ARP and name cache are flushed.
C:\>arp -d
C:\>ipconfig /flushdns
Windows IP Configuration

Successfully flushed the DNS Resolver Cache.

! The ping command lists the IP address (198.133.219.25), meaning that the DNS request
  worked.
! However, the ping does not complete, probably due to ACLs filtering ICMP traffic.
C:\>ping www.cisco.com

Pinging www.cisco.com [198.133.219.25] with 32 bytes of data:
Request timed out.
Request timed out.
Request timed out.
Request timed out.

Ping statistics for 192.133.219.25:
    Packets: Sent = 4, Received = 0, Lost = 4 (100% loss),

! Next, the ARP cache lists an entry for the default gateway.
C:\>arp -a

Interface: 192.168.1.102 --- 0x2
  Internet Address      Physical Address      Type
  192.168.1.1           00-13-10-d4-de-08     dynamic
! Next, the local name cache lists the name used in the ping command and the IP address
```

continues

Example 15-1 *Example Use of Host Networking Commands (Continued)*

```
! learned from the DNS server.
C:\>ipconfig /displaydns

Windows IP Configuration

        www.cisco.com
        ----------------------------------------
        Record Name . . . . . : www.cisco.com
        Record Type . . . . . : 1
        Time To Live  . . . . : 26190
        Data Length . . . . . : 4
        Section . . . . . . . : Answer
        A (Host) Record . . . : 198.133.219.25
! Lines omitted for brevity
```

> **NOTE**   At press time, the simulator used on the Cisco exams did not include host networking commands; however, the exam can still require you to interpret the output of host commands, and the simulator could include these commands in the future.

In addition to these commands, Figure 15-2 shows an example of the windows used to statically configure a host's IP address, mask, default gateway, and DNS server IP addresses. These details can be configured with commands as well, but most people prefer the easier graphical interface.

Figure 15-2 *Configuring Static IP Addresses on Windows XP*

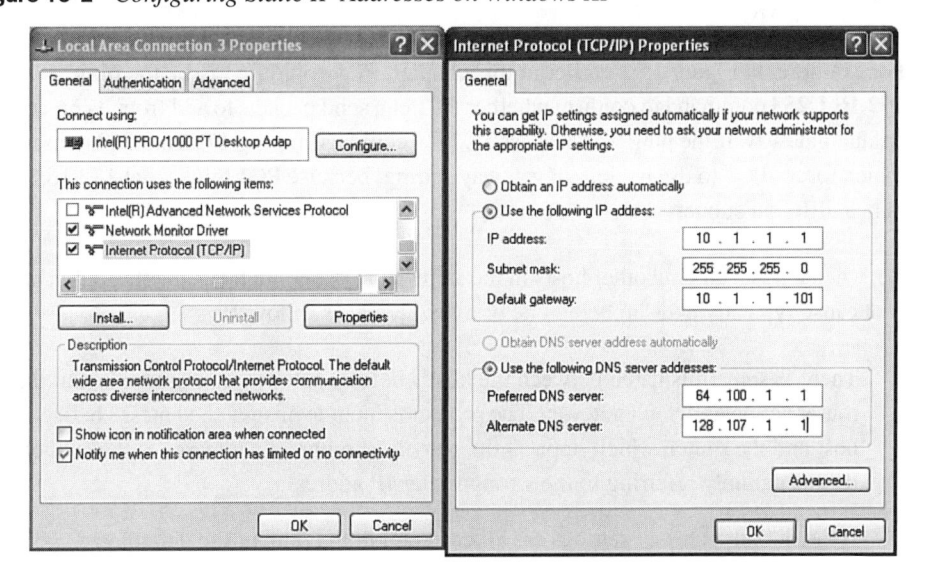

Troubleshooting Host Routing Problems

Troubleshooting host routing problems should begin with the same two-step routing logic used by a host. The first question to ask is whether the host can ping other hosts inside the same subnet. If a ping of a same-subnet host fails, the root cause typically falls into one of two categories:

■   The two hosts have incorrect IP address and mask configurations, typically so that at least one of the two hosts thinks it is in a different subnet.

■   The two hosts have correct IP address and mask configurations, but the underlying Ethernet has a problem.

For the exam, start by looking at the host's addresses and masks, and determine the subnet number and range of addresses for each. If the subnets are the same, then move on to Layer 1 and 2 Ethernet troubleshooting as covered in Chapter 10, "Ethernet Switch Troubleshooting," and in the *CCNA ICND2 Exam Certification Guide*, Chapter 3, "Troubleshooting LAN Switching."

If the host can ping other hosts in the same subnet, the next step is to confirm if the host can ping IP addresses in other subnets, thereby testing the second branch of a host's routing logic. Two different pings can be helpful at this step:

■   Ping the default gateway IP address to confirm that the host can send packets over the LAN to and from the default gateway.

■   Ping a different IP address on the default gateway/router, but not the IP address on the same LAN.

For example, in Figure 15-1 earlier in this chapter, PC1 could first issue the **ping 172.16.1.253** command to confirm whether PC1 can send packets to and from its presumed default gateway. If the ping was successful, PC1 could use a **ping 172.16.2.253** command, which forces PC1 to use its default gateway setting, because PC1 thinks that 172.16.2.253 is in a different subnet.

So, when a host can ping other hosts in the same subnet, but not hosts in other subnets, the root cause typically ends up being one of a few items, as follows:

■   There is some mismatch between the host's default gateway configuration and the router acting as default gateway. The problems include mismatched masks between the host and the router, which impacts the perceived range of addresses in the subnet, or the host simply referring to the wrong router IP address.

■   If the default gateway settings are all correct, but the ping of the default gateway IP address fails, there is probably some Layer 1 or 2 problem on the LAN.

■   If the default gateway settings are all correct and the ping of the default gateway works, but the ping of one of the other router interface IP addresses fails (like the **ping 172.16.2.253** command based on Figure 15-1), then the router's other interface may have failed.

While all the details in this section can be helpful when troubleshooting problems on hosts, keep in mind that many of the problems stem from incorrect IP address and mask combinations. For the exam, be ready to find the IP address and masks, and apply the math from Chapter 12 to quickly determine where these types of problems exist.

Finding the Matching Route on a Router

Chapter 5 summarized the process by which a router forwards a packet. A key part of that process is how a router compares the destination IP address of each packet with the existing contents of that router's IP routing table. The route that matches the packet's destination tells the router out which interface to forward the packet and, in some cases, the IP address of the next-hop router.

In some cases, a particular router's routing table might have more than one route that matches an individual destination IP address. Some legitimate and normal reasons for the overlapping routes in a routing table include auto-summary, route summarization, and the configuration of static routes.

The exams can test your understanding of IP routing by asking questions about which route would be matched for a packet sent to particular IP addresses. To answer such questions, you should keep the following important facts in mind:

■   When a particular destination IP address matches more than one route in a router's routing table, the router uses the most specific route—in other words, the route with the longest prefix length.

Key
Topic

■   Although the router uses binary math to compare the destination IP address to the routing table entries, you can simply compare the destination IP address to each subnet in the routing table. If a subnet's implied address range includes the packet's destination address, the route matches the packet's destination.

■   If the question includes a simulator, you can easily find the matched route by using the **show ip route** *address* command, which lists the route matched for the IP address listed in the command.

Example 15-2 shows a sample IP routing table for a router, with many overlapping routes. Read the example, and before reading the explanations after the example, predict which route this router would match for packets destined to the following IP addresses: 172.16.1.1, 172.16.1.2, 172.16.2.2, and 172.16.4.3.

Example 15-2   show ip route *Command with Overlapping Routes*

```
R1#show ip route rip
Codes: C - connected, S - static, R - RIP, M - mobile, B - BGP
       D - EIGRP, EX - EIGRP external, O - OSPF, IA - OSPF inter area
       N1 - OSPF NSSA external type 1, N2 - OSPF NSSA external type 2
       E1 - OSPF external type 1, E2 - OSPF external type 2
       i - IS-IS, su - IS-IS summary, L1 - IS-IS level-1, L2 - IS-IS level-2
       ia - IS-IS inter area, * - candidate default, U - per-user static route
       o - ODR, P - periodic downloaded static route

Gateway of last resort is not set

     172.16.0.0/16 is variably subnetted, 5 subnets, 4 masks
R       172.16.1.1/32 [120/1] via 172.16.25.2, 00:00:04, Serial0/1/1
R       172.16.1.0/24 [120/2] via 172.16.25.129, 00:00:09, Serial0/1/0
R       172.16.0.0/22 [120/1] via 172.16.25.2, 00:00:04, Serial0/1/1
R       172.16.0.0/16 [120/2] via 172.16.25.129, 00:00:09, Serial0/1/0
R       0.0.0.0/0 [120/3] via 172.16.25.129, 00:00:09, Serial0/1/0
R1#show ip route 172.16.4.3
Routing entry for 172.16.0.0/16
  Known via "rip", distance 120, metric 2
  Redistributing via rip
  Last update from 172.16.25.129 on Serial0/1/0, 00:00:19 ago
  Routing Descriptor Blocks:
  * 172.16.25.129, from 172.16.25.129, 00:00:19 ago, via Serial0/1/0
      Route metric is 2, traffic share count is 1
```

For the exam, to find the matching route, all you need to know is the destination IP address of the packet and the router's IP routing table. By examining each subnet and mask in the routing table, you can determine the range of IP addresses in each subnet. Then, you can compare the packet's destination to the ranges of addresses, and find all matching routes. In cases where a particular destination IP address falls within the IP address range for multiple routes, then you pick the route with the longest prefix length. In this case:

■   Destination address 172.16.1.1 matches all five routes, but the host route for specific IP address 172.16.1.1, prefix length /32, has the longest prefix length.

■   Destination address 172.16.1.2 matches four of the routes (all except the host route for 172.16.1.1), but the route to 172.16.1.0/24 has the longest prefix.

■   Destination address 172.16.2.2 matches the last three routes listed in R1's routing table in the example, with the route for 172.16.0.0/22 having the longest prefix length.

■   Destination address 172.16.4.3 matches the last two routes listed in R1's routing table in the example, with the route for 172.16.0.0/16 having the longest prefix length.

Finally, note the output of the **show ip route 172.16.4.3** command at the end of Example 15-2. This command shows which route the router would match to reach IP address 172.16.4.3—a very handy command for both real life and for Sim questions on the exams. In this case, a packet sent to IP address 172.16.4.3 would match the route for the entire Class B network 172.16.0.0/16, as highlighted near the end of the example.

Troubleshooting Commands

The most popular troubleshooting command on a router or switch is the **ping** command. Chapter 14, "Routing Protocol Concepts and Configuration," already introduced this command, in both its standard form and the extended form. Basically, the **ping** command sends a packet to another host, and the receiving host sends back a packet to the original host, testing to see if packets can be routed between the two hosts.

This section introduces three additional Cisco IOS commands that can be useful when troubleshooting routing problems, namely the **show ip arp**, **traceroute**, and **telnet** commands.

The show ip arp Command

The **show ip arp** command lists the contents of a router's ARP cache. Example 15-3 lists sample output from this command, taken from router R1 in Figure 15-1, after the router and hosts were changed to all use a /24 mask.

Example 15-3 *Sample **show ip arp** Command Output*

```
R1#show ip arp
Protocol  Address          Age (min)  Hardware Addr   Type   Interface
Internet  172.16.1.1              8   0013.197b.2f58  ARPA   FastEthernet0/0
Internet  172.16.1.253           -    0013.197b.5004  ARPA   FastEthernet0/0
Internet  172.16.2.253           -    0013.197b.5005  ARPA   FastEthernet0/1
```

The most important parts of each entry are the IP address, MAC address, and interface. When a router needs to send a packet out a particular interface, the router will only use entries associated with that interface. For example, for R1 to send a packet to host PC1 in Figure 15-1 (address 172.16.1.1), R1 needs to forward the packet out its Fa0/0 interface, so R1 will only use ARP cache entries associated with Fa0/0.

Additionally, the Age heading includes a few interesting facts. If it lists a number, the Age value represents the number of minutes since the router last received a packet from the host. For example, it had been 8 minutes since R1 had received a packet from host PC1, source IP address 172.16.1.1, source MAC address 0013.197b.2f58. The Age does not mean how long it has been since the ARP request/reply; the timer is reset to 0 each time a matching packet is received. If the Age is listed as a dash, the ARP entry actually represents an IP address assigned to the router—for example, R1's Fa0/0 interface in Figure 15-1 is shown as 172.16.1.253, which is the second entry in Example 15-3.

The traceroute Command

The Cisco IOS **traceroute** command, like the Cisco IOS **ping** command, tests the route between a router and another host or router. However, the **traceroute** command also identifies the IP addresses of the routers in the route. For example, consider Figure 15-3 and Example 15-4. The figure shows an internetwork with three routers, with the **traceroute 172.16.2.7** command being used on router R1. The arrowed lines show the three IP addresses identified by the command output, which is shown in Example 15-4.

Figure 15-3 *Internetwork Used in* **traceroute** *Example*

Example 15-4 *Sample* **traceroute** *Command Output*

```
R1#traceroute 172.16.2.7

Type escape sequence to abort.
Tracing the route to 172.16.2.7

  1 10.1.13.3   8 msec 4 msec 4 msec
  2 172.16.1.4   24 msec 25 msec 26 msec
  3 172.16.2.7   26 msec 26 msec 28 msec
```

The example shows a working **traceroute** command. However, if a routing problem exists, the command will not complete. For example, imagine that R1 had a route that matched 172.16.2.7, so R1 could forward packets to R2. However, R2 does not have a route that matches destination 172.16.2.7. In that case, the **traceroute** command would list the first line that refers to a router (highlighted in Example 15-4). However, no other routers would be listed, and the user would have to stop the command, typically by pressing the Ctrl-Shift-6 key sequence a few times. However, 10.1.13.3 is an IP address on the router that has a routing problem (R2), so the next step would be to telnet to R2 and find out why it does not have a route matching destination 172.16.2.7.

It is important to note that the **traceroute** command lists the IP addresses considered to be the next-hop device. For example, in Example 15-4, the first IP address (R2, 10.1.13.3) is the next-hop IP address in the route R1 uses to route the packet. Similarly, the next IP address (R3, 172.16.1.4) is the next-hop router in the route used by R2. (Chapter 7, "Troubleshooting IP Routing," in the *CCNA ICND2 Official Exam Certification Guide* explains how the **traceroute** command finds these IP addresses.)

> **NOTE** Many operating systems have a similar command, including the Microsoft OS **tracert** command, which achieves the same goal.

Telnet and Suspend

Many engineers troubleshoot network problems sitting at their desks. To get access to a router or switch, the engineer just needs to use Telnet or SSH on their desktop PC to connect to each router or switch, oftentimes opening multiple Telnet or SSH windows to connect to multiple devices. As an alternative, the engineer could connect to one router or switch using a Telnet or SSH client on their desktop computer, and then use the **telnet** or **ssh** Cisco IOS EXEC commands to connect to other routers and switches. These commands acts as a Telnet or SSH client, respectively, so that you can easily connect to other devices when troubleshooting. When finished, the user could just use the **exit** command to disconnect the Telnet or SSH session.

Frankly, many people who rarely troubleshoot just use multiple windows on their desktop and ignore the Cisco IOS **telnet** and **ssh** commands. However, those who do a lot more troubleshooting tend to use these commands because, with practice, they enable you to move between routers and switches more quickly.

One of the most important advantages of using the Cisco IOS **telnet** and **ssh** commands is the suspend feature. The suspend feature allows a Telnet or SSH connection to remain active while creating another Telnet or SSH connection, so that you can make many concurrent connections, and then easily switch between the connections. Figure 15-4 shows a sample internetwork with which the text will demonstrate the suspend feature and its power.

The router administrator is using the PC named Bench to telnet into the Cincy router. When connected to the Cincy CLI, the user telnets to router Milwaukee. When in Milwaukee, the user suspends the Telnet session by pressing Ctrl-Shift-6, followed by pressing the letter x. The user then telnets to New York and again suspends the connection. At the end of the example, the user is concurrently telnetted into all three routers, with the ability to switch between the connections with just a few keystrokes. Example 15-5 shows example output, with annotations to the side.

Figure 15-4 *Telnet Suspension*

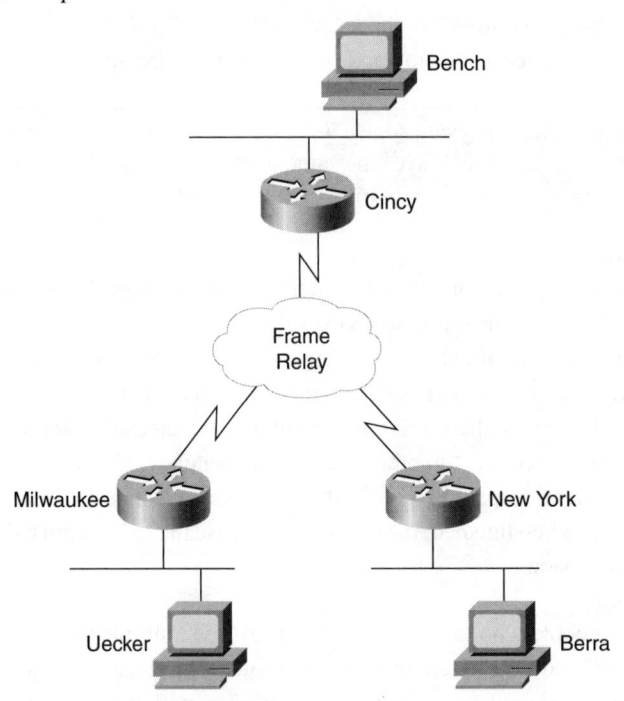

Example 15-5 *Telnet Suspensions*

```
Cincy#telnet milwaukee                    (User issues command to Telnet to Milwaukee)
Trying Milwaukee (10.1.4.252)... Open


User Access Verification

Password:                    (User plugs in password, can type commands at Milwaukee)
Milwaukee>
Milwaukee>
Milwaukee>
                    (Note: User pressed Ctrl-Shift-6 and then x)
Cincy#telnet NewYork                (User back at Cincy because Telnet was suspended)
Trying NewYork (10.1.6.253)... Open
                    (User is getting into New York now, based on telnet NewYork command)


User Access Verification

                                                                        continues
```

Example 15-5 *Telnet Suspensions (Continued)*

```
Password:
NewYork>                              (User can now type commands on New York)
NewYork>
NewYork>
NewYork>

                        (Note: User pressed Ctrl-Shift-6 and then x)

Cincy#show sessions              (This command lists suspended Telnet sessions)
Conn Host            Address          Byte  Idle Conn Name
   1 Milwaukee       10.1.4.252          0     0 Milwaukee
*  2 NewYork         10.1.6.253          0     0 NewYork

Cincy#where                    (where does the same thing as show sessions)
Conn Host            Address          Byte  Idle Conn Name
   1 Milwaukee       10.1.4.252          0     0 Milwaukee
*  2 NewYork         10.1.6.253          0     0 NewYork

Cincy#resume 1         (Resume connection 1 (see show session) to Milwaukee)
[Resuming connection 1 to milwaukee ... ]

Milwaukee>                           (User can type commands on Milwaukee)
Milwaukee>
Milwaukee>
! (Note: User pressed Ctrl-Shift-6 and then x, because the user wants to
!  go back to Cincy)
Cincy#        (WOW! User just pressed Enter and resumes the last Telnet)
 [Resuming connection 1 to milwaukee ... ]

Milwaukee>
Milwaukee>
Milwaukee>
                        (Note: User pressed Ctrl-Shift-6 and then x)
Cincy#disconnect 1              (No more need to use Milwaukee  Telnet terminated!)
Closing connection to milwaukee [confirm]        (User presses Enter to confirm)
Cincy#
[Resuming connection 2 to NewYork ... ]
                (Pressing Enter resumes most recently suspended active Telnet)

NewYork>
NewYork>
NewYork>
                        (Note: User pressed Ctrl-Shift-6 and then x)
Cincy#disconnect 2                  (Done with New York, terminate Telnet)
Closing connection to NewYork [confirm]          (Just press Enter to confirm)
Cincy#
```

The play-by-play notes in the example explain most of the details. Example 15-5 begins with the Cincy command prompt that would be seen in the Telnet window from host Bench. After telnetting to Milwaukee, the Telnet connection was suspended because the user pressed Ctrl-Shift-6, let go, and then pressed x and let go. Then, after establishing a Telnet connection to New York, that connection was suspended with the same key sequence.

The two connections can be suspended or resumed easily. The **resume** command can be used to resume any suspended connection. To reconnect to a particular session, the **resume** command can list a connection ID, which is shown in the **show sessions** command. (The **where** command provides the same output.) If the **resume** command is used without a connection ID, the command reconnects the user to the most recently suspended connection. Also, instead of using the **resume** command, you can just use the session number as a command. For instance, just typing the command **2** does the same thing as typing the command **resume 2**.

The interesting and potentially dangerous nuance here is that if a Telnet session is suspended and you simply press Enter, Cisco IOS Software resumes the connection to the most recently suspended Telnet connection. That is fine, until you realize that you tend to press the Enter key occasionally to clear some of the clutter from the screen. With a suspended Telnet connection, pressing Enter a few times to unclutter the screen might reconnect to another router. This is particularly dangerous when you are changing the configuration or using potentially damaging EXEC commands, so be careful about what router you are actually using when you have suspended Telnet connections.

If you want to know which session has been suspended most recently, look for the session listed in the **show sessions** command that has an asterisk (*) to the left of the entry. The asterisk marks the most recently suspended session.

In addition to the commands in Example 15-5 that show how to suspend and resume Telnet and SSH connections, two other commands can list useful information about sessions for users logged into a router. The **show users** command lists all users logged into the router on which the command is used. This command lists all sessions, including users at the console, and those connecting using both Telnet and SSH. The **show ssh** command lists the same kind of information, but only for users that connected using SSH. Note that these commands differ from the **show sessions** command, which lists suspended Telnet/SSH sessions from the local router to other devices.

This concludes the first half of the chapter. The remainder of the chapter focuses on how to apply many of the troubleshooting tips covered earlier in this chapter by analyzing an internetwork that has a few problems.

A Routing Troubleshooting Scenario

This section describes a three-part scenario. Each part (A, B, and C) uses figures, examples, and text to explain part of what is happening in an internetwork and asks you to complete some tasks and answer some questions. For each part, the text shows sample answers for the tasks and questions.

The goal of this scenario is to demonstrate how to use some of the troubleshooting tips covered earlier in this chapter. The scenario is not designed to match any particular type of question you might see on the CCNA exams. Instead, it is just one more tool to help you learn how to apply your knowledge to new unique scenarios, which is exactly what the exam will require you to do.

Note that Appendix F, "Additional Scenarios," has two additional scenarios about other topics in this book. Appendix F, "Additional Scenarios," in the *ICND2 Official Exam Certification Guide* has five additional scenarios, again with the goal of providing more practice with troubleshooting and analysis skills for new scenarios.

Scenario Part A: Tasks and Questions

The scenario begins with an internetwork that has just been installed, but the documentation is incomplete. Your job is to examine the existing documentation (in the form of an internetwork diagram), along with the output of several **show** commands. From that information, you should

■   Determine the IP address and subnet mask/prefix length of each router interface.

■   Calculate the subnet number for each subnet in the diagram.

■   Complete the internetwork diagram, listing router IP addresses and prefix lengths, as well as the subnet numbers.

■   Identify any existing problems with the IP addresses or subnets shown in the existing figure.

■   Suggest solutions to any problems you find.

Examples 15-6 through 15-8 list command output from routers R1, R2, and R3 in Figure 15-5. Example 15-9 lists commands as typed into a text editor, which were later pasted into R4's configuration mode.

Figure 15-5 *Scenario 3: Incomplete Network Diagram*

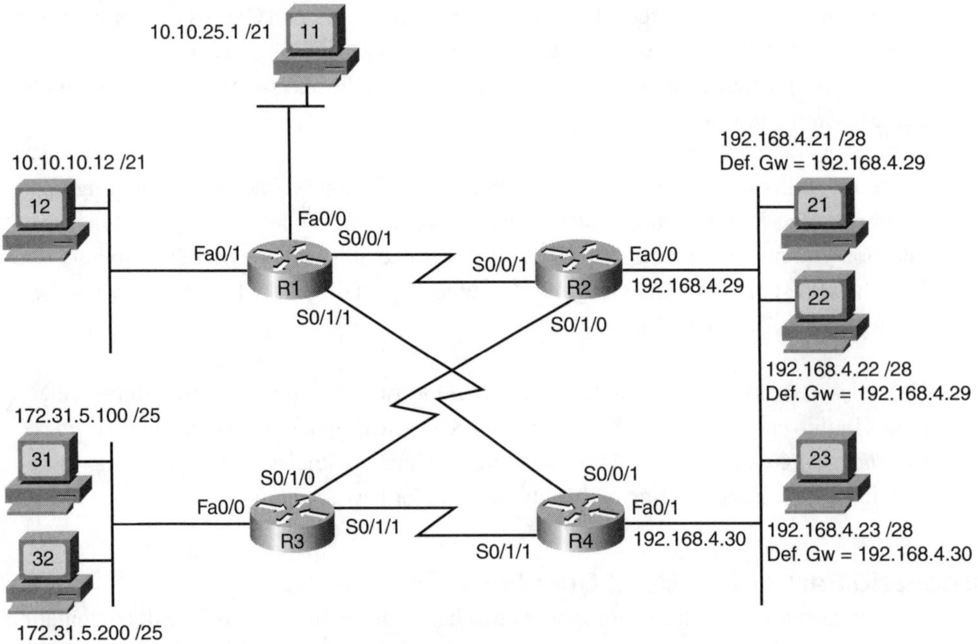

Example 15-6 *Scenario Output: Router R1*

```
R1#show ip interface brief
Interface              IP-Address      OK? Method Status                Protocol
FastEthernet0/0        10.10.24.1      YES NVRAM  up                    up
FastEthernet0/1        10.10.15.1      YES NVRAM  up                    up
Serial0/0/0            unassigned      YES NVRAM  administratively down  down
Serial0/0/1            192.168.1.1     YES NVRAM  up                    up
Serial0/1/0            unassigned      YES NVRAM  administratively down  down
Serial0/1/1            192.168.1.13    YES NVRAM  up                    up
R1#show protocols
Global values:
  Internet Protocol routing is enabled
FastEthernet0/0 is up, line protocol is up
  Internet address is 10.10.24.1/21
FastEthernet0/1 is up, line protocol is up
  Internet address is 10.10.15.1/21
Serial0/0/0 is administratively down, line protocol is down
Serial0/0/1 is up, line protocol is up
  Internet address is 192.168.1.1/30
Serial0/1/0 is administratively down, line protocol is down
Serial0/1/1 is up, line protocol is up
  Internet address is 192.168.1.13/30
```

Example 15-7 *Scenario Output: Router R2*

```
R2#show protocols
Global values:
  Internet Protocol routing is enabled
FastEthernet0/0 is up, line protocol is up
  Internet address is 192.168.4.29/28
FastEthernet0/1 is administratively down, line protocol is down
Serial0/0/0 is administratively down, line protocol is down
Serial0/0/1 is up, line protocol is up
  Internet address is 192.168.1.2/30
Serial0/1/0 is up, line protocol is up
  Internet address is 192.168.1.6/30
Serial0/1/1 is administratively down, line protocol is down
```

Example 15-8 *Scenario Output: Router R3*

```
R3#show ip interface brief
Interface              IP-Address      OK? Method Status                Protocol
FastEthernet0/0        172.31.5.1      YES NVRAM  up                    up
FastEthernet0/1        unassigned      YES NVRAM  administratively down down
Serial0/0/0            unassigned      YES NVRAM  administratively down down
Serial0/0/1            unassigned      YES NVRAM  administratively down down
Serial0/1/0            192.168.1.5     YES NVRAM  up                    up
Serial0/1/1            192.168.1.18    YES NVRAM  up                    up
R3#show ip route connected
     172.31.0.0/25 is subnetted, 1 subnets
C       172.31.5.0 is directly connected, FastEthernet0/0
     192.168.1.0/24 is variably subnetted, 5 subnets, 2 masks
C       192.168.1.4/30 is directly connected, Serial0/1/0
C       192.168.1.16/30 is directly connected, Serial0/1/1
```

Example 15-9 *Scenario Output: Router R4*

```
! The following commands are in a text editor, and will be pasted into
! configuration mode on R4.
interface fa0/1
 ip address 192.168.4.30 255.255.255.240
!
interface serial 0/0/1
 ip address 192.168.1.14 255.255.255.252
!
interface serial 0/1/1
 ip address 192.168.1.19 255.255.255.252
!
! The following three lines correctly configure RIP Version 2
router rip
 version 2
 network 192.168.1.0
 network 192.168.4.0
```

Scenario Part A: Answers

Examples 15-6, 15-7, and 15-8 list the IP addresses of each interface on routers R1, R2, and R3, respectively. However, some of the commands used in the examples do not provide mask information. In particular, the **show ip interface brief** command—a great command for getting a quick look at interfaces, their IP addresses, and the status—does not list the mask. The **show protocols** command lists that same information, as well as the subnet mask.

Example 15-8 (R3) does list the mask information directly, but it may take a little work to find it. You can see the interfaces and their configured IP addresses in the **show ip interfaces brief** command output, and then compare that information to the output of the **show ip route connected** command. This command does list the mask information, and the subnet number connected to an interface. A router determines the subnet number and mask for each connected route based on the configured **ip address** interface subcommand on each interface. From these facts, you can determine the mask used on each of R3's interfaces.

Finally, Example 15-9 lists configuration commands that will be pasted into router R4. These commands explicitly list the IP addresses and subnet masks in the various **ip address** configuration commands.

Figure 15-6 shows the answers to the first three tasks in Part A, listing the IP addresses and masks of each interface, as well as the subnet numbers.

Figure 15-6 *Scenario Part A: Subnet Numbers*

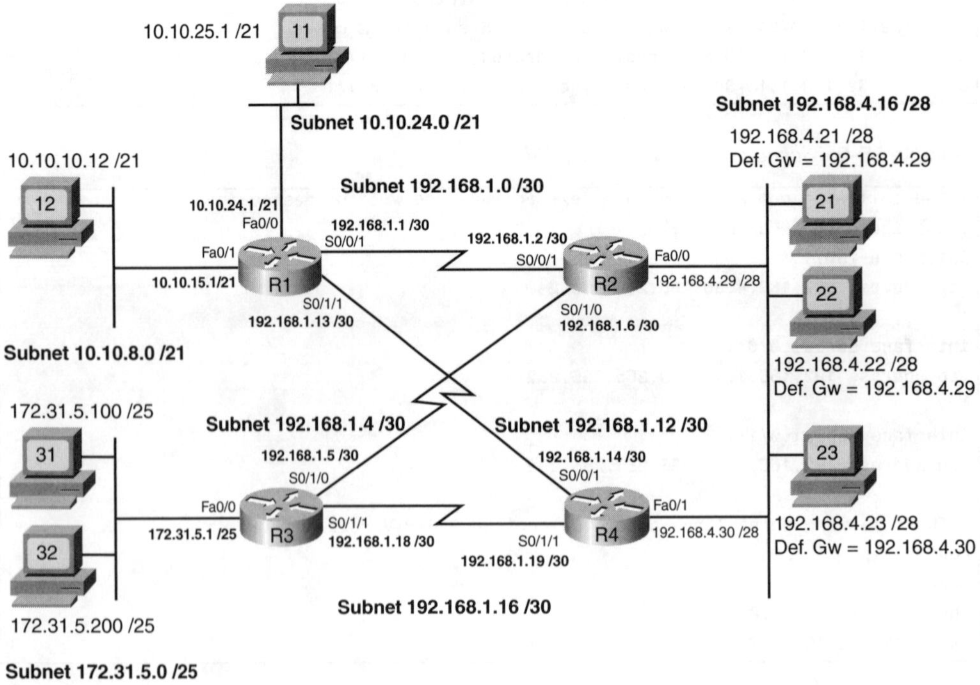

With all the information listed in one internetwork diagram, you can use the suggestions and tips from earlier in this chapter to analyze the IP addresses and subnets. In this case, you should have found two different addressing problems. The first of the two IP addressing problems is the disagreement between PC31 and PC32 regarding the subnet numbers and range of addresses on the lower-left LAN in Figure 15-6. In this case, PC32, with IP address 172.31.5.200 and a prefix length of /25, thinks it is in subnet 172.31.5.128/25, with a range of addresses from 172.31.5.129 to 172.31.5.254. PC31 and R3, attached to the same LAN, think they are attached to subnet 172.31.5.0/25, with the range of addresses being 172.31.5.1–172.31.5.126.

This particular problem results in R3 not being able to forward packets to PC32, because R3's connected route for that interface will refer to subnet 172.31.5.0/25. As a result, packets sent to PC32's IP address would not match that connected route. Additionally, PC32's setting for its default gateway IP address (172.31.5.1) is invalid, because the default gateway IP address should be in the same subnet as the host.

The second addressing problem in this scenario is that on the serial link between routers R3 and R4, R4's IP address and mask (192.168.1.19/30) is actually a broadcast address in subnet 192.168.1.16/30. Subnet 192.168.1.16/30 has an address range of 192.168.1.17–192.168.1.18, with a subnet broadcast address of 192.168.1.19. Note that the scenario suggested that the commands in Example 15-9 would be pasted into R4's configuration mode; R4 would actually reject the **ip address 192.168.1.19 255.255.255.252** command because it is a subnet broadcast address.

Several possible working solutions exist for both problems, but the simple solution in each case is to assign a valid but unused IP address from the correct subnets. In PC32's case, any IP address between 172.31.5.1 and 172.31.5.126, not already used by PC31 or R3, would work fine. For R4, IP address 192.168.1.17 would be the only available IP address, because R3 has already been assigned 192.168.1.18.

Scenario Part B: Analyze Packet/Frame Flow

Part B of this scenario continues with the network shown in Figure 15-6—including the IP addressing errors from Part A. However, no other problems exist. In this case, all physical connections and links are working, and RIP-2 has been correctly configured, and is functional.

With those assumptions in mind, answer the following questions. Note that to answer some questions, you need to refer to MAC addresses that are not otherwise specified. In these cases, a pseudo MAC address is listed—for example, R1-Fa0/1-MAC for R1's Fa0/1 interface's MAC address.

1.   PC12 successfully pings PC21, with the packet flowing over the R1-R2 link. What ARP table entries are created to support the forwarding of the ICMP Echo Request packet?

2.   Assume when PC12 pings PC23 that the ICMP echo request goes over the R1-R4 path. What ARP table entries are required on PC12? R1? R4?

3.   Assume when PC12 pings PC23 that the ICMP echo request goes over the R1-R2 path. What ARP table entries are required in support of the ICMP echo reply from PC23, on PC23? R2? R4? R1?

4.   PC31 sends a packet to PC22. When the packet passes over the Ethernet on the right side of the figure, what is the source MAC address? Destination MAC address? Source IP address? Destination IP address?

5.   PC31 sends a packet to PC22. When the packet passes over the serial link between R3 and R2, what is the source MAC address? Destination MAC address? Source IP address? Destination IP address?

6.   PC21 sends a packet to PC12, with the packet passing over the R2-R1 path. When the packet passes over the Ethernet on the right side of the figure, what is the source MAC address? Destination MAC address? Source IP address? Destination IP address?

7.   PC21 sends a packet to PC12, with the packet passing over the R2-R1 path. When the packet passes over the Ethernet on the left side of the figure, what is the source MAC address? Destination MAC address? Source IP address? Destination IP address?

Scenario Part B: Answers

Scenario Part B requires that you think about the theory behind the IP forwarding process. That process includes many details covered in Chapter 5. In particular, to answer the questions in Part B correctly, you need to remember the following key facts:

Key Topic

- The IP packet flows from the sending host to the receiving host.

- The data link header and trailer, which encapsulate the packet, do not flow over the complete end-to-end route—instead, each individual data link helps move the packet from a host to a router, between two routers, or from a router to the destination host.

- For the process to work, the data link frame's destination address lists the next device's data link address.

- The IP header lists the IP address of the sending host and receiving host.

- Routers discard the data link header and trailer for received frames and build a new data link header and trailer—appropriate for the outgoing interface—before forwarding the frame.

- On LANs, hosts and routers use ARP to discover the Ethernet MAC address used by other devices on the same LAN.

- On point-to-point WAN links, ARP is not needed, and the data link addressing is uninteresting and can be ignored.

If your reading of this list caused you to doubt some of your answers, feel free to go back and reevaluate your answers before looking at the actual answers.

Scenario Part B: Question 1

This question focuses on the packet flow from PC12 to PC21, assuming the packet passes over the R1-R2 link. The fact that the packet is created due to a **ping** command, and contains an ICMP echo request, does not impact the answer at all. The question specifically asks about which ARP table entries must be used by each device.

To answer the question, you need to remember how a host or router will choose to which device it sends the frame. PC12 sends the frame to R1 because the destination IP address is in a different subnet than PC12. R1 then sends a new frame to R2. Finally, R2 sends yet another new frame (with new data link header and trailer) to PC21. Figure 15-7 shows the frames, with just the destination MAC address and destination IP address shown.

To analyze the frame sent by PC12, remember that PC12's logic is basically "the destination IP address is on another subnet, so send this packet to my default gateway." To do so, PC12 needs to encapsulate the IP packet in an Ethernet frame so that the frame arrives at R1, PC12's default gateway. So, PC12 must find the MAC address of its default gateway (10.10.15.1) in PC12's ARP table. If the ARP table entry exists, PC12 can immediately build the frame shown in Figure 15-7 at step 1. If not, PC12 must first send an ARP broadcast, and receive a reply, to build the correct entry in its ARP table.

Also, note that PC12 does not need to know PC21's MAC address, because PC12 is not trying to send the packet directly to PC21. Instead, PC12 is trying to send the packet to its default gateway, so PC12 needs to know its default gateway's MAC address.

Figure 15-7   *Scenario Part B: Answer to Question 1*

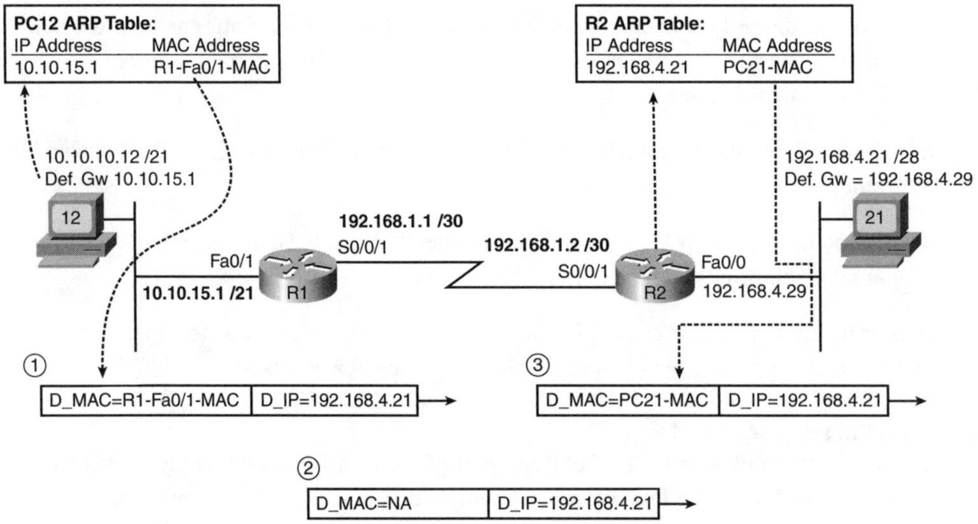

Step 2, as marked in Figure 15-7, shows the frame after R1 has stripped off the incoming frame's Ethernet header and trailer, R1 has decided to forward the packet out R1's S0/0/1 interface to R2 next, and R1 has added a (default) HDLC header and trailer to encapsulate the IP packet. The packet's destination IP address (192.168.4.21) is unchanged. HDLC, used only on point-to-point links, does not use MAC addresses, so it does not need ARP at all. So, no ARP table entries are needed on R1 for forwarding this packet.

Finally, step 3 again shows the frame after the router (R2) has stripped off the incoming HDLC frame's header and trailer and built the new Ethernet header and trailer. R2 needs to forward the packet out R2's Fa0/0 interface, directly to PC21, so R2 builds a header with PC21's MAC address as the destination. To make that happen, R2 needs an ARP table entry listing PC21's IP address (192.168.4.21) and its corresponding MAC address. Again, if R2 does not have an ARP table entry for IP address 192.168.4.21, R2 will send an ARP request (broadcast), and wait for a reply, before R2 would forward the packet.

Scenario Part B: Question 2

The answer to question 2 uses the same logic and reasoning as the answer to question 1. In this case, PC12, R1, and R4 will forward the packet in three successive steps, as follows:

1. PC12 decides to send the packet to its default gateway, because the destination (192.16.4.23) is on a different subnet than PC12. So, PC12 needs an ARP table entry listing the MAC address of its default gateway (10.10.15.1, or R1).

2. R1 receives the frame, strips off the data link header and trailer, and decides to forward the packet over the serial link to R4. The link uses HDLC, so R1 does not need ARP at all.

3. R4 receives the frame and strips off the incoming frame's HDLC header and trailer. R4 then decides to forward the packet directly to PC23, out R4's Fa0/1 interface, so R4 needs an ARP table entry listing the MAC address of host 192.168.4.23 (PC23).

Figure 15-8 shows the ARP table entries required for the flow of a packet from PC12 to PC23. Note that the figure also shows the correlation between the next-hop IP address and the MAC address, with the MAC address then being added to a new Ethernet data link header.

Figure 15-8 *Required ARP Table Entries: Question 2*

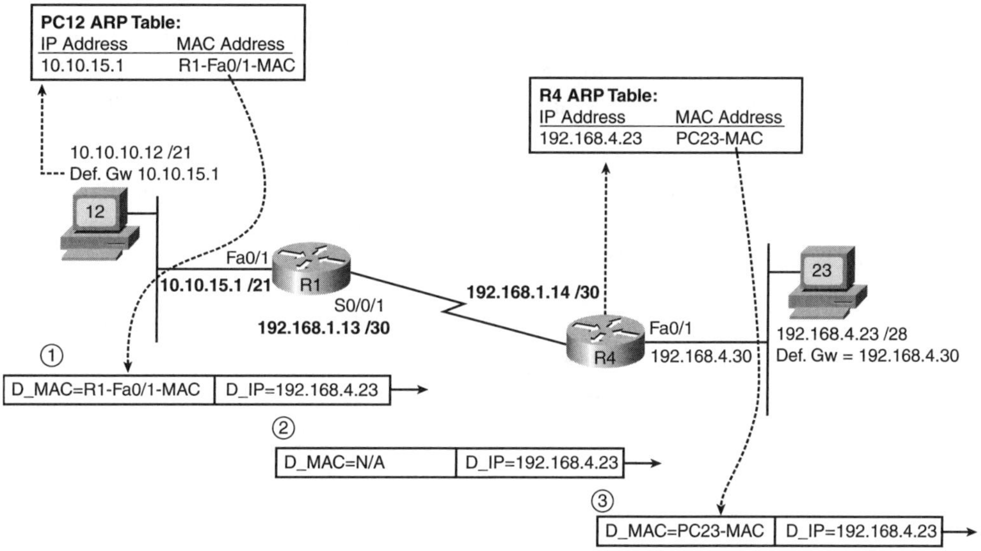

Scenario Part B: Question 3

The tricky part of this particular question relates to the fact that two routers connect to the subnet on the right of Figure 15-6, so PC23 appears to have two possible routers to use as its default gateway. The question suggests that an ICMP echo request packet goes from PC12, through R1, then R2, and over the LAN to PC23. PC23 then needs to send the ICMP echo reply to PC12, so to answer the question fully, you need to understand where the packet flows, and then determine the required ARP table entries on each device.

PC23 still uses the same familiar host logic when sending a packet—if the destination is on a different subnet, PC23 will send the packet to its default gateway. In this case, PC23 needs to send the ICMP echo reply to PC12, which is in another subnet, so PC23 will send the packet to 192.168.4.30 (R4)—PC23's configured default gateway. Presumably, R4 would then forward the packet to R1, and then R1 would forward the packet directly to PC12.

The ARP entries required for sending packets from PC23, to R4, to R1, and then to PC12 are as follows:

1.   PC23 decides to send the packet to its default gateway, R4. So, PC23 needs an ARP table entry listing the MAC address of its default gateway (192.168.4.30).

2.   R4 receives the frame, strips off the data link header and trailer, and decides to forward the packet over the serial link to R1. This links uses HDLC, so R4 does not need ARP at all.

3.   R1 receives the frame from R4 and strips off the incoming frame's HDLC header and trailer. R1 then decides to forward the packet directly to PC12, out R1's Fa0/1 interface, so R1 needs an ARP table entry listing the MAC address of host 10.10.10.12 (PC12).

Figure 15-9 shows the ARP table entries required for the flow of a packet from PC23 to PC12. Note that the figure also shows the correlation between the next-hop IP address and the MAC address, with the MAC address then being added to a new Ethernet data link header.

Figure 15-9   *Required ARP Table Entries: Question 3*

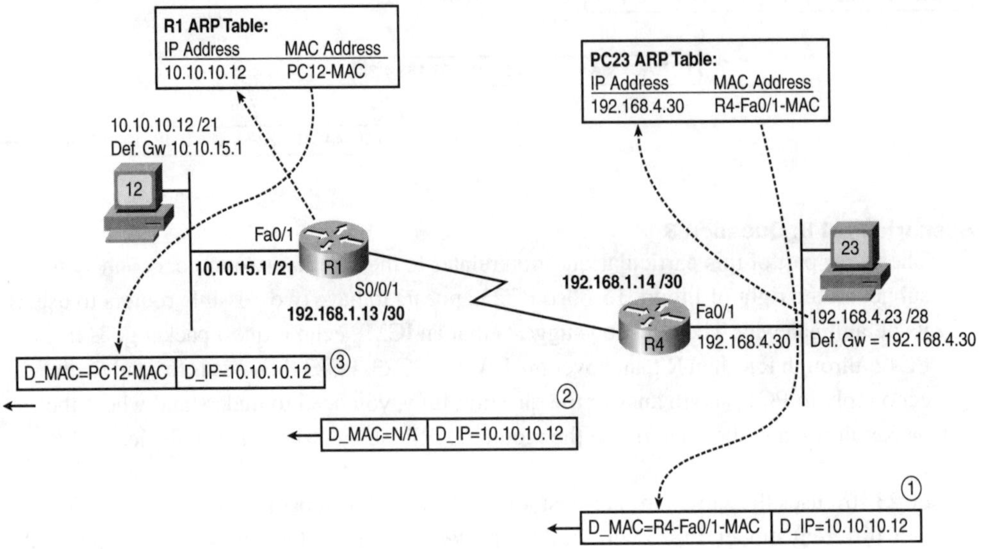

Scenario Part B: Question 4

This question uses a packet sent from PC31 to PC22, but with the question focusing on the packet as it crosses the LAN on the right side of Figure 15-6. To answer this question fully, you need to recall that while the source and destination IP addresses of the packet remain unchanged from sending host to receiving host, the data link source and destination addresses change each time a router builds a new data link header when forwarding a packet. Additionally, you need to realize that the R3→R4 serial link has been misconfigured (R4's proposed IP address of 192.168.1.19 was invalid), so no IP packets can be forwarded over the link between R3 and R4. As a result, the packet will go over this path: PC31→R3→R2→PC22.

The packet in question here (from PC31 to PC22) passes over the LAN on the right side of the figure when R2 forwards the packet over the LAN to PC22. In this case, R2 will build a new Ethernet header, with a source MAC address of R2's Fa0/0 interface MAC address. The destination MAC address will be PC22's MAC address. The source and destination IP addresses of 172.31.5.100 (PC31) and 192.168.4.22 (PC22), respectively, remain unchanged.

Figure 15-10 shows both data link addresses and both network layer addresses in each frame sent from PC31 to PC22. Note that the figure shows the addresses in the data link and network layer headers for each stage of its passage from PC31 to PC22.

Scenario Part B: Question 5

This question uses the same packet flow as question 4, but it focuses on the frame that passes the serial link between R3 and R2. The question can be easily answered as long as you remember that the router discards the data link headers of received frames, and then encapsulates the packet in a new data link header and trailer before forwarding the packet. This new data link header and trailer must be appropriate for the outgoing interface.

In this case, the routers use HDLC, which is the default point-to-point serial data link protocol on Cisco routers. HDLC headers do not include MAC addresses at all—in fact, HDLC addressing is completely uninteresting, because any frame sent by R3 on that link must be destined for R2, because R2 is the only other device on the other end of the link. As a result, there are no MAC addresses, but the source and destination IP addresses of 172.31.5.100 (PC31) and 192.168.4.22 (PC22), respectively, remain unchanged. Figure 15-9, found in the previous answer, shows a representation of the HDLC frame, mainly pointing out that it does not contain MAC addresses.

Figure 15-10   *Required ARP Table Entries: Question 4*

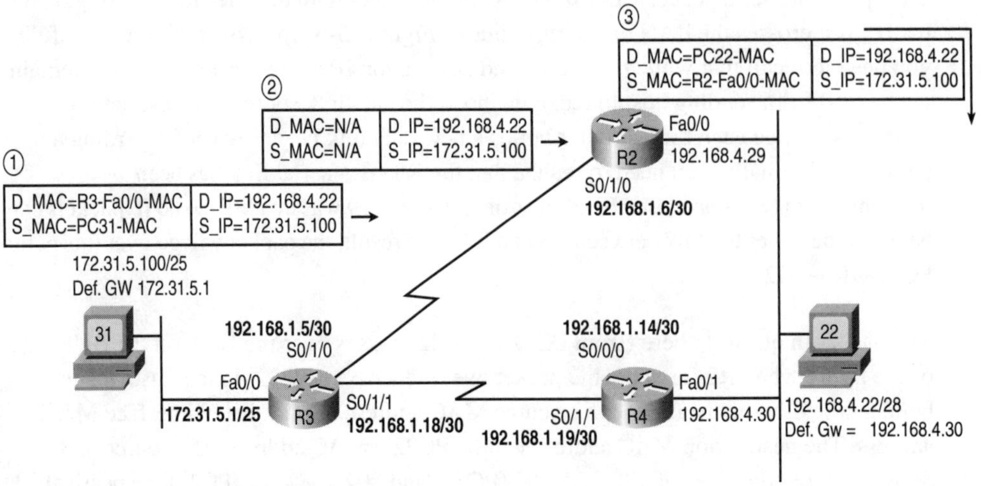

Scenario Part B: Question 6

This question focuses on a packet sent from PC21 to PC12, as the packet crosses the LAN on the right side of Figure 15-6. Also, the question tells you that the packet goes from PC21 to R2, then to R1, then to PC12.

In this case, PC21 forwards the packet, encapsulated in an Ethernet frame, to R2. To do so, the Ethernet header lists PC21 as the source MAC address, and R2's Fa0/0 interface MAC address as the destination MAC address. The IP addresses—a source of 192.168.4.21 (PC21) and a destination of 10.10.10.12 (PC12)—remain the same for the entire journey from PC21 to PC12. Figure 15-11 summarizes the frame contents for both this question and the next.

Figure 15-11   *Required ARP Table Entries: Questions 6 and 7*

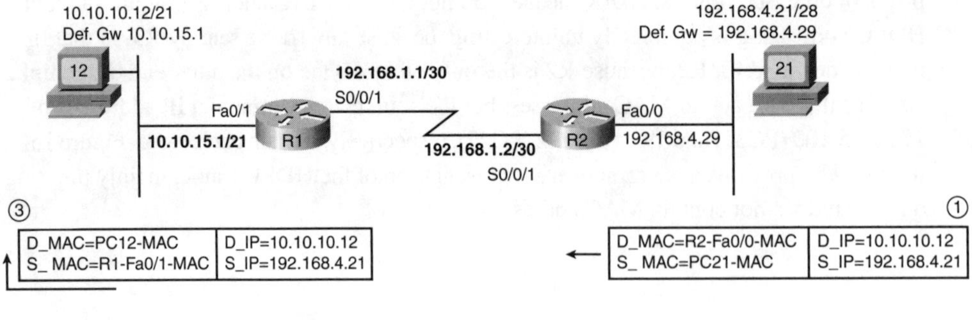

Scenario Part B: Question 7

Question 7 continues question 6 by examining the same packet, sent from PC21 to PC12, as the packet crosses the LAN on the upper-left part of Figure 15-6. The route taken by this packet is from PC21 to R2, then to R1, then to PC12.

To begin, PC21 sends the IP packet, with a source of 192.168.4.21 (PC21) and a destination of 10.10.10.12 (PC12). To send this packet, PC21 encapsulates the packet in an Ethernet frame to deliver the packet to its default gateway (R2). R2 strips off the Ethernet header of the received frame, and before forwarding the packet to R1, R2 encapsulates the packet in an HDLC frame. When R1 receives the HDLC frame, R1 removes the HDLC header and trailer, deciding to forward the packet out R1's Fa0/1 interface to PC12. As usual, the packet's source and destination address do not change at all during this process.

Before R1 forwards the packet out its Fa0/1 interface, R1 adds an Ethernet header and trailer. The source MAC address is R1's Fa0/1 interface MAC address, and the destination, found in R1's ARP table, is PC12's MAC address. Note that Figure 15-11, shown in the previous section, shows this frame on the left side of the figure.

Scenario Part C: Analyze Connected Routes

For Part C of this scenario, predict the output that would be displayed of the **show ip route connected** command on R4 and R1. You may continue to assume that any IP addressing problems found in Part A still have *not* been corrected. You may refer back to Example 15-5 through Example 15-9, as well as the completed IP address reference of Figure 15-6, for reference.

Scenario Part C: Answers

Routers add connected IP routes to their IP routing tables, referencing the subnet that is connected to an interface, assuming the following are true:

■ The interface's two status codes are "up" and "up."

■ The interface has an IP address correctly configured.

Key Topic

For each interface meeting these two requirements, the router calculates the subnet number based on the IP address and subnet mask listed in the **ip address** interface subcommand. Based on details included in Parts A and B of this scenario, all router interfaces shown in Figure 15-5 have an IP address and are up/up, with the exception of R4's S0/1/1 interface. This one serial interface was to be assigned an IP address that was really a subnet broadcast address, so the router would have rejected the **ip address** command. Table 15-5 lists the location and connected routes added to R1 and R4.

Table 15-5   *Connected Routes Added to R1 and R4*

Location	IP Address	Subnet	Outgoing Interface
R1 Fa0/0	10.10.24.1/21	10.10.24.0/21	Fa0/0
R1 Fa0/1	10.10.15.1/21	10.10.8.0/21	Fa0/1
R1 S0/0/1	192.168.1.1/30	192.168.1.0/30	S0/0/1
R1 S0/1/1	192.168.1.13/30	192.168.1.12/30	S0/1/1
R4 S0/0/1	192.168.1.14/30	192.168.1.12/30	S0/0/1
R4 Fa0/1	192.168.4.30/28	192.168.4.16/28	Fa0/1

To see the connected routes in a concise command, you can use the **show ip route connected** EXEC command. This command simply lists a subset of the routes in the routing table—those that are connected routes. Example 15-10 and Example 15-11 show the contents of the **show ip route connected** command on both R1 and R4, respectively.

Example 15-10   show ip route connected *Command Output for R1*

```
R1#show ip route connected
     10.0.0.0/21 is subnetted, 2 subnets
C       10.10.8.0 is directly connected, FastEthernet0/1
C       10.10.24.0 is directly connected, FastEthernet0/0
     192.168.1.0/24 is variably subnetted, 5 subnets, 2 masks
C       192.168.1.12/30 is directly connected, Serial0/1/1
C       192.168.1.0/30 is directly connected, Serial0/0/1
```

Example 15-11   show ip route connected *Command on R4*

```
R4#show ip route connected
     192.168.4.0/28 is subnetted, 1 subnets
C       192.168.4.16 is directly connected, FastEthernet0/1
     192.168.1.0/24 is variably subnetted, 5 subnets, 2 masks
C       192.168.1.12/30 is directly connected, Serial0/0/1
```

If you compare the highlighted portions of Example 15-11 with Example 15-9's **ip address 192.168.4.30 255.255.255.240** command, a subcommand under R4's Fa0/1 interface, you can correlate the information. The mask from the **ip address** command can be used to determine the prefix notation version of the same mask—/28. The address and mask together can be used to determine the subnet number of 192.168.4.16. These same pieces of information are highlighted in the output of the **show ip route connected** command in Example 15-11.

Exam Preparation Tasks

Review All the Key Topics

Review the most important topics from inside the chapter, noted with the key topics icon in the outer margin of the page. Table 15-6 lists a reference of these key topics and the page numbers on which each is found.

Table 15-6 *Key Topics for Chapter 15*

Key Topic Element	Description	Page Number
List	First octet values of addresses that are always reserved and cannot be assigned to hosts	475
Table 15-2	Summary of reasons why an exam question should or should not allow the use of the zero and broadcast subnets	476
List	Summary of four tips when approaching IP addressing related questions on the exams	478
List	Summary of how a host thinks about routing, address assignment, name resolution, and ARP	478
List	Two typical reasons why a host cannot ping other hosts in the same subnet	482
List	Three typical reasons why a host can ping other hosts in the same subnet, but not hosts in other subnets	482-483
List	Tips regarding how a router matches a packet's destination IP address as part of the routing process	483
Figure 15-3	Shows the IP addresses discovered by the Cisco IOS **traceroute** command	486
List	Reminders that are helpful when thinking about the source and destination MAC and IP addresses used at various points in an internetwork	496
List	Two key requirements for a router to add a connected route	503

Complete the Tables and Lists from Memory

Print a copy of Appendix H, "Memory Tables" (found on the CD-ROM), or at least the section for this chapter, and complete the tables and lists from memory. Appendix I, "Memory Tables Answer Key," also on the CD-ROM, includes completed tables and lists to check your work.

Command Reference

Table 15-7 lists the EXEC commands used in this chapter and a brief description of their use. Additionally, you might want to review the host commands listed earlier in the chapter in Table 15-4. (This chapter did not introduce any new configuration commands.)

Table 15-7   *Chapter 15* **show** *and* **debug** *Command Reference*

Command	Purpose
show sessions	Lists the suspended Telnet and SSH session on the router from which the Telnet and SSH sessions were created
where	Does the same thing as the **show sessions** command
telnet {*hostname* | *ip_address*}	Connects the CLI to another host using Telnet
ssh –l *username* {*hostname* | *ip_address*}	Connects the CLI to another host using SSH
disconnect [*connection_number*]	Disconnects a currently suspended Telnet or SSH connection, based on the connection number as seen with the **show sessions** command
resume [*connection_number*]	Connects the CLI to a currently suspended Telnet or SSH connection, based on the connection number as seen with the **show sessions** command
traceroute {*hostname* | *ip_address*}	Discovers if a path from the router to a destination IP address is working, listing each next-hop router in the route
Ctrl-Shift-6, **x**	The key sequence required to suspend a Telnet or SSH connection
show ip arp	Lists the contents of the router's ARP cache
show arp	Lists the contents of the router's ARP cache
show ssh	Lists information about the users logged in to the router using SSH
show users	Lists information about users logged in to the router, including Telnet, SSH, and console users

Cisco Published ICND1 Exam Topics* Covered in This Part:

Describe the operation of data networks

- Interpret network diagrams

- Determine the path between two hosts across a network

- Describe the components required for network and Internet communications

- Identify and correct common network problems at Layers 1, 2, 3, and 7 using a layered model approach

- Differentiate between LAN/WAN operation and features

Implement an IP addressing scheme and IP services to meet network requirements for a small branch office

- Explain the basic uses and operation of NAT in a small network connecting to one ISP

- Describe the operation and benefits of using private and public IP addressing

- Enable NAT for a small network with a single ISP and connection using SDM and verify operation using CLI and ping

Implement and verify WAN links

- Describe different methods for connecting to a WAN

- Configure and verify a basic WAN serial connection

*Always recheck http://www.cisco.com for the latest posted exam topics.

Part IV: Wide-Area Networks

This chapter covers the following subjects:

WAN Technologies: This section examines several additional WAN technologies that were not covered in Chapter 4, namely modems, DSL, cable, and ATM.

IP Services for Internet Access: This section examines how an Internet access router uses DHCP client and server functions, as well as NAT.

CHAPTER 16

WAN Concepts

Chapter 4, "Fundamentals of WANs," introduced two important WAN technologies common in enterprise networks today:

- Leased lines, which use either High-Level Data Link Control (HDLC) or Point-to-Point Protocol (PPP)

- Frame Relay

Part IV of this book covers the remainder of the WAN-specific topics in this book. In particular, this chapter examines a broader range of WAN technologies, including commonly used Internet access technologies. Chapter 17, "WAN Configuration," focuses on how to implement several features related to WAN connections, including several Layer 3 services required for a typical Internet connection from a small office or home (SOHO) today.

"Do I Know This Already?" Quiz

The "Do I Know This Already?" quiz allows you to assess if you should read the entire chapter. If you miss no more than one of these eight self-assessment questions, you might want to move ahead to the "Exam Preparation Tasks" section. Table 16-1 lists the major headings in this chapter and the "Do I Know This Already?" quiz questions covering the material in those headings so you can assess your knowledge of these specific areas. The answers to the "Do I Know This Already?" quiz appear in Appendix A.

Table 16-1 *"Do I Know This Already?" Foundation Topics Section-to-Question Mapping*

Foundation Topics Section	Questions
WAN Technologies	1–5
IP Services for Internet Access	6–8

1. Which of the following best describes the function of demodulation by a modem?

    a. Encoding an incoming analog signal from the PC as a digital signal for transmission into the PSTN

    b. Decoding an incoming digital signal from the PSTN into an analog signal

    c. Encoding a set of binary digits as an analog electrical signal

    d. Decoding an incoming analog electrical signal from the PSTN into a digital signal

    e. Encoding a set of binary digits as a digital electrical signal

2. Which of the following standards has a limit of 18,000 feet for the length of the local loop?

    a. ADSL

    b. Analog modems

    c. ISDN

    d. Cable Internet service

3. Which of the following is true regarding the location and purpose of a DSLAM?

    a. Typically used at a home or small office to connect the phone line to a DSL router

    b. Typically used at a home or small office instead of a DSL router

    c. Typically used inside the telco's CO to prevent any voice traffic from reaching the ISP's router

    d. Typically used inside the telco's CO to separate the voice traffic from the data traffic

4. Which of the following remote-access technologies support specifications that allow both symmetric speeds and asymmetric speeds?

    a. Analog modems

    b. WWW

    c. DSL

    d. Cable modems

5. Which of the following remote-access technologies, when used to connect to an ISP, is considered to be an "always on" Internet service?

    a. Analog modems

    b. DSL

    c. Cable modems

    d. All of these answers are correct.

6. For a typical Internet access router, using either cable or DSL, which of the following does the router typically do on the router interface connected to the LAN with the PCs in the small or home office?

    a. Acts as a DHCP server

    b. Acts as a DHCP client

    c. Performs NAT/PAT for the source address of packets that exit the interface

    d. Acts as DNS server

7. For a typical Internet access router, using either cable or DSL, which of the following does the router typically do on the router interface connected toward the Internet?

    a. Acts as a DHCP server

    b. Acts as a DHCP client

    c. Performs NAT/PAT for the source address of packets that exit the interface

    d. Acts as DNS server

8. This question examines a home-based network with a PC, a DSL router, and a DSL line. The DSL router uses typical default settings and functions. The PC connected to the router has IP address 10.1.1.1. This PC opens a browser and connects to the www.cisco.com web server. Which of the following are true in this case?

    a. The web server can tell it is communicating with a host at IP address 10.1.1.1.

    b. The PC learns the IP address of the www.cisco.com web server as a public IP address.

    c. The 10.1.1.1 address would be considered an inside local IP address.

    d. The 10.1.1.1 address would be considered an inside global IP address.

Foundation Topics

WANs differ from LANs in several ways. Most significantly, WAN links typically go much longer distances, with the WAN cabling being installed underground in many cases to prevent accidental damage by people walking on them or cars driving over them. Governments typically do not let the average person dig around other people's property, so WAN connections use cabling installed by a service provider, with the service provider having permission from the appropriate government agencies to install and maintain the cabling. The service provider then sells the WAN services to various enterprises. This difference between WANs and LANs can be summed up with the old adage "You own LANs, but you lease WANs."

This chapter has two major sections. The first section examines a broad range of WAN connectivity options, including switched circuits, DSL, cable, and ATM. The second half then explains how Internet connections from a home or small office often need several Layer 3 services before the WAN connection can be useful. The second section goes on to explain why DHCP and NAT are needed for routers connecting to the Internet, with particular attention to the NAT function.

WAN Technologies

This section introduces four different types of WAN technologies in addition to the leased-line and Frame Relay WANs introduced in Chapter 4. The first of these technologies, analog modems, can be used to communicate between most any two devices, and can be used to connect to the Internet through an ISP. The next two technologies, DSL and cable Internet, are almost exclusively used for Internet access. The last of these, ATM, is a packet-switching service used like Frame Relay to connect enterprise routers, as well as for other purposes not discussed in this book.

Before introducing each of these types of WANs, this section starts by explaining a few details about the telco's network, particularly because modems and DSL use the phone line installed by the telco.

Perspectives on the PSTN

The term Public Switched Telephone Network (PSTN) refers to the equipment and devices that telcos use to create basic telephone service between any two phones in the world. This term refers to the combined networks of all telephone companies. The "public" part of PSTN refers to the fact that it is available for public use (for a fee), and the "switched" part refers to the fact that you can change or switch between phone calls with different people at will. Although the PSTN was originally built to support voice traffic, two of the three Internet access technologies covered in this chapter happen to use the PSTN to send data, so a basic understanding of the PSTN can help you appreciate how modems and DSL work.

Sound waves travel through the air by vibrating the air. The human ear hears the sound because the ear vibrates as a result of the air inside the ear moving, which, in turn, causes the brain to process the sounds that were heard by the ear.

The PSTN, however, cannot forward sound waves. Instead, a telephone includes a microphone, which simply converts the sound waves into an analog electrical signal. (The electrical signal is called analog because it is analogous to the sound waves.) The PSTN can send the analog electrical signal between one phone and another using an electrical circuit. On the receiving side, the phone converts the analog electrical signal back to sound waves using a speaker that is inside the part of the phone that you put next to your ear.

The original PSTN predated the invention of the digital computer by quite a while, with the first telephone exchanges being created in the 1870s, soon after the invention of the telephone by Alexander Graham Bell. In its original form, a telephone call required an electrical circuit between the two phones. With the advent of digital computers, however, in the mid-1950s telcos began updating the core of the PSTN to use digital electrical signals, which gave the PSTN many advantages in speed, quality, manageability, and capability to scale to a much larger size.

Next, consider what the telco has to do to make your home phone work. Between your home and some nearby telco central office (CO), the telco typically installs a cable with a pair of wires, called the *local loop*. (In the United States, if you have ever seen a two- to three-foot-high light-green post in your neighborhood, that is the collection point for the local loop cables that connect to the houses on that street.) One end of the cable enters your house and connects to the phone outlets in your house. The other end (possibly miles away) connects to a computer in the CO, generically called a voice switch. Figure 16-1 shows the concept, along with some other details.

The local loop supports analog electrical signals to create a voice call. The figure shows two local loops, one connected to Andy's phone, and the other connected to Barney's. Andy and Barney happen to live far enough apart that their local loops connect to different COs.

Figure 16-1   *Analog Voice Calls Through a Digital PSTN*

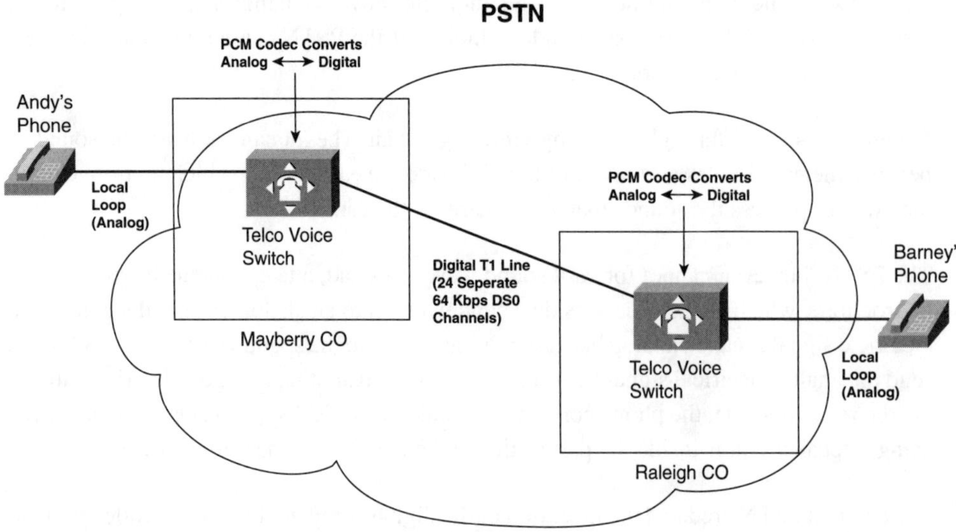

When Andy calls Barney, the phone call works, but the process is more complicated than just setting up an electrical circuit between the two phones. In particular, note that

■   The phones use analog electrical signals only.

■   The voice switches use a digital circuit to forward the voice (a T1 in this case).

■   The voice switch must convert between analog electricity and digital electricity in both directions.

To make it all work, the phone company switch in the Mayberry CO performs analog-to-digital (A/D) conversion of Andy's incoming analog voice. When the switch in Raleigh gets the digital signal from the Mayberry switch, before sending it out the analog line to Barney's house, the Raleigh switch reverses the A/D process, converting the digital signal back to analog. The analog signal going over the local line to Barney's house is roughly the same analog signal that Andy's phone sent over his local line; in other words, it is the same sounds.

The original standard for converting analog voice to a digital signal is called *pulse-code modulation (PCM)*. PCM defines that an incoming analog voice signal should be sampled 8000 times per second by the A/D converter, using an 8-bit code for each sample. As a result, a single voice call requires 64,000 bits per second—which amazingly fits perfectly into 1 of the 24 available 64-kbps DS0 channels in a T1. (As you may recall from Chapter 4, a T1 holds 24 separate DS0 channels, 64 kbps each, plus 8 kbps of management overhead, for a total of 1.544 Mbps.)

The details and complexity of the PSTN as it exists today go far beyond this brief introduction. However, these few pages do introduce a few key points that will give you some perspectives on how other WAN technologies work. In summary:

- The telco voice switch in the CO expects to send and receive analog voice over the physical line to a typical home (the *local loop*).

- The telco voice switch converts the received analog voice to the digital equivalent using a codec.

- The telco converts the digital voice back to the analog equivalent for transmission over the local loop at the destination.

- The voice call, with the PCM codec in use, consumes 64 kbps through the digital part of the PSTN (when using links like T1s and T3s inside the telco).

Analog Modems

Analog modems allow two computers to send and receive a serial stream of bits over the same voice circuit normally used between two phones. The modems can connect to a normal local phone line (local loop), with no physical changes required on the local loop cabling and no changes required on the voice switch at the telco's CO. Because the switch in the CO expects to send and receive analog voice signals over the local loop, modems simply send an analog signal to the PSTN and expect to receive an analog signal from the PSTN. However, that analog signal represents some bits that the computer needs to send to another computer, instead of voice created by a human speaker. Similar in concept to a phone converting sound waves into an analog electrical signal, a modem converts a string of binary digits on a computer into a representative analog electrical signal.

To achieve a particular bit rate, the sending modem could modulate (change) the analog signal at that rate. For instance, to send 9600 bps, the sending modem would change the signal (as necessary) every 1/9600th of a second. Similarly, the receiving modem would sample the incoming analog signal every 1/9600th of a second, interpreting the signal as a binary 1 or 0. (The process of the receiving end is called *demodulation*. The term *modem* is a shortened version of the combination of the two words *modulation* and *demodulation*.)

Because modems represent data as an analog electrical signal, modems can connect to a PSTN local loop, make the equivalent of a phone call to another site that has a modem connected to its phone line, and send data. As a result, modems can be used at most any location that has a phone line installed.

The PSTN refers to a communications path between the two modems as a circuit. Because the modems can switch to a different destination just by hanging up and dialing another phone number, this type of WAN service is called a *switched circuit*. Figure 16-2 shows an example, now with Andy and Barney connecting their PCs to their home phone lines using a modem.

Figure 16-2 *Basic Operation of Modems over PSTN*

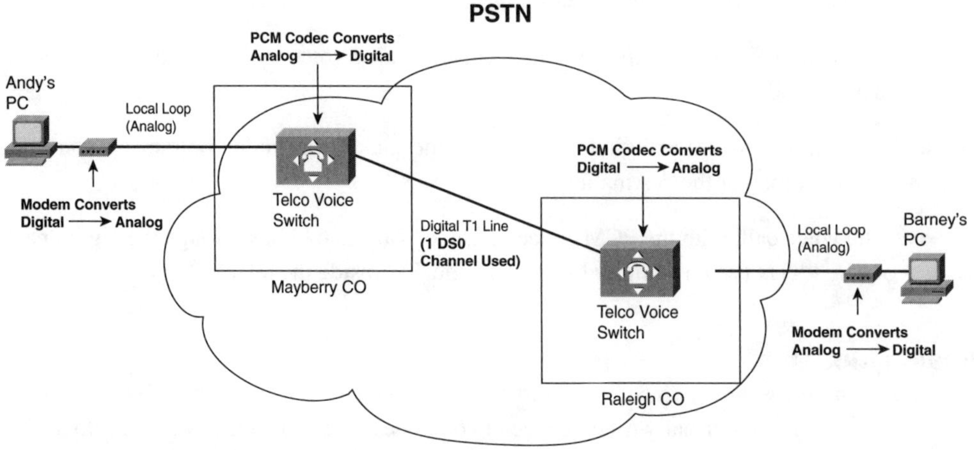

Once the circuit has been established, the two computers have a Layer 1 service, meaning that they can pass bits between each other. The computers also need to use some data link layer protocol on the circuit, with PPP being a popular option today. The telco has no need to try and interpret what the bits sent by the modem mean—in fact, the telco does not even care to know if the signal represents voice or data.

To be used as an Internet access WAN technology, the home-based user connects via a modem to a router owned by an ISP. The home user typically has a modem in their computer (internal modem) or outside the computer (external modem). The ISP typically has a large bank of modems. The ISP then publishes a phone number for the phone lines installed into the ISP router's modem bank, and the home user dials that number to connect to the ISP's router.

The circuit between two modems works and acts like a leased line in some regards; however, the link differs in regards to clocking and synchronization. The CSU/DSUs on the ends of a leased line create what is called a synchronous circuit, because not only do the CSU/DSUs try to run at the same speed, they adjust their speeds to match or synchronize with the other CSU/DSU. Modems create an asynchronous circuit, which means that the two modems try to use the same speed, but they do not adjust their clock rates to match the other modem.

Modems have the great advantage of being the most pervasively available remote-access technology, usable most anywhere that a local phone line is available. The cost is relatively low, particularly if the phone line is already needed for basic voice service; however, modems run at a relatively slow speed. Even with modern compression technologies, the bit rate for modems is only a little faster than 100 kbps. Additionally, you cannot concurrently talk on the phone and send data with a modem on the same phone line.

Digital Subscriber Line

By the time *digital subscriber line (DSL)* came around in the mid- to late 1990s, the main goal for remote-access WAN technology had changed. The need to connect to any other computer anywhere had waned, but the need to connect to the Internet was growing quickly. In years past, modems were used to dial a large variety of different computers, which was useful. Today you can think of the Internet as a utility, just like you think of the electric company, the gas company, and so on. The Internet utility provides IP connectivity to the rest of the world, so if you can just get connected to the Internet, you can communicate with anyone else in the world.

Because most people today just want access to the utility—in other words, the Internet— DSL was defined a little differently than modems. In fact, DSL was designed to provide high-speed access between a home or business and the local CO. By limiting the scope of where DSL needed to work, design engineers were able to define DSL to support much faster speeds than modems.

DSL's basic services have some similarities, as well as differences, to analog modems. Some of the key features are as follows:

- DSL allows analog voice signals and digital data signals to be sent over the same local loop wiring at the same time.

- The local loop must be connected to something besides a traditional voice switch at the local CO, in this case a device called a *DSL access multiplexer (DSLAM)*.

- DSL allows for a concurrent voice call to be up at the same time as the data connection.

- Unlike modems, DSL's data component is always on; in other words, you do not have to signal or dial a phone number to set up a data circuit.

DSL really does provide some great benefits—you can use the same old phones that you already have, you can keep the same phone number, and, once DSL is installed, you can just sit down and start using your "always on" Internet service without having to dial a number. Figure 16-3 shows some of the details of a typical DSL connection.

Key
Topic

Figure 16-3 *DSL Connection from the Home to an ISP*

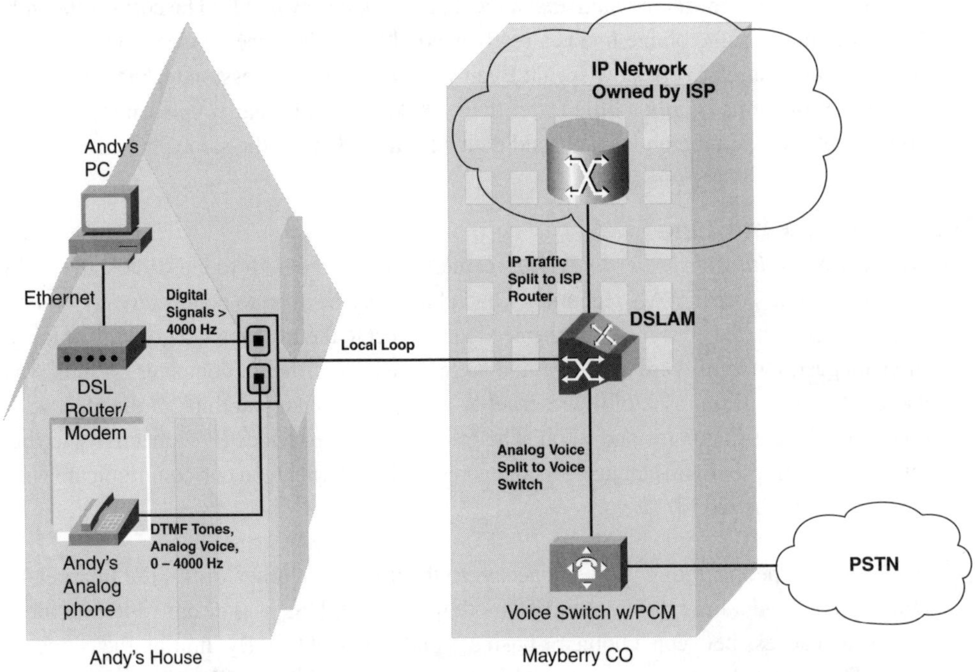

The figure shows a generic-looking device labeled "DSL Router/Modem" which connects via a standard telephone cable to the same phone jack on the wall. Many options exist for the DSL hardware at the home: There could be a separate router and DSL modem, the two could be combined as shown in the figure, or the two could be combined along with a LAN switch and a wireless AP. (Figure 13-4 and Figure 13-5 in Chapter 13, "Operating Cisco Routers," show a couple of the cabling options for the equivalent design when using cable Internet, which has the same basic hardware options.)

In the home, a DSL modem or DSL-capable router is connected to the phone line (the local loop) using a typical telephone cable, as shown on the left side of Figure 16-3. The same old analog telephones can be connected to any other available phone jacks, at the same time. The cable from the phone or DSL modem to the telephone wall jack uses RJ-11 connectors, as is typical for a cable for an analog phone or a modem.

DSL supports concurrent voice and data, so you can make a phone call without disrupting the always-on DSL Internet connection. The phone generates an analog signal at frequency ranges between 0 and 4000 Hz; the DSL modem uses frequencies higher than 4000 Hz so that the phone and DSL signals do not interfere with each other very much. You typically need to put a filter, a small device about the size of a small packet of chewing gum, between each phone and the wall socket (not shown) to prevent interference from the higher-frequency DSL signals.

The DSLAM at the local CO plays a vitally important role in allowing the digital data and analog voice to be processed correctly. When migrating a customer from just using voice to instead support voice and DSL, the phone company has to disconnect the local loop cable from the old voice switch and move it to a DSLAM. The local loop wiring itself does not have to change. The DSLAM directs (multiplexes) the analog voice signal—the frequency range between 0 Hz and 4000 Hz—to a voice switch, and the voice switch treats that signal just like any other analog voice line. The DSLAM multiplexes the data traffic to a router owned by the ISP providing the service in Figure 16-3.

The design with a local loop, DSLAM, and ISP router enables a business model in which you buy Internet services from an ISP that is not the local phone company. The local telco owns the local loop. However, many ISPs that are not a local telco sell DSL Internet access. The way it works is that you pay the ISP a monthly fee for DSL service, and the ISP works with the telco to get your local loop connected to the telco's DSLAM. The telco then configures the DSLAM to send data traffic from your local loop to that ISP's router. You pay the ISP for high-speed DSL Internet service, and the ISP keeps part of the money and gives part of the money to the local telco.

DSL Types, Speeds, and Distances

DSL technology includes many options at many speeds, with some variations getting more attention in the marketplace. So, it is helpful to consider at least a few of the options.

One key difference in the types of DSL is whether the DSL service is symmetric or asymmetric. *Symmetric* DSL means that the link speed in each direction is the same, whereas *asymmetric* means that the speeds are different. As it turns out, SOHO users tend to need to receive much more data than they need to send. For example, a home user might type in a URL in a browser window, sending a few hundred bytes of data to the ISP. The web page returned from the Internet may be many megabytes large. Asymmetric DSL allows for much faster downstream (Internet toward home) speeds, but with lower upstream (home toward Internet) speeds, as compared with symmetric DSL. For example, an ADSL connection might use a 1.5-Mbps speed downstream (toward the end user), and a 384-Kbps speed upstream toward the Internet. Table 16-2 lists some of the more popular types of DSL, and whether each is asymmetric or symmetric.

Table 16-2 *DSL Types*

Acronym	Spelled Out	Type
ADSL	Asymmetric DSL	Asymmetric
CDSL (G.lite)	Consumer DSL	Asymmetric
VDSL	Very-high-data-rate DSL	Asymmetric

continues

Table 16-2   *DSL Types (Continued)*

Acronym	Spelled Out	Type
SDSL	Symmetric DSL	Symmetric
HDSL	High-data-rate DSL	Symmetric
IDSL	ISDN DSL	Symmetric

Typically, most consumer DSL installations in the United States use ADSL.

The speed of a DSL line is a difficult number to pin down. DSL standards list maximum speeds, but in practice the speed can vary widely, based on many factors, including:

■ The distance between the CO and the consumer (the longer the distance, the slower the speed)

■ The quality of the local loop cabling (the worse the wiring, the slower the speed)

■ The type of DSL (each standard has different maximum theoretical speeds)

■ The DSLAM used in the CO (older equipment may not have recent improvements that allow for faster speeds on lower-grade local loops)

For example, ADSL has theoretical downstream speeds of close to 10 Mbps, with the Cisco ICND1 course currently making a minor reference to a maximum of 8.192 Mbps. However, most ISPs, if they quote any numbers at all, state that the lines will run at about 1.5 Mbps downstream, and 384 kbps upstream—numbers much more realistic compared to the actual speeds experienced by their customers. Regardless of the actual speeds, these speeds are significantly faster than modem speeds, making DSL very popular in the marketplace for high-speed Internet access.

Besides the factors that limit the speed, DSL lines typically do not work at all if the local loop exceeds that particular DSL standard's maximum cabling length. For example, ADSL has become popular in part because it supports local loops that are up to 18,000 feet (a little over 3 miles/5 kilometers). However, if you live in the country, far away from the CO, chances are DSL is not an option.

DSL Summary

DSL brings high-speed remote-access capabilities to the home. It supports concurrent voice and data, using the same old analog phones and same old local loop cabling. The Internet data service is always on—no dialing required. Furthermore, the speed of the DSL service itself does not degrade when more users are added to the network.

DSL has some obvious drawbacks. DSL simply will not be available to some people, particularly those in rural areas, based on the distance from the home to the CO. The local telco must have DSL equipment in the CO before it, or any ISP, can offer DSL services. Even when the home is close enough to the CO, sites farther from the CO might run slower than sites closer to the CO.

Cable Internet

Of all the Internet access technologies covered in this chapter, cable modem technology is the only one that does not use a phone line from the local telco for physical connectivity. Many homes also have a cable TV service supplied by a coaxial cable—in other words, over the cable TV (CATV) cabling. Cable modems provide an always-on Internet access service, while allowing you to surf the Internet over the cable and make all the phone calls you want over your telephone line—and you can watch TV at the same time!

NOTE   Cable companies today also offer digital voice services, competing with the local telcos. The voice traffic also passes over the same CATV cable.

Cable modems (and cable routers with integrated cable modems, similar in concept to DSL) use some of the capacity in the CATV cable that otherwise might have been allocated for new TV channels, using those frequency bands for transferring data. It is a little like having an "Internet" channel to go along with CNN, TBS, ESPN, The Cartoon Network, and all your other favorite cable channels.

To appreciate how cable modems work, you need a little perspective on some cable TV terminology. Cable TV traditionally has been a one-way service—the cable provider sends electrical signals down the cable for all the channels. All you have to do, after the physical installation is complete, is choose the channel you want to watch. While you are watching The Cartoon Network, the electrical signals for CNN still are coming into your house over the cable—your TV is just ignoring that part of the signal. If you have two TVs in your house, you can watch two different channels because the signals for all the channels are being sent down the cable.

Cable TV technology has its own set of terminology, just like most of the other access technologies covered in this chapter. Figure 16-4 outlines some of the key terms.

The cable modem or cable router connects to the CATV cable, shown as a dotted line in the figure. In a typical house or apartment, there are several cable wall plates installed, so the cable modem/router just connects to one of those wall jacks. And like DSL modems/routers, the cable modem/router connects to the PCs in the home using an Ethernet connection.

Figure 16-4   *Cable TV Terminology*

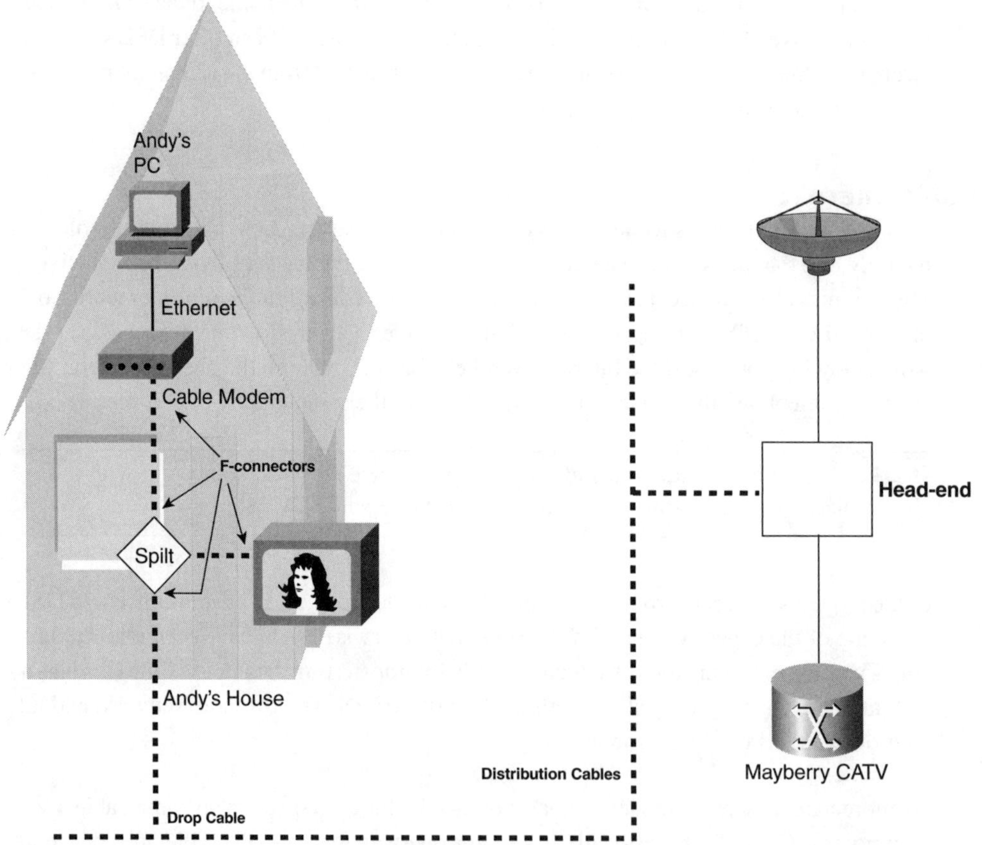

The other end of the cable connects to equipment in the cable company's facilities, generally called the head-end. Equipment on the head-end can split the channels used for Internet over to an ISP router, much like a DSLAM splits data off the telco local loop over to an ISP's router. That same equipment collects TV signals (typically from a satellite array) and feeds those over other channels on the cable to provide TV service.

Cable Internet service has many similarities to DSL services. It is intended to be used to access some ISP's router, with that service being always on and available. It is asymmetric, with much faster downstream speeds. The SOHO user needs a cable modem and router, which may be in a single device or in separate devices.

There are some key differences, as you might imagine. Cable Internet service runs faster than DSL, with practical speeds from two to five times faster than the typically quoted 1.5 Mbps for DSL. Cable speeds do not degrade due to the length of the cable (distance from the cable company's facilities). However, the effective speed of cable Internet does degrade as more and more traffic is sent over the cable by other users, because the cable is shared among users in certain parts of the CATV cable plant, whereas DSL does not suffer from this problem. To be fair, the cable companies can engineer around these contention problems and improve the effective speed for those customers.

> **NOTE**   Pinning down exact answers to the questions "how fast is cable?" and "how fast is DSL?" is difficult because the speeds vary depending on many factors. However, you can test the actual amount of data transferred using one of many speed-testing websites. I tend to use CNET's website, which can be found by searching the web for "Internet speed test CNET" or at http://reviews.cnet.com/7004-7254_7-0.html.

Comparison of Remote-Access Technologies

This chapter scratches the surface of how modems, cable, and DSL work. Consumers choose between these options for Internet access all the time, and network engineers choose between these options for supporting their work-at-home users as well. So, Table 16-3 lists some of the key comparison points for these options.

Table 16-3   *Comparison of Modems, DSL, and Cable*

Key Topic

	Analog Modems	DSL	Cable Modems
Transport	Telco local loop	Telco local loop	CATV cable
Supports symmetric speeds	Yes	Yes	No
Supports asymmetric speeds	Yes	Yes	Yes
Typical practical speeds (may vary)	Up to 100 kbps	1.5 Mbps downstream	3 to 6 Mbps downstream
Allows concurrent voice and data	No	Yes	Yes
Always-on Internet service	No	Yes	Yes
Local loop distance issues	No	Yes	No
Throughput degrades under higher loads	No	No	Yes

ATM

The other WAN technologies introduced in this book can all be used for Internet access from the home or a small office. Asynchronous Transfer Mode (ATM) is most often used today either as a packet-switching service, similar in purpose to Frame Relay, or as a switching technology used inside the core network built by telcos. This section introduces ATM as a packet-switching service.

To use ATM, routers connect to an ATM service via an access link to an ATM switch inside the service provider's network—basically the same topology as Frame Relay. For multiple sites, each router would need a single access link to the ATM network, with a virtual circuit (VC) between sites as needed. ATM can use permanent VCs (PVC) like Frame Relay.

Of course, there are differences between Frame Relay and ATM; otherwise, you would not need both! First, ATM typically supports much higher-speed physical links, especially those using a specification called Synchronous Optical Network (SONET). The other big difference is that ATM does not forward frames—it forwards *cells*. A cell, just like a packet or frame, is a string of bits sent over some network. The difference is that while packets and frames can vary in size, ATM cells are always a fixed 53 bytes in length.

ATM cells contain 48 bytes of payload (data) and a 5-byte header. The header contains two fields that together act like the data-link connection identifier (DLCI) for Frame Relay by identifying each VC. The two fields are named *Virtual Path Identifier (VPI)* and *Virtual Channel Identifier (VCI)*. Just like Frame Relay switches forward frames based on the DLCI, devices called ATM switches, resident in the service provider network, forward cells based on the VPI/VCI pair.

The end users of a network typically connect using Ethernet, and Ethernet devices do not create cells. So, how do you get traffic off an Ethernet and onto an ATM network? A router connects both to the LAN and to the ATM WAN service via an access link. When a router receives a packet from the LAN and decides to forward the packet over the ATM network, the router creates the cells by breaking the packet into smaller pieces. This cell-creation process involves breaking up a data link layer frame into 48-byte-long segments. Each segment is placed in a cell along with the 5-byte header. Figure 16-5 shows the general idea, as performed on R2.

Figure 16-5 *ATM Segmentation and Reassembly*

R1 actually reverses the segmentation process after receiving all the cells—a process called *reassembly.* The entire concept of segmenting a frame into cells, and reassembling them, is called *segmentation and reassembly (SAR).* Cisco routers use specialized ATM interfaces to support ATM. The ATM cards include special hardware to perform the SAR function quickly. They also often include special hardware to support SONET.

Because of its similar function to Frame Relay, ATM also is considered to be a type of packet-switching service. However, because it uses fixed-length cells, it more often is called a *cell-switching* service.

Packet Switching Versus Circuit Switching

Many WAN technologies can be categorized as either a circuit-switching service or a packet-switching service. In traditional telco terminology, a circuit provides the physical ability to send voice or data between two endpoints. The origins of the term circuit relate to how the original phone systems actually created an electrical circuit between two telephones in order to carry the voice signal. The leased lines explained in Chapter 4 are circuits, providing the physical ability to transfer bits between two endpoints.

Packet switching means that the devices in the WAN do more than pass the bits or electrical signal from one device to another. With packet switching, the provider's networking devices interpret the bits sent by the customers by reading some type of address field in the header. The service makes choices, switching one packet to go in one direction, and the next packet to go in another direction to another device. Table 16-4 summarizes a few of the key comparison points between these two types of WANs.

Table 16-4   *Comparing Circuits and Packet Switching*

Key
Topic

Feature	Circuits	Packet Switching
Service implemented as OSI layer . . .	1	2
Point-to-point (two devices) or more	Point-to-point	Multipoint (more than two)

Ethernet as a WAN Service

Before moving on to a discussion of some Internet access issues, it is useful to note a major development in WAN services: Ethernet as a WAN service, or Metropolitan Ethernet (Metro E). To supply a Metro E service, the service provider provides an Ethernet cable, oftentimes optical to meet the longer distance requirements, into the customer site. The customer can then connect the cable to a LAN switch or router.

Additionally, the service provider can offer both Fast Ethernet and Gigabit Ethernet speeds, but, like Frame Relay, offer a lower committed information rate (CIR). For example, a customer might need 20 Mbps of bandwidth between routers located at large data centers on either side of a city. The provider installs a Fast Ethernet link between the sites, contracting with the customer for 20 Mbps. The customer then configures the routers so that they will purposefully send only 20 Mbps, on average, using a feature called shaping. The end result is that the customer gets the bandwidth, typically at a better price than other options (like using a T3).

Metro E offers many design options as well, including simply connecting one customer site to an ISP, or connecting all of a customer's sites to each other using various VLANs over a single Ethernet access link. Although the details are certainly beyond the CCNA exams, it is an interesting development to watch as it becomes more popular in the marketplace.

Next, this chapter changes focus completely, examining several features that are required for a typical Internet connection using DSL and cable.

IP Services for Internet Access

DSL and cable Internet access have many similar features. In particular, both use a router, with that router being responsible for forwarding packets from the computers in the home or office to a router on the other side of the cable/DSL line, and vice versa. This second major section of this chapter examines several IP-related functions that must be performed by the DSL/cable router, in particular a couple of ways to use DHCP, as well as a feature called Network Address Translation (NAT).

The equipment used at a SOHO to connect to the Internet using DSL or cable may be a single integrated device, or several separate devices, as introduced in Figures 13-4 and 13-5 in Chapter 13. For the sake of explaining the details in this chapter, the figures will show separate devices, as in Figure 16-6.

Figure 16-6 *Internet Access Equipment, Separate Devices*

Thinking about the flow of data left-to-right in the figure, a PC sends data to its default gateway, which is the local access router. The LAN switch just forwards frames to the access router. The router makes a routing decision to forward the packet to the ISP router as the next-hop router. Then, the cable modem converts the Ethernet frame received from the router to meet cable specifications, the details of which are beyond the scope of this book. Finally, the ISP router has a routing table for all routes in the Internet, so it can forward the packet to wherever the packet needs to go.

Of the three devices at the small office, this section examines the router in detail. Besides basic routing, the access router needs to perform three additional important functions, as will be explained in this section: assign addresses, learn routes, and translate addresses (NAT).

Address Assignment on the Internet Access Router

The Internet access router in Figure 16-6 has two LAN interfaces—one facing the Internet and one facing the devices at that site. As was mentioned in Part III of this book on many occasions, to be able to route packets on those two interfaces, the router needs an IP address on each interface. However, instead of choosing and statically configuring the IP addresses with the **ip address** interface subcommand, the IP addresses are chosen per the following rules:

- The Internet-facing interface needs one public IP address so that the routers in the Internet know how to route packets to the access router.

- The ISP typically assigns that public (and globally routable) IP address dynamically, using DHCP.

- The local PCs typically need to dynamically learn IP addresses with DHCP, so the access router will act as a DHCP server for the local hosts.

- The router needs a statically configured IP address on the local subnet, using a private network number.

- The local LAN subnet will use addresses in a private network number.

> **NOTE**   The section "Public and Private Addressing" in Chapter 12, "IP Addressing and Subnetting," introduces the concept of private networks and lists the ranges of addresses in private networks.

Figure 16-7 shows the net results of the DHCP exchanges between the various devices, ignoring some of the cabling details.

Figure 16-7 *DHCP Server and Client Functions on an Internet Access Router*

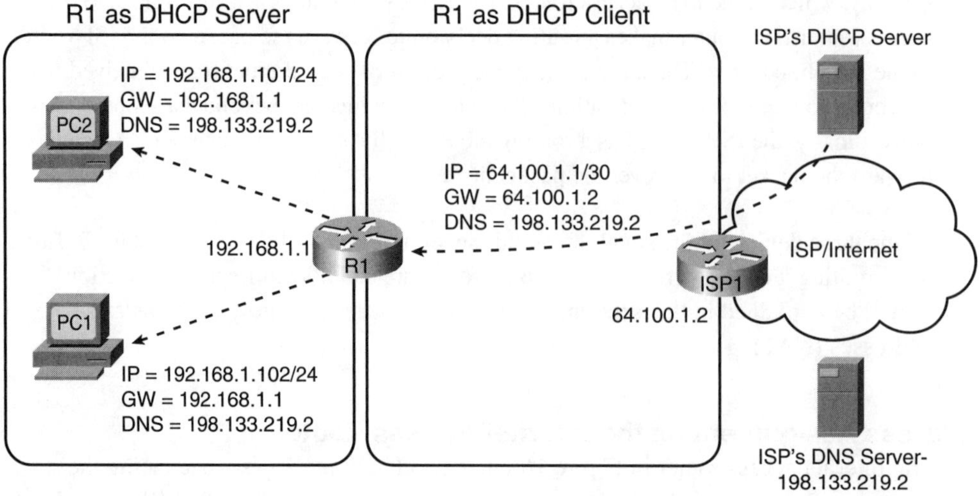

For the process in Figure 16-7 to work, the access router (R1) needs a statically configured IP address on the local interface, a DHCP server function enabled on that interface, and a DHCP client function enabled on the Internet interface. R1 learns its Internet interface IP address from the ISP, in this case 64.100.1.1. After being configured with IP address 192.168.1.1/24 on the local interface, R1 starts answering DHCP requests, assigning IP addresses in that same subnet to PC1 and PC2. Note that R1's DHCP messages list the DNS IP address (198.133.219.2) learned from the ISP's DHCP server.

Routing for the Internet Access Router

Besides the IP address details, router R1 needs to be able to route packets to and from the Internet. R1 has two connected routes, as normal. However, instead of learning all the routes in the global Internet using a routing protocol, R1 can use a default route. In fact, the topology is a classic case for using a default route—the access router has one possible physical route to use to reach the rest of the Internet, namely the route connecting the access router to the ISP's router.

Instead of requiring a static route configuration, the access router can add a default route based on the default gateway learned by the DHCP client function. For example, in Figure 16-7, R1 learned a default gateway IP address of 64.100.1.2, which is router ISP1's interface connected to the DSL or cable service. The access router creates a default route with that default gateway IP address as the next-hop router. Figure 16-8 shows this default route, along with a few other important routes, as solid lines with arrows.

Figure 16-8 *Routing in an Internet Access Router*

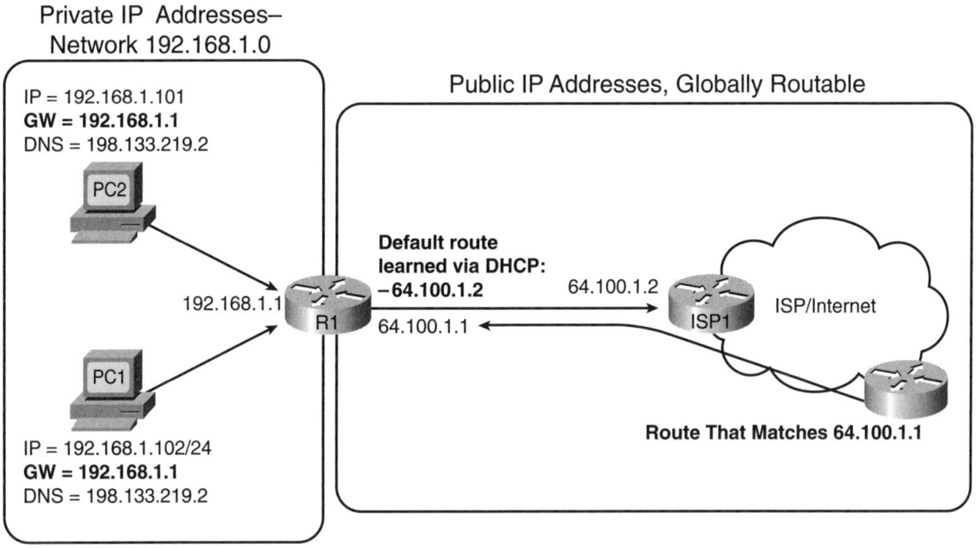

The default gateway settings on the local PCs, along with the default route on the access router (R1), allow the PCs to send packets that reach the Internet. At that point, the Internet routers should be able to forward the packets anywhere in the Internet. However, the routes pointing in the reverse direction, from the Internet back to the small office, seem incomplete at this point. Because R1's Internet-facing IP address (64.100.1.1 in Figure 16-8) is from the public registered IP address range, all the routers in the Internet should have a matching route, enabling them to forward packets to that address. However, Internet routers should never have any routes for private IP addresses, like those in private networks, such as private network 192.168.1.0/24 as used in Figure 16-8.

The solution to this problem is not related to routing; instead, the solution is to make the local hosts on the LAN look as if they are using R1's publicly registered IP address by using NAT and PAT. Hosts in the Internet will send the packets to the access router's public IP address (64.100.1.1 in Figure 16-8), and the access router will translate the address to match the correct IP address on the hosts on the local LAN.

NAT and PAT

Before getting to the details of how NAT and Port Address Translation (PAT) solve this last part of the puzzle, a few other related perspectives can help you to understand NAT and PAT—one related to IP address conservation, and one related to how TCP and UDP use ports.

First, the Internet Corporation for Assigned Names and Numbers (ICANN) manages the process of assigning public IP addresses in the global IPv4 address space—and we are slowly running out of addresses. So, when an ISP adds a new DSL or cable customer, the ISP wants to assign as few public IP addresses to that customer as possible. Additionally, the ISP prefers to assign the address dynamically, so if a customer decides to move to another ISP, the ISP can quickly reclaim and reuse the IP address for another customer. So, for a typical DSL or cable connection to the Internet, the ISP assigns a single publicly routable IP address, using DHCP, as was shown earlier in Figure 16-7. In particular, the ISP does not want to assign multiple public IP addresses to each PC (like PC1 and PC2 in Figure 16-7), again to conserve the public IPv4 address space.

The second thing to think about is that, from a server's perspective, there is no important difference between some number of TCP connections from different hosts, versus the same number of TCP connections from the same host. Figure 16-9 details an example that helps make the logic behind PAT more obvious.

Figure 16-9 *Three TCP Connections: From Three Different Hosts, and from One Host*

Three Connections from Three PCs

64.100.1.1

64.100.1.1, port 1024   128.107.1.1, port 80   Server

64.100.1.2

64.100.1.2, port 1024   Internet   128.107.1.1, port 80

64.100.1.3

64.100.1.3, port 1033   128.107.1.1, port 80   128.107.1.1

Three Connections from One PC

64.100.1.1, port 1024   128.107.1.1, port 80   Server

64.100.1.1

64.100.1.1, port 1025   Internet   128.107.1.1, port 80

64.100.1.1, port 1026   128.107.1.1, port 80   128.107.1.1

The top part of the figure shows a network with three different hosts connecting to a web server using TCP. The bottom half of the figure shows the same network later in the day, with three TCP connections from one client. All six connections connect to the server IP address (128.107.1.1) and port (80, the well-known port for web services). In each case, the server is able to differentiate between the various connections because each has a unique combination of IP address and port number.

Keeping the address conservation and port number concepts in mind, next examine how PAT allows the local hosts to use private IP addresses while the access router uses a single public IP address. PAT takes advantage of the fact that a server really does not care if it has one connection each to three different hosts or three connections to a single host IP address. So, to support lots of local hosts at the small office, using a single publicly routable IP address on the router, PAT translates the local hosts' private IP addresses to the one registered public IP address. To tell which packets need to be sent back to which local host, the router keeps track of both the IP address and TCP or UDP port number. Figure 16-10 shows an example, using the same IP addresses and routers shown previously in Figure 16-7.

Figure 16-10 *PAT Function on an Internet Access Router*

NAT Translation Table

Inside Local	Inside Global
192.168.1.101:1024	64.100.1.1: 1024
192.168.1.102:1024	64.100.1.1: 1025

The figure shows a packet sent by PC1 to the server in the Internet on the right. The top part of the figure (steps 1 and 2) shows the packet's source IP address and source port both before and after R1 performs PAT. The lower part of the figure (steps 3 and 4) shows the return packet from the server, which shows the destination IP address and destination port, again both before and after R1 performs the PAT function. (The server, when replying to a packet with a particular source IP address and port, uses those same values in the response packet.) The numbered steps in the figure follow this logic:

1. PC1 sends a packet to server 128.107.1.1 and, per PC1's default gateway setting, sends the packet to access router R1.

2. R1 performs PAT, based on the details in the router's NAT translation table, changing the local host's IP from the private IP address used on the local LAN to the one globally routable public IP address available to R1, namely 64.100.1.1 in this case. R1 forwards the packet based on its default route.

3. When the server replies to the packet sent from PC1, the server sends the packet to destination address 64.100.1.1, destination port 1024, because those were the values in the source fields of the packet at step 2. The Internet routers know how to forward this packet back to R1, because the destination is a globally routable public IP address.

4. R1 changes the destination IP address and port per the NAT table, switching from destination address/port 64.100.1.1/1024 to 192.168.1.101/1024. R1 knows a route to reach 192.168.1.101, because this address is in a subnet connected to R1.

More generally, the PAT feature causes the router to translate the source IP address and port for packets leaving the local LAN, and to translate the destination IP address and port on packets returning to the local LAN. The end result is that, as far as hosts in the Internet are concerned, all the packets coming from this one customer are from one host (64.100.1.1 in Figure 16-10), for which all the routers in the Internet should have a matching route. This allows the ISP to conserve public IPv4 addresses.

The terms *inside local* and *inside global*, as listed in the NAT translation table in Figure 16-10, have some very specific and important meanings in the world of NAT. When speaking of NAT, the terms have the perspective of the enterprise network engineer, rather than someone working at the ISP. Keeping that in mind, NAT uses the following terms (and many others):

Inside host: Refers to a host in the enterprise network, like PC1 and PC2 in the last few figures.

Inside local: Refers to an IP address in an IP header, with that address representing a local host as the packet passes over the local enterprise network (not the Internet). In this case, 192.168.1.101 and .102 are inside local IP addresses, and the packets at steps 1 and 4 in Figure 16-10 show inside local IP addresses.

Inside global: Refers to an IP address in an IP header, with that address representing a local host as the packet passes over the global Internet (not the enterprise). In this case, 64.100.1.1 is the one inside global IP address, and the packets at steps 2 and 3 in Figure 16-10 show the inside global IP address.

Inside interface: The router interface connected to the same LAN as the inside hosts.

Outside interface: The router interface connected to the Internet.

Now that you have seen an example of how PAT works, a more exact definition of the terms NAT and PAT can be described. So, when using the terms in a very specific, formal manner, NAT refers to the translation of network layer (IP) addresses, with no translation of ports, whereas PAT refers to the translation of IP addresses as well as transport layer (TCP and UDP) port numbers. However, with a broader definition of the term NAT, PAT is simply one of several ways to configure and use NAT. In real life, in fact, most people refer to this broader definition of NAT. So, an engineer might say "we use NAT with our Internet connection to conserve our public IP addresses"; technically the function is PAT, but most everyone simply calls it NAT.

In closing, some of you who have installed a cable router or DSL router in your home may have found that it was easy to get that router to work—much easier than trying to understand the details explained in this chapter. If you buy a consumer-grade cable router or DSL router, it comes preconfigured to use a DHCP client, DHCP server, and PAT as described in this section. (In fact, your product may have one RJ-45 port labeled "Internet" or "Uplink"—that is the port that by default acts as a DHCP client, and it would be the Internet-facing interface in the figures presented toward the end of this chapter.) So, these functions happen, but they happen with no effort required on your part. However, to do the same functions with an enterprise-class Cisco router, the router needs to be configured, because the Cisco enterprise routers ship from the factory with no initial configuration. Chapter 17 will show how to configure the features described in this section on Cisco routers.

Exam Preparation Tasks

Review All the Key Topics

Key
Topic

Review the most important topics from inside the chapter, noted with the key topics icon in the outer margin of the page. Table 16-5 lists a reference of these key topics and the page numbers on which each is found.

Table 16-5 *Key Topics for Chapter 16*

Key Topic Element	Description	Page Number
List	Comparison points between DSL and modems	519
Figure 16-3	Typical topology and devices used for DSL	520
List	Factors that affect the speed of a DSL line	522
Figure 16-4	Typical topology and devices used for cable	524
Table 16-3	Comparison points for Internet access technologies	525
Table 16-4	Comparison of circuit switching and packet switching	527
List	Factors that impact the IP addresses used by Internet access routers	529
Figure 16-7	Depicts DHCP client and server functions in an Internet access router	530
Figure 16-10	Shows how PAT translates IP addresses in Internet access routers	533
List	Definitions of several key NAT terms	534

Complete the Tables and Lists from Memory

Print a copy of Appendix H, "Memory Tables" (found on the CD-ROM), or at least the section for this chapter, and complete the tables and lists from memory. Appendix I, "Memory Tables Answer Key," also on the CD-ROM, includes completed tables and lists to check your work.

Definitions of Key Terms

Define the following key terms from this chapter and check your answers in the glossary.

ADSL, asymmetric, ATM, DSL, inside global, inside local, modem, NAT, PAT, PSTN, symmetric, telco

This chapter covers the following subjects:

Configuring Point-to-Point WANs: This section examines how to configure leased lines between two routers using HDLC and PPP.

Configuring and Troubleshooting Internet Access Routers: This section shows how to configure DHCP client, DHCP server, and PAT functions on an Internet access router using SDM.

CHAPTER 17

WAN Configuration

This chapter examines the configuration details for how to configure a few of the types of wide-area networks (WANs) covered in Chapter 4, "Fundamentals of WANs," and Chapter 16, "WAN Concepts." The first section of this chapter examines leased-line configuration using both High-Level Data Link Control (HDLC) and Point-to-Point Protocol (PPP). The second section of the chapter shows how to configure the Layer 3 features required for an Internet access router to connect to the Internet, specifically Dynamic Host Configuration Protocol (DHCP) and Network Address Translation/Port Address Translation (NAT/PAT). However, the configuration in the second half of the chapter does not use the command-line interface (CLI), but instead focuses on using the web-based router Security Device Manager (SDM) interface.

For those of you preparing specifically for the CCNA 640-802 exam by using the reading plan in the introduction to this book, note that you should move on to Part IV of the *CCNA ICND2 Official Exam Certification Guide* after completing this chapter.

"Do I Know This Already?" Quiz

The "Do I Know This Already?" quiz allows you to assess if you should read the entire chapter. If you miss no more than one of these seven self-assessment questions, you might want to move ahead to the "Exam Preparation Tasks" section. Table 17-1 lists the major headings in this chapter and the "Do I Know This Already?" quiz questions covering the material in those headings so you can assess your knowledge of these specific areas. The answers to the "Do I Know This Already?" quiz appear in Appendix A.

Table 17-1   *"Do I Know This Already?" Foundation Topics Section-to-Question Mapping*

Foundation Topics Section	Questions
Configuring and Troubleshooting Point-to-Point WANs	1–3
Configuring and Troubleshooting Internet Access Routers	4–7

1. Routers R1 and R2 connect using a leased line, with both routers using their respective Serial 0/0 interfaces. The routers can currently route packets over the link, which uses HDLC. Which of the following commands would be required to migrate the configuration to use PPP?

    a. **encapsulation ppp**

    b. **no encapsulation hdlc**

    c. **clock rate 128000**

    d. **bandwidth 128000**

2. Routers R1 and R2 have just been installed in a new lab. The routers will connect using a back-to-back serial link, using interface serial 0/0 on each router. Which of the following is true about how to install and configure this connection?

    a. If the DCE cable is installed in R1, the **clock rate** command must be configured on R2's serial interface.

    b. If the DTE cable is installed in R1, the **clock rate** command must be configured on R2's serial interface.

    c. If the **clock rate 128000** command is configured on R1, the **bandwidth 128** command must be configured on R2.

    d. None of the answers are correct.

3. Two brand new Cisco routers have been ordered and installed in two different sites, 100 miles apart. A 768-kbps leased line has been installed between the two routers. Which of the following commands is required on at least one of the routers in order to forward packets over the leased line, using PPP as the data link protocol?

    a. **no encapsulation hdlc**

    b. **encapsulation ppp**

    c. **clock rate 768000**

    d. **bandwidth 768**

    e. **description this is the link**

4. When configuring a DHCP server on an Internet access router using SDM, which of the following settings is typically configured on the Internet access router?

    a. The MAC addresses of the PCs on the local LAN

    b. The IP address of the ISP's router on the common cable or DSL link

    c.   The range of IP addresses to be leased to hosts on the local LAN

    d.   The DNS server IP address(es) learned via DHCP from the ISP

5.   When configuring an access router with SDM, to use DHCP client services to learn an IP address from an ISP, and configure PAT at the same time, which of the following is true?

    a.   The SDM configuration wizard requires PAT to be configured if the DHCP client function has been chosen to be configured.

    b.   The SDM configuration wizard considers any interfaces that already have IP addresses configured as candidates to become inside interfaces for PAT.

    c.   The SDM configuration wizard assumes the interface on which DHCP client services have been enabled should be an inside interface.

    d.   None of the answers are correct.

6.   Which of the following is true about the configuration process using SDM?

    a.   SDM uses an SSH connection via the console or an IP network to configure a router.

    b.   SDM uses a web interface from the IP network or from the console.

    c.   SDM loads configuration commands into a router at the end of each wizard (after the user clicks the Finish button), saving the configuration in the running-config and startup-config files.

    d.   None of these answers are correct.

7.   Which of the following are common problems when configuring a new Internet access router's Layer 3 features?

    a.   Omitting commonly used but optional information from the DHCP server features—for example, the IP address(es) of the DNS server(s)

    b.   Setting the wrong interfaces as the NAT inside and outside interfaces

    c.   Forgetting to configure the same routing protocol that the ISP uses

    d.   Forgetting to enable CDP on the Internet-facing interface

Foundation Topics

Configuring Point-to-Point WANs

This brief section explains how to configure leased lines between two routers, using both HDLC and PPP. The required configuration is painfully simply—for HDLC, do nothing, and for PPP, add one interface subcommand on each router's serial interface (**encapsulation ppp**). However, several optional configuration steps can be useful, so this section explains those optional steps and their impact on the links.

> **NOTE**   This chapter assumes all serial links use an external channel service unit/data service unit (CSU/DSU). The configuration details of the external CSU/DSU, or an internal CSU/DSU, are beyond the scope of the book.

Configuring HDLC

Considering the lowest three layers of the OSI reference model on router Ethernet interfaces for a moment, there are no required configuration commands related to Layers 1 and 2 for the interface to be up and working, forwarding IP traffic. The Layer 1 details occur by default once the cabling has been installed correctly. Router IOS defaults to use Ethernet as the data link protocol on all types of Ethernet interfaces, so no Layer 2 commands are required. To make the interface operational for forwarding IP packets, the router needs one command to configure an IP address on the interface, and possibly a **no shutdown** command if the interface is in an "administratively down" state.

Similarly, serial interfaces on Cisco routers that use HDLC typically need no specific Layer 1 or 2 configuration commands. The cabling needs to be completed as described in Chapters 4 and 16, but there are no required configuration commands related to Layer 1. IOS defaults to use HDLC as the data link protocol, so there are no required commands that relate to Layer 2. As on Ethernet interfaces, the only required command to get IP working on the interface is the **ip address** command and possibly the **no shutdown** command.

However, many optional commands exist for serial links. The following list outlines some configuration steps, listing the conditions for which some commands are needed, plus commands that are purely optional:

Key Topic

Step 1   Configure the interface IP address using the **ip address** interface subcommand.

Step 2   The following tasks are required only when the specifically listed conditions are true:

   a.   If an **encapsulation** *protocol* interface subcommand that lists a protocol besides HDLC already exists on the interface, use the **encapsulation hdlc** interface subcommand to enable HDLC.

b. If the interface line status is administratively down, enable the interface using the **no shutdown** interface subcommand.

c. If the serial link is a back-to-back serial link in a lab (or a simulator), configure the clocking rate using the **clock rate** *speed* interface subcommand, but only on the one router with the DCE cable (per the **show controllers serial** *number* command).

Step 3 The following steps are always optional, and have no impact on whether the link works and passes IP traffic:

a. Configure the link's speed using the **bandwidth** *speed-in-kbps* interface subcommand.

b. For documentation purposes, configure a description of the purpose of the interface using the **description** *text* interface subcommand.

In practice, when you configure a Cisco router with no pre-existing interface configuration, and install a normal production serial link with CSU/DSUs, the **ip address** command is likely the one configuration command you would need. Figure 17-1 shows a sample internetwork, and Example 17-1 shows the configuration. In this case, the serial link was created with a back-to-back serial link in a lab, requiring Steps 1 (**ip address**) and 2c (**clock rate**) from the preceding list, plus optional Step 3b (**description**).

Figure 17-1 *Typical Serial Link Between Two Routers*

Example 17-1 *HDLC Configuration*

```
R1#show running-config
! Note - only the related lines are shown
interface FastEthernet0/0
 ip address 192.168.1.1 255.255.255.0
!
interface Serial0/1/1
 ip address 192.168.2.1 255.255.255.0
 description link to R2
 clockrate 1536000
```

continues

Example 17-1 *HDLC Configuration (Continued)*

```
!
router rip
 version 2
 network 192.168.1.0
 network 192.168.2.0
!
R1#show controllers serial 0/1/1
Interface Serial0/1/1
Hardware is GT96K
DCE V.35, clock rate 1536000
! lines omitted for brevity
R1#show interfaces s0/1/1
Serial0/1/1 is up, line protocol is up
  Hardware is GT96K Serial
  Description: link to R2
  Internet address is 192.168.2.1/24
  MTU 1500 bytes, BW 1544 Kbit, DLY 20000 usec,
     reliability 255/255, txload 1/255, rxload 1/255
  Encapsulation HDLC, loopback not set
  Keepalive set (10 sec)
  Last input 00:00:06, output 00:00:03, output hang never
  Last clearing of "show interface" counters never
  Input queue: 0/75/0/0 (size/max/drops/flushes); Total output drops: 0
  Queueing strategy: weighted fair
  Output queue: 0/1000/64/0 (size/max total/threshold/drops)
     Conversations  0/1/256 (active/max active/max total)
     Reserved Conversations 0/0 (allocated/max allocated)
     Available Bandwidth 1158 kilobits/sec
  5 minute input rate 0 bits/sec, 0 packets/sec
  5 minute output rate 0 bits/sec, 0 packets/sec
     70 packets input, 4446 bytes, 0 no buffer
     Received 50 broadcasts, 0 runts, 0 giants, 0 throttles
     0 input errors, 0 CRC, 0 frame, 0 overrun, 0 ignored, 0 abort
     73 packets output, 5280 bytes, 0 underruns
     0 output errors, 0 collisions, 5 interface resets
     0 output buffer failures, 0 output buffers swapped out
     0 carrier transitions
     DCD=up  DSR=up  DTR=up  RTS=up  CTS=up
R1#show ip interface brief
Interface              IP-Address      OK? Method Status                Protocol
FastEthernet0/0        192.168.1.1     YES manual up                    up
FastEthernet0/1        unassigned      YES NVRAM  administratively down down
Serial0/0/0            unassigned      YES NVRAM  administratively down down
Serial0/0/1            unassigned      YES manual administratively down down
Serial0/1/0            unassigned      YES manual administratively down down
Serial0/1/1            192.168.2.1     YES manual up                    up
```

Example 17-1 *HDLC Configuration (Continued)*

```
R1#show interfaces description
Interface                     Status          Protocol Description
Fa0/0                         up              up
Fa0/1                         admin down      down
Se0/0/0                       admin down      down
Se0/0/1                       admin down      down
Se0/1/0                       admin down      down
Se0/1/1                       up              up       link to R2
```

The configuration on R1 is relatively simple. The matching configuration on R2's S0/0/1 interface simply needs an **ip address** command, plus the default settings of **encapsulation hdlc** and **no shutdown**. The **clock rate** command would not be needed on R2, as R1 has the DCE cable, so R2 must be connected to a DTE cable.

The rest of the example lists the output of a few **show** commands. First, the output from the **show controllers** command for S0/1/1 confirms that R1 indeed has a DCE cable installed. The **show interfaces S0/1/1** command lists the various configuration settings near the top, including the default encapsulation value (HDLC) and default bandwidth setting on a serial interface (1544, meaning 1544 kbps or 1.544 Mbps). At the end of the example, the **show ip interface brief** and **show interfaces description** commands display a short status of the interfaces, with both listing the line status and protocol status codes.

Configuring PPP

Configuring the basics of PPP is just as simple as for HDLC, except that whereas HDLC is the default serial data-link protocol and requires no additional configuration, you must configure the **encapsulation ppp** command for PPP. Other than that, the list of possible and optional configuration steps is exactly the same as for HDLC. So, to migrate from a working HDLC link to a working PPP link, the only command needed is an **encapsulation ppp** command on each of the two routers' serial interfaces. Example 17-2 shows the serial interface configuration on both R1 and R2 from Figure 17-1, this time using PPP.

Example 17-2 *PPP Configuration*

```
R1#show running-config interface s0/1/1
Building configuration...

Current configuration : 129 bytes
!
interface Serial0/1/1
 description link to R2
 ip address 192.168.2.1 255.255.255.0
 encapsulation ppp
```

continues

Example 17-2 *PPP Configuration (Continued)*

```
 clockrate 1536000
end
```

```
! R2's configuration next
R2#show run interface s0/0/1
Building configuration...

Current configuration : 86 bytes
!
interface Serial0/0/1
 ip address 192.168.2.2 255.255.255.0
 encapsulation ppp
end
```

The example lists a new variation on the **show running-config** command as well as the PPP-related configuration. The **show running-config interface S0/1/1** command on R1 lists the interface configuration for interface S0/1/1, and none of the rest of the running-config. Note that on both routers, the **encapsulation ppp** command has been added; it is important that both routers use the same data link protocol, or the link will not work.

Configuring and Troubleshooting Internet Access Routers

As covered in Chapter 16, Internet access routers often connect to the Internet using one LAN interface, and to the local LAN using another interface. Routers that are built specifically for consumers as Internet access routers ship from the factory with DHCP client services enabled on the Internet-facing interface, DHCP server functions enabled on the local interface, and PAT functions enabled. Enterprise routers, which have many features and may not necessarily be used as Internet access routers, ship from the factory without these features enabled by default. This section shows how to configure these functions on a Cisco enterprise-class router.

Cisco routers support another configuration method besides using the CLI. In keeping with the exam topics published by Cisco for the ICND1 exam, this chapter shows how to configure the rest of the features in this chapter using this alternative tool, called *Cisco Router and Security Device Manager (SDM)*. Instead of using Telnet or SSH, the user connects to the router using a web browser. (To support the web browser, the router must first be configured from the CLI with at least one IP address, typically on the local LAN, so that the engineer's computer can connect to the router.) From there, SDM allows the engineer to configure a wide variety of router features, including the DHCP client, DHCP server, and PAT.

> **NOTE** Cisco switches also allow web access for configuration, using a tool called *Cisco Device Manager (CDM)*. The general concept of CDM matches the concepts of SDM.

Note that the features configured through SDM in the remainder of this chapter can also be done with the CLI.

Internet Access Router: Configuration Steps

You can configure the DHCP client, DHCP server, and PAT functions with SDM using the following five major steps:

Step 1   **Establish IP connectivity.** Plan and configure (from the CLI) IP addresses on the local LAN so that a PC on the LAN can ping the router's LAN interface.

Step 2   **Install and access SDM.** Install SDM on the router and access the router SDM interface using a PC that can ping the router's IP address (as implemented at Step 1).

Step 3   **Configure DHCP and PAT.** Use SDM to configure both DHCP client services and the PAT service on the router.

Step 4   **Plan for DHCP services.** Plan the IP addresses to be assigned by the router to the hosts on the local LAN, along with the DNS IP addresses, domain name, and default gateway settings that the router will advertise.

Step 5   **Configure the DHCP server.** Use SDM to configure the DHCP server features on the router.

The sections that follow examine each step in order in greater detail. The configuration will use the same internetwork topology that was used in the Chapter 16 discussion of Internet access routers, repeated here as Figure 17-2.

Step 1: Establish IP Connectivity

The Internet access router needs to use a private IP network on the local LAN, as mentioned in Chapter 16. For this step, you should choose the following details:

Step a   Choose any private IP network number.

Step b   Choose a mask that allows for enough hosts (typically the default mask is fine).

Step c   Choose a router IP address from that network.

> Key
> Topic

Figure 17-2   *Internet Access Router: Sample Network*

It does not really matter which private network you use, as long as it is a private network. Many consumer access routers use Class C network 192.168.1.0, as will be used in this chapter, and the default mask. If you work at a small company with a few sites, all connecting to the Internet, you can use the same private network at each site, because NAT/PAT will translate the addresses anyway.

Step 2: Install and Access SDM

To be able to install the SDM software on the router (if it is not already installed on the router), and to allow the engineer's host to access the router using a web browser, the engineer needs to use a host with IP connectivity to reach the router. Typically, the engineer would use a host on the local LAN, configure the router's local LAN interface with the IP address planned at Step 1, and configure the host with another IP address in that same network. Note that SDM does not use Telnet or SSH, and the PC must be connected via an IP network—the console can only be used to access the CLI.

The network engineer must configure several additional commands on the router before a user can access and use it, the details of which are beyond the scope of this book. If you are curious, you can look for more details by searching www.cisco.com for "SDM installation." This configuration step was listed just in case you try using SDM with your own lab gear, to make you aware that there is more work to do. By the end of the process, a web browser should be able to connect to the router and see the SDM Home page for that router, like the example shown in Figure 17-3.

Figure 17-3 *SDM Home Page*

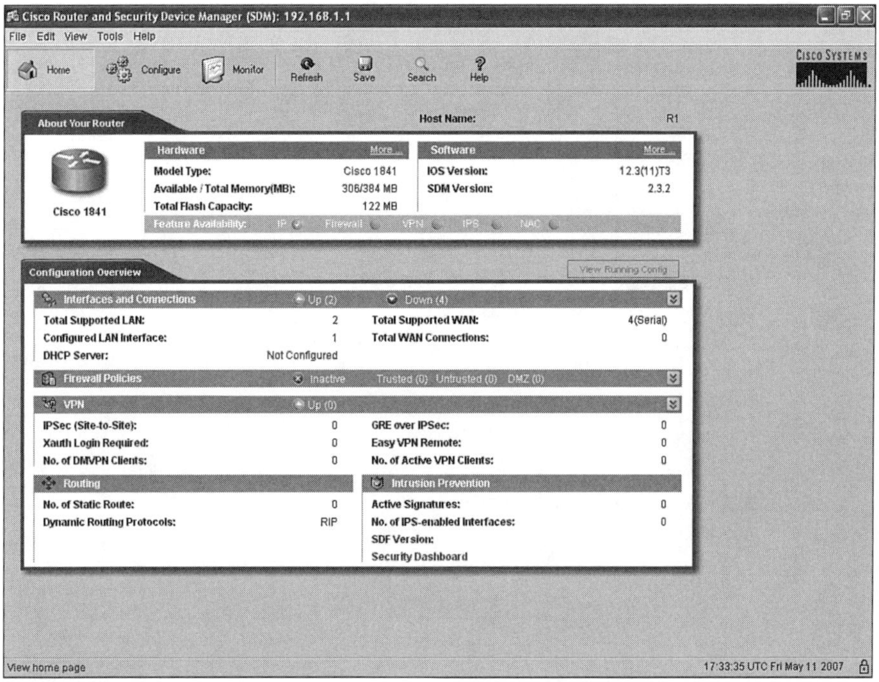

Step 3: Configure DHCP and PAT

The SDM user interface has a wide variety of configuration wizards that guide you through a series of web pages, asking for input. At the end of the process, SDM loads the corresponding configuration commands into the router.

One such wizard allows you to configure the DHCP client feature on the Internet-facing interface and, optionally, configure the PAT feature. This section shows sample windows for the configuration of router R1 in Figure 17-2.

From the SDM Home page shown in Figure 17-3:

1. Click **Configure** near the top of the window.

2. Click **Interfaces and Connections** at the top of the Tasks pane on the left side of the window.

Figure 17-4 shows the resulting Interfaces and Connections window, with the Create Connection tab displayed. (Note that the heavy arrowed lines are overlaid on the image of the page to point out the items referenced in the text.)

Figure 17-4 *SDM Configure Interfaces and Connections Window*

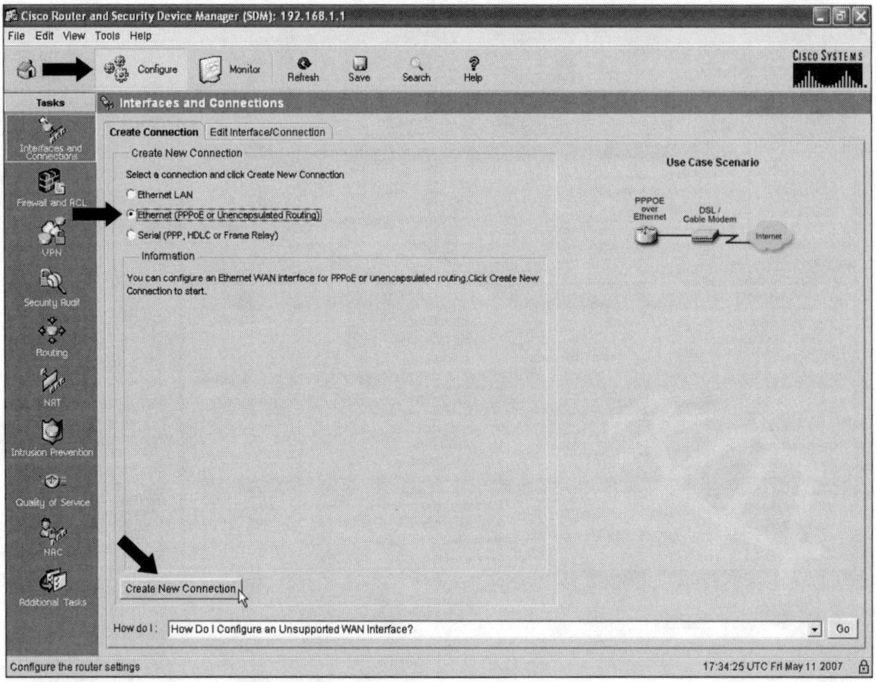

The network topology on the right side of this tab should look familiar, as it basically matches Figure 17-2, with a router connected to a cable or DSL modem. On the Create Connection tab, do the following:

1.   Choose the **Ethernet (PPPoE or Unencapsulated Routing)** radio button.

2.   Click the **Create New Connection** button near the bottom of the tab.

These actions open the SDM Ethernet Wizard, shown in Figure 17-5. The page in Figure 17-5 has no options to choose, so just click **Next** to keep going.

The next page of the wizard, shown in Figure 17-6, has only one option, a check box that, if checked, enables the protocol PPP over Ethernet (PPPoE). If the ISP asks that you use PPPoE, then check this box. Ordinarily, you simply leave this box unchecked, which implies unencapsulated routing. (Unencapsulated routing means that the router forwards Ethernet frames onto the interface, with an IP packet inside the Ethernet frame, as was covered in several places in Part III of this book.)

Figure 17-5 *SDM Ethernet Wizard Welcome Page*

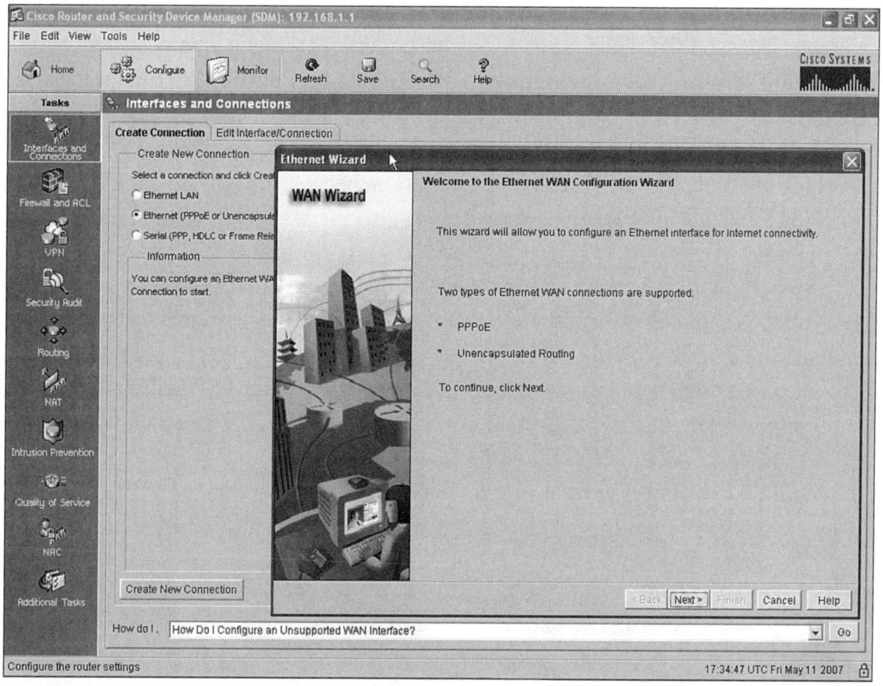

Figure 17-6 *SDM Ethernet Wizard: Choice to Use Encapsulation with PPPoE*

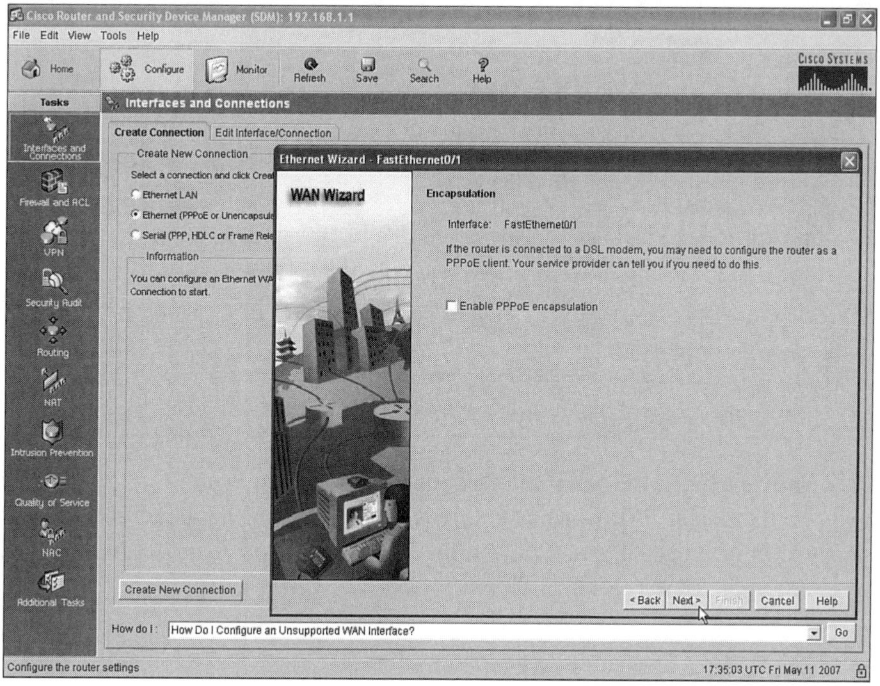

As you can see near the top of Figure 17-6, the wizard picked a Fast Ethernet interface, Fa0/1 in this case, as the interface to configure. The router used in this example has two LAN interfaces, one of which already has an IP address assigned from Step 1 (Fa0/0). Because this wizard will be configuring DHCP client services on this router, the wizard picked the only LAN interface that did not already have an IP address, namely Fa0/1, as the interface on which it will enable the DHCP client function. This choice is particularly important when troubleshooting a new installation, because this must be the LAN interface connected to the cable or DSL modem. This is also the NAT/PAT outside interface.

Click **Next**. Figure 17-7 shows the next page of the wizard, the IP Address page. This page gives you the option of statically configuring this interface's IP address. However, as explained in Chapter 16, the goal is to use a dynamically assigned IP address from the ISP—an address that happens to come from the globally routable IP address space. So, you want to use the default radio button option of **Dynamic (DHCP Client)**.

Figure 17-7 *SDM Ethernet Wizard: Static or DHCP Address Assignment*

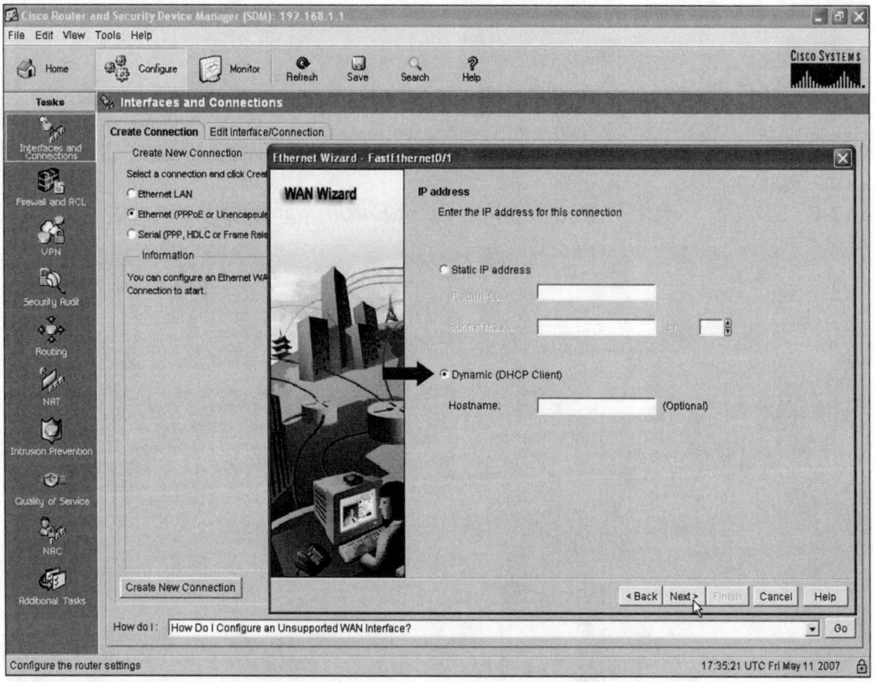

Click **Next** to move to the Advanced Options page, shown in Figure 17-8. This page asks if you want to enable PAT, which of course is also desired on an Internet access router. Simply click the **Port Address Translation** check box. If you do not want to enable PAT for some reason, do not check this box.

Figure 17-8 *SDM Ethernet Wizard: Enable PAT and Choose Inside Interface*

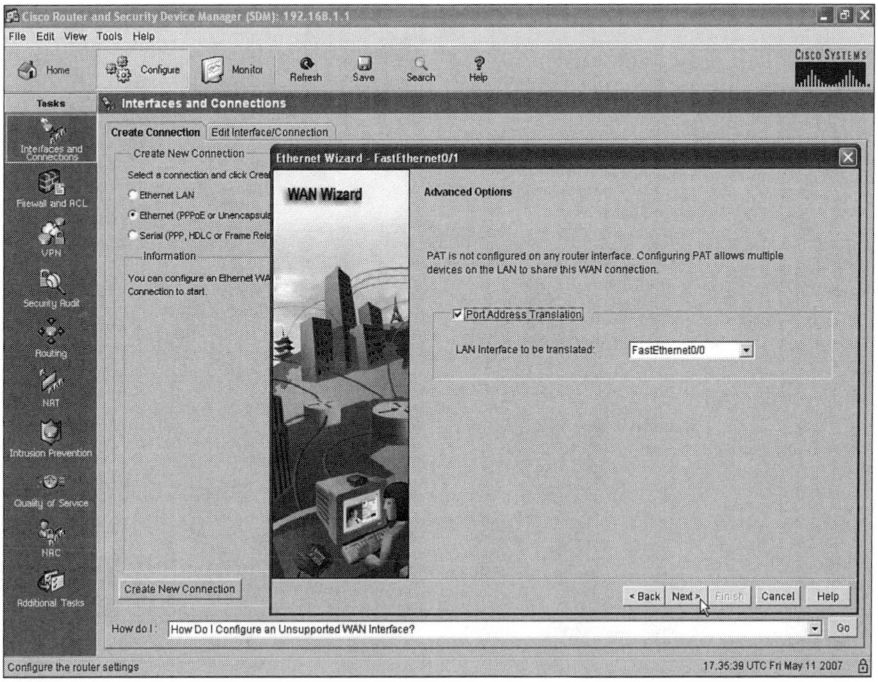

It is particularly important to note the LAN Interface to Be Translated drop-down box near the middle of the page. In NAT terminology, this box lists the inside interface, which means that the listed interface is connected to the local LAN. This example shows FastEthernet0/0 as the inside interface, as intended. Almost as important in this case is that the interface being configured for the DHCP client by this wizard, in this case FastEthernet0/1, is assumed to be the outside interface by the NAT feature, again exactly as intended.

Click **Next** to move to the Summary page shown in Figure 17-9, which summarizes the choices you made when using this wizard. The text on the screen is particularly useful, as it reminds you that:

■ The interface being configured is FastEthernet0/1.

■ FastEthernet0/1 will use DHCP client services to find its IP address.

■ PPPoE encapsulation is disabled, which means that unencapsulated routing is used.

■ PAT is enabled, with FastEthernet0/0 as the inside interface, and FastEthernet0/1 as the outside interface.

Figure 17-9   *SDM Ethernet Wizard: Request that the Configuration Changes Be Made*

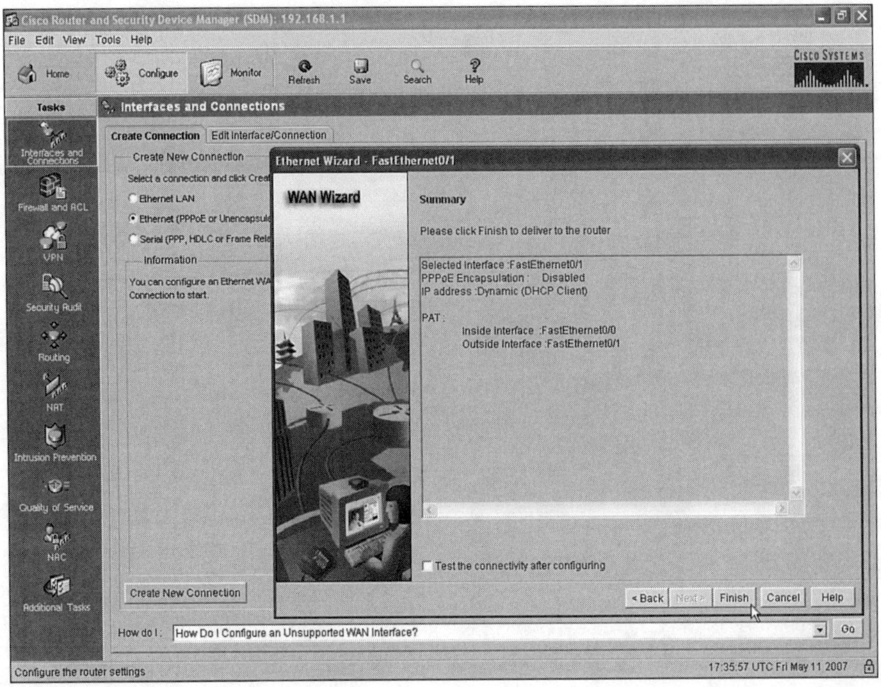

Click **Finish**. SDM builds the configuration and loads it into the router's running-config file. If you want to save the configuration, click the save button near the top of the SDM home page to make the router do a **copy running-config startup-config** command to save the configuration. However, without this extra action, the configuration will only be added to the running-config file.

At this point, the DHCP client and PAT functions have been configured. The remaining tasks are to plan the details of what to configure for the DHCP server function on the router for the local LAN, and to use SDM to configure that feature.

Step 4: Plan for DHCP Services

Before configuring the DHCP server function on the router, to support the local LAN, you need to plan a few of the values to be configured in the server. In particular, you need to choose the subset of the private IP network on the local LAN that you intend to allow to be assigned using DHCP. For the example in this chapter, part of the work at Step 1 was to choose a private IP network for the local LAN, in this case 192.168.1.0, and default mask 255.255.255.0. It makes sense to allow only a subset of the IP addresses in this network to be assigned with DHCP, leaving some IP addresses for static assignment. For example, router R1's Fa0/0 interface, connected to the local LAN, has already been configured with IP address 192.168.1.1, so that address should not be included in the range of addresses allowed to be assigned by the DHCP server.

The following list outlines the key items that you need to gather before you configure the router as a DHCP server. The first two items in the list relate to planning on the local LAN, and the last two items are just values learned from the ISP that need to be passed on to the hosts on the local LAN.

Key Topic

1. Recall the private IP network and mask used on the local LAN and then choose a subset of that network that can be assigned to hosts using DHCP.

2. Make a note of the router's IP address in that network; this address will be the local hosts' default gateway.

3. Find the DNS server IP addresses learned by the router using DHCP client services, using the **show dhcp server** EXEC command; the routers will then be able to inform the DHCP clients on the local LAN about the DNS server IP address(es).

4. Find the domain name, again with the **show dhcp server** EXEC command.

> **NOTE**   Cisco uses the term *DHCP pool* for the IP addresses that can be assigned using DHCP.

For the example in this chapter, the first two items, IP network 192.168.1.0 with mask /24, have already been chosen back in Step 1 of the overall configuration process. The range 192.168.1.101–192.168.1.254 has been reserved for DHCP clients, leaving range 192.168.1.1–192.168.1.100 for static IP addresses. The router's 192.168.1.1 IP address, which was configured back at Step 1 so that the engineer could connect to the router using SDM, will be assigned as the local hosts' default gateway.

For the last two items in the planning list, the DNS server IP addresses and the domain name, Example 17-3 shows how to find those values using the **show dhcp server** command. This command lists information on a router acting as a DHCP client, information learned from each DHCP server from which the router has learned an IP address. The pieces of information needed for the DHCP server SDM configuration are highlighted in the example.

Example 17-3   *Finding the DNS Server IP Addresses and Domain Name*

```
R1#show dhcp server
  DHCP server: ANY (255.255.255.255)
    Leases:    8
    Offers:    8      Requests: 8    Acks: 8     Naks: 0
    Declines: 0       Releases: 21   Bad:  0
    DNS0:    198.133.219.2,   DNS1:  0.0.0.0
    Subnet: 255.255.255.252   DNS Domain: example.com
```

Step 5: Configure the DHCP Server

To configure the DHCP server with SDM, click **Configure** near the top of the SDM window and then click **Additional Tasks** at the bottom of the Tasks pane to open the Additional Tasks window, shown in Figure 17-10.

Figure 17-10 *SDM Additional Tasks Configuration Window*

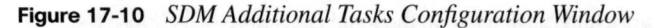

Select the **DHCP Pools** option on the left (as noted with one of the heavy arrows) and then click the **Add** button to open the Add DHCP Pool dialog box, shown in Figure 17-11. This dialog box has a place to type all the information gathered in the previous step, along with other settings. Figure 17-11 shows the screen used to configure router R1 in the ongoing example in this chapter.

The four planning items discussed in the previous overall configuration step (Step 4) are typed in obvious places in this dialog box:

■ Range of addresses to be assigned with DHCP

■ DNS server IP addresses

■ Domain name

■ Default router settings

Figure 17-11 *SDM DHCP Pool Dialog Box*

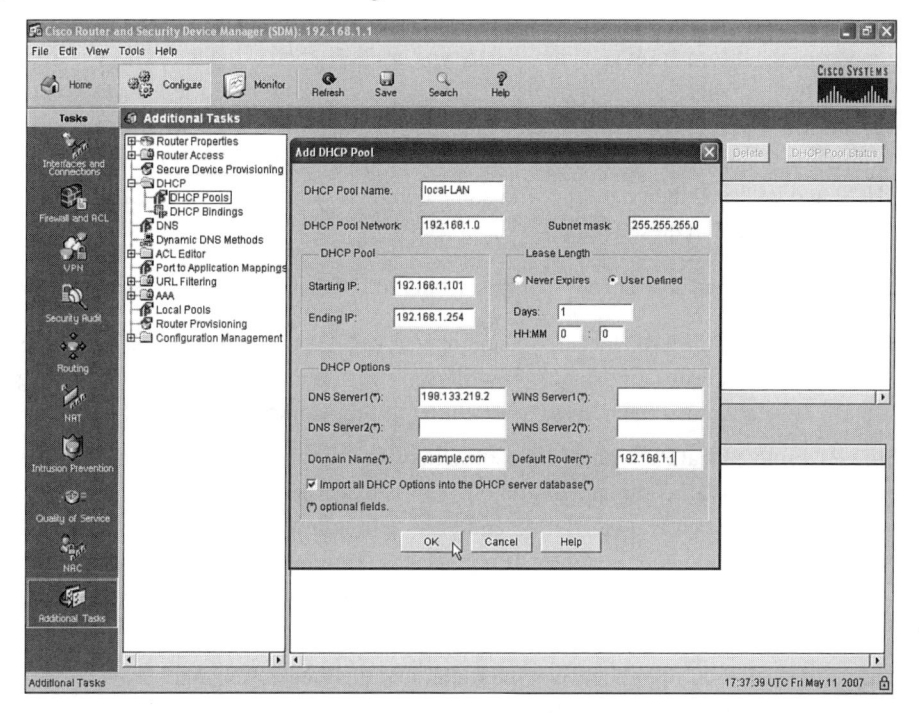

Additionally, the dialog box wants to know the subnet number and mask used on the subnet in which the addresses will be assigned. Also, you need to make up a name for this pool of DHCP addresses—the name can be most anything, but choose a meaningful name for that installation.

Whew! Configuring an Internet access router with SDM might seem to require a lot of steps and navigating through a lot of windows; however, it is certainly less detailed than configuring the same features from the CLI. The next section examines a few small verification and troubleshooting tasks.

Internet Access Router Verification

The choice to cover SDM configuration for DHCP and NAT/PAT, instead of the CLI configuration commands, has both some positives and negatives. The positives include the fact that the ICND1 exam, meant for entry-level network engineers, can cover a common set of features seen on Internet access routers, which are commonly used by smaller companies. Also, because the underlying configuration can be large (the configuration added by SDM for the examples in this chapter required about 20 configuration commands), the use of SDM avoided the time and effort to go over a lot of configuration options, keeping the topic a little more focused.

One negative of using SDM is that troubleshooting becomes a little more difficult because the configuration has not been covered in detail. As a result, true troubleshooting requires a review of the information you intended to type or click when using the SDM wizards, and double-checking that configuration from SDM. Showing all the SDM screens used to check each item would itself be a bit laborious. Instead of showing all those SDM screens, this section points out a few of the most common oversights when using SDM to configure DHCP and PAT, and then it closes with some comments about a few key CLI EXEC commands related to these features.

To perform some basic verification of the installation of the access router, try the following:

Step 1   Go to a PC on the local LAN and open a web browser. Try your favorite Internet-based website (for example, www.cisco.com). If a web page opens, that is a good indication that the access router configuration worked. If not, go to Step 2.

Step 2   From a local PC with a Microsoft OS, open a command prompt and use the **ipconfig /all** command to find out if the PC learned an IP address, mask, default gateway, and DNS IP addresses as configured in the DHCP server configuration on the router. If not, use the commands listed in the Chapter 15 section "Host Networking Commands" to try and successfully lease an IP address from a host.

Step 3   Check the cabling between the router and the local LAN, and between the router and the cable or DSL modem, noting which router interface connects to which part of the network. Then check the SDM configuration to ensure that the inside interface per the PAT configuration is the interface connected to the local LAN, and the outside interface per the PAT configuration is connected to the DSL/cable modem.

Step 4   Test the PAT function by generating traffic from a local PC to a host in the Internet. (More details on this item are given in the next few pages.)

The last item in the list provides a good opportunity to examine a few EXEC commands from the CLI. Example 17-4 lists the output of several CLI commands related to the access router configuration in this chapter, with some comments following the example.

Example 17-4   *Interesting EXEC Commands on the Access Router*

```
R1#show ip dhcp binding
Bindings from all pools not associated with VRF:
IP address       Client-ID/Hardware address/User name  Lease expiration      Type
192.168.1.101    0063.6973.636f.2d                      May 12 2007 08:24 PM  Automatic
192.168.1.111    0100.1517.1973.2c                      May 12 2007 08:26 PM  Automatic
R1#show ip nat translations
Pro Inside global      Inside local        Outside local      Outside global
tcp 64.100.1.1:36486   192.168.1.101:36486 192.168.7.1:80     192.168.7.1:80
udp 64.100.1.1:1027    192.168.1.111:1027  198.133.219.2:53   198.133.219.2:53
```

Example 17-4 *Interesting EXEC Commands on the Access Router (Continued)*

```
R1#clear ip nat translation *
R1#show ip nat translations

R1#
```

The **show ip dhcp binding** command output lists information about the IP addresses assigned to hosts on the local LAN by the DHCP server function in the access router. This command output can be compared to the results when trying to get hosts on the local LAN to acquire an IP address from the router's DHCP server function.

The **show ip nat translations** command output provides a few insights that confirm the normal operation of NAT and PAT. The output shown in Example 17-4 lists one heading line plus two actual NAT translation table entries. The two highlighted parts of the heading line refer to the inside global address and the inside local address. The inside local address should always be the IP address of a host on the local LAN, in this case 192.168.1.101. The router translates that IP address to the one globally routable public address known to the router—the 64.100.1.1 IP address learned via DHCP from the ISP.

The last command in the example, **clear ip nat translation ***, can be useful when the problem symptom is that some users' connections that need to use NAT work fine, and other users' connection that need to use NAT do not work at all. NAT table entries might need to be removed before a host can start sending data again, although this is probably a rare occurrence today. However, this command clears out all the entries in the table, and then the router creates new entries as the ensuing packets arrive. Note that this **clear** command could impact some applications.

Exam Preparation Tasks

Review All the Key Topics

Key
Topic

Review the most important topics from inside the chapter, noted with the key topics icon in the outer margin of the page. Table 17-2 lists a reference of these key topics and the page numbers on which each is found.

Table 17-2 *Key Topics for Chapter 17*

Key Topic Element	Description	Page Number
List	Optional and required configuration steps for a serial link between two routers	542
List	IP addressing details planned and configured on the local LAN for an Internet access router	547
List	Planning items before configuring the DHCP server	555
List	Common items to check when troubleshooting access router installation	558

Complete the Tables and Lists from Memory

Print a copy of Appendix H, "Memory Tables" (found on the CD-ROM), or at least the section for this chapter, and complete the tables and lists from memory. Appendix I, "Memory Tables Answer Key," also on the CD-ROM, includes completed tables and lists to check your work.

Definitions of Key Terms

Define the following key terms from this chapter, and check your answers in the glossary.

Cisco Router and Security Device Manager

Command References

Although you should not necessarily memorize the information in the tables in this section, this section does include a reference for the configuration commands (Table 17-3) and EXEC commands (Table 17-4) covered in this chapter. Practically speaking, you should memorize the commands as a side effect of reading the chapter and doing all the activities in this exam preparation section. To check to see how well you have memorized the commands as a side effect of your other studies, cover the left side of the table with a piece of paper, read the descriptions in the right side, and see if you remember the command.

Table 17-3 *Chapter 17 Configuration Command Reference*

Command	Description
encapsulation {**hdlc** | **ppp** | **frame-relay**}	Serial interface subcommand that defines the data-link protocol to use on the link
clock rate *speed*	Serial interface subcommand that, when used on an interface with a DCE cable, sets the clock speed in bps
bandwidth *speed-kbps*	Interface subcommand that sets the router's opinion of the link speed, in kbps, but has no effect on the actual speed
description *text*	Interface subcommand that can set a text description of the interface

Table 17-4 *Chapter 17 EXEC Command Reference*

Command	Description
show ip nat translations	Lists the NAT/PAT translation table entries
show dhcp server	Lists information learned from a DHCP server, by a router acting as a DHCP client
clear ip nat translation *	Clears (removes) all dynamic entries in the NAT table
show interfaces	Lists several important settings on serial links, including encapsulation, bandwidth, keepalives, the two status codes, description, and IP address/ mask
show controllers serial *number*	Lists whether a cable is connected to the interface, and if so, whether it is a DTE or DCE cable
show interfaces [*type number*] **description**	Lists a single line per interface (or if the interface is included, just one line of output total) that lists the interface status and description
show ip interface brief	Lists a single line per interface, listing the IP address and interface status

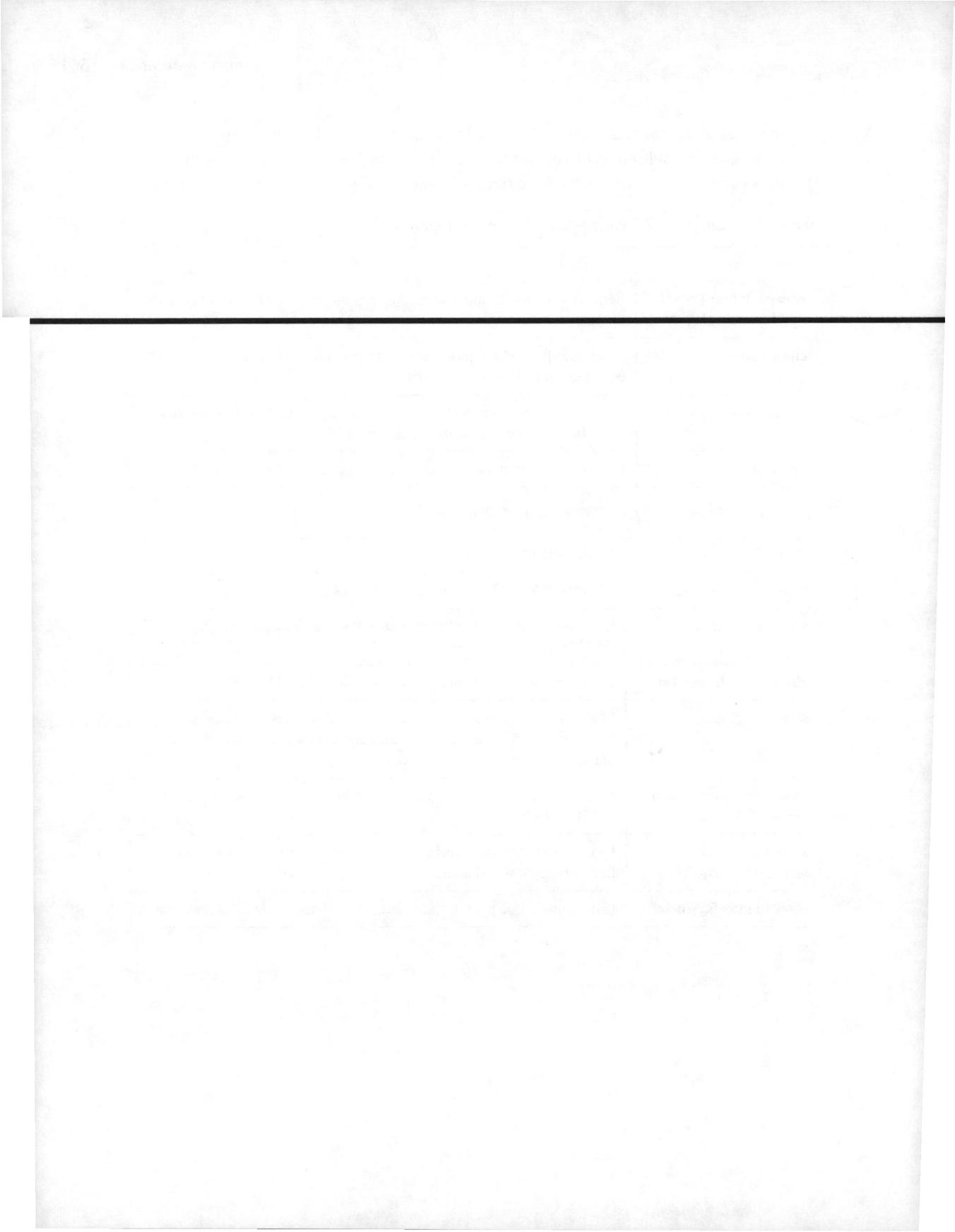

Part V: Final Preparation

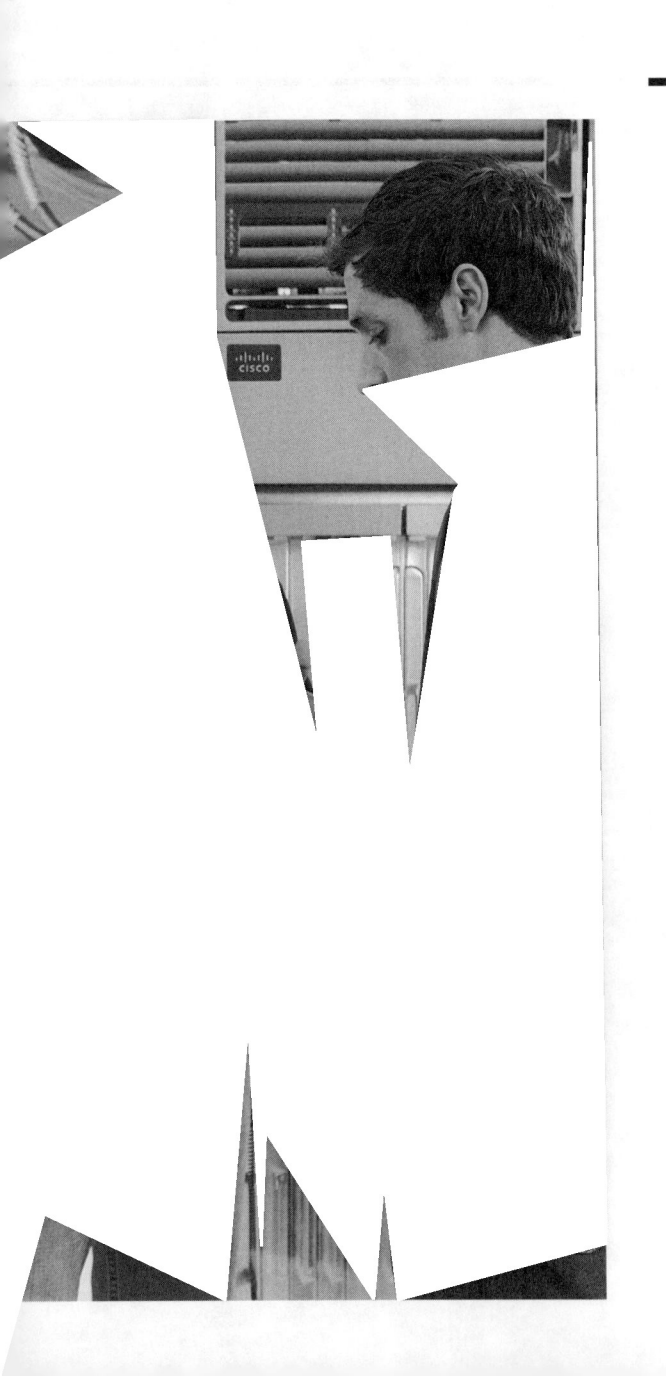

CHAPTER 18

Final Preparation

The first 17 chapters of this book cover the technologies, protocols, commands, and features you need to understand to pass the ICND2 exam. Although these chapters supply the detailed information, most people need more preparation than simply reading the first 17 chapters. This chapter details a set of tools and a study plan to help you complete your preparation for the exams.

If you're preparing for the CCNA exam by reading both this book and the *CCNA ICND2 Official Exam Certification Guide*, you know that both books have a final preparation chapter. However, you can refer to just this chapter to read about the suggested study plan, because this chapter refers to the tools in both this book and the ICND2 book. Just look for the text highlighted in gray, like this sentence, for suggestions that apply to CCNA (640-802) exam preparation, but not to ICND1 (640-816) exam preparation.

This short chapter has two main sections. The first section lists the exam preparation tools that can be useful at this point in your study process. The second section lists a suggested study plan now that you have completed all the earlier chapters.

> **NOTE** This chapter refers to many of the book's chapters and appendixes, as well as tools available on the CD. Some of the appendixes, beginning with Appendix D, are included only on the CD that comes with this book. To access those, just insert the CD and make the appropriate selection from the opening interface.

Tools for Final Preparation

This section lists some information about the available tools and how to access them.

Exam Engine and Questions on the CD

The CD includes an exam engine—software that displays and then grades a set of exam-realistic questions. These include simulation (sim) questions, drag-and-drop, and many scenario-based questions that require the same level of analysis as the questions on the ICND1 and CCNA exams. Using the exam engine, you can either practice with the questions in Study Mode or take a simulated (timed) ICND1 or CCNA exam.

The installation process has two major steps. The CD includes a recent copy of the exam engine software, supplied by Boson Software (http://www.boson.com). The practice exam—the database of ICND1 exam questions—is not on the CD. Instead, the practice exam resides on the http://www.boson.com web server, so the second major step is to activate and download the practice exam.

> **NOTE**   The cardboard CD case in the back of this book includes the CD and a piece of paper. The paper lists the activation key for the practice exam associated with this book. *Do not lose the activation key.*

Install the Software from the CD

The software installation process is pretty routine as compared with other software installation processes. The following steps outline the process:

Step 1   Insert the CD into your PC.

Step 2   The software that automatically runs is the Cisco Press software to access and use all CD-based features, including the exam engine, viewing a PDF file of this book, and viewing the CD-only appendixes. From the main menu, click the option to **Install the Exam Engine**.

Step 3   Respond to prompt windows, as you would with any typical software installation process.

The installation process might give you the option to register the software. This process requires that you establish a login at the http://www.boson.com website. You will need this login to activate the exam, so feel free to register when prompted. If you already have a login at the http://www.boson.com site, you don't need to register again. Just use your existing login.

Activate and Download the Practice Exam

After the exam engine is installed, you should activate the exam associated with this book:

Step 1   Start the Boson Exam Environment (BEE) software from the Start menu. It should be installed in a Cisco Press folder on your computer.

Step 2   The first time you start the software, it should ask you to either log in or register an account. If you do not already have an account with Boson, select the option to register a new account. (You must register to download and use the exam.)

Step 3   After you are registered, the software might prompt you to download the latest version of the software, which you should do. Note that this process updates the exam engine software (formally called the Boson Exam Environment). It doesn't activate the practice exam.

Step 4   To activate and download the exam associated with this book, from the exam engine main window, click the **Exam Wizard** button.

Step 5   From the Exam Wizard pop-up window, select **Activate a purchased exam** and click the **Next** button. (Although you did not purchase the exam directly, you purchased it indirectly when you purchased this book.)

Step 6   On the next screen, enter the Activation Key from the paper inside the cardboard CD holder, and click the **Next** button.

Step 7   The activation process downloads the practice exam. When this is done, the main exam engine menu should list a new exam, with a name such as "ExSim for Cisco Press ICND1 ECG." If you do not see the exam, be sure you have selected the **My Exams** tab on the menu. You may need to click the plus sign icon (+) to expand the menu and see the exam.

At this point, the software and practice exam are ready to use.

Activating Other Exams

You need to go through the exam software installation process and the registration process only once. After that, for each new exam, only a few steps are required. For instance, if you bought both this book and the *CCNA ICND2 Official Exam Certification Guide*, you could follow the steps just listed to install the software and activate the exam associated with this book. Then, for the practice exam associated with the ICND2 book, which has about 150 exam-realistic ICND2 questions, you need to follow only a few more steps. All you have to do is start the Boson exam environment (if it is not still up and running) and follow Steps 4 through 6 in the preceding list. In fact, if you purchase other Cisco Press books, or purchase a practice exam from Boson, you just need to activate each new exam as described in Steps 4 through 6.

You can also purchase additional practice exams from Boson directly from its website. When you purchase an exam, you receive an activation key, and then you can activate and download the exam—again without requiring any additional software installation.

The Cisco CCNA Prep Center

Cisco provides a wide variety of CCNA preparation tools at a Cisco Systems website called the CCNA Prep Center. The CCNA Prep Center includes demonstrations of the exam's user interface, sample questions, informational videos, discussion forums, and other tools.

To use the CCNA Prep Center, you need a registered login at http://www.cisco.com. To register, simply go to http://www.cisco.com, click **Register** at the top of the page, and supply some information. (You do not need to work for Cisco or one of its partners to get a login.)

After you have registered, proceed to http://www.cisco.com/go/prepcenter, and look for the link to the CCNA Prep Center. There you can log in and explore the many features.

Subnetting Videos, Reference Pages, and Practice Problems

Being able to analyze the IP addressing and subnetting used in any IPv4 network may be the single most important skill for all the CCNA exams. This book's Chapter 12, "IP Addressing and Subnetting," covers most of those details. The ICND2 book's Chapter 5, "VLSM and Route Summarization," adds to the puzzle by explaining VLSM.

This book includes several tools to help you practice and refine your subnetting skills:

- **Subnetting reference pages:** CD-only Appendix E, "Subnetting Reference Pages," summarizes the binary and decimal shortcut processes explained in Chapter 12. Each reference page lists a single process related to subnetting, along with reference information useful for that process. These summarized processes may be a more convenient tool when you're practicing subnetting, as compared to flipping pages in the subnetting chapters, looking for the correct process.

- **Subnetting videos:** The DVD included with this book has a series of subnetting videos. These videos show you how to use the shortcut processes to find the answers to popular subnetting questions. You can select and play the videos from a simple menu that starts when you insert the DVD into a DVD drive.

- **Subnetting practice:** CD-only Appendix D, "Subnetting Practice," contains a variety of subnetting practice problems, including 25 problems for which you need to find the subnet number, subnet broadcast address, and range of valid IP addresses. This appendix shows you how to use both binary and shortcut processes to find the answers.

Scenarios

As mentioned in the Introduction to this book, some of the exam questions require you to use the same skills commonly used to troubleshoot problems in real networks. The troubleshooting sections and chapters of both the ICND1 and ICND2 books help prepare you for those kinds of questions.

Another way to prepare for troubleshooting questions on the exams is to think through many different network scenarios, predicting what should occur, and investigating whether the network is performing as it should. Appendix F, "Additional Scenarios," in both books includes some tasks that you should attempt before reading the suggested solutions listed later in the appendix. By reading these scenarios and doing the exercises, you can practice some of the skills required when analyzing and troubleshooting networks.

Study Plan

You could simply study using all the available tools, as mentioned earlier in this chapter. However, this section suggests a particular study plan, with a sequence of tasks that may work better than just using the tools randomly. However, feel free to use the tools in any way and at any time that helps you fully prepare for the exam.

If you are preparing for only the ICND1 exam, you can ignore the gray highlighted portions of this study plan. If you are studying for the CCNA exam by using the ICND2 book as well, include the tasks highlighted in gray.

The suggested study plan separates the tasks into four categories:

- **Recall the facts.** Activities that help you remember all the details from the first 17 chapters of this book.

- **Practice subnetting.** You must master subnetting to succeed on the ICND1, ICND2, and CCNA exams. This category lists the items you can use to practice subnetting skills.

- **Build troubleshooting skills using scenarios.** To answer some exam questions that present a scenario, you may need to recall facts, do subnetting math quickly and accurately, and use a hands-on simulator—all to answer a single question. This plan section suggests activities that help you pull together these different skills.

- **Use the exam engine to practice realistic questions.** You can use the exam engine on the CD to study using a bank of unique exam-realistic questions available only with this book.

Recall the Facts

As with most exams, you must recall many facts, concepts, and definitions to do well on the test. This section suggests a couple of tasks that should help you remember all the details:

Step 1 **Review and repeat, as needed, the activities in the "Exam Preparation Tasks" section at the end of each chapter.** Most of these activities help you refine your knowledge of a topic while also helping you memorize the facts. For CCNA exam preparation, do this for Chapters 2 through 17 in this book as well as Chapters 1 through 17 in the ICND2 book.

Step 2 **Review all the "Do I Know This Already?" quiz questions at the beginning of the chapters.** Although the questions may be familiar, reading through them again will help improve your recall of the topics covered in the questions. Also, the DIKTA questions tend to cover the most important topics from the chapter, and it never hurts to drill on those topics.

Practice Subnetting

Without question, absolutely the most important skill you need to succeed in passing the ICND1, ICND2, and CCNA exams is to be able to accurately, confidently, and quickly answer subnetting questions. The CCNA exams all have some element of time pressure; the most stressful questions are the sim, simlet, and subnetting questions. So, you should practice subnetting math and processes until you can consistently find the correct answer in a reasonable amount of time.

Before I suggest how you should prepare for subnetting questions, please note that there are many alternative methods for finding the answers to subnetting questions. For example, you can use binary math for all 32 bits of the addresses and subnet numbers. Alternatively, you could recognize that 3 of the 4 octets in most subnetting problems are easily predicted without binary math, and then use binary math in the final interesting octet. Another option would be to use decimal shortcuts. (This topic is covered in this book's Chapter 12, which is included in the ICND2 book's Appendix H.) Shortcuts require no binary math but do require you to practice a process until you've memorized it. You can even use variations on these processes as taught in other books or classes.

Whichever process you prefer, you should practice it until you can use it accurately, confidently, and quickly.

The following list of suggested activities includes practice activities that you can use regardless of the process you choose. In some cases, this list includes items that help you learn the shortcuts included with this book:

Step 1   **View or Print Appendix E, "Subnetting Reference Pages."** This short CD-only appendix includes a series of single-page summaries of the subnetting processes found in Chapter 12. Appendix E includes reference pages that summarize both the binary and decimal shortcut subnetting processes.

Step 2   **Watch the subnetting videos found on the CCNA video DVD found in the back of this book.** These videos show examples of how to use some of the more detailed shortcut processes to help ensure that you know how to use the processes. CCNA exam candidates: The subnetting videos are on DVDs included with both books. They are identical, so you can watch the videos from either DVD.

Step 3   **View or print Appendix D, "Subnetting Practice."** This CD-only appendix includes enough subnetting practice problems so that, through repetition, you can significantly improve your speed and internalize the shortcut processes. Plan on working on these problems until you can consistently get the right answer, quickly, and you no longer have to sit back and think about the process for finding the answer. The goal is to make the process of finding the answers to such problems automatic. CCNA exam candidates: The ICND2 Appendix D contains all the problems from ICND1's Appendix D, plus a few others, so use ICND2's Appendix D.

Step 4 **Practice subnetting with Cisco's subnetting game.** Cisco has a subnetting game, available at the Cisco CCNA Prep Center. It prompts you with various subnetting scenarios and makes practicing subnetting fun. Just go to the CCNA Prep Center (http://www.cisco.com/go/prepcenter), log in with your Cisco.com User ID, select the **Additional Information** tab, and look for the link to download the game. (If you do not have a login, you can establish one from this web page.)

Step 5 **Develop your own practice problems using a subnet calculator.** You can download many free subnet calculators from the Internet, including one available from Cisco as part of the CCNA Prep Center. You can make up your own subnetting problems like those in Appendix D, do the problems, and then test your answers by using the subnet calculator.

Build Troubleshooting Skills Using Scenarios

Just as a real problem in a real network may be caused by a variety of issues—a routing protocol, a bad cable, spanning tree, an incorrect ACL, or even errors in your documentation about the internetwork—the exam makes you apply a wide range of knowledge to answer individual questions. The one activity for this section is as follows:

■ **Review the scenarios included in Appendix F of this book.** These scenarios make you think about issues covered in multiple chapters of the book. They also require more abstract thought to solve the problem. CCNA exam candidates should review the scenarios in Appendix F of both books.

Use the Exam Engine

The exam engine includes two basic modes:

■ **Study mode** is most useful when you want to use the questions to learn and practice. In study mode, you can select options such as whether you want to randomize the order of the questions, randomize the order of the answers, automatically see the answers, refer to specific sections of the text that reside on the CD, and many other options.

■ **Simulation mode** presents questions in a timed environment, providing you with a more exam-realistic experience. However, it restricts your ability to see your score as you progress through the exam, view the answers as you are taking the exam, and refer to sections of the text. These timed exams not only allow you to study for the actual ICND1 and CCNA exams, they also help you simulate the time pressure of the actual exam.

Choosing Study or Simulation Mode

Both study mode and simulation mode are useful for preparing for the exams. It's easy to choose one of the modes from the exam engine's user interface. The following steps show you how to move to the screen where you select study or simulation mode:

Step 1   Click the **Choose Exam** button. The exam should be listed under the title **ExSim for Cisco Press ICND1 ECG**.

Step 2   Click the exam's name to highlight it.

Step 3   Click the **Load Exam** button.

The engine should display a window. Here you can choose **Study Mode** or **Simulation Mode** using the radio buttons.

Choosing the Right Exam Option

The exam engine has many options. You need to choose from one of the three listed exams on the left side of the window, and select either simulation or study mode. Additionally, depending on these two choices, you can potentially modify many other small settings. Although this is a useful tool, it can be difficult to figure out which options to choose to perform the following four primary tasks:

- Study for the ICND1 exam

- Study for the CCNA exam

- Simulate the ICND1 exam

- Simulate the CCNA exam

To support the ability to study for and simulate both the ICND1 and CCNA exams, the practice test includes two separate question banks. The first bank includes about 150 unique questions written specifically for the ICND1 exam. The second bank includes a subset of the ICND2 question bank written for the *CCNA ICND2 Official Exam Certification Guide*.

When studying for or simulating the CCNA exam, you have to choose an option that includes both the ICND2 and ICND1 questions. To study for or simulate the ICND1 exam, you need to choose an exam option that includes only ICND1 questions. The following list outlines the three options on the menu and the questions served by the exam engine for each choice:

- **Cisco ICND1 Exam:** ICND1 questions only

- **Custom Exam:** ICND1 questions only

- **Full CCNA Exam:** Both ICND1 and ICND2 questions

You might want to experiment with some of the options. After you have chosen to either study using these questions or simulate an exam, Table 18-1 lists the four main options, along with how to pick the right options from the user interface.

Table 18-1 *Directions for What to Choose from the Menu to Study or Simulate the Exam*

If you want to:	. . . choose this exam:	. . . and this mode:	. . . and modify these additional settings:
Study for ICND1	Cisco ICND1 CD Exam	Study	No specific settings are required.
Simulate ICND1	Custom Exam	—	Select the timed exam option, 55 questions, 75 minutes. Deselect **Show current score during exam**, and select **Never** under **Show answers and explanations**.
Study for CCNA	Full CCNA Exam	Study	No specific settings are required.
Simulate CCNA	Full CCNA Exam	Simulation	No specific settings are required.

In addition to these main four study options, the custom exam option has a particularly useful feature for exam study. With this option, by clicking the **Modify Settings** button, you can select the questions to study by chapter. So, if you want to use the question bank for study, and you are studying by chapter or groups of chapters, you can select the questions associated with those chapters.

Summary

The tools and suggestions listed in this chapter were designed with one goal in mind: to help you develop the skills required to pass the ICND1 and CCNA exams. This book, and its companion ICND2 book, were developed not just to tell you the facts, but to help you learn how to apply the facts. No matter what your experience level when you take the exams, it is our hope that the broad range of preparation tools, and even the structure of the books and the focus on troubleshooting, will help you pass the exams with ease. I wish you well on the exams.

Part VI: Appendixes

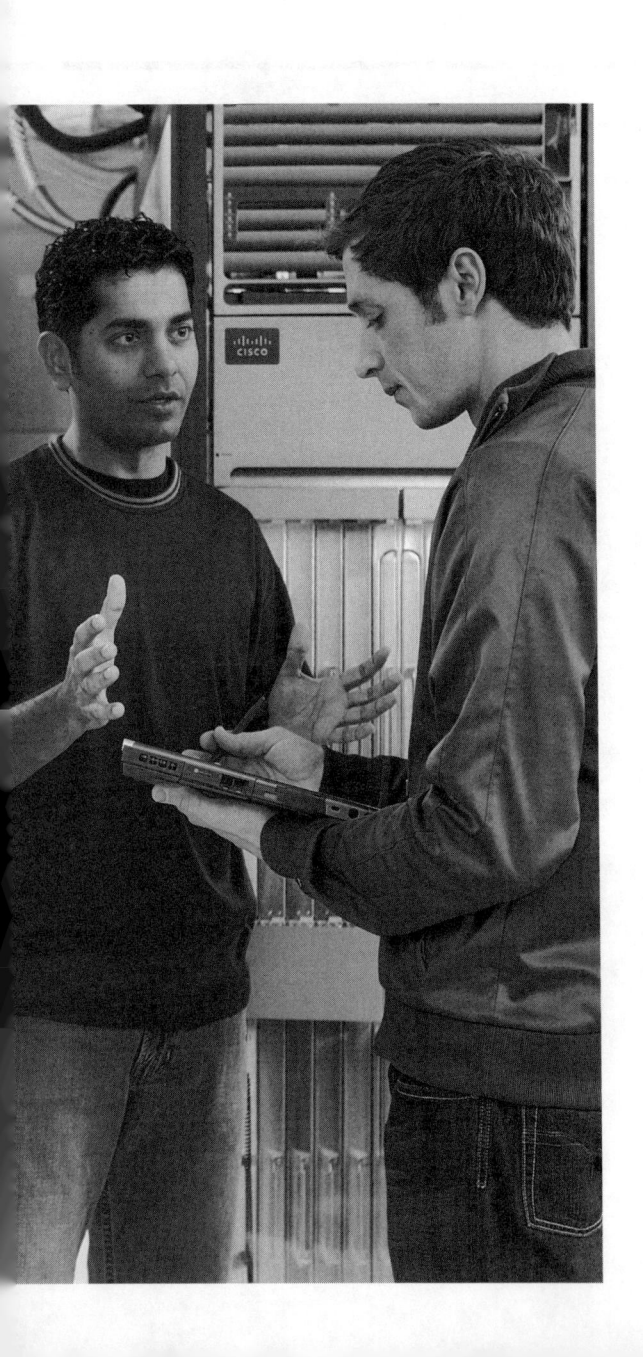

Answers to the "Do I Know This Already?" Quizzes

Chapter 2

"Do I Know This Already?"

1. D and F

2. A and G

3. B. Adjacent-layer interaction occurs on one computer, with two adjacent layers in the model. The higher layer requests services from the next lower layer, and the lower layer provides the services to the next higher layer.

4. B. Same-layer interaction occurs on multiple computers. The functions defined by that layer typically need to be accomplished by multiple computers—for example, the sender setting a sequence number for a segment, and the receiver acknowledging receipt of that segment. A single layer defines that process, but the implementation of that layer on multiple devices is required to accomplish the function.

5. A. Encapsulation is defined as the process of adding a header in front of data supplied by a higher layer (and possibly adding a trailer as well).

6. D

7. C

8. A

9. F

10. C and E. OSI includes the transport layer (not transmission layer) and the network layer (not Internet layer).

Chapter 3

"Do I Know This Already?"

1. D

2. A

3. B

4. B, D, and E. Routers, wireless access point Ethernet ports, and PC NICs all send using pins 1 and 2, whereas hubs and switches send using pins 3 and 6. Straight-through cables are used when connecting devices that use the opposite pairs of pins to transmit data.

5. B

6. A

7. A and C

8. C and D

9. A

10. B, C, and E

11. C

Chapter 4

"Do I Know This Already?"

1. B

2. B

3. B

4. A

5. E

6. E. Although HDLC has an Address field, its value is immaterial on a point-to-point link, as there is only one intended recipient, the device on the other end of the circuit.

7. A

8. B. One of the main advantages of Frame Relay is that a router can use a single access link to support multiple VCs, with each VC allowing the router to send data to a different remote router. To identify each VC, the router must use a different DLCI, because the DLCI identifies the VC.

Chapter 5

"Do I Know This Already?"

1. A and C. The network layer defines logical addressing, in contrast to physical addressing. The logical address structure allows for easy grouping of addresses, which makes routing more efficient. Path selection refers to the process of choosing the best routes to use in the network. Physical addressing and arbitration typically are data link layer functions, and error recovery typically is a transport layer function.

2. C and E

3. A

4. B. 224.1.1.1 is a class D address. 223.223.223.255 is the network broadcast address for class C network 223.223.223.0, so it cannot be assigned to a host.

5. D

6. D and F. Without any subnetting in use, all addresses in the same network as 10.1.1.1—all addresses in Class A network 10.0.0.0—must be on the same LAN. Addresses separated from that network by some router cannot be in network 10.0.0.0. So, the two correct answers are the only two answers that list a valid unicast IP address that is not in network 10.0.0.0.

7. D

8. F

9. C

10. B and C

11. A and C

12. C

13. D

Chapter 6

"Do I Know This Already?"

1. D. PC1 interprets the absence of an acknowledgement to mean that PC1 cannot tell if PC2 got any of the segments. As a result, PC1 resends all segments.

2. D

3. D and E

4. D and E

5. C. TCP, not UDP, performs windowing, error recovery, and ordered data transfer. Neither performs routing or encryption.

6. C and F. The terms packet and L3PDU refer to the data encapsulated by Layer 3. Frame and L2PDU refer to the data encapsulated by Layer 2.

7. B. Note that the hostname is all the text between the // and the /. The text before the // identifies the application layer protocol, and the text after the / represents the name of the web page.

8. A and D. VoIP flows need better delay, jitter, and loss, with better meaning less delay, jitter, and loss, as compared with all data applications. VoIP typically requires less bandwidth than data applications.

9. C. Intrusion Detection Systems (IDS) monitor packets, comparing the contents of single packets, or multiple packets, to known combinations (signatures) that typically imply that a network attack is occurring.

10. A. A virtual private network (VPN) is a security feature in which two endpoints encrypt data before forwarding it through a public network such as the Internet, providing privacy of the data inside the packets.

Chapter 7

"Do I Know This Already?"

1. A. A switch compares the destination address to the MAC address table. If a matching entry is found, the switch knows out which interface to forward the frame. If no matching entry is found, the switch floods the frame.

2. C. A switch floods broadcast frames, multicast frames (if no multicast optimizations are enabled), and unknown unicast destination frames (frames whose destination MAC address is not in the MAC address table).

3. A. A switch floods broadcast frames, multicast frames (if no multicast optimizations are enabled), and unknown unicast destination frames (frames whose destination MAC address is not in the MAC address table).

4. B. Switches learn MAC table entries by noting the source MAC address of each received frame and the interface in which the frame was received, adding an entry that contains both pieces of information (MAC address and interface).

5. A and B. When the frame sent by PC3 arrives at the switch, the switch has learned a MAC address table entry for only 1111.1111.1111, PC1's MAC address. PC3's

frame, addressed to 2222.2222.2222, is flooded, which means it is forwarded out all interfaces except for the interface on which the frame arrived.

6. A. A collision domain contains all devices whose frames could collide with frames sent by all the other devices in the domain. Bridges, switches, and routers separate or segment a LAN into multiple collision domains, whereas hubs and repeaters do not.

7. A, B, and C. A broadcast domain contains all devices whose sent broadcast frames should be delivered to all the other devices in the domain. Hubs, repeaters, bridges, and switches do not separate or segment a LAN into multiple broadcast domains, whereas routers do.

8. B and D

Chapter 8

"Do I Know This Already?"

1. A and B

2. B

3. B

4. A

5. F

6. D

7. B and C

Chapter 9

"Do I Know This Already?"

1. B. If both commands are configured, IOS accepts only the password as configured in the **enable secret** command.

2. B and C

3. B. The first nonblank character after the **banner login** phrase is interpreted as the beginning delimiter character. In this case, it's the letter "t." So, the second letter "t"— the first letter in "the"—is interpreted as the ending delimiter. The resulting login banner is the text between these two "t"s—namely, "his is."

4. A. The setting for the maximum number of MAC addresses has a default of 1, so the **switchport port-security maximum** command does not have to be configured.

5. **A, D, and F.** To allow access via Telnet, the switch must have password security enabled, at a minimum using the **password** vty line configuration subcommand. Additionally, the switch needs an IP address (configured under the VLAN 1 interface) and a default gateway when the switch needs to communicate with hosts in a different subnet.

6. **F**

7. **E**

8. **A.** VLAN names are case-sensitive, so the **name MY-VLAN** command, while using the correct syntax, would set a different VLAN name than the name shown in the question. The **interface range** command in one of the answers includes interfaces Fa0/13, Fa0/14, and Fa0/15. Because Fa0/14 is not assigned to VLAN 2, this command would not have allowed the right VLAN assignment. To assign a port to a VLAN, the **switchport access vlan 2** command would have been required (not the **switchport vlan 2** command, which is syntactically incorrect).

Chapter 10

"Do I Know This Already?"

1. **E and F.** CDP discovers information about neighbors. **show cdp** gives you several options that display more or less information, depending on the parameters used.

2. **E and F**

3. **A, B, and D.** The disabled state in the **show interfaces status** command is the same as an "administratively down and down" state shown in the **show interfaces** command. The interface must be in a connect state (per the **show interfaces status** command) before the switch can send frames out the interface.

4. **A and D.** SW2 has effectively disabled IEEE standard autonegotiation by configuring both speed and duplex. However, Cisco switches can detect the speed used by the other device, even with autonegotiation turned off. Also, at 1 Gbps, the IEEE autonegotiation standard says to use full duplex if the duplex setting cannot be negotiated, so both ends use 1 Gbps, full duplex.

5. **B and D.** The **show interfaces** command lists the actual speed and duplex setting, but it does not imply anything about how the settings were configured or negotiated. The **show interfaces status** command lists a prefix of **a-** in front of the speed and duplex setting to imply that the setting was autonegotiated, leaving off this prefix if the setting was configured.

6. **A, B, and D.** For Fa0/1, autonegotiation should work normally, with both switches choosing the faster speed (100) and better duplex setting (full). Autonegotiation also works on SW1's Fa0/2, with both switches choosing the 100 Mbps and FDX setting.

Fa0/3 disables autonegotiation as a result of having both the speed and duplex configured. The other switch still automatically senses the speed (100 Mbps), but the autonegotiation failure results in the other switch using half duplex.

7. A and C. Switch forwarding logic and MAC table entries are separated per VLAN. Because the frame came in an interface in VLAN 2, it will only be forwarded based on VLAN 2's MAC table entries, and it will only cause the addition of MAC table entries in VLAN 2. The output from the **show mac address-table dynamic** command lists only dynamic MAC table entries, so you cannot definitively state how the frame will be forwarded, because the static entries are not listed.

8. B and C. IOS adds MAC addresses configured by the port security feature as static MAC addresses, so they do not show up in the output of the **show mac address-table dynamic** command. **show mac address-table port-security** is not a valid command.

Chapter 11

"Do I Know This Already?"
1. A. 802.11a uses the U-NNI band of frequencies (around 5.4 GHz). 802.11b and 802.11g use the ISM band (around 2.4 GHz). 802.11i is a security standard.

2. B. 802.11a uses only OFDM, and 802.11b uses only DSSS. 802.11g runs at a maximum of 54 Mbps using OFDM encoding.

3. C

4. A. The Extended Service Set (ESS) mode uses multiple access points, which then allows roaming between the APs. BSS uses a single AP, and IBSS (ad hoc mode) does not use an AP, so roaming between different APs cannot be done with BSS and IBSS.

5. A and C. APs need to know the SSID for the WLAN the AP is supporting and, if an AP is capable of multiple standards, the wireless standard to use. The AP uses the best speed to each device based on the signal quality between the AP and that device; the speed can vary from device to device. The size of the coverage area is not configured; instead, it is impacted by antenna choice, antenna gain, interference, and the wireless standard used.

6. B. The AP connects to a LAN switch using a straight-through cable, just like an end-user device. All APs in the same ESS should connect to the same VLAN, because all clients connected to the same WLAN should be in the same subnet. Like LAN switches, APs do not need IP configuration to forward traffic, although it is useful for managing and accessing the AP. The standard or speed used on the WLAN does not require any particular Ethernet speed on the wired side of the AP, although overall performance is better when using faster WLAN speeds by using at least 100-Mbps Ethernet.

7. C and D. Ethernet cabling does not typically give off any radio frequency interference, so the cabling should not affect the WLAN communications. Clients discover APs by listening on all channels, so a configuration setting to a particular channel on an AP does not prevent the client from discovering the AP.

8. B and D. The standard is IEEE 802.11i. The Wi-Fi alliance defined the term WPA2 to refer to that same standard.

9. A, C, and D

Chapter 12

"Do I Know This Already?"

1. A and C

2. B

3. D

4. E. Class B networks imply 16 network bits; the mask implies 7 host bits (7 binary 0s in the mask), leaving 9 subnet bits. 2^9 yields 512 subnets, and $2^7 - 2$ yields 126 hosts per subnet.

5. B. The design requirements mean that at least 7 subnet bits are needed, because $2^6 = 64$ and $2^7 = 128$. Similarly, 7 host bits are also needed, because $2^6 - 2 = 62$ (not enough) and $2^7 - 2 = 126$ (enough). Masks of /23, /24, and /25 (255.255.254.0, 255.255.255.0, and 255.255.255.128, respectively), when used with a Class B network, have at least 7 subnet bits and 7 host bits. The /23 mask maximizes the number of host bits (9 host bits in this case).

6. C. Class C networks imply 24 network bits; the mask implies 4 host bits (4 binary 0s in the mask), leaving 4 subnet bits. 2^4 yields 16 subnets, and $2^4 - 2$ yields 14 hosts per subnet.

7. C. You need 8 bits to number up to 150 hosts because $2^7 - 2$ is less than 150, but $2^8 - 2$ is greater than 150. Similarly, you need 8 subnet bits, because 2^7 is less than 164, but 2^8 is greater than 164. The only valid Class B subnet mask with 8 host and 8 subnet bits is 255.255.255.0.

8. B, C, D, and E. To meet these requirements, the mask needs at least 8 subnet bits, because $2^8 = 256$, but $2^7 = 128$, which is not enough subnets. The mask also needs at least 8 host bits, because $2^8 - 2 = 254$, but $2^7 - 2 = 126$, which is not enough hosts per subnet. Because a Class A network is in use, the mask needs 8 network bits. As a result, the first 16 bits in the mask must be binary 1s, and the last 8 bits binary 0s, with any valid combination in the third octet.

9. E and F. IP address 190.4.80.80, with mask 255.255.255.0, is in subnet number 190.4.80.0, with broadcast address 190.4.80.255, and a range of valid addresses of 190.4.80.1 through 190.4.80.254.

10. F. 190.4.80.80, mask 255.255.240.0, is in subnet 190.4.80.0, broadcast address 190.4.95.255, with a range of valid addresses of 190.4.80.1 through 190.4.95.254.

11. D, E, F. 190.4.80.80, mask 255.255.255.128 (/25), is in subnet 190.4.80.0, broadcast address 190.4.80.127, with a range of valid addresses of 190.4.80.1 through 190.4.80.126.

12. B and D. To find the answer, you should use the presumed address and mask and try to find the subnet number and subnet broadcast address of that subnet. If the subnet number or broadcast address happens to be the same number you started with, as listed in the answer, then you have identified the fact that the number is a subnet number or broadcast address. For this question, note that 10.0.0.0 is a Class A network number, which is the same value as the zero subnet, no matter what mask is used—so it is definitely reserved. For 172.27.27.27, mask 255.255.255.252, you will find subnet 172.27.27.24, valid address range 172.27.27.25–26, and a subnet broadcast address of 172.27.27.27.

13. C, D, E, and F. In this case, the subnet numbers begin with 180.1.0.0 (subnet zero), and then 180.1.8.0, 180.1.16.0, 180.1.24.0, and so on, increasing by 8 in the third octet, up to 180.1.248.0 (broadcast subnet).

14. A. In this case, the subnet numbers begin with 180.1.0.0 (subnet zero), and then 180.1.1.0, 180.1.2.0, 180.1.3.0, and so on, increasing by 1 in the third octet, up to 180.1.255.0 (broadcast subnet).

Chapter 13

"Do I Know This Already?"

1. B and E. Cisco routers have an on/off switch, but Cisco switches generally do not.

2. B and C. SOHO routers oftentimes expect to connect users to the Internet, so they use DHCP client services to learn a publicly routable IP address from an ISP, and then use DHCP server functions to lease IP addresses to the hosts in the small office.

3. A. Both switches and routers configure IP addresses, so the **ip address** *address mask* and **ip address dhcp** commands could be used on both routers and switches. The **interface vlan 1** command applies only to switches.

4. B and D. To route packets, a router interface must have an IP address assigned and be in an "up and up" interface state. For a serial link created in a lab, without using

CSU/DSUs, one router must be configured with a **clock rate** command to the speed of the link. The **bandwidth** and **description** commands are not required to make a link operational.

5. C. If the first of the two status codes is "down," it typically means that a Layer 1 problem exists (for example, the physical cable is not connected to the interface).

6. C and E

7. B and C. A router has one IP address for each interface in use, whereas a LAN switch has a single IP address that is just used for accessing the switch. Setup mode prompts for some different details in routers and switches; in particular, routers ask for IP addresses and masks for each interface.

8. D and F. The router boot process considers the low-order 4 bits of the configuration register, called the boot field, as well as any configured **boot system** global configuration commands. This process allows an engineer to specify which IOS is loaded when the router is initialized.

9. A

Chapter 14

"Do I Know This Already?"

1. A and C. A router will add a static route to the routing table as long as the outgoing interface or next-hop information is currently valid.

2. A

3. A and B

4. E and F

5. B, D, E, and F

6. D, E, and F

7. A, D, E, and H. The configuration consists of the **router rip** command, the **version 2** command, and the **network 10.0.0.0** and **network 11.0.0.0** commands. The **network** command uses classful network numbers as the parameter, and the **version 2** command is required to make the router use only RIP Version 2. Router2 does not need a **network 9.0.0.0** command, because a router needs only **network** commands that match directly connected subnets.

8. A. The **network** command uses classful network numbers as the parameter, matching all of that router's interfaces whose addresses are in the classful network. The parameter must list the full network number, not just the network octets.

9. B

10. B and C. The bracketed numbers include first the administrative distance, and then the metric. The time counter (value 00:00:13) is an increasing counter that lists the time since this route was last included in a received RIP update. The counter resets to 00:00:00 upon receipt of each periodic routing update.

Chapter 15

1. C and D. Addresses that begin with 225 are Class D multicast IP addresses, so they cannot be assigned to interfaces to be used as unicast IP addresses. 10.43.53.63 255.255.255.192 is actually a subnet broadcast address for subnet 10.43.53.0 255.255.255.192.

2. B

3. C. The asterisk beside connection 2 identifies the connection number to which the **resume** command will connect the user if the **resume** command does not have any parameters.

4. A and D. LAN-based hosts ARP to find the MAC addresses of other hosts they perceive to be in the same subnet. PC1 thinks that 10.1.1.130 is in the same subnet, so PC1 will ARP looking for that host's MAC address. PC3 would not ARP for 10.1.1.10, because PC3's subnet, per its address and mask, is 10.1.1.128/25, range 10.1.1.129–10.1.1.254. R1 would have a connected route for subnet 10.1.1.0/24, range 10.1.1.1–10.1.1.254, so R1 would ARP looking for 10.1.1.130's MAC address.

5. A. A ping of a host's own IP address does not test whether the LAN is working or not, because the packet does not have to traverse the LAN. A ping that requires the packet to go from PC1 to the default gateway (R1) proves the LAN works, at least between PC1 and R1. The only answer that lists a command that causes a packet to need to cross the LAN from PC1 to R1 (although that process fails) is the **ping 10.1.1.1** command.

6. A, C, and E. The **tracert** (Microsoft operating systems) and **traceroute** (Cisco IOS Software) commands list the IP address of the intermediate routers and end host. The commands list the router's IP address closest to the host that issued the command.

7. B and C. A host only ARPs to find MAC addresses of other hosts in the same subnet. PC1 would need its default gateway's MAC address, and likewise, R1 would need PC1's MAC address in its ARP cache to send the return packet.

8. A and D. A host only ARPs to find MAC addresses of other hosts in the same subnet. However, a host learns the IP address to MAC address mapping information from a received ARP request. PC1 would send an ARP broadcast for R1's 10.1.1.1 IP address, which would cause PC1 to learn about R1's MAC address, and R1 to learn PC1's MAC address. Similarly, because the first packet is going from PC1 to PC2, R2 will need

to send an ARP broadcast looking for PC2's MAC address, through which PC2 will learn R2's MAC address, meaning that PC2 does not need to send an ARP broadcast looking for R2's MAC address.

9. A, C, and E. The IP header has a source IP address of 10.1.1.10 and a destination of 172.16.2.7 for the packets going left-to-right, with those addresses reversed for the ping reply packets that go right-to-left. The MAC addresses always represent the addresses of the devices on that local LAN. Note that HDLC, on the serial link, does not use MAC addresses.

Chapter 16

"Do I Know This Already?"

1. D. Modems demodulate an analog signal sent by the phone company into a digital signal. The goal is to re-create the original bits sent by the other modem, so the demodulation function converts the analog signal into the bits that it was intended to represent.

2. A. Of the Internet access options covered in this book, only DSL has distance limitations based on the length of the local telco loop.

3. D. The DSLAM separates, or multiplexes, the voice traffic from the data, splitting the voice traffic off to a voice switch, and the data traffic to a router.

4. A and C. Cable Internet supports only asymmetric speeds.

5. B and C

6. A. The router acts as a DHCP server on the local LAN segment, with a static IP address on the interface. It performs NAT/PAT, changing the source IP address of packets entering the interface. It does not act as a DNS server; although as DHCP server, it does tell the PCs on the local LAN the IP address(es) of any known DNS servers.

7. B and C. The router acts as a DHCP server on the local LAN segment, and as a DHCP client on the Internet-facing interface. It performs NAT/PAT, changing the source IP address of packets entering the local LAN interface and exiting the Internet-facing interface. It does not act as a DNS server; although as DHCP server, it does tell the PCs on the local LAN the IP address(es) of any known DNS servers.

8. B and C. In a typical installation, the router translates (with NAT/PAT) the local hosts' IP addresses, so the server would receive packets from a public IP address (known to the access router) instead of from private IP address 10.1.1.1. The PC user will use normal DNS services to learn the IP address of www.cisco.com, which would be a public IP address in the Internet. In NAT terminology, the inside local IP address is the

private IP address for a local host in the enterprise network, whereas the inside global IP address is the public Internet IP address to which the inside local IP address is translated by NAT/PAT.

Chapter 17

1. A. The **encapsulation** command resets the encapsulation (data-link), so only the **encapsulation ppp** command is required. The **clock rate** command only matters if a back-to-back serial link is used, and if that link already works, that means the clock rate command has already been configured. The **bandwidth** command is never required to make the link work.

2. B. For a back-to-back serial link, the **clock rate** command is required on the router with the DCE cable installed. If R1 connects to a DTE cable, R2 must use a DCE cable, requiring the **clock rate** command on R2. The **bandwidth** command is never needed to make any interface work; it is merely a reference for other functions, such as for defaults for choosing routing protocol metrics for EIGRP and OSPF.

3. B. The **clock rate** command is needed only when a back-to-back serial link is created in a lab, and this link uses a real leased line installed by a telco. Although the **bandwidth** command may be recommended, it is not required to make the link work. Because the routers are brand new, having not been configured before, the serial interfaces still have their default encapsulation of HDLC, so the **encapsulation ppp** command is required, on both routers, to make PPP operational.

4. C and D. Other settings include the DHCP clients' default gateway, which is the access router's local LAN interface IP address, the subnet number, and subnet mask.

5. B. The SDM configuration wizard allows DHCP client services to be configured, with an option to add PAT configuration or not. The PAT configuration option assumes all interfaces that already have IP addresses are candidates to be inside interfaces, with DHCP-client interfaces assumed to be outside interfaces.

6. D. SDM uses a web browser on a PC and a web server function on the router, requiring the user to connect through an IP network rather than from the console. SDM does not use SSH at all. SDM loads the configuration into the router only after the user clicks the Finish button on any of the configuration wizards, but the configuration is added only to the running-config file.

7. A and B. To enable a local host user to type names instead of IP addresses to access the Internet, the access router DHCP server needs to be configured with several details, including the IP addresses of the DNS servers advertised by the ISPs. Also, mixing up which interface should be the inside interface and which should be the outside interface is common. The other two answers have nothing to do with the required configuration on an Internet access router.

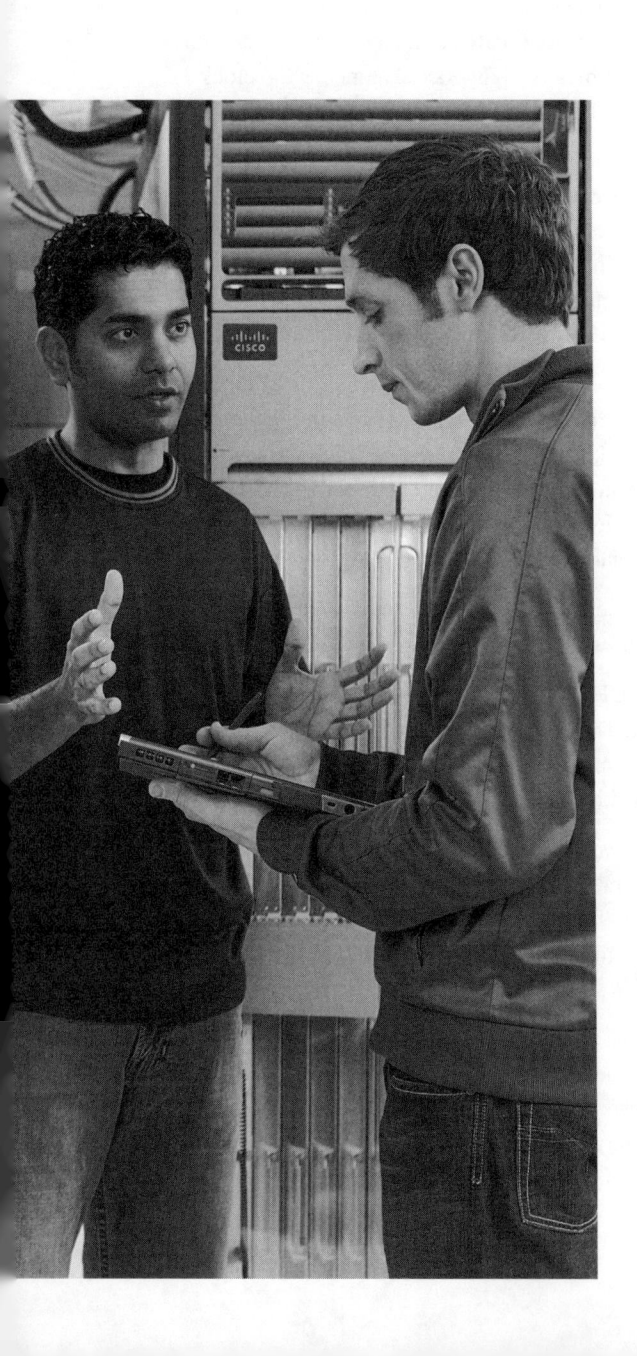

Decimal to Binary Conversion Table

This appendix provides a handy reference for converting between decimal and binary formats for the decimal numbers 0 through 255. Feel free to refer to this table when practicing any of the subnetting problems found in this book and on the CD-ROM.

Although this appendix is useful as a reference tool, note that if you plan to convert values between decimal and binary when doing the various types of subnetting problems on the exams, instead of using the shortcut processes that mostly avoid binary math, you will likely want to practice converting between the two formats before the exam. For practice, just pick any decimal value between 0 and 255, convert it to 8-bit binary, and then use this table to find out if you got the right answer. Also, pick any 8-bit binary number, convert it to decimal, and again use this table to check your work.

Decimal Value	Binary Value	Decimal Value	Binary Value	Decimal Value	Binary Value	Decimal Value	Binary Value
0	00000000	32	00100000	64	01000000	96	01100000
1	00000001	33	00100001	65	01000001	97	01100001
2	00000010	34	00100010	66	01000010	98	01100010
3	00000011	35	00100011	67	01000011	99	01100011
4	00000100	36	00100100	68	01000100	100	01100100
5	00000101	37	00100101	69	01000101	101	01100101
6	00000110	38	00100110	70	01000110	102	01100110
7	00000111	39	00100111	71	01000111	103	01100111
8	00001000	40	00101000	72	01001000	104	01101000
9	00001001	41	00101001	73	01001001	105	01101001
10	00001010	42	00101010	74	01001010	106	01101010
11	00001011	43	00101011	75	01001011	107	01101011
12	00001100	44	00101100	76	01001100	108	01101100
13	00001101	45	00101101	77	01001101	109	01101101
14	00001110	46	00101110	78	01001110	110	01101110
15	00001111	47	00101111	79	01001111	111	01101111
16	00010000	48	00110000	80	01010000	112	01110000
17	00010001	49	00110001	81	01010001	113	01110001
18	00010010	50	00110010	82	01010010	114	01110010
19	00010011	51	00110011	83	01010011	115	01110011
20	00010100	52	00110100	84	01010100	116	01110100
21	00010101	53	00110101	85	01010101	117	01110101
22	00010110	54	00110110	86	01010110	118	01110110
23	00010111	55	00110111	87	01010111	119	01110111
24	00011000	56	00111000	88	01011000	120	01111000
25	00011001	57	00111001	89	01011001	121	01111001
26	00011010	58	00111010	90	01011010	122	01111010
27	00011011	59	00111011	91	01011011	123	01111011
28	00011100	60	00111100	92	01011100	124	01111100
29	00011101	61	00111101	93	01011101	125	01111101
30	00011110	62	00111110	94	01011110	126	01111110
31	00011111	63	00111111	95	01011111	127	01111111

Decimal Value	Binary Value	Decimal Value	Binary Value	Decimal Value	Binary Value	Decimal Value	Binary Value
128	10000000	160	10100000	192	11000000	224	11100000
129	10000001	161	10100001	193	11000001	225	11100001
130	10000010	162	10100010	194	11000010	226	11100010
131	10000011	163	10100011	195	11000011	227	11100011
132	10000100	164	10100100	196	11000100	228	11100100
133	10000101	165	10100101	197	11000101	229	11100101
134	10000110	166	10100110	198	11000110	230	11100110
135	10000111	167	10100111	199	11000111	231	11100111
136	10001000	168	10101000	200	11001000	232	11101000
137	10001001	169	10101001	201	11001001	233	11101001
138	10001010	170	10101010	202	11001010	234	11101010
139	10001011	171	10101011	203	11001011	235	11101011
140	10001100	172	10101100	204	11001100	236	11101100
141	10001101	173	10101101	205	11001101	237	11101101
142	10001110	174	10101110	206	11001110	238	11101110
143	10001111	175	10101111	207	11001111	239	11101111
144	10010000	176	10110000	208	11010000	240	11110000
145	10010001	177	10110001	209	11010001	241	11110001
146	10010010	178	10110010	210	11010010	242	11110010
147	10010011	179	10110011	211	11010011	243	11110011
148	10010100	180	10110100	212	11010100	244	11110100
149	10010101	181	10110101	213	11010101	245	11110101
150	10010110	182	10110110	214	11010110	246	11110110
151	10010111	183	10110111	215	11010111	247	11110111
152	10011000	184	10111000	216	11011000	248	11111000
153	10011001	185	10111001	217	11011001	249	11111001
154	10011010	186	10111010	218	11011010	250	11111010
155	10011011	187	10111011	219	11011011	251	11111011
156	10011100	188	10111100	220	11011100	252	11111100
157	10011101	189	10111101	221	11011101	253	11111101
158	10011110	190	10111110	222	11011110	254	11111110
159	10011111	191	10111111	223	11011111	255	11111111

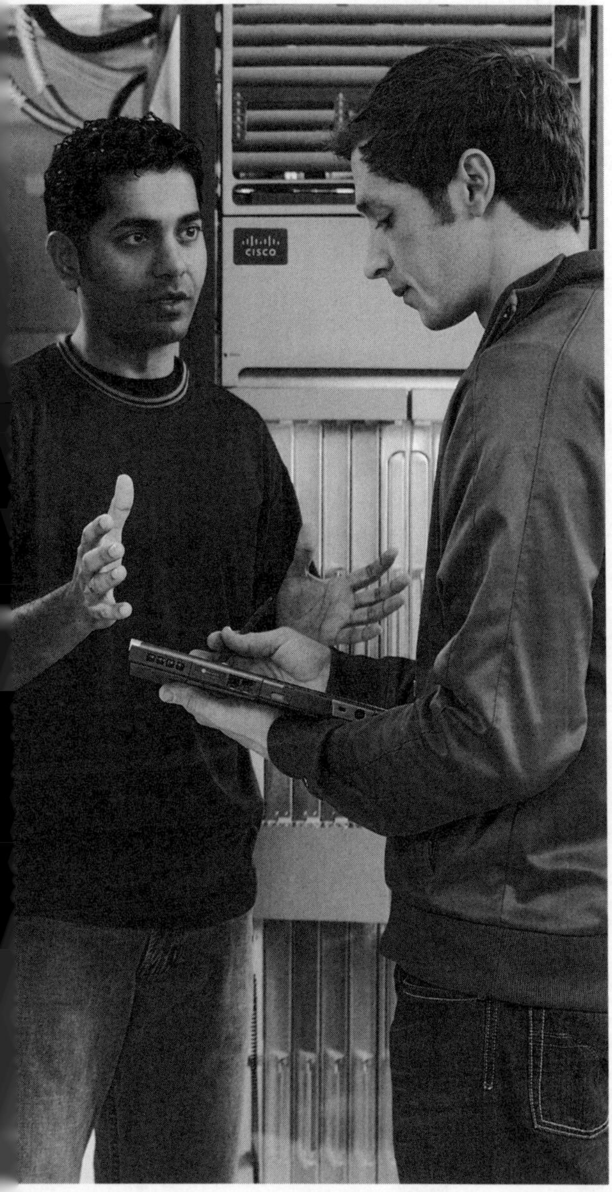
CISCO

ICND1 Exam Updates: Version 1.0

Over time, reader feedback allows Cisco Press to gauge which topics give our readers the most problems when taking the exams. Additionally, Cisco may make small changes in the breadth of exam topics or in emphasis of certain topics. To assist readers with those topics, the author creates new materials clarifying and expanding upon those troublesome exam topics. As mentioned in the introduction, the additional content about the exam is contained in a PDF document on this book's companion website at http://www.ciscopress.com/title/ 1587201828. The document you are viewing is Version 1.0 of this appendix.

This appendix presents all the latest update information available at the time of this book's printing. To make sure you have the latest version of this document, you should be sure to visit the companion website to see if any more recent versions have been posted since this book went to press.

This appendix attempts to fill the void that occurs with any print book. In particular, this appendix does the following:

1. Mentions technical items that might not have been mentioned elsewhere in the book

2. Covers new topics when Cisco adds topics to the ICND1 or CCNA exam blueprints

3. Provides a way to get up-to-the-minute current information about content for the exam

Always Get the Latest at the Companion Website

You are reading the version of this appendix that was available when your book was printed. However, given that the main purpose of this appendix is to be a living, changing document, it is very important that you look for the latest version online at the book's companion website. To do so:

1. Browse to http://www.ciscopress.com/title/1587201828.

2. Select the **Downloads** option under the **More Information** box.

3. Download the latest "ICND1 Appendix C" document.

> **NOTE**   Note that the downloaded document has a version number. If the version of the PDF on the website is the same version as this appendix in your book, your book has the latest version, and there is no need to download or use the online version.

Technical Content

The current version of this appendix does not contain any additional technical coverage. This appendix is here simply to provide the instructions to check online for a later version of this appendix.

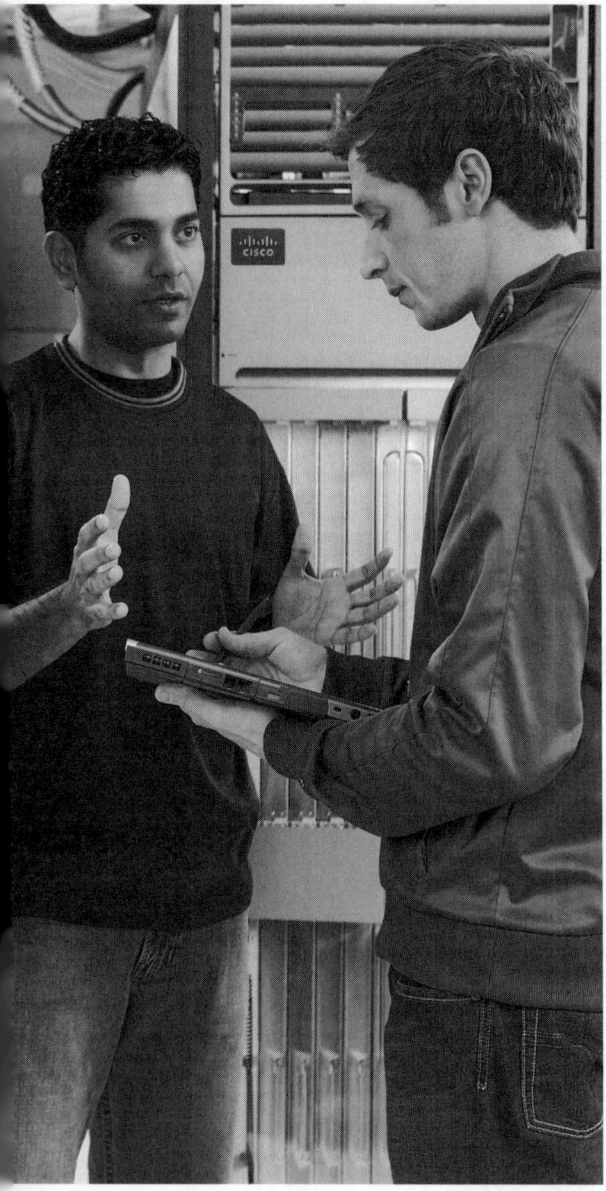
cisco

10BASE-T   The 10-Mbps baseband Ethernet specification using two pairs of twisted-pair cabling (Categories 3, 4, or 5): One pair transmits data and the other receives data. 10BASE-T, which is part of the IEEE 802.3 specification, has a distance limit of approximately 100 m (328 feet) per segment.

100BASE-TX   A name for the IEEE Fast Ethernet standard that uses two-pair copper cabling, a speed of 100 Mbps, and a maximum cable length of 100 meters.

1000BASE-T   A name for the IEEE Gigabit Ethernet standard that uses four-pair copper cabling, a speed of 1000 Mbps (1 Gbps), and a maximum cable length of 100 meters.

802.1Q   The IEEE standardized protocol for VLAN trunking.

802.11a   The IEEE standard for wireless LANs using the U-NII spectrum, OFDM encoding, at speeds of up to 54 Mbps.

802.11b   The IEEE standard for wireless LANs using the ISM spectrum, DSSS encoding, and speeds of up to 11 Mbps.

802.11g   The IEEE standard for wireless LANs using the ISM spectrum, OFDM or DSSS encoding, and speeds of up to 54 Mbps.

802.11i   The IEEE standard for wireless LAN security, including authentication and encryption.

A

AAA   Authentication, Authorization, and Accounting. Authentication confirms the identity of the user or device. Authorization determines what the user or device is allowed to do. Accounting records information about access attempts, including inappropriate requests.

access interface   A LAN network design term that refers to a switch interface connected to end-user devices.

access link   In Frame Relay, the physical serial link that connects a Frame Relay DTE device, usually a router, to a Frame Relay switch. The access link uses the same physical layer standards as do point-to-point leased lines.

access point   A wireless LAN device that provides a means for wireless clients to send data to each other and to the rest of a wired network, with the AP connecting to both the wireless LAN and the wired Ethernet LAN.

accounting   In security, the recording of access attempts. *See* AAA.

ad hoc mode   In wireless LANs, a method or mode of operation in which clients send data directly to each other without the use of a wireless access point (AP).

adjacent-layer interaction   The general topic of how on one computer, two adjacent layers in a networking architectural model work together, with the lower layer providing services to the higher layer.

administrative distance   In Cisco routers, a means for one router to choose between multiple routes to reach the same subnet when those routes were learned by different routing protocols. The lower the administrative distance, the better the source of the routing information.

ADSL   Asymmetric digital subscriber line. One of many DSL technologies, ADSL is designed to deliver more bandwidth downstream (from the central office to the customer site) than upstream.

Anti-X   The term used by Cisco to refer to a variety of security tools that help prevent various attacks, including antivirus, anti-phishing, and anti-spam.

ARP   Address Resolution Protocol. An Internet protocol used to map an IP address to a MAC address. Defined in RFC 826.

asymmetric   A feature of many Internet access technologies, including DSL, cable, and modems, in which the downstream transmission rate is higher than the upstream transmission rate.

asynchronous   The lack of an imposed time ordering on a bit stream. Practically, both sides agree to the same speed, but there is no check or adjustment of the rates if they are slightly different. However, because only 1 byte per transfer is sent, slight differences in clock speed are not an issue.

ATM   Asynchronous Transfer Mode. The international standard for cell relay in which multiple service types (such as voice, video, and data) are conveyed in fixed-length (53-byte) cells. Fixed-length cells allow cell processing to occur in hardware, thereby reducing transit delays.

authentication   In security, the verification of the identity of a person or a process. *See* AAA.

authorization   In security, the determination of the rights allowed for a particular user or device. *See* AAA.

autonomous system   An internetwork in the administrative control of one organization, company, or governmental agency, inside which that organization typically runs an Interior Gateway Protocol (IGP).

auxiliary port   A physical connector on a router that is designed to be used to allow a remote terminal, or PC with a terminal emulator, to access a router using an analog modem.

B

back-to-back link   A serial link between two routers, created without CSU/DSUs, by connecting a DTE cable to one router and a DCE cable to the other. Typically used in labs to build serial links without the expense of an actual leased line from the telco.

balanced hybrid   A term that refers to a general type of routing protocol algorithm, the other two being distance vector and link state. The Enhanced Interior Gateway Routing Protocol (EIGRP) is the only routing protocol that Cisco classifies as using a balanced hybrid algorithm.

bandwidth   A reference to the speed of a networking link. Its origins come from earlier communications technology in which the range, or width, of the frequency band dictated how fast communications could occur.

basic service set (BSS)   In wireless LANs, a WLAN with a single access point.

bitwise Boolean AND   A Boolean AND between two numbers of the same length in which the first bit in each number is ANDed, and then the second bit in each number, and then the third, and so on.

Boolean AND   A math operation performed on a pair of one-digit binary numbers. The result is another one-digit binary number. 1 AND 1 yields 1; all other combinations yield a 0.

boot field   The low-order 4 bits of the configuration register in a Cisco router. The value in the boot field in part tells the router where to look for a Cisco IOS image to load.

BRI   Basic Rate Interface. An ISDN interface composed of two 64-kbps bearer (B) channels and one 16-kbps data (D) channel for circuit-switched communication of voice, video, and data.

broadcast address   *See* subnet broadcast address.

broadcast domain   A set of all devices that receive broadcast frames originating from any device within the set. Devices in the same VLAN are in the same broadcast domain.

broadcast frame   An Ethernet frame sent to destination address FFFF.FFFF.FFFF, meaning that the frame should be delivered to all hosts on that LAN.

broadcast subnet   When subnetting a Class A, B, or C network, the one subnet in each classful network for which all subnet bits have a value of binary 1. The subnet broadcast address in this subnet has the same numeric value as the classful network's network-wide broadcast address.

bus   A common physical signal path composed of wires or other media across which signals can be sent from one part of a computer to another.

C

CDP   Cisco Discovery Protocol. A media- and protocol-independent device-discovery protocol that runs on most Cisco-manufactured equipment, including routers, access servers, and switches. Using CDP, a device can advertise its existence to other devices and receive information about other devices on the same LAN or on the remote side of a WAN.

CDP neighbor   A device on the other end of some communications cable that is advertising CDP updates.

CIDR notation   *See* prefix notation.

circuit switching   A generic reference to network services, typically WAN services, in which the provider sets up a (layer 1) circuit between two devices, and the provider makes no attempt to interpret the meaning of the bits. *See also* packet switching.

classful network   An IPv4 Class A, B, or C network; called a classful network because these networks are defined by the class rules for IPv4 addressing.

classful routing protocol   Does not transmit the mask information along with the subnet number, and therefore must consider Class A, B, and C network boundaries and perform autosummarization at those boundaries. Does not support VLSM.

classless routing protocol   An inherent characteristic of a routing protocol, specifically that the routing protocol does send subnet masks in its routing updates, thereby removing any need to make assumptions about the addresses in a particular subnet or network, making it able to support VLSM and manual route summarization.

CLI   Command-line interface. An interface that enables the user to interact with the operating system by entering commands and optional arguments.

clock rate   The speed at which a serial link encodes bits on the transmission medium.

clock source   The device to which the other devices on the link adjust their speed when using synchronous links.

clocking   The process of supplying a signal over a cable, either on a separate pin on a serial cable or as part of the signal transitions in the transmitted signal, so that the receiving device can keep synchronization with the sending device.

codec   Coder-decoder. An integrated circuit device that transforms analog voice signals into a digital bit stream and then transforms digital signals back into analog voice signals.

collision domain   A set of network interface cards (NICs) for which a frame sent by one NIC could result in a collision with a frame sent by any other NIC in the same collision domain.

command-line interface   *See* CLI.

configuration mode   A part of the Cisco IOS Software CLI in which the user can type configuration commands that are then added to the device's currently used configuration file (running-config).

configuration register   In Cisco routers, a 16-bit, user-configurable value that determines how the router functions during initialization. In software, the bit position is set by specifying a hexadecimal value using configuration commands.

connection establishment   The process by which a connection-oriented protocol creates a connection. With TCP, a connection is established by a three-way transmission of TCP segments.

console port   A physical socket on a router or switch to which a cable can be connected between a computer and the router/switch, for the purpose of allowing the computer to use a terminal emulator and use the CLI to configure, verify, and troubleshoot the router/switch.

convergence   The time required for routing protocols to react to changes in the network, removing bad routes and adding new, better routes so that the current best routes are in all the routers' routing tables.

CPE   Customer premises equipment. Any equipment related to communications that is located at the customer site, as opposed to inside the telephone company's network.

crossover cable   An Ethernet cable that swaps the pair used for transmission on one device to a pair used for receiving on the device on the opposite end of the cable. In 10BASE-T and 100BASE-TX networks, this cable swaps the pair at pins 1,2 to pins 3,6 on the other end of the cable, and the pair at pins 3,6 to pins 1,2 as well.

CSMA/CA   Carrier sense multiple access with collision avoidance. A media-access mechanism that defines how devices decide when they can send, with a goal of avoiding collisions as much as possible. IEEE WLANs use CSMA/CA.

CSMA/CD   Carrier sense multiple access collision detect. A media-access mechanism in which devices ready to transmit data first check the channel for a carrier. If no carrier is sensed for a specific period of time, a device can transmit. If two devices transmit at once, a collision occurs and is detected by all colliding devices. This collision subsequently delays retransmissions from those devices for some random length of time.

CSU/DSU   Channel service unit/data service unit. A device that understands the Layer 1 details of serial links installed by a telco and how to use a serial cable to communicate with networking equipment such as routers.

cut-through switching   One of three options for internal processing on some models of Cisco LAN switches in which the frame is forwarded as soon as possible, including forwarding the first bits of the frame before the whole frame is received.

D

DCE   Data communications equipment. From a physical layer perspective, the device providing the clocking on a WAN link, typically a CSU/DSU, is the DCE. From a packet-switching perspective, the service provider's switch, to which a router might connect, is considered the DCE.

decapsulation   On a computer that receives data over a network, the process in which the device interprets the lower-layer headers and, when finished with each header, removes the header, revealing the next-higher-layer PDU.

default gateway/default router   On an IP host, the IP address of some router to which the host sends packets when the packet's destination address is on a subnet other than the local subnet.

default mask   The mask used in a Class A, B, or C network that does not create any subnets; specifically, mask 255.0.0.0 for Class A networks, 255.255.0.0 for Class B networks, and 255.255.255.0 for Class C networks.

default route   On a router, the route that is considered to match all packets that are not otherwise matched by some more specific route.

demarc   The legal term for the demarcation or separation point between the telco's equipment and the customer's equipment.

denial of service (DoS)   A type of attack whose goal is to cause problems by preventing legitimate users from being able to access services, thereby preventing the normal operation of computers and networks.

DHCP   Dynamic Host Configuration Protocol. A protocol used by hosts to dynamically discover and lease an IP address, and learn the correct subnet mask, default gateway, and DNS server IP addresses.

Direct Sequence Spread Spectrum (DSSS)   A method of encoding data for transmission over a wireless LAN in which the device uses 1 of 11 (in the USA) nearby frequencies in the 2.4-GHz range.

directed broadcast address   *See* subnet broadcast address.

distance vector   The logic behind the behavior of some interior routing protocols, such as RIP. Distance vector routing algorithms call for each router to send its entire routing table in each update, but only to its neighbors. Distance vector routing algorithms can be prone to routing loops but are computationally simpler than link-state routing algorithms.

DNS   Domain Name System. An application layer protocol used throughout the Internet for translating hostnames into their associated IP addresses.

DS0   Digital signal level 0. A 64-kbps line or channel of a faster line inside a telco whose origins are to support a single voice call using the original voice (PCM) codecs.

DS1   Digital signal level 1. A 1.544-Mbps line from the telco, with 24 DS0 channels of 64 kbps each, plus an 8-kbps management and framing channel. Also called a T1.

DSL   Digital subscriber line. Public network technology that delivers high bandwidth over conventional telco local-loop copper wiring at limited distances. Typically used as an Internet access technology, connecting a user to an ISP.

DTE   Data terminal equipment. From a Layer 1 perspective, the DTE synchronizes its clock based on the clock sent by the DCE. From a packet-switching perspective, the DTE is the device outside the service provider's network, typically a router.

E

E1   Similar to a T1, but used in Europe. It uses a rate of 2.048 Mbps and 32 64-kbps channels, with one channel reserved for framing and other overhead.

enable mode   A part of the Cisco IOS CLI in which the user can use the most powerful and potentially disruptive commands on a router or switch, including the ability to then reach configuration mode and reconfigure the router.

encapsulation   The placement of data from a higher-layer protocol behind the header (and in some cases, between a header and trailer) of the next-lower-layer protocol. For example, an IP packet could be encapsulated in an Ethernet header and trailer before being sent over an Ethernet.

encryption   Applying a specific algorithm to data to alter the appearance of the data, making it incomprehensible to those who are not authorized to see the information.

error detection   The process of discovering whether or not a data-link level frame was changed during transmission. This process typically uses a Frame Check Sequence (FCS) field in the data-link trailer.

error disabled   An interface state on LAN switches that is the result of one of many security violations.

error recovery   The process of noticing when some transmitted data was not successfully received and resending the data until it is successfully received.

Ethernet   A series of LAN standards defined by the IEEE, originally invented by Xerox Corporation and developed jointly by Xerox, Intel, and Digital Equipment Corporation.

Extended Service Set (ESS)   In wireless LANs, a WLAN with multiple access points to create one WLAN, allowing roaming between the APs.

Exterior Gateway Protocol (EGP)   A routing protocol that was designed to exchange routing information between different autonomous systems.

F

filter   Generally, a process or a device that screens network traffic for certain characteristics, such as source address, destination address, or protocol, and determines whether to forward or discard that traffic based on the established criteria.

firewall   A device that forwards packets between the less secure and more secure parts of the network, applying rules that determine which packets are allowed to pass, and which are not.

Flash   A type of read/write permanent memory that retains its contents even with no power applied to the memory, and uses no moving parts, making the memory less likely to fail over time.

flooding   The result of the LAN switch forwarding process for broadcasts and unknown unicast frames. Switches forward these frames out all interfaces, except the interface in which the frame arrived. Switches also forward multicasts by default, although this behavior can be changed.

flow control   The process of regulating the amount of data sent by a sending computer toward a receiving computer. Several flow control mechanisms exist, including TCP flow control, which uses windowing.

forward   To send a frame received in one interface out another interface, toward its ultimate destination.

forward acknowledgment   A process used by protocols that do error recovery in which the number that acknowledges data lists the next data that should be sent, not the last data that was successfully received.

four-wire circuit   A line from the telco with four wires, composed of two twisted-pair wires. Each pair is used to send in one direction, so a four-wire circuit allows full-duplex communication.

fragment-free switching   One of three internal processing options on some Cisco LAN switches in which the first bits of the frame may be forwarded before the entire frame is received, but not until the first 64 bytes of the frame are received, in which case, in a well-designed LAN, collision fragments should not occur as a result of this forwarding logic.

frame   A term referring to a data-link header and trailer, plus the data encapsulated between the header and trailer.

Frame Relay   An international standard data-link protocol that defines the capabilities to create a frame-switched (packet-switched) service, allowing DTE devices (typically routers) to send data to many other devices using a single physical connection to the Frame Relay service.

Frequency Hopping Spread Spectrum   A method of encoding data on a wireless LAN in which consecutive transmissions occur on different nearby frequency bands as compared with the prior transmission. Not used in modern WLAN standards.

full duplex   Generically, any communication in which two communicating devices can concurrently send and receive data. In Ethernet LANs, the allowance for both devices to send and receive at the same time, allowed when both devices disable their CSMA/CD logic.

full mesh   A network topology in which more than two devices can physically communicate and, by choice, all pairs of devices are allowed to communicate directly.

H

half duplex   Generically, any communication in which only one device at a time can send data. In Ethernet LANs, the normal result of the CSMA/CD algorithm that enforces the rule that only one device should send at any point in time.

HDLC   High-Level Data Link Control. A bit-oriented synchronous data link layer protocol developed by the International Organization for Standardization (ISO).

head end   The upstream, transmit end of a cable TV (CATV) installation.

host   Any device that uses an IP address.

host address   The IP address assigned to a network card on a computer.

host part   A term used to describe a part of an IPv4 address that is used to uniquely identify a host inside a subnet. The host part is identified by the bits of value 0 in the subnet mask.

host route   A route with a /32 mask, which by virtue of this mask represents a route to a single host IP address.

HTML   Hypertext Markup Language. A simple document-formatting language that uses tags to indicate how a given part of a document should be interpreted by a viewing application, such as a web browser.

HTTP   Hypertext Transfer Protocol. The protocol used by web browsers and web servers to transfer files, such as text and graphic files.

hub   A LAN device that provides a centralized connection point for LAN cabling, repeating any received electrical signal out all other ports, thereby creating a logical bus. Hubs do not interpret the electrical signals as a frame of bits, so hubs are considered to be Layer 1 devices.

I

ICMP   Internet Control Message Protocol. A TCP/IP network layer protocol that reports errors and provides other information relevant to IP packet processing.

IEEE   Institute of Electrical and Electronics Engineers. A professional organization that develops communications and network standards, among other activities.

IEEE 802.2   An IEEE LAN protocol that specifies an implementation of the LLC sublayer of the data link layer.

IEEE 802.3   A set of IEEE LAN protocols that specifies the many variations of what is known today as an Ethernet LAN.

inactivity timer   For switch MAC address tables, a timer associated with each entry, which counts time upwards from 0 and is reset to 0 each time a switch receives a frame with the same MAC address. The entries with the largest timers can be removed to make space for additional MAC address table entries.

infrastructure mode   A mode of wireless LAN (WLAN) operation in which WLAN clients send and receive data with an access point (AP), which allows the clients to communicate with the wired infrastructure through the AP. Clients do not send data to each other directly; the AP must receive the data from one client, and then send the data to the other WLAN client.

inside global   For packets sent to and from a host that resides inside the trusted part of a network that uses NAT, a term referring to the IP address used in the headers of those packets when those packets traverse the global (public) Internet.

inside local   For packets sent to and from a host that resides inside the trusted part of a network that uses NAT, a term referring to the IP address used in the headers of those packets when those packets traverse the Enterprise (private) part of the network.

Interior Gateway Protocol (IGP)   *See* interior routing protocol.

interior routing protocol   A routing protocol designed for use within a single organization.

intrusion detection system (IDS)   A security function that examines more complex traffic patterns against a list of both known attack signatures and general characteristics of how attacks may be carried out, rating each perceived threat and reporting the threats.

intrusion prevention system (IPS)   A security function that examines more complex traffic patterns against a list of both known attack signatures and general characteristics of how attacks may be carried out, rating each perceived threat and reacting to prevent the more significant threats.

IOS   Cisco operating system software that provides the majority of a router's or switch's features, with the hardware providing the remaining features.

IOS Image   A file that contains the IOS.

IP   Internet Protocol. The network layer protocol in the TCP/IP stack, providing routing and logical addressing standards and services.

IP address   In IP Version 4 (IPv4), a 32-bit address assigned to hosts using TCP/IP. Each address consists of a network number, an optional subnetwork number, and a host number. The network and subnetwork numbers together are used for routing, and the host number is used to address an individual host within the network or subnetwork.

ISDN   Integrated Services Digital Network. A service offered by telephone companies that permits telephone networks to carry data, voice, and other traffic. Often used as an Internet access technology, as well as dial backup when routers lose their normal WAN communications links.

ISL   Inter-Switch Link. A Cisco-proprietary protocol that maintains VLAN information as traffic flows between switches and routers.

ISO   International Organization for Standardization. An international organization that is responsible for a wide range of standards, including many standards relevant to networking. The ISO developed the OSI reference model, a popular networking reference model.

K

keepalive   A proprietary feature of Cisco routers in which the router sends messages on a periodic basis as a means of letting the neighboring router know that the first router is still alive and well.

L

L4PDU   The data compiled by a Layer 4 protocol, including Layer 4 headers and encapsulated high-layer data, but not including lower-layer headers and trailers.

Layer 3 protocol   A protocol that has characteristics like OSI Layer 3, which defines logical addressing and routing. IP, IPX, and AppleTalk DDP are all Layer 3 protocols.

learning   The process used by switches for discovering MAC addresses, and their relative location, by looking at the source MAC address of all frames received by a bridge or switch.

leased line   A serial communications circuit between two points, provided by some service provider, typically a telephone company (telco). Because the telco does not sell a physical cable between the two endpoints, instead charging a monthly fee for the ability to send bits between the two sites, the service is considered to be a leased service.

link state   A classification of the underlying algorithm used in some routing protocols. Link-state protocols build a detailed database that lists links (subnets) and their state (up, down), from which the best routes can then be calculated.

LLC   Logical Link Control. The higher of the two data link layer sublayers defined by the IEEE. Synonymous with IEEE 802.2.

local loop   A line from the premises of a telephone subscriber to the telephone company CO.

logical address   A generic reference to addresses as defined by Layer 3 protocols, which do not have to be concerned with the physical details of the underlying physical media. Used mainly to contrast these addresses with data-link addresses, which are generically considered to be physical addresses because they differ based on the type of physical medium.

M

MAC   Media Access Control. The lower of the two sublayers of the data link layer defined by the IEEE. Synonymous with IEEE 802.3 for Ethernet LANs.

MAC address   A standardized data link layer address that is required for every device that connects to a LAN. Ethernet MAC addresses are 6 bytes long and are controlled by the IEEE. Also known as a *hardware address*, a *MAC layer address*, and a *physical address*.

metric   A unit of measure used by routing protocol algorithms to determine the best route for traffic to use to reach a particular destination.

microsegmentation   The process in LAN design by which every switch port connects to a single device, with no hubs connected to the switch ports, creating a separate collision domain per interface. The term's origin relates to the fact that one definition for the word "segment" is "collision domain," with a switch separating each switch port into a separate collision domain or segment.

modem   Modulator-demodulator. A device that converts between digital and analog signals so that a computer may send data to another computer using analog telephone lines. At the source, a modem converts digital signals to a form suitable for transmission over analog communication facilities. At the destination, the analog signals are returned to their digital form.

multimode   A type of fiber-optic cabling with a larger core than single-mode cabling, allowing light to enter at multiple angles. Such cabling has lower bandwidth than single-mode fiber but requires a typically cheaper light source, such as an LED rather than a laser.

N

name server   A server connected to a network that resolves network names into network addresses.

NAT   Network Address Translation. A mechanism for reducing the need for globally unique IP addresses. NAT allows an organization with addresses that are not globally unique to connect to the Internet by translating those addresses into public addresses in the globally routable address space.

network   A collection of computers, printers, routers, switches, and other devices that can communicate with each other over some transmission medium.

network address   *See* network number.

network broadcast address   In IPv4, a special address in each classful network that can be used to broadcast a packet to all hosts in that same classful network. Numerically, the address has the same value as the network number in the network part of the address, and all 255s in the host octets—for example, 10.255.255.255 is the network broadcast address for classful network 10.0.0.0.

network number   A number that uses dotted decimal notation like IP addresses, but the number itself represents all hosts in a single Class A, B, or C IP network.

network part   The portion of an IPv4 address that is either 1, 2, or 3 octets/bytes long, based on whether the address is in a Class A, B, or C network.

networking model   A generic term referring to any set of protocols and standards collected into a comprehensive grouping that, when followed by the devices in a network, allows all the devices to communicate. Examples include TCP/IP and OSI.

NVRAM   Nonvolatile RAM. A type of random-access memory (RAM) that retains its contents when a unit is powered off.

O

ordered data transfer   A networking function, included in TCP, in which the protocol defines how the sending host should number the data transmitted, defines how the receiving device should attempt to reorder the data if it arrives out of order, and specifies to discard the data if it cannot be delivered in order.

Orthogonal Frequency Division Multiplexing   A method of encoding data in wireless LANs that allows for generally higher data rates than the earlier FHSS and DSSS encoding methods.

OSI   Open System Interconnection reference model. A network architectural model developed by the ISO. The model consists of seven layers, each of which specifies particular network functions, such as addressing, flow control, error control, encapsulation, and reliable message transfer.

P

packet   A logical grouping of information that includes the network layer header and encapsulated data, but specifically does not include any headers and trailers below the network layer.

packet switching   A generic reference to network services, typically WAN services, in which the service examines the contents of the transmitted data to make some type of forwarding decision. This term is mainly used to contrast with the WAN term *circuit switching*, in which the provider sets up a (Layer 1) circuit between two devices, and the provider makes no attempt to interpret the meaning of the bits.

partial mesh   A network topology in which more than two devices could physically communicate but, by choice, only a subset of the pairs of devices connected to the network is allowed to communicate directly.

PCM   Pulse code modulation. A technique of encoding analog voice into a 64-kbps data stream by sampling with 8-bit resolution at a rate of 8000 times per second.

PDU   Protocol data unit. An OSI term to refer generically to a grouping of information by a particular layer of the OSI model. More specifically, an LxPDU would imply the data and headers as defined by Layer x.

ping   Packet Internet groper. An Internet Control Message Protocol (ICMP) echo message and its reply; ping often is used in IP networks to test the reachability of a network device.

pinout   The documentation and implementation of which wires inside a cable connect to each pin position in any connector.

port   In TCP and UDP, a number that is used to uniquely identify the application process that either sent (source port) or should receive (destination port) data. In LAN switching, another term for switch interface.

Port Address Translation (PAT)   A NAT feature in which one inside global IP address supports over 65,000 concurrent TCP and UDP connections.

port number   A field in a TCP or UDP header that identifies the application that either sent (source port) or should receive (destination port) the data inside the data segment.

positive acknowledgment and retransmission (PAR)   A generic reference to how the error recovery feature works in many protocols, including TCP, in which the receiver must send an acknowledgment that either implies that the data was (positively) received, or send an acknowledgement that implies that some data was lost, so the sender can then resend the lost data.

Power-on Self Test (POST)   The process on any computer, including routers and switches, in which the computer hardware first runs diagnostics on the required hardware before even trying to load a bootstrap program.

PPP   Point-to-Point Protocol. A protocol that provides router-to-router and host-to-network connections over synchronous point-to-point and asynchronous point-to-point circuits.

prefix notation   A shorter way to write a subnet mask in which the number of binary 1s in the mask is simply written in decimal. For instance, /24 denotes the subnet mask with 24 binary 1 bits in the subnet mask. The number of bits of value binary 1 in the mask is considered to be the prefix length.

PRI   Primary Rate Interface. An Integrated Services Digital Network (ISDN) interface to primary rate access. Primary rate access consists of a single 64-kbps D channel plus 23 (T1) or 30 (E1) B channels for voice or data.

private addresses   IP addresses in several Class A, B, and C networks that are set aside for use inside private organizations. These addresses, as defined in RFC 1918, are not routable through the Internet.

problem isolation   The part of the troubleshooting process in which the engineer attempts to rule out possible causes of the problem until the root cause of the problem can be identified.

protocol data unit (PDU)   A generic term referring to the header defined by some layer of a networking model, and the data encapsulated by the header (and possibly trailer) of that layer, but specifically not including any lower-layer headers and trailers.

Protocol Type field   A field in a LAN header that identifies the type of header that follows the LAN header. Includes the DIX Ethernet Type field, the IEEE 802.2 DSAP field, and the SNAP protocol Type field.

PSTN   Public Switched Telephone Network. A general term referring to the variety of telephone networks and services in place worldwide. Sometimes called *POTS*, or Plain Old Telephone Service.

PTT   Post, telephone, and telegraph. A government agency that provides telephone services. PTTs exist in most areas outside of North America and provide both local and long-distance telephone services.

public IP address   An IP address that is part of a registered network number, as assigned by an Internet Assigned Numbers Authority (IANA) member agency, so that only the organization to which the address is registered is allowed to use the address. Routers in the Internet should have routes allowing them to forward packets to all the publicly registered IP addresses.

R

RAM   Random-access memory. A type of volatile memory that can be read and written by a microprocessor.

RFC   Request For Comments. A document used as the primary means for communicating information about the TCP/IP protocols. Some RFCs are designated by the Internet Architecture Board (IAB) as Internet standards, and others are informational. RFCs are available online from numerous sources, including http://www.rfc-editor.org/.

RIP   Routing Information Protocol. An Interior Gateway Protocol (IGP) that uses distance vector logic and router hop count as the metric. RIP Version 1 (RIP-1) has become unpopular, with RIP Version 2 (RIP-2) providing more features, including support for VLSM.

RJ-45   A popular type of cabling connector used for Ethernet cabling. It is similar to the RJ-11 connector used for telephone wiring in homes in the United States. RJ-45 allows the connection of eight wires.

ROM   Read-only memory. A type of nonvolatile memory that can be read but not written by the microprocessor.

ROMMON   A shorter name for ROM Monitor, which is a low-level operating system that can be loaded into Cisco routers for several seldom needed maintenance tasks, including password recovery and loading a new IOS when Flash memory has been corrupted.

root cause   A troubleshooting term that refers to the reason why a problem exists, specifically a reason for which, if changed, the problem would either be solved or changed to a different problem.

routed protocol   A protocol which defines packets that can be routed by a router. Examples of routed protocols include AppleTalk, DECnet, and IP.

Router Security Device Manager   The administrative web-based interface on a router that allows for configuration and monitoring of the router, including the configuration of DHCP and NAT/PAT.

routing protocol   A set of messages and processes with which routers can exchange information about routes to reach subnets in a particular network. Examples of routing protocols include the Enhanced Interior Gateway Routing Protocol (EIGRP), the Open Shortest Path First (OSPF) protocol, and the Routing Information Protocol (RIP).

routing table   A list of routes in a router, with each route listing the destination subnet and mask, the router interface out which to forward packets destined to that subnet, and, as needed, the next-hop router's IP address.

routing update   A generic reference to any routing protocol's messages in which it sends routing information to a neighbor.

running-config file   In Cisco IOS switches and routers, the name of the file that resides in RAM memory, holding the device's currently used configuration.

RxBoot   A limited-function version of IOS stored in ROM in some older models of Cisco routers, for the purpose of performing some seldom needed low-level functions, including loading a new IOS into Flash memory when Flash has been deleted or corrupted.

S

same-layer interaction   The communication between two networking devices for the purposes of the functions defined at a particular layer of a networking model, with that communication happening by using a header defined by that layer of the model. The two devices set values in the header, send the header and encapsulated data, with the receiving device(s) interpreting the header to decide what action to take.

Secure Shell (SSH)   A TCP/IP application layer protocol that supports terminal emulation between a client and server, using dynamic key exchange and encryption to keep the communications private.

segment   In TCP, a term used to describe a TCP header and its encapsulated data (also called an *L4PDU*). Also in TCP, the process of accepting a large chunk of data from the application layer and breaking it into smaller pieces that fit into TCP segments. In Ethernet, a segment is either a single Ethernet cable or a single collision domain (no matter how many cables are used).

segmentation   The process of breaking a large piece of data from an application into pieces appropriate in size to be sent through the network.

serial cable   A type of cable with many different styles of connectors used to connect a router to an external CSU/DSU on a leased-line installation.

Service Set Identifier (SSID)   A text value used in wireless LANs to uniquely identify a single WLAN.

setup mode   An option on Cisco IOS switches and routers that prompts the user for basic configuration information, resulting in new running-config and startup-config files.

shared Ethernet   An Ethernet that uses a hub, or even the original coaxial cabling, which results in the devices having to take turns sending data, sharing the available bandwidth.

single-mode   A type of fiber-optic cabling with a narrow core that allows light to enter only at a single angle. Such cabling has a higher bandwidth than multimode fiber but requires a light source with a narrow spectral width (such as a laser).

sliding windows   For protocols such as TCP that allow the receiving device to dictate the amount of data the sender can send before receiving an acknowledgment—a concept called a window—a reference to the fact that the mechanism to grant future windows is typically just a number that grows upwards slowly after each acknowledgment, sliding upward.

SONET   Synchronous Optical Network. A standard format for transporting a wide range of digital telecommunications services over optical fiber.

Spanning Tree Protocol   A bridge protocol that uses the Spanning Tree algorithm, allowing a switch to dynamically work around loops in a network topology by creating a spanning tree. Switches exchange bridge protocol data unit (BPDU) messages with other bridges to detect loops and then remove the loops by shutting down selected bridge interfaces.

star   A network topology in which endpoints on a network are connected to a common central device by point-to-point links.

startup-config file   In Cisco IOS switches and routers, the name of the file that resides in NVRAM memory, holding the device's configuration that will be loaded into RAM as the running-config file when the device is next reloaded or powered on.

store-and-forward switching   One of three internal processing options on some Cisco LAN switches in which the Ethernet frame must be completely received before the switch can begin forwarding the first bit of the frame.

STP   Shielded twisted pair. Shielded twisted-pair cabling has a layer of shielded insulation to reduce electromagnetic interference (EMI).

straight-through cable   In Ethernet, a cable that connects the wire on pin 1 on one end of the cable to pin 1 on the other end of the cable, pin 2 on one end to pin 2 on the other end, and so on.

subnet   Subdivisions of a Class A, B, or C network, as configured by a network administrator. Subnets allow a single Class A, B, or C network to be used instead of multiple networks, and still allow for a large number of groups of IP addresses, as is required for efficient IP routing.

subnet address   *See* subnet number.

subnet broadcast address   A special address in each subnet, specifically the largest numeric address in the subnet, designed so that packets sent to this address should be delivered to all hosts in that subnet.

subnet mask   A 32-bit number that numerically describes the format of an IP address by representing the combined network and subnet bits in the address with mask bit values of 1, and representing the host bits in the address with mask bit values of 0.

subnet number   In IP v4, a dotted decimal number that represents all addresses in a single subnet. Numerically, the smallest value in the range of numbers in a subnet, reserved so that it cannot be used as a unicast IP address by a host.

subnet part   In a subnetted IPv4 address, interpreted with classful addressing rules, one of three parts of the structure of an IP address, with the subnet part uniquely identifying different subnets of a classful IP network.

subnetting   The process of subdividing a Class A, B, or C network into smaller groups called subnets.

switch   A network device that filters, forwards, and floods Ethernet frames based on the destination address of each frame.

switched Ethernet   An Ethernet that uses a switch, and particularly not a hub, so that the devices connected to one switch port do not have to contend to use the bandwidth available on another port. This term contrasts with *shared Ethernet*, in which the devices must share bandwidth, whereas switched Ethernet provides much more capacity, as the devices do not have to share the available bandwidth.

symmetric   A feature of many Internet access technologies in which the downstream transmission rate is the same as the upstream transmission rate.

synchronous   The imposition of time ordering on a bit stream. Practically, a device will try to use the same speed as another device on the other end of a serial link. However, by examining transitions between voltage states on the link, the device can notice slight variations in the speed on each end and can adjust its speed accordingly.

T

T1   A line from the telco that allows transmission of data at 1.544 Mbps, with the ability to treat the line as 24 different 64-kbps DS0 channels (plus 8 kbps of overhead).

TCP   Transmission Control Protocol. A connection-oriented transport layer TCP/IP protocol that provides reliable data transmission.

TCP/IP   Transmission Control Protocol/Internet Protocol. A common name for the suite of protocols developed by the U.S. Department of Defense in the 1970s to support the construction of worldwide internetworks. TCP and IP are the two best-known protocols in the suite.

telco   A common abbreviation for telephone company.

Telnet   The standard terminal-emulation application layer protocol in the TCP/IP protocol stack. Telnet is used for remote terminal connection, enabling users to log in to remote systems and use resources as if they were connected to a local system. Telnet is defined in RFC 854.

trace   Short for traceroute. A program available on many systems that traces the path that a packet takes to a destination. It is used mostly to debug routing problems between hosts.

transparent bridge   The name of a networking device that was a precursor to modern LAN switches. Bridges forward frames between LAN segments based on the destination MAC address. Transparent bridging is so named because the presence of bridges is transparent to network end nodes.

trunk interface   On a LAN switch, an interface that is currently using either 802.1Q or ISL trunking.

trunking   Also called *VLAN trunking*. A method (using either the Cisco ISL protocol or the IEEE 802.1q protocol) to support multiple VLANs that have members on more than one switch.

twisted pair   Transmission medium consisting of two insulated wires, with the wires twisted around each other in a spiral. An electrical circuit flows over the wire pair, with the current in opposite directions on each wire, which significantly reduces the interference between the two wires.

U

UDP   User Datagram Protocol. Connectionless transport layer protocol in the TCP/IP protocol stack. UDP is a simple protocol that exchanges datagrams without acknowledgments or guaranteed delivery.

unknown unicast frame   An Ethernet frame whose destination MAC address is not listed in a switch's MAC address table, so the switch must flood the frame.

up and up   Jargon referring to the two interface states on a Cisco IOS router or switch (line status and protocol status), with the first "up" referring to the line status, and the second "up" referring to the protocol status. An interface in this state should be able to pass data-link frames.

update timer   A timer used by a router to indicate when to send the next routing update.

URL   Universal Resource Locator. A standard for how to refer to any piece of information retrievable via a TCP/IP network, most notably used to identify web pages. For example, http://www.cisco.com/univercd is a URL that identifies the protocol (HTTP), hostname (www.cisco.com), and web page (/univercd).

user mode   A mode of the user interface to a router or switch in which the user can type only nondisruptive EXEC commands, generally just to look at the current status, but not to change any operational settings.

UTP   Unshielded twisted pair. A type of cabling, standardized by the Electronics Industry Alliance (EIA) and Telecommunications Industry Association (TIA), that holds twisted pairs of copper wires (typically four pair), and does not contain any shielding from outside interference.

V

variable-length subnet masks (VLSM)   The capability to specify a different subnet mask for the same Class A, B, or C network number on different subnets. VLSM can help optimize available address space.

virtual circuit   In packet-switched services like Frame Relay, VC refers to the ability of two DTE devices (typically routers) to send and receive data directly to each other, which supplies the same function as a physical leased line (leased circuit), but doing so without a physical circuit. This term is meant as a contrast with a leased line or leased circuit.

virtual LAN (VLAN)   A group of devices, connected to one or more switches, with the devices grouped into a single broadcast domain through switch configuration. VLANs allow switch administrators to separate the devices connected to the switches into separate VLANs without requiring separate physical switches, gaining design advantages of separating the traffic without the expense of buying additional hardware.

virtual private network (VPN)   The process of securing communication between two devices whose packets pass over some public and unsecured network, typically the Internet. VPNs encrypt packets so that the communication is private and authenticate the identity of the endpoints.

VoIP   Voice over IP. The transport of voice traffic inside IP packets over an IP network.

W

web server   Software, running on some computer, that stores web pages and sends those web pages to web clients (web browsers) that request the web pages.

well-known port   A TCP or UDP port number reserved for use by a particular application. The use of well-known ports allows a client to send a TCP or UDP segment to a server, to the correct destination port for that application.

Wi-Fi Alliance   An organization formed by many companies in the wireless industry (an industry association) for the purpose of getting multivendor certified-compatible wireless products to market in a more timely fashion than would be possible by simply relying on standardization processes.

Wi-Fi Protected Access (WPA)   A trademarked name of the Wi-Fi Alliance that represents a set of security specifications that predated the standardization of the IEEE 802.11i security standard.

window   The term window represents the number of bytes that can be sent without receiving an acknowledgment.

wired equivalent privacy (WEP)   An early WLAN security specification that used relatively weak security mechanisms, using only preshared keys and either no encryption or weak encryption.

WLAN client   A wireless device that wants to gain access to a wireless access point for the purpose of communicating with other wireless devices or other devices connected to the wired internetwork.

WPA2   The Wi-Fi Alliance trademarked name for the same set of security specifications defined in the IEEE 802.11i security standard.

Z

zero subnet   For every classful IPv4 network that is subnetted, the one subnet whose subnet number has all binary 0s in the subnet part of the number. In decimal, the zero subnet can be easily identified because it is the same number as the classful network number.

Index

CCNA ICND2
Official Exam Certification Guide
Second Edition

Wendell Odom, CCIE No. 1624

Cisco Press

800 East 96th Street
Indianapolis, IN 46240 USA

CCNA ICND2 Official Exam Certification Guide, Second Edition

Wendell Odom

Copyright © 2008 Cisco Systems, Inc.

Published by:
Cisco Press
800 East 96th Street
Indianapolis, IN 46240 USA

Printed in the United States of America

Seventh Printing September 2009

Library of Congress Cataloging-in-Publication Data:

Odom, Wendell.

　CCNA ICND2 official exam certification guide / Wendell Odom. -- 2nd ed.

　　p. cm.

　ISBN 978-1-58720-181-3 (hbk : CD-ROM)

　1. Electronic data processing personnel--Certification. 2. Computer network protocols--Study guides. 3. Internetworking (Telecommunication)--Study guides. I. Title.

　QA76.3.O3618 2004

　004.6--dc22

2007029471

ISBN-13: 978-1-58720-181-3

ISBN-10: 1-58720-181-x

Warning and Disclaimer

Trademark Acknowledgments

Corporate and Government Sales

The publisher offers excellent discounts on this book when ordered in quantity for bulk purchases or special sales, which may include electronic versions and/or custom covers and content particular to your business, training goals, marketing focus, and branding interests. For more information, please contact:

U.S. Corporate and Government Sales
1-800-382-3419   corpsales@pearsontechgroup.com

For sales outside the United States please contact:
International Sales
international@pearsoned.com

Feedback Information

At Cisco Press, our goal is to create in-depth technical books of the highest quality and value. Each book is crafted with care and precision, undergoing rigorous development that involves the unique expertise of members from the professional technical community.

Readers' feedback is a natural continuation of this process. If you have any comments regarding how we could improve the quality of this book, or otherwise alter it to better suit your needs, you can contact us through email at feedback@ciscopress.com. Please make sure to include the book title and ISBN in your message.

We greatly appreciate your assistance.

Publisher: Paul Boger

Associate Publisher: David Dusthimer

Executive Editor: Brett Bartow

Managing Editor: Patrick Kanouse

Development Editor: Andrew Cupp

Senior Project Editor: Meg Shaw and Tonya Simpson

Editorial Assistant: Vanessa Evans

Designer: Louisa Adair

Composition: Mark Shirar

Indexer: Ken Johnson

Cisco Representative: Anthony Wolfenden

Cisco Press Program Manager: Jeff Brady

Copy Editors: Written Elegance and Gayle Johnson

Technical Editors: Teri Cook and Steve Kalman

Proofreader: Susan Eldridge

Americas Headquarters
Cisco Systems, Inc.
170 West Tasman Drive
San Jose, CA 95134-1706
USA
www.cisco.com
Tel: 408 526-4000
800 553-NETS (6387)
Fax: 408 527-0883

Asia Pacific Headquarters
Cisco Systems, Inc.
168 Robinson Road
#28-01 Capital Tower
Singapore 068912
www.cisco.com
Tel: +65 6317 7777
Fax: +65 6317 7799

Europe Headquarters
Cisco Systems International BV
Haarlerbergpark
Haarlerbergweg 13-19
1101 CH Amsterdam
The Netherlands
www-europe.cisco.com
Tel: +31 0 800 020 0791
Fax: +31 0 20 357 1100

Cisco has more than 200 offices worldwide. Addresses, phone numbers, and fax numbers are listed on the Cisco Website at **www.cisco.com/go/offices.**

©2007 Cisco Systems, Inc. All rights reserved. CCVP, the Cisco logo, and the Cisco Square Bridge logo are trademarks of Cisco Systems, Inc.; Changing the Way We Work, Live, Play, and Learn is a service mark of Cisco Systems, Inc.; and Access Registrar, Aironet, BPX, Catalyst, CCDA, CCDP, CCIE, CCIP, CCNA, CCNP, CCSP, Cisco, the Cisco Certified Internetwork Expert logo, Cisco IOS, Cisco Press, Cisco Systems, Cisco Systems Capital, the Cisco Systems logo, Cisco Unity, Enterprise/Solver, EtherChannel, EtherFast, EtherSwitch, Fast Step, Follow Me Browsing, FormShare, GigaDrive, GigaStack, HomeLink, Internet Quotient, IOS, IP/TV, iQ Expertise, the iQ logo, iQ Net Readiness Scorecard, iQuick Study, LightStream, Linksys, MeetingPlace, MGX, Networking Academy, Network Registrar, Packet, PIX, ProConnect, RateMUX, ScriptShare, SlideCast, SMARTnet, StackWise, The Fastest Way to Increase Your Internet Quotient, and TransPath are registered trademarks of Cisco Systems, Inc. and/or its affiliates in the United States and certain other countries.

All other trademarks mentioned in this document or Website are the property of their respective owners. The use of the word partner does not imply a partnership relationship between Cisco and any other company. (0609R)

About the Author

Wendell Odom, CCIE No. 1624, has been in the networking industry since 1981. He currently teaches QoS, MPLS, and CCNA courses for Skyline Advanced Technology Services (http://www.skyline-ats.com). Wendell also has worked as a network engineer, consultant, and systems engineer, and as an instructor and course developer. He is the author of all prior editions of *CCNA Exam Certification Guide*, as well as the *Cisco QoS Exam Certification Guide*, Second Edition, *Computer Networking First-Step*, *CCIE Routing and Switching Official Exam Certification Guide*, Second Edition, and *CCNA Video Mentor*, all from Cisco Press.

About the Technical Reviewers

Teri Cook (CCSI, CCDP, CCNP, CCDA, CCNA, MCT, and MCSE 2000/2003: Security) has more than 10 years of experience in the IT industry. She has worked with different types of organizations within the private business and DoD sectors, providing senior-level network and security technical skills in the design and implementation of complex computing environments. Since obtaining her certifications, Teri has been committed to bringing quality IT training to IT professionals as an instructor. She is an outstanding instructor that utilizes real-world experience to present complex networking technologies. As an IT instructor, Teri has been teaching Cisco classes for more than five years.

Stephen Kalman is a data security trainer and the author or tech editor of more than 20 books, courses, and CBT titles. His most recent book is *Web Security Field Guide*, published by Cisco Press. In addition to those responsibilities he runs a consulting company, Esquire Micro Consultants, which specializes in network security assessments and forensics.

Mr. Kalman holds SSCP, CISSP, ISSMP, CEH, CHFI, CCNA, CCSA (Checkpoint), A+, Network+, and Security+ certifications and is a member of the New York State Bar.

Dedications

For my wonderful, lovely, giving wife. Thanks so much for all your support, encouragement, love, and respect.

Acknowledgments

The team that helped produce this book has simply been awesome. Everyone who has touched the book has made it better, and the team has been particularly great at helping catch the errors that always creep into the manuscript.

Both Teri and Steve did great jobs as technical editors. Teri's ability to see each phrase in the context of an entire chapter, or whole book, was awesome, helping to catch things that no one would otherwise catch. Steve did his usual great job—something like 5–6 books of mine that he's done now—and as always, I get to learn a lot just by reading Steve's input. The depth of the reviews for this book was better than any of my other books because of Teri and Steve; thanks very much!

Drew Cupp got the "opportunity" to develop one of my books for the first time in a long time. Drew's insights and edits worked wonders, and a fresh set of eyes on the materials copied from the previous edition strengthened those parts a lot. All while juggling things in the middle of a whirlwind schedule—thanks, Drew, for doing a great job!

The wonderful and mostly hidden production folks did their usual great job. When I saw how they reworded something, and thought "Wow, why didn't I write that?" it made me appreciate the kind of team we have at Cisco Press. The final copy edit, figure review, and pages review process required a fair amount of juggling and effort as well—especially for the extra quality initiatives we've implemented. Thanks to you all!

Brett Bartow again was the executive editor on the book, as has been the case for almost all the books I've helped write. Brett did his usual great and patient job, being my advocate in so many ways. Brett, thanks for doing so many things on so many levels to help us be successful together.

Additionally, there are several folks who don't have any direct stake in the book who also helped it along. Thanks to Frank Knox for the discussions on the exams, why they're so difficult, and how to handle troubleshooting. Thanks to Rus Healy for the help with wireless. Thanks to the Mikes at Skyline for making my schedule work to get this book (and the ICND1 book) out the door. And thanks to the course and exam teams at Cisco for the great early communications and interactions about the changes to the courses and exams.

And as always, a special thanks to my Lord and Savior Jesus Christ—thanks for helping me rejoice in you even while doing the final reviews of 1400 pages of manuscript in just a few weeks!

This Book Is Safari Enabled

The Safari® Enabled icon on the cover of your favorite technology book means the book is available through Safari Bookshelf. When you buy this book, you get free access to the online edition for 45 days.

Safari Bookshelf is an electronic reference library that lets you easily search thousands of technical books, find code samples, download chapters, and access technical information whenever and wherever you need it.

To gain 45-day Safari Enabled access to this book:

- Go to http://www.ciscopress.com/safarienabled

- Complete the brief registration form

- Enter the coupon code 37R6-7E1Q-6HAX-5YQZ-G6KW

If you have difficulty registering on Safari Bookshelf or accessing the online edition, please e-mail customer-service@safaribooksonline.com.

Contents at a Glance

Contents

Icons Used in This Book

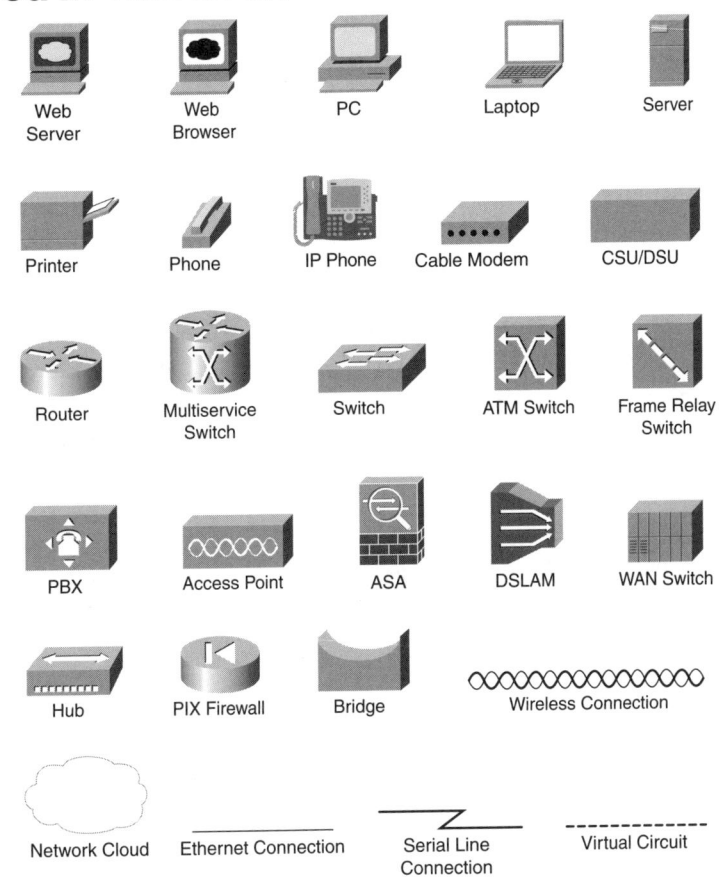

Command Syntax Conventions

The conventions used to present command syntax in this book are the same conventions used in the IOS Command Reference. The Command Reference describes these conventions as follows:

- **Boldface** indicates commands and keywords that are entered literally as shown. In actual configuration examples and output (not general command syntax), boldface indicates commands that are manually input by the user (such as a **show** command).

- *Italics* indicate arguments for which you supply actual values.

- Vertical bars (|) separate alternative, mutually exclusive elements.

- Square brackets [ ] indicate optional elements.

- Braces { } indicate a required choice.

- Braces within brackets [{ }] indicate a required choice within an optional element.

Foreword

CCNA ICND2 Official Exam Certification Guide, Second Edition, is an excellent self-study resource for the CCNA ICND2 exam. Passing the ICND2 exam validates the knowledge and skills required to successfully install, operate, and troubleshoot a small- to medium-size enterprise branch network. It is one of two exams required for CCNA certification.

Gaining certification in Cisco technology is key to the continuing educational development of today's networking professional. Through certification programs, Cisco validates the skills and expertise required to effectively manage the modern enterprise network.

Cisco Press exam certification guides and preparation materials offer exceptional—and flexible—access to the knowledge and information required to stay current in your field of expertise, or to gain new skills. Whether used as a supplement to more traditional training or as a primary source of learning, these materials offer users the information and knowledge validation required to gain new understanding and proficiencies.

Developed in conjunction with the Cisco certifications and training team, Cisco Press books are the only self-study books authorized by Cisco, and they offer students a series of exam practice tools and resource materials to help ensure that learners fully grasp the concepts and information presented.

Additional authorized Cisco instructor-led courses, e-learning, labs, and simulations are available exclusively from Cisco Learning Solutions Partners worldwide. To learn more, visit http://www.cisco.com/go/training.

I hope that you find these materials to be an enriching and useful part of your exam preparation.

Erik Ullanderson
Manager, Global Certifications
Learning@Cisco
August, 2007

Introduction

Congratulations! If you're reading far enough to look at the introduction to this book, you've probably already decided to go for your Cisco certification. If you want to succeed as a technical person in the networking industry, you need to know Cisco. Cisco has a ridiculously high market share in the router and switch marketplace, with more than 80 percent market share in some markets. In many geographies and markets around the world, networking equals Cisco. If you want to be taken seriously as a network engineer, Cisco certification makes perfect sense.

Historically speaking, the first entry-level Cisco certification has been the Cisco Certified Network Associate (CCNA) certification, first offered in 1998. The first three versions of the CCNA certification (1998, 2000, and 2002) required that you pass a single exam to become certified. However, over time, the exam kept growing, both in the amount of material covered and in the difficulty level of the questions. So, for the fourth major revision of the exams, announced in 2003, Cisco continued with a single certification (CCNA), but offered two options for the exams to get certified: a single-exam option and a two-exam option. The two-exam option allowed people to study roughly half of the material, and take and pass one exam, before moving on to the next.

Cisco announced changes to the CCNA certification and exams in June 2007. This announcement includes many changes, most notably:

- The exams collectively cover a broader range of topics.

- The exams increase the focus on proving the test taker's skills (as compared with just testing knowledge).

- Cisco created a new entry-level certification: the Cisco Certified Entry Network Technician (CCENT) certification.

For the current certifications, announced in June 2007, Cisco created the ICND1 (640-822) and ICND2 (640-816) exams, along with the CCNA (640-802) exam. To become CCNA certified, you can pass both the ICND1 and ICND2 exams, or just pass the CCNA exam. The CCNA exam simply covers all the topics on the ICND1 and ICND2 exams, giving you two options for gaining your CCNA certification. The two-exam path gives those people with less experience a chance to study for a smaller set of topics at a time, whereas the one-exam option provides a more cost-effective certification path for those who want to prepare for all the topics at once.

Although the two-exam option will be useful for some certification candidates, Cisco designed the ICND1 exam with a much more important goal in mind. The CCNA certification has grown to the point that it tested knowledge and skills beyond what an xxviii

entry-level network technician would need to have. Cisco needed a certification that was more reflective of the skills required for entry-level networking jobs. So, Cisco designed its Interconnecting Cisco Networking Devices 1 (ICND1) course, and the corresponding ICND1 640-822 exam, to include the knowledge and skills most needed by an entry-level technician in a small enterprise network. And to show that you have the skills required for those entry-level jobs, Cisco created a new certification, CCENT, which is attained by passing the ICND1 exam.

Figure I-1 shows the basic organization of the certifications and the exams used for getting your CCENT and CCNA certifications. (Note that no separate certification exists for passing the ICND2 exam.)

Figure I-1 *Cisco Entry-Level Certifications and Exams*

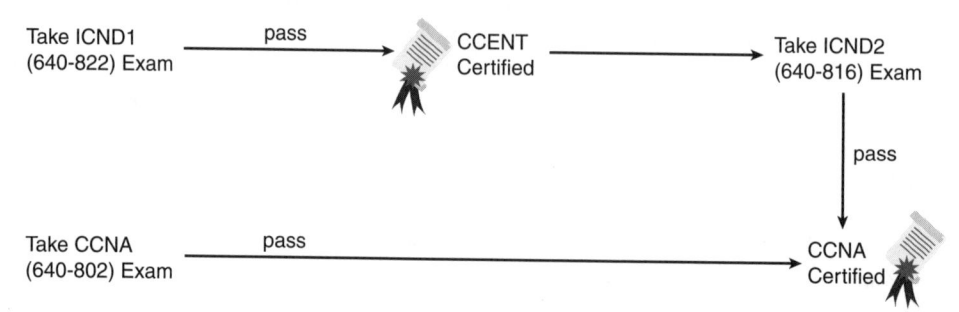

As you can see from the figure, while the CCENT certification is available by taking the ICND1 exam, you do not have to first be CCENT certified before getting your CCNA certification—you can choose to just take the CCNA exam and bypass the CCENT certification.

The ICND1 and ICND2 exams cover different sets of topics, with a minor amount of overlap. For example, ICND1 covers IP addressing and subnetting, while ICND2 covers a more complicated use of subnetting called variable-length subnet masking (VLSM), so ICND2 must then cover subnetting to some degree. The CCNA exam covers all the topics covered on both the ICND1 and ICND2 exams.

While the popularity of the CCENT certification cannot be seen until a few years have passed, certainly the Cisco CCNA certification enjoys a position as the most popular entry-level networking certification program. A CCNA certification proves that you have a firm foundation in the most important components of the Cisco product line—namely, routers and switches. It also proves that you have a broad knowledge of protocols and networking technologies.

Format of the CCNA Exams

The ICND1, ICND2, and CCNA exams all follow the same general format. When you get to the testing center and check in, the proctor will give you some general instructions and then take you into a quiet room with a PC. When you're at the PC, you have a few things to do before the timer starts on your exam. For example, you can take a sample quiz, just to get accustomed to the PC and to the testing engine. Anyone who has user-level skills in getting around a PC should have no problems with the testing environment. Additionally, Chapter 18, "Final Preparation," points to a Cisco website at which you can see a demo of the Cisco test engine.

When you start the exam, you are asked a series of questions. You answer a question and then move on to the next question. *The exam engine does not let you go back and change your answer.* Yes, that's true—when you move on to the next question, that's it for the earlier question.

The exam questions can be in one of the following formats:

- Multiple-choice (MC)

- Testlet

- Drag-and-drop (DND)

- Simulated lab (Sim)

- Simlet

The first three types of questions are relatively common in many testing environments. The multiple-choice format simply requires that you point and click a circle beside the correct answer(s). Cisco traditionally tells you how many answers you need to choose, and the testing software prevents you from choosing too many answers. Testlets are questions with one general scenario, with multiple MC questions about the overall scenario. Drag-and-drop questions require you to click and hold the mouse button, move a button or icon to another area, and release the mouse button to place the object somewhere else—typically into a list. So, for some questions, to get the question correct, you might need to put a list of five things into the proper order.

The last two types both use a network simulator to ask questions. Interestingly, the two types allow Cisco to assess two very different skills. First, Sim questions generally describe a problem, and your task is to configure one or more routers and switches to fix the problem. The exam then grades the question based on the configuration you changed or added. Interestingly, Sim questions are the only questions that Cisco (to date) has openly confirmed that partial credit is given.

The Simlet questions might well be the most difficult style of question on the exams. Simlet questions also use a network simulator, but instead of answering the question by changing the configuration, the question includes one or more MC questions. The questions require that you use the simulator to examine the current behavior of a network, interpreting the output of any **show** commands that you can remember to answer the question. While Sim questions require you to troubleshoot problems related to a configuration, Simlets require you to both analyze working networks and networks with problems, correlating **show** command output with your knowledge of networking theory and configuration commands.

What's on the CCNA Exam(s)?

Ever since I was in grade school, whenever the teacher announced that we were having a test soon, someone would always ask, "What's on the test?" Even in college, people would try to get more information about what would be on the exams. At heart, the goal is to know what to study hard, what to study a little, and what not to study.

Cisco does want the public to know both the variety of topics, and an idea about the kinds of knowledge and skills required for each topic, for every Cisco certification exam. To that end, Cisco publishes a set of exam objectives for each exam. The objectives list the specific topics, like IP addressing, RIP, and VLANs. The objectives also imply the kinds of skills required for that topic. For example, one objective might start with "Describe..." and another might begin with "Describe, configure, and troubleshoot...." The second objective clearly states that you need a thorough and deep understanding of that topic. By listing the topics and skill level, Cisco helps us all prepare for its exams.

While the exam objectives are helpful, keep in mind that Cisco adds a disclaimer that the posted exam topics for all its certification exams are *guidelines*. Cisco makes the effort to keep the exam questions within the confines of the stated exam objectives, and I know from talking to those involved that every question is analyzed for whether it fits within the stated exam topics.

ICND1 Exam Topics

Table I-1 lists the exam topics for the ICND1 exam, with the ICND2 exam topics following in Table I-2. Although the posted exam topics are not numbered at Cisco.com, Cisco Press does number the exam topics for easier reference. The table also notes the book parts in which each exam topic is covered. Because the exam topics might change over time, double-check the exam topics as listed on Cisco.com (specifically, http://www.cisco.com/go/ccna). If Cisco does happen to add exam topics at a later date, note that Appendix C of this book describes how to go to http://www.ciscopress.com and download additional information about those newly added topics.

Table I-1 *ICND1 Exam Topics*

Reference Number	ICND1 Book Part(s) Where Topic Is Covered	Exam Topic
		Describe the operation of data networks
1	I	Describe the purpose and functions of various network devices
2	I	Select the components required to meet a given network specification
3	I, II, III	Use the OSI and TCP/IP models and their associated protocols to explain how data flows in a network
4	I	Describe common networking applications including web applications
5	I	Describe the purpose and basic operation of the protocols in the OSI and TCP models
6	I	Describe the impact of applications (Voice Over IP and Video Over IP) on a network
7	I–IV	Interpret network diagrams
8	I–IV	Determine the path between two hosts across a network
9	I, III, IV	Describe the components required for network and Internet communications
10	I–IV	Identify and correct common network problems at layers 1, 2, 3 and 7 using a layered model approach
11	II, III	Differentiate between LAN/WAN operation and features
		Implement a small switched network
12	II	Select the appropriate media, cables, ports, and connectors to connect switches to other network devices and hosts
13	II	Explain the technology and media access control method for Ethernet technologies
14	II	Explain network segmentation and basic traffic management concepts
15	II	Explain the operation of Cisco switches and basic switching concepts
16	II	Perform, save and verify initial switch configuration tasks including remote access management
17	II	Verify network status and switch operation using basic utilities (including: ping, traceroute, telnet, SSH, arp, ipconfig), SHOW & DEBUG commands

Table I-1 *ICND1 Exam Topics (Continued)*

Reference Number	ICND1 Book Part(s) Where Topic Is Covered	Exam Topic
18	II	Implement and verify basic security for a switch (port security, deactivate ports)
19	II	Identify, prescribe, and resolve common switched network media issues, configuration issues, autonegotiation, and switch hardware failures
		Implement an IP addressing scheme and IP services to meet network requirements for a small branch office
20	I, III	Describe the need and role of addressing in a network
21	I, III	Create and apply an addressing scheme to a network
22	III	Assign and verify valid IP addresses to hosts, servers, and networking devices in a LAN environment
23	IV	Explain the basic uses and operation of NAT in a small network connecting to one ISP
24	I, III	Describe and verify DNS operation
25	III, IV	Describe the operation and benefits of using private and public IP addressing
26	III, IV	Enable NAT for a small network with a single ISP and connection using SDM and verify operation using CLI and ping
27	III	Configure, verify and troubleshoot DHCP and DNS operation on a router. (including: CLI/SDM)
28	III	Implement static and dynamic addressing services for hosts in a LAN environment
29	III	Identify and correct IP addressing issues
		Implement a small routed network
30	I, III	Describe basic routing concepts (including: packet forwarding, router lookup process)
31	III	Describe the operation of Cisco routers (including: router bootup process, POST, router components)
32	I, III	Select the appropriate media, cables, ports, and connectors to connect routers to other network devices and hosts
33	III	Configure, verify, and troubleshoot RIPv2
34	III	Access and utilize the router CLI to set basic parameters
35	III	Connect, configure, and verify operation status of a device interface

Table I-1 *ICND1 Exam Topics (Continued)*

Reference Number	ICND1 Book Part(s) Where Topic Is Covered	Exam Topic
36	III	Verify device configuration and network connectivity using ping, traceroute, telnet, SSH or other utilities
37	III	Perform and verify routing configuration tasks for a static or default route given specific routing requirements
38	III	Manage IOS configuration files (including: save, edit, upgrade, restore)
39	III	Manage Cisco IOS
40	III	Implement password and physical security
41	III	Verify network status and router operation using basic utilities (including: ping, traceroute, telnet, SSH, arp, ipconfig), SHOW & DEBUG commands
		Explain and select the appropriate administrative tasks required for a WLAN
42	II	Describe standards associated with wireless media (including: IEEE, WI-FI Alliance, ITU/FCC)
43	II	Identify and describe the purpose of the components in a small wireless network. (including: SSID, BSS, ESS)
44	II	Identify the basic parameters to configure on a wireless network to ensure that devices connect to the correct access point
45	II	Compare and contrast wireless security features and capabilities of WPA security (including: open, WEP, WPA-1/2)
46	II	Identify common issues with implementing wireless networks
		Identify security threats to a network and describe general methods to mitigate those threats
47	I	Explain today's increasing network security threats and the need to implement a comprehensive security policy to mitigate the threats
48	I	Explain general methods to mitigate common security threats to network devices, hosts, and applications
49	I	Describe the functions of common security appliances and applications
50	I, II, III	Describe security recommended practices including initial steps to secure network devices
		Implement and verify WAN links
51	IV	Describe different methods for connecting to a WAN
52	IV	Configure and verify a basic WAN serial connection

ICND2 Exam Topics

Table I-2 lists the exam topics for the ICND2 (640-816) exam, along with the book parts in *CCNA ICND2 Official Exam Certification Guide* in which each topic is covered.

Table I-2 *ICND2 Exam Topics*

Reference Number	ICND2 Book Part(s) Where Topic Is Covered	Exam Topic
		Configure, verify and troubleshoot a switch with VLANs and interswitch communications
101	I	Describe enhanced switching technologies (including: VTP, RSTP, VLAN, PVSTP, 802.1q)
102	I	Describe how VLANs create logically separate networks and the need for routing between them
103	I	Configure, verify, and troubleshoot VLANs
104	I	Configure, verify, and troubleshoot trunking on Cisco switches
105	II	Configure, verify, and troubleshoot interVLAN routing
106	I	Configure, verify, and troubleshoot VTP
107	I	Configure, verify, and troubleshoot RSTP operation
108	I	Interpret the output of various show and debug commands to verify the operational status of a Cisco switched network
109	I	Implement basic switch security (including: port security, unassigned ports, trunk access, etc.)
		Implement an IP addressing scheme and IP Services to meet network requirements in a medium-size Enterprise branch office network
110	II	Calculate and apply a VLSM IP addressing design to a network
111	II	Determine the appropriate classless addressing scheme using VLSM and summarization to satisfy addressing requirements in a LAN/WAN environment
112	V	Describe the technological requirements for running IPv6 (including: protocols, dual stack, tunneling, etc)
113	V	Describe IPv6 addresses
114	II, III	Identify and correct common problems associated with IP addressing and host configurations
		Configure and troubleshoot basic operation and routing on Cisco devices
115	III	Compare and contrast methods of routing and routing protocols
116	III	Configure, verify and troubleshoot OSPF

Table I-2 *ICND2 Exam Topics (Continued)*

Reference Number	ICND2 Book Part(s) Where Topic Is Covered	Exam Topic
117	III	Configure, verify and troubleshoot EIGRP
118	II, III	Verify configuration and connectivity using ping, traceroute, and telnet or SSH
119	II, III	Troubleshoot routing implementation issues
120	II, III, IV	Verify router hardware and software operation using SHOW & DEBUG commands
121	II	Implement basic router security
		Implement, verify, and troubleshoot NAT and ACLs in a medium-size Enterprise branch office network.
122	II	Describe the purpose and types of access control lists
123	II	Configure and apply access control lists based on network filtering requirements
124	II	Configure and apply an access control list to limit telnet and SSH access to the router
125	II	Verify and monitor ACLs in a network environment
126	II	Troubleshoot ACL implementation issues
127	V	Explain the basic operation of NAT
128	V	Configure Network Address Translation for given network requirements using CLI
129	V	Troubleshoot NAT implementation issues
		Implement and verify WAN links
130	IV	Configure and verify Frame Relay on Cisco routers
131	IV	Troubleshoot WAN implementation issues
132	IV	Describe VPN technology (including: importance, benefits, role, impact, components)
133	IV	Configure and verify PPP connection between Cisco routers

CCNA Exam Topics

In the previous version of the exams, the CCNA exam covered a lot of what was in the ICND (640-811) exam, plus some coverage of topics in the INTRO (640-821) exam. The new CCNA exam (640-802) covers all the topics on both the ICND1 (640-822) and ICND2 (640-816) exams. One of the reasons for a more balanced coverage in the exams is that some of the topics that used to be in the second exam have been moved to the first exam.

The new CCNA (640-802) exam covers all topics in both the ICND1 and ICND2 exams. The official CCNA 640-802 exam topics, posted at http://www.cisco.com, include all the topics listed in Table I-2 for the ICND2 exam, plus most of the exam topics for the ICND1 exam listed in Table I-1. The only exam topics from these two tables that are not listed as CCNA exam topics are the topics highlighted in gray in Table I-1. However, note that the gray topics are still covered on the CCNA 640-802 exam. Those topics are just not listed in the CCNA exam topics because one of the ICND2 exam topics refers to the same concepts.

ICND1 and ICND2 Course Outlines

Another way to get some direction about the topics on the exams is to look at the course outlines for the related courses. Cisco offers two authorized CCNA-related courses: Interconnecting Cisco Network Devices 1 (ICND1) and Interconnecting Cisco Network Devices 2 (ICND2). Cisco authorizes Certified Learning Solutions Providers (CLSP) and Certified Learning Partners (CLP) to deliver these classes. These authorized companies can also create unique custom course books using this material, in some cases to teach classes geared toward passing the CCNA exam.

About the *CCENT/CCNA ICND1 Official Exam Certification Guide* and *CCNA ICND2 Official Exam Certification Guide*

As mentioned earlier, Cisco has separated the content covered by the CCNA exam into two parts: topics typically used by engineers who work in a small enterprise network (ICND1), with the additional topics commonly used by engineers in medium-sized enterprises being covered by the ICND2 exam. Likewise, the Cisco Press CCNA Exam Certification Guide series includes two books for CCNA—*CCENT/CCNA ICND1 Official Exam Certification Guide* and *CCNA ICND2 Official Exam Certification Guide*. These two books cover the breadth of topics on each exam, typically to a little more depth than is required for the exams, just to ensure that the books prepare you for the more difficult exam questions.

The following sections list the variety of features in both this book and *CCENT/CCNA ICND1 Official Exam Certification Guide*. Both books have the same basic features, so if you are reading both this book and the ICND1 book, you don't need to read the introduction to both books. Also, for those of you who are using both books to prepare for the CCNA 640-802 exam (rather than taking the two-exam option), the end of this introduction lists a suggested reading plan.

Objectives and Methods

The most important and somewhat obvious objective of this book is to help you pass the ICND2 exam or the CCNA exam. In fact, if the primary objective of this book were different, the book's title would be misleading! However, the methods used in this book to help you pass the exams are also designed to make you much more knowledgeable about how to do your job.

This book uses several key methodologies to help you discover the exam topics on which you need more review, to help you fully understand and remember those details, and to help you prove to yourself that you have retained your knowledge of those topics. So, this book does not try to help you pass the exams only by memorization, but by truly learning and understanding the topics. The CCNA certification is the foundation for many of the Cisco professional certifications, and it would be a disservice to you if this book did not help you truly learn the material. Therefore, this book helps you pass the CCNA exam by using the following methods:

- Helping you discover which exam topics you have not mastered

- Providing explanations and information to fill in your knowledge gaps

- Supplying exercises that enhance your ability to recall and deduce the answers to test questions

- Providing practice exercises on the topics and the testing process through test questions on the CD

Book Features

To help you customize your study time using these books, the core chapters have several features that help you make the best use of your time:

- **"Do I Know This Already?" Quizzes:** Each chapter begins with a quiz that helps you determine the amount of time you need to spend studying that chapter.

- **Foundation Topics:** These are the core sections of each chapter. They explain the protocols, concepts, and configuration for the topics in that chapter.

- **Exam Preparation Tasks:** At the end of the Foundation Topics section of each chapter, the Exam Preparation Tasks section lists a series of study activities that should be done at the end of the chapter. Each chapter includes the activities that make the most sense for studying the topics in that chapter. The activities include the following:

  — **Key Topics Review:** The Key Topics icon is shown next to the most important items in the Foundation Topics section of the chapter. The Key Topics Review activity lists the key topics from the chapter, and the page number. While the contents of the entire chapter could be on the exam, you should definitely know the information listed in each key topic, so these should be reviewed.

— **Complete Tables and Lists from Memory:** To help you exercise your memory and memorize some lists of facts, many of the more important lists and tables from the chapter are included in Appendix J on the CD. This document lists only partial information, allowing you to complete the table or list. Appendix K lists the same tables and lists, completed, for easy comparison.

— **Definition of Key Terms:** While the exams are unlikely to ask a question like "Define this term," the CCNA exams do require that you learn and know a lot of networking terminology. This section lists the most important terms from the chapter, asking you to write a short definition and compare your answer to the glossary at the end of the book.

— **Command Reference Tables:** Some book chapters cover a large amount of configuration and EXEC commands. These tables list the commands introduced in the chapter, along with an explanation. For exam preparation, use them for reference, but also read the tables once when performing the Exam Preparation Tasks to make sure that you remember what all the commands do.

■ **CD-based Practice Exam:** The companion CD contains an exam engine (from Boson software, http://www.boson.com) that includes a large number of exam-realistic practice questions. You can take simulated ICND2 exams, as well as simulated CCNA exams, with the CD in this book. (You can take simulated ICND1 and CCNA exams with the CD in *CCENT/CCNA ICND1 Official Exam Certification Guide*.)

■ **Subnetting Videos:** The companion DVD contains a series of videos that show how to calculate various facts about IP addressing and subnetting, in particular using the shortcuts described in this book.

■ **Subnetting Practice:** CD Appendix D contains a large set of subnetting practice problems, with the answers and with explanations of how the answers were found. This is a great resource to get ready to do subnetting well and fast.

■ **CD-based Practice Scenarios:** CD Appendix F contains several networking scenarios for additional study. These scenarios describe various networks and requirements, taking you through conceptual design, configuration, and verification. These scenarios are useful for building your hands-on skills, even if you do not have lab gear.

■ **Companion Website:** The website http://www.ciscopress.com/title/1587201828 posts up-to-the-minute materials that further clarify complex exam topics. Check this site regularly for new and updated postings written by the author that provide further insight into the more troublesome topics on the exam.

How This Book Is Organized

This book contains 18 core chapters—Chapters 1 through 18, with Chapter 18 including some summary materials and suggestions for how to approach the exams. Each core chapter covers a subset of the topics on the ICND2 exam. The core chapters are organized into sections and cover the following topics:

■ Part I: LAN Switching

— **Chapter 1, "Virtual LANs"**: This chapter explains the concepts and configuration surrounding virtual LANs, including VLAN trunking and VLAN Trunking Protocol.

— **Chapter 2, "Spanning Tree Protocol"**: This chapter dives deeply into the concepts behind the original Spanning Tree Protocol (STP), as well as the newer Rapid STP (RSTP), including concepts, configuration, and troubleshooting.

— **Chapter 3, "Troubleshooting LAN Switching"**: This chapter explains some general ideas about how to troubleshoot networking problems, with most of the chapter focusing on the forwarding process used by LAN switches.

■ Part II: IP Routing

— **Chapter 4, "IP Routing: Static and Connected Routes"**: This chapter examines how routers add both static routes and connected routes to the routing table, while also reviewing the concepts behind how routers route, or forward, packets.

— **Chapter 5, "VLSM and Route Summarization"**: This chapter explains how IP routing and routing protocols can support the use of different subnet masks in a single classful network (VLSM), as well as the math concepts behind how routers can summarize multiple routes into one routing table entry.

— **Chapter 6, "IP Access Control Lists"**: This chapter examines how ACLs can filter packets so that a router will not forward the packet. The chapter examines the concepts and configuration for standard and extended ACLs, including named and numbered ACLs.

- — **Chapter 7, "Troubleshooting IP Routing"**: This chapter shows a structured plan for how to isolate problems related to two hosts that should be able to send packets to each other, but cannot. The chapter also includes a variety of tips and tools for helping attack routing problems.

- Part III: Routing Protocols Configuration and Troubleshooting

  - — **Chapter 8, "Routing Protocol Theory"**: This chapter explains the theory behind distance vector and link-state protocols.

  - — **Chapter 9, "OSPF"**: This chapter examines OSPF, including more detail about link-state theory as implemented by OSPF, and OSPF configuration.

  - — **Chapter 10, "EIGRP"**: This chapter examines EIGRP, including a description of the theory behind EIGRP, as well as EIGRP configuration and verification.

  - — **Chapter 11, "Troubleshooting Routing Protocols"**: This chapter explains some of the typical reasons why routing protocols fail to exchange routing information, showing specific examples of common problems with both OSPF and EIGRP.

- Part IV: Wide-Area Networks

  - — **Chapter 12, "Point-to-Point WANs"**: This short chapter reviews the basics of WANs and examines PPP, including CHAP, in more detail.

  - — **Chapter 13, "Frame Relay Concepts"**: This chapter focuses on the terminology and theory behind the Frame Relay protocol, including the IP addressing options when using Frame Relay.

  - — **Chapter 14, "Frame Relay Configuration and Troubleshooting"**: This chapter shows a variety of configuration options for Frame Relay, including both point-to-point and multipoint subinterfaces. It also explains how to best use **show** commands to isolate the root cause of common Frame Relay problems.

  - — **Chapter 15, "Virtual Private Networks"**: This chapter examines the concepts and protocols used to create secure VPNs over the Internet. This chapter includes the basics of IPsec.

- Part V: Scaling the IP Address Space

  — **Chapter 16, "Network Address Translation"**: This chapter closely examines the concepts behind the depletion of the IPv4 address space, and how NAT, in particular the Port Address Translation (PAT) option, helps solve the problem. The chapter also shows how to configure NAT on routers using the IOS CLI.

  — **Chapter 17, "IP Version 6"**: This chapter introduces the basics of IPv6, including the 128-bit address format, OSPF and EIGRP support for IPv6, and basic native IPv6 configuration. It also introduces the concept of IPv6 tunneling and migration strategies.

- Part VI: Final Preparation

  — **Chapter 18, "Final Preparation"**: This chapter suggests a plan for final preparation after you have finished the core parts of the book, in particular explaining the many study options available in the book.

- Part VII: Appendixes (in Print)

  — **Appendix A, "Answers to the 'Do I Know This Already?' Quizzes"**: Includes the answers to all the questions from Chapters 1 through 17.

  — **Appendix B, "Decimal-to-Binary Conversion Table"**: Lists decimal values 0 through 255, along with the binary equivalents.

  — **Appendix C, "ICND2 Exam Updates: Version 1.0"**: This appendix covers a variety of short topics that either clarify or expand upon topics covered earlier in the book. This appendix is updated from time to time and posted at http://www.ciscopress.com/ccna, with the most recent version available at the time of printing included here as Appendix C. (The first page of the appendix includes instructions on how to check whether a later version of Appendix C is available online.)

  — **Glossary**: The glossary contains definitions for all the terms listed in the "Definitions of Key Terms" section at the conclusion of Chapters 1–17.

- Part VII: Appendixes (on CD)

The following appendixes are available in PDF format on the CD that accompanies this book:

— **Appendix D, "Subnetting Practice"**: Although not covered in any of the chapters printed in this book, subnetting is easily the most important prerequisite assumed skill for the ICND2 exam. This appendix, as well as Appendixes E, H, and I, include materials from *CCENT/CCNA ICND1 Official Exam Certification Guide* for those of you that bought this book, but not the ICND1 book. In particular, this appendix includes a large number of subnetting practice problems, with the answers listed. The answers use both binary and decimal-shortcut processes described in the ICND1 book's Chapter 12; Appendix H of this book is a duplicate of ICND1's Chapter 12.

— **Appendix E, "Subnetting Reference Pages"**: This appendix summarizes the process to find the answer to several key subnetting questions, with the details on a single page. The goal is to give you a handy reference page to refer to when practicing subnetting.

— **Appendix F, "Additional Scenarios"**: One method to improve your troubleshooting and network analysis skills is to examine as many unique network scenarios as is possible, think about them, and then get some feedback as to whether you came to the right conclusions. This appendix provides several such scenarios.

— **Appendix G, "Video Scenario Reference"**: The DVD includes several subnetting videos that show how to use the processes covered in Appendix H (copied from ICND1's Chapter 12). This appendix contains copies of the key elements from those videos, which can be useful when watching the videos (so that you do not have to keep moving back and forth in the video).

— **Appendix H, "ICND1 Chapter 12: IP Addressing and Subnetting"**: This appendix is a duplicate of Chapter 12 from *CCENT/CCNA ICND1 Official Exam Certification Guide*. This chapter explains IP addressing and subnetting, which is considered prerequisite knowledge for the ICND2 exam. Appendix H is included with this book for those of you who do not have a copy of *CCENT/CCNA ICND1 Official Exam Certification Guide*, but you need to review and learn more about subnetting.

— **Appendix I, "ICND1 Chapter 17: WAN Configuration"**: This appendix is a duplicate of Chapter 17 from *CCENT/CCNA ICND1 Official Exam Certification Guide*. Chapter 12 of this book (ICND2), "Point-to-Point WANs," makes a suggestion to review a few prerequisite points as listed in this chapter. This chapter is included in this book for those of you who do not have a copy of *CCENT/CCNA ICND1 Official Exam Certification Guide*.

— **Appendix J, "Memory Tables"**: This appendix holds the key tables and lists from each chapter, with some of the content removed. You can print this appendix and, as a memory exercise, complete the tables and lists. The goal is to help you memorize facts that can be useful on the exams.

— **Appendix K, "Memory Tables Answer Key"**: This appendix contains the answer key for the exercises in Appendix J.

— **Appendix L, "ICND2 Open-Ended Questions"**: This appendix is a holdover from previous editions of this book. The older edition had some open-ended questions for the purpose of helping you study for the exam, but the newer features make these questions unnecessary. For convenience, the old questions are included here, unedited since the last edition.

How to Use This Book to Prepare for the ICND2 (640-816) Exam

This book was designed with two primary goals in mind: to help you study for the ICND2 exam and to help you study for the CCNA exam by using both this book and the *CCENT/ CCNA ICND1 Official Exam Certification Guide*. Using this book to prepare for the ICND2 exam is straightforward—read each chapter in succession, and follow the study suggestions in Chapter 18, "Final Preparation."

For the core chapters of this book (Chapters 1–17), you do have some choices as to how much of the chapter you read. In some cases, you might already know most of or all the information covered in a given chapter. To help you decide how much time to spend on each chapter, the chapters begin with a "Do I Know This Already?" quiz. If you get all the quiz questions correct, or just miss one question, you might want to skip to the end of the chapter and the "Exam Preparation Tasks" section, and do those activities. Figure I-2 shows the overall plan.

Figure I-2 *How to Approach Each Chapter of This Book*

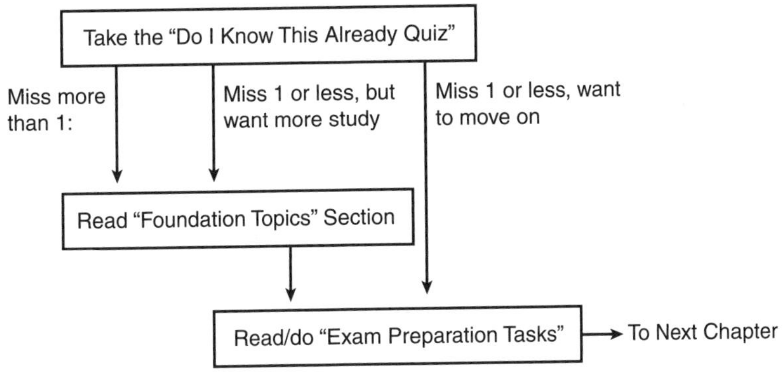

When you have completed Chapters 1–17, you can then use the guidance listed in Chapter 18 to detail the rest of the exam preparation tasks. That chapter includes the following suggestions:

- Check http://www.ciscopress.com for the latest copy of Appendix C, which can include additional topics for study.

- Practice subnetting using the tools available in the CD appendixes.

- Repeat the tasks in all chapters' "Exam Preparation Tasks" chapter-ending sections.

- Review the scenarios in CD Appendix F.

- Review all the "Do I Know This Already?" questions.

- Practice the exam using the exam engine.

How to Use These Books to Prepare for the CCNA 640-802 Exam

If you plan to get your CCNA certification using the one-exam option of taking the CCNA 640-802 exam, you can use this book along with *CCENT/CCNA ICND1 Official Exam Certification Guide*. If you've not yet bought either book, you can generally get the pair cheaper by buying both books as a two-book set, called the CCNA Certification Library.

These two books were designed to be used together when studying for the CCNA exam. You have two options for the order in which to read the two books. The first and most obvious option is to read the ICND1 book, and then move on to this (ICND2) book. The other option is to read all of ICND1's coverage of one topic area, then read ICND2's coverage of the same topics, and then go back to ICND1 again. Figure I-3 outlines my suggested option for reading the two books.

Figure I-3 *Reading Plan When Studying for CCNA Exam*

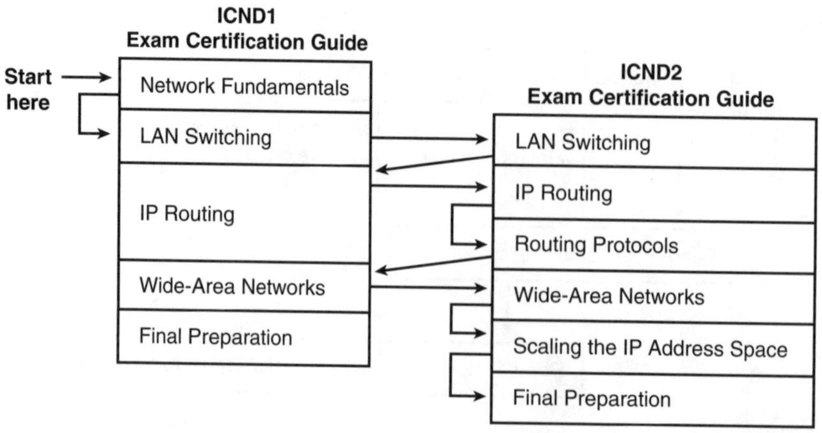

Both reading-plan options have some benefits. Moving back and forth between books can help you to focus on one general topic at a time. However, note that some overlap exists between the two exams, so you find some overlap between the two books as well. From reader comments about the previous edition of these books, those readers who were new to networking tended to do better by completing all of the first book and then moving on to the second, while readers that had more experience and knowledge before starting the books tended to prefer to follow a reading plan like the one shown in Figure I-3.

Note that for final preparation, you can use the final chapter (Chapter 18) of this book, rather than the final preparation chapter (Chapter 18) of the ICND1 book.

In addition to the flow shown in Figure I-3, when studying for the CCNA exam (rather than for the ICND1 and ICND2 exams), you must master IP subnetting before moving on to the IP routing and routing protocol parts (Parts II and III) of this book. This book does not review subnetting or the underlying math in the printed text, assuming that you know how to find the answers. Those ICND2 chapters, particularly Chapter 5 ("VLSM and Route Summarization"), will be much easier to understand if you can easily do the related subnetting math.

For More Information

If you have any comments about the book, you can submit those through Ciscopress.com. Just go to the website, click the Contact Us link, and type in your message.

Cisco might make changes that affect the CCNA certification from time to time. You should always check http://www.cisco.com/go/ccna for the latest details.

The CCNA certification is arguably the most important Cisco certification, with the new CCENT certification possibly surpassing CCNA in the future. CCNA certainly is the most popular Cisco certification, is required for several other certifications, and is the first step in distinguishing yourself as someone who has proven knowledge of Cisco.

CCNA ICND2 Official Exam Certification Guide is designed to help you attain CCNA certification. This is the CCNA ICND2 certification book from the only Cisco-authorized publisher. We at Cisco Press believe that this book certainly can help you achieve CCNA certification—but the real work is up to you! I trust that your time will be well spent.

Cisco Published ICND2 Exam Topics*
Covered in This Part

Configure, verify and troubleshoot a switch with VLANs and interswitch communications

- Describe enhanced switching technologies (including: VTP, RSTP, VLAN, PVSTP, 802.1q)

- Describe how VLANs create logically separate networks and the need for routing between them

- Configure, verify, and troubleshoot VLANs

- Configure, verify, and troubleshoot trunking on Cisco switches

- Configure, verify, and troubleshoot VTP

- Configure, verify, and troubleshoot RSTP operation

- Interpret the output of various show and debug commands to verify the operational status of a Cisco switched network

- Implement basic switch security (including: port security, unassigned ports, trunk access, etc.)

* Always recheck http://www.cisco.com for the latest posted exam topics.

Part I: LAN Switching

This chapter covers the following subjects:

Virtual LAN Concepts: This section explains the meaning and purpose for VLANs, VLAN trunking, and the VLAN Trunking Protocol (VTP).

VLAN and VLAN Trunking Configuration and Verification: This section shows how to configure VLANs and trunks on Cisco catalyst switches.

VTP Configuration and Verification: This final section explains how to configure and troubleshoot VTP installations.

CHAPTER 1

Virtual LANs

The first part of this book, which includes Chapters 1, 2, and 3, focuses on the world of LANs. Chapter 1 examines the concepts and configurations related to virtual LANs (VLANs), while Chapter 2, "Spanning Tree Protocol," covers how the Spanning Tree Protocol (STP) prevents loops in a switched network. Finally, Chapter 3, "Troubleshooting LAN Switching," pulls many LAN-related concepts together while exploring the process of troubleshooting common LAN problems.

As mentioned in the Introduction, this book assumes that you have a solid mastery of the most important topics covered on the ICND1 exam. If you are unclear about these prerequisites, you might want to glance over the list of prerequisite knowledge required by this book, under the heading "ICND1 Exam Topics" in the Introduction.

"Do I Know This Already?" Quiz

The "Do I Know This Already?" quiz allows you to assess whether you should read the entire chapter. If you miss no more than one of these ten self-assessment questions, you might want to move ahead to the "Exam Preparation Tasks" section. Table 1-1 lists the major headings in this chapter and the "Do I Know This Already?" quiz questions covering the material in those headings so that you can assess your knowledge of these specific areas. The answers to the "Do I Know This Already?" quiz appear in Appendix A.

Table 1-1 *"Do I Know This Already?" Foundation Topics Section-to-Question Mapping*

Foundation Topics Section	Questions
Virtual LAN Concepts	1–5
VLAN and VLAN Trunking Configuration and Verification	6–8
VTP Configuration and Verification	9–10

1. In a LAN, which of the following terms best equates to the term *VLAN*?

   a. Collision domain

   b. Broadcast domain

   c. Subnet domain

   d. Single switch

   e. Trunk

2. Imagine a switch with three configured VLANs. How many IP subnets are required, assuming that all hosts in all VLANs want to use TCP/IP?

   a. 0

   b. 1

   c. 2

   d. 3

   e. You can't tell from the information provided.

3. Which of the following fully encapsulates the original Ethernet frame in a trunking header rather than inserting another header inside the original Ethernet header?

   a. VTP

   b. ISL

   c. 802.1Q

   d. Both ISL and 802.1Q

   e. None of the other answers are correct.

4. Which of the following adds the trunking header for all VLANs except one?

   a. VTP

   b. ISL

   c. 802.1Q

   d. Both ISL and 802.1Q

   e. None of the other answers are correct.

5. Which of the following VTP modes allow VLANs to be configured on a switch?

   a. Client

   b. Server

   c. Transparent

   d. Dynamic

   e. None of the other answers are correct.

6. Imagine that you are told that switch 1 is configured with the **auto** parameter for trunking on its Fa0/5 interface, which is connected to switch 2. You have to configure switch 2. Which of the following settings for trunking could allow trunking to work?

    a. Trunking turned **on**

    b. **Auto**

    c. **Desirable**

    d. **Access**

    e. None of the other answers are correct.

7. A switch has just arrived from Cisco. The switch has never been configured with any VLANs, VTP configuration, or any other configuration. An engineer gets into configuration mode and issues the **vlan 22** command, followed by the **name Hannahs-VLAN** command. Which of the following are true?

    a. VLAN 22 is listed in the output of the **show vlan brief** command.

    b. VLAN 22 is listed in the output of the **show running-config** command.

    c. VLAN 22 is not created by this process.

    d. VLAN 22 does not exist in that switch until at least one interface is assigned to that VLAN.

8. Which of the following commands list the operational state of interface Gigabit 0/1 in regard to VLAN trunking?

    a. **show interfaces gi0/1**

    b. **show interfaces gi0/1 switchport**

    c. **show interfaces gi0/1 trunk**

    d. **show trunks**

9. An engineer has just installed four new 2960 switches and connected the switches to each other using crossover cables. All the interfaces are in an "up and up" state. The engineer configures each switch with the VTP domain name Fred and leaves all four switches in VTP server mode. The engineer adds VLAN 33 at 9:00 a.m., and then within 30 seconds, issues a **show vlan brief** command on the other three switches, but does not find VLAN 33 on the other three switches. Which answer gives the most likely reason for the problem in this case?

    a. VTP requires that all switches have the same VTP password.

    b. The engineer should have been more patient and waited for SW1 to send its next periodic VTP update.

    c. None of the links between the switches trunk because of the default 2960 trunking administrative mode of auto.

    d. None of the other answers are correct.

10. Switches SW1 and SW2 connect through an operational trunk. The engineer wants to use VTP to communicate VLAN configuration changes. The engineer configures a new VLAN on SW1, VLAN 44, but SW2 does not learn about the new VLAN. Which of the following configuration settings on SW1 and SW2 would *not* be a potential root cause why SW2 does not learn about VLAN 44?

- **a.** VTP domain names of larry and LARRY, respectively
- **b.** VTP passwords of bob and BOB, respectively
- **c.** VTP pruning enabled and disabled, respectively
- **d.** VTP modes of server and client, respectively

Foundation Topics

A Cisco Catalyst switch uses default settings that allow it to work with no additional configuration, right out of the box. However, most installations configure three major types of switch features: VLANs, as covered in this chapter; Spanning Tree, as covered in Chapter 2; and a variety of administrative settings that do not impact the forwarding behavior of the switch, which are explained in *CCENT/CCNA ICND1 Official Exam Certification Guide*.

All published objectives for the ICND1 exam are considered to be prerequisites for the ICND2 exam, although the ICND2 exam does not cover those topics as an end to themselves. For example, as described in the ICND1 book, switches learn MAC addresses by examining the source MAC address of incoming frames, and make forwarding/filtering decisions based on the destination MAC address of the frames. That book's LAN chapters (Chapter 3 plus Chapters 7 through 11) also explain the concepts of autonegotiation, collisions, collision domains, and broadcast domains. So, while the ICND2 exam might not have a specific question on these topics, these topics might be required to answer a question related to the exam objectives for the ICND2 exam. And, of course, the CCNA exam covers all the topics and objectives for both the ICND1 and ICND2 exams.

Besides the base concepts, the ICND1 book also describes a wide variety of small configuration tasks that either provide access to each switch or then help secure the switch when access has been granted. A switch should be configured with an IP address, subnet mask, and default gateway, allowing remote access to the switch. Along with that access, Cisco recommends several actions for better security beyond simply physically securing the router to prevent access from the switch console. In particular, passwords should be configured, and for remote access, Secure Shell (SSH) should be used instead of Telnet, if possible. The HTTP service should also be disabled, and banners should be configured to warn potential attackers away. Additionally, each switch's syslog messages should be monitored for any messages relating to various types of attacks.

The three chapters in this first part of the book pick up the LAN story, explaining the topics specifically related to ICND2 exam objectives. In particular, this chapter examines the concepts related to VLANs, and then covers the configuration and operation of VLANs. The first major section of this chapter explains the core concepts, including how to pass VLAN traffic between switches using VLAN trunks, and how the Cisco-proprietary VLAN Trunking Protocol (VTP) aids the process of configuring VLANs in a campus LAN. The second major section of this chapter shows how to configure VLANs and VLAN trunks, how to statically assign interfaces to a VLAN, and how to configure a switch so that a phone and PC on the same interface are in two different VLANs. The final major section covers VTP configuration and troubleshooting.

Virtual LAN Concepts

Before understanding VLANs, you must first have a specific understanding of the definition of a LAN. Although you can think about LANs from many perspectives, one perspective in particular can help you understand VLANs:

> A LAN includes all devices in the same broadcast domain.

A broadcast domain includes the set of all LAN-connected devices that when any of the devices sends a broadcast frame, all the other devices get a copy of the frame. So, you can think of a LAN and a broadcast domain as being basically the same thing.

Without VLANs, a switch considers all its interfaces to be in the same broadcast domain; in others words, all connected devices are in the same LAN. With VLANs, a switch can put some interfaces into one broadcast domain and some into another, creating multiple broadcast domains. These individual broadcast domains created by the switch are called virtual LANs. Figure 1-1 shows an example, with two VLANs and two devices in each VLAN.

Figure 1-1   *Sample Network with Two VLANs Using One Switch*

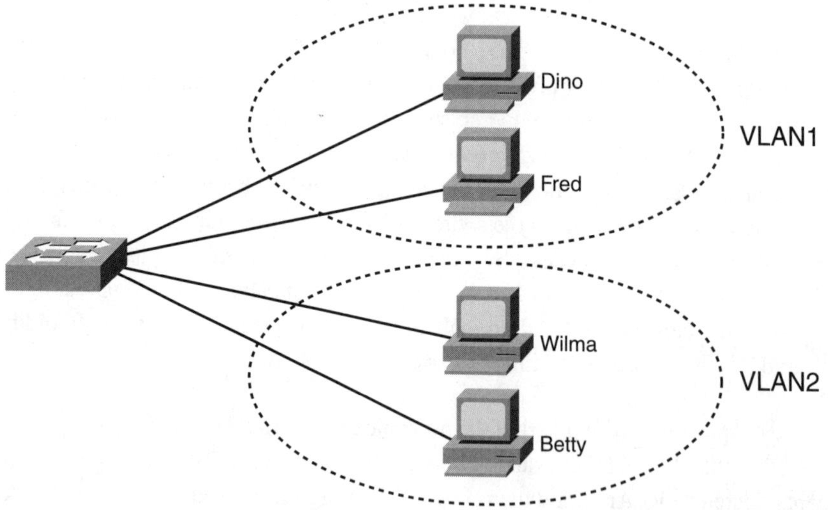

Putting hosts into different VLANs provides many benefits, although the reasons might not be obvious from Figure 1-1. The key to appreciating these benefits is to realize that a broadcast sent by one host in a VLAN will be received and processed by all the other hosts in the VLAN, but not by hosts in a different VLAN. The more hosts in a single VLAN, the larger the number of broadcasts, and the greater the processing time required by each host in the VLAN. Additionally, anyone can download several free software packages, generically called protocol analyzer software, which can capture all the frames received by a host. (Visit Wireshark, at http://www.wireshark.org, for a good free analyzer package.) As a result, larger VLANs expose larger numbers and types of broadcasts to other hosts, exposing more frames to hosts that could be used by an attacker that uses protocol analyzer software to try and perform a reconnaissance attack. These are just a few reasons for separating hosts into different VLANs. The following summarizes the most common reasons:

- To create more flexible designs that group users by department, or by groups that work together, instead of by physical location

- To segment devices into smaller LANs (broadcast domains) to reduce overhead caused to each host in the VLAN

- To reduce the workload for the Spanning Tree Protocol (STP) by limiting a VLAN to a single access switch

- To enforce better security by keeping hosts that work with sensitive data on a separate VLAN

- To separate traffic sent by an IP phone from traffic sent by PCs connected to the phones

This chapter does not examine the reasons for VLANs in any more depth, but it does closely examine the mechanics of how VLANs work across multiple Cisco switches, including the required configuration. To that end, the next section examines VLAN trunking, a feature required when installing a VLAN that exists on more than one LAN switch.

Trunking with ISL and 802.1Q

When using VLANs in networks that have multiple interconnected switches, the switches need to use *VLAN trunking* on the segments between the switches. VLAN trunking causes the switches to use a process called *VLAN tagging*, by which the sending switch adds another header to the frame before sending it over the trunk. This extra VLAN header includes a *VLAN identifier* (VLAN ID) field so that the sending switch can list the VLAN ID and the receiving switch can then know in what VLAN each frame belongs. Figure 1-2 outlines the basic idea.

Figure 1-2   *VLAN Trunking Between Two Switches*

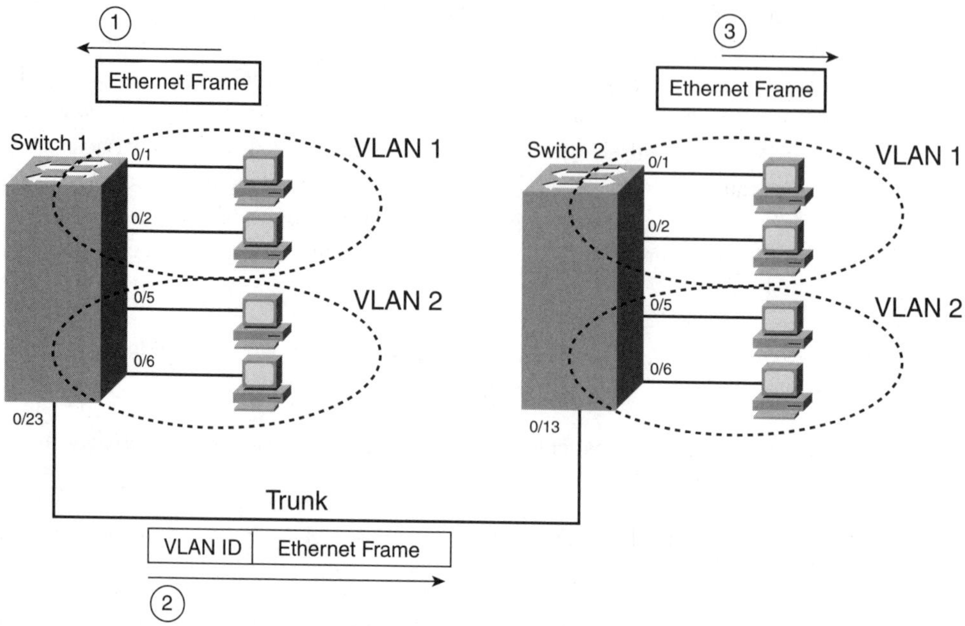

The use of trunking allows switches to pass frames from multiple VLANs over a single physical connection. For example, Figure 1-2 shows switch 1 receiving a broadcast frame on interface Fa0/1 at Step 1. To flood the frame, switch 1 needs to forward the broadcast frame to switch 2. However, switch 1 needs to let switch 2 know that the frame is part of VLAN 1. So, as shown at Step 2, before sending the frame, switch 1 adds a VLAN header to the original Ethernet frame, with the VLAN header listing a VLAN ID of 1 in this case. When switch 2 receives the frame, it sees that the frame was from a device in VLAN 1, so switch 2 knows that it should only forward the broadcast out its own interfaces in VLAN 1. Switch 2 removes the VLAN header, forwarding the original frame out its interfaces in VLAN 1 (Step 3).

For another example, consider the case when the device on switch 1's Fa0/5 interface sends a broadcast. Switch 1 sends the broadcast out port Fa0/6 (because that port is in VLAN 2) and out Fa0/23 (because it is a trunk, meaning that it supports multiple different VLANs). Switch 1 adds a trunking header to the frame, listing a VLAN ID of 2. Switch 2 strips off the trunking header after noticing that the frame is part of VLAN 2, so switch 2 knows to forward the frame out only ports Fa0/5 and Fa0/6, and not ports Fa0/1 and Fa0/2.

Cisco switches support two different trunking protocols: Inter-Switch Link (ISL) and IEEE 802.1Q. Trunking protocols provide several features, most importantly that they define headers which identify the VLAN ID, as shown in Figure 1-2. They do have some differences as well, as discussed next.

ISL

Cisco created ISL many years before the IEEE created the 802.1Q standard VLAN trunking protocol. Because ISL is Cisco proprietary, it can be used only between two Cisco switches that support ISL. (Some newer Cisco switches do not even support ISL, instead supporting only the standardized alternative, 802.1Q.) ISL fully encapsulates each original Ethernet frame in an ISL header and trailer. The original Ethernet frame inside the ISL header and trailer remains unchanged. Figure 1-3 shows the framing for ISL.

Figure 1-3 *ISL Header*

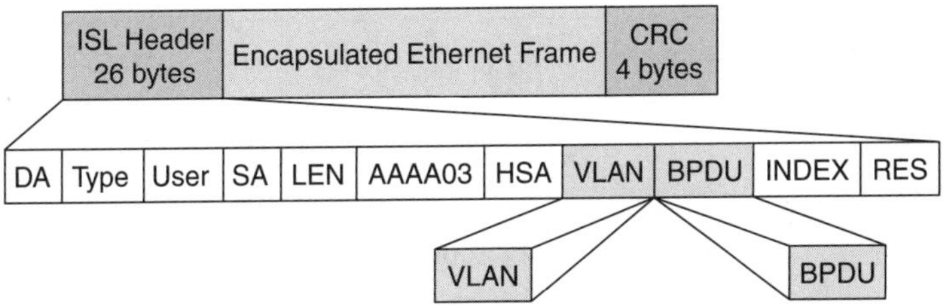

The ISL header includes several fields, but most importantly, the ISL header VLAN field provides a place to encode the VLAN number. By tagging a frame with the correct VLAN number inside the header, the sending switch can ensure that the receiving switch knows to which VLAN the encapsulated frame belongs. Also, the source and destination addresses in the ISL header use MAC addresses of the sending and receiving switch, as opposed to the devices that actually sent the original frame. Other than that, the details of the ISL header are not that important.

IEEE 802.1Q

The IEEE standardizes many of the protocols that relate to LANs today, and VLAN trunking is no exception. Years after Cisco created ISL, the IEEE completed work on the 802.1Q standard, which defines a different way to do trunking. Today, 802.1Q has become the more popular trunking protocol, with Cisco not even supporting ISL in some of its newer models of LAN switches, including the 2960 switches used in the examples in this book.

802.1Q uses a different style of header than does ISL to tag frames with a VLAN number. In fact, 802.1Q does not actually encapsulate the original frame in another Ethernet header and trailer. Instead, 802.1Q inserts an extra 4-byte VLAN header into the original frame's Ethernet header. As a result, unlike ISL, the frame still has the same original source and destination MAC addresses. Also, because the original header has been expanded, 802.1Q encapsulation forces a recalculation of the original frame check sequence (FCS) field in the

Ethernet trailer, because the FCS is based on the contents of the entire frame. Figure 1-4 shows the 802.1Q header and framing of the revised Ethernet header.

Figure 1-4 *802.1Q Trunking Header*

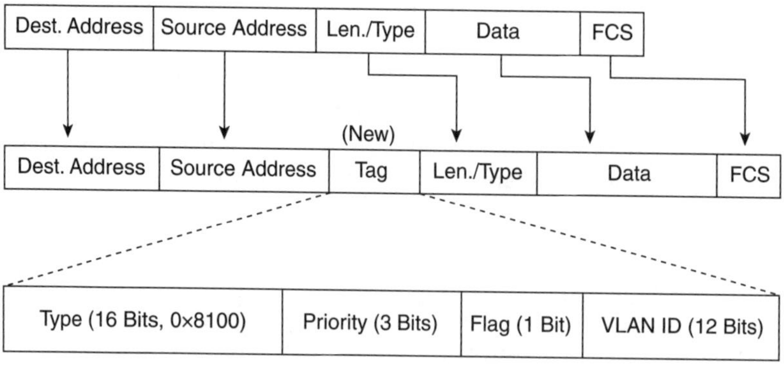

ISL and 802.1Q Compared

So far, the text has described one major similarity between ISL and 802.1Q, with a couple of differences. The similarity is that both ISL and 802.1Q define a VLAN header that has a VLAN ID field. However, each trunking protocol uses a different overall header, plus one is standardized (802.1Q) and one is proprietary (ISL). This section points out a few other key comparison points between the two.

Both trunking protocols support the same number of VLANs, specifically 4094 VLANs. Both protocols use 12 bits of the VLAN header to number VLANs, supporting 2^{12}, or 4096, VLAN IDs, minus two reserved values (0 and 4095). Of the supported VLANs, note that VLAN IDs 1–1005 are considered to be *normal range* VLANs, whereas values higher than 1005 are called *extended range* VLANs. This distinction matters in regard to the VLAN Trunking Protocol (VTP), which is covered in the next section.

ISL and 802.1Q both support a separate instance of Spanning Tree Protocol (STP) for each VLAN, but with different implementation details, as explained in Chapter 2. For campus LANs with redundant links, using only one instance of STP means that some links sit idle under normal operations, with those links only being used when another link fails. By supporting multiple instances of STP, engineers can tune the STP parameters so that under normal operations, some VLANs' traffic uses one set of links and other VLANs' traffic uses other links, taking advantage of all the links in the network.

NOTE   802.1Q has not always supported multiple instances of STP, so some older references might have accurately stated that, at that time, 802.1Q only supported a single instance of STP.

One final key difference between ISL and 802.1Q covered here relates to a feature called the *native VLAN*. 802.1Q defines one VLAN on each trunk as the native VLAN, whereas ISL does not use the concept. By default, the 802.1Q native VLAN is VLAN 1. By definition, 802.1Q simply does not add an 802.1Q header to frames in the native VLAN. When the switch on the other side of the trunk receives a frame that does not have an 802.1Q header, the receiving switch knows that the frame is part of the native VLAN. Note that because of this behavior, both switches must agree which VLAN is the native VLAN.

The 802.1Q native VLAN provides some interesting functions, mainly to support connections to devices that do not understand trunking. For example, a Cisco switch could be cabled to a switch that does not understand 802.1Q trunking. The Cisco switch could send frames in the native VLAN—meaning that the frame has no trunking header—so the other switch would understand the frame. The native VLAN concept gives switches the capability of at least passing traffic in one VLAN (the native VLAN), which can allow some basic functions, like reachability to telnet into a switch.

Table 1-2 summarizes the key features and points of comparison between ISL and 802.1Q.

Table 1-2 *ISL and 802.1Q Compared*

Key Topic

Function	ISL	802.1Q
Defined by	Cisco	IEEE
Inserts another 4-byte header instead of completely encapsulating the original frame	No	Yes
Supports normal-range (1–1005) and extended-range (1006–4094) VLANs	Yes	Yes
Allows multiple spanning trees	Yes	Yes
Uses a native VLAN	No	Yes

IP Subnets and VLANs

When including VLANs in a design, the devices in a VLAN need to be in the same subnet. Following the same design logic, devices in different VLANs need to be in different subnets.

Because of these design rules, many people think that a VLAN is a subnet and that a subnet is a VLAN. Although not completely true, because a VLAN is a Layer 2 concept and a subnet is a Layer 3 concept, the general idea is reasonable because the same devices in a single VLAN are the same devices in a single subnet.

As with all IP subnets, for a host in one subnet to forward packets to a host in another subnet, at least one router must be involved. For example, consider Figure 1-5, which shows a switch with three VLANs, shown inside the dashed lines, with some of the logic used when a host in VLAN 1 sends an IP packet to a host in VLAN 2.

Figure 1-5 *Routing Between VLANs*

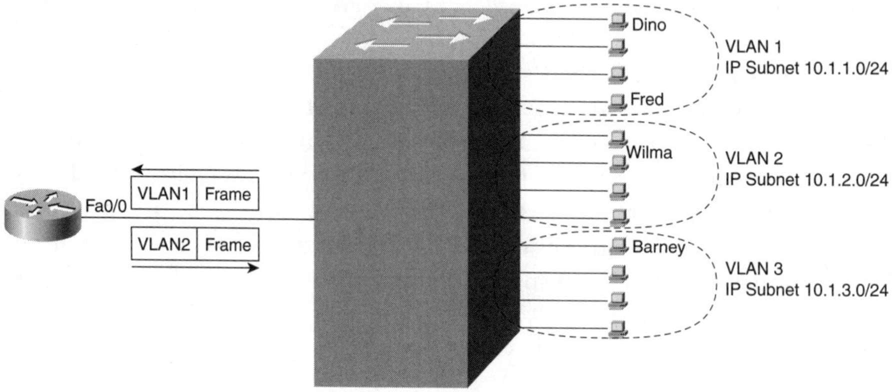

In this case, when Fred sends a packet to Wilma's IP address, Fred sends the packet to his default router, because Wilma's IP address is in a different subnet. The router receives the frame, with a VLAN header that implies the frame is part of VLAN 1. The router makes a forwarding decision, sending the frame back out the same physical link, but this time with a VLAN trunking header that lists VLAN 2. The switch forwards the frame in VLAN 2 to Wilma.

It might seem a bit inefficient to send the packet from the switch, to the router, and right back to the switch—and it is. A more likely option in real campus LANs today is to use a switch called either a multilayer switch or a Layer 3 switch. These switches can perform both Layer 2 switching and Layer 3 routing, combining the router function shown in Figure 1-5 into the switch.

VLAN Trunking Protocol (VTP)

The Cisco-proprietary VLAN Trunking Protocol (VTP) provides a means by which Cisco switches can exchange VLAN configuration information. In particular, VTP advertises about the existence of each VLAN based on its VLAN ID and the VLAN name. However, VTP does not advertise the details about which switch interfaces are assigned to each VLAN.

Because this book has not yet shown how to configure VLANs, to better appreciate VTP, consider this example of what VTP can do. Imagine that a network has ten switches connected somehow using VLAN trunks, and each switch has at least one port assigned to a VLAN with VLAN ID 3 and the name Accounting. Without VTP, an engineer would have to log in to all ten switches and enter the same two config commands to create the VLAN and define its name. With VTP, you would create VLAN 3 on one switch, and the other nine switches would learn about VLAN 3 and its name using VTP.

VTP defines a Layer 2 messaging protocol that the switches use to exchange VLAN configuration information. When a switch changes its VLAN configuration—in other words, when a VLAN is added or deleted, or an existing VLAN is changed—VTP causes all the switches to synchronize their VLAN configuration to include the same VLAN IDs and VLAN names. The process is somewhat like a routing protocol, with each switch sending periodic VTP messages. Switches also send VTP messages as soon as their VLAN configuration changes. For example, if you configured a new VLAN 3, with the name Accounting, the switch would immediately send VTP updates out all trunks, causing the distribution of the new VLAN information to the rest of the switches.

Each switch uses one of three VTP modes: server mode, client mode, or transparent mode. To use VTP, an engineer sets some switches to use server mode and the rest to use client mode. Then, VLAN configuration can be added on the servers, with all other servers and clients learning about the changes to the VLAN database. Clients cannot be used to configure VLAN information.

Oddly enough, Cisco switches cannot disable VTP. The closest option is to use transparent mode, which causes a switch to ignore VTP, other than to forward VTP messages so that any other clients or servers can receive a copy.

The next section explains the normal operations when the engineer uses server and client modes to take advantage of VTP's capabilities, followed by an explanation of the rather unusual way to essentially disable VTP by enabling VTP transparent mode.

Normal VTP Operation Using VTP Server and Client Modes

The VTP process begins with VLAN creation on a switch called a VTP server. The VTP server then distributes VLAN configuration changes through VTP messages, sent only over ISL and 802.1Q trunks, throughout the network. Both VTP servers and clients process the received VTP messages, update their VTP configuration database based on those messages, and then independently send VTP updates out their trunks. At the end of the process, all switches learn the new VLAN information.

VTP servers and clients choose whether to react to a received VTP update, and update their VLAN configurations based on whether the *VLAN database configuration revision number* increases. Each time a VTP server modifies its VLAN configuration, the VTP server increments the current configuration revision number by 1. The VTP update messages list the new configuration revision number. When another client or server switch receives a VTP message with a higher configuration revision number than its own, the switch updates its VLAN configuration. Figure 1-6 illustrates how VTP operates in a switched network.

Figure 1-6   *VTP Configuration Revision Numbers and the VTP Update Process*

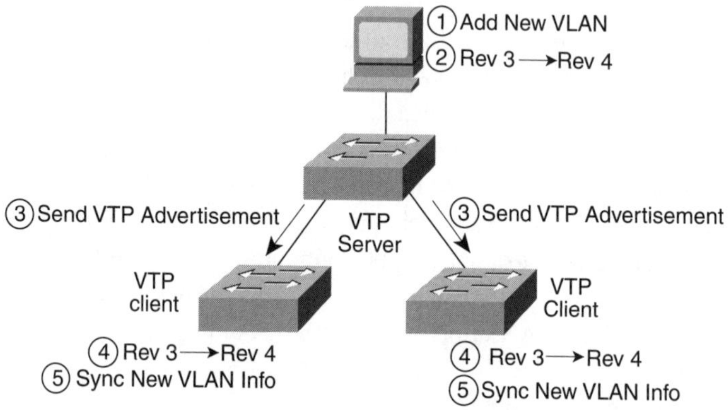

Figure 1-6 begins with all switches having the same VLAN configuration revision number, meaning that they have the same VLAN configuration database; this means that all switches know about the same VLAN numbers and VLAN names. The process begins with each switch knowing that the current configuration revision number is 3. The steps shown in Figure 1-6 are as follows:

1.   Someone configures a new VLAN from the command-line interface (CLI) of a VTP server.

2.   The VTP server updates its VLAN database revision number from 3 to 4.

3.   The server sends VTP update messages out its trunk interfaces, stating revision number 4.

4.   The two VTP client switches notice that the updates list a higher revision number (4) than their current revision numbers (3).

5.   The two client switches update their VLAN databases based on the server's VTP updates.

While this example shows a very small LAN, the process works the same for larger networks. When a VTP server updates the VLAN configuration, the server immediately sends VTP messages out all trunks. The neighboring switches on the other end of the trunks process the received messages and update their VLAN databases, and then they send VTP messages to their neighbors. The process repeats on the neighboring switches, until eventually, all switches have heard of the new VLAN database.

> **NOTE**   The complete process by which a server changes the VLAN configuration, and all VTP switches learn the new configuration, resulting in all switches knowing the same VLAN IDs and name, is called *synchronization*.

VTP servers and clients also send periodic VTP messages every 5 minutes, in case any newly added switches need to know the VLAN configuration. Additionally, when a new trunk comes up, switches can immediately send a VTP message asking the neighboring switch to send its VLAN database.

So far, this chapter has referred to VTP messages as either VTP updates or VTP messages. In practice, VTP defines three different types of messages: summary advertisements, subset advertisements, and advertisement requests. The summary advertisements list the revision number, domain name, and other information, but no VLAN information. The periodic VTP messages that occur every five minutes are VTP summary advertisements. If something changes, as indicated by a new 1-larger revision number, the summary advertisement message is followed by one or more subset advertisements, each of which advertises some subset of the VLAN database. The third message, the advertisement request message, allows a switch to immediately request VTP messages from a neighboring switch as soon as a trunk comes up. However, the examples shown for the purposes of this book do not make distinctions about the use of the messages.

Three Requirements for VTP to Work Between Two Switches

When a VTP client or server connects to another VTP client or server switch, Cisco IOS requires that the following three facts be true before the two switches can exchange VTP messages:

- The link between the switches must be operating as a VLAN trunk (ISL or 802.1Q).

- The two switches' case-sensitive VTP domain name must match.

- If configured on at least one of the switches, the two switches' case-sensitive VTP password must match.

Key Topic

The VTP domain name provides a design tool by which engineers can create multiple groups of VTP switches, called domains, whose VLAN configurations are autonomous. To do so, the engineer can configure one set of switches in one VTP domain and another set in another VTP domain, and switches in the different domains will ignore each other's VTP messages. VTP domains allow engineers to break up the switched network into different administrative domains. For example, in a large building with a large IT staff, one division's

IT staff might use a VTP domain name of Accounting, while another part of the IT staff might use a domain name of Sales, maintaining control of their configurations but still being able to forward traffic between divisions through the LAN infrastructure.

The VTP password mechanism provides a means by which a switch can prevent malicious attackers from forcing a switch to change its VLAN configuration. The password itself is never transmitted in clear text.

Avoiding VTP by Using VTP Transparent Mode

Interestingly, to avoid using VTP to exchange VLAN information in Cisco switches, switches cannot simply disable VTP. Instead, switches must use the third VTP mode: VTP transparent mode. Transparent mode gives a switch autonomy from the other switches. Like VTP servers, VTP transparent mode switches can configure VLANs. However, unlike servers, transparent mode switches never update their VLAN databases based on incoming VTP messages, and transparent mode switches never try to create VTP messages to tell other switches about their own VLAN configuration.

VTP transparent mode switches essentially behave as if VTP does not exist, other than one small exception: Transparent mode switches forward VTP updates received from other switches, just to help out any neighboring VTP server or client switches.

From a design perspective, because of the dangers associated with VTP (as covered in the next section), some engineers just avoid VTP altogether by using VTP transparent mode on all switches. In other cases, engineers might make a few switches transparent mode switches to give autonomy to the engineers responsible for those switches, while using VTP server and client modes on other switches.

Storing VLAN Configuration

To forward traffic for a VLAN, a switch needs to know the VLAN's VLAN ID and its VLAN name. VTP's job is to advertise these details, with the full set of configuration for all VLANs being called the *VLAN configuration database*, or simply VLAN database.

Interestingly, Cisco IOS stores the information in the VLAN database differently than for most other Cisco IOS configuration commands. When VTP clients and servers store VLAN configuration—specifically, the VLAN ID, VLAN name, and other VTP configuration settings—the configuration is stored in a file called vlan.dat in flash memory. (The filename is short for "VLAN database.") Even more interesting is the fact that Cisco IOS does not put this VLAN configuration in the running-config file or the startup-config file. No command exists to view the VTP and VLAN configuration directly; instead, you need to use several **show** commands to list the information about VLANs and VTP output.

The process of storing the VLAN configuration in flash in the vlan.dat file allows both clients and servers to dynamically learn about VLANs, and have the configuration automatically stored, therefore making both client and server prepared for their next reload. If the dynamically learned VLAN configuration was only added to the running config file, the campus LAN could be exposed to cases in which all switches lost power around the same time (easily accomplished with a single power source into the building), resulting in loss of all VLAN configuration. By automatically storing the configuration in the vlan.dat file in flash memory, each switch has at least a recent VLAN configuration database, and can then rely on VTP updates from other switches if any VLAN configuration has changed recently.

An interesting side effect of this process is that when you use a VTP client or server switch in a lab, and you want to remove all the configuration to start with a clean switch, you must issue more than the **erase startup-config** command. If you only erase the startup-config and reload the switch, the switch remembers all VLAN config and VTP configuration that is instead stored in the vlan.dat file in flash. To remove those configuration details before reloading a switch, you would have to delete the vlan.dat file in flash with a command such as **delete flash:vlan.dat**.

Switches in transparent mode store VLAN configuration in both the running-config file as well as the vlan.dat file in flash. The running-config can be saved to the startup-config as well.

> **NOTE**   In some older switch Cisco IOS versions, VTP servers stored VLAN configuration in both vlan.dat and the running-config file.

VTP Versions

Cisco supports three VTP versions, aptly named versions 1, 2, and 3. Most of the differences between these versions are unimportant to the discussions in this book. However, VTP version 2 made one important improvement over version 1 relative to VTP transparent mode, an improvement that is briefly described in this section.

The section "Avoiding VTP by Using VTP Transparent Mode," earlier in this chapter, described how a switch using VTP version 2 would work. However, in VTP version 1, a VTP transparent mode switch would first check a received VTP update's domain name and password. If the transparent mode switch did not match both parameters, the transparent mode switch discarded the VTP update, rather than forwarding the update. The problem with VTP version 1 is that in cases where a transparent mode switch existed in a network with multiple VTP domains, the switch wouldn't forward all VTP updates. So, VTP version

2 changed transparent mode logic, ignoring the domain name and password, allowing a VTP version 2 transparent mode switch to forward all received VTP updates.

> **NOTE**   Version 3 is available only in higher-end Cisco switches today, and will be ignored for the purposes of this book.

VTP Pruning

By default, Cisco switches flood broadcasts (and unknown destination unicasts) in each active VLAN out all trunks, as long as the current STP topology does not block the trunk. (You find more on STP in Chapter 2.) However, in most campus networks, many VLANs exist on only a few switches, but not all switches. Therefore, it is wasteful to forward broadcasts over all trunks, causing the frames to arrive at switches that do not have any ports in that VLAN.

Switches support two methods by which an engineer can limit which VLAN's traffic flows over a trunk. One method requires the manual configuration of the *allowed VLAN list* on each trunk; this manual configuration is covered later in the chapter. The second method, VTP pruning, allows VTP to dynamically determine which switches do not need frames from certain VLANs, and then VTP prunes those VLANs from the appropriate trunks. Pruning simply means that the appropriate switch trunk interfaces do not flood frames in that VLAN. Figure 1-7 shows an example, with the dashed-line rectangles denoting the trunks from which VLAN 10 has been automatically pruned.

Figure 1-7   *VTP Pruning*

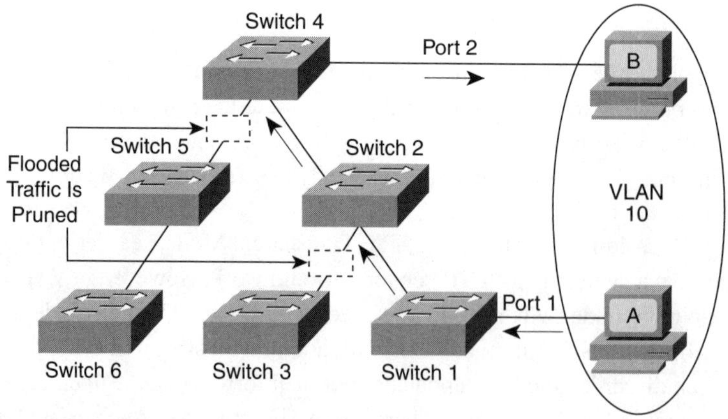

In Figure 1-7, switches 1 and 4 have ports in VLAN 10. With VTP pruning enabled network-wide, switch 2 and switch 4 automatically use VTP to learn that none of the switches in the lower-left part of the figure have any ports assigned to VLAN 10. As a result, switch 2 and switch 4 prune VLAN 10 from the trunks as shown. The pruning causes switch 2 and switch 4 to not send frames in VLAN 10 out these trunks. For example, when station A sends a broadcast, the switches flood the broadcast, as shown by the arrowed lines in Figure 1-7.

VTP pruning increases the available bandwidth by restricting flooded traffic. VTP pruning is one of the two most compelling reasons to use VTP, with the other reason being to make VLAN configuration easier and more consistent.

Summary of VTP Features

Table 1-3 offers a comparative overview of the three VTP modes.

Table 1-3 *VTP Features*

Function	Server	Client	Transparent
Only sends VTP messages out ISL or 802.1Q trunks	Yes	Yes	Yes
Supports CLI configuration of VLANs	Yes	No	Yes
Can use normal-range VLANs (1–1005)	Yes	Yes	Yes
Can use extended-range VLANs (1006–4095)	No	No	Yes
Synchronizes (updates) its own config database when receiving VTP messages with a higher revision number	Yes	Yes	No
Creates and sends periodic VTP updates every 5 minutes	Yes	Yes	No
Does not process received VTP updates, but does forward received VTP updates out other trunks	No	No	Yes
Places the VLAN ID, VLAN name, and VTP configuration into the running-config file	No	No	Yes
Places the VLAN ID, VLAN name, and VTP configuration into the vlan.dat file in flash	Yes	Yes	Yes

Key Topic

VLAN and VLAN Trunking Configuration and Verification

Cisco switches do not require any configuration to work. You can purchase Cisco switches, install devices with the correct cabling, and turn on the switches, and they work. You would never need to configure the switch and it would work fine, even if you interconnected switches, until you needed more than one VLAN. Even the default STP settings would likely work just fine, but if you want to use VLANs—and most every enterprise network does—you need to add some configuration.

This chapter separates the VLAN configuration details into two major sections. The current section focuses on configuration and verification tasks when VTP is ignored, either by using the default VTP settings or if using VTP transparent mode. The final major section of this chapter, "VTP Configuration and Verification," examines VTP specifically.

Creating VLANs and Assigning Access VLANs to an Interface

This section shows how to create a VLAN, give the VLAN a name, and assign interfaces to a VLAN. To focus on these basic details, this section shows examples using a single switch, so VTP and trunking are not needed.

For a Cisco switch to forward frames in a particular VLAN, the switch must be configured to believe that the VLAN exists. Additionally, the switch must have nontrunking interfaces (called *access interfaces*) assigned to the VLAN and/or trunks that support the VLAN. The configuration steps for creating the VLAN, and assigning a VLAN to an access interface, are as follows. (Note that the trunk configuration is covered in the section "VLAN Trunking Configuration," later in this chapter.)

Key Topic

Step 1 To configure a new VLAN, follow these steps:

    a. From configuration mode, use the **vlan** *vlan-id* global configuration command to create the VLAN and to move the user into VLAN configuration mode.

    b. (Optional) Use the **name** *name* VLAN subcommand to list a name for the VLAN. If not configured, the VLAN name is VLANZZZZ, where ZZZZ is the 4-digit decimal VLAN ID.

Step 2 To configure a VLAN for each access interface, follow these steps:

    a. Use the **interface** command to move into interface configuration mode for each desired interface.

    b. Use the **switchport access vlan** *id-number* interface subcommand to specify the VLAN number associated with that interface.

    c. (Optional) To disable trunking on that same interface, ensuring that the interface is an access interface, use the **switchport mode access** interface subcommand.

> **NOTE** VLANs can be created and named in configuration mode (as described in Step 1) or by using a configuration tool called VLAN database mode. The VLAN database mode is not covered in this book, and it is typically not covered for other Cisco exams, either.

> **NOTE** Cisco switches also support a dynamic method of assigning devices to VLANs, based on the device's MAC addresses, using a tool called the VLAN Management Policy Server (VMPS). This tool is seldom if ever used.

The previous process can be used on a switch either configured to be a transparent mode switch or a switch with all default VTP settings. For reference, the following list outlines the key Cisco switch defaults related to VLANs and VTP. For now, this chapter assumes either default VTP settings or a setting of VTP transparent mode. Later in this chapter, the section "Caveats When Moving Away from Default VTP Configuration" revisits Cisco switch defaults and the implication of how to go from not using VTP, based on the default settings, to how to use VTP.

Key Topic

■ VTP server mode.

■ No VTP domain name.

■ VLAN 1 and VLANs 1002–1005 are automatically configured (and cannot be deleted).

■ All access interfaces are assigned to VLAN 1 (an implied **switchport access vlan 1** command).

VLAN Configuration Example 1: Full VLAN Configuration

Example 1-1 shows the configuration process of adding a new VLAN and assigning access interfaces to that VLAN. Figure 1-8 shows the network used in the example, with one LAN switch (SW1) and two hosts in each of three VLANs (1, 2, and 3). The example shows the details of the two-step process for VLAN 2 and the interfaces in VLAN 2, with the configuration of VLAN 3 deferred until the next example.

Figure 1-8 *Network with One Switch and Three VLANs*

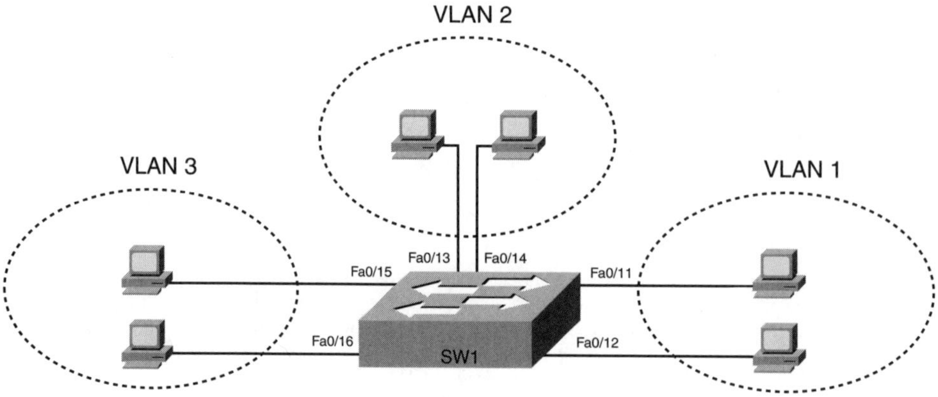

Example 1-1 *Configuring VLANs and Assigning VLANs to Interfaces*

```
sw1-2960#show vlan brief

VLAN Name                             Status    Ports
---- -------------------------------- --------- -------------------------------

1    default                          active    Fa0/1, Fa0/2, Fa0/3, Fa0/4
                                                 Fa0/5, Fa0/6, Fa0/7, Fa0/8
                                                 Fa0/9, Fa0/10, Fa0/11, Fa0/12
                                                 Fa0/13, Fa0/14, Fa0/15, Fa0/16
                                                 Fa0/17, Fa0/18, Fa0/19, Fa0/20
                                                 Fa0/21, Fa0/22, Fa0/23, Fa0/24
                                                 Gi0/1, Gi0/2
1002 fddi-default                     act/unsup
1003 token-ring-default               act/unsup
1004 fddinet-default                  act/unsup
1005 trnet-default                    act/unsup
! Above, VLAN 2 did not yet exist. Below, VLAN 2 is added, with name Freds-vlan,
! with two interfaces assigned to VLAN 2.
sw1-2960#configure terminal
Enter configuration commands, one per line.  End with CNTL/Z.
sw1-2960(config)#vlan 2
sw1-2960(config-vlan)#name Freds-vlan
sw1-2960(config-vlan)#exit
sw1-2960(config)#interface range fastethernet 0/13 - 14
sw1-2960(config-if)#switchport access vlan 2
sw1-2960(config-if)#exit
! Below, the show running-config command lists the interface subcommands on
! interfaces Fa0/13 and Fa0/14. The vlan 2 and name Freds-vlan commands do
! not show up in the running-config.
sw1-2960#show running-config
! lines omitted for brevity
interface FastEthernet0/13
```

Example 1-1 *Configuring VLANs and Assigning VLANs to Interfaces (Continued)*

```
 switchport access vlan 2
 switchport mode access
!
interface FastEthernet0/14
 switchport access vlan 2
 switchport mode access
!
SW1#show vlan brief

VLAN Name                             Status    Ports
---- -------------------------------- --------- -------------------------------
1    default                          active    Fa0/1, Fa0/2, Fa0/3, Fa0/4
                                                Fa0/5, Fa0/6, Fa0/7, Fa0/8
                                                Fa0/9, Fa0/10, Fa0/11, Fa0/12
                                                Fa0/15, Fa0/16, Fa0/17, Fa0/18
                                                Fa0/19, Fa0/20, Fa0/21, Fa0/22
                                                Fa0/23, Fa0/24, Gi0/1, Gi0/2
2    Freds-vlan                       active    Fa0/13, Fa0/14
1002 fddi-default                     act/unsup
1003 token-ring-default               act/unsup
1004 fddinet-default                  act/unsup
1005 trnet-default                    act/unsup
```

The example begins with the **show vlan brief** command, confirming the default settings of five nondeletable VLANs, with all interfaces assigned to VLAN 1. In particular, note that this 2960 switch has 24 Fast Ethernet ports (Fa0/1–Fa0/24) and two Gigabit Ethernet ports (Gi0/1 and Gi0/2), all of which are listed as being in VLAN 1.

Next, the example shows the process of creating VLAN 2 and assigning interfaces Fa0/13 and Fa0/14 to VLAN 2. Note in particular that the example uses the **interface range** command, which causes the **switchport access vlan 2** interface subcommand to be applied to both interfaces in the range, as confirmed in the **show running-config** command output at the end of the example.

After the configuration has been added, to list the new VLAN, the example repeats the **show vlan brief** command. Note that this command lists VLAN 2, name Freds-vlan, and the interfaces assigned to that VLAN (Fa0/13 and Fa0/14).

> **NOTE** Example 1-1 uses default VTP configuration. However, if the switch had been configured for VTP transparent mode, the **vlan 2** and **name Freds-vlan** configuration commands would have also been seen in the output of the **show running-config** command. Because this switch is in VTP server mode (default), the switch stores these two commands only in the vlan.dat file.

A switch might not use the VLAN assigned by the **switchport access vlan** *vlan-id* command in some cases, depending on the operational mode of an interface. A Cisco switch's operational mode relates to whether the interface is currently using a trunking protocol. An interface that is currently using trunking is called a *trunk interface*, and all other interfaces are called *access interfaces*. So, engineers use phrases like "Fa0/12 is a trunk port" or "Fa0/13 is an access interface," referring to whether the design intends to use a particular interface to trunk (trunk mode) or to connect to just one VLAN (access mode).

The optional interface subcommand **switchport mode access** tells the switch to only allow the interface to be an access interface, which means that the interface will not use trunking and it will use the assigned access VLAN. If you omit the optional **switchport mode access** interface subcommand, the interface could negotiate to use trunking, becoming a trunk interface and ignoring the configured access VLAN.

VLAN Configuration Example 2: Shorter VLAN Configuration

Example 1-1 shows several of the optional configuration commands, with a side effect of being a bit longer than is required. Example 1-2 shows a much briefer alternative configuration, picking up the story where Example 1-1 ended, showing the addition of VLAN 3 (as seen in Figure 1-8). Note that SW1 does not know about VLAN 3 at the beginning of this example.

Example 1-2 *Shorter VLAN Configuration Example (VLAN 3)*

```
SW1#configure terminal
Enter configuration commands, one per line.  End with CNTL/Z.
SW1(config)#interface range Fastethernet 0/15 - 16
SW1(config-if-range)#switchport access vlan 3
% Access VLAN does not exist. Creating vlan 3
SW1(config-if-range)#^Z
SW1#show vlan brief

VLAN Name                             Status    Ports
---- -------------------------------- --------- -------------------------------
1    default                          active    Fa0/1, Fa0/2, Fa0/3, Fa0/4
                                                Fa0/5, Fa0/6, Fa0/7, Fa0/8
                                                Fa0/9, Fa0/10, Fa0/11, Fa0/12
                                                Fa0/17, Fa0/18, Fa0/19, Fa0/20
                                                Fa0/21, Fa0/22, Fa0/23, Fa0/24
                                                Gi0/1, Gi0/2
2    Freds-vlan                       active    Fa0/13, Fa0/14
3    VLAN0003                         active    Fa0/15, Fa0/16
1002 fddi-default                     act/unsup
1003 token-ring-default               act/unsup
1004 fddinet-default                  act/unsup
1005 trnet-default                    act/unsup
SW1#
```

Example 1-2 shows how a switch can dynamically create a VLAN—the equivalent of the **vlan** *vlan-id* global config command—when the **switchport access vlan** interface subcommand refers to a currently unconfigured VLAN. This example begins with SW1 not knowing about VLAN 3. When the **switchport access vlan 3** interface subcommand was used, the switch realized that VLAN 3 did not exist, and as noted in the shaded message in the example, the switch created VLAN 3, using a default name (VLAN0003). No other steps are required to create the VLAN. At the end of the process, VLAN 3 exists in the switch, and interfaces Fa0/15 and Fa0/16 are in VLAN 3, as noted in the shaded part of the **show vlan brief** command output.

As a reminder, note that some of the configuration shown in Examples 1-1 and 1-2 ends up only in the vlan.dat file in flash memory, and some ends up only in the running-config file. In particular, the interface subcommands are in the running-config file, so a **copy running-config startup-config** command would be needed to save the configuration. However, the definitions of new VLANs 2 and 3 have already been automatically saved in the vlan.dat file in flash. Table 1-7, later in this chapter, lists a reference of the various configuration commands, where they are stored, and how to confirm the configuration settings.

VLAN Trunking Configuration

Trunking configuration on Cisco switches involves two important configuration choices, as follows:

- The type of trunking: IEEE 802.1Q, ISL, or negotiate which one to use

- The *administrative mode*: Whether to trunk, not trunk, or negotiate

Cisco switches can either negotiate or configure the type of trunking to use (ISL or 802.1Q). By default, Cisco switches negotiate the type of trunking with the switch on the other end of the trunk, using the Dynamic Trunk Protocol (DTP). When negotiating, if both switches support both ISL and 802.1Q, they choose ISL. If one switch is willing to use either type, and the other switch is only willing to use one type of trunking, the two switches agree to use that one type of trunking supported by both switches. The type of trunking preferred on an interface, for switches that support both types, is configured using the **switchport trunk encapsulation** {**dot1q** | **isl** | **negotiate**} interface subcommand. (Many of the most recently developed Cisco switches, including 2960s, only support the IEEE-standard 802.1Q trunking today, so these switches simply default to a setting of **switchport trunk encapsulation dot1q**.)

The administrative mode refers to the configuration setting for whether trunking should be used on an interface. The term *administrative* refers to what is configured, whereas an interface's *operational* mode refers to what is currently happening on the interface. Cisco switches use an interface's *administrative mode*, as configured with the **switchport mode** interface subcommand, to determine whether to use trunking. Table 1-4 lists the options of the **switchport mode** command.

Key Topic

Table 1-4 *Trunking Administrative Mode Options with the **switchport mode** Command*

Command Option	Description
access	Prevents the use of trunking, making the port always act as an access (nontrunk) port
trunk	Always uses trunking
dynamic desirable	Initiates negotiation messages and responds to negotiation messages to dynamically choose whether to start using trunking, and defines the trunking encapsulation
dynamic auto	Passively waits to receive trunk negotiation messages, at which point the switch will respond and negotiate whether to use trunking, and if so, the type of trunking

For example, consider the two switches shown in Figure 1-9. This figure shows an expansion of the network of Figure 1-8, with a trunk to a new switch (SW2) and with parts of VLANs 1 and 3 on ports attached to SW2. The two switches use a Gigabit Ethernet link for the trunk. In this case, the trunk does not dynamically form by default, because both (2960) switches default to an administrative mode of *dynamic auto*, meaning that neither switch initiates the trunk negotiation process. By changing one switch to use *dynamic desirable* mode, which does initiate the negotiation, the switches negotiate to use trunking, specifically 802.1Q because the 2960s only support 802.1Q.

Figure 1-9 *Network with Two Switches and Three VLANs*

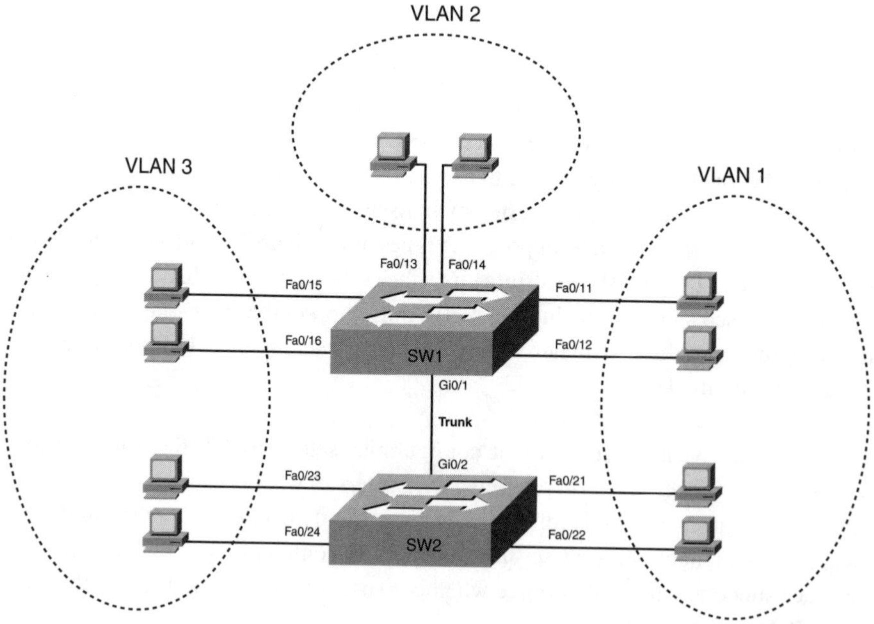

Example 1-3 begins by showing the two switches with the default configuration so that the two switches do not trunk. The example then shows the configuration of SW1 so that the two switches negotiate and use 802.1Q trunking.

Example 1-3 *Trunking Configuration and **show** Commands on 2960 Switches*

```
SW1#show interfaces gigabit 0/1 switchport
Name: Gi0/1
Switchport: Enabled
Administrative Mode: dynamic auto
Operational Mode: static access
Administrative Trunking Encapsulation: dot1q
Operational Trunking Encapsulation: native
Negotiation of Trunking: On
Access Mode VLAN: 1 (default)
Trunking Native Mode VLAN: 1 (default)
Administrative Native VLAN tagging: enabled
Voice VLAN: none
Access Mode VLAN: 1 (default)
Trunking Native Mode VLAN: 1 (default)
Administrative Native VLAN tagging: enabled
Voice VLAN: none
Administrative private-vlan host-association: none
Administrative private-vlan mapping: none
Administrative private-vlan trunk native VLAN: none
Administrative private-vlan trunk Native VLAN tagging: enabled
Administrative private-vlan trunk encapsulation: dot1q
Administrative private-vlan trunk normal VLANs: none
Administrative private-vlan trunk private VLANs: none
Operational private-vlan: none
Trunking VLANs Enabled: ALL
Pruning VLANs Enabled: 2-1001
Capture Mode Disabled
Capture VLANs Allowed: ALL

Protected: false
Unknown unicast blocked: disabled
Unknown multicast blocked: disabled
Appliance trust: none
! Note that the next command results in a single empty line of output.
SW1#show interfaces trunk

SW1#
! Next, the administrative mode is set to dynamic desirable.
SW1#configure terminal
Enter configuration commands, one per line.  End with CNTL/Z.
SW1(config)#interface gigabit 0/1
SW1(config-if)#switchport mode dynamic desirable
```

continues

Example 1-3 *Trunking Configuration and **show** Commands on 2960 Switches (Continued)*

```
SW1(config-if)#^Z
SW1#
01:43:46: %LINEPROTO-5-UPDOWN: Line protocol on Interface GigabitEthernet0/1, changed
state to down
SW1#
01:43:49: %LINEPROTO-5-UPDOWN: Line protocol on Interface GigabitEthernet0/1, changed
state to up
SW1#show interfaces gigabit 0/1 switchport
Name: Gi0/1
Switchport: Enabled
Administrative Mode: dynamic desirable
Operational Mode: trunk
Administrative Trunking Encapsulation: dot1q
Operational Trunking Encapsulation: dot1q
Negotiation of Trunking: On
Access Mode VLAN: 1 (default)
Trunking Native Mode VLAN: 1 (default)
! lines omitted for brevity
! The next command formerly listed a single empty line of output; now it lists
! information about the 1 operational trunk.
SW1#show interfaces trunk

Port        Mode        Encapsulation  Status      Native vlan
Gi0/1       desirable   802.1q         trunking    1


Port        Vlans allowed on trunk
Gi0/1       1-4094


Port        Vlans allowed and active in management domain
Gi0/1       1-3


Port        Vlans in spanning tree forwarding state and not pruned
Gi0/1       1-3
```

First, focus on important items from the output of the **show interfaces switchport** command at the beginning of Example 1-3. The output lists the default administrative mode setting of dynamic auto. Because SW2 also defaults to dynamic auto, the command lists SW1's operational status as access, meaning that it is not trunking. The third shaded line points out the only supported type of trunking (802.1Q) on this 2960 switch. (On a switch that supports both ISL and 802.1Q, this value would by default list "negotiate," to mean that the type or encapsulation is negotiated.) Finally, the operational trunking type is listed as "native," which is a subtle way to say that the switch does not add any trunking header to forwarded frames on this port, treating frames as if they are in an 802.1Q native VLAN.

To enable trunking, the two switches' administrative modes must be set to a combination of values that result in trunking. By changing SW1 to use dynamic desirable mode, as shown next in Example 1-3, SW1 will now initiate the negotiations, and the two switches will use trunking. Of particular interest is the fact that the switch brings the interface to a down state, and then back up again, as a result of the change to the administrative mode of the interface.

To verify that trunking is working now, the end of Example 1-3 lists the **show interfaces switchport** command. Note that the command still lists the administrative settings, which denote the configured values, along with the operational settings, which list what the switch is currently doing. In this case, SW1 now claims to be in an operational mode of trunk, with an operational trunking encapsulation of dot1Q.

For the ICND2 and CCNA exams, you should be ready to interpret the output of the **show interfaces switchport** command, realize the administrative mode implied by the output, and know whether the link should operationally trunk based on those settings. Table 1-5 lists the combinations of the trunking administrative modes and the expected operational mode (trunk or access) resulting from the configured settings. The table lists the administrative mode used on one end of the link on the left, and the administrative mode on the switch on the other end of the link across the top of the table.

Table 1-5 *Expected Trunking Operational Mode Based on the Configured Administrative Modes*

Key Topic

Administrative Mode	Access	Dynamic Auto	Trunk	Dynamic Desirable
access	Access	Access	Access	Access
dynamic auto	Access	Access	Trunk	Trunk
trunk	Access	Trunk	Trunk	Trunk
dynamic desirable	Access	Trunk	Trunk	Trunk

Controlling Which VLANs Can Be Supported on a Trunk

The *allowed VLAN list* feature provides a mechanism for engineers to administratively disable a VLAN from a trunk. By default, switches include all possible VLANs (1–4094) in each trunk's allowed VLAN list. However, the engineer can then limit the VLANs allowed on the trunk by using the following interface subcommand:

```
switchport trunk allowed vlan {add | all | except | remove} vlan-list
```

This command provides a way to easily add and remove VLANs from the list. For example, the **add** option permits the switch to add VLANs to the existing allowed VLAN list, and the **remove** option permits the switch to remove VLANs from the existing list. The **all** option means all VLANs, so you can use it to reset the switch to its original default setting (permitting VLANs 1–4094 on the trunk). The **except** option is rather tricky: It adds all

VLANs to the list that are not part of the command. For example, the **switchport trunk allowed vlan except 100-200** interface subcommand adds VLANs 1 through 99 and 201 through 4094 to the existing allowed VLAN list on that trunk.

In addition to the allowed VLAN list, a switch has three other reasons to prevent a particular VLAN's traffic from crossing a trunk. All four reasons are summarized in the following list:

- A VLAN has been removed from the trunk's *allowed VLAN* list.

- A VLAN does not exist, or is not active, in the switch's VLAN database (as seen with the **show vlan** command).

- A VLAN has been automatically pruned by VTP.

- A VLAN's STP instance has placed the trunk interface into a state other than a Forwarding State.

Of these additional three reasons, the second reason needs a little more explanation. (The third reason, VTP pruning, has already been covered in this chapter, and the fourth reason, STP, is covered thoroughly in Chapter 2.) If a switch does not know that a VLAN exists, as evidenced by the VLAN's absence from the output of the **show vlan** command, the switch will not forward frames in that VLAN over any interface. Additionally, a VLAN can be administratively shut down on any switch by using the **shutdown vlan** *vlan-id* global configuration command, which also causes the switch to no longer forward frames in that VLAN, even over trunks. So, switches do not forward frames in a nonexistent or shutdown VLAN over any of the switch's trunks.

The book lists the four reasons for limiting VLANs on a trunk in the same order in which IOS describes these reasons in the output of the **show interfaces trunk** command. This command includes a progression of three lists of the VLANs supported over a trunk. These three lists are as follows:

- VLANs in the allowed VLAN list on the trunk

- VLANs in the previous group that are also configured and active (not shut down) on the switch

- VLANs in the previous group that are also not pruned and are in an STP Forwarding State

To get an idea of these three lists inside the output of the **show interfaces trunk** command, Example 1-4 shows how VLANs might be disallowed on a trunk for various reasons. The command output is taken from SW1 in Figure 1-9, after the completion of the configuration as shown in Examples 1-1, 1-2, and 1-3. In other words, VLANS 1 through 3 exist, and trunking is operational. Then, during the example, the following items are configured on SW1:

Step 1   VLAN 4 is added.

Step 2   VLAN 2 is shut down.

Step 3   VLAN 3 is removed from the trunk's allowed VLAN list.

Example 1-4   *Allowed VLAN List and the List of Active VLANs*

```
! The three lists of VLANs in the next command list allowed VLANs (1-4094),
! Allowed and active VLANs (1-3), and allowed/active/not pruned/STP forwarding
! VLANs (1-3)
SW1#show interfaces trunk

Port        Mode         Encapsulation  Status       Native vlan
Gi0/1       desirable    802.1q         trunking     1

Port        Vlans allowed on trunk
Gi0/1       1-4094

Port        Vlans allowed and active in management domain
Gi0/1       1-3

Port        Vlans in spanning tree forwarding state and not pruned
Gi0/1       1-3
! Next, the switch is configured with new VLAN 4; VLAN 2 is shutdown;
! and VLAN 3 is removed from the allowed VLAN list on the trunk.
SW1#configure terminal
Enter configuration commands, one per line.  End with CNTL/Z.
SW1(config)#vlan 4
SW1(config-vlan)#vlan 2
SW1(config-vlan)#shutdown
SW1(config-vlan)#interface gi0/1
SW1(config-if)#switchport trunk allowed vlan remove 3
SW1(config-if)#^Z
! The three lists of VLANs in the next command list allowed VLANs (1-2, 4-4094),
! allowed and active VLANs (1,4), and allowed/active/not pruned/STP forwarding
! VLANs (1,4)
SW1#show interfaces trunk

Port        Mode         Encapsulation  Status       Native vlan
Gi0/1       desirable    802.1q         trunking     1

! VLAN 3 is omitted next, because it was removed from the allowed VLAN list.
Port        Vlans allowed on trunk
```

continues

Example 1-4 *Allowed VLAN List and the List of Active VLANs (Continued)*

```
Gi0/1       1-2,4-4094

! VLAN 2 is omitted below because it is shutdown. VLANs 5-4094 are omitted below
! because SW1 does not have them configured.
Port        Vlans allowed and active in management domain
Gi0/1       1,4

Port        Vlans in spanning tree forwarding state and not pruned
Gi0/1       1,4
```

Trunking to Cisco IP Phones

Cisco IP phones use Ethernet to connect to the IP network for the purpose of sending Voice over IP (VoIP) packets. Cisco IP phones can send VoIP packets to other IP phones to support voice calls, as well as send VoIP packets to voice gateways, which in turn connect to the existing traditional telephone network, supporting the ability to call most any phone in the world.

Cisco anticipated that each desk in an enterprise might have both a Cisco IP phone and a PC on it. To reduce cabling clutter, Cisco includes a small LAN switch in the bottom of each Cisco IP phone. The small switch allows one cable to run from the wiring closet to the desk and connect to the IP phone, and then the PC can connect to the switch by connecting a short Ethernet (straight-through) cable from the PC to the bottom of the IP phone. Figure 1-10 shows the cabling as well as a few more details.

Figure 1-10 *Typical Connection of a Cisco IP Phone and PC to a Cisco Switch*

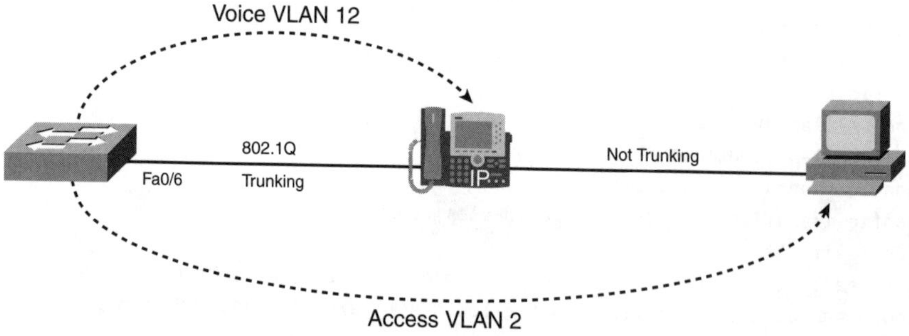

Cisco IP telephony design guidelines suggest that the link between the phone and switch should use 802.1Q trunking, and that the phone and PC should be in different VLANs (and therefore in different subnets). By placing the phones in one VLAN, and the PCs connected to the phones in a different VLAN, engineers can more easily manage the IP address space, more easily apply quality of service (QoS) mechanisms to the VoIP packets, and provide better security by separating the data and voice traffic.

Cisco calls the VLAN used for the phone's traffic the voice VLAN and the VLAN used for data the data or access VLAN. For the switch to forward traffic correctly, Cisco switches need to know the VLAN ID of both the voice VLAN and the data VLAN. The data (or access) VLAN is configured just as seen in the last few examples, using the **switchport access vlan** *vlan-id* command. The voice vlan is configured with the **switchport voice vlan** *vlan-id* interface subcommand. For example, to match Figure 1-10, interface Fa0/6 would need both the **switchport access vlan 2** interface subcommand and the **switchport voice vlan 12** subcommand.

Table 1-6 summarizes the key points about the voice VLAN.

Table 1-6 *Voice and Data VLAN Configuration*

Device	Name of the VLAN	Configured With This Command
Phone	Voice or auxiliary VLAN	**switchport voice vlan** *vlan-id*
PC	Data or access VLAN	**switchport access vlan** *vlan-id*

Securing VLANs and Trunking

Switches are exposed to several types of security vulnerabilities over both used ports and unused ports. For example, an attacker could connect a computer to a wall plug cabled to a switch port and cause problems on the VLAN assigned to that port. Additionally, the attacker could negotiate trunking and cause many other types of problems, some related to VTP.

Cisco makes some recommendations for how to protect unused switch ports. Instead of using default settings, Cisco recommends configuring these interfaces as follows:

- Administratively disable the unused interface, using the **shutdown** interface subcommand.

- Prevent trunking from being negotiated when the port is enabled by using the **switchport nonegotiate** interface subcommand to disable negotiation, or the **switchport mode access** interface subcommand to statically configure the interface as an access interface.

- Assign the port to an unused VLAN, sometimes called a *parking lot VLAN*, using the **switchport access vlan** *number* interface subcommand.

Frankly, if you just shut down the interface, the security exposure goes away, but the other two tasks prevent any immediate problems if some other engineer enables the interface by configuring a **no shutdown** command.

Besides these recommendations on unused ports, Cisco recommends that the negotiation of trunking be disabled on all in-use access interfaces, with all trunks being manually configured to trunk. The exposure is that an attacker could disconnect a legitimate user's computer from the RJ-45 port, connect the attacker's PC, and try to negotiate trunking. By configuring all in-use interfaces that should not be trunking with the **switchport nonnegotiate** interface subcommand, these interfaces will not dynamically decide to trunk, reducing the exposure to trunking-related problems. For any interfaces that need to trunk, Cisco recommends manually configuring trunking.

VTP Configuration and Verification

VTP configuration requires only a few simple steps, but VTP has the power to cause significant problems, either by accidental poor configuration choices or by malicious attacks. The following sections first examine the overall configuration, followed by some comments about potential problems created by the VTP process. These sections then end with a discussion of how to troubleshoot problems related to VTP.

Using VTP: Configuring Servers and Clients

Before configuring VTP, several VTP settings must be chosen. In particular, assuming that the engineer wants to make use of VTP, the engineer needs to decide which switches will be in the same VTP domain, meaning that these switches will learn VLAN configuration information from each other. The VTP domain name must be chosen, along with an optional but recommended VTP password. (Both values are case sensitive.) The engineer must also choose which switches will be servers (usually at least two for redundancy), and which will be clients.

After the planning steps are completed, the following steps can be used to configure VTP:

Step 1   Configure the VTP mode using the **vtp mode** {**server** | **client**} global configuration command.

Step 2   Configure the VTP (case-sensitive) domain name using the **vtp domain** *domain-name* global configuration command.

Step 3   (Optional) On both clients and servers, configure the same case-sensitive password using the **vtp password** *password-value* global configuration command.

Step 4   (Optional) Configure VTP pruning on the VTP servers using the **vtp pruning** global configuration command.

Step 5   (Optional) Enable VTP version 2 with the **vtp version 2** global configuration command.

Step 6   Bring up trunks between the switches.

Example 1-5 shows a sample configuration, along with a **show vtp status** command, for the two switches in Figure 1-11. The figure points out the configuration settings on the two switches before Example 1-5 shows VTP configuration being added. In particular, note that both switches use default VTP configuration settings.

Figure 1-11   *Switch Configuration Before Example 1-5*

SW1
Gi0/1

VLANs:	1, 2, 3,1002-1005
VTP Mode:	Server
VTP Domain:	<null>
VTP Password:	<null>
VTP Revision:	5
IP Address:	192.168.1.105

Trunk

Gi0/2
SW2

VLANs:	1,1002-1005
VTP Mode:	Server
VTP Domain:	<null>
VTP Password:	<null>
Revision:	1
IP Address:	192.168.1.106

Example 1-5 shows the following configuration on both SW1 and SW2, and the results:

- **SW1:** Configured as a server, with VTP domain name Freds-domain, VTP password Freds-password, and VTP pruning enabled

- **SW2:** Configured as a client, with VTP domain name Freds-domain and VTP password Freds-password

Example 1-5   *Basic VTP Client and Server Configuration*

```
! IOS generates at least one informational message after each VTP command listed
! below. The comments added by the author begin with an exclamation point.
SW1#configure terminal
Enter configuration commands, one per line.  End with CNTL/Z.
SW1(config)#vtp mode server
Setting device to VTP SERVER mode
SW1(config)#vtp domain Freds-domain
Changing VTP domain name from NULL to Freds-domain
SW1(config)#vtp password Freds-password
Setting device VLAN database password to Freds-password
SW1(config)#vtp pruning
Pruning switched on
```

continues

Example 1-5 *Basic VTP Client and Server Configuration (Continued)*

```
SW1(config)#^Z
! Switching to SW2 now
SW2#configure terminal
Enter configuration commands, one per line.  End with CNTL/Z.
SW2(config)#vtp mode client
Setting device to VTP CLIENT mode.
SW2(config)#vtp domain Freds-domain
Domain name already set to Freds-domain.
SW2(config)#vtp password Freds-password
Setting device VLAN database password to Freds-password
SW2(config)#^Z
! The output below shows configuration revision number 5, with 7 existing VLANs
! (1 through 3, 1002 through 1005), as learned from SW1
SW2#show vtp status
VTP Version                     : 2
Configuration Revision          : 5
Maximum VLANs supported locally : 255
Number of existing VLANs        : 7
VTP Operating Mode              : Client
VTP Domain Name                 : Freds-domain
VTP Pruning Mode                : Enabled
VTP V2 Mode                     : Disabled
VTP Traps Generation            : Disabled
MD5 digest                      : 0x22 0x07 0xF2 0x3A 0xF1 0x28 0xA0 0x5D
Configuration last modified by 192.168.1.105 at 3-1-93 00:28:35
! The next command lists the known VLANs, including VLANs 2 and 3, learned
! from SW1
SW2#show vlan brief


VLAN Name                             Status    Ports
---- -------------------------------- --------- -------------------------------
1    default                          active    Fa0/1, Fa0/2, Fa0/3, Fa0/4
                                                Fa0/5, Fa0/6, Fa0/7, Fa0/8
                                                Fa0/9, Fa0/10, Fa0/11, Fa0/12
                                                Fa0/13, Fa0/14, Fa0/15, Fa0/16
                                                Fa0/17, Fa0/18, Fa0/19, Fa0/20
                                                Fa0/21, Fa0/22, Fa0/23, Fa0/24
                                                Gi0/1
2    Freds-vlan                       active
3    VLAN0003                         active
1002 fddi-default                     act/unsup
1003 token-ring-default               act/unsup
1004 fddinet-default                  act/unsup
1005 trnet-default                    act/unsup
! Switching to SW1 now
! Back on SW1, the output below confirms the same revision number as SW2, meaning
! that the two switches have synchronized their VLAN databases.
```

Example 1-5 *Basic VTP Client and Server Configuration (Continued)*

```
SW1#show vtp status
VTP Version                    : 2
Configuration Revision         : 5
Maximum VLANs supported locally : 255
Number of existing VLANs       : 7
VTP Operating Mode             : Server
VTP Domain Name                : Freds-domain
VTP Pruning Mode               : Enabled
VTP V2 Mode                    : Disabled
VTP Traps Generation           : Disabled
MD5 digest                     : 0x22 0x07 0xF2 0x3A 0xF1 0x28 0xA0 0x5D
Configuration last modified by 192.168.1.105 at 3-1-93 00:28:35
Local updater ID is 192.168.1.105 on interface Vl1 (lowest numbered VLAN interface found)
SW1#show vtp password
VTP Password: Freds-password
```

The example is relatively long, but the configuration is straightforward. Both switches were configured with the VTP mode (server and client), the same domain name, and the same password, with trunking already having been configured. The configuration resulted in SW2 (client) synchronizing its VLAN database to match SW1 (server).

Cisco IOS switches in VTP server or client mode store the **vtp** configuration commands, and some other configuration commands, in the vlan.dat file in flash, and the switches do not store the configuration commands in the running-config file. Instead, to verify these configuration commands and their settings, the **show vtp status** and **show vlan** commands are used. For reference, Table 1-7 lists the VLAN-related configuration commands, the location in which a VTP server or client stores the commands, and how to view the settings for the commands.

Table 1-7 *Where VTP Clients and Servers Store VLAN-Related Configuration*

Configuration Commands	Where Stored	How to View
vtp domain	vlan.dat	**show vtp status**
vtp mode	vlan.dat	**show vtp status**
vtp password	vlan.dat	**show vtp password**
vtp pruning	vlan.dat	**show vtp status**
vlan *vlan-id*	vlan.dat	**show vlan [brief]**
name *vlan-name*	vlan.dat	**show vlan [brief]**
switchport access vlan *vlan-id*	running-config	**show running-config, show interfaces switchport**
switchport voice vlan *vlan-id*	running-config	**show running-config, show interfaces switchport**

Key
Topic

Any analysis of VTP and VLANs on Cisco switches depends on two important commands: the **show vtp status** and **show vlan** commands. First, note that when the domain is synchronized, the **show vtp status** command on all switches should have the same configuration revision number. Additionally, the **show vlan** command should list the same VLANs and VLAN names. For example, both SW1 and SW2 end Example 1-5 with a revision number of 5, and both know about seven VLANs: 1–3 and 1002–1005. Both instances of the **show vtp status** command in Example 1-5 list the IP address of the last switch to modify the VLAN database—namely SW1, 192.168.1.105—so it is easier to find which switch last changed the VLAN configuration. Only on VTP servers, the **show vtp status** command ends with a line that lists that switch's IP address that identifies itself when advertising VTP updates, making it easier to confirm which switch last changed the VLAN configuration.

Note that the VTP password can only be displayed with the **show vtp password** command. The **show vtp status** command displays an MD5 digest of the password.

> **NOTE**   Cisco switches send VTP messages and Cisco Discovery Protocol (CDP) messages on trunks using VLAN 1.

Caveats When Moving Away from Default VTP Configuration

The default behavior of VTP introduces the possibility of problems when first configuring VTP. To see why, consider the following five points about VTP:

- The default VTP configuration on Cisco switches is VTP server mode with a null domain name.

- With all default settings, a switch does not send VTP updates, even over trunks, but the switch can be configured with VLANs because it is in server mode.

- After configuring a domain name, that switch immediately starts sending VTP updates over all its trunks.

- If a switch that still has a (default) null domain name receives a VTP update—which by definition lists a domain name—and no password was used by the sending switch, the receiving switch starts using that VTP domain name.

- When the previous step occurs, the switch with the higher VLAN database revision number causes the switch with the lower revision number to overwrite its VLAN database.

Example 1-5 progresses through these same five facts. Example 1-5 begins with trunking enabled between the two switches, but with default VTP settings (items 1 and 2 from the list preceding this paragraph). As soon as SW1 configures its VTP domain name, SW1 sends VTP messages over the trunk to SW2 (item 3). SW2 reacts by starting to use the VTP domain name listed in the received VTP update (Freds-domain, in this case). By the time the **vtp domain Freds-domain** command was issued on SW2 in Example 1-5, SW2 was already using the dynamically learned domain name Freds-domain, so Cisco IOS on SW2 issued the response "Domain name already set to Freds-domain" (item 4). Finally, SW2, with a lower VTP revision number, synchronized its VLAN database to match SW1 (item 5).

The process worked exactly as intended in Example 1-5. However, this same process allows an engineer to innocently configure a switch's VTP domain name and completely crash a switched LAN. For example, imagine that SW2 had configured VLAN 4 and assigned several interfaces to VLAN 4, but SW1 does not have a definition for VLAN 4. Following this same process, when SW2 synchronizes its VLAN database to match SW1, SW2 overwrites the old database, losing the definition of VLAN 4. At that point, SW2 can no longer forward frames in VLAN 4, and all the users of VLAN 4 might start calling the help desk.

This same process could be used to perform a denial of service (DoS) attack using VTP. With only default VTP settings, any attacker that can manage to bring up a trunk between an attacking switch and the existing legitimate switch can cause the existing switches to synchronize to the attacking switch's VLAN database, which may well have no VLANs configured. So, for real networks, if you do not intend to use VTP when installing a switch, it is worth the effort to simply configure it to be a VTP transparent mode switch, as is covered in the next section. By doing so, the configuration of a VTP domain name on that new switch will not impact the existing switches, and the configuration of a domain name on another switch will not impact this new switch.

NOTE The section titled "Troubleshooting VTP" explains how to recognize when VTP might have caused problems like those mentioned in this section.

Avoiding VTP: Configuring Transparent Mode

To avoid using VTP, you need to configure VTP transparent mode. In transparent mode, a switch never updates its VLAN database based on a received VTP message, and never causes other switches to update their databases based on the transparent mode switch's VLAN database. The only VTP action performed by the switch is to forward VTP messages received on one trunk out all the other trunks, which allows other VTP clients and servers to work correctly.

Configuring VTP transparent mode is simple: Just issue the **vtp mode transparent** command in global configuration mode. You do not need a domain name or a password.

Troubleshooting VTP

VTP can have an enormous impact on a campus LAN built using Cisco switches, both a negative and positive impact. The following sections examine three aspects of VTP troubleshooting. First, the text suggests a process by which to troubleshoot VTP when VTP does not appear to be distributing VLAN configuration information (adds/deletions/changes). Following that, the text examines a common class of problems that occur when a trunk comes up, possibly triggering the neighboring switches to send VTP updates and overwrite one of the switch's VLAN database. This topic ends with suggested best practices for preventing VTP problems.

Determining Why VTP Is Not Currently Working

The first step in troubleshooting VTP should be to determine whether a problem exists in the first place. For switches that should be using VTP, in the same domain, a problem can first be identified when any two neighboring switches have different VLAN databases. In other words, they know about different VLAN IDs, with different names, and with a different configuration revision number. After identifying two neighboring switches whose VLAN databases do not match, the next step is to check the configuration and the operational trunking mode (not the administrative mode), and to correct any problems. The following list details the specific steps:

Key Topic

Step 1   Confirm the switch names, topology (including which interfaces connect which switches), and switch VTP modes.

Step 2   Identify sets of two neighboring switches that should be either VTP clients or servers whose VLAN databases differ with the **show vlan** command.

Step 3   On each pair of two neighboring switches whose databases differ, verify the following:

a.   At least one operational trunk should exist between the two switches (use the **show interfaces trunk**, **show interfaces switchport**, or **show cdp neighbors** command).

b.   The switches must have the same (case-sensitive) VTP domain name (**show vtp status**).

c.   If configured, the switches must have the same (case-sensitive) VTP password (**show vtp password**).

d. While VTP pruning should be enabled or disabled on all servers in the same domain, having two servers configured with opposite pruning settings does not prevent the synchronization process.

Step 4 For each pair of switches identified in Step 3, solve the problem by either troubleshooting the trunking problem or reconfiguring a switch to correctly match the domain name or password.

> **NOTE**   For real campus LANs, besides the items in this list, also consider the intended VTP design as well.

While the process does spell out several steps, it mainly shows how to attack the problem with knowledge covered earlier in this chapter. The process basically states that if the VLAN databases differ, and the switches should be either VTP clients or servers, that a VTP problem exists—and the root cause is usually some VTP configuration problem. However, on the exam, you might be forced to figure out the answer based on **show** command output. For example, consider a problem in which three switches (SW1, SW2, and SW3) all connect to each other. An exam question might require that you find any VTP problems in the network, based on the output of **show** commands like those in Example 1-6.

> **NOTE**   It would be a good exercise to read the example and apply the troubleshooting steps listed at the beginning of this section before reading any of the explanations that follow the example.

Example 1-6 *VTP Troubleshooting Example*

```
SW1#show cdp neighbors
Capability Codes: R - Router, T - Trans Bridge, B - Source Route Bridge
                  S - Switch, H - Host, I - IGMP, r - Repeater, P - Phone

Device ID           Local Intrfce     Holdtme   Capability    Platform   Port ID
SW2                 Gig 0/1           163         S I         WS-C2960-2Gig 0/2
SW3                 Gig 0/2           173         S I         WS-C3550-2Gig 0/1
SW1#show vlan brief

VLAN Name                         Status    Ports
---- ----------------------------- --------- -------------------------------
1    default                      active    Fa0/1, Fa0/2, Fa0/3, Fa0/4
                                            Fa0/5, Fa0/6, Fa0/7, Fa0/8
                                            Fa0/9, Fa0/10, Fa0/13, Fa0/14
                                            Fa0/15, Fa0/16, Fa0/17, Fa0/18
                                            Fa0/19, Fa0/20, Fa0/21, Fa0/22
                                            Fa0/23, Fa0/24, Gi0/2
```

continues

Example 1-6 *VTP Troubleshooting Example (Continued)*

```
3    VLAN0003                          active      Fa0/11
4    VLAN0004                          active
5    VLAN0005                          active
49   VLAN0049                          active
50   VLAN0050                          active
1002 fddi-default                      act/unsup
1003 trcrf-default                     act/unsup
1004 fddinet-default                   act/unsup
1005 trbrf-default                     act/unsup
SW1#show interfaces trunk


Port        Mode         Encapsulation  Status       Native vlan
Gi0/1       desirable    802.1q         trunking     1


Port        Vlans allowed on trunk
Gi0/1       1-4094


Port        Vlans allowed and active in management domain
Gi0/1       1,3-5,49-50


Port        Vlans in spanning tree forwarding state and not pruned
Gi0/1       3-5,49-50
SW1#show vtp status
VTP Version                    : 2
Configuration Revision         : 131
Maximum VLANs supported locally : 255
Number of existing VLANs       : 10
VTP Operating Mode             : Client
VTP Domain Name                : Larry
VTP Pruning Mode               : Disabled
VTP V2 Mode                    : Enabled
VTP Traps Generation           : Disabled
MD5 digest                     : 0x1D 0x27 0xA9 0xF9 0x46 0xDF 0x66 0xCF
Configuration last modified by 1.1.1.3 at 3-1-93 00:33:38
! SW2 next
SW2#show cdp neighbors
Capability Codes: R - Router, T - Trans Bridge, B - Source Route Bridge
                 S - Switch, H - Host, I - IGMP, r - Repeater, P - Phone


Device ID          Local Intrfce    Holdtme  Capability  Platform    Port ID
SW1                Gig 0/2          175         S I      WS-C2960-2Gig 0/1
SW3                Gig 0/1          155         S I      WS-C3550-2Gig 0/2
SW2#show vlan brief


VLAN Name                           Status     Ports
---- ------------------------------ ---------- ------------------------------
1    default                        active     Fa0/1, Fa0/2, Fa0/3, Fa0/4
```

Example 1-6 *VTP Troubleshooting Example (Continued)*

```
                                           Fa0/5, Fa0/6, Fa0/7, Fa0/8
                                           Fa0/9, Fa0/10, Fa0/11, Fa0/12
                                           Fa0/13, Fa0/14, Fa0/15, Fa0/16
                                           Fa0/17, Fa0/18, Fa0/19, Fa0/20
                                           Fa0/21, Fa0/22, Fa0/23, Fa0/24
3    VLAN0003                active
1002 fddi-default            act/unsup
1003 trcrf-default           act/unsup
1004 fddinet-default         act/unsup
1005 trbrf-default           act/unsup
SW2#show vtp status
VTP Version                   : 2
Configuration Revision        : 0
Maximum VLANs supported locally : 255
Number of existing VLANs      : 6
VTP Operating Mode            : Server
VTP Domain Name               : larry
VTP Pruning Mode              : Disabled
VTP V2 Mode                   : Enabled
VTP Traps Generation          : Disabled
MD5 digest                    : 0x8C 0x75 0xC5 0xDE 0xE9 0x7C 0x2D 0x8B
Configuration last modified by 1.1.1.2 at 0-0-00 00:00:00
Local updater ID is 1.1.1.2 on interface Vl1 (lowest numbered VLAN interface found)
! SW3 next
SW3#show vlan brief

VLAN Name                        Status    Ports
---- -------------------------------- --------- -------------------------------
1    default                     active    Fa0/1, Fa0/2, Fa0/3, Fa0/4
                                           Fa0/5, Fa0/6, Fa0/7, Fa0/8
                                           Fa0/9, Fa0/10, Fa0/11, Fa0/12
                                           Fa0/14, Fa0/15, Fa0/16, Fa0/17
                                           Fa0/18, Fa0/19, Fa0/20, Fa0/21
                                           Fa0/22, Fa0/23, Fa0/24, Gi0/1
3    VLAN0003                    active    Fa0/13
4    VLAN0004                    active
5    VLAN0005                    active
20   VLAN20                      active
1002 fddi-default                act/unsup
1003 trcrf-default               act/unsup
1004 fddinet-default             act/unsup
1005 trbrf-default               act/unsup
SW3#show interfaces trunk

Port       Mode        Encapsulation Status       Native vlan
Gi0/2      desirable   n-802.1q      trunking     1
```

continues

Example 1-6 *VTP Troubleshooting Example (Continued)*

```
Port        Vlans allowed on trunk
Gi0/2        1-4094


Port        Vlans allowed and active in management domain
Gi0/2        1,3-5,20


Port        Vlans in spanning tree forwarding state and not pruned
Gi0/2        1,3-5,20
SW3#show vtp status
VTP Version                   : 2
Configuration Revision        : 134
Maximum VLANs supported locally : 1005
Number of existing VLANs      : 9
VTP Operating Mode            : Server
VTP Domain Name               : Larry
VTP Pruning Mode              : Disabled
VTP V2 Mode                   : Enabled
VTP Traps Generation          : Disabled
MD5 digest                    : 0x76 0x1E 0x06 0x1E 0x1C 0x46 0x59 0x75
Configuration last modified by 1.1.1.3 at 3-1-93 01:07:29
Local updater ID is 1.1.1.3 on interface Vl1 (lowest numbered VLAN interface found)
```

For Step 1, the **show cdp neighbors** and **show interfaces trunk** commands provide enough information to confirm the topology as well as show which links are operating as trunks. The **show interfaces trunk** command lists only interfaces in an operationally trunking state. Alternately, the **show interfaces switchport** command lists the operational mode (trunk or access) as well. Figure 1-12 shows the network diagram. Note also that the link between SW1 and SW3 does not currently use trunking.

Figure 1-12 *Switched Network Topology in Example 1-6*

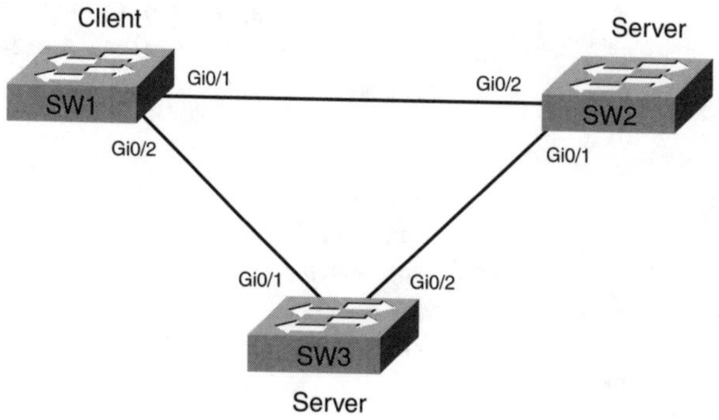

For Step 2, a quick review of the **show vlan brief** command output from each switch shows that all three switches have different VLAN databases. For example, all three switches know about VLAN 3, whereas SW1 is the only switch that knows about VLAN 50, and SW3 is the only switch that knows about VLAN 20.

Because all three pairs of neighboring switches have different VLAN databases, Step 3 of the troubleshooting process suggests that each pair be examined. Starting with SW1 and SW2, a quick look at the **show vtp status** command on both switches identifies the problem: SW1 uses the domain name Larry, whereas SW2 uses larry, and the names differ because of the different case of the first letter. Similarly, SW3 and SW2 have difficulties because of the mismatched VTP domain name. Because SW2 is the only switch with lowercase larry, a solution would be to reconfigure SW2 to use Larry as the domain name.

Continuing Step 3 for SW1 and SW3, the two switches have the same domain name (Step 3B), but a look at Step 3A shows that no trunk is connecting SW1 to SW3. CDP confirms that SW1's Gi0/2 interface connects to SW3, but the **show interfaces trunk** command on SW1 does not list the Gi0/2 interface. As a result, neither switch can send VTP messages to each other. The root cause of this problem is most likely an oversight in the configuration of the **switchport mode** interface subcommand.

While the example did not have any problems because of VTP password mismatches, it is important to know how to check the passwords. First, the password can be displayed on each switch with the **show vtp password** command. Additionally, the **show vtp status** command lists an MD5 hash derived from both the VTP domain name and VTP password. So, if two switches have the same case-sensitive domain name and password, the MD5 hash value listed in the **show vtp status** command output will be the same. However, if two switches list different MD5 hash values, you then need to examine the domain names. If the domain names are the same, the passwords must have been different because the MD5 hashes are different.

Before moving on to the next topic, here is a quick comment about VTP version and how it should not prevent switches from working. If you examine the **show vtp status** command output again in Example 1-6, note the headings VTP Version and V2 Mode Enabled. The first line lists the highest VTP version supported by that switch's software. The other line shows what the switch is currently using. If a switch has the VTP version 2 command configured, overriding the default of version 1, the switch will use **vtp version 2**—but only if the other switches in the domain also support version 2. So, a mismatch of the configured VTP version means that the switches work, but they would use VTP version 1, and the line reading "VTP V2 Mode" would list the word *disabled*, meaning that VTP version 1 is used.

Problems When Connecting New Switches and Bringing Up Trunks

VTP can be running just fine for months, and then one day, a rash of calls to the help desk describe cases in which large groups of users can no longer use the network. After further examination, it appears that most every VLAN in the campus has been deleted. The switches still have many interfaces with **switchport access vlan** commands that refer to the now-deleted VLANs. None of the devices on those now-deleted VLANs work, because Cisco switches do not forward frames for nonexistent VLANs.

This scenario can and does happen occasionally, mainly when a new switch is connected to an existing network. Whether this problem happens by accident or as a denial of service (DoS) attack, the root cause is that when a new VLAN trunk (ISL or 802.1Q) comes up between two switches, and the two switches are either VTP servers or clients, the switches send VTP updates to each other. If a switch receives a VTP advertisement that has the same domain name and was generated with the same VTP password, one or the other switch overwrites its VLAN database as part of the synchronization process. Specifically, the switch that had the lower revision number synchronizes its VLAN database to match the neighboring switch (which has the higher revision number). Summarizing the process more formally:

Step 1   Confirm that trunking will occur on the new link (refer to Table 1-5 for details).

Step 2   Confirm that the two switches use the same case-sensitive VTP domain name and password.

Step 3   If Steps 1 and 2 confirm that VTP will work, the switch with the lower revision number updates its VLAN database to match the other switch.

For example, Example 1-6 and Figure 1-12 show that the SW1-to-SW3 link is not trunking. If this link were to be configured to trunk, SW1 and SW3 would send VTP messages to each other, using the same VTP domain name and the same VTP password. So, one switch would update its VLAN database to match the other. Example 1-6 shows SW1 with revision number 131 and SW3 with revision number 134, so SW1 will overwrite its VLAN database to match SW3, thereby deleting VLANs 49 and 50. Example 1-7 picks up the story at the end of Example 1-6, showing the trunk between SW1 and SW3 coming up, allowing VTP synchronization, and resulting in changes to SW1's VLAN database.

Example 1-7   *VTP Troubleshooting Example*

```
SW1#configure terminal
Enter configuration commands, one per line.  End with CNTL/Z.
SW1(config)#interface gi0/2
SW1(config-if)#switchport mode dynamic desirable
SW1(config-if)#^Z
SW1#
01:43:46: %SYS-5-CONFIG_I: Configured from console by console
```

Example 1-7 *VTP Troubleshooting Example (Continued)*

```
01:43:46: %LINEPROTO-5-UPDOWN: Line protocol on Interface GigabitEthernet0/2, changed
state to down
SW1#01:43:49: %LINEPROTO-5-UPDOWN: Line protocol on Interface GigabitEthernet0/2,
changed state to up
SW1#show vlan brief

VLAN Name                             Status    Ports
---- -------------------------------- --------- -------------------------------
1    default                          active    Fa0/1, Fa0/2, Fa0/3, Fa0/4
                                                Fa0/5, Fa0/6, Fa0/7, Fa0/8
                                                Fa0/9, Fa0/10, Fa0/13, Fa0/14
                                                Fa0/15, Fa0/16, Fa0/17, Fa0/18
                                                Fa0/19, Fa0/20, Fa0/21, Fa0/22
                                                Fa0/23, Fa0/24, Gi0/1
3    VLAN0003                         active    Fa0/11
4    VLAN0004                         active
5    VLAN0005                         active
20   VLAN20                           active
1002 fddi-default                     act/unsup
1003 trcrf-default                    act/unsup
1004 fddinet-default                  act/unsup
1005 trbrf-default                    act/unsup
```

In real life, you have several ways to help reduce the chance of such problems when installing a new switch to an existing VTP domain. In particular, before connecting a new switch to an existing VTP domain, reset the new switch's VTP revision number to 0 by one of the following methods:

■ Configure the new switch for VTP transparent mode and then back to VTP client or server mode.

■ Erase the new switch's vlan.dat file in flash and reload the switch. This file contains the switch's VLAN database, including the revision number.

Avoiding VTP Problems Through Best Practices

Besides the suggestion of resetting the VLAN database revision number before installing a new switch, a couple of other good VTP conventions, called best practices, can help avoid some of the pitfalls of VTP. These are as follows:

■ If you do not intend to use VTP, configure each switch to use transparent mode.

■ If using VTP server or client mode, always use a VTP password.

Key
Topic

- Disable trunking with the **switchport mode access** and **switchport nonegotiate** commands on all interfaces except known trunks, preventing VTP attacks by preventing the dynamic establishment of trunks.

By preventing the negotiation of trunking to most ports, the attacker can never see a VTP update from one of your switches. With a VTP password set, even if the attacker manages to get trunking working to an existing switch, the attacker would then have to know the password to do any harm. And by using transparent mode, you can avoid the types of problems described earlier, in the section "Caveats When Moving Away from Default VTP Configuration."

Exam Preparation Tasks

Review All the Key Topics

Review the most important topics from inside the chapter, noted with the Key Topics icon in the outer margin of the page. Table 1-8 lists these key topics and the page numbers on which each is found.

Key Topic

Table 1-8 *Key Topics for Chapter 1*

Key Topic Element	Description	Page Number
List	Reasons for using VLANs	11
Figure 1-2	Diagram of VLAN trunking	12
Figure 1-4	802.1Q header	14
Table 1-2	Comparisons of 802.1Q and ISL	15
Figure 1-6	VTP synchronization process concepts	18
List	Requirements for VTP to work between two switches	19
Table 1-3	VTP features summary	23
List	Configuration checklist for configuring VLANs and assigning to interfaces	24
List	Default VTP and VLAN configuration	25
Table 1-4	Options of the **switchport mode** command	30
Table 1-5	Expected trunking results based on the configuration of the **switchport mode** command	33
List	Four reasons why a trunk does not pass traffic for a VLAN	34
Table 1-6	Voice and data VLAN configuration and terms	37
List	Recommendations for how to protect unused switch ports	37
List	VTP configuration checklist	38
Table 1-7	VTP and VLAN configuration commands, and where they are stored	41
List	VTP troubleshooting process used when VTP is not performing as desired	44
List	Predicting what will happen with VTP when a new switch connects to a network	50
List	VTP best practices for preventing VTP problems	51

Complete the Tables and Lists from Memory

Print a copy of Appendix J, "Memory Tables," (found on the CD) or at least the section for this chapter, and complete the tables and lists from memory. Appendix K, "Memory Tables Answer Key," also on the CD, includes completed tables and lists to check your work.

Definitions of Key Terms

Define the following key terms from this chapter, and check your answers in the glossary:

> 802.1Q, ISL, trunk, trunking administrative mode, trunking operational mode, VLAN, VLAN configuration database, vlan.dat, VTP, VTP client mode, VTP pruning, VTP server mode, VTP transparent mode

Command Reference to Check Your Memory

While you should not necessarily memorize the information in the tables in this section, this section does include a reference for the configuration and EXEC commands covered in this chapter. Practically speaking, you should memorize the commands as a side effect of reading the chapter and doing all the activities in this exam preparation section. To check to see how well you have memorized the commands as a side effect of your other studies, cover the left side of the table with a piece of paper, read the descriptions in the right side, and see whether you remember the command.

Table 1-9 *Chapter 1 Configuration Command Reference*

Command	Description
vlan *vlan-id*	Global config command that both creates the VLAN and puts the CLI into VLAN configuration mode
name *vlan-name*	VLAN subcommand that names the VLAN
shutdown	VLAN subcommand that prevents that one switch from forwarding traffic in that VLAN
shutdown vlan *vlan-id*	Global config command that administratively disables a VLAN, preventing the switch from forwarding frames in that VLAN
vtp domain *domain-name*	Global config command that defines the VTP domain name
vtp password *password*	Global config command that defines the VTP password
vtp {server | client | transparent}	Global config command that defines the VTP mode

Table 1-9 *Chapter 1 Configuration Command Reference (Continued)*

Command	Description
vtp pruning	Global config command that tells the VTP server to tell all switches to use VTP pruning
**switchport mode {access	dynamic {auto	desirable}	trunk}**	Interface subcommand that configures the trunking administrative mode on the interface
**switchport trunk allowed vlan {add	all	except	remove}** *vlan-list*	Interface subcommand that defines the list of allowed VLANs
switchport access vlan *vlan-id*	Interface subcommand that statically configures the interface into that one VLAN
**switchport trunk encapsulation {dot1q	isl	negotiate}**	Interface subcommand that defines which type of trunking to use, assuming that trunking is configured or negotiated
switchport voice vlan *vlan-id*	Interface subcommand that defines the VLAN used for frames sent to and from a Cisco IP phone
switchport nonnegotiate	Interface subcommand that disables the negotiation of VLAN trunking

Table 1-10 *Chapter 1 EXEC Command Reference*

Command	Description
show interfaces *interface-id* **switchport**	Lists information about any interface regarding administrative settings and operational state
show interfaces *interface-id* **trunk**	Lists information about all operational trunks (but no other interfaces), including the list of VLANs that can be forwarded over the trunk
**show vlan [brief	id** *vlan-id*	**name** *vlan-name*	**summary]**	Lists information about the VLAN
show vlan [*vlan***]**	Displays VLAN information
show vtp status	Lists VTP configuration and status information
show vtp password	Lists the VTP password

This chapter covers the following subjects:

Spanning Tree Protocol (IEEE 802.1d): This section explains the core concepts behind the operation of the original IEEE STP protocols.

Rapid STP (IEEE 802.1w): This section focuses on the differences between the earlier 802.1d STP standard and the new 802.1w RSTP standard.

STP Configuration and Verification: This section explains how to configure STP on Cisco IOS switches, and how to verify the current STP status on each switch and interface.

STP Troubleshooting: This section suggests an approach for how to predict the port role of each STP interface, thereby predicting the topology of the spanning tree.

CHAPTER 2

Spanning Tree Protocol

When LAN designs require multiple switches, most network engineers include redundant Ethernet segments between the switches. The goal is simple. The switches might fail, and cables might be cut or unplugged, but if redundant switches and cables are installed, the network service might still be available for most users.

LANs with redundant links introduce the possibility that frames might loop around the network forever. These looping frames would cause network performance problems. Therefore, LANs use Spanning Tree Protocol (STP), which allows the redundant LAN links to be used while preventing frames from looping around the LAN indefinitely through those redundant links. This chapter covers STP, along with a few configuration commands used to tune how STP behaves.

This chapter covers the details of STP, plus a newer variation called Rapid Spanning Tree Protocol (RSTP). The end of the chapter covers STP configuration on 2960 series switches, along with some suggestions on how to approach STP problems on the exams.

"Do I Know This Already?" Quiz

The "Do I Know This Already?" quiz allows you to assess whether you should read the entire chapter. If you miss no more than one of these ten self-assessment questions, you might want to move ahead to the "Exam Preparation Tasks" section. Table 2-1 lists the major headings in this chapter and the "Do I Know This Already?" quiz questions that cover the material in those headings so that you can assess your knowledge of these specific areas. The answers to the "Do I Know This Already?" quiz appear in Appendix A.

Table 2-1 *"Do I Know This Already?" Foundation Topics Section-to-Question Mapping*

Foundation Topics Section	Questions
Spanning Tree Protocol (IEEE 802.1d)	1–5
Rapid STP (IEEE 802.1w)	6–7
STP Configuration and Verification	8–9
STP Troubleshooting	10

1.   Which of the following IEEE 802.1d port states are stable states used when STP has completed convergence?

   a.   Blocking

   b.   Forwarding

   c.   Listening

   d.   Learning

   e.   Discarding

2.   Which of the following are transitory IEEE 802.1d port states used only during the process of STP convergence?

   a.   Blocking

   b.   Forwarding

   c.   Listening

   d.   Learning

   e.   Discarding

3.   Which of the following bridge IDs would win election as root, assuming that the switches with these bridge IDs were in the same network?

   a.   32768:0200.1111.1111

   b.   32768:0200.2222.2222

   c.   200:0200.1111.1111

   d.   200:0200.2222.2222

   e.   40,000:0200.1111.1111

4.   Which of the following facts determines how often a nonroot bridge or switch sends an 802.1d STP Hello BPDU message?

   a.   The Hello timer as configured on that switch.

   b.   The Hello timer as configured on the root switch.

   c.   It is always every 2 seconds.

   d.   The switch reacts to BPDUs received from the root switch by sending another BPDU 2 seconds after receiving the root BPDU.

5. What STP feature causes an interface to be placed in the Forwarding State as soon as the interface is physically active?

   a. STP

   b. RSTP

   c. Root Guard

   d. 802.1w

   e. PortFast

   f. EtherChannel

6. Which answer lists the name of the IEEE standard that improves the original STP standard and lowers convergence time?

   a. STP

   b. RSTP

   c. Root Guard

   d. 802.1w

   e. PortFast

   f. Trunking

7. Which of the following RSTP port states have the same name as a similar port state in traditional STP?

   a. Blocking

   b. Forwarding

   c. Listening

   d. Learning

   e. Discarding

   f. Disabled

8. On a 2960 switch, which of the following commands change the value of the bridge ID?

   a. **spanning-tree bridge-id** *value*

   b. **spanning-tree vlan** *vlan-number* **root** {**primary** I **secondary**}

   c. **spanning-tree vlan** *vlan-number* **priority** *value*

   d. **set spanning-tree priority** *value*

9. Examine the following extract from the **show spanning-tree** command on a Cisco switch:

```
Bridge ID  Priority    32771   (priority 32768 sys-id-ext 3)
           Address     0019.e86a.6f80
```

Which of the following answers is true regarding the switch on which this command output was gathered?

a. The information is about the STP instance for VLAN 1.

b. The information is about the STP instance for VLAN 3.

c. The command output confirms that this switch cannot possibly be the root switch.

d. The command output confirms that this switch is currently the root switch.

10. Switch SW3 is receiving only two Hello BPDUs, both from the same root switch, received on the two interfaces listed as follows:

```
SW3#show interfaces status
Port       Name       Status      Vlan   Duplex   Speed    Type
Fa0/13                connected   1      a-half   a-100    10/100BaseTX
Gi0/1                 connected   1      a-full   a-1000   1000BaseTX
```

SW3 has no STP-related configuration commands. The Hello received on Fa0/13 lists cost 10, and the Hello received on Gi0/1 lists cost 20. Which of the following is true about STP on SW3?

a. SW3 will choose Fa0/13 as its root port.

b. SW3 will choose Gi0/1 as its root port.

c. SW3's Fa0/13 will become a designated port.

d. SW3's Gi0/1 will become a designated port.

Foundation Topics

Without Spanning Tree Protocol (STP), a LAN with redundant links would cause Ethernet frames to loop for an indefinite period of time. With STP enabled, some switches block ports so that these ports do not forward frames. STP chooses which ports block so that only one active path exists between any pair of LAN segments (collision domains). As a result, frames can be delivered to each device, without causing the problems created when frames loop through the network.

This chapter begins by explaining the need for the original IEEE standard for STP and how the standard works. The second major section explains how the new and much faster Rapid STP (RSTP) works in comparison. The last two major sections examine the configuration and troubleshooting of STP, respectively.

Spanning Tree Protocol (IEEE 802.1d)

IEEE 802.1d, the first public standard for STP, defined a reasonable solution to the problem of frames looping around redundant links forever. The following sections begin with a more detailed description of the problem, followed by a description of the end result of how 802.1d STP solves the problem. The sections end with a lengthy description of how STP works, as a distributed process on all LAN switches, to prevent loops.

The Need for Spanning Tree

The most common problem that can be avoided by using STP is broadcast storms. Broadcast storms cause broadcasts (or multicasts or unknown-destination unicasts) to loop around a LAN indefinitely. As a result, some links can become saturated with useless copies of the same frame, crowding out good frames, as well as significantly impacting end-user PC performance by making the PCs process too many broadcast frames. To see how this occurs, Figure 2-1 shows a sample network in which Bob sends a broadcast frame. The dashed lines show how the switches forward the frame when STP does not exist.

Figure 2-1 *Broadcast Storm*

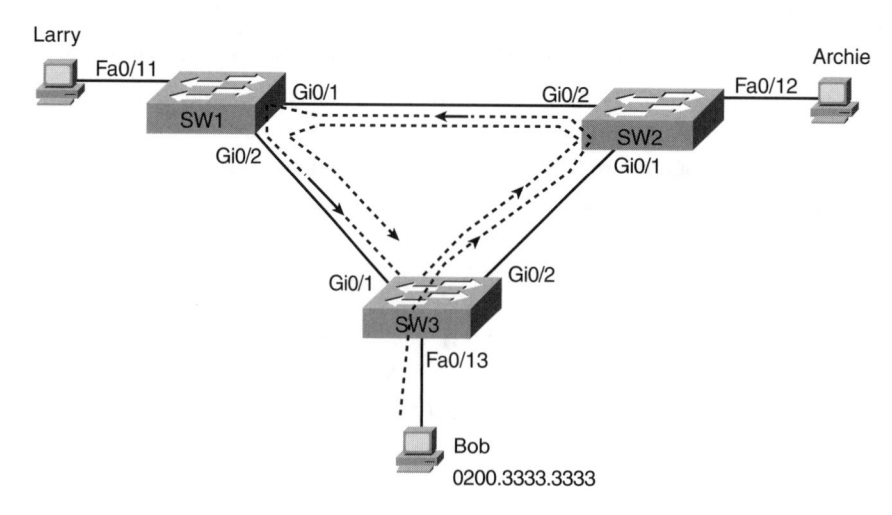

Switches flood broadcasts out all interfaces in the same VLAN, except the interface in which the frame arrived. In the figure, that means SW3 will forward Bob's frame to SW2; SW2 will forward the frame to SW1; SW1 will forward the frame back to SW3; and SW3 will forward it back to SW2 again. This frame will loop until something changes—someone shuts down an interface, reloads a switch, or does something else to break the loop. Also note that the same event happens in the opposite direction. When Bob sends the original frame, SW3 also forwards a copy to SW1, SW1 forwards it to SW2, and so on.

MAC table instability also occurs as a result of the looping frames. MAC table instability means that the switches' MAC address tables will keep changing the information listed for the source MAC address of the looping frame. For example, SW3 begins Figure 2-1 with a MAC table entry as follows:

    0200.3333.3333   Fa0/13   VLAN 1

However, now think about the switch-learning process that occurs when the looping frame goes to SW2, then SW1, and then back into SW3's Gi0/1 interface. SW3 thinks, "Hmmm… the source MAC address is 0200.3333.3333, and it came in my Gi0/1 interface. Update my MAC table!" resulting in the following entry on SW3:

    0200.3333.3333   Gi0/1   VLAN 1

At this point, if a frame arrives at SW3—a different frame than the looping frame that causes the problems—destined to Bob's MAC address of 0200.3333.3333, SW3 would incorrectly forward the frame out Gi0/1 to SW1. This new frame can also loop, or the frame might simply never be delivered to Bob.

The third class of problem caused by not using STP in a network with redundancy is that working hosts get multiple copies of the same frame. Consider a case in which Bob sends a frame to Larry, but none of the switches know Larry's MAC address. (Switches flood frames sent to unknown destination unicast MAC addresses.) When Bob sends the frame (destined to Larry's MAC address), SW3 sends a copy to SW1 and SW2. SW1 and SW2 also flood the frame, causing copies of the frame to loop. SW1 also sends a copy of each frame out Fa0/11 to Larry. As a result, Larry gets multiple copies of the frame, which may result in an application failure, if not more pervasive networking problems.

Table 2-2 summarizes the main three classes of problems that occur when STP is not used in a LAN with redundancy.

Table 2-2 *Three Classes of Problems Caused by Not Using STP in Redundant LANs*

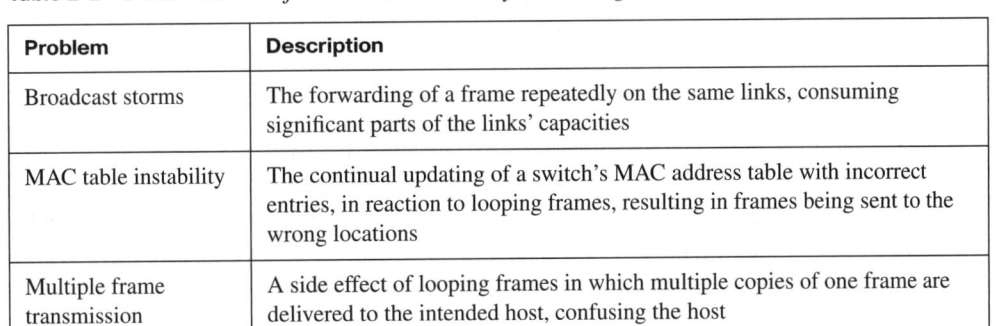
Key Topic

Problem	Description
Broadcast storms	The forwarding of a frame repeatedly on the same links, consuming significant parts of the links' capacities
MAC table instability	The continual updating of a switch's MAC address table with incorrect entries, in reaction to looping frames, resulting in frames being sent to the wrong locations
Multiple frame transmission	A side effect of looping frames in which multiple copies of one frame are delivered to the intended host, confusing the host

What IEEE 802.1d Spanning Tree Does

STP prevents loops by placing each bridge/switch port in either a Forwarding State or a Blocking State. Interfaces in the Forwarding State act as normal, forwarding and receiving frames, but interfaces in a Blocking State do not process any frames except STP messages. All the ports in Forwarding State are considered to be in the current *spanning tree*. The collective set of forwarding ports creates a single path over which frames are sent between Ethernet segments.

Figure 2-2 shows a simple STP tree that solves the problem shown in Figure 2-1 by placing one port on SW3 in the Blocking State.

Figure 2-2 *Network with Redundant Links and STP*

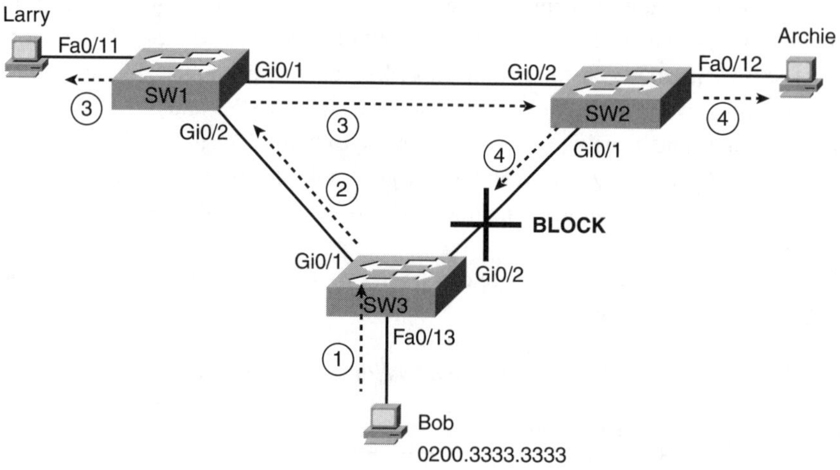

Now when Bob sends a broadcast frame, the frame does not loop. Bob sends the frame to SW3 (Step 1), which then forwards the frame only to SW1 (Step 2), because SW3's Gi0/2 interface is in a Blocking State. SW1 floods the frame out both Fa0/11 and Gi0/1 (Step 3). SW2 floods the frame out Fa0/12 and Gi0/1 (Step 4). However, SW3 ignores the frame received from SW2, again because that frame enters SW3's Gi0/2 interface, which is in a Blocking State.

With the STP topology in Figure 2-2, the switches simply do not use the link between SW2 and SW3 for traffic in this VLAN, which is the minor negative side effect of STP. However, if the link between SW1 and SW3 fails, STP converges so that SW3 forwards instead of blocks on its Gi0/2 interface.

> **NOTE** The term *STP convergence* refers to the process by which the switches collectively realize that something has changed in the LAN topology, so the switches might need to change which ports block and which ports forward.

How does STP manage to make switches block or forward on each interface? And how does it converge to change state from Blocking to Forwarding to take advantage of redundant links in response to network outages? The following sections answer these questions.

How Spanning Tree Works

The STP algorithm creates a spanning tree of interfaces that forward frames. The tree structure creates a single path to and from each Ethernet segment, just like you can trace a single path in a living, growing tree from the base of the tree to each leaf.

> **NOTE**   Because Ethernet bridges are seldom used today, this chapter refers only to switches. However, both bridges and switches use STP.

The process used by STP, sometimes called the *Spanning Tree Algorithm (STA)*, chooses the interfaces that should be placed into a Forwarding State. For any interfaces not chosen to be in a Forwarding State, STA places the interfaces in Blocking State. In other words, STP simply picks which interfaces should forward.

STP uses three criteria to choose whether to put an interface in Forwarding State:

- STP elects a root switch. STP puts all working interfaces on the root switch in Forwarding State.

- Each nonroot switch considers one of its ports to have the least administrative cost between itself and the root switch. STP places this least-root-cost interface, called that switch's root port (RP), in Forwarding State.

- Many switches can attach to the same Ethernet segment. The switch with the lowest administrative cost from itself to the root bridge, as compared with the other switches attached to the same segment, is placed in Forwarding State. The lowest-cost switch on each segment is called the designated bridge, and that bridge's interface, attached to that segment, is called the *designated port (DP)*.

> **NOTE**   The real reason the root places all working interfaces in a Forwarding State is that all its interfaces will become DPs, but it is easier to just remember that the all the root switches' working interfaces will forward frames.

All other interfaces are placed in Blocking State. Table 2-3 summarizes the reasons STP places a port in Forwarding or Blocking State.

Key
Topic

Table 2-3 *STP: Reasons for Forwarding or Blocking*

Characterization of Port	STP State	Description
All the root switch's ports	Forwarding	The root switch is always the designated switch on all connected segments.
Each nonroot switch's root port	Forwarding	The port through which the switch has the least cost to reach the root switch.
Each LAN's designated port	Forwarding	The switch forwarding the lowest-cost BPDU onto the segment is the designated switch for that segment.
All other working ports	Blocking	The port is not used for forwarding frames, nor are any frames received on these interfaces considered for forwarding.

NOTE   STP only considers working interfaces. Failed interfaces (for example, interfaces with no cable installed) or administratively shut down interfaces are instead placed into an STP Disabled State. So, this section uses the term *working ports* to refer to interfaces that could forward frames if STP placed the interface into a Forwarding State.

The STP Bridge ID and Hello BPDU

The Spanning Tree Algorithm (STA) begins with an election of one switch to be the root switch. To better understand this election process, you need to understand the STP messages sent between switches as well as the concept and format of the identifier used to uniquely identify each switch.

The STP bridge ID (BID) is an 8-byte value unique to each switch. The bridge ID consists of a 2-byte priority field and a 6-byte system ID, with the system ID being based on a burned-in MAC address in each switch. Using a burned-in MAC address ensures that each switch's bridge ID will be unique.

STP defines messages called *bridge protocol data units* (BPDU), which bridges and switches use to exchange information with each other. The most common message, called a Hello BPDU, lists the sending switch's bridge ID. By listing its own unique bridge ID, switches can tell the difference between BPDUs sent by different switches. This message also lists the bridge ID of the current root switch.

STP defines several types of BPDU messages, with the Hello BPDU being the message that does most of the work. The Hello BPDU includes several fields, but most importantly, it contains the fields listed in Table 2-4.

Table 2-4 *Fields in the STP Hello BPDU*

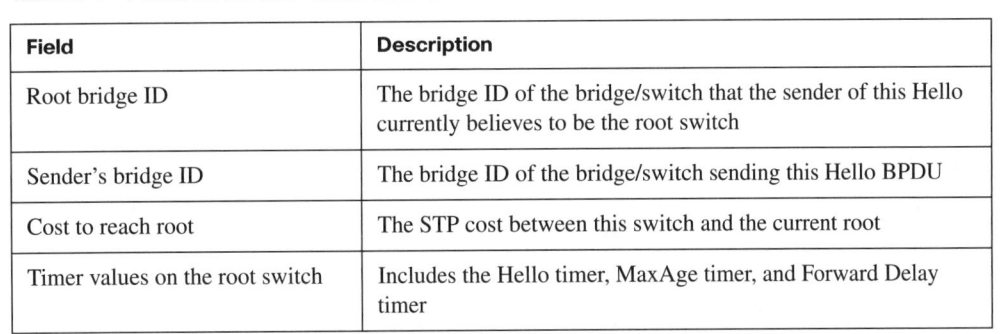
Key
Topic

Field	Description
Root bridge ID	The bridge ID of the bridge/switch that the sender of this Hello currently believes to be the root switch
Sender's bridge ID	The bridge ID of the bridge/switch sending this Hello BPDU
Cost to reach root	The STP cost between this switch and the current root
Timer values on the root switch	Includes the Hello timer, MaxAge timer, and Forward Delay timer

For the time being, just keep the first three items from Table 2-4 in mind as the following sections work through the three steps in how STP chooses the interfaces to place into a Forwarding State. Next, the text examines the three main steps in the STP process.

Electing the Root Switch

Switches elect a root switch based on the bridge IDs in the BPDUs. The root switch is the switch with the lowest numeric value for the bridge ID. Because the two-part bridge ID starts with the priority value, essentially the switch with the lowest priority becomes the root. For example, if one switch has priority 100, and another switch has priority 200, the switch with priority 100 wins, regardless of what MAC address was used to create the bridge ID for each bridge/switch.

If a tie occurs based on the priority portion of the bridge ID, the switch with the lowest MAC address portion of the bridge ID is the root. No other tiebreaker should be needed because switches use one of their own burned-in MAC addresses as the second part of their bridge IDs. So if the priorities tie, and one switch uses a MAC address of 0020.0000.0000 as part of the bridge ID, and the other uses 0FFF.FFFF.FFF, the first switch (MAC 0200.0000.0000) becomes the root.

STP elects a root switch in a manner not unlike a political election. The process begins with all switches claiming to be the root by sending Hello BPDUs listing their own bridge ID as the root bridge ID. If a switch hears a Hello that lists a better (lower) bridge ID—called a Superior Hello—that switch stops advertising itself as root and starts forwarding the superior Hello. The Hello sent by the better switch lists the better switch's bridge ID as the root. It works like a political race in which a less-popular candidate gives up and leaves the race, throwing her support behind another candidate. Eventually everyone agrees which switch has the best (lowest) bridge ID, and everyone supports the elected switch—which is where the political race analogy falls apart.

Figure 2-3 shows the beginning of the root election process. In this case, SW1 has advertised itself as root, as have SW2 and SW3. However, SW2 now believes that SW1 is a better root, so SW2 is now forwarding the Hello originating at SW1. This forwarded Hello lists SW1's BID as the root BID. However, at this point, SW1 and SW3 both still believe that they each are the best, so they still list their own BID as the root in their Hello BPDUs.

Figure 2-3 *Beginnings of the Root Election Process*

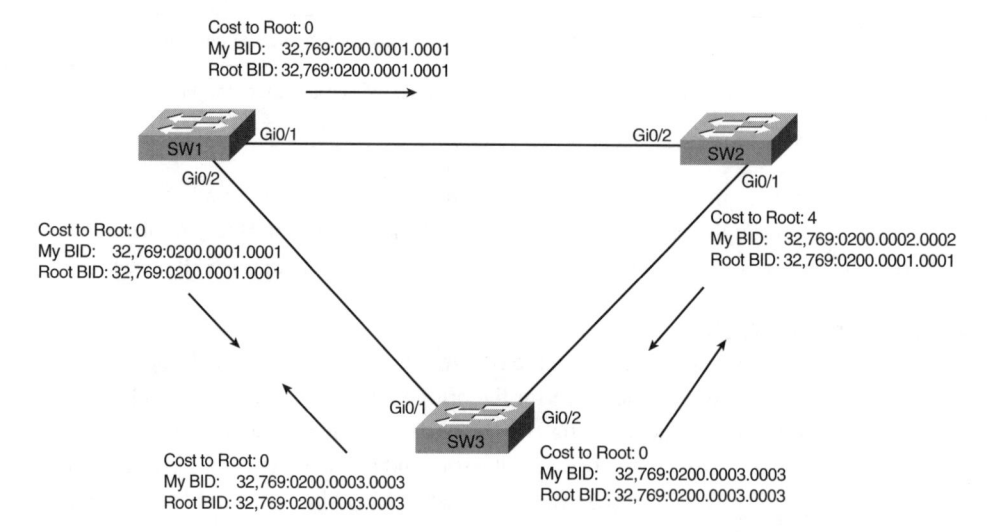

Two candidates still exist in Figure 2-3: SW1 and SW3. So who wins? Well, from the bridge ID, the lower-priority switch wins; if a tie occurs, the lower MAC address wins. As shown in the figure, SW1 has a lower bridge ID (32769:0200.0000.0001) than SW3 (32769:0200.0003.0003), so SW1 wins, and SW3 now also believes that SW1 is the better switch. Figure 2-4 shows the resulting Hello messages sent by the switches.

After the election is complete, only the root switch continues to originate STP Hello BPDU messages. The other switches receive the Hellos, update the sender's BID field (and cost-to-reach-the-root field), and forward the Hellos out other interfaces. The figure reflects this fact, with SW1 sending Hellos at Step 1, and SW2 and SW3 independently forwarding the Hello out their other interfaces at Step 2.

Figure 2-4   *SW1 Wins Election*

Cost to Root: 0
My BID: 32,769:0200.0001.0001
Root BID: 32,769:0200.0001.0001

Cost 4

Gi0/1   Gi0/2
SW1   SW2
Gi0/2   Cost 4 Gi0/1

Cost to Root: 0   Cost 4
My BID: 32,769:0200.0001.0001   Cost to Root: 4
Root BID: 32,769:0200.0001.0001   My BID: 32,769:0200.0002.0002
                                                    Root BID: 32,769:0200.0001.0001

Cost 4

Gi0/1   Gi0/2
Cost 5   SW3
                        Cost to Root: 5
                        My BID: 32,769:0200.0003.0003
                        Root BID: 32,769:0200.0001.0001

Choosing Each Switch's Root Port

The second part of the STP process occurs when each nonroot switch chooses its one and only *root port*. A switch's root port (RP) is its interface through which it has the least STP cost to reach the root switch.

To calculate the cost, a switch adds the cost listed in a received Hello to the STP port cost assigned to that same interface. The STP port cost is simply an integer value assigned to each interface for the purpose of providing an objective measurement that allows STP to choose which interfaces to add to the STP topology.

Figure 2-5 shows an example of how SW3 calculates its cost to reach the root over the two possible paths by adding the advertised cost (in Hello messages) to the interface costs listed in the figure.

Figure 2-5   *SW3 Calculating Cost to Reach the Root and Choosing Its RP*

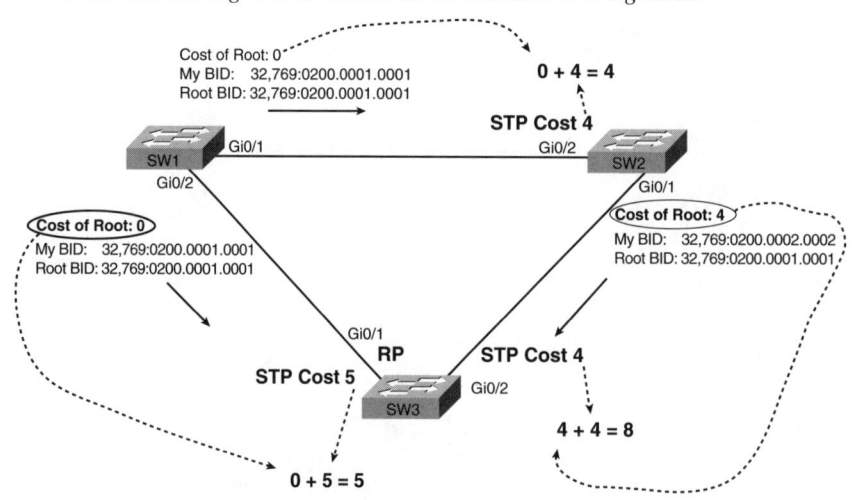

As a result of the process depicted in Figure 2-5, SW3 chooses Gi0/1 as its RP, because the cost to reach the root switch through that port (5) is lower than the other alternative (Gi0/2, cost 8). Similarly, SW2 will choose Gi0/2 as its RP, with a cost of 4 (SW1's advertised cost of 0 plus SW2's Gi0/2 interface cost of 4). Each switch places its root port into a Forwarding State.

In more complex topologies, the choice of root port will not be so obvious. The section "STP Troubleshooting," later in this chapter, shows an example in which the root port choice requires a little more thought.

Choosing the Designated Port on Each LAN Segment

STP's final step to choose the STP topology is to choose the designated port on each LAN segment. The designated port on each LAN segment is the switch port that advertises the lowest-cost Hello onto a LAN segment. When a nonroot switch forwards a Hello, the nonroot switch sets the cost field in the Hello to that switch's cost to reach the root. In effect, the switch with the lower cost to reach the root, among all switches connected to a segment, becomes the DP on that segment.

For example, in Figure 2-4, both SW2 and SW3 forward Hello messages onto the segment. Note that both SW2 and SW3 list their respective cost to reach the root switch (cost 4 on SW2 and cost 5 on SW3.) As a result, SW2's Gi0/1 port is the designated port on that LAN segment.

All DPs are placed into a forwarding state, so in this case, SW2's Gi0/1 interface will be in a forwarding state.

If the advertised costs tied, the switches break the tie by choosing the switch with the lower bridge ID. In this case, SW2 would have won, with a bridge ID of 32769:0200.0002.0002 versus SW3's 32769:0200.0003.0003.

> **NOTE** A switch can connect two or more interfaces to the same collision domain if hubs are used. In such cases, another tiebreaker is needed: The switch chooses the interface with the lower internal interface number.

The only interface that does not have a reason to be in a Forwarding State on the three switches in the examples shown in Figures 2-3, 2-4, and 2-5 is SW3's Gi0/2 port. So, the STP process is now complete. Table 2-5 outlines the state of each port and shows why it is in that state.

Table 2-5 *State of Each Interface*

Switch Interface	State	Reason Why the Interface Is in Forwarding State
SW1, Gi0/1	Forwarding	The interface is on the root switch.
SW1, Gi0/2	Forwarding	The interface is on the root switch.
SW2, Gi0/2	Forwarding	The root port.
SW2, Gi0/1	Forwarding	The designated port on the LAN segment to SW3.
SW3, Gi0/1	Forwarding	The root port.
SW3, Gi0/2	Blocking	Not the root port and not designated port.

Port costs can be configured, or you can use the default values. Table 2-6 lists the default port costs defined by IEEE; Cisco uses these same defaults. The IEEE revised the cost values because the original values, set in the early 1980s, did not anticipate the growth of Ethernet to support 10-Gigabit Ethernet.

Table 2-6 *Default Port Costs According to IEEE*

Key
Topic

Ethernet Speed	Original IEEE Cost	Revised IEEE Cost
10 Mbps	100	100
100 Mbps	10	19
1 Gbps	1	4
10 Gbps	1	2

With STP enabled, all working switch interfaces will settle into an STP Forwarding or Blocking State, even access ports. For switch interfaces connected to hosts or routers, which do not use STP, the switch will still forward Hellos onto those interfaces. By virtue of being the only device sending a Hello onto that LAN segment, the switch is sending the least-cost Hello onto that LAN segment, making the switch become the designated port on that LAN segment. So, STP puts working access interfaces into a Forwarding State as a result of the designated port part of the STP process.

Reacting to Changes in the Network

After the STP topology—the set of interfaces in a forwarding state—has been determined, this set of forwarding interfaces does not change unless the network topology changes. This section examines the ongoing operation of STP while the network is stable, and then it examines how STP converges to a new topology when something changes.

The root switch sends a new Hello BPDU every 2 seconds by default. Each switch forwards the Hello on all DPs, but only after changing two items. The cost is changed to reflect that switch's cost to reach the root, and the sender's bridge ID field is also changed. (The root's bridge ID field is not changed.) By forwarding the received (and changed) Hellos out all DPs, all switches continue to receive Hellos about every 2 seconds. The following list summarizes the steady-state operation when nothing is currently changing in the STP topology:

Key Topic

1. The root creates and sends a Hello BPDU, with a cost of 0, out all its working interfaces (those in a Forwarding State).

2. The nonroot switches receive the Hello on their root ports. After changing the Hello to list their own bridge ID as the sender's BID, and listing that switch's root cost, the switch forwards the Hello out all designated ports.

3. Steps 1 and 2 repeat until something changes.

Each switch relies on these periodic received Hellos from the root as a way to know that its path to the root is still working. When a switch ceases to receive the Hellos, something has failed, so the switch reacts and starts the process of changing the spanning-tree topology. For various reasons, the convergence process requires the use of three timers. Note that all switches use the timers as dictated by the root switch, which the root lists in its periodic Hello BPDU messages. The timer and their descriptions are listed in Table 2-7.

Table 2-7 *STP Timers*

Key
Topic

Timer	Description	Default Value
Hello	The time period between Hellos created by the root.	2 sec.
Max Age	How long any switch should wait, after ceasing to hear Hellos, before trying to change the STP topology.	10 times Hello
Forward Delay	Delay that affects the process that occurs when an interface changes from Blocking State to Forwarding State. A port stays in an interim Listening State, and then an interim Learning State, for the number of seconds defined by the forward delay timer.	15 sec.

If a switch does not get an expected Hello BPDU within the Hello time, the switch continues as normal. However, if the Hellos do not show up again within MaxAge time, the switch reacts by taking steps to change the STP topology. At that point, the switch essentially reevaluates which switch should be the root switch, and if it is not the root, which port should be its RP, and which ports should be DPs, assuming that the Hellos it was formerly receiving have stopped arriving.

The best way to describe STP convergence is to show an example using the same familiar topology. Figure 2-6 shows the same familiar figure, with SW3's Gi0/2 in a Blocking State, but SW1's Gi0/2 interface has just failed.

Figure 2-6   *Reacting to Link Failure Between SW1 and SW3*

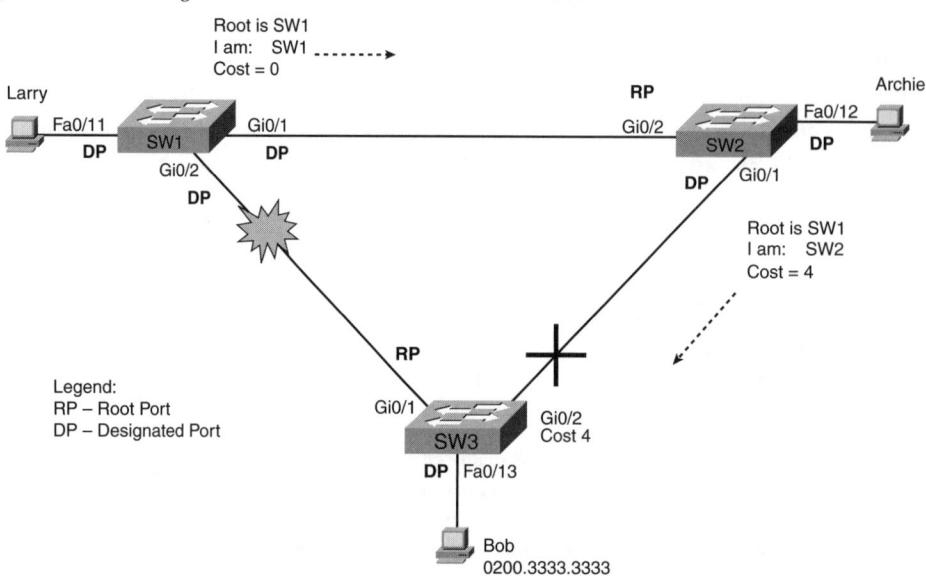

SW3 reacts to the change because SW3 fails to receive its expected Hellos on its Gi0/1 interface. However, SW2 does not need to react because SW2 continues to receive its periodic Hellos in its Gi0/2 interface. In this case, SW3 reacts either when MaxAge time passes without hearing the Hellos, or as soon as SW3 notices that interface Gi0/1 has failed. (If the interface fails, the switch can assume that the Hellos will not be arriving anymore.)

Now that SW3 can act, it begins by reevaluating the choice of root switch. SW3 still receives the Hello from SW1, forwarded by SW2, and SW1 has a lower bridge ID; otherwise, SW1 would not have already been the root. So, SW3 decides that SW1 is still the best switch and that SW3 is not the root.

Next, SW3 reevaluates its choice of RP. At this point, SW3 is only receiving Hellos on one interface, interface Gi0/2. Whatever the calculated cost, Gi0/2 will become SW3's new RP. (The cost would be 8: SW2's advertised cost of 4 plus Gi0/2's interface cost of 4.)

SW3 then reevaluates its role as DP on any other interfaces. In this example, no real work needs to be done. SW3 was already DP on interface Fa0/13, and it continues to be the DP, because no other switches connect to that port.

When STP converges, a switch chooses transition interfaces from one state to another. However, a transition from blocking to forwarding cannot be done immediately because an immediate change to forwarding could temporarily cause frames to loop. To prevent these temporary loops, STP transitions an interface through two intermediate interface states, as follows:

- **Listening**: Like the Blocking State, the interface does not forward frames. Old, now-incorrect MAC table entries are timed out during this state, because the old incorrect MAC table entries would be the root cause of the temporary loops.

- **Learning**: Interfaces in this state still do not forward frames, but the switch begins to learn the MAC addresses of frames received on the interface.

STP moves an interface from Blocking to Listening, then to Learning, and then to Forwarding State. STP leaves the interface in each interim state for a time equal to the forward delay timer. As a result, a convergence event that causes an interface to change from Blocking to Forwarding requires 30 seconds to transition from Blocking to Forwarding. Additionally, a switch might have to wait MaxAge seconds before even choosing to move an interface from Blocking to Forwarding state. Following the same example shown in the last several figures, SW3 might wait MaxAge seconds before deciding that it is no longer receiving the same root BPDU on its root port (20 seconds is the default), and then wait 15 seconds each in Listening and Learning States on interface Gi0/2, resulting in a 50-second convergence delay.

Table 2-8 summarizes Spanning Tree's various interface states for easier review.

Table 2-8   *IEEE 802.1d Spanning-Tree States*

State	Forwards Data Frames?	Learns MACs Based on Received Frames?	Transitory or Stable State?
Blocking	No	No	Stable
Listening	No	No	Transitory
Learning	No	Yes	Transitory
Forwarding	Yes	Yes	Stable
Disabled	No	No	Stable

Optional STP Features

STP has been around for over 20 years. Cisco switches implement the standard IEEE 802.1d STP, but over the intervening years, Cisco added proprietary features to make improvements to STP. In some cases, the IEEE added these improvements, or something like them, to later IEEE standards, whether as a revision of the 802.1d standard or as an additional standard. The following sections examine three of the proprietary additions to STP: EtherChannel, PortFast, and BPDU Guard.

> **NOTE**   If you plan to work on a production campus LAN network, you should probably learn more about STP features than is covered in this book. To do so, go to the Cisco software configuration guide for 2960 switches and look at the chapters on STP, RSTP, and optional STP features. The introduction to this book lists information about how to find Cisco documentation.

EtherChannel

One of the best ways to lower STP's convergence time is to avoid convergence altogether. EtherChannel provides a way to prevent STP convergence from being needed when only a single port or cable failure occurs.

EtherChannel combines multiple parallel segments of equal speed (up to eight) between the same pair of switches, bundled into an EtherChannel. The switches treat the EtherChannel as a single interface with regard to the frame-forwarding process as well as for STP. As a result, if one of the links fails, but at least one of the links is up, STP convergence does not have to occur. For example, Figure 2-7 shows the familiar three-switch network, but now with two Gigabit Ethernet connections between each pair of switches.

Figure 2-7   *Two-Segment EtherChannels Between Switches*

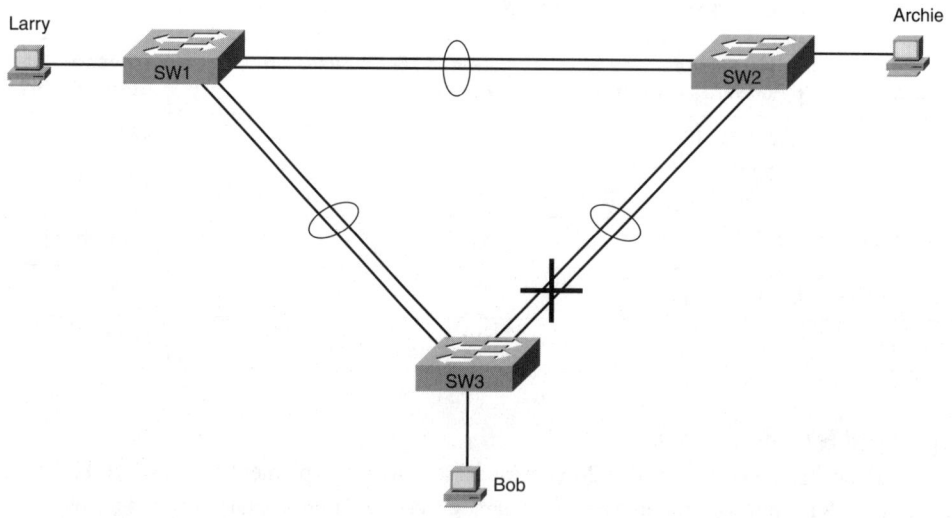

With each pair of Ethernet links configured as an EtherChannel, STP treats each EtherChannel as a single link. In other words, both links to the same switch must fail for a switch to need to cause STP convergence. Without EtherChannel, if you have multiple parallel links between two switches, STP blocks all the links except one. With EtherChannel, all the parallel links can be up and working at the same time, while reducing the number of times STP must converge, which in turn makes the network more available.

EtherChannel also provides more network bandwidth. All trunks in an EtherChannel are either forwarding or blocking, because STP treats all the trunks in the same EtherChannel as one trunk. When an EtherChannel is in Forwarding State, the switches load-balance traffic over all the trunks, providing more bandwidth.

PortFast

PortFast allows a switch to immediately place a port in Forwarding State when the port becomes physically active, bypassing any choices about the STP topology and bypassing the Listening and Learning States. However, the only ports on which you can safely enable PortFast are ports on which you know that no bridges, switches, or other STP-speaking devices are connected.

PortFast is most appropriate for connections to end-user devices. If you turn on PortFast on ports connected to end-user devices, when an end-user PC boots, as soon as the PC NIC is active, the switch port can move to an STP Forwarding State and forward traffic. Without PortFast, each port must wait while the switch confirms that the port is a DP, and then wait while the interface sits in the temporary Listening and Learning States before settling into the Forwarding State.

STP Security

Switch interfaces that connect to end-user locations in the LAN have some security exposures. An attacker could connect a switch to one of these ports, with a low STP priority value, and become the root switch. Also, by connecting the attacker's switch to multiple legitimate switches, the attacker's switch could end up forwarding a lot of traffic in the LAN, and the attacker could use a LAN analyzer to copy large numbers of data frames sent through the LAN. Also, users could innocently harm the LAN. For example, a user could buy and connect an inexpensive consumer LAN switch to an existing switch, possibly creating a loop, or possibly causing the new, relatively-low-powered switch to become the root.

The Cisco BPDU Guard feature helps defeat these kinds of problems by disabling a port if any BPDUs are received on the port. So, this feature is particularly useful on ports that should only be used as an access port and never connected to another switch. Additionally, the BPDU Guard feature is often used on the same interface that has PortFast enabled, because a PortFast-enabled port will already be in a Forwarding State, which increases the possibility for forwarding loops.

The Cisco Root Guard feature helps defeat the problem where the new rogue switch tries to become the root switch. The Root Guard feature allows another switch to be connected to the interface, and participate in STP by sending and receiving BPDUs. However, when the switch interface with Root Guard enabled receives a superior BPDU from the neighboring switch—a BPDU that has a lower/better bridge ID—the switch with Root Guard reacts. Not only does the switch ignore the superior BPDU, but the switch also disables the interface, not sending or receiving frames, as long as the superior BPDUs keep arriving. If the superior BPDUs stop arriving, the switch can start using the interface again.

Rapid STP (IEEE 802.1w)

As mentioned earlier in this chapter, the IEEE defines STP in the 802.1d IEEE standard. The IEEE has improved the 802.1d protocol with the definition of Rapid Spanning Tree Protocol (RSTP), as defined in standard 802.1w.

RSTP (802.1w) works just like STP (802.1d) in several ways:

Key Topic

- It elects the root switch using the same parameters and tiebreakers.

- It elects the root port on nonroot switches with the same rules.

- It elects designated ports on each LAN segment with the same rules.

- It places each port in either Forwarding or Blocking State, although RSTP calls the Blocking State the Discarding State.

RSTP can be deployed alongside traditional 802.1d STP switches, with RSTP features working in switches that support it, and traditional 802.1d STP features working in the switches that support only STP.

With all these similarities, you might be wondering why the IEEE bothered to create RSTP in the first place. The overriding reason is convergence. STP takes a relatively long time to converge (50 seconds with the default settings). RSTP improves network convergence when topology changes occur.

RSTP improves convergence by either eliminating or significantly reducing the waiting periods that 802.1d STP needs to avoid loops during convergence. 802.1d STP requires a waiting period of MaxAge (default 20 seconds) before reacting to some events, whereas RSTP only has to wait 3*Hello (default 6 seconds). Additionally, RSTP eliminates the forward delay (default 15 seconds) time in both Listening and Learning States. Traditional STP convergence has essentially three time periods, each of which RSTP improves upon. These three waiting periods of (by default) 20, 15, and 15 seconds create 802.1d STP's relatively slow convergence, and the reduction or elimination of these waiting periods makes RSTP convergence occur quickly.

RSTP convergence times are typically less than 10 seconds. In some cases, they can be as low as 1 to 2 seconds. The following sections explain the terminology and processes used by RSTP to overcome the shortcomings of 802.1d STP and improve convergence time.

> **NOTE**   Like most texts, when needing to distinguish between the older 802.1d and newer 802.1w standards, STP refers to 802.1d, and RSTP refers to 802.1w.

RSTP Link and Edge Types

RSTP characterizes the types of physical connectivity in a campus LAN into three different types:

- Link-type point-to-point

- Link-type shared

- Edge-type

Figure 2-8 shows each type.

Figure 2-8 *RSTP Link and Edge Types*

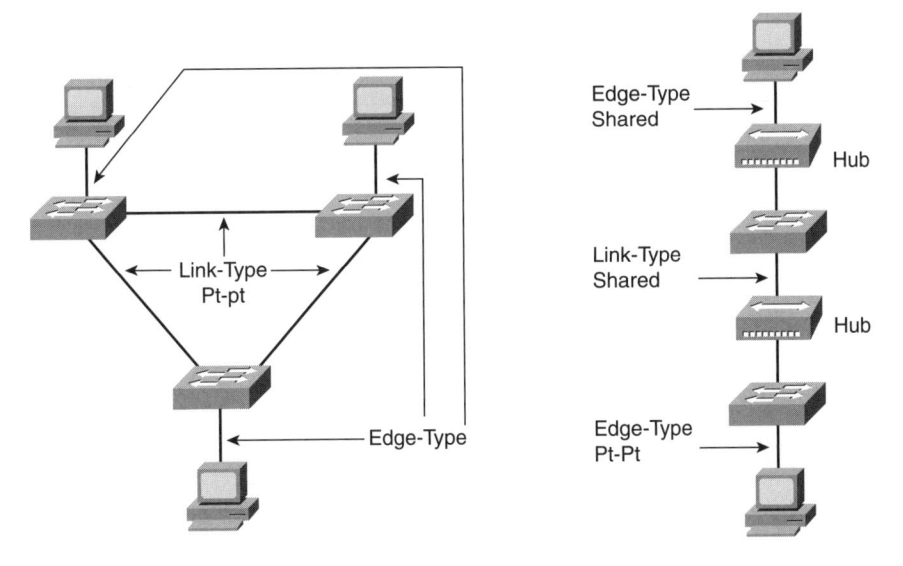

Figure 2-8 shows two sample networks. The network on the left is a typical campus design today, with no hubs. All the switches connect with Ethernet cables, and all the end-user devices also connect with Ethernet cables. The IEEE defined RSTP to improve convergence in these types of networks.

In the network on the right side of the figure, hubs are still in use for connections between the switches, as well as for connections to end-user devices. Most networks do not use hubs anymore. The IEEE did not attempt to make RSTP work in networks that use shared hubs, and RSTP would not improve convergence in the network on the right.

RSTP calls Ethernet connections between switches *links* and calls Ethernet connections to end-user devices *edges*. Two types of links exist: point-to-point, as shown on the left side of Figure 2-8, and shared, as shown on the right side. RSTP does not distinguish between point-to-point and shared types for edge connections.

RSTP reduces convergence time for link-type point-to-point and edge-type connections. It does not improve convergence over link-type shared connections. However, most modern networks do not use hubs between switches, so the lack of RSTP convergence improvements for link-type shared doesn't really matter.

RSTP Port States

You should also be familiar with RSTP's new terms to describe a port's state. Table 2-9 lists the states, with some explanation following the table.

Key Topic

Table 2-9 *RSTP and STP Port States*

Operational State	STP State (802.1d)	RSTP State (802.1w)	Forwards Data Frames in This State?
Enabled	Blocking	Discarding	No
Enabled	Listening	Discarding	No
Enabled	Learning	Learning	No
Enabled	Forwarding	Forwarding	Yes
Disabled	Disabled	Discarding	No

Similar to STP, RSTP stabilizes with all ports either in Forwarding State or Discarding State. *Discarding* means that the port does not forward frames, process received frames, or learn MAC addresses, but it does listen for BPDUs. In short, it acts just like the STP Blocking State. RSTP uses an interim Learning State when moving an interface from a Discarding State to Forwarding State. However, RSTP needs to use Learning State for only a short time.

RSTP Port Roles

Both STP (802.1d) and RSTP (802.1w) use the concepts of port states and port roles. The STP process determines the role of each interface. For example, STP determines which interfaces are currently in the role of a root port or designated port. Then, STP determines the stable port state to use for interfaces in certain roles: the Forwarding State for ports in the RP or DP roles, and the Blocking State for ports in other roles.

RSTP adds three more port roles, two of which are shown in Figure 2-9. (The third new role, the disabled role, is not shown in the figure; it simply refers to shutdown interfaces.)

Figure 2-9 *RSTP Port Roles*

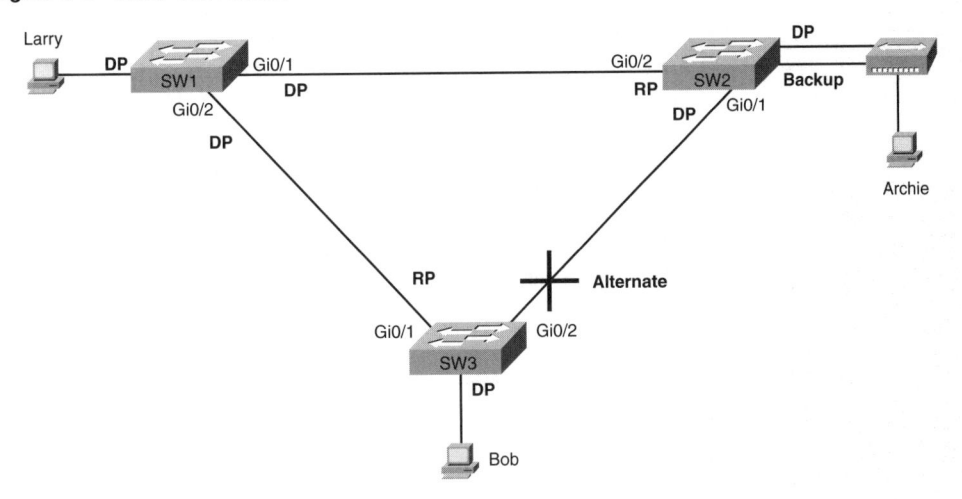

The RSTP *alternate* port role identifies a switch's best alternative to its current RP. In short, the alternate port role is an alternate RP. For example, SW3 lists Gi0/1 as its RP, but SW3 also knows that it is receiving Hello BPDUs on interface Gi0/2. Switch SW3 has a root port, just as it would with STP. (See Figure 2-4 for a reminder of the steady-state flow of BPDUs.) RSTP designates ports that receive suboptimal BPDUs (BPDUs that are not as "good" as the ones received on the root port) as alternate ports. If SW3 stops getting Hellos from the root bridge, RSTP on SW3 chooses the best alternate port as its new root port to begin the speedier convergence process.

The other new RSTP port type, *backup* port, applies only when a single switch has two links to the same segment (collision domain) . To have two links to the same collision domain, the switch must be attached to a hub, as shown in Figure 2-9 off SW2. In the figure, switch SW2 places one of the two ports into the designated port role (and eventually into a Forwarding State) and the other interface into the backup role (and eventually into the Discarding State). SW2 forwards BPDUs out the port in Forwarding State and gets the same BPDU back on the port that is in Discarding State. So SW2 knows it has an extra connection to that segment, called a *backup port*. If the DP port in Forwarding State fails, SW2 can quickly move that backup port from a Discarding State to a Learning State and then a Forwarding State.

Table 2-10 lists the port role terms for both STP and RSTP.

Table 2-10 *RSTP and STP Port Roles*

RSTP Role	STP Role	Definition
Root port	Root port	A single port on each nonroot switch in which the switch hears the best BPDU out of all the received BPDUs
Designated port	Designated port	Of all switch ports on all switches attached to the same segment/collision domain, the port that advertises the "best" BPDU
Alternate port	—	A port on a switch that receives a suboptimal BPDU
Backup port	—	A nondesignated port on a switch that is attached to the same segment/collision domain as another port on the same switch
Disabled	—	A port that is administratively disabled or is not capable of working for other reasons

RSTP Convergence

This section on RSTP started by telling you how similar RSTP is to STP: how they both choose a root using the same rules, choose designated ports using the same rules, and so forth. If RSTP did only the same things as STP, there would have been no need to update the original 802.1d STP standard with the new 802.1w RSTP standard. The main reason for the new standard is to improve convergence time.

The RSTP Spanning Tree Algorithm (STA) works somewhat differently than its older predecessor. For example, under stable conditions, every switch independently generates and sends Hello BPDUs, rather than only changing and forwarding the Hellos sent by the root switch. However, under stable conditions, the end results are the same: A switch that continues to hear the same Hellos, with the same cost and root switch BID listed, leaves the STP topology as is.

The main changes with RSTP's version of the STA occur when changes occur in the network. RSTP acts differently on some interfaces based on RSTP's characterization of the interface based on what is connected to the interface.

Edge-Type Behavior and PortFast

RSTP improves convergence for edge-type connections by immediately placing the port in Forwarding State when the link is physically active. In effect, RSTP treats these ports just like the Cisco-proprietary PortFast feature. In fact, on Cisco switches, to enable RSTP on edge interfaces, you simply configure PortFast.

Link-Type Shared

RSTP doesn't do anything differently from STP on link-type shared links. However, because most of the links between switches today are not shared, but are typically full-duplex point-to-point links, it doesn't matter.

Link-Type Point-to-Point

RSTP improves convergence over full-duplex links between switches—the links that RSTP calls "link-type point-to-point." The first improvement made by RSTP over these types of links relates to how STP uses MaxAge. STP requires that a switch that no longer receives root BPDUs in its root port must wait for MaxAge seconds before starting convergence. MaxAge defaults to 20 seconds. RSTP recognizes the loss of the path to the root bridge, through the root port, in 3 times the Hello timer, or 6 seconds with a default Hello timer value of 2 seconds. So RSTP recognizes a lost path to the root much more quickly.

RSTP removes the need for Listening State and reduces the time required for Learning State by actively discovering the network's new state. STP passively waits on new BPDUs and reacts to them during the Listening and Learning States. With RSTP, the switches negotiate with neighboring switches by sending RSTP messages. The messages enable the switches to quickly determine whether an interface can be immediately transitioned to a Forwarding State. In many cases, the process takes only a second or two for the entire RSTP domain.

An Example of Speedy RSTP Convergence

Rather than explain every nuance of RSTP convergence, one example can give you plenty of knowledge about the process. Figure 2-10 shows a network that explains RSTP convergence.

Figure 2-10 *RSTP Convergence Example: Steps 1 and 2*

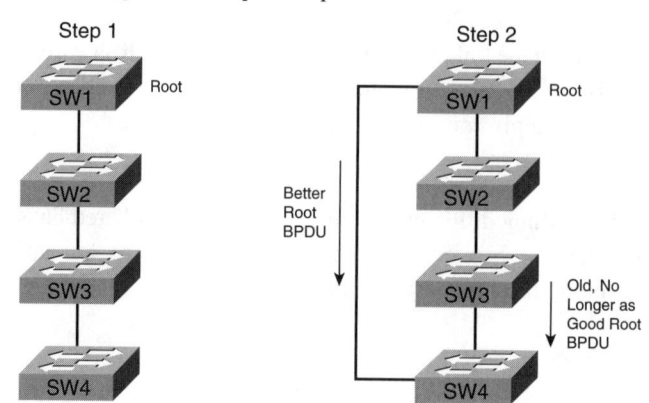

Figure 2-10 sets up the problem. On the left, in Step 1, the network has no redundancy. RSTP has placed all link-type point-to-point links in Forwarding State. To add redundancy, the network engineer adds another link-type point-to-point link between SW1 and SW4, as shown on the right as Step 2. So, RSTP convergence needs to occur.

The first step of convergence occurs when SW4 realizes that it is receiving a better BPDU than the one that entered from SW3. Because both the old and new root BPDUs advertise the same switch, SW1, the new, "better" BPDU coming over the direct link from SW1 must be better because of lower cost. Regardless of the reason, SW4 needs to transition to Forwarding State on the new link to SW1, because it is now SW4's root port.

At this point, RSTP behavior diverges from STP. RSTP on SW4 now temporarily blocks all other link-type ports. By doing so, SW4 prevents the possibility of introducing loops. Then SW4 negotiates with its neighbor on the new root port, SW1, using RSTP proposal and agreement messages. As a result, SW4 and SW1 agree that they can each place their respective ends of the new link into Forwarding State immediately. Figure 2-11 shows this third step.

Why can SW1 and SW4 place their ends of the new link in Forwarding State without causing a loop? Because SW4 blocks on all other link-type ports. In other words, it blocks on all other ports connected to other switches. That's the key to understanding RSTP convergence. A switch knows it needs to change to a new root port. It blocks on all other links and then negotiates to bring the new root port to Forwarding State. Essentially, SW4 tells SW1 to trust it and start forwarding, because SW4 promises to block all other ports until it is sure that it can move some of them back to Forwarding State.

Figure 2-11 *RSTP Convergence Example: Steps 3 and 4*

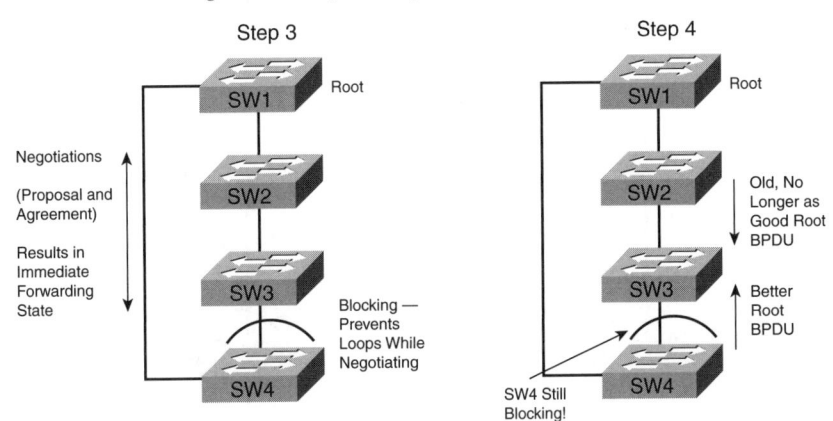

The process is not yet complete, however. The RSTP topology currently shows SW4 blocking, which in this example is not the final, best topology.

SW4 and SW3 repeat the same process that SW1 and SW4 just performed. In Step 4, SW4 still blocks, preventing loops. However, SW4 forwards the new root BPDU to SW3, so SW3 hears two BPDUs now. In this example, assume that SW3 thinks that the BPDU from SW4 is better than the one received from SW2; this makes SW3 repeat the same process that SW4 just performed. It follows this general flow from this point:

1. SW3 decides to change its root port based on this new BPDU from SW4.

2. SW3 blocks all other link-type ports. (RSTP calls this process *synchronization*.)

3. SW3 and SW4 negotiate.

4. As a result of the negotiation, SW4 and SW3 can transition to forwarding on their interfaces on either end of the link-type point-to-point link.

5. SW3 maintains Blocking State on all other link-type ports until the next step in the logic.

Figure 2-12 shows some of these steps in the Step 5 portion on the left and the resulting behavior in Step 6 on the right.

Figure 2-12   *RSTP Convergence Example: Steps 5 and 6*

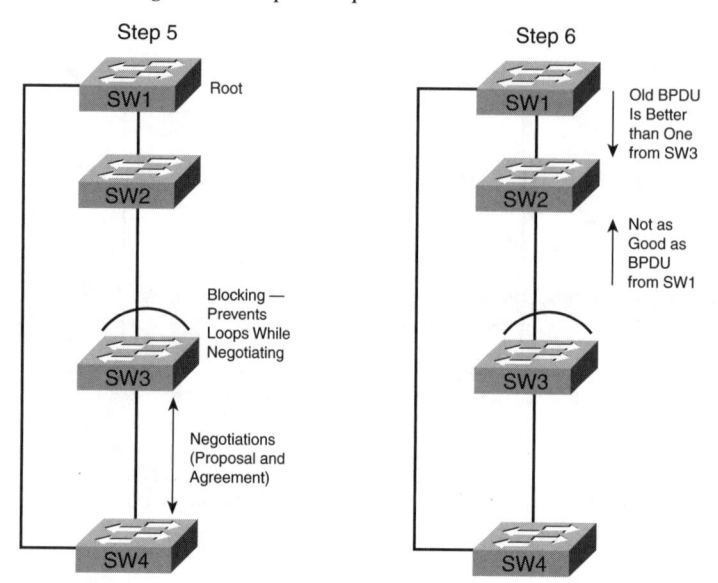

SW3 stills blocks on its upper interface at this point. Notice that SW2 is now receiving two BPDUs, but the same old BPDU it had been receiving all along is still the better BPDU. So SW2 takes no action. And RSTP is finished converging!

Although it took several pages to explain, the process in this example might take as little as 1 second to complete. For the CCNA exams, you should remember the terms relating to RSTP, as well as the concept that RSTP improves convergence time compared to STP.

STP Configuration and Verification

Cisco switches use STP (IEEE 802.1d) by default. You can buy some switches and connect them with Ethernet cables in a redundant topology, and STP will ensure that no loops exist. And you never even have to think about changing any settings!

Although STP works without any configuration, you should understand how STP works, understand how to interpret the STP-related **show** commands, and know how to tune STP by configuring various parameters. For example, by default, all switches use the same priority, so the switch with the lowest burned-in MAC address becomes the root. Instead, a switch can be configured with a lower priority, so the engineer always knows which switch is root, assuming that that switch is up and running.

The following sections begin by discussing several options for load-balancing traffic by using multiple instances of STP, followed by a short description of how to configure STP to take advantage of those multiple STP instances. The remainder of these sections show various configuration examples for both STP and RSTP.

Multiple Instances of STP

When IEEE standardized STP, VLANs did not yet exist. When VLANs were later standardized, the IEEE did not define any standards that allowed more than one instance of STP, even with multiple VLANs. At that time, if a switch only followed IEEE standards, the switch applied one instance of STP to all VLANs. In other words, if an interface was forwarding, it did so for all VLANs, and if it blocked, again it did so for all VLANs.

By default, Cisco switches use IEEE 802.1d, not RSTP (802.1w), with a Cisco-proprietary feature called Per-VLAN Spanning Tree Plus (PVST+). PVST+ (often abbreviated as simply PVST today) creates a different instance of STP for each VLAN. So, before looking at the tunable STP parameters, you need to have a basic understanding of PVST+, because the configuration settings can differ for each instance of STP.

PVST+ gives engineers a load-balancing tool. By changing some STP configuration parameters in different VLANs, the engineer could cause switches to pick different RPs and DPs in different VLANs. As a result, some traffic in some VLANs can be forwarded over one trunk, and traffic for other VLANs to be forwarded over a different trunk. Figure 2-13 shows the basic idea, with SW3 forwarding odd-numbered VLAN traffic over the left trunk (Gi0/1) and even-numbered VLANs over the right trunk (Gi0/2).

Figure 2-13 *Load Balancing with PVST+*

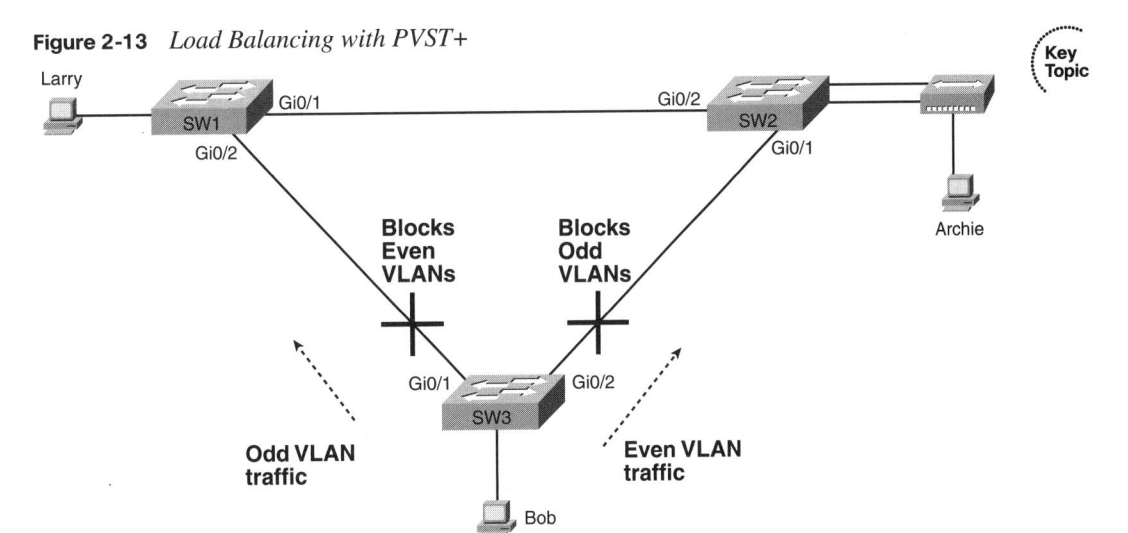

Later, when the IEEE introduced 802.1W RSTP, the IEEE still did not have a standard for using multiple instances of STP. So, Cisco implemented another proprietary solution to support one VLAN per RSTP spanning tree. Cisco has called this option both Rapid Per-VLAN Spanning Tree (RPVST) and Per-VLAN Rapid Spanning Tree (PVRST). Regardless of the acronyms, the idea is just like PVST+, but as applied to RSTP: one instance of RSTP to control each VLAN. So, not only do you get fast convergence, but you can also load-balance as shown in Figure 2-13.

Later, the IEEE created a standardized option for multiple spanning trees. The IEEE standard (802.1s) is often called either Multiple Spanning Trees (MST) or Multiple Instances of Spanning Trees (MIST). MIST allows the definition of multiple instances of RSTP, with each VLAN being associated with a particular instance. For example, to achieve the load-balancing effect in Figure 2-13, MIST would create two instances of RSTP: one for the even-numbered VLANs and one for the odd-numbered VLANs. If 100 VLANs existed, the switches still would only need two instances of RSTP, instead of the 100 instances used by PVRST. However, MIST requires more configuration on each switch, mainly to define the RSTP instances and associate each VLAN with an instance of STP.

Table 2-11 summarizes these three options for multiple spanning trees.

Key Topic

Table 2-11   *Comparing Three Options for Multiple Spanning Trees*

Option	Supports STP	Supports RSTP	Configuration Effort	Only One Instance Required for Each Redundant Path
PVST+	Yes	No	small	No
PVRST	No	Yes	small	No
MIST	No	Yes	medium	Yes

Configuration Options That Influence the Spanning Tree Topology

Regardless of whether PVST+, PVRST, or MIST is used, two main configuration options can be used to achieve the kind of load-balancing effects described around Figure 2-13: the bridge ID and the port cost. These options impact the per-VLAN STP topology as follows:

- The bridge IDs influence the choice of root switch, and for nonroot switches, their choice of root port.

- Each interface's (per-VLAN) STP cost to reach the root, which influences the choice of designated port on each LAN segment.

The following sections point out a few details particular to the implementation of STP on Cisco switches, beyond the generic concepts covered earlier in this chapter.

The Bridge ID and System ID Extension

As mentioned earlier in this chapter, a switch's bridge ID (BID) is formed by combining the switch's 2-byte priority and 6-byte MAC address. In practice, Cisco switches use a more detailed IEEE BID format that separates the priority into two parts. Figure 2-14 shows the more detailed format, with the former 16-bit priority field now including a 12-bit subfield called the *system ID extension*.

Figure 2-14 *STP System ID Extension*

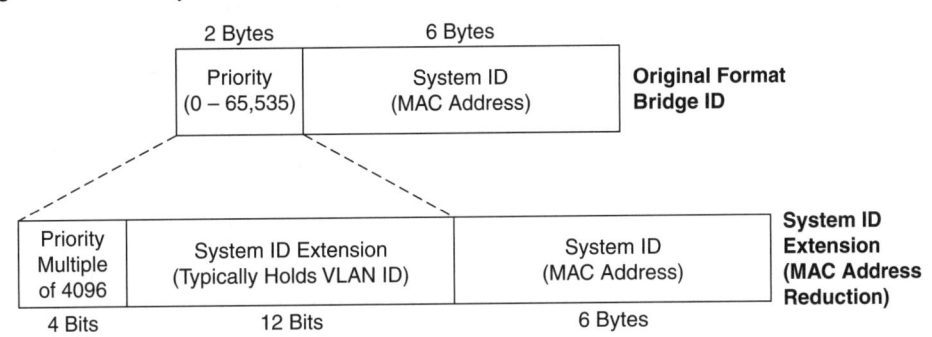

To build a switch's BID for a particular per-VLAN STP instance, the switch must use a base priority setting of a multiple of decimal 4096. (These multiples of 4096, when converted to binary, all end with 12 binary 0s.) To create the first 16 bits of the BID for a particular VLAN, the switch starts with a 16-bit version of the base priority value, which has all binary 0s in the last 12 digits. The switch then adds its base priority value to the VLAN ID. The result is that the low-order 12 bits in the original priority field then list the VLAN ID.

A nice side effect of using the system ID extension is that PVST+ then uses a different BID in each VLAN. For example, a switch configured with VLANs 1 through 4, with a default base priority of 32,768, has a default STP priority of 32,769 in VLAN 1, 32,770 in VLAN 2, 32,771 in VLAN 3, and so on.

Per-VLAN Port Costs

Each switch interface defaults its per-VLAN STP cost to the values shown earlier in Table 2-6 as the revised IEEE cost values. On Cisco switches, the STP cost is based on the actual speed of the interface, so if an interface negotiates to use a lower speed, the default STP cost reflects that lower speed per Table 2-6. If the interface negotiates to use a different speed, the switch dynamically changes the STP port cost as well.

Alternatively, a switch's port cost can be configured, either for all VLANs or for one VLAN at a time. After being configured, the switch ignores the negotiated speed on the interface, instead using the configured cost.

STP Configuration Option Summary

Table 2-12 summarizes the default settings for both the BID and the port costs, as well as lists the optional configuration commands covered in this chapter.

Key Topic

Table 2-12 *STP Defaults and Configuration Options*

Setting	Default	Command(s) to Change Default
Bridge ID	Priority: 32,768 + VLAN ID System: A burned-in MAC on the switch	**spanning-tree vlan** *vlan-id* **root** {**primary** | **secondary**} **spanning-tree vlan** *vlan-id* **priority** *priority*
Interface cost	Per Table 2-6: 100 for 10 Mbps, 19 for 100 Mbps, 4 for 1 Gbps, 2 for 10 Gbps	**spanning-tree vlan** *vlan-id* **cost** *cost*
PortFast	Not enabled	**spanning-tree portfast**
BPDU Guard	Not enabled	**spanning-tree bpduguard enable**

Next, the configuration section shows how to examine the operation of STP in a simple network, along with how to change these optional settings.

Verifying Default STP Operation

The following examples were taken from a small network with two switches, as shown in Figure 2-15. In this network, using default settings, all interfaces should forward except one interface on one switch on the links connecting the switches. Example 2-1 lists several **show** commands. The text following the example explains how the **show** command output identifies the details of the STP topology created in this small network.

Figure 2-15 *Two-Switch Network*

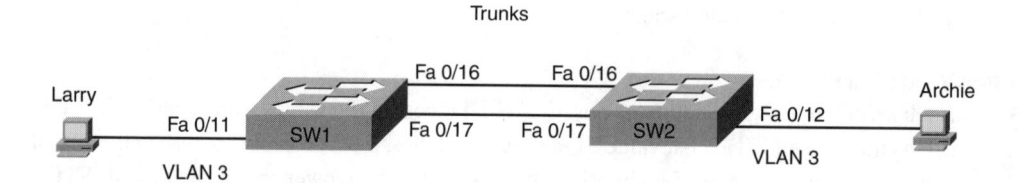

Example 2-1 *STP Status with Default STP Parameters*

```
SW1#show spanning-tree vlan 3

VLAN0003
  Spanning tree enabled protocol ieee
  Root ID    Priority    32771
             Address     0019.e859.5380
             Cost        19
             Port        16 (FastEthernet0/16)
             Hello Time   2 sec  Max Age 20 sec  Forward Delay 15 sec

  Bridge ID  Priority    32771  (priority 32768 sys-id-ext 3)
             Address     0019.e86a.6f80
             Hello Time   2 sec  Max Age 20 sec  Forward Delay 15 sec
             Aging Time 300


Interface        Role Sts Cost      Prio.Nbr Type
---------------- ---- --- --------- -------- --------------------------------
Fa0/11           Desg FWD 19        128.11   P2p
Fa0/16           Root FWD 19        128.16   P2p
Fa0/17           Altn BLK 19        128.17   P2p
SW1#show spanning-tree root

                                    Root  Hello Max Fwd
Vlan                   Root ID      Cost  Time  Age Dly  Root Port
---------------------- ------------------- -------- ----- --- --- ------------
VLAN0001    32769 0019.e859.5380       19    2   20  15 Fa0/16
VLAN0002    32770 0019.e859.5380       19    2   20  15 Fa0/16
VLAN0003    32771 0019.e859.5380       19    2   20  15 Fa0/16
VLAN0004    32772 0019.e859.5380       19    2   20  15 Fa0/16
! The next command supplies the same information as the show spanning-tree vlan 3
! command about the local switch, but in slightly briefer format
SW1#show span vlan 3 bridge

                                             Hello  Max  Fwd
Vlan                        Bridge ID        Time   Age  Dly  Protocol
------------- -------------------------------- ----- --- --- --------
VLAN0003    32771 (32768,   3) 0019.e86a.6f80    2   20  15  ieee
```

Example 2-1 begins with the output of the **show spanning-tree vlan 3** command on SW1. This command first lists three major groups of messages: one group of messages about the root switch, followed by another group about the local switch, and ending with interface role and status information. By comparing the shaded root ID and bridge ID in the first two groups of messages, you can quickly tell whether the local switch is root because the bridge ID and root ID would be the same. In this example, the local switch (SW1) is not the root.

The third group of messages in the **show spanning-tree vlan 3** command output identifies part of the STP topology in this example by listing all interfaces in that VLAN (both access interfaces and trunks that could possibly support the VLAN), their STP port roles, and their STP port states. For example, SW1 determines that Fa0/11 plays the role of a designated port because no other switches compete to become the DP on that port, as shown with the role of 'desg' in the command output. Therefore, SW1 must be advertising the lowest-cost Hello onto that segment. As a result, SW1 places Fa0/11 into a Forwarding State.

While the command output shows that SW1 chose interface Fa0/16 as its RP, SW1's logic in making this choice is not apparent from the command output. SW1 receives Hello BPDUs from SW2 on Fast Ethernet ports 0/16 and 0/17, both from SW2. Because both Fa0/16 and Fa0/17 default to the same port cost (19), SW1's path to the root is the same (19) over both paths. When a switch experiences a tie in regard to the cost to reach the root, the switch first uses the interfaces' *port priority* values as a tiebreaker. If the port priority values tie, the switch uses the lowest internal interface number. The interface priority and internal port number are listed under the heading "Prio.Nbr" in Example 2-1. In this case, SW1 is using the default port priority of 128 on each interface, so SW1 uses the lower port number, Fa0/16, as its root port, therefore placing Fa0/16 into a Forwarding State.

Note also that the command output shows Fa0/17 to be playing the role of an alternate (root) port, as shown with the "Altn" abbreviation in the command output. While the alternate port role is an RSTP concept, the Cisco 802.1d STP implementation also uses this concept, so the **show** command lists the alternate port role. However, because this port is neither an RP or DP, SW1 places this port into a Blocking State.

The next command in the example, **show spanning-tree root**, lists the bridge ID of the root switch in each VLAN. Note that both switches are using all default settings, so SW2 becomes root in all four existing VLANs. This command also lists the priority portion of the bridge ID separately, showing the differing priority values (32,769, 32,770, 32,771, and 32,772) based on the system ID extension explained earlier in this chapter. The last command in the example, **show spanning-tree vlan 3 bridge**, simply lists information about the local switch's bridge ID in VLAN 3.

Configuring STP Port Costs and Switch Priority

Example 2-2 shows how to impact the STP topology by configuring port cost and switch priority. First, on SW1, the port cost is lowered on FastEthernet 0/17, which makes SW1's path to the root through Fa0/17 better than the path out Fa0/16, therefore changing SW1's root port. Following that, the example shows SW1 becoming the root switch by changing SW1's bridge priority.

Example 2-2 *Manipulating STP Port Cost and Bridge Priority*

```
SW1#debug spanning-tree events
Spanning Tree event debugging is on
SW1#configure terminal
Enter configuration commands, one per line.  End with CNTL/Z.
SW1(config)#interface Fa0/17
SW1(config-if)#spanning-tree vlan 3 cost 2
00:45:39: STP: VLAN0003 new root port Fa0/17, cost 2
00:45:39: STP: VLAN0003 Fa0/17 -> listening
00:45:39: STP: VLAN0003 sent Topology Change Notice on Fa0/17
00:45:39: STP: VLAN0003 Fa0/16 -> blocking
00:45:54: STP: VLAN0003 Fa0/17 -> learning
00:46:09: STP: VLAN0003 sent Topology Change Notice on Fa0/17
00:46:09: STP: VLAN0003 Fa0/17 -> forwarding
SW1(config-if)#^Z
SW1#show spanning-tree vlan 3


VLAN0003
  Spanning tree enabled protocol ieee
  Root ID    Priority    32771
             Address     0019.e859.5380
             Cost        2
             Port        17 (FastEthernet0/17)
             Hello Time   2 sec  Max Age 20 sec  Forward Delay 15 sec

  Bridge ID  Priority    32771   (priority 32768 sys-id-ext 3)
             Address     0019.e86a.6f80
             Hello Time   2 sec  Max Age 20 sec  Forward Delay 15 sec
             Aging Time 15


Interface        Role Sts Cost      Prio.Nbr Type
---------------- ---- --- --------- -------- --------------------------------
Fa0/11           Desg FWD 19        128.11   P2p
Fa0/16           Altn BLK 19        128.16   P2p
Fa0/17           Root FWD 2         128.17   P2p
SW1#configure terminal
Enter configuration commands, one per line.  End with CNTL/Z.
SW1(config)#spanning-tree vlan 3 root primary
00:46:58: setting bridge id (which=1) prio 24579 prio cfg 24576 sysid 3
  (on) id 6003.0019.e86a.6f80
00:46:58: STP: VLAN0003 we are the spanning tree root
00:46:58: STP: VLAN0003 Fa0/16 -> listening
00:46:58: STP: VLAN0003 Topology Change rcvd on Fa0/16
00:47:13: STP: VLAN0003 Fa0/16 -> learning
00:47:28: STP: VLAN0003 Fa0/16 -> forwarding
```

This example starts with the **debug spanning-tree events** command on SW1. This command tells the switch to issue informational log messages whenever STP performs changes to an interface's role or state. These messages show up in the example as a result of the commands shown later in the example output.

Next, the port cost of the SW1 interface FastEthernet 0/17, in VLAN 3 only, is changed using the **spanning-tree vlan 3 cost 2** command, in interface Fa0/17 configuration mode. Immediately following this command, SW1 displays the first meaningful debug messages. These messages basically state that Fa0/17 is now SW1's root port, that Fa0/16 immediately transitions to a Blocking State, and that Fa0/17 slowly transitions to a Forwarding State by first going through the Listening and Learning States. You can see the timing of 15 seconds (per the default forward delay setting) in both the Learning and Listening States as shown in the shaded timestamps in the example.

> **NOTE**   Most of the configuration commands for setting STP parameters can omit the **vlan** parameter, thereby changing a setting for all VLANs. For example, the **spanning-tree cost 2** command would make an interface's STP cost be 2 for all VLANs.

Following the first set of debug messages, the output of the **show spanning-tree** command lists FastEthernet 0/16 as Blocking and FastEthernet 0/17 as Forwarding, with the cost to the root bridge now only 2, based on the changed cost of interface FastEthernet 0/17.

The next change occurs when the **spanning-tree vlan 3 root primary** command is issued on SW1. This command changes the base priority to 24,576, making SW1's VLAN 3 priority be 24,576 plus 3, or 24,579. As a result, SW1 becomes the root switch, as shown in the debug messages that follow.

The **spanning-tree vlan** *vlan-id* **root primary** command tells a switch to use a particular priority value in that VLAN only, with the switch choosing a value that will cause the switch to become the root switch in that VLAN. To do so, this command sets the base priority—the priority value that is then added to the VLAN ID to calculate the switch's priority—to a value lower than the current root switch's base priority. This command chooses the base priority as follows:

Key Topic

- 24,576, if the current root has a base priority higher than 24,576

- 4096 less than the current root's base priority if the current root's priority is 24,576 or lower

The **spanning-tree vlan** *vlan-id* **root secondary** command tells a switch to use a base priority value so that the local switch will become root if the primary root switch fails. This command sets the switch's base priority to 28,672 regardless of the current root's current priority value.

Note that the priority can also be explicitly set with the **spanning-tree vlan** *vlan-id* **priority** *value* global configuration command, which sets the base priority of the switch. However, because many LAN designs rely on one known root, with one backup to the root, the other commands are typically preferred.

Configuring PortFast and BPDU Guard

The PortFast and BPDU Guard features can be easily configured on any interface. To configure PortFast, just use the **spanning-tree portfast** interface subcommand. To also enable BPDU Guard, add the **spanning-tree bpduguard enable** interface subcommand.

Configuring EtherChannel

Finally, the two switches do have parallel Ethernet connections that could be configured for EtherChannel. By doing so, STP does not block on either interface, because STP treats both interfaces on each switch as one link. Example 2-3 shows the SW1 configuration and **show** commands for the new EtherChannel.

Example 2-3 *Configuring and Monitoring EtherChannel*

```
SW1#configure terminal
Enter configuration commands, one per line.  End with CNTL/Z.
SW1(config)#interface fa 0/16
SW1(config-if)#channel-group 1 mode on
SW1(config)#int fa 0/17
SW1(config-if)#channel-group 1 mode on
SW1(config-if)#^Z
00:32:27: STP: VLAN0001 Po1 -> learning
00:32:42: STP: VLAN0001 Po1 -> forwarding

SW1#show spanning-tree vlan 3


VLAN0003
  Spanning tree enabled protocol ieee
  Root ID    Priority    28675
             Address     0019.e859.5380
             Cost        12
             Port        72 (Port-channel1)
             Hello Time   2 sec  Max Age 20 sec  Forward Delay 15 sec

  Bridge ID  Priority    28675  (priority 28672 sys-id-ext 3)
             Address     0019.e86a.6f80
             Hello Time   2 sec  Max Age 20 sec  Forward Delay 15 sec
             Aging Time 300

Interface        Role Sts Cost      Prio.Nbr Type
---------------- ---- --- --------- -------- ---------------------------------
```

continues

Example 2-3 *Configuring and Monitoring EtherChannel (Continued)*

```
Fa0/11            Desg FWD 19        128.11    P2p
Po1               Root FWD 12        128.72    P2p
SW1#show etherchannel 1 summary
Flags:  D - down         P - in port-channel
        I - stand-alone  s - suspended
        H - Hot-standby (LACP only)
        R - Layer3       S - Layer2
        U - in use       f - failed to allocate aggregator
        u - unsuitable for bundling
        w - waiting to be aggregated
        d - default port


Number of channel-groups in use: 1
Number of aggregators:            1

Group  Port-channel  Protocol    Ports
------+-------------+-----------+---------------------------------------------
1         Po1(SU)        -        Fa0/16(P)   Fa0/17(P)
```

On 2960 switches, any port can be part of an EtherChannel, with up to eight on a single EtherChannel, so the EtherChannel commands are interface subcommands. The **channel-group 1 mode on** interface subcommands enable EtherChannel on interfaces FastEthernet 0/16 and 0/17. Both switches must agree on the number for the EtherChannel, 1 in this case, so SW2's portchannel configuration is identical to SW1's.

The **channel-group** command allows for configuring an interface to always be in a port channel (using the **on** keyword), or to be dynamically negotiated with the other switch using the **auto** or **desirable** keywords. With the **on** keyword used on SW1, if for some reason SW2 was not configured correctly for EtherChannel, the switches would not forward traffic over the interfaces. Alternatively, the EtherChannel **channel-group** configuration commands on each switch could use parameters of **auto** or **desirable** instead of **on**. With these other parameters, the switches negotiate whether to use EtherChannel. If negotiated, an EtherChannel is formed. If not, the ports can be used without forming an EtherChannel, with STP blocking some interfaces.

The use of the **auto** and **desirable** parameters can be deceiving. If you configure **auto** on both switches, the EtherChannel never comes up! The **auto** keyword tells the switch to wait for the other switch to start the negotiations. As long as one of the two switches is configured with as either **on** or **desirable**, the EtherChannel can be successfully negotiated.

In the rest of Example 2-3, you see several references to "port-channel" or "Po." Because STP treats the EtherChannel as one link, the switch needs some way to represent the entire

EtherChannel. The 2960 IOS uses the term "Po," short for "port channel," as a way to name the EtherChannel. (EtherChannel is sometimes called port channel.) For example, near the end of the example, the **show etherchannel 1 summary** command references Po1, for port channel/EtherChannel 1.

Configuring RSTP

RSTP configuration and verification are incredibly anticlimactic after fully understanding the STP configuration options covered in this chapter. Each switch requires a single global command, **spanning-tree mode rapid-pvst**. As you can tell from the command, it not only enables RSTP but also PVRST, running one RSTP instance for all defined VLANs.

The rest of the configuration commands covered in this section apply to RSTP and PVRST with no changes. The same commands impact the BID, the port cost, and EtherChannels. In fact, the **spanning-tree portfast** interface subcommand even works, technically making the interface an RSTP edge-type interface, instead of a link-type, and instantly moving the interface to a Forwarding State.

Example 2-4 shows an example of how to migrate from STP and PVST+ to RSTP and PVRST, and how to tell whether a switch is using RSTP or STP.

Example 2-4 *RSTP and PVRST Configuration and Verification*

```
SW1#configure terminal
Enter configuration commands, one per line.  End with CNTL/Z.
SW1(config)#spanning-tree mode ?
  mst        Multiple spanning tree mode
  pvst       Per-Vlan spanning tree mode
  rapid-pvst Per-Vlan rapid spanning tree mode

! The next line configures this switch to use RSTP and PVRST.
!
SW1(config)#spanning-tree mode rapid-pvst
SW1(config)#^Z
! The "protocol RSTP" shaded text means that this switch uses RSTP, not IEEE STP.
SW1#show spanning-tree vlan 4


VLAN0004
  Spanning tree enabled protocol rstp
  Root ID    Priority    32772
             Address     0019.e859.5380
             Cost        19
             Port        16 (FastEthernet0/16)
             Hello Time   2 sec  Max Age 20 sec  Forward Delay 15 sec

  Bridge ID  Priority    32772  (priority 32768 sys-id-ext 4)
```

continues

Example 2-4 *RSTP and PVRST Configuration and Verification (Continued)*

```
                Address       0019.e86a.6f80
                Hello Time    2 sec  Max Age 20 sec  Forward Delay 15 sec
                Aging Time 300

Interface        Role Sts Cost      Prio.Nbr Type
---------------- ---- --- --------- -------- --------------------------------
Fa0/16           Root FWD 19        128.16   P2p Peer(STP)
Fa0/17           Altn BLK 19        128.17   P2p Peer(STP)
```

Of particular importance, take the time to compare the "protocol rstp" phrase shaded in the example with the earlier examples' output from the **show spanning-tree** command. The earlier examples all used the default setting of STP and PVST+, listing the text "protocol ieee," referring to the original IEEE 802.1d STP standard.

STP Troubleshooting

The final sections focus on how to apply the information covered in the earlier parts of this chapter to new scenarios. While this section helps you prepare to troubleshoot STP problems in real networks, the main goal for this section is to prepare you to answer STP questions on the CCNA exams. (Note that these sections do not introduce any new facts about STP.)

STP questions tend to intimidate many test takers. One reason STP causes exam takers more problems is that even those with on-the-job experience might not have ever needed to troubleshoot STP problems. STP runs by default and works well using default configuration settings in medium to small networks, so engineers seldom need to troubleshoot STP problems. Also, while the theory and commands covered in this chapter might be understandable, applying many of those concepts and commands to a unique problem on the exam takes time.

This section describes and summarizes a plan of attack for analyzing and answering different types of STP problems on the exam. Some exam questions might require you to determine which interfaces should forward or block. Other questions might want to know which switch is the root, which ports are root ports, and which ports are designated ports. Certainly, other variations of questions exist as well. Regardless of the type of question, the following three steps can be used to analyze STP in any LAN, and then, in turn, answer any STP questions on the exam:

Key Topic

Step 1 Determine the root switch.

Step 2 For each nonroot switch, determine its one root port (RP) and cost to reach the root switch through that RP.

Step 3 For each segment, determine the designated port (DP) and the cost advertised by the DP onto that segment.

The following sections review the key points about each of these steps, and then list some tips for helping you quickly find the answer for exam questions.

Determining the Root Switch

Determining the STP root switch is easy if you know all the switches' BIDs; just pick the lowest value. If the question lists the priority and MAC address separately, as is common in **show** command output, pick the switch with the lowest priority, or in the case of a tie, pick the lower MAC address value.

Much like with real networks, if a question requires you to issue **show** commands on various switches to find the root switch, an organized strategy can help you answer questions faster. First, remember that many variations of the **show spanning-tree** command list the root's BID, with priority on one line and the MAC address on the next, in the first part of the output; the local switch's BID is listed in the next section. (See Example 2-1 for a shaded example.) Also remember that Cisco switches default to use PVST+, so be careful to look at STP details for the correct VLAN. With these facts in mind, the following list outlines a good strategy:

Step 1 Pick a switch at which to begin, and find the root switch's BID and the local switch's BID in the VLAN in question using the **show spanning-tree vlan** *vlan-id* exec command.

Step 2 If the root BID and local BID are equal, the local switch is the root switch.

Step 3 If the root BID is not equal to the local switch's BID, follow these steps:

    a. Find the RP interface on the local switch (also in the **show spanning-tree** command output).

    b. Using Cisco Discovery Protocol (CDP) or other documentation, determine which switch is on the other end of the RP interface found in Step 3A.

    c. Log in to the switch on the other end of the RP interface and repeat this process, starting at Step 1.

Example 2-5 shows the output of a **show spanning-tree vlan 1** command. Without even knowing the topology of the LAN, take the time now to try this troubleshooting strategy based on the output in the example, and compare your thoughts to the explanations following this example.

Example 2-5 *Finding the Root Switch*

```
SW2#show spanning-tree vlan 1
VLAN0001
  Spanning tree enabled protocol ieee
  Root ID    Priority    32769
             Address     000a.b7dc.b780
             Cost        19
             Port        1 (FastEthernet0/1)
             Hello Time   2 sec  Max Age 20 sec  Forward Delay 15 sec

  Bridge ID  Priority    32769  (priority 32768 sys-id-ext 1)
             Address     0011.92b0.f500
             Hello Time   2 sec  Max Age 20 sec  Forward Delay 15 sec
             Aging Time 300

Interface        Role Sts Cost      Prio.Nbr Type
---------------- ---- --- --------- -------- --------------------------------
Fa0/1            Root FWD 19        128.1    P2p
Fa0/19           Desg FWD 100       128.19   Shr
Fa0/20           Desg FWD 100       128.20   Shr
SW2#show spanning-tree vlan 1 bridge id
VLAN0001         8001.0011.92b0.f500
```

The shaded portions of the example point out the root's BID (priority and address) as well as SW2's differing BID. Because the root switch's BID is different, the next step should be to find the root port, which is listed in two different places in the command output (Fa0/1). The next step would be to repeat the process on the switch on the other end of SW2's Fa0/1 interface, but the example does not identify that switch.

Determining the Root Port on Nonroot Switches

Each nonroot switch has one, and only one, root port (RP). (Root switches do not have an RP.) To choose its RP, a switch listens for incoming Hello BPDUs. For each received Hello, the switch adds the cost listed in the Hello BPDU to that switch's port cost for the port on which the Hello was received. The least-calculated cost wins; in case of a tie, the switch picks the interface with the lower port priority, and if that ties, the switch picks the lower internal port number.

While the previous paragraph truly summarizes how a nonroot switch picks its RP, when an exam question supplies information about the root switch and interface port costs, a slightly different approach can possibly speed your way to an answer. For example, consider the following question, asked about the network shown in Figure 2-16:

> In the switched network shown in Figure 2-16, all switches and segments are up and working, with STP enabled in VLAN 1. SW1 has been elected root. SW2's Fa0/1 interface uses a cost setting of 20, with all other interfaces using the default STP cost. Determine the RP on SW4.

Figure 2-16 *STP Analysis Example 1*

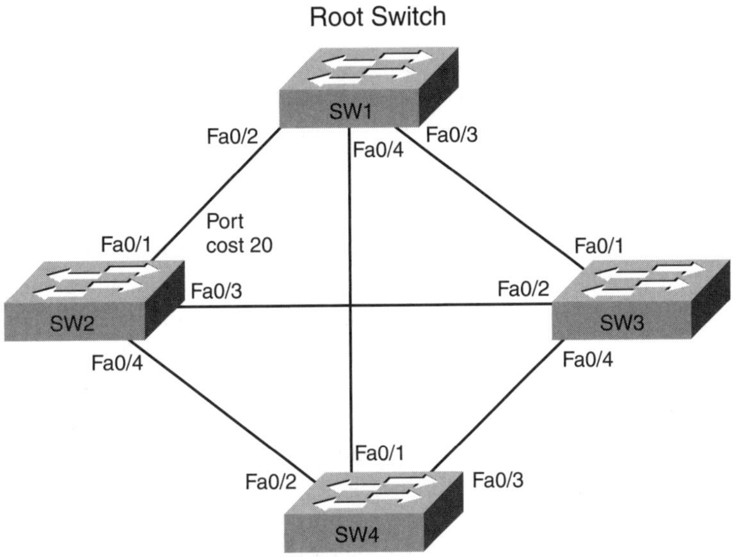

One way to go about solving this particular problem is to just apply the STP concepts as summarized in the first paragraph in this section. Alternately, you might find the solution a little more quickly with the following process, starting with a nonroot switch:

Step 1   Determine all possible paths over which a frame, sent by the nonroot switch, can reach the root switch.

Step 2   For each possible path in Step 1, add the costs of all outgoing interfaces in that path.

Step 3   The lowest cost found is the cost to reach the root, and the outgoing interface is that switch's RP.

Step 4   If the cost ties, use the port priority tiebreaker, and if that ties, use the lowest port number tiebreaker.

Table 2-13 shows the work done for Steps 1 and 2 of this process, listing the paths and the respective costs to reach the root over each path. In this network, SW4 has five possible paths to the root switch. The cost column lists the interface costs in the same order as in the first column, along with the total cost.

Table 2-13   *Finding SW4's RP: Calculating the Cost*

Physical Path (Outgoing Interfaces)	Cost
SW4 (Fa0/2) –> SW2 (Fa0/1) –> SW1	19 + 20 = 39
SW4 (Fa0/3) –> SW3 (Fa0/1) –> SW1	19 + 19 = 38
SW4 (Fa0/1) –> SW1	19 = 19
SW4 (Fa0/2) –> SW2 (Fa0/3) –> SW3 (Fa0/1) –> SW1	19 + 19 + 19 = 57
SW4 (Fa0/3) –> SW3 (Fa0/2) –> SW2 (Fa0/1) –> SW1	19 + 19 + 20 = 58

Just to ensure that the contents of the table are clear, examine the SW4 (Fa0/2) –> SW2 (Fa0/1) –> SW1 physical path for a moment. For this path, the outgoing interfaces are SW4's Fa0/2 interface, defaulting cost 19, and SW2's Fa0/1 interface, configured for cost 20, for a total of 39.

You should also realize which interfaces' costs are ignored with this process. Using the same example, the frame sent by SW4 toward the root would enter SW2's Fa0/4 interface and SW1's Fa0/2 interface. Neither interfaces' costs would be considered.

In this case, SW4's RP would be its FA0/1 interface, because the least-cost path (cost 19) begins with that interface.

Beware of making assumptions with questions that require you to find a switch's RP. For example, in this case, it might be intuitive to think that SW4's RP would be its Fa0/1 interface, because it is directly connected to the root. However, if SW4's Fa0/3 and SW3's Fa0/1 interfaces were changed to a port cost of 4 each, the SW4 (Fa0/3) –> SW3 (Fa0/1) –> SW1 path would total a cost of 8, and SW4's RP would be its Fa0/3 interface. So, just because the path looks better in the diagram, remember that the deciding point is the total cost.

Determining the Designated Port on Each LAN Segment

Each LAN segment has a single switch that acts as the designated port (DP) on that segment. On segments that connect a switch to a device that does not even use STP—for example, segments connecting a switch to a PC or a router—the switch port is elected as the DP because the only device sending a Hello onto the segment is the switch. However, segments that connect multiple switches require a little more work to discover which should be the DP. By definition, the DP for a segment is determined as follows:

> The switch interface that forwards the lowest-cost Hello BPDU onto the segment is the DP. In case of a tie, among the switches sending the Hellos whose cost tied, the switch with the lowest BID wins.

Again, the formal definition describes what STP does, and you can apply that concept to any STP question. However, for the exams, if you just finished finding the RP of each nonroot switch, and you noted the cost to reach the root on each switch (for example, as shown in Table 2-13), you can easily find the DP as follows:

Step 1   For switches connected to the same LAN segment, the switch with the lowest cost to reach the root is the DP on that segment.

Step 2   In case of a tie, among the switches that tied on cost, the switch with the lowest BID becomes the DP.

For example, consider Figure 2-17. This figure shows the same switched network as in Figure 2-16, but with the RPs and DPs noted, as well as each switch's least cost to reach the root over its respective RP.

Figure 2-17   *Picking the Designated Ports*

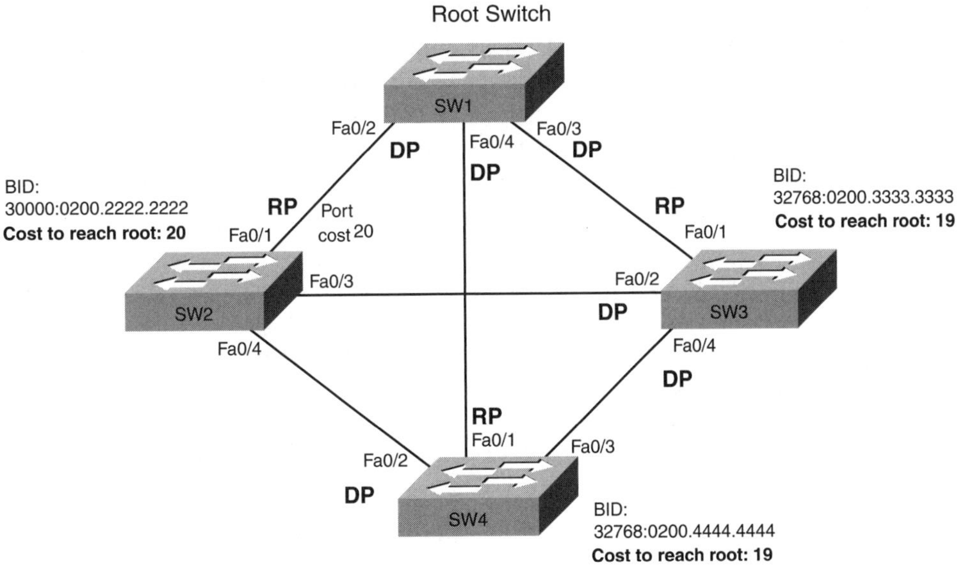

Focus on the segments that connect the nonroot switches for a moment. For the SW2–SW4 segment, SW4 wins by virtue of having a cost 19 path to the root, whereas SW2's best path is cost 20. For the same reason, SW3 becomes the DP on the SW2–SW3 segment. For the SW3–SW4 segment, both SW3 and SW4 tie on cost to reach the root. The figure lists the BIDs of the nonroot switches, so you can see that SW3's BID is lower. As a result, SW3 wins the tiebreaker, making SW3 the DP on that segment.

Note also that the root switch (SW1) becomes the DP on all its segments by virtue of the fact that the root switch always advertises Hellos of cost 0, and all other switches' calculated cost must be at least 1, because the lowest allowed port cost is 1.

For the exams, you should be able to find the root switch, then the RP on each switch, and then the DP on each segment, after you know the BIDs, port costs, and topology of the LAN. At that point, you also know which interfaces forward—those interfaces that are RPs or DPs—with the rest of the interfaces blocking.

STP Convergence

The STP topology—the set of interfaces in a Forwarding State—should remain stable as long as the network remains stable. When interfaces and switches go up or down, the resulting STP topology can change; in other words, STP convergence will occur. This section points out a few common-sense strategies for attacking these types of problems on the exams.

Some STP exam questions might ignore the transition details when convergence occurs, instead focusing on which interfaces change from Forwarding to Blocking, or Blocking to Forwarding, when a particular change happens. For example, a question might list details of a scenario and then ask, "Which interfaces change from a Blocking to a Forwarding State?" For these questions that compare the topologies both before and after a change, just apply the same steps already covered in this section, but twice: once for the conditions before the changes and once for the conditions that caused the change.

Other STP questions might focus on the transition process, including the Hello timer, MaxAge timer, forward delay timer, Listening and Learning States, and their usage, as described earlier in this chapter. For these types of questions, remember the following facts about what occurs during STP convergence:

- For interfaces that stay in the same STP state, nothing needs to change.

- For interfaces that need to move from a Forwarding State to a Blocking State, the switch immediately changes the state to Blocking.

- For interfaces that need to move from a Blocking State to a Forwarding State, the switch first moves the interface to Listening State, then Learning State, each for the time specified by the forward delay timer (default 15 seconds). Only then will the interface be placed into Forwarding State.

Exam Preparation Tasks

Review All the Key Topics

Review the most important topics from this chapter, noted with the Key Topics icon in the outer margin of the page. Table 2-14 lists a reference of these key topics and the page numbers on which each is found.

Key Topic

Table 2-14 *Key Topics for Chapter 2*

Key Topic Element	Description	Page Number
Table 2-2	Lists the three main problems that occur when not using STP in a LAN with redundant links	63
Table 2-3	Lists the reasons why a switch chooses to place an interface into Forwarding or Blocking State	66
Table 2-4	Lists the most important fields in Hello BPDU messages	67
Figure 2-5	Shows how switches calculate their root cost	70
Table 2-6	Lists the original and current default STP port costs for various interface speeds	71
List	A summary description of steady-state STP operations	72
Table 2-7	STP timers	73
List	Definitions of what occurs in the Listening and Learning States	75
Table 2-8	Summary of 802.1d states	75
List	Similarities between RSTP and STP	78
Table 2-9	Lists 802.1d and corresponding 802.1w interface states	80
Table 2-10	Lists STP and RSTP port roles and comparisons	82
Figure 2-13	Conceptual view of load-balancing benefits of PVST+	87
Table 2-11	Compares three options for multiple spanning trees	88
Figure 2-14	Shows the format of the system ID extension of the STP priority field	89
Table 2-12	Lists default settings for STP optional configuration settings and related configuration commands	90

continues

Table 2-14 *Key Topics for Chapter 2 (Continued)*

Key Topic Element	Description	Page Number
List	Two branches of logic in how the **spanning-tree root primary** command picks a new base STP priority	94
List	Strategy for solving STP problems on the exams	98

Complete the Tables and Lists from Memory

Print a copy of Appendix J, "Memory Tables," (found on the CD) or at least the section for this chapter, and complete the tables and lists from memory. Appendix K, "Memory Tables Answer Key," also on the CD, includes completed tables and lists to check your work.

Definitions of Key Terms

Define the following key terms from this chapter, and check your answers in the glossary.

Alternate port, backup port, Blocking State, BPDU Guard, bridge ID, bridge protocol data unit (BPDU), designated port, disabled port, Discarding State, EtherChannel, forward delay, Forwarding State, Hello BPDU, IEEE 802.1d, IEEE 802.1s, IEEE 802.1w, Inferior Hello, Learning State, Listening State, MaxAge, PortFast, Rapid Spanning Tree Protocol (RSTP), root port, root switch, Spanning Tree Protocol (STP)

Command Reference to Check Your Memory

While you should not necessarily memorize the information in the tables in this section, this section does include a reference for the configuration and EXEC commands covered in this chapter. Practically speaking, you should memorize the commands as a side effect of reading the chapter and doing all the activities in this exam preparation section. To check to see how well you have memorized the commands as a side effect of your other studies, cover the left side of the table with a piece of paper, read the descriptions in the right side, and see whether you remember the command.

Table 2-15 *Chapter 2 Configuration Command Reference*

Command	Description
spanning-tree vlan *vlan-number* **root primary**	Global configuration command that changes this switch to the root switch. The switch's priority is changed to the lower of either 24,576 or 4096 less than the priority of the current root bridge when the command was issued.

Table 2-15 *Chapter 2 Configuration Command Reference (Continued)*

Command	Description
spanning-tree vlan *vlan-number* **root secondary**	Global configuration command that sets this switch's STP base priority to 28,672.
spanning-tree [**vlan** *vlan-id*] {**priority** *priority*}	Global configuration command that changes the bridge priority of this switch for the specified VLAN.
spanning-tree [**vlan** *vlan-number*] **cost** *cost*	Interface subcommand that changes the STP cost to the configured value.
channel-group *channel-group-number* **mode** {**auto** | **desirable** | **on**}	Interface subcommand that enables EtherChannel on the interface.
spanning-tree portfast	Interface subcommand that enables PortFast on the interface.
spanning-tree bpduguard enable	Interface subcommand to enable BPDU Guard on an interface
spanning-tree mode {**mst** | **rapid-pvst** | **pvst**}	Global command to enable PVST+ and 802.1d (**pvst**), PVRST and 802.1w (**rapid-pvst**), or IEEE 802.1s (multiple spanning trees) and 802.1w (**mst**).

Table 2-16 *Chapter 2 EXEC Command Reference*

Command	Description
show spanning-tree	Lists details about the state of STP on the switch, including the state of each port
show spanning-tree *interface interface-id*	Lists STP information only for the specified port
show spanning-tree vlan *vlan-id*	Lists STP information for the specified VLAN
show spanning-tree [**vlan** *vlan-id*] **root**	Lists information about each VLAN's root or for just the specified VLAN
show spanning-tree [**vlan** *vlan-id*] **bridge**	Lists STP information about the local switch for each VLAN or for just the specified VLAN
debug spanning-tree events	Causes the switch to provide informational messages about changes in the STP topology
show etherchannel [*channel-group-number*] {**brief** | **detail** | **port** | **port-channel** | **summary**}	Lists information about the state of EtherChannels on this switch.

This chapter covers the following subjects:

Generalized Troubleshooting Methodologies:
This section presents discussions and opinions
about how to approach a networking problem
when a general examination of the problem does
not quickly identify the root cause.

**Troubleshooting the LAN Switching Data
Plane**: This section suggests several organized
steps for troubleshooting Ethernet LAN
problems, with a detailed review of commands
and methods.

**Predicting Normal Operation of the LAN
Switching Data Plane**: This section suggests
how to analyze switch **show** command output and
figures to predict where a frame should be
forwarded in an example switched LAN.

CHAPTER 3

Troubleshooting LAN Switching

This chapter, along with Chapter 7, "Troubleshooting IP Routing," and Chapter 11, "Troubleshooting Routing Protocols," has an important job: to help you develop the troubleshooting skills required to quickly and confidently answer certain types of questions on the exams. At the same time, this chapter can hopefully make you better prepared to solve real networking problems.

> **NOTE** For some thoughts about why troubleshooting is so important for the exams, refer to the section "Format of the CCNA Exams" in the introduction to this book.

The troubleshooting chapters in this book do not have the same primary goal as the other chapters. Simply put, the nontroubleshooting chapters focus on individual features and facts about an area of technology, whereas the troubleshooting chapters pull a much broader set of concepts together. These troubleshooting chapters take a broader look at the networking world, focusing on how the parts work together, assuming that you already know about the individual components.

This chapter covers the same technology covered in the other chapters in this part of the book (Chapter 1, "Virtual LANs," and Chapter 2, "Spanning Tree Protocol") and the related prerequisite materials (as covered in *CCENT/CCNA ICND1 Official Exam Certification Guide*). Also, because this chapter is the first troubleshooting chapter in this book, it also explains some general concepts about troubleshooting methodology.

"Do I Know This Already?" Quiz

Because the troubleshooting chapters of this book pull in concepts from many other chapters, including some chapters in *CCENT/CCNA ICND1 Official Exam Certification Guide*, as well as show how to approach some of the more challenging questions on the CCNA exams, you should read these chapters regardless of your current knowledge level. For these reasons, the troubleshooting chapters do not include a "Do I Know This Already?" quiz. However, if you feel particularly confident about troubleshooting LAN switching features covered in this book and *CCENT/CCNA ICND1 Official Exam Certification Guide*, feel free to move to the "Exam Preparation Tasks" section, near the end of this chapter, to bypass the majority of the chapter.

Foundation Topics

This chapter has three major sections. The first section focuses on the troubleshooting process as an end to itself. The second section explains how to apply the general troubleshooting methods specifically to a LAN switching data plane. The last section then lists some hints and ideas about specific types of problems related to LAN switching.

Generalized Troubleshooting Methodologies

> **NOTE**   The generic troubleshooting strategies and methods described here are a means to an end. You don't need to study these processes or memorize them for the purposes of the exam. Instead, these processes can help you think through problems on the exam so that you can answer the questions a little more quickly and with a little more confidence.

When faced with a need to solve a networking problem, everyone uses some troubleshooting methodology, whether informal or formal. Some people like to start by checking the physical cabling and interface status of all the physical links that could affect the problem. Some people like to start by pinging everything that could tell you more about the problem, and then drilling deeper into the details. Some people might even just try whatever comes to mind until they intuitively know the general problem. None of these methods is inherently bad or good; I've tried all these methods, and others, and had some success with each approach.

While most people develop troubleshooting habits and styles that work well based on their own experiences and strengths, a more systematic troubleshooting methodology can help anyone learn to troubleshoot problems with better success. The following sections describe one such systematic troubleshooting methodology for the purpose of helping you prepare to troubleshoot networking problems on the CCNA exams. This troubleshooting methodology has three major branches, which generally occur in the order shown here:

- **Analyzing/predicting normal operation**: The description and prediction of the details of what should happen if the network is working correctly, based on documentation, configuration, and **show** and **debug** command output.

- **Problem isolation**: When some problem might be occurring, find the component(s) that do not work correctly as compared to the predicted behavior, again based on documentation, configuration, and **show** and **debug** command output.

- **Root cause analysis**: Identify the underlying causes of the problems identified in the previous step, specifically the causes that have a specific action with which the problem can be fixed.

Following these three steps should result in the engineer knowing how to fix the problem, not just the problem symptoms. Next, the text explains some thoughts about how to approach each step of the troubleshooting process.

Analyzing and Predicting Normal Network Operation

Any network's job is to deliver data from one end-user device to another. To analyze a network, an engineer needs to understand the logic used by each successive device as it forwards the data to the next device. By thinking about what should happen at each device, the engineer can describe the entire flow of data.

The term *data plane* refers to any actions taken by networking devices for the forwarding of an individual frame or packet. To forward each frame or packet, a device applies its data plane logic and processes to the frame or packet. For example, when a LAN switch receives a frame in an interface in VLAN 3, the switch will make a forwarding decision based on the VLAN 3 entries in the MAC address table, and forward the packet. All this logic is part of a switch's data plane processing.

The term *control plane* refers to the overhead processes that do not need to be done for each packet or frame. Instead, some control plane processes support the forwarding process. For example, VLAN Trunking Protocol (VTP) and IP routing protocols are examples of control plane processes. Other control plane processes can only be indirectly related to the data plane. For example, Cisco Discovery Protocol (CDP) can be useful for confirming the accuracy of network documentation, but CDP can be disabled with no effect on the data plane forwarding processes.

To predict the expected operation of a network, or to explain the details of how a correctly functioning network is currently working, it can be helpful to begin by looking at either the control plane or data plane. This text shows the data plane first, but in real life, you can pick one or the other in part based on the known symptoms of the problem.

Data Plane Analysis

Data plane troubleshooting examines each device in the expected forwarding path for the data, in order. The analysis begins with the host creating the original data. That host sends the data to some other device, which then sends the data to another device, and so on, until the data reaches the endpoint host. The receiving host typically sends some sort of reply, so to fully understand how useful communications happen, you also need to analyze the reverse process as well. In particular, the outward problem symptoms typically identify two end-user devices that cannot communicate, but the underlying problem might only be related to frames or packets going in one direction.

Unless a particular problem's symptoms already suggest a specific problem, data plane troubleshooting should begin with an analysis of the Layer 3 data plane. If you start with Layer 3, you can see the major steps in sending and receiving data between two hosts. You can then examine each individual Layer 3 forwarding step more closely, looking at the underlying Layer 1 and 2 details. For example, Figure 3-1 shows the six major IP forwarding (data plane) steps in a small network.

Figure 3-1 *Major Steps in an IP Forwarding Example*

When understanding the expected behavior of Layer 3 in this case, you would need to consider how the packet flows from left to right, and then how the reply flows from right to left. Using the six steps in the figure, the following analysis could be done:

Step 1 Think about PC1's IP address and mask, the IP address and mask of PC2, and PC1's logic to realize that PC2 is in another subnet. This causes PC1 to choose to send the packet to its default gateway (R1).

Step 2 Consider R1's forwarding logic for matching the packet's destination IP address with R1's routing table, with the expectation that R1 chooses to send the packet to R2 next.

Step 3 On R2, consider the same routing table matching logic as used on R1 in the previous step, using R2's routing table. The matching entry should be a connected route on R2.

Step 4 This step relates to PC2's reply packet, which uses the same basic logic as Step 1. Compare PC2's IP address/mask with PC1's IP address, noting that they are in different subnets. As a result, PC2 should send the packet to its default gateway, R2.

Step 5   Consider R2's forwarding logic for packets destined to PC1's IP address, with the expectation that the matching route would cause R2 to send these packets to R1 next.

Step 6   The final routing step, on R1, should show that a packet destined to PC1's IP address matches a connected route on R1, which causes R1 to send the packet directly to PC1's MAC address.

After you have a good grasp of the expected behaviors of each step at Layer 3, you could then more closely examine Layer 2. Following the same ordering again, you could take a closer look at the first Layer 3 routing step in Figure 3-1 (PC1 sending a packet to R1), examining the Layer 1 and 2 details of how the frame is sent by PC1 to be delivered to R1, as shown in Figure 3-2.

Figure 3-2   *Major Steps in a LAN Switching Forwarding Example*

For this analysis, you would again begin with PC1, this time considering the Ethernet header and trailer, particularly the source and destination MAC addresses. Then, at Step 2, you would consider SW1's forwarding logic, which compares the frame's destination MAC address to SW1's MAC address table, telling SW1 to forward the frame to SW2. Steps 3 and 4 would repeat Step 2's logic from SW2 and SW3, respectively.

Control Plane Analysis

Many control plane processes directly affect the data plane process. For example, IP routing cannot work without appropriate IP routes, so routers typically use a dynamic routing protocol—a control plane protocol—to learn the routes. Routing protocols are considered to be control plane protocols in part because the work done by a routing protocol does not have to be repeated for each frame or packet.

While the data plane processes lend themselves to a somewhat generic troubleshooting process of examining the forwarding logic at each device, control plane processes differ too much to allow such a generalized troubleshooting process. However, it is helpful to consider a specific set of troubleshooting steps for each specific control plane protocol. For example, Chapter 1 explains how to approach troubleshooting various types of VTP problems.

Predicting Normal Operations: Summary of the Process

On the exams, some questions will simply require that you analyze and predict the normal operation of a working network. In other cases, predicting the normal behavior is just a precursor to isolating and fixing a problem. Regardless, if the question gives you no specific clues about the part of the network on which to focus, the following list summarizes a suggested approach for finding the answers:

Step 1   Examine the data plane as follows:

   a. Determine the major Layer 3 steps—including origin host to default router, each router to the next router, and last router to the destination host—in both directions.

   b. For each Layer 2 network between a host and router or between two routers, analyze the forwarding logic for each device.

Step 2   Examine the control plane as follows:

   a. Identify the control plane protocols that are used and vital to the forwarding process.

   b. Examine each vital control plane protocol for proper operation; the details of this analysis differ for each protocol.

   c. Defer any analysis of control plane protocols that do not affect the data plane's correct operation until you clearly see a need for the protocol to answer that question (for example, CDP).

Problem Isolation

The troubleshooting process is seldom a sequential process. For organizational purposes, this chapter lists problem isolation as the second of three troubleshooting steps. However, this step is more likely to happen as soon as the first step (predicting normal behavior) finds a problem. So, while the generic lists shown in this section help provide structure about how to troubleshoot a problem, the actual practice can be messy.

When you have no clues as to how to proceed, other than maybe that two hosts cannot communicate, it is again best to start with the Layer 3 data plane—in other words, IP forwarding logic. Then, when you find an IP forwarding step that doesn't work, examine that step more closely to further isolate where the problem is occurring. For example, consider Figure 3-1 again, which shows a packet being delivered from PC1 to PC2, and back, in six routing steps. In this case, however, you determine that R2 gets the packet, but the packet is never delivered to PC2. So, you take closer look at everything from R2 to PC2 to further isolate the problem.

After you isolate the problem to one IP forwarding step (as shown in Figure 3-1), you should continue to further isolate the problem to as small a number of components as possible. For example, if R2 gets the packet, but PC2 does not, the problem might be in R2, SW4, SW5, PC2, the cabling, or possibly devices left out of the network documentation.

The process to further isolate the problem typically requires thinking about functions at many layers of the OSI model, as well as both data plane and control plane functions. Continuing with the same example problem scenario, to be able to forward packets to PC2, R2 will need to know PC2's MAC address as learned using Address Resolution Protocol (ARP). If you discover that R2 does not have an ARP entry to PC2, you might be tempted to think that some sort of IP-related problem exists. However, this problem might be caused by the SW4–SW5 trunk being down, which means that R2's IP ARP request—a LAN broadcast—cannot be delivered by SW4 to SW5, and then to PC2. So, the problem with the packet-forwarding process from R2 to PC2 might be related to a control protocol (ARP), but the failed ARP request might be caused by yet other devices (SW4–SW5 trunk down), which might well be a Layer 2 or a Layer 1 problem.

If an exam question gives no hints as to where to start, the following process summarizes a good general systematic problem isolation strategy:

Step 1   Begin by examining the Layer 3 data plane (IP forwarding), comparing the results to the expected normal behavior, until you identify the first major routing step that fails.

Step 2   Further isolate the problem to as few components as possible:

   a.   Examine functions at all layers, but focusing on Layers 1, 2, and 3.

   b.   Examine both data plane and control plane functions.

On the exams, remember that you get no extra points for good troubleshooting methods, so just find the answer any way you can, even if that means you guessed a bit based on the context of the question. For example, the suggested process in Step 2A says to focus on Layers 1, 2, and 3; that suggestion is based on the fact that the CCNA exams focus mainly on these three layers. But you should look to shortcut this process as much as possible based on what the question says.

Root Cause Analysis

The final of the three steps, root cause analysis, strives to finish the troubleshooting process to identify the specific device and function that needs to be fixed. The root cause is the true reason the problem has occurred, and more importantly, it is the function that, when fixed, solves that particular problem.

Finding the root cause is vitally important because the root cause, unlike many of the problems identified by the problem isolation process, has a specific solution associated with it. For example, continuing the same problem with R2 not being able to forward packets to PC2, consider the list of problems identified through problem isolation:

■ R2 cannot forward packets to PC2.

■ R2 gets no ARP reply from PC2.

■ SW4's interface for the trunk to SW5 is in a down/down state.

■ The cable used between SW4 and SW5 uses the wrong cabling pinouts.

All these statements might be true about a particular problem scenario, but only the last item has an obvious actionable solution (replace with a correctly wired cable). While the other statements are valid and important facts found during problem isolation, they do not imply the specific action to take to solve the problem. As a result, the root cause analysis step reduces to two simple statements:

Step 1 Continue isolating the problem until you identify the true root cause, which in turn has an obvious solution.

Step 2 If you cannot reduce the problem to its true root cause, isolate the problem as much as is possible, and change something in the network, which will hopefully change the symptoms and help you identify the root cause.

Real World Versus the Exams

On the exam, you should look for clues as to the general topic for which you need to do some part of the troubleshooting process. For example, if the figure shows a network like the one in Figure 3-1, but all the multiple-choice answers refer to VLANs and VTP, start by looking at the LAN environment. Note that you might still want to consider Layers 1 through 3, and both the data and control plane details, to help you find the answers.

NOTE This section applies generally to troubleshooting, but it is included only in this chapter because this is the first chapter in the book dedicated to troubleshooting.

Troubleshooting the LAN Switching Data Plane

The generic troubleshooting strategies explained so far in this chapter suggest beginning with the IP routing process at Layer 3. If the engineer identifies a problem at a particular step in the IP forwarding process, the next step should be to examine that routing step more closely, including looking at the underlying Layer 1 and 2 status.

The following sections examine the tools and processes used to troubleshoot the LAN data plane processes at Layers 1 and 2. The rest of this chapter assumes that no Layer 3 problems exist; Chapters 7 and 11 examine Layer 3 troubleshooting. This chapter also makes some references to control plane protocols, specifically VTP and Spanning Tree Protocol (STP), but VTP and STP have already been well covered in the two previous chapters. So, these sections focus specifically on the LAN switching data plane.

These sections begin with a review of the LAN switch forwarding processes and an introduction to the four major steps in the LAN switching troubleshooting process as suggested in this chapter. Next, the text examines each of these four steps in succession. Finally, an example of how to apply the troubleshooting process is shown.

An Overview of the Normal LAN Switch Forwarding Process

The LAN switch forwarding process, described in detail in *CCENT/CCNA ICND1 Official Exam Certification Guide* Chapter 7, is relatively simple. However, before taking a closer look at how to use **show** command output to both predict normal operations and isolate the root cause of a forwarding problem, it is helpful to review how a switch thinks about the forwarding process when no problems exist. The following process steps outline that logic:

Step 1   Determine the VLAN in which the frame should be forwarded, as follows:

   a.   If the frame arrives on an access interface, use the interface's access VLAN.

   b.   If the frame arrives on a trunk interface, use the VLAN listed in the frame's trunking header.

Step 2   If the incoming interface is in an STP Learning or Forwarding State in that VLAN, add the source MAC address to the MAC address table, with incoming interface and VLAN ID (if not already in the table).

Step 3   If the incoming interface is not in an STP Forwarding State in that VLAN, discard the frame.

Step 4   Look for the destination MAC address of the frame in the MAC address table, but only for entries in the VLAN identified at Step 1. If the destination MAC is found or not found, follow these steps:

a. **Found:** Forward the frame out the only interface listed in the matched address table entry

b. **Not found:** Flood the frame out all other access ports in that same VLAN that are in an STP Forwarding State, and out all trunk ports that list this VLAN as fully supported (active, in the allowed list, not pruned, STP Forwarding)

To forward a frame, a switch must first determine in which VLAN the frame should be forwarded (Step 1), learn the source MAC addresses as needed (Step 2), and then choose where to forward the frame. Just to make sure that the process is clear, consider an example using Figure 3-3, in which PC1 sends a frame to its default gateway, R1, with the MAC addresses shown in the figure.

Figure 3-3   *Switched Network Used in Data Plane Analysis in Chapter 3*

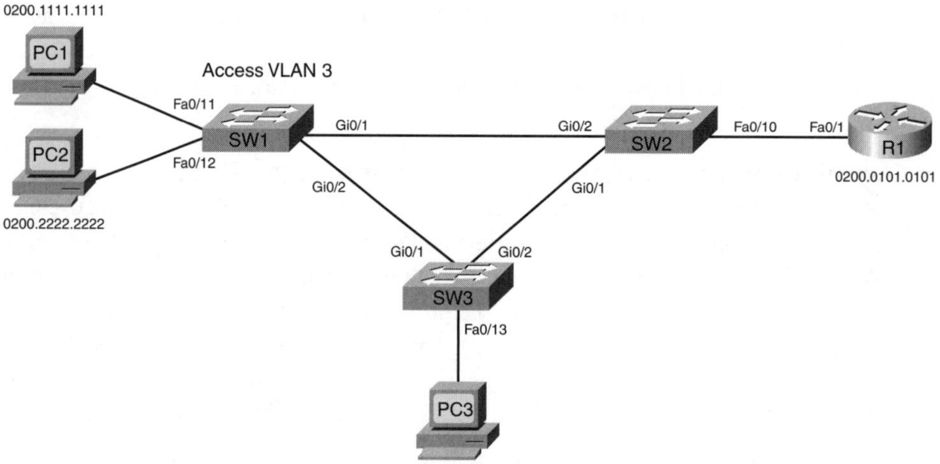

In this case, consider the frame as sent from PC1 (source MAC 0200.1111.1111) to R1 (destination MAC 0200.0101.0101). SW1, using Step 1 of the summarized forwarding logic, determines whether interface Fa0/11 is operating as an access interface or a trunk. In this case, it is an access interface assigned to VLAN 3. For Step 2, SW1 adds an entry to its MAC address table, listing MAC address 0200.1111.1111, interface Fa0/11, and VLAN 3. At Step 3, SW1 confirms that the incoming interface, Fa0/11, is in an STP Forwarding State. Finally, at Step 4, SW1 looks for an entry with MAC address 0200.0101.0101 in VLAN 3. If SW1 finds an entry that lists interface Gigabit 0/1, SW1 then forwards the frame only out Gi0/1. If the outgoing interface (Gi0/1) is a trunk interface, SW1 adds a VLAN trunking header that lists VLAN 3, the VLAN ID determined at Step 1.

For another slightly different example, consider a broadcast sent by PC1. Steps 1 through 3 occur as before, but at Step 4, SW1 floods the frame. However, SW3 only floods the frame out access ports in VLAN 3 and trunk ports that support VLAN 3, with the restriction that SW1 will not forward a copy of the frame out ports not in an STP Forwarding State.

Although this forwarding logic is relatively simple, the troubleshooting process requires the application of most every LAN-related concept in both the ICND1 and ICND2 books, plus other topics as well. For example, knowing that PC1 first sends frames to SW1, it makes sense to check the interface's status, ensure that the interface is "up and up," and fix the problem with the interface if it is not. Dozens of individual items might need to be checked to troubleshoot a problem. So, this chapter suggests a LAN data plane troubleshooting process that organizes the actions into four main steps:

Step 1 Confirm the network diagrams using CDP.

Step 2 Isolate interface problems.

Step 3 Isolate filtering and port security problems.

Step 4 Isolate VLANs and trunking problems.

The next four sections review and explain the concepts and tools to perform each of these four steps. While some facts and information are new, most of the specific underlying concepts have already been covered, either in *CCENT/CCNA ICND1 Official Exam Certification Guide* or in Chapters 1 and 2 of this book. The main goal is to help you pull all the concepts together so that analyzing unique scenarios—as will be required on the exams—takes a little less time, with a much better chance for success.

NOTE The next two sections, "Step 1: Confirm the Network Diagrams Using CDP," and "Step 2: Isolate Interface Problems," are also covered in the ICND1 book's Chapter 10. If you are reading both books to prepare for the CCNA exam, you don't need to read these sections of this chapter as well as the similarly named sections of ICND1's Chapter 10. If you are reading both books, feel free to skip to the section "Step 3: Isolate Filtering and Port Security Problems."

Step 1: Confirm the Network Diagrams Using CDP

The Cisco Discovery Protocol (CDP) can be useful to verify the information in the network diagram as well as to complete the rest of the necessary information about the devices and topology. In real life, the network diagrams can be old and outdated, and a problem might be caused because someone moved some cables and didn't update the diagrams. I doubt that Cisco would write a question with purposefully inaccurate information in the figure associated with the question, but the exam might easily include questions for which the network diagram does not list all the required information, and you need to use CDP to find the rest of the details. So, this section reviews CDP, and a good first LAN data plane troubleshooting step is as follows:

Step 1   Verify the accuracy of and complete the information listed in the network diagram using CDP.

> **NOTE**   This chapter shows a series of numbered troubleshooting steps for LAN switching, begun here with Step 1. The steps and their numbers are unimportant for the exam; the steps are just numbered in this chapter for easier reference.

Cisco routers, switches, and other devices use CDP for a variety of reasons, but routers and switches use it to announce basic information about themselves to their neighbors—information like the host name, device type, IOS version, and interface numbers. Three commands in particular list the CDP information learned from neighbors, as listed in Table 3-1. In fact, in cases for which no diagram exists, an engineer could create a diagram of routers and switches using **show cdp** command output.

Table 3-1   **show cdp** *Commands That List Information About Neighbors*

Command	Description
show cdp neighbors [*type number*]	Lists one summary line of information about each neighbor, or just the neighbor found on a specific interface if an interface was listed
show cdp neighbors detail	Lists one large set (approximately 15 lines) of information, one set for every neighbor
show cdp entry *name*	Lists the same information as the **show cdp neighbors detail** command, but only for the named neighbor

The only tricky part of the process of comparing CDP output to a diagram is that the output lists two interfaces or ports on many lines of output. Reading left to right, the output typically lists the host name of the neighboring device under the heading of "Device ID." However, the next heading of "Local Intrfce," meaning "local interface," is the local device's interface name/number. The neighboring device's interface name/number is on the right side of the command output under the heading "Port ID." Example 3-1 lists an example **show cdp neighbors** command from SW2 in Figure 3-3. Take the time to compare the shaded portions of the command output to the accurate details in Figure 3-3 to see which fields list interfaces for which devices.

Example 3-1 **show cdp** *Command Example*

```
SW2#show cdp neighbors
Capability Codes: R - Router, T - Trans Bridge, B - Source Route Bridge
                  S - Switch, H - Host, I - IGMP, r - Repeater, P - Phone

Device ID          Local Intrfce      Holdtme    Capability    Platform     Port ID
SW1                Gig 0/2            173          S I         WS-C2960-2   Gig 0/1
R1                 Fas 0/10           139        R S I         1841         Fas 0/1
```

CDP creates a security exposure when enabled. To avoid the exposure of allowing an attacker to learn details about each switch, CDP can be easily disabled. Cisco recommends that CDP be disabled on all interfaces that do not have a specific need for it. The most likely interfaces that need to use CDP are interfaces connected to other Cisco routers and switches and interfaces connected to Cisco IP phones. Otherwise, CDP can be disabled per interface using the **no cdp enable** interface subcommand. (The **cdp enable** interface subcommand reenables CDP.) Alternately, the **no cdp run** global command disables CDP for the entire switch, with the **cdp run** global command reenabling CDP globally.

Step 2: Isolate Interface Problems

A Cisco switch interface must be in a working state before the switch can process frames received on the interface or send frames out the interface. So, a somewhat obvious troubleshooting step should be to examine the state of each interface, specifically those expected to be used when forwarding frames, and verify that the interfaces are up and working.

This section examines the possible interface states on a Cisco IOS–based switch, lists root causes for the nonoperational states, and covers a popular problem that occurs even when the interface appears to be in a working state. The specific tasks for this step can be summarized with the following troubleshooting steps:

Step 2 Check for interface problems as follows:

    a. Determine interface status code(s) for each required interface, and if not in a connect or up/up state, resolve the problems until the interface reaches the connect or up/up state.

    b. For interfaces in a connect (up/up) state, also check for two other problems: duplex mismatches and some variations of port security purposefully dropping frames.

Interface Status Codes and Reasons for Nonworking States

Cisco switches use two different sets of status codes: one set of two codes (words) that uses the same conventions as do router interface status codes and another set with a single code (word). Both sets of status codes can determine whether an interface is working.

The switch **show interfaces** and **show interfaces description** commands list the two-code status just like routers. The two codes are named the *line status* and *protocol status*, with the codes generally referring to whether Layer 1 is working and whether Layer 2 is working, respectively. LAN switch interfaces typically show an interface with both codes as "up" or both codes as "down," because all switch interfaces use the same Ethernet data link layer protocols, so the data link layer protocol should never have a problem.

> **NOTE**   This book refers to these two status codes in shorthand by just listing the two codes with a slash between them, for example, "up/up."

The **show interfaces status** command lists a single interface status code. This single interface status code corresponds to different combinations of the traditional two-code interface status codes and can be easily correlated to those codes. For example, the **show interfaces status** command lists a "connect" state for working interfaces, which corresponds to the up/up state seen with the **show interfaces** and **show interfaces description** commands.

Any interface state other than connect or up/up means that the switch cannot forward or receive frames on the interface. Each nonworking interface state has a small set of root causes. Also, note that the exams could easily ask a question that only showed one or the other type of status code, so to be prepared for the exams, know the meanings of both sets of interface status codes. Table 3-2 lists the code combinations and some root causes that could have caused a particular interface status.

Table 3-2   *LAN Switch Interface Status Codes*

Line Status	Protocol Status	Interface Status	Typical Root Cause
admin. down	down	disabled	Interface is configured with the **shutdown** command.
down	down	notconnect	No cable; bad cable; wrong cable pinouts; speeds mismatched on the two connected devices; device on the other end of the cable is either powered off or the other interface is shut down.
up	down	notconnect	Not expected on LAN switch interfaces.

Key Topic

Table 3-2 *LAN Switch Interface Status Codes (Continued)*

Line Status	Protocol Status	Interface Status	Typical Root Cause
down	down (err-disabled)	err-disabled	Port security has disabled the interface.
up	up	connect	Interface is working.

The notconnect State and Cabling Pinouts

Table 3-2 lists several reasons why a switch interface can be in the notconnect state. Most of those reasons do not need much further explanation than the text in the table. For example, if an interface is connected to another switch, and the interface is in a notconnect state, check the other switch to find out whether the other switch's interface has been shut down. However, one of the reasons for a notconnect state—incorrect cable pinouts—deserves a little more attention because it is both a common mistake and is not otherwise covered in this book. (Ethernet cabling pinouts are covered in *CCENT/CCNA ICND1 Official Exam Certification Guide* Chapter 3.)

Ethernet unshielded twisted-pair (UTP) cabling standards specify the pins to which each of the wires should connect on the RJ-45 connectors on the ends of the cable. The devices transmit using pairs of wires, with 10BASE-T and 100BASE-Tx using two pairs: one to transmit and one to receive data. When connecting two devices that use the same pair of pins to transmit, the cable—a crossover cable—must connect or cross the wires connected to each device's transmit pair over to the other device's expected receive pair. Conversely, devices that already use opposite pairs for transmitting data need a straight-through cable that does not cross the pairs. Figure 3-4 shows an example in a typical switched LAN, with the types of cabling pinouts shown.

Figure 3-4 *Example Use of Crossover and Straight-Through Cables*

Effective troubleshooting requires knowledge of which devices transmit on which pairs. Table 3-3 lists the more common devices seen in the context of CCNA, along with the pairs used. Note that when connecting two types of devices from the same column, a crossover cable is required; when connecting two devices from different columns of the table, a straight-through cable is required.

Key Topic

Table 3-3 *10BASE-T and 100BASE-Tx Pin Pairs Used*

Devices That Transmit on 1,2 and Receive on 3,6	Devices That Transmit on 3,6 and Receive on 1,2
PC NICs	Hubs
Routers	Switches
Wireless access points (Ethernet interface)	—
Ethernet-connected network printers	—

Interface Speed and Duplex Issues

Switch interfaces can find their speed and duplex settings in several ways. By default, interfaces that use copper wiring and are capable of multiple speeds and duplex settings use the IEEE-standard (IEEE 802.3x) autonegotiation process. Alternately, switch interfaces, routers, and most network interface cards (NIC) can also be configured to use a specific speed or duplex setting. On switches and routers, the **speed {10 | 100 | 1000}** interface subcommand with the **duplex {half | full}** interface subcommand sets these values. Note that configuring both speed and duplex on a switch interface disables the IEEE-standard autonegotiation process on that interface.

The **show interfaces** and **show interfaces status** commands list both the speed and duplex settings on an interface, as shown in Example 3-2.

Example 3-2 *Displaying Speed and Duplex Settings on Switch Interfaces*

```
SW1#show interfaces status

Port      Name            Status       Vlan    Duplex  Speed Type
Fa0/1                     notconnect   1         auto   auto 10/100BaseTX
Fa0/2                     notconnect   1         auto   auto 10/100BaseTX
Fa0/3                     notconnect   1         auto   auto 10/100BaseTX
Fa0/4                     connected    1       a-full  a-100 10/100BaseTX
Fa0/5                     connected    1       a-full  a-100 10/100BaseTX
Fa0/6                     notconnect   1         auto   auto 10/100BaseTX
Fa0/7                     notconnect   1         auto   auto 10/100BaseTX
Fa0/8                     notconnect   1         auto   auto 10/100BaseTX
Fa0/9                     notconnect   1         auto   auto 10/100BaseTX
Fa0/10                    notconnect   1         auto   auto 10/100BaseTX
```

Example 3-2 *Displaying Speed and Duplex Settings on Switch Interfaces (Continued)*

```
Fa0/11                      connected      1          a-full      10 10/100BaseTX
Fa0/12                      connected      1            half     100 10/100BaseTX
Fa0/13                      connected      1          a-full   a-100 10/100BaseTX
Fa0/14                      disabled       1            auto    auto 10/100BaseTX
Fa0/15                      notconnect     3            auto    auto 10/100BaseTX
Fa0/16                      notconnect     3            auto    auto 10/100BaseTX
Fa0/17                      connected      1          a-full   a-100 10/100BaseTX
Fa0/18                      notconnect     1            auto    auto 10/100BaseTX
Fa0/19                      notconnect     1            auto    auto 10/100BaseTX
Fa0/20                      notconnect     1            auto    auto 10/100BaseTX
Fa0/21                      notconnect     1            auto    auto 10/100BaseTX
Fa0/22                      notconnect     1            auto    auto 10/100BaseTX
Fa0/23                      notconnect     1            auto    auto 10/100BaseTX
Fa0/24                      notconnect     1            auto    auto 10/100BaseTX
Gi0/1                       connected      trunk        full    1000 10/100/1000BaseTX
Gi0/2                       notconnect     1            auto    auto 10/100/1000BaseTX
SW1#show interfaces fa0/13
FastEthernet0/13 is up, line protocol is up (connected)
  Hardware is Fast Ethernet, address is 0019.e86a.6f8d (bia 0019.e86a.6f8d)
  MTU 1500 bytes, BW 100000 Kbit, DLY 100 usec,
     reliability 255/255, txload 1/255, rxload 1/255
  Encapsulation ARPA, loopback not set
  Keepalive set (10 sec)
  Full-duplex, 100Mb/s, media type is 10/100BaseTX
  input flow-control is off, output flow-control is unsupported
  ARP type: ARPA, ARP Timeout 04:00:00
  Last input 00:00:05, output 00:00:00, output hang never
  Last clearing of "show interface" counters never
  Input queue: 0/75/0/0 (size/max/drops/flushes); Total output drops: 0
  Queueing strategy: fifo
  Output queue: 0/40 (size/max)
  5 minute input rate 0 bits/sec, 0 packets/sec
  5 minute output rate 0 bits/sec, 0 packets/sec
     85022 packets input, 10008976 bytes, 0 no buffer
     Received 284 broadcasts (0 multicast)
     0 runts, 0 giants, 0 throttles
     0 input errors, 0 CRC, 0 frame, 0 overrun, 0 ignored
     0 watchdog, 281 multicast, 0 pause input
     0 input packets with dribble condition detected
     95226 packets output, 10849674 bytes, 0 underruns
     0 output errors, 0 collisions, 1 interface resets
     0 babbles, 0 late collision, 0 deferred
     0 lost carrier, 0 no carrier, 0 PAUSE output
     0 output buffer failures, 0 output buffers swapped out
```

While both commands can be useful, only the **show interfaces status** command implies how the switch determined the speed and duplex settings. The command output lists autonegotiated settings with an "a-". For example, "a-full" means full-duplex as autonegotiated, where as "full" means full-duplex but as manually configured. The example shades the command output that implies that the switch's Fa0/12 interfaces' speed and duplex were not found through autonegotiation, but Fa0/13 did use autonegotiation. Note that the **show interfaces Fa0/13** command (without the **status** option) simply lists the speed and duplex for interface Fa0/13, with nothing implying that the values were learned through autonegotiation.

Cisco switches have some interesting features related to interface speed that can help you determine some types of interface problems. If a Cisco switch interface has been configured to use a particular speed, and the speed does not match the device on the other end of the cable, the switch interface will be in a notconnect or down/down state. However, this kind of speed mismatch can only occur when the speed has been manually configured on the switch. Cisco switch interfaces that do not have the **speed** command configured can automatically detect the speed used by the other device—even if the other device turns off the IEEE autonegotiation process—and then use that speed.

For example, in Figure 3-3, imagine that SW2's Gi0/2 interface was configured with the **speed 100** and **duplex half** commands (not recommended settings on a Gigabit-capable interface, by the way). SW2 would use those settings and disable the IEEE-standard autonegotiation process because both the **speed** and **duplex** commands have been configured. If SW1's Gi0/1 interface did not have a **speed** command configured, SW1 would still recognize the speed (100 Mbps)—even though SW2 would not use IEEE-standard negotiation—and SW1 would also use a speed of 100 Mbps. Example 3-3 shows the results of this specific case on SW1.

Example 3-3 *Displaying Speed and Duplex Settings on Switch Interfaces*

```
SW1#show interfaces gi0/1 status

Port       Name             Status      Vlan     Duplex  Speed Type
Gi0/1                       connected   trunk    a-half  a-100 10/100/1000BaseTX
```

The speed and duplex still show up with a prefix of "a-" in the example, implying autonegotiation. The reason is that in this case, the speed was found automatically, and the duplex setting was chosen because of the default values used by the IEEE autonegotiation process. The IEEE standards state that for ports running at 100 Mbps, if autonegotiation fails, use a default half-duplex setting.

Finding a duplex mismatch can be much more difficult than finding a speed mismatch because *if the duplex settings do not match on the ends of an Ethernet segment, the switch interface will be in a connect (up/up) state.* In this case, the interface works, but it might work poorly, with poor performance and with symptoms of intermittent problems. The reason is that the device using half-duplex uses carrier sense multiple access collision detect (CSMA/CD) logic, waiting to send when receiving a frame, believing collisions occur when they physically do not, and stopping sending a frame because the switch thinks a collision occurred. With enough traffic load, the interface could be in a connect state, but essentially useless for passing traffic, even causing the loss of vital VTP and STP messages.

To identify duplex mismatch problems, try the following actions:

- Use commands like **show interfaces** on each end of the link to confirm the duplex setting on each end.

- Watch for increases to certain counters on half-duplex interfaces. The counters—runts, collisions, and late collisions—occur when the other device uses full duplex. (Note that these counters can also increment when legitimate collisions occur as well.)

Example 3-2 (earlier in this section) uses shading to indicate these counters in the output of the **show interfaces** command.

The root cause of duplex mismatches might be related to the defaults chosen by the IEEE autonegotiation process. When a device attempts autonegotiation, and the other device does not respond, the first device chooses the default duplex setting based on the current speed. The default duplex settings, per the IEEE, are chosen as follows:

- If the speed is 10 or 100 Mbps, default to use half-duplex.

- If the speed is 1000 Mbps, default to use full-duplex.

> **NOTE** Ethernet interfaces using speeds faster than 1 Gbps always use full-duplex.

Step 3: Isolate Filtering and Port Security Problems

Generally speaking, any analysis of the forwarding process should consider any security features that might discard some frames or packets. For example, both routers and switches can be configured with access control lists (ACL) that examine the packets and frames being sent or received on an interface, with the router or switch discarding those packets/frames.

The CCNA exams do not include coverage of switch ACLs, but the exams do cover a similar switch feature called port security. As covered in *CCENT/CCNA ICND1 Official Exam Certification Guide*, Chapter 9, the port security feature can be used to cause the switch to discard some frames sent into and out of an interface. Port security has three basic features with which it determines which frames to filter:

Key Topic

■   Limit which specific MAC addresses can send and receive frames on a switch interface, discarding frames to/from other MAC addresses.

■   Limit the number of MAC addresses using the interface, discarding frames to/from MAC addresses learned after the maximum limit was reached.

■   A combination of the previous two points.

The first port security troubleshooting step should be to find which interfaces have port security enabled, followed by a determination as to whether any violations are currently occurring. The trickiest part relates to the differences in what the IOS does in reaction to violations based on the **switchport port-security violation** *violation-mode* interface subcommand, which tells the switch what to do when a violation occurs. The general process is as follows:

Step 3   Check for port security problems as follows:

  a.   Identify all interfaces on which port security is enabled (**show running-config** or **show port-security**).

  b.   Determine whether a security violation is currently occurring based in part on the *violation mode* of the interface's port security configuration, as follows:

  —   **shutdown**: The interface will be in an err-disabled state.

  —   **restrict**: The interface will be in a connect state, but the **show port-security interface** command will show an incrementing violations counter.

  —   **protect**: The interface will be in a connect state, and the **show port-security interface** command will not show an incrementing violations counter.

  c.   In all cases, compare the port security configuration to the diagram as well as the "last source address" field in the output of the **show port-security interface** command.

One of the difficulties when troubleshooting port security relates to the fact that some port security configurations discard only the offending frames, but they do not disable the interface as a result, all based on the configured violation mode. All three violation modes discard the traffic as dictated by the configuration. For example, if only one predefined MAC address of 0200.1111.1111 is allowed, the switch discards all traffic on that interface, other than traffic to or from 0200.1111.1111. However, shutdown mode causes all future traffic to be discarded—even legitimate traffic from address 0200.1111.1111—after a violation has occurred. Table 3-4 summarizes some of these key points for easier study.

Table 3-4   *Port Security Behavior Based on Violation Mode*

Key Topic

Violation Mode	Discards Offending Traffic	Discards All Traffic After Violation Occurs	Violation Results in err-disabled Interface State	Counters Increment for Each New Violation
shutdown	Yes	Yes	Yes	Yes
restrict	Yes	No	No	Yes
protect	Yes	No	No	No

Troubleshooting Step 3B refers to the interface err-disabled (error disabled) state. This state verifies that the interface has been configured to use port security, that a violation has occurred, and that no traffic is allowed on the interface at the present time. This interface state implies that the shutdown violation mode is used, because it is the only one of the three port security modes that causes the interface to be disabled. To fix this problem, the interface must be shut down and then enabled with the **no shutdown** command. Example 3-4 lists an example in which the interface is in an err-disabled state.

Example 3-4   *Using Port Security to Define Correct MAC Addresses of Particular Interfaces*

```
! The first command lists all interfaces on which port security has been enabled,
! and the violation mode, under the heading "Security Action".
SW1#show port-security
Secure Port  MaxSecureAddr  CurrentAddr  SecurityViolation  Security Action
             (Count)        (Count)      (Count)
-------------------------------------------------------------------------------
   Fa0/13          1             1              1             Shutdown
-------------------------------------------------------------------------------
Total Addresses in System (excluding one mac per port)    : 0
Max Addresses limit in System (excluding one mac per port) : 8320
!
! The next command shows the err-disabled state, implying a security violation.
SW1#show interfaces Fa0/13 status

Port       Name            Status       Vlan    Duplex  Speed Type
Fa0/13                     err-disabled 1        auto    auto  10/100BaseTX
!
! The next command's output has shading for several of the most important facts.
SW1#show port-security interface Fa0/13
Port Security              : Enabled
Port Status                : Secure-shutdown
```

continues

Example 3-4   *Using Port Security to Define Correct MAC Addresses of Particular*
                   Interfaces (Continued)

```
Violation Mode             : Shutdown
Aging Time                 : 0 mins
Aging Type                 : Absolute
SecureStatic Address Aging : Disabled
Maximum MAC Addresses      : 1
Total MAC Addresses        : 1
Configured MAC Addresses   : 1
Sticky MAC Addresses       : 0
Last Source Address:Vlan   : 0200.3333.3333:2
Security Violation Count   : 1
```

The output of the **show port-security interface** command lists a couple of items helpful in the troubleshooting process. The port status of "secure-shutdown" means that the interface is disabled for all traffic as a result of a violation, and that the interface state should be "err-disabled." The end of the command output lists a violations counter, incremented by 1 for each new violation. Interestingly, with a violation mode of shutdown, the counter increments by 1, the interface is placed into err-disabled state, and the counter cannot increment anymore until the engineer uses the **shutdown** and **no shutdown** commands on the interface, in succession. Finally, note that the second-to-last line lists the source MAC address of the last frame received on the interface. This value can be useful in identifying the MAC address of the device that caused the violation.

The restrict and protect violation modes still cause frame discards, but with much different behavior. With these violation modes, the interface remains in a connect (up/up) state while still discarding the inappropriate frames because of port security. So, avoid the pitfall of assuming that an interface in a connect, or up/up, state cannot have any other reasons for not passing traffic.

Example 3-5 shows a sample configuration and **show** command when using protect mode. In this case, a PC with MAC address 0200.3333.3333 sent frames into port Fa0/13, with the port configured to restrict Fa0/13 to only receive frames sent by 0200.1111.1111.

Example 3-5   *Port Security Using Protect Mode*

```
SW1#show running-config
! Lines omitted for brevity
interface FastEthernet0/13
 switchport mode access
 switchport port-security
 switchport port-security mac-address 0200.1111.1111
 switchport port-security violation protect
! Lines omitted for brevity
```

Example 3-5 *Port Security Using Protect Mode (Continued)*

```
SW1#show port-security interface Fa0/13
Port Security                : Enabled
Port Status                  : Secure-up
Violation Mode               : Protect
Aging Time                   : 0 mins
Aging Type                   : Absolute
SecureStatic Address Aging   : Disabled
Maximum MAC Addresses        : 1
Total MAC Addresses          : 1
Configured MAC Addresses     : 1
Sticky MAC Addresses         : 0
Last Source Address:Vlan     : 0200.3333.3333:1
Security Violation Count     : 0
```

This **show** command output was gathered after many frames had been sent by a PC with MAC address 0200.3333.3333, with all the frames being discarded by the switch because of port security. The command output shows the disallowed PC's 0200.3333.3333 MAC address as the last source MAC address in a received frame. However, note that the port status is listed as secure-up and the violation count as 0—both indications that might make you think all is well. However, in protect mode, the **show port-security interface** command does not show any information confirming that an actual violation has occurred. The only indication is that end-user traffic does not make it to where it needs to go.

If this example had used violation mode restrict, the port status would have also stayed in a secure-up state, but the security violation counter would have incremented once for each violating frame.

For the exams, a port security violation might not be a problem; it might be the exact function intended. The question text might well explicitly state what port security should be doing. In these cases, it can be quicker to just immediately look at the port security configuration. Then, compare the configuration to the MAC addresses of the devices connected to the interface. The most likely problem on the exams is that the MAC addresses have been misconfigured or that the maximum number of MAC addresses has been set too low. (*CCENT/CCNA ICND1 Official Exam Certification Guide*, Chapter 9, explains the details of the configuration statements.)

One last security feature that needs a brief mention is IEEE 802.1x authentication. IEEE 802.1x (not to be confused with the IEEE 802.3x autonegotiation standard) defines a process to authenticate the user of the PC connected to a switch port. 802.1x can be used as part of an overall Network Admission Control (NAC) strategy, in which a user internal to an enterprise LAN cannot use the LAN until the user supplies some authentication credentials.

With 802.1x, each user communicates with a AAA server with a series of authentication messages. The access switch listens to the messages, discarding all frames on the link except for 802.1x messages to and from the PC. When the switch overhears the message from the AAA server that says that the user has been successfully authenticated, the switch then allows all traffic to flow on that port. If the user is not authenticated, the switch does not allow traffic on that interface. The details of how to configure 802.1x, and recognize an authentication failure as the root cause of a particular problem, is beyond the scope of this book.

Step 4: Isolate VLAN and Trunking Problems

A switch's forwarding process depends on both the definitions of access VLANs on access interfaces and on VLAN trunks that can pass traffic for many VLANs. Additionally, before a switch can forward frames in a particular VLAN, the switch must know about a VLAN, either through configuration or VTP, and the VLAN must be active. The following sections examine some of the tools regarding all these VLAN-related issues. This configuration step includes the following steps:

Step 4   Check VLANs and VLAN trunks as follows:

   a.   Identify all access interfaces and their assigned access VLANs, and reassign into the correct VLANs as needed.

   b.   Determine whether the VLANs both exist (configured or learned with VTP) and are active on each switch. If not, configure and activate the VLANs to resolve problems as needed.

   c.   Identify the operationally trunking interfaces on each switch, and determine the VLANs that can be forwarded over each trunk.

The next three sections discuss Steps 4A, 4B, and 4C in succession.

Ensuring That the Right Access Interfaces Are in the Right VLANs

To ensure that each access interface has been assigned to the correct VLAN, engineers simply need to determine which switch interfaces are access interfaces instead of trunk interfaces, determine the assigned access VLANs on each interface, and compare the information to the documentation. The three **show** commands listed in Table 3-5 can be particularly helpful in this process.

Key Topic

Table 3-5   *Commands That Can Find Access Ports and VLANs*

EXEC Command	Description
show vlan brief show vlan	Lists each VLAN and all interfaces assigned to that VLAN, but does not include trunks

Table 3-5 *Commands That Can Find Access Ports and VLANs (Continued)*

EXEC Command	Description
show interfaces *type number* **switchport**	Identifies an interface's access VLAN, voice VLAN, and the administrative (configured) mode and operational mode (access or trunking)
show mac address-table dynamic	Lists MAC table entries: MAC addresses with associated interfaces and VLANs

If possible, start this step with the **show vlan** and **show vlan brief** commands, because they list all the known VLANs and the access interfaces assigned to each VLAN. Be aware, however, that the output of these commands includes all interfaces that are not currently operationally trunking. So, these commands list interfaces in a notconnect state, err-disabled state, and most importantly in this case, interfaces that might trunk after the interface comes up. For example, these commands might include interface Gi0/2 in the list of interfaces in VLAN 1, but as soon as Gi0/1 comes up, the interface might negotiate trunking—at which point the interface would no longer be an access interface and would no longer be listed in the output of the **show vlan brief** command.

If the **show vlan** and **show interface switchport** commands are not available in a particular test question, the **show mac address-table** command can also help identify the access VLAN. This command lists the MAC address table, with each entry including a MAC address, interface, and VLAN ID. If the test question implies that a switch interface connects to a single device PC, you should only see one MAC table entry that lists that particular access interface; the VLAN ID listed for that same entry identifies the access VLAN. (You cannot make such assumptions for trunking interfaces.)

After you determine the access interfaces and associated VLANs, if the interface is assigned to the wrong VLAN, use the **switchport access vlan** *vlan-id* interface subcommand to assign the correct VLAN ID.

Access VLANs Not Being Defined or Being Active

The next troubleshooting step, Step 4B, examines the fact that a switch does not forward frames in an undefined VLAN or in a defined VLAN that is not in the active state. This section summarizes the best ways to confirm that a switch knows that a particular VLAN exists, and if it exists, determines the state of the VLAN.

VTP servers and clients only display their current list of known VLANs with the **show vlan** command. Neither the running-config nor the startup-config file holds the **vlan** *vlan-id* global configuration commands that define the VLAN, or the associated **name** commands that name a VLAN. Transparent mode switches do put these configuration commands in both the vlan.dat and the running-config file, so you can see the configuration using the **show running-config** command.

After you determine that a VLAN does not exist, the problem might be that the VLAN simply needs to be defined. If so, follow the VLAN configuration process as covered in detail in Chapter 1, summarized as follows:

■ **On VTP servers and clients, assuming that VTP is working**: The VLAN must be configured on a VTP server, typically with the **vlan** *vlan-id* global configuration command, with the other VTP servers and clients learning about the VLAN. The VLAN can also be configured as a result of the **switchport access vlan** *vlan-id* interface subcommand, on the VTP server at which the VLAN does not yet exist, causing the server to automatically create the VLAN.

■ **On VTP servers and client, assuming that VTP is not working**: Troubleshoot VTP as covered in the section "VTP Troubleshooting" in Chapter 1.

■ **On a VTP transparent switch**: The configuration is the same as on a server, but it must be done on each switch, because VTP transparent mode switches do not advertise the new VLAN to other switches.

For any existing VLANs, also verify that the VLAN is active. The **show vlan** command should list one of two VLAN state values: active and act/lshut. The second of these states means that the VLAN is shut down. To solve this problem, use the **no shutdown vlan** *vlan-id* global configuration command. Note that this command must be issued on each switch, because this shutdown state is not advertised by VTP.

Identify Trunks and VLANs Forwarded on Those Trunks

At this step (4C), you can separate problems into two general categories as you begin to isolate the problem: problems with the details of how an operational trunk works and problems caused when an interface that should trunk does not trunk.

The first category in this step can be easily done using the **show interfaces trunk** command, which only lists information about currently operational trunks. The best place to begin with this command is the last section of output, which lists the VLANs whose traffic will be forwarded over the trunk. Any VLANs that make it to this final list of VLANs in the command output meet the following criteria:

Key Topic

■   The VLAN exists and is active on this switch (as covered in the previous section and seen in the **show vlan** command).

■   The VLAN has not been removed from the allowed VLAN list on the trunk (as configured with the **switchport trunk allowed vlan** interface subcommand).

- The VLAN has not been VTP-pruned from the trunk (as done automatically by VTP, assuming that VTP pruning has been enabled with the **vtp pruning** global configuration command).

- The trunk is in an STP Forwarding State in that VLAN (as also seen in the **show spanning-tree vlan** *vlan-id* command).

Example 3-6 shows a sample of the command output from the **show interfaces trunk** command, with the final section of the command output shaded. In this case, the trunk only forwards traffic in VLANs 1 and 4.

Example 3-6 *Allowed VLAN List and List of Active VLANs*

```
SW1#show interfaces trunk

Port       Mode        Encapsulation  Status       Native vlan
Gi0/1      desirable   802.1q         trunking     1

Port       Vlans allowed on trunk
Gi0/1      1-2,4-4094

Port       Vlans allowed and active in management domain
Gi0/1      1,4

Port       Vlans in spanning tree forwarding state and not pruned
Gi0/1      1,4
```

The absence of a VLAN in this last part of the command's output does not necessarily mean that a problem has occurred. In fact, a VLAN might be legitimately excluded from a trunk for any of the reasons in the list just before Example 3-6. However, for a given exam question, it can be useful to know why traffic for a VLAN will not be forwarded over a trunk. The output of the **show interfaces trunk** command's three lists of VLANs shows a progression of reasons why a VLAN is not forwarded over a trunk. To remember the details, review the details surrounding Chapter 1's Example 1-4 and the few paragraphs before the example.

A trunk's native VLAN configuration should also be checked at this step. The native VLAN ID can be manually set to different VLANs on either end of the trunk. If the native VLANs differ, the switches will accidentally cause frames to leave one VLAN and enter another. For example, if switch SW1 sends a frame using native VLAN 1 on an 802.1Q trunk, SW1 does not add a VLAN header, as is normal for the native VLAN. When switch SW2 receives the frame, noticing that no 802.1Q header exists, SW2 assumes that the frame is part of SW2's configured native VLAN. If SW2 has been configured to think VLAN 2 is the native VLAN on that trunk, SW2 will try to forward the received frame into VLAN 2.

The second general class of trunking problem is that an interface that should trunk does not. The most likely cause of this problem is a misconfiguration of trunking on the opposite ends of the link. The **switchport mode {access | trunk | dynamic {desirable | auto}}** interface subcommand tells the interface whether to trunk and the rules with which to negotiate trunking. You can display any interface's administrative (configured) trunking mode, as set by this configuration command, using the **show interface switchport** command. Make sure that you know the meaning of each of this configuration command's options as listed in Table 1-4 in Chapter 1, and the combinations on either end of the segment that result in trunking, as listed in Chapter 1's Table 1-5.

In some cases, an interface can fail to use trunking because of a misconfiguration of the type of trunking—in other words, whether to use ISL or 802.1Q. For example, if two switches on opposite ends of a segment configured the **switchport trunk encapsulation isl** and **switchport trunk encapsulation dot1Q** commands, respectively, the trunk would not form, because the types of trunks (the encapsulation) do not match.

Example: Troubleshooting the Data Plane

This section shows an example of how to apply the steps to a particular network and scenario. The scenario includes several problems based on Figure 3-5. At the beginning, PC1, PC2, and PC3 cannot ping their default gateway, R1, at IP address 2.2.2.9. This section shows how to apply the troubleshooting processes covered so far in this chapter to uncover the problems and fix them. For easier reference, the steps have been summarized here as follows:

Key Topic

Step 1   Verify the accuracy of and complete the information listed in the network diagram using CDP.

Step 2   Check for interface problems as follows:

   a.   Determine the interface status code(s) for each required interface, and if not in a connect or up/up state, resolve the problems until the interface reaches the connect or up/up state.

   b.   For interfaces in a connect (up/up) state, also check for two other problems: duplex mismatches and some variations of port security purposefully dropping frames.

Step 3   Check for port security problems as follows:

   a.   Identify all interfaces on which port security is enabled (**show running-config** or **show port-security**).

b. Determine whether a security violation is currently occurring based in part on the *violation mode* of the interface's port security configuration, as follows:

— **shutdown**: The interface will be in an err-disabled state.

— **restrict**: The interface will be in a connect state, but the **show port-security interface** command will show an incrementing violations counter.

— **protect**: The interface will be in a connect state, and the **show port-security interface** command will not show an incrementing violations counter.

c. In all cases, compare the port security configuration to the diagram as well as the "last source address" field in the output of the **show port-security interface** command.

Step 4   Check VLANs and VLAN trunks as follows:

a. Identify all access interfaces and their assigned access VLANs, and reassign into the correct VLANs as needed.

b. Determine whether the VLANs both exist (configured or learned with VTP) and are active on each switch. If not, configure and activate the VLANs to resolve problems as needed.

c. Identify the operationally trunking interfaces on each switch, and determine the VLANs that can be forwarded over each trunk.

Figure 3-5 *Network Used in the Data Plane Troubleshooting Example*

Step 1: Verify the Accuracy of the Diagram Using CDP

Example 3-7 shows a variety of example output from the **show cdp neighbors** and **show cdp entry** commands on the three switches in Figure 3-5. A simple comparison confirms the names and interfaces in the figure, with the exception that SW2's Fa0/9 interface connects to router R1, instead of SW2's Fa0/10 interface shown in Figure 3-5.

Example 3-7   *Verifying Figure 3-5 Using CDP*

```
SW1#show cdp neighbors
Capability Codes: R - Router, T - Trans Bridge, B - Source Route Bridge
                  S - Switch, H - Host, I - IGMP, r - Repeater, P - Phone


Device ID         Local Intrfce      Holdtme   Capability    Platform    Port ID
SW2               Gig 0/1            122          S I        WS-C2960-2  Gig 0/2
SW3               Gig 0/2            144          S I        WS-C3550-2  Gig 0/1
! SW2 commands next
SW2#show cdp neighbors
Capability Codes: R - Router, T - Trans Bridge, B - Source Route Bridge
                  S - Switch, H - Host, I - IGMP, r - Repeater, P - Phone


Device ID         Local Intrfce      Holdtme   Capability    Platform    Port ID
SW1               Gig 0/2            125          S I        WS-C2960-2  Gig 0/1
SW3               Gig 0/1            170          S I        WS-C3550-2  Gig 0/2
R1                Fas 0/9            157         R S I       1841        Fas 0/1
SW2#show cdp entry R1
-------------------------
Device ID: R1
Entry address(es):
  IP address: 2.2.2.10
Platform: Cisco 1841,  Capabilities: Router Switch IGMP
Interface: FastEthernet0/9,  Port ID (outgoing port): FastEthernet0/1
Holdtime : 150 sec


Version :
Cisco IOS Software, 1841 Software (C1841-ADVENTERPRISEK9-M), Version 12.4(9)T, RELEASE
SOFTWARE (fc1)
Technical Support: http://www.cisco.com/techsupport
Copyright  1986-2006 by Cisco Systems, Inc.
Compiled Fri 16-Jun-06 21:26 by prod_rel_team


advertisement version: 2
VTP Management Domain: ''
Duplex: full
Management address(es):
! SW3 command next
SW3#show cdp neighbors
Capability Codes: R - Router, T - Trans Bridge, B - Source Route Bridge
                  S - Switch, H - Host, I - IGMP, r - Repeater, P - Phone
```

Example 3-7 *Verifying Figure 3-5 Using CDP (Continued)*

```
Device ID            Local Intrfce        Holdtme    Capability    Platform      Port ID
SW1                  Gig 0/1              154        S I           WS-C2960-2    Gig 0/2
SW2                  Gig 0/2              178        S I           WS-C2960-2    Gig 0/1
```

This mistake in documentation in Figure 3-5 (listing SW2 interface Fa0/10 instead of Fa0/9) does not affect the current network's operation. However, had trunking been required between SW2 and R1, SW2 interface Fa0/9—not Fa0/10—would have to have been explicitly configured to enable trunking, because routers cannot automatically negotiate to use trunking. Chapter 4, "IP Routing: Static and Connected Routes," covers the details of router trunking configuration.

Note that CDP does not identify documentation problems with the interfaces that connect to the end-user PCs; for the purposes of this example, know that the rest of the interfaces shown in Figure 3-5 are the correct interfaces.

Step 2: Check for Interface Problems

The next step examines the interface status on each of the interfaces that should currently be used. Example 3-8 lists several **show interface status** commands on both SW1 and SW3. (For this chapter's purposes, assume that all interfaces on SW2 are working correctly.) Examine the output, identify any problems you see, and make a list of other interface-related problems you might want to investigate further based on this output.

Example 3-8 *Interface Problems on SW1*

```
SW1#show interfaces fa0/11 status

Port      Name             Status        Vlan      Duplex  Speed Type
Fa0/11                     connected     3         a-full  a-100 10/100BaseTX
SW1#show interfaces fa0/12 status

Port      Name             Status        Vlan      Duplex  Speed Type
Fa0/12                     notconnect    3          auto    auto 10/100BaseTX
SW1#show interfaces Gi0/1 status

Port      Name             Status        Vlan      Duplex  Speed Type
Gi0/1                      connected     trunk     a-full a-1000 10/100/1000BaseTX
SW1#show interfaces Gi0/2 status

Port      Name             Status        Vlan      Duplex  Speed Type
Gi0/2                      connected     1         a-full a-1000 10/100/1000BaseTX
! Switching to SW3 next
SW3#sh interfaces fa0/13 status
```

continues

Example 3-8 *Interface Problems on SW1 (Continued)*

```
Port       Name                Status       Vlan    Duplex  Speed Type
Fa0/13                         connected    3       a-half  a-100 10/100BaseTX
SW3#show interfaces Gi0/1 status

Port       Name                Status       Vlan    Duplex  Speed Type
Gi0/1                          connected    1       a-full a-1000 1000BaseTX
SW3#show interfaces Gi0/2 status

Port       Name                Status       Vlan    Duplex  Speed Type
Gi0/2                          connected    trunk   a-full a-1000 1000BaseTX
```

One obvious problem exists on SW1, with interface Fa0/12 in a notconnect state. Many reasons for this state exist, almost all relating to some cabling problem—anything from a cable that is not fully inserted into the switch port to difficult-to-find interference problems on the cable. (See Table 3-2 for suggested reasons.)

SW3's interfaces appear not to have any problems. However, all three interfaces have a duplex setting that is the same setting as what the switch would use if the autonegotiation process failed, with the use of half-duplex on Fa0/13 being notable. That raises the possibility of one of the two interface problems mentioned earlier in the chapter that could occur when the interface is in a connect state, namely, a duplex mismatch.

You can determine that SW3's Gigabit 0/1 and 0/2 interfaces do not have a mismatch by simply using the **show interfaces** status command on SW1 and SW2 on the other end of those links, respectively. However, ports connected to a PC pose a troubleshooting problem in that you probably will not be near the PC, so you might have to guide the end user through some steps to verify the speed and duplex settings. However, it is helpful to look for the telltale signs of runts, collisions, and early collisions, as listed in the output of the **show interfaces** command in Example 3-9.

Example 3-9 *Signs of a Duplex Mismatch*

```
SW3#show interfaces fa0/13
FastEthernet0/13 is up, line protocol is up (connected)
  Hardware is Fast Ethernet, address is 000a.b7dc.b78d (bia 000a.b7dc.b78d)
  MTU 1500 bytes, BW 100000 Kbit, DLY 100 usec,
     reliability 255/255, txload 1/255, rxload 1/255
  Encapsulation ARPA, loopback not set
  Keepalive set (10 sec)
  Half-duplex, 100Mb/s, media type is 10/100BaseTX
  input flow-control is off, output flow-control is unsupported
  ARP type: ARPA, ARP Timeout 04:00:00
  Last input never, output 00:00:01, output hang never
  Last clearing of "show interface" counters never
```

Example 3-9 *Signs of a Duplex Mismatch (Continued)*

```
Input queue: 0/75/0/0 (size/max/drops/flushes); Total output drops: 0
Queueing strategy: fifo
Output queue: 0/40 (size/max)
5 minute input rate 0 bits/sec, 0 packets/sec
5 minute output rate 0 bits/sec, 0 packets/sec
   108 packets input, 6946 bytes, 0 no buffer
   Received 3 broadcasts (0 multicast)
   54 runs, 0 giants, 0 throttles
   0 input errors, 0 CRC, 0 frame, 0 overrun, 0 ignored
   0 watchdog, 2 multicast, 0 pause input
   0 input packets with dribble condition detected
   722 packets output, 52690 bytes, 0 underruns
   0 output errors, 114 collisions, 5 interface resets
   0 babbles, 78 late collision, 19 deferred
   0 lost carrier, 0 no carrier, 0 PAUSE output
   0 output buffer failures, 0 output buffers swapped out
```

In this case, a duplex mismatch does indeed exist. However, note that these same counters do increment under normal half-duplex operations, so these counters do not definitively identify the problem as a duplex mismatch.

In this case, SW3's configuration was changed to use full-duplex on interface Fa0/13, matching the manual setting on PC3.

Step 3: Check for Port Security Problems

The next step examines the port security configuration and status on each switch. Starting with the **show port-security** command is particularly helpful because it lists the interfaces on which the feature has been enabled. Example 3-10 shows this command on SW1 and SW2, plus a few other commands. Note that both SW2 and SW3 do not have the port security feature enabled.

Examine the output in Example 3-10, and before reading beyond the end of the example, make a few notes about what next steps you would take to either rule out port security as a potential problem, or what command you would use to further isolate a potential problem.

Example 3-10 *Port Security on SW1 and SW2*

```
SW1#show port-security
Secure Port  MaxSecureAddr  CurrentAddr  SecurityViolation  Security Action
             (Count)        (Count)      (Count)
---------------------------------------------------------------------------
   Fa0/11        1             1              97            Restrict
---------------------------------------------------------------------------
Total Addresses in System (excluding one mac per port)    : 0
```

continues

Example 3-10 *Port Security on SW1 and SW2 (Continued)*

```
Max Addresses limit in System (excluding one mac per port) : 8320
! On SW2 below, no interfaces have port security enabled.
SW2#show port-security
Secure Port  MaxSecureAddr  CurrentAddr  SecurityViolation  Security Action
             (Count)        (Count)      (Count)
---------------------------------------------------------------------------
---------------------------------------------------------------------------
Total Addresses in System (excluding one mac per port)    : 0
Max Addresses limit in System (excluding one mac per port) : 8320
```

The **show port-security** commands in the example list the interfaces on which port security has been enabled—specifically, SW1 interface Fa0/11 and no interfaces on SW2. On SW1, the notable items for troubleshooting are that the security action heading, which matches the violation mode setting, shows an action of restrict. With the restrict setting, SW1 interface Fa0/11 can be in the connect state (as seen in Example 3-8), but port security can be discarding traffic that violates the port security configuration. So, a closer examination of the port security configuration is in order, as shown in Example 3-11.

Example 3-11 *Port Security on SW1 and SW2*

```
SW1#show port-security interface fa0/11
Port Security                : Enabled
Port Status                  : Secure-up
Violation Mode               : Restrict
Aging Time                   : 0 mins
Aging Type                   : Absolute
SecureStatic Address Aging   : Disabled
Maximum MAC Addresses        : 1
Total MAC Addresses          : 1
Configured MAC Addresses     : 1
Sticky MAC Addresses         : 0
Last Source Address:Vlan     : 0200.1111.1111:3
Security Violation Count     : 97
!
! Next, the configuration shows that the configured MAC address does not
! match PC1's MAC address.
SW1#show running-config interface fa0/11

interface FastEthernet0/11
 switchport access vlan 3
 switchport mode access
 switchport port-security
 switchport port-security violation restrict
```

Example 3-11   *Port Security on SW1 and SW2 (Continued)*

```
switchport port-security mac-address 0200.3333.3333
!
! The following log message also points to a port security issue.
01:46:58: %PORT_SECURITY-2-PSECURE_VIOLATION: Security violation occurred, caused by MAC
address 0200.1111.1111 on port FastEthernet0/11.
```

The example begins by confirming the security mode and violation counter, as well as showing the last MAC address (0200.1111.1111) to send a frame into interface Fa0/11. PC1's MAC address (0200.1111.1111) does not match the port security configuration as seen in the second part of the example, a configuration that defaults to a maximum of one MAC address with an explicitly configured MAC address of 0200.3333.3333. A simple solution is to reconfigure port security to instead list PC1's MAC address. Note that the engineer would not need to use the **shutdown** and then the **no shutdown** commands on this interface to recover the interface, because the configuration uses violation mode restrict, which leaves the interface up while discarding the traffic to/from PC1.

Finally, the end of the example shows a log message generated by the switch for each violation when using restrict mode. This message would be seen from the console, or from a Telnet or Secure Shell (SSH) connection to the switch, if the remote user had issued the **terminal monitor** EXEC command.

Step 4: Check for VLAN and VLAN Trunk Problems

Step 4A begins by examining the access interfaces to ensure that the interfaces have been assigned to the correct VLANs. In this case, all interfaces connected to PCs and routers in Figure 3-5 should be assigned to VLAN 3. Example 3-12 provides some useful **show** command output. Take a few moments to read through the example, and look for any VLAN assignment problems.

Example 3-12   *Checking Access Interface VLAN Assignments*

```
SW1#show interfaces fa0/11 status

Port        Name              Status       Vlan     Duplex  Speed Type
Fa0/11                        connected    3        a-full  a-100 10/100BaseTX
SW1#show interfaces fa0/12 status

Port        Name              Status       Vlan     Duplex  Speed Type
Fa0/12                        notconnect   3          auto   auto 10/100BaseTX
! SW2 next
SW2#show interfaces status
! lines omitted for brevity
Fa0/9                         connected    1        a-full  a-100 10/100BaseTX
Fa0/10                        notconnect   3          auto   auto 10/100BaseTX
```

continues

Example 3-12 *Checking Access Interface VLAN Assignments (Continued)*

```
! SW3 next
SW3#show interfaces fa0/13 status

Port        Name              Status        Vlan      Duplex  Speed Type
Fa0/13                        connected     3          full   a-100 10/100BaseTX
```

The only problem in this case is the fact that while SW2's Fa0/10 interface was assigned to VLAN 3, per the drawing in Figure 3-5, SW2 connects to R1 using Fa0/9 (as seen with CDP in Example 3-7). Interface Fa0/9 defaults to be in VLAN 1. To solve this particular problem, on SW2, configure the **switchport access vlan 3** interface subcommand on interface Fa0/9.

The next part of Step 4 (Step 4B) suggests to check the VLANs to ensure that the VLANs are active on each switch. This ongoing example only uses VLAN 3, so Example 3-13 shows that VLAN 3 indeed is known on each switch. When reading the example, look for any problems with VLAN 3.

Example 3-13 *Finding a Half-Duplex Problem*

```
SW1#show vlan id 3

VLAN Name                            Status    Ports
---- -------------------------------- --------- -------------------------------
3    book-vlan3                       active    Fa0/11, Fa0/12, Gi0/1, Gi0/2
! lines omitted for brevity
! SW2 next
SW2#show vlan brief

VLAN Name                            Status    Ports
---- -------------------------------- --------- -------------------------------
1    default                          active    Fa0/1, Fa0/2, Fa0/3, Fa0/4
                                                Fa0/5, Fa0/6, Fa0/7, Fa0/8
                                                Fa0/11, Fa0/12, Fa0/13, Fa0/14
                                                Fa0/15, Fa0/16, Fa0/17, Fa0/18
                                                Fa0/19, Fa0/20, Fa0/21, Fa0/22
                                                Fa0/23, Fa0/24
3    VLAN0003                         active    Fa0/9, Fa0/10
! lines omitted for brevity
! SW3 next
SW3#show vlan brief

VLAN Name                            Status    Ports
---- -------------------------------- --------- -------------------------------
1    default                          active    Fa0/1, Fa0/2, Fa0/3, Fa0/4
                                                Fa0/5, Fa0/6, Fa0/7, Fa0/8
                                                Fa0/9, Fa0/10, Fa0/11, Fa0/12
```

Example 3-13 *Finding a Half-Duplex Problem (Continued)*

```
                                        Fa0/14, Fa0/15, Fa0/16, Fa0/17
                                        Fa0/18, Fa0/19, Fa0/20, Fa0/21
                                        Fa0/22, Fa0/23, Fa0/24
3    book-vlan3                active    Fa0/13
! lines omitted for brevity
```

In this case, VLAN 3 exists and is active on all three switches. However, SW2 lists a different name than do the other two switches. The name is unimportant to the operation of the VLAN, so this difference does not matter. As it turns out, SW2 is using VTP transparent mode, with SW1 and SW3 as VTP client and server mode switches, respectively. So, the name of VLAN 3 (book-vlan3) matches on SW1 and SW3.

Finally, the last part of troubleshooting Step 4 (Step 4C) suggests that you confirm the trunking status of all expected trunk interfaces. It is also helpful to determine on which trunks the VLANs will be forwarded. Example 3-14 lists output that helps supply the answers. Examine the output in the example, and before reading past the end of the example, list any trunks that do not currently forward traffic in VLAN 3, and make a list of possible reasons why VLAN 3 is omitted from the trunk.

Example 3-14 *Verifying Trunking and VLAN 3*

```
SW1#show interfaces trunk

Port        Mode          Encapsulation  Status       Native vlan
Gi0/1       desirable     802.1q         trunking     1
Gi0/2       desirable     802.1q         trunking     1


Port        Vlans allowed on trunk
Gi0/1       1-4094
Gi0/2       1-4094


Port        Vlans allowed and active in management domain
Gi0/1       1,3
Gi0/2       1,3


Port        Vlans in spanning tree forwarding state and not pruned
Gi0/1       3
Gi0/2       1,3
! SW2 next
SW2#show interfaces trunk

Port        Mode          Encapsulation  Status       Native vlan
Gi0/1       auto          802.1q         trunking     1
Gi0/2       auto          802.1q         trunking     1
```

continues

Example 3-14   *Verifying Trunking and VLAN 3 (Continued)*

```
Port            Vlans allowed on trunk
Gi0/1           1-4094
Gi0/2           1-4094


Port            Vlans allowed and active in management domain
Gi0/1           1,3
Gi0/2           1,3


Port            Vlans in spanning tree forwarding state and not pruned
Gi0/1           1,3
Gi0/2           1
! SW3 next
SW3#show interfaces trunk

Port        Mode        Encapsulation  Status      Native vlan
Gi0/1       auto        n-802.1q       trunking    1
Gi0/2       desirable   n-802.1q       trunking    1

Port        Vlans allowed on trunk
Gi0/1           1-4094
Gi0/2           1-4094


Port        Vlans allowed and active in management domain
Gi0/1           1,3
Gi0/2           1,3


Port        Vlans in spanning tree forwarding state and not pruned
Gi0/1           1,3
Gi0/2           1,3
```

By examining the end of the **show interfaces trunk** command on each switch, you can see that of both trunk interfaces on each switch, only SW2's Gi0/2 interface is not currently forwarding traffic in VLAN 3. Earlier in this chapter, the section "Identify Trunks and VLANs Forwarded on Those Trunks" listed four reasons a VLAN would be excluded from a trunk. However, three of the four reasons can be ruled out based on the output in the commands in Example 3-14 and in a few other examples in this chapter. First, if VLAN 3 were excluded because it was not in the allowed VLAN list, or because VLAN 3 was not active, VLAN 3 would be omitted from the first two lists of VLANs in SW2's **show interfaces trunk** command. Also, VTP pruning can be ruled out because earlier examples showed that all three switches have at least one interface in VLAN 3 and in a connect state, so even if all three switches used VTP correctly, with VTP pruning enabled, VLAN 3 would not be pruned. So, VLAN 3 is omitted in this case because of STP.

After finding all the problems in this ongoing example, and fixing the problems, PC1, PC3, and R1 can all ping each other. PC2, with an unspecified cabling problem, still does not work.

Predicting Normal Operation of the LAN Switching Data Plane

One of the steps in troubleshooting is to analyze what should be happening so that you can then compare that to what is happening—and hopefully isolate the root cause of any problems. These last sections of Chapter 3 complete this chapter's examination of how LANs should work by examining two examples of frames forwarded through a working version of the same sample network used in the just-completed troubleshooting example. The goal of these sections is to explain how to interpret the current **show** command output on switches to predict where the switches would each forward a particular frame. The first example shows a broadcast sent by PC1 in Figure 3-5, and the second example shows the forwarding process for a unicast frame sent by R1 to PC1's MAC address.

PC1 Broadcast in VLAN 3

The first working data plane example examines the path of a broadcast sent by PC1. PC1 might not have R1's MAC address in PC1's ARP cache, so in that case, PC1 sends an ARP broadcast, with an IP destination address of 255.255.255.255 and an Ethernet destination address of FFFF.FFFF.FFFF. This section examines what the various switches do to forward the broadcast to all parts of VLAN 3, as shown in Figure 3-6.

Figure 3-6 *Forwarding Path from PC1 to R1 per Example 3-14*

To analyze the flow of the broadcast, refer to the generic forwarding process, as summarized in the section "An Overview of the Normal LAN Switching Forwarding Process," earlier in this chapter. Earlier examples confirmed that SW1 port Fa0/11 is assigned to VLAN 3 and that SW1's Fa0/11 interface is an access interface. Because the frame is a broadcast, SW1 will flood the frame. Knowing these facts, Example 3-15 lists enough information to predict the interfaces out which SW1 will forward the broadcast frame sent by PC1 by listing the output of the **show spanning-tree vlan 3 active** command.

Example 3-15 *SW1's List of Active Interfaces*

```
SW1#show spanning-tree vlan 3 active

VLAN0003
  Spanning tree enabled protocol ieee
  Root ID    Priority    24579
             Address     000a.b7dc.b780
             Cost        1
             Port        26 (GigabitEthernet0/2)
             Hello Time   2 sec  Max Age 20 sec  Forward Delay 15 sec

  Bridge ID  Priority    32771  (priority 32768 sys-id-ext 3)
             Address     0019.e86a.6f80
             Hello Time   2 sec  Max Age 20 sec  Forward Delay 15 sec
             Aging Time 300

Interface         Role Sts Cost      Prio.Nbr Type
```

Example 3-15 *SW1's List of Active Interfaces (Continued)*

```
-----------------  ----  ---  ---------  --------  -------------------------------
Fa0/11            Desg  FWD  19          128.11    P2p
Gi0/1             Desg  FWD  4           128.25    P2p
Gi0/2             Root  FWD  1           128.26    P2p
```

Note that SW1 will not forward the frame back out Fa0/11, as the frame came in on Fa0/11. Also, SW1 will forward the frame out both trunk interfaces (Gi0/1 and Gi0/2). Also, earlier in this chapter, Example 3-14 shows evidence that both SW1's trunks use 802.1Q, with native VLAN 1, so SW1 will add an 802.1Q header, with VLAN ID 3, to each copy of the broadcast frame sent over those two trunks.

SW1's actions mean that both SW2 and SW3 should receive a copy of the broadcast frame sent by PC1. In SW2's case, SW2 happens to discard its copy of PC1's broadcast frame received on SW2's Gi0/2 interface. SW2 discards the frame because of Step 3 of the generic forwarding process from earlier in this chapter, because SW2's incoming interface (Gi0/2) is in a Blocking State in VLAN 3. (Example 3-14 and the text following that example showed SW2's Gi0/2 interface in a Blocking State for VLAN 3.) Note that SW2's Blocking State did not prevent SW1 from sending the frame to SW2; instead, SW2 silently discards the received frame.

For the copy of PC1's broadcast frame received by SW3 on its Gi0/1 interface, SW3 floods the frame. SW3 determines the frame's VLAN based on the incoming 802.1Q header and finds the incoming interface in an STP Forwarding State. Based on these facts, SW3 will forward the frame inside VLAN 3. Example 3-16 shows the information that's needed to know on which interfaces SW3 forwards the VLAN 3 broadcast.

Example 3-16 *SW3: Forwarding a Broadcast in VLAN 3*

```
SW3#show mac address-table dynamic vlan 3
          Mac Address Table
-------------------------------------------

Vlan    Mac Address      Type       Ports
----    -----------      --------   -----
   3    0200.0101.0101   DYNAMIC    Gi0/2
   3    0200.1111.1111   DYNAMIC    Gi0/1
   3    0200.3333.3333   DYNAMIC    Fa0/13
Total Mac Addresses for this criterion: 3

SW3#show spanning-tree vlan 3 active

VLAN0003
```

continues

Example 3-16   *SW3: Forwarding a Broadcast in VLAN 3 (Continued)*

```
 Spanning tree enabled protocol ieee
 Root ID    Priority    24579
            Address     000a.b7dc.b780
            This bridge is the root
            Hello Time   2 sec  Max Age 20 sec  Forward Delay 15 sec

 Bridge ID  Priority    24579  (priority 24576 sys-id-ext 3)
            Address     000a.b7dc.b780
            Hello Time   2 sec  Max Age 20 sec  Forward Delay 15 sec
            Aging Time 300


Interface        Role Sts Cost       Prio.Nbr Type
---------------- ---- --- ---------  -------- --------------------------------
Fa0/13           Desg FWD 19          128.13   P2p
Gi0/1            Desg FWD 4           128.25   P2p
Gi0/2            Desg FWD 4           128.26   P2p
```

As with SW1, SW3 does not forward the broadcast out the same interface in which the frame arrived (Gi0/1 in this case), but SW3 does flood the frame out all other interfaces in that VLAN and in an STP Forwarding State, namely Fa0/13 and Gi0/2. Also, because SW3's Gi0/2 interface currently uses 802.1Q trunking, with native VLAN 1, SW3 adds an 802.1Q header with VLAN ID 3 listed.

Finally, when SW2 receives the copy of the broadcast in SW2's Gi0/1 interface from SW3, SW2 follows the same generic process as the other switches. SW2 identifies the VLAN based on the incoming 802.1Q header, confirms that the incoming interface is in a Forwarding State, and floods the broadcast out all its interfaces that are both in a Forwarding State and in VLAN 3. In this case, SW2 forwards the frame only out interface Fa0/9, connected to router R1. Example 3-17 shows the supporting command output.

Example 3-17   *SW2: Forwarding a Broadcast in VLAN 3 Received from SW3*

```
! First, note that the broadcast address FFFF.FFFF.FFFF is not
! in the VLAN 3 MAC table.
SW2#show mac address-table dynamic vlan 3
          Mac Address Table
-------------------------------------------

Vlan    Mac Address       Type        Ports
----    -----------       --------    -----
   3    000a.b7dc.b79a    DYNAMIC     Gi0/1
   3    0200.0101.0101    DYNAMIC     Fa0/9
   3    0200.1111.1111    DYNAMIC     Gi0/1
   3    0200.3333.3333    DYNAMIC     Gi0/1
```

Example 3-17 *SW2: Forwarding a Broadcast in VLAN 3 Received from SW3 (Continued)*

```
Total Mac Addresses for this criterion: 4
! Next, note that on Fa0/9 and Gi0/1 are in an STP forwarding state,
! and the broadcast came in Gi0/1 - so SW2 floods the frame only out Fa0/9.
SW2#show spanning-tree vlan 3 active
!lines omitted for brevity

Interface        Role Sts Cost      Prio.Nbr Type
---------------- ---- --- --------- -------- --------------------------------
Fa0/9            Desg FWD 19        128.9    P2p
Gi0/1            Root FWD 4         128.25   P2p
Gi0/2            Altn BLK 4         128.26   P2p
```

SW2 does not forward the frame out Gi0/1, because the frame entered SW2's Gi0/1 interface.

Forwarding Path: Unicast from R1 to PC1

The second data plane example examines how switches forward unicast frames. To analyze the forwarding process for unicast frames, consider R1's ARP reply in response to PC1's ARP request/broadcast. The destination addresses (both IP and MAC) of R1's ARP reply are PC1's IP and MAC addresses, respectively. Figure 3-7 shows the forwarding path, with the examples that follow spelling out how the generic frame-forwarding process applies to this particular case.

Figure 3-7 *Forwarding Path from R1 to PC1 per Example 3-15*

When SW2 receives the frame from R1, SW2 notes that the frame entered interface Fa0/9, an access interface in VLAN 3. The end of Example 3-17 previously showed Fa0/9 in an STP Forwarding State in VLAN 3, so SW2 will attempt to forward the frame instead of discarding the frame. As seen next in Example 3-18, SW2's MAC address table lists PC1's MAC address—0200.1111.1111—off interface Gi0/1 and in VLAN 3, so SW2 forwards the frame out Gi0/1 to SW3.

Example 3-18 *SW2's Logic When Forwarding a Known Unicast to PC1*

```
SW2#show mac address-table dynamic vlan 3
          Mac Address Table
-------------------------------------------


Vlan    Mac Address       Type        Ports
----    -----------       --------    -----
   3    000a.b7dc.b79a    DYNAMIC     Gi0/1
   3    0200.0101.0101    DYNAMIC     Fa0/9
   3    0200.1111.1111    DYNAMIC     Gi0/1
Total Mac Addresses for this criterion: 3
```

When SW3 receives the frame from SW2, SW3 notes that the frame entered interface Gi0/2, a trunking interface, and that the trunking header listed VLAN ID 3. The end of Example 3-16 previously showed Gi0/2 in an STP Forwarding State in VLAN 3 (forwarding Step 3), so SW3 will not discard the received frame because of STP. As seen next in Example 3-19, SW3's MAC address table lists PC1's MAC address— 0200.1111.1111—off interface Gi0/1 and in VLAN 3, so SW3 forwards the frame out Gi0/1 to SW1.

Example 3-19 *SW3's Logic When Forwarding a Known Unicast to PC1*

```
SW3#show mac address-table dynamic vlan 3
          Mac Address Table
-------------------------------------------


Vlan    Mac Address       Type        Ports
----    -----------       --------    -----
   3    0200.0101.0101    DYNAMIC     Gi0/2
   3    0200.1111.1111    DYNAMIC     Gi0/1
   3    0200.3333.3333    DYNAMIC     Fa0/13
Total Mac Addresses for this criterion: 3
```

When SW1 receives the frame from SW3, SW1 notes that the frame entered interface Gi0/2, a trunking interface, and that the trunking header listed VLAN ID 3. The end of Example 3-15 previously showed SW1's Gi0/2 in an STP Forwarding State in VLAN 3, so SW1 will not discard the frame because of the interface not being in an STP Forwarding

State. As seen next in Example 3-20, SW1's MAC address table lists PC1's MAC address—0200.1111.1111—off interface Fa0/11 and VLAN 3, so SW1 forwards the frame out Fa0/11 to PC1. In this case, SW1 strips off the 802.1Q VLAN header, because interface Fa0/11 is an access interface.

Example 3-20 *SW1's Logic When Forwarding a Known Unicast to PC1*

```
SW1#show mac address-table dynamic vlan 3
          Mac Address Table
-------------------------------------------

Vlan    Mac Address       Type        Ports
----    -----------       --------    -----
   3    000a.b7dc.b799    DYNAMIC     Gi0/2
   3    0200.0101.0101    DYNAMIC     Gi0/2
   3    0200.3333.3333    DYNAMIC     Gi0/2
Total Mac Addresses for this criterion: 3
SW1#show mac address-table vlan 3
          Mac Address Table
-------------------------------------------

Vlan    Mac Address       Type        Ports
----    -----------       --------    -----
 All    0100.0ccc.cccc    STATIC      CPU
 All    0100.0ccc.cccd    STATIC      CPU
 All    0180.c200.0000    STATIC      CPU
 All    0180.c200.0001    STATIC      CPU
 All    0180.c200.0002    STATIC      CPU
 All    0180.c200.0003    STATIC      CPU
 All    0180.c200.0004    STATIC      CPU
 All    0180.c200.0005    STATIC      CPU
 All    0180.c200.0006    STATIC      CPU
 All    0180.c200.0007    STATIC      CPU
 All    0180.c200.0008    STATIC      CPU
 All    0180.c200.0009    STATIC      CPU
 All    0180.c200.000a    STATIC      CPU
 All    0180.c200.000b    STATIC      CPU
 All    0180.c200.000c    STATIC      CPU
 All    0180.c200.000d    STATIC      CPU
 All    0180.c200.000e    STATIC      CPU
 All    0180.c200.000f    STATIC      CPU
 All    0180.c200.0010    STATIC      CPU
 All    ffff.ffff.ffff    STATIC      CPU
   3    000a.b7dc.b799    DYNAMIC     Gi0/2
   3    0200.0101.0101    DYNAMIC     Gi0/2
   3    0200.1111.1111    STATIC      Fa0/11
Total Mac Addresses for this criterion: 23
```

This last step points out an important fact about the MAC address table and port security. Note that the **show mac address-table dynamic** command on SW1 does not list PC1's MAC address of 0200.1111.1111, so you might have been tempted to think that SW1 will flood the frame because it is an unknown unicast frame. However, because SW1 has configured port security on Fa0/11, including the **switchport port-security mac-address 0200.1111.1111** interface subcommand, IOS considers this MAC address a static MAC address. So, by leaving off the **dynamic** keyword, the **show mac address-table vlan 3** command lists all MAC addresses known in the VLAN, including 0200.1111.1111. This command output confirms that SW1 will forward the unicast to 0200.1111.1111 only out interface Fa0/11.

Exam Preparation Tasks

Review All the Key Topics

Review the most important topics from this chapter, noted with the Key Topics icon in the outer margin of the page. Table 3-6 lists a reference of these key topics and the page numbers on which each is found.

Key Topic

Table 3-6 *Key Topics for Chapter 3*

Key Topic Element	Description	Page Number
Table 3-2	Lists both sets of interface status codes and typical root causes for each state	122-123
Figure 3-4	Typical uses of Ethernet straight-through and crossover cables	123
Table 3-3	Lists devices and the pins on which they transmit for 10BASE-T and 100BASE-Tx	124
List	Suggestions for noticing duplex mismatch problems	127
List	Default IEEE autonegotiation duplex choices based on current speed	127
List	Port security features	128
Table 3-4	Port security violation modes with differences in behavior and **show** commands	129
Table 3-5	Lists **show** commands useful for finding access interfaces and their assigned VLANs	132-133
List	The four reasons a switch does not pass a VLAN's traffic over a particular trunk	134-135
List	Lists the troubleshooting steps explained in this chapter (does not need to be memorized)	136

Complete the Tables and Lists from Memory

Print a copy of Appendix J, "Memory Tables," (found on the CD) or at least the section for this chapter, and complete the tables and lists from memory. Appendix K, "Memory Tables Answer Key," also on the CD, includes completed tables and lists to check your work.

Cisco Published ICND2 Exam Topics*
Covered in This Part

Configure, verify and troubleshoot a switch with VLANs and interswitch communications

- Configure, verify, and troubleshoot interVLAN routing

Implement an IP addressing scheme and IP Services to meet network requirements in a medium-size Enterprise branch office network

- Calculate and apply a VLSM IP addressing design to a network

- Determine the appropriate classless addressing scheme using VLSM and summarization to satisfy addressing requirements in a LAN/WAN environment

- Identify and correct common problems associated with IP addressing and host configurations

Configure and troubleshoot basic operation and routing on Cisco devices

- Verify configuration and connectivity using ping, traceroute, and telnet or SSH

- Troubleshoot routing implementation issues

- Verify router hardware and software operation using SHOW & DEBUG commands

- Implement basic router security

Implement, verify, and troubleshoot NAT and ACLs in a medium-size Enterprise branch office network.

- Describe the purpose and types of access control lists

- Configure and apply access control lists based on network filtering requirements

- Configure and apply an access control list to limit telnet and SSH access to the router

- Verify and monitor ACL's in a network environment

- Troubleshoot ACL implementation issues

* Always recheck http://www.cisco.com for the latest posted exam topics.

Part II: IP Routing

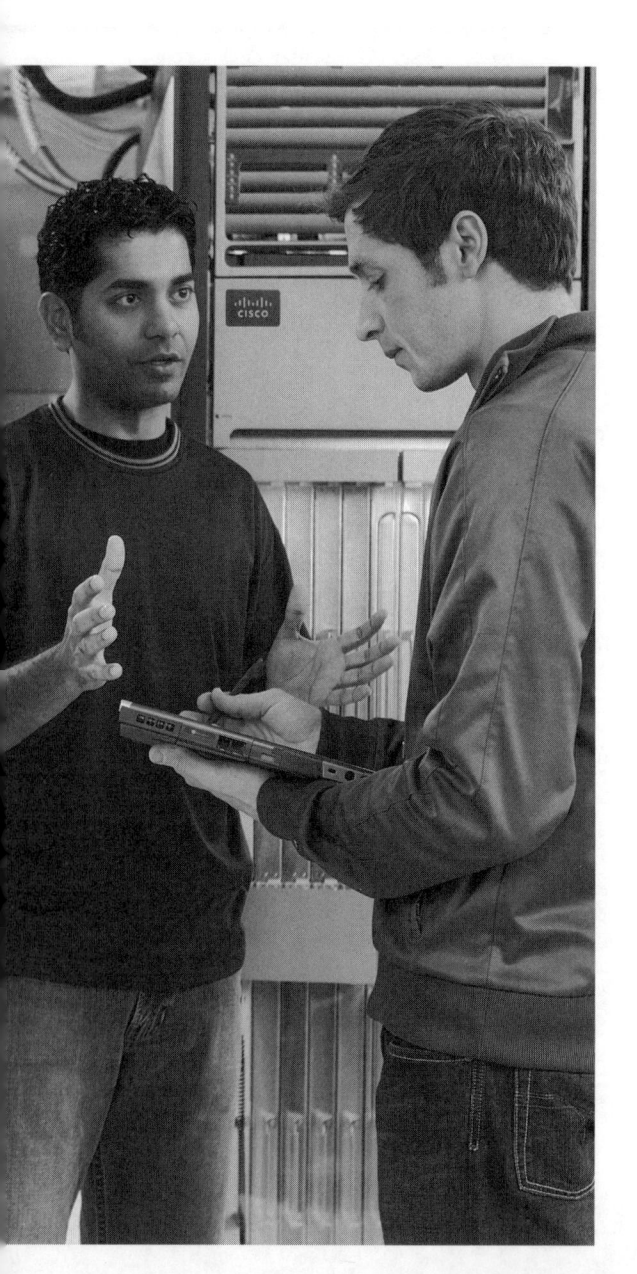

This chapter covers the following subjects:

IP Routing and Addressing: This section reviews the relationship between IP addressing and IP routing, and fills in more of the detail of how routing works with multiple overlapping routes.

Routes to Directly Connected Subnets: This section examines how routers add routes for subnets connected to a router's interfaces.

Static Routes: This section describes how to configure static routes, including static default routes.

CHAPTER 4

IP Routing: Static and Connected Routes

This chapter begins Part II, "IP Routing." The four chapters in this part focus on features that impact the IP routing process—also called IP forwarding—by which hosts and routers deliver packets from the source host to the destination host. These four chapters also occasionally explain topics related to IP routing protocols, in part because IP routing, a data plane feature, relies heavily on the control plane work done by routing protocols.

This chapter covers several topics related to connected routes, which are routes to reach subnet attached to a router interface. This chapter also explains static routes, including default routes, as well as reviews the basic codependent topics of IP addressing and IP routing.

"Do I Know This Already?" Quiz

The "Do I Know This Already?" quiz allows you to assess whether you should read the entire chapter. If you miss no more than one of these eight self-assessment questions, you might want to move ahead to the section "Exam Preparation Tasks." Table 4-1 lists the major headings in this chapter and the "Do I Know This Already?" quiz questions covering the material in those headings so that you can assess your knowledge of these specific areas. The answers to the "Do I Know This Already?" quiz appear in Appendix A.

Table 4-1 *"Do I Know This Already?" Foundation Topics Section-to-Question Mapping*

Foundation Topics Section	Questions
IP Routing and Addressing	1–2
Routes to Directly Connected Subnets	3–4
Static Routes	5–8

1. A PC user turns on her computer, and as soon as the computer is up and working, she opens a web browser to browse http://www.ciscopress.com. Which protocol(s) would definitely not be used by the PC during this process?

    a. DHCP

    b. DNS

    c. ARP

    d. ICMP

2. A PC user turns on her computer, and as soon as the computer is up and working, she opens a command prompt. From there, she issues the **ping 2.2.2.2** command, and the ping shows 100 percent success. The PC's IP address is 1.1.1.1 with mask 255.255.255.0. Which of the following settings would be required on the PC to support the successful ping?

    a. The IP address of a DNS server

    b. The IP address of a default gateway

    c. The IP address of an ARP server

    d. The IP address of a DHCP server

3. Router 1 has a Fast Ethernet interface 0/0 with IP address 10.1.1.1. The interface is connected to a switch. This connection is then migrated to use 802.1Q trunking. Which of the following commands could be part of a valid configuration for Router 1's Fa0/0 interface?

    a. **interface fastethernet 0/0.4**

    b. **dot1q enable**

    c. **dot1q enable 4**

    d. **trunking enable**

    e. **trunking enable 4**

    f. **encapsulation dot1q**

4. A router is configured with the **no ip subnet-zero** global configuration command. Which of the following interface subcommands would not be accepted by this router?

    a. **ip address 10.1.1.1 255.255.255.0**

    b. **ip address 10.0.0.129 255.255.255.128**

    c. **ip address 10.1.2.2 255.254.0.0**

    d. **ip address 10.0.0.5 255.255.255.252**

5. Which of the following must be true before IOS lists a route as "S" in the output of a **show ip route** command?

   a. The IP address must be configured on an interface.

   b. The router must receive a routing update from a neighboring router.

   c. The **ip route** command must be added to the configuration.

   d. The **ip address** command must use the **special** keyword.

   e. The interface must be up and up.

6. Which of the following commands correctly configures a static route?

   a. **ip route 10.1.3.0 255.255.255.0 10.1.130.253**

   b. **ip route 10.1.3.0 serial 0**

   c. **ip route 10.1.3.0 /24 10.1.130.253**

   d. **ip route 10.1.3.0 /24 serial 0**

7. Which of the following is affected by whether a router is performing classful or classless routing?

   a. When to use a default route

   b. When to use masks in routing updates

   c. When to convert a packet's destination IP address to a network number

   d. When to perform queuing based on the classification of a packet into a particular queue

8. A router has been configured with the **ip classless** global configuration command. The router receives a packet destined to IP address 168.13.4.1. The following text lists the contents of the router's routing table. Which of the following is true about how this router forwards the packet?

```
Gateway of last resort is 168.13.1.101 to network 0.0.0.0

     168.13.0.0/24 is subnetted, 2 subnets
C       168.13.1.0 is directly connected,  FastEthernet0/0
R       168.13.3.0 [120/1] via 168.13.100.3, 00:00:05, Serial0.1
```

   a. It is forwarded to 168.13.100.3.

   b. It is forwarded to 168.13.1.101.

   c. It is forwarded out interface Fa0/0, directly to the destination host.

   d. The router discards the packet.

Foundation Topics

This chapter introduces several straightforward concepts regarding how a router adds routes to its routing table without using a dynamic routing protocol. In particular, this chapter covers connected routes, including connected routes when a router uses LAN trunking. It also covers static routes, with some emphasis on how routers use special static routes called default routes. However, because this chapter is the first IP-centric chapter of this book, it begins with a brief review of two related topics: IP routing and IP addressing.

> **NOTE**   The introduction to this book describes an alternate reading plan for readers pursuing the CCNA 640-802 exam, which you move back and forth between *CCENT/ CCNA ICND1 Official Exam Certification Guide* and this book. If you are using this plan, note that the first major section reviews topics from the ICND1 book. If you are following that reading plan, feel free to skip ahead to the section "IP Forwarding by Matching the Most Specific Route."

IP Routing and Addressing

IP routing depends on the rules of IP addressing, with one of the original core design goals for IP addressing being the creation of efficient IP routing. IP routing defines how an IP packet can be delivered from the host at which the packet is created to the destination host. IP addressing conventions group addresses into consecutively numbered sets of addresses called subnets, which then aids the IP forwarding or IP routing process.

> **NOTE**   This book uses the terms *IP routing* and *IP forwarding* as synonymous terms. The term *IP routing protocols* refers to routing protocols that routers use to dynamically fill the routing tables with the currently best routes. Note that some texts and courses use the term *IP routing* when referring to both the packet-forwarding process and the protocols used to learn routes.

IP Routing

Both hosts and routers participate in the IP routing process. The next list summarizes a host's logic when forwarding a packet, assuming that the host is on an Ethernet LAN or wireless LAN:

1.   When sending a packet, compare the destination IP address of the packet to the sending host's perception of the range of addresses in the connected subnet, based on the host's IP address and subnet mask.

   a.   If the destination is in the same subnet as the host, send the packet directly to the destination host. Address Resolution Protocol (ARP) is needed to find the destination host's MAC address.

   b.   If the destination is not in the same subnet as the host, send the packet directly to the host's default gateway (default router). ARP is needed to find the default gateway's MAC address.

Routers use the following general steps, noting that with routers, the packet must first be received, whereas the sending host (as previously summarized) begins with the IP packet in memory:

1.   For each received frame, use the data-link trailer frame check sequence (FCS) field to ensure that the frame had no errors; if errors occurred, discard the frame (and do not continue to the next step).

Key
Topic

2.   Check the frame's destination data link layer address, and process only if addressed to this router or to a broadcast/multicast address.

3.   Discard the incoming frame's old data-link header and trailer, leaving the IP packet.

4.   Compare the packet's destination IP address to the routing table, and find the route that matches the destination address. This route identifies the outgoing interface of the router, and possibly the next-hop router.

5.   Determine the destination data-link address used for forwarding packets to the next router or destination host (as directed in the routing table).

6.   Encapsulate the IP packet inside a new data-link header and trailer, appropriate for the outgoing interface, and forward the frame out that interface.

For example, consider Figure 4-1, which shows a simple network with two routers and three hosts. In this case, PC1 creates a packet to be sent to PC3's IP address, namely 172.16.3.3. The figure shows three major routing steps, labeled A, B, and C: PC1's host routing logic that forwards the packet toward R1, R1's routing logic that forwards the packet toward R2, and R2's routing logic that forwards the packet toward PC3.

First, consider Step A from Figure 4-1. PC1 knows its own IP address of 172.16.1.1, mask 255.255.255.0. (All interfaces use an easy mask of 255.255.255.0 in this example.) PC1 can calculate its subnet number (172.16.1.0/24) and range of addresses (172.16.1.1–172.16.1.254). Destination address 172.16.3.3 is not in PC1's subnet, so PC1 uses Step 1B in the summary of host routing logic—namely, PC1 sends the packet, inside an Ethernet frame, to its default gateway IP address of 172.16.1.251.

Figure 4-1   *Example of the IP Routing Process*

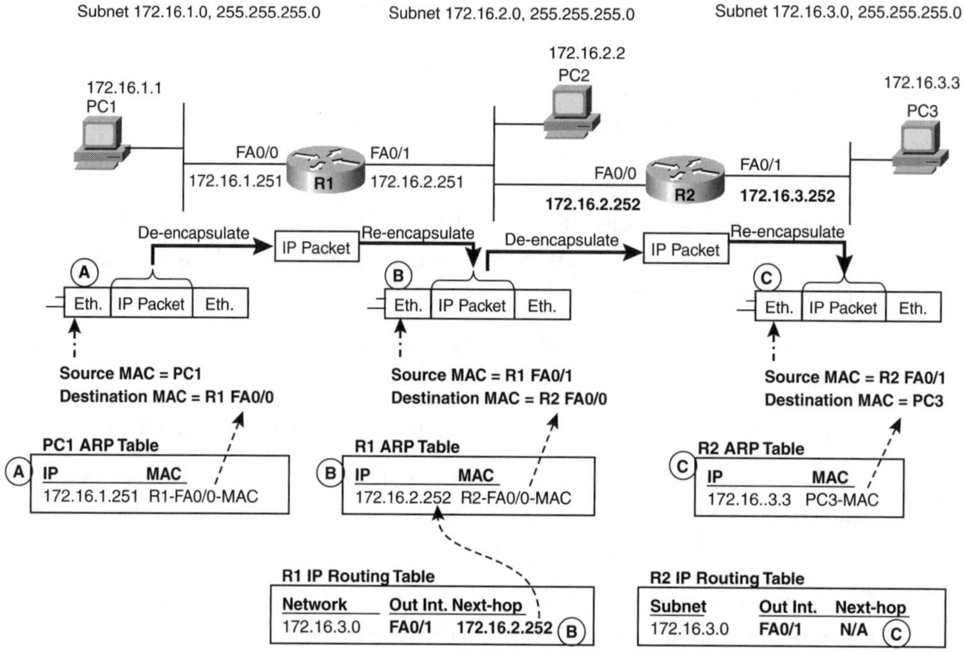

This first step (Step A) of PC1 sending the packet to its default gateway also reviews a couple of important concepts. As you can see from the lower part of the figure, PC1 uses its own MAC address as the source MAC address, but it uses R1's LAN MAC address as the destination MAC address. As a result, any LAN switches can deliver the frame correctly to R1's Fa0/0 interface. Also note that PC1 looked for and found 172.16.1.251's MAC address in PC1's ARP cache. If the MAC address had not been found, PC1 would have had to use ARP to dynamically discover the MAC address used by 172.16.1.251 (R1) before being able to send the frame shown in Figure 4-1.

Next focus on Step B from Figure 4-1, which is the work done by router R1 to forward the packet. Using the router's six summarized routing steps that preceded Figure 4-1, the following occurs at R1. Note that the figure denotes many of the details with letter *B*:

1.   R1 checks the FCS, and the frame has no errors.

2.   R1 finds its own Fa0/0 interface MAC address in the frame's destination MAC address field, so R1 should process the encapsulated packet.

3.   R1 discards the old data-link header and trailer, leaving the IP packet (as shown directly under the R1 icon in Figure 4-1).

4. (In the bottom center of Figure 4-1) R1 compares the destination IP address (172.16.3.3) to R1's routing table, finding the matching route shown in the figure, with outgoing interface Fa0/1 and next-hop router 172.16.2.252.

5. R1 needs to find the next-hop device's MAC address (R2's MAC address), so R1 looks and finds that MAC address in its ARP table.

6. R1 encapsulates the IP packet in a new Ethernet frame, with R1's Fa0/1 MAC address as the source MAC address, and R2's Fa0/0 MAC address (per the ARP table) as the destination MAC address. R1 sends the frame.

While the steps might seem laborious, you can think of briefer versions of this logic in cases where a question does not require this level of depth. For example, when troubleshooting routing problems, focusing on Step 4—the matching of the packet's destination IP address to a router's routing table—is probably one of the most important steps. So, a briefer summary of the routing process might be: Router receives a packet, matches the packet's destination address with the routing table, and forwards the packet based on that matched route. While this abbreviated version ignores some details, it can make for quicker work when troubleshooting problems or discussing routing issues.

To complete the example, consider the same six-step router forwarding logic as applied on router R2, listed with letter C in Figure 4-1, as follows:

1. R2 checks the FCS, and the frame has no errors.

2. R2 finds its own Fa0/0 interface MAC address in the frame's destination MAC address field, so R2 should process the encapsulated packet.

3. R2 discards the old data-link header and trailer, leaving the IP packet (as shown directly under the R2 icon in Figure 4-1).

4. (In the bottom right of Figure 4-1) R2 compares the destination IP address (172.16.3.3) to R2's routing table, finding the matching route shown in the figure, with outgoing interface Fa0/1 and no next-hop router listed.

5. Because no next-hop router exists, R2 needs to find the true destination host's MAC address (PC3's MAC address), so R2 looks and finds that MAC address in its ARP table.

6. R2 encapsulates the IP packet in a new Ethernet frame, with R2's Fa0/1 MAC address as the source MAC address, and PC3's MAC address (per the ARP table) as the destination MAC address. R1 sends the frame.

Finally, when this frame arrives at PC3, PC3 sees its own MAC address listed as the destination MAC address, so PC3 begins to process the frame.

The same general process works with WAN links as well, with a few different details. On point-to-point links, as shown in Figure 4-2, an ARP table is not needed. Because a point-to-point link can have at most one other router connected to it, you can ignore the data-link addressing. However, with Frame Relay, the routing process does consider the data-link addresses, called data-link connection identifiers (DLCI). The routing details regarding Frame Relay DLCIs are covered later in this book in Chapter 13.

Figure 4-2   *Example of the IP Routing Process*

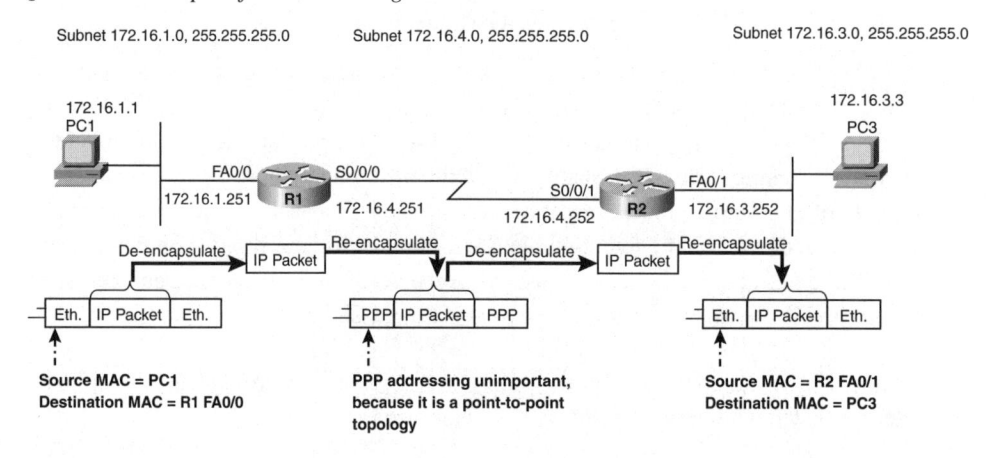

The IP routing process on both the hosts and the routers relies on these devices' abilities to understand IP addressing and predict which IP addresses are in each group or subnet. The next section provides a brief review of IP addresses and subnetting.

IP Addressing and Subnetting

IP addressing rules aid the IP routing processes by requiring that IP addresses be organized into groups of consecutively numbered IP addresses called subnets. To allow a concise way to refer to a subnet, IP addressing defines the concept of a subnet number and subnet mask, which together exactly identify the range of addresses in a subnet. For example, the routers in Figures 4-1 and 4-2 used routes that listed subnet number 172.16.3.0 when forwarding the packet destined for PC3 (172.16.3.3). The figures omitted the subnet mask to reduce clutter, but any device can look at subnet number 172.16.3.0, with mask 255.255.255.0, and know that these two numbers concisely represent the following subnet:

■   Subnet number 172.16.3.0

■   Range of usable addresses in the subnet: 172.16.3.1–172.16.3.254

■   Subnet broadcast address (not usable for individual hosts): 172.16.3.255

The following list provides a brief review of some of the major IP addressing concepts. Note that this chapter solely focuses on IP version 4 (IPv4) addresses, with Chapter 17, "IP Version 6," covering IPv6.

■ Unicast IP addresses are IP addresses that can be assigned to an individual interface for sending and receiving packets.

■ Each unicast IP address resides in a particular Class A, B, or C network, called a classful IP network.

■ If subnetting is used, which is almost always true in real life, each unicast IP address also resides in a specific subset of the classful network called a subnet.

■ The subnet mask, written in either dotted decimal form (for example, 255.255.255.0) or prefix notation form (for example, /24), identifies the structure of unicast IP addresses and allows devices and people to derive the subnet number, range of addresses, and broadcast address for a subnet.

■ Devices in the same subnet should all use the same subnet mask; otherwise, they have different opinions about the range of addresses in the subnet, which can break the IP routing process.

■ Devices in a single VLAN should be in the same single IP subnet.

■ Devices in different VLANs should be in different IP subnets.

■ To forward packets between subnets, a device that performs routing must be used. In this book, only routers are shown, but multilayer switches—switches that also perform routing functions—can also be used.

■ Point-to-point serial links use a different subnet than the LAN subnets, but these subnets only require two IP addresses, one for each router interface on either end of the link.

■ Hosts separated by a router must be in separate subnets.

Figure 4-3 shows an example internetwork that exhibits many of these features. Switch SW1 defaults to put all interfaces into VLAN 1, so all hosts on the left (PC1 included) are in a single subnet. Note that SW1's management IP address, also in VLAN 1, will be from that same subnet. Similarly, SW2 defaults to put all ports in VLAN 1, requiring a second subnet. The point-to-point link requires a third subnet. The figure shows the subnet numbers, masks, and range of addresses. Note that all addresses and subnets are part of the same single classful Class B network 172.16.0.0, and all subnets use a mask of 255.255.255.0.

Figure 4-3 *Example IP Addressing Design*

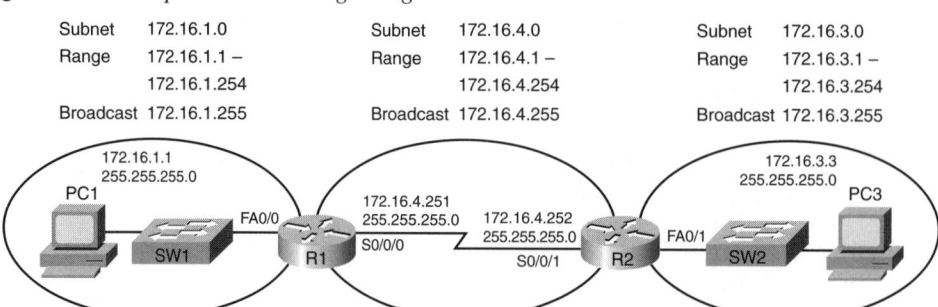

Subnet	172.16.1.0	Subnet	172.16.4.0	Subnet	172.16.3.0
Range	172.16.1.1 –	Range	172.16.4.1 –	Range	172.16.3.1 –
	172.16.1.254		172.16.4.254		172.16.3.254
Broadcast	172.16.1.255	Broadcast	172.16.4.255	Broadcast	172.16.3.255

Figure 4-3 lists the subnet numbers, ranges of addresses, and subnet broadcast addresses. However, each device in the figure can find the same information just based on its respective IP address and subnet mask configuration, deriving the subnet number, range of addresses, and broadcast address for each attached subnet.

The CCNA exams require mastery of these IP addressing and subnetting concepts, but more significantly, the exams require mastery of the math used to analyze existing IP networks and design new IP networks. If you have not already taken the time to master subnetting, it would be useful to study and practice before going further in your reading. While this section reviewed the basics of IP addressing, it does not cover subnetting math.

To learn about subnetting and the related math, you have a couple of options. For those of you who bought the two-book library that includes this book as well as *CCENT/CCNA ICND1 Official Exam Certification Guide*, dig into Chapter 12 of that book and do the practice problems listed. For those of you that bought this without the ICND1 book, all the resources for learning subnetting in the ICND1 book have been included on this book's CD. Refer to the following elements:

■   CD-only Appendix D, "Subnetting Practice"

■   CD-only Appendix E, "Subnetting Reference Pages"

■   CD-only Appendix H, "ICND1 Chapter 12: IP Addressing and Subnetting"

■   Subnetting videos

To be prepared to read the rest of this book without letting the subnetting math cause any difficulties, before reading any further in this book, you should be able to do the tasks in the following list, given plenty of time. You do not have to be able to find the answer quickly at this point in your preparation, but to be prepared for the exams, you need to be ready to do these tasks within the listed time limits:

■   Given a dotted decimal mask, convert it to prefix notation, or vice versa. (Suggested time for exam readiness: 5 seconds)

- Given an IP address and mask, find the subnet number, range of addresses, and subnet broadcast address. (Suggested time: 15 seconds)

- Given a subnet mask and class (A, B, or C) of a network, determine the number of subnets and hosts per subnet. (Suggested time: 15 seconds)

- Given a class of network (A, B, or C) and design requirements for a number of subnets and number of hosts per subnet, find all masks that meet the requirements, and choose the mask that either maximizes the number of subnets or the number of hosts per subnet. (Suggested time: 30 seconds)

- Given a classful network and a single subnet mask to use for all subnets, list the subnet numbers, and identify the zero subnet and broadcast subnet. (Suggested time: 30 seconds)

With these details of subnetting in mind, the next section examines how a router matches the routing table when the subnets listed in the routing table overlap so that one packet's destination matches more than one route.

IP Forwarding by Matching the Most Specific Route

Any router's IP routing process requires that the router compare the destination IP address of each packet with the existing contents of that router's IP routing table. Often, only one route matches a particular destination address. However, in some cases, a particular destination address matches more than one of the router's routes. Some legitimate and normal reasons for the overlapping routes in a routing table include the following:

- The use of autosummary

- Manual route summarization

- The use of static routes

- Incorrectly designed subnetting so that subnets overlap their address ranges

Chapter 5, "VLSM and Route Summarization," explains more detail about each of these reasons. While some cases of overlapping routes are problems, other cases are normal operation resulting from some other feature. This section focuses on how a router chooses which of the overlapping routes to use, with the features that cause the overlap being covered in Chapter 5.

The following statement summarizes a router's forwarding logic with overlapping routes:

> When a particular destination IP address matches more than one route in a router's routing table, the router uses the most specific route—in other words, the route with the longest prefix length.

Key
Topic

To see exactly what that means, the routing table listed in Example 4-1 shows a series of overlapping routes. First, before reading any text beneath the example, try to predict which route would be used for packets sent to the following IP addresses: 172.16.1.1, 172.16.1.2, 172.16.2.3, and 172.16.4.3.

Example 4-1   **show ip route** *Command with Overlapping Routes*

```
R1#show ip route rip

      172.16.0.0/16 is variably subnetted, 5 subnets, 4 masks
R        172.16.1.1/32 [120/1] via 172.16.25.2, 00:00:04, Serial0/1/1
R        172.16.1.0/24 [120/2] via 172.16.25.129, 00:00:09, Serial0/1/0
R        172.16.0.0/22 [120/1] via 172.16.25.2, 00:00:04, Serial0/1/1
R        172.16.0.0/16 [120/2] via 172.16.25.129, 00:00:09, Serial0/1/0
R        0.0.0.0/0 [120/3] via 172.16.25.129, 00:00:09, Serial0/1/0
R1#show ip route 172.16.4.3
Routing entry for 172.16.0.0/16
  Known via "rip", distance 120, metric 2
  Redistributing via rip
  Last update from 172.16.25.129 on Serial0/1/0, 00:00:19 ago
  Routing Descriptor Blocks:
  * 172.16.25.129, from 172.16.25.129, 00:00:19 ago, via Serial0/1/0
      Route metric is 2, traffic share count is 1
```

While a diagram of the internetwork might be supplied with the question, you really only need two pieces of information to determine which route will be matched: the destination IP address of the packet and the contents of the router's routing table. By examining each subnet and mask in the routing table, you can then determine the range of IP addresses in each subnet. In this case, the ranges defined by each route, respectively, are as follows:

■   172.16.1.1 (just this one address)

■   172.16.1.0–172.16.1.255

■   172.16.0.0–172.16.3.255

■   172.16.0.0–172.16.255.255

■   0.0.0.0–255.255.255.255 (all addresses)

NOTE   The route listed as 0.0.0.0/0 is the default route, which matches all IP addresses, and is explained later in this chapter.

As you can see from these ranges, several of the routes' address ranges overlap. When matching more than one route, the route with the longer prefix length is used. For example:

■ **172.16.1.1:** Matches all five routes; longest prefix is /32, the route to 172.16.1.1/32.

■ **172.16.1.2:** Matches last four routes; longest prefix is /24, the route to 172.16.1.0/24.

■ **172.16.2.3:** Matches last three routes; longest prefix is /22, the route to 172.16.0.0/22.

■ **172.16.4.3:** Matches the last two routes; longest prefix is /16, the route to 172.16.0.0/16.

Besides just doing the subnetting math on every route in the routing table, the **show ip route** *ip-address* command can also be particularly useful. This command lists detailed information about the route that the router matches for the IP address listed in the command. If multiple routes are matched for the IP address, this command lists the best route: the route with the longest prefix. For example, Example 4-1 lists the output of the **show ip route 172.16.4.3** command. The first line of (highlighted) output lists the matched route: the route to 172.16.0.0/16. The rest of the output lists the details of that particular route. This command can be handy command for both real life and for Sim questions on the exams.

DNS, DHCP, ARP, and ICMP

The IP routing process uses several related protocols, including the ARP protocol already mentioned in this chapter. Before moving on to the new topics for this chapter, this section reviews several related protocols.

Before a host can send any IP packets, the host needs to know several IP-related parameters. Hosts often use Dynamic Host Configuration Protocol (DHCP) to learn these key facts, including:

■ The host's IP address

■ The associated subnet mask

■ The IP address of the default gateway (router)

■ The IP address(es) of the DNS server(s)

Key
Topic

To learn this information, the host—a DHCP client—sends a broadcast that eventually reaches a DHCP server. The server can then lease an IP address to that host and supply the other information in the previous list. At that point, the host has an IP address with which to use as a source IP address, and enough information to make the simple host routing decision of whether to send packets directly to another host (same subnet) or to the default gateway (another subnet). (In Microsoft Windows XP, the **ipconfig /all** command lists the host's interfaces as the information listed before this paragraph.)

Typically the user either directly or indirectly refers to another host's host name, which in turn causes the host to need to send a packet to the other host. For example, opening a web browser and typing in **http://www.cisco.com** as the URL identifies the host name of a web server owned by Cisco. Opening an e-mail client like Microsoft Outlook indirectly references a host name. The e-mail client was likely configured to know the host name of both an incoming and outgoing e-mail server, so while the user does not look at the settings every day, the e-mail client software knows the name of the hosts with which to exchange mail.

Because hosts cannot send packets to a destination host name, most hosts use Domain Name System (DNS) protocols to resolve the name into its associated IP address. The host acts as a DNS client, sending messages to the unicast IP address of the DNS server. The DNS request lists the name (for example, www.cisco.com), with the server replying with the IP address that corresponds to that host name. After it is learned, the host can cache the name-to-address information, only needing to resolve that name again after the entry has timed out. (In Windows XP, the **ipconfig /displaydns** command lists the host's current list of names and addresses.)

Internet Control Message Protocol (ICMP) includes many different functions, all focused on the control and management of IP. ICMP defines a varied set of messages for different purposes, including the ICMP Echo Request and ICMP Echo Reply messages. The popular **ping** command tests the route to a remote host, and the reverse route back to the original host, by sending Echo Request messages to the destination IP address and with that destination host replying to each Echo Request message with an Echo Reply message. When the **ping** command receives the Echo Reply messages, the command knows that the route between the two hosts works.

All these protocols work together to help the IP routing process, but DHCP, DNS, ICMP, and ARP typically do not occur for every packet. For example, imagine a new host computer connects to a LAN, and the user types the **ping www.cisco.com** command. DHCP might well be used as the OS boots, when the PC uses DHCP to learn its IP address and other information, but then DHCP might not be used for days. The PC then uses DNS to resolve www.cisco.com into an IP address, but then the PC does not need to use DNS again until a new host name is referenced. If the host was pinging the remote host, the local host then creates an IP packet, with an ICMP Echo Request inside the packet, with a destination IP address of the addresses learned by the earlier DNS request. Finally, because the host just came up, it does not have an ARP entry for its default gateway, so the host must use ARP to find the default gateway's MAC address. Only then can the packet be sent to the true destination host, as described in the first part of this chapter. For subsequent packets sent to the same host name, these overhead protocols likely do not need to be used again, and the local host can just send the new packet.

The following list summarizes the steps used by a host, as needed, for the protocols mentioned in this section:

1. If not known yet, the host uses DHCP to learn its IP address, subnet mask, DNS IP addresses, and default gateway IP address. If already known, the host skips this step.

2. If the user references a host name not currently held in the host's name cache, the host makes a DNS request to resolve the name into its corresponding IP address. Otherwise, the host skips this step.

3. If the user issued the **ping** command, the IP packet contains an ICMP Echo Request; if the user instead used a typical TCP/IP application, it uses protocols appropriate to that application.

4. To build the Ethernet frame, the host uses the ARP cache's entry for the next-hop device—either the default gateway (when sending to a host on another subnet) or the true destination host (when sending to a host on the same subnet). If the ARP cache does not hold that entry, the host uses ARP to learn the information.

Fragmentation and MTU

TCP/IP defines a maximum length for an IP packet. The term used to describe that maximum length is *maximum transmission unit (MTU)*.

The MTU varies based on configuration and the interface's characteristics. By default, a computer calculates an interface's MTU based on the maximum size of the data portion of the data-link frame (where the packet is placed). For example, the default MTU value on Ethernet interfaces is 1500.

Routers, like any IP host, cannot forward a packet out an interface if the packet is longer than the MTU. If a router's interface MTU is smaller than a packet that must be forwarded, the router fragments the packet into smaller packets. Fragmentation is the process of breaking the packet into smaller packets, each of which is less than or equal to the MTU value. Figure 4-4 shows an example of fragmentation in a network where the MTU on the serial link has been lowered to 1000 bytes through configuration.

Figure 4-4 *IP Fragmentation*

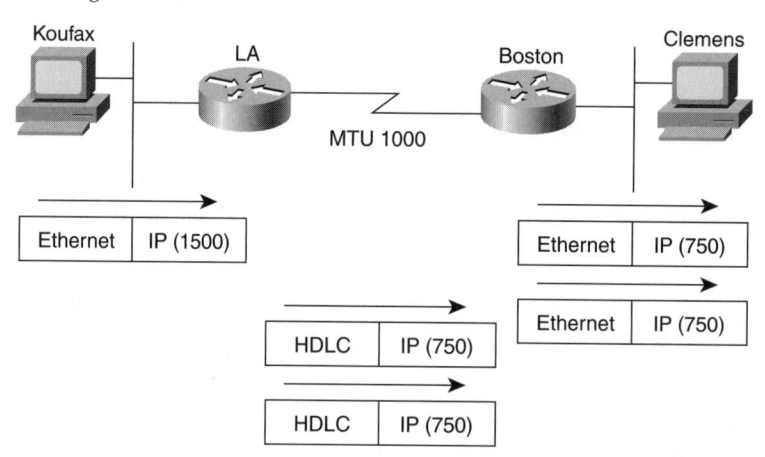

As Figure 4-4 illustrates, Koufax sends a 1500-byte packet toward Router LA. LA removes the Ethernet header but cannot forward the packet as is, because it is 1500 bytes and the High-Level Data Link Control (HDLC) link supports an MTU of only 1000. So LA fragments the original packet into two packets, each 750 bytes in length. The router does the math required to figure out the minimum number of fragments (two in this case) and breaks the original packet into equal-length packets. Because of this, any other routers the packets might go through are less likely to need to perform fragmentation. After forwarding the two packets, Boston receives the packets and forwards them *without reassembling them.* Reassembly is done by the endpoint host, which in this case is Clemens.

The IP header contains fields useful for reassembling the fragments into the original packet. The IP header includes an ID value that is the same in each fragmented packet, as well as an offset value that defines which part of the original packet is held in each fragment. Fragmented packets arriving out of order can be identified as a part of the same original packet and can be reassembled in the correct order using the offset field in each fragment.

Two configuration commands can be used to change the IP MTU size on an interface: the **mtu** interface subcommand and the **ip mtu** interface subcommand. The **mtu** command sets the MTU for all Layer 3 protocols; unless a need exists to vary the setting per Layer 3 protocol, this command is preferred. If a different setting is desired for IP, the **ip mtu** command sets the value used for IP. If both are configured on an interface, the IP MTU setting takes precedence on that interface. However, if the **mtu** command is configured after **ip mtu** is configured, the **ip mtu** value is reset to the same value as that of the **mtu** command. Use care when changing these values.

The review of IP routing and addressing is now complete. Next, this chapter examines connected routes, including connected routes related to VLAN trunking and secondary IP addresses.

Routes to Directly Connected Subnets

A router automatically adds a route to its routing table for the subnet connected to each interface, assuming that the following two facts are true:

■ The interface is in a working state—in other words, the interface status in the **show interfaces** command lists a line status of up and a protocol status of up.

■ The interface has an IP address assigned, either through the **ip address** interface subcommand or by using DHCP client services.

The concept of connected routes is relatively basic. The router of course needs to know the subnet number used on the physical network connected to each of its interfaces, but if the interface is not currently working, the router needs to remove the route from its routing table. The **show ip route** command lists these routes with a *c* as the route code, meaning connected, and the **show ip route connected** command lists only connected routes.

The following sections about connected routes focus on a couple of variations in configuration that affect connected routes, thereby affecting how routers forward packets. The first topic relates to a tool called secondary IP addressing, while the second relates to a router's configuration when using VLAN trunking.

Secondary IP Addressing

Imagine that you planned your IP addressing scheme for a network. Later, a particular subnet grows, and you have used all the valid IP addresses in the subnet. What should you do? Three main options exist:

■ Make the existing subnet larger

■ Migrate the hosts to use addresses in a different, larger subnet

■ Use secondary addressing

All three options are reasonable, but all have some problems.

To make the subnet larger, just change the mask used on that subnet. However, changing the mask could create overlapped subnets. For example, if subnet 10.1.4.0/24 is running out of addresses, and you make a change to mask 255.255.254.0 (9 host bits, 23 network/subnet bits), the new subnet includes addresses 10.1.4.0 to 10.1.5.255. If you have already assigned subnet 10.1.5.0/24, with assignable addresses 10.1.5.1 through 10.1.5.254, you would create an overlap, which is not allowed. However, if the 10.1.5.x addresses are unused, expanding the old subnet might be reasonable.

The second option is to simply pick a new, unused, but larger subnet. All the IP addresses would need to be changed. This is a relatively simple process if most or all hosts use DHCP, but a potentially laborious process if many hosts use statically configured IP addresses.

Note that both of the first two solutions imply a strategy of using different masks in different parts of the network. Use of these different masks is called variable-length subnet masking (VLSM), which introduces more complexity into the network, particularly for people who are monitoring and troubleshooting the network.

The third major option is to use a Cisco router features called *secondary IP addressing*. Secondary addressing uses multiple networks or subnets on the same data link. By using more than one subnet on the same medium, you increase the number of available IP addresses. To make it work, the router needs an IP address in each subnet so that the hosts in each subnet have a usable default gateway IP address in the same subnet. Additionally, packets that need to pass between these subnets must be sent to the router. For example, Figure 4-5 has subnet 10.1.2.0/24; assume that it has all IP addresses assigned. Assuming secondary addressing to be the chosen solution, subnet 10.1.7.0/24 also could be used on the same Ethernet. Example 4-2 shows the configuration for secondary IP addressing on Yosemite.

Figure 4-5 *TCP/IP Network with Secondary Addresses*

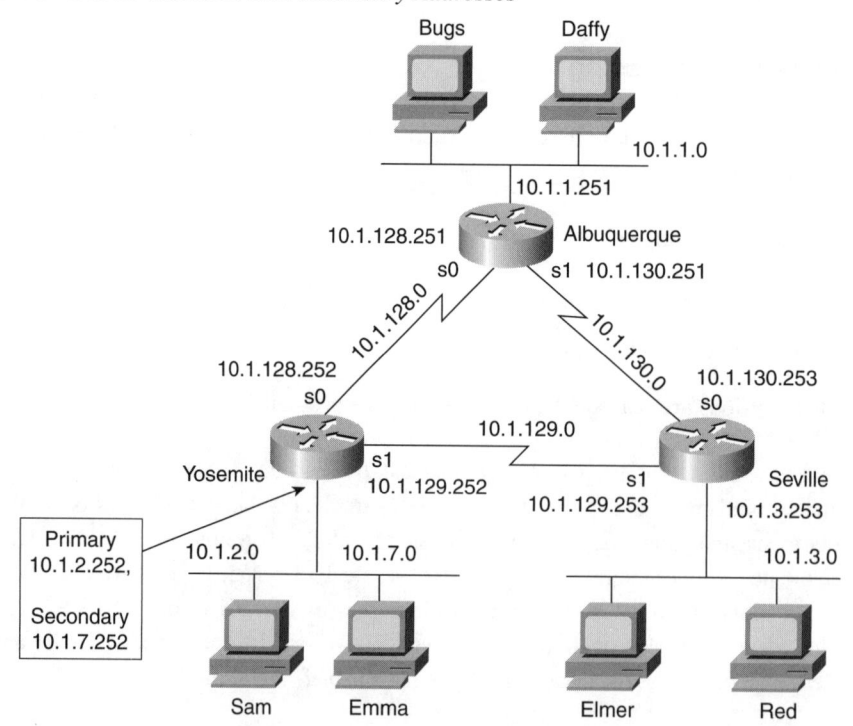

Example 4-2 *Secondary IP Addressing Configuration and the* **show ip route** *Command on Yosemite*

```
! Excerpt from show running-config follows...
Hostname Yosemite
ip domain-lookup
ip name-server 10.1.1.100 10.1.2.100
interface ethernet 0
 ip address 10.1.7.252  255.255.255.0 secondary
 ip address 10.1.2.252  255.255.255.0
interface serial 0
 ip address 10.1.128.252  255.255.255.0
interface serial 1
 ip address 10.1.129.252  255.255.255.0

Yosemite# show ip route connected
     10.0.0.0/24 is subnetted, 4 subnets
C       10.1.2.0 is directly connected, Ethernet0
C       10.1.7.0 is directly connected, Ethernet0
C       10.1.129.0 is directly connected, Serial1
C       10.1.128.0 is directly connected, Serial0
```

The router has connected routes to subnets 10.1.2.0/24 and 10.1.7.0/24, so it can forward packets to each subnet. The hosts in each subnet on the same LAN can use either 10.1.2.252 or 10.1.7.252 as their default gateway IP addresses, depending on the subnet in which they reside.

The biggest negative to secondary addressing is that packets sent between hosts on the LAN might be inefficiently routed. For example, when a host in subnet 10.1.2.0 sends a packet to a host in 10.1.7.0, the sending host's logic is to send the packet to its default gateway, because the destination is on a different subnet. So, the sending host sends the packet to the router, which then sends the packet back into the same LAN.

Supporting Connected Routes to Subnet Zero

IOS can restrict a router from configuring an **ip address** command with an address inside the zero subnet. The zero subnet (or subnet zero) is the one subnet in each classful network that has all binary 0s in the subnet part of the binary version of the subnet number. In decimal, the zero subnet happens to be the same number as the classful network number.

With the **ip subnet-zero** command configured, IOS allows the zero subnet to become a connected route as a result of an **ip address** command being configured on an interface. This command has been a default setting since at least IOS version 12.0, which was a relatively old IOS version by the time this book was published. So, for the exam, if you see the **ip subnet-zero** command configured, or if the question does not specify that the **no ip subnet-zero** command is configured, assume that the zero subnet can be configured.

> **NOTE**   Older editions of this book stated that you should assume that the zero subnet cannot be used, unless an exam question implied that the zero subnet was usable. The current CCNA exams, and therefore this book, allow the zero subnet to be used unless the exam question states or implies that it should not be used.

With the **no ip subnet-zero** command configured on a router, that router rejects any **ip address** command that uses an address/mask combination for the zero subnet. For example, the interface subcommand **ip address 10.0.0.1 255.255.255.0** implies zero subnet 10.0.0.0/24, so the router would reject the command if the **no ip subnet-zero** global configuration command was configured. Note that the error message simply says "bad mask," rather than stating that the problem was because of the zero subnet.

The **no ip subnet-zero** command on one router does not affect other routers, and it does not prevent a router from learning about a zero subnet through a routing protocol. It simply prevents the router from configuring an interface to be in a zero subnet.

Note that in today's CCNA exams, you can assume that the zero subnet is allowed to be used unless the question states that it should not be used. In particular, a question that uses a classful routing protocol (as discussed in Chapter 5), or uses the **no ip subnet-zero** command, implies that the zero and broadcast subnets should be avoided.

ISL and 802.1Q Configuration on Routers

As discussed in Chapter 1, "Virtual LANs," VLAN trunking can be used between two switches and between a switch and a router. By using trunking instead of using a physical router interface per VLAN, the number of required router interfaces can be reduced. Instead of a single physical interface on the router for each VLAN on the switch, one physical interface can be used, and the router can still route packets between the various VLANs.

Figure 4-6 shows a router with a single Fast Ethernet interface and a single connection to a switch. Either Inter-Switch Link (ISL) or 802.1Q trunking can be used, with only small differences in the configuration for each. For frames that contain packets that the router routes between the two VLANs, the incoming frame is tagged by the switch with one VLAN ID, and the outgoing frame is tagged by the router with the other VLAN ID. Example 4-3 shows the router configuration required to support ISL encapsulation and forwarding between these VLANs.

Figure 4-6 *Router Forwarding Between VLANs*

Example 4-3 *Router Configuration for the ISL Encapsulation Shown in Figure 4-6*

```
interface fastethernet 0/0.1
 ip address 10.1.1.1 255.255.255.0
 encapsulation isl 1
!
interface fastethernet 0/0.2
 ip address 10.1.2.1 255.255.255.0
 encapsulation isl 2
!
interface fastethernet 0/0.3
 ip address 10.1.3.1 255.255.255.0
 encapsulation isl 3
```

Example 4-3 shows the configuration for three *subinterfaces* of the Fast Ethernet interface on the router. A subinterface is a logical subdivision of a physical interface. The router assigns each subinterface an IP address and assigns the subinterface to a single VLAN. So, instead of three physical router interfaces, each attached to a different subnet/VLAN, the router uses one physical router interface with three logical subinterfaces, each attached to a different subnet/VLAN. The **encapsulation** command numbers the VLANs, which must match the configuration for VLAN IDs in the switch.

This example uses subinterface numbers that match the VLAN ID on each subinterface. There is no requirement that the numbers match, but most people choose to make them match, just to make the configuration more obvious and to make troubleshooting easier. In other words, the VLAN IDs can be 1, 2, and 3, but the subinterface numbers could have been 4, 5, and 6, because the subinterface numbers are just used internally by the router.

Example 4-4 shows the same network, but this time with 802.1Q used instead of ISL. IEEE 802.1Q has a concept called the native VLAN, which is a special VLAN on each trunk for which no 802.1Q headers are added to the frames. By default, VLAN 1 is the native VLAN. Example 4-4 shows the difference in configuration.

Example 4-4   *Router Configuration for the 802.1Q Encapsulation Shown in Figure 4-6*

```
interface fastethernet 0/0
 ip address 10.1.1.1 255.255.255.0
!
interface fastethernet 0/0.2
 ip address 10.1.2.1 255.255.255.0
 encapsulation dot1q 2
!
interface fastethernet 0/0.3
 ip address 10.1.3.1 255.255.255.0
 encapsulation dot1q 3
```

The configuration creates three VLANs on the router Fa0/0 interface. Two of the VLANs, VLANs 2 and 3, are configured just like Example 4-3, except that the **encapsulation** command lists 802.1Q as the type of encapsulation.

The native VLAN, VLAN 1 in this case, can be configured with two styles of configuration. Example 4-4 shows one style in which the native VLAN's IP address is configured on the physical interface. As a result, the router does not use VLAN trunking headers in this VLAN, as is intended for the native VLAN. The alternative is to configure the native VLAN's IP address on another subinterface and to use the **encapsulation dot1q 1 native** interface subcommand. This command tells the router that the subinterface is associated with VLAN 1, but the **native** keyword tells the router not to use any 802.1Q headers with that subinterface.

Routers do not perform dynamic negotiation of trunking. So, the switch connected to a router interface must manually configure trunking, as covered in Chapter 1. For example, a switch on the other end of the router's Fa0/0 interface would configure the **switchport mode trunk** interface subcommand (to enable trunking manually), and if the switch is capable of using either type of trunking, the **switchport trunk encapsulation dot1q** interface subcommand to statically configure the use of 802.1Q.

Static Routes

Routers use three main methods to add routes to their routing tables: connected routes, static routes, and dynamic routing protocols. Routers always add connected routes when interfaces have IP addresses configured and the interfaces are up and working. In most networks, engineers purposefully use dynamic routing protocols to cause each router to learn the rest of the routes in an internetwork. Using static routes—routes added to a routing table through direct configuration—is the least used of the three options.

Static routing consists of individual **ip route** global configuration commands that define a route to a router. The configuration command includes a reference to the subnet—the subnet number and mask—along with instructions about where to forward packets destined to that subnet. To see the need for static routes, and to see the configuration, look at Example 4-5, which shows two **ping** commands testing IP connectivity from Albuquerque to Yosemite (see Figure 4-7).

Figure 4-7   *Sample Network Used in Static Route Configuration Examples*

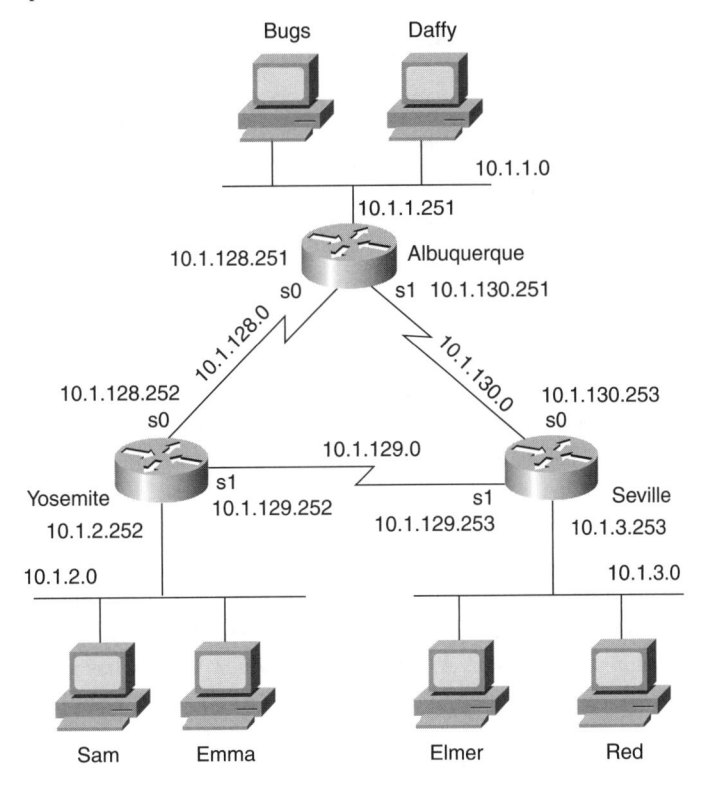

Example 4-5   *Albuquerque Router EXEC Commands with Only Connected Routers*

```
Albuquerque#show ip route
Codes: C - connected, S - static, I - IGRP, R - RIP, M - mobile, B - BGP
       D - EIGRP, EX - EIGRP external, O - OSPF, IA - OSPF inter area
       N1 - OSPF NSSA external type 1, N2 - OSPF NSSA external type 2
       E1 - OSPF external type 1, E2 - OSPF external type 2, E - EGP
```

continues

Example 4-5 *Albuquerque Router EXEC Commands with Only Connected Routers (Continued)*

```
       i - IS-IS, L1 - IS-IS level-1, L2 - IS-IS level-2, ia - IS-IS inter area
       * - candidate default, U - per-user static route, o - ODR
       P - periodic downloaded static route

Gateway of last resort is not set

     10.0.0.0/24 is subnetted, 3 subnets

C       10.1.1.0 is directly connected, Ethernet0
C       10.1.130.0 is directly connected, Serial1
C       10.1.128.0 is directly connected, Serial0
Albuquerque#ping 10.1.128.252
Type escape sequence to abort.
Sending 5, 100-byte ICMP Echos to 10.1.128.252, timeout is 2 seconds:
!!!!!
Success rate is 100 percent (5/5), round-trip min/avg/max = 4/4/8 ms

Albuquerque#ping 10.1.2.252
Type escape sequence to abort.
Sending 5, 100-byte ICMP Echos to 10.1.2.252, timeout is 2 seconds:
.....
Success rate is 0 percent (0/5)
```

The end of the example shows two different **ping** commands on router Albuquerque, one to 10.1.128.252 (Yosemite's S0 IP address) and one to 10.1.2.252 (Yosemite's LAN IP address). The IOS **ping** command sends five ICMP Echo Request packets by default, with the command output listing an exclamation point (!) to mean that an Echo Reply was received, and a period (.) to mean no reply was received. In the example, the first instance, **ping 10.1.128.252**, shows five responses (100%), and the second instance, **ping 10.1.2.252**, shows that no responses were received (0%). The first **ping** command works because Albuquerque has a route to the subnet in which 10.1.128.2 resides (subnet 10.1.128.0/24). However, the **ping** to 10.1.2.252 does not work because Albuquerque does not have a route that matches address 10.1.2.252. At this point, Albuquerque only has routes for its three connected subnets. So, Albuquerque's **ping 10.1.2.252** command creates the packets, but Albuquerque discards the packets because no routes exist.

Configuring Static Routes

One simple solution to the failure of the **ping 10.1.2.252** command is to enable an IP routing protocol on all three routers. In fact, in a real network, that is the most likely solution. As an alternative, you can configure static routes. Many networks have a few static routes, so you need to configure them occasionally. Example 4-6 shows the **ip route** command on Albuquerque, which adds static routes and makes the failed ping from Example 4-5 work.

Example 4-6 *Static Routes Added to Albuquerque*

```
ip route 10.1.2.0 255.255.255.0 10.1.128.252
ip route 10.1.3.0 255.255.255.0 10.1.130.253
```

The **ip route** command defines the static route by defining the subnet number and the next-hop IP address. One **ip route** command defines a route to 10.1.2.0 (mask 255.255.255.0), which is located off Yosemite, so the next-hop IP address as configured on Albuquerque is 10.1.128.252, which is Yosemite's Serial0 IP address. Similarly, a route to 10.1.3.0, the subnet off Seville, points to Seville's Serial0 IP address, 10.1.130.253. Note that the next-hop IP address is an IP address in a directly connected subnet; the goal is to define the next router to send the packet to. Now Albuquerque can forward packets to these two subnets.

The **ip route** command has two basic formats. The command can refer to a next-hop IP address, as shown in Example 4-6. Alternately, for static routes that use point-to-point serial links, the command can list the outgoing interface instead of the next-hop IP address. For example, Example 4-6 could instead use the **ip route 10.1.2.0 255.255.255.0 serial0** global configuration command instead of the first **ip route** command.

Unfortunately, adding the two static routes in Example 4-6 to Albuquerque does not solve all the network's routing problems. The static routes help Albuquerque deliver packets to these two subnets, but the other two routers don't have enough routing information to forward packets back toward Albuquerque. For example, PC Bugs cannot ping PC Sam in this network, even after the addition of the commands in Example 4-6. The problem is that although Albuquerque has a route to subnet 10.1.2.0, where Sam resides, Yosemite does not have a route to 10.1.1.0, where Bugs resides. The **ping** request packet goes from Bugs to Sam correctly, but Sam's ping response packet cannot be routed by the Yosemite router back through Albuquerque to Bugs, so the ping fails.

The Extended ping Command

In real life, you might not be able to find a user, like Bugs, to ask to test your network by pinging. Instead, you can use the extended **ping** command on a router to test routing in the same way that a ping from Bugs to Sam tests routing. Example 4-7 shows Albuquerque with the working **ping 10.1.2.252** command, but with an extended **ping 10.1.2.252** command that works similarly to a **ping** from Bugs to Sam—a ping that fails in this case (only the two static routes from Example 4-6 have been added at this point).

Example 4-7   *Albuquerque: Working Ping After Adding Default Routes, Plus Failing Extended* **ping** *Command*

```
Albuquerque#show ip route
Codes: C - connected, S - static, I - IGRP, R - RIP, M - mobile, B - BGP
       D - EIGRP, EX - EIGRP external, O - OSPF, IA - OSPF inter area
       N1 - OSPF NSSA external type 1, N2 - OSPF NSSA external type 2
       E1 - OSPF external type 1, E2 - OSPF external type 2, E - EGP
       i - IS-IS, L1 - IS-IS level-1, L2 - IS-IS level-2, ia - IS-IS inter area
       * - candidate default, U - per-user static route, o - ODR
       P - periodic downloaded static route

Gateway of last resort is not set

     10.0.0.0/24 is subnetted, 5 subnets
S        10.1.3.0 [1/0] via 10.1.130.253
S        10.1.2.0 [1/0] via 10.1.128.252
C        10.1.1.0 is directly connected, Ethernet0
C        10.1.130.0 is directly connected, Serial1
C        10.1.128.0 is directly connected, Serial0
Albuquerque#ping 10.1.2.252

Type escape sequence to abort.
Sending 5, 100-byte ICMP Echos to 10.1.2.252, timeout is 2 seconds:
!!!!!
Success rate is 100 percent (5/5), round-trip min/avg/max = 4/4/8 ms

Albuquerque#ping
Protocol [ip]:
Target IP address: 10.1.2.252
Repeat count [5]:
Datagram size [100]:
Timeout in seconds [2]:
Extended commands [n]: y
Source address or interface: 10.1.1.251
Type of service [0]:
Set DF bit in IP header? [no]:
Validate reply data? [no]:
Data pattern [0xABCD]:
Loose, Strict, Record, Timestamp, Verbose[none]:
Sweep range of sizes [n]:
Type escape sequence to abort.
Sending 5, 100-byte ICMP Echos to 10.1.2.252, timeout is 2 seconds:
. . . . .
Success rate is 0 percent (0/5)
```

The simple **ping 10.1.2.252** command works for one obvious reason and one not-so-obvious reason. First, Albuquerque can forward a packet to subnet 10.1.2.0 because of the static route. The return packet, sent by Yosemite, is sent to address 10.1.128.251—Albuquerque's Serial0 IP address—and Yosemite has a connected route to reach subnet 10.2.128.0. But why does Yosemite send the Echo Reply to Albuquerque's S0 IP address of 10.1.128.251? Well, the following points are true about the **ping** command on a Cisco router:

■ The Cisco **ping** command uses, by default, the output interface's IP address as the packet's source address, unless otherwise specified in an extended ping. The first ping in Example 4-7 uses a source of 10.1.128.251, because the route used to send the packet to 10.1.2.252 sends packets out Albuquerque's Serial0 interface, whose IP address is 10.1.128.251.

Key Topic

■ Ping response packets (ICMP Echo Replies) reverse the IP addresses used in the received ping request to which they are responding. So, in this example, Yosemite's Echo Reply, in response to the first ping in Example 4-7, uses 10.1.128.251 as the destination address and 10.1.2.252 as the source IP address.

Because the **ping 10.1.2.252** command on Albuquerque uses 10.1.128.251 as the packet's source address, Yosemite can send back a response to 10.1.128.251, because Yosemite happens to have a (connected) route to 10.1.128.0.

The danger when troubleshooting with the standard **ping** command is that routing problems can still exist, but the **ping 10.1.2.252** command, which worked, gives you a false sense of security. A more thorough alternative is to use the extended **ping** command to act like you issued a ping from a computer on that subnet, without having to call a user and ask to enter a **ping** command for you on the PC. The extended version of the **ping** command can be used to refine the problem's underlying cause by changing several details of what the ping command sends in its request. In fact, when a ping from a router works, but a ping from a host does not, the extended ping could help you re-create the problem without needing to work with the end user on the phone.

For example, in Example 4-7, the extended **ping** command on Albuquerque sends a packet from source IP address 10.1.1.251 (Albuquerque's Ethernet) to 10.1.2.252 (Yosemite's Ethernet). According to the output, Albuquerque did not receive a response. Normally, the **ping** command would be sourced from the IP address of the outgoing interface. With the use of the extended ping source address option, the source IP address of the echo packet is set to Albuquerque's Ethernet IP address, 10.1.1.251. Because the ICMP echo generated by the extended ping is sourced from an address in subnet 10.1.1.0, the packet looks more like a packet from an end user in that subnet. Yosemite builds an Echo Reply, with destination

10.1.1.251, but it does not have a route to that subnet. So Yosemite cannot send the ping reply packet back to Albuquerque.

To solve this problem, all routers could be configured to use a routing protocol. Alternatively, you could simply define static routes on all the routers in the network.

Static Default Routes

A default route is a special route that matches all packet destinations. Default routes can be particularly useful when only one physical path exists from one part of the network to another, and in cases for which one enterprise router provides connectivity to the Internet for that enterprise. For example, in Figure 4-8, R1, R2, and R3 are connected to the rest of the network only through R1's LAN interface. All three routers can forward packets to the rest of the network as long as the packets get to R1, which in turn forwards packets to router Dist1.

Figure 4-8 *Sample Network Using a Default Route*

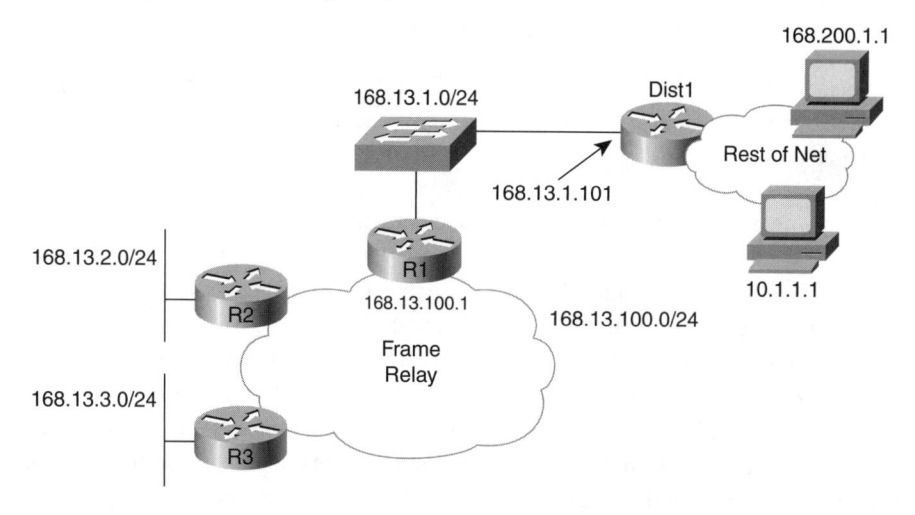

The following sections show two options for configuring static default routes: one using the **ip route** command and another using the **ip default-network** command.

Default Routes Using the ip route Command

By configuring a default route on R1, with next-hop router Dist1, and by having R1 advertise the default to R2 and R3, default routing can be accomplished. By using such a default route, R1, R2, and R3 should not need specific routes to the subnets to the right of router Dist1. Example 4-8 begins an examination of this design by showing the definition of a static default route on R1 and the resulting information in R1's IP routing table.

Example 4-8 *R1 Static Default Route Configuration and Routing Table*

```
R1(config)#ip route 0.0.0.0 0.0.0.0 168.13.1.101
R1#show ip route
Codes: C - connected, S - static, I - IGRP, R - RIP, M - mobile, B - BGP
       D - EIGRP, EX - EIGRP external, O - OSPF, IA - OSPF inter area
       N1 - OSPF NSSA external type 1, N2 - OSPF NSSA external type 2
       E1 - OSPF external type 1, E2 - OSPF external type 2, E - EGP
       i - IS-IS, L1 - IS-IS level-1, L2 - IS-IS level-2, ia - IS-IS inter area
       * - candidate default, U - per-user static route, o - ODR
       P - periodic downloaded static route

Gateway of last resort is 168.13.1.101 to network 0.0.0.0

     168.13.0.0/24 is subnetted, 4 subnets
C       168.13.1.0 is directly connected,  FastEthernet0/0
R       168.13.3.0 [120/1] via 168.13.100.3, 00:00:05, Serial0.1
R       168.13.2.0 [120/1] via 168.13.100.2, 00:00:21, Serial0.1
C       168.13.100.0 is directly connected, Serial0.1
S*   0.0.0.0/0 [1/0] via 168.13.1.101
```

R1 defines the default route with a static **ip route** command, with destination 0.0.0.0, mask 0.0.0.0. As a result, R1's **show ip route** command lists a static route to 0.0.0.0, mask 0.0.0.0, with next hop 168.13.1.101—essentially, the same information in the **ip route 0.0.0.0 0.0.0.0 168.13.1.101** global configuration command. A destination of 0.0.0.0, with mask 0.0.0.0, represents all destinations by convention. With just that configuration, R1 has a static route that matches any and all IP packet destinations.

Note also in Example 4-8 that R1's **show ip route** command output lists a "Gateway of last resort" as 168.13.1.101. When a router knows about at least one default route, the router notes that route with an asterisk in the routing table. If a router learns about multiple default routes—either through static configuration or from routing protocols—the router notes each default route with an asterisk in the routing table. Then, the router chooses the best default route, noting that choice as the gateway of last resort. (The administrative distance of the source of the routing information, as defined by the administrative distance setting, has some impact on this choice. Administrative distance is covered in Chapter 8, "Routing Protocol Theory," in the section "Administrative Distance.")

While the Routing Information Protocol (RIP) configuration is not shown, R1 also advertises this default route to R2 and R3, as shown in the output of the **show ip route** command on R3 in Example 4-9.

Example 4-9   *R3: Nuances of the Successful Use of the Static Route on R1*

```
R3#show ip route
Codes: C - connected, S - static, I - IGRP, R - RIP, M - mobile, B - BGP
       D - EIGRP, EX - EIGRP external, O - OSPF, IA - OSPF inter area
       N1 - OSPF NSSA external type 1, N2 - OSPF NSSA external type 2
       E1 - OSPF external type 1, E2 - OSPF external type 2, E - EGP
       i - IS-IS, L1 - IS-IS level-1, L2 - IS-IS level-2, ia - IS-IS inter area
       * - candidate default, U - per-user static route, o - ODR
       P - periodic downloaded static route

Gateway of last resort is 168.13.100.1 to network 0.0.0.0

     168.13.0.0/24 is subnetted, 4 subnets
R       168.13.1.0 [120/1] via 168.13.100.1, 00:00:13, Serial0.1
C       168.13.3.0 is directly connected, Ethernet0
R       168.13.2.0 [120/1] via 168.13.100.2, 00:00:06, Serial0.1
C       168.13.100.0 is directly connected, Serial0.1
```

Different routing protocols advertise default routes in a couple of different ways. As an example, when R3 learns a default route from R1 using RIP, R3 lists the destination of the default route (0.0.0.0) and the next-hop router, which is R1 in this case (168.13.100.1), as highlighted in Example 4-9. So, when R3 needs to use its default route, it forwards packets to R1 (168.13.100.1)

Default Routes Using the ip default-network Command

Another style of configuration for the default route uses the **ip default-network** command. This command lists a classful IP network as its parameter, telling the router to use the routing details of the route for that classful network as the forwarding details for a default route.

This command is most useful when the engineer wants to use the default route to reach networks besides the networks used inside that enterprise. For example, in Figure 4-8, imagine that all subnets of the enterprise's 168.13.0.0 Class B network are known; they exist only near routers R1, R2, and R3; and these routes are all in the routing tables of R1, R2, and R3. Also, none of the subnets of 168.13.0.0 are to the right of Router Dist1. If the engineer wants to use a default route for forwarding packets to destinations to the right of Dist1, the **ip default-network** command works well.

To use the **ip default-network** command to configure a default route, the engineer relies on her knowledge that Dist1 is already advertising a route for classful network 10.0.0.0 to R1. R1's route to network 10.0.0.0 points to Dist1's 168.13.1.101 address as the next-hop address. Knowing that, the engineer can configure the **ip default-network 10.0.0.0** command on R1, which tells R1 to build its default route based on its learned route for network 10.0.0.0/8. Example 4-10 shows several details about this scenario on R1.

Example 4-10 *R1's Use of the* **ip default-network** *Command*

```
R1#configure terminal
R1(config)#ip default-network 10.0.0.0
R1(config)#exit
R1#show ip route
Codes: C - connected, S - static, I - IGRP, R - RIP, M - mobile, B - BGP
       D - EIGRP, EX - EIGRP external, O - OSPF, IA - OSPF inter area
       N1 - OSPF NSSA external type 1, N2 - OSPF NSSA external type 2
       E1 - OSPF external type 1, E2 - OSPF external type 2, E - EGP
       i - IS-IS, L1 - IS-IS level-1, L2 - IS-IS level-2, ia - IS-IS inter area
       * - candidate default, U - per-user static route, o - ODR
       P - periodic downloaded static route

Gateway of last resort is 168.13.1.101 to network 10.0.0.0

     168.13.0.0/24 is subnetted, 5 subnets
R       168.13.200.0 [120/1] via 168.13.1.101, 00:00:12, FastEthernet0/0
C       168.13.1.0 is directly connected, FastEthernet0/0
R       168.13.3.0 [120/1] via 168.13.100.3, 00:00:00, Serial0.1
R       168.13.2.0 [120/1] via 168.13.100.2, 00:00:00, Serial0.1
C       168.13.100.0 is directly connected, Serial0.1
R*   10.0.0.0/8 [120/1] via 168.13.1.101, 00:00:12, FastEthernet0/0
```

R1 shows both the result of having normally learned a route to network 10.0.0.0 through RIP, plus the additional results of the **ip default-network 10.0.0.0** global command. R1's RIP route for 10.0.0.0/8 lists a next-hop IP address of 168.13.1.101, Dist1's IP address on their common LAN, as normal. Because of the **ip default-network 10.0.0.0** command, R1 decides to use the details in the route to network 10.0.0.0 as its default route. The last part of the line about the gateway of last resort lists the default network, 10.0.0.0. Also, R1 lists an asterisk beside the route referenced in the **ip default-network** command.

Default Route Summary

Remembering the details of configuring default routes, and in particular the resulting details in the output of the **show ip route** command, can be a challenge. However, make it a point to remember these key points regarding default routes:

- Default static routes can be statically configured using the **ip route 0.0.0.0 0.0.0.0** *next-hop-address* or the **ip default-network** *net-number* command.

- When a router only matches a packet with the default route, that router uses the forwarding details listed in the gateway of last resort line.

Regardless of how the default route shows up—whether it's a gateway of last resort, a route to 0.0.0.0, or a route to some other network with an * beside it in the routing table—it is used according to the rules of classless or classful routing, as is explained in the next section.

Classful and Classless Routing

Cisco routers have two configurable options for how a router uses an existing default route: classless routing and classful routing. Classless routing causes a router to use its default routes for any packet that does not match some other route. Classful routing places one restriction on when a router can use its default route, resulting in cases in which a router has a default route but the router chooses to discard a packet rather than forwarding the packet based on the default route.

The terms *classless* and *classful* also characterize both IP addressing and IP routing protocols, so a fair amount of confusion exists as to the meaning of the terms. Before explaining the details of classful routing and classless routing, the next section summarizes the other use of these terms.

Summary of the Use of the Terms Classless and Classful

The terms *classless addressing* and *classful addressing* refer to two different ways to think about IP addresses. Both terms refer to a perspective on the structure of a subnetted IP address. Classless addressing uses a two-part view of IP addresses, and classful addressing has a three-part view. With classful addressing, the address always has an 8-, 16-, or 24-bit network field, based on the Class A, B, and C addressing rules. The end of the address has a host part that uniquely identifies each host inside a subnet. The bits in between the network and host part comprise the third part, namely the subnet part of the address. With classless addressing, the network and subnet parts from the classful view are combined into a single part, often called the subnet or prefix, with the address ending in the host part.

The terms *classless routing protocol* and *classful routing protocol* refer to features of different IP routing protocols. These features cannot be enabled or disabled; a routing protocol is, by its very nature, either classless or classful. In particular, classless routing protocols advertise mask information for each subnet, giving classless protocols the ability to support both VLSM and route summarization. Classful routing protocols do not advertise mask information, so they do not support VLSM or route summarization.

The third use of the terms *classless* and *classful*—the terms *classful routing* and *classless routing*—have to do with how the IP routing process makes use of the default route. Interestingly, this is the only one of the three uses of the terms that can be changed based on router configuration. Table 4-2 lists the three uses of the classless and classful terms, with a brief explanation. A more complete explanation of classless and classful routing follows the table. Chapter 5 explains more background information about the terms *classless routing protocol* and *classful routing protocol*.

Table 4-2 *Comparing the Use of the Terms Classless and Classful*

Key
Topic

As Applied To	Classful	Classless
Addresses	Addresses have three parts: network, subnet, and host.	Addresses have two parts: subnet or prefix, and host.
Routing protocols	Routing protocol does not advertise masks nor support VLSM; RIP-1 and IGRP.	Routing protocol does advertise masks and support VLSM; RIP-2, EIGRP, OSPF.
Routing (forwarding)	IP forwarding process is restricted in how it uses the default route.	IP forwarding process has no restrictions on using the default route.

Classless and Classful Routing Compared

Classless IP routing works just like most people think IP routing would work when a router knows a default route. Compared to classful routing, classless routing's core concepts are straightforward. Classful routing restricts the use of the default route. The following two statements give a general description of each, with an example following the definitions:

- **Classless routing:** When a packet's destination only matches a router's default route, and does not match any other routes, forward the packet using that default route.

Key
Topic

- **Classful routing:** When a packet's destination only matches a router's default route, and does not match any other routes, only use the default route if this router does not know any routes in the classful network in which the destination IP address resides.

The use of the term *classful* refers to the fact that the logic includes some consideration of classful IP addressing rules—namely, the classful (Class A, B, or C) network of the packet's destination address. To make sense of this concept, Example 4-11 shows a router with a default route, but classful routing allows the use of the default route in one case, but not another. The example uses the same default routes examples from earlier in this chapter, based on Figure 4-8. Both R3 and R1 have a default route that could forward packets to Router Dist1. However, as seen in Example 4-11, on R3, the **ping 10.1.1.1** works, but the **ping 168.13.200.1** fails.

> **NOTE**   This example uses the default route on R1 as defined with the **ip route** command and as explained in Examples 4-8 and 4-9, but it would have worked the same regardless of how the default route was learned.

Example 4-11   *Classful Routing Causes One Ping on R3 to Fail*

```
R3#show ip route
Codes: C - connected, S - static, I - IGRP, R - RIP, M - mobile, B - BGP
       D - EIGRP, EX - EIGRP external, O - OSPF, IA - OSPF inter area
       N1 - OSPF NSSA external type 1, N2 - OSPF NSSA external type 2
       E1 - OSPF external type 1, E2 - OSPF external type 2, E - EGP
       i - IS-IS, L1 - IS-IS level-1, L2 - IS-IS level-2, ia - IS-IS inter area
       * - candidate default, U - per-user static route, o - ODR
       P - periodic downloaded static route

Gateway of last resort is 168.13.100.1 to network 0.0.0.0

     168.13.0.0/24 is subnetted, 4 subnets
R       168.13.1.0 [120/1] via 168.13.100.1, 00:00:13, Serial0.1
C       168.13.3.0 is directly connected, Ethernet0
R       168.13.2.0 [120/1] via 168.13.100.2, 00:00:06, Serial0.1
C       168.13.100.0 is directly connected, Serial0.1
R3#ping 10.1.1.1

Type escape sequence to abort.
Sending 5, 100-byte ICMP Echos to 10.1.1.1, timeout is 2 seconds:
!!!!!
Success rate is 100 percent (5/5), round-trip min/avg/max = 84/89/114 ms
R3#
R3#ping 168.13.200.1

Type escape sequence to abort.
Sending 5, 100-byte ICMP Echos to 168.13.200.1, timeout is 2 seconds:
.....
Success rate is 0 percent (0/5)
```

First, consider R3's attempt to match both destinations (10.1.1.1 and 168.13.200.1) against the routes in the routing table. R3's routing table does not have any routes that match either destination IP address, other than the default route. So, R3's only option is to use its default route.

R3 is configured to use classful routing. With classful routing, the router first matches the Class A, B, or C network number in which a destination resides. If the Class A, B, or C network is found, Cisco IOS Software then looks for the specific subnet number. If it isn't found, the packet is discarded, as is the case with the ICMP echoes sent with the **ping 168.13.200.1** command. However, with classful routing, if the packet does not match a Class A, B, or C network in the routing table, and a default route exists, the default route is indeed used—which is why R3 can forward the ICMP echoes sent by the successful **ping 10.1.1.1** command.

In short, with classful routing, the only time the default route is used is when the router does not know about any subnets of the packet's destination Class A, B, or C network.

You can toggle between classless and classful routing with the **ip classless** and **no ip classless** global configuration commands, respectively. With classless routing, Cisco IOS Software looks for the best match, ignoring class rules. If a default route exists, with classless routing, the packet always at least matches the default route. If a more specific route matches the packet's destination, that route is used. Example 4-12 shows R3 changed to use classless routing, and the successful ping of 168.13.200.1.

Example 4-12 *Classless Routing Allows Ping 168.13.200.1 to Now Succeed*

```
R3#configure terminal
Enter configuration commands, one per line.  End with CNTL/Z.
R3(config)#ip classless
R3(config)#^Z
R3#ping 168.13.200.1

Type escape sequence to abort.
Sending 5, 100-byte ICMP Echos to 168.13.200.1, timeout is 2 seconds:
!!!!!
Success rate is 100 percent (5/5), round-trip min/avg/max = 80/88/112 ms
```

Exam Preparation Tasks

Review All the Key Topics

Review the most important topics from this chapter, noted with the Key Topics icon in the outer margin of the page. Table 4-3 lists a reference of these key topics and the page numbers on which each is found.

Table 4-3 *Key Topics for Chapter 4*

Key Topic Element	Description	Page Number
List	Steps taken by a host when forwarding IP packets	162
List	Steps taken by a router when forwarding IP packets	163
List	Review of key points about IP addressing	167
Thought	Summary of the logic a router uses when a packet's destination matches more than one route	169
List	Items typically learned through DHCP	171
List	Steps and protocols used by a host when communicating with another host	173
List	Rules regarding when a router creates a connected route	175
List	Rules about the source address used for packets generated by the IOS **ping** command	185
List	Key facts regarding the definition of static default routes	190
Table 4-2	Summary of the three separate but related uses of the terms *classless* and *classful*	191
List	Definitions of classless routing and classful routing	191

Complete the Tables and Lists from Memory

Print a copy of Appendix J, "Memory Tables," (found on the CD) or at least the section for this chapter, and complete the tables and lists from memory. Appendix K, "Memory Tables Answer Key," also on the CD, includes completed tables and lists to check your work.

Definitions of Key Terms

Define the following key terms from this chapter, and check your answers in the glossary:

Classful addressing, classful routing, classful routing protocol, classless addressing, classless routing, classless routing protocol, extended ping, secondary IP address, zero subnet

Command Reference to Check Your Memory

While you should not necessarily memorize the information in the tables in this section, this section does include a reference for the configuration and EXEC commands covered in this chapter. Practically speaking, you should memorize the commands as a side effect of reading the chapter and doing all the activities in this exam preparation section. To check to see how well you have memorized the commands as a side effect of your other studies, cover the left side of the table with a piece of paper, read the descriptions on the right side, and see whether you remember the command.

Table 4-4 *Chapter 4 Configuration Command Reference*

Command	Description
encapsulation dot1q *vlan-id* [**native**]	A subinterface subcommand that tells the router to use 802.1Q trunking, for a particular VLAN, and with the **native** keyword, to not encapsulate in a trunking header
encapsulation isl *vlan-identifier*	A subinterface subcommand that tells the router to use ISL trunking, for a particular VLAN
[**no**] **ip classless**	Global command that enables (**ip classless**) or disables (**no ip classless**) classless routing
[**no**] **ip subnet-zero**	Global command that allows (**ip subnet-zero**) or disallows (**no ip subnet-zero**) the configuration of an interface IP address in a zero subnet
ip address *ip-address mask* [**secondary**]	Interface subcommand that assigns the interface's IP address, and optionally makes the address a secondary address
ip route *prefix mask* {*ip-address* | *interface-type interface-number*} [*distance*] [**permanent**]	Global configuration command that creates a static route
ip default-network *network-number*	Global command that creates a default route based on the router's route to reach the classful network listed in the command

Table 4-5 *Chapter 4 EXEC Command Reference*

Command	Description
show ip route	Lists the router's entire routing table
show ip route *ip-address*	Lists detailed information about the route that a router matches for the listed IP address
ping {*host-name* | *ip-address*}	Tests IP routes by sending an ICMP packet to the destination host
traceroute {*host-name* | *ip-address*}	Tests IP routes by discovering the IP addresses of the routes between a router and the listed destination

This chapter covers the following subjects:

VLSM: This section explains the issues and solutions when designing an internetwork that uses VLSM.

Manual Route Summarization: This section explains the concept of manual route summarization and describes how to design internetworks to allow easier summarization.

Autosummarization and Discontiguous Classful Networks: This section examines the autosummarization feature and explains how it must be considered in internetwork designs that use discontiguous networks.

VLSM and Route Summarization

While Chapter 4, "IP Routing: Static and Connected Routes," focuses on topics related to IP routing, this chapter focuses on topics related to IP addressing: variable-length subnet masking (VLSM), manual route summarization, and automatic route summarization. These features relate to IP addressing in that they all require some thought about the range of IP addresses implied by a given address and mask, or by a subnet that is part of a summarized route. So, this chapter requires a full understanding of IP addressing for a full understanding of the examples in this chapter.

This chapter mainly focuses on concepts and **show** commands, with only a few configuration commands of interest.

"Do I Know This Already?" Quiz

The "Do I Know This Already?" quiz allows you to assess whether you should read the entire chapter. If you miss no more than one of these eight self-assessment questions, you might want to move ahead to the section "Exam Preparation Tasks." Table 5-1 lists the major headings in this chapter and the "Do I Know This Already?" quiz questions covering the material in those headings so that you can assess your knowledge of these specific areas. The answers to the "Do I Know This Already?" quiz appear in Appendix A.

Table 5-1 *"Do I Know This Already?" Foundation Topics Section-to-Question Mapping*

Foundation Topics Section	Questions
VLSM	1–3
Manual Route Summarization	4–6
Autosummarization and Discontiguous Classful Networks	7–8

1. Which of the following routing protocols support VLSM?

   a. RIP-1

   b. RIP-2

   c. EIGRP

   d. OSPF

2. What does the acronym VLSM stand for?

   a. Variable-length subnet mask

   b. Very long subnet mask

   c. Vociferous longitudinal subnet mask

   d. Vector-length subnet mask

   e. Vector loop subnet mask

3. R1 has configured interface Fa0/0 with the **ip address 10.5.48.1 255.255.240.0** command. Which of the following subnets, when configured on another interface on R1, would not be considered to be an overlapping VLSM subnet?

   a. 10.5.0.0 255.255.240.0

   b. 10.4.0.0 255.254.0.0

   c. 10.5.32.0 255.255.224.0

   d. 10.5.0.0 255.255.128.0

4. Which of the following summarized subnets is the smallest (smallest range of addresses) summary route that includes subnets 10.3.95.0, 10.3.96.0, and 10.3.97.0, mask 255.255.255.0?

   a. 10.0.0.0 255.0.0.0

   b. 10.3.0.0 255.255.0.0

   c. 10.3.64.0 255.255.192.0

   d. 10.3.64.0 255.255.224.0

5. Which of the following summarized subnets is not a valid summary that includes subnets 10.1.55.0, 10.1.56.0, and 10.1.57.0, mask 255.255.255.0?

   a. 10.0.0.0 255.0.0.0

   b. 10.1.0.0 255.255.0.0

   c. 10.1.55.0 255.255.255.0

   d. 10.1.48.0 255.255.248.0

   e. 10.1.32.0 255.255.224.0

6. Which of the following routing protocols support manual route summarization?

   a. RIP-1

   b. RIP-2

   c. EIGRP

   d. OSPF

7. Which routing protocol(s) perform(s) autosummarization by default?

   a. RIP-1

   b. RIP-2

   c. EIGRP

   d. OSPF

8. An internetwork has a discontiguous network 10.0.0.0, and it is having problems. All routers use RIP-1 with all default configurations. Which of the following answers lists an action that, by itself, would solve the problem and allow the discontiguous network?

   a. Migrate all routers to use OSPF, using as many defaults as is possible.

   b. Disable autosummarization with the **no auto-summary** RIP configuration command.

   c. Migrate to EIGRP, using as many defaults as is possible.

   d. The problem cannot be solved without first making network 10.0.0.0 contiguous.

Foundation Topics

This chapter discusses three related topics: VLSM, manual route summarization, and automatic route summarization. These topics mainly relate to each other because of the underlying math, which requires that the engineer be able to look at a subnet number and mask to quickly determine the implied range of addresses. This chapter begins with VLSM, moving on to manual route summarization, and finally autosummarization.

VLSM

VLSM occurs when an internetwork uses more than one mask in different subnets of a single Class A, B, or C network. VLSM allows engineers to reduce the number of wasted IP addresses in each subnet, allowing more subnets and avoiding having to obtain another registered IP network number from regional IP address assignment authorities. Also, even when using private IP networks (as defined in RFC 1918), large corporations might still need to conserve the address space, again creating a need to use VLSM.

Figure 5-1 shows an example of VLSM used in class A network 10.0.0.0.

Figure 5-1   *VLSM in Network 10.0.0.0: Masks 255.255.255.0 and 255.255.255.252*

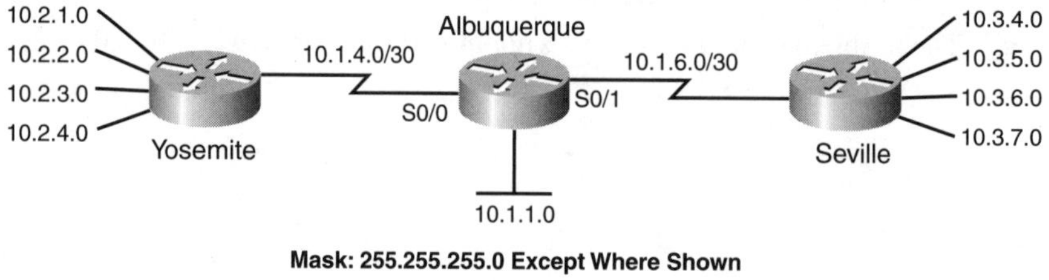

Mask: 255.255.255.0 Except Where Shown

Figure 5-1 shows a typical choice of using a /30 prefix (mask 255.255.255.252) on point-to-point serial links, with some other mask (255.255.255.0, in this example) on the LAN subnets. All subnets are of class A network 10.0.0.0, with two masks being used, therefore meeting the definition of VLSM.

Oddly enough, a common mistake occurs when people think that VLSM means "using more than one mask," rather than "using more than one mask in a single classful network." For example, if in one internetwork diagram, all subnets of network 10.0.0.0 use a 255.255.240.0 mask and all subnets of network 11.0.0.0 use a 255.255.255.0 mask, two different masks are used. However, only one mask is inside each respective classful network, so this particular design would not be using VLSM.

Example 5-1 lists the routing table on Albuquerque from Figure 5-1. Albuquerque uses two masks inside network 10.0.0.0, as noted in the highlighted line in the example.

Example 5-1 *Albuquerque Routing Table with VLSM*

```
Albuquerque#show ip route
Codes: C - connected, S - static, I - IGRP, R - RIP, M - mobile, B - BGP
       D - EIGRP, EX - EIGRP external, O - OSPF, IA - OSPF inter area
       N1 - OSPF NSSA external type 1, N2 - OSPF NSSA external type 2
       E1 - OSPF external type 1, E2 - OSPF external type 2, E - EGP
       i - IS-IS, L1 - IS-IS level-1, L2 - IS-IS level-2, ia - IS-IS inter area
       * - candidate default, U - per-user static route, o - ODR
       P - periodic downloaded static route

Gateway of last resort is not set

     10.0.0.0/8 is variably subnetted, 11 subnets, 2 masks
D       10.2.1.0/24 [90/2172416] via 10.1.4.2, 00:00:34, Serial0/0
D       10.2.2.0/24 [90/2172416] via 10.1.4.2, 00:00:34, Serial0/0
D       10.2.3.0/24 [90/2172416] via 10.1.4.2, 00:00:34, Serial0/0
D       10.2.4.0/24 [90/2172416] via 10.1.4.2, 00:00:34, Serial0/0
D       10.3.4.0/24 [90/2172416] via 10.1.6.2, 00:00:56, Serial0/1
D       10.3.5.0/24 [90/2172416] via 10.1.6.2, 00:00:56, Serial0/1
D       10.3.6.0/24 [90/2172416] via 10.1.6.2, 00:00:56, Serial0/1
D       10.3.7.0/24 [90/2172416] via 10.1.6.2, 00:00:56, Serial0/1
C       10.1.1.0/24 is directly connected, Ethernet0/0
C       10.1.6.0/30 is directly connected, Serial0/1
C       10.1.4.0/30 is directly connected, Serial0/0
```

Classless and Classful Routing Protocols

For a routing protocol to support VLSM, the routing protocol must advertise not only the subnet number but also the subnet mask when advertising routes. Additionally, a routing protocol must include subnet masks in its routing updates to support manual route summarization.

Each IP routing protocol is considered to be either classless or classful, based on whether the routing protocol does (classless) or does not (classful) send the mask in routing updates. Each routing protocol is either classless or classful by its very nature; no commands exist to enable or disable whether a particular routing protocol is a classless or classful routing protocol. Table 5-2 lists the routing protocols, shows whether each is classless or classful, and offers reminders of the two features (VLSM and route summarization) enabled by the inclusion of masks in the routing updates.

Table 5-2 *Classless and Classful Interior IP Routing Protocols*

Routing Protocol	Is It Classless?	Sends Mask in Updates	Supports VLSM	Supports Manual Route Summarization
RIP-1	No	No	No	No
IGRP	No	No	No	No
RIP-2	Yes	Yes	Yes	Yes
EIGRP	Yes	Yes	Yes	Yes
OSPF	Yes	Yes	Yes	Yes

Overlapping VLSM Subnets

The subnets chosen to be used in any IP internetwork design must not overlap their address ranges. With a single subnet mask in a network, the overlaps are somewhat obvious; however, with VLSM, the overlapping subnets might not be as obvious. When multiple subnets overlap, a router's routing table entries overlap. As a result, routing becomes unpredictable, and some hosts can be reached from only particular parts of the internetwork. In short, a design that uses overlapping subnets is considered to be an incorrect design, and should not be used.

Two general types of problems exist that relate to overlapping VLSM subnets, both in real jobs and for the exams: analyzing an existing design to find overlaps and choosing new VLSM subnets so that you do not create an overlapped subnet. To appreciate what the exam might cover for VLSM and overlapping subnets, consider Figure 5-2, which shows a single Class B network (172.16.0.0), using a VLSM design that includes three different masks, /23, /24, and /30.

Figure 5-2 *VLSM Design with Possible Overlap*

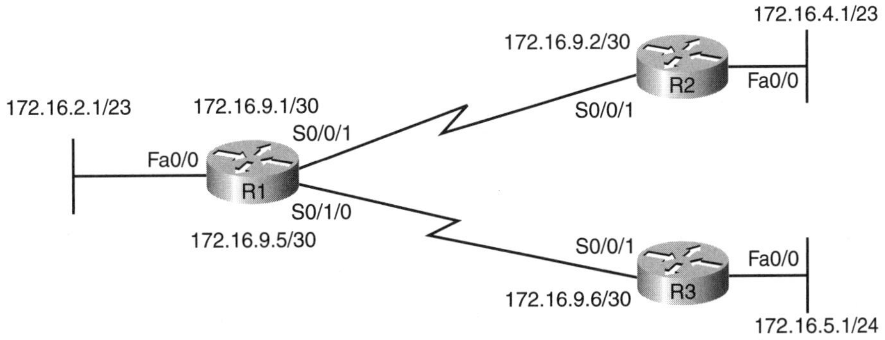

Now imagine that an exam question shows you the figure, and either directly or indirectly asks whether overlapping subnets exist. This type of question might simply tell you that some hosts cannot ping each other, or it might not even mention that the root cause could be that some of the subnets overlap. To answer such a question, you could follow this simple but possibly laborious task:

Step 1   Calculate the subnet number and subnet broadcast address of each subnet; this gives you the range of addresses in that subnet.

Step 2   Compare the ranges of addresses in each subnet and look for cases in which the address ranges overlap.

For example, in Figure 5-2, you would look at the five subnets, and using Step 1, calculate the subnet numbers, broadcast addresses, and range of addresses, with the answers listed in Table 5-3.

Table 5-3 *Subnets and Address Ranges in Figure 5-2*

Subnet Location	Subnet Number	First Address	Last Address	Broadcast Address
R1 LAN	172.16.2.0	172.16.2.1	172.16.3.254	172.16.3.255
R2 LAN	172.16.4.0	172.16.4.1	172.16.5.254	172.16.5.255
R3 LAN	172.16.5.0	172.16.5.1	172.16.5.254	172.16.5.255
R1-R2 serial	172.16.9.0	172.16.9.1	172.16.9.2	172.16.9.3
R1-R3 serial	172.16.9.4	172.16.9.5	172.16.9.6	172.16.9.7

Step 2 states the somewhat obvious step of comparing the address ranges to see whether any overlaps occur. Note that none of the subnet numbers are identical; however, a closer look at the R2 LAN and R3 LAN subnets shows that these two subnets overlap. In this case, the design is invalid because of the overlap, and one of the two subnets would need to be changed.

Designing a Subnetting Scheme Using VLSM

CCENT/CCNA ICND1 Official Exam Certification Guide explains how to design the IP addressing scheme for a new internetwork by choosing IP subnets when using a single subnet mask throughout a classful network. To do so, the process first analyzes the design requirements to determine the number of subnets and the number of hosts in the largest subnet. Then, a subnet mask is chosen. Finally, all possible subnets of the network, using that mask, are identified, and then the actual subnets used in the design are picked from that list. For example, in Class B network 172.16.0.0, a design might call for ten subnets, with a largest subnet of 200 hosts. Mask 255.255.255.0 meets the requirements, with 8 subnet bits and 8 host bits, supporting 256 subnets and 254 hosts per subnet. The subnet numbers would be 172.16.0.0, 172.16.1.0, 172.16.2.0, and so on.

When using VLSM in a design, the design process starts by deciding how many subnets of each size are required. For example, most installations use subnets with a /30 prefix for serial links because these subnets support exactly two IP addresses, which are all the addresses needed on a point-to-point link. The LAN-based subnets often have different requirements, with shorter prefix lengths (meaning more host bits) for larger numbers of hosts/subnet, and longer prefix lengths (meaning fewer host bits) for smaller numbers of hosts/subnet.

> **NOTE**   To review subnetting design when using static-length subnet masks (SLSM), refer to *CCENT/CCNA ICND1 Official Exam Certification Guide*, Chapter 12, or the CD-only version of that chapter in this book's CD (Appendix H). (The CD-only Appendix D, "Subnetting Practice," of this book also includes some related practice problems.)

After the number of subnets with each mask has been determined, the next step is to find subnet numbers that match those requirements. This task is not particularly difficult if you already understand how to find subnet numbers when using static-length masks. However, a more formal process can help, which is outlined as follows:

Step 1   Determine the number of subnets needed for each mask/prefix based on the design requirements.

Step 2   Using the shortest prefix length (largest number of host bits), identify the subnets of the classful network when using that mask, until the required number of such subnets has been identified.

Step 3   Identify the next numeric subnet number using the same mask as in the previous step.

Step 4   Starting with the subnet number identified at the previous step, identify smaller subnets based on the next-longest prefix length required for the design, until the required number of subnets of that size have been identified.

Step 5   Repeat Steps 3 and 4 until all subnets of all sizes have been found.

Frankly, using the above process, as written, can be a little difficult, but an example can certainly help make sense of the process. So, imagine a network design for which the following design requirements were determined, per Step 1 of the previous process. The design calls for the use of Class B network 172.16.0.0:

■   Three subnets with mask /24 (255.255.255.0)

■   Three subnets with mask /26 (255.255.255.192)

■   Four subnets with mask /30 (255.255.255.252)

Step 2 in this case means that the first three subnets of network 172.16.0.0 should be identified, with mask /24, because /24 is the shortest prefix length of the three prefix lengths listed in the design requirements. Using the same math covered in detail in the ICND1 book, the first three subnets would be 172.16.0.0/24, 172.16.1.0/24, and 172.16.2.0/24:

■   172.16.0.0/24: Range 172.16.0.1–172.16.0.254

■   172.16.1.0/24: Range 172.16.1.1–172.16.1.254

■   172.16.2.0/24: Range 172.16.2.1–172.16.2.254

Step 3 in this case says to identify one more subnet using the /24 mask, so the next numeric subnet would be 172.16.3.0/24.

Before moving on to Step 4, take a few minutes to review Figure 5-3. The figure shows the results of Step 2 on the top part of the figure, listing the three subnets identified at this step as "allocated" because they will be used for subnets in this design. It also lists the next subnet, as found at Step 3, listing it as unallocated, because it has not yet been chosen to be used for a particular part of the design.

Figure 5-3   *Designing to Use VLSM Subnets*

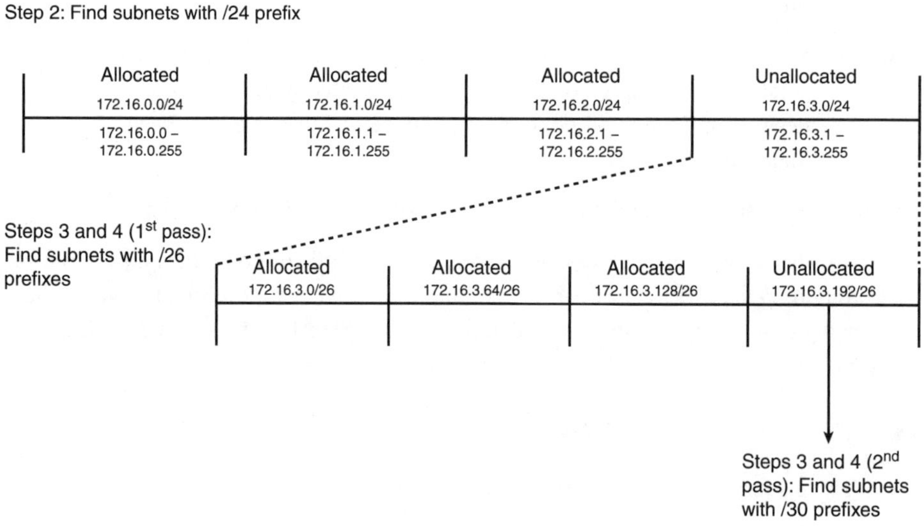

Step 2: Find subnets with /24 prefix

To find the subnets at Step 4, start with the unallocated subnet number found at Step 3 (172.16.3.0), but with Step 4 applying the next longer prefix length, or /26 in this example. The process always results in the first subnet number being the subnet number found at the previous step, or 172.16.3.0 in this case. The three subnets are as follows:

- 172.16.3.0/26: Range 172.16.3.1–172.16.3.62

- 172.16.3.64/26: Range 172.16.3.65–172.16.3.126

- 172.16.3.128/26: Range 172.16.3.129–172.16.3.190

Finally, Step 5 says to repeat Steps 3 and 4 until all subnets have been found. In this case, repeating Step 3, the next subnet is found, using the /26 prefix length—namely subnet 172.16.3.192/26. This subnet is considered unallocated for the time being. To repeat Step 4 for the next longest prefix length, Step 4 uses the /30 prefix, starting with subnet number 172.16.3.192. The first subnet will be 172.16.3.192, with mask /30, plus the next three subnets with that same mask, as follows:

- 172.16.3.192/30: Range 172.16.3.193–172.16.3.194

- 172.16.3.196/30: Range 172.16.3.197–172.16.3.198

- 172.16.3.200/30: Range 172.16.3.201–172.16.3.202

- 172.16.3.204/30: Range 172.16.3.205–172.16.3.206

The wording in the formalized process might seem to be a bit laborious, but it does result in a set of VLSM subnets that do not overlap. By using a structured approach of essentially allocating the larger subnets first, then the smaller subnets, you can generally choose subnets so that the address ranges do not overlap.

Adding a New Subnet to an Existing Design

Another task required when working with VLSM-based internetworks is to choose a new subnet number for an existing internetwork. In particular, extra care must be taken when choosing new subnet numbers to avoid causing an overlap between the new subnet and any existing subnets. For example, consider the internetwork in Figure 5-2, with classful network 172.16.0.0. An exam question might suggest that a new subnet, with a /23 prefix length, needs to be added to the design. The question might also say "Pick the smallest subnet number that can be used for the new subnet." So, the subnets must be identified, and a nonoverlapping subnet must be chosen.

To attack such a problem, you would essentially need to find all the subnet numbers that could be created in that classful network, using the stated or implied mask. Then, you would have to ensure that the new subnet did not overlap with any existing subnets. Specifically, you could use the following steps:

Step 1 If not already listed as part of the question, pick the subnet mask (prefix length) based on the design requirements, typically based on the number of hosts needed in the subnet.

Step 2 Calculate all possible subnet numbers of the classful network, using the mask determined at Step 1. (If the exam question asks for the numerically largest or smallest subnet number, you might choose to only do this math for the first few or last few subnets.)

Step 3 For the subnets found at Step 2, calculate the subnet broadcast address and range of addresses for each assumed subnet.

Step 4 Compare the lists of potential subnets and address ranges to the existing subnets and address ranges. Rule out any of the potential subnets that overlap with an existing subnet.

Step 5 Pick a subnet number from the list found at Step 2 that does not overlap with any existing subnets, noting whether the question asks for the smallest or largest subnet number.

Using this five-step process with the example started just before the step list with Figure 5-2, the question supplied the prefix length of /23 (Step 1). Table 5-4 lists the results for Steps

2 and 3, listing the subnet numbers, broadcast addresses, and range of addresses for the first five of the possible /23 subnets.

Table 5-4 *First Five Possible /23 Subnets*

Subnet	Subnet Number	First Address	Last Address	Broadcast Address
First (zero)	172.16.0.0	172.16.0.1	172.16.1.254	172.16.1.255
Second	172.16.2.0	172.16.2.1	172.16.3.254	172.16.3.255
Third	172.16.4.0	172.16.4.1	172.16.5.254	172.16.5.255
Fourth	172.16.6.0	172.16.6.1	172.16.7.254	172.16.7.255
Fifth	172.16.8.0	172.16.8.1	172.16.9.254	172.16.9.255

Step 4 compares the information in the table with the existing subnets. In this case, the second, third, and fourth subnets in Table 5-4 overlap with existing subnets in Figure 5-2.

Step 5 has more to do with the exam than with real networks. Multiple-choice questions sometimes need to force the question to have only a single answer, so asking for the numerically smallest or largest subnet solves the problem. This particular example problem asks for the smallest subnet number, and the zero subnet is still available (172.16.0.0/23, with broadcast address 172.16.1.255). If the question allowed the use of the zero subnet, the zero subnet (172.16.0.0/23) would be the correct answer. However, if the zero subnet was prohibited from use, the first three subnets listed in Table 5-4 would not be available, making the fourth subnet (172.16.8.0/23) the correct answer. Note that Scenario 5 in the CD-only Appendix F, "Additional Scenarios," gives you an opportunity to practice using this particular process.

NOTE   For the exam, the zero subnet should be avoided if (a) the question implies the use of classful routing protocols or (b) the routers are configured with the **no ip subnet-zero** global configuration command. Otherwise, assume that the zero subnet can be used.

VLSM Configuration

Routers do not enable or disable VLSM as a configuration feature. From a configuration perspective, VLSM is simply a side effect of the **ip address** interface subcommand. Routers configure VLSM by virtue of having at least two router interfaces, on the same router or among all routers in the internetwork, with IP addresses in the same classful network but with different masks. Example 5-2 shows a simple example on Router R3 from Figure 5-2, with interface Fa0/0 being assigned IP address 172.16.5.1/24, and interface S0/0/1 being assigned IP address 172.16.9.6/30, thereby using at least two different masks in network 172.16.0.0.

Example 5-2 *Configuring VLSM*

```
R3#configure terminal
R3(config)#interface Fa0/0
R3(config-if)#ip address 172.16.5.1 255.255.255.0
R3(config-if)#interface S0/0/1
R3(config-if)#ip address 172.16.9.6 255.255.255.252
```

Classless routing protocols, which support VLSM, do not have to be configured to enable VLSM. Support for VLSM is simply a feature inherent to those routing protocols.

Next, the text moves on to the second major section of this chapter, the topic of manual route summarization.

Manual Route Summarization

Small networks might have only a few dozen routes in their routers' routing tables. The larger the network, the larger the number of routes. In fact, Internet routers have more than 100,000 routes in some cases.

The routing table might become too large in large IP networks. As routing tables grow, they consume more memory in a router. Also, each router can take more time to route a packet, because the router has to match a route in the routing table, and searching a larger table generally takes more time. And with a large routing table, it takes more time to troubleshoot problems, because the engineers working on the network need to sift through more information.

Route summarization reduces the size of routing tables while maintaining routes to all the destinations in the network. As a result, routing performance can be improved and memory can be saved inside each router. Summarization also improves convergence time, because the router that summarizes the route no longer has to announce any changes to the status of the individual subnets. By advertising only that the entire summary route is either up or down, the routers that have the summary route do not have to reconverge every time one of the component subnets goes up or down.

This chapter refers to route summarization as manual route summarization, in contrast to the last major topic in this chapter, autosummarization. The term *manual* refers to the fact that manual route summarization only occurs when an engineer configures one or more commands. Autosummarization occurs automatically without a specific configuration command.

The following sections first examine the concepts behind route summarization, followed by some suggestions of how to determine good summary routes. Note that while the concepts are covered, the configuration of manually summarized routes is not covered as an end to itself in this book.

Route Summarization Concepts

Engineers use route summarization to reduce the size of the routing tables in the network. Route summarization causes some number of more-specific routes to be replaced with a single route that includes all the IP addresses covered by the subnets in the original routes.

Summary routes, which replace multiple routes, must be configured by a network engineer. Although the configuration command does not look exactly like a **static ip route** command, the same basic information is configured. Now the routing protocol advertises just the summary route, as opposed to the original routes.

Route summarization works much better when the network was designed with route summarization in mind. For example, Figure 5-1, earlier in this chapter, shows the results of good planning for summarization. In this network, the engineer planned his choices of subnet numbers relative to his goal of using route summarization. All subnets off the main site (Albuquerque), including WAN links, start with 10.1. All LAN subnets off Yosemite start with 10.2, and likewise, all LAN subnets off Seville start with 10.3.

Earlier, Example 5-1 showed a copy of Albuquerque's routing table without summarization. That example shows Albuquerque's four routes to subnets that begin with 10.2, all pointing out its serial 0/0 interface to Yosemite. Similarly, Albuquerque shows four routes to subnets that begin with 10.3, all pointing out its serial 0/1 interface to Seville. This design allows the Yosemite and Seville routers to advertise a single summary route instead of the four routes they currently advertise to Albuquerque, respectively.

Example 5-3 shows the results of the configuration of manual route summarization on both Yosemite and Seville. In this case, Yosemite is advertising a summary route for 10.2.0.0/16, which represents address range 10.2.0.0–10.2.255.255 (all addresses that begin with 10.2). Seville advertises a summary route for 10.3.0.0/16, which represents the address range 10.3.0.0–10.3.255.255 (all addresses that begin 10.3).

Example 5-3 *Albuquerque Routing Table After Route Summarization*

```
Albuquerque#show ip route
Codes: C - connected, S - static, I - IGRP, R - RIP, M - mobile, B - BGP
       D - EIGRP, EX - EIGRP external, O - OSPF, IA - OSPF inter area
       N1 - OSPF NSSA external type 1, N2 - OSPF NSSA external type 2
       E1 - OSPF external type 1, E2 - OSPF external type 2, E - EGP
       i - IS-IS, L1 - IS-IS level-1, L2 - IS-IS level-2, ia - IS-IS inter area
```

Example 5-3 *Albuquerque Routing Table After Route Summarization (Continued)*

```
       * - candidate default, U - per-user static route, o - ODR
       P - periodic downloaded static route

Gateway of last resort is not set

     10.0.0.0/8 is variably subnetted, 5 subnets, 3 masks
D       10.2.0.0/16 [90/2172416] via 10.1.4.2, 00:05:59, Serial0/0
D       10.3.0.0/16 [90/2172416] via 10.1.6.3, 00:05:40, Serial0/1
C       10.1.1.0/24 is directly connected, Ethernet0/0
C       10.1.6.0/30 is directly connected, Serial0/1
C       10.1.4.0/30 is directly connected, Serial0/0
```

The resulting routing table on Albuquerque still routes packets correctly, but with more efficiency and less memory. Frankly, improving from 11 routes to 5 routes does not help much, but the same concept, applied to larger networks, does help.

The effects of route summarization can also be seen on the other two routers in the figure. Example 5-4 shows Yosemite, including both the route summarization configuration and Yosemite's routing table. Example 5-5 shows the same kind of information on Seville.

Example 5-4 *Yosemite Configuration and Routing Table After Route Summarization*

```
Yosemite#configure terminal
Enter configuration commands, one per line.  End with CNTL/Z.
Yosemite(config)#interface serial 0/0
Yosemite(config-if)#ip summary-address eigrp 1 10.2.0.0 255.255.0.0
Yosemite(config-if)#^Z

Yosemite#show ip route
Codes: C - connected, S - static, I - IGRP, R - RIP, M - mobile, B - BGP
       D - EIGRP, EX - EIGRP external, O - OSPF, IA - OSPF inter area
       N1 - OSPF NSSA external type 1, N2 - OSPF NSSA external type 2
       E1 - OSPF external type 1, E2 - OSPF external type 2, E - EGP
       i - IS-IS, L1 - IS-IS level-1, L2 - IS-IS level-2, ia - IS-IS inter area
       * - candidate default, U - per-user static route, o - ODR
       P - periodic downloaded static route

Gateway of last resort is not set

     10.0.0.0/8 is variably subnetted, 9 subnets, 3 masks
D       10.2.0.0/16 is a summary, 00:04:57, Null0
D       10.3.0.0/16 [90/2684416] via 10.1.4.1, 00:04:30, Serial0/0
C       10.2.1.0/24 is directly connected, FastEthernet0/0
D       10.1.1.0/24 [90/2195456] via 10.1.4.1, 00:04:52, Serial0/0
C       10.2.2.0/24 is directly connected, Loopback2
C       10.2.3.0/24 is directly connected, Loopback3
```

continues

Example 5-4 *Yosemite Configuration and Routing Table After Route Summarization (Continued)*

```
C       10.2.4.0/24 is directly connected, Loopback4
D       10.1.6.0/30 [90/2681856] via 10.1.4.1, 00:04:53, Serial0/0
C       10.1.4.0/30 is directly connected, Serial0/0
```

Example 5-5 *Seville Configuration and Routing Table After Route Summarization*

```
Seville#configure terminal
Enter configuration commands, one per line.  End with CNTL/Z.
Seville(config)#interface serial 0/0
Seville(config-if)#ip summary-address eigrp 1 10.3.0.0 255.255.0.0
Seville(config-if)#^Z
Seville#show ip route
Codes: C - connected, S - static, I - IGRP, R - RIP, M - mobile, B - BGP
       D - EIGRP, EX - EIGRP external, O - OSPF, IA - OSPF inter area
       N1 - OSPF NSSA external type 1, N2 - OSPF NSSA external type 2
       E1 - OSPF external type 1, E2 - OSPF external type 2, E - EGP
       i - IS-IS, L1 - IS-IS level-1, L2 - IS-IS level-2, ia - IS-IS inter area
       * - candidate default, U - per-user static route, o - ODR
       P - periodic downloaded static route

Gateway of last resort is not set

     10.0.0.0/8 is variably subnetted, 9 subnets, 3 masks
D       10.2.0.0/16 [90/2684416] via 10.1.6.1, 00:00:36, Serial0/0
D       10.3.0.0/16 is a summary, 00:00:38, Null0
D       10.1.1.0/24 [90/2195456] via 10.1.6.1, 00:00:36, Serial0/0
C       10.3.5.0/24 is directly connected, Loopback5
C       10.3.4.0/24 is directly connected, FastEthernet0/0
C       10.1.6.0/30 is directly connected, Serial0/0
C       10.3.7.0/24 is directly connected, Loopback7
D       10.1.4.0/30 [90/2681856] via 10.1.6.1, 00:00:36, Serial0/0
C       10.3.6.0/24 is directly connected, Loopback6
```

Route summarization configuration differs with different routing protocols; Enhanced
IGRP (EIGRP) is used in this example. The summary routes for EIGRP are created by the
ip summary-address interface subcommands on Yosemite and Seville in this case. Each
command defines a new summarized route and tells EIGRP to only advertise the summary
out this interface and not to advertise any routes contained in the larger summary. For
example, Yosemite defines a summary route to 10.2.0.0, mask 255.255.0.0, which defines
a route to all hosts whose IP addresses begin with 10.2. In effect, this command causes
Yosemite and Seville to advertise routes 10.2.0.0 255.255.0.0 and 10.3.0.0 255.255.0.0,
respectively, and not to advertise their original four LAN subnets.

Note that back in Example 5-3, Albuquerque's routing table now contains a route to 10.2.0.0 255.255.0.0 (the mask is listed in prefix notation as /16), but none of the original four subnets that begin with 10.2. The same thing occurs for route 10.3.0.0/16.

The routing tables on Yosemite and Seville look a little different from Albuquerque. Focusing on Yosemite (Example 5-4), notice that the four routes to subnets that begin with 10.2 show up because they are directly connected subnets. Yosemite does not see the four 10.3 routes. Instead, it sees a summary route, because Albuquerque now advertises the 10.3.0.0/16 summarized route only. The opposite is true on Seville (Example 5-5), which lists all four connected routes that begin with 10.3 and a summary route for 10.2.0.0/16.

The most interesting part of Yosemite's routing tables is the route to 10.2.0.0/16, with the outgoing interface set to **null0**. Routes referring to an outgoing interface of the null0 interface mean that packets matching this route are discarded. EIGRP added this route, with interface null0, as a result of the **ip summary-address** command. The logic works like this:

Yosemite needs this odd-looking route because now it might receive packets destined for other 10.2 addresses besides the four existing 10.2 subnets. If a packet destined for one of the four existing 10.2.x subnets arrives, Yosemite has a correct, more specific route to match the packet. If a packet whose destination starts with 10.2 arrives, but it is not in one of those four subnets, the null route matches the packet, causing Yosemite to discard the packet—as it should.

The routing table on Seville is similar to Yosemite's in terms of the table entries and why they are in the table.

Route Summarization Strategies

As mentioned earlier, manual route summarization works best when the network engineer plans his choice of subnet numbers anticipating route summarization. For example, the earlier examples assumed a well-thought-out plan, with the engineers only using subnets beginning with 10.2 for subnets off the Yosemite router. That convention allowed the creation of a summary route for all addresses beginning with 10.2 by having Yosemite advertise a route describing subnet 10.2.0.0, mask 255.255.0.0.

Some summarized routes combine many routes into one route, but that might not be the "best" summarization. The word *best*, when applied to choosing what summary route to configure, means that the summary should include all the subnets specified in the question but as few other addresses as is possible. For example, in the earlier summarization example, Yosemite summarized four subnets (10.2.1.0, 10.2.2.0, 10.2.3.0, and 10.2.4.0, all with mask 255.255.255.0) into the 10.2.0.0/16 summary route. However, this summary includes a lot of IP addresses that are not in those four subnets. Does the summary work given that network's design goals? Sure. However, instead of just defining a summary that encompasses lots of additional addresses that do not yet exist in a network, the engineer might instead want to configure the tightest, or most concise, or best summary: the summary that includes all the subnets but as few extra subnets (the ones that have not been assigned yet) as possible. This section describes a strategy for finding those concise best summary routes.

The following list describes a generalized binary process by which you can find a best summary route for a group of subnets:

Step 1 List all to-be-summarized subnet numbers in binary.

Step 2 Find the first N bits of the subnet numbers for which every subnet has the same value, moving from left to right. (For our purposes, consider this first part the "in-common" part.)

Step 3 To find the summary router's subnet number, write down the in-common bits from Step 2 and binary 0s for the remaining bits. Convert back to decimal, 8 bits at a time, when finished.

Step 4 To find the summary route's subnet mask, write down N binary 1s, with N being the number of in-common bits found at Step 2. Complete the subnet mask with all binary 0s. Convert back to decimal, 8 bits at a time, when finished.

Step 5 Check your work by calculating the range of valid IP addresses implied by the new summary route, comparing the range to the summarized subnets. The new summary should encompass all IP addresses in the summarized subnets.

By looking at the subnet numbers in binary, you can more easily discover the bits in common among all the subnet numbers. By using the longest number of bits in common, you can find the best summary. The next two sections show two examples using this process to find the best, most concise, tightest summary routes for the network shown in Figure 5-1.

Sample "Best" Summary on Seville

Seville has subnets 10.3.4.0, 10.3.5.0, 10.3.6.0, and 10.3.7.0, all with mask 255.255.255.0. You start the process by writing down all the subnet numbers in binary:

```
0000 1010 0000 0011 0000 01|00 0000 0000 - 10.3.4.0
0000 1010 0000 0011 0000 01|01 0000 0000 - 10.3.5.0
0000 1010 0000 0011 0000 01|10 0000 0000 - 10.3.6.0
0000 1010 0000 0011 0000 01|11 0000 0000 - 10.3.7.0
```

Step 2 requires that you find all in-common bits at the beginning of all the subnets. Even before looking at the numbers in binary, you can guess that the first two octets are identical in all four subnets. So, a quick look at the first 16 bits of all four subnet numbers confirms that all have the same value. This means that the in-common part (Step 2) is at least 16 bits long. Further examination shows that the first 6 bits of the third octet are also identical, but the seventh bit in the third octet has some different values among the different subnets. So the in-common part of these four subnets is the first 22 bits.

Step 3 says to create a subnet number for the summary by taking the same bits in the in-common part, and write down binary 0s for the rest. In this case:

    0000 1010 0000 0011 0000 01|00 0000 0000 - 10.3.4.0

Step 4 creates the mask by using binary 1s for the same bits as the in-common part, which is the first 22 bits in this case, and then binary 0s for the remaining bits, as follows:

    1111 1111 1111 1111 1111 11|00 0000 0000 - 255.255.252.0

So, the summary route uses subnet 10.3.4.0, mask 255.255.252.0.

Step 5 suggests a method to check your work. The summary route should include all the IP addresses in the summarized routes. In this case, the range of addresses for the summary route starts with 10.3.4.0. The first valid IP address is 10.3.4.1, the final valid IP address is 10.3.7.254, and the broadcast address is 10.3.7.255. In this case, the summary route includes all the IP addresses in the four routes it summarizes and no extraneous IP addresses.

Sample "Best" Summary on Yosemite

The four subnets on Yosemite cannot be summarized quite as efficiently as those on Seville. On Seville, the summary route itself covers the same set of IP addresses as the four subnets with no extra addresses. As you will see, the best summary route at Yosemite includes twice as many addresses in the summary as exist in the original four subnets.

Yosemite has subnets 10.2.1.0, 10.2.2.0, 10.2.3.0, and 10.2.4.0, all with mask 255.255.255.0. The process starts at Step 1 by writing down all the subnet numbers in binary:

    0000 1010 0000 0010 0000 0|001 0000 0000 - 10.2.1.0
    0000 1010 0000 0010 0000 0|010 0000 0000 - 10.2.2.0
    0000 1010 0000 0010 0000 0|011 0000 0000 - 10.2.3.0
    0000 1010 0000 0010 0000 0|100 0000 0000 - 10.2.4.0

At Step 2, it appears that the first two octets are identical in all four subnets, plus the first 5 bits of the third octet. So, the first 21 bits of the four subnet numbers are in common.

Step 3 says to create a subnet number for the summary route by taking the same value for the in-common part and binary 0s for the rest. In this case:

0000 1010 0000 0010 0000 0|000 0000 0000 - 10.2.0.0

Step 4 creates the mask used for the summary route by using binary 1s for the in-common part and binary 0s for the rest. The in-common part in this example is the first 21 bits:

1111 1111 1111 1111 1111 1|000 0000 0000 - 255.255.248.0

So, the best summary is 10.2.0.0, mask 255.255.248.0.

Step 5 suggests a method to check your work. The summary route should define a superset of the IP addresses in the summarized routes. In this case, the range of addresses starts with 10.2.0.0. The first valid IP address is 10.2.0.1, the final valid IP address is 10.2.7.254, and the broadcast address is 10.2.7.255. In this case, the summary route summarizes a larger set of addresses than just the four subnets, but it does include all addresses in all four subnets.

Autosummarization and Discontiguous Classful Networks

As covered in the previous sections, manual route summarization can improve routing efficiency, reduce memory consumption, and improve convergence by reducing the length of routing tables. The final sections of this chapter examine the automatic summarization of routes at the boundaries of classful networks, using a feature called autosummarization.

Because classful routing protocols do not advertise subnet mask information, the routing updates simply list subnet numbers but no accompanying mask. A router receiving a routing update with a classful routing protocol looks at the subnet number in the update, but the router must make some assumptions about what mask is associated with the subnet. For example, with Cisco routers, if R1 and R2 have connected networks of the same single Class A, B, or C network, and if R2 receives an update from R1, R2 assumes that the routes described in R1's update use the same mask that R2 uses. In other words, the classful routing protocols require a static-length subnet mask (SLSM) throughout each classful network so that each router can then reasonably assume that the mask configured for its own interfaces is the same mask used throughout that classful network.

When a router has interfaces in more than one Class A, B, or C network, it can advertise a single route for an entire Class A, B, or C network into the other classful network. This feature is called *autosummarization*. It can be characterized as follows:

> When advertised on an interface whose IP address is not in network X, routes related to subnets in network X are summarized and advertised as one route. That route is for the entire Class A, B, or C network X.

Key Topic

In other words, if R3 has interfaces in networks 10.0.0.0 and 11.0.0.0, when R3 advertises routing updates out interfaces with IP addresses that start with 11, the updates advertise a single route for network 10.0.0.0. Similarly, R3 advertises a single route to 11.0.0.0 out its interfaces whose IP addresses start with 10.

An Example of Autosummarization

As usual, an example makes the concept much clearer. Consider Figure 5-4, which shows two networks in use: 10.0.0.0 and 172.16.0.0. Seville has four (connected) routes to subnets of network 10.0.0.0. Example 5-6 shows the output of the **show ip route** command on Albuquerque, as well as RIP-1 **debug ip rip** output.

Figure 5-4 *Autosummarization*

Example 5-6 *Albuquerque Routes and RIP Debugs*

```
Albuquerque#show ip route
Codes: C - connected, S - static, I - IGRP, R - RIP, M - mobile, B - BGP
       D - EIGRP, EX - EIGRP external, O - OSPF, IA - OSPF inter area
       N1 - OSPF NSSA external type 1, N2 - OSPF NSSA external type 2
       E1 - OSPF external type 1, E2 - OSPF external type 2, E - EGP
       i - IS-IS, L1 - IS-IS level-1, L2 - IS-IS level-2, ia - IS-IS inter area
       * - candidate default, U - per-user static route, o - ODR
       P - periodic downloaded static route

Gateway of last resort is not set

     172.16.0.0/24 is subnetted, 2 subnets
C       172.16.1.0 is directly connected, Ethernet0/0
```

continues

Example 5-6   *Albuquerque Routes and RIP Debugs (Continued)*

```
C        172.16.3.0 is directly connected, Serial0/1
R     10.0.0.0/8 [120/1] via 172.16.3.3, 00:00:28, Serial0/1


Albuquerque#debug ip rip
RIP protocol debugging is on

00:05:36: RIP: received v1 update from 172.16.3.3 on Serial0/1
00:05:36:      10.0.0.0 in 1 hops
```

As shown in Example 5-6, Albuquerque's received update on Serial0/1 from Seville advertises only the entire Class A network 10.0.0.0 because autosummarization is enabled on Seville (by default). As a result, the Albuquerque IP routing table lists just one route to network 10.0.0.0.

This example also points out another feature of how classful routing protocols make assumptions. Albuquerque does not have any interfaces in network 10.0.0.0. So, when Albuquerque receives the routing update, it assumes that the mask used with 10.0.0.0 is 255.0.0.0, the default mask for a Class A network. In other words, classful routing protocols expect autosummarization to occur.

Discontiguous Classful Networks

Autosummarization does not cause any problems as long as the summarized network is contiguous rather than discontiguous. U.S. residents can appreciate the concept of a discontiguous network based on the common term *contiguous 48*, referring to the 48 U.S. states besides Alaska and Hawaii. To drive to Alaska from the contiguous 48, for example, you must drive through another country (Canada, for the geographically impaired!), so Alaska is not contiguous with the 48 states. In other words, it is discontiguous.

To better understand what the terms *contiguous* and *discontiguous* mean in networking, refer to the following two formal definitions when reviewing the example of a discontiguous classful network that follows:

```
Key
Topic
```

- **Contiguous network:** A classful network in which packets sent between every pair of subnets can pass only through subnets of that same classful network, without having to pass through subnets of any other classful network.

- **Discontiguous network:** A classful network in which packets sent between at least one pair of subnets must pass through subnets of a different classful network.

Figure 5-5 shows an example of a discontiguous network 10.0.0.0. In this case, packets sent from the subnets of network 10.0.0.0 on the left, near Yosemite, to the subnets of network 10.0.0.0 on the right, near Seville, have to pass through subnets of network 172.16.0.0.

Figure 5-5 *Discontiguous Network 10.0.0.0*

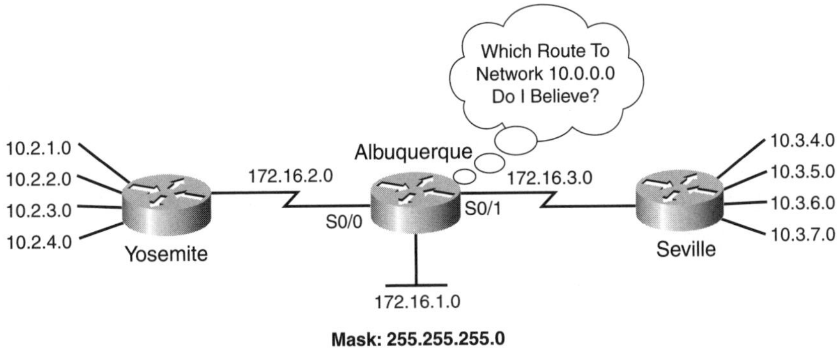

Autosummarization prevents an internetwork with a discontiguous network from working properly. Example 5-7 shows the results of using autosummarization in the internetwork shown in Figure 5-5, in this case using the classful RIP-1 routing protocol.

Example 5-7 *Albuquerque Routing Table: Autosummarization Causes Routing Problem with Discontiguous Network 10.0.0.0*

```
Albuquerque#show ip route
Codes: C - connected, S - static, I - IGRP, R - RIP, M - mobile, B - BGP
       D - EIGRP, EX - EIGRP external, O - OSPF, IA - OSPF inter area
       N1 - OSPF NSSA external type 1, N2 - OSPF NSSA external type 2
       E1 - OSPF external type 1, E2 - OSPF external type 2, E - EGP
       i - IS-IS, L1 - IS-IS level-1, L2 - IS-IS level-2, ia - IS-IS inter area
       * - candidate default, U - per-user static route, o - ODR
       P - periodic downloaded static route

Gateway of last resort is not set

     172.16.0.0/24 is subnetted, 3 subnets
C       172.16.1.0 is directly connected, Ethernet0/0
C       172.16.2.0 is directly connected, Serial0/0
C       172.16.3.0 is directly connected, Serial0/1
R    10.0.0.0/8 [120/1] via 172.16.3.3, 00:00:13, Serial0/1
                 [120/1] via 172.16.2.2, 00:00:04, Serial0/0
```

As shown in Example 5-7, Albuquerque now has two routes to network 10.0.0.0/8: one pointing left toward Yosemite and one pointing right toward Seville. Instead of sending packets destined for Yosemite's subnets out Serial 0/0, Albuquerque sends some packets out

S0/1 to Seville! Albuquerque simply balances the packets across the two routes, because as far as Albuquerque can tell, the two routes are simply equal-cost routes to the same destination: the entire network 10.0.0.0. So, applications would cease to function correctly in this network.

The solution to this problem is to disable the use of autosummarization. Because classful routing protocols must use autosummarization, the solution requires migration to a classless routing protocol and disabling the autosummarization feature. Example 5-8 shows the same internetwork from Figure 5-5 and Example 5-7, but this time with (classless) EIGRP, with autosummarization disabled.

Example 5-8   *Classless Routing Protocol with No Autosummarization Allows Discontiguous Network*

```
Albuquerque#show ip route
Codes: C - connected, S - static, I - IGRP, R - RIP, M - mobile, B - BGP
       D - EIGRP, EX - EIGRP external, O - OSPF, IA - OSPF inter area
       N1 - OSPF NSSA external type 1, N2 - OSPF NSSA external type 2
       E1 - OSPF external type 1, E2 - OSPF external type 2, E - EGP
       i - IS-IS, L1 - IS-IS level-1, L2 - IS-IS level-2, ia - IS-IS inter area
       * - candidate default, U - per-user static route, o - ODR
       P - periodic downloaded static route

Gateway of last resort is not set

     172.16.0.0/24 is subnetted, 3 subnets
C       172.16.1.0 is directly connected, Ethernet0/0
C       172.16.2.0 is directly connected, Serial0/0
C       172.16.3.0 is directly connected, Serial0/1
     10.0.0.0/24 is subnetted, 8 subnets
D       10.2.1.0/24 [90/2172416] via 172.16.2.2, 00:00:01, Serial0/0
D       10.2.2.0/24 [90/2297856] via 172.16.2.2, 00:00:01, Serial0/0
D       10.2.3.0/24 [90/2297856] via 172.16.2.2, 00:00:01, Serial0/0
D       10.2.4.0/24 [90/2297856] via 172.16.2.2, 00:00:01, Serial0/0
D       10.3.5.0/24 [90/2297856] via 172.16.3.3, 00:00:29, Serial0/1
D       10.3.4.0/24 [90/2172416] via 172.16.3.3, 00:00:29, Serial0/1
D       10.3.7.0/24 [90/2297856] via 172.16.3.3, 00:00:29, Serial0/1
D       10.3.6.0/24 [90/2297856] via 172.16.3.3, 00:00:29, Serial0/1
```

With autosummarization disabled on both Yosemite and Seville, neither router advertises an automatic summary of network 10.0.0.0/8 to Albuquerque. Instead, each router advertises the known subnets, so now Albuquerque knows the four LAN subnets off Yosemite as well as the four LAN subnets off Seville.

Autosummarization Support and Configuration

Classful routing protocols must use autosummarization. Some classless routing protocols support autosummarization, defaulting to use it, but with the ability to disable it with the **no auto-summary** router subcommand. Other classless routing protocols, notably Open Shortest Path First (OSPF), simply do not support autosummarization. Table 5-5 summarizes the facts about autosummarization on Cisco routers.

Table 5-5 *Autosummarization Support and Defaults*

Routing Protocol	Classless?	Supports Autosummarization?	Defaults to Use Autosummarization?[1]	Can Disable Autosummarization?
RIP-1	No	Yes	Yes	No
RIP-2	Yes	Yes	Yes	Yes
EIGRP	Yes	Yes	Yes	Yes
OSPF	Yes	No	—	—

[1] As of IOS 12.4 mainline.

Also note that the autosummary feature impacts routers that directly connect to parts of more than one classful network, but it has no impact on routers whose interfaces all connect to the same single classful network. For example, in Figure 5-5, the solution (as shown in Example 5-8) required the **no auto-summary** EIGRP subcommand on both Yosemite and Seville. However, Albuquerque, whose interfaces all sit inside a single network (Class B network 172.16.0.0), would not change its behavior with either the **auto-summary** or **no auto-summary** command configured in this case.

Exam Preparation Tasks

Review All the Key Topics

Key Topic

Review the most important topics from this chapter, noted with the Key Topics icon in the outer margin of the page. Table 5-6 lists a reference of these key topics and the page numbers on which each is found.

Table 5-6   *Key Topics for Chapter 5*

Key Topic Element	Description	Page Number
Table 5-2	List of IP routing protocols, with facts about classless/classful, VLSM support, and summarization support	204
List	Two-step strategy for finding overlapping VLSM subnets	205
List	Five-step strategy for choosing a new nonoverlapping VLSM subnet	209
List	Five-step process for finding the best manual summary route	216
Definition	Generalized definition of autosummarization	219
Definitions	Definitions for contiguous network and discontiguous network	220
Table 5-5	List of routing protocols and facts related to autosummarization	223

Complete the Tables and Lists from Memory

Print a copy of Appendix J, "Memory Tables," (found on the CD) or at least the section for this chapter, and complete the tables and lists from memory. Appendix K, "Memory Tables Answer Key," also on the CD, includes completed tables and lists to check your work.

Definitions of Key Terms

Define the following key terms from this chapter, and check your answers in the glossary:

Autosummarization, classful network, classful routing protocol, classless routing protocol, contiguous network, discontiguous network, overlapping subnets, summary route, variable-length subnet masking

Read Appendix F Scenarios

Appendix F, "Additional Scenarios," contains five detailed scenarios that both give you a chance to analyze different designs, problems, and command output, and show you how concepts from several different chapters interrelate. Appendix F Scenario 1, Part A, and all of Scenario 5 provide an opportunity to practice and develop skills with VLSM.

Command Reference to Check Your Memory

This chapter introduces only one new command that has not already been introduced in this book, namely the [no] **auto-summary** router configuration mode command. This command enables autosummarization (omitting the **no** option) or disables autosummarization (using the **no** option).

This chapter includes this command reference section just as a reminder of the one command to remember from this chapter.

This chapter covers the following subjects:

Standard IP Access Control Lists: This section explains how standard IP ACLs work and how to configure them.

Extended IP Access Control Lists: This section examines the deeper complexity of extended IP ACLs, including how to configure them.

Advances in Managing ACL Configuration: This section examines the nuances of two major enhancements to ACL configuration over the years: named ACLs and sequence numbers.

Miscellaneous ACL Topics: This section explains a few additional ACL concepts.

CHAPTER 6

IP Access Control Lists

Network security is one of the hottest topics in networking today. Although security has always been important, the explosion of the size and scope of the Internet has created more security exposures. In years past, most companies were not permanently connected to a global network—a network through which others could attempt to illegally access their networks. Today, because most companies connect to the Internet, many companies receive significant income through their network-based facilities—facts that increase the exposure and increase the impact when security is breached.

Cisco routers can be used as part of a good overall security strategy. One of the most important tools in Cisco IOS software used as part of that strategy are access control lists (ACL). ACLs define rules that can be used to prevent some packets from flowing through the network. Whether you simply want to restrict access to the payroll server to only people in the payroll department, or whether you are trying to stop Internet hackers from bringing your e-commerce web server to its knees, IOS ACLs can be a key security tool that is part of a larger security strategy.

This chapter is in Part II of this book, which is oriented toward IP routing topics. The reason that it is in Part II is that the most typical use of ACLs on the CCNA exams is to filter packets. So, whereas Chapters 4 and 5 discuss various features that impact the IP routing process to allow packets to flow, this chapter examines ACLs that then prevent selected packets from flowing.

"Do I Know This Already?" Quiz

The "Do I Know This Already?" quiz allows you to assess whether you should read the entire chapter. If you miss no more than one of these ten self-assessment questions, you might want to move ahead to the "Exam Preparation Tasks" section. Table 6-1 lists the major headings in this chapter and the "Do I Know This Already?" quiz questions covering the material in those sections. This helps you assess your knowledge of these specific areas. The answers to the "Do I Know This Already?" quiz appear in Appendix A.

Table 6-1   *"Do I Know This Already?" Foundation Topics Section-to-Question Mapping*

Foundation Topics Section	Questions
Standard IP Access Control Lists	1–3
Extended IP Access Control Lists	4–6
Advances in Managing ACL Configuration	7 and 8
Miscellaneous ACL Topics	9 and 10

1. Barney is a host with IP address 10.1.1.1 in subnet 10.1.1.0/24. Which of the following are things that a standard IP ACL could be configured to do?

    a. Match the exact source IP address

    b. Match IP addresses 10.1.1.1 through 10.1.1.4 with one **access-list** command without matching other IP addresses

    c. Match all IP addresses in Barney's subnet with one **access-list** command without matching other IP addresses

    d. Match only the packet's destination IP address

2. Which of the following wildcard masks is most useful for matching all IP packets in subnet 10.1.128.0, mask 255.255.255.0?

    a. 0.0.0.0

    b. 0.0.0.31

    c. 0.0.0.240

    d. 0.0.0.255

    e. 0.0.15.0

    f. 0.0.248.255

3. Which of the following wildcard masks is most useful for matching all IP packets in subnet 10.1.128.0, mask 255.255.240.0?

    a. 0.0.0.0

    b. 0.0.0.31

    c. 0.0.0.240

    d. 0.0.0.255

    e. 0.0.15.255

    f. 0.0.248.255

4. Which of the following fields cannot be compared based on an extended IP ACL?

   a. Protocol

   b. Source IP address

   c. Destination IP address

   d. TOS byte

   e. URL

   f. Filename for FTP transfers

5. Which of the following **access-list** commands permits traffic that matches packets going from host 10.1.1.1 to all web servers whose IP addresses begin with 172.16.5?

   a. **access-list 101 permit tcp host 10.1.1.1 172.16.5.0 0.0.0.255 eq www**

   b. **access-list 1951 permit ip host 10.1.1.1 172.16.5.0 0.0.0.255 eq www**

   c. **access-list 2523 permit ip host 10.1.1.1 eq www 172.16.5.0 0.0.0.255**

   d. **access-list 2523 permit tcp host 10.1.1.1 eq www 172.16.5.0 0.0.0.255**

   e. **access-list 2523 permit tcp host 10.1.1.1 172.16.5.0 0.0.0.255 eq www**

6. Which of the following **access-list** commands permits traffic that matches packets going to any web client from all web servers whose IP addresses begin with 172.16.5?

   a. **access-list 101 permit tcp host 10.1.1.1 172.16.5.0 0.0.0.255 eq www**

   b. **access-list 1951 permit ip host 10.1.1.1 172.16.5.0 0.0.0.255 eq www**

   c. **access-list 2523 permit tcp any eq www 172.16.5.0 0.0.0.255**

   d. **access-list 2523 permit tcp 172.16.5.0 0.0.0.255 eq www 172.16.5.0 0.0.0.255**

   e. **access-list 2523 permit tcp 172.16.5.0 0.0.0.255 eq www any**

7. Which of the following fields can be compared using a named extended IP ACL but not a numbered extended IP ACL?

   a. Protocol

   b. Source IP address

   c. Destination IP address

   d. TOS byte

   e. None of the other answers are correct.

8. In a router running IOS 12.3, an engineer needs to delete the second line in ACL 101, which currently has four commands configured. Which of the following options could be used?

    a. Delete the entire ACL and reconfigure the three ACL statements that should remain in the ACL.

    b. Delete one line from the ACL using the **no access-list...** command.

    c. Delete one line from the ACL by entering ACL configuration mode for the ACL and then deleting only the second line based on its sequence number.

    d. Delete the last three lines from the ACL from ACL configuration mode, and then add the last two statements back into the ACL.

9. What general guideline should you follow when placing extended IP ACLs?

    a. Perform all filtering on output if at all possible.

    b. Put more-general statements early in the ACL.

    c. Filter packets as close to the source as possible.

    d. Order the ACL commands based on the source IP addresses, lowest to highest, to improve performance.

10. Which of the following tools requires the end user to telnet to a router to gain access to hosts on the other side of the router?

    a. Named ACLs

    b. Reflexive ACLs

    c. Dynamic ACLs

    d. Time-based ACLs

Foundation Topics

Cisco IOS has supported IP ACLs almost since the original commercial Cisco routers were introduced in the late 1980s. IOS identified these ACLs with a number. Years later, as part of the introduction of IOS 11.2, Cisco added the ability to create named ACLs. These named ACLs provide some other minor benefits as compared to numbered ACLs, but both could be used to filter the exact same packets with the exact same rules. Finally, with the introduction of IOS 12.3, Cisco improved ACL support again, particularly with how IOS allows engineers to edit existing ACLs. This latest major step in the progression of ACLs over the years makes numbered and named ACLs support the exact same features, other than the one obvious difference of using either a number or a name to identify the ACL.

Because of the historical progression of Cisco's support for ACLs, the CCNA exams still cover a lot of the same information and configuration commands that have been used with Cisco routers for almost 20 years. To support all that history, this chapter spends most of its time explaining IP ACLs—numbered IP ACLs—using the same commands and syntax available in IOS for a long time. In particular, this chapter begins with a description of the simplest types of numbered IP ACLs—standard IP ACLs. The second major section then examines the more-complex extended IP ACLs, which can be used to examine many more fields inside an IP packet. Following that, the next section of the chapter describes the deepening support for ACLs in IOS—both the introduction of support for named ACLs with IOS version 11.2, and the later addition of support for ACL sequence numbers and enhanced ACL editing with IOS 12.3. The chapter concludes by covering miscellaneous ACL topics.

Standard IP Access Control Lists

IP ACLs cause a router to discard some packets based on criteria defined by the network engineer. The goal of these filters is to prevent unwanted traffic in the network—whether preventing hackers from penetrating the network or just preventing employees from using systems they shouldn't. Access lists should simply be part of an organization's security policy.

By the way, IP access lists can also be used to filter routing updates, to match packets for prioritization, to match packets for VPN tunneling, and to match packets for implementing quality-of-service features. You will also see ACLs used as part of configuring Network Address Translation (NAT) in Chapter 16, "Network Address Translation." So you will see ACLs in most of the other Cisco certification exams as you move on in your career.

This chapter covers two main categories of IOS IP ACLs—standard and extended. Standard ACLs use simpler logic, and extended ACLs use more-complex logic. The first section of this chapter covers standard IP ACLs, followed by a section on extended IP ACLs. Several sections related to both types of ACLs close the chapter.

Standard IP ACL Concepts

Engineers need to make two major choices for any ACL that will filter IP packets: which packets to filter, and where in the network to place the ACL. Figure 6-1 serves as an example. In this case, imagine that Bob is not allowed to access Server1, but Larry is.

Figure 6-1   *Locations Where Access List Logic Can Be Applied in the Network*

Filtering logic could be configured on any of the three routers and on any of their interfaces. The dotted arrowed lines in the figure show the most appropriate points at which to apply the filtering logic in an ACL. Because Bob's traffic is the only traffic that needs to be filtered, and the goal is to stop access to Server1, the access list could be applied at either R1 or R3. And because Bob's attempted traffic to Server1 would not need to go through R2, R2 would not be a good place to put the access list logic. For the sake of discussion, assume that R1 should have the access list applied.

Cisco IOS software applies the filtering logic of an ACL either as a packet enters an interface or as it exits the interface. In other words, IOS associates an ACL with an interface, and specifically for traffic either entering or exiting the interface. After you have chosen the router on which you want to place the access list, you must choose the interface on which to apply the access logic, as well as whether to apply the logic for inbound or outbound packets.

For instance, imagine that you want to filter Bob's packets sent to Server1. Figure 6-2 shows the options for filtering the packet.

Figure 6-2 *Internal Processing in R1 in Relation to Where R1 Can Filter Packets*

Key
Topic

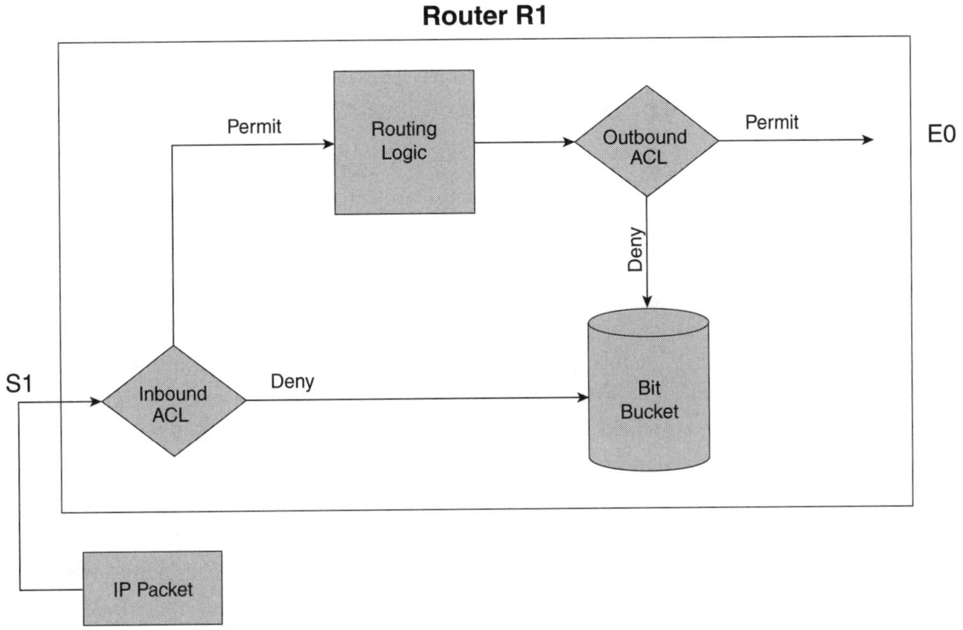

Filtering logic can be applied to packets entering S1 or to packets exiting E0 on R1 to match the packet sent by Bob to Server1. In general, you can filter packets by creating and enabling access lists for both incoming and outgoing packets on each interface. Here are some key features of Cisco access lists:

■ Packets can be filtered as they enter an interface, before the routing decision.

■ Packets can be filtered before they exit an interface, after the routing decision.

■ *Deny* is the term used in Cisco IOS software to imply that the packet will be filtered.

■ *Permit* is the term used in Cisco IOS software to imply that the packet will not be filtered.

■ The filtering logic is configured in the access list.

■ At the end of every access list is an implied "deny all traffic" statement. Therefore, if a packet does not match any of your access list statements, it is blocked.

For example, you might create an access list in R1 and enable it on R1's S1 interface. The access list would look for packets that came from Bob. Therefore, the access list would need to be enabled for inbound packets, because in this network, packets from Bob enter S1, and packets to Bob exit S1.

Access lists have two major steps in their logic: matching and action. Matching logic examines each packet and determines whether it matches the **access-list** statement. For instance, Bob's IP address would be used to match packets sent from Bob. IP ACLs tell the router to take one of two actions when a statement is matched: deny or permit. Deny means to discard the packet, and permit implies that the packet should continue on its way.

So the access list for preventing Bob's traffic to the server might go something like this:

> Look for packets with Bob's source IP address and Server1's destination IP address. When you see them, discard them. If you see any other packets, do not discard them.

Not surprisingly, IP ACLs can get a lot more difficult than those in real life. Even a short list of matching criteria can create complicated access lists on a variety of interfaces in a variety of routers. I've even heard of a couple of large networks with a few full-time people who do nothing but plan and implement access lists!

Cisco calls its packet-filtering features "access control lists" in part because the logic is created with multiple configuration commands that are considered to be in the same list. When an access list has multiple entries, IOS searches the list sequentially until the first statement is matched. The matched statement determines the action to be taken. The two diamond shapes in Figure 6-2 represent the application of access list logic.

The logic that IOS uses with a multiple-entry ACL can be summarized as follows:

Key Topic

1. The matching parameters of the **access-list** statement are compared to the packet.

2. If a match is made, the action defined in this **access-list** statement (permit or deny) is performed.

3. If a match is not made in Step 2, repeat Steps 1 and 2 using each successive statement in the ACL until a match is made.

4. If no match is made with an entry in the access list, the deny action is performed.

Wildcard Masks

IOS IP ACLs match packets by looking at the IP, TCP, and UDP headers in the packet. Extended access lists can check source and destination IP addresses, as well as source and destination port numbers, along with several other fields. However, standard IP access lists can examine only the source IP address.

Regardless of whether you use standard or extended IP ACLs, you can tell the router to match based on the entire IP address or just a part of the IP address. For instance, if you wanted to stop Bob from sending packets to Server1, you would look at the entire IP address of Bob and Server1 in the access list. But what if the criteria were to stop all hosts in Bob's subnet from getting to Server1? Because all hosts in Bob's subnet have the same numbers in their first 3 octets, the access list could just check the first 3 octets of the address to match all packets with a single **access-list** command.

Cisco *wildcard masks* define the portion of the IP address that should be examined. When defining the ACL statements, as you'll see in the next section of this chapter, you can define a wildcard mask along with the IP address. The wildcard mask tells the router which part of the IP address in the configuration statement must be compared with the packet header.

For example, suppose that one mask implies that the whole packet should be checked and another implies that only the first 3 octets of the address need to be examined. (You might choose to do that to match all IP hosts in the same subnet when using a subnet mask of 255.255.255.0.) To perform this matching, Cisco access lists use wildcard masks.

Wildcard masks look similar to subnet masks, but they are not the same. Wildcard masks represent a 32-bit number, as do subnet masks. However, the wildcard mask's 0 bits tell the router that those corresponding bits in the address must be compared when performing the matching logic. The binary 1s in the wildcard mask tell the router that those bits do not need to be compared. In fact, many people call these bits the "don't care" bits.

To get a sense of the idea behind a wildcard mask, Table 6-2 lists some of the more popular wildcard masks, along with their meanings.

Table 6-2   *Sample Access List Wildcard Masks*

Wildcard Mask	Binary Version of the Mask	Description
0.0.0.0	00000000.00000000.00000000.00000000	The entire IP address must match.
0.0.0.255	00000000.00000000.00000000.11111111	Just the first 24 bits must match.
0.0.255.255	00000000.00000000.11111111.11111111	Just the first 16 bits must match.
0.255.255.255	00000000.11111111.11111111.11111111	Just the first 8 bits must match.

continues

Table 6-2 *Sample Access List Wildcard Masks (Continued)*

Wildcard Mask	Binary Version of the Mask	Description
255.255.255.255	11111111.11111111.11111111.11111111	Automatically considered to match any and all addresses.
0.0.15.255	00000000.00000000.00001111.11111111	Just the first 20 bits must match.
0.0.3.255	00000000.00000000.00000011.11111111	Just the first 22 bits must match.

The first several examples show typical uses of the wildcard mask. As you can see, it is not a subnet mask. A wildcard of 0.0.0.0 means that the entire IP address must be examined, and be equal, to be considered a match. 0.0.0.255 means that the last octet automatically matches, but the first 3 must be examined, and so on. More generally, the wildcard mask means the following:

> Bit positions of binary 0 mean that the access list compares the corresponding bit position in the IP address and makes sure it is equal to the same bit position in the address configured in the **access-list** statement. Bit positions of binary 1 are "don't care" bits. Those bit positions are immediately considered to be a match.

The last two rows of Table 6-2 show two reasonable, but not obvious, wildcard masks. 0.0.15.255 in binary is 20 binary 0s followed by 12 binary 1s. This means that the first 20 bits must match. Similarly, 0.0.3.255 means that the first 22 bits must be examined to find out if they match. Why are these useful? If the subnet mask is 255.255.240.0, and you want to match all hosts in the same subnet, the 0.0.15.255 wildcard means that all network and subnet bits must be matched, and all host bits are automatically considered to match. Likewise, if you want to filter all hosts in a subnet that uses subnet mask 255.255.252.0, the wildcard mask 0.0.3.255 matches the network and subnet bits. In general, if you want a wildcard mask that helps you match all hosts in a subnet, invert the subnet mask, and you have the correct wildcard mask.

A Quicker Alternative for Interpreting Wildcard Masks

Both IP standard ACLs (source IP address only) and extended ACLs (both source and destination addresses) can be configured to examine all or part of an IP address based on the wildcard mask. However, particularly for the exams, working with the masks in binary may be slow and laborious unless you master binary-to-decimal and decimal-to-binary conversions. This section suggests an easier method of working with ACL wildcard masks that works well if you have already mastered subnetting math.

In many cases, an ACL needs to match all hosts in a particular subnet. To match a subnet with an ACL, you can use the following shortcut:

■   Use the subnet number as the address value in the **access-list** command.

■   Use a wildcard mask found by subtracting the subnet mask from 255.255.255.255.

Key Topic

For example, for subnet 172.16.8.0 255.255.252.0, use the subnet number (172.16.8.0) as the *address* parameter, and then do the following math to find the wildcard mask:

$$
\begin{array}{r}
255.255.255.255 \\
- \ 255.255.252.0 \\
\hline
0. \quad 0. \quad 3.255
\end{array}
$$

Some exam questions may not ask that you pick the ACL statement that needs to be configured, instead asking that you interpret some existing **access-list** commands. Typically, these questions list preconfigured ACL statements, or you need to display the contents of an ACL from a router simulator, and you need to decide which statement a particular packet matches. To do that, you need to determine the range of IP addresses matched by a particular address/wildcard mask combination in each ACL statement.

If you have mastered subnetting math using any of the decimal shortcuts, avoiding binary math, another shortcut can be used to analyze each existing address/wildcard pair in each ACL command. To do so:

Step 1   Use the address in the **access-list** command as if it were a subnet number.

Key Topic

Step 2   Use the number found by subtracting the wildcard mask from 255.255.255.255 as a subnet mask.

Step 3   Treat the values from the first two steps as a subnet number and subnet mask, and find the broadcast address for the subnet. The ACL matches the range of addresses between the subnet number and broadcast address, inclusively.

The range of addresses identified by this process is the same range of addresses matched by the ACL. So, if you can already find a subnet's range of addresses quickly and easily, using this process to change an ACL's math may help you find the answer more quickly on the exams. For example, with the command **access-list 1 permit 172.16.200.0 0.0.7.255**, you would first think of 172.16.200.0 as a subnet number. Then you could calculate the assumed subnet mask of 255.255.248.0, as follows:

```
  255.255.255.255
–   0.  0.  7.255
  255.255.248.0
```

From there, using any process you like, use subnetting math to determine that the broadcast address of this subnet would be 172.16.207.255. So, the range of addresses matched by this ACL statement would be 172.16.200.0 through 172.16.207.255.

NOTE   CD-only Appendix F, Scenario 3, provides an opportunity to practice choosing a wildcard mask to match hosts in a particular subnet.

Standard IP Access List Configuration

ACL configuration tends to be simpler than the task of interpreting the meaning and actions taken by an ACL. To that end, this section presents a plan of attack for configuring ACLs. Then it shows a couple of examples that review both the configuration and the concepts implemented by those ACLs.

The generic syntax of the standard ACL configuration command is

access-list *access-list-number* {**deny** | **permit**} *source* [*source-wildcard*]

A standard access list uses a series of **access-list** commands that have the same number. The **access-list** commands with the same number are considered to be in the same list, with the commands being listed in the same order in which they were added to the configuration. Each **access-list** command can match a range of source IP addresses. If a match occurs, the ACL either allows the packet to keep going (**permit** action) or discards the packet (**deny** action). Each standard ACL can match all, or only part, of the packet's source IP address. Note that for standard IP ACLs, the number range for ACLs is 1 to 99 and 1300 to 1999.

The following list outlines a suggested configuration process. You do not need to memorize the process itself for the exam; it is simply listed here as a convenient study review aid.

Step 1 Plan the location (router and interface) and direction (in or out) on that interface:

    a. Standard ACLs should be placed near to the destination of the packets so that it does not unintentionally discard packets that should not be discarded.

    b. Because standard ACLs can only match a packet's source IP address, identify the source IP addresses of packets as they go in the direction that the ACL is examining.

Step 2 Configure one or more **access-list** global configuration commands to create the ACL, keeping the following in mind:

    a. The list is searched sequentially, using first-match logic. In other words, when a packet matches one of the **access-list** statements, the search is over, even if the packet would match subsequent statements.

    b. The default action, if a packet does not match any of the **access-list** commands, is to **deny** (discard) the packet.

Step 3 Enable the ACL on the chosen router interface, in the correct direction, using the **ip access-group** *number* {**in** | **out**} interface subcommand.

Next, two examples of standard ACLs are shown.

Standard IP ACL: Example 1

Example 6-1 attempts to stop Bob's traffic to Server1. As shown in Figure 6-1, Bob is not allowed to access Server1. In Example 6-1, the configuration enables an ACL for all packets going out R1's Ethernet0 interface. The ACL matches the source address in the packet—Bob's IP address. Note that the **access-list** commands are at the bottom of the example because the **show running-config** command also lists them near the bottom, after the interface configuration commands.

Example 6-1   *Standard Access List on R1 Stopping Bob from Reaching Server1*

```
interface Ethernet0
 ip address 172.16.1.1 255.255.255.0
 ip access-group 1 out
!
access-list 1 remark stop all traffic whose source IP is Bob
access-list 1 deny 172.16.3.10 0.0.0.0
access-list 1 permit 0.0.0.0 255.255.255.255
```

First, focus on the basic syntax of the commands. Standard IP access lists use a number in the range of 1 to 99 or 1300 to 1999. This example uses ACL number 1 versus the other available numbers for no particular reason. (There is absolutely no difference in using one number or another, as long as it is in the correct range. In other words, list 1 is no better or worse than list 99.) The **access-list** commands, under which the matching and action logic are defined, are global configuration commands. To enable the ACL on an interface and define the direction of packets to which the ACL is applied, the **ip access-group** command is used. In this case, it enables the logic for ACL 1 on Ethernet0 for packets going out the interface.

ACL 1 keeps packets sent by Bob from exiting R1's Ethernet interface, based on the matching logic of the **access-list 1 deny 172.16.3.10 0.0.0.0** command. The wildcard mask of 0.0.0.0 means "match all 32 bits," so only packets whose IP address exactly matches 172.16.3.10 match this statement and are discarded. The **access-list 1 permit 0.0.0.0 255.255.255.255** command, the last statement in the list, matches all packets, because the wildcard mask of 255.255.255.255 means "don't care" about all 32 bits. In other words, the statement matches all IP source addresses. These packets are permitted.

Finally, note that the engineer also added an **access-list 1 remark** command to the ACL. This command allows the addition of a text comment, or remark, so that you can track the purpose of the ACL. The remark only shows up in the configuration; it is not listed in **show** command output.

Although it's a seemingly simple example, in this case access list 1 also prevents Bob's packets sent to Server2 from being delivered. With the topology shown in Figure 6-1, an outbound standard ACL on R1's E0 interface cannot somehow deny Bob access to Server1 while permitting access to Server2. To do that, an extended ACL is needed that can check both the source and destination IP addresses.

Interestingly, if the commands in Example 6-1 are entered in configuration mode, IOS changes the configuration syntax of a couple of commands. The output of the **show running-config** command in Example 6-2 shows what IOS actually places in the configuration file.

Example 6-2 *Revised Standard Access List Stopping Bob from Reaching Server1*

```
interface Ethernet0
 ip address 172.16.1.1 255.255.255.0
 ip access-group 1 out

access-list 1 remark stop all traffic whose source IP is Bob
access-list 1 deny host 172.16.3.10
access-list 1 permit any
```

The commands in Example 6-1 are changed based on three factors. Cisco IOS allows both an older style and newer style of configuration for some parameters. Example 6-1 shows the older style, and the router changes to the equivalent newer-style configuration in Example 6-2. First, the use of a wildcard mask of 0.0.0.0 does indeed mean that the router should match that specific host IP address. The newer-style configuration uses the **host** keyword in *front* of the specific IP address. The other change to the newer-style configuration involves the use of wildcard mask 255.255.255.255 to mean "match anything." The newer-style configuration uses the keyword **any** to replace both the IP address and 255.255.255.255 wildcard mask. **any** simply means that any IP address is matched.

Standard IP ACL: Example 2

The second standard IP ACL example exposes more ACL issues. Figure 6-3 and Examples 6-3 and 6-4 show a basic use of standard IP access lists, with two typical oversights in the first attempt at a complete solution. The criteria for the access lists are as follows:

- Sam is not allowed access to Bugs or Daffy.

- Hosts on the Seville Ethernet are not allowed access to hosts on the Yosemite Ethernet.

- All other combinations are allowed.

Figure 6-3   *Network Diagram for Standard Access List Example*

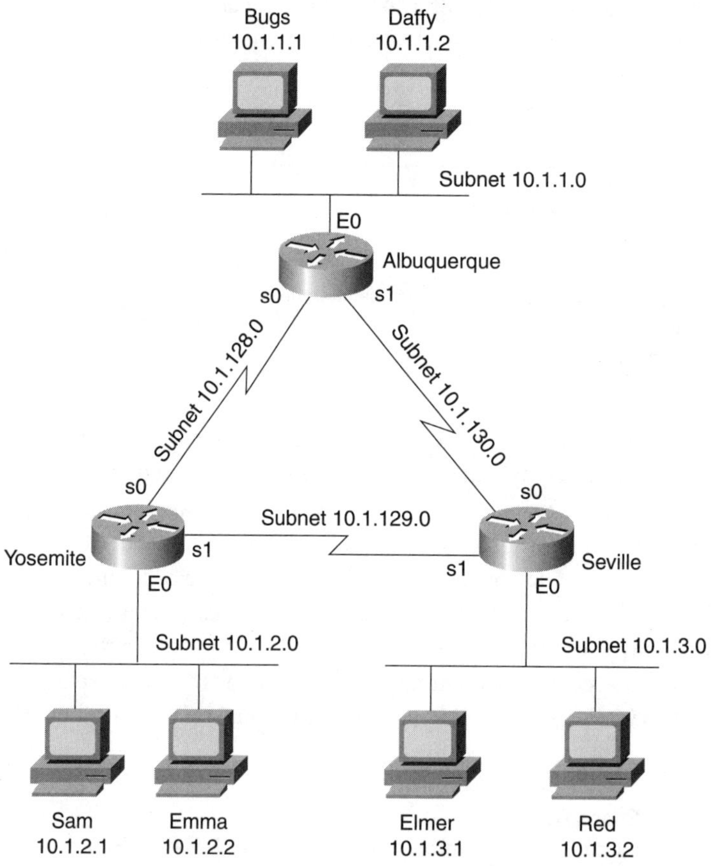

Example 6-3   *Yosemite Configuration for Standard Access List Example*

```
interface serial 0
 ip access-group 3 out
!
access-list 3 deny host 10.1.2.1
access-list 3 permit any
```

Example 6-4   *Seville Configuration for Standard Access List Example*

```
interface serial 1
 ip access-group 4 out
!
access-list 4 deny 10.1.3.0    0.0.0.255
access-list 4 permit any
```

At first glance, these two access lists seem to perform the desired function. ACL 3, enabled for packets exiting Yosemite's S0 interface, takes care of criterion 1, because ACL 3 matches Sam's IP address exactly. ACL 4 in Seville, enabled for packets exiting its S1 interface, takes care of criterion 2, because ACL 4 matches all packets coming from subnet 10.1.3.0/24. Both routers meet criterion 3: A wildcard **permit any** is used at the end of each access list to override the default, which is to discard all other packets. So all the criteria appear to be met.

However, when one of the WAN links fails, some holes can appear in the ACLs. For example, if the link from Albuquerque to Yosemite fails, Yosemite learns a route to 10.1.1.0/24 through Seville. Packets from Sam, forwarded by Yosemite and destined for hosts in Albuquerque, leave Yosemite's serial 1 interface without being filtered. So criterion 1 is no longer met. Similarly, if the link from Seville to Yosemite fails, Seville routes packets through Albuquerque, routing around the access list enabled on Seville, so criterion 2 is no longer met.

Example 6-5 illustrates an alternative solution, with all the configuration on Yosemite—one that works even when some of the links fail.

Example 6-5 *Yosemite Configuration for Standard Access List Example: Alternative Solution to Examples 6-3 and 6-4*

```
interface serial 0
 ip access-group 3 out
!
interface serial 1
 ip access-group 3 out
!
interface ethernet 0
 ip access-group 4 out
!
access-list 3 remark meets criteria 1
access-list 3 deny host 10.1.2.1
access-list 3 permit any
!
access-list 4 remark meets criteria 2
access-list 4 deny 10.1.3.0 0.0.0.255
access-list 4 permit any
```

The configuration shown in Example 6-5 solves the problem from Examples 6-3 and 6-4. ACL 3 checks for Sam's source IP address, and it is enabled on both serial links for outbound traffic. So, of the traffic that is rerouted because of a WAN link failure, the packets from Sam are still filtered. To meet criterion 2, Yosemite filters packets as they exit its

Ethernet interface. Therefore, regardless of which of the two WAN links the packets enter, packets from Seville's subnet are not forwarded to Yosemite's Ethernet.

Extended IP Access Control Lists

Extended IP access lists have both similarities and differences compared to standard IP ACLs. Just like standard lists, you enable extended access lists on interfaces for packets either entering or exiting the interface. IOS searches the list sequentially. The first statement matched stops the search through the list and defines the action to be taken. All these features are true of standard access lists as well.

The one key difference between the two is the variety of fields in the packet that can be compared for matching by extended access lists. A single extended ACL statement can examine multiple parts of the packet headers, requiring that all the parameters be matched correctly to match that one ACL statement. That matching logic is what makes extended access lists both much more useful and much more complex than standard IP ACLs.

This section starts with coverage of the extended IP ACL concepts that differ from standard ACLs—namely, the matching logic. Following that, the configuration details are covered.

Extended IP ACL Concepts

Extended access lists create powerful matching logic by examining many parts of a packet. Figure 6-4 shows several of the fields in the packet headers that can be matched.

Figure 6-4 *Extended Access List Matching Options*

The top set of headers shows the IP protocol type, which identifies what header follows the IP header. You can specify all IP packets, or those with TCP headers, UDP headers, ICMP, and so on, by checking the Protocol field. You can also check both the source and destination IP addresses, as shown. The lower part of the figure shows an example with a TCP header following the IP header, pointing out the location of the TCP source and destination port numbers. These port numbers identify the application. For instance, the web uses port 80 by default. If you specify a protocol of TCP or UDP, you can also check the port numbers.

Table 6-3 summarizes the most commonly used fields that can be matched with an extended IP ACL, as compared with standard IP ACLs.

Table 6-3 *Standard and Extended IP Access Lists: Matching*

Key
Topic

Type of Access List	What Can Be Matched
Both standard and extended ACLs	Source IP address
	Portions of the source IP address using a wildcard mask
Only extended ACLs	Destination IP address
	Portions of the destination IP address using a wildcard mask
	Protocol type (TCP, UDP, ICMP, IGRP, IGMP, and others)
	Source port
	Destination port
	All TCP flows except the first
	IP TOS
	IP precedence

Knowing what to look for is just half the battle. IOS checks all the matching information configured in a single **access-list** command. Everything must match for that single command to be considered a match and for the defined action to be taken. The options start with the protocol type (IP, TCP, UDP, ICMP, and others), followed by the source IP address, source port, destination IP address, and destination port number. Table 6-4 lists several sample **access-list** commands, with several options configured and some explanations. Only the matching options are shaded.

Table 6-4 *Extended **access-list** Commands and Logic Explanations*

access-list Statement	What It Matches
access-list 101 deny ip any host 10.1.1.1	Any IP packet, any source IP address, with a destination IP address of 10.1.1.1.
access-list 101 deny tcp any gt 1023 host 10.1.1.1 eq 23	Packets with a TCP header, any source IP address, with a source port greater than (**gt**) 1023, a destination IP address of exactly 10.1.1.1, and a destination port equal to (**eq**) 23.
access-list 101 deny tcp any host 10.1.1.1 eq 23	The same as the preceding example, but any source port matches, because that parameter is omitted in this case.
access-list 101 deny tcp any host 10.1.1.1 eq telnet	The same as the preceding example. The **telnet** keyword is used instead of port 23.
access-list 101 deny udp 1.0.0.0 0.255.255.255 lt 1023 any	A packet with a source in network 1.0.0.0, using UDP with a source port less than (**lt**) 1023, with any destination IP address.

Matching TCP and UDP Port Numbers

Extended IP ACLs allow for the matching of the IP header protocol field, as well as matching the source and destination TCP or UDP port numbers. However, many people have difficulty when first configuring ACLs that match port numbers, particularly when matching the source port number.

When considering any exam question that involves TCP or UDP ports, keep the following key points in mind:

■ The **access-list** command must use protocol keyword **tcp** to be able to match TCP ports and the **udp** keyword to be able to match UDP ports. The **ip** keyword does not allow for matching the port numbers.

■ The source port and destination port parameters on the **access-list** command are positional. In other words, their location in the command determines if the parameter examines the source or destination port.

■ Remember that ACLs can match packets sent to a server by comparing the destination
port to the well-known port number. However, ACLs need to match the source port for
packets sent by the server.

■ It is useful to memorize the most popular TCP and UDP applications, and their well-
known ports, as listed in Table 6-5, as shown later in this chapter.

For example, consider the simple network shown in Figure 6-5. The FTP server sits on the
right, with the client on the left. The figure shows the syntax of an ACL that matches

■ Packets that include a TCP header

■ Packets sent from the client subnet

■ Packets sent to the server subnet

■ Packets with TCP destination port 21

Figure 6-5   *Filtering Packets Based on Destination Port*

access-list 101 permit tcp 172.16.1.0 0.0.0.255 172.16.3.0 0.0.0.255 eq 21

To fully appreciate the matching of the destination port with the **eq 21** parameter, consider
packets moving left to right, from PC1 to the server. If the server is using well-known port
21 (FTP control port), the packet sent by PC1, in the TCP header, has a destination port
value of 21. The ACL syntax includes the **eq 21** parameter *after* the destination IP address,
with this position in the command implying that this parameter matches the destination
port. As a result, the ACL statement shown in the figure would match this packet, and the
destination port of 21, if used in any of the four locations implied by the four thick arrowed
lines in the figure.

Conversely, Figure 6-6 shows the reverse flow, with a packet sent by the server back toward
PC1. In this case, the packet's TCP header has a source port of 21, so the ACL must check
the source port value of 21, and the ACL must be located on different interfaces.

Key Topic

Figure 6-6 *Filtering Packets Based on Source Port*

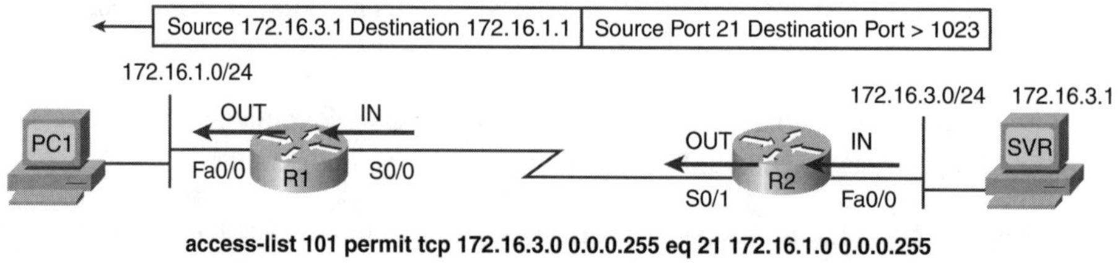
Source 172.16.3.1 Destination 172.16.1.1
Source Port 21 Destination Port > 1023
172.16.1.0/24
OUT
IN
PC1
Fa0/0
R1
S0/0
172.16.3.0/24
172.16.3.1
OUT
IN
R2
S0/1
Fa0/0
SVR
access-list 101 permit tcp 172.16.3.0 0.0.0.255 eq 21 172.16.1.0 0.0.0.255

For exam questions that require ACLs and matching of port numbers, first consider whether the question requires that the ACL be placed in a certain location and direction. If so, you can then determine if that ACL would process packets either sent to the server or sent by the server. At that point, you can decide whether you need to check the source or destination port in the packet.

For reference, Table 6-5 lists many of the popular port numbers and their transport layer protocols and applications. Note that the syntax of the **access-list** commands accepts both the port numbers and a shorthand version of the application name.

Table 6-5 *Popular Applications and Their Well-Known Port Numbers*

Port Number(s)	Protocol	Application	Application Name Keyword in access-list Command Syntax
20	TCP	FTP data	**ftp-data**
21	TCP	FTP control	**ftp**
22	TCP	SSH	—
23	TCP	Telnet	**telnet**
25	TCP	SMTP	**smtp**
53	UDP, TCP	DNS	**domain**
67, 68	UDP	DHCP	**bootps(67)** **bootpc(68)**
69	UDP	TFTP	**tftp**
80	TCP	HTTP (WWW)	**www**
110	TCP	POP3	**pop3**
161	UDP	SNMP	**snmp**
443	TCP	SSL	—
16,384–32,767	UDP	RTP-based voice (VoIP) and video	—

Extended IP ACL Configuration

Because extended ACLs can match so many different fields in the various headers in an IP packet, the command syntax cannot be easily summarized in a single generic command. For reference, Table 6-6 lists the syntax of the two most common generic commands.

Table 6-6 *Extended IP Access List Configuration Commands*

Command	Configuration Mode and Description
access-list *access-list-number* {**deny** | **permit**} *protocol source source-wildcard destination destination-wildcard* [**log** | **log-input**]	Global command for extended numbered access lists. Use a number between 100 and 199 or 2000 and 2699, inclusive.
access-list *access-list-number* {**deny** | **permit**} {**tcp** | **udp**} *source source-wildcard* [*operator* [*port*]] *destination destination-wildcard* [*operator* [*port*]] [**established**] [**log**]	A version of the **access-list** command with TCP-specific parameters.

The configuration process for extended ACLs mostly matches the same process used for standard ACLs. The location and direction should be chosen first so that the ACL's parameters can be planned based on the information in the packets flowing in that direction. The ACL should be configured with **access-list** commands. Then the ACL should be enabled with the same **ip access-group** command used with standard ACLs. All these steps remain the same as with standard ACLs. However, the differences in configuration are summarized as follows:

- Extended ACLs should be placed as close as possible to the source of the packets to be filtered, because extended ACLs can be configured so that they do not discard packets that should not be discarded. So filtering close to the source of the packets saves some bandwidth.

- All fields in one **access-list** command must match a packet for the packet to be considered to match that **access-list** statement.

- The extended **access-list** command uses numbers between 100–199 and 2000–2699, with no number being inherently better than another.

The extended version of the **access-list** command allows for matching of port numbers using several basic operations, such as equal-to and less-than. However, the commands use abbreviations, so Table 6-7 lists the abbreviations and a fuller explanation.

Key
Topic

Table 6-7   *Operators Used When Matching Port Numbers*

Operator in the access-list Command	Meaning
eq	Equal to
neq	Not equal to
lt	Less than
gt	Greater than
range	Range of port numbers

Extended IP Access Lists: Example 1

This example focuses on understanding the basic syntax. In this case, Bob is denied access to all FTP servers on R1's Ethernet, and Larry is denied access to Server1's web server. Figure 6-7 is a reminder of the network topology. Example 6-6 shows the configuration on R1.

Figure 6-7   *Network Diagram for Extended Access List Example 1*

Example 6-6   *R1's Extended Access List: Example 1*

```
interface Serial0
 ip address 172.16.12.1 255.255.255.0
 ip access-group 101 in
!
interface Serial1
 ip address 172.16.13.1 255.255.255.0
 ip access-group 101 in
!
access-list 101 remark Stop Bob to FTP servers, and Larry to Server1 web
access-list 101 deny tcp host 172.16.3.10 172.16.1.0 0.0.0.255 eq ftp
access-list 101 deny tcp host 172.16.2.10 host 172.16.1.100 eq www
access-list 101 permit ip any any
```

In Example 6-6, the first ACL statement prevents Bob's access to FTP servers in subnet 172.16.1.0. The second statement prevents Larry's access to web services on Server1. The final statement permits all other traffic.

Focusing on the syntax for a moment, there are several new items to review. First, the access list number for extended access lists falls in the range of 100 to 199 or 2000 to 2699. Following the **permit** or **deny** action, the *protocol* parameter defines whether you want to check for all IP packets or just those with TCP or UDP headers. When you check for TCP or UDP port numbers, you must specify the TCP or UDP protocol.

This example uses the **eq** parameter, meaning "equals," to check the destination port numbers for FTP control (keyword **ftp**) and HTTP traffic (keyword **www**). You can use the numeric values—or, for the more popular options, a more obvious text version is valid. (If you were to enter **eq 80**, the config would show **eq www**.)

In this first extended ACL example, the access lists could have been placed on R2 and R3 instead of on R1. As you will read near the end of this chapter, Cisco makes some specific recommendations about where to locate IP ACLs. With extended IP ACLs, Cisco suggests that you locate them as close as possible to the source of the packet. Therefore, Example 6-7 achieves the same goal as Example 6-6 of stopping Bob's access to FTP servers at the main site, and it does so with an ACL on R3.

Example 6-7 *R3's Extended Access List Stopping Bob from Reaching FTP Servers Near R1*

```
interface Ethernet0
 ip address 172.16.3.1 255.255.255.0
 ip access-group 101 in

access-list 101 remark deny Bob to FTP servers in subnet 172.16.1.0/24
access-list 101 deny tcp host 172.16.3.10 172.16.1.0 0.0.0.255 eq ftp
access-list 101 permit ip any any
```

ACL 101 looks a lot like ACL 101 from Example 6-6, but this time, the ACL does not bother to check for the criteria to match Larry's traffic, because Larry's traffic will never enter R3's Ethernet 0 interface. Because the ACL has been placed on R3, near Bob, it watches for packets Bob sends that enter its Ethernet0 interface. Because of the ACL, Bob's FTP traffic to 172.16.1.0/24 is denied, with all other traffic entering R3's E0 interface making it into the network. Example 6-7 does not show any logic for stopping Larry's traffic.

Extended IP Access Lists: Example 2

Example 6-8, based on the network shown in Figure 6-8, shows another example of how to use extended IP access lists. This example uses the same criteria and network topology as the second standard IP ACL example, as repeated here:

■   Sam is not allowed access to Bugs or Daffy.

■   Hosts on the Seville Ethernet are not allowed access to hosts on the Yosemite Ethernet.

■   All other combinations are allowed.

Figure 6-8   *Network Diagram for Extended Access List Example 2*

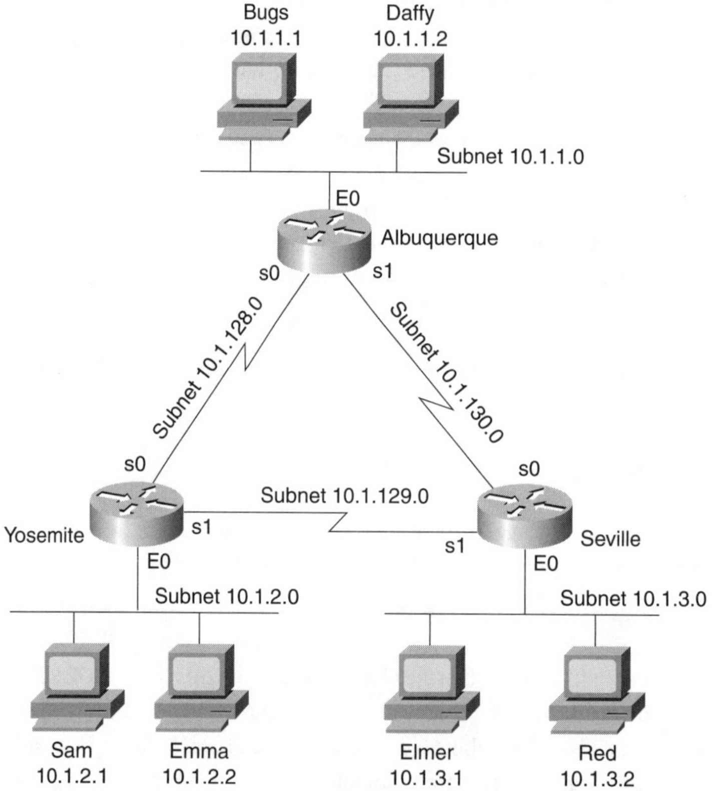

Example 6-8   *Yosemite Configuration for Extended Access List Example 2*

```
interface ethernet 0
 ip access-group 110 in
!
access-list 110 deny ip host 10.1.2.1 10.1.1.0 0.0.0.255
access-list 110 deny ip 10.1.2.0 0.0.0.255 10.1.3.0 0.0.0.255
access-list 110 permit ip any any
```

This configuration solves the problem with few statements while keeping to Cisco's design guideline of placing extended ACLs as close as possible to the source of the traffic. The ACL filters packets that enter Yosemite's E0 interface, which is the first router interface that packets sent by Sam enter. The issue of having packets "routed around" access lists on serial interfaces is taken care of with the placement on Yosemite's only Ethernet interface. Also, the filtering mandated by the second requirement (to disallow Seville's LAN hosts from accessing Yosemite's) is met by the second **access-list** statement. Stopping packet flow from Yosemite's LAN subnet to Seville's LAN subnet stops effective communication between the two subnets. Alternatively, the opposite logic could have been configured at Seville.

Advances in Managing ACL Configuration

Now that you have a good understanding of the core concepts in IOS IP ACLs, this next section examines a couple of enhancements to IOS support for ACLs: named ACLs and ACL sequence numbers. Although both features are useful and important, neither adds any function as to what a router can and cannot filter, as compared to the numbered ACLs already covered in this chapter. Instead, named ACLs and ACL sequence numbers provide the engineer with configuration options that make it easier to remember ACL names and easier to edit existing ACLs when an ACL needs to change.

Named IP Access Lists

Named ACLs, introduced with IOS version 11.2, can be used to match the same packets, with the same parameters, that can be matched with standard and extended IP ACLs. Named IP ACLs do have some differences, however, some of which make them easier to work with. The most obvious difference is that IOS identifies named ACLs using names you make up, as opposed to numbers—and you have a better chance of remembering names.

In addition to using more memorable names, the other major advantage of named ACLs over numbered ACLs, at the time they were introduced into IOS, was that you could delete individual lines in a named IP access list. Throughout the history of numbered IP ACLs and the **ip access-list** global command, until the introduction of IOS 12.3, a single line in a numbered ACL could not be deleted. For example, if you had earlier configured the **ip access-list 101 permit tcp any any eq 80** command, and then you entered the **no ip access-list 101 permit tcp any any eq 80** command, the whole ACL 101 would be deleted! The advantage of the introduction of named ACLs is that you can enter a command that removes individual lines in an ACL.

> **NOTE**   With IOS 12.3, Cisco expanded IOS to be able to delete individual lines in numbered ACLs, making IOS support for editing both named and numbered ACLs equivalent. These details are explained in the next section.

The configuration syntax is very similar between named and numbered IP access lists. The items that can be matched with a numbered standard IP access list are identical to the items that can be matched with a named standard IP access list. Likewise, the items are identical with both numbered and named extended IP access lists.

Two important configuration differences exist between old-style numbered ACLs and the newer named access lists. One key difference is that named access lists use a global command that places the user in a named IP access list submode, under which the matching and permit/deny logic is configured. The other key difference is that when a named matching statement is deleted, only that one statement is deleted.

Example 6-9 shows an example that uses named IP ACLs. It shows the changing command prompt in configuration mode, showing that the user has been placed in ACL configuration mode. It also lists the pertinent parts of the output of a **show running-config** command. It ends with an example of how you can delete individual lines in a named ACL.

Example 6-9   *Named Access List Configuration*

```
conf t
Enter configuration commands, one per line.  End with Ctrl-Z.
Router(config)#ip access-list extended barney
Router(config-ext-nacl)#permit tcp host 10.1.1.2 eq www any
Router(config-ext-nacl)#deny udp host 10.1.1.1 10.1.2.0 0.0.0.255
Router(config-ext-nacl)#deny ip 10.1.3.0 0.0.0.255 10.1.2.0 0.0.0.255
! The next statement is purposefully wrong so that the process of changing
! the list can be seen.
Router(config-ext-nacl)#deny ip 10.1.2.0 0.0.0.255 10.2.3.0 0.0.0.255

Router(config-ext-nacl)#deny ip host 10.1.1.130 host 10.1.3.2
Router(config-ext-nacl)#deny ip host 10.1.1.28 host 10.1.3.2
Router(config-ext-nacl)#permit ip any any
Router(config-ext-nacl)#interface serial1
Router(config-if)#ip access-group barney out
Router(config-if)#^Z
Router#show running-config
Building configuration...
```

Example 6-9 *Named Access List Configuration (Continued)*

```
Current configuration:

.
. (unimportant statements omitted)
.
interface serial 1
 ip access-group barney out
!
ip access-list extended barney
 permit tcp host 10.1.1.2 eq www any
 deny   udp host 10.1.1.1 10.1.2.0 0.0.0.255
 deny   ip 10.1.3.0 0.0.0.255 10.1.2.0 0.0.0.255
 deny   ip 10.1.2.0 0.0.0.255 10.2.3.0 0.0.0.255
 deny   ip host 10.1.1.130 host 10.1.3.2
 deny   ip host 10.1.1.28 host 10.1.3.2
 permit ip any any
Router#conf t
Enter configuration commands, one per line.  End with Ctrl-Z.
Router(config)#ip access-list extended barney
Router(config-ext-nacl)#no deny ip 10.1.2.0 0.0.0.255 10.2.3.0 0.0.0.255
Router(config-ext-nacl)#^Z
Router#show access-list

Extended IP access list barney
    10 permit tcp host 10.1.1.2 eq www any
    20 deny   udp host 10.1.1.1 10.1.2.0 0.0.0.255
    30 deny   ip 10.1.3.0 0.0.0.255 10.1.2.0 0.0.0.255
    50 deny   ip host 10.1.1.130 host 10.1.3.2
    60 deny   ip host 10.1.1.28 host 10.1.3.2
    70 permit ip any any
```

Example 6-9 begins with the creation of an ACL named barney. The **ip access-list extended barney** command creates the ACL, naming it barney and placing the user in ACL configuration mode. This command also tells the IOS that barney is an extended ACL. Next, seven different **permit** and **deny** statements define the matching logic and action to be taken upon a match. The **permit** and **deny** commands use the exact same syntax that the numbered **access-list** commands use, starting with the **deny** and **permit** keywords. In this example, a comment is added just before the command that is deleted later in the example.

The **show running-config** command output lists the named ACL configuration before the single entry is deleted. Next, the **no deny ip...** command deletes a single entry from the ACL. Notice that the output of the **show access-list** command still lists the ACL, with six **permit** and **deny** commands instead of seven.

Editing ACLs Using Sequence Numbers

Numbered ACLs have existed in IOS since the early days of Cisco routers. From their creation, up through IOS version 12.2, the only way to edit an existing numbered ACL—for example, to simply delete a line from the ACL—was to delete the whole ACL and then reconfigure the entire ACL. Besides being an inconvenience to the engineer, this process also caused some unfortunate side effects. When deleting the ACL, it is important to disable the ACL from all interfaces, and then delete it, reconfigure it, and enable it on the interface. Otherwise, during the reconfiguration process, before all the statements have been reconfigured, the ACL will not perform all the checks it should, sometimes causing problems, or exposing the network to various attacks.

As mentioned in the preceding section, the original IOS support for named ACLs, introduced in IOS 11.2, solved some of the editing problem. The original commands for named ACLs allowed the engineer to delete a line from an ACL, as shown in the preceding section in Example 6-9. However, the configuration commands did not allow the user to insert a new **permit** or **deny** command into the list. All new commands were added to the end of the ACL.

With IOS 12.3, Cisco introduced several more configuration options for ACLs—options that apply to both named and numbered IP ACLs. These options take advantage of an ACL sequence number that is added to each ACL **permit** or **deny** statement, with the numbers representing the sequence of statements in the ACL. ACL sequence numbers provide the following features for both numbered and named ACLs:

Key Topic

■ An individual ACL **permit** or **deny** statement can be deleted just by referencing the sequence number, without deleting the rest of the ACL.

■ Newly added **permit** and **deny** commands can be configured with a sequence number, dictating the location of the statement within the ACL.

■ Newly added **permit** and **deny** commands can be configured *without* a sequence number, with IOS creating a sequence number and placing the command at the end of the ACL.

To take advantage of the ability to delete and insert lines in an ACL, both numbered and named ACLs must use the same overall configuration style and commands used for named ACLs. The only difference in syntax is whether a name or number is used. Example 6-10 shows the configuration of a standard numbered IP ACL, using this alternative configuration style. The example shows the power of the ACL sequence number for editing. In this example, the following occurs:

Step 1 Numbered ACL 24 is configured, using this new-style configuration, with three **permit** commands.

Step 2 The **show ip access-list** command shows the three permit commands, with sequence numbers 10, 20, and 30.

Step 3   The engineer deletes only the second **permit** command, using the **no 20** ACL subcommand, which simply refers to sequence number 20.

Step 4   The **show ip access-list** command confirms that the ACL now has only two lines (sequence numbers 10 and 30).

Step 5   The engineer adds a new **permit** command to the beginning of the ACL, using the **5 deny 10.1.1.1** ACL subcommand.

Step 6   The **show ip access-list** command again confirms the changes, this time listing three **permit** commands, sequence numbers 5, 10, and 30.

> **NOTE**   For this example, note that the user does not leave configuration mode, instead using the **do** command to tell IOS to issue the **show ip access-list** EXEC command from configuration mode.

Example 6-10   *Editing ACLs Using Sequence Numbers*

```
! Step 1: The 3-line Standard Numbered IP ACL is configured.
R1#configure terminal
Enter configuration commands, one per line.  End with Ctrl-Z.
R1(config)#ip access-list standard 24
R1(config-std-nacl)#permit 10.1.1.0 0.0.0.255
R1(config-std-nacl)#permit 10.1.2.0 0.0.0.255
R1(config-std-nacl)#permit 10.1.3.0 0.0.0.255
! Step 2: Displaying the ACL's contents, without leaving configuration mode.
R1(config-std-nacl)#do show ip access-list 24
Standard IP access list 24
    10 permit 10.1.1.0, wildcard bits 0.0.0.255
    20 permit 10.1.2.0, wildcard bits 0.0.0.255
    30 permit 10.1.3.0, wildcard bits 0.0.0.255
! Step 3: Still in ACL 24 configuration mode, the line with sequence number 20 is deleted.
R1(config-std-nacl)#no 20
! Step 4: Displaying the ACL's contents again, without leaving configuration mode.
! Note that line number 20 is no longer listed.
R1(config-std-nacl)#do show ip access-list 24
Standard IP access list 24
    10 permit 10.1.1.0, wildcard bits 0.0.0.255
    30 permit 10.1.3.0, wildcard bits 0.0.0.255
! Step 5: Inserting a new first line in the ACL.
R1(config-std-nacl)#5 deny 10.1.1.1
! Step 6: Displaying the ACL's contents one last time, with the new statement (sequence
! number 5) listed first.
R1(config-std-nacl)#do show ip access-list 24
Standard IP access list 24
    5 deny    10.1.1.1
    10 permit 10.1.1.0, wildcard bits 0.0.0.255
    30 permit 10.1.3.0, wildcard bits 0.0.0.255
```

Interestingly, numbered ACLs can be configured with the new-style configuration, as shown in Example 6-10, or with the old-style configuration, using **access-list** global configuration commands, as shown in the first several examples in this chapter. In fact, you can use both styles of configuration on a single ACL. However, no matter which style of configuration is used, the **show running-config** command output still shows the old-style configuration commands. Example 6-11 demonstrates these facts, picking up where Example 6-10 ended, with the following additional steps:

Step 7   The engineer lists the configuration (**show running-config**), which lists the old-style configuration commands—even though the ACL was created with the new-style commands.

Step 8   The engineer adds a new statement to the end of the ACL, using the old-style **access-list 24 permit 10.1.4.0 0.0.0.255** global configuration command.

Step 9   The **show ip access-list** command confirms that the old-style **access-list** command from the previous step followed the rule of being added only to the end of the ACL.

Step 10 The engineer displays the configuration to confirm that the parts of ACL 24 configured with both new-style commands and old-style commands are all listed in the same old-style ACL (**show running-config**).

Example 6-11   *Adding to and Displaying a Numbered ACL Configuration*

```
! Step 7: A configuration snippet for ACL 24.
R1#show running-config
! The only lines shown are the lines from ACL 24
access-list 24 deny    10.1.1.1
access-list 24 permit 10.1.1.0 0.0.0.255
access-list 24 permit 10.1.3.0 0.0.0.255


! Step 8: Adding a new access-list 24 command
R1#configure terminal
Enter configuration commands, one per line.  End with CNTL/Z.
R1(config)#access-list 24 permit 10.1.4.0 0.0.0.255
R1(config)#^Z
! Step 9: Displaying the ACL's contents again, with sequence numbers. Note that even
! the new statement has been automatically assigned a sequence number.
R1#show ip access-list 24
Standard IP access list 24
    5 deny    10.1.1.1
    10 permit 10.1.1.0, wildcard bits 0.0.0.255
    30 permit 10.1.3.0, wildcard bits 0.0.0.255
    40 permit 10.1.4.0, wildcard bits 0.0.0.255
!
```

Example 6-11 *Adding to and Displaying a Numbered ACL Configuration (Continued)*

```
! Step 10: The numbered ACL configuration remains in old-style configuration commands.
R1#show running-config
! The only lines shown are the lines from ACL 24
access-list 24 deny    10.1.1.1
access-list 24 permit 10.1.1.0 0.0.0.255
access-list 24 permit 10.1.3.0 0.0.0.255
access-list 24 permit 10.1.4.0 0.0.0.255
```

Miscellaneous ACL Topics

This short section covers a couple of small topics: how to filter Telnet and SSH traffic using ACLs, and some general implementation guidelines.

Controlling Telnet and SSH Access with ACLs

An engineer can control remote access to a router by using ACLs that look for the well-known ports used by both Telnet (23) and SSH (22). However, to do the job by enabling ACLs on interfaces using the **ip access-group** interface subcommand, the ACL would need to check for all the router's IP addresses, and both the Telnet and SSH port. As new interfaces are configured, the ACL would need to be updated.

IOS provides a much easier option for protecting access into and out of the virtual terminal line (vty) ports. Telnet and SSH users connect to vty lines on a router, so to protect that access, an IP ACL can be applied to the vty lines. You can use ACLs to limit the IP hosts that can telnet into the router, and you can also limit the hosts to which a user of the router can telnet.

For instance, imagine that only hosts in subnet 10.1.1.0/24 are supposed to be able to telnet into any of the Cisco routers in a network. In such a case, the configuration shown in Example 6-12 could be used on each router to deny access from IP addresses not in that subnet.

Example 6-12 *vty Access Control Using the **access-class** Command*

```
line vty 0 4
 login
 password cisco
 access-class 3 in
!
! Next command is a global command
 access-list 3 permit 10.1.1.0 0.0.0.255
```

The **access-class** command refers to the matching logic in **access-list 3**. The keyword **in** refers to Telnet connections into this router—in other words, people telnetting into this router. As configured, ACL 3 checks the source IP address of packets for incoming Telnet connections.

If the command **access-class 3 out** had been used, it would have checked for not only outgoing Telnets, but also the packets' destination IP address. When filtering outbound Telnet and SSH connections, checking the source IP address, which by definition must be one of the interface IP addresses in that router, would not really make any sense. For filtering outgoing Telnet sessions, it makes the most sense to filter based on the destination IP address. So, the use of the **access-class 3 out** command, particularly the **out** keyword, is one of those rare cases in which a standard IP ACL actually looks at the destination IP address and not the source.

ACL Implementation Considerations

In production IP networks, IP ACL creation, troubleshooting, and updates can consume a large amount of time and effort. The ICND2 exam does not have many questions about things to watch for when you implement IP ACLs in live networks, but it does cover a few small items, which are discussed in this section.

Cisco makes the following general recommendations in the courses on which the CCNA exams are based:

- Create your ACLs using a text editor outside the router, and copy and paste the configurations into the router. (Even with the ability to delete and insert lines into an ACL, creating the commands in an editor will still likely be an easier process.)

- Place extended ACLs as close as possible to the source of the packet to discard the packets quickly.

- Place standard ACLs as close as possible to the packet's destination, because standard ACLs often discard packets that you do not want discarded when they are placed close to the source.

- Place more-specific statements early in the ACL.

- Disable an ACL from its interface (using the **no ip access-group** command) before making changes to the ACL.

The first suggestion states that you should create the ACLs outside the router using an editor. That way, if you make mistakes when typing, you can fix them in the editor. This suggestion is not as important as it was before IOS version 12.3, because IOS 12.3 supports

ACL line numbers and the deletion and insertion of single lines in an ACL, as described earlier, in the section "Editing ACLs Using Sequence Numbers."

NOTE   If you create all your ACLs in a text editor, it may be useful to begin each file with the **no access-list** *number* command, followed by the configuration commands in the ACL. Then, each time you edit the text file to change the ACL, all you have to do is copy/paste the entire file's contents, with the first line deleting the entire existing ACL, and the rest of the statements re-creating the new ACL.

The second and third points deal with the concept of where to locate your ACLs. If you intend to filter a packet, filtering closer to the packet's source means that the packet takes up less bandwidth in the network, which seems to be more efficient—and it is. Therefore, Cisco suggests locating extended ACLs as close to the source as possible.

However, Cisco also suggests, at least in the CCNA-related courses, to locate standard ACLs close to the destination. Why not close to the source of the packets? Well, because standard ACLs look only at the source IP address, they tend to filter more than you want filtered when placed close to the source. For instance, imagine that Fred and Barney are separated by four routers. If you filter Barney's traffic sent to Fred on the first router, Barney can't reach any hosts near the other three routers. So the Cisco ICND2 course makes a blanket recommendation to locate standard ACLs closer to the destination to avoid filtering traffic you don't mean to filter.

By placing more-specific matching parameters early in each list, you are less likely to make mistakes in the ACL. For instance, imagine that you have a statement that permits all traffic from 10.1.1.1 to 10.2.2.2, destined for port 80 (the web), and another statement that denies all other packets sourced in subnet 10.1.1.0/24. Both statements would match packets sent by host 10.1.1.1 to a web server at 10.2.2.2, but you probably meant to match the more-specific statement (permit) first. In general, placing the more-specific statements first tends to ensure that you don't miss anything.

Finally, Cisco recommends that you disable the ACLs on the interfaces before you change the statements in the list. Thankfully, if you have an IP ACL enabled on an interface with the **ip access-group** command, and you delete the entire ACL, IOS does not filter any packets. (That was not always the case in earlier IOS versions!) Even so, as soon as you add a command to the ACL, the IOS starts filtering packets. Suppose you have ACL 101 enabled on S0 for output packets. You delete list 101 so that all packets are allowed through. Then you enter a single **access-list 101** command. As soon as you press Enter, the list exists, and the router filters all packets exiting S0 based on the one-line list. If you want to enter a long ACL, you might temporarily filter packets you don't want to filter! Therefore, the better way is to disable the list from the interface, make the changes to the list, and then reenable it on the interface.

Reflexive Access Lists

Reflexive ACLs, also called IP session filtering, provide a way to prevent a class of security attacks by permitting each allowed TCP or UDP session on an individual basis. To do so, the router reacts when seeing the first packet in a new session between two hosts. It reacts to the packet to add a permit statement to the ACL, allowing that session's traffic based on the source and destination IP address and TCP/UDP port.

Figure 6-9 shows a classic case in which traditional ACLs create a security hole, but reflexive ACLs could plug the hole. Most Enterprises want to allow users to use a web browser to connect to Internet-based web servers. A traditional extended ACL could permit the traffic by allowing traffic to and from any two IP addresses, but with the additional check on the TCP port used by HTTP (port 80). In this case, the figure shows an ACL that checks source port 80 for packets coming into the Enterprise, meaning that the packets came from a web server.

Figure 6-9   *The Need for Reflexive ACLs*

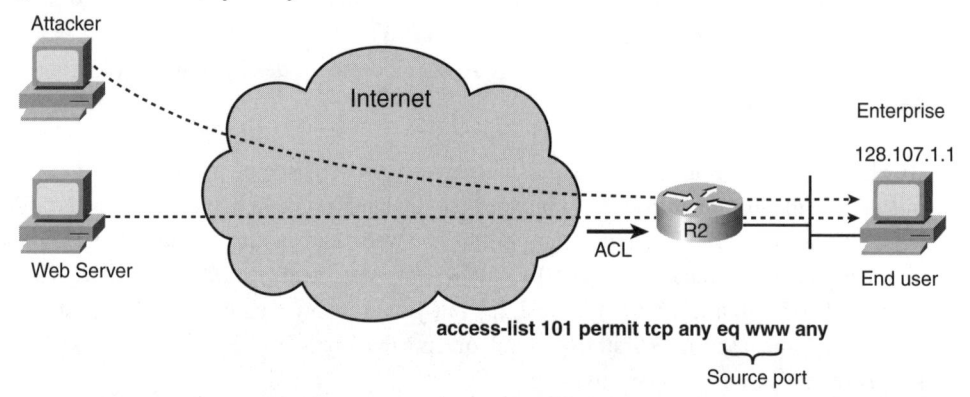

The ACL used on R2 filters all incoming traffic except traffic from web servers. This allows the Internet-based web server on the left to send packets to the user in the Enterprise on the right. However, it also allows the attacker to send packets, with source port 80, with the router allowing the packets through. Although these packets may not be part of an existing TCP connection, several known attacks can be made using these packets—from a simple DoS attack by flooding packets into the Enterprise, to the leveraging of known bugs in the operating system.

Reflexive ACLs still allow legitimate users to send and receive packets through the router, while discarding the packets from other hosts, like packets from the attacker shown in Figure 6-9. With reflexive ACLs, when the Enterprise user first creates a new session, the router notices the new session and records the source and destination IP addresses and ports used for that session. The reflexive ACL on R2 would not allow all port 80 traffic in. Instead, it would allow only packets whose addresses and ports matched the original packet. For example, if the PC on the right started a session with the legitimate web server, source port 1030, R2 would allow packets in from the Internet if they had the following characteristics: source IP address 64.100.2.2, destination IP address 128.107.1.1, source port 80, destination port 1030. As a result, only the packets from that legitimate session are allowed through the router, and the packets sent by the attacker are discarded.

Reflexive ACLs require some additional configuration, as well as the use of named extended ACL configuration.

Dynamic ACLs

Dynamic ACLs solve a different problem that also cannot be easily solved using traditional ACLs. Imagine a set of servers that need to be accessed by a small set of users. With ACLs, you can match the IP addresses of the hosts used by the users. However, if the user borrows another PC, or leases a new address using DHCP, or takes her laptop home, and so on, the legitimate user now has a different IP address. So a traditional ACL would have to be edited to support each new IP address. Over time, maintaining an ACL that checked for all these IP addresses would be painful. Additionally, it would introduce the possibility of security holes when other users' hosts start using one of the old IP addresses.

Dynamic ACLs, also called Lock-and-Key Security, solve this problem by tying the ACL to a user authentication process. Instead of starting by trying to connect to the server, the users must be told to first telnet to a router. The router asks for a username/password combination. If it is authentic, the router dynamically changes its ACL, permitting traffic from the IP address of the host that just sent the authentication packets. After a period of inactivity, the router removes the dynamic entry in the ACL, closing the potential security hole. Figure 6-10 shows the idea.

Figure 6-10 *Dynamic ACLs*

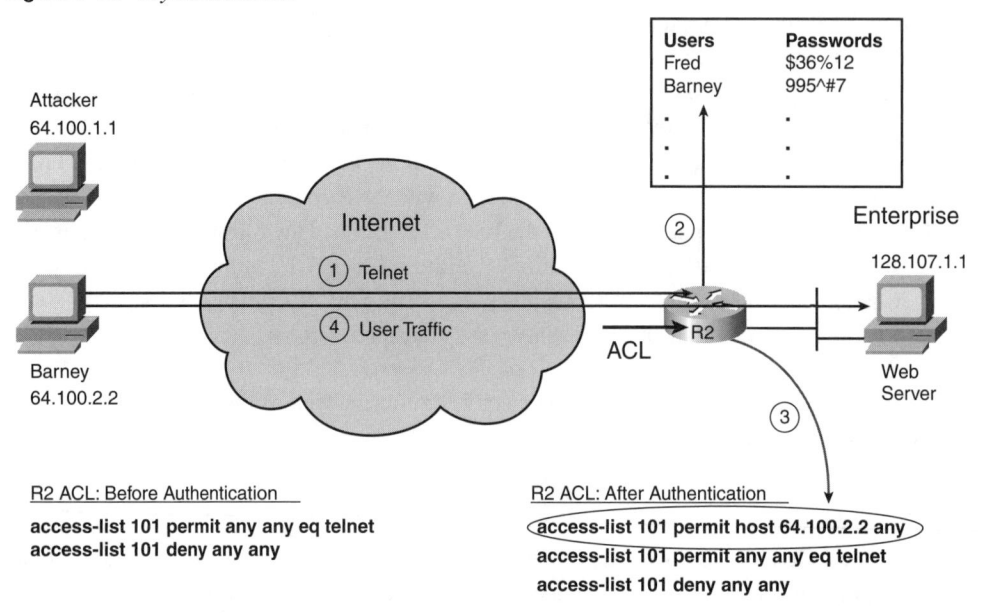

R2 ACL: Before Authentication

access-list 101 permit any any eq telnet
access-list 101 deny any any

R2 ACL: After Authentication

access-list 101 permit host 64.100.2.2 any
access-list 101 permit any any eq telnet
access-list 101 deny any any

The process shown in the figure begins with the router denying all traffic except Telnet. (Although the figure shows an ACL that allows telnetting to any IP address, in practice, the Telnet traffic only needs to be allowed into a router IP address.) To trigger the process, the following steps occur:

Step 1 The user connects to the router using Telnet.

Step 2 The user supplies a username/password, which the router compares to a list, authenticating the user.

Step 3 After authentication, the router dynamically adds an entry to the beginning of the ACL, permitting traffic sourced by the authenticated host.

Step 4 Packets sent by the permitted host go through the router to the server.

Time-Based ACLs

The term time-based ACL refers to a feature of normal IP ACLs (both numbered and named) in which a time constraint can be added to the configuration commands. In some cases, it may be useful to match packets in an ACL, but only at certain times in the day, or even on particular days of the week. Time-based ACLs allow the addition of time constraints, with IOS keeping or removing the statements from the ACL during the appropriate times of day.

Exam Preparation Tasks

Review All the Key Topics

Review the most important topics from this chapter, noted with the key topics icon. Table 6-8 lists these key topics and where each is discussed.

Table 6-8   Key Topics for Chapter 6

Key Topic Element	Description	Page Number
Figure 6-2	Logic diagram showing when a router examines packets with inbound and outbound ACLs	233
List	Four steps that describe how a router processes a multiline ACL	234
Table 6-2	Explains sample wildcard masks and their meanings	235-236
List	Shortcut to find values in the **access-list** command to match a subnet number, given the subnet number and subnet mask	237
List	Shortcut to interpret the address and wildcard mask in an **access-list** command as a subnet number and mask	237
List	ACL planning and configuration checklist	239
Table 6-3	List of IP packet fields matchable with standard and extended ACLs	245
List	Hints and tips on matching TCP and UDP ports using IP ACLs	246
Figure 6-6	Shows a packet with source and destination port, with the corresponding location of the source port parameter in the **access-list** command	248
List	Three items that differ between standard and extended IP ACLs	249
Table 6-7	List of operators that can be used when comparing port numbers in extended **access-list** commands	250
List	Features for both numbered and named ACLs provided by ACL sequence numbers	256
List	List of suggested best practices for ACLs according to the authorized Cisco CCNA courses	260

Complete the Tables and Lists from Memory

Print a copy of Appendix J, "Memory Tables" (found on the CD), or at least the section for this chapter, and complete the tables and lists from memory. Appendix K, "Memory Tables Answer Key," also on the CD, includes completed tables and lists for you to check your work.

Read the Appendix F Scenarios

Appendix F, "Additional Scenarios," contains five detailed scenarios that give you a chance to analyze different designs, problems, and command output. They also demonstrate how concepts from several different chapters interrelate. Scenario 3 focuses on IP ACLs, including practice with how to choose ACL wildcard masks to match all hosts in a single subnet.

Definitions of Key Terms

Define the following key terms from this chapter, and check your answers in the glossary:

Extended access list, named access list, standard access list, wildcard mask, dynamic ACL, reflexive ACL

Command Reference to Check Your Memory

Although you should not necessarily memorize the information in the tables in this section, this section does include a reference for the configuration and EXEC commands covered in this chapter. Practically speaking, you should memorize the commands as a side effect of reading the chapter and doing all the activities in this exam preparation section. To see how well you have memorized the commands as a side effect of your other studies, cover the left side of the table, read the descriptions on the right side, and see if you remember the command.

Table 6-9 *Chapter 6 Configuration Command Reference*

Command	Description
access-list *access-list-number* {**deny** | **permit**} *source* [*source-wildcard*] [**log**]	Global command for standard numbered access lists. Use a number between 1 and 99 or 1300 and 1999, inclusive.
access-list *access-list-number* {**deny** | **permit**} *protocol source source-wildcard destination destination-wildcard* [**log**]	Global command for extended numbered access lists. Use a number between 100 and 199 or 2000 and 2699, inclusive.

Table 6-9 *Chapter 6 Configuration Command Reference (Continued)*

Command	Description
access-list *access-list-number* {**deny**	**permit**} **tcp** *source source-wildcard* [*operator* [*port*]] *destination destination-wildcard* [*operator* [*port*]] [**log**]	A version of the **access-list** command with TCP-specific parameters.
access-list *access-list-number* **remark** *text*	Defines a remark that helps you remember what the ACL is supposed to do.
ip access-group {*number*	*name* [**in**	**out**]}	Interface subcommand to enable access lists.
access-class *number*	*name* [**in**	**out**]	Line subcommand to enable either standard or extended access lists.
ip access-list {**standard**	**extended**} *name*	Global command to configure a named standard or extended ACL and enter ACL configuration mode.
{**deny**	**permit**} *source* [*source-wildcard*] [**log**]	ACL mode subcommand to configure the matching details and action for a standard named ACL.
{**deny**	**permit**} *protocol source source-wildcard destination destination-wildcard* [**log**]	ACL mode subcommand to configure the matching details and action for an extended named ACL.
{**deny**	**permit**} **tcp** *source source-wildcard* [*operator* [*port*]] *destination destination-wildcard* [*operator* [*port*]] [**log**]	ACL mode subcommand to configure the matching details and action for a named ACL that matches TCP segments.
remark *text*	ACL mode subcommand to configure a description of a named ACL.

Table 6-10 *Chapter 6 EXEC Command Reference*

Command	Description
show ip interface [*type number*]	Includes a reference to the access lists enabled on the interface.
show access-lists [*access-list-number*	*access-list-name*]	Shows details of configured access lists for all protocols.
show ip access-list [*access-list-number*	*access-list-name*]	Shows IP access lists.

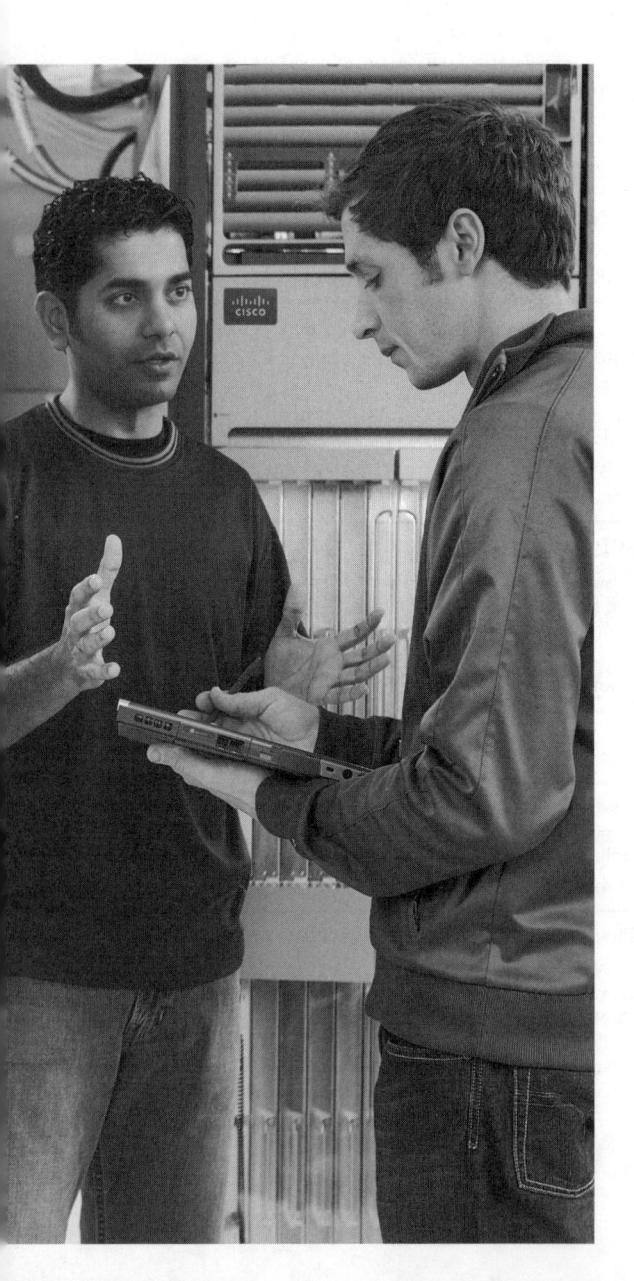

This chapter covers the following subjects:

The ping and traceroute Commands: This section explains how the **ping** and **traceroute** commands work, along with the nuances of how they can be used to better troubleshoot routing problems.

Troubleshooting the Packet Forwarding Process: This section examines the packet forwarding process, focusing on host routing and how routers route packets. It also covers issues related to forwarding packets in both directions between two hosts.

Troubleshooting Tools and Tips: This section covers a wide variety of topics that have some effect on the packet forwarding process. It includes many tips about various commands and concepts that can aid the troubleshooting process.

CHAPTER 7

Troubleshooting IP Routing

This troubleshooting chapter has several goals. First, it explains several tools and functions not covered in Chapters 4 through 6—specifically, tools that can be very helpful when you're analyzing problems. This chapter also reviews concepts from all three of the other chapters in Part II, "IP Routing." It pulls together the concepts by showing a suggested process for troubleshooting routing problems, as well as examples of how to use the process. The second half of the chapter focuses on a series of troubleshooting tips for many of the specific topics covered in Chapters 4 through 6.

"Do I Know This Already?" Quiz

The troubleshooting chapters of this book pull in concepts from many other chapters, including some chapters in *CCENT/CCNA ICND1 Official Exam Certification Guide*. They also show you how to approach some of the more challenging questions on the CCNA exams. Therefore, it is useful to read these chapters regardless of your current knowledge level. For these reasons, the troubleshooting chapters do not include a "Do I Know This Already?" quiz. However, if you feel particularly confident about troubleshooting IP routing features covered in this book and *CCENT/CCNA ICND1 Official Exam Certification Guide*, feel free to move to the "Exam Preparation Tasks" section near the end of this chapter to bypass the majority of the chapter.

Foundation Topics

This chapter focuses on troubleshooting the IP routing process. To that end, it begins with a section about two important troubleshooting tools: ping and traceroute. Following that, the chapter examines the IP routing process from a troubleshooting perspective, particularly focusing on how to isolate routing problems to identify the root cause of the problem. The final section covers a wide variety of small topics, all of which can be useful when you're troubleshooting IP routing problems.

> **NOTE**   This chapter, and Chapter 15 in *CCENT/CCNA ICND1 Official Exam Certification Guide*, both explain details of how to troubleshoot the IP routing process. IP routing is vitally important on both the ICND1 and ICND2 exams, as well as on the CCNA exam, so there is overlap between the exams, requiring some overlap in the books. However, this chapter covers many topics that go beyond the details required for the ICND1 exam. To be fully prepared, read this entire chapter, but feel free to skim portions if the chapter seems repetitive with the ICND1 book.

The ping and traceroute Commands

This section examines a suggested process of troubleshooting IP routing—in other words, the data plane process of how hosts and routers forward IP packets. To that end, this section first examines a set of useful tools and protocols—in particular, ICMP, **ping**, and **traceroute**. Following that, the text suggests a good general troubleshooting process for IP problems, with a few examples to show how to use the processes.

Internet Control Message Protocol (ICMP)

TCP/IP includes ICMP, a protocol designed to help manage and control the operation of a TCP/IP network. The ICMP protocol provides a wide variety of information about a network's health and operational status. *Control Message* is the most descriptive part of the name. ICMP helps control and manage IP's work by defining a set of messages and procedures about the operation of IP. Therefore, ICMP is considered part of TCP/IP's network layer. Because ICMP helps control IP, it can provide useful troubleshooting information. In fact, the ICMP messages sit inside an IP packet, with no transport layer header, so ICMP is truly an extension of the TCP/IP network layer.

RFC 792 defines ICMP. The following excerpt from RFC 792 describes the protocol well:

> Occasionally a gateway (router) or destination host will communicate with a source host, for example, to report an error in datagram processing. For such

purposes, this protocol, the Internet Control Message Protocol (ICMP), is used. ICMP uses the basic support of IP as if it were a higher level protocol; however, ICMP is actually an integral part of IP and must be implemented by every IP module.

ICMP defines several different types of messages to accomplish its varied tasks, as summarized in Table 7-1.

Table 7-1 *ICMP Message Types*

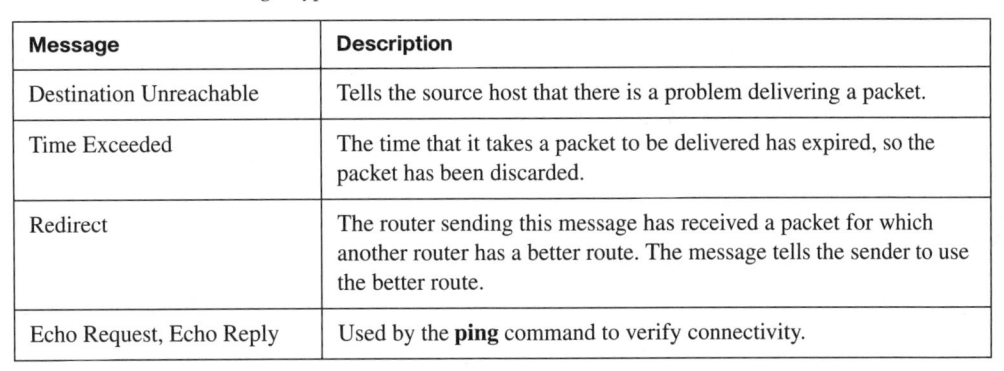

Message	Description
Destination Unreachable	Tells the source host that there is a problem delivering a packet.
Time Exceeded	The time that it takes a packet to be delivered has expired, so the packet has been discarded.
Redirect	The router sending this message has received a packet for which another router has a better route. The message tells the sender to use the better route.
Echo Request, Echo Reply	Used by the **ping** command to verify connectivity.

The ping Command and the ICMP Echo Request and Echo Reply

The **ping** command uses the ICMP Echo Request and Echo Reply messages. In fact, when people say they sent a ping packet, they really mean that they sent an ICMP Echo Request. These two messages are somewhat self-explanatory. The Echo Request simply means that the host to which it is addressed should reply to the packet. The Echo Reply is the ICMP message type that should be used in the reply. The Echo Request includes some data that can be specified by the **ping** command; whatever data is sent in the Echo Request is sent back in the Echo Reply.

The **ping** command itself supplies many creative ways to use Echo Requests and Replies. For instance, the **ping** command lets you specify the length as well as the source and destination addresses, and it also lets you set other fields in the IP header. Chapter 4, "IP Routing: Static and Connected Routes," shows an example of the extended **ping** command that lists the various options.

The Destination Unreachable ICMP Message

This book focuses on IP. But if you take a broader view, the role of the entire set of TCP/IP protocols is to deliver data from the sending application to the receiving application. Hosts and routers send ICMP Destination Unreachable messages back to the sending host when that host or router cannot deliver the data completely to the application at the destination host.

To aid in troubleshooting, the ICMP Unreachable message includes five separate unreachable functions (codes) that further identify the reason why the packet cannot be delivered. All five code types pertain directly to an IP, TCP, or UDP feature.

For example, the internetwork shown in Figure 7-1 can be used to better understand some of the Unreachable codes. Assume that Fred is trying to connect to the web server, called Web. (Web uses HTTP, which in turn uses TCP as the transport layer protocol.) Three of the ICMP unreachable codes can possibly be used by Routers A and B. The other two codes are used by the web server. These ICMP codes are sent to Fred as a result of the packet originally sent by Fred.

Figure 7-1 *Sample Network for Discussing ICMP Unreachable Codes*

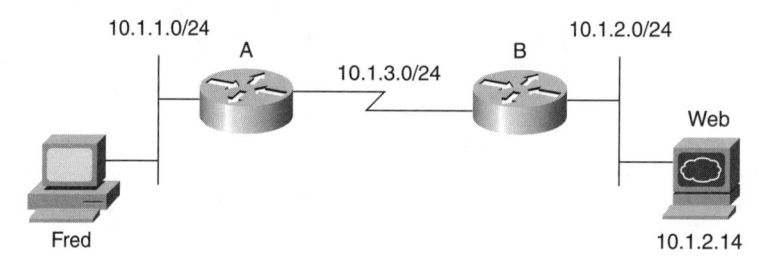

Table 7-2 summarizes the more common ICMP unreachable codes. After the table, the text explains how each ICMP code might be needed for the network shown in Figure 7-1.

Table 7-2 *ICMP Unreachable Codes*

Unreachable Code	When It Is Used	What Typically Sends It
Network unreachable	There is no match in a routing table for the packet's destination.	Router
Host unreachable	The packet can be routed to a router connected to the destination subnet, but the host is not responding.	Router
Can't fragment	The packet has the Don't Fragment bit set, and a router must fragment to forward the packet.	Router
Protocol unreachable	The packet is delivered to the destination host, but the transport layer protocol is not available on that host.	Host
Port unreachable	The packet is delivered to the destination host, but the destination port has not been opened by an application.	Host

The following list explains each code in Table 7-2 in greater detail using the network in Figure 7-1 as an example:

- **Network unreachable:** Router A uses this code if it does not have a route telling it where to forward the packet. In this case, Router A needs to route the packet to subnet 10.1.2.0/24. If it cannot, Router A sends Fred the ICMP Destination Unreachable message with the code "network unreachable" in response to Fred's packet destined for 10.1.2.14.

- **Host unreachable:** This code implies that the single destination host is unavailable. If Router A has a route to 10.1.2.0/24, the packet is delivered to Router B. If Router B's LAN interface is working, B also has a connected route to 10.1.2.0/24, so B tries to ARP and learn the web server's MAC address. However, if the web server is down, Router B does not get an ARP reply from the web server. Router B sends Fred the ICMP Destination Unreachable message with the code "host unreachable," meaning that B has a route but cannot forward the packet directly to 10.1.2.14.

- **Can't fragment:** This code is the last of the three ICMP unreachable codes that a router might send. Fragmentation defines the process in which a router needs to forward a packet, but the outgoing interface allows only packets that are smaller than the packet. The router is allowed to fragment the packet into pieces, but the packet header can be set with the "Do Not Fragment" bit in the IP header. In this case, if Router A or B needs to fragment the packet, but the Do Not Fragment bit is set in the IP header, the router discards the packet and sends Fred an ICMP Destination Unreachable message with the code "can't fragment."

- **Protocol unreachable:** If the packet successfully arrives at the web server, two other unreachable codes are possible. One implies that the protocol above IP, typically TCP or UDP, is not running on that host. This is highly unlikely, because most operating systems that use TCP/IP use a single software package that provides IP, TCP, and UDP functions. But if the host receives the IP packet and TCP or UDP is unavailable, the web server host sends Fred the ICMP Destination Unreachable message with the code "protocol unreachable" in response to Fred's packet destined for 10.1.2.14.

- **Port unreachable:** This final code field value is more likely today. If the server—the computer—is up and running, but the web server software is not running, the packet can get to the server but cannot be delivered to the web server software. In effect, the server is not listening on that application protocol's well-known port. So, host 10.1.2.14 sends Fred the ICMP Destination Unreachable message with the code "port unreachable" in response to Fred's packet destined for 10.1.2.14.

NOTE   Most security policies today filter these various unreachable messages to help bolster the network's security profile.

The **ping** command lists various responses that in some cases imply that an unreachable message was received. Table 7-3 lists the various unreachable codes that may be displayed by the Cisco IOS Software **ping** command.

Table 7-3   *Codes That the* **ping** *Command Receives in Response to Its ICMP Echo Request*

ping Command Code	Description
!	ICMP Echo Reply received
.	Nothing was received before the **ping** command timed out
U	ICMP unreachable (destination) received
N	ICMP unreachable (network/subnet) received
M	ICMP Can't Fragment message received
?	Unknown packet received

The Redirect ICMP Message

The ICMP Redirect message provides a means by which routers can tell hosts to use another router as default gateway for certain destination addresses. Most hosts use the concept of a default router IP address, sending packets destined for subnets to their default router. However, if multiple routers connect to the same subnet, a host's default gateway may not be the best router on that subnet to which to forward packets sent to some destinations. The default gateway can recognize that a different router is a better option. Then it can send ICMP redirect messages to the host to tell it to send the packets for that destination address to this different router.

For example, in Figure 7-2, the PC uses Router B as its default router. However, Router A's route to subnet 10.1.4.0 is a better route. (Assume the use of mask 255.255.255.0 in each subnet in Figure 7-2.) The PC sends a packet to Router B (Step 1 in Figure 7-2). Router B then forwards the packet based on its own routing table (Step 2); that route points through Router A, which has a better route. Finally, Router B sends the ICMP redirect message to the PC (Step 3), telling it to forward future packets destined for 10.1.4.0 to Router A instead. Ironically, the host can ignore the redirect and keep sending the packets to Router B, but in this example, the PC believes the redirect message, sending its next packet (Step 4) directly to Router A.

The ICMP Time Exceeded Message

The ICMP Time Exceeded message notifies a host when a packet it sent has been discarded because it was "out of time." Packets are not actually timed, but to prevent them from being forwarded forever when there is a routing loop, each IP header uses a Time to Live (TTL) field. Routers decrement the TTL by 1 every time they forward a packet; if a router decrements the TTL to 0, it throws away the packet. This prevents packets from rotating forever. Figure 7-3 shows the basic process.

Figure 7-2 *ICMP Redirect*

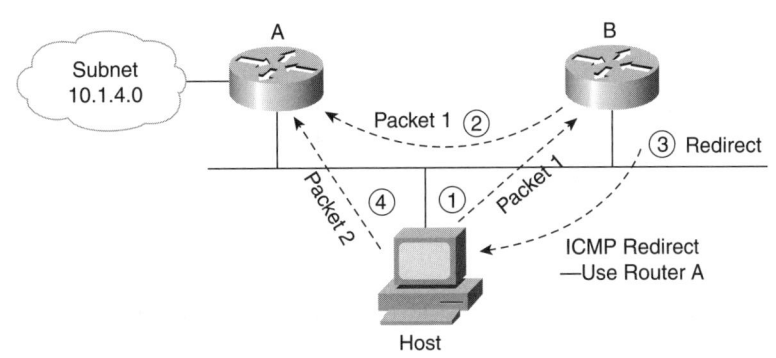

Figure 7-3 *TTL Decremented to 0*

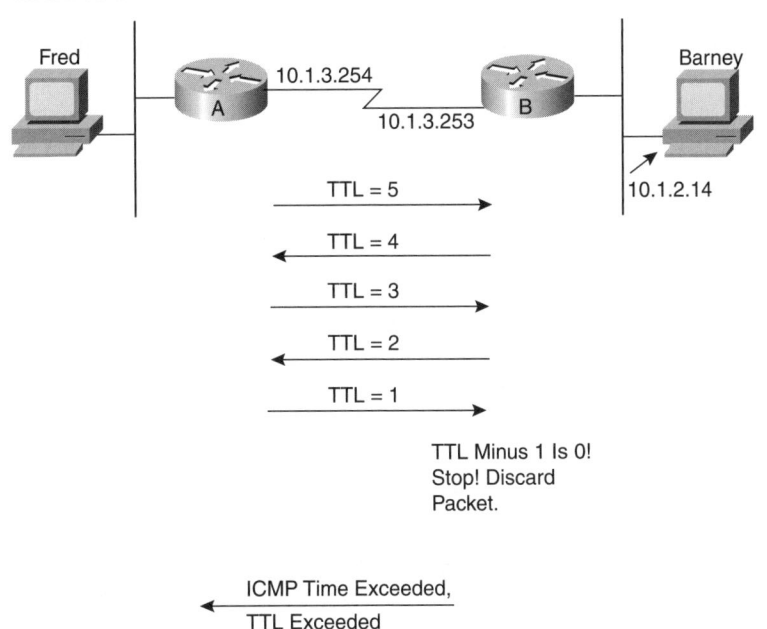

As you can see in the figure, the router that discards the packet also sends an ICMP Time Exceeded message, with a Code field of "time exceeded" to the host that sent the packet. That way, the sender knows that the packet was not delivered. Getting a Time Exceeded message can also help you when you troubleshoot a network. Hopefully, you do not get too many of these; otherwise, you have routing problems.

The traceroute Command

The **ping** command is a powerful troubleshooting tool that can be used to answer the question "Does the route from here to there work?" The **traceroute** command provides an arguably better troubleshooting tool because not only can it determine if the route works, but it can supply the IP address of each router in the route. If the route is not working, **traceroute** can identify the best places to start troubleshooting the problem.

The IOS **traceroute** command uses the Time Exceeded message and the IP TTL field to identify each successive router in a route. The **traceroute** command sends a set of messages with increasing TTL values, starting with 1. The **traceroute** command expects these messages to be discarded when routers decrement the TTL to 0, returning Time Exceeded messages to the **traceroute** command. The source IP addresses of the Time Exceeded messages identify the routers that discarded the messages, which can then be displayed by the **traceroute** command.

To see how this command works, consider the first set of packets (three packets by default) sent by the **traceroute** command. The packets are IP packets, with a UDP transport layer, and with the TTL set to 1. When the packets arrive at the next router, the router decrements the TTL to 0 in each packet, discards the packet, and sends a Time Exceeded message back to the host that sent the discarded packet. The **traceroute** command looks at the first router's source IP address in the received Time Exceeded packet.

Next, the **traceroute** command sends another set of three IP packets, this time with TTL = 2. The first router decrements TTL to 1 and forwards the packets, and the second router decrements the TTL to 0 and discards the packets. This second router sends Time Exceeded messages back to the router where the **traceroute** command was used, and the **traceroute** command now knows the second router in the route.

The **traceroute** command knows when the test packets arrive at the destination host because the host sends back an ICMP Port Unreachable message. The original packets sent by the IOS **traceroute** command use a destination UDP port number that is very unlikely to be used on the destination host, so as soon as the TTL is large enough to allow the packet to arrive at the destination host, the host notices that it does not have an application listening at that particular UDP port. So, the destination host returns a Port Unreachable message, which tells the **traceroute** command that the complete route has been found, and the command can stop.

Figure 7-4 shows an example, but with only one of the three messages at each TTL setting (to reduce clutter). Router A uses the **traceroute** command to try to find the route to Barney. Example 7-1 shows this **traceroute** command on Router A, with debug messages from Router B, showing the three resulting Time Exceeded messages.

Figure 7-4 *Cisco IOS Software* **traceroute** *Command: Messages Generated*

Key
Topic

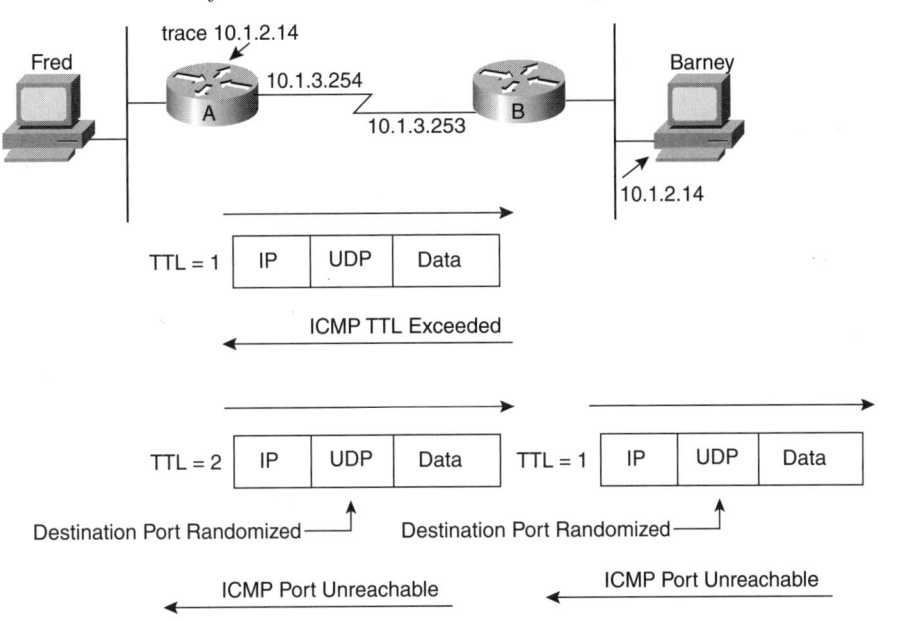

Example 7-1 *ICMP* **debug** *on Router B When Running the* **traceroute** *Command on Router A*

```
RouterA#traceroute 10.1.2.14

Type escape sequence to abort.
Tracing the route to 10.1.2.14

  1 10.1.3.253 8 msec 4 msec 4 msec
  2 10.1.2.14 12 msec 8 msec 4 msec
RouterA#
! Moving to Router B now
! The following output occurs in reaction to the traceroute command on A
RouterB#debug ip icmp
RouterB#
ICMP: time exceeded (time to live) sent to 10.1.3.254 (dest was 10.1.2.14)
ICMP: time exceeded (time to live) sent to 10.1.3.254 (dest was 10.1.2.14)
ICMP: time exceeded (time to live) sent to 10.1.3.254 (dest was 10.1.2.14)
```

The **traceroute** command lists the IP address of Router B in the first line and the IP address of the destination host in the second line. Note that it lists Router B's left-side IP address. B replies with the Time Exceeded message, using B's outgoing interface IP address as the source address in that packet. As a result, the **traceroute** command lists that IP address. If the address is known to a DNS server, or if it's in Router A's hostname table, the command can list the hostname instead of the IP address.

Similar to the extended **ping** command as described in the section titled, "The Extended **ping** Command" in Chapter 4, the extended version of the **traceroute** command does a much better job of simulating packets sent by end-user hosts, especially for testing reverse routes. For example, in Example 7-1, A's **traceroute** command uses A's 10.1.3.254 IP address as the source address of sent packets, because A uses the interface with address 10.1.3.254 to send the packets generated by the **traceroute** command. So, the **traceroute** command in Example 7-1 tests the forward route toward 10.1.2.14 and the reverse route to 10.1.3.254. By using the extended **traceroute** command, the command can be used to test a more appropriate reverse route, such as the route to the LAN subnet on the left side of Router A. Example 7-2, later in this chapter, shows an example of the extended **traceroute** command.

> **NOTE**   The **tracert** command on Microsoft operating systems works much like the IOS **traceroute** command. However, it is important to note that the Microsoft **tracert** command sends ICMP Echo Requests and does not use UDP. So, IP ACLs could cause the IOS **traceroute** to fail while the Microsoft **tracert** worked, and vice versa.

Troubleshooting the Packet Forwarding Process

Troubleshooting the IP routing process is one of the more complex tasks faced by network engineers. As usual, using a structured approach can help. Chapter 4 in particular, as well as Chapters 5 and 6, have already explained a lot about the first major part of the troubleshooting process—namely, what should happen in a network. This section focuses on the second major step: problem isolation. (For a more general reference on troubleshooting techniques, refer to Chapter 3, "Troubleshooting LAN Switching.")

> **NOTE**   This chapter defers any detailed troubleshooting of routing protocols until Chapter 11, "Troubleshooting Routing Protocols."

Isolating IP Routing Problems Related to Hosts

The troubleshooting process outlined in this chapter separates the troubleshooting steps— one part for the hosts, and one part for the routers. Essentially, for any problem in which two hosts cannot communicate, the first part of this troubleshooting process examines the issues that might impact each host's ability to send packets to and from its respective default gateway. The second part isolates problems related to how routers forward packets.

The following list outlines the troubleshooting steps focused on testing the host's connectivity to the first router:

Step 1   Check the host's ability to send packets inside its own subnet. Either ping the host's default gateway IP address from the host, or ping the host's IP address from the default gateway. If the ping fails, do the following:

    a.   Ensure that the router's interface used at the default gateway is in an "up and up" state.

    b.   Check the source host's IP address and mask setting as compared to the router's interface used as the default gateway. Ensure that both agree as to the subnet number and mask, and therefore agree to the range of valid addresses in the subnet.

    c.   If the router uses VLAN trunking, solve any trunk configuration issues, ensuring that the router is configured to support the same VLAN in which the host resides.

    d.   If the other steps do not lead to a solution, investigate Layer 1/2 problems with the LAN, as covered in Chapter 3. For example, look for an undefined VLAN.

Step 2   Verify the default gateway setting on the host by pinging one of the default router's other interface IP addresses. Or, from the default router, use an extended ping of the host's IP address with a source address from another of the router's interfaces.

For example, in Figure 7-5, the problem symptoms may be that PC1 cannot browse the web server at PC4. To test PC1's ability to send packets over its local subnet, PC1 could use the **ping 10.1.1.1** command to test connectivity to the default router in its same subnet. Or the engineer could simply **ping 10.1.1.10** from R1 (Step 1). Either location for the **ping** works fine, because both ping locations require that a packet be sent in each direction. If the **ping** fails, further problem isolation should uncover the two specific problem areas listed in Steps 1A, 1B, and 1C. If not, the problem is likely to be some Layer 1 or 2 problem, as discussed in Chapter 3.

Figure 7-5   *Sample Network for Troubleshooting Scenarios*

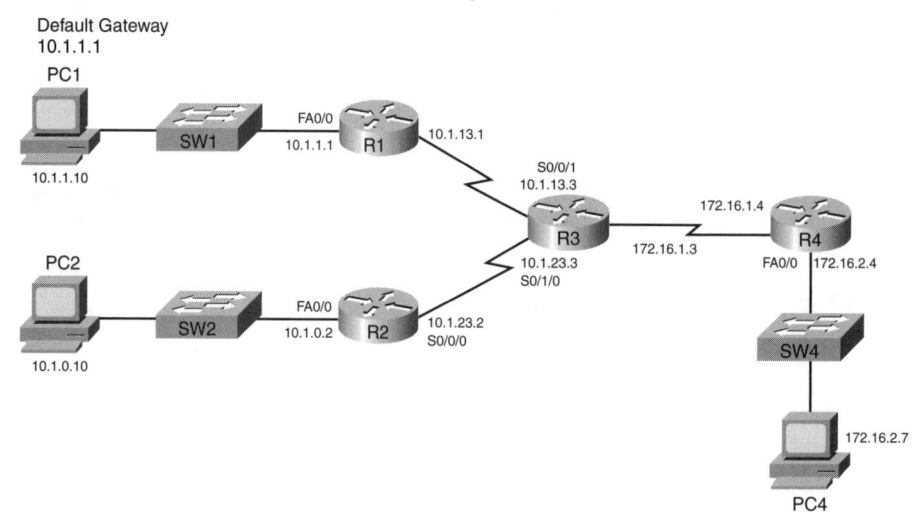

Step 2 stresses an often-overlooked troubleshooting concept to verify that the default gateway setting is working. Neither **ping** option listed in Step 1 requires the host to use its default gateway setting, because the source and destination address in each packet are in the same subnet. Step 2 forces the host to send a packet to an IP address in another subnet, thereby testing the host's default gateway setting. Also, by pinging an IP address on the default gateway (router), instead of some faraway host IP address, this step removes much of the IP routing complexity from the test. Instead, the focus is on whether the host's default gateway setting works. For example, in Figure 7-5, a **ping 10.1.13.1** command on PC1 forces PC1 to use its default gateway setting because 10.1.13.1 is not in PC1's subnet (10.1.1.0/24). But the IP address is on router R1, which removes most of the rest of the network as being a possible cause if the ping fails.

Isolating IP Routing Problems Related to Routers

When the host problem isolation process is complete, and the pings all work, on both the sending and receiving hosts, any remaining IP routing issues should be between the first and last router in both the forward and reverse route between the two hosts. The following list picks up the troubleshooting process with the source host's default gateway/router, relying on the **traceroute** command on the router. (Note that the host's equivalent command, such as **tracert** on Microsoft operating systems, can also be used.)

NOTE Although the following list may be useful for reference, it is rather long. Do not get bogged down in the details, but do read the examples of its use that follow this list; that should clarify many of the steps. As usual, you do not need to memorize any troubleshooting processes listed here. They are meant as learning tools to help you build your skills.

Step 3   Test connectivity to the destination host by using the extended **traceroute** command on the host's default gateway, using the router's interface attached to the source host for the source IP address of the packets. If the command successfully completes:

    a.   No routing problems exist in the forward route or reverse route directions.

    b.   If the end-user traffic still does not work (even though the **traceroute** worked), troubleshoot any ACLs on each interface on each router in the route, in both directions.

Step 4   If the **traceroute** command in Step 3 does not complete, test the *forward route* as follows:

    a.   **telnet** to the last traced router (the last router listed in the **traceroute** command).

    b.   Find that router's route that matches the destination IP address that was used in the original **traceroute** command (**show ip route**, **show ip route** *ip-address*).

    c.   If no matching route is found, investigate why the expected route is missing. Typically it's either a routing protocol issue or a static route misconfiguration. It could also be related to a missing connected route.

    d.   If a matching route is found, and the route is a default route, confirm that it will be used based on the setting for the **ip classless/no ip classless** commands.

    e.   If a matching route is found, **ping** the next-hop IP address listed in the route. Or, if the route is a connected route, **ping** the true destination IP address.

       •   If the **ping** fails, investigate Layer 2 problems between this router and the IP address that was pinged, and investigate possible ACL problems.

       •   If the **ping** works, investigate ACL issues.

Key
Topic

      f. If a matching route is found, and no other problems are found, confirm that the route is not errantly pointing in the wrong direction.

Step 5 If Step 4 does not identify a problem in the forward route, test the *reverse route*:

      a. If the forward route on the last traced router refers to another router as the next-hop router, repeat the substeps of Step 3 from that next-hop router. Analyze the reverse route—the route to reach the source IP address used by the failed **traceroute** command.

      b. If the forward route on the last traced router refers to a connected subnet, check the destination host's IP settings. In particular, confirm the settings for the IP address, mask, and default gateway.

For example, if PC1 cannot communicate with PC4 in Figure 7-5, and the hosts can both communicate through their respective default gateways, Step 3 of the router-oriented problem isolation process could start with a **traceroute 172.16.2.7**, using R1's Fa0/0 IP address (10.1.1.1) as the source IP address. If that **traceroute** command lists 10.1.13.3 as the last IP address in the command output, rather than completing, you would then start Step 4, which examines R3's forward route toward 172.16.2.7. If the analysis at Step 4 does not uncover the problem, Step 5 would then move on to the next-hop router, R4 in this case, and examine R4's reverse route—its route back to the original source address of 10.1.1.1.

Next, two separate scenarios show how to use these troubleshooting steps to isolate some sample problems.

Troubleshooting Scenario 1: Forward Route Problem

This first example of the router troubleshooting process uses the same internetwork shown in Figure 7-5. In this case, PC1 cannot use a web browser to connect to the web service running on PC4. After further investigation, PC1 cannot ping 172.16.2.7 (PC4). Example 7-2 shows the commands used on R1 and R4 for the host-oriented Steps 1 and 2, as well as a beginning of the router-oriented Step 3.

Example 7-2 *Troubleshooting Scenario 1: Steps 1 and 2 and Part of Step 3*

```
R1#ping 10.1.1.10

Type escape sequence to abort.
Sending 5, 100-byte ICMP Echos to 10.1.1.10, timeout is 2 seconds:
!!!!!
Success rate is 100 percent (5/5), round-trip min/avg/max = 1/2/4 ms
R1#ping
Protocol [ip]:
Target IP address: 10.1.1.10
Repeat count [5]:
```

Example 7-2 *Troubleshooting Scenario 1: Steps 1 and 2 and Part of Step 3 (Continued)*

```
Datagram size [100]:
Timeout in seconds [2]:
Extended commands [n]: y
Source address or interface: 10.1.13.1
Type of service [0]:
Set DF bit in IP header? [no]:
Validate reply data? [no]:
Data pattern [0xABCD]:
Loose, Strict, Record, Timestamp, Verbose[none]:
Sweep range of sizes [n]:
Type escape sequence to abort.
Sending 5, 100-byte ICMP Echos to 10.1.1.10, timeout is 2 seconds:
Packet sent with a source address of 10.1.13.1
!!!!!
Success rate is 100 percent (5/5), round-trip min/avg/max = 1/2/4 ms
R1#
! Now moving to R4 to repeat the test
R4#ping 172.16.2.7

Type escape sequence to abort.
Sending 5, 100-byte ICMP Echos to 172.16.2.7, timeout is 2 seconds:
.....
Success rate is 0 percent (0/5)
R4#show ip interface brief
Interface              IP-Address      OK? Method Status                Protocol
FastEthernet0/0        172.16.2.4      YES manual administratively down down
FastEthernet0/1        172.16.1.4      YES manual up                    up
Serial0/0/0            unassigned      YES unset  administratively down down
Serial0/0/1            unassigned      YES unset  administratively down down
Serial0/1/0            unassigned      YES unset  administratively down down
```

The standard and extended pings on R1 at the beginning of the example essentially perform Steps 1 and 2, the host-oriented steps, to confirm that PC1 seems to be working well. However, the example next shows that R4 cannot reach PC4 because R4's LAN interface has been shut down, as shown at the end of the example. Although this scenario may seem a bit simple, it provides a good starting point for troubleshooting a problem.

To get a fuller view of the troubleshooting process, next consider this same scenario, with the same root problem, but now you do not have access to router R4. So, you can only perform Steps 1 and 2 for PC1, which work, but you cannot do those same steps for PC4 from R4. So, Example 7-3 moves on to Steps 3 and 4. The beginning of the example shows Step 3, where R1 uses **traceroute 172.16.2.7**, with a source IP address of 10.1.1.1. This command does not complete, referencing 10.1.13.3 (R3) as the last router. Step 4 proceeds by looking at how R3 then routes packets destined for 172.16.2.7.

Example 7-3   *Troubleshooting Scenario 1: Step 4*

```
R1#traceroute
Protocol [ip]:
Target IP address: 172.16.2.7
Source address: 10.1.1.1
Numeric display [n]:
Timeout in seconds [3]:
Probe count [3]:
Minimum Time to Live [1]:
Maximum Time to Live [30]:
Port Number [33434]:
Loose, Strict, Record, Timestamp, Verbose[none]:
Type escape sequence to abort.
Tracing the route to 172.16.2.7

  1 10.1.13.3 0 msec 4 msec 0 msec
  2 10.1.13.3 !H  *  !H
! Note above that the command did stop by itself, but it does not list the
! destination host 172.16.2.7
R3#show ip route 172.16.2.7
% Subnet not in table
R3#show ip route
Codes: C - connected, S - static, R - RIP, M - mobile, B - BGP
       D - EIGRP, EX - EIGRP external, O - OSPF, IA - OSPF inter area
       N1 - OSPF NSSA external type 1, N2 - OSPF NSSA external type 2
       E1 - OSPF external type 1, E2 - OSPF external type 2
       i - IS-IS, su - IS-IS summary, L1 - IS-IS level-1, L2 - IS-IS level-2
       ia - IS-IS inter area, * - candidate default, U - per-user static route
       o - ODR, P - periodic downloaded static route

Gateway of last resort is not set

     172.16.0.0/24 is subnetted, 1 subnets
C       172.16.1.0 is directly connected, FastEthernet0/0
     10.0.0.0/24 is subnetted, 4 subnets
C       10.1.13.0 is directly connected, Serial0/0/1
R       10.1.1.0 [120/1] via 10.1.13.1, 00:00:04, Serial0/0/1
R       10.1.0.0 [120/1] via 10.1.23.2, 00:00:01, Serial0/1/0
C       10.1.23.0 is directly connected, Serial0/1/0
```

The extended **traceroute** command at the beginning of the example shows output identifying R3 (10.1.13.3) as the last listed device in the command output (Step 3). Step 4 then proceeds with an examination of the forward route on R3 toward IP address 172.16.2.7. The **show ip route 172.16.2.7** command gets right to the point. The message "subnet not in table" means that R3 does not have a route matching destination address 172.16.2.7. If the question does not supply access to a simulator, only the output of the **show ip route** command, you would need to examine the routes to determine that none of them refer to a range of addresses that includes 172.16.2.7.

Any time the problem isolation process points to a missing route, the next step is to determine how the router should have learned about the route. In this case, R3 should have used RIP-2 to learn the route. So, the next steps would be to troubleshoot any problems with the dynamic routing protocol.

The root cause of this problem has not changed—R4 has shut down its Fa0/0 interface—but the symptoms are somewhat interesting. Because the interface is shut down, R4 does not advertise a route for subnet 172.16.2.0/24 to R3. However, R3 advertises an autosummarized route to network 172.16.0.0/16 to both R1 and R2, so both R1 and R2, because of RIP-2's default autosummary setting, can forward packets destined for 172.16.2.7 to R3. As a result, the **traceroute** command on R1 can forward packets to R3.

Troubleshooting Scenario 2: Reverse Route Problem

This next example uses the same network diagram as shown in Figure 7-5, with all the information shown in the figure still being true. However, the details mentioned in the previous section may have changed—particularly the problem that exists to make the example more interesting. So, approach this second problem only relying on the figure as being true.

In this scenario, PC1 again cannot ping 172.16.2.7 (PC4). The host default gateway checks suggested in Steps 1 and 2 again work for PC1, but the tests cannot be performed for the reverse direction, because the engineer cannot access PC4 or router R4. So, Example 7-4 picks up the suggested troubleshooting process at Step 3, showing the result of the extended **traceroute** command on R1. Note that the command does not even list R3's 10.1.13.3 IP address in this case. So, the rest of Example 7-4 shows the investigations into the specific substeps of Step 4.

Example 7-4   *Troubleshooting Scenario 2: Steps 3 and 4*

```
R1#traceroute ip 172.16.2.7 source fa0/0

Type escape sequence to abort.
Tracing the route to 172.16.2.7

  1  *  *  *
  2  *  *  *
  3  *
```

continues

Example 7-4 *Troubleshooting Scenario 2: Steps 3 and 4 (Continued)*

```
R1#show ip route 172.16.2.7
Routing entry for 172.16.0.0/16
  Known via "rip", distance 120, metric 1
  Redistributing via rip
  Last update from 10.1.13.3 on Serial0/1/0, 00:00:05 ago
  Routing Descriptor Blocks:
  * 10.1.13.3, from 10.1.13.3, 00:00:05 ago, via Serial0/1/0
      Route metric is 1, traffic share count is 1

R1#ping 10.1.13.3

Type escape sequence to abort.
Sending 5, 100-byte ICMP Echos to 10.1.13.3, timeout is 2 seconds:
!!!!!
Success rate is 100 percent (5/5), round-trip min/avg/max = 1/2/4 ms
R1#show ip access-lists

! Switching to router R3 next
R3#show ip access-lists

R3#
```

The example starts by showing the Step 3 part of the process, with the **traceroute** command only listing lines of asterisks. This means that the command did not successfully identify even the very next router in the route.

Next, moving on to Step 4, the following list outlines the substeps of Step 4 as applied to this example:

Step 4a   The example had already begun with a Telnet into R1, so no extra work is required.

Step 4b   The next command, **show ip route 172.16.2.7**, shows that R1 has a nondefault route for network 172.16.0.0, pointing to R3 (10.1.13.3) as the next hop.

Step 4c   This step does not apply in this case, because a matching route was found in Step 4B.

Step 4d   This step does not apply in this case, because the matching route is not a route to 0.0.0.0/0 (the default route).

Step 4e   The next listed command, **ping 10.1.13.3**, tests R1's ability to send packets over the link to the next-hop router identified in Step 4B. The ping works.

Step 4f   On both R1 and the next-hop router (R3), the **show ip access-lists** command confirms that neither router has any IP ACLs configured.

Because all the steps to examine the forward route passed, the process then moves on to Step 5. The original **traceroute** command in Example 7-4 used R1's Fa0/0 interface IP address, 10.1.1.1, as the source IP address. For Step 5, the process begins at R3 with an analysis of R3's reverse route to reach 10.1.1.1. Examine the output in Example 7-5, and look for any problems before reading the explanations following the example.

Example 7-5   *Troubleshooting Scenario 2: Step 5*

```
! The next command shows the matched route, for subnet 10.1.1.0/26,
! with next-hop 10.1.23.2.
R3#show ip route 10.1.1.1
Routing entry for 10.1.1.0/26
  Known via "static", distance 1, metric 0
  Routing Descriptor Blocks:
  * 10.1.23.2
      Route metric is 0, traffic share count is 1

! The next command shows the overlapping subnets - 10.1.1.0/26 and 10.1.1.0/24.
R3#show ip route
Codes: C - connected, S - static, R - RIP, M - mobile, B - BGP
       D - EIGRP, EX - EIGRP external, O - OSPF, IA - OSPF inter area
       N1 - OSPF NSSA external type 1, N2 - OSPF NSSA external type 2
       E1 - OSPF external type 1, E2 - OSPF external type 2
       i - IS-IS, su - IS-IS summary, L1 - IS-IS level-1, L2 - IS-IS level-2
       ia - IS-IS inter area, * - candidate default, U - per-user static route
       o - ODR, P - periodic downloaded static route

Gateway of last resort is not set

     172.16.0.0/24 is subnetted, 2 subnets
C       172.16.1.0 is directly connected, FastEthernet0/0
R       172.16.2.0 [120/1] via 172.16.1.4, 00:00:18, FastEthernet0/0
     10.0.0.0/8 is variably subnetted, 5 subnets, 2 masks
C       10.1.13.0/24 is directly connected, Serial0/0/1
S       10.1.1.0/26 [1/0] via 10.1.23.2
R       10.1.1.0/24 [120/1] via 10.1.13.1, 00:00:10, Serial0/0/1
R       10.1.0.0/24 [120/1] via 10.1.23.2, 00:00:11, Serial0/1/0
C       10.1.23.0/24 is directly connected, Serial0/1/0
```

R3 has an incorrectly configured static route for subnet 10.1.1.0/26. This subnet includes the address range 10.1.1.0–10.1.1.63, which includes IP address 10.1.1.1. When R3 attempts to send a packet back to 10.1.1.1, R3 has two routes that match the destination address. But R3 picks the more specific (longer prefix) route for subnet 10.1.1.0/26. This route causes R3 to forward packets intended for 10.1.1.1 out R3's link to R2, instead of to R1.

Although you cannot necessarily determine the true intent of this static route, this process has identified the root cause—the static route to 10.1.1.0/26 on R3. If the LAN off R1 should include all addresses between 10.1.1.0 and 10.1.1.255, the static route should just be deleted.

An Alternative Problem Isolation Process for Steps 3, 4, and 5

The router-oriented steps of the IP routing problem isolation process depend on the **traceroute** command, relying on this command's ability to identify on which router the router-oriented troubleshooting should begin. As an alternative, the **ping** and **telnet** commands can be used. However, because these commands cannot quickly identify the most likely routers on which the problem exists, using **ping** and **telnet** requires that you perform a set of tasks on the first router (the host's default gateway/router) in a route, and then the next router, and the next, and so on, until the problem is identified.

So, just to be complete, note that you can do the same specific subtasks as already explained in Steps 4 and 5, but when using **ping**, just repeat the steps at each successive router. For example, to apply this revised process to the first of the two just-completed scenarios, the process would begin with router R1, PC1's default router. In the first scenario, R1 did not have any forward route issues for forwarding packets to 172.16.2.7 (PC4), and R1 had no reverse route issues and no ACLs. This new alternative process would then suggest moving on to the next router (R3). In this example, R3's forward route problem—not having a route that matches destination address 172.16.2.7—would be found.

Troubleshooting Tools and Tips

The second half of this chapter covers a wide variety of troubleshooting tools and tips that can be helpful when you're troubleshooting real networks. Some of the information in this section may apply directly to the CCNA exams. Other parts of this section will be indirectly useful for the exams. The information may help you learn as you work with networks in your job, making you better prepared for the unique scenarios on the exams.

Host Routing Tools and Perspectives

This section covers two short topics related to how hosts process IP packets. The first topic lists several tips for troubleshooting hosts. The second topic reviews information covered in *CCENT/CCNA ICND1 Official Exam Certification Guide* on how a LAN switch's IP configuration works like a host.

Host Troubleshooting Tips

When you're trying to isolate the cause of networking problems, the tips in Table 7-4 may help you more quickly find problems related to hosts. The tips are organized by typical symptoms, along with common root causes. Note that the table does not list all possible causes, just the more common ones.

Table 7-4 *Common Host Problem Symptoms and Typical Reasons*

Symptom	Common Root Cause
The host can send packets to hosts in the same subnet, but not to other subnets.	The host does not have a default gateway configured, or the default gateway IP address is incorrect.
The host can send packets to hosts in the same subnet, but not to other subnets.	The host's default gateway is in a different subnet than the host's IP address (according to the host's perception of the subnet).
Some hosts in a subnet can communicate with hosts in other subnets, but others cannot.	This may be caused by the default gateway (router) using a different mask than the hosts. This may result in the router's connected route not including some of the hosts on the LAN.
Some hosts on the same VLAN can send packets to each other, but others cannot.	The hosts may not be using the same mask.

When troubleshooting networking problems in real life, it's helpful to get used to thinking about the symptoms, because that's where the problem isolation process typically begins. However, for the exams, most host communication problems are caused by just a handful of issues:

Step 1 Check all hosts and routers that should be in the same subnet to ensure that they all use the same mask and that their addresses are indeed all in the same subnet.

Key
Topic

Step 2 Compare each host's default gateway setting with the router's configuration to ensure that it is the right IP address.

Step 3 If the first two items are correct, next look at Layer 1/2 issues, as covered in Chapters 1 through 3.

LAN Switch IP Support

Ethernet switches do not need to know anything about Layer 3 to perform their basic Layer 2 function of forwarding Ethernet frames. However, to support several important features, such as the ability to telnet and SSH to the switch to troubleshoot problems, LAN switches need an IP address.

Switches act like hosts when it comes to IP configuration. As compared to a PC, a Cisco switch does not use a NIC. Instead, it uses an internal virtual interface associated with VLAN 1 that essentially gives the switch itself an interface in VLAN 1. Then, the same kinds of items that can be configured on a host for IP can be configured on this VLAN interface: IP address, mask, and default gateway. DNS server IP addresses can also be configured.

The following list repeats the LAN switch IP configuration checklist from *CCENT/CCNA ICND1 Official Exam Certification Guide*. Following the list, Example 7-6 shows the IP address configuration for switch SW1 in Figure 7-5 from earlier in the chapter.

Step 1 Enter VLAN 1 configuration mode using the **interface vlan 1** global configuration command (from any config mode).

Step 2 Assign an IP address and mask using the **ip address** *ip-address mask* interface subcommand.

Step 3 Enable the VLAN 1 interface using the **no shutdown** interface subcommand.

Step 4 Add the **ip default-gateway** *ip-address* global command to configure the default gateway.

Example 7-6 *Switch Static IP Address Configuration*

```
SW1#configure terminal
SW1(config)#interface vlan 1
SW1(config-if)#ip address 10.1.1.200 255.255.255.0
SW1(config-if)#no shutdown
00:25:07: %LINK-3-UPDOWN: Interface Vlan1, changed state to up
00:25:08: %LINEPROTO-5-UPDOWN: Line protocol on Interface Vlan1, changed
  state to up
SW1(config-if)#exit
SW1(config)#ip default-gateway 10.1.1.1
```

> **NOTE** The VLAN interface on a switch stays in an administratively down state until the user issues the **no shutdown** command; the switch cannot send IP packets until the VLAN 1 interface is up.

A common oversight when configuring or troubleshooting IP connectivity problems to LAN switches relates to VLAN trunking. Cisco generally suggests that you avoid putting end-user devices into VLAN 1, but the switch IP address may well be configured in VLAN 1. To support the ability for the switch to send and receive packets to hosts in different subnets, thereby supporting Telnet into the switch from those end-user subnets, the router's trunking configuration must include configuration for VLAN 1 as well as the end-user VLANs.

show ip route Reference

The **show ip route** command plays a huge role in troubleshooting IP routing and IP routing protocol problems. Many chapters in this book and in the ICND1 book mention various facts about this command. This section pulls the concepts together in one place for easier reference and study.

Figure 7-6 shows the output of the **show ip route** command from back in Example 7-3. The figure numbers various parts of the command output for easier reference, with Table 7-5 describing the output noted by each number.

Figure 7-6 **show ip route** *Command Output Reference*

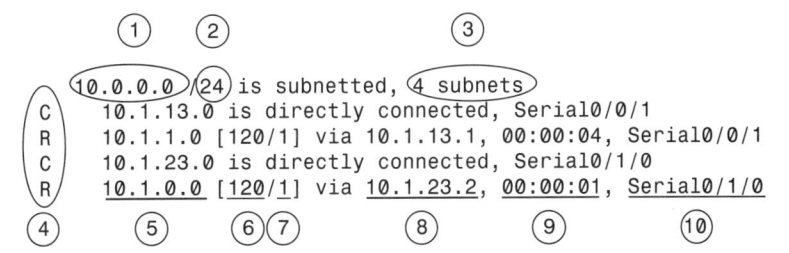

Table 7-5 *Descriptions of the* **show ip route** *Command Output*

Item Number	Item	Value in the Figure	Description
1	Classful network	10.0.0.0	The routing table is organized by classful network. This line is the heading line for classful network 10.0.0.0.
2	Prefix length	/24	When this router knows only one subnet mask for all subnets of the network, this location lists that one mask, by default in prefix notation.
3	Number of subnets	4 subnets	Lists the number of routes for subnets of the classful network known to this router.
4	Legend code	R, C	A short code that identifies the source of the routing information. R is for RIP, and C is for connected. The figure omits the legend text at the top of the **show ip route** command output, but it can be seen in Example 7-3.
5	Subnet number	10.1.0.0	The subnet number of this particular route.
6	Administrative distance	120	If a router learns routes for the listed subnet from more than one source of routing information, the router uses the source with the lowest AD.
7	Metric	1	The metric for this route.
8	Next-hop router	10.1.23.2	For packets matching this route, the IP address of the next router to which the packet should be forwarded.
9	Timer	00:00:01	Time since this route was learned in a routing update.
10	Outgoing interface	Serial0/1/0	For packets matching this route, the interface out which the packet should be forwarded.

The output of the command differs slightly when VLSM is used. The figure shows an example in which VLSM is not used in network 10.0.0.0, with mask /24 used for all subnets of that network. So, IOS lists the mask once, in the heading line (/24 in this case). If VLSM were in use, the heading line would simply note that the network is variably subnetted, and each route would list the mask. For an example, see Example 5-1 in Chapter 5, "VLSM and Route Summarization."

Interface Status

One of the steps in the IP routing troubleshooting process described earlier, in the "Troubleshooting the Packet Forwarding Process" section, says to check the interface status, ensuring that the required interface is working. For a router interface to be working, the two interface status codes must both be listed as "up," with engineers usually saying the interface is "up and up."

This chapter does not explain the troubleshooting steps for router interfaces, simply assuming that each interface is indeed in an up/up state. Chapter 12's section titled "Troubleshooting Serial Links" covers many of the details for troubleshooting router interfaces. For router LAN interfaces connected to a LAN switch, the main items to check on routers are that the router and switch match each other's duplex and speed settings, and that if trunking is configured, both the router and switch have been manually configured for trunking, because routers do not dynamically negotiate LAN trunking.

VLSM Issues

This section examines several issues when using VLSM:

■   Recognizing whether VLSM is used and, if so, which routing protocols can be used

■   Understanding the conditions in which routers can allow the misconfiguration of overlapping VLSM subnets

■   Understanding the outward symptoms that can occur when overlapping VLSM subnets exist

Recognizing When VLSM Is Used

One common oversight when troubleshooting a problem in an unfamiliar internetwork is failing to recognize whether VLSM is used. As defined in Chapter 5, an internetwork uses VLSM when multiple subnet masks are used for different subnets of *a single classful network*. For example, if in one internetwork all subnets of network 10.0.0.0 use a 255.255.240.0 mask, and all subnets of network 172.16.0.0 use a 255.255.255.0 mask, the design does not use VLSM. If multiple masks were used for subnets of network 10.0.0.0, VLSM would be in use.

The follow-on concept is that only classless routing protocols (RIP-2, EIGRP, OSPF) can support VLSM; classful routing protocols (RIP-1, IGRP) cannot. So, a quick determination of whether VLSM is actually used can then tell you whether a classless routing protocol is required. Note that the routing protocol does not require any special configuration to support VLSM. It is just a feature of the routing protocol.

Configuring Overlapping VLSM Subnets

IP subnetting rules require that the address ranges in the subnets used in an internetwork should not overlap. IOS can recognize when a new **ip address** command creates an overlapping subnet, but only in some cases. This section examines the conditions under which overlapping subnets can be configured, beginning with the following general statements about when the overlaps cannot and can be configured:

- **Preventing the overlap:** IOS detects the overlap when the **ip address** command implies an overlap with another **ip address** command *on the same router.* If the interface being configured is up/up, IOS rejects the **ip address** command. If not, IOS accepts the **ip address** command, but IOS will never bring up the interface.

- **Allowing the overlap:** IOS cannot detect an overlap when an **ip address** command overlaps with an **ip address** command on another router.

Key Topic

The router shown in Example 7-7 prevents the configuration of an overlapping VLSM subnet. The example shows router R3 configuring Fa0/0 with IP address 172.16.5.1/24, and Fa0/1 with 172.16.5.193/26. The ranges of addresses in each subnet are:

Subnet 172.16.5.0/24:   172.16.5.1– 172.16.5.254
Subnet 172.16.5.192/26: 172.16.5.193–172.16.5.254

Example 7-7 *Single Router Rejects Overlapped Subnets*

```
R3#configure terminal
R3(config)#interface Fa0/0
R3(config-if)#ip address 172.16.5.1 255.255.255.0
R3(config-if)#interface Fa0/1
R3(config-if)#ip address 172.16.5.193 255.255.255.192
% 172.16.5.192 overlaps with FastEthernet0/0
R3(config-if)#
```

IOS knows that it is illegal to overlap the ranges of addresses implied by a subnet. In this case, because both subnets would be connected subnets, this single router knows that these two subnets should not coexist, because that would break subnetting rules, so IOS rejects the second command.

However, it is possible to configure overlapping subnets if they are connected to different routers. Figure 7-7 shows a figure very similar to Figure 5-2 in Chapter 5—used in that chapter to explain the problem of overlapping subnets. Example 7-8 shows the configuration of the two overlapping subnets on R2 and R3.

Figure 7-7 *Internetwork That Allows the Configuration of Overlapped Subnets*

Example 7-8 *Two Routers Accept Overlapped Subnets*

```
R2#configure terminal
R2(config)#interface Fa0/0
R2(config-if)#ip address 172.16.4.1 255.255.254.0
R3#configure terminal
R3(config)#interface Fa0/0
R3(config-if)# ip address 172.16.5.1 255.255.255.0
```

For the exams, keep in mind that overlapped subnets can be configured if the subnets do not connect to the same router. So, if a question asks you to pick a new subnet number and configure an interface to be in that subnet, the router's acceptance of your **ip address** command does not necessarily tell you that you did the math correctly.

The next topic explains some of the problem symptoms you might see if such an overlap exists.

Symptoms with Overlapping Subnets

NOTE   Although this section is included for the sake of completeness, the types of problems described here may well be beyond the scope of the CCNA exams.

The outward problem symptoms differ depending on whether the address in question is in the overlapped portion of the subnets and if multiple hosts are attempting to use the exact same IP address. The addresses in the nonoverlapped parts of the subnet typically work fine, whereas those in the overlapped area may or may not work at all. For example, continuing with the overlapped subnets shown in Figure 7-7, subnets 172.16.4.0/23 and 172.16.5.0/24 overlap—specifically, addresses 172.16.5.0–172.16.5.255. Hosts in the nonoverlapped range of 172.16.4.0–172.16.4.255 probably work fine.

For the addresses in the overlapped address range, in many cases, hosts in the smaller of the two overlapped subnets work fine, but hosts in the larger of the two subnets do not. To see why, consider the case in which PC1 in Figure 7-7 tries to ping both 172.16.5.2 (PC2, off R2) and 172.16.5.3 (PC3, off R3). (For the sake of this example, assume that PC2's and PC3's IP addresses are not duplicated in the opposite overlapped subnet.) As you can see from the routing tables on R1 and R3 and the **traceroute 172.16.5.2** command in Example 7-9, the packet sent by PC1 to PC2 would actually be delivered from R1 to R3, and then onto R3's LAN.

Example 7-9   *Two Routers Accept Overlapped Subnets*

```
! R1's route to reach 172.16.5.2, off R2, points to R3
R1#show ip route 172.16.5.2
Routing entry for 172.16.5.0/24
  Known via "rip", distance 120, metric 1
  Redistributing via rip
  Last update from 172.16.9.6 on Serial0/1/0, 00:00:25 ago
  Routing Descriptor Blocks:
  * 172.16.9.6, from 172.16.9.6, 00:00:25 ago, via Serial0/1/0
      Route metric is 1, traffic share count is 1
! R1's route to reach 172.16.5.3, off R3, points to R3
R1#show ip route 172.16.5.3
Routing entry for 172.16.5.0/24
  Known via "rip", distance 120, metric 1
```

continues

Example 7-9   *Two Routers Accept Overlapped Subnets (Continued)*

```
 Redistributing via rip
 Last update from 172.16.9.6 on Serial0/1/0, 00:00:01 ago
 Routing Descriptor Blocks:
 * 172.16.9.6, from 172.16.9.6, 00:00:01 ago, via Serial0/1/0
     Route metric is 1, traffic share count is 1

! The traceroute to PC2 shows R3, not R2, as the first router, so the packet never
! reaches PC2, and the command never completes until stopped by the user.
R1#traceroute 172.16.5.2

Type escape sequence to abort.
Tracing the route to 172.16.5.2

  1 172.16.9.6 4 msec 0 msec 4 msec
  2  *   *   *
  3  *   *   *
  4
R1#traceroute 172.16.5.3

Type escape sequence to abort.
Tracing the route to 172.16.5.3

  1 172.16.9.6 0 msec 4 msec 0 msec
  2 172.16.5.3 4 msec *  0 msec
```

The example shows that R1 forwards packets to hosts 172.16.5.2 (PC2) and 172.16.5.3 (PC3) by sending them to R3 next. R3 then tries to send them onto R3's LAN subnet, which works well for PC3 but not so well for PC2. So, PC3, in the smaller of the two overlapped subnets, works fine, whereas PC2, in the larger of the two overlapped subnets, does not.

The symptoms can get even worse when addresses are duplicated. For example, imagine that PC22 has been added to R2's LAN subnet, with IP address 172.16.5.3 duplicating PC3's IP address. Now when the PC22 user calls to say that his PC cannot communicate with other devices, the network support person uses a **ping 172.16.5.3** to test the problem—and the ping works! The ping works to the wrong instance of 172.16.5.3, but it works. So, the symptoms may be particularly difficult to track down.

Another difficultly with overlapped VLSM subnets is that the problem may not show up for a while. In this same example, imagine that all addresses in both subnets were to be assigned by a DHCP server, beginning with the smallest IP addresses. For the first six months, the server assigned only IP addresses that began with 172.16.4.*x* on the R2 LAN subnet. Finally, enough hosts were installed on the R2 LAN to require the use of addresses that begin with 172.16.5, like PC2's address of 172.16.5.2 used in the preceding example.

Unfortunately, no one can send packets to those hosts. At first glance, the fact that the problem showed up long after the installation and configuration were complete may actually cloud the issue.

VLSM Troubleshooting Summary

The following list summarizes the key troubleshooting points to consider when you're troubleshooting potential VLSM problems on the exams:

- Pay close attention to whether the design really uses VLSM. If it does, note whether a classless routing protocol is used.

- Be aware that overlapping subnets can indeed be configured.

- The outward problem symptoms may be that some hosts in a subnet work well, but others cannot send packets outside the local subnet.

- Use the **traceroute** command to look for routes that direct packets to the wrong part of the network. This could be a result of the overlapped subnets.

- On the exams, you might see a question you think is related to VLSM and IP addresses. In that case, the best plan of attack may well be to analyze the math for each subnet and ensure that no overlaps exist, rather than troubleshooting using **ping** and **traceroute**.

Key Topic

Discontiguous Networks and Autosummary

Chapter 5 explained the concept of discontiguous networks, along with the solution: using a classless routing protocol with autosummarization disabled. This section examines one particular case in which a discontiguous network exists only part of the time. Figure 7-8 shows an internetwork with two classful networks: 10.0.0.0 and 172.16.0.0. The design shows two contiguous networks because a route consisting of only subnets of each network exists between all subnets of that network.

Figure 7-8   *Internetwork with (Currently) Contiguous Networks*

In this figure, with all links up and working, using a routing protocol with autosummary enabled by default, all hosts can ping all other hosts. In this design, packets for network 172.16.0.0 flow over the high route, and packets for network 10.0.0.0 flow over the low route.

Unfortunately, a problem can occur later when one of the four links between routers fails. If any link between the routers fails, one of the two classful networks becomes discontiguous. For example, if the link between R3 and R4 fails, the route from R1 to R4 passes through subnets of network 172.16.0.0, so network 10.0.0.0 is discontiguous. Even with a classless routing protocol, but with autosummarization enabled, both R1 and R4 advertise a route for 10.0.0.0/8 to R2, and R2 sees two routes to all of network 10.0.0.0— one through R1, and another through R4. The solution, as always, is to use a classless routing protocol with autosummary disabled.

Although the design in Figure 7-8 may seem a bit contrived, it happens more often than you might think—particularly as companies are bought and sold. Both for real life and the exams, keep the concept of discontiguous networks in mind for normal working cases and for cases in which redundant links fail.

Access List Troubleshooting Tips

Troubleshooting problems that are impacted by ACLs may well be one of the most difficult tasks for real networking jobs. One of the major difficulties is that the traditional troubleshooting tools such as **ping** and **traceroute** do not send packets that look like the packets matched by the variety of fields in extended ACLs. So, although a **ping** may work, the end-user host may not be able to get to the right application, or vice versa.

This section summarizes some tips for attacking ACL-related problems in real life and on the exams:

Key Topic

Step 1   Determine on which interfaces ACLs are enabled, and in which direction (**show running-config, show ip interfaces**).

Step 2   Determine which ACL statements are matched by test packets (**show access-lists, show ip access-lists**).

Step 3   Analyze the ACLs to predict which packets should match the ACL, focusing on the following points:

  a. Remember that the ACL uses first-match logic.

  b. Consider using the (possibly) faster math described in Chapter 6, "IP Access Control Lists," which converts ACL address/wildcard mask pairs into address/subnet mask pairs that allow the use of the same math as subnetting.

  c. Note the direction of the packet in relation to the server (going to the server, coming from the server). Make sure that the packets have particular values as either the source IP address and port, or as the destination IP address and port, when processed by the ACL enabled for a particular direction (in or out).

  d. Remember that the **tcp** and **udp** keywords must be used if the command needs to check the port numbers. (See Table 6-5 in Chapter 6 for a list of popular TCP and UDP port numbers.)

  e. Note that ICMP packets do not use UDP or TCP. ICMP is considered to be another protocol matchable with the **icmp** keyword (instead of **ip**, **tcp**, and **udp**).

  f. Instead of using the implicit deny any at the end of each ACL, use an explicit configuration command to deny all traffic at the end of the ACL so that the **show** command counters increment when that action is taken.

Chapter 6 covered the background information behind the tips listed in Step 3. The remainder of this section focuses on commands available for you to investigate problems in the first two steps.

If a problem in forwarding IP packets is occurring, and existing ACLs may be impacting the problem, the first problem isolation step is to find the location and direction of the ACLs. The fastest way to do this is to look at the output of the **show running-config** command and to look for **ip access-group** commands under each interface. However, in some cases, enable mode access may not be allowed, and **show** commands are required. The only way to find the interfaces and direction for any IP ACLs is the **show ip interfaces** command, as shown in Example 7-10.

Example 7-10 *Sample* **show ip interface** *Command*

```
R1>show ip interface s0/0/1
Serial0/0/1 is up, line protocol is up
  Internet address is 10.1.2.1/24
  Broadcast address is 255.255.255.255
  Address determined by setup command
  MTU is 1500 bytes
  Helper address is not set
  Directed broadcast forwarding is disabled
  Multicast reserved groups joined: 224.0.0.9
  Outgoing access list is not set
  Inbound  access list is 102
! roughly 26 more lines omitted for brevity
```

Note that the command output lists whether an ACL is enabled, in both directions, and which ACL it is. The example shows an abbreviated version of the **show ip interface S0/0/1** command, which lists messages for just this one interface. The **show ip interface** command would list the same messages for every interface in the router.

Step 2 then says that the contents of the ACL must be found. Again, the most expedient way to look at the ACL is to use the **show running-config** command. If enable mode is not allowed, the **show access-lists** and **show ip access-lists** commands give the same output. The only difference is that if other non-IP ACLs have been configured, the **show access-lists** command lists the non-IP ACLs as well. The output provides the same details shown in the configuration commands, as well as a counter for the number of packets matching each line in the ACL. Example 7-11 shows an example.

Example 7-11 *Sample* **show ip access-lists** *Command*

```
R1#show ip access-lists
Extended IP access list 102
    10 permit ip 10.1.2.0 0.0.0.255 10.1.1.0 0.0.0.255 (15 matches)
```

After the locations, directions, and configuration details of the various ACLs have been discovered in Steps 1 and 2, the hard part begins—interpreting what the ACL really does. Of particular interest is the last item in the troubleshooting tips list, item 3E. In the ACL shown in Example 7-11, some packets (15 so far) have matched the single configured **access-list** statement in ACL 102. However, some packets have probably been denied because of the implied deny all packets logic at the end of an ACL. By configuring the **access-list 102 deny ip any any** command at the end of the ACL, which explicitly matches all packets and discards them, the **show ip access-lists** command would then show the number of packets being denied at the end of the ACL. Cisco sometimes recommends adding the explicit deny all statement at the end of the ACL for easier troubleshooting.

Exam Preparation Tasks

Review All the Key Topics

Review the most important topics from this chapter, noted with the key topics icon. Table 7-6 lists these key topics and where each is discussed.

Table 7-6 *Key Topics for Chapter 7*

Key Topic Element	Description	Page Number
Table 7-1	Popular ICMP messages and their purpose	271
Figure 7-3	Diagram of how the TTL IP header field and the ICMP Time Exceeded message work	275
Figure 7-4	Demonstration of how the **traceroute** command uses the TTL field and Time Exceeded message	277
List	Two major steps and several substeps in a suggested host routing problem isolation process	279
List	Three major steps for problem isolation with IP routing in routers, with the list numbered as a continuation of the host routing problem isolation list	281
List	Three tips for general items to check when troubleshooting host connectivity problems	289
List	Configuration step list for LAN switch IP details	290
List	Conditions under which overlapping subnets can be configured, and when IOS can prevent this error	293
List	Summary of troubleshooting tips for questions in which VLSM may be causing a problem	297
List	Three steps for troubleshooting ACL problems, particularly when the configuration cannot be displayed	298-299

Complete the Tables and Lists from Memory

Print a copy of Appendix J, "Memory Tables" (found on the CD), or at least the section for this chapter, and complete the tables and lists from memory. Appendix K, "Memory Tables Answer Key," also on the CD, includes completed tables and lists for you to check your work.

Definitions of Key Terms

Define the following key terms from this chapter, and check your answers in the glossary:

Forward route, reverse route

Cisco Published ICND2 Exam Topics*
Covered in This Part

Implement an IP addressing scheme and IP Services to meet network requirements in a medium-size Enterprise branch office network

- Identify and correct common problems associated with IP addressing and host configurations

Configure and troubleshoot basic operation and routing on Cisco devices

- Compare and contrast methods of routing and routing protocols

- Configure, verify and troubleshoot OSPF

- Configure, verify and troubleshoot EIGRP

- Verify configuration and connectivity using ping, traceroute, and telnet or SSH

- Troubleshoot routing implementation issues

- Verify router hardware and software operation using SHOW & DEBUG commands

* Always recheck http://www.cisco.com for the latest posted exam topics.

Part III: Routing Protocols Configuration and Troubleshooting

This chapter covers the following subjects:

Dynamic Routing Protocol Overview: This section introduces the core concepts behind how routing protocols work and many terms related to routing protocols.

Distance Vector Routing Protocol Features: This section explains how distance vector routing protocols work, focusing on the loop-avoidance features.

Link-State Routing Protocol Features: This section explains how link-state routing protocols work, using OSPF as a specific example.

CHAPTER 8

Routing Protocol Theory

Part II, "IP Routing," focused on the IP routing (packet forwarding) process, with some coverage of how routers fill their routing tables. Part III, "Routing Protocols Configuration and Troubleshooting," which begins with this chapter, changes the focus to how routers fill their routing tables by using dynamic routing protocols.

IP routing protocols work on a set of routers, sending messages to nearby routers to help those routers learn all the best routes to reach each subnet. Although this core goal is simple, the processes used by routing protocols tend to be some of the more complex and detailed topics on the CCNA exams. This chapter begins this book's examination of IP routing protocols by explaining the fundamental concepts and theory behind how routing protocols work. Chapters 9 and 10 go on to provide much more detail about how OSPF and EIGRP work, respectively. Chapter 11 ends this part of the book by examining some troubleshooting processes and tips for OSPF and EIGRP.

"Do I Know This Already?" Quiz

The "Do I Know This Already?" quiz allows you to assess whether you should read the entire chapter. If you miss no more than one of these ten self-assessment questions, you might want to move ahead to the "Exam Preparation Tasks" section. Table 8-1 lists the major headings in this chapter and the "Do I Know This Already?" quiz questions covering the material in those sections. This helps you assess your knowledge of these specific areas. The answers to the "Do I Know This Already?" quiz appear in Appendix A.

Table 8-1 *"Do I Know This Already?" Foundation Topics Section-to-Question Mapping*

Foundation Topics Section	Questions
Dynamic Routing Protocol Overview	1–5
Distance Vector Routing Protocol Features	6–8
Link-State Routing Protocol Features	9 and 10

1. Which of the following routing protocols are considered to use distance vector logic?

    a. RIP-1

    b. RIP-2

    c. EIGRP

    d. OSPF

    e. BGP

    f. Integrated IS-IS

2. Which of the following routing protocols are considered to use link-state logic?

    a. RIP-1

    b. RIP-2

    c. EIGRP

    d. OSPF

    e. BGP

    f. Integrated IS-IS

3. Which of the following routing protocols use a metric that is, by default, at least partially affected by link bandwidth?

    a. RIP-1

    b. RIP-2

    c. EIGRP

    d. OSPF

    e. BGP

4. Which of the following interior routing protocols support VLSM?

    a. RIP-1

    b. RIP-2

    c. EIGRP

    d. OSPF

    e. Integrated IS-IS

5. Which of the following situations would cause a router using RIP-2 to remove all the routes learned from a particular neighboring router?

   a. RIP keepalive failure

   b. No longer receiving updates from that neighbor

   c. Updates received 5 or more seconds after the last update was sent to that neighbor

   d. Updates from that neighbor have the global "route bad" flag

6. Which of the following distance vector features prevents routing loops by causing the routing protocol to advertise only a subset of known routes, as opposed to the full routing table, under normal stable conditions?

   a. Counting to infinity

   b. Poison reverse

   c. Holddown

   d. Split horizon

   e. Route poisoning

7. Which of the following distance vector features prevents routing loops by advertising an infinite metric route when a route fails?

   a. Holddown

   b. Full updates

   c. Split horizon

   d. Route poisoning

8. A router that is using a distance vector protocol just received a routing update that lists a route as having an infinite metric. The previous routing update from that neighbor listed a valid metric. Which of the following is not a normal reaction to this scenario?

   a. Immediately send a partial update that includes a poison route for the failed route

   b. Put the route into holddown state

   c. Suspend split horizon for that route and send a poison reverse route

   d. Send a full update listing a poison route for the failed route

9. An internetwork is using a link-state routing protocol. The routers have flooded all LSAs, and the network is stable. Which of the following describes what the routers will do to reflood the LSAs?

    a. Each router refloods each LSA using a periodic timer that has a time similar to distance vector update timers.

    b. Each router refloods each LSA using a periodic timer that is much longer than distance vector update timers.

    c. The routers never reflood the LSAs as long as the LSAs do not change.

    d. The routers reflood all LSAs whenever one LSA changes.

10. Which of the following is true about how a router using a link-state routing protocol chooses the best route to reach a subnet?

    a. The router finds the best route in the link-state database.

    b. The router calculates the best route by running the SPF algorithm against the information in the link-state database.

    c. The router compares the metrics listed for that subnet in the updates received from each neighbor and picks the best (lowest) metric route.

Foundation Topics

Routing protocols define various ways that routers chat among themselves to determine the best routes to each destination. As networks grew more complex over time, routers gained both processing power and RAM. As a result, engineers designed newer routing protocols, taking advantage of faster links and faster routers, transforming routing protocols. This chapter follows that progression to some degree, starting with an introduction to routing protocols. Following that, the theory behind distance vector routing protocols, used with the earliest IP routing protocols, is explained. The final section of this chapter examines the theory behind link-state routing protocols, which is used by some of the more recently defined routing protocols.

Dynamic Routing Protocol Overview

NOTE If you are using the reading plan suggested in the Introduction, you should have already read about routing protocols in *CCENT/CCNA ICND1 Official Exam Certification Guide*. If so, you may want to skim the text from here to the heading "IGP Comparisons: Summary," because the next several pages cover topics already covered in Chapter 14 of the ICND1 book.

Routers add IP routes to their routing tables using three methods: connected routes, static routes, and routes learned by using dynamic routing protocols. Before we get too far into the discussion, however, it is important to define a few related terms and clear up any misconceptions about the terms *routing protocol*, *routed protocol*, and *routable protocol*. The concepts behind these terms are not that difficult, but because the terms are so similar, and because many documents pay poor attention to when each of these terms is used, they can be a bit confusing. These terms are generally defined as follows:

- **Routing protocol:** A set of messages, rules, and algorithms used by routers for the overall purpose of learning routes. This process includes the exchange and analysis of routing information. Each router chooses the best route to each subnet (path selection) and finally places those best routes in its IP routing table. Examples include RIP, EIGRP, OSPF, and BGP.

Key Topic

- **Routed protocol** and **routable protocol:** Both terms refer to a protocol that defines a packet structure and logical addressing, allowing routers to forward or route the packets. Routers forward, or route, packets defined by routed and routable protocols. Examples include IP and IPX (a part of the Novell NetWare protocol model).

NOTE The term *path selection* sometimes refers to part of the job of a routing protocol, in which the routing protocol chooses the best route.

Even though routing protocols (such as RIP) are different from routed protocols (such as IP), they do work together very closely. The routing process forwards IP packets, but if a router does not have any routes in its IP routing table that match a packet's destination address, the router discards the packet. Routers need routing protocols so that the routers can learn all the possible routes and add them to the routing table so that the routing process can forward (route) routable protocols such as IP.

Routing Protocol Functions

Cisco IOS software supports several IP routing protocols, performing the same general functions:

Key Topic

1.   Learn routing information about IP subnets from other neighboring routers.

2.   Advertise routing information about IP subnets to other neighboring routers.

3.   If more than one possible route exists to reach one subnet, pick the best route based on a metric.

4.   If the network topology changes—for example, a link fails—react by advertising that some routes have failed, and pick a new currently best route. (This process is called convergence.)

> **NOTE**   A neighboring router connects to the same link (for example, the same WAN link or the same Ethernet LAN) as another router, with the two routers being neighbors.

Figure 8-1 shows an example of three of the four functions in the list. Both R1 and R3 learn about a route to subnet 172.16.3.0/24 from R2 (function 1). After R3 learns about the route to 172.16.3.0/24 from R2, R3 advertises that route to R1 (function 2). Then R1 must make a decision about the two routes it learned about for reaching subnet 172.16.3.0/24: one with metric 1 from R2, and one with metric 2 from R3. R1 chooses the lower metric route through R2 (function 3).

Convergence is the fourth routing protocol function listed here. The term *convergence* refers to a process that occurs when the topology changes—that is, when either a router or link fails or comes back up again. When something changes, the best routes available in the network may change. Convergence simply refers to the process by which all the routers collectively realize something has changed, advertise the information about the changes to all the other routers, and all the routers then choose the currently best routes for each subnet. The ability to converge quickly, without causing loops, is one of the most important considerations when choosing which IP routing protocol to use.

Figure 8-1 *Three of the Four Basic Functions of Routing Protocols*

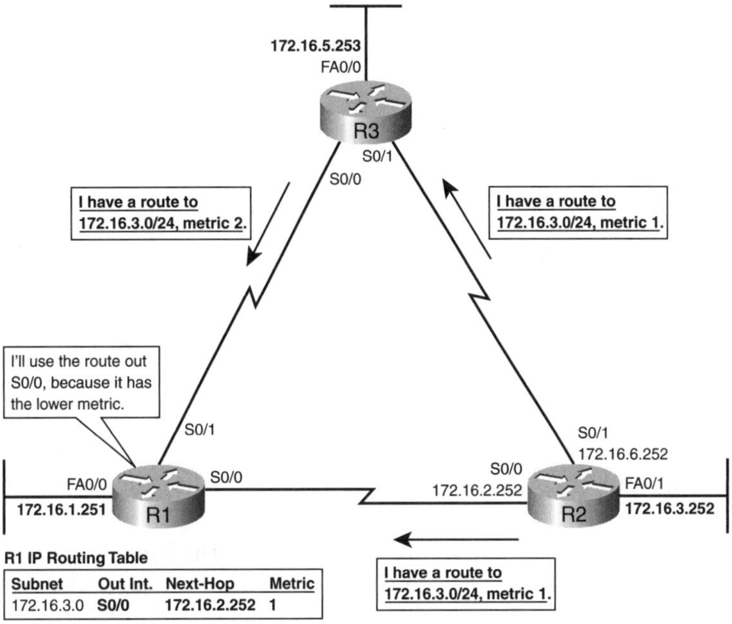

In Figure 8-1, convergence might occur if the link between R1 and R2 failed. In that case, R1 should stop using its old route for subnet 172.16.3.0/24 (directly through R2), instead sending packets to R3.

Interior and Exterior Routing Protocols

IP routing protocols fall into one of two major categories: *Interior Gateway Protocols (IGP)* or *Exterior Gateway Protocols (EGP)*. The definitions of each are as follows:

- **IGP:** A routing protocol that was designed and intended for use inside a single autonomous system (AS)

- **EGP:** A routing protocol that was designed and intended for use between different autonomous systems

> **NOTE** The terms IGP and EGP include the word gateway because routers used to be called gateways.

These definitions use another new term: autonomous system (AS). An AS is an internetwork under the administrative control of a single organization. For instance, an internetwork created and paid for by a single company is probably a single AS, and an internetwork created by a single school system is probably a single AS. Other examples include large divisions of a state or national government, where different government agencies may be able to build their own internetworks. Each ISP is also typically a single different AS.

Some routing protocols work best inside a single AS by design, so these routing protocols are called IGPs. Conversely, routing protocols designed to exchange routes between routers in different autonomous systems are called EGPs. (Currently, only one legitimate EGP exists: the Border Gateway Protocol [BGP]).

Each AS can be assigned a number called (unsurprisingly) an *AS number (ASN)*. Like public IP addresses, the Internet Corporation for Assigned Network Numbers (ICANN, http://www.icann.org) controls the worldwide rights to assigning ASNs. It delegates that authority to other organizations around the world, typically to the same organizations that assign public IP addresses. For example, in North America, the American Registry for Internet Numbers (ARIN, http://www.arin.net/) assigns public IP address ranges and ASNs.

Figure 8-2 shows a small view of the worldwide Internet. The figure shows two Enterprises and three ISPs using IGPs (OSPF and EIGRP) inside their own networks, and with BGP being used between the ASNs.

Figure 8-2 *Comparing Locations for Using IGPs and EGPs*

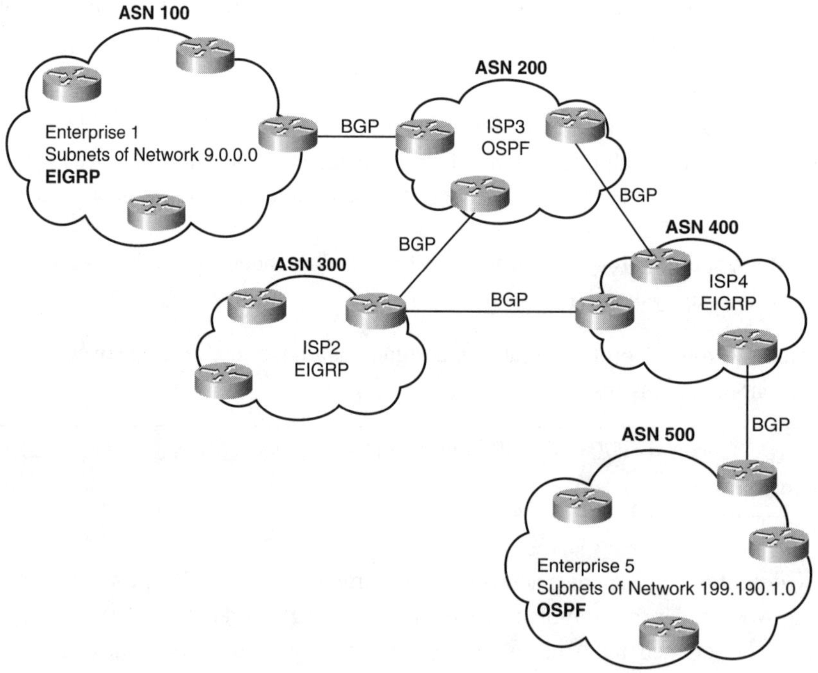

Comparing IGPs

Today, there is no real choice of what EGP to use: you simply use BGP. However, when choosing an IGP to use inside a single organization, you have several choices. The most reasonable choices today are RIP-2, EIGRP, and OSPF. Of these three IGPs, RIP-2 has already been covered to some depth in *CCENT/CCNA ICND1 Official Exam Certification Guide*, and this book covers OSPF and EIGRP in more depth in Chapters 9 and 10, respectively. This section introduces a few key comparison points between the various IP IGPs.

IGP Routing Protocol Algorithms

A routing protocol's underlying algorithm determines how the routing protocol does its job. The term *routing protocol algorithm* simply refers to the logic and processes used by different routing protocols to solve the problem of learning all routes, choosing the best route to each subnet, and converging in reaction to changes in the internetwork. Three main branches of routing protocol algorithms exist for IGP routing protocols:

- Distance vector (sometimes called Bellman-Ford after its creators)

- Link-state

- Balanced hybrid (sometimes called enhanced distance vector)

Key
Topic

Historically speaking, distance vector protocols were invented first, mainly in the early 1980s. RIP was the first popularly used IP distance vector protocol, with the Cisco-proprietary Interior Gateway Routing Protocol (IGRP) being introduced a little later. By the early 1990s, distance vector protocols' somewhat slow convergence and potential for routing loops drove the development of new alternative routing protocols that used new algorithms. Link-state protocols—in particular, OSPF and Integrated IS-IS—solved the main issues with distance vector protocols, but they required a fair amount more planning in medium- to larger-sized networks.

Around the same time as the introduction of OSPF, Cisco created a proprietary routing protocol called Enhanced Interior Gateway Routing Protocol (EIGRP), which used some features of the earlier IGRP protocol. EIGRP solved the same problems as did link-state routing protocols, but less planning was required when implementing the network. As time went on, EIGRP was classified as a unique type of routing protocol—neither distance vector nor link state—so EIGRP is called either a balanced hybrid protocol or an advanced distance vector protocol.

The second and third major sections of this chapter examine distance vector and link-state algorithms in more detail. Chapter 10 explains balanced hybrid concepts in the context of the discussion of EIGRP.

Metrics

Routing protocols choose the best route to reach a subnet by choosing the route with the lowest metric. For example, RIP uses a counter of the number of routers (hops) between a router and the destination subnet. Table 8-2 lists the most important IP routing protocols for the CCNA exams and some details about the metric in each case.

Table 8-2 *IP IGP Metrics*

IGP	Metric	Description
RIP-1, RIP-2	Hop count	The number of routers (hops) between a router and the destination subnet.
OSPF	Cost	The sum of all interface cost settings for all links in a route, with the cost defaulting to be based on interface bandwidth.
EIGRP	Composite of bandwidth and delay	Calculated based on the route's slowest link and the cumulative delay associated with each interface in the route.

Unlike RIP-1 and RIP-2, both the OSPF and EIGRP metrics are impacted by the various interface bandwidth settings. Figure 8-3 compares the impact of the metrics used by RIP and EIGRP.

Figure 8-3 *RIP and EIGRP Metrics Compared*

RIP, Regardless of Bandwidth

Routing Table Subnet

Subnet	Output Interface
10.1.1.0	S0

EIGRP

Routing Table Subnet

Subnet	Output Interface
10.1.1.0	S1

As shown at the top of the figure, Router B's RIP route to 10.1.1.0 points through Router A because that route has a lower hop count (1) than the route through Router C (2). However, in the lower half of the figure, Router B chooses the two-hop route through Router C when using EIGRP because the bandwidths of the two links in the route are much faster (better) than that of the single-hop route. Note that so that EIGRP would make the right choice, the engineer correctly configured the interface bandwidth to match the actual link speeds, thereby allowing EIGRP to choose the faster route. (The **bandwidth** interface subcommand does not change the actual physical speed of the interface. It just tells the IOS what speed to assume the interface is using.)

IGP Comparisons: Summary

For convenient comparison and study, Table 8-3 summarizes many of the features supported by various IGPs. The table includes items specifically mentioned in this chapter or in earlier chapters in this book.

Table 8-3 *Interior IP Routing Protocols Compared*

Feature	RIP-1	RIP-2	EIGRP	OSPF	IS-IS
Classless	No	Yes	Yes	Yes	Yes
Supports VLSM	No	Yes	Yes	Yes	Yes
Sends mask in update	No	Yes	Yes	Yes	Yes
Distance vector	Yes	Yes	No[1]	No	No
Link-state	No	No	No[1]	Yes	Yes
Supports autosummarization	Yes	Yes	Yes	No	No
Supports manual summarization	No	Yes	Yes	Yes	Yes
Proprietary	No	No	Yes	No	No
Routing updates are sent to a multicast IP address	No	Yes	Yes	Yes	—
Supports authentication	No	Yes	Yes	Yes	Yes
Convergence	Slow	Slow	Very fast	Fast	Fast

[1]EIGRP is often described as a balanced hybrid routing protocol, instead of link-state or distance vector. Some documents refer to EIGRP as an advanced distance vector protocol.

In addition to Table 8-3, Table 8-4 lists several other items about RIP-2, OSPF, and EIGRP. The items in Table 8-4 are explained more fully in Chapters 9 and 10, but they are included here for your reference when studying.

Key Topic

Table 8-4 *Comparing Features of IGPs: RIP-2, EIGRP, and OSPF*

Features	RIP-2	OSPF	EIGRP
Metric	Hop count	Link cost	Function of bandwidth, delay
Sends periodic updates	Yes (30 seconds)	No	No
Full or partial routing updates	Full	Partial	Partial
Where updates are sent	(224.0.0.9)[1]	(224.0.0.5, 224.0.0.6)	(224.0.0.10)
Metric considered to be "infinite"	16	$(2^{24} - 1)$	$(2^{32} - 1)$
Supports unequal-cost load balancing	No	No	Yes

[1]This table specifically refers to features of RIP-2, but the only difference with RIP-1 in this table is that RIP-1 broadcasts updates to IP address 255.255.255.255.

Administrative Distance

Many companies and organizations use a single routing protocol. However, in some cases, a company needs to use multiple routing protocols. For instance, if two companies connect their networks so that they can exchange information, they need to exchange some routing information. If one company uses RIP, and the other uses EIGRP, on at least one router, both RIP and EIGRP must be used. Then, that router can take routes learned by RIP and advertise them into EIGRP, and vice versa, through a process called route redistribution.

Depending on the network topology, the two routing protocols might learn routes to the same subnets. When a single routing protocol learns multiple routes to the same subnet, the metric tells it which route is best. However, when two different routing protocols learn routes to the same subnet, because each routing protocol's metric is based on different information, IOS cannot compare the metrics. For instance, RIP might learn a route to subnet 10.1.1.0 with metric 1, and EIGRP might learn a route to 10.1.1.0 with metric 2,195,416, but the EIGRP may be the better route—or it may not. There is simply no basis for comparison between the two metrics.

When IOS must choose between routes learned using different routing protocols, IOS uses a concept called *administrative distance*. Administrative distance is a number that denotes how believable an entire routing protocol is on a single router. The lower the number, the better, or more believable, the routing protocol. For instance, RIP has a default administrative distance of 120, and EIGRP defaults to 90, making EIGRP more believable than RIP. So, when both routing protocols learn routes to the same subnet, the router adds only the EIGRP route to the routing table.

The administrative distance values are configured on a single router and are not exchanged with other routers. Table 8-5 lists the various sources of routing information, along with the default administrative distances.

Table 8-5 *Default Administrative Distances*

Route Type	Administrative Distance
Connected	0
Static	1
BGP (external routes)	20
EIGRP (internal routes)	90
IGRP	100
OSPF	110
IS-IS	115
RIP	120
EIGRP (external routes)	170
BGP (internal routes)	200
Unusable	255

Key
Topic

> **NOTE**   The **show ip route** command lists each route's administrative distance as the first of the two numbers inside the brackets. The second number in brackets is the metric.

The table shows the default administrative distance values, but IOS can be configured to change the administrative distance of a particular routing protocol, a particular route, or even a static route. For instance, the command **ip route 10.1.3.0 255.255.255.0 10.1.130.253** defines a static route with a default administrative distance of 1, but the command **ip route 10.1.3.0 255.255.255.0 10.1.130.253 210** defines the same static route with an administrative distance of 210.

Distance Vector Routing Protocol Features

This section explains the basics of distance vector routing protocols, using RIP as an example. This section begins by examining the basic normal operations of distance vector protocols, followed by a thorough explanation of the many distance vector loop-avoidance features.

The Concept of a Distance and a Vector

The term *distance vector* describes what a router knows about each route. At the end of the process, when a router learns about a route to a subnet, all the router knows is some measurement of distance (the metric) and the next-hop router and outgoing interface to use for that route (a vector, or direction). To show you more exactly what a distance vector protocol does, Figure 8-4 shows a view of what a router learns with a distance vector routing protocol. The figure shows an internetwork in which R1 learns about three routes to reach subnet X:

■   The four-hop route through R2

■   The three-hop route through R5

■   The two-hop route through R7

Figure 8-4   *Information Learned Using Distance Vector Protocols*

R1 learns about the subnet, and a metric associated with that subnet, and nothing more. R1 must then pick the best route to reach subnet X. In this case, it picks the two-hop route through R7, because that route has the lowest metric. To further appreciate the meaning of the term distance vector, consider Figure 8-5, which shows what R1 really knows about subnet X in Figure 8-4.

Figure 8-5 *Graphical Representation of the Distance Vector Concept*

Key Topic

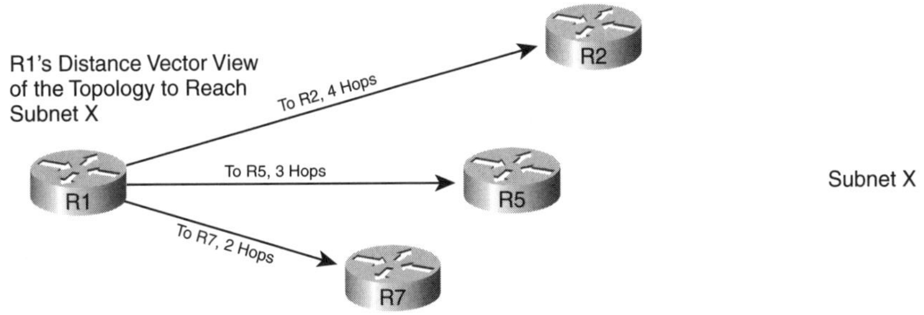

Effectively, all R1 knows about subnet X is three vectors. The length of the vectors represents the metric, which describes how good (or bad) each route is. The direction of the vector represents the next-hop router. So, with distance vector logic, routing protocols do not learn much about the network when they receive routing updates. All the routing protocols know is some concept of a vector: a vector's length is the distance (metric) to reach a subnet, and a vector's direction is through the neighbor that advertised the route.

Distance Vector Operation in a Stable Network

Distance vector routing protocols send periodic full routing updates. Figure 8-6 illustrates this concept in a simple internetwork with two routers, three LAN subnets, and one WAN subnet. The figure shows both routers' full routing tables, listing all four routes, and the periodic full updates sent by each router.

Figure 8-6 *Normal Steady-State RIP Operations*

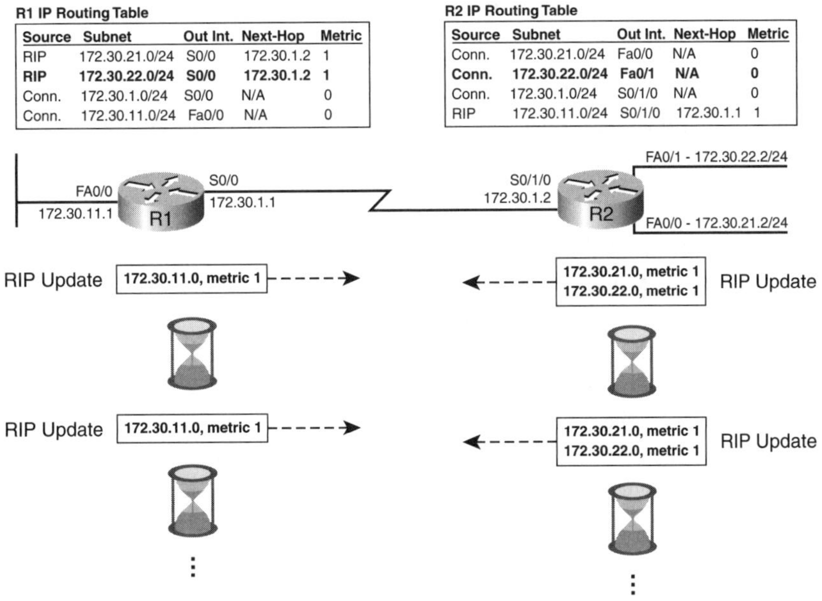

R1 IP Routing Table

Source	Subnet	Out Int.	Next-Hop	Metric
RIP	172.30.21.0/24	S0/0	172.30.1.2	1
RIP	**172.30.22.0/24**	**S0/0**	**172.30.1.2**	**1**
Conn.	172.30.1.0/24	S0/0	N/A	0
Conn.	172.30.11.0/24	Fa0/0	N/A	0

R2 IP Routing Table

Source	Subnet	Out Int.	Next-Hop	Metric
Conn.	172.30.21.0/24	Fa0/0	N/A	0
Conn.	**172.30.22.0/24**	**Fa0/1**	**N/A**	**0**
Conn.	172.30.1.0/24	S0/1/0	N/A	0
RIP	172.30.11.0/24	S0/1/0	172.30.1.1	1

To more fully understand distance vector operations in this figure, focus on some of the more important facts about what router R1 learns for subnet 172.30.22.0/24, which is the subnet connected to R2's Fa0/1 interface:

1.   R2 considers itself to have a 0 hop route for subnet 172.30.22.0/24, so in the routing update sent by R2 (shown below the R2 router icon), R2 advertises a metric 1 (hop count 1) route.

2.   R1 receives the RIP update from R2, and because R1 has learned of no other possible routes to 172.30.22.0/24, this route must be R1's best route to the subnet.

3.   R1 adds the subnet to its routing table, listing it as a RIP learned route.

4.   For the learned route, R1 uses an outgoing interface of S0/0, because R1 received R2's routing update on R1's S0/0 interface.

5.   For the learned route, R1 uses a next-hop router of 172.30.1.2, because R1 learned the route from a RIP update whose source IP address was 172.30.1.2.

At the end of this process, R1 has learned a new route. The rest of the RIP learned routes in this example follow the same process.

Besides the process of advertising and learning routes, Figure 8-6 also highlights a few other particularly important facts about distance vector protocols:

- **Periodic:** The hourglass icons represent the fact that the updates repeat on a regular cycle. RIP uses a 30-second update interval by default.

- **Full updates:** The routers send full updates every time instead of just sending new or changed routing information.

- **Full updates limited by split-horizon rules:** The routing protocol omits some routes from the periodic full updates because of split-horizon rules. Split horizon is a loop-avoidance feature that is covered in the next few pages.

Distance Vector Loop Prevention

As you can see, the actual distance vector process is pretty simple. Unfortunately, the simplicity of distance vector protocols introduced the possibility of routing loops. Routing loops occur when the routers forward packets such that the same single packet ends up back at the same routers repeatedly, wasting bandwidth and never delivering the packet. In production networks, the number of looping packets could congest the network to the point that the network becomes unusable, so routing loops must be avoided as much as possible. The rest of this chapter's coverage of distance vector protocols is devoted to describing a variety of distance vector features that help prevent loops.

Key
Topic

Route Poisoning

When a route fails, distance vector routing protocols risk causing routing loops until every router in the internetwork believes and knows that the original route has failed. As a result, distance vector protocols need a way to specifically identify which routes have failed.

Distance vector protocols spread the bad news about a route failure by poisoning the route. *Route poisoning* refers to the practice of advertising a route, but with a special metric value called *infinity*. Simply put, routers consider routes advertised with an infinite metric to have failed. Note that each distance vector routing protocol uses the concept of an actual metric value that represents infinity. RIP defines infinity as 16.

Figure 8-7 shows an example of route poisoning with RIP, with R2's Fa0/1 interface failing, meaning that R2's route for 172.30.22.0/24 has failed.

> **NOTE**   Even though routes poisoned by RIP have a metric of 16, the **show ip route** command does not list the metric's value. Instead, it lists the phrase "possibly down."

Figure 8-7 *Route Poisoning*

Figure 8-7 shows the following process:

1. R2's Fa0/1 interface fails.

2. R2 removes its connected route for 172.30.22.0/24 from its routing table.

3. R2 advertises 172.30.22.0 with an infinite metric, which for RIP is metric 16.

4. R1 keeps the route in its routing table, with an infinite metric, until it removes the route from the routing table.

Any metric value below infinity can be used as a valid metric for a valid route. With RIP, that means that a 15-hop route would be a valid route. Some of the largest enterprise networks in the world have at most four or five routers in the longest route between any two subnets, so a valid maximum metric of 15 hops is enough.

Problem: Counting to Infinity over a Single Link

Distance vector routing protocols risk causing routing loops during the time between when the first router realizes a route has failed until all the routers know that the route has failed. Without the loop-prevention mechanisms explained in this chapter, distance vector protocols can experience a problem called counting to infinity. Certainly, routers could never literally count to infinity, but they can count to their version of infinity—for example, to 16 with RIP.

Counting to infinity causes two related problems. Several of the distance vector loop-prevention features focus on preventing these problems:

- Packets may loop around the internetwork while the routers count to infinity, with the bandwidth consumed by the looping packets crippling an internetwork.
- The counting-to-infinity process may take several minutes, meaning that the looping could cause users to believe that the network has failed.

When routers count to infinity, they collectively keep changing their minds about the metric of a failed route. The metric grows slowly until it reaches infinity, at which point the routers finally believe that the route has failed. The best way to understand this concept is to see an example; Figure 8-8 shows the beginnings of the counting-to-infinity problem.

Figure 8-8 *R2 Incorrectly Believes That R1 Has a Route to 172.30.22.0/24*

R1 IP Routing Table (After Step 4)

Source	Subnet	Out Int.	Next-Hop	Metric
RIP	172.30.21.0/24	S0/0	172.30.1.2	1
RIP	**172.30.22.0/24**	**S0/0**	**172.30.1.2**	**16**
Conn.	172.30.1.0/24	S0/0	N/A	0
Conn.	172.30.11.0/24	Fa0/0	N/A	0

R2 IP Routing Table (After Step 3)

Source	Subnet	Out Int.	Next-Hop	Metric
Conn.	172.30.21.0/24	Fa0/0	N/A	0
RIP	**172.30.22.0/24**	**S0/1/0**	**172.30.1.1**	**2**
Conn.	172.30.1.0/24	S0/1/0	N/A	0
RIP	172.30.11.0/24	S0/1/0	172.30.1.1	1

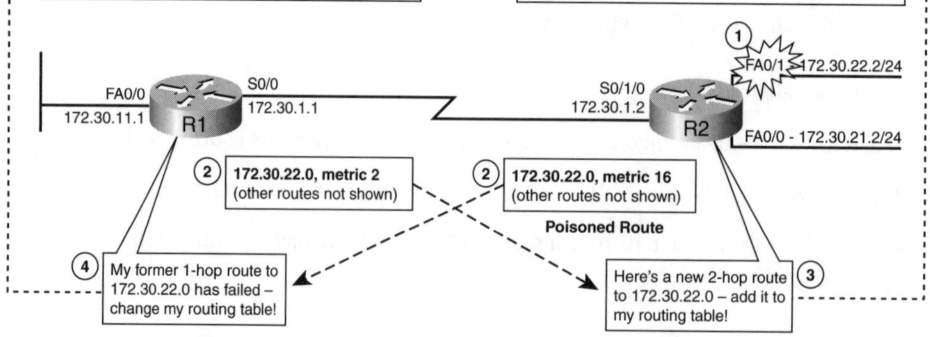

The key to this example is to know that R1's periodic update to R2 (left-to-right in Figure 8-8) occurs at almost the same instant as R2's poison route advertisement to R1. Figure 8-8 shows the following process:

1. R2's Fa0/1 interface fails, so R2 removes its connected route for 172.30.22.0/24 from its routing table.

2. R2 sends a poisoned route advertisement (metric 16 for RIP) to R1, but *at about the same time*, R1's periodic update timer expires, so R1 sends its regular update, including an advertisement about 172.30.22.0, metric 2.

3. R2 hears about the metric 2 route to reach 172.30.22.0 from R1. Because R2 no longer has a route for subnet 172.30.22.0, it adds the two-hop route to its routing table, next-hop router R1.

4. At about the same time as Step 3, R1 receives the update from R2, telling R1 that its former route to 172.30.22.0, through R2, has failed. As a result, R1 changes its routing table to list a metric of 16 for the route to 172.30.22.0.

At this point, R1 and R2 forward packets destined for 172.30.22.0/24 back and forth to each other. R2 has a route for 172.30.22.0/24, pointing to R1, and R1 has the reverse. The looping occurs until R1 and R2 both count to infinity. Figure 8-9 shows the next step in their cooperative march toward infinity.

Figure 8-9 *R1 and R2 Count to Infinity*

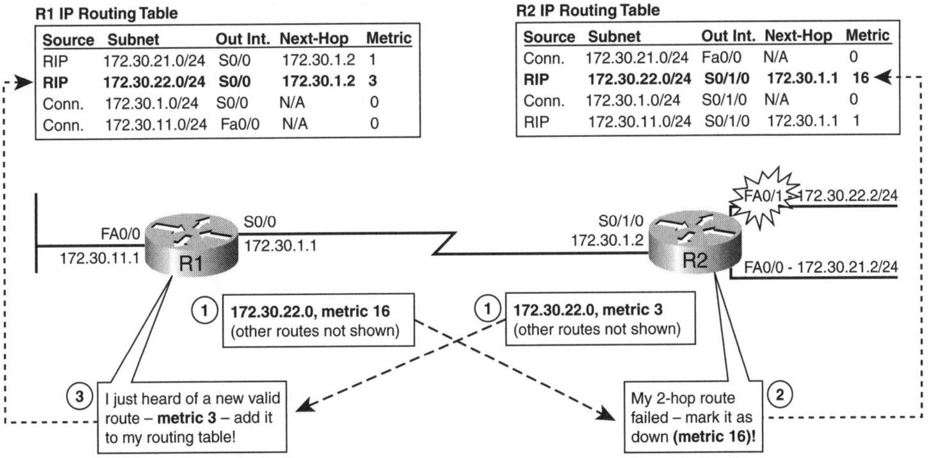

Figure 8-9 shows both routers' next periodic updates, as follows:

1. Both R1's and R2's update timers expire at about the same time. R1 advertises a poison (metric 16) route, and R2 advertises a metric 3 route. (Remember, RIP routers add 1 to the metric before advertising the route.)

2. R2 receives R1's update, so R2 changes its route for 172.30.22.0 to use a metric of 16.

3. At about the same time as Step 2, R1 receives R2's update, so R1 changes its route for 172.30.22.0 to use a metric of 3.

The process continues through each periodic update cycle, with both routers eventually reaching metric 16. At that point, the routers could time out the routes and remove them from their routing tables.

Split Horizon

In the simple internetwork used in Figures 8-8 and 8-9, router R2 has a connected route to 172.30.22.0, and R1 learns the route because of a routing update sent by R2. However, there is little need for R1 to advertise that same route back to R2, because R1 learned that route from R2 in the first place. So, one way to prevent the counting-to-infinity problem shown in these figures is to have R1 simply not advertise subnet 172.30.22.0, using a feature called split horizon. Split horizon is defined as follows:

> **Key Topic**
>
> In routing updates sent out interface X, do not include routing information about routes that refer to interface X as the outgoing interface.

Distance vector protocols work a lot like how people in a neighborhood spread rumors. People tell their neighbors, who tell other neighbors, until eventually everyone in the neighborhood learns the latest gossip. Following that analogy, if you heard a rumor from your neighbor Fred, you wouldn't turn around and tell him the same rumor. Likewise, split horizon means that when router R1 learns a route from router R2, R1 has no need to advertise that same route back to router R2.

Figure 8-10 shows the effect of split horizon on routers R1 and R2 in the same familiar internetwork. R1's routing table (at the top of the figure) lists four routes, three of which have R1's S0/0 interface as the outgoing interface. So, split horizon prevents R1 from including those three routes in the update sent by R1 out its S0/0 interface.

Figure 8-10 *Effects of Split Horizon Without Poison Reverse*

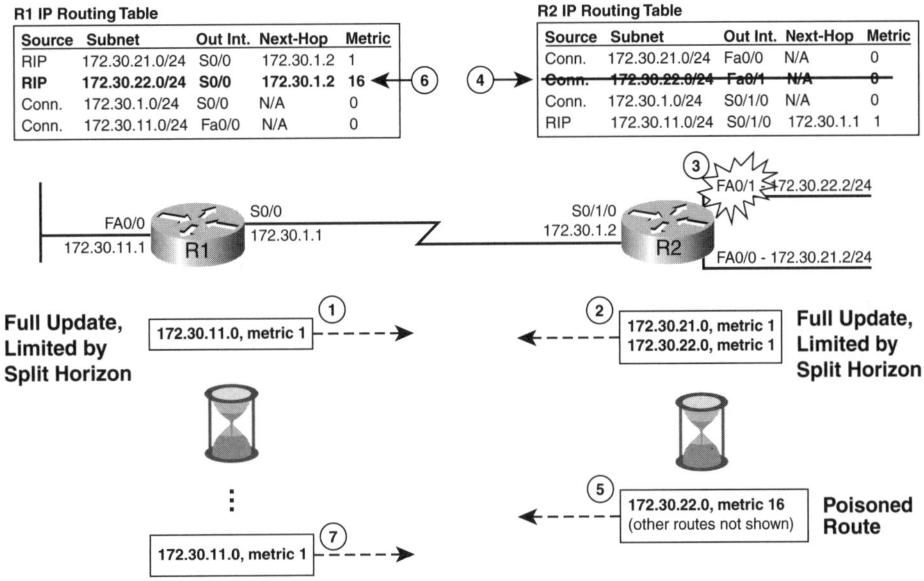

Figure 8-10 shows the following process:

1. R1 sends its normal periodic full update, which, because of split-horizon rules, includes only one route.

2. R2 sends its normal periodic full update, which, because of split-horizon rules, includes only two routes.

3. R2's Fa0/1 interface fails.

4. R2 removes its connected route for 172.30.22.0/24 from its routing table.

5. R2 advertises 172.30.22.0 with an infinite metric, which for RIP is metric 16.

6. R1 temporarily keeps the route for 172.30.22.0 in its routing table, later removing the route from the routing table.

7. In its next regular update, R1, because of split horizon, still does not advertise the route for 172.30.22.0.

Split horizon prevents the counting-to-infinity problem shown in Figures 8-8 and 8-9 because R1 does not advertise 172.30.22.0 to R2 at all. As a result, R2 never hears about an (incorrect) alternative route to 172.30.22.0. Cisco IOS defaults to use split horizon on most interfaces.

> **NOTE**   RIP implementation with Cisco IOS does not act exactly as described in Step 7 of this particular example. Instead, it uses a feature called poison reverse, as described in the next section.

Poison Reverse and Triggered Updates

Distance vector protocols can attack the counting-to-infinity problem by ensuring that every router learns that the route has failed, through every means possible, as quickly as possible. The next two loop-prevention features do just that and are defined as follows:

Key Topic

- **Triggered update:** When a route fails, do not wait for the next periodic update. Instead, send an immediate triggered update listing the poisoned route.

- **Poison reverse:** When learning of a failed route, suspend split-horizon rules for that route, and advertise a poisoned route.

Figure 8-11 shows an example of each of these features, with R2's interface Fa0/1 failing yet again. Note that the figure begins with all interfaces working, and all routes known.

Figure 8-11   *R2 Sending a Triggered Update, with R1 Advertising a Poison Reverse Route*

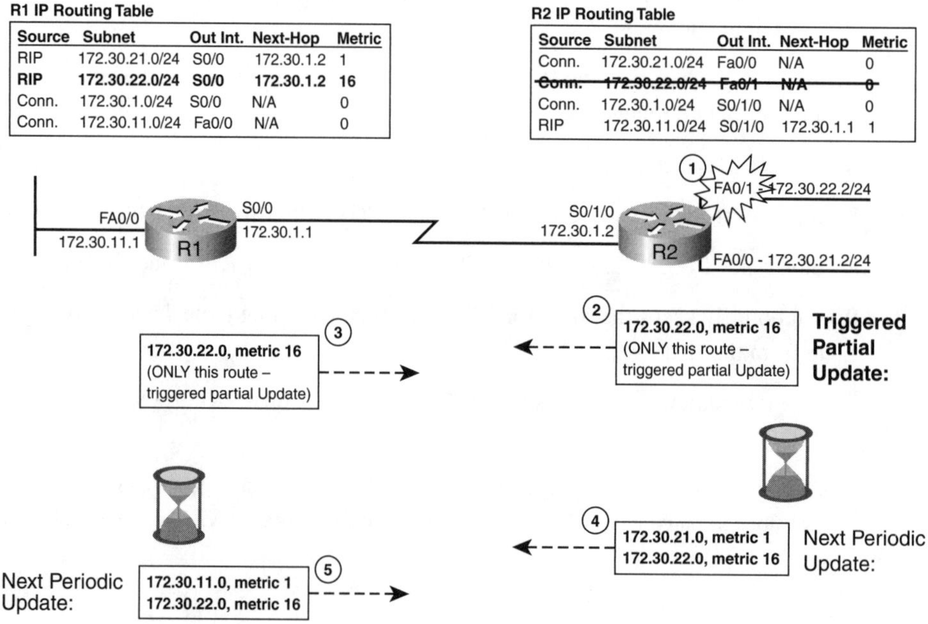

The process shown in Figure 8-11 runs as follows:

1. R2's Fa0/1 interface fails.

2. R2 immediately sends a triggered partial update with only the changed information—in this case, a poison route for 172.30.22.0.

3. R1 responds by changing its routing table and sending back an immediate (triggered) partial update, listing only 172.30.22.0 with an infinite metric (metric 16). This is a poison reverse route.

4. On R2's next regular periodic update, R2 advertises all the typical routes, including the poison route for 172.30.22.0, for a time.

5. On R1's next regular periodic update, R1 advertises all the typical routes, plus the poison reverse route for 172.30.22.0, for a time.

In this example, R2 reacts immediately by sending the triggered update. R1 also reacts immediately, suspending split-horizon rules for the failed route to send a poison reverse route. In fact, R2's poison route is not considered to be a poison reverse route, because R2 was already advertising a route for 172.30.22.0. However, R1's poison route is a poison reverse route because it was advertised back to the router from which R1 learned about the failed route. In fact, some books also refer to poison reverse as *split horizon with poison reverse*, because the router suspends the split-horizon rule for the failed route.

Problem: Counting to Infinity in a Redundant Network

Split horizon prevents the counting-to-infinity problem from occurring between two routers. However, with redundant paths in an internetwork, which is true of most internetworks today, split horizon alone does not prevent the counting-to-infinity problem. To see the problem, Figure 8-12 shows the new working network in its normal, stable, everything-working state. Figures 8-13 and 8-14 show in a moment how the counting-to-infinity problem occurs, even when split horizon is enabled.

Figure 8-12 *Periodic Updates in a Stable Triangle Internetwork*

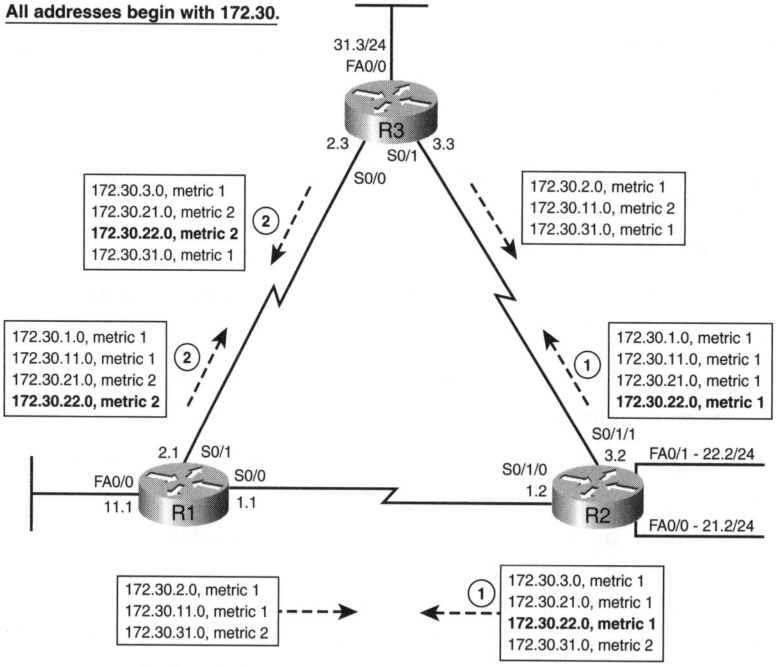

> **NOTE** Figure 8-12 omits the RIP updates that would be sent out the LAN interfaces to make the figure less cluttered.

Besides showing the normal operation of another network, Figure 8-12 provides a good example of how split horizon works. Again using subnet 172.30.22.0 as an example, the following process occurs in this internetwork:

1. R2 advertises a metric 1 route in its updates to both R1 and R3.
2. R1 then advertises a metric 2 route for 172.30.22.0 to R3, and R3 advertises a metric 2 route for 172.30.22.0 to R1.
3. Both R1 and R3 add the metric 1 route, learned directly from R2, to their routing tables, and ignore the two-hop routes they learn from each other. For example, R1 places route 172.30.22.0, using outgoing interface S0/0, next-hop router 172.30.1.2 (R2), in its routing table.

Split horizon prevents R1 and R3 from advertising subnet 172.30.22.0 back to R2. Note that Figure 8-12 shows all the route advertisements for 172.30.22.0 in bold text. R1 and R3 do not list 172.30.22.0 in their updates sent back to R2. In fact, all the routing updates shown in Figure 8-12 show the effects of split horizon.

Now that you have a good understanding of the internetwork shown in Figure 8-12, Figure 8-13 shows the same internetwork, but with the beginning of the counting-to-infinity problem, even though split horizon is enabled. Again, R2's fa0/1 begins the example by failing.

Figure 8-13 *Counting to Infinity in a Redundant Internetwork*

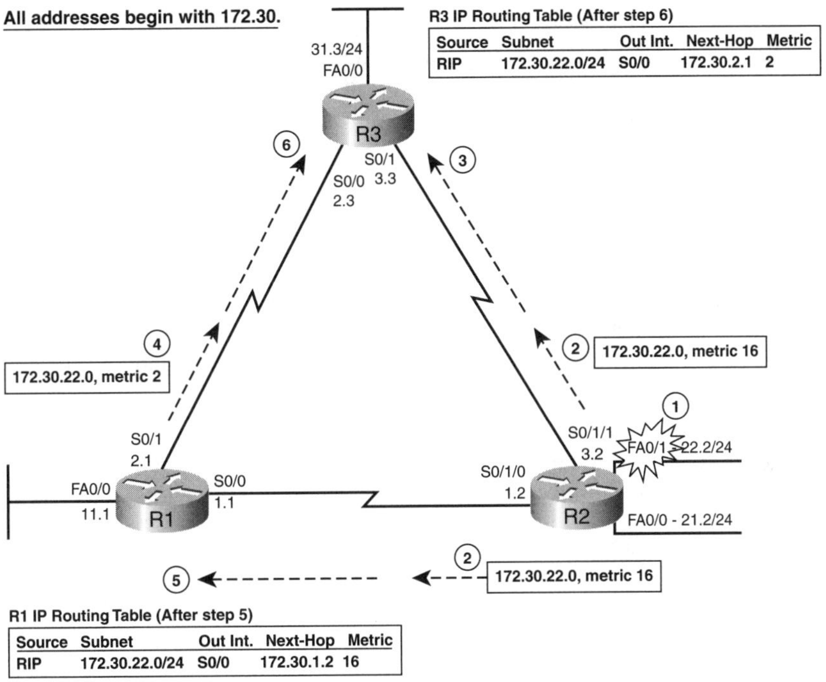

The process shown in Figure 8-13 is as follows. As usual, this example relies on some unfortunate timing of periodic routing updates around the time that the route fails.

1. R2's Fa0/1 interface fails.

2. R2 immediately sends a triggered partial update, poisoning the route for 172.30.22.0. R2 sends the updates out all still-working interfaces.

3. R3 receives R2's triggered update that poisons the route for 172.30.22.0, so R3 updates its routing table to list metric 16 for this route.

4.   Before the update described in Step 2 arrives at R1, R1 sends its normal periodic update to R3, listing 172.30.22.0, metric 2, as normal. (Note that Figure 8-13 omits some of what would be in R1's periodic update to reduce clutter.)

5.   R1 receives R2's triggered update (described in Step 2) that poisons the route for 172.30.22.0, so R1 updates its routing table to list metric 16 for this route.

6.   R3 receives the periodic update sent by R1 (described in Step 4), listing a metric 2 route for 172.30.22.0. As a result, R3 updates its routing table to list a metric 2 route, through R1 as the next-hop router, with outgoing interface S0/0.

At this point, R3 has an incorrect metric 2 route for 172.30.22.0, pointing back to R1. Depending on the timing of when the entries enter and leave the routing table, the routers may end up forwarding the packets sent to subnet 172.30.22.0/24 through the network, possibly looping some packets around the network several times, while the counting-to-infinity process continues.

The Holddown Process and Holddown Timer

The last loop-prevention feature covered in this chapter, a process called *holddown*, prevents the looping and counting-to-infinity problem shown in Figure 8-13. Distance vector protocols use holddown to specifically prevent the loops created by the counting-to-infinity problems that occur in redundant internetworks. The term holddown gives a hint as to its meaning:

> As soon as the route is considered to be down, *hold it down for a while* to give the routers time to make sure every router knows that the route has failed.

The holddown process tells a router to ignore new information about the failed route, for a time period called the holddown time, as counted using the *holddown timer*. The holddown process can be summarized as follows:

Key Topic

> After hearing a poisoned route, start a holddown timer for that one route. Until the timer expires, do not believe any other routing information about the failed route, because believing that information may cause a routing loop. However, information learned from the neighbor that originally advertised the working route can be believed before the holddown timer expires.

The holddown concept may be better understood with an example. Figure 8-14 repeats the example of Figure 8-13, but with R3's holddown process preventing the counting-to-infinity problem. The figure shows how R3 ignores any new information about subnet 172.30.22.0 because of holddown. As usual, the figure begins with all interfaces up and working, and all routes known, and with Step 1 being the failure of the same interface off router R2.

Figure 8-14 *Using Holddown to Prevent Counting to Infinity*

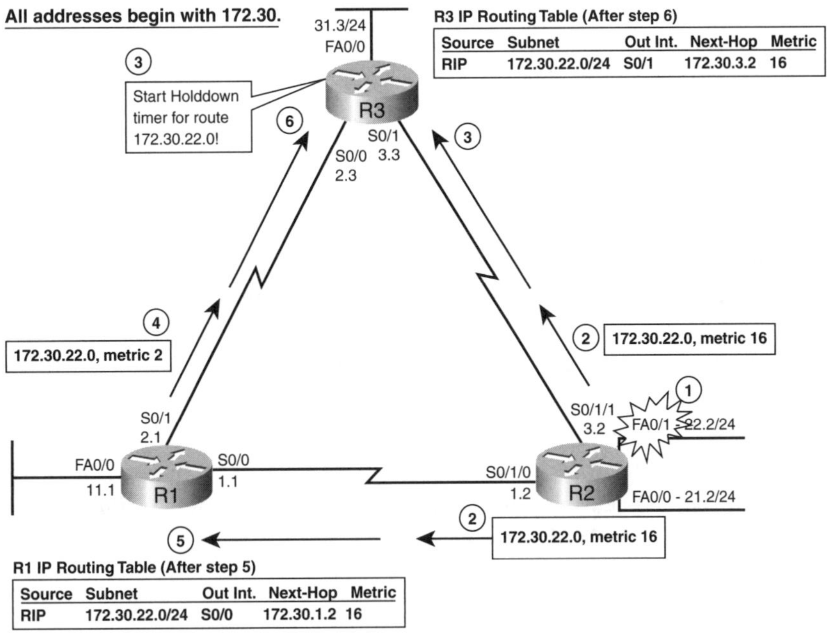

The process shown in Figure 8-14 is as follows, with Steps 3 and 6 differing from Figure 8-13's steps:

1. R2's Fa0/1 interface fails.

2. R2 immediately sends a triggered partial update, poisoning the route for 172.30.22.0. R2 sends the updates out all still-working interfaces.

3. R3 receives R2's triggered update that poisons the route for 172.30.22.0, so R3 updates its routing table to list metric 16 for this route. R3 also puts the route for 172.30.22.0 in holddown and starts the holddown timer for the route (the default is 180 seconds with RIP).

4. Before the update described in Step 2 arrives at R1, R1 sends its normal periodic update to R3, listing 172.30.22.0, metric 2, as normal. (Note that Figure 8-14 omits some details in R1's periodic update to reduce clutter.)

5. R1 receives R2's triggered update (described in Step 2) that poisons the route for 172.30.22.0, so R1 updates its routing table to list metric 16 for this route.

6. R3 receives the update from R1 (described in Step 4), listing a metric 2 route for 172.30.22.0. Because R3 has placed this route in a holddown state, and this new metric 2 route was learned from a different router (R1) than the original route (R2), R3 ignores the new routing information.

As a result of R3's holddown logic described in Step 6, all three routers have a metric 16 route for 172.30.22.0. At this point, any future routing updates will list only metric 16 routes for this subnet—at least until a real route to the subnet becomes available again.

The definition of holddown allows the routers to believe the same router that originally advertised the route, even before the holddown timer expires. For example, the entire process of Figure 8-14 may occur within just a few seconds because of all the triggered updates. If R2's Fa0/1 interface comes up again, R2 then advertises a metric 1 route for 172.30.22.0 again. If R1 and R3 would believe R2's advertisement, they could avoid waiting almost 3 more minutes for their holddown timers to expire for subnet 172.30.22.0. As it turns out, believing the routing update from the same router that originally advertised the route does not risk causing a loop. Therefore, holddown allows the routers (in this case R1 and R3) to believe R2's advertisement.

Distance Vector Summary

Before closing the coverage of distance vector loop avoidance, it is useful to review the concepts covered here. This section covered a lot of theory, some of which can be a little tricky, but the main features can be summarized easily:

■ During periods of stability, routers send periodic full routing updates based on a short update timer (the RIP default is 30 seconds). The updates list all known routes except the routes omitted because of split-horizon rules.

■ When changes occur that cause a route to fail, the router that notices the failure reacts by immediately sending triggered partial updates, listing only the newly poisoned (failed) routes, with an infinite metric.

■ Other routers that hear the poisoned route also send triggered partial updates, poisoning the failed route.

■ Routers suspend split-horizon rules for the failed route by sending a poison reverse route back toward the router from which the poisoned route was learned.

■ All routers place the route in holddown state and start a holddown timer for that route after learning that the route has failed. Each router ignores all new information about this route until the holddown timer expires, unless that information comes from the same router that originally advertised the good route to that subnet.

Link-State Routing Protocol Features

Like distance vector protocols, link-state protocols send routing updates to neighboring routers, which in turn send updates to their neighboring routers, and so on. At the end of the process, like distance vector protocols, routers that use link-state protocols add the best routes to their routing tables, based on metrics. However, beyond this level of explanation, these two types of routing protocol algorithms have little in common.

This section covers the most basic mechanics of how link-state protocols work, with the examples using Open Shortest Path First (OSPF), the first link-state IP routing protocol, in the examples. The section begins by showing how link-state routing protocols flood routing information throughout the internetwork. Then it describes how link-state protocols process the routing information to choose the best routes.

Building the Same LSDB on Every Router

Routers using link-state routing protocols need to collectively advertise practically every detail about the internetwork to all the other routers. At the end of the process, called flooding, every router in the internetwork has the exact same information about the internetwork. Routers use this information, stored in RAM inside a data structure called the link-state database (LSDB), to perform the other major link-state process to calculate the currently best routes to each subnet. Flooding a lot of detailed information to every router sounds like a lot of work, and relative to distance vector routing protocols, it is.

Open Shortest Path First (OSPF), the most popular link-state IP routing protocol, advertises information in routing update messages of various types, with the updates containing information called link-state advertisements (LSA). LSAs come in many forms, including the following two main types:

- **Router LSA:** Includes a number to identify the router (router ID), the router's interface IP addresses and masks, the state (up or down) of each interface, and the cost (metric) associated with the interface.

- **Link LSA:** Identifies each link (subnet) and the routers that are attached to that link. It also identifies the link's state (up or down).

Some routers must first create the router and link LSAs, and then flood the LSAs to all other routers. Each router creates a router LSA for itself and then floods that LSA to other routers in routing update messages. To flood an LSA, a router sends the LSA to its neighbors. Those neighbors in turn forward the LSA to their neighbors, and so on, until all the routers have learned about the LSA. For the link LSAs, one router attached to a subnet also creates and floods a link LSA for each subnet. (Note that in some cases, a link LSA is not required, typically when only one router connects to the subnet.) At the end of the process, every router has every other router's router LSA and a copy of all the link LSAs as well.

Figure 8-15 shows the general idea of the flooding process, with R8 creating and flooding its router LSA. Note that Figure 8-15 actually shows only a subset of the information in R8's router LSA.

Figure 8-15   *Flooding LSAs Using a Link-State Routing Protocol*

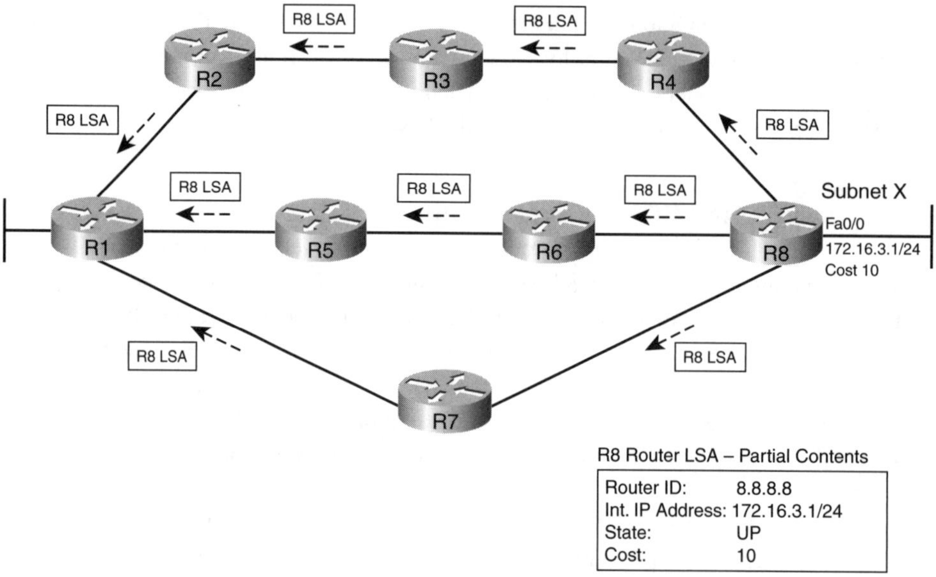

Figure 8-15 shows the rather basic flooding process, with R8 sending the original LSA for itself, and the other routers flooding the LSA by forwarding it until every router has a copy. To prevent looping LSA advertisements, a router that knows about the LSA first asks its neighbor if that neighbor already knows about this LSA. For example, R8 would begin by separately asking R4, R6, and R7 if they know about the router LSA for R8. Those three routers would reply, stating that they do not know about the R8 router LSA. Only at that point does R8 send the LSA to each of those neighboring routers. The process repeats with every neighbor. If a router has already learned the LSA—no matter over what path—it could politely say that it already has the LSA, thereby preventing the LSA from being advertised in loops around the network.

The origins of the term *link state* can be explained by considering the (partial) contents of the router LSA shown in Figure 8-15. The figure shows one of the four interface IP addresses that would be listed in R8's router LSA, along with the interface's state. Link-state protocols get their name from the fact that the LSAs advertise each interface (link) and whether the interface is up or down (state). So, the LSDB contains information about not only the up and working routers and interfaces and links (subnets), but all routers and interfaces and links (subnets), even if the interfaces are down.

After the LSA has been flooded, even if the LSAs do not change, link-state protocols do require periodic reflooding of the LSAs, similar to the periodic updates sent by distance vector protocols. However, distance vector protocols typically use a short timer; for example, RIP sends periodic updates every 30 seconds and RIP sends a full update listing all normally advertised routes. OSPF refloods each LSA based on each LSA's separate aging timer (default 30 minutes). As a result, in a stable internetwork, link-state protocols actually use less network bandwidth to send routing information than do distance vector protocols. If an LSA changes, the router immediately floods the changed LSA. For example, if Figure 8-15's Router R8's LAN interface failed, R8 would need to reflood the R8 LSA, stating that the interface is now down.

Applying Dijkstra SPF Math to Find the Best Routes

The link-state flooding process results in every router having an identical copy of the LSDB in memory, but the flooding process alone does not cause a router to learn what routes to add to the IP routing table. Although incredibly detailed and useful, the information in the LSDB does not explicitly state each router's best route to reach a destination. Link-state protocols must use another major part of the link-state algorithm to find and add routes to the IP routing table—routes that list a subnet number and mask, an outgoing interface, and a next-hop router IP address. This process uses something called the Dijkstra Shortest Path First (SPF) algorithm.

The SPF algorithm can be compared to how humans think when taking a trip using a road map. Anyone can buy the same road map, so anyone can know all the information about the roads. However, when you look at the map, you first find your starting and ending locations, and then you analyze the map to find the possible routes. If several routes look similar in length, you may decide to take a longer route if the roads are highways rather than country roads. Someone else may own the same map, but they might be starting from a different location, and going to a different location, so they may choose a totally different route.

In the analogy, the LSDB works like the map, and the SPF algorithm works like the person reading the map. The LSDB holds all the information about all the possible routers and links. The SPF algorithm defines how a router should process the LSDB, with each router considering itself to be the starting point for the route. Each router uses itself as the starting point because each router needs to put routes in its own routing table. The SPF algorithm calculates all the possible routes to reach a subnet, and the cumulative metric for each entire route, for each possible destination subnet. In short, each router must view itself as the starting point, and each subnet as the destination, and use the SPF algorithm to look at the LSDB road map to find and pick the best route to each subnet.

Figure 8-16 shows a graphical view of the results of the SPF algorithm run by router R1 when trying to find the best route to reach subnet 172.16.3.0/24 (based on Figure 8-15). Figure 8-16 shows R1 at the top of the figure rather than on the left because SPF creates a mathematical tree. These trees are typically drawn with the base or root of the tree at the top of the figure, and the leaves (subnets) at the bottom.

Key Topic

Figure 8-16 *SPF Tree to Find R1's Route to 172.16.3.0/24*

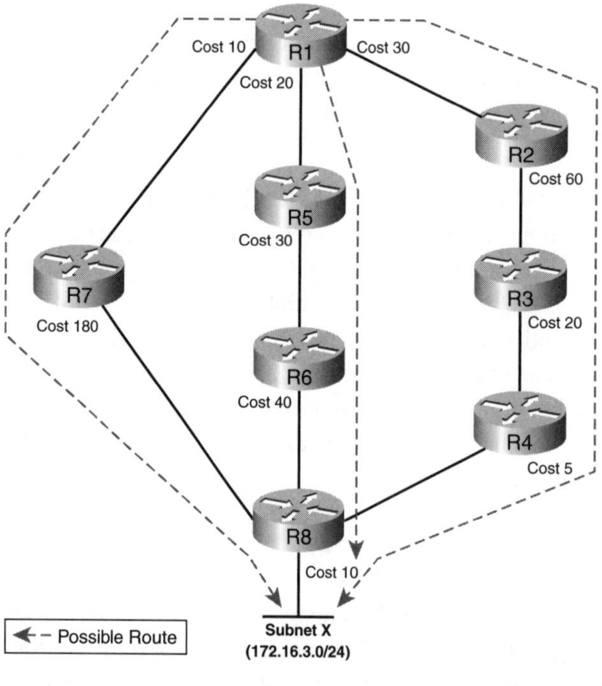

Figure 8-16 does not show the SPF algorithm's math (frankly, almost no one bothers looking at the math), but it does show a drawing of the kind of analysis done by the SPF algorithm on R1. Generally, each router runs the SPF process to find all routes to each subnet, and then the SPF algorithm can pick the best route. To pick the best route, a router's SPF algorithm adds the cost associated with each link between itself and the destination subnet, over each possible route. Figure 8-16 shows the costs associated with each route beside the links, with the dashed lines showing the three routes R1 finds between itself and subnet X (172.16.3.0/24).

Table 8-6 lists the three routes shown in Figure 8-16, with their cumulative costs, showing that R1's best route to 172.16.3.0/24 starts by going through R5.

Table 8-6 *Comparing R1's Three Alternatives for the Route to 172.16.3.0/24*

Route	Location in Figure 8-16	Cumulative Cost
R1–R7–R8	Left	10 + 180 + 10 = 200
R1–R5–R6–R8	Middle	20 + 30 + 40 + 10 = 100
R1–R2–R3–R4–R8	Right	30 + 60 + 20 + 5 + 10 = 125

As a result of the SPF algorithm's analysis of the LSDB, R1 adds a route to subnet 172.16.3.0/24 to its routing table, with the next-hop router of R5.

Convergence with Link-State Protocols

As soon as the internetwork is stable, link-state protocols reflood each LSA on a regular basis. (OSPF defaults to 30 minutes.) However, when an LSA changes, link-state protocols react swiftly, converging the network and using the currently best routes as quickly as possible. For example, imagine that the link between R5 and R6 fails in the internetwork of Figures 8-15 and 8-16. The following list explains the process R1 uses to switch to a different route. (Similar steps would occur for changes to other routers and routes.)

1. R5 and R6 flood LSAs that state that their interfaces are now in a "down" state. (In a network of this size, the flooding typically takes maybe a second or two.)

2. All routers run the SPF algorithm again to see if any routes have changed. (This process may take another second in a network this size.)

3. All routers replace routes, as needed, based on the results of SPF. (This takes practically no additional time after SPF has completed.) For example, R1 changes its route for subnet X (172.16.3.0/24) to use R2 as the next-hop router.

These steps allow the link-state routing protocol to converge quickly—much more quickly than distance vector routing protocols.

Summary and Comparisons to Distance Vector Protocols

Link-state routing protocols provide fast convergence, which is probably the most important feature of a routing protocol, with built-in loop avoidance. Link-state routing protocols do not need to use the large variety of loop-avoidance features used by distance vector protocols, which in itself greatly reduces the convergence time. The main features of a link-state routing protocol are as follows:

■   All routers learn the same detailed information about all routers and subnets in the internetwork.

■   The individual pieces of topology information are called LSAs. All LSAs are stored in RAM in a data structure called the link-state database (LSDB).

■   Routers flood LSAs when 1) they are created, 2) on a regular (but long) time interval if the LSAs do not change over time, and 3) immediately when an LSA changes.

■   The LSDB does not contain routes, but it does contain information that can be processed by the Dijkstra SPF algorithm to find a router's best route to reach each subnet.

■   Each router runs the SPF algorithm, with the LSDB as input, resulting in the best (lowest-cost/lowest-metric) routes being added to the IP routing table.

■   Link-state protocols converge quickly by immediately reflooding changed LSAs and rerunning the SPF algorithm on each router.

One of the most important comparison points between different routing protocols is how fast the routing protocol converges. Certainly, link-state protocols converge much more quickly than distance vector protocols. The following list summarizes some of the key comparison points for different routing protocols, comparing the strengths of the underlying algorithms:

■   **Convergence:** Link-state protocols converge much more quickly.

■   **CPU and RAM:** Link-state protocols consume much more CPU and memory than distance vector protocols, although with proper design, this disadvantage can be reduced.

■   **Avoiding routing loops:** Link-state protocols inherently avoid loops, whereas distance vector protocols require many additional features (for example, split horizon).

■   **Design effort:** Distance vector protocols do not require much planning, whereas link-state protocols require much more planning and design effort, particularly in larger networks.

■   **Configuration:** Distance vector protocols typically require less configuration, particularly when the link-state protocol requires the use of more-advanced features.

Exam Preparation Tasks

Review All the Key Topics

Review the most important topics from this chapter, noted with the key topics icon. Table 8-7 lists these key topics and where each is discussed.

Key Topic

Table 8-7 *Key Topics for Chapter 8*

Key Topic Element	Description	Page Number
List	Definitions and comparison of the terms routing protocol, routed protocol, and routable protocol	309
List	List of the main functions of a routing protocol	310
List	Definitions of IGP and EGP	311
List	Three types of IGP routing protocol algorithms	313
Table 8-3	Comparison points for IGP protocols	315
Table 8-4	More comparisons between RIP-2, OSPF, and EIGRP	316
Table 8-5	List of routing information sources and their respective administrative distance	317
Figure 8-5	Graphical view of the meaning of distance vector	319
List	Description of distance vector periodic updates, full updates, and full updates limited by split horizon	320
Figure 8-7	Example of route poisoning	321
Definition	Split horizon	324
Definitions	Triggered updates, poison reverse	326
Definition	Holddown	330
Figure 8-16	Graphical representation of a link-state SPF calculation	336
List	Summary of link-state operations	338

Complete the Tables and Lists from Memory

Print a copy of Appendix J, "Memory Tables" (found on the CD), or at least the section for this chapter, and complete the tables and lists from memory. Appendix K, "Memory Tables Answer Key," also on the CD, includes completed tables and lists for you to check your work.

Definitions of Key Terms

Define the following key terms from this chapter, and check your answers in the glossary:

Balanced hybrid, convergence, counting to infinity, Dijkstra Shortest Path First (SPF) algorithm, distance vector, exterior gateway protocol (EGP), full update, holddown (holddown timer), infinity, interior gateway protocol (IGP), link state, link-state advertisement (LSA), link-state database (LSDB), metric, partial update, periodic update, poison reverse, poisoned route, routable protocol, routed protocol, routing protocol, split horizon, triggered update

Command Reference to Check Your Memory

This chapter does not refer to any commands that are not otherwise covered more fully in another chapter. Therefore, this chapter, unlike most others in this book, does not have any command reference tables.

This chapter covers the following subjects:

OSPF Protocols and Operation: This section completes the discussion of link-state protocols begun in Chapter 8, "Routing Protocol Theory," by describing the specifics of OSPF operation.

OSPF Configuration: This section examines how to configure OSPF in a single area and in multiple areas, OSPF authentication, and a few other small features.

CHAPTER 9

OSPF

Link-state routing protocols were originally developed mainly in the early to mid-1990s. The protocol designers assumed that link speeds, router CPUs, and router memory would continue to improve over time, so the protocols were designed to provide much more powerful features by taking advantage of these improvements. By sending more information, and requiring the routers to perform more processing, link-state protocols gain some important advantages over distance vector protocols—in particular, much faster convergence. The goal remains the same—adding the currently best routes to the routing table—but these protocols use different methods to find and add those routes.

This chapter explains the most commonly used IP link-state routing protocol—Open Shortest Path First (OSPF). The other link-state protocol for IP, Integrated IS-IS, is mainly ignored on the CCNA exams.

"Do I Know This Already?" Quiz

The "Do I Know This Already?" quiz allows you to assess whether you should read the entire chapter. If you miss no more than one of these ten self-assessment questions, you might want to move ahead to the "Exam Preparation Tasks" section. Table 9-1 lists the major headings in this chapter and the "Do I Know This Already?" quiz questions covering the material in those sections. This helps you assess your knowledge of these specific areas. The answers to the "Do I Know This Already?" quiz appear in Appendix A.

Table 9-1 *"Do I Know This Already?" Foundation Topics Section-to-Question Mapping*

Foundation Topics Section	Questions
OSPF Protocols and Operation	1–5
OSPF Configuration	6–10

1. Which of the following affects the calculation of OSPF routes when all possible default values are used?

   a. Bandwidth

   b. Delay

c. Load

d. Reliability

e. MTU

f. Hop count

2. OSPF runs an algorithm to calculate the currently best route. Which of the following terms refer to that algorithm?

a. SPF

b. DUAL

c. Feasible successor

d. Dijkstra

e. Good old common sense

3. Two OSPF routers connect to the same VLAN using their Fa0/0 interfaces. Which of the following settings on the interfaces of these two potentially neighboring routers would prevent the two routers from becoming OSPF neighbors?

a. IP addresses of 10.1.1.1/24 and 10.1.1.254/25, respectively

b. The addition of a secondary IP address on one router's interface, but not the other

c. Both router interfaces assigned to area 3

d. One router is configured to use MD5 authentication, and the other is not configured to use authentication

4. Which of the following OSPF neighbor states is expected when the exchange of topology information is complete so that neighboring routers have the same LSDB?

a. Two-way

b. Full

c. Exchange

d. Loading

5. Which of the following is true about an existing OSPF designated router?

a. A newly connected router in the same subnet, with a higher OSPF priority, preempts the existing DR to become the new DR.

b. A newly connected router in the same subnet, with a lower OSPF priority, preempts the existing DR to become the new DR.

c. The DR may be elected based on the lowest OSPF Router ID.

d. The DR may be elected based on the highest OSPF Router ID.

e. The DR attempts to become fully adjacent with every other neighbor on the subnet.

6. Which of the following **network** commands, following the command **router ospf 1**, tells this router to start using OSPF on interfaces whose IP addresses are 10.1.1.1, 10.1.100.1, and 10.1.120.1?

   a. **network 10.0.0.0 255.0.0.0 area 0**

   b. **network 10.0.0.0 0.255.255.255 area 0**

   c. **network 10.0.0.1 255.0.0.255 area 0**

   d. **network 10.0.0.1 0.255.255.0 area 0**

7. Which of the following **network** commands, following the command **router ospf 1**, tells this router to start using OSPF on interfaces whose IP addresses are 10.1.1.1, 10.1.100.1, and 10.1.120.1?

   a. **network 0.0.0.0 255.255.255.255 area 0**

   b. **network 10.0.0.0 0.255.255.0 area 0**

   c. **network 10.1.1.0 0.x.1x.0 area 0**

   d. **network 10.1.1.0 255.0.0.0 area 0**

   e. **network 10.0.0.0 255.0.0.0 area 0**

8. Which of the following commands list the OSPF neighbors off interface serial 0/0?

   a. **show ip ospf neighbor**

   b. **show ip ospf interface**

   c. **show ip neighbor**

   d. **show ip interface**

   e. **show ip ospf neighbor serial 0/0**

9. OSPF routers R1, R2, and R3 attach to the same VLAN. R2 has been configured with the **ip ospf authentication message-digest** interface subcommand on the LAN interface connected to the common VLAN. The **show ip ospf neighbor** command lists R1 and R3 as neighbors, in an Init and Full state, respectively. Which of the following are true?

   a. R3 must have an **ip ospf message-digest** interface subcommand configured.

   b. R3 must have an **ip ospf message-digest-key** interface subcommand configured.

   c. R1's failure must be because of having configured an incorrect OSPF authentication type.

   d. R1's failure may or may not be related to authentication.

10. An OSPF router learns about six possible routes to reach subnet 10.1.1.0/24. All six routes have a cost of 55, and all six are interarea routes. By default, how many of these routes are placed in the routing table?

    a.   1

    b.   2

    c.   3

    d.   4

    e.   5

    f.   6

Foundation Topics

This chapter examines Open Shortest Path First (OSPF) concepts and configuration, picking up where the link-state coverage in Chapter 8 ended. In particular, the first half of this chapter explains a variety of the basics related to how OSPF works. The second half examines how to configure OSPF on Cisco routers.

OSPF Protocols and Operation

The OSPF protocol has a wide variety of sometimes-complex features. To aid the learning process, OSPF features can be broken into three major categories: neighbors, database exchange, and route calculation. OSPF routers first form a neighbor relationship that provides a foundation for all continuing OSPF communications. After routers become neighbors, they exchange the contents of their respective LSDBs, through a process called database exchange. Finally, as soon as a router has topology information in its link-state database (LSDB), it uses the Dijkstra Shortest Path First (SPF) algorithm to calculate the now-best routes and add those to the IP routing table.

Interestingly, the IOS **show** commands also support this same structure. IOS has an OSPF neighbor table (**show ip ospf neighbor**), an OSPF LSDB (**show ip ospf database**), and of course an IP routing table (**show ip route**). The processes explained in the first half of this chapter can then be seen in action on routers by displaying the contents of these three tables.

OSPF Neighbors

Although some variations exist, a general definition of an OSPF neighbor is, from one router's perspective, another router that connects to the same data link with which the first router can and should exchange routing information using OSPF. Although this definition is correct, you can better understand the true meaning of the OSPF neighbor concept by thinking about the purpose of OSPF neighbor relationships. First, neighbors check and verify basic OSPF settings before exchanging routing information—settings that must match for OSPF to work correctly. Second, the ongoing process of one router knowing when the neighbor is healthy, and when the connection to a neighbor has been lost, tells the router when it must recalculate the entries in the routing table to reconverge to a new set of routes. Additionally, the OSPF Hello process defines how neighbors can be dynamically discovered, which means that new routers can be added to a network without requiring every router to be reconfigured.

The OSPF Hello process by which new neighbor relationships are formed works somewhat like when you move to a new house and meet your various neighbors. When you see each other outside, you might walk over, say hello, and learn each others' names. After talking a bit, you form a first impression, particularly as to whether you think you'll enjoy chatting with this neighbor occasionally, or whether you may just wave and not take the time to talk the next time you see him outside. Similarly, with OSPF, the process starts with messages called OSPF Hello messages. The Hellos in turn list each router's Router ID (RID), which serves as each router's unique name or identifier for OSPF. Finally, OSPF does several checks of the information in the Hello messages to ensure that the two routers should become neighbors.

Identifying OSPF Routers with a Router ID

OSPF needs to uniquely identify each router for many reasons. First, neighbors need a way to know which router sent a particular OSPF message. Additionally, the OSPF LSDB lists a set of Link State Advertisements (LSA), some of which describe each router in the internetwork, so the LSDB needs a unique identifier for each router. To that end, OSPF uses a concept called the *OSPF router ID* (RID).

OSPF RIDs are 32-bit numbers written in dotted decimal, so using an IP address is a convenient way to find a default RID. Alternatively, the OSPF RID can be directly configured, as covered in the later section "Configuring the OSPF Router ID."

Meeting Neighbors by Saying Hello

As soon as a router has chosen its OSPF RID, and some interfaces come up, the router is ready to meet its OSPF neighbors. OSPF routers can become neighbors if they are connected to the same subnet (and in some other special cases not covered on the CCNA exams). To discover other OSPF-speaking routers, a router sends multicast OSPF Hello packets to each interface and hopes to receive OSPF Hello packets from other routers connected to those interfaces. Figure 9-1 outlines the basic concept.

Figure 9-1 *Link-State Hello Packets*

Routers A and B both send Hello messages onto the LAN. They continue to send Hellos based on their Hello Timer settings. Soon afterward, the two routers can begin exchanging topology information with each other. Then they run the Dijkstra algorithm to fill the routing table with the best routes. The Hello messages themselves have the following features:

- The Hello message follows the IP packet header, with IP packet protocol type 89.

- Hello packets are sent to multicast IP address 224.0.0.5, a multicast IP address intended for all OSPF-speaking routers.

- OSPF routers listen for packets sent to IP multicast address 224.0.0.5, in part hoping to receive Hello packets and learn about new neighbors.

Routers learn several important pieces of information from looking at the received Hello packets. The Hello message includes the sending router's RID, Area ID, Hello interval, dead interval, router priority, the RID of the designated router, the RID of the backup designated router, and a list of neighbors that the sending router already knows about on the subnet. (There's more to come on most of these items.)

The list of neighbors is particularly important to the Hello process. For example, when Router A receives a Hello from Router B, Router A needs to somehow tell Router B that Router A got the Hello. To do so, Router A adds Router B's RID to the list of OSPF neighbors inside the next (and future) Hello that Router A multicasts onto the network. Likewise, when Router B receives Router A's Hello, Router B's next (and ongoing) Hellos include Router A's RID in the list of neighbors.

As soon as a router sees its own RID in a received Hello, the router believes that *two-way* communication has been established with that neighbor. The two-way state for a neighbor is important, because at that point, more detailed information, such as LSAs, can be exchanged. Also, in some cases on LANs, neighbors might reach the two-way state and stop there. You'll read more about that in the section "Choosing a Designated Router."

Potential Problems in Becoming a Neighbor

Interestingly, receiving a Hello from a router on the same subnet does not always result in two routers becoming neighbors. It's like meeting a new neighbor in real life. If you disagree about a lot of things, and you don't get along, you might not talk all that much. Similarly, with OSPF, routers on the same subnet must agree about several of the parameters exchanged in the Hello; otherwise, the routers simply do not become neighbors. Specifically, the following must match before a pair of routers become neighbors:

- Subnet mask used on the subnet

- Subnet number (as derived using the subnet mask and each router's interface IP address)

- Hello interval

Key
Topic

- Dead interval

- OSPF area ID

- Must pass authentication checks (if used)

- Value of the stub area flag

If any one of these parameters differs, the routers do not become neighbors. In short, if you're troubleshooting OSPF when routers should be neighbors, and they are not, check this list!

> **NOTE**   The stub area flag relates to concepts outside the scope of the CCNA exams, but it is listed as a requirement for two routers to become neighbors just so the list will be complete.

A couple of the items in the list need further explanation. First, a potential neighbor confirms that it is in the same subnet by comparing the neighboring router's IP address and subnet mask, as listed in the Hello message, with its own address and mask. If they are in the exact same subnet, with the same range of addresses, this check passes.

Next, two timer settings, the Hello Interval and Dead Interval, must match. OSPF routers send Hello messages every Hello Interval. When a router no longer hears a Hello from a neighbor for the time defined by the Dead Interval, the router believes the neighbor is no longer reachable, and the router reacts and reconverges the network. For instance, on Ethernet interfaces, Cisco routers default to a Hello interval of 10 seconds and a dead interval of 4 times the Hello interval, or 40 seconds. If a router does not hear any Hello messages from that neighbor for 40 seconds, it marks the now-silent router as "down" in its neighbor table. At that point, the routers can react and converge to use the now-currently best routes.

Neighbor States

OSPF defines a large set of potential actions that two neighbors use to communicate with each other. To keep track of the process, OSPF routers set each neighbor to one of many OSPF neighbor states. An OSPF neighbor state is the router's perception of how much work has been completed in the normal processes done by two neighboring routers. For example, if Routers R1 and R2 connect to the same LAN and become neighbors, R1 lists a neighbor state for R2, which is R1's perception of what has happened between the two routers so far. Likewise, R2 lists a neighbor state for R1, representing R2's view of what has happened between R2 and R1 so far. (The most common command to list the neighbors and states is **show ip ospf neighbor**.)

Because the neighbor states reflect various points in the normal OSPF processes used between two routers, it is useful to discuss neighbor states along with these processes and OSPF messages. Also, by understanding the OSPF neighbor states and their meanings, an engineer can more easily determine if an OSPF neighbor is working normally, or if a problem exists.

Figure 9-2 shows several of the neighbor states used by the early formation of a neighbor relationship. The figure shows the Hello messages and the resulting neighbor states.

Figure 9-2 *Early Neighbor States*

The first two states, the Down state and the Init state, are relatively simple. In cases when a router previously knew about a neighbor, but the interface failed, the neighbor is listed as a Down state. As soon as the interface comes up, the two routers can send Hellos, transitioning that neighbor to an Init state. Init means that the neighbor relationship is being initialized.

A router changes from Init to a two-way state when two major facts are true: a received Hello lists that router's RID as having been seen, and that router has checked all parameters for the neighbor and they look good. These two facts mean that the router is willing to communicate with this neighbor. To make the process work, when each router receives a Hello from a new neighbor, the router checks the neighbor's configuration details, as described earlier. If all looks good, the router's next Hello lists the neighbor's RID in the list of "seen" routers. After both routers have checked the parameters and sent a Hello listing the other router's RID as "seen," both routers should have reached the two-way state.

For example, in Figure 9-2, R2 receives the first Hello, which lists "Seen [null]." This notation means that R1 has not yet seen any approved potential neighbors. When R2 sends its Hello, R2 lists R1's RID, implying that R2 has seen R1's Hello and has verified that all parameters look good. R1 returns the favor in the third Hello, sent one Hello-interval later than R1's first Hello.

After they are in a two-way state, the two routers are ready to exchange topology information, as covered in the next section.

OSPF Topology Database Exchange

OSPF routers exchange the contents of their LSDBs so that both neighbors have an exact copy of the same LSDB at the end of the database exchange process—a fundamental principle of how link-state routing protocols work. The process has many steps, with much more detail than is described here. This section begins by explaining an overview of the entire process, followed by a deeper look at each of the steps.

Overview of the OSPF Database Exchange Process

Interestingly, after two OSPF routers become neighbors and reach a two-way state, the next step may not be to exchange topology information. First, based on several factors, the routers must first decide if they should directly exchange topology information, or if the two neighbors should learn each other's topology information, in the form of LSAs, indirectly. As soon as a pair of OSPF neighbors knows that they should share topology information directly, they exchange the topology data (LSAs). After this is completed, the process moves to a relatively quiet maintenance state in which the routers occasionally reflood the LSAs and watch for changes to the network.

The overall process flows as follows, with each step explained in the following pages:

Step 1   Based on the OSPF interface type, the routers may or may not collectively elect a Designated Router (DR) and Backup Designated Router (BDR).

Step 2   For each pair of routers that need to become fully adjacent, mutually exchange the contents of their respective LSDBs.

Step 3   When completed, the neighbors monitor for changes and periodically reflood LSAs while in the Full (fully adjacent) neighbor state.

Choosing a Designated Router

OSPF dictates that a subnet either should or should not use a Designated Router (DR) and Backup Designated Router (BDR) based on the OSPF interface type (also sometimes called the OSPF network type). Several OSPF interface types exist, but for the CCNA exams you should be aware of two main types: point-to-point and broadcast. (These types can be configured with the **ip ospf network** *type* command.) These OSPF interface types make a general reference to the type of data-link protocol used. As you might guess from the names, the point-to-point type is intended for use on point-to-point links, and the broadcast type is for use on data links that support broadcast frames, such as LANs.

Figure 9-3 shows a classic example of two sets of neighbors—one using the default OSPF interface type of point-to-point on a serial link, and the other using the default OSPF interface type of broadcast on a LAN. The end result of the DR election is that topology information is exchanged only between neighbors shown with arrowed lines in the figure. Focus on the lower-right part of the figure.

Figure 9-3 *No DR on a Point-to-Point Link, with a DR on the LAN*

When a DR is not required, neighboring routers can go ahead and start the topology exchange process, as shown on the left side of the figure. In OSPF terminology, the two routers on the left should continue working to exchange topology information and become fully adjacent. On the right side of the figure, the top part shows a LAN topology where a DR election has been held, with Router A winning the election. With a DR, the topology exchange process happens between the DR and every other router, but not between every pair of routers. As a result, all routing updates flow to and from Router A, with Router A essentially distributing the topology information to the other routers. All routers learn all topology information from all other routers, but the process only causes a direct exchange of routing information between the DR and each of the non-DR routers.

The DR concept prevents overloading a subnet with too much OSPF traffic when many routers are on a subnet. Of course, lots of routers could be attached to one LAN, which is why a DR is required for routers attached to a LAN. For instance, if ten routers were attached to the same LAN subnet, and they were allowed to forward OSPF updates to each of the other nine routers, topology updates would flow between 45 different pairs of neighbors—with almost all the information being redundant. With the DR concept, as shown on the right side of Figure 9-3, that same LAN would require routing updates only between the DR and the nine other routers, significantly reducing the flooding of OSPF information across the LAN.

Because the DR is so important to the exchange of routing information, the loss of the elected DR could cause delays in convergence. OSPF includes the concept of a *Backup DR* (BDR) on each subnet, so when the DR fails or loses connectivity to the subnet, the BDR can take over as the DR. (All routers except the DR and BDR are typically called "DROther" in IOS **show** command output.)

> **NOTE**   All non-DR and non-BDR routers attempt to become fully adjacent with both the DR and BDR, but Figure 9-3 shows only the relationships with the DR to reduce clutter.

When a DR is required, the neighboring routers hold an election. To elect a DR, the neighboring routers look at two fields inside the Hello packets they receive and choose the DR based on the following criteria:

Key Topic

- The router sending the Hello with the *highest OSPF priority* setting becomes the DR.

- If two or more routers tie with the highest priority setting, the router sending the Hello with the *highest RID* wins.

- It's not always the case, but typically the router with the second-highest priority becomes the BDR.

- A priority setting of 0 means that the router does not participate in the election and can never become the DR or BDR.

- The range of priority values that allow a router to be a candidate are 1 through 255.

- If a new, better candidate comes along after the DR and BDR have been elected, the new candidate does not preempt the existing DR and BDR.

Database Exchange

The database exchange process can be quite involved with several OSPF messages. The details of the process can be ignored for the purposes of this book, but a brief overview can help give some perspective on the overall process.

After two routers decide to exchange databases, they do not simply send the contents of the entire database. First, they tell each other a list of LSAs in their respective databases—not all the details of the LSAs, just a list. Each router then compares the other router's list to its own LSDB. For any LSAs that a router does not have a copy of, the router asks the neighbor for a copy of the LSA, and the neighbor sends the full LSA.

When two neighbors complete this process, they are considered to have *fully completed* the database exchange process. So OSPF uses the *Full* neighbor state to mean that the database exchange process has been completed.

Maintaining the LSDB While Being Fully Adjacent

Neighbors in a Full state still do some maintenance work. They keep sending Hellos every Hello interval. The absence of Hellos for a time equal to the Dead Interval means that the connection to the neighbor has failed. Also, if any topology changes occur, the neighbors send new copies of the changed LSAs to each neighbor so that the neighbor can change its LSDBs. For example, if a subnet fails, a router updates the LSA for that subnet to reflect its state as being down. That router then sends the LSA to its neighbors, and they in turn send it to their neighbors, until all routers again have an identical copy of the LSDB. Each router can then also use SPF to recalculate any routes affected by the failed subnet.

The router that creates each LSA also has the responsibility to reflood the LSA every 30 minutes (the default), even if no changes occur. This process is quite different than the distance vector concept of periodic updates. Distance vector protocols send full updates over a short time interval, listing all routes (except those omitted due to loop-avoidance tools such as split horizon). OSPF does not send all routes every 30 minutes. Instead, each LSA has a separate timer, based on when the LSA was created. So, there is no single moment when OSPF sends a lot of messages to reflood all LSAs. Instead, each LSA is reflooded by the router that created the LSA, every 30 minutes.

As a reminder, some routers do not attempt to become fully adjacent. In particular, on interfaces on which a DR is elected, routers that are neither DR nor BDR become neighbors, but they do not become fully adjacent. These non-fully adjacent routers do not directly exchange LSAs. Also, the **show ip ospf neighbor** command on such a router lists these neighbors in a two-way state as the normal stable neighbor state, and Full as the normal stable state for the DR and BDR.

Summary of Neighbor States

For easier reference and study, Table 9-2 lists and briefly describes the neighbor states mentioned in this chapter.

Table 9-2 *OSPF Neighbor States and Their Meanings*

Neighbor State	Meaning
Down	A known neighbor is no longer reachable, often because of an underlying interface failure.
Init	An interim state in which a Hello has been heard from the neighbor, but that Hello does not list the router's RID as having been seen yet.
Two-way	The neighbor has sent a Hello that lists the local router's RID in the list of seen routers, also implying that neighbor verification checks all passed.
Full	Both routers know the exact same LSDB details and are fully adjacent.

Key
Topic

Building the IP Routing Table

OSPF routers send messages to learn about neighbors, listing those neighbors in the OSPF neighbor table. OSPF routers then send messages to exchange topology data with these same neighbors, storing the information in the OSPF topology table, more commonly called the LSDB or the OSPF database. To fill the third major table used by OSPF, the IP routing table, OSPF does not send any messages. Each router runs the Dijkstra SPF algorithm against the OSPF topology database, choosing the best routes based on that process.

The OSPF topology database consists of lists of subnet numbers (called *links*, hence the name *link-state database*). It also contains lists of routers, along with the links (subnets) to which each router is connected. Armed with the knowledge of links and routers, a router can run the SPF algorithm to compute the best routes to all the subnets. The concept is very much like putting together a jigsaw puzzle. The color and shape of each piece help you identify what pieces might fit next to it. Similarly, the detailed information in each LSA—things such as a *link LSA* listing the routers attached to the subnet, and a *router LSA* listing its IP addresses and masks—gives the SPF algorithm enough information to figure out which routers connect to each subnet and create the mathematical equivalent of a network diagram.

Each router independently uses the Dijkstra SPF algorithm, as applied to the OSPF LSDB, to find the best route from that router to each subnet. The algorithm finds the shortest path from that router to each subnet in the LSDB. Then the router places the best route to each subnet in the IP routing table. It sounds simple, and it is with a drawing of an internetwork that lists all the information. Fortunately, although the underlying math of the SPF algorithm can be a bit daunting, you do not need to know SPF math for the exams or for real networking jobs. However, you do need to be able to predict the routes SPF will choose using network diagrams and documentation.

OSPF chooses the least-cost route between the router and a subnet by adding up the outgoing interfaces' OSPF costs. Each interface has an OSPF cost associated with it. The router looks at each possible route, adds up the costs on the interfaces out which packets would be forwarded on that route, and then picks the least-cost route. For example, Figure 9-4 shows a simple internetwork with the OSPF cost values listed beside each interface. In this figure, router R4 has two possible paths with which to reach subnet 10.5.1.0/24. The two routes are as follows, listing each router and its outgoing interface:

R4 Fa0/0—R1 S0/1—R5 Fa0/0
R4 Fa0/0—R2 S0/1—R5 Fa0/0

Figure 9-4   *Sample OSPF Network with Costs Shown*

Route R4 – R1 – R5 : cost 1 + 100 + 10 = 111
Route R4 – R2 – R5 : cost 1 + 64 + 10 = 75

If you add up the cost associated with each interface, the first of the two routes totals a cost of 111, and the second totals 75. So, R4 adds the route through R2 as the best route and lists R2's IP address as the next-hop IP address.

Now that you have seen how OSPF routers perform the most fundamental functions of OSPF, the next section takes a broader look at OSPF, particularly some important design points.

Scaling OSPF Through Hierarchical Design

OSPF can be used in some networks with very little thought about design issues. You just turn on OSPF in all the routers, and it works! However, in large networks, engineers need to think about and plan how to use several OSPF features that allow it to scale well in larger networks. To appreciate the issues behind OSPF scalability, and the need for good design to allow scalability, examine Figure 9-5.

Figure 9-5   *Single-Area OSPF*

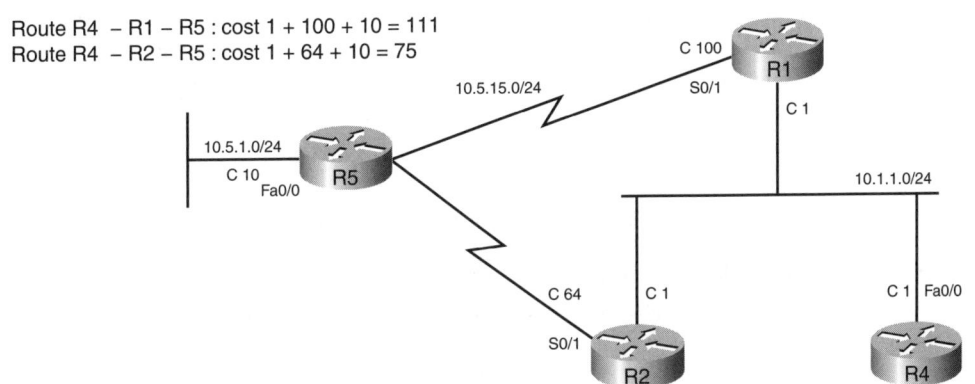

In the network shown in Figure 9-5, the topology database on all nine routers is the same full topology that matches the figure. With a network that size, you can just enable OSPF, and it works fine. But imagine a network with 900 routers instead of only nine, and several thousand subnets. In that size of network, the sheer amount of processing required to run the complex SPF algorithm might cause convergence time to be slow, and the routers might experience memory shortages. The problems can be summarized as follows:

- A larger topology database requires more memory on each router.

- Processing the larger-topology database with the SPF algorithm requires processing power that grows exponentially with the size of the topology database.

- A single interface status change (up to down or down to up) forces every router to run SPF again!

Although there is no exact definition of "large" in this context, in networks with at least 50 routers and at least a few hundred subnets, engineers should use OSPF scalability features to reduce the problems just described. These numbers are gross generalizations. They depend largely on the network design, the power of the router CPU, the amount of RAM, and so on.

OSPF Areas

Using OSPF areas solves many, but not all, of the most common problems with running OSPF in larger networks. OSPF areas break up the network so that routers in one area know less topology information about the subnets in the other area—and they do not know about the routers in the other area at all. With smaller-topology databases, routers consume less memory and take less processing time to run SPF. Figure 9-6 shows the same network as Figure 9-5, but with two OSPF areas, labeled Area 1 and Area 0.

The same topology is shown in the upper part of the figure, but the lower part of the figure shows the topology database on Routers 1, 2, and 4. By placing part of the network in another area, the routers inside Area 1 are shielded from some of the details. Router 3 is known as an OSPF Area Border Router (ABR), because it is on the border between two different areas. Router 3 does not advertise full topology information about the part of the network in Area 0 to Routers 1, 2, and 4. Instead, Router 3 advertises summary information about the subnets in Area 0, effectively making Routers 1, 2, and 4 think the topology looks like the lower part of Figure 9-6. Therefore, Routers 1, 2, and 4 view the world as if it has fewer routers. As a result, the SPF algorithm takes less time, and the topology database takes less memory.

Figure 9-6 *Two-Area OSPF*

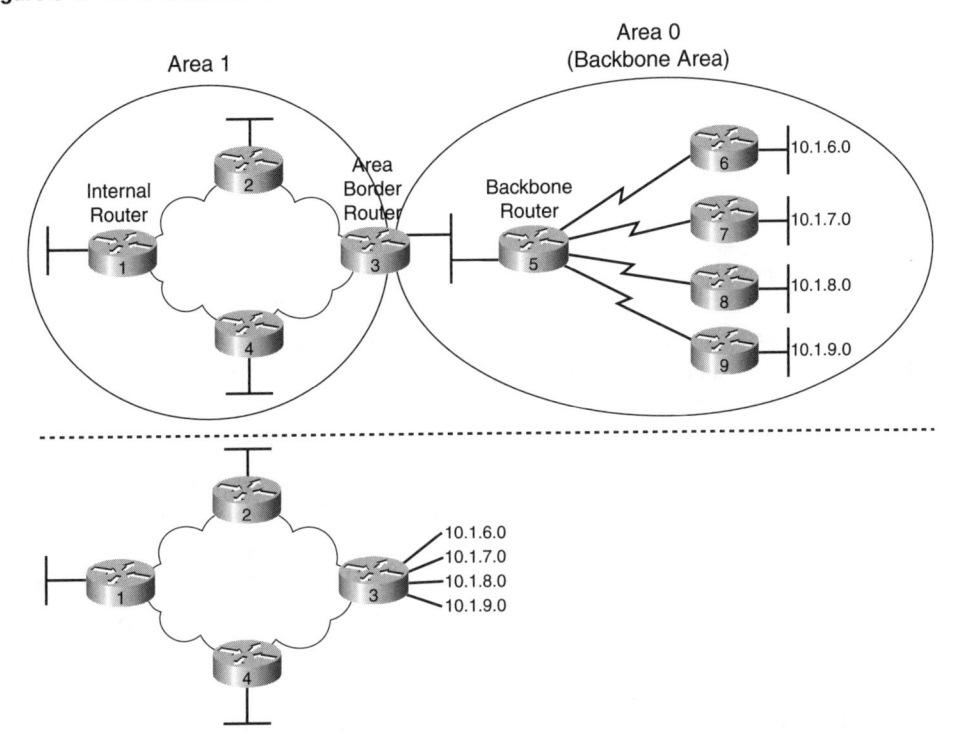

OSPF design introduces a few important terms you should know for the exams; they are defined in Table 9-3.

Table 9-3 *OSPF Design Terminology*

Term	Description
Area Border Router (ABR)	An OSPF router with interfaces connected to the backbone area and to at least one other area.
Autonomous System Border Router (ASBR)	An OSPF router that connects to routers that do not use OSPF for the purpose of exchanging external routes into and out of the OSPF domain.
Backbone router	A router in one area, the backbone area.
Internal router	A router in a single nonbackbone area.
Area	A set of routers and links that share the same detailed LSDB information, but not with routers in other areas, for better efficiency.
Backbone area	A special OSPF area to which all other areas must connect. Area 0.

continues

Table 9-3 *OSPF Design Terminology (Continued)*

Term	Description
External route	A route learned from outside the OSPF domain and then advertised into the OSPF domain.
Intra-area route	A route to a subnet inside the same area as the router.
Interarea route	A route to a subnet in an area of which the router is not a part.
Autonomous system	In OSPF, a reference to a set of routers that use OSPF.

It is very important to note the difference between the summarized information shown in Figure 9-6 versus summarized routes as covered in Chapter 5, "VLSM and Route Summarization." In this case, the term "summary" just means that a router inside one area receives briefer information in the LSA for a subnet, thereby decreasing the amount of memory needed to store the information. For example, in Figure 9-6, router R1 (in Area 1) learns only a very brief LSA about subnets in Area 0. This process reduces the size and complexity of the SPF algorithm. In addition, the term "summary" can refer to a summary route configured in OSPF, with the general concepts covered in Chapter 5. OSPF manual route summarization reduces the number of subnets, which in turn also reduces the size and effort of the SPF calculation.

> **NOTE**   Although the perspectives of the routers in Area 1 are shown in Figure 9-6, the same thing happens in reverse—routers in Area 0 do not know the details of Area 1's topology.

Notice that the dividing line between areas is not a link, but a router. In Figure 9-6, Router 3 is in both Area 1 and Area 0. OSPF uses the term Area Border Router (ABR) to describe a router that sits in both areas. An ABR has the topology database for both areas and runs SPF when links change status in either area. So, although using areas helps scale OSPF by reducing the size of the LSDB and the time to compute a routing table, the amount of RAM and CPU consumed on ABRs can actually increase. As a result, the routers acting as ABRs should be faster routers with relatively more memory.

OSPF Area Design Advantages

Using areas improves OSPF operations in many ways, particularly in larger internetworks:

■ The smaller per-area LSDB requires less memory.

■ The router requires fewer CPU cycles to process the smaller per-area LSDB with the SPF algorithm, reducing CPU overhead and improving convergence time.

- The SPF algorithm has to be run on internal routers only when an LSA inside the area changes, so routers have to run SPF less often.

- Less information must be advertised between areas, reducing the bandwidth required to send LSAs.

- Manual summarization can only be configured on ABRs and ASBRs, so areas allow for smaller IP routing tables by allowing for the configuration of manual route summarization.

OSPF Configuration

OSPF configuration includes only a few required steps, but it has many optional steps. After an OSPF design has been chosen—a task that may be complex in larger IP internetworks—the configuration may be as simple as enabling OSPF on each router interface and placing that interface in the correct OSPF area.

This section shows several configuration examples, starting with a single-area OSPF internetwork and then a multiarea OSPF internetwork. Following those examples, the text goes on to cover several of the additional optional configuration settings. For reference, the following list outlines the configuration steps covered in this chapter, as well as a brief reference to the required commands:

Step 1 Enter OSPF configuration mode for a particular OSPF process using the **router ospf** *process-id* global command.

Step 2 (Optional) Configure the OSPF router ID by:

    a. Configuring the **router-id** *id-value* router subcommand.

    b. Configuring an IP address on a loopback interface.

Step 3 Configure one or more **network** *ip-address wildcard-mask* **area** *area-id* router subcommands, with any matched interfaces being added to the listed area.

Step 4 (Optional) Change the interface Hello and Dead intervals using the **ip ospf hello-interval** *time* and **ip ospf dead-interval** *time* interface subcommands.

Step 5 (Optional) Impact routing choices by tuning interface costs as follows:

    a. Configure costs directly using the **ip ospf cost** *value* interface subcommand.

    b. Change interface bandwidths using the **bandwidth** *value* interface subcommand.

c. Change the numerator in the formula to calculate the cost based on the interface bandwidth, using the **auto-cost reference-bandwidth** *value* router subcommand.

Step 6 (Optional) Configure OSPF authentication:

a. On a per-interface basis using the **ip ospf authentication** interface subcommand.

b. For all interfaces in an area using the **area authentication** router subcommand.

Step 7 (Optional) Configure support for multiple equal-cost routes using the **maximum-paths** *number* router subcommand.

OSPF Single-Area Configuration

OSPF configuration differs only slightly from RIP configuration when a single OSPF area is used. The best way to describe the configuration, and the differences with the configuration of the other routing protocols, is to use an example. Figure 9-7 shows a sample network, and Example 9-1 shows the configuration on Albuquerque.

Figure 9-7 *Sample Network for OSPF Single-Area Configuration*

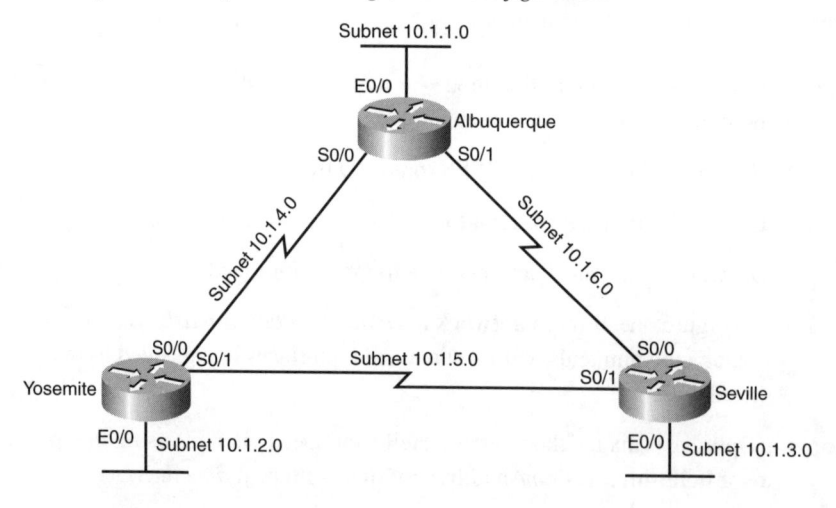

Example 9-1 *OSPF Single-Area Configuration on Albuquerque*

```
interface ethernet 0/0
 ip address 10.1.1.1 255.255.255.0
interface serial 0/0
 ip address 10.1.4.1 255.255.255.0
interface serial 0/1
 ip address 10.1.6.1 255.255.255.0
```

Example 9-1 *OSPF Single-Area Configuration on Albuquerque (Continued)*

```
!
router ospf 1
 network 10.0.0.0 0.255.255.255 area 0
```

The configuration correctly enables OSPF on all three interfaces on Albuquerque. First, the **router ospf 1** global command puts the user in OSPF configuration mode. The **router ospf** command has a parameter called the OSPF *process-id*. In some instances, you might want to run multiple OSPF processes in a single router, so the **router** command uses the *process-id* to distinguish between the processes. The *process-id* does not have to match on each router, and it can be any integer between 1 and 65,535.

The **network** command tells a router to enable OSPF on each matched interface, discover neighbors on that interface, assign the interface to that area, and advertise the subnet connected to each interface. In this case, the **network 10.0.0.0 0.255.255.255 area 0** command matches all three of Albuquerque's interfaces because the OSPF **network** command matches interfaces using an address and a wildcard-style mask like those used with IP ACLs. The wildcard mask shown in Example 9-1 is 0.255.255.255, with address 10.0.0.0. From the details included in Chapter 6, "IP Access Control Lists," this combination matches all addresses that begin with 10 in the first octet. So, this one **network** command matches all three of Albuquerque's interfaces, puts them in Area 0, and causes Albuquerque to try to discover neighbors on those interfaces. It also causes Albuquerque to advertise the three connected subnets.

The wildcard mask in the OSPF **network** command works like an ACL wildcard mask, but there is one restriction on the values used. The OSPF wildcard mask must have only one string of consecutive binary 1s and one string of consecutive binary 0s. For example, a mask of 0.0.255.255 represents 16 binary 0s and 16 binary 1s and would be allowed. Likewise, a mask of 255.255.255.0 would be allowed, because it has a string of 24 binary 1s followed by eight binary 0s. However, a value of 0.255.255.0 would not be allowed, because it has two sets of eight binary 0s, separated by a string of 16 binary 1s.

Example 9-2 shows an alternative configuration for Albuquerque that also enables OSPF on every interface. In this case, the IP address for each interface is matched with a different **network** command. The wildcard mask of 0.0.0.0 means that all 32 bits must be compared, and they must match—so the **network** commands include the specific IP address of each interface, respectively. Many people prefer this style of configuration in production networks, because it removes any ambiguity about the interfaces on which OSPF is running.

Example 9-2 *OSPF Single-Area Configuration on Albuquerque Using Three **network***
Commands

```
interface ethernet 0/0
 ip address 10.1.1.1 255.255.255.0
interface serial 0/0
 ip address 10.1.4.1 255.255.255.0
interface serial 0/1
 ip address 10.1.6.1 255.255.255.0
!
router ospf 1
 network 10.1.1.1 0.0.0.0 area 0
 network 10.1.4.1 0.0.0.0 area 0
 network 10.1.6.1 0.0.0.0 area 0
```

OSPF Configuration with Multiple Areas

Configuring OSPF with multiple areas is simple when you understand OSPF configuration
in a single area. Designing the OSPF network by making good choices about which subnets
should be placed in which areas is the hard part! After the area design is complete, the
configuration is easy. For instance, consider Figure 9-8, which shows some subnets in Area
0 and some in Area 1.

Figure 9-8 *Multiarea OSPF Network*

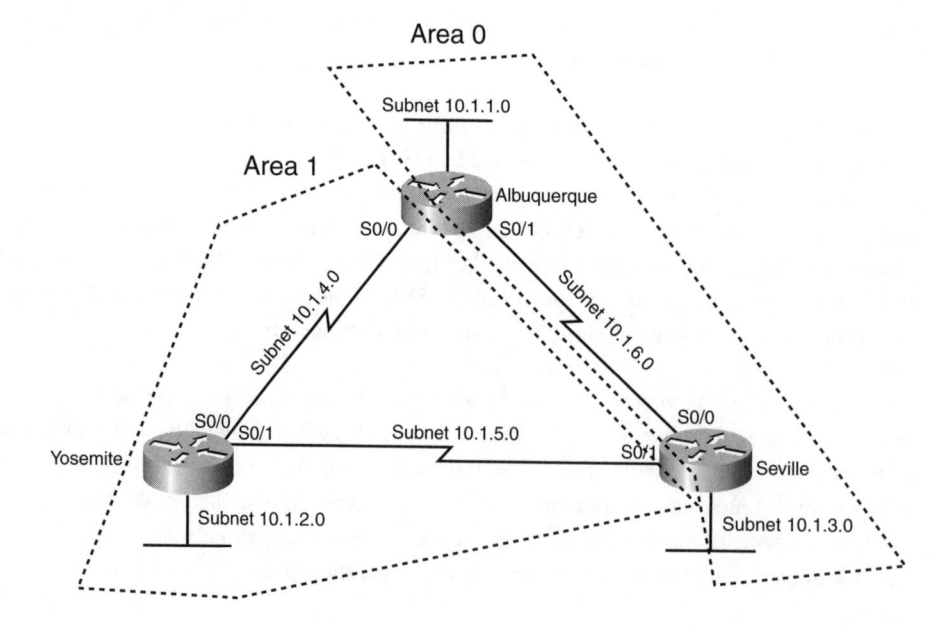

Multiple areas are not needed in such a small network, but two areas are used in this example to show the configuration. Note that Albuquerque and Seville are both ABRs, but Yosemite is totally inside Area 1, so it is not an ABR. Examples 9-3 and 9-4 show the configuration on Albuquerque and Yosemite, along with several **show** commands.

Example 9-3 *OSPF Multiarea Configuration and* **show** *Commands on Albuquerque*

```
! Only the OSPF configuration is shown to conserve space
!
router ospf 1
 network 10.1.1.1 0.0.0.0 area 0
 network 10.1.4.1 0.0.0.0 area 1
 network 10.1.6.1 0.0.0.0 area 0
Albuquerque#show ip route
Codes: C - connected, S - static, I - IGRP, R - RIP, M - mobile, B - BGP
       D - EIGRP, EX - EIGRP external, O - OSPF, IA - OSPF inter area
       N1 - OSPF NSSA external type 1, N2 - OSPF NSSA external type 2
       E1 - OSPF external type 1, E2 - OSPF external type 2, E - EGP
       i - IS-IS, L1 - IS-IS level-1, L2 - IS-IS level-2, ia - IS-IS inter area
       * - candidate default, U - per-user static route, o - ODR
       P - periodic downloaded static route

Gateway of last resort is not set

     10.0.0.0/24 is subnetted, 6 subnets
O       10.1.3.0 [110/65] via 10.1.6.3, 00:01:04, Serial0/1
O       10.1.2.0 [110/65] via 10.1.4.2, 00:00:39, Serial0/0
C       10.1.1.0 is directly connected, Ethernet0/0
C       10.1.6.0 is directly connected, Serial0/1
O       10.1.5.0 [110/128] via 10.1.4.2, 00:00:39, Serial0/0
C       10.1.4.0 is directly connected, Serial0/0

Albuquerque#show ip route ospf
     10.0.0.0/24 is subnetted, 6 subnets
O       10.1.3.0 [110/65] via 10.1.6.3, 00:01:08, Serial0/1
O       10.1.2.0 [110/65] via 10.1.4.2, 00:00:43, Serial0/0
O       10.1.5.0 [110/128] via 10.1.4.2, 00:00:43, Serial0/0
```

Example 9-4 *OSPF Multiarea Configuration and* **show** *Commands on Yosemite*

```
! Only the OSPF configuration is shown to conserve space
router ospf 1
 network 10.0.0.0 0.255.255.255 area 1
Yosemite#show ip route
Codes: C - connected, S - static, I - IGRP, R - RIP, M - mobile, B - BGP
       D - EIGRP, EX - EIGRP external, O - OSPF, IA - OSPF inter area
       N1 - OSPF NSSA external type 1, N2 - OSPF NSSA external type 2
       E1 - OSPF external type 1, E2 - OSPF external type 2, E - EGP
```

continues

Example 9-4   *OSPF Multiarea Configuration and* **show** *Commands on Yosemite (Continued)*

```
        i - IS-IS, L1 - IS-IS level-1, L2 - IS-IS level-2, ia - IS-IS inter area
        * - candidate default, U - per-user static route, o - ODR
        P - periodic downloaded static route

Gateway of last resort is not set

     10.0.0.0/24 is subnetted, 6 subnets
IA      10.1.3.0 [110/65] via 10.1.5.1, 00:00:54, Serial0/1
IA      10.1.1.0 [110/65] via 10.1.4.1, 00:00:49, Serial0/0
C       10.1.2.0 is directly connected, Ethernet0/0
C       10.1.5.0 is directly connected, Serial0/1
IA      10.1.6.0 [110/128] via 10.1.4.1, 00:00:38, Serial0/0
C       10.1.4.0 is directly connected, Serial0/0
```

The configuration needs to set the correct area number on the appropriate interfaces. For instance, the **network 10.1.4.1 0.0.0.0 area 1** command at the beginning of Example 9-3 matches Albuquerque's Serial 0/0 interface IP address, placing that interface in Area 1. The **network 10.1.6.1 0.0.0.0 area 0** and **network 10.1.1.1 0.0.0.0 area 0** commands place Serial 0/1 and Ethernet 0/0, respectively, in Area 0. Unlike Example 9-1, Albuquerque cannot be configured to match all three interfaces with a single **network** command, because one interface (Serial 0/0) is in a different area than the other two interfaces.

Continuing with Example 9-3, the **show ip route ospf** command just lists OSPF-learned routes, as opposed to the entire IP routing table. The **show ip route** command lists all three connected routes, as well as the three OSPF learned routes. Note that Albuquerque's route to 10.1.2.0 has the **O** designation beside it, meaning *intra-area,* because that subnet resides in Area 1, and Albuquerque is part of Area 1 and Area 0.

In Example 9-4, notice that the OSPF configuration in Yosemite requires only a single **network** command because all interfaces in Yosemite are in Area 1. Also note that the routes learned by Yosemite from the other two routers show up as *interarea (IA) routes,* because those subnets are in Area 0, and Yosemite is in Area 1.

Configuring the OSPF Router ID

OSPF-speaking routers must have a Router ID (RID) for proper operation. To find its RID, a Cisco router uses the following process when the router reloads and brings up the OSPF process. Note that when one of these steps identifies the RID, the process stops.

1.   If the **router-id** *rid* OSPF subcommand is configured, this value is used as the RID.

2. If any loopback interfaces have an IP address configured and the interface has a line and protocol status of up/up, the router picks the highest numeric IP address among the up/up loopback interfaces.

3. The router picks the highest numeric IP address from all other working (up/up) interfaces.

The first and third criteria should make some sense right away: the RID is either configured or is taken from a working interface's IP address. However, this book has not yet explained the concept of a *loopback interface*, as mentioned in Step 2. A loopback interface is a virtual interface that can be configured with the **interface loopback** *interface-number* command, where *interface-number* is an integer. Loopback interfaces are always in an "up and up" state unless administratively placed in a shutdown state. For instance, a simple configuration of the command **interface loopback 0**, followed by **ip address 192.168.200.1 255.255.255.0**, would create a loopback interface and assign it an IP address. Because loopback interfaces do not rely on any hardware, these interfaces can be up/up whenever IOS is running, making them good interfaces on which to base an OSPF RID.

Each router chooses its OSPF RID when OSPF is initialized. Initialization happens during the initial load of IOS. So, if OSPF comes up, and later other interfaces come up that happen to have higher IP addresses, the OSPF RID does not change until the OSPF process is restarted. OSPF can be restarted with the **clear ip ospf process** command as well, but depending on circumstances, IOS still may not change its OSPF RID until the next IOS reload.

Many commands list the OSPF RID of various routers. For instance, in Example 9-5, the first neighbor in the output of the **show ip ospf neighbor** command lists Router ID 10.1.5.2, which is Yosemite's RID. Following that, **show ip ospf** lists Albuquerque's own RID.

Example 9-5 *Displaying OSPF-Related Information in Albuquerque*

```
Albuquerque#show ip ospf neighbor

Neighbor ID     Pri   State          Dead Time   Address       Interface
10.1.6.3          1   FULL/  -       00:00:35    10.1.6.3      Serial0/1
10.1.5.2          1   FULL/  -       00:00:37    10.1.4.2      Serial0/0
Albuquerque#show ip ospf
Routing Process "ospf 1" with ID 10.1.6.1
! lines omitted for brevity
```

OSPF Hello and Dead Timers

The default settings for the OSPF Hello and dead timers typically work just fine. However, it is important to note that a mismatch on either setting causes two potential neighbors to never become neighbors, never reaching the two-way state. Example 9-6 lists the most common way to see the current settings using the **show ip ospf interface** command, as taken from Albuquerque, when configured as shown in the multiarea OSPF example (Examples 9-3 and 9-4).

Example 9-6 *Displaying the Hello and Dead Timers on Albuquerque*

```
Albuquerque#show ip ospf interface
Serial0/1 is up, line protocol is up
  Internet Address 10.1.6.1/24, Area 0
  Process ID 1, Router ID 10.1.6.1, Network Type POINT_TO_POINT, Cost: 64
  Transmit Delay is 1 sec, State POINT_TO_POINT,
  Timer intervals configured, Hello 10, Dead 40, Wait 40, Retransmit 5
    Hello due in 00:00:07
  Index 2/3, flood queue length 0
  Next 0x0(0)/0x0(0)
  Last flood scan length is 2, maximum is 2
  Last flood scan time is 0 msec, maximum is 0 msec
  Neighbor Count is 1, Adjacent neighbor count is 1
    Adjacent with neighbor 10.1.6.3
  Suppress hello for 0 neighbor(s)
Ethernet0/0 is up, line protocol is up
  Internet Address 10.1.1.1/24, Area 0
  Process ID 1, Router ID 10.1.6.1, Network Type BROADCAST, Cost: 10
  Transmit Delay is 1 sec, State DR, Priority 1
  Designated Router (ID) 10.1.6.1, Interface address 10.1.1.1
  No backup designated router on this network
  Timer intervals configured, Hello 10, Dead 40, Wait 40, Retransmit 5
    Hello due in 00:00:08
  Index 1/1, flood queue length 0
  Next 0x0(0)/0x0(0)
  Last flood scan length is 0, maximum is 0
  Last flood scan time is 0 msec, maximum is 0 msec
  Neighbor Count is 0, Adjacent neighbor count is 0
  Suppress hello for 0 neighbor(s)
Serial0/0 is up, line protocol is up
  Internet Address 10.1.4.1/24, Area 1
  Process ID 1, Router ID 10.1.6.1, Network Type POINT_TO_POINT, Cost: 64
  Transmit Delay is 1 sec, State POINT_TO_POINT,
  Timer intervals configured, Hello 10, Dead 40, Wait 40, Retransmit 5
    Hello due in 00:00:01
  Index 1/2, flood queue length 0
  Next 0x0(0)/0x0(0)
  Last flood scan length is 1, maximum is 1
  Last flood scan time is 0 msec, maximum is 0 msec
  Neighbor Count is 1, Adjacent neighbor count is 1
    Adjacent with neighbor 10.1.5.2
  Suppress hello for 0 neighbor(s)
```

Note also that the **show ip ospf interface** command lists more detailed information about OSPF operation on each interface. For instance, this command lists the area number, OSPF cost, and any neighbors known on each interface. The timers used on the interface, including the Hello and dead timer, are also listed.

To configure the Hello and Dead intervals, you can use the **ip ospf hello-interval** *value* and **ip ospf dead-interval** *value* interface subcommands. Interestingly, if the Hello interval is configured, IOS automatically reconfigures the interface's dead interval to be 4 times the Hello interval.

OSPF Metrics (Cost)

OSPF calculates the metric for each possible route by adding up the outgoing interfaces' OSPF costs. The OSPF cost for an interface can be configured, or a router can calculate the cost based on the interface's bandwidth setting.

As a reminder, the bandwidth setting on an interface can be configured using the **bandwidth** interface subcommand. This command sets the router's perception of interface speed, with a unit of Kbps. Note that the interface's bandwidth setting does not have to match the physical interface speed, but it usually makes sense to set the bandwidth to match the physical interface speed. On Ethernet interfaces, the bandwidth reflects the current negotiated speed—10,000 (meaning 10,000 Kbps or 10 Mbps) for 10 Mbps Ethernet, and 100,000 (meaning 100,000 Kbps or 100 Mbps) for 100 Mbps. For serial interfaces, the bandwidth defaults to 1544 (meaning 1544 Kbps, or T1 speed), but IOS cannot adjust this setting dynamically.

IOS chooses an interface's cost based on the following rules:

1. The cost can be explicitly set using the **ip ospf cost** *x* interface subcommand, to a value between 1 and 65,535, inclusive.

2. IOS can calculate a value based on the generic formula *Ref-BW* / *Int-BW*, where *Ref-BW* is a reference bandwidth that defaults to 100 Mbps, and *Int-BW* is the interface's bandwidth setting.

3. The reference bandwidth can be configured from its default setting of 100 (100 Mbps) using the router OSPF subcommand **auto-cost reference-bandwidth** *ref-bw*, which in turn affects the calculation of the default interface cost.

The simple formula to calculate the default OSPF cost has one potentially confusing part. The calculation requires that the numerator and denominator use the same units, whereas the **bandwidth** and **auto-cost reference-bandwidth** commands use different units. For instance, Cisco IOS software defaults Ethernet interfaces to use a bandwidth of 10,000, meaning 10,000 Kbps, or 10 Mbps. The reference bandwidth defaults to a value of 100, meaning 100 Mbps. So, the default OSPF cost on an Ethernet interface would be 100 Mbps / 10 Mbps, after making both values use a unit of Mbps. Higher-speed serial interfaces default to a bandwidth of 1544, giving a default cost of 10^8 bps / 1,544,000 bps, which is rounded down to a value of 64, as shown for interface S0/1 in Example 9-6. If the reference bandwidth had been changed to 1000, using the router OSPF subcommand **auto-cost reference-bandwidth 1000**, the calculated metric would be 647.

The main motivation for changing the reference bandwidth is so that routers can have different cost values for interfaces running at speeds of 100 Mbps and higher. With the default setting, an interface with a 100 Mbps bandwidth setting (for example, an FE interface) and an interface with a 1000 Mbps bandwidth (for example, a GE interface) would both have a default cost of 1. By changing the reference bandwidth to 1000, meaning 1000 Mbps, the default cost on a 100-Mbps bandwidth interface would be 10, versus a default cost of 1 on an interface with a bandwidth of 1000 Mbps.

> **NOTE**   Cisco recommends making the OSPF reference bandwidth setting the same on all OSPF routers in a network.

OSPF Authentication

Authentication is arguably the most important of the optional configuration features for OSPF. The lack of authentication opens the network to attacks in which an attacker connects a router to the network, with the legitimate routers believing the OSPF data from the rogue router. As a result, the attacker can easily cause a denial-of-service (DoS) attack by making all routers remove the legitimate routes to all subnets, instead installing routes that forward packets to the attacking router. The attacker can also perform a reconnaissance attack, learning information about the network by listening for and interpreting the OSPF messages.

OSPF supports three types of authentication—one called null authentication (meaning no authentication), one that uses a simple text password and therefore is easy to break, and one that uses MD5. Frankly, if you bother to configure an option in real life, the MD5 option is the only reasonable option. As soon as a router has configured OSPF authentication on an interface, that router must pass the authentication process for every OSPF message, with every neighboring router on that interface. This means that each neighboring router on that interface must also have the same authentication type and the same authentication password configured.

The configuration can use two interface subcommands on each interface—one to enable the particular type of authentication, and one to set the password used for the authentication.

Example 9-7 shows a sample configuration in which simple password authentication is configured on interface Fa0/0, and MD5 authentication is configured on Fa0/1.

Example 9-7   *OSPF Authentication Using Only Interface Subcommands*

```
! The following commands enable OSPF simple password authentication and
! set the password to a value of "key-t1".
R1#show running-config
! lines omitted for brevity
interface FastEthernet0/0
 ip ospf authentication
 ip ospf authentication-key key-t1
! Below, the neighbor relationship formed, proving that authentication worked.
R1# show ip ospf neighbor fa 0/0
Neighbor ID     Pri   State          Dead Time   Address       Interface
2.2.2.2           1   FULL/BDR       00:00:37    10.1.1.2      FastEthernet0/0
! Next, each interface's OSPF authentication type can be seen in the last line
! or two in the output of the show ip ospf interface command.
R1# show ip ospf interface fa 0/0
! Lines omitted for brevity
 Simple password authentication enabled

! Below, R1's Fa0/1 interface is configured to use type 2 authentication.
! Note that the key must be defined with
! the ip ospf message-digest-key interface subcommand.
R1#show running-config
! lines omitted for brevity
interface FastEthernet0/1
 ip ospf authentication message-digest
 ip ospf message-digest-key 1 md5 key-t2
! Below, the command confirms type 2 (MD5) authentication, key number 1.
R1# show ip ospf interface fa 0/1
! Lines omitted for brevity
 Message digest authentication enabled
 Youngest key id is 1
```

The trickiest part of the configuration is to remember the command syntax used on two interface subcommands. Note the interface subcommands used to configure the authentication keys, with the syntax differing depending on the type of authentication. For reference, Table 9-4 lists the three OSPF authentication types and the corresponding commands.

Table 9-4 *OSPF Authentication Types*

Type	Meaning	Command to Enable Authentication	What the Password Is Configured With
0	None	**ip ospf authentication null**	—
1	Clear text	**ip ospf authentication**	**ip ospf authentication-key** *key-value*
2	MD5	**ip ospf authentication message-digest**	**ip ospf message-digest-key** *key-number* **md5** *key-value*

Note that the passwords, or authentication keys, are kept in clear text in the configuration, unless you add the **service password-encryption** global command to the configuration. (If you have a copy of *CCENT/CCNA ICND1 Official Exam Certification Guide*, you might want to refer to Chapter 9 of that book for more information on the **service password-encryption** command.)

The default setting to use type 0 authentication—which really means no authentication—can be overridden on an area-by-area basis by using the **area authentication** router command. For example, Router R1 in Example 9-7 could be configured with the **area 1 authentication message-digest** router subcommand, which makes that router default to use MD5 authentication on all its interfaces in Area 1. Similarly, the **area 1 authentication** router subcommand enables simple password authentication for all interfaces in Area 1, making the **ip ospf authentication** interface subcommand unnecessary. Note that the authentication keys (passwords) must still be configured with the interface subcommands listed in Table 9-4.

OSPF Load Balancing

When OSPF uses SPF to calculate the metric for each of several routes to reach one subnet, one route may have the lowest metric, so OSPF puts that route in the routing table. However, when the metric is a tie, the router can put up to 16 different equal-cost routes in the routing table (the default is four different routes) based on the setting of the **maximum-paths** *number* router subcommand. For example, if an internetwork had six possible paths between some parts of the network, and the engineer wanted all routes to be used, the routers could be configured with the **maximum-paths 6** subcommand under **router ospf**.

The more challenging concept relates to how the routers use those multiple routes. A router could load-balance the packets on a per-packet basis. For example, if the router had three equal-cost OSPF routes for the same subnet in the routing table, the router could send the next packet over the first route, the next packet over the second route, the next packet over the third route, and then start over with the first route for the next packet. Alternatively, the load balancing could be on a per-destination IP address basis.

Exam Preparation Tasks

Review All the Key Topics

Review the most important topics from this chapter, noted with the key topics icon. Table 9-5 lists these key topics and where each is discussed.

Key
Topic

Table 9-5 *Key Topics for Chapter 9*

Key Topic Element	Description	Page Number
List	Items that must match on OSPF neighbors before they will become neighbors and reach the two-way state (at least)	349
Figure 9-2	Neighbor states and messages during OSPF neighbor formation	351
List	Three-step summary of the OSPF topology database exchange process	352
Figure 9-3	Drawing comparing full adjacencies formed with and without a DR	353
List	Rules for electing a designated router	354
Table 9-2	OSPF neighbor states and their meanings	355
List	List of reasons why OSPF needs areas to scale well	358
Table 9-3	OSPF design terms and definitions	359-360
List	Configuration checklist for OSPF	361-362
List	Details of how IOS determines an interface's OSPF cost	366
Table 9-4	OSPF authentication types and configuration commands	372

Definitions of Key Terms

Define the following key terms from this chapter, and check your answers in the glossary:

Two-way state, Area Border Router (ABR), Autonomous System Border Router (ASBR), Backup Designated Router, database description, dead interval, designated router, Full state, fully adjacent, Hello interval, link-state advertisement, link-state request, link-state update, neighbor, neighbor table, router ID (RID), topology database

Command Reference to Check Your Memory

Although you should not necessarily memorize the information in the tables in this section, this section does include a reference for the configuration and EXEC commands covered in this chapter. Practically speaking, you should memorize the commands as a side effect of reading the chapter and doing all the activities in this exam preparation section. To see how well you have memorized the commands as a side effect of your other studies, cover the left side of the table, read the descriptions on the right side, and see if you remember the command.

Table 9-6 *Chapter 9 Configuration Command Reference*

Command	Description
router ospf *process-id*	Enters OSPF configuration mode for the listed process.
network *ip-address wildcard-mask* **area** *area-id*	Router subcommand that enables OSPF on interfaces matching the address/wildcard combination and sets the OSPF area.
ip ospf cost *interface-cost*	Interface subcommand that sets the OSPF cost associated with the interface.
bandwidth *bandwidth*	Interface subcommand that directly sets the interface bandwidth (Kbps).
auto-cost reference-bandwidth *number*	Router subcommand that tells OSPF the numerator in the *Ref-BW/Int-BW* formula used to calculate the OSPF cost based on the interface bandwidth.
ip ospf hello *number*	Interface subcommand that sets the OSPF Hello interval, and also resets the Dead interval to 4 times this number.
ip ospf dead-interval *number*	Interface subcommand that sets the OSPF dead timer.
ip ospf network *type*	Interface subcommand that defines the OSPF network type.

Table 9-6 *Chapter 9 Configuration Command Reference (Continued)*

Command	Description
router-id *id*	OSPF command that statically sets the router ID.
ip ospf hello-interval *seconds*	Interface subcommand that sets the interval for periodic Hellos.
ip ospf priority *number-value*	Interface subcommand that sets the OSPF priority on an interface.
maximum-paths *number-of-paths*	Router subcommand that defines the maximum number of equal-cost routes that can be added to the routing table.
ip ospf authentication [null | message-digest]	Interface subcommand that enables type 0 (null), type 1 (no optional parameter listed), or type 2 (message-digest) authentication.
ip ospf message-digest-key *key-number* **md5** *key-value*	Interface subcommand that sets the OSPF authentication key if MD5 authentication is used.
ip ospf authentication-key *key-value*	Interface subcommand that sets the OSPF authentication key if simple password authentication is used.
area *area* **authentication [message-digest | null]**	Router subcommand that configures the default authentication service for interfaces in the listed area.

Table 9-7 *Chapter 9 EXEC Command Reference*

Command	Description
show ip route ospf	Lists routes in the routing table learned by OSPF.
show ip protocols	Shows routing protocol parameters and current timer values.
show ip ospf interface	Lists the area in which the interface resides, neighbors adjacent on this interface, and Hello and dead timers.
show ip ospf neighbor [*neighbor-RID*]	Lists neighbors and current status with neighbors, per interface, and optionally lists details for the router ID listed in the command.
debug ip ospf events	Issues log messages for each OSPF packet.
debug ip ospf packet	Issues log messages describing the contents of all OSPF packets.
debug ip ospf hello	Issues log messages describing Hellos and Hello failures.

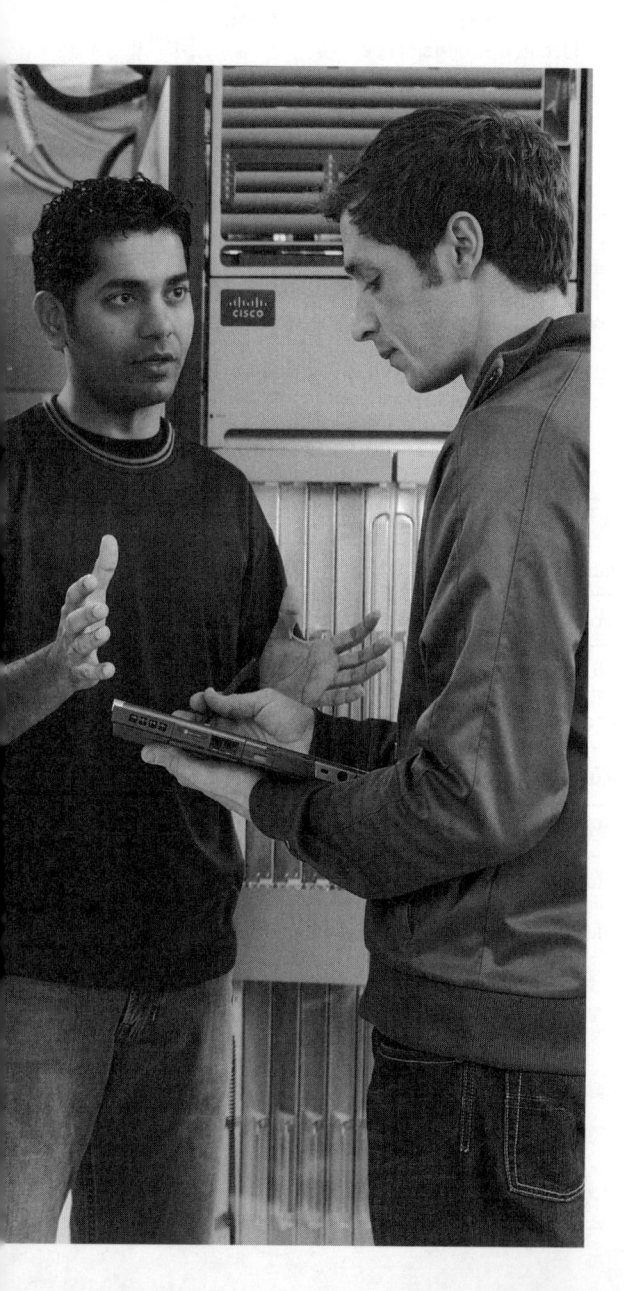

This chapter covers the following subjects:

EIGRP Concepts and Operation: This section explains the concepts behind EIGRP neighbors, exchanging topology information, and calculating routes.

EIGRP Configuration and Verification: This section shows how to configure EIGRP, including authentication and tuning the metric, as well as how to determine the successor and feasible successor routes in the output of **show** commands.

CHAPTER 10

EIGRP

Enhanced Interior Gateway Routing Protocol (EIGRP) provides an impressive set of features and attributes for its main purpose of learning IP routes. EIGRP converges very quickly, on par with or even faster than OSPF, but without some of the negatives of OSPF. In particular, EIGRP requires much less processing time, much less memory, and much less design effort than OSPF. The only significant negative is that EIGRP is Cisco-proprietary, so if an internetwork uses some non-Cisco routers, EIGRP cannot be used on those routers.

EIGRP does not fit neatly into the general categories of distance vector and link-state routing protocols. Sometimes Cisco refers to EIGRP as simply an advanced distance vector protocol, but in other cases, Cisco refers to EIGRP as a new type: a balanced hybrid routing protocol. Regardless of the category, the underlying concepts and processes used by EIGRP may have some similarities with other routing protocols, but EIGRP has far more differences, making EIGRP a unique routing protocol unto itself.

This chapter begins by examining some of the key concepts behind how EIGRP does its work. The second half of this chapter explains EIGRP configuration and verification.

"Do I Know This Already?" Quiz

The "Do I Know This Already?" quiz allows you to assess whether you should read the entire chapter. If you miss no more than one of these nine self-assessment questions, you might want to move ahead to the "Exam Preparation Tasks" section. Table 10-1 lists the major headings in this chapter and the "Do I Know This Already?" quiz questions covering the material in those sections. This helps you assess your knowledge of these specific areas. The answers to the "Do I Know This Already?" quiz appear in Appendix A.

Table 10-1 *"Do I Know This Already?" Foundation Topics Section-to-Question Mapping*

Foundation Topics Section	Questions
EIGRP Concepts and Operation	1–4
EIGRP Configuration and Verification	5–9

1.   Which of the following affect the calculation of EIGRP metrics when all possible default values are used?

   a.   Bandwidth

   b.   Delay

   c.   Load

   d.   Reliability

   e.   MTU

   f.   Hop count

2.   How does EIGRP notice when a neighboring router fails?

   a.   The failing neighbor sends a message before failing.

   b.   The failing neighbor sends a "dying gasp" message.

   c.   The router notices a lack of routing updates for a period of time.

   d.   The router notices a lack of Hello messages for a period of time.

3.   Which of the following is true about the concept of EIGRP feasible distance?

   a.   A route's feasible distance is the calculated metric of a feasible successor route.

   b.   A route's feasible distance is the calculated metric of the successor route.

   c.   The feasible distance is the metric of a route from a neighboring router's perspective.

   d.   The feasible distance is the EIGRP metric associated with each possible route to reach a subnet.

4.   Which of the following is true about the concept of EIGRP reported distance?

   a.   A route's reported distance is the calculated metric of a feasible successor route.

   b.   A route's reported distance is the calculated metric of the successor route.

   c.   A route's reported distance is the metric of a route from a neighboring router's perspective.

   d.   The reported distance is the EIGRP metric associated with each possible route to reach a subnet.

5.   Which of the following **network** commands, following the command **router eigrp 1**, tells this router to start using EIGRP on interfaces whose IP addresses are 10.1.1.1, 10.1.100.1, and 10.1.120.1?

   a.   **network 10.0.0.0**

   b.   **network 10.1.1x.0**

   c.   **network 10.0.0.0 0.255.255.255**

   d.   **network 10.0.0.0 255.255.255.0**

6. Routers R1 and R2 attach to the same VLAN with IP addresses 10.0.0.1 and 10.0.0.2, respectively. R1 is configured with the commands **router eigrp 99** and **network 10.0.0.0.** Which of the following commands might be part of a working EIGRP configuration on R2 that ensures that the two routers become neighbors and exchange routes?

   a. **network 10**

   b. **router eigrp 98**

   c. **network 10.0.0.2 0.0.0.0**

   d. **network 10.0.0.0**

7. Examine the following excerpt from a router's CLI:

```
P 10.1.1.0/24, 1 successors, FD is 2172416
        via 10.1.6.3 (2172416/28160), Serial0/1
        via 10.1.4.2 (2684416/2284156), Serial0/0
        via 10.1.5.4 (2684416/2165432), Serial1/0
```

   Which of the following identifies a next-hop IP address on a feasible successor route?

   a. 10.1.6.3

   b. 10.1.4.2

   c. 10.1.5.4

   d. It cannot be determined from this command output.

8. Which of the following must occur to configure MD5 authentication for EIGRP?

   a. Setting the MD5 authentication key via some interface subcommand

   b. Configuring at least one key chain

   c. Defining a valid lifetime for the key

   d. Enabling EIGRP MD5 authentication on an interface

9. In the **show ip route** command, what code designation implies that a route was learned with EIGRP?

   a. E

   b. I

   c. G

   d. R

   e. P

   f. D

Foundation Topics

EIGRP Concepts and Operation

Like OSPF, EIGRP follows three general steps to be able to add routes to the IP routing table:

1. **Neighbor discovery**: EIGRP routers send Hello messages to discover potential neighboring EIGRP routers and perform basic parameter checks to determine which routers should become neighbors.

2. **Topology exchange**: Neighbors exchange full topology updates when the neighbor relationship comes up, and then only partial updates as needed based on changes to the network topology.

3. **Choosing routes**: Each router analyzes its respective EIGRP topology tables, choosing the lowest-metric route to reach each subnet.

As a result of these three steps, IOS maintains three important EIGRP tables. The EIGRP neighbor table lists the neighboring routers and is viewed with the **show ip eigrp neighbor** command. The EIGRP topology table holds all the topology information learned from EIGRP neighbors and is displayed with the **show ip eigrp topology** command. Finally, the IP routing table holds all the best routes and is displayed with the **show ip route** command.

The next few sections describe some details about how EIGRP forms neighbor relationships, exchanges routes, and adds entries to the IP routing table. In addition to these three steps, this section explains some unique logic EIGRP uses when converging and reacting to changes in an internetwork—logic that is not seen with the other types of routing protocols.

EIGRP Neighbors

An EIGRP neighbor is another EIGRP-speaking router, connected to a common subnet, with which the router is willing to exchange EIGRP topology information. EIGRP uses EIGRP Hello messages, sent to multicast IP address 224.0.0.10, to dynamically discover potential neighbors. A router learns of potential neighbors by receiving a Hello.

Routers perform some basic checking of each potential neighbor before that router becomes an EIGRP neighbor. A potential neighbor is a router from which an EIGRP Hello has been received. Then the router checks the following settings to determine if the router should be allowed to be a neighbor:

■ It must pass the authentication process.

■ It must use the same configured AS number.

■ The source IP address used by the neighbor's Hello must be in the same subnet.

NOTE   The router's EIGRP K values must also match, but this topic is outside the scope of this book.

The verification checks are relatively straightforward. If authentication is configured, the two routers must be using the same type of authentication and the same authentication key. EIGRP configuration includes a parameter called an autonomous system number (ASN), which must be the same on two neighboring routers. Finally, the IP addresses used to send the EIGRP Hello messages—the routers' respective interface IP addresses—must be in the range of addresses on the other routers' respective connected subnet.

The EIGRP neighbor relationship is much simpler than OSPF. EIGRP does not have an additional concept of being fully adjacent like OSPF, and there are no neighbor states like OSPF. As soon as an EIGRP neighbor is discovered and passes the basic verification checks, the router becomes a neighbor. At that point, the two routers can begin exchanging topology information. The neighbors send Hellos every EIGRP Hello interval. A router considers its EIGRP neighbor to no longer be reachable after the neighbor's Hellos cease to occur for the number of seconds defined by the EIGRP Hold Timer—the rough equivalent of the OSPF Dead Interval.

Exchanging EIGRP Topology Information

EIGRP uses EIGRP *Update messages* to send topology information to neighbors. These Update messages can be sent to multicast IP address 224.0.0.10 if the sending router needs to update multiple routers on the same subnet; otherwise, the updates are sent to the unicast IP address of the particular neighbor. (Hello messages are always sent to the 224.0.0.10 multicast address.) Unlike OSPF, there is no concept of a Designated Router (DR) or Backup Designated Router (BDR), but the use of multicast packets on LANs allows EIGRP to exchange routing information with all neighbors on the LAN efficiently.

The update messages are sent using *Reliable Transport Protocol (RTP)*. The significance of RTP is that, like OSPF, EIGRP resends routing updates that are lost in transit. By using RTP, EIGRP can better avoid loops.

> **NOTE**   The acronym RTP also refers to a different protocol, Real-time Transport
> Protocol (RTP), which is used to transmit voice and video IP packets.

Neighbors use both full routing updates and partial updates, as shown in Figure 10-1. A full
update means that a router sends information about all known routes, whereas a partial
update includes only information about recently changed routes. Full updates occur when
neighbors first come up. After that, the neighbors send only partial updates in reaction to
changes to a route. From top to bottom, Figure 10-1 shows neighbor discovery with Hellos,
the sending of full updates, the maintenance of the neighbor relationship with ongoing
Hellos, and partial updates.

Figure 10-1   *Full and Partial EIGRP Updates*

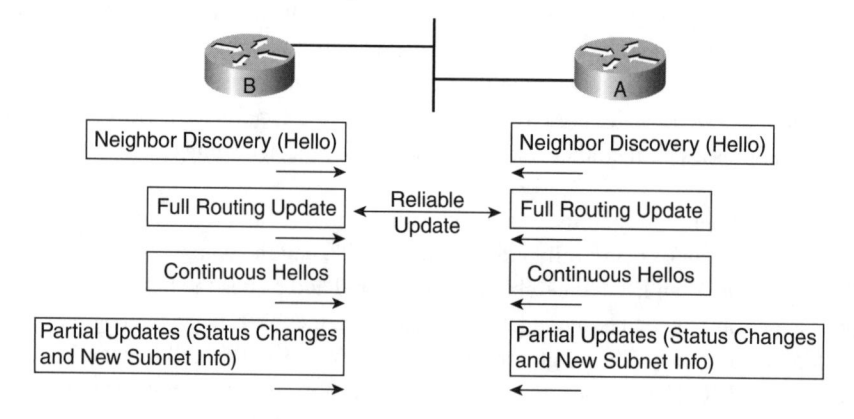

Calculating the Best Routes for the Routing Table

Metric calculation is one of the more interesting features of EIGRP. EIGRP uses a
composite metric, calculated as a function of bandwidth and delay by default. The
calculation can also include interface load and interface reliability, although Cisco
recommends against using either. EIGRP calculates the metric for each possible route by
inserting the values of the composite metric into a formula.

> **NOTE**   Past documents and books often stated that EIGRP, and its predecessor, IGRP,
> also could use MTU as a part of the metric, but MTU cannot be used and was never
> considered as part of the calculation.

EIGRP's metric calculation formula actually helps describe some of the key points about the metric. The formula, assuming that the default settings use just bandwidth and delay, is as follows:

$$\text{Metric} = \left(\left(\frac{10^7}{\text{least-bandwidth}} \right) + \text{cumulative-delay} \right) * 256$$

In this formula, the term *least-bandwidth* represents the lowest-bandwidth link in the route, using a unit of kilobits per second. For instance, if the slowest link in a route is a 10-Mbps Ethernet link, the first part of the formula is $10^7 / 10^4$, which equals 1000. You use 10^4 in the formula because 10 Mbps is equal to 10,000 kbps (10^4 kbps). The cumulative-delay value used in the formula is the sum of all the delay values for all links in the route, with a unit of "tens of microseconds." You can set both bandwidth and delay for each link, using the cleverly named **bandwidth** and **delay** interface subcommands.

> **NOTE**   Most **show** commands, including **show ip eigrp topology** and **show interfaces**, list delay settings as the number of microseconds of delay. The metric formula uses a unit of tens of microseconds.

EIGRP updates list the subnet number and mask, along with the cumulative delay, minimum bandwidth, along with the other typically unused portions of the composite metric. The router then considers the bandwidth and delay settings on the interface on which the update was received and calculates a new metric. For example, Figure 10-2 shows Albuquerque learning about subnet 10.1.3.0/24 from Seville. The update lists a minimum bandwidth of 100,000 kbps, and a cumulative delay of 100 microseconds. R1 has an interface bandwidth set to 1544 kbps—the default bandwidth on a serial link—and a delay of 20,000 microseconds.

Figure 10-2   *How Albuquerque Calculates Its EIGRP Metric for 10.1.3.0/24*

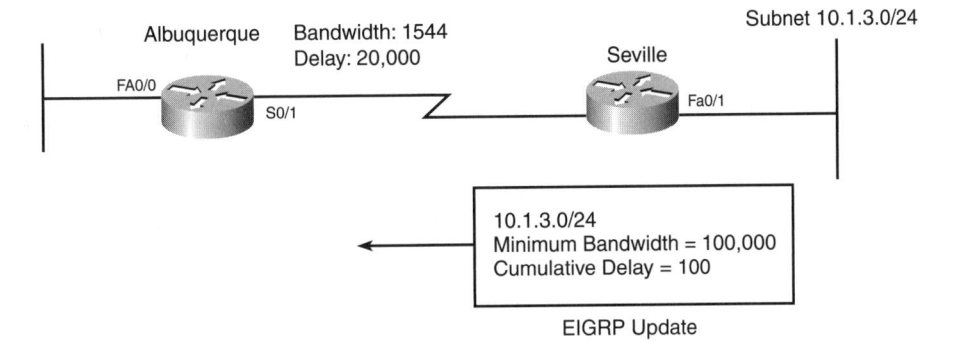

In this case, Albuquerque discovers that its S0/1 interface bandwidth (1544) is less than the advertised minimum bandwidth of 100,000, so Albuquerque uses this new, slower bandwidth in the metric calculation. (If Albuquerque's S0/1 interface had a bandwidth of 100,000 or more in this case, Albuquerque would instead use the minimum bandwidth listed in the EIGRP Update from Seville.) Albuquerque also adds the interface S0/1 delay (20,000 microseconds, converted to 2000 tens-of-microseconds for the formula) to the cumulative delay received from Seville in the update (100 microseconds, converted to 10 tens-of-microseconds). This results in the following metric calculation:

$$\text{Metric} = \left(\left(\frac{10^7}{1544}\right) + (10 + 2000)\right) * 256 = 2{,}172{,}416$$

> **NOTE**   IOS rounds down the division in this formula to the nearest integer before performing the rest of the formula. In this case, $10^7 / 1544$ is rounded down to 6476.

If multiple possible routes to subnet 10.1.3.0/24 existed, Albuquerque would also calculate the metric for those routes and would choose the route with the best (lowest) metric to be added to the routing table. If the metric is a tie, by default a router would place up to four equal-metric routes into the routing table, sending some traffic over each route. The later section "EIGRP Maximum Paths and Variance" explains a few more details about how EIGRP can add multiple equal-metric routes, and multiple unequal-metric routes, to the routing table.

Feasible Distance and Reported Distance

The example described for Figure 10-2 provides a convenient backdrop to define a couple of EIGRP terms:

- **Feasible Distance (FD)**: The metric of the best route to reach a subnet, as calculated on a router

- **Reported Distance (RD)**: The metric as calculated on a neighboring router and then reported and learned in an EIGRP Update

For example, in Figure 10-2, Albuquerque calculates an FD of 2,172,416 to reach subnet 10.1.3.0/24 through Seville. Seville also calculates its own metric to reach subnet 10.1.3.0/24. Seville also lists that metric in its EIGRP update sent to Albuquerque. In fact, based on the information in Figure 10-2, Seville's FD to reach subnet 10.1.3.0/24, which is then known by Albuquerque as Seville's RD to reach 10.1.3.0/24, could be easily calculated:

$$\left(\left(\frac{10^7}{100{,}000}\right) + (10)\right) * 256 = 28{,}160$$

FD and RD are mentioned in an upcoming discussion of how EIGRP reacts and converges when a change occurs in an internetwork.

Caveats with Bandwidth on Serial Links

EIGRP's robust metric gives it the ability to choose routes that include more router hops but with faster links. However, to ensure that the right routes are chosen, engineers must take care to configure meaningful bandwidth and delay settings. In particular, serial links default to a bandwidth of 1544 and a delay of 20,000 microseconds, as used in the example shown in Figure 10-2. However, IOS cannot automatically change the bandwidth and delay settings based on the Layer 1 speed of a serial link. So, using default bandwidth settings on serial links can lead to problems.

Figure 10-3 shows the problem with using default bandwidth settings and how EIGRP uses the better (faster) route when the bandwidth is set correctly. The figure focuses on router B's route to subnet 10.1.1.0/24 in each case. In the top part of the figure, all serial interfaces use defaults, even though the top serial link is a slow 64 kbps. The bottom figure shows the results when the slow serial link's **bandwidth** command is changed to reflect the correct (slow) speed.

Figure 10-3 *Impact of the Bandwidth on EIGRP's Metric Calculation*

EIGRP Convergence

Loop avoidance poses one of the most difficult problems with any dynamic routing protocol. Distance vector protocols overcome this problem with a variety of tools, some of which create a large portion of the minutes-long convergence time after a link failure. Link-state protocols overcome this problem by having each router keep a full topology of the network, so by running a rather involved mathematical model, a router can avoid any loops.

EIGRP avoids loops by keeping some basic topological information, but it avoids spending too much CPU and memory by keeping the information brief. When a router learns multiple routes to the same subnet, it puts the best route in the IP routing table. EIGRP keeps some topological information for the same reason as OSPF—so that it can very quickly converge and use a new route without causing a loop. Essentially, EIGRP keeps a record of each possible next-hop router, and some details related to those routes, but no information about the topology beyond the next-hop routers. This sparser topology information does not require the sophisticated SPF algorithm, resulting in quick convergence and less overhead, with no loops.

The EIGRP convergence process uses one of two branches in its logic, based on whether the failed route does or does not have a *feasible successor* route. If a feasible successor route exists, the router can immediately use that route. If not, the router must use a *query and response* process to find a loop-free alternative route. Both processes result in fast convergence, typically quicker than 10 seconds, but the query and response process takes slightly longer.

EIGRP Successors and Feasible Successors

EIGRP calculates the metric for each route to reach each subnet. For a particular subnet, the route with the best metric is called the successor, with the router filling the IP routing table with this route. (This route's metric is called the feasible distance, as introduced earlier.)

Of the other routes to reach that same subnet—routes whose metrics were larger than the FD for the route—EIGRP needs to determine which can be used immediately if the currently best route fails, without causing a routing loop. EIGRP runs a simple algorithm to identify which routes could be used, keeping these loop-free backup routes in its topology table and using them if the currently best route fails. These alternative, immediately usable routes are called *feasible successor* routes, because they can feasibly be used when the successor route fails. A router determines if a route is a feasible successor based on the feasibility condition:

> If a nonsuccessor route's RD is less than the FD, the route is a feasible successor route.

Although it is technically correct, this definition is much more understandable with the example shown in Figure 10-4. The figure illustrates how EIGRP figures out which routes are feasible successors for subnet 1. In the figure, Router E learns three routes to Subnet 1, from Routers B, C, and D. After calculating each route's metric, based on bandwidth and delay information received in the routing update and on E's corresponding outgoing interfaces, Router E finds that the route through Router D has the lowest metric, so Router E adds that route to its routing table, as shown. The FD is the metric calculated for this route, a value of 14,000 in this case.

Figure 10-4 *Successors and Feasible Successors with EIGRP*

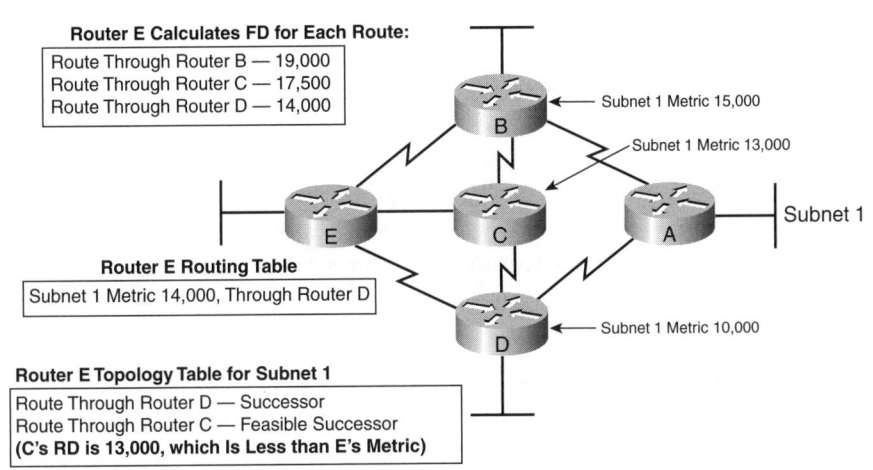

EIGRP decides if a route can be a feasible successor if the reported distance for that route (the metric as calculated on that neighbor) is less than its own best computed metric (the FD). When that neighbor has a lower metric for its route to the subnet in question, that route is said to have met the *feasibility condition*. For example, Router E computes a metric (FD) of 14,000 on its best route (through Router D). Router C's computed metric—its reported distance for this route—is lower than 14,000 (it's 13,000). As a result, E knows that C's best route for this subnet could not possibly point toward router E, so Router E believes that it could start using the route through Router C and not cause a loop. As a result, Router E adds a route through Router C to the topology table as a feasible successor route. Conversely, Router B's reported distance is 15,000, which is larger than Router E's FD of 14,000, so Router E does not consider the route through Router B a feasible successor.

If the route to Subnet 1 through Router D fails, Router E can immediately put the route through Router C into the routing table without fear of creating a loop. Convergence occurs almost instantly in this case.

The Query and Reply Process

When a route fails and has no feasible successor, EIGRP uses a distributed algorithm called *Diffusing Update Algorithm (DUAL)*. DUAL sends queries looking for a loop-free route to the subnet in question. When the new route is found, DUAL adds it to the routing table.

The EIGRP DUAL process simply uses messages to confirm that a route exists, and would not create a loop, before deciding to replace a failed route with an alternative route. For instance, in Figure 10-4, imagine that both Routers C and D fail. Router E does not have a feasible successor route for subnet 1, but there is an obvious physically available path through Router B. To use the route, Router E sends EIGRP *query* messages to its working neighbors (in this case, Router B). Router B's route to subnet 1 is still working fine, so Router B replies to Router E with an EIGRP *reply* message, simply stating the details of the working route to subnet 1 and confirming that it is still viable. Router E can then add a new route to subnet 1 to its routing table, without fear of a loop.

Replacing a failed route with a feasible successor takes a very short amount of time, typically less than a second or two. When queries and replies are required, convergence can take slightly longer, but in most networks, convergence can still occur in less than 10 seconds.

EIGRP Summary and Comparisons with OSPF

EIGRP is a popular IGP for many reasons. It works well, converging quickly while avoiding loops as a side effect of its underlying balanced hybrid/advanced distance vector algorithms. It does not require a lot of configuration or a lot of planning, even when scaling to support larger internetworks.

EIGRP also has another advantage that is not as important today as in years past: the support of Novell's IPX and Apple's AppleTalk Layer 3 protocols. Routers can run EIGRP to learn IP routes, IPX routes, and AppleTalk routes, with the same wonderful performance features. However, like many other Layer 3 protocols, IP has mostly usurped IPX and AppleTalk, making support for these Layer 3 protocols a minor advantage.

Table 10-2 summarizes several important features of EIGRP as compared to OSPF.

Table 10-2   *EIGRP Features Compared to OSPF*

Feature	EIGRP	OSPF
Converges quickly	Yes	Yes
Built-in loop prevention	Yes	Yes
Sends partial routing updates, advertising only new or changed information	Yes	Yes
Classless; therefore, supports manual summarization and VLSM	Yes	Yes
Allows manual summarization at any router	Yes	No
Sends routing information using IP multicast on LANs	Yes	Yes

Table 10-2 *EIGRP Features Compared to OSPF (Continued)*

Key
Topic

Feature	EIGRP	OSPF
Uses the concept of a designated router on a LAN	No	Yes
Flexible network design with no need to create areas	Yes	No
Supports both equal-metric and unequal-metric load balancing	Yes	No
Robust metric based on bandwidth and delay	Yes	No
Can advertise IP, IPX, and AppleTalk routes	Yes	No
Public standard	No	Yes

EIGRP Configuration and Verification

Basic EIGRP configuration closely resembles RIP and OSPF configuration. The **router eigrp** command enables EIGRP and puts the user in EIGRP configuration mode, in which one or more **network** commands are configured. For each interface matched by a **network** command, EIGRP tries to discover neighbors on that interface, and EIGRP advertises the subnet connected to the interface.

This section examines EIGRP configuration, including several optional features. It also explains the meaning of the output of many **show** commands to help connect the theory covered in the first part of this chapter with the reality of the EIGRP implementation in IOS. The following configuration checklist outlines the main configuration tasks covered in this chapter:

Step 1   Enter EIGRP configuration mode, and define the EIGRP ASN by using the **router eigrp** *as-number* global command.

Key
Topic

Step 2   Configure one or more **network** *ip-address* [*wildcard-mask*] router subcommands. This enables EIGRP on any matched interface and causes EIGRP to advertise the connected subnet.

Step 3   (Optional) Change the interface Hello and hold timers using the **ip hello-interval eigrp** *asn time* and **ip hold-time eigrp** *asn time* interface subcommands.

Step 4   (Optional) Impact metric calculations by tuning bandwidth and delay using the **bandwidth** *value* and **delay** *value* interface subcommands.

Step 5   (Optional) Configure EIGRP authentication.

Step 6 (Optional) Configure support for multiple equal-cost routes using the **maximum-paths** *number* and **variance** *multiplier* router subcommands.

Basic EIGRP Configuration

Example 10-1 shows a sample EIGRP configuration, along with **show** commands, on Albuquerque in Figure 10-5. The EIGRP configuration required on Yosemite and Seville matches exactly the two lines of EIGRP configuration on Albuquerque.

Figure 10-5 *Sample Internetwork Used in Most of the EIGRP Examples*

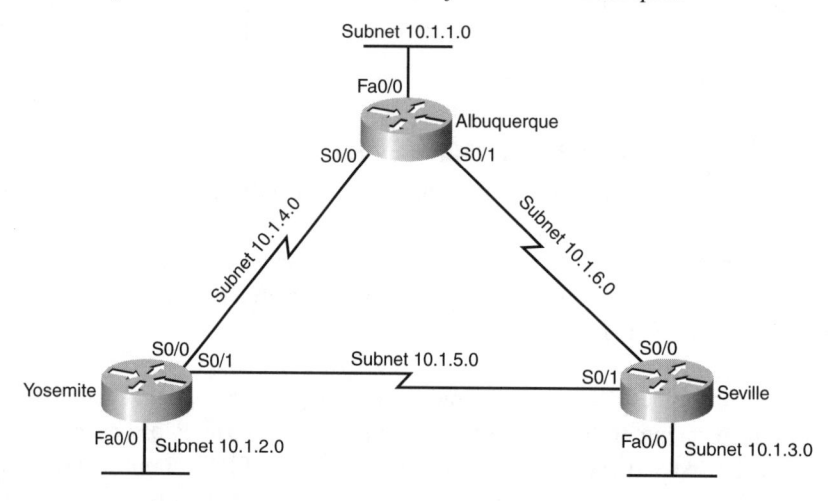

Example 10-1 *Sample Router Configuration with EIGRP Enabled*

```
router eigrp 1
 network 10.0.0.0
Albuquerque#show ip route
Codes: C - connected, S - static, I - IGRP, R - RIP, M - mobile, B - BGP
       D - EIGRP, EX - EIGRP external, O - OSPF, IA - OSPF inter area
       N1 - OSPF NSSA external type 1, N2 - OSPF NSSA external type 2
       E1 - OSPF external type 1, E2 - OSPF external type 2, E - EGP
       i - IS-IS, L1 - IS-IS level-1, L2 - IS-IS level-2, ia - IS-IS inter area
       * - candidate default, U - per-user static route, o - ODR
       P - periodic downloaded static route

Gateway of last resort is not set

     10.0.0.0/24 is subnetted, 6 subnets
D       10.1.3.0 [90/2172416] via 10.1.6.3, 00:00:43, Serial0/1
D       10.1.2.0 [90/2172416] via 10.1.4.2, 00:00:43, Serial0/0
C       10.1.1.0 is directly connected, FastEthernet0/0
C       10.1.6.0 is directly connected, Serial0/1
```

Example 10-1 *Sample Router Configuration with EIGRP Enabled (Continued)*

```
D        10.1.5.0 [90/2681856] via 10.1.6.3, 00:00:45, Serial0/1
                  [90/2681856] via 10.1.4.2, 00:00:45, Serial0/0
C        10.1.4.0 is directly connected, Serial0/0

Albuquerque#show ip route eigrp
     10.0.0.0/24 is subnetted, 6 subnets
D        10.1.3.0 [90/2172416] via 10.1.6.3, 00:00:47, Serial0/1
D        10.1.2.0 [90/2172416] via 10.1.4.2, 00:00:47, Serial0/0
D        10.1.5.0 [90/2681856] via 10.1.6.3, 00:00:49, Serial0/1
                  [90/2681856] via 10.1.4.2, 00:00:49, Serial0/0

Albuquerque#show ip eigrp neighbors
IP-EIGRP neighbors for process 1
H    Address                 Interface    Hold Uptime    SRTT    RTO  Q   Seq Type
                                          (sec)          (ms)         Cnt Num
0    10.1.4.2                Se0/0         11 00:00:54    32     200  0   4
1    10.1.6.3                Se0/1         12 00:10:36    20     200  0   24

Albuquerque#show ip eigrp interfaces
IP-EIGRP interfaces for process 1

                    Xmit Queue    Mean    Pacing Time    Multicast    Pending
Interface    Peers  Un/Reliable   SRTT    Un/Reliable    Flow Timer   Routes
Fa0/0        0          0/0        0          0/10           0           0
Se0/0        1          0/0        32         0/15           50          0
Se0/1        1          0/0        20         0/15           95          0
Albuquerque#show ip eigrp topology summary
IP-EIGRP Topology Table for AS(1)/ID(10.1.6.1)
Head serial 1, next serial 9
6 routes, 0 pending replies, 0 dummies
IP-EIGRP(0) enabled on 3 interfaces, 2 neighbors present on 2 interfaces
Quiescent interfaces:  Se0/1/0 Se0/0/1
```

For EIGRP configuration, all three routers must use the same AS number in the **router eigrp** command. For instance, they all use **router eigrp 1** in this example. The actual number used doesn't really matter, as long as it is the same on all three routers. (The range of valid AS numbers is 1 through 65,535, as is the range of valid Process IDs with the **router ospf** command.) The **network 10.0.0.0** command enables EIGRP on all interfaces whose IP addresses are in network 10.0.0.0, which includes all three interfaces on Albuquerque. With the identical two EIGRP configuration statements on the other two routers, EIGRP is enabled on all three interfaces on those routers as well, because those interfaces are also in network 10.0.0.0.

The **show ip route** and **show ip route eigrp** commands both list the EIGRP-learned routes with a "D" beside them. "D" signifies EIGRP. The letter E was already being used for Exterior Gateway Protocol (EGP) when Cisco created EIGRP, so Cisco chose the next-closest unused letter, D, to denote EIGRP-learned routes.

You can see information about EIGRP neighbors with the **show ip eigrp neighbors** command and information about the number of active neighbors (called peers in the command output) with the **show ip eigrp interfaces** command, as shown in the last part of the example. These commands also provide some insight into EIGRP's underlying processes, such as the use of RTP for reliable transmission. For instance, the **show ip eigrp neighbors** command shows a "Q Cnt" (Queue Count) column, listing either the number of packets waiting to be sent to a neighbor or packets that have been sent but for which no acknowledgment has been received. The **show ip eigrp interfaces** command lists similar information in the "Xmit Queue Un/Reliable" column, which separates statistics for EIGRP messages that are sent with RTP (reliable) or without it (unreliable).

Finally, the end of the example displays Albuquerque's RID. EIGRP allocates its RID just like OSPF—based on the configured value, or the highest IP address of an up/up loopback interface, or the highest IP address of a nonloopback interface, in that order of precedence. The only difference compared to OSPF is that the EIGRP RID is configured with the **eigrp router-id** *value* router subcommand.

The EIGRP **network** command can be configured without a wildcard mask, as shown in Example 10-1. Without a wildcard mask, the **network** command must use a classful network as the lone parameter, and all interfaces in the classful network are matched. Example 10-2 shows an alternative configuration that uses a **network** command with an address and wildcard mask. In this case, the command matches an interface IP address that would be matched if the address and mask in the **network** command were part of an ACL. The example shows three **network** commands on Albuquerque, one matching each of the three interfaces.

Example 10-2   *Using Wildcard Masks with EIGRP Configuration*

```
Albuquerque#router eigrp 1
Albuquerque(config-router)#network 10.1.1.0 0.0.0.255
Albuquerque(config-router)#network 10.1.4.0 0.0.0.255
Albuquerque(config-router)#network 10.1.6.0 0.0.0.255
```

EIGRP Metrics, Successors, and Feasible Successors

As defined earlier in this chapter, an EIGRP successor route is a route that has the best metric for reaching a subnet, and a Feasible Successor (FS) route is a route that could be used if the successor route failed. This section examines how to see successor and FS routes with EIGRP, along with the calculated metrics. To that end, Example 10-3 shows Albuquerque's single best route to reach subnet 10.1.3.0/24, both in the routing table and as the successor route in the EIGRP topology table. It also lists the two equal-metric successor routes for subnet 10.1.5.0/24, with both of these successor routes being highlighted in the EIGRP topology table. Some of the explanations are listed in the example, and the longer explanations follow the example.

Example 10-3 *Using Wildcard Masks with EIGRP Configuration, and Feasible Successor Examination*

```
! Below, note the single route to subnet 10.1.3.0, and the two
! equal-metric routes to 10.1.5.0.
Albuquerque#show ip route
Codes: C - connected, S - static, R - RIP, M - mobile, B - BGP
       D - EIGRP, EX - EIGRP external, O - OSPF, IA - OSPF inter area
       N1 - OSPF NSSA external type 1, N2 - OSPF NSSA external type 2
       E1 - OSPF external type 1, E2 - OSPF external type 2
       i - IS-IS, L1 - IS-IS level-1, L2 - IS-IS level-2, ia - IS-IS inter area
       * - candidate default, U - per-user static route, o - ODR
       P - periodic downloaded static route

Gateway of last resort is not set

     10.0.0.0/24 is subnetted, 6 subnets
D       10.1.3.0 [90/2172416] via 10.1.6.3, 00:00:57, Serial0/1
D       10.1.2.0 [90/2172416] via 10.1.4.2, 00:00:57, Serial0/0
C       10.1.1.0 is directly connected, Ethernet0/0
C       10.1.6.0 is directly connected, Serial0/1
D       10.1.5.0 [90/2681856] via 10.1.4.2, 00:00:57, Serial0/0
                 [90/2681856] via 10.1.6.3, 00:00:57, Serial0/1
C       10.1.4.0 is directly connected, Serial0/0
! Next, the EIGRP topology table shows one successor for the route to 10.1.3.0,
! and two successors for 10.1.5.0, reconfirming that EIGRP installs successor
! routes (not feasible successor routes) into the IP routing table.
Albuquerque#show ip eigrp topology
IP-EIGRP Topology Table for AS(1)/ID(10.1.6.1)

Codes: P - Passive, A - Active, U - Update, Q - Query, R - Reply,
       r - reply Status, s - sia Status

P 10.1.3.0/24, 1 successors, FD is 2172416
         via 10.1.6.3 (2172416/28160), Serial0/1
P 10.1.2.0/24, 1 successors, FD is 2172416
         via 10.1.4.2 (2172416/28160), Serial0/0
P 10.1.1.0/24, 1 successors, FD is 281600
         via Connected, Ethernet0/0
P 10.1.6.0/24, 1 successors, FD is 2169856
         via Connected, Serial0/1
```

continues

Example 10-3 *Using Wildcard Masks with EIGRP Configuration, and Feasible Successor Examination (Continued)*

```
P 10.1.5.0/24, 2 successors, FD is 2681856
         via 10.1.4.2 (2681856/2169856), Serial0/0
         via 10.1.6.3 (2681856/2169856), Serial0/1
P 10.1.4.0/24, 1 successors, FD is 2169856
         via Connected, Serial0/0
```

The comments in the example explain the main key points, most of which are relatively straightforward. However, a closer look at the **show ip eigrp topology** command can provide a few insights. First, focus on the EIGRP topology table's listing of the number of successor routes. The entry for 10.1.3.0/24 states that there is one successor, so the IP routing table lists one EIGRP-learned route for subnet 10.1.3.0/24. In comparison, the EIGRP topology table entry for subnet 10.1.5.0/24 states that two successors exist, so the IP routing table shows two EIGRP-learned routes for that subnet.

Next, focus on the numbers in brackets for the EIGRP topology table entry for 10.1.3.0/24. The first number is the metric calculated by Albuquerque for each route. The second number is the RD—the metric as calculated on neighboring router 10.1.6.3 (Seville) and as reported to Albuquerque. Because these routers have defaulted all bandwidth and delay settings, the metric values match the sample metric calculations shown in the earlier section "Calculating the Best Routes for the Routing Table."

Creating and Viewing a Feasible Successor Route

With all default settings in this internetwork, none of Albuquerque's routes meet the feasibility condition, in which an alternative route's RD is less than the FD (the metric of the best route). Example 10-4 changes the bandwidth on one of Yosemite's interfaces, lowering Yosemite's FD to reach subnet 10.1.3.0/24. In turn, Yosemite's RD for this same route, as reported to Albuquerque, will now be lower, meeting the feasibility condition, so Albuquerque will now have an FS route.

Example 10-4 *Creating a Feasible Successor Route on Albuquerque*

```
! Below, the bandwidth of Yosemite's link to Seville (Yosemite's S0/1 interface)
! is changed from 1544 to 2000, which lowers Yosemite's metric for
! subnet 10.1.3.0.
Yosemite(config)#interface S0/1
Yosemite(config-if)#bandwidth 2000
! Moving back to Albuquerque
! Below, the EIGRP topology table shows a single successor route for 10.1.3.0,
! but two entries listed - the new entry is a feasible successor route. The new
! entry shows a route to 10.1.3.0 through 10.1.4.2 (which is Yosemite).
Albuquerque#show ip eigrp topology
IP-EIGRP Topology Table for AS(1)/ID(10.1.6.1)
```

Example 10-4 *Creating a Feasible Successor Route on Albuquerque (Continued)*

```
Codes: P - Passive, A - Active, U - Update, Q - Query, R - Reply,
       r - reply Status, s - sia Status

P 10.1.3.0/24, 1 successors, FD is 2172416
        via 10.1.6.3 (2172416/28160), Serial0/1
        via 10.1.4.2 (2684416/1794560), Serial0/0
! the rest of the lines omitted for brevity
! Moving back to Yosemite here
Yosemite#show ip route eigrp
     10.0.0.0/24 is subnetted, 5 subnets
D       10.1.3.0 [90/1794560] via 10.1.5.3, 00:40:14, Serial0/1
D       10.1.1.0 [90/2195456] via 10.1.4.1, 00:42:19, Serial0/0
```

To see the feasible successor route, and why it is a feasible successor, look at the two numbers in parentheses in the second highlighted line from the **show ip eigrp topology** command on Albuquerque. The first of these is Albuquerque's router's calculated metric for the route, and the second number is the neighbor's RD. Of the two possible routes—one through 10.1.6.3 (Seville) and one through 10.1.4.2 (Yosemite)—the route through Seville has the lowest metric (2,172,416), making it the successor route, and making the FD also be 2,172,416. Albuquerque puts this route into the IP routing table. However, note the RD on the second of the two routes (the route through Yosemite), with an RD value of 1,794,560. The feasibility condition is that the route's RD must be smaller than that router's best calculated metric—its FD—for that same destination subnet. So, the route through Yosemite meets this condition, making it a feasible successor route. The following points summarize the key information about the successor and feasible successor routes in this example:

■ The route to 10.1.3.0 through 10.1.6.3 (Seville) is the successor route, because the calculated metric (2,172,416), shown as the first of the two numbers in parentheses, is the best calculated metric.

Key Topic

■ The route to 10.1.3.0 through 10.1.4.2 (Yosemite) is a feasible successor route, because the neighbor's Reported Distance (1,794,560, shown as the second number in parentheses) is lower than Albuquerque's FD.

■ Although both the successor and feasible successor routes are in the EIGRP topology table, only the successor route is added to the IP routing table.

NOTE The **show ip eigrp topology** command lists only successor and feasible successor routes. To see other routes, use the **show ip eigrp topology all-links** command.

Convergence Using the Feasible Successor Route

One of the advantages of EIGRP is that it converges very quickly. Example 10-5 shows one such example, using **debug** messages to show the process. Some of the **debug** messages may not make a lot of sense, but the example does highlight a few interesting and understandable **debug** messages.

For this example, the link between Albuquerque and Seville is shut down, but this is not shown in the example. The **debug** messages on Albuquerque show commentary about EIGRP's logic in changing from the original route for 10.1.3.0/24 to the new route through Yosemite. Pay particular attention to the time stamps, which show that the convergence process takes less than 1 second.

Example 10-5 *Debug Messages During Convergence to the Feasible Successor Route for Subnet 10.1.3.0/24*

```
!!!!!!!!!!!!!!!!!!!!!!!!!!!!!!!!!!!!!!!!!!!!!!!!!!!!!!!!!!!!!!!!!!!!!!!!!!!!!!!!!!!
! Below, debug eigrp fsm is enabled, and then Seville's link to Albuquerque
! (Seville's S0/0 interface) will be disabled, but not shown in the example text.
! SOME DEBUG MESSAGES are omitted to improve readability.
Albuquerque#debug eigrp fsm
EIGRP FSM Events/Actions debugging is on
Albuquerque#
*Mar  1 02:35:31.836: %LINK-3-UPDOWN: Interface Serial0/1, changed state to down
*Mar  1 02:35:31.848: DUAL: rcvupdate: 10.1.6.0/24 via Connected metric 42949672
95/4294967295
*Mar  1 02:35:31.848: DUAL: Find FS for dest 10.1.6.0/24. FD is 2169856, RD is 2
169856
*Mar  1 02:35:31.848: DUAL: 0.0.0.0 metric 4294967295/4294967295 not found D
min is 4294967295
*Mar  1 02:35:31.848: DUAL: Peer total/stub 2/0 template/full-stub 2/0
*Mar  1 02:35:31.848: DUAL: Dest 10.1.6.0/24 entering active state.
*Mar  1 02:35:31.852: DUAL: Set reply-status table. Count is 2.
*Mar  1 02:35:31.852: DUAL: Not doing split horizon
!
! Next, Albuquerque realizes that neighbor 10.1.6.3 (Seville) is down, so
! Albuquerque can react.
!
*Mar  1 02:35:31.852: %DUAL-5-NBRCHANGE: IP-EIGRP(0) 1: Neighbor 10.1.6.3
   (Serial0/1) is down: interface down
!
! The next two highlighted messages imply that the old route to 10.1.3.0 is
! removed, and the new successor route (previously the feasible successor route)
! is added to the "RT" (routing table).
!
*Mar  1 02:35:31.852: DUAL: Destination 10.1.3.0/24
*Mar  1 02:35:31.852: DUAL: Find FS for dest 10.1.3.0/24. FD is 2172416,
  RD is 2172416
```

Example 10-5 *Debug Messages During Convergence to the Feasible Successor Route for Subnet 10.1.3.0/24 (Continued)*

```
*Mar  1 02:35:31.856: DUAL: 10.1.6.3 metric 4294967295/4294967295
*Mar  1 02:35:31.856: DUAL: 10.1.4.2 metric 2684416/1794560 found Dmin is 2684416
!
! The next two highlighted messages state that the old route is removed, and the
! new route through Yosemite is added to the "RT" (routing table).
!
*Mar  1 02:35:31.856: DUAL: Removing dest 10.1.3.0/24, nexthop 10.1.6.3
*Mar  1 02:35:31.856: DUAL: RT installed 10.1.3.0/24 via 10.1.4.2
*Mar  1 02:35:31.856: DUAL: Send update about 10.1.3.0/24.  Reason: metric chg
*Mar  1 02:35:31.860: DUAL: Send update about 10.1.3.0/24.  Reason: new if
```

EIGRP Authentication

EIGRP supports one type of authentication: MD5. Configuring MD5 authentication requires several steps:

Step 1 Create an (authentication) key chain:

> **a.** Create the chain and give it a name with the **key chain** *name* global command (this also puts the user into key chain config mode).
>
> **b.** Create one or more key numbers using the **key** *number* command in key chain configuration mode.
>
> **c.** Define the authentication key's value using the **key-string** *value* command in key configuration mode.
>
> **d.** (Optional) Define the lifetime (time period) for both sending and accepting this particular key.

Step 2 Enable EIGRP MD5 authentication on an interface, for a particular EIGRP ASN, using the **ip authentication mode eigrp** *asn* **md5** interface subcommand.

Step 3 Refer to the correct key chain to be used on an interface using the **ip authentication key-chain eigrp** *asn name-of-chain* interface subcommand.

The configuration in Step 1 is fairly detailed, but Steps 2 and 3 are relatively simple. Essentially, IOS configures the key values separately, then requires an interface subcommand to refer to the key values. To support the ability to have multiple keys, and even multiple sets of keys, the configuration includes the concept of a key chain and multiple keys on each key chain.

Key
Topic

The IOS key chain concept resembles key chains and keys used in everyday life. Most people have at least one key chain, with the keys they typically use every day. If you have a lot of keys for work and home, you might have two key chains to make it a little easier to find the right key. You might even have a key chain with seldom-used keys that you keep on a shelf somewhere. Similarly, IOS allows lets you configure multiple key chains so that different key chains can be used on different interfaces. Each key chain can include multiple keys. Having multiple keys in one key chain allows neighbors to still be up and working while the keys are being changed. (As with all passwords and authentication keys, changing the keys occasionally enhances security.) To configure these main details, follow Steps 1A, 1B, and 1C to create the key chain, create one or more keys, and assign the text key (password).

The last and optional item that can be configured for EIGRP authentication is the useful lifetime of each key. If this isn't configured, the key is valid forever. However, if it is configured, the router uses the key only during the listed times. This feature allows the key chain to include several keys, each with different successive lifetimes. For example, 12 keys could be defined, one for each month of the year. The routers then automatically use the lowest-numbered key whose time range is valid, changing keys automatically every month in this example. This feature allows an engineer to configure the keys once and have the routers use new keys occasionally, improving security.

To support the useful lifetime concept, a router must know the time and date. Routers can set the time and date with the **clock set** EXEC command. Routers can also use Network Time Protocol (NTP), a protocol that allows routers to synchronize their time-of-day clocks.

The best way to appreciate the configuration is to see an example. Example 10-6 shows a sample configuration that uses two key chains. Key chain "carkeys" has two keys, each with different lifetimes, so that the router will use new keys automatically over time. It also shows the two key chains being referenced on two different interfaces.

Example 10-6 *EIGRP Authentication*

```
! Chain "carkeys" will be used on R1's Fa0/0 interface. R1 will use key "fred"
! for about a month and then start using "wilma."
!
key chain carkeys
  key 1
  key-string fred
  accept-lifetime 08:00:00 Jan 11 2005 08:00:00 Feb 11 2005
  send-lifetime 08:00:00 Jan 11 2005 08:00:00 Feb 11 2005
 key 2
  key-string wilma
  accept-lifetime 08:00:00 Feb 10 2005 08:00:00 Mar 11 2005
  send-lifetime 08:00:00 Feb 10 2005 08:00:00 Mar 11 2005
```

Example 10-6 *EIGRP Authentication (Continued)*

```
! Next, key chain "anothersetofkeys" defines the key to be used on
! interface Fa0/1.
key chain anothersetofkeys
 key 1
 key-string barney
 !
! Next, R1's interface subcommands are shown. First, the key chain is referenced
! using the ip authentication key-chain command, and the ip authentication mode eigrp
! command causes the router to use an MD5 digest of the key string.
interface FastEthernet0/0
 ip address 172.31.11.1 255.255.255.0
 ip authentication mode eigrp 1 md5
 ip authentication key-chain eigrp 1 carkeys
 !
! Below, R1 enables EIGRP authentication on interface Fa0/1,
! using the other key chain.
interface FastEthernet0/1
 ip address 172.31.12.1 255.255.255.0
 ip authentication mode eigrp 1 md5
 ip authentication key-chain eigrp 1 anothersetofkeys
```

For authentication to work, neighboring routers must both have EIGRP MD5 authentication enabled, and the key strings they currently use must match. Note that the key chain name does not need to match. The most common problems relate to when the useful lifetime settings do not match, or one of the router's clocks has the wrong time. For real-life implementations, NTP should be enabled and used before restricting keys to a particular time frame.

To verify that the authentication worked, use the **show ip eigrp neighbors** command. If the authentication fails, the neighbor relationship will not form. Also, if you see routes learned from a neighbor on that interface, it also proves that authentication worked. You can see more details about the authentication process using the **debug eigrp packets** command, particularly if the authentication fails.

EIGRP Maximum Paths and Variance

Like OSPF, EIGRP supports the ability to put multiple equal-metric routes in the routing table. Like OSPF, EIGRP defaults to support four such routes for each subnet, and it can be configured to support up to 16 using the **maximum-paths** *number* EIGRP subcommand. However, EIGRP's metric calculation often prevents competing routes from having the exact same metric. The formula may result in similar metrics, but given that the metric values can easily be in the millions, calculating the exact same metric is statistically unlikely.

IOS includes the concept of EIGRP variance to overcome this problem. Variance allows routes whose metrics are relatively close in value to be considered equal, allowing multiple unequal-metric routes to the same subnet to be added to the routing table.

The **variance** *multiplier* EIGRP router subcommand defines an integer between 1 and 128. The router then multiplies the variance times a route's FD—the best metric with which to reach that subnet. Any FS routes whose metric is less than the product of the variance times the FD are considered to be equal routes and may be placed in the routing table, depending on the setting of the **maximum-paths** command.

An example of variance can make this concept clear. To keep the numbers more obvious, Table 10-3 lists an example with small metric values. The table lists the metric for three routes to the same subnet, as calculated on router R4. The table also lists the neighboring routers' RD, and the decision to add routes to the routing table based on various variance settings.

Table 10-3   *Example of Routes Chosen as Equal Because of Variance*

Next Hop	Metric	RD	Added to RT at Variance 1?	Added to RT at Variance 2?	Added to RT at Variance 3?
R1	50	30	Yes	Yes	Yes
R2	90	40	No	Yes	Yes
R3	120	60	No	No	No

Before considering the variance, note that in this case, the route through R1 is the successor route because it has the lowest metric. This also means that the metric for the route through R1, 50, is the FD. The route through R2 is an FS route because its RD of 40 is less than the FD of 50. The route through R3 is not an FS route, because R3's RD of 60 is more than the FD of 50.

At a default variance setting of 1, the metrics must be exactly equal to be considered equal, so only the successor route is added to the routing table. With variance 2, the FD (50) is multiplied by the variance (2) for a product of 100. The route through R2, with FD 90, is less than 100, so R4 adds the route through R2 to the routing table as well. The router can then load-balance traffic across these two routes.

In the third case, with variance 3, the product of the FD (50) times 3 results in a product of 150, and all three routes' calculated metrics are less than 150. However, the route through R3 is not an FS route, so it cannot be added to the routing table for fear of causing a routing loop.

The following list summarizes the key points about variance:

■ The variance is multiplied by the current FD (the metric of the best route to reach the subnet).

Key
Topic

■ Any FS routes whose calculated metric is less than or equal to the product of variance times the FD are added to the IP routing table, assuming that the **maximum-paths** setting allows more routes.

■ Routes that are neither successor nor feasible successor can never be added to the IP routing table, regardless of the variance setting.

As soon as the routes have been added to the routing table, the router supports a variety of options for how to load-balance traffic across the routes. The router can balance the traffic proportionally with the metrics, meaning that lower metric routes send more packets. The router can send all traffic over the lowest-metric route, with the other routes just being in the routing table for faster convergence in case the best route fails. However, the details of the load-balancing process require a much deeper discussion of the internals of the forwarding process in IOS, and this topic is outside the scope of this book.

Tuning the EIGRP Metric Calculation

By default, EIGRP calculates an integer metric based on the composite metric of bandwidth and delay. Both settings can be changed on any interface using the **bandwidth** *value* and the **delay** *value* interface subcommands.

Cisco recommends setting each interface's bandwidth to an accurate value, rather than setting the bandwidth to change EIGRP's metric calculation. Although LAN interfaces default to accurate bandwidth settings, router serial links should be configured with the **bandwidth** *speed* command, with a speed value in kbps, matching the interface's actual speed.

Because fewer features rely on the interface delay setting, Cisco recommends that if you want to tune EIGRP metric, change the interface delay settings. To change an interface's delay setting, use the **delay** *value* command, where the value is the delay setting with an unusual unit: tens-of-microseconds. Interestingly, the EIGRP metric formula also uses the unit of tens-of-microseconds; however, **show** commands list the delay with a unit of microseconds. Example 10-7 shows an example, with the following details:

1. The router's Fa0/0 has a default delay setting of 100 microseconds (usec).

2. The **delay 123** command is configured on the interface, meaning 123 tens-of-microseconds.

3.   The **show interfaces fa0/0** command now lists a delay of 1230 microseconds.

Example 10-7   *Configuring Interface Delay*

```
Yosemite#show interfaces fa0/0
FastEthernet0/0 is up, line protocol is up
  Hardware is Gt96k FE, address is 0013.197b.5026 (bia 0013.197b.5026)
  Internet address is 10.1.2.252/24
  MTU 1500 bytes, BW 100000 Kbit, DLY 100 usec,
! lines omitted for brevity

Yosemite#configure terminal
Enter configuration commands, one per line.  End with CNTL/Z.
Yosemite(config)#interface fa0/0
Yosemite(config-if)#delay 123
Yosemite(config-if)#^Z

Yosemite#show interfaces fa0/0
FastEthernet0/0 is up, line protocol is up
  Hardware is Gt96k FE, address is 0013.197b.5026 (bia 0013.197b.5026)
  Internet address is 10.1.2.252/24
  MTU 1500 bytes, BW 100000 Kbit, DLY 1230 usec,
! lines omitted for brevity
```

Exam Preparation Tasks

Review All the Key Topics

Review the most important topics from this chapter, noted with the key topics icon. Table 10-4 lists these key topics and where each is discussed.

Key Topic

Table 10-4 *Key Topics for Chapter 10*

Key Topic Element	Description	Page Number
List	Reasons why EIGRP routers are prevented from becoming neighbors	381
Figure 10-1	Depicts the normal progression through neighbor discovery, full routing updates, ongoing Hellos, and partial updates	382
List	Definitions of Feasible Distance and Reported Distance	384
Figure 10-4	Example of how routers determine which routes are feasible successors	387
Table 10-2	Comparisons of EIGRP and OSPF features	388
List	EIGRP configuration checklist	389
List	Key points about how to determine a feasible successor route from **show** command output	395
List	EIGRP MD5 authentication configuration checklist	397
List	Key points about EIGRP variance	401

Complete the Tables and Lists from Memory

Print a copy of Appendix J, "Memory Tables" (found on the CD), or at least the section for this chapter, and complete the tables and lists from memory. Appendix K, "Memory Tables Answer Key," also on the CD, includes completed tables and lists for you to check your work.

Definitions of Key Terms

Define the following key terms from this chapter, and check your answers in the glossary:

feasibility condition, feasible distance, feasible successor, full update, partial update, reported distance, successor

Command Reference to Check Your Memory

Although you should not necessarily memorize the information in the tables in this section, this section does include a reference for the configuration and EXEC commands covered in this chapter. Practically speaking, you should memorize the commands as a side effect of reading the chapter and doing all the activities in this exam preparation section. To see how well you have memorized the commands as a side effect of your other studies, cover the left side of the table, read the descriptions on the right side, and see if you remember the command.

Table 10-5   *Chapter 10 Configuration Command Reference*

Command	Description
router eigrp *autonomous-system*	Global command to move the user into EIGRP configuration mode for the listed ASN.
network *network-number* [*wildcard-mask*]	EIGRP router subcommand that matches either all interfaces in a classful network, or a subset of interfaces based on the ACL-style wildcard mask, enabling EIGRP on those interfaces.
maximum-paths *number-paths*	Router subcommand that defines the maximum number of equal-cost routes that can be added to the routing table.
variance *multiplier*	Router subcommand that defines an EIGRP multiplier used to determine if a feasible successor route's metric is close enough to the successor's metric to be considered equal.
bandwidth *bandwidth*	Interface subcommand directly sets the interface bandwidth (kbps).
delay *delay-value*	Interface subcommand to set the interface delay value, with a unit of tens-of-microseconds.
ip hello-interval eigrp *as-number timer-value*	Interface subcommand that sets the EIGRP Hello interval for that EIGRP process.
ip hold-time eigrp *as-number timer-value*	Interface subcommand that sets the EIGRP hold time for the interface.
maximum-paths *number-of-paths*	Router subcommand that defines the maximum number of equal-cost routes that can be added to the routing table.

Table 10-5 *Chapter 10 Configuration Command Reference (Continued)*

Command	Description
ip authentication key-chain eigrp *asn chain-name*	Interface subcommand that references the key chain used for MD5 authentication with EIGRP.
ip authentication mode eigrp *asn* **md5**	Interface subcommand that enables EIGRP MD5 authentication for all neighbors reached on the interface.
key chain *name*	Global command to create and name an authentication key chain.
key *integer-number*	Key chain mode command to create a new key number.
key-string *text*	Key chain mode command to create the authentication key's value.
accept-lifetime *start-time* {**infinite** | *end-time* | **duration** *seconds*}	Key chain mode command to set the time frame during which a router will accept the use of a particular key.
send-lifetime *start-time* {**infinite** | *end-time* | **duration** *seconds*}	Key chain mode command to set the time frame during which a router will send EIGRP messages using a particular key.

Table 10-6 *Chapter 10 EXEC Command Reference*

Command	Description
show ip route eigrp	Lists routes in the routing table learned by EIGRP.
show ip route *ip-address* [*mask*]	Shows the entire routing table, or a subset if parameters are entered.
show ip protocols	Shows routing protocol parameters and current timer values.
show ip eigrp neighbors	Lists EIGRP neighbors and status.
show ip eigrp topology	Lists the contents of the EIGRP topology table, including successors and feasible successors.
show ip eigrp traffic	Lists statistics on the number of EIGRP messages sent and received by a router.
debug eigrp packets	Displays the contents of EIGRP packets.
debug eigrp fsm	Displays changes to the EIGRP successor and feasible successor routes.
debug ip eigrp	Displays similar output to the **debug eigrp packets** command, but specifically for IP.

This chapter covers the following subjects:

Perspectives on Troubleshooting Routing Protocol Problems: This short introductory section explains the troubleshooting process this book suggests for routing protocol problems.

Interfaces Enabled with a Routing Protocol: This section shows how to determine the interfaces on which a router attempts to form neighbor relationships and whose connected subnets to advertise.

Neighbor Relationships: This section examines why routers may fail to become neighbors with routers they should become neighbors with.

CHAPTER 11

Troubleshooting Routing Protocols

Chapters 3 and 7, the other two chapters of this book that are dedicated to troubleshooting, focus on the process of forwarding data. In particular, Chapter 7, "Troubleshooting IP Routing," mostly ignores how routes are added to the routing table, focusing entirely on the data plane process of IP packet forwarding and how to troubleshoot that process. Chapter 7 assumes that the control plane processes related to filling the routing table will be covered elsewhere—mainly in Part III of this book.

This chapter wraps up the coverage of the IPv4 control plane—the process of filling routers' routing tables with good routes—by examining how to troubleshoot problems with OSPF and EIGRP. The troubleshooting process itself is relatively straightforward, at least to the depth required for the CCNA exams. However, as usual, you need to think about many different details while troubleshooting, so the process can help ensure that you verify each component before moving on to the next function.

This chapter concludes Part III of this book. If you are preparing specifically for the CCNA exam by using the reading plan mentioned in the Introduction, note that after this chapter, you should go back to *CCENT/CCNA ICND1 Official Exam Certification Guide*, Part IV.

"Do I Know This Already?" Quiz

The troubleshooting chapters of this book pull in concepts from many other chapters, including some chapters in *CCENT/CCNA ICND1 Official Exam Certification Guide*. They also show you how to approach some of the more challenging questions on the CCNA exams. Therefore, it is useful to read these chapters regardless of your current knowledge level. For these reasons, the troubleshooting chapters do not include a "Do I Know This Already?" quiz. However, if you feel particularly confident about troubleshooting OSPF and EIGRP, feel free to move to the "Exam Preparation Tasks" section near the end of this chapter to bypass the majority of the chapter.

Foundation Topics

The best first step when troubleshooting a routing protocol is to examine the configuration on the various routers. Comparing the routing protocol configuration, particularly the **network** subcommands, to the interface IP addresses can quickly confirm whether the routing protocol has been enabled on all the intended interfaces. If it is enabled on all the correct interfaces on all the routers, further examination of interface configuration and authentication configuration can verify whether some configuration settings might prevent two routers on the same subnet from becoming neighbors. A failure to pass all the requirements to become neighbors will prevent two routers from exchanging routing information.

Chapter 9, "OSPF," and Chapter 10, "EIGRP," cover routing protocol configuration in depth, so this chapter makes no attempt to explain how to troubleshoot a problem by looking for configuration mistakes. However, the configuration may not always be available for the exams or in real life. This chapter focuses on how to troubleshoot routing protocol problems using only **show** and **debug** commands. First, this chapter discusses some options for troubleshooting routing protocol problems, including a suggested process that has two major steps. The other two major sections of this chapter examine how to perform each of the major troubleshooting steps, for both EIGRP and OSPF.

Perspectives on Troubleshooting Routing Protocol Problems

Because a routing protocol's job is to fill a router's routing table with the currently best routes, it makes sense that troubleshooting potential problems with routing protocols could begin with the IP routing table. Given basic information about an internetwork, including the routers, their IP addresses and masks, and the routing protocol, you could calculate the subnet numbers that should be in the router's routing table and list the likely next-hop router(s) for each route. For example, Figure 11-1 shows an internetwork with six subnets. Router R1's routing table should list all six subnets, with three connected routes, two routes learned from R2 (172.16.4.0/24 and 172.16.5.0/24), and one route learned from R3 (172.16.6.0/24).

So, one possible troubleshooting process would be to analyze the internetwork, look at the routing table, and look for missing routes. If one or more expected routes are missing, the next step would be to determine if that router has learned any routes from the expected next-hop (neighbor) router. The next steps to isolate the problem differ greatly if a router is having problems forming a neighbor relationship with another router, versus having a working neighbor relationship but not being able to learn all routes.

Figure 11-1 *Internetwork with Six Subnets*

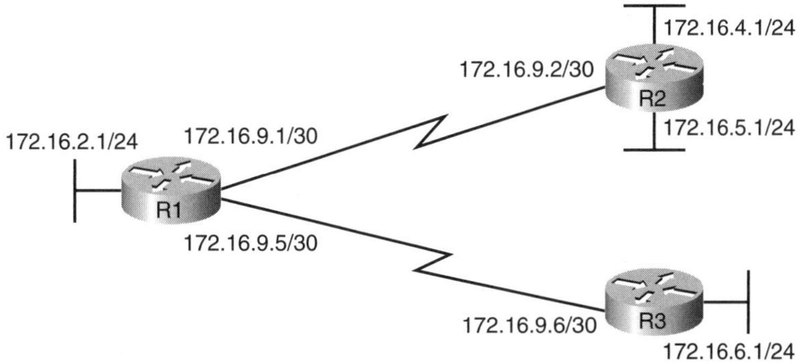

For example, imagine that R1 in Figure 11-1 has learned a route for subnet 172.16.4.0/24 in Figure 11-1 but not for subnet 172.16.5.0/24. In this case, it is clear that R1 has a working neighbor relationship with R2. In these cases, the root cause of this problem may still be related to the routing protocol, or it might be unrelated to the routing protocol. For example, the problem may be that R2's lower LAN interface is down. However, if R1 did not have a route for either 172.16.4.0/24 or 172.16.5.0/24, R1's neighbor relationship with R2 could be the problem.

Troubleshooting routing protocol problems in real internetworks can be very complex—much more complex than even the more difficult CCNA exam questions. Defining a generic troubleshooting process with which to attack both simple and complex routing protocol problems would require a lot of space, and be counter-productive for preparing for the CCNA exams. This chapter offers a straightforward process for attacking routing protocol problems—specifically, problems similar to the depth and complexity of the CCNA exams.

If an exam question appears to be related to a problem with a routing protocol, you can quickly identify some common configuration errors with the following process—even without the configuration or the ability to use the **show running-config** command. The process has three main branches:

Step 1 Examine the internetwork design to determine on which interfaces the routing protocol should be enabled and which routers are expected to become neighbors.

Step 2 Verify whether the routing protocol is enabled on each interface (as per Step 1). If it isn't, determine the root cause and fix the problem.

Step 3   Verify that each router has formed all expected neighbor relationships. If it hasn't, find the root cause and fix the problem.

At this point, having completed chapters 9 and 10, Step 1 should not require any further explanation. The two remaining major sections of this chapter examine Steps 2 and 3. By completing these steps and fixing any problems found throughout this process, you should have fixed the CCNA-level routing protocol problems.

Interfaces Enabled with a Routing Protocol

This section examines the second major troubleshooting step outlined in the previous section of the chapter: how to verify the interfaces on which the routing protocol has been enabled. Both EIGRP and OSPF configuration enables the routing protocol on an interface by using the **network** router subcommand. For any interfaces matched by the **network** commands, the routing protocol tries the following two actions:

- Attempt to find potential neighbors on the subnet connected to the interface

- Advertise the subnet connected to that interface

At the same time, the **passive-interface** router subcommand can be configured so that the router does not attempt to find neighbors on the interface (the first action just listed) but still advertises the connected subnet (the second action).

Three **show** commands are all that is needed to know exactly which interfaces have been enabled with EIGRP and OSPF and which interfaces are passive. In particular, the **show ip eigrp interfaces** command lists all EIGRP-enabled interfaces that are not passive interfaces. The **show ip protocols** command essentially lists the contents of the configured **network** commands for each routing protocol, as well as a separate list of the passive interfaces. Comparing these two commands identifies all EIGRP-enabled interfaces and those that are passive. For OSPF, the command works slightly differently, with the **show ip ospf interface brief** command listing all OSPF-enabled interfaces (including passive interfaces). Table 11-1 summarizes these commands for easier reference.

Table 11-1   *Key Commands to Find Routing Protocol Enabled Interfaces*

Command	Key Information
show ip eigrp interfaces	Lists the interfaces on which the routing protocol is enabled (based on the **network** commands), except passive interfaces.
show ip ospf interface brief	Lists the interfaces on which the OSPF is enabled (based on the **network** commands), including passive interfaces.
show ip protocols	Lists the contents of the **network** configuration commands for each routing process, and lists enabled but passive interfaces.

NOTE   All the commands in Table 11-1 list the interfaces regardless of interface status, in effect telling you the results of the **network** and **passive-interface** configuration commands.

So, for the major troubleshooting step covered in this section, the task is to use the commands in Table 11-1 and analyze the output. First an EIGRP example will be shown, followed by an OSPF example.

EIGRP Interface Troubleshooting Example

This section shows a few examples of the commands in the context of Figure 11-2, which is used in all the examples in this chapter.

Figure 11-2   *Sample Internetwork for EIGRP/OSPF Troubleshooting Examples*

This example includes four routers, with the following scenario in this case:

■ R1 and R2 are configured correctly on both LAN interfaces.

■ R3 is mistakenly not enabled with EIGRP on its Fa0/1 interface.

■ R4 meant to use a **passive-interface fa0/1** command, because no other routers are off R4's Fa0/1 LAN, but instead R4 has configured a **passive-interface fa0/0** command.

Example 11-1 begins by showing the pertinent commands, with an example on either R1 or on R2. It also shows the configuration on R1 for the sake of comparison.

Example 11-1   *EIGRP Problems with Interfaces*

```
R1#show running-config
! only pertinent lines shown
router eigrp 99
 network 10.0.0.0
!
R1>show ip eigrp interfaces
```

continues

Example 11-1 *EIGRP Problems with Interfaces (Continued)*

```
IP-EIGRP interfaces for process 99

                    Xmit Queue   Mean   Pacing Time   Multicast    Pending
Interface    Peers  Un/Reliable  SRTT   Un/Reliable   Flow Timer   Routes
Fa0/0          2      0/0         620      0/10           50          0
Fa0/1          0      0/0           0      0/10            0          0
R1>show ip protocols
Routing Protocol is "eigrp 99"
  Outgoing update filter list for all interfaces is not set
  Incoming update filter list for all interfaces is not set
  Default networks flagged in outgoing updates
  Default networks accepted from incoming updates
  EIGRP metric weight K1=1, K2=0, K3=1, K4=0, K5=0
  EIGRP maximum hopcount 100
  EIGRP maximum metric variance 1
  Redistributing: eigrp 99
  EIGRP NSF-aware route hold timer is 240s
  Automatic network summarization is in effect
  Maximum path: 4
  Routing for Networks:
    10.0.0.0
  Routing Information Sources:
    Gateway         Distance      Last Update
    10.1.1.2              90      00:13:11
    10.1.1.3              90      00:13:09
  Distance: internal 90 external 170
! The next commands are on router R2
!
R2>show ip eigrp interfaces
IP-EIGRP interfaces for process 99

                    Xmit Queue   Mean   Pacing Time   Multicast    Pending
Interface    Peers  Un/Reliable  SRTT   Un/Reliable   Flow Timer   Routes
Fa0/0          2      0/0         736      0/1          3684          0
Fa0/1          0      0/0           0      0/1             0          0
R2>show ip protocols
Routing Protocol is "eigrp 99"
  Outgoing update filter list for all interfaces is not set
  Incoming update filter list for all interfaces is not set
  Default networks flagged in outgoing updates
  Default networks accepted from incoming updates
  EIGRP metric weight K1=1, K2=0, K3=1, K4=0, K5=0
  EIGRP maximum hopcount 100
  EIGRP maximum metric variance 1
  Redistributing: eigrp 99
  EIGRP NSF-aware route hold timer is 240s
  Automatic network summarization is in effect
```

Example 11-1 *EIGRP Problems with Interfaces (Continued)*

```
 Maximum path: 4
 Routing for Networks:
   10.0.0.0
 Routing Information Sources:
   Gateway         Distance      Last Update
   10.1.1.3             90       00:13:25
   10.1.1.1             90       00:13:25
 Distance: internal 90 external 170


R2>show ip route eigrp
     10.0.0.0/24 is subnetted, 3 subnets
D       10.1.11.0 [90/30720] via 10.1.1.1, 00:13:38, FastEthernet0/0
```

The **show ip eigrp interfaces** command output on both R1 and R2 shows how both R1 and R2 have configured EIGRP using process ID 99, and that EIGRP has been enabled on both Fa0/0 and Fa0/1 on R1 and R2. This command lists only interfaces on which EIGRP has been enabled, excluding passive interfaces.

The highlighted parts of the **show ip protocols** command output on each router are particularly interesting. These sections show the parameters of the configured **network** commands. For each **network** command, the **show ip protocols** command lists a separate line under the header "Routing for Networks," with each line listing the contents of the various **network** router subcommands. For example, R1 uses the **network 10.0.0.0** configuration command (shown at the beginning of the example), which matches the "10.0.0.0" line in the output of the **show ip protocols** command.

The end of the example gives brief insight into the current problem on R3 from R2's perspective. The end of the **show ip protocols** command on R2 lists two routing information sources: 10.1.1.1 (R1) and 10.1.1.3 (R3). However, R2 has learned only one EIGRP route (10.1.11.0/24), as shown in the **show ip route eigrp** command output. When working properly, R2 should learn three EIGRP routes—one for each of the outer LAN subnets shown in Figure 11-2.

Next, Example 11-2 shows the problems on R3 and R4 that prevent R1 and R2 from learning about subnets 10.1.33.0/24 and 10.1.44.0/24. The example shows the pertinent configuration on each router for perspective, as well as **show** commands that point out the problems.

Example 11-2 *EIGRP Problems on R3 and R4*

```
R3#show running-config
! lines omitted for brevity
router eigrp 99
```

continues

Example 11-2   *EIGRP Problems on R3 and R4 (Continued)*

```
 network 10.1.1.3 0.0.0.0
 network 10.1.13.3 0.0.0.0
 auto-summary
R3#show ip eigrp interfaces
IP-EIGRP interfaces for process 99

                      Xmit Queue   Mean   Pacing Time   Multicast    Pending
Interface      Peers  Un/Reliable  SRTT   Un/Reliable   Flow Timer   Routes
Fa0/0          2          0/0      1          0/10          50          0
R3#show ip protocols
Routing Protocol is "eigrp 99"
  Outgoing update filter list for all interfaces is not set
  Incoming update filter list for all interfaces is not set
  Default networks flagged in outgoing updates
  Default networks accepted from incoming updates
  EIGRP metric weight K1=1, K2=0, K3=1, K4=0, K5=0
  EIGRP maximum hopcount 100
  EIGRP maximum metric variance 1
  Redistributing: eigrp 99
  EIGRP NSF-aware route hold timer is 240s
  Automatic network summarization is in effect
  Maximum path: 4
  Routing for Networks:
     10.1.1.3/32
     10.1.13.3/32
  Routing Information Sources:
    Gateway         Distance       Last Update
    10.1.1.2             90        00:28:16
    10.1.1.1             90        00:28:14
  Distance: internal 90 external 170
! R4 output starts here

R4#show running-config
! lines omitted for brevity
router eigrp 99
 passive-interface FastEthernet0/0
 network 10.0.0.0
 auto-summary

R4#show ip eigrp interfaces
IP-EIGRP interfaces for process 99

                      Xmit Queue   Mean   Pacing Time   Multicast    Pending
Interface      Peers  Un/Reliable  SRTT   Un/Reliable   Flow Timer   Routes
Fa0/1          0          0/0      0          0/1           0           0
R4#show ip protocols
Routing Protocol is "eigrp 99"
```

Example 11-2 *EIGRP Problems on R3 and R4 (Continued)*

```
Outgoing update filter list for all interfaces is not set
Incoming update filter list for all interfaces is not set
Default networks flagged in outgoing updates
Default networks accepted from incoming updates
EIGRP metric weight K1=1, K2=0, K3=1, K4=0, K5=0
EIGRP maximum hopcount 100
EIGRP maximum metric variance 1
Redistributing: eigrp 99
EIGRP NSF-aware route hold timer is 240s
Automatic network summarization is in effect
Maximum path: 4
Routing for Networks:
   10.0.0.0
Passive Interface(s):
  FastEthernet0/0
Routing Information Sources:
  Gateway         Distance      Last Update
Distance: internal 90 external 170
```

The root cause of R3's problem is that R3 has a **network 10.1.13.3 0.0.0.0** configuration command, which does not match R3's 10.1.33.3 Fa0/1 IP address. If the configuration was not available in the exam question, the **show ip protocols** command could be used to essentially see the same configuration details. In this case, the **show ip protocols** command on R3 lists the text "10.1.13.3/32" as a reference to the contents of the incorrect **network** command's parameters. As a result, R3 does not try to find neighbors on its Fa0/1 interface, which is not a big deal in this case, but R3 also does not advertise subnet 10.1.33.0/24, the connected subnet off its Fa0/1 interface. Also note that R3's **show ip eigrp interfaces** command omits interface Fa0/1, which does not by itself determine the root cause, but it can help you isolate the problem.

On R4, the engineer could have correctly used a **passive-interface fastethernet0/1** router subcommand, because no other routers should exist off R4's Fa0/1 interface. However, the engineer mistakenly referred to R4's Fa0/0 interface instead of Fa0/1. R4's **show ip eigrp interfaces** command purposefully omits the (Fa0/0) passive interface, and the highlighted part of R4's **show ip protocols** command output lists Fa0/0 as a passive interface. Because R4's Fa0/0 is passive, R4 does not even attempt to become neighbors with other routers on the same LAN.

OSPF Interface Troubleshooting Example

OSPF has the same basic requirements as EIGRP for interfaces, with a few exceptions. First, EIGRP routers need to use the same ASN or process ID as their neighboring routers, as configured in the **router** global configuration command. OSPF routers can use any process ID, with no need to match their neighbors. Second, OSPF requires that the interfaces connected to the same subnet be assigned to the same OSPF area, whereas EIGRP has no concept of areas.

Example 11-3 shows a mostly working OSPF internetwork, again based on Figure 11-2. The following problems exist:

> R2 has been configured to put both interfaces in area 1. R1, R3, and R4 have been configured to put their common LAN interfaces (Fa0/0 in each case) in area 0, breaking OSPF design rules.

Example 11-3 shows how to isolate the root cause of the problem. It also shows the normal working output, with the **show ip ospf interface brief** and **show ip protocols** commands.

Example 11-3   *OSPF Problems on R2*

```
R1>show ip ospf interface brief
Interface    PID   Area           IP Address/Mask     Cost  State Nbrs F/C
Fa0/1        11    0              10.1.11.1/24        1     DR    0/0
Fa0/0        11    0              10.1.1.1/24         1     DROTH 2/2
R1>show ip protocols
Routing Protocol is "ospf 11"
  Outgoing update filter list for all interfaces is not set
  Incoming update filter list for all interfaces is not set
  Router ID 1.1.1.1
  Number of areas in this router is 1. 1 normal 0 stub 0 nssa
  Maximum path: 4
  Routing for Networks:
    10.0.0.0 0.255.255.255 area 0
  Routing Information Sources:
    Gateway         Distance      Last Update
    3.3.3.3              110      00:01:12
    4.4.4.4              110      00:01:12
    1.1.1.1              110      00:01:12
  Distance: (default is 110)
R1>show ip route ospf
     10.0.0.0/24 is subnetted, 5 subnets
O       10.1.44.0 [110/2] via 10.1.1.4, 00:01:19, FastEthernet0/0
O       10.1.33.0 [110/2] via 10.1.1.3, 00:01:19, FastEthernet0/0
! Now moving to router R2
R2>show ip ospf interface brief
Interface    PID   Area           IP Address/Mask     Cost  State Nbrs F/C
Fa0/1        22    1              10.1.22.2/24        1     DR    0/0
Fa0/0        22    1              10.1.1.2/24         1     DR    0/0
R2>show ip protocols
Routing Protocol is "ospf 22"
```

Example 11-3   *OSPF Problems on R2 (Continued)*

```
 Outgoing update filter list for all interfaces is not set
 Incoming update filter list for all interfaces is not set
 --More--  _____          _____     Router ID 2.2.2.2
 Number of areas in this router is 1. 1 normal 0 stub 0 nssa
 Maximum path: 4
 Routing for Networks:
    10.0.0.0 0.255.255.255 area 1
 Reference bandwidth unit is 100 mbps
 Routing Information Sources:
    Gateway          Distance      Last Update
 Distance: (default is 110)
R2>
!!!!!!!!!!!!!!!!!!!!!!!!!!!!!!!!!!!!!!!!!!!!!!!!!!!!!!!!!!!!!!!!!!!!!!!!!!!!!!!!!
May 28 18:30:26.659: %OSPF-4-ERRRCV: Received invalid packet: mismatch area ID,
from backbone area must be virtual-link but not found from 10.1.1.4,
FastEthernet0/0
```

For OSPF, the **show ip ospf interface brief** command lists output similar to the **show ip eigrp interface** command, with one line for each enabled interface. (The **show ip ospf interface** command, not shown in the example, lists detailed OSPF information for each interface.) In this example, both R1 and R2 have OSPF enabled on both LAN interfaces, but this command also lists the area number for each interface, with R2 having both LAN interfaces in area 1. As a result, R2's Fa0/0 interface is in a different area than the other three routers' interfaces on the same LAN.

A closer look at R2's **show ip protocols** command output, particularly the highlighted portion, points out the configuration error. The highlighted phrase "10.0.0.0 0.255.255.255 area 1" is actually the exact syntax of the one **network** command on router R2, minus the word "network." Reconfiguring R2 so that its Fa0/0 interface matches the other three routers would solve this particular problem.

The end of the example shows an unsolicited log message generated by router R2, notifying the console user that this router has received a Hello from a router in a different area.

As you check the interfaces, you could also check several other details mentioned in Chapter 7's IP troubleshooting coverage. It makes sense to go ahead and check the interface IP addresses, masks, and interface status, using the **show interfaces** and **show ip interface brief** commands. In particular, it is helpful to note which interfaces are up/up, because a routing protocol will not attempt to find neighbors or advertise connected subnets for an interface that is not in an up/up state. These verification checks were discussed in detail in Chapter 7, so they are not repeated here.

Neighbor Relationships

As mentioned near the beginning of this chapter, when a routing protocol has been enabled on an interface, and the interface is not configured as a passive interface, the routing protocol attempts to discover neighbors and form a neighbor relationship with each neighbor that shares the common subnet. This section examines the large number of facts that each router must check with each potential neighbor before the two routers become neighbors.

OSPF and EIGRP both use Hello messages to learn about new neighbors and to exchange information used to perform some basic verification checks. For example, as just shown in Example 11-3, an OSPF router should not become neighbors with another router in another area, because all routers on a common subnet should be in the same area by design. (The border between areas is a router, not a link.)

After an EIGRP or OSPF router hears a Hello from a new neighbor, the routing protocol examines the information in the Hello, along with some local settings, to decide if the two neighbors should even attempt to become neighbors. Because there is no formal term for all these items that a routing protocol considers, this book just calls them *neighbor requirements*. Table 11-2 lists the neighbor requirements for both EIGRP and OSPF. Following the table, the next few pages examine some of these settings for both EIGRP and OSPF, again using examples based on Figure 11-2.

Key Topic

Table 11-2   *Neighbor Requirements for EIGRP and OSPF*

Requirement	EIGRP	OSPF
Interfaces must be in an up/up state	Yes	Yes
Interfaces must be in the same subnet	Yes	Yes
Must pass neighbor authentication (if configured)	Yes	Yes
Must use the same ASN/process-ID on the **router** configuration command	Yes	No
Hello and hold/dead timers must match	No	Yes
IP MTU must match	No	Yes
Router IDs must be unique	No[1]	Yes
K-values must match	Yes	N/A
Must be in the same area	N/A	Yes

[1]Having duplicate EIGRP RIDs does not prevent routers from becoming neighbors, but it can cause problems when external EIGRP routes are added to the routing table.

NOTE   Even though it is important to study and remember the items in this table, it may be best not to study this table right now. Instead, read the rest of the chapter first, because the items in the table will be mentioned and reviewed throughout the rest of this chapter.

Unlike the rest of the neighbor requirements listed in Table 11-2, the first requirement has very little to do with the routing protocols themselves. The two routers must be able to send packets to each other over the physical network to which they are both connected. To do that, the router interfaces must be up/up. In practice, before examining the rest of the details of why two routers do not become neighbors, confirm that the two routers can ping each other on the local subnet. If the ping fails, investigate all the Layer 1, 2, and 3 issues that could prevent the ping from working (such as an interface not being up/up), as covered in various chapters of this book and in *CCENT/CCNA ICND1 Official Exam Certification Guide*.

Because the details differ slightly between the two routing protocols, this section first examines EIGRP, followed by OSPF.

NOTE   This section assumes that the routing protocol has actually been enabled on each required interface, as covered earlier in this chapter in the section titled "Interfaces Enabled with a Routing Protocol."

EIGRP Neighbor Requirements

Any two EIGRP routers that connect to the same data link, and whose interfaces have been enabled for EIGRP and are not passive, will at least consider becoming neighbors. To quickly and definitively know which potential neighbors have passed all the neighbor requirements for EIGRP, just look at the output of the **show ip eigrp neighbors** command. This command lists only neighbors that have passed all the neighbor verification checks. Example 11-4 shows an example, with the four routers from Figure 11-2 again, but with all earlier EIGRP configuration problems having been fixed.

Example 11-4 *R1* **show ip eigrp neighbors** *Command with All Problems Fixed*

```
R1#show ip eigrp neighbors
IP-EIGRP neighbors for process 99
H   Address              Interface      Hold Uptime   SRTT   RTO  Q   Seq
                                        (sec)         (ms)        Cnt Num
2   10.1.1.3             Fa0/0          13 00:00:04   616   3696  0   8
1   10.1.1.4             Fa0/0          12 00:00:54    1     200  0   45
0   10.1.1.2             Fa0/0          14 00:01:19   123    738  0   43
```

If the **show ip eigrp neighbors** command does not list one or more expected neighbors, and the two routers can ping each other's IP address on their common subnet, the problem is probably related to one of the neighbor requirements listed in Tables 11-2 and 11-3. Table 11-3 summarizes the EIGRP neighbor requirements and notes the best commands with which to determine which requirement is the root cause of the problem.

Table 11-3   *EIGRP Neighbor Requirements and the Best* **show/debug** *Commands*

Requirement	Best Command(s) to Isolate the Problem
Must be in the same subnet	**show interfaces**
Must pass any neighbor authentication	**debug eigrp packets**
Must use the same ASN on the **router** configuration command	**show ip eigrp interfaces, show protocols**
K-values must match	**show protocols**

All the requirements listed in Table 11-3, except the last one, were explained in Chapter 10. EIGRP K-values refer to the parameters that can be configured to change what EIGRP uses in its metric calculation. Cisco recommends leaving these values at their default settings, using only bandwidth and delay in the metric calculation. Because Cisco recommends that you not change these values, this particular problem is not very common. However, you can check the K-values on both routers with the **show ip protocols** command.

Example 11-5 shows three problems that can cause two routers that should become EIGRP neighbors to fail to do so. For this example, the following problems have been introduced:

■   R2 has been configured with IP address 10.1.2.2/24, in a different subnet than R1, R3, and R4.

■   R3 has been configured to use ASN 199 with the **router eigrp 199** command, instead of ASN 99, as used on the other three routers.

■   R4 has been configured to use MD5 authentication, like the other routers, but R4 has a key value of "FRED" instead of the value "fred," used by the other three routers.

R1 can actually detect two of the problems without having to use commands on the other routers. R1 generates an unsolicited log message for the mismatched subnet problem, and a **debug** command on R1 can reveal the authentication failure. A quick examination of a few **show** commands on R3 can identify that the wrong ASN has been used in the **router** configuration command. Example 11-5 shows the details.

Example 11-5 *Common Problems Preventing the Formation of EIGRP Neighbors*

```
! First, R1 has no neighbor relationships yet. R1 uses ASN (process) 99.
R1#show ip eigrp neighbors
IP-EIGRP neighbors for process 99


R1#
! Next, R1 generates a log message, which shows up at the console, stating
! that the router with IP address 10.1.2.2 is not on the same subnet as R1.
!
*May 28 20:02:22.355: IP-EIGRP(Default-IP-Routing-Table:99): Neighbor
    10.1.2.2 not on common subnet for FastEthernet0/0


! Next, R1 enables a debug that shows messages for each packet received from R4,
! which uses the wrong password (authentication key string)
!
R1#debug eigrp packets
EIGRP Packets debugging is on
    (UPDATE, REQUEST, QUERY, REPLY, HELLO, IPXSAP, PROBE, ACK, STUB, SIAQUERY,
     SIAREPLY)
*May 28 20:04:00.931: EIGRP: pkt key id = 1, authentication mismatch
*May 28 20:04:00.931: EIGRP: FastEthernet0/0: ignored packet from 10.1.1.4,
    opcode = 5 (invalid authentication)
! The rest of the output is from R3
! The first line of output from the show ip protocols command lists ASN 199
!
R3#show ip protocols
Routing Protocol is "eigrp 199"
!
! The first line of output from show ip eigrp interfaces lists ASN 199
!
R3#show ip eigrp interfaces
IP-EIGRP interfaces for process 199

                  Xmit Queue   Mean   Pacing Time   Multicast   Pending
Interface   Peers  Un/Reliable  SRTT   Un/Reliable   Flow Timer  Routes
Fa0/0         0       0/0         0        0/10          0          0
Fa0/1         0       0/0         0        0/10          0          0
```

OSPF Neighbor Requirements

Similar to EIGRP, a router's **show ip ospf neighbor** command lists all the neighboring routers that have met all the requirements to become an OSPF neighbor as listed in Table 11-2—with one minor exception (mismatched MTU). (If the MTU is mismatched, the two routers are listed in the **show ip ospf neighbor** command. This particular problem is discussed later, in the section "The MTU Matching Requirement.") So, the first step in troubleshooting OSPF neighbors is to look at the list of neighbors.

Example 11-6 lists the output of a **show ip ospf neighbor** command on router R2, from Figure 11-2, with the configuration correct on each of the four routers in the figure.

Example 11-6 *Normal Working* **show ip ospf neighbors** *Command on Router R2*

```
R2#show ip ospf neighbor

Neighbor ID     Pri   State         Dead Time   Address      Interface
1.1.1.1           1   FULL/BDR      00:00:37    10.1.1.1     FastEthernet0/0
3.3.3.3           1   2WAY/DROTHER  00:00:37    10.1.1.3     FastEthernet0/0
4.4.4.4           1   FULL/DR       00:00:31    10.1.1.4     FastEthernet0/0
```

A brief review of OSPF neighbor states (as explained in Chapter 9) can help you understand a few of the subtleties of the output in the example. A router's listed status for each of its OSPF neighbors—the neighbor's state—should settle into either a *two-way* or *Full* state under normal operation. For neighbors that do not need to directly exchange their databases, typically two non-DR routers on a LAN, the routers should settle into a *two-way* neighbor state. In most cases, two neighboring routers need to directly exchange their complete full LSDBs with each other. As soon as that process has been completed, the two routers settle into a Full neighbor state. In Example 11-6, router R4 is the DR, and R1 is the BDR, so R2 and R3 (as non-DRs) do not need to directly exchange routes. Therefore, R2's neighbor state for R3 (RID 3.3.3.3) in Example 11-6 is listed as two-way.

> **NOTE**   Notably, OSPF neighbors do not have to use the same process ID on the **router ospf** *process-id* command to become neighbors. In Example 11-6, all four routers use different process IDs.

If the **show ip ospf neighbor** command does not list one or more expected neighbors, before moving on to look at OSPF neighbor requirements, you should confirm that the two routers can ping each other on the local subnet. As soon as the two neighboring routers can ping each other, if the two routers still do not become OSPF neighbors, the next step is to examine each of the OSPF neighbor requirements. Table 11-4 summarizes the requirements, listing the most useful commands with which to find the answers.

Key Topic

Table 11-4 *OSPF Neighbor Requirements and the Best* **show/debug** *Commands*

Requirement	Best Command(s) to Isolate the Problem
Must be in the same subnet	**show interfaces**, **debug ip ospf hello**
Must pass any neighbor authentication	**debug ip ospf adj**
Hello and hold/dead timers must match	**show ip ospf interface**, **debug ip ospf hello**

Table 11-4 *OSPF Neighbor Requirements and the Best* **show/debug** *Commands (Continued)*

Key
Topic

Requirement	Best Command(s) to Isolate the Problem
Must be in the same area	**debug ip ospf adj, show ip ospf interface brief**
Router IDs must be unique	**show ip ospf**

The rest of this section looks at a couple of examples in which two OSPF routers could become neighbors but do not because of some of the reasons in the table. This is followed by information on the MTU matching requirement.

OSPF Neighbor Example 1

In this first example of OSPF neighbor problems, the usual four-router network from Figure 11-2 is used. This internetwork is designed to use a single area, area 0. In this case, the following problems have been introduced into the design:

■ R2 has been configured with both LAN interfaces in area 1, whereas the other three routers' Fa0/0 interfaces are assigned to area 0.

■ R3 is using the same RID (1.1.1.1) as R1.

■ R4 is using MD5 authentication like the other three routers, but R4 has misconfigured its authentication key value (FRED instead of fred).

Example 11-7 shows the evidence of the problems, with comments following the example.

Example 11-7 *Finding Mismatch Area, Same RID, and Authentication Problems*

```
R1#debug ip ospf adj
OSPF adjacency events debugging is on
R1#
*May 28 23:59:21.031: OSPF: Send with youngest Key 1
*May 28 23:59:24.463: OSPF: Rcv pkt from 10.1.1.2, FastEthernet0/0, area 0.0.0.0
     mismatch area 0.0.0.1 in the header
*May 28 23:59:24.907: OSPF: Rcv pkt from 10.1.1.4, FastEthernet0/0 :
  Mismatch Authentication Key - Message Digest Key 1


R1#undebug all
All possible debugging has been turned off
R1#show ip ospf interface brief
Interface    PID   Area        IP Address/Mask    Cost  State Nbrs F/C
Fa0/1        11    0           10.1.11.1/24       1     DR    0/0
Fa0/0        11    0           10.1.1.1/24        1     DR    0/0
! Now to R2
! R2 shows that Fa0/0 is in area 1
!
R2#show ip ospf interface brief
```

continues

Example 11-7 *Finding Mismatch Area, Same RID, and Authentication Problems (Continued)*

```
Interface    PID   Area                IP Address/Mask   Cost  State Nbrs F/C
Fa0/1        22    1                   10.1.22.2/24      1     DR    0/0
Fa0/0        22    1                   10.1.1.2/24       1     DR    0/0
! Next, on R3
! R3 lists the RID of 1.1.1.1
!
R3#show ip ospf
 Routing Process "ospf 33" with ID 1.1.1.1
 Supports only single TOS(TOS0) routes
! lines omitted for brevity
! Back to R1 again
! Next command confirms that R1 is also trying to use RID 1.1.1.1
!
R1#show ip ospf
 Routing Process "ospf 11" with ID 1.1.1.1
 Supports only single TOS(TOS0) routes
 ! lines omitted for brevity
*May 29 00:01:25.679: %OSPF-4-DUP_RTRID_NBR: OSPF detected duplicate router-id
1.1.1.1 from 10.1.1.3 on interface FastEthernet0/0
```

As noted in Table 11-4, the **debug ip ospf adj** command helps troubleshoot mismatched OSPF area problems as well as authentication problems. The highlighted messages in the first few lines of the example point out that the router with address 10.1.1.2 (R2) has a mismatched area ID 0.0.0.1, meaning area 1. Indeed, R2 was misconfigured to put its Fa0/0 interface in area 1. Immediately following is a reference to a "mismatched authentication key," meaning that the correct authentication type was used, but the configured keys have different values, specifically for router 10.1.1.4 (R4).

> **NOTE**   Routers treat debug messages as log messages, which IOS sends to the console by default. To see these messages from a Telnet or SSH connection, use the **terminal monitor** command. To disable the display of these messages, use the **terminal no monitor** command.

The next part of the example shows the **show ip ospf interface brief** command on both R1 and R2, pointing out how each router's Fa0/0 interface is in a different OSPF area.

The end of the example lists the information that shows R1 and R3 both trying to use RID 1.1.1.1. Interestingly, both routers automatically generate a log message for the duplicate OSPF RID problem between R1 and R3. A duplicate RID causes significant problems with OSPF, far beyond just whether two routers can become neighbors. The end of Example 11-7 shows the (highlighted) log message. The **show ip ospf** commands on both R3 and R1 also show how you can easily list the RID on each router, noting that they both use the same value.

OSPF Neighbor Example 2

In this next example, the same network from Figure 11-2 is used again. The problems on R2, R3, and R4 from the previous example have been fixed, but new problems have been introduced on R2 and R4 to show the symptoms. In this case, the following problems have been introduced into the design:

- R2 has been configured with a Hello/Dead timer of 5/20 on its Fa0/0 interface, instead of the 10/40 used (by default) on R1, R3, and R4.

- R3's problems have been solved; no problems related to OSPF neighbors exist.

- R4 is now using the correct key string (fred), but with clear-text authentication instead of the MD5 authentication used by the other three routers.

Example 11-8 shows the evidence of the problems, with comments following the example. As usual, the **debug ip ospf adj** command helps discover authentication problems. Also, the **debug ip ospf hello** command helps uncover mismatches discovered in the Hello message, including mismatched IP addresses/masks and timers.

Example 11-8 *Finding Mismatched Hello/Dead Timers and Wrong Authentication*
Types

```
R1#debug ip ospf adj
OSPF adjacency events debugging is on
R1#
*May 29 10:41:30.639: OSPF: Rcv pkt from 10.1.1.4, FastEthernet0/0 :
  Mismatch Authentication type. Input packet specified type 1, we use type 2
R1#
R1#undebug all
All possible debugging has been turned off
R1#debug ip ospf hello
OSPF hello events debugging is on
R1#
*May 29 10:41:42.603: OSPF: Rcv hello from 2.2.2.2 area 0 from
  FastEthernet0/0 10.1.1.2
*May 29 10:41:42.603: OSPF: Mismatched hello parameters from 10.1.1.2
*May 29 10:41:42.603: OSPF: Dead R 20 C 40, Hello R 5 C 10
  Mask R 255.255.255.0 C 255.255.255.0
R1#undebug all
All possible debugging has been turned off
R1#show ip ospf interface fa0/0
FastEthernet0/0 is up, line protocol is up
  Internet Address 10.1.1.1/24, Area 0
  Process ID 11, Router ID 1.1.1.1, Network Type BROADCAST, Cost: 1
```

continues

Example 11-8   *Finding Mismatched Hello/Dead Timers and Wrong Authentication*
Types (Continued)

```
Transmit Delay is 1 sec, State DR, Priority 1
Designated Router (ID) 1.1.1.1, Interface address 10.1.1.1
Backup Designated router (ID) 3.3.3.3, Interface address 10.1.1.3
Timer intervals configured, Hello 10, Dead 40, Wait 40, Retransmit 5
! lines omitted for brevity
! Moving on to R2 next
!
R2#show ip ospf interface fa0/0
FastEthernet0/0 is up, line protocol is up
  Internet Address 10.1.1.2/24, Area 0
  Process ID 22, Router ID 2.2.2.2, Network Type BROADCAST, Cost: 1
  Transmit Delay is 1 sec, State DR, Priority 1
  Designated Router (ID) 2.2.2.2, Interface address 10.1.1.2
  No backup designated router on this network
  Timer intervals configured, Hello 5, Dead 20, Wait 20, Retransmit 5
! lines omitted for brevity
```

The example begins with the debug messages related to the authentication problem
between R1, which uses MD5 authentication, and R4, which now uses clear-text
authentication. As listed in Chapter 9's Table 9-4, IOS considers OSPF clear-text
authentication to be type 1 authentication and MD5 to be type 2. The highlighted debug
message confirms that thinking, stating that R1 received a packet from 10.1.1.4 (R4), with
type 1 authentication, but with R1 expecting type 2 authentication.

Next, the example shows the messages generated by the **debug ip ospf hello** command—
specifically, those related to the Hello/Dead timer mismatch. The highlighted message uses
a "C" to mean "configured value"—in other words, the value on the local router, or R1 in
this case. The "R" in the message means "Received value," or the value listed in the
received Hello. In this case, the phrase "Dead R 20 C 40" means that the router that
generated this message, R1, received a Hello with a Dead timer set to 20, but R1's
configured value on the interface is 40, so the values don't match. Similarly, the message
shows the mismatch in the Hello timers as well. Note that any IP subnet mismatch problems
could also be found with this same debug, based on the received and configured subnet
masks.

The majority of the space in the example shows the output of the **show ip ospf interface**
command on both R1 and R2, which lists the Hello and Dead timers on each interface,
confirming the details listed in the debug messages.

The MTU Matching Requirement

Of all the potential problems between two potential OSPF neighbors listed in Table 11-2, only one problem, the mismatched MTU problem, allows the neighbor to be listed in the other router's **show ip ospf neighbor** command output. When two routers connect to the same subnet, with different interface IP MTU settings, the two routers can become neighbors and reach the two-way state. However, when the two routers attempt to exchange LSDBs, the database exchange process fails because of the MTU mismatch.

When the MTU mismatch occurs, the routers typically move between a few neighbor states while trying to overcome the problem. The most common state is the Exchange state, as shown in Example 11-9. In this case, R1 and R3 have no other problems that prevent them from becoming OSPF neighbors, except that R3 has been configured with an IP MTU of 1200 bytes on its Fa0/0 interface, instead of the default 1500 used by R1.

Example 11-9 *Results of Mismatched MTUs on OSPF Neighbors*

```
R1#show ip ospf neighbor

Neighbor ID     Pri   State         Dead Time   Address       Interface
3.3.3.3          1    EXCHANGE/DR   00:00:36    10.1.1.3      FastEthernet0/0
```

The state typically cycles from Exchange state, back to Init state, and then back to Exchange state.

Exam Preparation Tasks

Review All the Key Topics

Review the most important topics from this chapter, noted with the key topics icon.
Table 11-5 lists these key topics and where each is discussed.

Table 11-5 *Key Topics for Chapter 11*

Key Topic Element	Description	Page Number
List	Two things that happen when EIGRP or OSPF is enabled on a router's interface	410
Table 11-1	List of three commands that are useful when determining on which interfaces EIGRP or OSPF has been enabled	410
Table 11-2	List of neighbor requirements for both EIGRP and OSPF	418
Table 11-3	List of EIGRP neighbor requirements and useful commands to isolate that requirement as the root cause of a neighbor problem	420
Table 11-4	The same information as Table 11-3, but for OSPF	422-423

Complete the Tables and Lists from Memory

Print a copy of Appendix J, "Memory Tables" (found on the CD), or at least the section for this chapter, and complete the tables and lists from memory. Appendix K, "Memory Tables Answer Key," also on the CD, includes completed tables and lists for you to check your work.

Command Reference to Check Your Memory

Although you should not necessarily memorize the information in the tables in this section, this section does include a reference for the configuration and EXEC commands covered in this chapter. Practically speaking, you should memorize the commands as a side effect of reading the chapter and doing all the activities in this exam preparation section. To see how well you have memorized the commands as a side effect of your other studies, cover the left side of the table, read the descriptions on the right side, and see if you remember the command.

Table 11-6 *Chapter 11 Configuration Command Reference*

Command	Description
ip hello-interval eigrp *as-number timer-value*	Interface subcommand that sets the EIGRP Hello interval for that EIGRP process.
ip hold-time eigrp *as-number timer-value*	Interface subcommand that sets the EIGRP hold time for the interface.
ip ospf hello-interval *seconds*	Interface subcommand that sets the interval for periodic Hellos.
ip ospf dead-interval *number*	Interface subcommand that sets the OSPF Dead Timer.

Table 11-7 *Chapter 11 EXEC Command Reference*

Command	Description
show ip protocols	Shows routing protocol parameters and current timer values, including an effective copy of the routing protocols' **network** commands, and a list of passive interfaces.
show ip eigrp interfaces	Lists the interfaces on which EIGRP has been enabled for each EIGRP process, except passive interfaces.
show ip route eigrp	Lists only EIGRP-learned routes from the routing table.
debug eigrp packets	Displays the contents of EIGRP packets, including many useful notices about reasons why neighbor relationships fail to form.
show ip eigrp neighbors	Lists EIGRP neighbors and status.
show ip ospf interface brief	Lists the interfaces which the OSPF protocol is enabled (based on the **network** commands), including passive interfaces.
show ip ospf interface [*type number*]	Lists detailed OSPF settings for all interfaces, or the listed interface, including Hello and Dead timers and OSPF area.
show ip route ospf	Lists routes in the routing table learned by OSPF.
show ip ospf neighbor	Lists neighbors and current status with neighbors, per interface.
debug ip ospf events	Issues log messages for each action taken by OSPF, including the receipt of messages.
debug ip ospf packet	Issues log messages describing the contents of all OSPF packets.
debug ip ospf hello	Issues log messages describing Hellos and Hello failures.

Cisco Published ICND2 Exam Topics*
Covered in This Part

Configure and troubleshoot basic operation and routing on Cisco devices

- Verify router hardware and software operation using SHOW & DEBUG commands

Implement and verify WAN links

- Configure and verify Frame Relay on Cisco routers

- Troubleshoot WAN implementation issues

- Describe VPN technology (including: importance, benefits, role, impact, components)

- Configure and verify PPP connection between Cisco routers

* Always recheck http://www.cisco.com for the latest posted exam topics.

Part IV: Wide-Area Networks

This chapter covers the following subjects:

PPP Concepts: This section examines PPP concepts, including control protocols and PAP/CHAP.

PPP Configuration: This section looks at how to configure a simple PPP serial link, as well as how to configure CHAP.

Troubleshooting Serial Links: This section examines the overall serial link troubleshooting process, including typical reasons why an interface has a particular status code.

CHAPTER 12

Point-to-Point WANs

This chapter is the first of four chapters in Part IV of this book. This part focuses on WAN technologies. This chapter completes the examination of point-to-point links by examining more details about how PPP works, along with a wide variety of troubleshooting topics related to point-to-point leased lines. Chapter 13, "Frame Relay Concepts," and Chapter 14, "Frame Relay Configuration and Troubleshooting," explore Frame Relay technologies. Chapter 15, "Virtual Private Networks," looks at the concepts behind virtual private networks (VPN). VPNs let you create secure communication paths that work like WAN links, while using other, less-secure networks, such as the Internet.

"Do I Know This Already?" Quiz

The "Do I Know This Already?" quiz allows you to assess whether you should read the entire chapter. If you miss no more than one of these seven self-assessment questions, you might want to move ahead to the "Exam Preparation Tasks" section. Table 12-1 lists the major headings in this chapter and the "Do I Know This Already?" quiz questions covering the material in those sections. This helps you assess your knowledge of these specific areas. The answers to the "Do I Know This Already?" quiz appear in Appendix A.

Table 12-1 *"Do I Know This Already?" Foundation Topics Section-to-Question Mapping*

Foundation Topics Section	Questions
PPP Concepts	1 and 2
PPP Configuration	3–5
Troubleshooting Serial Links	6 and 7

1. Which of the following PPP authentication protocols authenticates a device on the other end of a link without sending any password information in clear text?

   a. MD5

   b. PAP

   c. CHAP

   d. DES

2. Which of the following PPP protocols controls the operation of CHAP?

    a. CDPCP

    b. IPCP

    c. LCP

    d. IPXCP

3. Two routers have no initial configuration whatsoever. They are connected in a lab using a DTE cable connected to R1 and a DCE cable connected to R2, with the DTE and DCE cables then connected to each other. The engineer wants to create a working PPP link. Which of the following commands are required on R1 for the link to reach a state in which R1 can ping R2's serial IP address, assuming that the physical back-to-back link physically works?

    a. **encapsulation ppp**

    b. **no encapsulation hdlc**

    c. **clock rate**

    d. **ip address**

4. Imagine that two routers, R1 and R2, have a leased line between them. Each router had its configuration erased and was then reloaded. R1 was then configured with the following commands:

```
hostname R1
interface s0/0
 encapsulation ppp
 ppp authentication chap
```

Which of the following configuration commands can complete the configuration on R1 so that CHAP can work correctly? Assume that R2 has been configured correctly and that the password is fred.

    a. No other configuration is needed.

    b. **ppp chap** (global command)

    c. **username R1 password fred**

    d. **username R2 password fred**

    e. **ppp chap password fred**

5. Consider the following excerpt from the output of a **show** command:

```
Serial0/0/1 is up, line protocol is up
  Hardware is GT96K Serial
  Internet address is 192.168.2.1/24
  MTU 1500 bytes, BW 1544 Kbit, DLY 20000 usec,
     reliability 255/255, txload 1/255, rxload 1/255
  Encapsulation PPP, LCP Open
  Open: CDPCP, IPCP, loopback not set
```

Which of the following are true about this router's S0/0/1 interface?

a.   The interface is using HDLC.

b.   The interface is using PPP.

c.   The interface currently cannot pass IPv4 traffic.

d.   The link should be able to pass PPP frames at the present time.

6.   Consider the following excerpt from the output of a **show interfaces** command on an interface configured to use PPP:

```
Serial0/0/1 is up, line protocol is down
  Hardware is GT96K Serial
  Internet address is 192.168.2.1/24
```

A ping of the IP address on the other end of the link fails. Which of the following are reasons for the failure, assuming that the problem listed in that answer is the only problem with the link?

a.   The CSU/DSU connected to the other router is not powered on.

b.   The IP address on the router at the other end of the link is not in subnet 192.168.2.0/24.

c.   CHAP authentication failed.

d.   The router on the other end of the link has been configured to use HDLC.

e.   None of the other answers is correct.

7.   Two routers have a serial link between them, with the link configured to use PPP, and with EIGRP configured correctly for all interfaces. The engineer can ping the IP address on the other end of the link, but not the IP address of the other router's LAN interface. Which of the following answers is a likely cause of the problem?

a.   The CSU/DSU connected to the other router is not powered on.

b.   The serial IP address on the router at the other end of the link is not in the same subnet as the local router.

c.   CHAP authentication failed.

d.   The router on the other end of the link has been configured to use HDLC.

Foundation Topics

Point-to-Point Protocol (PPP) defines a data-link protocol with many features besides just helping two devices send data over the link. This chapter starts by explaining the many PPP features available on routers, followed by PPP configuration, including the configuration of PPP authentication. The chapter ends with a section on troubleshooting serial links, covering a wide variety of topics, including PPP.

> **NOTE**   WAN options such as leased lines, packet switching, and CSUs/DSUs, as well as basic knowledge of HDLC and PPP, are all considered prerequisite knowledge for the ICND2 exam and for this book. However, if you do not have a copy of *CCENT/CCNA ICND1 Official Exam Certification Guide*, this book's CD includes a copy of that book's Chapter 17 as an appendix; it covers this prerequisite information. The appendix on the CD is Appendix I, "ICND1 Chapter 17: WAN Configuration and Troubleshooting." If you have not yet read Chapter 17 in the ICND1 book, or if you do not have that book, now may be a good time to review Appendix I before continuing with this chapter.

PPP Concepts

PPP provides several basic but important functions that are useful on a leased line that connects two devices, as reviewed in the following list:

Key Topic

■ Definition of a header and trailer that allows delivery of a data frame over the link

■ Support for both synchronous and asynchronous links

■ A protocol type field in the header, allowing multiple Layer 3 protocols to pass over the same link

■ Built-in authentication tools: Password Authentication Protocol (PAP) and Challenge Handshake Authentication Protocol (CHAP)

■ Control protocols for each higher-layer protocol that rides over PPP, allowing easier integration and support of those protocols

The next several pages take a closer look at the protocol field, authentication, and the control protocols.

The PPP Protocol Field

One of the more important features included in the PPP standard, but not in the HDLC standard, is the protocol field. The protocol field identifies the type of packet inside the frame. When PPP was created, this field allowed packets from the many different Layer 3 protocols to pass over a single link. Today, the protocol type field still provides the same function, even for the support of two different versions of IP (IPv4 and IPv6). Figure 12-1 compares the framing details of HDLC and PPP, showing the proprietary HDLC Protocol field and the standardized PPP Protocol field.

Figure 12-1 *PPP and HDLC Framing*

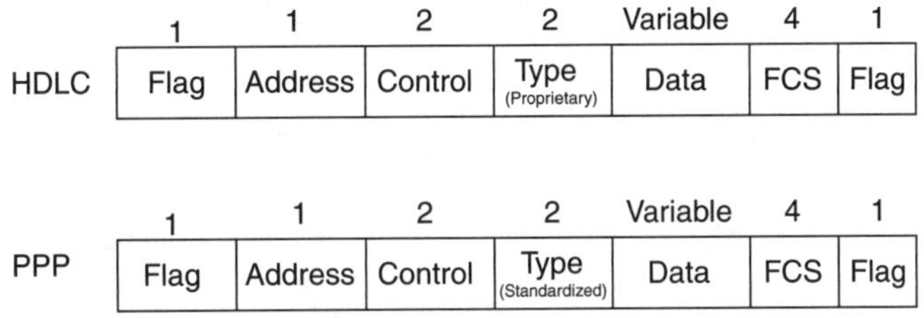

PPP defines a set of Layer 2 control messages that perform various link control functions. These control functions fall into two main categories:

■ Those needed regardless of the Layer 3 protocol sent across the link

■ Those specific to each Layer 3 protocol

The PPP *Link Control Protocol* (LCP) implements the control functions that work the same regardless of the Layer 3 protocol. For features related to any higher-layer protocols, typically Layer 3 protocols, PPP uses a series of PPP *control protocols* (CP), such as IP Control Protocol (IPCP). PPP uses one instance of LCP per link, and one CP for each Layer 3 protocol defined on the link. For example, on a PPP link using IPv4, IPv6, and Cisco Discovery Protocol (CDP), the link uses one instance of LCP, plus IPCP (for IPv4), IPv6CP (for IPv6), and CDPCP (for CDP).

The next section first summarizes the functions of LCP and then explains one of those functions, authentication, in more detail.

PPP Link Control Protocol (LCP)

LCP provides four notable features, which are covered in this chapter. Table 12-2 summarizes the functions, gives the LCP feature names, and describes the features briefly. Following the table, the text explains each feature in more detail. Note that the features listed in the table are optional and are disabled by default.

Table 12-2 *PPP LCP Features*

Function	LCP Feature	Description
Looped link detection	Magic number	Detects if the link is looped, and disables the interface, allowing rerouting over a working route.
Error detection	Link Quality Monitoring (LQM)	Disables an interface that exceeds an error percentage threshold, allowing rerouting over better routes.
Multilink support	Multilink PPP	Load-balances traffic over multiple parallel links.
Authentication	PAP and CHAP	Exchanges names and passwords so that each device can verify the identity of the device on the other end of the link.

Looped Link Detection

Error detection and looped link detection are two key features of PPP. Looped link detection allows for faster convergence when a link fails because it is looped. What does "looped" mean? Well, to test a circuit, the phone company might loop the circuit. The telco technician can sit at his desk and, using commands, cause the phone company's switch to loop the circuit. This means that the phone company takes the electrical signal sent by the CPE device and sends the same electrical current right back to the same device.

The routers cannot send bits to each other while the link is looped, of course. However, the router might not notice that the link is looped, because the router is still receiving something over the link! PPP helps the router recognize a looped link quickly so that it can bring down the interface and possibly use an alternative route.

In some cases, routing protocol convergence can be sped up by LCP's recognition of the loop. If the router can immediately notice that the link is looped, it can put the interface in a "down and down" status, and routing protocols can change their routing updates based on the fact that the link is down. If a router does not notice that the link has been looped, the routing protocol must wait for timeouts—things such as not hearing from the router on the other end of the link for some period of time.

LCP notices looped links quickly using a feature called *magic numbers*. When using PPP, the router sends PPP LCP messages instead of Cisco-proprietary keepalives across the link; these messages include a magic number, which is different on each router. If a line is looped, the router receives an LCP message with its own magic number instead of getting a message with the other router's magic number. When a router receives its own magic number, that router knows that the frame it sent has been looped back, so the router can take down the interface, which speeds convergence.

Enhanced Error Detection

Similar to many other data-link protocols, PPP uses an FCS field in the PPP trailer to determine if an individual frame has an error. If a frame is received in error, it is discarded. However, PPP can monitor the frequency with which frames are received in error so that it can take down an interface if too many errors occur.

PPP LCP analyzes the error rates on a link using a PPP feature called Link Quality Monitoring (LQM). LCP at each end of the link sends messages describing the number of correctly received packets and bytes. The router that sent the packets compares this number of correctly-received frames to the number of frames and bytes it sent, and it calculates percentage loss. The router can take down the link after a configured error rate has been exceeded.

The only time LQM helps is when you have redundant routes in the network. By taking down a link that has many errors, you can cause packets to use an alternative path that might not have as many errors.

PPP Multilink

When multiple PPP links exist between the same two routers—referred to as parallel links—the routers must then determine how to use those links. With HDLC links, and with PPP links using the simplest configuration, the routers must use Layer 3 load balancing. This means that the routers have multiple routes for the same destination subnets. For example, the upper part of Figure 12-2 shows the load-balancing effect on R1 when forwarding packets to subnet 192.168.3.0/24.

Figure 12-2 *Load Balancing Without Multilink PPP*

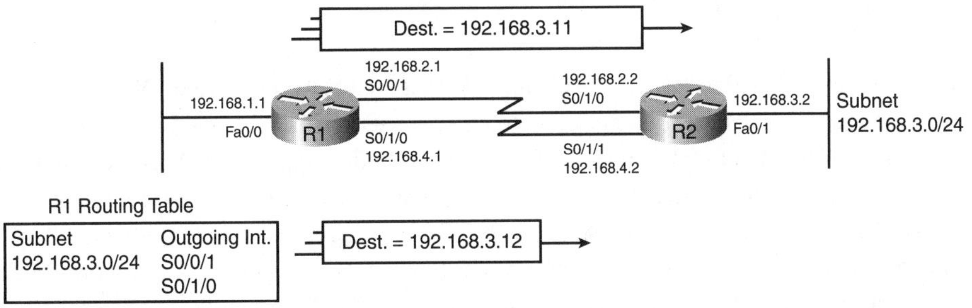

The figure shows two packets, one large and one small. Using Layer 3 logic, the router may choose to send one packet over one link, and the next packet over another. However, because the packets might be of different sizes, the router may not balance the traffic equally over each link. In some cases, particularly when most packets are sent to just a few destination hosts, the numbers of packets sent over each link might not even be balanced, which may overload one of the links and leave another link idle.

Multilink PPP load-balances the traffic equally over the links while allowing the Layer 3 logic in each router to treat the parallel links as a single link. When encapsulating a packet, PPP fragments the packet into smaller frames, sending one fragment over each link. For example, for the network shown in Figure 12-2, with two links, R1 would create two frames for each Layer 3 packet, with each frame holding roughly half the original packet. Then, PPP sends one fragment of each original packet over each of the two links. By sending about half of each packet over each link, multilink PPP can more evenly load-balance the traffic. As an added benefit, multilink PPP allows the Layer 3 routing tables to use a single route that refers to the combined links, keeping the routing table smaller. For example, in Figure 12-2, R1 would instead use one route for subnet 192.168.3.0/24, referring to the group of interfaces as a concept called a *multilink group*.

PPP Authentication

The term *authentication* refers to a set of security functions that help one device confirm that the other device should be allowed to communicate and is not some imposter. For instance, if R1 and R2 are supposed to be communicating over a serial link, R1 might want R2 to somehow prove that it really is R2. Authentication provides a way to prove one's identity.

WAN authentication is most often needed when dial lines are used. However, the configuration of the authentication features remains the same whether a leased line or dial line is used.

PAP and CHAP authenticate the endpoints on either end of a point-to-point serial link. CHAP is the preferred method today because the identification process uses values hidden with a Message Digest 5 (MD5) one-way hash, which is more secure than the clear-text passwords sent by PAP.

Both PAP and CHAP require the exchange of messages between devices. When a dialed line is used, the dialed-to router expects to receive a username and password from the dialing router with both PAP and CHAP. With a leased line, typically both routers mutually authenticate the other router. Whether leased line or dial, with PAP, the username and password are sent in the first message. With CHAP, the protocol begins with a message called a *challenge*, which asks the other router to send its username and password. Figure 12-3 outlines the different processes in the case where the links are dialed. The process works the same when the link uses a leased line.

Figure 12-3 *PAP and CHAP Authentication Process*

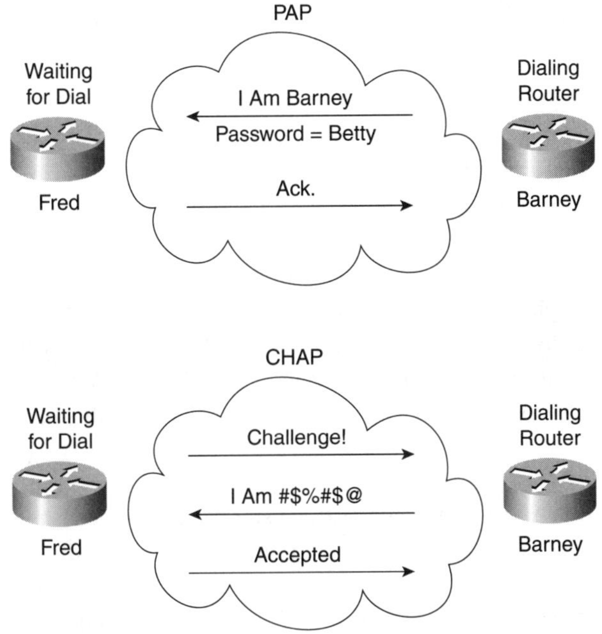

PAP flows are much less secure than CHAP because PAP sends the hostname and password in clear text in the message. These can be read easily if someone places a tracing tool in the circuit. CHAP instead uses a one-way hash algorithm, with input to the algorithm being a password that never crosses the link, plus a shared random number. The CHAP challenge states the random number; both routers are preconfigured with the password. The challenged router runs the hash algorithm using the just-learned random number and the secret password and sends the results back to the router that sent the challenge. The router that sent the challenge runs the same algorithm using the random number (sent across the link) and the password (not sent across the link). If the results match, the passwords must match.

The most interesting part of the CHAP process is that at no time does the password itself ever cross the link. With the random number, the hash value is different every time. So even if someone sees the calculated hash value using a trace tool, the value is meaningless as a way to break in next time. CHAP authentication is difficult to break, even with a tracing tool on the WAN link.

PPP Configuration

This section examines how to configure PPP and then how to add CHAP configuration. At the same time, this section also examines a couple of commands that help verify if PPP is up and working.

Basic PPP Configuration

Configuring PPP requires only the **encapsulation ppp** command on both ends of the link. To change back to use the default of HDLC, the engineer just needs to use the **encapsulation hdlc** command on both ends of the link as well. However, besides this basic configuration, the physical serial link needs to be ordered and installed. This section assumes that the physical link has been installed and is working. If you want to read more details about the physical link, refer to Chapter 17 of *CCENT/CCNA ICND1 Official Exam Certification Guide*, or to the copy of that chapter included as this book's CD-only Appendix I.

Example 12-1 shows a simple configuration using the two routers shown in Figure 12-4. The example includes the IP address configuration, but the IP addresses do not have to be configured for PPP to work. Because most installations will use IP, the configuration is added for some perspectives in the **show** commands in the second part of the example.

Figure 12-4 *Two-Router Internetwork Used in PPP Examples*

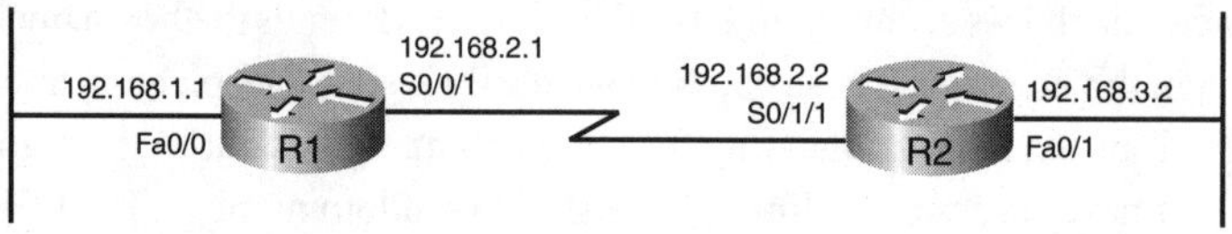

Example 12-1 *Basic PPP Configuration*

```
! The example starts with router R1
interface Serial0/0/1
 ip address 192.168.2.1 255.255.255.0
 encapsulation ppp
 clockrate 1536000
! Next, the configuration on router R2
interface Serial0/1/1
 ip address 192.168.2.2 255.255.255.0
 encapsulation ppp
! Back to router R1 again
R1#show interfaces serial 0/0/1
Serial0/0/1 is up, line protocol is up
  Hardware is GT96K Serial
```

Example 12-1 *Basic PPP Configuration (Continued)*

```
Internet address is 192.168.2.1/24
MTU 1500 bytes, BW 1544 Kbit, DLY 20000 usec,
   reliability 255/255, txload 1/255, rxload 1/255
Encapsulation PPP, LCP Open
Open: CDPCP, IPCP, loopback not set
! lines omitted for brevity
```

This example shows the simple configuration, with both routers needing to use PPP encapsulation. If either router defaulted to use HDLC, and the other configured PPP as shown, the link would not come up, staying in an "up and down" interface state.

The **show interfaces** command at the bottom of the example shows the normal output when the link is up and working. The second interface status code typically refers to the data-link status, with the "up" value meaning that the data link is working. Additionally, a few lines into the output, the highlighted phrases show that PPP is indeed configured, and that LCP has completed its work successfully, as noted with the "LCP Open" phrase. Additionally, the output lists the fact that two CPs, CDPCP and IPCP, have also successfully been enabled—all good indications that PPP is working properly.

CHAP Configuration and Verification

The simplest version of CHAP configuration requires only a few commands. The configuration uses a password configured on each router. As an alternative, the password could be configured on an external Authentication, Authorization, and Accounting (AAA) server outside the router. The configuration steps are as follows:

Step 1 Configure the routers' hostnames using the **hostname** *name* global configuration command.

Step 2 Configure the name of the other router, and the shared secret password, using the **username** *name* **password** *password* global configuration command.

Step 3 Enable CHAP on the interface on each router using the **ppp authentication chap** interface subcommand.

Example 12-2 shows a sample configuration, using the same two routers as the previous example (see Figure 12-4).

Key
Topic

Example 12-2 *CHAP Configuration Example*

```
hostname R1                              hostname R2

username R2 password mypass              username R1 password mypass
!                                        !
interface serial 0/0/1                   interface serial 0/1/1
 encapsulation ppp                        encapsulation ppp
 ppp authentication chap                  ppp authentication chap
```

The commands themselves are not complicated, but it is easy to misconfigure the hostnames and passwords. Notice that each router refers to the other router's hostname in the **username** command, but both routers must configure the same password value. Also, not only are the passwords (mypass in this case) case-sensitive, but the hostnames, as referenced in the **username** command, also are also case-sensitive.

Because CHAP is a function of LCP, if the authentication process fails, LCP does not complete, and the interface falls to an "up and down" interface state.

PAP Configuration

PAP uses the exact same configuration commands as CHAP, except that the **ppp authentication pap** command is used instead of **ppp authentication chap**. The rest of the verification commands work the same, regardless of which of the two types of authentication are used. For example, if PAP authentication fails, LCP fails, and the link settles into an "up and down" state.

Cisco IOS Software also supports the capability to configure the router to first try one authentication method and, if the other side does not respond, try the other option. For example, the **ppp authentication chap pap** interface subcommand tells the router to send CHAP messages, and if no reply is received, to try PAP. Note that the second option is not tried if the CHAP messages flow between the two devices, and the result is that authentication failed. It uses the other option only if the other device does not send back any messages.

The next section discusses a wide range of WAN troubleshooting topics, including a few more details about troubleshooting CHAP issues.

Troubleshooting Serial Links

This section discusses how to isolate and find the root cause of problems related to topics covered earlier in this chapter, as well as some point-to-point WAN topics covered in *CCENT/CCNA ICND1 Official Exam Certification Guide*. Also, this section does not attempt to repeat the IP troubleshooting coverage in Parts II and III of this book, but it does point out some of the possible symptoms on a serial link when a Layer 3 subnet mismatch occurs on opposite ends of a serial link, which prevents the routers from routing packets over the serial link.

A simple **ping** command can determine whether a serial link can or cannot forward IP packets. A **ping** of the other router's serial IP address—for example, a working **ping 192.168.2.2** command on R1 in Figure 12-4—proves that the link either works or does not.

If the **ping** does not work, the problem could be related to functions at OSI Layer 1, 2, or 3. The best way to isolate which layer is the most likely cause is to examine the interface status codes described in Table 12-3. (As a reminder, router interfaces have two status codes—line status and protocol status.)

Table 12-3 *Interface Status Codes and Typical Meanings When a Ping Does Not Work*

Line Status	Protocol Status	Likely Reason/Layer
Administratively down	Down	Interface is shut down
Down	Down	Layer 1
Up	Down	Layer 2
Up	Up	Layer 3

The serial link verification and troubleshooting process should begin with a simple three-step process:

Step 1 From one router, ping the other router's serial IP address.

Step 2 If the ping fails, examine the interface status on both routers, and investigate problems related to the likely problem areas listed in Table 12-4 (shown later in this chapter).

Step 3 If the ping works, also verify that any routing protocols are exchanging routes over the link.

> **NOTE** The interface status codes can be found using the **show interfaces**, **show ip interface brief**, and **show interfaces description** commands.

The rest of this chapter explores the specific items to be examined when the ping fails, based on the combinations of interface status codes listed in Table 12-3.

Troubleshooting Layer 1 Problems

The interface status codes, or interface state, play a key role in isolating the root cause of problems on serial links. In fact, the status on both ends of the link may differ, so it is important to examine the status on both ends of the link to help determine the problem.

One simple and easy-to-find Layer 1 problem occurs when either one of the two routers has administratively disabled its serial interface with the **shutdown** interface subcommand. If a router's serial interface is in an administratively down line status, the solution is simple— just configure a **no shutdown** interface configuration command on the interface. Also, if one router's interface has a line status of down, the other router may be shut down, so check both sides of the link.

The combination of a *down* line status on both ends of the serial link typically points to a Layer 1 problem. The following list describes the most likely reasons:

Key Topic

- The leased line is down (a telco problem).

- The line from the telco is not plugged in to either or both CSU/DSUs.

- A CSU/DSU has failed or is misconfigured.

- A serial cable from a router to its CSU/DSU is disconnected or faulty.

The details of how to further isolate these four problems is beyond the scope of this book.

Interestingly, one other common physical layer problem can occur that results in both routers' interfaces being in an up/down state. On a back-to-back serial link, if the required **clock rate** command is missing on the router with a DCE cable installed, both routers' serial interfaces will fail and end up with a line status of up but a line protocol status of down. Example 12-3 shows just such an example, pointing out a couple of ways to check to see if a missing **clock rate** command is the problem. The two best ways to find this problem are to notice the absence of the **clock rate** command on the router with the DCE cable, and to note the "no clock" phrase in the output of the **show controllers serial** command. (This example shows R1 from Figure 12-4, with the **clock rate** command removed.)

Example 12-3   *Problem: No* **clock rate** *Command on the DCE End*

```
R1#show controller s0/0/1
Interface Serial0/0/1
Hardware is PowerQUICC MPC860
  Internet address is 192.168.2.1/24
DCE V.35, no clock
! lines omitted for brevity
R1#show running-config interface S0/0/1
```

Example 12-3 *Problem: No **clock rate** Command on the DCE End (Continued)*

```
Building configuration...

Current configuration : 42 bytes
!
interface Serial0/0/1
 ip address 192.168.2.1 255.255.255.0
end
```

> **NOTE** Some recent IOS releases actually prevent the user from removing the **clock rate** command on the interface if a DCE cable or no cable is installed, in an effort to prevent the unintentional omission of the **clock rate** command. Also, IOS sometimes spells the **clock rate** command as the **clockrate** command; both are acceptable.

Troubleshooting Layer 2 Problems

When both routers' serial line status is up, but at least one of the routers' line protocol status (the second interface status code) either is down or continually switches between up and down, the interface probably has one of two types of data link layer problems. This section explains both problems, which are summarized in Table 12-4.

Table 12-4 *Likely Reasons for Data-Link Problems on Serial Links*

Line Status	Protocol Status	Likely Reason
Up	Down (stable) on both ends or Down (stable) on one end, flapping between up and down on the other	Mismatched **encapsulation** commands
Up	Down on one end, up on the other	Keepalive is disabled on the end in an up state
Up	Down (stable) on both ends	PAP/CHAP authentication failure

> **NOTE** As with the other troubleshooting topics in this book, Table 12-4 lists some of the more common types of failures but not all.

The first of these two problems—a mismatch between the configured data-link protocols—is easy to identify and fix. The **show interfaces** command lists the encapsulation type in the seventh line of the output, so using this command on both routers can quickly identify the problem. Alternatively, a quick look at the configuration, plus remembering that HDLC is the default serial encapsulation, can confirm whether the encapsulations are mismatched. The solution is simple—reconfigure one of the two routers to match the other router's **encapsulation** command.

The other two root causes require a little more discussion to understand the issue and determine if they are the real root cause. The next two headings take a closer look at each.

Keepalive Failure

The second item relates to a feature called *keepalive*. The *keepalive* feature helps a router recognize when a link is no longer functioning so that the router can bring down the interface, hoping to then use an alternative IP route.

The keepalive function (by default) causes routers to send keepalive messages to each other every 10 seconds (the default setting). (Cisco defines a proprietary HDLC keepalive message, with PPP defining a keepalive message as part of LCP.) This 10-second timer is the keepalive interval. If a router does not receive any keepalive messages from the other router for a number of keepalive intervals (three or five intervals by default, depending on the IOS version), the router brings down the interface, thinking that the interface is no longer working.

For real networks, it is useful to just leave keepalives enabled. However, you can make a mistake and turn off keepalives on one end of a serial link, leave them enabled on the other, and cause the link to fail. For example, if R1 were configured with the **no keepalive** interface subcommand, disabling keepalives, R1 would no longer send the keepalive messages. If R2 continued to default to use keepalives, R2 would keep sending keepalive messages, plus R2 would expect to receive keepalive messages from R1. After several keepalive intervals pass, R2, having not received any keepalive messages from R1, would change the interface to an "up and down" state. Then, R2 would continually bring the link back up, still not get any keepalives from R1, and then fall back to an "up and down" state again, and flapping up and down repeatedly. R1, not caring about keepalives, would leave the interface in an "up and up" state the whole time. Example 12-4 shows this exact example, again with the routers in Figure 12-4.

Example 12-4 *Line Problems Because of Keepalive Only on R2*

```
! R1 disables keepalives, and remains in an up/up state.
R1#configure terminal
Enter configuration commands, one per line.  End with CNTL/Z.
R1(config)#interface s 0/0/1
R1(config-if)#no keepalive
R1(config-if)#^Z
R1#show interfaces s0/0/1
Serial0/0/1 is up, line protocol is up
  Hardware is PowerQUICC Serial
```

Example 12-4 *Line Problems Because of Keepalive Only on R2 (Continued)*

```
  Internet address is 192.168.2.1/24  MTU 1500 bytes, BW 1544 Kbit, DLY 20000 usec,
     reliability 255/255, txload 1/255, rxload 1/255
  Encapsulation HDLC, loopback not set
  Keepalive not set
! lines omitted for brevity
! Below, R2 still has keepalives enabled (default)
R2#show interfaces S0/1/1
Serial0/1/1 is up, line protocol is down
  Hardware is PowerQUICC Serial
  Internet address is 192.168.2.2/24
  MTU 1500 bytes, BW 1544 Kbit, DLY 20000 usec,
     reliability 255/255, txload 1/255, rxload 1/255
  Encapsulation HDLC, loopback not set
  Keepalive set (10 sec)
! lines omitted for brevity
```

NOTE It is a configuration mistake to enable keepalives on only one end of a point-to-point serial link. It appears that some very recent IOS versions notice when the keepalives are mistakenly disabled on one end of a link and prevent the problem described here from happening. For the CCNA exams, just be aware that keepalives should be enabled on both ends of the link, or disabled on both ends.

PAP and CHAP Authentication Failure

As mentioned earlier, a failure in the PAP/CHAP authentication process results in both routers falling to an "up and down" state. To discover whether a PAP/CHAP failure is really the root cause, you can use the **debug ppp authentication** command. For perspective, Example 12-5 shows the output of this command when CHAP has been configured as in earlier Example 12-2, with CHAP working correctly in this case.

Example 12-5 *Debug Messages Confirming the Correct Operation of CHAP*

Key Topic

```
R1#debug ppp authentication
PPP authentication debugging is on
R1#
*May 21 18:26:55.731: Se0/0/1 PPP: Using default call direction
*May 21 18:26:55.731: Se0/0/1 PPP: Treating connection as a dedicated line
*May 21 18:26:55.731: Se0/0/1 PPP: Authorization required
*May 21 18:26:55.731: Se0/0/1 CHAP: O CHALLENGE id 16 len 23 from "R1"
*May 21 18:26:55.731: Se0/0/1 CHAP: I CHALLENGE id 49 len 23 from "R2"
*May 21 18:26:55.735: Se0/0/1 CHAP: Using hostname from unknown source
*May 21 18:26:55.735: Se0/0/1 CHAP: Using password from AAA
*May 21 18:26:55.735: Se0/0/1 CHAP: O RESPONSE id 49 len 23 from "R1"
*May 21 18:26:55.735: Se0/0/1 CHAP: I RESPONSE id 16 len 23 from "R2"
*May 21 18:26:55.735: Se0/0/1 PPP: Sent CHAP LOGIN Request
```

continues

Example 12-5 *Debug Messages Confirming the Correct Operation of CHAP (Continued)*

```
*May 21 18:26:55.735: Se0/0/1 PPP: Received LOGIN Response PASS
*May 21 18:26:55.735: Se0/0/1 PPP: Sent LCP AUTHOR Request
*May 21 18:26:55.735: Se0/0/1 PPP: Sent IPCP AUTHOR Request
*May 21 18:26:55.735: Se0/0/1 LCP: Received AAA AUTHOR Response PASS
*May 21 18:26:55.739: Se0/0/1 IPCP: Received AAA AUTHOR Response PASS
*May 21 18:26:55.739: Se0/0/1 CHAP: O SUCCESS id 16 len 4
*May 21 18:26:55.739: Se0/0/1 CHAP: I SUCCESS id 49 len 4
```

CHAP uses a three-message exchange, as shown back in Figure 12-3, with a set of messages flowing for authentication in each direction by default. The three highlighted lines show the authentication process by which R1 authenticates R2; it begins with R1 sending a challenge message. The first highlighted message in Example 12-5 lists an "O," meaning "output." This indicates that the message is a challenge message and that it was sent from R1. The next highlighted message is the received response message (noted with an "I" for input), from R2. The last highlighted line is the third message, sent by R1, stating that the authentication was successful. You can see the same three messages for R2's authentication of R1 in the output as well, but those messages are not highlighted in the example.

When CHAP authentication fails, the **debug** output shows a couple of fairly obvious messages. Example 12-6 shows the results using the same two-router internetwork shown in Figure 12-4, this time with the passwords misconfigured, so CHAP fails.

Example 12-6 *Debug Messages Confirming the Failure of CHAP*

```
R1#debug ppp authentication
PPP authentication debugging is on
! Lines omitted for brevity
*May 21 18:24:03.171: Se0/0/1 PPP: Sent CHAP LOGIN Request
*May 21 18:24:03.171: Se0/0/1 PPP: Received LOGIN Response FAIL
*May 21 18:24:03.171: Se0/0/1 CHAP: O FAILURE id 15 len 25 msg is "Authentication failed"
```

Troubleshooting Layer 3 Problems

This chapter suggests that the best starting place to troubleshoot serial links is to ping the IP address of the router on the other end of the link—specifically, the IP address on the serial link. Interestingly, the serial link can be in an "up and up" state but the ping can still fail because of Layer 3 misconfiguration. In some cases, the ping may work, but the routing protocols may not be able to exchange routes. This short section examines the symptoms, which are slightly different depending on whether HDLC or PPP is used, and the root cause.

First, consider an HDLC link on which the physical and data-link details are working fine. In this case, both routers' interfaces are in an "up and up" state. However, if the IP addresses configured on the serial interfaces on the two routers are in different subnets, a ping to the IP address on the other end of the link will fail, because the routers do not have a matching route. For example, in Figure 12-4, if R1's serial IP address remained 192.168.2.1, and R2's was changed to 192.168.3.2 (instead of 192.168.2.2), still with a mask of /24, the two routers would have connected routes to different subnets. They would not have a route matching the opposite router's serial IP address.

Finding and fixing a mismatched subnet problem with HDLC links is relatively simple. You can find the problem by doing the usual first step of pinging the IP address on the other end of the link, and failing. If both interface status codes on both routers' interfaces are up, the problem is likely this mismatched IP subnet.

For PPP links, with the same IP address/mask misconfiguration, both routers' interfaces also are in an "up and up" state, but the ping to the other router's IP address actually works. As it turns out, a router using PPP advertises its serial interface IP address to the other router, with a /32 prefix, which is a route to reach just that one host. So, both routers have a route with which to route packets to the other end of the link, even though two routers on opposite ends of a serial link have mismatched their IP addresses. For example, in Figure 12-4 again, if R2's IP address were 192.168.4.2/24, while R1's remained 192.168.2.1/24, the two addresses would be in different subnets, but the pings would work because of PPP's advertisement of the host routes. Example 12-7 shows this exact scenario.

NOTE A route with a /32 prefix, representing a single host, is called a *host route*.

Example 12-7 *PPP Allowing a Ping over a Serial Link, Even with Mismatched Subnets*

```
R1#show ip route
Codes: C - connected, S - static, R - RIP, M - mobile, B - BGP
       D - EIGRP, EX - EIGRP external, O - OSPF, IA - OSPF inter area
       N1 - OSPF NSSA external type 1, N2 - OSPF NSSA external type 2
       E1 - OSPF external type 1, E2 - OSPF external type 2
       i - IS-IS, su - IS-IS summary, L1 - IS-IS level-1, L2 - IS-IS level-2
       ia - IS-IS inter area, * - candidate default, U - per-user static route
       o - ODR, P - periodic downloaded static route

C    192.168.1.0/24 is directly connected, FastEthernet0/0
C    192.168.2.0/24 is directly connected, Serial0/0/1
     192.168.4.0/32 is subnetted, 1 subnets
C       192.168.4.2 is directly connected, Serial0/0/1
R1#ping 192.168.4.2

Type escape sequence to abort.
Sending 5, 100-byte ICMP Echos to 192.168.4.2, timeout is 2 seconds:
!!!!!
Success rate is 100 percent (5/5), round-trip min/avg/max = 1/2/4 ms
```

The first highlighted line in the example shows the normal connected route on the serial link, for network 192.168.2.0/24. R1 thinks this subnet is the subnet connected to S0/0/1 because of R1's configured IP address (192.168.2.1/24). The second highlighted line shows the host route created by PPP, specifically for R2's new serial IP address (192.168.4.2). (R2 will have a similar route for 192.168.2.1/32, R1's serial IP address.) So, both routers have a route to allow them to forward packets to the IP address on the other end of the link, which allows the **ping** to the other side of the serial link to work in spite of the addresses on each end being in different subnets.

Although the **ping** to the other end of the link works, the routing protocols still do not advertise routes because of the IP subnet mismatch on the opposite ends of the link. So, when troubleshooting a network problem, do not assume that a serial interface in an up/up state is fully working, or even that a serial interface over which a ping works is fully working. Also make sure the routing protocol is exchanging routes and that the IP addresses are in the same subnet. Table 12-5 summarizes the behavior on HDLC and PPP links when the IP addresses on each end do not reside in the same subnet but no other problems exist.

Table 12-5 *Summary of Symptoms for Mismatched Subnets on Serial Links*

Symptoms When IP Addresses on a Serial Link Are in Different Subnets	HDLC	PPP
Does a ping of the other router's serial IP address work?	No	Yes
Can routing protocols exchange routes over the link?	No	No

Exam Preparation Tasks

Review All the Key Topics

Review the most important topics from this chapter, noted with the key topics icon. Table 12-6 lists these key topics and where each is discussed.

Key Topic

Table 12-6 *Key Topics for Chapter 12*

Key Topic Element	Description	Page Number
List	PPP features	436
Table 12-2	PPP LCP features	438
Figure 12-3	Comparison of messages sent by PAP and CHAP	441
List	Configuration checklist for CHAP	443
Table 12-3	List of typical combinations of serial interface status codes, and the typical general reason for each combination	445
List	Common reasons for Layer 1 serial link problems	446
Table 12-4	Common symptoms and reasons for common Layer 2 problems on serial links	447
Example 12-5	Sample **debug** messages showing a successful CHAP authentication process	449

Complete the Tables and Lists from Memory

Print a copy of Appendix J, "Memory Tables" (found on the CD), or at least the section for this chapter, and complete the tables and lists from memory. Appendix K, "Memory Tables Answer Key," also on the CD, includes completed tables and lists for you to check your work.

Definitions of Key Terms

Define the following key terms from this chapter, and check your answers in the glossary:

CHAP, IP control protocol, keepalive, Link Control Protocol, PAP

Command Reference to Check Your Memory

Although you should not necessarily memorize the information in the tables in this section, this section does include a reference for the configuration and EXEC commands covered in this chapter. Practically speaking, you should memorize the commands as a side effect of reading the chapter and doing all the activities in this exam preparation section. To see how well you have memorized the commands as a side effect of your other studies, cover the left side of the table, read the descriptions on the right side, and see if you remember the command.

Table 12-7 *Chapter 12 Configuration Command Reference*

Command	Description
**encapsulation {hdlc	ppp}**	Interface subcommand that defines the serial data-link protocol.
**ppp authentication {pap	chap	pap chap	chap pap}**	Interface subcommand that enables only PAP, only CHAP, or both (order-dependent).
username *name* **password** *secret*	Global command that sets the password that this router expects to use when authenticating the router with the listed hostname.

Table 12-8 *Chapter 12 EXEC Command Reference*

Command	Description
show interfaces [*type number*]	Lists statistics and details of interface configuration, including the encapsulation type.
debug ppp authentication	Generates messages for each step in the PAP or CHAP authentication process.
debug ppp negotiation	Generates **debug** messages for the LCP and NCP negotiation messages sent between the devices.

This chapter covers the following subjects:

Frame Relay Overview: This section introduces the terminology, functions, and purpose of Frame Relay protocols.

Frame Relay Addressing: This section examines the DLCI, the Frame Relay data-link address, and how it is used to transfer frames over the Frame Relay cloud.

Network Layer Concerns with Frame Relay: This section mainly examines the various options for the use of Layer 3 subnets over a Frame Relay network.

Controlling Speed and Discards in the Frame Relay Cloud: This short section explains a few features related to controlling the flow of data over the Frame Relay network.

CHAPTER 13

Frame Relay Concepts

Frame Relay remains the most popular WAN technology used today. However, its popularity is waning. It is being replaced mainly by virtual private network (VPN) technology of two main types: Internet VPNs, which use the Internet to transport packets, and Multiprotocol Label Switching (MPLS) VPNs, which follow the same basic service model as Frame Relay, typically offered by the same Frame Relay providers, but with significant technical advantages. However, Frame Relay is still used by many companies today, and it can also be used to connect to MPLS and Internet VPNs, so Frame Relay will be an important networking topic for some time.

Frame Relay most closely compares to the OSI data link layer (Layer 2). If you remember that the word "frame" describes the data link layer protocol data unit (PDU), it will be easy to remember that Frame Relay relates to OSI Layer 2. Like other data-link protocols, Frame Relay can be used to deliver packets (Layer 3 PDUs) between routers. Frame Relay protocol headers and trailers are simply used to let a packet traverse the Frame Relay network, just like Ethernet headers and trailers are used to help a packet traverse an Ethernet segment.

This chapter describes Frame Relay protocol details. Chapter 14, "Frame Relay Configuration and Troubleshooting," examines the configuration, verification, and troubleshooting of Frame Relay networks.

"Do I Know This Already?" Quiz

The "Do I Know This Already?" quiz allows you to assess whether you should read the entire chapter. If you miss no more than one of these eight self-assessment questions, you might want to move ahead to the "Exam Preparation Tasks" section. Table 13-1 lists the major headings in this chapter and the "Do I Know This Already?" quiz questions covering the material in those sections. This helps you assess your knowledge of these specific areas. The answers to the "Do I Know This Already?" quiz appear in Appendix A.

Table 13-1 *"Do I Know This Already?" Foundation Topics Section-to-Question Mapping*

Foundation Topics Section	Questions
Frame Relay Overview	1–3
Frame Relay Addressing	4 and 5
Network Layer Concerns with Frame Relay	6 and 7
Controlling Speed and Discards in the Frame Relay Cloud	8

1. Which of the following is a protocol used between the Frame Relay DTE and the Frame Relay switch?

   a. VC

   b. CIR

   c. LMI

   d. Q.921

   e. DLCI

   f. FRF.5

   g. Encapsulation

2. Which of the following statements about Frame Relay are true?

   a. The DTE typically sits at the customer site.

   b. Routers send LMI messages to each other to signal the status of a VC.

   c. A frame's source DLCI must remain unchanged, but the frame's destination DLCI is allowed to change, as the frame traverses the Frame Relay cloud.

   d. The Frame Relay encapsulation type on the sending router should match the encapsulation type on the receiving router for the receiving router to be able to understand the frame's contents.

3. What does DLCI stand for?

   a. Data-link connection identifier

   b. Data-link connection indicator

   c. Data-link circuit identifier

   d. Data-link circuit indicator

4. Router R1 receives a frame from router R2 with DLCI value 222 in it. Which of the following statements about this network is the most accurate?

   a. 222 represents Router R1.

   b. 222 represents Router R2.

   c. 222 is the local DLCI on R1 that represents the VC between R1 and R2.

   d. 222 is the local DLCI on R2 that represents the VC between R1 and R2.

5. A Frame Relay planning diagram shows the number 101 beside R1, 102 by R2, 103 by R3, and 104 by R4. No other DLCIs are listed. The lead network engineer tells you that the planning diagram uses global DLCI addressing and that a full mesh of VCs exists. Which of the following are true?

   a. Frames sent by R1 to R2, as they cross R2's access link, have DLCI 102.

   b. Frames sent by R1 to R2, as they cross R2's access link, have DLCI 101.

   c. Frames sent by R3 to R2, as they cross R3's access link, have DLCI 102.

   d. Frames sent by R3 to R1, as they cross R3's access link, have DLCI 102.

6. FredsCo has five sites, with routers connected to the same Frame Relay network. Virtual circuits (VC) have been defined between each pair of routers. What is the fewest subnets that FredsCo could use on the Frame Relay network?

   a. 1

   b. 2

   c. 3

   d. 4

   e. 5

   f. 10

7. BarneyCo has five sites, with routers connected to the same Frame Relay network. VCs have been defined between each pair of routers. Barney, the company president, will fire anyone who configures Frame Relay without using point-to-point subinterfaces. What is the fewest subnets that BarneyCo could use on the Frame Relay network?

   a. 1

   b. 4

   c. 8

   d. 10

   e. 12

   f. 15

8. R1 sends a Frame Relay frame over a VC to router R2. About the same time, a Frame Relay switch notices that too many packets are trying to exit the Frame Relay network over the access link connected to R2. Which of the following is the most likely result that could be caused by this scenario?

a. R1 eventually receives a frame with BECN set.

b. R1 eventually receives a frame with FECN set.

c. R1 eventually receives a frame with DE set.

d. None of the other answers is correct.

Foundation Topics

With point-to-point serial links, a company orders a leased line, or circuit, between two points. The telco creates the circuit, installing a two-pair (four-wire) cable into the buildings on either end of the circuit. The telco creates the circuit so that it will run at the preset speed requested by the customer, typically some multiple of 64 kbps. As soon as the Telcos' cable has been connected to a CSU/DSU, and a router, on each end of the circuit, the routers have a dedicated physical link, with the ability to send data in both directions simultaneously.

Frame Relay is a set of WAN standards that create a more efficient WAN service as compared to point-to-point links, while still allowing pairs of routers to send data directly to each other. With leased lines, each leased line requires a serial interface on each router and a separate (and expensive) physical circuit built by the telco. Frame Relay supports the ability to send data to multiple remote routers over a single physical WAN circuit. For example, a company with one central site and ten remote sites would require ten leased lines to communicate with the main site and ten serial interfaces on the central site router. With Frame Relay, the main site could have a single leased line connecting it to the Frame Relay service, and a single serial interface on the router at the central site, and still be able to communicate with each of the ten remote-site routers.

The first section of this chapter focuses on the basics of Frame Relay, including a lot of new terminology. The second section examines Frame Relay data-link addressing. This topic requires some attention because Frame Relay addresses are needed for both router configuration and troubleshooting. The last two major sections of this chapter examine some network layer concerns when using Frame Relay, along with a few features that impact the speed and frame discard rates inside the Frame Relay cloud.

Frame Relay Overview

Frame Relay networks provide more features and benefits than simple point-to-point WAN links, but to do that, Frame Relay protocols are more detailed. For example, Frame Relay networks are multiaccess networks, which means that more than two devices can attach to the network, similar to LANs. Unlike with LANs, you cannot send a data link layer broadcast over Frame Relay. Therefore, Frame Relay networks are called *nonbroadcast multiaccess (NBMA)* networks. Also, because Frame Relay is multiaccess, it requires the use of an address that identifies to which remote router each frame is addressed.

Figure 13-1 outlines the basic physical topology and related terminology in a Frame Relay network.

Figure 13-1 *Frame Relay Components*

Figure 13-1 shows the most basic components of a Frame Relay network. A leased line is installed between the router and a nearby Frame Relay switch; this link is called the *access link*. To ensure that the link is working, the device outside the Frame Relay network, called the *data terminal equipment* (*DTE*), exchanges regular messages with the Frame Relay switch. These keepalive messages, along with other messages, are defined by the Frame Relay *Local Management Interface* (*LMI*) protocol. The routers are considered DTE, and the Frame Relay switches are *data communications equipment* (*DCE*).

Whereas Figure 13-1 shows the physical connectivity at each connection to the Frame Relay network, Figure 13-2 shows the logical, or virtual, end-to-end connectivity associated with a virtual circuit (VC).

Figure 13-2 *Frame Relay PVC Concepts*

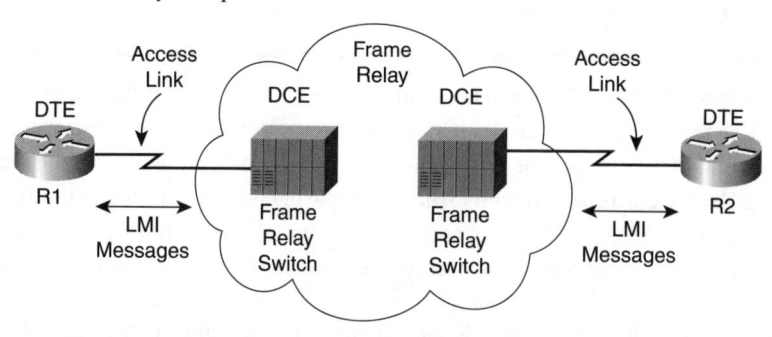

The logical communications path between each pair of DTEs is a VC. The dashed line in the figure represents a single VC; this book uses a thick dashed line style to make sure you notice the line easily. Typically, the service provider preconfigures all the required details of a VC; predefined VCs are called permanent virtual circuits (PVC).

Routers use the data-link connection identifier (DLCI) as the Frame Relay address; it identifies the VC over which the frame should travel. So, in Figure 13-2, when R1 needs to forward a packet to R2, R1 encapsulates the Layer 3 packet into a Frame Relay header and trailer and then sends the frame. The Frame Relay header includes the correct DLCI so that the provider's Frame Relay switches correctly forward the frame to R2.

Table 13-2 lists the components shown in Figures 13-1 and 13-2 and some associated terms. After the table, the most important features of Frame Relay are described in further detail.

Table 13-2 *Frame Relay Terms and Concepts*

Key Topic

Term	Description
Virtual circuit (VC)	A logical concept that represents the path that frames travel between DTEs. VCs are particularly useful when you compare Frame Relay to leased physical circuits.
Permanent virtual circuit (PVC)	A predefined VC. A PVC can be equated to a leased line in concept.
Switched virtual circuit (SVC)	A VC that is set up dynamically when needed. An SVC can be equated to a dial connection in concept.
Data terminal equipment (DTE)	DTEs are connected to a Frame Relay service from a telecommunications company. They typically reside at sites used by the company buying the Frame Relay service.
Data communications equipment (DCE)	Frame Relay switches are DCE devices. DCEs are also known as data circuit-terminating equipment. DCEs are typically in the service provider's network.
Access link	The leased line between the DTE and DCE.
Access rate (AR)	The speed at which the access link is clocked. This choice affects the connection's price.
Committed Information Rate (CIR)	The speed at which bits can be sent over a VC, according to the business contract between the customer and provider.
Data-link connection identifier (DLCI)	A Frame Relay address used in Frame Relay headers to identify the VC.
Nonbroadcast multiaccess (NBMA)	A network in which broadcasts are not supported, but more than two devices can be connected.
Local Management Interface (LMI)	The protocol used between a DCE and DTE to manage the connection. Signaling messages for SVCs, PVC status messages, and keepalives are all LMI messages.

Frame Relay Standards

The definitions for Frame Relay are contained in documents from the International Telecommunications Union (ITU) and the American National Standards Institute (ANSI). The Frame Relay Forum (http://www.frforum.com), a vendor consortium, also defines several Frame Relay specifications, many of which predate the original ITU and ANSI specifications, with the ITU and ANSI picking up many of the forum's standards. Table 13-3 lists the most important of these specifications.

Table 13-3 *Frame Relay Protocol Specifications*

What the Specification Defines	ITU Document	ANSI Document
Data-link specifications, including LAPF header/trailer	Q.922 Annex A (Q.922-A)	T1.618
PVC management, LMI	Q.933 Annex A (Q.933-A)	T1.617 Annex D (T1.617-D)
SVC signaling	Q.933	T1.617
Multiprotocol encapsulation (originated in RFC 1490/2427)	Q.933 Annex E (Q.933-E)	T1.617 Annex F (T1.617-F)

Virtual Circuits

Frame Relay provides significant advantages over simply using point-to-point leased lines. The primary advantage has to do with virtual circuits. Consider Figure 13-3, which shows a typical Frame Relay network with three sites.

Figure 13-3 *Typical Frame Relay Network with Three Sites*

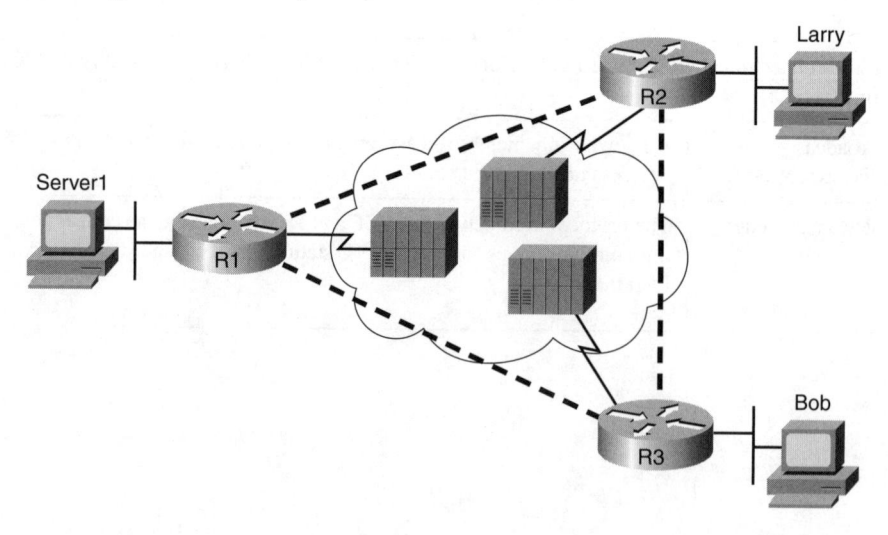

A virtual circuit defines a logical path between two Frame Relay DTEs. The term *virtual circuit* describes the concept well. It acts like a point-to-point circuit, providing the ability to send data between two endpoints over a WAN. There is no physical circuit directly between the two endpoints, so it's virtual. For example, R1 terminates two VCs—one whose other endpoint is R2, and one whose other endpoint is R3. R1 can send traffic directly to either of the other two routers by sending it over the appropriate VC.

VCs share the access link and the Frame Relay network. For example, both VCs terminating at R1 use the same access link. In fact, many customers share the same Frame Relay network. Originally, people with leased-line networks were reluctant to migrate to Frame Relay, because they would be competing with other customers for the provider's capacity inside the cloud. To address these fears, Frame Relay is designed with the concept of a committed information rate (CIR). Each VC has a CIR, which is a guarantee by the provider that a particular VC gets at least that much bandwidth. So you can migrate from a leased line to Frame Relay, getting a CIR of at least as much bandwidth as you previously had with your leased line.

Interestingly, even with a three-site network, it's probably less expensive to use Frame Relay than to use point-to-point links. Imagine an organization with 100 sites that needs any-to-any connectivity. How many leased lines are required? 4950! And besides that, the organization would need 99 serial interfaces per router if it used point-to-point leased lines. With Frame Relay, an organization could have 100 access links to local Frame Relay switches, one per router, and have 4950 VCs running over them. That requires a lot fewer actual physical links, and you would need only one serial interface on each router!

Service providers can build their Frame Relay networks more cost-effectively than for leased lines. As you would expect, that makes it less expensive for the Frame Relay customer as well. For connecting many WAN sites, Frame Relay is simply more cost-effective than leased lines.

Two types of VCs are allowed—permanent (PVC) and switched (SVC). PVCs are predefined by the provider; SVCs are created dynamically. PVCs are by far the more popular of the two. Frame Relay providers seldom offer SVCs as a service. (The rest of this chapter and Chapter 14 ignore SVCs.)

When the Frame Relay network is engineered, the design might not include a VC between each pair of sites. Figure 13-3 includes PVCs between each pair of sites; this is called a full-mesh Frame Relay network. When not all pairs have a direct PVC, it is called a partial-mesh network. Figure 13-4 shows the same network as Figure 13-3, but this time with a partial mesh and only two PVCs. This is typical when R1 is at the main site and R2 and R3 are at remote offices that rarely need to communicate directly.

Figure 13-4   *Typical Partial-Mesh Frame Relay Network*

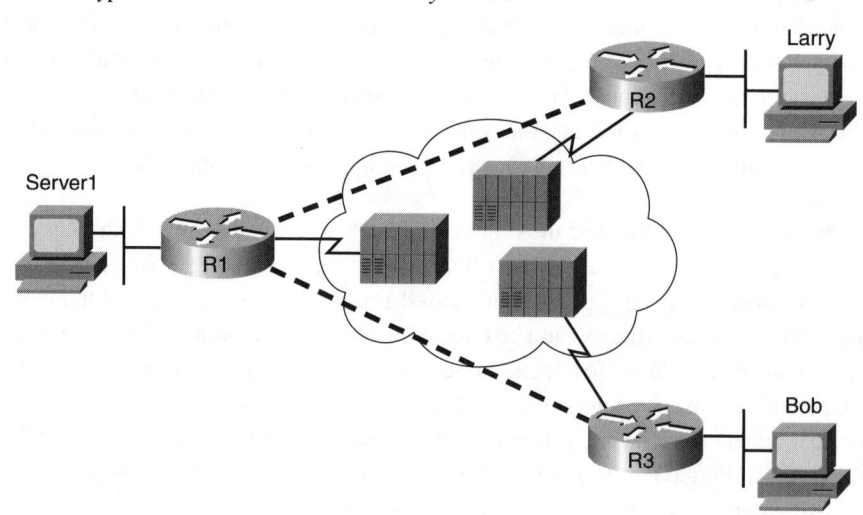

The partial mesh has some advantages and disadvantages compared to a full mesh. The primary advantage is that partial mesh is cheaper, because the provider charges per VC. The downside is that traffic from R2's site to R3's site must go to R1 first and then be forwarded. If that's a small amount of traffic, it's a small price to pay. If it's a lot of traffic, a full mesh is probably worth the extra money, because traffic going between two remote sites would have to cross R1's access link twice.

One conceptual hurdle with PVCs is that there is typically a single access link across which multiple PVCs flow. For example, consider Figure 13-4 from R1's perspective. Server1 sends a packet to Larry. It comes across the Ethernet. R1 gets it and matches Larry's routing table, which tells him to send the packet out Serial0, which is R1's access link. He encapsulates the packet in a Frame Relay header and trailer and then sends it. Which PVC does it use? The Frame Relay switch should forward it to R2, but why does it?

To solve this problem, Frame Relay uses an address to differentiate one PVC from another. This address is called a data-link connection identifier (DLCI). The name is descriptive: The address is for an OSI Layer 2 (data-link) protocol, and it identifies a VC, which is sometimes called a *virtual connection*. So, in this example, R1 uses the DLCI that identifies the PVC to R2, so the provider forwards the frame correctly over the PVC to R2. To send frames to R3, R1 uses the DLCI that identifies the VC for R3. DLCIs and how they work are covered in more detail later in this chapter.

LMI and Encapsulation Types

When you're first learning about Frame Relay, it's often easy to confuse the LMI and the encapsulation used with Frame Relay. The LMI is a definition of the messages used between the DTE (for example, a router) and the DCE (for example, the Frame Relay switch owned by the service provider). The encapsulation defines the headers used by a DTE to communicate some information to the DTE on the other end of a VC. The switch and its connected router care about using the same LMI; the switch does not care about the encapsulation. The endpoint routers (DTE) do care about the encapsulation.

The most important LMI message relating to topics on the exam is the LMI status inquiry message. Status messages perform two key functions:

- They perform a keepalive function between the DTE and DCE. If the access link has a problem, the absence of keepalive messages implies that the link is down.

- They signal whether a PVC is active or inactive. Even though each PVC is predefined, its status can change. An access link might be up, but one or more VCs could be down. The router needs to know which VCs are up and which are down. It learns that information from the switch using LMI status messages.

Three LMI protocol options are available in Cisco IOS software: Cisco, ITU, and ANSI. Each LMI option is slightly different and therefore is incompatible with the other two. As long as both the DTE and DCE on each end of an access link use the same LMI standard, LMI works fine.

The differences between LMI types are subtle. For example, the Cisco LMI calls for the use of DLCI 1023, whereas ANSI T1.617-D and ITU Q.933-A specify DLCI 0. Some of the messages have different fields in their headers. The DTE simply needs to know which of the three LMIs to use so that it can use the same one as the local switch.

Configuring the LMI type is easy. Today's most popular option is to use the default LMI setting. This setting uses the LMI autosense feature, in which the router simply figures out which LMI type the switch is using. So you can simply let the router autosense the LMI and never bother coding the LMI type. If you choose to configure the LMI type, the router disables the autosense feature.

Table 13-4 outlines the three LMI types, their origin, and the keyword used in the Cisco IOS software **frame-relay lmi-type** interface subcommand.

Table 13-4   *Frame Relay LMI Types*

Name	Document	IOS LMI-Type Parameter
Cisco	Proprietary	**cisco**
ANSI	T1.617 Annex D	**ansi**
ITU	Q.933 Annex A	**q933a**

A Frame Relay-connected router encapsulates each Layer 3 packet inside a Frame Relay header and trailer before it is sent out an access link. The header and trailer are defined by the Link Access Procedure Frame Bearer Services (LAPF) specification, ITU Q.922-A. The sparse LAPF framing provides error detection with an FCS in the trailer, as well as the DLCI, DE, FECN, and BECN fields in the header (which are discussed later). Figure 13-5 diagrams the frame.

Figure 13-5   *LAPF Header*

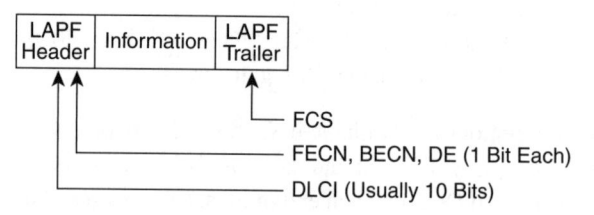

However, the LAPF header and trailer do not provide all the fields typically needed by routers. In particular, Figure 13-5 does not show a Protocol Type field. Each data-link header needs a field to define the type of packet that follows the data-link header. If Frame Relay is using only the LAPF header, DTEs (including routers) cannot support multiprotocol traffic, because there is no way to identify the type of protocol in the Information field.

Two solutions were created to compensate for the lack of a Protocol Type field in the standard Frame Relay header:

■   Cisco and three other companies created an additional header, which comes between the LAPF header and the Layer 3 packet shown in Figure 13-5. It includes a 2-byte Protocol Type field, with values matching the same field Cisco uses for HDLC.

■   RFC 1490 (which was later superceded by RFC 2427; you should know both numbers), *Multiprotocol Interconnect over Frame Relay*, defined the second solution. RFC 1490 was written to ensure multivendor interoperability between Frame Relay DTEs. This RFC defines a similar header, also placed between the LAPF header and

Layer 3 packet, and includes a Protocol Type field as well as many other options. ITU and ANSI later incorporated RFC 1490 headers into their Q.933 Annex E and T1.617 Annex F specifications, respectively.

Figure 13-6 outlines these two alternatives.

Figure 13-6   *Cisco and RFC 1490/2427 Encapsulation*

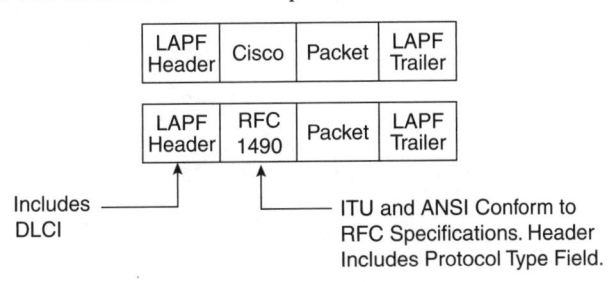

DTEs use and react to the fields specified by these two types of encapsulation, but Frame Relay switches ignore these fields. *Because the frames flow from DTE to DTE, both DTEs should agree on the encapsulation used. The switches don't care.* However, each VC can use a different encapsulation. In the configuration, the encapsulation created by Cisco is called **cisco**, and the other one is called **ietf**.

Now that you have a broad understanding of Frame Relay concepts and terminology, the next section takes a much closer look at Frame Relay DLCIs.

Frame Relay Addressing

Frame Relay defines the rules by which devices deliver Frame Relay frames across a Frame Relay network. Because a router uses a single access link that has many VCs connecting it to many routers, there must be something to identify each of the remote routers—in other words, an address. The DLCI is the Frame Relay address.

DLCIs work slightly differently from the other data-link addresses covered on the CCNA exams. This difference is mainly because of the use of the DLCI and the fact that *the header has a single DLCI field, not both Source and Destination DLCI fields.*

Frame Relay Local Addressing

You should understand a few characteristics of DLCIs before we get into their use. Frame Relay DLCIs are locally significant; this means that the addresses need to be unique only on the local access link. A popular analogy that explains local addressing is that there can be only a single street address of 2000 Pennsylvania Avenue in Washington, DC, but there can be a 2000 Pennsylvania Avenue in every town in the United States. Likewise, DLCIs must be unique on each access link, but the same DLCI numbers can be used on every access link in your network. For example, in Figure 13-7, notice that DLCI 40 is used on two access links to describe two different PVCs. No conflict exists, because DLCI 40 is used on two different access links.

Figure 13-7   *Frame Relay Addressing with Router A Sending to Routers B and C*

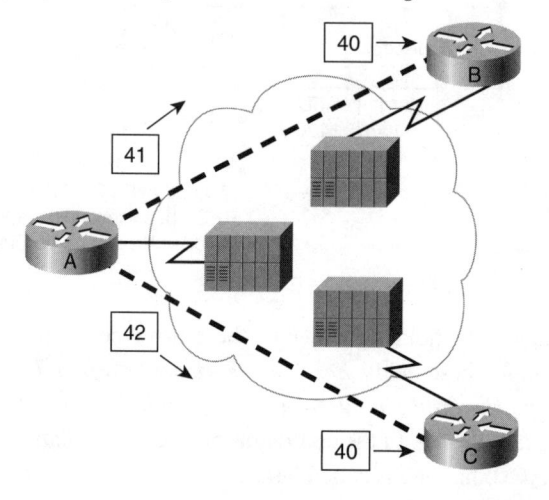

Local addressing, which is the common term for the fact that DLCIs are locally significant, is a fact. It is how Frame Relay works. Simply put, a single access link cannot use the same DLCI to represent multiple VCs on the same access link. Otherwise, the Frame Relay switch would not know how to forward frames correctly. For instance, in Figure 13-7, Router A must use different DLCI values for the PVCs on its local access link (41 and 42 in this instance).

Frame Relay Global Addressing

Most people get confused about DLCIs the first time they think about the local significance of DLCIs and the existence of only a single DLCI field in the Frame Relay header. Global addressing solves this problem by making DLCI addressing look like LAN addressing in concept. Global addressing is simply a way of choosing DLCI numbers when planning a Frame Relay network so that working with DLCIs is much easier. Because local addressing is a fact, global addressing does not change these rules. Global addressing just makes DLCI assignment more obvious—as soon as you get used to it.

Here's how global addressing works: The service provider hands out a planning spreadsheet and a diagram. Figure 13-8 is an example of such a diagram, with the global DLCIs shown.

Figure 13-8   *Frame Relay Global DLCIs*

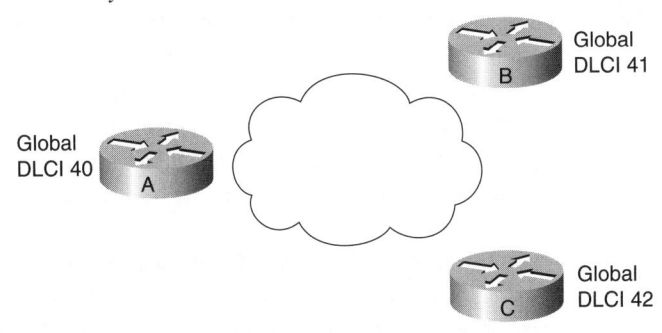

Global addressing is planned as shown in Figure 13-8, with the DLCIs placed in Frame Relay frames as shown in Figure 13-9. For example, Router A uses DLCI 41 when sending a frame to Router B, because Router B's global DLCI is 41. Likewise, Router A uses DLCI 42 when sending frames over the VC to Router C. The nice thing is that global addressing is much more logical to most people, because it works like a LAN, with a single MAC address for each device. On a LAN, if the MAC addresses are MAC-A, MAC-B, and MAC-C for the three routers, Router A uses destination address MAC-B when sending frames to Router B and uses MAC-C as the destination to reach Router C. Likewise, with global DLCIs 40, 41, and 42 used for Routers A, B, and C, respectively, the same concept applies. Because DLCIs address VCs, the logic is something like this when Router A sends a frame to Router B: "Hey, local switch! When you get this frame, send it over the VC that we agreed to number with DLCI 41." Figure 13-9 outlines this example.

Figure 13-9   *Frame Relay Global Addressing from the Sender's Perspective*

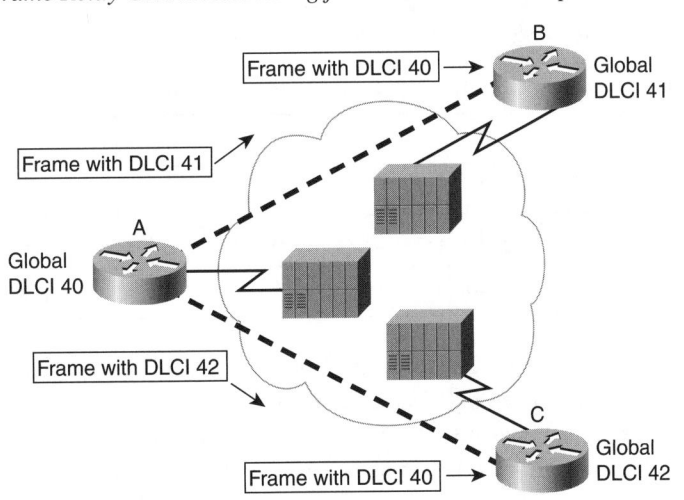

Key Topic

Router A sends frames with DLCI 41, and they reach the local switch. The local switch sees the DLCI field and forwards the frame through the Frame Relay network until it reaches the switch connected to Router B. Then Router B's local switch forwards the frame out the access link to Router B. The same process happens between Router A and Router C when Router A uses DLCI 42. The beauty of global addressing is that you think of each router as having an address, like LAN addressing. If you want to send a frame to someone, you put his or her DLCI in the header, and the network delivers the frame to the correct DTE.

The final key to global addressing is that the Frame Relay switches actually change the DLCI value before delivering the frame. Did you notice that Figure 13-9 shows a different DLCI value as the frames are received by Routers B and C? For example, Router A sends a frame to Router B, and Router A puts DLCI 41 in the frame. The last switch changes the field to DLCI 40 before forwarding it to Router B. The result is that when Routers B and C receive their frames, the DLCI value is actually the sender's DLCI. Why? Well, when Router B receives the frame, because the DLCI is 40, it knows that the frame came in on the PVC between itself and Router A. In general, the following are true:

- The sender treats the DLCI field as a destination address, using the destination's global DLCI in the header.

- The receiver thinks of the DLCI field as the source address, because it contains the global DLCI of the frame's sender.

Figure 13-9 describes what happens in a typical Frame Relay network. Service providers supply a planning spreadsheet and diagrams with global DLCIs listed. Table 13-5 gives you an organized view of what DLCIs are used in Figure 13-9.

Table 13-5 *DLCI Swapping in the Frame Relay Cloud of Figure 13-9*

The Frame Sent by Router	With DLCI Field	Is Delivered to Router	With DLCI Field
A	41	B	40
A	42	C	40
B	40	A	41
C	40	A	42

Global addressing makes DLCI addressing more intuitive for most people. It also makes router configuration more straightforward and lets you add new sites more conveniently. For instance, examine Figure 13-10, which adds Routers D and E to the network shown in Figure 13-9. The service provider simply states that global DLCIs 43 and 44 are used for these two routers. If these two routers also have only one PVC to Router A, all the DLCI planning is complete. You know that Router D and Router E use DLCI 40 to reach Router A and that Router A uses DLCI 43 to reach Router D and DLCI 44 to reach Router E.

Figure 13-10 *Adding Frame Relay Sites: Global Addressing*

The remaining examples in this chapter use global addressing in any planning diagrams unless otherwise stated. One practical way to determine whether the diagram lists the local DLCIs or the global DLCI convention is this: If two VCs terminate at the same DTE, and a single DLCI is shown, it probably represents the global DLCI convention. If one DLCI is shown per VC, local DLCI addressing is depicted.

Now that you have a better understanding of how Frame Relay uses DLCIs to address each VC, causing the correct delivery of frames over a Frame Relay cloud, the next section moves up to Layer 3, examining the IP addressing conventions that can be used over Frame Relay.

Network Layer Concerns with Frame Relay

Frame Relay networks have both similarities and differences as compared to LAN and point-to-point WAN links. These differences introduce some additional considerations for passing Layer 3 packets across a Frame Relay network. You need to concern yourself with a couple of key issues relating to Layer 3 flows over Frame Relay:

■   Choices for Layer 3 addresses on Frame Relay interfaces

■   Broadcast handling

In particular, the Frame Relay implementation in Cisco defines three different options for assigning subnets and IP addresses on Frame Relay interfaces:

- One subnet containing all Frame Relay DTEs

- One subnet per VC

- A hybrid of the first two options

This section examines the three main options for IP addressing over Frame Relay, as well as broadcast handling, which impacts how routing protocols work over Frame Relay.

Frame Relay Layer 3 Addressing: One Subnet Containing All Frame Relay DTEs

Figure 13-11 shows the first alternative, which is to use a single subnet for the Frame Relay network. This figure shows a fully meshed Frame Relay network because the single-subnet option is typically used when a full mesh of VCs exists. In a full mesh, each router has a VC to every other router, meaning that each router can send frames directly to every other router. This more closely resembles how a LAN works. So, a single subnet can be used for all the routers' Frame Relay interfaces, as configured on the routers' serial interfaces. Table 13-6 summarizes the addresses used in Figure 13-11.

Figure 13-11 *Full Mesh with IP Addresses*

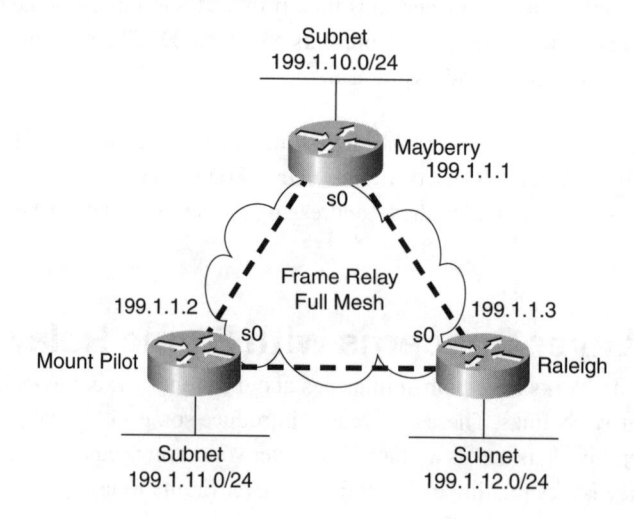

Table 13-6 *IP Addresses with No Subinterfaces*

Router	IP Address of Frame Relay Interface
Mayberry	199.1.1.1
Mount Pilot	199.1.1.2
Raleigh	199.1.1.3

The single-subnet alternative is straightforward, and it conserves your IP address space. It also looks like what you are used to with LANs, which makes it easier to conceptualize. Unfortunately, most companies build partial-mesh Frame Relay networks, and the single-subnet option has some deficiencies when the network is a partial mesh.

Frame Relay Layer 3 Addressing: One Subnet Per VC

The second IP addressing alternative, having a single subnet for each VC, works better with a partially meshed Frame Relay network, as shown in Figure 13-12. Boston cannot forward frames directly to Charlotte, because no VC is defined between the two. This is a more typical Frame Relay network, because most organizations with many sites tend to group applications on servers at a few centralized locations, and most of the traffic is between each remote site and those servers.

Figure 13-12 *Partial Mesh with IP Addresses*

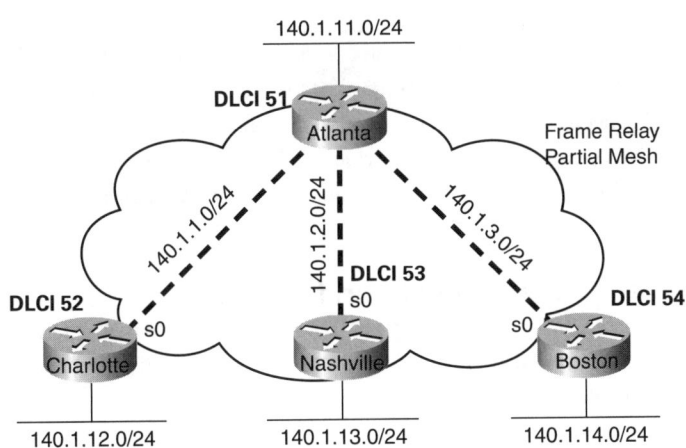

The single-subnet-per-VC alternative matches the logic behind a set of point-to-point links. Using multiple subnets instead of one larger subnet wastes some IP addresses, but it overcomes some issues with distance vector routing protocols.

Table 13-7 shows the IP addresses for the partially meshed Frame Relay network shown in Figure 13-12.

Table 13-7   *IP Addresses with Point-to-Point Subinterfaces*

Router	Subnet	IP Address
Atlanta	140.1.1.0	140.1.1.1
Charlotte	140.1.1.0	140.1.1.2
Atlanta	140.1.2.0	140.1.2.1
Nashville	140.1.2.0	140.1.2.3
Atlanta	140.1.3.0	140.1.3.1
Boston	140.1.3.0	140.1.3.4

Cisco IOS Software has a configuration feature called *subinterfaces* that creates a logical subdivision of a physical interface. Subinterfaces allow the Atlanta router to have three IP addresses associated with its Serial0 physical interface by configuring three separate subinterfaces. A router can treat each subinterface, and the VC associated with it, as if it were a point-to-point serial link. Each of the three subinterfaces of Serial0 on Atlanta would be assigned a different IP address from Table 13-7 (Chapter 14 shows several sample configurations).

> **NOTE**   The example uses IP address prefixes of /24 to keep the math simple. In production networks, point-to-point subinterfaces typically use a prefix of /30 (mask 255.255.255.252), because that allows for only two valid IP addresses—the exact number needed on a point-to-point subinterface. Of course, using different masks in the same network means your routing protocol must also support VLSM.

Frame Relay Layer 3 Addressing: Hybrid Approach

The third alternative for Layer 3 addressing is a hybrid of the first two alternatives. Consider Figure 13-13, which shows a trio of routers with VCs between each of them, as well as two other VCs to remote sites.

Two options exist for Layer 3 addressing in this case. The first is to treat each VC as a separate Layer 3 group. In this case, five subnets are needed for the Frame Relay network. However, Routers A, B, and C create a smaller full mesh between each other. This allows Routers A, B, and C to use one subnet. The other two VCs—one between Routers A and D and one between Routers A and E—are treated as two separate Layer 3 groups. The result is a total of three subnets.

Figure 13-13 *Hybrid of Full and Partial Mesh*

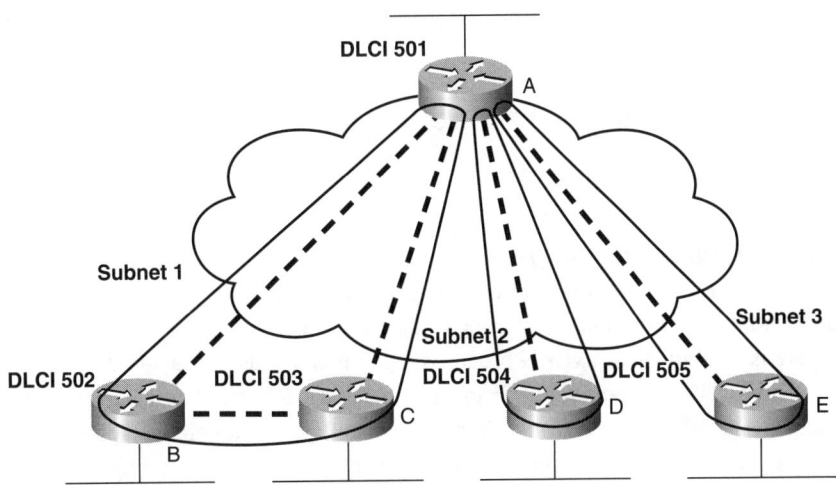

To accomplish either style of Layer 3 addressing in this third and final case, subinterfaces are used. Point-to-point subinterfaces are used when a single VC is considered to be all that is in the group—for instance, between Routers A and D and between Routers A and E. Multipoint subinterfaces are used when more than two routers are considered to be in the same group—for instance, with Routers A, B, and C.

Multipoint subinterfaces logically terminate more than one VC. In fact, the name "multipoint" implies the function, because more than one remote site can be reached via a VC associated with a multipoint subinterface.

Table 13-8 summarizes the addresses and subinterfaces that are used in Figure 13-13.

Table 13-8 *IP Addresses with Point-to-Point and Multipoint Subinterfaces*

Router	Subnet	IP Address	Subinterface Type
A	140.1.1.0/24	140.1.1.1	Multipoint
B	140.1.1.0/24	140.1.1.2	Multipoint
C	140.1.1.0/24	140.1.1.3	Multipoint
A	140.1.2.0/24	140.1.2.1	Point-to-point
D	140.1.2.0/24	140.1.2.4	Point-to-point
A	140.1.3.0/24	140.1.3.1	Point-to-point
E	140.1.3.0/24	140.1.3.5	Point-to-point

What will you see in a real network? Most of the time, point-to-point subinterfaces are used, with a single subnet per PVC. However, you should understand all options for the CCNA exams.

> **NOTE**   Chapter 14 provides full configurations for all three cases illustrated in Figures 13-11, 13-12, and 13-13.

Layer 3 Broadcast Handling

After contending with Layer 3 addressing over Frame Relay, the next consideration is how to deal with Layer 3 broadcasts. Frame Relay can send copies of a broadcast over all VCs, but there is no equivalent to LAN broadcasts. In other words, no capability exists for a Frame Relay DTE to send a single frame into the Frame Relay network and have that frame replicated and delivered across multiple VCs to multiple destinations. However, routers need to send broadcasts for several features to work. In particular, routing protocol updates are either broadcasts or multicasts.

The solution to the Frame Relay broadcast dilemma has two parts. First, Cisco IOS software sends copies of the broadcasts across each VC, assuming that you have configured the router to forward these necessary broadcasts. If there are only a few VCs, this is not a big problem. However, if hundreds of VCs terminate in one router, for each broadcast, hundreds of copies could be sent.

As the second part of the solution, the router tries to minimize the impact of the first part of the solution. The router places the copies of the broadcasts in a different output queue than the one for user traffic so that the user does not experience a large spike in delay each time a broadcast is replicated and sent over every VC. Cisco IOS software can also be configured to limit the amount of bandwidth that is used for these replicated broadcasts.

Although such scalability issues are more likely to appear on the CCNP Routing exam, a short example shows the significance of broadcast overhead. If a router knows 1000 routes, uses RIP, and has 50 VCs, 1.072 MB of RIP updates is sent every 30 seconds. That averages out to 285 kbps. (The math is as follows: 536-byte RIP packets, with 25 routes in each packet, for 40 packets per update, with copies sent over 50 VCs. 536 * 40 * 50 = 1.072 MB per update interval. 1.072 * 8 / 30 seconds = 285 kbps.) That's a lot of overhead!

Knowing how to tell the router to forward these broadcasts to each VC is covered in the section "Frame Relay Configuration and Verification" in Chapter 14. The issues that relate to dealing with the volume of these updates are more likely a topic for the CCNP and CCIE exams.

Controlling Speed and Discards in the Frame Relay Cloud

This chapter has already examined the most important topics in Frame Relay relative to how Frame Relay delivers frames over the network. This final short section examines a few strategies you can use to fine-tune the operation of a Frame Relay network.

The Frame Relay header includes three single-bit flags that Frame Relay can use to help control what occurs inside the Frame Relay cloud. These bits can be particularly useful when one or more sites use an access rate—the clock rate of the access link—that far exceeds the CIR of a VC. For example, if a router has a T1 Frame Relay access link, but only a 128-kbps committed information rate (CIR) on a VC that goes over that link, the router can send a lot more data into the Frame Relay network than the business contract with the Frame Relay provider allows. This section examines 3 bits that impact how the switches might help control the network when the network gets congested because of these speed mismatches—namely, the Forward Explicit Congestion Notification (FECN), Backward Explicit Congestion Notification (BECN), and Discard Eligibility (DE) bits.

FECN and BECN

To deal with instances in which a router can send more data than the VC allows, IOS includes a feature called *Traffic Shaping*, which enables a router to send some packets, wait, send more, wait again, and so on. Traffic Shaping allows the router to decrease the overall rate of sending bits to a speed slower than the access rate, and maybe even as low as the CIR of a VC. For instance, with a T1 access link and a 128-kbps CIR, Traffic Shaping could be defined to send an average of only 256 kbps over that VC. The idea is that the Frame Relay provider will probably discard a lot of traffic if the router averages sending data over that VC at close to T1 speed, which is 12 times the CIR in this case. However, the Frame Relay provider may not discard traffic if the average rate is only 256 kbps—twice the CIR in this case.

You can set Traffic Shaping to use a single speed, or to adapt to range between two speed settings. When it's configured to adapt between two speeds, if the network is not congested, the higher speed is used; when the network is congested, the router adapts so that it shapes using the lower rate.

To adapt the shaping rates, the routers need a way to know whether congestion is occurring—and that's where FECN and BECN are used. Figure 13-14 shows the basic use of the FECN and BECN bits.

Figure 13-14   *Basic Operation of FECN and BECN*

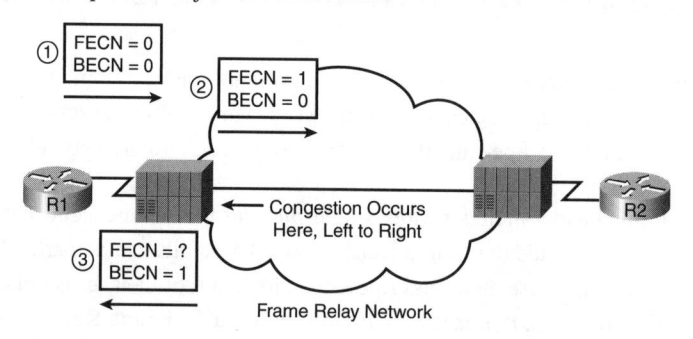

FECN and BECN are bits in the Frame Relay header. At any point—either in a router or inside the Frame Relay cloud—a device can set the FECN bit, meaning that this frame itself has experienced congestion. In other words, congestion exists in the forward direction of that frame. In Figure 13-14, in Step 1, the router sends a frame, with FECN=0. The Frame Relay switch notices congestion and sets FECN=1 in Step 2.

The goal of the whole process, however, is to get the sending router—R1 in this figure—to slow down. So, knowing that it set FECN in a frame in Step 2 in the figure, the Frame Relay switch *can* set the BECN bit in the next frame going back to R1 on that VC, shown as Step 3 in the figure. The BECN tells R1 that congestion occurred in the direction opposite, or backward, of the direction of the frame. In other words, it says that congestion occurred for the frame sent by R1 to R2. R1 can then choose to slow down (or not), depending on how Traffic Shaping is configured.

The Discard Eligibility (DE) Bit

When the provider's network becomes congested, it seems reasonable for the provider to try to discard the frames sent by customers that are causing the congestion. The providers typically build their networks to handle traffic loads far in excess of the collective CIRs for all VCs. However, if one or more customers abuse the right to send data at speeds far in advance of their contracted CIR speeds, the provider rightfully could discard only traffic sent by those customers.

Frame Relay protocols define a means to lessen the blow when the customer sends more than CIR bits per second over a VC, causing the provider to discard some frames. The customer can set the DE bit in some frames. If the provider's switches need to discard frames because of congestion, the switches can discard the frames with the DE bit set. If the customer sets the DE bit in the right frames, such as for less important traffic, the customer can ensure that the important traffic gets through the Frame Relay network, even when the provider has to discard traffic. When the provider's network is not so congested, the customer can send lots of extra data through the Frame Relay network without its being discarded.

Exam Preparation Tasks

Review All the Key Topics

Review the most important topics from this chapter, noted with the key topics icon. Table 13-9 lists these key topics and where each is discussed.

Key Topic

Table 13-9 *Key Topics for Chapter 13*

Key Topic Element	Description	Page Number
Figure 13-1	Figure listing several terms related to a Frame Relay topology	462
Table 13-2	Table listing key Frame Relay terms and definitions	463
List	Two important functions of the Frame Relay LMI	467
Table 13-4	Frame Relay LMI types and LMI type configuration keywords	468
Figure 13-6	Figure showing headers and positions for the Cisco and IETF additional Frame Relay headers	469
Figure 13-9	Figure showing the concept of Frame Relay global addressing	471
List	Three options of subnets used on a Frame Relay network	474
Figure 13-14	Operation and use of the FECN and BECN bits	480

Complete the Tables and Lists from Memory

Print a copy of Appendix J, "Memory Tables" (found on the CD), or at least the section for this chapter, and complete the tables and lists from memory. Appendix K, "Memory Tables Answer Key," also on the CD, includes completed tables and lists for you to check your work.

Definitions of Key Terms

Define the following key terms from this chapter, and check your answers in the glossary:

Access link, access rate, Committed Information Rate (CIR), data-link connection identifier (DLCI), Frame Relay DCE, Frame Relay DTE, Frame Relay mapping, Inverse ARP, Local Management Interface (LMI), nonbroadcast multiaccess (NBMA), permanent virtual circuit (PVC), virtual circuit (VC)

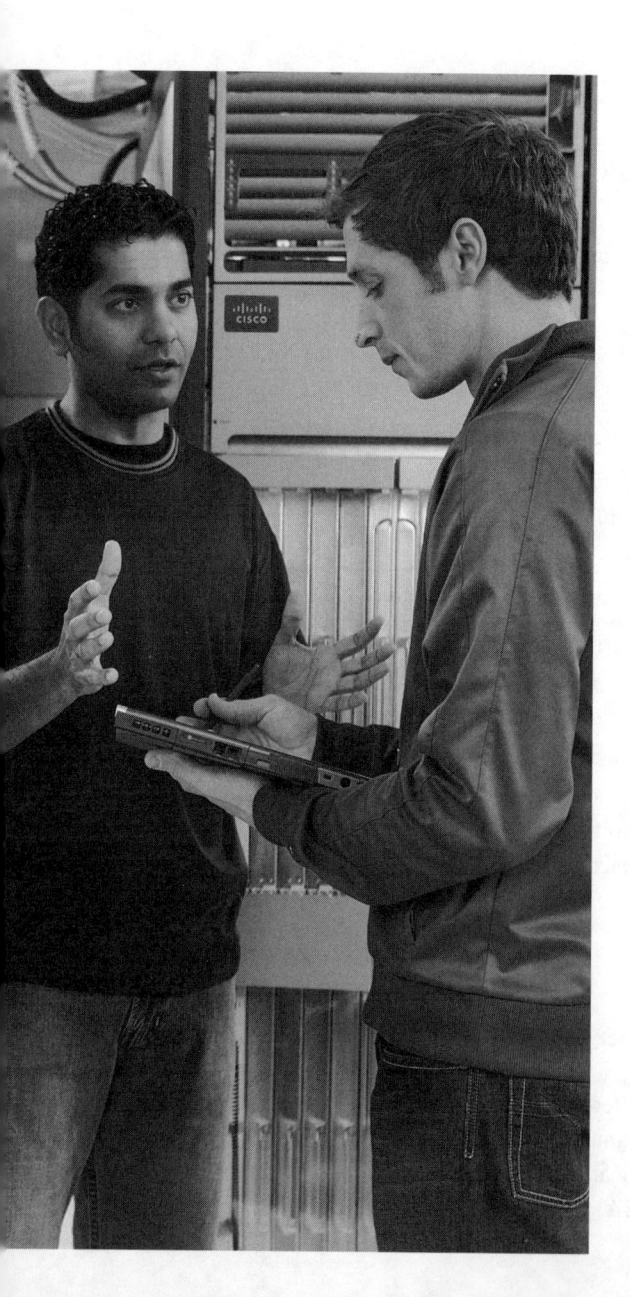

This chapter covers the following subjects:

Frame Relay Configuration and Verification:
This section shows you how to configure the required and optional Frame Relay features, with basic verification of each feature.

Frame Relay Troubleshooting: This section examines a process by which an engineer can find the root cause of why one Frame Relay router cannot ping another Frame Relay router.

CHAPTER 14

Frame Relay Configuration and Troubleshooting

Chapter 13, "Frame Relay Concepts," introduced and explained the main concepts behind Frame Relay. This chapter shows you how to configure the features on Cisco routers, how to verify that each feature works, and how to troubleshoot problems with forwarding packets over a Frame Relay network.

"Do I Know This Already?" Quiz

The "Do I Know This Already?" quiz allows you to assess whether you should read the entire chapter. If you miss no more than one of these eight self-assessment questions, you might want to move ahead to the "Exam Preparation Tasks" section. Table 14-1 lists the major headings in this chapter and the "Do I Know This Already?" quiz questions covering the material in those sections. This helps you assess your knowledge of these specific areas. The answers to the "Do I Know This Already?" quiz appear in Appendix A.

Table 14-1   *"Do I Know This Already?" Foundation Topics Section-to-Question Mapping*

Foundation Topics Section	Questions
Frame Relay Configuration and Verification	1–5
Frame Relay Troubleshooting	6–8

1. Imagine two Cisco routers, R1 and R2, using a Frame Relay service. R1 connects to a switch that uses LMI type ANSI T1.617, and R2 connects to a switch that uses ITU Q.933a. What keywords could be used in the R1 and R2 configuration so that the LMIs work correctly?

    a. **ansi** and **itu**

    b. **T1617** and **q933a**

    c. **ansi** and **q933a**

    d. **T1617** and **itu**

    e. This won't work with two different types.

2. BettyCo has five sites, with routers connected to the same Frame Relay network. VCs have been defined between each pair of routers. Betty, the company president, will fire anyone who configures anything that could just as easily be left as a default. Which of the following configuration commands, configured for the Frame Relay network, would get the engineer fired?

    a. **ip address**

    b. **encapsulation**

    c. **lmi-type**

    d. **frame-relay map**

    e. **frame-relay inverse-arp**

3. WilmaCo has some routers connected to a Frame Relay network. R1 is a router at a remote site, with a single VC back to WilmaCo's headquarters. The R1 configuration currently looks like this:

```
interface serial 0/0
  ip address 10.1.1.1 255.255.255.0
  encapsulation frame-relay
```

Wilma, the company president, has heard that point-to-point subinterfaces are cool, and she wants you to change the configuration to use a point-to-point subinterface. Which of the following commands do you need to use to migrate the configuration?

    a. **no ip address**

    b. **interface-dlci**

    c. **no encapsulation**

    d. **encapsulation frame-relay**

    e. **frame-relay interface-dlci**

4. WilmaCo has another network, with a main site router that has ten VCs connecting to the ten remote sites. Wilma now thinks that multipoint subinterfaces are even cooler than point-to-point. The current main site router's configuration looks like this:

```
interface serial 0/0
  ip address 172.16.1.1 255.255.255.0
  encapsulation frame-relay
```

Wilma wants you to change the configuration to use a multipoint subinterface. Which of the following do you need to use to migrate the configuration? (Note: DLCIs 101 through 110 areused for the ten VCs.)

a.   **interface-dlci 101 110**

b.   **interface dlci 101-110**

c.   Ten different **interface-dlci** commands

d.   **frame-relay interface-dlci 101 110**

e.   **frame-relay interface dlci 101-110**

f.   Ten different **frame-relay interface-dlci** commands

5.   Which of the following commands lists the information learned by Inverse ARP?

a.   **show ip arp**

b.   **show arp**

c.   **show inverse arp**

d.   **show frame-relay inverse-arp**

e.   **show map**

f.   **show frame-relay map**

6.   Which of the following are Frame Relay PVC status codes for which a router sends frames for the associated PVC?

a.   Up

b.   Down

c.   Active

d.   Inactive

e.   Static

f.   Deleted

7.   Central site router RC has a VC connecting to ten remote routers (R1 through R10), with RC's local DLCIs being 101 through 110, respectively. RC has grouped DLCIs 107, 108, and 109 into a single multipoint subinterface S0/0.789, whose current status is "up and up." Which of the following must be true?

a.   Serial 0/0 could be in an up/down state.

b.   The PVC with DLCI 108 could be in an inactive state.

c.   The **show frame-relay map** command lists mapping information for all three VCs.

d.   At least one of the three PVCs is in an active or static state.

8. Frame Relay router R1 uses interface S0/0 to connect to a Frame Relay access link. The physical interface is in an up/down state. Which of the following could cause this problem?

   a. The access link has a physical problem and cannot pass bits between the router and switch.

   b. The switch and router are using different LMI types.

   c. The router configuration is missing the **encapsulation frame-relay** command on interface S0/0.

   d. The router received a valid LMI status message that listed some of the DLCIs as inactive.

Foundation Topics

This chapter has two main sections. The first section examines Frame Relay configuration, along with explanations of several **show** commands. The second section discusses how to approach and troubleshoot Frame Relay problems.

Frame Relay Configuration and Verification

Frame Relay configuration can be very basic or somewhat detailed, depending on how many default settings can be used. By default, Cisco IOS automatically senses the LMI type and automatically discovers the mapping between DLCI and next-hop IP addresses (using Inverse ARP). If you use all Cisco routers, the default to use Cisco encapsulation works without any additional configuration. If you also design the Frame Relay network to use a single subnet, you can configure the routers to use their physical interfaces without any subinterfaces—making the configuration shorter still. In fact, using as many default settings as possible, the only new configuration command for Frame Relay, as compared to point-to-point WANs, is the **encapsulation frame-relay** command.

The CCNA exams' Frame Relay questions can be difficult for a couple of reasons. First, Frame Relay includes a variety of optional settings that can be configured. Second, for network engineers who already have some experience with Frame Relay, that experience may be with one of the three main options for Frame Relay configuration (physical, multipoint, or point-to-point), but the exams cover all options. So, it is important for the exams that you take the time to look at samples of all the options, which are covered here.

Planning a Frame Relay Configuration

Engineers must do a fair amount of planning before knowing where to start with the configuration. Although most modern Enterprises already have some Frame Relay connections, when planning for new sites, you must consider the following items and communicate them to the Frame Relay provider, which in turn has some impact on the routers' Frame Relay configurations:

- Define which physical sites need a Frame Relay access link installed, and define the clock rate (access rate) used on each link

- Define each VC by identifying the endpoints and setting the CIR

- Agree to an LMI type (usually dictated by the provider)

Additionally, the engineer must choose the particular style of configuration based on the following. For these items, the enterprise engineer does not need to consult the Frame Relay provider:

■ Choose the IP subnetting scheme: one subnet for all VCs, one subnet for each VC, or a subnet for each fully meshed subset.

■ Pick whether to assign the IP addresses to physical, multipoint, or point-to-point subinterfaces.

■ Choose which VCs need to use IETF encapsulation instead of the default value of "cisco." IETF encapsulation is typically used when one router is not a Cisco router.

After the planning has been completed, the configuration steps flow directly from the choices made when planning the network. The following list summarizes the configuration steps, mainly as a tool to help remind you of all the steps when you're doing your final exam preparation. Feel free to refer to this list as the upcoming examples show you how to configure the various options. (There is no need to memorize the steps; the list is just a tool to help organize your thinking about the configuration.)

Key
Topic

Step 1 Configure the physical interface to use Frame Relay encapsulation (**encapsulation frame-relay** interface subcommand).

Step 2 Configure an IP address on the interface or subinterface (**ip address** subcommand).

Step 3 (Optional) Manually set the LMI type on each physical serial interface (**frame-relay lmi-type** interface subcommand).

Step 4 (Optional) Change from the default encapsulation of **cisco** to **ietf** by doing the following:

   a. For all VCs on the interface, add the **ietf** keyword to the **encapsulation frame-relay** interface subcommand.

   b. For a single VC, add the **ietf** keyword to the **frame-relay interface-dlci** interface subcommand (point-to-point subinterfaces only) or to the **frame-relay map** command.

Step 5 (Optional) If you aren't using the (default) Inverse ARP to map the DLCI to the next-hop router's IP address, define static mapping using the **frame-relay map ip** *ip-address dlci* **broadcast** subinterface subcommand.

Step 6   On subinterfaces, associate one (point-to-point) or more (multipoint) DLCIs with the subinterface in one of two ways:

    a.   Using the **frame-relay interface-dlci** *dlci* subinterface subcommand

    b.   As a side effect of static mapping using the **frame-relay map ip** *ip-address dlci* **broadcast** subinterface subcommand

The rest of this section shows examples of all these configuration steps, along with some discussion about how to verify that the Frame Relay network is working correctly.

A Fully Meshed Network with One IP Subnet

The first example shows the briefest possible Frame Relay configuration, one that uses just the first two steps of the configuration checklist in this chapter. The design for the first example includes the following choices:

■   Install an access link into three routers.

■   Create a full mesh of PVCs.

■   Use a single subnet (Class C network 199.1.1.0) in the Frame Relay network.

■   Configure the routers using their physical interfaces.

Take the default settings for LMI, Inverse ARP, and encapsulation. Examples 14-1, 14-2, and 14-3 show the configuration for the network shown in Figure 14-1.

Figure 14-1   *Full Mesh with IP Addresses*

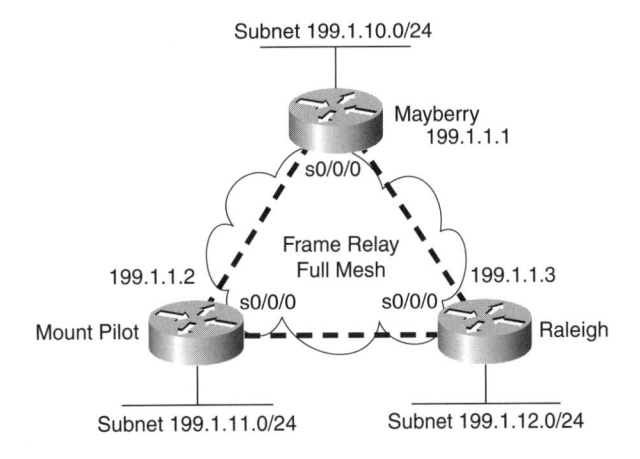

Example 14-1 *Mayberry Configuration*

```
interface serial0/0/0
 encapsulation frame-relay
 ip address  199.1.1.1  255.255.255.0
!
interface fastethernet 0/0
 ip address  199.1.10.1  255.255.255.0
!
router eigrp 1
 network 199.1.1.0
 network 199.1.10.0
```

Example 14-2 *Mount Pilot Configuration*

```
interface serial0/0/0
 encapsulation frame-relay
 ip address  199.1.1.2  255.255.255.0
!
interface fastethernet 0/0
 ip address  199.1.11.2  255.255.255.0
!
router eigrp 1
 network 199.1.1.0
 network 199.1.11.0
```

Example 14-3 *Raleigh Configuration*

```
interface serial0/0/0
 encapsulation frame-relay
 ip address  199.1.1.3  255.255.255.0
!
interface fastethernet 0/0
 ip address  199.1.12.3  255.255.255.0
!
router eigrp 1
 network 199.1.1.0
 network 199.1.12.0
```

The configuration is simple in comparison with the protocol concepts. The **encapsulation frame-relay** command tells the routers to use Frame Relay data-link protocols instead of the default, which is HDLC. Note that the IP addresses on the three routers' serial interfaces are all in the same Class C network. Also, this simple configuration takes advantage of the following IOS default settings:

- The LMI type is automatically sensed.

- The (default) encapsulation is Cisco instead of IETF.

- PVC DLCIs are learned via LMI status messages.

- Inverse ARP is enabled (by default) and is triggered when the status message declaring that the VCs are up is received.

Configuring the Encapsulation and LMI

In some cases, the default values are inappropriate. For example, you must use IETF encapsulation if one router is not a Cisco router. For the purpose of showing an alternative configuration, suppose that the following requirements were added:

- The Raleigh router requires IETF encapsulation on both VCs.

- Mayberry's LMI type should be ANSI, and LMI autosense should not be used.

To change these defaults, the steps outlined as optional configuration Steps 3 and 4 in the configuration checklist should be used. Examples 14-4 and 14-5 show the changes that would be made to Mayberry and Raleigh.

Example 14-4 *Mayberry Configuration with New Requirements*

```
interface serial0/0/0
 encapsulation frame-relay
 frame-relay lmi-type ansi
 frame-relay map ip 199.1.1.3 53 ietf
 ip address 199.1.1.1  255.255.255.0
! rest of configuration unchanged from Example 14-1.
```

Example 14-5 *Raleigh Configuration with New Requirements*

```
interface serial0/0/0
 encapsulation frame-relay ietf
 ip address  199.1.1.3  255.255.255.0

! rest of configuration unchanged from Example 14-3.
```

These configurations differ from the previous ones (in Examples 14-1 and 14-3) in two ways. First, Raleigh changed its encapsulation for both its PVCs with the **ietf** keyword on the **encapsulation** command. This keyword applies to all VCs on the interface. However, Mayberry cannot change its encapsulation in the same way, because only one of the two VCs terminating in Mayberry needs to use IETF encapsulation, and the other needs to use Cisco encapsulation. So Mayberry is forced to code the **frame-relay map** command, referencing the DLCI for the VC to Raleigh, with the **ietf** keyword. With that command, you can change the encapsulation setting per VC, as opposed to the configuration on Raleigh, which changes the encapsulation for all VCs.

The second major change is the LMI configuration. The LMI configuration in Mayberry would be fine without any changes, because the default use of LMI autosense would recognize ANSI as the LMI type. However, by coding the **frame-relay lmi-type ansi** interface subcommand, Mayberry must use ANSI, because this command not only sets the LMI type, it also disables autonegotiation of the LMI type.

> **NOTE**   The LMI setting is a per-physical-interface setting, even if subinterfaces are used, so the **frame-relay lmi-type** command is always a subcommand under the physical interface.

Mount Pilot needs to configure a **frame-relay map** command with the **ietf** keyword for its VC to Raleigh, just like Mayberry. This change is not shown in the examples.

Frame Relay Address Mapping

Figure 14-1 does not even bother listing the DLCIs used for the VCs. The configurations work as stated, and frankly, if you never knew the DLCIs, this network would work! However, for the exams, and for real networking jobs, you need to understand an important concept related to Frame Relay—Frame Relay address mapping. Figure 14-2 shows the same network, this time with global DLCI values shown.

Figure 14-2   *Full Mesh with Global DLCIs Shown*

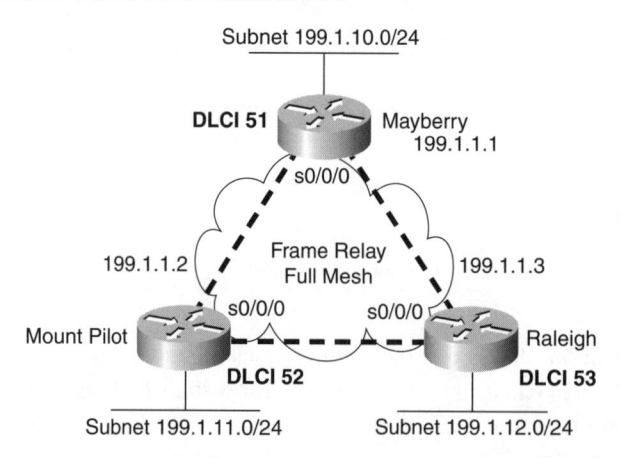

Frame Relay "mapping" creates a correlation between a Layer 3 address and its corresponding Layer 2 address. The concept is similar to the ARP cache for LAN interfaces. For example, the IP Address Resolution Protocol (ARP) cache used on LANs is an example of Layer 3-to-Layer 2 address mapping. With IP ARP, you know the IP address of another device on the same LAN, but not the MAC address; when the ARP completes, you know another device's LAN (Layer 2) address. Similarly, routers that use Frame Relay need a mapping between a router's Layer 3 address and the DLCI used to reach that other router.

This section discusses the basics of why mapping is needed for LAN connections and Frame Relay, with a focus on Frame Relay. Here's a more general definition of mapping:

> The information that correlates to the next-hop router's Layer 3 address, and the Layer 2 address used to reach it, is called mapping. Mapping is needed on multiaccess networks.

Key Topic

Thinking about routing helps make the need for mapping more apparent. Imagine that a host on the Mayberry Ethernet sends an IP packet to a host on the Mount Pilot Ethernet. The packet arrives at the Mayberry router over the LAN, and Mayberry discards the Ethernet header and trailer. Mayberry looks at the routing table, which lists a route to 199.1.11.0, outgoing interface Serial 0/0/0, and next-hop router 199.1.1.2, which is Mount Pilot's Frame Relay IP address.

The next decision that the router must make to complete the process points out the need for mapping: What DLCI should Mayberry put in the Frame Relay header? We configured no DLCIs. However, it would work as configured! To see the answer, consider Example 14-6, which shows some important commands that can be used to see how Mayberry makes the right choice for the DLCI.

Example 14-6 **show** *Commands on Mayberry, Showing the Need for Mapping*

```
Mayberry#show ip route
Codes: C - connected, S - static, I - IGRP, R - RIP, M - mobile, B - BGP
       D - EIGRP, EX - EIGRP external, O - OSPF, IA - OSPF inter area
       N1 - OSPF NSSA external type 1, N2 - OSPF NSSA external type 2
       E1 - OSPF external type 1, E2 - OSPF external type 2, E - EGP
       i - IS-IS, L1 - IS-IS level-1, L2 - IS-IS level-2, ia - IS-IS inter area
       * - candidate default, U - per-user static route, o - ODR
       P - periodic downloaded static route

Gateway of last resort is not set

D    199.1.11.0/24 [90/2195456] via 199.1.1.2, 00:00:26, Serial0/0/0
C    199.1.10.0/24 is directly connected, Fastethernet0/0
D    199.1.12.0/24 [90/2185984] via 199.1.1.3, 00:01:04, Serial0/0/0
C    199.1.1.0/24 is directly connected, Serial0/0/0
C    192.68.1.0/24 is directly connected, Fastethernet0/0
C    192.168.1.0/24 is directly connected, Fastethernet0/0

Mayberry#show frame-relay pvc
```

continues

Example 14-6 **show** *Commands on Mayberry, Showing the Need for Mapping (Continued)*

```
PVC Statistics for interface Serial0/0/0 (Frame Relay DTE)

                Active     Inactive     Deleted       Static
 Local            2           0            0             0
 Switched         0           0            0             0
 Unused           0           0            0             0

DLCI = 52, DLCI USAGE = LOCAL, PVC STATUS = ACTIVE, INTERFACE = Serial0/0/0

  input pkts 46          output pkts 22          in bytes 2946
  out bytes 1794         dropped pkts 0          in FECN pkts 0
  in BECN pkts 0         out FECN pkts 0         out BECN pkts 0
  in DE pkts 0           out DE pkts 0
  out bcast pkts 21      out bcast bytes 1730
  pvc create time 00:23:07, last time pvc status changed 00:21:38

DLCI = 53, DLCI USAGE = LOCAL, PVC STATUS = ACTIVE, INTERFACE = Serial0/0/0

  input pkts 39          output pkts 18          in bytes 2564
  out bytes 1584         dropped pkts 0          in FECN pkts 0
  in BECN pkts 0         out FECN pkts 0         out BECN pkts 0
  in DE pkts 0           out DE pkts 0
  out bcast pkts 18      out bcast bytes 1584
  pvc create time 00:23:08, last time pvc status changed 00:21:20

Mayberry#show frame-relay map
Serial0/0/0 (up): ip 199.1.1.2 dlci 52(0x34,0xC40), dynamic,
             broadcast,, status defined, active
Serial0/0/0 (up): ip 199.1.1.3 dlci 53(0x35,0xC50), dynamic,
             broadcast,, status defined, active
```

The example highlights all the related information on Mayberry for sending packets to network 199.1.11.0/24 off Mount Pilot. Mayberry's route to 199.1.11.0 refers to outgoing interface Serial 0/0/0 and to 199.1.1.2 as the next-hop address. The **show frame-relay pvc** command lists two DLCIs, 52 and 53, and both are active. How does Mayberry know the DLCIs? Well, the LMI status messages tell Mayberry about the VCs, the associated DLCIs, and the status (active).

Which DLCI should Mayberry use to forward the packet? The **show frame-relay map** command output holds the answer. Notice the highlighted phrase "ip 199.1.1.2 dlci 52" in the output. Somehow, Mayberry has mapped 199.1.1.2, which is the next-hop address in the route, to the correct DLCI, which is 52. So, Mayberry knows to use DLCI 52 to reach next-hop IP address 199.1.1.2.

Mayberry can use two methods to build the mapping shown in Example 14-6. One uses a statically configured mapping, and the other uses a dynamic process called *Inverse ARP*. The next two small sections explain the details of each of these options.

Inverse ARP

Inverse ARP dynamically creates a mapping between the Layer 3 address (for example, the IP address) and the Layer 2 address (the DLCI). The end result of Inverse ARP is the same as IP ARP on a LAN: The router builds a mapping between a neighboring Layer 3 address and the corresponding Layer 2 address. However, the process used by Inverse ARP differs for ARP on a LAN. After the VC is up, each router announces its network layer address by sending an Inverse ARP message over that VC. This works as shown in Figure 14-3.

Figure 14-3 *Inverse ARP Process*

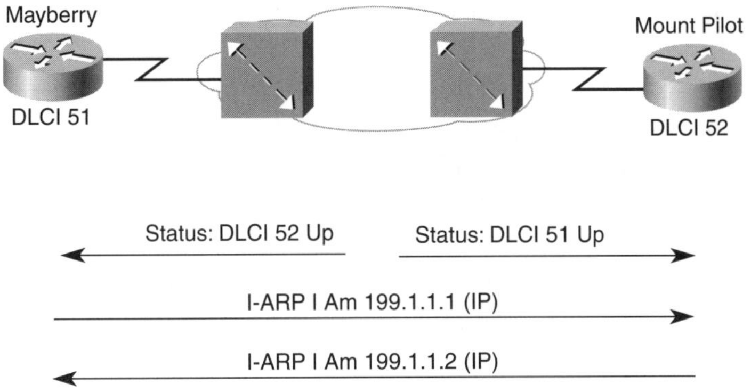

As shown in Figure 14-3, Inverse ARP announces its Layer 3 addresses as soon as the LMI signals that the PVCs are up. Inverse ARP starts by learning the DLCI data link layer address (via LMI messages), and then it announces its own Layer 3 addresses that use that VC. Inverse ARP is enabled by default.

In Example 14-6, Mayberry shows two different entries in the **show frame-relay map** command output. Mayberry uses Inverse ARP to learn that DLCI 52 is mapped to next-hop IP address 199.1.1.2 and that DLCI 53 is mapped to next-hop IP address 199.1.1.3. Interestingly, Mayberry learns this information by receiving an Inverse ARP from Mount Pilot and Raleigh, respectively.

Table 14-2 summarizes what occurs with Inverse ARP in the network shown in Figure 14-2.

Table 14-2 *Inverse ARP Messages for Figure 14-2*

Sending Router	DLCI When the Frame Is Sent	Receiving Router	DLCI When the Frame Is Received	Information in the Inverse ARP Message
Mayberry	52	Mount Pilot	51	I am 199.1.1.1.
Mayberry	53	Raleigh	51	I am 199.1.1.1.
Mount Pilot	51	Mayberry	52	I am 199.1.1.2.
Mount Pilot	53	Raleigh	52	I am 199.1.1.2.
Raleigh	51	Mayberry	53	I am 199.1.1.3.
Raleigh	52	Mount Pilot	53	I am 199.1.1.3.

To understand Inverse ARP, focus on the last two columns of Table 14-2. Each router receives some Inverse ARP "announcements." The Inverse ARP message contains the sender's Layer 3 address, and the Frame Relay header, of course, has a DLCI in it. These two values are placed in the Inverse ARP cache on the receiving router. For example, in the third row, Mayberry receives an Inverse ARP. The DLCI is 52 when the frame arrives at Mayberry, and the IP address is 199.1.1.2. This is added to the Frame Relay map table in Mayberry, which is shown in the highlighted part of the **show frame-relay map** command in Example 14-6.

Static Frame Relay Mapping

You can statically configure the same mapping information instead of using Inverse ARP. In a production network, you probably would just go ahead and use Inverse ARP. For the exams, you need to know how to configure the static map command statements. Example 14-7 lists the static Frame Relay map for the three routers shown in Figure 14-2, along with the configuration used to disable Inverse ARP.

Example 14-7 **frame-relay map** *Commands*

```
Mayberry
interface serial 0/0/0
 no frame-relay inverse-arp
 frame-relay map ip 199.1.1.2 52 broadcast
 frame-relay map ip 199.1.1.3 53 broadcast
Mount Pilot
interface serial 0/0/0
 no frame-relay inverse-arp
 frame-relay map ip 199.1.1.1 51 broadcast
 frame-relay map ip 199.1.1.3 53 broadcast
```

Example 14-7 **frame-relay map** *Commands (Continued)*

```
Raleigh
interface serial 0/0/0
 no frame-relay inverse-arp
 frame-relay map ip 199.1.1.1 51 broadcast
 frame-relay map ip 199.1.1.2 52 broadcast
```

The **frame-relay map** command entry for Mayberry, referencing 199.1.1.2, is used for packets in Mayberry going to Mount Pilot. When Mayberry creates a Frame Relay header, expecting it to be delivered to Mount Pilot, Mayberry must use DLCI 52. Mayberry's **frame-relay map** statement correlates Mount Pilot's IP address, 199.1.1.2, to the DLCI used to reach Mount Pilot—namely, DLCI 52. Likewise, a packet sent back from Mount Pilot to Mayberry causes Mount Pilot to use its **map** statement to refer to Mayberry's IP address of 199.1.1.1. Mapping is needed for each next-hop Layer 3 address for each Layer 3 protocol being routed. Even with a network this small, the configuration process can be laborious.

NOTE The **broadcast** keyword is required when the router needs to send broadcasts or multicasts to the neighboring router—for example, to support routing protocol messages such as Hellos.

A Partially Meshed Network with One IP Subnet Per VC

The second sample network, based on the environment shown in Figure 14-4, uses point-to-point subinterfaces. Examples 14-8 through 14-11 show the configuration for this network. The command prompts are included in the first example because they change when you configure subinterfaces.

Figure 14-4 *Partial Mesh with IP Addresses*

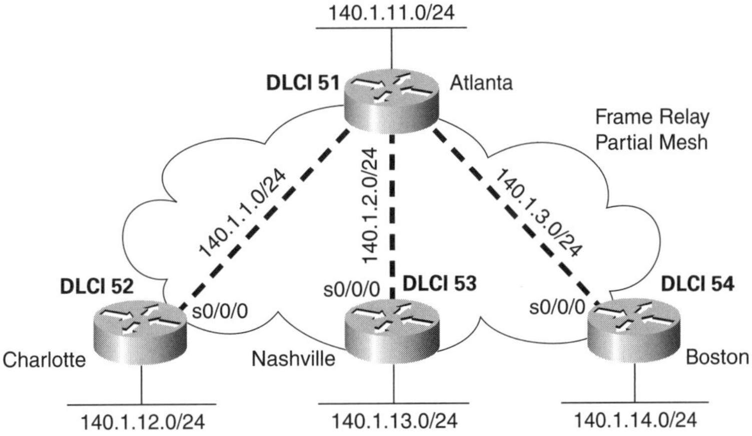

Example 14-8 *Atlanta Configuration*

```
Atlanta(config)#interface serial0/0/0
Atlanta(config-if)#encapsulation frame-relay

Atlanta(config-if)#interface serial 0/0/0.1 point-to-point
Atlanta(config-subif)#ip address 140.1.1.1  255.255.255.0
Atlanta(config-subif)#frame-relay interface-dlci 52

Atlanta(config-fr-dlci)#interface serial 0/0/0.2 point-to-point
Atlanta(config-subif)#ip address 140.1.2.1 255.255.255.0
Atlanta(config-subif)#frame-relay interface-dlci 53

Atlanta(config-fr-dlci)#interface serial 0/0/0.3 point-to-point
Atlanta(config-subif)#ip address 140.1.3.1 255.255.255.0
Atlanta(config-subif)#frame-relay interface-dlci 54

Atlanta(config-fr-dlci)#interface fastethernet 0/0
Atlanta(config-if)#ip address 140.1.11.1 255.255.255.0
```

Example 14-9 *Charlotte Configuration*

```
interface serial0/0/0
 encapsulation frame-relay
!
interface serial 0/0/0.1 point-to-point
 ip address 140.1.1.2  255.255.255.0
 frame-relay interface-dlci 51
!
interface fastethernet 0/0
 ip address 140.1.12.2 255.255.255.0
```

Example 14-10 *Nashville Configuration*

```
interface serial0/0/0
 encapsulation frame-relay
!
interface serial 0/0/0.2 point-to-point
 ip address 140.1.2.3 255.255.255.0
 frame-relay interface-dlci 51
!
interface fastethernet 0/0
 ip address 140.1.13.3 255.255.255.0
```

Example 14-11 *Boston Configuration*

```
interface serial0/0/0
 encapsulation frame-relay
!
interface serial 0/0/0.3 point-to-point
 ip address 140.1.3.4 255.255.255.0
 frame-relay interface-dlci 51
!
interface fastethernet 0/0
 ip address 140.1.14.4  255.255.255.0
```

Again, defaults abound in this configuration, but some defaults are different than when you're configuring on the physical interface. The LMI type is autosensed, and Cisco encapsulation is used, which is just like the fully meshed examples. Inverse ARP is not really needed on point-to-point subinterfaces, but it is enabled by default in case the router on the other end of the VC needs to use Inverse ARP, as explained later in this section.

Two new commands create the configuration required with point-to-point subinterfaces. First, the **interface serial 0/0/0.1 point-to-point** command creates logical subinterface number 1 under physical interface Serial 0/0/0. The **frame-relay interface-dlci** subinterface subcommand then tells the router which single DLCI is associated with that subinterface.

An example of how the **frame-relay interface-dlci** command works can help. Consider router Atlanta in Figure 14-4. Atlanta receives LMI messages on Serial0/0/0 stating that three PVCs, with DLCIs 52, 53, and 54, are up. Which PVC goes with which subinterface? Cisco IOS software needs to associate the correct PVC with the correct subinterface. This is accomplished with the **frame-relay interface-dlci** command.

The subinterface numbers do not have to match on the router on the other end of the PVC, nor does the DLCI number. In this example, I just numbered the subinterfaces to be easier to remember. In real life, it is useful to encode some information about your network numbering scheme into the subinterface number. For example, a company might encode part of the carrier's circuit ID in the subinterface number so that the operations staff could find the correct information to tell the telco when troubleshooting the link. Many sites use the DLCI as the subinterface number. Of course, useful troubleshooting information, such as the DLCI, the name of the router on the other end of the VC, and so on, could be configured as text with the **description** command as well. In any case, there are no requirements for matching subinterface numbers. This example just matches the subinterface number to the third octet of the IP address.

Assigning a DLCI to a Particular Subinterface

As mentioned in the configuration checklist at the beginning of the "Frame Relay Configuration and Verification" section, when configuring subinterfaces, the DLCIs must be associated with each subinterface in one of two ways. Examples 14-8 through 14-11 showed how to associate the DLCIs using the **frame-relay interface-dlci** subinterface subcommand. The alternative configuration would be to use the **frame-relay map** command as a subinterface subcommand on multipoint subinterfaces or as a physical interface subcommand. This command would both associate a DLCI with the subinterface and statically configure a mapping of Layer 3 next-hop IP address to that DLCI.

The router disables Inverse ARP on a subinterface when the **frame-relay map** command is configured. So, when using static maps on the router on one end of the VC, keep in mind that the router on the other end of the VC will not receive any Inverse ARP messages and may also then need to be configured with the **frame-relay map** command.

Comments About Global and Local Addressing

When you take the Cisco CCNA exams, if a figure for a question shows three or more routers, you should be able to easily decide whether the figure implies local or global DLCI values. For instance, Figure 14-4 shows a main site with three PVCs, one to each remote site. However, only one DLCI is shown beside the main site router, implying the use of global addressing. If local DLCIs were used, the figure would need to show a DLCI for each PVC beside the main site router.

In cases where a figure for a question shows only two routers, the figure might not imply whether local or global DLCI addressing is used. In those cases, look for clues in the question, answers, and any configuration. The best clues relate to the following fact:

> On any given router, only local DLCI values are in the configuration or **show** commands.

Again, consider Figure 14-4 along with Examples 14-8 through 14-11. The figure shows global DLCIs, with DLCI 51 beside the Atlanta router. However, the **frame-relay interface-dlci** commands on the Atlanta router (Example 14-8) and the Atlanta **show** commands in upcoming Example 14-12 list DLCIs 52, 53, and 54. Although Figure 14-4 makes it obvious that global addressing is used, even if only two routers had been shown, the **show** commands and configuration commands could have helped identify the correct DLCIs to use.

Frame Relay Verification

Example 14-12 shows the output from the most popular Cisco IOS software Frame Relay EXEC commands for monitoring Frame Relay, as issued on router Atlanta.

Example 14-12 *Output from EXEC Commands on Atlanta*

```
Atlanta#show frame-relay pvc

PVC Statistics for interface Serial0/0/0 (Frame Relay DTE)

               Active      Inactive     Deleted       Static
  Local          3            0            0            0
  Switched       0            0            0            0
  Unused         0            0            0            0
DLCI = 52, DLCI USAGE = LOCAL, PVC STATUS = ACTIVE, INTERFACE = Serial0/0/0.1

  input pkts 843          output pkts 876         in bytes 122723
  out bytes 134431        dropped pkts 0          in FECN pkts 0
  in BECN pkts 0          out FECN pkts 0         out BECN pkts 0
  in DE pkts 0            out DE pkts 0
  out bcast pkts 876       out bcast bytes 134431
  pvc create time 05:20:10, last time pvc status changed 05:19:31
  --More--
DLCI = 53, DLCI USAGE = LOCAL, PVC STATUS = ACTIVE, INTERFACE = Serial0/0/0.2

  input pkts 0            output pkts 875         in bytes 0
  out bytes 142417        dropped pkts 0          in FECN pkts 0
  in BECN pkts 0          out FECN pkts 0         out BECN pkts 0
  in DE pkts 0            out DE pkts 0
  out bcast pkts 875       out bcast bytes 142417
  pvc create time 05:19:51, last time pvc status changed 04:55:41
  --More--
DLCI = 54, DLCI USAGE = LOCAL, PVC STATUS = ACTIVE, INTERFACE = Serial0/0/0.3

  input pkts 10           output pkts 877         in bytes 1274
  out bytes 142069        dropped pkts 0          in FECN pkts 0
  in BECN pkts 0          out FECN pkts 0         out BECN pkts 0
  in DE pkts 0            out DE pkts 0
  out bcast pkts 877       out bcast bytes 142069
  pvc create time 05:19:52, last time pvc status changed 05:17:42

Atlanta#show frame-relay map
Serial0/0/0.3 (up): point-to-point dlci, dlci 54(0x36,0xC60), broadcast
          status defined, active
Serial0/0/0.2 (up): point-to-point dlci, dlci 53(0x35,0xC50), broadcast
          status defined, active
Serial0/0/0.1 (up): point-to-point dlci, dlci 52(0x34,0xC40), broadcast
          status defined, active
```

continues

Example 14-12 *Output from EXEC Commands on Atlanta (Continued)*

```
Atlanta#debug frame-relay lmi
Frame Relay LMI debugging is on
Displaying all Frame Relay LMI data

Serial0/0/0(out): StEnq, myseq 163, yourseen 161, DTE up
datagramstart = 0x45AED8, datagramsize = 13
FR encap = 0xFCF10309
00 75 01 01 01 03 02 A3 A1

Serial0/0/0(in): Status, myseq 163
RT IE 1, length 1, type 1
KA IE 3, length 2, yourseq 162, myseq 163
```

The **show frame-relay pvc** command lists useful management information. For instance, the packet counters for each VC, plus the counters for FECN and BECN, can be particularly useful. Likewise, comparing the packets/bytes sent on one router versus the counters of what is received on the router on the other end of the VC is also quite useful. This reflects the number of packets/bytes lost inside the Frame Relay cloud. Also, the PVC status is a great place to start when troubleshooting.

The **show frame-relay map** command lists mapping information. With the earlier example of a fully meshed network, in which the configuration did not use any subinterfaces, a Layer 3 address was listed with each DLCI. In this example, a DLCI is listed in each entry, but no mention of corresponding Layer 3 addresses is made. The whole point of mapping is to correlate a Layer 3 address to a Layer 2 address, but there is no Layer 3 address in the **show frame-relay map** command output! The reason is that the information is stored somewhere else. Subinterfaces require the use of the **frame-relay interface-dlci** configuration command. Because these subinterfaces are point-to-point, when a route points out a single subinterface, the DLCI to use to send frames is implied by the configuration. Mapping via Inverse ARP or static **frame-relay map** statements is needed only when more than two VCs terminate on the interface or subinterface, because those are the only instances in which confusion about which DLCI to use might occur.

The **debug frame-relay lmi** output lists information for the sending and receiving LMI inquiries. The switch sends the status message, and the DTE (router) sends the status inquiry. The default setting with Cisco IOS software is to send, and to expect to receive, these status messages. The Cisco IOS software **no keepalive** command is used to disable the use of LMI status messages. Unlike other interfaces, Cisco keepalive messages do not flow from router to router over Frame Relay. Instead, they are simply used to detect whether the router has connectivity to its local Frame Relay switch.

A Partially Meshed Network with Some Fully Meshed Parts

You can also choose to use multipoint subinterfaces for a Frame Relay configuration. This last sample network, based on the network shown in Figure 14-5, uses both multipoint and point-to-point subinterfaces. Examples 14-13 through 14-17 show the configuration for this network. Table 14-3 summarizes the addresses and subinterfaces used.

Figure 14-5 *Hybrid of Full and Partial Mesh*

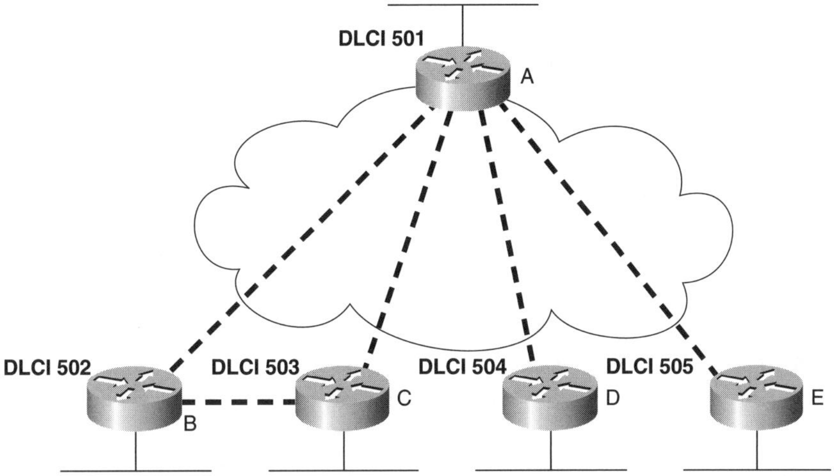

Example 14-13 *Router A Configuration*

```
interface serial0/0/0
 encapsulation frame-relay
!
interface serial 0/0/0.1 multipoint
 ip address 140.1.1.1  255.255.255.0
 frame-relay interface-dlci 502
 frame-relay interface-dlci 503
!
interface serial 0/0/0.2 point-to-point
 ip address 140.1.2.1 255.255.255.0
 frame-relay interface-dlci 504
!
interface serial 0/0/0.3 point-to-point
 ip address 140.1.3.1 255.255.255.0
 frame-relay interface-dlci 505
```

Example 14-14 *Router B Configuration*

```
interface serial0/0/0
 encapsulation frame-relay
!
interface serial 0/0/0.1 multipoint
 ip address 140.1.1.2  255.255.255.0
 frame-relay interface-dlci 501
 frame-relay interface-dlci 503
```

Example 14-15 *Router C Configuration*

```
interface serial0/0/0
 encapsulation frame-relay
!
interface serial 0/0/0.1 multipoint
 ip address 140.1.1.3  255.255.255.0
 frame-relay interface-dlci 501
 frame-relay interface-dlci 502
```

Example 14-16 *Router D Configuration*

```
interface serial0/0/0
encapsulation frame-relay
!
interface serial 0/0/0.1 point-to-point
 ip address 140.1.2.4  255.255.255.0
 frame-relay interface-dlci 501
```

Example 14-17 *Router E Configuration*

```
interface serial0/0/0
 encapsulation frame-relay
!
interface serial 0/0/0.1 point-to-point
 ip address 140.1.3.5 255.255.255.0
 frame-relay interface-dlci 501
```

Table 14-3 *IP Addresses with Point-to-Point and Multipoint Subinterfaces*

Router	Subnet	IP Address	Subinterface Type
A	140.1.1.0/24	140.1.1.1	Multipoint
B	140.1.1.0/24	140.1.1.2	Multipoint
C	140.1.1.0/24	140.1.1.3	Multipoint
A	140.1.2.0/24	140.1.2.1	Point-to-point

Table 14-3 *IP Addresses with Point-to-Point and Multipoint Subinterfaces (Continued)*

Router	Subnet	IP Address	Subinterface Type
D	140.1.2.0/24	140.1.2.4	Point-to-point
A	140.1.3.0/24	140.1.3.1	Point-to-point
E	140.1.3.0/24	140.1.3.5	Point-to-point

Multipoint subinterfaces work best when you have a full mesh between a set of routers. On Routers A, B, and C, a multipoint subinterface is used for the configuration referencing the other two routers, because you can think of these three routers as forming a fully meshed subset of the network.

The term multipoint simply means that there is more than one VC, so you can send and receive to and from more than one VC on the subinterface. Like point-to-point subinterfaces, multipoint subinterfaces use the **frame-relay interface-dlci** command. Notice that there are two commands for each multipoint subinterface in this case, because each of the two PVCs associated with this subinterface must be identified as being used with that subinterface.

Router A is the only router using both multipoint and point-to-point subinterfaces. On Router A's multipoint Serial0/0/0.1 interface, DLCIs for Router B and Router C are listed. On Router A's other two subinterfaces, which are point-to-point, only a single DLCI needs to be listed. In fact, only one **frame-relay interface-dlci** command is allowed on a point-to-point subinterface, because only one VC is allowed. Otherwise, the configurations between the two types are similar.

No mapping statements are required for the configurations shown in Examples 14-13 through 14-17, because Inverse ARP is enabled on the multipoint subinterfaces by default. No mapping is ever needed for the point-to-point subinterface, because the only DLCI associated with the interface is statically configured with the **frame-relay interface-dlci** command.

Example 14-18 lists another **show frame-relay map** command, showing the mapping information learned by Inverse ARP for the multipoint subinterface. Notice that the output now includes the Layer 3 addresses, whereas the same command when using point-to-point subinterfaces (in Example 14-12) did not. The reason is that the routes might refer to a next-hop IP address reachable out a multipoint interface, but because more than one DLCI is

associated with the interface, the router needs mapping information to match the next-hop
IP address to the correct DLCI.

Example 14-18 *Frame Relay Maps and Inverse ARP on Router C*

```
RouterC#show frame-relay map
Serial0/0/0.1 (up): ip 140.1.1.1 dlci 501(0x1F5,0x7C50), dynamic,
              broadcast,, status defined, active
Serial0/0/0.1 (up): ip 140.1.1.2 dlci 502(0x1F6,0x7C60), dynamic,
              broadcast,, status defined, active


RouterC#debug frame-relay events
Frame Relay events debugging is on

RouterC#configure terminal
Enter configuration commands, one per line.  End with Ctrl-Z.
RouterC(config)#interface serial 0/0/0.1
RouterC(config-subif)#shutdown
RouterC(config-subif)#no shutdown
RouterC(config-subif)#^Z
RouterC#

Serial0/0/0.1: FR ARP input
Serial0/0/0.1: FR ARP input
Serial0/0/0.1: FR ARP input
datagramstart = 0xE42E58, datagramsize = 30
FR encap = 0x7C510300
80 00 00 00 08 06 00 0F 08 00 02 04 00 09 00 00
8C 01 01 01 7C 51 8C 01 01 03

datagramstart = 0xE420E8, datagramsize = 30
FR encap = 0x7C610300
80 00 00 00 08 06 00 0F 08 00 02 04 00 09 00 00
8C 01 01 02 7C 61 8C 01 01 03
```

The messages about Inverse ARP in the **debug frame-relay events** output are not so
obvious. One easy exercise is to search for the hex version of the IP addresses in the output.
These addresses are highlighted in Example 14-18. For example, the first 4 bytes of
140.1.1.1 are 8C 01 01 01in hexadecimal. This field starts on the left side of the output, so
it is easy to recognize.

Frame Relay Troubleshooting

Frame Relay has many features and options that can be configured. For both real life and the exams, troubleshooting Frame Relay problems often means that you need to look at all the routers' configurations and make sure that the configurations meet the requirements. The LMI types must match or be autosensed, the Layer 3 mapping information has been learned or statically mapped, the right DLCI values have been associated with each subinterface, and so on. So, to be well prepared for the CCNA exams, you should review and memorize the many Frame Relay configuration options and what each option means.

However, the exams may have Frame Relay questions that require you to determine a problem without looking at the configuration. This second major section of this chapter examines Frame Relay troubleshooting, with emphasis on how to use **show** commands, along with the symptoms of a problem, to isolate the root cause of the problem.

A Suggested Frame Relay Troubleshooting Process

To isolate a Frame Relay problem, the process should start with some pings. Optimally, pings from an end-user host on a LAN, to another host on a remote LAN, can quickly determine if the network currently can meet the true end goal of delivering packets between computers. If that ping fails, a ping from one router to the other router's Frame Relay IP address is the next step. If that ping works, but the end user's ping failed, the problem probably has something to do with Layer 3 issues, and troubleshooting those issues was well covered in Chapters 7 and 11. However, if a ping from one router to another router's Frame Relay IP address fails, the problem is most likely related to the Frame Relay network.

This section focuses on troubleshooting problems when a Frame Relay router cannot ping another router's Frame Relay IP address. At that point, the engineer should ping the Frame Relay IP addresses of all the other routers on the other end of each VC to determine the following:

> Do the pings fail for all remote routers' Frame Relay IP addresses, or do some pings fail and some pings work?

For example, Figure 14-6 shows a sample Frame Relay network that will be used with the remaining examples in this chapter. If R1 tried to **ping** R2's Frame Relay IP address (10.1.2.2 in this case) and failed, the next question is whether R1's pings to R3 (10.1.34.3) and R4 (10.1.34.4) work.

Figure 14-6 *Sample Frame Relay Network for the Troubleshooting Examples*

This chapter organizes its explanations of how to troubleshoot Frame Relay based on this first problem isolation step. The following list summarizes the major actions, with each step in the following list being examined in order following the list.

Key Topic

If a Frame Relay router's pings fail for all remote routers whose VCs share a single access link, do the following:

Step 1 Check for Layer 1 problems on the access link between the router and the local Frame Relay switch (all routers).

Step 2 Check for Layer 2 problems on the access link, particularly encapsulation and LMI.

After resolving any problems in the first two steps, or if the original ping tests showed that the Frame Relay router can ping some, but not all, of the other Frame Relay routers whose VCs share a single access link, follow these steps:

Step 3 Check for PVC problems based on the PVC status and subinterface status.

Step 4 Check for Layer 2/3 problems with both static and dynamic (Inverse ARP) mapping.

Step 5 Check for Layer 2/3 problems related to a mismatch of end-to-end encapsulation (cisco or ietf).

Step 6 Check for other Layer 3 issues, including mismatched subnets.

The rest of this chapter explains some of the details of each step of this suggested troubleshooting process.

Layer 1 Issues on the Access Link (Step 1)

If a router's physical interface used for the Frame Relay access link is not in an "up and up" state, the router cannot send any frames over the link. If the interface has a line status (the first interface status code) of down, the interface most likely has a Layer 1 issue.

From a Layer 1 perspective, a Frame Relay access link is merely a leased line between a router and a Frame Relay switch. As such, the exact same Layer 1 issues exist for this link as for a point-to-point leased line. Because the possible root causes and suggested troubleshooting steps mirror what should be done on a leased line, refer to the section "Troubleshooting Layer 1 Problems" in Chapter 12, "Point-to-Point WANs," for more information about this step.

Layer 2 Issues on the Access Link (Step 2)

If a router's physical interface line status is up, but the line protocol status (second status code) is down, the link typically has a Layer 2 problem between the router and the local Frame Relay switch. With Frame Relay interfaces, the problem is typically related to either the **encapsulation** command or the Frame Relay LMI.

The potential problem related to the **encapsulation** command is very simple to check. If a router's serial interface configuration omits the **encapsulation frame-relay** interface subcommand, but the physical access link is working, the physical interface settles into an up/down state. If the configuration is unavailable, the **show interfaces** command can be used to see the configured encapsulation type, which is listed in the first few lines of command output.

The other potential problem relates to the LMI. LMI status messages flow in both directions between a router (DTE) and Frame Relay switch (DCE) for two main purposes:

■   For the DCE to inform the DTE about each VC's DLCI and its status

■   To provide a keepalive function so that the DTE and DCE can easily tell when the access link can no longer pass traffic

Key Topic

A router places the physical link in an up/down state when the link physically works but the router ceases to hear LMI messages from the switch. With the interface not in an up/up state, the router does not attempt to send any IP packets out the interface, so all pings should fail at this point.

A router might cease to receive LMI messages from the switch because of both legitimate reasons and mistakes. The normal legitimate purpose for the LMI keepalive function is that if the link really is having problems, and cannot pass any data, the router can notice the loss of keepalive messages and bring the link down. This allows the router to use an alternative route, assuming that an alternative route exists. However, a router might cease to receive LMI messages and bring down the interface because of the following mistakes:

■ Disabling LMI on the router (with the **no keepalive** physical interface subcommand), but leaving it enabled on the switch—or vice versa

■ Configuring different LMI types on the router (with the **frame-relay lmi-type** *type* physical interface subcommand) and the switch

You can easily check for both encapsulation and LMI using the **show frame-relay lmi** command. This command lists only output for interfaces that have the **encapsulation frame-relay** command configured, so you can quickly confirm whether the **encapsulation frame-relay** command is configured on the correct serial interfaces. This command also lists the LMI type used by the router, and it shows counters for the number of LMI messages sent and received. Example 14-19 shows an example from router R1 in Figure 14-6.

Example 14-19   show frame-relay lmi *Command on R1*

```
R1#show frame-relay lmi

LMI Statistics for interface Serial0/0/0 (Frame Relay DTE) LMI TYPE = ANSI
  Invalid Unnumbered info 0        Invalid Prot Disc 0
  Invalid dummy Call Ref 0         Invalid Msg Type 0
  Invalid Status Message 0         Invalid Lock Shift 0
  Invalid Information ID 0         Invalid Report IE Len 0
  Invalid Report Request 0         Invalid Keep IE Len 0
  Num Status Enq. Sent 122         Num Status msgs Rcvd 34
  Num Update Status Rcvd 0         Num Status Timeouts 88
  Last Full Status Req 00:00:04    Last Full Status Rcvd 00:13:24
```

For this example, router R1 was statically configured with the **frame-relay lmi-type ansi** interface subcommand, with switch S1 still using LMI type cisco. When the LMI configuration was changed, the router and switch had exchanged 34 LMI messages (of type cisco). After that change, R1's counter of the number of status enquiry messages sent kept rising (122 when the **show frame-relay lmi** command output was captured), but the counter of the number of LMI status messages received from the switch remained at 34. Just below that counter is the number of timeouts, which counts the number of times the router expected to receive a periodic LMI message from the switch but did not. In this case, the router was actually still receiving LMI messages, but they were not ANSI LMI messages so the router did not understand or recognize them.

If repeated use of the **show frame-relay lmi** command shows that the number of status messages received remains the same, the likely cause, other than a truly nonworking link, is that the LMI types do not match. The best solution is to allow for LMI autosense by configuring the **no frame-relay lmi-type** *type* physical interface subcommand, or alternatively, configuring the same LMI type that is used by the switch.

If you troubleshoot and fix any problems found in Steps 1 and 2, on all Frame Relay connected routers, all the routers' access link physical interfaces should be in an up/up state. The last four steps examine issues that apply to individual PVCs and neighbors.

PVC Problems and Status (Step 3)

The goal at this step in the troubleshooting process is to discover the DLCI of the PVC used to reach a particular neighbor and then find out if the PVC is working. To determine the correct PVC, particularly if little or no configuration or documentation is available, you have to start with the failed **ping** command. The **ping** command identifies the IP address of the neighboring router. Based on the neighbor's IP address, a few **show** commands can link the neighbor's IP address with the associated connected subnet, the connected subnet with the local router's interface, and the local router's interface with the possible DLCIs. Also, the Frame Relay mapping information can identify the specific PVC. Although this book has covered all the commands used to find these pieces of information, the following list summarizes the steps that take you from the neighbor's IP address to the correct local DLCI used to send frames to that neighbor:

Step 3a   Discover the IP address and mask of each Frame Relay interface/ subinterface (**show interfaces**, **show ip interface brief**), and calculate the connected subnets.

Step 3b   Compare the IP address in the failed **ping** command, and pick the interface/subinterface whose connected subnet is the same subnet.

Step 3c   Discover the PVC(s) assigned to that interface or subinterface (**show frame-relay pvc**).

Step 3d   If more than one PVC is assigned to the interface or subinterface, determine which PVC is used to reach a particular neighbor (**show frame-relay map**).

NOTE   As a reminder, lists like this one are meant for convenient reference when you read the chapter. It's easy to find the list when you study and want to remember a particular part of how to attack a given problem. You do not need to memorize the list, or practice it until you internalize the information.

Steps 3a, 3b, 3c, and 3d discover the correct PVC to examine. After it is discovered, Step 3 in the suggested troubleshooting process interprets the status of that PVC, and the associated interface or subinterface, to determine the cause of any problems.

This section takes a closer look at an example in which R1 cannot ping R2's 10.1.2.2 Frame Relay IP address. Before focusing on the process to determine which VC is used, it is helpful to see the final answer, so Figure 14-7 lists some of the details. For this example, R1's **ping 10.1.2.2** command fails in this case.

Figure 14-7 *Configuration Facts Related to R1's Failed **ping 10.1.2.2** Command*

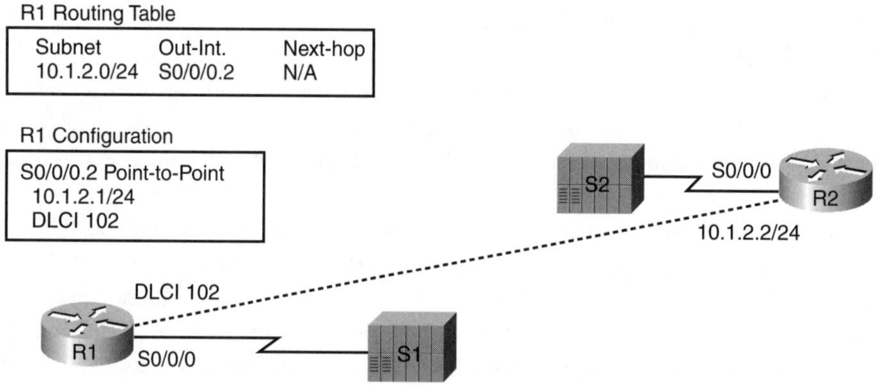

Find the Connected Subnet and Outgoing Interface (Steps 3a and 3b)

The first two substeps to find R1's PVC (DLCI) connecting to R2 (Substeps 3a and 3b) should be relatively easy assuming that you have already finished Parts II and III of this book. Any time you ping the Frame Relay IP address of a neighboring router, that IP address should be in one of the subnets also connected to the local router. To find the interface used on a local router when forwarding packets to the remote router, you just have to find that common connected subnet.

In this example, with R1 pinging 10.1.2.2, Example 14-20 shows a few commands that confirm that R1's S0/0/0.2 subinterface is connected to subnet 10.1.2.0/24, which includes R2's 10.1.2.2 IP address.

Example 14-20 *Finding Subnet 10.1.2.0/24 and Subinterface S0/0/0.2*

```
R1>show ip interface brief
Interface            IP-Address      OK? Method Status                 Protocol
FastEthernet0/0      10.1.11.1       YES NVRAM  up                     up
FastEthernet0/1      unassigned      YES NVRAM  administratively down  down
Serial0/0/0          unassigned      YES NVRAM  up                     up
Serial0/0/0.2        10.1.2.1        YES NVRAM  down                   down
```

Example 14-20 *Finding Subnet 10.1.2.0/24 and Subinterface S0/0/0.2 (Continued)*

```
Serial0/0/0.5         10.1.5.1        YES manual down                down
Serial0/0/0.34        10.1.34.1       YES NVRAM  up                  up
R1#show interfaces s 0/0/0.2
Serial0/0/0.2 is down, line protocol is down
  Hardware is GT96K Serial
  Internet address is 10.1.2.1/24
  MTU 1500 bytes, BW 1544 Kbit, DLY 20000 usec,
     reliability 255/255, txload 1/255, rxload 1/255
  Encapsulation FRAME-RELAY
  Last clearing of "show interface" counters never
```

Find the PVCs Assigned to That Interface (Step 3c)

The **show frame-relay pvc** command directly answers the question of which PVCs have been assigned to which interfaces and subinterfaces. If the command is issued with no parameters, the command lists about ten lines of output for each VC, with the end of the first line listing the associated interface or subinterface. Example 14-21 lists the beginning of the command output.

Example 14-21 *Correlating Subinterface S0/0/0.2 to the PVC with DLCI 102*

```
R1>show frame-relay pvc

PVC Statistics for interface Serial0/0/0 (Frame Relay DTE)

               Active    Inactive   Deleted      Static
  Local          1          2          0           0
  Switched       0          0          0           0
  Unused         0          0          0           0

DLCI = 102, DLCI USAGE = LOCAL, PVC STATUS = INACTIVE, INTERFACE = Serial0/0/0.2

  input pkts 33          output pkts 338        in bytes 1952
  out bytes 29018        dropped pkts 0         in pkts dropped 0
  out pkts dropped 0          out bytes dropped 0
  in FECN pkts 0         in BECN pkts 0         out FECN pkts 0
  out BECN pkts 0        in DE pkts 0           out DE pkts 0
  out bcast pkts 332     out bcast bytes 28614
  5 minute input rate 0 bits/sec, 0 packets/sec
  5 minute output rate 0 bits/sec, 0 packets/sec
  pvc create time 00:30:05, last time pvc status changed 00:04:14


DLCI = 103, DLCI USAGE = LOCAL, PVC STATUS = INACTIVE, INTERFACE = Serial0/0/0.34

  input pkts 17          output pkts 24         in bytes 1106
  out bytes 2086         dropped pkts 0         in pkts dropped 0
  out pkts dropped 0          out bytes dropped 0
```

continues

Example 14-21   *Correlating Subinterface S0/0/0.2 to the PVC with DLCI 102 (Continued)*

```
  in FECN pkts 0          in BECN pkts 0          out FECN pkts 0
  out BECN pkts 0         in DE pkts 0            out DE pkts 0
  out bcast pkts 11       out bcast bytes 674
  5 minute input rate 0 bits/sec, 0 packets/sec
  5 minute output rate 0 bits/sec, 0 packets/sec
  pvc create time 00:30:07, last time pvc status changed 00:02:57

DLCI = 104, DLCI USAGE = LOCAL, PVC STATUS = ACTIVE, INTERFACE = Serial0/0/0.34

  input pkts 41           output pkts 42          in bytes 2466
  out bytes 3017          dropped pkts 0          in pkts dropped 0
  out pkts dropped 0             out bytes dropped 0
  in FECN pkts 0          in BECN pkts 0          out FECN pkts 0
  out BECN pkts 0         in DE pkts 0            out DE pkts 0
  out bcast pkts 30       out bcast bytes 1929
  5 minute input rate 0 bits/sec, 0 packets/sec
  5 minute output rate 0 bits/sec, 0 packets/sec
  pvc create time 00:30:07, last time pvc status changed 00:26:17
```

To find all the PVCs associated with an interface or subinterface, just scan the highlighted parts of the output in Example 14-21. In this case, S0/0/0.2 is listed with only one PVC, the one with DLCI 102, so only one PVC is associated with S0/0/0.2 in this case.

Determine Which PVC Is Used to Reach a Particular Neighbor (Step 3d)

If the router's configuration associates more than one PVC with one interface or subinterface, the next step is to figure out which of the PVCs is used to send traffic to a particular neighbor. For instance, Example 14-21 shows R1 uses a multipoint subinterface S0/0/0.34 with DLCIs 103 and 104, with DLCI 103 used for the PVC to R3, and DLCI 104 for the PVC connecting to R4. So, if you were troubleshooting a problem in which the **ping 10.1.34.3** command failed on R1, the next step would be to determine which of the two DLCIs (103 or 104) identifies the VC connecting R1 to R3.

Unfortunately, you cannot always find the answer without looking at other documentation. The only **show** command that can help is **show frame-relay map**, which can correlate the next-hop IP address and DLCI. Unfortunately, if the local router relies on Inverse ARP, the local router cannot learn the mapping information right now either, so the mapping table may not have any useful information in it. However, if static mapping is used, the correct PVC/DLCI can be identified.

In the example of R1 failing when pinging 10.1.2.2 (R2), because only one PVC is associated with the correct interface (S0/0/0.2), the PVC has already been identified, so you can ignore this step for now.

PVC Status

At this point in major troubleshooting Step 3, the correct outgoing interface/subinterface and correct PVC/DLCI have been identified. Finally, the PVC status can be examined to see if it means that the PVC has a problem.

Routers use four different PVC status codes. A router learns about two of the possible status values, *active* and *inactive*, via LMI messages from the Frame Relay switch. The switch's LMI message lists all DLCIs for all configured PVCs on the access link, and whether the PVC is currently usable (active) or not (inactive).

The first of the two PVC states that is not learned using LMI is called the *static* state. If the LMI is disabled, the router does not learn any information from the switch about PVC status. So, the router lists all its configured DLCIs in the *static* state, meaning statically configured. The router does not know if the PVCs will work, but it can at least send frames using those DLCIs and hope that the Frame Relay network can deliver them.

The other PVC state, *deleted*, is used when LMI is working but the switch's LMI message does not mention anything about a particular DLCI value. If the router has configuration for a DLCI (for example, in a **frame-relay interface-dlci** command), but the switch's LMI message does not list that DLCI, the router lists that DLCI in a deleted state. This state means that the router has configured the DLCI, but the switch has not. In real life, the deleted state may mean that the router or switch has been misconfigured, or that the Frame Relay switch has not yet been configured with the correct DLCI. Table 14-4 summarizes the four Frame Relay PVC status codes.

Table 14-4 *PVC Status Values*

Status	Active	Inactive	Deleted	Static
The PVC is defined to the Frame Relay network	Yes	Yes	No	Unknown
The router will attempt to send frames on a VC in this state	Yes	No	No	Yes

Key Topic

As noted in the last row of the table, routers only send data over PVCs in an active or static state. Also, even if the PVC is in a static state, there is no guarantee that the Frame Relay network can actually send frames over that PVC, because the static state implies that LMI is turned off, and the router has not learned any status information.

The next step in the troubleshooting process is to find the status of the PVC used to reach a particular neighbor. Continuing with the problem of R1 failing when pinging R2 (10.1.2.2), Example 14-22 shows the status of the PVC with DLCI 102, as identified earlier.

Example 14-22   show frame-relay pvc *Command on R1*

```
R1>show frame-relay pvc 102


PVC Statistics for interface Serial0/0/0 (Frame Relay DTE)


DLCI = 102, DLCI USAGE = LOCAL, PVC STATUS = INACTIVE, INTERFACE = Serial0/0/0.2

  input pkts 22            output pkts 193          in bytes 1256
  out bytes 16436          dropped pkts 0           in pkts dropped 0
  out pkts dropped 0              out bytes dropped 0
  in FECN pkts 0           in BECN pkts 0           out FECN pkts 0
  out BECN pkts 0          in DE pkts 0             out DE pkts 0
  out bcast pkts 187       out bcast bytes 16032
  5 minute input rate 0 bits/sec, 0 packets/sec
  5 minute output rate 0 bits/sec, 0 packets/sec
  pvc create time 01:12:56, last time pvc status changed 00:22:45
```

In this case, R1 cannot ping R2 because the PVC with DLCI 102 is in an inactive state.

To further isolate the problem and find the root cause, you need to look deeper into the reasons why a PVC can be in an inactive state. First, as always, repeat the same troubleshooting steps on the other router—in this case, R2. If no problems are found on R2, other than an inactive PVC, the problem may be a genuine problem in the Frame Relay provider's network, so a call to the provider may be the next step. However, you may find some other problem on the remote router. For example, to create the failure and **show** commands in this section, R2's access link was shut down, so a quick examination of troubleshooting Step 1 on router R2 would have identified the problem. However, if further troubleshooting shows that both routers list their ends of the PVC in an inactive state, the root cause lies within the Frame Relay provider's network.

Finding the root cause of a problem related to a PVC in a deleted state is relatively easy. The deleted status means that the Frame Relay switch's configuration and the router's configuration do not match, with the router configuring a DLCI that is not also configured on the switch. Either the provider said it would configure a PVC with a particular DLCI, and did not, or the router engineer configured the wrong DLCI value.

Subinterface Status

Subinterfaces have a line status and protocol status code, just like physical interfaces. However, because subinterfaces are virtual, the status codes and their meanings differ a bit from physical interfaces. This section briefly examines how Frame Relay subinterfaces work and how IOS decides if a Frame Relay subinterface should be in an up/up state or a down/down state.

Frame Relay configuration associates one or more DLCIs with a subinterface using two commands: **frame-relay interface-dlci** and **frame-relay map**. Of all the DLCIs associated with a subinterface, IOS uses the following rules to determine the status of a subinterface:

■ **down/down:** All the DLCIs associated with the subinterface are inactive or deleted, or the underlying physical interface is not in an up/up state.

■ **up/up:** At least one of the DLCIs associated with the subinterface is active or static.

For example, to cause the problems shown in Example 14-22, R2 and R3 simply shut down their Frame Relay access links. Figure 14-8 shows the next LMI status message that switch S1 sends to R1.

Figure 14-8 *Results of Shutting Down R2 and R3 Access Links*

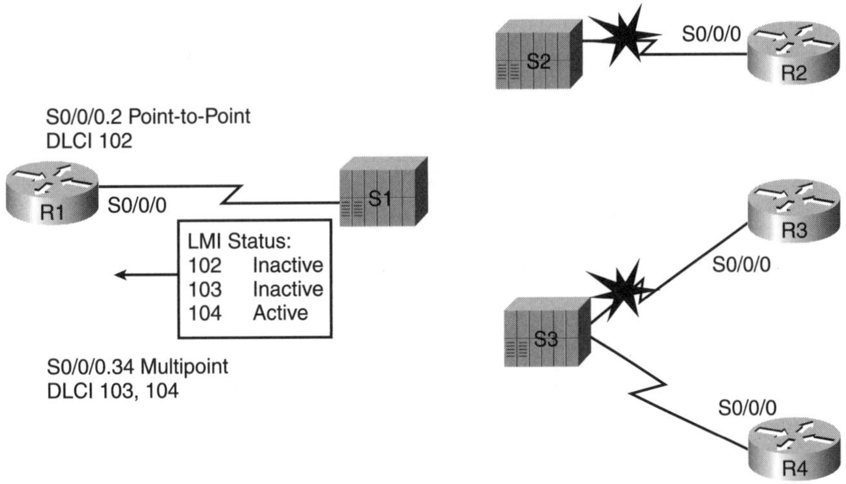

As shown in the figure, R1 uses a point-to-point subinterface (S0/0/0.2) for the VC connecting to R2, and a multipoint subinterface (S0/0/0.34) associated with the VCs to R3 and R4 (103 and 104, respectively). The beginning of Example 14-20 shows that S0/0/0.2 is in a down/down state, which is because the only DLCI associated with the subinterface (102) is inactive. However, S0/0/0.34 has two DLCIs, one of which is active, so IOS leaves S0/0/0.34 in an up/up state.

It is useful to look at subinterface status when troubleshooting, but keep in mind that just because a subinterface is up, if it is a multipoint subinterface, the up/up state does not necessarily mean that all DLCIs associated with the subinterface are working.

Frame Relay Mapping Issues (Step 4)

If you follow the first three steps of the troubleshooting process suggested in this chapter and resolve the problems at each step, at this point each router's access link interfaces should be in an up/up state, and the PVC between the two routers should be in an active (or static) state. If the routers still cannot ping each other's Frame Relay IP addresses, the next thing to check is the Frame Relay address mapping information, which maps DLCIs to next-hop IP addresses.

This section does not repeat the detailed coverage of address mapping that appears in both Chapter 13 and this chapter. However, for perspective, the following list points out some tips and hints as reminders when you perform this troubleshooting step:

Key Topic

On point-to-point subinterfaces:

- These subinterfaces do not need Inverse ARP or static mapping, because IOS simply thinks that the subnet defined on the subinterface is reachable via the only DLCI on the subinterface.

- The **show frame-relay map** command output still lists these subinterfaces, but with no next-hop IP address.

Key Topic

On physical interfaces and multipoint subinterfaces:

- They need to use either Inverse ARP or static mapping.

- The **show frame-relay map** command should list the remote router's Frame Relay IP address and the local router's local DLCI for each PVC associated with the interface or subinterface.

- If you're using static mapping, the **broadcast** keyword is needed to support a routing protocol.

For completeness, Example 14-23 shows the output of the **show frame-relay map** command on router R1 from Figure 14-6, with no problems with the mapping. (The earlier problems that were introduced have been fixed.) In this case, interface S0/0/0.2 is a point-to-point subinterface, and S0/0/0.34 is a multipoint, with one Inverse ARP-learned mapping and one statically configured mapping.

Example 14-23 **show frame-relay map** *Command on R1*

```
R1#show frame-relay map
Serial0/0/0.34 (up): ip 10.1.34.4 dlci 104(0x68,0x1880), static,
              broadcast,
              CISCO, status defined, active
Serial0/0/0.34 (up): ip 10.1.34.3 dlci 103(0x67,0x1870), dynamic,
              broadcast,, status defined, active
Serial0/0/0.2 (up): point-to-point dlci, dlci 102(0x66,0x1860), broadcast
          status defined, active
```

End-to-End Encapsulation (Step 5)

The end-to-end encapsulation on a PVC refers to the headers that follow the Frame Relay header, with two options: the Cisco-proprietary header and an IETF standard header. The configuration details were covered earlier in this chapter, in the section "Configuring the Encapsulation and LMI."

As it turns out, a mismatched encapsulation setting on the routers on opposite ends of the link might cause a problem in one particular case. If one router is a Cisco router, using Cisco encapsulation, and the other router is a non-Cisco router, using IETF encapsulation, pings may fail because of the encapsulation mismatch. However, two Cisco routers can understand both types of encapsulation, so it should not be an issue in networks with only Cisco routers.

Mismatched Subnet Numbers (Step 6)

At this point, if the problems found in the first five of the six troubleshooting steps have been resolved, all the Frame Relay problems should be resolved. However, if the two routers on either end of the PVC have mistakenly configured IP addresses in different subnets, the routers will not be able to ping one another, and the routing protocols will not become adjacent. So, as a last step, you should confirm the IP addresses on each router, and the masks, and ensure that they connect to the same subnet. To do so, just use the **show ip interface brief** and **show interfaces** commands on the two routers.

Exam Preparation Tasks

Review All the Key Topics

Review the most important topics from this chapter, noted with the key topics icon. Table 14-5 lists these key topics and where each is discussed.

Table 14-5   *Key Topics for Chapter 14*

Key Topic Element	Description	Page Number
List	Frame Relay configuration checklist	488
List	Default Frame Relay settings in IOS	490
Definition	Frame Relay address mapping concept and definition	493
Figure 14-3	Frame Relay Inverse ARP process	495
List	Six-step Frame Relay troubleshooting checklist	508
List	Summary of the two main functions of LMI	509
Table 14-4	List of PVC status values and their meanings	515
List	Reasons for subinterfaces to be up/up or down/down	517
List	Summary of mapping information seen on point-to-point subinterfaces	518
List	Summary of mapping information seen on multipoint subinterfaces	518

Complete the Tables and Lists from Memory

Print a copy of Appendix J, "Memory Tables" (found on the CD), or at least the section for this chapter, and complete the tables and lists from memory. Appendix K, "Memory Tables Answer Key," also on the CD, includes completed tables and lists for you to check your work.

Read the Appendix F Scenarios

Appendix F, "Additional Scenarios," contains five detailed scenarios. They give you a chance to analyze different designs, problems, and command output and show you how concepts from several different chapters interrelate. Scenario 4 examines a variety of options and issues related to implementing Frame Relay.

Command Reference to Check Your Memory

Although you should not necessarily memorize the information in the tables in this section, this section does include a reference for the configuration and EXEC commands covered in this chapter. Practically speaking, you should memorize the commands as a side effect of reading the chapter and doing all the activities in this exam preparation section. To see how well you have memorized the commands as a side effect of your other studies, cover the left side of the table, read the descriptions on the right side, and see if you remember the command.

Table 14-6 *Chapter 14 Configuration Command Reference*

Command	Description
encapsulation frame-relay [ietf]	Interface configuration mode command that defines the Frame Relay encapsulation that is used rather than HDLC, PPP, and so on.
**frame-relay lmi-type {ansi	q933a	cisco}**	Interface configuration mode command that defines the type of LMI messages sent to the switch.
bandwidth *num*	Interface subcommand that sets the router's perceived interface speed.
frame-relay map {*protocol protocol-address dlci***} [broadcast] [ietf	cisco]**	Interface configuration mode command that statically defines a mapping between a network layer address and a DLCI.
keepalive *sec*	Interface configuration mode command that defines whether and how often LMI status inquiry messages are sent and expected.
interface serial *number.sub* **[point-to-point	multipoint]**	Global configuration mode command that creates a subinterface or references a previously created subinterface.
frame-relay interface-dlci *dlci* **[ietf	cisco]**	Subinterface configuration mode command that links or correlates a DLCI to the subinterface.

Table 14-7 *Chapter 14 EXEC Command Reference*

Command	Description
show interfaces [*type number*]	Shows the physical interface status.
show frame-relay pvc [**interface** *interface*][*dlci*]	Lists information about the PVC status.
show frame-relay lmi [*type number*]	Lists LMI status information.
debug frame-relay lmi	Displays the contents of LMI messages.
debug frame-relay events	Lists messages about certain Frame Relay events, including Inverse ARP messages.

This chapter covers the following subjects:

VPN Fundamentals: This section describes the main goals and benefits of VPNs.

IPsec VPNs: This section explains how the IP Security (IPsec) protocol architecture provides the main features needed in both site-to-site and access VPNs.

SSL VPNs: This final section examines the use of the Secure Socket Layer (SSL) protocol that is included in common web browsers today.

CHAPTER 15

Virtual Private Networks

A company with one main site and ten remote sites could buy ten T1 lines, one each from the central site to each remote office. A more cost-effective solution would be to use Frame Relay. However, especially because the remote sites often need access to the Internet, it is even more cost effective to simply connect each office to the Internet, and send traffic between sites over the Internet, using the Internet as a WAN.

Unfortunately, the Internet is not nearly as secure as leased lines and Frame Relay. For example, for an attacker to steal a copy of data frames passing over a leased line, the attacker would have to physically tap into the cable, oftentimes inside a secure building, under the street, or at the telco central office (CO); all of these actions can result in a jail sentence. With the Internet, an attacker can find less intrusive ways to get copies of packets, without even having to leave his home computer, and with a much smaller risk of getting carted off to jail.

Virtual private networks (VPN) solve the security problems associated with using the Internet as a WAN service. This chapter explains the concepts and terminology related to VPNs.

"Do I Know This Already?" Quiz

The "Do I Know This Already?" quiz allows you to assess whether you should read the entire chapter. If you miss no more than one of these six self-assessment questions, you might want to move ahead to the section "Exam Preparation Tasks." Table 15-1 lists the major headings in this chapter and the "Do I Know This Already?" quiz questions covering the material in those headings so that you can assess your knowledge of these specific areas. The answers to the "Do I Know This Already?" quiz appear in Appendix A.

Table 15-1   *"Do I Know This Already?" Foundation Topics Section-to-Question Mapping*

Foundation Topics Section	Questions
VPN Fundamentals	1–2
IPsec VPNs	3–5
SSL VPNs	6

1. Which of the following terms refers to a VPN that uses the Internet to connect the sites of a single company, rather than using leased lines or Frame Relay?

   a. Intranet VPN

   b. Extranet VPN

   c. Access VPN

   d. Enterprise VPN

2. Which of the following are not considered to be desirable security goals for a site-to-site VPN?

   a. Message integrity checks

   b. Privacy (encryption)

   c. Antivirus

   d. Authentication

3. Which of the following functions could be performed by the IPsec IP Authentication Header?

   a. Authentication

   b. Encryption

   c. Message integrity checks

   d. Anti-replay

4. Which of the following is considered to be the best encryption protocol for providing privacy in an IPsec VPN as compared to the other answers?

   a. AES

   b. HMAC-MD5

   c. HMAC-SHA-1

   d. DES

   e. 3DES

5. Which three of the following options would be the most commonly used options for newly purchased and installed VPN components today?

   a. ASA

   b. PIX firewall

   c. VPN concentrator

   d. Cisco router

   e. Cisco VPN client

6. When using the Cisco Web VPN solution, with the client using a normal web browser without any special client software, which of the following are true?

   a. The user creates a TCP connection to a Web VPN server using SSL.

   b. If the user connects to a normal web server inside the enterprise, and that server only supports HTTP and not SSL, those packets pass over the Internet unencrypted.

   c. The Web VPN server connects to internal web servers on behalf of the Web VPN client, translating between HTTP and SSL as need be.

   d. The web VPN client cannot connect without at least thin-client SSL software installed on the client.

Foundation Topics

This chapter has three main sections. The first section introduces the basic concept of a VPN. The second (and largest) section examines some of the details of building VPNs using the rules defined in the IP Security (IPsec) RFCs. The last section explains the basics of an alternative VPN technology called SSL.

VPN Fundamentals

Leased lines have some wonderful security features. The router on one ends knows with confidence the identity of the device on the other end of the link. The receiving router also has good reason to believe that no attackers saw the data in transit, or even changed the data to cause some harm.

Virtual private networks (VPN) try to provide these same secure features as a leased line. In particular, they provide the following:

Key Topic

■ **Privacy:** Preventing anyone in the middle of the Internet (man in the middle) who copies the packet in the Internet from being able to read the data

■ **Authentication:** Verifying that the sender of the VPN packet is a legitimate device and not a device used by an attacker

■ **Data integrity:** Verifying that the packet was not changed as the packet transited the Internet

■ **Antireplay:** Preventing a man in the middle from copying packets sent by a legitimate user, and then later resending the packets to appear to be a legitimate user

To accomplish these goals, two devices near the edge of the Internet create a VPN, sometimes called a *VPN tunnel*. These devices add headers to the original packet, with these headers including fields that allow the VPN devices to perform all the functions. The VPN devices also encrypt the original IP packet, meaning that the original packet's contents are undecipherable to anyone who happens to see a copy of the packet as it traverses the Internet.

Figure 15-1 shows the general idea of what typically occurs with a VPN tunnel. The figure shows a VPN created between a branch office router and a Cisco Adaptive Security Appliance (ASA). In this case, the VPN is called a site-to-site VPN, because it connects two sites of a company, in particular. This VPN is also called site-to-site *intranet* VPN, because it connects sites that belong inside a single company.

Figure 15-1 *VPN Tunnel Concepts for a Site-to-Site Intranet VPN*

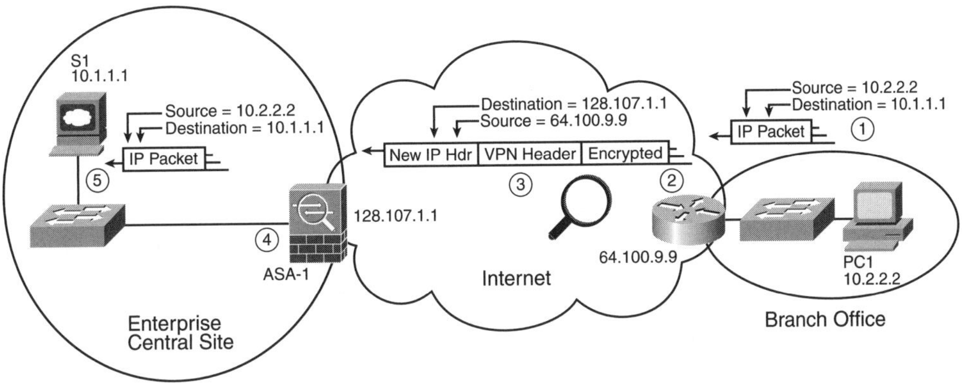

The figure shows the following steps, which explain the overall flow in the figure:

1. Host PC1 (10.2.2.2) on the right sends a packet to the web server (10.1.1.1), just as it would without a VPN.

2. The router encrypts the packet, adds some VPN headers, adds another IP header (with public IP addresses), and forwards the packet.

3. A man in the middle copies the packet but cannot change the packet without being noticed, and cannot read the contents of the packet.

4. ASA-1 receives the packet, confirms the authenticity of the sender, confirms that the packet has not been changed, and then decrypts the original packet.

5. Server S1 receives the unencrypted packet.

The benefits of using an Internet-based VPN as shown in Figure 15-1 are many. The cost of a high-speed Internet connection is typically much less than that of either a leased line or a Frame Relay WAN. The Internet is seemingly everywhere, making this kind of solution available worldwide. And by using VPN technology and protocols, the communications are secure.

NOTE   The term *tunnel* generically refers to any protocol's packet that is sent by encapsulating the packet inside another packet. The term *VPN tunnel* implies that the encapsulated packet has been encrypted, whereas the term *tunnel* does not imply whether the packet has been encrypted.

VPNs can be built with a variety of devices and for a variety of purposes. Figure 15-2 shows an example of three of the primary reasons for building an Internet VPN today.

Figure 15-2 *Intranet, Extranet, and Access VPNs*

In the top part of the figure, the central site and a remote branch office of a fictitious company (Fredsco) are connected with an intranet VPN. The middle of the figure shows Fredsco connecting to another company that supplies parts to Fredsco, making that VPN an extranet VPN. Finally, when Fred brings his laptop home at the end of the day and connects to the Internet, the secure VPN connection from the laptop back into the Fredsco network is called a remote access VPN, or simply an access VPN. In this case, the laptop itself is the end of the VPN tunnel, rather than the Internet access router. Table 15-2 summarizes the key points about these three types of VPNs.

Key
Topic

Table 15-2 *Types of VPNs*

Type	Typical Purpose
Intranet	Connects all the computers at two sites of the same organization, typically using one VPN device at each site
Extranet	Connects all the computers at two sites of different but partnering organizations, typically using one VPN device at each site
Access	Connects individual Internet users to the enterprise network

To build a VPN, one device at each site needs to have hardware and/or software that understand a chosen set of VPN security standards and protocols. The devices include the following:

■ **Routers:** In addition to packet forwarding, the router can provide VPN functions as well. The router can have specialized add-on cards that help the router perform the encryption more quickly.

■ **Adaptive Security Appliances (ASA):** The Cisco leading security appliance that can be configured for many security functions, including VPNs.

■ **PIX firewalls:** The older product line of Cisco firewall products that can perform VPN functions in addition to working as a firewall. New installations today would instead use an ASA.

■ **VPN concentrators:** An older product line from Cisco, these devices provide a hardware platform to specifically act as the endpoint of a VPN tunnel. New installations today would instead use an ASA.

■ **VPN client:** For access VPNs, the PC might need to do the VPN functions; the laptop needs software to do those functions, with that software being called a *VPN client*.

Next, the text examines the use of a set of protocols called IPsec to create VPNs.

IPsec VPNs

IPsec is an architecture or framework for security services for IP networks. The name itself is not an acronym, but rather a shortened version of the title of the RFC that defines it (RFC 4301, *Security Architecture for the Internet Protocol*), more generally called IP Security, or IPsec.

IPsec defines a set of functions, for example, authentication and encryption, and some rules regarding each of those functions. However, like the TCP/IP protocol architecture defines many protocols, some of which are alternatives to each other, IPsec allows the use of several different protocol options for each VPN feature. One of IPsec's strengths is that its role as an architecture allows it to be added to and changed over time as improvements to security protocols are made.

The following sections examine the components of IPsec, beginning with encryption, followed by key exchange, message integrity, and authentication.

IPsec Encryption

If you ignore the math—and thankfully, you can—IPsec encryption is not too difficult to understand. IPsec encryption uses a pair of encryption algorithms, which are essentially math formulas, that meet a couple of requirements. First, the two math formulas are a matched set:

■   One to hide (encrypt) the data

■   Another to re-create (decrypt) the original data from the encrypted data

Besides those somewhat obvious functions, the two math formulas were chosen so that if you intercept the encrypted text, but do not have the secret password (called an encryption key), decrypting that one packet would be difficult. Additionally, the formulas are also chosen so that if an attacker did happen to decrypt one packet, that information would not give the attacker any advantages in decrypting the other packets.

The process for encrypting data for an IPsec VPN works generally as shown in Figure 15-3. Note that the encryption key is also known as the session key, shared key, or shared session key.

Figure 15-3   *Basic IPsec Encryption Process*

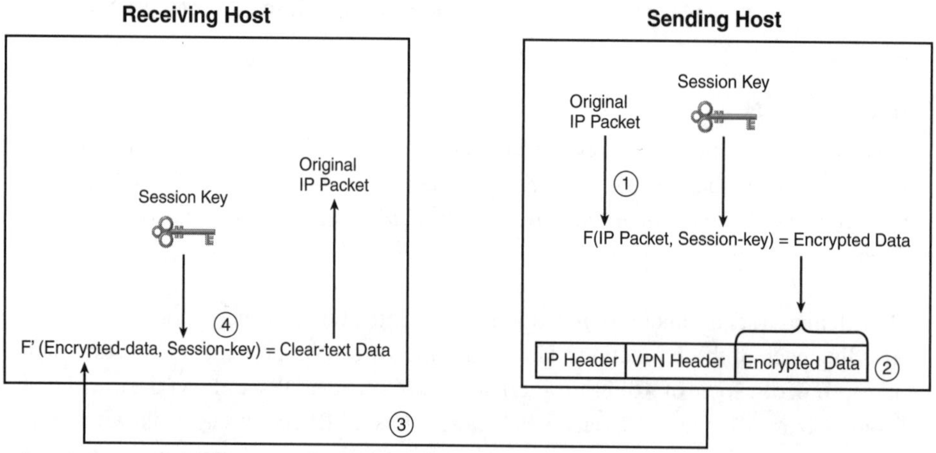

The four steps highlighted in the figure are as follows:

1.   The sending VPN device (like the remote office router in Figure 15-1) feeds the original packet and the session key into the encryption formula, calculating the encrypted data.

2. The sending device encapsulates the encrypted data into a packet, which includes the new IP header and VPN header.

3. The sending device sends this new packet to the destination VPN device (ASA-1 back in Figure 15-1).

4. The receiving VPN device runs the corresponding decryption formula, using the encrypted data and session key—the same value as was used on the sending VPN device—to decrypt the data.

IPsec supports several variations on the encryption algorithms, some of which are simply more recently developed and better, while some have other trade-offs. In particular, the length of the keys has some impact on both the difficulty for attackers to decrypt the data, with longer keys making it more difficult, but with the negative result of generally requiring more processing power. Table 15-3 summarizes several of these options and the lengths of the keys.

Table 15-3 *Comparing VPN Encryption Algorithms*

Encryption Algorithm	Key Length (Bits)	Comments
Data Encryption Standard (DES)	56	Older and less secure than the other options listed here
Triple DES (3DES)	56 x 3	Applies three different 56-bit DES keys in succession, improving the encryption strength versus DES
Advanced Encryption Standard (AES)	128 and 256	Considered the current best practice, with strong encryption and less computation than 3DES

Key Topic

IPsec Key Exchange

The use of a shared common key value (also called symmetric keys) for encryption causes a bit of chicken-and-egg problem: If both devices need to know the same key value before they can encrypt/decrypt the data, how can the two devices send the key values to each over the network without having to send the keys as clear text, open to being stolen by an attacker?

The problem related to *key distribution* has existed since the idea of encryption was first created. One simple but problematic option is to use Pre-Shared Keys (PSK), a fancy term for the idea that you manually configure the values on both devices. With PSKs, you might just exchange keys by calling the engineer at the remote site, or sending a letter, or (don't do this at home) sending an unsecure e-mail with the key value.

The problem with PSKs is that even if no one steals the shared encryption key, it is only human nature that the PSKs will almost never change. It's like changing your password on a website that never requires you to change your password: You might never think about it, no one makes you change it, and you do not want to have to remember a new password. However, for better security, the keys need to be changed occasionally because even though the encryption algorithms make it difficult to decrypt the data, it is technically possible for an attacker to break a key, and then be able to decrypt the packet. Dynamic key exchange protocols allow frequent changes to encryption keys, significantly reducing the amount of lost data if an attacker compromises an encryption key.

IPsec, as a security architecture, calls for the use of *dynamic key exchange* through a process defined by RFC 4306 and called Internet Key Exchange (IKE). IKE (RFC 4306) calls for the use of a specific process called Diffie-Hellman (DH) key exchange, named after the inventors of the process. DH key exchange overcomes the chicken-and-egg problem with an algorithm that allows the devices to make up and exchange keys securely, preventing anyone who can see the messages from deriving the key value.

The primary configuration option for DH key exchange is the length of the keys used by the DH key exchange process to encrypt the key exchange messages. The longer the encryption key that needs to be exchanged, the longer the DH key needs to be. Table 15-4 summarizes the main three options.

Key Topic

Table 15-4 *DH Options*

Option	Key Length
DH-1	768-bit
DH-2	1024-bit
DH-5	1536-bit

IPsec Authentication and Message Integrity

IPsec has several options for the authentication and message integrity process as well. Authentication generally refers to the process by which a receiving VPN device can confirm that a received packet was really sent by a trusted VPN peer. Message integrity, sometimes referred to as message authentication, allows the receiver to confirm that the message was not changed in transit.

IPsec authentication and message integrity checks use some of the same general concepts as does the encryption and key exchange process, so this text does not go into a lot of detail. However, it is useful to understand the basics.

Message integrity checks can be performed by the IPsec Authentication Header (AH) protocol using a shared (symmetric) key concept, like the encryption process, but using a hash function rather than an encryption function. The hash works similarly to the frame check sequence (FCS) concept in the trailer of most data-link protocols, but in a much more secure manner. The hash (a type of math function), with the formal name of Hashed-based Message Authentication Code (HMAC), results in a small number that can then be stored in one of the VPN headers. The sender calculates the hash and sends the results in the VPN header. The receiver recomputes the hash, using a shared key (same key value on both ends), and compares the computed value with the value listed in the VPN header. If the two values match, it means that the data fed into the formula by the sender matches what was fed into the formula by the receiver, so the receiver knows that the message did not change in transit.

These integrity check functions with HMAC typically use a secret key that needs to be at least twice as long as the encryption key that encrypts the message. As a result, several HMAC options have been created over the years. For example, the long-supported message digest algorithm 5 (MD5) standard uses a 128-bit key, allowing it to support VPNs that use the 56-bit DES encryption key length.

NOTE   If the VPN uses ESP to encrypt the packets, the HMAC message integrity function is not needed, because the attacker would have had to break the encryption key before she could have possibly altered the contents of the message.

The authentication process uses a public/private key concept similar to DH key exchange, relying on the idea that a value encrypted with the sender's private key can be decrypted with the sender's public key. Like the message integrity check, the sender calculates a value and puts it in the VPN header, but this time using the sender's private key. The receiver uses the sender's public key to decrypt the transmitted value, comparing it to the value listed in the header. If the values match, the receiver knows that the sender is authentic.

Table 15-5 summarizes a few of the specific protocols and tools available for IPsec authentication and message integrity.

Table 15-5 *IPsec Authentication and Message Integrity Options*

Function	Method	Description
Message integrity	HMAC-MD5	HMAC-MD5 uses a 128-bit shared key, generating a 128-bit hash value.
Message integrity	HMAC-SHA	HMAC–Secure Hash Algorithm defines different key sizes (for example, SHA-1 [160], SHA-256 [256], and SHA-512 [512]) to support different encryption key sizes. Considered better than MD5 but with more compute time required.
Authentication	Pre-Shared Keys	Both VPN devices must be preconfigured with the same secret key.
Authentication	Digital signatures	Also called Rivest, Shamir, and Adelman (RSA) signatures. The sender encrypts a value with its private key; the receiver decrypts with the sender's public key and compares with the value listed by the sender in the header.

The ESP and AH Security Protocols

To perform the VPN functions described in this chapter, IPsec defines two security protocols, with each protocol defining a header. These headers are shown in generic form back in Figure 15-1 as the VPN header. These headers simply provide a place to store information that is needed for the various VPN functions. For example, the message integrity process requires that the sender place the results of the hash function into a header and transmit the header (as part of the entire message) to the receiving VPN device, which then uses the value stored in that header to complete the message integrity check.

Two of the protocols defined by IPsec are the Encapsulating Security Payload (ESP) and the IP Authentication Header (AH). ESP defines rules for performing the main four functions for VPNs, as mentioned throughout this chapter and as summarized in Table 15-6. AH supports two features, namely, authentication and message integrity. A particular IPsec VPN might only use one of the two headers, or both. For example, AH could provide authentication and message integrity, with ESP providing data privacy (encryption).

Table 15-6 *Summary of Functions Supported by ESP and AH*

Key
Topic

Feature	Supported by ESP?	Supported by AH?
Authentication	Yes (weak)	Yes (strong)
Message integrity	Yes	Yes
Encryption	Yes	No
Antireplay	Yes	No

IPsec Implementation Considerations

IPsec VPNs provide a secure connection through the unsecure Internet so that hosts can behave as if they are connected directly to the corporate network. For site-to-site VPNs, the end-user hosts have no idea that a VPN even exists, just as would be the case with a leased line or Frame Relay WAN. The user can use any application, just as if he were connected to the LAN at the main office.

IPsec remote access VPN users enjoy the same functions as do site-to-site VPN users, providing the user access to any and all allowed applications. However, remote access VPNs do require some additional effort in that each host needs to use the Cisco VPN client software. This software implements the IPsec standards on the PC, rather than requiring VPN support on a separate device. The installation is not difficult, but it is an additional bit of work for each host, whereas compared to a site-to-site VPN implemented with an already installed Cisco router, the only requirement might be an upgrade of the Cisco IOS.

To ease the installation and configuration of VPNs, Cisco provides a framework and a set of functions called *Easy VPN*. The problem solved by Easy VPN can be easily understood by considering the following example. A company has 200 remote sites with which it wants to create an intranet VPN using the Internet. Additionally, this company wants extranet site-to-site VPN connections to a dozen partners. Finally, 2000 employees own laptops, and they all at least occasionally bring home their laptops and connect to the enterprise network through the Internet. And, IPsec has many options for each function, requiring configuration at each site.

Easy VPN helps solve the administration headaches in such an environment by allowing a Cisco Easy VPN server, typically the central site VPN device (for example, an ASA), to dynamically inform the remote site devices as to their IPsec VPN configurations. The remote devices—routers, ASAs, laptops with Cisco VPN client software, and so on—act as Easy VPN clients, connecting to the Easy VPN server and downloading the configuration settings.

Next, the final section of this chapter briefly examines an alternative VPN technology called SSL.

SSL VPNs

Today's commonly used web browsers all support a protocol called *Secure Socket Layer (SSL)*. These same browsers also typically support a follow-on but less-well-known standard called *Transport Layer Security (TLS)*. This section explains how SSL can be used to create access VPNs.

> **NOTE**   Rather than refer to both SSL and TLS throughout this section, the text uses the more popular SSL term alone. SSL and TLS are not truly equivalent protocols, but they perform the same functions, and they are equal to the level of depth described in this chapter.

Web browsers use HTTP to connect to web servers. However, when the communications with the web server need to be secure, the browser switches to use SSL. SSL uses well-known port 443, encrypting data sent between the browser and the server, and authenticating the user. Then, the HTTP messages flow over the SSL connection.

Most people have used SSL, oftentimes without knowing it. If you have ever used a website on the Internet, and needed to supply some credit card information or other personal information, the browser probably switched to using SSL. Most browsers show an icon that looks like a padlock, with the padlock open when not using SSL and the padlock closed (locked) when using SSL.

Web servers can choose when and how to implement SSL. Because SSL requires more work, many web servers just use HTTP for supplying general information, switching to use SSL only when the user needs to supply sensitive information, such as login credentials and financial information. However, when an enterprise's internal web servers need to send data to a home user on the other side of the Internet, rather than a user on the enterprise's local LAN, the server might need to secure all communications to the client to prevent the loss of data.

Cisco solves some of the problems associated with internal web access for Internet-based users with a feature called Web VPN. Unlike IPsec VPNs, Web VPN typically only allows web traffic, as opposed to all traffic. However, a large majority of enterprise applications today happen to be web-enabled. For example, most end users need access to internal applications, which run from internal web servers and possibly to an e-mail server. If a user can check her e-mail from a web browser, most if not all the functions needed by that user can be performed from a web browser, and Web VPN can provide a reasonable solution.

Web VPN secures an enterprise home user's connection to the enterprise network by using SSL between the end user and a special Web VPN server. Figure 15-4 shows the general idea.

Figure 15-4 *Web VPN Using SSL*

To use Web VPN, the Internet-based user opens any web browser and connects to a Cisco Web VPN server. The Web VPN server can be implemented by many devices, including an ASA. This connection uses SSL for all communications, using the built-in SSL capabilities in the web browser, so that all communications between the client and the Web VPN server are secure.

The Web VPN server acts as a web server, presenting a web page back to the client. The web page lists the enterprise applications available to the client. For example, it might list all the typical enterprise web-based applications, the e-mail server's web-based server, and other web-based services. When the user selects an option, the Web VPN server connects to that service, using either HTTP or SSL, as required by the server. The Web VPN server then passes the HTTP/SSL traffic to and from the real server over the SSL-only connection back to the Internet-based client. As a result, all communications over the Internet are secured with SSL.

The strength of this Web VPN solution is that it requires no software or special effort from the client. Employees can even use their home computer, someone else's computer, or any Internet-connected computer, and connect to the host name of the Web VPN server.

The negative with Web VPN is that it only allows the use of a web browser. If you need to use an application that cannot be accessed using a browser, you have a couple of options. First, you could implement IPsec VPNs, as already discussed. Alternately, you could use a variation on Web VPN in which the client computer loads an SSL-based thin client, much in concept like the IPsec-based Cisco VPN client used with IPsec VPNs. The client computer could then connect to the Web VPN server using the thin client, and the Web VPN server would simply pass the traffic from the PC through to the local LAN, allowing access as if the client were connected to the main enterprise network.

Exam Preparation Tasks

Review All the Key Topics

Review the most important topics from this chapter, noted with the Key Topics icon in the outer margin of the page. Table 15-7 lists a reference of these key topics and the page numbers on which each is found.

Table 15-7 *Key Topics for Chapter 15*

Key Topic Element	Description	Page Number
List	Desired security features for VPNs	528
Table 15-2	Three types of VPNs and their typical purpose	530
Figure 15-3	Significant parts of the VPN encryption process	532
Table 15-3	Facts about the three IPsec VPN encryption algorithms for encrypting the entire packet	533
Table 15-4	Three DH key exchange options and key lengths	534
Table 15-6	Summary of functions supported by the IPsec ESP and AH protocols	537

Complete the Tables and Lists from Memory

Print a copy of Appendix J, "Memory Tables," (found on the CD) or at least the section for this chapter, and complete the tables and lists from memory. Appendix K, "Memory Tables Answer Key," also on the CD, includes completed tables and lists to check your work.

Definitions of Key Terms

Define the following key terms from this chapter, and check your answers in the glossary:

Diffie-Hellman key exchange, IPsec, shared key, SSL, VPN, VPN client, Web VPN

Cisco Published ICND2 Exam Topics*
Covered in This Part

Implement an IP addressing scheme and IP Services to meet network requirements in a medium-size Enterprise branch office network

- Describe the technological requirements for running IPv6 (including: protocols, dual stack, tunneling, etc)

- Describe IPv6 addresses

Implement, verify, and troubleshoot NAT and ACLs in a medium-size Enterprise branch office network.

- Explain the basic operation of NAT

- Configure Network Address Translation for given network requirements using CLI

- Troubleshoot NAT implementation issues

* Always recheck http://www.cisco.com for the latest posted exam topics.

Part V: Scaling the IP Address Space

This chapter covers the following subjects:

Perspectives on IPv4 Address Scalability: This section explains the most significant need that drove the requirement for NAT back in the 1990s.

Network Address Translation Concepts: This section explains how several different variations of NAT work.

NAT Configuration and Troubleshooting: This section describes how to configure NAT, as well as how to use **show** and **debug** commands to troubleshoot NAT problems.

CHAPTER 16

Network Address Translation

This chapter begins Part V, "Scaling the IP Address Space." The two chapters in this part of the book relate to each other in that they explain the two most important solutions to what was a huge obstacle for the growth of the Internet. The problem was that the IPv4 address space would have been completely consumed by the mid-1990s without some significant solutions. One of the most significant short-term solutions was Network Address Translation (NAT), which is the focus of this chapter. The most significant long-term solution is IPv6, which attacks the problem by making the address space very large. IPv6 is covered in the next chapter.

This chapter begins with brief coverage of Classless Interdomain Routing (CIDR), which helps Internet service providers (ISP) manage the IP address space, and private IP addressing. The remaining majority of the chapter explains the concepts and configurations related to NAT.

"Do I Know This Already?" Quiz

The "Do I Know This Already?" quiz allows you to assess whether you should read the entire chapter. If you miss no more than one of these nine self-assessment questions, you might want to move ahead to the section "Exam Preparation Tasks." Table 16-1 lists the major headings in this chapter and the "Do I Know This Already?" quiz questions covering the material in those headings so that you can assess your knowledge of these specific areas. The answers to the "Do I Know This Already?" quiz appear in Appendix A.

Table 16-1 *"Do I Know This Already?" Foundation Topics Section-to-Question Mapping*

Foundation Topics Section	Questions
Perspectives on IPv4 Address Scalability	1–3
Network Address Translation Concepts	4–5
NAT Configuration and Troubleshooting	6–9

1. What does CIDR stand for?

   a. Classful IP Default Routing

   b. Classful IP D-class Routing

   c. Classful Interdomain Routing

   d. Classless IP Default Routing

   e. Classless IP D-class Routing

   f. Classless Interdomain Routing

2. Which of the following summarized subnets represent routes that could have been created for CIDR's goal to reduce the size of Internet routing tables?

   a. 10.0.0.0 255.255.255.0

   b. 10.1.0.0 255.255.0.0

   c. 200.1.1.0 255.255.255.0

   d. 200.1.0.0 255.255.0.0

3. Which of the following are not private addresses according to RFC 1918?

   a. 172.31.1.1

   b. 172.33.1.1

   c. 10.255.1.1

   d. 10.1.255.1

   e. 191.168.1.1

4. With static NAT, performing translation for inside addresses only, what causes NAT table entries to be created?

   a. The first packet from the inside network to the outside network

   b. The first packet from the outside network to the inside network

   c. Configuration using the **ip nat inside source** command

   d. Configuration using the **ip nat outside source** command

5. With dynamic NAT, performing translation for inside addresses only, what causes NAT table entries to be created?

   a. The first packet from the inside network to the outside network

   b. The first packet from the outside network to the inside network

   c. Configuration using the **ip nat inside source** command

   d. Configuration using the **ip nat outside source** command

6. NAT has been configured to translate source addresses of packets received from the inside part of the network, but only for some hosts as identified by an Access Control List. Which of the following commands identifies the hosts?

   a. **ip nat inside source list 1 pool barney**

   b. **ip nat pool barney 200.1.1.1 200.1.1.254 netmask 255.255.255.0**

   c. **ip nat inside**

   d. **ip nat inside 200.1.1.1 200.1.1.2**

   e. None of the other answers are correct.

7. NAT has been configured to translate source addresses of packets received from the inside part of the network, but only for some hosts. Which of the following commands identifies the outside local IP addresses that are translated?

   a. **ip nat inside source list 1 pool barney**

   b. **ip nat pool barney 200.1.1.1 200.1.1.254 netmask 255.255.255.0**

   c. **ip nat inside**

   d. **ip nat inside 200.1.1.1 200.1.1.2**

   e. None of the other answers are correct

8. Examine the following configuration commands:

   ```
   interface Ethernet0/0
    ip address 10.1.1.1 255.255.255.0
    ip nat inside
   interface Serial0/0
    ip address 200.1.1.249 255.255.255.252
   ip nat inside source list 1 interface Serial0/0
   access-list 1 permit 10.1.1.0 0.0.0.255
   ```

   If the configuration is intended to enable source NAT overload, which of the following commands could be useful to complete the configuration?

   a. The **ip nat outside** command

   b. The **ip nat pat** command

   c. The **overload** keyword

   d. The **ip nat pool** command

9. Examine the following **show** command output on a router configured for dynamic NAT:

```
-- Inside Source
access-list 1 pool fred refcount 2288
 pool fred: netmask 255.255.255.240
    start 200.1.1.1 end 200.1.1.7
    type generic, total addresses 7, allocated 7 (100%), misses 965
```

Users are complaining about not being able to reach the Internet. Which of the following is the most likely cause?

a. The problem is not related to NAT, based on the information in the command output.

b. The NAT pool does not have enough entries to satisfy all requests.

c. Standard ACL 1 cannot be used; an extended ACL must be used.

d. The command output does not supply enough information to identify the problem.

Foundation Topics

This chapter covers the details of NAT using three major sections. The first section explains the challenges to the IPv4 address space caused by the Internet revolution of the 1990s. The second section explains the basic concept behind NAT, how several variations of NAT work, and how the Port Address Translation (PAT) option conserves the IPv4 address space. The final section shows how to configure NAT from the Cisco IOS Software command-line interface (CLI), and how to troubleshoot NAT.

For those of you following the optional reading plan for which you move back and forth between this book and *CCENT/CCNA ICND1 Official Exam Certification Guide*, note that Chapter 17 of that book also covers NAT and PAT, with the configuration performed from the Security Device Manager (SDM). This chapter necessarily covers some of the same underlying concepts, but with a much fuller description of the concepts and configuration.

Perspectives on IPv4 Address Scalability

The original design for the Internet required every organization to ask for, and receive, one or more registered classful IP network numbers. The people administering the program ensured that none of the IP networks were reused. As long as every organization used only IP addresses inside its own registered network numbers, IP addresses would never be duplicated, and IP routing could work well.

Connecting to the Internet using only a registered network number, or several registered network numbers, worked well for a while. In the early to mid-1990s, it became apparent that the Internet was growing so fast that all IP network numbers would be assigned by the mid-1990s! Concern arose that the available networks would be completely assigned, and some organizations would not be able to connect to the Internet.

The main long-term solution to the IP address scalability problem was to increase the size of the IP address. This one fact was the most compelling reason for the advent of IP version 6 (IPv6). (Version 5 was defined much earlier, but was never deployed, so the next attempt was labeled as version 6.) IPv6 uses a 128-bit address, instead of the 32-bit address in IPv4. With the same or improved process of assigning unique address ranges to every organization connected to the Internet, IPv6 can easily support every organization and individual on the planet, with the number of IPv6 addresses theoretically reaching above 10^{38}.

Many short-term solutions to the addressing problem were suggested, but three standards worked together to solve the problem. Two of the standards work closely together: Network Address Translation (NAT) and private addressing. These features together allow organizations to use unregistered IP network numbers internally and still communicate well with the Internet. The third standard, Classless Interdomain Routing (CIDR), allows ISPs to reduce the wasting of IP addresses by assigning a company a subset of a network number rather than the entire network. CIDR also can allow ISPs to summarize routes such that multiple Class A, B, or C networks match a single route, which helps reduce the size of Internet routing tables.

CIDR

CIDR is a global address assignment convention, defining how the Internet Assigned Numbers Authority (IANA), its member agencies, and ISPs should assign the globally unique IPv4 address space to individual organizations. CIDR, defined in RFC 4632 (http://www.ietf.org/rfc/rfc4632.txt), has two main goals. First, its policies dictate that address assignment choices should aid the process of aggregating (summarizing) multiple network numbers into a single routing entity, reducing the size of Internet routers' routing tables. The second goal is to allow ISPs to assign address ranges to their customers of sizes other than an entire Class A, B, or C network, reducing waste, and putting off the date at which no more IPv4 addresses are available to assign to new organizations and people wanting to connect to the Internet. The following sections explain a little more detail about each of CIDR's two main goals.

Route Aggregation for Shorter Routing Tables

One of the main goals of CIDR is to allow easier route aggregation in the Internet. Imagine a router in the Internet with a route to every Class A, B, and C network on the planet! More than 2 million Class C networks exist! If Internet routers had to list every classful network in their routing tables, the routers would have to have a lot of memory, and routing table searches would require a lot of processing power. By aggregating the routes, fewer routes would need to exist in the routing table.

Figure 16-1 shows a typical case of how CIDR might be used to consolidate routes to multiple Class C networks into a single route. In the figure, imagine that ISP 1 owns Class C networks 198.0.0.0 through 198.255.255.0 (these might look funny, but they are valid Class C network numbers). Without CIDR, all other ISPs' routing tables would have a separate route to each of the 2^{16} Class C networks that begin with 198. With CIDR, as shown in the figure, the other ISPs' routers have a single route to 198.0.0.0/8—in other words, a route to all hosts whose IP address begins with 198. More than 2 million Class C networks alone exist, but CIDR has helped Internet routers reduce their routing tables to a more manageable size—in the range of a little over 200,000 routes by early 2007.

Figure 16-1 *Typical Use of CIDR*

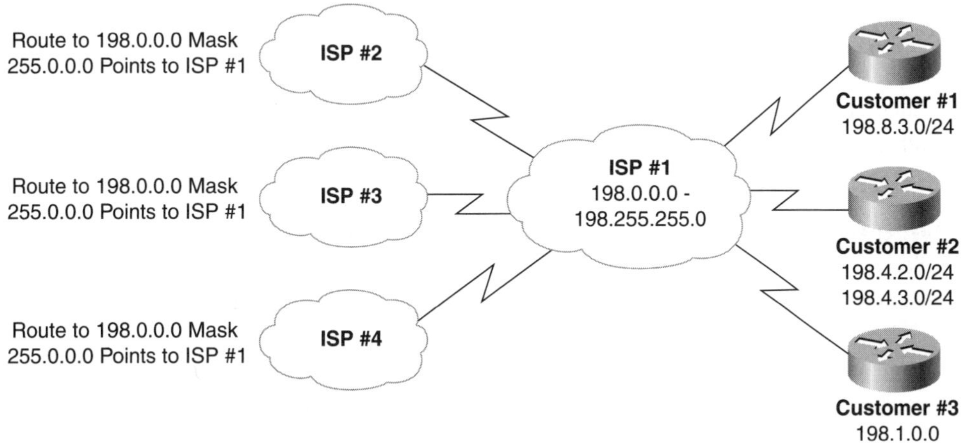

By using a routing protocol that exchanges the mask as well as the subnet/network number, a *classless* view of the number can be attained. In other words, treat the grouping as a math problem, ignoring the Class A, B, and C rules. For example, 198.0.0.0/8 (198.0.0.0, mask 255.0.0.0) defines a set of addresses whose first 8 bits are equal to decimal 198. ISP 1 advertises this route to the other ISPs, which need a route only to 198.0.0.0/8. In its routers, ISP 1 knows which Class C networks are at which customer sites. This is how CIDR gives Internet routers a much more scalable routing table—by reducing the number of entries in the tables.

For CIDR to work as shown in Figure 16-1, ISPs need to be in control of consecutive network numbers. Today, IP networks are allocated by administrative authorities for various regions of the world. The regions in turn allocate consecutive ranges of network numbers to particular ISPs in those regions. This allows summarization of multiple networks into a single route, as shown in Figure 16-1.

IPv4 Address Conservation

CIDR also helps reduce the chance of our running out of IPv4 addresses for new companies connecting to the Internet. Furthermore, CIDR allows an ISP to allocate a subset of a Class A, B, or C network to a single customer. For example, imagine that ISP 1's customer 1 needs only ten IP addresses and that customer 3 needs 25 IP addresses. ISP 1 does something like this: It assigns IP subnet 198.8.3.16/28, with assignable addresses 198.8.3.17 to 198.8.3.30, to customer 1. For customer 3, ISP 1 suggests 198.8.3.32/27, with 30 assignable addresses (198.8.3.33 to 198.8.3.62). The ISP has met the customers' needs and still not used all of Class C network 198.8.3.0.

CIDR helps prevent the wasting of IP addresses, thereby reducing the need for registered IP network numbers. Instead of two customers consuming two entire Class C networks, each consumes a small portion of a single Class C network. At the same time, CIDR, along with the intelligent administration of consecutive network numbers to each ISP, allows the Internet routing table to support a much smaller routing table in Internet routers than would otherwise be required.

Private Addressing

Some computers might never be connected to the Internet. These computers' IP addresses could be duplicates of registered IP addresses in the Internet. When designing the IP addressing convention for such a network, an organization could pick and use any network number(s) it wanted, and all would be well. For example, you can buy a few routers, connect them in your office, and configure IP addresses in network 1.0.0.0, and it would work. The IP addresses you use might be duplicates of real IP addresses in the Internet, but if all you want to do is learn on the lab in your office, everything will be fine.

When building a private network that will have no Internet connectivity, you can use IP network numbers called *private internets*, as defined in RFC 1918, *Address Allocation for Private Internets* (http://www.ietf.org/rfc/rfc1918.txt). This RFC defines a set of networks that will never be assigned to any organization as a registered network number. Instead of using someone else's registered network numbers, you can use numbers in a range that are not used by anyone else in the public Internet. Table 16-2 shows the private address space defined by RFC 1918.

Key Topic

Table 16-2   *RFC 1918 Private Address Space*

Range of IP Addresses	Class of Networks	Number of Networks
10.0.0.0 to 10.255.255.255	A	1
172.16.0.0 to 172.31.255.255	B	16
192.168.0.0 to 192.168.255.255	C	256

In other words, any organization can use these network numbers. However, no organization is allowed to advertise these networks using a routing protocol on the Internet.

You might be wondering why you would bother to reserve special private network numbers when it doesn't matter whether the addresses are duplicates. Well, as it turns out, you can use private addressing in an internetwork, and connect to the Internet at the same time, as long as you use Network Address Translation (NAT). The rest of the chapter examines and explains NAT.

Network Address Translation Concepts

NAT, defined in RFC 3022, allows a host that does not have a valid, registered, globally unique IP address to communicate with other hosts through the Internet. The hosts might be using private addresses or addresses assigned to another organization. In either case, NAT allows these addresses that are not Internet-ready to continue to be used and still allows communication with hosts across the Internet.

NAT achieves its goal by using a valid registered IP address to represent the private address to the rest of the Internet. The NAT function changes the private IP addresses to publicly registered IP addresses inside each IP packet, as shown in Figure 16-2.

Figure 16-2 *NAT IP Address Swapping: Private Addressing*

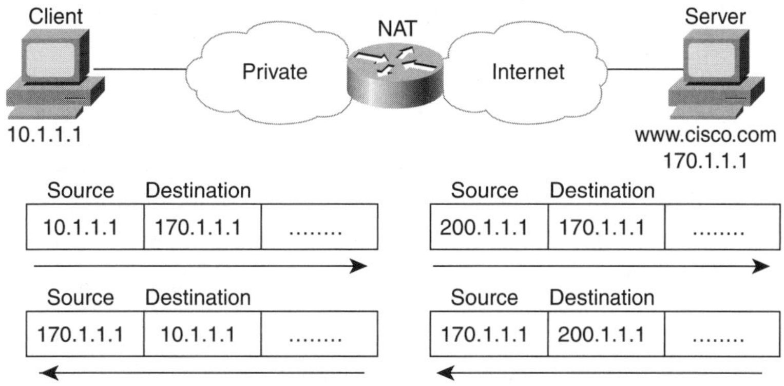

Notice that the router, performing NAT, changes the packet's source IP address when the packet leaves the private organization. The router performing NAT also changes the destination address in each packet that is forwarded back into the private network. (Network 200.1.1.0 is a registered network in Figure 16-2.) The NAT feature, configured in the router labeled NAT, performs the translation.

Cisco IOS Software supports several variations of NAT. The next few pages cover the concepts behind several of these variations. The section after that covers the configuration related to each option.

Static NAT

Static NAT works just like the example shown in Figure 16-2, but with the IP addresses statically mapped to each other. To help you understand the implications of static NAT, and to explain several key terms, Figure 16-3 shows a similar example with more information.

Figure 16-3 *Static NAT Showing Inside Local and Global Addresses*

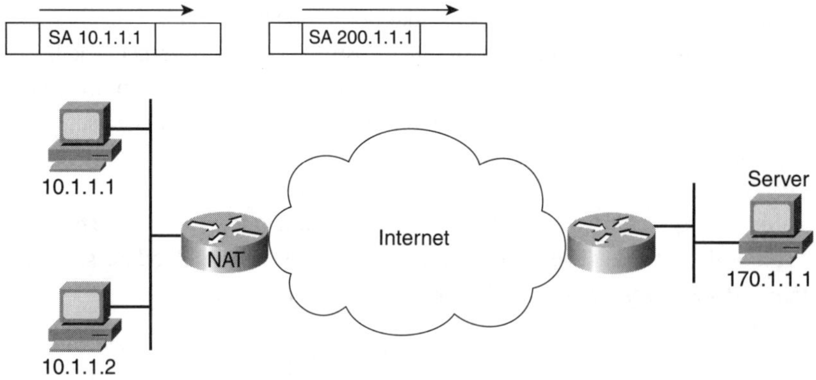

Private Address	Public Address
10.1.1.1	200.1.1.1
10.1.1.2	200.1.1.2

First, the concepts: The company's ISP has assigned it registered network 200.1.1.0. Therefore, the NAT router must make the private IP addresses look like they are in network 200.1.1.0. To do so, the NAT router changes the source IP addresses in the packets going from left to right in the figure.

In this example, the NAT router changes the source address ("SA" in the figure) of 10.1.1.1 to 200.1.1.1. With static NAT, the NAT router simply configures a one-to-one mapping between the private address and the registered address that is used on its behalf. The NAT router has statically configured a mapping between private address 10.1.1.1 and public, registered address 200.1.1.1.

Supporting two IP hosts in the private network requires a second static one-to-one mapping using a second IP address in the public address range. For example, to support 10.1.1.2, the router statically maps 10.1.1.2 to 200.1.1.2. Because the enterprise has a single registered Class C network, it can support at most 254 private IP addresses with NAT, with the usual two reserved numbers (the network number and network broadcast address).

The terminology used with NAT, particularly with configuration, can be a little confusing. Notice in Figure 16-3 that the NAT table lists the private IP addresses as "private" and the public, registered addresses from network 200.1.1.0 as "public." Cisco uses the term *inside local* for the private IP addresses in this example and *inside global* for the public IP addresses.

In Cisco terminology, the enterprise network that uses private addresses, and therefore needs NAT, is the "inside" part of the network. The Internet side of the NAT function is the "outside" part of the network. A host that needs NAT (such as 10.1.1.1 in the example) has the IP address it uses inside the network, and it needs an IP address to represent it in the outside network. So, because the host essentially needs two different addresses to represent it, you need two terms. Cisco calls the private IP address used in the inside network the *inside local* address and the address used to represent the host to the rest of the Internet the *inside global* address. Figure 16-4 repeats the same example, with some of the terminology shown.

Figure 16-4 *Static NAT Terminology*

Key Topic

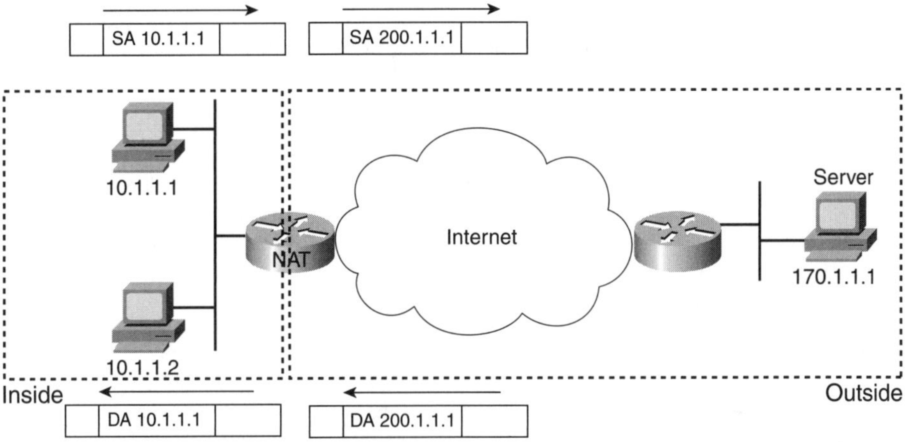

Inside Local	Inside Global
10.1.1.1	200.1.1.1
10.1.1.2	200.1.1.2

Most typical NAT configurations change only the IP address of inside hosts. Therefore, the current NAT table shown in Figure 16-4 shows the inside local and corresponding inside global registered addresses. However, the outside host IP address can also be changed with NAT. When that occurs, the terms *outside local* and *outside global* denote the IP address used to represent that host in the inside network and the outside network, respectively. Table 16-3 summarizes the terminology and meanings.

Key Topic

Table 16-3 *NAT Addressing Terms*

Term	Meaning
Inside local	In a typical NAT design, the term *inside* refers to an address used for a host inside an enterprise. An inside local is the actual IP address assigned to a host in the private enterprise network. A more descriptive term might be *inside private*.
Inside global	In a typical NAT design, the term *inside* refers to an address used for a host inside an enterprise. NAT uses an inside global address to represent the inside host as the packet is sent through the outside network, typically the Internet. A NAT router changes the source IP address of a packet sent by an inside host from an inside local address to an inside global address as the packet goes from the inside to the outside network. A more descriptive term might be *inside public*, because when using RFC 1918 addresses in an enterprise, the inside global address represents the inside host with a public IP address that can be used for routing in the public Internet.
Outside global	In a typical NAT design, the term *outside* refers to an address used for a host outside an enterprise—in other words, in the Internet. An outside global address is the actual IP address assigned to a host that resides in the outside network, typically the Internet. A more descriptive term might be *outside public*, because the outside global address represents the outside host with a public IP address that can be used for routing in the public Internet.
Outside local	NAT can translate the outside IP address—the IP address that represents the host outside the enterprise network—although this is not a popular option. When a NAT router forwards a packet from the inside network to the outside, when using NAT to change the outside address, the IP address that represents the outside host as the destination IP address in the packet header is called the outside local IP address. A more descriptive term might be *outside private*, because when using RFC 1918 addresses in an enterprise, the outside local address represents the outside host with a private IP address from RFC 1918.

Dynamic NAT

Dynamic NAT has some similarities and differences compared to static NAT. Like static NAT, the NAT router creates a one-to-one mapping between an inside local and inside global address and changes the IP addresses in packets as they exit and enter the inside network. However, the mapping of an inside local address to an inside global address happens dynamically.

Dynamic NAT sets up a pool of possible inside global addresses and defines matching criteria to determine which inside local IP addresses should be translated with NAT. For example, in Figure 16-5, a pool of five inside global IP addresses has been established: 200.1.1.1 through 200.1.1.5. NAT has also been configured to translate any inside local addresses that start with 10.1.1.

Figure 16-5 *Dynamic NAT*

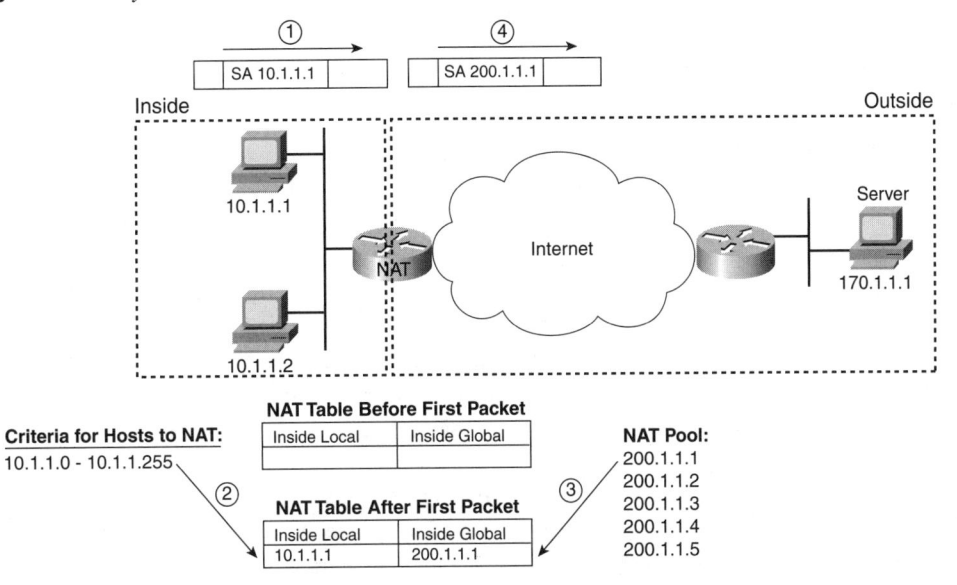

Criteria for Hosts to NAT:
10.1.1.0 - 10.1.1.255

NAT Table Before First Packet

Inside Local	Inside Global

NAT Table After First Packet

Inside Local	Inside Global
10.1.1.1	200.1.1.1

NAT Pool:
200.1.1.1
200.1.1.2
200.1.1.3
200.1.1.4
200.1.1.5

The numbers 1, 2, 3, and 4 in the figure refer to the following sequence of events:

1. Host 10.1.1.1 sends its first packet to the server at 170.1.1.1.

2. As the packet enters the NAT router, the router applies some matching logic to decide whether the packet should have NAT applied. Because the logic has been configured to match source IP addresses that begin with 10.1.1, the router adds an entry in the NAT table for 10.1.1.1 as an inside local address.

3. The NAT router needs to allocate an IP address from the pool of valid inside global addresses. It picks the first one available (200.1.1.1, in this case) and adds it to the NAT table to complete the entry.

4. The NAT router translates the source IP address and forwards the packet.

The dynamic entry stays in the table as long as traffic flows occasionally. You can configure a timeout value that defines how long the router should wait, having not translated any packets with that address, before removing the dynamic entry. You can also manually clear the dynamic entries from the table using the **clear ip nat translation** * command.

NAT can be configured with more IP addresses in the inside local address list than in the inside global address pool. The router allocates addresses from the pool until all are allocated. If a new packet arrives from yet another inside host, and it needs a NAT entry, but all the pooled IP addresses are in use, the router simply discards the packet. The user must try again until a NAT entry times out, at which point the NAT function works for the next host that sends a packet. Essentially, the inside global pool of addresses needs to be as large as the maximum number of concurrent hosts that need to use the Internet at the same time—unless you use PAT, as is explained in the next section.

Overloading NAT with Port Address Translation (PAT)

Some networks need to have most, if not all, IP hosts reach the Internet. If that network uses private IP addresses, the NAT router needs a very large set of registered IP addresses. With static NAT, for each private IP host that needs Internet access, you need a publicly registered IP address, completely defeating the goal of reducing the number of public IPv4 addresses needed for that organization. Dynamic NAT lessens the problem to some degree, because every single host in an internetwork should seldom need to communicate with the Internet at the same time. However, if a large percentage of the IP hosts in a network will need Internet access throughout that company's normal business hours, NAT still requires a large number of registered IP addresses, again failing to reduce IPv4 address consumption.

The NAT Overload feature, also called Port Address Translation (PAT), solves this problem. Overloading allows NAT to scale to support many clients with only a few public IP addresses. The key to understanding how overloading works is to recall how hosts use TCP and User Datagram Protocol (UDP) ports. Figure 16-6 details an example that helps make the logic behind overloading more obvious.

The top part of the figure shows a network with three different hosts connecting to a web server using TCP. The bottom half of the figure shows the same network later in the day, with three TCP connections from the same client. All six connections connect to the server IP address (170.1.1.1) and port (80, the well-known port for web services). In each case, the server differentiates between the various connections because their combined IP address and port numbers are unique.

NAT takes advantage of the fact that the server doesn't care whether it has one connection each to three different hosts or three connections to a single host IP address. So, to support lots of inside local IP addresses with only a few inside global, publicly registered IP addresses, NAT overload (PAT) translates both the address and possibly the port numbers as well. Figure 16-7 outlines the logic.

Figure 16-6 *Three TCP Connections: From Three Different Hosts and from One Host*

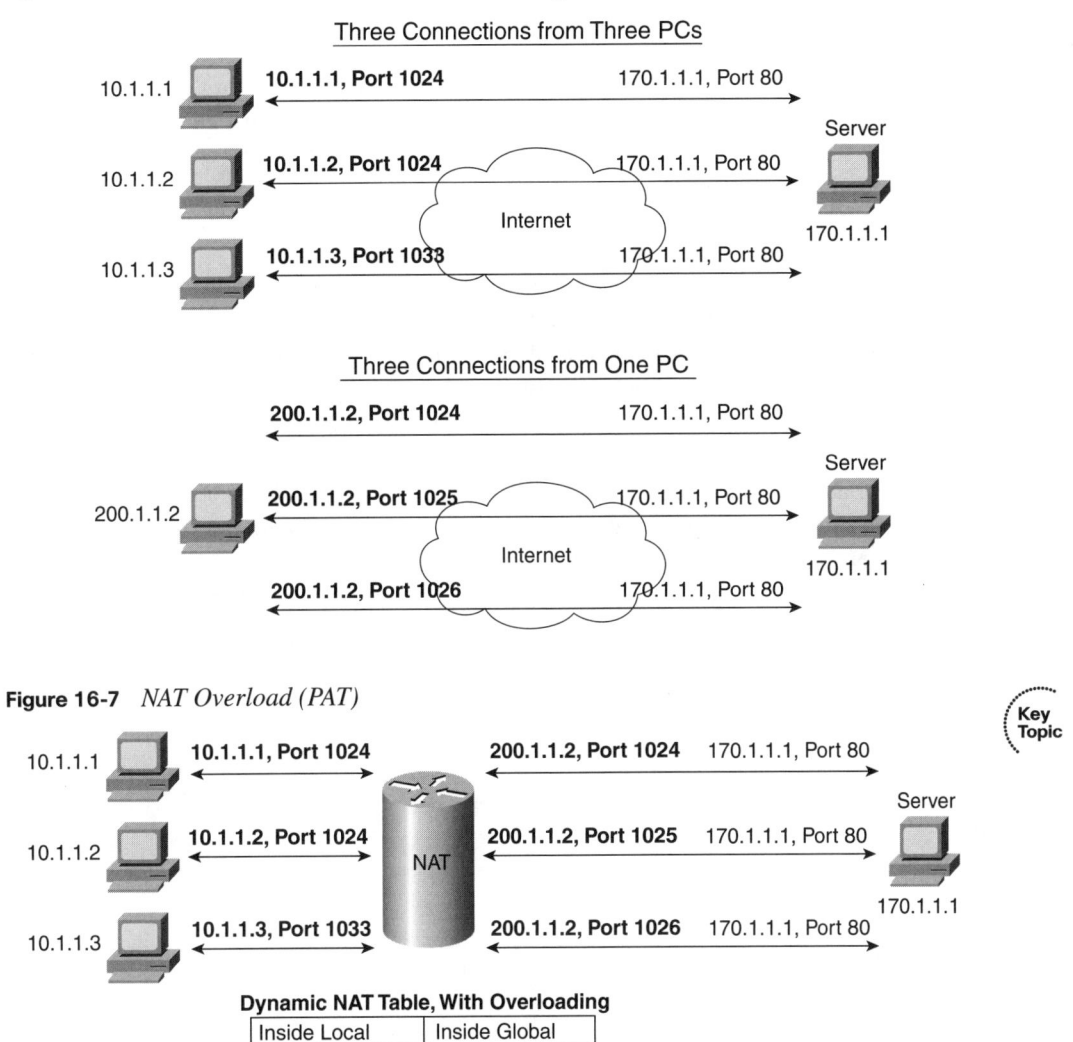

Figure 16-7 *NAT Overload (PAT)*

Key
Topic

Dynamic NAT Table, With Overloading

Inside Local	Inside Global
10.1.1.1:1024	200.1.1.2:1024
10.1.1.2:1024	200.1.1.2:1025
10.1.1.3:1033	200.1.1.2:1026

When PAT creates the dynamic mapping, it selects not only an inside global IP address but also a unique port number to use with that address. The NAT router keeps a NAT table entry for every unique combination of inside local IP address and port, with translation to the inside global address and a unique port number associated with the inside global address. And because the port number field has 16 bits, NAT overload can use more than 65,000 port numbers, allowing it to scale well without needing many registered IP addresses—in many cases, needing only one outside global IP address.

Of the three types of NAT covered in this chapter so far, PAT is by far the most popular option. Static NAT and Dynamic NAT both require a one-to-one mapping from the inside local to the inside global address. PAT significantly reduces the number of required registered IP addresses compared to these other NAT alternatives.

Translating Overlapping Addresses

The first three NAT options explained in the previous sections are the most likely to be used in most networks. However, yet another variation of NAT exists, one that allows translation of both the source and destination IP address. This option is particularly helpful when two internetworks use overlapping IP address ranges, for example, when one organization is not using private addressing but instead is using a network number registered to another company. If one company inappropriately uses a network number that is registered appropriately to a different company, and they both connect to the Internet, NAT can be used to allow both companies to communicate to hosts in the Internet and to each other. To do so, NAT translates both the source and the destination IP addresses in this case. For example, consider Figure 16-8, in which company A uses a network that is registered to Cisco (170.1.0.0).

Figure 16-8 *NAT IP Address Swapping: Unregistered Networks*

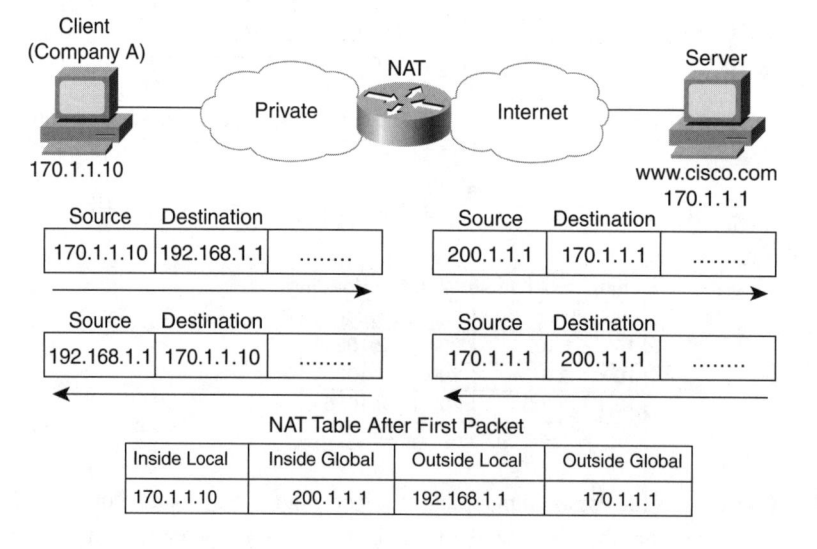

NAT Table After First Packet

Inside Local	Inside Global	Outside Local	Outside Global
170.1.1.10	200.1.1.1	192.168.1.1	170.1.1.1

With an overlapping address space, a client in company A cannot send a packet to the legitimate IP host 170.1.1.1—or, if it did, the packet would never get to the real 170.1.1.1. Why? The routing tables inside the company (on the left) probably have a route matching 170.1.1.1 in its routing table. For host 170.1.1.10 in the figure, it is in the subnet in which the "private" 170.1.1.1 would reside, so host 170.1.1.10 would not even try to forward packets destined for 170.1.1.1 to a router. Instead, it would forward them directly to host 170.1.1.1, assuming that it was on the same LAN! NAT can solve this problem, but both the source and the destination addresses must be changed as the packet passes through the NAT router. In Figure 16-8, notice that the original packet sent by the client has a destination address of 192.168.1.1. That address, called the *outside local* address, represents the server outside the company. *Outside* means that the address represents the host that physically sits in the "outside" part of the network. *Local* means that this address represents the host on the private side of the network.

As the packet passes through the NAT router (from left to right), the source address is changed, just like in the previous examples. However, the destination address is also changed, in this case, to 170.1.1.1. The destination address is also called the *outside global* address at this point, because it represents a host that is always physically on the outside network, and the address is the global, publicly registered IP address that can be routed through the Internet.

The NAT configuration includes a static mapping between the real IP address (outside global), 170.1.1.1, and the private IP address (outside local) used to represent it inside the private network—192.168.1.1.

Because the client initiates a connection to the server on the right, the NAT router not only must translate addresses, but it also must modify Domain Name System (DNS) responses. The client, for example, performs a DNS request for www.cisco.com. When the DNS reply comes back (from right to left) past the NAT router, NAT changes the DNS reply so that the client in the company thinks that www.cisco.com's IP address is 192.168.1.1.

Today, given a choice, companies tend to simply use private addressing to avoid the need to translate both IP addresses in each packet. Also, the NAT router needs a static entry for every server in the overlapped network number—a potentially painstaking task. By using private addresses, you can use NAT to connect the network to the Internet and reduce the number of registered IP addresses needed, and have to perform only the NAT function for the private address in each packet.

Table 16-4 summarizes the use of NAT terminology in Figure 16-8.

Table 16-4   *NAT Addressing Terms as Used in Figure 16-8*

Term	Value in Figure 16-8
Inside local	170.1.1.10
Inside global	200.1.1.1
Outside global	170.1.1.1
Outside local	192.168.1.1

NAT Configuration and Troubleshooting

In the following sections, you read about how to configure the three most common variations of NAT: static NAT, dynamic NAT, and PAT, along with the **show** and **debug** commands used to troubleshoot NAT.

Static NAT Configuration

Static NAT configuration, as compared to the other variations of NAT, requires the fewest configuration steps. Each static mapping between a local (private) address and a global (public) address must be configured. Additionally, the router must be told on which interfaces it should use NAT, because NAT does not have to be enabled on every interface. In particular, the router needs to know each interface and whether the interface is an inside or outside interface. The specific steps are as follows:

Step 1   Configure interfaces to be in the inside part of the NAT design using the **ip nat inside** interface subcommand.

Step 2   Configure interfaces to be in the outside part of the NAT design using the **ip nat outside** interface subcommand.

Step 3   Configure the static mappings with the **ip nat inside source static** *inside-local inside-global* global configuration command.

Figure 16-9 shows the familiar network used in the description of static NAT earlier in this chapter, which is also used for the first several configuration examples. In Figure 16-9, you can see that FredsCo has obtained Class C network 200.1.1.0 as a registered network number. That entire network, with mask 255.255.255.0, is configured on the serial link between FredsCo and the Internet. With a point-to-point serial link, only two of the 254 valid IP addresses in that network are consumed, leaving 252 addresses.

Figure 16-9 *NAT IP Address Swapping: Private Networks*

Registered Network: 200.1.1.0

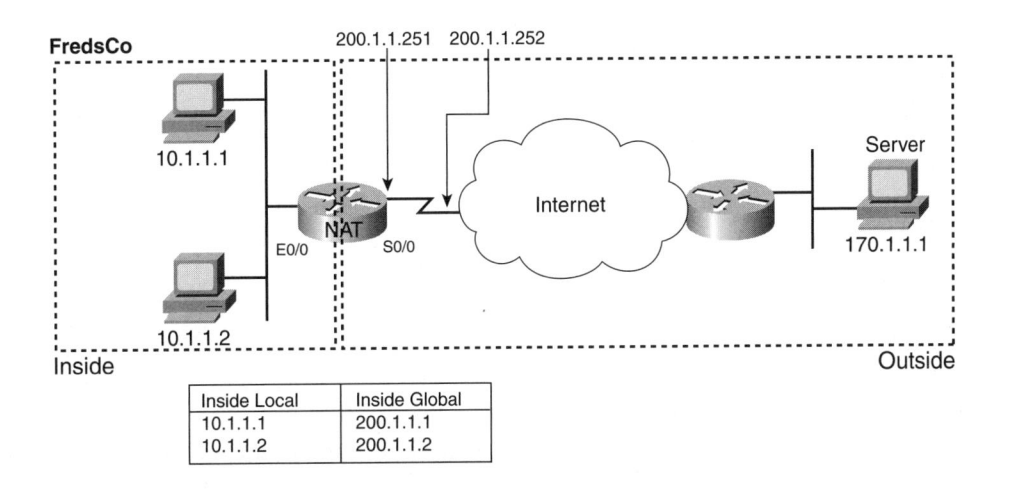

When planning a NAT configuration, you must find some IP addresses to use as inside global IP addresses. Because these addresses must be part of some registered IP address range, it is common to use the extra addresses in the subnet connecting the enterprise to the Internet—for example, the extra 252 IP addresses in network 200.1.1.0 in this case. The router can also be configured with a loopback interface and assigned an IP address that is part of a globally unique range of registered IP addresses.

Example 16-1 lists the NAT configuration, using 200.1.1.1 and 200.1.1.2 for the two static NAT mappings.

Example 16-1 *Static NAT Configuration*

```
NAT# show running-config
!
! Lines omitted for brevity
!
interface Ethernet0/0
 ip address 10.1.1.3 255.255.255.0
 ip nat inside
!
interface Serial0/0
 ip address 200.1.1.251 255.255.255.0
 ip nat outside
!
ip nat inside source static 10.1.1.2 200.1.1.2
ip nat inside source static 10.1.1.1 200.1.1.1
```

continues

Example 16-1 *Static NAT Configuration (Continued)*

```
NAT# show ip nat translations
Pro Inside global       Inside local      Outside local     Outside global
--- 200.1.1.1           10.1.1.1          ---               ---
--- 200.1.1.2           10.1.1.2          ---               ---

NAT# show ip nat statistics
Total active translations: 2 (2 static, 0 dynamic; 0 extended)
Outside interfaces:
  Serial0/0
Inside interfaces:
  Ethernet0/0
Hits: 100  Misses: 0
Expired translations: 0
Dynamic mappings:
```

The static mappings are created using the **ip nat inside source static** command. The **inside** keyword means that NAT translates addresses for hosts on the inside part of the network. The **source** keyword means that NAT translates the source IP address of packets coming into its inside interfaces. The **static** keyword means that the parameters define a static entry, which should never be removed from the NAT table because of timeout. Because the design calls for two hosts, 10.1.1.1 and 10.1.1.2, to have Internet access, two **ip nat inside** commands are needed.

After creating the static NAT entries, the router needs to know which interfaces are "inside" and which are "outside." The **ip nat inside** and **ip nat outside** interface subcommands identify each interface appropriately.

A couple of **show** commands list the most important information about NAT. The **show ip nat translations** command lists the two static NAT entries created in the configuration. The **show ip nat statistics** command lists statistics, listing things such as the number of currently active translation table entries. The statistics also include the number of hits, which increments for every packet for which NAT must translate addresses.

Dynamic NAT Configuration

As you might imagine, dynamic NAT configuration differs in some ways from static NAT, but it has some similarities as well. Dynamic NAT still requires that each interface be identified as either an inside or outside interface, and of course static mapping is no longer required. Dynamic NAT uses an access control list (ACL) to identify which inside local (private) IP addresses need to have their addresses translated, and it defines a pool of registered public IP addresses to allocate. The specific steps are as follows:

Step 1 As with static NAT, configure interfaces to be in the inside part of the NAT design using the **ip nat inside** interface subcommand.

Step 2 As with static NAT, configure interfaces to be in the outside part of the NAT design using the **ip nat outside** interface subcommand.

Step 3 Configure an ACL that matches the packets coming in inside interfaces for which NAT should be performed.

Step 4 Configure the pool of public registered IP addresses using the **ip nat pool** *name first-address last-address* **netmask** *subnet-mask* global configuration command.

Step 5 Enable dynamic NAT by referencing the ACL (Step 3) and pool (Step 4) with the **ip nat inside source list** *acl-number* **pool** *pool-name* global configuration command.

The next example uses the same network topology as the previous example (see Figure 16-9). In this case, the same two inside local addresses, 10.1.1.1 and 10.1.1.2, need translation. The same inside global addresses used in the static mappings in the previous example, 200.1.1.1 and 200.1.1.2, are instead placed in a pool of dynamically assignable inside global addresses. Example 16-2 shows the configuration as well as some **show** commands.

Example 16-2 *Dynamic NAT Configuration*

```
NAT# show running-config
!
! Lines omitted for brevity
!
interface Ethernet0/0
 ip address 10.1.1.3 255.255.255.0
 ip nat inside
!
interface Serial0/0
 ip address 200.1.1.251 255.255.255.0
 ip nat outside
!
ip nat pool fred 200.1.1.1 200.1.1.2 netmask 255.255.255.252
ip nat inside source list 1 pool fred
!
access-list 1 permit 10.1.1.2
access-list 1 permit 10.1.1.1
! The next command lists one empty line because no entries have been dynamically
! created yet.
NAT# show ip nat translations
```

continues

Example 16-2 *Dynamic NAT Configuration (Continued)*

```
NAT# show ip nat statistics
Total active translations: 0 (0 static, 0 dynamic; 0 extended)
Outside interfaces:
  Serial0/0
Inside interfaces:
  Ethernet0/0
Hits: 0  Misses: 0
Expired translations: 0
Dynamic mappings:
-- Inside Source
access-list 1 pool fred refcount 0
 pool fred: netmask 255.255.255.252
    start 200.1.1.1 end 200.1.1.2
    type generic, total addresses 2, allocated 0 (0%), misses 0
```

The configuration for dynamic NAT includes a pool of inside global addresses as well as an IP access list to define the inside local addresses for which NAT is performed. The **ip nat pool** command lists the first and last numbers in a range of inside global addresses. For example, if the pool needed ten addresses, the command might have listed 200.1.1.1 and 200.1.1.10. The required **netmask** parameter performs a kind of verification check on the range of addresses. If the address range would not be in the same subnet assuming the configured **netmask** was used, then IOS will reject the **ip nat pool** command. In this case, subnet 200.1.1.0, mask 255.255.255.252 (the configured **netmask**) would include 200.1.1.1 and 200.1.1.2 in the range of valid addresses, so IOS accepts this command.

Like static NAT, dynamic NAT uses the **ip nat inside source** command. Unlike static NAT, the dynamic NAT version of this command refers to the name of the NAT pool it wants to use for inside global addresses—in this case, fred. It also refers to an IP ACL, which defines the matching logic for inside local IP addresses. The **ip nat inside source list 1 pool fred** command maps between hosts matched by ACL 1 and the pool called fred, which was created by the **ip nat pool fred** command.

Example 16-2 ends with a couple of **show** commands that confirm that the router does not yet have any NAT translation table entries. At first, the **show ip nat translations** and **show ip nat statistics** commands display either nothing or minimal configuration information. At this point, neither host 10.1.1.1 nor 10.1.1.2 has sent any packets, and NAT has not created any dynamic entries in the NAT table or translated addresses in any packets.

The **show ip nat statistics** command at the end of the example lists some particularly interesting troubleshooting information with two different counters labeled "misses," as highlighted in the example. The first occurrence of this counter counts the number of times a new packet comes along, needing a NAT entry, and not finding one. At that point, dynamic NAT reacts and builds an entry. The second misses counter at the end of the command output lists the number of misses in the pool. This counter only increments when dynamic NAT tries to allocate a new NAT table entry and finds no available addresses, so the packet cannot be translated—probably resulting in an end user not getting to the application.

To see the misses counter and several other interesting facts, Example 16-3 continues the example started in Example 16-2. This example shows the results when hosts 10.1.1.1 and 10.1.1.2 start creating TCP connections, in this case with Telnet. This example picks up where Example 16-2 left off.

Example 16-3 *Verifying Normal Dynamic NAT Operation*

```
! A Telnet from 10.1.1.1 to 170.1.1.1 happened next; not shown
!
NAT# show ip nat statistics
Total active translations: 1 (0 static, 1 dynamic; 0 extended)
Outside interfaces:
  Serial0/0
Inside interfaces:
  Ethernet0/0
Hits: 69  Misses: 1
Expired translations: 0
Dynamic mappings:
-- Inside Source
access-list 1 pool fred refcount 1
 pool fred: netmask 255.255.255.252
    start 200.1.1.1 end 200.1.1.2
    type generic, total addresses 2, allocated 1 (50%), misses 0
NAT# show ip nat translations
Pro Inside global      Inside local      Outside local      Outside global
--- 200.1.1.1          10.1.1.1          ---                ---
NAT# clear ip nat translation *


!
! telnet from 10.1.1.2 to 170.1.1.1 happened next; not shown
!
NAT# show ip nat translations
Pro Inside global      Inside local      Outside local      Outside global
--- 200.1.1.1          10.1.1.2          ---                ---
!
! Telnet from 10.1.1.1 to 170.1.1.1 happened next; not shown
!
NAT# debug ip nat
IP NAT debugging is on

01:25:44: NAT: s=10.1.1.1->200.1.1.2, d=170.1.1.1 [45119]
01:25:44: NAT: s=170.1.1.1, d=200.1.1.2->10.1.1.1 [8228]
01:25:56: NAT: s=10.1.1.1->200.1.1.2, d=170.1.1.1 [45120]
01:25:56: NAT: s=170.1.1.1, d=200.1.1.2->10.1.1.1 [0]
```

The example begins with host 10.1.1.1 telnetting to 170.1.1.1 (not shown), with the NAT router creating a NAT entry. The NAT table shows a single entry, mapping 10.1.1.1 to 200.1.1.1. Note that the first misses counter in the **show ip nat statistics** command lists 1 miss, meaning that the first packet in host 10.1.1.1's TCP connection to 170.1.1.1 occurred and caused the router to not find a NAT table entry, incrementing the counter. The misses counter at the end of the output did not increment, because the router was able to allocate a pool member and add a NAT table entry. Also note that the last line lists statistics on the number of pool members allocated (1) and the percentage of the pool currently in use (50%).

The NAT table entry times out after a period of inactivity. However, to force the entry out of the table, the **clear ip nat translation *** command can be used. As shown in Table 16-7 at the end of the chapter, this command has several variations. Example 16-3 uses the brute force option—**clear ip nat translation *** —which removes all dynamic NAT table entries. The command can also delete individual entries by referencing the IP addresses.

After clearing the NAT entry, host 10.1.1.2 telnets to 170.1.1.1. The **show ip nat translations** command now shows a mapping between 10.1.1.2 and 200.1.1.1. Because 200.1.1.1 is no longer allocated in the NAT table, the NAT router can allocate it for the next NAT request. (Cisco IOS tends to pick the lowest available IP address when choosing the next IP address from the pool.)

Finally, at the end of Example 16-3, you see that host 10.1.1.1 has telnetted to another host in the Internet, plus the output from the **debug ip nat** command. This **debug** command causes the router to issue a message every time a packet has its address translated for NAT. You generate the output results by entering a few lines from the Telnet connection from 10.1.1.1 to 170.1.1.1. Notice that the output implies a translation from 10.1.1.1 to 200.1.1.2, but it does not imply any translation of the outside address.

NAT Overload (PAT) Configuration

NAT overload, as mentioned earlier, allows NAT to support many inside local IP addresses with only one or a few inside global IP addresses. By essentially translating the private IP address and port number to a single inside global address, but with a unique port number, NAT can support many (over 65,000) private hosts with only a single public, global address.

Two variations of PAT configuration exist in IOS. If PAT uses a pool of inside global addresses, the configuration looks exactly like dynamic NAT, except the **ip nat inside source list** global command has an **overload** keyword added to the end. If PAT just needs to use one inside global IP address, PAT can use one of its interface IP addresses. Because NAT can support over 65,000 concurrent flows with a single inside global address, a single public IP address can support an entire organization's NAT needs.

The following checklist details the configuration when using a NAT pool:

Use the same steps for configuring dynamic NAT, as outlined in the previous section, but include the **overload** keyword at the end of the **ip nat inside source list** global command.

The following checklist details the configuration when using an interface IP address as the sole inside global IP address:

Step 1   As with dynamic and static NAT, configure inside interfaces with the **ip nat inside** interface subcommand.

Step 2   As with dynamic and static NAT, configure outside interfaces with the **ip nat outside** interface subcommand.

Step 3   As with dynamic NAT, configure an ACL that matches the packets coming in inside interfaces.

Step 4   Configure the **ip nat source list** *acl-number* **interface** *interface name/ number* **overload** global configuration command, referring to the ACL created in Step 3 and to the interface whose IP address will be used for translations.

Example 16-2 shows a dynamic NAT configuration. To convert it to a PAT configuration, the **ip nat inside source list 1 pool fred overload** command would be used instead, simply adding the **overload** keyword.

The next example shows PAT configuration using a single interface IP address. Figure 16-10 shows the same familiar network, with a few changes. In this case, the ISP has given FredsCo a subset of network 200.1.1.0: CIDR subnet 200.1.1.248/30. In other words, this subnet has two usable addresses: 200.1.1.249 and 200.1.1.250. These addresses are used on either end of the serial link between FredsCo and its ISP. The NAT feature on FredsCo's router translates all NAT addresses to its serial IP address, 200.1.1.249.

In Example 16-4, which shows the NAT overload configuration, NAT translates using inside global address 200.1.1.249 only, so the NAT pool is not required. In the example, as implied in Figure 16-10, host 10.1.1.1 creates two Telnet connections, and host 10.1.1.2 creates one Telnet connection, causing three dynamic NAT entries, each using inside global address 200.1.1.249, but each with a unique port number.

Figure 16-10   *NAT Overload and PAT*

Registered Subnet: 200.1.1.248, Mask 255.255.255.252

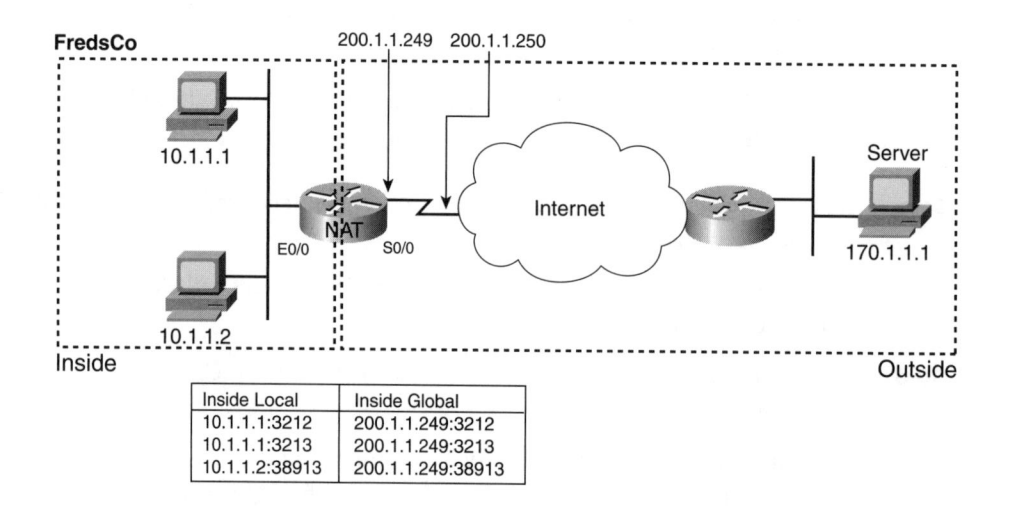

Inside Local	Inside Global
10.1.1.1:3212	200.1.1.249:3212
10.1.1.1:3213	200.1.1.249:3213
10.1.1.2:38913	200.1.1.249:38913

Example 16-4   *NAT Overload Configuration*

```
NAT# show running-config
!
! Lines Omitted for Brevity
!
interface Ethernet0/0
 ip address 10.1.1.3 255.255.255.0
 ip nat inside
!
interface Serial0/0
 ip address 200.1.1.249 255.255.255.252
 ip nat outside
!
ip nat inside source list 1 interface Serial0/0 overload
!
access-list 1 permit 10.1.1.2
access-list 1 permit 10.1.1.1
!

NAT# show ip nat translations
Pro Inside global       Inside local     Outside local     Outside global
tcp 200.1.1.249:3212    10.1.1.1:3212    170.1.1.1:23      170.1.1.1:23
tcp 200.1.1.249:3213    10.1.1.1:3213    170.1.1.1:23      170.1.1.1:23
tcp 200.1.1.249:38913   10.1.1.2:38913   170.1.1.1:23      170.1.1.1:23
NAT# show ip nat statistics
```

Example 16-4 *NAT Overload Configuration (Continued)*

```
Total active translations: 3 (0 static, 3 dynamic; 3 extended)
Outside interfaces:
  Serial0/0
Inside interfaces:
  Ethernet0/0
Hits: 103  Misses: 3
Expired translations: 0
Dynamic mappings:
-- Inside Source
access-list 1 interface Serial0/0 refcount 3
```

The **ip nat inside source list 1 interface serial 0/0 overload** command has several parameters, but if you understand the dynamic NAT configuration, the new parameters shouldn't be too hard to grasp. The **list 1** parameter means the same thing as it does for dynamic NAT: Inside local IP addresses matching ACL 1 have their addresses translated. The **interface serial 0/0** parameter means that the only inside global IP address available is the IP address of the NAT router's interface serial 0/0. Finally, the **overload** parameter means that overload is enabled. Without this parameter, the router does not perform overload, just dynamic NAT.

As you can see in the output of the **show ip nat translations** command, three translations have been added to the NAT table. Before this command, host 10.1.1.1 creates two Telnet connections to 170.1.1.1, and host 10.1.1.2 creates a single Telnet connection. Three entries are created, one for each unique combination of inside local IP address and port.

NAT Troubleshooting

The first three major parts of this book devote an entire chapter to troubleshooting. In each of those parts, the chapters cover a wide variety of topics that are related in regard to the technical topics covered in each chapter. The troubleshooting chapters (3, 7, and 11) explain the details of troubleshooting each technology area, but they also help pull some of the related concepts together.

The majority of NAT troubleshooting issues relate to getting the configuration correct. The following list summarizes some hints and tips about how to find the most common NAT configuration problems. Following the list, the text explains one common routing problem that can prevent NAT from working, which relates mainly to ensuring that the configuration is correct.

■ Ensure that the configuration includes the **ip nat inside** or **ip nat outside** interface subcommand. These commands enable NAT on the interfaces, and the inside/outside designation is important.

Key
Topic

- For static NAT, ensure that the **ip nat source static** command lists the inside local address first and the inside global IP address second.

- For dynamic NAT, ensure that the ACL configured to match packets sent by the inside host match that host's packets, before any NAT translation has occurred. For example, if an inside local address of 10.1.1.1 should be translated to 200.1.1.1, ensure that the ACL matches source address 10.1.1.1, not 200.1.1.1.

- For dynamic NAT without PAT, ensure that the pool has enough IP addresses. Symptoms of not having enough addresses include a growing value in the second misses counter in the **show ip nat statistics** command output, as well as seeing all the addresses in the range defined in the NAT pool in the list of dynamic translations.

- For PAT, it is easy to forget to add the **overload** option on the **ip nat inside source list** command. Without it, NAT works, but PAT does not, often resulting in users' packets not being translated and hosts not being able to get to the Internet.

- Perhaps NAT has been configured correctly, but an ACL exists on one of the interfaces, discarding the packets. Note that IOS processes ACLs before NAT for packets entering an interface, and after translating the addresses for packets exiting an interface.

Finally, the NAT function on one router can be impacted by a routing problem that occurs on another router. The routers in the outside part of the network, oftentimes the Internet, need to be able to route packets to the inside global IP addresses configured on the NAT router. For example, Figure 16-4, earlier in this chapter, shows the flow of packets from inside to outside, and outside to inside. Focusing on the outside-to-inside flow, the routers in the Internet needed to know how to route packets to public registered IP address 200.1.1.1. Typically, this address range would be advertised by a dynamic routing protocol. So, if a review of the NAT configuration shows that the configuration looks correct, look at the routes in both the NAT router and other routers to ensure that the routers can forward the packets, based on the addresses used on both sides of the router performing the NAT function.

Exam Preparation Tasks

Review All the Key Topics

Review the most important topics from this chapter, noted with the Key Topics icon in the outer margin of the page. Table 16-5 lists a reference of these key topics and the page numbers on which each is found. Also, note that any configuration checklists should be reviewed and studied for the content, but you don't need to memorize the step numbers or order—they are just convenient tools for remembering all the steps.

Key Topic

Table 16-5 *Key Topics for Chapter 16*

Key Topic Element	Description	Page Number
Figure 16-1	CIDR global IPv4 address assignment and route aggregation concept	551
Table 16-2	List of private IP network numbers	552
Figure 16-2	Main concept of NAT translating private IP addresses into publicly unique global addresses	553
Figure 16-4	Typical NAT network diagram with key NAT terms listed	555
Table 16-3	List of four key NAT terms and their meanings	556
Figure 16-7	Concepts behind address conservation achieved by NAT Overload (PAT)	559
List	Configuration checklist for static NAT	562
List	Configuration checklist for dynamic NAT	565
List	Summary of differences between dynamic NAT configuration and PAT using a pool	569
List	Configuration checklist for PAT configuration using an interface IP address	569
List	The most common NAT errors	571-572

Complete the Tables and Lists from Memory

Print a copy of Appendix J, "Memory Tables," (found on the CD) or at least the section for this chapter, and complete the tables and lists from memory. Appendix K, "Memory Tables Answer Key," also on the CD, includes completed tables and lists to check your work.

Definitions of Key Terms

Define the following key terms from this chapter, and check your answers in the glossary:

> CIDR, inside global, inside local, NAT overload, outside global, outside local, PAT, private IP network

Command Reference to Check Your Memory

While you should not necessarily memorize the information in the tables in this section, this section does include a reference for the configuration and EXEC commands covered in this chapter. Practically speaking, you should memorize the commands as a side effect of reading the chapter and doing all the activities in this exam preparation section. To check to see how well you have memorized the commands as a side effect of your other studies, cover the left side of the table with a piece of paper, read the descriptions on the right side, and see whether you remember the command.

Table 16-6   *Chapter 16 Configuration Command Reference*

Command	Description
ip nat {inside | outside}	Interface subcommand to enable NAT and identify whether the interface is in the inside or outside of the network
ip nat inside source {list {*access-list-number* | *access-list-name*}} {**interface** *type number* | **pool** *pool-name*} [**overload**]	Global command that enables NAT globally, referencing the ACL that defines which source addresses to NAT, and the interface or pool from which to find global addresses
ip nat pool *name start-ip end-ip* {**netmask** *netmask* | **prefix-length** *prefix-length*}	Global command to define a pool of NAT addresses

Table 16-7   *Chapter 16 EXEC Command Reference*

Command	Description
show ip nat statistics	Lists counters for packets and NAT table entries, as well as basic configuration information
show ip nat translations [**verbose**]	Displays the NAT table
clear ip nat translation {*	[**inside** *global-ip local-ip*] [**outside** *local-ip global-ip*]}	Clears all or some of the dynamic entries in the NAT table, depending on which parameters are used
clear ip nat translation *protocol* **inside** *global-ip global-port local-ip local-port* [**outside** *local-ip global-ip*]	Clears some of the dynamic entries in the NAT table, depending on which parameters are used
debug ip nat	Issues a log message describing each packet whose IP address is translated with NAT

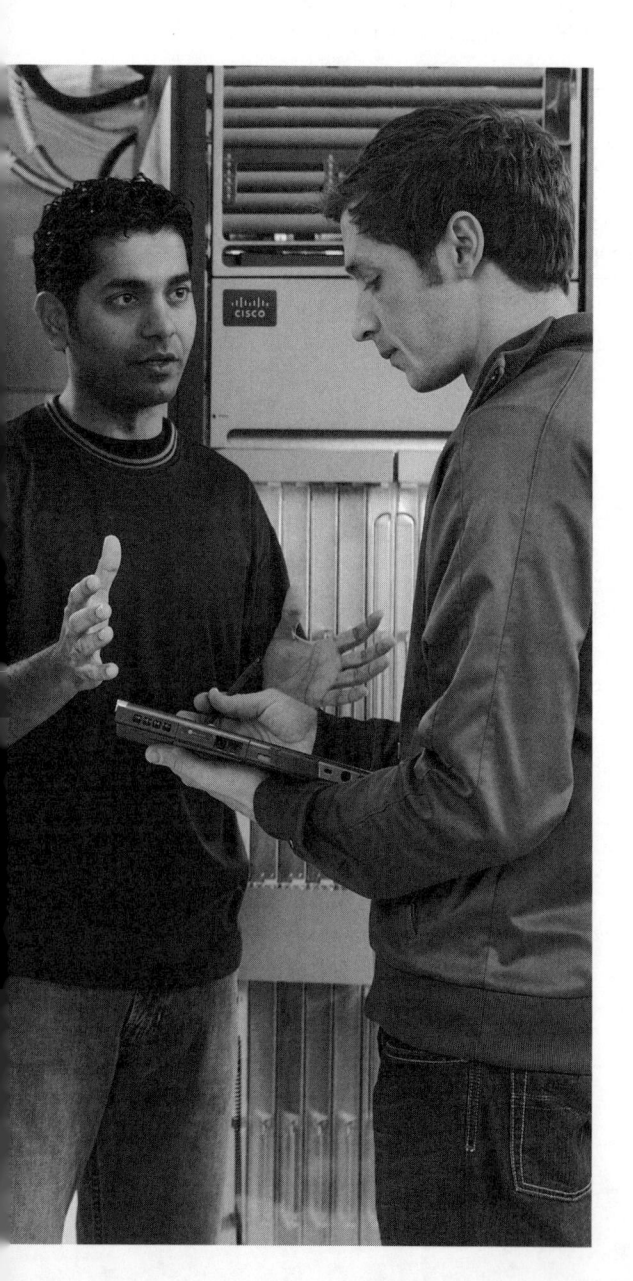

This chapter covers the following subjects:

Global Unicast Addressing, Routing, and Subnetting: This section introduces the concepts behind unicast IPv6 addresses, IPv6 routing, and subnetting using IPv6, all in comparison to IPv4.

IPv6 Protocols and Addressing: This section examines the most common protocols used in conjunction with IPv6.

Configuring IPv6 Routing and Routing Protocols: This section shows how to configure IPv6 routing and routing protocols on Cisco routers.

IPv6 Transition Options: This section explains some of the options for migrating from IPv4 to IPv6.

CHAPTER 17

IP Version 6

IP version 6 (IPv6), the replacement protocol for IPv4, is well known for a couple of reasons. IPv6 provides the ultimate solution for the problem of running out of IPv4 addresses in the global Internet by using a 128-bit address—approximately 10^{38} total addresses, versus the mere (approximate) $4*10^9$ total addresses in IPv4. However, IPv6 has been the ultimate long-term solution for over ten years, in part because the interim solutions, including Network Address Translation/Port Address Translation (NAT/PAT), have thankfully delayed the day in which we truly run out of public unicast IP addresses.

This chapter focuses on IPv6 addressing and routing, in part because the primary motivation for the eventual migration to IPv6 is to relieve the address constraints of IPv4. This chapter also briefly introduces some of the other features of IPv6, as well as explains some of the reasons for the need for IPv6.

"Do I Know This Already?" Quiz

The "Do I Know This Already?" quiz allows you to assess whether you should read the entire chapter. If you miss no more than one of these nine self-assessment questions, you might want to move ahead to the section "Exam Preparation Tasks." Table 17-1 lists the major headings in this chapter and the "Do I Know This Already?" quiz questions covering the material in those headings so that you can assess your knowledge of these specific areas. The answers to the "Do I Know This Already?" quiz appear in Appendix A.

Table 17-1 *"Do I Know This Already?" Foundation Topics Section-to-Question Mapping*

Foundation Topics Section	Questions
Global Unicast Addressing, Routing, and Subnetting	1, 2
IPv6 Protocols and Addressing	3–5
Configuring IPv6 Routing and Routing Protocols	6–8
IPv6 Transition Options	9

1. Which of the following is the most likely organization from which an enterprise could obtain an administrative assignment of a block of IPv6 global unicast IP addresses?

   a. An ISP

   b. ICANN

   c. An RIR

   d. Global unicast addresses are not administratively assigned by an outside organization.

2. Which of the following is the shortest valid abbreviation for FE80:0000:0000:0100:0000:0000:0000:0123?

   a. FE80::100::123

   b. FE8::1::123

   c. FE80::100:0:0:0:123:4567

   d. FE80:0:0:100::123

3. Which of the following answers lists a multicast IPv6 address?

   a. 2000::1:1234:5678:9ABC

   b. FD80::1:1234:5678:9ABC

   c. FE80::1:1234:5678:9ABC

   d. FF80::1:1234:5678:9ABC

4. Which of the following answers list either a protocol or function that can be used by a host to dynamically learn its own IPv6 address?

   a. Stateful DHCP

   b. Stateless DHCP

   c. Stateless autoconfiguration

   d. Neighbor Discovery Protocol

5. Which of the following help allow an IPv6 host to learn the IP address of a default gateway on its subnet?

   a. Stateful DHCP

   b. Stateless RS

   c. Stateless autoconfiguration

   d. NDP

6. Which of the following are routing protocols that support IPv6?

    a. RIPng

    b. RIP-2

    c. OSPFv2

    d. OSPFv3

    e. OSPFv4

7. In the following configuration, this router's Fa0/0 interface has a MAC address of 4444.4444.4444. Which of the following IPv6 addresses will the interface use?

```
ipv6 unicast-routing
ipv6 router rip tag1
interface FastEthernet0/0
 ipv6 address 3456::1/64
```

    a. 3456::C444:44FF:FE44:4444

    b. 3456::4444:44FF:FE44:4444

    c. 3456::1

    d. FE80::1

    e. FE80::4644:44FF:FE44:4444

    f. FE80::4444:4444:4444

8. In the configuration text in the previous question, RIP was not working on interface Fa0/0. Which of the following configuration commands would enable RIP on Fa0/0?

    a. **network 3456::/64**

    b. **network 3456::/16**

    c. **network 3456::1/128**

    d. **ipv6 rip enable**

    e. **ipv6 rip tag1 enable**

9. Which of the following IPv4-to-IPv6 transition methods allows an IPv4-only host to communicate with an IPv6-only host?

    a. Dual-stack

    b. 6to4 tunneling

    c. ISATAP tunneling

    d. NAT-PT

Foundation Topics

The world has changed tremendously over the last 10–20 years as a result of the growth and maturation of the Internet and networking technologies in general. Twenty years ago, no global network existed to which the general populace could easily connect. Ten years ago, the public Internet had grown to the point where people in most parts of the world could connect to the Internet, but with most Internet users being the more computer-savvy people. Today, practically everyone seems to have access, through their PCs, handheld devices, phones, or even the refrigerator.

The eventual migration to IPv6 will likely be driven by the need for more addresses. Practically every mobile phone supports Internet traffic, requiring the use of an IP address. Most new cars have the ability to acquire and use an IP address, along with wireless communications, allowing the car dealer to contact the customer when the car's diagnostics detect a problem with the car. Some manufacturers have embraced the idea that all their appliances need to be IP enabled.

Besides the sheer growth in the need for IPv4 addresses, edicts from governmental agencies could drive demand for IPv6. As of this writing, the U.S. government had set a date in 2008 by which all government agencies should be running IPv6 in their core IP networks. Such initiatives can help drive adoption of IPv6.

While the two biggest reasons why networks might migrate to IPv6 are the need for more addresses and mandates from government organizations, at least IPv6 includes some attractive features and migration tools. Some of those advantages are as follows:

- **Address assignment features:** IPv6 address assignment allows easier renumbering, dynamic allocation, and recovery of addresses, with nice features for mobile devices to move around and keep their IP address (thereby avoiding having to close and reopen an application).

- **Aggregation:** IPv6's huge address space makes for much easier aggregation of blocks of addresses in the Internet.

- **No need for NAT/PAT:** Using publicly registered unique addresses on all devices removes the need for NAT/PAT, which also avoids some of the application layer and VPN-tunneling issues caused by NAT.

- **IPsec:** IPsec works with both IPv4 and IPv6, but it is required on IPv6 hosts, so you can rely on support for IPsec as needed for VPN tunneling.

- **Header improvements:** While it might seem like a small issue, the IPv6 header improves several things compared to IPv4. In particular, routers do not need to recalculate a header checksum for every packet, reducing per-packet overhead. Additionally, the header includes a flow label that allows easy identification of packets sent over the same single TCP or User Datagram Protocol (UDP) connection.

- **Transition tools:** As is covered in the last major section of this chapter, IPv6 has many tools to help with the transition from IPv4 to IPv6.

The worldwide migration from IPv4 to IPv6 will not be an event, or even a year on the calendar. Rather, it will be a long process, a process that has already begun. Network engineers have a growing need to learn more about IPv6. This chapter covers the basics of IPv6, ending with some discussions about the issues of living in a world in which both IPv4 and IPv6 will likely coexist for quite a long time.

> **NOTE** *Information Week* (http://www.informationweek.com) published an interesting article about the need to migrate to IPv6, around the time this book was being completed. To see the article, search the website for the article "The Impending Internet Address Shortage."

Global Unicast Addressing, Routing, and Subnetting

One of the original design goals for the Internet was that all organizations would register and be assigned one or more public IP networks (Class A, B, or C). By registering to use a particular public network number, the company or organization using that network was assured by the numbering authorities that no other company or organization in the world would be using the addresses in that network. As a result, all hosts in the world would have globally unique IP addresses.

From the perspective of the Internet infrastructure, in particular the goal of keeping Internet routers' routing tables from getting too large, assigning an entire network to each organization helped to some degree. The Internet routers could ignore all subnets, instead having a route for each classful network. For example, if a company registered and was assigned Class B network 128.107.0.0/16, the Internet routers just needed one route for that entire network.

Over time, the Internet grew tremendously. It became clear by the early 1990s that something had to be done, or the growth of the Internet would grind to a halt when all the public IP networks were assigned, and no more existed. Additionally, the IP routing tables in Internet routers were becoming too large for the router technology of that day. So, the Internet community worked together to come up with both some short-term and long-term solutions to two problems: the shortage of public addresses and the size of the routing tables.

The short-term solutions included a much smarter public address assignment policy, where public addresses were not assigned as only Class A, B, and C networks, but as smaller subdivisions (prefixes), reducing waste. Additionally, the growth of the Internet routing tables was reduced by smarter assignment of the address ranges. For example, assigning the Class C networks that begin with 198 to only a particular Internet service provider (ISP) in a particular part of the world allowed other ISPs to use one route for 198.0.0.0/8—in other words, all addresses that begin with 198—rather than a route for each of the 65,536 different Class C networks that begin with 198. Finally, NAT/PAT achieved amazing results by allowing a typical home or small office to consume only one public IPv4 address, greatly reducing the need for public IPv4 addresses.

The ultimate solution to both problems is IPv6. The sheer number of IPv6 addresses takes care of the issue of running out of addresses. The address assignment policies already used with IPv4 have been refined and applied to IPv6, with good results for keeping the size of IPv6 routing tables smaller in Internet routers. The following sections provide a general discussion of both issues, in particular how global unicast addresses, along with good administrative choices for how to assign IPv6 address prefixes, aid in routing in the global Internet. These sections conclude with a discussion of subnetting in IPv6.

Global Route Aggregation for Efficient Routing

By the time IPv6 was being defined in the early 1990s, it was clear that thoughtful choices about how to assign the public IPv4 address space could help with the efficiency of Internet routers by keeping their routing tables much smaller. By following those same well-earned lessons, IPv6 public IP address assignment can make for even more efficient routing as the Internet migrates to IPv6.

The address assignment strategy for IPv6 is elegant, but simple, and can be roughly summarized as follows:

■ Public IPv6 addresses are grouped (numerically) by major geographic region.

■ Inside each region, the address space is further subdivided by ISP inside that region.

■ Inside each ISP in a region, the address space is further subdivided for each customer.

The same organizations handle this address assignment for IPv6 as for IPv4. The Internet Corporation for Assigned Network Numbers (ICANN, http://www.icann.org) owns the process. ICANN assigns one or more IPv6 address ranges to each Regional Internet Registry (RIR), of which five exist at the time of publication, roughly covering North America, Central/South America, Europe, Asia/Pacific, and Africa. These RIRs then subdivide their assigned address space into smaller portions, assigning prefixes to different

ISPs and other smaller registries, with the ISPs then assigning even smaller ranges of addresses to their customers.

> **NOTE**   The Internet Assigned Numbers Authority (IANA) formerly owned the address assignment process, but it was transitioned to ICANN.

The IPv6 global address assignment plan results in more efficient routing, as shown in Figure 17-1. The figure shows a fictitious company (Company1) that has been assigned an IPv6 prefix by a fictitious ISP, NA-ISP1 (standing for North American ISP number 1). The figure lists the American Registry for Internet Numbers (ARIN), which is the RIR for North America.

Figure 17-1   *Conceptual View of IPv6 Global Routes*

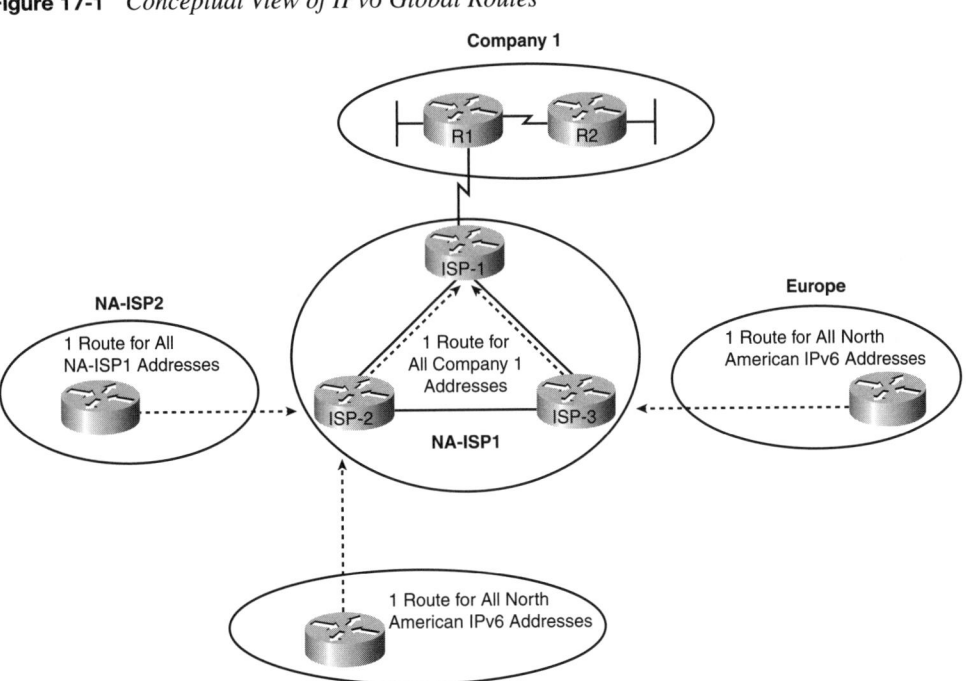

As shown in the figure, the routers installed by ISPs in other major geographies of the world can have a single route that matches all IPv6 addresses in North America. While hundreds of ISPs might be operating in north America, and hundreds of thousands of enterprise customers of those ISPs, and tens of millions of individual customers of those ISPs, all the public IPv6 addresses can be from one (or a few) very large address blocks—requiring only one (or a few) routes on the Internet routers in other parts of the world. Similarly, routers inside other ISPs in North America (for example, NA-ISP2, indicating North American ISP number 2 in the figure) can have one route that matches all address ranges assigned to NA-ISP1. And the routers inside NA-ISP1 just need to have one route that matches the entire address range assigned to Company1, rather than needing to know about all the subnets inside Company1.

Besides keeping the routers' routing table much smaller, this process also results in fewer changes to Internet routing tables. For example, if NA-ISP1 signed a service contract with another enterprise customer, NA-ISP1 could assign another prefix inside the range of addresses already assigned to NA-ISP1 by ARIN. The routers outside NA-ISP1's network—the majority of the Internet—do not need to know any new routes, because their existing routes already match the address range assigned to the new customer. The NA-ISP2 routers (another ISP) already have a route that matches the entire address range assigned to NA-ISP1, so they do not need any more routes. Likewise, the routers in ISPs in Europe and South America already have a route that works as well.

While the general concept might not be too difficult, a specific example can help. Before seeing a specific example, however, it helps to know a bit about how IPv6 addresses and prefixes are written.

Conventions for Representing IPv6 Addresses

IPv6 conventions use 32 hexadecimal numbers, organized into 8 quartets of 4 hex digits separated by a colon, to represent a 128-bit IPv6 address. For example:

2340:1111:AAAA:0001:1234:5678:9ABC:1234

Each hex digit represents 4 bits, so if you want to examine the address in binary, the conversion is relatively easy if you memorize the values shown in Table 17-2.

Table 17-2 *Hexadecimal/Binary Conversion Chart*

Hex	Binary	Hex	Binary
0	0000	8	1000
1	0001	9	1001
2	0010	A	1010
3	0011	B	1011
4	0100	C	1100
5	0101	D	1101
6	0110	E	1110
7	0111	F	1111

Writing or typing 32 hexadecimal digits, while more convenient than doing the same with 128 binary digits, can still be a pain. To make things a little easier, two conventions allow you to shorten what must be typed for an IPv6 address:

■ Omit the leading 0s in any given quartet.

■ Represent 1 or more consecutive quartets of all hex 0s with a double colon (::), but only for one such occurrence in a given address.

> **NOTE**   For IPv6, a quartet is one set of 4 hex digits in an IPv6 address. Eight quartets are in each IPv6 address.

For example, consider the following address. The bold digits represent digits in which the address could be abbreviated.

FE00:0000:0000:0001:0000:0000:0000:0056

This address has two different locations in which one or more quartets have 4 hex 0s, so two main options exist for abbreviating this address, using the :: abbreviation in one or the other location. The following two options show the two briefest valid abbreviations:

■ FE00::1:0:0:0:56

■ FE00:0:0:1::56

In particular, note that the :: abbreviation, meaning "one or more quartets of all 0s," cannot be used twice, because that would be ambiguous. So, the abbreviation FE00::1::56 would not be valid.

Conventions for Writing IPv6 Prefixes

IPv6 prefixes represent a range or block of consecutive IPv6 addresses. The number that represents the range of addresses, called a *prefix*, is usually seen in IP routing tables, just like you see IP subnet numbers in IPv4 routing tables.

Before examining IPv6 prefixes in more detail, it is helpful to review a few terms used with IPv4. IPv4 addresses can be analyzed and understood using either *classful addressing* rules or *classless addressing* rules. (This book and *CCENT/CCNA ICND1 Official Exam Certification Guide* both use classful terminology for the most part.) Classful addressing means that the analysis of an IP address or subnet includes the idea of a classful network number, with a separate network part of the address. The top part of Figure 17-2 reviews these concepts.

Figure 17-2   *IPv4 Classless and Classful Addressing, and IPv6 Addressing*

Thinking about IPv4 addressing as classful addresses helps to fully understand some issues in networking. With classful addressing, for example, the written value 128.107.3.0/24 means 16 network bits (because the address is in a Class B network) and 8 host bits (because the mask has 8 binary 0s), leaving 8 subnet bits. The same value, interpreted with classless rules, means prefix 128.107.3.0, prefix length 24. Same subnet/prefix, same meaning, same router operation, same configuration—it's just two different ways to think about the meaning of the numbers.

IPv6 uses a classless view of addressing, with no concept of classful addressing. Like IPv4, IPv6 prefixes list some value, a slash, and then a numeric prefix length. Like IPv4 prefixes, the last part of the number, beyond the length of the prefix, is represented by binary 0s. And finally, IPv6 prefix numbers can be abbreviated with the same rules as IPv4 addresses. For example, consider the following IPv6 address that is assigned to a host on a LAN:

2000:1234:5678:9ABC:1234:5678:9ABC:1111/64

This value represents the full 128-bit IP address; in fact, you have no opportunities to abbreviate this address. However, the /64 means that the prefix (subnet) in which this address resides is the subnet that includes all addresses that begin with the same first 64 bits as the address. Conceptually, it is the same logic as an IPv4 address. For example, address 128.107.3.1/24 is in the prefix (subnet) whose first 24 bits are the same values as address 128.107.3.1.

Like with IPv4, when writing or typing a prefix, the bits past the end of the prefix length are all binary 0s. In the IPv6 address shown previously, the prefix in which the address resides would be as follows:

2000:1234:5678:9ABC:**0000:0000:0000:0000**/64

When abbreviated, this would be:

2000:1234:5678:9ABC::/64

Next, one last fact about the rules for writing prefixes before seeing some examples and moving on. If the prefix length is not a multiple of 16, the boundary between the prefix and the host part of the address is inside a quartet. In such cases, the prefix value should list all the values in the last octet in the prefix part of the value. For example, if the address just shown with a /64 prefix length instead had a /56 prefix length, the prefix would include all the first 3 quartets (a total of 48 bits), plus the first 8 bits of the fourth octet. The last 8 bits (last 2 hex digits) of the fourth octet should now be binary 0s. So, by convention, the rest of the fourth octet should be written, after being set to binary 0s, as follows:

2000:1234:5678:9A00::/56

The following list summarizes some key points about how to write IPv6 prefixes:

Key Topic

■ The prefix has the same value as the IP addresses in the group for the first number of bits, as defined by the prefix length.

■ Any bits after the prefix-length number of bits are binary 0s.

■ The prefix can be abbreviated with the same rules as IPv6 addresses.

■ If the prefix length is not on a quartet boundary, write down the value for the entire quartet.

Examples can certainly help a lot in this case. Table 17-3 shows several sample prefixes, their format, and a brief explanation.

Table 17-3 *Example IPv6 Prefixes and Their Meanings*

Prefix	Explanation	Incorrect Alternative
2000::/3	All addresses whose first 3 bits are equal to the first 3 bits of hex number 2000 (bits are 001)	2000/3 (omits ::) 2::/3 (omits the rest of the first quartet)
2340:1140::/26	All addresses whose first 26 bits match the listed hex number	2340:114::/26 (omits the last digit in the second quartet)
2340:1111::/32	All addresses whose first 32 bits match the listed hex number	2340:1111/32 (omits ::)

Almost as important to this convention is to note which options are not allowed. For example, 2::/3 is not allowed instead of 2000::/3, because it omits the rest of the octet, and a device could not tell whether 2::/3 means "hex 0002" or "hex 2000." Only leading 0s in a quartet, and not trailing 0s, can be omitted when abbreviating an IPv6 address or prefix.

Now that you understand a few of the conventions about how to represent IPv6 addresses and prefixes, a specific example can show how ICANN's IPv6 global unicast IP address assignment strategy can allow the easy and efficient routing shown back in Figure 17-1.

Global Unicast Prefix Assignment Example

IPv6 standards reserve the 2000::/3 prefix—which, when interpreted more fully, means all addresses that begin with binary 001 or either a hex 2 or 3—as global unicast addresses. Global unicast addresses are addresses that have been assigned as public and globally unique IPv6 addresses, allowing hosts using those addresses to communicate through the Internet without the need for NAT. In other words, these addresses fit the purest design for how to implement IPv6 for the global Internet.

Figure 17-3 shows an example set of prefixes that could result in a company (Company1) being assigned a prefix of 2340:1111:AAAA::/48.

Figure 17-3 *Example IPv6 Prefix Assignment in the Internet*

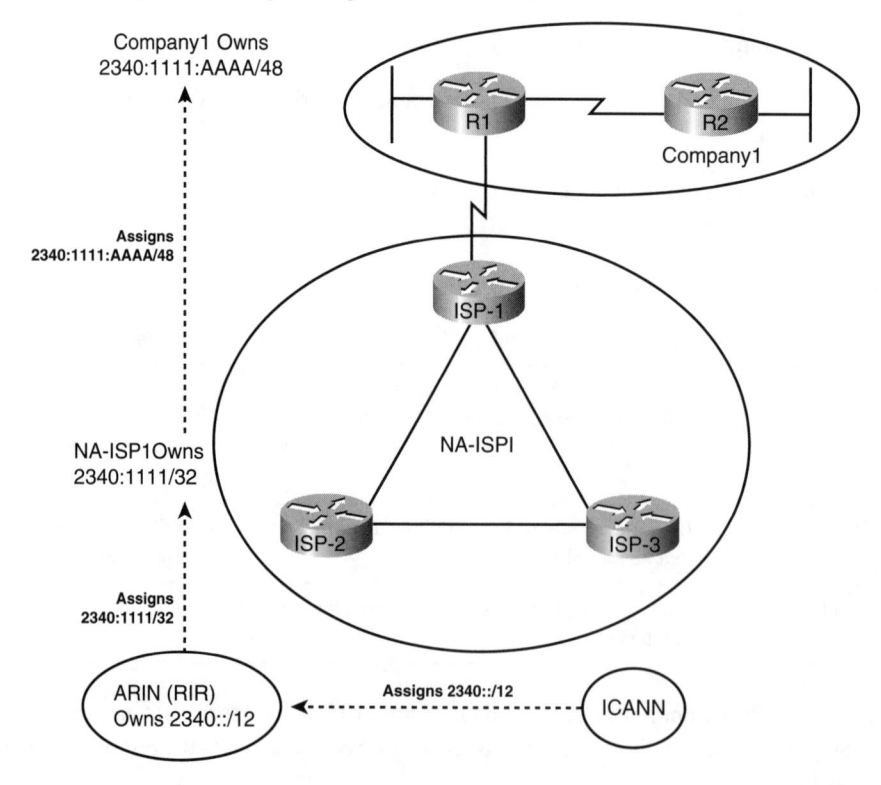

Company1 Owns
2340:1111:AAAA/48

Company1

Assigns
2340:1111:AAAA/48

ISP-1

NA-ISPI

NA-ISP1Owns
2340:1111/32

ISP-2   ISP-3

Assigns
2340:1111/32

ARIN (RIR)   Assigns 2340::/12   ICANN
Owns 2340::/12

The process starts with ICANN, which owns the entire IPv6 address space, and assigns the rights to *registry prefix* 2340::/12 to one of the RIRs, ARIN in this case (North America). This means that ARIN has the rights to assign any IPv6 addresses that begin with the first 12 bits of hex 2340 (binary value 0010 0011 0100). For perspective, that's a large group of addresses—2^{116} to be exact.

Next, NA-ISP1 asks ARIN for a prefix assignment. After ARIN ensures that NA-ISP1 meets some requirements, ARIN might assign *ISP prefix* 2340:1111::/32 to NA-ISP1. This too is a large group—2^{96} addresses to be exact. For perspective, this one address block might well be enough public IPv6 addresses for even the largest ISP, without that ISP ever needing another IPv6 prefix.

Finally, Company1 asks its ISP, NA-ISP1, for the assignment of an IPv6 prefix. NA-ISP1 assigns Company1 the site prefix 2340:1111:AAAA::/48, which is again a large range of addresses—2^{80} in this case. In the next paragraph, the text shows what Company1 could do with that prefix, but first, examine Figure 17-4, which presents the same concepts as shown in Figure 17-1, but now with the prefixes shown.

Figure 17-4 *IPv6 Global Routing Concepts*

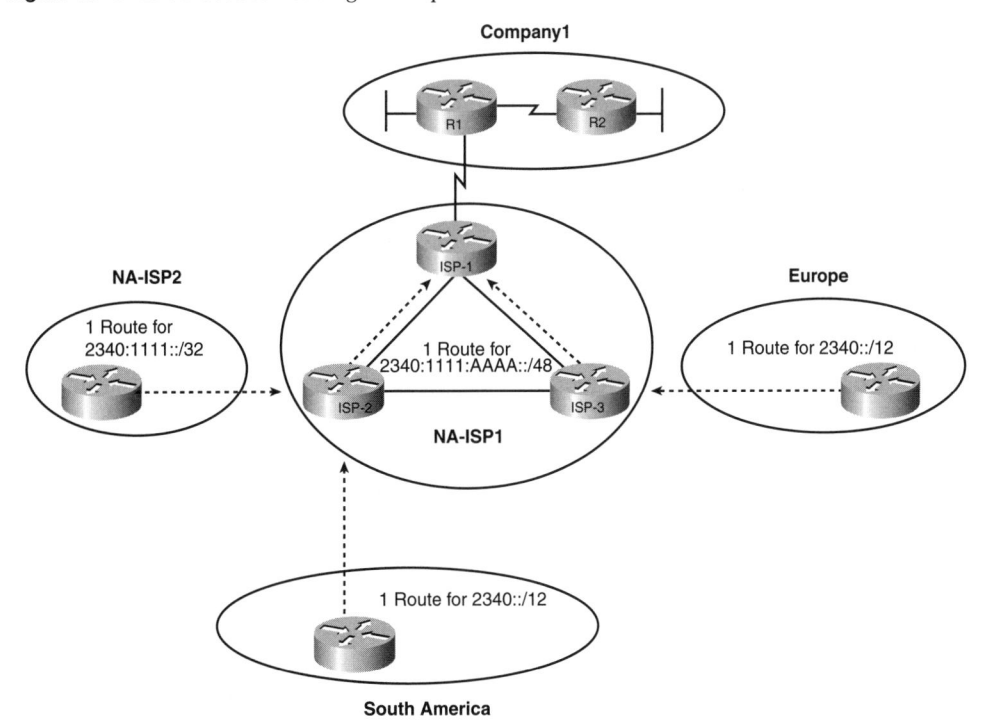

The figure shows the perspectives of routers outside North America, routers from another ISP in North America, and other routers in the same ISP. Routers outside North America can use a route for prefix 2340::/12, knowing that ICANN assigned this prefix to be used only by ARIN. This one route could match all IPv6 addresses assigned in North America. Routers in NA-ISP2, an example alternative ISP in North America, need one route for 2340:1111::/32, the prefix assigned to NA-ISP1. This one route could match all packets destined for all customers of NA-ISP1. Inside NA-ISP1, its routers need to know to which NA-ISP1 router to forward packets to for that particular customer (the router named ISP-1 in this case), so the routes inside NA-ISP1's routers lists a prefix of 2340:1111:AAAA/48.

Subnetting Global Unicast IPv6 Addresses Inside an Enterprise

The original IPv4 Internet design called for each organization to be assigned a classful network number, with the enterprise subdividing the network into smaller address ranges by subnetting the classful network. This same concept of subnetting carries over from IPv4 to IPv6, with the enterprise subnetting the prefix assigned by its ISP into smaller prefixes. When thinking about the IPv6 subnetting concept, you could make the following general analogies with classful IPv4 subnetting to help understand the process:

■ The prefix assigned to the enterprise by the ISP, which must be the same for all IPv6 addresses in one enterprise, is like the IPv4 network part of an address.

■ The enterprise engineer extends the length of the prefix, borrowing host bits, to create a subnet part of the address.

■ The last/third major part is the host part of the address, called the *interface ID* in IPv6, and is meant to uniquely identify a host inside a subnet.

For example, Figure 17-5 shows a more detailed view of the Company1 enterprise network shown in several of the earlier figures in this chapter. The design concepts behind how many subnets are needed with IPv6 are identical to those for IPv4: A subnet is needed for each VLAN and for each serial link, with the same options for subnets with Frame Relay. In this case, two LANs and two serial links exist, so Company1 needs four subnets.

The figure also shows how the enterprise engineer extended the length of the prefix as assigned by the ISP (/48) to /64, thereby creating a 16-bit subnet part of the address structure. The /48 prefix is generally called the *site prefix*, and the longer prefix used on each link is called a *subnet prefix*. To create this extra 16-bit subnet field, the engineer uses the same concept as with IPv4 when choosing a subnet mask by borrowing bits from the host field of an IPv4 address. In this case, think of the host field as having 80 bits (because the prefix assigned by the ISP is 48 bits long, leaving 80 bits), and the design in Figure 17-5 borrows 16 bits for the subnet field, leaving a measly 64 bits for the host field.

Figure 17-5 *Company1 Needs Four Subnets*

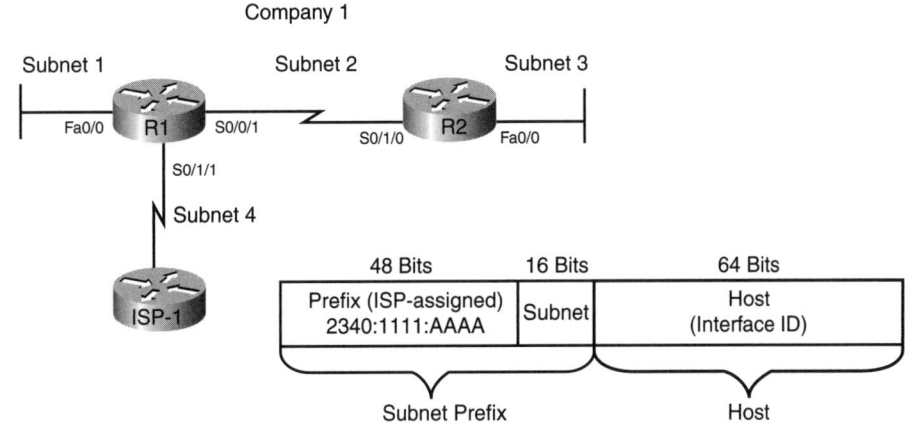

A bit of math about the design choices can help provide some perspective on the scale of IPv6. The 16-bit subnet field allows 2^{16}, or 65,536, subnets—overkill for all but the very largest organizations or companies. (There are also no worries about a zero or broadcast subnet in IPv6!) The host field is seemingly even more overkill: 2^{64} hosts per subnet, which is more than 1,000,000,000,000,000,000 addresses per subnet. However, a good reason exists for this large host or interface ID part of the address, because it allows one of the automatic IPv6 address assignment features to work well, as is covered in the section "IPv6 Host Address Assignment," later in this chapter.

Figure 17-6 takes the concept to the final conclusion, assigning the specific four subnets to be used inside Company1. Note that the figure shows the subnet fields and prefix lengths (64 in this case) in bold.

Figure 17-6 *Company1 with Four Subnets Assigned*

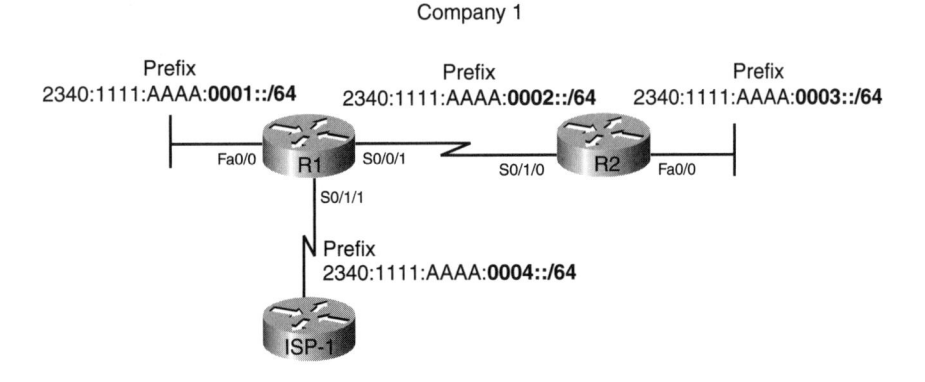

NOTE   The subnet numbers in the figure could be abbreviated slightly, removing the three leading 0s from the last shown quartets.

Figure 17-6 just shows one option for subnetting the prefix assigned to Company1. However, any number of subnet bits could be chosen, as long as the host field retained enough bits to number all hosts in a subnet. For example, a /112 prefix length could be used, extending the /48 prefix by 64 bits (4 hex quartets). Then, for the design in Figure 17-6, you could choose the following four subnets:

- 2340:1111:AAAA::0001:0000/112

- 2340:1111:AAAA::0002:0000/112

- 2340:1111:AAAA::0003:0000/112

- 2340:1111:AAAA::0004:0000/112

By using global unicast IPv6 addresses, Internet routing can be very efficient and enterprises can have plenty of IP addresses and plenty of subnets, with no requirement for NAT functions to conserve the address space.

Prefix Terminology

Before wrapping up this topic, a few new terms need to be introduced. The process of global unicast IPv6 address assignment examines many different prefixes, with many different prefix lengths. The text scatters a couple of more specific terms, but for easier study, Table 17-4 summarizes the four key terms, with some reminders of what each means.

Table 17-4 *Example IPv6 Prefixes and Their Meanings*

Term	Assignment	Example from Chapter 17
Registry prefix	By ICANN to an RIR	2340::/12
ISP prefix	By an RIR to an ISP[1]	2340:1111/32
Site prefix	By an ISP to a customer (site)	2340:1111:AAAA/48
Subnet prefix	By an enterprise engineer for each individual link	2340:1111:AAAA:0001/64

[1]While an RIR can assign a prefix to an ISP, an RIR can also assign a prefix to other Internet registries, which can subdivide and assign additional prefixes, until eventually an ISP and then its customers are assigned some unique prefix.

The next sections of this chapter broaden the discussion of IPv6 to include additional types of IPv6 addresses, along with the protocols that control and manage several common functions for IPv6.

IPv6 Protocols and Addressing

IPv4 hosts need to know several basic facts before they can succeed in simple tasks like opening a web browser to view a web page. IPv4 hosts typically need to know the IP address of one or more Domain Name System (DNS) servers so that they can use DNS protocol messages to ask a DNS server to resolve that name into an IPv4 address. They need to know an IP address of a router to use as a default gateway (default router), with the host sending packets destined to a host in a different subnet to that default router. The host, of course, needs to know its unicast IPv4 IP address and mask—or, as stated with classless terminology, its IPv4 address and prefix length—from which the host can calculate the prefix (subnet) on that link.

IPv6 hosts need the same information—DNS IP addresses, default router IP address, and their own address/prefix length—for the same reasons. IPv6 hosts still use host names, and they need to have the host name resolved into an IPv6 address. IPv6 hosts still send packets directly to hosts on the same subnet, but they send packets to the default router for off-subnet destinations.

While IPv6 hosts need to know the same information, IPv6 changes the mechanisms for learning some of these facts compared to IPv4. The following sections examine the options and protocols through which a host can learn these key pieces of information. At the same time, these sections introduce several other types of IPv6 addresses that are used by the new IPv6 protocols. The end of these sections summarizes the details and terminology for the various types of IPv6 addresses.

DHCP for IPv6

IPv6 hosts can use Dynamic Host Configuration Protocol (DHCP) to learn and lease an IP address and corresponding prefix length (mask), the IP address of the default router, and the DNS IP address(es). The concept works basically like DHCP for IPv4: The host sends a (multicast) IPv6 packet searching for the DHCP server. When a server replies, the DHCP client sends a message asking for a lease of an IP address, and the server replies, listing an IPv6 address, prefix length, default router, and DNS IP addresses. The names and formats of the actual DHCP messages have changed quite a bit from IPv4 to IPv6, so DHCPv4 and DHCPv6 differ in detail, but the basic process remains the same. (DHCPv4 refers to the version of DHCP used for IPv4, and DHCPv6 refers to the version of DHCP used for IPv6.)

DHCPv4 servers retain information about each client, like the IP address leased to that client and the length of time for which the lease is valid. This type of information is called *state information*, because it tracks the state or status of each client. DHCPv6 servers happen to have two operational modes: stateful, in which the server tracks state information, and stateless, in which the server does not track state information. Stateful DHCPv6 servers fill the same role as the older DHCPv4 servers, while stateless DHCPv6 servers fill one role in an IPv6 alternative to stateful DHCP. (Stateless DHCP, and its purpose, is covered in the upcoming section "Learning the IP Address(es) of DNS Servers.")

One difference between DHCPv4 and stateful DHCPv6 is that IPv4 hosts send IP broadcasts to find DHCP servers, while IPv6 hosts send IPv6 multicasts. IPv6 multicast addresses have a prefix of FF00::/8, meaning that the first 8 bits of an address are binary 11111111, or FF in hex. The multicast address FF02::1:2 (longhand FF02:0000:0000:0000:0000:0000:0001:0002) has been reserved in IPv6 to be used by hosts to send packets to an unknown DHCP server, with the routers working to forward these packets to the appropriate DHCP server.

IPv6 Host Address Assignment

When using IPv4 in enterprise networks, engineers typically configure static IPv4 addresses on each router interface with the **ip address** interface subcommand. At the same time, most end-user hosts use DHCP to dynamically learn their IP address and mask. For Internet access, the router can use DHCP to learn its own public IPv4 address from the ISP.

IPv6 follows the same general model, but with routers using one of two options for static IPv6 address assignment, and with end-user hosts using one of two options for dynamic IPv6 address assignment. The following sections examine all four options. But first, to appreciate the configuration options, you need a little more information about the low-order 64 bits of the IPv6 address format: the interface ID.

The IPv6 Interface ID and EUI-64 Format

Earlier in this chapter, Figure 17-5 shows the format of an IPv6 global unicast address, with the second half of the address called the host or interface ID. The value of the interface ID portion of a global unicast address can be set to any value, as long as no other host in the same subnet attempts to use the same value. (IPv6 includes a dynamic method for hosts to find out whether a duplicate address exists on the subnet before starting to use the address.) However, the size of the interface ID was purposefully chosen to allow easy autoconfiguration of IP addresses by plugging the MAC address of a network card into the interface ID field in an IPv6 address.

MAC addresses are 6 bytes (48 bits) in length, so for a host to automatically decide on a value to use in the 8-byte (64-bit) interface ID field, IPv6 cannot simply copy just the MAC address. To complete the 64-bit interface ID, IPv6 fills in 2 more bytes. Interestingly, to do so, IPv6 separates the MAC address into two 3-byte halves, and inserts hex FFFE in between the halves, to form the interface ID field, as well as setting 1 special bit to binary 1. This format, called the EUI-64 format, is shown in Figure 17-7.

Figure 17-7 *IPv6 Address Format with Interface ID and EUI-64*

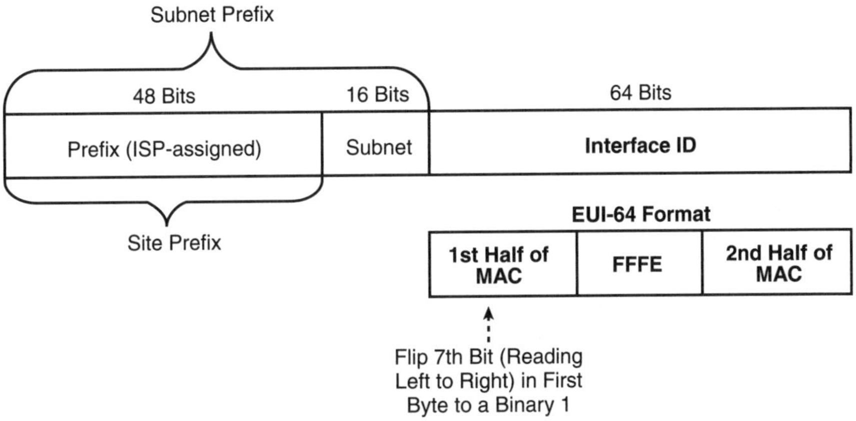

Although it might seem a bit convoluted, it works. Also, with a little practice, you can look at an IPv6 address and quickly notice the FFFE late in the address, and then easily find the two halves of the corresponding interface's MAC address.

To be complete, the figure points out one other small detail regarding the EUI-64 interface ID value. Splitting the MAC address into two halves, and injecting FFFE, is easy. However, the EUI-64 format requires setting the seventh bit in the first byte of the value to binary 1. The underlying reason is that Ethernet MAC addresses are listed with the low-order bits of each byte on the left, and the high-order bits on the right. So, the eighth bit in a byte (reading from left to right) is the highest-order bit in the address, and the seventh bit (reading from left to right) is the second highest-order bit. This second highest-order bit in the first byte—the seventh bit reading from left to right—is called the universal/local (U/L) bit. Set to binary 0, it means that the MAC address is a burned-in MAC address. Set to 1, it means that the MAC address has been configured locally. EUI-64 says that the U/L bit should be set to 1, meaning local.

For example, the following two lines list a host's MAC address and corresponding EUI-64 format interface ID, assuming the use of an address configuration option that uses the EUI-64 format:

■   0034:5678:9ABC

■   0234:56FF:FE78:9ABC

> **NOTE**   To change the seventh bit (reading left-to-right) in the example, convert hex 00 to binary 00000000, change the seventh bit to 1 (00000010), and then convert back to hex, for hex 02 as the first two digits.

Static IPv6 Address Configuration

Two options for static IPv6 address configuration are covered in this book, and both are available on both routers and hosts: static configuration of the entire address, and static configuration of a /64 prefix with the host calculating its EUI-64 interface ID to complete the IP address. This section shows the concept using routers.

To configure an IPv6 address on an interface, the router needs an **ipv6 address** *address/prefix-length* [**eui-64**] interface subcommand on each interface. If the **eui-64** keyword is not included, the address must represent the entire 128-bit address. If the **eui-64** keyword is included, the address should represent the 64-bit prefix, with the router creating the interface ID using the EUI-64 format. The *prefix-length* parameter should be the length of the subnet prefix. For example, Example 17-1 lists the commands on Router R1 from Figure 17-6 earlier in this chapter, which is one of Company1's enterprise routers. It uses the site prefix length of /64. The example shows both versions of the command (with and without the **eui-64** keyword.)

Example 17-1   *Configuring Static IPv6 Addresses*

```
! The first interface is in subnet 1, and will use EUI-64 as the Interface ID
!
interface FastEthernet0/0
 ipv6 address 2340:1111:AAAA:1::/64 eui-64
! The next interface spells out the whole 128 bits, abbreviated. The longer
! version is 2340:1111:AAAA:0002:0000:0000:0000:0001/64. It is in subnet 2.
!
interface Serial0/0/1
 ipv6 address 2340:1111:AAAA:2::1/64
! The third interface is in subnet 4, with EUI-64 format Interface ID again.
!
interface Serial0/1/1
 ipv6 address 2340:1111:AAAA:4::/64 eui-64
!
R1#show ipv6 interface fa0/0
FastEthernet0/0 is up, line protocol is up
  IPv6 is enabled, link-local address is FE80::213:19FF:FE7B:5004
  Global unicast address(es):
    2340:1111:AAAA:1:213:19FF:FE7B:5004, subnet is 2340:1111:AAAA:1::/64 [EUI]
! Lines omitted for brevity
R1#show ipv6 interface S0/0/1
Serial0/0/1 is up, line protocol is up
  IPv6 is enabled, link-local address is FE80::213:19FF:FE7B:5004
  Global unicast address(es):
    2340:1111:AAAA:2::1, subnet is 2340:1111:AAAA:2::/64
! Lines omitted for brevity
R1#show ipv6 interface s0/1/1
Serial0/1/1 is up, line protocol is up
```

Example 17-1 *Configuring Static IPv6 Addresses (Continued)*

```
IPv6 is enabled, link-local address is FE80::213:19FF:FE7B:5004
Global unicast address(es):
  2340:1111:AAAA:4:213:19FF:FE7B:5004, subnet is 2340:1111:AAAA:4::/64 [EUI]
! Lines omitted for brevity
```

The end of the example lists the full global unicast IPv6 address as part of the **show ipv6 interface** command. When using the EUI-64 option, this command is particularly useful, because the configuration command does not list the entire IPv6 address. Note that if the EUI format is used, the **show ipv6 interface** command notes that fact (see interfaces Fa0/0 and S0/1/1, versus S0/0/1). Also, routers do not have MAC addresses associated with some interfaces, including serial interfaces, so to form the EUI-64–formatted interface ID on those interfaces, routers use the MAC address of a LAN interface. In this case, S0/1/1's interface ID is based on Fa0/0's MAC address.

Stateless Autoconfiguration and Router Advertisements

IPv6 supports two methods of dynamic configuration of IPv6 addresses. One uses a stateful DHCPv6 server, which as mentioned earlier, works the same as DHCP in IPv4 in concept, although many details in the messages differ between DHCPv4 and DHCPv6. IPv6 also supplies an alternative called *stateless autoconfiguration* (not to be confused with stateless DHCP). With stateless autoconfiguration, a host dynamically learns the /64 prefix used on the subnet, and then calculates the rest of its address by using an EUI-64 interface ID based on its network interface card (NIC) MAC address.

The stateless autoconfiguration process uses one of many features of the IPv6 Neighbor Discovery Protocol (NDP) to discover the prefix used on the LAN. NDP performs many functions for IPv6, all related to something that occurs between two hosts in the same subnet. For example, one part of NDP replaces the IPv4 ARP protocol. IPv4 ARP allows devices on the same subnet—neighbors—to learn each other's MAC address. Because this and many other activities occur only inside the local subnet between neighbors on the same link, IPv6 collected these basic functions into one protocol suite, called NDP.

Stateless autoconfiguration uses two NDP messages, namely router solicitation (RS) and router advertisement (RA) messages, to discover the IPv6 prefix used on a LAN. The host sends the RS message as an IPv6 multicast message, asking all routers to respond to the questions "What IPv6 prefix(s) is used on this subnet?" and "What is the IPv6 address(s) of any default routers on this subnet?" Figure 17-8 shows the general idea, on subnet 1 from Figure 17-6, with PC1 sending an RS, and router R1 replying with the IPv6 prefix used on the LAN and R1's own IPv6 address as a potential default router.

Figure 17-8 *Example NDP RS/RA Process to Find the Default Routers*

> **NOTE** IPv6 allows multiple prefixes and multiple default routers to be listed in the RA message; the figure just shows one of each for simplicity's sake.

IPv6 does not use broadcasts. In fact, there is no such thing as a subnet broadcast address, a network-wide broadcast address, or an equivalent of the all-hosts 255.255.255.255 broadcast IPv4 address. Instead, IPv6 uses multicast addresses. By using a different multicast IPv6 address for different functions, a computer that has no need to participate in a particular function can simply ignore those particular multicasts, reducing the impact to the host. For example, the RS message only needs to be received and processed by routers, so the RS message's destination IP address is FF02::2, which is the address reserved in IPv6 to be used only by IPv6 routers. RA messages are sent to a multicast address intended for use by all IPv6 hosts on the link (FF02::1), so not only will the host that sent the RS learn the information, but all other hosts on the link will also learn the details.

Table 17-5 summarizes some of the key details about the RS/RA messages.

Table 17-5 *Details of the RS/RA Process*

Message	RS	RA
Multicast destination	FF02::2	FF02::1
Meaning of multicast address	All routers on this link	All IPv6 nodes on this link

IPv6 Address Configuration Summary

This chapter covers four methods for assigning IPv6 addresses to hosts or router interfaces. Two variations use static configuration, while two dynamically learn the address. However, with both static and dynamic configuration, two alternatives exist—one that supplies the entire IPv6 address and one that allows the host to calculate the EUI-64 interface ID. Table 17-6 summarizes the configuration methods.

Table 17-6 *IPv6 Address Configuration Options*

Static or Dynamic	Option	Portion Configured or Learned
Static	Do not use EUI-64	Entire 128-bit address
Static	Use EUI-64	Just the /64 prefix
Dynamic	Stateful DHCPv6	Entire 128-bit address
Dynamic	Stateless autoconfiguration	Just the /64 prefix

Discovering the Default Router with NDP

In IPv4, hosts discover their default router (default gateway) either through static configuration on the host or, more typically, with DHCP. IPv6 can use both of these same options as well, plus the NDP RS/RA messages as explained in the previous section. The NDP router discovery process occurs by default on IPv6 hosts and routers, so while the stateful DHCPv6 server can supply the IP address(es) of the possible default routers, it is perfectly reasonable in IPv6 to simply not bother to configure these details in a stateful DHCP server, allowing the built-in NDP RS/RA messages to be used instead.

The default router discovery process is relatively simple. Routers automatically send RA messages on a periodic basis. These messages list not only the sending router's IPv6 address but also all the known routers on that subnet. A host can wait for the next periodic RA message or request that all local routers send an RA immediately by soliciting the routers using the RS message.

Learning the IP Address(es) of DNS Servers

Like IPv4 hosts, IPv6 hosts typically need to know the IP address of one or more DNS servers to resolve names into the corresponding IP address. Oftentimes, the host also needs to learn the DNS domain name to use. And like IPv4 hosts, IPv6 hosts can be told these IP addresses using (stateful) DHCP. When a host (or router for that matter) learns its IPv6 address using stateful DHCP, the host can also learn the DNS server IP addresses and the domain name, taking care of this particular detail.

Stateless DHCP, which is most useful in conjunction with stateless autoconfiguration, is an alternative method for finding the DNS server IP addresses and the domain name. A host that uses stateless autoconfiguration can learn its IPv6 address and prefix automatically, as well as learn its default router IP address, in both cases using NDP RS/RA messages. However, the stateless autoconfiguration process does not help a host learn the DNS IP addresses and domain name. So, stateless DHCP supplies that information using the same messages as stateful DHCP. However, to supply this information, the server does not need to track any state information about each client, so a stateless DHCP server can be used.

Table 17-7 summarizes some of the key features of stateful and stateless DHCPv6.

Table 17-7   *Comparison of Stateless and Stateful DHCPv6 Services*

Feature	Stateful DHCP	Stateless DHCP
Remembers IPv6 address (state information) of clients that make requests	Yes	No
Assigns IPv6 address to client	Yes	No
Supplies useful information, like DNS server IP addresses	Yes	Yes
Is most useful in conjunction with stateless autoconfiguration	No	Yes

IPv6 Addresses

This chapter has already introduced the concepts behind the general format of IPv6 addresses, the ideas behind global unicast IPv6 addresses, and some details about multicast IPv6 addresses. The following sections round out the coverage of addressing, specifically the three categories of IPv6 address:

■ **Unicast:** IP addresses assigned to a single interface for the purpose of allowing that one host to send and receive data.

■ **Multicast:** IP addresses that represent a dynamic group of hosts for the purpose of sending packets to all current members of the group. Some multicast addresses are used for special purposes, like with NDP messages, while most support end-user applications.

■ **Anycast:** A design choice by which servers that support the same function can use the same unicast IP address, with packets sent by clients being forwarded to the nearest server, allowing load balancing across different servers.

Unicast IPv6 Addresses

IPv6 supports three main classes of unicast addresses. One of these classes, global unicast IP addresses, closely matches the purpose of IPv4 public IP addresses. Global unicast addresses are assigned by ICANN and the RIRs for the purpose of allowing globally unique IPv6 addresses for all hosts. These addresses come from inside the 2000::/3 prefix, which includes all addresses that begin with 2 or 3 (hex).

The next class of IPv6 unicast addresses covered here, *unique local* unicast addresses, have the same function as IPv4 RFC 1918 private addresses. In IPv4, most every enterprise, and most every Internet-connected small or home office, uses IPv4 private networks. *Unique local* unicast addresses begin with hex FD (FD00::/8), with the format shown in Figure 17-9.

> **NOTE**   The original IPv6 RFCs defined a private address class called *site local*, meaning local within a site (organization). The original site local address class has been deprecated and replaced with unique local unicast addresses.

Figure 17-9   *Unique Local Address Format*

To use these addresses, an enterprise engineer would choose a 40-bit global ID in a pseudorandom manner, with the goal that hopefully the addresses will be unique in the universe. In reality, pseudorandom is probably a number made up by the engineer. The 16-bit subnet field and 64-bit interface ID work just like with global unicast addresses, numbering different subnets and hosts and allowing EUI-64 assignment of the interface ID. As usual, the engineer could avoid using EUI-64, using easier-to-remember values like 0000:0000:0000:0001 as the interface ID.

Link local addresses are the third class of unicast IPv6 addresses covered here. IPv4 has no concepts like the link local IP address. IPv6 uses these addresses when sending packets over the local subnet; routers never forward packets destined for link local addresses to other subnets.

Link local addresses can be useful for functions that do not need to leave the subnet, in particular because a host can automatically derive its own link local IP address without sending packets over the subnet. So, before sending the first packets, the host can calculate its own link local address so that the host has an IPv6 address to use when doing its first overhead messages. For example, before a host sends an NDP RS (router solicitation) message, the host will have already calculated its link local address. The host uses its link local address as the source IP address in the RS message.

Link local addresses come from the FE80::/10 range. No specific configuration is required, because a host forms these addresses by using the first 10 bits of hex FE80 (binary 1111111010), 54 more binary 0s, and the last 64 bits being the host's EUI-64 format interface ID. Figure 17-10 shows the format.

Figure 17-10 *Link Local Address Format*

10 Bits	54 Bits	64 Bits
FE80/10 1111111010	All 0s	Interface ID

Routers also use link local addresses on each interface enabled to support IPv6. Like hosts, routers automatically calculate their link local IP addresses. In fact, Example 17-1 earlier in this chapter listed the (R1) router's link local IP addresses in the output of the **show ipv6 interface** command output. Interestingly, routers normally use link local addresses as the next-hop IP address in IPv6 routes, rather than the neighboring router's global unicast or unique local unicast address.

Multicast and Other Special IPv6 Addresses

Multicast addresses can be used to communicate to dynamic groupings of hosts, with the sender sending a single packet and with the network replicating that packet as needed so that all hosts listening for packets sent to that multicast address receive a copy of the packet. IPv6 can limit the scope of where routers forward multicasts based on the value in the first quartet of the address. This book only examines multicasts that should stay on a local link; these addresses all begin with FF02::/16, so they are easily recognized.

For reference, Table 17-8 lists some of the more commonly seen IPv6 multicast addresses. Of particular interest are the addresses chosen for use by Routing Information Protocol (RIP), Open Shortest Path First (OSPF), and Enhanced IGRP (EIGRP), which somewhat mirror the multicast addresses each protocol uses for IPv4.

Table 17-8 *Common Link Local Multicast Addresses*

Purpose	IPv6 Address	IPv4 Equivalent
All IP nodes on the link	FF02::1	Subnet broadcast address
All routers on the link	FF02::2	N/A
OSPF messages	FF02::5, FF02::6	224.0.0.5, 224.0.0.6
RIP-2 messages	FF02::9	224.0.0.9
EIGRP messages	FF02::A	224.0.0.10
DHCP relay agents (routers that forward to the DHCP server)	FF02::1:2	N/A

Before completing the discussion of IPv6 addressing, you should know about a couple of special IPv6 addresses. First, IPv6 supports the concept of a loopback IP address, as follows:

::1 (127 binary 0s and a 1)

Just like the IPv4 127.0.0.1 loopback address, this address can be used to test a host's software. A packet sent by a host to this address goes down the protocol stack, and then right back up the stack, with no communication with the underlying network card. This allows testing of the software on a host, particularly when testing new applications.

The other special address is the :: address (all binary 0s). This address represents the unknown address, which hosts can use when sending packets in an effort to discover their IP addresses.

Summary of IP Protocols and Addressing

This chapter has covered a lot of concepts and details about IPv6 addresses, many of which require some work to remember or memorize. This short section pulls several concepts from throughout this major section on IPv6 protocols and addresses together before moving on to some details about routing protocols and router configuration.

When an IPv6 host first boots, it needs to do several tasks before it can send packets through a router to another host. When using one of the two methods of dynamically learning an IPv6 address that can be used to send packets past the local routers to the rest of a network, the first few initialization steps are the same, with some differences in the later steps. The following list summarizes the steps a host takes when first booting, at least for the functions covered in this chapter:

Step 1   The host calculates its IPv6 link local address (begins with FE80::/10).

Step 2   The host sends an NDP router solicitation (RS) message, with its link local address as the source address and the all-routers FF02::2 multicast destination address, to ask routers to supply a list of default routers and the prefix/length used on the LAN.

Step 3   The router(s) replies with an RA message, sourced from the router's link local address, sent to the all-IPv6-hosts-on-the-link multicast address (FF02::1), supplying the default router and prefix information.

Step 4   If the type of dynamic address assignment is stateless autoconfiguration, the following occur:

  a.   The host builds the unicast IP address it can use to send packets through the router by using the prefix learned in the RA message and calculating an EUI-64 interface ID based on the NIC MAC address.

  b.   The host uses DHCP messages to ask a stateless DHCP server for the DNS server IP addresses and domain name.

Key
Topic

Step 4   If the type of dynamic address assignment is stateful DHCP, the host uses DHCP messages to ask a stateful DHCP server for a lease of an IP address/prefix length, as well as default router addresses, the DNS server IP addresses, and domain name.

> **NOTE**   Other tasks occur when a host initializes as well, but they are beyond the scope of this book.

IPv6 includes many different types of addresses, including unicast and multicast. By way of summary, Table 17-9 lists the types of IPv6 addresses mentioned by this chapter, with a few details, for easier reference when studying.

Key Topic

Table 17-9   *Common Link Local Multicast Addresses*

Type of Address	Purpose	Prefix	Easily Seen Hex Prefix(es)
Global unicast	Unicast packets sent through the public Internet	2000::/3	2 or 3
Unique local	Unicast packets inside one organization	FD00::/8	FD
Link Local	Packets sent in the local subnet	FE80::/10	FE8, FE9, FEA, FEB
Multicast (link local scope)	Multicasts that stay on the local subnet	FF02::/16	FF02

Configuring IPv6 Routing and Routing Protocols

To support IPv6, all the IPv4 routing protocols had to go through varying degrees of changes, with the most obvious being that each had to be changed to support longer addresses and prefixes. The following sections first examine a few details about routing protocols and then show how to configure IPv6 routing and routing protocols on Cisco routers.

IPv6 Routing Protocols

As with IPv4, most IPv6 routing protocols are interior gateway protocols (IGP), with Border Gateway Protocol (BGP) still being the only exterior gateway protocol (EGP) of note. All these current IGPs and BGP have been updated to support IPv6. Table 17-10 lists the routing protocols and their new RFCs (as appropriate).

Table 17-10 *Updates to Routing Protocols for IPv6*

Routing Protocol	Full Name	RFC
RIPng	RIP Next Generation	2080
OSPFv3	OSPF version 3	2740
MP-BGP4	Multiprotocol BGP-4	2545/4760
EIGRP for IPv6	EIGRP for IPv6	Proprietary

Each of these routing protocols has to make several changes to support IPv6. The actual messages used to send and receive routing information have changed, using IPv6 headers instead of IPv4 headers and using IPv6 addresses in those headers. For example, RIPng sends routing updates to the IPv6 destination address FF02::9, instead of the old RIP-2 IPv4 224.0.0.9 address. Also, the routing protocols typically advertise their link local IP address as the next hop in a route, as will be shown in the upcoming Example 17-2.

The routing protocols still retain many of the same internal features. For example, RIPng, being based on RIP-2, is still a distance vector protocol, with hop count as the metric and 15 hops as the longest valid route (16 is infinity). OSPFv3, created specifically to support IPv6, is still a link-state protocol, with cost as the metric but with many of the internals, including link-state advertisement (LSA) types, changed. As a result, OSPFv2, as covered in Chapter 9, "OSPF," is not compatible with OSPFv3. However, the core operational concepts remain the same.

IPv6 Configuration

Cisco router IOS enables the routing (forwarding) of IPv4 packets by default, with IPv4 being enabled on an interface when the interface has an IPv4 address configured. For IPv4 routing protocols, the routing protocol must be configured, with the **network** command indirectly enabling the routing protocol on an interface.

IPv6 configuration follows some of these same guidelines, with the largest difference being how to enable a routing protocol on an interface. Cisco router IOS does not enable IPv6 routing by default, so a global command is required to enable IPv6 routing. The unicast IP addresses need to be configured on the interfaces, similar to IPv4. The routing protocol needs to be globally configured, similar to IPv4. Finally, the routing protocol has to be configured on each interface as needed, but with IPv6, the process does not use the **network** router subcommand.

This section shows an example configuration, again showing Router R1 from the Company1 enterprise network shown in earlier figures in this chapter. The example uses

RIPng as the routing protocol. The following list outlines the four main steps to configure IPv6:

Step 1   Enable IPv6 routing with the **ipv6 unicast-routing** global command.

Step 2   Enable the chosen routing protocol. For example, for RIPng, use the **ipv6 router rip** *name* global configuration command.

Step 3   Configure an IPv6 unicast address on each interface using the **ipv6 address** *address/prefix-length* [**eui-64**] interface command.

Step 4   Enable the routing protocol on the interface, for example, with the **ipv6 rip** *name* **enable** interface subcommand (where the name matches the **ipv6 router rip** *name* global configuration command).

Example 17-2 shows the configuration, plus a few **show** commands. Note that the IP address configuration matches the earlier Example 17-1. Because Example 17-1 showed the address configuration, this example shows gray highlights on the new configuration commands only.

Example 17-2   *Configuring IPv6 Routing and Routing Protocols on R1*

```
R1#show running-config
! output is edited to remove lines not pertinent to this example
ipv6 unicast-routing
!
interface FastEthernet0/0
 ipv6 address 2340:1111:AAAA:1::/64 eui-64
 ipv6 rip atag enable
!
interface Serial0/0/1
 ipv6 address 2340:1111:AAAA:2::1/64
 ipv6 rip atag enable
!
interface Serial0/1/1
 ipv6 address 2340:1111:AAAA:4::/64 eui-64
 ipv6 rip atag enable
!
ipv6 router rip atag
!
R1#show ipv6 route
IPv6 Routing Table - 10 entries
Codes: C - Connected, L - Local, S - Static, R - RIP, B - BGP
       U - Per-user Static route
       I1 - ISIS L1, I2 - ISIS L2, IA - ISIS interarea, IS - ISIS summary
       O - OSPF intra, OI - OSPF inter, OE1 - OSPF ext 1, OE2 - OSPF ext 2
       ON1 - OSPF NSSA ext 1, ON2 - OSPF NSSA ext 2
R    ::/0 [120/2]
```

Example 17-2 *Configuring IPv6 Routing and Routing Protocols on R1 (Continued)*

```
      via FE80::213:19FF:FE7B:2F58, Serial0/1/1
C    2340:1111:AAAA:1::/64 [0/0]
      via ::, FastEthernet0/0
L    2340:1111:AAAA:1:213:19FF:FE7B:5004/128 [0/0]
      via ::, FastEthernet0/0
C    2340:1111:AAAA:2::/64 [0/0]
      via ::, Serial0/0/1
L    2340:1111:AAAA:2::1/128 [0/0]
      via ::, Serial0/0/1
R    2340:1111:AAAA:3::/64 [120/2]
      via FE80::213:19FF:FE7B:5026, Serial0/0/1
C    2340:1111:AAAA:4::/64 [0/0]
      via ::, Serial0/1/1
L    2340:1111:AAAA:4:213:19FF:FE7B:5004/128 [0/0]
      via ::, Serial0/1/1
L    FE80::/10 [0/0]
      via ::, Null0
L    FF00::/8 [0/0]
      via ::, Null0
R1#show ipv6 interface brief
FastEthernet0/0          [up/up]
    FE80::213:19FF:FE7B:5004
    2340:1111:AAAA:1:213:19FF:FE7B:5004
FastEthernet0/1          [up/up]
    unassigned
Serial0/0/0              [administratively down/down]
    unassigned
Serial0/0/1              [up/up]
    FE80::213:19FF:FE7B:5004
    2340:1111:AAAA:2::1
Serial0/1/0              [administratively down/down]
    unassigned
Serial0/1/1              [up/up]
    FE80::213:19FF:FE7B:5004
    2340:1111:AAAA:4:213:19FF:FE7B:5004
```

The configuration itself does not require a lot of work beyond the IPv6 address configuration shown previously in Example 17-1. The **ipv6 router rip** *name* command requires a name (formally called a tag) that is just a text name for the routing process. Example 17-2 shows the configuration, using a RIP tag named "atag". This tag does not have to match between the various routers. Otherwise, the configuration itself is straightforward.

The **show ipv6 route** command lists all the IPv6 routes, listing some important differences as highlighted in the command output. First, note the first few lines of highlighted output in that command, and the new routing code "L". For each interface with a unicast address, the router adds the usual connected route for the prefix connected to that interface. For example, the first highlighted line inside this command lists 2340:1111:AAAA:1::/64, which is the subnet connected to R1's Fa0/0 interface. The output also lists a host route— a /128 prefix length route—as a local route. Each of these local routes, as noted with the code "L," lists the specific address on each interface, respectively.

The next highlighted lines in that same **show ipv6 route** command list some interesting next-hop information in a RIP-learned route. The example highlights the route to subnet 3, listing outgoing interface S0/0/1, but the next-hop address is R2's link local IP address of FE80::213:19FF:FE7B:5026. IPv6 routing protocols typically advertise the link local addresses as next-hop addresses.

Finally, the last part of the example shows the output of the **show ipv6 interface brief** command, which lists the unicast IP addresses on each interface. The highlighted lines first show the link local address (each starts with FE8), and then the global unicast address, on R1's Fa0/0 interface. Each of the three interfaces used in this example has both the link local address, which is automatically generated, and the global unicast addresses configured, as shown in the first part of Example 17-2.

Configuring host names and DNS servers on routers for IPv4 can be a small convenience, but for IPv6, it might well be a necessity. Because of the length of IPv6 addresses, even a simple **ping** command requires a fair amount of typing and referring to other command output or documentation. So, just as with IPv4, you might want to configure static host names on routers, or refer to a DNS server, with the following two commands. Note that the commands and syntax are the same as the commands for IPv4, just with IPv6 addresses used as parameters.

- **ip host** *name ipv6-address* [*second-address* [*third-address* [*fourth-address*]]]

- **ip name-server** *server-address1* [*server-address2...server-address6*]

The first command configures a host name only known to the local routers, while the second refers to a DNS server. Note that the router attempts to act as a DNS client by default, based on the default **ip domain-lookup** global configuration command. However, if the **no ip domain-lookup** command has been configured, change the command back to **ip domain-lookup** to begin using DNS services.

While the configuration and **show** commands in Example 17-2 can be useful for learning the basics, much more is required before an internetwork can be ready for an IPv6 deployment. (*Deploying IPv6 Networks*, by Ciprian Popoviciu et al., published by Cisco Press, is a great resource if you want to read more.) The next section takes a brief look at one of the larger deployment issues, namely, how to support users during a worldwide migration from IPv4 to IPv6, which might take decades.

IPv6 Transition Options

While IPv6 solves a lot of problems, an overnight migration from IPv4 to IPv6 is ridiculous. The number of devices on Earth that use IPv4 number is well into the billions, and in some cases, even if you wanted to migrate to IPv6, the devices or their software might not even have IPv6 support, or at least well-tested IPv6 support. The migration from IPv4 to IPv6 will at least take years, if not decades.

Thankfully, much time and effort have been spent thinking about the migration process and developing standards for how to approach the migration or transition issue. The following sections introduce the main options and explain the basics. In particular, these sections examine the idea of using dual stacks, tunneling, and translation between the two versions of IP. Note that no one solution is typically enough to solve all problems; in all likelihood, a combination of these tools will need to be used in most every network.

IPv4/IPv6 Dual Stacks

The term *dual stacks* means that the host or router uses both IPv4 and IPv6 at the same time. For hosts, this means that the host has both an IPv4 and IPv6 address associated with each NIC, that the host can send IPv4 packets to other IPv4 hosts, and that the host can send IPv6 packets to other IPv6 hosts. For routers, it means that in addition to the usual IPv4 IP addresses and routing protocols covered in many of the other chapters of this book, the routers would also have IPv6 addresses and routing protocols configured, as shown in this chapter. To support both IPv4 and IPv6 hosts, the router could then receive and forward both IPv4 packets and IPv6 packets.

The dual stack approach can be a reasonable plan of attack to migrate an enterprise to IPv6 for communications inside the enterprise. The routers could be easily migrated to use dual stacks, and most desktop operating systems (OS) support IPv6 today. In some cases, the upgrade may require new software or hardware, but this approach allows a slower migration, which is not necessarily a bad thing, because the support staff needs time to learn how IPv6 works.

Tunneling

Another tool to support the IPv4-to-IPv6 transition is tunneling. Many types of tunneling exist, but in this case, the tunnel function typically takes an IPv6 packet sent by a host and encapsulates it inside an IPv4 packet. The IPv4 packet can then be forwarded over an existing IPv4 internetwork, with another device removing the IPv4 header, revealing the original IPv6 packet. The concept is very much like a VPN tunnel, as explained in Chapter 15, "Virtual Private Networks."

Figure 17-11 shows a typical example with a type of tunnel generically called an IPv6-to-IPv4 tunnel, meaning IPv6 inside IPv4. The figure shows a sample enterprise internetwork in which hosts on some of the LANs have migrated to IPv6, but the core of the network still runs IPv4. This might be the case during an initial testing phase inside an enterprise, or it could be commonly done with an IPv4-based ISP that has customers wanting to migrate to IPv6.

Figure 17-11   *Example IPv6-to-IPv4 Tunnel, Physical and Logical View*

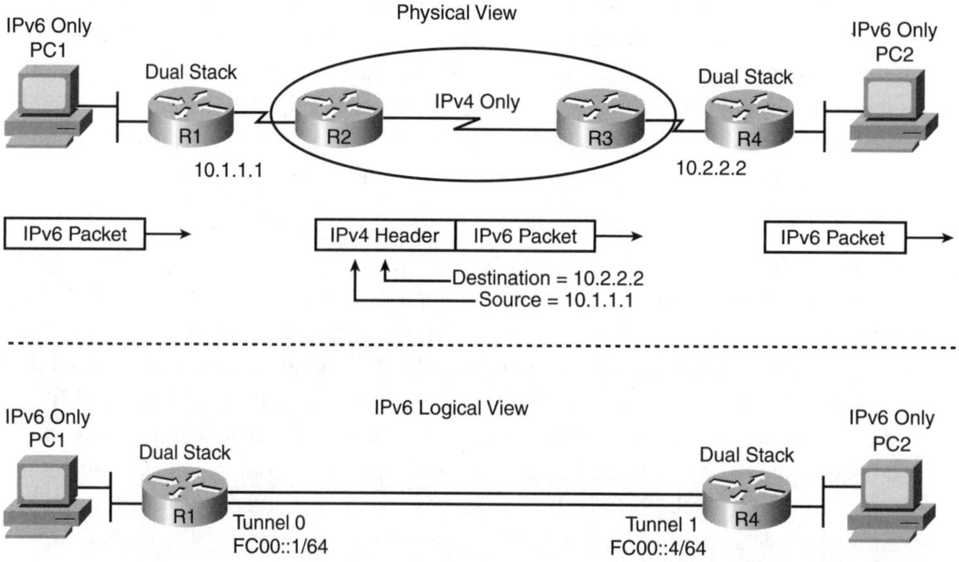

In the figure, the IPv6-based PC1 sends an IPv6 packet. Router R1 then encapsulates or tunnels the IPv6 packet into a new IPv4 header, with a destination IPv4 address of an address on Router R4. Routers R2 and R3 happily forward the packet, because it has a normal IPv4 header, while R4 de-encapsulates the original IPv6 packet, forwarding it to IPv6-based PC2. It's called a tunnel in part because the IPv6 packets inside the tunnel can't be seen while traversing the tunnel; the routers in the middle of the network, R2 and R3 in this case, perceive the packets as IPv4 packets.

Several types of IPv6-to-IPv4 tunnels exist. To perform the tunneling shown by the routers in Figure 17-11, the first three of the following types of tunnels could be used, with the fourth type (Teredo tunnels) being used by hosts:

- **Manually configured tunnels (MCT):** A simple configuration in which tunnel interfaces, a type of virtual router interface, are created, with the configuration referencing the IPv4 addresses used in the IPv4 header that encapsulates the IPv6 packet.

- **Dynamic 6to4 tunnels**: This term refers to a specific type of dynamically created tunnel, typically done on the IPv4 Internet, in which the IPv4 addresses of the tunnel endpoints can be dynamically found based on the destination IPv6 address.

- **Intra-site Automatic Tunnel Addressing Protocol (ISATAP):** Another dynamic tunneling method, typically used inside an enterprise. Unlike 6to4 tunnels, ISATAP tunnels do not work if IPv4 NAT is used between the tunnel endpoints.

- **Teredo tunneling:** This method allows dual-stack hosts to create a tunnel to another host, with the host itself both creating the IPv6 packet and encapsulating the packet inside an IPv4 header.

Figure 17-12 shows the basic idea behind the Teredo tunnel.

Figure 17-12 *Example Encapsulation for a Teredo Host-Host Tunnel*

Translating Between IPv4 and IPv6 with NAT-PT

Both classes of IPv6 transition features mentioned so far in this chapter, dual stack and tunnels, rely on the end hosts to at least support IPv6, if not both IPv4 and IPv6. However, in some cases, an IPv4-only host needs to communicate with an IPv6-only host. A third class of transition features needs to be used in this case: a tool that translates the headers of an IPv6 packet to look like an IPv4 packet, and vice versa.

In Cisco routers, Network Address Translation–Protocol Translation (NAT-PT), defined in RFC 2766, can be used to perform the translation. To do its work, a router configured with NAT-PT must know what IPv6 address to translate to which IPv4 address and vice versa, the same kind of information held in the traditional NAT translation table. And like traditional NAT, NAT-PT allows static definition, dynamic NAT, and dynamic PAT, which can be used to conserve IPv4 addresses.

Transition Summary

Table 17-11 summarizes the transition options for IPv6 for easier reference and study.

Table 17-11 *Summary of IPv6 Transition Options*

Name	Particular Type	Description
Dual stack	—	Supports both protocols, and sends IPv4 to IPv4 hosts and IPv6 to IPv6 hosts
Tunnel	MCT	Tunnel is manually configured; sends IPv6 through IPv4 network, typically between routers
Tunnel	6to4	Tunnel endpoints are dynamically discovered; sends IPv6 through IPv4 network, typically between routers
Tunnel	ISATAP	Tunnel endpoints are dynamically discovered; sends IPv6 through IPv4 network between routers; does not support IPv4 NAT
Tunnel	Teredo	Typically used by hosts; host creates IPv6 packet and encapsulates in IPv4
NAT-PT	—	Router translates between IPv4 and IPv6; allows IPv4 hosts to communicate with IPv6 hosts

Exam Preparation Tasks

Review All the Key Topics

Review the most important topics from this chapter, noted with the Key Topics icon in the outer margin of the page. Table 17-12 lists a reference of these key topics and the page numbers on which each is found.

Key
Topic

Table 17-12 *Key Topics for Chapter 17*

Key Topic Element	Description	Page Number
Figure 17-1	Route aggregation concepts in the global IPv6 Internet	583
List	Rules for abbreviating IPv6 addresses	585
List	Rules for writing IPv6 prefixes	587
Figure 17-3	Example prefix assignment process	588
List	Major steps in subdividing a prefix into a subnet prefix in an enterprise	590
Figure 17-5	Example and structure of IPv6 subnets	591
Figure 17-7	Structure of IPv6 addresses and EUI-64 formatted interface ID	595
Table 17-6	List of four main options to IPv6 address configuration	599
Table 17-7	Comparisons of IPv6 stateful and stateless DHCP services	600
List	Different types and purposes of IPv6 addresses	600
Figure 17-10	Format and structure of link local addresses	602
List	Summary of the steps a host takes to learn its address, prefix length, DNS, and default router	603
Table 17-9	Summary of prefixes and purpose of most common types of IPv6 addresses	604
List	Configuration checklist for IPv6 configuration	606
Table 17-11	List of IPv6 transition options	612

Complete the Tables and Lists from Memory

Print a copy of Appendix J, "Memory Tables," (found on the CD) or at least the section for this chapter, and complete the tables and lists from memory. Appendix K, "Memory Tables Answer Key," also on the CD, includes completed tables and lists to check your work.

Definitions of Key Terms

Define the following key terms from this chapter, and check your answers in the glossary:

Dual stacks, global unicast address, ISP prefix, link local address, NAT-PT, Neighbor Discovery Protocol (NDP), Regional Internet Registry (RIR), registry prefix, site prefix, stateful DHCP, stateless autoconfiguration, stateless DHCP, subnet prefix, unique local address

Command Reference to Check Your Memory

While you should not necessarily memorize the information in the tables in this section, this section does include a reference for the configuration and EXEC commands covered in this chapter. Practically speaking, you should memorize the commands as a side effect of reading the chapter and doing all the activities in this exam preparation section. To check to see how well you have memorized the commands as a side effect of your other studies, cover the left side of the table with a piece of paper, read the descriptions on the right side, and see whether you remember the command.

Table 17-13 *Chapter 17 Configuration Command Reference*

Command	Description
ipv6 unicast-routing	Global command that enables IPv6 routing on the router
ipv6 router rip *tag*	Global command that enables RIPng
ipv6 rip *name* **enable**	Interface subcommand that enables RIPng on the interface
ipv6 address {*ipv6-address/prefix-length* | *prefix-name sub-bits/prefix-length*} **eui-64**	Interface subcommand that manually configures either the entire interface IP address, or a /64 prefix with the router building the EUI-64 format interface ID automatically
ipv6 host *name ipv6-address1* [*ipv6-address2...ipv6-address4*]	Global command to create a static host name definition
ip name-server *server-address1* [*server-address2...server-address6*]	Global command to point to one or more name servers, to resolve a name into either an IPv4 or IPv6 address
[**no**] **ip domain-lookup**	Global command that enables the router as a DNS client, or with the **no** option, disables the router as a DNS client

Table 17-14 *Chapter 17 EXEC Command Reference*

Command	Description
show ipv6 route	Lists IPv6 routes
show ipv6 route *ip-address*	Lists the route(s) this router would match for packets sent to the listed address
show ipv6 route [*prefix/prefix-length*]	Lists the route for the specifically listed prefix/length
show ipv6 interface [*type number*]	Lists IPv6 settings on an interface, including link local and other unicast IP addresses
show ipv6 interface brief	Lists interface status and IPv6 addresses for each interface

Part VI: Final Preparation

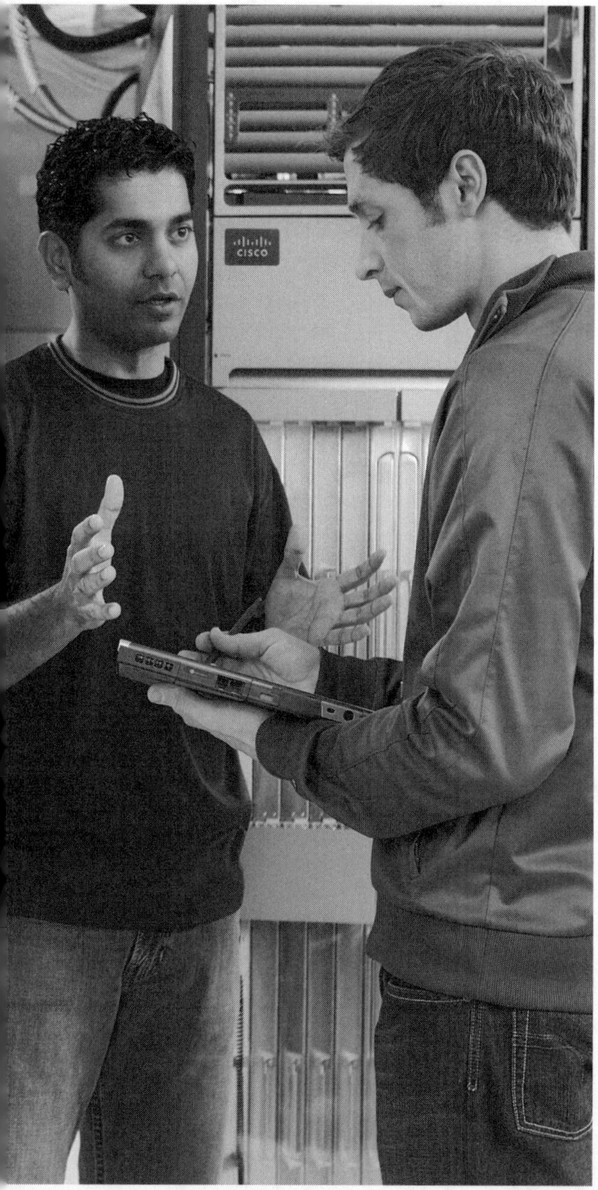

CHAPTER 18

Final Preparation

The first 17 chapters of this book cover the technologies, protocols, commands, and features you need to understand to pass the ICND2 exam. Although these chapters supply the detailed information, most people need more preparation than simply reading the first 17 chapters. This chapter details a set of tools and a study plan to help you complete your preparation for the exams.

If you're preparing for the CCNA exam by reading both this book and the *CCENT/CCNA ICND1 Official Exam Certification Guide*, you know that both books have a final preparation chapter. However, you can refer to just this chapter to read about the suggested study plan, because this chapter refers to the tools in both this book and the ICND1 book. Just look for the text highlighted in gray, like this sentence, for suggestions that apply to CCNA (640-802) exam preparation, but not to ICND2 (640-816) exam preparation.

This short chapter has two main sections. The first section lists the exam preparation tools that can be useful at this point in your study process. The second section lists a suggested study plan now that you have completed all the earlier chapters.

> **NOTE** This chapter references many of the book's chapters and appendixes, as well as tools available on the CD. Some of the appendixes, beginning with Appendix D, are included only on the CD that comes with this book. To access those, just insert the CD and make the appropriate selection from the opening interface.

Tools for Final Preparation

This section lists some information about the available tools and how to access them.

Exam Engine and Questions on the CD

The CD includes an exam engine—software that displays and then grades a set of exam-realistic questions. These include simulation (sim) questions, drag-and-drop, and many scenario-based questions that require the same level of analysis as the questions on the ICND2 and CCNA exams. Using the exam engine, you can either practice using the questions in Study Mode or take a simulated (timed) ICND2 or CCNA exam.

The installation process has two major steps. The CD includes a recent copy of the exam engine software, supplied by Boson Software (http://www.boson.com). The practice exam—the database of ICND2 exam questions—is not on the CD. Instead, the practice exam resides on the http://www.boson.com web server, so the second major step is to activate and download the practice exam.

> **NOTE**   The cardboard CD case in the back of this book includes the CD and a piece of paper. The paper lists the activation key for the practice exam associated with this book. *DO NOT LOSE THE ACTIVATION KEY.*

Install the Software from the CD

The software installation process is pretty routine compared with other software installation processes. The following steps outline the process:

Step 1   Insert the CD into your PC.

Step 2   The software that automatically runs is the Cisco Press software to access and use all CD-based features, including the exam engine, viewing a PDF of this book, and viewing the CD-only appendices. From the main menu, click the option to **Install the Exam Engine**.

Step 3   Respond to prompt windows, as you would with any typical software installation process.

The installation process might give you the option to register the software. This process requires that you establish a login at the http://www.boson.com website. You will need this login to activate the exam, so feel free to register when prompted. If you already have a login at the http://www.boson.com site, you don't need to register again. Just use your existing login.

Activate and Download the Practice Exam

After the exam engine is installed, you should activate the exam associated with this book:

Step 1   Start the Boson Exam Environment (BEE) software from the Start menu. It should be installed in a Cisco Press folder on your computer.

Step 2   The first time you start the software, it should ask you to either log in, or register an account. If you do not already have an account with Boson, select the option to register a new account. (You must register to download and use the exam.)

Step 3   After you are registered, the software might prompt you to download the latest version of the software, which you should do. Note that this process updates the exam engine software (formally called the Boson Exam Environment). It does not activate the practice exam.

Step 4   To activate and download the exam associated with this book, from the exam engine main window, click the **Exam Wizard** button.

Step 5   From the Exam Wizard pop-up window, select **Activate a purchased exam** and click the **Next** button. (Although you did not purchase the exam directly, you purchased it indirectly when you purchased this book.)

Step 6   On the next screen, enter the Activation Key from the paper inside the cardboard CD holder in the back of the book, and click the **Next** button.

Step 7   The activation process downloads the practice exam. When this is done, the main exam engine menu should list a new exam, with a name such as "ExSim for Cisco Press ICND2 ECG." If you do not see the exam, be sure you have selected the My Exams tab on the menu. You may need to click the plus sign icon (+) to expand the menu to see the exam.

At this point, the software and practice exam are ready to use.

Activating Other Exams

You need to go through the exam software installation process and the registration process only once. After that, for each new exam, only a few steps are required. For example, if you bought both this book and the *CCENT/CCNA ICND1 Official Exam Certification Guide*, you could follow the steps listed here to install the software and activate the exam associated with this book. Then, for the practice exam associated with the ICND1 book, which has about 150 exam-realistic ICND1 questions, you need to follow only a few more steps. All you have to do is start the exam engine (if it is not still up and running) and follow Steps 4 through 6 from the preceding list. In fact, if you purchase other Cisco Press books, or purchase a practice exam from Boson, you just need to activate each new exam as described in Steps 4 through 6.

You can also purchase additional practice exams from Boson directly from its website. When you purchase an exam, you receive an activation key, and then you can activate and download the exam—again without requiring any additional software installation.

The Cisco CCNA Prep Center

Cisco provides a wide variety of CCNA preparation tools at a Cisco Systems website called the CCNA Prep Center. The CCNA Prep Center includes demonstrations of the exam's user interface, sample questions, informational videos, discussion forums, and other tools.

To use the CCNA Prep Center, you need a registered login at http://www.cisco.com. To register, simply go to http://www.cisco.com, click **Register** at the top of the page, and supply some information. (You do not need to work for Cisco or one of its partners to get a login.)

After you have registered, proceed to http://www.cisco.com/go/prepcenter, and look for the link to the CCNA Prep Center. There, you can log in and explore the many features.

Subnetting Videos, Reference Pages, and Practice Problems

Being able to analyze the IP addressing and subnetting used in any IPv4 network may be the single most important skill for all the CCNA exams. The *CCENT/CCNA ICND1 Official Exam Certification Guide*'s Chapter 12, "IP Addressing and Subnetting," covers most of those details, with this book's Chapter 5, "VLSM and Route Summarization," adding to the puzzle by explaining VLSM. (In case you do not have the ICND1 book, ICND1's Chapter 12 is included with this book as CD-only Appendix H, "ICND1 Chapter 12: IP Addressing and Subnetting.")

This book includes several tools to help you practice and refine your subnetting skills:

- **Subnetting Reference Pages:** CD-only Appendix E, "Subnetting Reference Pages," summarizes the binary and decimal shortcut processes explained in both ICND1's Chapter 12 and this book's Chapter 5. Each reference page lists a single process related to subnetting, along with reference information useful for that process. These summarized processes may be a more convenient tool when you're practicing subnetting, as compared to flipping pages in the subnetting chapters, looking for the correct process.

- **Subnetting Videos:** The DVD included with this book has a series of subnetting videos. These videos show you how to use the shortcut processes to find the answers to popular subnetting questions. You can select and play the videos from a simple menu that starts when you insert the DVD into a DVD drive.

- **Subnetting Practice:** CD-only Appendix D, "Subnetting Practice," contains a variety of subnetting practice problems, including 25 problems for which you need to find the subnet number, subnet broadcast address, and range of valid IP addresses. This appendix shows you how to use both binary and shortcut processes to find the answers.

Scenarios

As mentioned in the introduction to this book, some of the exam questions require you to use the same skills commonly used to troubleshoot problems in real networks. The troubleshooting sections and chapters of both the ICND1 and ICND2 books help prepare you for those kinds of questions.

Another way to prepare for troubleshooting questions on the exams is to think through many different network scenarios, predicting what should occur, and investigating whether the network is performing as it should. Appendix F, "Additional Scenarios," in both this book and the ICND1 book, includes several scenarios that include some tasks you should attempt before reading the suggested solution listed later in the appendix. By reading these scenarios and doing the exercises, you can practice some of the skills required when analyzing and troubleshooting networks.

Study Plan

You could simply study using all the available tools, as mentioned earlier in this chapter. However, this section suggests a particular study plan, with a sequence of tasks that may work better than just using the tools randomly. However, feel free to use the tools in any way and at any time that helps you fully prepare for the exam.

If you are only preparing for the ICND2 exam, you can ignore the gray highlighted portions of this study plan. If you are studying for the CCNA exam by using the ICND1 book as well, include the tasks highlighted in gray.

The suggested study plan separates the tasks into four categories:

- **Recall the Facts:** Activities that help you remember all the details from the first 17 chapters of this book.

- **Practice Subnetting:** You must master subnetting to succeed on the ICND1, ICND2, and CCNA exams. This category lists the items you can use to practice subnetting skills.

- **Build Troubleshooting Skills Using Scenarios:** To answer some exam questions that present a scenario, you may need to recall facts, do subnetting math quickly and accurately, and use a hands-on simulator—all to answer a single question. This plan section suggests activities that help you pull together these different skills.

- **Use the Exam Engine to Practice Realistic Questions:** You can use the exam engine on the CD to study using a bank of unique exam-realistic questions available only with this book.

Recall the Facts

As with most exams, you must recall many facts, concepts, and definitions to do well on the test. This section suggests a couple of tasks that should help you remember all the details:

Step 1   **Review and repeat, as needed, the activities in the "Exam Preparation Tasks" section at the end of each chapter.** Most of these activities help you refine your knowledge of a topic while also helping you memorize the facts. For CCNA exam preparation, do this for Chapters 2 through 17 in the ICND1 book, as well as Chapters 1 through 17 in this book.

Step 2   **Review all the "Do I Know This Already?" quiz questions at the beginning of the chapters.** Although the questions might be familiar, reading through them again will help improve your recall of the topics covered in the questions. Also, the DIKTA questions tend to cover the most important topics from the chapter, and it never hurts to drill on those topics.

Practice Subnetting

Without question, absolutely the most important skill you need to succeed in passing the ICND1, ICND2, and CCNA exams is to be able to accurately, confidently, and quickly answer subnetting questions. The CCNA exams all have some element of time pressure; the most stressful questions are the sim, simlet, and subnetting questions. So, you should practice subnetting math and processes until you can consistently find the correct answer in a reasonable amount of time.

Before I suggest how you should prepare for subnetting questions, please note that there are many alternative methods for finding the answers to subnetting questions. For example, you can use binary math for all 32 bits of the addresses and subnet numbers. Alternatively, you could recognize that 3 of the 4 octets in most subnetting problems are easily predicted without binary math, and then use binary math in the final interesting octet. Another option would be to use decimal shortcuts. (This topic is covered in ICND1's Chapter 12 and this book's Appendix H.) Shortcuts require no binary math, but they do require you to practice a process until you've memorized it. You can even use variations on these processes as taught in other books or classes.

Whichever process you prefer, you should practice it until you can use it accurately, confidently, and quickly.

The following list of suggested activities includes practice activities that you can use regardless of the process you choose. In some cases, this list includes items that help you learn the shortcuts included with this book:

Step 1 **View or Print Appendix E, "Subnetting Reference Pages."** This short CD-only appendix includes a series of single-page summaries of the subnetting processes found in ICND1's Chapter 12 (and this book's Appendix H, which is a copy of ICND1's Chapter 12.) Appendix E includes reference pages that summarize both the binary and decimal shortcut subnetting processes.

Step 2 **Watch the subnetting videos found on the CCNA video DVD found in the back of this book.** These videos show examples of how to use some of the more detailed shortcut processes to help ensure that you know how to use the processes. CCNA exam candidates: The subnetting videos are on DVDs included with both books. They are identical, so you can watch the videos from either DVD.

Step 3 **View or print Appendix D, "Subnetting Practice."** This CD-only appendix includes enough subnetting practice problems so that, through repetition, you can significantly improve your speed and internalize the shortcut processes. Plan on working on these problems until you can consistently get the right answer, quickly, and you no longer have to sit back and think about the process for finding the answer. The goal is to make the process for finding the answers to such problems automatic. CCNA exam candidates: the ICND2 Appendix D contains all the problems from ICND1's Appendix D, plus a few others, so use ICND2's Appendix D.

Step 4 **Practice Subnetting with Cisco's Subnetting Game.** Cisco has a subnetting game, available at the Cisco CCNA Prep Center. It prompts you with various subnetting scenarios, and makes practicing subnetting fun. Just go to the CCNA Prep Center (http://www.cisco.com/go/ prepcenter), log in with your Cisco.com User ID, select the **Additional Information** tab, and look for the link to download the game. (If you do not have a login, you can establish one from this web page.)

Step 5 **Develop your own practice problems using a subnet calculator.** You can download many free subnet calculators from the Internet, including one available from Cisco as part of the CCNA Prep Center. You can make up your own subnetting problems like those in Appendix D, do the problems, and then test your answers by using the subnet calculator.

Build Troubleshooting Skills Using Scenarios

Just as a real problem in a real network may be caused by a variety of issues—a routing protocol, a bad cable, Spanning Tree, an incorrect ACL, or even errors in your documentation about the internetwork—the exam makes you apply a wide range of knowledge to answer individual questions. The one activity for this section is as follows:

- **Review the scenarios included in Appendix F of this book.** These scenarios make you think about issues covered in multiple chapters of the book. They also require more abstract thought to solve the problem. CCNA exam candidates should review the scenarios in Appendix F of both books.

Use the Exam Engine

The exam engine includes two basic modes:

- **Study mode** is most useful when you want to use the questions to learn and practice. In study mode, you can select options such as whether you want to randomize the order of the questions, randomize the order of the answers, automatically see the answers, refer to specific sections of the text that reside on the CD, and many other options.

- **Simulation mode** presents questions in a timed environment, providing you with a more exam realistic experience. However, it restricts your ability to see your score as you progress through the exam, view the answers as you are taking the exam, and refer to sections of the text. These timed exams not only allow you to study for the actual ICND2 and CCNA exams, they also help you simulate the time pressure of the actual exam.

Choosing Study or Simulation Mode

Both study mode and simulation mode are useful for preparing for the exams. It's easy to choose one of the modes from the exam engine's user interface. The following steps show you how to move to the screen where you select study or simulation mode:

Step 1 Click the **Choose Exam** button. The exam should be listed under the title **ExSim for Cisco Press ICND2 ECG**.

Step 2 Click the exam's name once, to highlight it.

Step 3 Click the **Load Exam** button.

The engine should display a window. Here you can choose **Simulation Mode** or **Study Mode** using the radio buttons on the right side of the window.

Choosing the Right Exam Option

The exam engine has many options. You need to choose from one of the three listed exams on the left side of the window, and select either simulation or study mode. Additionally, depending on these two choices, you can potentially modify many other small settings. Although this is a useful tool, it can be difficult to figure out which options to choose to perform the following four primary tasks:

- Study for the ICND2 exam

- Study for the CCNA exam

- Simulate the ICND2 exam

- Simulate the CCNA exam

To support the ability to study for and simulate both the ICND2 and CCNA exams, the practice test includes two separate hidden question banks. The first bank includes about 150 unique questions written specifically for the ICND2 exam. The second bank includes a subset of the ICND1 question bank written for the *CCENT/CCNA ICND1 Official Exam Certification Guide*.

When studying for or simulating the CCNA exam, you must choose an option that includes both the ICND2 and ICND1 questions. To study for or simulate the ICND2 exam, you must choose an exam option that includes only ICND2 questions. The following list outlines the three options from the menu, and the questions served by the exam engine for each choice:

- **Cisco ICND2 Exam:** ICND2 questions only

- **Custom Exam:** ICND2 questions only

- **Full CCNA Exam:** Both ICND1 and ICND2 questions

You might want to experiment with some of the options. After you have chosen to either study using these questions or simulate an exam, Table 18-1 lists the four main options, along with how to pick the right options from the user interface.

Table 18-1 *Directions for What to Choose from the Menu to Study or Simulate the Exam*

If you want to...	choose this exam...	...and this mode...	...and modify these additional settings:
Study for ICND2	Cisco ICND2 Book Exam	Study	No specific settings required
Simulate ICND2	Custom Exam	—	Select the timed exam option, 55 questions, 75 minutes. Deselect **Show current score during exam** and select **Never** under **Show answers and explanations**.
Study for CCNA	Full CCNA Exam	Study	No specific settings are required
Simulate CCNA	Full CCNA Exam	Simulation	No specific settings are required

In addition to these main four study options, the custom exam option has a particularly useful feature for exam study. With this option, by clicking the **Modify Settings** button, you can select the questions to study by chapter. So, if you want to use the question bank for study, and you are studying by chapter or groups of chapters, you can select the questions associated with those chapters.

Summary

The tools and suggestions listed in this chapter were designed with one goal in mind: to help you develop the skills required to pass the ICND2 and CCNA exams. This book, and its companion ICND1 book, were developed not just to tell you the facts, but to help you learn how to apply the facts. No matter what your experience level when you take the exams, it is our hope that the broad range of preparation tools, and even the structure of the books and the focus on troubleshooting, will help you pass the exams with ease. I wish you well on the exams.

Part VII: Appendixes

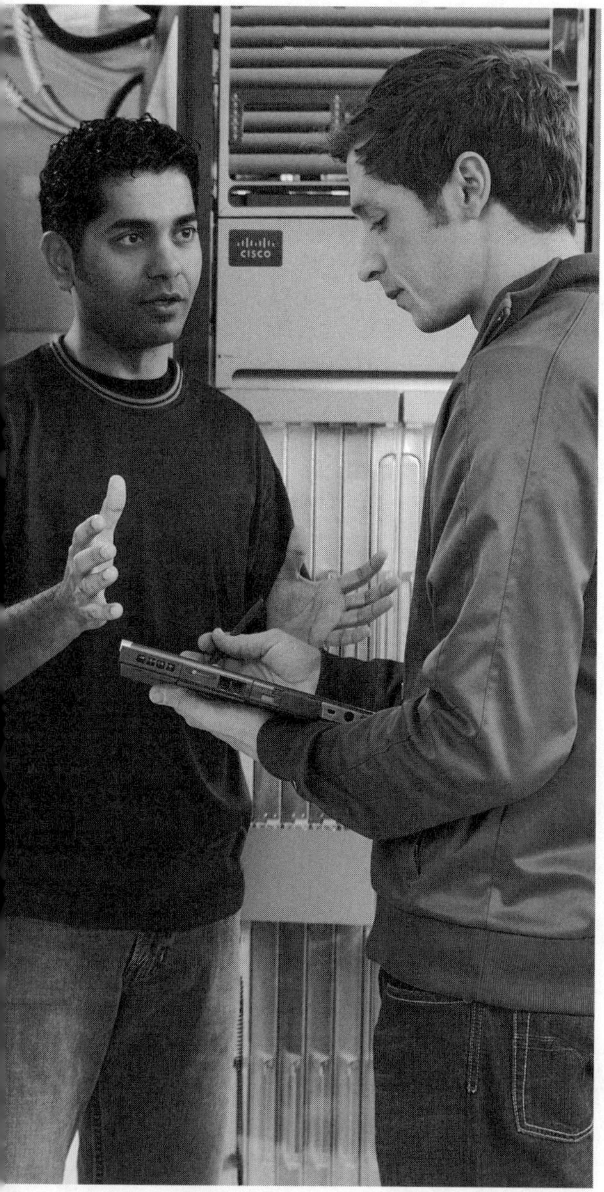

Answers to the "Do I Know This Already?" Quizzes

Chapter 1

1. B

2. D. While a subnet and a VLAN are not equivalent concepts, the devices in one VLAN are typically in the same subnet, and vice versa.

3. B

4. C

5. B and C

6. A and C. The **auto** setting means that the switch can negotiate trunking, but it can only respond to negotiation messages, and it cannot initiate the negotiation process. So, the other switch must be configured to trunk or to initiate the negotiation process (based on being configured with the **dynamic desirable** option.)

7. A. The default VTP setting of VTP server mode means that the switch can configure VLANs, so the VLAN is configured. However, being in server mode, the configuration commands only show up in the show vlan brief command output, and are not listed as part of the running-config file.

8. B and C

9. C. VTP does not require a password, although if a password is used, the password must match. VTP sends VTP updates immediately after a VLAN database change. However, VTP only sends VTP messages over trunks, and 2960s default to using a trunking administrative mode of **auto**, which does not initiate the trunking negotiation process. So, none of the switches automatically form a trunk, and no VTP messages are sent.

10. C and D. The domain name and password must be equal, and the switches must connect using a trunk before VTP will work. It is normal to have some switches as servers and some as clients. A mismatched pruning configuration setting does not prevent the synchronization of VLAN databases.

Chapter 2

1. A and B. Listening and Learning are transitory port states, used only when moving from the Blocking to the Forwarding State. Discarding is not an 802.1d STP port state.

2. C and D. Listening and Learning are transitory port states, used only when moving from the Blocking to the Forwarding state. Discarding is not an 802.1d STP port state. Forwarding and Blocking are stable states.

3. C. The smallest numeric bridge ID wins the election.

4. B. Nonroot switches forward Hellos received from the root; the root sends these Hellos based on the root's configured Hello timer.

5. E

6. B and D. The IEEE 802.1w standard, called Rapid STP, provides much faster STP convergence.

7. B and D. RSTP uses port states of Forwarding, Learning, and Discarding, with Forwarding and Learning States performing the same basic functions as the STP port states with the same name.

8. B and C

9. B. Cisco switches use the extended system ID format for bridge IDs by default, in which the priority field is broken down into a base priority value (32,768 in this case) plus the VLAN ID. The priority of this switch allows it to be capable of being the root switch, but the command output does not supply enough information to know whether this switch is currently root.

10. B. The two interfaces default to a port cost of 19 (Fa0/13) and 4 (Gi0/1), making SW3's cost to reach the root 10 + 19 = 29 out Fa0/13, and 20 + 4 = 24 over Gi0/1. SW3 therefore chooses Gi0/1 as its root port. SW3 could then advertise a cost of 24 (cost to reach the root) Hello out Fa0/13, but it would be inferior to the Hello already being received on Fa0/13 (cost 10), so SW3 would not choose Fa0/13 as a designated port.

Chapter 4

1. D. The host might need to use Dynamic Host Configuration Protocol (DHCP) to acquire an IP address, and it would likely use Domain Name System (DNS) to resolve www.ciscopress.com into an IP address. It would also use Address Resolution Protocol (ARP) to find the default gateway's MAC address, because the ARP cache would have been cleared as part of the boot process.

2. B. The **ping 2.1.1.2** command does not use a host name, so no DNS server is required. A DHCP client does not need to know the DHCP server's IP address to use DHCP. There's no such thing as an ARP server. However, to send the packet to another subnet, the PC needs to know the IP address of its default gateway.

3. A and F

4. C. With the **no ip subnet-zero** command configured, the router will not allow any interfaces to be configured with an IP address in the zero subnet. Of the listed answers, subnet 10.0.0.0 255.254.0.0 is a zero subnet, with a range of addresses from 10.0.01 to 10.1.255.254. The **ip address 10.1.2.2 255.254.0.0** command would be rejected.

5. A, C, E. The **ip route** command must define the static route; the "s" in the output means "static". However, the interface referenced or implied by the route must also be up/up, and IP must be enabled on the outgoing interface as well, typically with the configuration of the **ip address** command.

6. A. The correct syntax lists a subnet number, then a subnet mask in dotted decimal form, and then either an outgoing interface or a next-hop IP address.

7. A

8. B. With classless routing enabled, the router uses the default route if no other routes are matched. The line beginning "Gateway of last resort . . ." lists the IP address of the next-hop router, 168.13.1.101, which will be used as the default route.

Chapter 5

1. B, C, and D

2. A. Note that sometimes VLSM stands for variable-length subnet masking, which refers to the process of using different masks in the same classful network, whereas variable-length subnet mask refers to the subnet masks themselves.

3. C and D. Subnet 10.5.0.0 255.255.240.0 implies range 10.5.0.0–10.5.15.255, which does not overlap. 10.4.0.0 255.254.0.0 implies range 10.4.0.0–10.5.255.255, which does overlap. 10.5.32.0 255.255.224.0 implies range 10.5.32.0–10.5.63.255, which does overlap. 10.5.0.0 255.255.128.0 implies range 10.5.0.0– 10.5.127.255, which does overlap.

4. C. All the listed answers include the range of all three subnets, except for 10.3.64.0 255.255.224.0, which implies an address range of 10.3.64.0–10.3.95.255. Of the other three answers, 10.3.64.0 255.255.192.0 is the smallest range (10.3.64.0– 10.3.127.255). It also happens to be the smallest single summary route that includes all three subnets listed in the question.

5. C and D. 10.0.0.0 255.0.0.0 implies a range of all addresses that begin with 10, and 10.1.0.0 255.255.0.0 implies a range of all addresses that begin with 10.1, so both these answers include all the address ranges listed in the question. 10.1.32.0 255.255.224.0 implies a range of 10.1.32.0–10.1.63.255, which includes all addresses listed in the question. 10.1.55.0 255.255.255.0 implies a range of only 10.1.55.0–10.1.55.255, which does not include all addresses. 10.1.48.0 255.255.248.0 implies a range of 10.1.48.0–10.1.55.255, which omits two of the subnets listed in the question.

6. B, C, and D

7. A, B, and C

8. A. Discontiguous networks are allowed as long as autosummarization is disabled. OSPF does not even support autosummarization, so using OSPF would solve the problem. RIP-1 cannot disable autosummarization. EIGRP can disable autosummarization, but it is on by default.

Chapter 6

1. A and C. Standard ACLs check the source IP address. The address range 10.1.1.1–10.1.1.4 can be matched by an ACL, but it requires multiple **access-list** commands. Matching all hosts in Barney's subnet can be accomplished with the **access-list 1 permit 10.1.1.0 0.0.0.255** command.

2. D. 0.0.0.255 matches all packets that have the same first 3 octets. This is useful when you want to match a subnet in which the subnet part comprises the first 3 octets, as in this case.

3. E. 0.0.15.255 matches all packets with the same first 20 bits. This is useful when you want to match a subnet in which the subnet part comprises the first 20 bits, as in this case.

4. E and F. Extended ACLs can look at the Layer 3 (IP) and Layer 4 (TCP, UDP) headers, and a few others, but not any application layer information. Named extended ACLs can look for the same fields as a numbered extended ACL.

5. A and E. The correct range of ACL numbers for extended IP access lists is 100 to 199 and 2000 to 2699. The answers that list the **eq www** parameter after 10.1.1.1 match the source port number, and the packets are going toward the web server, not away from it.

6. E. Because the packet is going toward any web client, you need to check for the web server's port number as a source port. The client IP address range is not specified in the question, but the servers are, so the source address beginning with 172.16.5 is the correct answer.

7. E. Named extended IP ACLs can match the exact same set of fields as can numbered extended IP ACLs.

8. A and C. Before IOS 12.3, numbered ACLs must be removed and then reconfigured to remove a line from the ACL. As of IOS 12.3, you can also use ACL configuration mode and sequence numbers to delete one ACL line at a time.

9. C. The authorized Cisco curriculum makes the suggestion in answer C for extended IP ACLs, suggesting that standard ACLs be placed as close to the destination as possible.

10. C. Dynamic ACLs require the user to telnet to the router and authenticate using a username and password, which then causes the router to permit packets sent by the host.

Chapter 8

1. A and B

2. D and F

3. C and D

4. B, C, D, and E

5. B. Distance vector protocols rely on periodic full routing updates from their neighbors to confirm that the neighbor is still working.

6. D. Split horizon causes a router to not advertise routes out an interface if the route would cause packets to be sent out that same interface.

7. D. Route poisoning means advertising the failed route with an "infinite" metric, as opposed to simply ceasing to advertise the route. Poison reverse is route poisoning by advertising a route that previously was not advertised because of split horizon.

8. D. The router should not immediately send a full update. Instead, distance vector protocols immediately send a partial routing update, listing just the poisoned route.

9. B. Link-state protocols reflood each LSA on a periodic but longer timer. With RIP, the update timer is 30 seconds, and with OSPF, the timer is 30 minutes.

10. B. Link-state protocols collect information about the internetwork in the form of LSAs, which sit in memory in the link-state database. The router then runs the SPF algorithm to calculate that router's best metric route to reach each subnet.

Chapter 9

1. A. OSPF calculates metrics based on the cost associated with each interface. OSPF, by default, calculates interface cost based on the bandwidth setting.

2. A and D. OSPF uses the SPF algorithm, conceived by a mathematician named Dijkstra.

3. A and D. Routers must use the same authentication type and, if so, the same authentication key. Additionally, the subnet number and range of addresses, as calculated from the interfaces' IP addresses and masks, must be the same subnet.

4. B. Neighboring OSPF routers that complete the database exchange are considered fully adjacent and rest in a Full neighbor state.

5. D and E. The DR is elected based on the highest OSPF priority. If there is a tie, it is based on the highest OSPF RID. However, after the DR is elected, the DR role cannot be taken over by a better router until the DR and BDR have lost connectivity to the subnet. The DR attempts to be fully adjacent to all other routers on the subnet as part of the optimized database exchange process.

6. B. The **network 10.0.0.0 0.255.255.255 area 0** command works, because it matches all interfaces whose first octet is 10. The **network 10.0.0.1 0.255.255.0 area 0** command uses matching logic that matches all interfaces whose first octet is 10 and last octet is 1, which matches all three interface IP addresses. However, the wildcard mask used in OSPF **network** commands can have only one string of consecutive binary 1s, with all other digits as binary 0s, and this wildcard mask breaks that rule.

7. A. The **network 0.0.0.0 255.255.255.255 area 0** command matches all IP addresses as a result of the 255.255.255.255 wildcard mask, so this command enables OSPF in Area 0 on all interfaces. The answer with wildcard mask 0.255.255.0 is illegal, because it represents more than one string of binary 0s separated by binary 1s. The answer with x's is syntactically incorrect. The answer with wildcard mask 255.0.0.0 means "Match all addresses whose last 3 octets are 0.0.0," so none of the three interfaces are matched.

8. A, B, and E

9. B and D. For R2's neighbor state for R3 to be Full, R2 and R3 must have passed the authentication process as required by R2's configuration. The only way to configure a matching authentication key is with the **ip ospf message-digest-key** command, so answer B is correct. However, R3 may enable MD5 authentication in two ways: one using the command listed in answer A and also by configuring the OSPF subcommand **area x authentication message-digest**, which changes the default for all interfaces in that area. So Answer A is not correct, because that command is not required. R1's failure could be for many reasons, making D correct and C incorrect.

10. D. The OSPF **maximum-paths** *number* router subcommand sets the number of equal-cost routes added to the routing table. This command defaults to a setting of 4.

Chapter 10

1. A and B

2. D

3. B. The Feasible Distance (FD) is, for all known routes to reach a subnet, the metric for the best of those routes. The best route is called the successor route, and it is added to the IP routing table.

4. C. A route's reported distance (RD) is the metric used by the neighbor that advertised the route. A router uses it to determine which routes meet the feasibility condition for whether the route can be a feasible successor route.

5. A and C. The EIGRP **network** command supports a parameter of a classful network, enabling EIGRP on all interfaces in that classful network, or an address and wildcard mask. In the latter case, interface IP addresses that match the configured address, when applying ACL-like logic with the wildcard mask, match the command.

6. C and D. The EIGRP **network 10.0.0.2 0.0.0.0** command exactly matches the interface with address 10.0.0.2 because of the wildcard mask, enabling EIGRP on that interface. The EIGRP ASN value must match on both routers. The **network 10** command is syntactically incorrect; the entire classful network must be configured.

7. C. The first number in parentheses is the computed metric for a route, and the second number is the reported distance (RD) for the route. The route through 10.1.6.3 is the successor route, so it is not a feasible successor route. For the other two routes, only the third route's RD is less than or equal to the feasible distance (the metric of the successor route).

8. B and D. The MD5 key must be configured. It is not configured with an interface subcommand, but rather as part of a key chain. The useful lifetime of a key may be configured, but it is not required.

9. F

Chapter 12

1. C. Of the possible answers, only PAP and CHAP are PPP authentication protocols. PAP sends the password as clear text between the two devices.

2. C. The PPP Link Control Protocol (LCP) controls functions that apply to the link regardless of the Layer 3 protocol, including looped link detection, link quality monitoring, and authentication.

3. A and D. Both routers need an **encapsulation ppp** command, and both also will need IP addresses, before the ping will work. R1 does not need a **clock rate** command, because R2 is connected to the DCE cable.

4. D. The **username** command on one router should refer to the case-sensitive hostname of the other router.

5. B and D. The output lists encapsulation PPP, meaning that it is configured to use PPP. The line and protocol status are both up, LCP is open, and both CDPCP and IPCP are open, meaning that IP and CDP packets can be sent over the link.

6. C and D. Physical layer problems typically result in a line status (first status code) value of "down." A remote router IP address in a different subnet would not prevent a PPP-configured interface from reaching a protocol status (second line status) of "up." If the other end of the link was misconfigured to use HDLC, or if it was configured for PPP but CHAP authentication failed, the interface could be in an "up and down" state, as shown.

7. B. With PPP, two routers can use IP addresses in different subnets on opposite ends of the links, and a ping to the other router's serial IP address works. However, this subnet mismatch causes routing protocols to fail when forming neighbor relationships to exchange routes, so neither router learns EIGRP routes from the other.

Chapter 13

1. C. The LMI manages the link between the DTE and the switch, including noticing when a virtual circuit (VC) comes up or goes down.

2. A and D. The DTE typically sits at the customer site, and the DCE sits at the service provider site. Frame Relay switches send LMI messages to DTEs (typically routers) to signal VC status. A Frame Relay frame does not have a source and destination DLCI, but a single DLCI field.

3. A

4. C. The DLCI addresses a VC, not a router. The DLCI value in the frame as it crosses the local link represents that VC on that link. Because the question refers to a frame crossing the access link connected to R1, 222 is the local DLCI on R1 that identifies that VC.

5. B and C. The global DLCIs represent the DLCI the other routers use when sending frames over their local access links. So, when R1 sends a frame to R2, when the frame crosses R2's access link, the network has changed the DLCI to R1's global DLCI, 101. Similarly, when R3 sends a frame to R1, as the frame crosses R3's access link, the frame has R1's global DLCI in it, 101.

6. A. A single subnet can be used in any Frame Relay topology, but with a full mesh, a single subnet can be used with no tricky issues related to routing protocols.

7. D. BarneyCo has a total of ten VCs. With all of them configured on point-to-point subinterfaces, you need ten subnets, because you need one subnet per VC.

8. A. The frame that experienced the congestion was going from R1 to R2, so the frame with the Backward (opposite direction) Explicit Congestion Notification (BECN) bit set would go in the opposite direction, from R2 back to R1.

Chapter 14

1. C. The correct keywords are **ansi** and **q933**. However, the routers autodetect the LMI type by default, so not configuring the LMI also works.

2. C, D, and E. The LMI type is autosensed by default. Inverse ARP is on by default as well, meaning that it does not need to be enabled with the **frame-relay inverse-arp** command, nor do any static mapping statements need to be added.

3. A and E. The IP address moves to the subinterface, so it needs to be removed from the serial interface first (with the **no ip address** command). The encapsulation stays on the physical interface. The **frame-relay interface-dlci** command must be used on the subinterface so that the router knows which DLCI goes with which subinterface—even if only one DLCI exists.

4. F. You can code only one DLCI on a **frame-relay interface-dlci** command, and you need one for each VC under the multipoint interface.

5. F

6. C and E. Up and down are not PVC status codes. Inactive means that the switch thinks a defined PVC is not working, and deleted means that the DLCI is not defined at the switch.

7. D. For a Frame Relay subinterface to be in an up/up state, the underlying physical interface must be in an up/up state, and at least one of the PVCs associated with the subinterface must be in one of the two working PVC states (active or static).

8. B and C. For a Frame Relay physical interface to have a line status of "up," the same physical layer features as used on leased lines must be working. To also have a protocol status of "down," either the router is missing the **encapsulation frame-relay** command, or the router and switch disagree about the LMI type.

Chapter 15

1. A. Extranet VPNs connect sites in different but cooperating companies. Access VPNs provide access to individual users, typically from home or while traveling. The term "enterprise VPN" is not generally used to describe a type of VPN.

2. C. Antivirus software is an important security function, but it is not a function provided by the VPN itself.

3. A and C. Encapsulating Security Payload (ESP) headers support all four of the functions listed in the answers, whereas the Authentication Header (AH) only supports authentication and message integrity.

4. A. Of these answers, only Data Encryption Standard (DES), Triple DES (3DES), and Advanced Encryption Standard (AES) are encryption tools for encrypting the entire packet. AES provides better encryption and less computation time among the three options.

5. A, D, and E. All the devices and software listed in the answers can be used to terminate a VPN tunnel. However, ASAs have replaced PIX firewalls and VPN concentrators in the Cisco product line.

6. A and C. The client always uses Secure Socket Layer (SSL) to connect to the Web VPN server, so all Internet communications are encrypted. One major advantage of Web VPN is that the client does not need to have any client software, just using the built-in SSL capabilities of typical web browsers.

Chapter 16

1. F

2. D. CIDR's original intent was to allow the summarization of multiple Class A, B, and C networks to reduce the size of Internet routing tables. Of the answers, only 200.1.0.0 255.255.0.0 summarizes multiple networks.

3. B and E. RFC 1918 identifies private network numbers. It includes Class A network 10.0.0.0, Class B networks 172.16.0.0 through 172.31.0.0, and Class C networks 192.168.0.0 through 192.168.255.0.

4. C. With static NAT, the entries are statically configured. Because the question mentions translation for inside addresses, the **inside** keyword is needed in the command.

5. A. With dynamic NAT, the entries are created as a result of the first packet flow from the inside network.

6. A. The **list 1** parameter references an IP ACL, which matches packets, identifying the inside local addresses.

7. E. When translating inside addresses, the outside address is not translated, so the outside local address does not need to be identified in the configuration.

8. A and C. The configuration is missing the **overload** keyword in the **ip nat inside source** command and in the **ip nat outside** interface subcommand on the serial interface.

9. B. The last line mentions that the pool has seven addresses, with all seven allocated, with the misses counter close to 1000—meaning that close to 1000 new flows were rejected because of insufficient space in the NAT pool.

Chapter 17

1. A. One method for IPv6 global unicast address assignment is that ICANN allocates large address blocks to RIRs, RIRs assign smaller address blocks to ISPs, and ISPs assign even smaller address blocks to their customers.

2. D. Inside a quartet, any leading 0s can be omitted, and one sequence of 1 or more quartets of all 0s can be replaced with double colons (::). The correct answer replaces the longer 3-quartet sequence of 0s with ::.

3. D. Global unicast addresses begin with 2000::/3, meaning that the first 3 bits match the value in hex 2000. Similarly, unique local addresses match FD00::/8, and link local addresses match FE80::/10 (values that begin with FE8, FE9, FEA, and FEB hex). Multicast IPv6 addresses begin with FF00::/8, meaning that the first 2 hex digits are F.

4. A and C. IPv6 supports stateful DHCP, which works similarly to IPv4's DHCP protocol to dynamically assign the entire IP address. Stateless autoconfiguration also allows the assignment by finding the prefix from some nearby router and calculating the interface ID using the EUI-64 format.

5. A and D. Stateless autoconfiguration only helps a host learn and form its own IP address, but it does not help the host learn a default gateway. Stateless RS is not a valid term or feature. Neighbor Discovery Protocol (NDP) is used for several purposes, including the same purpose as ARP in IPv4, and for learning configuration parameters like a default gateway IP address.

6. A and D. OSPFv3, RIPng, EIGRP for IPv6, and MP-BGP4 all support IPv6.

7. C and E. The configuration explicitly assigns the 3456::1 IP address. The interface also forms the EUI-64 interface ID (4644:44FF:FE44:4444), adding it to FE80::/64, to form the link local IP address.

8. E. RIPng configuration does not use a **network** command; instead, the **ipv6 rip** command is configured on the interface, listing the same tag as on the **ipv6 router rip** command, and the **enable** keyword.

9. D. Network Address Translation–Protocol Translation (NAT-PT) translates between IPv4 and IPv6, and vice versa. The two tunneling methods allow IPv6 hosts to communicate with other IPv6 hosts, sending the packets through an IPv4 network. Dual-stack allows a host or router to concurrently support both protocols.

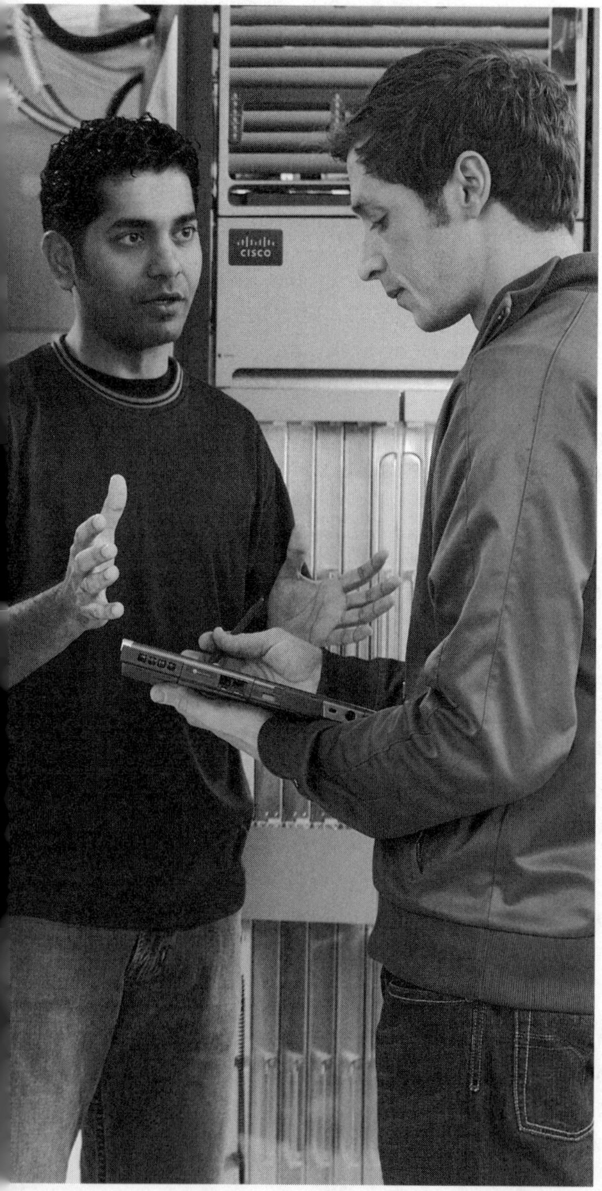
cisco

Decimal to Binary Conversion Table

This appendix provides a handy reference for converting between decimal and binary formats for the decimal numbers 0 through 255. Feel free to refer to this table when practicing any of the subnetting problems found in this book and on the CD-ROM.

Although this appendix is useful as a reference tool, note that if you plan to convert values between decimal and binary when doing the various types of subnetting problems on the exams, instead of using the shortcut processes that mostly avoid binary math, you will likely want to practice converting between the two formats before the exam. For practice, just pick any decimal value between 0 and 255, convert it to 8-bit binary, and then use this table to find out if you got the right answer. Also, pick any 8-bit binary number, convert it to decimal, and again use this table to check your work.

Decimal Value	Binary Value	Decimal Value	Binary Value	Decimal Value	Binary Value	Decimal Value	Binary Value
0	00000000	32	00100000	64	01000000	96	01100000
1	00000001	33	00100001	65	01000001	97	01100001
2	00000010	34	00100010	66	01000010	98	01100010
3	00000011	35	00100011	67	01000011	99	01100011
4	00000100	36	00100100	68	01000100	100	01100100
5	00000101	37	00100101	69	01000101	101	01100101
6	00000110	38	00100110	70	01000110	102	01100110
7	00000111	39	00100111	71	01000111	103	01100111
8	00001000	40	00101000	72	01001000	104	01101000
9	00001001	41	00101001	73	01001001	105	01101001
10	00001010	42	00101010	74	01001010	106	01101010
11	00001011	43	00101011	75	01001011	107	01101011
12	00001100	44	00101100	76	01001100	108	01101100
13	00001101	45	00101101	77	01001101	109	01101101
14	00001110	46	00101110	78	01001110	110	01101110
15	00001111	47	00101111	79	01001111	111	01101111
16	00010000	48	00110000	80	01010000	112	01110000
17	00010001	49	00110001	81	01010001	113	01110001
18	00010010	50	00110010	82	01010010	114	01110010
19	00010011	51	00110011	83	01010011	115	01110011
20	00010100	52	00110100	84	01010100	116	01110100
21	00010101	53	00110101	85	01010101	117	01110101
22	00010110	54	00110110	86	01010110	118	01110110
23	00010111	55	00110111	87	01010111	119	01110111
24	00011000	56	00111000	88	01011000	120	01111000
25	00011001	57	00111001	89	01011001	121	01111001
26	00011010	58	00111010	90	01011010	122	01111010
27	00011011	59	00111011	91	01011011	123	01111011
28	00011100	60	00111100	92	01011100	124	01111100
29	00011101	61	00111101	93	01011101	125	01111101
30	00011110	62	00111110	94	01011110	126	01111110
31	00011111	63	00111111	95	01011111	127	01111111

Decimal Value	Binary Value	Decimal Value	Binary Value	Decimal Value	Binary Value	Decimal Value	Binary Value
128	10000000	160	10100000	192	11000000	224	11100000
129	10000001	161	10100001	193	11000001	225	11100001
130	10000010	162	10100010	194	11000010	226	11100010
131	10000011	163	10100011	195	11000011	227	11100011
132	10000100	164	10100100	196	11000100	228	11100100
133	10000101	165	10100101	197	11000101	229	11100101
134	10000110	166	10100110	198	11000110	230	11100110
135	10000111	167	10100111	199	11000111	231	11100111
136	10001000	168	10101000	200	11001000	232	11101000
137	10001001	169	10101001	201	11001001	233	11101001
138	10001010	170	10101010	202	11001010	234	11101010
139	10001011	171	10101011	203	11001011	235	11101011
140	10001100	172	10101100	204	11001100	236	11101100
141	10001101	173	10101101	205	11001101	237	11101101
142	10001110	174	10101110	206	11001110	238	11101110
143	10001111	175	10101111	207	11001111	239	11101111
144	10010000	176	10110000	208	11010000	240	11110000
145	10010001	177	10110001	209	11010001	241	11110001
146	10010010	178	10110010	210	11010010	242	11110010
147	10010011	179	10110011	211	11010011	243	11110011
148	10010100	180	10110100	212	11010100	244	11110100
149	10010101	181	10110101	213	11010101	245	11110101
150	10010110	182	10110110	214	11010110	246	11110110
151	10010111	183	10110111	215	11010111	247	11110111
152	10011000	184	10111000	216	11011000	248	11111000
153	10011001	185	10111001	217	11011001	249	11111001
154	10011010	186	10111010	218	11011010	250	11111010
155	10011011	187	10111011	219	11011011	251	11111011
156	10011100	188	10111100	220	11011100	252	11111100
157	10011101	189	10111101	221	11011101	253	11111101
158	10011110	190	10111110	222	11011110	254	11111110
159	10011111	191	10111111	223	11011111	255	11111111

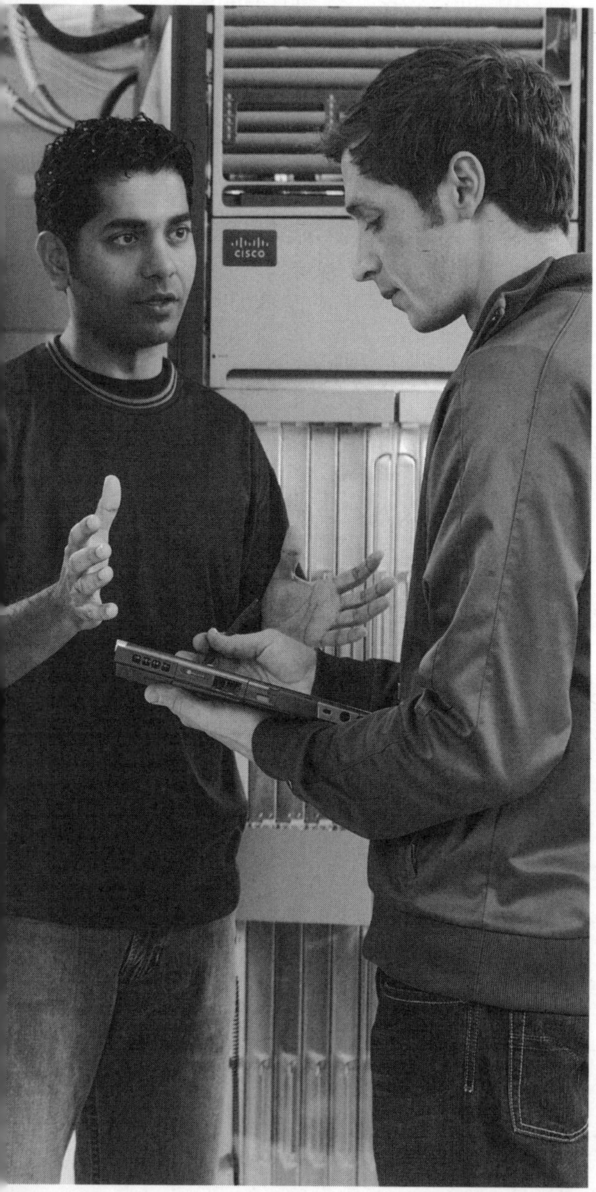
CISCO

ICND2 Exam Updates: Version 1.0

Over time, reader feedback allows Cisco Press to gauge which topics give our readers the most problems when taking the exams. Additionally, Cisco may make small changes in the breadth of exam topics or in emphasis of certain topics. To assist readers with those topics, the author creates new materials clarifying and expanding upon those troublesome exam topics. As mentioned in the introduction, the additional content about the exam is contained in a PDF document on this book's companion website at http://www.ciscopress.com/title/158720181x. The document you are viewing is Version 1.0 of this appendix.

This appendix presents all the latest update information available at the time of this book's printing. To make sure you have the latest version of this document, you should be sure to visit the companion website to see if any more recent versions have been posted since this book went to press.

This appendix attempts to fill the void that occurs with any print book. In particular, this appendix does the following:

- Mentions technical items that might not have been mentioned elsewhere in the book

- Covers new topics when Cisco adds topics to the ICND2 or CCNA exam blueprints

- Provides a way to get up-to-the-minute current information about content for the exam

Always Get the Latest at the Companion Website

You are reading the version of this appendix that was available when your book was printed. However, given that the main purpose of this appendix is to be a living, changing document, it is very important that you look for the latest version online at the book's companion website. To do so:

1. Browse to http://www.ciscopress.com/title/158720181x.

2. Select the **Downloads** option under the **More Information** box.

3. Download the latest "ICND2 Appendix C" document.

> **NOTE**   Note that the downloaded document has a version number. If the version of the PDF on the website is the same version as this appendix in your book, your book has the latest version, and there is no need to download or use the online version.

Technical Content

The current version of this appendix does not contain any additional technical coverage. This appendix is here simply to provide the instructions to check online for a later version of this appendix.

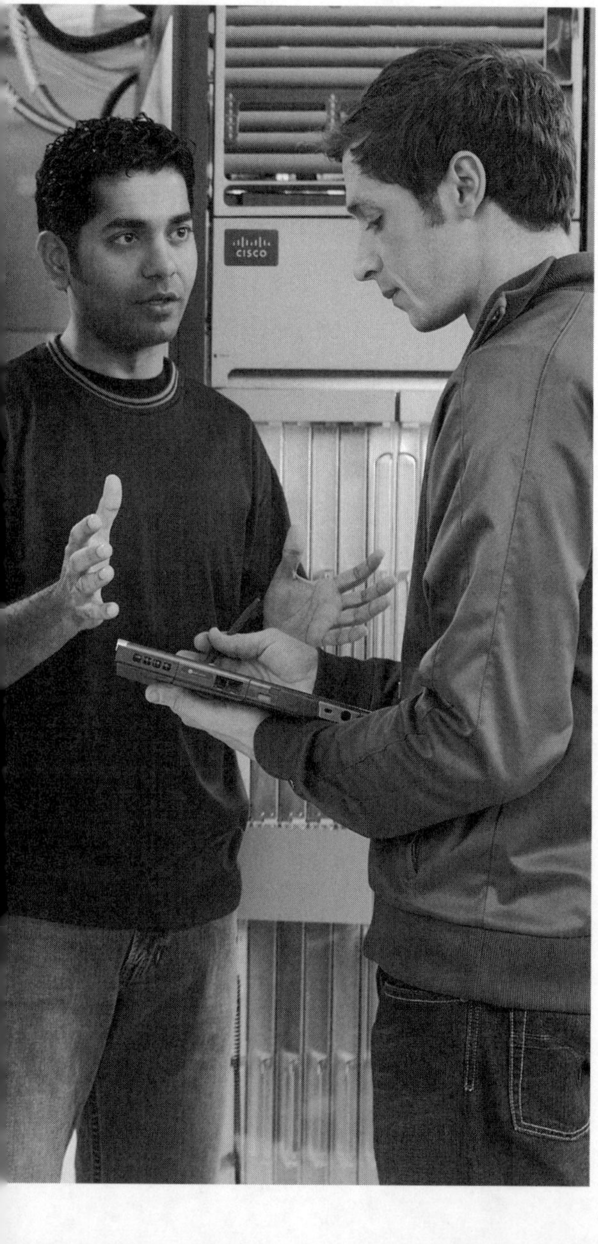
CISCO

GLOSSARY

ABR   Area Border Router. A router using OSPF in which the router has interfaces in multiple OSPF areas.

access link   In Frame Relay, the physical serial link that connects a Frame Relay DTE, usually a router, to a Frame Relay switch. The access link uses the same physical layer standards as do point-to-point leased lines.

access rate   See AR.

ACL   Access control list. A list configured on a router to control packet flow through the router, such as to prevent packets with a certain IP address from leaving a particular interface on the router.

administrative distance   In Cisco routers, a means for one router to choose between multiple routes to reach the same subnet when those routes are learned by different routing protocols. The lower the administrative distance, the more preferred the source of the routing information.

administrative mode   See trunking administrative mode.

alternate port   In RSTP 802.1w, a port role used to denote an interface that is currently receiving an inferior Hello BPDU, making it a possible replacement for the root port. Also used in the Cisco 802.1d STP implementation.

AR   Access Rate. In Frame Relay, the speed at which bits are sent over an access link.

Area Border Router   See ABR.

ARP   Address Resolution Protocol. An Internet protocol used to map an IP address to a MAC address. Defined in RFC 826.

ASBR   Autonomous System Border Router. A router using OSPF in which the router learns routes via another source, typically another routing protocol, exchanging routes that are external to OSPF with the OSPF domain.

asynchronous   Describes a convention for sending data with digital signals. The sender and receiver operate at the same speeds, but no attempt is made to dynamically cause the sender and receiver to adjust their speeds based on the other device's speed.

Autonomous System Border Router   See ASBR.

autosummarization   A routing protocol feature in which a router that connects to more than one classful network advertises summarized routes for each entire classful network when sending updates out interfaces connected to other classful networks.

B

backup designated router   An OSPF router connected to a multiaccess network that monitors the work of the designated router (DR) and takes over the work of the DR if the DR fails.

backup port   In RSTP 802.1w, a port role used when multiple interfaces on one switch connect to a single collision domain. This makes one interface the designated port (DP), and one or more others become available to replace the DP (backup role).

balanced hybrid   Refers to one of three general types of routing protocol algorithms. The other two are distance vector and link-state. EIGRP is the only routing protocol that Cisco classifies as using a balanced hybrid algorithm.

Bc   Committed burst. A Frame Relay term referring to the number of bits that can be sent during a defined time interval. This helps measure if/when the DTE has, on average, sent more data over a VC than the speed defined in the traffic contract.

BECN   Backward explicit congestion notification. The bit in the Frame Relay header that implies that congestion is occurring in the opposite (backward) direction from the frame. Switches and DTEs can react by slowing the rate at which data is sent in that direction.

Blocking State   In 802.1d STP, a port state in which no received frames are processed, and the switch forwards no frames out the interface, with the exception of STP messages.

Boolean AND   A math operation performed on a pair of one-digit binary numbers. The result is another one-digit binary number. 1 AND 1 yields 1; all other combinations yield 0.

BPDU   Bridge protocol data unit. The generic name for Spanning Tree Protocol messages.

BPDU Guard   A Cisco switch feature that listens for incoming STP BPDU messages, disabling the interface if any are received. The goal is to prevent loops when a switch connects to a port expected to only have a host connected to it.

BRI   Basic Rate Interface. An ISDN interface composed of two bearer channels and one data (D) channel for circuit-switched communication of voice, video, and data.

bridge ID (BID)   An 8-byte identifier for bridges and switches used by STP and RSTP. It is composed of a 2-byte priority field followed by a 6-byte System ID field that is usually filled with a MAC address.

bridge protocol data unit   See BPDU.

broadcast address   See subnet broadcast address.

broadcast domain   A set of all devices that receive broadcast frames originating from any device in the set. Devices in the same VLAN are in the same broadcast domain.

broadcast subnet   When subnetting a Class A, B, or C network, the one subnet in each classful network for which all subnet bits have a value of binary 1. The subnet broadcast address in this subnet has the same numeric value as the classful network's network-wide broadcast address.

C

CHAP   Challenge Handshake Authentication Protocol. A security feature defined by PPP that allows either or both endpoints on a link to authenticate the other device as a particular authorized device.

CIDR   An RFC-standard tool for global IP address range assignment. CIDR reduces the size of Internet routers' IP routing tables, helping deal with the rapid growth of the Internet. The term classless refers to the fact that the summarized groups of networks represent a group of addresses that do not confirm to IPv4 classful (Class A, B, and C) grouping rules.

CIDR notation   See prefix notation.

CIR   Committed Information Rate. In Frame Relay and ATM, the average speed at which bits can be transferred over a virtual circuit according to the business contract between the customer and the service provider.

circuit switching   The switching system in which a dedicated physical circuit path must exist between the sender and the receiver for the duration of the "call." Used heavily in the telephone company network.

classful addressing   A concept in IPv4 addressing that defines a subnetted IP address as having three parts: network, subnet, and host.

classful network   An IPv4 Class A, B, or C network. It is called a classful network because these networks are defined by the class rules for IPv4 addressing.

classful routing   A variation of the IPv4 forwarding (routing) process that defines the particulars of how the default route is used. The default route is used only if the classful network in which the packet's destination address resides is missing from the router's routing table.

classful routing protocol   An inherent characteristic of a routing protocol. Specifically, the routing protocol does not send subnet masks in its routing updates. This requires the protocol to make assumptions about classful networks and makes it unable to support VLSM and manual route summarization.

classless addressing   A concept in IPv4 addressing that defines a subnetted IP address as having two parts: a prefix (or subnet) and a host.

classless interdomain routing (CIDR)   See CIDR.

classless routing   A variation of the IPv4 forwarding (routing) process that defines the particulars of how the default route is used. The default route is always used for packets whose destination IP address does not match any other routes.

classless routing protocol   An inherent characteristic of a routing protocol. Specifically, the routing protocol sends subnet masks in its routing updates, thereby removing any need to make assumptions about the addresses in a particular subnet or network. This allows the protocol to support VLSM and manual route summarization.

Committed Information Rate (CIR)   See CIR.

contiguous network   In IPv4, a internetwork design in which packets being forwarded between any two subnets of a single classful network only pass through the subnets of that classful network.

convergence   The time required for routing protocols to react to changes in the network, removing bad routes and adding new, better routes so that the current best routes are in all the routers' routing tables.

counting to infinity   An unfortunate side effect of distance vector routing protocols in which the routers slowly increase the metric for a failed route until the metric reaches that routing protocol's finite definition of a maximum metric (called infinity).

CSU/DSU   Channel service unit/data service unit. A device that connects a physical circuit installed by the telco to some CPE device, adapting between the voltages, current, framing, and connectors used on the circuit to the physical interface supported by the DTE.

D

Database Description   An OSPF packet type that lists brief descriptions of the LSAs in the OSPF LSDB.

data-link connection identifier (DLCI)   See DLCI.

DCE   Data communications equipment. From a physical layer perspective, the device providing the clocking on a WAN link, typically a CSU/DSU, is the DCE. From a packet-switching perspective, the service provider's switch, to which a router might connect, is considered the DCE.

DE   Discard eligible. The bit in the Frame Relay header that, if frames must be discarded, signals a switch to choose this frame to discard instead of another frame without the DE bit set.

Dead Timer   In OSPF, a timer used for each neighbor. A router considers the neighbor to have failed if no Hellos are received from that neighbor in the time defined by the timer.

deny   An action taken with an ACL that implies that the packet is discarded.

designated port   In both STP and RSTP, a port role used to determine which of multiple interfaces, each connected to the same segment or collision domain, should forward frames to the segment. The switch advertising the lowest-cost Hello BPDU onto the segment becomes the DP.

designated router   In OSPF, on a multiaccess network, the router that wins an election and is therefore responsible for managing a streamlined process for exchanging OSPF topology information between all routers attached to that network.

Diffie-Hellman Key Exchange   A key exchange protocol in which two devices can exchange information over a public network. Combined with some preexisting secrets, this allows them to calculate a symmetric key known only to them.

Diffusing Update Algorithm (DUAL)   See DUAL.

Dijkstra Shortest Path First (SPF) algorithm   The name of the algorithm used by link-state routing protocols to analyze the LSDB and find the least-cost routes from that router to each subnet.

directed broadcast address   The same as a subnet broadcast address.

disabled port   In STP, a port role for nonworking interfaces—in other words, interfaces that are not in a connect or up/up interface state.

Discarding State   An RSTP interface state in which no received frames are processed, and the switch forwards no frames out the interface, with the exception of RSTP messages.

discontiguous network   In IPv4, a internetwork design in which packets being forwarded between two subnets of a single classful network must pass through the subnets of another classful network.

distance vector   The logic behind the behavior of some interior routing protocols, such as RIP and IGRP. Distance vector routing algorithms call for each router to send its entire routing table in each update, but only to its neighbors. Distance vector routing algorithms can be prone to routing loops but are computationally simpler than link-state routing algorithms. Also called Bellman-Ford routing algorithm.

DLCI   Data-Link Connection Identifier. The Frame Relay address that identifies a VC on a particular access link.

DTE   Data terminal equipment. From a Layer 1 perspective, the DTE synchronizes its clock based on the clock sent by the DCE. From a packet-switching perspective, the DTE is the device outside the service provider's network, typically a router.

DUAL   Diffusing Update Algorithm. A convergence algorithm used in EIGRP when a route fails and a router does not have a feasible successor route. DUAL causes the routers to send EIGRP Query and Reply messages to discover alternate loop-free routes.

dual stacks   In IPv6, a mode of operation in which a host or router runs both IPv4 and IPv6.

dynamic ACL   A type of ACL that goes beyond traditional IP ACLs to dynamically permit traffic from a host if the host's user first connects to the router via Telnet and passes an authentication process.

E

EIGRP   Enhanced Interior Gateway Routing Protocol. An advanced version of IGRP developed by Cisco. Provides superior convergence properties and operating efficiency and combines the advantages of link-state protocols with those of distance vector protocols.

encoding   The conventions for how a device varies the electrical or optical signals sent over a cable to imply a particular binary code. For instance, a modem might encode a binary 1 or 0 by using one frequency to mean 1 and another to mean 0.

EtherChannel   A Cisco-proprietary feature in which up to eight parallel Ethernet segments between the same two devices, each using the same speed, can be combined to act as a single link for forwarding and Spanning Tree Protocol logic.

extended access list   A list of IOS **access-list** global configuration commands that can match multiple parts of an IP packet, including the source and destination IP address and TCP/UDP ports, for the purpose of deciding which packets to discard and which to allow through the router.

extended ping   An IOS command in which the **ping** command accepts many other options besides just the destination IP address.

exterior gateway protocol (EGP)   A routing protocol that was designed to exchange routing information between different autonomous systems.

F

feasibility condition   In EIGRP, when a router has learned of multiple routes to reach one subnet, if the best route's metric is X, the feasibility condition is another route whose reported distance is <= X.

feasible distance   In EIGRP, the metric of the best route to reach a subnet.

feasible successor   In EIGRP, a route that is not the best route (successor route) but that can be used immediately if the best route fails, without causing a loop. Such a route meets the feasibility condition.

FECN   Forward explicit congestion notification. The bit in the Frame Relay header that signals to anything receiving the frame (switches and DTEs) that congestion is occurring in the same direction as the frame.

FTP   File Transfer Protocol. An application protocol, part of the TCP/IP protocol stack, used to transfer files between network nodes. FTP is defined in RFC 959.

filter   Generally, a process or a device that screens network traffic for certain characteristics, such as source address, destination address, or protocol. This process determines whether to forward or discard that traffic based on the established criteria.

forward   To send a frame toward its ultimate destination by way of an internetworking device.

forward delay   An STP timer, defaulting to 15 seconds, used to dictate how long an interface stays in both the Listening state and Learning state. Also called the forward delay timer.

Forwarding State   An STP and RSTP port state in which an interface operates unrestricted by STP.

forward route   From one host's perspective, the route over which a packet travels from that host to some other host.

Frame Relay   An international standard data-link protocol that defines the capabilities to create a frame-switched (packet-switched) service, allowing DTE devices (typically routers) to send data to many other devices using a single physical connection to the Frame Relay service.

Frame Relay DCE   The Frame Relay switch.

Frame Relay DTE   The customer device connected to a Frame Relay access link, typically a router.

Frame Relay mapping   The information that correlates, or maps, a Frame Relay DLCI to the Layer 3 address of the DTE on the other end of the VC identified by the local DLCI.

framing   The conventions for how Layer 2 interprets the bits sent according to OSI Layer 1. For example, after an electrical signal has been received and converted to binary, framing identifies the information fields inside the data.

full duplex   Generically, any communication in which two communicating devices can concurrently send and receive data. Specifically for Ethernet LANs, the ability of both devices to send and receive at the same time. This is allowed when there are only two stations in a collision domain. Full duplex is enabled by turning off the CSMA/CD collision detection logic.

Full State   In OSPF, a neighbor state that implies that the two routers have exchanged the complete (full) contents of their respective LSDBs.

full update   With IP routing protocols, the general concept that a routing protocol update lists all known routes. See also partial update.

fully adjacent   In OSPF, a characterization of the state of a neighbor in which the two neighbors have reached the Full state.

G

global unicast address   A type of unicast IPv6 address that has been allocated from a range of public globally unique IP addresses as registered through ICANN, its member agencies, and other registries or ISPs.

H

HDLC   High-Level Data-Link Control. A bit-oriented synchronous data link layer protocol developed by the International Organization for Standardization (ISO). Derived from synchronous data-link control (SDLC), HDLC specifies a data encapsulation method on synchronous serial links using frame characters and checksums.

Hello   (Multiple definitions) 1) A protocol used by OSPF routers to discover, establish, and maintain neighbor relationships. 2) A protocol used by EIGRP routers to discover, establish, and maintain neighbor relationships. 3) In STP, refers to the name of the periodic message sourced by the root bridge in a spanning tree.

Hello BPDU   The STP and RSTP message used for the majority of STP communications, listing the root's Bridge ID, the sending device's Bridge ID, and the sending device's cost with which to reach the root.

Hello interval   With OSPF and EIGRP, an interface timer that dictates how often the router should send Hello messages.

Hello timer   In STP, the time interval at which the root switch should send Hello BPDUs.

holddown   A Distance Vector protocol state assigned to a route placed so that routers neither advertise the route nor accept advertisements about it for a specific length of time (the holddown timer). Holddown is used to flush bad information about a route from all routers in the network. A route typically is placed in holddown when a link in that route fails.

I

IEEE 802.11   The IEEE base standard for wireless LANs.

IEEE 802.1ad   The IEEE standard for the functional equivalent of the Cisco-proprietary EtherChannel.

IEEE 802.1d   The IEEE standard for the original Spanning Tree Protocol.

IEEE 802.1Q   The IEEE-standard VLAN trunking protocol. 802.1Q includes the concept of a native VLAN, for which no VLAN header is added, and a 4-byte VLAN header is inserted after the original frame's type/length field.

IEEE 802.1s   The IEEE standard for Multiple Instances of Spanning Tree (MIST), which allows for load balancing of traffic among different VLANs.

IEEE 802.1w   The IEEE standard for an enhanced version of STP, called Rapid STP, which speeds convergence.

IEEE 802.3   The IEEE base standard for Ethernet-like LANs.

IGRP   Interior Gateway Routing Protocol. An old, no-longer-supported Interior Gateway Protocol (IGP) developed by Cisco.

inferior Hello   When comparing two or more received Hello BPDUs, a Hello that lists a numerically larger root Bridge ID than another Hello, or a Hello that lists the same root Bridge ID but with a larger cost.

infinity   In the context of IP routing protocols, a finite metric value defined by the routing protocol that is used to represent an unusable route in a routing protocol update.

inside global   A NAT term referring to the IP address used for a host inside the trusted part of the network, but in packets as they traverse the global (untrusted) part of the network.

inside local   A NAT term referring to the IP address used for a host inside the trusted part of the network, but in packets as they traverse the local (trusted) part of the network.

interior gateway protocol (IGP)   A routing protocol designed to be used to exchange routing information inside a single autonomous system.

Inter-Switch Link (ISL)   The Cisco-proprietary VLAN trunking protocol that predated 802.1Q by many years. ISL defines a 26-byte header that encapsulates the original Ethernet frame.

Inverse ARP   A Frame Relay protocol with which a router announces its Layer 3 address over a VC, thereby informing the neighbor of useful Layer-3-to-Layer-2 mapping information.

IP Control Protocol (IPCP)   A control protocol defined as part of PPP for the purpose of initializing and controlling the sending of IPv4 packets over a PPP link.

IPsec   The term referring to the IP Security Protocols, which is an architecture for providing encryption and authentication services, typically when creating VPN services through an IP network.

ISDN   Integrated Services Digital Network. A communication protocol offered by telephone companies that permits telephone networks to carry data, voice, and video.

ISL   See Inter-Switch Link.

ISP prefix　In IPv6, the prefix that describes an address block that has been assigned to an ISP by some Internet registry.

K

keepalive　A feature of many data-link protocols in which the router sends messages periodically to let the neighboring router know that the first router is still alive and well.

L

LAPF　Link Access Procedure Frame Bearer Services. Defines the basic Frame Relay header and trailer. The header includes DLCI, FECN, BECN, and DE bits.

learn　Transparent bridges and switches learn MAC addresses by examining the source MAC addresses of frames they receive. They add each new MAC address, along with the port number of the port on which it learned of the MAC address, to an address table.

Learning State　In STP, a temporary port state in which the interface does not forward frames, but it can begin to learn MAC addresses from frames received on the interface.

leased line　A transmission line reserved by a communications carrier for a customer's private use. A leased line is a type of dedicated line.

Link Control Protocol　A control protocol defined as part of PPP for the purpose of initializing and maintaining a PPP link.

link local address　A type of unicast IPv6 address that represents an interface on a single data link. Packets sent to a link local address cross only that particular link and are never forwarded to other subnets by a router. Used for communications that do not need to leave the local link, such as neighbor discovery.

link-state　A classification of the underlying algorithm used in some routing protocols. Link-state protocols build a detailed database that lists links (subnets) and their state (up, down), from which the best routes can then be calculated.

link-state advertisement (LSA)　In OSPF, the name of the data structure that resides inside the LSDB and describes in detail the various components in a network, including routers and links (subnets).

link-state database (LSDB)　In OSPF, the data structure in RAM of a router that holds the various LSAs, with the collective LSAs representing the entire topology of the network.

link-state request   An OSPF packet used to ask a neighboring router to send a particular LSA.

link-state update   An OSPF packet used to send an LSA to a neighboring router.

Listening State   A temporary STP port state that occurs immediately when a blocking interface must be moved to a Forwarding state. The switch times out MAC table entries during this state. It also ignores frames received on the interface and doesn't forward any frames out the interface.

Local Management Interface (LMI)   A Frame Relay protocol used between a DTE (router) and DCE (Frame Relay switch). LMI acts as a keepalive mechanism. The absence of LMI messages means that the other device has failed. It also tells the DTE about the existence of each VC and DLCI, along with its status.

LSA   See link-state advertisement.

M

mask   See subnet mask.

MaxAge   In STP, a timer that states how long a switch should wait when it no longer receives Hellos from the root switch before acting to reconverge the STP topology. Also called the MaxAge Timer.

metric   A numeric measurement used by a routing protocol to determine how good a route is as compared to other alternate routes to reach the same subnet.

MLP   Multilink Point-to-Point Protocol. A method of splitting, recombining, and sequencing frames across multiple point-to-point WAN links.

MTU   Maximum transmission unit. The maximum packet size, in bytes, that a particular interface can handle.

N

named access list   An ACL that identifies the various statements in the ACL based on a name, rather than a number.

NAT   Network Address Translation. A mechanism for reducing the need for globally unique IPv4 addresses. NAT allows an organization with addresses that are not globally unique to connect to the Internet by translating those addresses into globally routable address space.

NAT overload   See Port Address Translation (PAT).

NAT-PT   An IPv6 feature in which packets are translated between IPv4 and IPv6.

NBMA   See nonbroadcast multiaccess.

neighbor   In routing protocols, another router with which a router decides to exchange routing information.

Neighbor Discovery Protocol (NDP)   A protocol that is part of the IPv6 protocol suite, used to discover and exchange information about devices on the same subnet (neighbors). In particular, it replaces the IPv4 ARP protocol.

neighbor table   For OSPF and EIGRP, a list of routers that have reached neighbor status.

nonbroadcast multiaccess (NBMA)   A characterization of a type of Layer 2 network in which more than two devices connect to the network, but the network does not allow broadcast frames to be sent to all devices on the network.

O

OSPF   Open Shortest Path First. A popular link-state IGP that uses a link-state database and the Shortest Path First (SPF) algorithm to calculate the best routes to reach each known subnet.

outside global   A NAT term referring to an IP address used for a host in the outside (untrusted) part of the network, for packets as they traverse the outside part of the network, which is usually the global Internet.

outside local   A NAT term referring to an IP address used for a host in the outside (untrusted) part of the network, for packets as they traverse the inside (trusted), or local, part of the network.

overlapping subnets   An (incorrect) IP subnet design condition in which one subnet's range of addresses includes addresses in the range of another subnet.

P

packet switching   A WAN service in which each DTE device connects to a telco using a single physical line, with the possibility of being able to forward traffic to all other sites connected to the same service. The telco switch makes the forwarding decision based on an address in the packet header.

PAP   Password Authentication Protocol. A PPP authentication protocol that allows PPP peers to authenticate one another.

partial mesh   A network topology in which more than two devices could physically communicate, but by choice, only a subset of the pairs of devices connected to the network are allowed to communicate directly.

partial update   With IP routing protocols, the general concept that a routing protocol update lists a subset of all known routes. See also full update.

PAT   See Port Address Translation.

periodic update   With routing protocols, the concept that the routing protocol advertises routes in a routing update on a regular periodic basis. This is typical of distance vector routing protocols.

permanent virtual circuit (PVC)   A preconfigured communications path between two Frame Relay DTEs, identified by a local DLCI on each Frame Relay access link, that provides the functional equivalent of a leased circuit, but without a physical leased line for each VC.

permit   An action taken with an ACL that implies that the packet is allowed to proceed through the router and be forwarded.

poisoned route   A route in a routing protocol's advertisement that lists a subnet with a special metric value, called an infinite metric, that designates the route as a failed route.

poison reverse   A distance vector poisoned route advertisement for a subnet that would not have been advertised because of split-horizon rules but is now advertised as a poison route.

port   (Multiple definitions) 1) In TCP and UDP, a number that is used to uniquely identify the application process that either sent (source port) or should receive (destination port) data. 2) In LAN switching, another term for switch interface.

Port Address Translation (PAT)   A NAT feature in which one Inside Global IP address supports more than 65,000 concurrent TCP and UDP connections.

PortFast   A switch STP feature in which a port is placed in an STP Forwarding state as soon as the interface comes up, bypassing the Listening and Learning states. This feature is meant for ports connected to end-user devices.

PPP   Point-to-Point Protocol. A data-link protocol that provides router-to-router and host-to-network connections over synchronous and asynchronous circuits.

prefix notation   A shorter way to write a subnet mask in which the number of binary 1s in the mask is simply written in decimal. For instance, /24 denotes the subnet mask with 24 binary 1 bits in the subnet mask. The number of bits of value binary 1 in the mask is considered to be the prefix.

PRI   Primary Rate Interface. An ISDN interface to primary rate access. Primary rate access consists of a single 64-kbps D channel plus 23 (T1) or 30 (E1) B channels for voice or data.

private address   Several Class A, B, and C networks that are set aside for use inside private organizations. These addresses, as defined in RFC 1918, are not routable through the Internet.

private IP network   One of several classful IPv4 network numbers that will never be assigned for use in the Internet, meant for use inside a single enterprise.

private key   A secret value used in public/private key encryption systems. Either encrypts a value that can then be decrypted using the matching public key, or decrypts a value that was previously encrypted with the matching public key.

problem isolation   The part of the troubleshooting process in which the engineer attempts to rule out possible causes of the problem, narrowing the possible causes until the root cause of the problem can be identified.

protocol type   A field in the IP header that identifies the type of header that follows the IP header, typically a Layer 4 header, such as TCP or UDP. ACLs can examine the protocol type to match packets with a particular value in this header field.

public key   A secret value used in public/private key encryption systems. Either encrypts a value that can then be decrypted using the matching private key, or decrypts a value that was previously encrypted with the matching private key.

PVC   See permanent virtual circuit.

R

Rapid Spanning Tree Protocol (RSTP)   Defined in IEEE 802.1w. Defines an improved version of STP that converges much more quickly and consistently than STP (802.1d).

reflexive ACL   A type of ACL that goes beyond traditional IP ACLs to monitor the addition of new user sessions. The router reacts to add an ACL entry that matches that session's IP addresses and TCP or UDP port numbers.

Regional Internet Registry (RIR)   The generic term for one of five current organizations that are responsible for assigning the public, globally unique IPv4 and IPv6 address space.

registry prefix   In IPv6, the prefix that describes a block of public, globally unique IPv6 addresses assigned to a Regional Internet Registry by ICANN.

reported distance   From one EIGRP router's perspective, the metric for a subnet as calculated on a neighboring router and reported in a routing update to the first router.

reverse route   From one host's perspective, for packets sent back to the host from another host, the route over which the packet travels.

RIP   Routing Information Protocol. An Interior Gateway Protocol (IGP) that uses distance vector logic and router hop count as the metric. RIP version 1 (RIP-1) has become unpopular. RIP version 2 (RIP-2) provides more features, including support for VLSM.

root bridge   See root switch.

root port   In STP, the one port on a nonroot switch in which the least-cost Hello is received. Switches put root ports in a Forwarding state.

root switch   In STP, the switch that wins the election by virtue of having the lowest Bridge ID, and, as a result, sends periodic Hello BPDUs (the default is 2 seconds).

routable protocol   See routed protocol.

routed protocol   A Layer 3 protocol that defines a packet that can be routed, such as IPv4 and IPv6.

router ID (RID)   In OSPF, a 32-bit number, written in dotted decimal, that uniquely identifies each router.

route summarization   The process of combining multiple routes into a single advertised route, for the purpose of reducing the number of entries in routers' IP routing tables.

routing protocol   A set of messages and processes with which routers can exchange information about routes to reach subnets in a particular network. Examples of routing protocols include Enhanced Interior Gateway Routing Protocol (EIGRP), Open Shortest Path First (OSPF), and Routing Information Protocol (RIP).

RSTP   See Rapid Spanning Tree Protocol.

S

secondary IP address   The second (or more) IP address configured on a router interface, using the **secondary** keyword on the **ip address** command.

Secure Sockets Layer (SSL)   A security protocol that is integrated into commonly used web browsers that provides encryption and authentication services between the browser and a website.

segment   (Multiple definitions) 1) In TCP, a term used to describe a TCP header and its encapsulated data (also called an L4PDU). 2) Also in TCP, the set of bytes formed when TCP breaks a large chunk of data given to it by the application layer into smaller pieces that fit into TCP segments. 3) In Ethernet, either a single Ethernet cable or a single collision domain (no matter how many cables are used).

shared key   A reference to a security key whose value is known by both the sender and receiver.

site prefix   In IPv6, the prefix that describes a public globally unique IPv6 address block that has been assigned to an end-user organization (for example, an Enterprise or government agency). The assignment typically is made by an ISP or Internet registry.

SLSM   Static-length subnet mask. The usage of the same subnet mask for all subnets of a single Class A, B, or C network.

Spanning Tree Protocol (STP)   A protocol defined by IEEE standard 802.1d. Allows switches and bridges to create a redundant LAN, with the protocol dynamically causing some ports to block traffic, so that the bridge/switch forwarding logic will not cause frames to loop indefinitely around the LAN.

split horizon   A distant vector routing technique in which information about routes is prevented from exiting the router interface through which that information was received. Split-horizon updates are useful in preventing routing loops.

SSL   See Secure Sockets Layer.

standard access list   A list of IOS global configuration commands that can match only a packet's source IP address for the purpose of deciding which packets to discard and which to allow through the router.

stateful DHCP   A term used in IPv6 to contrast with stateless DHCP. Stateful DHCP keeps track of which clients have been assigned which IPv6 addresses (state information).

stateless autoconfiguration   A feature of IPv6 in which a host or router can be assigned an IPv6 unicast address without the need for a stateful DHCP server.

stateless DHCP   A term used in IPv6 to contrast with stateful DHCP. Stateless DHCP servers don't lease IPv6 addresses to clients. Instead, they supply other useful information, such as DNS server IP addresses, but with no need to track information about the clients (state information).

subinterface   One of the virtual interfaces on a single physical interface.

subnet   A subdivision of a Class A, B, or C network, as configured by a network administrator. Subnets allow a single Class A, B, or C network to be used and still allow for a large number of groups of IP addresses, as is required for efficient IP routing.

subnet broadcast address   A special address in each subnet—specifically, the largest numeric address in the subnet—designed so that packets sent to this address should be delivered to all hosts in that subnet.

subnet mask   A 32-bit number that describes the format of an IP address. It represents the combined network and subnet bits in the address with mask bit values of 1 and represents the host bits in the address with mask bit values of 0.

subnet prefix   In IPv6, a term for the prefix that is assigned to each data link, acting like a subnet in IPv4.

successor   In EIGRP, the route to reach a subnet that has the best metric and should be placed in the IP routing table.

summary route   A route created via configuration commands to represent routes to one or more subnets with a single route, thereby reducing the size of the routing table.

SVC   Switched virtual circuit. A VC that is set up dynamically when needed.

switch   A network device that filters, forwards, and floods frames based on each frame's destination address. The switch operates at the data link layer of the Open System Interconnection (OSI) reference model.

synchronous   The imposition of time ordering on a bit stream. Practically, a device tries to use the same speed as another device on the other end of a serial link. However, by examining transitions between voltage states on the link, the device can notice slight variations in the speed on each end and can adjust its speed accordingly.

T

TFTP Trivial File Transfer Protocol. An application protocol that allows files to be transferred from one computer to another over a network, but with only a few features, making the software require little storage space.

topology database The structured data that describes the network topology to a routing protocol. Link-state and balanced hybrid routing protocols use topology tables, from which they build the entries in the routing table.

triggered update A routing protocol feature in which the routing protocol does not wait for the next periodic update when something changes in the network, instead immediately sending a routing update.

trunk In campus LANs, an Ethernet segment over which the devices add a VLAN header that identifies the VLAN in which the frame exists.

trunking Also called VLAN trunking. A method (using either the Cisco ISL protocol or the IEEE 802.1Q protocol) to support multiple VLANs that have members on more than one switch.

trunking administrative mode The configured trunking setting on a Cisco switch interface, as configured with the **switchport mode** command.

trunking operational mode The current behavior of a Cisco switch interface for VLAN trunking.

two-way state In OSPF, a neighbor state that implies that the router has exchanged Hellos with the neighbor, and all required parameters match.

U

unique local address A type of IPv6 unicast address meant as a replacement for IPv4 private addresses.

update timer The time interval that regulates how often a routing protocol sends its next periodic routing updates. Distance vector routing protocols send full routing updates every update interval.

V

variable-length subnet mask(ing)   See VLSM.

variance   IGRP and EIGRP compute their metrics, so the metrics for different routes to the same subnet seldom have the exact same value. The variance value is multiplied with the lower metric when multiple routes to the same subnet exist. If the product is larger than the metrics for other routes, the routes are considered to have "equal" metric, allowing multiple routes to be added to the routing table.

VC   Virtual circuit. A logical concept that represents the path that frames travel between DTEs. VCs are particularly useful when comparing Frame Relay to leased physical circuits.

virtual LAN (VLAN)   A group of devices connected to one or more switches that are grouped into a single broadcast domain through configuration. VLANs allow switch administrators to place the devices connected to the switches in separate VLANs without requiring separate physical switches. This creates design advantages of separating the traffic without the expense of buying additional hardware.

virtual private network (VPN)   A set of security protocols that, when implemented by two devices on either side of an unsecure network such as the Internet, can allow the devices to send data securely. VPNs provide privacy, device authentication, anti-replay services, and data integrity services.

VLAN   See virtual LAN.

VLAN configuration database   The name of the collective configuration of VLAN IDs and names on a Cisco switch.

vlan.dat   The default file used to store a Cisco switch's VLAN configuration database.

VLAN Trunking Protocol (VTP)   A Cisco-proprietary messaging protocol used between Cisco switches to communicate configuration information about the existence of VLANs, including the VLAN ID and VLAN name.

VLSM   Variable-length subnet mask(ing). The ability to specify a different subnet mask for the same Class A, B, or C network number on different subnets. VLSM can help optimize available address space.

VoIP   Voice over IP. The transport of voice traffic inside IP packets over an IP network.

VPN   See virtual private network.

VPN client   Software that resides on a PC, often a laptop, so that the host can implement the protocols required to be an endpoint of a VPN.

VTP   See VLAN Trunking Protocol.

VTP client mode   One of three VTP operational modes for a switch with which switches learn about VLAN numbers and names from other switches, but which does not not allow the switch to be directly configured with VLAN information.

VTP pruning   The VTP feature by which switches dynamically choose interfaces on which to prevent the flooding of frames in certain VLANs when the frames do not need to go to every switch in the network.

VTP server mode   One of three sets of operating characteristics (modes) in VTP. Switches in server mode can configure VLANs, tell other switches about the changes, and learn about VLAN changes from other switches.

VTP transparent mode   One of three sets of operating characteristics (modes) in VTP. Switches in transparent mode can configure VLANs, but they do not tell other switches about the changes, and they do not learn about VLAN changes from other switches.

W

web VPN   A tool offered by Cisco in which a user can use any common web browser to securely connect using SSL to a web VPN server, which then connects to the user's Enterprise web-based applications—applications that may or may not support SSL.

wildcard mask   The mask used in Cisco IOS ACL commands and OSPF and EIGRP **network** commands.

Z

zero subnet   For every classful IPv4 network that is subnetted, the one subnet whose subnet number has all binary 0s in the subnet part of the number. In decimal, the 0 subnet can be easily identified because it is the same number as the classful network number.

Index

B - C

G - H - I

U -V

W -X -Y -Z

SEARCH THOUSANDS OF BOOKS FROM LEADING PUBLISHERS

Safari® Bookshelf

Safari® Bookshelf is a searchable electronic reference library for IT professionals that features more than 2,000 titles from technical publishers, including Cisco Press.

With Safari Bookshelf you can

- **Search** the full text of thousands of technical books, including more than 70 Cisco Press titles from authors such as Wendell Odom, Jeff Doyle, Bill Parkhurst, Sam Halabi, and Karl Solie.

- **Read** the books on My Bookshelf from cover to cover, or just flip to the information you need.

- **Browse** books by category to research any technical topic.

- **Download** chapters for printing and viewing offline.

With a customized library, you'll have access to your books when and where you need them—and all you need is a user name and password.

TRY SAFARI BOOKSHELF FREE FOR 14 DAYS!

You can sign up to get a 10-slot Bookshelf free for the first 14 days. Visit **http://safari.ciscopress.com** to register.

Safari
BOOKS ONLINE
ENABLED

THIS BOOK IS SAFARI ENABLED

INCLUDES FREE 45-DAY ACCESS TO THE ONLINE EDITION

The Safari® Enabled icon on the cover of your favorite technology book means the book is available through Safari Bookshelf. When you buy this book, you get free access to the online edition for 45 days.

Safari Bookshelf is an electronic reference library that lets you easily search thousands of technical books, find code samples, download chapters, and access technical information whenever and wherever you need it.

TO GAIN 45-DAY SAFARI ENABLED ACCESS TO THIS BOOK:

- Go to **http://www.ciscopress.com/safarienabled**
- Complete the brief registration form
- Enter the coupon code found in the front of this book before the "Contents at a Glance" page

If you have difficulty registering on Safari Bookshelf or accessing the online edition, please e-mail customer-service@safaribooksonline.com.

CCNA Wireless

Official Exam Certification Guide

Brandon James Carroll

Cisco Press

800 East 96th Street

Indianapolis, IN 46240

CCNA Wireless Official Exam Certification Guide

Brandon James Carroll

Copyright© 2009 Cisco Systems, Inc.

Published by:
Cisco Press
800 East 96th Street
Indianapolis, IN 46240 USA

Printed in the United States of America

Second Printing February 2009

Library of Congress Cataloging-in-Publication Data:

Carroll, Brandon.
  CCNA wireless official exam certification guide / Brandon James Carroll.
    p. cm.
  ISBN 978-1-58720-211-7 (hbk. : CD-ROM)
  1. Wireless LANs--Examinations--Study guides. 2. Electronic data
processing personnel--Certification--Study guides. I. Title.
  TK5105.78C37 2009
  004.6'8076--dc22

                        2008038512

ISBN-13: 978-1-58720-211-7

ISBN-10: 1-58720-211-5

Warning and Disclaimer

This book is designed to provide information about the 640-721 Implementing Cisco Unified Wireless Networking Essentials (IUWNE) certification exam. Every effort has been made to make this book as complete and as accurate as possible, but no warranty or fitness is implied.

The information is provided on an "as is" basis. The authors, Cisco Press, and Cisco Systems, Inc., shall have neither liability nor responsibility to any person or entity with respect to any loss or damages arising from the information contained in this book or from the use of the discs or programs that may accompany it.

The opinions expressed in this book belong to the author and are not necessarily those of Cisco Systems, Inc.

Trademark Acknowledgments

All terms mentioned in this book that are known to be trademarks or service marks have been appropriately capitalized. Cisco Press or Cisco Systems, Inc., cannot attest to the accuracy of this information. Use of a term in this book should not be regarded as affecting the validity of any trademark or service mark.

Corporate and Government Sales

The publisher offers excellent discounts on this book when ordered in quantity for bulk purchases or special sales, which may include electronic versions and/or custom covers and content particular to your business, training goals, marketing focus, and branding interests. For more information, please contact:

U.S. Corporate and Government Sales
1-800-382-3419
corpsales@pearsontechgroup.com

For sales outside the United States please contact:
International Sales
international@pearsoned.com

Feedback Information

At Cisco Press, our goal is to create in-depth technical books of the highest quality and value. Each book is crafted with care and precision, undergoing rigorous development that involves the unique expertise of members from the professional technical community.

Readers' feedback is a natural continuation of this process. If you have any comments regarding how we could improve the quality of this book or otherwise alter it to better suit your needs, you can contact us through email at feedback@ciscopress.com. Please make sure to include the book title and ISBN in your message.

We greatly appreciate your assistance.

Publisher: Paul Boger	**Associate Publisher:** Dave Dusthimer
Executive Editor: Brett Bartow	**Cisco Representative:** Anthony Wolfenden
Managing Editor: Patrick Kanouse	**Cisco Press Program Manager:** Jeff Brady
Senior Development Editor: Christopher Cleveland	**Copy Editors:** Karen A. Gill, Gayle Johnson
Project Editor: Mandie Frank	**Technical Editors:** Bobby Corcoran, Robert Marg
Editorial Assistant: Vanessa Evans	**Proofreader:** Sheri Cain, Water Crest Publishing, Inc.
Book and Cover Designer: Louisa Adair	**Indexer:** Tim Wright
Composition: Mark Shirar	

CISCO.

Americas Headquarters	Asia Pacific Headquarters	Europe Headquarters
Cisco Systems, Inc.	Cisco Systems (USA) Pte. Ltd.	Cisco Systems International BV
San Jose, CA	Singapore	Amsterdam, The Netherlands

Cisco has more than 200 offices worldwide. Addresses, phone numbers, and fax numbers are listed on the Cisco Website at **www.cisco.com/go/offices.**

CCDE, CCENT, Cisco Eos, Cisco Lumin, Cisco Nexus, Cisco StadiumVision, the Cisco logo, DCE, and Welcome to the Human Network are trademarks; Changing the Way We Work, Live, Play, and Learn is a service mark; and Access Registrar, Aironet, AsyncOS, Bringing the Meeting To You, Catalyst, CCDA, CCDP, CCIE, CCIP, CCNA, CCNP, CCSP, CCVP, Cisco, the Cisco Certified Internetwork Expert logo, Cisco IOS, Cisco Press, Cisco Systems, Cisco Systems Capital, the Cisco Systems logo, Cisco Unity, Collaboration Without Limitation, EtherFast, EtherSwitch, Event Center, Fast Step, Follow Me Browsing, FormShare, GigaDrive, HomeLink, Internet Quotient, IOS, iPhone, iQ Expertise, the iQ logo, iQ Net Readiness Scorecard, iQuick Study, IronPort, the IronPort logo, LightStream, Linksys, MediaTone, MeetingPlace, MGX, Networkers, Networking Academy, Network Registrar, PCNow, PIX, PowerPanels, ProConnect, ScriptShare, SenderBase, SMARTnet, Spectrum Expert, StackWise, The Fastest Way to Increase Your Internet Quotient, TransPath, WebEx, and the WebEx logo are registered trademarks of Cisco Systems, Inc. and/or its affiliates in the United States and certain other countries.

All other trademarks mentioned in this document or Website are the property of their respective owners. The use of the word partner does not imply a partnership relationship between Cisco and any other company. (0805R)

About the Author

Brandon James Carroll, CCNA, CCNP, CCSP, is one of the leading instructors for Cisco security technologies in the country, teaching classes that include the CCNA, CCNP, and CCSP courses, numerous CCVP courses, and custom developed courseware. In his eight years with Ascolta, Brandon has developed and taught many private Cisco courses for companies such as Boeing, Intel, and Cisco. He is a certified Cisco instructor and the author of *Cisco Access Control Security*, in addition to several Quick Reference Sheets.

Prior to becoming a technical instructor for Ascolta, Brandon was a technician and an ADSL specialist for GTE Network Services and Verizon Communications. His duties involved ISP router support and network design. As a lead engineer, he tested and maintained Frame Relay connections between Lucent B-STDX and Cisco routers. His team was in charge of troubleshooting ISP Frame Relay to ATM cut-overs for ADSL customers. Brandon trained new employees at Verizon to the EPG in ADSL testing and troubleshooting procedures and managed a Tekwizard database for technical information and troubleshooting techniques. He majored in information technology at St. Leo University.

About the Technical Reviewers

Bobby Corcoran, CCNA, is a systems engineer responsible for the design, configuration, implementation, and support of LAN, WAN, wireless, voice, and security infrastructures for a health care organization, including two acute care hospitals and several ancillary health care facilities. His recent wireless experience includes the migration of a multicampus Cisco SWAN to CUWN architecture. Bobby holds a bachelor's degree in business administration from Southern Oregon University.

Robert Marg is a wireless consulting systems engineer with Cisco. In his position at Cisco, he is a technical leader in wireless and mobility and has worked closely with enterprise, commercial, federal and transportation marketing, and product management teams to develop and deliver solutions for numerous customers and various transportation and federal agencies. Robert holds a bachelor's degree in bacteriology from the University of Wisconsin-Madison.

Dedication

I would like to dedicate this book to all those engineers out there who are going to spend many hours away from friends and family just to learn this material, advance their careers, and accelerate the network world. It's because of you that I have done the same in writing this book.

Acknowledgments

I would like to thank Brett Bartow for giving me another wonderful opportunity to work on this book and to work with a handful of exceptional people.

I'd also like to thank my technical editors, Robert Marg and Bobby Corcoran, for the extremely difficult task that they underwent and for the continued support. Thanks for responding to all my extra emails! You truly have made this a better book.

I would like to give special recognition to Christopher Cleveland, Dayna Isley, Andrew Cupp, Mandie Frank, and all the good people at Cisco Press, for keeping this publication on track.

In addition, I would like to thank Ascolta Training for giving me the opportunity to explore areas of technology that I really love. And I want to recognize Ted Wagner and Kevin Marz for their constant encouragement and support. Finally, thanks to Tony DeSimone, William Kivlen, Jack Wood, Kevin Masui, and the other instructors at Ascolta for being there when I needed to bounce ideas off of someone.

Contents at a Glance

Contents

Icons Used in This Book

Router   Gateway   Multilayer Switch   Switch   Wireless Router   Wireless Bridge

Access Point   WLAN Controller   LWAPP Access Point   PC   Laptop   Server

Wireless Connection   Ethernet Connection   Serial Line Connection   Network Cloud

Command Syntax Conventions

The conventions used to present command syntax in this book are the same conventions used in the IOS Command Reference. The Command Reference describes these conventions as follows:

- **Boldface** indicates commands and keywords that are entered literally as shown. In actual configuration examples and output (not general command syntax), boldface indicates commands that are manually input by the user (such as a **show** command).

- *Italic* indicates arguments for which you supply actual values.

- Vertical bars (|) separate alternative, mutually exclusive elements.

- Square brackets [ ] indicate optional elements.

- Braces { } indicate a required choice.

- Braces within brackets [{ }] indicate a required choice within an optional element.

Foreword

CCNA Wireless Official Exam Certification Guide is an excellent self-study resource for the Cisco IUWNE (640-721) exam. Passing the IUWNE exam validates the knowledge and skills required to successfully secure Cisco network devices.

Gaining certification in Cisco technology is key to the continuing educational development of today's networking professional. Through certification programs, Cisco validates the skills and expertise required to effectively manage the modern enterprise network.

Cisco Press exam certification guides and preparation materials offer exceptional—and flexible—access to the knowledge and information required to stay current in your field of expertise or to gain new skills. Whether used as a supplement to more traditional training or as a primary source of learning, these materials offer users the information and knowledge validation required to gain new understanding and proficiencies.

Developed in conjunction with the Cisco certifications and training team, Cisco Press books are the only self-study books authorized by Cisco, and they offer students a series of exam practice tools and resource materials to help ensure that learners fully grasp the concepts and information presented.

Additional authorized Cisco instructor-led courses, e-learning, labs, and simulations are available exclusively from Cisco Learning Solutions Partners worldwide. To learn more, visit http://www.cisco.com/go/training.

I hope that you find these materials to be an enriching and useful part of your exam preparation.

Erik Ullanderson
Manager, Global Certifications
Learning@Cisco
May 2008

Introduction

Welcome to the world of Cisco Certified Network Associate (CCNA) Wireless! As technology continues to evolve, wireless technologies are finding their way to the forefront. This clearly indicates the progression from a fixed wired type of connectivity to a more fluid, mobile workforce that can work when, where, and how they want. Regardless of your background, one of the primary goals of the new CCNA Wireless certification is to introduce you to the Cisco Unified Wireless Network (CUWN).

In June 2008, Cisco announced new CCNA specialties, including CCNA Security, CCNA Wireless, and CCNA Voice. These certifications, released 10 years after the initial CCNA, represent the growth of Cisco into new and emerging industries. Certification candidates can now specialize into specific areas of study. Figure I-1 shows the basic organization of the certifications and exams used to achieve your CCNA Wireless certification.

Figure I-1   *Cisco Certifications and CCNA Wireless Certification Path*

As you can see from the figure, a traditional CCNA certification is a prerequisite before you venture into the CCNA Wireless certification.

Goals and Methods

The most important and somewhat obvious goal of this book is to help you pass the Implementing Cisco Unified Wireless Networking Essentials (IUWNE) exam (640-721). In fact, if the primary objective of this book were different, the book title would be misleading; however, the methods used in this book to help you pass the IUWNE exam are designed to also make you much more knowledgeable about how to do your job.

This book uses several key methodologies to help you discover the exam topics that you need to review in more depth so that you can fully understand and remember those details and prove to yourself that you have retained your knowledge of those topics. This book does not try to help you pass by memorization but helps you truly learn and understand the topics. The CCNA Wireless exam is the foundation for Cisco professional certifications to come, and it would be a disservice to you if this book did not help you truly learn the material. Therefore, this book will help you pass the CCNA Wireless exam by using the following methods:

■   Helping you discover which test topics you have not mastered

■   Providing explanations and information to fill in your knowledge gaps

■   Supplying exercises and scenarios that enhance your ability to recall and deduce the answers to test questions

■   Providing practice exercises on the topics and the testing process via test questions on the CD

In addition, this book uses quite a different style from typical certification-preparation books. The newer Cisco certification exams have adopted a style of testing that essentially says, "If you do not know how to do it, you will not pass this exam." This means that most of the questions on the certification exam require you to deduce the answer through reasoning or configuration rather than just memorization of facts, figures, or syntax from a book. To accommodate this newer testing style, I have written this book as a "real-world" explanation of Cisco wireless topics. Whenever possible, key concepts are explained using real-world examples rather than showing tables full of syntax options and explanations, which are freely available at Cisco.com. As you read through this book, you will definitely get a feeling of, "This is how I can *do* this" rather than, "There is the general syntax I need to memorize," which is exactly what you need for the newer Cisco exams.

Who Should Read This Book?

This book is designed to provide a twofold purpose. The primary purpose is to tremendously increase your chances of passing the CCNA Wireless certification exam. The secondary purpose is to provide the information necessary to deploy a CUWN and a Cisco Mobility Express (CME) network as part of the Smart Business Communications System (SBCS). The new Cisco exam approach provides an avenue to write the book with both a real-world and certification-study approach at the same time. As you read through this book and study the configuration examples and exam tips, you will truly understand how you can deploy a wireless network, while at the same time feel equipped to pass the CCNA Wireless certification exam.

Strategies for Exam Preparation

Strategies for exam preparation will vary depending on your existing skills, knowledge, and equipment available. Of course, the ideal exam preparation would consist of building a small wireless lab with a 2106 wireless LAN controller and an 1131AP, as well as a Cisco Mobility Express (CME) 526 controller and 521 AP. You would also need a switch and a few wireless clients so that you could work through configurations as you read through this book. However, not everyone has access to this equipment, so the next best step you can take is to read through the chapters in this book, jotting notes down with key concepts or configurations on a separate notepad. Each chapter begins with a "Do I Know This Already?" quiz designed to give you a good idea of the chapter content. In some cases, you might already know most of or all the information covered in a given chapter.

After you have read this book, look at the current exam objectives for the CCNA Wireless exam listed on the Cisco website (http://www.cisco.com/certification). If you see areas shown in the certification exam outline that you would still like to study, find those sections in the book and review them. When you feel confident in your skills, attempt the practice exam included on the book CD. As you work through the practice exam, note the areas where you lack confidence, and review those concepts or configurations in the book. After you have reviewed the areas, work through the practice exam a second time and rate your skills. Keep in mind that the more you work through the practice exam, the more familiar the questions will become and the less accurate the practice exam will measure your skills. After you have worked through the practice exam a second time and feel confident with your skills, schedule the real IUWNE (640-721) exam through VUE (www.vue.com). You should typically take the exam within a week from when you consider yourself ready to take it so the information is fresh in your mind.

Cisco exams are difficult. Even if you have a solid grasp of the information, many other factors play into the testing environment (stress, time constraints, and so on). If you pass the exam on the first attempt, fantastic! If not, know that this is happens to many people. The next time you attempt the exam, you have a major advantage: You have experienced the exam firsthand. Although future exams might have different questions, the topics and general "feel" of the exam will remain the same. Take some time to study areas from the book where you felt weak on the exam. You must wait a certain period between attempts, so use that time to make yourself more prepared in the areas in which you scored low.

640-721 IUWNE Exam Topics

Table I-1 lists the exam topics for the 640-721 IUWNE exam. This table also lists the book parts where each exam topic is covered.

Table I-1 *Exam Topics for 640-721 IUWNE Exam*

Book Part(s) Where Topic Is Covered	Exam Topic
Describe WLAN fundamentals	
Part I	Describe basics of spread spectrum technology (modulation, DSS, OFDM, MIMO, Channels reuse and overlap, Rate-shifting, CSMA/CA)

Table I-1   *Exam Topics for 640-721 IUWNE Exam   (continued)*

Book Part(s) Where Topic Is Covered	Exam Topic
Part I	Describe the impact of various wireless technologies (Bluetooth, WiMAX, ZigBee, cordless phone)
Part I	Describe wireless regulatory bodies, standards and certifications (FCC, ETSI, 802.11a/b/g/n, WiFi Alliance)
Part I	Describe WLAN RF principles (antenna types, RF gain/loss, EIRP, refraction, reflection, ETC)
Part I	Describe networking technologies used in wireless (SSID —> WLAN_ID —> Interface — >VLAN, 802.1Q trunking)
Part I	Describe wireless topologies (IBSS, BSS, ESS, Point-to-Point, Point-to-Multipoint, basic Mesh, bridging)
Part III	Describe 802.11 authentication and encryption methods (Open, Shared, 802.1X, EAP, TKIP, AES)
Part I	Describe frame types (associated/unassociated, management, control, data)
Install a basic Cisco wireless LAN	
Part II	Describe the basics of the Cisco Unified Wireless Network architecture (Split MAC, LWAPP, stand-alone AP versus controller-based AP, specific hardware examples)
Part II	Describe the Cisco Mobility Express Wireless architecture (Smart Business Communication System — SBCS, Cisco Config Agent — CCA, 526WLC, 521AP - stand-alone and controller-based)
Part II	Describe the modes of controller-based AP deployment (local, monitor, HREAP, sniffer, rogue detector, bridge)
Part II	Describe controller-based AP discovery and association (OTAP, DHCP, DNS, Master-Controller, Primary-Secondary-Tertiary, n+1 redundancy)
Part II	Describe roaming (Layer 2 and Layer 3, intra-controller and inter-controller, mobility groups)
Part II	Configure a WLAN controller and access points WLC: ports, interfaces, WLANs, NTP, CLI and Web UI, CLI wizard, LAG AP: Channel, Power
Part II	Configure the basics of a stand-alone access point (no lab) (Express setup, basic security)
Part II	Describe RRM

Table I-1 *Exam Topics for 640-721 IUWNE Exam* *(continued)*

Book Part(s) Where Topic Is Covered	Exam Topic
Install Wireless Clients	
Part II	Describe client OS WLAN configuration (Windows, Apple, and Linux.)
Part II	Install Cisco ADU
Part II	Describe basic CSSC
Part II	Describe CCX versions 1 through 5
Implement basic WLAN Security	
Part III	Describe the general framework of wireless security and security components (authentication, encryption, MFP, IPS)
Part III	Describe and configure authentication methods (Guest, PSK, 802.1X, WPA/WPA2 with EAP- TLS, EAP-FAST, PEAP, LEAP)
Part III	Describe and configure encryption methods (WPA/WPA2 with TKIP, AES)
Part III	Describe and configure the different sources of authentication (PSK, EAP-local or -external, Radius)
Operate basic WCS	
Part III	Describe key features of WCS and Navigator (versions and licensing)
Part III	Install/upgrade WCS and configure basic administration parameters (ports, O/S version, strong passwords, service vs. application)
Part III	Configure controllers and APs (using the Configuration tab not templates)
Part III	Configure and use maps in the WCS (add campus, building, floor, maps, position AP)
Part III	Use the WCS monitor tab and alarm summary to verify the WLAN operations
Conduct basic WLAN Maintenance and Troubleshooting	
Part III	Identify basic WLAN troubleshooting methods for controllers, access points, and clients methodologies
Part III	Describe basic RF deployment considerations related to site survey design of data or VoWLAN applications, Common RF interference sources such as devices, building material, AP location Basic RF site survey design related to channel reuse, signal strength, cell overlap

Table I-1   *Exam Topics for 640-721 IUWNE Exam   (continued)*

Book Part(s) Where Topic Is Covered	Exam Topic
Part III	Describe the use of WLC show, debug and logging
Part III	Describe the use of the WCS client troubleshooting tool
Part III	Transfer WLC config and O/S using maintenance tools and commands
Part III	Describe and differentiate WLC WLAN management access methods (console port, CLI, telnet, ssh, http, https, wired versus wireless management)

How This Book Is Organized

Although you can read this book cover to cover, it is designed to be flexible and allow you to easily move between chapters and sections of chapters to cover just the material that you need more work with. If you do intend to read all the chapters, the order in the book is an excellent sequence to use.

Part I, "Wireless LAN Fundamentals," consists of Chapters 1 through 9, which cover the following topics:

■ **Chapter 1, "Introduction to Wireless Networking Concepts":** This chapter discusses the basics of wireless networking along with some of the challenges you may face. It is intended to be an introductory chapter to what you will be covering in chapters to come.

■ **Chapter 2, "Standards Bodies":** This chapter focuses primarily on the standards bodies involved in wireless technology.

■ **Chapter 3, "WLAN RF Principles":** This chapter discusses WLAN transmissions along with some of the influences on WLAN transmissions. You will also learn how to determine your signal strength and determine what may be influencing your wireless deployment.

■ **Chapter 4, "WLAN Technologies and Topologies":** This chapter covers the various wireless topologies that you may come across, from Wireless Personal Area Networks (WPAN) to wireless LANs (WLAN). It also offers a further look at 802.11 topologies, including Ad-hoc mode and Infrastructure mode. In addition, you get a look at roaming and some vendor-specific topologies.

■ **Chapter 5, "Antennae Communications":** This chapter focuses on antennas. It covers everything from how antennas work to how they are regulated. It even discusses the different types of antennas that Cisco offers.

■ **Chapter 6, "Overview of the 802.11 WLAN Protocols":** This chapter examines each of the 802.11 protocols, including 802.11a, 802.11b. 802.11g, and even 802.11n.

- Chapter 7, "Wireless Traffic Flow and AP Discovery": This chapter disusses how traffic flows in a wireless network and shows you the various headers and communications. You will also learn how a client discovers an AP.

- Chapter 8, "Additional Wireless Technologies": This chapter takes into account the other wireless technologies that are seen in the market today, including Bluetooth, ZigBee, and WiMax.

- Chapter 9, "Delivering Packets from the Wireless to Wired Network": This chapter dives into the flow of a packet. You will actually experience the journey of a packet as it travels from the wireless to the wired network.

Part II, "Cisco Wireless LANs," which focuses primarily on configuration and consists of Chapters 10 through 16, covers the following topics:

- Chapter 10, "Cisco Wireless Networks Architecture": This chapter discusses the CUWN architecutre and the devices involved.

- Chapter 11, "Controller Discovery and Association": In this chapter, you will learn how an AP discovers a controller and associates with it. You will also learn what steps to take to provide controller redundancy.

- Chapter 12, "Adding Mobility with Roaming": This chapter discusses how clients roam, how the controllers are configured to support roaming, and all that is involved in asymmetric roaming, symmetric roaming, and mobility anchors.

- Chapter 13, "Simple Network Configuration and Monitoring with the Cisco Controller": This chapter is your first configuration chapter that gets into allowing client access. In this chapter, you will learn how to build a WLAN with open authentication.

- Chapter 14, "Migrating Standalone APs to LWAPP": This chapter discusses the process of migrating a standalone AP to LWAPP using various tools.

- Chapter 15, "Cisco Mobility Express": This chapter discusses the Mobility Express solution for small environments. In this chapter, you will learn how to configure the Cisco 526 controller and 521 AP.

- Chapter 16, "Wireless Clients": This chapter discusses the Windows wireless clients with the Wireless Zero Configuration utility, the Apple Airport utility, and the Linux Network Configuration utility. You will also learn how to set up the Aironet Desktop Utility (ADU) and the Cisco Secure Services Client (CSSC). Finally, you will learn about the Cisco Compatible Extensions Program (CCX).

Part III, "WLAN Maintenance and Administration," which consists of Chapters 17 through 20, covers the following topics:

- Chapter 17, "Securing the Wireless Network": This chapter discusses the various methods of securing wireless networks. This chapter covers the many EAP methods, 802,.1x, Wired Equivalent Privacy (WEP), and Wi-Fi Protected Access (WPA)/WPA2.

- **Chapter 18, "Enterprise Wireless Management with the WCS and the Location Appliance":** This chapter introduces the Wireless Control System (WCS) that can be used to manage large depolyments with many controllers.

- **Chapter 19, "Maintaining Wireless Networks":** This chapter discusses the management side of things. Here you learn how to perform mainentance tasks, including upgrades.

- **Chapter 20, "Troubleshooting Wireless Networks":** This chapter discusses troubleshooting techniques for wireless networks using the various tools that are available. You will learn to use the command-line interface (CLI) of the controller as well as the WCS.

In addition to the 20 main chapters, this book includes tools to help you verify that you are prepared to take the exam. Chapter 21, "Final Preparation," includes guidelines that you can follow in the final days before the exam. Appendix A, "Answers to the 'Do I Know This Already?' Quizzes," will help you verify your knowledge based on the self-assessment quizzes at the beginning of each chapter. The Glossary helps to navigate you through the many terms associated with wireless networking. Also, the CD-ROM includes quiz questions and memory tables (refer to Appendix B and C on the CD-ROM) that you can work through to verify your knowledge of the subject matter.

Cisco Published 640-721 IUWNE Exam Topics Covered in This Part

Describe WLAN fundamentals

- Describe basics of spread spectrum technology (modulation, DSS, OFDM, MIMO, Channels reuse and overlap, Rate-shifting, CSMA/CA)

- Describe the impact of various wireless technologies (Bluetooth, WiMAX, ZigBee, cordless phone)

- Describe wireless regulatory bodies, standards and certifications (FCC, ETSI, 802.11a/b/g/n, WiFi Alliance)

- Describe WLAN RF principles (antenna types, RF gain/loss, EIRP, refraction, reflection, ETC)

- Describe networking technologies used in wireless (SSID —> WLAN_ID —> Interface — >VLAN, 802.1q trunking)

- Describe wireless topologies (IBSS, BSS, ESS, Point-to-Point, Point-to-Multipoint, basic Mesh, bridging)

- Describe frame types (associated/unassociated, management, control, data)

Part I: Wireless LAN Fundamentals

This chapter covers the following subjects:

Wireless Local-Area Networks: A brief history of wireless networking and some of the basic concepts.

How Bandwidth Is Achieved from RF Signals: The frequency spectrum used in RF transmissions.

Modulation Techniques and How They Work: How binary data is represented and transmitted using RF technology.

CHAPTER 1

Introduction to Wireless Networking Concepts

Perhaps this is the first time you have ever delved into the world of wireless networking. Or maybe you have been in networking for some time and are now beginning to see the vast possibilities that come with wireless networking. Either way, this chapter can help you understand topics that are not only tested on the CCNA Wireless exam but provide a good foundation for the chapters to come. If you are comfortable with the available frequency bands, the modulation techniques used in wireless LANs, and some of the standards and regulatory bodies that exist for wireless networking, you may want to skip to Chapter 2, "Standards Bodies."

This chapter provides a brief history of wireless networks and explores the basics of radio technology, the modulation techniques used, and some of the issues seen in wireless LANs.

You should do the "Do I Know This Already?" quiz first. If you score 80 percent or higher, you might want to skip to the section "Exam Preparation Tasks." If you score below 80 percent, you should spend the time reviewing the entire chapter. Refer to Appendix A, "Answers to the 'Do I Know This Already?' Quizzes" to confirm your answers.

"Do I Know This Already?" Quiz

The "Do I Know This Already?" quiz helps you determine your level of knowledge of this chapter's topics before you begin. Table 1-1 details the major topics discussed in this chapter and their corresponding quiz questions.

Table 1-1   *"Do I Know This Already?" Section-to-Question Mapping*

Foundation Topics Section	Questions
Wireless Local-Area Networks	1–2
How Bandwidth Is Achieved from RF Signals	3–6
Modulation Techniques and How They Work	7–10

1. Which of the following accurately describes the goal of RF technology?

   a. To send as much data as far as possible and as fast as possible

   b. To send secure data to remote terminals

   c. To send small amounts of data periodically

   d. To send data and voice short distances using encryption

2. Which of the following is a significant problem experienced with wireless networks?

   a. Infection

   b. Policing

   c. Transmission

   d. Interference

3. Which two of the following are unlicensed frequency bands used in the United Stated? (Choose two.)

   a. 2.0 MHz

   b. 2.4 GHz

   c. 5.0 GHz

   d. 6.8 GHz

4. Each 2.4-GHz channel is how many megahertz wide?

   a. 22 MHz

   b. 26 MHz

   c. 24 MHz

   d. 28 MHz

5. How many nonoverlapping channels exist in the 2.4-GHz ISM range?

   a. 9

   b. 3

   c. 17

   d. 13

6. The 5.0-GHz range is used by which two of the following 802.11 standards? (Choose two.)

   a. 802.11

   b. 802.11b/g

   c. 802.11n

   d. 802.11a

7. Which three of the following modulation techniques do WLANs today use? (Choose three.)

   a. OFDM

   b. AM

   c. FM

   d. DSSS

   e. MIMO

8. DSSS uses a chipping code to encode redundant data into the modulated signal. Which two of the following are examples of chipping codes that DSSS uses? (Choose two.)

   a. Barker code

   b. Baker code

   c. Complementary code keying (CCK)

   d. Cypher block chaining (CBC)

9. DSSS binary phase-shift keying uses what method of encoding at the 1-Mbps data rate?

   a. 11-chip Barker code

   b. 8-chip CCK

   c. 11-chip CCK

   d. 8-chip Barker code

10. With DRS, when a laptop operating at 11 Mbps moves farther away from an access point, what happens?

   a. The laptop roams to another AP.

   b. The laptop loses its connection.

   c. The rate shifts dynamically to 5.5 Mbps.

   d. The rate increases, providing more throughput.

Foundation Topics

Wireless Local-Area Networks

Although wireless networking began to penetrate the market in the 1990s, the technology has actually been around since the 1800s. A musician and astronomer, Sir William Herschel (1738 to 1822) made a discovery that infrared light existed and was beyond the visibility of the human eye. The discovery of infrared light led the way to the electromagnetic wave theory, which was explored in-depth by a man named James Maxwell (1831 to 1879). Much of his discoveries related to electromagnetism were based on research done by Michael Faraday (1791 to 1867) and Andre-Marie Ampere (1775 to 1836), who were researchers that came before him. Heinrich Hertz (1857 to 1894) built on the discoveries of Maxwell by proving that electromagnetic waves travel at the speed of light and that electricity can be carried on these waves.

Although these discoveries are interesting, you might be asking yourself how they relate to wireless local-area networks (WLANs). Here is the tie-in: In standard LANs, data is propagated over wires such as an Ethernet cable, in the form of electrical signals. The discovery that Hertz made opens the airways to transfer the same data, as electrical signals, without wires. Therefore, the simple answer to the relationship between WLANs and the other discoveries previously mentioned is that a WLAN is a LAN that does not need cables to transfer data between devices, and this technology exists because of the research and discoveries that Herschel, Maxwell, Ampere, and Hertz made. This is accomplished by way of Radio Frequencies (RF).

With RF, the goal is to send as much data as far as possible and as fast as possible. The problem is the numerous influences on radio frequencies that need to be either overcome or dealt with. One of these problems is interference, which is discussed at length in Chapter 5, "Antennae Communications." For now, just understand that the concept of wireless LANs is doable, but it is not always going to be easy. To begin to understand how to overcome the issues, and for that matter what the issues are, you need to understand how RF is used.

How Bandwidth Is Achieved from RF Signals

To send data over the airwaves, the IEEE has developed the 802.11 specification, which defines half-duplex operations using the same frequency for send and receive operations on a WLAN. No licensing is required to use the 802.11 standards; however, you must follow the rules that the FCC has set forth. The IEEE defines standards that help to operate within the FCC rules. The FCC governs not only the frequencies that can be used without licenses but the power levels at which WLAN devices can operate, the transmission technologies that can be used, and the locations where certain WLAN devices can be deployed.

> **Note:** The FCC is the regulatory body that exists in the United States. The *European Telecommunications Standards Institute* (ETSI) is the European equivalent to the FCC. Other countries have different regulatory bodies.

To achieve bandwidth from RF signals, you need to send data as electrical signals using some type of emission method. One such emission method is known as Spread Spectrum. In 1986, the FCC agreed to allow the use of spread spectrum in the commercial market using what is known as the industry, scientific, and medical (ISM) frequency bands. To place data on the RF signals, you use a modulation technique. Modulation is the addition of data to a carrier signal. You are probably familiar with this already. To send music, news, or speech over the airwaves, you use *frequency modulation* (FM) or *amplitude modulation* (AM). The last time you were sitting in traffic listening to the radio, you were using this technology.

Unlicensed Frequency Bands Used in WLANs

As you place more information on a signal, you use more frequency spectrum, or bandwidth. You may be familiar with using terms like *bits*, *kilobits*, megabits, and gigabits when you refer to bandwidth. In wireless networking, the word *bandwidth* can mean two different things. In one sense of the word, it can refer to data rates. In another sense of the word, it can refer to the width of an RF channel.

> **Note:** This book uses the term *bandwidth* to refer to the width of the RF channel and not to data rates.

When referring to bandwidth in a wireless network, the standard unit of measure is the Hertz (Hz). A Hertz measures the number of cycles per second. One Hertz is one cycle per second. In radio technology, a *Citizens' Band* (CB) radio is pretty low quality. It uses about 3 kHz of bandwidth. FM radio is generally a higher quality, using about 175 kHz of bandwidth. Compare that to a television signal, which sends both voice and video over the air. The TV signal you receive uses almost 4500 kHz of bandwidth.

Figure 1-1 shows the entire electromagnetic spectrum. Notice that the frequency ranges used in CB radio, FM radio, and TV broadcasts are only a fraction of the entire spectrum. Most of the spectrum is governed by folks like the FCC. This means that you cannot use the same frequencies that FM radio uses in your wireless networks.

As Figure 1-1 illustrates, the electromagnetic spectrum spans from Extremely Low Frequency (ELF) at 3 to 30 Hz to Extremely High Frequency (EHF) at 30 GHz to 300 GHz. The data you send is not done so in either of these ranges. In fact, the data you send using WLANs is either in the 900-MHz, 2.4-GHz, or 5-GHz frequency ranges. This places you in the Ultra High Frequency (UHF) or Super High Frequency (SHF) ranges. Again, this is just a fraction of the available spectrum, but remember that the FCC controls it. You are locked into the frequency ranges you can use. Table 1-2 lists the ranges that can be used in the United States, along with the frequency ranges allowed in Japan and Europe.

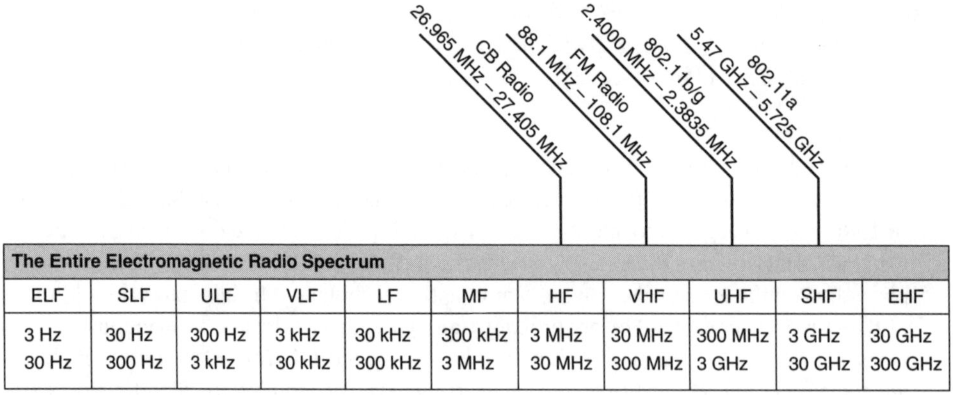

Figure 1-1 *Electromagnetic Spectrum*

Table 1-2 *Usable Frequency Bands in Europe, the United States, and Japan*

Europe	USA	Japan	Frequency
2.4 GHz	900 MHz		
	2.4 GHz ISM		2.0–2.4835 GHz
		2.4 GHz	2.0–2.495 GHz
CEPT A	UNII-1	5.15–5.25 GHz	5.15–5.25 GHz
CEPT A	UNII-2		5.25–5.35 GHz
CEPT B	UNII-2 Extended		5.47–5.7253 GHz
	ISM		5.725–5.850 GHz
		5.0 GHz	5.038–5.091 GHz
		4.9 GHz	4.9–5.0 GHz

Table 1-2 clearly shows that not all things are equal, depending on which country you are in. In Europe, the 2.4-GHz range and the 5.0-GHz range are used. The 5.0-GHz frequency ranges that are used in Europe are called the Conference of European Post and Telecommunication (CEPT) A, CEPT B, CEPT C, and CEPT C bands. In the United States, the 900-MHz, 2.4-GHz ISM, and 5.0-GHz Unlicensed National Information Infrastructure (UNII) bands are used. Japan has its own ranges in the 2.4- and 5.0-GHz range. The following sections explain the U.S. frequency bands in more detail.

900 MHz

The 900-MHz band starts at 902 MHz and goes to 928 MHz. This frequency range is likely the most familiar to you because you probably had a cordless phone that operated in this range. This is a good way to understand what wireless channels are. You might have picked up your cordless phone only to hear a lot of static or even a neighbor on his cordless phone. If this happened, you could press the Channel button to switch to a channel that did not have as much interference. When you found a clear channel, you could make your call. The channel you were changing to was simply a different range of frequencies. This way, even though both your phone and your neighbor's were operating in the 900-MHz range, you could select a channel in that range and have more than one device operating at the same time.

2.4 GHz

The 2.4-GHz range is probably the most widely used frequency range in WLANs. It is used by the 802.11, 802.11b, 802.11g, and 802.11n IEEE standards. The 2.4-GHz frequency range that can be used by WLANs is subdivided into channels that range from 2.4000 to 2.4835 GHz. The United States has 11 channels, and each channel is 22-MHz wide. Some channels overlap with others and cause interference. For this reason, channels 1, 6, and 11 are most commonly used because they do not overlap. In fact, many consumer-grade wireless devices are hard set so you can choose only one of the three channels. Figure 1-2 shows the 11 channels, including overlap. Again, notice that channels 1, 6, and 11 do not overlap.

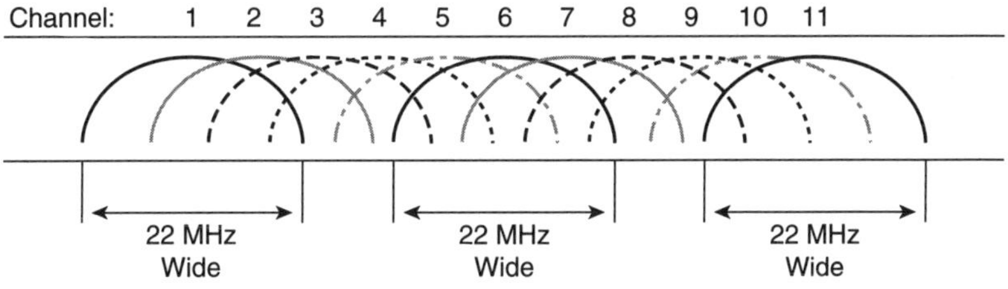

Figure 1-2 *2.4-GHz Channels*

With 802.11b and 802.11g, the energy is spread out over a wide area of the band. With 802.11b or 802.11g products, the channels have a bandwidth of 22 MHz. This allows three nonoverlapping, noninterfering channels to be used in the same area.

The 2.4-GHz range uses *direct sequence spread spectrum* (DSSS) modulation. DSSS is discussed later in this chapter in the section "DSSS." Data rates of 1 Mbps, 2 Mbps, 5.5 Mbps, and 11 Mbps are defined for this range.

5 GHz

The 5-GHz range is used by the 802.11a standard and the new 802.11n draft standard. In the 802.11a standard, data rates can range from 6 Mbps to 54 Mbps. 802.11a devices were not seen in the market until 2001, so they do not have quite the market penetration as 2.4-GHz range 802.11 b devices. The 5-GHz range is also subdivided into channels, each being 20-MHz wide. A total of 23 nonoverlapping channels exist in the 5-GHz range.

The 5-GHz ranges use *Orthogonal Frequency Division Multiplexing* (OFDM). OFDM is discussed later in this chapter in the section "OFDM." Data rates of 6, 9, 12, 18, 24, 36, 48, and 54 Mbps are defined.

Modulation Techniques and How They Work

In short, the process of *modulation* is the varying in a signal or a tone called a *carrier signal*. Data is then added to this carrier signal in a process known as *encoding*.

Imagine that you are singing a song. Words are written on a sheet of music. If you just read the words, your tone is soft and does not travel far. To convey the words to a large group, you use your vocal chords and modulation to send the words farther. While you are singing the song, you encode the written words into a waveform and let your vocal cords modulate it. People hear you singing and decode the words to understand the meaning of the song.

Modulation is what wireless networks use to send data. It enables the sending of encoded data using radio signals. Wireless networks use modulation as a carrier signal, which means that the modulated tones carry data. A modulated waveform consists of three parts:

Amplitude: The volume of the signal

Phase: The timing of the signal between peaks

Frequency: The pitch of the signal

Wireless networks use a few different modulation techniques, including these:

DSSS

OFDM

Multiple-Input Multiple-Output (MIMO)

The sections that follow cover these modulation techniques in further detail.

DSSS

DSSS is the modulation technique that 802.11b devices use to send the data. In DSSS, the transmitted signal is spread across the entire frequency spectrum that is being used. For example, an access point that is transmitting on channel 1 spreads the carrier signal across the 22-MHz-wide channel range of 2.401 to 2.423 GHz.

To encode data using DSSS, you use a chip sequence. A chip and a bit are essentially the same thing, but a bit represents the data, and a chip is used for the carrier encoding. Encoding is the process of transforming information from one format to another. To understand how data is encoded in a wireless network and then modulated, you must first understand chipping codes.

Chipping Codes

Because of the possible noise interference with a wireless transmission, DSSS uses a sequence of chips. When DSSS spreads information across a frequency range, it sends a single data bit as a string of chips or a *chip stream*. With redundant data being sent, if some of the signal is lost to noise, the data can likely still be understood. The chipping code process takes each data bit and then expands it into a string of bits.

Figure 1-3 illustrates this process for better understanding.

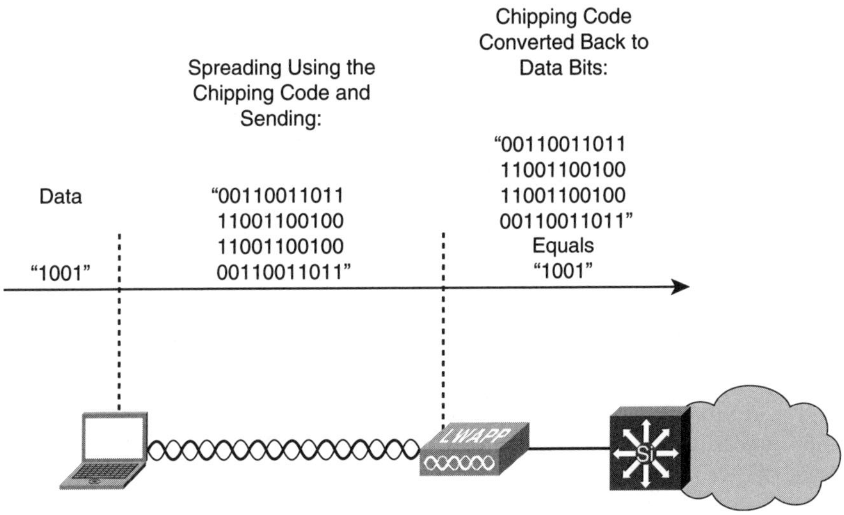

Figure 1-3 *Chipping Sequence*

As the laptop in the figure sends data over the wireless network, the data must be encoded using a chip sequence and then modulated over the airwaves. In the figure, the chipping code for the bit value of **1** is expanded to the chip sequence of 00110011011, and the chipping code for the bit value of **0** is 11001100100. Therefore, after the data bits are sent, **1001** creates the chip sequence.

00110011011	11001100100	11001100100	00110011011
1	0	0	1

You can decode this chip sequence back to the value of 1001 at the receiving access point. Remember, because of interference, it is still possible that some of the bits in the chip sequence will be lost or inverted. This means that a 1 could become a 0 and a 0 could become a 1. This is okay, because more than five bits need to be inverted to change the value between a 1 and a 0. Because of this, using a chipping sequence makes 802.11 networks more resilient against interference.

Also, because more bits are sent for chipping (carrier) than there is actual data, the chipping rate is higher than the data rate.

Barker Code

To achieve rates of 1 Mbps and 2 Mbps, 802.11 uses a Barker code. This code defines the use of 11 chips when encoding the data. The 11-chip Barker code used in 802.11 is 10110111000. Certain mathematical details beyond the scope of this book make the Barker code ideal for modulating radio waves. In the end, and for the exam, each bit of data sent is encoded into an 11-bit Barker code and then modulated with DSSS.

Complementary Code Keying

When you are using DSSS, the Barker code works well for lower data rates such as 1-Mbps, 2-Mbps, 5.5-Mbps, and 11-Mbps. DSSS uses a different method for higher data rates, which allows the 802.11 standard to achieve rates of 5.5 and 11 Mbps. Complementary code keying (CCK) uses a series of codes called complementary sequences. There are 64 unique code words. Up to 6 bits can be represented by a code word, as opposed to the 1 bit represented by a Barker code.

DSSS Modulation Techniques and Encoding

Now that the data has been encoded using Barker code or CCK, it needs to be transmitted or modulated out of the radio antennas. You can think of it this way:

- Encoding is how the changes in RF signal translate to the 1s and 0s.
- Modulation is the characteristic of the RF signal that is manipulated.

For example, amplitude modulation, frequency modulation, and phase-shift keying are modulations. The encoding would be that a 180-degree phase shift is a 1, and 0-degree phase shift is a 0. This is binary phase-shift keying. In 802.11b, the data is modulated on a carrier wave, and that carrier wave is spread across the frequency range using DSSS. 802.11b can modulate and encode the data using the methods seen in Table 1-3.

Key Topic

Table 1-3 *DSSS Encoding Methods*

Data Rate	Encoding	Modulation
1	11 chip Barker coding	DSSS Binary Phase Shift Keying
2	11 chip Barker coding	DSSS Quadrature Phase Shift Keying
5.5	8 chip encoding 8 bits CCK coding	DSSS Quadrature Phase Shift Keying
11	8 chip encoding 4 bits CCK coding	DSSS Quadrature Phase Shift Keying

One method of modulation that is simple to understand is amplitude modulation. With amplitude modulation, the information sent is based on the amplitude of the signal. For example, +5 volts is a 1, and −5 volts is a 0. Because of external factors, the amplitude of a signal is likely changed, and this in turn modifies the information you are sending. This makes AM a "not-so-good" solution for sending important data. However, other factors, such as frequency and phase, are not likely to change. 802.11b uses phase to modulate the data. Specifically, in 802.11b, BPSK and QPSK are used.

BPSK

Remember that phase is timing between peaks in the signal. Actually, that needs to be expanded further so you can really grasp the concept of BPSK and QPSK. To begin, look at Figure 1-4, which shows a waveform. This waveform, or motion, is happening over a period of time.

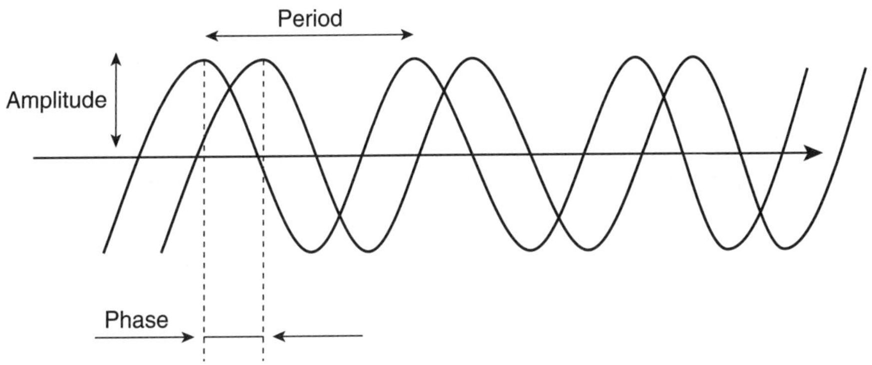

Figure 1-4   *Waveform*

Figure 1-4 illustrates the next step in determining phase. The phase is the difference between the two waveforms at the same frequency. If the waveforms peak at the same time, they are said to be *in-phase*, or 0 degrees. If the two waves peak at different times, they are said to be *out-of-phase*. Phase-shift keying (PSK) represents information by changing the phase of the signal.

BPSK is the simplest method of PSK. In BPSK, two phases are used that are separated by 180 degrees. BPSK can modulate 1 bit per symbol. To simplify this, a phase shift of 180 degrees is a 1, and a phase shift of 0 degrees is a 0, as illustrated in Figure 1-5.

802.11 also uses quadrature phase-shift keying (QPSK), which is discussed in the following section.

QPSK

In BPSK, 1 bit per symbol is encoded. This is okay for lower data rates. QPSK has the capability to encode 2 bits per symbol. This doubles the data rates available in BPSK while staying within the same bandwidth. At the 2-Mbps data rate, QPSK is used with Barker encoding. At the 5.5-Mbps data rate, QPSK is also used, but the encoding is CCK-16. At the 11-Mbps data rate, QPSK is also used, but the encoding is CCK-128.

OFDM

OFDM is not considered a spread spectrum technology, but it is used for modulation in wireless networks. Using OFDM, you can achieve the highest data rates with the maximum resistance to corruption of the data caused by interference. OFDM defines a number of channels in a frequency range. These channels are further divided into a larger number of small-bandwidth subcarriers. The channels are 20 MHz, and the subcarriers are

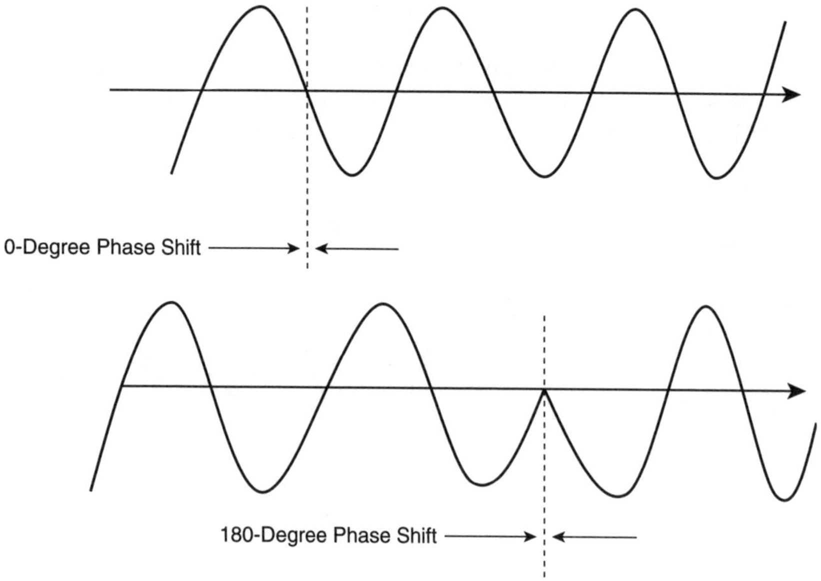

Figure 1-5   *Encoding with Phase Shifting*

300 kHz wide. You end up with 52 subcarriers per channel. Each of the subcarriers has a low data rate, but the data is sent simultaneously over the subcarriers in parallel. This is how you can achieve higher data rates.

OFDM is not used in 802.11b because 802.11b devices use DSSS. 802.11g and 802.11a both used OFDM. The way they are implemented is a little different because 802.11g is designed to operate in the 2.4-MHz range along with 802.11b devices. Chapter 2, "Standards Bodies," covers the differences in the OFDM implementations.

MIMO

MIMO is a technology that is used in the new 802.11n specification. Although at press time, the 802.11n specification had not yet been ratified by the IEEE, many vendors are already releasing products into the market that claim support for it. Here is what you need to know about it, though. A device that uses MIMO technology uses multiple antennas for receiving signals (usually two or three) in addition to multiple antennas for sending signals. MIMO technology can offer data rates higher than 100 Mbps by multiplexing data streams simultaneously in one channel. In other words, if you want data rates higher than 100-Mbps, then multiple streams are sent over a bonded channel, not just one. Using advanced signal processing, the data can be recovered after being sent on two or more spatial streams.

With the use of MIMO technology, an access point (AP) can talk to non-MIMO-capable devices and still offer about a 30 percent increase in performance of standard 802.11a/b/g networks.

Dynamic Rate Shifting

Now that you have an idea of how data is encoded and modulated, things will start to get a little easier. Another important aspect to understand, not only for the exam but for actual wireless deployments, is that the farther away you get from the access point, the lower the data rates are that you can achieve. This is true regardless of the technology. Although you can achieve higher data rates with different standards, you still have this to deal with.

All Cisco wireless products can perform a function called dynamic rate shifting (DRS). In 802.11 networks, operating in the 2.4-GHz range, the devices can rate-shift from 11 Mbps to 5.5 Mbps, and further to 2 and 1 Mbps depending on the circumstances. It even happens without dropping your connection. Also, it is done on a transmission-by-transmission basis, so if you shift from 11 Mbps to 5.5 Mbps for one transmission and then move closer to the AP, it can shift back up to 11 Mbps for the next transmission.

This process also occurs with 802.11g and 802.11a. In all deployments, DRS supports multiple clients operating at multiple rates.

Sending Data Using CSMA/CA

Wireless networks have to deal with the possibility of collisions. This is because, in a wireless topology, the behavior of the AP is similar to that of a hub. Multiple client devices can send at the same time. When this happens, just like in a wired network where a hub exists, a collision can occur. The problem with wireless networks is that they cannot tell when a collision has occurred. If you are in a wired network, a jam signal is heard by listening to the wire. To listen for a jam signal, wireless devices need two antennas. They can send using one antenna while listening for a jam signal with the other. Although this sounds feasible, especially because MIMO technology defines the use of multiple antennas, the transmitting signal from one antenna would drown out the received signal on the other, so the jam signal would not be heard.

To avoid collisions on a wireless network, carrier sense multiple access collision avoidance (CSMA/CA) is used. You are probably familiar with carrier sense multiple access collision detect (CSMA/CD), which is used on wired networks. Although the two are similar, collision avoidance means that when a device wishes to send, it must listen first. If the channel is considered idle, the device sends a signal informing others that it is going to send data and that they should not send. It then listens again for a period before sending. Another way to supplement this is using request to send (RTS) and clear to send (CTS) packets. With the RTS/CTS method, the sending device uses an RTS packet, and the intended receiver uses a CTS packet. This alerts other devices that they should not send for a period.

Exam Preparation Tasks

Review All Key Concepts

Review the most important topics from this chapter, noted with the Key Topics icon in the outer margin of the page. Table 1-4 lists a reference of these key topics and the page number where you can find each one.

Table 1-4   *Key Topics for Chapter 1*

Key Topic Item	Description	Page Number
Figure 1-1	The electromagnetic spectrum	10
Table 1-2	The usable frequency bands for WLANs in the United States, Europe, and Japan	10
Figure 1-2	The 2.4-GHz channels	11
Figure 1-3	Understanding chipping sequences	13
Table 1-3	DSSS encoding methods	14
Figure 1-5	Phase-shift encoding and how it works	16

Complete the Tables and Lists from Memory

Print a copy of Appendix B, "Memory Tables," (found on the CD) or at least the section for this chapter, and complete the tables and lists from memory. Appendix C, "Memory Tables Answer Key," also on the CD, includes completed tables and lists to check your work.

Definition of Key Terms

Define the following key terms from this chapter, and check your answers in the Glossary:

FCC, IEEE, ETSI, bandwidth, Hz, ISM, UNII, channels, DSSS, OFDM, amplitude, phase, frequency, chipping code, Barker code, CCK, BPSK, QPSK, MIMO, DRS, CSMA/CA, RTS, CTS

This chapter covers the following subjects:

Wireless Standards and Regulatory Commit-tees: Looks at the wireless regulatory committess and some of their requirements.

Wi-Fi Certification: Discusses how Wi-Fi devices are certified for interoperability.

CHAPTER 2

Standards Bodies

It took a long time for wireless to come together as we know it today. If it weren't for the standards bodies and committees, there's no telling where the technology would be. In this chapter, you will look at the standards bodies as well as the bodies that regulate the airwaves.

Take the "Do I Know This Already?" quiz first. If you do well on the quiz, you may want to skim through this chapter and continue to the next. If you score low on the quiz, you should spend some time reading through the chapter. These standards are important because they are something you will deal with on a day-to-day basis in wireless networking. Refer to Appendix A, "Answers to the 'Do I Know This Already?' Quizzes" to confirm your answers.

"Do I Know This Already?" Quiz

The "Do I Know This Already?" quiz helps you determine your level of knowledge of this chapter's topics before you begin. Table 2-1 details the major topics discussed in this chapter and their corresponding quiz questions.

Table 2-1 *"Do I Know This Already?" Section-to-Question Mapping*

Foundation Topics Section	Questions
Wireless Standards and Regulatory Committees	1–8
Wi-Fi Certification	9–10

1. The FCC regulates wireless usage in which of the following countries?

    a. United States of America

    b. United Arab Emirates

    c. United Kingdom

    d. Europe, Asia, and Asia

2. True or false: The U.S. complies with ETSI standards of EIRP.

    a. True

    b. False

3. What is the maximum EIRP for point-to-multipoint in Europe? (Choose all that apply.)

    a. 20 dBm

    b. 17 dBi

    c. 17 dBm

    d. 36 dBm

4. The FCC regulates EIRP in the U.S. to a maximum of _____ for point-to-point and _____ for point-to-multipoint.

    a. 36 dBm, 36 dBm

    b. 30 dBm, 17 dBm

    c. 17 dBm, 36, dBm

    d. 36 dBm, 17 dBm

5. The IEEE committees work on which of the following wireless standards? (Choose all that apply.)

    a. 802.11a

    b. 802.11g

    c. 802.11x

    d. 802.1q

    e. 802.11b

6. True or false: The IEEE is a regulatory body in the U.S. that controls the usage of wireless frequencies.

    a. True

    b. False

7. In Europe, can a professional installer increase the gain on wireless antennas?

    a. Yes, provided that he or she decreases the transmit power using a 1:1 ratio.

    b. No; this is illegal.

    c. Only with a wavier.

    d. Antennas don't have anything to do with gain.

8. The FCC regulates that professional installers maintain what ratio of gain to transmit power when increasing the gain of an antenna?

    a. 3:1

    b. 1:1

    c. 6:1

    d. 1:3

9. Which organization certifies interoperability for wireless equipment?

    a. Wi-Max Alliance

    b. IEEE

    c. Wi-Fi Alliance

    d. FRF.12

10. Certification of wireless equipment includes which protocols and standards for interoperability? (Choose two.)

    a. 802.11a/b/g

    b. IPsec

    c. WPA/WPA2

    d. Zigbee

Foundation Topics

Wireless Standards and Regulatory Committees

Many people benefit from the availability of wireless Internet access as they travel to various parts of the world. Without regulatory committees and organizations to ensure the proper use and interoperability of equipment, it's likely that people could not connect from place to place. To ensure that certain rules governing the use of wireless RF are adhered to, numerous country-specific organizations and global committees monitor standards and usage. This chapter discusses some of them.

FCC

The Federal Communications Commission (FCC) is an independent agency in the United States that regulates communication methods. It is held directly responsible by Congress. It is the FCC in the United States that governs the frequency ranges that can be used without a license, the transmit power of devices, the types of devices that can be used indoors as well as outdoors, and how the various types of hardware can be used. The FCC exists because of the Communications Act of 1934.

Note: The FCC website is http://www.fcc.gov.

When it comes to the FCC and Cisco wireless, it's important to know the requirements defined in *FCC - Part 15 - Antenna Requirements*. This federal requirement states that antennas must use a unique nonstandard connector that cannot be acquired easily. The reason for not being acquired easily is to ensure that home users and noncertified installers cannot easily deploy an antenna that goes beyond the regulated values. For this reason, Cisco uses a connector known as the Reverse-Polarity-Threaded Neil-Concelman (RP-TNC) connector, as shown in Figure 2-1.

RP-TNC PLUG

Figure 2-1 *RP-TNC Connector*

What makes this connector unique is that the center contacts are reversed so that you can't use a store-bought antenna with a Cisco wireless device. If you did so, you might violate the FCC regulatory requirements.

In addition to the antenna rules, the FCC defines power output rules that must be followed. There are rules for everyday people to follow, and rules for people who are considered professionals in the field. A professional has a little more leeway than someone who buys a wireless device at the local electronics store. To get an idea of these rules, you can look at the 2.4-GHz EIRP Output Rules. Effective Isotropic Radiated Power (EIRP) is a way to measure the amount of energy radiated from an antenna. EIRP is an important concept to understand, especially when you're dealing with regulatory bodies. It's important that the EIRP not exceed that mandated by the governing bodies. These rules are designed for point-to-point scenarios as well as point-to-multipoint. The point-to-point rules are as follows:

- You can have a maximum of 36-dBm EIRP.

- You can have a maximum of 30-dBm transmitter power with 6-dBi gain of antenna and cable combined.

- You are allowed a 1:1 ratio of power to gain.

For point-to-multipoint scenarios, you are allowed the same maximum EIRP and the same maximum transmitter power and antenna gain; however, you can exceed the 36-dBm EIRP rule using a 3:1 ratio of power to gain.

Table 2-2 compares the FCC maximum requirements for point-to-point to the Cisco maximum.

Table 2-2   *FCC Antenna Requirements Versus Cisco Standards for Point-to-Point Environments*

	Transmitter Power	**Maximum Gain**	**EIRP**
FCC Maximum	30-dBm	6-dBm	36-dBm
Cisco Maximum	20-dBm	36-dBm	56-dBm

Key Topic

Table 2-3 compares the FCC maximum requirements for point-to-multipoint to the Cisco maximum.

Table 2-3   *FCC Antenna Requirements Versus Cisco Standards for Point-to-Multipoint Environments*

	Transmitter Power	**Maximum Gain**	**EIRP**
FCC Maximum	30-dBm	6-dBm	36-dBm
Cisco Maximum	20-dBm	36-dBm	36-dBm

Key Topic

ETSI

The European Telecommunication Standards Institute (ETSI) is the not-for-profit organization that standardizes the frequencies and power levels used in Europe as well as many other countries. The European Commission (EC) recognizes ETSI as an official European Standards Organization. Many of the mandates for wireless usage come from the EC. Then, ETSI defines various standards based on these mandates. According to the ETSI website, the ETSI has almost 700 members in 60 countries.

Similar to the FCC, the ETSI has 2.4-GHz EIRP output rate standards that you should be familiar with. The ETSI's rules, however, are different from the FCC's rules. ETSI defines 20-dBm EIRP on point-to-multipoint and on point-to-point with 17-dBm maximum transmit power with 3-dBi gain. In a way, this is easier to remember, because these numbers are the same value for both point-to-point and point-to-multipoint connections. Of course, a professional installer can increase the gain as long as he or she lowers the transmit power below 17 dBm at a ratio of 1:1. Therefore, a professional installer could drop the transmit power by 1 dBm and increase the gain by 1 dBm and still stay within the guidelines.

Table 2-4 compares the Cisco standards to the ETSI standards for EIRP. The table shows the governing body maximum transmitted power, maximum gain, and EIRP compared to that of the Cisco integated antennas. You can see that the Cisco antenna has a transmit power of 17 dBm and a maximum gain of 2.2 dBi and ends up with an EIRP of 19.2 dBm, which is lower than the 20 dBm allowed by the governing bodies. If you reduced the transmit power to 15 dBm and increased the maximum gain to 5 dBi, the resulting EIRP would be 20 dBm, which is still within the guidelines of the governing body. Likewise, reducing the transmit power to 13 dBm and increasing the gain to 7 dBi keeps the EIRP at 20 dBm—within the guidelines.

Key Topic

Table 2-4 *Cisco Versus ETSI EIRP Standards for Point-to-Point and Point-to-Multipoint Environments*

	Transmitter Power (dBm)	Maximum Gain (dBi)	EIRP (dBm)
Governing Body Maximum	17	3	20
Cisco Integrated Antennas	17	2.2	19.2
Reduced Tx Power	15	5	20
Reduced Tx Power	13	7	20
Reduced Tx Power	7	13	20
Reduced Tx Power	0	20	20

IEEE

The Institute of Electrical and Electronics Engineers (IEEE) is a not-for-profit organization that has more than 370,000 members globally. It has 319 sections in ten geographic areas. It has defined more than 900 standards and has another 400 in development.

Note: For a history of the IEEE, see http://ieee.org/web/aboutus/history/index.html.

The IEEE's "Wireless Standards Zone" is dedicated to standards that are related to wireless technology. Here you can find information about the 802 protocols, such as the following:

- **802.11:** The Working Group for Wireless LAN

- **802.15:** The Working Group for Wireless PAN

- **802.16:** The Working Group for Broadband Wireless Access Standards

Note: You can find the Wireless Standards Zone at http://standards.ieee.org/wireless/ and an overview of the aforementioned working groups at http://standards.ieee.org/wireless/overview.html.

This book focuses mainly on the 802.11a, 802.11b, 802.11g, and 802.11n protocols. These protocols are for wireless LANs.

Wi-Fi Certification

Into the arena of interoperability testing enters the Wi-Fi Alliance. The Wi-Fi Alliance is a not-for-profit organization that certifies the interoperability of more than 4200 products. The Wi-Fi Alliance was formed in 1999 and currently has more than 300 members in more than 20 countries. What makes this organization different from the ETSI, FCC, and IEEE is that it gives its seal of approval to devices that plan in interoperability. The next time you're at the electronics shop, flip over one of the wireless products; you might find it to be Wi-Fi Certified. If so, you will notice that the 802.11a, 802.11b, and 802.11g protocols are certified if the device can use them as well as security protocols such as WPA and WPA2. Usually, the label has a checkmark next to what the device is certified for.

Note: The Wi-Fi alliance can be found at http://www.wi-fi.org.

Exam Preparation Tasks

Review All the Key Topics

Review the most important topics from this chapter, denoted with the Key Topic icon. Table 2-5 lists these key topics and the page number where you can find each one.

Table 2-5   *Key Topics for Chapter 2*

Key Topic Item	Description	Page Number
Table 2-2	FCC antenna requirements versus Cisco standards (point-to-point)	25
Table 2-3	FCC antenna requirements versus Cisco standards (point-to-multipoint)	25
Table 2-4	Cisco versus ETSI EIRP standards (point-to-point and point-to-multipoint)	26

Complete the Tables and Lists from Memory

Print a copy of Appendix B, "Memory Tables," (found on the CD) or at least the section for this chapter, and complete the tables and lists from memory. Appendix C, "Memory Tables Answer Key," also on the CD, includes completed tables and lists to check your work.

Definition of Key Terms

Define the following key terms from this chapter, and check your answers in the glossary:

FCC, IEEE, ETSI, W-Fi Alliance, EIRP

This chapter covers the following subjects:

Characteristics of Wireless Networks:
Provides a review of wireless transmissions.

Influences on Wireless Transmissions:
Covers the different elements that can affect wireless transmissions.

Determining Signal Strength Influences:
Describes how to determine your signal strength and what might be influencing your wireless deployment.

CHAPTER 3

WLAN RF Principles

In wireless technologies, you need to understand what influences act on wireless transmissions. This chapter reviews the characteristics of wireless transmissions and the influences that act on them, sometimes causing problems. Some of the material covered in the first section, "Characteristics of Wireless Networks," is a review of information you learned in Chapter 1, "Introduction to Wireless Networking Concepts." If you are comfortable with your knowledge of this information, you can just review the key topics at the end of this chapter.

The second section of this chapter covers influences on wireless transmissions. These are usually drawbacks, so you should become familiar with them. The third part of this chapter discusses ways to determine signal strength and other influences on wireless signals.

You should do the "Do I Know This Already?" quiz first. If you score 80% or higher, you might want to skip to the section "Exam Preparation Tasks." If you score below 80%, you should spend the time reviewing the entire chapter. Refer to Appendix A, "Answers to the 'Do I Know This Already?' Quizzes" to confirm your answers.

"Do I Know This Already?" Quiz

The "Do I Know This Already?" quiz helps you determine your level of knowledge of this chapter's topics before you begin. Table 3-1 details the major topics discussed in this chapter and their corresponding quiz questions.

Table 3-1 *"Do I Know This Already?" Section-to-Question Mapping*

Foundation Topics Section	Questions
Characteristics of Wireless Networks	1–3
Influences on Wireless Transmissions	4–9
Determining Signal Strength Influences	10–11

1. Which of the following best describes a frequency that is seen 1 million times per second?

   a.   1 Hz

   b.   1000000 Mb

   c.   1 joule

   d.   1 MHz

2. What does amplitude measure?

   a.   Distance from high crest to high crest horizontally in a waveform

   b.   Distance between two access points

   c.   Distance from low crest to midspan in a waveform

   d.   Height of wave from lowest crest to highest crest

3. EIRP is calculated using which of the following formulas?

   a.   EIRP = transmitter power – cable loss + antenna gain

   b.   EIRP = interference – cable loss + antenna gain

   c.   EIRP = cable gain – cable loss + antenna gain

   d.   EIRP = transmitter loss + cable loss + antenna gain

4. Metal desks, glass, light fixtures, and computer screens can contribute to which influence on wireless transmissions?

   a.   Scattering

   b.   Refraction

   c.   Reflection

   d.   Absorption

5. Carpet, human bodies, and walls can contribute to which influence on wireless transmission?

   a.   Scattering

   b.   Refraction

   c.   Reflection

   d.   Absorption

6. In the Free Path Loss model, objects that are farther away from a transmitter receive the same amount of signal as those that are closer to the transmitter. True or False?

   a.   True

   b.   False

7. If a signal is being spread about by microparticles, it is experiencing which influence on wireless transmissions?

   a. Scattering

   b. Spreading

   c. Scarring

   d. Splitting

   e. Refracting

8. Multipath causes which of the following issues? (Choose all that apply.)

   a. Redundant connectivity

   b. The signal becoming out of phase, which can potentially cancel the signal

   c. The signal being received by multiple devices in the path, causing security concerns

   d. Portions of the signal being reflected and arriving out of order

9. Scattering is caused by humidity. True or False?

   a. True

   b. False

10. For line of sight (LOS) transmissions, what can determine where signals can become out of phase?

    a. Free Path Zone

    b. EIRP

    c. Fresnel Zone

    d. Phase Zone

11. Link budget is used to do which of the following? (Choose two.)

    a. Account for all the receivers on a link

    b. Account for all the gains and losses

    c. Determine how much money you can spend on a wireless deployment

    d. Factor in EIRP and attenuation for a transmission

Foundation Topics

Characteristics of Wireless Networks

Many influences can act on a wireless transmission. For that reason, it is important to understand what is actually involved in a wireless transmissions so you know exactly what is being affected. This section reviews what a wavelength is, how frequency it is used in wireless transmission, and what the purpose of amplitude is. In addition, it covers how Effective Isotropic Radiated Power (EIRP) is calculated and what it defines.

Review of Wavelength

A *wavelength* is the distance between successive crests of a wave. This is how wavelength is measured. Most people have seen examples of sound waves. By measuring the distance between the crest of each wave, you can determine the wavelength. This is a distinctive feature of radio waves that are sent from a transmitter. Thinking back to what was discussed in Chapter 1, the waveform takes on a form called a *sine wave*.

The waveform starts as an AC signal that is generated by a transmitter inside an access point (AP) and is then sent to the antenna, where it is radiated as a sine wave. During this process, current changes the *electromagnetic field* around the antenna, so it transmits electric and magnetic signals.

The wavelength is a certain size, measured from one point in the AC cycle to the next point in the AC cycle. This in turn is called a *waveform*. Following are some quick facts about waveforms that you may relate to:

■   AM radio waveforms are 400 to 500 meters long.

■   Wireless waveforms in wireless LANS are only a few centimeters.

■   Waveforms sent by satellites are approximately 1 mm long.

Review of Frequency

Because the term *frequency* is thrown around quite a bit in wireless networking, you need to have a clear understanding of it. Frequency, as discussed in Chapter 1, determines how often the signal is seen. It is the rate at which something occurs or is repeated over a particular period or in a given sample or period. It is insufficient to say that frequency is how often a signal is seen. If you are going to measure frequency, you need a period of time to look at it. Frequency, which is usually measured in seconds, is the rate at which a vibration occurs that constitutes a wave; this can be either in some form of material, as in sound waves, or it can be in an electromagnetic field, as you would see in radio waves and light.

Because frequency refers to cycles, following are some quick facts to help you to understand how it is measured:

■   1 cycle = 1 Hz

■   Higher frequencies travel shorter distances

- When a waveform is seen once in a second = 1 Hz

- 10 times in a second = 10 Hz

- 1 million times in a second = 1 MHz

- 1 billion times in a second = 1 GHz

These are useful numbers that you can see throughout wireless networks.

Review of Amplitude

The vertical distance between crests in the wave is called *amplitude*. Different amplitude can exist for the same wavelength and the same frequency. Amplitude is the quantity or amount of energy that is put into a signal. Folks like the FCC and European Telecommunications Standards Institute (ETSI) regulate the amplitude.

Note: You can find a neat visualization of amplitude at http://id.mind.net/~zona/mstm/physics/waves/introduction/introductionWaves.html.

What Is Effective Isotropic Radiated Power?

When an access point sends energy to an antenna to be radiated, a cable might exist between the two. A certain degree of loss in energy is expected to occur in the cable. To counteract this loss, an antenna adds gain, thus increasing the energy level. The amount of gain you use depends on the antenna type. Note that both the FCC and ETSI regulate the power that an antenna radiates. Ultimately, Effective Isotropic Radiated Power (EIRP) is the power that results. EIRP is what you use to estimate the service area of a device.

To calculate EIRP, use the following formula:

EIRP = transmitter output power – cable loss + antenna gain

Influences on Wireless Transmissions

Now that you clearly understand wireless transmissions and what is involved, it is a good time to discuss the influences on wireless signals. Some influences can stop a wireless signal from propagating altogether, whereas others might simply shorten the transmission distance. Either way, you should be aware of these factors so you can plan and adjust your deployment accordingly. In this section, you learn about the Free Path Loss model, absorption, reflection, scattering, multipath, refraction, and line of sight.

Understanding the Free Path Loss Model

To understand *Free Path Loss*, you can think of jumping smack into the middle of a puddle. This would cause a sort of wave effect to spread in all directions away from you. The closer to you that the wave is, the larger it is. Likewise, the farther away from you that wave travels, the smaller it gets. After a certain distance, the wave widens so much that it just disappears.

You might recall learning that an object that is in motion stays in motion until something stops it. But nothing stops the wave. It just disappears. This is where you get the term *free*. Take a look at Figure 3-1, and you can see that as the wave—or, in this case, the radiated wireless signal—travels away from the source, it thins out. This is represented by the bold dots becoming less and less bold.

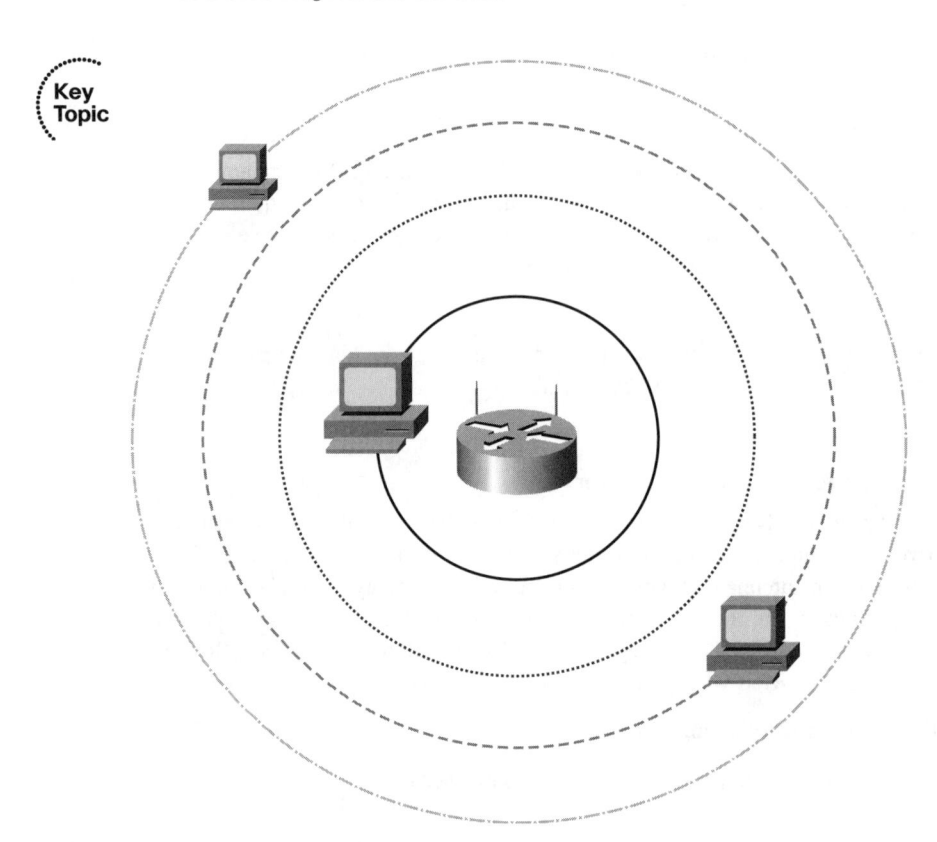

Figure 3-1   *The Free Path Loss Model*

You might also notice that the farther away the signal gets from the center, the sparser the dots are. Figure 3-1 has a single transmitting device (you could relate that to an access point) and many receiving devices. Not all the receiving stations get each one of the dots or signals that the transmitter sent. A device closer to the transmitter usually gets a more concentrated signal, and a receiver farther away might get only one dot.

Determining the range involves a determination of the energy loss and the distance. If you place receivers outside of that range, they cannot receive wireless signals from the access point and, in a nutshell, your network does not work.

Understanding Absorption

Earlier in this chapter, you learned that amplitude allowed a wave to travel farther. This can be good, because you can cover a greater area, potentially requiring fewer access points for your wireless deployment. By removing or reducing amplitude in a wave, you essentially reduce the distance a wave can travel. A factor that influences wireless transmission by reducing amplitude is called *absorption*.

An effect of absorption is heat. When something absorbs a wave, it creates heat in whatever absorbed the wave. This is seen in microwaves. They create waves that are absorbed by your food. The result is hot food. A problem you can encounter is that if a wave is entirely absorbed, it stops. While this effect reduces the distance the wave can travel, it does not change the wavelength or the frequency of the wave. These two values do not change as a wave is absorbed.

You might be asking what some possible sources of absorption are. Walls, bodies, and carpet can absorb signals. Relate it to sound. If you had really loud neighbors who were barbecuing outside your bedroom window, how could you deaden the sound? You could hang a blanket on the window or board up the window. Things that absorb sound waves also absorb data waves.

How can this affect your wireless deployment? Looking at Figure 3-2, you can see an office that has just been leased and ready to move in. After a quick site survey, you determine that four APs will provide plenty of coverage. This is because you cannot see absorption. Nothing causes the issue.

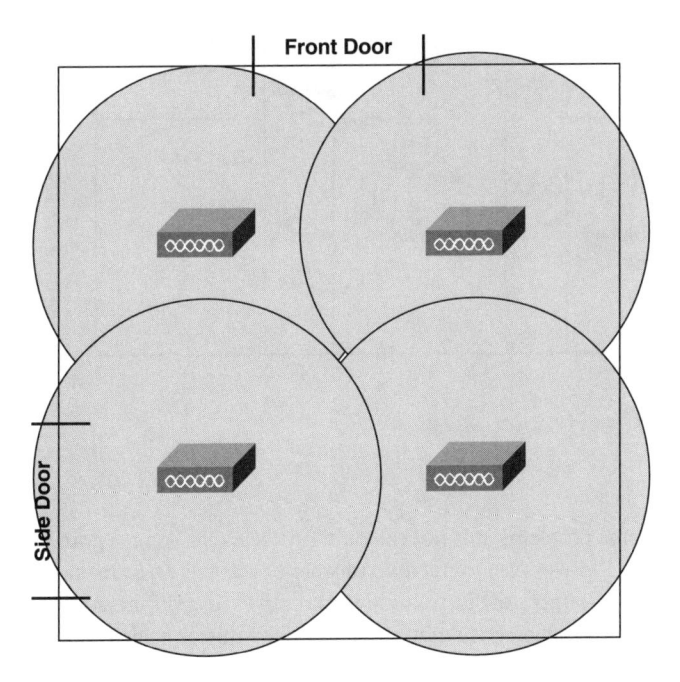

Figure 3-2   *Absorption Before Office Move-In*

Now look at Figure 3-3, which shows the same office after move-in. Notice that with the furniture, cubicle walls, and other obstacles, the four APs that you originally thought would be sufficient no longer provide the proper coverage because of the signal being absorbed. This is an illustration of absorption.

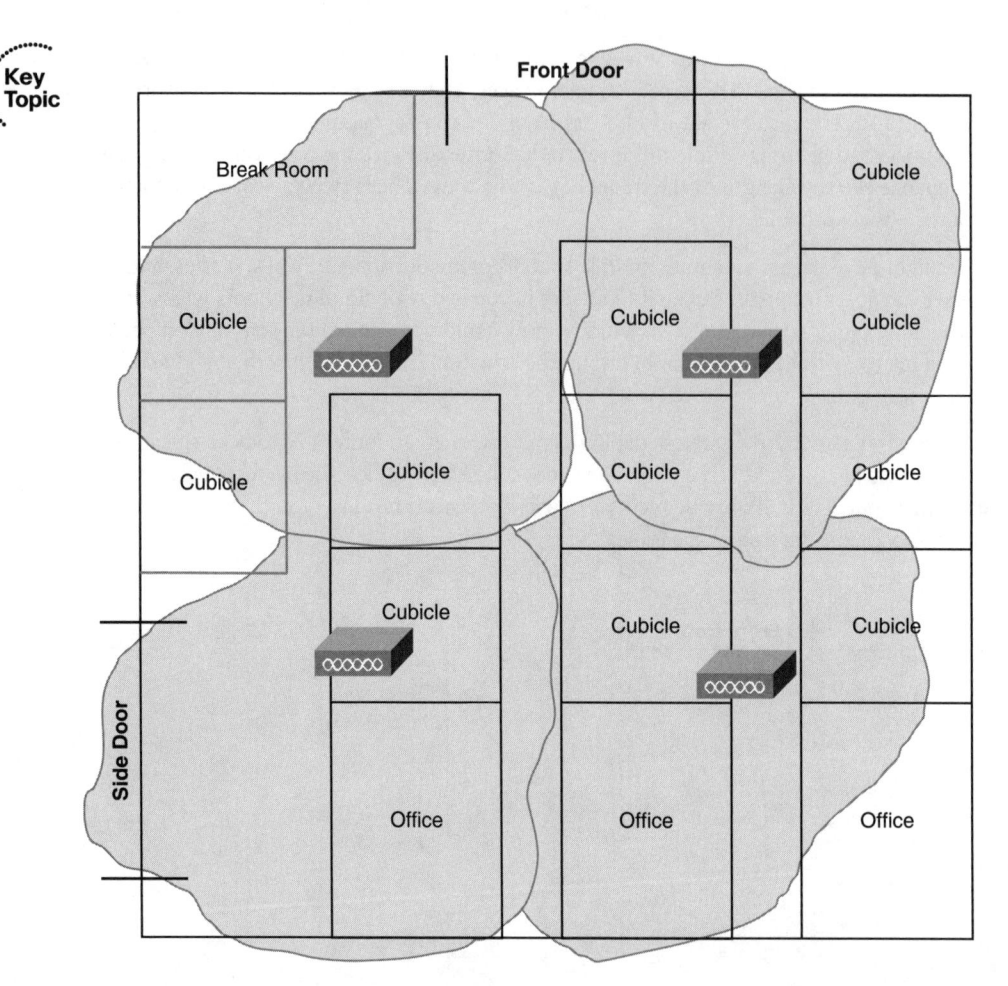

Figure 3-3 *Absorption After Office Move-In*

Understanding Reflection

Although absorption causes some problems, it is not the only obstacle that you are going to encounter that will affect your wireless deployments. Another obstacle is *reflection*. Reflection happens when a signal bounces off of something and travels in a different direction. This can be illustrated by shining a flashlight on an angle at a mirror, which causes it to reflect on an opposite wall. The same concept is true with wireless waveforms. You can see this effect in Figure 3-4, where the reflection of the signal is reflected at the same angle that it hits the mirror. You can also relate this to sources of interference in an office environment. Although offices do not usually have mirrors lying around, they do have other objects with similar reflective qualities, such as monitors and framed artwork with glass facing.

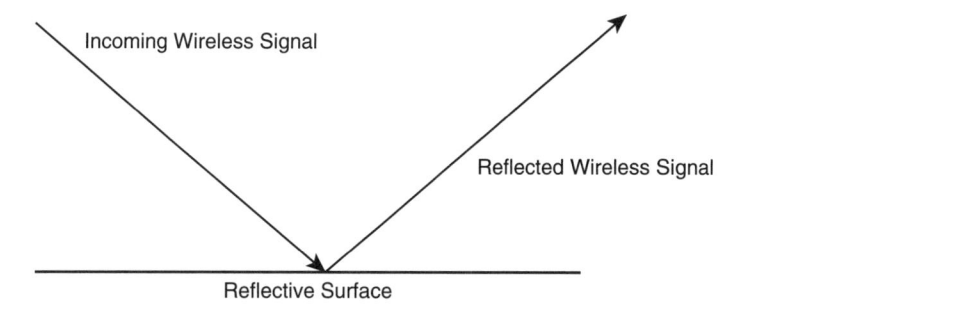

Figure 3-4   *The Reflection Issue*

Reflection depends on the frequency. You will encounter some frequencies that are not affected as much as others. This is because objects that reflect some frequencies might not reflect others.

Understanding Multipath

Multipath is what happens when portions of signals are reflected and then arrive out of order at the receiver, as illustrated in Figure 3-5.

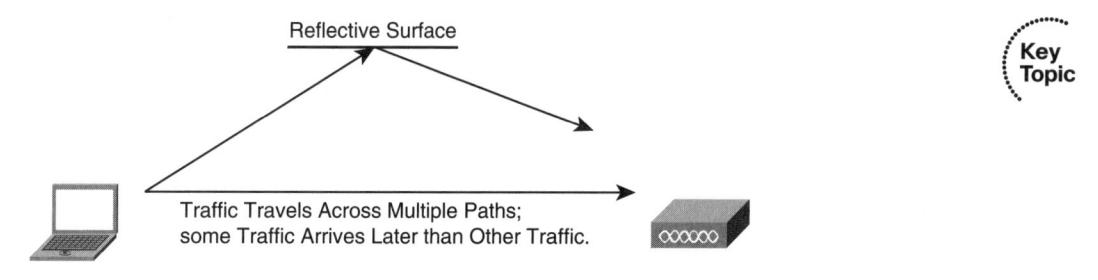

Figure 3-5   *The Multipath Issue*

One characteristic of multipath is that a receiver might get the same signal several times over. This is dependent on the wavelength and the position of the receiver.

Another characteristic of multipath is that it can cause the signal to become out of *phase*. When you receive out-of-phase signals, they can cancel each other out, resulting in a null signal.

Understanding Scattering

The issue of wireless signals scattering happens when the signal is sent in many different directions. This can be caused by some object that has reflective, yet jagged edges, such as dust particles in the air and water. One way to illustrate the effects would be to consider shining a light onto a pile of broken glass. The light that is reflected shoots off in many different directions. The same is true with wireless, only the pile of glass is replaced with microparticles of dust or water.

On a large scale, imagine that it is raining. Large raindrops have reflective capabilities. When a waveform travels through those microparticles, it is reflected in many directions. This is *scattering*. To visualize this, notice that Figure 3-6 involves a waveform traveling between two sites on a college campus. During a heavy downpour of rain, the wireless signal would be scattered in transit from one antenna to the next.

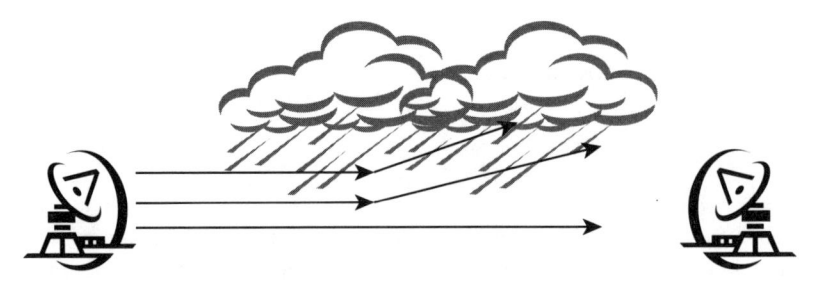

Figure 3-6   *Wireless Signal Scattering*

Scattering has more of an effect on shorter wavelengths, and the effect depends on frequency. The result is that the signal weakens.

Understanding Refraction

Refraction is the change in direction of, or the bending of, a waveform as it passes through something that is a different density. This behavior causes some of the signal to be reflected away and part to be bent through the object. To better understand this concept, Figure 3-7 demonstrates the effect of refraction. A waveform is being passed through a glass of water. Notice that, because the glass is reflective, some of the light is reflected, yet some still passes through.

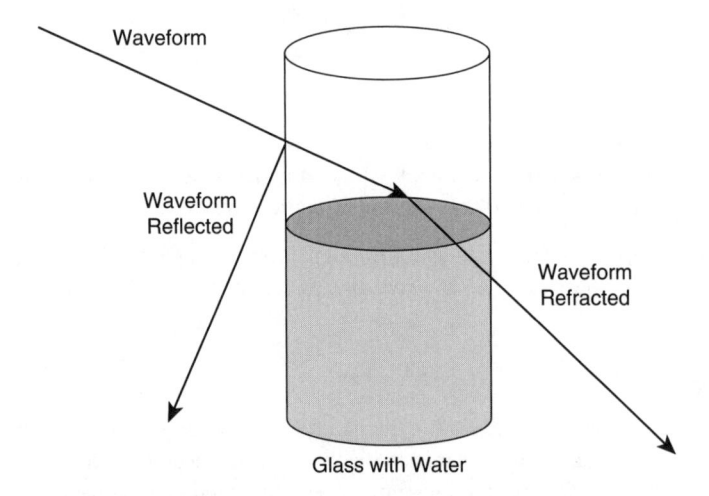

Figure 3-7   *The Refraction Issue*

The waveform that is passed through the glass is now at a different angle.

Note: You can find a neat Java-based example of refraction at http://www.phy.hk/wiki/ englishhtm/RefractionByPrism.htm.

Because refraction usually has the most effect on outdoor signals, dryness refracts away from the earth (as seen in dust particles), and humidity refracts toward the earth.

Understanding Line of Sight

As an object travels toward a receiver, it might have to deal with various obstructions that are directly in the path. These obstructions in the path cause many of the issues just discussed—absorption, reflection, refraction, scattering. As wireless signals travel farther distances, the signal widens near the midpoint and slims down nearer to the receiver. Figure 3-8 illustrates where two directional antennas are sending a signal between the two points. The fact that it appears to be a straight shot is called *visual line of sight (LOS)*. Although the path has no obvious obstacles, at greater distances the earth itself becomes an obstacle. This means that the curvature of the earth, as well as mountains, trees, and any other environmental obstacles, can actually interfere with the signal.

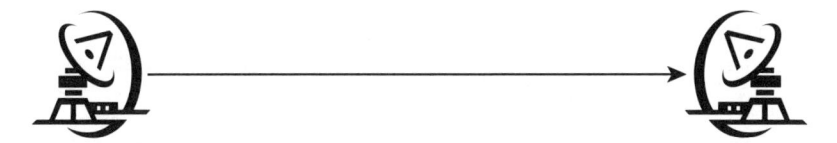

Figure 3-8   *Directional Antennas and Line of Sight*

Even though you see the other endpoint as a direct line, you must remember that the signal does not. The signal in fact widens, as illustrated in Figure 3-9. What was not an obvious obstruction in Figure 3-8 is more clearly highlighted in Figure 3-9.

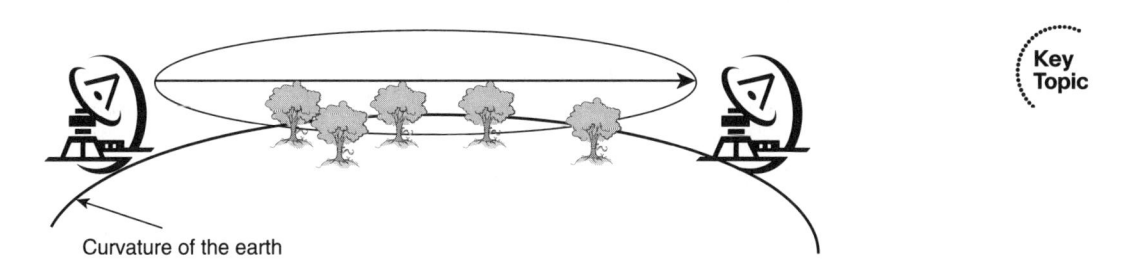

Curvature of the earth

Figure 3-9   *Directional Antennas and LOS with Obstructions*

Key
Topic

When you plan for LOS, you should factor in the closest obstacle.

Determining Signal Strength Influences

Although it might seem hopeless to deploy a network that is susceptible to various forms of interference, you can fight back. To fight back, you need to know what tools are available out there for you to determine signal strength, noise levels, and potential sources of interference in the path. This section discusses these tools.

The Fresnel Zone

To give you a little background, Augustin-Jean Fresnel was a French physicist and civil engineer who lived from 1788 to 1827. He correctly assumed that light moved in a wavelike motion transverse to the direction of propagation. His assumption, or claim, was correct. Because of his work, a method for determining where reflections will be in phase and out of phase between sender and receiver is based on his name. This method determines what is called the *Fresnel zone*.

Here is how Fresnel did it. First he divided the path into zones. The first zone should be at least 60 percent clear of obstructions. To visualize this, you can think of the shape of a football, which is wider in the middle. However, with the Fresnel zone calculation, you use an equation to determine what the size of the ball is at the middle. This helps to determine the width that a wave will be so you can make sure that no obstacles are in the path.

Note: While at the CCNA wireless level, you should not need to calculate the Fresnel zone. You can find the actual formula at http://en.wikipedia.org/wiki/Fresnel_zone#Determining_Fresnel_zone_clearance.

Also, you can find an online Fresnel zone clearance calculator at http://www.terabeam.com/support/calculations/fresnel-zone.php.

Note: Indoor signals are too short to be affected.

Figure 3-10 illustrates the height an antenna would need to be at different distances to overcome this. For example, for a 2.4-GHz system, at 7 miles you need to have the antennas mounted at 45 to 50 feet.

Although this is just an example, the numbers are pretty close, and at least you can get more of a visual of what you are up against in the real world. Again, do not spend too much time on this in preparation for the CCNA wireless exam, because it is not a concept you will be tested on.

Received Signal Strength Indicator

The Received Signal Strength Indicator (RSSI) measurement uses vendor-specified values. Because of this, you cannot rely on it to compare different vendors. In the end, all this gives you is a grading of how much signal was received.

Keep in mind that the measurement is vendor specific, so the scale that is used might vary. For example, one vendor might use a scale of 0 to 100, whereas another might use a scale

2.4 GHz Systems			
Wireless Link-Distance in Miles	Approximate Value "F" (60% Fresnal Zone at 2.4 GHz)	Approximate Value "C" Earth Curvature	Value "H" Antenna Mounting Height with No Obstructions
1	14	3	17
5	31	5	36
10	43	13	56
15	53	28	81
20	61	50	111
25	68	78	146
5 GHz Systems			
1	9	3	12
5	20	5	25
10	28	13	41
15	35	28	63
20	40	50	90
25	45	78	123

Figure 3-10 *Sample Bridge Calculator*

of 0 to 60. The scale is usually represented in dBm, so the two scales would not match up. It is also up to the vendor to determine what dBm is represented by 0 and what dBm is represented by 100.

One tool that is used in wireless networks to give RSSI values is called Network Stumbler.

Note: You can find the free Network Stumbler software at http://www.netstumbler.com/.

RSSI is acquired during the preamble stage of receiving an 802.11 frame. RSSI has been replaced with Receive Channel Power Indicator (RCPI), which is a functional measurement covering the entire received frame with defined absolute levels of accuracy and resolution. To gain these measurements, you can use a CB21AG card and the Aironet Desktop Utility (ADU), which are covered in Chapter 16, "Wireless Clients." The CB21AG card is the most widely adopted card used by Airmagnet and OmniPeek.

Signal-to-Noise Ratio

Signal-to-noise ratio (SNR) is the term used to describe how much stronger the signal is compared to the surrounding noise that corrupts the signal. To understand this, suppose you walk into a crowded park with many screaming kids and speak in a normal voice while on the phone. The odds are that the noise is going to be so loud that the person on the other end will not be able to distinguish your words from all the noise around you that is also being transmitted over the phone. This is how the wireless network operates. If the outside influences are causing too much noise, the receivers cannot understand the transmissions.

When the software that runs your wireless card reports this measurement, it is best to have a higher number, but this is also built on the RSSI value, so it is vendor determined.

Note: You can explore SNR levels in the Network Stumbler application previously mentioned. Remember that the values are valid only for the Network Stumbler application. Other applications might report different SNR values.

Link Budget

Link budget is a value that accounts for all the gains and losses between sender and receiver, including attenuation, antenna gain, and other miscellaneous losses that might occur. This can be useful in determining how much power is needed to transmit a signal that the receiving end can understand.

The following is a simple equation to factor link budget:

Received Power (dBm) = Transmitted Power (dBm) + Gains (dB) − Losses (dB)

Exam Preparation Tasks

Review All Key Concepts

Review the most important topics from this chapter, noted with the Key Topics icon in the outer margin of the page. Table 3-2 lists a reference of these key topics and the page number where you can find each one.

Table 3-2   *Key Topics for Chapter 3*

Key Topic Item	Description	Page Number
Figure 3-1	The Free Path Loss model	36
Figure 3-3	The absorption issue	38
Figure 3-4	The reflection issue	39
Figure 3-5	The multipath issue	39
Figure 3-9	Line of sight	45

Definition of Key Terms

Define the following key terms from this chapter, and check your answers in the Glossary:

wavelength, frequency, amplitude, EIRP, Free Path Loss, absorption, reflection, multipath, phase (in-phase/out-of-phase), scattering, refraction, line of sight, SNR, link budget

This chapter covers the following subjects:

General Wireless Topologies: Discusses wireless LAN topologies from a high-level perspective.

Original 802.11 Topologies: Discusses wireless network topologies defined by the IEEE.

Vendor-Specific Topology Extensions: Explains how vendors extend network topologies.

CHAPTER 4

WLAN Technologies and Topologies

When you work in a wireless network, you can encounter a number of technologies and deployment options. Sometimes your situation calls for a peer-to-peer connection, and other times you will want to connect to users who are in another room or on another floor, yet on the same network. In this chapter you will learn what these networks are and when they are appropriate. You will also look at which types of equipment are appropriate for certain situations and environments.

Use the "Do I Know This Already?" quiz to gauge whether you should read the entire chapter or if you should simply jump to the "Exam Preparation Tasks" section and review. If in doubt, read through the whole chapter!

"Do I Know This Already?" Quiz

The "Do I Know This Already?" quiz helps you determine your level of knowledge of this chapter's topics before you begin. Table 4-1 details the major topics discussed in this chapter and their corresponding quiz questions.

Table 4-1 *"Do I Know This Already?" Section-to-Question Mapping*

Foundation Topics Section	Questions
General Wireless Topologies	1–7
Original 802.11 Topologies	8–20
Vendor-Specific Topology Extensions	21–26

1. Which of the following topologies can be used with clients closer than 20 feet?

   a. WLAN

   b. WWAN

   c. WPAN

   d. WMAN

2. True or false: A WLAN uses 802.16b.

   a. True

   b. False

3. What topology is most often seen in a LAN and is designed to connect multiple devices to the network?

   a. WMAN

   b. WPAN

   c. WLAN

   d. WWAN

4. In what frequency ranges does a wireless LAN operate? (Choose two.)

   a. 2.2 GHz

   b. 2.4 GHz

   c. 2.4 MHz

   d. 5 GHz

   e. 5 MHz

5. What type of speed can you expect from a WMAN?

   a. Broadband

   b. WAN

   c. Ethernet

   d. Dialup modem

6. What is the name of the common WMAN technology?

   a. WiMAN

   b. WiMAX

   c. Wi-Fi

   d. WiNET

7. True or false: Deploying a WWAN is relatively inexpensive, so it's common for enterprise customers to deploy their own.

   a. True

   b. False

8. Which of the following are 802.11 topologies for LANs? (Choose all that apply.)

   a. Adsense

   b. Ad hoc

   c. Infrastructure

   d. Internal

9. What does BSS stand for?

   a. Basic Service Signal

   b. Basic Service Separation

   c. Basic Service Set

   d. Basic Signal Server

10. If an AP is not used in a wireless network, this is called which of the following?

   a. Independent Basic Service Set

   b. Solitary Service Set

   c. Single-Mode Set (SMS)

   d. Basic Individual Service Set

11. For two devices to communicate without an access point, you must define which of the following?

   a. A group name

   b. A password

   c. A network number

   d. A key

12. True or false: When operating in infrastructure mode, an AP is operating in full-duplex mode.

   a. True

   b. False

13. What device does an access point act as to connect wireless clients to a wired network?

   a. Hub

   b. Bridge

   c. Router

   d. Repeater

14. What is another name for wireless clients?

   a. Stations

   b. End nodes

   c. Clients

   d. Mobile APs

15. An access point is what kind of device?

   a. Support device

   b. Network device

   c. Perimeter device

   d. Infrastructure device

16. What is the name for the area of coverage offered by a single access point?

  a. VSA

  b. MSA

  c. TSA

  d. BSA

17. When more than one AP connects to a common distribution, what is the network called?

  a. Extended Service Area

  b. Basic Service Area

  c. Local Service Area

  d. WMAN

18. Clients connect to which of the following to access the LAN via a wireless AP?

  a. SSID

  b. SCUD

  c. BSID

  d. BSA

19. When one area exists, what is the name of the service set advertised by an AP?

  a. BBSM

  b. BSUP

  c. BSSID

  d. SSIG

20. Using MBSSIDs indicates which of the following?

  a. More than one AP is advertising SSIDs.

  b. More than one SSID is being advertised by one AP.

  c. The AP sees more than one SSID.

  d. There are multiple MACs on one SSID.

21. What can you use to connect an isolated wired network to a LAN?

  a. WLAN

  b. WGB

  c. Repeater

  d. Hub

22. Cisco offers which types of wireless bridges? (Choose two.)

  a. aWGB

  b. bWGB

  c. uWGB

  d. cWGB

23. For topologies where cable lengths prohibit placing an AP in certain locations, what solution can be used?

  a. Install a new switch that's closer.

  b. Install a hub instead.

  c. Install a repeater.

  d. Install a wireless client.

24. How much overlap is needed with an AP when a wireless repeater is used?

  a. 10 to 15 percent

  b. 100 percent

  c. 50 percent

  d. 40 to 80 percent

25. True or false: Outdoor mesh networks support only point-to-point topologies.

  a. True

  b. False

26. Mesh deployments are appropriate when _____ is a major concern.

  a. Connectivity

  b. Security

  c. Cost

  d. Speed

Foundation Topics

General Wireless Topologies

When you're talking about wireless topologies, there are a number of ways it could go. If you are talking about how your wireless network looks next to your wired network, you are most likely talking about a wireless local-area network (WLAN). The goal of a WLAN versus a wireless personal-area network (WPAN) is quite different. The following sections discuss the purpose of each network type, what they try to accomplish, and what types of wireless technologies you might encounter there. Figure 4-1 shows the various wireless topologies.

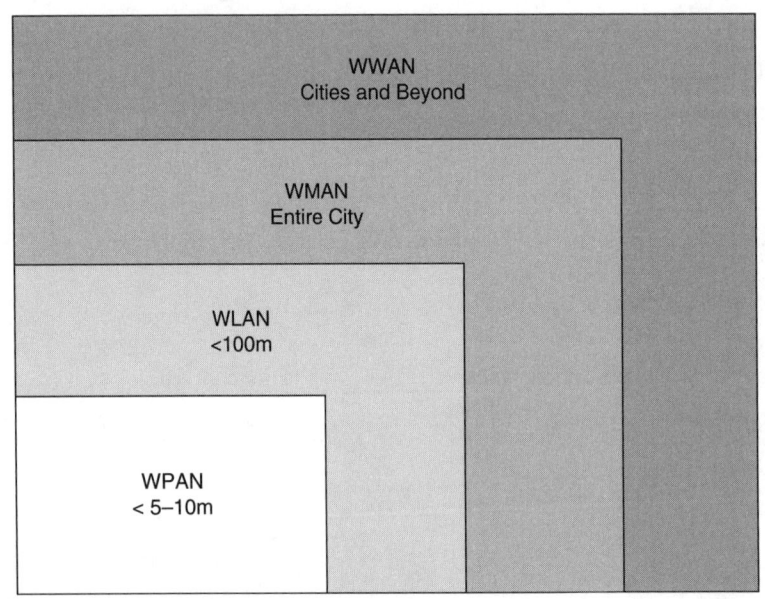

Figure 4-1   *Wireless Topology Overview*

WPAN

If you were to consider all the options, a WPAN would be the solution to choose if you wanted to wirelessly connect to something that is very close to you. It seems funny to put it that way, because if something close to you needs to be networked, you might as well just walk over and grab it, right? Wrong. Even though this is called a network, its form can mislead you into thinking that it's not a networking technology. What forms are we talking about? Headsets, headphones—even a mouse.

A WPAN has the following characteristics:

■   The range is short—about 20 feet.

- Eight active devices

- Unlicensed 2.4-GHz spectrum

- Called a piconet

A WPAN is a network that is designed to operate within a 20-foot range. The most common WPAN is Bluetooth. In a Bluetooth network, you communicate on the 2.4-GHz spectrum. Thinking about how many people have Bluetooth headsets and mice and such, you would expect a lot of interference, but that's not the case. Bluetooth uses Frequency Hopping Spread Spectrum (FHSS). Although this book doesn't discuss FHSS, it's good to understand that even though Bluetooth operates on the same frequency as 802.11b and 802.11g, they don't interfere *as much as* another AP in the same frequency spectrum would, but they *do* interfere. The fact that Bluetooth communicates with a shared hopping sequence in a local area is what makes it a *piconet*.

Bluetooth piconets consist of up to eight active devices but can have many inactive devices. WPANs usually fall into the unlicensed 2.4-GHz spectrum and are standardized by the 802.15 IEEE workgroup. A WPAN study group was formed in 1998, and two months later a Bluetooth Special Interest Group (SIG) was formed. Shortly thereafter the study group became the IEEE 802.15 group. The Bluetooth SIG has more than 9000 members and continues to further the technology.

Note: You can find out more about the Bluetooth SIG at http://www.bluetooth.com/Bluetooth/SIG/.

WLAN

WLANs are designed for a larger area than that of a WPAN. These can scale from very small home offices to large enterprise networks. The fact that they are local-area means that the organization where the WLAN exists also manages and probably owns the equipment. WLANs have the following characteristics:

- 2.4-GHz or 5-GHz spectrum.

- A larger range than a WPAN—close to 100 meters from AP to client.

- To achieve further distance, more power output is required.

- It's not personal; rather, more clients are expected.

- WLANs are very flexible, so more than eight active devices/clients are expected, unlike a WPAN.

Normally you find a mix of dual-band wireless access points, laptops, and desktops in a WLAN. A WLAN operates in either the 2.4-GHz spectrum for 802.11b/g or the 5-GHz spectrum for 802.11a. Of the protocols seen in WLANs, 802.11b was the first to really get market penetration. Others, such as the 802.11a, have followed. Now the 802.11a, b, g, and n WLAN standards are commonly found in networks around the world. The frequency spectrums used by 802.11a/b, g, and n are all unlicensed.

Because WLANs cover larger areas, they require more power output than a WPAN. The issue to watch in WLANs is that you don't exceed the power rules that the government sets forth. For example, in the U.S., the Federal Communications Commission (FCC) mandates radiated power levels.

WLANs are designed to give mobile clients access to network resources. For this reason, a WLAN expects to see multiple users. In addition to wireless users, there are wireless print servers, presentation servers, and storage devices. You end up with many devices connecting to each other or sharing information with each other, usually over a common distribution system such as the local-area network. This makes WLANs much more complex than WPANs.

What makes WLANs flexible is the fact that the APs and clients are dual-band. This makes it easy to deploy different transmission methods in different areas, and most clients can still operate.

WMAN

A wireless metropolitan-area network (WMAN) covers a large geographic area and has the following characteristics:

- Speeds decrease as the distance increases.

- Close to broadband speeds versus Ethernet speeds.

- Used as a backbone, point-to-point, or point-to-multipoint.

- Most well-known is WiMax.

WMANs are used as backbone services, point-to-point, or even point-to-multipoint links that can be a replacement for technologies such as T1 and T3. Sometimes, a WMAN can use unlicensed frequencies. However, this isn't always a preferred solution, because others could use the same frequency, thus causing interference. Instead, many prefer to use a licensed frequency range; however, this requires payment for exclusive rights.

It's normal for the speeds in a WMAN to decrease with distance. This places them in a closer category to broadband than to Ethernet. The most widely known WMAN is WiMax (802.16b). WiMax can be used to offer last-mile access as an alternative to broadband services such as DSL or cable connections. WiMax is an excellent solution where facilities or distance are a limitation. With WiMax, you pay a service provider for access, because the cost of deployment is normally very high.

Note: Cisco offers a WiMax solution; however, this is not covered in this book. For more information on the Cisco WiMax solution, visit http://www.cisco.com/go/wimax.

WWAN

A wireless wide-area network (WWAN) covers a large geographic area. WWANs have the following characteristics:

- Low data rates

- Pay-for-use

■   High cost of deployment

Because they cover a large geographic area, WWANs usually are very expensive to deploy. To better understand what a WWAN is, consider your cellular service. Your cell service is a WWAN and probably offers data access as well as voice access. The data rates are probably around 115 kbps, although some providers offer higher data rates. The most widely deployed WWAN technologies are Global System for Mobile Communication (GSM) and Code Division Multiple Access (CDMA). Payment for data access or even voice access is typically based on usage.

Original 802.11 Topologies

Although the previous sections discussed network topologies that you might encounter, it was a very general discussion. You also need to understand the original topologies, defined by the 802.11 committees, including the following:

■   Ad hoc mode

■   Infrastructure mode

The following sections give more details on these topologies.

Overview of Ad Hoc Networks

When two computers want to communicate directly with one another, they do so in the form of an *ad hoc* network. Ad hoc networks don't require a central device to allow them to communicate. Rather, one device sets a group name and radio parameters, and the other uses it to connect. This is called a *Basic Service Set (BSS)*, which defines the area in which a device is reachable. Because the two machines don't need a central device to speak to each other, it is called an *Independent Basic Service Set (IBSS)*. This type of ad hoc network exists as soon as two devices see each other. Figure 4-2 shows an ad hoc network.

Each computer has only one radio. Because there is only one radio, the throughput is lower and acts as a half-duplex device, because you can't send and receive at the same time.

You don't have much control in these networks, so you're stuck when it comes to methods such as authentication. In addition, you need to address who starts the conversation and who decides on the order of communication, to name just a couple issues.

Network Infrastructure Mode

In wireless networks, an access point acts as a connection point for clients. An AP is actually a cross between a hub and a bridge. Here's why:

■   There is one radio, which cannot send and receive at the same time. This is where the AP is likened to a hub. It's a half-duplex operation.

■   APs have some intelligence that is similar to that of a bridge. That is how an AP can see a frame and decide to forward it based on MAC addresses.

What is different on an AP versus a bridge is that wireless frames are more complex. Standard Ethernet frames have a source MAC address and a destination MAC address. Wireless frames can have three or four MAC addresses. Two of them are the source and destination MAC addresses, and one is the AP's MAC address that is tied to a workgroup.

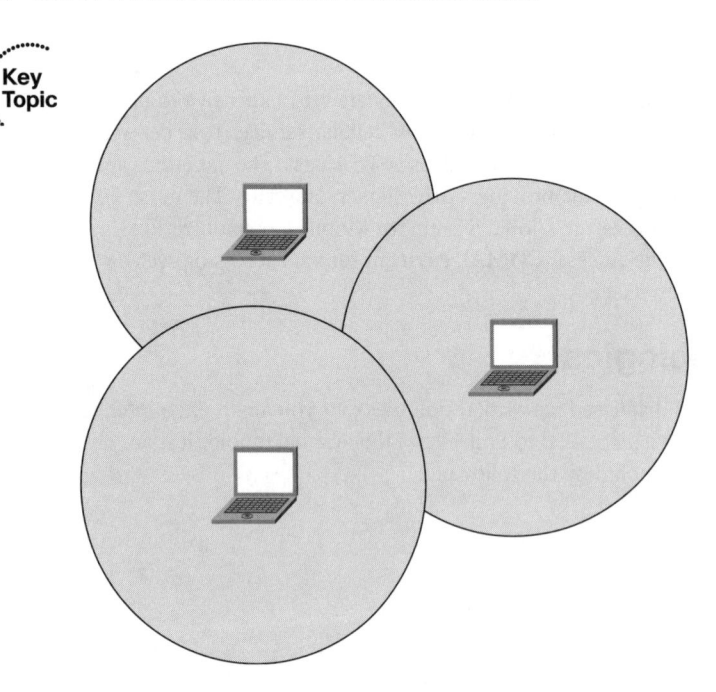

Figure 4-2   *Ad Hoc Network*

The fourth that could be present is a NEXT_HOP address in the event that you are using a workgroup bridge (WGB).

An AP is actually just one type of wireless station. This terminology could cause some confusion between an AP and a client on a network, so to differentiate between them, a client is called a *station (STA)*, and an AP is called an *infrastructure device.*

So what does a typical wireless topology look like? Of course, wireless clients are associated with an AP. In the wireless space, the coverage area of the AP is called a *Basic Service Area (BSA)*, which is also sometimes known as a *wireless cell*. They mean the same thing. When only one AP exists, this coverage area is called a BSA, as shown in Figure 4-3. That AP then usually has an Ethernet connection to an 802.3 LAN, depending on the function of the AP.

Note: Some APs can function in a repeater mode, in which they don't need an Ethernet connection.

Assuming that the AP has an Ethernet connection, it bridges the 802.11 wireless traffic from the wireless clients to the 802.3 wired network on the Ethernet side.

The wired network attached to the AP's Ethernet port is a path to a wireless LAN controller (or controller for short). The client traffic is passed through the controller and then is forwarded to the wired network, called the *distribution system*. The distribution system is how a client accesses the Internet, file servers, printers, and anything else available on the wired network.

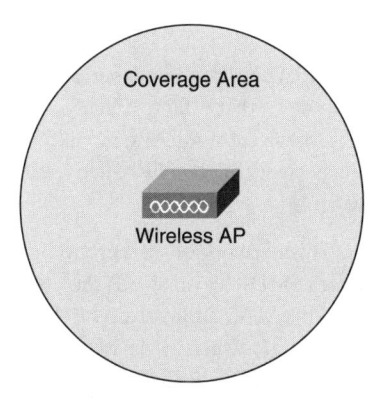

Figure 4-3   *Basic Service Area*

When more than one AP is connected to a common distribution system, as shown in
Figure 4-4, the coverage area is called an *Extended Service Area (ESA)*.

Figure 4-4   *Extended Service Area*

Why would you want more than one AP connected to the same LAN? There are a few
reasons:

■   To provide adequate coverage in a larger area.

■   To allow clients to move from one AP to the other and still be on the same LAN.

■   To provide more saturation of APs, resulting in more bandwidth per user.

This process of a client moving from one AP to another is called *roaming*. For roaming to
work, the APs must overlap. You might wonder why they need to overlap, because interference in a wireless network is a common issue. The reason for the overlap is so that a
client can see both APs and associate to the one with the stronger signal. As soon as the
signal from the associated AP hits the threshold built into the client, the client looks for
another AP with a better signal.

Service Set Identifiers

Think about how you connect to a wireless network. On your laptop, you might see a popup that says "Wireless networks are available" or something to that effect. When you look at the available networks, you see names. On older Cisco autonomous APs, the network was called "Tsunami." On a store-bought Linksys, the network is actually called "linksys." So the client sees a name that represents a network.

On the AP, the network is associated with a MAC address. This network or workgroup that your clients connect to is called a *Service Set Identifier (SSID)*. So on an AP, the SSID is a combination of MAC address and network name. This MAC address can be that of the wireless radio or another MAC address generated on the AP. When an AP offers service for only one network, it is called a *Basic Service Set Identifier (BSSID)*. APs offer the ability to use more than one SSID. This would let you offer a Guest Network and a Corporate Network and still use the same AP. When the AP has more than one network, it is called a *Multiple Basic Service Set Identifier (MBSSID)*. You can think of it as a virtual AP. It offers service for multiple networks, but it's the same hardware. Because it's the same hardware and the same frequency range, users on one network share with users on another and can collide if they send at the same time.

Now let's return to the roaming discussion. To get roaming to work, the BSA of each AP must overlap. The APs also need to be configured for the same SSID. This enables the client to see that the same network is offered by different MAC addresses, as illustrated in Figure 4-5.

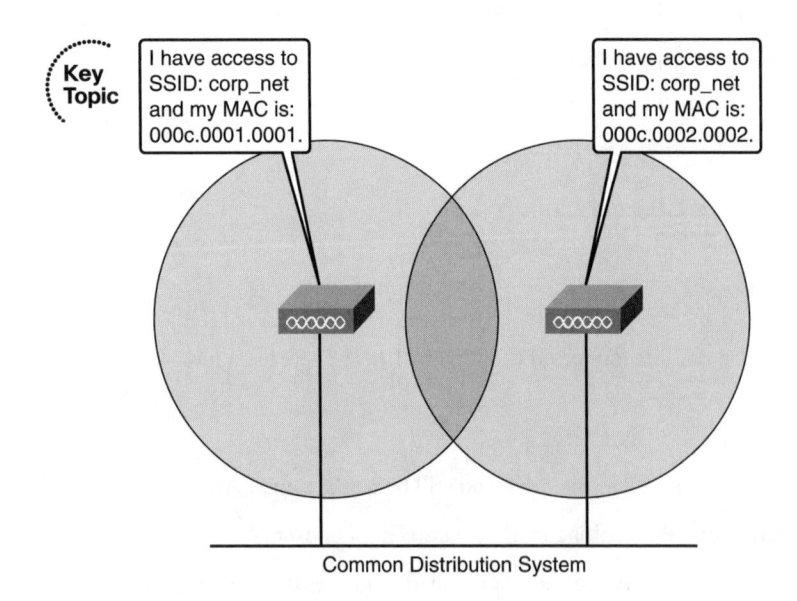

Figure 4-5   *Wireless Roaming*

When a client roams and moves from one AP to the other, the SSID remains the same, but the MAC address changes to the new AP with a better signal.

Another issue to consider when roaming is the possibility of interference between the two overlapping APs. Even though they offer the same SSID, they need to be on different *channels*, or frequency ranges, that do not overlap. This prevents *co-channel interference*, which should be avoided. The 2.4 spectrum allows only three nonoverlapping channels. You must consider this fact when placing APs.

Vendor-Specific Topology Extensions

The vendor-specific topology extensions are an enablement of additional network functionality by way of vendor-defined protocols, devices, and topologies. In this section you will learn how workgroup bridges, wireless repeaters, outdoor wireless bridges, and wireless mesh networks through the use of wireless controllers can enhance the functionality and capability of your wireless deployment.

Workgroup Bridges

You will most likely have times when you have an isolated network that needs access to the rest of the network for access to the server farm and the Internet. You might not be able to run an Ethernet cable to the isolated network, or you might not own the property so you can't drill holes in the walls, and so on. In this scenario, you would use a WGB topology such as the one shown in Figure 4-6.

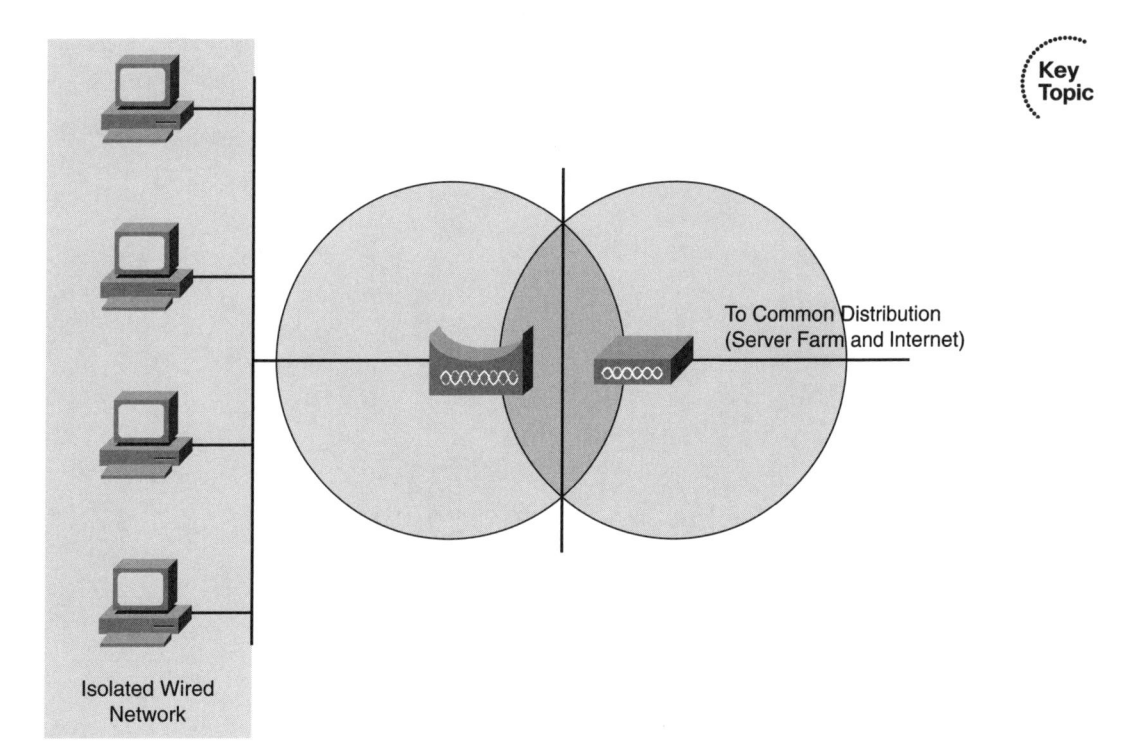

Figure 4-6 *Workgroup Bridge Topology*

Notice that the WGB is used to bridge a wired network to an AP that connects to a distribution system.

Cisco offers two types of workgroup bridges:

■ **Autonomous Workgroup Bridge (aWGB):** The aWGB was originally just called a workgroup bridge, but Cisco later changed the name when it introduced the Universal WGB. The aWGB is supported in IOS AP version 12.4(3G)JA and later. The aWGB connects only to upstream Cisco APs, and the AP sees multiple Ethernet clients.

■ **Universal Workgroup Bridge (uWGB):** The uWGB is supported on IOS AP version 12.4(11)XJ and later. It allows bridging to upstream non-Cisco APs and appears as a single client.

Repeaters

Recall that in an Extended Service Set (ESS), multiple APs connect clients. This is all well and good until you have clients roaming about who get into areas where coverage is necessary but not possible. The solution of a WGB doesn't work, because a WGB connects users who are wired. An example is a worker at a warehouse who carries a barcode scanner or even a wireless Cisco IP Phone. There are scenarios where you can't run a cable into a location to install an AP. This is where you want to use a *wireless repeater*. A wireless repeater is simply an AP that doesn't connect to a wired network for its connectivity to the distribution network. Instead, it overlaps with an AP that does physically connect to the distribution network. The overlap needs to be 50 percent for optimal performance. Figure 4-7 shows an example. A repeater is allowing a client to connect to the network when in fact the client would normally be out of the service area of the AP.

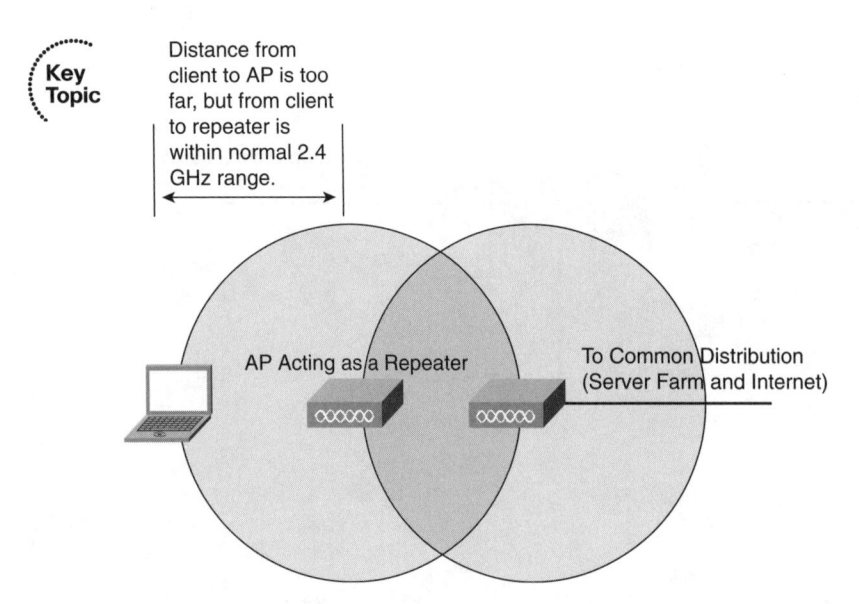

Key Topic

Distance from client to AP is too far, but from client to repeater is within normal 2.4 GHz range.

AP Acting as a Repeater

To Common Distribution (Server Farm and Internet)

Figure 4-7   *Wireless Repeater Topology*

You can get APs that act as a repeater as well, which is how the Cisco solution works. The catch is that you need a Cisco AP as the upstream "root" device, and only one SSID is supported in repeater mode. Additionally, the overall throughput is cut in half for each repeater hop.

Outdoor Wireless Bridges

When you have two or more LANs within a few miles of each other and you want to link them, you can use a wireless bridge. Because you are "bridging," the technology works at Layer 2. This means that the LANs do not route traffic and do not have a routing table.

You can connect one LAN directly to another in a point-to-point configuration, as shown in Figure 4-8, or you can connect many LANs through a central hub, as shown in Figure 4-9.

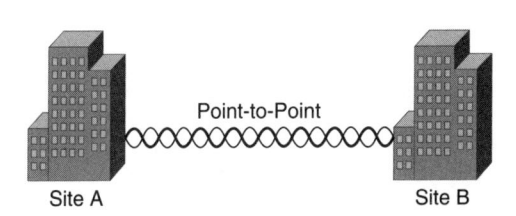

Figure 4-8   *Point-to-Point Wireless Bridge Topology*

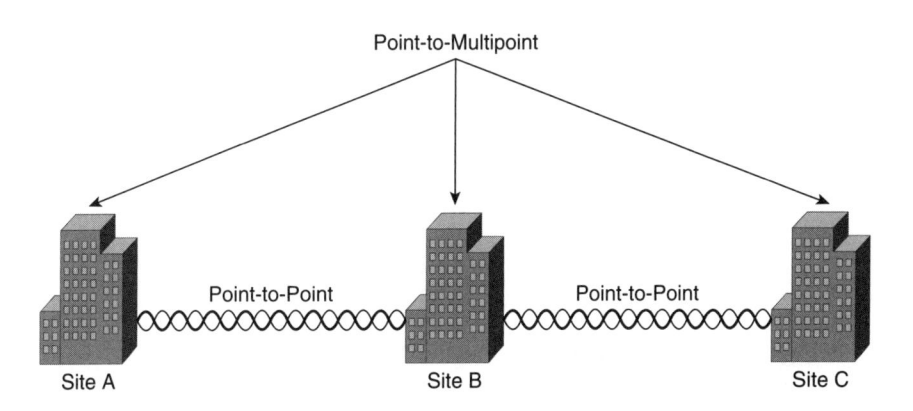

Figure 4-9   *Point-to-Multipoint Wireless Bridge Topology*

Each end of a point-to-multipoint topology would have to communicate through the hub if it wanted to communicate with the others. Cisco offers the Cisco Aironet 1300 series wireless bridge and the Cisco Aironet 1400 series wireless bridge. When using a 1400 series, you can bridge only networks, but if you use a 1300 series, you can allow clients to connect as well as bridge networks. The 1300 series operates in the 2.4-GHz range, and the 1400 series operates in the 5-GHz range.

Outdoor Mesh Networks

As you can see, bridges are a good way to connect remote sites. However, suppose that you are operating in a point-to-multipoint topology, and the central site experiences congestion. Who suffers? Just the central site? Just the remote site? No; the answer is everyone. When two remote sites communicate through a central site, the central site makes all the difference.

Assume that the central site goes down, as shown in Figure 4-10.

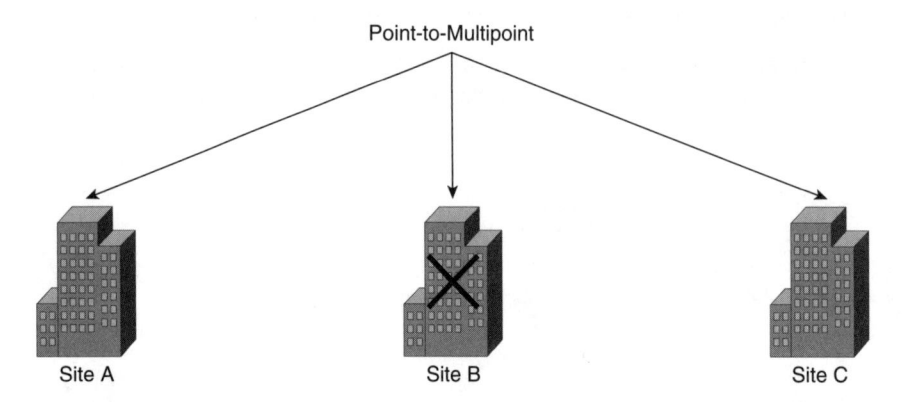

Figure 4-10 *Wireless Bridge Issues*

Now the remote sites can't communicate with each other or the central site. This can be a major issue to contend with. The solution is to deploy a mesh network such as the one illustrated in Figure 4-11.

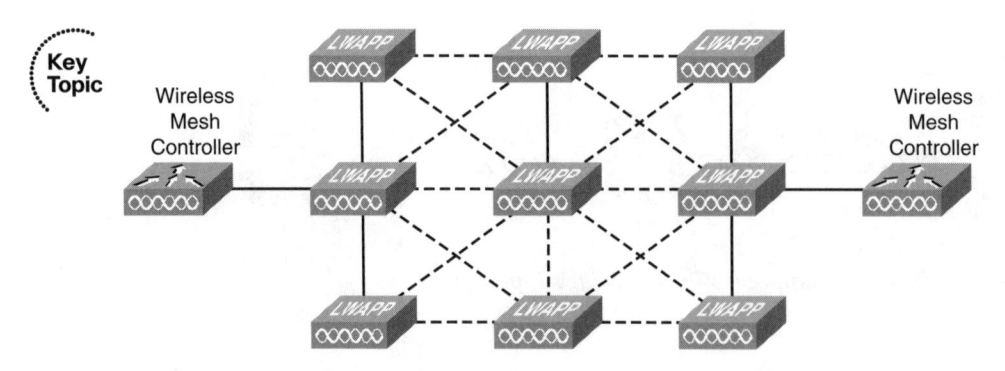

Figure 4-11 *Wireless Mesh Solution*

The mesh solution is appropriate when connectivity is important, because multiple paths can be used. The IEEE is currently working on a mesh standard (802.11s). However, the solution discussed here is a Cisco solution in which a wireless controller, also shown in Figure 4-11, is involved.

When you have a mesh network, some *nodes* (another term for APs in a mesh network) are connected to a wired network. Some nodes simply act as repeaters. A mesh node repeats data to nearby nodes. More than one path is available, so a special algorithm is used to determine the best path. The alternative paths can be used when there is congestion or when a wireless mesh node goes down.

Exam Preparation Tasks

Review All the Key Topics

Review the most important topics from this chapter, denoted with the Key Topic icon. Table 4-2 lists these key topics and the page number where you can find each one.

Table 4-2 *Key Topics for Chapter 4*

Key Topic Item	Description	Page Number
Figure 4-1	Wireless topology overview	52
Figure 4-2	Ad hoc network	56
Figure 4-3	Basic service area	57
Figure 4-4	Extended service area	57
Figure 4-5	Wireless roaming	58
Figure 4-6	Workgroup bridge topology	59
Figure 4-7	Wireless repeater topology	60
Figure 4-8	Point-to-point wireless bridge topology	61
Figure 4-9	Point-to-multipoint wireless bridge topology	61
Figure 4-11	Wireless mesh solution	62

Definition of Key Terms

Define the following key terms from this chapter, and check your answers in the glossary:

WPAN, SIG, WLAN, IEEE, WMAN, WiMax, WWAN, GSM, CDMA, ad hoc, infrastructure, distribution system, BSS, IBSS, STA, infrastructure device, BSA, ESA, roaming, SSID, BSSID, MBSSID, co-channel interference, WGB, aWGB, uWGB, repeater, node

This chapter covers the following subjects:

Principles of Antennas: Covers antenna concepts.

Common Antenna Types: Describes omnidirectional and directional antennas.

Antenna Connectors and Hardware: Looks at some of the connectors used in wireless deployments as well as other common hardware.

CHAPTER 5

Antenna Communications

In any wireless network, the capability to propagate the signal is key. Without that capability, the whole concept of a wireless network falls apart. In this chapter, you will learn about antenna principles, along with some common antenna and connector types.

You should take the "Do I Know This Already Quiz?" first. If you score 80 percent or higher, you may want to skip to the section "Exam Preparation Tasks." If you score below 80 percent, you should review the entire chapter.

"Do I Know This Already?" Quiz

The "Do I Know This Already?" quiz helps you determine your level of knowledge of this chapter's topics before you begin. Table 5-1 details the major topics discussed in this chapter and their corresponding quiz questions.

Table 5-1 *"Do I Know This Already?" Section-to-Question Mapping*

Foundation Topics Section	Questions
Principles of Antennas	1–7
Common Antenna Types	8–16
Antenna Connectors and Hardware	17–20

1. Which of the following are types of polarization? (Choose all that apply.)

   a. Vertical

   b. Horizontal

   c. Nautical

   d. Circular

2. All Cisco antennas use what type of polarization?

   a. Linear

   b. Circular

   c. Magnetic

   d. Perpendicular

3. In an electromagnetic wave, where is the magnetic wave found in relation to the electric wave?

    a. Parallel to the electric wave.

    b. At a 45-degree angle to the electric wave.

    c. Perpendicular (at a 90-degree angle).

    d. There is no magnetic wave.

4. How many antennas are used with diversity?

    a. Three

    b. Four

    c. One

    d. Two

5. What does diversity listen to when choosing a better antenna to use?

    a. The destination MAC address

    b. The preamble

    c. The data

    d. The source MAC address

6. How far apart should antennas be placed when using diversity?

    a. 2 meters

    b. Two wavelengths

    c. One wavelength

    d. 1 meter

7. True or false: Two antennas using diversity can cover two areas.

    a. True

    b. False

8. What are the main families of antennas? (Choose all that apply.)

    a. Omnidirectional

    b. Unidirectional

    c. Directional

    d. Yagi

9. In relation to sending a linear waveform, the horizontal plane (H-plane) is also called what?

    a. Vertical plane

    b. Azimuth

    c. Axis

    d. Linear plane

10. To display the coverage from top to bottom, what plane is represented?

    a. A-plane

    b. E-plane

    c. C-plane

    d. Airplane

11. The 2.2 dipole antenna is designed for what type of deployment?

    a. Indoor omnidirectional

    b. Indoor directional

    c. Outdoor point-to-point

    d. Outdoor omnidirectional

12. Which antenna is considered a "special" omnidirectional antenna?

    a. AIR-ANT1728

    b. AIR-ANT3338

    c. AIR-ANT2485P-R

    d. AIR-ANT3213

13. A yagi antenna is best used in what setting or settings? (Choose all that apply.)

    a. Warehouse where multiple antennas are lined up

    b. Conference room

    c. Point-to-point over long distances

    d. Long hallways

14. True or false: A parabolic dish antenna uses a wide RF path.

    a. True

    b. False

15. For mounting reasons, what can be changed on a parabolic antenna?

    a. Polarity

    b. Diversity

    c. Shape

    d. Radiation pattern

16. The AIR-ANT3213 uses how many antennas?

    a. Two

    b. Four

    c. Six

    d. One

17. Cisco uses which types of connectors? (Choose all that apply.)

   a. SMA

   b. N-connector

   c. RP-TNC

   d. TNC

18. To lower the amount of energy being sent to the antenna, which of the following devices could be used?

   a. Amplifier

   b. Attenuator

   c. Lightning arrestor

   d. Fiber-patch

19. To increase the amount of energy, which of the following devices could be used?

   a. Amplifier

   b. Attenuator

   c. Lightning arrestor

   d. Fiber-patch

20. True or false: Lightning arrestors are designed to withstand a full lightning strike.

   a. True

   b. False

Foundation Topics

Principles of Antennas

If someone asked you what the most important part of a wireless network is, what would you say? I'd have to say the antenna. Why? Without it, you have a nice little AP that can offer network services for anyone within about 3 feet. But that's not what you want. You want to make sure that your space is properly covered. You need antennas to do this. In fact, you need the *right* antennas to do this. In this section you will learn about the factors involved in dealing with antennas, which include *polarity* and *diversity*.

Polarization

The goal of an antenna is to emit electromagnetic waves. The electro portion of the term electromagnetic describes the wave and that it can move in different ways. The way that it moves is its polarization. There are three types of polarization:

■ Vertical

■ Horizontal

■ Circular

As shown in Figure 5-1, *vertical polarization* means that the wave moves up and down in a linear way. *Horizontal polarization* means that the wave moves left and right in a linear way.

The third type of polarization, *circular polarization*, indicates that the wave circles as it moves forward, as illustrated in Figure 5-2.

The electric field is generated by stationary charges, or current. There is also a magnetic field—hence the term electromagnetic. The magnetic field is found perpendicular (at a 90-degree angle) to the electric field. This magnetic field is generated at the same time as the electric field; however, the magnetic field is generated by moving charges. Cisco antennas are always vertically polarized in wireless networks. This makes the electric field vertical. Why is this important? The importance is that the antenna is designed to propagate signals in a certain direction. Here is where installation errors can hurt you. For example, if you have a long tube-like antenna, it would face up/down. If you placed it flat instead, the signal would propagate in a different direction and would end up degraded.

Although this is not a huge factor in indoor deployments, it can be in outdoor deployments. Usually other factors degrade your wireless signal propagation on indoor deployments.

Diversity

By now you should understand what the multipath issue is. Traffic takes different paths because of the obstacles in the wireless path. One way to deal with multipath issues is to use two antennas on one AP. *Diversity* is the use of two antennas for each radio to increase the odds that you receive a better signal on either of the antennas.

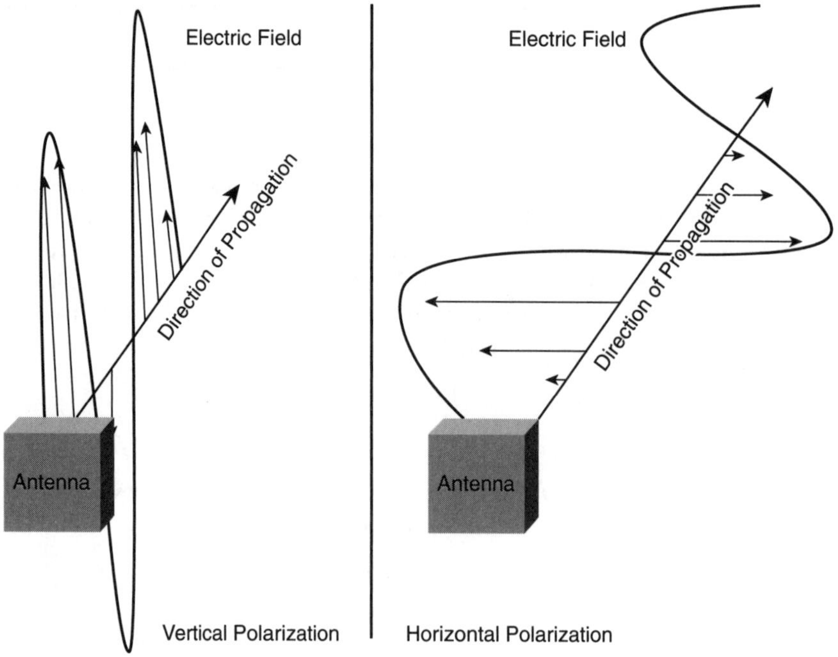

Figure 5-1   *Vertical and Horizontal Polarization*

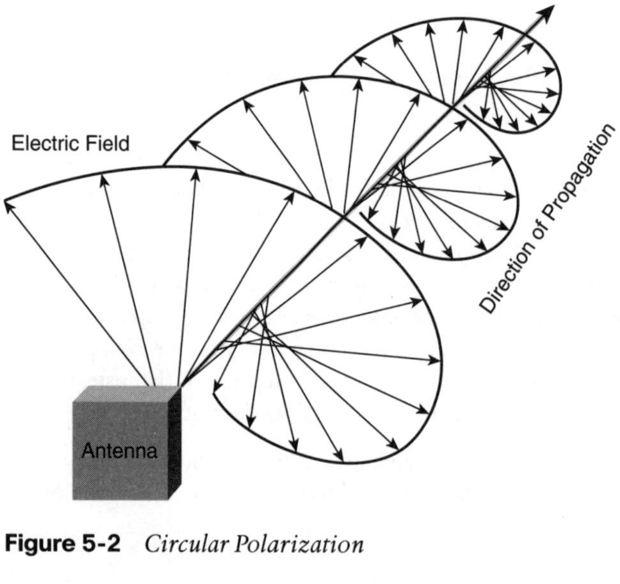

Figure 5-2   *Circular Polarization*

Here is how it works: The two antennas are placed one wavelength apart. When the AP hears a preamble of a frame, it switches between the two antennas and uses an algorithm to determine which antenna has the better signal. After an antenna is chosen, it is used for the rest of that frame. You can switch antennas and listen to the preamble because it has no real data. As soon as the real data gets there, it uses only one of the antennas.

Most of the time this happens with a single radio in the AP and two antennas connected to it. This is important because the two antennas cover the same area. You wouldn't try to cover two different areas with the same radio. Additionally, the antennas need to be the same. If you used a weaker antenna on one side versus the other, the coverage area would not be the same.

Common Antenna Types

The two main types of antennas are directional and omnidirectional. In this section you will learn the difference between the two types and look at some of the antennas that Cisco offers. Both send the same amount of energy; the difference is in how the beam is focused. To understand this, imagine that you have a flashlight. By twisting the head of the light, you can make the beam focus in a specific area. When the beam has a wider focus, it doesn't appear to be as bright. While you twist the head of the light, you never change its output. The batteries are the same. The power is the same. The light is the same. You simply focus it in different ways. The same goes for wireless antennas. When you look at a directional antenna, it appears to be a stronger signal in one direction, but it's still emitting the same amount of energy. To increase power in a particular direction, you add gain.

The angles of coverage are fixed with each antenna. When you buy high-gain antennas, it is usually to focus a beam.

Omnidirectional Antennas

There are two ways to determine the coverage area of an antenna. The first is to place the AP in a location and walk around with a client recording the signal-to-noise ratio (SNR) and Received Signal Strength Indicator (RSSI). This could take a really long time. The second method is a little easier. In fact, the manufacturer does it for you. Figures 5-3 and 5-4 show different views of the wireless signal. Figure 5-3 shows how the wireless signal might propagate if you were standing above it and looking down on the antenna.

Note: We say "might" because these values are different for each type of antenna.

This is called the *horizontal plane (H-plane)* or *azimuth*. When you look at an omnidirectional antenna from the top (H-plane), you should see that it propagates evenly in a 360-degree pattern.

The vertical pattern does not propagate evenly, though. Figure 5-4 shows the *elevation plane (E-plane)*. This is how the signal might propagate in a vertical pattern, or from top to bottom. As you can see, it's not a perfect 360 degrees. This is actually by design. It's what is known as the "one floor" concept. The idea is that the signal propagates wider from side to side than it does from top to bottom so that it can offer coverage to the floor it is placed on rather than to the floor above or below the AP.

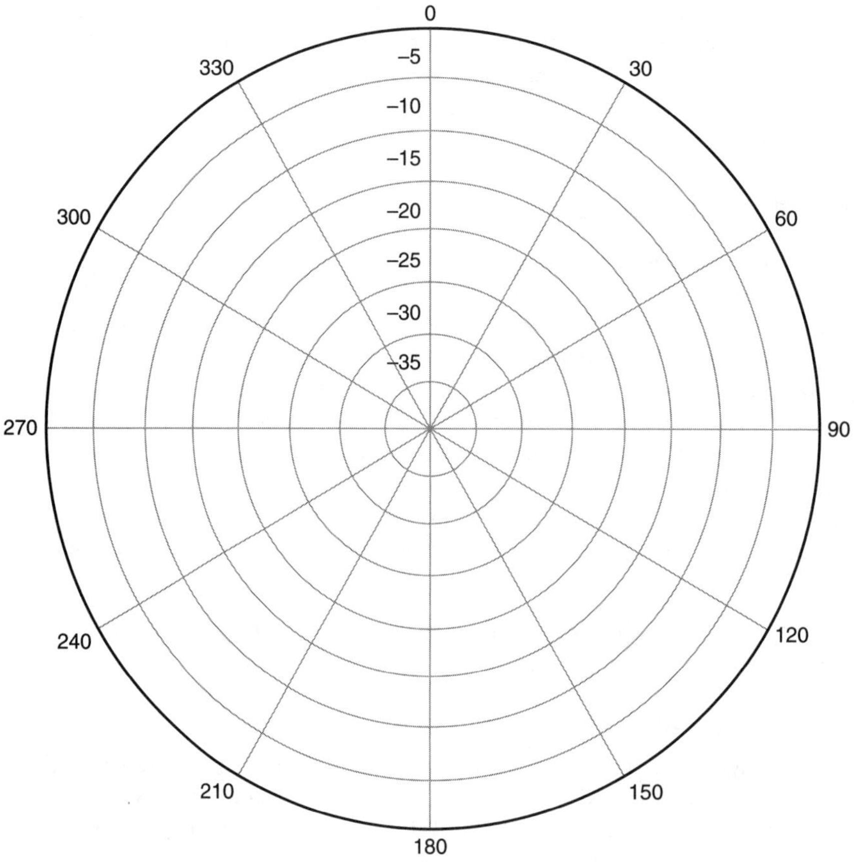

Figure 5-3   *H-plane*

Another way to look at this is to imagine an AP, as shown in Figure 5-5. If you draw in the H-plane and E-plane, you can relate the signal to each plane.

Now that you have a better understanding of how to determine the propagation patterns of an antenna, let's look at some antennas.

2.2-dBi Dipole

The 2.2-dBi *dipole*, or rubber duck, shown in Figure 5-6, is most often seen indoors because it is a very weak antenna. In fact, it's actually designed for a client or AP that doesn't cover a large area. Its radiation pattern resembles a doughnut, because vertically it doesn't propagate much. Instead, it's designed to propagate on the H-plane. The term *dipole* may be new to you. The dipole antenna was developed by Heinrich Rudolph Hertz and is considered the simplest type of antenna. Dipoles have a doughnut-shaped *radiation pattern*. Many times, an antenna is compared to an isotropic radiator. An *isotropic radiator* assumes that the signal is propagated evenly in all directions. This would be a perfect 360-degree sphere in all directions, on the H and E planes. The 2.2-dBi dipole antenna doesn't work this way; rather, it has a doughnut shape.

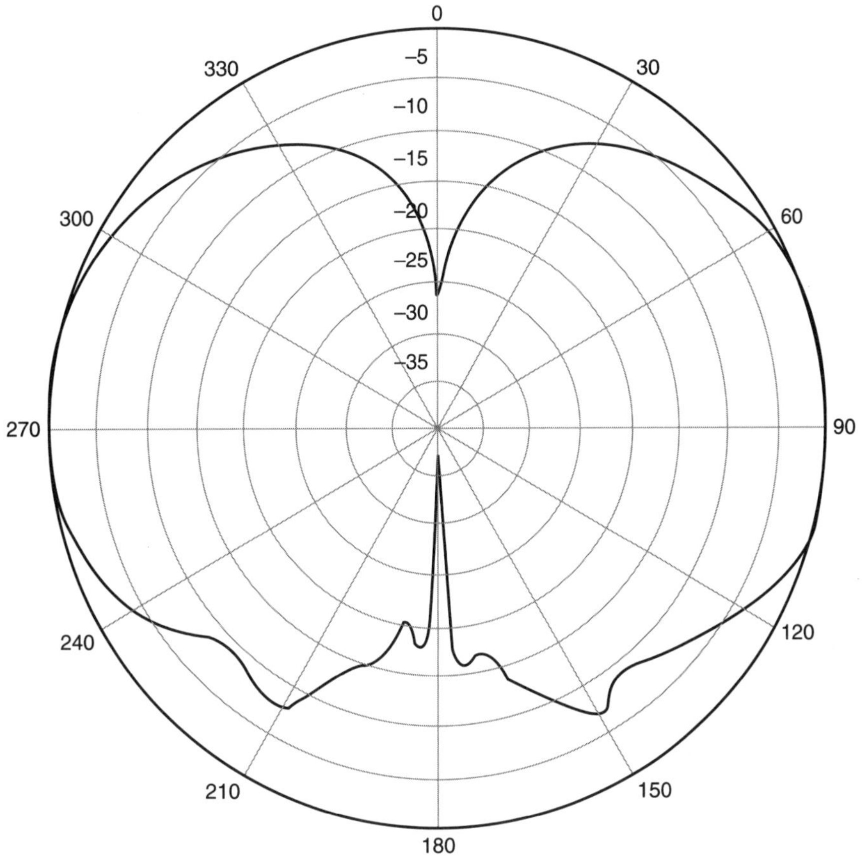

Figure 5-4 *E-plane*

AIR-ANT1728

The AIR-ANT1728, shown in Figure 5-7, is a ceiling-mounted omnidirectional antenna operating at 5.2 dBi.

You would use this when a 2.14-dBi dipole doesn't provide adequate coverage for an area. This antenna has more gain, thus increasing the H-plane, as shown in Figure 5-8.

The easiest way to express the effect of adding gain—in this case, 5.2 dBi versus 2.2 dBi—is to imagine squeezing a balloon from the top and the bottom, as shown in Figure 5-9.

The squeezing represents the addition of gain. The H-plane widens and the E-plane shortens, as shown in Figure 5-10.

Table 5-2 details the statistics of the AIR-ANT1728.

Key Topic

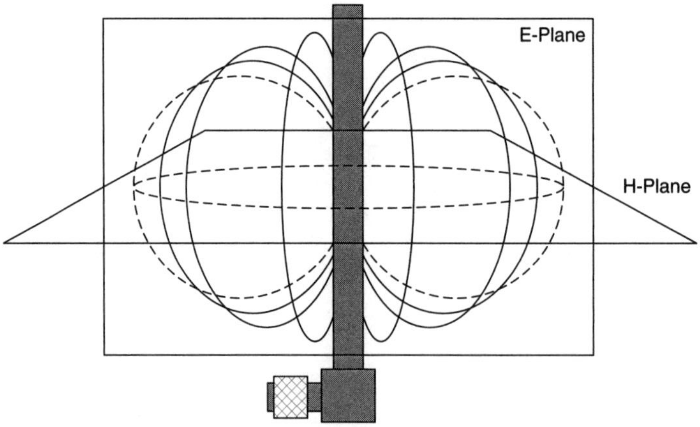

*This figure is based on an original image from the Wikipedia entry: http://en.wikipedia.org/wiki/E-plane_and_H-plane

Figure 5-5 *H-plane and E-plane*

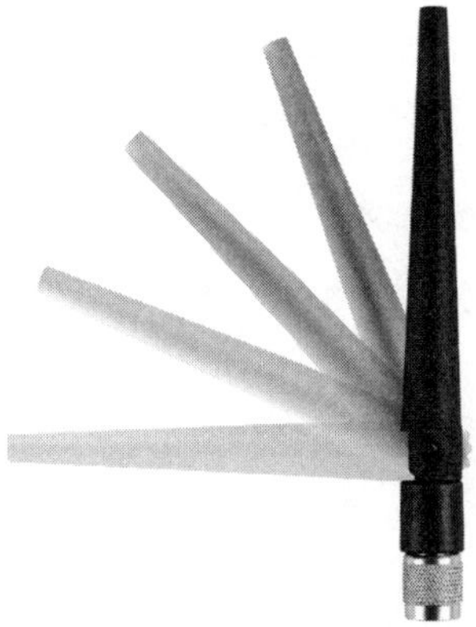

Figure 5-6 *2.14-dBi Dipole Antenna (Rubber Duck)*

Key Topic

Table 5-2 *AIR-ANT1728 Statistics*

Gain	5.2 dBi
Polarization	5.2 dBi
H-plane	Vertical
E-plane	Omnidirectional 360 degrees
Antenna connector type	RP-TNC
Mounting	Drop ceiling cross-member indoor only
*This connector type is covered later, in the section "Antenna Connectors and Hardware."	

Key Topic

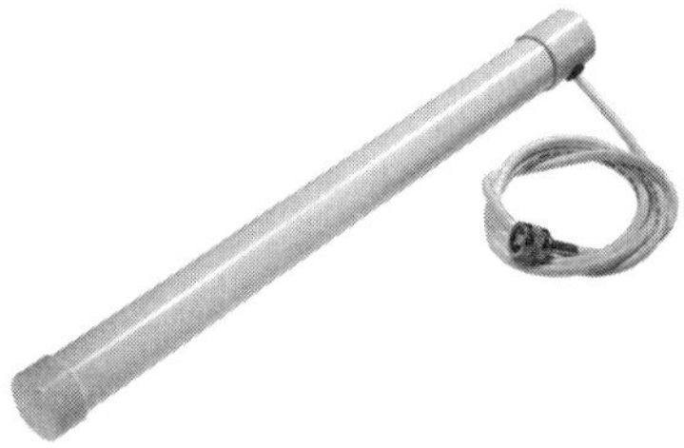

Figure 5-7 *AIR-ANT1728*

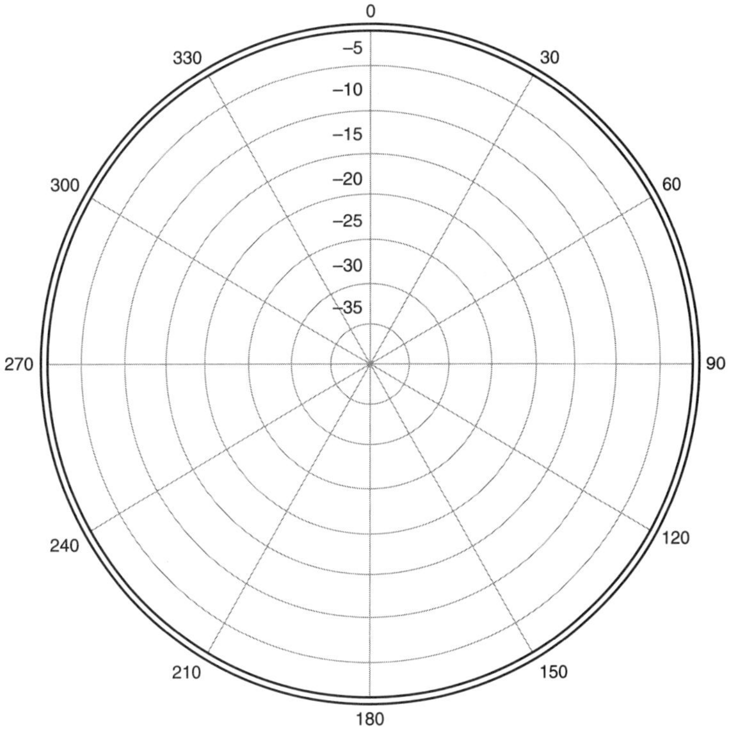

Figure 5-8 *H-plane of the AIR-ANT1728*

Key Topic

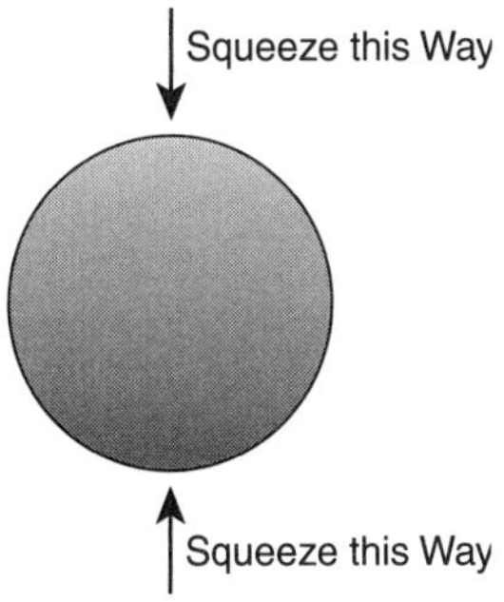

Figure 5-9 *Effect of Adding Gain*

Squeeze this Way

Wider after adding gain!

Squeeze this Way

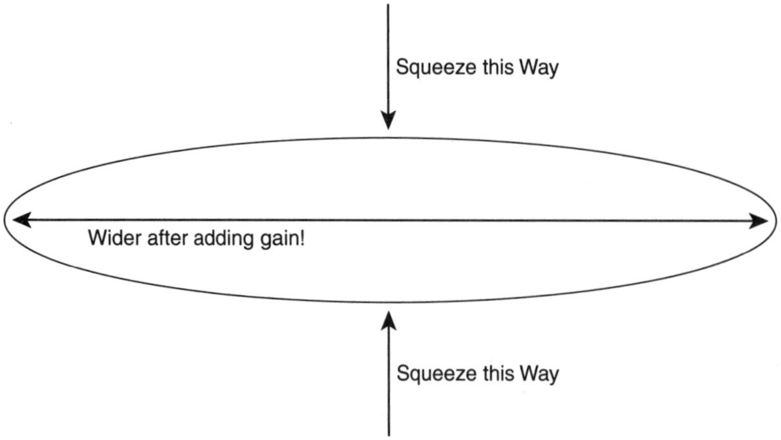

Figure 5-10   *H-plane and E-plane After Gain Is Added*

AIR-ANT2506

The AIR-ANT2506, shown in Figure 5-11, is a mast-mount indoor/outdoor antenna that you mount on a round mast. It is a 5.2-dBi antenna and is omnidirectional.

Table 5-3 gives details on the antenna.

Table 5-3   *AIR-ANT2506*

Gain	5.2 dBi
Polarization	Vertical
H-plane	Omnidirectional 360 degrees
E-plane	RP-TNC
Antenna connector type	Mast-mount indoor/outdoor
Mounting	

*This connector type is covered later, in the section "Antenna Connectors and Hardware."

AIR-ANT24120

The AIR-ANT24120, shown in Figure 5-12, is an omnidirectional antenna that is designed to offer higher gain at 12 dBi. Like the 2506, it is a mast-mount antenna.

Table 5-4 provides more details on the AIR-ANT24120.

Table 5-4   *AIR-ANT24120*

Gain	12 dBi
Polarization	Linear Vertical
H-plane	Omnidirectional 360 degrees
E-plane	7 degrees
Antenna connector type	RP-TNC
Mounting	Mast-mount

*This connector type is covered later, in the section "Antenna Connectors and Hardware."

Figure 5-11   *AIR-ANT2506*

Directional Antennas

Directional antennas are usually mounted on walls and have their radiation patterns focused in a certain direction. This is similar to the earlier example of a flashlight (see the section "Common Antenna Types"). The goal is to provide coverage for areas such as long hallways, a warehouse, or anywhere you need a more directed signal. When used in an indoor environment, this kind of antenna usually is placed on walls and pillars. In an outdoor environment it can be seen on rooftops in the form of a parabolic dish.

This kind of antenna provides more gain than an omnidirectional, but again, the shape or radiation pattern is focused. They employ the "one floor" logic discussed earlier (see the section "Omnidirectional Antennas"). This means that they do not have much of a range vertically.

8.5-dBi Patch, Wall Mount

The 8.5-dBi patch is a wall-mounted directional antenna that provides more gain than a basic omnidirectional rubber duck. This results in 8.5 dBi for directional instead of 2.14 omnidirectional. Figure 5-13 shows the Cisco AIR-ANT2485P-R 8.5-dBi wall-mounted patch antenna.

Notice that this is a flat antenna. It is designed to radiate directionally, as illustrated in Figure 5-14. You place this antenna on a wall. By its form factor, it is very discreet.

Figures 5-15 and 5-16 show the H-plane and E-plane. Notice that the radiation pattern is not 360 degrees, even on the H-plane. However, a bit of signal is seen behind the antenna. This is normal and usually is absorbed by the wall that the antenna is mounted to. When

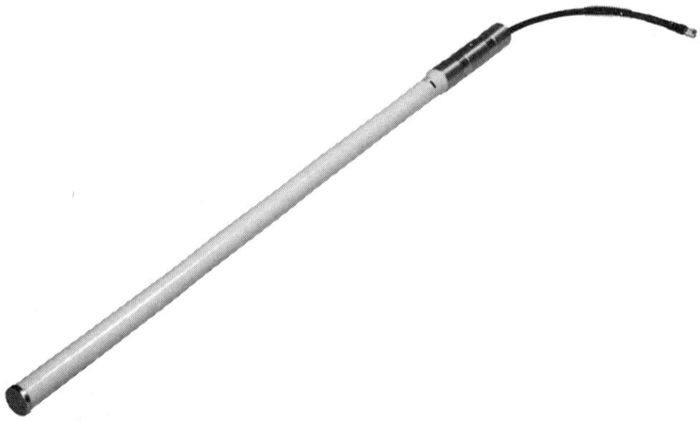

Figure 5-12   *AIR-ANT24120*

Figure 5-13   *AIR-ANT2485P-R Wall-Mounted Patch Antenna*

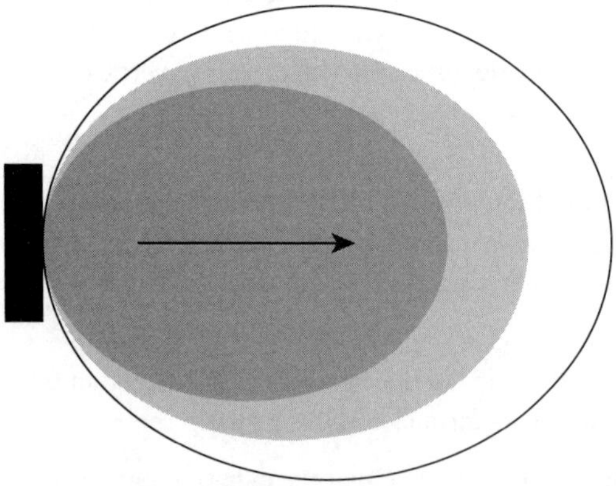

Figure 5-14   *Radiation Pattern of the AIR-ANT2485P-R*

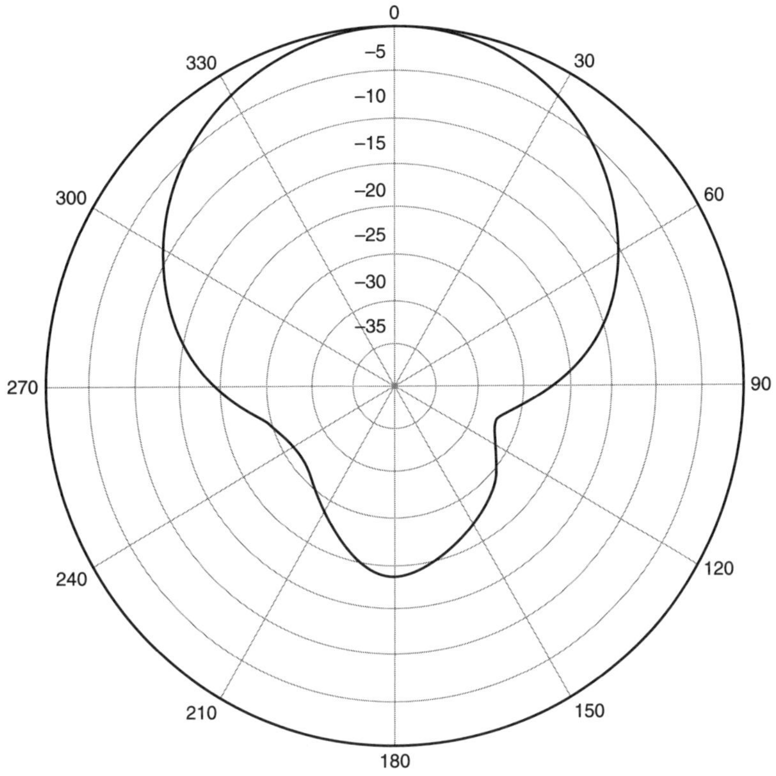

Figure 5-15 *H-plane of the AIR-ANT-2485P-R*

the antenna is mounted above a doorway, the back signal lets a client get the signal from the antenna just as he or she gets to the doorway.

Table 5-5 provides the details of the AIR-ANT2485P-R.

Table 5-5 *AIR-ANT2485P-R*

Gain	8.5 dBi
Polarization	Vertical
H-plane	66 degrees
E-plane	56 degrees
Antenna connector type	RP-TNC
Mounting	Wall mount

*This connector type is covered later, in the section "Antenna Connectors and Hardware."

Key Topic

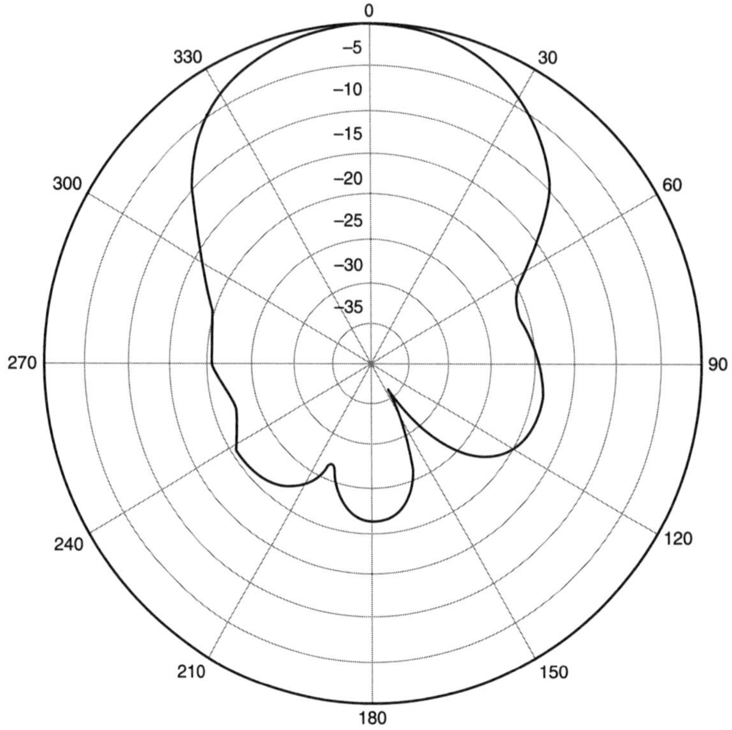

Figure 5-16   *E-plane of the AIR-ANT-2485P-R*

13.5 Yagi Antenna

The 13.5 yagi antenna is a directional antenna that offers a very direct radiation pattern. Sometimes you see these mounted above doorways to cover a long hallway. You can also put a number of them side by side on a wall to cover a large open space such as a warehouse or convention center.

Yagi antennas are sometimes called Yagi-Uda antennas, after their two creators.

Note: For more information on the history of the Yagi-Uda antenna, see http://en. wikipedia.org/wiki/Yagi_antenna#History.

Yagi antennas have a butterfly effect that is an effect of their polarization, as illustrated in Figure 5-17.

You can clearly see the butterfly-type pattern in the figure. Notice that there is also some coverage on the back side of the antenna, even though it is designed as a directional antenna. This fact can be useful if you want to test under the antenna.

Figure 5-18 shows the 10-dBi yagi, one of the yagi antennas offered by Cisco.

Although it is enclosed in an aesthetically pleasing cylinder, the antenna inside is a "comb" that resembles old UHF television antennas that you used to see on the roofs of houses.

68–78 Degrees at 900 MHz

28–80 Degrees at 2.4 GHz

Directional Yagi

Key Topic

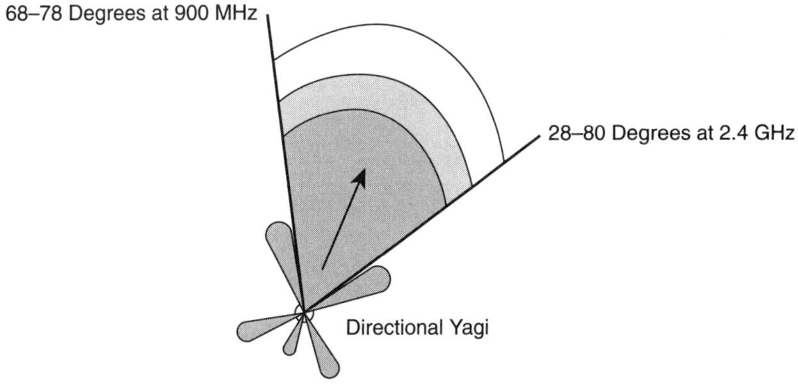

Figure 5-17 *Radiation Pattern of a Yagi Antenna*

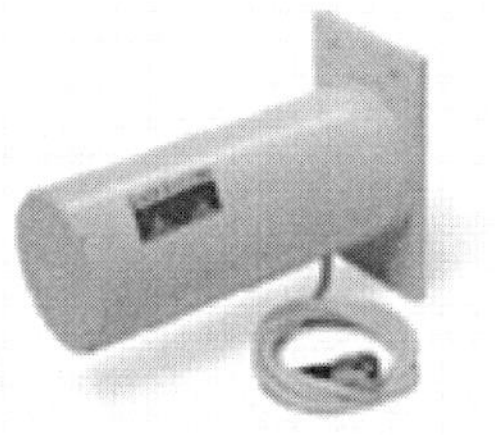

Figure 5-18 *AIR-ANT2410Y-R*

Figure 5-19 shows the AIR-ANT1949, another yagi antenna offered by Cisco.

This yagi is a high-gain antenna at 13.5 dBi. Its H-plane and E-plane are shown in Figures 5-20 and 5-21, respectively.

Table 5-6 shows the details of the AIR-ANT1949 yagi.

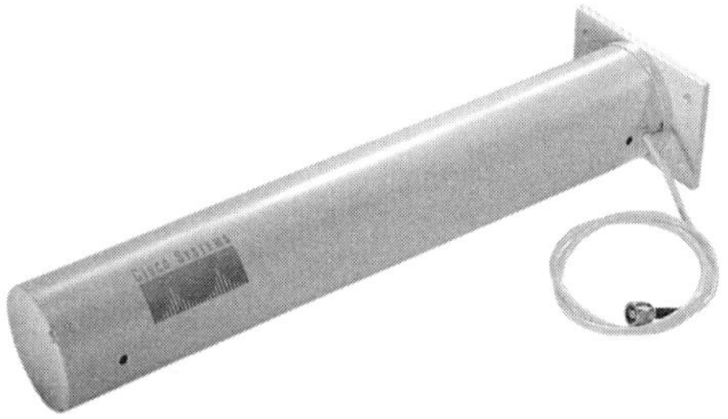

Figure 5-19 *AIR-ANT1949 Yagi*

Table 5-6   *AIR-ANT1949 Yagi*

Frequency range	2.4 to 2.83 GHz
Gain	13.5 dBi
Polarization	Vertical
H-plane	30 degrees
E-plane	25 degrees
Antenna connector type	RP-TNC
Mounting	Mast/wall mount

*This connector type is covered later, in the section "Antenna Connectors and Hardware."

Figure 5-20   *H-plane of the AIR-ANT1949 Yagi*

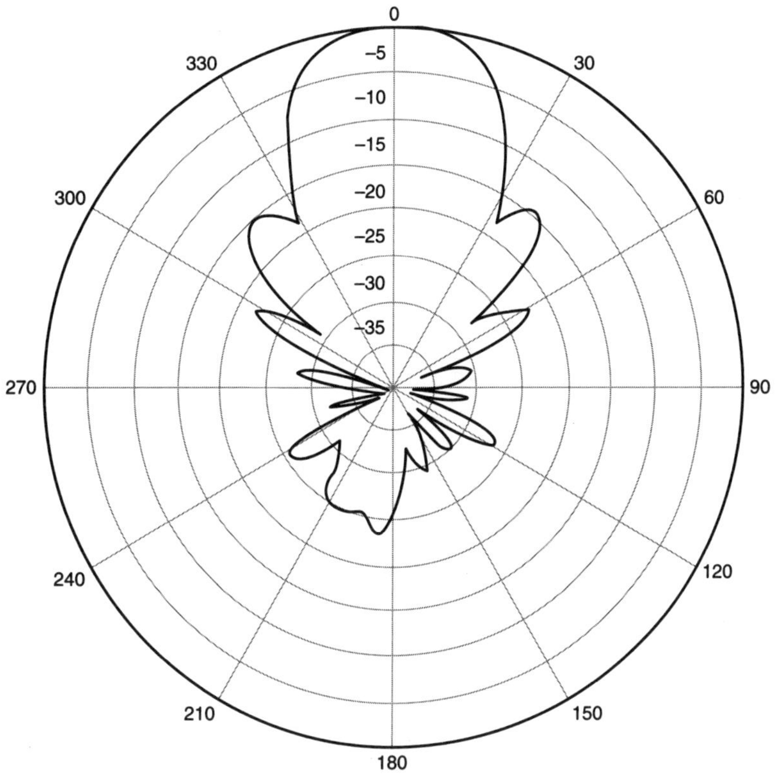

Figure 5-21   *E-plane of the AIR-ANT1949 Yagi*

When you mount a yagi, the polarity is important to consider. Because the antenna is enclosed in a protective casing, you might not be able to look at it and know the radiation pattern. Read the manufacturer documentation or look for manufacturer markings that indicate how to mount the antenna. On a Cisco yagi, the bottom usually is indicated by a black dot. Remember that if you mount it incorrectly, you will degrade the signal.

21-dBi Parabolic Dish

The 21-dBi *parabolic dish* antenna, shown in Figure 5-22, is almost 100 times more powerful than the rubber duck (discussed in the section "2.2-dBi Dipole").

Parabolic dish antennas have a very narrow path. Their radiation pattern is very focused. When you install these, you have to be very accurate in the direction you point them. You would use a parabolic dish in point-to-point scenarios. Distances of up to 25 miles at 2.4 GHz and 12 miles at 5 GHz can be reached using parabolic dish antennas. Parabolic dish antennas have a butterfly effect similar to yagi antennas. Also, some parabolic dish antennas allow polarity to be changed. This is important, because they can be mounted at different angles, and polarity changes how the RF is propagated. Table 5-7 shows the details of the Cisco AIR-ANT3338.

Figure 5-22 *Parabolic Dish Antenna*

Table 5-7 *AIR-ANT3338 Parabolic Dish Antenna*

Power	5 Watts
Gain	21 dBi
Polarization	Vertical
H-plane	12 degrees
E-plane	12 degrees
Antenna connector type	RP-TNC
Mounting	Mast mount

*This connector type is covered later, in the section "Antenna Connectors and Hardware."

Dual-Patch "Omnidirectional" 5.2 dBi, Pillar Mount

Another special type of antenna to consider is the dual-patch 5.2-dBi pillar-mount omni-directional, shown in Figure 5-23.

It is considered "special" because it has two patch directional antennas placed back to back, making it "omnidirectional." Because there are actually two antennas, you can use diversity with this antenna.

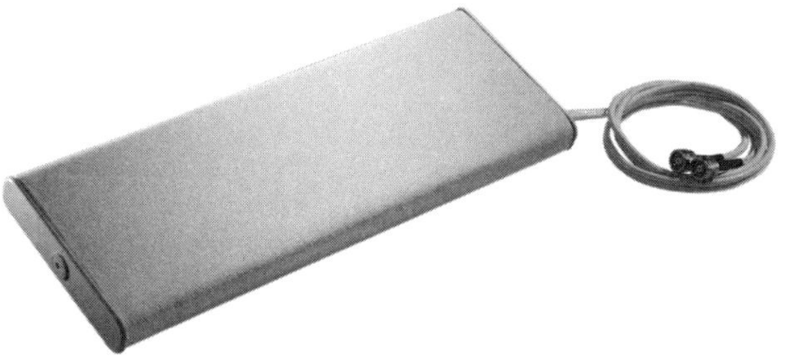

Figure 5-23   *AIR-ANT3213 Dual-Patch 5.2-dBi Pillar-Mount Omnidirectional*

You would use this type of antenna to provide access to a hall, because it's usually mounted to a pillar in the middle of the hall. Figures 5-24 and 5-25 show this antenna's radiation patterns.

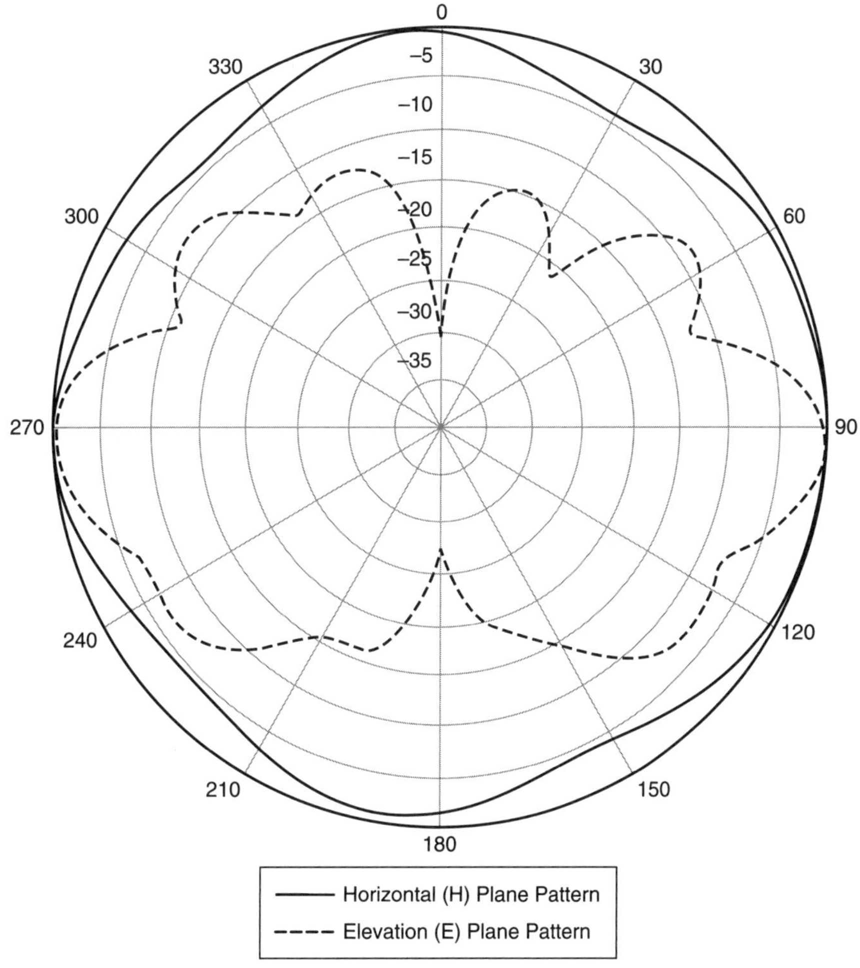

Figure 5-24   *AIR-ANT3213 Left Antenna Radiation Pattern*

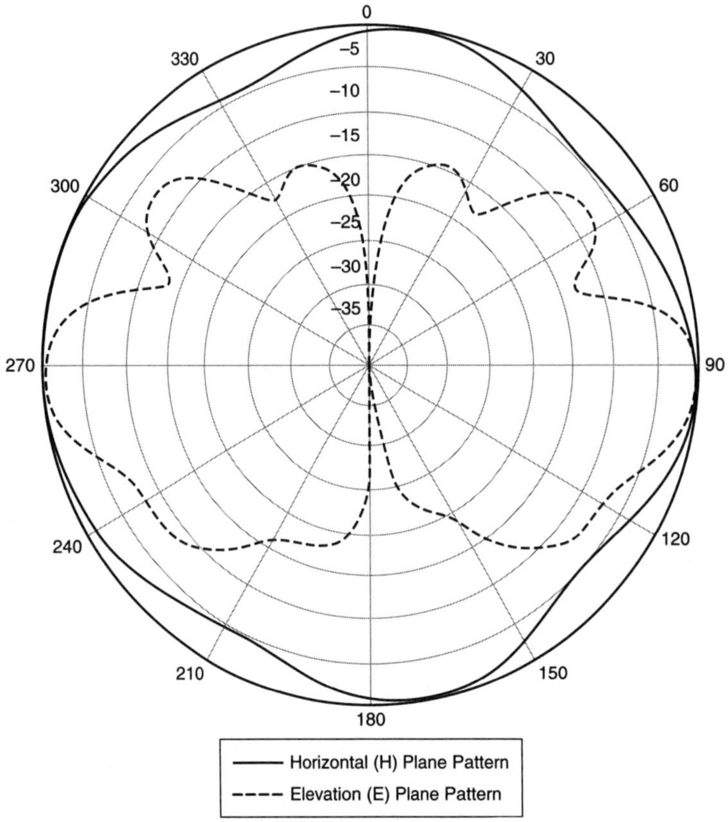

Figure 5-25   *AIR-ANT3213 Right Antenna Radiation Pattern*

In these two figures, the outer line is the H-plane, and the inner, dashed line is the E-plane.

Table 5-8 shows the details of the AIR-ANT3213.

Table 5-8   *AIR-ANT3213 Antenna*

Frequency range	2.4 to 2.83 GHz
Gain	5.2 dBi
Polarization	Vertical
H-plane	Omnidirectional
E-plane	25 degrees
Antenna connector type	RP-TNC
*This connector type is covered in the next section.	

Antenna Connectors and Hardware

Cisco uses a connector called the *RP-TNC*, which stands for *Reverse-Polarity Threaded Neill-Concelman*, named for its inventor. Another type that Cisco uses is the *N connector*, invented in the 1940s by Paul Neill at Bell Labs. Different connecters are required because of government regulations. The vendor has to ensure that you use the right antenna with the right product. This doesn't mean that people can't make an antenna, but by using vendor-designed antennas, you can be sure that you are within government guidelines for EIRP.

Other vendors use connectors such as the Subminiature version A (SMA) and its variants, the RP-SMA and SMA-RS. You also find MC and MMCX connectors on PCMCIA cards. There are a number of others; these are only a few. The important thing, though, is that both sides need to match the type.

If the antenna isn't a direct connect, you need to get a cable from the vendor. When you add a cable between the radio and the antenna, you also add loss. The specific vendor documentation should tell you how much loss.

Attenuators

If custom cabling is used, you can end up with too much signal, thus causing bleedover into other networks. You can use an *attenuator* to reduce the signal. You would place an attenuator between the radio and the antenna.

Amplifiers

If you add a cable between an antenna and its radio, you add loss. To make up for this loss, you add gain. However, you may not be able to add enough gain to compensate. In this scenario, you add an *amplifier* between the AP and antenna to strengthen the signal. This method is called an active amplifier because it strengthens the antenna.

Lightning Arrestors

One of the types of antennas discussed in this chapter is a parabolic dish. These antennas offer point-to-point capability between two networks that are far away. This calls for mounting the antenna outdoors, usually on a roof. The antenna cables back to a radio on a bridge or AP and from there makes its way back to the common distribution. In other words, the parabolic dish provides a path back to your wired LAN. So, logically, if a lightning bolt were to hit the antenna or an access point, it could transfer its energy back along the copper cable. This would result in damage to your entire wired LAN as well.

The good news is that you can protect against this by using a *lightning arrestor*. The Cisco Aironet Lightning Arrestor, illustrated in Figure 5-26, prevents surges from reaching the RF equipment by its shunting effect.

Surges are limited to less than 50 volts in about 100 nanoseconds. Because a typical lightning surge is 2 microseconds, this should provide adequate protection from indirect strikes. Lightning arrestors do not try to stop direct strikes. They also require a ground, as shown in Figure 5-26.

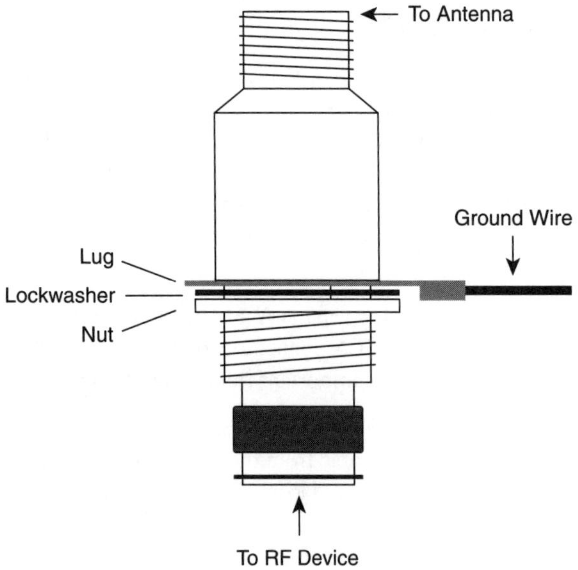

Figure 5-26   *Lightning Arrestor*

Splitters

The final topic of this chapter is installing a *splitter*. Splitters are used mainly in outdoor wireless deployments to split in two a signal coming from a cable and to send it in two directions. You could also use it to receive a signal coming from one direction and forward it through another antenna, connected to the same access point, toward another direction. Although this technique can be useful, the drawback is that it greatly reduces the range and throughput by about 50 percent.

Exam Preparation Tasks

Review All the Key Topics

Review the most important topics from this chapter, denoted with the Key Topic icon. Table 5-9 lists these key topics and the page number where each one can be found.

Table 5-9 *Key Topics for Chapter 5*

Key Topic Item	Description	Page Number
Figure 5-5	H-plane and E-plane	76
Figure 5-6	2.14-dBi dipole	76
Figure 5-9	effect of adding gain	77
Figure 5-10	H-plane and E-plane after adding gain	78
Table 5-2	AIR-ANT1728 statistics	76
Table 5-3	AIR-ANT2506	78
Table 5-4	AIR-ANT24120	79
Table 5-5	AIR-ANT2485P-R	81
Figure 5-17	Radiation pattern of a yagi	83
Table 5-6	AIR-ANT1949 yagi	84
Table 5-7	AIR-ANT3338 parabolic dish antenna	86
Table 5-8	AIR-ANT3213 antenna	88
Figure 5-26	Lightning arrestor	90

Complete the Tables and Lists from Memory

Print a copy of Appendix B, "Memory Tables," (found on the CD) or at least the section for this chapter, and complete the tables and lists from memory. Appendix C, "Memory Tables Answer Key," also on the CD, includes completed tables and lists so that you can check your work.

Definition of Key Terms

Define the following key terms from this chapter, and check your answers in the Glossary:

polarity, diversity vertical polarization, horizontal polarization, circular polarization, omnidirectional antenna, horizontal (H) plane, azimuth, elevation (E) plane, one-floor concept, dipole, radiation pattern, isotropic radiator, directional antenna, rubber duck, Yagi-Uda, parabolic dish, dual-patch "omnidirectional," Reverse-Polarity Threaded Neill-Concelman (RP-TNC), N connector, attenuator, amplifier, lightning arrestor, splitter

References in This Chapter

Cisco Systems, "Cisco Aironet Antennas and Accessories Reference Guide," http://tinyurl.com/2v2dp2

This chapter covers the following subjects:

The 802.11 Protocol Family Overview: A brief overview of the 802.11 family of WLAN protocols.

The Original 802.11 Protocol: A look at the original 802.11 protocol.

The 802.11b Protocol: A look at the 802.11b protocol.

The 802.11g Protocol: A look at the 802.11g protocol and how it operates with 802.11b clients.

The 802.11a Protocol: A look at the 802.11a protocol.

The 802.11n Protocol: A look at the 802.11n draft standard.

CHAPTER 6

Overview of the 802.11 WLAN Protocols

The wireless space consists of numerous protocols. Specifically in the WLAN area, the Institute of Engineers Electrical and Electronic Engineers (IEEE) has created several protocols within the 802.11 category to facilitate the networking process. These protocols define the data rates, the modulation techniques, and more. An understanding of these protocols is essential for any administrator of wireless networks.

In this chapter, you will learn about the 802.11 family of protocols, including 802.11, 802.11a, b, and g. In addition, you will gain an introduction to the 802.11n draft standard.

You should do the "Do I Know This Already?" quiz first. If you score 80 percent or higher, you might want to skip to the section "Exam Preparation Tasks." If you score below 80 percent, you should spend the time reviewing the chapter. Refer to Appendix A, "Answers to the 'Do I Know This Already?' Quizzes" to confirm your answers.

"Do I Know This Already?" Quiz

The "Do I Know This Already?" quiz helps you determine your level of knowledge of this chapter's topics before you begin. Table 6-1 details the major topics discussed in this chapter and their corresponding quiz questions.

Table 6-1 *"Do I Know This Already?" Section-to-Question Mapping*

Foundation Topics Section	Questions
The 802.11 Protocol Family Overview	1
The Original 802.11	2–5
The 802.11b Protocol	6–10
The 802.11g Protocol	11–14
The 802.11a Protocol	16–20
The 802.11n Protocol	21–25

1. What organization standardizes the 802.11 set of protocols?

   a. IANA

   b. IEEE

   c. FCC

   d. ETSI

2. What is the maximum data rate that the original 802.11 protocol supports?

   a. 1 Mbps

   b. 5 Mbps

   c. 2 Mbps

   d. 3 Mbps

3. The original 802.11 protocol supported which two RF technologies? (Choose two.)

   a. FHSS

   b. CDMA

   c. IETF

   d. DSSS

4. The original 802.11 protocol operates in which frequency range?

   a. 2.0 GHz

   b. 900 MHz

   c. 5.0 GHz

   d. 2.4 GHz

5. The original 802.11 protocol operates in the ISM bands. True or false?

   a. True

   b. False

6. 802.11b operates on which frequency range?

   a. 2.0 GHz

   b. 900 MHz

   c. 5.0 GHz

   d. 2.4 GHz

7. 802.11b has how many nonoverlapping channels?

   a. 2

   b. 3

   c. 4

   d. 8

8. Which of the following modulation techniques are used by 802.11b? (Choose all that apply.)

    a. DBPSK

    b. 16-QAM

    c. DQPSK

    d. 64-QAM

9. What coding method is used by 802.11b? (Choose all that apply.)

    a. Barker 11

    b. CCK

    c. Barker 8

    d. QAM-CCK

10. Which 802.11b channels do not overlap? (Choose all that apply.)

    a. 1

    b. 3

    c. 6

    d. 11

11. What modulation technique is used by the 802.11g protocol? (Choose all that apply.)

    a. DBPSK

    b. DQPSK

    c. QAM

    d. Barker

12. What is the maximum data rate that the 802.11g protocol supports?

    a. 22 Mbps

    b. 48 Mbps

    c. 54 Mbps

    d. 90 Mbps

13. When no 802.11b clients are in an 802.11b/g cell, what information will be in the AP beacon?

    a. NON_ERP present: yes; Use Protection: no

    b. NON_ERP present: no; Use Protection: yes

    c. NON_ERP present: yes; Use Protection: yes

    d. NON_ERP present: no; Use Protection: no

14. What are two protection methods used by 802.11g clients when an 802.11b client is in the cell? (Choose two.)

    a. RTS/CTS

    b. LMI

    c. CTS to self

    d. RTS to self

15. The 802.11a protocol is backward compatible only with 802.11g because they support the same maximum data rates. True or false?

    a. True

    b. False

16. An 802.11a client must support which data rates?

    a. 6, 12, 24 Mbps

    b. 11, 24, 54 Mbps

    c. 6, 9, 12, 18, 24, 36, 48, 54 Mbps

    d. 6, 11, 24, 48 Mbps

17. The 802.11a protocol operates in which frequency spectrum?

    a. 2.0 GHz

    b. 900 MHz

    c. 5.0 GHz

    d. 2.4 GHz

18. Which is not a valid modulation technique for 802.11a?

    a. BPSK

    b. QPSK

    c. Barker 11

    d. QAM

19. 802.11a uses the UNII-1, UNII-2, and UNII-3 bands. Which bands are usable without a license in Europe? (Choose all that apply.)

    a. UNII-1

    b. UNII-2

    c. UNII-3

    d. UNII-4.1

20. The FCC and ETSI have imposed what requirements for use in the UNII-2 and UNII-3 bands? (Choose all that apply.)

   a. DFC

   b. TPC

   c. CSMA/CA

   d. MIMO

21. 802.11n supports multiple antennas using what technology?

   a. MIMO

   b. MAO

   c. Multi-scan antenna output

   d. Spatial coding

22. What type of multiplexing does 802.11n use?

   a. Spatial

   b. OFDM

   c. DSSS

   d. FHSS

23. What task does TxBF accomplish in 802.11n networks?

   a. The signal is sent over multiple transmit antennas, improving performance at the receiver.

   b. The signal increases in gain to accomplish greater distances.

   c. The signal is spread across multiple channels and then re-created at the receiver to negate interference issues on sidebands.

   d. The signal is bonded on a 40-MHz channel, giving you more bandwidth.

24. How does 802.11n improve the throughput with acknowledgments?

   a. It uses a 1-for-1 acknowledgment option; 1 sent = 1 acknowledged.

   b. It does not use acknowledgments.

   c. It uses block acknowledgments.

   d. It uses a 2-to-1 ratio of sent frames to acknowledgments.

25. A device that has two transmit antennas and two receive antennas is referred to as which of the following?

   a. Dual TxRx

   b. 2X2

   c. 2x

   d. A double

Foundation Topics

The 802.11 Protocol Family Overview

The IEEE helps to standardize wireless protocols. Those that you must be familiar with for the CCNA Wireless Exam are the 802.11 a/b/g and n protocols. These four IEEE standards define the wireless family that is used in almost all wireless LANS today. The standardization of wireless networking started with the original 802.11 protocol in 1997, and each protocol thereafter has simply added to the benefit of wireless technologies. This chapter looks at the 802.11 protocol families, their history, and how they operate. The 802.11 protocols encompass the 2.4-GHz and 5-GHz range.

The Original 802.11 Protocol

The original 802.11 protocol was where wireless LANs find there beginnings. It is rare to find this original protocol in new hardware today, probably because it only operates at 1 and 2 Mbps. The 802.11 standard describes frequency-hopping spread spectrum (FHSS), which operates only at 1 and 2 Mbps. The standard also describes direct sequence spread spectrum (DSSS), which operates only at 1 and 2 Mbps. If a client operates at any other data rate, it is considered non-802.11 compliant, even if it can use the 1- and 2-Mbps rates.

Table 6-2 highlights the characteristics of the original 802.11 protocol.

Key Topic

Table 6-2 *The 802.11 Protocol*

Ratified	1997
RF Technology	FHSS and DSSS
Frequency Spectrum	2.4-GHz

The original 802.11 protocol falls within the industry, scientific, and medical (ISM) bands and operates only in the 2.4-GHz range. The 2.4-GHz range has up to 14 channels depending on the country you are in. In the United States, the FCC allows channels 1 through 11 to be used. This gives you 3 nonoverlapping channels: 1, 6, and 11. This is important because you do not want to have APs and clients operating on the same channel placed near each other for interference reasons.

The 802.11b Protocol

802.11b is a supplement to the 802.11 protocol. To get an better feel for how the 802.11 protocols progressed, understand that technology moves faster than the standards do. 802.11 was quickly outgrown because wired networks offered 10 Mbps versus the 1 and 2 Mbps of 802.11. Vendors developed methods of achieving higher data rates. The danger in vendor-designed protocols, of course, is *interoperability*. The job of the IEEE was simply to define a standard that all vendors could follow based on the proprietary implementations that they were using.

802.11b offers higher data rates—up to 11 Mbps—with backward compatibility at 1 and 2 Mbps. At 1 and 2 Mbps, the same coding and modulation as 802.11 is used. When operating at the new speeds—5.5 Mbps and 11 Mbps—a different modulation and coding is used. 802.11 uses Barker 11 coding, as covered in Chapter 1, "Introduction to Wireless Networking Concepts," and 802.11b uses complementary code keying (CCK) for coding. For modulation, 802.11 uses differential binary phase-shift keying (DBPSK), whereas 802.11b uses differential quadrature phase-shift keying (DQPSK). The result is more data sent in the same period.

802.11b was ratified in September 1999. The United States has 11 channels, the same as 802.11. In Europe, the ETSI defines 13 channels, and Japan has 14. 802.11b allows dynamic rate shifting (DRS) to enable clients to shift rates to lower rates as they travel farther away from an AP and higher rates as they get closer to an AP. Today, 802.11b is the most popular and most widely deployed wireless standard. Table 6-3 gives some basic information on the 802.11b standard.

Table 6-3   *The 802.11b Protocol*

Ratified	1999
RF Technology	DSSS
Frequency Spectrum	2.4-GHz
Coding	Barker 11 and CCK
Modulation	DBPSK and DQPSK
Data Rates	1, 2, 5.5, 11 Mbps
Nonoverlapping Channels	1, 6, 11

Key Topic

The 802.11g Protocol

The IEEE ratified 802.11g in June 2003. In addition to the four data rates of 802.11b, it added eight more. The maximum data rate of 54 Mbps places 802.11g in the same speed range as 802.11a; however, it remains in the 2.4-Ghz frequency range. On the lower end, 802.11g is still compatible with 802.11b, using the same modulation and coding as 802.11b for the 1-, 2-, 5.5-, and 11-Mbps rates. To achieve the higher data rates, 802.11g uses orthogonal frequency division multiplexing (OFDM) for modulation. OFDM is the same modulation that 802.11a uses.

There are still only three nonoverlapping channels. With OFDM, you must be careful about power outputs; the power needs to be reduced to handle the peaks in the modulation technique and still fall within governmental regulations. Table 6-4 shows some details about 802.11g.

Key Topic

Table 6-4 *The 802.11g Protocol*

Ratified	June 2003
RF Technology	DSSS and OFDM
Frequency Spectrum	2.4 GHz
Coding	Barker 11 and CCK
Modulation	DBPSK and DQPSK
Data Rates	1, 2, 5.5, 11 Mbps with DSSS 6, 9, 12, 18, 24, 36, 48, 54 Mbps with OFDM
Nonoverlapping Channels	1, 6, 11

How 802.11g Interacts with 802.11b

One interesting point about 802.11g is that, although it is backward compatible with 802.11b clients, you probably do not want it to be because if you must support 802.11b clients, the entire cell suffers. In fact, if the average bandwidth is 22 Mbps in an 802.11g cell and an 802.11b client shows up, the cell performance could degrade. This degradation in performance is because 802.11b clients do not understand OFDM. If an 802.11b client sends when an 802.11g client is sending, a collision will occur, and both clients will have to resend.

However, protection mechanisms are built in. To understand how this protection works, examine Figure 6-1.

Beacon:
Non-ERP Present: No
Use Protection: No

Client A
802.11g

802.11g
Access Point

Client B
802.11g

Figure 6-1 *802.11g Cell with No 802.11b Clients*

Assume that initially 802.11b clients do not exist. The default behavior of an AP is to send beacons that include information about the AP and the wireless cell. Without 802.11b clients, the AP sends the following information in a beacon:

NON_ERP present: no

Use Protection: no

ERP is Extended Rate Physical. These are devices that have extended data rates. In other words, NON_ERP is talking about 802.11b clients. If they were ERP, that would support the higher data rates, making them 802.11g clients.

Now, going back to Figure 6-1 with no 802.11b clients, the AP tells everyone that 802.11b clients are unavailable and that they do not need to use protection mechanisms.

After an 802.11b client associates with the AP, things change. In Figure 6-2, the AP alerts the rest of the network about the NON_ERP client. This is done in the beacon that the AP sends.

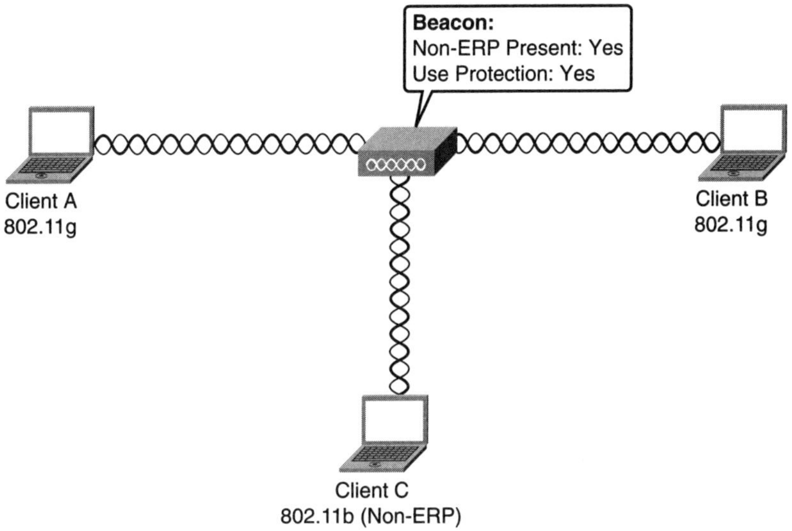

Figure 6-2   *802.11g Cell with an 802.11b Client*

Now that the cell knows about the 802.11b clients, the way that data is sent within the cell changes. When an 802.11g client sends a frame, it first must warn the 802.11b clients by sending a request to send (RTS) message at 802.11b speed so the 802.11b clients can hear and understand it. The RTS is not a broadcast as you might think, but rather a unicast that is sent to the recipient of the frame that the 802.11g client wants to send to. The recipient then responds with a clear to send (CTS) at 802.11b speed. Figure 6-3 illustrates this process.

In Step 1, the client knows that the 802.11b client is present; therefore, before sending, it issues an RTS at 802.11b speeds.

In Figure 6-4, the 802.11b client hears the RTS (Step 2), which includes the duration, and it waits until the duration is over before sending its data even though it cannot hear the 802.11g data that will be sent during the duration. Client B also hears the RTS and decides to send a CTS (Step 3).

In Step 4, shown in Figure 6-5, Client B sends a CTS back to Client A. Client C hears the CTS in Step 5.

In Step 6, Figure 6-6, Client A sends data to Client B at 802.11g speeds. The 802.11b client (Client C) cannot hear the data that it perceived as noise, but it still waits the duration seen in the RTS/CTS before sending data.

This protection mechanism works well because the 802.11b client can hear the RTS and the CTS no matter which client he is closest to. Another protection mechanism exists,

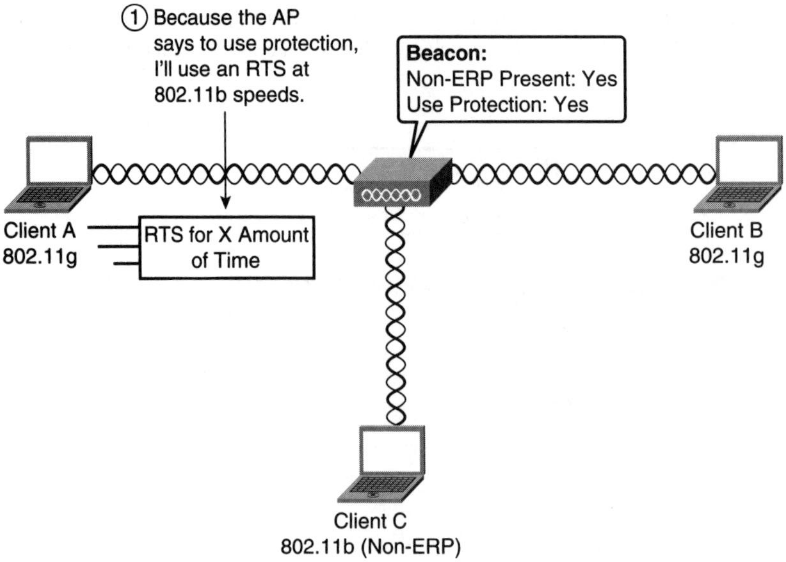

Figure 6-3   *802.11g Cell Using Protection: Part 1*

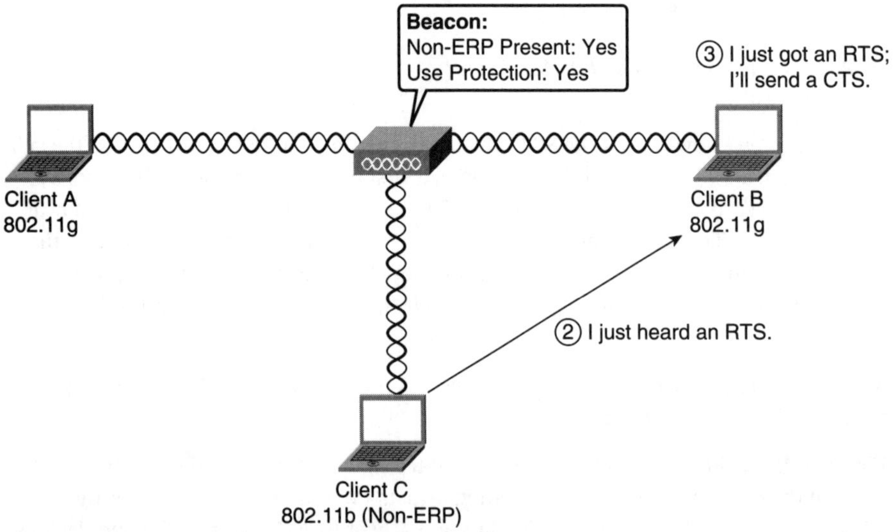

Figure 6-4   *802.11g Cell Using Protection: Part 2*

clear to send to self (CTS to self), but this is not a preferred method because a client that is not close to the sender might not hear the CTS to self.

Another bad side effect of 802.11b clients in an 802.11g cell is sort of a domino effect. As one AP advertises:

NON_ERP present: yes

Use Protection: yes

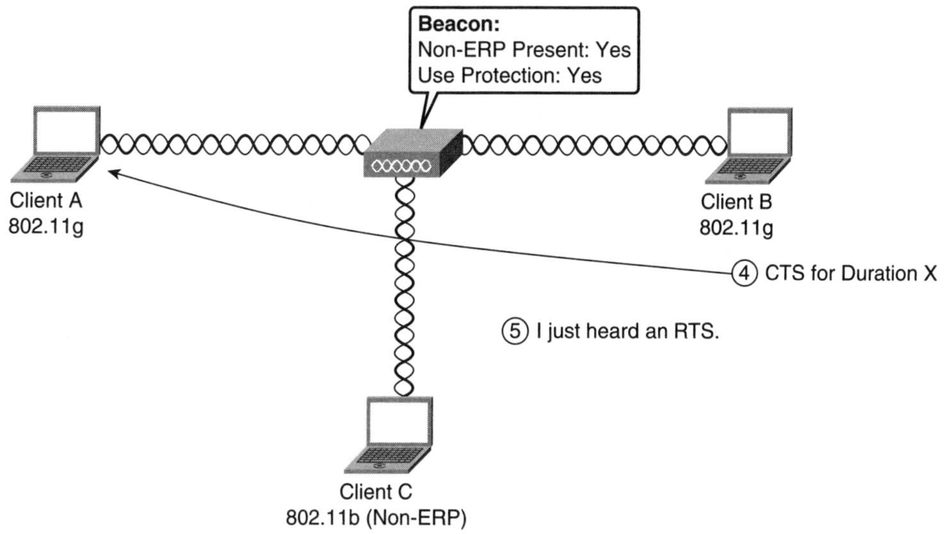

Figure 6-5 *802.11g Cell Using Protection: Part 3*

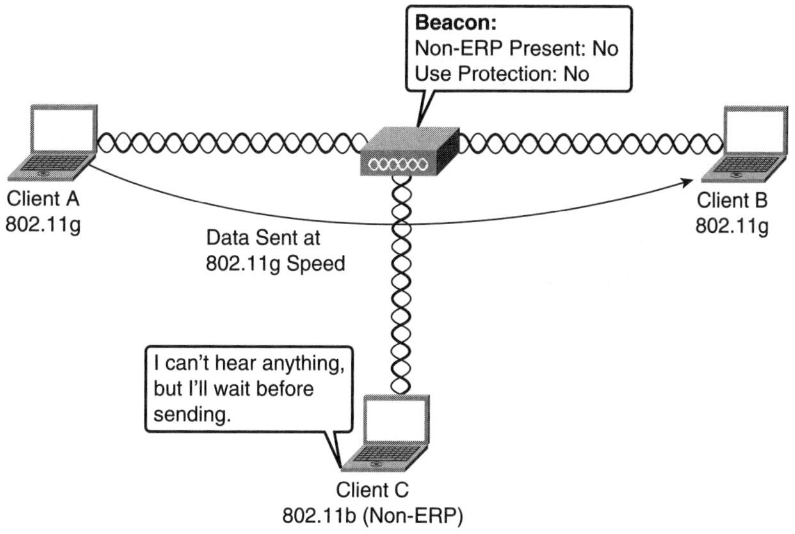

Figure 6-6 *802.11g Cell Using Protection: Part 4*

Nearby APs that hear this beacon start to advertise:

NON_ERP present: no

Use Protection: yes

The nearby cell advertises NON_ERP present to indicate that it did not hear NON_ERP devices, yet it advertises "Use Protection: yes" to be safe. This in effect forces the cell to use protection even without 802.11b clients in that particular cell, thus degrading performance for everyone in the cell. This is why APs have the option to use 802.11g only.

The 802.11a Protocol

802.11a was ratified in 1999 and operates in the 5-GHz frequency range. This makes it incompatible with 802.11, 802.11b, and 802.11g, while avoiding interference from these devices in addition to microwaves, Bluetooth devices, and cordless phones. 802.11a had late-market adoption, so it is not as widely deployed as the 802.11b and g protocols.

Another difference is that 802.11a supports anywhere from 12 to 23 nonoverlapping channels as opposed to the 3 nonoverlapping channels in 802.11b/g. Because OFDM is used, subchannels can overlap. 802.11a requires that the data rates of 6, 12, and 24 Mbps be supported but allows for data rates up to 54 Mbps.

Table 6-5 shows some details on the 802.11a standard.

Table 6-5   *The 802.11a Protocol*

Ratified	1999
RF Technology	OFDM
Frequency Spectrum	5.0 GHz
Coding	Convolution Coding
Modulation	BPSK, QPSK, 16-QAM, 64-QAM depending on the subcarrier.
Data Rates	6, 9, 12, 18, 24, 36, 48, 54 Mbps with OFDM
Nonoverlapping Channels	Each band has a 4; the middle 8 are used with 52 subcarriers on each channel.

Key Topic

*Convolution coding is a form of error correction in which redundant information analogous to a parity bit in a file system is added to the data. The error correction is calculated across all the subcarriers, so if narrowband interference corrupts data on one subcarrier, the receiver can reconstruct that data using the convolution coding on another subcarrier.[1]

The rules under ETSI specifications are a little different. ETSI allows 19 channels and requires that dynamic frequency control (DFC) and transmit power control (TPC) be used.

What makes 802.11a unique is the way the 5-GHz frequency band is divided into multiple parts. These parts, the Unlicensed National Information Infrastructure (UNII), were designed for different uses. UNII-1 was designed for indoor use with a permanent antenna. UNII-2 was designed for indoor or outdoor use with an external antenna, and UNII-3 was designed for outdoor bridges and external antennas.

The FCC revised the use of the frequency in 2004 by adding channels and requiring compliance of DFC and TPC to avoid radar. The revision also allows all three parts of the UNII to be used indoors. This is not the case with ETSI, however, because it does not allow unlicensed use of UNII-3.

Table 6-6 shows the frequency ranges of each of the UNII bands.

Table 6-6 *The UNII Frequency Bands*

Band	Frequency	Use
UNII-1	5.15–5.25 GHz (UNII Indoor)	FCC allows indoor and outdoor use.
UNII-2	5.25–5.35 GHz (UNII Low)	Outdoor/indoor with DFC and TPC
UNII-3	5.725–5.825 GHz (U-NII/ISM)	FCC allows indoor and outdoor use.
		ETSI does not allow unlicensed use.

In the 802.11a spectrum, the higher-band channels are 30 MHz apart. This includes UNII-2 and above. The lower bands are 20 MHz apart.

802.11a Power Requirements

Table 6-7 details the rules for power as stated by the FCC in the United States. The "Output Power Not to Exceed" column in the table reflects the output power when using an omnidirectional antenna with 6-dBi gain.

Table 6-7 *FCC Regulations on Output and EIRP for UNII*

Band	Output Power Not to Exceed	EIRP Maximum
UNII-1	50 mW	22 dBm
UNII-2	250 mW	29 dBm
UNII-2 Extended	1 W	36 dBm
UNII-3	1W	36 dBm

As you can see from the table, UNII-1 is not to exceed 50 mW of output power or 22 dBm EIRP. UNII-2 is not to exceed 250 mW of output power and 29 dBm EIRP, whereas the extended UNII-2 and UNII-3 should be no more than 1 Watt of output power and 36 dBm EIRP. The FCC states that the responsibility of staying within output power regulations for wireless networks falls on the operator. For this reason, understanding the EIRP maximum values will help keep you within the guidelines.

The ETSI, of course, has its own rules, as seen in Table 6-8.

Table 6-8 *ETSI Regulations on Output and EIRP for UNII* *(continued)*

Band	Output Power Not to Exceed	EIRP Maximum
UNII-1	200 mW	23 dBm
UNII-2	200 mW	23 dBm

continues

Table 6-8 *ETSI Regulations on Output and EIRP for UNII*   *(continued)*

Band	Output Power Not to Exceed	EIRP Maximum
UNII-2 Extended	1 W	30 dBm
UNII-3	Licensed use only	—

The IEEE rules are a bit more strict but should keep you within the federal regulations.

The 802.11n Protocol

802.11n is currently a draft standard. Again, technology has progressed more rapidly than the standards, because vendors are already shipping 802.11n APs and clients. What makes 802.11n special is that in a pure 802.11n environment, you can get speeds up to 300 Mbps, but most documentation says it will provide 100 Mbps. This is probably because the expectation is that other 802.11 clients will be present. 802.11n is, in fact, backward compatible with 802.11b/g and a.

The backward compatibility and speed capability of 802.11n come from its use of multiple antennas and a technology called Multiple-Input, Multiple-Output (MIMO). MIMO, pronounced Mee-Moh, uses different antennas to send and receive, thus increasing throughput and accomplishing more of a full duplex operation.

MIMO comes in three types:

■ Precoding

■ Spatial multiplexing

■ Diversity coding

Precoding is a function that takes advantage of multiple antennas and the multipath issue that was discussed in Chapter 3, "WLAN RF Principles." 802.11n uses transmit beamforming (TxBF), which is a technique that is used when more than one transmit antenna exists where the signal is coordinated and sent from each antenna so that the signal at the receiver is dramatically improved, even if it is far from the sender. This technique is something that you would use when the receiver has only a single antenna and is not moving. If the receiver is moving, then the reflection characteristics change, and the beamforming can no longer be coordinated. This coordination is called channel state information (CSI).

Spatial multiplexing takes a signal, splits it into several lower rate streams, and then sends each one out of different antennas. Each one of the lower rate streams are sent on the same frequency. The number of streams is limited to the lowest number of antennas on either the transmitter or the receiver. If an AP has four antennas and a client has two, you are limited to two.

Currently, the Wi-Fi Alliance is certifying 802.11n devices even though they are still in draft status. The Wi-FI Alliance is doing this using the interim IEEE 802.11n draft 2.0.

802.11n and the other 802.11 protocol standards are different in other ways, too. For example, at the physical layer, the way a signal is sent considers reflections and interferences an advantage instead of a problem. Another way that throughput is increased is by aggregation of channels. In 802.11n, two channels are aggregated to increase throughput. 802.11n uses 20-MHz and 40-MHz channels. The 40-MHz channels in 802.11n are actually two 20-MHz channels that are adjacent to each other and bonded.

Clients in 802.11n environments are pretty complex, so 802.11n is combined with OFDM. This enables the use of more subcarriers that range from 48 to 52.

With 802.11n, you can get up to 32 data rates.

Sending Frames

For the allocated time to send frames, only CTS to self is used with 802.11n; the RTS/CTS that was discussed earlier in this chapter is not used.

Another feature of 802.11n that makes it much more efficient is the way it uses block acknowledgments as opposed to acknowledging each unicast packet like the other 802.11 protocols do. A block acknowledgment works by sending a number of frames before having them acknowledged. This is similar to the way TCP works.

Another aspect of sending requires knowledge of how frames are sent in a normal 802.11 a/b/g world. You will learn more about this in Chapter 7, "Wireless Traffic Flow and AP Discovery," but the following is a quick look:

> Each sending station must wait until a frame is sent before sending the next frame; this is called distributed interframe space (DIFS).

This DIFS can cause more overhead than necessary. 802.11n improves on this DIFS mechanism by using a smaller interframe space called reduced interframe space (RIFS). This reduces delay and overhead.

Antenna Considerations

The number of antennas that the sender and the receiver have can differ. Here is how they work.

If a transmitter can emit over three antennas, it has three data streams. If it can receive over three antennas, it has three receive chains. In documentation, this is called a 3×3. Two receive chains and two data streams is called a 2×2.

This is important because the Cisco 1250 AP is a 2×3 device. If you have a laptop that is a 2×2, you can start to see how this takes on meaning. When using special multiplexing, you are limited to the same number of streams as the lowest number of antennas. In this scenario, you would have two streams.

Finally, note that even if you do not have 802.11n clients, you can expect to see about a 30 percent improvement, based on these features.

Exam Preparation Tasks

Review All Key Concepts

Review the most important topics from this chapter, noted with the Key Topics icon in the outer margin of the page. Table 6-9 lists a reference of these key topics and the page number where you can find each one.

Table 6-9   *Key Topics for Chapter 6*

Key Topic Item	Description	Page Number
Table 6-2	The 802.11 protocol	100
Table 6-3	The 802.11b protocol	101
Table 6-4	The 802.11g protocol	102
Table 6-5	The 802.11a protocol	106
Table 6-6	The UNII frequency bands	107

Complete the Tables and Lists from Memory

Print a copy of Appendix B, "Memory Tables" (found on the CD) or at least the section for this chapter, and complete the tables and lists from memory. Appendix C, "Memory Tables Answer Key," also on the CD, includes completed tables and lists to check your work.

Definition of Key Terms

Define the following key terms from this chapter, and check your answers in the Glossary:

FHSS, DSSS, ISM, OFDM, beacons, ERP, RTS/CTS, CTS to self, DFC, TPC, MIMO, precoding, transmit beamforming, spatial multiplexing, channel state information, block acknowledgments, DIFS, RIFS

End Notes

[1]CWNA Certified Wireless Network Administrator; Official Study Guide, Planet 3 Wireless, McGraw Hill/Osborne 2005

This chapter covers the following subjects:

Wireless Frame Transmission: A discussion of how frames are transmitted on a wireless LAN.

Wireless Frame Headers: A look at the headers used in wireless transmissions.

Frame Types: Putting together how the frame types are used in managing and connecting to a network.

A Wireless Connection: A look at a wireless connection.

CHAPTER 7

Wireless Traffic Flow and AP Discovery

It is not likely that in your everyday activity you will be following the flow of traffic. At least the hope is that you will not have to. On occasion, however, you will need to analyze the flow of traffic in troubleshooting network issues. For this reason and just so that you have a complete understanding of what is involved in wireless transmissions, you need to understand wireless traffic flow and the process of discovering an AP. In this chapter, you will learn how a client finds an AP, associates, and sends traffic.

You should do the "Do I Know This Already?" quiz first. If you score 80 percent or higher, you may want to skip to the section "Exam Preparation Tasks." If you score below 80 percent, you should spend the time reviewing the entire chapter. Refer to Appendix A, "Answers to the 'Do I Know This Already?' Quizzes" to confirm your answers.

"Do I Know This Already?" Quiz

The "Do I Know This Already?" quiz helps you determine your level of knowledge of this chapter's topics before you begin. Table 7-1 details the major topics discussed in this chapter and their corresponding quiz questions.

Table 7-1 *"Do I Know This Already?" Section-to-Question Mapping*

Foundation Topics Section	Questions
Wireless Frame Transmission	1–5
Wireless Frame Headers	6–7
Frame Types	8–12

1. What are the three frame types seen in a wireless LAN? (Choose three.)

   a. Management

   b. Control

   c. Data

   d. Contention

2. What type of frame is used for acknowledging receipt of data?

   a. Control

   b. Reply

   c. Null

   d. Management

3. What frame type is used to send beacons?

   a. Control

   b. Management

   c. Informational

   d. Data

4. To determine if the medium is in use, which of the following are used? (Choose all that apply.)

   a. CCA

   b. CAS

   c. VCA

   d. VCS

5. Which interframe space is used for quickly sending a frame?

   a. UIFS

   b. DIFS

   c. SIFS

   d. PIFS

6. How many MAC addresses can be present in a wireless header?

   a. 1

   b. 2

   c. 3

   d. 4

7. Which of the following is a management frame type?

   a. Probe response

   b. ACK

   c. RTS

   d. Null function

8. Beacons contain information to assist clients in accessing the network. Which of the following is *not* in a beacon?

   a. Beacon interval

   b. Capability information

   c. A reference time for the cell

   d. The WEP passphrase

9. A client that connects by hearing a beacon is said to use what type of scanning?

   a. Passive

   b. Classic

   c. Active

   d. Fast

10. A client that sends a probe request is said to use what type of scanning?

   a. Preemptive

   b. Dynamic

   c. Passive

   d. Active

11. A client that sends a deauthentication message must reauthenticate when it returns to the cell. True or false?

   a. True

   b. False

12. A client that sends a disassociation message must reauthenticate when it returns to the cell. True or false?

   a. True

   b. False

Foundation Topics

Wireless Frame Transmission

When people talk about wireless networks, they often say that they are just like wired 802.3 LANs. This is actually incorrect, aside from the fact that they use MAC addresses. Wireless LANs use the 802.11 frame structure, and you can encounter multiple types of frames. To get a better understanding, you can begin by learning the three types of wireless frames. Once you are familiar with the three types of wireless frames, you can further your knowledge by taking a deeper look at interframe spacing (IFS) and why it is necessary.

Wireless Frame Types

Wireless LANs come in three frame types:

- **Management frames:** Used for joining and leaving a wireless cell. Management frame types include association request, association response, and reassociation request, just to name a few. (See Table 7-2 for a complete list.)

- **Control frames:** Used to acknowledge when data frames are received.

- **Data frames:** Frames that contain data.

Now that you have an idea of what frames are used, it is helpful to see how these frames are sent. For this, you need to understand a few more terms that might be new to you. Because all the terms meld together to some degree, they are explained in context throughout the next section.

Sending a Frame

Recall that wireless networks are half-duplex networks. If more than one device were to send at the same time, a collision would result. If a collision occurs, the data from both senders would be unreadable and would need to be resent. This is a waste of time and resources. To overcome this issue, wireless networks use multiple steps to access the network. Wireless LANs use carrier sense multiple access collision avoidance (CSMA/CA), which is similar to the way 802.3 LANs work. The *carrier sense* part means that a station has to determine if anyone else is sending. This is done with clear channel assessment (CCA), and what it means is that you listen. You can, however, run into an issue where two devices cannot hear each other. This is called the hidden node problem. This issue is overcome using virtual carrier sense (VCS). The medium is not considered available until both the physical and virtual carrier report that it is clear.

Each station must also observe IFS. IFS is a period that a station has to wait before it can send. Not only does IFS ensure that the medium is clear, but it ensures that frames are not sent so close together that they are misinterpreted. The types of IFS periods are as follows:

- **Short interframe space (SIFS):** For higher priority and used for ACKs, among other things

- **Point-coordination interframe space (PIFS):** Used when an AP is going to control the network

- **Distributed-coordination interframe space (DIFS):** Used for data frames and is the normal spacing between frames

Each of these has a specific purpose as defined by the IEEE.

SIFS is used when you must send a frame quickly. For example, when a data frame is sent and must be acknowledged (ACK), the ACK should be sent before another station sends other data. Data frames use DIFS. The time value of DIFS is longer than SIFS, so the SIFS would preempt DIFS because it has a higher priority.

Figure 7-1 illustrates the transmission of a frame. In the figure, Station A wants to send a frame. As the process goes, both the physical and virtual carrier need to be free. This means the client has to listen. To listen, the client chooses a random number and begins a countdown process, called a *backoff timer*. The speed at which the countdown occurs is called a *slottime* and is different for 802.11a, b, and g.

① Select a random timer (29), 28, 27, 26....

② Listen during countdown.

④ I was at 18; add 45 to that and continue (63, 62, 61...).

Figure 7-1 *Sending a Frame: Part 1*

It works like this:

1. Station A selects the random timer value of 29.

2. Station A starts counting at 29, 28, 27, 26, and so on. While Station A is counting down, it is also listening for whether anyone else is sending a frame.

3. When the timer is at 18, Station B sends a frame, having a duration value in the header of 45.

4. The duration of 45 that is in the header of the frame sent by Station B is called a *network allocation vector (NAV)* and is a reservation of the medium that includes the amount of time to send its frame, wait for the SIFS, and then receive an ACK from the AP.

5. Station A adds 45 to the 18 that is left and continues counting down, 63, 62, 61, and so on. The total time that Station A waits before sending is called the *contention window*.

6. After the timer on Station A reaches 0, it can send its frame as illustrated in Figure 7-2. At this point, the medium should be clear.

If Station A sends but fails, it resets the backoff timer to a new random number and counts down again. The backoff timer gets larger as the frames fail in transmission. For example, the initial timer can be any number between 0 and 31. After the first failure, it jumps to any number between 0 and 127. It doubles for the next failure, then again, then again.

This entire process is known as the *distributed coordination function* (DCF). This simply means that each station is responsible for coordinating the sending of its data. The alternative to DCF is *point coordination function (PCF)*, which means the AP is responsible for coordination of data transmission.

Figure 7-2   *Sending a Frame: Part 2*

If the frame is successful, an ACK must be sent. The ACK uses the SIFS timer value to make sure it is sent quickly. Some amount of silence between frames is natural. The SIFS is the shortest period of silence. The NAV reserves this time. A normal silence time is the DIFS. Again, the ACK uses SIFS because you want it to be sent immediately. The station that sends the ACK waits for the SIFS and then ACKs with the duration of 0. This is how the end of the transmission is indicated.

Wireless Frame Headers

Figure 7-3 shows a wireless frame. Each of the fields has been expanded so you can see it more clearly. It is beneficial to understand these fields and how they play a part in the sending and receiving of wireless frames.

```
▶ Frame 217 (66 bytes on wire, 66 bytes captured)
▼ IEEE 802.11 Data, Flags: ....R.F.
     Type/Subtype: Data (0x20)
   ▼ Frame Control: 0x0A08 (Normal)
        Version: 0
        Type: Data frame (2)
        Subtype: 0
      ▼ Flags: 0xA
           DS status: Frame from DS to a STA via AP(To DS: 0 From DS: 1) (0x02)
           .... .0.. = More Fragments: This is the last fragment
           .... 1... = Retry: Frame is being retransmitted
           ...0 .... = PWR MGT: STA will stay up
           ..0. .... = More Data: No data buffered
           .0.. .... = Protected flag: Data is not protected
           0... .... = Order flag: Not strictly ordered
     Duration: 44
     Destination address: Apple_ab:14:26 (00:1e:c2:ab:14:26)
     BSS Id: Cisco-Li_0d:21:3d (00:12:17:0d:21:3d)
     Source address: Cisco-Li_0d:21:3b (00:12:17:0d:21:3b)
     Fragment number: 0
     Sequence number: 1419
```

Figure 7-3 *Wireless Frame Capture 1*

As you can see from the capture, a preamble is present, denoted with the Type/Subtype label, followed by a Frame Control field. The preamble can be anywhere from 76 to 156 bytes. The Frame Control field is 2 bytes. It tells what type of frame it is, represented with 2 bytes. In this case, it is a data frame.

The Flags field indicates that the frame is traveling *from* the DS, not toward the DS. This is represented with a single byte. In the figure, this is a frame that is coming back to the client.

Following the Flags field is a Duration field. The Duration field indicates how long the medium is reserved while this frame is being sent and includes time for an ACK to be sent in reply. The idea behind this process is to prevent collisions.

A wireless frame can have up to three MAC addresses following the Duration field. This is a total of 18 bytes. In the figure, you can see the following:

■ Destination MAC address

■ BSS ID, which is also a MAC address

■ Source MAC address

The source address (SA) is the station that sent the frame. The transmitter address (TA) is the address of the station that is emitting the frame; in Figure 7-3, a TA is not shown. In some scenarios, a TA might vary from an SA. For example, if a wireless frame is relayed through a repeater, the TA would be the radio of the repeater, and the SA would be the sending device. The destination address (DA) is the final destination of the frame; in this case, it is the wireless client.

The Sequence Control field (2 bytes) indicates whether the frame is a fragment. Again, in Figure 7-3, the Sequence Control field is indicated with *Fragment Number* and shows that this is number 0, or the last fragment. This leads to an interesting topic—fragmentation. When and why would you fragment on a wireless network? The answer is that a wireless frame is, by default, 2346 bytes long. Considering that the frame is going to move to or from an Ethernet distribution that has a maximum transmission unit (MTU) of 1500 bytes and can see frames as big as 1518 bytes or slightly larger (depending on the trunking used), the frames on the wireless side are too big and need to be chopped up.

Optionally, you can see a fourth MAC address, a receiving address (RA), which is the address of the *direct* station that this frame is sent to; however, this is not seen in the figure. The frame could be relayed through a wireless bridge or repeater. This additional address adds six more bytes.

Finally, the frame body follows (not seen in the figure). It can be up to 2306 bytes and references only two MAC addresses, just like any other L2 frame. The frame body is encapsulated inside the last header shown in the figure.

In addition, you might see a 4-byte frame check sequence (FCS) following the L2 frame. This is common but not required.

Frame Types

For the most part, all frames are going to have the same type of header. The difference is in the body of the frame. The body is more specific and indicates what the frame is all about. Table 7-2 shows some frame types.

Table 7-2   *Frame Types Table*

Management	Control	Data
Beacon	Request to Send (RTS)	Simple data
Probe Request	Clear to Send (CTS)	Null function
Probe Response	Acknowledgment	Data+CF-ACK
Association Request	Power-Save-Poll (PS-Poll)	Data+CF-Poll
Association Response	Contention Free End (CF-End)	Data+CF-Ack
Authentication Request	Contention Free End + Acknowledgment (CF-End +ACK)	ACK+CF-Poll
Authentication Response	CF-ACK	
Deauthentication	CF-ACK+CF-Poll	
Reassociation request		
Reassociation response		
Announcement traffic indication message (ATIM)		
Each frame type merits its own discussion to follow.		

Management Frames

Management frames, as their name indicates, are used to manage the connection. In looking at a frame capture, the Type field indicates Management, and the subtype tells what kind of management frame it is. As Table 7-2 listed, there are 11 Management frame types. There are some more-often seen frames that you should be familiar with. These frame types are discussed in the following sections.

Beacons and Probes

Figure 7-4 shows a management frame with a subtype of 8. This indicates that it is a beacon frame, which is used to help clients find the network.

Figure 7-4 *Management Frame Capture*

Figure 7-5 shows a sample network where the AP is sending a beacon frame.

Figure 7-5 *Sample Network Using Beacon Frames*

When the client hears the beacon frame, it can learn a great deal of information about the cell. In Figure 7-6, you can see that the beacon frame includes a timestamp that gives a reference time for the cell, the beacon interval, and a field called Capability Information, which provides specifics for this cell. The Capability Information field includes information regarding power save mode, authentication, and preamble information.

A beacon frame also includes the SSIDs that the AP supports, the rates that are supported, and six fields called Parameter Set that indicate modulation methods and such.

Another field you will find is Traffic Indication Map (TIM), which indicates whether the AP is buffering traffic for clients in power-save mode.

When a client sees a beacon frame, it should be able to use that information to determine if it is able to connect to the wireless Cell. Chapter 16, "Wireless Clients," covers the

```
▽ IEEE 802.11 wireless LAN management frame
  ▽ Fixed parameters (12 bytes)
      Timestamp: 0x0000000A7341A18A
      Beacon Interval: 0.102400 [Seconds]
    ▽ Capability Information: 0x0401
        .... .... .... ...1 = ESS capabilities: Transmitter is an AP
        .... .... .... ..0. = IBSS status: Transmitter belongs to a BSS
        .... ..0. .... 00.. = CFP participation capabilities: No point coordinator at AP (0x0000)
        .... .... ...0 .... = Privacy: AP/STA cannot support WEP
        .... .... ..0. .... = Short Preamble: Short preamble not allowed
        .... .... .0.. .... = PBCC: PBCC modulation not allowed
        .... .... 0... .... = Channel Agility: Channel agility not in use
        .... ..0 .... .... = Spectrum Management: dot11SpectrumManagementRequired FALSE
        .... .1.. .... .... = Short Slot Time: Short slot time in use
        .... 0... .... .... = Automatic Power Save Delivery: apsd not implemented
        ..0. .... .... .... = DSSS-OFDM: DSSS-OFDM modulation not allowed
        .0.. .... .... .... = Delayed Block Ack: delayed block ack not implemented
        0... .... .... .... = Immediate Block Ack: immediate block ack not implemented
  ▽ Tagged parameters (52 bytes)
    ▷ SSID parameter set: "carroll"
    ▷ Supported Rates: 1.0(B) 2.0(B) 5.5(B) 11.0(B) 18.0 24.0(B) 36.0 54.0
    ▷ DS Parameter set: Current Channel: 6
    ▷ Traffic Indication Map (TIM): DTIM 0 of 1 bitmap empty
```

Figure 7-6 *Beacon Frame Details*

process of how a client searches channels and displays connection capability information. For now, just understand that the beacon frame allows a client to passively scan a network.

Sometimes, however, you do not want to passively scan a network. Perhaps you know exactly what cell you want to connect to. In this situation, you can actively scan a network to determine if the cell you are looking for is accessible. When a client actively scans a network, it uses probe request and probe response messages. Figure 7-7 shows a client actively scanning.

Figure 7-7 *Active Scanning*

As you can tell in the figure, the client is looking for a wireless cell with the SSID of "Carroll." This client sends a probe request and the AP, upon receiving the probe request, issues a probe response. The probe response is similar to the beacon frame, including capability information, authentication information, and so on. The difference is that a beacon frame is sent frequently and a probe response is sent only in response to a probe request.

Connecting After a Probe or Beacon

After a client has located an AP and understands the capabilities, it tries to connect using an authentication frame. This frame has information about the algorithm used to authenticate, a number for the authentication transaction, and information on whether authentication has succeeded or failed.

One thing to note is that authentication can be *Open*, meaning that no authentication algorithm such as WEP is being used. The only reason an authentication message is used is to indicate that the client has the capability to connect. In Figure 7-8, the client is sending an authentication request, and the AP is sending an authentication response. Upon authentication, the client sends an association request, and the AP responds with an association response.

Figure 7-8 *Authentications and Association*

Leaving and Returning

When a client is connected to a wireless cell, either the client or the AP can leave the connection by sending a deauthentication message. The deauthentication message has information in the body as to why it is leaving. In addition, a client can send a disassociation message, which disassociates the client from the cell but keeps the client authenticated. The next time a client comes back to the wireless cell, it can simply send a reassociation message, and the AP would send a reassociation response—eliminating the need for authentication to reconnect to the cell.

Note: Cisco Unified Wireless networks use deauthentication and disassociation messages to contain rogue APs. This concept is a little outside of this discussion but will be covered in Chapter 10, "Cisco Wireless Networks Architecture."

Control Frames

One of the most common control frames is the ACK, which helps the connection by acknowledging receipt of frames. Other control frames include the request to send (RTS) and clear to send (CTS), which were discussed in Chapter 6, "Overview of the 802.11 WLAN Protocols." The ACK, RTS, and CTS frames are used in DCF mode.

The control frames that are used in PCF mode are as follows:

■ Contention Free End (CF+End)

■ Contention Free End Ack (CF +end_ack_)

- CF-Ack

- CF Ack+CF Poll

- CF-Poll

These frames are also discussed in the paragraphs to follow.

When an AP takes control of a network and shifts from DCF mode (every station for itself) to PCF mode (the AP is responsible for everyone sending), the AP lets all stations know that they should stop sending by issuing a beacon frame with a duration of 32768. When this happens and everyone stops sending, there is no longer a contention for the medium, because the AP is managing it. This is called a *contention free window (CFW)*. The AP then sends poll messages to each client asking if they have anything to send. This is called a CF-Poll, as illustrated in Figure 7-9.

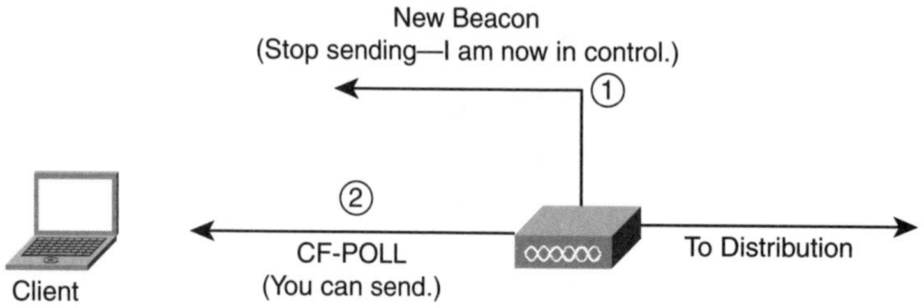

Figure 7-9   *CF-Poll in PCF Mode*

Figure 7-10 illustrates how the AP might control communication. Here, the AP has data to deliver to the client (DATA). It allows the client to send data (CF-Poll) and acknowledges receipt of the client data (CF-ACK).

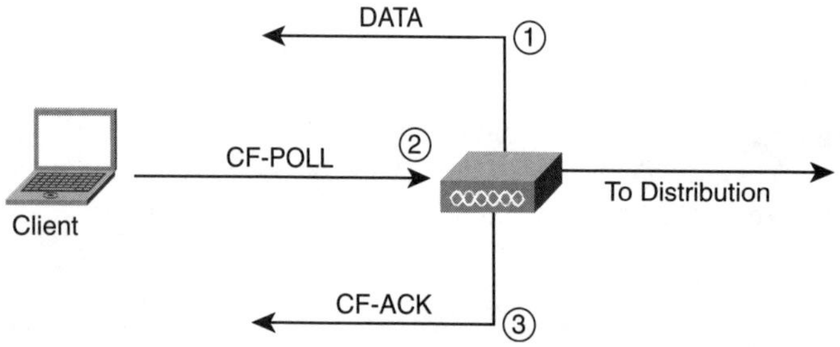

Figure 7-10   *Data + CF-Poll + CF-ACK*

Other variations exist, but from these examples you should have a decent understanding of PCF operation.

Power Save Mode and Frame Types

Another mode of operation mostly seen on laptops is called power save mode. Looking back at Table 7-2, you can see that a control frame is related to a power save (PS-Poll). In a power save, a client notifies an AP that it is falling asleep by using a null function frame. The client wakes up after a certain period of time, during which the AP buffers any traffic for it. When the client wakes up and sees a beacon frame with the TIM listing that it has frames buffered, the client sends a PS-Poll requesting the data.

Frame Speeds

One final item to discuss before putting it together is frame speed. The AP advertises mandatory speeds at which a client must be able to operate. You can use other speeds, but they are not mandatory. For example, 24 Mbps might be mandatory, but an AP might also be capable of 54 Mbps. A client *must* support 24 Mbps but is allowed to use the best rate possible, in this example 54 Mbps. When data is sent at one rate, the ACK is always sent at 1 data rate lower.

A Wireless Connection

Using Figures 7-11 through 7-18, you can step through a simple discovery and association process.

1. The AP sends beacons every 2 seconds, as shown in Figure 7-11.

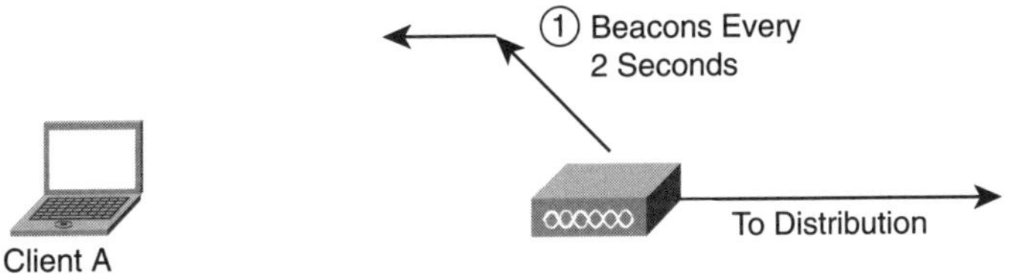

Figure 7-11   *AP Beacons*

2. Client A is passively scanning and hears the beacon. This enables the client to determine whether it can connect. You can see this in Figure 7-12.

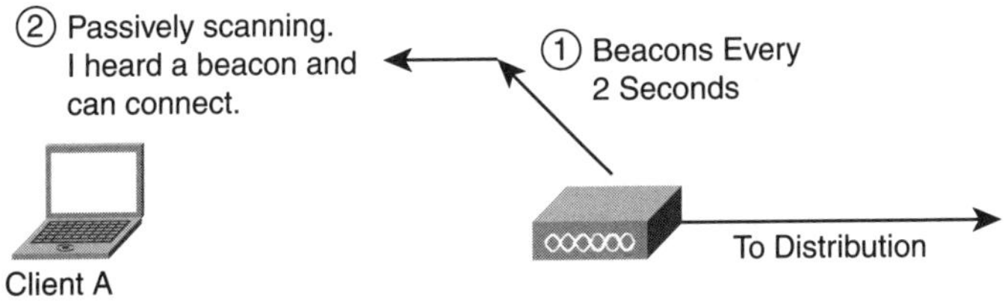

Figure 7-12   *Passive Scanning*

3. A new client (Client B) arrives. Client B is already configured to look for the AP, so instead of passive scanning, it sends a probe request for the specific AP (see Figure 7-13).

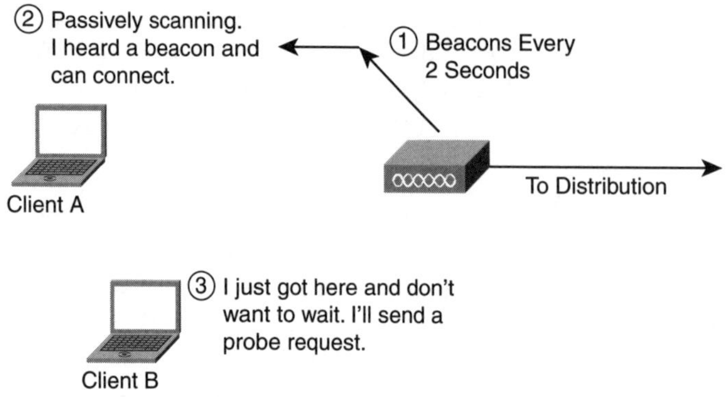

② Passively scanning.
I heard a beacon and
can connect.

① Beacons Every
2 Seconds

Client A

To Distribution

③ I just got here and don't
want to wait. I'll send a
probe request.

Client B

Figure 7-13   *Active Scanning Probe Request*

4. The AP sends a probe response, seen in Figure 7-14, which is similar to a beacon. This lets Client B determine if it can connect.

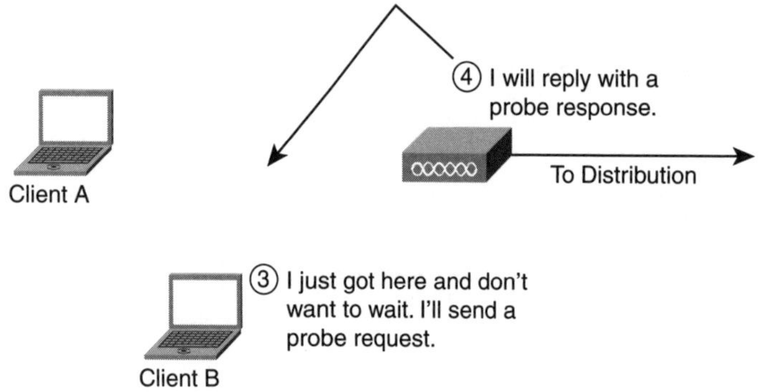

Client A

④ I will reply with a
probe response.

To Distribution

③ I just got here and don't
want to wait. I'll send a
probe request.

Client B

Figure 7-14   *Probe Response*

5. From this point on, the process would be the same for Client A and Client B. In Figure 7-15, Client B sends an authentication request.

Client A

⑥ Authentication Response

To Distribution

⑤ Authentication Request

Client B

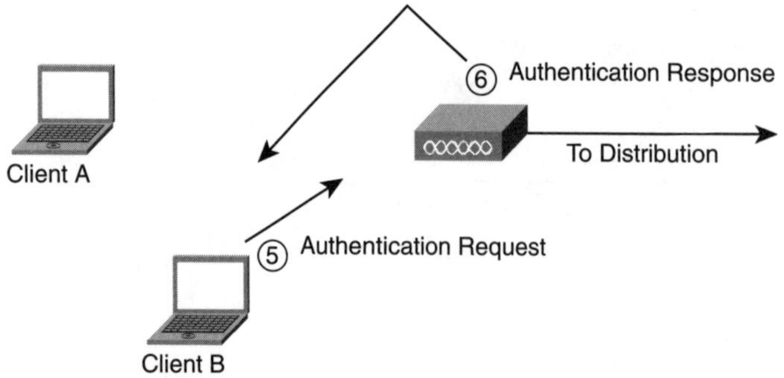

Figure 7-15   *Association Request and Response*

6. Also seen in Figure 7-15, the AP returns an authentication response to the client.

7. The client then sends an association request, as seen in Figure 7-16.

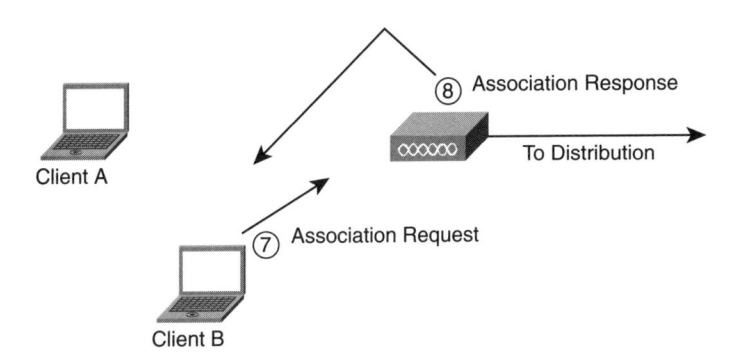

Figure 7-16 *Association Request and Response*

8. Now the AP sends an association response, also seen in Figure 7-16.

9. When the client wants to send, it uses an RTS, assuming this is a mixed b/g cell. The RTS includes the duration, as you can see in Figure 7-17.

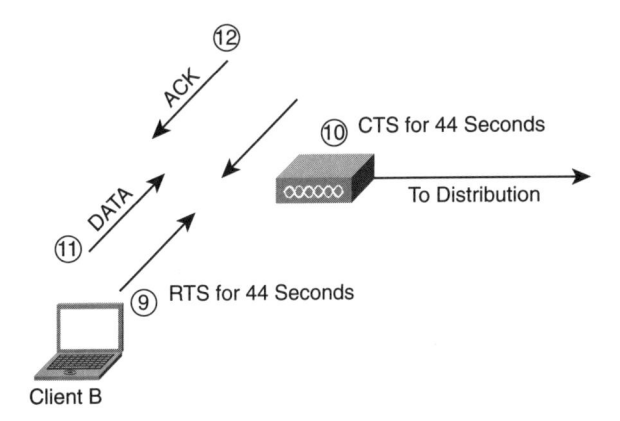

Figure 7-17 *RTS/CTS*

10. Also seen in Figure 7-17, the AP returns a CTS.

11. The client sends the data (see Figure 7-17).

12. The AP sends an ACK after each frame is received (Figure 7-17).

13. In Figure 7-18, the client sends a disassociation message.

14. The AP replies with a disassociation response (Figure 7-18).

15. The client returns and sends a reassociation message (Figure 7-18).

16. The AP responds with a reassociation response (Figure 7-18).

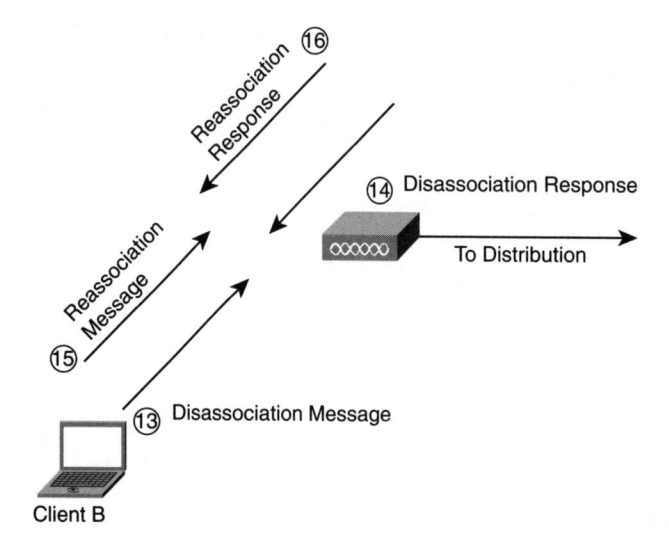

Figure 7-18 *Reassociation*

Again, this process has other variations, but this should give you a pretty good understanding of how to manage a connection.

Exam Preparation Tasks

Review All the Key Concepts

Review the most important topics from this chapter, noted with the Key Topics icon in the outer margin of the page. Table 7-3 lists a reference of these key topics and the page number where you can find each one.

Table 7-3 *Key Topics for Chapter 7*

Key Topic Item	Description	Page Number
Figure 7-1	Sending a frame: part 1	117
Figure 7-2	Sending a frame: part 2	118
Figure 7-3	Wireless frame capture	119
Table 7-2	Frame types table	120
Figure 7-4	Management frame capture	121
Figure 7-6	Beacon frame details	122
Figure 7-8	Authentication and association	123

Complete the Tables and Lists from Memory

Print a copy of Appendix B, "Memory Tables," (found on the CD) or at least the section for this chapter, and complete the tables and lists from memory. Appendix C, "Memory Tables Answer Key," also on the CD, includes completed tables and lists to check your work.

Definition of Key Terms

Define the following key terms from this chapter, and check your answers in the Glossary:

management frames, control frames, data frames, CSMA/CA, CCA, hidden node problem, virtual carrier sense, IFS, SIFS, DIFS, ACK, backoff timer, NAV, slottime, contention window, DCF, PCF, SA, RA, TA, DA, MTU, beacon, probe request, probe response, authentication request, authentication response, association request, association response, TIM, ATIM, passive scan, active scan, deauthentication message, deauthentication response, disassociation message, disassociation response, null function frame, PS-Poll

This chapter covers the following subjects:

Cordless Phones: Briefly looks at cordless phone technology and why it interferes with WLANs.

Bluetooth: Discusses Bluetooth and its standardization progression.

ZigBee: Shows how ZigBee is used and how it interferes with WLANs.

WiMax: Describes WiMax technology as it compares to Wi-Fi.

Other Types of Interference: Covers additional sources of wireless interference.

CHAPTER 8

Additional Wireless Technologies

Although the 802.11 wireless spectrum is the best-known technology, others are in use and, believe it or not, are very popular. The purpose of this chapter is to discuss some, not all, of the other wireless technologies and how they might interfere or interact with the 802.11 WLAN standards. These technologies include cordless phone technology, Bluetooth, ZigBee, WiMax, and some other odds and ends.

You should take the "Do I Know This Already?" quiz first. If you score 80 percent or higher, you might want to skip to the section "Exam Preparation Tasks." If you score below 80 percent, you should review the entire chapter.

"Do I Know This Already?" Quiz

The "Do I Know This Already?" quiz helps you determine your level of knowledge of this chapter's topics before you begin. Table 8-1 details the major topics discussed in this chapter and their corresponding quiz questions.

Table 8-1 *"Do I Know This Already?" Section-to-Question Mapping*

Foundation Topics Section	Questions
Cordless Phones	1–2
Bluetooth	3–7
ZigBee	8–9
WiMax	10–14
Other Types of Interference	15

1. Who developed the DECT standard?

    a. FCC

    b. IEEE

    c. ITUT

    d. ETSI

2. DECT devices in the U.S. use what designation to differentiate them from European DECT devices?

   a. DECT 1.0

   b. DECT 2.0

   c. DECT 6.0

   d. US-DECT

3. Bluetooth is designed to cover what type of area?

   a. Metropolitan

   b. Wide area

   c. Local area

   d. Personal area

4. How many Bluetooth devices can be paired?

   a. Two

   b. Four

   c. Six

   d. Eight

5. Bluetooth operates in which frequency band?

   a. 2.4 GHz

   b. 5.0 GHz

   c. 900 MHz

   d. 10 GHz

6. What is the current Bluetooth standard?

   a. Bluetooth 2008

   b. Bluetooth 2.1 + EDR

   c. Bluetooth 2.0

   d. Bluetooth 1.1

7. Which group is responsible for Bluetooth development?

   a. IEEE

   b. Bluetooth SIG

   c. Bluetooth Forum

   d. Bluetooth Inc.

8. ZigBee is used for what common deployments? (Choose all that apply.)

   a. Home automation

   b. Monitoring

   c. GPS location

   d. Control systems

9. ZigBee operates in which frequency band?

   a. 2.4 GHz

   b. 5.0 GHz

   c. 900 MHz

   d. 10 GHz

10. True or false: WiMax interferes with 802.11 LANs because it operates on the same frequency band.

   a. True

   b. False

11. WiMax is designed for what type of connections?

   a. Last-mile access

   b. Wireless mesh LANs

   c. Point-to-multipoint WANs

   d. Single-cell

12. WiMax is defined in which IEEE specification?

   a. 802.15.1

   b. 802.16e

   c. 802.1

   d. 802.3

13. Fixed line of sight (LOS) offers which data rate?

   a. 40 Mbps

   b. 100 Mbps

   c. 1 Gbps

   d. 10 Mbps

14. NLOS advertises which data rate?

   a. 30 to 40 Mbps

   b. 100 Mbps

   c. 70 Mbps

   d. 1 Gbps

15. Which of the following are potential sources of interference for WLANs? (Choose all that apply.)

   a. Microwave

   b. Fluorescent light

   c. Magnet

   d. Microphone

Foundation Topics

Cordless Phones

Cordless phones have been around as long as I can remember—or at least since I was in junior high. Cordless phones sometimes operate in the wireless spectrum as WLANs, which can cause interference issues. Visit an electronics store, and you'll find some phones that operate at 2.4 GHz and others that operate at 5.8 GHz. This should be a consideration when you purchase cordless phones. If you have 802.11a deployed, a 2.4-GHz phone should suffice. If you have 802.11b/g, you should avoid a phone that operates in the 2.4-GHz range and go with a 5.8-GHz phone. With that said, let's look at cordless phone technology in more detail.

To begin with, cordless phones can use *Time Division Multiple Access (TDMA)* or *Frequency Division Multiple Access (FDMA)*. The Multiple Access technology is used to allow more than one handset to access the frequency band at the same time, as shown in Figure 8-1. As you can see, a cordless phone communicates with the base station. Multiple cordless phones can use the same base station at the same time by using TDMA or FDMA.

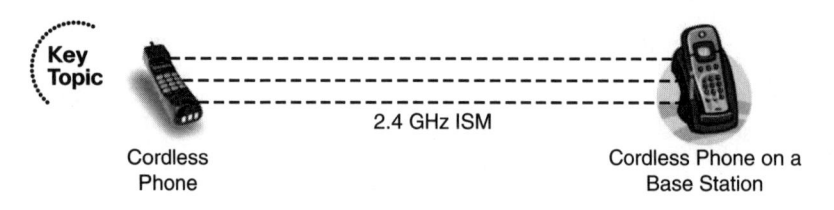

2.4 GHz ISM

Cordless
Phone

Cordless Phone on a
Base Station

Figure 8-1 *Standard Cordless Phone Usage*

It's common for cordless phones to use the *Digital Enhanced Cordless Telecommunications (DECT)* standard. DECT is an ETSI standard for digital portable phones and is found in cordless technology that is deployed in homes and businesses. Currently, the DECT standard is a good alternative for avoiding interference issues with any 802.11 technologies. The original DECT frequency band was 1880 to 1900 MHz. It's used in all European countries. It is also used in most of Asia, Australia, and South America.

In 2005, the FCC changed channelization and licensing costs in the 1920 to 1930 MHz, or 1.9 GHz, band. This band is known as Unlicensed Personal Communications Services (UPCS). This change by the FCC allowed the use of DECT devices in the U.S. with few changes. The modified DECT devices are called DECT 6.0. This allows a distinction to be made between DECT devices used overseas and other cordless devices that operate at 900 MHz, 2.4 GHz, and 5.8 GHz.

Bluetooth

Bluetooth is a personal-area technology that was named after a king of Denmark, Harald "Bluetooth" Gormson. It is said that the use of his name is based on his role in unifying Denmark and Norway. Bluetooth technology was intended to unify the telecom and computing industries. Today, Bluetooth can be found integrated into cell phones, PDAs, laptops, desktops, printers, headsets, cameras, and video game consoles. Bluetooth has low power consumption, making it a good choice for mobile, battery-powered devices.

The Bluetooth Special Interest Group (SIG) was formed in 1998, and the name "Bluetooth" was officially adopted. In 1999, Bluetooth 1.0 and 1.0b were released, although they were pretty much unusable. Bluetooth 1.1 followed and was much more functional. Eventually, based on Bluetooth 1.1, the 802.15.1 specification was approved by the IEEE to conform with Bluetooth technology.

Bluetooth 1.2 was then adopted in 2003 with faster connections and discovery of devices as well as the use of adaptive Frequency Hopping Spread Spectrum technology. In 2004, Bluetooth 2.0 + *Enhanced Data Rate (EDR)*, supporting speeds up to 2 Mbps, was adopted by the Bluetooth SIG. The IEEE followed with 802.15.1-2005, which is the specification that relates to Bluetooth 1.2. After the 802.15-2005 standard, the IEEE severed ties to the Bluetooth SIG because the Bluetooth SIG wanted to pursue functionality with other standards.

As of July 26, 2007, the adopted standard according to the Bluetooth SIG is Bluetooth 2.1 + EDR. One of the key features of the 2.1 standard is an improved quick-pairing process, in which you simply hold two devices close together to start the quick-pairing process. Also, a new technology called "sniff subrating" increases battery life up to five times. Bluetooth 2.1 + EDR is backward-compatible with Bluetooth 1.1.

Bluetooth technology might interfere with 802.11 LANs, because it operates in the 2.4-GHz range. However, because it is designed for a proximity of about 35 feet, has low transmit power, and uses Frequency Hopping Spread Spectrum, it is unlikely that Bluetooth will interfere.

Bluetooth is considered a piconet; it allows eight devices (one master and seven slaves) to be paired, as shown in Figure 8-2. Although the figure is a little extreme, it shows you just how many devices can be paired with a laptop or desktop. You can download photos you've taken, while listening to music with your headphones, synchronizing your cell phone's contacts and PDA calendar with Outlook, and using your mouse to print that new white paper on Cisco.com, all while playing a video game. Imagine the wire mess you would have without Bluetooth.

ZigBee

Many people have never heard of ZigBee, but it's a technology that is well-designed and very useful. ZigBee was developed by the ZigBee Alliance. It consists of small, low-power digital radios based on the IEEE 802.15.4 standard for *wireless personal-area networks (WPAN)*, such as wireless headphones connecting to cell phones via short-range radio. If you look at the ZigBee Alliance home page at http://www.zigbee.org, you'll likely notice

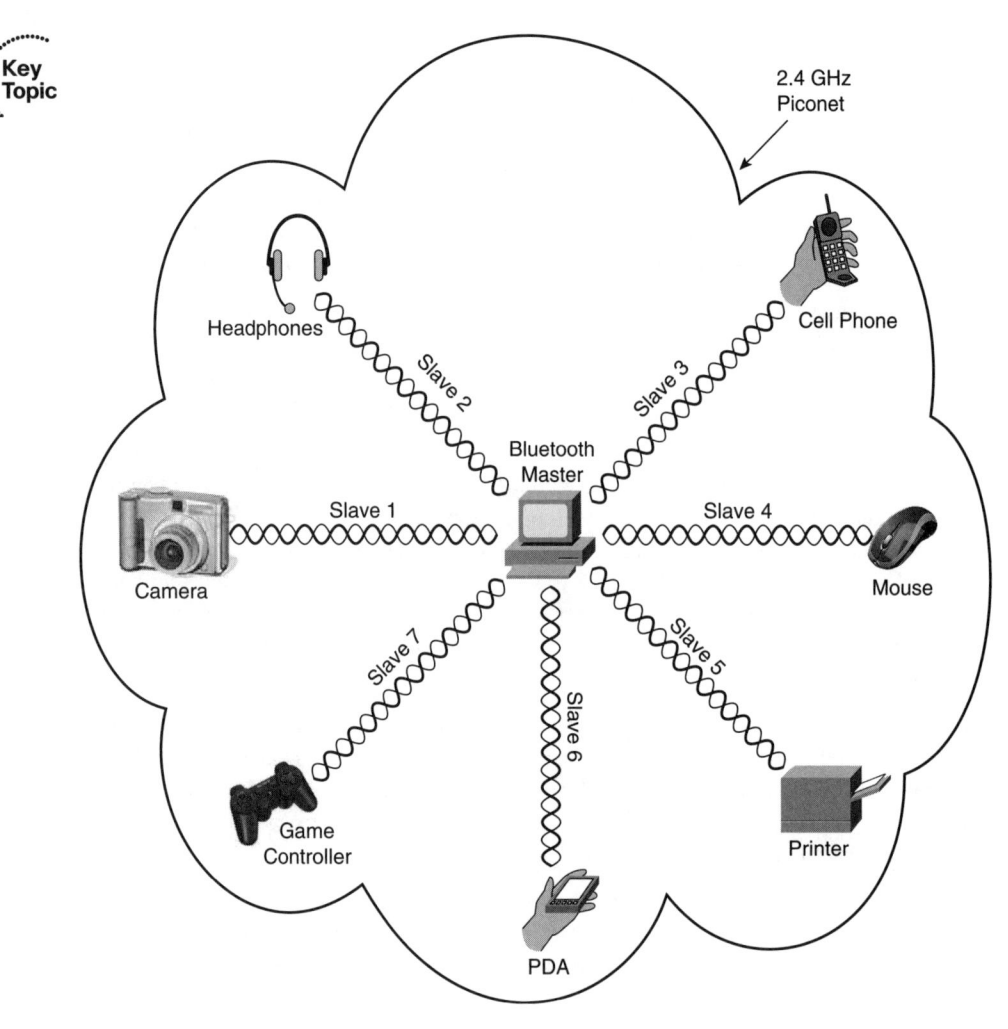

Figure 8-2   *Bluetooth Piconet*

that ZigBee relates much of its use to control and monitoring. In fact, ZigBee is often used for monitoring, building automation, control devices, personal healthcare devices, and computer peripherals.

The ZigBee website says:

> "ZigBee was created to address the market need for a cost-effective, standards-based wireless networking solution that supports low data-rates, low-power consumption, security, and reliability.

> "ZigBee is the only standards-based technology that addresses the unique needs of most remote monitoring and control and sensory network applications.

> "The initial markets for the ZigBee Alliance include Energy Management and Efficiency, Home Automation, Building Automation and Industrial Automation."[1]

You might be wondering how this technology relates to WLANs and how it might interfere. The answer is that ZigBee operates in the ISM bands: 868 MHz in Europe, 915 MHz in countries such as the U.S. and Australia, and 2.4 GHz pretty much everywhere. The 2.4 GHz operation range is where the issue lies, because that is the range in which 802.11b/g WLANs operate.

Figures 8-3, 8-4, and 8-5 show some common ZigBee topologies. Figure 8-3 shows the star topology, in which the center device is a network coordinator (NC). Every network has an NC. Other devices can be full-function devices, and still others can be reduced-function devices. Full-function devices can send, receive, and so on. A reduced-function device doesn't have as much capability and could do something like report the temperature of a system back to a controller.

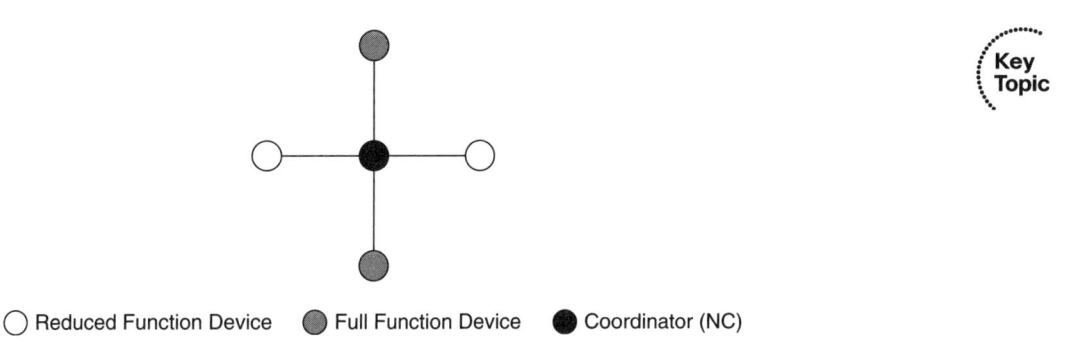

○ Reduced Function Device   ● Full Function Device   ● Coordinator (NC)

Figure 8-3   *ZigBee Star Topology*

The cluster topology shown in Figure 8-4 also has an NC, as well as some full-function devices and reduced-function devices. This cluster topology resembles an extended star in LAN terms.

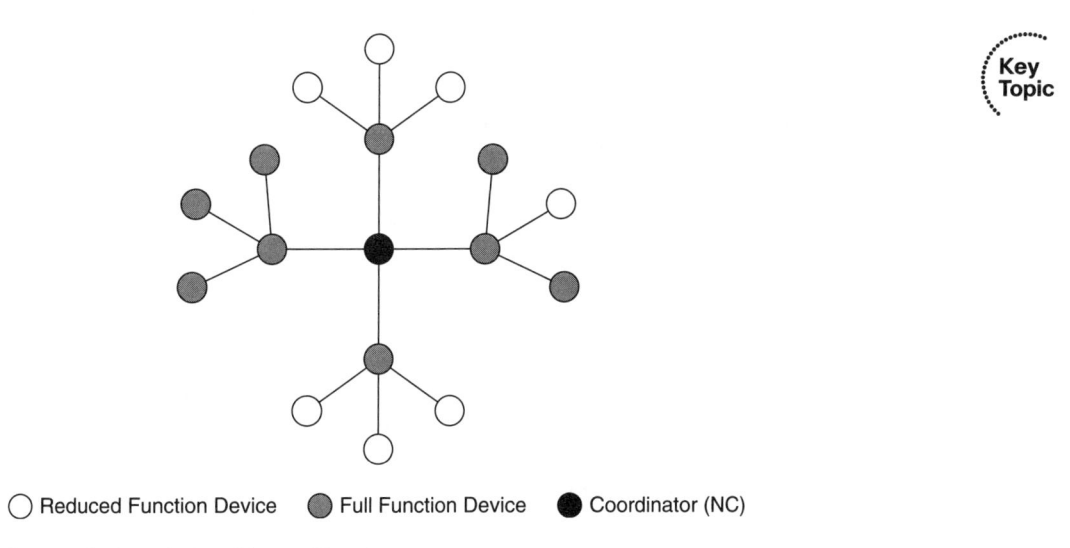

○ Reduced Function Device   ● Full Function Device   ● Coordinator (NC)

Figure 8-4   *ZigBee Cluster Topology*

Certain scenarios call for all devices to communicate with each other in a coordinated effort to provide some sort of information. This is where you find a mesh topology, as shown in Figure 8-5.

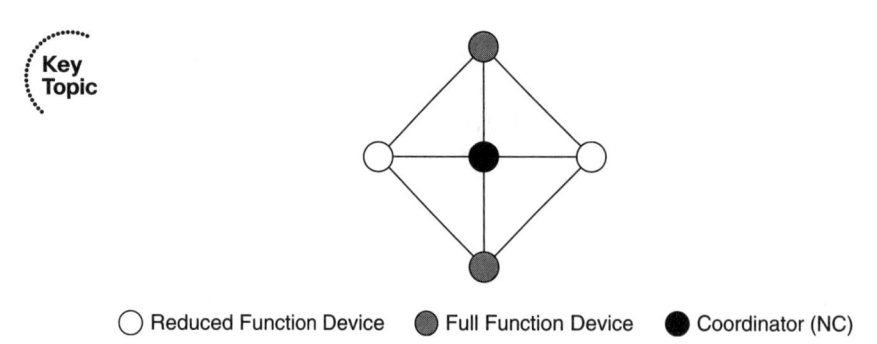

○ Reduced Function Device   ● Full Function Device   ● Coordinator (NC)

Figure 8-5   *ZigBee Mesh Topology*

WiMax

Worldwide Interoperability for Microwave Access (WiMax) is defined by the WiMax forum and standardized by the IEEE 802.16 suite. The most current standard is 802.16e.

According to the WiMax Forum:

> "WiMAX is a standards-based technology enabling the delivery of last mile wireless broadband access as an alternative to wired broadband like cable and DSL. WiMAX provides fixed, nomadic, portable and, soon, mobile wireless broadband connectivity without the need for direct line-of-sight with a base station. In a typical cell radius deployment of three to ten kilometers, WiMAX Forum Certified systems can be expected to deliver capacity of up to 40 Mbps per channel, for fixed and portable access applications.

> "This is enough bandwidth to simultaneously support hundreds of businesses with T-1 speed connectivity and thousands of residences with DSL speed connectivity. Mobile network deployments are expected to provide up to 15 Mbps of capacity within a typical cell radius deployment of up to three kilometers. It is expected that WiMAX technology will be incorporated in notebook computers and PDAs by 2007, allowing for urban areas and cities to become 'metro zones' for portable outdoor broadband wireless access."[2]

You must understand a few aspects of WiMax; the first is the concept of being fixed line of sight (LOS) or non-LOS (mobile). In non-LOS, *mobile* doesn't mean mobile in the sense that most of us think. WiMax mobility is more like the ability to travel and then set up shop temporarily. When you are done, you pack up and move on. A few service providers use this technology to provide end-user access as an alternative to DSL or cable modem. Your signal range in this Non-LOS scenario is about 3 to 4 miles, and data rates are advertised at around 30 Mbps, but you can expect less—closer to 15 Mbps.

Other service providers are targeting business customers in a fixed LOS WiMax deployment in which the topology most closely resembles that of a traditional T1, being a point-to-point type of topology and providing backhaul or backbone services. This fixed LOS advertises 30 to 70 Mbps throughput, but you can expect around 40 Mbps.

Note   I know of a company in the Seattle area that advertises a 100-Mbps connection point-to-point with 10 Gbps of bandwidth per month at no additional charge. If you go over the 10 Gbps limit, you are charged additional fees.

As the IEEE standardizes WiMax technology, it has progressed from the original 802.16 to 802.16a, c, d, and finally 802.16e.

As mentioned, the WiMax defines last-mile access. Figure 8-6 shows a sample topology in which subscribers have a point-to-point connection back to a service provider and from there have access to the public Internet.

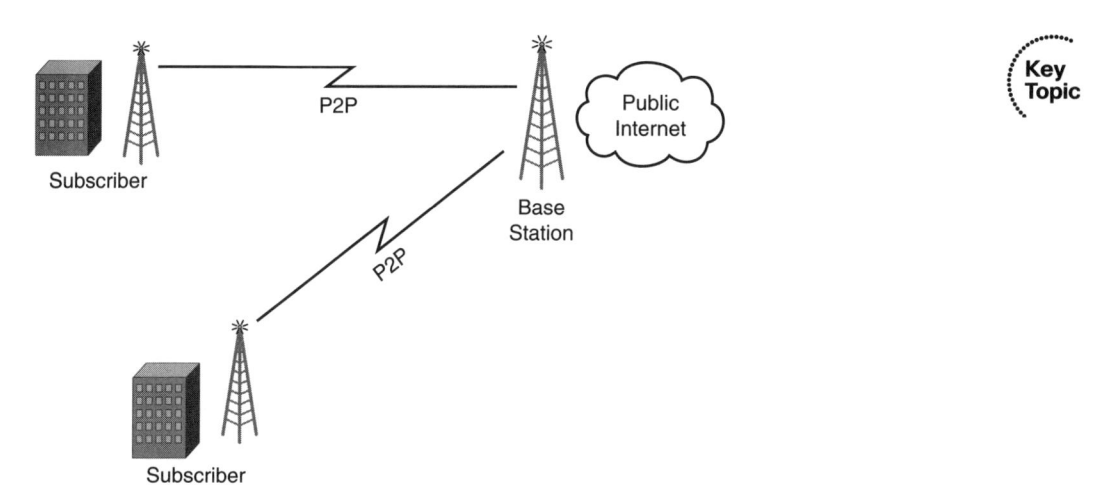

Key Topic

Figure 8-6   *WiMax Deployment*

WiMax operates on the 10- to 66-GHz frequency band, so it doesn't interfere with 802.11 LANs. So why is it discussed in this section? The school of thought here is that, with some planning, a device acting as a gateway can be deployed offering 802.11 LAN access with 802.16 last-mile access or upstream access to a service provider, thus removing the need for wires. The question of how feasible this is lies in the hands of the vendors developing the products and the standards committees ensuring interoperability. Some vendors, however, have tested this technology in lab environments with much success.

Other Types of Interference

Other types of interference can occur in the same frequency ranges. These devices might not be the most obvious, but they should be considered. They can include the following:

- Microwaves (operate at 1 to 40 GHz)

- Wireless X11 cameras (operate at 2.4 GHz)

- Radar systems (operate at 2 to 4 GHz for moderate-range surveillance, terminal traffic control, and long-range weather and at 4 to 8 GHz for long-range tracking and airborne weather systems)

- Motion sensors (operate at 2.4 GHz)

- Fluorescent lighting (operates at 20000 Hz or higher)

- Game controllers and adapters (usually operate at 2.5 GHz)

When dealing with wireless deployments, you can use tools to determine signal strength and coverage, but just knowing about these additional sources of interference will save you some time in determining where to place APs and clients.

Exam Preparation Tasks

Review All the Key Topics

Review the most important topics from this chapter, denoted with the Key Topic icon. Table 8-2 lists these key topics and the page number where each one can be found.

Table 8-2   *Key Topics for Chapter 8*

Key Topic Item	Description	Page Number
Figure 8-1	Standard cordless phone usage	134
Figure 8-2	A Bluetooth piconet	136
Figure 8-3	ZigBee star topology	137
Figure 8-4	ZigBee cluster topology	137
Figure 8-5	ZigBee mesh topology	138
Figure 8-6	A WiMax deployment	139

Definition of Key Terms

Define the following key terms from this chapter, and check your answers in the Glossary:

Bluetooth, ZigBee, WiMax, Time Division Multiple Access (TDMA), Frequency Division Multiple Access (FDMA), Digital Enhanced Cordless Telecommunications (DECT), Special Interest Group (SIG), adaptive Frequency Hopping Spread Spectrum technology, Enhanced Data Rate (EDR), 802.15.1, 802.15.1-2005, sniff subrating, wireless personal-area network (WPAN), 802.16e, WiMax

Endnotes

[1]About ZigBee, http://www.zigbee.org/en/markets/index.asp

[2]About WiMax, http://www.wimaxforum.org/technology/

References in This Chapter

Digital Enhanced Cordless Telecommunications, Wikipedia.org, http://en.wikipedia.org/wiki/Digital_Enhanced_Cordless_Telecommunications, December 2006

Bluetooth, Wikipedia.org, http://en.wikipedia.org/wiki/Bluetooth

ZigBee, Wikipedia.org, http://en.wikipedia.org/wiki/Zigbee, February 2008

This chapter covers the following subjects:

The Wireless Network Road Trip: A look at the packet delivery process on a wireless-to-wired network.

Using VLANs to Add Control: How VLANs are used in wireless networks to separate subnets.

Configuring VLANs and Trunks: How to apply a configuration of VLANs and trunks on a Cisco switch.

CHAPTER 9

Delivering Packets from the Wireless to Wired Network

Much coordination is involved with the delivery of wireless packets to and from the wireless networks. This chapter focuses on delivery of packets to the wired network and the path that traffic will traverse. It is intended to give you a good understanding of what devices are involved and how they manipulate packets as they are transmitted.

You should do the "Do I Know This Already?" quiz first. If you score 80 percent or higher, you may way to skip to the section "Exam Preparation Tasks." If you score below 80 percent, you should spend the time reviewing the entire chapter.

"Do I Know This Already?" Quiz

The "Do I Know This Already?" quiz helps you determine your level of knowledge of this chapter's topics before you begin. Table 9-1 details the major topics discussed in this chapter and their corresponding quiz questions.

Table 9-1 *"Do I Know This Already?" Section-to-Question Mapping*

Foundation Topics Section	Questions
The Wireless Network Road Trip	1–4
Using VLANs to Add Control	5–8
Configuring VLANs and Trunks	9–12

1. When a client wants to send traffic to another device, it must use what protocol to resolve the MAC addresses?

    a. ARP

    b. CDP

    c. NPR

    d. OFDM

2. If a client wants to communicate with a device on another subnet, what device handles the communication?

  a. WLC

  b. Switch

  c. AP

  d. Gateway router

3. How many MAC addresses can be seen in an 802.11 frame?

  a. 1

  b. 2

  c. 3

  d. 4

4. What protocol is the 802.11 frame encapsulated in when it is sent from the AP to the WLC?

  a. LDAP

  b. CDP

  c. 802.3

  d. LWAPP

5. A VLAN is used to define a _____ and isolate a _____ . (Choose two.)

  a. Logical broadcast domain

  b. Transparent network

  c. Virtual trunk

  d. Subnet

6. Clients see VLANs. True or False?

  a. True

  b. False

7. How many VLANs typically are assigned to an access port on a switch?

  a. 2

  b. 4

  c. 256

  d. 1

8. What are trunks normally used for?

   a. Connections between APs

   b. Connections between switches and clients

   c. Connections between switches

   d. Switches do not support trunks

9. Which of the following configurations is used to create a Layer 2 (nonrouted) VLAN on a Cisco IOS–based switch?

   a.
```
config t
interface fa0/1
vlan enable
vlan 5
```

   b.
```
config t
vlan database
vlan
vlan enable 7
```

   c.
```
config t
vlan 7
end
```

   d.
```
config t
interface vlan 1
no shut
end
```

10. Which of the following commands is used to create a trunk?

   a. `switchport mode trunk`

   b. `switchport trunk enable`

   c. `switchport trunk`

   d. `trunk enable`

11. Which of the following commands defines the native VLAN?

   a. `native vlan 1`

   b. `switchport native vlan 1`

   c. `switchport mode native 1`

   d. `switchport trunk native vlan 1`

12. Which of the following configurations applies VLAN 25 to FastEthernet interface 0/3?

a. ```
    conf t
    interface f0/1
    switchport mode trunk
    vlan 25
    ```

b.  ```
    conf t
    interface f0/3
    switchport mode access
    vlan 25
    ```

c. ```
    conf t
    interface f0/3
    switchport mode access
    switchport access vlan 25
    ```

d.  ```
    conf t
    interface f0/4
    switchport mode trunk
    vlan 25
    ```

Foundation Topics

The Wireless Network Road Trip

At this point, you already have an understanding of how frames are sent on a wireless network. In the Cisco Unified Wireless Network, frames do not stay on the wireless network; rather, they travel from a lightweight AP to a wireless LAN controller (WLC). The WLC and lightweight APs are discussed in Chapter 10, "Cisco Wireless Networks Architecture." The purpose of this chapter is to familiarize you with how traffic is kept separate as it travels from the AP to the WLC and then to the wired network. To better understand this process, you must understand how a network typically looks and the process that each device uses to send and receive data.

The Association Process

To begin, you need a network. This chapter uses the common logical topology seen in Figure 9-1. As you can see, multiple wireless clients are in range of an AP that is advertising multiple service set identifiers (SSID). One SSID puts users on a network that is offered to guest users called Guest. The other SSID is called UserNet and is designed for authenticated users of the corporate network. Naturally, more security is going to be applied to users of UserNet, such as authentication and encryption, as opposed to the network Guest. The Guest network places users on the 172.30.1.0/24 subnet. The UserNet places users on the 10.99.99.0/24 network. Although these two networks are on different subnets and users associate with different SSIDs, recall that an AP can advertise multiple SSIDs but actually uses the same wireless radio. In the wireless space, the SSID and IP subnet keep the networks logically separated.

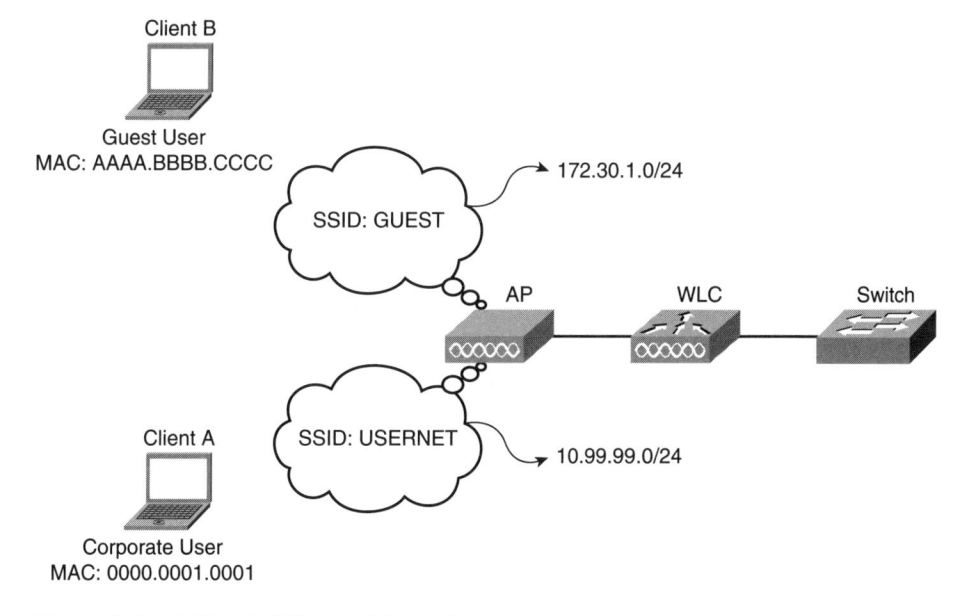

Figure 9-1 *A Simple Wireless Network*

Clients have more than one way to find an AP and associate with it. A client can passively scan the network and listen on each frequency for beacons being sent by an AP, or it can use an active scan process and send a probe request in search of a specific AP. Users of the UserNet would likely actively scan the network, whereas a guest would passively scan. The detailed method of client interaction is covered in Chapter 16, "Wireless Clients."

Getting back to the association process, a client scans the channels hoping to hear a beacon from an AP or actively sends a probe request. If a probe response is received or a beacon is heard, the client can attempt to associate with the SSID received in that probe response or beacon.

The next step is to authenticate and associate with the AP. When the client chooses an SSID, it sends an authentication request. The AP should reply with an authentication response. After this occurs and a "Success" message is received, an association request is sent, including the data rates and capabilities of the client, followed by an association response from the AP. The association response from the AP includes the data rates that the AP is capable of, other capabilities, and an identification number for the association.

Next, the client must determine the speed. It does this by determining the Received Signal Strength Indicator (RSSI) and signal-to-noise ratio (SNR), and it chooses the best speed to send at based on these determinations. All management frames are sent at the lowest rate, whereas the data headers can be sent faster than management frames, and the actual data frames at the fastest possible rate. Just as the client determines its rates to send, the AP, in turn, does the same. Now that the client is associated, it can attempt to send data to other devices on the network.

Sending to a Host on Another Subnet

When a client is associated with an AP, the general idea is to send data to other devices. To illustrate this, first try to send data between Client A in Figure 9-2, which is on the User-Net network, and Client B, which is on the Guest network. Although a typical network would not allow guest users to send traffic to internal WLAN users for security purposes, this will provide an example of how the connection works.

The two clients are clearly on two different subnets, so the rules of how IP works are still in play. The clients cannot send traffic directly to each other. Based on normal IP rules, they would first determine that the other is *not* on the same subnet and then decide to use a default gateway to relay the information. If a client has never communicated with the default gateway, it uses Address Resolution Protocol (ARP) to resolve its MAC address. The process would appear as follows:

Step 1.   Client A wants to send traffic to Client B.

Step 2.   Client A determines that the IP address of Client B is not on the same subnet.

Step 3.   Client A decides to send the traffic to the default gateway of 10.99.99.5.

Step 4.   Client A looks in its ARP table for a mapping to the gateway, but it is not there.

Step 5.   Client A creates an ARP request and sends to the AP, as seen in Figure 9-3.

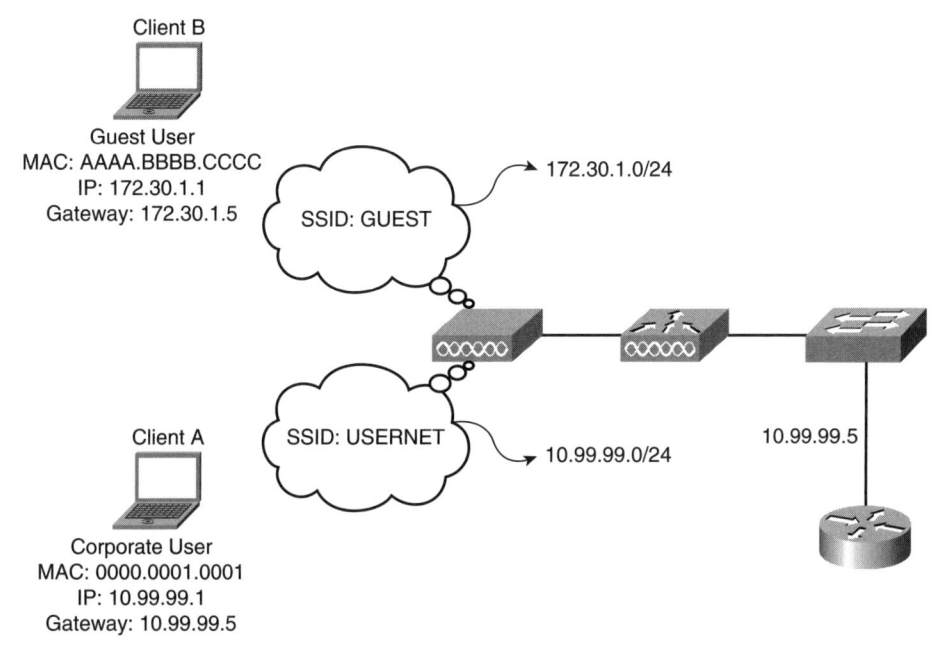

Figure 9-2 *Client A Communicating with Client B*

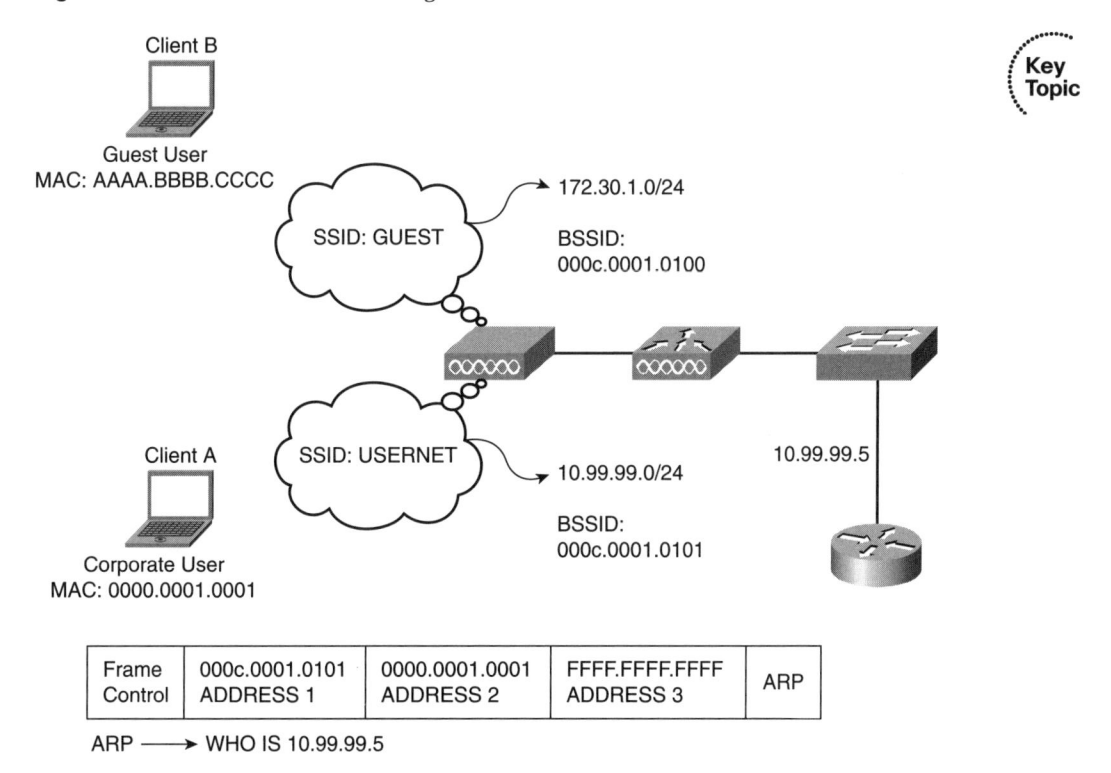

Frame Control	000c.0001.0101 ADDRESS 1	0000.0001.0001 ADDRESS 2	FFFF.FFFF.FFFF ADDRESS 3	ARP

ARP ⟶ WHO IS 10.99.99.5

Figure 9-3 *ARPing for the Gateway*

When the ARP request is sent to the AP, it is an interesting process and actually works a little bit differently than on a wired network. Remember that on a wired network, the header has only two MAC addresses: the source address and the destination address. An 802.11 frame can have four addresses: the source address (SA), destination address (DA), transmitter address (TA), and receiving address (RA). In this situation, the SA is the MAC of the client sending the ARP request, the DA is broadcast (for the ARP), and the RA is the AP. No TA is present in this example.

Figure 9-4 shows the ARP request.

Key Topic

Frame Control	ADDRESS 1 000c.0001.0101	ADDRESS 2 0000.0001.0001	ADDRESS 3 FFFF.FFFF.FFFF	ARP REQUEST

Figure 9-4 *ARP Request*

The AP receives the ARP and sees its MAC address. It verifies the frame check sequence (FCS) in the frame and waits the short interframe space (SIFS) time. When the SIFS time expires, it sends an ACK back to the wireless client that sent the ARP request. This ACK is not an ARP response; rather, it is an ACK for the wireless frame transmission.

The AP then forwards the frame to the WLC using the Lightweight Access Point Protocol (LWAPP), as illustrated in Figure 9-5.

Key Topic

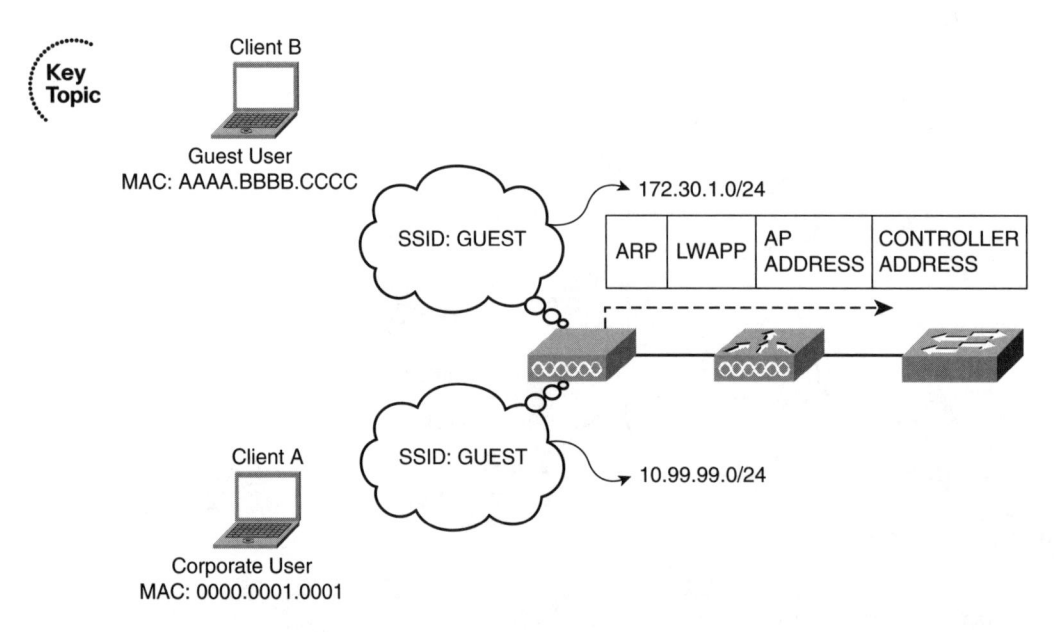

Figure 9-5 *ARP Forwarded in LWAPP Frame*

The LWAPP frame that travels from the AP to the WLC is traveling on a wired network. This brings forth the question, "What happened to the 802.11 frame format?" LWAPP simply encapsulates the frame inside a 6-byte header. The new 6-byte header has the AP IP and MAC address as the source and the WLC IP and MAC address as the destination. Encapsulated inside of that header is the original 802.11 frame with the three MAC addresses, including the broadcast MAC address for the ARP process. When the WLC receives the LWAPP frame, it opens the frame revealing the ARP request and rewrites the ARP request in an 802.3 frame that can be sent across the wired network. The first address from the 802.11 frame is dropped, the second address is placed as the source address in the new 802.3 frame, and the third address, the broadcast address, is placed as the destination address. The WLC then forwards the ARP request, in 802.3 format, across the wired network, as seen in Figure 9-6. Here you can see how the frame appears between the wireless Client A and the AP, how the AP encapsulates the frame and sends it to the WLC, and how the WLC rewrites the frame and sends it to the wired network.

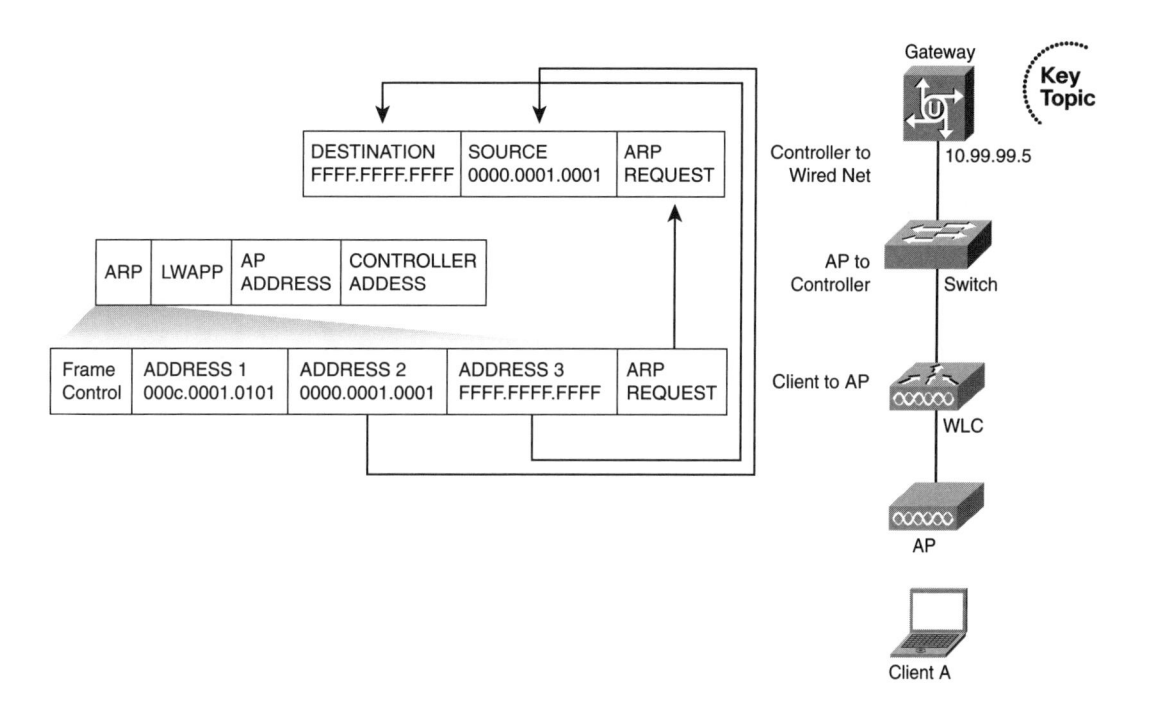

Figure 9-6   *WLC Forwarding the ARP Toward the Gateway*

As switches receive the ARP request, they read the destination MAC address, which is a broadcast, and flood the frame out all ports except the one it came in on. The exception to this rule is if VLANs are in use, in which case the frame would be flooded to all ports that are members of the same VLAN. Assuming that VLANs are not in use, the frame, as stated, is flooded out all ports except the one it came in on.

At some point, the frame will be received by a Layer 3 device, hopefully the default gateway. In Figure 9-7, the router has received the ARP request and will respond to it with its MAC address.

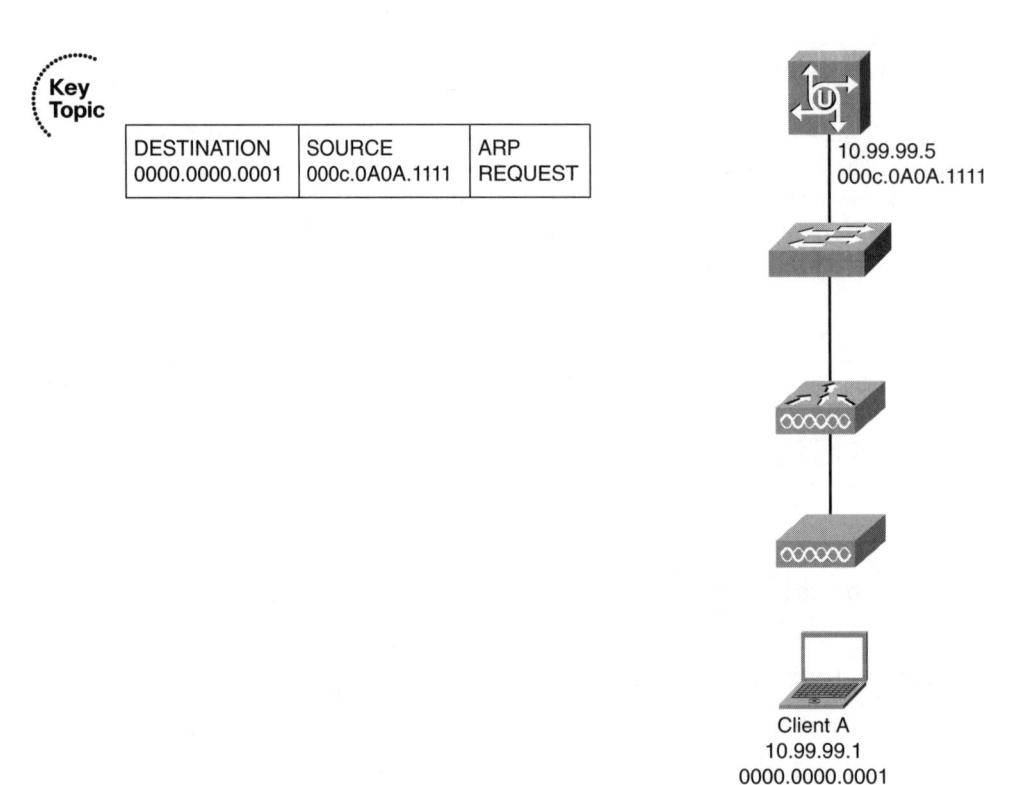

DESTINATION	SOURCE	ARP
0000.0000.0001	000c.0A0A.1111	REQUEST

Figure 9-7 *Gateway Responds to ARP*

That ARP response is sent back as a unicast message, so the switches in the path are going to forward it directly to the port that leads back to the wireless client, rather than flooding the frame out all ports. Eventually the frame is received by the WLC, and it must be rebuilt as an 802.11 frame. When the WLC rewrites the frame, it places the DA as address 1, the SA as address 3, and the TA as address 2, which is the SSID of the AP. Figure 9-8 illustrates this process.

As illustrated in Figure 9-9, the newly formed 802.11 frame is placed inside an LWAPP header where the AP IP and MAC is the destination and the WLC IP and MAC is the source. The LWAPP frame is forwarded to the AP.

Next, the AP must remove the LWAPP header, exposing the 802.11 frame. The 802.11 frame is buffered, and the process of sending a frame on the wireless network begins. The AP starts a backoff timer and begins counting down. If a wireless frame is heard during the countdown, the reservation in the heard frame is added to the countdown and the AP continues. Eventually, the timer expires, and the frame can be sent an 802.11 frame.

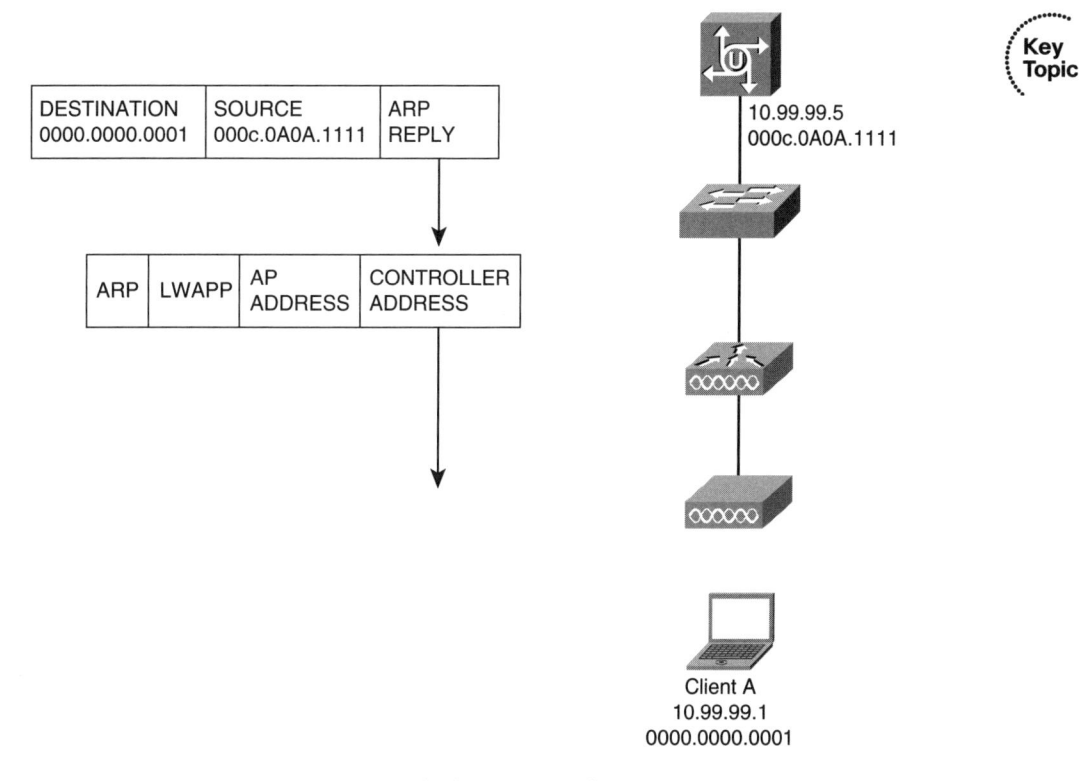

Key
Topic

Figure 9-8 *WLC Receives ARP Reply from GW and Converts It to LWAPP*

The client, upon receiving the frame, sends an ACK after waiting the SIFS value.

The ARP process of the client now has a mapping to the GW MAC address and can dispatch the awaiting frame. Remember that it still must follow the rules, a backoff timer, and a contention window and eventually transmit the frame following the ARP response.

Using VLANs to Add Control

Here is where things get a little tricky, which brings out the real purpose for this section. According to the topology that this example is using, the client is trying to communicate with another device that is connected to the same AP, but it just associates with a different SSID and on a different subnet. The question is, "How do the AP and WLC keep the two subnets separate when they are on the wired network?" The answer is VLANs. A *VLAN* is a concept in switched networks that allows segmentation of users at a logical level. By using VLANs on the wired side of the AP and WLC, the client subnet can be logically segmented, just as it is on the wireless space. The results look like this:

> SSID = Logical Subnet = Logical VLAN or Logical Broadcast Domain

After the wireless frames move from the AP to the wired network, they must share a single physical wire. You may think this is hard because having multiple BSSIDs means there is more than one network, but it is not hard. The way this is accomplished is by using the 802.1Q protocol. 802.1Q places a 4-byte tag in each 802.3 frame to indicate which VLAN

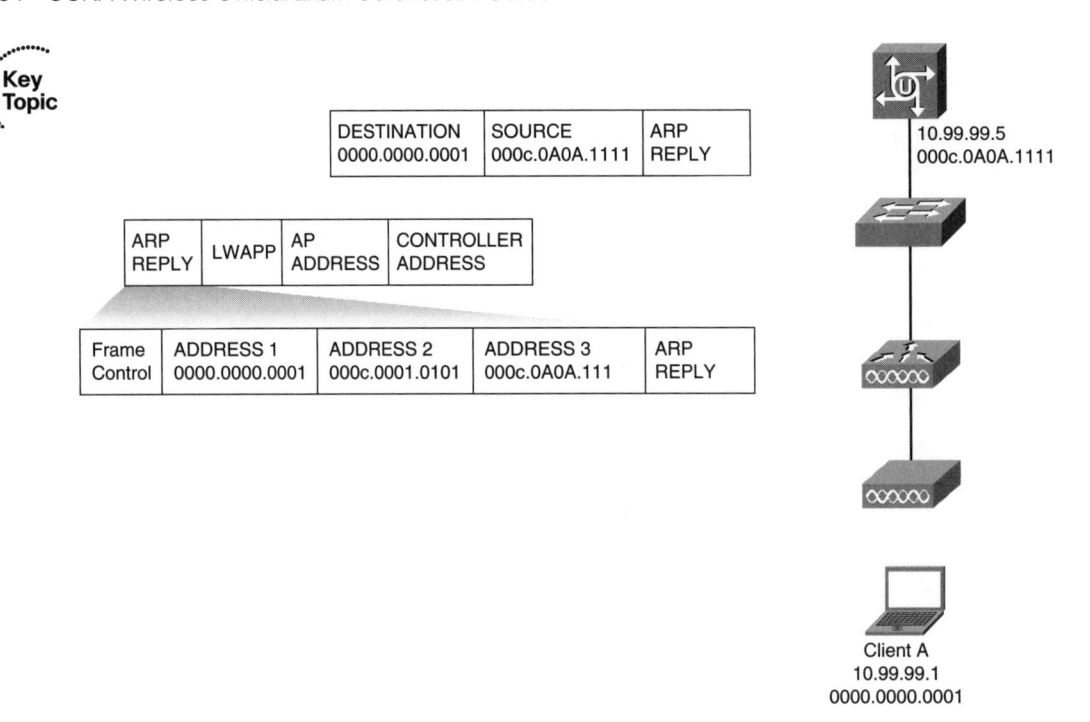

Figure 9-9   *WLC Forwards LWAPP Frame to AP*

the frame is a member of. If the frames from the Guest network are on VLAN 10, the tag indicates VLAN 10; in turn, the frames from the UserNet network would be tagged with VLAN 20. Although they ride the same wire, they are logically segmented by their VLAN membership. The switches on either end of the "trunk link" know which VLAN frames belong to based on their 802.1Q tag.

VLAN Membership Modes

Ports on switches are either going to be access ports that are associated with one VLAN or trunk ports that allow traffic for more than one VLAN to traverse them provided they are tagged by 802.1Q. The only exception to the rule is when frames are on the native VLAN, which is discussed in the next section.

When in access mode, no VLAN tag exists; rather, the port is assigned the VLAN membership. When traffic comes off that port and is destined for another port that connects to another switch, the 802.1Q protocol uses the VLAN membership information to create the tag. Therefore, all traffic that is sent on a trunk link includes a tag, with the exception of the native VLAN. But what is a native VLAN?

The native VLAN is an IEEE stipulation to the 802.1Q protocol that states that frames on the native VLAN are not modified when they are sent over trunk links. In Cisco switches, the default native VLAN is VLAN 1. An administrator can change this, however. Because you can modify it, it is important to ensure that the native VLAN is the same VLAN on both ends of the link. Because the traffic for the native VLAN is not tagged, the switches assume that the frames are on the native VLAN. If the native VLAN is different on either side, traffic can hop from one VLAN to another, as seen in Figure 9-10.

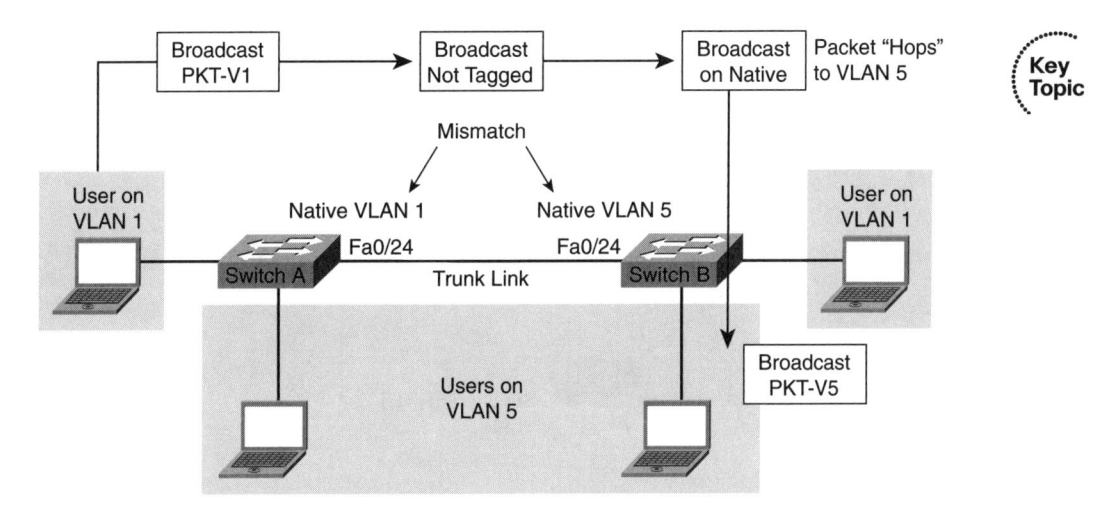

Figure 9-10   *Native VLAN Mismatch*

Because the native VLAN on Switch A port Fa0/24 is sent to VLAN 1, all traffic on VLAN 1 will not be tagged. On Switch B, port Fa0/24, the native VLAN is 5. This means that all traffic coming across the link from Switch A, without a tag, is assumed to be in VLAN 5. When the user attached to a VLAN 1 interface on Switch A sends a broadcast, it is forwarded across the trunk link without a tag. Switch B believes the broadcast to be for VLAN 5 users because that is the native VLAN on that interface, and it forwards the frame to users of VLAN 5. Again, this is to be avoided because it can be a security concern in one aspect, and it can break overall connectivity in another. In the end, the easiest way to avoid this is to ensure that both interfaces between switches are configured for the same native VLAN.

Configuring VLANs and Trunks

To configure VLANs and trunks to support your wireless topology, first understand your topology. By understanding your topology, you will see where to use access ports, where to use trunk ports, and how the configuration will come together. Figure 9-11 shows a sample topology that is used for the remainder of the configuration examples given in this chapter.

Although a switched network has additional design aspects, do not concern yourself with them for the CCNA wireless certification. Understand that you simply need to be proficient in configuring the ports. To do so, you need to perform the following tasks:

Step 1.   Create a VLAN on the switch.

Step 2.   Assign ports to the VLAN that you create.

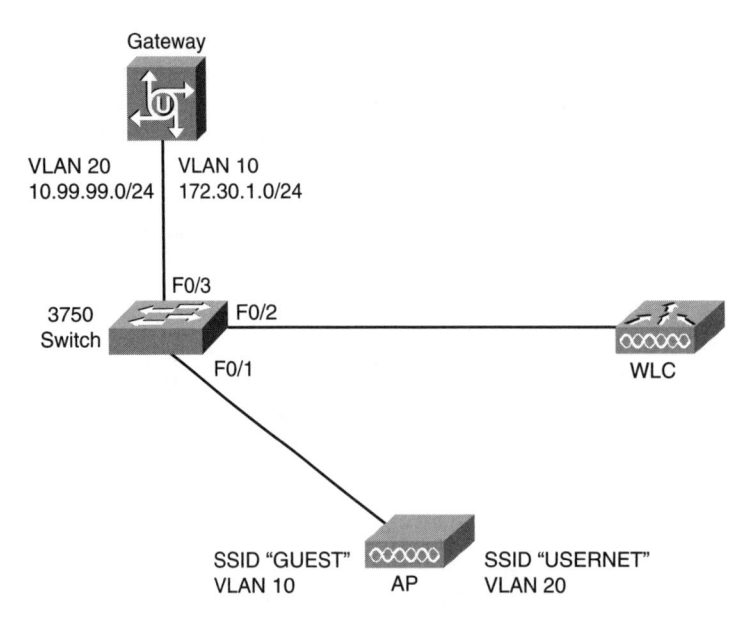

Figure 9-11 *VLAN Topology*

Step 3. Save the configuration.

Step 4. Configure trunk ports where necessary.

Using the standard topology in Figure 9-11, the first step is to create the VLANs that you will use. In the figure, VLANs 10 and 20 are in use. You will then assign a VLAN to an interface on the switch or configure the proper interface as a trunk. You should begin with the VLAN configuration.

Creating VLANs

VLANs are identified by a number ranging from 1 to 4094 on most switch platforms. VLANs ranging from 1 to 1001 are stored in a VLAN database. VLANs 1002 through 1005 are reserved for Token Ring and FDDI VLANs and are created by default. You cannot remove them. VLANs greater than 1005 are considered extended-range VLANs and are not stored in the VLAN database.

Follow these guidelines when defining VLANs:

■ The switch supports 1005 VLANs in VTP client, server, and transparent modes.

Note: VTP is the VLAN Trunk Protocol, designed to maintain consistency of VLANs in a network. This topic is beyond the scope of this book and will not be discussed. For more information on VLANs, see *Interconnecting Cisco Network Devices, Part 2 (ICND2): (CCNA Exam 640-802 and ICND Exam 640-816)*, 3rd Edition, published by Cisco Press.

■ Normal-range VLANs are identified with a number between 1 and 1001. VLAN numbers 1002 through 1005 are reserved for Token Ring and FDDI VLANs.[1]

- VLAN configuration for VLANs 1 to 1005 is always saved in the VLAN database. If the VTP mode is transparent, VTP and VLAN configuration are also saved in the switch running configuration file.[1]

- The switch also supports VLAN IDs 1006 through 4094 in VTP transparent mode (VTP disabled). These are extended-range VLANs, and configuration options are limited. Extended-range VLANs are not saved in the VLAN database.

- Before you can create a VLAN, the switch must be in VTP server mode or VTP transparent mode. If the switch is a VTP server, you must define a VTP domain, or VTP will not function.[1]

Cisco switches have default VLAN values. VLAN 1 is assigned to each interface, and the port is configured to dynamically determine if trunking is being used.

To add a VLAN to a switch, use the command **vlan** *vlan-id*. You can see this in Table 9-2.

Table 9-2 *VLAN Creation Commands*

Command	Action
vlan *vlan-id*	Enter a VLAN ID, and enter config-vlan mode. Enter a new VLAN ID to create a VLAN, or enter an existing VLAN ID to modify that VLAN.
name *vlan-name*	(Optional) Enter a name for the VLAN. If no name is entered for the VLAN, the default is to append the VLAN ID with leading zeros to the word *VLAN*.

The steps to create a VLAN are as follows:

Step 1. Access global configuration mode using the **configure terminal** command.

Step 2. Create the VLAN using the **vlan** command.

Step 3. Optionally give the VLAN a name using the **name** command.

Step 4. Exit to privileged EXEC mode using the **end** command.

You can verify your work using the **show vlan** command.

In Example 9-1, VLANs 10 and 20 are created on the 3750 switch seen in Figure 9-11. These VLANs are used for the trunk interfaces between the AP and switch, switch and controller, and switch and GW router.

Example 9-1 *Creating the VLANs*

```
Switch#configure terminal
Enter configuration commands, one per line. End with CNTL/Z.

Switch(config)#vlan 10
Switch(config-vlan)#exit

Switch(config)#vlan 20
Switch(config-vlan)#exit
```

```
Switch(config)#end
Switch#
00:01:07: %SYS-5-CONFIG_I: Configured from console by consol

Switch#show vlan brief

VLAN Name                     Status  Ports
-- -----------------------  -----  ---------------------.
1   default                  active  Fa0/1, Fa0/2, Fa0/3, Fa0/4
                                     Fa0/5, Fa0/6, Fa0/7, Fa0/8
                                     Fa0/9, Fa0/10, Fa0/11, Fa0/12
                                     Fa0/13, Fa0/14, Fa0/15, Fa0/16
                                     Fa0/17, Fa0/18, Fa0/19, Fa0/20
                                     Fa0/21, Fa0/22, Gi0/1, Gi0/2

10  VLAN0010                 active

20  VLAN0020                 active
1002 fddi-default              act/unsup
1003 token-ring-default          act/unsup
1004 fddinet-default         act/unsup
1005 trnet-default           act/unsup
```

The next step is to assign ports to a VLAN.

Assigning Ports to a VLAN

After you have created the VLANs you plan to use, you need to manually assign them to a port and place the port in access mode. To do this, use the **switchport access** and **switchport mode** commands, as seen in Table 9-3.

Key Topic

Table 9-3 *Port Assignment Commands*

Command	Action
switchport mode access	Defines the VLAN membership mode for the port
switchport access vlan *vlan-id*	Assigns the port to a VLAN

The steps to assign a port to a VLAN are as follows:

Step 1.   Access global configuration mode using the **configure terminal** command.

Step 2.   Access the interface using the **interface** command.

Step 3.   Set the membership mode to access using the **switchport mode access** command.

Step 4.   Assign a VLAN to the port using the **switchport access vlan** *vlan-id* command.

Step 5.   Exit to privileged EXEC mode using the **end** command.

Step 6.   You can verify your work using the **show interface status** and **show interface** *interface* **switchoprt** commands.

In Figure 9-11, no ports will be made access ports, but if you needed to do this, your configuration would resemble Example 9-2. Notice that you can use the **show interface status** command to verify the VLAN assignment.

Example 9-2   *Assigning a Port to a VLAN*

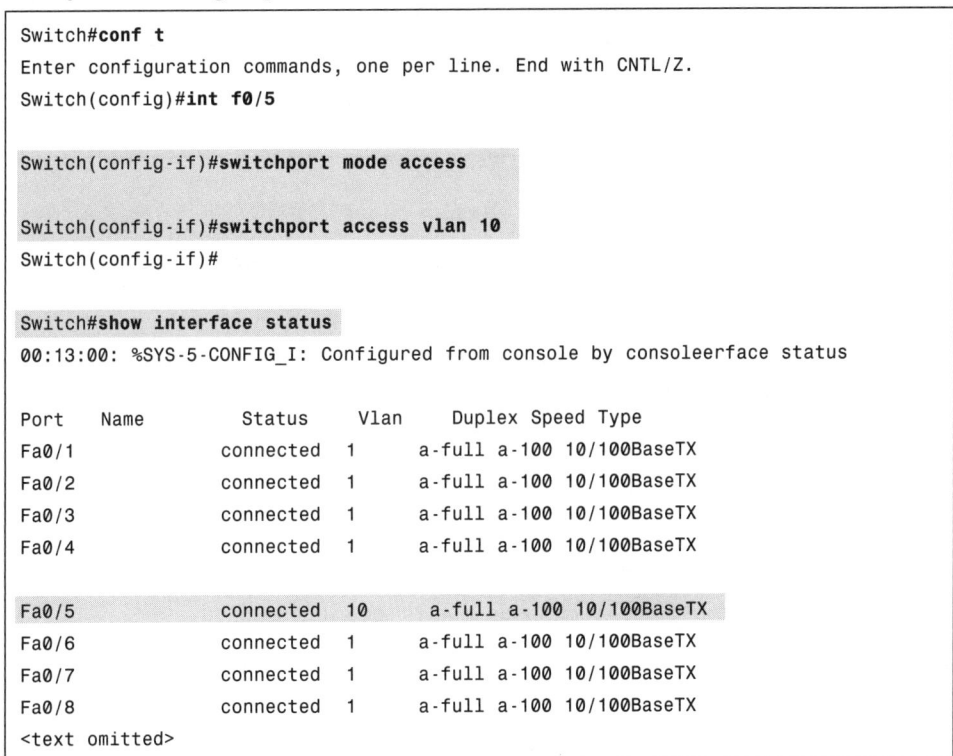

```
Switch#conf t
Enter configuration commands, one per line. End with CNTL/Z.
Switch(config)#int f0/5

Switch(config-if)#switchport mode access

Switch(config-if)#switchport access vlan 10
Switch(config-if)#

Switch#show interface status
00:13:00: %SYS-5-CONFIG_I: Configured from console by consoleerface status

Port    Name        Status    Vlan    Duplex Speed Type
Fa0/1               connected  1      a-full a-100 10/100BaseTX
Fa0/2               connected  1      a-full a-100 10/100BaseTX
Fa0/3               connected  1      a-full a-100 10/100BaseTX
Fa0/4               connected  1      a-full a-100 10/100BaseTX

Fa0/5               connected  10       a-full a-100 10/100BaseTX
Fa0/6               connected  1      a-full a-100 10/100BaseTX
Fa0/7               connected  1      a-full a-100 10/100BaseTX
Fa0/8               connected  1      a-full a-100 10/100BaseTX
<text omitted>
```

After you save the configuration, the next step is to create the trunks.

Creating Trunk Ports

The next task to accomplish is the trunk configuration. You normally perform this configuration on interfaces that connect between switches, on AP-to-controller interfaces where an AP is supporting more than on SSID, and on controller-to-switch interfaces, where the controller is supporting multiple SSIDs mapped to multiple dynamic interfaces.

To enable trunking in the interface, use the **switchport mode** command. Next, use the **switchport trunk** command to set the native VLAN and the encapsulation type. Most switches default to use 802.1Q trunking, but on some switches, you might have other options. Table 9-4 lists the commands that you use to enable trunking.

Table 9-4   *Enable Trunking Commands*

Command	Action
switchport mode trunk	Defines the interface as a trunk
switchport trunk encapsulation dot1q	Defines the trunking protocol as 802.1Q
switchport trunk native *vlan#*	Configures the native VLAN is using something other than VLAN 1
switchport nonegotiate	Tells the switch that either side of the link must be hard coded to trunk and no type of dynamic negotiation is taking place

The steps to create a trunk port are as follows:

Step 1.   Access global configuration mode using the **configure terminal** command.

Step 2.   Access the interface using the **interface** command.

Step 3.   Set the interface to use 802.1Q encapsulation using the **switchport trunk encapsulation dot1q** command.

Step 4.   Set the interface to trunk using the **switchport mode trunk** command.

Step 5.   (Optional) Set the trunk's native VLAN using the **switchport trunk native** *vlan#* command.

Step 6.   Tell the switch not to negotiate using the **switchport nonegotiate** command.

Step 7.   Exit to privileged EXEC mode using the **end** command.

Step 8.   You can verify your work using the **show interface status** and **show interface** *interface* **switchport** and **show interface** *interface* **trunk** commands.

With these configuration items in place, you can successfully control the flow of traffic and keep subnets segmented in your switches. For Figure 9-11, the trunk configuration takes place on interface Fa0/1, Fa0/2, and Fa0/3, as seen in Example 9-3.

Example 9-3   *Trunk Configuration*

```
Switch#enable
! To simplify configuration, you can set the parameters on a range of interfaces
rather than one at a time

Switch(config)#interface range f0/1 - 3

Switch(config-if-range)#switchport trunk encapsulation dot1q
```

```
Switch(config-if-range)#switchport mode trunk
Switch(config-if-range)#
00:15:42: %LINEPROTO-5-UPDOWN: Line protocol on Interface FastEthernet0/1, changed
   state to down
00:15:42: %LINEPROTO-5-UPDOWN: Line protocol on Interface FastEthernet0/2, changed
   state to down
00:15:42: %LINEPROTO-5-UPDOWN: Line protocol on Interface FastEthernet0/3, changed
   state to downswitchpoer
00:15:45: %LINEPROTO-5-UPDOWN: Line protocol on Interface FastEthernet0/1, changed
   state to up
00:15:46: %LINEPROTO-5-UPDOWN: Line protocol on Interface FastEthernet0/2, changed
   state to up
00:15:46: %LINEPROTO-5-UPDOWN: Line protocol on Interface FastEthernet0/3, changed
   state to up

Switch(config-if-range)#switchport nonegotiate

Switch(config-if-range)#switchport trunk native vlan 1
Switch(config-if-range)#
! Exit Back to Priviledge EXEC to verify

Switch(config-if-range)#end
!Use the following command to verify what interfaces are enabled for trunking
Switch#show interface trunk
00:19:55: %SYS-5-CONFIG_I: Configured from console by consoleow interface trunk

Port     Mode     Encapsulation Status     Native vlan

Fa0/1    on       802.1q        trunking   1

Fa0/2    on       802.1q        trunking   1

Fa0/3    on       802.1q        trunking   1
Fa0/23   desirable 802.1q        trunking   1
Fa0/24   desirable 802.1q        trunking   1
! Output omitted for brevity
```

With this minimal switch configuration, the APs, controllers, and gateway should all be able to communicate.

Note: The **native vlan** statement is only required to switch configurations on controllers when the value is left to "0" in the controller.

Exam Preparation Tasks

Review All the Key Concepts

Review the most important topics from this chapter, noted with the Key Topics icon in the outer margin of the page. Table 9-5 lists a reference of these key topics and the page number where you can find each one.

Table 9-5   *Key Topics for Chapter 9*

Key Topic Item	Description	Page Number
Figure 9-3	ARPing for the gateway	149
Figure 9-4	ARP request	150
Figure 9-5	ARP forwarded in LWAPP frame	150
Figure 9-6	WLC forwarding the ARP toward the gateway	151
Figure 9-7	Gateway responds to ARP	152
Figure 9-8	WLC receives ARP reply from GW and converts it to LWAPP	153
Figure 9-9	WLC forwards LWAPP frame to AP	154
Figure 9-10	Native VLAN mismatch	155
Table 9-2	VLAN creation commands	157
Example 9-2	Creating VLANs	159
Table 9-3	Port assignment commands	158
Example 9-3	Assigning a port to a VLAN	160
Table 9-4	Enable trunking commands	160

Complete the Tables and Lists from Memory

Print a copy of Appendix B, "Memory Tables," (found on the CD) or at least the section for this chapter, and complete the tables and lists from memory. Appendix C, "Memory Tables Answer Key," also on the CD, includes completed tables and lists to check your work.

Definition of Key Terms

Define the following key terms from this chapter, and check your answers in the Glossary:

lightweight AP, WLC, ARP, SA, TA, RA, DA, LWAPP, VLAN, access port, trunk port, 802.1Q, native VLAN

Command Reference to Check Your Memory

This section includes the most important configuration and EXEC commands covered in this chapter. To check to see how well you have memorized the commands as a side effect of your other studies, cover the left side of Table 9-6 with a piece of paper, read the descriptions on the right side, and see whether you remember the command.

Table 9-6   *Chapter 9 Command Reference*

Command	Description
vlan *vlan-id*	Creates a VLAN
switchport mode access	Configures a port as an access port
switchport access vlan *vlan-id*	Assigns a VLAN to a port
switchport mode trunk	Enables a port to act as a trunk port
switchport trunk native vlan *vlan-id*	Sets the native VLAN on a trunk
show interface status	Verifies VLAN assignments
show interface trunk	Verifies trunk configurations

End Notes

[1]Configuring VLANs, http://tinyurl.com/588kw9

Cisco Published 640-721 IUWNE Exam Topics Covered in This Part

Install a basic Cisco wireless LAN

- Describe the basics of the Cisco Unified Wireless Network architecture (Split MAC, LWAPP, stand-alone AP versus controller-based AP, specific hardware examples)

- Describe the Cisco Mobility Express Wireless architecture (Smart Business Communication System — SBCS, Cisco Config Agent — CCA, 526WLC, 521AP - stand-alone and controller-based)

- Describe the modes of controller-based AP deployment (local, monitor, HREAP, sniffer, rogue detector, bridge)

- Describe controller-based AP discovery and association (OTAP, DHCP, DNS, Master-Controller, Primary-Secondary-Tertiary, n+1 redundancy)

- Describe roaming (Layer 2 and Layer 3, intra-controller and inter-controller, mobility groups)

- Configure a WLAN controller and access points WLC: ports, interfaces, WLANs, NTP, CLI and Web UI, CLI wizard, LAG AP: Channel, Power

- Configure the basics of a stand-alone access point (no lab) (Express setup, basic security)

- Describe RRM

Install Wireless Clients

- Describe client OS WLAN configuration (Windows, Apple, and Linux.)

- Install Cisco ADU

- Describe basic CSSC

- Describe CCX versions 1 through 5

Part II: Cisco Wireless LANs

This chapter covers the following subjects:

The Need for Centralized Control: Briefly discusses the need for centralized control in a wireless deployment.

The Cisco Solution: Looks at the Cisco Unified Wireless Network.

The CUWN Architecture: Covers the devices in a Cisco Unified Wireless Network.

CHAPTER 10

Cisco Wireless Networks Architecture

In the past, wireless networks were deployed on an AP-by-AP basis, and the configuration for each AP was stored on the AP itself. Management solutions existed, but all in all this is not a scalable solution. The Cisco Unified Wireless Solution involves an AP that is managed by a controller device. The controller devices can manage multiple APs. The AP configuration is performed on the controller, and each AP added to the network gets its configuration from a controller. This makes it a more viable solution for large enterprise networks.

You should do the "Do I Know This Already?" quiz first. If you score 80 percent or higher, you might want to skip to the section "Exam Preparation Tasks." If you score below 80 percent, you should review the entire chapter. Refer to Appendix A, "Answers to the 'Do I Know This Already?' Quizzes," to confirm your answers.

"Do I Know This Already?" Quiz

The "Do I Know This Already?" quiz helps you determine your level of knowledge of this chapter's topics before you begin. Table 10-1 details the major topics discussed in this chapter and their corresponding quiz questions.

Table 10-1 *"Do I Know This Already?" Section-to-Question Mapping*

Foundation Topics Section	Questions
The Need for Centralized Control	1
The Cisco Solution	2–7
The CUWN Architecture	8–17

1. What kind of AP does a controller manage?

    a. Lightweight AP

    b. Managed AP

    c. LDAP AP

    d. Autonomous AP

2. Which of the following is not a functional area of the Cisco Unified Wireless Network?

   a. AP

   b. Controller

   c. Client

   d. ACS

3. Of all the Cisco Wireless LAN Controllers, what is the greatest number of APs you can support?

   a. Up to 50

   b. Up to 150

   c. Up to 300

   d. Up to 30,000

4. What protocol is used for communication between an AP and a WLC?

   a. STP

   b. LWAPP

   c. LDAP

   d. TCP

5. Which of the following functions does the controller handle? (Choose all that apply.)

   a. Association

   b. Reassociation when you have clients that are roaming

   c. The authentication process

   d. Frame exchange and the handshake between the clients

6. Which of the following functions does the AP handle? (Choose all that apply.)

   a. Buffer and transmit the frames for clients that are in power-save mode

   b. Frame bridging

   c. Send responses to probe requests from different clients on the network

   d. Forward notifications of received probe requests to the controller

7. How many VLANs does an AP typically handle?

   a. 13

   b. 15

   c. 16

   d. 512

8. How many elements comprise the CUWN architecture?

   a. 5

   b. 10

   c. 15

   d. 20

9. Which of the following APs support 802.11a/b and g? (Choose all that apply.)

   a. 1130AG

   b. 1240AG

   c. 1300 series

   d. 1400 series

10. Which AP supports the 802.11n draft version 2.0?

   a. 1250 series AP

   b. 1240 AG

   c. 1300 series

   d. 1130 AG

11. When an AP operates in H-REAP mode, where would it be seen?

   a. In a campus

   b. At the remote edge of a WAN

   c. In the data center

   d. Bridging site-to-site

12. The 4400 series WLC, model AIR-WLC4404-100-K9, can support up to how many APs?

   a. 50

   b. 100

   c. 300

   d. 600

13. True or false: An AP must run the same version of code as the controller.

   a. True

   b. False

14. What type of device is the 3750G series Wireless LAN Controller integrated into?

   a. A router as a module

   b. A router as part of the code

   c. A 3750 series switch

   d. It's a blade for the 6500 series.

15. How many APs can the Cisco WiSM manage?

   a.   100

   b.   150

   c.   300

   d.   600

16. How many lightweight APs can you have in a mobility domain?

   a.   512

   b.   1024

   c.   3068

   d.   7200

17. With wireless network management, what device is used to track more than one device at a time?

   a.   WCS

   b.   WCS navigator

   c.   Location appliance

   d.   Rogue AP detector

Foundation Topics

The Need for Centralized Control

There is certainly a need for centralized control in wireless deployments today. Initial wireless deployments were based on standalone access points called *autonomous access or fat APs*. An autonomous AP is one that does not rely on a central control device. Although this is a great start, the problem lies in scalability. Eventually, you will have problems keeping your configurations consistent, monitoring the state of each AP, and actually taking action when a change occurs. You end up with holes in your coverage area, and there is no real dynamic method to recover from that. There is certainly a need for centralized control, and the Cisco Unified Wireless Network (CUWN) is based on centralized control.

Eventually you will want or need to convert those standalone APs, if possible, to lightweight APs. A lightweight AP is managed with a controller.

Traditionally after a site survey, you would deploy your wireless network based on the information you gathered. As time passes, the environment you did the original site survey in will change. These changes, although sometimes subtle, will affect the wireless coverage. The CUWN addresses these issues.

An AP operating in lightweight mode gets its configuration from the controller. This means that you will perform most of your configuration directly on the controller. It dynamically updates the AP as the environment changes. This also allows all the APs to share a common configuration, increasing the uniformity of your wireless network and eliminating inconsistencies in your AP configurations.

The Cisco Solution

The CUWN solution is based on a centralized control model. Figure 10-1 illustrates the numerous components of the CUWN.

Figure 10-1 *Quick Look at the CUWN*

As you can see, five functional areas exist:

■   Wireless clients

- Access points

- Network unification

- Network management

- Network services

APs in the CUWN

Another type of device in a CUWN is a lightweight access point (AP). The lightweight AP is controlled and monitored by the Cisco Wireless LAN Controller (WLC). The AP communicates using a special protocol called the *Lightweight AP Protocol (LWAPP)* to relay information to the WLC about the coverage, the interference that the AP is experiencing, and client data about associations, among other pieces of information. This is a management type of communication, and via LWAPP it is encrypted. Client data is also sent inside these LWAPP frame headers. Client data travels from the wireless space to an AP, and then through a WLC and off to the rest of the network. When client data is encapsulated into an LWAPP header, you have not only the data, but also information about the Received Signal Strength Indicator (RSSI) and signal-to-noise ratio (SNR). The WLC uses this information to make decisions that can improve coverage areas.

WLCs in the CUWN

A single WLC can manage from six to 300 access points. You can create groupings of controllers for more scalability. This type of network could easily get out of hand if you had more than 300, 600, or 900 APs. In cases such as this, a WCS application can manage a number of controllers as well as a location appliance that can help track where devices are in the network.

Note: There is obviously more to the solution that what has been discussed in this section. For more information on the Unified Wireless Solution, visit http://www.cisco.com/go/wireless. This is the home page for the Cisco Unified Wireless Network. Here you can dig into the white papers, configuration guides, and much more.

The major point to understand is that in the CUWN, the AP uses LWAPP to exchange control message information with the controller. Client data is also encapsulated into LWAPP between the AP and the controller. The controller then forwards the data frames from those wireless clients to the wired network to get that traffic back and forth.

Features of the Cisco Controllers

One of the implemented designs of the Cisco Wireless LAN Controllers is the *split MAC* design. This means that you split 802 protocols between the controller and the APs. On one side, the APs handle the real-time portion and time-sensitive packets. On the other side, the controller handles the packets that are not time-sensitive.

The AP handles the following operations:

Key Topic

- Frame exchange and the handshake between clients

- Transmits beacons

- Buffers and transmits the frames for clients that are in power-save mode

- Sends responses to probe requests from different clients on the network

- Forwards notifications of received probe requests to the controller

- Provides real-time quality information to the controller

- Monitors all channels for noise and interference

The controller handles pretty much everything else. Remember that the controller handles packets that are not considered time-sensitive. This includes the following:

- Association

- Reassociation when you have clients that are roaming

- The authentication process

- Frame translation

- Frame bridging

Part of the control traffic that is sent back and forth via LWAPP is information that provides radio resource management (RRM). This RRM engine monitors the radio resources, performs dynamic channel assignments, provides detection and avoidance of interference, and provides the dynamic transmit power control (TPC) that was discussed in Chapter 1, "Introduction to Wireless Networking Concepts." Also, whenever coverage holes (such as when one AP goes down) are detected by another access point, the controller can actually adjust power settings on other APs in the area to correct the coverage hole.

LWAPP can operate in two modes:

- **Layer 2 LWAPP mode:** This mode deals only with MAC addresses. This makes sense, because this is the only type of addressing at Layer 2. In Layer 2 mode, the AP needs to be in the same subnet as the controller and hence does not provide much flexibility for large customer installations.

- **Layer 3 LWAPP mode:** When operating in Layer 3 mode, the LWAPP can see and use Layer 2 addresses (MAC addresses) and Layer 3 addresses (IP addresses). Layer 3 mode LWAPP allows the network administrator to place APs in different subnet boundaries, and the protocol traverses those boundaries.

Supporting Multiple Networks

Previous chapters discussed that an AP can actually advertise multiple SSIDs, which lets the AP offer guest access as well as corporate user access and maybe even access for wireless IP phones. Each Wireless LAN Controller actually can support 512 different VLAN instances. Remember that on the connection between the AP and the Wireless LAN Controller, all your wireless client data is passed via the LWAPP tunnel as it travels toward the wired domain.

To review, recall that an SSID exists only in the wireless space. An SSID is then tied to a VLAN within the controller. Each lightweight AP can support 512 different VLANs, but you don't very often see that many on one AP.

On the other hand, your Wireless LAN Controller can have up to 16 wireless LANs (WLAN) tied to each AP. Each WLAN is assigned a wireless LAN identification (WLANID) by the controller. This is a number between 1 and 16, and you don't get to choose which one to use.

So, now you have a WLAN that brings together the concept of an SSID on the wireless space and a VLAN on the wired space. By having separate WLANs, you can assign different quality-of-service (QoS) policies to the type of traffic encountered on each of them. An example of this would be to have a WLAN for IP Phones and a different WLAN for regular network users.

Each AP supports up to 16 SSIDs; generally, one SSID is mapped to one VLAN. With that said, even though a Wireless LAN Controller can support up to 512 VLANs per AP, you see a maximum of only 16 VLANs in most situations.

The CUWN Architecture

The Cisco Unified Wireless Network defines a total of five functional areas or interconnected elements, as shown in Figure 10-2.

The five elements or components all work together. It's no longer about point products, where you can buy a standalone AP and deploy it and then later get management software to handle it. Today it is all about everything working together to create a smarter, more functional network. To illustrate how it all comes together, consider a Cisco wireless network. This type of network includes the following wireless clients (the first component of the CUWN):

■   Cisco Aironet client devices

■   Cisco-compatible client devices (not necessarily Cisco products, but still compatible)

■   Cisco Secure Services Client (SSC)

The client devices get a user connected.

The second component, the access point, is dynamically managed by your controllers, and they use LWAPP to communicate. The AP bridges the client device to the wired network. A number of APs that could be discussed here are as follows:

■   The 1130AG

■   The 1240AG

■   The 1250AG

■   The 1300 series bridge

■   The 1400 series bridge

■   The 1500 series outdoor mesh

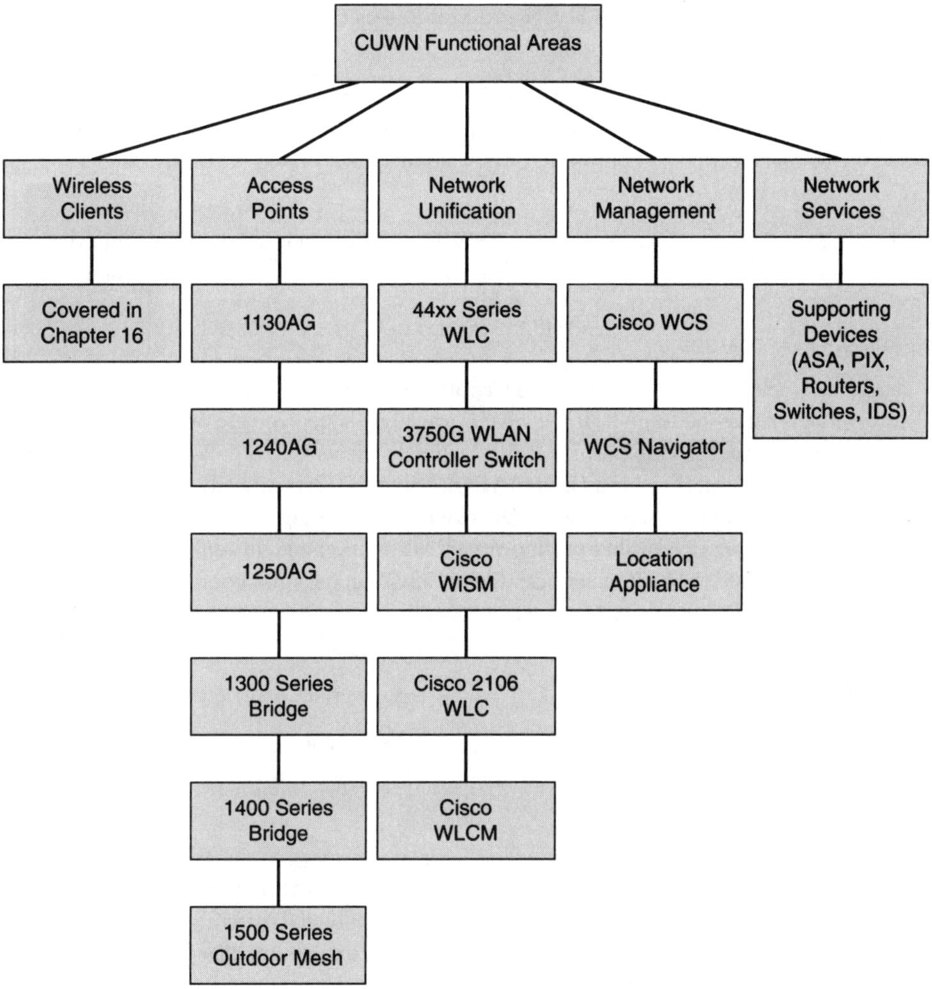

Figure 10-2 *CUWN Architecture*

Each of these access points is discussed in further detail in the section "Access Points."

The next functional area of the CUWN architecture—network unification—is the module that includes your controllers, including the following:

■ The 6500 series Catalyst switch Wireless Services Module (WiSM)

■ Cisco Wireless LAN Controller module (WLCM)

■ Cisco Catalyst 3750 series integrated WLC

■ Cisco 4400 series WLC

■ Cisco 2000 series WLC

The next functional area of the CUWN architecture—network management—is provided by the Cisco wireless control module.

The final functional area of the CUWN architecture—network services—includes everything else: the self-defending network, enhanced network support, such as location services, intrusion detection and prevention, firewalls, network admission control, and all those other services.

Those are the five functional areas of the CUWN. The following sections highlight the topics that you will want to be the most familiar with for the CCNA Wireless exam.

Client Devices

The Cisco wireless clients are covered in Chapter 16, "Wireless Clients," in greater detail. However, it is still good to understand what is available. When you are on a Cisco wireless network, you can actually use most vendors' wireless clients. Cisco provides wireless software called the Aironet Desktop Utility (ADU). The ADU is specifically used to manage and configure the Cisco wireless cards. Those wireless cards are discussed in more detail in Chapter 16. There is a cardbus version as well as a PCI version. In addition to the ADU, another client called the Secure Services Client (SSC) can help you configure security profiles for wired and wireless use on a Cisco network.

<img>Key Topic</img>

Access Points

As previously mentioned, there are two types of access points:

- Autonomous APs

- Lightweight APs

Some APs are built into modules and deployed in ISR routers at branch sites; other APs are deployed as just standalone devices. Cisco APs are known to offer the best range and throughput in the industry, as well as a number of security features that you do not find with other vendors.

Cisco APs offer multiple configuration options. Some of them support external antennas, some support internal antennas, and some are to be deployed outdoors. Still others are designed to be deployed indoors. Some APs are designed to be implemented for wide-area networking and bridging purposes and, while operating as a bridge, may also allow client connections. The point is that Cisco APs can serve a number of purposes.

The benefit of the CUWN APs is that they are zero-touch management, assuming that Layer 2 connectivity is already in place. As soon as they are plugged in and powered on, you don't have to do anything else at the AP level. The models that you need to be familiar with for the CCNA Wireless exam include the 1130AG, 1240AG, 1250AG, 1300, and 1400 series wireless bridges.

Note: Currently, the 1400 series bridge cannot be managed by the controller and is not considered an AP.

The 1130, 1240, and 1250 can be both autonomous and lightweight APs. Whereas the 1300 and 1400 series are designed to operate as bridges, the 1300 series can also support wireless clients. In turn, the 1400 series supports bridging only. Another model is the outdoor mesh 1500 series, which supports only LWAPP, so that would be designed for a lightweight scenario only.

Cisco is known for being ahead of the curve. That's where the special functionality of the 1250AG comes in. The 1250AG is one of the first access points to support the 802.11n draft version 2.0 standard and is the basis for all 802.11 Wi-Fi interoperability testing. For a client vendor to get the v2.0 stamp of approval, it must be validated against the 1250, and the 1250 is the only AP used during this validation.

The 1130AG

The 1130AG, shown in Figure 10-3, is a dual-band 802.11 a/b or g AP that has integrated antennas.

Courtesy of Cisco Systems, Inc. Unauthorized use not permitted.

Figure 10-3   *Cisco 1130AG Series AP*

The 1130AG can operate as a standalone device or in lightweight AP mode. It also can operate as a Hybrid Remote Edge AP (H-REAP) device. An H-REAP device operates on the far side of a WAN, and its controller is back at the core site.

The 1130AG is 802.11i/WPA2-compliant, and it has 32 MB of RAM and 16 MB of flash memory. The 1130 AP typically is deployed in office or hospital environments. Naturally, the internal antennas do not offer the same coverage and distance as APs that are designed for external antennas. Consider the 1130s. They have 3 dB gain and 4.5 dB gain for the 2.4- and 5-GHz frequencies, respectively. If you were to compare the 1131 to the 1242 with the 2.2 dipole antennas, you would see a larger coverage area than with the 1242.

The 1240AG

The 1240AG series AP, shown in Figure 10-4, is also a dual-band 802.11 a/b or g device, similar to the 1130AG; however, it supports only external antennas.

Courtesy of Cisco Systems, Inc. Unauthorized use not permitted.

Figure 10-4 *Cisco 1240AG Series AP*

Those external antennas would connect using the RP-TNC connectors. The 1240AG can operate as an autonomous AP and in lightweight AP mode. Like the 1130AG, it also can operate in H-REAP mode. It too is 802.11i/WPA2-compliant.

The 1250 Series AP

Shown in Figure 10-5, the 1250 series AP is one of the first enterprise APs to support the 802.11n draft version 2.0.

Because it supports the 802.11n draft standard, you can get data rates of about 300 Mbps on each radio and the 2-by-3 multiple input and multiple output technology. The 2-by-3 is discussed in Chapter 6, "Overview of the 802.11 WLAN Protocols." Also, because the 1250 is modular, it can easily be upgraded in the field. It operates in controller-based and standalone mode and is also 802.11i/WPA2-compliant.

The 1250 is designed for a more rugged type of indoor environment. You might see this at more hazardous locations such as packaging plants, or in situations where you might need

Courtesy of Cisco Systems, Inc. Unauthorized use not permitted.

Figure 10-5 *Cisco 1250 Series AP*

to place an antenna in a hazardous location and the AP elsewhere. You might see this type of AP in factories and hospitals. It has 64 MB of DRAM and 32 MB of flash memory. It has 2.4-GHz and 5-GHz radios.

The 1300 Series AP/Bridge

The Cisco Aironet 1300 series outdoor access point/bridge, shown in Figure 10-6, is designed to act as an AP for clients as well as act as a bridge.

The 1300 operates in only 802.11b or g modes because it does not have a 5-GHz radio. It has a NEMA-4-compliant enclosure, so you can deploy it in an outdoor environment and it can withstand the elements.

The 1300 series is available in two versions—one with integrated antennas and one with antenna connectors so that you can add your own antennas to it. The connectors would be 2.4-GHz antennas, because the 1300 series does not support 802.11a.

You would expect to find the 1300 series on a college campus in a quad-type area with outdoor users or mobile clients. You might also see it in public settings, such as a park, or as a temporary type of network access for a trade show. The 1300 requires a special power supply, provided and shipped by Cisco when the product is purchased. The power supply provides power to the 1300 via coaxial. You should place it indoors or at least in an enclosure to protect it, because it is *not* NEM-4-compliant. The 1300 is a very good point-to-point and point-to-multipoint bridge that can be used to interconnect buildings and to connect buildings that do not have a wired infrastructure in place.

Courtesy of Cisco Systems, Inc. Unauthorized use not permitted.

Figure 10-6   *Cisco 1300 Series AP*

The 1400 Series Wireless Bridge

The Cisco Aironet 1400 series wireless bridge, shown in Figure 10-7, is designed for outdoor environments.

It has a rugged enclosure that can withstand the elements. It is designed for point-to-point or point-to-multipoint networks. It can be mounted on poles, walls, or even roofs. You can also change the polarization, which, depending on how the wireless bridge is mounted, could be a very important aspect of deploying this wireless bridge. As far as the antennas go, it has a high-gain internal radio, and you can also get a version of this hardware that allows you to do a professional installation of radios with N-type connectors. This means that you can actually connect a high-gain dish. The 1400 series does not support LWAPP and operates only in standalone mode.

Note: Currently the 1400 series bridge cannot be managed by the controller and is not considered an AP.

Cisco Access Point Summary

Table 10-2 summarizes the Cisco APs.

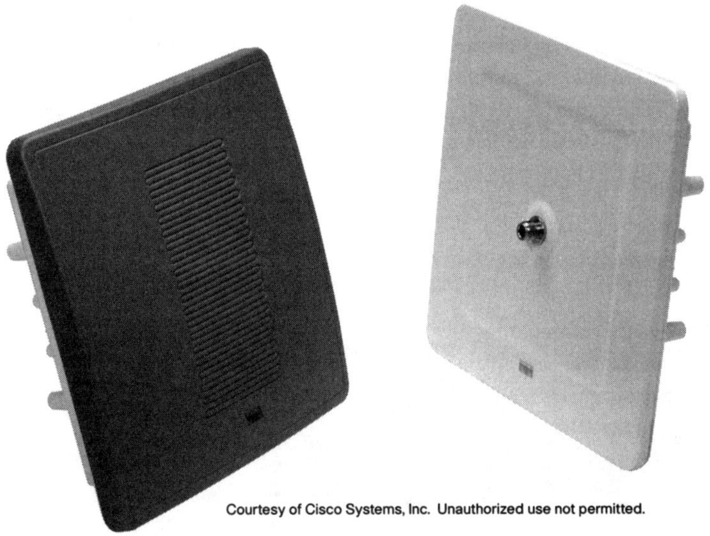

Courtesy of Cisco Systems, Inc. Unauthorized use not permitted.

Figure 10-7   *Cisco 1400 Series AP*

Table 10-2   *Summary of Cisco APs*

AP	Modes Supported	Environment	Antennas Supported	802.11 Protocols Supported	Max Data Rates Supported
1130AG	Autonomous/ lightweight AP.HREAP	Indoor	Integrated	a/b/g	54 Mbps
1240AG	Autonomous/ lightweight AP.HREAP	Rugged Indoor	External	a/b/g	54 Mbps
1250 AP	Autonomous/ lightweight AP	Rugged Indoor	External	a/b/g/n	300 Mbps
1300 AP/bridge	Autonomous/ lightweight AP, bridge	Outdoor	Internal or External	b/g	54 Mbps
1400	Bridge only (not an AP)	Outdoor	Internal or External	a/b/g	N/A

Wireless LAN Controllers

The entire design of the Wireless LAN Controllers is for scalability. The communication between a lightweight AP can happen over any type of Layer 2 or Layer 3 infrastructure using LWAPP. There are integrated controller platforms designed for installation in switches. The 3750-G actually comes as an integrated 2RU switch with either a 25 or 50 AP controller, as well as the WiSM and the WLCM. These are both modular controllers that can be installed in 6500 series switches or in Integrated Services Routers (ISR). There are also appliance-based controllers, which include the 44xx series WLC as well as the 2100 series WLC. Which controller you require depends on how many APs you need deployed. This can be anywhere from six to 300 access points per controller. This is a fixed value and can't be upgraded via licensing. If you need to support more APs, you need another controller or a controller that supports more APs.

The Cisco 44xx Series WLC

The Cisco 44xx series Wireless LAN Controller, shown in Figure 10-8, is a standalone appliance.

Courtesy of Cisco Systems, Inc. Unauthorized use not permitted.

Figure 10-8   *Cisco 4400 Series Wireless LAN Controller*

It is designed to take up one rack unit. It has either two or four Gigabit Ethernet uplinks, and they use mini-GBIC FSG slots. It can support 12, 25, 50, or 100 APs, depending on the model. And it can support up to 5000 MAC addresses in its database.

The 4400 series has a 10/100 interface called a service port; it is used for SSH and SSL connections for management purposes. The service port can be used for out-of-band management, but it is not required to manage the device. You can manage the device via the controller's logical management interface. There is also a console port that you can use to connect via HyperTerminal or Teraterm Pro.

Depending on the country you are in, power requirements vary, but the chassis has two power supply slots.

The controller code version used for the CCNA Wireless exam is version 5.x, and the AP runs the same version. It's actually a requirement that they run the same version, so when an AP joins with a controller, the controller upgrades or downgrades the AP. The controller upgrades four APs at a time. The 4400 series can support up to 100 access points. So, a 4400 would upgrade ten APs at a time until they are all upgraded.

The 3750-G WLC

The 3750-G Wireless LAN Controller, shown in Figure 10-9, is integrated into a switch.

There are two assemblies—the WS-C3750G-24PS-E and the AIR-WLC4402-*-K9. The two assemblies are connected to the SEPAPCB assembly, which has two Gigabit Ethernet links connecting through SFP cables and two GPIO control cables. The major benefits of this integration into the switching platform include the following:

■   Conservation of space

Courtesy of Cisco Systems, Inc. Unauthorized use not permitted.

Figure 10-9 *Cisco 3750-G Series Wireless LAN Controller*

■ Integration of the backplane of the controller and switch

■ It saves ports

The 3750G is stackable with the 3750G switches, so you can stack it with other 3750s that do not have the controller in them. The features it supports are the same as with the 4402 controllers; the only difference is the physical ports.

The Cisco WiSM

The Cisco WiSM, shown in Figure 10-10, is a services module that installs in the 6500 series switch or 7600 series router with the Cisco Supervisor Engine 720.

Courtesy of Cisco Systems, Inc. Unauthorized use not permitted.

Figure 10-10 *Cisco WiSM*

It has the same functionality as the 4400 series standalone controllers; the difference is that it supports up to 300 APs. The WiSM supports 150 access points per controller, with each blade having two controllers. Thus, you can have a total of 300 access points. You can also cluster 12 of them into a mobility domain. This allows up to 7200 lightweight APs in a mobility domain.

The Cisco 2106 WLC

The Cisco 2106 Wireless LAN Controller, shown in Figure 10-11, is also a single-rack unit design with eight 10/100 Ethernet ports.

Courtesy of Cisco Systems, Inc. Unauthorized use not permitted.

Figure 10-11 *Cisco 2106 Series Wireless LAN Controller*

It can support up to six primary access points. It has an RJ-45 console port and two RJ-45 ports that support PoE. It has nearly all the same features as the 4400 series controllers but has eight built-in switch ports. You can expect to see this controller in a small branch environment.

The Cisco WLCM

The Wireless LAN Controller Module (WLCM), shown in Figure 10-12, is designed for the ISR routers. You would see this controller in a small office.

Courtesy of Cisco Systems, Inc. Unauthorized use not permitted.

Figure 10-12 *Cisco WLCM*

It has the same functionality as the 2106, but it does not have the directly connected AP and console port. It supports six APs. The WLCM-Enhanced (WLCM-E) supports eight or 12 APs, depending on which module you get.

Of course, some limitations apply. Most of the features are similar to the 4000 series:

■   LWAPP

■   RF control

■   The ability to be a DHCP server

■   Layer 2 security

The differences are things such as the following:

■   Lack of PoE ports

■   The number of APs supported

■   The LWAPP modes supported

For these reasons, you see the WLCM deployed in smaller branches.

Wireless LAN Controller Summary

Table 10-3 summarizes the Cisco Wireless LAN Controller models.

Table 10-3   *Controller Summary*

Controller Mode	Number of APs Supported	Environment Deployed In
4400	Up to 100	Enterprise
3750G	—	Enterprise
WiSM	300 per WiSM, up to 3600	Enterprise (service module)
2106	6	Branch
WLCM	6	Branch

Wireless Network Management

In very large networks, a single wireless controller isn't enough to manage all your APs. This type of scenario might call for the Cisco Wireless Control System (WCS). The WCS is a single point of management for up to 3000 lightweight APs and 1250 autonomous APs. The WCS runs on a Windows or Red Hat Linux server. To scale beyond 3000 APs, you would need the WCS Navigator. The WCS Navigator enables you to navigate between different wireless control systems. It is a manager of managers, so to speak. You can use the WCS Navigator to navigate between different WCS servers. You can then scale it up to 30,000 APs in a single deployment and support up to 20 WCS deployments, all within the WCS Navigator. There is also an additional appliance you can use, called the Cisco Wireless Location Appliance, as shown in Figure 10-13.

Courtesy of Cisco Systems, Inc. Unauthorized use not permitted.

Figure 10-13 *Cisco Location Appliance*

This is designed to do location tracking for Wi-Fi devices and RFID tags. It helps track thousands of devices.

Exam Preparation Tasks

Review All the Key Topics

Review the most important topics from this chapter, denoted with the Key Topic icon. Table 10-4 lists these key topics and the page number where each one can be found.

Table 10-4 *Key Topics for Chapter 10*

Key Topic Item	Description	Page Number
Paragraph from the section "Features of the Cisco Controllers"	Lists detailing access point and Cisco controller responsibilities	172
Figure 10-2	The CUWN architecture	175
List from the section "Access Points"	Description of the two types of access points	176
Paragraphs from the section "The Cisco 44xx Series WLC"	Description of the specifications and capabilities of the Cisco 44xx series WLC	182

Complete the Tables and Lists from Memory

Print a copy of Appendix B, "Memory Tables" (found on the CD) or at least the section for this chapter, and complete the tables and lists from memory. Appendix C, "Memory Tables Answer Key," also on the CD, includes completed tables and lists to check your work.

Definition of Key Terms

Define the following key terms from this chapter, and check your answers in the glossary:

Lightweight AP, Autonomous AP, WLCM, WLCS

References

Cisco Wireless Services Module (WiSM): http://tinyurl.com/6mngkj

Migrate to the Cisco Unified Wireless Network: http://tinyurl.com/5uo78w

Cisco Unified Wireless Network: Secure Wireless Access for Business-Critical Mobility: http://tinyurl.com/687nff

This chapter covers the following subjects:

Understanding the Different LWAPP Modes: A discussion of Layer 2 and Layer 3 LWAPP.

How an LWAPP AP Discovers a Controller: A discussion regarding the process that an AP goes through when finding a controller.

How an LWAPP AP Chooses a Controller and Joins It: The process an AP takes when it chooses a controller to join.

How an LWAPP AP Receives Its Configuration: The process an AP takes when it retrieves its configuration.

Redundancy for APs and Controllers: How to provide redundancy for your APs.

The AP Is Joined, Now What?: A discussion on the different functions an AP can perform.

CHAPTER 11

Controller Discovery and Association

When a lightweight AP boots up, it cannot function without a controller. In this chapter, you will learn about the Lightweight Access Point Protocol (LWAPP) and the modes in which it can operate. You will also learn about how an AP finds controllers on the network, chooses one to join with, and then retrieves its configuration. In addition, you will look at the ways to provide redundancy for your AP in the event that a controller goes down. Finally, when an AP is joined with a controller, it can operate in certain modes that can be used for different reasons. You will learn these operational modes and when they are used.

You should do the "Do I Know This Already?" quiz first. If you score 80 percent or higher, you may want to skip to the section "Exam Preparation Tasks." If you score below 80 percent, you should spend the time reviewing the entire chapter. Refer to Appendix A, "Answers to the 'Do I Know This Already?' Quizzes," to confirm your answers.

"Do I Know This Already?" Quiz

The "Do I Know This Already?" quiz helps you determine your level of knowledge of this chapter's topics before you begin. Table 11-1 details the major topics discussed in this chapter and their corresponding quiz questions.

Table 11-1 *"Do I Know This Already?" Section-to-Question Mapping*

Foundation Topics Section	Questions
Understanding the Different LWAPP Modes	1–3
How an LWAPP AP Discovers a Controller	4–5
How an LWAPP AP Chooses a Controller and Joins It	6–8
How an LWAPP AP Receives Its Configuration	9
Redundancy for APs and Controllers	10–11
The AP Is Joined, Now What?	12–14

1. What two modes can LWAPP operate in? (Choose two.)

   a. Layer 2 LWAPP mode

   b.   Joint LWAPP mode

   c.   Autonomous LWAPP mode

   d.   Layer 3 LWAPP mode

2. When LWAPP communication between the access point and the wireless LAN controller happens in native, Layer 2 Ethernet frames, what is this known as?

   a.   EtherWAPP

   b.   Hybrid mode

   c.   Native mode LWAPP

   d.   Layer 2 LWAPP mode

3. What is the only requirement for Layer 3 LWAPP mode?

   a.   IP connectivity must be established between the access points and the WLC.

   b.   You must know the IP addressing on the AP.

   c.   Client devices must be in the same VLAN.

   d.   Each device in the Layer 3 domain must be on the same subnet.

4. Which state is not a valid state of an AP that is discovering and joining a controller?

   a.   Discover

   b.   Join

   c.   Image Data

   d.   Hybrid-REAP

5. What is the first step in a Layer 3 LWAPP discovery?

   a.   Priming

   b.   AP Join Request

   c.   Subnet broadcast of Layer 3 LWAPP discovery message

   d.   OATAP

6. AP-Priming is used for which of the following?

   a.   Prime an AP prior to bootup with complex algorithms

   b.   Deliver a list of controllers to the AP using a hunting process and discovery algorithm

   c.   Perform basic setup of controller configurations delivered to the AP

   d.   Provision an AP over the air

7. Which of the following is not contained in a join response message?

   a.   Type of controller

   b.   Interfaces in the controller

   c.   Number and type of radios

   d.   AP name

8. The join request message is sent to the primary controller only under what condition?

   a.   The controller is reachable.

   b.   The AP has an IP address.

   c.   The primary controller has low load.

   d.   The AP is primed.

9. If no primed information is available, what does the AP look for next when trying to join a controller?

   a.   A master controller

   b.   A primer controller

   c.   A new controller

   d.   A new subnet

10. When an AP retrieves its configuration file, where is it applied?

   a.   RAM

   b.   ROM

   c.   NVRAM

   d.   Flash

11. How many backup controllers are in an N + 1 design?

   a.   1

   b.   2

   c.   3

   d.   4

12. Which method is considered the most redundant?

   a.   N + 1

   b.   N + N

   c.   N + N + 1

   d.   N * N + 1

13. Which AP mode can you use for site surveys?

   a.   Local mode

   b.   H-REAP mode

   c.   Bridge mode

   d.   Rogue Detection mode

14. In Monitor mode, which command can you use to change the value of the channels monitored?

   a.   `config advanced channel-list`

   b.   `config advanced 802.11b channel-list monitor`

   c.   `config advanced 802.11b monitor channel-list`

   d.   `config advanced monitor channel-list`

Foundation Topics

Understanding the Different LWAPP Modes

LWAPP can operate in either Layer 2 LWAPP mode or Layer 3 LWAPP mode. The Layer 2 mode is considered out of date, and Cisco prefers and recommends Layer 3 mode. Layer 3 mode is the default LWAPP mode on most Cisco devices.

At a high level, and after the AP has an IP address, the phases of LWAPP operation include these:

Step 1.   An AP sends an LWAPP discovery request message. This is a broadcast that is sent at Layer 2.

Step 2.   Assuming that a controller is operating in Layer 2 LWAPP mode, the wireless LAN controller (WLC) receives the LWAPP discovery request and responds with an LWAPP discovery response message.

Note: Only Cisco 1000 Series LAPs support Layer 2 LWAPP mode. Also, Layer 2 LWAPP mode is not supported on Cisco 2000 Series WLCs. These WLCs support only Layer 3 LWAPP mode.

Step 3.   The AP chooses a controller based on the response received and sends a join request.

Step 4.   The WLC receiving the LWAPP join request responds to the AP join request with an LWAPP join response. This process is going to include a mutual authentication. An encryption key is created to secure the rest of the join process and any future LWAPP control messages.

Step 5.   After the AP has joined the WLC, LWAPP messages are exchanged, and the AP initiates a firmware download from the WLC (if the AP and WLC have a version mismatch). If the onboard firmware of the AP is not the same as that of the WLC, the AP downloads firmware to stay in sync with the WLC. The firmware download mechanism utilizes LWAPP.

Step 6.   After the WLC and AP match firmware revisions, the WLC provisions the AP with the appropriate settings. These settings might include service set identifiers (SSID), security parameters, 802.11 parameters such as data rates and supported PHY types, radio channels, and power levels.

Step 7.   After the provisioning phase is completed, the AP and WLC enter the LWAPP runtime state and begin servicing data traffic.

Step 8.   During runtime operations, the WLC might issue various commands to the AP through LWAPP control messages. These commands might be provisioning commands or requests for statistical information that the AP collects and maintains.

Step 9. During runtime operations, LWAPP keepalive messages are exchanged between the AP and WLC to preserve the LWAPP communication channel. When an AP misses a sufficient number of keepalive message exchanges, it attempts to discover a new WLC.

LWAPP Layer 2 Transport Mode

When operating in Layer 2 mode, LWAPP has the following characteristics and requirements:

■ LWAPP communication between the AP and the WLC is in native, Layer 2 Ethernet frames. This is known as Layer 2 LWAPP mode.

■ In Layer 2 LWAPP mode, although the APs might get an IP address via DHCP, all LWAPP communications between the AP and WLC are in Ethernet encapsulated frames, not IP packets.

■ The APs must be on the same Ethernet network as the WLC. This means that Layer 2 mode is not very scalable.

The source and destination MAC addresses depend on the direction of the frame:

■ An LWAPP control frame sent from the AP to the WLC uses the AP Ethernet MAC address as the source address and the WLC MAC address as the destination address.

■ An LWAPP control frame sent from the WLC to the AP uses the WLC MAC address as the source address and the AP MAC address as the destination address.

Data packets between wireless LAN clients and other hosts are typically IP packets. Figure 11-1 illustrates the process of clients sending frames in a logical topology. Do not be concerned with the underlying network here, but rather the process between devices that will occur.

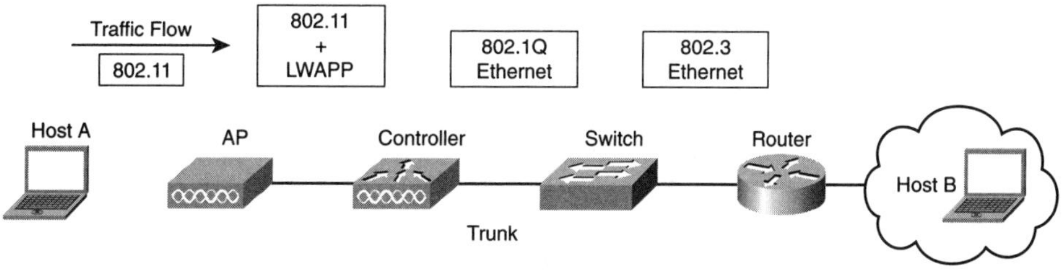

Figure 11-1 *Host A Sending to Host B*

In this figure, a host, Host A, is seen sending a packet to Host B. The following sequence occurs:

Step 1. Host A transmits an IP packet over the 802.11 RF interface after it is encapsulated in an 802.11 frame with the Host A MAC address as the source address and the access point radio interface MAC address as the destination address.

Step 2.   At the AP, the AP adds an LWAPP header to the frame with the C-bit set to 0 and then encapsulates the LWAPP header and 802.11 frame into an Ethernet frame. This Ethernet frame uses the AP Ethernet MAC address as the source MAC address and the WLC MAC address as the destination MAC address.

Step 3.   At the WLC, the Ethernet and LWAPP headers are removed, and the original 802.11 frame is processed.

Step 4.   After processing the 802.11 MAC header, the WLC extracts the payload (the IP packet), encapsulates it into an Ethernet frame, and then forwards the frame onto the appropriate wired network, typically adding an 802.1Q VLAN tag.

Step 5.   The packet then travels through the wired switching and routing infrastructure to Host B.

After receiving the frame, Host B will likely reply. When Host B returns an IP packet to Host A, the following sequence occurs:

Step 1.   The packet is carried from Host B over the wired switching and routing network to the WLC, where an Ethernet frame arrives with the Host A MAC address as the destination MAC address. The IP packet from Host B is encapsulated inside this Ethernet frame.

Step 2.   The WLC takes the entire Ethernet frame, adds the LWAPP header with the C-bit set to 0, and then encapsulates the combined frame inside an LWAPP Ethernet frame. This LWAPP Ethernet frame uses the WLC MAC address as the source MAC address and the access point Ethernet MAC address as the destination MAC address. This frame is sent out over the switched network to the AP.

Step 3.   At the AP, the Ethernet and LWAPP headers are removed and processed.

Step 4.   The payload (the IP packet) is then encapsulated in an 802.11 MAC frame and transmitted over the air by the AP to Host A.

LWAPP Layer 3 Transport Mode

As previously mentioned, Cisco prefers Layer 3 LWAPP mode. This is because it is more scalable than Layer 2 LWAPP. Layer 3 LWAPP control and data messages are transported over the IP network in User Datagram Protocol (UDP) packets. Layer 3 LWAPP is supported on all Cisco WLC platforms and lightweight APs.

The only requirement is established IP connectivity between the APs and the WLC. The LWAPP tunnel uses the IP address of the AP and the AP-Manager interface IP address of the WLC as endpoints. On the AP side, both LWAPP control and data messages use an ephemeral port that is derived from a hash of the AP MAC address as the UDP port. On the WLC side, LWAPP data messages always use UDP port 12222, and LWAPP control messages always use UDP port 12223. The process of clients sending frames in Layer 3

LWAPP mode is similar to that of Layer 2 mode; however, the frames are now encapsulated in UDP. The process is as follows:

Step 1. Host A transmits the packet over the 802.11 RF interface. This packet is encapsulated in an 802.11 frame with the MAC address of Host A as the source address and the radio interface MAC address of the AP as the destination address.

Step 2. At the AP, the AP adds an LWAPP header to the frame with the C-bit set to 0 and then encapsulates the LWAPP header and 802.11 frame into a UDP packet that is transmitted over IP. The source IP address is the IP address of the AP, and the destination IP address is the AP Manager Address of the WLC. The source UDP port is the ephemeral port based on a hash of the access point MAC address. The destination UDP port is 12222.

Step 3. The IP packet is encapsulated in Ethernet as it leaves the AP and is transported by the switching and routed network to the WLC.

Step 4. At the WLC, the Ethernet, IP, UDP, and LWAPP headers are removed from the original 802.11 frame.

Step 5. After processing the 802.11 MAC header, the WLC extracts the payload (the IP packet from Host A), encapsulates it into an Ethernet frame, and then forwards the frame onto the appropriate wired network, typically adding an 802.1Q VLAN tag.

Step 6. The packet is then transmitted by the wired switching and routing infrastructure to Host B.

When Host B receives the packet, it is likely to respond, so the reverse process is as follows:

Step 1. The packet is delivered by the wired switching and routing network to the WLC, where an Ethernet frame arrives with the MAC address of Host A as the destination MAC address.

Step 2. The WLC removes the Ethernet header and extracts the payload (the IP packet destined for Host A).

Step 3. The original IP packet from Host A is encapsulated with an LWAPP header, with the C-bit set to 0, and then transported in a UDP packet to the AP over the IP network. The packet uses the WLC AP Manager IP address as the source IP address and the AP IP address as the destination address. The source UDP port is 12222, and the destination UDP port is the ephemeral port derived from the AP MAC address hash.

Step 4. This packet is carried over the switching and routing network to the AP.

Step 5. The AP removes the Ethernet, IP, UDP, and LWAPP headers, and it extracts the payload, which is then encapsulated in an 802.11 frame and delivered to Host A over the RF network.

For Layer 3 LWAPP, a 1500-byte maximum transmission unit (MTU) is assumed. You can change this, but 1500 is the default.

How an LWAPP AP Discovers a Controller

When an AP discovers and joins a controller, the AP proceeds through several states. In Figure 11-2, you can see these states and when they happen.

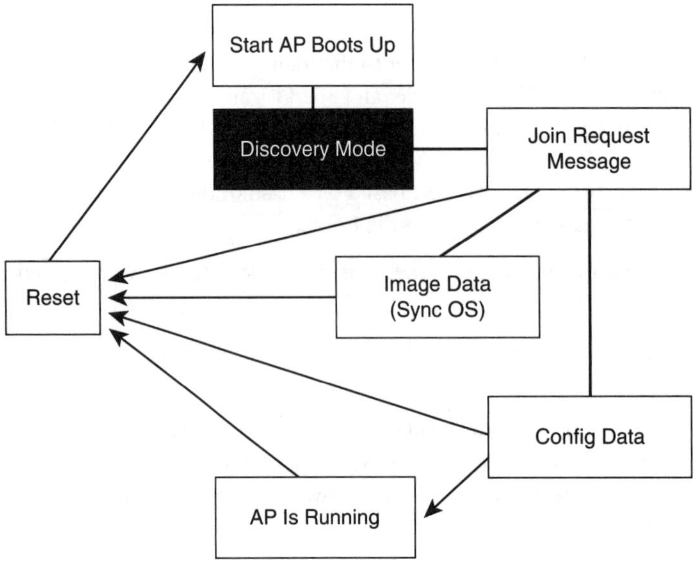

Figure 11-2   *AP States*

The process begins with the discovery of a controller. Because the lightweight APs are by definition "zero-touch" when deployed, you should only need to plug them in and let them do the rest. On the back end, the part you do not see is a little more complex. The steps in this process, beginning with discovery, are as follows:

Step 1.   The APs send LWAPP discovery request messages to WLCs. This is broadcast at Layer 2. Because Layer 3 mode is what you want to use, this should fail.

Step 2.   Upon failing, the AP proceeds to Layer 3 by checking its configuration for an IP address. If no IP address exists, the client uses DHCP to obtain one.

Step 3.   The AP uses information obtained in the DHCP response to contact a controller.

Step 4.   Any WLC receiving the LWAPP discovery request message responds with an LWAPP discovery response message. If no controller responds, the AP reverts to Layer 2 broadcasts and starts the process again.

The Cisco implementation uses the hunting process and discovery algorithm to find as many controllers as possible. The AP builds a list of WLCs using the search and discovery process, and then it selects a controller to join from the list.

The controller search process repeats continuously until at least one WLC is found and joined. IOS-based APs only do a Layer 3 discovery.

The Layer 3 discovery process follows a certain order:

Step 1.   The AP does a subnet broadcast to see if a controller is operating in Layer 3 mode on the local subnet.

Step 2.   The AP does an over-the-air provisioning (OTAP).

Note: Although OTAP is not fully covered here, you can find a detailed document at http://tinyurl.com/5hah9q.

Step 3.   When other APs exist and are in a joined state with a controller, they send messages that are used for resource management. These messages have the IP address of the controller in it. The AP can listen to these messages and get the controller IP address. The AP can then send a directed discovery message to the controller.

Step 4.   The next process is called *AP priming*.

AP priming is something that happens after an AP is associated with at least one controller. The AP then gets a list of other controllers that it can associate with from the one it is already associated with. These other controllers are part of a *mobility group*. This information then gets stored in NVRAM and can be used if the AP reboots. To contact these controllers, the AP sends a broadcast to the primary controller and all the other controllers in the group.

Another method of discovering a controller is via DHCP using Vendor Option mode. This simply uses DHCP option 43 to learn the IP address of the management interface of a controller.

The final method of discovering a controller is using Domain Name System (DNS). You use DHCP to get IP information, including a DNS server entry. Then the AP looks for a DNS entry for CISCO-LWAPP-CONTROLLER. This should return the IP address of a controller management interface. The AP can use this address to send a unicast query. This process results in an AP finding a controller, all of which happens during the Discovery mode indicated in Figure 11-2.

Note: With APs running 12.3.11-JX1 and later, you can manually prime the APs with a console cable to aid in the join process.

How an LWAPP AP Chooses a Controller and Joins It

Now that the AP potentially has numerous controllers to join, it must choose one and send it a join request message. Figure 11-3 illustrates this portion of communication.

A join request message contains the following information:

- Type of controller

- MAC of controller

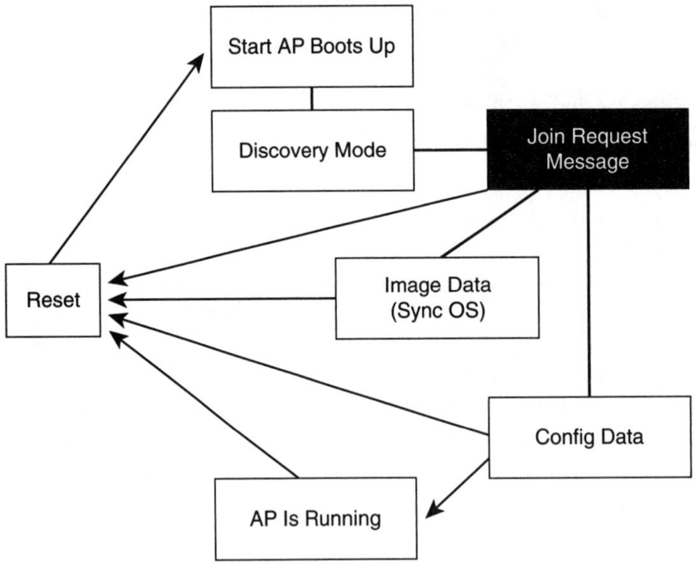

Figure 11-3   *AP Join State*

- AP hardware version

- AP software version

- AP name

- Number and type of radios

- Certificate payload (x.509)

- Session payload to set up the session values

- Test payload to see if jumbo frames can be used

This join request message is sent using a predefined method consisting of the following steps:

Step 1.   An AP chooses the primary controller (if primed).

This can be defined in each AP and stored in flash to survive a reboot. Using the controller GUI, go to **WIRELESS > Access Points > All APs > ***SelectedAp*** > Details**, as seen in Figure 11-4.

Step 2.   Choose the secondary controller, tertiary (if primed).

Step 3.   If no primed information is available, then look for a master controller.

The definition of a controller as master is configured in the GUI under **CONTROLLER > Advanced > Master Controller Mode**, as shown in Figure 11-5.

Key Topic

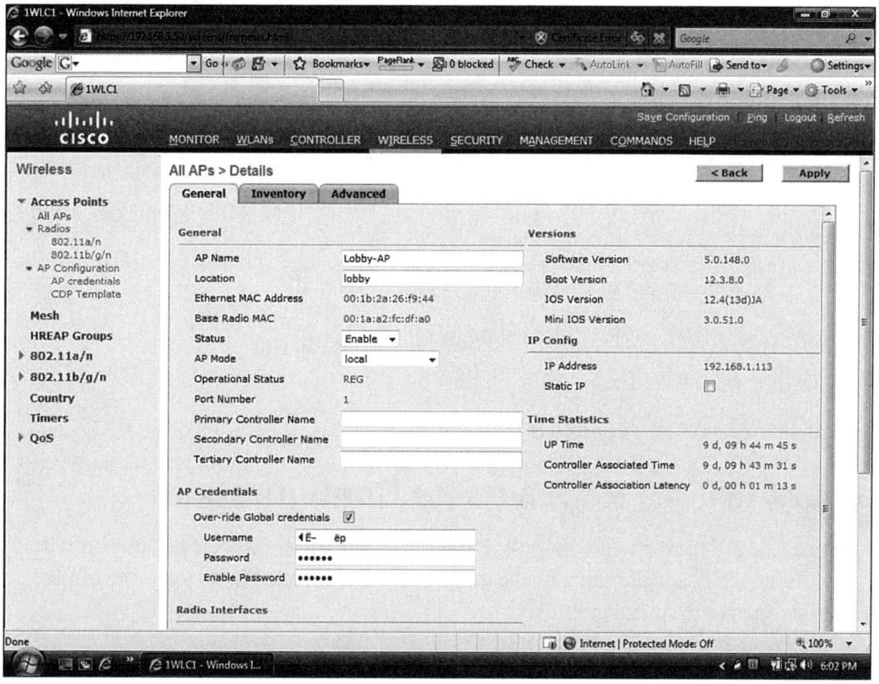

Figure 11-4 *Define Primary Controller*

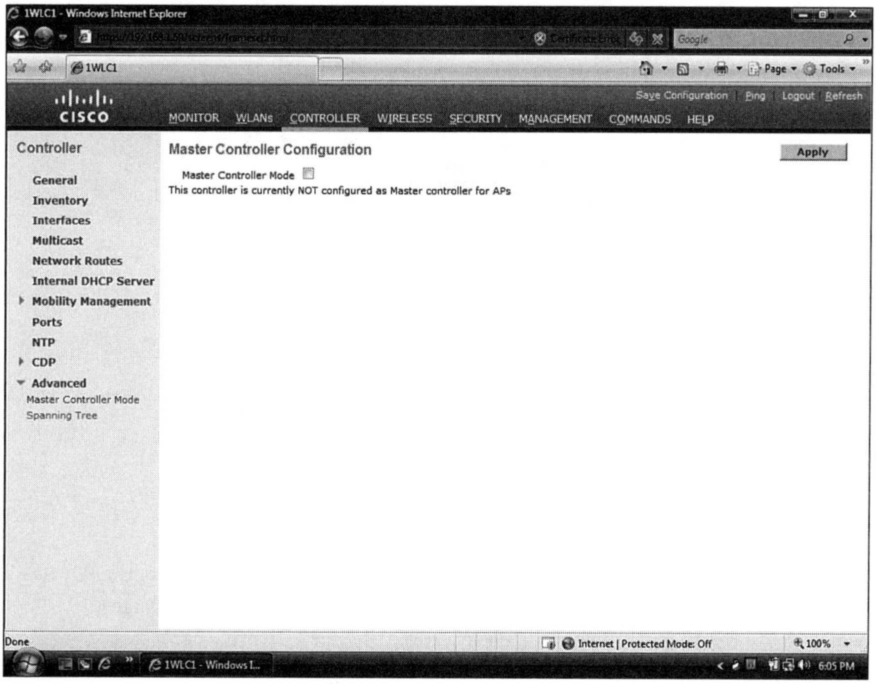

Figure 11-5 *Enable Master Controller Mode*

A mobility group should have only one master controller. Turn this feature off after you have added all new APs. After you have added the new APs, they will be primed and will no longer need a master.

Step 4.   When all else fails, look for the least loaded AP-Manager interface based on how many APs each is currently managing.

Upon receiving a join request message, a controller should respond with a join reply message. This includes the following information:

■ Result code, which is the green light that says they can talk

■ Controller certificate payload response

■ Test payload for jumbo frames

This process joins an AP to a controller.

How an LWAPP AP Receives Its Configuration

After joining, the AP moves to an image data phase, as shown in Figure 11-6, but only if the image on the AP is not the same as the image on the controller. If they are the same, this step is skipped and the image is used.

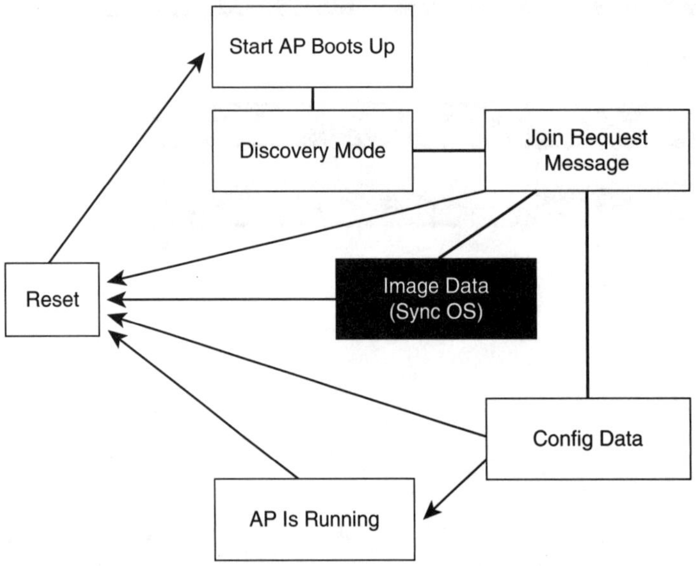

Figure 11-6   *The Image Data State*

The controller upgrades or downgrades the AP at this point, and then it resets the AP. After a reset, the process begins again. The code is downloaded in LWAPP messages.

After the process of discovery and join happen and the image is the same on the controller and the AP, the AP gets its configuration from the controller. This happens during the config data stage, as illustrated in Figure 11-7.

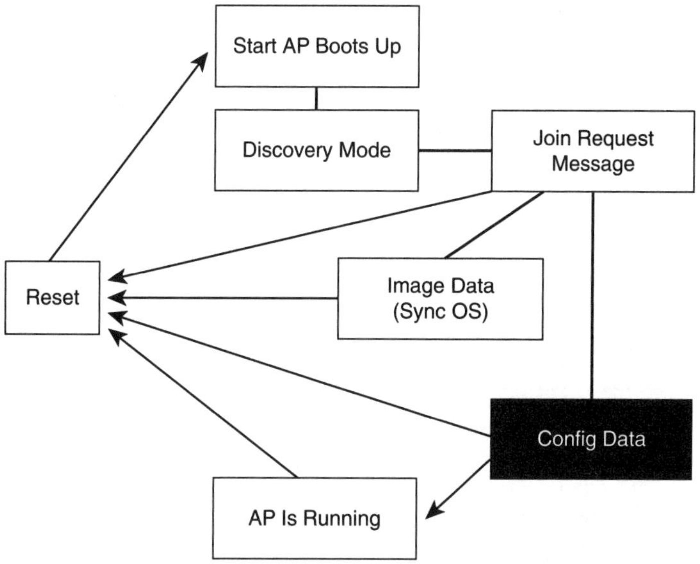

Figure 11-7   *AP Gets Config*

The AP then prompts the controller for a config by sending an LWAPP configure request message that contains parameters that can be configured as well as any values that are currently set; however, most of these values are empty.

When the controller gets the request, it sends a configure response message, which has the configuration values.

The AP then applies the configuration values in RAM. It is important to understand that these values are not stored in flash. If the AP reboots, the process begins again.

After applying the configuration, the AP is up and running.

Redundancy for APs and Controllers

Networks today involve a mix of critical forms of data, be it voice traffic or business transactions. Redundancy is a part life. You need to be familiar with two forms of redundancy for the CCNA Wireless exam:

- AP redundancy
- Controller redundancy

AP redundancy is seen when APs exist in the same RF domain. They are designed to self-heal when poor coverage exists. This involves increasing power levels by stepping up one or two levels or even changing the channel on which they operate.

Controller redundancy is seen in multiple forms. One form of controller redundancy is having a primary, secondary, and tertiary controller, as shown in Figure 11-8. As you can see in the figure, Controller A is the primary controller for WLAN A. Controller C is acting as the secondary controller for WLAN A, and Controller B is acting as the tertiary controller for WLAN A. Each WLAN has a different primary, secondary, and tertiary controller.

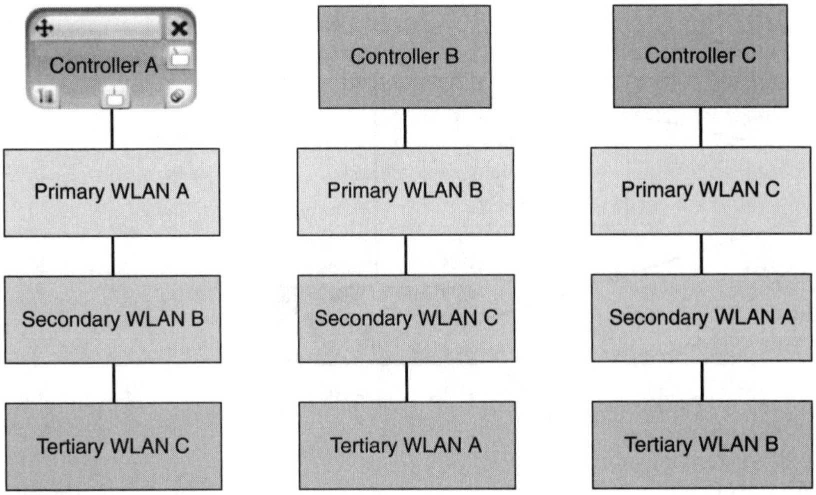

Figure 11-8 *Controller Redundancy*

Another form of controller redundancy is using link aggregation (LAG) or multiple AP managers.

You can also have a primary and backup port on a controller. If the primary goes down, you can use the backup.

Common designs for controller redundancy include the following:

- **N + 1:** This design has a single backup for multiple controllers. If you have five controllers with one backup for all of them to share, the backup can easily become overwhelmed if more than one controller is down at a time.

- **N + N:** This design allows each controller to back up the other. For example, AP-1 points to WLC1 as its primary and WLC2 as its secondary. AP-2 points to WLC2 as its primary and WLC1 as its secondary. Load balancing is desired between APs and controllers. Also, if one controller is maxed out with APs, the design is no good.

- **N + N + 1:** This is the most redundant design. Each controller backs up the other, and an extra is designed as a backup. Take the same example as N + N but add a third controller, WLC-BACKUP, that every AP points to as the tertiary.

The AP Is Joined, Now What?

You can change the mode by navigating to **Wireless > APs > All APs > Detail**.

Now that you have an AP joined with a controller, what can it do? Most people expect it to get them to the Internet. Your AP can actually serve numerous roles based on the mode it is in. Different APs support different modes. An AP can operate in each of the following modes:

- Local

- Monitor

- Sniffer

- Rogue Detector

- Hybrid REAP

- Bridge

The sections that follow describe each of these modes in greater detail.

Local Mode

This is business as usual for an AP. In this mode, the AP scans all channels over a 180-second period for monitoring services, and it inspects management packets for intrusion detection system (IDS) signature matches.

You can also use this mode for site surveys.

When the AP scans channels, it jumps to each unassigned channel for 60 ms and then goes back to its assigned channel for 13 seconds. The purpose of scanning channels is to monitor traffic.

Monitor Mode

Monitor mode is passive. When in this mode, the AP does not send traffic out of its radios, and it does not allow client connections. This mode is used for finding rogue APs or IDS matches, troubleshooting, or site surveys. Monitor mode APs can be used with the location appliance to increase accuracy. Scanning is based on the country, and the command **config advanced 802.11b monitor channel-list** can change the value of the channels monitored.

Sniffer Mode

This mode operates with an OmniPeak, Airmagnet, or Wireshark server to capture data. The encapsulation of the captured data is specific to the product with which it is used. The AP sends the data to the specified device for review. This mode is used to gather time stamps, signal strength, packet size, and other relevant information. You can use this mode as a troubleshooting tool for forensics.

Rogue Detection Mode

This special role communicates rogue AP information between WLCs. In this mode, the radios on the AP are turned off, and it listens for ARP messages on the wired network. It compares the MAC information to a rogue AP and client MAC list that it receives from the controller. The AP forwards this to other controllers. If an ARP is heard on the wired LAN, the controller generates an alarm.

H-REAP Mode

H-REAP mode is designed to be used when you have APs across a WAN and you want to use the controller at a central site. The big issue is that the controller is connected via a WAN link, so you must follow certain guidelines:

■ The link cannot be any slower than 128 kbps.

■ Roundtrip latency cannot be more than 100 ms roundtrip.

■ The AP needs to get a 4-MB code update across the WAN link.

The AP needs to communicate with the controller for only a short time during the initial phase, and then it can function without it but with reduced functionality. The two modes of operation are as follows:

■ **Connected mode:** In Connected mode, the AP can communicate with the controller.

■ **Standalone mode:** In Standalone mode, the AP is disconnected and is unable to reach the controller. All client requests are based on a configuration that is local to the AP. This mode is supported on the AP 1130, AP 1240, and AP 1250.

Bridge Mode

In Bridge mode, the AP can act as a bridge and allow client access. APs can use point-to-point or point-to-multipoint links. To determine the best path, the APs use a protocol called Adaptive Wireless Path Protocol (AWPP). Cisco calls this an iMesh for indoor APs and a mesh for outdoor APs.

Exam Preparation Tasks

Review All the Key Concepts

Review the most important topics from this chapter, noted with the Key Topics icon in the outer margin of the page. Table 11-2 lists a reference of these key topics and the page number where you can find each one.

Table 11-2   *Key Topics for Chapter 11*

Key Topic Item	Description	Page Number
List in the section "Understanding the Different LWAPP Modes"	Steps of LWAPP	193
Figure 11-2	AP states	196
List in the section "How an LWAPP AP Discovers a Controller"	AP states process	200
Figure 11-4	How the AP gets its image	199

Definition of Key Terms

Define the following key terms from this chapter, and check your answers in the Glossary:

Lightweight Access Point Protocol (LWAPP), Layer 3 LWAPP mode, LWAPP discovery request, LWAPP discovery response, AP priming, join request message, master controller, N + 1, N + N, N + N + 1, Local mode, Monitor mode, Sniffer mode, Rogue Detection mode, Hybrid REAP mode, Bridge mode, over-the-air provisioning (OTAP)

This chapter covers the following subjects:

Understanding Roaming: Looks at the concept of roaming and how it should work.

Types of Roaming: Discusses Layer 2 and Layer 3 roaming as well as mobility anchor configurations.

CHAPTER 12

Adding Mobility with Roaming

More and more frequently, end users are expecting the ability to begin a transfer and then change locations seamlessly. This is where roaming functionality comes into play. Roaming is a big part of wireless networks. To facilitate this process, you need to be aware of some terms and options. This chapter introduces you to those terms and how the roaming process is configured.

You should take the "Do I Know This Already?" quiz first. If you score 80 percent or higher, you might want to skip to the section "Exam Preparation Tasks." If you score below 80 percent, you should review the entire chapter.

"Do I Know This Already?" Quiz

The "Do I Know This Already?" quiz helps you determine your level of knowledge of this chapter's topics before you begin. Table 12-1 details the major topics discussed in this chapter and their corresponding quiz questions.

Table 12-1 *"Do I Know This Already?" Section-to-Question Mapping*

Foundation Topics Section	Questions
Understanding Roaming	1–5
Types of Roaming	6–11

1. Which of the following describes a mobility group?

   a. A set of users with rights to roam

   b. A group of controllers configured with the same hostname

   c. A group of controllers configured in the same mobility group

   d. A set of controllers that roam

2. Controllers that are aware of each other but that are in different mobility groups are said to be in what?

   a. Mobility chain

   b. Mobility mode

   c. Mobility-aware mode

   d. Mobility domain

3. How many mobility domains can a controller be a member of?

   a. One

   b. Two

   c. Three

   d. Four

4. True or false: A client can roam from one mobility group to another in the same mobility domain.

   a. True

   b. False

5. True or false: A client can roam between two controllers in different mobility domains.

   a. True

   b. False

6. Which of the following are valid roaming types? (Choose two.)

   a. Layer 2 roaming

   b. Seamless AP roaming

   c. Layer 3 roaming

   d. Layer 4 roaming

7. Which of the following statements is not true?

   a. For roaming to work, the controllers need to be in the same mobility domain.

   b. For roaming to work, the controllers need to run the same code version.

   c. For roaming to work, the controllers need to operate in the same LWAPP mode.

   d. For roaming to work, the SSID (WLAN) does not necessarily need to be the same.

8. What is the term for roaming from one AP to another AP managed by the same controller?

    a. Same-controller roaming

    b. Intercontroller roaming

    c. Intracontroller roaming

    d. This is not roaming.

9. What is the term for roaming from one AP to another AP managed by a different controller?

    a. Same-controller roaming

    b. Intercontroller roaming

    c. Intracontroller roaming

    d. This is not roaming.

10. What is it called when client traffic is tunneled back to the anchor controller before being sent to its destination?

    a. Symmetric tunneling

    b. Asymmetric tunneling

    c. Anchor roaming

    d. Layer 2 roaming

11. What is it called when client traffic is sent directly to a destination and return traffic goes to an anchor controller before being sent back to the client on a foreign controller?

    a. Symmetric tunneling

    b. Asymmetric tunneling

    c. Anchor roaming

    d. Layer 3 roaming

Foundation Topics

Understanding Roaming

It's probably safe to say that most people understand the concept of roaming at a high level. You want to move from your desk to the conference room. The conference room is on the other side of the building, but you are in the middle of a large upload. You don't sweat it because you are on a wireless network and wireless is..."everywhere"!

That sounds nice, and that's what wireless networks have to offer, but how does wireless get "everywhere"? From what you have learned so far, you know that a wireless signal can't travel "everywhere" because of absorption, refraction, scattering, and more. You've also learned a little about roaming and how an AP needs some overlap to facilitate the process. But there is still more to it. If you step back and look at the big picture, you start to see that the controller has to be involved in this lightweight AP deployment. How is the controller involved? To understand that, you need to understand mobility groups.

Understanding Mobility Groups

In simple terms, a *mobility group* is a setting on a controller that defines the controller as a member of a group. Other controllers would also be members of that group. These controllers share information about the clients that are roaming. In Figure 12-1, two controllers are in the same mobility group. They can exchange information about the client that is roaming. Figure 12-2 shows a network with three controllers. Controller1 and Controller2 are in the same mobility group, and Controller3 is in a different one. When this scenario occurs, the three controllers are considered to be in the same *mobility domain*. A controller can be aware of another controller in a different mobility group as long as they are in the same mobility domain. This allows them to exchange information regarding their clients. This allows clients in different mobility groups to roam between the different mobility domains. If the controllers were in different mobility groups and did not have knowledge of each other, roaming could not occur. To provide this knowledge, you as an administrator need to enter the MAC address and management IP address of the other controller in the first controller, and vice versa. In other words, Controller2 needs to be configured with Controller3's MAC and management IP addresses, and Controller3 needs to be configured with Controller2's MAC and IP addresses.

To set this up in the controller, first you need to configure the controller's mobility domain. Remember that multiple controllers share the same mobility group, and controllers in different mobility groups can communicate with each other if they are part of the same mobility domain. To configure the mobility *domain* using the controller web interface, choose **CONTROLLER > General**.

A controller can be in only one mobility group and one mobility domain. To configure the mobility group, choose **CONTROLLER > Mobility Management**. Controllers that are in the same mobility group have the same virtual gateway IP address. You can add these controllers by clicking **New** and then adding the IP address, MAC address, and mobility group of the other controller, as shown in Figure 12-3. In Figure 12-3, Controller2 is added to Controller1. If you have more than one controller to add, you can do it all at once. First you create a text file that includes the controller MAC address and IP address for each

Key Topic

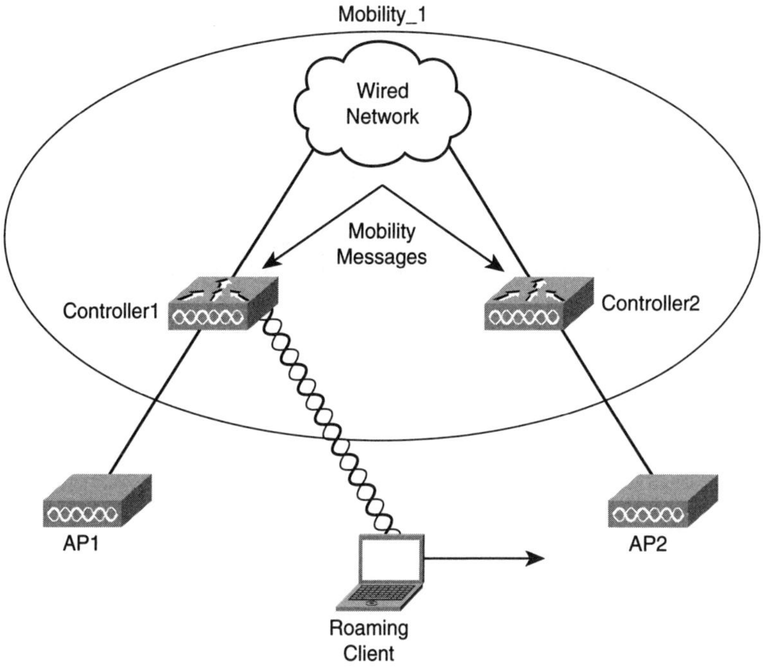

Figure 12-1 *Mobility Group*

Key Topic

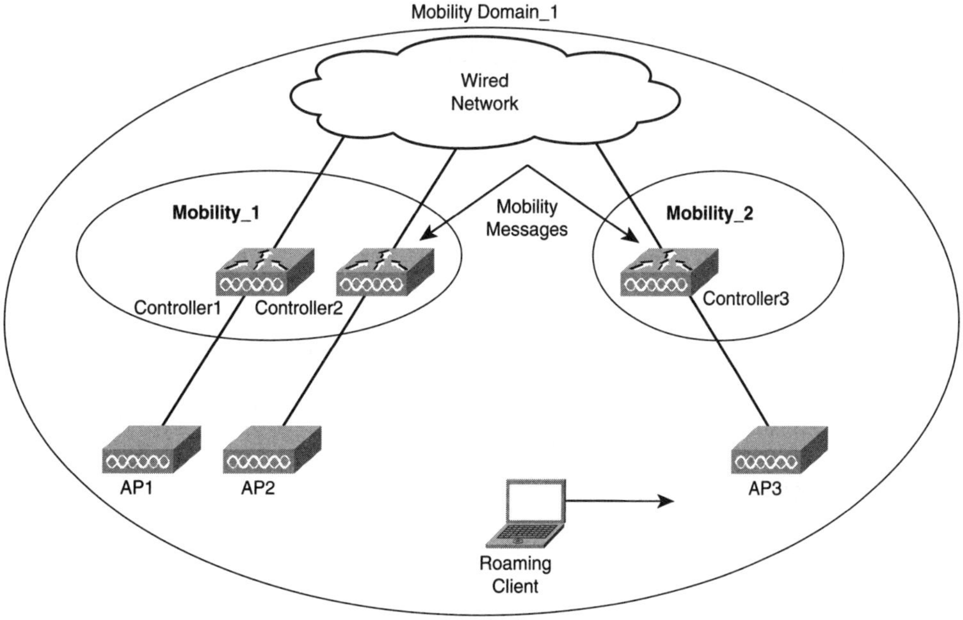

Figure 12-2 *Mobility Domain*

controller you want to add. Then you paste the contents of the text file into the Edit All page. In Figure 12-3, two controllers are listed on the Edit All page. You can have up to 24 controllers in a mobility group.

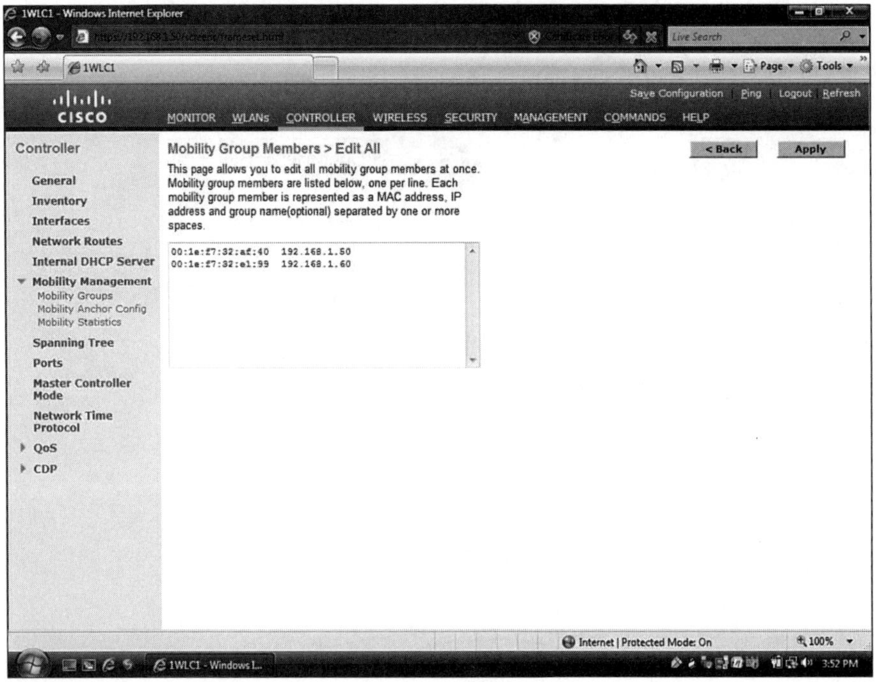

Figure 12-3 *Edit All Page*

So what happens if a user moves to another mobility domain? Because a controller in a different mobility domain does not have information about the client, the client must reassociate. When the client reassociates, it will most likely get a new IP address, and any sessions it currently has will need to be restarted.

So now you understand the part that controllers play in roaming. In truth, they play an even bigger part, depending on the type of roaming that is happening. Cisco controllers can support a Layer 2 or Layer 3 roaming process, as detailed in the following sections.

Types of Roaming

Before we dive into roaming as a Layer 2 or 3 process, let's define it. Roaming is the movement of a client from one AP to another while still transmitting. Roaming can be done across different mobility groups, but must remain inside the same mobility domain. Consider the following examples.

Figure 12-4 shows a client transmitting data and moving from AP1 to AP2. These two APs are in the same mobility domain. This is roaming.

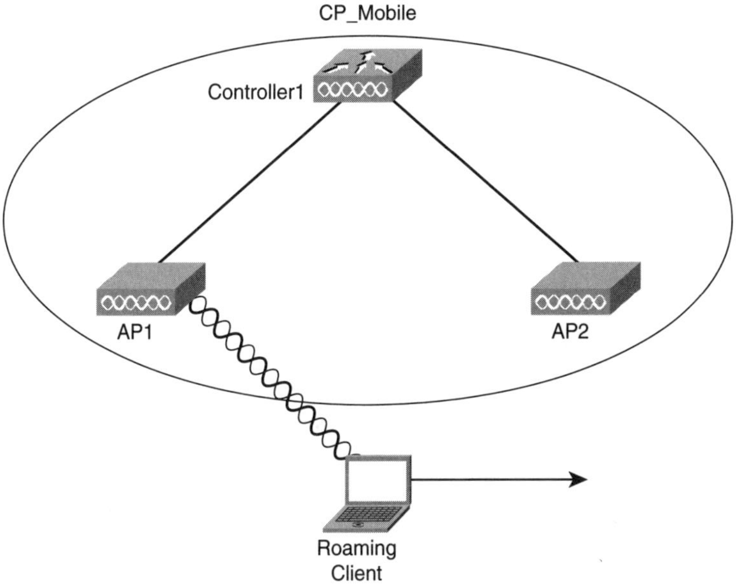

Figure 12-4   *Client Roaming in the Same Mobility Group*

Figure 12-5 shows a client transmitting data and moving from AP2 to AP3. These two APs are in different mobility groups but are in the same mobility domain. This too is roaming.

Now here is where roaming breaks. In Figure 12-6, a user is transmitting data and decides to go work at a local coffee shop that offers wireless network access. After buying a $5 cup of coffee and settling down into a cushy sofa, he fires up his laptop and continues surfing the net. This is *not* roaming. In this case, the user has a new IP address, and any sessions that were active before need to be restarted.

The following must occur for your controllers to support roaming:

■   The controllers need to be in the same mobility domain.

■   The controllers need to run the same code version.

■   The controllers need to operate in the same LWAPP mode.

■   Access control lists (ACL) in the network need to be the same.

■   The SSID (WLAN) needs to be the same.

Let's return to Layer 2 versus Layer 3 roaming. Here is the simple explanation. Layer 2 roaming happens when the user roams to a different AP and keeps his existing IP address. Layer 3 roaming occurs when a client leaves an AP on one subnet and associates with another AP on a different subnet, but using the same SSID.

The following section takes a closer look at the Layer 2 roaming process.

Key Topic

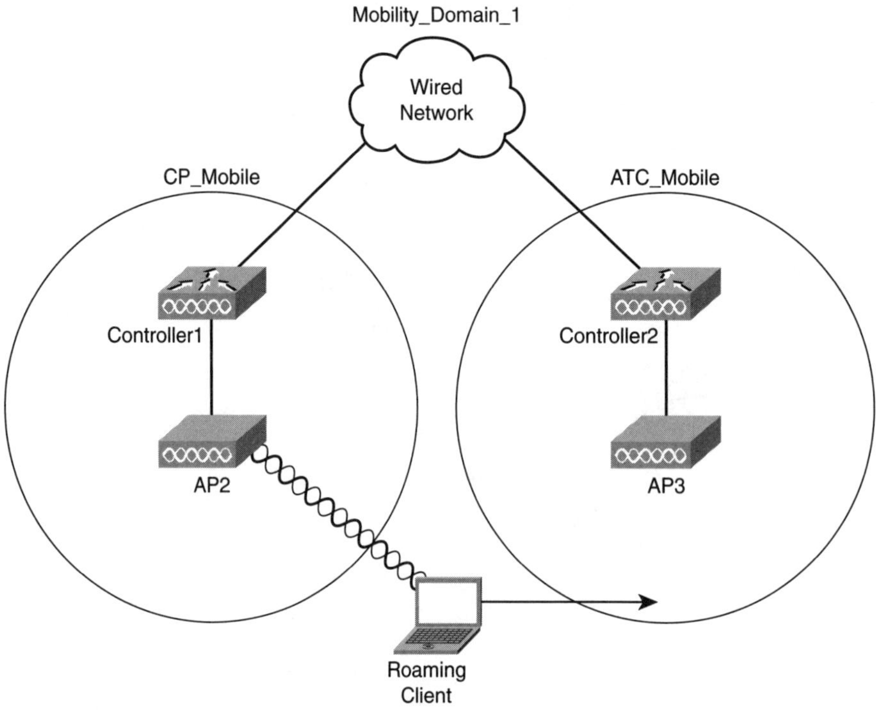

Figure 12-5 *Client Roaming in the Same Mobility Domain*

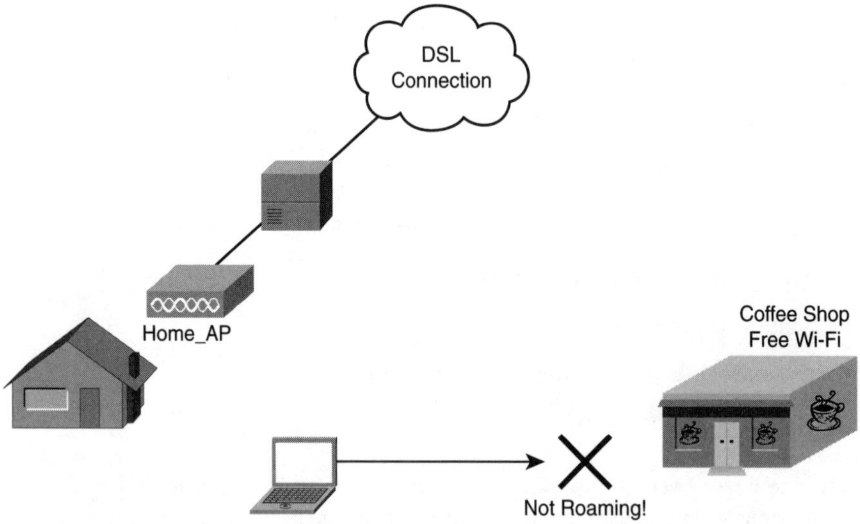

Figure 12-6 *Client Not Roaming*

The Layer 2 Roaming Process

As previously discussed, Layer 2 roaming happens when a user moves to another AP but stays on the same VLAN and the same IP subnet. As far as the user is concerned, nothing special has happened. The client isn't notified that he is roaming. He also keeps his IP address, and all active transmissions stay active. This process is handled within a single controller. This process is called *intracontroller roaming* and takes less than 10 ms. Behind the scenes, the client, when roaming to a new AP, sends a query to request authentication. The query is sent from the AP to the controller, where the controller realizes that the client is already authenticated, just via another AP. The client is then registered as roaming in the controller, although you do not see this in the controller or in the WCS, and life goes on. Figure 12-7 depicts this scenario.

10.10.0.0/24
VLAN 5
Guest_Access

Guest_Access

Controller1

Guest_Access

AP1

AP2

Roaming
Client

10.10.0.107/24
Guest_Access

Key
Topic

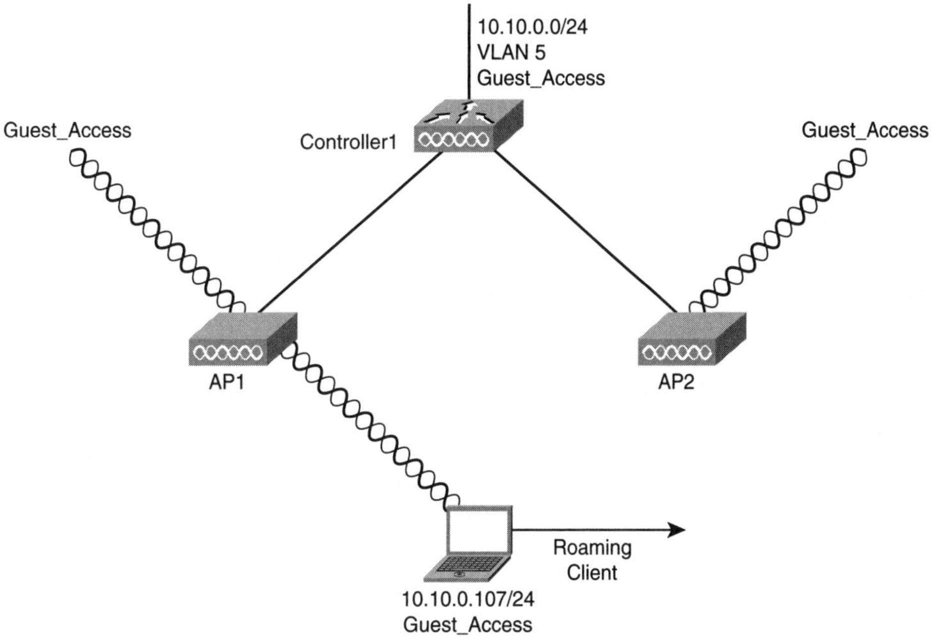

Figure 12-7 *Intracontroller Roaming*

Now take that same scenario and add another controller, as shown in Figure 12-8. Here, the client associated with Controller1 is on VLAN10. Upon roaming to AP3, which is managed by Controller2, the connection stays active. What happened? In this situation, *intercontroller roaming* happened. This occurs when a user roams from one controller to another but remains on the same VLAN and does not have to perform a DHCP process again, which would force the session to break. The two controllers are configured with the same mobility group. The two controllers then exchange mobility messages. Using mobility messages, the client database entry on Controller1 is moved to Controller2. This happens in less than 20 ms. Again, the process is transparent to the user. He roams, data keeps flowing, sessions stay active, and life is good.

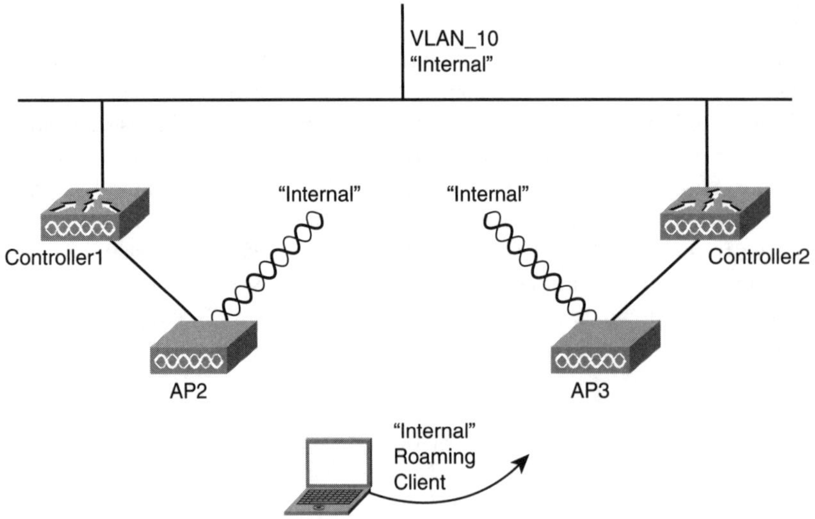

Figure 12-8 *Intercontroller Roaming*

Both intracontroller roaming and intercontroller roaming allow the user to roam and remain on the same IP subnet. This is Layer 2 roaming. Now let's explore Layer 3 roaming.

The Layer 3 Roaming Process

As with Layer 2 roaming, the goal of Layer 3 roaming is for a client to roam transparently. The difference is that you are working with multiple controllers on different subnets. The catch is that although the controllers are on different subnets, the user does not change IP addresses. Instead, the controllers tunnel the traffic back to the original controller. So it's a smoke-and-mirrors configuration. You are literally making the network believe that the user hasn't roamed. The two tunneling methods are as follows:

- **Asymmetric tunneling:** In asymmetric tunneling, traffic from the client is routed to the destination, regardless of its source address, and the return traffic is sent to its original controller, called an *anchor*, and is tunneled to the new controller.

- **Symmetric tunneling:** In symmetric tunneling, all traffic is tunneled from the client to the anchor controller, sent to the destination, returned to the anchor controller, and then tunneled back to the client via the foreign controller.

The following sections discuss these two types of tunneling in more detail.

Asymmetric Tunneling

When a client roams in an intercontroller roam, the database entry moves to the new controller. That's not the case with Layer 3 roaming. In the case of Layer 3 roaming, the client's entry in the original controller is marked as an anchor entry. Then the database entry is not moved; instead, it is copied to the foreign controller. On the foreign controller, the entry is marked "Foreign." The client is then reauthenticated, the entry is updated in the new AP, and the client is good to go. The client's IP address doesn't change. All this is transparent to the user. Figure 12-9 depicts this process.

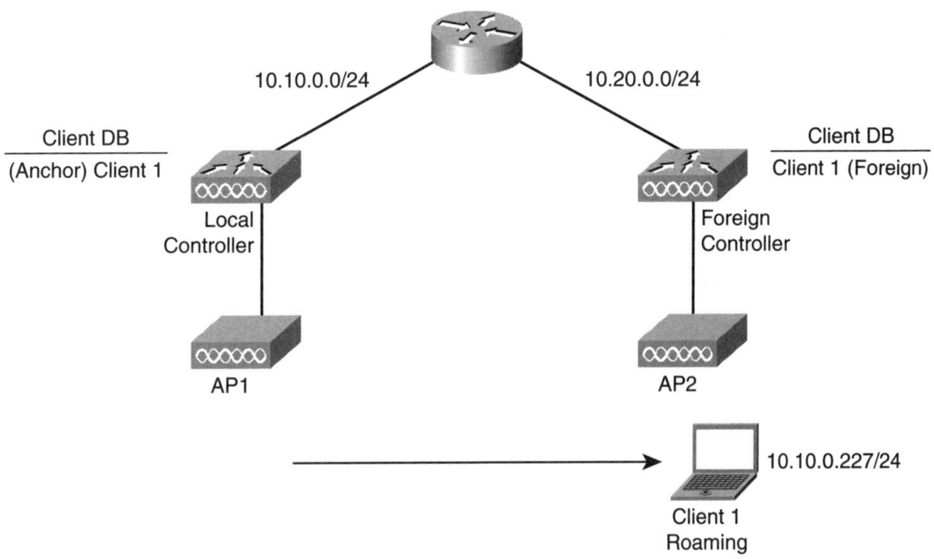

Figure 12-9 *Layer 3 Roaming*

Normally when a client sends traffic, it is sent to a default gateway, assuming that it is leaving the subnet, and then on to the destination. The traffic makes its way back to the client, taking the reverse path that it traveled to get there. This means that if Controller1 sends traffic to Router1 and then to Server1, Server1 returns the traffic via Router1 and then Controller1, as shown in Figure 12-10.

After the client roams to a new controller and a new AP, the return traffic is not delivered to the correct controller. So the anchor controller sees that the return traffic is for a client with an entry marked anchor and knows that it needs to tunnel it to the foreign controller. The foreign controller, upon receiving the packet, forwards it to the client, and all is well. This is how asymmetric tunneling works.

However, this configuration has some problems. Today's networks are taking more and more security precautions; one of these precautions is Reverse Path Filtering (RPF), a function used by routers. The router examines all packets received as input on that interface to make sure that the source address and source interface appear in the routing table and match the interface on which the packet was received. Also, following RFC 3837 and some other antispoofing ACL recommendations, the source address would not match what is expected to be seen, and it would be dropped. So what do you do when this happens? The answer is symmetric tunneling.

Symmetric Tunneling

In general, when a client sends a packet for Server1, much like what is shown in Figure 12-10, the following occurs:

The foreign controller tunnels the packet to the anchor controller rather than forwarding it. Then the anchor controller forwards the packet to Server1. Server1 replies, sending the traffic back to the anchor controller. The anchor controller tunnels it back to the foreign

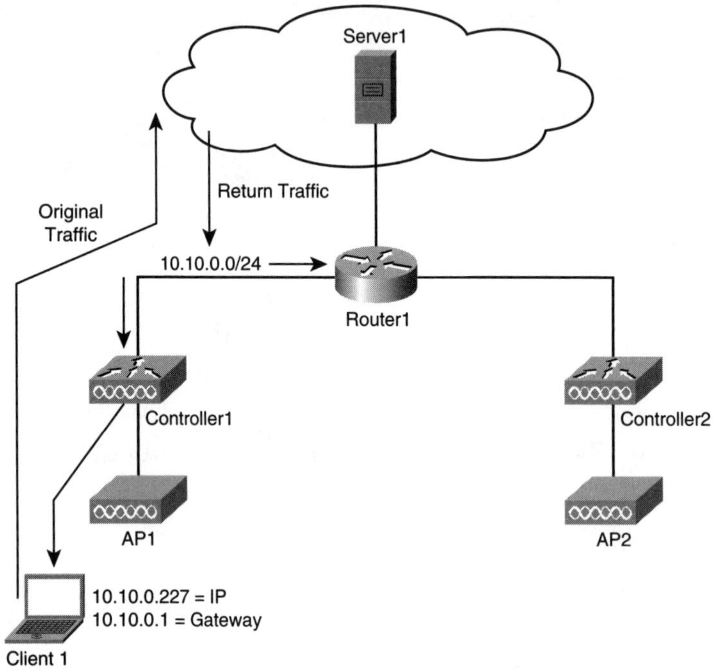

Figure 12-10 *Original Traffic Flow*

controller. The foreign controller delivers the packet back to the client. If the client roams to another foreign controller, the database is moved to the new foreign controller, but the anchor controller does not change.

Configuring Tunneling

To begin the tunneling configuration, first you must decide which type of tunneling you will do. The default mode is asymmetric, and the controllers must match in their configuration. Select **CONTROLLER > Mobility Management > Mobility Anchor Config**. Figure 12-11 shows the resulting configuration page.

This configuration page enables you to configure a Keep Alive Count and Keep Alive Interval. There also is a checkbox for symmetric mobility tunneling mode, which is not enabled by default. The Keep Alive Count is the number of times a ping request is sent to an anchor controller before the anchor is considered unreachable. The default value is 3. The Keep Alive Interval is the amount of time (in seconds—the default is 10) between each ping request sent to an anchor controller.

Mobility Anchors

With mobility anchors, also called guest tunneling or auto anchor mobility, all the client traffic that belongs to a WLAN (especially the Guest WLAN) is tunneled to a predefined WLC or set of controllers that are configured as an anchor for that specific WLAN. This feature helps restrict clients to a specific subnet and have more control over the user

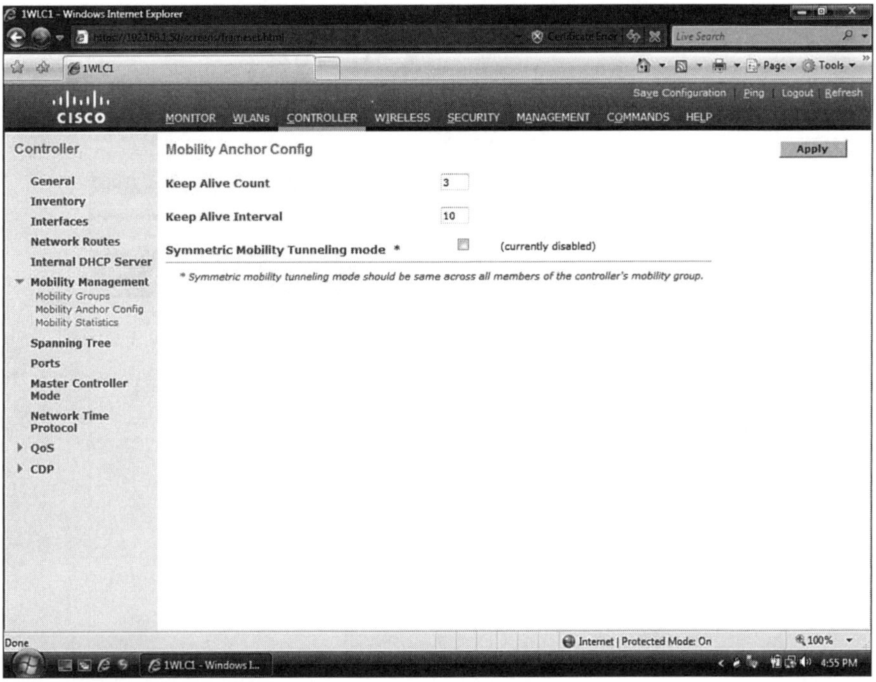

Figure 12-11 *Mobility Anchor Configuration*

traffic. Normally what happens is that a client anchors to the first controller it associates through. But what if you want clients anchored to a controller on a DMZ interface of a firewall? Using a mobility anchor forces clients to be anchored to a controller other than the one they first associate with. This forces their traffic to be tunneled to the DMZ. Then it must pass through the firewall and its associated policies before getting anywhere. This is done on a per-WLAN basis.

Note: The protocol used for tunneling is known as EoIP. It's beyond the scope of the CCNA Wireless exam, but you can find more information in RFC 3439.

You should configure the same mobility anchors for a WLAN. If a client associates with a WLAN in which the local controller is the mobility anchor, the client is anchored locally.

The whole mobility anchor concept might seem strange at first, but think of it as roaming ahead of time. That's basically what it is. As soon as the client associates to a WLAN, it is known to be anchored somewhere else, and a tunnel is set up. This means that the foreign controller sets up the tunnel before the client has an IP address. So the foreign controller doesn't have any knowledge of the client's IP address. This tunnel is the same type of tunnel that is created when Layer 3 roaming occurs between controllers.

To configure a controller to act as mobility anchor, follow these steps:

Step 1.   Click **WLANs** to open the WLANs page.

Step 2.   Click the blue down arrow for the desired WLAN or wired guest LAN, and choose **Mobility Anchors,** as shown in Figure 12-12.

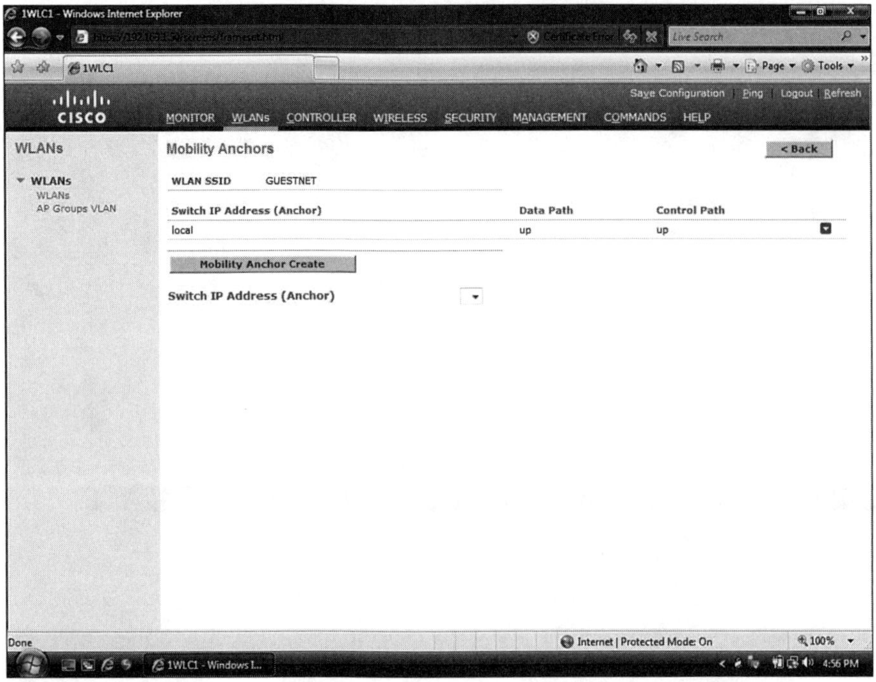

Figure 12-12   *Selecting a Mobility Anchor*

Note: On a WiSM running controller code 4.1.185.0, you do not click the blue down arrow; you just hover the mouse pointer over it.

Step 3.   Select the IP address of the controller to be designated a mobility anchor in the Switch IP Address (Anchor) drop-down box.

Step 4.   Click **Mobility Anchor Create.** The selected controller becomes an anchor for this WLAN or wired guest LAN.

Step 5.   Click **Save Configuration** to save your changes.

Step 6.   Repeat this process for any other mobility anchors you want to designate for this WLAN.

Step 7.   Repeat this process on *every* controller where this WLAN exists.

Exam Preparation Tasks

Review All the Key Topics

Review the most important topics from this chapter, denoted with the Key Topic icon. Table 12-2 lists these key topics and the page number where each one can be found.

Table 12-2   *Key Topics for Chapter 12*

Key Topic Item	Description	Page Number
Figure 12-1	A mobility group	211
Figure 12-2	A mobility domain	211
Figure 12-4	A client roaming in the same mobility group	213
Figure 12-5	A client roaming in the same mobility domain	214
List from the section "Types of Roaming"	Requirements for controllers to support roaming	213
Figure 12-7	Intracontroller roaming	215
Figure 12-8	Intercontroller roaming	216

Definition of Key Terms

Define the following key terms from this chapter, and check your answers in the glossary:

mobility group, mobility domain, roaming, intracontroller roaming, intercontroller roaming, asymmetric tunneling, symmetric tunneling, anchor, mobility anchor

This chapter covers the following subjects:

Controller Terminology: A discussion of the terminology used with Cisco controllers.

Connecting to the Controller: How to connect to a Cisco controller via the CLI and web interfaces.

Configuring the Controller Using the Web Interface: How to build a simple guest network, allow connections, and control where access is permitted.

Monitoring with the Controller: A look at the Monitor interface and how to perform various monitoring tasks.

CHAPTER 13

Simple Network Configuration and Monitoring with the Cisco Controller

One essential task of a CCNA Wireless certification candidate is being able to create a basic configuration. This involves tasks such as accessing the controller interface, creating a WLAN, and making sure that the WLAN is active on the access points (AP). The ultimate goal is to be able to send traffic from a client on that WLAN to some destination on the wired side of the network. To do this, you need to understand some terminology used with the controllers, how to connect to a controller, how to configure the WLAN from the GUI utility of the controller, and how to perform basic monitoring of the controller. These topics are discussed in this chapter.

You should do the "Do I Know This Already?" quiz first. If you score 80 percent or higher, you might want to skip to the section "Exam Preparation Tasks." If you score below 80 percent, you should spend the time reviewing the entire chapter. Refer to Appendix A, "Answers to the 'Do I Know This Already?' Quizzes," to confirm your answers.

"Do I Know This Already?" Quiz

The "Do I Know This Already?" quiz helps you determine your level of knowledge of this chapter's topics before you begin. Table 13-1 details the major topics discussed in this chapter and their corresponding quiz questions.

Table 13-1 *"Do I Know This Already?" Section-to-Question Mapping*

Foundation Topics Section	Questions
Controller Terminology	1–4
Connecting to the Controller	5–9
Configuring the Controller Using the Web Interface	10–13
Monitoring with the Controller	14–19

1. Which of the following describes a port as related to the controller terminology?

 a. It is a logical interface.

 b. It is a physical interface.

 c. It is not an interface; it is a slot.

 d. A port is a connection to an application; for example, port 23 would connect to Telnet.

2. What command configures a static route on the controller?

 a. route add

 b. ip route

 c. default route

 d. config route

3. Which port is active during the boot process?

 a. Service

 b. Management

 c. AP-Manager

 d. Virtual

4. Which of the following best defines a mobility group?

 a. A group of APs that allow roaming

 b. A group of controllers that communicate

 c. A group of traveling clients

 d. A group of mobile AP configurations

5. How was the following menu accessed?

```
Please choose an option from below:
1. Run primary image (version 4.1.192.17) (active)

2. Run backup image (version 4.2.99.0)

3. Manually update images

4. Change active boot image

5. Clear Configuration

Please enter your choice:
```

 a. During bootup, this menu automatically shows.

 b. A break sequence was entered from the CLI.

 c. The Controllers menu command was used.

 d. The Esc key was pressed during bootup.

6. What is the default password for the Cisco controller CLI?

   a. Cisco

   b. cisco

   c. admin

   d. San-Fran

7. Which command is used to save the configuration from the Cisco controller CLI?

   a. wr em

   b. copy run start

   c. save config

   d. save

8. What is the default IP address of the Cisco controller?

   a. 10.1.1.1

   b. 10.1.209.1

   c. 172.16.1.1

   d. 192.168.1.1

9. Which is not a top-level menu of the Cisco controller?

   a. MONITOR

   b. COMMANDS

   c. SECURITY

   d. PING

10. Which is the correct path to create an interface?

   a. CONTROLLER > Interfaces > New

   b. CONTROLLER > Inventory > New Interface

   c. INTERFACES > New

   d. CONTROLLER > Ports > New

11. When creating the WLAN profile, what two pieces of information do you need? (Choose two.)

   a. Name

   b. SSID

   c. Port

   d. Interface

12. What does it mean if the Radio Policy is set to **All** in the Configuration tab of the WLAN?

    a.   All WLANs are on.

    b.   The WLAN supports all radio types.

    c.   The WLAN has all radios in it.

    d.   Users must have all radios.

13. You have selected **WIRELESS > Access Points > Radios > 802.11a/n.** From there, you select the **Configure** option for one of the listed APs. What does the WLAN Override drop-down control?

    a.   The WLAN mode of the radio

    b.   Whether the WLAN SSID is broadcast via the radio

    c.   Whether a WLAN is accessible via the radio

    d.   Whether you can change the settings on this radio

14. Which management area provides information about APs that are not authorized in your network?

    a.   Access Point Summary

    b.   Client Summary

    c.   Top WLANs

    d.   Rogue Summary

15. Which three pieces of information can you find on the controller Summary page? (Choose all that apply.)

    a.   Software version

    b.   Internal temperature

    c.   Port speeds

    d.   System name

16. A radio power level of 3 indicates what?

    a.   Three times the power

    b.   The third level of power

    c.   25% of the maximum power

    d.   1/3 power

17. What criteria defined a wireless client, thus adding it to the Clients list?

    a.   A probe is seen.

    b.   It is associated.

    c.   It is authenticated.

    d.   It is statically defined.

18. How many rogue APs can one AP contain?

    a. 1

    b. 2

    c. 3

    d. 4

19. What would cause a client to be excluded?

    a. The client has passed 802.11 authentication five times.

    b. The client has passed 802.11 association five times.

    c. The client has failed 802.11 authentication five times.

    d. The client has attempted 802.11 association five times.

Foundation Topics

Controller Terminology

Now that you have some understanding about the different types of controllers that are available, it is helpful to understand some of the terminology that goes along with them. The term *interface*, when related to a Cisco controller, is not the same as you would experience on a router. With Cisco routers, an interface can be a physical or logical (loopback) entity. With Cisco controllers, an interface is logical. It can include VLANs, which in turn have a port association. Some interfaces are static, because your controller must always have them.

The next term to understand is port. A *port* is a physical interface on your controller. It is something that you can touch.

The second term that you need to understand is interface. An *interface* can be logical and dynamic.

Another term to understand is WLAN. A *WLAN* consists of a service set identifier (SSID) and all the parameters that go along with it. A WLAN ties to a port.

A port ties together a VLAN and SSIDs. A 4404 has four ports, and a 4402 has two. The Cisco Wireless Service Manager (WiSM) has eight virtual ports. Some interfaces are static, and others are virtual. Some static interfaces cannot be removed because they serve a specific purpose. The static interfaces include these:

- Management interface
- AP-Manager
- Service port
- Virtual

The dynamic interfaces include a user-defined list. These interfaces are similar to subinterfaces and use 802.1 Q headers.

If you allow users to roam, you are going to have a mobility group. A *mobility group* is numerous APs configured with common interfaces. These interfaces must be defined on all the controllers within the mobility group. If one controller does not have an interface configured, a user cannot roam to that controller.

So far, you seen that both static and dynamic interfaces exist. Further discussion of these interfaces might help to clarify how to use them.

Dynamic Interfaces

Administrators define dynamic interfaces, and the system defines static interfaces. Static interfaces have specific system roles and are required.

Static Interfaces

The *management interface* is one that controls communications in your network for all the physical ports. It can be untagged, which means that the VLAN identifier is set to 0. By leaving the VLAN identifier set to 0, the controller does not include an 802.1Q tag with the frame; rather, the frame is sent untagged. This means that if the traffic for the management interface travels across a trunk port on the switch where the controller is connected, the traffic is on the native VLAN of that trunk. Your APs use the management interfaces to discover the controller. Mobility groups also exchange information using the management interface.

The AP manager interface is another static interface. The address that is assigned to this interface is used as the source for communications between the wireless controller and the Cisco access point. That means that this address has to be unique, but it can be in the same subnet as the management interfaces.

Another static interface is what is known as a *virtual interface*. The virtual interface controls the Layer 3 security and mobility manager communications for all of the physical ports of the controller. The virtual interface also has the DNS gateway hostname used by the Layer 3 security and mobility managers so they can verify the source of the certificates. When Layer 3 web authorization is enabled, the virtual interface will be used on the wireless side to force an authorization. For example, a user associates to an AP that is configured for web authorization. Next, the user opens a web browser, which attempts to access the default home page. With web authorization enabled, the web browser is redirected to the virtual interface IP address, which is commonly set to 1.1.1.1.

At this point, the user needs to enter credentials for the web authorization. After the user is authorized, he is redirected to his home page. Alternatively, he could be redirected to a Terms of Use page instead of his home page.

Another static interface is the service port. The service port of the 4400 series controller is a 10/100 copper Ethernet interface. This service port is designed for out-of-band management and can also be used for system recovery and maintenance purposes. This is the only port that will be active when the controller is in its boot mode. Note that the service port is not autosensing—you must use the right type of cable with it. Therefore, if you were going to plug in between a switch and a service port, you would have to use the right cable, because it does not autosense. Also, no VLAN tag is assigned to the port, so the port should not be a configured as a trunk port on the switch.

Another interesting feature of the service port is that you cannot configure a default gateway for the port via the web interface, but you can go into the CLI and define a static route. To define a static route, use the **config route** command.

This new terminology might seem a little overwhelming at first, but after you get into the controller interface and start to create wireless LANs, much of your understanding will fall into place.

Connecting to the Controller

To begin configuring the controller, you need a connection to it. You can access the controller in more than one way; however, this section focuses on creating a command-line interface (CLI) connection. After you have CLI access, you can observe the boot sequence and run though a basic configuration. Doing so provides an IP address that you can use later to browse to the HTML interface.

You will be connecting to the serial interface, so you will use a DB9 serial cable. You will also need a laptop with a serial connection. Many new laptops do not have serial connections, although you can purchase an adapter that connects to a USB port.

After you set up the connection from the laptop to the serial port, you need to use a terminal emulation application such as HyperTerminal, SecureCRT, or ZTerm (for Mac OSX). Using the terminal emulation application, you can boot the controller to view the boot process.

Controller Boot Sequence

As you boot the controller, you are given an option to press Esc for boot options, along with other information regarding the device, as seen in Example 13-1.

Example 13-1   *Controller Bootup Sequence as Seen from the CLI*

```
Bootloader 4.1.171.0 (Apr 27 2007 - 05:19:36)
Motorola PowerPC ProcessorID=00000000 Rev. PVR=80200020
CPU: 833 MHz
CCB: 333 MHz
DDR: 166 MHz
LBC: 41 MHz
L1 D-cache 32KB, L1 I-cache 32KB enabled.
I2C: ready
DTT: 1 is 20 C
DRAM: DDR module detected, total size:512MB.
512 MB
8540 in PCI Host Mode.
8540 is the PCI Arbiter.
Memory Test PASS
FLASH:
Flash Bank 0: portsize = 2, size = 8 MB in 142 Sectors
8 MB
L2 cache enabled: 256KB
Card Id: 1540
Card Revision Id: 1
Card CPU Id: 1287
Number of MAC Addresses: 32
Number of Slots Supported: 4
Serial Number: FOC1206F03A
Unknown command Id: 0xa5
```

```
Unknown command Id: 0xa4
Unknown command Id: 0xa3
Manufacturers ID: 30464
Board Maintenance Level: 00
Number of supported APs: 12
In: serial
Out: serial
Err: serial


.o88b. d888888b .d8888. .o88b. .d88b.
d8P Y8 `88' 88' YP d8P Y8 .8P Y8.
8P 88 `8bo. 8P 88 88
8b 88 `Y8b. 8b 88 88
Y8b d8 .88. db 8D Y8b d8 `8b d8'
`Y88P' Y888888P `8888Y' `Y88P' `Y88P'
Model AIR-WLC4402-12-K9 S/N: FOC1206F03A
Net:
PHY DEVICE : Found Intel LXT971A PHY at 0x01
FEC ETHERNET
IDE: Bus 0: OK
Device 0: Model: STI Flash 8.0.0 Firm: 01/17/07 Ser#: STI1M75607342054704
Type: Removable Hard Disk
Capacity: 245.0 MB = 0.2 GB (501760 x 512)
Device 1: not available
Booting Primary Image...
Press <ESC> now for additional boot options...
***** External Console Active *****
Boot Options
Please choose an option from below:
1. Run primary image (version 4.1.192.17) (active)
2. Run backup image (version 4.2.99.0)
3. Manually update images
4. Change active boot image
5. Clear Configuration
Please enter your choice:
```

The Esc key was issued in Example 13-1. From the highlighted output, you can do the following:

Step 1.   Run the primary image.

Step 2.   Run the backup image.

Step 3. Manually update images.

Step 4. Change the active boot image.

Step 5. Clear the configuration.

The correct choice at this point is to run the primary image. When the HTML interface is accessible, you can upgrade the code on the controller. Because this is covered in Chapter 19, "Maintaining Wireless Networks," it will not be covered now. Of course, you can also manually update the image, as seen in Step 3. Alternatively, you can change the active boot image or clear the configuration file.

Performing Initial CLI Configurations

Initially, the controller looks for a configuration file. If the controller finds such a file, it loads it and then prompts you for a username and password. If no configuration exists, you see a prompt to run through a dialog and a message stating that the certificate was not found, as in Example 13-2.

Example 13-2 *Certificate Not Found Message*

```
Starting LOCP: ok
Starting CIDS Services: ok
Starting Ethernet-over-IP: ok
Starting Management Services:
Web Server: ok
CLI: ok


Secure Web: Web Authentication Certificate not found (error).
(Cisco Controller)



Welcome to the Cisco Wizard Configuration Tool
Use the '-' character to backup
System Name [Cisco_32:af:43]:
```

For the CCNA Wireless exam, you should be familiar with the CLI Wizard Configuration tool. This tool is designed for quick setup of the controller. Example 13-3 shows a CLI Wizard configuration.

> **Note**   During the startup script, any time that you make a mistake after pressing the **Enter** key, you can move back a step to fix the error by pressing the (-) key.

Example 13-3 *CLI Wizard Configuration*

```
Welcome to the Cisco Wizard Configuration Tool
Use the '-' character to backup
System Name [Cisco_32:af:43]: WLC_1
Enter Administrative User Name (24 characters max): admin
```

```
Enter Administrative Password (24 characters max): *****
Re-enter Administrative Password : *****
Service Interface IP Address Configuration [none][DHCP]: 10.1.1.1
Invalid response

Service Interface IP Address Configuration [none][DHCP]: none
Service Interface IP Address: 10.1.1.1
Service Interface Netmask: 255.255.255.0
Enable Link Aggregation (LAG) [yes][NO]:
Management Interface IP Address: 192.168.1.75
Management Interface Netmask: 255.255.255.0
Management Interface Default Router: 192.168.1.1
Management Interface VLAN Identifier (0 = untagged):
Management Interface Port Num [1 to 2]: 1
Management Interface DHCP Server IP Address: 192.168.1.1
AP Transport Mode [layer2][LAYER3]:
AP Manager Interface IP Address: 192.168.1.80
AP-Manager is on Management subnet, using same values
AP Manager Interface DHCP Server (192.168.1.1):
Virtual Gateway IP Address: 1.1.1.1
Mobility/RF Group Name: CP_Mobile1
Enable Symmetric Mobility Tunneling [yes][NO]: no
Network Name (SSID): OpenAccess
Allow Static IP Addresses [YES][no]:
Configure a RADIUS Server now? [YES][no]:
Enter the RADIUS Server's Address: -
Configure a RADIUS Server now? [YES][no]: no
Warning! The default WLAN security policy requires a RADIUS server.
Please see documentation for more details.
Enter Country Code list (enter 'help' for a list of countries) [US]:
Enable 802.11b Network [YES][no]:
Enable 802.11a Network [YES][no]:
Enable 802.11g Network [YES][no]:
Enable Auto-RF [YES][no]:
Configuration saved!
Resetting system with new configuration...

Configuration saved!
Resetting system with new configuration...
Bootloader 4.1.171.0 (Apr 27 2007 - 05:19:36)
Motorola PowerPC ProcessorID=00000000 Rev. PVR=80200020
CPU: 833 MHz
CCB: 333 MHz
DDR: 166 MHz
LBC: 41 MHz
```

continues

```
L1 D-cache 32KB, L1 I-cache 32KB enabled.
I2C: ready`
DTT: 1 is 31 C
DRAM: DDR module detected, total size:512MB.
512 MB
8540 in PCI Host Mode.
8540 is the PCI Arbiter.
Memory Test PASS
```

After the controller reboots, you are prompted for a username. This, of course, is the username that you created in the CLI Wizard:

```
Enter User Name (or 'Recover-Config' this one-time only to reset configura-
tion to factory defaults)
User: admin
Password:*****
(Cisco Controller) >
```

After you are authenticated, you can become familiar with some of the commands available to you in the CLI. Press the question mark key (?) to get a list of commands. Similar to the Cisco routers and security appliances, the ? can follow a letter to give you a list of commands that begin with that letter. For example, issuing the **p?** command shows that **ping** is available. Use the space key to complete the command if it is unique. Ping is a common utility that helps to verify connectivity. Another common command is the command to save your work. Unlike Cisco routers, **copy run start** does not work here. Instead, you use the **save config** command. In Example 13-4, you can see the process of saving the configuration. After you issue the command, you are asked to verify. You need not press **Enter** after making your selection. Simply press the letter **y** for yes and press **n** for no.

Example 13-4 *Saving Your Configuration from the CLI*

```
(Cisco Controller) >save config
Are you sure you want to save? (y/n) y

Configuration Saved!
(Cisco Controller) >
```

Just as routers have a global configuration mode, so does the controller. Accessing the configuration mode of the controller is a little different from what you might expect. You use the **config** command followed by what it is you want to configure. For example, if you want to configure 802.11a parameters, you type **config 802.11a ?**. You need to type the **?** because you have to enter the complete string, and the question mark helps you find the syntax, as demonstrated in Example 13-5.

Example 13-5 *Using the ? Help Facility*

```
(Cisco Controller) >config 802.11a ?
11nSupport Configure 802.11n-5Ghz parameters.
antenna Configures the 802.11a antenna
beaconperiod Configures the 802.11a beacon interval (20..1000)
cac Configure Call Admission Control parameters for 802.11a radios.
channel Configures the 802.11a channel
chan_width Configure 802.11a channel width
disable Disables 802.11a.
dtim Configures the 802.11a DTIM Period
enable Enables 802.11a.
fragmentation Configures the 802.11a Fragmentation Threshold
l2roam Configures 802.11a l2roam information.
pico-cell Configures the 802.11a pico-cell mode
picocell-V2 Configures the 802.11a picocell-V2 mode
rate Configures 802.11a operational rates.
txPower Configures the 802.11a Tx Power Level
dtpc Configures the 802.11a DTPC Setting
tsm Configures the 802.11a Traffic stream Metrics option
exp-bwreq Configures the 802.11a Expedited BW Request option
(Cisco Controller) >config 802.11a
```

You can also perform **debug** commands from the CLI interface. This is important because these commands are not available from the web interface.

Note: debug commands, although useful, can be dangerous. They take up a lot of resources, so use them sparingly. Also, they turn off when your session times out.

Performing Initial Web Configurations

You can connect to the web interface without ever running though the CLI by browsing to the default IP address on the controller, which is 192.168.1.1. Assume, for the purposes of demonstration, that the controller IP address is 192.168.1.50. This is the IP address that has been assigned to the management interface. When you browse to the controller after using the Setup dialog, you use HTTPS, as seen in Figure 13-1.

After you have accessed the Controller Login page, click the **Login** button. You then see the controller Summary page, shown in Figure 13-2.

Navigating the Web Interface of the Controller

It is beneficial to take time to understand the controller interface. The main menus along the top of the interface are as follows:

■ MONITOR

■ WLANs

Figure 13-1 *Browsing to the Controller*

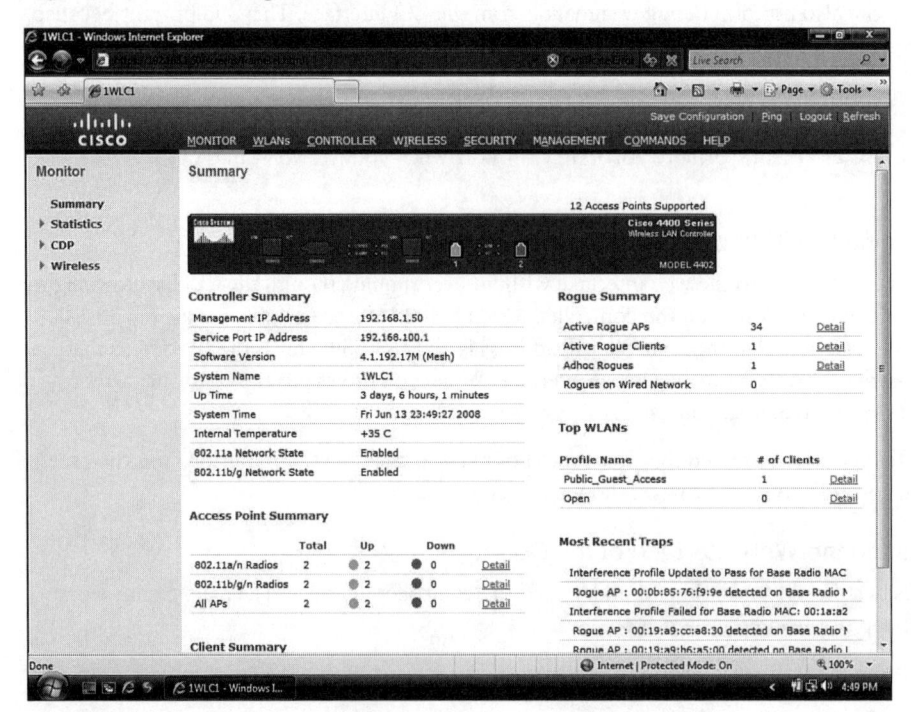

Figure 13-2 *Controller Summary*

- CONTROLLER

- WIRELESS

- SECURITY

- MANAGEMENT

- COMMANDS

- HELP

Also, along the top right you have access to links that save your configuration, access a ping utility, log out, and refresh the page.

When you select one of the top-level configuration tabs, the menu in the left margin of the screen changes. The change enables configuration and monitoring options that pertain to the main level with which you are working. For example, if you are working in the WIRELESS tab, the left menus include the following configuration areas, as seen in Figure 13-3:

- Access Points

- Mesh

- HREAP Groups

- 802.11a/n

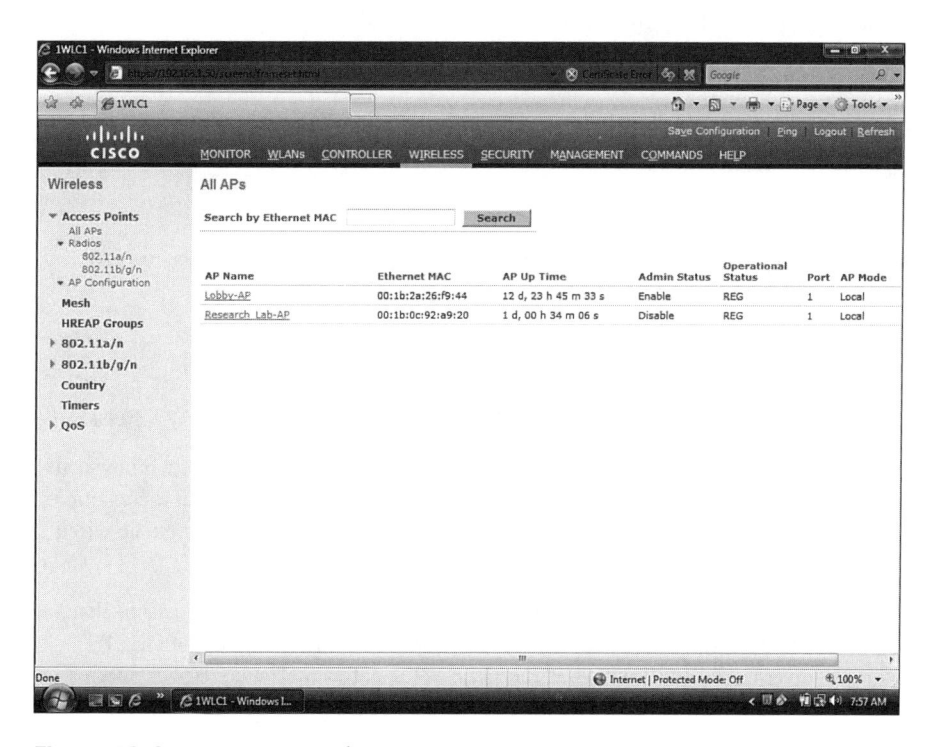

Figure 13-3 *WIRELESS Submenus*

- 802.11b/g/n

- QoS

Each top-level heading you change results in a new side menu.

Configuring the Controller Using the Web Interface

For this example, you build basic wireless connectivity. The process is as follows:

- Build the controller interface.

- Create the WLAN and tie it to the interface.

- Modify security settings.

Building the controller interface is required because, as you might recall from the beginning of this chapter, the interface is a logical entity. It is not a physical port that you can touch, although the interface you create will end up having access to the network via one of the physical ports. After you have created the interface, you need to create the WLAN. The WLAN defines the wireless side, whereas the interface creates the wired side of the configuration. You then need to bind these two to each other so that users on the wireless side can access the wired side of the network.

The default settings for a WLAN apply certain security settings that prohibit a user from connecting without additional configuration. The last step in creating a functional WLAN allowing anyone access with no security is to modify the security settings of the WLAN. The following sections detail the process.

Building the Controller Interface

Step 1. Create an interface in the controller that ties to the VLAN that you want the GUESTNET users on.

CONTROLLER > Interfaces > New

Step 2. Populate the fields with the appropriate values for the Interface Name and VLAN Id fields, as shown in Figure 13-4. Click **Apply**.

Step 3. Define the IP address for this interface. This should be an address that resides on the same subnet as the GUEST_LAN network.

In Figure 13-5, the IP address is 172.30.1.50, and the gateway is 172.30.1.1.

Step 4. Next, on the same configuration page shown in Figure 13-5, select a physical port for this GUEST_LAN to use to access the wired network. In the example, port 1 is used because it is a trunk back to the switch that accesses the wired network.

Step 5. The next step involves defining the DHCP servers. These servers assign IP addresses to the clients that access the network. In the example, the DHCP server is 172.30.1.1, which is the same as the gateway. The controller queries this DHCP server when clients need IP addresses.

Step 6. Click **Apply**.

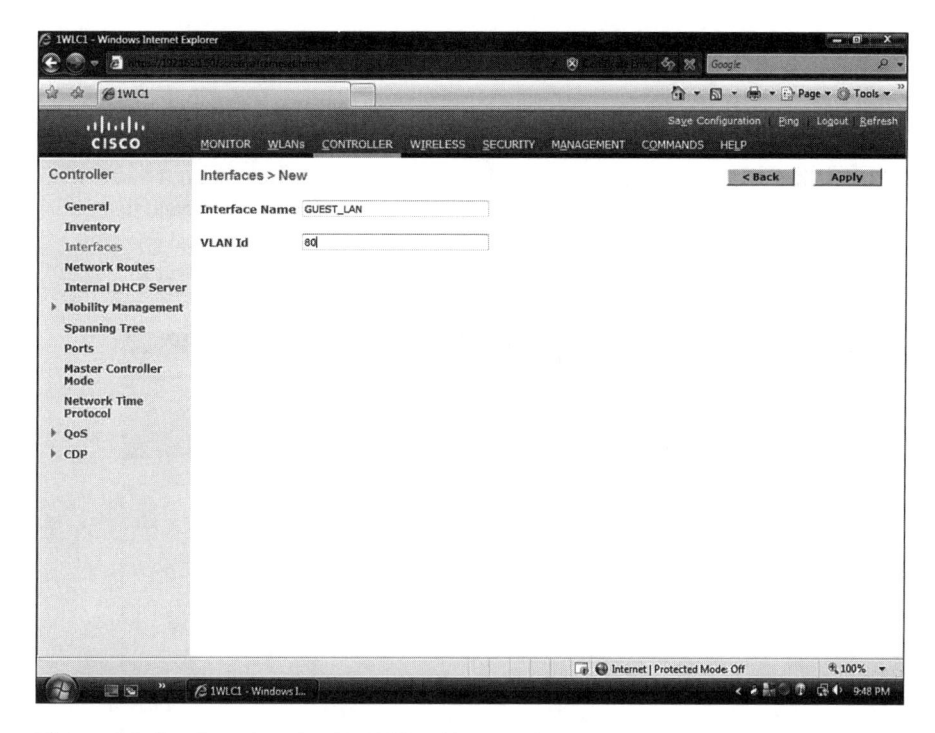

Figure 13-4   *Creating the GUEST_LAN Interface*

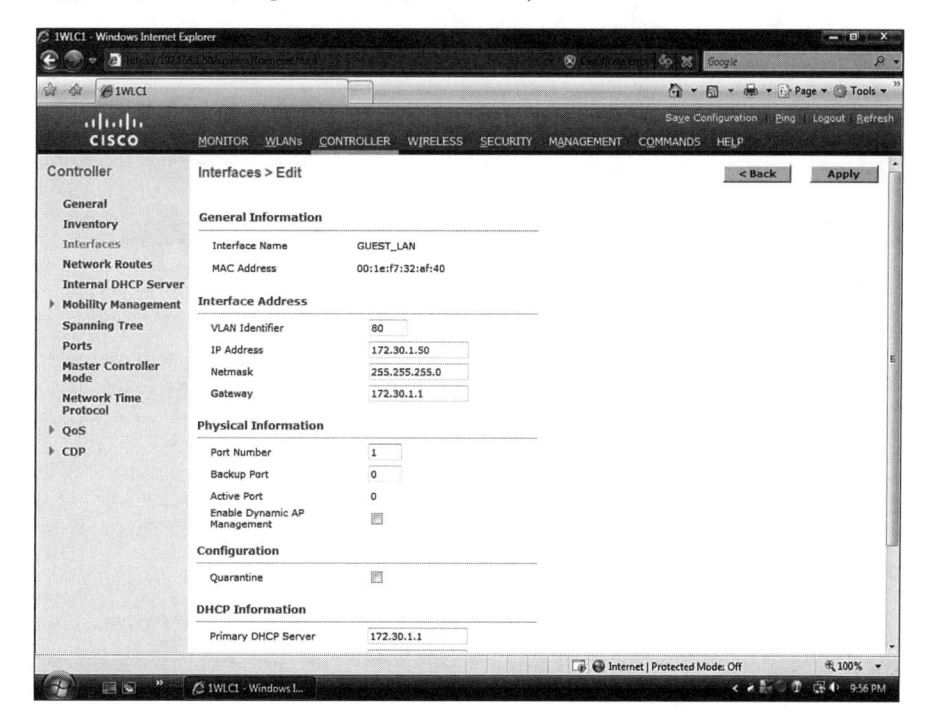

Figure 13-5   *Adding an IP Address to the GUEST_LAN Interface*

> **Note**   You will receive a message indicating that WLANS are disabled temporarily when you click Apply. This is normal.

After you click Apply, you are returned to the list of interfaces seen in Figure 13-6. Notice that physical interfaces are listed here, such as the service-port, ap-manager, and management. These interfaces are tied to VLANs that you can access via the physical connection—port 1. Port 1 is connected to a switch and is operating as an 802.1Q trunk.

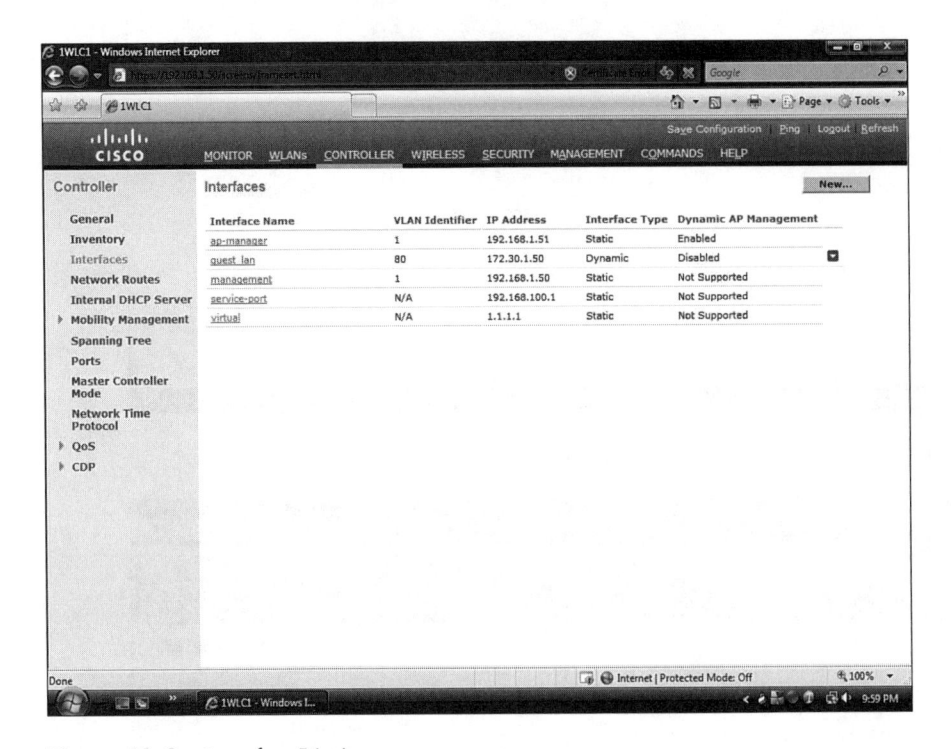

Figure 13-6   *Interface Listing*

The GUEST_LAN interface that you created ties the controller to the wired network over port 1 on VLAN 80. No WLAN is associated with it, and no AP is sending beacons advertising GUEST_LAN access. That part has yet to be configured.

Creating the WLAN and Tying It to the Interface

The next piece of the configuration is creating the wireless side.

Step 1.   Choose **WLANs > New**.

You see a configuration page that assigns an arbitrary WLAN ID to the WLAN that you are creating. In the case of Figure 13-7, the WLAN ID is 2.

Step 2.   Give the WLAN a profile name.

Step 3.   Give the WLAN an SSID. In this case, the SSID chosen is GUESTNET.

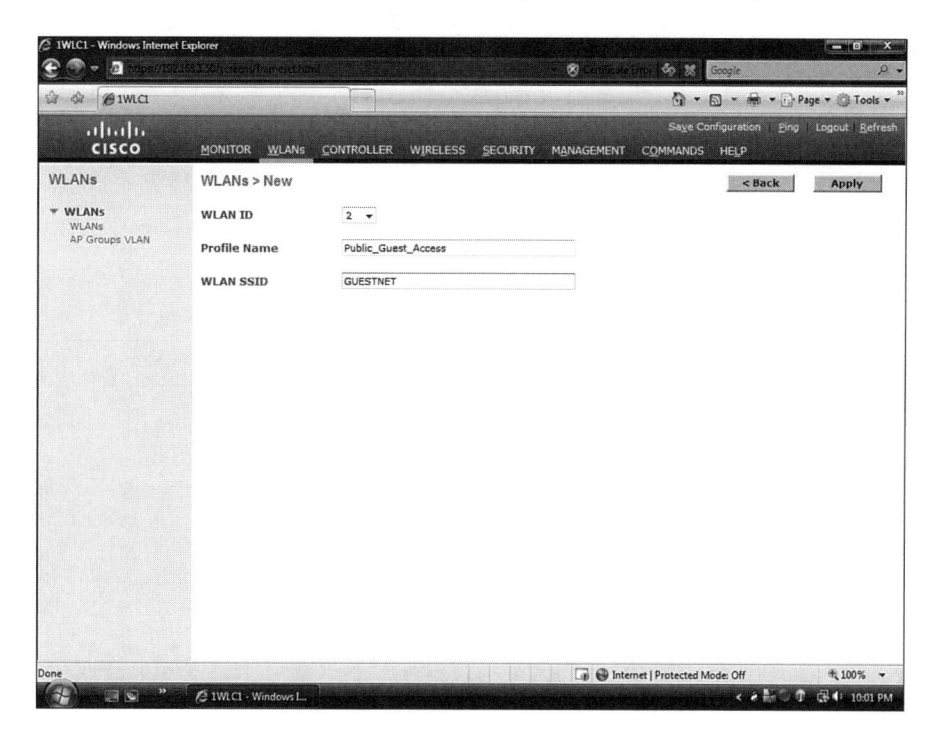

Figure 13-7   *Creating the WLAN Profile Name*

Step 4.   Click **Apply**.

The next page that you arrive at has four tabs, seen in Figure 13-8. These tabs allow you to configure the General, Security, QoS, and Advanced settings for the WLAN.

Step 5.   On the General tab, make sure of the following:

■ The WLAN Status is **Enabled**. If it is not, the WLAN settings are not sent to all APs.

Note: Skip the Security Policies field. You will change this in the Security tab.

■ For the Radio Policy, if **All** is left selected, all radios are available for the GUESTNET network. It is common to allow 802.11b/g for guests and then use 802.11a for private WLANs, because 802.11b/g usually experience more interference than 802.11a. For guests, quality of service is probably not the highest concern; however, it is for internal users. For now, just leave Radio Policy at the default value of **All**.

Step 6.   Next is the important step of choosing the interface in the Interface drop-down that ties this GUESTNET WLAN to the **guest_lan** physical interface on VLAN 80. If you choose the wrong interface here, people can end up on the wrong network.

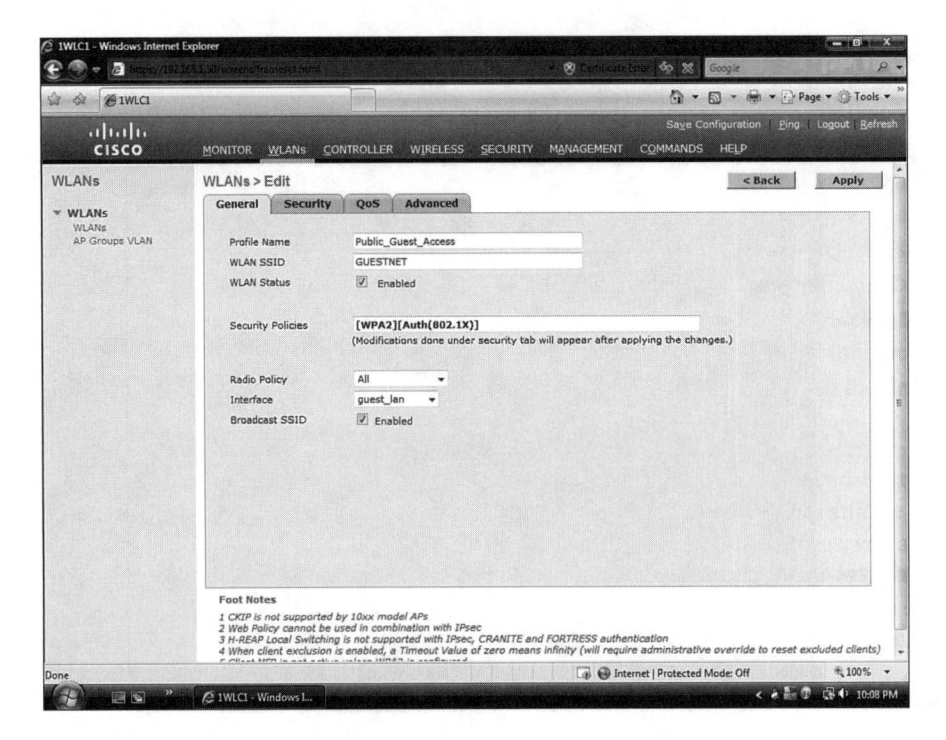

Figure 13-8   *WLAN Configuration Tabs*

Step 7.   Choose not to broadcast the SSID by deselecting the Broadcast SSID check box. This adds a little security, but, as you will learn in Chapter 17, "Securing the Wireless Network," it is not a high degree of security. The default value is to broadcast the SSID.

Step 8.   Do not click **Apply** yet.

Modifying the Security Settings

Before you apply the configuration, you need to modify the security settings. Follow these steps:

Step 1.   Click the Security tab within the WLAN configuration window.

You are presented with three additional tabs:

■ Layer 2

■ Layer 3

■ AAA Servers

For now, you should only be concerned with the Layer 2 policy, because the Layer 3 policy defaults to None.

Step 2.   Choose **None** as the Layer 2 security method.

Step 3.   Click **Apply**.

Success! You now have a functional WLAN, as Figure 13-9 illustrates. That is, it is functional as long as the wired network behind it is good to go.

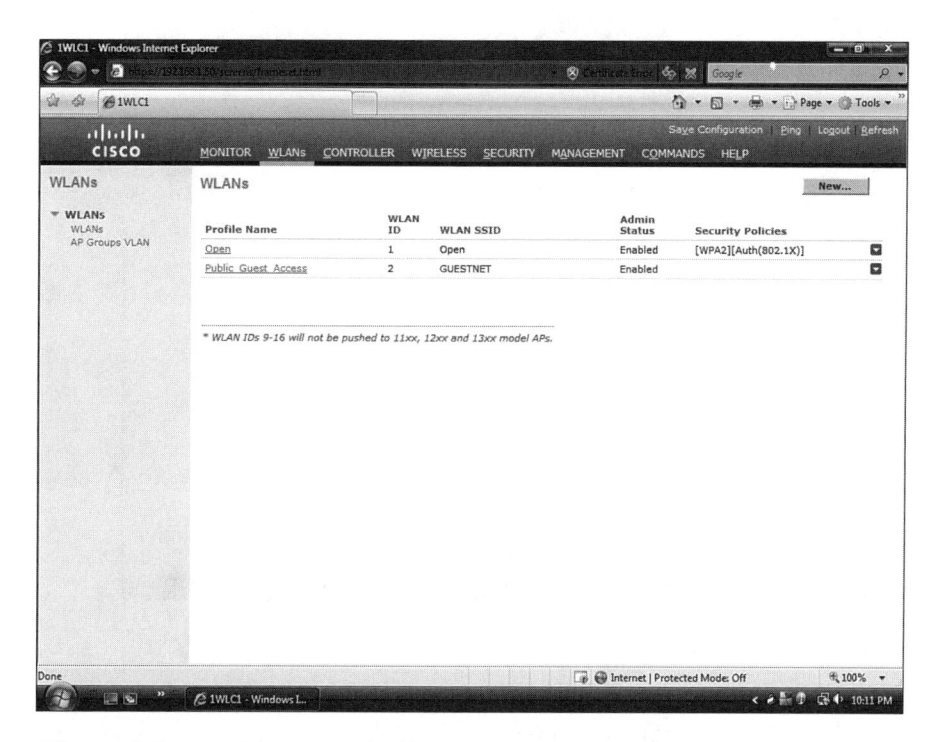

Figure 13-9   *Listing WLAN Profiles*

Naming Access Points

Still, you might want to do some tweaks to the network. For example, suppose that you have two APs. One AP is in the lobby, and the other is in the research lab. You do not want anyone to access the AP in the research lab using the GUESTNET. What do you do? You just control the APs that allow GUESTNET access. To begin, though, you should identify which AP is in the lobby and which is in the research lab. Figure 13-10 shows that the two APs are identified by a MAC address as the AP name.

This can be confusing. I recommend changing the name of the AP to something that makes sense. Here is how to do it:

Step 1.   Find the MAC address of the AP in the lobby. It is printed on the bottom of the AP.

Step 2.   After you have the MAC of the lobby AP, go to the WLC interface and browse to **WIRELESS > Access Points > All APs**.

Step 3.   Select the AP that matches the MAC address. The AP name begins with "AP" followed by the MAC address.

Step 4.   Change the Name in the General tab to **Lobby-AP**.

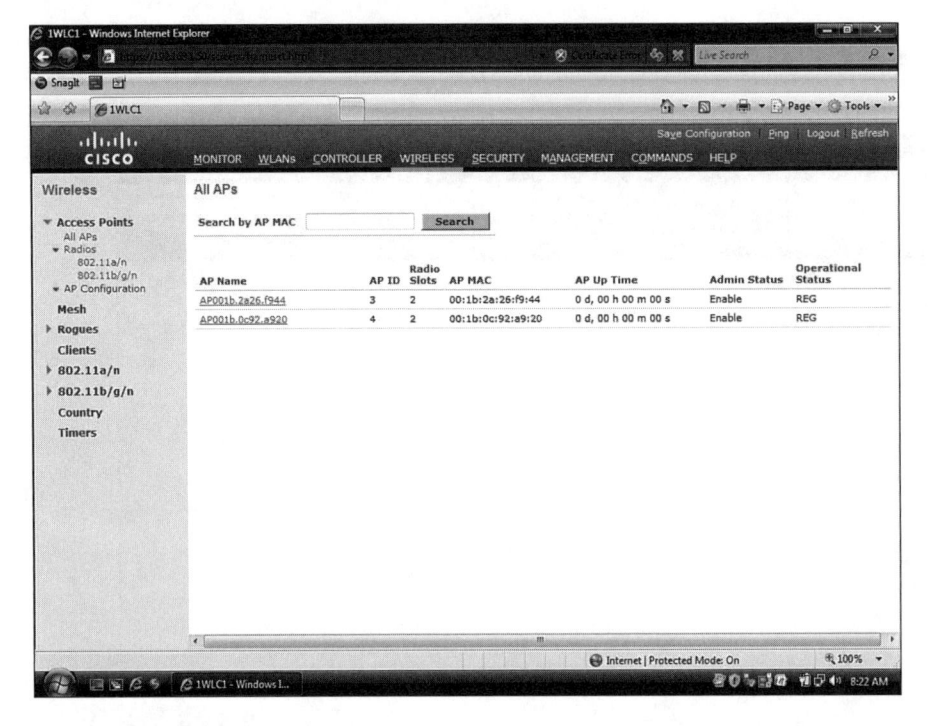

Figure 13-10 *Listing All APs*

Note: This name follows the AP when you move it within your network, so it is important to update the name on the controller if you ever move the AP or swap it out. Also, it is good practice to label the Cisco PoE switch port with the same name. This helps when you are troubleshooting any issues and might need to remotely power cycle the AP by shutting its switch port.

Step 5.   Optionally add a location. These steps are seen in Figure 13-11.

Step 6.   Click **Apply**.

Step 7.   Next, select the other AP.

Note: You might have more than two APs in your own deployment. The term *other AP* in this case simply refers to the only other AP used in the example.

Step 8.   Repeat Steps 5 through 7 to assign a different name and location for the Research_Lab AP.

When completed, you should see two APs that are easy to identify based on their name.

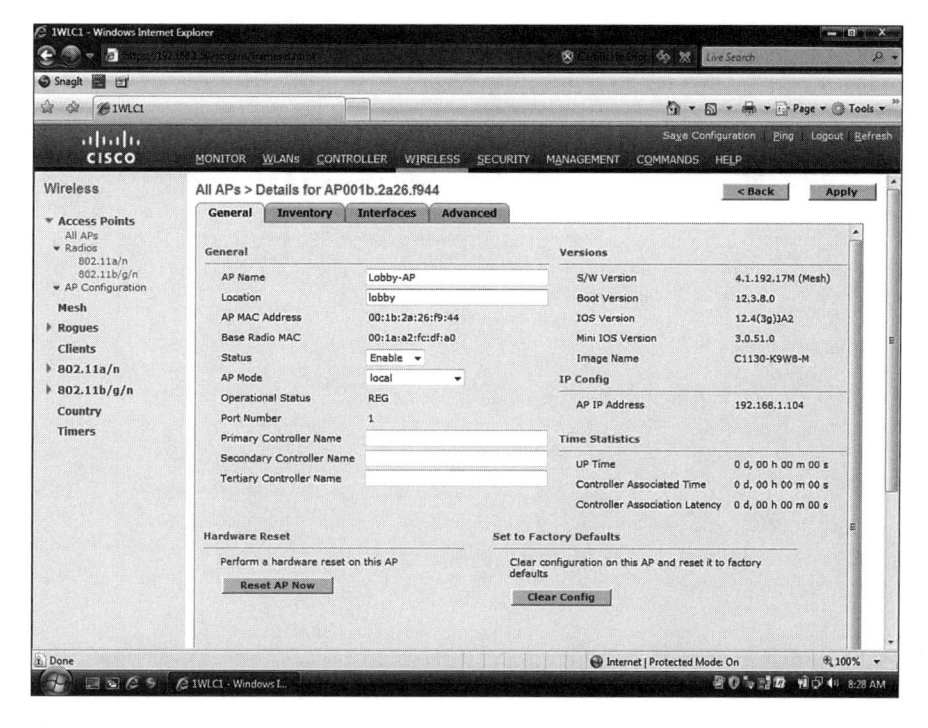

Figure 13-11 *Naming the AP*

Restricting Access to Access Points

Now is where the control part comes in. Remember that you do not want the GUESTNET access going through the Research_Lab-AP. Following is how to prevent it:

Step 1. Start by selecting **WIRELESS > Access Points > Radios > 802.11a/n.**

Step 2. Find the Research_Lab-AP seen in Figure 13-12.

Step 3. To the right of the entry, hover your mouse over the arrow seen in Figure 13-13, and select **Configure.**

Step 4. Select the WLAN Override by selecting **enable**, as seen in Figure 13-14. A new list of WLANS appears.

Step 5. Select the WLAN that you want this AP to support.

In this case, leaving the GUESTNET WLAN unchecked removes that access through this AP.

Step 6. Click **Apply.**

Step 7. Repeat these steps for the 802.11b/g/n radio.

After you have done this for the Research_Lab-AP, you probably want to do the same for the Lobby_AP, but only allow GUESTNET access though it, removing any other networks.

Figure 13-12 *802.11a/n Radios*

Figure 13-13 *802.11a/n Radio Options Menu*

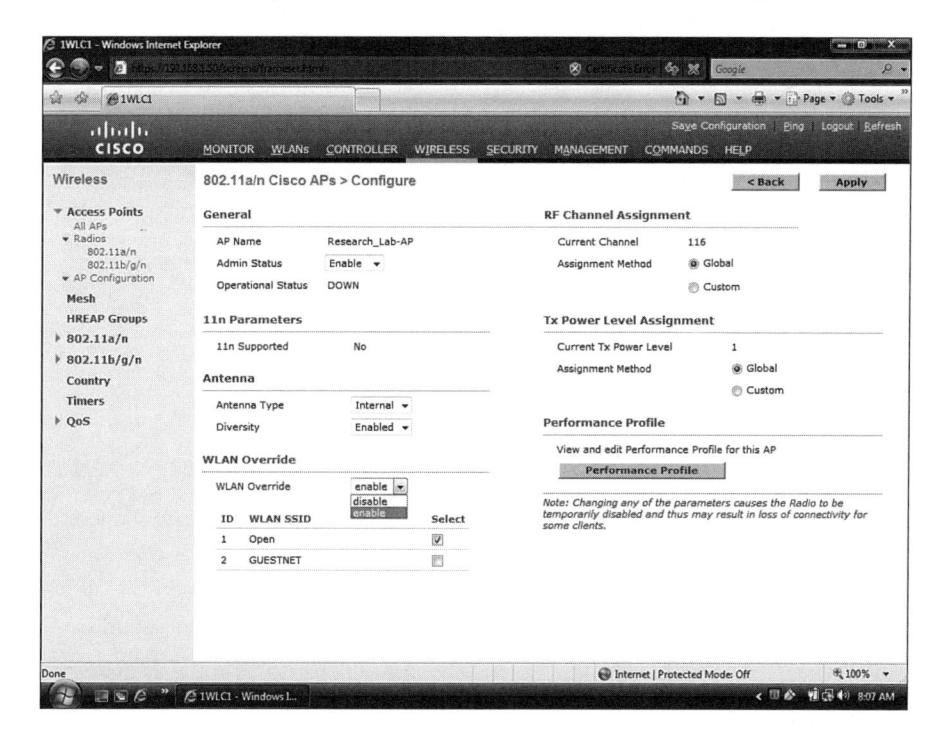

Figure 13-14   *Enabling WLAN Override*

Summary of Controller Configuration Using the Web Interface

At this point you have accomplished much by way of your controller. Through one interface, you can see how much power in configuration you have. What did you do? Here is the list:

■   You set up multiple APs at the same time.

■   You easily configured a WLAN connection to provide GUESTNET access.

■   You controlled which APs allows GUESTNET access.

Of course, more options are available that you might want to understand, and many relate to security. First, however, it is beneficial to understand how to monitor the network from the interface of the controller, view your APs, and simply get a better picture of what is going on in the network. The following sections discuss these aspects.

Monitoring with the Controller

As far as the management and monitoring of the network go, you have much power by way of the controller. The controller is a central point of intelligence that can give you valuable information regarding the network overall as well as specifics related to APs, clients, rogues, and more. The main login page of the controller provides an excellent starting point.

General Monitoring

The Controller Summary page is the first thing you see when you log in. At first glance, it might seem like a simple overview, but it has much more than that. Examine Figure 13-15, where you will notice the following functional areas of the Summary page:

- Controller Summary

- Access Point Summary

- Client Summary

- Rogue Summary

- Top WLANs

- Most Recent Traps

Each area provides a wealth of information, as described in the sections that follow.

Controller Summary

Controller Summary provides the management IP address and the service port address. You can also see the software version. In Figure 13-15, you can see that the version is 4.1.192.17M (Mesh). Eventually you will learn to upgrade it to version 5.x. For now, this version is acceptable.

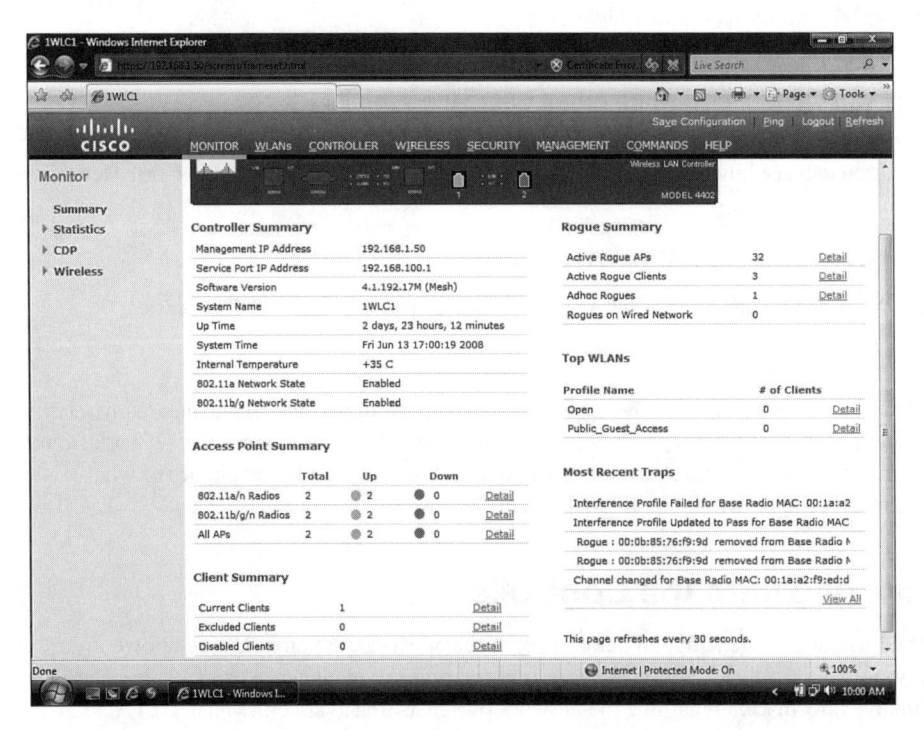

Figure 13-15 *Monitor Summary*

You can also gather the name of the controller and its uptime. Next, you can see the up time and system time on the controller, as well as the internal temperature. In addition, you can see that the 802.11a and 802.11b/g networks are enabled.

Access Point Summary

The next functional area is Access Point Summary, which shows the total number of 802.11a.n and 802.11b/g/n radios that are present, how many are up, and how many are down. You can click **Detail** for more information. 802.11b/g/n Radios details have been selected, and you are presented with a list of APs, as seen in Figure 13-16.

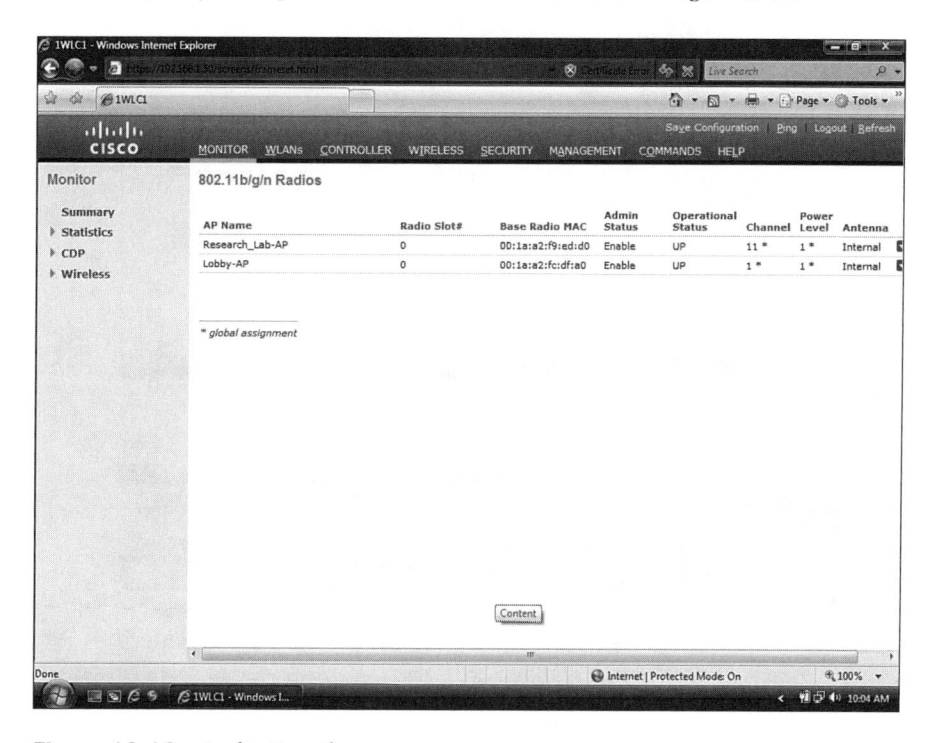

Figure 13-16 *Radio Details*

This list provides valuable information regarding the administrative status of the APs as well as the channel they are operating on and their power level. A power level of 1 indicates the highest level of power legal in the country you are in. You can change these levels by hovering your mouse over the blue arrow on the right and selecting the **Configure** link, as seen in Figure 13-17.

After you select **Configure**, you are taken to the page shown in Figure 13-18 that allows you to set General parameters, including enabling and disabling the radios, 11n parameters if available, and antenna type and diversity.

You can also gather information about management frame protection and perform a WLAN override. A WLAN override lets you control which SSIDs are made available by this AP. You saw this in the section "Configuring the Controller Using the Web Interface."

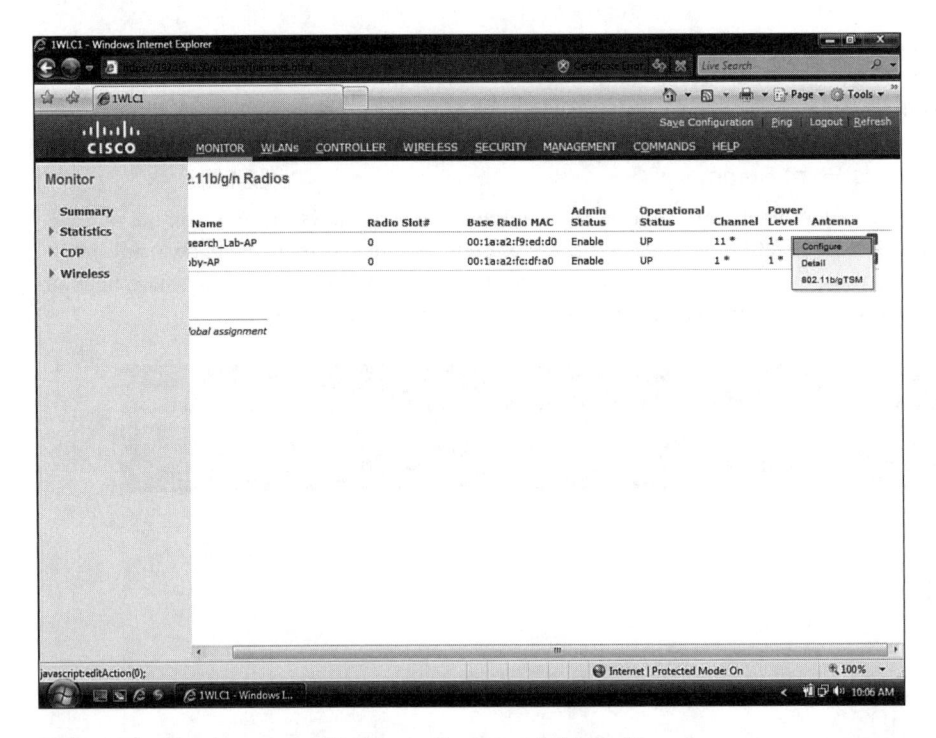

Figure 13-17   *Access the Configure Options of the Radios*

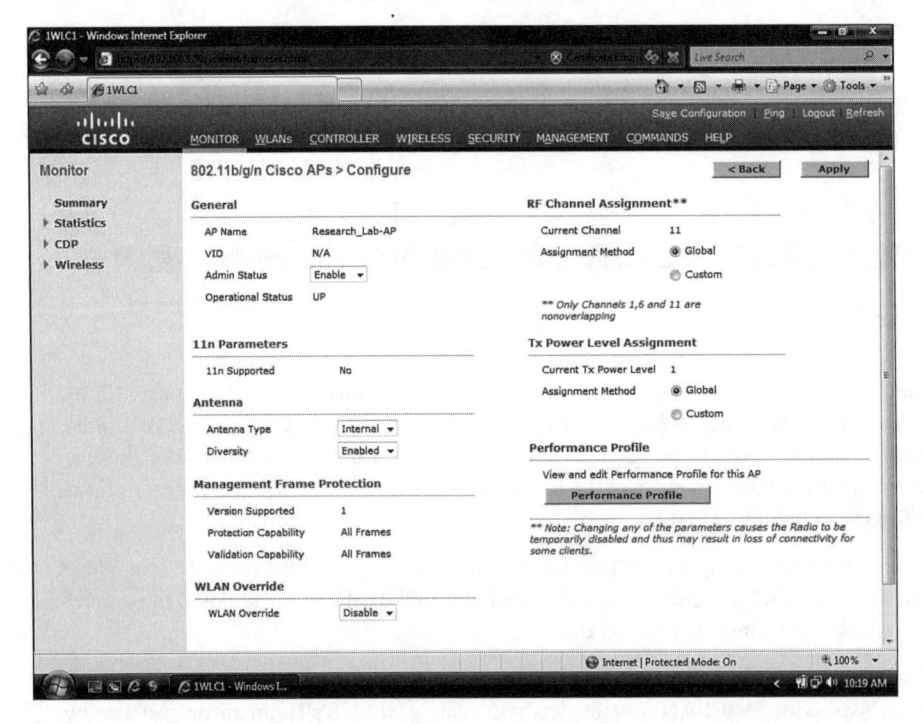

Figure 13-18   *802.11b/g/n Cisco APs > Configure Screen*

On the right side of the page, you can change the RF channel assignment and the TX (transmit) power level assignment. The higher the number of the power setting, the lower the power level is. For example, changing the level from 1 to 2 decreases the power by 50 percent. Changing it to 3 decreases it by 25 percent, and 4 decreases it by 12.5 percent. Each level halves the one before it.

You can also change and edit a performance profile. The Performance Profile link takes you to a page that lets you define RF values and thresholds. Additionally, from the Monitor page, you can select the Wireless link on the left side of the page, as shown in Figure 13-19.

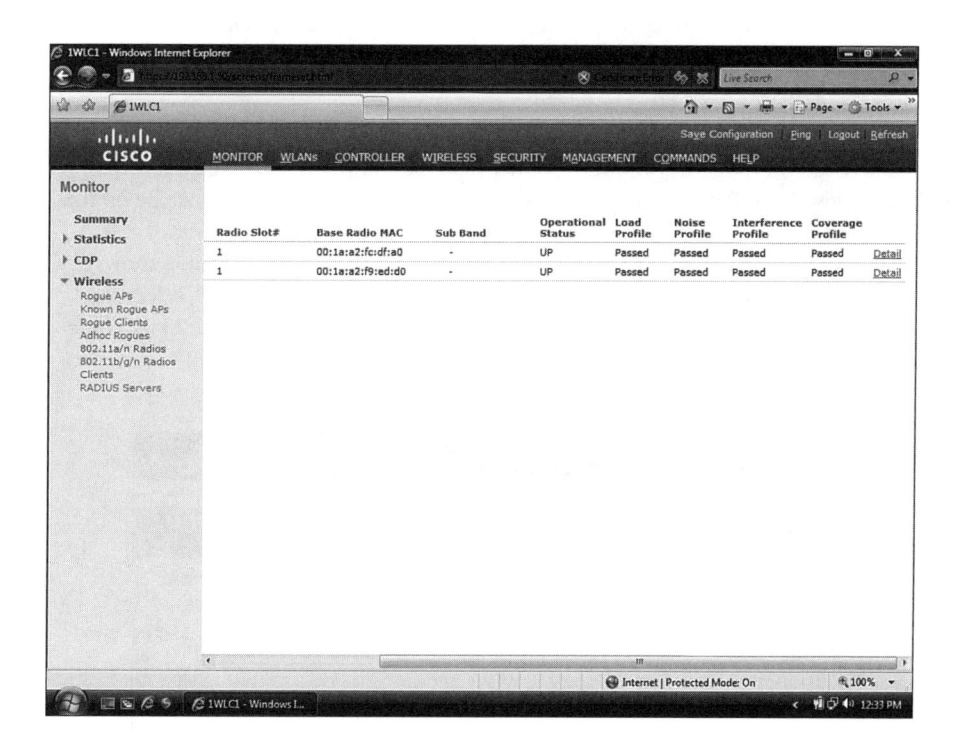

Figure 13-19   *Viewing 802.11a/n Radios*

In the figure, you can see a list containing the following links:

- **Rogue APs:** Selecting **Rogue APs** takes you to a page that lists the rogue APs.

- **Known Rogue APs:** Selecting **Known Rogue APs** takes you to a page of known rogue APs.

- **Rogue Clients:** The **Rogue Clients** link takes you to a list of rogue clients.

- **Adhoc Rogues:** **Adhoc Rogues** takes you to a list of clients that are creating ad-hoc networks. This can pose a serious security risk, because it can enable access to the wired infrastructure.

- **802.11a/n Radios / 802.11b/g/n Radios:** The 802 Radios links provide a list of APs with that specific type of radio.

- **Clients:** This link ties you to a page that provides a list of clients and lets you search by MAC address for clients.

- **RADIUS Servers:** This link provides a list of RADUIS Authentication and Accounting servers.

Looking further into the 802.11a/n Radios and 802.11b/g/n Radios options, you can gain even more information by selecting the **Details** link for a radio from the Monitor Summary page. Here is what you get. You see the slot that the radio is in and the base radio MAC address. Looking more closely at Figure 13-19, you can see that Operational Status is UP. You can gain information regarding a load profile, noise profile, interference profile, and coverage profile.

Load Profile is set to 80% by default. If the load of this particular AP goes over that threshold, Load Profile shows a warning rather than the status Passed. Likewise, if the SNR is too low, Load Profile indicates a warning. Should too much interference be on the same channel that this AP is operating on, the Interference Profile shows a warning. If clients roam away and are not able to relay off another AP, the Coverage Profile shows a warning. To see the details of these profiles, from the screen in Figure 13-18, select the **Details** link at the right side of the page. This causes a page similar to Figure 13-20 to be displayed.

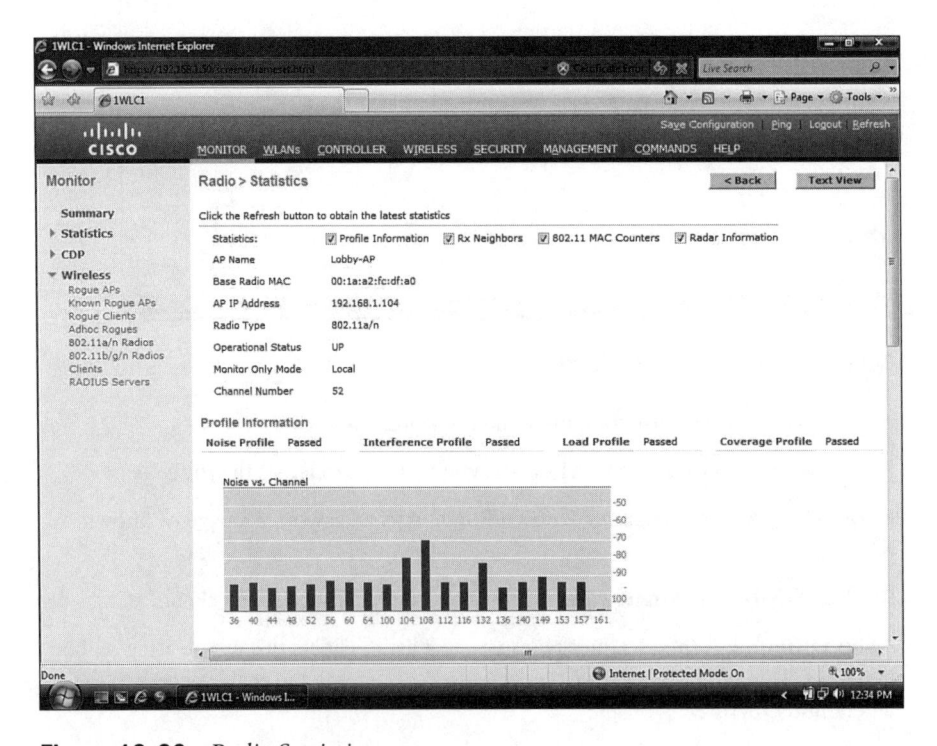

Figure 13-20 *Radio Statistics*

The resulting page is Radio Statistics. Numerous items are of interest here that are not seen in the figure:

■   The Noise vs. Channel chart shows each channel of the AP and the level of non-802.11 noise interference on that particular channel.

■   The Interference by Channel shows statistics for other 802.11 interference.

■   The Load Statistics section provides information about transmit and receive utilization, channel utilization, and attached clients.

■   Two charts exist: % Client Count vs. RSSI and % Client Count vs. SNR.

■   The next section covers the Rx Neighbors Information. This section displays neighboring APs along with their IP address and Received Signal Strength Indicator (RSSI). The controller uses this to allocate channels and ensure adequate coverage by shaping the coverage area.

As far as the CCNA Wireless exam is concerned, you should be familiar with the overall concept, but you do not need to understand each area in great detail. Still, with all this information for monitoring the APs that this controller manages and their radios, you must contend with those rogue devices. Rogue devices include *any* wireless device that can interfere with the managed APs. The following section discusses how to manage them.

Managing Rogue APs

You can manage rogue APs from the controller interface. Recall that on the Monitor page, the second column has information on rogue devices. This is a good place to start. Reviewing the Monitor page, seen in Figure 13-21, notice that the first line below Rogue Summary is Active Rogue APs.

A rogue AP is an AP that is unknown to the controller. You want to avoid jumping to conclusions here. It might simply be an AP in a neighboring business. It does not necessarily represent the bad guys. This takes a little work to figure out, however.

The next line is Active Rogue Clients. This is a wireless device that sends an unexpected frame. This is usually from a default configuration on client devices.

Next is Adhoc Rogues, which is, as previously mentioned, any device setting up an Adhoc network.

Finally, you have the Rogues on a Wired Network field. This is a count of rogues that a Rogue Detector AP has discovered. It works by the AP detecting ARP requests on the wired network for APs marked as rogue.

You can gather more information by selecting the **Detail** link on the right. Selecting this for the Active Rogue APs presents a list of the designated rogue APs. The key on this page is the number of detecting radios. Examine Figure 13-22. Notice that 20 of 32 rogues are

Figure 13-21 *Review Rogues from the Monitor Page*

listed. Also key in on the number of detecting radios. The fewer radios, the better. That is because if only one or two detect the rogue, the rogue is probably on the edge of the network, most likely coming from a neighboring business, as is the case with this figure.

If the number of detecting radios is high, the rogue is being seen by a number of APs and most likely is within your network, probably sitting under a desk exactly where it should not be.

You can click on the rogue that you are concerned with and select **Contain Rogue**, as seen in Figure 13-23.

When you contain the rogue, your AP spoofs its MAC address and sends deauthentication frames that appear to come from the contained AP. When clients see this, they are unable to stay associated with the contained AP. This should stress the importance of ensuring that it is not the AP of your neighbor.

Another note related to containment relates to the number of devices you can contain. You cannot contain more than three rogues per AP because the AP that is performing containment takes a CPU hit of up to 10 percent per contained AP. The system cap is 30 percent. This means that if an AP contains two rogues, it takes a 20 percent CPU hit. With the system cap of 30 percent, it can contain only one more rogue.

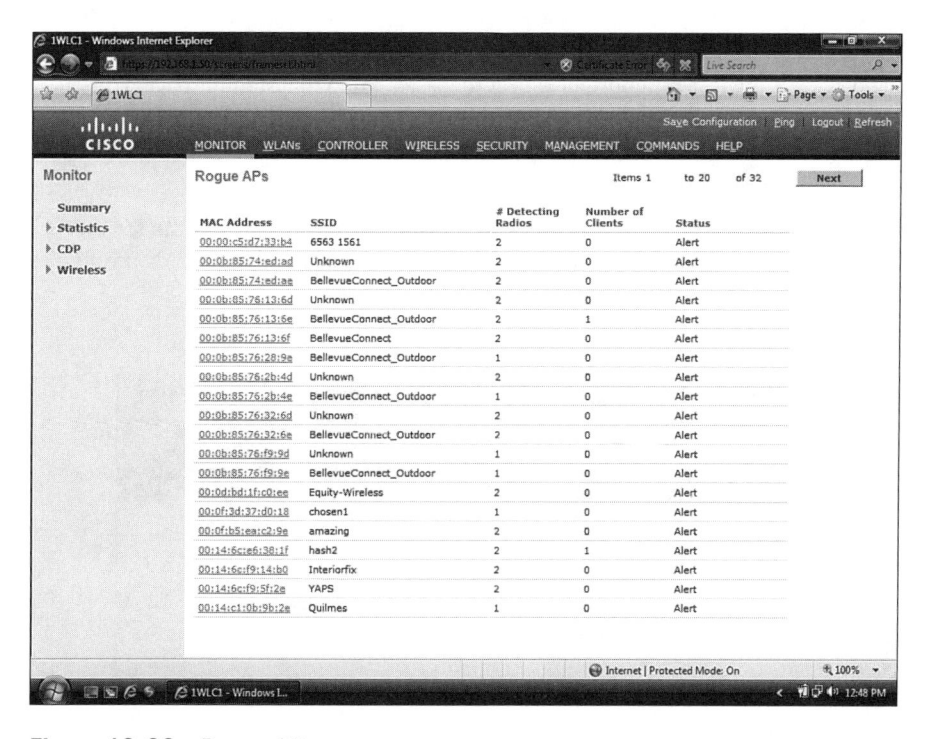

Figure 13-22   *Rogue APs*

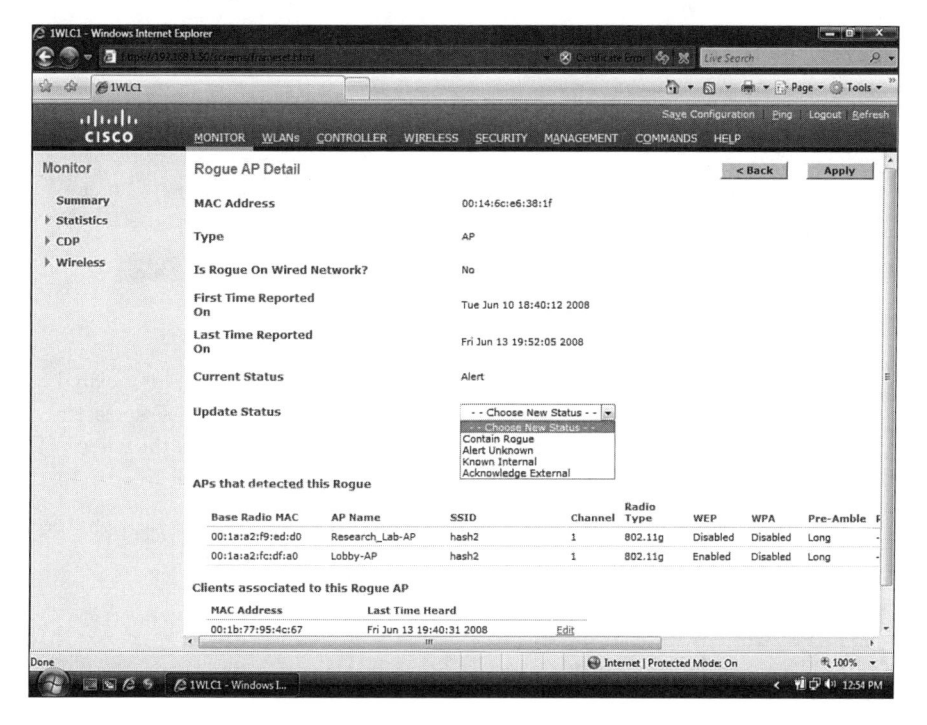

Figure 13-23   *Contain the Rogue AP*

Managing Clients

Managing clients is another important aspect to master. From the Monitor page, you can see the client summary. This gives a total of current clients, excluded clients, and disabled clients. Any device that sends a probe is considered a current client, so this number might be inflated even if the client does not associate with the AP.

Clicking on **details** provides a list of clients, as shown in Figure 13-24. You can see the MAC address of the clients, the AP with which they are associated, the WLAN profile they are using, and the protocol they are using.

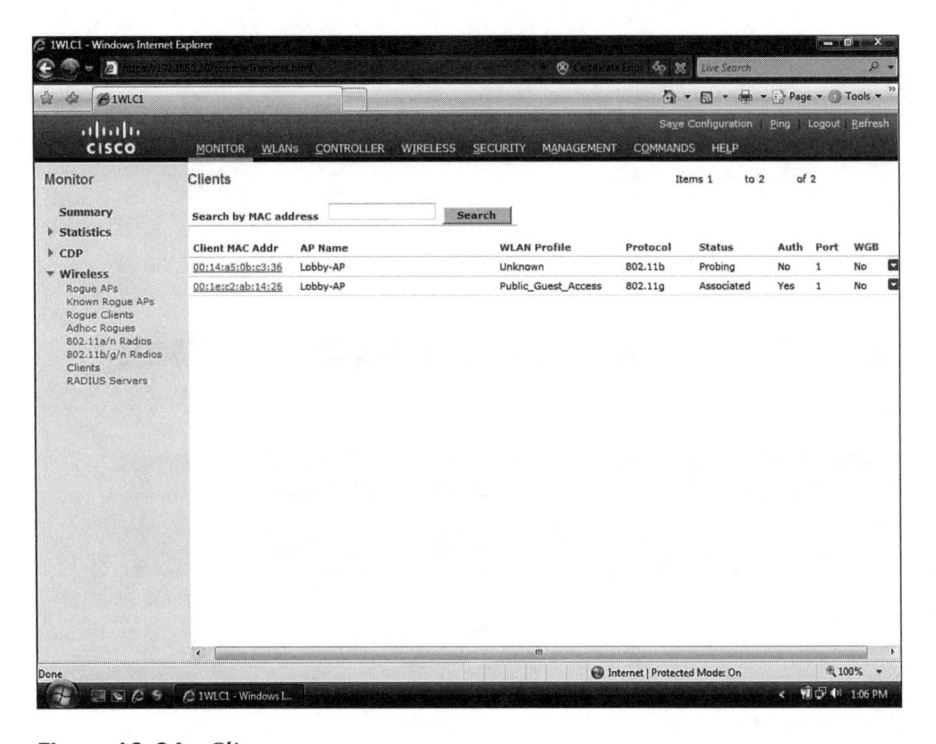

Figure 13-24 *Clients*

In the case of Figure 13-24, the client with MAC address 00:1e:c2:ab:14:26 is associated with the Public_Guest_Access profile. Next you have the status, in this case Associated. Also, the client is authenticated, and port 1 on the controller is the means to the wired network. This client is not a workgroup bridge.

As seen in other examples, you can hover your mouse over the blue arrow to the right for a list of options, including these:

- LinkTest
- Disable
- Remove

- 802.11aTSM

- 802.11b/gTSM

The LinkTest provides a way to test the link of the client by reporting the number of sent and received packets, the signal strength, and the signal-to-noise ratio (SNR).

Disabling the client puts it into a Disabled Client list and bans it until it is manually removed. To view this list, select **Security > Disabled Clients.** To manually add clients, click **New.**

The **Remove** link disassociates the client. However, this does not prevent it from attempting association again, like disabling would.

For more details, click the client MAC address. This presents the Detail page, as seen in Figure 13-25. The five sections are as follows:

- Client Properties

- Security Information

- Quality of Service Properties

- Client Statistics

- AP Properties

Finally, there are excluded clients. Clients can be excluded for the following reasons:

- The client has failed 802.11 authentication five times.

- The client has failed 802.11 association five times.

- The client has failed 802.1x authentication three times.

- The client has failed the policy on an external server.

- The client has an IP that is already in use.

- The client has failed three web authentication attempts.

By default, these clients are excluded for 60 seconds. Think of it as a waiting period. If a client retries after that 60 seconds and does not fail any of the criteria in the preceding list, the client is no longer excluded.

Using Internal DHCP

One reason for exclusion is that the client might be trying to use an IP that is in use already. You can solve this issue using DHCP. If your network does not have a DHCP server, the controller can act as one for you. To configure the controller as a DHCP server, go to **CONTROLLER > Internal DHCP Server > New.** The rest of the DHCP server configuration is pretty self-explanatory.

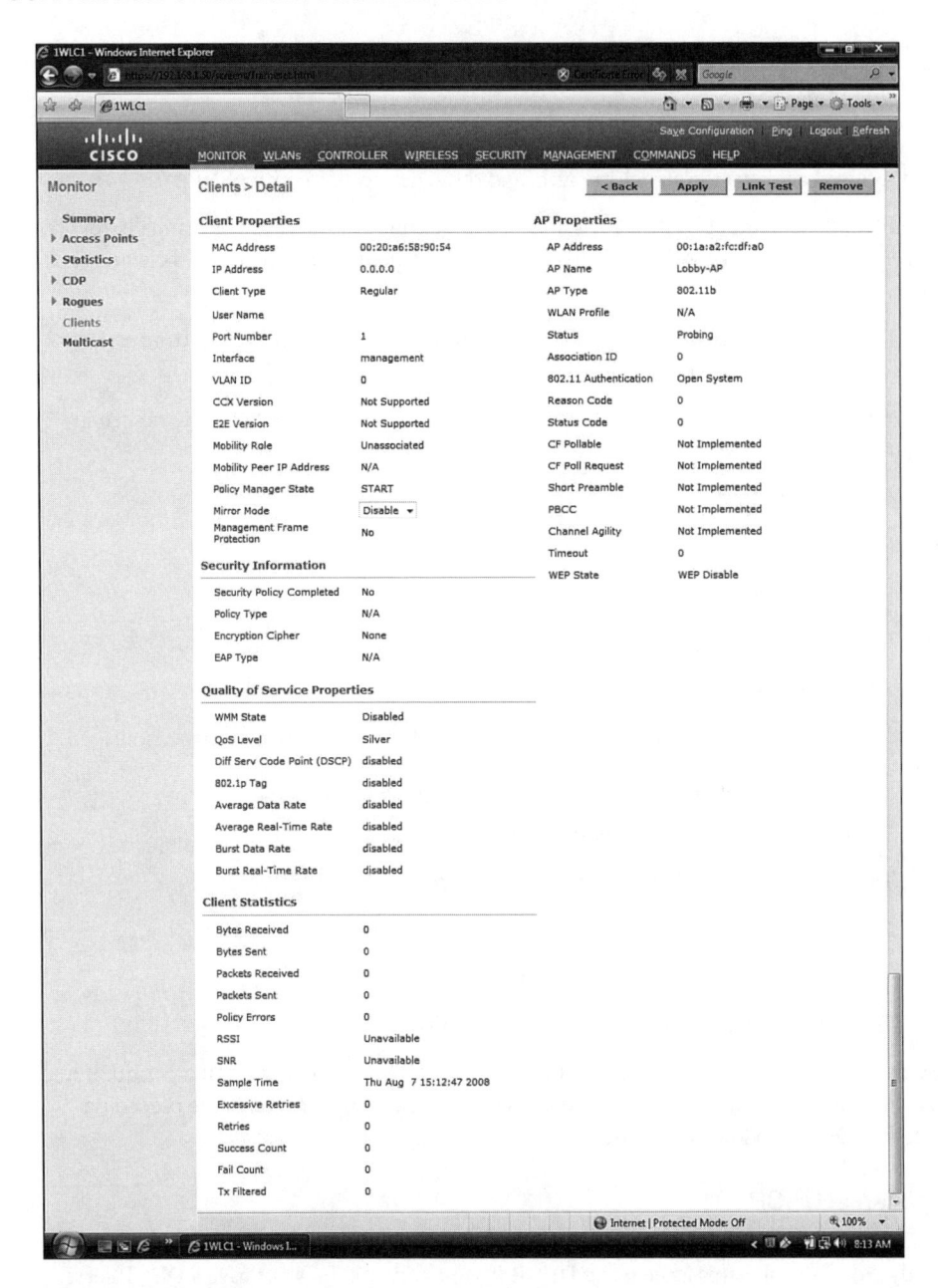

Figure 13-25 *Clients > Detail*

Exam Preparation Tasks

Review All the Key Concepts

Review the most important topics from this chapter, noted with the Key Topics icon in the outer margin of the page. Table 13-2 lists a reference of these key topics and the page number where you can find each one.

Table 13-2   *Key Topics for Chapter 13*

Key Topic Item	Description	Page Number
Controller Terminology	Section defining controller terms	228
Example 13-3	Setup Wizard	232
Configuring the Controller Using the Web Interface	Creating an interface and creating a WLAN	238
Figure 13-12	802.11a/n radios	246
Figure 13-13	802.11a/n Radio Options menu	246
Figure 13-19	Viewing 802.11a/n radios	251
Figure 13-21	Review rogues from the Monitor page	254

Definition of Key Terms

Define the following key terms from this chapter, and check your answers in the Glossary:

port, interface, WLAN, static interface, dynamic interface, roaming, mobility group

This chapter covers the following subjects:

Connecting to a Standalone AP: A brief discussion on how to gain access to a standalone AP using various methods.

Using the Express Setup and Express Security for Basic Configuration: How to set up the standalone AP for wireless access using the Express Setup and Express Security configurations.

Converting to LWAPP: How to convert a standalone AP to lightweight mode using the Upgrade tool.

CHAPTER 14

Migrating Standalone APs to LWAPP

Many Cisco APs are capable of operating in both autonomous mode and lightweight mode. APs that can do both usually ship in standalone mode. Some may choose to use these APs in standalone mode. Others might immediately convert them to Lightweight Access Point Protocol (LWAPP)–capable APs and integrate them into a network designed after the Cisco Unified Wireless Network (CUWN). In this chapter, you will learn how to access a standalone AP, how to configure it in standalone mode, and how to convert it to lightweight mode.

You should do the "Do I Know This Already?" quiz first. If you score 80 percent or higher, you might want to skip to the section "Exam Preparation Tasks." If you score below 80 percent, you should spend the time reviewing the entire chapter. Refer to Appendix A, "Answers to the 'Do I Know This Already?' Quizzes," to confirm your answers.

"Do I Know This Already?" Quiz

The "Do I Know This Already?" quiz helps you determine your level of knowledge of this chapter's topics before you begin. Table 14-1 details the major topics discussed in this chapter and their corresponding quiz questions.

Table 14-1 *"Do I Know This Already?" Section-to-Question Mapping*

Foundation Topics Section	Questions
Connecting to a Standalone AP	1–4
Using the Express Setup and Express Security for Basic Configuration	5–6
Converting to LWAPP	7–10

1. A standalone AP has a console port. True or False?

    a. True

    b. False

2. Which methods can be used to assign an IP address to a standalone AP? (Choose all that apply.)

    a. DHCP

    b. Static through the CLI

    c. TFTP

    d. DNS

3. What are three methods that require an IP address? (Choose all that apply.)

    a. Console to it using a console cable and the console port.

    b. Telnet into it if it has an IP address.

    c. Web browse to it if it has an IP address.

    d. SSH into it if it has an IP address.

4. Which of the following methods can be used to obtain the IP address of the AP? (Choose all that apply.)

    a. DHCP server logs

    b. CDP

    c. NTP server statistics

    d. IP Setup Utility

5. You can apply a separate SSID to different radios. True or False?

    a. True

    b. False

6. More than one authentication server can be configured. True or False?

    a. True

    b. False

7. What is required if you are converting from standalone to lightweight mode? (Choose all that apply.)

    a. An upgrade image

    b. A DHCP server

    c. An upgrade tool

    d. A WLC

8. If you are using the Autonomous to Lightweight Mode Upgrade tool, what else must you obtain from Cisco?

   a. A TFTP server

   b. A WCS

   c. The correct LWAPP software (version 12.3(JA) or better)

   d. Autonomous to Lightweight Mode Upgrade image

9. What protocol is used for the upgrade from autonomous to lightweight?

   a. FTP

   b. TFTP

   c. SCP

   d. SSH

10. A controller must be reachable after the AP is upgraded for the AP to function. True or False?

   a. True

   b. False

Foundation Topics

Connecting to a Standalone AP

Almost any AP that is capable of operating in both autonomous and lightweight mode ships in autonomous mode. You need to convert the device to lightweight mode if you plan to use it in that mode. Luckily, you can accomplish this conversion in two ways. You can get a Windows application called the Upgrade tool to do it, and you can get it done using the Cisco Wireless Control System (WCS). Either method accomplishes the same task; it is simply a matter of what you prefer and what you have access to. After the device is in lightweight mode, you can manage it through the Cisco wireless LAN controllers (WLC). Understand, however, that Cisco provides customers with the flexibility of running either IOS or LWAPP, and an AP can be purchased in whatever form as needed.

Accessing the AP in Autonomous Mode

Key Topic

You can access an autonomous AP in four ways:

■ Console to it using a console cable and the console port.

■ Telnet into it if it has an IP address.

■ Browse to it with a web browser if it has an IP address.

■ SSH into it if configured (preferred over Telnet).

You might be wondering how to get an IP address for an autonomous AP. The answer is simple: use DHCP. You just plug in the autonomous AP, and it grabs an address on its own. Note, however, that the device does not have a service set identifier (SSID) configured by default, and the radio is disabled by default; this is true for any IOS release later than 12.3(4)JA. In fact, the autonomous AP has a yellow sticker right on the outside of the box that indicates this. When you consider why, you begin to realize that it is a good security mechanism. You do not have to worry about people associating with the AP while you are scrambling to set it up.

If you are wondering how you are going the find the AP when it has a dynamic address, you can try to get the IP from the DHCP server, which you might or might not have access to. You can also use Cisco Discovery Protocol (CDP) on the switch that the AP is connected to, and you can sometimes use the command **show arp | include** *mac-address* (assuming that the IP address is in the CAM table), or you can use a tool created by Cisco called the IP Setup Utility, seen in Figure 14-1. The IP Setup Utility takes the MAC address of the AP and resolves the IP address associated with it. You can get the MAC address from a sticker on the AP.

After you obtain the IP address, you can access the AP via a web browser. Figure 14-2 shows the initial page when you log in to the AP.

To quickly configure the settings of the AP, you can use the Express Setup and Express Security Pages.

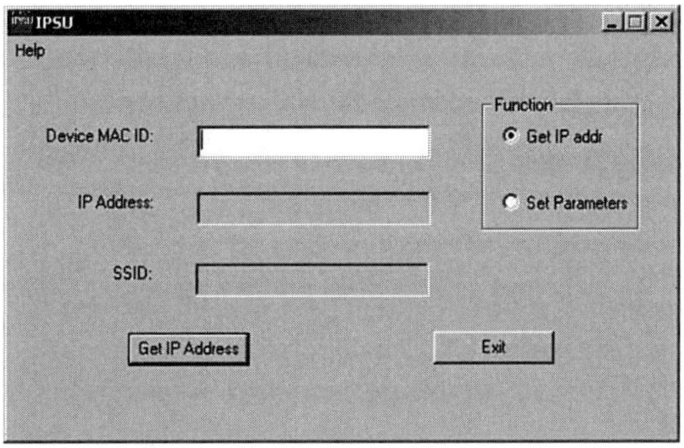

Figure 14-1 *IP Setup Utility*

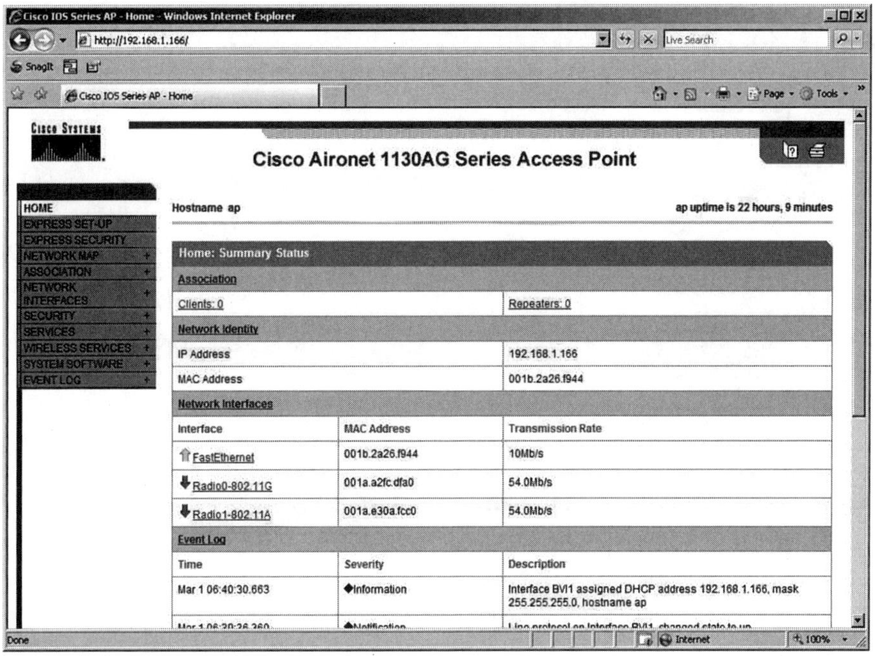

Figure 14-2 *Initial Login to the AP*

Using the Express Setup and Express Security for Basic Configuration

From the initial login screen, you quickly can gain valuable information about clients, repeaters, interfaces, and events.

To quickly set up the AP, use the EXPRESS SET-UP and EXPRESS SECURITY links in the left menu. You are prompted for the following:

■ Hostname of the device

- Method of IP address assignment

- IP address

- Subnet mask

- Default gateway

- SNMP community

- Radio properties, as seen in Figure 14-3

- 802.11G properties, including its role

- 802.11A properties, including its role

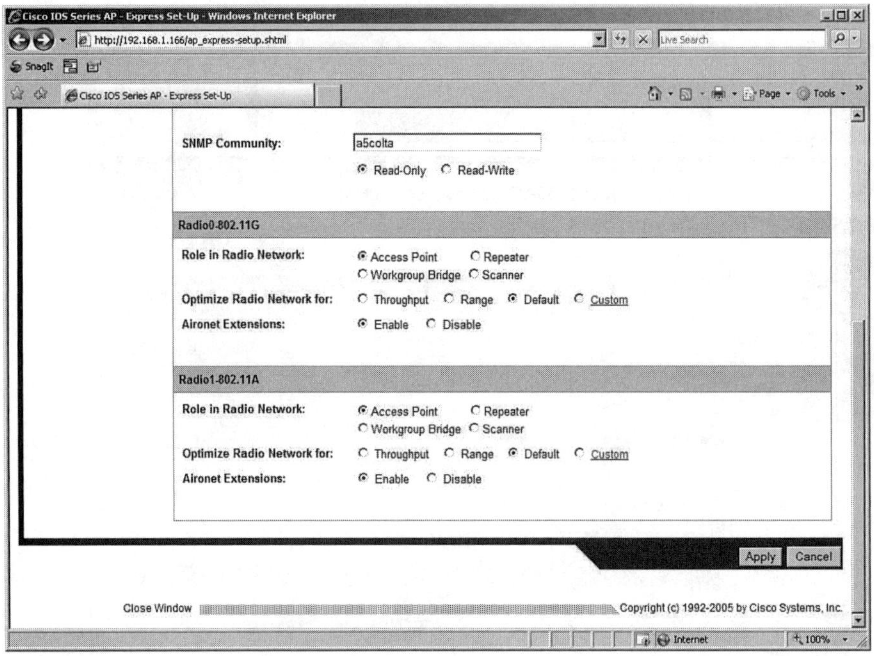

Figure 14-3   *Express Setup Radio Properties*

It is that easy. Simply click **Apply** for the settings in the Express Setup page to take effect.

As for the Express Security configuration, this is where you assign an SSID, determine whether it will be broadcast, apply VLANs, and define the security settings such as Wired Equivalent Privacy (WEP), Wi-Fi Protected Access (WPA), and WPA2. If you enable VLAN IDs, you can have more than one SSID and apply the security settings differently to each VLAN. Again, you need to apply the changes with the **Apply** button. Figure 14-4 shows a sample of the Express Security page.

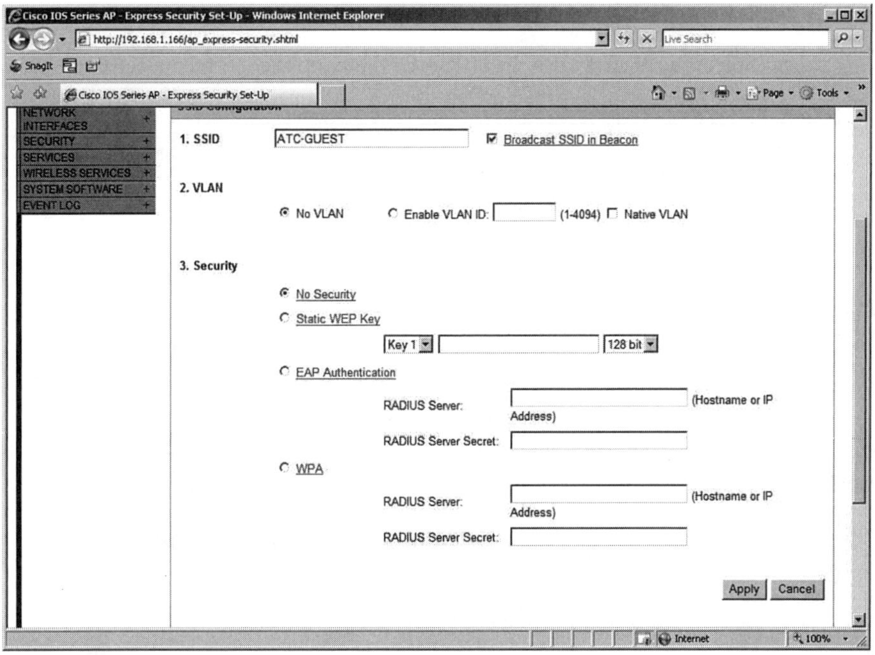

Figure 14-4   *Express Security Setup*

Following are some other important facts related to the configuration of SSIDS and security:

■   You cannot tie an SSID to a particular radio; the SSID configured applies to both radios.

■   You cannot set up more than one authentication server.

■   You cannot combine authentication types.

After applying the Express Setup and Express Security configuration, you can use the web interface for additional configuration.

Working with the Web Interface

At this point, assuming you have followed along through the section, "Using the Express Setup and Express Security for Basic Configuration," you do not necessarily have a functional AP. As mentioned previously, the radios are now disabled by default. You can see this from the home page:

Step 1.   Click **HOME** from the left menu.

Step 2.   View the status of the radios under the Network Interfaces section.

You can use two different methods to enable the radios:

■ Select the **NETWORK INTERFACES** link on the left menu, select the radio, and then select the Settings button and enable the radio with the **Enable** radio button.

■ Click on the radio link on the home page, as seen in Figure 14-5 (in this case, Radio0-802.11G or Radio1-802-802.11A).

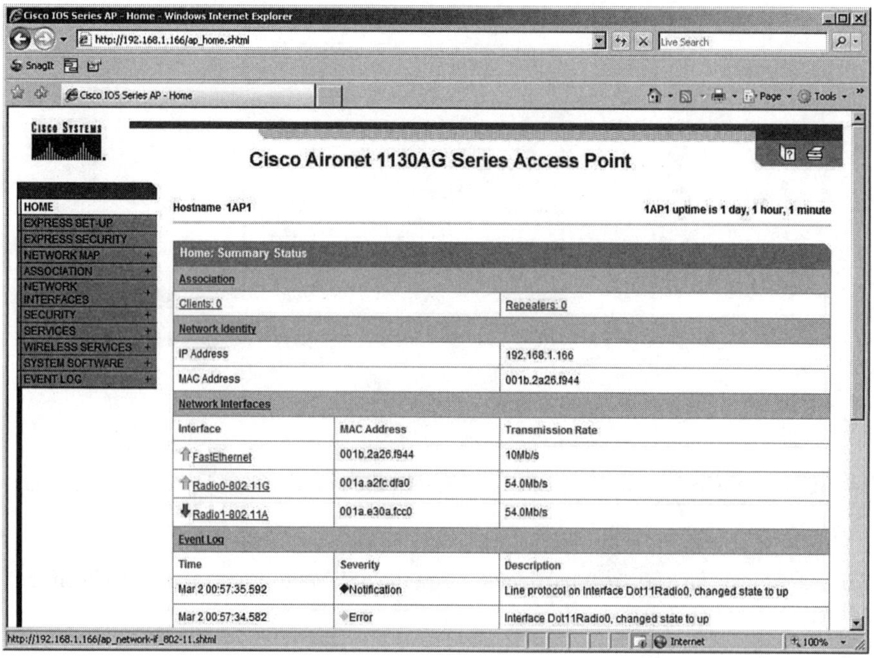

Figure 14-5   *Radio Configuration*

After you have accessed the Settings page, you can enable the radio following the same process as the first method described. When the radio is enabled, you have a working AP.

Note: You might want to spend some time getting familiar with the options in the web interface; however, for the CCNA wireless exam, it is not as significant of a topic as the lightweight configurations.

That being said, with a functional AP, you can allow users access to the network. Recall, however, that the goal is to use this AP with a controller. This means you need to convert this autonomous AP to a lightweight AP.

Converting to LWAPP

Three methods you can use to convert the AP to lightweight mode are as follows:

■ Use the IOS to LWAPP conversion utility. This is an installable application that you can download from Cisco.com.

■ Use the WCS. If you have a WCS, this method is probably preferred; however, it is not covered as part of the CCNA wireless certification.

■ As of July 2005, simply archive the image to the AP to convert it to LWAPP.

The section that follows examines the IOS-to-LWAPP conversion.

Converting to LWAPP Using the IOS-to-LWAPP Conversion Utility

Before you can use the IOS-to-LWAPP conversion utility, you need to obtain the software. To do so, you need to access the AP download page at Cisco.com. To do so, follow these steps:

Step 1. Go to www.cisco.com/go/wireless.

Step 2. Click the AP you are working with. The list of APs is at the bottom of the page.

Step 3. On the AP page, from the right side of the page in a box labeled **Support**, click the **Download Software** link.

Step 4. Using the menu tree, find the AP you are looking for, and expand the folder.

Step 5. Select the link to the AP inside that folder.

Step 6. Enter your Cisco username and password.

When you have authenticated to Cisco, you will see a page similar to the one in Figure 14-6. Notice that this page offers four links:

■ Autonomous to Lightweight Mode Upgrade Image

■ Autonomous to Lightweight Mode Upgrade Tool

■ IOS Software

■ IP Setup Utility (IPSU)

The first link is to the Autonomous to Lightweight Mode Upgrade Image. You need this image to perform the upgrade. It is not the same image that runs on the controller. Recall that the controller and AP need to be on the same version; however, any mismatch is corrected when an AP finds a controller. If the code versions are different, the controller either upgrades or downgrades the AP. This Autonomous to Lightweight Mode Upgrade image simply gets LWAPP functionality on the AP. From there, the controller can handle the rest.

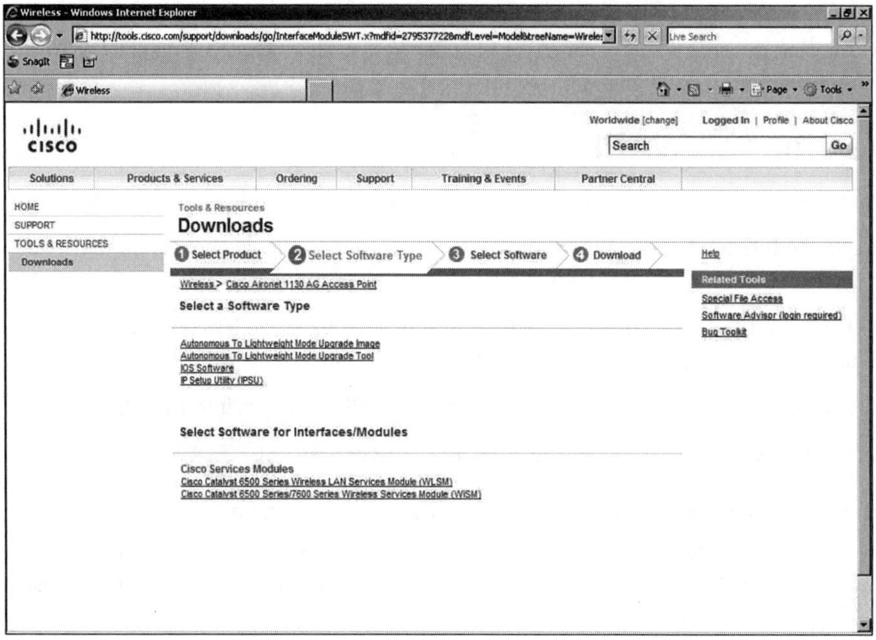

Figure 14-6 *Download Area of Cisco.com*

The second link on the Downloads page is to the Autonomous to Lightweight Mode Upgrade Tool. This is the software application you need to perform the upgrade. This software installs on a Windows computer.

The third link on the Downloads page is to IOS Software, and the fourth link is for the IP Setup Utility. Select the link to download the software you need. Because you want the IP Setup Utility for this task, click that link.

After you have the Autonomous to Lightweight Mode Upgrade Tool software and the Autonomous to Lightweight Mode Upgrade image, you are ready to install it on a Windows PC. After it is installed, you can perform the upgrade.

Before performing the upgrade, however, you must meet the following requirements:

■ IOS on the AP must be version 12.3(7)JA or above. If it is not, upgrade it first by selecting the IOS Software link on the Downloads page.

■ The WLC must be running version 3.1 or later. Keep in mind that after you do the upgrade from autonomous to lightweight, the AP cannot function without the controller, and the console port is no longer useful. Also, the upgrade supports only Layer 3 LWAPP mode.

To begin the upgrade, first check to see if you are running a code version on the AP that is capable of being upgraded. In Figure 14-7, the code version is 12.3(7)JA4. This indicates that the version is compatible.

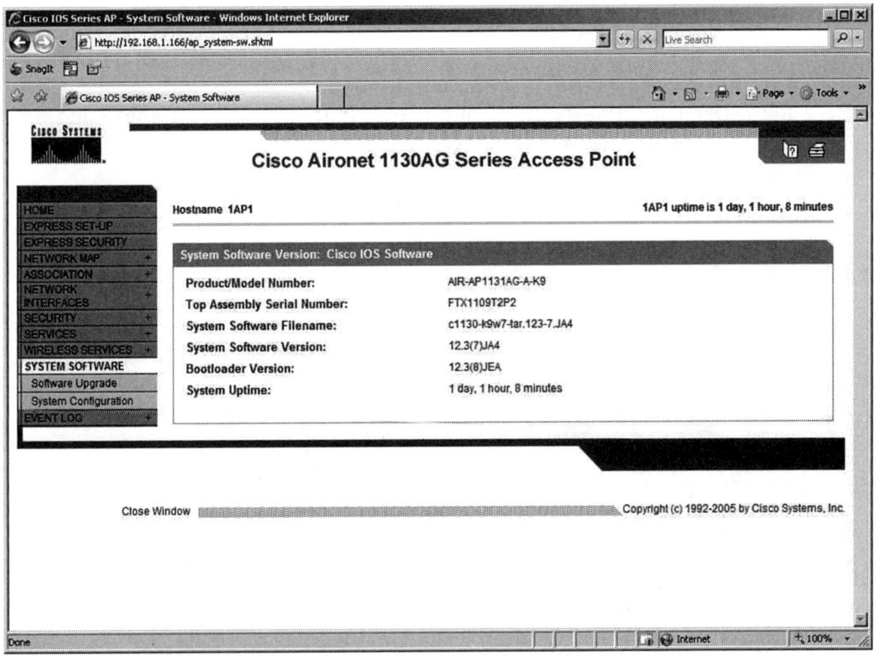

Figure 14-7   *Verify the IOS Version*

Note: You can order new LWAPP-capable APs with the lightweight code already installed if desired.

After you have verified the IOS version, you need to make sure that the controller and the AP are on the same subnet or that the controller is reachable after the upgrade. You can do this via DHCP option 43 or DNS.

The next step is to prepare a text file of APs that you want to upgrade. I recommend using Notepad so that you can save it as a .txt file. In the text file, the format should resemble the following:

ap-ip-address, telnet-username, telnet-Password, enable-password

Create a new line for each AP that you want to convert. When you are finished with the text file, save it somewhere that you can find it, and name it something like **APList.txt**. You are going to browse to this file in the Upgrade tool interface.

As a final preparation step, you need to make sure that the upgrade code is on the local machine. The steps described in the preceding paragraphs detailed where you can obtain this, so make sure you have it.

You will be using the TFTP protocol to upgrade the AP, so you can use Tftpd32, which you can download for free from http://tftpd32.jounin.net, or you can use the TFTP service that is integrated in the Upgrade tool.

Key Topic

The overall upgrade process is as follows:

Step 1. Open the Upgrade tool.

Step 2. In the IP File field, select the ... button (this button is called an ellipsis and looks like three dots), select the **APList.txt** file, and click **Open**, as demonstrated in Figure 14-8.

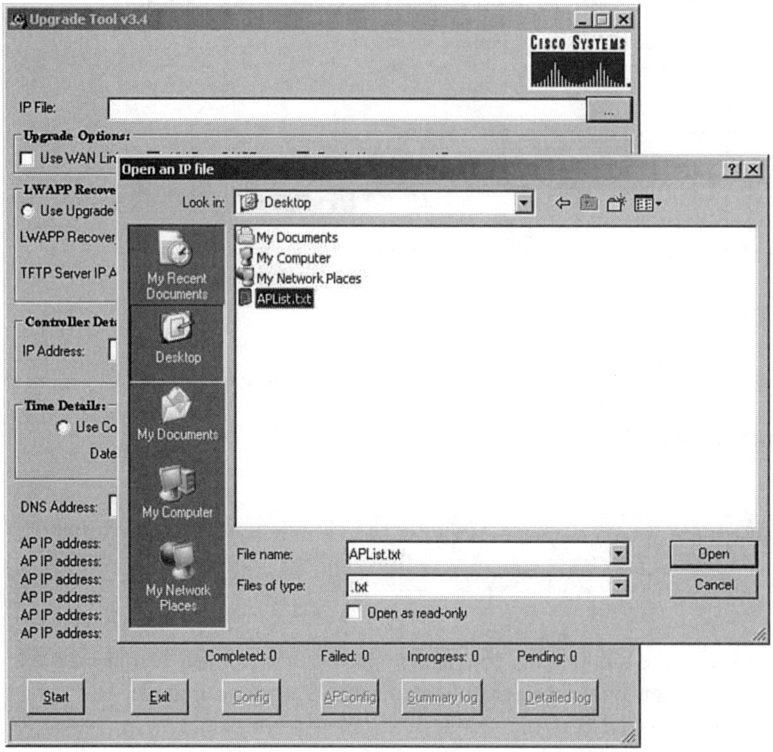

Figure 14-8 *Selecting the APList.txt File*

Step 3. In the Upgrade Options field, choose any options that apply. These pertain to how to handle the upgrade. Are the APs being upgraded over a WAN link? Should the AP be converted to DHCP after the upgrade? Should they keep their existing hostname after the upgrade? Select the check box to indicate your choice based on your preferences and network situation. In Figure 14-9, the APs are going to retain their hostnames.

Step 4. In the LWAPP Recovery Image section shown in Figure 14-9, select the method of TFTP you want to use, whether it is internal to the Upgrade tool or using an external application such as Tftpd32. Then select the LWAPP Recovery image. Choose how many APs can upgrade at once in the Max. AP at run field.

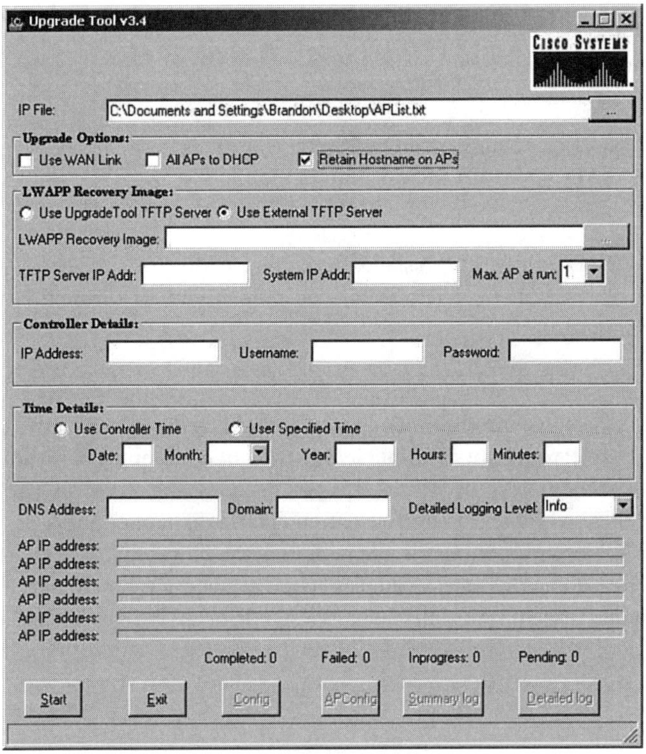

Figure 14-9 *Upgrade Options*

Step 5.   In the Controller Details section, define the controllers management IP address, username, and password.

Step 6.   In the Time Details section, select the User Controller Time radio button.

Step 7.   If resolving by DNS, enter the DNS address and domain name. Optionally, change the logging level if you want to see more verbose information.

Step 8.   Click the **Start** button to begin the process.

The upgrade process verifies each parameter you have entered and errors out if inconsistencies are noted. After the conversion, the AP reboots. After the reboot, the AP behaves like any lightweight AP and tries to find a controller.

Note: During the upgrade process to the lightweight code, a self-signed certificate is generated for each AP and sent to the WLC if the AP is an older AP without a Cisco signed certificate. It is important that all the controllers that the AP may associate with have this certificate. In this case, if the CUWN has a WCS server, you would import the self-signed certificate to WCS from the controller the AP is currently associated with. You would do this by refreshing the controller config to WCS from the controller the AP is associated to and then push it to all other controllers.

This is an important note for those who are upgrading from older APs that support the upgrade path from autonomous APs to the lightweight code for the CUWN, but it is not so important for those looking to take the CCNA Wireless Exam.

You can read more about it in the article "Self-Signed Certificate Manual Addition to the Controller for LWAPP-Converted APs" at http://tinyurl.com/4l3p3c.

If you want to convert an AP from lightweight to standalone, you can do so via the command-line interface (CLI) or by resetting the AP to factory defaults. If you do it from the CLI, you use the following command:

```
config ap tftp-downgrade tftp-server-ip-address filename apname
```

If you are resetting to factory defaults, use the **mode** button by holding it down until the LED turns red. This causes the AP to reboot, ignoring its lightweight code, apply an IP address of 10.0.0.1, and broadcast for an IOS file. This means you need a TFTP server on that subnet and a default file on there with the naming convention **cplatform_name-k9w7-tar.default**. This is what the AP looks for. If the file can be found, the downgrade will take place. You probably will not be doing this unless you plan to move a lightweight AP out of the lightweight deployment and place it somewhere else as a standalone AP.

Exam Preparation Tasks

Review All the Key Concepts

Review the most important topics from this chapter, noted with the Key Topics icon in the outer margin of the page. Table 14-2 lists a reference of these key topics and the page number where you can find each one.

Table 14-2 *Key Topics for Chapter 14*

Key Topic Item	Description	Page Number
Paragraph/list in the section "Accessing the AP in Autonomous Mode"	List of methods used to access the AP	264
Paragraph/list in the section "Using the Express Setup and Express Security for Basic Configuration"	List of requirements for Express Setup	265
Paragraph/list in the section "Converting to LWAPP	List of requirements to meet before upgrading to lightweight mode	269
List in the section "Converting to LWAPP	Steps to perform the upgrade using the Upgrade tool	272

Definition of Key Terms

Define the following key terms from this chapter, and check your answers in the Glossary:

Upgrade tool, IP Setup Utility

This chapter covers the following subjects:

Overview of the Small Business Communication System: An introduction to the Small Business Communication System, its components, and how mobility fits in.

Configuring the 521 AP and 526 Controller: A look at three methods used to configure the Cisco Mobility Express solution.

CHAPTER 15

Cisco Mobility Express

Cisco Mobility Express was designed to offer wireless services to small businesses in a form factor similar to the lightweight architecture. It is not the full Lightweight Access Point Protocol (LWAPP) but rather a subset of LWAPP functionality. This means that although the 521 AP runs the subset of LWAPP, it cannot communicate with enterprise controllers. The Cisco Mobility Express solution delivers best-in-class wireless capabilities that until recently had been reserved for enterprises. The solution is sold at a premium accessible to small to medium-sized business (SMB) customers who are seeking to gain a competitive edge without having to compromise between price and sophistication. SMBs now have an alternative to consumer-grade products and can benefit from the latest enterprise-class services available over Wi-Fi. Also of noteworthiness is that Linksys offers an upgrade program for businesses that want to get enterprise-class devices into the network. This is a key type of business to see this in.

You should do the "Do I Know This Already?" quiz" first. If you score 80 percent or higher, you might want to skip to the section "Exam Preparation Tasks." If you score below 80 percent, you should spend the time reviewing the entire chapter. Refer to Appendix A, "Answers to the 'Do I Know This Already?' Quizzes," to confirm your answers.

"Do I Know This Already?" Quiz

The "Do I Know This Already?" quiz helps you determine your level of knowledge of this chapter's topics before you begin. Table 15-1 details the major topics discussed in this chapter and their corresponding quiz questions.

Table 15-1 *"Do I Know This Already?" Section-to-Question Mapping*

Foundation Topics Section	Questions
Overview of the Small Business Communication System	1–5
Configuring the 521 AP and 526 Controller	6–10

1. The Cisco Mobility Express solution is part of what system?

   a. ACCID

   b. SBCS

   c. SAFE

   d. IOS

2. Which of the following devices is *not* part of the Cisco Smart Business Communication System?

   a. Cisco Unified Communications 500 Series for Small Businesses

   b. Cisco Unified IP Phones

   c. The Cisco 4402 Wireless LAN controller

   d. The Cisco 521 Wireless Express Access Point

3. What protocol manages the Cisco 521 AP when operating in lightweight mode?

   a. LWAPP

   b. CDP

   c. IP Discovery

   d. A subset of LWAPP

4. The Cisco 521 AP supports which of the following protocols? (Choose all that apply.)

   a. 802.11a

   b. 802.11b

   c. 802.11g

   d. WPA2

5. The Cisco 526 Express Controller supports RRM. True or False?

   a. True

   b. False

6. The Cisco Mobility Express solution can be managed by which of the following?
   (Choose all that apply.)

   a. Cisco Security Manager

   b. Command-line interface

   c. Web interface

   d. CCA

7. From the CLI, which is not a valid boot option?

   a. Run the primary image (Version 4.2.61.8) (active).

   b. Run the backup image (Version 4.1.154.22).

   c. Manually upgrade the primary image.

   d. Manually downgrade the primary image.

e. Change the active boot image.

f. Clear the configuration.

8. The Cisco 526 Express Controller supports NTP. True or False?

a. True

b. False

9. Which of the following is the correct way to access the web interface of a Cisco 526 Express Controller if you have never performed CLI setup?

a. http://10.1.1.1

b. https://10.1.1.1

c. http://192.168.1.1

d. https://192.168.1.1

10. What is the PC application that manages the Cisco Mobility Express solution?

a. CCA

b. CSA

c. ACS

d. AAA

Foundation Topics

Overview of the Small Business Communication System

The Cisco Mobility Express solution, seen in Figure 15-1, is either a standalone or a controller-based access point (AP) and a controller-based solution.

Application-based
Access points,
controllers, and
application servers

Controller-based
Access points and controllers

Standalone
Access points

Adapt to your level of sophistication

Grow with your business

Offer a mobile foundation for all

Figure 15-1   *Cisco Mobility Express Solution*

You manage the solution through a configuration assistant software application. The Cisco Mobility Express solution is only a portion, however, of the Cisco Smart Business Communication System (SBCS). This SBCS includes the following:

Key Topic

- Cisco Unified Communications 500 Series for Small Businesses

  This device can support up to 48 users and acts as a DHCP server. This DHCP functionality is important because it is a requirement of the AP, and the controller does not act as a DHCP server. Only the Cisco UC 500 series and the Cisco 870W router support DHCP.

- Cisco Unified IP Phones

- Cisco Monitor Director

- The Cisco Mobility Solution, including the following:

  The Cisco 526 Wireless Express Controller

  The Cisco 521 Wireless Express Access Point

The design of this solution is perfect for small businesses that want a controller-based AP deployment but do not plan to grow to more than 12 APs, because the architecture allows one controller to support six APs, with two controllers able to communicate with each other. The devices are managed by a central application called the Cisco Configuration Assistant (CCA), which is a Windows application that you can download from

Cisco.com and install locally. Along with the Cisco Configuration Assistant and the Radio Resource Management (RRM) capabilities of the Cisco Mobility Solution, this network is self-configuring, self-optimizing, and self-healing in the event of interference.

521 AP

The Cisco 521 AP has a form factor that is similar to the 1130 series AP. The Cisco 521 AP, seen in Figure 15-2, has internal 802.11 b/g antennas.

Figure 15-2   *The Cisco 521 AP*

When managed by the Cisco 526 controller, the Cisco 521 AP uses a protocol subset of LWAPP. The Cisco 521 AP cannot communicate with the CUWN controllers because a hardware check during the AP bootup process does not allow it to join any other controller besides the 526.

Features of the Cisco 521 AP include the following:

- 802.11g radio

- Industry-leading radio design

- Variable transmit power settings

- Integrated antennas

- Hardware-assisted Advanced Encryption Standard (AES) encryption

- IEEE 802.11i-compliant; WPA2 and WPA certified

- Low-profile design

- Multipurpose and lockable mounting bracket

- Power over Ethernet (IEEE 802.3af and Cisco Inline Power)

- Field-upgradeable from standalone to controller mode

- Inclusion of Cisco Configuration Assistant management software

526 Wireless Express Controller

The Cisco 526 Wireless Express Mobility controller harnesses the power of Cisco LWAPP technology, best-in-class automatic radio optimization, mobility performance, and multiaccess point management. On top of the basic transport layer, the controller supports Cisco Secure Guest Access and Voice-over-WLAN advanced mobility services. As part of the Smart Business Communications System, this controller is managed by the Cisco Configuration Assistant, easing deployment and decreasing the cost of ongoing maintenance. A single Cisco 526 controller supports up to six Cisco 521 access points, and up to two controllers can be deployed per network, delivering the capacity, simplicity, and price point that is appropriate for the SMB.[1]

The Cisco 526 Wireless Express controller supports the following features:

■ Secure network access for guest users

■ Support for Cisco voice-over-WLAN optimization

■ Easy management with CCA

■ Support for Cisco LWAPP

■ Support for up to six access points per controller and up to 2 controllers per network, for a total of 12 access points

■ Multiaccess point RRM

■ Support for a wide range of authentication mechanisms to enable scalable security architectures and minimize security interoperability issues (WEP, MAC filtering, WPA, WPA2, WebAuth, 802.1X, and EAP)

■ Wired/wireless network virtualization

Comparing the Cisco Mobility Express Architecture to the CUWN

When you compare the Cisco Mobility Express Architecture to the Cisco Unified Wireless Network, you will find that the model is similar; however, the protocols are different. The Mobility Express solution does not use the full enterprise class version of LWAPP; rather, it uses a subset of LWAPP. In addition, the Cisco 521 AP cannot communicate with CUWN wireless LAN controllers. Likewise, the Cisco 526 cannot communicate with APs from the 1100 series or higher. The 526 supports control of up to 12 APs in a small network.

Configuring the 521 AP and 526 Controller

In general, you can configure the Mobility Express solution in three ways, none of which are performed on the AP. You do not even need to directly access the AP. Instead, on the controller itself, use either the CLI, which is normally used for basic setup and initialization, or the web interface. After a basic setup on the controller, you can use the Configuration Assistant management tool. Each of these methods is discussed in the following sections.

Using the CLI to Configure the Controller

To configure the Cisco Mobility Express solution, you need a console connection to the Cisco 526. You do not need to do anything on the AP because the controller takes care of it. After you have a console connection, you can power on the device and view the boot process. In Example 15-1, notice that if you press the **Esc** key, you are presented with multiple boot options. The normal selection is to run the primary image.

Example 15-1   *Booting the Cisco 526 Controller*

```
Booting Primary Image...
Press <ESC> now for additional boot options...


Boot Options


Please choose an option from below:


1. Run primary image (Version 4.2.61.8) (active)
2. Run backup image (Version 4.1.154.22)
3. Manually upgrade primary image
4. Change active boot image
5. Clear Configuration


Please enter your choice:
```

Continuing with the boot process, Example 15-2 shows the tests that are performed as the device initializes.

Example 15-2   *Tests During the Boot Process*

```
CISCO SYSTEMS
Embedded BIOS Version 1.0(12)6 08/21/06 17:26:53.43


Low Memory: 632 KB
High Memory: 251 MB
PCI Device Table.
Bus Dev Func VendID DevID Class Irq
00 01 00 1022 2080 Host Bridge
00 01 02 1022 2082 Chipset En/Decrypt 11
00 0C 00 1148 4320 Ethernet 11
00 0D 00 177D 0003 Network En/Decrypt 10
00 0F 00 1022 2090 ISA Bridge
00 0F 02 1022 2092 IDE Controller
00 0F 03 1022 2093 Audio 10
00 0F 04 1022 2094 Serial Bus 9
00 0F 05 1022 2095 Serial Bus 9


Evaluating BIOS Options ...
Launch BIOS Extension to setup ROMMON


Cisco Systems ROMMON Version (1.0(12)7) #2: Fri Oct 13 10:52:36 MDT 2006
```

continues

```
Platform AIR-WLC526-K9


Launching BootLoader...

Cisco Bootloader (Version 4.0.191.0)



.o88b. d888888b .d8888. .o88b. .d88b.
d8P Y8 `88' 88' YP d8P Y8 .8P Y8.
8P 88 `8bo. 8P 88 88
8b 88 `Y8b. 8b 88 88
Y8b d8 .88. db 8D Y8b d8 `8b d8'
`Y88P' Y888888P `8888Y' `Y88P' `Y88P'


Booting Primary Image...
Press <ESC> now for additional boot options...
Detecting hardware . . . .

Generating Secure Shell DSA Host Key ...
Generating Secure Shell RSA Host Key ...
Generating Secure Shell version 1.5 RSA Host Key ...
XML config selected
Cisco is a trademark of Cisco Systems, Inc.
Software Copyright Cisco Systems, Inc. All rights reserved.

Cisco AireOS Version 4.2.61.8
Initializing OS Services: ok
Initializing Serial Services: ok
Initializing Network Services: ok
Starting ARP Services: ok
Starting Trap Manager: ok
Starting Network Interface Management Services: ok
Starting System Services: ok
Starting FIPS Features: Not enabled
Starting Fast Path Hardware Acceleration: ok
Starting Switching Services: ok
Starting QoS Services: ok
Starting Policy Manager: ok
Starting Data Transport Link Layer: ok
Starting Access Control List Services: ok
Starting System Interfaces: ok
Starting Client Troubleshooting Service: ok
```

```
Starting Management Frame Protection: ok
Starting LWAPP: ok
Starting Certificate Database: ok
Starting VPN Services: ok
Starting Security Services: ok
Starting Policy Manager: ok
Starting Authentication Engine: ok
Starting Mobility Management: ok
Starting Virtual AP Services: ok
Starting AireWave Director: ok
Starting Network Time Services: ok
Starting Cisco Discovery Protocol: ok
Starting Broadcast Services: ok
Starting Power Over Ethernet Services: ok
Starting Logging Services: ok
Starting DHCP Server: ok
Starting IDS Signature Manager: ok
Starting RFID Tag Tracking: ok
Starting Mesh Services: ok
Starting TSM: ok
Starting LOCP: ok


Starting CIDS Services: ok
Starting Ethernet-over-IP: ok
Starting Management Services:
Web Server: ok
CLI: ok
Secure Web: Web Authentication Certificate not found (error).
dhcp pool 192.168.1.100(0xc0a80164) — 192.168.1.102(0xc0a80166), network
192.168.1.0(0xc0a80100) netmask 255.255.255.0(0xffffff00), default gateway 0xc0
internal dhcp server is config successfully

(Cisco Controller)
```

Upon completing the boot sequence, a controller with no configuration prompts you to perform the setup using the Cisco Wizard Configuration tool, as demonstrated in Example 15-3. Be prepared to provide the following information:

■ Hostname of the device

■ Username of the administrator

■ Password for the administrator

■ Management interface information

■ AP-Manager interface information

■ Virtual gateway IP address

Example 15-3   *Cisco Wizard Configuration*

```
Welcome to the Cisco Wizard Configuration Tool
Use the '-' character to backup
System Name [Cisco_be:7a:e0]: 526-3
Enter Administrative User Name (24 characters max): admin3
Enter Administrative Password (24 characters max): *****
Re-enter Administrative Password : *****

Management Interface IP Address: 10.30.1.100
Management Interface Netmask: 255.255.255.0
Management Interface Default Router: 10.30.1.254
Management Interface VLAN Identifier (0 = untagged): 0
Management Interface Port Num [1 to 2]: 1
Management Interface DHCP Server IP Address: 10.30.1.253

AP Manager Interface IP Address: 10.30.1.101

AP-Manager is on Management subnet, using same values
AP Manager Interface DHCP Server (10.30.1.253):

Virtual Gateway IP Address: 1.1.1.1

Mobility/RF Group Name: CP-POD3

Enable Symmetric Mobility Tunneling [yes][NO]: NO

Network Name (SSID): IUWNE-301
Allow Static IP Addresses [YES][no]: YES

Configure a RADIUS Server now? [YES][no]: no
Warning! The default WLAN security policy requires a RADIUS server.
Please see documentation for more details.

Enter Country Code list (enter 'help' for a list of countries) [US]: US

Enable 802.11b Network [YES][no]: yes
Enable 802.11g Network [YES][no]: yes
Enable Auto-RF [YES][no]: yes

Configure a NTP server now? [YES][no]: no
Configure the system time now? [YES][no]: no

Warning! No AP will come up unless the time is set.
Please see documentation for more details.

Configuration correct? If yes, system will save it and reset. [yes][NO]: yes
```

After you have completed the configuration from the CLI, you can browse to the IP address of the management interface.

Using the Web Browser to Configure the Controller

To access the controller via a web browser, enter the IP address of the management interface of the controller preceded by **https://**. This is either the IP address you configured in the CLI Wizard or the default address of 192.168.1.1. In Figure 15-3, you can see the login page for the controller that will appear.

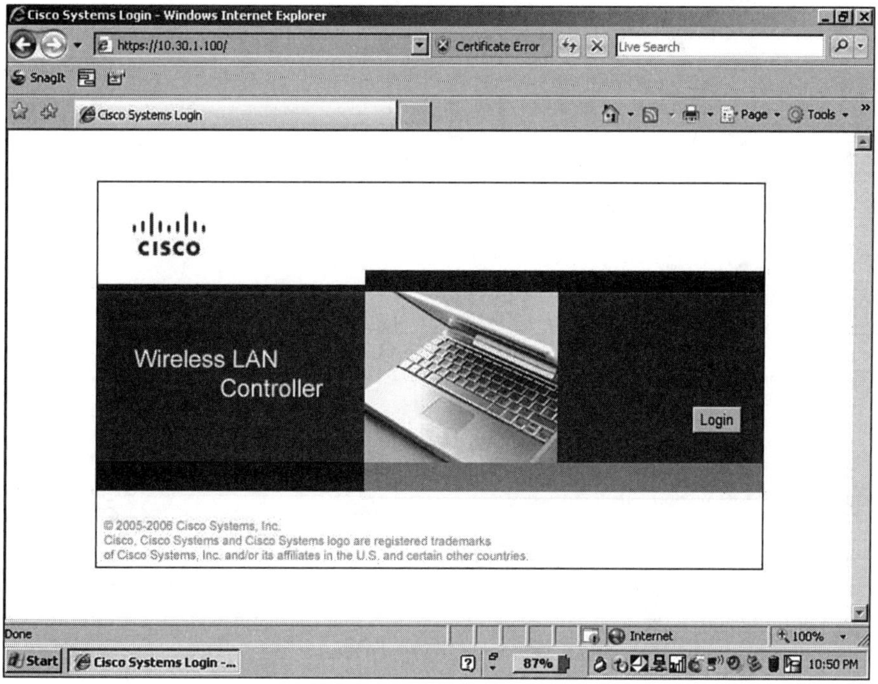

Figure 15-3   *Login Screen to the 526 Controllers*

Notice that the connection is secure via HTTPS. Click the **Login** button and enter a username and password before performing any configuration. After you are logged in, you are presented with a Summary page, as seen in Figure 15-4.

The Summary page gives you a look at the controller status, the AP status, and the top WLANs. Changes are logged as you make them, and you can see them on the Summary page.

Figure 15-4   *Summary Page*

Note: The Wireless Express controller web interface is quite similar to the WLC web interface used in the CUWN architecture.

When it comes to the controllers, you do not need to do much work. The AP and controllers will find each other. You can see in Figure 15-5 that the All APs option from the WIRELESS menu is showing an AP that has been discovered.

When you select the AP name, you are taken to a page that allows you to enter details specific to that AP, such as its name and its primary controller, as shown in Figure 15-6. You can also enable or disable the AP from this menu. Other options include resetting the AP and clearing the AP configuration.

Using the Cisco Configuration Assistant

With the configuration as is, you can access the Configuration Assistant. The Cisco Configuration Assistant (CCA) is a management tool that installs on a Windows computer and is based on an application called Cisco Network Assistant, which has been modified to support the Cisco Mobility solution. After you have installed the CCA, you can access it via a desktop shortcut. When the application launches, you need to connect to or create a community. When you log in for the first time, you create a community. A *community* is a group name for your Mobility Express network. Figure 15-7 shows the configuration page that you see when creating a community.

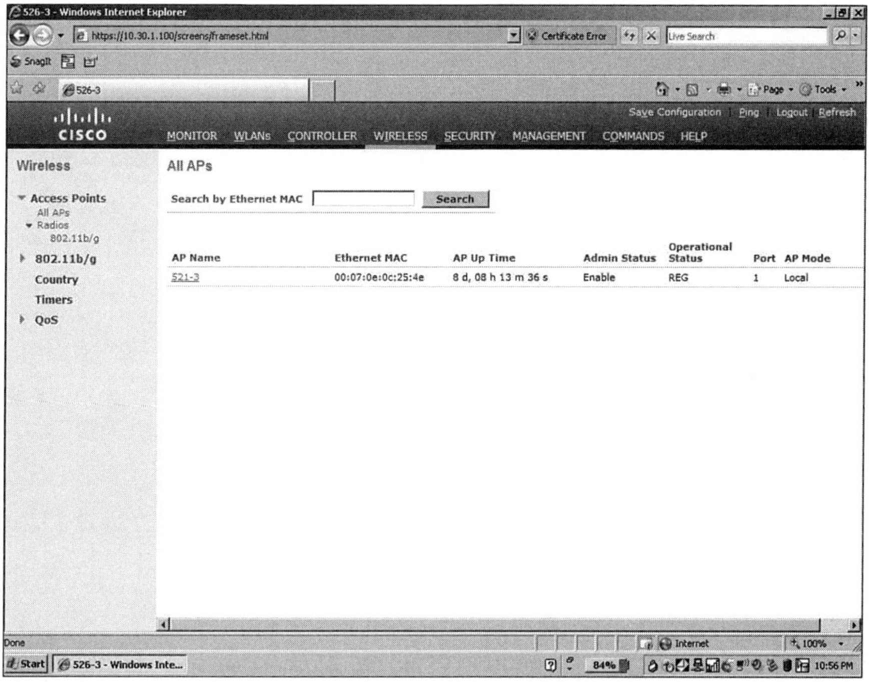

Figure 15-5 *The All APs List*

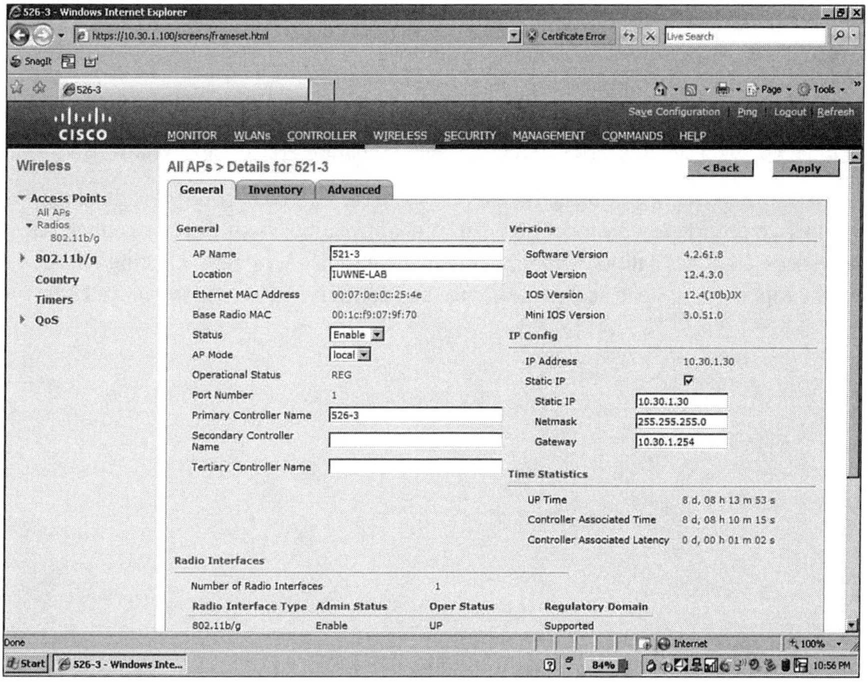

Figure 15-6 *Details Page for AP Configuration*

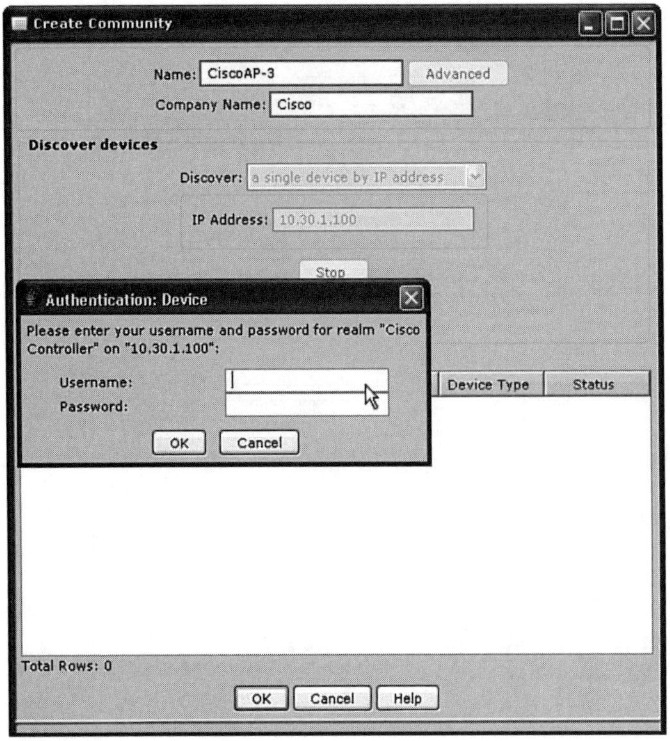

Figure 15-7   *Creating a Community*

CCA will discover the standalone APs. The APs will appear in the CCA interface. If you are running CCA 1.5 or later, you can migrate the standalone APs to lightweight APs.

CCA will also discover WLCs using IP discovery and the Cisco Discovery Protocol (CDP). CDP is a Cisco proprietary protocol that can gain information about directly connected Cisco devices. CCA has a topology view shown in Figure 15-8; by right-clicking on a device in the topology, you can access the device and configure it, as seen in Figure 15-9.

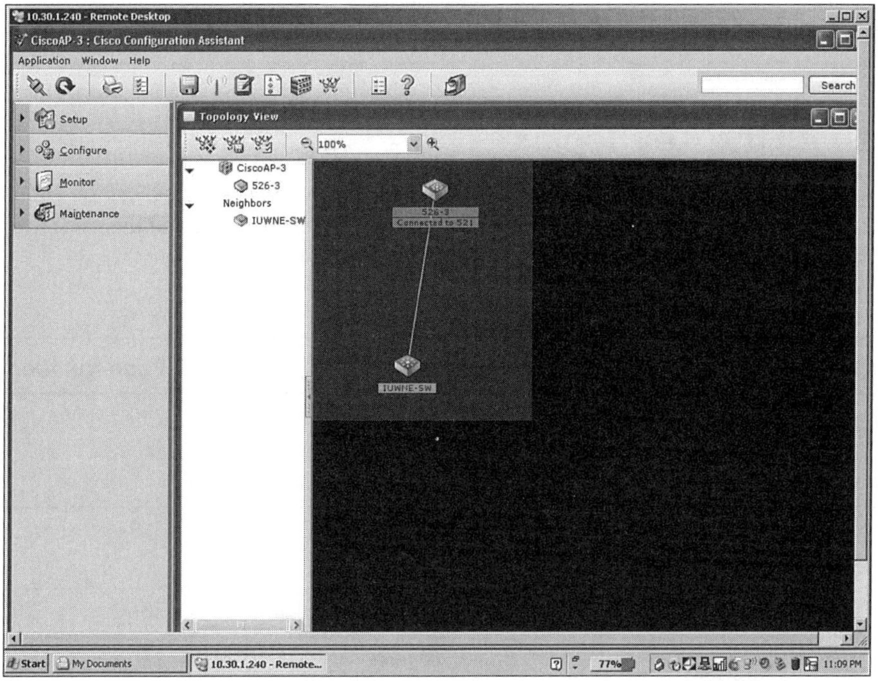

Figure 15-8 *CCA Topology View*

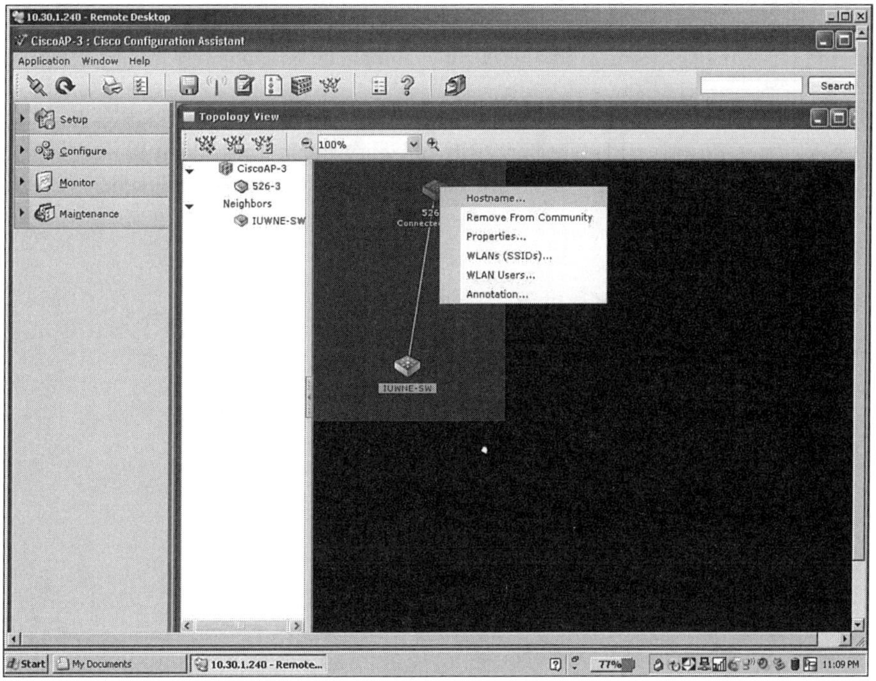

Figure 15-9 *Configuration Menu in Topology View*

Exam Preparation Tasks

Review All the Key Topics

Review the most important topics from this chapter, noted with the Key Topics icon in the outer margin of the page. Table 15-2 lists a reference of these key topics and the page number where you can find each one.

Table 15-2   *Key Topics for Chapter 15*

Key Topic Item	Description	Page Number
Paragraph from the section, "Overview of the Small Business Communication System"	Bullet points detailing the components of the solution	280
Example 15-1	Booting the Cisco 526 controller	283
Example 15-3	Cisco Wizard configuration	286
Figure 15-4	Summary page	288

Definition of Key Terms

Define the following key terms from this chapter, and check your answers in the Glossary:

SMB, Cisco Smart Business Communication System (SBCS), Cisco Configuration Assistant (CCA), Radio Resource Management (RRM), Lightweight Access Point Protocol (LWAPP), Cisco Wizard Configuration tool, community, Cisco Discovery Protocol (CDP)

References

[1]Cisco 526 Wireless Express Mobility Controller: http://tinyurl.com/2rbfxg

Cisco 521 Wireless Express Access Point: http://tinyurl.com/6bxhze

This chapter covers the following subjects:

Using Windows to Connect to a Wireless LAN: Looks at using the Windows Wireless Zero Configuration Utility to connect to a wireless LAN.

Using a Mac to Connect to a Wireless LAN: Shows how to use Mac OSX to connect to a wireless LAN.

Using Linux to Connect to a Wireless LAN: Covers how to use Linux NetworkManager to connect to a wireless LAN.

Using the ADU to Connect to a Wireless LAN: Describes how to install a Cisco wireless card and use the ADU to manage enterprise class profiles.

The ACAU: Covers using the Aironet Client Administration Utility to deploy profiles to the enterprise.

The Cisco Secure Services Client: Shows how to use the Cisco Secure Services Client to manage customer and guest access to Cisco networks.

The Cisco Client Extension Program: Looks at free licensing to Cisco extensions for third-party vendors.

CHAPTER 16

Wireless Clients

Networks today have many different types of clients. Users with PCs and laptops running Linux or the Mac OS are becoming more common. In a mobile environment, these devices must support connectivity to wireless networks. This chapter introduces the network configuration tools found in Windows, Linux, and Mac devices. In addition to these packaged clients, Cisco provides the Aironet Desktop Utility (ADU), discussed in this chapter, along with some of its available utilities.

You should do the "Do I Know This Already?" quiz first. If you score 80 percent or higher, you might want to skip to the section "Exam Preparation Tasks." If you score below 80 percent, you should review the entire chapter. Refer to Appendix A, "Answers to the 'Do I Know This Already?' Quizzes," to confirm your answers.

"Do I Know This Already?" Quiz

The "Do I Know This Already?" quiz helps you determine your level of knowledge of this chapter's topics before you begin. Table 16-1 details the major topics discussed in this chapter and their corresponding quiz questions.

Table 16-1 *"Do I Know This Already?" Section-to-Question Mapping*

Foundation Topics Section	Questions
Using Windows to Connect to a Wireless LAN	1–4
Using a Mac to Connect to a Wireless LAN	5
Using Linux to Connect to a Wireless LAN	6
Using the ADU to Connect to a Wireless LAN	7–9
The ACAU	10
The Cisco Secure Services Client	11
The Cisco Client Extension Program	12

1. What is the name of the Windows utility for configuring wireless profiles?

   a. Zero Day Configuration

   b. Wireless Zero NetworkManager

   c. AirPort Zero Configuration

   d. Wireless Zero Configuration Utility

2. The Windows Wireless Zero Configuration Utility can set up which of the following enterprise class profiles? (Choose all that apply.)

   a. 802.1x

   b. WPA/WPA2/CCKM

   c. WEP static keys

   d. None of these

3. True or false: When the WZC is in use, the ADU can also be used.

   a. True

   b. False

4. True or false: The WZC will choose the most secure network available when starting up.

   a. True

   b. False

5. What configuration tool is used to set up wireless profiles on Mac OSX?

   a. WZC

   b. AirPort

   c. AirWave

   d. Aironet

6. What graphical configuration tool is used in Linux to set up wireless networks?

   a. iwconfig

   b. NetworkManager

   c. WZC

   d. Ubuntu ADU

7. Cisco offers which types of wireless cards? (Choose all that apply.)

   a. Cardbus

   b. PCI

   c. USB

   d. Flash

   e. PCMCIA

8. What does the term CAM refer to in the ADU advanced parameters?

   a. Constant Awake Mode

   b. Content Addressable Memory

   c. Confidential Aironet Module

   d. Constant Airwave Mode

9. When you perform a site survey with the CSSU, what indicates a good SNR?

   a. A higher number in dBm

   b. A lower number in dBm

   c. The CSSU can't determine the SNR.

   d. An equal receive strength

10. What software lets you create profiles for deployment with the ADU?

   a. ACCU

   b. ASSCU

   c. ACAU

   d. SSC

11. What software is designed for both wired and wireless profile management and access to Cisco enterprise networks?

   a. SSC

   b. SSM

   c. ASA

   d. ADU

12. What program is designed for vendors to create compatible hardware?

   a. CCX

   b. Compatibility Program

   c. CCA

   d. Cisco Client Portability Program

Foundation Topics

Using Windows to Connect to a Wireless LAN

The wireless configuration tool for Microsoft Windows is called the Windows Wireless Zero Configuration Utility (WZC). The WZC is designed to provide the basic capabilities necessary to access most WLANs; however, it is not very powerful when it comes to troubleshooting utilities. Many vendors such as IBM/Lenovo install a custom client that can be used to create and manage profiles as an alternative to the WZC. So when you use these vendor-installed clients, you cannot use the Windows WZC.

WZC is a pretty basic client. It's designed to set up the connection for you and take some of the workload off the end user—hence the "Zero Configuration" part of the name. When a computer boots without a WLAN profile preconfigured, the WZC detects any wireless networks that are broadcasting and informs the user that a wireless network is available.

If a profile has already been created, the WZC tries to join it automatically. This WZC behavior can cause confusion when you have a WZC profile configured with the same SSID as another network that is within range. This is why changing default SSIDs such as "linksys" is recommended.

Configuring a Profile

You can set up a profile using Windows Vista in many ways. One method is to follow these steps:

Step 1.   Click **Start** (that's the little round Windows logo if you're running Vista).

Step 2.   Right-click **Network**.

Step 3.   Click **Properties**. You see the Network and Sharing Center window, as shown in Figure 16-1.

Step 4.   Click **Manage wireless networks** in the left panel. The Manage wireless networks window appears. Here you can see all available wireless network connection profiles. If you have yet to create any, this window looks like Figure 16-2.

Step 5.   Double-click an existing profile to view or change its setting. Click the **Add** button to create a new profile.

If you decide to add a new network, you see a new window that allows you to do so in a wizard-style setup.

Another way to add a wireless profile is to connect to one that is within range of your computer and that Windows has discovered. In Figure 16-3, Windows has detected a wireless network within range.

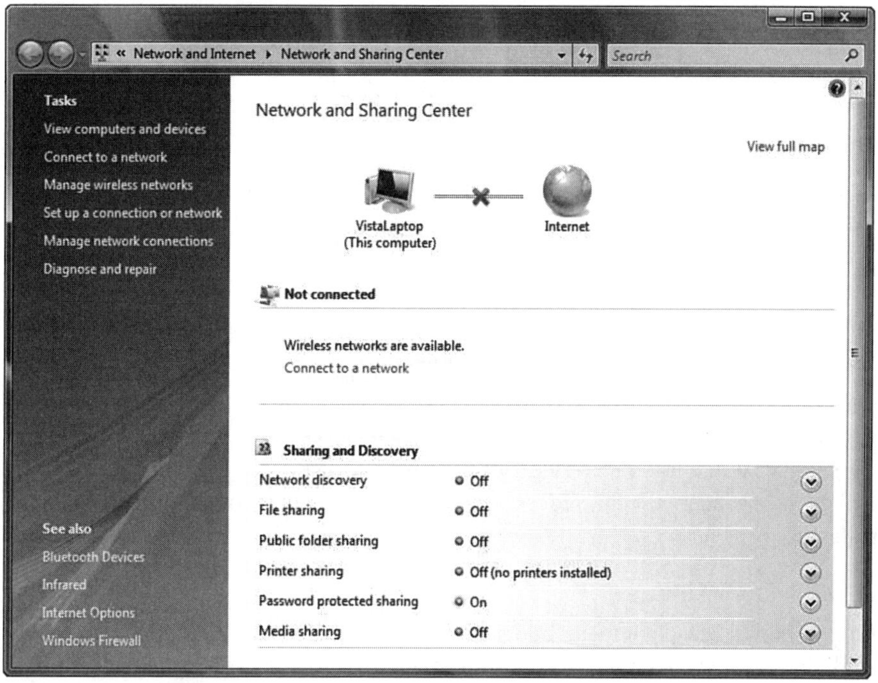

Figure 16-1 *Network and Sharing Center*

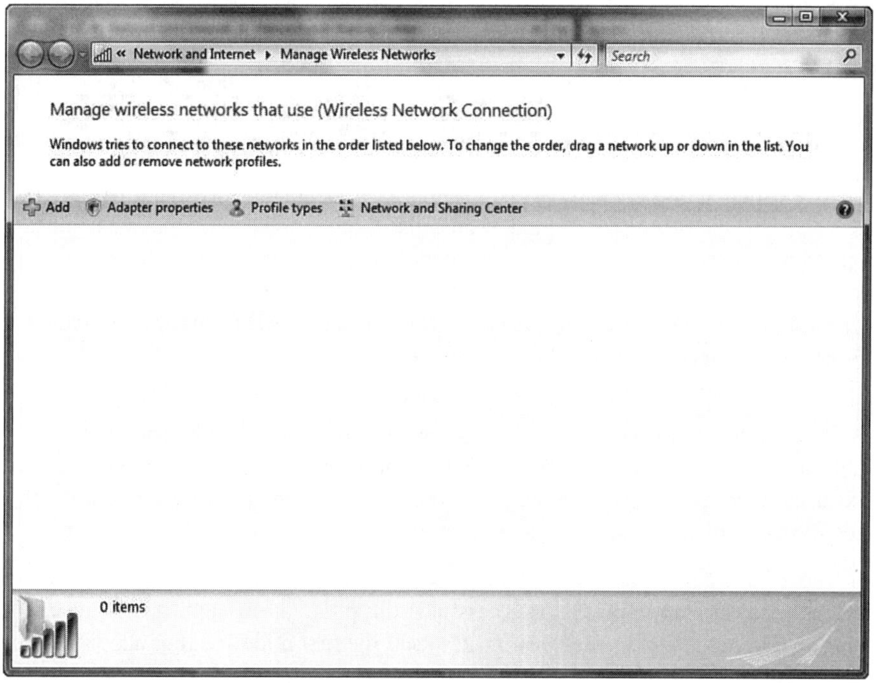

Figure 16-2 *Managing Wireless Networks*

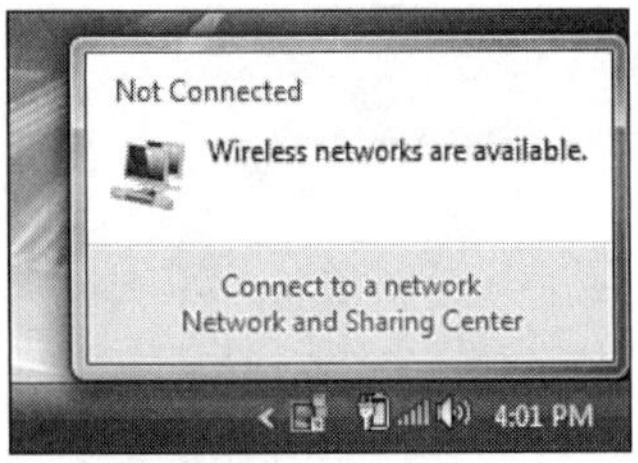

Figure 16-3 *Wireless Networks Detected*

When you click the link, a new window appears, allowing you to connect one of the available networks, as shown in Figure 16-4.

You can select one of the available networks and click the **Connect** button. If there are any security settings, you are prompted for that information. You will probably find the profile setup in Windows to be very easy, especially because it detects networks for you. You might also wonder how this process works. The next section covers the process in more detail.

How the WZC Tool Works

When a Windows-based computer boots up, the Wireless Zero Configuration reports any network that is being broadcast, usually via a balloon window at the bottom right of the screen. This is because when a WZC client attempts to access a network, it uses an active scanning process. This differs from other methods, such as passive scanning, which is used by other clients.

Note: The concept of passive scanning simply involves the client's waiting until it hears a beacon from an access point.

With active scanning, the WZC sends probe requests with a blank SSID field. This is called *active null scanning*. This type of scan causes access points (AP) that are in range to respond with a list of available service set identifiers (SSID). If one of the received SSIDs exists on the preferred networks list in the WZC, the WZC connects to it, or at least tries to. If that connection fails, the WZC tries the next SSID from the preferred networks list that was seen to be available from the scan.

If none of the SSIDs that were learned from the active null scan or in the preferred networks list result in a successful connection, the WZC looks for any ad hoc network in the available networks list. If the WZC finds an ad hoc network, it connects to it, which could be a security issue. This happens in the background without any user intervention. When you set up the profile, you can select an option to connect to only infrastructure networks.

If the connection attempts are still unsuccessful at this point (and assuming that you *are* allowing ad hoc connections), the WZC makes itself the first node and thus allows others

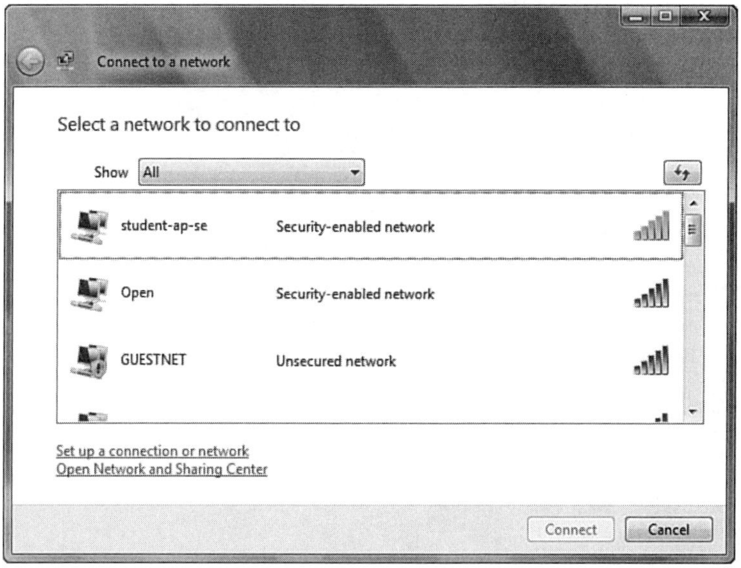

Figure 16-4   *Connecting to a Network*

to connect to it. Then the WZC sends out beacons that others on the network can see, allowing other devices to connect to the WZC sending the beacons.

If the WZC finds no preferred network and no ad hoc network to connect to, it checks the setting **Automatically Connect to non-preferred networks.** This is not enabled by default. If it were enabled, the WZC would try each non-preferred network in the available networks list.

If this setting is left at its default value, the WZC assigns itself a random network name and places the card in infrastructure mode. From this point on, it scans all the channels every 60 seconds, looking for new networks.

Using a Mac to Connect to a Wireless LAN

You can configure WLAN profiles on a Mac using AirPort or AirPort Extreme. This section describes AirPort Extreme, its software interface, and how to configure a profile on a Mac to connect to a WLAN.

AirPort, which really refers to the old version that supported only 802.11b networks, provides a software interface used to configure the WLAN profile, connect to detected networks, and perform advanced configurations and troubleshooting.

Configuring a Profile

To configure a profile in Mac OSX, follow these steps:

Step 1.   Click the **Open Apple** icon in the top-right corner of the screen.

Step 2.   Select **System Preferences.**

Step 3.   Select **Network**. This opens the network configuration page, as shown in Figure 16-5. From here you can select **AirPort**.

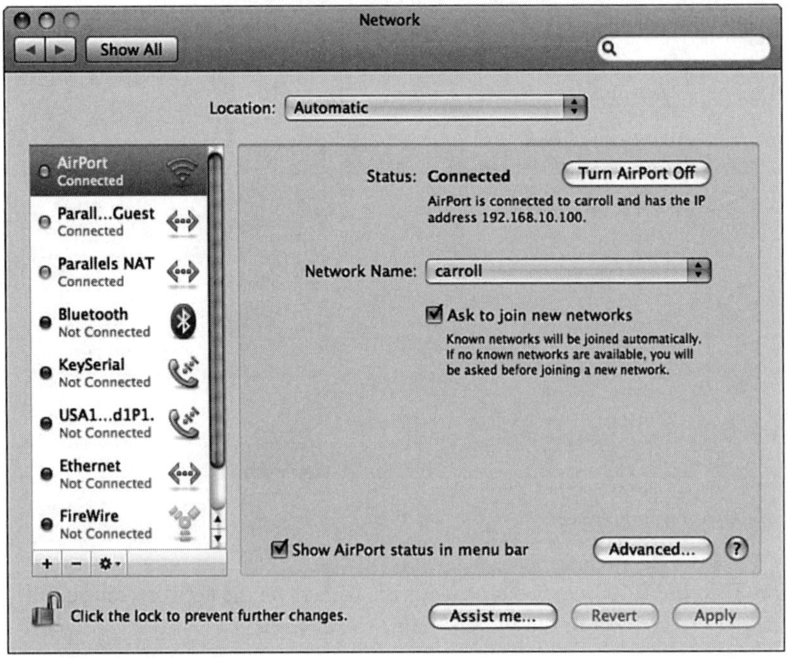

Figure 16-5   *Network Configuration on the Mac OSX*

Step 4.   You can access any already discovered network, create an ad hoc network, or join another network.

How the AirPort Extreme Tool Works

When you access the main AirPort configuration interface in Mac OSX 10.5 and above, you can disable the card, join networks, and even perform advanced configurations. To access the main AirPort interface, click the **Open Apple** icon and select **System Preferences > Network**.

If you want to create a profile, select the **Network Name** drop-down menu. Here you can choose **Join Other Network** or **Create Network**. The **Create Network** option allows you to set up an ad hoc network of computer-to-computer connectivity without using an AP. By selecting the **Join Other Network** option, you can enter an SSID and use the drop-down to select any security settings that may be necessary, as shown in Figure 16-6.

As an alternative, you can join any networks that AirPort has already discovered by selecting the **Network Name** drop-down and choosing one of the networks, as shown in Figure 16-7. If security settings are required, you are prompted.

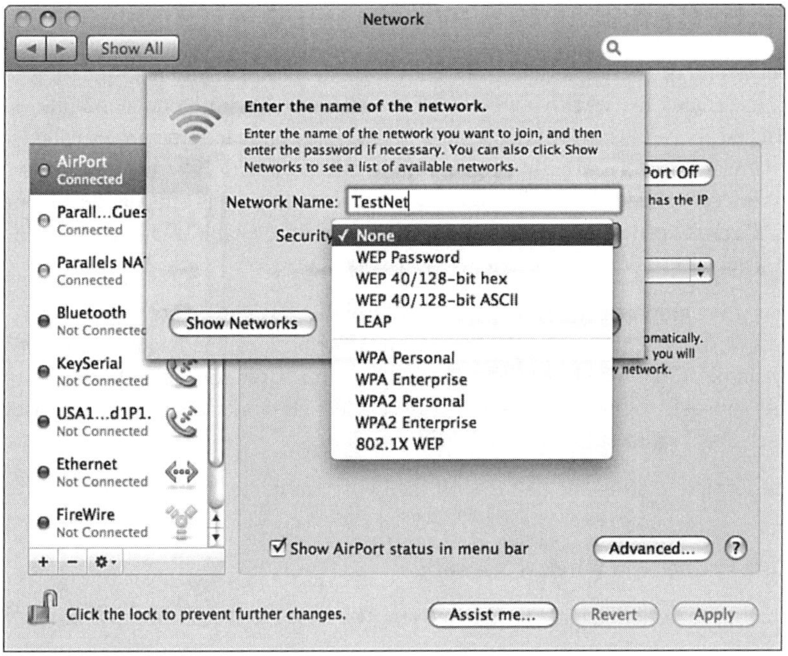

Figure 16-6   *Wireless Security Settings on Mac OSX*

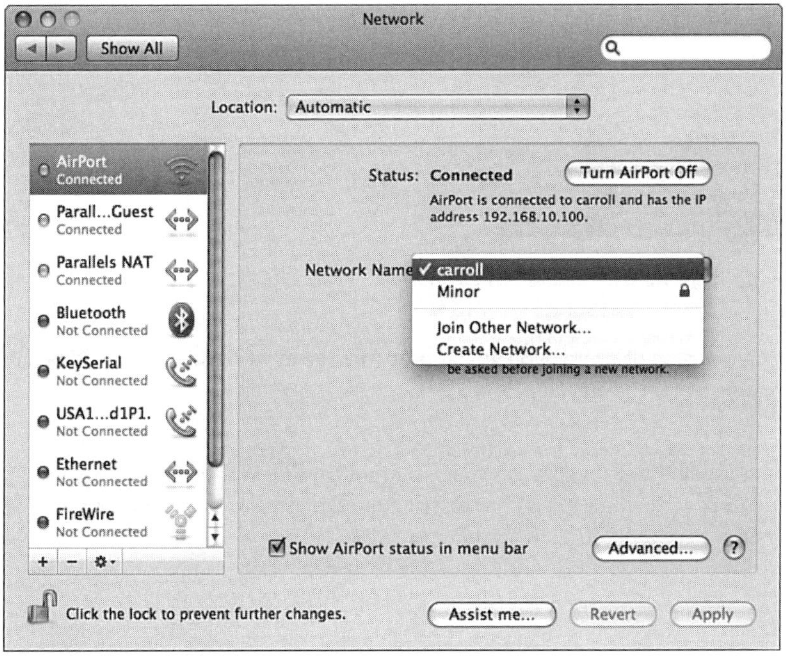

Figure 16-7   *Selecting the Network Name*

Using Linux to Connect to a Wireless LAN

If you or a user within the network that you are involved in is using the Linux operating system, you can certainly use it with a wireless network. Linux has both command-line and GUI interface-type tools for working with WLANs. The command-line tool is called iwconfig. It is similar to the ifconfig that you would use to work with Ethernet interfaces. Although this tool offers many capabilities, Cisco has decided that it is outside the scope of the CCNA Wireless certification. Still, you need to be able to enable a Linux-based device for WLAN access. To do this, you can use NetworkManager.

NetworkManager is a graphical user interface (GUI) tool that lets you create wireless profiles in Linux. It works on a number of different Linux distributions. Finding available networks is fairly simple. Click the network connection icon in what is equivalent to the System Tray. As shown in Figure 16-8, a number of wireless networks are available. To use one of them, select the radio button next to the network name.

You can create a simple profile, one that is most likely used at home, by following these steps:

Step 1.   Click **Create New Wireless Network**.

Step 2.   Enter a network name in the **Create New Wireless Network** pop-up box.

Step 3.   Click **Connect**.

Figure 16-8   *Available Networks in NetworkManager*

Again, this is not the type of profile you would probably see at work, so you should be familiar with creating a more advanced profile.

Note: If you want to try this, I suggest using an Ubuntu Live CD. You can use it to boot your computer to Linux without harming your existing operating system. Best of all, you can download Ubuntu for free at http://www.ubuntu.com.

Configuring a Profile

Don't be alarmed when you see the term "enterprise profile." It just means that the profile contains more options, most likely security options and such. Setting up an advanced profile is not difficult, nor is it too time-consuming. You just have to know the parameters and plug them in. Assuming that you know these parameters, you can select **Connect to Other Wireless Network**, as shown in Figure 16-9, to begin the process of configuring a profile.

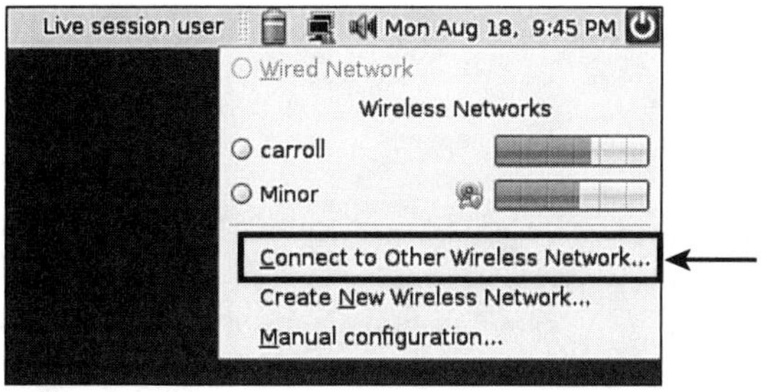

Figure 16-9   *Connecting to Other Wireless Network*

Next you need to enter the network name and use the drop-down menu to select the type of profile. In Figure 16-10, the network MySecureNet is using WPA2 Enterprise. After you make this selection, a number of other options are available to you, such as the EAP method, key type, identity, and password (see Figure 16-11). The values here are the defaults, but they can and usually are changed, depending on the security you have set up in your network.

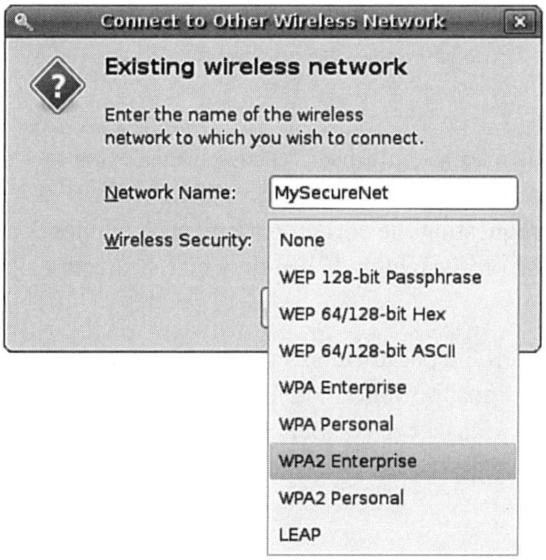

Figure 16-10   *Creating the Profile MySecureNet*

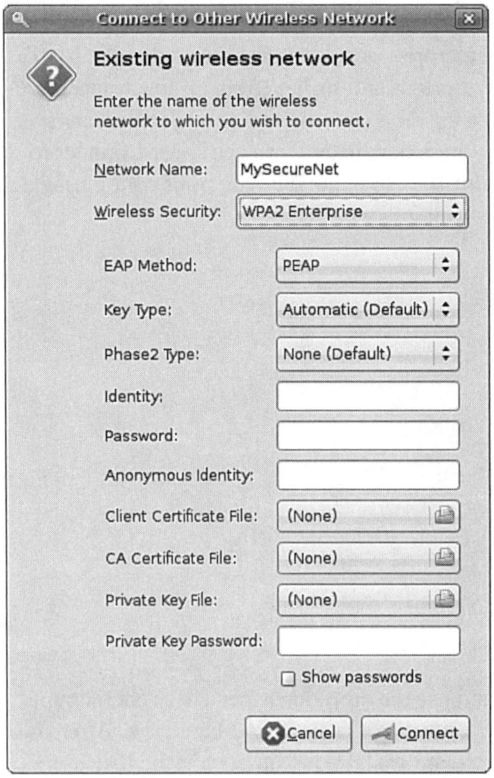

Figure 16-11 *WPA2 Enterprise Options*

Another option you have in the advanced settings is Awake Mode. If you place a card into Constant Awake Mode (CAM), the card is active at all times. This consumes more power.

How the NetworkManager Tool Works

When you click **Connect**, the NetworkManager tool sends discovery messages using the selected profile parameters. If for some reason an invalid parameter is entered in the NetworkManager tool, a message box appears, requesting the correct parameter. A connection does not take place until the parameters in the profile match. When they match, a connection can take place.

When a connection cannot take place due to invalid parameters, it is still added to the list of available networks. However, it indicates a signal power of 0. On the next boot, or if you restart the network daemon, the NetworkManager remembers the parameters.

Using the ADU to Connect to a Wireless LAN

You have a number of ways to connect to a WLAN. Cisco provides software to manage a single a/b/g wireless card called the Aironet Desktop Utility (ADU). As an administrator, you might be called on to use the Aironet Client Administration Utility (ACAU) to deploy across multiple clients. Additionally, you may use the Cisco Aironet Site Survey Utility (CASSU) when performing site surveys. The following sections cover these topics.

Cisco Wireless LAN Adapters

Cisco offers enterprise class wireless LAN adapters in the PCI and cardbus form factors. The AIR-CB21AG-X-K9 is a cardbus model, and the AIR-PI21AG-A-K9 is the PCI model. These adapters support most advanced wireless security configurations when you use Cisco software to manage them. You can, however, use the Windows WZC, but it's better to use the ADU and Aironet System Tray Utility (ASTU) if you want all the features of the cards to be available to you. The ADU has more configuration capability compared to WZC and also includes diagnostic tools, which don't come with the WZC.

With the ADU and a Cisco wireless card, you can

- Scan different channels.

- Determine which APs are on which channels.

- Determine the authentication and security configurations of each detected AP.

- Get Received Signal Strength Indicator (RSSI) information.

- Get signal-to-noise ratio (SNR) information.

Table 16-2 compares the WZC and the ADU.

The Aironet System Tray Utility (ASTU) is a smaller subset of the ADU that lives in your computer's system tray. Right-click it to access more information or even to launch the ADU.

Table 16-2   *Comparing the WZC and the ADU*

Capability	WZC	ADU
Scan different channels	No	Yes
Determine which APs are on which channels	No	Yes
Determine the authentication and security configurations of each detected AP	No	Yes
Get RSSI information	No	Yes
Get SNR information	No	Yes

Key Topic

Installing the ADU

When you install the ADU, you have three options, as shown in Figure 16-12:

■ **Install Client Utilities and Driver:** Installs the drivers for the card and the ADU software.

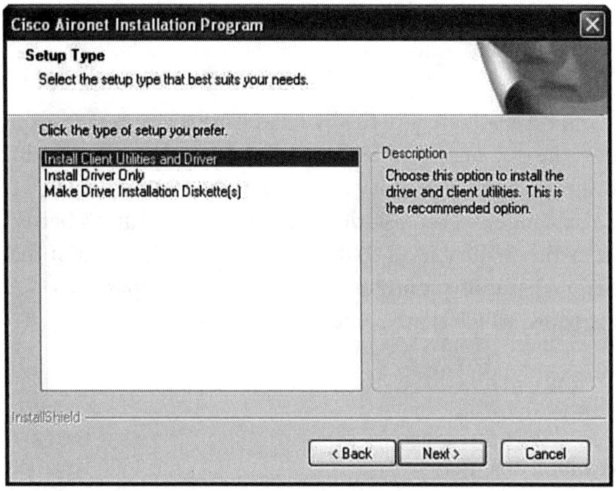

Figure 16-12   *Three Options When Installing the ADU*

■ **Install Driver Only:** Indicates that you will manage profiles and connect to networks with the WZC.

■ **Make Driver Installation Diskette(s):** Indicates that you will export these to a re-movable device such as a USB drive and take it with you.

In the following example, you will install the drivers and the client utility.

The process is pretty simple. It's best to start by inserting the card. You may see the Win-dows Found New Hardware Wizard, as shown in Figure 16-13. If you see this, close it. You don't need it.

After you have closed the Found New Hardware Wizard, continue with the installation by selecting the type of install you want to perform. In this case, it's the default option: **Install Client Utilities and Driver**, as shown previously in Figure 16-12.

As the installation progresses (as you click the **Next** button), you are given the option to install the CASSU, as shown in Figure 16-14.

One thing to point out with this site survey utility is that it's by no means a complete site survey tool because it has no mapping capability. It can, however, be used along with other site survey tools that do provide mapping capability. As a free utility that comes with the purchase of a Cisco network adapter, it's a good site survey tool. Some customers might not be able to afford the higher-priced tools provided by Ekahau, Wireless Valley, or Air-Magnet, so a free survey tool is better than no survey tool. However, if you can afford the

Figure 16-13   *Found New Hardware Wizard*

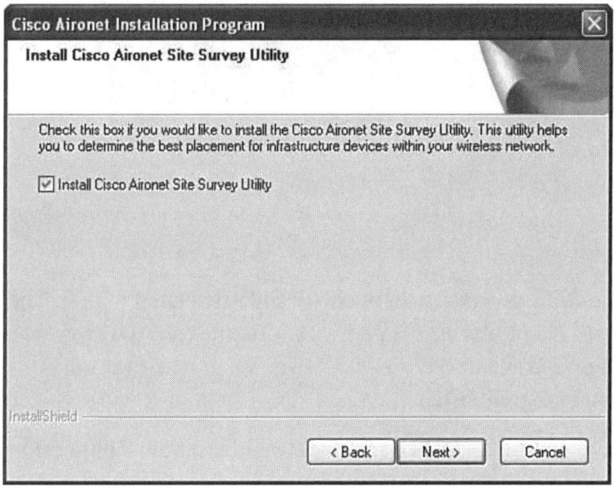

Figure 16-14   *Site Survey Utility Install Option*

higher-priced tools, the CSSU wouldn't provide any additional benefits over the higher-end tools.

The next option you have in the install program is the use of the ADU or third-party tools such as the WZC. This still installs the ADU. Again, you can choose to use the WZC, although it's not recommended. Later you can switch to the ADU by deselecting the **Use Windows to configure my wireless network settings** option in the WZC, as shown in Figure 16-15.

You need to reboot when the install is finished. If there are any open APs, the ADU finds them when the computer is restarted. You will most likely want to create an actual profile with security settings and such. The next section discusses the profile configuration.

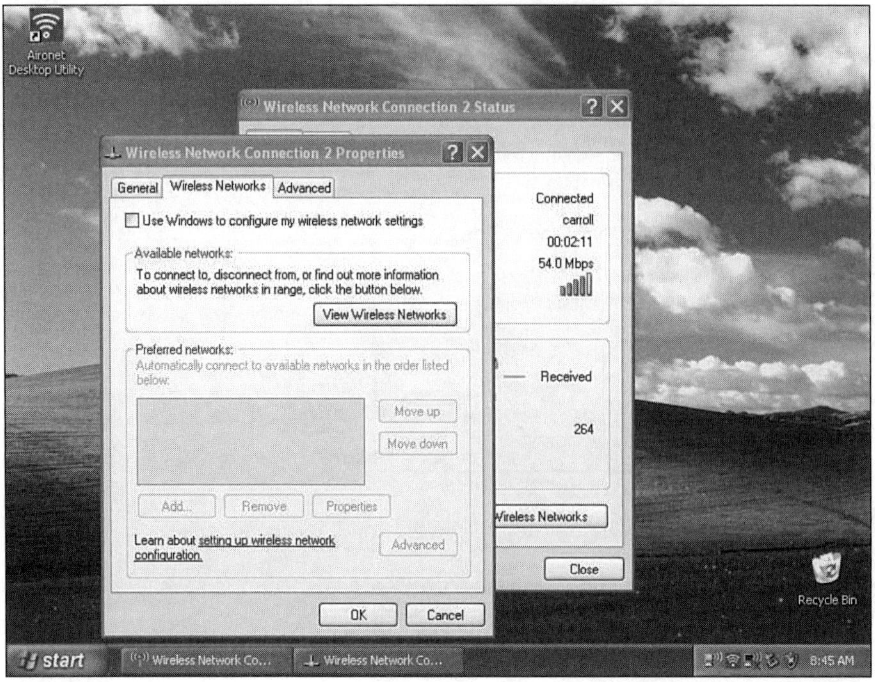

Figure 16-15 *Deselecting WZC as the Default Wireless Network Connection Tool*

Configuring a Profile

In this example, after a reboot, the ADU picked up an open AP and associated with it. The ADU did this because the Windows client was associated with it before the ADU was even installed. To get information on a connection, you can hover the mouse over the ADU icon on the systray, as shown in Figure 16-16.

You can also right-click this icon, which is the ASTU, and choose either **Show Connection Status** or **Open Aironet Desktop Utility**. Figure 16-17 shows these options as well as others available in the ASTU.

As you become more familiar with the ADU, you will see that these options in the ASTU are merely a subset of what is available in the actual ADU interface.

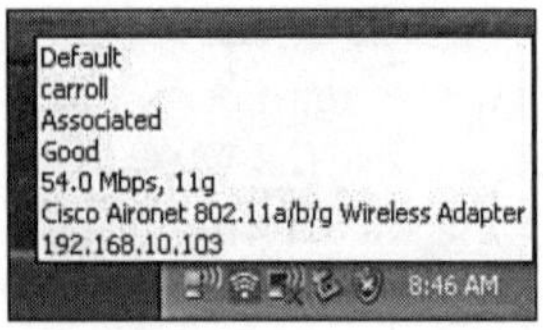

Figure 16-16 *Getting Information About a Connection*

Figure 16-18 shows the ADU interface for a connected profile called Default.

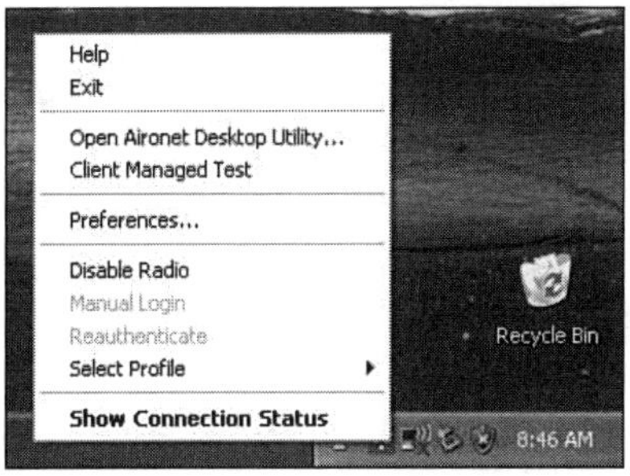

Figure 16-17   *ASTU Options*

If you don't access the ADU from the ASTU, you can start it by choosing **Start > All Programs > Cisco Aironet > Aironet Desktop Utility**. If you use the classic Start menu in Windows XP, choose **Start > Programs > Cisco Aironet > Aironet Desktop Utility**.

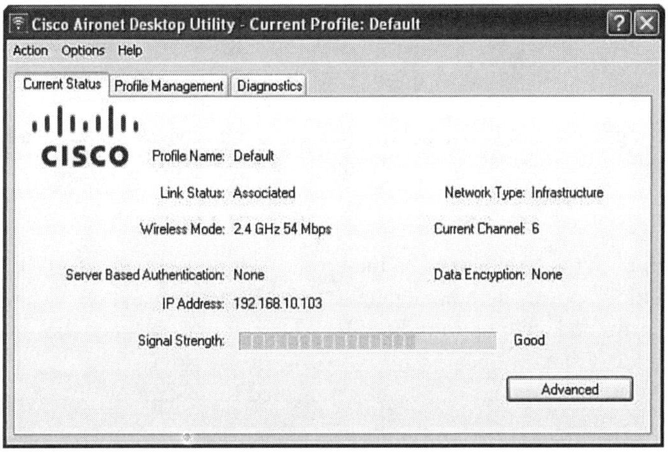

Figure 16-18   *ADU Interface*

Connecting to Preferred Networks

You can connect to preferred networks that the ADU has scanned for and found. In this case, you can enter security information and save it as a profile, or you can create a profile manually. To see what APs are nearby, select the Profile Management tab in ADU (see Figure 16-19), and then click the **Scan** button.

To connect to an AP in the scan list, select it and click **Activate**. A Profile Management window appears. Its three tabs—General, Security, and Advanced—allow any special AP settings to be entered into the profile and saved. The General tab sets up options such as the name of the connection and general parameters. The Security tab is where you

Figure 16-19   *Profile Management in ADU*

configure the security settings for the WLAN, and the Advanced tab is where you configure advanced settings such as power levels and wireless modes for the WLAN.

Manually Creating a Profile

To create a profile, you can click the **New** button on the Profile Management tab of ADU. A Profile Management window appears with three tabs—General, Security, and Advanced. Give the profile a name and enter up to three SSIDs. After you have named the profile, select the Security tab. From the Security tab, you can choose from WPA/WPA2/CCKM, WPA/WPA2 Passphrase, 802.1x, Pre-Shared Key (Static WEP), or None, as shown in Figure 16-20.

Unsecure Profiles

By leaving the default option (None), you would essentially be creating an unsecure profile. This is not a recommended practice.

802.1x Profiles

You can also create an 802.1x profile, but understand that it is authentication only. This means that your data is not encrypted. It does, however, use a central authentication server. To talk to this server, you must choose between Lightweight Extensible Authentication Protocol (LEAP), which is the default, Extensible Authentication Protocol Transport Layer Security (EAP-TLS), Protected Extensible Authentication Protocol (PEAP),

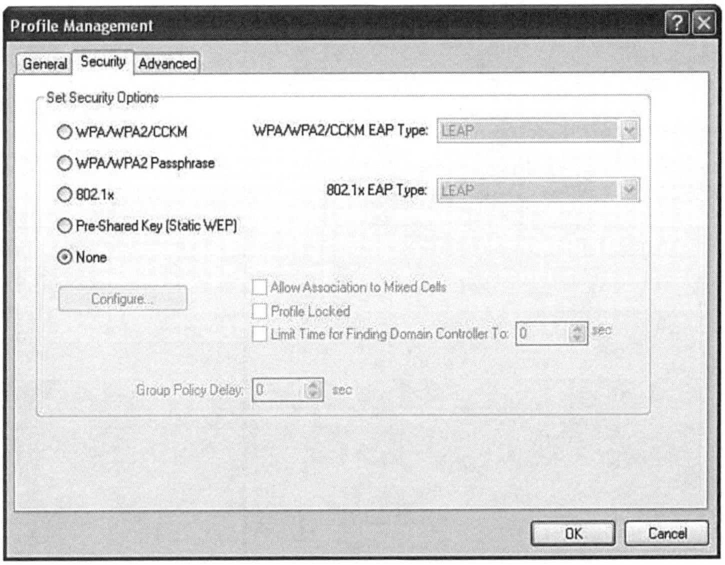

Figure 16-20   *Security Options*

Extensible Authentication Protocol Generic Token Card (EAP-GTC), PEAP with EAP Microsoft Challenge Handshake Authentication Protocol Version 2 (EAP MS-CHAP V2), EAP Flexible Authentication via Secure Tunneling (EAP-FAST), and Host-Based EAP.

Click **Configure** to add a temporary username and password or to use a saved username and password.

WPA/WPA2/CCKM Profiles

WPA/WPA2/CCKM lets you select an EAP type, as shown in Figure 16-21.

This method performs encryption with a rotated encryption key and authentication with 802.1x.

WPA/WPA2 Passphrase Profiles

You can choose to use WPA/WPA2 Passphrase. This method uses encryption with a rotated encryption key and a common authentication key, called a passphrase. To configure the passphrase, click the **Configure** button and enter the ASCII or hexadecimal passphrase, as shown in Figure 16-22.

By following the preceding steps, you can create any of the available profiles. Table 16-3 compares the different security options.

Key Topic

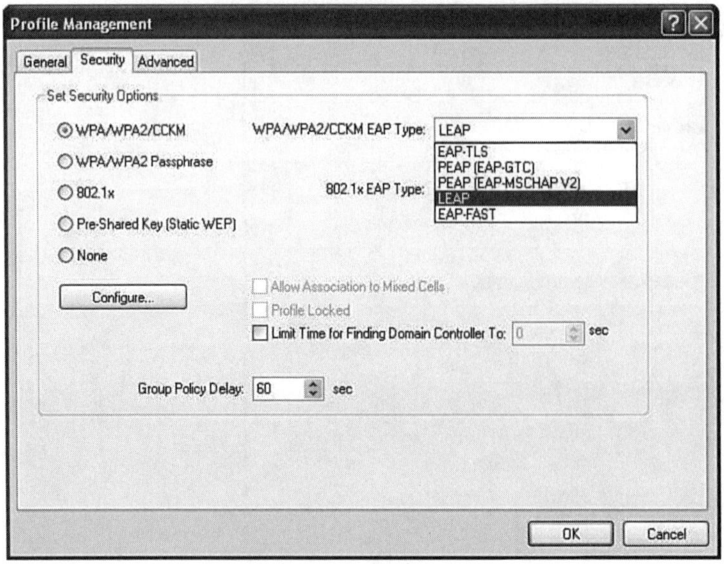

Figure 16-21 *WPA/WPA2/CCKM*

Key Topic

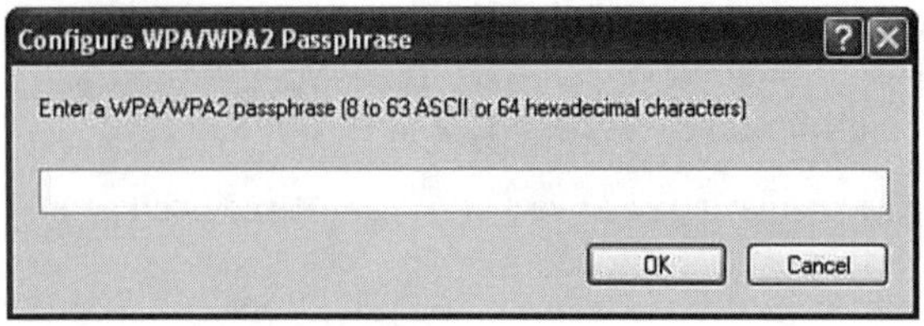

Figure 16-22 *WPA/WPA2 Passphrase*

Key Topic

Table 16-3 *Security Options Comparison*

Security Option	Encryption	Authentication
WPA/WPA2/CCKM	Rotating key	EAP methods (see 802.1x)
WPA/WPA2 Passphrase	Rotating key	8 to 63 ASCII or 64 hexadecimal passphrase
802.1x	None	EAP-TLS, PEAP, LEAP, EAP-FAST, host-based EAP (host-based is not an option for WPA/WPA2/CCKM)
Pre-Shared Key (Static WEP)	Weak	None
None	None	None

Managing Profiles

You can manage profiles from the Profile Management tab in ADU. You can create a new profile, as already discussed. You can also modify existing profiles. You can import existing profiles by clicking the **Import** button and browsing to the location of a .prf file. You can also export profiles and move them to other computers. To do this, simply click the **Export** button, define a name for the profile (if you want to change it), and browse to where you want to save it. This might be an external USB drive or even the desktop. As soon as you have the location where you want it, click **Save**.

As discussed previously in this chapter, you can scan for nearby networks. You also can change the order of your profiles by clicking the **Order Profiles** button and moving them up or down in the order you want.

Using Diagnostic Tools

After you have created a profile and it is in use, there are likely times when you will need to troubleshoot connectivity issues. If this is the case, a number of tools are available in the ADU. The following sections discuss options that you may find helpful in troubleshooting.

Adapter Information

Begin by looking at the adapter information shown in Figure 16-23. You find this information by clicking the **Adapter Information** button on the Diagnostics tab in the ADU interface. Two important pieces of information that you get from this output are the driver version and the card's MAC address. These can be used in troubleshooting. On the controller, you can enable a debug based on the client's MAC address to get specific information for that client. Also, the driver information can be used to look for bug reports in Cisco's support center.

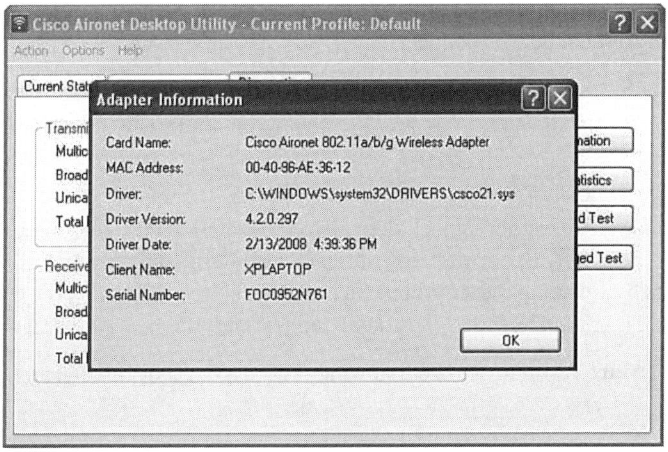

Figure 16-23 *Adapter Information*

Advanced Statistics

The Advanced Statistics button gives information about the frames transmitted and received, as demonstrated in the sample output shown in Figure 16-24.

Key Topic

| Advanced Statistics | | | ? | X |

Transmit

Frames Transmitted OK:	445	RTS Frames:	49
Frames Retried:	65	CTS Frames:	8
Frames Dropped:	0	No CTS Frames:	41
No ACK Frames:	284	Retried RTS Frames:	41
ACK Frames:	445	Retried Data Frames:	65

Receive

Beacons Received:	245	Authentication Time-Out:	0
Frames Received OK:	739	Authentication Rejects:	0
Frames Received with Errors:	63	Association Time-Out:	0
CRC Errors:	903	Association Rejects:	0
Encryption Errors:	0	Standard MIC OK:	0
Duplicate Frames:	2	Standard MIC Errors:	0
AP Mismatches:	0	CKIP MIC OK:	0
Data Rate Mismatches:	0	CKIP MIC Errors:	0

OK

Figure 16-24 *Advanced Statistics*

If you note a high count of retries, it is probably due to a high number of collisions. High numbers of RTS/CTS (provided in relation to the total number of frames transmitted) may indicate frame errors and bad link quality. You can use the Advanced Statistics to troubleshoot authentication issues as well as encryption problems. Authentication Rejects indicates that you are in fact talking to a server that is rejecting the authentication attempt. Authentication Time-Outs could indicate a connectivity issue with the AAA server.

Choose **Options > Display Settings** to change how the values appear, selecting either relative or cumulative values. For the most part, the default values (cumulative) are preferred.

Test Utility

An additional set of tools for troubleshooting includes a driver installation test, card insertion test, card enable test, radio test, association test, authentication test, and network test. You access these tests by selecting the **Action** menu in ADU and then choosing the **Client Managed Test** link. Figure 16-25 shows the completed test output.

To begin the test, click the **Start Test** button. The following tests are run sequentially:

1. Driver Installation test
2. Card Insertion test
3. Card Enable test
4. Radio test

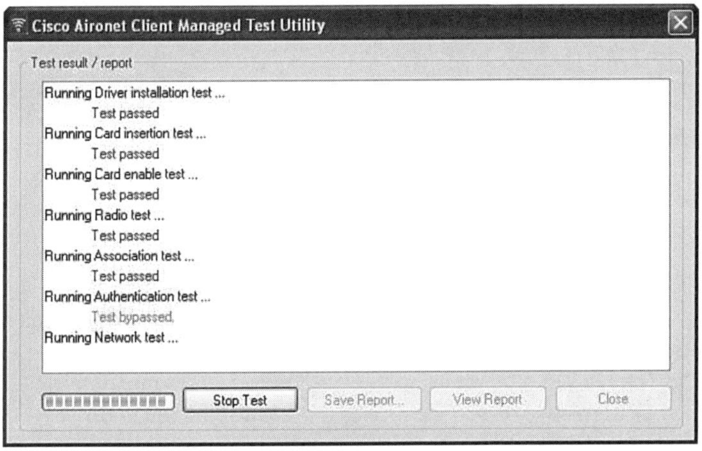

Figure 16-25 *Client Managed Tests*

5. Association test

6. Authentication test

7. Network test

The information gained from each of these tests can quickly point you in the direction of the issue. If the driver is not installed, this could indicate that it was inadvertently removed. If the driver is not installed, the ADU does not work. If the card is not inserted, it does not work. If the card has been disabled, it does not work. Also, if the radio is disabled, it does not function.

The Association test indicates if open association is functioning; the same goes for the Authentication test. These two tests can indicate where the connection is failing.

Finally, the Network test helps determine if the issue lies with the network rather than the wireless connection. Sometimes you get associated but still can't send if the network itself is having issues. Troubleshooting is discussed more in Chapter 20, "Troubleshooting Wireless Networks."

Site Survey Utility

The Site Survey Utility (CSSU) is the optional software set that you select using a checkbox during installation. This can be a handy tool for troubleshooting. As stated earlier in this chapter, it doesn't link to a map; however, it can give you handy information about the signal you are receiving.

To access the CSSU, choose **Start > All Programs > Cisco Aironet > Aironet Site Survey Utility**.

The utility dynamically represents your connection to the wireless network. As shown in Figure 16-26, it displays the AP MAC address, channel, signal strength (RSSI), noise level,

SNR, and speed of the connection. The connection quality is represented with the following colors:

- Green = excellent

- Yellow = good

- Orange = fair

- Red = poor

By default, the output is displayed in dB or dBm, as shown in Figure 16-26. You can change this to display as a percentage, as shown in Figure 16-27. The decibels display unit is recommended because it gives a much more precise view. You can also maximize the window and increase the **Time in seconds** value (up to 60 seconds) to view more information over a greater period of time. Also, Cisco's TAC asks for the information in dB or dBm.

Key Topic

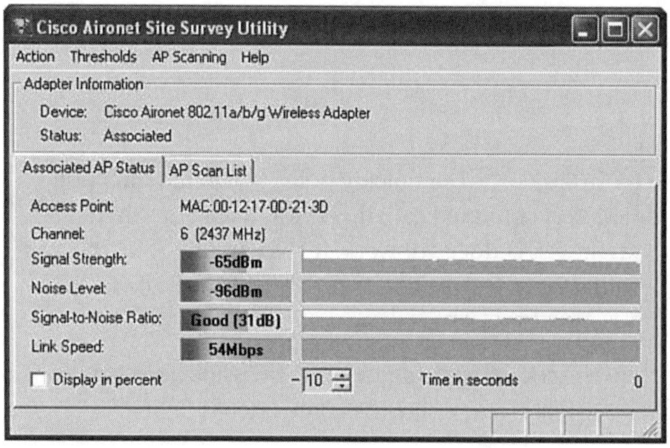

Figure 16-26   *CSSU Display in dBm*

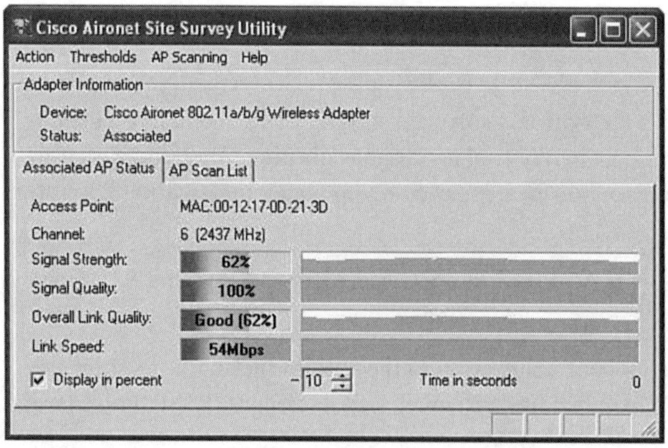

Figure 16-27   *CSSU Display in Percentage*

You can configure the CSSU with thresholds that can trigger an alert or logging. You set thresholds by choosing **Thresholds > Configure Thresholds**.

The AP scan list reports all the APs that your adapter detects. You don't use this information to associate with an AP. Instead, you would use this information to determine the characteristics of the APS around you. Again, this is a troubleshooting utility, so it can help you determine sources of interference.

Another neat feature of the CSSU is the ability to enable a proximity beeper. It beeps more quickly as you get a better signal. To enable it, choose **Action > enable proximity beeper**.

You can change what triggers the proximity beeper under the **Action** drop-down menu by selecting **Options**.

The ACAU

The Aironet Configuration Administration Utility (ACAU) is designed to help automate the process of deploying the ADU and client profiles. The main interface, shown in Figure 16-28, has four configuration families under the Global Settings tab. These configuration families include Setup Settings, User Settings, Profile Settings, and ASTU Settings. If you double-click these, they expand, allowing you to use radio buttons to control the capabilities of the ADU and how it is installed.

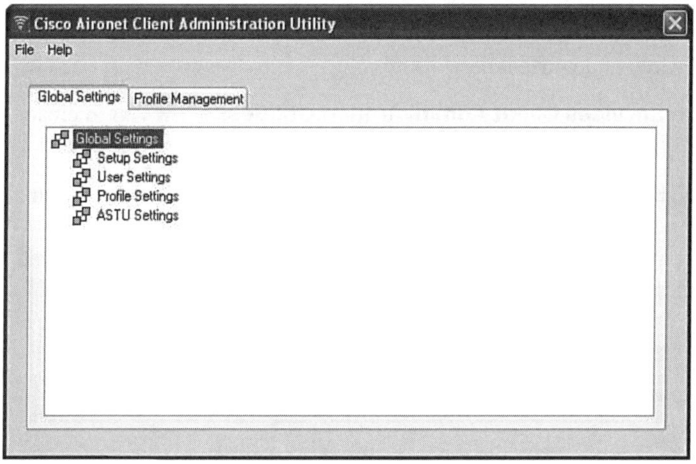

Figure 16-28 *ACAU Interface*

On the Profile Management tab, you can add up to 16 new profiles, modify them, remove them, import and export them, and reorder them. The profile configuration looks very similar to that of the ADU profile configuration. The difference between the two is that these profiles are not considered local. When you have the Global Settings arranged the way you want them, and then the Profiles set up the way you want them, choose **File >**

Save As. The default name for the file is CiscoAdminConfig.dat. Save this file and then place it in the same directory as the ADU installation executable. When the ADU install executes, it looks for a .dat file and uses it for its setup, automatically bringing in the profiles you configured in the ACAU.

The Cisco Secure Services Client

The Cisco Secure Services Client (SSC) is client software that provides 802.1x (Layer 2) user and device authentication for access to both wired and wireless networks. The SSC does not need a Cisco wireless card to operate the software. It's really an alternative to the WZC, with some major benefits. From the wired network side, it provides 802.1x capabilities for user and device authentication, which is more extensive than the standard wired LAN connection. On the wireless side, it provides all the security capabilities needed for enterprise class connectivity. The interface is very simple, making it easy for customers and guests to connect to a Cisco network.

The CSSC provides a unified wired and wireless supplicant that can provide services across many different vendor network cards as well as provide the ability to centralize management of client adapters. The CSSC also provides a tremendous amount of flexibility for authenticating to the wired and wireless network, not restricted to simply open, WEP, PEAP, and EAP-TLS. One other key advantage is the client's capability to disable the wired interface automatically if the wireless adapter associates to a wireless network. This ensures that IP address space is used efficiently and split tunneling is avoided.

There are three pieces of SSC software:

■ **The SSC itself:** Client software that provides 802.1x user and device authentication for access to both wired and wireless networks.

■ **The Cisco Secure Services Client Administration Utilities:** Allow you to create complex profiles.

■ **The Cisco Secure Services Client Log Packager:** Connects system information for support. An administrator would create profiles using the Cisco Secure Services Client Administration Utilities, which then generate an XML file that can be deployed network-wide to all the client machines.

Licensing

There are three SSC license types:

■ 90-day trial

■ Nonexpiring wired only

■ Nonexpiring wired and wireless

The 90-day trial offers full features for wired and wireless. When the 90 days are up, you must purchase a license, or it will automatically convert to a nonexpiring wired only. This is a limited feature set. If you purchase a license for the wireless features, you will have the full set of capabilities for both wired and wireless enabled.

Installation

The installation process uses a Microsoft Installer (MSI), which you can obtain from Cisco.com. You must have administrative rights on the computer you are installing on. Figure 16-29 shows the install wizard of the SSC.

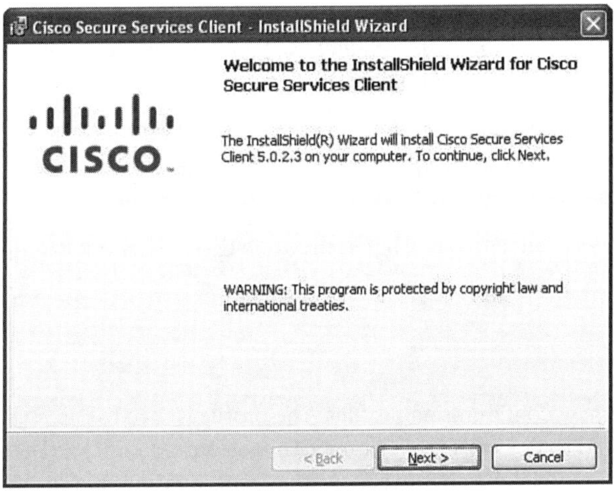

Figure 16-29   *Installing the SSC*

Configuring Profiles

The SSC runs as a service and appears in the systray whether or not it is connected. You can hover the mouse cursor over the systray icons to find out the status. Right-click to access the menu. Any existing profiles or networks that have been detected appear, as shown in Figure 16-30.

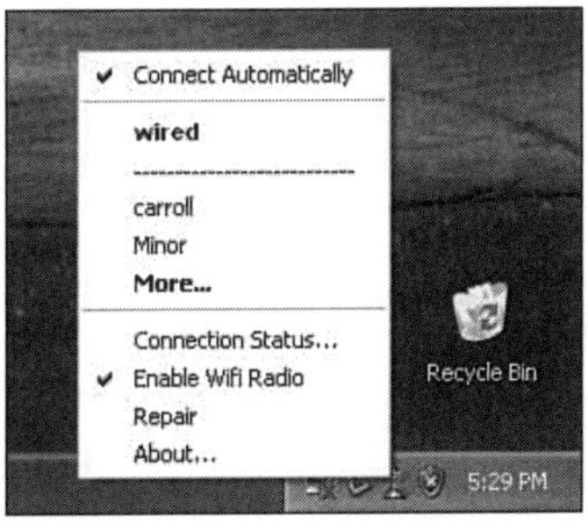

Figure 16-30   *Right-Click Menu of SSC*

SSC Groups

In the SSC, connections are logically grouped with a name. You can create your own groups, as well as move connections between groups. You can also add basic wireless connections (PSK-based), but not secured or wired connections.

> **Note:** The user interface of SSC talks about profiles. For administrators, the Secure Services Client Administration Utility (SSCAU) talks about networks.
>
> A network can be a wireless connection, a home type like the ones created with the SSC, or an enterprise type, based on individual authentication instead of a common passphrase. A network can also be a wired connection.
>
> The significance of this is that all profiles are networks, but at the same time a network can be more than just an SSC profile.

SSCAU Overview

With the SSCAU, you can create new configuration profiles. The profile is saved as an XML file and then can be deployed to devices in the network. You also can modify existing configuration profiles. Furthermore, you can process existing configuration profiles to verify the profile's policy logic, encrypt the credentials, and sign the file.

There are two ways to deploy the generated profiles:

- To existing clients

- Via an MSI that will also install the SSC

The Cisco Client Extension Program

The Cisco Client Extension (CCX) program is no-cost licensing of technology for use in WLAN adapters and devices. This allows for the following:

- Independent testing to ensure interoperability with the Cisco infrastructure's latest innovation

- Marketing of compliant products by Cisco and product suppliers under the "Cisco Compatible" brand

CCX for Wi-Fi RFID Tags allows vendors to have a common set of features. More information on the Cisco Compatible Extension Program can be found at http://www.cisco.com/web/partners/pr46/pr147/partners_pgm_concept_home.html.

Exam Preparation Tasks

Review All the Key Topics

Review the most important topics from this chapter, denoted with the Key Topic icon. Table 16-4 lists these key topics and the page number where each one can be found.

Table 16-4   *Key Topics for Chapter 16*

Key Topic Item	Description	Page Number
Table 16-2	Comparison between WZC and ADU	307
Figure 16-12	Three options when installing the ADU	308
Figure 16-19	Profile management in ADU	312
Figure 16-20	Security options	313
Figure 16-21	WPA/WPA2/CCKM	314
Figure 16-22	WPA/WPA2 passphrase	314
Table 16-3	Security options comparison	314
Figure 16-24	Advanced statistics	316
Figure 16-26	CSSU display in dBm	318
Figure 16-28	ACAU interface	319

Complete the Tables and Lists from Memory

Print a copy of Appendix B, "Memory Tables" (found on the CD) or at least the section for this chapter, and complete the tables and lists from memory. Appendix C, "Memory Tables Answer Key," also on the CD, includes completed tables and lists to check your work.

Definition of Key Terms

Define the following key terms from this chapter, and check your answers in the glossary:

WZC, SSID, AirPort Extreme, NetworkManager, iwconfig, WPA, WPA2, ADU, ACAU, 802.1x, CSSU, CSSC, SSCAU, CCX

Cisco Published 640-721 IUWNE Exam Topics Covered in This Part

Describe WLAN fundamentals

- Describe 802.11 authentication and encryption methods (Open, Shared, 802.1X, EAP, TKIP, AES)

Implement basic WLAN Security

- Describe the general framework of wireless security and security components (authentication, encryption, MFP, IPS)

- Describe and configure authentication methods (Guest, PSK, 802.1X, WPA/WPA2 with EAP-TLS, EAP-FAST, PEAP, LEAP)

- Describe and configure encryption methods (WPA/WPA2 with TKIP, AES)

- Describe and configure the different sources of authentication (PSK, EAP-local or - external, Radius)

Operate basic WCS

- Describe key features of WCS and Navigator (versions and licensing)

- Install/upgrade WCS and configure basic administration parameters (ports, O/S version, strong passwords, service vs. application)

- Configure controllers and APs (using the Configuration tab not templates)

- Configure and use maps in the WCS (add campus, building, floor, maps, position AP)

- Use the WCS monitor tab and alarm summary to verify the WLAN operations

Conduct basic WLAN Maintenance and Troubleshooting

- Identify basic WLAN troubleshooting methods for controllers, access points, and clients methodologies

- Describe basic RF deployment considerations related to site survey design of data or VoWLAN applications, Common RF interference sources such as devices, building material, AP location Basic RF site survey design related to channel reuse, signal strength, cell overlap

- Describe the use of WLC show, debug and logging

- Describe the use of the WCS client troubleshooting tool

- Transfer WLC config and O/S using maintenance tools and commands

- Describe and differentiate WLC WLAN management access methods (console port, CLI, telnet, ssh, http, https, wired versus wireless management)

Part III: WLAN Maintenance and Administration

This chapter covers the following subjects:

Threats to Wireless Networks: Discusses threats to wireless networks.

Simple Authentications: Looks at basic wireless security.

Centralized Authentication: Shows how centralized authentication works using various EAP methods.

Authentication and Encryption: Describes WPA and WPA2.

CHAPTER 17

Securing the Wireless Network

It's usually obvious that wireless networks can be less secure than wired networks. This calls for a great deal of thought when you deploy a wireless network. What security do you need? What security measures can you perform? What are the security capabilities of your equipment? Should you authenticate users when they access the network? Should you encrypt traffic over the wireless space? As you can see, there are many options to think about. But let's break this into small parts. First, who are your users? The answer will be different for networks that allow guest access versus those that don't. Second, how hidden do you need to make your users' traffic? Again, this answer will differ depending on the users. If you are offering guest access, encryption probably is not a big concern. If all or even a portion of your users are internal, encryption probably is a concern. In this chapter, you will learn about various methods of securing a wireless network. Some methods provide a way to identify the user. Others offer a way to hide user data. Still other methods do both.

You should take the "Do I Know This Already?" quiz first. If you score 80 percent or higher, you might want to skip to the section "Exam Preparation Tasks." If you score below 80 percent, you should review the entire chapter. Refer to Appendix A, "Answers to the 'Do I Know This Already?' Quizzes," to confirm your answers.

"Do I Know This Already?" Quiz

The "Do I Know This Already?" quiz helps you determine your level of knowledge of this chapter's topics before you begin. Table 17-1 details the major topics discussed in this chapter and their corresponding quiz questions.

Table 17-1 *"Do I Know This Already?" Section-to-Question Mapping*

Foundation Topics Section	Questions
Threats to Wireless Networks	1–4
Simple Authentications	5–7
Centralized Authentication	8–12
Authentication and Encryption	13–14

1. Threats to wireless networks include which of the following? (Choose all that apply.)

   a. Rogue APs

   b. Client misassociation

   c. Unauthorized port access

   d. Stateful inspection

2. Which of the following can be used to prevent misassociation attacks? (Choose all that apply.)

   a. Client MFP

   b. Spoofing

   c. Infrastructure MFP

   d. Rogue-AP containment

3. Client MFP allows clients to perform what function?

   a. Detect invalid clients

   b. Detect invalid APs

   c. Detect invalid controllers

   d. Detect invalid SSIDs

4. To perform Client MFP, what version of CCX is required?

   a. v1.x

   b. v2.x

   c. v5.x

   d. v6.x

5. WEP uses which of the following encryption algorithms?

   a. AES

   b. TKIP

   c. MD5

   d. RC4

6. What key size should be selected to perform 128-bit WEP with a Windows client?

   a. 40-bit

   b. 104-bit

   c. 128-bit

   d. 192-bit

7. How many bits does an IV add to a WEP key?

    a. 24 bits

    b. 48 bits

    c. 188 bits

    d. 8 bits

8. In centralized authentication, a certificate is used based on information from a trusted third party. What information is *not* included in a certificate?

    a. Username

    b. Public key

    c. Validity dates

    d. Session keys

9. Central authentication uses which IEEE specification?

    a. 802.11a

    b. 802.1q

    c. 802.1d

    d. 802.1x

10. Which protocol is used for the authentication server?

    a. RADIUS

    b. Active Directory

    c. LDAP

    d. TACACS+

11. Which EAP method uses certificates on both the client and the server?

    a. EAP-FAST

    b. EAP-MD5

    c. EAP-TLS

    d. PEAP

12. Which EAP method uses a PAC instead of certificates?

    a. EAP-FAST

    b. EAP-MD5

    c. EAP-TLS

    d. PEAP

13. Which protocol requires the use of TKIP, but can optionally use AES?

    a. WPA2

    b. GTK

    c. MS-CHAPv2

    d. WPA

14. Which protocol mandates that AES must be supported but not TKIP?

    a. WPA2

    b. GTK

    c. MS-CHAPv2

    d. WPA

Foundation Topics

Threats to Wireless Networks

Throughout this book, you have learned about the many threats to wireless networks. If you really wanted to simplify the threats, you could think of it like this: You want legitimate clients to connect to legitimate APs and access corporate resources. Some attacks are formed from the perspective of an AP trying to gain information from clients. Other attacks are from the perspective of getting illegitimate clients onto the network to use corporate resources at no charge or to actually steal data or cause harm to the network.

These threats include the following:

- Ad hoc networks

- Rogue APs

- Client misassociation

- Wireless attacks

Ad Hoc Networks

An ad hoc network is a wireless network formed between two clients. The security risk involves bypassing corporate security policies. An attacker could form an ad hoc network with a trusted client, steal information, and even use it as a means of attacking the corporate network by bridging to the secure wired LAN.

Rogue APs

A rogue AP is not part of the corporate infrastructure. It could be an AP that's been brought in from home or an AP that's in a neighboring network. A rogue AP is not always bad. It could be an AP that's part of the corporate domain yet still operating in autonomous mode. Part of an administrator's job is determining if the AP is supposed to be there. Fortunately, you don't have to do all the work yourself. A few functions of the AP's software can detect rogue APs and even indicate if they are on your network.

Something to consider when looking for rogue APs is what happens to clients that can connect to those rogue APs. If a client connects to a rogue AP, it should be considered a rogue client. The reason is that rogue APs typically are installed with default configurations, meaning that any client that connects bypasses any corporate security policy. So you do not know if the client is a corporate user or an attacker.

Client Misassociation

When a client connects to an AP, operating system utilities normally allow the client to save the SSID. In the future, when that SSID is seen again, the client can create a connection automatically. There is a possibility that clients will be unaware of the connection. If the SSID is being spoofed, the client could connect to a potentially unsafe network. Consider the following scenario. An attacker learns the SSID of your corporate network. Using this information, he sends beacons advertising your SSID. A wireless station in the range of the rogue AP connects to the AP. The AP allows connectivity to the Internet but is not actually on your corporate wired network. Using tools that are easily available on the Internet, another client connected to the same rogue AP attacks the misassociated client and steals valuable corporate data.

This scenario employs multiple attack methods. It uses a method known as *management frame spoofing* as well as an active attack against a misassociated client. So how can this be prevented? The answer begins with a function called Management Frame Protection.

Management Frame Protection

One method of Management Frame Protection (MFP) is *Infrastructure MFP*. With this method, each management frame includes a cryptographic hash called a Message Integrity Check (MIC). The MIC is added to each frame before the Frame Check Sequence (FCS). When this is enabled, each WLAN has a unique key sent to each radio on the AP. Then, the AP sends management frames, and the network knows that this AP is in protection mode. If the frame were altered, or if someone spoofs the SSID of the WLAN and doesn't have the unique key, it invalidates the message. This causes other APs that hear the invalid frames to report them to the controller.

The other method of MFP is called *Client MFP*. If the client is running Cisco Compatible Extensions (CCX) 5 or better, it can talk to the AP and find out what the MIC is. Then it can verify management frames it hears in addition to the APs that provide this function. The major benefit of this mode is the extension of detection. In Figure 17-1, the APs are in the middle of the network, and clients are on the outside. The clients can detect the AP called BAD_AP that is generating invalid frames, even though BAD_AP is out of the range of the APs that are in protection mode.

With MFP version 1, all local mode APs are protectors. They digitally sign all frames they send. Any other AP, or the same local mode AP, for that matter, could be a validator.

With MFP version 2, clients must run the Cisco Secure Services Client (CSSC) or a client that is capable of CCXv5. This enables the client to hear the rogue and report illegitimate frames. You don't have to worry about your client associating with the rogue AP, because it drops invalid frames.

Client MFP has another benefit. Suppose a neighboring AP performed containment as a denial-of-service (DoS) method against your network because it's a deauthentication frame that is used for containment. The client would see that the containment frame doesn't have the MIC and would ignore the deauthentication frame. This would keep people from containing your network as a form of DoS attack.

To enable MFP, choose **SECURITY > Wireless Protection Policies > AP Authentication/MFP**. You view MFP with the Wireless LAN Controller by choosing **SECURITY > Wireless Protection Policies > Management Frame Protection**, as shown in Figure 17-2.

Wireless Attacks

It's not news that networks in general are constantly bombarded with attacks. Some of these attacks are unique to wireless networks, as is the case with management frame spoofing. With management frame spoofing, a rogue AP advertises an SSID known to the

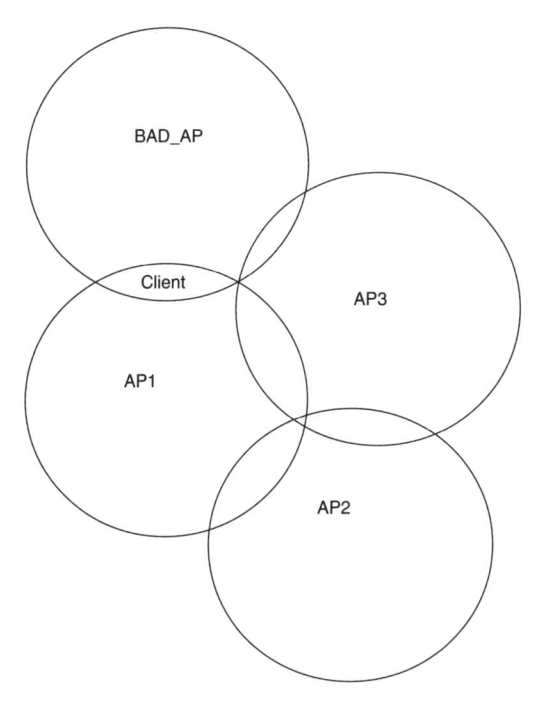

Figure 17-1   *Client MFP in Action*

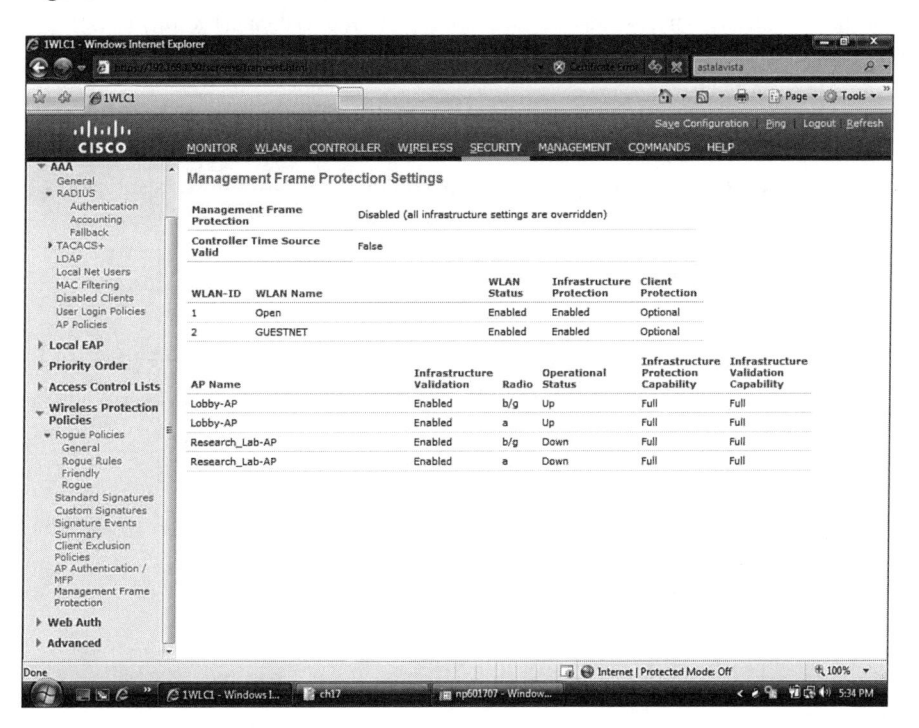

Figure 17-2   *Configuring MFP*

client in an attempt to get the client to connect to the rogue AP. Other attacks apply to both wired and wireless networks:

- **Reconnaissance attacks:** An attacker attempts to gain information about your network. Initially, the method of mitigating recon attacks involved hiding the SSID by not broadcasting it in beacon frames.

- **Access attacks:** An attacker tries to gain access to data, devices, and/or the network. Initially the method of preventing access to the network involved MAC-based authentication as well as static Wired Equivalent Privacy (WEP). The problem with WEP today is that the keys can be broken in 4 to 7 minutes.

- **Denial-of-service (DoS) attacks:** An attacker attempts to keep legitimate users from gaining services they require. Today, the use of intrusion detection system/intrusion prevention system (IDS/IPS) sensors on the wired network can help mitigate these attacks. You also can use MFP to prevent containment DoS attacks.

The mitigation methods used to prevent attacks mentioned here are not very advanced and are considered weak by today's standards. However, you might be wondering how these methods work. What alternatives are there if these mitigation methods are weak? What other options exist? The following sections discuss these aspects.

Simple Authentications

One of the first items to discuss involves users being allowed to connect to the network. Many methods of authenticating users exist, as discussed in the following sections.

Open Authentication

Open authentication is a simple as it gets. The term "authentication" is used loosely here because it's part of the association process, although there really isn't any authentication per se. Figure 17-3 illustrates this process, picking up after the initial probe request and response. The client sends an authentication request to the AP, and the AP replies with a confirmation and registers the client. Then the association request and confirmation take place. WEP is taking place in the figure. Everything is "open."

This type of open authentication is commonly used at hot spots. This is a Layer 2 security method. You choose the **None** option under the **Security** tab while configuring a WLAN, as shown in Figure 17-4.

Preshared Key Authentication with Wired Equivalent Privacy

With static WEP you don't authenticate users; you simply verify that they have a key. You don't know who they are, just that they know your key.

The process of WEP authentication is as follows:

Step 1.   A client sends an authentication request.

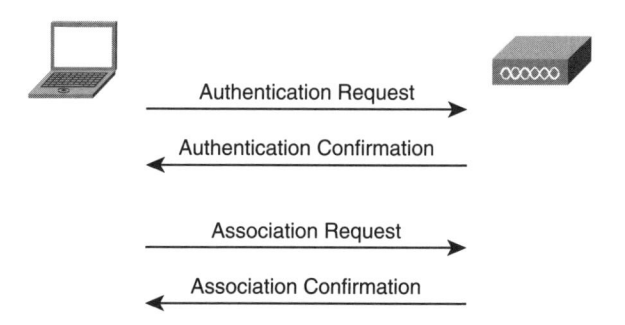

Figure 17-3 *Open Authentication*

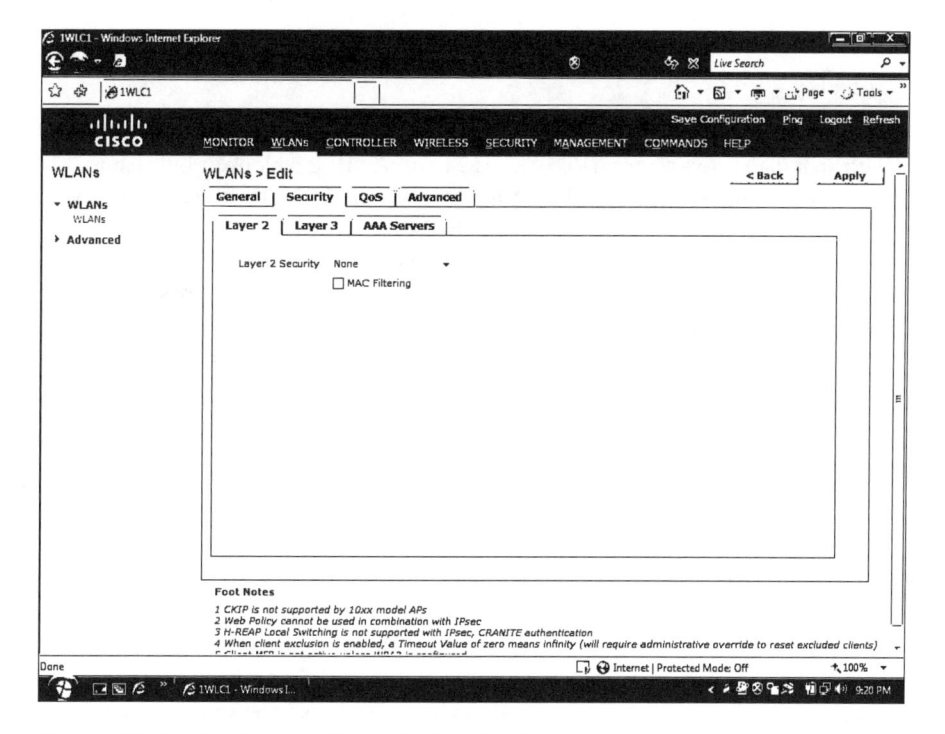

Figure 17-4 *Configuring Open Authentication*

Step 2.   The AP sends an authentication response containing clear-text challenge text.

Step 3.   The client uses the text received to respond with an encrypted authentication packet. The encryption is done using one of the client's static WEP keys.

Step 4.   The AP compares what it received to the AP's own copy of what the response should look like based on the static WEP keys. If they match, the client moves on to association.

This method is actually considered weaker than open authentication, because an attacker could capture the challenge text and then the reply that is encrypted. Because the challenge is clear text, the attacker could easily use it to derive the static WEP key used to create the encrypted packet. They simply use the challenge along with the response to re-create the key. WEP uses the RC4 encryption method.

Note: It is important to note that although the WEP key is used to encrypt the challenge text, it is used only for authentication purposes. WEP is not used to hide, protect, or encrypt any user data after it is associated with the AP.

Some other interesting caveats about using WEP involve the key size. Three key lengths can be used:

■   40-bit key

■   104-bit key

■   128-bit key

I can't stress enough that these values are not what you think. You see, the key is combined with an *initialization vector (IV)*, which is 24 bits. An IV is a block of bits that is used to produce a unique encryption key. When you add the 24-bit IV to the 40-bit key, the resulting size is 64 bits. When you combine the 24-bit IV with the 104-bit key, the result is 128 bits. When you combine the 24-bit IV with the 128-bit key, the result is 152 bits. This has been a sore spot for Windows users, because the maximum key size supported with the native client is 128 bits. If you choose the key size of 128 bits, when combined with the IV, it yields a 152-bit key, and the authentication fails. Therefore, you should use a 104-bit key for Windows, or it won't work.

After it is authenticated, the client is issued an association identifier and can begin sending data. From this point on, WEP is used to encrypt traffic.

Figure 17-5 shows the configuration of static WEP.

MAC Address Filtering

MAC address filtering is a simple form of authenticating the device that is connecting. MAC address filtering entails defining MAC addresses that are allowed to connect. Although this is an easy way to ensure that people with the defined MAC address are allowed on the network, the danger is that MAC addresses can easily be spoofed. This method is not recommended. To configure MAC address filtering, you simply check a box on the Static WEP configuration page, as shown in Figure 17-6.

Centralized Authentication

Centralized authentication is the act of verifying the user's identity by a means other than the local definitions. In this scenario, a Public Key Infrastructure (PKI) is usually in place. PKI uses digital certificates that are cryptographically signed by a trusted third party. The trusted third party is called a Certificate Authority (CA). If you have ever been pulled over for speeding, you have most likely experienced a PKI infrastructure, so to speak. When the trooper comes to your window, he usually wants to see your driver's license. The trooper did not issue that identification to you; rather, a third party that the trooper trusts did. The concept is the same in the PKI world.

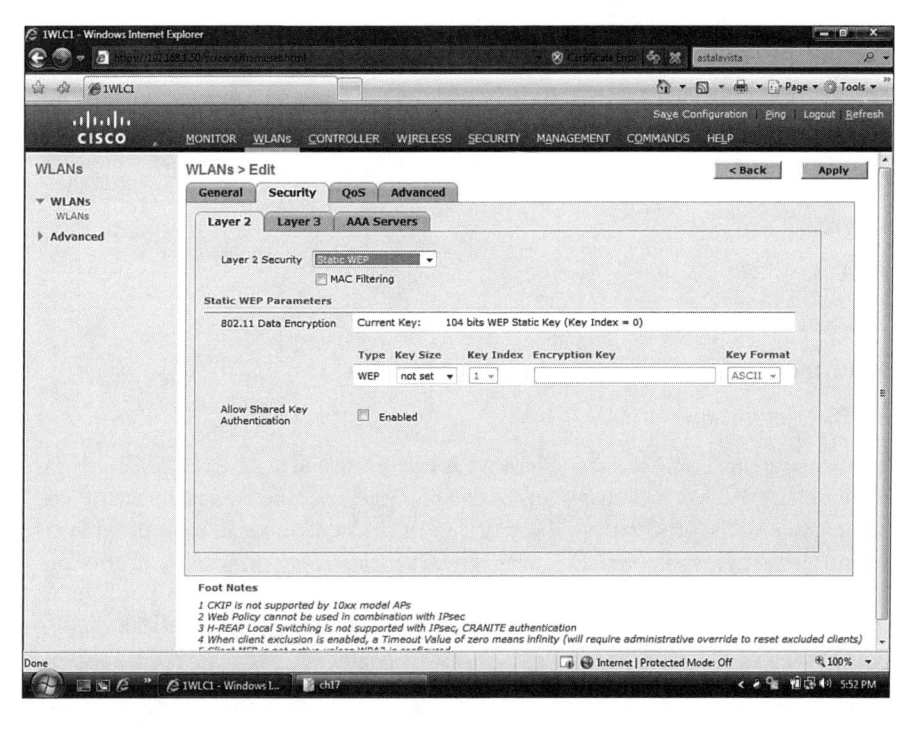

Figure 17-5   *Configuring WEP*

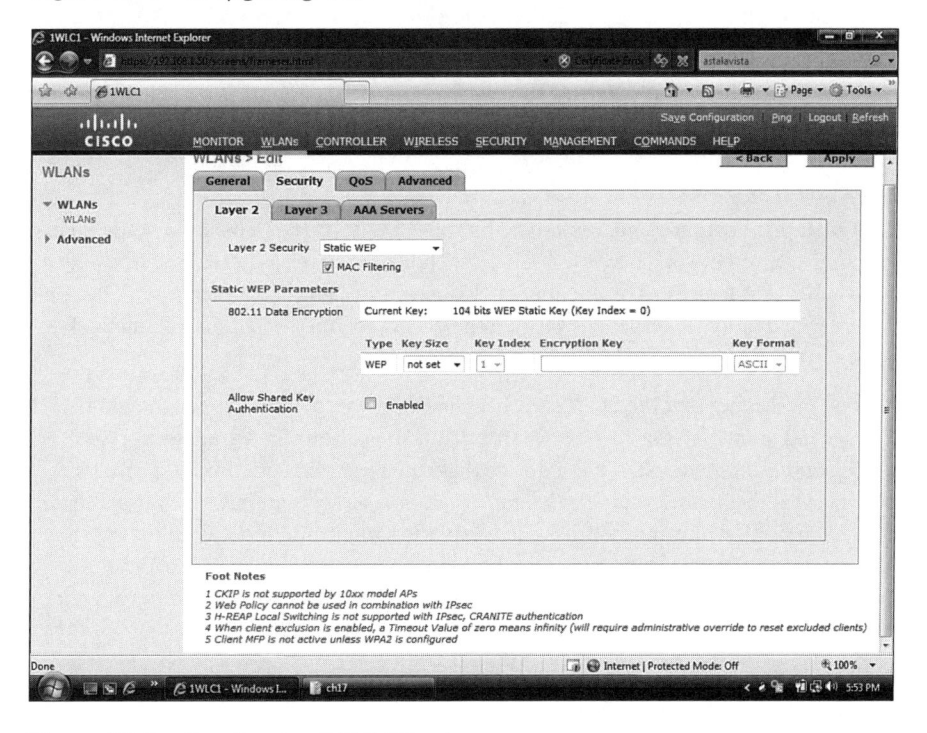

Figure 17-6   *Configuring MAC Filtering*

So to get this to work, the first thing you need is a certificate that identifies who you are. You can get an identity certificate from folks like VeriSign or Entrust. You also can get an identity certificate from a CA server that you have set up. It just so happens that Microsoft Server has a CA that you can manage on your own.

A certificate contains the following information:

- Username

- Public key

- Serial number

- Valid dates

- The CA's information

When you use digital certificates, you have a CA certificate and a server certificate that is issued by the CA. Each device that wants to communicate uses the CA certificate to verify the signature of the other party's ID certificate. If the signature matches, you authenticate. As an alternative, you could use a self-signed certificate, but this causes an error on the initial connection, because you might not trust the issuer. It's an easy fix; you simply view the certificate and add it to your certificate store. Then accept the certificate, and you are in business.

These certificates are used for 802.1x authentication. This is a centralized method of authentication that can use various Extensible Authentication Protocol (EAP) methods of authenticating a client to an Authentication, Authorization, and Accounting (AAA) server.

Certificates can also be used for LWAPP control data, but it's not the same certificate that is used for 802.1x. Additionally, certificates are used for web authentication, but again, it's not the same certificate as the one used by 802.1x.

802.1x and How It Is Used

802.1x is an authentication standard defined by the IEEE. It has been used for some time on the wired side of networks, so it was a logical choice for wireless networks. At its most basic level, 802.1x is a method of opening or closing a port based on a condition. The condition here is that an AAA server has verified the client's identity. 802.1x is a framework that uses various EAP methods in its communication.

Elaborating on the fact that the 802.1x has been used on wired networks for some time, you can see in Figure 17-7 that the device that wants to get onto the wired network is called the *supplicant*. A supplicant is a device that can use an EAP method to prove its identity to the authentication server. The *authentication server* is an AAA server that has a list of users in one form or another that can verify the supplicant. In between the two is the *authenticator*, which in this network is the switch. The switch uses EAP over LAN (EAPoL) between the supplicant and itself and then RADIUS (with EAP in it) between itself and the authentication server.

Now swap out that switch with an AP, as shown in Figure 17-8, and you have the same scenario as before, except that the protocol between the wireless supplicant and the AP is EAPoWLAN.

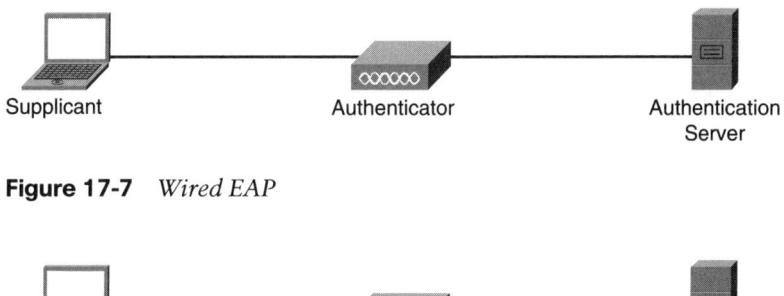

Figure 17-7 *Wired EAP*

Figure 17-8 *Wireless EAP*

Until the user authenticates, no frames can be passed to the wireless network.

The process of authentication involves the following steps:

Step 1.   The client associates with an AP.

Step 2.   The client receives an authentication request.

Step 3.   The client returns an authentication response.

Step 4.   The client receives an association request.

Step 5.   The client sends an association response.

After open authentication takes place, either side can begin the 802.1x process. During this time, the "port" is still blocked for user traffic, and the following happens:

1. The supplicant sends credentials to the authenticator.
2. The AP sends the authentication information to the server via a RADIUS packet.
3. RADIUS traffic returns from the authentication server and is forwarded by the AP back to the client.
4. During the communication, the client and the AP derive unique session keys.
5. The RADIUS server sends an access success message back to the client, along with a session WEP key.
6. The AP keeps the session WEP key to use between the AP and itself.
7. The AP sends the session WEP key, along with a broadcast/multicast WEP key, to the client.
8. The client and AP can use the session WEP keys to encrypt traffic.

The AP keeps the session WEP key so that it can encrypt traffic between the AP and the client protecting the connection. The AP sends a broadcast/multicast WEP key because each session WEP key is unique. So if the client were to use it to encrypt a broadcast or multicast, only the AP would be able to see it.

The EAP Process

Now that you understand the 802.1x process, it's good to remind you at this point that 802.1x is nothing more than a framework. 802.1x does not define how the user credentials are sent, only that they are sent.

EAP controls how the user credentials are sent under the premise that no matter what EAP method you use, they will all use the same process. It involves the following steps:

Step 1.   The client requests access.

Step 2.   The client is queried for its identity.

Step 3.   The client provides the proof.

Step 4.   The client gets an answer from the server.

Figure 17-9 illustrates the EAP process.

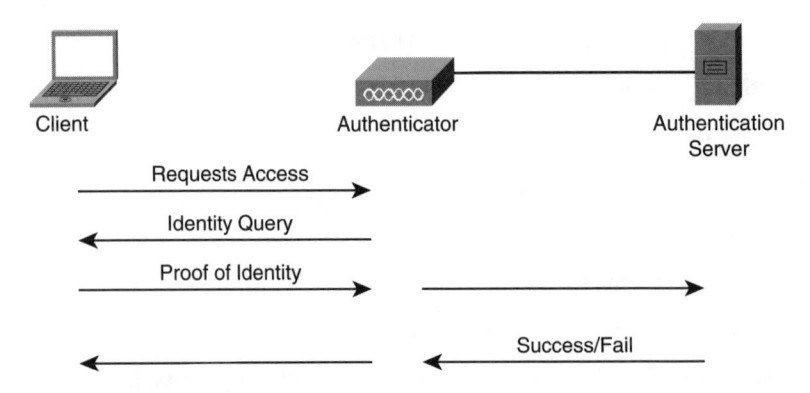

Figure 17-9   *EAP Process*

The Authentication Server

The authentication server can be external and can be a Cisco Secure Access Control Server (ACS) or perhaps a Free RADIUS server. It really doesn't matter what you use as an authentication server, as long as it supports the EAP method configured on the controller and used by the supplicant and AP. You need to define the location of the RADIUS server in the interface of the controller. To do this, choose **SECURITY > RADIUS Authentication Servers > New**, as shown in Figure 17-10.

When you define the RADIUS server, enter the server's IP address and the shared secret (a predefined passphrase that you determine and configure) to be used with the server. Then click **Next**.

You see the server listed on the RADIUS Authentication Servers page, as shown in Figure 17-11.

The next step in enabling the 802.1x authentication is to define the EAP method, as described in the following sections.

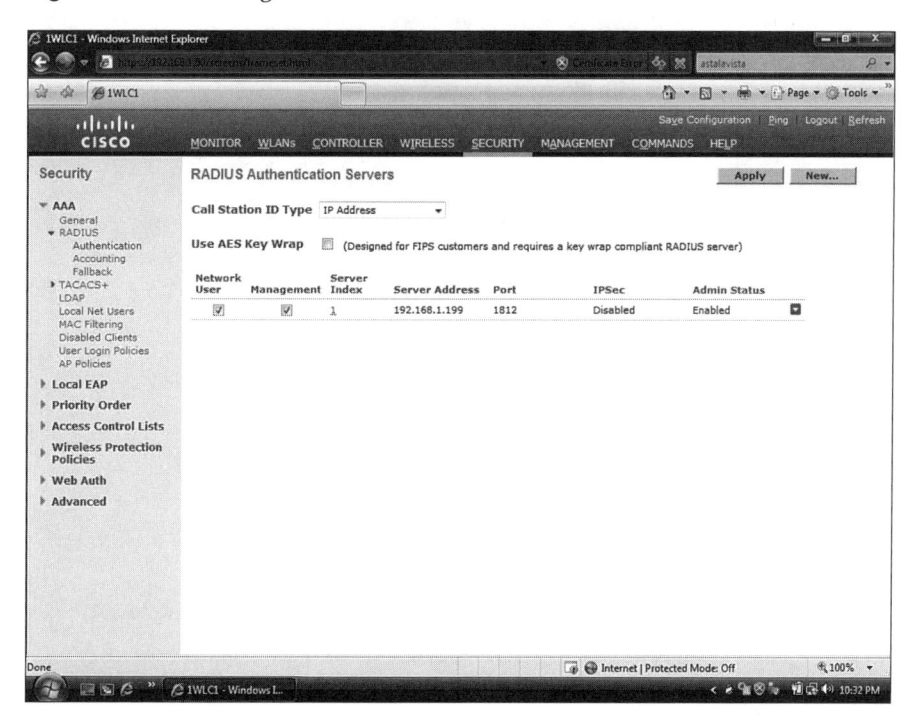

Figure 17-10 *Adding a RADIUS Server*

Figure 17-11 *List of RADIUS Servers*

EAP-TLS

Extensible Authentication Protocol-Transport Layer Security (EAP-TLS) is a commonly used EAP method for wireless networks. In EAP-TLS, a certificate must be installed on both the authentication server and the supplicant. For this reason, it is considered one of the most secure methods available. This would require both client and server key pairs to be generated first and then signed by a CA server. The communication used by EAP-TLS is similar to SSL encryption; however, TLS is considered the successor to SSL. EAP-TLS establishes an encrypted tunnel in which a user certificate is sent inside it.

Note: EAP-TLS is defined in RFC 2716.

Figure 17-12 shows the process of EAP-TLS.

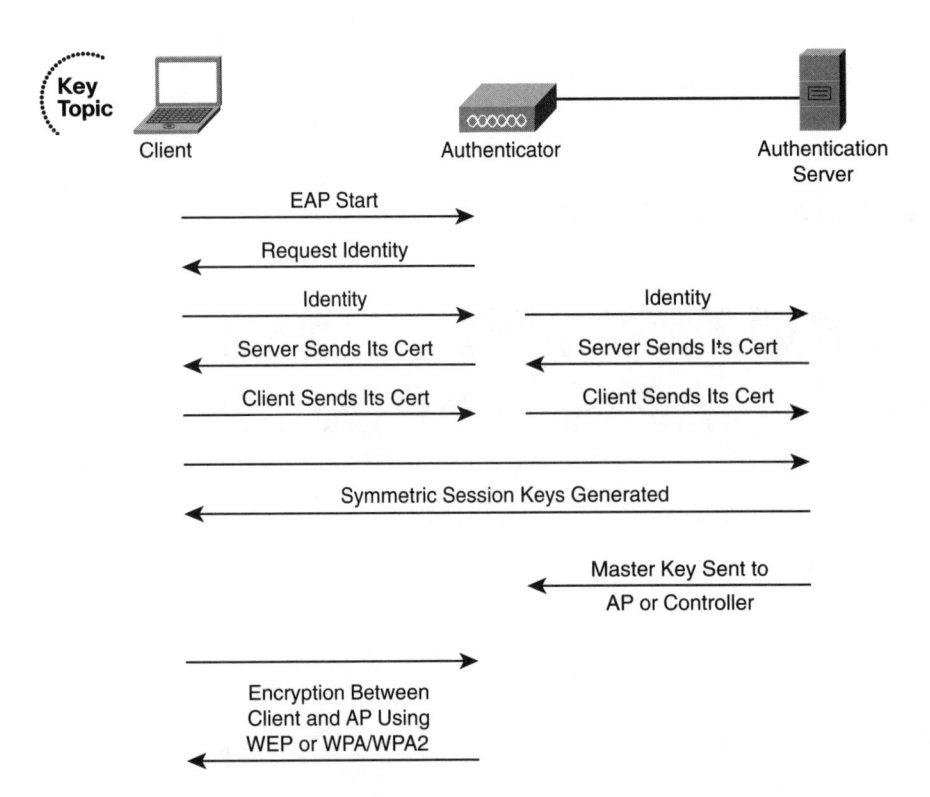

Figure 17-12   *EAP-TLS Process*

As you can see, the process begins with an EAP Start message. Next, the AP requests the client's identity. The client responds with its identity, and this is sent via EAP over RADIUS to the authentication server. The authentication server sends its certificate, and the client sends its certificate, thus proving their identity to each other. Next, symmetric session keys (also called master session keys) are created. The authentication server sends the master session key to the AP or controller to be used for either WEP or WPA/WPA2 encryption between the AP and the client. You configure EAP-TLS in the same location as WEP by selecting 802.1x in the Layer 2 security drop-down (refer to Figure 17-6). The EAP method is between the server and the client, so the AP really doesn't care. You simply select 802.1x.

EAP-FAST

Extensible Authentication Protocol-Flexible Authentication via Secure Tunnel (EAP-FAST) is a protocol that was developed by Cisco Systems. Its purpose was to address weaknesses in Lightweight Extensible Authentication Protocol (LEAP), another Cisco-developed EAP method. The concept of EAP-FAST is similar to EAP-TLS; however, EAP-FAST does not use PKI. Instead, EAP-FAST uses a strong shared secret key called a Protected Access Credential (PAC) that is unique on every client.

EAP-FAST negotiation happens in two phases, phase 1 and phase 2, but it is during phase 0 that the PAC is provisioned. After the PAC has been distributed, phase 1 can happen. In phase 1, the AAA server and the client establish a TLS tunnel after authenticating each other using the PAC. After phase 1 establishes the secure TLS tunnel, phase 2 authenticates the user to the AAA server using another EAP method, with either passwords or generic token cards.

Figure 17-13 shows the details of EAP-FAST negotiation using generic token card authentication for the user.

EAP-FAST negotiation occurs as follows:

1. The client sends an EAPoL start to the AP.
2. The AP, which is the authenticator, sends back an EAP Identity Request Message.
3. The client sends a response to the authenticator. It is forwarded to the authentication server (AAA server) in a RADIUS packet.
4. The authentication server sends an EAP-FAST start message that includes an Authority ID (A-ID).
5. The client sends a PAC based on the received A-ID. The client also sends a *PAC Opaque* reply to the server. The PAC Opaque is a variable-length field that can be interpreted only by the authentication server. The PAC Opaque is used to validate the client's credentials.
6. The authentication server decrypts the PAC Opaque using a master key that was used to derive the PAC key. The authentication server sends an EAP-TLS Server hello along with the *Cipher Trust Protocol Set.*
7. If the keys match, a TLS tunnel is established, with the client sending a confirmation.
8. The server sends an identity request inside the TLS tunnel using a protocol such as Extensible Authentication Protocol-Generic Token Card (EAP-GTC).
9. The client sends an authentication response.
10. The server sends a Pass or Fail message. The Pass message indicates that the client is successfully authenticated.

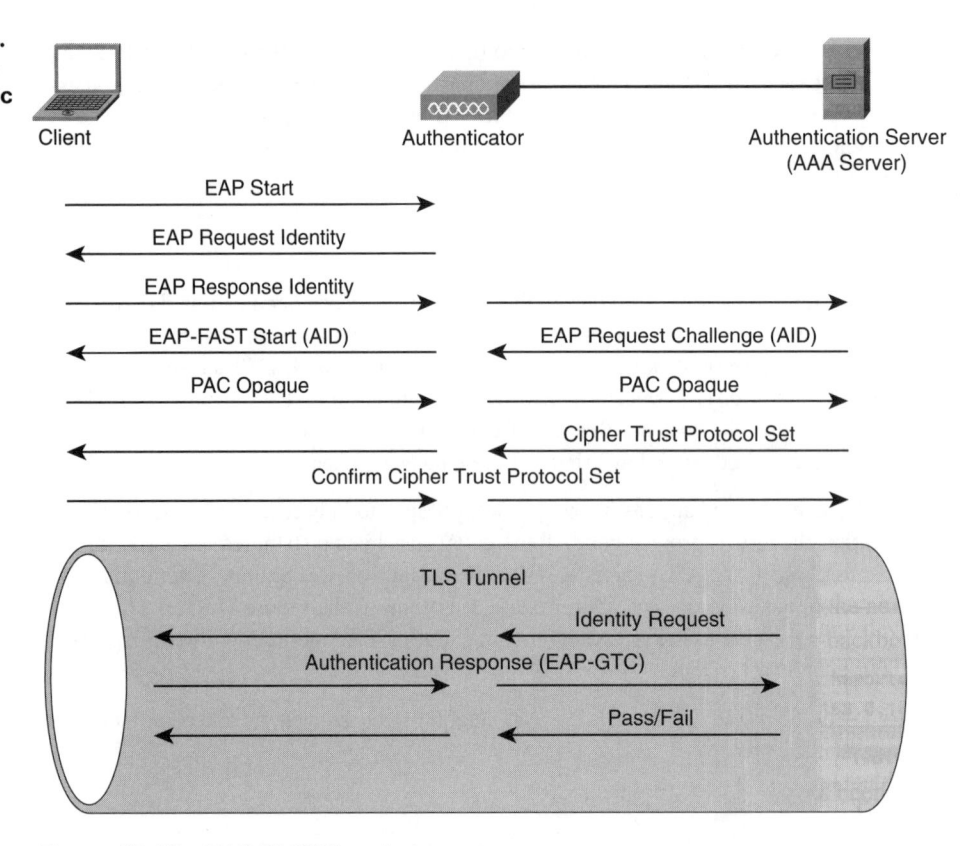

Figure 17-13 *EAP-FAST Negotiation*

PEAP

As you've seen with EAP-TLS, certificates are required on both the client and the server. With EAP-FAST, no certificates are required; rather, the PAC takes care of things. With Protected EAP (PEAP), only a server-side certificate is used. This server-side certificate is used to create a tunnel, and then the real authentication takes place inside. The PEAP method was jointly developed by Cisco Systems, Microsoft, and RSA. PEAP uses Microsoft Challenge Handshake Authentication Protocol version 2 (MS-CHAPv2) or Generic Token Card (GTC) to authenticate the user inside an encrypted tunnel.

To authenticate to Microsoft Windows Active Directory, you would use MS-CHAPv2.

Figure 17-14 shows the PEAP process.

In PEAP, the following occurs:

1. The client sends an EAPoL start, and the authenticator returns a request for identity. This is similar to the other EAP methods.
2. The client returns its identity, and it is forwarded to the AAA server.
3. The AAA server sends a server certificate and begins establishing a TLS tunnel.
4. The client returns a premaster secret.

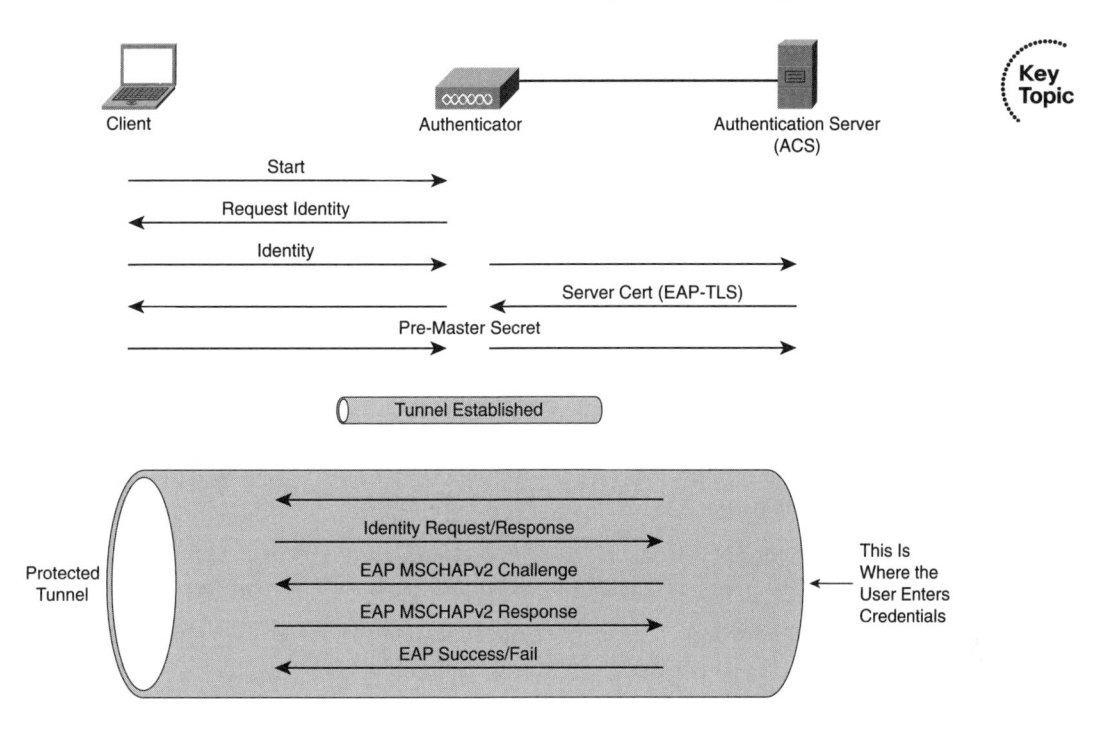

Figure 17-14   *PEAP Process*

5. The tunnel is established.

6. The AAA server sends an identity request to the client.

7. The AAA client sends an identity response.

8. The server sends an EAP-MS-CHAPv2 challenge.

9. The client enters credentials into a popup, and that is sent back as an EAP-MS-CHAPv2 response.

10. The server returns a pass or fail. If it's a pass, the user can send traffic.

LEAP

Lightweight Extensible Authentication Protocol (LEAP) gets honorable mention here mainly because it is a Cisco EAP method that is still seen in 802.11b networks. LEAP is vulnerable to an offline exploit, and you should avoid it if possible. LEAP uses a proprietary algorithm to create the initial session key.

Authentication and Encryption

Now that you understand some of the methods used to authenticate users, it's time to explore some encryption methods. The beginning of this chapter discussed WEP. The problem with WEP is that it can be broken easily. Therefore, other methods have been established in an effort to provide more strength in encryption. In the following sections, you will learn about Wi-Fi Protected Access (WPA) and Wi-Fi Protected Access 2 (WPA2).

WPA Overview

WPA was introduced in 2003 by the Wi-Fi Alliance as a replacement for WEP. WPA uses Temporal Key Integrity Protocol (TKIP) to automatically change the keys. TKIP still uses RC4; it just improves how it's done. This is a major improvement over static WEP. WPA can optionally support Advanced Encryption Standard (AES), but it's not mandatory. WPA is based on 802.11i draft version 3. WEP uses RC4 encryption, which is very weak. The better alternative was to use AES encryption, but that would have required an equipment upgrade. To avoid an equipment upgrade, WPA was developed to use TKIP and a larger IV than WEP. This would make it more difficult to guess the keys while not requiring new hardware. Instead, you could simply perform a firmware upgrade in most cases.

WPA offers two authentication modes:

■ **Enterprise mode:** Enterprise mode WPA requires an authentication server. RADIUS is used for authentication and key distribution, and TKIP is used with the option of AES available as well.

■ **Personal mode:** Personal mode WPA uses preshared keys, making it the weaker option, but the one that is most likely to be seen in a home environment.

Figure 17-15 shows the process of WPA authentication.

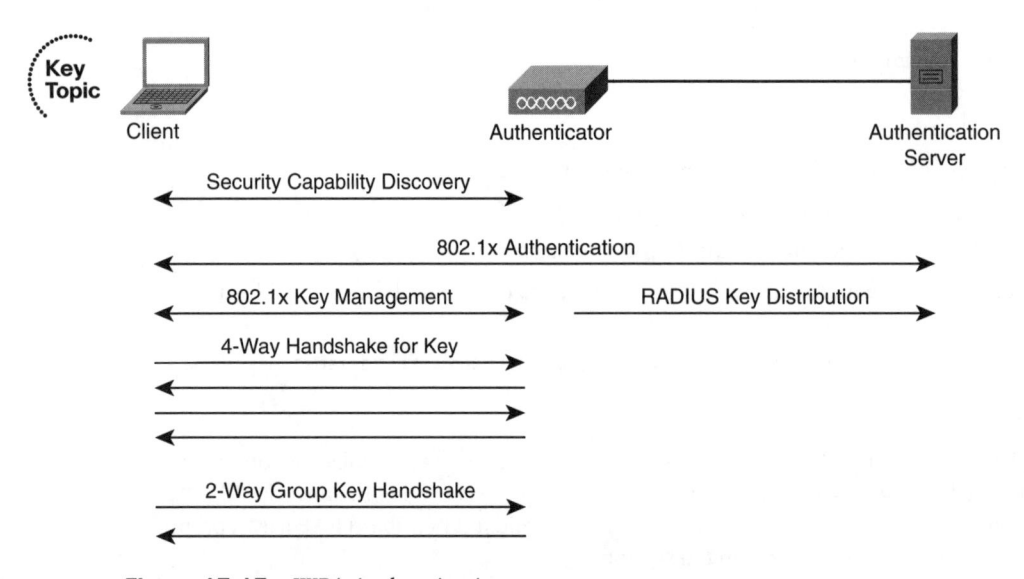

Figure 17-15   *WPA Authentication*

At the beginning of negotiations, the client and AP must agree on security capabilities. After the two agree on the same level of security, the 802.1x process starts. This is the standard 802.1x process, as outlined previously. After successful 802.1x authentication, the authentication server derives a master key and sends it to the AP. The same key is derived from the client. Now the client and the AP have the same *Pairwise Master Key (PMK)*, which will last for the duration of the session.

Next, a four-way handshake occurs (see Figure 17-16), in which the client and authenticator communicate and a new key called a *Pairwise Transient Key (PTK)* is derived. This key
confirms the PMK between the two, establishes a temporal key to be used for message
encryption, authenticates the negotiated parameters, and creates keying material for the
next phase, called the two-way group key handshake.

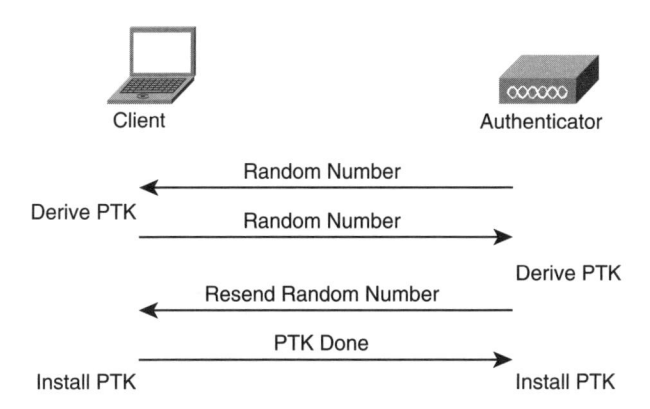

Figure 17-16   *WPA Four-Way Handshake*

When the two-way group key handshake occurs, the client and authenticator negotiate
the *Group Transient Key (GTK)*, which is used to decrypt broadcast and multicast transmissions.

In Figure 17-16, you can see that the AP first generates a random number and sends it to
the client. The client then uses a common passphrase along with this random number to
derive a key that is used to encrypt data to the AP. The client then sends its own random
number to the AP, along with a *Message Integrity Code (MIC)*, which is used to ensure
that the data is not tampered with. The AP generates a key used to encrypt unicast traffic
to the client. To validate, the AP sends the random number again, encrypted using the derived key. A final message is sent, indicating that the temporal key (TK) is in place on both
sides.

The two-way handshake that exchanges the group key involves the generation of a *Group
Master Key (GMK)*, usually by way of a random number. After the AP generates the
GMK, it generates a group random number. This is used to generate a *Group Temporal
Key (GTK)*. The GTK provides a group key and a MIC. This key changes when it times out
or when a client leaves the network.

To configure WPA, set the Layer 2 security method by choosing **WLANs > Edit**. Then
select the Security tab and choose **WPA+WPA2** from the drop-down, as shown in Figure
17-17. To allow WPA, ensure that TKIP is selected. This is automatically done for you
when you select the **WPA Policy** check box.

WPA2 Overview

WPA2, as its name implies, is the second attempt at WPA. WPA was not designed to be
just a firmware upgrade; instead, you might need new hardware to use it. The reason for

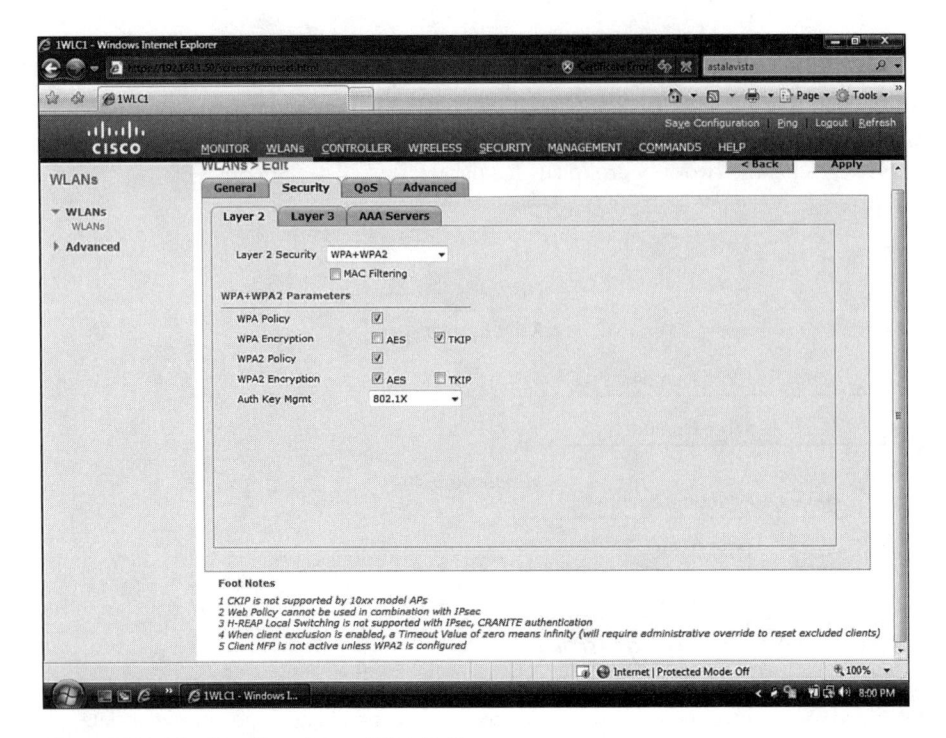

Figure 17-17   *Configuring a WPA Policy*

the more-capable hardware requirement is that WPA2 was designed to use AES encryption. WPA was designed based on the 802.11a draft but was released in 2003, whereas 802.11i was released in 2004. By the time 802.11i was ratified, it had added more support for 802.1x methods and AES/CCMP for encryption. The Wi-Fi Alliance then released WPA2 to be compatible with the 802.11i standard.

It was mentioned that AES is used for encryption. Advanced Encryption Standard-Cipher Block Chaining Message Authentication Code Protocol (AES/CCMP) still uses the IV and MIC, but the IV increases after each block of cipher.

Comparing WPA to WPA2, you can see that

- WPA mandates TKIP, and AES is optional.

- WPA2 mandates AES and doesn't allow TKIP.

- WPA allows AES in its general form.

- WPA2 only allows the AES/CCMP variant.

- With WPA2, key management allows keys to be cached to allow for faster connections.

To configure WPA2, from the **WLANs > Edit** page, select the **WPA2 Policy** option. Then select either **AES** and **TKIP** or just **AES** as the default value, as shown in Figure 17-18. Then select the authentication key management option; the choices are 802.1x, CCKM, PSK, and 802.1X+CCKM.

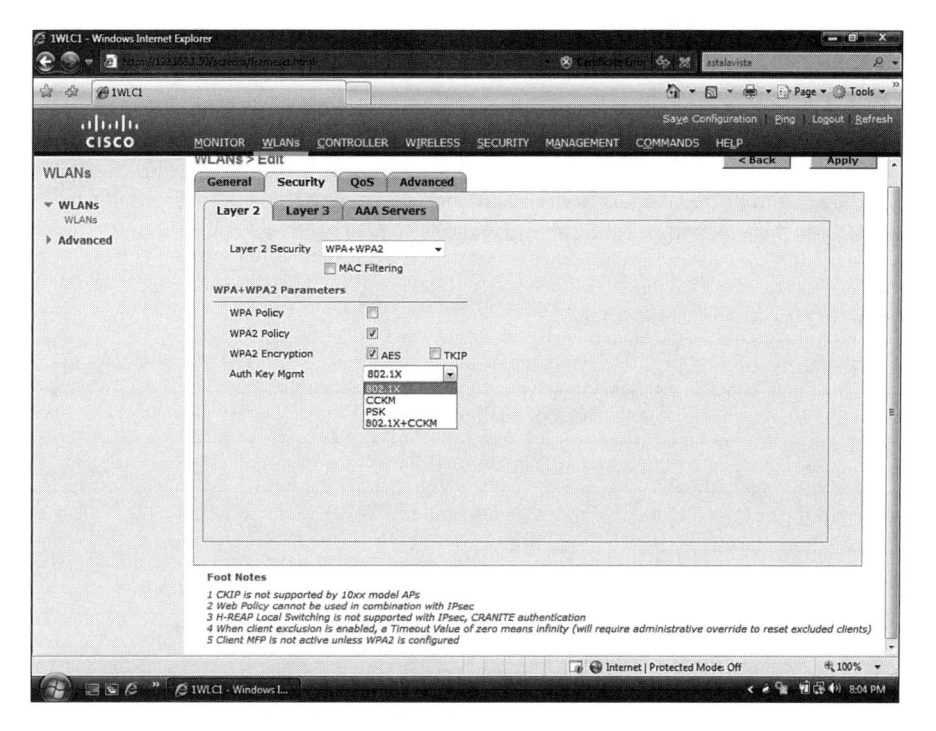

Figure 17-18   *Configuring a WPA2 Policy*

Exam Preparation Tasks

Review All the Key Topics

Review the most important topics from this chapter, denoted with the Key Topic icon. Table 17-2 lists these key topics and the page number where each one can be found.

Table 17-2   *Key Topics for Chapter 17*

Key Topic Item	Description	Page Number
Figure 17-1	Client MFP in action	333
Figure 17-2	Configuring MFP	333
Paragraph from the section "Pre-shared Key Authentication with Wired Equivalent Privacy"	Steps describing the WEP process	334
Figure 17-5	Configuring WEP	337
Figure 17-12	The EAP-TLS process	342
Figure 17-13	The EAP-FAST process	344
Figure 17-14	The PEAP process	345
Figure 17-15	The WPA process	346
Figure 17-18	Configuring WPA2 policy	349

Complete the Tables and Lists from Memory

Print a copy of Appendix B, "Memory Tables" (found on the CD) or at least the section for this chapter, and complete the tables and lists from memory. Appendix C, "Memory Tables Answer Key," also on the CD, includes completed tables and lists to check your work.

Definition of Key Terms

Define the following key terms from this chapter, and check your answers in the glossary:

Management Frame Protection (MFP), Infrastructure MFP, Message Integrity Check (MIC), Frame Check Sequence (FCS), Client MFP, Initialization Vector (IV), supplicant, authentication server, authenticator, Extensible Authentication Protocol (EAP), Extensible Authentication Protocol-Transport Layer Security (EAP-TLS), Extensible Authentication Protocol-Flexible Authentication via Secure Tunnel (EAP-FAST), Protected EAP (PEAP), Microsoft Challenge Handshake Authentication Protocol version 2 (MS-CHAPv2), Generic Token Card (GTC), Lightweight Extensible Authentication Protocol (LEAP), Wi-Fi Protected Access (WPA), Wi-Fi Protected Access 2 (WPA2), Temporal Key Integrity Protocol (TKIP), Advanced Encryption Standard (AES), Pairwise Master Key (PMK), Pairwise Transient Key (PTK), Group Transient Key (GTK), Message Integrity Code (MIC), Group Master Key (GMK), Group Temporal Key (GTK)

References

Infrastructure Management Frame Protection (MFP) with WLC and LAP Configuration Example: http://tinyurl.com/5zbe2o

This chapter covers the following subjects:

Introduction to the WCS: An introduction to the Wireless Control System (WCS).

Installing and Configuring the WCS: An overview of how to install the WCS, log in, and perform basic tasks.

Administration Options in the WCS: A discussion of various options involved in administering the WCS.

Adding Controllers to the WCS: How to add controllers to the WCS and manage them in the WCS.

Maps and APs in the WCS: Viewing and working with maps and APs in the WCS interface.

Monitoring with the WCS: Using WCS to monitor the wireless network.

CHAPTER 18

Enterprise Wireless Management with the WCS and the Location Appliance

In the management scheme of things, the design of the Cisco Unified Wireless Networking (CUWN) enables management of lightweight access points (AP) via a controller. This central form of management allows for consistent policy among all devices from, the controller. However, when a company scales beyond the scope of management with a single controller, the Wireless Control System (WCS) steps in. In addition, the Cisco Wireless Location Appliance can help keep things under control. This chapter is a brief overview of the WCS, how it is installed, how it is managed, how it manages controllers, and how it manages APs.

You should do the "Do I Know This Already?" quiz first. If you score 80 percent or higher, you might want to skip to the section "Exam Preparation Tasks." If you score below 80 percent, you should spend the time reviewing the entire chapter. Refer to Appendix A, "Answers to the 'Do I Know This Already?' Quizzes," to confirm your answers.

"Do I Know This Already?" Quiz

The "Do I Know This Already?" quiz helps you determine your level of knowledge of this chapter's topics before you begin. Table 18-1 details the major topics discussed in this chapter and their corresponding quiz questions.

Table 18-1 *"Do I Know This Already?" Section-to-Question Mapping*

Foundation Topics Section	Questions
Introduction to the WCS	1–3
Installing and Configuring the WCS	4–8
Administration Options in the WCS	9–12
Adding Controllers to the WCS	13–19
Maps and APs in the WCS	20–25
Monitoring with the WCS	26

1. What are three benefits of the WCS?

   a. Wireless planning

   b. Wireless design

   c. Wireless management

   d. Wireless RF tagging

2. The Cisco Wireless Location Appliance can provide real-time tracking of up to how many clients?

   a. 1500

   b. 2500

   c. 3500

   d. 5000

3. WCS licensing can enable up to how many supported APs?

   a. 5500

   b. 2500

   c. 2000

   d. 5000

4. On which two operating systems can the WCS be installed?

   a. Windows Server

   b. Red Hat Linux

   c. Solaris 9

   d. Ubuntu Linux

5. Following recommended hardware requirements, you will be able to support how many controllers in a single WCS?

   a. 500

   b. 2500

   c. 5000

   d. 250

6. What type of web server does the WCS run?

   a. IIS

   b. Apache

   c. Sun Java Web Server

   d. A Proprietary Web Service

7. What action can you take if IIS is running on the server where you are installing the WCS? (Choose all that apply.)

   a. Nothing; they do not conflict.

   b. Just change to the port where you used the WCS.

   c. Disable the IIS Server.

   d. Uninstall IIS.

8. What is the first action when accessing the WCS for the first time?

   a. Enter a license key.

   b. Add a controller.

   c. Save the configuration.

   d. Archive the server.

9. What is the first page you come to upon logging into the WCS?

   a. WCS Start

   b. WCS Home

   c. WCS Summary

   d. WCS Monitor

10. The Client tab provides information about which of the following? (Choose all that apply.)

   a. Top APs by client count

   b. Clients that are associated

   c. Security configuration of the AP

   d. Rogue AP counts

11. Which menu allows you to add users of the WCS system?

   a. **Administration > AAA**

   b. **Configuration > Users**

   c. **Authentication > AAA**

   d. **Monitor > AAA**

12. Logging options can be changed in which menu?

   a. **Administration > SNMP > Logging**

   b. **Administration > Syslog**

   c. **Configuration > Logging**

   d. **Administration > Logging**

13. You can add a controller to the WCS through which menu?

   a.   Configure > Controllers

   b.   Controllers > Add

   c.   Administration > Controllers > Add

   d.   Management > Controllers

14. What are the two ways to add a controller to the WCS?

   a.   Use a CSV file

   b.   Use SNMP discovery

   c.   Use Device Info

   d.   Import from CiscoWorks DCR

15. APs are configured from which menu?

   a.   Configure > APs

   b.   Configure > Controllers > APs

   c.   Configure > Access Points

   d.   You do not configure APs, just controllers. APs automatically synch their config-
            uration with that of the controller.

16. How can you verify that the configuration on the controller is consistent with the in-
       formation in the WCS database?

   a.   Use the Compare tool.

   b.   Use the Sync button.

   c.   Use the Audit Config page.

   d.   You cannot verify this information.

17. You want to configure general settings for a controller once and then apply those set-
       tings to all the controllers in your network. This is a perfect opportunity to use what
       feature of the WCS?

   a.   Copy/Paste

   b.   TFTP

   c.   FTP

   d.   Templates

18. You can use the WCS templates only for controllers. True or False?

   a.   True

   b.   False

19. Auto provisioning relies on which DHCP option?

   a.   66

   b.   53

    c.   20

    d.   150

20. Which of the following WCS menu options enables you to find a list of maps?

    a.   Monitor > Maps

    b.   Configure > Maps

    c.   Administration > Maps

    d.   WCS > Maps

21. The WCS maps consist of which of the following elements? (Choose all that apply.)

    a.   Campus

    b.   Building

    c.   Floor

    d.   Room

22. When you create a map, what important characteristics should you add? (Choose all that apply.)

    a.   Obstructions

    b.   Walls

    c.   Doors

    d.   People

23. By adding certain elements to the WCS maps, you aid which process?

    a.   RF modeling

    b.   RF surveys

    c.   Site survey

    d.   Imaging

24. Planning mode lets you generate heat maps of theoretical APs placed on your map. The heat map then lets you generate what?

    a.   A new map

    b.   A summary of equipment used

    c.   A proposal of equipment required and deployment locations

    d.   Log messages in the WCS

25. Which of the following is a valuable tool accessible from the Monitoring menu?

    a.   Site survey

    b.   Reset controllers

    c.   Client troubleshooting

    d.   SNMP traps

Foundation Topics

Introduction to the WCS

The Cisco WCS is a browser-based software application that offers the capability to manage multiple controller deployments through a single interface. Benefits of the WCS include the following:

■ Wireless planning

■ Wireless design

■ Wireless management

The WCS is based on a licensing system. Licensing enables single-server deployments of up to 500 APs to 2500 APs being supported. You can even obtain a 30-day demo license that is fully functional for up to 10 APs.

The Cisco Wireless Location Appliance, accessed via the WCS interface, provides mapping of clients and assistance in enforcing security policies. Using the Location Appliance with the WCS can provide much information to network administrators, including the following:

■ Real-time tracking of up to 2500 clients

■ Historical information

■ RF fingerprinting

■ A single point of management

Models include the WCS Base and the WCS Base plus location. You can find detailed product information at http://www.cisco.com/go/wireless.

Installing and Configuring the WCS

The WCS has two deployment possibilities: a Linux-based deployment and a Windows-based deployment. In large deployments, Cisco recommends the Linux-based deployment.

The requirements for the Linux-based deployment are as follows:

■ Red Hat Enterprise ES/AS Linux Release 4 (the Cisco WCS can be installed as a service under Linux)

■ Intel Xeon Quad 3.15-GHz CPU

■ 8-GB RAM, 200-GB HD

Meeting these requirements allows for support of 3000 APs and 250 controllers and really cannot be stressed enough. If you want to be happy with the deployment, make sure you meet the Cisco recommendations on the machine.

In a smaller deployment, you can use the following:

- Windows Server 2003

- Pentium 4/3.06 GHz (minimum) 2-GB RAM, 30-GB hard drive

- Intel dual-core 3.2-GHz CPU 4-GB RAM, 80-GB hard drive

With a deployment using these specifications, you can support up to 2000 APs and 150 controllers.

Other considerations should include the protocol traffic that the WCS uses to manage the controllers. This means you need to consider the transit path and any firewalls, IPS devices, and IOS firewall routers.

In addition to those ports, you need to allow HTTP port 80 and port 443, because the WCS runs an Apache web server, along with port 21 for FTP, port 69 for TFTP, and 162 for Simple Network Management Protocol (SNMP) traps.

The Java portion of the WCS uses ports 1299, 8009, 8456, and 8457. Table 18-2 provides a recap of these ports.

Table 18-2 *WCS Ports*

Key
Topic

Port	Use
HTTP: Configurable during install (80 by default)	Web access
HTTPS: Configurable during install (443 by default)	Secure web access
1315	Java
1299	Java
6789	—
8009	Java
8456	Java
8005	—
69	TFTP
21	FTP
162	SNMP traps
8457	—

The easiest way to obtain the WCS software is from Cisco.com, which means you need to log in to the Cisco website with valid credentials (a CCO account) and then download the software. Cisco provides a Quick Install guide for both Linux and Windows versions. The

CCNA Wireless exam focuses primarily on the Windows version, but you should view both versions on the Cisco website to see the entire process.

For a Windows-based installation, you simply launch the executable file and follow the prompts. The install takes you through several pages that relate to the web server, passwords, directories, and so on. The WCS first checks to see if it is already installed. If the WCS is already installed, and depending on the version, you might be able to upgrade rather than do a fresh install. It is always a good idea to back up the WCS prior to an upgrade. If you are performing a fresh install, you need to do the following:

- Accept the license agreement.

- Verify the server ports.

- Enter the passwords.

- Choose the FTP and TFTP root folders.

- Select whether this is a multihomed server (two NIC cards).

- Define the Install folder.

- Verify with a summary page.

- Wait for the installation to complete.

You can access the WCS locally by going to **Start > All Programs >** and then selecting the WCS group. The WCS is installed as a service, and the service should automatically start. You might encounter problems if the WCS and IIS are installed on the same machine, because both would try to secure port 80. To combat this issue, either make sure IIS is not installed prior to installing the WCS or shut down Internet Information Service (IIS). Open a web browser and browse to the IP address of the WCS server. Use the passwords that you defined during the setup process. After you are logged in, you see the main page of the WCS, called WCS Home. As Figure 18-1 illustrates, the WCS home page includes numerous tabs as well as some items that are commonly used for monitoring.

The first thing you want to do after the install and upon the first login is to add a license key to the WCS. The license key should be available in digital format. You need to select **Help > Licensing** and then browse to and upload the key. You cannot add controllers until you do this.

Administration Options in the WCS

In the WCS interface, you have tabs or horizontal menus across the top that access various configuration elements, including these:

- Monitor

- Reports

- Administration

Each of these menus cascade to drop-down submenus that you can access.

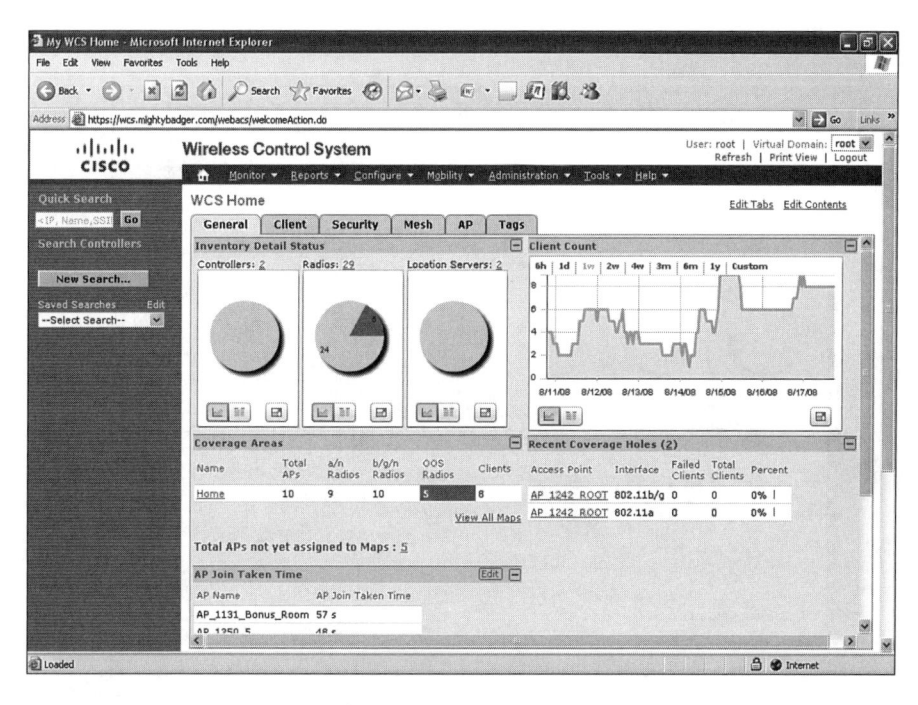

Figure 18-1 *The WCS Interface*

When you log in, the page you see is called the WCS Home, which has four primary tabs that we will discuss out of the six seen in Figure 18-2:

- **General:** Provides information about the inventory, the coverage, and the client count

- **Client:** Provides information about the top APs by client count, clients that are associated, and other information related to clients

- **Security:** Includes information about rogue APs, alarms, and attacks

- **Mesh:** Provides information about the signal-to-noise ratio (SNR) of the backhaul link and the node hop count

Figure 18-2 shows these tabs on the WCS home page.

The Administration drop-down menu provides access to control over the various background tasks that the WCS performs. This includes the logging settings, the system settings, and user preferences.

The Administration drop-down menu also enables configuration of AAA. To access AAA settings, go to **Administration > AAA**. Add users by going to **Administration > AAA > Users > Add Users**. To configure groups, go to **Administration > AAA > Groups**. To see a list of who is logging into the WCS, go to **Administration > AAA > Users > Audit Trail**. To change the WCS logging options, go to **Administration > Logging**.

Because the WCS tracks wireless networks, the volume of information can get overwhelming, and space can become an issue. To configure aggregation settings, go to

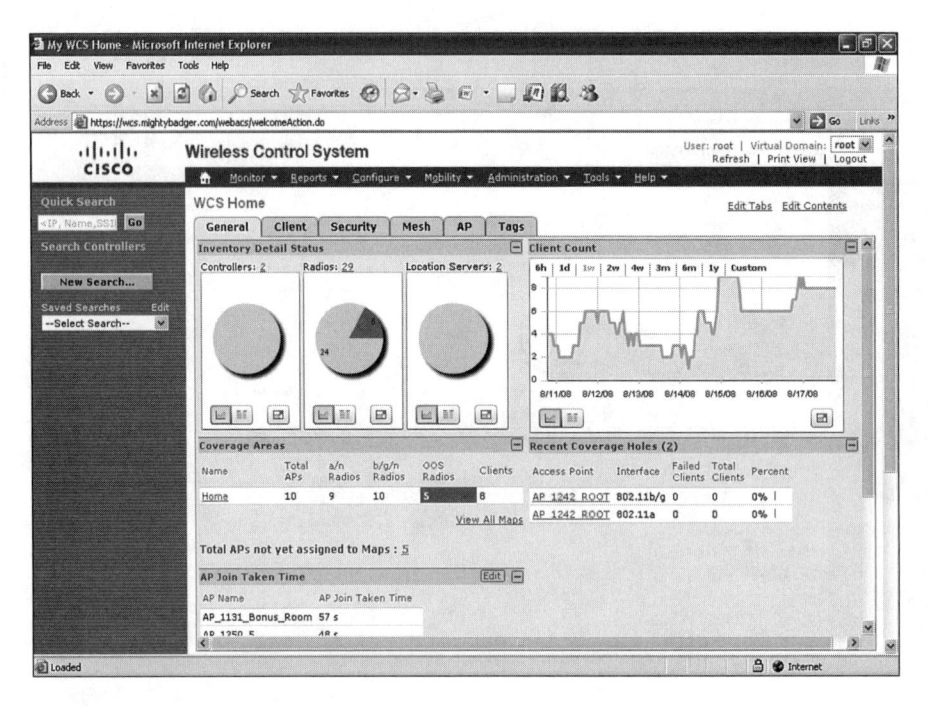

Figure 18-2 *WCS Home Page Tabs*

Administration > Settings > Data Management. You can also configure the WCS to send email to a user when an event is triggered. To configure the email preferences, go to **Administration > Settings > Mail Server**.

Adding Controllers to the WCS

To add controllers to the WCS, use the Configure tab. From there, you cannot only add controllers, but you can configure APs. You can also create templates here that allow the deployment of common configurations among multiple devices. To add controllers, browse to **Configure > Controllers**, as shown in Figure 18-3.

The Configure Controllers page summarizes all the controllers in the WCS and allows you to add controllers. Using the **Select a command** drop-down (seen in Figure 18-3), select **Add Controller**, and then select **GO**. This takes you to the configuration page shown in Figure 18-4.

Notice that the Add Format Type is configured for **Device Info**. The other option is **File**. You use the **File** option if you want to bring in several devices from a CSV file. When you add a controller to the WCS using the **Device Info** option, you use SNMP. You need to enter the IP address of the device as well as the SNMP version, retries, timeout in seconds, and community string. Click **OK** to apply. After you have added the controller, you can configure it on an individual basis. This is good, but the power of using the WCS comes in using templates. This is the second way you can configure the controller. The next section, "Working with Templates," provides more information.

Key Topic

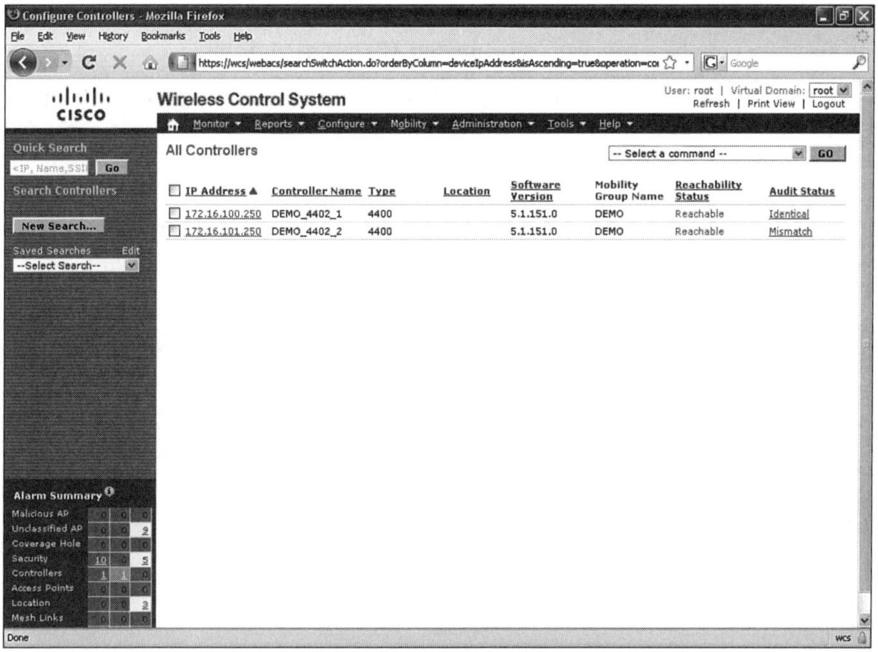

Figure 18-3 *Configuring Controllers in the WCS*

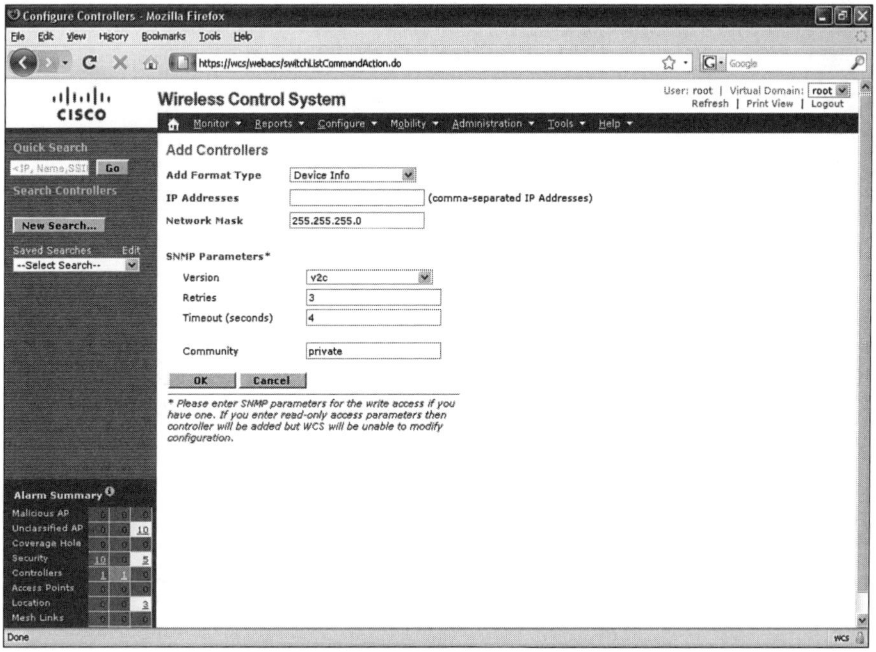

Figure 18-4 *Add Controller to the WCS*

You can also configure APs from the Configure menu by selecting **Configure > Access Points.** As with controllers, you can configure the APs using templates.

You now have the WCS, designed to manage many devices. It is important for the configuration on the controller to be the same as the configuration in the WCS database. To make sure all the configurations are consistent, you should run an audit regularly. You run an audit by going to **Configure > Controllers.** Select a controller and then, using the dropdown, choose **Audit Now** and click **Go.** Figure 18-5 shows the resulting Audit Report page.

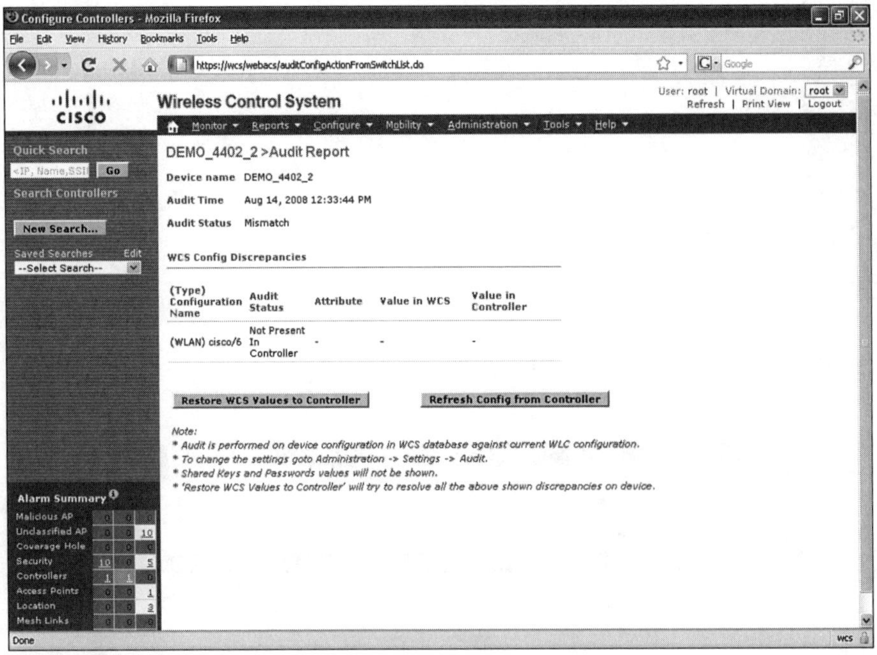

Figure 18-5   *Controller Audit Report*

Working with Templates

Key Topic

Everyone likes to save time, and templates can help with that. WCS templates allow administrators to save time by configuring them once and then applying them to more than one device.

To add templates, follow these steps:

Step 1.   Choose **Configure > Controller Templates.**

Step 2.   Choose **Add Template** from the **Select a command** drop-down menu and click **GO.**

Step 3.   Enter the template name.

Step 4.   Provide a description of the template.

Step 5.   Click **Save**.

You have several templates available. Some of the common ones include the following:

- Configure WLAN Templates

- Configure a RADIUS Authentication Template

- Configure a Local EAP General Template

- Configure a Local EAP Profile Template

- Configure an EAP-FAST Template

- Configure Access Control List Templates

- Configure a TFTP Server Template

- Configure a Telnet SSH Template

- Configure a Local Management User Template

- Configure Radio Templates

Again, the benefit is that you can save the template and apply it to multiple controllers.

You can apply a controller template to a controller by following these steps:

Step 1.   Go to **Configure > Controller Templates**.

Step 2.   Using the left sidebar menu, choose the category of templates to apply.

Step 3.   Select the box next to the template from the Template Name column that you want to apply to the controller. In Figure 18-6, you can see several WLAN templates.

Step 4.   Click the **Apply to Controllers** button. (You may need to scroll down to see it.)

Taking things a step further, you can create what is known as a configuration group. A *configuration group* is a way to apply configuration to many controllers as if they were one. The design here is for consistent configuration of a mobility group. A change in configuration changes all controllers in the group. You can also apply controller templates to a configuration group. You can access the configuration groups by selecting **Configure > Config Groups**. Figure 18-7 shows the Config Groups page. Notice that the group name **Config** is applied to one controller and 105 templates are applied to it. The 105 templates applied represent a great deal of manual configuration that was not necessary because templates were used.

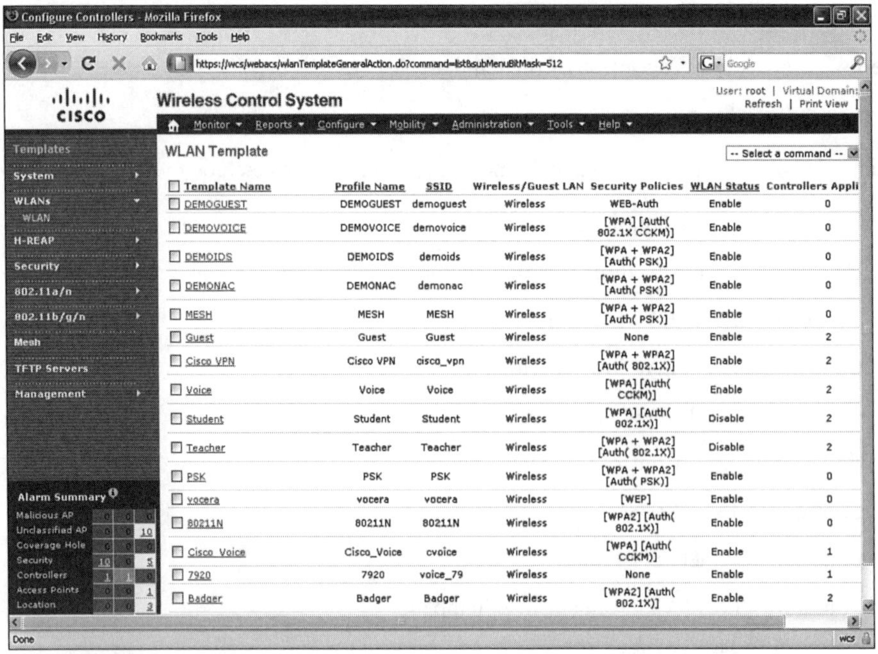

Figure 18-6 *WLAN Templates*

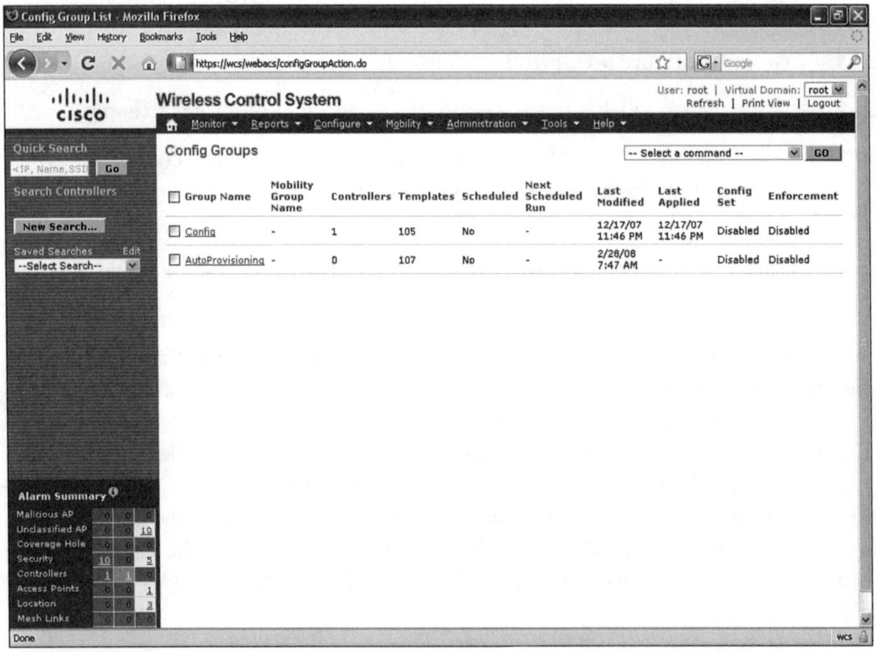

Figure 18-7 *Config Groups*

Auto Provisioning

You can configure auto provisioning to simplify deployments when you have many controllers. To set up auto provisioning, browse to **Configure > Auto Provisioning** to access the page shown in Figure 18-8.

Start by creating a filter to define which devices will be auto provisioned. To do this, use the **Select a command** drop-down and select **Add Filter**. Then click **Go**.

Next, select the desired filter properties.

After the filter is created, configure how the controller is detected on the network. You do this from the Auto Provisioning Setting page, the link for which you can find on the left side of the Auto Provisioning page. When you click on the Auto Provisioning Setting link, you are taken to the Auto Provisioning Primary Search Key Setting page, shown in Figure 18-9.

What happens when auto provisioning is configured? When a controller running version 5.0 or later is connected to the network for the first time, if it does not have a valid configuration, it first gets an IP address from a DHCP server. The DHCP server then returns through option 150, the IP address of a server with the configuration file of the controller. The server address is the WCS server.

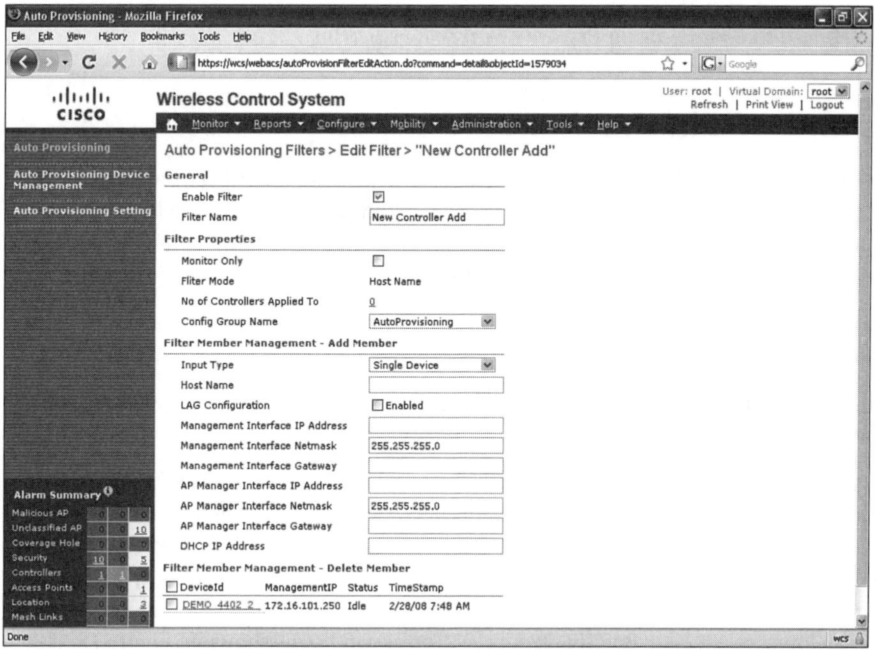

Figure 18-8   *Auto Provisioning*

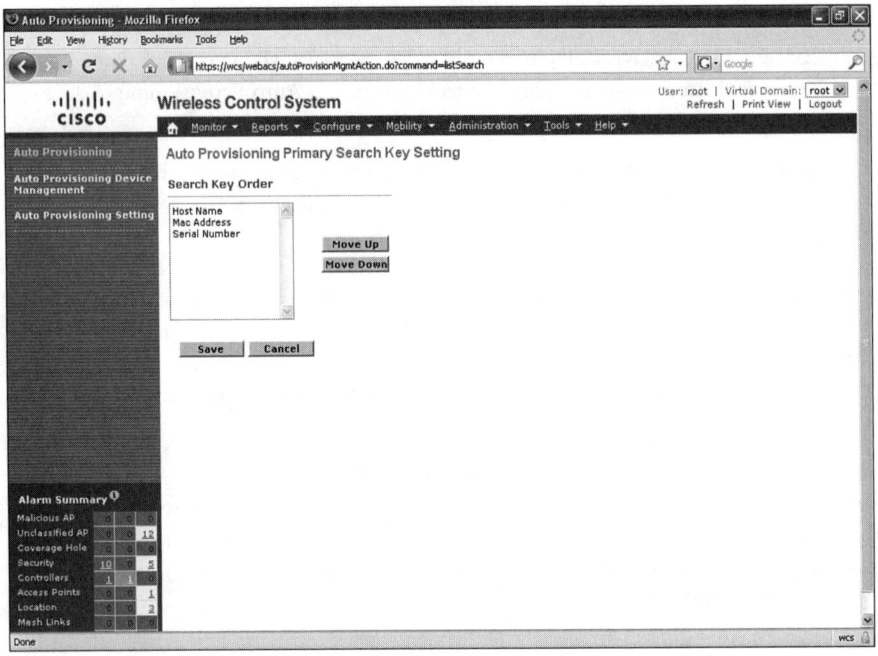

Figure 18-9 *Auto Provisioning Primary Search Key Setting Page*

Maps and APs in the WCS

Maps in the WCS are designed to give you a visual representation of the wireless network. Not only do maps help with monitoring after a deployment, but they help in the implementation and deployment process. You can use planning mode to determine how many APs you need in an area and where to place them.

To access the maps, browse to **Monitor > Maps**. From here you can see a list of maps, as illustrated in Figure 18-10.

You start by adding a building and then adding floors. After you have the building and floors, you add APs.

The maps begin in the context of a campus. To create a new campus, use the drop-down and select **New Campus**. Then click **GO**. This brings you to a page where you enter the campus name and contact and browse to the image file. After you have created the campus, it appears in the list of maps. You can now add a building to the campus; however, buildings do not necessarily need to be added to a campus. They can be standalone. To add a building, select **New Building** from the drop-down list, as shown in Figure 18-11.

Key Topic

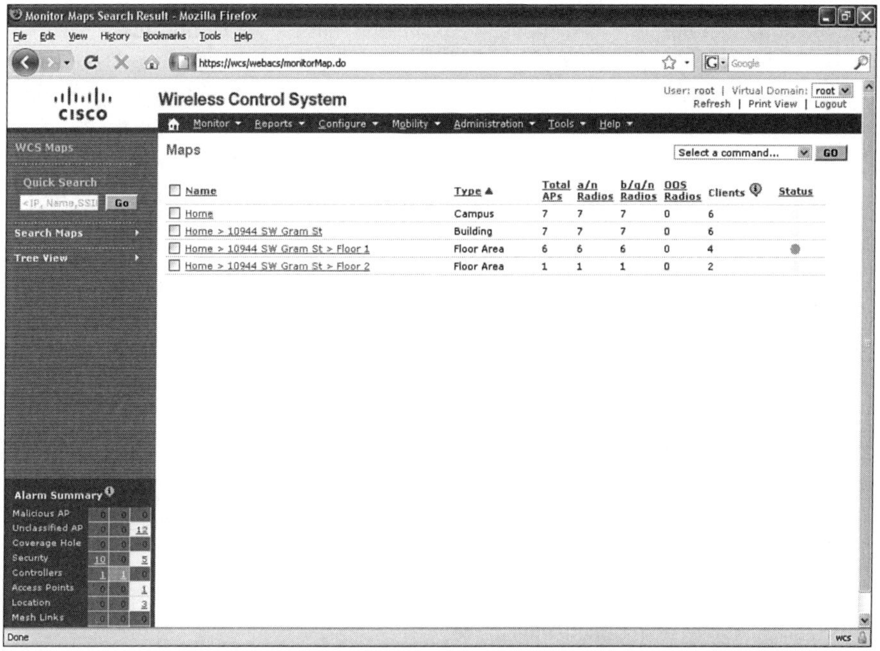

Figure 18-10 *Maps in the WCS*

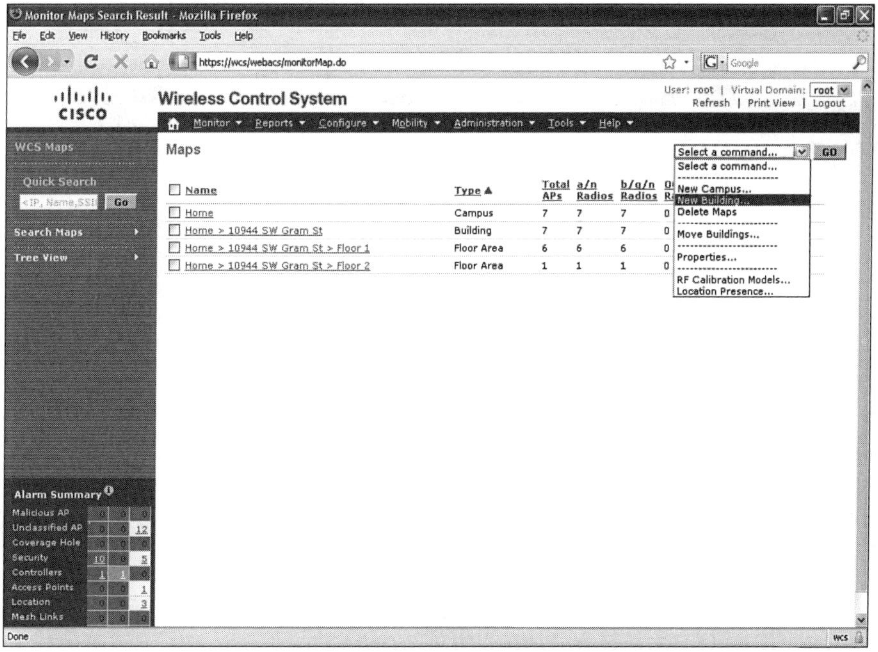

Figure 18-11 *Add Building*

Note: When adding buildings to a campus map, consider that the horizontal and vertical span should be larger than or the same size as any floors that you might add later. This can be a problem later when you build a map for the basement of a building and then work your way up to the first floor. If the first floor is larger than the basement, you cannot create the first floor. In fact, you cannot create any floor if it is larger than the basement. The WCS will not allow the larger level to then be added. You can find more information in the section "Adding and Using Maps" in the *Cisco Wireless Control System Configuration Guide, Release 4.1* at http://tinyurl.com/6f8apm.

When you add a building, you need to enter the following information:

■ Building name

■ Contact

■ Number of floors

■ Number of basements

■ Horizontal and vertical dimensions in feet

Figure 18-12 shows a two-floor building.

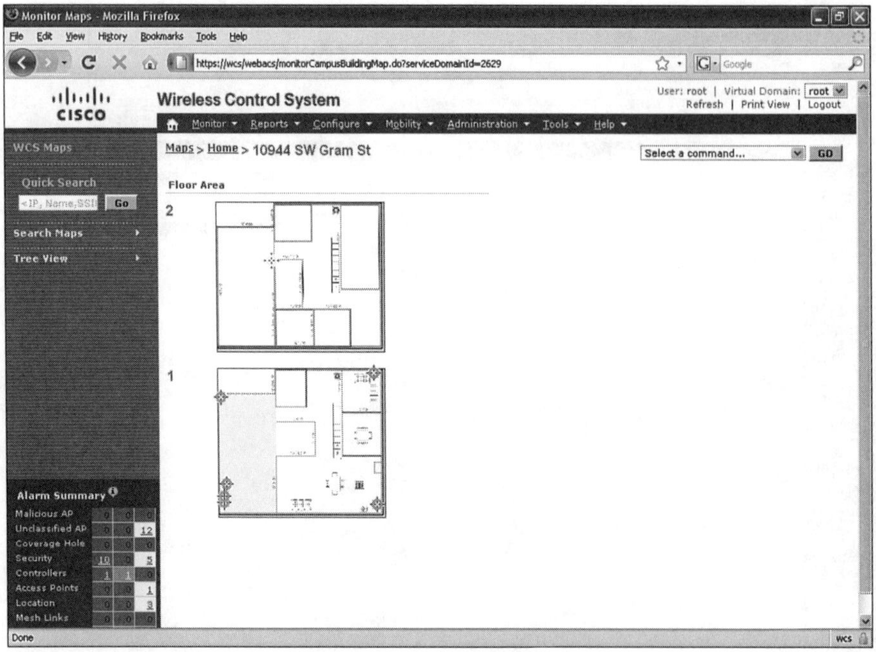

Figure 18-12   *Two Floor Building*

You can add a new floor area from the drop-down list. A floor area is what gives you a view of the environment and lets you add valuable information such as the floor type, the height, and the image file. Figure 18-13 shows this configuration page. The floor types include Cubes and Walled Offices, Drywall Office Only, and Outdoor Open Space. This is important because it assists the WCS with RF modeling.

Key
Topic

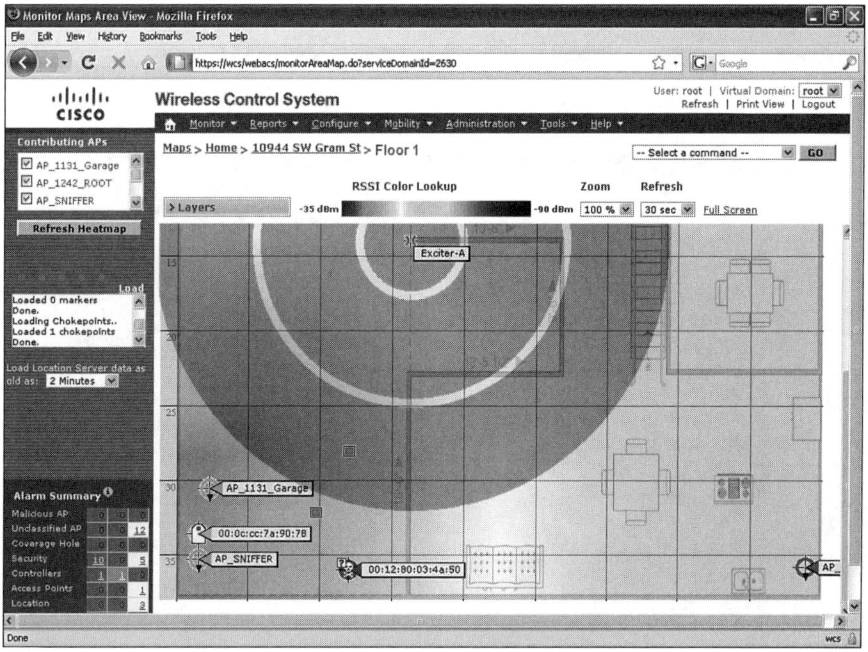

Figure 18-13   *Heat Maps in the WCS*

After you have created the floor area, you can add APs to it. As you can tell, each element is layered on top of the prior (for example, Campus > Building > Floor Area > AP). It is really a logical method. Now when you add the AP, take care in your accuracy. Make sure you add them as the correct AP type, antenna configuration, location, and so on. When you place each AP on the floor area, RF prediction can take place. RF prediction generates heat maps and includes APs, clients, and rogues.

When you create the map as an administrator, you add obstructions, walls, windows, and doors. This information as well as the placement of the APs is used for RF prediction. The usage of the heat map created by RF prediction is to accurately display coverage. You can click on elements of the map to get more information. Figure 18-13 shows a sample of a heat map.

You might be wondering what the difference is between the RF prediction and the site survey. It is simple really. A *site survey* is a measurement of a certain point in time. That point in time is when you did the site survey. The values you determine from the site survey can change as influences to RF are added to the area where you performed the site survey.

In contrast, the WCS *RF prediction* uses information entered in the map and the map editor to predict how the AP will react in the environment. The WCS can base its information on what you tell it the environment *will* look like.

Using the drop-down list, you can access the map editor, as shown in Figure 18-14.

The map editor loads as shown in Figure 18-15.

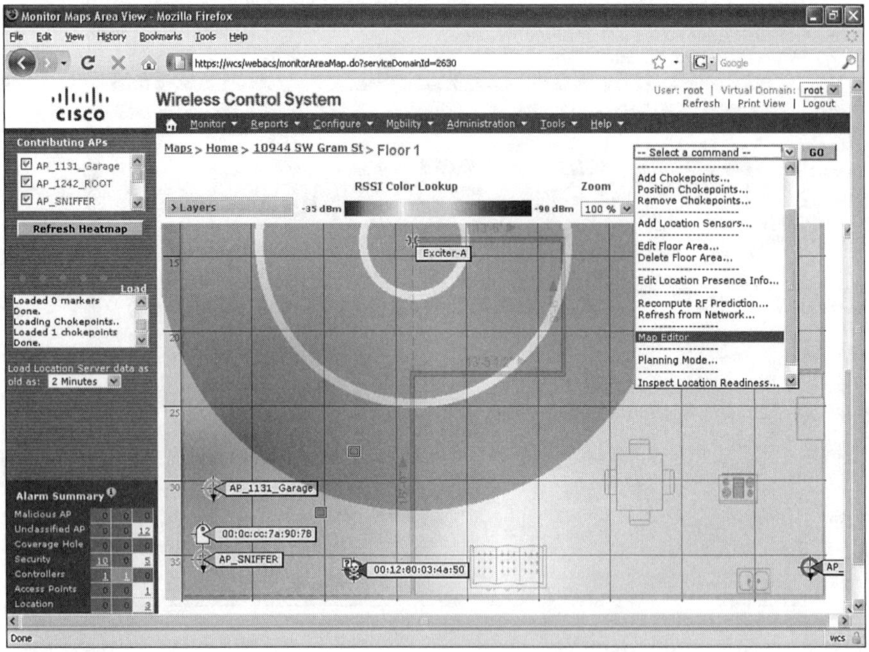

Figure 18-14 *Accessing the Map Editor*

Planning Mode

WCS Planning Mode lets you determine how many APs you need for a given coverage area. It places hypothetical APs on the map and lets you view the coverage area based on the placement of the hypothetical APs. From the **Monitor > Maps** page, use the **Select a command** drop-down to select Planning Mode. Click on **Add APs** to add the hypothetical APs to the map. When you do so, a blue dotted line appears on the map.

Note: If you do not want to use the square blue dotted area, you can select **perimeter** and then trace the exact area that you want to model off of.

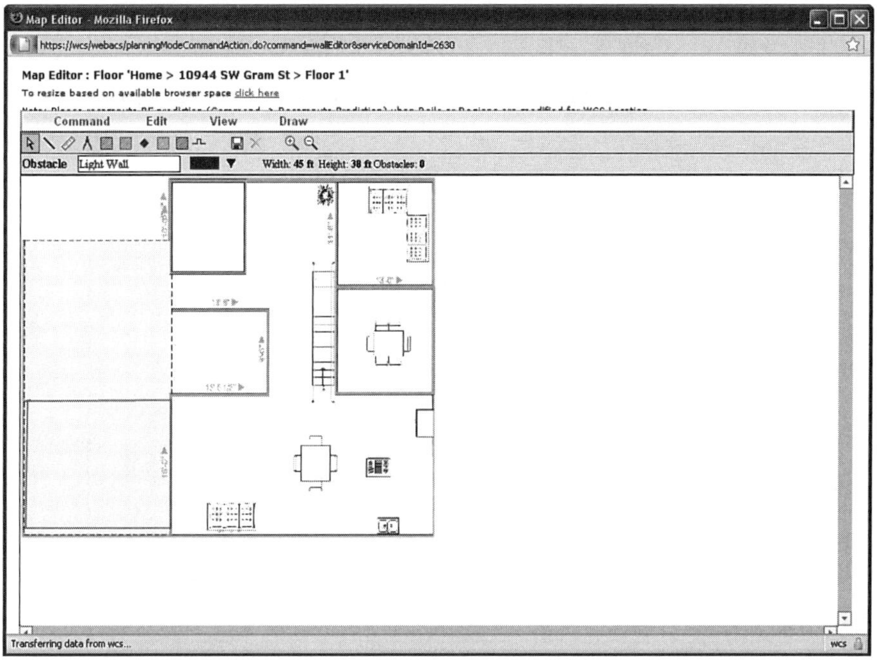

Figure 18-15   *Map Editor*

You move this around to determine the coverage area. You probably do not want it to trace the outer edge of the floor because it might place APs on the edge walls. This extends coverage beyond the outside of the building. If you want to extend the capabilities for radio frequency identification (RFID) and asset tracking, this might be something you want to do. It does help more accurately pinpoint the location of assets. However, if you are just talking about a WLAN used for employee or guest access, you would not want to extend the coverage to the outside.

In the menu on the left, select the AP type along with other criteria to be used and click the **Calculate** button. You can see this in Figure 18-16, where the AP type selected is a 1250 and "N" support is enabled.

You must also select at least one service type. The service type in the figure is Data/Coverage. Clicking the **Calculate** button shows that one AP is recommended, and clicking the **Apply** button displays a heat map identifying the coverage areas, as shown in Figure 18-17.

Now that you have an AP placed on the map and an accurate heat map depicting the coverage area, you can generate a proposal by clicking the **Generate Proposal** link at the top of the page in Figure 18-17. As Figure 18-18 shows, you first select the protocols you want to support and click **Generate**. This creates the proposal in Figure 18-19.

Key Topic

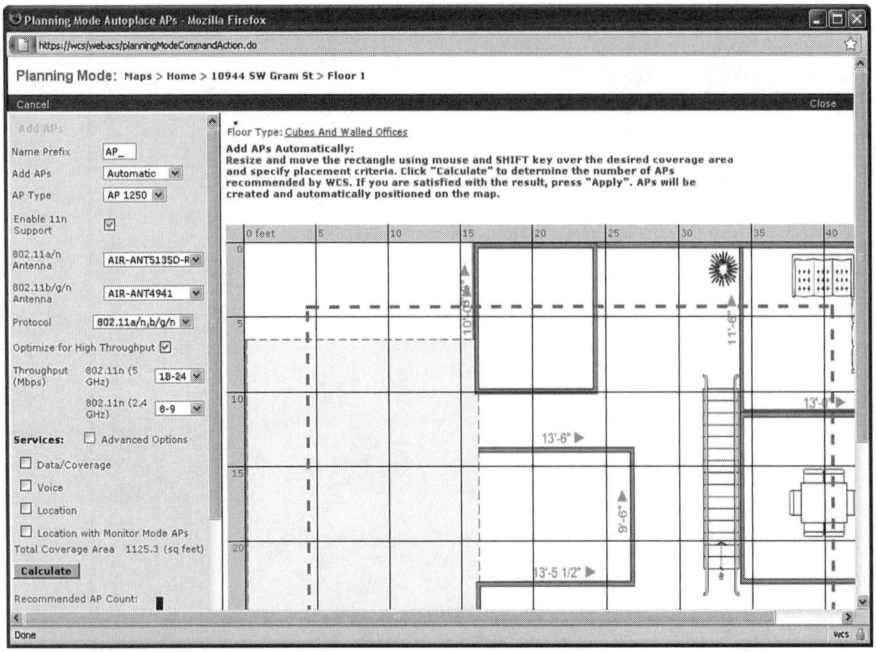

Figure 18-16 *Adding APs to the Map in Planning Mode*

Key Topic

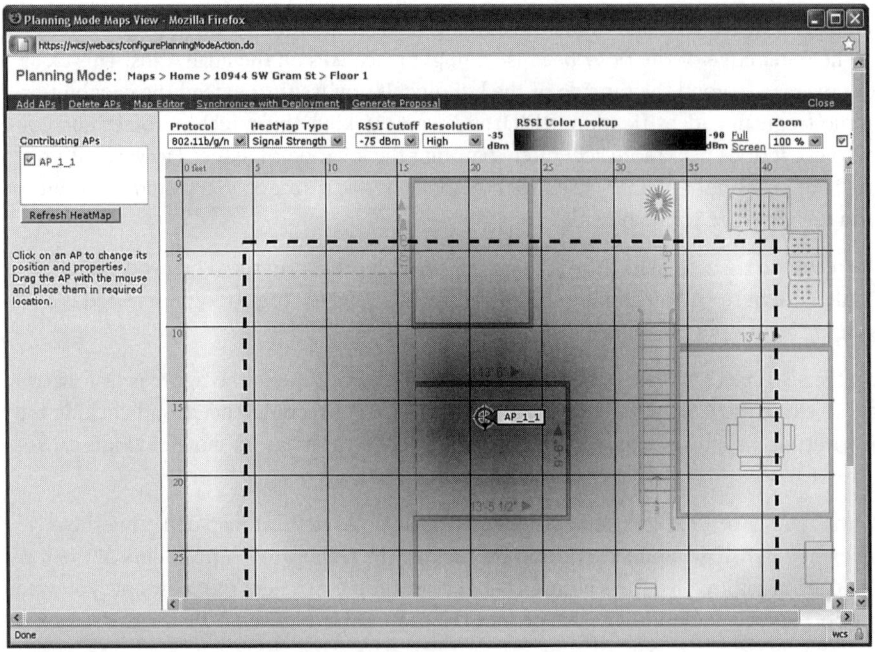

Figure 18-17 *Heat Map in Planning Mode*

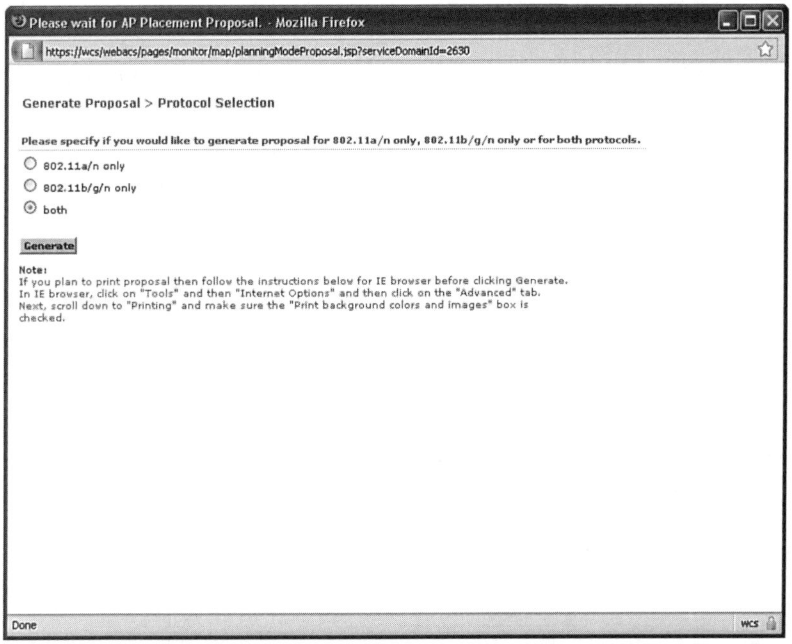

Figure 18-18   *Generating a Proposal*

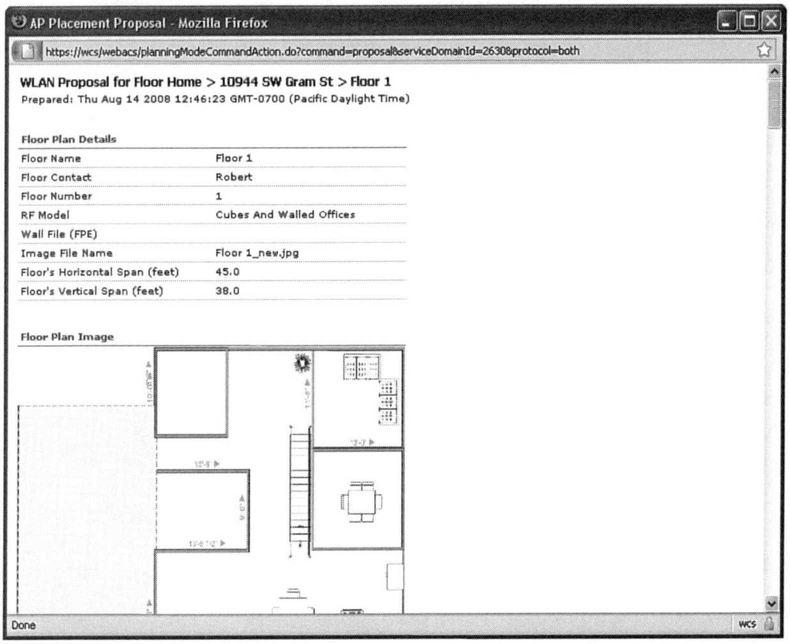

Figure 18-19   *Viewing the First Portion of the Proposal*

Monitoring with the WCS

You can use the WCS to monitor the wireless network. You can use the monitoring pages to view controllers, APs, and more. Figure 18-20 shows the Monitor menu.

An alarm summary, shown in Figure 18-20, is available and refreshes every 15 seconds. Fields that are clear indicate no alarms. Red is critical, orange is a major alarm, and yellow is a minor alarm.

By clicking an alarm, you can get more details on the situation.

Another valuable resource in the WCS is the capability to troubleshoot clients. Select **Monitor > Clients**. Next, place a Client MAC address into the **Client MacAddress** field and click the **Troubleshoot** button, as shown in Figure 18-21. This allows you to focus your troubleshooting efforts on the specified client.

You can also monitor rogue APs, security settings, and Radio Resource Management (RRM). In addition, you can monitor Location Appliances. The Location Appliance tightly integrates with the WCS and can provide real-time location tracking within about 30 feet. This is an added benefit when troubleshooting issues related to interference and rogues.

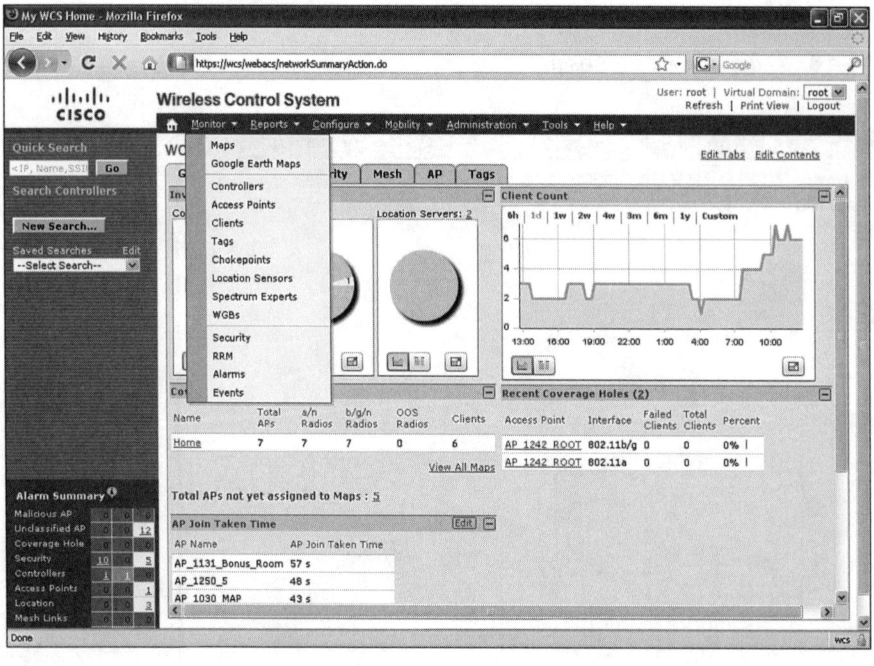

Figure 18-20   *Monitor Menu*

Key Topic

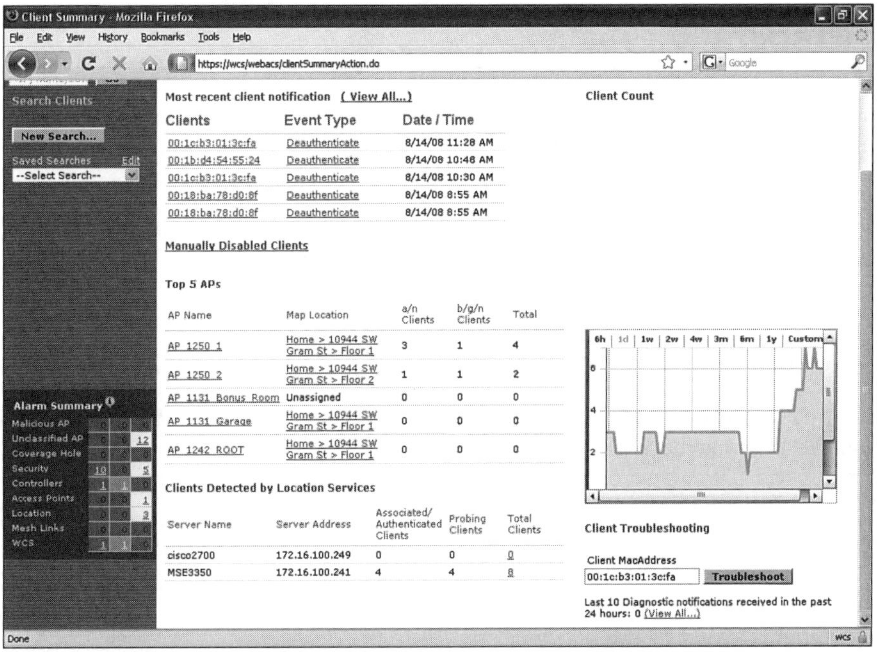

Figure 18-21 *Client Troubleshooting*

Exam Preparation Tasks

Review All the Key Topics

Review the most important topics from this chapter, noted with the Key Topics icon in the outer margin of the page. Table 18-3 lists a reference of these key topics and the page number where you can find each one.

Table 18-3 *Key Topics for Chapter 18*

Key Topic Item	Description	Page Number
Paragraph from the section "Installing and Configuring the WCS"	Lists detailing the requirements for install	358
Table 18-2	WCS ports	359
Figure 18-1	The WCS interface	361
Figure 18-3	Configuring controllers in the WCS	363
Paragraph from the section "Working with Templates"	Steps to create a template	364
Paragraph from the section "Working with Templates"	Steps to apply a template to a controller	365
Figure 18-10	Maps in the WCS	369
Figure 18-13	Heat maps in the WCS	371
Figure 18-14	Accessing the map editor	372
Figure 18-16	Adding APs to the map in Planning Mode	374
Figure 18-17	Heat map in Planning Mode	374
Figure 18-20	Monitor menu	376
Figure 18-21	Client troubleshooting	377

Complete the Tables and Lists from Memory

Print a copy of Appendix B, "Memory Tables" (found on the CD) or at least the section for this chapter, and complete the tables and lists from memory. Appendix C, "Memory Tables Answer Key," also on the CD, includes completed tables and lists to check your work.

Definition of Key Terms

Define the following key terms from this chapter, and check your answers in the Glossary:

WCS, Cisco Wireless Location Appliance, WCS templates, auto provisioning, site survey, WCS RF prediction, WCS Planning Mode

References

Chapter 10, "Using Templates," from the *Cisco Wireless Control System Configuration Guide, Release 5.0:* http://tinyurl.com/5ust42.

This chapter covers the following subjects:

Upgrading a Controller: Describes how to upgrade a Cisco controller.

Upgrading an AP: Looks at how an AP upgrades its image.

Upgrading WCS: Describes how to manage an upgrade of WCS.

Managing Configurations: Covers how to manage configuration files with the controller.

CHAPTER 19

Maintaining Wireless Networks

Part of the day-to-day management of a wireless network involves working with images of the controllers and access points (AP). Cisco recommends that all controllers run the same version of code. In turn, the APs associated with a controller run the same version of code as the controller. Hence, upgrading or downgrading a controller puts all the APs on the same version as well. In this chapter, you will learn the steps required to upgrade a controller, upgrade an AP, upgrade the Wireless Control System (WCS), and manage configuration files.

You should do the "Do I Know This Already?" quiz first. If you score 80 percent or higher, you may want to skip to the section "Exam Preparation Tasks." If you score below 80 percent, you should spend the time reviewing the entire chapter.

"Do I Know This Already?" Quiz

The "Do I Know This Already?" quiz helps you determine your level of knowledge of this chapter's topics before you begin. Table 19-1 details the major topics discussed in this chapter and their corresponding quiz questions.

Table 19-1 *"Do I Know This Already?" Section-to-Question Mapping*

Foundation Topics Section	Questions
Upgrading a Controller	1–5
Upgrading an AP	6–7
Upgrading WCS	8
Managing Configurations	9–11

1. According to the following figure, what version of controller code is in use?

a. 5.0.148.0

b. 192.168.1.50

c. +38 C

d. 4.1.2.60 (Mesh)

2. What do you choose to verify the version of hardware?

a. Controller > General

b. Controller > Inventory

c. Management > Summary

d. Monitor > Summary

3. Which statement about the following figure is true?

a. The AP being viewed is the Lobby-AP.

b. The AP is running in autonomous mode.

c. The AP has a static IP address.

d. The AP is running software version 5.0.148.0.

4. Which extension is used in controller upgrade files?

a. .bin

b. .exe

c. .cfg

d. .aes

5. Which protocols are used to upgrade a controller? (Choose two.)

a. FTP

b. TFTP

c. HTTP

d. SCP

6. What does an AP do if a controller is running a higher version of software?

    a. It does nothing; they don't need to be the same.

    b. It automatically upgrades to the same version as the controller.

    c. It causes the controller to downgrade to the same version as the AP.

    d. It reboots continuously and keeps searching for a controller with the same version.

7. If an AP leaves one controller and associates with another, what does it check?

    a. The controller's hardware version

    b. How many licenses the controller has

    c. The version the controller is running

    d. The version that other APs are running

8. The WCS is upgraded using what method?

    a. WCS code upgrade script

    b. FTP

    c. TFTP

    d. SCP

9. How do you save the controller's configuration using the web interface?

    a. Choose **Commands > Save**.

    b. Click the Save **Configuration** link.

    c. Choose **Commands > Copy-Run-Start**.

    d. Choose **Controllers > Save**.

10. If you clicked the **Upload** button on the page shown in the following figure, what would happen?

a. The controller software would get backed up to an FTP server.

b. The controller configuration would be archived to an NFS server at the IP address 192.168.2.96.

c. The controller configuration would be uploaded in clear text using a TFTP server.

d. The controller configuration would be encrypted and uploaded to 192.168.2.96 using TFTP.

11. In what format is the controller configuration file?

a. XML

b. XHTML

c. DHTML

d. Clear text

Foundation Topics

Upgrading a Controller

Management tasks in the controller involve upgrading or downgrading images as well as managing configuration files. You can begin working with these files by verifying the version currently running on the controller. Figure 19-1 shows the **MONITOR > Summary** page, which indicates that the version of code on this particular controller is software version 4.1.192.17M (Mesh). 5.x is the current version of code, so you need to obtain the version you want to have loaded before performing the upgrade.

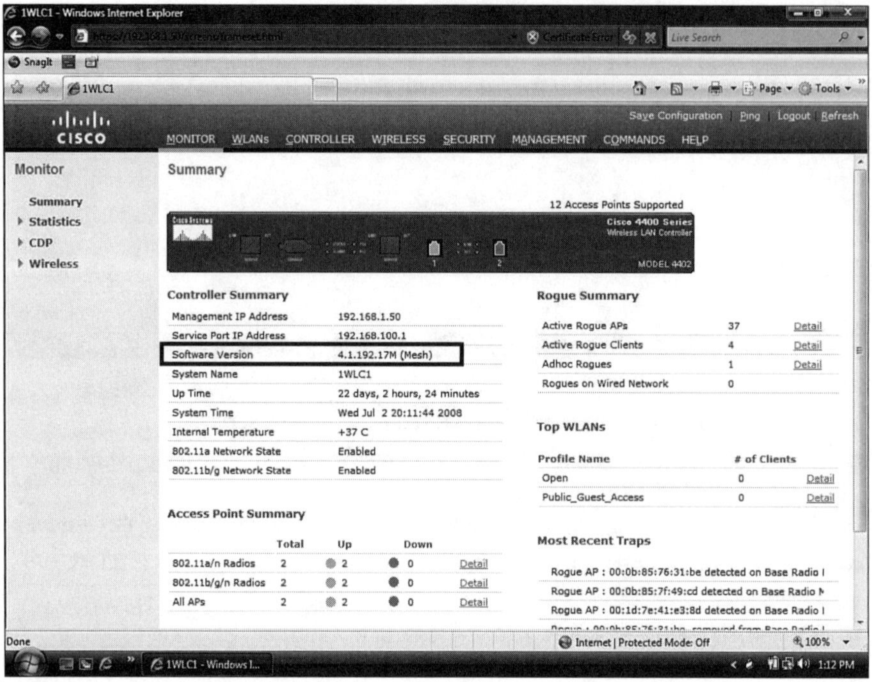

Figure 19-1   *Verify the Controller Software Version*

You also need to know the hardware with which you are working. You can find the hardware information by choosing **CONTROLLER > Inventory** and verifying the platform. The platform used in this example is an AIR-WLC4402-12-K9, as shown in Figure 19-2.

For the record, you might as well verify the AP hardware being used. To verify the AP software version, choose **WIRELESS > All APs**, and click the AP name you want to verify. In Figure 19-3, the Lobby-AP has been selected. You see a configuration page with four tabs:

■   General

■   Inventory

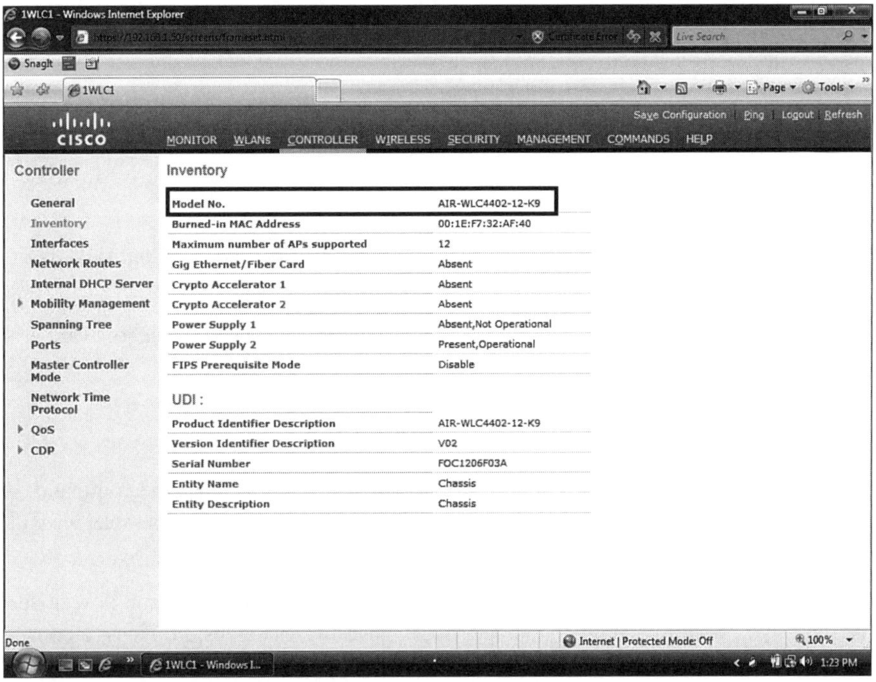

Figure 19-2 *Verify the Hardware Version*

Key
Topic

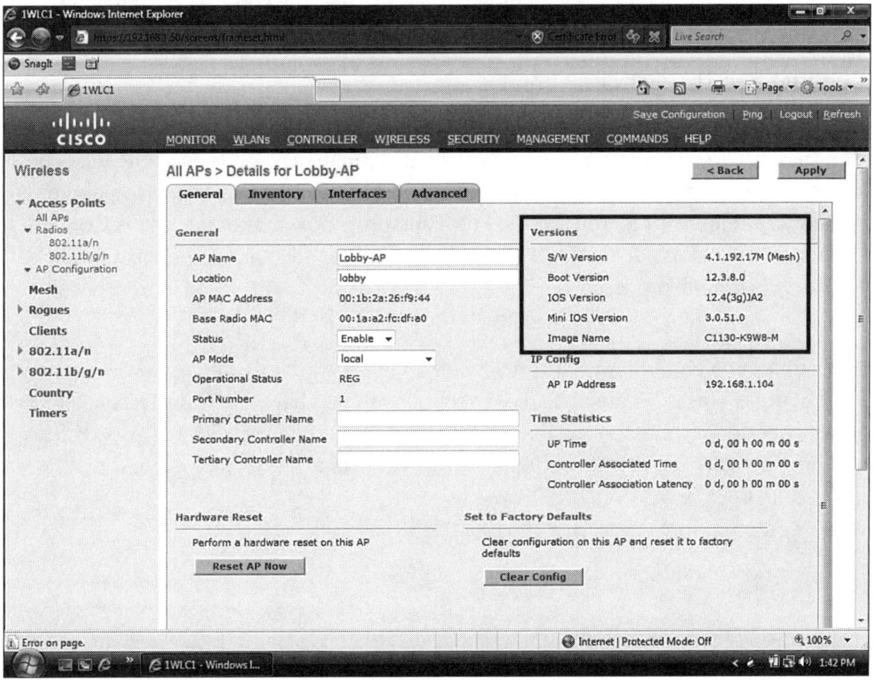

Figure 19-3 *General Details for the Lobby-AP*

- Interfaces

- Advanced

The General tab displays the software (S/W) version, as shown in Figure 19-3.

In the figure, the version on the AP is 4.1.192.17M (Mesh), which is the same version that is running on the controller.

Selecting the Inventory tab displays the hardware version. In this case, the Lobby-AP is an AIR-AP1131AG-A-K9, as shown in Figure 19-4.

Now you have all the version information you need to upgrade the controller software version. The next step is to determine which upgrade approach you will take.

Controller Upgrade Approaches

You can take two approaches when upgrading the controller. You can use the command-line interface (CLI), or you can use the web-based interface. To keep things simple, we will focus on the web interface method.

Key Topic

Start by going to the Cisco Software Center (www.cisco.com/go/software) and download-ing the image you want to install. The image should have an .aes extension. This is a com-pressed archive file. Three files are included in the .aes compressed file:

- **RTOS:** The controller's Real-Time Operating System

- **CODE:** Airwave Director, command-line interface, and the controller's switch web interface

- **ppcboot.bin:** The controller's bootloader

The next step is to place the .aes file on a TFTP server. Tftpd32 is a common TFTP server program that can you can obtain from http://tftpd32.jounin.net. As soon as the file is on the server, and the controller can reach the server, choose **COMMANDS > Download File**, as shown in Figure 19-5. You see the File Type drop-down. The file type is **Code**. Next, enter the IP address of the TFTP server, as well as the file path and filename. Click **Download** to begin the process.

Note   Sometimes you have to upgrade through prior releases of software up to the version you ultimately want. This is because the older versions of code have a built-in TFTP client that does not support file transfers greater than 32 MB. The following URL is a good refer-ence for helping network engineers or administrators determine an upgrade path: http:/ /www.cisco.com/en/US/tech/tk722/tk809/ technologies_configuration_example09186a00805f381f.shtml.

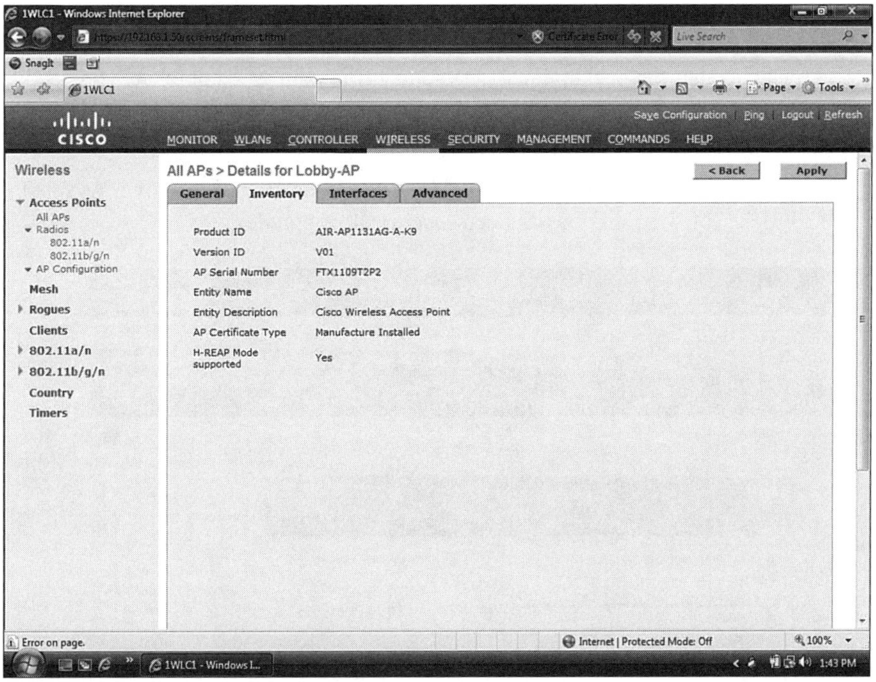

Figure 19-4 *AP Hardware Version*

Key Topic

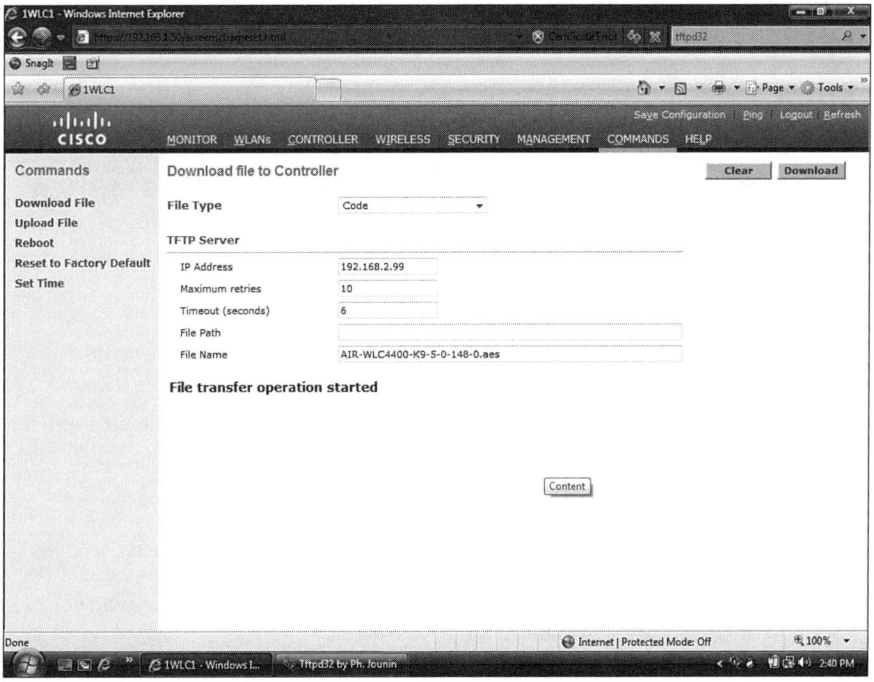

Figure 19-5 *Upgrade the Controller via the Web Interface*

As the transfer begins, the page continues to refresh every few seconds. The controller copies the file to RAM. When it's finished, the controller puts the file in flash. The existing image then becomes the backup image. As soon as the transfer is complete, you need to reboot the controller. You can click the link displayed on the Download file to Controller page. This redirects you to the Reboot page.

After the reboot, log back in, and verify that the new code has been transferred. As shown in Figure 19-6, the software version has been successfully upgraded.

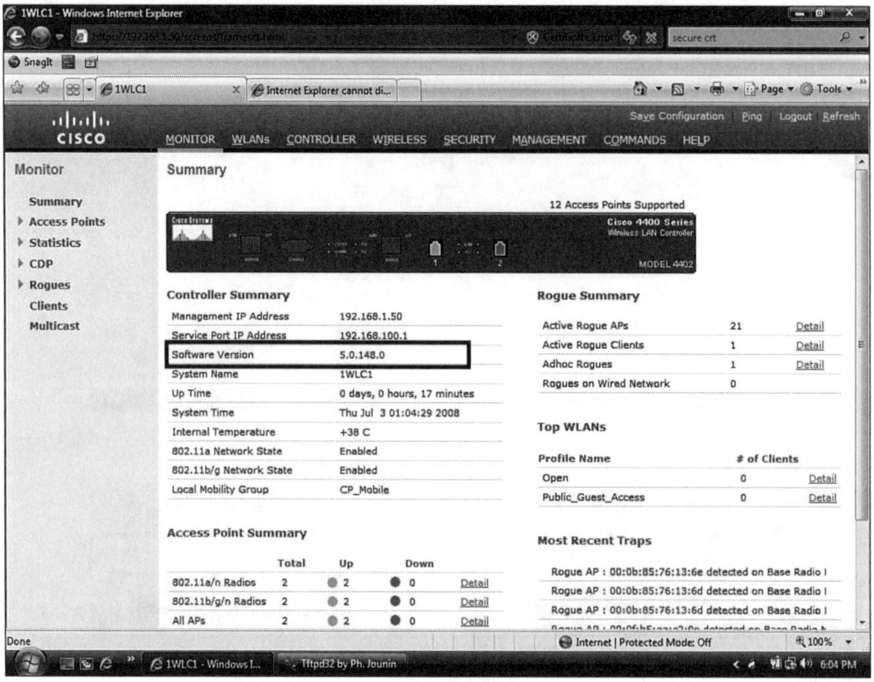

Figure 19-6   *Verify the Upgrade of the Controller*

Upgrade Using WCS

You can also use WCS to upgrade the controller. Upgrading the controller also upgrades the APs, because they sync to the same code. To perform the upgrade, follow these steps:

Step 1.   Verify connectivity before you start the upgrade process. Use the ping utility from the WCS to be sure that the WCS server can contact the controller. Also, if you use an external TFTP server, ping it as well.

Note   The ping utility is a Windows function, not a function or utility in WCS. To access the ping utility, you need to open a command prompt in Windows and enter the **ping** command followed by the address you want to ping.

Step 2. Click **Configure > Controllers** to navigate to the All Controllers page.

Step 3. Select the check box of the controller you want to upgrade. Choose **Select a Command > Download Software**, and click **GO**. WCS displays the Download Software to Controller page.

Step 4. If you use the built-in WCS TFTP server, check the **TFTP Server on WCS System** check box. If you use an external TFTP server, uncheck this check box and add the external TFTP server IP address.

Step 5. Click **Browse** and navigate to the software update file. The files are uploaded to the root directory that was configured for use by the TFTP server. You can change to a different directory.

Note You should always double-check the software file you plan to use for your controller. Selecting the wrong file can cause problems. Be sure that you have the correct software file for your controller.

Step 6. Click **Download**. WCS downloads the software to the controller, and the controller writes the code to flash RAM. As WCS performs this function, it displays its progress in the Status field.

Upgrading an AP

Upgrading an AP is pretty easy. In fact, if you followed the process described in the preceding section, you are already done, because the AP synchronizes to the controller. Recall that in Figure 19-3 you verified the version of AP software, and it was the same as the controller—version 4.1.192.17M (Mesh). After upgrading the controller to software version 5.0.148.0, you can again verify the client by choosing **WIRELESS > All APs** and clicking the AP name that you want to verify. In Figure 19-7, the Lobby-AP has been selected. According to the information in the Software Version field, it has been upgraded to version 5.0.148.0, matching that of the controller. Remember that after upgrading the software on the controller, the APs automatically upgrade their software as well, but only 20 APs can upgrade at any given time.

Remember that APs synchronize to the controller. This means the following:

Key Topic

■ If the controller is a higher version, the AP upgrades.

■ If the controller is a lower version, the AP downgrades.

■ If the AP leaves one controller and associates with another, the AP checks the controller version and upgrades/downgrades as needed.

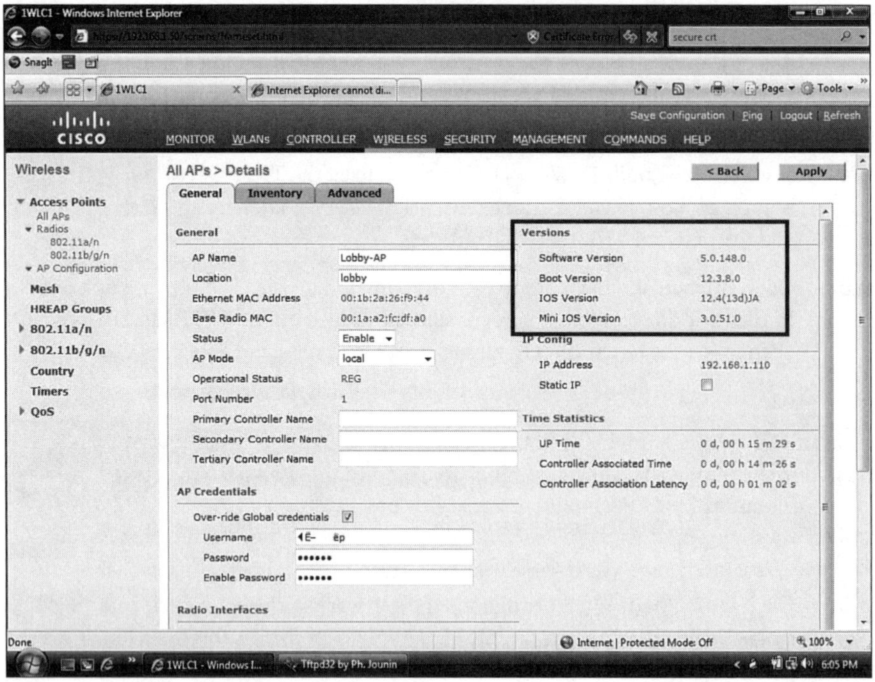

Figure 19-7   *Verify the AP Upgrade*

Upgrading WCS

Beginning in WCS version 4.2, the WCS code upgrade script made it possible to upgrade the WCS while retaining the directories, root password, and license information. The operation is automated and simply involves downloading the install file from the Cisco website and running it on the machine on which the WCS is installed. During the install process, you are informed that a previous install has been detected, and you're asked to choose between upgrading and installing. Upgrading retains all the information from the previous install. If you choose the install option, it will be as if WCS was not previously there; in other words, it's a fresh install.

Managing Configurations

When working in the Cisco Unified Wireless Environment, you deal with a number of configuration files. You potentially have numerous controller configurations as well as AP configurations. When you're working with the controller, it's a good idea to save your configuration often. Clicking the Save Configuration link can save a controller's configuration. It is found in the top-right corner of the web interface, as shown in Figure 19-8.

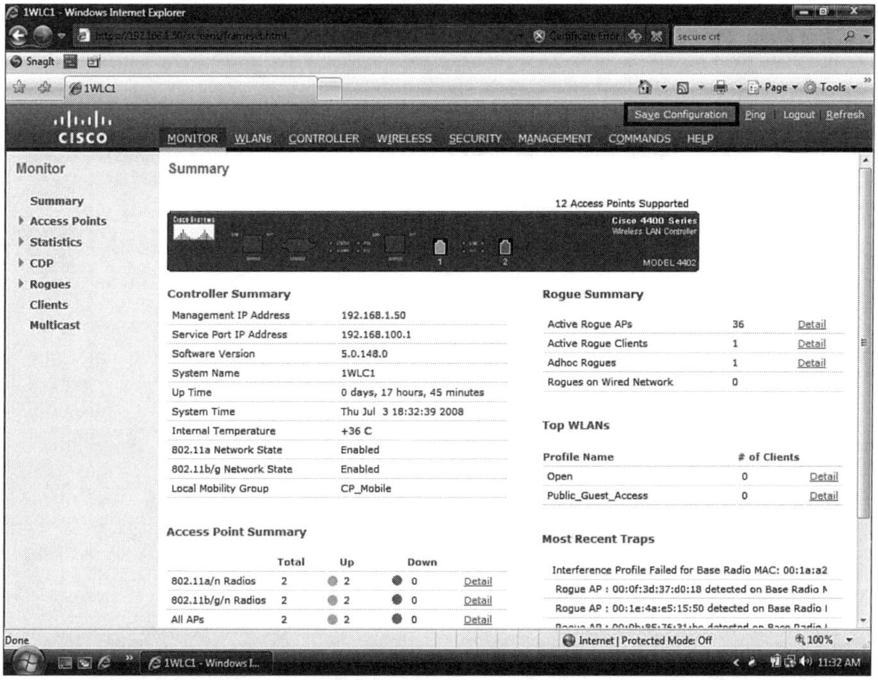

Figure 19-8 *Save the Configuration*

In addition to saving the configuration to NVRAM, you can back up the configuration on a remote TFTP server. Saving to a TFTP server is similar to how you upgraded the controller, only this time you are moving a file in the opposite direction. The setup requires the use of TFTP server software installed on the destination computer where you want to back up the file. TFTP uses UDP port 69, so make sure that nothing in the transit path, such as a firewall, might block that type of traffic. If you have already upgraded from the TFTP server, you probably won't have any issues.

The next step is to choose **COMMANDS > Upload File.** In the drop-down box, choose **Configuration.** Select the option to encrypt the file is you want, enter the server's address and configuration file name, and click upload. If you don't choose to encrypt it, you get a pop-up warning when you click **Upload.**

After you upload the configuration file, you can download this file to other controllers. However, you cannot read it as you would a configuration file from a router or switch, because it is an XML file.

Suppose you wanted to back up the controller configuration to 192.168.2.99. Simply enter the IP address 192.168.2.99 in the IP Address field and give it a name, as shown in Figure 19-9. In this example, the file name is 1WLC1.cfg.

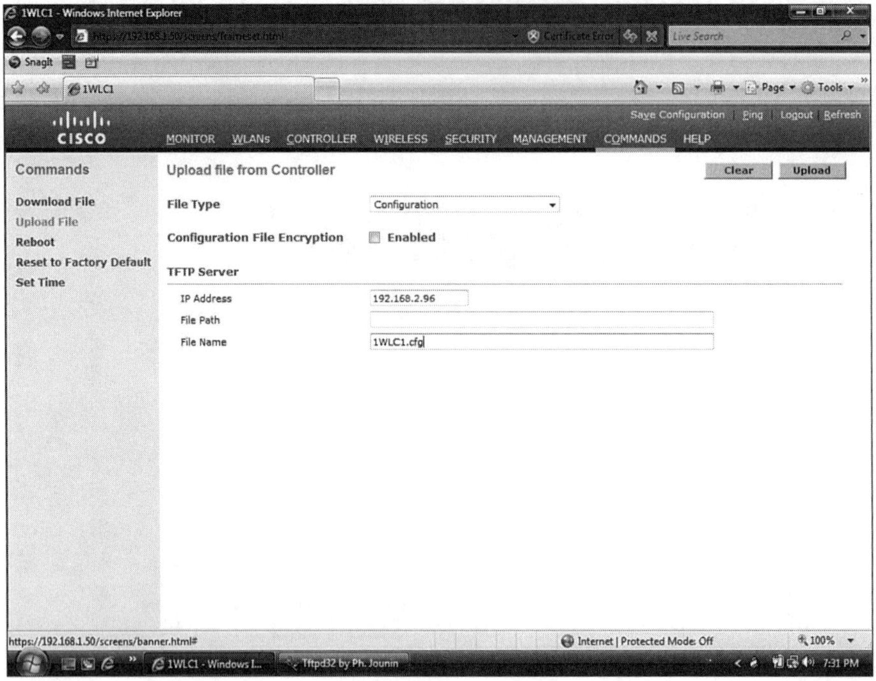

Figure 19-9 *Backing Up the Controller Configuration to TFTP*

Click the Upload button to begin the process. This takes a short time. After completion, you can verify by viewing the directory on the TFTP server where the files are stored, as shown in Figure 19-10. After viewing the directory on the TFTP server, you can see that the upload was successful. The file has been backed up and can now be used on other controllers.

Further exploration shows that the file can be opened and viewed but is not very readable, as shown in Figure 19-11.

If you do want to view the configuration in a readable format, you could issue the **show running-config** command from the CLI on the controller. In Example 19-1, the **show running-config** command has been entered on the controller. Using this command you can see line by line how the controller is configured. It's important to note the difference between this command and the **show run-config** command, because they produce very different output. **show running-config** displays the contents of the configuration line by line. **show run-config** provides information about the state of the system.

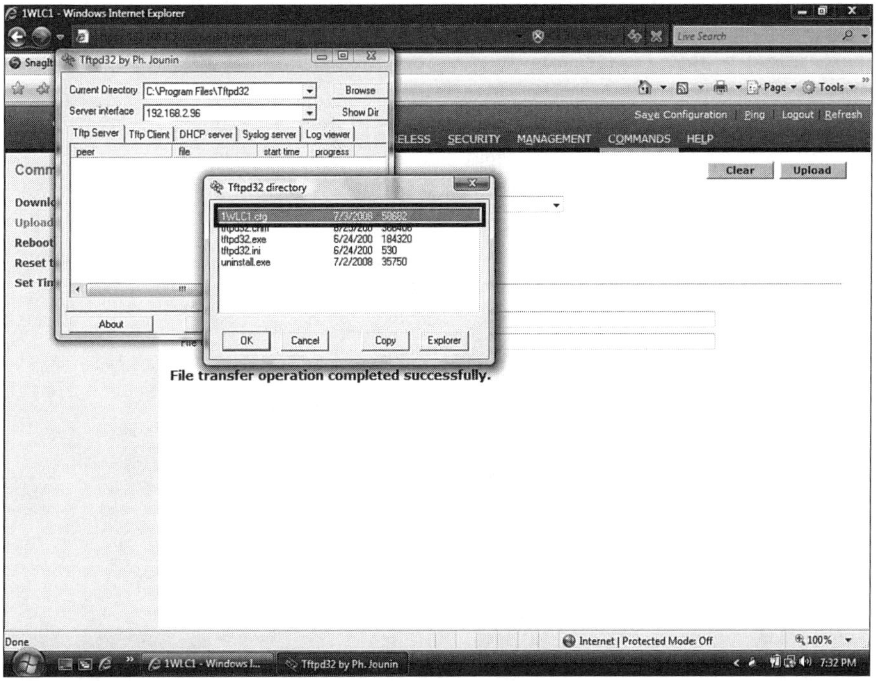

Figure 19-10   *TFTP Directory*

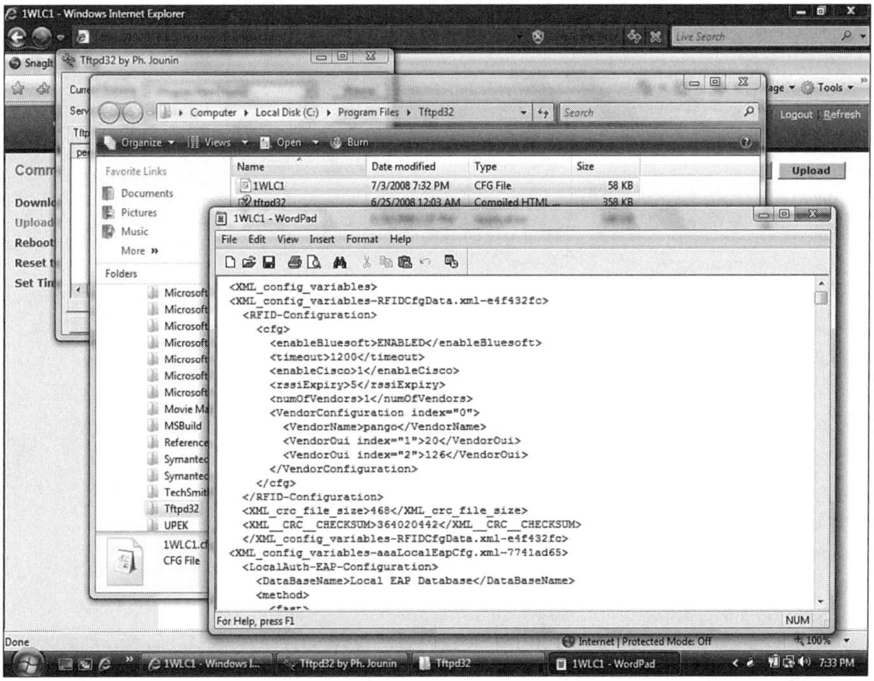

Figure 19-11   *Viewing the File on the TFTP Server*

Example 19-1 show running-config *Command Output*

```
(Cisco Controller) > show running-config

 802.11a 11nSupport a-mpdu tx priority 0 disable
 802.11a cac voice tspec-inactivity-timeout ignore
 802.11a cac video tspec-inactivity-timeout ignore
 802.11a cac voice stream-size 84000 max-streams 2
 802.11b 11nSupport a-mpdu tx priority 0 disable
 802.11b cac voice tspec-inactivity-timeout ignore
 802.11b cac video tspec-inactivity-timeout ignore
 802.11b cac voice stream-size 84000 max-streams 2
 aaa auth mgmt local radius
 advanced 802.11a receiver pico-cell-V2 rx_sense_thrld 0 0 0
 advanced 802.11a receiver pico-cell-V2 cca_sense_thrld 0 0 0
advanced 802.11a receiver pico-cell-V2 sta_tx_pwr 0 0 0
 Location Summary
 Algorithm used:              Average
 Client
         RSSI expiry timeout: 150 sec
         Half life:                60 sec
         Notify Threshold:         0 db
 Calibrating Client
         RSSI expiry timeout: 30 sec
         Half life:                0 sec
 Rogue AP
         RSSI expiry timeout:    120 sec
         Half life:                0 sec
         Notify Threshold:         0 db
 RFID Tag
         RSSI expiry timeout: 5 sec
         Half life:                0 sec
         Notify Threshold:         0 db
 location rssi-half-life tags 0
location rssi-half-life rogue-aps 0
 location expiry tags 5
 location expiry client 150
 location expiry calibrating-client 30
 location expiry rogue-aps 120
 advanced eap identity-request-timeout 1
 advanced eap identity-request-retries 20
 advanced eap request-timeout 1
 ap syslog host global 255.255.255.255
interface create guest_lan 80
interface address ap-manager 192.168.1.51 255.255.255.0 192.168.1.1
interface address dynamic-interface guest_lan 172.30.1.50 255.255.255.0 172.30.1.1
 interface address management 192.168.1.50 255.255.255.0 192.168.1.1
```

```
interface address service-port 192.168.100.1 255.255.255.0
interface address virtual 1.1.1.1
interface dhcp ap-manager primary 192.168.1.1
interface dhcp dynamic-interface guest_lan primary 172.30.1.1
interface dhcp management primary 192.168.1.1
interface dhcp service-port disable
interface vlan ap-manager 1
interface vlan guest_lan 80
interface vlan management 1
interface port ap-manager 1
interface port guest_lan 1
interface port management 1
 load-balancing window 5
 logging buffered 1
 mesh security eap
 mgmtuser add admin **** read-write
 mobility group domain CP_Mobile
 mobility group anchor wlan add 2 192.168.1.50
 mobility dscp value for inter-controller mobility packets 0
 network webmode enable
 network rf-network-name CP_Mobile
 radius fallback-test mode off
 radius fallback-test username cisco-probe
 radius fallback-test interval 300
 snmp version v2c enable
 snmp version v3 enable
 sysname 1WLC1
 wlan create 1 Open Open
 wlan create 2 Public_Guest_Access GUESTNET
 wlan interface 2 guest_lan
 wlan session-timeout 1 1800
 wlan session-timeout 2 disable
 wlan wmm allow 1
 wlan wmm allow 2
 wlan security wpa disable 2
 wlan security web-auth server-precedence 1
 wlan security web-auth server-precedence 2
 wlan security wpa akm ft reassociation-time 0 1
 wlan security wpa akm ft over-the-air disable 1
 wlan security wpa akm ft over-the-ds disable 1
 wlan security wpa akm ft reassociation-time 0 2
 wlan security wpa akm ft over-the-air disable 2
 wlan security wpa akm ft over-the-ds disable 2
 wlan enable 1
 wlan enable 2
```

Working with AP Configuration Files

Keeping in mind that the AP gets its configuration from the controller should make it clear that you don't really have to do much to manage AP configurations. However, you might encounter scenarios where you want to reset an AP to its factory default. You can do this at the AP itself, but you require physical access to the AP. To reset the AP from the controller, simply choose **WIRELESS**, choose the AP you want to reset, and scroll to the bottom. You have two options, as shown in Figure 19-12. You can click **Clear All Config** or **Clear Config Except Static IP**. The choice depends on what you want to happen. If you use static IPs and want to reset the AP and remove it from the network, choose the second option.

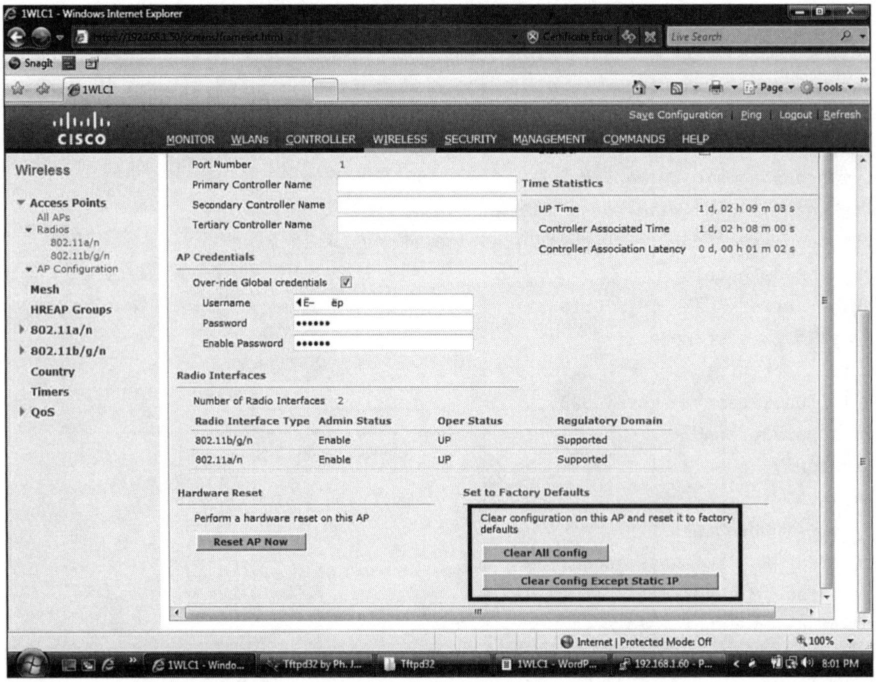

Figure 19-12 *Options for Resetting the AP*

Resetting the Controller to the Defaults

Finally, if you decide to reset the controller to its factory defaults, you can choose **COMMANDS > Reset to Factory Default**. This page presents a message similar to the one shown in Figure 19-13; it explains what happens when you reset the controller to the defaults. The controller needs to reboot for this to occur, because the configuration is not only stored in NVRAM, but it is also active in RAM and is cleared only with a reboot. You will lose connectivity when you do this.

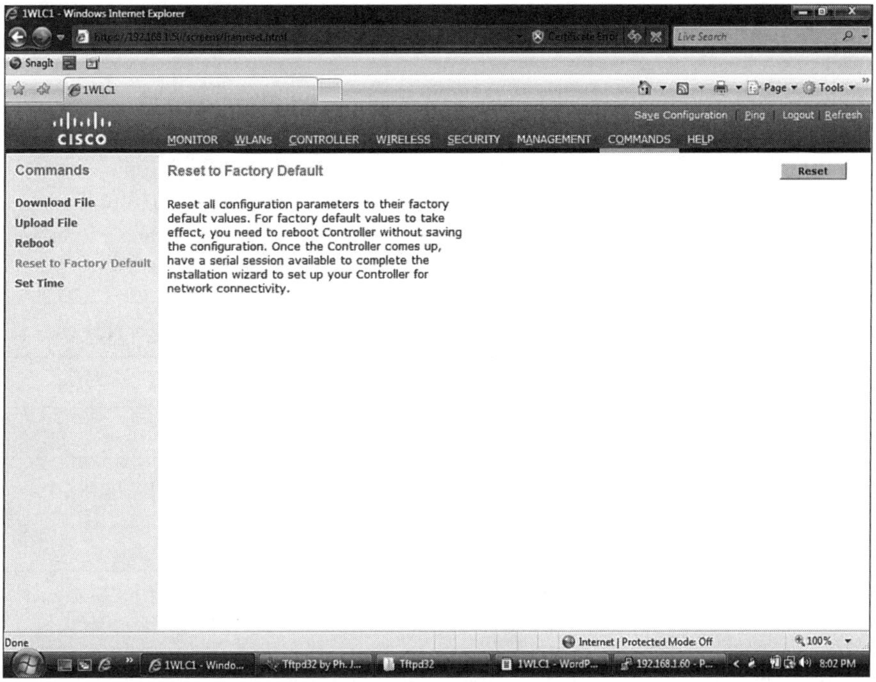

Figure 19-13   *Reset the Controller to the Factory Defaults*

Exam Preparation Tasks

Review All the Key Topics

Review the most important topics from this chapter, denoted with the Key Topic icon. Table 19-2 lists these key topics and the page number where each one can be found.

Table 19-2   *Key Topics for Chapter 19*

Key Topic Item	Description	Page Number
Figure 19-1	Verifying the software version	386
Figure 19-3	General details for the Lobby-AP	387
Paragraph from the section "Controller Upgrade Approaches"	A list of files contained in the compressed upgrade file	388
Figure 19-5	Upgrading the controller via the web interface	389
Paragraph from the section "Upgrading an AP"	Bullet points about AP upgrades and downgrades	391
Figure 19-9	Backing up the controller configuration to TFTP	394

Definition of Key Terms

Define the following key terms from this chapter, and check your answers in the Glossary:

RTOS, RAM, NVRAM, TFTP

References

Cisco Wireless Control System Configuration Guide, Release 5.0: http://www.cisco.com/en/US/docs/wireless/wcs/5.0/configuration/guide/wcstasks.html#wp1076844

Cisco Wireless LAN Controller Configuration Guide, Release 5.0: http://www.cisco.com/en/US/docs/wireless/controller/5.0/configuration/guide/c5mfw.html

This chapter covers the following subjects:

Physical Connections and LEDs: A look at troubleshooting using physical features of the network.

Common Client-Side Issues: A discussion of common client issues.

Using the CLI to Troubleshoot: A look at CLI commands for viewing and debugging using the CLI.

Using the Controller Interface: Details of troubleshooting using various web interface pages.

Using WCS Version 5.x to Troubleshoot Clients: Overview of techniques used to troubleshoot clients using WCS.

Using the Cisco Spectrum Expert: A brief introduction to the Cisco Spectrum Expert and its use.

CHAPTER 20

Troubleshooting Wireless Networks

Trouble tends to be something everyone runs into at some point in time. People make typos. Cables mysteriously go bad. Stuff happens. This chapter discusses numerous issues that can happen in a wireless network along with some of the techniques, commands, configuration pages, and methods that you can use to correct them. Although everyone has a unique style, this chapter helps you hone your skills at recognizing misconfigurations and making corrections, using the command-line interface (CLI), the controller interface, and the Wireless Control System (WCS).

You should do the "Do I Know This Already?" quiz first. If you score 80 percent or higher, you might want to skip to the section "Exam Preparation Tasks." If you score below 80 percent, you should spend the time reviewing the entire chapter. Refer to Appendix A, "Answers to the 'Do I Know This Already?' Quizzes," to confirm your answers.

"Do I Know This Already?" Quiz

The "Do I Know This Already?" quiz helps you determine your level of knowledge of this chapter's topics before you begin. Table 20-1 details the major topics discussed in this chapter and their corresponding quiz questions.

Table 20-1 *"Do I Know This Already?" Section-to-Question Mapping*

Foundation Topics Section	Questions
Physical Connections and LEDs	1–2
Common Client-Side Issues	3–5
Using the CLI to Troubleshoot	6–11
Using the Controller Interface	12–13
Using WCS Version 5.x to Troubleshoot Clients	14
Using the Cisco Spectrum Expert	15

1. At what layers of the OSI model does trouble happen most often?

    a. Layer 1
    b. Layers 1 through 3
    c. Layers 2 through 6
    d. Above Layer 7

2. What are some actions regarding physical characteristics that you can use for troubleshooting? (Choose all that apply.)

    a. Analyze port LEDs
    b. Verify wiring
    c. Check the internal fans
    d. View debugs

3. Which of the following accurately describes the hidden node issue?

    a. A node is hidden under a desk and used to attack the wireless network.
    b. A node is accessing the network from the parking lot.
    c. Two nodes are attempting to send at the same time. They are out of range of each other but not of the AP.
    d. Nodes on the network access hidden APs.

4. Which of the following best describes the exposed node issue?

    a. Two nodes are sending on the same channel to different APs. The cells are too close, so a collision occurs.
    b. A node is attacking the network in plain view.
    c. A node is on the wireless network without antivirus software.
    d. A node is listening on undesired ports.

5. When an AP has a greater RF range than a client, the client can see the AP but annot associate with it because the client frames do not reach the AP. What is this situation known as?

    a. The Weak Antenna syndrome
    b. The Weak Link issue
    c. The Half Duplex situation
    d. The Near/Far issue

6. From where can you execute **debug** commands?

    a. The GUI
    b. The CLI
    c. The GUI and the CLI
    d. The WCS only

7. What command provides a summary of clients?

   a. show clients

   b. show client summary

   c. show summary

   d. show ap client summary

8. Examine the following output and then answer the question.

```
(Cisco Controller) >show client detail 00:15:af:0a:0b:71
Client MAC Address.............................. 00:15:af:0a:0b:71
Client Username ................................ N/A
AP MAC Address.................................. 00:1a:a2:fc:df:a0
Client State................................... Probing
Wireless LAN Id................................. N/A
BSSID.......................................... 00:1a:a2:fc:df:9f
Channel........................................ 11
IP Address..................................... Unknown
Association Id................................. 0
Authentication Algorithm....................... Open System
Reason Code.................................... 0
Status Code.................................... 0
Session Timeout................................ 0
Client CCX version............................. No CCX support
Mirroring...................................... Disabled
QoS Level...................................... Silver
Diff Serv Code Point (DSCP).................... disabled
802.1P Priority Tag............................ disabled
WMM Support.................................... Disabled
Mobility State................................. None
Mobility Move Count............................ 0
Security Policy Completed...................... No
--More-- or (q)uit
Policy Manager State........................... START
Policy Manager Rule Created.................... Yes
NPU Fast Fast Notified......................... No
Policy Type.................................... N/A
```

Based on this output, does the client have full IP connectivity?

   a. Yes.

   b. No, the client has partial connectivity but no DNS.

   c. No, the client has no IP connectivity because he has no IP address.

   d. Yes, but the network is down.

9. If you leave a debug turned on, what happens?

 a. It consumes all the resources on the controller.

 b. It runs continuously.

 c. It turns off when the controller reloads.

 d. It becomes disabled when the session times out.

10. Look at the following output and answer the question.

```
(Cisco Controller) >debug ?

aaa Configures the AAA debug options.
airewave-director Configures the Airewave Director debug options
ap Configures debug of Cisco AP.
arp Configures debug of ARP.
bcast Configures debug of broadcast.
cac Configures the call admission control (CAC) debug options.
cdp Configures debug of cdp.
crypto Configures the Hardware Crypto debug options.
dhcp Configures the DHCP debug options.
client Enables debugs for common client problems.
disable-all Disables all debug messages.
dot11 Configures the 802.11 events debug options.
dot1x Configures the 802.1X debug options.
iapp Configures the IAPP debug options.
ccxrm Configures the CCX_RM debug options.
ccxdiag Configures the CCX Diagnostic debug options.
```

Which debug would be used to troubleshoot issues with port-based authentication?

 a. arp

 b. cdp

 c. dot11

 d. dot1x

11. How do you enable client troubleshooting?

 a. Issue the CLI command **debug mac addr** *mac_address_of_client*.

 b. Click the **Troubleshoot** button from the Clients Summary page of the WCS.

 c. Select the client from the **Clients** drop-down menu.

 d. Use an access list to match a client and tie it to a debug.

12. Where would you find information equivalent to the **show client summary** command within the controller interface?

 a. MANAGEMENT > Clients

 b. CONTROLLER > Clients

 c. MONITOR > Clients > Detail

 d. WLANs > Clients

13. Facility Level 5 is what?

   a. USENET

   b. SYSLOG

   c. FTP DAEMONS

   d. KERNEL

14. WCS is used to troubleshoot client-to-AP connectivity. True or false?

   a. True

   b. False

15. Which of the following devices does the Cisco Spectrum Expert provide information about?

   a. Microwave ovens

   b. RC cars

   c. Controllers

   d. Wired clients

Foundation Topics

Physical Connections and LEDs

Trouble usually happens between Layer 1 and Layer 3 of the OSI reference model. That is not to say that trouble does not occur at Layers 4 through 7, but Layers 1 through 3 are the layers where network administrators have the most hands on. Working your way up can often prove to be a time saver. Starting at Layer 1, physical connectivity can often save valuable time. You can begin by visually examining the physical connections. Keep in mind all that is involved in the path of your traffic. This can include areas related to the following:

- AP to switch

- Switch to switch

- Switch to controller

- Controller to distribution

While you are examining the physical connectivity, note the port LED status of each device. What do the LEDs indicate? Are they green? Are they amber? Are they red? Each device has different LEDs; for example, the LEDs on a controller are different from the LEDs on an AP, yet they all have somewhat of a common color coding. Usually red is bad, amber is not so good, and green is okay. Look up the Cisco documentation for details for each product that you work with. The "References" section at the end of this chapter includes some valuable links that can help you determine issues in the network and correct them, some using the port LEDs for verification.

After you have verified the physical connections, you can work in one of two directions:

- Verification from the client back to the controller

- Verification from the controller to the client

In either case, common issues arise. You might find that connectivity issues are not related to the wireless network at all, but rather the distribution network, gateway, or Internet service provider (ISP). Regardless, the ability to isolate problems is a requirement of those seeking the CCNA Wireless certification. The next section explores some common client-side issues.

Common Client-Side Issues

Client-side issues arise frequently and are often expressed in vague ways, for example, "I cannot get to the Internet." "Okay," you might think, "What does that mean?" The answer might not always be clear, but you can verify some values to quickly restore connectivity for end users.

Note: When I worked for a large service provider, we went through a transition from bridges to switches. During the initial deployment, none of the administrators on the local-area network knew about the Spanning Tree Protocol (STP) or the effects it had when a device was connected to a switchport.

I recall that first week, sitting in my little cubicle at 7:55 a.m. and hearing the voices of my colleagues say, "The Internet is down." And then, of course, someone would call IT and say that *nobody* could get to the Internet and that he thought the Internet was down. I felt sorry for the IT guys, because nobody called them and said, "When I came in this morning and turned on my computer, Spanning Tree put all the ports into a blocking mode while verifying that there was no loop, so none of us could get to the Internet for about one minute." Had someone done that, the IT guys could have simply enabled PortFast on all the client ports and solved the problem. My point? Users do not call and give you the answer to the problem. Instead, they give you a symptom, and it is up to you to decipher the true issue regardless of how vague the symptom they described is. Now enough of my reminiscing. What can you do to isolate these issues?

Some of the more common issues that you can verify include the following:

- Check that the client card is enabled. Many laptops have a hardware switch that disables the wireless card internally, which can cause issues.

- Check that service set identifiers (SSIDs) are not incorrectly configured.

- Verify whether the client is using a radio that is not enabled on the AP.

- Verify whether the MAC address of the client is being "blacklisted" on the network.

- If using 802.1x, verify whether the client side is configured to support the network method, such as Extensible Authentication Protocol-Transport Layer Security (EAP-TLS) with certificates.

- Verify whether the client is getting an IP address that is blocked by an access control list (ACL) somewhere else in the network.

- Check the client firewall or antivirus software, because it might be blocking access. There might not be much you can do other than asking the client to turn each of these off temporarily for testing.

- If performing Network Access Control (NAC), check whether the client is posturing properly. Check the Authentication, Authorization, and Accounting (AAA) server or the Monitoring, Analysis, and Response System (MARS) logs to determine this. From a wireless perspective, there is not much you can do except have the users access a "Guest" type of network that does not require security posturing.

Note: Cisco Security MARS provides security monitoring for network devices and host applications supporting both Cisco and other vendors. You can find out more about it at http://tinyurl.com/bfr64.

- If you are using preshared keys for wireless authentication, verify that they are correctly configured on the client side. Also, verify that they are configured for the correct length.

Checking these common issues can shorten the time that you spend troubleshooting.

Other problems, however, include one issue called the *Hidden Node issue*. This happens when more than one client tries to send on the same channel at the same time. This issue arises because the two clients are in range of the AP but not each other. The result is that they both send, and a collision occurs.

Methods of mitigating this issue include reducing the maximum frame size, forcing a request to send/clear to send (RTS/CTS), and reducing the transmit power of the AP and shrinking the cell. In some cases, obstacles cause the devices not to see each other. In these scenarios, you might need to remove the obstacle; however, sometimes removing a wall is not an option. In these cases, take the other measures mentioned. The goal is to either get the clients to hear each other (or an RTS/CTS) so they do not sent at the same time or to get them onto different APs and operating on different channels. By shrinking the cell, you get the clients on different channels, but by lowering the transmit power, you might need to add more APs to fully cover the area. By forcing an RTS/CTS, the clients still might be on the same channel, but at least they are not stepping on the toes of the other.

Another common issue is called the *Exposed Node issue*, which occurs when you have two wireless cells on the same channel and they are too close to each other. This happens often in Wireless B/G networks because only three nonoverlapping channels exist. If clients in either of the overlapping cells transmit packets, a collision can occur. The simple fix to this is to change your topology, or at least the channel allocation. In some cases this is not a possibility, so you might consider a change to an 802.11a deployment, where more channels are available for allocation.

Another issue that happens between clients and APs is the *Near/Far issue*, which is caused by an AP transmitter being more powerful than the client transmitter. When a client sees an AP, because of its strong signal, it attempts to associate with it. Because the client transmitter is weaker than the AP, it does not have the range that the AP does. This means that the client transmission does not reach the AP, and the association fails. You can solve this problem using features of the controller. The controller can help monitor the client signal and adjust the radio resources as needed.

Additionally, as you might have been expecting, backward compatibility is an issue. This issue occurs when an 802.11b client joins the 802.11g cell and when an 802.11b/g/a client enters an 802.11n cell. The normal symptom is overall degraded data rates. To solve this issue, you can lock in a G-only cell for G clients.

Using the CLI to Troubleshoot

Sometimes resolving the common issues is not easy and they require further research. In these cases, you can use the CLI or the GUI tool to gather additional information. From the CLI, you have a few options for troubleshooting. First, you can use **show** commands on the CLI to gain valuable information related to the operational status of the controller, the APs, and the clients. Many of these **show** commands are available in various pages of the GUI tool, as you will see in later sections of this chapter.

Some of the **show** commands you should be familiar with include the following:

- **show client summary**

- **show client detail**

Example 20-1 shows the output from a **show client summary** command. In this output, you can see clients that are associated or trying to associate to the network. The example has an 802.11b client with the MAC address 0:13:e8:a9:e1:29 that is probing but not associated with an AP. Furthermore, the client is seen by the AP "Lobby-AP."

Example 20-1 *Viewing the Client Summary*

```
(Cisco Controller) >show client summary


Number of Clients................................ 1


MAC Address AP Name Status WLAN Auth Protocol Port
---------------- ----------------- ------------- ---- ---- -------- ----


00:13:e8:a9:e1:29 Lobby-AP Probing N/A No 802.11b 1


 (Cisco Controller) >
```

How can this assist you in the troubleshooting process? Well, suppose that a client reports a problem associating, and as you further research the issue, you find that the AP MAC address is seen by the Lobby-AP, and it is usually associated with the Research-Lab AP. You might then ask if the client is trying to connect while in the lobby. Who knows where this might lead you, but at least you have more information than when you started—information that might lead to a resolution.

If you wanted to dig even deeper into the client information, you might use the **show client detail** command. Example 20-2 shows the output of this command. Note the additional information you can gain there. Information includes the client username if applicable, mobility information if applicable, and much more.

Example 20-2 *Viewing Client Details*

```
(Cisco Controller) >show client detail 00:15:af:0a:0b:71
Client MAC Address............................. 00:15:af:0a:0b:71
Client Username ............................... N/A
AP MAC Address................................. 00:1a:a2:fc:df:a0
Client State................................... Probing
Wireless LAN Id................................ N/A
BSSID.......................................... 00:1a:a2:fc:df:9f
Channel........................................ 11
IP Address..................................... Unknown
Association Id................................. 0
Authentication Algorithm....................... Open System
Reason Code.................................... 0
```

continues

Example 20-2   *Viewing Client Details*   *(continued)*

```
Status Code..................................... 0
Session Timeout................................ 0
Client CCX version............................. No CCX support
Mirroring...................................... Disabled
QoS Level...................................... Silver
Diff Serv Code Point (DSCP).................... disabled
802.1P Priority Tag............................ disabled
WMM Support.................................... Disabled
Mobility State................................. None
Mobility Move Count............................ 0
Security Policy Completed...................... No
—More— or (q)uit
Policy Manager State........................... START
Policy Manager Rule Created.................... Yes
NPU Fast Fast Notified......................... No
Policy Type.................................... N/A
Encryption Cipher.............................. None
Management Frame Protection.................... No
EAP Type....................................... Unknown
Interface...................................... management
VLAN........................................... 0
Client Capabilities:
CF Pollable.............................. Not implemented
CF Poll Request.......................... Not implemented
Short Preamble........................... Not implemented
PBCC..................................... Not implemented
Channel Agility.......................... Not implemented
Listen Interval.......................... 0
Client Statistics:
Number of Bytes Received.................. 0
Number of Bytes Sent...................... 0
Number of Packets Received................ 0
Number of Packets Sent.................... 0
Number of Policy Errors................... 0
Radio Signal Strength Indicator........... Unavailable
—More— or (q)uit
Signal to Noise Ratio..................... Unavailable
Nearby AP Statistics:
TxExcessiveRetries: 0
TxRetries: 0
RtsSuccessCnt: 0
RtsFailCnt: 0
TxFiltered: 0
TxRateProfile: [0,0,0,0,0,0,0,0,0,0,0,0]
Research_Lab-AP(slot 0) ...................
```

Example 20-2   *Viewing Client Details*   *(continued)*

```
antenna0: 5 seconds ago -93 dBm................. antenna1: 4293918453 seconds ago
-128 dBm
Lobby-AP(slot 0) ........................
antenna0: 4293918453 seconds ago -128 dBm........ antenna1: 5 seconds ago -94 dBm
```

Although this information is valuable, it is important to note that it is static. In other words, the information you gain from **show** commands gives you the state or the conditions of the network at the time that you enter the command. If you require real-time information, debugs come in handy.

If you have come from the routing world, you are probably familiar with the use of **debug** commands and how invaluable they are in troubleshooting. If you are working your way through the certification program, and you are doing it in order (CCNA > CCNA Wireless), then you learned in the CCNA curriculum how a **debug** command is used in some basic troubleshooting scenarios. The concept of **debug** commands carries over here to the wireless space. Available only from the CLI, **debug** commands can be used on the controller to help troubleshoot issues. The principle in the use of **debug** commands is the same:

■ Do not leave them on, because they are CPU intensive.

■ Be prepared to turn them off. Sometimes the output is overwhelming.

■ **Debug** commands take priority over other processes on the controller.

If you think that some **debug** commands might already be enabled, use the **show debug** command to verify that notion. One fail-safe that is in place is that if you do turn on a **debug** command and forget about it, the **debug** becomes disabled when the CLI session times out. Although this is a good fail-safe, you should still turn your **debug** commands off when you are done with them. To see a list of the available **debug** commands, use the **debug ?** command, as seen in Example 20-3. You can use this to determine which **debug** command is appropriate for the situation; for example, if you are troubleshooting a port-based authentication problem, you might enable **debug dot1x**.

Example 20-3   *Viewing Available* **debug** *Commands*

```
(Cisco Controller) >debug ?

aaa Configures the AAA debug options.
airewave-director Configures the Airewave Director debug options
ap Configures debug of Cisco AP.
arp Configures debug of ARP.
bcast Configures debug of broadcast.
cac Configures the call admission control (CAC) debug options.
cdp Configures debug of cdp.
crypto Configures the Hardware Crypto debug options.
dhcp Configures the DHCP debug options.
client Enables debugs for common client problems.
disable-all Disables all debug messages.
```

continues

Example 20-3 *Viewing Available* **debug** *Commands* *(continued)*

```
dot11 Configures the 802.11 events debug options.
dot1x Configures the 802.1X debug options.
iapp Configures the IAPP debug options.
ccxrm Configures the CCX_RM debug options.
ccxdiag Configures the CCX Diagnostic debug options.
locp Configures the LOCP debug options.
l2roam Configures the L2 Roam debug options.
l2age Configures debug of Layer 2 Ago Timeout Messages.
lwapp Configures the LWAPP debug options
mac Configures MAC debugging
--More-- or (q)uit
```

To really hone in on where the issues are, you can use **debug** commands for a specific AP or a specific client. This requires placing the controller into client troubleshooting mode. To do this, begin by telling the controller, by way of a CLI command, that you want to debug for a specific MAC address. For example, to tell the controller that it will be debugging for MAC address 00:1a:a2:f9:ed:d0, enter the following:

Key Topic

```
(Cisco Controller) >debug mac addr 00:1a:a2:f9:ed:d0
```
The next step is to tell the controller which debug to use for that particular MAC address. For example, if you want to debug LWAPP events for the MAC address 00:1a:a2:f9:ed:d0, use the **debug lwapp** command as shown here:

Key Topic

```
(Cisco Controller) >debug lwapp events enable
```
To verify that the **debug** command is enabled, use the **show debug** command, as seen in Example 20-4.

Key Topic

Example 20-4 *Verifying Enabled Debugs*

```
(Cisco Controller) >show debug
MAC address ............................. 00:1a:a2:f9:ed:d0

Debug Flags Enabled:
arp error enabled.
bcast error enabled.
lwapp events enabled.
lwapp errors enabled.
```

Then you wait for an LWAPP event to occur. In Example 20-5, an LWAPP event has occurred, and a message has been sent to the console.

Example 20-5 *Controller Debug Output*

```
(Cisco Controller) >Wed Jun 25 19:50:50 2008: 00:1a:a2:f9:ed:d0 Received LWAPP
  ECHO_REQUEST from AP 00:1a:a2:f9:ed:d0
Wed Jun 25 19:50:50 2008: 00:1a:a2:f9:ed:d0 Successfully transmission of LWAPP
  Echo-Response to AP 00:1a:a2:f9:ed:d0
Wed Jun 25 19:50:50 2008: 00:1a:a2:f9:ed:d0 Received LWAPP PRIMARY_DISCOVERY_REQ
  from AP 00:1a:a2:f9:ed:d0
```

Example 20-5   *Controller Debug Output   (continued)*

```
Wed Jun 25 19:50:50 2008: 00:1a:a2:f9:ed:d0 Received LWAPP RRM_DATA_REQ from AP
  00:1a:a2:f9:ed:d0
Wed Jun 25 19:50:50 2008: 00:1a:a2:f9:ed:d0 Successfully transmission of LWAPP
  Airewave-Director-Data Response to AP 00:1a:a2:f9:ed:d0
Wed Jun 25 19:51:14 2008: 00:1a:a2:f9:ed:d0 Received LWAPP RRM_DATA_REQ from AP
  00:1a:a2:f9:ed:d0
Wed Jun 25 19:51:14 2008: 00:1a:a2:f9:ed:d0 Successfully transmission of LWAPP
  Airewave-Director-Data Response to AP 00:1a:a2:f9:ed:d0
```

The actual output of the debug in the example is pretty normal. What is important, however, is that you understand how to enable the debug process, verify it, and turn it off. To
disable the debug process, use the **debug disable-all** command, as seen in Example 20-6.
First the debug process was verified with the **show debug** command, and then it was disabled. After the debug process was disabled, the command **show debug** was again used to
verify that it was in fact disabled.

Example 20-6   *Verify the Enabled Debugs*

```
(Cisco Controller) >show debug
MAC address ............................... 00:1a:a2:f9:ed:d0

Debug Flags Enabled:
arp error enabled.
bcast error enabled.
lwapp events enabled.
lwapp errors enabled.



(Cisco Controller) >debug disable-all

 (Cisco Controller) >show debug
MAC debugging ............................ disabled

Debug Flags Enabled:



 (Cisco Controller) >
```

When you let the session time out, even though it turns off the **debug** command, it still
leaves the command to perform client troubleshooting, as seen in Example 20-7. This
means that if you enable a new **debug** command, it only debugs for the client you specify.

Example 20-7   *Command to Perform Client Troubleshooting Remains*

```
Connection to 192.168.1.50 closed.
terminal$:
terminal$:
terminal$:ssh 192.168.1.50
```

continues

Example 20-5 *Command to Perform Client Troubleshooting Remains* *(continued)*

```
(Cisco Controller)
User: admin
Password:*****
(Cisco Controller) >show debug
MAC address ............................. 00:1a:a2:f9:ed:d0

Debug Flags Enabled:
```

As you can see, the connection was closed, essentially timing out. After authenticating again to the CLI of the controller, the **show debug** command was entered. This command output indicates that the MAC address 00:1a:a2:f9:ed:d0 is still enabled for client debugging. The point here is that it is always best to turn off **debug** commands when you are finished using them. You can also turn off a specific **debug** command using the **disable** option at the end of the command. For example, to turn off the LWAPP debug that was used in the previous examples, you would use the **debug lwapp events disable** command.

When you are comfortable turning **debug** commands on and off, you can explore **debug** commands such as **debug dot11**. The **debug dot11** command helps you troubleshoot 802.11 parameters, such as these:

- Mobility
- Rogue detection
- Load balancing events

In Example 20-8, you can see a client that has successfully associated.

Example 20-8 *A Successful Association*

```
Fri Aug 8 15:32:54 2008: 00:1e:c2:ab:14:26 apfPemAddUser2 (apf_policy.c:209)
  Changing state for mobile 00:1e:c2:ab:14:26 on AP 00:1a:a2:f9:ed:d0 from
  Associated to Associated

Fri Aug 8 15:32:54 2008: 00:1e:c2:ab:14:26 New client (policy)

Fri Aug 8 15:32:54 2008: 00:1e:c2:ab:14:26 Stopping deletion of Mobile Station:
  (callerId: 48)

Fri Aug 8 15:32:54 2008: 00:1e:c2:ab:14:26 Sending Assoc Response to station on
  BSSID 00:1a:a2:f9:ed:d0 (status 0)

Fri Aug 8 15:32:54 2008: 00:1e:c2:ab:14:26 apfProcessAssocReq (apf_80211.c:4149)
  Changing state for mobile 00:1e:c2:ab:14:26 on AP 00:1a:a2:f9:ed:d0 from
  Associated to Associated

Fri Aug 8 15:32:54 2008: 00:1e:c2:ab:14:26 802 new client 00:1e:c2:ab:14:26
```

Example 20-8 *A Successful Association* *(continued)*

```
Fri Aug 8 15:32:55 2008: 00:1e:c2:ab:14:26 LBS Client data rcvd from AP
00:1a:a2:f9:ed:d0(0) with RSSI (A -128, B -36), SNR 57

Fri Aug 8 15:32:55 2008: 00:1e:c2:ab:14:26 LBS change cur RSSI B -44 , prev -47,
  send notify
```

In this small output, you can see that the client has become associated. One aspect of troubleshooting might involve connectivity. With this output, you can see that the client is in fact associated. If the client still has connectivity issues, you would want to start looking at the wired network, working your way from the controller, then to the switch, then to the next hop router, and so on.

You can also use debugs such as **debug dhcp** if you are having issues with clients obtaining IP addresses. If you are having authentication issues, you might use the **debug aaa** or **debug dot1x** commands.

Using the Controller Interface

The controller has several tools to help troubleshoot. From the controller interface, you can use controller logs, SNMP to alert administrators to current issues, and the Tech Support Pages. In the section "Using the CLI to Troubleshoot," you looked at output of a client that was trying to associate. You can see a web interface equivalent to the **show client summary** command in Figure 20-1.

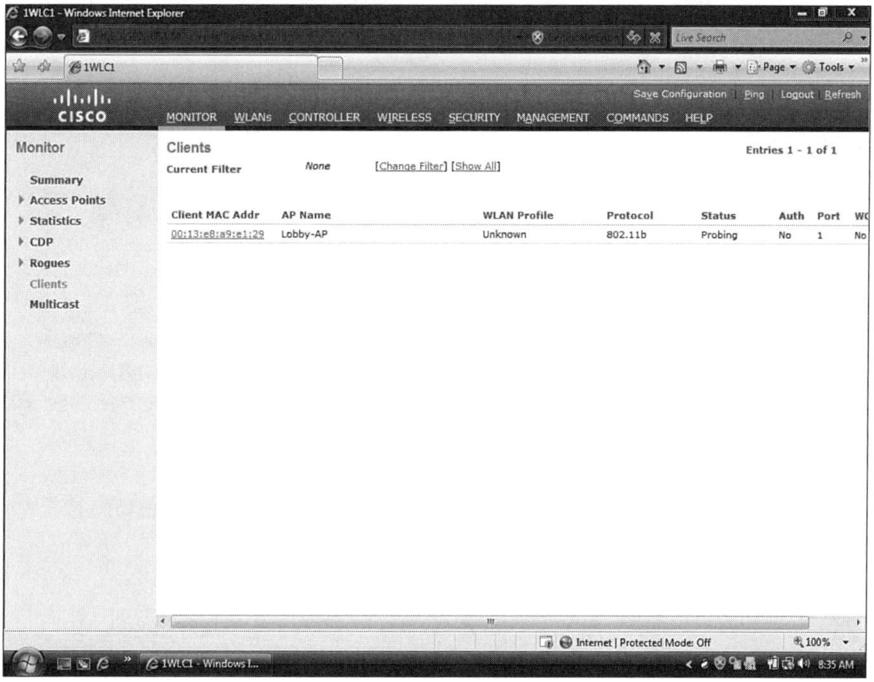

Figure 20-1 *Viewing the Client Summary*

Here you can gain information about the client, the WLAN the client is on, and other valuable information for troubleshooting.

Using the Controller Logs

Another valuable resource is the controller logs. Controller logs allow you to see events that have occurred at various levels. You probably want to send these to a Syslog server, but you can view them on the controller by going to **MANAGEMENT > Logs > Message logs**. Figure 20-2 shows just a sample of the information that you can obtain here.

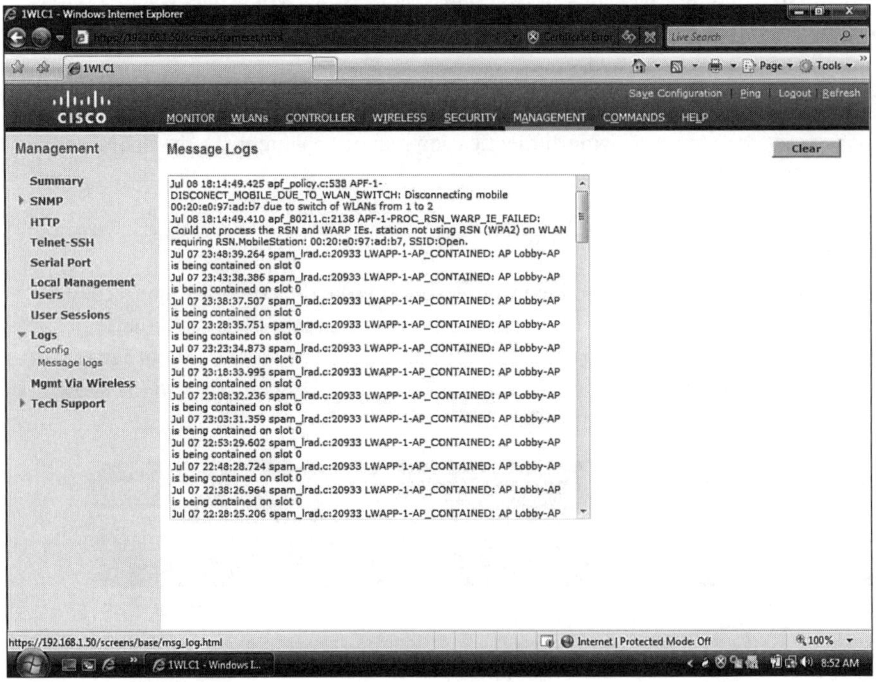

Figure 20-2 *Viewing the Controller Logs*

To change the way logging is configured, browse to **MANAGEMENT > Logs > Config**. This configuration page is shown in Figure 20-3. You cant see it inf Figure 20-3, but by selecting the **Syslog** check box, you can point to an external server by entering the address in the Syslog Server IP Address field.

> **Note:**   If you do not already have a Syslog server, you can download kiwi from http:/ /www.kiwisyslog.com. Kiwi is a free Syslog server that many people use.

In addition, from the Syslog Configuration page, you can set the level of logging by changing the facility levels. These levels control how much information is captured. In general, the larger the facility number, the more information that is recorded; however, this is not always the case. Table 20-2 shows the available facility levels.

Table 20-2   *Available Facility Levels*

Facility Name	Facility Level
Kernel	0
User Process	1
Mail	2
System Daemons	3
Authorization	4
Syslog	5
Line Printer	6
USENET	7
Unix-to-Unix Copy	8
Cron	9
—	10
FTP Daemons	11
System Use 1	12
System Use 2	13
System Use 3	14
System Use 4	15
Local Use 0	16
Local Use 1	17
Local Use 2	18
Local Use 3	19
Local Use 4	20
Local Use 5	21
Local Use 6	22
Local Use 7	23

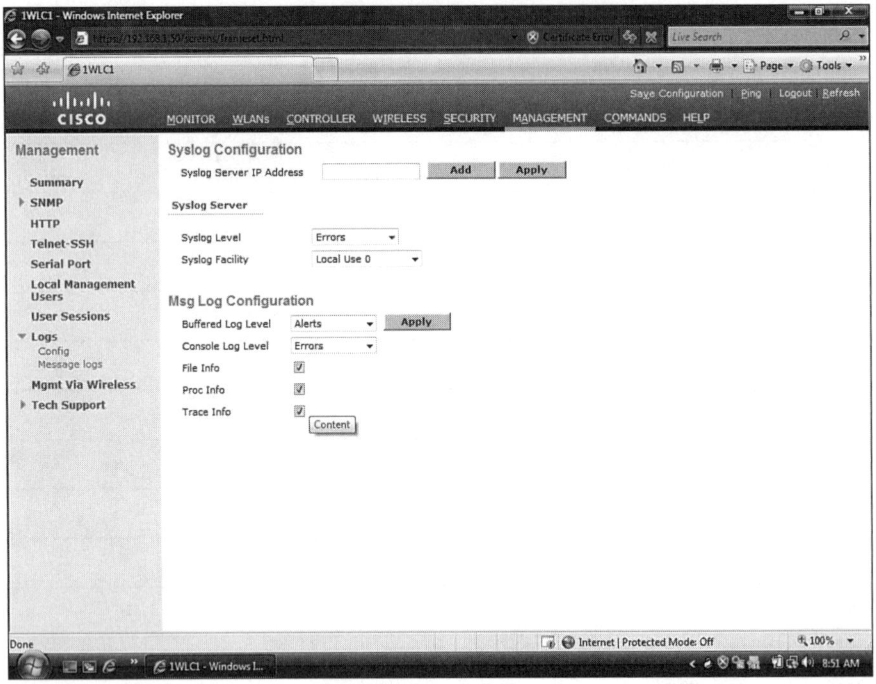

Figure 20-3 *Configuring Syslog*

You can locally view the logs by selecting **MANAGEMENT > Logs > Message logs**. The message logs include information related to the network infrastructure, client issues, authentication issues, and AP association issues. These have relevance to the controller.

Using SNMP

When using SNMP gets/sets, you can obtain information about the status of the controller and allows you to remotely manage the controller. To set up SNMP, go to **MANAGEMENT > SNMP > General**. Here you configure the following parameters, as shown in Figure 20-4:

- Name
- Location
- Contact
- System Description
- System Object ID
- SNMP Port Number
- Trap Port Number
- SNMP v1 Mode
- SNMP v2c Mode
- SNMP v3 Mode

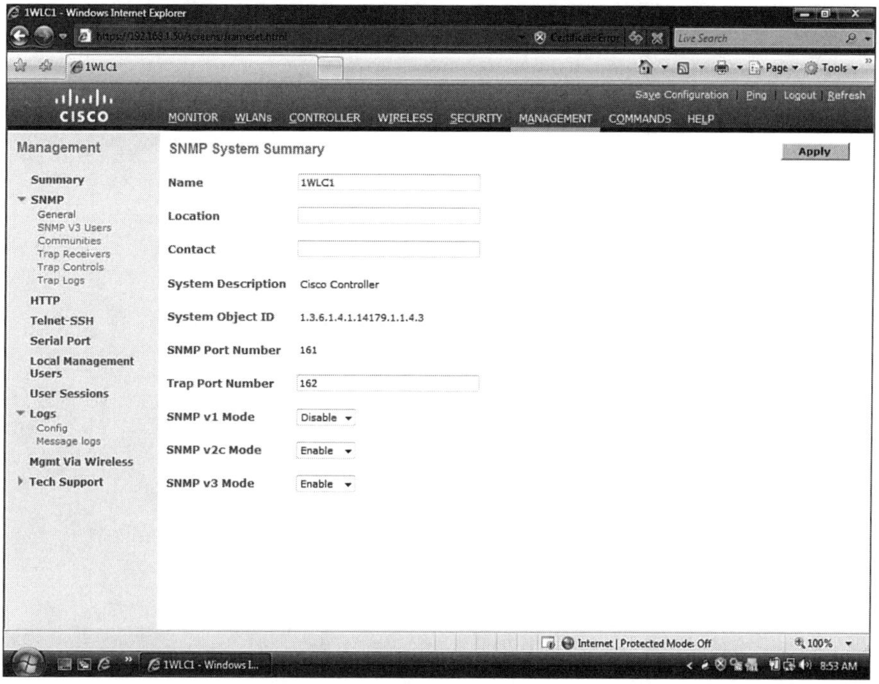

Figure 20-4   *SNMP Configuration on Controllers*

Configuring the Community Strings

When you set up SNMP, two community names exist by default. Public is for read-only access, and Private is for read/write access. If you have any involvement in security, you already know that you should change these values. They are well-known values that an attacker can use to gain control of your controller. You can modify the values in the controller by choosing **MANAGEMENT > SNMP > Communities**.

You can also set the SNMPv3 users and trap receivers. Although it is not covered here, it is recommended that you use SNMPv3, because it is the most secure method at the moment.

To view the SNMP trap logs, go to **MANAGEMENT > SNMP > Trap Logs**. Figure 20-5 shows a sample of the SNMP trap logs.

You can use these trap logs to troubleshoot client association failures and AP association failures. The trap logs generate a reason code that can point you in the right direction to correct the issue. Another way to refine the information you receive is by using the Trap Controls found at **MANAGEMENT > SNMP > Trap Controls**. Here you can control what events generate a trap.

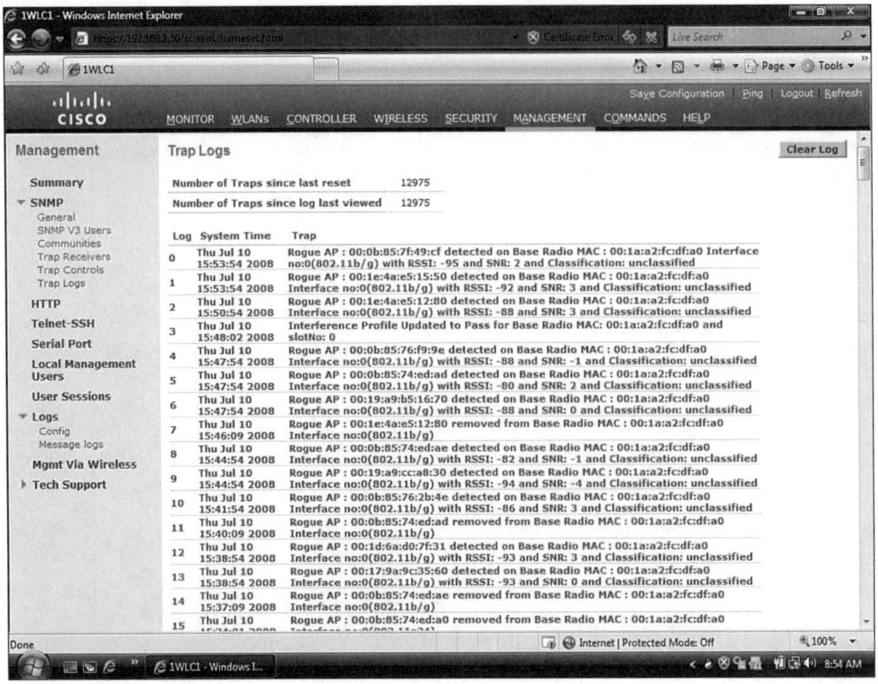

Figure 20-5   *SNMP Trap Logs*

Using Tech Support

You might also find the Tech Support Pages, found at **MANAGEMENT > Tech Support**, to be of benefit. Although Cisco TAC uses most of what you do here, you might find it beneficial information for troubleshooting.

Crash logs, which the controller maintains, are created when a system fails. You cannot use most of the information found in the logs without Cisco TAC assistance. If Cisco TAC request these logs, you can access them by going to **MANAGEMENT > Tech Support > Controller Crash**. Five crash dump files can be stored on a controller at any given time.

APs also create a crash log file that the controller can download. Go to **MANAGEMENT > Tech Support >AP Crash Log > Get Log** to retrieve it. TAC also uses the AP crash logs.

Using WCS Version 5.x to Troubleshoot Clients

You can use WCS to troubleshoot wireless deployments. Use the **Monitor > Client** page to troubleshoot clients. You can see this page in Figure 20-6. When you use this tool, you get a Summary page with a list of problems and corresponding solutions. The page also has a log analysis and a detailed event history.

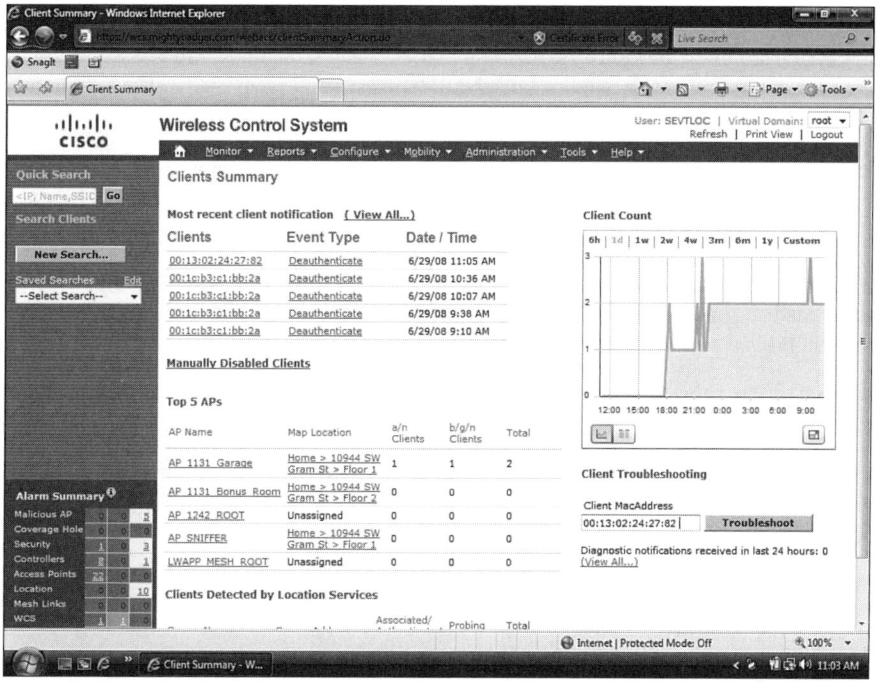

Figure 20-6   *Critical Alarms*

You can use the alarms to troubleshoot. In the Clients Summary page, click the numerous alarms in the lower left to be taken to that Alarm page. Figure 20-6 shows several critical alarms.

Using the Cisco Spectrum Expert

Cisco Spectrum Expert addresses the problem of RF interference in wireless networks. With Cisco Spectrum Expert, you can detect, classify, locate, and manually mitigate sources of wireless interference.

The Cisco Spectrum Expert Wi-Fi is the industry-leading spectrum intelligence product for Wi-Fi networks. Cisco Spectrum Expert Wi-Fi offers complete visibility into the RF physical layer in the 2.4-GHz and 5-GHz frequencies, allowing for enhanced performance, security, and reliability of WLAN services.

The Cisco Spectrum Expert Wi-Fi includes the following components:

■ Cisco Spectrum Expert Wi-Fi sensor

■ Cisco Spectrum Expert software

■ Cisco Spectrum Expert antenna

The Cisco Spectrum Expert Wi-Fi sensor is a sensor in the CardBus card form factor for notebooks. It is supported on Microsoft Windows–based laptops and delivers comprehensive spectrum intelligence. Network administrators can streamline wireless network troubleshooting with better visibility into the RF spectrum and can easily identify and detect sources of wireless interference.

Cisco Spectrum Expert provides a comprehensive list of all access points, ad hoc networks, and interferer devices (for example, microwave ovens, cordless phones, wireless security cameras, Bluetooth devices, and RF jammers).

Cisco Spectrum Expert also gives you a Channel Summary that provides visibility of RF activity—such as power levels and presence of 802.11 and interferer devices—on a channel-by-channel basis.

The Devices View provides a deeper look at each device and its impact to the wireless network, including power level, channel coverage, and other data.

A Device Finder tracks down the location of devices, causing wireless interference throughout your enterprise. The Device Classifier offers the most comprehensive classification of the RF devices, which include the following:

■ Wi-Fi access points

■ In-network devices

■ Known devices

■ Unknown devices

■ Ad hoc devices

■ Wi-Fi stations

■ A variety of Bluetooth devices

■ A variety of cordless phones[1]

■ Microwave ovens

■ Generic fixed-frequency devices

■ Generic frequency-hopped devices

■ Generic continuous transmitters (for example, FM phones, NTSC video devices)

■ RF jamming devices

■ 802.11FH devices

■ Analog video devices

The Spectrum Views create plots and charts for a direct view into the RF spectrum, including measurements of RF power and network device activity. The plots are especially useful to trained RF engineers, and the charts are informative for both the expert RF engineer and the generalist network engineer.

An Alarms Setting configures enterprise-specific alerts and alarm triggers to notify you when wireless network is at critical utilization points.

All this is integrated with Cisco WCS and is based on obtaining a license to integrate it.

Exam Preparation Tasks

Review All the Key Topics

Review the most important topics from this chapter, noted with the Key Topics icon in the outer margin of the page. Table 20-3 lists a reference of these key topics and the page number where you can find each one.

Table 20-3 *Key Topics for Chapter 20*

Key Topic Item	Description	Page Number
Paragraph from the section "Common Client-Side Issues"	Discussion of the Hidden Node issue	410
Paragraph from the section "Common Client-Side Issues"	Discussion of the Exposed Node issue	410
Paragraph from the section "Common Client-Side Issues"	Discussion of the Near/Far issue	410
Example 20-1	Viewing the client summary	411
Example 20-2	Viewing client details	411
Command syntax	Enable client troubleshooting	414
Command syntax	Debug LWAPP events	414
Example 20-4	Verify enabled debugs	414
Figure 20-1	Viewing the client summary	417
Figure 20-2	Viewing the controller logs	418

Complete the Tables and Lists from Memory

Print a copy of Appendix B, "Memory Tables," (found on the CD) or at least the section for this chapter, and complete the tables and lists from memory. Appendix C, "Memory Tables Answer Key," also on the CD, includes completed tables and lists to check your work.

Definition of Key Terms

Define the following key terms from this chapter, and check your answers in the Glossary:

Hidden Node issue, Exposed Node issue

References

"Troubleshooting TechNotes" at Cisco.com: http://tinyurl.com/6dqxj2

"Troubleshooting Connectivity in a Wireless LAN Network" at Cisco.com: http://tinyurl.com/6l2ob2

The Cisco Spectrum Expert at Cisco.com: http://tinyurl.com/5eja7f

Part IV: Final Preparation

CHAPTER 21

Final Preparation

This book has covered the technologies, protocols, commands, and features required for you to be prepared to pass the CCNA Wireless exam. Although this book supplies detailed information, most people need more preparation than simply reading a book. This chapter details a set of tools and a study plan that can help you complete your preparation for the exam.

If you're preparing for the CCNA Wireless exam, you should have already passed the CCNA level exams, either the CCNA exam or the ICND1 and ICND2 exams. For information on passing the CCNA exams, refer to *CCENT/CCNA ICND1 Official Exam Certification Guide* or *CCNA ICND2 Official Exam Certification Guide*, or go to http://www.cisco.com/go/ccna.

This short chapter has two main sections. The first lists the exam preparation tools that are useful at this point in your study process. The second section lists a suggested study plan now that you have completed the rest of the chapters.

Note: This chapter refers to many of the chapters and appendixes included with this book, as well as tools available on the CD. Appendixes B and C are included only on the CD that comes with this book. To access those, just insert the CD and make the appropriate selection from the opening interface.

Tools for Final Preparation

This section describes the available tools and how to access them.

Exam Engine and Questions on the CD

The CD in the back of the book includes an exam engine—software that displays and grades a set of exam-realistic questions. The question database includes simulation (sim) questions, drag-and-drop questions, and many scenario-based questions that require the same level of analysis as the questions on the CCNA Wireless exam. Using the exam engine, you can either study by practicing using the questions in Study Mode, or take a simulated (timed) CCNA Wireless exam.

The installation process has two major steps. The CD in the back of this book has a recent copy of the exam engine software, supplied by Boson Software (http://www.boson.com). The practice exam—the database of CCNA Wireless exam questions—is not on the CD. Instead, the practice exam resides on the www.boson.com web server, so the second major step is to activate and download the practice exam.

Note: The cardboard CD case in the back of this book includes the CD and a piece of pa-per. The paper lists the activation key for the practice exam associated with this book. *Do not lose this activation key.*

Install the Software from the CD

The software installation process is pretty routine as compared with other software instal-lation processes. The following list outlines the steps:

Step 1.   Insert the CD into your PC.

Step 2.   The software that automatically runs is the Cisco Press software to access and use all CD-based features, including the exam engine, viewing a PDF of this book, and viewing the CD-only appendixes. From the main menu, click the op-tion to **Install the Exam Engine**.

Step 3.   Respond to the prompt windows as you would with any typical software in-stallation process.

The installation process might give you the option to register the software. This process requires that you establish a login at the www.boson.com website. You need this login to activate the exam, so feel free to register when prompted.

Activate and Download the Practice Exam

After the exam engine is installed, you should activate the exam associated with this book:

Step 1.   Start the Boson Exam Engine (BEE) software from the Start menu.

Step 2.   The first time you start the software, it should ask you to either log in or register an account. If you do not already have an account with Boson, select the option to register a new account. (You must register to download and use the exam.)

Step 3.   After you are registered, the software might prompt you to download the lat-est version of the software, which you should do. Note that this process up-dates the exam engine software (formally called the Boson Exam Environment), not the practice exam.

Step 4.   To activate and download the exam associated with this book, from the exam engine main window, click the **Exam Wizard** button.

Step 5.   From the Exam Wizard pop-up window, select **Activate a purchased exam** and click the **Next** button. (Although you did not purchase the exam directly, you purchased it indirectly when you bought the book.)

Step 6.   At the next screen, enter the Activation Key from the paper inside the card-board CD holder in the back of the book and click the **Next** button.

Step 7.   The activation process downloads the practice exam. When it is done, the main exam engine menu should list a new exam, with a name like "ExSim for Cisco Press CCNA Wireless ECG." If you do not see the exam, make sure you have selected the My Exams tab on the menu. You may need to click the plus sign icon (+) to expand the menu and see the exam.

At this point, the software and practice exam are ready to use.

Activating Other Exams

You need to install the exam software and register only once. Then, for each new exam, only a few steps will be required. For instance, if you bought both this book along with *CCENT/CCNA ICND1 Official Exam Certification Guide* or *CCNA ICND2 Official Exam Certification Guide*, you could follow the steps listed on the last page or so to install the software and activate the exam associated with this book. Then, for the practice exam associated with the ICND1 book and ICND2 book, you would need to follow only a few more steps. All you have to do is start the exam engine (if it's not still up and running) and follow Steps 4 and 5 in the preceding list. If fact, if you purchase other Cisco Press books, or purchase a practice exam from Boson, you just need to activate each new exam as described in Steps 4 and 5.

You can also purchase additional practice exams from Boson directly from its website. When you purchase an exam, you receive an activation key, and then you can activate and download the exam—again without requiring any additional software installation.

Cisco Learning Network

Cisco provides a wide variety of CCNA wireless preparation tools at a Cisco Systems website called the Cisco Learning Network. The Cisco Learning Network includes Quick Learning Modules, interviews with Cisco's Portfolio Manager for Wireless Certifications, documents that give you a sneak peek of what's included in the Instructor-Led Training Course, and blogs and discussion forums to help you on your way.

To use the Cisco Learning Network, you do not need a registered login at http://www. cisco.com, but you can register as a member of the learning network. This gives you access to additional content. To register, simply go to https://cisco.hosted.jivesoftware.com/ create-account.jspa and supply some information. (You do not need to work for Cisco or one of its Partners to get a login.)

After you have registered, proceed to the Certifications area, and look for the link to the CCNA Wireless pages.

Study Plan

You could simply study using all the available tools, as mentioned earlier in this chapter. However, this section suggests a particular study plan, with a sequence of tasks that may work better than just using the tools randomly. However, feel free to use the tools in any way and at any time that helps you get fully prepared for the exam.

The suggested study plan separates the tasks into three categories:

- **Recall the facts:** Activities that help you remember all the details from this book.

- **Practice configurations:** You must master configurations on various devices to pass the CCNA Wireless exam. This category lists the items you can use to master configuration skills.

- **Use the exam engine to practice realistic questions:** You can use the exam engine on the CD to study using a bank of unique exam-realistic questions available only with this book.

Recall the Facts

As with most exams, you must recall many facts, concepts, and definitions to do well on the test. This section suggests a couple of tasks that should help you remember all the details:

- Review and repeat, as needed, the activities in the Exam Preparation Tasks section at the end of each chapter. Most of these activities help refine your knowledge of a topic while also helping you memorize the facts.

- Using the Exam Engine, answer all the questions in the Book database. This question database includes all the questions at the beginning of each chapter. Although some of the questions may be familiar, repeating them will help improve your recall of the topics covered in the questions.

Practice Configurations

A large part of CCNA wireless involves performing configurations on various devices. You might need to work on a controller, AP, or even WCS. Understanding these interfaces and various configurations is a must. This means that hands-on experience can take you over the edge to confidently and accurately build or verify configurations.

There are a number of sources of lab access. Some of these sources include rack rentals from trusted Cisco Partners. If you are a Cisco Partner, you might even have access to the Partner E-learning Connection (PEC). If you have access to a lab provided by your company, take advantage of it. Nothing beats hands-on experience.

Additionally, you can review the key topics in each chapter. These often refer to key configuration elements.

Use the Exam Engine

The exam engine includes two basic modes:

- **Study mode:** Study mode is most useful when you want to use the questions to learn and practice. In study mode, you can select options such as whether you want to randomize the order of the questions, randomize the order of the answers, automatically see the answers, and many other options.

- **Simulation mode:** Simulation mode simulates an actual CCNA Wireless exam by either requiring or allowing a set number of questions and a set time period. These timed exams not only allow you to study for the actual exam, but they also help you simulate the time pressure that can occur on the actual exam.

Choosing Study or Simulation Mode

Both study mode and simulation mode are useful for preparing for the exams. Picking the correct mode from the exam engine's user interface is pretty obvious, but you should still spend some time experimenting with the exam engine.

Passing Scores for the Cisco CCNA Wireless Exams

When scoring your simulated exam using this book's exam engine, you should strive to get a score of 85 percent or better. However, the scoring on the book's exam engine does not match how Cisco scores the actual CCNA Wireless exam. As it turns out, Cisco does not publish many details about how the actual exam is scored. Therefore, you cannot reasonably deduce which questions you got right or wrong, and how many points are assigned to each question.

Cisco does publish some specific guidance about how it scores the exam, and other details have been mentioned by Cisco personnel during public presentations about the CCNA Wireless exam. Here are some key facts about scoring:

- Cisco does give partial credit on simulation questions, so complete as much of a simulation question as you can.

- Cisco may or may not give more weight to some questions.

- The test does not adapt based on your answers to early questions in the test. For example, if you miss a RIP question, and it is question 1, the test does not start giving you more RIP questions.

- Cisco's scores range from 300 to 1000, with a passing grade usually (but not always) around 849 for the CCNA Wireless exam.

- The 849 out of 1000 does not necessarily mean that you got 84.9 percent of the questions correct.

Part V: Appendixes

Answers to the "Do I Know This Already?" Quizzes

Chapter 1

1. A
2. D
3. B and C
4. A
5. B
6. C and D
7. A, D, and E
8. A and C
9. A
10. C

Chapter 2

1. A
2. B
3. A and C
4. A
5. A, B, and E
6. B
7. A
8. A
9. C
10. A and C

Chapter 3

1. D
2. D
3. A
4. C
5. D
6. B
7. A
8. B and D
9. A
10. C
11. B and D

Chapter 4

1. C
2. B
3. C
4. B and D
5. A
6. B
7. B
8. B and C
9. D
10. A
11. A
12. B
13. B
14. A
15. D
16. D
17. A
18. A
19. C
20. B
21. B
22. A and C

23. C

24. C

25. B

26. A

Chapter 5

1. A, B, and D

2. A

3. C

4. D

5. B

6. C

7. B

8. A and C

9. B

10. B

11. A

12. D

13. A, C, and D

14. B

15. A

16. A

17. B and C

18. B

19. A

20. B

Chapter 6

1. B

2. C

3. A and D

4. D

5. A

6. D

7. B

8. A and C

9. A and B

10. A, C, and D

11. A and B

12. C

13. D

14. A and C

15. B

16. A

17. C

18. C

19. A and B

20. A and B

21. A

22. A

23. A

24. C

25. B

Chapter 7

1. A, B, and C

2. A

3. B

4. A and D

5. C

6. D

7. A

8. D

9. A

10. D

11. A

12. B

Chapter 8

1. D

2. C

3. D

4. D
5. A
6. B
7. B
8. A, B, and D
9. A
10. B
11. A
12. B
13. A
14. A
15. A and B

Chapter 9

1. A
2. D
3. D
4. D
5. A and B. A VLAN is used to define a logical broadcast domain and isolate a subnet.
6. B
7. D
8. C
9. C
10. A
11. D
12. C

Chapter 10

1. A
2. D
3. C
4. B
5. A, B, and C
6. A, C, and D
7. C
8. A

9. A and B
10. A
11. B
12. B
13. A
14. C
15. C
16. D
17. C

Chapter 11

1. A and D
2. D
3. A
4. D
5. C
6. B
7. B
8. D
9. A
10. A
11. A
12. C
13. A
14. C

Chapter 12

1. C
2. D
3. A
4. A
5. B
6. A and C
7. D
8. C
9. B

10. A
11. B

Chapter 13

1. B
2. D
3. A
4. A
5. D
6. A
7. C
8. D
9. D
10. A
11. A and B
12. B
13. C
14. D
15. A, B, and D
16. C
17. A
18. C
19. C

Chapter 14

1. A
2. A and B
3. B, C, and D
4. A, B, and D
5. B
6. B
7. A and D
8. D
9. B
10. A

Chapter 15

1. B
2. C
3. D
4. B, C, and D
5. A
6. B, C, and D
7. D
8. A
9. D
10. A

Chapter 16

1. D
2. A and C
3. B
4. B
5. B
6. B
7. A and B
8. A
9. A
10. C
11. A and B
12. A

Chapter 17

1. A and B
2. A and C
3. B
4. C
5. D
6. B
7. A
8. D
9. D

10. A
11. C
12. A
13. D
14. A

Chapter 18

1. A, B, and C
2. B
3. B
4. A and B
5. D
6. B
7. C and D
8. A
9. B
10. A and B
11. A
12. D
13. A
14. A and C
15. C
16. C
17. D
18. B. There are AP templates as well.
19. D
20. A
21. A, B, and C
22. A, B, and C
23. A
24. C
25. C

Chapter 19

1. A
2. B
3. D
4. D
5. A and B
6. B
7. C
8. A
9. B
10. D
11. A

Chapter 20

1. B
2. A and B
3. C
4. A
5. D
6. B
7. B
8. C
9. D
10. D
11. A
12. C
13. B
14. A
15. A

GLOSSARY

This glossary defines many of the terms, abbreviations, and acronyms related to networking. It includes all the key terms used throughout the book. As with any growing technical field, some terms evolve and take on several meanings. Where necessary, multiple definitions and abbreviation expansions are provided.

Numbers

802.1q   An IEEE form of trunking.

802.1x   An IEEE definition of port-based authentication.

802.15.1   An IEEE definition of personal-area networks.

802.15.1-2005   An IEEE definition of personal-area networks that includes additions incorporated in Bluetooth v1.2.

802.16e   An IEEE standard defining point-to-multipoint broadband wireless definitions and an amendment to 802.16.

A

absorption   Removes amplitude from a wave, essentially reducing the distance it can travel.

access port   A port connected to a host rather than to another switch and normally on only one VLAN.

acknowledged (ACK)   A response to some form of request.

active scan   The process of actively scanning for available wireless networks.

Adaptive Frequency Hopping Spread Spectrum Technology   A spread spectrum method used to improve resistance to RF, often used in Bluetooth technology.

ad hoc   When two computers communicate directly with one another.

Advanced Encryption Standard (AES)   Also known as Rijndael. A block cipher adopted as an encryption standard by the U.S. government.

Aironet Client Administration Utility (ACAU)   A Cisco software utility designed to configure the Aironet Desktop Utility before deployment.

Aironet Desktop Utility (ADU)   Cisco software used to manage a single a/b/g wireless card.

Airport Extreme   The MAC-OSX wireless client.

amplifier   Added between the AP and the antenna to strengthen the signal.

amplitude   The volume of the signal.

anchor   The original controller.

Announcement Traffic Indication Message (ATIM)   Used in IEEE 802.11 ad hoc or independent BSS networks to announce the existence of buffered frames when a client is in sleep mode.

AP priming   After the AP is associated with at least one controller, the AP gets a list of other controllers it can associate with from the one that is already associated with.

ARP   Address Resolution Protocol. Used to resolve a MAC address to an IP address.

association request   A request from a client to the AP for association.

association response   A response from an AP to a client during open association.

asymmetric tunneling   Traffic from the client is routed to the destination, regardless of its source address. The return traffic is sent to its original controller, called an anchor, and is tunneled to the new controller.

attenuator   Reduces the signal if there is too much signal, causing bleed-over into other networks.

authentication request   A request from a client to an AP during open authentication.

authentication response   A response from an AP to a client during open authentication.

authentication server   An AAA server that has a list of users in one form or another that can verify the supplicant.

authenticator   The switch.

Autonomous Workgroup Bridge (aWGB)   A wireless bridge operating autonomously.

autoprovisioning   Simplifies deployments when you have a large number of controllers.

azimuth   The angle measured in degrees between a reference plane and a point.

B

backoff timer   A random number that begins a countdown process while listening.

bandwidth   The frequency spectrum, measured in Hertz. Bandwidth can refer to data rates or the width of an RF channel.

barker code   Defines the use of 11 chips when encoding data.

Basic Service Area (BSA)   The coverage area of the AP.

Basic Service Set (BSS)   One device sets a network name and radio parameters, and the other uses it to connect.

Basic Service Set Identifier (BSSID)   Only one network that an AP is offering service for.

beacon   An announcement of services from an AP.

Binary Phase Shift Keying (BPSK)   A modulation technique used in 802.11 networks.

block acknowledgment   The confirmation from the recipient station, stating which frames have been received. Used in 802.11n networks.

Bluetooth   A personal-area technology.

bridge mode   A mode that an AP can operate in, in which it bridges traffic from source to destination.

C

Carrier Sense Multiple Access/Collision Avoidance (CSMA/CA)   When a device wants to send, it must listen first. Similar to CSMA/CD.

channel   A defined frequency range.

Channel State Information (CSI)   If the receiver is moving, the reflection characteristics change, and the beamforming can no longer be coordinated.

chipping code   A code used to represent bits.

circular polarization   Indicates that the wave circles as it moves forward.

Cisco Client Extension Program (CCX)   A no-cost licensing of technology for use in WLAN adapters and devices.

Cisco Configuration Assistant (CCA)   A software application used to set up mobility express networks.

Cisco Discovery Protocol (CDP)   A Cisco-proprietary protocol that can gain information about directly connected Cisco devices.

Cisco Site Survey Utility (CSSU)   The optional software set that you select with a checkbox during installation.

Cisco Smart Business Communication System (SBCS)   The Cisco solution for voice, video, and wireless for the small business.

Cisco Wireless Location Appliance   Maps clients and helps enforce security policies.

Cisco Wizard Configuration Tool   A wizard-type menu used to perform basic configuration.

Clear Channel Assessment (CCA)   A function found within physical layers that determines the current state of use of a wireless medium.

Clear-To-Send (CTS)   A message indicating that it is clear to send data on the wireless medium.

Clear-To-Send to self (CTS to self)   A method indicating that it is clear to send data on a wireless network.

client MFP   If the client is running CCX 5 or better, it can actually talk to the AP and find out what the MIC is.

co-channel interference   Crosstalk between channels that are next to each other.

Code Division Multiple Access (CDMA)   A channel access method.

community   A group name for your mobility express network.

Complementary Code Keying (CCK)   Uses a series of codes called complementary sequences.

contention window   The total amount of time that Station A waits before sending.

control frame   Used to acknowledge when data frames are received.

CSSC   Cisco Secure Services Client software.

D

data frame   A frame that contains data.

deauthentication message   When a client is connected to a wireless cell, either the client or the AP can leave the connection by sending this message. This message has information in the body about why it is leaving.

deauthentication response   A response to a deauthentication message.

destination address (DA)   A frame's final destination.

Digital Enhanced Cordless Telecommunications (DECT)   An ETSI standard for digital portable phones. Found in cordless technology that is deployed in homes or business.

dipole   See rubber duck.

directional antenna   Mounted on a wall. Its radiation pattern is focused in a certain direction.

Direct Sequence Spread Spectrum (DSSS)   The modulation technique used by 802.11b devices to send data. The transmitted signal is spread across the entire frequency spectrum that is being used.

disassociation message   Disassociates from the cell but keeps the client authenticated.

disassociation response   A response to a disassociation message.

Distributed Coordination Function (DCF)   Each station is responsible for coordinating the sending of its data.

Distributed Interframe Space (DIFS)   Each sending station must wait after a frame is sent before sending the next frame.

distribution system   The AP connects to a distribution system to get to server farms, the Internet, and other subnets.

diversity vertical polarization   The use of two antennas for each radio to increase the odds of receiving a better signal on either of the antennas.

dual-patch "omnidirectional"   Two patch directional antennas are placed back to back, making it "omnidirectional."

Dynamic Frequency Control (DFC)   The ability to change frequency to avoid radar signals.

dynamic interface   Includes the user-defined list.

Dynamic Rate Shifting (DRS)   The capability of a wireless network to shift to a lower rate as a client moves farther away from the AP.

E

Effective Isotropic Radiated Power (EIRP)   Used to estimate the service area of a device. The formula is as follows:

EIRP = transmitter − cable loss + antenna gain

elevation plane (E-plane)   The vertical pattern does not propagate evenly.

Enhanced Data Rate (EDR)   A Bluetooth 2.0 feature providing up to three times the bandwidth for Bluetooth clients.

exposed node issue   When there are two wireless cells on the same channel and they are too close to each other.

Extended Rate Physical (ERP)   Devices that have extended data rates.

Extended Service Area (ESA)   More than one AP is connected to a common distribution system.

Extensible Authentication Protocol (EAP)   Controls the authentication process under the premise that no matter what EAP method you use, the basic steps will reamain the same.

Extensible Authentication Protocol-Flexible Authentication via Secure Tunnel (EAP-FAST)   Created to address weaknesses in Lightweight Extensible Authentication Protocol (LEAP). Uses PAC, not PKI.

Extensible Authentication Protocol-Transport Layer Security (EAP-TLS)   A commonly used EAP method for wireless networks.

European Telecommunications Standards Institute (ETSI)   Produces globally applicable standards for Information and Communications Technologies (ICT), including fixed, mobile, radio, converged, broadcast, and Internet technologies.

F

Federal Communications Commission (FCC)   An independent U.S. government agency established by the Communications Act of 1934. It regulates interstate and international communications by radio, television, wire, satellite, and cable. The FCC's jurisdiction covers the 50 states, the District of Columbia, and U.S. possessions.

Frame Check Sequence (FCS)   Extra checksum characters added to a frame in a communication protocol for error detection and correction.

free path loss   The loss in signal strength of an electromagnetic wave that results from a line-of-sight path through free space, where no obstacles are nearby to cause reflection or diffraction.

frequency   The pitch of the signal.

Frequency Division Multiple Access (FDMA)   An access technology that radio systems use to share the radio spectrum, commonly found in 802.11 networks.

Frequency Hopping Spread Spectrum (FHSS)   A spread spectrum method in which the signal hops between channels. If a channel experiences interference, it can be skipped.

G

Generic Token Card (GTC)   Authenticates the user inside an encrypted tunnel.

Global System for Mobile Communication (GSM)   A digital mobile telephony system that uses a variation of time-division multiple access (TDMA). The most widely used of the three digital wireless telephony technologies (TDMA, GSM, and CDMA). GSM operates at either the 900-MHz or 1800-MHz frequency band.

Group Master Key (GMK)   Used by the AP to generate a group random number.

Group Temporal Key (GTK)   Generated by the GMK random number. Provides a group key and a MIC. This key changes when it times out or when a client leaves the network.

Group Transient Key (GTK)   Used to decrypt broadcast and multicast.

H

Hertz (Hz)   Used to measure bandwidth. Hertz measures the number of cycles per second. One Hertz is one cycle per second.

hidden node issue   When more than one client tries to send on the same channel at the same time. They are in range of the AP but not each other.

hidden node problem   When two devices cannot hear each other.

horizontal plane (H-plane)   The horizontal plane of an omnidirectional polarized antenna, opposite the E-plane.

horizontal polarization   The wave goes left and right in a linear way.

hybrid REAP mode   Hybrid Remote Edge Access Point (H-REAP) is a solution for branch office and remote office deployments. It lets you configure access points (AP) in a branch or remote office from the corporate office through a wide-area network (WAN) link without the need to deploy a controller in each office.

I

Independent Basic Service Set (IBSS)   When two machines do not need a central device to speak to each other.

Industry, Scientific, and Medical (ISM) frequency bands   Use of spread spectrum in the commercial market.

infrastructure Refers to assets that support a network.

infrastructure device The access point (AP).

infrastructure MFP Management Frame Protection performed by APs.

initialization vector (IV) A block of bits that is used to produce a unique encryption key.

Institute for Electrical and Electronics Engineers (IEEE) A nonprofit organization, IEEE is the world's leading professional association for the advancement of technology.

intercontroller roaming When a user roams from one controller to another but remains on the same VLAN.

interface The logical, dynamic, or static port of a network device. Also refers to VLANs.

interframe spacing (IFS) A period of time that a station has to wait before it can send.

intracontroller roaming When roaming is handled within a single controller.

IP Setup utility Takes the MAC address of the AP and resolves the IP address associated with it.

isotropic radiator A reference that assumes that the signal is propagated evenly in all directions. This would be a perfect 360-degree sphere in all directions, on the H- and E-planes.

iwconfig The command-line tool for Linux to work with WLANs.

J–K

join request message A message sent by an AP to join a wireless controller.

L

Layer 3 LWAPP mode The default LWAPP mode on most Cisco devices.

lightning arrestor Prevents surges from reaching the RF equipment by the device's shunting effect.

Lightweight Access Point Protocol (LWAPP) A protocol used for communication between a lightweight AP and a wireless controller.

lightweight AP An AP that receives configuration from a controller and cannot function without the controller.

Lightweight Extensible Authentication Protocol (LEAP) Uses a proprietary algorithm to create the initial session key.

Line-of-Sight (LOS) The signal between the two points that appears to be a straight shot.

link budget A value that accounts for all the gains and losses between sender and receiver. It accounts for attenuation, antenna gain, and other miscellaneous losses that may occur.

local mode The standard operating mode of an access point.

LWAPP discovery request An LWAPP message used to discover a controller.

LWAPP discovery response A response from a controller to an AP during discovery.

M

management frame   Used to join and leave a wireless cell.

Management Frame Protection (MFP)   A method used to detect spoofed management frames in which valid frames contain a hash that spoofed frames would not.

master controller   Configured in the GUI interface by choosing CONTROLLER > Advanced > Master Controller Mode.

Maximum Transmission Unit (MTU)   The largest frame size supported on an interface.

Message Integrity Check (MIC)   A cryptographic hash in each management frame used to ensure that data is not tampered with.

Microsoft Challenge Handshake Authentication Protocol version 2 (MS-CHAPv2)   A protocol used to authenticate the user inside an encrypted tunnel in Microsoft Windows Active Directory.

mobility anchor   A feature in which all the client traffic that belongs to a WLAN (especially the guest WLAN) is tunneled to a predefined WLC or a set of controllers that are configured as an anchor for that specific WLAN. Also called guest tunneling or auto-anchor mobility.

mobility domain   A controller can be aware of another controller in a different mobility group.

mobility group   A setting that defines the controller as a member of a group.

monitor mode   A mode that an AP can operate in where it constantly scans all channels to perform rouge detection. When in this mode, the AP cannot service clients.

multipath   Defines when portions of signals are reflected and then arrive out of order at the receiver.

Multiple Basic Service Set Identifier (MBSSID)   Used when the AP has more than one network.

Multiple-Input Multiple-Output (MIMO)   A technology that is used in the new 802.11n specification. A device that uses MIMO technology uses multiple antennas to receive signals, usually two or three, as well as multiple antennas to send signals.

N

N+1   A method of controller redundancy—a controller plus one for backup.

N+N   Two active controllers that can back each other up.

N+N+1   Two controllers backing each other up, with a dedicated backup as a last resort.

native VLAN   The VLAN on a trunk that does not get tagged.

NAV   Norton AntiVirus.

N connector   A type of antenna connector.

network manager   A graphical user interface (GUI) tool that enables the creation of wireless profiles in Linux.

node   Another term for an access point in a mesh network.

null function frame   The client wakes up after a certain period of time, during which the AP buffers any traffic for it.

NVRAM   Nonvolatile RAM. A storage location used to keep configuration files.

O

omnidirectional antenna   An antenna type that does not focus a signal in one direction.

one-floor concept   The signal propagates wider from side to side than from top to bottom. Therefore, the signal can offer coverage to the floor it is placed on rather than to the floor above or below the AP.

Orthogonal Frequency Division Multiplexing (OFDM)   Defines a number of channels in a frequency range. Not considered a spread spectrum technology but is used for modulation in a wireless network.

Over-the-Air Provisioning (OTAP)   A method for APs to discover the management IP of a controller over the air.

P

Pairwise Master Key (PMK)   A wireless security key.

Pairwise Transient Key (PTK)   This type of key confirms the PMK between two devices, establishes a temporal key to be used for message encryption, authenticates the negotiated parameters, and creates keying material for the next phase, called the two-way group key handshake.

parabolic dish   Has a very narrow path and is very focused in its radiation pattern.

passive scan   A scan in which wireless clients mark the channels on which a beacon is heard.

phase   The timing of the signal between peaks.

Point Coordination Function (PCF)   The AP is responsible for coordinating the sending of its data.

polarity   The direction in which the RF is sent from an antenna—horizontal or vertical.

port   A physical interface on your controller.

precoding   A function that takes advantage of multiple antennas and the multipath issue.

probe request   A client request for an AP.

probe response   A response to a probe request.

protected EAP (PEAP)   Only a server-side certificate is used to create a tunnel, and then the real authentication takes place inside.

PS-poll   Power-save poll.

Q–R

Quadrature Phase Shift Keying (QPSK)   A version of frequency modulation in which the phase of the carrier wave is modulated to encode bits of digital information in each phase change.

radiation pattern   The direction of the RF propagation.

Radio Resource Management (RRM)   A software feature of the Cisco controller that acts as a built-in RF engineer to consistently provide real-time RF management of your wireless network.

RAM   Random-access memory, used during operation. Lost when the system reloads.

Real-Time Operating System (RTOS)   The controller's operating system.

Receiving Address (RA)   The address of the direct station that this frame is sent to.

Reduced Interframe Space (RIFS)   A smaller interframe space, reducing delay and overhead.

reflection   Happens when a signal bounces off something and travels in a different direction.

refraction   The change in direction or the bending of a waveform as it passes through something that has a different density.

repeater   A device that repeats a signal to extend distance.

Request-To-Send (RTS)   A request to send on a wireless network.

response   In a wireless LAN, a response to a request for connectivity.

Reverse-Polarity Threaded Neill-Concelman (RP-TNC)   A type of antenna connector.

roaming   A client moving from one AP to another AP, overlapping.

rogue detector mode   A mode an AP can operate in to look for rogue devices. When operating in this mode, an AP looks on the wireless network for ARP messages from rogue devices.

rubber duck   A common wireless antenna in a rubber sheath.

S

scattering   The signal is sent in many different directions. This can be caused by an object that has reflective yet jagged edges, or dust particles in the air and water.

Secure Services Client Administration Utilities (SSCAU)   A component of Cisco Secure Services Client (SSC) client software that enables the administrator to create complex profiles.

Service Set Identifier (SSID)   The name of a wireless network.

Short Interframe Space (SIFS)   For higher priority. Used for ACKs, among other things.

Signal-to-Noise Ratio (SNR)   How much stronger the signal is compared to the surrounding noise that corrupts it.

site survey   A measurement of a certain point in time—the time when you did the site survey.

slottime   The speed at which the backoff timer countdown occurs.

Small to Mid-Size Business (SMB)   A business that has customers seeking to gain a competitive edge without having to compromise between price and sophistication.

sniffer mode   A mode that an AP can operate in to capture data and forward 802.11 packets to an application such as Wireshark for analysis.

sniff subrating   Increases battery life up to five times.

source address (SA)   The stations that sent the frame.

spatial multiplexing   Takes a signal, splits it into a bunch of lower-rate streams, and then sends each one out different antennas.

Special Interest Group (SIG)   A Bluetooth group.

splitter   Used in outdoor wireless deployments to split in two a signal coming from a cable, and send it in two directions.

static interface   Includes management interface, AP-Manager, service port.

station (STA)   The client on a network.

supplicant   A device that can use an EAP method to prove its identity to the authentication server.

symmetric tunneling   All traffic is tunneled from the client to the anchor controller, sent to the destination, returned to the anchor controller, and then tunneled back to the client via the foreign controller.

T

Temporal Key Integrity Protocol (TKIP)   A method of automatically changing the keys.

TFTP   Trivial File Transfer Protocol. Used to copy files between a client and server using UDP port 69.

Time Division Multiple Access (TDMA)   An access method that allocates time slots to access the network.

Traffic Indication Map (TIM)   This field indicates whether the AP is buffering traffic for clients in power-save mode.

Transmit Beamforming (TxBF)   A technique that is used when there is more than one transmit antenna. The signal is coordinated and sent from each antenna so that the signal at the receiver is dramatically improved, even if it is far from the sender.

Transmit Power Control (TPC)   The ability to adjust power dynamically, and a requirement for use in the UNII bands.

Transmitter Address (TA)   The address of the station that is emitting the frame.

trunk port   A port that carries traffic for multiple VLANs by tagging traffic from each VLAN.

U

Universal Workgroup Bridge (uWGB)   A wireless bridge.

Unlicensed National Information Infrastructure (UNII)   Frequency ranges used in wireless networks that don't require licensing.

upgrade tool   A Windows application that converts the device to lightweight mode.

V

vertical polarization   The wave moves up and down in a linear way.

virtual carrier sense   A method of verifying link integrity.

virtual local-area network (VLAN)   A concept in switched networks that allows segmentation of users at a logical level.

W

wavelength   The distance between successive crests of a wave.

WCS planning mode   Determines how many APs are needed for a given coverage area by placing hypothetical APs on the map. Lets you view the coverage area.

WCS RF prediction   Uses information entered into the map and the map editor to predict how the AP will react in the environment.

WCS template   Allows administrators to save time by configuring it once and then being able to apply it to more than one device.

Wi-Fi Alliance   A nonprofit organization that certifies the interoperability of more than 4200 products.

Wi-Fi Protected Access (WPA)   Uses the Temporal Key Integrity Protocol (TKIP) as a way to automatically change the keys.

Wi-Fi Protected Access 2 (WPA2)   Allows for the AES/CCMP variant and allows keys to be cached for faster connections.

Windows Wireless Zero Configuration Utility (WZC)   The wireless configuration tool for Microsoft Windows.

Wireless Control System (WCS)   A browser-based software application control element that offers the ability to manage multicontroller deployments through a single interface.

Wireless LAN Controller (WLC)   A Cisco wireless controller used to configure wireless networks and deliver configurations to lightweight APs.

wireless local-area network (WLAN)   The wireless portion of a local-area network.

wireless metropolitan-area network (WMAN)   A wireless network that encompasses a metropolitan area.

wireless personal-area network (WPAN)   A wireless network covering a very small area.

wireless wide-area network (WWAN)   A wireless network that covers a wide area.

workgroup bridge (WGB)   A device that bridges traffic.

Worldwide Interoperability for Microwave Access (WiMax)   A method of wide-area or last-mile wireless access.

WPA   A Wi-Fi protected access, authentication, and encryption method using the TKIP protocol.

WPA2   A Wi-Fi protected access, authentication, and encryption method using AES encryption.

X–Y–Z

Yagi-Uda   A directional antenna that offers a very direct radiation pattern.

ZigBee   A technology consisting of small, low-power digital radios based on the IEEE 802.15.4 standard for wireless personal-area networks.

Index